Toward Benevolent Neutrality: Church, State, and the Supreme Court

(Fifth Edition)

by

Robert T. Miller
Baylor University

and

Ronald B. Flowers
Texas Christian University

MARKHAM PRESS FUND OF
BAYLOR UNIVERSITY PRESS
Waco, Texas

Library of Congress Cataloging-in-Publication Data

Miller, Robert Thomas, 1920-
Toward benevolent neutrality : church, state and the Supreme Court / Robert T. Miller and Ronald B. Flowers. — 5th ed.
p. cm.
Includes bibliographical references.
ISBN 0-918954-63-0 Printed case ISBN: 978-1-4813-1457-2
1. Church and state—United States—Cases. 2. Freedom of religion—United States—Cases. I. Fowers, Ronald B. (Ronald Bruce), 1935- II. Title.
KF4865.A7M54 1996
342.73 0852—dc20 96–18086
[347.302852} CIP

Library of Congress Catalog Card Number: 96-18086
International Standard Book Number: 0-918954-63-0

TABLE OF CONTENTS

Volume II

ALPHABETICAL TABLE OF CONTENTS

PREFACE AND GUIDE TO THE FIFTH EDITION

Religious freedom and separation of church and state have been embodied within the First Amendment of the Constitution of the United States of America since the ratification of the Bill of Rights in 1791. These important constitutional guarantees were uncommon in the world of the late eighteenth century and are far from universal even today. The interpretation of the First Amendment's Establishment and Free Exercise Clauses is primarily a function of the judiciary, and the final word on First Amendment issues comes from the United States Supreme Court. The process of explaining the meanings and marking the boundaries of these constitutional provisions was described and summarized by the late Chief Justice Warren Burger in WALZ v. TAX COMMISSION:

> The general principle deducible from the First Amendment and all that has been said by the Court is this: that we will not tolerate either governmentally established religion or governmental interference with religion. Short of those expressly proscribed governmental acts there is room for play in the joints productive of a benevolent neutrality which will permit religious exercise to exist without sponsorship and without interference (397 U.S. 664, 669).

As it has worked toward "benevolent neutrality," the Court has produced a body of fascinating literature that is of great value to those who seek to understand this important facet of American constitutional development. This collection presents virtually every Supreme Court decision concerning religious freedom and separation of church and state. It also contains essays designed to assist readers in understanding the historical background and legal issues involved in each case. In previous editions we expressed the hope that this book will meet a wide range of needs: those of members of the university community pursuing studies in political science, religion, history, or law; ministers, priests, rabbis, imams, and other professionals in the field of religion; lawyers and judges; politicians and public administrators; writers and editors engaged in diverse areas of publication; and everyone who seeks deeper understanding of the Court's thinking on church-state issues affecting the lives of all Americans. Given that there has been demand enough that we have been able to issue this updated Fifth Edition, it is apparent that the book has met at least some of the needs just mentioned. For that we are glad and hope that this edition will be equally utilitarian.

Realizing that legal specialists will have access to law libraries and in order to keep the book to a manageable size (although in this Fifth Edition we have had to go to two volumes), cases have been edited to remove technical material. The cases are supplied with cross references to the appropriate page numbers in *United States Reports,* the official reporting service of the Federal Government for Supreme Court opinions. The points where page breaks occur are marked in the text itself, in bold face type, with the symbol ⊥ and the appropriate page number, e.g., **⊥357**. Recent cases, those not yet published in *United States Reports,* i.e., those that have a citation from the *Supreme Court Reporter* (such as 115 S.Ct. 2508), are also cross referenced in the same manner.

Although this edition is arranged in two volumes, pages are numbered consecutively throughout the work so that one can easily find a case or an essay by looking in the two tables of contents at the front of each volume. There is a Topical Table of Contents, in which cases and essays are arranged by major topics and subtopics. Cases are arranged chronologically within each subtopic. The Alphabetical Table of Contents enables one to find the location of a case, essay, or appendix even if one does not know its topic.

An introductory essay deals in historical fashion with the major events leading to adoption of the First Amendment. The two principal sections of the book deal with the Establishment Clause and Free Exercise Clause. An essay precedes each of these sections and gives an historical overview describing the legal principles employed in the interpretation of each clause and explaining how these principles developed. Other essays are designed to assist the reader by describing how the Court has dealt with constitutional issues and by outlining the chronological sequence in which cases were decided. In all the essays in the book, references to cases published in the book are printed in CAPITAL LETTERS while other case titles are printed in *italics*.

Included in the final pages of the book, in Volume II, are various aids to facilitate study of the case literature contained in this work:

First, Appendices A and B provide the texts of Thomas Jefferson's "A Bill for Establishing Religious Freedom" and James Madison's "Memorial and Remonstrance Against Religious Assessments." These historic documents figure prominently in the development of religious freedom in this country and both are referred to repeatedly by the Court in its various majority, concurring, and dissenting opinions. Appendix C contains the text of the "Religious Freedom Restoration Act" (RFRA) of 1993. This act of Congress was designed to undo what the Court did in its Free Exercise Clause decision in EMPLOYMENT DIVISION OF OREGON v. SMITH (1990).

Second, there is a glossary of legal terms. Although neither extensive nor comprehensive, the glossary does contain the most frequently used technical legal terms appearing in this collection of cases.

Third, a bibliography lists many important books and articles that form part of the vast literature on church-state relations. This bibliography has been updated and expanded since the Fourth Edition.

Fourth, the reader is provided with an alphabetical Table of Cases in two parts: Supreme Court cases and lower court cases, both Federal and State. These tables list all the cases cited in the introductory essays and in the Supreme Court cases themselves. Because many of the leading cases are frequently cited both in opinions and essays, full citations are given only in this two-part Table of Cases, in order to conserve space and to provide a minimum of distraction for the reader. In addition to the legal citation for each case, the Table of Cases lists each page number in this work where a case is mentioned. Thus the Table of Cases serves as an Index to the book, as well as the repository of legal citations. In this table, the names of cases published in the book appear in **BOLD CAPITAL LETTERS**. The page number where the text of that case is printed is also in **bold**. Names of cases which are not published in the book are in *italics*.

Fifth, a Table of Supreme Court Opinions by Justice identifies opinions written by each of the Supreme Court Justices in the ninety-two cases edited and reprinted in this work. This tabulation is designed to facilitate tracing the church-state thought of each jurist without having to scan the entire collection of opinions.

Sixth, a Table of Supreme Court Constituencies shows the make-up of the Court during the terms that the cases included in the book were handed down. Please read the explanation at the top of the first page of the chart.

We acknowledge gratefully the assistance of several persons who have helped in producing these volumes. First and foremost is Mrs. Janet Burton, Academic Publications Coordinator for Baylor University Press. As with the Fourth Edition, she was the glue that held this project together. From reconceiving the format, to mastering scanning technology, to proofreading, to gently but firmly calling attention to mistakes and the deadline, to maintaining a lively sense of humor through it all, Janet Burton was wonderful! Without her, this edition would not have come into being. We express our thanks to Mrs. Sharon Edwards, Secretary of the Department of Political Science at Baylor University and Ms. Susan Kendrick, Assistant Law Librarian at the Baylor University School of Law, who was especially helpful in looking up case citations and titles for the bibliography. We owe a good deal of gratitude to Carolyn Allen and Hillary Wright, student assistants in the Department of Religion at Texas Christian University for their help in inputting text, particularly for the various tables and the bibliography, and to Brian Rodecap, student assistant for the Baylor University Press, whose skills with the computer and attention to detail proved invaluable. Mrs. Annice Ipser, Secretary of the Religion Department helped in a variety of ways, particularly time management for the student assistants and the TCU side of the author team, who is also Chair of the Department.

Finally, but far from least, wives and other family members provided needed encouragement and sacrificed "family times" in the interest of this project. To Leah Flowers, sincere appreciation is expressed for who you are and for your support of my scholarly endeavors. I hope that my love may even somehow be reflected in the pages of a book of Supreme Court opinions.

Just as this edition was going to press, indeed, after virtually all the type was set, Robert T. Miller died; July 2, 1996. Even though Bob had been battling serious illness for several years, he was completely dedicated to the project until the end. Consequently, this editon is dedicated to the life and memory of Bob Miller and to his beloved Ann, who supported every edition of this book and who nurtured and nursed him during his long illness. Staunch defender of religious liberty, faithful Christian, careful and energetic scholar, outstanding teacher, family man, loyal employee, supporter, and "work horse" of Baylor University and the *Journal of Church and State*, Bob Miller was a phenomenon. Rest in peace, Good Friend.

Ronald B. Flowers
Professor of Religion
Chair of the Department
Texas Christian University

This work is the thirty-first published by the Markham Press Fund of Baylor University Press, established in memory of Dr. L. N. and Princess Finch Markham of Longview, Texas, by their daughters, Mrs. R. Matt Dawson of Waco, Texas and Mrs. B. Reid Clanton of Longview, Texas.

1 INTRODUCTION

The broad religious freedom that is today enjoyed and largely taken for granted in the United States is not part of our European heritage. This freedom is primarily native to these shores and is the evolutionary outcome of a distinctly American experience. In his classic treatise on the development of religious freedom in America, Sanford H. Cobb asserted that

> this revolutionary principle, declarative of the complete separation of Church from State, so startlingly in contrast with the principles which had dominated in the past—this pure Religious Liberty—may be confidently reckoned as of distinctly American origin. . . . Here, among all the benefits to mankind to which this soil has given rise, this pure religious liberty may be justly rated as the great gift of America to civilization and the world. . . .[1]

Although there were scattered advocates of religious toleration and even a few bold thinkers who argued for the inherent right of the individual to worship freely according to the dictates of conscience, the prevailing pattern in the Europe from which the early American colonists came was one of close cooperation between state and church in the maintenance of religious as well as political orthodoxy. Establishment was the order of the day: the state was the defender and sponsor of the church, and the church was a bulwark of the existing political order. Persecution of domestic dissenters and bloody foreign wars in the name of religion were frequent in the sixteenth and seventeenth centuries.

[1] *The Rise of Religious Liberty in America: A History* (New York: Macmillan Co., 1902), p. 2. Despite its date of publication, this is still perhaps the most thorough and frequently cited single work on the history of the development of religious freedom from the early colonial period to the adoption of the first state constitutions. Another valuable study of the period is William W. Sweet, *Religion in Colonial America* (New York: Charles Scribner's Sons, 1942).

The exact part played by religion in the settlement of the English colonies in America is impossible to determine. In times past its role has perhaps been exaggerated. Undoubtedly there were a number of motives, and these were mixed. However, many individuals and congregations—Puritans, Quakers, Mennonites, Roman Catholics, Brethren (Dunkers)—did come in search of a "Zion in the wilderness" where they could practice their religious beliefs without fear of the persecution to which they had been subjected.

The missionary spirit also impelled some to make the hazardous voyage. Even those colonies not ordinarily associated with religion paid at least lip service to this objective. The royal charter of 1606, granted to the commercial corporation that colonized Virginia, emphasized a commitment to the propagation of the Christian faith to the aborigines "who yet live in Darkness and miserable Ignorance of the true Knowledge and Worship of God," and expressed the hope that in time those who went might "bring the Infidels and Savages, living in those parts, to human Civility, and to a settled and quiet government."[2]

While economic considerations may well have lurked behind the rhetoric, it is still significant that in practically every statement of purpose, appeal for settlers, and charter issued, missionary and other religious purposes were given a prominent position.

One should not assume, however, that all of those who appealed for religious tolerance and Christian love while undergoing persecution in their homeland became practitioners of those virtues when they came into authority in the new land. Too often their concept of religious freedom proved to mean freedom for their own particular beliefs and practices only, and they set out to reproduce the European model of establishment and oppression.

[2] Benjamin P. Poore, ed., *The Federal and State Constitutions, Colonial Charters, and Other Organic Laws of the United States*, 2 vols. (Washington, D.C.: Government Printing Office, 1878), 2:1888.

The scene shifted but the scenario remained largely the same.

In Massachusetts Bay, Plymouth, Connecticut, and New Hampshire, Congregationalism was the established church. In North and South Carolina, as well as Virginia, the Church of England was the official church just as in the England from which most of the settlers came. New York, Maryland, and Georgia passed through various stages of establishment and disestablishment during the colonial period. The status of New Jersey is subject to considerable debate as to whether there was ever a formal establishment or whether it was simply an informal arrangement without benefit of legislative enactment. Only in William Penn's Pennsylvania and Delaware and in Roger Williams's Rhode Island was there never an established church.

The fate of dissenters in most of the early colonies was little different from what it would have been in England, except perhaps even more unpleasant. Such fellow Congregationalists as Roger Williams, Anne Hutchinson, and John Wheelwright were banished from Massachusetts because of their failure to conform to the prescribed orthodoxy of the dominant church leadership. Roman Catholics were forbidden to enter the colony under threat of death. Baptists and Quakers were frequently fined, imprisoned, whipped, and banished; at least four Quakers were executed. Settlement of Rhode Island, Connecticut, and New Hampshire can be attributed primarily to the intolerant actions of Massachusetts authorities. One of the supreme ironies of the entire colonial period occurred when in 1662 Charles II wrote the legislature of the Bay Colony criticizing that colony's officials for excessive acts of persecution against religious dissenters and demanding that Church of England worship be permitted.[3]

Though physical persecution was never as prevalent outside Massachusetts, the spirit of intolerance was likely just as strong in most other colonies as is evidenced by the repressive legislative acts and executive proclamations which sprinkle the early colonial records. Even the more secular southern colonies had repressive laws that were not infrequently enforced. For example, a considerable number of Quakers were arrested, fined, and ordered to leave Virginia under a law passed by that colony's legislature in 1663. A strange repetition of this repression occurred a hundred years later on the very eve of the Revolution.

During the years from 1768 to 1770, Baptists bore the brunt of this belated persecution for their refusal to comply with a requirement of licenses for meeting houses and for their outspoken criticism of the established church. At one point some thirty Baptist ministers were imprisoned, to the great anger of Patrick Henry, who rode fifty miles on horseback to make a successful, dramatic appearance on behalf of three defendants in a Spotsylvania County trial.

The colonies of Roger Williams and William Penn—and Maryland in its early years—were striking exceptions in a society that demanded religious conformity. These soon became havens for the religiously harassed of both the Old and New Worlds. Penn and the Baltimores are rightly commended for their practice of toleration. Roger Williams, however, argued, not for mere toleration, but rather for complete religious freedom and disestablishment based on the natural rights of man as well as biblical authority.

Though Williams's concept of religious rights was far ahead of his day, the success of his "livelie experiment" inevitably had an effect outside Rhode Island. As persecution gradually subsided in all the colonies, a great variety of sects began to appear, spelling the eventual doom of any single established church. There was also a steadily growing number of persons without church affiliation who obviously had no taste for either persecution or establishment: William Warren Sweet has estimated that even in stern New England only one in eight persons was a church member by the end of the colonial era.[4]

In addition, many Deists began to come to positions of prominence and added their influence to that of Baptists, Presbyterians, Quakers, and other opponents of establishment and oppression.

By the time of the Revolution, conditions were ripe for enunciation of religious liberty and separation of church and state. Each colony had its own specific experiences, but there was now a common and growing feeling as to the desirability of incorporating in the new fundamental laws to be framed as states the more tolerant attitude which existed in the minds of the people, notwithstanding the severity of the codes under which they lived. The religious movement known as the Great Awakening, which swept the country just prior to the Revolution, resulted in new alignments. It placed great emphasis on individual conversion and thus tended to make church membership more a matter of personal decision and less a matter of family inheritance. It also produced church leaders who subsequently urged disestablishment and advocated religious freedom.

The war itself had a liberalizing and unifying effect on the country; it tended to submerge internal differ-

[3]Cobb, *The Rise of Religious Liberty in America*, p. 224.

[4]Sweet, *Religion in Colonial America*, p. 229. Other scholars question the seeming significance of Sweet's statement on the ground that church membership in the colonial period was very strict and the aggregate of sympathizers and attenders of any given church was likely much more numerous than the actual membership.

ences. Ideologically, thinking persons could not fail to see the inconsistency of the natural rights philosophy proclaimed on all sides and the practices of religious discrimination. More important, perhaps, was the necessity of making concessions to dissenting church members and the unchurched to ensure their cooperation in the war effort.

Between 1776 and 1780 all of the states except Rhode Island and Connecticut adopted new written constitutions. Seven of these Revolutionary state constitutions contained separate bills of rights, while the remainder had within them various sections guaranteeing individual liberties. The provisions that relate to religion point up both the advances made toward the achievement of complete freedom and the restrictions still present. Most of the documents expressed support for religious liberty; half provided for separation of church and state. However, the liberty proclaimed, while broader than anywhere else in the world at that time, fell short of granting complete freedom and equality to all beliefs. For example, the Pennsylvania Constitution, though it declared the "unalienable right" of all to worship God "according to the dictates of their own consciences and understanding," required members of the State Assembly to profess belief in God and the divine inspiration of both the Old and New Testaments.

Though religious liberty, at least for Protestants, was guaranteed in these first state constitutions, the struggle for disestablishment proved long and bitter. The last vestiges of official establishment did not disappear until 1833, when Massachusetts finally adopted an amendment providing for separation. Even in Virginia, whose 1776 Declaration of Rights contained a stirring and comprehensive statement of religious freedom, supporters of the Episcopal Church fiercely resisted the combined efforts of Thomas Jefferson and James Madison to disestablish that church. Indeed, Jefferson was to record the struggle as the most severe contest in which he had ever been engaged.

In December 1776 the legislature passed a bill that exempted dissenters from supporting the established church. In June 1779, Jefferson presented his Bill for Establishing Religious Freedom (see Appendix A), but Virginia was not yet ready to take the final step. Session after session of the legislature passed without action, and in 1784 the forces of establishment counterattacked by introducing a bill providing for a general assessment for the teaching of religion. Madison, who assumed the primary role of leadership on Jefferson's departure to France, finally brought about the narrow defeat of the Assessment Bill by circulating his celebrated "Memorial and Remonstrance Against Religious Assessment" (see Appendix B). He then reintroduced Jefferson's bill for religious liberty; it became law in January 1786, the year before the Philadelphia Convention, at which Madison would come to be known as the "Father of the Constitution."

In view of all that had gone before, one might assume that those who in 1787 framed the federal Constitution would have devoted substantial time and attention to the issue of religion. Actually, there was remarkably little discussion of the question. A few days after the sessions began, Charles C. Pinckney submitted his draft of a proposed constitution providing that "the Legislature of the United States shall pass no law on the subject of religion. . . ." This draft was not accepted, but toward the end of the convention he submitted another more limited proposal which passed on 30 August. Ultimately, Pinckney's proposal became the last clause of Article VI, which provides that, while all state and national officers are bound by oath or affirmation to support the U.S. Constitution, "no religious test shall ever be required as a qualification to any office or public trust under the United States." Only Roger Sherman of Connecticut spoke against this single reference to religion in the original Constitution. He thought it unnecessary, "the prevailing liberality being a sufficient security against such tests."

In the state ratifying conventions there was some complaint because of the omission of any reference to God, and in at least two conventions fear was expressed at the inclusion of Pinckney's "no test oath" clause. In Massachusetts, Major T. Lusk said balefully that he "shuddered at the idea that Roman Catholics, Papists, and Pagans might be introduced into office, and that Popery and the Inquisition may be established in America."[5]

The strongest and most persistent criticism of the Constitution during the entire ratification struggle, however, concerned the absence of a bill of rights containing a specific guarantee of religious liberty as well as other fundamental rights. From his diplomatic post in France, Jefferson wrote his friend Madison, "I will now add what I do not like. First the omission of a bill of rights providing clearly and without the aid of sophisms for freedom of religion. . . ."[6]

Supporters of the Constitution responded to the criticism by contending that the inclusion of a bill of rights was not only unnecessary but that, if included, it might prove dangerous to the rights of the people. The national government, they reasoned, was one of delegated authority only: it possessed no powers except those given it in the Constitution, and no

[5]Jonathan Elliot, ed., *The Debates in the Several State Conventions on the Adoption of the Federal Constitution*, 2d ed., 5 vols. (Philadelphia: J. P. Lippincott Company, 1891), 2:148.

[6]Julian P. Boyd, ed., *The Papers of Thomas Jefferson* (Princeton, N.J.: Princeton University Press, 1950-), 12:440.

such grant of power to impinge on the rights of individuals had been made. The danger of inclusion of a bill of rights lay in the fact that no listing of such rights could possibly be all-inclusive, and the inadvertent failure to include a particular right could be taken to mean that it had been intentionally omitted. As Alexander Hamilton warned in *Federalist* 84, such a bill of rights "would contain various exceptions to powers not granted; and on this very account, would afford a colorable pretext to claim more than was granted. For why declare that things shall not be done which there is no power to do?"

Notwithstanding the assurances that they gave, advocates of the Constitution respected the apprehensions of the people and committed themselves at various state conventions to work for adoption of a bill of rights by amendment when the new government was established. In his inaugural address, President Washington called for congressional response to the commitments made; and on 8 June 1789 Madison, now a congressman from Virginia, submitted a series of amendments prepared largely from those suggested by the ratifying conventions of his own and other states. Debate on the proposals was lengthy in both houses of Congress. Action was finally completed by the Senate on 25 September, and twelve amendments were submitted to the states for ratification. During the next two years, ten of the twelve proposals received requisite state legislative approval and were added to the Constitution by proclamation on 15 December 1791. Significantly, the First Amendment begins with restrictions concerning religion: "Congress shall make no law respecting an establishment of religion, or prohibiting the free exercise thereof. . . ." In this brief but emphatic statement the long and bitter struggle toward the goal of constitutionally protected freedom of religion was brought to fruition. Of these clauses, Justice Wiley Rutledge wrote in 1947 (EVERSON v. BOARD OF EDUCATION): "No provision of the Constitution is more closely tied to or given content by its generating history than the religious clause of the First Amendment. It is at once the refined product and the terse summation of that history" (330 U.S. 1, 33).

Important as the religious guarantee of the First Amendment was, however, the circle of protection drawn around the individual was not yet complete. Although the national government was thus denied any power to interfere with the free exercise of religion or to establish religion, such actions on the part of the states were not prohibited by the terms of the amendment.

By this time, to be sure, all of the states had either bills of rights or other specific constitutional provisions assuring religious freedom. These were strengthened as the states amended their original constitutions or adopted new ones. As has been noted, the last establishment provision was taken from a state constitution in 1833; and as new states applied for admission to the Union, Congress insisted on adequate constitutional guarantees of freedom of religion and separation. However, state judges sometimes failed to apply vigorously the protective guarantees of the state constitutions; and, because no federal question was involved, there was no recourse to the U.S. Supreme Court from their decisions.

In 1810 Chief Justice John Marshall suggested that the Court might be ready to extend the prohibitions of the federal Bill of Rights to the states when he said, "The Constitution of the United States contains what may be deemed a Bill of Rights for the people of each state" (*Fletcher* v. *Peck*, 6 Cranch 87, 138). But in 1833 the great chief justice removed any question as to the applicability of the Bill of Rights when he wrote: "These amendments contain no expression indicating an intention to apply them to the State governments. This Court cannot so apply them" (*Barron* v. *Baltimore*, 7 Peters 243, 250).

Eleven years later (*Permoli* v. *First Municipality of New Orleans*) the Court again rejected an opportunity to expand its jurisdiction when it held specifically with respect to the free exercise clause of the First Amendment: "The Constitution makes no provision for protecting the citizens of the respective States in their religious liberties; this is left to the State constitutions and laws; nor is there any inhibition imposed by the Constitution of the United States in this respect on the States" (3 How. 589, 609).

Here the question rested until 1868 when the Fourteenth Amendment, which did unquestionably apply to the states, was adopted. This amendment forbids the states to "make or enforce any law which shall abridge the privileges or immunities of citizens of the United States" or to "deprive any person of life, liberty, or property without due process of law." Almost from the time of its adoption there were persons, sometimes members of the Court itself, who contended that the purpose, or at least the effect, of the amendment was to "incorporate," "absorb," or "nationalize" the federal Constitution's Bill of Rights, thus making its guarantees applicable to the states.

Historical evidence supporting this contention gives it some credence. However, the Court consistently rejected the argument in case after case until 1925. Then, in a landmark decision (*Gitlow* v. *New York*) involving questions of free speech and press, Justice Sanford opened the door to "selective incorporation" when he wrote, "for present purposes we may and do assume that freedom of speech and press—which are protected by the First Amendment from abridgement by Congress—are among the fundamental personal rights and 'liberties' protected by the due process clause of the Fourteenth Amendment from impairment by the states" (268 U.S. 666).

This assumption heralded what has become one of the most significant movements in American constitutional law. Although even today the argument made with great force by such justices as Black and Douglas for *in toto* "incorporation" has not been accepted by a majority of the Court, virtually all provisions of the Bill of Rights have been brought to bear against the states. In 1940 the free exercise clause of the First Amendment was specifically incorporated in one of the leading Jehovah's Witnesses cases, CANTWELL v. CONNECTICUT.[7]

In EVERSON v. BOARD OF EDUCATION, the 1947 New Jersey "Bus Case," the establishment clause was similarly applied to the states.

Thus the protective circle thrown around the rights of the individual by constitutional mandate was completed. Insofar as formal documents can guarantee religious liberty, it is secure. But as Anson Phelps Stokes has warned, "It is one thing to secure 'rights,' a very different thing to see that they are preserved inviolate."[8]

In a democracy, it is incumbent upon the people themselves and all agencies of government to see that these constitutional provisions are respected and implemented. Perhaps oddly, for a country which rightfully boasts of its democratic institutions, the United States has most often ultimately imposed this awesome, and generally onerous, burden upon its least "democratic" institution—the nonelective, life-tenured Supreme Court. As in no other country, the judiciary has been called upon to interpret and defend the constitutional pronouncements.

Constitutional clauses such as "free exercise" of religion and "establishment of religion" are obviously not self-defining. They are emotion-laden and susceptible to varied and contradictory definitions. The conflicts which result must sooner or later be submitted to a recognized arbiter if they are to be resolved peacefully. In large part because of its power to pass on the constitutionality of the action of other governmental agencies, this role of arbiter has fallen to the Supreme Court. Because the arbiter must defend as well as interpret constitutional guarantees of fundamental religious rights, it is fortunate that the Court has assumed the role. Though the idea is now generally accepted that the Court is a political as well as judicial institution, its more insulated position often permits members to make necessary but unpopular decisions that their more politically vulnerable associates in the other branches cannot, or think they cannot, afford.

Many of the decisions have been subjected to heavy criticism. Presidents have called for corrective actions; literally hundreds of constitutional amendments designed to modify the rulings have been introduced by incensed members of Congress. Still, compliance—though grudging—has eventually been forthcoming, likely because, as Justice Robert Jackson wrote in 1954: "The people have seemed to feel that the Supreme Court, whatever its defects, is still the most detached, dispassionate, and trustworthy custodian that our system affords for the translation of abstract into constitutional commands."[9]

More than their counterparts in the elective branches, the judges are expected to spell out and to justify their decisions in understandable written opinions not only for the benefit of the parties to the immediate litigation but also for the enlightenment and guidance of other judges, lawyers, and laymen of this and subsequent generations. Even those judges whose arguments do not at the moment prevail frequently feel an obligation to offer alternatives for the future in the form of dissenting and concurring opinions. These, too, make up the subject matter for the continuing national constitutional seminar that the educational function of the Court requires it to conduct. Speaking to the difficult problems inevitably involved in determining the proper relationship of religion and the state, these opinions (majority, dissenting, and concurring) form the substance of this volume.

---

[7]It is contended by some authorities, such as Henry J. Abraham, that the religious exercise guarantee was incorporated in 1934 in HAMILTON v. REGENTS OF THE UNIVERSITY OF CALIFORNIA. In that case, Justice Cardozo said in a concurring opinion: "I assume for present purposes that the religious liberty protected by the First Amendment against invasion by the nation is protected by the Fourteenth Amendment against invasion by the states" (293 U.S. 245, 265). An excellent discussion of the entire incorporation movement is found in Chapter 3 of Abraham's *Freedom and the Court: Civil Rights and Liberties in the United States*, 4th ed. (New York: Oxford University Press, 1982). Chapter 6 is devoted in its entirety to the Court's interpretation of the religion clauses.

[8]*Church and State in the United States*, 3 vols. (New York: Harper & Brothers, Publishers, 1950), 1:593. This is the most definitive work on the entire topic of church and state in this country. A revised one-volume edition has been prepared by Leo Pfeffer: Anson Phelps Stokes and Leo Pfeffer, *Church and State in the United States* (New York: Harper & Row, 1964).

[9]*The Supreme Court in the American System of Government* (Cambridge, Mass.: Harvard University Press, 1955), p. 23.

2 THE ESTABLISHMENT OF RELIGION

The development of the Establishment Clause and some aspects of its application have been described in the opening essay of this book. Now the clause must be examined more extensively in preparation for the cases which have been argued and decided specifically on establishment grounds. Interpretation of the Establishment Clause has not been easy; its meaning is not self-evident. Part of the problem of interpretation stems from lack of clarity concerning what the framers of the Constitution intended when they wrote the clause. Although the justices of the Supreme Court have on occasion appealed to the intentions of the authors of the Constitution in arriving at their decisions, there is no unanimity about what the authors had in mind when they composed the clause. Clearly, they intended to eliminate the possibility of an established church in the new nation, but when one gets beyond that, agreement as to their intent ceases. According to one authority, "Historical data can throw some light on the purposes behind such language, but all too often 'intention of the framers' has been a rhetorical device employed by partisans to read their own policy preferences into the Constitution."[1]

The uncertainty of determining the founders' intent has resulted in two basic approaches to the interpretation of the Establishment Clause. One of these may be labeled the "accommodationist" or "no preference" approach. This viewpoint argues that so long as the state does not single out one religious group for support to the exclusion of all others, there is nothing wrong with a cooperative relationship between government and religious institutions. In this interpretation, government can provide aid for religious institutions as long as the aid is imparted fairly and without favoritism.

The accommodationist view gained great visibility, at both the scholarly and popular levels, in the 1980s. Some scholars examined the debates leading up to the writing and ratification of the Constitution and the Bill of Rights and concluded that the founders intended only to remove religious requirements for public office, prevent the creation of a national church or religion, protect freedom of conscience in matters of religion against invasion by the national government, and leave the states to deal with questions of religion as they saw fit.[2] Consequently,

> there appears to be no historical evidence that the First Amendment was intended to preclude Federal government aid to religion when it was provided on a nondiscriminatory basis. Nor does there appear to be any historical evidence that the First Amendment was intended to provide an *absolute separation or independence* of religion and the national state.[3]

This view was also adopted by the administration of Ronald Reagan. Attorney General Edwin Meese III explicitly said "It has been and will continue to be the policy of this administration to press for a Jurisprudence of Original Intention." He applied this con-

---

[1]Charles H. Pritchett, *The American Constitution*, 3rd ed. (New York: McGraw-Hill, 1977), p. 32; see also Arthur Sutherland, "Historians, Lawyers, and 'Establishment of Religion,'" in *Religion and the Public Order*, Donald A. Gianella, ed., no. 5 (Ithaca, N.Y.: Cornell University Press, 1969), pp. 45–46.

[2]Robert L. Cord, *Separation of Church and State: Historical Fact and Current Fiction* (New York: Lambeth Press, 1982), p. 15. This book is one of the principal exponents of the "intentionalist" position, which is also accommodationist, and argues it forcefully. For a more systematically argued statement of the same position, see Stephen V. Monsma, *Positive Neutrality: Letting Religious Freedom Ring* (Westport, CT: Greenwood Press, 1993).

[3]Cord, p. 15 (emphasis in original).

cept to religion just as Professor Cord had done.[4] The Bush administration continued to endorse this philosophy.[5]

Accommodationism gained popular recognition and support as a result of the rise of the "New Christian Right," which gained high visibility because of the outspokenness of its leaders (many of whom were television evangelists), because of its alleged impact on politics (beginning with the election of 1980), and because of the attention given to it by the media. Here the accommodationism went beyond that of most scholars, for many in the "New Christian Right" believed that the nation was founded on Christian or, somewhat more broadly, Judaeo-Christian principles, although they acknowledged that the founders never intended to give government support to any particular denomination of Christianity.[6]

The other major approach to interpreting the Establishment Clause is the "separationist" or "no aid" approach. According to this view, not only should the state not aid or support one religious group, it should not aid any, even if this could be done on a basis of equality. Government and religion should neither depend upon nor aid each other. There is to be strict separation between government and religion.[7] This view is said to grow out of the views of many of the framers of the Constitution, notably Jefferson and Madison. For example, in Jefferson's "A Bill for Establishing Religious Freedom" and Madison's "Memorial and Remonstrance" (see Appendices A and B), the idea is clearly expressed, in a variety of ways, that religion should be independent of government interference. This has been interpreted to mean that not even nondiscriminatory, even-handed aid is permissible. In the words of one leading exponent of this view, "in the minds of the fathers of our Constitution, independence of religion and government was the alpha and omega of democracy and freedom."[8] In the late 1980s considerable scholarly work was done to endorse this interpretation and to answer nonpreferentialists such as Professor Cord and Chief Justice Rehnquist and the Reagan/Bush appointees to the Supreme Court.[9]

Many would say that to place all views of church-state relationships in these two categories only is an over-simplification. Professor Carl H. Esbeck has provided five very useful categories to delineate various perceptions of the proper relationship between religion and civil authority which go beyond Establishment Clause analysis, but which nonetheless are useful in this context. Although his article spells out the categories in great detail, he summarizes them as follows:

> *Strict separationists* are alone in regarding religion as principally a private and an individualistic phenomenon that should little influence public affairs and matters of state. Strict separationism is the only model unwilling to recognize ontological status in the law for churches and other religious organizations. To the extent that religious societies have legal defenses against interference by the state, these defenses are merely the sum of the individual rights derived from the organization's members.
>
> *Pluralistic separationists* reject the notion that the state is subject to and beneficiary of any "higher law," regarding such talk as civil religion, that is, a tendency toward self-righteous nationalism fueled by nativist religion. They view the modern nation-state as strictly a human invention, not an entity divinely instituted.
>
> *Institutional separationists* maintain that an ultimate worldview transcends and unifies the state, and thus limits it by holding the state accountable to this "higher law." This overarching public philosophy is deemed properly theistic and heavily influenced by Judeo-Christian thought, as is the history and tradition of all Western nations.
>
> *Nonpreferentialists* would permit government to favor religion on a basis that does

[4]Address before the American Bar Association, Washington, D.C., July 9, 1985, transcript, Superintendent of Documents classification number J1.34:M47, p. 17. In the same year a judicial statement of the accommodationist, no preference, position was made in Justice (later Chief Justice) Rehnquist's dissent in WALLACE v. JAFFREE.

[5]An explicit example is the "Brief for the United States as Amicus Curiae" in LEE v. WEISMAN, February 1991.

[6]Cf. Tim LaHaye, *Battle for the Mind* (Old Tappan, N.J.: Fleming H. Revell Co., 1980), pp. 37–38; Jerry Falwell, *Listen America!* (Garden City, N.Y.: Doubleday and Co., 1980), pp. 16, 27. Rus Walton, *One Nation Under God* (Old Tappan, N.J.: Fleming H. Revell Co., 1975), at p. 23, says "The Constitution was designed to perpetuate a Christian order" (emphasis in original).

[7]Richard E. Morgan, *The Politics of Religious Conflict* (New York: Pegasus, 1968), pp. 20-26.

[8]Leo Pfeffer, *Church, State, and Freedom*, rev. ed. (Boston: Beacon Press, 1987), p. 127.

[9]Examples are Leonard W. Levy, *The Establishment Clause: Religion and the First Amendment* (New York: Macmillan, 1986, 2nd, revised edition. Chapel Hill: University of North Carolina Press, 1994) and the work of Douglas Laycock; see his "'Nonpreferential' Aid to Religion: A False Claim About Original Intent," *William and Mary Law Review* 27 (Special Issue, 1985–1986): 875–923, and his "Original Intent and the Constitution Today," in James E. Wood, Jr., ed., *The First Freedom: Religion and the Bill of Rights* (Waco, TX: J. M. Dawson Institute of Church-State Studies, Baylor University, 1990), pp. 87–112. See also the explicit arguing of this view in Justice Souter's concurring opinion in LEE v. WEISMAN.

not prefer one religion over another. Thus, unlike the three separationist models, non-preferentialists would allow the state to aid religion in general while not aiding those professing no religious belief.

Restorationists, finally, are the only type that would bind the state to a particular confession of faith and would assign civil officials limited duties in defense of the dominant religion.[10]

The judicial interpretation of the Establishment Clause has a relatively short history that dates from EVERSON v. BOARD OF EDUCATION, decided in 1947. Prior to *Everson* there were a few cases which seemed to raise Establishment Clause questions, but they were decided on other grounds. In 1899 the Court considered BRADFIELD v. ROBERTS, in which a challenge was made to the expenditure of federal money for the improvement of a hospital owned and operated by an order of Catholic nuns. The case was handled as a matter of corporation law. So long as the hospital fulfilled its contract (i.e., to treat illness), the Court held that its operation by a religious order was of no consequence. The Establishment Clause was not used as a basis for the decision.

In 1908 the Court decided *Quick Bear* v. *Leupp*, which involved the federal government's holding in trust some money which belonged to Indians. The Court decided that the money could be used to pay for the education of Indian children in Catholic schools because it was the Indians' money, not the government's.

The 1925 case of PIERCE v. SOCIETY OF SISTERS challenged an Oregon law requiring that all able-bodied children of school age attend public school, thus potentially threatening the existence of church-related (and secular private) schools. The Court held that the law was unconstitutional, but the decision was made on the basis of the Fourteenth Amendment, not the First.

A final case which seemed to raise Establishment Clause issues was COCHRAN v. BOARD OF EDUCATION, decided in 1930. The question was whether Louisiana could use state funds to provide textbooks for students attending parochial schools. Holding that the program was constitutional, the Court again based its argument upon the Fourteenth Amendment, rather than the First.

One can surmise that there were at least three reasons why no explicitly Establishment Clause litigation was decided by the Court prior to 1947. First, persons who wanted to challenge the use of tax monies in support of religious institutions or practices encountered extreme difficulty in obtaining standing to sue. (See the section entitled "Standing to Sue.") Second, many states have statutory or constitutional provisions that are more specific than those of the federal Constitution in prohibiting use of governmental funds for particular religious activities. These prohibitions tend to minimize state involvement in religious matters. Third, the application of the Establishment Clause to the states had not happened prior to that time.[11] Indeed, it is commonly understood that the *Everson* case was the first in which the Establishment Clause was incorporated into the Fourteenth Amendment. The case setting the precedent for incorporation, *Gitlow* v. *New York*, had been decided in 1925. In 1940, in CANTWELL v. CONNECTICUT, the Court made the following observation:

> The First Amendment declares that Congress shall make no law respecting an establishment of religion or prohibiting the free exercise thereof. The Fourteenth Amendment has rendered the legislatures of the states as incompetent as Congress to enact such laws (310 U.S. 296, 303).

In spite of this broad language, *Cantwell* was decided solely on a free exercise question. As a result, the Establishment Clause was not specifically applied to the states until *Everson*.

The issue in *Everson* was whether state tax money could be used to reimburse parents for the cost of transporting children by bus to parochial schools. A New Jersey taxpayer sued in a state court (taxpayer suits being permissible under New Jersey law), claiming that such use of state money was a violation of the Establishment Clause made applicable to the states by the Fourteenth Amendment. The plaintiff based his argument on the broad language in *Cantwell*. The Supreme Court accepted the case because it raised a compelling federal question.

In writing the opinion of the Court, Justice Black included a paragraph defining the limits of the Establishment Clause, a paragraph which is frequently quoted, which, indeed, has served as the baseline for subsequent Establishment Clause litigation:

> The "establishment of religion" clause of the First Amendment means at least this: Neither a state nor the Federal Government can set up a church. Neither can pass laws which aid one religion, aid all religions, or prefer one religion over another. Neither can force nor in-

[10]Carl H. Esbeck, "Five Views of Church-State Relations in Contemporary American Thought," *Brigham Young University Law Review* (1986): 378–379 (emphasis added).

[11]See "Introduction" in this book for a discussion of the incorporation of the First Amendment into the Fourteenth. For a much more extensive treatment of this topic, see Henry J. Abraham and Barbara A. Perry, *Freedom and the Court: Civil Rights and Liberties in the United States* (New York: Oxford University Press, 6th edition, 1994), pp. 49–83.

> fluence a person to go to or to remain away from church against his will or force him to profess a belief or disbelief in religion. No person can be punished for entertaining or professing religious beliefs or disbeliefs, for church attendance or non-attendance. No tax in any amount, large or small, can be levied to support any religious activities or institutions, whatever they may be called, or whatever form they may adopt to teach or practice religion. Neither a state nor the Federal Government can, openly or secretly, participate in the affairs of any religious organizations or groups and *vice versa*. In the words of Jefferson, the clause against establishment of religion by law was intended to erect "a wall of separation between church and State" (330 U.S. 1, 15-16 (1947)).

In the light of this separationist language, many were surprised when Justice Black and four colleagues found that reimbursements for transportation were not a violation of the Establishment Clause.

In the paragraph quoted above, as elsewhere in the majority opinion, Justice Black simply assumed that the precedent of incorporation of the Establishment Clause into the Fourteenth Amendment was well established. He did not argue in support of the concept. For him the Establishment Clause should be applied to the states: the Court has followed that procedure in all subsequent Establishment Clause cases since *Everson*.

It should be noted that since *Everson* many have raised both theoretical and practical objections to the concept of incorporation. How can the Due Process and Equal Protection Clauses of the Fourteenth Amendment apply the Establishment Clause to the states if the aid challenged under that clause does not oppress anyone either in beliefs or religious exercise? How can a state's right be imposed as a prohibition on a state (thus showing that the Fourteenth Amendment is logically inconsistent with reference to the Establishment Clause)? Incorporation interposes federal judges between the people and their local and state legislatures and state courts.[12] Objections to incorporation, particularly as it applies to religion, were expressed forcefully as a part of the Reagan administration's "jurisprudence of original intent."

> And nowhere else has the principle of federalism been dealt so politically violent and constitutionally suspect a blow as by the theory of incorporation. . . . The point, of course, is that the Establishment Clause of the First Amendment was designed to prohibit Congress from establishing a national church. The belief was that the Constitution should not allow Congress to designate a particular faith or sect as politically above the rest. But to have argued, as is popular today, that the amendment demands a strict neutrality between religion and irreligion would have struck the founding generation as bizarre. The purpose was to prohibit religious tyranny, not to undermine religion generally.[13]

However, several commentators have pointed out that no Supreme Court Justice since 1925 (*Gitlow* v. *New York*) has questioned the validity of incorporation. That is true. Not even the most accommodationist of the justices writing in the cases included in this book have questioned the correctness of the concept of incorporation.

Although *Everson* articulated a strict separationist view of the Establishment Clause, subsequent cases have followed it with varying degrees of rigidity. In McCOLLUM v. BOARD OF EDUCATION (1948), Justice Black again wrote the opinion for the Court and adhered to the separationism of the *Everson* rhetoric. The *McCollum* opinion declared that a plan to offer released time religious education on public school premises during the school day was unconstitutional. Four years later, however, in ZORACH v. CLAUSON, Justice Douglas's majority opinion rather dramatically departed from a strict separationist approach to the Establishment Clause. This opinion found a New York program of released time instruction constitutional because the classes were taught away from school premises and there was no coercion to get the children to go, although three dissenters, including Justice Black, disagreed with the contention that there was no coercion. Justice Douglas began with the assumption that we are a religious people and concluded that state encouragement and cooperation with religion is not state aid but rather "follows the best of our traditions."

In 1962 the Court decided the first of the prayer cases, ENGEL v. VITALE. Here the Court returned to the more absolutist view of the Establishment Clause articulated, but not implemented, by *Everson*, which is not surprising since Justice Black

---

[12]As representative of this literature see Mark DeWolfe Howe, *The Garden and the Wilderness: Religion and Government in American Constitutional History* (Chicago: University of Chicago Press, 1965), pp. 136-139, and Joseph M. Snee, S.J., "Religious Disestablishment and the Fourteenth Amendment," *Washington University Law Quarterly* (December 1954): 371-407. For a review of objections to incorporating the Establishment Clause and attempts to answer them, see Justice Brennan's concurring opinion in ABINGTON TOWNSHIP SCHOOL DISTRICT v. SCHEMPP 373 U.S. 203 at 253-258.

[13]Edwin Meese III, address before the American Bar Association, p. 14.

wrote the *Engel* opinion. In finding government-written prayer unconstitutional, Justice Black wrote:

> The Establishment Clause, unlike the Free Exercise Clause, does not depend upon any showing of direct governmental compulsion and is violated by the enactment of laws which establish official religion whether those laws operate directly to coerce nonobserving individuals or not (370 U.S. 421, 430).

From *Everson* to *Engel* there is not a clear line of interpretation of the Establishment Clause. *Everson*, *McCollum*, and *Engel* represent a hard-line separationist, "no aid" approach; but *Zorach* represents a much more flexible, almost accommodationist, "no preference" approach. In this period there were no clear guidelines as to how the clause should be interpreted.

Clarification of the situation began with ABINGTON TOWNSHIP SCHOOL DISTRICT v. SCHEMPP, decided in 1963. In that case, involving compulsory prayer and Bible reading in the public schools, Justice Clark set forth two tests which were to be applied in order to determine a program's constitutionality under the Establishment Clause. Concerning such legislation, Justice Clark wrote:

> The test may be stated as follows: what are the purpose and the primary effect of the enactment? If either is the advancement or inhibition of religion then the enactment exceeds the scope of legislative power as circumscribed by the Constitution. That is to say that to withstand the strictures of the Establishment Clause there must be a secular legislative purpose and a primary effect that neither advances nor inhibits religion (374 U.S. 203, 222).

Some have suggested that the "secular purpose" part of this test had been used two years before in the Sunday closing law cases, particularly McGOWAN v. MARYLAND, in which the laws, which originally had the purpose of compelling observance of the Christian day of worship, were found constitutional because they now had a secular purpose of providing a day of rest. But in those cases the secular purpose of only Sunday closing laws was at issue, whereas in the *Schempp* opinion the test was generalized to apply not solely to the cases at bar but to all legislation involving the Establishment Clause.

In 1970 a third test was set forth, this time by Chief Justice Burger in WALZ v. TAX COMMISSION. This case challenged the legality of tax exemptions for properties used for religious worship. In finding tax exemptions constitutional, the Chief Justice declared that the elimination of exemptions would cause government officials to evaluate church property for tax purposes and, in the case of default, to initiate legal proceedings against the churches, thus causing "excessive entanglement" between government and religion. He reasoned:

> Granting tax exemptions to churches necessarily operates to afford all indirect economic benefit and also gives rise to some, but yet a lesser, involvement than taxing them. In analyzing either alternative the questions are whether it is a continuing one calling for official and continuing surveillance leading to an impermissible degree of entanglement (397 U.S. 664, 674).

(The "secular purpose," "primary effect," and "excessive entanglement" tests are frequently called the *Lemon* test because they were first used together in LEMON v. KURTZMAN.)

In *Walz*, Justice Harlan mentioned that practices such as tax exemption may also cause political controversy, a different kind of government involvement in religious life that also ought to be avoided. In some of the cases subsequent to *Walz*, the possibility of political divisiveness was mentioned, e.g., proponents of government aid to parochial schools trying to influence legislatures and/or candidates while opponents try to blunt their efforts. In these cases the warning was given that political division along religious lines was the very kind of thing the Establishment Clause was intended to avoid. From time to time different justices, usually when writing in dissent, have argued that the political divisiveness dimension of the entanglement test should be raised to the level of a fourth test for interpreting the Establishment Clause. But the suggestion has never been implemented.

Through 1982, the Court steered a middle course between the rigid separationism of *Everson and Engel* and the flexible accommodationism of *Zorach*. The three tests were applied in such a way that there can be indirect aid to a religious institution if the purpose of that legislation is secular, if its primary effect is neither to aid nor to inhibit religion, and if the involvement between a religious institution and government is not excessive. Words such as "primary" and "excessive" are not totally clear in meaning, but they allowed courts a measure of flexibility in interpreting the Establishment Clause, thus permitting them to avoid hostility to religion without lowering the bars to direct aid to religion.

The three components of the test are independent of each other. Thus, a law may pass two of the tests, fail one, and be declared unconstitutional.

The purpose of the "secular purpose" test is to ascertain the government's intent in a piece of legislation, to see whether or not it was designed to advance or inhibit religion. If either purpose is present, the law is unconstitutional. Since its introduction, however, the "secular purpose" test has not been the deciding factor in most of the cases that have come before the Court, primarily because legislatures have become more sophisticated in writing a secular purpose into their legislative enactments, although as recently as EDWARDS v. AGUILLARD (1987) and TEXAS MONTHLY v. BULLOCK (1989) state statutes were struck down because they lacked a secular purpose.[14]

The "primary effect" test goes beyond the intent of the law to determine its effect as it is implemented and enforced. The primary effect of the law must be neither to advance nor to inhibit religion, although this language leaves open the possibility of some slight or indirect aid. The effect of a law may be determined first by an analysis of the religious permeation of the recipient institution. That is, how religious is the institution receiving aid? There are some institutions which are pervasively religious, e.g., churches. Others are less thoroughly permeated by religion, e.g., parochial schools. Still others are only slightly permeated by religion; they are collaterally religious, e.g., many church-affiliated colleges and universities. The more pervasively religious the institution receiving government aid, the more likely it is that the law will be found unconstitutional as a violation of the establishment clause.

A second factor in the application of the "primary effect" test is that of severability. That is, how independent of its religious function is the secular function of the institution receiving aid. Are the functions sufficiently distinct from each other so that state aid flows only to the secular function and not to the religious function? If so, the program under scrutiny will probably pass the "primary effect" test;[15] if not, it will fail.

The "excessive entanglement" test is related, at least in part, to the "primary effect" test. That is, if a program is of such a nature that it requires regular government inspection or surveillance to make sure the effect of the program is not aiding or hindering religion, that surveillance itself is a violation of the Establishment Clause because it brings government and religion into too much interaction. Supervisory observation to remedy the impermissible effect of the aid program, if done on a continual and extensive basis, constitutes excessive and forbidden entanglement.[16]

Between *Walz* and LARSON v. VALENTE (1982), the three tests were used in all Establishment Clause cases. The Court's attitude during that period is summarized in COMMITTEE FOR PUBLIC EDUCATION v. NYQUIST, referring to the three-part test: "these [previous Establishment Clause] decisions dictate that to pass muster under the Establishment Clause the law in question must" conform to the test.[17] And in 1982, in LARKIN v. GRENDEL'S DEN: "This Court has consistently held that a statute must satisfy three criteria to pass muster under the Establishment Clause. . . ."[18] But earlier in that same year, the Court's consistent use of the tests had begun to waver. In *Larson*, the Court declared that the tests were applicable to laws "affording a uniform benefit to *all* religions," not to laws "that discriminate *among* religions."[19] The case was decided on equal protection grounds: the statute was given strict scrutiny and judged to be discriminating between religions.

In subsequent cases, the results and the rhetoric showed much less commitment to the use of the *Lemon* test. In MARSH v. CHAMBERS the Court did not even mention the three-part test, much less apply it. Rather, an argument from history was used to find the employment of chaplains in state legislatures to be constitutional. In MUELLER v. ALLEN and LYNCH v. DONNELLY the tests were utilized to reach the decision, but in the process language was used which made it appear that the tests were used more out of convenience than commitment. In referring to the three-part test, *Mueller* says: "While this principle is well settled, our cases have also emphasized that it provides 'no more than [a] helpful signpost' in dealing with Establishment Clause challenges."[20] In *Lynch*: "But, we have repeatedly emphasized our unwillingness to be confined to any single test or criterion in this sensitive area."[21] In that same case, Justice O'Connor, concurring, suggested a redefinition of the three-part test, in which the purpose and effect prongs would prohibit government endorsement or disapproval of religion, i.e., when a law makes adherence to religion relevant to a person's standing in the political community. The entanglement prong would prohibit only institutional entanglement of religion with government, not any and all kinds of entanglement. She repeated this view in WALLACE v. JAFFREE (1986), adding, over against Justice Rehnquist, who proposed that the three-part test be abandoned, that she was not yet ready to discard the test. However, by the time of her dissent in AGUILAR v. FELTON, her thinking had changed to the point that she was virtually willing to abandon the entanglement part of the test. Justice Stevens, writing for the majority in *Jaffree*, employed the three-part test and used Justice

[14]Cf. also STONE v. GRAHAM (1980) and WALLACE v. JAFFREE (1985).

[15]Cf. the reasoning in BOARD OF EDUCATION v. ALLEN (1968).

[16]An example of this process is LEMON v. KURTZMAN (1971). These principles of interpreting the Establishment Clause are derived in part from the very helpful article by Denise Cote, "Establishment Clause Analysis of Legislative and Administrative Aid to Religion," *Columbia Law Review* 74 (1974): 1175–1202.

[17]413 U.S. 756 at 772-773 (emphasis added).

[18]459 U.S. 116 at 123 (emphasis added).

[19]456 U.S. 228 at 252. However, the Court did go on to say that the statute at issue in *Larson* was violative of the entanglement test.

[20]463 U.S. 388 at 394, quoting *Hunt* v. *McNair* 413 U.S. 734 at 741 (1973).

[21]465 U.S. 668 at 679.

O'Connor's concept that the secular purpose prong is violated if the law endorses religion. He called that the dispositive point in the case. In a concurring opinion, Justice Powell described the three-part test as "the only coherent test a majority of the Court has ever adopted." Far from wanting to abandon it or even to reinterpret it, he counseled against criticizing the test.

Taken together, the cases between 1982 and 1986 show that there developed among the justices a lack of unanimity about the meaning and applicability of the "*Lemon* test." Consistency was the loser in this development. Interestingly, the cases between 1987 and 1991 do not show the same inconsistency. Of the nine Establishment Clause cases added to the fourth edition of this book, eight explicitly utilize the three-part test in reaching their decisions, or at least refer to it.[22] One was decided on statutory, rather than constitutional, grounds.[23] However, of those eight, three[24] used Justice O'Connor's reinterpretation from *Lynch* to describe the functioning of the three-part test. This terminology is best summarized in a statement in *Texas Monthly*, which says that the "core notion" of the *Lemon* test

> is not only that government may not be overtly hostile to religion but also that it may not place its prestige, coercive authority, or resources behind a single religious faith or behind religion in general, compelling nonadherents to support the practices or proselytizing of favored religious organizations and conveying the message that those who do not contribute gladly are less than full members of the community (489 U.S. 1, 9).

Concurrently with the emergence of evidence that the justices did not agree on how to apply the three-part test, the Court began to waver between a separationist interpretation of the Establishment Clause, which had been its tendency prior to 1982, and an accommodationist one. In *Marsh* the Court found state-paid chaplains to legislatures to be consistent with the Constitution. *Mueller* allowed state income tax deductions to help finance children's tuitions to both public and private, including church-related, schools. *Lynch* declared that cities may constitutionally finance the erection and display of a nativity scene and went so far as to say: "Nor does the Constitution require complete separation of church and state: it *affirmatively mandates accommodation*, not merely tolerance, of all religions, and forbids hostility toward any."[25] However, the Court did not completely adopt an accommodationist stance. In *Jaffree* a law mandating a minute of silence for meditation or voluntary prayer was declared unconstitutional, as were plans to provide government-paid teachers in parochial schools in AGUILAR v. FELTON and GRAND RAPIDS SCHOOL DISTRICT v. BALL.

The cases since 1987 exhibited a similar ambivalence. Six of them are separationist, denying government aid to religion.[26] But BOWEN v. KENDRICK held that a law allowing federal funds to be used by religious organizations in programs of sex education was not facially unconstitutional, ALLEGHENY v. ACLU held that a religious symbol on public property is not an establishment of religion (so long as it is accompanied by symbols that communicate that Chanukah/Christmas is a cultural holiday), and BOARD OF EDUCATION v. MERGENS acquiesced in the "equal access" of religious clubs in public schools, under specified conditions.

However, what many thought was more portentous of change in the Court's Establishment Clause doctrine were dissents by some of the Reagan appointees. In the same vein as Chief Justice Rehnquist's extremely accommodationist dissent in *Jaffree*, Justice Scalia's dissents in EDWARDS v. AGUILLARD and TEXAS MONTHLY v. BULLOCK argue strongly for accommodationism, as does Justice Kennedy's stinging dissent in ALLEGHENY v. ACLU, in which he argues for a reversal of the Court's Establishment Clause doctrine since *Everson* and the adoption of a new standard which would allow all government participation in religion except coercion to religious behavior or direct benefits which create a state religion (492 U.S. 573, 658-660).

However, in his opinion for the Court in LEE v. WEISMAN, Justice Kennedy seemed to be much more traditional in his approach to the Establishment Clause than his revisionist dissent in *Allegheny* would have led one to anticipate. Although he thought there was an element of coercion in the offering of prayers in the commencement context,

> We can decide the case without reconsidering the general constitutional framework by which public schools' efforts to accommodate religion are measured. Thus we do not accept the invitation of petitioners and amicus the United States to reconsider our decision

[22]HERNANDEZ v. COMMISSIONER, TEXAS MONTHLY v. BULLOCK, ALLEGHENY v. ACLU, CHURCH OF LATTER-DAY SAINTS v. AMOS, BOARD OF EDUCATION v. MERGENS, EDWARDS v. AGUILLARD, BOWEN v. KENDRICK, and LEE v. WEISMAN. In addition, JIMMY SWAGGART MINISTRIES v. CALIFORNIA, although decided primarily on free exercise grounds, also refers to the *Lemon* test in holding that the state tax does not create excessive entanglement between California and the ministry.

[23]DAVIS v. UNITED STATES.

[24]ALLEGHENY v. ACLU, BOARD OF EDUCATION v. MERGENS, and TEXAS MONTHLY v. BULLOCK.

[25]465 U.S. 668 at 673 (emphasis added).

[26]HERNANDEZ v. COMMISSIONER, TEXAS MONTHLY v. BULLOCK, CHURCH OF LATTER-DAY SAINTS v. AMOS, EDWARDS v. AGUILLARD, DAVIS v. UNITED STATES, and LEE v. WEISMAN.

> in *Lemon* v. *Kurtzman*. The government involvement with religious activity in this case is pervasive, to the point of creating a state-sponsored and state-directed religious exercise in a public school. Conducting this formal religious observance conflicts with settled rules pertaining to prayer exercises for students, and that suffices to determine the question before us (505 U.S. 577, 587).[27]

Interestingly, in separate concurring opinions Justice Blackmun explicitly criticized the coercion standard and Justice Souter did the same for both a "nonpreferentialist" interpretation of the Establishment Clause and the coercion standard. It is as if they were staking out positions for future Establishment Clause battles.

In LAMB'S CHAPEL v. CENTER MORICHES SCHOOL DISTRICT (1993), the Court held that a public school district which had allowed other outside groups to use its facilities could not deny such access to churches. More to the point, given that the school district had allowed other groups to use the facilities to communicate about the role of families in society but had denied that opportunity to a group who wanted to address that subject from a religious point of view, the school district was guilty of impermissible viewpoint discrimination. In reaching that conclusion, Justice White, for the Court, very briefly, in an almost off-hand comment, wrote that permission to use the school property would not constitute establishment of religion as measured by the *Lemon* test.

Justice Scalia, joined by Justice Thomas, concurred in the judgment but failed to accept most of the reasoning. He expressed in scathing terms his dislike for the Court's use of the *Lemon* test:

> Like some ghoul in a late-night horror movie that repeatedly sits up in its grave and shuffles abroad after being repeatedly killed and buried, *Lemon* stalks our Establishment Clause jurisprudence once again, frightening the little children and school attorneys of Center Moriches Union Free School District. . . . The secret of the *Lemon* test's survival, I think, is that it is so easy to kill. It is there to scare us (and our audience) when we wish it to do so, but we can command it to return to the tomb at will (508 U.S. 384, 398-399).

The Court, he said, uses the test to invalidate a practice it forbids but ignores the test when it wishes to uphold a practice. Justice Scalia took his stand with the many critics of the test in stating that he would refuse to apply *Lemon*. He also took issue with the Court's use of the "endorsement of religion" concept.

Justice White, in a footnote in the majority opinion, responded to Justice Scalia:

> While we are somewhat diverted by Justice Scalia's evening at the cinema, we return to the reality that there is a proper way to inter an established decision and *Lemon*, however frightening it might be to some, has not been overruled. This case, like *Corporation of Presiding Bishop of Church of Jesus Christ of Latter-day Saints* v. *Amos*, presents no occasion to do so. Justice Scalia apparently was less haunted by the ghosts of the living when he joined the opinion of the Court in that case (508 U.S. 384, 395).

Justice Scalia responded with a footnote of his own, in which he said that in *Amos* there was no majority in favor of discarding *Lemon*, so he joined the Court's opinion. But in this case, the lower courts did not invoke, or even mention, *Lemon* in reaching their decisions, so it was inappropriate for the Supreme Court to invoke it.

Justice Kennedy, concurring in part in a brief opinion, agreed with the judgment. Like Justice Scalia, he thought the case should have been decided on the basis of free speech, without consideration of the Establishment Clause or of endorsement of religion, that the citation of *Lemon* was "unsettling and unnecessary."

In ZOBREST v. CATALINA FOOTHILLS SCHOOL DISTRICT, the Court arrived at essentially an accommodationist decision by ignoring the *Lemon* test. Although it relied on two cases which utilized the test, *Mueller* and *Witters*, *Zobrest* did not even mention it. Chief Justice Rehnquist decided that the plaintiff could be provided a sign language interpreter in his parochial school under a federal program because "We have never said that 'religious institutions are disabled by the First Amendment from participating in publicly sponsored social welfare programs.'"[28] Because the government program made money available to disabled students generally and because the school they attended was solely at the discretion of their parents, rather than any government agency, the program was constitutional. Like *Zobrest* before it, KIRYAS JOEL SCHOOL DISTRICT v. GRUMET was decided without reference to the *Lemon* test. *Kiryas Joel* tested the constitutionality of a public school district created by the New York legislature for a community composed entirely of Satmar Hasidic Jews. The Court concluded that such a public school district was a violation of the Establishment Clause. In reaching that decision it relied heavily on LARKIN v. GRENDEL'S DEN (1982), in which the granting of what amounted to legislative

---

[27]The *amicus* to which he refers was a request by the Bush Administration that the Court adopt the Establishment Clause jurisprudence articulated by Justice Kennedy in *Allegheny* as its procedure for interpreting the clause.

[28]509 U.S.1, 8, quoting BOWEN v. KENDRICK.

authority to churches was declared unconstitutional. *Larkin* said that intermixing of religious and governmental functions had the impermissible primary effect of advancing religion and creating an excessive entanglement between religion and government, two prongs of the *Lemon* test. However, *Kiryas Joel* reached similar conclusions without relying on the test at all. In short, *Kiryas Joel* relied heavily on the result of *Grendel's Den* while ignoring its reasoning.

However, this nonemployment of the *Lemon* test did not go unnoticed by other members of the Court, who explicitly commented on it. Justice Blackmun, in a concurring opinion, wrote to say that the Court's slighting of *Lemon* did not signify a departure from the principles contained therein. He seemed to be saying that the Court in fact utilized the second and third prongs of *Lemon*, it just did not explicitly mention them. He concluded by stressing his commitment to "the general validity of the basic principles stated in *Lemon*."[29]

Justice O'Connor's concurring opinion contained extensive comments about her increasing disenchantment with the *Lemon* test. Although she had written in concurring in WALLACE v. JAFFREE that she was "not yet ready to abandon all aspects of the *Lemon* test," she now appeared to be ready to make that move. She expressed doubt about the validity of a unified theory which would be applicable in all Establishment Clause cases, since they are not all the same. Because the *Lemon* test was once thought to be such an all-encompassing theory, her skepticism now caused her to have serious doubts about it.

> As the Court's opinion today shows, the slide away from *Lemon*'s unitary approach is well under way. A return to *Lemon*, even if possible, would likely be futile, regardless of where one stands on the substantive Establishment Clause questions. I think a less unitary approach provides a better structure for analysis. . . . And abandoning the *Lemon* framework need not mean abandoning some of the insights that the test reflected, nor the insights of the cases that applied it (114 S.Ct. 2481, 2500).

Justice Scalia, in his long dissent, devoted two paragraphs to the status of the *Lemon* test. He declared it to be "inefficient" and altogether not worth much. But he would differ from Justice O'Connor, who, he said, would replace *Lemon* with nothing. He would interpret the Establishment Clause with historical precedent. "The foremost principle I would apply is fidelity to the longstanding traditions of our people, which surely provide the diversity of treatment that Justice O'Connor seeks, but do not leave us to our own devices." (114 S.Ct. 2481, 2515.)

In ROSENBERGER v. UNIVERSITY OF VIRGINIA (1995), the Court again decided an Establishment Clause case without mentioning the *Lemon* test. The University had denied *Wide Awake*, a student publication with distinctly Christian content, support from student activity funds on the grounds that to give that support would violate the Establishment Clause. Justice Kennedy, writing for the Court, held that the University had improperly denied those funds because the denial amounted to viewpoint discrimination, impermissible under the Free Speech Clause. But it remained to be decided whether such discrimination was mandated by the Establishment Clause.

Justice Kennedy began his analysis by writing:

> If there is to be assurance that the Establishment Clause retains its force in guarding against those governmental actions it was intended to prohibit, we must in each case inquire first into the purpose and object of the governmental action in question and then into the practical details of the program's operation (115 S.Ct. 2510, 2521).

That sounds very much like the "secular purpose" and the "primary effect" prongs of the *Lemon* test in different terminology. If Justice Kennedy was aware of that, he did not reveal it. He proceeded to analyze the case without any mention of the three-part test. The "purpose and object" of the student activities fund program was to provide a limited open forum and to support various student activities, including publications, to the end of fostering free speech and intellectual stimulation which reflected the diversity of the student body. Within that framework, the school's policy was neutral toward religion, seeking neither to advance nor to inhibit religion. The "practical details of the program's operation" were that the University denied student activities funding to *Wide Awake*. That was impermissible under the neutrality required by the Establishment Clause because "*[Wide Awake]* did not seek subsidy because of its Christian editorial viewpoint; it sought funding as a student journal, which it was." (115 S.Ct. 2510, 2522.) Given that the University had created a category of student publications of a wide variety for funding from student activity funds, it was not required by the Establishment Clause to deny funds to *Wide Awake*. "There is no Establishment Clause violation in the University's honoring its duties under the Free Speech Clause" (115 S.Ct. 2510, 2525).

Consequently, the Court decided this case on the basis of the first two prongs of the *Lemon* test without acknowledging it and, perhaps, without realizing it. But, at least in the view of Justice Souter and

---

[29]Of course, Justice Blackmun retired at the end of the Court's 1994–95 term. Consequently, his voice of commitment to *Lemon* is no longer heard.

Justices Ginsburg, Stevens, and Breyer, who joined in his dissent, in the process the Court had weakened the Establishment Clause beyond anything the *Lemon* test had ever permitted. It allowed the Clause to approve government financial support of explicitly theological, sectarian speech.

CAPITOL SQUARE REVIEW BOARD v. PINETTE (1995) was very much like *Rosenberger.* It dealt with the question of whether religious speech on public property violates the Establishment Clause. That the speech involved was of a private group, the Ku Klux Klan, in an area long used as a traditional public forum, was dispositive of the case. The Establishment Clause does not forbid a government entity from allowing private religious speech, so long as the private group meets the same time, place, and manner restrictions imposed by the state on all other expressions on the state's property. Petitioners, the board responsible for the supervision of Capitol Square, argued that the close proximity of the Klan's cross to the seat of government would be seen by observers to be the endorsement of religion by government. This gave Justice Scalia, the author of the plurality opinion, opportunity to reject the idea of "the" endorsement test or even "an" endorsement test for interpreting the Establishment Clause. He did not even mention the *Lemon* test, for which he had expressed contempt in the past, and denied any kind of status to the endorsement test originally proposed by Justice O'Connor in LYNCH v. DONNELLY (1984) and used in some cases since then. He alleged the petitioners were urging on the Court a "transferred endorsement" test, i.e., one that would attribute governmental status to private religious speech. He refused to accept the invitation. The case could be, and was, decided on the principle that it is not a violation of the no establishment principle for the government to enact neutral policies that happen to benefit religion. That was the case when the Capitol Square Review Board allowed the Klan to erect its cross in what was clearly an open public forum, available to all.

In separate opinions concurring in part and in the judgment, Justices O'Connor and Souter lamented Justice Scalia's dismissal of the endorsement test for a *per se* rule for adjudicating Establishment Clause cases. They each argued that the endorsement test would have had applicability in the case at bar and that it provided a more principled way courts can deal with acceptability under the Establishment Clause of private religious expression in public fora. Likewise, Justice Stevens, in his dissent, chided the plurality for not applying the endorsement test. Unlike Justices O'Connor and Souter, however, he contended that if the Court had been willing to apply the endorsement standard, it would have had to have held the action of the Review Board, in approving of the Klan's cross in Capitol Square, unconstitutional.

STANDING TO SUE

With good reason the American people have looked upon the Supreme Court of the United States as the ultimate defender of the dual constitutional principles of religious liberty and separation of church and state. However, the Court has not always proved receptive to challenges to governmental actions alleged to violate those principles, especially when brought by individuals or groups in the absence of criminal prosecution by the state.

All courts exercise a measure of control over their dockets, but the Supreme Court possesses a unique discretion as to what will be considered. Constitutional and statutory provisions fix some jurisdictional and procedural limits; but to a remarkable degree the Court, through self-imposed restraints, determines the cases and issues it will hear on appeal from state and lower federal courts. Through this supervisory power and the governing judicial precedents, the Court also exerts great control over the dockets of the lower federal courts. Judicial answers to significant constitutional questions have frequently been avoided or delayed because the courts declined to take jurisdiction over the cases in which they were raised. Since the restraints are largely self-imposed, the Court is free to overlook or reconsider them should it become convinced either that the query has become so critical as to demand response or that the times are more propitious for that response.

In the exercise of control over its work load, the Supreme Court has developed over the years a considerable number of rules, understandings, and procedural techniques that can be invoked.[1] The Court, for example, will not render "advisory opinions," that is, will not give answers to hypothetical questions. It insists that there be an actual "case or controversy" with a concrete set of facts in which adverse parties have a substantial legal interest. An appeal may also be rejected as involving a "political," as opposed to a "justiciable," question.

"Standing to sue" is the procedural requirement that has most often created a problem for those seeking to question the constitutionality of a practice of government as infringing one or both of the religion clauses. This important but complicated and nebulous concept has been held to mean that the party bringing the suit must convince the Court that the interest presented is a substantial and legally

[1]A helpful discussion of the "maxims of judicial self-restraint" can be found in Henry J. Abraham, *The Judicial Process: An Introductory Analysis of the Courts of the United States, England, and France*, 6th ed. (New York: Oxford University Press, 1993), pp. 348–70; cf. also C. Herman Pritchett, *The American Constitution*, 3rd ed. (New York: McGraw-Hill Book Co., 1977), pp. 129–36.

protected interest; that it has been injured or is in direct danger of such injury; and that it is a personal right peculiar to him or her—not just one shared with all other persons generally. Obviously, proof of these requisites is a formidable assignment, particularly if the Court is not sympathetic to the substance of the appellant's cause.

One avenue of attack, which was until 1968 unavailable in federal courts due to the Supreme Court's interpretation of standing, is the taxpayer's suit. This is a rather commonly used method of contesting the constitutionality of municipal and state actions. The theory of such litigation is that the taxpayer has standing because if tax money taken by government is used for an unconstitutional purpose, the taxpayer, in effect, has been deprived of property without due process of law.

In 1923 the Supreme Court was confronted with such a suit when Mrs. Frothingham, a citizen of the District of Columbia, challenged the constitutionality of the Federal Maternity Act of 1921. A unanimous Court denied Mrs. Frothingham's standing to sue, saying with respect to the status of a United States taxpayer: "His interest in the moneys of the Treasury—partly realized from taxation and partly from other sources—is shared with millions of others; is comparatively minute and indeterminable; and the effect upon future taxation of any payment out of the funds, so remote, fluctuating and uncertain that no basis is afforded for an appeal to the preventive powers of a court of equity" (262 U.S. 447, 487).

Because *Frothingham* v. *Mellon* related only to federal taxpayers' suits, it did not inhibit continued use of such litigation at the state level. Appeals of these decisions to the Supreme Court have sometimes been accepted, sometimes rejected. The Court has never enunciated a clear doctrine as to what extent the standing issue is resolved through acceptance of a case by the state court. In 1952, for example, two residents of New Jersey challenged the practice of Bible reading in a public high school. One sued as a taxpayer, the other both as a taxpayer and as a parent of a pupil in the school. When the New Jersey court ruled in favor of the challenged practice, appeal was made to the Supreme Court. The appeal was denied on the basis of lack of standing in *Doremus* v. *Board of Education*, the Court noting that one plaintiff was only a taxpayer and that the other plaintiff's child was no longer a student in the school. Justice Jackson distinguished the situation in *Doremus*, where there was no increase in cost of education, from that in EVERSON v. BOARD OF EDUCATION, in which the Court had accepted an appeal of the same state's school busing practices. *Everson*, he said, "showed a measurable appropriation or disbursement of school-district funds occasioned solely by the activities complained of." He made no mention of COCHRAN v. LOUISIANA STATE BOARD OF EDUCATION, where the Court had seemingly accepted jurisdiction because the state court had assumed the presence of standing.

Although the theoretical position of the Court was thus left rather unclear, it soon became evident that the Court was substantially relaxing its standing requirement with respect to the review of state taxpayers' suits in which there was an allegation of denial of constitutional rights. The same year the Court rejected the *Doremus* case, it accepted jurisdiction in ZORACH v. CLAUSON. There the petitioners sought appeal based on their status as parents of children in a school in which released time was used. It would have been difficult to show any added tax burden resulting from the practice involved. Ten years later the Court took and decided ENGEL v. VITALE without even discussing the question of standing.

The body of the text of the Court's opinion in ABINGTON TOWNSHIP SCHOOL DISTRICT v. SCHEMPP (1963) was likewise silent as to the question of standing. The only reference to the issue is found in a footnote to Justice Clark's opinion. There, in this rather inconspicuous spot, he indicated that the Court had made a major concession with respect to standing for those presenting challenges based on the Establishment Clause. He wrote: "But the requirements for standing to challenge state action under the Establishment Clause, unlike those relating to the Free Exercise Clause, do not include proof that particular religious freedoms are infringed" (374 U.S. 844, 859). He then commented that the interests of the school children and the parents who were affected by the laws and practices in question would "surely suffice" to give them standing.

In 1968 the appeal of a young school teacher, who had sought an injunction from a state court seeking to prevent enforcement of the Arkansas "monkey law" against her, was accepted and upheld in EPPERSON v. ARKANSAS, although the state had neither undertaken to enforce the statute nor given any evidence that it ever intended to. It is most unlikely that an earlier Court would have seriously considered the appeal.[2]

In the early 1960s, *Frothingham* v. *Mellon* took on added significance for both supporters and opponents of state aid to parochial schools as bills providing for federal aid to education were hotly debated in each session of Congress. Separationists feared that the holding in the 1923 case would prevent any judicial review as to the constitutionality of the provi-

[2]Leo Pfeffer says that *Epperson* illustrates the point "that there is no way to make the Supreme Court take a case when it does not want to, and not much of a way to stop it from taking a case when it wants to take it." *God, Caesar, and the Constitution: The Court as Referee of Church-State Confrontation* (Boston: Beacon Press, 1975), p. 222.

sions for parochial aid, which the act would almost certainly contain. Amendments were repeatedly attached to the proposals to provide for judicial review by means of taxpayers' suits, but the comprehensive Federal Elementary and Secondary Aid to Education Act was passed in 1965 without any such condition. Under the leadership of Senator Sam Ervin of North Carolina, new measures that would have granted standing to challenge alleged violations of the First Amendment were introduced in the Senate, only to die in the House.[3]

In the face of these legislative defeats, seven taxpayers in 1967 brought suit against the 1965 act in a federal district court in New York. They sought to enjoin the Secretary of Health, Education, and Welfare, on constitutional grounds, from spending funds under the act for services and textbooks for religious schools. The district court dismissed the case (*Flast* v. *Gardner*) for lack of standing under the *Frothingham* rule, but the Supreme Court granted certiorari and heard the case in 1968 as FLAST v. COHEN.[4]

Without passing on the constitutionality of the Elementary and Secondary Education Act itself, and without expressly overruling *Frothingham*, the Supreme Court, by an eight-to-one vote, lowered the barrier against taxpayer suits challenging federal expenditures as violations of the Establishment Clause. Such suits could be entertained, said Chief Justice Warren, provided a taxpayer could demonstrate a two-point "nexus": "First, the taxpayer must establish a logical link between that status and the type of legislative enactment attacked. . . . Secondly, the taxpayer must establish a nexus between that status and the precise nature of the constitutional infringement alleged" (392 U.S. 83, 102). To establish the second nexus the taxpayer must prove that the challenged statute exceeds limits imposed by the Constitution on the exercise of the taxing and spending power. Appellants here had met all the tests and were now free to pursue their suits on its merits in the appropriate court.

Justice Douglas concurred in the opinion but would have preferred to go further and overturn *Frothingham* completely. That the majority of the Court was not willing to do so but, instead, rather narrowly limited the breach in the *Frothingham* rule to First Amendment establishment claims is significant in itself. It indicates the high priority the justices attached to those claims.

The Supreme Court has never passed on the constitutionality of the Elementary and Secondary Education Act since the 1968 decision. Nevertheless, FLAST v. COHEN is a landmark decision. It not only removed an almost insurmountable barrier to challenges of federal aid to church-related schools, but also opened more widely the doors of federal courts to taxpayer suits against state aid. The significance of the latter development is attested to by the number of such cases subsequently accepted and decided.

In 1982 the Burger Court backed away from the door opened in *Flast* by a narrow vote of five-to-four in VALLEY FORGE CHRISTIAN COLLEGE v. AMERICANS UNITED FOR SEPARATION OF CHURCH AND STATE. The *Valley Forge* case arose in 1978 when Americans United and four of its employees filed suit in a United States district court in Pennsylvania. They challenged the action of the then Department of Health, Education, and Welfare when that government agency conveyed, without charge, seventy acres of land and the buildings of a "surplus" government hospital to a denominational school then called Northeast Bible College. The suit charged violation of the Establishment Clause and alleged that each member of the organization dedicated to separation of church and state "would be deprived of the fair and constitutional use of his (her) tax dollars." The district court failed to find standing and dismissed the complaint. Appeal was sought, and the Third Circuit Court of Appeals held that the claimants had standing as citizens who had shown a "particular and concrete injury" to a "personal, constitutional right," if not as taxpayers.

Justice Rehnquist wrote the majority opinion of the Supreme Court and was joined by Justices Burger, White, Powell, and O'Connor. Rehnquist agreed with the district court that those seeking to bring the suit had "failed to allege that they have suffered any actual or concrete injury beyond a generalized grievance common to all tax-payers." On rather narrow technical grounds, he distinguished the fact situation here from that in *Flast*: in that case it was congressional action and exercise of the Taxing and Spending Clause of Article I which was challenged;

[3]However, Representative Emanuel Celler, at the insistence of the National Council of Churches, read into the record an assurance that judicial review would be available to resolve any constitutional issues arising under the act.

[4]The significance attached to the case is indicated by the individuals and interest groups that were involved in the Supreme Court hearing. Senator Ervin filed an *amicus curiae* brief for The Americans for Public Schools et al. and joined Leo Pfeffer and other attorneys in arguing the case for the appellants. *Amicus curiae* briefs were also filed on behalf of appellants by the National Council of Churches, Americans United for Separation of Church and State, the American Jewish Committee, and Council of Chief State School Officers. Solicitor General E. N. Griswold argued on behalf of Cohen and *amicus curiae* briefs were filed for the A.F.L.-C.I.O, the National Jewish Commission on Law and Public Affairs, and various private parties. Because of the practical requirement of legal expertise and substantial sums of money to bring such suits, participation of such groups is essential.

in the instant case it was action by an executive department and an exercise of congressional power under the Property Clause of Article IV.

The opinion saw no basis for creation of a "hierarchy of constitutional values" that would justify a standard of easier court access to those invoking religious rights. Justice Rehnquist also struck out at amicus groups such as Americans United:

> Their claim that the government has violated the Establishment Clause does not provide a special license to roam the country in search of governmental wrongdoing and to reveal their discoveries in federal court. The federal courts were simply not constituted as ombudsmen of the general welfare (454 U.S. 464, 487).

At another point he commented that "standing is not measured by the intensity of the litigant's interest or the fervor of his advocacy." Joined by Justices Marshall and Blackmun, Justice Brennan wrote a vigorous dissent, citing the majority opinion as "a stark example of the unfortunate trend of resolving cases at the 'threshold' while obscuring the nature of the underlying rights and interests at stake." Brennan charged that the Court was "blind to history" when it sought to distinguish the case from *Flast*, and he contended, "Surely . . . a taxpayer must have standing at the time that he learns of the Government's alleged Establishment Clause violation to seek equitable relief in order to halt the continuing and intolerable burden on his pocketbook, his conscience, and his constitutional rights" (454 U.S. 464, 490-91, 509).

In a separate dissent, Justice Stevens argued that *Flast* has given a special position to establishment claims and would not allow for the "drawing of a tenuous distinction between the Spending Clause and the Property Clause." The *Valley Forge* decision, by limiting access to those able to prove direct, personal, actual injury, undoubtedly made suits against federal action on establishment grounds much more difficult and therefore much less likely to be brought.

The degree to which the Court will ultimately retreat toward its pre-*Flast* stance is not yet clear. However, there is no doubt that the Burger Court continued to move away from the more liberalized standing policy of the Warren Court. For example, in 1984, in a case not involving church-state issues, the Court in *Allen* v. *Wright* denied standing to parents with black children in public schools undergoing desegregation who sought to challenge regulations of the IRS concerning tax-exemption entitlement of private schools that discriminate against blacks. Justice Brennan, as in the *Valley Forge* case, complained bitterly that "Once again the Court 'uses' standing to slam the court house door against plaintiffs who are entitled to full consideration of their claims on the merits" (468 U.S. 764). Justice Stevens also filed a dissenting opinion in which Justice Blackmun joined.

Two years later the Court again invoked lack of standing to avoid ruling, at least temporarily, on the highly controversial issue of "equal access," a practice that will be discussed at a later point. The voting alignment of the judges was noticeably different in *Bender* v. *Williamsport Area School District* from that in *Valley Forge* and *Allen* v. *Wright*. In *Bender* it was Justices Stevens, Brennan, Blackmun, and Marshall, joined this time by Justice O'Connor, who used standing to refrain from a decision on the merits of an appellant's claim.

In 1981, a group of high school students in Williamsport, Pennsylvania, organized "Petros," a club that they said would promote "spiritual growth and positive attitudes in the lives of its members." After consulting with the school district's legal counsel, the principal and superintendent denied the request of members of the organization to meet on campus during the school's activity period to read scripture, discuss religious matters, and pray. When the negative decision was upheld by the school board, the students and their parents filed suit in the United States District Court for the Middle District of Pennsylvania, alleging that the exclusion of Petros because of its religious activities violated the First Amendment.

The district court ruled that the school board would not have violated the Establishment Clause by authorizing Petros to meet on the same basis as other student groups. Rather, refusal to allow meetings had impermissibly infringed upon the students' right of free speech. The school board voted eight-to-one not to appeal the ruling, and Petros resumed its meetings.

Later, however, John C. Youngman, Jr., the only school board dissenter, appealed to the United States Court of Appeals for the Third Circuit. In 1984 that court held that the board authorization ultimately given to the club to meet had the primary effect of advancing religion and that teacher monitoring of the meetings involved an excessive entanglement of government and religion.

The Supreme Court granted the students' petition for certiorari and the case was argued 15 October 1985, at which time it became evident that the question of Mr. Youngman's standing to bring suit was a crucial issue. On 25 March 1986 the Court, by a vote of five-to-four, decided that he did not have standing to appeal as an individual, as a member of the board, or as a parent, and that the Court of Appeals had no jurisdiction to hear the appeal. The judgment of the appellate court was therefore vacated. Mr. Youngman, said Justice Stevens for the majority, had been sued not as an individual or a parent but in his official capacity as a member of the school board. As the lone dissenter, he had no standing to appeal a decision of the board, and he had not asserted a parental interest during the district court proceedings. The action taken by the Supreme Court reverted the issue to the District Court's decision, which was limited to only the Williamsport Area School District.

Chief Justice Burger, writing for Justices White and Rehnquist, would have accepted Youngman's standing as a parent of a student at Williamsport High and would have proceeded to the constitutional issue of granting the religious group equal access to the student activity forum. He, as did Justice Powell in a separate dissent, saw WIDMAR v. VINCENT as controlling.

Justice Powell made his position quite clear when he wrote, "I do not believe—particularly in this age of massive media information—that the few years difference in age between high school and college students justifies departing from Widmar" (475 U.S. 534, 559). Although Justice O'Connor voted with the majority in failing to find standing, her earlier interpretations of the Establishment Clause indicated that she would likely vote to uphold an equal access statute if it were decided by the Court on substantive grounds. Indeed, she wrote the majority opinion in the 1990 case, BOARD OF EDUCATION v. MERGENS. There the Court finally reached a decision on the merits of the "equal access" issue, holding that, under certain conditions, student-organized and student-led religious clubs in the public schools are not in violation of the Establishment Clause.

In 1985, in WALLACE v. JAFFREE, the Court held that a minute of silence in a public school classroom for purposes of prayer was contrary to the Establishment Clause. However, the law at bar in that case specifically mentioned prayer as a purpose of the minute of silence. Because even the justices who found the silence unconstitutional hinted broadly that they supported a strictly neutral moment of silence, many wondered what would be the fate of a law that mandated such a minute without explicitly mentioning prayer. It appeared that *Karcher* v. *May* would provide the answer, but it turned out to be what amounted to another standing case.

In 1982 the New Jersey legislature passed a law that would permit primary and secondary schools to begin the instructional day with a minute of silence. The statute specified that the silence was "to be used solely at the discretion of the individual student, . . . for quiet and private contemplation or introspection."[5] However, many must have had anxieties about the law, for it was passed over the governor's veto and the state attorney general announced that he would not defend the law if it were challenged. It was challenged by a variety of plaintiffs, including a school teacher and some parents of students, who named as defendants the state Department of Education, its commissioner, and the boards of education of two townships. They chose not to defend the law, either.

At that point, Alan Karcher, Speaker of the State General Assembly, and Carmen Orechio, President of the Senate, intervened as defendants on behalf of the legislature. The United States District Court for New Jersey found the law unconstitutional because it failed all three prongs of the *Lemon* test, *sub nom. May* v. *Cooperman.* The Court of Appeals affirmed the lower court's decision. Karcher and Orechio appealed the case to the Supreme Court, but prior to that, they had lost their positions as presiding legislative officers: they were still legislators, but they were no longer Speaker and President, respectively. In addition, the legislature, under its new leadership, withdrew its appeal. In fact, the legislature that had passed the minute of silence law had expired.

The question thus before the Supreme Court was whether two officers of a state legislature could pursue an appeal of a case when they no longer held those offices and the legislature itself had declined to continue its appeal. It decided that they could not. Justice O'Connor for the Court:

> In sum, Karcher and Orechio participated in this lawsuit in their official capacities as presiding officers of the New Jersey Legislature, but since they no longer hold those offices, they lack authority to pursue this appeal on behalf of the legislature. Karcher and Orechio as individual legislators and representatives of the 200th New Jersey Legislature are not "parties" entitled to appeal the Court of Appeals' judgment under 28 U.S.C. § 1254(2). Accordingly, we must dismiss their appeal for lack of jurisdiction (*Karcher* v. *May* 484 U.S. 72, 81).

However, the Court held that its ruling did not vacate the judgments of the lower courts, so the end result of this case was that the moment of silence, without the mention of prayer, was unconstitutional, at least in New Jersey.

FLAST v. COHEN

392 U.S. 83
ON APPEAL FROM THE UNITED STATES DISTRICT COURT FOR
THE SOUTHERN DISTRICT OF NEW YORK
Argued March 12, 1968 — Decided June 10, 1968

⊥85 Mr. *Chief Justice WARREN* delivered the opinion of the Court.

In *Frothingham* v. *Mellon* this Court ruled that a federal taxpayer is without standing to challenge the constitutionality of a federal statute. That ruling has stood for 45 years as an impenetrable barrier to suits against Acts of Congress brought by individuals who can assert

[5] N. J. Stat. Ann. § 18A:36–4 (West Supp. 1987).

only the interest of federal taxpayers. In this case, we must decide whether the *Frothingham* barrier should be lowered when a taxpayer attacks a federal statute on the ground that it violates the Establishment and Free Exercise Clauses of the First Amendment.

Appellants filed suit in the United States District Court for the Southern District of New York to enjoin the allegedly unconstitutional expenditure of federal funds under Titles I and II of the Elementary and Secondary Education Act of 1965. The complaint alleged that the seven appellants had as a common attribute that "each pay[s] income taxes of the United States," and it is clear from the complaint that the appellants were resting their standing to maintain the action solely on their status as federal taxpayers. The appellees, who are charged by Congress with administering the Elementary and Secondary Education Act of 1965, were sued in their official capacities.

The gravamen of the appellants' complaint was that federal funds appropriated under the Act were being used to finance instruction in reading, arithmetic, and other subjects in religious schools, and to purchase textbooks ⊥**86** and other instructional materials for use in such schools. Such expenditures were alleged to be in contravention of the Establishment and Free Exercise Clauses of the First Amendment. Appellants' constitutional attack focused on the statutory criteria which state and local authorities must meet to be eligible for federal grants under the Act. Title I of the Act establishes a program for financial assistance to local educational agencies for the education of low-income families. Federal payments are made to state educational agencies, which pass the payments on in the form of grants to local educational agencies. Under § 205 of the Act, a local educational agency wishing to have a plan or program funded by a grant must submit the plan or program to the appropriate state educational agency for approval. The plan or program must be "consistent with such basic criteria as the [appellee United States Commissioner of Education] may establish." The specific criterion of that section attacked by the appellants is the requirement "that, to the extent consistent with the number of educationally deprived children in the school district of the local educational agency who are enrolled in private elementary and secondary schools, such agency has made provision for including special educational services and arrangements (such as dual enrollment, educational radio and television, and mobile educational services and equipment) in which such children can participate. . . ."

Under § 206 of the Act, the Commissioner of Education is given broad powers to supervise a State's participation in Title I programs and grants. Title II of the Act establishes a program of federal grants for the acquisition of school library resources, textbooks, ⊥**87** and other printed and published instructional materials "for the use of children and teachers in public and private elementary and secondary schools." A State wishing to participate in the program must submit a plan to the Commissioner for approval, and the plan must "provide assurance that to the extent consistent with law such library resources, textbooks, and other instructional materials will be provided on an equitable basis for the use of children and teachers in private elementary and secondary schools in the State. . . ."

While disclaiming any intent to challenge as unconstitutional all programs under Title I of the Act, the complaint alleges that federal funds have been disbursed under the Act, "with the consent and approval of the [appellees]," and that such funds have been used and will continue to be used to finance "instruction in reading, arithmetic and other subjects and for guidance in religious and sectarian schools" and "the purchase of textbooks and instructional and library materials for use in religious and sectarian schools." Such expenditures of federal tax funds, appellants alleged, violate the First Amendment because "they constitute a law respecting an establishment of religion" and because "they prohibit the free exercise of religion on the part of the [appellants] . . . by reason of the fact that they constitute compulsory taxation for religious purposes." The complaint asked for a declaration that appellees' actions in approving the expenditure of federal funds for the alleged purposes were not authorized by the Act or, in the alternative, that if appellees' actions are deemed within the authority and intent of the Act, "the Act is to that extent unconstitutional and void." The complaint also prayed for an injunction to enjoin appel⊥**88**lees from approving any expenditure of federal funds for the allegedly unconstitutional purposes. The complaint further requested that a three-judge court be convened.

The Government moved to dismiss the complaint on the ground that appellants lacked standing to maintain the action. District Judge Frankel, who considered the motion, recognized that *Frothingham* v. *Mellon* provided "powerful" support for the Government's position, but he ruled that the standing question was of sufficient substance to warrant the convening of a three-judge court to decide the question. The three-judge court received briefs and heard arguments limited to the standing question, and the court ruled on the authority of *Frothingham* that appellants lacked standing. Judge Frankel dissented. From the dismissal of their complaint on that ground, appellants appealed directly to this Court and we noted probable jurisdiction. For reasons explained at length below, we hold that appellants do have standing as federal taxpayers to maintain this action, and the judgment below must be reversed. . . .

⊥**91** This Court first faced squarely the question whether a litigant asserting only his status as a taxpayer has standing to maintain a suit in a federal court in *Frothingham* v. *Mellon*, and that decision must be the starting point for analysis in this case. The taxpayer in *Frothingham* attacked as unconstitutional the Maternity Act of 1921, which established a federal program of grants to those States which would undertake programs to reduce maternal and infant mortality. The taxpayer alleged that Congress, in enacting the challenged statute, had exceeded the powers delegated to it under Article I of the Constitution and had invaded the legislative province reserved to the several States by the Tenth Amendment. The taxpayer complained that the result of the allegedly unconstitutional enactment would be to increase her future federal tax ⊥**92** liability and "thereby take her property without due process of law." The Court noted that a federal taxpayer's "interest in the moneys of the Treasury . . . is comparatively minute and indeterminable" and that the "effect upon future taxation, of any payment out of the [Treasury's] funds, . . . [is] remote, fluctuating and uncertain." As a result, the Court ruled that the taxpayer had failed to allege the type of "direct injury" necessary to confer standing.

Although the barrier *Frothingham* erected against federal taxpayer suits has never been breached, the decision has been the source of some confusion and the object of considerable criticism. The confusion has developed as commentators have tried to determine whether *Frothingham* establishes a constitutional bar to taxpayer suits or whether the Court was simply imposing a rule of self-restraint which was not constitutionally compelled. The conflicting viewpoints are reflected in the arguments made to this Court by the parties in this case. The Government has pressed upon us the view that *Frothingham* announced a constitutional rule, compelled by the Article III limitations on federal court jurisdiction and grounded in considerations of the doctrine of separation of powers. Appellants, however, insist that ⊥**93** *Frothingham* expressed no more than a policy of judicial self-restraint which can be disregarded when compelling reasons for assuming jurisdiction over a taxpayer's suit exist. The opinion delivered in *Frothingham* can be read to support either position. The concluding sentence of the opinion states that, to take jurisdiction of the taxpayer's suit, "would be not to decide a judicial controversy, but to assume a position of authority over the governmental acts of another and co-equal department, an authority which plainly we do not possess." Yet the concrete reasons given for denying standing to a federal taxpayer suggest that the Court's holding rests on something less than a constitutional foundation. For example, the Court conceded that standing had previously been conferred on municipal taxpayers to sue in that capacity. However, the Court viewed the interest of a federal taxpayer in total federal tax revenues as "comparatively minute and indeterminable" when measured against a municipal taxpayer's interest in a smaller city treasury. This suggests that the petitioner in *Frothingham* was denied standing not because she was a taxpayer but because her tax bill was not large enough. In addition, the Court spoke of the "attendant inconveniences" of entertaining that taxpayer's suit because it might open the door of federal courts to countless such suits "in respect of every other appropriation act and statute whose administration requires the outlay of public money, and whose validity may be questioned." Such a statement suggests pure policy considerations.

⊥**94** To the extent that *Frothingham* has been viewed as resting on policy considerations, it has been criticized as depending on assumptions not consistent with modern conditions. For example, some commentators have pointed out that a number of corporate taxpayers today have a federal tax liability running into hundreds of millions of dollars, and such taxpayers have a far greater monetary stake in the Federal Treasury than they do in any municipal treasury. To some degree, the fear expressed in *Frothingham* that allowing one taxpayer to sue would inundate the federal courts with countless similar suits has been mitigated by the ready availability of the devices of class actions and joinder under the Federal Rules of Civil Procedure, adopted subsequent to the decision in *Frothingham*. Whatever the merits of the current debate over *Frothingham*, its very existence suggests that we should undertake a fresh examination of the limitations upon standing to sue in a federal court and the application of those limitations to taxpayer suits. . . .

⊥**101** Thus, in terms of Article III limitations on federal court jurisdiction, the question of standing is related only to whether the dispute sought to be adjudicated will be presented in an adversary context and in a form historically viewed as capable of judicial resolution. It is for that reason that the emphasis in standing problems is on whether the party invoking federal court jurisdiction has "a personal stake in the outcome of the controversy" and whether the dispute touches upon "the legal relations of parties having adverse legal interests." A taxpayer may or may not have the requisite personal stake in the outcome, depending upon the circumstances of the particular case. Therefore, we find no absolute bar in Article III to suits by federal taxpayers challenging allegedly unconstitutional federal taxing and spending programs. There remains, however, the problem of determining the circumstances under which a federal taxpayer will be deemed to have the personal stake and interest that impart the necessary concrete adverseness to such litigation so that standing can be conferred on the taxpayer *qua* taxpayer consistent with the constitutional limitations of Article III.

The various rules of standing applied by federal courts have not been developed in the abstract. Rather, they have been fashioned with specific reference to the status asserted by the party whose standing is challenged and to the type of question he wishes to have adjudicated. We have noted that, in deciding the question of standing, it is not relevant that the substantive issues in the litigation might be nonjustifiable. However, our decisions ⊥**102** establish that, in ruling on standing, it is both appropriate and necessary to look to the substantive issues for another purpose, namely, to determine whether there is a logical nexus between the status asserted and the claim sought to be adjudicated. For example, standing requirements will vary in First Amendment religion cases depending upon whether the party raises an Establishment Clause claim or a claim under the Free Exercise Clause. Such inquiries into the nexus between the status asserted by the litigant and the claim he presents are essential to assure that he is a proper and appropriate party to invoke federal judicial power. Thus, our point of reference in this case is the standing of individuals who assert only the status of federal taxpayers and who challenge the constitutionality of a federal spending program. Whether such individuals have standing to maintain that form of action turns on whether they can demonstrate the necessary stake as taxpayers in the outcome of the litigation to satisfy Article III requirements.

The nexus demanded of federal taxpayers has two aspects to it. First, the taxpayer must establish a logical link between that status and the type of legislative enactment attacked. Thus, a taxpayer will be a proper party to allege the unconstitutionality only of exercises of congressional power under the taxing and spending clause of Art. I, § 8, of the Constitution. It will not be sufficient to allege an incidental expenditure of tax funds in the administration of an essentially regulatory statute. This requirement is consistent with the limitation imposed upon state taxpayer standing in federal courts in *Doremus* v. *Board of Education*. Secondly, the taxpayer must establish a nexus between that status and the precise nature of the constitutional infringement alleged. Under this requirement, the taxpayer must show that the challenged enactment exceeds ⊥**103** specific constitutional limitations imposed upon the exercise of the congressional taxing and spending power and not simply that the enactment is generally beyond the powers delegated to Congress by Art. I, § 8. When both nexuses are established, the litigant will have shown a taxpayer's stake in the outcome of the controversy and will be a proper and appropriate party to invoke a federal court's jurisdiction.

The taxpayer-appellants in this case have satisfied both nexuses to support their claim of standing under the test we announce today. Their constitutional challenge is made to an exercise by Congress of its power under Art. I, § 8, to spend for the general welfare, and the challenged program involves a substantial expenditure of federal tax funds. In addition, appellants have alleged that the challenged expenditures violate the Establishment and Free Exercise Clauses of the First Amendment. Our history vividly illustrates that one of the specific evils feared by those who drafted the Establishment Clause and fought for its adoption was that the taxing and spending power would be used to favor one religion over another or to support religion in general. James Madison, who is generally recognized as the leading architect of the religion clauses of the First Amendment, observed in his famous Memorial and Remonstrance Against Religious Assessments that "the same authority which can force a citizen to contribute three pence only of his property for the support of any one establishment, may force him to conform to any other establishment in all cases whatsoever." The concern of Madison and his supporters was quite clearly that religious liberty ultimately would be the victim if ⊥**104** government could employ its taxing and spending powers to aid one religion over another or to aid religion in general. The Establishment Clause was designed as a specific bulwark against such potential abuses of governmental power, and that clause of the First Amendment operates as a specific constitutional limitation upon the exercise by Congress of the taxing and spending power conferred by Art. I, § 8.

The allegations of the taxpayer in *Frothingham* v. *Mellon* were quite different from those made in this case, and the result in *Frothingham* is consistent with the test of taxpayer standing announced today. The taxpayer in *Frothingham* attacked a federal spending program and she, therefore, established the first nexus ⊥**105** required. However, she lacked standing because her constitutional attack was not based on an allegation that Congress, in enacting the Maternity Act of 1921, had breached a specific limitation upon its taxing and spending power. The taxpayer in *Frothingham* alleged essentially that Congress, by enacting the challenged statute, had exceeded the general powers delegated to it by Art. I, § 8, and that Congress had thereby invaded the legislative province reserved to the States by the Tenth Amendment. To be sure, Mrs. Frothingham made the additional allegation that her tax liability would be increased as a result of the allegedly unconstitutional enactment, and she framed that allegation in terms of a deprivation of property without due process of law. However, the Due Process Clause of the Fifth Amendment does not protect taxpayers against increases in tax liability, and the taxpayer in *Frothingham* failed to make any additional claim that the harm she alleged resulted from a breach by Congress of the specific constitutional limitations imposed upon an exercise of the taxing and spending power. In essence, Mrs. Frothingham was attempting to assert the States' interest in their legislative prerogatives and not a federal taxpayer's interest in being free of taxing and spending in contravention of specific constitutional limitations imposed upon Congress' taxing and spending power.

We have noted that the Establishment Clause of the First Amendment does specifically limit the taxing and spending power conferred by Art. I, § 8. Whether the Constitution contains other specific limitations can be determined only in the context of future cases. However, whenever such specific limitations are found, we believe a taxpayer will have a clear stake as a taxpayer in assuring that they are not breached by Congress. Consequently, we hold that a taxpayer will have stand⊥**106**ing consistent with Article III to invoke federal judicial power when he alleges that congressional action under the taxing and spending clause is in derogation of those constitutional provisions which operate to restrict the exercise of the taxing and spending power. The taxpayer's allegation in such cases would be that his tax money is being extracted and spent in violation of specific constitutional protections against such abuses of legislative power. Such an injury is appropriate for judicial redress, and the taxpayer has established the necessary nexus between his status and the nature of the allegedly unconstitutional action to support his claim of standing to secure judicial review. Under such circumstances, we feel confident that the questions will be framed with the necessary specificity, that the issues will be contested with the necessary adverseness and that the litigation will be pursued with the necessary vigor to assure that the constitutional challenge will be made in a form traditionally thought to be capable of judicial resolution. We lack that confidence in cases such as *Frothingham* where a taxpayer seeks to employ a federal court as a forum in which to air his generalized grievances about the conduct of government or the allocation of power in the Federal System.

While we express no view at all on the merits of appellants' claims in this case, their complaint contains sufficient allegations under the criteria we have outlined to give them standing to invoke a federal court's jurisdiction for an adjudication on the merits.

Reversed.

⊥**107** Mr. *Justice DOUGLAS*, concurring.

While I have joined the opinion of the Court, I do not think that the test it lays down is a durable one for the reasons stated by my *Brother HARLAN*. I think, therefore, that it will suffer erosion and in time result in the demise of *Frothingham* v. *Mellon*. It would therefore be the part of wisdom, as I see the problem, to be rid of *Frothingham* here and now.

I do not view with alarm, as does my *Brother HARLAN*, the consequences of that course. *Frothingham*, decided in 1923, was in the heyday of substantive due process, when courts were sitting in judgment on the wisdom or reasonableness of legislation. The claim in *Frothingham* was that a federal regulatory Act dealing with maternity deprived the plaintiff of property without due process of law. When the Court used substantive due process to determine the wisdom or reasonableness of legislation, it was indeed transforming itself into the Council of Revision which was rejected by the Constitutional Convention. It was that judicial attitude, not the theory of standing to sue rejected in *Frothingham*, that involved "important hazards for the continued effectiveness of the federal judiciary," to borrow a phrase from my *Brother HARLAN*. A contrary result in *Frothingham* in that setting might well have accentuated an ominous trend to judicial supremacy.

But we no longer undertake to exercise that kind of power. Today's problem is in a different setting.

Most laws passed by Congress do not contain even a ghost of a constitutional question. The "political" decisions, as distinguished from the "justiciable" ones, occupy most of the spectrum of congressional action. The case or controversy requirement comes into play only when the Federal Government does something that affects a person's life, his liberty, or his property. The wrong may be slight or it may be grievous. Madison in denouncing ⊥**108** state support of churches said the principle was violated when even "three pence" was appropriated to that cause by the Government. It therefore does not do to talk about taxpayers' interest as "infinitesimal." The restraint on "liberty" may be fleeting and passing and still violate a fundamental constitutional guarantee. The "three pence" mentioned by Madison may signal a monstrous invasion by the Government into church affairs, and so on. . . .

⊥**111** The judiciary is an indispensable part of the operation of our federal system. With the growing complexities of government it is often the one and only place where effective relief can be obtained. If the judiciary were to become a super-legislative group sitting in judgment on the affairs of people, the situation would be intolerable. But where wrongs to individuals are done by violation of specific guarantees, it is abdication for courts to close their doors.

Marshall wrote in *Marbury* v. *Madison* that if the judiciary stayed its hand in deference to the legislature, it would give the legislature "a practical and real omnipotence." My *Brother HARLAN's* view would do just that, for unless Congress created a procedure through which its legislative creation could be challenged quickly and with ease, the momentum of what it had done would grind the dissenter under.

We have a Constitution designed to keep government out of private domains. But the fences have often been broken down; and *Frothingham* denied effective machinery to restore them. The Constitution even with the judicial gloss it has acquired plainly is not adequate to protect the individual against the growing bureaucracy in the Legislative and Executive Branches. He faces a formidable opponent in government, even when he is endowed with funds and with courage. The individual is almost certain to be plowed under, unless he has a well-organized active political group to speak for him. The church is one. The press is another. The union is a third. But if a powerful sponsor is lacking, individual liberty withers—in spite of glowing opinions and resounding constitutional phrases.

I would not be niggardly therefore in giving private attorneys general standing to sue. I would certainly not ⊥**112** wait for Congress to give its blessing to our deciding cases clearly within our Article III jurisdiction. To wait for a sign from Congress is to allow important constitutional questions to go undecided and personal liberty unprotected.

There need be no inundation of the federal courts if taxpayers' suits are allowed. There is a wise judicial discretion that usually can distinguish between the frivolous question and the substantial question, between cases ripe for decision and cases that need prior administrative processing, and the like. When the judiciary is no longer "a great rock" in the storm, as Lord Sankey once put it, when the courts are niggardly in the use of their power and reach great issues only timidly and reluctantly, the force of the Constitution in the life of the Nation is greatly weakened. . . .

We have recently reviewed the host of devices ⊥**113** used by the States to avoid opening to Negroes public facilities enjoyed by whites. There is a like process at work at the federal level in respect to aid to religion. The efforts made to insert in the law an express provision which would allow federal aid to sectarian schools to be reviewable in the courts was defeated. The mounting federal aid to sectarian schools is notorious and the subterfuges numerous.

⊥**114** I would be as liberal in allowing taxpayers standing to object to these violations of the First Amendment as I would in granting standing to people to complain of any invasion of their rights under the Fourth Amendment or the Fourteenth or under any other guarantee in the Constitution itself or in the Bill of Rights.

Mr. *Justice* STEWART, concurring.

I join the judgment and opinion of the Court, which I understand to hold only that a federal taxpayer has standing to assert that a specific expenditure of federal funds violates the Establishment Clause of the First Amendment. Because that clause plainly prohibits taxing and spending in aid of religion, every taxpayer can claim a personal constitutional right not to be taxed for the support of a religious institution. The present case is thus readily distinguishable from *Frothingham* v. *Mellon* where the taxpayer did not rely on an explicit constitutional prohibition but instead questioned the scope of the powers delegated to the national legislature by Article I of the Constitution.

As the Court notes, "one of the specific evils feared by those who drafted the Establishment Clause and fought for its adoption was that the taxing and spending power would be used to favor one religion over another or to support religion in general." Today's decision no more than recognizes that the appellants have a clear stake as taxpayers in assuring that they not be compelled to contribute even "three pence . . . of [their] property for the support of any one establishment." In concluding that the appellants therefore have standing to sue, we do not undermine the salutary principle, established by *Frothingham* and reaffirmed today, that a taxpayer may not "employ a federal court as a forum in which to air his generalized grievances about the conduct of government or the allocation of power in the Federal System."

⊥**115** Mr. *Justice* FORTAS, concurring.

I would confine the ruling in this case to the proposition that a taxpayer may maintain a suit to challenge the validity of a federal expenditure on the ground that the expenditure violates the Establishment Clause. As the Court's opinion recites, there is enough in the constitutional history of the Establishment Clause to support the thesis that this Clause includes a *specific* prohibition upon the use of the power to tax to support an establishment of religion. There is no reason to suggest, and no basis in the logic of this decision for implying, that there may be other types of congressional expenditures which may be attacked by a litigant solely on the basis of his status as a taxpayer.

I agree that *Frothingham* does not foreclose today's result. I agree that the congressional powers to tax and spend are limited by the prohibition upon Congress to enact laws "respecting an establishment of religion." This thesis, slender as its basis is, provides a direct nexus, as the Court puts it, between the use and collection of taxes and the congressional action here. Because of this unique "nexus," in my judgment, it is not far-fetched to recognize that a taxpayer has a special claim to status as a litigant in a case raising the "establishment" issue. This special claim is enough, I think, to permit us to allow the suit, coupled, as it is, with the interest which the taxpayer and all other citizens have in the church-state issue. In terms of the structure and basic philosophy of our constitutional government, it would be difficult to point to any issue that has a more intimate, pervasive, and fundamental impact upon the life of the taxpayer—and upon the life of all citizens.

Perhaps the vital interest of a citizen in the establishment issue, without reference to his taxpayer's status, ⊥**116** would be acceptable as a basis for this challenge. We need not decide this. But certainly, I believe, we must recognize that our principle of judicial scrutiny of legislative acts which raise important constitutional questions requires that the issue here presented—the separation of state and church—which the Founding Fathers regarded as fundamental to our constitutional system—should be subjected to judicial testing. This is not a question which we, if we are to be faithful to our trust, should consign to limbo, unacknowledged, unresolved, and undecided.

On the other hand, the urgent necessities of this case and the precarious opening through which we find our way to confront it, do not demand that we open the door to a general assault upon exercises of the spending power. The status of taxpayer should not be accepted as a launching pad for an attack upon any target other than legislation affecting the Establishment Clause.

Mr. *Justice* HARLAN, dissenting.

The problems presented by this case are narrow and relatively abstract, but the principles by which they must be resolved involve nothing less than the proper functioning of the federal courts, and so run to the roots of our constitutional system. The nub of my view is that the end result of *Frothingham* v. *Mellon* was correct, even though, like others, I do not subscribe to all of its reasoning and premises. Although I therefore agree with certain of the conclusions reached today by the Court, I cannot accept the standing doctrine ⊥**117** that it substitutes for *Frothingham*, for it seems to me that this new doctrine rests on premises that do not withstand analysis. Accordingly, I respectfully dissent.

I

It is desirable first to restate the basic issues in this case. The question here is not, as it was not in *Frothingham*, whether "a federal taxpayer is without standing to challenge the constitutionality of a federal statute." It could hardly be disputed that federal taxpayers may, as taxpayers, contest the constitutionality of tax obligations imposed severally upon them by federal statute. Such a challenge may be made by way of defense to an action by the United States to recover the amount of a challenged tax debt, or to a prosecution for willful failure to pay or to report the tax. Moreover, such a challenge may provide the basis of an action by a taxpayer to obtain the refund of a previous tax payment.

The lawsuits here and in *Frothingham* are fundamentally different. They present the question whether federal taxpayers *qua* taxpayers may, in suits in which they do not contest the validity of their previous or existing tax obligations, challenge the constitutionality of the uses for which Congress has authorized the expenditure of public funds. These differences in the purposes of the cases are reflected in differences in the litigants' interests. An action brought to contest the validity of tax liabilities assessed to the plaintiff is designed to vindicate interests that are personal and proprietary. The wrongs alleged and the relief sought by such a plaintiff are unmistakably private; only secondarily are his interests representative of those of the general population. I take **⊥118** it that the Court, although it does not pause to examine the question, believes that the interests of those who as taxpayers challenge the constitutionality of public expenditures may, at least in certain circumstances, be similar. Yet this assumption is surely mistaken.

The complaint in this case, unlike that in *Frothingham*, contains no allegation that the contested expenditures will in any fashion affect the amount of these taxpayers' own existing or foreseeable tax obligations. Even in cases in which such an allegation is made, the suit cannot result in an adjudication either of the plaintiff's tax liabilities or of the propriety of any particular level of taxation. The relief available to such a plaintiff consists entirely of the vindication of rights held in common by all citizens. It is thus scarcely surprising that few of the state courts that permit such suits require proof either that the challenged expenditure is consequential in amount or that it is likely to affect significantly the plaintiff's own tax bill; these courts have at least impliedly recognized that such allegations are surplusage, useful only to preserve the form of an obvious fiction.

Nor are taxpayers' interests in the expenditure of public funds differentiated from those of the general public by any special rights retained by them in their tax payments. The simple fact is that no such rights can sensibly be said to exist. Taxes are ordinarily levied by the United States without limitations of purpose; absent such a limitation, payments received by the Treasury in satisfaction of tax obligations lawfully created become part of the Government's general funds. The national legislature is required by the Constitution to **⊥119** exercise its spending powers to "provide for the common Defence and general Welfare." Whatever other implications there may be to that sweeping phrase, it surely means that the United States holds its general funds, not as stakeholder or trustee for those who have paid its imposts, but as surrogate for the population at large. Any rights of a taxpayer with respect to the purposes for which those funds are expended are thus subsumed in, and extinguished by, the common rights of all citizens. To characterize taxpayers' interests in such expenditures as proprietary or even personal either deprives those terms of all meaning or postulates for taxpayers a *scintilla juris* in funds that no longer are theirs. . . .

II

⊥121 As I understand it, the Court's position is that it is unnecessary to decide in what circumstances public actions should be permitted, for it is possible to identify situations in which taxpayers who contest the constitutionality of federal expenditures assert "personal" rights and interests. This position, if supportable, would of course avoid many of the difficulties of this case; indeed, if the Court is correct, its extended exploration of the subtleties of Article III is entirely unnecessary. But, for reasons that follow, I believe that the Court's position is untenable.

The Court's analysis consists principally of the observation that the requirements of standing are met if a taxpayer has the "requisite personal stake in the outcome" of his suit. This does not, of course, resolve the standing problem; it merely restates it. The Court implements this standard with the declaration that taxpayers will be "deemed" to have the necessary personal interest if their suits satisfy two criteria; *first*, the challenged expenditure must form part of a federal spending program, and not merely be "incidental" to a regulatory program; and *second*, the constitutional provision under which the plaintiff claims must be a "specific limitation" upon Congress' spending powers. The difficulties with these criteria are many and severe, but it is enough for the moment to emphasize that they are not in any sense a measurement of any plaintiff's interest in the outcome of any suit. As even a cursory examination of **⊥122** the criteria will show, the Court's standard for the determination of standing and its criteria for the satisfaction of that standard are entirely unrelated.

It is surely clear that a plaintiff's interest in the outcome of a suit in which he challenges the constitutionality of a federal expenditure is not made greater or smaller by the unconnected fact that the expenditure is, or is not, "incidental" to an "essentially regulatory" program. An example will illustrate the point. Assume that two independent federal programs are authorized by Congress, that the first is designed to encourage a specified religious group by the provision to it of direct grants-in-aid, and that the second is designed to discourage all other religious groups by the imposition of various forms of discriminatory regulation. Equal amounts are appropriated by Congress for the two programs. If a taxpayer challenges their constitutionality in separate suits, are we to suppose, as evidently does the Court, that his ⊥**123** "personal stake" in the suit involving the second is necessarily smaller than it is in the suit involving the first, and that he should therefore have standing in one but not the other?

Presumably the Court does not believe that regulatory programs are necessarily less destructive of First Amendment rights, or that regulatory programs are necessarily less prodigal of public funds than are grants-in-aid, for both these general propositions are demonstrably false. The Court's disregard of regulatory expenditures is not even a logical consequence of its apparent assumption that taxpayer-plaintiffs assert essentially monetary interests, for it surely cannot matter to a taxpayer *qua* taxpayer whether an unconstitutional expenditure is used to hire the services of regulatory personnel or is distributed among private and local governmental agencies as grants-in-aid. His interest as taxpayer arises, if at all, from the fact of an unlawful expenditure, and not as a consequence of the expenditure's form. Apparently the Court has repudiated the emphasis in *Frothingham* upon the amount of the plaintiff's tax bill, only to substitute an equally irrelevant emphasis upon the form of the challenged expenditure.

The Court's second criterion is similarly unrelated to its standard for the determination of standing. The intensity of a plaintiff's interest in a suit is not measured, even obliquely, by the fact that the constitutional provision under which he claims is, or is not, a "specific limitation" upon Congress' spending powers. Thus, among the claims in *Frothingham* was the assertion that the Maternity Act deprived the petitioner of property without due process of law. The Court has evidently concluded that this claim did not confer standing because the Due Process Clause of the Fifth Amendment is not a specific limitation upon the spending ⊥**124** powers. Disregarding for the moment the formidable obscurity of the Court's categories, how can it be said that Mrs. Frothingham's interests in her suit were, as a consequence of her choice of a constitutional claim, necessarily less intense than those, for example, of the present appellants? I am quite unable to understand how, if a taxpayer believes that a given public expenditure is unconstitutional, and if he seeks to vindicate that belief in a federal court, his interest in the suit can be said necessarily to vary according to the constitutional provision under which he states his claim. . . .

⊥**125** Although the Court does not altogether explain its position, the essence of its reasoning is evidently that a taxpayer's claim under the Establishment Clause is "not merely one of ultra vires," but one which instead asserts "an abridgment of individual religious liberty" and a "governmental infringement of individual rights protected by the Constitution." It must first be emphasized that this is apparently not founded upon any "preferred" position for the First Amendment, or upon any asserted unavailability of other plaintiffs. The Court's position is instead that, because of the Establishment Clause's historical purposes, taxpayers retain rights under it quite different from those held by them under other constitutional provisions.

The difficulties with this position are several. First, we have recently been reminded that the historical purposes of the religious clauses of the First Amendment are significantly more obscure and complex than this Court has heretofore acknowledged. Careful students ⊥**126** of the history of the Establishment Clause have found that "it is impossible to give a dogmatic interpretation of the First Amendment, and to state with any accuracy the intention of the men who framed it. . . ." Above all, the evidence seems clear that the First Amendment was not intended simply to enact the terms of Madison's Memorial and Remonstrance against Religious Assessments. I do not suggest that history is without relevance to these questions, or that the use of federal funds for religious purposes was not a form of establishment that many in the 18th century would have found objectionable. I say simply that, given the ultimate obscurity of the Establishment Clause's historical purposes, it is inappropriate for this Court to draw fundamental distinctions among the several constitutional commands upon the supposed authority of isolated dicta extracted from the clause's complex history. In particular, I have not found, and the opinion of the Court has not adduced, historical evidence that properly permits the Court to distinguish, as it has here, among the Establishment Clause, the Tenth Amendment, and the Due Process Clause of the Fifth Amendment as limitations upon Congress' taxing and spending powers.

⊥**127** The Court's position is equally precarious if it is assumed that its premise is that the Establishment Clause is in some uncertain fashion a more "specific" limitation upon Congress' powers than are the various other constitutional commands. It is obvious, first, that only in some Pickwickian sense are any of the provisions with which the Court is concerned "specific[ally]" limitations upon spending, for they contain nothing that is expressly directed at the expenditure of public funds. The specificity to which the Court repeatedly refers must therefore arise, not from the provisions' language, but from something implicit in their purposes. But this Court has often emphasized that Congress' powers to spend are coterminous with the purposes for which, and methods by which, it may act, and that the various constitutional commands applicable to the central government, including those implicit both in the Tenth Amendment and in the General Welfare Clause, thus operate as limitations upon spending. I can attach no constitutional significance to the various degrees of specificity with which these limitations appear in the terms or history of the Constitution. If the Court accepts the proposition, as I do, ⊥**128** that the number and scope of public actions should be restricted, there are, as I shall show, methods more appropriate, and more nearly permanent, than the creation of an amorphous category of constitutional provisions that the Court has deemed, without adequate foundation, "specific limitations" upon Congress' spending powers.

Even if it is assumed that such distinctions may properly be drawn, it does not follow that federal taxpayers hold any "personal constitutional right" such that they may each contest the validity under the Establishment Clause of all federal expenditures. The difficulty, with which the Court never comes to grips, is that taxpayers' suits under the Establishment Clause are not in these circumstances meaningfully different from other public actions. If this case involved a tax specifically designed for the support of religion, as was the Virginia tax opposed by Madison in his Memorial and Remonstrance, I would agree that taxpayers have rights under the religious clauses of the First Amendment that would permit them standing to challenge the tax's validity in the federal courts. But this is not such a case, and appellants challenge an expenditure, not a tax. Where no such tax is involved, a taxpayer's complaint can consist only of an allegation that public funds have been, or shortly will be, expended for purposes inconsistent with the Constitution. The taxpayer cannot ask the return of any portion of his previous tax payments, cannot prevent the collection of any existing tax debt, and cannot demand an adjudication of the propriety of any particular level of taxation. His tax payments are received for the general purposes of the United States, and are, upon proper receipt, lost in the general revenues. The interests he ⊥**129** represents, and the rights he espouses, are, as they are in all public actions, those held in common by all citizens. To describe those rights and interests as personal, and to intimate that they are in some unspecified fashion to be differentiated from those of the general public, reduces constitutional standing to a word game played by secret rules.

⊥**130** Apparently the Court, having successfully circumnavigated the issue, has merely returned to the proposition from which it began. A litigant, it seems, will have standing if he is "deemed" to have the requisite interest, and "if you . . . have standing, then you can be confident you are" suitably interested.

III

It seems to me clear that public actions, whatever the constitutional provisions on which they are premised, may involve important hazards for the continued effectiveness of the federal judiciary. Although I believe such actions to be within the jurisdiction conferred upon the federal courts by Article III of the Constitution, there surely can be little doubt that they strain the judicial function and press to the limit judicial authority. There is every reason to fear that unrestricted public actions might well alter the allocation of authority among the three branches of the Federal Government. It is not, I submit, enough to say that the present members of the Court would not seize these opportunities for abuse, for such actions would, even without conscious abuse, go far toward the final transformation of this Court into the Council of Revision which, despite Madison's support, was rejected by the Constitutional Convention. I do not doubt that there must be "some effectual power in the government to restrain or correct the infractions" of ⊥**131** the Constitution's several commands, but neither can I suppose that such power resides only in the federal courts. We must as judges recall that, as Mr. Justice Holmes wisely observed, the other branches of the Government "are ultimate guardians of the liberties and welfare of the people in quite as great a degree as the courts." *Missouri, Kansas & Texas R. Co.* v. *May*. The powers of the federal judiciary will be adequate for the great burdens placed upon them only if they are employed prudently, with recognition of the strengths as well as the hazards that go with our kind of representative government.

Presumably the Court recognizes at least certain of these hazards, else it would not have troubled to impose limitations upon the situations in which, and purposes for which, such suits may be brought. Nonetheless, the limitations adopted by the Court are, as I have endeavored to indicate, wholly untenable. This is the more unfortunate because there is available a resolution of this problem that entirely satisfies the demands of the principle of separation of powers. This Court has previously held that individual litigants have standing to represent the public interest, despite their lack of economic or other personal interests, if Congress has appropriately authorized such suits. I would adhere to that principle. Any hazards to the ⊥**132** proper allocation of authority among the three branches of the Government would be substantially diminished if public actions had been pertinently authorized by Congress and the President. I appreciate that this Court does not ordinarily await the mandate of other branches of the Government, but it seems to me that the extraordinary character of public actions, and of the mischievous, if not dangerous, consequences they involve for the proper functioning of our constitutional system, and in particular of the federal courts, makes such judicial forbearance the part of wisdom. It must be emphasized ⊥**133** that the implications of these questions of judicial policy are of fundamental significance for the other branches of the Federal Government.

Such a rule could readily be applied to this case. Although various efforts have been made in Congress to authorize public actions to contest the validity of federal expenditures in aid of religiously affiliated schools and other institutions, no such authorization has yet been given.

This does not mean that we would, under such a rule, be enabled to avoid our constitutional responsibilities, or that we would confine to limbo the First Amendment or any other constitutional command. The question here is not, despite the Court's unarticulated premise, whether the religious clauses of the First Amendment are hereafter to be enforced by the federal courts; the issue is simply whether an *additional* category of plaintiffs, heretofore excluded from those courts, are to be permitted to maintain suits. The recent history of this Court is replete with illustrations that questions involving the religious clauses will not, if federal taxpayers are prevented from contesting federal expenditures, be left "unacknowledged, unresolved, and undecided."

Accordingly, for the reasons contained in this opinion, I would affirm the judgment of the District Court.

VALLEY FORGE CHRISTIAN COLLEGE v. AMERICANS UNITED FOR SEPARATION OF CHURCH AND STATE

454 U.S. 464
ON WRIT OF CERTIORARI TO THE UNITED STATES COURT OF APPEALS FOR THE THIRD CIRCUIT
Argued November 4, 1981 — Decided January 12,1982

⊥**466** *Justice REHNQUIST* delivered the opinion of the Court.

I

Article IV, Section 3, Clause 2 of the Constitution vests Congress with the "Power to dispose of and make all needful Rules and Regulations respecting the . . . Property belonging to the United States." Shortly after the termination of hostilities in the Second World War, Congress enacted the Federal Property and Administrative Services Act of 1949, 63 Stat. 377, 40 U. S. C. § 471 *et seq.* (1976 ed. and Supp. III). The Act was designed, in part, to provide "an economical and efficient system for . . . the disposal of surplus property." 63 Stat. 378, 40 U. S. C. § 471. In furtherance of this policy, federal agencies are directed to maintain adequate inventories of the property under their control and to identify excess property for transfer to other agencies able to use it. See 63 Stat. 384, 40 U. S. C. § 483(b), (c). Property that has outlived its usefulness to the federal government is declared "surplus" and may be transferred to pri⊥**467**vate or other public entities. See generally 63 Stat. 385, as amended, 40 U. S. C. § 484.

The Act authorizes the Secretary of Health, Education, and Welfare (now the Secretary of Education) to assume responsibility for disposing of surplus real property "for school, classroom, or other educational use." 63 Stat. 387, as amended, 40 U. S. C. § 484(k)(1). Subject to the disapproval of the Administrator of General Services, the Secretary may sell or lease the property to nonprofit, tax exempt educational institutions for consideration that takes into account "any benefit which has accrued or may accrue to the United States" from the transferee's use of the property. 63 Stat. 387, 40 U. S. C. § 484(k)(1)(A), (C). By regulation, the Secretary has provided for the computation of a "public benefit allowance," which discounts the transfer price of the property "on the basis of benefits to the United States from the use of such property for educational purposes." 34 CFR § 12.9(a)(1980).

The property which spawned this litigation was acquired by the Department of the Army in 1942, as part of a larger tract of approximately 181 acres of land northwest of Philadelphia. The Army built on that land the Valley Forge General Hospital, and for 30 years thereafter, that hospital provided medical care for members of the Armed Forces. In April 1973, as part of a plan to reduce the number of military ⊥**468** installations in the United States, the Secretary of Defense proposed to close the hospital, and the General Services Administration declared it to be "surplus property."

The Department of Health, Education, and Welfare (HEW) eventually assumed responsibility for disposing of portions of the property, and in August 1976, it conveyed a 77-acre tract to petitioner, the Valley Forge Christian College. The appraised value of the property at the time of conveyance was $577,500. This appraised value was discounted, however, by the Secretary's computation of a 100% public benefit allowance, which permitted petitioner to acquire the property without making any financial payment for it. The deed from HEW conveyed the land in fee simple with certain conditions subsequent, which required petitioner to use the property for 30 years solely for the educational purposes described in petitioner's application. In that description, petitioner stated its intention to conduct "a program of education . . . meeting the accrediting standards of the State of Pennsylvania, The American Association of Bible Colleges, the Division of Education of the General Council of the Assemblies of God and the Veterans Administration."

Petitioner is a nonprofit educational institution operating under the supervision of a religious order known as the Assemblies of God. By its own description, petitioner's purpose is "to offer systematic training on the collegiate level to men and women for Christian service as either ministers or laymen." Its degree programs reflect this orientation by providing courses of study "to train leaders for church related ministries." Faculty members ⊥**469** must "have been baptized in the Holy Spirit and be living consistent Christian lives," and all members of the college administration must be affiliated with the Assemblies of God. In its application for the 77-acre tract, petitioner represented that, if it obtained the property, it would make "additions to its offerings in the arts and humanities," and would strengthen its "psychology" and "counselling" courses to provide services in inner city areas.

In September 1976, respondents Americans United for Separation of Church and State, Inc. (Americans United), and four of its employees, learned of the conveyance through a news release. Two months later, they brought suit in the United States District Court for the Eastern District of Pennsylvania to challenge the conveyance on the ground that it violated the Establishment Clause of the First Amendment. In its amended complaint, Americans United described itself as a nonprofit organization composed of 90,000 "taxpayer members." The complaint asserted that each member "would be deprived of the fair and constitutional use of his (her) tax dollar for constitutional purposes in violation of his (her) rights under the First Amendment of the United States Constitution." Respondents sought a declaration that the conveyance was null and void, and an order compelling petitioner to transfer the property back to the United States.

On petitioner's motion, the District Court granted summary judgment and dismissed the complaint. The court found that respondents lacked standing to sue as taxpayers under *Flast* v. *Cohen*, and had "failed to allege that they have suffered any actual or concrete injury beyond a generalized grievance common to all taxpayers."

⊥470 Respondents appealed to the Court of Appeals for the Third Circuit, which reversed the judgment of the District Court by a divided vote. All members of the court agreed that respondents lacked standing as taxpayers to challenge the conveyance under *Flast* v. *Cohen* since that case extended standing to taxpayers *qua* taxpayers only to challenge congressional exercises of the power to tax and spend conferred by Art. I, § 8, of the Constitution, and this conveyance was authorized by legislation enacted under the authority of the Property Clause, Art. IV, § 3, cl. 2. Notwithstanding this significant factual difference from *Flast*, the majority of the Court of Appeals found that respondents also had standing merely as "citizens," claiming "'injury in fact' to their shared individuated right to a government that 'shall make no law respecting the establishment of religion.'" In the majority's view, this "citizen standing" was sufficient to satisfy the "case or controversy" requirement of Art. III. One judge, perhaps sensing the doctrinal difficulties with the majority's extension of standing, wrote separately, expressing his view that standing was necessary to satisfy "the need for an available plaintiff," without whom "the Establishment Clause would be rendered virtually unenforceable" by the Judiciary. The dissenting judge expressed the view that respondents' allegations constituted a "generalized grievance . . . too abstract to satisfy the injury in fact component of standing." He therefore concluded that their standing to contest the transfer was barred by this Court's decisions in *Schlesinger* v. *Reservists Committee to Stop the War* and *United States* v. *Richardson*.

Because of the unusually broad and novel view of standing to litigate a substantive question in the federal courts adopted by the Court of Appeals, we granted certiorari, and we now reverse.

II

⊥471 Article III of the Constitution limits the "judicial power" of the United States to the resolution of "cases" and "controversies." The constitutional power of federal courts cannot be defined, and indeed has no substance, without reference to the necessity "to adjudge the legal rights of litigants in actual controversies." *Liverpool Steamship Co.* v. *Commissioners of Emigration*. The requirements of Art. III are not satisfied merely because a party requests a court of the United States to declare its legal rights, and has couched that request for forms of relief historically associated with courts of law in terms that have a familiar ring to those trained in the legal process. The judicial power of the United States defined by Art. III is not an unconditioned authority to determine the constitutionality of legislative or executive acts. The power to declare the rights of individuals and to measure the authority of governments, this Court said 90 years ago, "is legitimate only in the last resort, and as a necessity in the determination of real, earnest and vital controversy." *Chicago & Grand Trunk R. Co.* v. *Wellman*. Otherwise, the power "is not judicial . . . in the sense in which judicial power is granted by the Constitution to the courts of the United States." *United States* v. *Ferreira*.

As an incident to the elaboration of this bedrock requirement, this Court has always required that a litigant have "standing" to challenge the action sought to be adjudicated in the lawsuit. The term "standing" subsumes a blend of constitutional requirements and prudential considerations, see *Warth* v. *Seldin*, and it has not always been clear in the opinions of this Court whether particular features of the "standing" requirement have been required by Art. III *ex proprio vigore*, or whether they are requirements that the Court itself has erected and which were not compelled by the language of the Constitution. See *Flast* v. *Cohen*.

⊥472 A recent line of decisions, however, has resolved that ambiguity, at least to the following extent: at an irreducible minimum, Art. III requires the party who invokes the court's authority to "show that he personally has suffered some actual or threatened injury as a result of the putatively illegal conduct of the defendant," *Gladstone, Realtors* v. *Village of Bellwood*, and that the injury "fairly can be traced to the challenged action" and "is likely to be redressed by a favorable decision," *Simon* v. *Eastern Kentucky Welfare Rights Org*. In this manner does Art. III limit the federal judicial power "to those disputes which confine federal courts to a role consistent with a system of separated powers and which are traditionally thought to be capable of resolution through the judicial process." *Flast* v. *Cohen*.

The requirement of "actual injury redressable by the court," *Simon*, serves several of the "implicit policies embodied in Article III," *Flast*. It tends to assure that the legal questions presented to the court will be resolved, not in the rarefied atmosphere of a debating society, but in a concrete factual context conducive to a realistic appreciation of the consequences of judicial action. The "standing" requirement serves other purposes. Because it assures an actual factual setting in which the litigant asserts a claim of injury in fact, a court may decide the case with some confidence that its decision will not pave the way for lawsuits which have some, but not all, of the facts of the case actually decided by the court.

⊥473 The Art. III aspect of standing also reflects a due regard for the autonomy of those persons likely to be most directly affected by a judicial order. The federal courts have abjured appeals to their authority which would convert the judicial process into "no more than a vehicle for the vindication of the value interests of concerned bystanders." *United States* v. *SCRAP*. Were the federal courts merely publicly funded forums for the ventilation of public grievances or the refinement of jurisprudential understanding, the concept of "standing" would be quite unnecessary. But the "cases and controversies" language of Art. III forecloses the conversion of courts of the United States into judicial versions of college debating forums. As we said in *Sierra Club* v. *Morton*: "The requirement that a party seeking review must allege facts showing that he is himself adversely affected . . . does serve as at least a rough attempt to put the decision as to whether review will be sought in the hands of those who have a direct stake in the outcome."

The exercise of judicial power, which can so profoundly affect the lives, liberty, and property of those to whom it extends, is therefore restricted to litigants who can show "injury in fact" resulting from the action which they seek to have the Court adjudicate.

The exercise of the judicial power also affects relationships between the coequal arms of the national government. The effect is, of course, most vivid when a federal court declares unconstitutional an act of the Legislative or Executive branch. While the exercise of that "ultimate and supreme function," *Chicago & Grand Trunk R. Co.* v. *Wellman*, is a formidable means of vindicating individual rights, when employed unwisely or unnecessarily it is also the ultimate threat to the continued effectiveness of the federal courts performing that role. While the propriety of such action by a federal court has been recognized since **⊥474** *Marbury* v. *Madison*, it has been recognized as a tool of last resort on the part of the federal judiciary throughout its nearly 200 years of existence: "[R]epeated and essentially head-on confrontations between the life-tenured branch and the representative branches of government will not, in the long run, be beneficial to either. The public confidence essential to the former and the vitality critical to the latter may well erode if we do not exercise self-restraint in the utilization of our power to negative the actions of the other branches." *United States* v. *Richardson*. Proper regard for the complex nature of our constitutional structure requires neither that the judicial branch shrink from a confrontation with the other two coequal branches of the federal government, nor that it hospitably accept for adjudication claims of constitutional violation by other branches of government where the claimant has not suffered cognizable injury. Thus this Court has "refrain[ed] from passing upon the constitutionality of an act [of the representative branches] unless obliged to do so in the proper performance of our judicial function, when the question is raised by a party whose interests entitle him to raise it." *Blair* v. *United States*. The importance of this precondition should not be underestimated as a means of "defin[ing] the role assigned to the judiciary in a tripartite allocation of power." *Flast* v. *Cohen*.

Beyond the constitutional requirements, the federal judiciary has also adhered to a set of prudential principles that bear on the question of standing. Thus, this Court has held that "the plaintiff generally must assert his own legal rights and interests, and cannot rest his claim to relief on the legal rights or interests of third parties." *Warth* v. *Seldin*. In addition, even when the plaintiff has al**⊥475**leged redressable injury sufficient to meet the requirements of Art. III, the Court has refrained from adjudicating "abstract questions of wide public significance" which amount to "generalized grievances," pervasively shared and most appropriately addressed in the representative branches. Finally, the Court has required that the plaintiff's complaint fall within "the zone of interests to be protected or regulated by the statute or constitutional guarantee in question." *Data Processing Service* v. *Camp*.

Merely to articulate these principles is to demonstrate their close relationship to the policies reflected in the Art. III requirement of actual or threatened injury amenable to judicial remedy. But neither the counsels of prudence nor the policies implicit in the "case or controversy" requirement should be mistaken for the rigorous Art. III requirements themselves. Satisfaction of the former cannot substitute for a demonstration of "'distinct and palpable injury' . . . that is likely to be redressed if the requested relief is granted." *Gladstone, Realtors* v. *Village of Bellwood*. That requirement states a limitation on judicial power, not merely a factor to be balanced in the weighing of so-called "prudential" considerations.

We need not mince words when we say that the concept of "Art. III standing" has not been defined with complete consistency in all of the various cases decided by this Court which have discussed it, nor when we say that this very fact is probably proof that the concept cannot be reduced to a one-sentence or one-paragraph definition. But of one thing we may be sure: Those who do not possess Art. III standing may **⊥476** not litigate as suitors in the courts of the United States. Art. III, which is every bit as important in its circumscription of the judicial power of the United States as in its granting of that power, is not merely a troublesome hurdle to be overcome if possible so as to reach the "merits" of a lawsuit which a party desires to have adjudicated; it is a part of the basic charter promulgated by the framers of the Constitution at Philadelphia in 1787, a charter which created a general government, provided for the interaction between that government and the governments of the several States, and was later amended so as to either enhance or limit its authority with respect to both States and individuals.

III

The injury alleged by respondents in their amended complaint is the "depriv[ation] of the fair and constitutional use of [their] tax dollar." As a result, our discussion ⊥**477** must begin with *Frothingham* v. *Mellon*. In that action a taxpayer brought suit challenging the constitutionality of the Maternity Act of 1921, which provided federal funding to the States for the purpose of improving maternal and infant health. The injury she alleged consisted of the burden of taxation in support of an unconstitutional regime, which she characterized as a deprivation of property without due process. "Looking through forms of words to the substance of [the] complaint," the Court concluded that the only "injury" was the fact "that officials of the executive branch of the government are executing and will execute an act of Congress asserted to be unconstitutional." Any tangible effect of the challenged statute on the plaintiff's tax burden was "remote, fluctuating, and uncertain." In rejecting this as a cognizable injury sufficient to establish standing, the Court admonished: "The party who invokes the power [of judicial review] must be able to show not only that the statute is invalid but that he has sustained or is immediately in danger of sustaining some direct injury as the result of its enforcement, and not merely that he suffers in some indefinite way in common with people generally. . . . Here the parties plaintiff have no such case."

Following the decision in *Frothingham*, the Court confirmed that the expenditure of public funds in an allegedly unconstitutional manner is not an injury sufficient to confer standing, even though the plaintiff contributes to the public coffers as a taxpayer. In *Doremus* v. *Board of Education* plaintiffs brought suit as citizens and taxpayers, claiming that a New Jersey law which authorized public school teachers in the classroom to read passages from ⊥**478** the Bible violated the Establishment Clause of the First Amendment. The Court dismissed the appeal for lack of standing: "This Court has held that the interests of a taxpayer in the moneys of the federal treasury are too indeterminable, remote, uncertain and indirect to furnish a basis for an appeal to the preventive powers of the Court over their manner of expenditure. . . . Without disparaging the availability of the remedy by taxpayer's action to restrain unconstitutional acts which result in direct pecuniary injury, we reiterate what the Court said of a federal statute as equally true when a state Act is assailed: The party who invokes the power must be able to show not only that the statute is invalid but that he has sustained or is immediately in danger of sustaining some direct injury as the result of its enforcement, and not merely that he suffers in some indefinite way in common with people generally." In short, the Court found that plaintiffs' grievance was "not a direct dollars-and-cents injury but is a religious difference." A case or controversy did not exist, even though the "clash of interests [was] real and . . . strong."

The Court again visited the problem of taxpayer standing in *Flast* v. *Cohen*. The taxpayer plaintiffs in *Flast* sought to enjoin the expenditure of federal funds under the Elementary and Secondary Education Act of 1965, which they alleged were being used to support religious schools in violation of the Establishment Clause. The Court developed a two-part test to determine whether the plaintiffs had standing to sue. First, because a taxpayer alleges injury only by virtue of his liability for taxes, the Court held that "a taxpayer will be a proper party to allege the unconstitutionality only of exercises of congressional power under the taxing and spending clause of Art. I, § 8, of the Constitu⊥**479**tion." Second, the Court required the taxpayer to "show that the challenged enactment exceeds specific constitutional limitations upon the exercise of the taxing and spending power and not simply that the enactment is generally beyond the powers delegated to Congress by Art. I, § 8."

The plaintiffs in *Flast* satisfied this test because "[t]heir constitutional challenge [was] made to an exercise by Congress of its power under Art. I, § 8, to spend for the general welfare," and because the Establishment Clause, on which plaintiffs' complaint rested, "operates as a specific constitutional limitation upon the exercise by Congress of the taxing and spending power conferred by Art. I, § 8." The Court distinguished *Frothingham* v. *Mellon* on the ground that Mrs. Frothingham had relied, not on a specific limitation on the power to tax and spend, but on a more general claim based on the Due Process Clause. Thus, the Court reaffirmed that the "case or controversy" aspect of standing is unsatisfied "where a taxpayer seeks to employ a federal court as a forum in which to air his generalized grievances about the conduct of government or the allocation of power in the Federal System."

Unlike the plaintiffs in *Flast*, respondents fail the first prong of the test for taxpayer standing. Their claim is deficient in two respects. First, the source of their complaint is not a congressional action, but a decision by HEW to transfer a parcel of federal property. *Flast* limited taxpayer standing to challenges directed "only [at] exercises of congressional power." See *Schlesinger* v. *Reservists Committee to Stop the War* (denying standing because the taxpayer plaintiffs "did not challenge an enactment under Art. I, § 8, but rather the action of the Executive Branch").

⊥480 Second, and perhaps redundantly, the property transfer about which respondents complain was not an exercise of authority conferred by the taxing and spending clause of Art. I, § 8. The authorizing legislation, the Federal Property and Administrative Services Act of 1949, was an evident exercise of Congress' power under the Property Clause, Art. IV, § 3, cl. 2. Respondents do not dispute this conclusion, and it is decisive of any claim of taxpayer standing under the *Flast* precedent.

⊥481 Any doubt that once might have existed concerning the rigor with which the *Flast* exception to the *Frothingham* principle ought to be applied should have been erased by this Court's recent decisions in *United States* v. *Richardson* and *Schlesinger* v. *Reservists Committee to Stop the War*. In *Richardson*, the question was whether the plaintiff had standing as a federal taxpayer to argue that legislation which permitted the Central Intelligence Agency to withhold from the public detailed information about its expenditures violated the Accounts Clause of the Constitution. We rejected plaintiff's claim of standing because "his challenge [was] not addressed to the taxing or spending power, but to the statutes regulating the CIA." The "mere recital" of those claims "demonstrate[d] how far he [fell] short of the standing criteria of *Flast* and how neatly he [fell] within the *Frothingham* holding left undisturbed."

The claim in *Schlesinger* was marred by the same deficiency. Plaintiffs in that case argued that the Incompatibility Clause of Art. I prevented certain Members of Congress from holding commissions in the Armed Forces Reserve. We summarily rejected their assertion of standing as taxpayers because they "did not challenge an enactment under Art. I, § 8, but rather the action of the Executive Branch in permitting Members of Congress to maintain their Reserve status."

⊥482 Respondents, therefore, are plainly without standing to sue as taxpayers. The Court of Appeals apparently reached the same conclusion. It remains to be seen whether respondents have alleged any other basis for standing to bring this suit.

IV

Although the Court of Appeals properly doubted respondents' ability to establish standing solely on the basis of their taxpayer status, it considered their allegations of taxpayer injury to be "essentially an assumed role." "Plaintiffs have no reason to expect, nor perhaps do they care about, any personal tax saving that might result should they prevail. The crux of the interest at stake, the plaintiffs argue, is found in the Establishment Clause, not in the supposed loss of money as such. As a matter of primary identity, therefore, the plaintiffs are not so much taxpayers as separationists. . . ." In the court's view, respondents had established standing by virtue of an "'injury in fact' to their shared individuated right to a government that 'shall make no law respecting the establishment of religion.'" The court distinguished this "injury" from "the question of 'citizen standing' as such." Although citizens generally could not establish standing simply by claiming an interest in governmental observance of the Constitution, respondents had "set forth instead a particular and concrete injury" to a "personal constitutional right."

The Court of Appeals was surely correct in recognizing that the Art. III requirements of standing are not satisfied by "the abstract injury in nonobservance of the Constitution asserted by . . . citizens." *Schlesinger* v. *Reservists Committee to Stop the War*. This Court repeatedly has rejected claims of standing predicated on "'the right, possessed by every citizen, to require that the **⊥483** Government be administered according to law. . . .' *Fairchild* v. *Hughes*." *Baker* v. *Carr*. See *Schlesinger* v. *Reservists Committee to Stop the War; Laird* v. *Tatum; Ex parte Levitt*. Such claims amount to little more than attempts "to employ a federal court as a forum in which to air . . . generalized grievances about the conduct of government." *Flast* v. *Cohen*.

In finding that respondents had alleged something more than "the generalized interest of all citizens in constitutional governance," *Schlesinger*, the Court of Appeals relied on factual differences which we do not think amount to legal distinctions. The court decided that respondents' claim differed from those in *Schlesinger* and *Richardson*, which were predicated, respectively, on the Incompatibility and Accounts Clauses, because "it is at the very least arguable that the Establishment Clause creates in each citizen a 'personal constitutional right' to a government that does not establish religion." The court found it unnecessary to determine whether this "arguable" proposition was correct, since it judged the mere allegation of a legal right sufficient to confer standing.

This reasoning process merely disguises, we think with a rather thin veil, the inconsistency of the court's result with our decisions in *Schlesinger* and *Richardson*. The plaintiffs in those cases plainly asserted a "personal right" to have the government act in accordance with their views of the Constitution; indeed, we see no barrier to the *assertion* of such claims with respect to any constitutional provision. But assertion of a right to a particular kind of government conduct, which the government has violated by acting differently, cannot alone satisfy the requirements of Art. III without draining those requirements of meaning.

⊥484 Nor can *Schlesinger* and *Richardson* be distinguished on the ground that the Incompatibility and Accounts Clauses are in some way less "fundamental" than the Establishment Clause. Each establishes a norm of conduct which the federal government is bound to honor—to no greater or lesser extent than any other inscribed in the Constitution. To the extent the Court of Appeals relied on a view of standing under which the Art. III burdens diminish as the "importance" of the claim on the merits increases, we reject that notion. The requirement of standing "focuses on the party seeking to get his complaint before a federal court and not on the issues he wishes to have adjudicated." *Flast* v. *Cohen*. Moreover, we know of no principled basis on which to create a hierarchy of constitutional values or a complementary "sliding scale" of standing which might permit respondents to invoke the judicial power of the United States. ⊥**485** "The proposition that all constitutional provisions are enforceable by any citizen simply because citizens are the ultimate beneficiaries of those provisions has no boundaries." *Schlesinger* v. *Reservists Committee to Stop the War*.

The complaint in this case shares a common deficiency with those in *Schlesinger* and *Richardson*. Although they claim that the Constitution has been violated, they claim nothing else. They fail to identify any personal injury suffered by the plaintiffs *as a consequence* of the alleged constitutional error, other than the psychological consequence presumably produced by observation of conduct with which one disagrees. That is not an injury sufficient to confer standing under Art. III, even though the disagreement is phrased in ⊥**486** constitutional terms. It is evident that respondents are firmly committed to the constitutional principle of separation of church and State, but standing is not measured by the intensity of the litigant's interest or the fervor of his advocacy. "[T]hat concrete adverseness which sharpens the presentation of issues," *Baker* v. *Carr*, is the anticipated consequence of proceedings commenced by one who has been injured in fact; it is not a permissible substitute for the showing of injury itself.

In reaching this conclusion, we do not retreat from our earlier holdings that standing may be predicated on noneconomic injury. See, *e.g.*, *United States* v. *SCRAP*; *Data Processing Service* v. *Camp*. We simply cannot see that respondents have alleged an *injury* of *any* kind, economic or otherwise, sufficient to confer standing. Respondents com⊥**487**plain of a transfer of property located in Chester County, Pennsylvania. The named plaintiffs reside in Maryland and Virginia; their organizational headquarters are located in Washington, D.C. They learned of the transfer through a news release. Their claim that the government has violated the Establishment Clause does not provide a special license to roam the country in search of governmental wrongdoing and to reveal their discoveries in federal court. The federal courts were simply not constituted as ombudsmen of the general welfare.

V

⊥**488** The Court of Appeals in this case ignored unambiguous limitations on taxpayer and citizen standing. It appears to have done so out of the conviction that enforcement of the Establishment Clause demands special exceptions from the requirement that a plaintiff allege "'distinct and palpable injury to himself,' . . . that is likely to be redressed if the requested relief is granted." *Gladstone, Realtors* v. *Village of Bellwood* (quoting *Warth* v. *Seldin*). The court derived precedential comfort from *Flast* v. *Cohen*: "The underlying justification for according standing in *Flast* it seems, was the implicit recognition that the Establishment Clause does create in every citizen a personal constitutional right, such that any citizen, including taxpayers, may contest under that clause the constitutionality of federal expenditures." The concurring opinion was even more direct. In its view, "statutes alleged to violate the Establishment Clause may not have an ⊥**489** individual impact sufficient to confer standing in the traditional sense." To satisfy "the need for an available plaintiff," and thereby to assure a basis for judicial review, respondents should be granted standing because, "as a practical matter, no one is better suited to bring this lawsuit and thus vindicate the freedoms embodied in the Establishment Clause."

Implicit in the foregoing is the philosophy that the business of the federal courts is correcting constitutional errors, and that "cases and controversies" are at best merely convenient vehicles for doing so and at worst nuisances that may be dispensed with when they become obstacles to that transcendent endeavor. This philosophy has no place in our constitutional scheme. It does not become more palatable when the underlying merits concern the Establishment Clause. Respondents' claim of standing implicitly rests on the presumption that violations of the Establishment Clause typically will not cause injury sufficient to confer standing under the "traditional" view of Art. III. But "[t]he assumption that if respondents have no standing to sue, no one would have standing, is not a reason to find standing." *Schlesinger* v. *Reservists Committee to Stop the War*. This view would convert standing into a requirement that must be observed only when satisfied. Moreover, we are unwilling to assume that injured parties are nonexistent simply because they have not joined respondents in their suit. The law of averages is not a substitute for standing.

Were we to accept respondents' claim of standing in this case, there would be no principled basis for confining our exception to litigants relying on the Establishment Clause. Ultimately, that exception derives from the idea that the judicial power requires nothing more for its invocation than important issues and able litigants. The existence of injured ⊥**490** parties who might not wish to bring suit becomes irrelevant. Because we are unwilling to countenance such a departure from the limits on judicial power contained in Art. III, the judgment of the Court of Appeals is reversed.

It is so ordered.

Justice BRENNAN, with whom *Justice* MARSHALL and *Justice* BLACKMUN join, dissenting.

A plaintiff's standing is a jurisdictional matter for Article III courts, and thus a "threshold question" to be resolved before turning attention to more "substantive" issues. See *Linda R. S.* v. *Richard D.* But in consequence there is an impulse to decide difficult questions of substantive law obliquely in the course of opinions purporting to do nothing more than determine what the Court labels "standing"; this accounts for the phenomenon of opinions, such as the one today, that tend merely to obfuscate, rather than inform, our understanding of the meaning of rights under the law. The serious by-product of that practice is that the Court disregards its constitutional responsibility when, by failing to acknowledge the protections afforded by the Constitution, it uses "standing to slam the courthouse door against plaintiffs who are entitled to full consideration of their claims on the merits."

The opinion of the Court is a stark example of this unfortunate trend of resolving cases at the "threshold" while obscur⊥**491**ing the nature of the underlying rights and interests at stake. The Court waxes eloquent on the blend of prudential and constitutional considerations that combine to create our misguided "standing" jurisprudence. *But not one word is said about the Establishment Clause right that the plaintiff seeks to enforce*. And despite its past recitation of our standing decisions, the opinion utterly fails, except by the sheerest form of *ipse dixit*, to explain why this case is unlike *Flast* v. *Cohen*, and is controlled instead by *Frothingham* v. *Mellon*.

I

There is now much in the way of settled doctrine in our understanding of the injury-in-fact requirement of Article III. At the core is the irreducible minimum that persons seeking judicial relief from an Article III court have "such a personal stake in the outcome of the controversy as to assure that concrete adverseness which sharpens the presentation of issues upon which the court so largely depends. . . ." *Baker* v. *Carr*. See *Duke Power Co.* v. *Carolina Environmental Study Group*. Cases of this Court have identified the two essential components of this "personal stake" requirement. Plaintiff must have suffered, or be threatened with, some "distinct and palpable injury." *Warth* v. *Seldin*. In addition, there must be some causal connection between plaintiff's asserted injury and defendant's challenged action. *Simon* v. *Eastern Ky. Welfare Rights Org.*; *Arlington Heights* v. *Metropolitan Housing Development Corp*. The Constitution requires an Article III court to ascertain that both requirements are met before proceeding to exercise its authority on behalf of any plaintiff, whether the form of relief requested is equitable or monetary.

But the existence of Article III injury "often turns on the nature and source of the claim asserted." *Warth* v. *Seldin*. ⊥**492** Neither "palpable injury" nor "causation" is a term of unvarying meaning. There is much in the way of "mutual understandings" and "common law traditions" that necessarily guides the definitional inquiry. *In addition*, the Constitution, and by legislation the Congress, may impart a new, and on occasion unique, meaning to the terms "injury" and "causation" in particular statutory or constitutional contexts. The Court makes a fundamental mistake when it determines that a plaintiff has failed to satisfy the two-pronged "injury-in-fact" test, or indeed any other test of "standing," without first determining whether the Constitution or a statute defines injury, and creates a cause of action for redress of that injury, in precisely the circumstance presented to the Court.

It may of course happen that a person believing himself injured in some obscure manner by government action will be held to have no legal right under the constitutional or statutory provision upon which he relies, and will not be permitted to complain of the invasion of another person's "rights." It ⊥**493** is quite another matter to employ the rhetoric of "standing" to deprive a person, whose interest is clearly protected by the law, of the opportunity to prove that his own rights have been violated. It is in precisely that dissembling enterprise that the Court indulges today.

The "case and controversy" limitation of Article III overrides no other provision of the Constitution. To construe that Article to deny standing "to the class for whose sake [a] constitutional protection is given," *Jones* v. *United States*, quoting *Hatch* v. *Reardon*, simply turns the Constitution on its head. Article III was designed to provide a ⊥**494** hospitable forum in which persons enjoying rights under the Constitution could assert those rights. How are we to discern whether a particular person is to be afforded a right of action in the courts? The Framers did not, of course, employ the modern vocabulary of standing. But this much is clear: The drafters of the Bill of Rights surely intended that the particular beneficiaries of their legacy should enjoy rights legally enforceable in courts of law. See *West Virginia State Bd. of Educ.* v. *Barnette*.

With these observations in mind, I turn to the problem of taxpayer standing in general, and this case in particular.

II

A

Frothingham v. *Mellon* involved a challenge to the Maternity Act of 1921, which provided financial grants to states that agreed to cooperate in programs designed to reduce infant and maternal mortality. Appellant contended that Congress, in enacting the program, had exceeded its authority under Article I, and had intruded on authority reserved to the States. The Court described Mrs. Frothingham's claim as follows: "[T]his plaintiff alleges . . . that she is a taxpayer of the United States; and her contention, though not clear, seems to be that the effect of the appropriations complained of will be to increase the burden of future taxation and thereby take her property without due process of law. The right of a taxpayer to enjoin the execution ⊥**495** of a federal appropriation act, on the ground that it is invalid and will result in taxation for illegal purposes, has never been passed upon by this Court."

The Court conceded that it had historically treated the interest of a *municipal* taxpayer in the application of the municipality's funds as sufficiently direct and immediate to warrant injunctive relief to prevent misuse. *Bradfield* v. *Roberts*, in which the Court permitted a federal taxpayer to present an Establishment Clause challenge to the use of federal money for the construction of hospital buildings in the District of Columbia, was held to fall within this rule because it was appropriate to treat the District of Columbia as a municipality. But the Court distinguished Mrs. Frothingham's action against the United States: "[T]he relation of a taxpayer of the United States to the Federal Government is very different. His interest in the moneys of the Treasury—partly realized from taxation and partly from other sources—is shared with millions of others; is comparatively minute and indeterminable; and the effect upon future taxation, of any payment out of the funds, so remote, fluctuating and uncertain, that no basis is afforded for an appeal to the preventive powers of a court of equity.

⊥**496** "The administration of any statute, likely to produce additional taxation to be imposed upon a vast number of taxpayers, the extent of whose several liability is indefinite and constantly changing, is essentially a matter of public and not of individual concern."

After noting the importance of judicial restraint, the Court concluded: "The party who invokes the [judicial] power must be able to show not only that the statute is invalid but that he has sustained or is immediately in danger of sustaining some direct injury as the result of its enforcement, and not merely that he suffers in some indefinite way in common with people generally."

Frothingham's reasoning remains obscure. The principal interpretive difficulty lies in the manner in which *Frothingham* chose to blend the language of policy with seemingly absolute statements about jurisdiction. For example, the Court commented with significance on the sheer number of taxpayers who might have raised a claim similar to that of Mrs. Frothingham. Yet it can hardly be argued that the Constitution bars from federal court a plaintiff who has suffered injury merely because others are similarly aggrieved. "[S]tanding is not to be denied simply ⊥**497** because many people suffer the same injury." *United States* v. *SCRAP*. And it is equally clear that the Constitution draws no distinction between injuries that are large, and those that are comparatively small. The line between more dollars and less is no valid constitutional measure. Cf. *Everson* v. *Board of Education* (Rutledge, J., dissenting). The only distinction that a Constitution guaranteeing justice to all can recognize is one between some injury and none at all.

Frothingham also stressed the indirectness of the taxpayer's injury. But, *as a matter of Article III standing*, if the causal relationship is sufficiently certain, the length of the causal chain is irrelevant. See *Warth* v. *Seldin*. The financial stake of a federal taxpayer in the outcome of a lawsuit challenging an allegedly unlawful federal expenditure is not qualitatively different from that of a state or a municipal taxpayer attacking a local expenditure. More importantly, the injury suffered by a taxpayer is not dependent on the extent of his tax payment. The concept of taxpayer injury necessarily recognizes the continuing stake of the taxpayer in the disposition of the Treasury to which he ⊥**498** has contributed his taxes, and his right to have those funds put to lawful uses. Until *Frothingham* there was nothing in our precedents to indicate that this concept, so comfortably applied to municipal taxpayers, was inconsistent with the framework of rights and remedies established by the Federal Constitution.

The explanation for the limit on federal taxpayer "standing" imposed by *Frothingham* must be sought in more substantive realms. *Justice HARLAN*, dissenting in *Flast*, came close to identifying what I consider the unstated premise of the *Frothingham* rule: "[The] taxpayer's complaint can consist only of an allegation that public funds have been, or shortly will be, expended for purposes inconsistent with the Constitution. The taxpayer cannot ask the return of any portion of his previous tax payments, cannot prevent the collection of any existing tax debt, and cannot demand an adjudication of the propriety of any particular level of taxation. His tax payments are received for the general purposes of the United States, and are, upon proper receipt, lost in the general revenues."

⊥**499** In a similar vein, the Government argued in *Flast* that taxpayer suits involve only a disagreement by the taxpayer with the uses to which tax revenues were committed, and that the resolution of such disagreements is entrusted to branches of the Federal Government other than the judiciary. The arguments of both the Government and *Justice HARLAN* are phrased, as they must be, not in the language of "standing," but of "legal rights" and "justiciable issues."

The *Frothingham* rule may be seen as founded solely on the prudential judgment by the Court that precipitate and unnecessary interference in the activities of a coequal branch of government should be avoided. Alternatively, *Frothingham* may be construed as resting upon an unarticulated, constitutionally established barrier between Congress' power to tax and its power to spend, which barrier makes it analytically impossible to mount an assault on the former through a challenge to the latter. But it is sufficient for present purposes to say that *Frothingham* held that the federal taxpayer has no continuing legal interest in the affairs of the Treasury analogous to a shareholder's continuing interest in the conduct of a corporation.

Whatever its provenance, the general rule of *Frothingham* displays sound judgment: Courts must be circumspect in dealing with the taxing power in order to avoid unnecessary intrusion into the functions of the legislative and executive branches. Congress' *purpose* in taxing will not ordinarily effect the validity of the tax. Unless the tax *operates* unconstitutionally, see *e.g*, *Murdock* v. *Pennsylvania*, the taxpayer may not object to the use of his funds. Mrs. Frothingham's argument, that the use of tax funds for purposes unauthorized by the Constitution amounted to a violation of due process, did not provide her with the required legal interest because the Due Process Clause of the Fifth Amendment does not protect taxpayers against increases in tax liability. See *Flast* v. *Cohen*. Mrs. Frothingham's claim was thus reduced **⊥500** to an assertion of "the States' interest in their legislative prerogatives," a third-party claim that could properly be barred. But in *Flast* the Court faced a different sort of constitutional claim, and found itself compelled to retreat from the general assertion in *Frothingham* that taxpayers have *no* interest in the disposition of their tax payments. To understand why *Frothingham's* bar necessarily gave way in the face of an Establishment Clause claim, we must examine the right asserted by a taxpayer making such a claim.

B

In 1947, nine Justices of this Court recognized that the Establishment Clause does impose a very definite restriction on the power to tax. The Court held in *Everson* v. *Board of Education* that the "'establishment of religion' clause of the First Amendment means at least this:" **⊥501** "No tax in any amount, large or small, can be levied to support any religious activities or institutions, whatever they may be called, or whatever form they may adopt, to teach or practice religion."

The members of the Court could not have been more explicit. "One of our basic rights is to be free of taxation to support a transgression of the constitutional command that the authorities 'shall make no law respecting an establishment of religion, or prohibiting the free exercise thereof.'" "[A]part from efforts to inject religious training or exercises and sectarian issues into the public schools, the only serious threat to maintaining that complete and permanent separation of religion and civil power which the First Amendment commands is through the use of the taxing power to support religion, religious establishments, or establishments having a religious foundation whatever their form or special religious function. . . . [M]oney taken by taxation from one is not to be used or given to support another's religious training or belief, or indeed one's own."

In determining whether the law challenged in *Everson* was one "respecting an establishment of religion," the Court did not fail to examine the historic meaning of the constitutional language, "particularly with respect to the imposition of taxes." For as *Justice RUTLEDGE* pointed out in his dissent, "No provision of the Constitution is more closely tied to or given content by its generating history than the religious clause of the First Amendment. It is at once the refined product and the terse summation of that history." That history bears a brief repetition in the present context.

Many of the early settlers of this Nation came here to escape the tyranny of laws that compelled the support of government-sponsored churches and that inflicted punishments for the failure to pay establishment taxes and tithes. But the inhabitants of the various colonies soon dis**⊥502**played a capacity to recreate the oppressive practices of the countries that they had fled. Once again persons of minority faiths were persecuted, and again such persons were subjected—this time by the colonial governments—to tithes and taxes for support of religion. *Reynolds* v. *United States*.

"These practices became so commonplace as to shock the freedom-loving colonials into a feeling of abhorrence. The imposition of taxes to pay ministers' salaries and to build and maintain churches and church property aroused their indignation. It was these feelings which found expression in the First Amendment." *Everson*.

In 1784-1785, before the adoption of the Constitution, the continuing conflict between those who saw state aid to religion as but the natural expression of "commonly shared" religious sentiments, and those who saw such support as a threat to the very notion of civil government, culminated in the battle fought in the Virginia House of Delegates over "a bill establishing provision for teachers of the Christian religion." *Reynolds*. The introduction of that bill in the state assembly prompted James Madison to prepare and circulate his famous "Memorial and Remonstrance Against Religious Assessments," imploring the legislature to establish and maintain the complete separation of religion and civil authority, and thus to reject the bill. In the end, the bill was rejected by the Virginia legislature, and in its place Madison succeeded in securing the enactment of a "A Bill for Establishing Religious Freedom," first introduced in the Virginia General Assembly seven years earlier by Thomas Jefferson. **⊥503** Because Madison and Jefferson played such leading roles in the events leading to the adoption of the First Amendment, the *Everson* opinions did not hesitate to reproduce the partial text of their Virginia bill as a primary source for understanding the objectives, and protections, afforded by the more concise phrasing of the Establishment Clause. Extracts from that bill also bear repeating in the present context. The preamble provided, in part: "[T]o compel a man to furnish contributions of money for the propagation of opinions which he disbelieves, is sinful and tyrannical; that even the forcing him to support this or that teacher of his own religious persuasion, is depriving him of the comfortable liberty of giving his contributions to the particular pastor, whose morals he would make his pattern." 12 Hennings Stat. 85.

Its operative language emphatically stated: "That no man shall be compelled to frequent or support any religious worship, place or ministry whatsoever, nor shall be enforced, restrained, molested, or burthened in his body or goods, nor shall otherwise suffer on account of his religious opinions or belief. . . ." *Id.*, at 86.

Justice RUTLEDGE summed up Madison's views in the following terms: "In no phase was he more unrelentingly absolute than in opposing state support or aid by taxation. Not even 'three pence' contribution was thus to be exacted from ⊥**504** any citizen for such a purpose. Tithes had been the lifeblood of establishment before and after other compulsions disappeared. Madison and his coworkers made no exceptions or abridgments to the complete separation [between church and state] they created. Their objection was not to small tithes. It was to any tithes whatsoever. 'If it were lawful to impose a small tax for religion, the admission would pave the way for oppressive levies.' Not the amount, but 'the principle of the assessment' was wrong." *Everson*.

It is clear in the light of this history, that one of the primary purposes of the Establishment Clause was to prevent the use of tax monies for religious purposes. *The taxpayer was the direct and intended beneficiary of the prohibition on financial aid to religion.* This basic understanding of the meaning of the Establishment Clause explains why the Court in *Everson*, while rejecting appellant's claim on the merits, ⊥**505** perceived the issue presented there as it did. The appellant sued "in his capacity as a district taxpayer" challenging the actions of the Board of Education in passing a resolution providing reimbursement to parents for the cost of transporting their children to parochial schools, and seeking to have that resolution "set aside." Appellant's Establishment Clause claim was precisely that the "statute . . . forced inhabitants to pay taxes to help support and maintain" church schools. It seems obvious that all the Justices who participated in *Everson* would have agreed with *Justice* JACKSON's succinct statement of the question presented: "Is it constitutional to tax this complainant to pay the cost of carrying pupils to Church schools of one specified denomination?" Given this view of the issues, could it fairly be doubted that this taxpayer alleged injury in precisely the form that the Establishment Clause sought to make actionable?

C

In *Flast* v. *Cohen* federal taxpayers sought to challenge the Department of Health, Education, and Welfare's administration of the Elementary and Second⊥**506**ary Education Act of 1965: specifically the Department's practice of allowing funds distributed under that Act to be used to finance instruction in religious schools. Appellants urged that the use of federal funds for such a purpose violated the Establishment and Free Exercise Clauses of the First Amendment, and sought a declaration that this use of federal funds was not authorized by the Act, or that to the extent the use was authorized, the Act was "unconstitutional and void." Appellants further sought an injunction to bar appellees from approving any expenditure of funds for the allegedly unconstitutional purposes. The *Frothingham* rule stood as a seemingly absolute barrier to the maintenance of the claim. The Court held, however, that the *Frothingham* barrier could be overcome by any claim that met both requirements of a two part "nexus" test.

The Justices who participated in *Flast* were not unaware of the Court's continued recognition of a federally cognizable "case or controversy" when a *local* taxpayer seeks to challenge as unconstitutional the use of a *municipality's* funds—⊥**507** the propriety of which had, of course, gone unquestioned in *Everson*. The Court was aware as well of the rule stated in *Doremus* v. *Board of Education* that the interest of a taxpayer, even one raising an Establishment Clause claim, was limited to the actions of a government involving the expenditure of funds. But in reaching its holding, it is also quite clear that the Court was responding, not only to *Everson's* continued acceptance of municipal taxpayer actions but also to *Everson's* exposition of the history and meaning of the Establishment Clause. See *Flast*.

It is at once apparent that the test of standing formulated by the Court in *Flast* sought to reconcile the developing doctrine of taxpayer "standing" with the Court's historical understanding that the Establishment Clause was intended to prohibit the Federal Government from using tax funds for the advancement of religion, and thus the constitutional imperative of taxpayer standing in certain cases brought pursuant to the Establishment Clause. The two-pronged "nexus" test offered by the Court, despite its general language, is ⊥**508** best understood as "a determinant of standing of plaintiffs alleging only injury as taxpayers who challenge alleged violations of the Establishment and Free Exercise Clauses of the First Amendment," and not as a general statement of standing principles. *Schlesinger* v. *Reservists Committee to Stop the War; Flast*. The test explains what forms of governmental action may be attacked by someone alleging *only* taxpayer status, and, without ruling out the possibility that history might reveal another similarly founded provision, explains why an Establishment Clause claim is treated differently from any other assertion that the federal government has exceeded the bounds of the law in allocating its largesse. Thus, consistent with *Doremus*, *Flast* required, as the first prong of its test, that the taxpayer demonstrate a logical connection between his taxpayer status and the type of legislation attacked. Appellants' challenge to a program of grants to educational institutions clearly satisfied this first requirement. As the second prong, consistent with the prohibition of taxpayer claims of the kind advanced in *Frothingham*, appellants were required to show a connection between their status and the precise nature of the infringement alleged. They had no difficulty meeting this requirement: the Court agreed that the Establishment Clause jealously protects taxpayers from diversion of their funds to the support of religion through the offices of the Federal Government.

⊥**509** The nexus test that the Court "announced" sought to maintain necessary continuity with prior cases, and set forth principles to guide future cases involving taxpayer standing. But *Flast* did not depart from the principle that no judgment about standing should be made without a fundamental understanding of the rights at issue. The two-part *Flast* test did not supply the rationale for the Court's decision, but rather its exposition: That rationale was supplied by an understanding of the nature of the restrictions on government power imposed by the Constitution and the intended beneficiaries of those restrictions.

It may be that Congress can tax for *almost* any reason, or for no reason at all. There is, so far as I have been able to discern, but one constitutionally imposed limit on that authority. Congress cannot use tax money to support a church, or to encourage religion. That is "*the* forbidden exaction." *Everson* v. *Board of Education* (emphasis added). See *Flast*. In absolute terms the history of the Establishment Clause of the First Amendment makes this clear. History also makes it clear that the federal taxpayer is a singularly "proper and appropriate party to invoke a federal court's jurisdiction" to challenge a federal bestowal of largesse as a violation of the Establishment Clause. Each, and indeed every, federal taxpayer suffers precisely the injury that the Establishment Clause guards against when the Federal Government directs that funds be taken from the pocketbooks of the citizenry and placed into the coffers of the ministry.

A taxpayer cannot be asked to raise his objection to such use of his funds at the time he pays his tax. Apart from the unlikely circumstance in which the Government announced in advance that a particular levy would be used for religious subsidies, taxpayers could hardly assert that they were being injured until the Government actually lent its support to a religious venture. Nor would it be reasonable to require him to address his claim to those officials charged with the collec⊥**510**tion of federal taxes. Those officials would be without the means to provide appropriate redress—there is no practical way to segregate the complaining taxpayer's money from that being devoted to the religious purpose. Surely, then, a taxpayer must have standing at the time that he learns of the Government's alleged Establishment Clause violation to seek equitable relief in order to halt the continuing and intolerable burden on his pocketbook, his conscience, and his constitutional rights.

III

Blind to history, the Court attempts to distinguish this case from *Flast* by wrenching snippets of language from our opinions, and by perfunctorily applying that language under color of the first prong of *Flast's* two-part nexus test. The tortuous distinctions thus produced are specious, at best: at worst, they are pernicious to our constitutional heritage.

First, the Court finds this case different from *Flast* because here the "source of [plaintiff's] complaint is not a *congressional* action, but a decision by HEW to transfer a parcel of federal property" (emphasis added). This attempt at distinction cannot withstand scrutiny. *Flast* involved a challenge to the actions of the Commissioner of Education, and other officials of HEW, in disbursing funds under the Elementary and Secondary Education Act of 1965 to "religious and sectarian" schools. Plaintiffs disclaimed "any intention to challenge all programs under . . . the Act." *Flast*. Rather, they claimed that defendant-administrators' approval of such expenditures was not authorized by the Act, or alternatively, to the extent the expenditure was authorized, the Act was "unconstitutional and void." In the present case, respondents challenge HEW's grant of property pursuant to the Federal Property and Administrative Services Act of 1949, seeking to enjoin HEW "from making a grant of this and other property to the [defendant] so long as such grant will violate the Establishment Clause." It may be that the Court is concerned with the adequacy of respondents' pleading; re⊥**511**spondents have not, in so many words, asked for a declaration that the "Federal Property and Administrative Services Act is unconstitutional and void to the extent that it authorizes HEW's actions." I would not construe their complaint so narrowly.

More fundamentally, no clear division can be drawn in this context between actions of the legislative branch and those of the executive branch. To be sure, the First Amendment is phrased as a restriction on Congress' legislative authority; this is only natural since the Constitution assigns the authority to legislate and appropriate only to the Congress. But it is difficult to conceive of an expenditure for which the last governmental actor, either implementing directly the legislative will, or acting within the scope of legislatively delegated authority, is not an Executive Branch official. The First Amendment binds the Government as a whole, regardless of which branch is at work in a particular instance.

The Court's second purported distinction between this case and *Flast* is equally unavailing. The majority finds it "decisive" that the Federal Property and Administrative Services Act of 1949 "was an evident exercise of Congress' power under the Property Clause, Art. IV, § 3, cl. 2," while the government action in *Flast* was taken under the Art. I, § 8. The Court relies on *United States* v. *Richardson* and *Schlesinger* v. *Reservists Committee to Stop the War* to support the distinction between the two clauses, noting that those cases involved alleged deviations from the requirements of Art. I, § 9, cl. 7, and Art. I, § 6, cl. 2, respectively. The standing defect in each case was *not*, however, the failure to allege a violation of the Spending Clause; rather, the taxpayers in those cases had not complained of the distribution of government largesse, and thus failed to meet the essential requirement of taxpayer standing recognized in *Doremus*.

It can make no constitutional difference in the case before us whether the donation to the defendant here was in the form of a cash grant to build a facility, see *Tilton* v. *Richard*⊥**512***son*, or in the nature of a gift of property including a facility already built. That this is a meaningless distinction is illustrated by *Tilton*. In that case, taxpayers were afforded standing to object to the fact that the

Government had not received adequate assurance that if the property that it financed for use as an educational facility was later converted to religious uses, it would receive full value for the property, as the Constitution requires. The complaint here is precisely that, although the property at issue is actually being used for a sectarian purpose, the government has not received, nor demanded, full value payment. Whether undertaken pursuant to the Property Clause or the Spending Clause, the breach of the Establishment Clause, and the relationship of the taxpayer to that breach, is precisely the same.

IV

⊥513 Plainly hostile to the Framers' understanding of the Establishment Clause, and *Flast's* enforcement of that understanding, the Court vents that hostility under the guise of standing, "to slam the courthouse door against plaintiffs who [as the Framers intended] are entitled to full consideration of their [Establishment Clause] claims on the merits." *Barlow* v. *Collins*. Therefore, I dissent.

Justice STEVENS, dissenting.

In Parts I, II, and III of his dissenting opinion, *Justice BRENNAN* demonstrates that respondent taxpayers have standing to mount an Establishment Clause challenge against the Federal Government's transfer of property worth $1,300,000 to the Assembly of God. For the Court to hold that plaintiffs' **⊥514** standing depends on whether the Government's transfer was an exercise of its power to spend money, on the one hand, or its power to dispose of tangible property, on the other, is to trivialize the standing doctrine.

One cannot read the Court's opinion and the concurring opinions of *Justice STEWART* and *Justice FORTAS* in *Flast* v. *Cohen* without forming the firm conclusion that the plaintiffs' invocation of the Establishment Clause was of decisive importance in resolving the standing issue in that case. *Justice FORTAS* made this point directly: "I agree that the congressional powers to tax and spend are limited by the prohibition upon Congress to enact laws 'respecting an establishment of religion.' This thesis, slender as its basis is, provides a direct 'nexus,' as the Court puts it, between the use and collection of taxes and the congressional action here. Because of this unique 'nexus,' in my judgment, it is not farfetched to recognize that a taxpayer has a special claim to status as a litigant in a case raising the 'establishment' issue. This special claim is enough, I think, to permit us to allow the suit, coupled, as it is, with the interest which the taxpayer and all other citizens have in the church-state issue. In terms of the structure and basic philosophy of our constitutional government, it would be difficult to point to any issue that has a more intimate, pervasive, and fundamental impact upon the life of the taxpayer—and upon the life of all citizens.

"Perhaps the vital interest of a citizen in the establishment issue, without reference to his taxpayer's status, would be acceptable as a basis for this challenge. We need not decide this. But certainly, I believe, we must recognize that our principle of judicial scrutiny of legislative acts which raise important constitutional questions requires that the issue here presented—the separation of state and church—which the Founding Fathers re**⊥515**garded as fundamental to our constitutional system—should be subjected to judicial testing. This is not a question which we, if we are to be faithful to our trust, should consign to limbo, unacknowledged, unresolved, and undecided.

"On the other hand, the urgent necessities of this case and the precarious opening through which we find our way to confront it, do not demand that we open the door to a general assault upon exercises of the spending power. The status of taxpayer should not be accepted as a launching pad for an attack upon any target other than legislation affecting the Establishment Clause."

Today the Court holds, in effect, that the Judiciary has no greater role in enforcing the Establishment Clause than in enforcing other "norm[s] of conduct which the federal government is bound to honor," such as the Accounts Clause, *United States* v. *Richardson*, and the Incompatibility Clause, *Schlesinger* v. *Reservists Committee to Stop the War*. Ironically, however, its decision rests on the premise that the difference between a disposition of funds pursuant to the Spending Clause and a disposition of realty pursuant to the Property Clause is of fundamental jurisprudential significance. With all due respect, I am persuaded that the essential holding of *Flast* v. *Cohen* attaches special importance to the Establishment Clause and does not permit the drawing of a tenuous distinction between the Spending Clause and the Property Clause.

For this reason, and for the reasons stated in Parts I, II, and III of *Justice BRENNAN's* opinion, I would affirm the judgment of the Court of Appeals.

TAX EXEMPTION TO RELIGIOUS INSTITUTIONS

Although the United States Supreme Court has given attention to a wide range of Establishment and Free Exercise Clause questions, the relationship between churches and taxation remains largely unexplored. The reason for this is primarily historical.

Tax exemption for religious institutions and leaders is an ancient and virtually universal concept, nearly always to be found wherever an establishment of religion has existed. Consequently, tax exemption for the established church was found in all but a few of the early American colonies. Even after the First Amendment was ratified most states continued to grant tax exemptions to religious institutions. So it is today: many states have constitutional or statutory provisions for exemption. A major rationale for this practice is that the state's power to tax is the power to control and thus the concept of separation of church and state demands that churches should be tax-exempt. Another justification for exemption is that it has been widely assumed that churches perform a valuable service for the community in that they promote a moral ideology necessary to a stable society. Furthermore, it is often noted that churches perform certain social functions which otherwise would require state performance at public expense (e.g., care of the aged and orphans). Tax exemptions, it has been argued, are in exchange for these services. Opponents of exemptions have contended that to exempt churches is to give them an indirect state subsidy: a violation of the Establishment Clause. But, because of the long-standing historical precedent for tax exemption and the rationale behind it, until recently the Supreme Court refused to accept any cases challenging the practice.

In 1970, the Court agreed to hear a case involving the issue of property tax exemptions for churches. Frederick Walz, a New York lawyer, bought a piece of property in New York City specifically for the purpose of initiating a case that would eliminate such exemptions. He claimed that because the churches in New York were tax-exempt, he, as a taxpayer, was required to make an indirect contribution to those religious bodies. Thus, he claimed that tax exemptions on property used for religious worship were a violation of the Establishment Clause.

The Court, in WALZ v. TAX COMMISSION, sustained the tax exemption on the basis of three arguments. First, Chief Justice Burger, the author of the opinion, pointed out that legislation creating the tax exemption did not grant it to churches only, but rather that churches were part of a large class of eleemosynary institutions which provide helpful services to the community. Consequently, the legislation had the effect of neither advancing nor inhibiting religion. Second, if the civil authority were to levy taxes on churches, it would be necessary to assess the taxable property, collect the taxes, and proceed with tax foreclosures in case of nonpayment. This kind of activity would bring churches and civil authorities into close proximity and foster an excessive entanglement between them. By not taxing the churches, the involvement between church and state was kept to a lesser, and more acceptable, level. (This excessive entanglement argument became the third part of the test for interpreting the Establishment Clause.) Finally, the argument from history was used. American churches had been exempt from property taxes for two centuries and it could be demonstrated that exemption had not led to an established church.

Dealing only with property used solely for religious worship, the *Walz* case left untouched an area fraught with controversy, that of "unrelated business income." Since the inception of income taxes, churches have been exempt from paying taxes on money earned from businesses that are totally unrelated to the religious mission of the church. Until 1950, in the federal tax system, unrelated business income of educational institutions and other charitable organizations was also exempt from income taxes. But in that year Congress took the exemption away from all organizations except churches. Churches operated radio stations, gasoline stations, apartment houses, steel mills, and even, in one instance, a girdle and brassiere factory. No other charitable institutions except churches were exempted from paying federal taxes on such income. Naturally, there was opposition to such preferential treatment of churches, even among most church leaders. However, the Supreme Court has never ruled on the constitutionality of such exemption.

The closest the Court has come to dealing with this issue was the case of *Diffenderfer* v. *Central Baptist Church of Miami, Florida* (1972). The church owned a parking lot on which its members parked when they came to Sunday worship. The rest of the week the church sold spaces on its lot, which made it a commercial enterprise exempt from city and state property taxes. A suit was filed claiming that such an arrangement violated the Establishment Clause. In 1971 the Court agreed to hear the case. Between acceptance of the case and oral arguments, Florida changed its law so that the parking lot in question and other religious properties would be subject to taxation in proportion to the time they were operated commercially. Because of the change in the law, the Court declared the case moot and passed up its chance to grapple with the question of whether government may constitutionally exempt from taxation church-owned property used for commercial purposes.

Meanwhile, Congress passed the Tax Reform Act of 1969. Under this statute, churches were placed in the same category as other charitable institutions, namely, their unrelated businesses and the income derived therefrom were made subject to federal taxes. However, the effective date of the act for churches was 1 January 1976, thus giving them time to adjust their activities to the provisions of the act and, of course, more years to enjoy paying no taxes on unrelated business income. In creating the legislation, Congress determined that all § 501(c)(3) organizations,[1] including religious organizations,

[1]Section 501(c)(3) of the Internal Revenue Code (26 U.S.C. §501(c)(3)) is the section which defines organizations which are exempt from income taxes because of

must file Internal Revenue Service (IRS) Form 990.[2] Given the amount and type of information required, churches were greatly concerned about the necessity to file the form. Furthermore, they believed that it would involve the government in internal church affairs, impermissible under the Establishment Clause.

In response to the concern of religious leaders, Congress initially agreed to exempt churches and conventions and associations of churches from having to file the form. In response to a Utah senator's concern that some units in the Mormon church known as "auxiliaries" be included in the exemption, the Senate added that word to the exempting legislation. Later, when a conference committee met to resolve differences between the House and Senate versions of the bill, the qualifying word "integrated" was added. Thus the amended §6033 limited the mandatory exemption from filing informational returns to "churches, their integrated auxiliaries, and conventions or associations of churches."[3]

Because the term "integrated auxiliaries" was not the subject of extensive hearings or debate, the interpretation and application of its meaning was left to the IRS. To determine which church organizations were to be recognized as integrated auxiliaries, in 1977 the IRS devised a three-part test:

(5)(i) For the purposes of this title, the term "integrated auxiliary of a church" means an organization:

(a) Which is exempt from taxation as an organization described in section 501(c)(3);
(b) Which is affiliated . . . with a church; and
(c) Whose principal activity is exclusively religious.[4]

The definition went on to ascribe the following meaning to "exclusively religious":

(ii) An organization's principal activity will not be considered to be exclusively religious if that activity is educational, literary, charitable, or of another nature (other than religious) that would serve as a basis for exemption under section 501(c)(3).[5]

An "affiliated" organization is one "either controlled by or associated with a church or a convention or association of churches."[6]

Since the IRS did not consider the "principal activity" of an organization to be "exclusively religious" if that activity itself would have qualified the organization for tax exemption under § 501(c)(3), an organization such as a denominational children's home or retirement home, or a church-related college was not considered an integrated auxiliary of a church body. That meant that such organizations had to file Form 990. Much worse, in the minds of most leaders of religious groups, the government was now in the position of defining the ministry of organizations related to churches.

The case of the Tennessee Baptist Children's Homes (TBCH) is illustrative of the problem.[7] The child care facility was established in 1891 and was, from the first, committed to providing a Christian environment for homeless or neglected children. It has had the goal of providing a highly regimented environment within which it could develop the physical, intellectual, and spiritual growth of children, including indoctrinating them in or converting them to the Baptist faith. At the time of the litigation, TBCH operated four childcare facilities in Tennessee.

In 1977, shortly after the IRS promulgated its definition of "integrated auxiliary," it informed TBCH that the homes conformed to the first two criteria, mentioned above, to be considered an integrated auxiliary of its parent church, but it did not meet the third, i.e., TBCH's principal activity was not exclusively religious because its services were dedicated to the entire community and, in addition, because its operation of childcare facilities would qualify it for § 501(c)(3) status on a basis other than religious. Consequently, TBCH would have to file Form 990.

their public service nature. It says, in pertinent part, that the following are exempt from paying income tax: "Corporations, any community chest, fund, or foundation, organized and operated exclusively for religious, charitable, scientific, testing for public safety, literary, or educational purposes, . . . no part of the net earnings of which inures to the benefit of any private shareholder or individual, no substantial part of the activities of which is carrying on propaganda, or otherwise attempting, to influence legislation . . . and which does not participate in, or intervene in . . . any political campaign on behalf of any candidate for public office."

[2]26 U.S.C. § 6033 requires that Form 990, a financial information form, should be filed annually and requires disclosure of, among other things, gross income; costs incurred in obtaining income; expenditures for exempt purposes; assets; liabilities; net worth; total contributions; names and addresses of substantial contributors; names, addresses, and compensation of officers, directors, trustees, and highly paid employees; a detailed description of any activities engaged in that have not previously been reported to the IRS; copies of all governing instruments; and amounts spent directly or indirectly on behalf of a candidate for public office.

It should be noted that this requirement imposed no taxes on the affected exempt organizations, but merely compelled churches, in this case, to disclose information that the IRS thought necessary to implement the Internal Revenue laws.

[3]26 U.S.C. § 6033(a)(2)(A).

[4]Treasury Regulation § 1.6033-2(g)(5).

[5]Treasury Regulation § 1.6033-2(g)(5)(ii).

[6]Treasury Regulation § 1.6033-2(g)(5)(iii).

[7]*Tennessee Baptist Children's Homes* v. *United States*. For another example, cf. *Lutheran Social Services of Minnesota* v. *United States*.

The administrators of TBCH refused to accept the IRS's definition and to file the required form. The IRS assessed penalties and interest, which TBCH paid. The Homes also requested refund of the penalty payments, which the IRS denied. In 1983 TBCH filed suit in federal district court, requesting recovery of the penalty payments and a redefinition of their activity, insisting that their principal activity was exclusively religious. TBCH also requested that the IRS pay all its attorney's fees and court costs and that the court declare that Treasury Regulation § 1.6033-2(g)(1)(i) & (g)(5), which required TBCH to file Form 990, is unconstitutional. The trial court found in TBCH's favor on the main issue, i.e., that TBCH's principal activity is exclusively religious, that it did not have to file Form 990, and that the IRS should return the penalty payments. However, the court denied the request for attorney's fees and refused to rule on the constitutionality of the regulation. On appeal by the IRS, a court of appeals affirmed all parts of the district court's decision.

The testimony by the government in this case illustrated exactly what church leaders feared as the worst result of the "exclusively religious" requirement of the regulations. Government lawyers argued that because TBCH provided for children such nonreligious services as food, shelter, medical expenses, and education, it is not exclusively religious, since similar services would be provided by a secular childcare facility. In the appeal, a government lawyer declared that "religious activity is limited only to the conduct of worship." That, of course, puts the government in the position of defining the ministry of a church-related institution and prevents all but places where worship is conducted from being exempt from filing Form 990. Fortunately, from the viewpoint of churches, the courts found against the government's position.[8]

The court of appeals decision in the *Tennessee Homes* case was handed down 14 May 1986. Just prior to that, on 6 May 1986, the IRS announced a change in policy which may have made the bulk of that litigation moot. When the detrimental aspects of the "integrated auxiliary" and "exclusively religious" dimensions of the IRS code became clear to church leaders, they formed a committee of representatives from a number of denominations and requested a dialogue with IRS officials. The result of those conversations was a modification of the IRS rules about exemption from having to file Form 990 (although some believe that the change would not have come about solely because of the conversations, but that litigation such as the *Tennessee Homes* case and some decisions against the government helped considerably). The change was the issuance of Revenue Procedure 86-23, which asserted that internally supported affiliates of churches or conventions or associations of churches would be exempt from filing. Under this interpretation, an organization is considered internally supported unless it both:

(1) Offers admissions, goods, services, or facilities for sale, other than on an incidental basis, to the general public (except goods, services, or facilities sold at a nominal charge or substantially less than cost), and

(2) normally receives more than 50 percent of its support from a combination of governmental sources; public solicitation of contributions (such as through a community fund drive); and receipts from the sale of admissions, goods, performance of services, or furnishing of facilities in activities that are not unrelated trades or businesses.[9]

This change was widely hailed by religious leaders as again making institutions such as denominational orphanages and church-related colleges exempt from having to file Form 990 and, perhaps more importantly, effectively prevents the government from declaring the ministry of such organizations to be nonreligious. Although the Supreme Court had never heard a tax case involving governmental definitions of religion and ministry, it may be that the new attitude on the part of the IRS will effectively remove that issue from the possibility of litigation.

In its 1988-89 and 1989-90 terms, the Supreme Court heard three cases involving the taxation of religion that had Establishment Clause implications. The first was TEXAS MONTHLY v. BULLOCK. The State of Texas passed a law that exempted from sales tax subscriptions to periodicals consisting "wholly of writings promulgating the teaching of [religious] faith" and books consisting "wholly of writings sacred to a religious faith." Secular periodicals were not exempt from the collection of sales tax. *Texas Monthly,* a secular magazine, filed suit, claiming that the state's limited tax exemption was a violation of the Establishment Clause.[10]

[8]A very similar result was found in a federal court of appeals in *Lutheran Social Services of Minnesota* v. *United States.*

[9]Revenue Procecure 86-23, 6 May 1986.

[10]Texas had exempted all magazine subscriptions of six months or more prior to 1984 and reinstated the comprehensive exemption in 1987. So the exemption singling out religious publications existed only for a three-year period and had been repealed by the time this case reached the Court. What prevented the case from being moot is that *Texas Monthly* had paid $149,107 in sales taxes during those three years. Texas did not return the money when the law was changed. The magazine thus had standing to sue to challenge the discriminatory exemption in order to recover its funds. In the words of the Court: "Texas cannot strip appellant of standing by changing the law after taking its money" (498 U.S. 1, 8).

A state district court held that the tax exemption was unconstitutional as a promotion of religion. The court of appeals reversed, finding that the tax exemption conformed to all three prongs of the *Lemon* test. The Supreme Court reversed that holding. Employing the "endorsement" language of Justice O'Connor's reinterpretation of the *Lemon* test in LYNCH v. DONNELLY, the Court, in an opinion written by Justice Brennan, held that Texas's law lacked a secular purpose. By exempting only religious publications, it had clearly endorsed religion over nonreligion. "It is difficult to view Texas' narrow exemption as anything but state sponsorship of religious belief, . . ." (498 U.S. 1, 15). The state could avoid this result by exempting all publications from taxation or by taxing them all. But it could not exempt only religious publications.[11]

Texas claimed that its exemption was consistent with the ruling in MURDOCK v. PENNSYLVANIA and *Follett* v. *McCormick,* two Jehovah's Witnesses cases from the 1940s which struck down flat license taxes applied to street preaching. The Court argued that those cases were not inconsistent with its holding in the case at bar, in which it held the selective sales tax exemption to be unconstitutional. In fact, the two cases were not on the point of the instant case. There the tax was on the missionaries; a tax that conditioned missionary activity on the payment, thus operating as a prior restraint on religious activity. Here the tax was a small percent of a purchase and payable by the *buyer,* consequently running small risk of curtailing missionary work through the sale of religious publications. To the extent that *Murdock* and *Follett* could be read to suggest that a government may never tax the sale of religious or other publications, the Court rejected such broad dicta.

"As a judicial demolition project, today's decision is impressive" (498 U.S. 1, 29). With those words Justice Scalia began a sharply worded dissent. He accused the majority of destroying what he claimed has been commonly done in the United States, i.e., provide tax exemptions for religious institutions without making them available to other types of nonprofit organizations. Furthermore, he argued that the decision is contrary to strong precedent, particularly WALZ v. TAX COMMISSION, in which the Court approved property tax exemptions for places of worship, and ZORACH v. CLAUSON, which upheld released-time religious education for public schools. Scalia wrote of an "accommodation principle," which, he believed, was articulated in HOBBIE v. UNEMPLOYMENT APPEALS COMMISSION. In that case the majority wrote that "the government may (and sometimes must) accommodate religious practices and that it may do so without violating the Establishment Clause." He believed that this "accommodation principle" is found in many of the Court's decisions and should have controlled here. Justice Scalia ended his dissent by saying that *Texas Monthly* "introduces a new strain of irrationality in our Religion Clause jurisprudence" (498 U.S. 1, 45).

In HERNANDEZ v. COMMISSIONER OF INTERNAL REVENUE the Court made a decision on the deductibility of payments to a religious organization. Section 170 of the Internal Revenue Code permits federal taxpayers to deduct from the gross income listed on their tax forms the amount of charitable contributions. Among those entities that qualify as legitimate recipients of charitable contributions are organizations "organized and operated exclusively for religious . . . purposes, . . ."[12]

The Church of Scientology provides for its devotees what may be described as psychological, or, better, counseling services. It has a procedure, known as "auditing," which is designed to help one identify areas of spiritual or psychic difficulty and to eliminate them. In the vocabulary of Scientology, these problems are known as "engrams." The condition of being free of engrams is known as "clear," i.e., being free from all psychological or spiritual malfunctions. Consequently, the person going through the auditing process, working toward the "clear" state, is known as a "preclear." The church also offers doctrinal courses, known as "training." The primary function of these instructions in the tenets of Scientology is to prepare people to become auditors.

Both "auditing" and "training" are offered sequentially. That is, one must grow in spiritual awareness and doctrinal knowledge. That cannot happen quickly, so there needs to be a series of sessions or courses, each with an increasing level of spiritual insight. The Church of Scientology charges fees for each of these various services. The church describes these charges as a "price," a "fixed donation," or a "fixed contribution." This price schedule is based on the church's "doctrine of exchange," a central tenet of Scientology. It is defined as the idea that anytime one receives something, one must pay something back. Under this doctrine, the revenue generated from auditing and training are the church's primary source of income.

[11]It is interesting to note that Justice Brennan, the author of the Court's opinion, quite clearly equates a tax exemption with a subsidy (cf. 498 U.S. 1, 14–15) whereas he argues in his concurring opinion in WALZ v. TAX COMMISSION that a tax exemption is not the same as a subsidy (cf. 379 U.S. 664, 690–691).

[12]26 U.S.C. § 170(a)(2)(B). The language in this statute is virtually identical to that in 26 U.S.C. § 501(c)(3).

People engaged in these procedures have routinely deducted the money they paid from their federal income tax as "charitable contributions." The IRS has disallowed those deductions—thus this case (and several others like it around the country). The Supreme Court, in its decision in this consolidated case, affirmed the decisions of the Tax Court and Court of Appeals and disallowed the contribution. Why? It was not because Scientology was not regarded as a religion, for the government stipulated that it is a religion and eligible to receive tax-deductible contributions under § 170.

The Court disallowed the payments as charitable contributions because it agreed with the IRS that they are not actually *contributions*. They are payments for specific services and in response to a specific fee schedule—they are given with the expectation of a *quid pro quo,* and consequently are not charitable contributions under the statute. "'The *sine qua non* of a charitable contribution is a transfer of money or property *without adequate consideration*'" (490 U.S. 680, 691).[13] The fatal flaw in Scientology's scheme, from the perspective of the deductibility of contributions, is that it has specific charges for specific courses in auditing or training.

The Court gave attention to constitutional arguments as well as statutory interpretation. Scientology argued that the law erected a harsher standard of deductibility for those religious groups that raise funds by imposing fixed costs for participation in some religious practices, thus violating the Establishment Clause. Also, § 170 promotes government entanglement with religion because it requires the IRS to evaluate the services of various religions. The Court disagreed. The statute does not discriminate between denominations. If the payment is a gift or contribution, it is deductible. If it is given with the expectation of a *quid pro quo,* it is not deductible. It is the same for all religions. Section 170 bears no animus to religion in general or to Scientology. As to entanglement, the IRS does have to obtain some information from the religious organization to determine if the payment is actually a gift. But that involves no inquiry into doctrine, nor does it require close administrative contact between the government and the religious group. Scientology claimed that the denial of deductibility interfered with the "doctrine of exchange." The Court responded that the doctrine does not prohibit the payment of taxes. At most, the denial means that adherents have less money available to purchase church services. But that is true of any taxing program and does not make taxation unconstitutional. Furthermore, the denial of deduction does not violate the doctrine of exchange. One may still equalize "outflow" with "inflow." One just has less money with which to do that.

Finally, Scientology argued that there had been selective enforcement of the tax code because the IRS had traditionally allowed the deductibility of payments made to other religious organizations when there appeared to be a *quid pro quo* relationship. (In a vigorous dissent joined by Justice Scalia, Justice O'Connor agreed with that argument.) The Court refused to rule on that argument because the record developed in the courts below was inadequate to show how the IRS had dealt with other religious groups on this question.

The deductibility of money under § 170 was the subject of the 1990 case DAVIS v. UNITED STATES. The Church of Jesus Christ of Latter-day Saints (Mormons) requires qualified young people to serve as missionaries for a two year period. The church decides who is qualified, where and when the missionaries will serve, and how much money it will take to sustain them during their years of service. That money is paid, except in unusual circumstances, by the missionaries' families. The money goes directly to the missionaries, but with the express understanding (articulated by the church) that the money is only to be used for expenses of the missionary work.

The two sons of Harold and Enid Davis went on missionary service and the parents provided them money to sustain them. But, because it was church work in which the sons were engaged, the Davis family deducted the amount of money given to the sons from their federal income tax—as a "charitable contribution" under § 170. When the IRS disallowed the deduction, the Davis family sued, only to lose at the district and appellate court levels.

The Supreme Court affirmed the judgments of the lower courts. A unanimous Court decided the case only on construction of the statutory language, without reaching any constitutional questions. Section 170(a)(1)(c) defines a charitable contribution as a contribution or gift "to or for the use of" a qualifying organization. The Court ruled that because the money went directly to the sons, who had total discretion over how the money was to be spent (albeit they had promised to use it only for their missionary work) and that the Mormon Church had no legal control over the money whatsoever, it was not money given "for the use of" the church. Consequently, the payments were not deductible under the statute.

The Court has dealt with other tax-related cases in which the Establishment Clause was not involved. Those are discussed in this book in the section entitled "Free Exercise and Taxation."

[13]Quoting *United States* v. *American Bar Endowment* 477 U.S. 105, 118 (1986), emphasis added in part.

WALZ v. TAX COMMISSION OF THE CITY OF NEW YORK

397 U.S. 664
ON APPEAL FROM THE COURT OF APPEALS OF THE STATE OF NEW YORK
Argued November 19, 1969 — Decided May 4, 1970

⊥**666** Mr. *Chief Justice BURGER* delivered the opinion of the Court.

Appellant, owner of real estate in Richmond County, New York, sought an injunction in the New York courts to prevent the New York City Tax Commission from granting property tax exemptions to religious organizations for religious properties used solely for religious worship. The exemption from state taxes is authorized by Art. 16, § 1, of the New York Constitution, which provides: "Exemptions from taxation may be granted only by general laws. Exemptions may be altered or repealed except those exempting real or personal property used exclusively for religious, educational or ⊥**667** charitable purposes as defined by law and owned by any corporation or association organized or conducted exclusively for one or more of such purposes and not operating for profit."

The essence of appellant's contention was that the New York State Tax Commission's grant of an exemption to church property indirectly requires the appellant to make a contribution to religious bodies and thereby violates provisions prohibiting establishment of religion under the First Amendment which under the Fourteenth Amendment is binding on the states.

Appellee's motion for summary judgment was granted and the Appellate Division, New York Supreme Court, and the New York Court of Appeals affirmed. We noted jurisdiction and affirm.

I

Prior opinions of this Court have discussed the development and historical background of the First Amendment in detail. It would therefore serve no useful purpose to review in detail the background of the Establishment and Free ⊥**668** Exercise Clauses of the First Amendment or to restate what the Court's opinions have reflected over the years.

It is sufficient to note that for the men who wrote the Religious Clauses of the First Amendment the "establishment" of a religion connoted sponsorship, financial support, and active involvement of the sovereign in religious activity. In England, and in some Colonies at the time of the separation in 1776, the Church of England was sponsored and supported by the Crown as a state, or established, church; in other countries "establishment" meant sponsorship by the sovereign of the Lutheran or Catholic Church. The exclusivity of established churches in the 17th and 18th centuries, of course, was often carried to prohibition of other forms of worship.

The Establishment and Free Exercise Clauses of the First Amendment are not the most precisely drawn portions of the Constitution. The sweep of the absolute prohibitions in the Religion Clauses may have been calculated; but the purpose was to state an objective, not to write a statute. In attempting to articulate the scope of the two Religion Clauses, the Court's opinions reflect the limitations inherent in formulating general principles on a case-by-case basis. The considerable internal inconsistency in the opinions of the Court derives from what, in retrospect, may have been too sweeping utterances on aspects of these clauses that seemed clear in relation to the particular cases but have limited meaning as general principles.

The Court has struggled to find a neutral course between the two Religion Clauses, both of which are cast in absolute terms, and either of which, if expanded to a ⊥**669** logical extreme, would tend to clash with the other. For example, in *Zorach* v. *Clauson*, Mr. *Justice DOUGLAS*, writing for the Court, noted: "The First Amendment however, does not say that in every and all respects there shall be a separation of Church and State."

"We sponsor an attitude on the part of government that shows no partiality to any one group and that lets each flourish according to the zeal of its adherents and the appeal of its dogma."

Mr. *Justice HARLAN* expressed something of this in his dissent in *Sherbert* v. *Verner*, saying that the constitutional neutrality imposed on us "is not so narrow a channel that the slightest deviation from an absolutely straight course leads to condemnation."

The course of constitutional neutrality in this area cannot be an absolutely straight line; rigidity could well defeat the basic purpose of these provisions, which is to insure that no religion be sponsored or favored, none commanded, and none inhibited. The general principle deducible from the First Amendment and all that has been said by the Court is this: that we will not tolerate either governmentally established religion or governmental interference with religion. Short of those expressly proscribed governmental acts there is room for play in the joints productive of a benevolent neutrality which will permit religious exercise to exist without sponsorship and without interference.

Each value judgment under the Religion Clauses must therefore turn on whether particular acts in question are intended to establish or interfere with religious beliefs and practices or have the effect of doing so. Adherence to the policy of neutrality that derives from an accommodation of the Establishment and Free Exercise Clauses ⊥**670** has prevented the kind of involvement that would tip the balance toward government control of churches or governmental restraint on religious practice.

Adherents of particular faiths and individual churches frequently take strong positions on public issues including, as this case reveals in the several briefs *amici*, vigorous advocacy of legal or constitutional positions. Of course, churches as much as secular bodies and private citizens have that right. No perfect or absolute separation is really possible; the very existence of the Religion Clauses is an involvement of sorts—one which seeks to mark boundaries to avoid excessive entanglement.

The hazards of placing too much weight on a few words or phrases of the Court is abundantly illustrated within the pages of the Court's opinion in *Everson*. Mr. *Justice* BLACK, writing for the Court's majority, having said the First Amendment "means at least this: Neither a state nor the Federal Government can . . . pass laws which aid one religion, aid all religions, or prefer one religion over another," yet had no difficulty in holding that "Measured by these standards, we cannot say that the First Amendment prohibits New Jersey from spending tax-raised funds to pay the bus fares of parochial school pupils as a part of a general program under which it pays the fares of pupils attending public and other schools. *It is undoubtedly true that children are helped to get to church schools. There is even a possibility that some of the children might not be sent to the church schools if the parents were compelled to pay their children's bus fares out of their own pockets*. . . ." (Emphasis added.)

⊥671 The Court did not regard such "aid" to schools teaching a particular religious faith as any more a violation of the Establishment Clause than providing "state-paid policemen, detailed to protect children . . . [at the schools] from the very real hazards of traffic. . . ."

Mr. *Justice* JACKSON, in perplexed dissent in *Everson*, noted that "the undertones of the opinion, advocating complete and uncompromising separation . . . seem utterly discordant with its conclusion. . . ."

Perhaps so. One can sympathize with Mr. *Justice* JACKSON's logical analysis but agree with the Court's eminently sensible and realistic application of the language of the Establishment Clause. In *Everson* the Court declined to construe the Religion Clauses with a literalness that would undermine the ultimate constitutional objective as illuminated by history. Surely, bus transportation and police protection to pupils who receive religious instruction "aid" that particular religion to maintain schools that plainly tend to assure future adherents to a particular faith by having control of their total education at an early age. No religious body that maintains schools would deny this as an affirmative if not dominant policy of church schools. But if as in *Everson* buses can be provided to carry and policemen to protect church school pupils, we fail to see how a broader range of police and fire protection given equally to all churches, along with nonprofit hospitals, art galleries, and libraries receiving the same tax exemption, is different for purposes of the Religion Clauses.

Similarly, making textbooks available to pupils in parochial schools in common with public schools was surely an "aid" to the sponsoring churches because it relieved those churches of an enormous aggregate cost **⊥672** for those books. Supplying of costly teaching materials was not seen either as manifesting a legislative purpose to aid or as having a primary effect of aid contravening the First Amendment. *Board of Education* v. *Allen*. In so doing the Court was heeding both its own prior holdings and our religious tradition. Mr. *Justice* DOUGLAS, in *Zorach* v. *Clauson*, after recalling that we "are a religious people whose institutions presuppose a Supreme Being," went on to say: "We make room for as wide a variety of beliefs and creeds as the spiritual needs of man deem necessary. . . . *When the state encourages religious instruction . . . it follows the best of our traditions*. For it then respects the religious nature of our people and accommodates the public service to their spiritual needs." (Emphasis added.)

With all the risks inherent in programs that bring about administrative relationships between public education bodies and church-sponsored schools, we have been able to chart a course that preserved the autonomy and freedom of religious bodies while avoiding any semblance of established religion. This is a "tight rope" and one we have successfully traversed.

II

The legislative purpose of the property tax exemption is neither the advancement nor the inhibition of religion; it is neither sponsorship nor hostility. New York, in common with the other States, has determined that certain entities that exist in a harmonious relationship to the community at large, and that foster its "moral or mental improvement," should not be inhibited in their activities by property taxation or the hazard of loss of those properties for nonpayment of taxes. It **⊥673** has not singled out one particular church or religious group or even churches as such; rather, it has granted exemption to all houses of religious worship within a broad class of property owned by nonprofit, quasi-public corporations which include hospitals, libraries, playgrounds, scientific, professional, historical and patriotic groups. The State has an affirmative policy that considers these groups as beneficial and stabilizing influences in community life and finds this classification useful, desirable, and in the public interest. Qualification for tax exemption is not perpetual or immutable; some tax-exempt groups lose that status when their activities take them outside the classification and new entities can come into being and qualify for exemption.

Governments have not always been tolerant of religious activity, and hostility toward religion has taken many shapes and forms—economic, political, and sometimes harshly oppressive. Grants of exemption historically reflect the concern of authors of constitutions and statutes as to the latent dangers inherent in the imposition of property taxes; exemption constitutes a reasonable and balanced attempt to guard against those dangers. The limits of permissible state accommodation to religion are by no means co-extensive with the noninterference mandated by the Free Exercise Clause. To equate the two would be to deny a national heritage with roots in the Revolution itself. We cannot read New

York's statute as attempting to establish religion; it is simply sparing the exercise of religion from the burden of property taxation levied on private profit institutions.

⊥**674** We find it unnecessary to justify the tax exemption on the social welfare services of "good works" that some churches perform for parishioners and others—family counselling, aid to the elderly and the infirm, and to children. Churches vary substantially in the scope of such services; programs expand or contract according to resources and need. As public-sponsored programs enlarge, private aid from the church sector may diminish. The extent of social services may vary, depending on whether the church serves an urban or rural, a rich or poor constituency. To give emphasis to so variable an aspect of the work of religious bodies would introduce an element of governmental evaluation and standards as to the worth of particular social welfare programs, thus producing a kind of continuing day-to-day relationship which the policy of neutrality seeks to minimize. Hence, the use of a social welfare yardstick as a significant element to qualify for tax exemption could conceivably give rise to confrontations that could escalate to constitutional dimensions.

Determining that the legislative purpose of tax exemption is not aimed at establishing, sponsoring, or supporting religion does not end the inquiry, however. We must also be sure that the end result—the effect—is not an excessive government entanglement with religion. The test is inescapably one of degree. Either course, taxation of churches or exemption, occasions some degree of involvement with religion. Elimination of exemption would tend to expand the involvement of government by giving rise to tax valuation of church property, tax liens, tax foreclosures, and the direct confrontations and conflicts that follow in the train of those legal processes.

Granting tax exemptions to churches necessarily operates to afford an indirect economic benefit and also gives rise to some, but yet a lesser, involvement than taxing ⊥**675** them. In analyzing either alternative the questions are whether the involvement is excessive, and whether it is a continuing one calling for official and continuing surveillance leading to an impermissible degree of entanglement. Obviously a direct money subsidy would be a relationship pregnant with involvement and, as with most governmental grant programs, could encompass sustained and detailed administrative relationships for enforcement of statutory or administrative standards, but that is not this case. The hazards of churches supporting government are hardly less in their potential than the hazards of governments supporting churches; each relationship carries some involvement rather than the desired insulation and separation. We cannot ignore the instances in history when church support of government led to the kind of involvement we seek to avoid.

The grant of a tax exemption is not sponsorship since the government does not transfer part of its revenue to churches but simply abstains from demanding that the church support the state. No one has ever suggested that tax exemption has converted libraries, art galleries, or hospitals into arms of the state or employees "on the public payroll." There is no genuine nexus between tax exemption and establishment of religion. As *Mr. Justice HOLMES* commented in a related context "a page of ⊥**676** history is worth a volume of logic." *New York Trust Co.* v. *Eisner*. The exemption creates only a minimal and remote involvement between church and state and far less than taxation of churches. It restricts the fiscal relationship between church and state, and tends to complement and reinforce the desired separation insulating each from the other.

Separation in this context cannot mean absence of all contact; the complexities of modern life inevitably produce some contact and the fire and police protection received by houses of religious worship are no more than incidental benefits accorded all persons or institutions within a State's boundaries, along with many other exempt organizations. The appellant has not established even an arguable quantitative correlation between the payment of an ad valorem property tax and the receipt of these municipal benefits.

All of the 50 States provide for tax exemption of places of worship, most of them doing so by constitutional guarantees. For so long as federal income taxes have had any potential impact on churches—over 75 years—religious organizations have been expressly exempt from the tax. Such treatment is an "aid" to churches no more and no less in principle than the real estate tax exemption granted by States. Few concepts are more deeply embedded in the fabric of our national life, beginning with pre-Revolutionary colonial times, than for the government to exercise at the very least this kind of benevolent neutrality toward churches and religious exer⊥**677**cise generally so long as none was favored over others and none suffered interference.

It is significant that Congress, from its earliest days, has viewed the Religion Clauses of the Constitution as authorizing statutory real estate tax exemption to religious bodies. In 1802 the 7th Congress enacted a taxing statute for the County of Alexandria, adopting the 1800 Virginia statutory pattern which provided tax exemptions for churches. As early as 1813 the 12th Congress refunded import duties paid by religious societies on the importation of religious articles. During this period the City Council of Washington, D.C., acting under congressional authority, enacted a series of real and personal property assessments which uniformly exempted church property. In 1870 the Congress specifically exempted all churches in the District of Colum⊥**678**bia and appurtenant grounds and property "from any and all taxes or assessments, national, municipal, or county."

It is obviously correct that no one acquires a vested or protected right in violation of the Constitution by long use, even when that span of time covers our entire national existence and indeed predates it. Yet an unbroken practice of according the exemption to churches, openly and by affirmative state action, not covertly or by state inaction, is not something to be lightly cast aside. Nearly 50 years ago Mr. *Justice HOLMES* stated: "If a thing has been practised for two hundred years by common consent, it will need a strong case for the Fourteenth Amendment to affect it." *Jackman* v. *Rosenbaum*.

Nothing in this national attitude toward religious tolerance and two centuries of uninterrupted freedom from taxation has given the remotest sign of leading to an established church or religion and on the contrary it has operated affirmatively to help guarantee the free exercise of all forms of religious beliefs. Thus, it is hardly useful to suggest that tax exemption is but the "foot in the door" or the "nose of the camel in the tent" leading to an established church. If tax exemption can be seen as the first step toward "establishment" of religion, as Mr. *Justice DOUGLAS* fears, the second step has been long in coming. Any move which realistically "establishes" a church or tends to do so can be dealt with "while this Court sits."

Mr. *Justice CARDOZO* commented in The Nature of the Judicial Process (1921) on the "tendency of a prin⊥**679**ciple to expand itself to the limit of its logic"; such expansion must always be contained by the historical frame of reference of the principle's purpose and there is no lack of vigilance on this score by those who fear religious entanglement in government.

The argument that making "fine distinctions" between what is and what is not absolute under the Constitution is to render us a government of men, not laws, gives too little weight to the fact that it is an essential part of adjudication to draw distinctions, including fine ones, in the process of interpreting the Constitution. We must frequently decide, for example, what are "reasonable" searches and seizures under the Fourth Amendment. Determining what acts of government tend to establish or interfere with religion falls well within what courts have long been called upon to do in sensitive areas.

It is interesting to note that while the precise question we now decide has not been directly before the Court previously, the broad question was discussed by the Court in relation to real estate taxes assessed nearly a century ago on land owned by and adjacent to a church in Washington, D.C. At the time Congress granted real estate tax exemptions to buildings devoted to art, to institutions of public charity, libraries, cemeteries, and "church buildings, and grounds actually occupied by such buildings." In denying tax exemption as to land owned by but not used for the church, but rather to produce income, the Court concluded: "In the exercise of this [taxing] power, Congress, like any State legislature unrestricted by constitutional provisions, may at its discretion wholly exempt certain classes of property from taxation, or ⊥**680** may tax them at a lower rate than other property." *Gibbons* v. *District of Columbia*.

It appears that at least up to 1885 this Court, reflecting more than a century of our history and uninterrupted practice, accepted without discussion the proposition that federal or state grants of tax exemption to churches were not a violation of the Religion Clauses of the First Amendment. As to the New York statute, we now confirm that view.

Affirmed.

Mr. *Justice BRENNAN*, concurring.

I concur for reasons expressed in my opinion in *Abington Township* v. *Schempp*. I adhere to the view there stated that to give concrete meaning to the Establishment Clause, "the line we must draw between the permissible and the impermissible is one which accords with history and faithfully reflects the understanding of the Founding Fathers. It is a line which the Court has consistently sought to mark in its decisions expounding the religious guarantees of the First Amendment. What the Framers meant to foreclose, and what our decisions under the Establishment Clause have forbidden, are those involvements of religious with secular institutions which (a) serve the essentially religious activities of religious institutions; (b) employ the organs of government for essentially religious purposes; or (c) use essentially religious means to serve governmental ends, where secular means would suffice. When the secular and religious institutions become involved in such manner, there inhere in the relationship precisely those ⊥**681** dangers—as much to church as to state—which the Framers feared would subvert religious liberty and the strength of a system of secular government. On the other hand, there may be myriad forms of involvements of government with religion which do not import such dangers and therefore should not, in my judgment, be deemed to violate the Establishment Clause." Thus, in my view, the history, purpose, and operation of real property tax exemptions for religious organizations must be examined to determine whether the Establishment Clause is breached by such exemptions.

I

The existence from the beginning of the Nation's life of a practice, such as tax exemptions for religious organizations, is not conclusive of its constitutionality. But such practice is a fact of considerable import in the interpretation of abstract constitutional language. On its face, the Establishment Clause is reasonably susceptible of different interpretations regarding the exemptions. This Court's interpretation of the clause, accordingly, is appropriately influenced by the reading it has received in the practices of the Nation. As Mr. *Justice HOLMES* observed in an analogous context, in resolving such questions of interpretation "a page of history is worth a volume of logic." *New York Trust Co.* v. *Eisner*. The more longstanding and widely accepted a practice, the greater its impact upon constitutional interpretation. History is particularly compelling in the present case because of the undeviating acceptance given religious tax exemptions from our earliest days as a Nation. Rarely if ever has this Court considered the constitutionality of a practice for which the historical support is so overwhelming.

⊥682 The Establishment Clause, along with the other provisions of the Bill of Rights, was ratified by the States in 1791. Religious tax exemptions were not an issue in the petitions calling for the Bill of Rights, in the pertinent congressional debates, or in the debates preceding ratification by the States. The absence of concern about the exemptions could not have resulted from failure to foresee the possibility of their existence, for they were widespread during colonial days. Rather, it seems clear that the exemptions were not among the evils which the Framers and Ratifiers of the Establishment Clause sought to avoid. Significantly, within a decade after ratification, at least four States passed statutes exempting the property of religious organizations from taxation.

Although the First Amendment may not have applied to the States during this period, practice in Virginia at the time is nonetheless instructive. The Commonwealth's efforts to separate church and state provided the direct antecedents of the First Amendment, ⊥683 and Virginia remained unusually sensitive to the proper relation between church and state during the years immediately following ratification of the Establishment Clause. Virginia's protracted movement to disestablish the Episcopal Church culminated in the passage on January 24, 1799, of "An ACT to repeal certain acts, and to declare the construction of the [Virginia] bill of rights and constitution, concerning religion." The 1799 Act stated that the Virginia Bill of Rights had "excepted from the powers given to the [civil] government the power of reviving any species of ecclesiastical or church government . . . by referring the subject of religion to conscience" and that the repealed measures had "bestowed property upon [the Anglican] church," had "asserted a legislative right to establish any religious sect" and had "incorporated religious sects, all of which is inconsistent with the principles of the constitution, and of religious freedom, and manifestly tends to the reestablishment of a national church." Yet just one year after the passage of this Act, Virginia reenacted a measure exempting from taxation property belonging to "any . . . college, houses for divine worship, or seminary of learning." This exemption dated at least from 1777 and had been reaffirmed immediately before and after ratification of the First Amendment. It may reasonably be inferred that the Virginians did not view the exemption for "houses of divine worship" as an establishment of religion.

Similarly, in 1784 the New York Legislature repealed colonial acts establishing the Episcopal Church in several counties of the State. ⊥684 Yet in 1799, the legislature provided that "no house or land belonging to . . . any church or place of public worship . . . nor any college or incorporated academy, nor any school house . . . alms house or property belonging to any incorporated library, shall be taxed by virtue of this act." And early practice in the District of Columbia—governed from the outset by the First Amendment—mirrored that in the States. In 1802 the Corporation of the City of Washington, under authority delegated by Congress, exempted "houses for public worship" from real property taxes.

Thomas Jefferson was President when tax exemption was first given Washington churches, and James Madison sat in sessions of the Virginia General Assembly which voted exemptions for churches in that Commonwealth. I have found no record of their personal views on the respective acts. The absence of such a record is itself ⊥685 significant. It is unlikely that two men so concerned with the separation of church and state would have remained silent had they thought the exemptions established religion. And if they had not either approved the exemptions, or been mild in their opposition, it is probable that their views would be known to us today. Both Jefferson and Madison wrote prolifically about issues they felt important, and their opinions were well known to contemporary chroniclers. See, for example, the record preserved of Madison's battle in 1784-1785 against the proposal in the Virginia Assembly to levy a general tax to support "teachers of the Christian religion," in the dissenting opinion of *Mr. Justice DOUGLAS*. Much the same can be said of the other Framers and Ratifiers of the Bill of Rights who remained active in public affairs during the late 18th and early 19th centuries. The adoption of the early exemptions without controversy, in other words, strongly suggests that they were not thought incompatible with constitutional prohibitions against involvements of church and state.

The exemptions have continued uninterrupted to the present day. They are in force in all 50 States. No judicial decision, state or federal, has ever held that they violate the Establishment Clause. In 1886, for example, this Court in *Gibbons* v. *District of Columbia*, rejected on statutory grounds a church's claim for the exemption of certain of its land under congressional statutes exempting Washington churches and appurtenant ground from real property taxes. But the Court ⊥686 gave not the slightest hint that it ruled against the church because, under the First Amendment, *any* exemption would have been unconstitutional. To the contrary, the Court's opinion implied that nothing in the Amendment precludes exemption of church property: "We are not disposed to deny that grounds left open around a church, not merely to admit light and air, but also used to add to its beauty and attractiveness, may, if not used or intended to be used for any other purpose, be exempt from taxation under these statutes."

Mr. Justice HOLMES said that "[i]f a thing has been practised for two hundred years by common consent, it will need a strong case for the Fourteenth Amendment to affect it. . . ." *Jackman* v. *Rosenbaum Co.* For almost 200 years the view expressed in the actions of legislatures and courts has been that tax exemptions for churches do not threaten "those consequences which the Framers deeply feared" or "tend to promote the type of interdependence between religion and state which the First Amendment was designed to prevent." An examination both of the governmental purposes for granting the exemptions and of the type of ⊥687 church-state relationship that has resulted from their existence makes clear that no "strong case" exists for holding unconstitutional this historic practice.

II

Government has two basic secular purposes for granting real property tax exemptions to religious organizations. First, these organizations are exempted because they, among a range of other private, nonprofit organizations contribute to the well-being of the community in a variety of nonreligious ways, and thereby bear burdens that would otherwise either have to be met by general taxation, or be left undone, to the detriment of the community. Thus, New York exempts "[r]eal property owned by a corporation or association ⊥688 organized exclusively for the moral or mental improvement of men and women, or for religious, bible, tract, charitable, benevolent, missionary, hospital, infirmary, educational, public playground, scientific, literary, bar association, library, patriotic, historical or cemetery purposes, for the enforcement of laws relating to children or animals, or for two or more such purposes. . . ."

Appellant seeks to avoid the force of this secular purpose of the exemptions by limiting his challenge to "exemptions from real property taxation to religious organizations on real property used exclusively for religious purposes." Appellant assumes, apparently, that church-owned property is used for exclusively religious purposes if it does not house a hospital, orphanage, weekday school or the like. Any assumption that a church building itself is used for exclusively religious activities, however, rests on a simplistic view of ordinary church operations. As the appellee's brief cogently observes, "the public welfare activities and the sectarian activities of religious institutions are . . . intertwined. . . . Often a particular church will use the same personnel, facilities and source of funds to carry out both its secular and religious activities." Thus, the same people who gather in church facilities for religious worship and study may return to these facilities to participate in Boy Scout activities, to promote antipoverty causes, to discuss public issues, or to listen to chamber music. Accordingly, the funds used to maintain the facilities as a place for religious worship and study also maintain them as a place for secular activities beneficial to the community as a whole. Even during formal worship services, churches frequently collect the funds used to finance ⊥689 their secular operations and make decisions regarding their nature.

Second, government grants exemptions to religious organizations because they uniquely contribute to the pluralism of American society by their religious activities. Government may properly include religious institutions among the variety of private, nonprofit groups which receive tax exemptions, for each group contributes to the diversity of association, viewpoint and enterprise essential to a vigorous, pluralistic society. To this end, New York extends its exemptions not only to religious and social service organizations but also to scientific, literary, bar, library, patriotic and historical groups, and generally to institutions "organized exclusively for the moral or mental improvement of men and women." The very breadth of this scheme of exemptions negates any suggestion that the State intends to single out religious organizations for special preference. The scheme is not designed to inject any religious activity into a nonreligious context, as was the case with school prayers. No particular activity of a religious organization—for example, the propagation of its beliefs—is specially promoted by the exemptions. They merely facilitate the existence of a broad range of private, non-profit organizations, among them religious groups, by leaving each free to come into existence, then to flourish or wither, without being burdened by real property taxes.

III

Although governmental purposes for granting religious exemptions may be wholly secular, exemptions can nonetheless violate the Establishment Clause if they result in ⊥690 extensive state involvement with religion. Accordingly, those who urge the exemptions' unconstitutionality argue that exemptions are the equivalent of governmental subsidy of churches. General subsidies of religious activities would, of course, constitute impermissible state involvement with religion.

Tax exemptions and general subsidies, however, are qualitatively different. Though both provide economic assistance, they do so in fundamentally different ways. A subsidy involves the direct transfer of public monies to the subsidized enterprise and uses resources exacted from taxpayers as a whole. An exemption, on the other hand, involves no such transfer. It assists the exempted enterprise only passively, by relieving a privately funded venture of the burden of paying taxes. In other words, ⊥691 "[i]n the case of direct subsidy, the state forcibly diverts the income of both believers and nonbelievers to churches," while "[i]n the case of an exemption, the state merely refrains from diverting to its own uses income independently generated by churches through voluntary contributions." Giannella, Religious Liberty, Nonestablishment, and Doctrinal Development, 81 Harv. L. Rev. 513, 553 (1968). Thus, "the symbolism of tax exemption is significant as a manifestation that organized religion is not expected to support the state; by the same token the state is not expected to support the church." Freund, Public Aid to Parochial Schools, 82 Harv. L. Rev. 1680, 1687, n. 16 (1969). Tax exemptions, accordingly, constitute mere passive state involvement with religion and not the affirmative involvement characteristic of outright governmental subsidy.

Even though exemptions produce only passive state involvement with religion, nonetheless some argue that their termination would be desirable as a means of reducing the level of church-state contact. But it cannot realistically be said that termination of religious tax exemptions would quantitatively lessen the extent of state involvement with religion. Appellee contends that "[a]s a practical matter, the public welfare activities and the sectarian activities of religious institutions are so intertwined that they cannot be separated for the purpose of determining eligibility for tax exemptions." If not impossible, the separation would certainly involve extensive state investigation into church operations and finances. Moreover, the termination of exemptions would give rise, as the Court says, to the necessity for "tax valuation of church property, tax liens, tax foreclosures and the direct confrontations and conflicts which follow in the train of those legal processes." ⊥**692** Taxation, further, would bear unequally on different churches, having its most disruptive effect on those with the least ability to meet the annual levies assessed against them. And taxation would surely influence the allocation of church resources. By diverting funds otherwise available for religious or public service purposes to the support of the Government, taxation would necessarily affect the extent of church support for the enterprises which they now promote. In many instances, the public service activities would bear the brunt of the reallocation, as churches looked first to maintain their places and programs of worship. In short, the cessation of exemptions would have a significant impact on religious organizations. Whether Government grants or withholds the exemptions, it is going to be involved with religion.

IV

Against the background of this survey of the history, purpose and operation of religious tax exemptions, I must conclude that the exemptions do not "serve the essentially religious activities of religious institutions." Their principal effect is to carry out secular purposes—the encouragement of public service activities and of a pluralistic society. During their ordinary operations, most churches engage in activities of a secular nature⊥**693** which benefit the community; and all churches by their existence contribute to the diversity of association, viewpoint, and enterprise so highly valued by all of us.

Nor do I find that the exemptions "employ the organs of government for essentially religious purposes." To the extent that the exemptions further secular ends, they do not advance "essentially religious purposes." To the extent that purely religious activities are benefited by the exemptions, the benefit is passive. Government does not affirmatively foster these activities by exempting religious organizations from taxes, as it would were it to subsidize them. The exemption simply leaves untouched that which adherents of the organization bring into being and maintain.

Finally, I do not think that the exemptions "use essentially religious means to serve governmental ends, where secular means would suffice." The means churches use to carry on their public service activities are not "essentially religious" in nature. They are the same means used by any purely secular organization—money, human time and skills, physical facilities. It is true that each church contributes to the pluralism of our society through its purely religious activities, but the state encourages these activities not because it champions religion *per se* but because it values religion among a variety of private, nonprofit enterprises which contribute to the diversity of the Nation. Viewed in this light, there is no nonreligious substitute for religion as an element in our societal mosaic, just as there is no nonliterary substitute for literary groups.

As I said in *Schempp*, the First Amendment does not invalidate "the propriety of certain tax . . . exemptions which incidentally benefit churches and religious institutions, along with many secular charities and nonprofit organizations. . . . [R]eligious institutions simply share benefits which government makes generally available ⊥**694** to educational, charitable, and eleemosynary groups. There is no indication that taxing authorities have used such benefits in any way to subsidize worship or foster belief in God."

Opinion of *Mr. Justice* HARLAN.

While I entirely subscribe to the result reached today and find myself in basic agreement with what *The CHIEF JUSTICE* has written, I deem it appropriate, in view of the radiations of the issues involved, to state those considerations that are, for me, controlling in this case and lead me to conclude that New York's constitutional provision, as implemented by its real property law, does not offend the Establishment Clause. Preliminarily, I think it relevant to face up to the fact that it is far easier to agree on the purpose that underlies the First Amendment's Establishment and Free Exercise Clauses than to obtain agreement on the standards that should govern their application. What is at stake as a matter of policy is preventing that kind and degree of government involvement in religious life that, as history teaches us, is apt to lead to strife and frequently strain a political system to the breaking point. . . .

⊥**700** *Mr. Justice* DOUGLAS, dissenting.

Petitioner is the owner of real property in New York and is a Christian. But he is not a member of any of the religious organizations, "rejecting them as hostile." The New York statute exempts from taxation real property "owned by a corporation or association organized exclusively for . . . religious . . . purposes" and used "exclusively for carrying out" such purpose. Yet nonbelievers who own realty are taxed at the usual rate. The question in the case therefore is whether believers—organized in church groups—can be made exempt from real estate taxes, merely because they are believers, while nonbelievers, whether organized or not, must pay the real estate taxes.

My *Brother HARLAN* says he "would suppose" that the tax exemption extends to "groups whose avowed tenets may be antitheological, atheistic and agnostic." If it does, then the line between believers and nonbelievers has not been drawn. But, with all respect, there is not even a suggestion in the present record that the statute covers property used exclusively by organizations for "antitheological purposes," "atheistic purposes" or "agnostic purposes."

In *Torcaso* v. *Watkins* we held that ⊥**701** a State could not bar an atheist from public office in light of the freedom of belief and religion guaranteed by the First and Fourteenth Amendments. Neither the State nor the Federal Government, we said, "can constitutionally pass laws or impose requirements which aid all religions as against nonbelievers, and neither can aid those religions based on a belief in the existence of God as against those religions founded on different beliefs."

That principle should govern this case.

There is a line between what a State may do in encouraging "religious" activities, *Zorach* v. *Clauson*, and what a State may not do by using its resources to promote "religious" activities, *McCollum* v. *Board of Education*, or bestowing benefits because of them. Yet that line may not always be clear. Closing public schools on Sunday is in the former category; subsidizing churches, in my view, is in the latter. Indeed I would suppose that in common understanding one of the best ways to "establish" one or more religions is to subsidize them, which a tax exemption does. The State may not do that any more than it may prefer "those who believe in no religion over those who do believe." *Zorach* v. *Clauson*.

In affirming this judgment the Court largely overlooks the revolution initiated by the adoption of the Fourteenth Amendment. That revolution involved the imposition of new and far-reaching constitutional restraints on the States. Nationalization of many civil liberties has been the consequence of the Fourteenth Amendment, reversing the historic position that the foundations of those liberties rested largely in state law.

The process of the "selective incorporation" of various provisions of the Bill of Rights into the Fourteenth Amendment, although often provoking lively disagree- ⊥**702**ment at large as well as among the members of this Court, has been a steady one. It started in 1896 with *Chicago, B. & Q. R. Co.* v. *Chicago* in which the Court held that the Fourteenth Amendment precluded a State from taking private property for public use without payment of just compensation, as provided in the Fifth Amendment. The first direct holding as to the incorporation of the First Amendment into the Fourteenth occurred in 1931 in *Stromberg* v. *California*, a case involving the right of free speech, although that holding in *Stromberg* had been foreshadowed in 1925 by the Court's opinion in *Gitlow* v. *New York*. As regards the religious guarantees of the First Amendment, the Free Exercise Clause was expressly deemed incorporated into the Fourteenth Amendment in 1940 in *Cantwell* v. *Connecticut*, although that holding had been foreshadowed in 1923 and 1934 by the Court's dicta in *Meyer* v. *Nebraska* and *Hamilton* v. *Regents*. The Establishment Clause was not incorporated in the Fourteenth Amendment until *Everson* v. *Board of Education* was decided in 1947.

Those developments in the last 30 years have had unsettling effects. It was, for example, not until 1962 that state-sponsored, sectarian prayers were held to violate the Establishment Clause. *Engel* v. *Vitale*. That decision brought many protests, for the habit of putting one sect's prayer in public schools had long been practiced. Yet if the Catholics, controlling one school board, could put their prayer into one group of public schools, the Mormons, Baptists, Moslems, Presbyterians, and others could do the same, once they got control. And so the seeds of Establishment would grow and a secular institution would be used to serve a sectarian end.

⊥**703** *Engel* was as disruptive of traditional state practices as was *Stromberg*. Prior to *Stromberg*, a State could arrest an unpopular person who made a rousing speech on the charge of disorderly conduct. Since *Stromberg*, that has been unconstitutional. And so the revolution occasioned by the Fourteenth Amendment has progressed as Article after Article in the Bill of Rights has been incorporated in it and made applicable to the States. Hence the question in the present case makes irrelevant the "two centuries of uninterrupted freedom from taxation," referred to by the Court. If history be our guide, then tax exemption of church property in this country is indeed highly suspect, as it arose in the early days when the church was an agency of the state. The question here, though, concerns the meaning of the Establishment Clause and the Free Exercise Clause made applicable to the States for only a few decades at best.

With all due respect the governing principle is not controlled by *Everson* v. *Board of Education*. *Everson* involved the use of public funds to bus children to parochial as well as to public schools. Parochial schools teach religion; yet they are also educational institutions offering courses competitive with public schools. They prepare students for the professions and for activities in all walks of life. Education in the secular sense was combined with religious indoctrination at the parochial schools involved in *Everson*. Even so, the *Everson* decision was five to four and, though one of the five, I have since had grave doubts about it, because I have become convinced that grants to institutions teaching a sectarian creed violate the Establishment Clause.

⊥**704** This case, however, is quite different. Education is not involved. The financial support rendered here is to the church, the place of worship. A tax exemption is a subsidy. Is my *Brother BRENNAN* correct in saying that we would hold that state or federal grants to churches, say, to construct the edifice itself would be unconstitutional? What is the difference between that kind of subsidy and the present subsidy?

The problem takes us back where Madison was in 1784 and 1785 when he battled the *Assessment Bill* in Virginia. That bill levied a tax for the support of Christian churches, leaving to each taxpayer the choice as to "what society of Christians" he wanted the tax paid; and absent such designation, the tax was to go for education. Even so, Madison was unrelenting in his opposition. As stated by Mr. *Justice RUTLEDGE*: "The modified Assessment Bill passed second reading in December, 1784, and was all but enacted. ⊥**705** Madison and his followers, however, maneuvered deferment of final consideration until November, 1785. And before the Assembly reconvened in the fall he issued his historic Memorial and Remonstrance." *Everson* v. *Board of Education*.

The *Remonstrance* stirred up such a storm of popular protest that the Assessment Bill was defeated.

The *Remonstrance* covers some aspects of the present subsidy, including Madison's protest in paragraph 3 to a requirement that any person be compelled to contribute even "three pence" to support a church. All men, he maintained in ¶ 4, enter society "on equal conditions" including the right to free exercise of religion: "Whilst we assert for ourselves a freedom to embrace, to profess and to observe the Religion which we believe to be of divine origin, we cannot deny an equal freedom to those whose minds have not yet yielded to the evidence which has convinced us. If this freedom be abused, it is an offence against God, not against man: To God, therefore, not to men, must an account of it be rendered. As the Bill violates equality by subjecting some to peculiar burdens; so it violates the same principle, by granting to others peculiar exemptions."

Madison's assault on the *Assessment Bill* was in fact an assault based on both the concepts of "free exercise" and "establishment" of religion later entered into the First Amendment. ⊥**706** Madison, whom we recently called "the leading architect of the religious clauses of the First Amendment," *Flast* v. *Cohen*, was indeed their author and chief promoter. As Mr. *Justice RUTLEDGE* said: "All the great instruments of the Virginia struggle for religious liberty thus became warp and woof of our constitutional tradition, not simply by the course of history, but by the common unifying force of Madison's life, thought and sponsorship. He epitomized the whole of that tradition in the Amendment's compact, but nonetheless comprehensive, phrasing." *Everson* v. *Board of Education*.

The Court seeks to avoid this historic argument as to the meaning of "establishment" and "free exercise" by relying on the long practice of the States in granting the subsidies challenged here.

Certainly government may not lay a tax on either worshiping or preaching. In *Murdock* v. *Pennsylvania* we ruled on a state license tax levied on religious colporteurs as a condition to pursuit of their activities. In holding the tax unconstitutional we said "The power to tax the exercise of a privilege is the power to control or suppress its enjoyment. *Magnano Co.* v. *Hamilton*. Those who can tax the exercise of this religious practice can make its exercise so costly as to deprive it of the resources necessary for its maintenance. Those who can tax the privilege of engaging in this form of missionary evangelism can close its doors to all those who do not have a full purse. Spreading religious beliefs in this ancient and honorable manner would thus be denied the needy. Those who can deprive religious groups of their colporteurs can take from them a part of ⊥**707** the vital power of the press which has survived from the Reformation."

Churches, like newspapers also enjoying First Amendment rights, have no constitutional immunity from all taxes. As we said in *Murdock:*

"We do not mean to say that religious groups and the press are free from all financial burdens of government. We have here something quite different, for example, from a tax on the income of one who engages in religious activities or a tax on property used or employed in connection with those activities. It is one thing to impose a tax on the income or property of a preacher. It is quite another thing to exact a tax from him for the privilege of delivering a sermon."

State aid to places of worship, whether in the form of direct grants, or tax exemption, takes us back to the *Assessment Bill* and the *Remonstrance*. The church *qua* church would not be entitled to that support from believers and from nonbelievers alike. Yet the church *qua* nonprofit, charitable institution is one of many that receives a form of subsidy through tax exemption. To be sure, the New York statute does not single out the church for grant or favor. It includes churches in a long list of nonprofit organizations: for the moral or mental improvement of men and women; for charitable, hospital, or educational purposes; for playgrounds; for scientific or literary objects; for bar associations; for medical societies; for libraries; for patriotic and historical purposes; for cemeteries; for the enforcement of laws relating to children or animals; for opera ⊥**708** houses, fraternal organizations; for academies of music; for veterans' organizations; pharmaceutical societies; and for dental societies. While the beneficiaries cover a wide range, "atheistic," "agnostic," or "antitheological" groups do not seem to be included.

Churches perform some functions that the State would constitutionally be empowered to perform. I refer to nonsectarian social welfare operations such as the care for orphaned children and the destitute and people who are sick. A tax exemption to agencies performing those functions would therefore be as constitutionally proper as the grant of direct subsidies to them. Under the First Amendment the State may not, however, provide worship if private groups fail to do so. As Mr. *Justice JACKSON* said: "[A State] may socialize utilities and economic enterprises and make taxpayers' business out of what conventionally had been private business. It may make public business of individual welfare, health, education, entertainment or security. But it cannot make public business of religious worship or instruction, or of attendance at religious institutions of any character. . . . That is a difference which the Constitution sets up between religion and almost every other subject matter of legislation, a difference which goes to the very root of religious freedom and which the Court is overlooking today." *Everson* v. *Board of Education*.

That is a major difference between churches on the one hand and the rest of the nonprofit organizations on the other. Government could provide or finance operas, hospitals, historical societies, and all the rest because they represent social welfare programs within ⊥**709** the reach of the police power. In contrast, government may not provide or finance worship because of the Establishment Clause any more than it may single out "atheistic" or "agnostic" centers or groups and create or finance them.

The Brookings Institution, writing in 1933, before the application of the Establishment Clause of the First Amendment to the States, said about tax exemptions of religious groups: "Tax exemption, no matter what its form, is essentially a government grant or subsidy. Such grants would seem to be justified only if the purpose for which they are made is one for which the legislative body would *be equally willing to make* a direct appropriation from public funds equal to the amount of the exemption. This test would not be met except in the case where the exemption is granted to encourage certain activities of private interests, which, if not thus performed, would have to be assumed by the government at an expenditure at least as great as the value of the exemption."

Since 1947 when the Establishment Clause was made applicable to the States, that Report would have to state that the exemption would be justified only where "the legislative body *could make*" an appropriation for the cause.

On the record of this case, the church *qua* nonprofit, charitable organization is intertwined with the church *qua* church. A church may use the same facilities, resources, and personnel in carrying out both its secular and its sectarian activities. The two are unitary and on the present record have not been separated one from ⊥**710** the other. The state has a public policy of encouraging private public welfare organizations, which it desires to encourage through tax exemption. Why may it not do so and include churches *qua* welfare organizations on a nondiscriminatory basis? That avoids, it is argued, a discrimination against churches and in a real sense maintains neutrality toward religion which the First Amendment was designed to foster. Welfare services, whether performed by churches or by nonreligious groups, may well serve the public welfare.

Whether a particular church seeking an exemption for its welfare work could constitutionally pass muster would depend on the special facts. The assumption is that the church is a purely private institution, promoting a sectarian cause. The creed, teaching, and beliefs of one may be undesirable or even repulsive to others. Its sectarian faith sets it apart from all others and makes it difficult to equate its constituency with the general public. The extent that its facilities are open to all may only indicate the nature of its proselytism. Yet though a church covers up its religious symbols in welfare work, its welfare activities may merely be a phase of sectarian activity. I have said enough to indicate the nature of this tax exemption problem.

Direct financial aid to churches or tax exemptions to the church *qua* church is not, in my view, even arguably permitted. Sectarian causes are certainly not antipublic and many would rate their own church or perhaps all churches as the highest form of welfare. The difficulty is that sectarian causes must remain in the private domain not subject to public control or subsidy. That seems to me to be the requirement of the Establishment Clause. As Edmond Cahn said: "In America, Madison submitted most astutely, the rights of conscience must be kept not only free but *equal* as well. And in view of the endless varia⊥**711**tions—not only among the numerous sects, but also among the organized activities they pursued and the relative emotional values they attached to their activities—how could any species of government assistance be considered genuinely equal from sect to sect? If, for example, a state should attempt to subsidize all sectarian schools without discrimination, it would necessarily violate the principle of equality because certain sects felt impelled to conduct a large number of such schools, others few, others none. How could the officers of government begin to measure the intangible factors that a true equality of treatment would involve, i.e., the relative intensity of religious attachment to parochial education that the respective groups required of their lay and clerical members? It would be presumptuous even to inquire. Thus, just as in matters of race our belated recognition of intangible factors has finally led us to the maxim 'separate therefore unequal,' so in matters of religion Madison's immediate recognition of intangible factors led us promptly to the maxim 'equal therefore separate.' Equality was out of the question without total separation." E. Cahn, Confronting Injustice 186-187 (1966).

The exemptions provided here insofar as welfare projects are concerned may have the ring of neutrality. But subsidies either through direct grant or tax exemption for sectarian causes, whether carried on by church *qua* church or by church *qua* welfare agency, must be treated differently, lest we in time allow the church *qua* church to be on the public payroll, which, I fear, is imminent.

⊥**712** As stated by my *Brother BRENNAN* in *Abington School Dist.* v. *Schempp* (concurring opinion), "It is not only the nonbeliever who fears the injection of sectarian doctrines and controversies into the civil polity, but in as high degree it is the devout believer who fears the secularization of a creed which becomes too deeply involved with and dependent upon the government."

Madison as President vetoed a bill incorporating the Protestant Episcopal Church in Alexandria, Virginia, as being a violation of the Establishment Clause. He said, *inter alia:* ". . . the bill vests in the said incorporated church an authority to provide for the support of the poor and the education of poor children of the same, an authority which, being altogether superfluous if the provision is to be the result of pious charity, would be a precedent for giving to religious societies as such a legal agency in carrying into effect a public and civil duty."

He also vetoed a bill which reserved a parcel of federal land "for the use" of the Baptist Church, as violating the Establishment Clause.

What Madison would have thought of the present state subsidy to churches—a tax exemption as distinguished from an outright grant—no one can say with certainty. The fact that Virginia early granted church tax exemptions cannot be credited to Madison. Certainly he seems to have been opposed. In his paper "Monopolies, Perpetuities, Corporations, Ecclesiastical Endowments" he wrote: "Strongly guarded as is the separation between Religion & Govt in the Constitution of the United ⊥**713** States the danger of encroachment by Ecclesiastical Bodies, may be illustrated by precedents already furnished in their short history." And he referred, *inter alia*, to the "attempt in Kentucky for example, where it was proposed to exempt Houses of Worship from taxes." From these three statements, Madison, it seems, opposed all state subsidies to churches.

We should adhere to what we said in *Torcaso* v. *Watkins*, that neither a State nor the Federal Government "can constitutionally pass laws or impose requirements *which aid all religions as against nonbelievers*, and neither can aid those religions based on a belief in the existence of God as against those religions founded on different beliefs." (Emphasis added.)

Unless we adhere to that principle, we do not give full support either to the Free Exercise Clause or to the Establishment Clause.

If a church can be exempted from paying real estate taxes, why may not it be made exempt from paying special assessments? The benefits in the two cases differ only in degree; and the burden on nonbelievers is likewise no different in kind.

⊥**714** The religiously used real estate of the churches today constitutes a vast domain. Their assets total over $141 billion and their annual income at least $22 billion. And the extent to which they are feeding from the public trough in a variety of forms is alarming.

We are advised that since 1968 at least five States have undertaken to give subsidies to parochial and other private schools—Pennsylvania, Ohio, New York, Connecticut, and Rhode Island. And it is reported that under two federal Acts, the Act of April 11, 1965, 79 Stat. 27, and the Act of November 8, 1965, 79 Stat. 1219, *billions of dollars* have been granted to parochial and other private schools.

The federal grants to elementary and secondary schools under 79 Stat. 27 were made to the States which in turn made advances to elementary and secondary schools. Those amounts are not available.

But the federal grants to private institutions of higher education are revealed in Department of Health, Education, and Welfare, Digest of Educational Statistics. These show in billions of dollars the following:

1965-66.............$1.4
1966-67.............$1.6
1967-68.............$1.7
1968-69.............$1.9
1969-70.............$2.1

⊥**715** It is an old, old problem. Madison adverted to it: "Are there not already examples in the U.S. of ecclesiastical wealth equally beyond its object and the foresight of those who laid the foundation of it? In the U.S. there is a double motive for fixing limits in this case, because wealth may increase not only from additional gifts, but from exorbitant advances in the value of the primitive one. In grants of vacant lands, and of lands in the vicinity of growing towns & Cities the increase of value is often such as if forseen, would essentially controul the liberality confirming them. The people of the U. S. owe their Independence & their liberty, to the wisdom of descrying in the minute tax of 3 pence on tea, the magnitude of the evil comprized in the precedent. Let them exert the same wisdom, in watching agst every evil lurking under plausible disguises, and growing up from small beginnings."

⊥**716** If believers are entitled to public financial support, so are nonbelievers. A believer and nonbeliever under the present law are treated differently because of the articles of their faith. Believers are doubtless comforted that the cause of religion is being fostered by this legislation. Yet one of the mandates of the First Amendment is to promote a stable, pluralistic society and to keep government neutral, not only between sects but between believers and nonbelievers. The present involvement of government in religion may seem *de minimis*. But it is, I fear, a long step down the Establishment path. Perhaps I have been misinformed. But as I have read the Constitution and its philosophy, I gathered that independence was the price of liberty.

I conclude that this tax exemption is unconstitutional.

TEXAS MONTHLY v. BULLOCK

489 U.S. 1
ON APPEAL FROM THE COURT OF APPEALS OF TEXAS, THIRD DISTRICT
Argued November 1, 1988 — Decided February 21, 1989

⊥**5** *Justice BRENNAN* announced the judgment of the Court and delivered an opinion, in which *Justice MARSHALL* and *Justice STEVENS* join.

Texas exempts from its sales tax "[p]eriodicals that are published or distributed by a religious faith and that consist wholly of writings promulgating the teaching of the faith and books that consist wholly of writings sacred to a religious faith." Tex. Tax Code Ann. § 151.312 (1982). The question presented is whether this exemption violates the Establishment Clause or the Free Press Clause of the First Amendment when the State denies a like exemption for other publications. We hold that, when confined exclusively to publications advancing the tenets of a religious faith, the exemption runs afoul of the Establishment Clause; accordingly, we need not reach the question whether it contravenes the Free Press Clause as well.

I

Prior to October 2, 1984, Texas exempted from its sales and use tax magazine subscriptions running half a year or longer and entered as second class mail. Tex. Tax Code Ann. § 151.320 (1982). This exemption was repealed as of October 2, 1984, before being reinstated effective October 1, 1987. Tex. Tax Code Ann. § 151.320 (Supp. 1988-1989). Throughout this 3-year period, Texas continued to exempt from its sales and use tax periodicals published or distributed by a religious faith consisting entirely of writings promulgating the teaching of the faith, along with books consisting ⊥**6** solely of writings sacred to a religious faith. Tex. Tax Code Ann. § 151.312 (1982).

Appellant Texas Monthly Inc., publishes a general interest magazine of the same name. Appellant is not a religious faith, and its magazine does not contain only articles promulgating the teaching of a religious faith. Thus, it was required during this 3-year period to collect and remit to the State the applicable sales tax on the price of qualifying subscription sales. Tex. Tax Code Ann. §§ 151.051, 151.052 151.401 (1982 and Supp. 1988-1989). In 1985, appellant paid sales taxes of $149,107.74 under protest and sued to recover those payments in state court.

The District Court of Travis County, Texas, ruled that an exclusive exemption for religious periodicals had "no basis . . . other than the promotion of religion itself, a prohibited reason," under the Establishment Clause. The court also found the exemption unconstitutional because it discriminated on the basis of the content of publications, presumably in violation of the Free Press Clause. Declaring itself "without power to rewrite the statute to make religious periodicals subject to tax," the court struck down the tax as applied to nonreligious periodicals and ordered the State to refund the amount of tax Texas Monthly had paid, plus interest.

The Court of Appeals, Third Supreme Judicial District of Texas, reversed by a 2-1 vote. 731 S. W. 2d 160 (1987). Applying the tripartite test enunciated in *Lemon* v. *Kurtzman*, the court held, first, that the exemption served the secular purpose of preserving separation between church and state. Second, the court asserted that the exemption did not have the primary effect of advancing or inhibiting religion, because "the effect of religious tax exemptions such as § 151.312 is to permit religious organizations to be independent of government support or sanction." The court considered it irrele⊥**7**vant that the exemption did not extend to other nonprofit or secular publications, because "the *neutrality* toward religion effected by the grant of an exemption for religious periodicals" remained unaffected by the provision or denial of a similar exemption for nonreligious publications. Finally, the court concluded that the exemption did not produce impermissible government entanglement with religion. Rather than scrutinize each publication for which a publisher sought an exemption for conformity with the statute's terms, the court found, the Comptroller's Office merely required that a group applying for an exemption demonstrate that it was a religious organization. Once a satisfactory showing had been made, the Comptroller's Office did not later reassess the group's status as a religious organization. It further allowed the group to determine, without review by the State, which of its publications promulgated the teaching of its faith. Because the exemption was administered to minimize state entanglement with religion, the court thought it consistent with *Lemon's* third prong.

In addition, the court rejected Texas Monthly's claim that the exemption violated the Free Press Clause because it discriminated among publications on the basis of their content. The court read our decision in *Arkansas Writers' Project, Inc.* v. *Ragland* to preclude only those taxes that are imposed solely on the press or targeted at a small group within the press. Because Texas' exemption encompassed only a minority of publications, leaving the bulk of subscription sales subject to tax, the court reasoned that it escaped the strictures of the Free Press Clause as we had interpreted it.

We noted probable jurisdiction and now reverse.

II

As a preliminary matter, Texas argues that appellant lacks standing to challenge the constitutionality of the exemption. It claims that if this Court were to declare the exemption ⊥**8** invalid, the proper course under state law would be to remove the exemption for religious publications, rather than extend it to nonreligious periodicals or strike down the sales and use tax in its entirety. If Texas is right, appellant cannot obtain a refund of the tax it paid under protest. Nor can it qualify for injunctive relief, because its subscription sales are no longer taxed. Hence, Texas contends, appellant cannot show that it has suffered or is threatened with redressable injury, which this Court declared to be a prerequisite for standing in *Valley Forge Christian College* v. *Americans United for Separation of Church and State, Inc.*

The State's contention is misguided. In *Arkansas Writers' Project* we rejected a similar argument, "for it would effectively insulate underinclusive statutes from constitutional challenge, a proposition we soundly rejected in *Orr* v. *Orr.*" It is not for us to decide whether the correct response as a matter of state law to a finding that a state tax exemption is unconstitutional is to eliminate the exemption, to curtail it, to broaden it, or to invalidate the tax altogether. Nor does it make any difference—contrary to the State's suggestion—that Texas Monthly seeks only a refund and not prospective relief, as did the appellant in *Arkansas Writers' Project*. A live controversy persists over Texas Monthly's right to recover the $149,107.74 it paid, plus interest. Texas cannot strip appellant of standing by changing the law after taking its money.

III

In proscribing all laws "respecting an establishment of religion," the Constitution prohibits, at the very least, legislation that constitutes an endorsement of one or another set of religious beliefs or of religion generally. It is part of our settled jurisprudence that "the Establishment Clause prohibits government from abandoning secular purposes in order to put an imprimatur on one religion, or on religion as such, or **⊥9** to favor the adherents of any sect or religious organization." *Gillette* v. *United States*. The core notion animating the requirement that a statute possess "a secular legislative purpose" and that "its principal or primary effect . . . be one that neither advances nor inhibits religion," *Lemon* v. *Kurtzman*, is not only that government may not be overtly hostile to religion, but also that it may not place its prestige, coercive authority, or resources behind a single religious faith or behind religious belief in general, compelling nonadherents to support the practices or proselytizing of favored religious organizations and conveying the message that those who do not contribute gladly are less than full members of the community.

⊥10 It does not follow, of course, that government policies with secular objectives may not incidentally benefit religion. The nonsectarian aims of government and the interests of religious groups often overlap, and this Court has never required that public authorities refrain from implementing reasonable measures to advance legitimate secular goals merely because they would thereby relieve religious groups of costs they would otherwise incur. Nor have we required that legislative categories make no explicit reference to religion. See *Wallace* v. *Jaffree* (O'Connor, J., concurring in judgment) ("The endorsement test does not preclude government from acknowledging religion or from taking religion into account in making law and policy"); *Lynch* v. *Donnelly* (Brennan, J., dissenting). Government need not resign itself to ineffectual diffidence because of exaggerated fears of contagion of or by religion, so long as neither intrudes unduly into the affairs of the other.

Thus, in *Widmar* v. *Vincent*, we held that a state university that makes its facilities available to registered student groups may not deny equal access to a registered student group desiring to use those facilities for religious worship or discussion. Although religious groups benefit from access to university facilities, a state university may not discriminate against them based on the content of their speech, and the university need not ban all student group meetings on campus in order to avoid providing any assistance to religion. Similarly, in *Mueller* v. *Allen*, we upheld a state income tax deduction for the cost of tuition, transportation, and nonreligious textbooks paid by a taxpayer for the benefit of a dependent. To be sure, the deduction aided parochial schools and parents whose children attended them, as well as nonsectarian private schools and their pupils' parents. We did not conclude, however, that **⊥11** this subsidy deprived the law of an overriding secular purpose or effect. And in the case most nearly on point, *Walz* v. *Tax Comm'n of New York City*, we sustained a property tax exemption that applied to religious properties no less than to real estate owned by a wide array of nonprofit organizations, despite the sizable tax savings it accorded religious groups.

In all of these cases, however, we emphasized that the benefits derived by religious organizations flowed to a large number of nonreligious groups as well. Indeed, were those benefits confined to religious organizations, they could not have appeared other than as state sponsorship of religion; if that were so, we would not have hesitated to strike them down for lacking a secular purpose and effect.

In *Widmar* v. *Vincent*, we noted that an open forum in a public university would not betray state approval of religion so long as the forum was available "to a broad class of nonreligious as well as religious speakers." "The provision of benefits to so broad a spectrum of groups," we said, "is an important index of secular effect." We concluded that the primary effect of an open forum would not be to advance religion, "[a]t least in the absence of empirical evidence that religious groups will dominate" it. Likewise, in *Mueller* v. *Allen*, we deemed it "particularly significant," that "the deduction is available for educational expenses incurred by *all* parents, including those whose children attend public schools and those whose children attend nonsectarian private schools or sectarian private schools."

⊥12 Finally, we emphasized in *Walz* that in granting a property tax deduction, the State "has not singled out one particular church or religious group or even churches as such; rather, it has granted exemption to all houses of religious worship within a broad class of property owned by nonprofit, quasipublic corporations which include hospitals, libraries, playgrounds, scientific, professional, historical, and patriotic groups." The breadth of New York's property tax exemption was essential to our holding that it was "not aimed at establishing, sponsoring, or supporting religion," but rather possessed the legitimate secular purpose and effect of contributing to the community's moral and intellectual diversity and encouraging private groups to undertake projects that advance the community's well-being and that would otherwise have to be funded by tax revenues or left undone. Moreover, "[t]he scheme [was] **⊥13** not designed to inject any religious activity into a nonreligious context, as was the case with school prayers. No particular activity of a religious organization—for example, the propagation of its beliefs—[was] specially promoted by the exemptions." As *Justice HARLAN* observed:

"To the extent that religious institutions sponsor the secular activities that this legislation is designed to promote, it is consistent with neutrality to grant them an exemption just as other organizations devoting resources to these projects receive exemptions. . . . As long as the breadth of exemption includes groups that pursue cultural, moral, or spiritual improvement in multifarious secular ways, including, I would suppose, groups whose avowed tenets may be antitheological, atheistic or agnostic, I can see no lack of neutrality in extending the benefit of the exemption to organized religious groups."

⊥**14** Texas' sales tax exemption for periodicals published or distributed by a religious faith and consisting wholly of writings promulgating the teaching of the faith lacks sufficient breadth to pass scrutiny under the Establishment Clause. Every tax exemption constitutes a subsidy that affects nonqualifying taxpayers, forcing them to become "indirect and vicarious 'donors.'" *Bob Jones University* v. *United States*. Insofar as that subsidy is conferred upon a wide array of nonsectarian groups as well as religious organizations in pursuit of some legitimate secular end, the fact that religious groups ⊥**15** benefit incidentally does not deprive the subsidy of the secular purpose and primary effect mandated by the Establishment Clause. However, when government directs a subsidy exclusively to religious organizations that is not required by the Free Exercise Clause and that either burdens nonbeneficiaries markedly or cannot reasonably be seen as removing a significant state-imposed deterrent to the free exercise of religion, as Texas has done, it "provide[s] unjustifiable awards of assistance to religious organizations" and cannot but "conve[y] a message of endorsement" to slighted members of the community. *Corporation of Presiding Bishop* v. *Amos*. This is particularly true where, as here, the subsidy is targeted at writings that promulgate the teachings of religious faiths. It is difficult to view Texas' narrow exemption as anything but state sponsorship of religious belief, regardless of whether one adopts the perspective of beneficiaries or of uncompensated contributors.

How expansive the class of exempt organizations or activities must be to withstand constitutional assault depends upon the State's secular aim in granting a tax exemption. If the State chose to subsidize, by means of a tax exemption, all groups that contributed to the community's cultural, intellectual, and moral betterment, then the exemption for religious publications could be retained, provided that the exemption swept as widely as the property tax exemption we upheld in ⊥**16** *Walz*. By contrast, if Texas sought to promote reflection and discussion about questions of ultimate value and the contours of a good or meaningful life, then a tax exemption would have to be available to an extended range of associations whose publications were substantially devoted to such matters; the exemption could not be reserved for publications dealing solely with religious issues, let alone restricted to publications advocating rather than criticizing religious belief or activity, without signaling an endorsement of religion that is offensive to the principles informing the Establishment Clause. See *Estate of Thornton* v. *Caldor* (O'Connor, J., concurring) (because the statute bestows an advantage on Sabbath observers "without according similar accommodation to ethical and religious beliefs and practices of other private employees," "[t]he message conveyed is one of endorsement of a particular religious belief, to the detriment of those who do not share it"; the statute therefore "has the effect of advancing religion, and cannot withstand Establishment Clause scrutiny"); *Welsh* v. *United States* (Harlan, J., concurring in result) (conscientious objector status cannot be limited to those whose opposition to war has religious roots, but must extend to those whose convictions have purely moral or philosophical sources).

It is not our responsibility to specify which permissible secular objectives, if any, the State should pursue to justify a tax exemption for religious periodicals. That charge rests with the Texas legislature. Our task, and that of the Texas courts, is rather to ensure that any scheme of exemptions ⊥**17** adopted by the legislature does not have the purpose or effect of sponsoring certain tenets or religious belief in general. As *Justice HARLAN* remarked: "The Court must survey meticulously the circumstances of governmental categories to eliminate, as it were, religious gerrymanders. In any particular case the critical question is whether the circumference of legislation encircles a class so broad that it can be fairly concluded that religious institutions could be thought to fall within the natural perimeter." *Walz*. Because Texas' sales tax exemption for periodicals promulgating the teachings of any religious sect lacks a secular objective that would justify this preference along with similar benefits for nonreligious publications or groups, and because it effectively endorses religious belief, the exemption manifestly fails this test.

IV

A

In defense of its sales tax exemption for religious publications, Texas claims that it has a compelling interest in avoiding violations of the Free Exercise and Establishment Clauses, and that the exemption serves that end. Without such an exemption, Texas contends, its sales tax might trammel free exercise rights, as did the flat license tax this Court struck down as applied to proselytizing by Jehovah's Witnesses in *Murdock* v. *Pennsylvania*. In addition, Texas argues that an exemption for religious publications neither advances nor inhibits religion, as required by the Establishment Clause, and that its elimination would entangle church and state to a greater degree than the exemption itself.

⊥18 We reject both parts of this argument. Although Texas may widen its exemption consonant with some legitimate secular purpose, nothing in our decisions under the Free Exercise Clause prevents the State from eliminating altogether its exemption for religious publications. "It is virtually self-evident that the Free Exercise Clause does not require an exemption from a governmental program unless, at a minimum, inclusion in the program actually burdens the claimant's freedom to exercise religious rights." *Tony & Susan Alamo Foundation* v. *Secretary of Labor*. In this case, the State has adduced no evidence that the payment of a sales tax by subscribers to religious periodicals or purchasers of religious books would offend their religious beliefs or inhibit religious activity. The State therefore cannot claim persuasively that its tax exemption is compelled by the Free Exercise Clause in even a single instance, let alone in every case. No concrete need to accommodate religious activity has been shown.

⊥19 Moreover, even if members of some religious group succeeded in demonstrating that payment of a sales tax—or, less plausibly, of a sales tax when applied to printed matter—would violate their religious tenets, it is by no means obvious that the State would be required by the Free Exercise Clause to make individualized exceptions for them.

In *United States* v. *Lee*, we ruled unanimously that the Federal Government need not exempt an Amish employer from the payment of Social Security taxes, notwithstanding our recognition that compliance would offend his religious beliefs. We noted that "[n]ot all burdens on religion are unconstitutional," and held that "[t]he state may justify a limitation on religious liberty by showing that it is essential to accomplish an overriding government interest." Although the balancing test we set forth in *Lee* must be performed on a case-by-case basis, a State's interest in the uniform collection of a ⊥20 sales tax appears comparable to the Federal Government's interest in the uniform collection of Social Security taxes, and mandatory exemptions under the Free Exercise Clause are arguably as difficult to prove. No one has suggested that members of any of the major religious denominations in the United States—the principal beneficiaries of Texas' tax exemption—could demonstrate an infringement of their free exercise rights sufficiently serious to overcome the State's countervailing interest in collecting its sales tax.

B

Texas' further claim that the Establishment Clause mandates or at least favors its sales tax exemption for religious periodicals is equally unconvincing. Not only does the exemption seem a blatant endorsement of religion, but it appears, on its face, to produce greater state entanglement with religion than the denial of an exemption. As *Justice STEVENS* has noted:

"[There exists an] overriding interest in keeping the government—whether it be the legislature or the courts—out of the business of evaluating the relative merits of differing religious claims. The risk that governmental approval of some and disapproval of others will be perceived as favoring one religion over another is an important risk the Establishment Clause was designed to preclude." The prospect of inconsistent treatment and government embroilment in controversies over religious doctrine seems especially baleful where, as in the case of Texas' sales tax exemption, a statute requires that public officials determine whether some message or activity is consistent with "the teaching of the faith."

⊥21 While Texas is correct in pointing out that compliance with government regulations by religious organizations and the monitoring of their compliance by government agencies would itself enmesh the operations of church and state to some degree, we have found that such compliance would generally not impede the evangelical activities of religious groups and that the "routine and factual inquiries" commonly associated with the enforcement of tax laws "bear no resemblance to the kind of government surveillance the Court has previously held to pose an intolerable risk of government entanglement with religion." *Tony & Susan Alamo Foundation* v. *Secretary of Labor*.

On the record before us, neither the Free Exercise Clause nor the Establishment Clause prevents Texas from withdrawing its current exemption for religious publications if it chooses not to expand it to promote some legitimate secular aim.

C

Our conclusion today is admittedly in tension with some unnecessarily sweeping statements in *Murdock* v. *Pennsylvania* and *Follett* v. *McCormick*. To the extent that language in those opinions is inconsistent with our decision here, based on the evolution in our thinking about the Religion Clauses over the last 45 years, we disavow it.

⊥22 In *Murdock*, the Court ruled that a city could not impose a flat license tax payable by "all persons canvassing for or soliciting . . . orders for goods, paintings, pictures, wares, or merchandise of any kind" on Jehovah's Witnesses who "went about from door to door . . . distributing literature and soliciting people to 'purchase' certain religious books and pamphlets." In *Follett*, the Court ruled similarly that a Jehovah's Witness who "went from house to house distributing certain books" was exempt under the Free Exercise Clause from payment of a flat business and occupation tax on booksellers. In both cases, the majority stated that the "sale" of religious pamphlets by itinerant evangelists was a form of *preaching*, and that imposing a license or occupation tax on such a preacher was tantamount to exacting "a tax from him for the privilege of delivering a sermon." *Murdock*. The Court acknowledged that imposing an income or property tax on preachers would not be unconstitutional. It emphasized, however, that a flat license or occupation tax poses a greater threat to the free exercise of religion than do those other taxes, because it is "levied and collected as a condition to the pursuit of activities whose enjoyment is guaranteed by the First Amendment" and thus "restrains in advance those constitutional liberties . . . and inevitably tends to suppress their exercise."

If one accepts the majority's characterization of the critical issues in *Murdock* and *Follett*, those decisions are easily compatible with our holding here. In striking down application of the town ordinance to Jehovah's Witnesses in *Follett*—an ordinance the Court found to be "in all material respects the same" as the one whose application it restricted in *Murdock*—the Court declared that only a single "narrow" question was presented: "It is whether a flat license tax as applied to one who earns his livelihood as an evangelist or preacher in his home town is constitutional." ⊥**23** Regarding *Follett* in this light, we must agree that "we have quite a different case from that of a merchant who sells books at a stand or on the road." There is no doubt that the First Amendment prevents both the States and the Federal Government from imposing a special occupation tax exclusively on those who devote their days to spreading religious messages. Moreover, it is questionable whether, consistent with the Free Exercise Clause, government may exact a facially neutral license fee designed for commercial salesmen from religious missionaries whose principal work is preaching and who only occasionally sell religious tracts for small sums, so long as "the fee is not a nominal one, imposed as a regulatory measure and calculated to defray the expense of protecting those on the streets and at home against the abuses of solicitors." In such a case, equal treatment of commercial and religious solicitation might result in an unconstitutional imposition on religious activity warranting judicial relief, particularly where that activity is deemed central to a given faith, as the Court found this form of proselytizing to be in *Murdock* and *Follett*, and where the tax burden is far from negligible.

⊥**24** Insofar as the Court's holdings in *Murdock* and *Follett* are limited to these points, they are plainly consistent with our decision today. The sales tax that Texas imposes is not an occupation tax levied on religious missionaries. Nor is it a flat tax that "restrains in advance" the free exercise of religion. On the contrary, because the tax is equal to a small fraction of the value of each sale and payable by the buyer, it poses little danger of stamping out missionary work involving the sale of religious publications, and in view of its generality it can hardly be viewed as a covert attempt to curtail religious activity. We therefore see no inconsistency between our former decisions and our present holding.

To the extent that our opinions in *Murdock* and *Follett* might be read, however, to suggest that the States and the Federal Government may never tax the sale of religious or other publications, we reject those dicta. Our intervening decisions make clear that even if the denial of tax benefits "will inevitably have a substantial impact" on religious groups, the refusal to grant such benefits does not offend the Free Exercise Clause when it does not prevent those groups "from observing their religious tenets." *Bob Jones Univer*⊥**25***sity* v. *United States*. In *Murdock* and *Follett*, the application of a flat license or occupation tax to Jehovah's Witnesses arguably did prevent adherents of that sect from acting in accordance with some of their central religious beliefs, in the absence of any overriding government interest in denying them an exemption. In the much more common circumstances exemplified by this case, however, taxes or regulations would not subject religious organizations to undue burdens and the government's interest in their uniform application is far weightier. Hence, there is no bar to Texas' imposing a general sales tax on religious publications.

V

We conclude that Texas' sales tax exemption for religious publications violates the First Amendment, as made applicable to the States by the Fourteenth Amendment. Accordingly, the judgment of the Texas Court of Appeals is reversed, and the case is remanded for further proceedings.

It is so ordered.

Justice WHITE, concurring in the judgment.

The Texas law at issue here discriminates on the basis of the content of publications: it provides that "periodicals . . . that consist wholly of writings promulgating the teachings of (a religious faith) . . . are exempted" from the burdens of the sales tax law. Tex. Tax Code Ann. § 151.312. Thus, ⊥**26** the content of a publication determines whether its publisher is exempt or non-exempt. Appellant is subject to the tax, but other publications are not because of the message they carry. This is plainly forbidden by the Press Clause of the First Amendment. *Arkansas Writer's Project* v. *Ragland*, our most recent decision to this effect, is directly applicable here, and is the proper basis for reversing the judgment below.

Justice BLACKMUN, with whom *Justice* O'CONNOR joins, concurring in the judgment.

The Texas statute at issue touches upon values that underlie three different clauses of the First Amendment: the Free Exercise Clause, the Establishment Clause, and the Press Clause. As indicated by the number of opinions issued in this case today, harmonizing these several values is not an easy task.

The Free Exercise Clause value suggests that a State may not impose a tax on spreading the gospel. See *Follett* v. *Town of McCormick* and *Murdock* v. *Pennsylvania*. The Establishment Clause value suggests that a State may not give a tax break to those who spread the gospel that it does not also give to others who actively might advocate disbelief in religion. See *Torcaso* v. *Watkins*, *Everson* v. *Board of Education*. The Press Clause value suggests that a State may not tax the sale of some publications, but not others based on their content absent a compelling reason for doing so. See *Arkansas Writers' Project, Inc.* v. *Ragland*.

It perhaps is fairly easy to reconcile the Free Exercise and Press Clause values. If the Free Exercise Clause suggests that a State may not tax the sale of religious literature by a religious organization, this fact alone would give a State a compelling reason to exclude this category of sales from an otherwise general sales tax. In this respect, I agree gener**⊥27**ally with what *Justice SCALIA* says in Part II of his dissenting opinion. I find it more difficult to reconcile in this case the Free Exercise and Establishment Clause values. The Free Exercise Clause suggests that a special exemption for religious books is required. The Establishment Clause suggests that a special exemption for religious books is forbidden. This tension between mandated and prohibited religious exemptions is well recognized. Of course, identifying the problem does not resolve it.

Justice BRENNAN's opinion, in its Part IV, would resolve the tension between the Free Exercise and Establishment Clause values simply by subordinating the Free Exercise value, even, it seems to me, at the expense of longstanding precedents. *Justice SCALIA's* opinion, conversely, would subordinate the Establishment Clause value. This position, it seems to me, runs afoul of the previously settled notion that government may not favor religious belief over disbelief

Perhaps it is a vain desire, but I would like to decide the present case without necessarily sacrificing either the Free Exercise Clause value or the Establishment Clause value. It is possible for a State to write a tax-exemption statute consistent with both values; for example, a state statute might exempt the sale not only of religious literature distributed by a religious organization but also of philosophical literature distributed by nonreligious organizations devoted to such matters of conscience as life and death, good and evil, being **⊥28** and nonbeing, right and wrong. Such a statute, moreover, should survive Press Clause scrutiny because its exemption would be narrowly tailored to meet the compelling interests that underlie both the Free Exercise and Establishment Clauses.

To recognize this possible reconciliation of the competing First Amendment considerations is one thing; to impose it upon a State as its only legislative choice is something else. *Justice SCALIA* rightly points out that the Free Exercise and Establishment Clauses often appear like Scylla and Charybdis, leaving a State little room to maneuver between them. The Press Clause adds yet a third hazard to a State's safe passage through the legislative waters concerning the taxation of books and journals. We in the judiciary must be wary of interpreting these three constitutional clauses in a manner that negates the legislative role altogether.

I believe we can avoid most of these difficulties with a narrow resolution of the case before us. We need not decide today the extent to which the Free Exercise Clause requires a tax exemption for the sale of religious literature by a religious organization; in other words, defining the ultimate scope of *Follett* and *Murdock* may be left for another day. We need decide here only whether a tax exemption *limited to* the sale of religious literature by religious organizations violates the Establishment Clause. I conclude that it does.

In this case, by confining the tax exemption exclusively to the sale of religious publications, Texas engaged in preferential support for the communication of religious messages. Although some forms of accommodating religion are constitutionally permissible, this one surely is not. A statutory preference for the dissemination of religious ideas offends our most basic understanding of what the Establishment Clause is all about and hence is constitutionally intolerable. **⊥29** Accordingly, whether or not *Follett* and *Murdock* prohibit taxing the sale of religious literature, the Establishment Clause prohibits a tax exemption limited to the sale of religious literature. Cf. *Estate of Thornton* v. *Caldor, Inc.* (the Establishment Clause prohibits a statute that grants employees an unqualified right not to work on their Sabbath), and *Hobbie* v. *Unemployment Appeals Comm'n of Fla.* (consistent with *Caldor*, the Free Exercise Clause prohibits denying unemployment compensation to employees who refuse to work on their Sabbath).

At oral argument, appellees suggested that the statute at issue here exempted from taxation the sale of atheistic literature distributed by an atheistic organization. If true, this statute might survive Establishment Clause scrutiny, as well as Free Exercise and Press Clause scrutiny. But as appellees were quick to concede at argument, the record contains nothing to support this facially implausible interpretation of the statute. Thus, constrained to construe this Texas statute as exempting religious literature alone, I concur in the holding that it contravenes the Establishment Clause, and in remanding the case for further proceedings not inconsistent with this holding.

Justice SCALIA, with whom *The CHIEF JUSTICE* and *Justice KENNEDY* join, dissenting.

As a judicial demolition project, today's decision is impressive. The machinery employed by the opinions of *Justice BRENNAN* and *Justice BLACKMUN* is no more substantial than the antinomy that accommodation of religion may be required but not permitted, and the bold but unsupportable assertion (given such realities as the text of the Declaration of Independence, the national Thanksgiving Day proclaimed by every President since Lincoln; the inscriptions on our coins, the words of our Pledge of Allegiance, the invocation with **⊥30** which sessions of our Court are opened and, come to think of it, the discriminatory protection of freedom of religion in the Constitution) that government may not "convey a message of endorsement of religion." With this frail equipment, the Court topples an exemption for religious publications of a sort that expressly appears in the laws of at least 15 of the 45 States that have sales and use taxes—States from Maine to Texas, from Idaho to New Jersey. In practice, a similar ⊥**31** exemption may well exist in even more States than that, since until today our case law has suggested that it is not only permissible but perhaps required. See *Follett* v. *McCormick*, *Murdock* v. *Pennsylvania*. I expect, for example, that even in States without express exemptions many churches, and many tax assessors, have thought sales taxes inapplicable to the religious literature typically offered for sale in church foyers.

When one expands the inquiry to sales taxes on items other than publications and to other types of taxes such as property, income, amusement, and motor vehicle taxes—all of which are likewise affected by today's holding—the Court's accomplishment is even more impressive. At least 45 state codes contain exemptions for religious groups without analogous exemptions for other types of nonprofit institutions.

For ⊥**32** over half a century the federal Internal Revenue Code has allowed "minister[s] of the gospel" (a term interpreted broadly enough to include cantors and rabbis) to exclude from gross ⊥**33** income the rental value of their parsonages. 26 U.S.C. § 107; see also § 213(b)(11) of the Revenue Act of 1921, ch. 136, 42 Stat. 239. In short, religious tax exemptions of the type the Court invalidates today permeate the state and federal codes, and have done so for many years.

I dissent because I find no basis in the text of the Constitution, the decisions of this Court or the traditions of our people for disapproving this longstanding and widespread practice.

I

The opinions of *Justice BRENNAN* and *Justice BLACKMUN* proceed as though this were a matter of first impression. It is not. Nineteen years ago, in *Walz* v. *Tax Comm'n of New York City*, we considered and rejected an Establishment Clause challenge that was in all relevant respects identical. Since today's opinions barely acknowledge the Court's decision in that case (as opposed to the separate concurrences of *Justices BRENNAN* and *HARLAN)*, it requires some discussion here. *Walz* involved ⊥**34** New York City's grant of tax exemptions, pursuant to a state statute and a provision of the State Constitution, to "religious organizations for religious properties used solely for religious worship." In upholding the exemption, we conducted an analysis that contains the substance of the three-pronged "test" adopted the following Term in *Lemon* v. *Kurtzman*. First, we concluded that "[t]he legislative purpose of the property tax exemption is neither the advancement nor the inhibition of religion." We reached that conclusion because past cases and the historical record established that property tax exemption "constitutes a reasonable and balanced attempt to guard against" the "latent dangers" of government hostility to religion. We drew a distinction between an unlawful intent to favor religion and a lawful intent to "'accommodat[e] the public service to [the people's] spiritual needs,'" (quoting *Zorach* v. *Clauson*), and found only the latter to be involved in "sparing the exercise of religion from the burden of property taxation levied on private profit institutions."

We further concluded that the exemption did not have the primary effect of sponsoring religious activity. We noted that, although tax exemptions may have the same economic effect as state subsidies, for the Establishment Clause purposes such "indirect economic benefit" is significantly different.

"The grant of a tax exemption is not sponsorship since the government does not transfer part of its revenue to churches but simply abstains from demanding that the church support the state. . . . There is no genuine nexus between tax exemption and establishment of religion."

Justice BRENNAN also recognized this distinction in his concurring opinion:

⊥**35** "Tax exemptions and general subsidies, however, are qualitatively different. Though both provide economic assistance, they do so in fundamentally different ways. A subsidy involves the direct transfer of public monies to the subsidized enterprise and uses resources exacted from taxpayers as a whole. An exemption, on the other hand, involves no such transfer." See also *id.* ("Tax exemptions . . . constitute mere passive state involvement with religion and not the affirmative involvement characteristic of outright governmental subsidy.")

Third, we held that the New York exemption did not produce unacceptable government entanglement with religion. In fact, quite to the contrary. Since the exemptions avoided the "tax liens, tax foreclosures, and the direct confrontations and conflicts that follow in the train of those legal processes," we found that their elimination would increase government's involvement with religious institutions. See also *id.* (Brennan, J., concurring) ("[I]t cannot realistically be said that termination of religious tax exemptions would quantitatively lessen the extent of state involvement with religion").

We recognized in *Walz* that the exemption of religion from various taxes had existed without challenge in the law of all 50 States and the National Government before, during, and after the framing of the First Amendment's Religion Clauses, and had achieved "undeviating acceptance" throughout the 200-year history of our Nation. "Few concepts," we said, "are more deeply embedded in the fabric of our national life, beginning with the pre-Revolutionary colonial times, than for the government to exercise at the very least this kind of benevolent neutrality toward churches and religious exercise generally so long as none was favored over others and none suffered interference." See also *id.*

(Brennan, J., concurring) (noting the "undeviating ac⊥**36**ceptance given religious tax exemptions from our earliest days as a Nation").

It should be apparent from this discussion that *Walz*, which we have reaffirmed on numerous occasions in the last two decades, is utterly dispositive of the Establishment Clause claim before us here. The Court invalidates § 151.312 of the Texas Tax Code only by distorting the holding of that case, and radically altering the well settled Establishment Clause jurisprudence which that case represents.

Justice BRENNAN explains away *Walz* by asserting that "[t]he breadth of New York's property tax exemption was essential to our holding that it was 'not aimed at establishing, sponsoring, or supporting religion.'" This is not a plausible reading of the opinion. At the outset of its discussion concerning the permissibility of the legislative purpose, the *Walz* Court did discuss the fact that the New York tax exemption applied not just to religions but to certain other "nonprofit" groups, including "hospitals, libraries, playgrounds, scientific, professional, historical, and patriotic groups." The finding of valid legislative purpose was not rested upon that, however, but upon the more direct proposition that "exemption constitutes a reasonable and balanced attempt to guard against" the "latent dangers" of governmental hostility towards religion "inherent in the imposition of property taxes." The venerable federal legislation that the Court cited to support its holding was not legislation that exempted religion along with other things, but legislation that exempted *religion alone*. See, *e.g.*, ch. 17, 6 Stat. 116 (1813) (remitting duties paid on the importation of plates for printing Bibles); ch. 91, 6 Stat. 346 (1826) (remitting duties paid on the importation of church vestments, furniture, and paintings); ch. 259, 6 Stat. 600 (1834)(remitting duties paid on the importation of church bells). Moreover, if the Court had in⊥**37**tended to rely upon a "breadth of coverage" rationale, it would have had to identify some characteristic that rationally placed religion within the same policy category as the other institutions. *Justice BRENNAN's* concurring opinion in *Walz* conducted such an analysis, finding the New York exemption permissible only because religions, like the other types on nonprofit organizations exempted, "contribute to the well-being of the community in a variety of nonreligious ways," and (incomprehensibly) because they "uniquely contribute to the pluralism of American society by their religious activities." (I say incomprehensibly because to favor religion for its "unique contribution" is to favor religion as religion.) *Justice HARLAN's* opinion conducted a similar analysis, finding that the New York statute "defined a class of nontaxable entities whose common denominator is their nonprofit pursuit of activities devoted to cultural and moral improvement and the doing of 'good works' by performing certain social services in the community that might otherwise have to be assumed by government." The Court's opinion in *Walz*, however, not only failed to conduct such an analysis, but—seemingly in reply to the concurrences—*explicitly and categorically disavowed reliance upon it*, concluding its discussion of legislative purpose with a paragraph that begins as follows: "We find it unnecessary to justify the tax exemption on the social welfare services or 'good works' that some churches perform for parishioners and others." This should be compared with today's rewriting of *Walz*: "[W]e concluded that the State might reasonably have determined that religious groups generally contribute to the cultural and moral improvement of the community, perform useful social services, and enhance a desirable pluralism of viewpoint and enterprise, just as do the host of other nonprofit organizations that qualified for the exemption." This is a marvelously accurate description of what *Justices BRENNAN* and *HARLAN* believed, and what the Court specifically re⊥**38**jected. The Court did not approve an exemption for charities that happened to benefit religion; it approved an exemption for religion as an exemption for religion.

Today's opinions go beyond misdescribing *Walz*, however. In repudiating what *Walz* in fact approved, they achieve a revolution in our Establishment Clause jurisprudence, effectively overruling other cases that were based, as *Walz* was, on the "accommodation of religion" rationale. According to *Justice BRENNAN's* opinion, no law is constitutional whose "benefits [are] confined to religious organizations,"—except, of course, those laws that are unconstitutional *unless* they contain benefits confined to religious organizations. See also *Justice BLACKMUN's* opinion. Our jurisprudence affords no support for this unlikely proposition. *Walz* is just one of a long line of cases in which we have recognized that "the government may (and sometimes must) accommodate religious practices and it may do so without violating the Establishment Clause." *Hobbie* v. *Unemployment Appeals Comm'n of Fla.*; see McConnell, Accommodation of Religion, 1985 Sup. Ct. Rev. 1, 3. In such cases as *Sherbert* v. *Verner*, *Wisconsin* v. *Yoder*, *Thomas* v. *Review Bd. of Indiana Employment Security Div.*, and *Hobbie* v. *Unemployment Appeals Comm'n of Fla.*, we held that the Free Exercise Clause of the First Amendment *required* religious beliefs to be accommodated by granting religion-specific exemptions from otherwise applicable laws. We have often made clear, however, that "[t]he limits of permissible state accommodation to religion are by no means coextensive with the noninterference mandated by the Free Exercise Clause." *Walz*.

⊥**39** We applied the accommodation principle, to permit special treatment of religion that was not required by the Free Exercise Clause, in *Zorach* v. *Clauson*, where we found no constitutional objection to a New York City program permitting public school children to absent themselves one hour a week for "religious observance and education outside the school grounds." We applied the same principle only two Terms ago in *Corporation of the Presiding Bishop*, where, citing *Zorach* and *Walz*, we upheld a section of the Civil Rights Act of 1964 exempting religious groups (and only religious groups) from Title VII's antidiscrimination provisions. We found that "it is a permissible legislative purpose to alleviate significant governmental interference with the ability of religious organizations to define and carry out their religious missions." We specifically rejected the District Court's conclusion identical to that which a majority of the Court endorses today: that invalidity followed from the fact that the exemption "singles out religious entities for a benefit, rather than benefiting a broad grouping of which religious organizations are only a part." We stated that the Court "has never indicated that statutes that give special consideration to religious groups are *per se* invalid." As discussed earlier, it was this same principle of permissible accommodation that we applied in *Walz*.

The novelty of today's holding is obscured by *Justice BRENNAN's* citation and description of many cases in which "breadth of coverage" *was* relevant to the First Amendment determination. Breadth of coverage is essential to constitutionality whenever a law's benefiting of religious activity is sought to be defended not specifically (or not exclusively) as an intentional and reasonable accommodation of religion, but as merely the incidental consequence of seeking to benefit *all* activity that achieves a particular secular goal. But that is a different rationale—more commonly invoked than accommodation of religion but, as our cases ⊥**40** show, not preclusive of it. Where accommodation of religion is the justification, by definition religion is being singled out. The same confusion of rationales explains the facility with which *Justice BRENNAN's* opinion can portray the present statute as violating the first prong of the *Lemon* test, which is usually described as requiring a "secular legislative purpose." That is an entirely accurate description of the governing rule when, as in *Lemon* and most other cases, government aid to religious institutions is sought to be justified on the ground that it is not religion *per se* that is the object of assistance, but rather the secular functions that the religious institutions, along with other institutions, provide. But as I noted earlier, the substance of the *Lemon* test (purpose, effect, entanglement) was first roughly set forth in *Walz*—and in *that* context, the "accommodation of religion" context, the purpose was said to be valid so long as it was "neither the advancement nor the inhibition of religion; . . . neither sponsorship nor hostility." Of course rather than reformulating the *Lemon* test in "accommodation" cases (the text of *Lemon* is not, after all, a statutory enactment), one might instead simply describe the protection of free exercise concerns, and maintenance of the necessary neutrality, as "secular purpose and effect," since they are a purpose and effect approved, and indeed to some degree mandated, by the Constitution. However the reconciliation with the *Lemon* terminology is achieved, our cases make plain that it is permissible for a State to act with the purpose and effect of "limiting governmental interference with the exercise of religion." *Corporation of Presiding Bishop*.

It is not always easy to determine when accommodation slides over into promotion, and neutrality into favoritism, but the withholding of a tax upon the dissemination of religious materials is not even a close case. The subjects of the exemption before us consist exclusively of "writings promulgating the teaching of the faith" and "writings sacred to a reli⊥**41**gious faith." If there is any close question it is not whether the exemption is permitted, but whether it is constitutionally compelled in order to avoid "interference with the dissemination of religious ideas." In *Murdock* v. *Pennsylvania*, we held that it was unconstitutional to apply a municipal license tax on door-to-door solicitation to sellers of religious books and pamphlets. One term later, in *Follett* v. *McCormick*, we held that it was unconstitutional to apply to such persons a municipal license tax on "[a]gents selling books." Those cases are not as readily distinguishable as *Justice BRENNAN* suggests. I doubt whether it would have made any difference (as he contends) if the municipalities had attempted to achieve the same result of burdening the religious activity through a sales tax rather than a license tax; surely such a distinction trivializes the holdings. And the other basis of distinction he proposes—that the persons taxed in those cases were "religious missionaries whose principal work is preaching"—is simply not available with respect to the first part of the statute at issue here (which happens to be the portion upon which petitioner placed its exclusive reliance). Unlike the Texas exemption for sacred books, which, on its face at least, applies to all sales, the exemption for periodicals applies to material that not only "consist[s] wholly of writings promulgating the teaching of [a religious] faith," but also is "published or distributed by [that] faith." Surely this is material distributed by missionaries. Unless, again, one wishes to trivialize the earlier cases, whether they are full-time or part-time missionaries can hardly make a difference, nor can the fact that they conduct their proselytizing through the mail or from a church or store instead of door-to-door.

I am willing to acknowledge, however, that *Murdock* and *Follett* are narrowly distinguishable. But what follows from that is not the facile conclusion that therefore the State has no "compelling interest in avoiding violations of the Free Ex⊥**42**ercise and Establishment Clauses," and thus the exemption is invalid. This analysis is yet another expression of *Justice BRENNAN's* repudiation of the accommodation principle—which, as described earlier, consists of recognition that "[t]he limits of permissible state accommodation to religion are by no means co-extensive with the noninterference mandated by the Free Exercise Clause." *Walz*. By saying that what is not required cannot be allowed, *Justice BRENNAN* would completely block off the already narrow "channel between the Scylla [of what the Free Exercise Clause demands] and the Charybdis [of what the Establishment

Clause forbids] through which any state or federal action must pass in order to survive constitutional scrutiny." *Thomas*. The proper lesson to be drawn from the narrow distinguishing of *Murdock* and *Follett* is quite different: If the exemption comes so close to being a constitutionally required accommodation, there is no doubt that it is at least a permissible one.

Although *Justice BRENNAN's* opinion places almost its entire reliance upon the "purpose" prong of *Lemon*, it alludes briefly to the second prong as well, finding that § 151.312 has the impermissible "effect of sponsoring certain religious tenets or religious belief in general." Once again, *Walz* stands in stark opposition to this assertion, but it may be useful to explain why. Quite obviously, a sales tax exemption aids religion, since it makes it less costly for religions to disseminate their beliefs. But that has never been enough to strike down an enactment under the Establishment Clause. "A law is not unconstitutional simply because it *allows* churches to advance religion, which is their very purpose." *Corporation of Presiding Bishop* (emphasis in original). The Court has consistently rejected "the argument that any program which in some manner aids an institution with a religious affiliation" violates the Establishment Clause. *Muel⊥**43**ler* v. *Allen* (quoting *Hunt* v. *McNair*). To be sure, we have set our face against the subsidizing of religion—and in other contexts we have suggested that tax exemptions and subsidies are equivalent. *E.g.*, *Bob Jones University* v. *United Sates*, *Regan* v. *Taxation With Representation of Wash*. We have not treated them as equivalent, however, in the Establishment Clause context, and with good reason. "In the case of direct subsidy, the state forcibly diverts the income of both believers and nonbelievers to churches. In the case of an exemption, the state merely refrains from diverting to its own uses income independently generated by the churches through voluntary contributions." Giannella, Religious Liberty, Nonestablishment, and Doctrinal Development, 81 Harv. L. Rev. 513, 553 (1968). In *Walz* we pointed out that the *primary* effect of a tax exemption was not to sponsor religious activity but to "restric[t] the fiscal relationship between church and state" and to "complement and reinforce the desired separation insulation each from the other."

Finally, and least persuasively of all, *Justice BRENNAN* suggests that § 151.312 violates the "excessive government entanglement" aspect of *Lemon*. It is plain that the exemption does not foster the sort of "comprehensive, discriminating, and continuing state surveillance" necessary to run afoul of that test. A state does not excessively involve itself in religious affairs merely by examining material to determine whether it is religious or secular in nature. *Mueller* v. *Allen*, *Meek* v. *Pittenger* (upholding loans of nonreligious textbooks to religious schools); *Board of Education of Central School Dist. No. I* v. *Allen* (same). In *Mueller*, for instance, we held that state officials' examination of textbooks to determine whether they were "books and materials used in the ⊥**44** teaching of religious tenets, doctrines or worship" did not constitute excessive entanglement. I see no material distinction between that inquiry and one Texas officials must make in this case. Moreover, here as in *Walz*, it is all but certain that elimination of the exemption will have the effect of *increasing* government's involvement with religion. The Court's invalidation of § 151.312 ensures that Texas churches selling publications that promulgate their religion will now be subject to numerous statutory and regulatory impositions, including audits, Tex. Tax Code Ann. § 151.023 (1982 and Supp. 1988-1989), requirements for the filing of security, § 151.251 *et seq.*, reporting requirements, § 151.401 *et seq.*, writs of attachment without bond, § 151.605, tax liens, § 151.608, and the seizure and sale of property to satisfy tax delinquencies, § 151.610.

II

Having found that this statute does not violate the Establishment Clause of the First Amendment, I must consider whether it violates the Press Clause, pursuant to our decision two terms ago in *Arkansas Writer's Project, Inc.* v. *Ragland*. Although I dissented in *Ragland*, even accepting it to be correct I cannot conclude as readily as does *Justice WHITE* that it applies here.

The tax exemption at issue in *Ragland*, which we held to be unconstitutional because content-based, applied to trade publications and sports magazines along with religious periodicals and sacred writings, and hence could not be justified as an accommodation of religion. If the purpose of accommodating religion can support action that might otherwise violate the Establishment Clause, I see no reason why it does not also support action that might otherwise violate the Press Clause or the Speech Clause. To hold otherwise would be to narrow the accommodation principle enormously, leaving it applicable to only nonexpressive religious worship. I do not ⊥**45** think that is the law. Just as the Constitution sometimes requires accommodation of religious expression despite not only the Establishment Clause but also the Speech and Press clauses, so also it sometimes *permits* accommodation despite all those clauses. Such accommodation is unavoidably content-based—because the Freedom of Religion clause is content-based.

It is absurd to think that a State which chooses to prohibit booksellers from making stories about seduction available to children of tender years cannot make an exception for stories contained in sacred writings (e.g., the story of Susanna and the Two Elders, Daniel 13:1-65). And it is beyond imagination that the sort of tax exemption permitted (indeed, required) by *Murdock* and *Follett* would have to be withdrawn if door-to-door salesmen of commercial magazines demanded equal treatment with Seventh-day Adventists on Press Clause grounds. And it is impossible to believe that the State is constitutionally prohibited from taxing Texas Monthly magazine more heavily than the Holy Bible.

. . . . .

Today's decision introduces a new strain of irrationality in our Religion Clause jurisprudence. I have no idea how to reconcile it with *Zorach* (which seems a much harder case of accommodation), with *Walz* (which seems precisely in point) and with *Corporation of Presiding Bishop* (on which the ink is hardly dry). It is not right—it is not constitutionally healthy—that this Court should feel authorized to refashion anew our civil society's relationship with religion, adopting a theory of church and state that is contradicted by current practice, tradition, and even our own case law. I dissent.

HERNANDEZ v. COMMISSIONER OF INTERNAL REVENUE

490 U.S. 680
ON WRIT OF CERTIORARI TO THE UNITED STATES COURT OF APPEALS FOR THE FIRST CIRCUIT

GRAHAM v. COMMISSIONER OF INTERNAL REVENUE

ON WRIT OF CERTIORARI TO THE UNITED STATES COURT OF APPEALS FOR THE NINTH CIRCUIT
Argued November 28, 1988 — Decided June 5, 1989

⊥683 *Justice* MARSHALL delivered the opinion of the Court.

Section 170 of the Internal Revenue Code of 1954, 26 U.S.C. § 170 (Code), permits a taxpayer to deduct from gross income the amount of a "charitable contribution." The Code defines that term as a "contribution or gift" to certain eligible donees, including entities organized and operated exclusively for religious purposes. We granted certiorari to determine **⊥684** whether taxpayers may deduct as charitable contributions payments made to branch churches of the Church of Scientology (Church) in order to receive services known as "auditing" and "training." We hold that such payments are not deductible.

I

Scientology was founded in the 1950's by L. Ron Hubbard. It is propagated today by a "mother church" in California and by numerous branch churches around the world. The mother church instructs laity, trains and ordains ministers, and creates new congregations. Branch churches, known as "franchises" or "missions," provide Scientology services at the local level, under the supervision of the mother church. *Church of Scientology of California* v. *Commissioner*.

Scientologists believe that an immortal spiritual being exists in every person. A person becomes aware of this spiritual dimension through a process known as "auditing." Auditing involves a one-to-one encounter between a participant (known as a "preclear") and a Church official (known as **⊥685** an "auditor"). An electronic device, the E-meter, helps the auditor identify the preclear's areas of spiritual difficulty by measuring skin responses during a question and answer session. Although auditing sessions are conducted one-on-one, the content of each session is not individually tailored. The preclear gains spiritual awareness by progressing through sequential levels of auditing, provided in short blocks of time known as "intensives."

The Church also offers members doctrinal courses known as "training." Participants in these sessions study the tenets of Scientology and seek to attain the qualifications necessary to serve as auditors. Training courses, like auditing sessions, are provided in sequential levels. Scientologists are taught that spiritual gains result from participation in such courses.

The Church charges a "fixed donation," also known as a "price" or a "fixed contribution," for participants to gain access to auditing and training sessions. These charges are set forth in schedules and prices vary with a session's length and level of sophistication. In 1972, for example, the general rates for auditing ranged from $625 for a 12½-hour auditing intensive, the shortest available, to $4,250 for a 100-hour intensive, the longest available. Specialized types of auditing required higher fixed donations: a 12½-hour "Integrity Processing" auditing intensive cost $750; a 12½-hour "Expanded Dianetics" auditing intensive cost $950. This system of mandatory fixed charges is based on a central tenet of Scientology known as the "doctrine of exchange," according to which any time a person receives something he must pay something back. In so doing, a Scientologist maintains "inflow" and "outflow" and avoids spiritual decline.

The proceeds generated from auditing and training sessions are the Church's primary source of income. The Church promotes these sessions not only through newspaper, **⊥686** magazine, and radio advertisements, but also through free lectures, free personality tests, and leaflets. The Church also encourages, and indeed rewards with a 5% discount, advance payment for these sessions. The Church often refunds unused portions of prepaid auditing or training fees, less an administrative charge.

The petitioners in these consolidated cases each made payments to a branch church for auditing or training sessions. They sought to deduct these payments on their federal income tax returns as charitable contributions under § 170. Respondent Commissioner of the Internal Revenue Service (Commissioner or IRS) disallowed these deductions, finding that the payments were not charitable contributions within the meaning of § 170.

The petitioners sought review of these determinations in the Tax Court. That court consolidated for trial the cases of the three petitioners in No. 87-1616: Katherine Jean Graham, Richard M. Hermann, and David Forbes

Maynard. The petitioner in No. 87-963, Robert L. Hernandez, agreed to be bound by the findings in the consolidated *Graham* trial, reserving his right to a separate appeal. Before trial, the Commissioner stipulated that the branch churches of Scientology are religious organizations entitled to receive tax-deductible charitable contributions under the relevant section of the Code. This stipulation isolated as the sole statutory issue whether payments for auditing or training sessions constitute "contribution[s] or gift[s]" under § 170.

⊥**687** The Tax Court held a 3-day bench trial during which the taxpayers and others testified and submitted documentary exhibits describing the terms under which the Church promotes and provides auditing and training sessions. Based on this record, the court upheld the Commissioner's decision. 83 T. C. 575 (1984). It observed first that the term "charitable contribution" in § 170 is synonymous with the word "gift," which case law had defined "as a *voluntary transfer* of property by the owner to another *without consideration* therefor," quoting *DeJong* v. *Commissioner* (emphasis in original). It then determined that petitioners had received consideration for their payments, namely, "the benefit of various religious services provided by the Church of Scientology." The Tax Court also rejected the taxpayers' constitutional challenges based on the Establishment and Free Exercise Clauses of the First Amendment.

The Court of Appeals for the First Circuit in petitioner Hernandez' case, and for the Ninth Circuit in Graham, Hermann, and Maynard's case, affirmed. The First Circuit rejected Hernandez' argument that under § 170, the IRS' ordinary inquiry into whether the taxpayer received consideration for his payment should not apply to "the return of a commensurate *religious* benefit, as opposed to an *economic or financial* benefit" (emphasis in original). ⊥**688** The court found "no indication that Congress intended to distinguish the religious benefits sought by Hernandez from the medical, educational, scientific, literary, or other benefits that could likewise provide the *quid* for the *quo* of a nondeductible payment to a charitable organization." The court also rejected Hernandez' argument that it was impracticable to put a value on the services he had purchased, noting that the Church itself had "established and advertised monetary prices" for auditing and training sessions, and that Hernandez had not claimed that these prices misstated the cost of providing these sessions.

Hernandez' constitutional claims also failed. Because § 170 created no denominational preference on its face, Hernandez had shown no Establishment Clause violation. As for the Free Exercise Clause challenge, the court determined that denying the deduction did not prevent Hernandez from paying for auditing and training sessions and thereby observing Scientology's doctrine of exchange. Moreover, granting a tax exemption would compromise the integrity and fairness of the tax system.

The Ninth Circuit also found that the taxpayers had received a "measurable, specific return . . . as a quid pro quo for the donation" they had made to the branch churches. The court reached this result by focusing on "the external features" of the auditing and training transactions, an analytic technique which "serves as an expedient for any more intrusive inquiry into the motives of the payor." Whether a particular exchange generated secular or religious benefits to the taxpayer was irrelevant, for under § 170 "[i]t is the structure of the transaction, and not the type of benefit received, that controls."

The Ninth Circuit also rejected the taxpayers' constitutional arguments. The tax deduction provision did not violate the Establishment Clause because § 170 is "neutral in its design" and reflects no intent "to visit a disability on a par⊥**689**ticular religion." Furthermore, that the taxpayers would "have less money to pay to the Church, or that the Church [would] receive less money, [did] not rise to the level of a burden on appellants' ability to exercise their religious beliefs." Indeed, because the taxpayers could still make charitable donations to the branch church, they were "not put to the choice of abandoning the doctrine of exchange or losing the government benefit, for they may have both." Finally, the court noted that the compelling governmental interest in "the maintenance of a sound and uniform tax system" counseled against granting a free exercise exemption.

We granted certiorari to resolve a circuit conflict concerning the validity of charitable deductions for auditing and training payments. We now affirm.

II

For over 70 years, federal taxpayers have been allowed to deduct the amount of contributions or gifts to charitable, religious, and other eleemosynary institutions. See 2 B. Bittker, Federal Taxation of Income, Estates and Gifts ¶ 35.1.1 (1981) (tracing history of charitable deduction). Section 170, the present provision, was enacted in 1954; it requires a taxpayer claiming the deduction to satisfy a number of conditions. The Commissioner's stipulation in this case, how⊥**690**ever, has narrowed the statutory inquiry to one such condition: whether petitioners' payments for auditing and training sessions are "contribution[s] or gift[s]" within the meaning of §170.

The legislative history of the "contribution or gift" limitation, though sparse, reveals that Congress intended to differentiate between unrequited payments to qualified recipients and payments made to such recipients in return for goods or services. Only the former were deemed deductible. The House and Senate Reports on the 1954 tax bill, for example, both define "gifts" as payments "made with no expectation of a financial return commensurate with the amount of the gift." S. Rep. No. 1622, 83d Cong., 2d Sess., 196 (1954); H. R. Rep. No. 1337, 83d Cong., 2d Sess., A44 (1954). Using payments to hospitals as an example, both Reports state that the gift characterization should not apply to "a payment by an individual to a hospital *in consideration of* a binding obligation to provide medical treatment for the individual's employees. It would apply only if there were no expectation of any quid pro quo from the hospital." S. Rep. No. 1622 (emphasis added); H. Rep. No. 1337 (emphasis added).

In ascertaining whether a given payment was made with "the expectation of any quid pro quo," S. Rep. No. 1622, H. Rep. No. 1337, the Internal Revenue Service (IRS) has customarily examined the external features of the transaction in question. This practice has the advantage of obviat⊥**691**ing the need for the IRS to conduct imprecise inquiries into the motivations of individual taxpayers. The lower courts have generally embraced this structural analysis. See, *e.g.*, *Singer Co.* v. *United States* (applying this approach and collecting cases), cited in *United States* v. *American Bar Endowment*; see also 2 B. Bittker, at ¶ 35.1.3 (collecting cases). We likewise focused on external features in *United States* v. *American Bar Endowment* to resolve the taxpayers' claims that they were entitled to partial deductions for premiums paid to a charitable organization for insurance coverage; the taxpayers contended that they had paid unusually high premiums in an effort to make a contribution along with their purchase of insurance. We upheld the Commissioner's disallowance of the partial deductions because the taxpayers had failed to demonstrate, at a minimum, the existence of comparable insurance policies with prices lower than those of the policy they had each purchased. In so doing, we stressed that "[t]he *sine qua non* of a charitable contribution is a transfer of money or property *without adequate consideration*" (emphasis added in part).

In light of this understanding of § 170, it is readily apparent that petitioners' payments to the Church do not qualify as "contribution[s] or gift[s]." As the Tax Court found, these payments were part of a quintessential *quid pro quo* exchange: in return for their money, petitioners received an identifiable benefit, namely, auditing and training sessions. The Church established fixed price schedules for auditing and training sessions in each branch church; it calibrated particular prices to auditing or training sessions of particular lengths and levels of sophistication; it returned a refund if auditing and training services went unperformed; it distributed "ac⊥**692**count cards" on which persons who had paid money to the Church could monitor what prepaid services they had not yet claimed; and it categorically barred provision of auditing or training sessions for free. Each of these practices reveals the inherently reciprocal nature of the exchange.

Petitioners do not argue that such a structural analysis is inappropriate under § 170, or that the external features of the auditing and training transactions do not strongly suggest a *quid pro quo* exchange. Indeed, the petitioners in the consolidated *Graham* case conceded at trial that they expected to receive specific amounts of auditing and training in return for their payments. Petitioners argue instead that they are entitled to deductions because a *quid pro quo* analysis is inappropriate under § 170 when the benefit a taxpayer receives is purely religious in nature. Along the same lines, petitioners claim that payments made for the right to participate in a religious service should be automatically deductible under § 170.

We cannot accept this statutory argument for several reasons. First, it finds no support in the language of § 170. Whether or not Congress could, consistent with the Establishment Clause, provide for the automatic deductibility of a payment made to a church that either generates religious benefits or guarantees access to a religious service, that is a choice Congress has thus far declined to make. Instead, Congress has specified that a payment to an organization operated exclusively for religious (or other eleemosynary) pur⊥**693**poses is deductible *only* if such a payment is a "contribution or gift." 26 U.S.C. § 170(c). The Code makes no special preference for payments made in the expectation of gaining religious benefits or access to a religious service. The House and Senate Reports on § 170, and the other legislative history of that provision, offer no indication that Congress' failure to enact such a preference was an oversight.

Second, petitioners' deductibility proposal would expand the charitable contribution deduction far beyond what Congress has provided. Numerous forms of payments to eligible donees plausibly could be categorized as providing a religious benefit or as securing access to a religious service. For example, some taxpayers might regard their tuition payments to parochial schools as generating a religious benefit or as securing access to a religious service; such payments, however, have long been held not to be charitable contributions under § 170. Taxpayers might make similar claims about payments for church-sponsored counseling sessions or for medical care at church-affiliated hospitals that otherwise might not be deductible. Given that, under the First Amendment, the IRS can reject otherwise valid claims of religious benefit only on the ground that a taxpayers' alleged beliefs are not sincerely held, but not on the ground that such beliefs are inherently irreligious, see *United States* v. *Ballard*, the resulting tax deductions would likely expand the charitable contribution provision far beyond its present size. We are loath to effect this result in the absence of supportive congressional intent.

⊥**694** Finally, the deduction petitioners seek might raise problems of entanglement between church and state. If framed as a deduction for those payments generating benefits of a religious nature for the payor, petitioners' proposal would inexorably force the IRS and reviewing courts to differentiate "religious" benefits from "secular" ones. If framed as a deduction for those payments made in connection with a religious service, petitioners' proposal would force the IRS and the judiciary into differentiating "religious" services from "secular" ones. We need pass no judgment now on the constitutionality of such hypothetical inquiries, but we do note that "pervasive monitoring" for "the subtle or overt presence of religious matter" is a central danger against which we have held the Establishment Clause guards. *Aguilar* v. *Felton*, see also *Widmar* v. *Vincent* ("[T]he University would risk greater 'entanglement' by attempting to enforce its exclusion of 'religious worship' and 'religious speech' than by opening its forum to religious as well as nonreligious speakers"); cf. *Thomas* v. *Review Bd. of Indiana Employment Security Div.*

Accordingly, we conclude that petitioners' payments to the Church for auditing and training sessions are not "contribution[s] or gift[s]" within the meaning of that statutory expression.

III

We turn now to petitioners' constitutional claims based on the Establishment Clause and the Free Exercise Clause of the First Amendment.

⊥**695** A

Petitioners argue that denying their requested deduction violates the Establishment Clause in two respects. First, § 170 is said to create an unconstitutional denominational preference by according disproportionately harsh tax status to those religions that raise funds by imposing fixed costs for participation in certain religious practices. Second, § 170 allegedly threatens governmental entanglement with religion because it requires the IRS to entangle itself with religion by engaging in "supervision of religious beliefs and practices" and "valuation of religious services."

Our decision in *Larson* v. *Valente* supplies the analytic framework for evaluating petitioners' contentions. *Larson* teaches that, when it is claimed that a denominational preference exists, the initial inquiry is whether the law facially differentiates among religions. If no such facial preference exists, we proceed to apply the customary three-pronged Establishment Clause inquiry derived from *Lemon* v. *Kurtzman*.

Thus analyzed, § 170 easily passes constitutional muster. The line which § 170 draws between deductible and nondeductible payments to statutorily qualified organizations does not differentiate among sects. Unlike the Minnesota statute at issue in *Larson*, which facially exempted from state registration and reporting requirements only those religious organizations that derived more than half their funds from members, § 170 makes no "explicit and deliberate distinctions between different religious organizations," ⊥**696** applying instead to all religious entities.

Section 170 also comports with the *Lemon* test. First, there is no allegation that § 170 was born of animus to religion in general or Scientology in particular. Cf. *Larson* (history of Minnesota restriction reveals hostility to "Moonies" and intent to "get at . . . people that are running around airports"). The provision is neutral both in design and purpose.

Second, the primary effect of § 170—encouraging gifts to charitable entities, including but not limited to religious organizations—is neither to advance nor inhibit religion. It is not alleged here that § 170 involves "[d]irect government action endorsing religion or a particular religious practice." *Wallace* v. *Jaffree* (O'Connor, J., concurring in judgment). It may be that a consequence of the *quid pro quo* orientation of the "contribution or gift" requirement is to impose a disparate burden on those charitable and religious groups that rely on sales of commodities or services as a means of fund-raising, relative to those groups that raise funds primarily by soliciting unilateral donations. But a statute primarily having a secular effect does not violate the Establishment Clause merely because it "happens to coincide or harmonize with the tenets of some or all religions." *McGowan* v. *Maryland*.

Third, § 170 threatens no excessive entanglement between church and state. To be sure, ascertaining whether a payment to a religious institution is part of a *quid pro quo* transaction may require the IRS to ascertain from the institution the prices of its services and commodities, the regularity with which payments for such services and commodities are waived, and other pertinent information about the transaction. But routine regulatory interaction which involves no inquiries into religious doctrine, see *Presbyterian Church in* ⊥**697** *U. S.* v. *Mary Elizabeth Blue Hull Mem. Presb. Church*, no delegation of state power to a religious body, see *Larkin* v. *Grendel's Den, Inc.*, and no "detailed monitoring and close administrative contact" between secular and religious bodies, see *Aguilar*, does not of itself violate the nonentanglement command. See *Tony and Susan Alamo Foundation* v. *Secretary of Labor* (stating that nonentanglement principle "does not exempt religious organizations from such secular governmental activity as fire inspections and building and zoning regulations" or the record-keeping requirements of the Fair Labor Standards Act) (citation omitted). As we have observed, it is petitioners' interpretation of § 170, requiring the Government to distinguish between "secular" and "religious" benefits or services, which may be "fraught with the sort of entanglement that the Constitution forbids." *Lemon*.

Nor does the application of § 170 to religious practices require the Government to place a monetary value on particular religious benefits. As an initial matter, petitioners' claim here raises no need for valuation, for they have alleged only that their payments are fully exempt from a *quid pro quo* analysis—not that some portion of these payments is deductible because it exceeds the value of the acquired service. Cf. *American Bar Endowment* (describing "dual character" payments) (citing, *inter alia*, Rev. Rul. 68-432, 1968-2 Cum. Bull. 104, 105). In any event, the need to ascertain what portion of a payment was a purchase and what portion was a contribution does not ineluctably create entanglement problems by forcing the government to place a monetary value on a religious benefit. In cases where the economic value of a good or service is elusive—where, for example, no comparable good or service is sold in the marketplace—the IRS has eschewed benefit-focused valuation. Instead, it has often employed as an al⊥**698**ternative method of valuation an inquiry into the cost (if any) to the donee of providing the good or service. See, *e. g.*, *Oppewal* v. *Commissioner of Internal Revenue* (cost of providing a "religiously-oriented" education). This valuation method, while requiring qualified religious institutions to disclose relevant information about church costs to the IRS, involves administrative inquiries that, as a general matter, "bear no resemblance to the kind of government surveillance the Court has previously held to pose an intolerable risk of government entanglement with religion." *Tony and Susan Alamo Foundation*, cf. *Lemon* (school-aid statute authorizing government inspection of parochial school records created impermissible "intimate and continuing relationship between church and state" because it required State "to determine which expenditures are religious and which are secular").

B

Petitioners also contend that disallowance of their § 170 deductions violates their right to the free exercise of religion by "plac[ing] a heavy burden on the central practice of Scientology." The precise nature of this claimed burden is unclear, but it appears to operate in two ways. First, the deduction disallowance is said to deter adherents from engaging in auditing and training sessions. Second, the deduction disallowance is said to interfere with observance of the doctrine of exchange, which mandates equality of an adherent's "outflow" and "inflow."

⊥**699** The free exercise inquiry asks whether government has placed a substantial burden on the observation of a central religious belief or practice and, if so, whether a compelling governmental interest justifies the burden. It is not within the judicial ken to question the centrality of particular beliefs or practices to a faith, or the validity of particular litigants' interpretations of those creeds. We do, however, have doubts as to whether the alleged burden imposed by the deduction disallowance on the Scientologists' practices is a substantial one. Neither the payment nor the receipt of taxes is forbidden by the Scientology faith generally, and Scientology does not proscribe the payment of taxes in connection with auditing or training sessions specifically. Cf. *United States* v. *Lee*. Any burden imposed on auditing or training therefore derives solely from the fact that, as a result of the deduction denial, adherents have less money available to gain access to such sessions. This burden is no different from that imposed by any public tax or fee; indeed, the burden imposed by the denial of the "contribution or gift" deduction would seem to pale by comparison to the overall federal income tax burden on an adherent. Likewise, it is unclear why the doctrine of exchange would be violated by a deduction disallowance so long as an adherent is free to equalize "outflow" with "inflow" by paying for as many auditing and training session as he wishes.

In any event, we need not decide whether the burden of disallowing the § 170 deduction is a substantial one, for our decision in *Lee* established that even a substantial burden would be justified by the "broad public interest in maintaining a sound tax system," free of "myriad exceptions flowing ⊥**700** from a wide variety of religious beliefs." In *Lee*, we rejected an Amish taxpayer's claim that the Free Exercise Clause commanded his exemption from Social Security tax obligations, noting that "[t]he tax system could not function if denominations were allowed to challenge the tax system" on the ground that it operated "in a manner that violates their religious belief." That these cases involve federal income taxes, not the Social Security system, is of no consequence. The fact that Congress has already crafted some deductions and exemptions in the Code also is of no consequence, for the guiding principle is that a tax "must be uniformly applicable to all, except as *Congress* provides explicitly otherwise" (emphasis added). Indeed, in one respect, the Government's interest in avoiding an exemption is more powerful here than in *Lee*; the claimed exemption in *Lee* stemmed from a specific doctrinal obligation not to pay taxes, whereas petitioners' claimed exemption stems from the contention that an incrementally larger tax burden interferes with their religious activities. This argument knows no limitation. We accordingly hold that petitioners' free exercise challenge is without merit.

IV

We turn, finally, to petitioners' assertion that disallowing their claimed deduction is at odds with the IRS' longstanding practice of permitting taxpayers to deduct payments made to other religious institutions in connection with certain religious practices. Through the appellate stages of this litigation, this claim was framed essentially as one of selective prosecution. The Courts of Appeals for the First and Ninth Circuits summarily rejected this claim, finding no evidence of the intentional governmental discrimination necessary to support such a claim. 822 F. 2d, at 853 (no showing of "the type of hostility to a target of law enforcement that would support a claim of selective enforcement"); 819 F. 2d, at 1223 (no "discriminatory intent" proved).

⊥**701** In their arguments to this Court, petitioners have shifted emphasis. They now make two closely related claims. First, the IRS has accorded payments for auditing and training disparately harsh treatment compared to payments to other churches and synagogues for their religious services. Recognition of a comparable deduction for auditing and training payments is necessary to cure this administrative inconsistency. Second, Congress, in modifying § 170 over the years, has impliedly acquiesced in the deductibility of payments to these other faiths; because payments for auditing and training are indistinguishable from these other payments, they fall within the principle acquiesced in by Congress that payments for religious services are deductible under § 170.

Although the Government demurred at oral argument as to whether the IRS, in fact, permits taxpayers to deduct payments made to purchase services from other churches and synagogues, the Commissioner's periodic revenue rulings have stated the IRS' position rather clearly. A 1971 ruling, still in effect, states: "Pew rents, building fund assessments, and periodic dues paid to a church . . . are all methods of making contributions to the church, and such payments are deductible as charitable contributions within the limitations set out in section 170 of the Code." Rev. Rul. 70-47, 1970-1 Cum. Bull. 49 (superseding A.R.M. 2, Cum. Bull. 150 (1919)). We also assume for purposes of argument that the IRS also allows taxpayers to deduct "specified payments for attendance at High Holy Day services, for tithes, for torah readings and for memorial plaques." *Foley* v. *Commissioner*.

The development of the present litigation, however, makes it impossible for us to resolve petitioners' claim that they have received unjustifiably harsh treatment compared to adherents of other religions. The relevant inquiry in determining whether a payment is a "contribution or gift" under § 170 is, as we have noted, not whether the payment secures reli⊥**702**gious benefits or access to religious services, but whether the transaction in which the payment is involved is structured as a *quid pro quo* exchange. To make such a determination in this case, the Tax Court heard testimony and received documentary proof as to the terms and structure of the auditing and training transactions; from this evidence it made factual findings upon which it based its conclusion of nondeductibility, a conclusion we have held consonant with § 170 and with the First Amendment.

Perhaps because the theory of administrative inconsistency emerged only on appeal, petitioners did not endeavor at trial to adduce from the IRS or other sources any specific evidence about other religious faiths' transactions. The IRS' revenue rulings, which merely state the agency's conclusions as to deductibility and which have apparently never been reviewed by the Tax Court or any other judicial body, also provide no specific facts about the nature of these other faiths' transactions. In the absence of such facts, we simply have no way (other than the wholly illegitimate one of relying on our personal experiences and observations) to appraise accurately whether the IRS' revenue rulings have correctly applied a *quid pro quo* analysis with respect to any or all of the religious practices in question. We do not know, for example, whether payments for other faiths' services are truly obligatory or whether any or all of these services are generally provided whether or not the encouraged "mandatory" payment is made.

The IRS' application of the "contribution or gift" standard may be right or wrong with respect to these other faiths, or it may be right with respect to some religious practices and wrong with respect to others. It may also be that some of these payments are appropriately classified as partially deductible "dual payments." With respect to those religions where the structure of transactions involving religious services is established not centrally but by individual congregations, the proper point of reference for a *quid pro quo* analy⊥**703**sis might be the individual congregation, not the religion as a whole Only upon a proper factual record could we make these determinations. Absent such a record, we must reject petitioners' administrative consistency argument.

Petitioners' congressional acquiescence claim fails for similar reasons. Even if one assumes that Congress has acquiesced in the IRS' ruling with respect to "[p]ew rents, building fund assessments, and periodic dues," Rev. Rul. 70-47, 1970-1 Cum. Bull. 49, the fact is that the IRS' 1971 ruling articulates no broad principle of deductibility, but instead merely identifies as deductible three discrete types of payments. Having before us no information about the nature or structure of these three payments, we have no way of discerning any possible unifying principle, let alone whether such a principle would embrace payments for auditing and training sessions.

V

For the reasons stated herein, the judgments of the Courts of Appeals are hereby

Affirmed.

Justice BRENNAN and *Justice* KENNEDY took no part in the consideration or decision of these cases.

⊥**704** *Justice* O'CONNOR, with whom *Justice* SCALIA joins, dissenting.

The Court today acquiesces in the decision of the Internal Revenue Service (IRS) to manufacture a singular exception to its 70-year practice of allowing fixed payments indistinguishable from those made by petitioners to be deducted as charitable contributions. Because the IRS cannot constitutionally be allowed to select which religions will receive the benefit of its past rulings, I respectfully dissent.

The cases before the Court have an air of artificiality about them that is due to the IRS' dual litigation strategy against the Church of Scientology. As the Court notes, the IRS has successfully argued that the mother Church of Scientology was not a tax-exempt organization from 1970 to 1972 because it had diverted profits to the founder of Scientology and others, conspired to impede collection of its taxes, and conducted almost all of its activities for a commercial purpose. In the cases before the Court today, however, the IRS decided to contest the payments made to Scientology under 26 U.S.C. § 170 rather than challenge the tax-exempt status of the various branches of the Church to which the payments were made. According to the Solicitor General, the IRS challenged the payments themselves in order to expedite matters. As part of its litigation strategy in these cases, the IRS agreed to several stipulations which, in my view, necessarily determine the proper approach to the questions presented by petitioners.

The stipulations, relegated to a single sentence by the Court, established that Scientology was at all relevant times a religion; that each Scientology branch to which payments were made was at all relevant times a "church" within the meaning of § 170(b)(1)(A)(i); and that ⊥**705** Scientology was at all times a "corporation" within the meaning of § 170(c)(2) and exempt from general income taxation under 26 U.S.C. § 501(a). As the Solicitor General recognizes, it follows from these stipulations that Scientology operates for " 'charitable purposes' " and puts the "public interest above the private interest." Moreover, the stipulations establish that the payments made by petitioners are fixed donations made by individuals to a tax-exempt religious organization in order to participate in religious services, and are not based on "market prices set to reap the profits of a commercial moneymaking venture." *Staples* v. *Commissioner*. The Tax Court, however, appears to have ignored the stipulations. It concluded, perhaps relying on its previous opinion in *Church of Scientology*, that "Scientology operates in a commercial manner in providing [auditing and training]. In fact, one of its articulated goals is to make money." The Solicitor General has duplicated the error here, referring on numerous occasions to the commercial nature of Scientology in an attempt to negate the effect of the stipulations.

It must be emphasized that the IRS' position here is *not* based upon the contention that a portion of the knowledge received from auditing or training is of secular, commercial, nonreligious value. Thus, the denial of a deduction in these cases bears no resemblance to the denial of a deduction for religious-school tuition up to the market value of the secularly useful education received. Here the IRS denies deductibility solely on the basis that the exchange is a *quid pro quo*, even though the *quid* is exclusively of spiritual or religious worth. Re⊥**706**spondent cites no instances in which this has been done before, and there are good reasons why.

When a taxpayer claims as a charitable deduction part of a fixed amount given to a charitable organization in exchange for benefits that have a commercial value, the allowable portion of that claim is computed by subtracting from the total amount paid the value of the physical benefit received. If at a charity sale one purchases for $1,000 a painting whose market value is demonstrably no more than $50, there has been a contribution of $950. The same would be true if one purchases a $1,000 seat at a charitable dinner where the food is worth $50. An identical calculation can be made where the *quid* received is not a painting or a meal, but an intangible such as entertainment, so long as that intangible has some market value established in a noncontributory context. Hence, one who purchases a ticket to a concert, at the going rate for concerts by the particular performers, makes a charitable contribution of zero even if it is announced in advance that all proceeds from the ticket sales will go to charity. The performers may have made a charitable contribution, but the audience has paid the going rate for a show.

It becomes impossible, however, to compute the "contribution" portion of a payment to a charity where what is received in return is not merely an intangible, but an intangible (or, for that matter a tangible) that is not bought and sold except in donative contexts so that the only "market" price against which it can be evaluated is a market price that always includes donations. Suppose, for example, that the charitable organization that traditionally solicits donations on Veterans' Day, in exchange for which it gives the donor an imitation poppy bearing its name, were to establish a flat rule that no one gets a poppy without a donation of at least $10. One would have to say that the "market" rate for such poppies was $10, but it would assuredly not be true that everyone who "bought" a poppy for $10 made no contribution. Similarly, if one buys a $100 seat at a prayer break⊥**707**fast—receiving as the *quid pro quo* food for both body and soul—it would make no sense to say that no charitable contribution whatever has occurred simply because the "going rate" for all prayer breakfasts (with equivalent bodily food) is $100. The latter may well be true, but that "going rate" *includes* a contribution.

Confronted with this difficulty, and with the constitutional necessity of not making irrational distinctions among taxpayers, and with the even higher standard of equality of treatment among *religions* that the First Amendment imposes, the Government has only two practicable options with regard to distinctively religious *quids pro quo*: to disregard them all or to tax them all. Over the years it has chosen the former course.

Congress enacted the first charitable contribution exception to income taxation in 1917. War Revenue Act of 1917, ch. 63, § 1201(2), 40 Stat. 330. A mere two years later, in A.R.M. 2, 1 Cum. Bull. 150 (1919), the IRS gave its first blessing to the deductions of fixed payments to religious organizations as charitable contributions:

"[T]he distinction of pew rents, assessments, church dues, and the like from basket collections is hardly warranted by the act. The act reads 'contributions' and 'gifts.' It is felt that all of these come within the two terms.

"In substance it is believed that these are simply methods of contributing although in form they may vary. Is a basket collection given involuntarily to be distinguished from an envelope system, the latter being regarded as 'dues'? From a technical angle, the pew rents may be differentiated, but in practice the so-called 'personal accommodation' they may afford is conjectural. It is believed that the real intent is to contribute and not to hire a seat or pew for personal accommodation. In fact, basket contributors sometimes receive the same accommodation informally."

⊥708 The IRS reaffirmed its position in 1970, ruling that "[p]ew rents, building fund assessments and periodic dues paid to a church . . . are all methods of making contributions to the church and such payments are deductible as charitable contributions." Rev. Rul. 70-47, 1970-1 Cum. Bull. 49. Similarly, notwithstanding the "form" of Mass stipends as fixed payments for specific religious services, the IRS has allowed charitable deductions of such payments. See Rev. Rul. 78-366, 1978-2 Cum. Bull. 241.

These rulings, which are "official interpretation[s] of [the tax laws] by the [IRS]," Rev. Proc. 78-24, 1978-2 Cum. Bull. 503, 504, flatly contradict the Solicitor General's claim that there "is no administrative practice recognizing that payments made in exchange for religious benefits are tax deductible." Indeed, an Assistant Commissioner of the IRS recently explained in a "question and answer guidance package" to tax-exempt organizations that "[i]n contrast to tuition payments, religious observances generally are not regarded as yielding private benefits to the donor, who is viewed as receiving only incidental benefits when attending the observances. The primary beneficiaries are viewed as being the general public and members of the faith. Thus, payments for saying masses, pew rents, tithes, and other payments involving fixed donations for similar religious services, are fully deductible contributions." IRS Official Explains New Examination-Education Program on Charitable Contributions to Tax-Exempt Organizations, B. N. A. Daily Tax Report for Executives 186:J-1, 186:J-3 (Sept. 26, 1988). Although this guidance package may not be as authoritative as IRS rulings, in the absence of any contrary indications it does reflect the continuing adherence of the IRS to its practice of allowing deductions for fixed payments for religious services.

There can be no doubt that at least some of the fixed payments which the IRS has treated as charitable deductions, or which the Court assumes the IRS would allow taxpayers to ⊥709 deduct, are as "inherently reciprocal," as the payments for auditing at issue here. In exchange for their payment of pew rents, Christians receive particular seats during worship services. See Encyclopedic Dictionary of Religion 2760 (1979). Similarly, in some synagogues attendance at the worship services for Jewish High Holy Days is often predicated upon the purchase of a general admission ticket or a reserved seat ticket. See J. Feldman, H. Fruhauf, & M. Schoen, Temple Management Manual, ch. 4, p. 10 (1984). Religious honors such as publicly reading from Scripture are purchased or auctioned periodically in some synagogues of Jews from Morocco and Syria. See H. Dobrinsky, A Treasury of Sephardic Laws and Customs 164, 175-177 (1986). Mormons must tithe ten percent of their income as a necessary but not sufficient condition to obtaining a "temple recommend," *i.e.*, the right to be admitted into the temple. See The Book of Mormon, 3 Nephi 24:7-12 (1921); Reorganized Church of Jesus Christ of Latter Day Saints, Book of Doctrine and Covenants § 106:1b (1978). A Mass stipend—a fixed payment given to a Catholic priest, in consideration of which he is obliged to apply the fruits of the Mass for the intention of the donor—has similar overtones of exchange. According to some Catholic theologians, the nature of the pact between a priest and a donor who pays a Mass stipend is "a bilateral contract known as *do ut facias*. One person agrees to give while the other party agrees to do something in return." 13 New Catholic Encyclopedia, Mass Stipend, p. 715 (1967). A finer example of a *quid pro quo* exchange would be hard to formulate.

This is not a situation where the IRS has explicitly and affirmatively reevaluated its longstanding interpretation of § 170 and decided to analyze *all* fixed religious contributions under a *quid pro quo* standard. There is no indication whatever that the IRS has abandoned its 70-year practice with re⊥710spect to payments made by those other than Scientologists. In 1978, when it ruled that payments for auditing and training were not charitable contributions under § 170, the IRS did not cite—much less try to reconcile—its previous rulings concerning the deductibility of other forms of fixed payments for religious services or practices. See Rev. Rul. 78-189, 1978-1 Cum. Bull. 68 (equating payments for auditing with tuition paid to religious schools).

Nevertheless, the Government now attempts to reconcile its previous rulings with its decision in these cases by relying on a distinction between direct and incidental benefits in exchange for payments made to a charitable organization. This distinction, adumbrated as early as the IRS' 1919 ruling, recognizes that even a deductible charitable contribution may generate certain benefits for the donor. As long as the benefits remain "incidental" and do not indicate that the payment was actually made for the "personal accommodation" of the donor, the payment will be deductible. It is the Government's view that the payments made by petitioners should not be deductible under § 170 because the "unusual facts in these cases . . . demonstrate that the payments were made primarily for 'personal accommodation.'" Specifically, the Solicitor General asserts that "the rigid connection between the provision of auditing and training services and payment of the fixed price" indicates a *quid pro quo* relationship and "reflect[s] the value that petitioners expected to receive for their money."

There is no discernible reason why there is a more rigid connection between payment and services in the religious practices of Scientology than in the religious practices of the faiths described above. Neither has the Government explained why the benefit received by a Christian who obtains the pew of his or her choice by paying a rental fee, a Jew who gains entrance to High Holy Day services by purchasing a ticket, a Mormon who makes the fixed payment necessary for a temple recommend, or a Catholic who pays a Mass stipend, ⊥711 is incidental to the real benefit conferred on the "general public and members of the faith," B. N. A. Daily Tax

Report, at 186:J-3, while the benefit received by a Scientologist from auditing is a personal accommodation. If the perceived difference lies in the fact that Christians and Jews worship in congregations, whereas Scientologists, in a manner reminiscent of Eastern religions, gain awareness of the "immortal spiritual being" within them in one-to-one sessions with auditors, such a distinction would raise serious Establishment Clause problems. The distinction is no more legitimate if it is based on the fact that congregational worship services "would be said anyway," without the payment of a pew rental or stipend or tithe by a particular adherent. The relevant comparison between Scientology and other religions must be between the Scientologist undergoing auditing or training on one hand and the congregation on the other. For some religions the central importance of the congregation achieves legal dimensions. In Orthodox Judaism, for example, certain worship services cannot be performed and Scripture cannot be read publicly without the presence of at least ten men. 12 Encyclopedia Judaica, Minyan, p. 67 (1971). If payments for participation occurred in such a setting, would the benefit to the tenth man be only incidental while for the personal accommodation of the eleventh? In the same vein, will the deductibility of a Mass stipend turn on whether there are other congregants to hear the Mass? And conversely, does the fact that the payment of a tithe by a Mormon is an absolute prerequisite to admission to the temple make that payment for admission a personal accommodation regardless of the size of the congregation?

Given the IRS' stance in these cases, it is an understatement to say that with respect to fixed payments for religious ⊥**712** services "the line between the taxable and the immune has been drawn by an unsteady hand." *United States* v. *Allegheny County*. This is not a situation in which a governmental regulation "happens to coincide or harmonize with the tenets of some or all religions," *McGowan* v. *Maryland*, but does not violate the Establishment Clause because it is founded on a neutral, secular basis. Rather, it involves the differential application of a standard based on constitutionally impermissible differences drawn by the Government among religions. As such, it is best characterized as a case of the Government "put[ting] an imprimatur on [all but] one religion." *Gillette* v. *United States*. That the Government may not do.

The Court attempts to downplay the constitutional difficulty created by the IRS' different treatment of other fixed payments for religious services by accepting the Solicitor General's invitation to let the IRS make case-specific *quid pro quo* determinations. ("The IRS' application of the 'contribution or gift' standard may be right or wrong with respect to these other faiths, or it may be right with respect to some religious practices and wrong with respect to others.") As a practical matter, I do not think that this unprincipled approach will prove helpful. The Solicitor General was confident enough in his brief to argue that, "even without making a detailed factual inquiry," Mormon tithing does not involve a *quid pro quo* arrangement. At oral argument, however, the Solicitor General conceded that if it was mandatory, tithing would be distinguishable from the "ordinary case of church dues." If the approach suggested by the Solicitor General is so malleable and indefinite, it is not a panacea, and cannot be trusted to secure First Amendment rights against arbitrary incursions by the Government.

⊥**713** On a more fundamental level, the Court cannot abjure its responsibility to address serious constitutional problems by converting a violation of the Establishment Clause into an "administrative consistency argument," with an inadequate record. It has chosen to ignore both longstanding, clearly articulated IRS practice, and the failure of the Government to offer any cogent, neutral explanation for the IRS' refusal to apply this practice to the Church of Scientology. Instead, the Court has pretended that whatever errors in application the IRS has committed are hidden from its gaze and will, in any event, be rectified in due time.

In my view, the IRS has misapplied its longstanding practice of allowing charitable contributions under § 170 in a way that violates the Establishment Clause. It has unconstitutionally refused to allow payments for the religious service of auditing to be deducted as charitable contributions in the same way it has allowed fixed payments to other religions to be deducted. Just as the Minnesota statute at issue in *Larson* v. *Valente* discriminated against the Unification Church, the IRS' application of the *quid pro quo* standard here—and only here—discriminates against the Church of Scientology. I would reverse the decisions below.

DAVIS v. UNITED STATES

495 U.S. 472
ON WRIT OF CERTIORARI TO THE UNITED STATES COURT OF APPEALS FOR THE NINTH CIRCUIT
Argued March 26, 1990 — Decided May 21, 1990

⊥**473***Justice* O'CONNOR delivered the opinion of the Court.

We are called upon in this case to determine whether the funds petitioners transferred to their two sons while they served as full-time, unpaid missionaries for the Church of ⊥**474** Jesus Christ of Latter-day Saints are deductible as charitable contributions "to or for the use of" the Church, pursuant to 26 U.S.C. § 170.

I

Petitioners, Harold and Enid Davis, and their sons, Benjamin and Cecil, are members of the Church of Jesus Christ of Latter-day Saints. According to the stipulated facts, the Church operates a worldwide missionary program involving 25,000 persons each year. Most of these missionaries are young men between the ages of 19 and 22. If the Church determines that a candidate is qualified to become a missionary, the president of the

Church sends a letter calling the candidate to missionary service in a specified geographical location. A follow-up letter from the Missionary Department lists the items of clothing the missionary will need, provides specific information relating to the mission, and sets forth the estimated amount of money needed to support the missionary service. This amount varies according to the location of the mission, and reflects an estimate of the amount the missionary will actually need.

The missionary's parents generally provide the necessary funds to support their son or daughter during the period of missionary service. If they are unable to do so, the Church will locate another donor from the local congregation or use money donated to the Church's general missionary funds. The Church believes that having individual donors send the necessary funds directly to the missionary benefits the Church in several important ways. Specifically, it "fosters the Church doctrine of sacrifice and consecration in the lives of its people" as well as reducing the administrative and bookkeeping requirements which would otherwise be imposed upon the Church.

After accepting the call, the missionary candidate receives priesthood ordinances to serve as an official missionary and minister of the Church. During the missionary service, the Mission President (leader of the mission) controls many as⊥**475**pects of the missionaries' lives, including the manner of dress and grooming. Missionaries are required to conform to a daily schedule which calls for at least 10 hours per day of actual missionary work in addition to study time, mealtime and planning time. Mission rules forbid dating, movies, plays, certain sports, and other activities; missionaries are not allowed to take vacations or travel for personal purposes.

Missionaries receive some supervision over their use of funds. The Missionary Handbook instructs missionaries that "[t]he money you receive for your support is sacred and should be spent wisely and only for missionary work. Keep expenses at a minimum. . . . Keep a financial record of all expenditures." The Mission Presidents give similar instructions to the missionaries under their supervision. Although missionaries are not required to obtain advance approval of each expenditure they make from their personal checking account, they do submit weekly reports to their group leader listing the amount of time spent in Church service, the type of missionary work accomplished, and a report of the total expenses for the week and month to date. If a missionary begins to accumulate surplus funds, he is expected to take action to reduce the amount of donations sent to him. The Mission President may alter his estimates of the amounts required each month to take into account changing circumstances.

Benjamin and Cecil Davis both applied to become missionaries. In 1979, the Church notified Benjamin by letter that he had been called to missionary service at the New York Mission. A second letter informed him of the estimated amount of money which would be needed to support his service. In 1980, Cecil Davis was notified that he had been called to missionary service at the New Zealand-Cook Island Mission. Cecil also received a second letter informing him about the mission and the amount of money he would need. Petitioners notified their bishop that they would provide the funds requested by the Church to meet their sons' mission ⊥**476** expenses. According to petitioners, both sons made a commitment with them to use the money only in accordance with the Church's instructions.

Petitioners transferred to Benjamin's personal checking account, on which he was the sole authorized signatory, $3,480.89 in 1980 and $4,135 in 1981. During 1981, petitioners transferred $1,518 to Cecil's personal checking account, on which he was the sole authorized signatory. Benjamin and Cecil used this money primarily to pay for rent, food, transportation, and personal needs while on their missions. Benjamin also spent approximately $20 per month to purchase religious tracts and other materials used during his missionary work. Neither Benjamin nor Cecil was required to or sought specific approval of each expenditure made from his personal checking account. However, each week Benjamin and Cecil submitted a report of the total expenses for the week and month to date. At the end of their service, Cecil had no money remaining in his account; Benjamin had $150 which he used to purchase a camera. (Petitioners do not claim a deduction for this amount.)

In their joint tax returns filed in 1980 and 1981, petitioners claimed their sons as dependents, but did not claim a charitable contribution deduction under 26 U.S.C. § 170 for the funds sent their sons during their missionary service. On April 16, 1984, petitioners filed an amended income tax return for the years 1980 and 1981, claiming additional charitable contributions of the $3,480.89 and $4,882 paid to their sons during the missionary service. In January 1985, the Internal Revenue Service disallowed the refunds. Petitioners filed a refund suit in the United States District Court for the District of Idaho. In September 1986, petitioners filed a second set of amended returns, limiting their charitable deductions to the amounts indicated by the Church and correcting the number of dependents claimed for each year.

In District Court petitioners and the United States both moved for summary judgment. ⊥**477** Petitioners argued that the payments they made to support their sons' missionary services were charitable contributions "for the use of" the Church. Alternatively, they claimed the payments were deductible under Treas. Reg. 1.170A-1(g), 26 CFR § 1.170A-1(g) (1989), which allows the deduction of "unreimbursed expenditures made incident to the rendition of services to an organization contributions to which are deductible." The District Court ruled in favor of the United States. It rejected petitioners' claimed deduction for unreimbursed expenditures because petitioners were not themselves performing donated services and it held that petitioners' payments to their sons were not "for the use of" the Church because the Church lacked sufficient possession and control of the funds.

The Court of Appeals for the Ninth Circuit affirmed. 861 F. 2d 558 (1988). The Court of Appeals rejected petitioners' claim that the transferred funds were deductible contributions because they conferred a benefit on the Church. Instead, the Court of Appeals held that contributions are deductible only when the recipient charity exercises control over the donated funds. The Court of Appeals reasoned that the beneficiary of a charitable contribution must be indefinite, see *Russell* v. *Allen*, and that this requirement cannot be met when the taxpayer makes a contribution directly to the intended beneficiary. In this case, the Court of Appeals concluded that the Church lacked actual control over the disposition of the funds and thus they were not deductible. The Court of Appeals agreed with the District Court that § 1.170A-1(g) did not apply to petitioners, as the regulation permits a deduction for unreimbursed expenses only by the taxpayer who performed the charitable service.

Because the Court of Appeals' decision conflicted with *White* v. *United States*, and *Brinley* v. *Commissioner*, ⊥**478** we granted certiorari, and now affirm.

II

Under § 170 of the Internal Revenue Code of 1954, 68A Stat. 58, as amended, 26 U.S.C. § 170 (1982 ed.), a taxpayer may claim a deduction for a charitable contribution only if the contribution is made "to or for the use of" a qualified organization. This section provides, in pertinent part:

"(a) Allowance of deduction.

"(1) General rule.—There shall be allowed as a deduction any charitable contribution (as defined in subsection (c)) payment of which is made within the taxable year. A charitable contribution shall be allowable as a deduction only if verified under regulations prescribed by the Secretary.

. . . . .

"(c) Charitable contribution defined.—For purposes of this section, the term 'charitable contribution' means a contribution or gift *to or for the use of*—

. . . . .

"(2) A corporation, trust, or community chest, fund, or foundation—

. . . . .

"(B) organized and operated exclusively for religious, charitable, scientific, literary, or educational purposes. . . ." (Emphasis added.)

Petitioners contend that the funds they transferred to their sons' accounts are deductible as contributions "for the use of" the Church. Alternatively, petitioners claim these funds are unreimbursed expenditures under Treasury Regulation § 1.170A-1(g), and therefore are deductible as contributions "to" the Church. We first consider whether the payments ⊥**479** at issue here are "for the use of" the Church within the meaning of § 170.

On its face, the phrase "for the use of" could support any number of different meanings. See, e.g, Webster's New International Dictionary (2d ed. 1950) ("use" defined in general usage as "to convert to one's service"; "to employ"; or, in law, "use imports a trust" relationship). Petitioners contend that the phrase "for the use of" must be given its broadest meaning as describing "the entire array of fiduciary relationships in which one person conveys money or property to someone else to hold or employ in some manner for the benefit of a third person." Under this reading, no legally enforceable relationship need exist between the recipient of the donated funds and the qualified donee; in effect, any intermediary may handle the funds in any way that would arguably benefit a charitable organization, regardless of how indirect or tangential the benefit might be. Petitioners also advance a second, somewhat narrower interpretation, specifically that a contribution is "for the use of" a qualified organization within the meaning of §170 so long as the donee has "a reasonable ability to ensure that the contribution primarily serves the organization's charitable purposes." In this case, petitioners argue that their payments at least meet this second interpretation. They point to the Church's role in requesting the funds, setting the amount to be donated, and requiring weekly expense sheets from the missionaries. The Service, on the other hand, has historically defined "for the use of" as conveying "a similar meaning as 'in trust for.'" See *e.g*, I. T. 1867, 11-2 Cum. Bull. 155 (1923).

Although the language of § 170 would support the interpretation of either the Service or petitioners, the events leading to the enactment of the 1921 amendment adding the phrase "for the use of" to § 170 indicate that Congress had a specific meaning of "for the use of" in mind. The original version of § 170, promulgated in the War Revenue Act of 1917, ch. 63, § 1201(2), 40 Stat. 330, did not allow deductions for gifts "for ⊥**480** the use of" a qualified donee. Rather, it allowed individuals to deduct only "[c]ontributions or gifts . . . to corporations or associations organized and operated exclusively for religious, charitable, scientific, or educational purposes. . . ." In interpreting this provision in the Act (and in the subsequent Revenue Act of 1918, ch. 18, § 214(a)(11), 40 Stat. 1068), the Bureau of Internal Revenue stated that "[c]ontributions to a trust company (a corporation) in trust to invest and disburse them for a charitable purpose are not allowable deductions under [§ 170]." O. D. 669, 3 Cum. Bull. 187 (1920). In hearings before the Senate Committee on Finance on the proposed Revenue Act of 1921, representatives of charitable foundations requested an amendment making gifts to trust companies and similar donees deductible even though a trustee, rather than a charitable organization, held legal title to the funds. Hearings on Proposed Revenue Act of 1921 before the Senate Committee on Finance, 67th Cong., 1st Sess., 521 (1921). Testimony before the Committee indicated that numerous communities had established charitable trusts, charitable foundations, or community chests so that individuals could donate money to a trustee who held, invested, and reinvested the principal, and then turned the principal over to a committee that distributed the funds for charitable purposes. See also H. R. Rep. No. 350, 67th Cong., 1st Sess., 12 (1921) (House Comm. on Ways and Means) (amendments "would allow the deduction, under proper restriction, of contributions or gifts to a community chest fund or foundation"); S. Rep. No. 275, 67th Cong., 1st Sess., 18 (1921). Responding to these concerns, Congress overruled the Service's interpretation of § 170 [then § 214(a)(11)] by adding the phrase "for the use of . . . any corporation, or community chest, fund, or foundation . . ." to the charitable deduction provision of the Revenue Act of 1921, ch. 136, § 214(a)(11), 42 Stat. 241. In light of these events, it can be inferred that Congress' use of the phrase "for the use of" related to its purpose in amending § 170 of allowing tax-⊥**481**payers to deduct contributions made to trusts, foundations, and similar donees. An interpretation of "for the use of" as conveying a similar meaning as "in trust for" would be consistent with this goal.

It would have been quite natural for Congress to use the phrase "for the use of" to indicate its intent of allowing deductions for donations in trust, as this phrase would have suggested a trust relationship to the members of the 67th Congress. From the dawn of English common law through the present, the word "use" has been employed to refer to various forms of trust arrangements. See 1 G. Bogert, Trusts and Trustees § 2, p. 9 (1935); Black's Law Dictionary 1382 (5th ed. 1979) ("*Use* and *trusts* are not so much different things as different aspects of the same subject. A use regards principally the beneficial interest; a trust regards principally the nominal ownership"). In the early part of this century, the word "use" was technically employed to refer to a passive trust, but less formally used as a synonym for the word "trust." See Bogert, at 9 ("The words 'use' and 'trust' are employed as synonyms frequently by writers and judges"); 1 R. Baldes, Perry on Trusts and Trustees § 298 (7th ed. 1929) ("A use, a trust, and a confidence is one and the same thing. . . ."); 1 Restatement of Trusts §§ 67-72 (Effect of Statute of Uses) (1935). The phrases "to the use of" or "for the use of" were frequently used in describing trust arrangements. See, *e.g*, *United States* v. *Bowling*, *Blanset* v. *Cardin*, *Rand* v. *United States*. Given that this meaning of the word "use" precisely corresponded with Congress' purpose for amending the statute, it appears likely that in choosing the phrase "for the use of" Congress was referring to donations made in trust or in a similar legal arrangement.

This understanding is confirmed by the Service's initial interpretation of the phrase. It is significant that almost immediately following the amendment of § 170, the Commis⊥**482**sioner interpreted the phrase "for the use of" as "intended to convey a similar meaning as 'in trust for.'" I. T. 1867, II-2 Cum. Bull. 155 (1923). Rejecting a taxpayer's claim that a gift to a volunteer fire company was deductible as a contribution for the use of the municipality, the Service noted that "[i]t does not appear that the municipality in any way has any control over the property of the incorporated volunteer fire company or that it has any voice in the manner in which such property should be used. Upon dissolution of the company, the property would not escheat to the State. A right of appropriation or enjoyment of the property of the fire company does not rest in the municipality." *Ibid.* The Service adhered to its interpretation that "for the use of" conveys "a similar meaning as 'in trust for'" in subsequent rulings permitting taxpayers to deduct the value of gifts irrevocably transferred to a trust for the benefit of qualified organizations. See, e.g., Rev. Rul. 55-275, 1955-1 Cum. Bull. 295; Rev. Rul. 194, 1953-2 Cum. Bull. 128; I. T. 3707, 1945 Cum. Bull. 114. Numerous judicial decisions have relied on this interpretation. See, *e.g.*, *Rockefeller* v. *Commissioner*, *Orr* v. *United States*, *Thomason* v. *Commissioner*, *Danz* v. *Commissioner*. Congress' reenactment of the statute in 1954, using the same language, indicates its apparent satisfaction with the prevailing interpretation of the statute. See *Cammarano* v. *United States*, *McCaughn* v. *Hershey Chocolate Co.*

The Commissioner's interpretation of "for the use of" thus appears to be entirely faithful to Congress' understanding and intent in using that phrase. Moreover, the Commissioner's interpretation is consistent with the purposes of § 170 as a whole. In enacting § 170, "Congress sought to provide tax benefits to charitable organizations, to encourage the de⊥**483**velopment of private institutions that serve a useful public purpose or supplement or take the place of public institutions of the same kind." *Bob Jones University* v. *United States*. The Commissioner's interpretation of "for the use of" assures that contributions will in fact foster such development because it requires contributions to be made in trust or in some similar legal arrangement. A defining characteristic of a trust arrangement is that the beneficiary has the legal power to enforce the trustee's duty to comply with the terms of the trust. See, *e.g.*, 3 W. Fratcher, Scott on Trusts § 200 (4th ed. 1988); 1 Restatement of Trusts § 200 (1935). A qualified beneficiary of a bona fide trust for charitable purposes would have both the incentive and legal authority to ensure that donated funds are properly used. If the trust contributes funds to a range of charitable organizations so that no single beneficiary could enforce its terms, the trustee's duty can be enforced by the Attorney General under the laws of most States. See 4A W. Fratcher, Scott on Trusts § 391 (4th ed. 1989); G. Bogert Trusts and Trustees § 411 (2d ed. 1977). Although the Service's interpretation does not require that the qualified organization take actual possession of the contribution, it nevertheless reflects that the beneficiary must have significant legal rights with respect to the disposition of donated funds.

Petitioners argue that any interpretation of "for the use of" that requires a qualified donee to have the same degree of control over contributed funds as a beneficiary would have over a trust *res*, would make "for the use of" redundant, meaning no more than "to." We disagree. When Congress amended § 170, it was fully aware of the Service's ruling that the original statutory deduction for contributions "to" a qualified organization could not be claimed for contributions made in trust for the organization. Accordingly, Congress amended the statute specifically to overcome this interpretation. Moreover, a contribution made in trust for a charity does not give the charity ⊥**484** immediate possession and control, as does a donation directly to a charity. Unlike a contribution that must go "to" a qualified organization, a contribution "for the use of" a donee may go to a trustee with the discretion to select among a number of qualified donees to whom the funds may be disbursed. Furthermore, a taxpayer may generally claim an immediate deduction for a gift to a trustee, even though receipt of the gift by the charity is delayed. Recognizing this characteristic of gifts in trust, Congress further amended § 170 in 1964 in order to encourage donations "to" a charity, because donations "in trust for" a charity "often do not find their way into operating philanthropic endeavors for extended periods of time." S. Rep. No. 830, 88th Cong., 2d Sess., 59-60 (1964).

Although the Service's interpretive rulings do not have the force and effect of regulations, we give an agency's interpretations and practices considerable weight where they involve the contemporaneous construction of a statute and where they have been in long use. Under the circumstances presented here, we think there is good reason to accept the Service's interpretation of "for the use of." The denial of deductions for donations in trust that prompted Congress to amend § 170, the accepted meaning of "use" as synonymous with the term "trust," and the Service's contemporaneous and longstanding construction of § 170 constitutes strong evidence in favor of this interpretation.

Although the language of the statute may also bear petitioners' interpretation, they have failed to establish that their interpretation is compelled by the statutory language. To the contrary, there is no evidence that Congress intended the phrase "for the use of" to be interpreted as referring to fiduciary relationships in general or as referring to a type of relationship that gives a qualified organization a reasonable abil⊥**485**ity to supervise the use of contributed funds. Rather, as noted above, there are strong indications that Congress intended a more specific meaning. Moreover, petitioners' interpretations would tend to undermine the purposes of § 170 by allowing taxpayers to claim deductions for funds transferred to children or other relatives for their own personal use. Because a recipient of donated funds need not have any legal relationship with a qualified organization, the Service would face virtually insurmountable administrative difficulties in verifying that any particular expenditure benefitted a qualified donee. Although there is no suggestion whatsoever in this case that the transferred funds were used for an improper purpose, it is clear that petitioners' interpretation would create an opportunity for tax evasion that others might be eager to exploit. We need not determine whether petitioners' interpretation of "for the use of" would have been a permissible one had the Service decided to adopt it, though we note that the Service may retain some flexibility to adopt other interpretations in the future. It is sufficient to decide this case that the Service's longstanding interpretation is both consistent with the statutory language and fully implements Congress' apparent purpose in adopting it. Accordingly, we conclude that a gift or contribution is "for the use of" a qualified organization when it is held in a legally enforceable trust for the qualified organization or in a similar legal arrangement.

Viewing the record here in the light most favorable to petitioners, as we must after a grant of summary judgment for the United States, we discern no evidence that petitioners ⊥**486** transferred funds to their sons "in trust for" the Church. It is undisputed that petitioners transferred the money to their sons' personal bank accounts on which the sons were the sole authorized signatories. Nothing in the record indicates that petitioners took any steps normally associated with creating a trust or similar legal arrangement. Although the sons may have promised to use the money "in accordance with Church guidelines," they did not have any legal obligation to do so; there is no evidence that the guidelines have any legally binding effect. Nor does the record support the assertion that the Church might have a legal entitlement to the money or a civil cause of action against missionaries who used their parents' money for purposes not approved by the Church. We conclude that, because petitioners did not donate the funds in trust for the Church, or in a similarly enforceable legal arrangement for the benefit of the Church, the funds were not donated "for the use of" the Church for purposes of § 170.

III

Petitioners contend, in the alternative, that their transfer of funds into their sons' account was a contribution "to" the Church under Treas. Reg. § 1.170A-1(g), 26 CFR § 1.170A-1(g) (1989), which provides:

"*Contributions of services*. No deduction is allowable under section 170 for a contribution of services. However, unreimbursed expenditures made incident to the rendition of services to an organization contributions to which are deductible may constitute a deductible contribution. For example, the cost of a uniform without general utility which is required to be worn in perform⊥**487**ing donated services is deductible. Similarly, out-of-pocket transportation expenses necessarily incurred in performing donated services are deductible. Reasonable expenditures for meals and lodging necessarily incurred while away from home in the course of performing donated services are also deductible. For the purposes of this paragraph, the phrase 'while away from home' has the same meaning as that phrase is used for purposes of section 162 and the regulations thereunder."

Petitioners assert that this regulation allows them to claim deductions for their sons' unreimbursed expenditures incident to their sons' contribution of services. We disagree. The plain language of § 1.170A-1(g) indicates that taxpayers may claim deductions only for expenditures made in connection with their own contributions of service to charities. Unless there is a specific statutory provision to the contrary, a taxpayer ordinarily reports his own income and takes his own deductions. See, *e.g.*, *Commissioner* v. *Culbertson* ("[T]he first principle of income taxation [is] that income must be taxed to him who earns it."); *New Colonial Ice Co.* v. *Helvering* ("[T]axpayer who sustain[s] the loss is the one to whom the deduction shall be allowed"). Section 1.170A-1(g) is thus most naturally read as referring to the individual taxpayer, who may deduct only those "unreimbursed expenditures" incurred in connection with the taxpayer's own "rendition of services to [a qualified] organization." This interpretation of the regulation is consistent with the Revenue Ruling that was the precursor to § 1.170A-1(g). See Rev. Rul. 55-4, 1955-1 Cum. Bull. 291 ("A taxpayer who gives his services gratuitously to an association, contributions to which are deductible under [§ 170] and who incurs unreimbursed traveling expenses . . . may deduct the amount of such unreimbursed expenses in computing his net income . . ."). It would strain the language of the regulation to read it, as petitioners suggest, as allowing a deduction for expenses made incident to a third party's rendition of services rather than to the taxpayer's own contribution of services. Similarly, the taxpayer is clearly intended to be the subject of the other provisions in the regulation. For example, it is most natural to read the regulation as referring to a taxpayer who incurs ⊥**488** expenditures for meals and lodging while away from his home, not while a third party is away from his home.

Petitioners' interpretation not only strains the language of the statute, but would also allow manipulation of § 1.170A-1(g) for tax evasion purposes. For example, parents might be tempted to transfer funds to their children in amounts greater than needed to reimburse reasonable expenses incurred in donating services to a charity. Parents and children might attempt to claim a deduction for the same expenditure. Controlling such abuses would place a heavy administrative burden on the Service which would not only have to monitor the taxpayer's records, but also correlate them with the records of the third party. To the extent petitioners' interpretation lessens the likelihood that claimed charitable contributions actually served a charitable purpose, it is inconsistent with § 170.

Petitioners cite judicial decisions that allowed taxpayers to claim deductions for the expenses of third parties who assisted the taxpayers in rendering services to qualified organizations. See, *e.g.*, *Rockefeller* v. *Commissioner*, *McCollum* v. *Commissioner*, *Smith* v. *Commissioner*. These cases are inapposite, as petitioners do not claim that they were independently rendering services to the Church, assisted by their sons.

We conclude that § 1.170A-1(g) does not allow taxpayers to claim a deduction for expenses not incurred in connection with the taxpayers' own rendition of services to a qualified organization. Therefore, petitioners are not entitled to a deduction under § 1.170A-1(g) .

Petitioners also assert that because their sons are agents of the Church authorized to receive payments to support their own ⊥**489** missionary efforts, payments made to their sons are payments to the Church. Because this argument was neither raised before nor decided by the Court of Appeals, we decline to address it here.

Accordingly, we hold that petitioners' transfer of funds into their sons' accounts was not a contribution "to or for the use of" the Church for purposes of § 170. The judgment of the Court of Appeals is

Affirmed.

SUNDAY WORK

A type of legislation that seems to be narrow in focus but which raises interesting church-state questions is that compelling observance of Sunday as a day of rest. Stated simply, this legislation prohibits most commercial activities on Sunday because of the state's strong interest in providing a day of rest for its population. These laws have been called a type of public welfare legislation.

There are, however, some exemptions from the general restrictions on Sunday labor. Exempted commercial enterprises are those involving "necessaries," i.e., those things which must be available to people all the time to enhance their safety, comfort, and enjoyment. Consequently, in addition to the sale of such items as food and drugs on Sunday, enterprises such as professional sports, amusement parks, and ice cream parlors are allowed to operate on the day of rest. The laws are intended to have the effect of prohibiting most people from working on Sunday so that they may rest, but allowing businesses which provide for basic human needs or which facilitate rest and recreation for the majority to remain open. The scope of this type of legislation and the extent and complexity of exemptions are clearly detailed in the cases that follow.

In the western world, the concept of a special day of rest goes back many centuries before the beginning of the Christian era. In the Ten Commandments one reads:

> Remember the sabbath day, to keep it holy.
> Six days you shall labor, and do all your

> work; but the seventh day is a sabbath to the Lord your God; in it you shall not do any work, you, or your son, or your daughter, your manservant, or your maidservant, or your cattle, or the sojourner who is within your gates; for in six days the Lord made heaven and earth, the sea, and all that is in them, and rested the seventh day; therefore the Lord blessed the sabbath day and hallowed it (Exodus 20:8-11, RSV).

As this passage indicates, the day of rest was to be the seventh day. It was of such strong religious significance that this rest day became obligatory for observant Jews.

Early in the second century of the Christian era a new day of rest gained widespread acceptance in the western world. The Christian religion, in commemoration of the resurrection of Jesus, adopted Sunday as its day of rest. Again, the day had very strong religious significance. In A.D. 321, as a part of the process which made Christianity the official religion of the Roman Empire, the Emperor Constantine decreed that Sunday be a day of rest. This law set the trend for most governments down to the present; the Sunday observance law has had a very wide acceptance.

In colonial America, the first Sunday observance law was promulgated in Virginia in 1610. It commanded that

> no man or woman shall dare to violate or breake the Sabboth by any gaming, publique or private abroad, or at home, but duly sanctifie and observe the same, both himselfe and his familie, by preparing themselves at home with private prayer, that they may be the better fitted for the publique, according to the commandments of God, and the orders of our Church, as also every man and woman shall repaire in the morning to the divine service, and Sermons preached upon the Sabboth day, and in the afternoon to divine service, and Catechising, upon paine of the first fault to lose their provision, and allowance for the whole weeke following, for the second to lose the said allowance, and also to be whipt, and for the third to suffer death.[1]

Later, laws were added which specifically prohibited the sale of merchandise and goods on Sunday. Statutes of this type were found in all the colonies. After the adoption of the First Amendment, provisions requiring church attendance were dropped, but prohibitions against commercial activities on Sunday were retained. A very comprehensive presentation of the history of this type of legislation is given in the Supreme Court decisions themselves, especially the concurring opinion of Justice Frankfurter in McGOWAN v. MARYLAND.[2]

The religious groups most directly affected by such laws are Jews and Seventh-day Adventists. Jews have always regarded the Biblical passage quoted above as divine law so that observant Jews believe that they have the obligation to observe the Sabbath (from sundown Friday to sundown Saturday, according to Biblical law) as a day of worship, meditation on religious themes, and cessation from work. Sabbath rest is a very important part of one's total religious life. Seventh-day Adventists, although definitely a Christian group, believe that the coming of Christ did not remove from the truly religious person the obligation to observe the seventh day as the day of worship. Because God, by resting from the labor of creation on the seventh day, established that pattern of life from the beginning of history, Adventists believe that it is a pattern which ought to be faithfully and carefully observed.

Observant Jews and Seventh-day Adventists have an obvious objection to Sunday laws: these statutes place an economic burden on Sabbatarians. The Sabbatarian refrains from doing business on Saturday because of religious belief while nonsabbatarian competitors proceed with business as usual; then one must not work on Sunday because of the Sunday law. While religion and the law have combined to allow him/her to work only five days in the week, nonsabbatarians have been able to work six. Consequently, the Sabbatarian argues that the Sunday law compels him/her to suffer an economic disadvantage because of religious belief.

In dealing with this issue, the Supreme Court, in 1961, handed down four decisions on the same day. Two of the cases dealt primarily with the Establishment Clause; two dealt primarily with the Free Exercise Clause. (Because the arguments were essentially the same in each type of case, only two cases, the most important of each type, are included in this book.)

In McGOWAN v. MARYLAND the establishment argument was raised by neither Jew nor Seventh-day Adventist, but by a discount store's employees who had been arrested for selling forbidden items on Sunday. Their argument was that the Sunday law was a violation of the Establishment Clause because it gave state sanction and coercion to the observance of the Christian day of worship. Because the

---

[1]H. Shelton Smith, Robert T. Handy, and Lefferts A. Loetscher, *American Christianity: An Historical Interpretation with Representative Documents*, 2 vols. (New York: Charles Scribner's Sons, 1960), 1:43.

[2]Additional historical material about Sunday laws may be found in Anson Phelps Stokes, *Church and State in the United States*, 3:153-76, and Leo Pfeffer, *Church, State, and Freedom* (Boston: Beacon Press, 1967), pp. 270-87.

state compelled the observance of the Christian day of worship, they had not been able to do business, thus suffering economic injury.[3]

The other case that raised primarily Establishment Clause consideration was *Two Guys from Harrison-Allentown, Inc.* v. *McGinley.* Essentially the same as the *McGowan* case, this case challenged a Pennsylvania statute. There were enough different facts, including questions about the term of a district attorney, to cause the Court to write a separate opinion, but its decision on the church-state issues was the same as in *McGowan.*

The primary case in which the free exercise issue was raised was BRAUNFELD v. BROWN. Here the appellants were Orthodox Jews challenging a Pennsylvania statute. Although they also raised equal protection and establishment objections to the law, the case was decided on their free exercise contention. Appellants argued that they suffered economic injury not only because the state gave its sanction to the Christian day of worship but because, as practicing Jews, they were put at a competitive disadvantage by requirements of their religion (the argument spelled out above).

The other free exercise case was *Gallagher* v. *Crown Kosher Super Market.* The appellees were Orthodox Jews engaged in the kosher food business in Massachusetts. Because most of their customers were Orthodox Jews who were required by their religion to eat kosher food, and because they had traditionally done about one-third of their weekly business on Sunday, they argued that the state's Sunday law prohibited the free exercise of both themselves and their customers.

In all four cases, the Court found the Sunday laws to be constitutional. In this series of cases the Court used the "argument from history." That is, from time to time the Court, in finding a law constitutional or unconstitutional, will base its findings on the history of the practice under scrutiny. Has this practice been engaged in for a long time or did it originate rather recently? In either case, has it always been done the same way, or has the purpose and/or effect of the law changed during its history? The Court found the laws constitutional in these cases because the original Sunday laws had changed with the passage of time. Although they originally had a religious purpose, i.e., to protect the Christian day of worship for its proper observance, they had been secularized in that they had come to be regarded only as laws to provide a day of rest for laboring people. They no longer had a religious purpose, so they could not be said to be a violation of the Establishment Clause. The argument from history is frequently used in conjunction with other arguments to determine the constitutionality of the act. (Cf. WALZ v. TAX COMMISSION, WISCONSIN v. YODER, and Justice Brennan's concurring opinion in ABINGTON SCHOOL DISTRICT v. SCHEMPP.) In these Sunday law cases, however, the argument from history is essentially the determining factor in declaring the statutes constitutional, as it is in the more recent MARSH v. CHAMBERS.

One should note that the dissent of Justice Douglas, which is included in the *McGowan* decision, applies to all four cases. It was the only dissent on the two Establishment Clause cases. In the free exercise cases, however, Justices Brennan and Stewart joined Douglas in dissent, making the vote six-to-three. The separate opinion of Justice Frankfurter, included in the *McGowan* case, was in essence a concurring opinion and was meant to apply to all four cases.

In these cases the Court mentioned that states could provide alternate ways of meeting their secular goals without imposing on the religious activities of Sabbatarians, e.g., they could designate Sunday as the day of rest but provide exemptions for those whose religion required rest on another day, but they were not constitutionally required to do so. In 1962, in *Arlan's Department Store* v. *Kentucky,* the Court considered a law which contained such an exemption. The plaintiffs argued that in allowing Sabbatarians to keep their stores open on Sunday, while compelling nonsabbatarians to close theirs, the state was preferring religion over nonreligion, a violation of the Establishment Clause. The Court dismissed the appeal, stating that it did not present a substantial federal question, allowing the state courts' affirmance of the exemption to stand.

In *Kentucky Commission on Human Rights* v. *Kerns Bakery* a bakery employee, who had experienced religious conversion, refused to work on Sunday. When he was fired he sought relief through the state's civil rights commission, which found that the company could have accommodated plaintiff's work without "undue hardship," which it was required to do by a state law which forbade discrimination against an employee whose religious belief prevented work on his/her Sabbath. When the bakery contested the commission's decision in state court, the court ruled that the law was a violation of the Establishment Clause. On appeal, the state's highest court reversed, ruling that the law had the purpose of advancing equal employment opportunities for members of all faiths, that the law did not pro-

[3]The appellants objected to the law on free exercise grounds also. But because they were challenging the law strictly on grounds of economic injury, and because they did not demonstrate that their own religious exercise had been affected, the Court set that question aside and dealt only with the establishment question. They also challenged the law on other than church-state grounds: specifically, that the Sunday law was a violation of the Equal Protection Clause of the Fourteenth Amendment. The opinions show that the Court was not persuaded by that argument.

mote any religion in terms of either state sanction or finances, and that it did not unduly entangle religion and state. The United States Supreme Court refused to grant certiorari in 1983, allowing this state statute, which was virtually identical with the federal Civil Rights Act of 1964, to stand as not being violative of the Establishment Clause.

Finally, in 1985 the Court decided THORNTON v. CALDOR, a case that dealt with the issue of whether a statute designed to accommodate the religious sensibilities of employees was contrary to Establishment Clause principles. (Between *McGowan* and *Braunfeld* in 1961 and *Thornton* the Court decided several other workplace cases, but they were decided on grounds other than establishment and are discussed elsewhere in this book.) In 1977 Connecticut revised its Sunday closing law and Caldor, Inc. began opening some of its stores on Sunday. One of those was where Donald E. Thornton worked. A Presbyterian, Thornton worked on Sundays for a while, but then asked to be relieved of Sunday work in line with a Connecticut law which exempted from work on their Sabbath all those who requested such relief. The company responded with suggestions for alternative work schedules which were to Thornton's disadvantage and, indeed, transferred him to a different store in the chain at a reduced salary. Thornton resigned and appealed to the State Board of Mediation and Arbitration, claiming that the company had acted contrary to the statute. The Board and a state court found in Thornton's favor. The Supreme Court of Connecticut reversed, holding that the statute itself violated all three parts of the *Lemon* test of the Establishment Clause.

The United States Supreme Court, voting eight-to-one, agreed with the Connecticut Supreme Court, although it focused only on the "primary effect" test, rather than all three. Chief Justice Burger argued for the majority that the law mandated that one who observed a Sabbath day as a matter of religious conviction *must* be free from work that day by request, no matter what sort of burden it placed on employers and fellow employees. "The statute arms Sabbath observers with an absolute and unqualified right not to work on whatever day they designate as their Sabbath." Consequently, the law effectively made the Sabbath concerns of workers dominant over all secular concerns at the workplace. Such a law has the impermissible primary effect of advancing religion.

It is interesting to note that Thornton had died before the case reached the State Supreme Court. The case was carried on by the administrator of his estate. Neither the state court nor the United States Supreme Court declared the case moot, probably because Connecticut had intervened on behalf of Thornton and thus remained as a party who could be affected by the result. The result was not what the state had hoped for, however.

McGOWAN v. MARYLAND

366 U.S. 420
ON APPEAL FROM THE COURT OF APPEALS OF MARYLAND
Argued December 8, 1960 — Decided May 29, 1961

⊥422 Mr. *Chief Justice WARREN* delivered the opinion of the Court.

The issues in this case concern the constitutional validity of Maryland criminal statutes, commonly known as Sunday Closing Laws or Sunday Blue Laws. These statutes, with exceptions to be noted hereafter, generally proscribe all labor, business and other commercial activities on Sunday. The questions presented are whether the classifications within the statutes bring about a denial of equal protection of the law, whether the laws are so vague as to fail to give reasonable notice of the forbidden conduct and therefore violate due process, and whether the statutes are laws respecting an establishment of religion or prohibiting the free exercise thereof.

Appellants are seven employees of a large discount department store located on a highway in Anne Arundel County, Maryland. They were indicted for the Sunday sale of a three-ring loose-leaf binder, a can of floor wax, a stapler and staples, and a toy submarine in violation of Md. Ann. Code, Art. 27, § 521. Generally, this section prohibited, throughout the State, the Sunday sale of all merchandise except the retail sale of tobacco products, confectioneries, milk, bread, fruits, gasoline, oils, greases, **⊥423** drugs and medicines, and newspapers and periodicals. Recently amended, this section also now excepts from the general prohibition the retail sale in Anne Arundel County of all foodstuffs, automobile and boating accessories, flowers, toilet goods, hospital supplies and souvenirs. It now further provides that any retail establishment in Anne Arundel County which does not employ more than one person other than the owner may operate on Sunday.

Although appellants were indicted only under § 521, in order properly to consider several of the broad constitutional contentions, we must examine the whole body of Maryland Sunday laws. Several sections of the Maryland statutes are particularly relevant to evaluation of the issues presented. Section 492 of Md. Ann. Code, Art. 27, forbids all persons from doing any work or bodily labor on Sunday and forbids permitting children or servants to work on that day or to engage in fishing, hunting and unlawful pastimes or recreations. The section excepts all works of necessity and charity. Section 522 of Md. Ann. Code, Art. 27, disallows the opening or use of any dancing saloon, opera house, bowling alley or barber shop on Sunday. However, in addition to the exceptions noted above, Md. Ann. Code, Art. 27, § 509, exempts, for Anne Arundel County, the Sunday operation of any bathing beach, bathhouse, dancing saloon and amusement park, and activities incident thereto and retail sales of merchandise customarily sold at, or incidental to, the operation of the aforesaid occupations and businesses. Section 90 of Md. Ann. Code, Art. 2B, makes generally unlawful the sale of alcoholic beverages on Sunday. However, this section, and immediately succeeding ones, provide various immunities for the Sunday sale of different kinds of alcoholic beverages, at different hours during the day, by vendors holding different types of licenses, in different political divisions of the State—particularly ⊥**424** in Anne Arundel County.

The remaining statutory sections concern a myriad of exceptions for various counties, districts of counties, cities and towns throughout the State. Among the activities allowed in certain areas on Sunday are such sports as football, baseball, golf, tennis, bowling, croquet, basketball, lacrosse, soccer, hockey, swimming, softball, boating, fishing, skating, horseback riding, stock car racing and pool or billiards. Other immunized activities permitted in some regions of the State include group singing or playing of musical instruments; the exhibition of motion pictures; dancing; the operation of recreation centers, picnic grounds, swimming pools, skating rinks and miniature golf courses. The taking of oysters and the hunting or killing of game is generally forbidden, but shooting conducted by organized rod and gun clubs is permitted in one county. In some of the subdivisions within the State, the exempted Sunday activities are sanctioned throughout the day; in others, they may not commence until early afternoon or evening; in many, the activities may only be conducted during the afternoon and late in the evening. Certain localities do not permit the allowed Sunday activity to be carried on within one hundred yards of any church where religious services are being held. Local ordinances and regulations concerning certain limited activities supplement the State's statutory scheme. In Anne Arundel County, for example, slot machines, pinball machines and bingo may be played on Sunday.

Among other things, appellants contended at the trial that the Maryland statutes under which they were charged were contrary to the Fourteenth Amendment for the reasons stated at the outset of this opinion. Appellants were convicted and each was fined five dollars and costs. The Maryland Court of Appeals affirmed; ⊥**425** on appeal, we noted probable jurisdiction.

I

Appellants argue that the Maryland statutes violate the "Equal Protection" Clause of the Fourteenth Amendment on several counts. First, they contend that the classifications contained in the statutes concerning which commodities may or may not be sold on Sunday are without rational and substantial relation to the object of the legislation. Specifically, appellants allege that the statutory exemptions for the Sunday sale of the merchandise mentioned above render arbitrary the statute under which they were convicted. Appellants further allege that § 521 is capricious because of the exemptions for the operation of the various amusements that have been listed and because slot machines, pin-ball machines, and bingo are legalized and are freely played on Sunday.

The standards under which this proposition is to be evaluated have been set forth many times by this Court. Although no precise formula has been developed, the Court has held that the Fourteenth Amendment permits the States a wide scope of discretion in enacting laws which affect some groups of citizens differently than others. The constitutional safeguard is offended only if the classification rests on grounds wholly irrelevant to the achievement of the State's objective. State legislatures are presumed to have acted within their constitutional power despite the fact that, in practice, their laws ⊥**426** result in some inequality. A statutory discrimination will not be set aside if any state of facts reasonably may be conceived to justify it.

It would seem that a legislature could reasonably find that the Sunday sale of the exempted commodities was necessary either for the health of the populace or for the enhancement of the recreational atmosphere of the day—that a family which takes a Sunday ride into the country will need gasoline for the automobile and may find pleasant a soft drink or fresh fruit; that those who go to the beach may wish ice cream or some other item normally sold there; that some people will prefer alcoholic beverages or games of chance to add to their relaxation; that newspapers and drug products should always be available to the public.

The record is barren of any indication that this apparently reasonable basis does not exist, that the statutory distinctions are invidious, that local tradition and custom might not rationally call for this legislative treatment. ⊥**427** Likewise, the fact that these exemptions exist and deny some vendors and operators the day of rest and recreation contemplated by the legislature does not render the statutes violative of equal protection since there would appear to be many valid reasons for these exemptions, as stated above, and no evidence to dispel them.

Secondly, appellants contend that the statutory arrangement which permits only certain Anne Arundel County retailers to sell merchandise essential to, or customarily sold at, or incidental to, the operation of bathing beaches, amusement parks et cetera is contrary to the "Equal Protection" Clause because it discriminates unreasonably against retailers in other Maryland counties. But we have held that the Equal Protection Clause relates to equality between persons as such, rather than between areas and that territorial uniformity is not a constitutional prerequisite. With particular reference to the State of Maryland, we have noted that the prescription of different substantive offenses in different counties is generally a matter for legislative discretion. We find no invidious discrimination here.

Thirdly, appellants contend that this same statutory provision, Art. 27, § 509, violates the "Equal Protection" Clause because it permits only certain merchants within Anne Arundel County (operators of bathing beaches and amusement parks et cetera) to sell merchandise customarily sold at these places while forbidding its sale by other vendors of this merchandise, such as appellants' employer. Here again, it would seem that a legislature ⊥**428** could reasonably find that these commodities, necessary for the health and recreation of its citizens, should only be sold on Sunday by those vendors at the locations where the commodities are most likely to be immediately put to use. Such a determination would seem to serve the consuming public and at the same time secure Sunday rest for those employees, like appellants, of all other retail establishments. In addition, the enforcement problems which would accrue if large retail establishments, like appellants' employer, were permitted to remain open on Sunday but were restricted to the sale of the merchandise in question would be far greater than the problems accruing if only beach and amusement park vendors were exempted. Here again, there has been no indication of the unreasonableness of this differentiation. On the record before us, we cannot say that these statutes do not provide equal protection of the laws.

II

Another question presented by appellants is whether Art. 27, § 509, which exempts the Sunday retail sale of "merchandise essential to, or customarily sold at, or incidental to, the operation of" bathing beaches, amusement parks et cetera in Anne Arundel County, is unconstitutionally vague. We believe that business people of ordinary intelligence in the position of appellants' employer would be able to know what exceptions are encompassed by the statute either as a matter of ordinary commercial knowledge or by simply making a reasonable investigation at a nearby bathing beach or amusement park within the county. Under these circumstances, there is no necessity to guess at the statute's meaning in order to determine what conduct it makes criminal. Questions concerning proof that the items appellants sold were customarily ⊥**429** sold at, or incidental to the operation of, a bathing beach or amusement park were not raised in the Maryland Court of Appeals, nor are they raised here. Thus, we cannot consider the matter.

III

The final questions for decision are whether the Maryland Sunday Closing Laws conflict with the Federal Constitution's provisions for religious liberty. First, appellants contend here that the statutes applicable to Anne Arundel County violate the constitutional guarantee of freedom of religion in that the statutes' effect is to prohibit the free exercise of religion in contravention of the First Amendment, made applicable to the States by the Fourteenth Amendment. But appellants allege only economic injury to themselves; they do not allege any infringement of their own religious freedoms due to Sunday closing. In fact, the record is silent as to what appellants' religious beliefs are. Since the general rule is that "a litigant may only assert his own constitutional rights or immunities," *United States* v. *Raines*, we hold that appellants have no standing to raise this contention. Furthermore, since appellants do not specifically allege that the statutes infringe upon the religious beliefs of the department store's present or prospective patrons, we ⊥**430** have no occasion here to consider the standing question of *Pierce* v. *Society of Sisters*. Those persons whose religious rights are allegedly impaired by the statutes are not without effective ways to assert these rights. Appellants present no weighty countervailing policies here to cause an exception to our general principles.

Secondly, appellants contend that the statutes violate the guarantee of separation of church and state in that the statutes are laws respecting an establishment of religion contrary to the First Amendment, made applicable to the States by the Fourteenth Amendment. If the purpose of the "establishment" clause was only to insure protection for the "free exercise" of religion, then what we have said above concerning appellants' standing to raise the "free exercise" contention would appear to be true here. However, the writings of Madison, who was the First Amendment's architect, demonstrate that the establishment of a religion was equally feared because of its tendencies to political tyranny and subversion of civil authority. Thus, in *Everson* v. *Board of Education*, the Court permitted a district taxpayer to challenge, on "establishment" grounds, a state statute which authorized district boards of education to reimburse parents for fares paid for the transportation of their children to both public and Catholic schools. Appellants here concededly have suffered direct economic injury, allegedly due to the imposition on them of the tenets of the Christian religion. We find that, in these circum⊥**431**stances, these appellants have standing to complain that the statutes are laws respecting an establishment of religion.

The essence of appellants' "establishment" argument is that Sunday is the Sabbath day of the predominant Christian sects; that the purpose of the enforced stoppage of labor on that day is to facilitate and encourage church attendance; that the purpose of setting Sunday as a day of universal rest is to induce people with no religion or people with marginal religious beliefs to join the predominant Christian sects; that the purpose of the atmosphere of tranquility created by Sunday closing is to aid the conduct of church services and religious observance of the sacred day. In substantiating their "establishment" argument, appellants rely on the wording of the present Maryland statutes, on earlier versions of the current Sunday laws and on prior judicial characterizations of these laws by the Maryland Court of Appeals. Although only the constitutionality of § 521, the section under which appellants have been convicted, is immediately before us in this litigation, inquiry into the history of Sunday Closing Laws in our country, in addition to an examination of the Maryland Sunday closing statutes in their entirety and of their history, is relevant to the decision of whether the Maryland Sunday law in question is one respecting an establishment of religion. There is no dispute that the original laws which dealt with Sunday labor were motivated by religious forces. But what we must decide is whether present Sunday legislation, having undergone extensive changes from the earliest forms, still retains its religious character.

Sunday Closing Laws go far back into American history, having been brought to the colonies with a background of English legislation dating to the thirteenth century. In 1237, Henry III forbade the frequenting of markets on ⊥**432** Sunday; the Sunday showing of wools at the staple was banned by Edward III in 1354; in 1409, Henry IV prohibited the playing of unlawful games on Sunday; Henry VI proscribed Sunday fairs in churchyards in 1444 and, four years later, made unlawful all fairs and markets and all showings of any goods or merchandise; Edward VI disallowed Sunday bodily labor by several injunctions in the mid-sixteenth century; various Sunday sports and amusements were restricted in 1625 by Charles I. The law of the colonies to the time of the Revolution and the basis of the Sunday laws in the States was 29 Charles II, c. 7 (1677). It provided, in part: "For the better observation and keeping holy the Lord's day, commonly called Sunday: be it enacted . . . that all the laws enacted and in force concerning the observation of the day, *and repairing to the church thereon*, be carefully put in execution; and that all and every person and persons whatsoever shall upon every Lord's day apply themselves to the observation of the same, by exercising themselves thereon in the duties of piety and true religion, publicly and privately; and that no tradesman, artificer, workman, laborer, or other person whatsoever, *shall do or exercise any worldly labor or business or work* of their ordinary callings upon the Lord's day, or any part thereof (works of necessity and charity only excepted); . . . and that no person or persons whatsoever shall publicly cry, show forth, or expose for sale any wares, merchandise, fruit, herbs, goods, or chattels, whatsoever, upon the Lord's day, or any part thereof. . . ." (Emphasis added.)

⊥**433** Observation of the above language, and of that of the prior mandates, reveals clearly that the English Sunday legislation was in aid of the established church.

The American colonial Sunday restrictions arose soon after settlement. Starting in 1650, the Plymouth Colony proscribed servile work, unnecessary traveling, sports, and the sale of alcoholic beverages on the Lord's day and enacted laws concerning church attendance. The Massachusetts Bay Colony and the Connecticut and New Haven Colonies enacted similar prohibitions, some even earlier in the seventeenth century. The religious orientation of the colonial statutes was equally apparent. For example, a 1629 Massachusetts Bay instruction began, "And to the end the Sabbath may be celebrated in a religious manner. . . ." A 1653 enactment spoke of Sunday activities "which things tend much to the dishonor of God, the reproach of religion, and the profanation of his holy Sabbath, the sanctification whereof is sometimes put for all duties immediately respecting the service of God. . . ." These laws persevered after the Revolution and, at about the time of the First Amendment's adoption, each of the colonies had laws of some sort restricting Sunday labor.

But, despite the strongly religious origin of these laws, beginning before the eighteenth century, nonreligious ⊥**434** arguments for Sunday closing began to be heard more distinctly and the statutes began to lose some of their totally religious flavor. In the middle 1700's, Blackstone wrote, "[T]he keeping one day in the seven holy, as a time of relaxation and refreshment as well as for public worship, is of admirable service to a state considered merely as a civil institution. It humanizes, by the help of conversation and society, the manners of the lower classes; which would otherwise degenerate into a sordid ferocity and savage selfishness of spirit; it enables the industrious workman to pursue his occupation in the ensuing week with health and cheerfulness."

A 1788 English statute dealing with chimney sweeps, in addition to providing for their Sunday religious affairs, also regulated their hours of work. The preamble to a 1679 Rhode Island enactment stated that the reason for the ban on Sunday employment was that "persons being evill minded, have presumed to employ in servile labor, more than necessity requireth, their servants. . . ." The New York law of 1788 omitted the term "Lord's day" and substituted "the first day of the week commonly called Sunday." Similar changes marked the Maryland statutes, discussed below. With the advent of the First Amendment, the colonial provisions requiring church attendance were soon repealed.

More recently, further secular justifications have been advanced for making Sunday a day of rest, a day when people may recover from the labors of the week just passed and may physically and mentally prepare for the week's work to come. In England, during the First World War, a committee investigating the health conditions of munitions workers reported that "if the maximum output is to be secured and maintained for any length of ⊥**435** time, a weekly period of rest must be allowed. . . . On economic and social grounds alike this weekly period of rest is best provided on Sunday."

The proponents of Sunday closing legislation are no longer exclusively representatives of religious interests. Recent New Jersey Sunday legislation was supported by labor groups and trade associations; modern English Sunday legislation was promoted by the National Federation of Grocers and supported by the National Chamber of Trade, the Drapers' Chamber of Trade, and the National Union of Shop Assistants.

Throughout the years, state legislatures have modified, deleted from and added to their Sunday statutes.

As evidenced by the New Jersey laws mentioned above, current changes are commonplace. Almost every State in our country presently has some type of Sunday regulation and over forty possess a relatively comprehensive system. Some of our States now enforce their Sunday legislation through Departments of Labor. Thus have Sunday laws evolved from the wholly religious sanctions that originally were enacted.

Moreover, litigation over Sunday closing laws is not novel. Scores of cases may be found in the state appellate courts relating to sundry phases of Sunday enactments. Religious objections have been raised there on numerous occasions but sustained only once, in *Ex parte Newman;* and that decision was overruled three years later, in *Ex parte Andrews*. A substantial number of cases in varying postures bearing ⊥**436** on state Sunday legislation have reached this Court. Although none raising the issues now presented have gained plenary hearing, language used in some of these cases further evidences the evolution of Sunday laws as temporal statutes. Mr. *Justice Field* wrote in *Soon Hing* v. *Crowley:* "Laws setting aside Sunday as a day of rest are upheld, not from any right of the government to legislate for the promotion of religious observances, but from its right to protect all persons from the physical and moral debasement which comes from uninterrupted labor. Such laws have always been deemed beneficent and merciful laws, especially to the poor and dependent, to the laborers in our factories and workshops and in the heated rooms of our cities; and their validity has been sustained by the highest courts of the States. . . ."

⊥**437** Before turning to the Maryland legislation now here under attack, an investigation of what historical position Sunday Closing Laws have occupied with reference to the First Amendment should be undertaken.

This Court has considered the happenings surrounding the Virginia General Assembly's enactment of "An act for establishing religious freedom," written by Thomas Jefferson and sponsored by James Madison, as best reflecting the long and intensive struggle for religious freedom in America, as particularly relevant in the search for the First Amendment's meaning. In 1776, nine years before the bill's ⊥**438** passage, Madison coauthored Virginia's Declaration of Rights which provided, *inter alia,* that "all men are equally entitled to the free exercise of religion, according to the dictates of conscience. . . ." Virginia had had Sunday legislation since early in the seventeenth century; in 1776, the laws penalizing "maintaining any opinions in matters of religion, *forbearing to repair to church,* or the exercising any mode of worship whatsoever" (emphasis added), were repealed, and all dissenters were freed from the taxes levied for the support of the established church. The Sunday labor prohibitions remained; apparently, they were not believed to be inconsistent with the newly enacted Declaration of Rights. Madison had sought also to have the Declaration expressly condemn the existing Virginia establishment. This hope was finally realized when "A Bill for Establishing Religious Freedom" was passed in 1785. In this same year, Madison presented to Virginia legislators "A Bill for Punishing . . . Sabbath Breakers" which provided, in part: "If any person on Sunday shall himself be found labouring at his own or any other trade or calling, or shall employ his apprentices, servants or slaves in labour, or other business, except it be in the ordinary houshold offices of daily necessity, or other work of necessity or charity, he shall forfeit the sum of ten shillings for every such offence, deeming every apprentice, servant, or slave so employed, and every day he shall be so employed as constituting a distinct offence."

This became law the following year and remained during the time that Madison fought for the First Amendment in the Congress. It was the law of Virginia, and similar ⊥**439** laws were in force in other States, when Madison stated at the Virginia ratification convention: "Happily for the states, they enjoy the utmost freedom of religion. . . . Fortunately for this commonwealth, a majority of the people are decidedly against any exclusive establishment. I believe it to be so in the other states. . . . I can appeal to my uniform conduct on this subject, that I have warmly supported religious freedom."

In 1799, Virginia pronounced "An act for establishing religious freedom" as "a true exposition of the principles of the bill of rights and constitution," and repealed all subsequently enacted legislation deemed inconsistent with it. Virginia's statute banning Sunday labor stood. . . .

⊥**440** But in order to dispose of the case before us, we must consider the standards by which the Maryland statutes are to be measured. Here, a brief review of the First Amendment's background proves helpful. The First Amendment states that "Congress shall make no law respecting an establishment of religion. . . ." The Amendment was proposed by James Madison on June 8, 1789, in the House of Representatives. It then read, in part: "The civil rights of none shall be abridged on account of religious belief or worship, *nor shall any national religion be established* nor shall the full and equal rights of conscience be in any manner, or on any pretext, infringed." (Emphasis added.)

We are told that Madison added the word "national" to meet the scruples of States which then had an established church. ⊥**441** After being referred to committee, it was considered by the House, on August 15, 1789, acting as a Committee of the Whole. Some assistance in determining the scope of the Amendment's proscription of establishment may be found in that debate.

In its report to the House, the committee, to which the subject of amendments to the Constitution had been submitted, recommended the insertion of the language, "no religion shall be established by law." Mr. Gerry "said it would read better if it was, that no religious doctrine shall be established by law." Mr. Madison "said, he apprehended the meaning of the words to be, that Congress should not establish a religion, and enforce the legal observation of it by law, nor compel men to worship God in any manner contrary to their conscience. . . . He believed that the people feared one sect might obtain a pre-eminence, or two combine together, and establish a religion to which they would compel others to conform."

The Amendment, as it passed the House of Representatives nine days later, read, in part: "Congress shall make no law establishing religion. . . ."

It passed the Senate on September 9, 1789, reading, in part: "Congress shall make no law establishing articles of faith, or a mode of worship. . . ."

An early commentator opined that the "real object of the amendment was . . . to prevent any national ecclesiastical establishment, which should give to an hierarchy the exclusive patronage of the national government." 3 Story, Commentaries on the Constitution of the United States, 728. But, the First Amendment, in its final form, **⊥442** did not simply bar a congressional enactment *establishing a church;* it forbade all laws *respecting an establishment of religion*. Thus, this Court has given the Amendment a "broad interpretation . . . in the light of its history and the evils it was designed forever to suppress. . . ." *Everson* v. *Board of Education*. It has found that the First and Fourteenth Amendments afford protection against religious establishment far more extensive than merely to forbid a national or state church. Thus, in *McCollum* v. *Board of Education*, the Court held that the action of a board of education, permitting religious instruction during school hours in public school buildings and requiring those children who chose not to attend to remain in their classrooms, to be contrary to the "Establishment" Clause.

However, it is equally true that the "Establishment" Clause does not ban federal or state regulation of conduct whose reason or effect merely happens to coincide or harmonize with the tenets of some or all religions. In many instances, the Congress or state legislatures conclude that the general welfare of society, wholly apart from any religious considerations, demands such regulation. Thus, for temporal purposes, murder is illegal. And the fact that this agrees with the dictates of the Judaeo-Christian religions while it may disagree with others does not invalidate the regulation. So too with the questions of adultery and polygamy. The same could be said of theft, fraud, etc., because those offenses were also proscribed in the Decalogue. . . .

⊥444 In light of the evolution of our Sunday Closing Laws through the centuries, and of their more or less recent emphasis upon secular considerations, it is not difficult to discern that as presently written and administered, most of them, at least, are of a secular rather than of a religious character, and that presently they bear no relationship to establishment of religion as those words are used in the Constitution of the United States.

Throughout this century and longer, both the federal and state governments have oriented their activities very largely toward improvement of the health, safety, recreation and general well-being of our citizens. Nu**⊥445**merous laws affecting public health, safety factors in industry, laws affecting hours and conditions of labor of women and children, week-end diversion at parks and beaches, and cultural activities of various kinds, now point the way toward the good life for all. Sunday Closing Laws, like those before us, have become part and parcel of this great governmental concern wholly apart from their original purposes or connotations. The present purpose and effect of most of them is to provide a uniform day of rest for all citizens; the fact that this day is Sunday, a day of particular significance for the dominant Christian sects, does not bar the State from achieving its secular goals. To say that the States cannot prescribe Sunday as a day of rest for these purposes solely because centuries ago such laws had their genesis in religion would give a constitutional interpretation of hostility to the public welfare rather than one of mere separation of church and State.

We now reach the Maryland statutes under review. The title of the major series of sections of the Maryland Code dealing with Sunday closing—Art. 27, §§ 492-534C—is "Sabbath Breaking"; § 492 proscribes work or bodily labor on the "Lord's day," and forbids persons to "profane the Lord's day," by gaming, fishing et cetera; § 522 refers to Sunday as the "Sabbath day." As has been mentioned above, many of the exempted Sunday activities in the various localities of the State may only be conducted during the afternoon and late evening; most Christian church services, of course, are held on Sunday morning and early Sunday evening. Finally, as previously noted, certain localities do not permit the allowed Sunday activities to be carried on within one hundred yards of any church where religious services are being held. This is the totality of the evidence of religious purpose which may be gleaned from the face of the present statute and from its operative effect.

⊥446 The predecessors of the existing Maryland Sunday laws are undeniably religious in origin. The first Maryland statute dealing with Sunday activities, enacted in 1649, was entitled "An Act concerning Religion." It made it criminal to "profane the Sabbath or Lords day called Sunday by frequent swearing, drunkennes or by any uncivill or disorderly recreation, or by working on that day when absolute necessity doth not require it." A 1692 statute entitled "An Act for the Service of Almighty God and the Establishment of the Protestant Religion within this Province," after first stating the importance of keeping the Lord's Day holy and sanctified and expressing concern with the breach of its observance throughout the State, then enacted a Sunday labor prohibition which was the obvious precursor of the present § 492. There was a re-enactment in 1696 entitled "An Act for Sanctifying & keeping holy the Lord's Day Commonly called Sunday." By 1723, the Sabbath-breaking section of the statute assumed the present form of § 492, omitting the specific prohibition against Sunday swearing and the patently religiously motivated title.

There are judicial statements in early Maryland decisions which tend to support appellants' position. In an 1834 case involving a contract calling for delivery on Sun⊥**447**day, the Maryland Court of Appeals remarked that "Ours is a christian community, and a day set apart as the day of rest, is the day consecrated by the resurrection of our Saviour, and embraces the twenty-four hours next ensuing the midnight of Saturday." *Kilgour* v. *Miles*. This language was cited with approval in *Judefind* v. *State*. It was also stated there: "It is undoubtedly true that rest from secular employment on Sunday does have a tendency to foster and encourage the Christian religion—of all sects and denominations that observe that day—as rest from work and ordinary occupation enables many to engage in public worship who probably would not otherwise do so. But it would scarcely be asked of a Court, in what professes to be a Christian land, to declare a law unconstitutional because it requires rest from bodily labor on Sunday, (except works of necessity and charity,) and thereby promotes the cause of Christianity. If the Christian religion is, incidentally or otherwise, benefited or fostered by having this day of rest, as it undoubtedly is, there is all the more reason for the enforcement of laws that help to preserve it. Whilst Courts have generally sustained Sunday laws as 'civil regulations,' their decisions will have no less weight if they are shown to be in accordance with divine law as well as human."

But it should be noted that, throughout the *Judefind* decision, the Maryland court specifically rejected the contention that the laws interfered with religious liberty and stated that the laws' purpose was to provide the "advantages of having a weekly day of rest, 'from a mere physical and political standpoint.'"

Considering the language and operative effect of the current statutes, we no longer find the blanket prohibition ⊥**448** against Sunday work or bodily labor. To the contrary we find that § 521 of Art. 27, the section which appellants violated, permits the Sunday sale of tobaccos and sweets and a long list of sundry articles which we have enumerated above; we find that § 509 of Art. 27 permits the Sunday operation of bathing beaches, amusement parks and similar facilities; we find that Art. 2B, § 28, permits the Sunday sale of alcoholic beverages, products strictly forbidden by predecessor statutes; we are told that Anne Arundel County allows Sunday bingo and the Sunday playing of pinball machines and slot machines, activities generally condemned by prior Maryland Sunday legislation. Certainly, these are not works of charity or necessity. Section 521's current stipulation that shops with only one employee may remain open on Sunday does not coincide with a religious purpose. These provisions, along with those which permit various sports and entertainments on Sunday, seem clearly to be fashioned for the purpose of providing a Sunday atmosphere of recreation, cheerfulness, repose and enjoyment. Coupled with the general proscription against other types of work, we believe that the air of the day is one of relaxation rather than one of religion.

The existing Maryland Sunday laws are not simply verbatim re-enactments of their religiously oriented antecedents. Only § 492 retains the appellation of "Lord's day" and even that section no longer makes recitation of religious purpose. It does talk in terms of "profan[ing] the Lord's day," but other sections permit the activities ⊥**449** previously thought to be profane. Prior denunciation of Sunday drunkenness is now gone. Contemporary concern with these statutes is evidenced by the dozen changes made in 1959 and by the recent enactment of a majority of the exceptions.

Finally, the relevant pronouncements of the Maryland Court of Appeals dispel any argument that the statutes' announced purpose is religious. In *Hiller* v. *Maryland*, the court had before it a Baltimore ordinance prohibiting Sunday baseball. The court said: "What the eminent chief judge said with respect to police enactments which deal with the protection of the public health, morals and safety apply with equal force to those which are concerned with the peace, order and quiet of the community on Sunday, for these social conditions are well recognized heads of the police power. Can the Court say that this ordinance has no real and substantial relation to the peace and order and quiet of Sunday, as a day of rest, in the City of Baltimore?"

And the Maryland court declared in its decision in the instant case: "The legislative plan is plain. It is to compel a day of rest from work, permitting only activities which are necessary or recreational." *McGowan* v. *State*. After engaging in the close scrutiny demanded of us when First Amendment liberties are at issue, we accept the State Supreme Court's determination that the statutes' present purpose and effect is not to aid religion but to set aside a day of rest and recreation.

But this does not answer all of appellants' contentions. We are told that the State has other means at its disposal ⊥**450** to accomplish its secular purpose, other courses that would not even remotely or incidentally give state aid to religion. On this basis, we are asked to hold these statutes invalid on the ground that the State's power to regulate conduct in the public interest may only be executed in a way that does not unduly or unnecessarily infringe upon the religious provisions of the First Amendment. However relevant this argument may be, we believe that the factual basis on which it rests is not supportable. It is true that if the State's interest were simply to provide for its citizens a periodic respite from work, a regulation demanding that everyone rest one day in seven, leaving the choice of the day to the individual, would suffice.

However, the State's purpose is not merely to provide a one-day-in-seven work stoppage. In addition to this, the State seeks to set one day apart from all others as a day of rest, repose, recreation and tranquility—a day which all members of the family and community have the opportunity to spend and enjoy together, a day on which there exists relative quiet and disassociation from the everyday intensity of commercial activities, a day on which people may visit friends and relatives who are not available during working days.

⊥**451** Obviously, a State is empowered to determine that a rest-one-day-in-seven statute would not accomplish this purpose; that it would not provide for a general cessation of activity, a special atmosphere of tranquility, a day which all members of the family or friends and relatives might spend together. Furthermore, it seems plain that the problems involved in enforcing such a provision would be exceedingly more difficult than those in enforcing a common-day-of-rest provision.

Moreover, it is common knowledge that the first day of the week has come to have special significance as a rest day in this country. People of all religions and ⊥**452** people with no religion regard Sunday as a time for family activity, for visiting friends and relatives, for late sleeping, for passive and active entertainments, for dining out, and the like. Sunday is a day apart from all others. The cause is irrelevant; the fact exists. It would seem unrealistic for enforcement purposes and perhaps detrimental to the general welfare to require a State to choose a common day of rest other than that which most persons would select of their own accord. For these reasons, we hold that the Maryland statutes are not laws respecting an establishment of religion.

The distinctions between the statutes in the case before us and the state action in *McCollum* v. *Board of Education*, the only case in this Court finding a violation of the "Establishment" Clause, lend further substantiation to our conclusion. In *McCollum*, state action permitted religious instruction in public school buildings during school hours and required students not attending the religious instruction to remain in their classrooms during that time. The Court found that this system had the effect of coercing the children to attend religious classes; no such coercion to attend church services is present in the situation at bar. In *McCollum*, the only alternative available to the nonattending students was to remain in their classrooms; the alternatives open to nonlaboring persons in the instant case are far more diverse. In *McCollum*, there was direct cooperation between state officials and religious ministers; no such direct participation exists under the Maryland laws. In *McCollum*, tax-supported buildings were used to aid religion; in the ⊥**453** instant case, no tax monies are being used in aid of religion.

Finally, we should make clear that this case deals only with the constitutionality of § 521 of the Maryland statute before us. We do not hold that Sunday legislation may not be a violation of the "Establishment" Clause if it can be demonstrated that its purpose—evidenced either on the face of the legislation, in conjunction with its legislative history, or in its operative effect—is to use the State's coercive power to aid religion.

Accordingly, the decision is *Affirmed*.

. . . . .

⊥**459** Separate opinion of Mr. *Justice* FRANKFURTER, whom Mr. *Justice* HARLAN joins.*

So deeply do the issues raised by these cases cut that it is not surprising that no one opinion can wholly express the views even of all the members of the Court who join in its result. Individual opinions in constitutional controversies have been the practice throughout the Court's history. Such expression of differences in view or even in emphasis converging toward the same result makes for the clarity of candor and thereby enhances the authority of the judicial process.

For me considerations are determinative here which call for separate statement. The long history of Sunday legislation, so decisive if we are to view the statutes now ⊥**460** attacked in a perspective wider than that which is furnished by our own necessarily limited outlook, cannot be conveyed by a partial recital of isolated instances or events. The importance of that history derives from its continuity and fullness—from the massive testimony which it bears to the evolution of statutes controlling Sunday labor and to the forces which have, during three hundred years of Anglo-American history at the least, changed those laws, transmuted them, made them the vehicle of mixed and complicated aspirations. Since I find in the history of these statutes insights controllingly relevant to the constitutional issues before us, I am constrained to set that history forth in detail. And I also deem it incumbent to state how I arrive at concurrence with *The CHIEF JUSTICE'S* principal conclusions without drawing on *Everson* v. *Board of Education*.

I

Because the long colonial struggle for disestablishment—the struggle to free all men, whatever their theological views, from state-compelled obligation to acknowledge and support state-favored faiths—made indisputably fundamental to our American culture the principle that the enforcement of religious belief as such is no legitimate concern of civil government, this Court has held that the Fourteenth Amendment embodies and applies against the States freedoms that are loosely indicated by the not rigidly precise but revealing phrase "separation of church and state." The general principles of church-state separation were found to be included in the Amendment's Due Process Clause in view of the meaning which the presuppositions of our society infuse into the concept of "liberty" protected by the clause. This is the source of the limitations imposed upon the States. To the extent that those limitations ⊥**461** are akin to the restrictions which the First Amendment places upon the action of the central government, it is because—as with the freedom of thought and speech of which Mr. *Justice* CARDOZO spoke in *Palko* v. *Connecticut*—it is accurate to say concerning the principle that a government must neither establish nor suppress religious belief, that "With rare aberrations a pervasive recognition of that truth can be traced in our history, political and legal."

*NOTE: This opinion applies also to *Two Guys from Harrison-Allentown, Inc.*, v. *McGinley*, *Braunfeld et al.* v. *Brown*, and *Gallagher* v. *Crown Kosher Super Market*.

But the several opinions in *Everson* and *McCollum*, and in *Zorach* v. *Clauson* make sufficiently clear that "separation" is not a self-defining concept. "[A]greement, in the abstract, that the First Amendment was designed to erect a 'wall of separation between church and State,' does not preclude a clash of views as to what the wall separates." By its nature, religion—in the comprehensive sense in which the Constitution uses that word—is an aspect of human thought and action which profoundly relates the life of man to the world in which he lives. Religious beliefs pervade, and religious institutions have traditionally regulated, virtually all human activity. It is a postulate of American life, reflected specifically in the First Amendment to the Constitution but not there alone, that those beliefs and institutions shall continue, as the needs and longings of the people shall inspire them, to exist, to function, to grow, to wither, and to exert with whatever innate strength they may contain their many influences upon men's conduct, free of the dictates and directions of the state. However, this freedom does not and cannot furnish the adherents of religious creeds entire insulation from every civic obligation. As the state's interest in the individual becomes more comprehensive, its concerns and the concerns of religion perforce overlap. State codes and the dictates of faith touch the same activities. ⊥**462** Both aim at human good, and in their respective views of what is good for man they may concur or they may conflict. No constitutional command which leaves religion free can avoid this quality of interplay.

Innumerable civil regulations enforce conduct which harmonizes with religious canons. State prohibitions of murder, theft and adultery reinforce commands of the decalogue. Nor do such regulations, in their coincidence with tenets of faith, always support equally the beliefs of all religious sects: witness the civil laws forbidding usury and enforcing monogamy. Because these laws serve ends which are within the appropriate scope of secular state interest, they may be enforced against those whose religious beliefs do not proscribe, and even sanction, the activity which the law condemns.

This is not to say that government regulations which find support in their appropriateness to the achievement of secular, civil ends are invariably valid under the First or Fourteenth Amendment, whatever their effects in the sphere of religion. If the value to society of achieving the object of a particular regulation is demonstrably outweighed by the impediment to which the regulation subjects those whose religious practices are curtailed by it, or if the object sought by the regulation could with equal effect be achieved by alternative means which do not substantially impede those religious practices, the regulation cannot be sustained. This was the ground upon which the Court struck down municipal license taxes as applied to religious colporteurs in *Follett* v. *Town of McCormick*, *Murdock* v. *Pennsylvania*, and *Jones* v. *Opelika*. In each of those cases it was believed that the State's need for revenue, which could be ⊥**463** satisfied by taxing any of a variety of sources, did not justify a levy imposed upon an activity which in the light of history could reasonably be viewed as sacramental. But see *Cox* v. *New Hampshire*, in which the Court, balancing the public benefits secured by a regulatory measure against the degree of impairment of individual conduct expressive of religious faith which it entailed, sustained the prohibition of an activity similarly regarded by its practicants as sacramental. And see *Prince* v. *Massachusetts*.

Within the discriminating phraseology of the First Amendment, distinction has been drawn between cases raising "establishment" and "free exercise" questions. Any attempt to formulate a bright-line distinction is bound to founder. In view of the competition among religious creeds, whatever "establishes" one sect disadvantages another, and vice versa. But it is possible historically, and therefore helpful analytically—no less for problems arising under the Fourteenth Amendment, illuminated as that Amendment is by our national experience, than for problems arising under the First—to isolate in general terms the two largely overlapping areas of concern reflected in the two constitutional phrases, "establishment" and "free exercise," and which emerge more ⊥**464** or less clearly from the background of events and impulses which gave those phrases birth.

In assuring the free exercise of religion, the Framers of the First Amendment were sensitive to the then recent history of those persecutions and impositions of civil disability with which sectarian majorities in virtually all of the Colonies had visited deviation in the matter of conscience. This protection of unpopular creeds, however, was not to be the full extent of the Amendment's guarantee of freedom from governmental intrusion in matters of faith. The battle in Virginia, hardly four years won, where James Madison had led the forces of disestablishment in successful opposition to Patrick Henry's proposed Assessment Bill levying a general tax for the support of Christian teachers, was a vital and compelling ⊥**465** memory in 1789. The lesson of that battle, in the words of Jefferson's Act for Establishing Religious Freedom, whose passage was its verbal embodiment, was "that to compel a man to furnish contributions of money for the propagation of opinions which he disbelieves, is sinful and tyrannical; that even the forcing him to support this or that teacher of his own religious persuasion, is depriving him of the comfortable liberty of giving his contributions to the particular pastor, whose morals he would make his pattern, and whose powers he feels most persuasive to righteousness, and is withdrawing from the ministry those temporal rewards, which proceeding from an approbation of their personal conduct, are an additional incitement to earnest and unremitting labours for the instruction of mankind. . . ." What Virginia had long practiced, and what Madison, Jefferson and others fought to end, was the extension of civil government's support to religion in a manner which made the two in some degree interdependent, and thus threatened the freedom of each. The purpose of the Establishment Clause was to assure that the national legislature would not exert its power in the service of any purely religious end; that it would not, as Virginia and virtually all of the Colonies had done, make of religion, as religion, an object of legislation.

Of course, the immediate object of the First Amendment's prohibition was the established church as it had been known in England and in most of the Colonies. But with foresight those who drafted and adopted the words, "Congress shall make no law respecting an establishment of religion," did not limit the constitutional proscription to any particular, dated form of state-supported theological venture. The Establishment Clause withdrew from **⊥466** the sphere of legitimate legislative concern and competence a specific, but comprehensive, area of human conduct: man's belief or disbelief in the verity of some transcendental idea and man's expression in action of that belief or disbelief. Congress may not make these matters, as such, the subject of legislation, nor, now, may any legislature in this country. Neither the National Government nor, under the Due Process Clause of the Fourteenth Amendment, a State may, by any device, support belief or the expression of belief for its own sake, whether from conviction of the truth of that belief, or from conviction that by the propagation of that belief the civil welfare of the State is served, or because a majority of its citizens, holding that belief, are offended when all do not hold it.

With regulations which have other objectives the Establishment Clause, and the fundamental separationist concept which it expresses, are not concerned. These regulations may fall afoul of the constitutional guarantee against infringement of the free exercise or observance of religion. Where they do, they must be set aside at the instance of those whose faith they prejudice. But once it is determined that a challenged statute is supportable as implementing other substantial interests than the promotion of belief, the guarantee prohibiting religious "establishment" is satisfied.

To ask what interest, what object, legislation serves, of course, is not to psychoanalyze its legislators, but to examine the necessary effects of what they have enacted. If the primary end achieved by a form of regulation is the affirmation or promotion of religious doctrine—primary, in the sense that all secular ends which it purportedly serves are derivative from, not wholly independent of, the advancement of religion—the regulation is beyond the power of the state. This was the case in *McCollum*. Or if a statute furthers both secular and religious ends **⊥467** by means unnecessary to the effectuation of the secular ends alone—where the same secular ends could equally be attained by means which do not have consequences for promotion of religion—the statute cannot stand. A State may not endow a church although that church might inculcate in its parishioners moral concepts deemed to make them better citizens, because the very *raison d'etre* of a church, as opposed to any other school of civilly serviceable morals, is the predication of religious doctrine. However, inasmuch as individuals are free, if they will, to build their own churches and worship in them, the State may guard its people's safety by extending fire and police protection to the churches so built. It was on the reasoning that parents are also at liberty to send their children to parochial schools which meet the reasonable educational standards of the State, *Pierce* v. *Society of Sisters*, that this Court held in the *Everson* case that expenditure of public funds to assure that children attending every kind of school enjoy the relative security of buses, rather than being left to walk or hitchhike, is not an unconstitutional "establishment," even though such an expenditure may cause some children to go to parochial schools who would not otherwise have gone. The close division of the Court in *Everson* serves to show what nice questions are involved in applying to particular governmental action the proposition, undeniable in the abstract, that not every regulation some of whose practical effects may facilitate the observance of a religion by its adherents affronts the requirement of church-state separation.

In an important sense, the constitutional prohibition of religious establishment is a provision of more comprehensive availability than the guarantee of free exercise, insofar as both give content to the prohibited fusion of church and state. The former may be invoked by the corporate operator of a seven-day department store whose **⊥468** state-compelled Sunday closing injures it financially—or by the department store's employees, whatever their faith, who are convicted for violation of a Sunday statute—as well as by the Orthodox Jewish retailer or consumer who claims that the statute prejudices him in his ability to keep his faith. But it must not be forgotten that the question which the department store operator and employees may raise in their own behalf is narrower than that posed by the case of the Orthodox Jew. Their "establishment" contention can prevail only if the absence of any substantial legislative purpose other than a religious one is made to appear.

In the present cases the Sunday retail sellers and their employees and customers, in attacking statutes banning various activities on a day which most Christian creeds consecrate, do assert that these statutes have no other purpose. They urge, first, that the legislators' motives **⊥469** were religious. But the private and unformulated influences which may work upon legislation are not open to judicial probing. "The decisions of this court from the beginning lend no support whatever to the assumption that the judiciary may restrain the exercise of lawful power on the assumption that a wrongful purpose or motive has caused the power to be exerted." *McCray* v. *United States*. "Inquiry into the hidden motives which may move [a legislature] to exercise a power constitutionally conferred upon it is beyond the competency of courts." *Sonzinsky* v. *United States*. These litigants also argue, however, that when the state statutory provisions are regarded in their legislative context religion is apparent on their face: they point to the use of the terms "Lord's day" and "Sabbath" and "desecration," to exceptions whose hours permit activities only at times on Sunday when religious services are customarily not held, to explicit prohibition of otherwise permitted activity in the vicinity of churches, to regulations which condition the allowance of conduct on its consistency with the "due observance" of the day. Of course, since these various provisions regarding exemption from the Sunday ban of certain recreational activities have no possible application to the litigants in the present cases, they are not themselves before the Court, and their constitutionality is not now in issue. But they are put forward as evidence of the purpose of the statutes which are attacked here, and as such we may properly look to them, and also to the history of the body of state Sunday regulations, which, it is urged, further demonstrates sectarian creedal purpose. As a basis for appraising these arguments that the statutes are religious legislation, and pre⊥**470**liminary to determining the claims of infringement of conscience raised in the *Gallagher* and *Braunfeld* cases, it is necessary to survey the long historical development and present-day position of civil Sunday regulation.

II

For these purposes the span of centuries which saw the enunciation of the Fourth Commandment, Constantine's edict proscribing labor on the venerable day of the Sun, and the Sunday prohibitions of Carlovingian, Merovingian and Saxon rulers, and later of the English kings of the thirteenth and fourteenth centuries, may be passed over. What is of concern here is the Sunday institution as it evolved in modern England, the American Colonies, and the States of the Union under the Constitution. The first significant English Sunday regulation, for this purpose, was the statute of Henry VI in 1448 which, after reciting "the abominable injuries and offences done to Almighty God, and to his Saints, . . . because of fairs and markets upon their high and principal feasts, . . . in which principal and festival days, for great earthly covetise, the people is more willingly vexed, and in bodily labour soiled, than in other . . . days, . . . as though they did nothing remember the horrible defiling of their souls in buying and selling, with many deceitful lies and false perjury, with drunkenness and strifes, and so spe⊥**471**cially withdrawing themselves and their servants from divine service . . . ," ordained that all fairs and markets should cease to show forth goods or merchandise on Sundays, Good Friday, and the principal feast days. A short-lived ordinance of Edward VI a century later, limiting the ban on bodily labor to Sundays and enumerated holy days, demonstrated in its preamble a similar sectarian purpose, and in 1625 Charles I, announcing that "there is nothing more acceptable to God than the true and sincere service and worship of him . . . and that the holy keeping of the Lord's day is a principal part of the true service of God," prohibited all meetings of the people out of their parishes for sports and pastimes on Sunday, and all bear-baiting, bull-baiting, interludes, common plays, and other unlawful exercises and pastimes on that day. Several years later the same king declared it reproachful of God and religion, and hence made it un⊥**472**lawful, for butchers to slaughter or carriers, drovers, waggoners, etc., to travel on the Lord's day; then, in 1677, "For the better Observation and keeping Holy the Lord's Day," the statute which is still the basic Sunday law of Britain, was enacted: "that all and every Person and Persons whatsoever, shall on every Lord's Day apply themselves to the Observation of the same, by exercising themselves thereon in the Duties of Piety and true Religion, publicly and privately; . . . and that no Tradesman, Artificer, Workman, Labourer or other Person whatsoever, shall do or exercise any worldly Labour, Business or Work of their ordinary Callings, upon the Lord's Day, or any part thereof (Works of Necessity and Charity only excepted;) . . . and that no Person or Persons whatsoever, shall publickly cry, shew forth, or expose to Sale, any Wares, Merchandizes, Fruit, Herbs, Goods or Chattels whatsoever, upon the Lord's Day. . . ." In 1781, a ⊥**473** statute reciting that various public entertainments and explications of scriptural texts by incompetent persons tended "to the great encouragement of irreligion and profaneness," closed all rooms and houses in which public entertainment, amusement or debates, for an admission charge, were held.

These Sunday laws were indisputably works of the English Establishment. Their prefatory language spoke their religious inspiration, exceptions made from time to time were expressly limited to preserve inviolable the hours of the divine service, and in their administration ⊥**474** a spirit of inquisitorial piety was evident. But even in this period of religious predominance, notes of a secondary civil purpose could be heard. Apart from the counsel of those who had from the time of the Reformation insisted that the Fourth Commandment itself embodied a precept of social rather than sacramental significance, claims ⊥**475** were asserted in the eighteenth century on behalf of Sunday rest, in part, in the service of health and welfare. Blackstone wrote that ". . . besides the notorious indecency and scandal of permitting any secular business to be publicly transacted on that day in a country professing Christianity, and the corruption of morals which usually follows its profanation, the keeping one day in the seven holy, as a time of relaxation and refreshment as well as for public worship, is of admirable service to a state, considered merely as a civil institution. It humanizes, by the help of conversation and society, the manners of the lower classes, which would otherwise degenerate into a sordid ferocity and savage selfishness of spirit; it enables the industrious workman to pursue his occupation in the ensuing week with health and cheerfulness; it imprints on the minds of the people that sense of their duty to God so necessary to make them good citizens, but which yet ⊥476 would be worn out and defaced by an unremitted continuance of labor, without any stated times of recalling them to the worship of their Maker." In 1788 the schedule to the act obligated master chimney sweeps to have their apprentices washed at least once a week, providing that on Sunday the master should send the apprentice to worship, should allow him to have religious instruction, and should not allow him to wear his sweeping dress; the act also regulated the sweeps' hours of work. In 1832 a Commons Select Committee on the Observance of the Sabbath heard the testimony of a medical doctor as to the physically injurious effects of seven-day unremitted labor, and although the report of the Committee reveals a primarily religious cast of mind, it discloses also a sensitivity to the plight of the journeyman bakers, seven thousand of whom had petitioned the House for one day's repose weekly, and to the wishes of shopkeepers and tradesmen forced by competition to work on Sunday, although "most desirous of a day of rest." The Committee recommended the enactment of severer sanctions for Lord's day violations: "The objects to be attained by Legislation may be considered to be, first, a solemn and decent outward Observance of the Lord's-day, as that portion of the week which is set apart by Divine Command for Public Worship; and next, the securing to every member of the Community without any exception, and however low his station, the uninterrupted enjoyment of that Day of Rest which has been in Mercy provided for him, and the privilege of employing it, as well in ⊥477 the sacred Exercises for which it was ordained, as in the bodily relaxation which is necessary for his well-being, and which, though a secondary end, is nevertheless, also of high importance."

But, whatever the nature of the propulsions underlying state-enforced Sunday labor stoppage during these centuries before the twentieth, it is clear that its effect was the creation of an institution of Sunday as a day apart. The origins of the institution were religious, certainly, but through long-established usage it had become a part of the life of the English people. It was a day of rest not merely in a physical, hygienic sense, but in the sense of a recurrent time in the cycle of human activity when the rhythms of existence changed, a day of particular associations which came to have their own autonomous value for life. When that value was threatened by the pressures of the Industrial Revolution, agitation began for new ⊥478 legislative action to preserve the traditional English Sunday.

At the turn of the century, the Factory and Workshop Act, 1901, prohibited the Sunday employment of women and children in industrial establishments. The Shops Act, 1912, in its institution of a five-and-a-half-day week for shop assistants, built upon the base of existing Sunday closing law. When during the war the pressures of ⊥479 national defense compelled continuous factory operation, a Committee of the Ministry of Munitions appointed to investigate industrial fatigue as this affected the health and efficiency of munitions workers, recommended to Parliament reinauguration of Sunday work stoppage. . . . ". . . [I]f the maximum output is to be secured and maintained for any length of time, a weekly period of rest must be allowed. . . . On economic and social grounds alike this weekly period of rest is best provided on Sunday. . . ."

⊥480 In 1936 the conflict between the economic pressures for seven-day commercial activity and the resistance to those pressures culminated in the Shops (Sunday Trading Restriction) Act of that year, which, with a complex pattern of exceptions, prohibited Sunday trading upon pain of penalties more severe, and hence better calculated to assure obedience, than the nominal fines which had obtained under the seventeenth century Lord's day ban. The Parliamentary Debates on the 1936 Act are instructive. With extremely rare exceptions, no intimation of religious purpose is to be discovered in them. The opening speech by Mr. Loftus who introduced the bill is representative: ". . . [I]t is a Bill which is necessary to secure the family life and liberty of hundreds of thousands of our people. . . .

. . . . .

⊥481 ". . . I will explain to the House that there are thousands of shopkeepers who hate opening on Sunday—they dislike the whole idea—but are forced to open because their neighbours open. They are forced to open not for the sake of the Sunday trading, but because if they let their customers get into the habit on Sunday of going to other shops they may lose their week-day custom. . . . They have the right to a holiday on Sunday, to be able to rest from work on that day and to go out into the parks or into the country on a summer day. That is the liberty for which they are asking, and that is the liberty which this Bill would give to them. As regards the support behind the Bill, it is promoted by the Early Closing Association, with 300 affiliated associations, and the National Federation of Grocers, representing 400,000 individual shops, and is supported by the National Chamber of Trade, the Drapers' Chamber of Trade, the National Federation of the Boot Trade, and as regards the employes—and this is important—it is supported by the National Union of Shop Assistants and by the National Union of Distributive Workers."

Speakers asserted the necessity for maintaining "the traditional quality of the Sunday in this country. . . ."

⊥482 Thus the English experience demonstrates the intimate relationship between civil Sunday regulation and the interest of a state in preserving to its people a recurrent time of mental and physical recuperation from the strains and pressures of their ordinary labors. It demonstrates also, of course, the intimate historical connection between the choice of Sunday as this time of rest and the doctrines ⊥483 of the Christian church. Long before the emergence of modern notions of government, religion had set Sunday apart. Through generations, the people were accustomed to it as a day when ordinary uses ceased. If it might once—or elsewhere—have been equally practicable to fulfill the same need of the workers and traders for periodic relaxation by the selection of some other cycle, it was no longer practicable in England. Some hypothetical man might do better with one-day-in-eight, or one-day-in-four, but the Englishman was used to one-day-in-seven. And that day was Sunday. Through associations fostered by tradition, that day had a character of its own which became in itself a cultural asset of importance: a release from the daily grind, a preserve of mental peace, an opportunity for self-disposition. Certainly, legislative fiat could have attempted to switch the day to Tuesday. But Parliament, naturally enough, concluded that such an attempt might prove as futile as the ephemeral decade of the French Republic of 1792.

III

⊥**484** In England's American settlements, too, civil Sunday regulation early became an institution of importance in shaping the colonial pattern of life. Every Colony had a law prohibiting Sunday labor. These had been enacted ⊥**485** in many instances prior to the last quarter of the seventeenth century, and they were continued in force throughout the period that preceded the adoption of the Federal ⊥**486** Constitution and the Bill of Rights. This is not in itself, of course, indicative of the purpose of those laws, or of their consistency with the guarantee of religious freedom which the First Amendment, restraining the power of the central Government, secured. Most of the States were only partly disestablished in 1789. Only in Virginia and in Rhode Island, which had never had an establishment, had the ideal of complete church-state separation been realized. Other States were fast approaching that ideal, however, and everywhere the spirit of liberty in religion was in the ascendant. Ratifying Conventions in New York, New Hampshire and North Carolina, as well as in Virginia and Rhode Island, proposed an antiestablishment amendment to the Constitution or signified that in their understanding the Constitution embodied such a safeguard. All of these five States had Sunday laws at the time that their Conventions spoke. Indeed, in four of the five, their legislatures had reaffirmed the Sunday labor ban within five years or less immediately prior to that date.

⊥**487** The earlier among the colonial Sunday statutes were unquestionably religious in purpose. Their preambles recite that profanation of the Lord's day "to the great Reproach of the Christian Religion," or "to the great offence of the Godly welafected among us," must be suppressed; that "the keeping holy the Lord's day, is a principal part of the true service of God"; that neglecting the Sabbath "pulls downe the judgments of God upon that place or people that suffer the same. . . ." The first Pennsylvania Sunday law announces a purpose "That Looseness, irreligion, and Atheism may not Creep in under pretense of Conscience. . . ." Sometimes ⊥**488** reproach of God is made an operative element of the offense. Prohibitions of Sunday labor are frequently coupled with admonitions that all persons shall "carefully apply themselves to Duties of Religion and Piety, publickly and privately . . . ," and are found in comprehensive ecclesiastical codes which also prohibit blasphemy, lay taxes for the support of the church, or compel attendance at divine services.

⊥**489** But even the seventeenth century legislation does not show an exclusively religious preoccupation. The same Pennsylvania law which speaks of the suppression of atheism also ordains Sunday rest "for the ease of the Creation," and shows solicitude that servants, as well as their masters, may be free on that day to attend such spiritual pursuits as they may wish. The Rhode Island Assembly in 1679 enacted: "Voted, Whereas there hath complaint been made that sundry persons being evill minded, have pre⊥**490**sumed to employ in servile labor, more than necessity requireth, their servants, and alsoe hire other mens' servants and sell them to labor on the first day of the week: . . . bee it enacted. . . . That if any person or persons shall employ his servants or hire and employ any other man's servant or servants, and set them to labor as aforesaid [he shall be penalized]."

⊥**491** In the latter half of the eighteenth century, the Sunday laws, while still giving evidence of concern for the "immorality" of the practices they prohibit, tend no longer to be prefixed by preambles in the form of theological treatises. Now it appears to be the community, rather than the Deity, which is offended by Sunday labor. New York's statute of 1788 no longer refers to the Lord's day, but to "the first day of the week commonly called Sunday." Where preambles do appear, they display a duplicity of purpose. . . .

⊥**492** More significant is the history of Sunday legislation in Virginia. Even before the English statute of 29 Charles II, that Colony had had laws compelling Sunday attendance at worship and forbidding Sunday labor. In 1776, the General Convention at Williamsburg adopted a Declaration of Rights, providing *inter alia*, that ". . . all men are equally entitled to the free exercise of religion, according to the dictates of conscience . . . ," and in the same year the acts of Parliament compelling church attendance and punishing deviation in belief were declared void, dissenters were exempted from the tax for support of the established church, and the levy of that tax was suspended. Eight years later came the battle over the Assessment Bill. Under Madison's leadership the forces supporting entire freedom of religion wrote the definitive quietus to the Virginia establishment, and Jefferson's Bill for Establishing Religious Freedom was enacted in 1786. . . . ⊥**493** In this bill breathed the full amplitude of the spirit which inspired the First Amendment, and this Court has looked ⊥**494** to the bill, and to the Virginia history which surrounded its enactment, as a gloss on the signification of the Amendment. The bill was drafted for the Virginia Legislature as No. 82 of the Revised Statutes returned to the Assembly by Jefferson and Wythe on June 18, 1779. Bill No. 84 of the Revision provided: "If any person on Sunday shall himself be found labouring at his own or any other trade or calling, or shall employ his apprentices, servants or slaves in labour, or other business, except it be in the ordinary household offices of daily necessity, or other work of necessity or charity, he shall forfeit the sum of ten shillings. . . ."

This bill was presented to the Assembly by Madison in 1785, and was enacted in 1786. Apparently neither Thomas Jefferson nor James Madison regarded it as ⊥**495** repugnant to religious freedom. Nor did the Virginia legislators who thirteen years later reaffirmed the Bill for Establishing Religious Freedom as "a true exposition of the principles of the bill of rights and constitution," by repealing all laws which they deemed inconsistent with it. The Sunday law of 1786 was not among those repealed.

IV

Legislation currently in force in forty-nine of the fifty States illegalizes on Sunday some form of conduct lawful if performed on weekdays. In several States only one or a few activities are banned—the sale of alcoholic beverages, hunting, barbering, pawnbroking, trad⊥**496**ing in automobiles—but thirty-four jurisdictions broadly ban Sunday labor, or the employment of labor, or selling or keeping open for sale, or some two or more of these comprehensive categories of affairs. In many of these States, and in others having no state-wide prohibition of industrial or commercial activity, municipal Sunday ordinances are ubiquitous. Most of these regulations are the product of many reenactments and amendments. Although some are still built upon the armatures ⊥**497** of earlier statutes, they are all, like the laws of Maryland, Massachusetts and Pennsylvania which are before us in these cases, recently reconsidered legislation. As expressions of state policy, they must be deemed as contemporary as their latest-enacted exceptions in favor of moving pictures or severer bans of Sunday motor vehicle trading. In all, they reflect a widely felt present-day need, for whose satisfaction old laws are shaped and new laws enacted.

To be sure, the Massachusetts statute now before the Court, and statutes in Pennsylvania and Maryland, still call Sunday the "Lord's day" or the "Sabbath." So do the Sunday laws in many other States. But the con⊥**498**tinuation of seventeenth century language does not of itself prove the continuation of the purposes for which the colonial governments enacted these laws, or that these are the purposes for which their successors of the twentieth have retained them and modified them. We know, ⊥**499** for example, that Committees of the New York Legislature, considering that State's Sabbath Laws on two occasions more than a century apart, twice recommended no repeal of those laws, both times on the ground that the laws did not involve "any partisan religious issue, but ⊥**500** rather economic and health regulation of the activities of the people on a universal day of rest," and that a Massachusetts legislative committee rested on the same views. Sunday legislation has been supported not only ⊥**501** by such clerical organizations as the Lord's Day Alliance, but also by labor and trade groups. The interlocking sections of the Massachusetts Labor Code construct their six-day-week provisions upon the basic premise of Sunday ⊥**502** rest. Other States have similar laws. When in Pennsylvania motion pictures were excepted from the Lord's day statute, a day-of-rest-in-seven clause for motion picture personnel was written into the exempting statute to ⊥**503** fill the gap. Puerto Rico's closing law, which limits the weekday hours of commercial establishments as well as proscribing their Sunday operation, does not express a religious purpose. Rhode Island and South Carolina now enforce portions of their Sunday employment bans through their respective Departments of Labor. It cannot be fairly denied that the institution of Sunday as a time whose occupations and atmosphere differ from those of other days of the week has now been a portion of the American cultural scene since well before the Constitution; that for many millions of people life has a hebdomadal rhythm in which this day, with all its particular associations, is the recurrent note of repose. Cultural history establishes not a few practices and prohibitions religious in origin which are retained as secular ⊥**504** institutions and ways long after their religious sanctions and justifications are gone. In light of these considerations, can it reasonably be said that no substantial non-⊥**505**ecclesiastical purpose relevant to a well-ordered social life exists for Sunday restrictions?

It is urged, however, that if a day of rest were the legislative purpose, statutes to secure it would take some other form than the prohibition of activity on Sunday. Such statutes, it is argued, would provide for one day's labor ⊥**506** stoppage in seven, leaving the choice of the day to the individual; or, alternatively, would fix a common day of rest on some other day—Monday or Tuesday. But, in all fairness, certainly, it would be impossible to call unreasonable a legislative finding that these suggested alternatives were unsatisfactory. A provision for one day's closing per week, at the option of every particular enterpriser, might be disruptive of families whose members are employed by different enterprises. Enforcement might be more difficult, both because violation would be less easily discovered and because such a law would not be seconded, as is Sunday legislation, by the community's moral temper. More important, one-day-a-week laws do not accomplish all that is accomplished by Sunday laws. They provide only a periodic physical rest, not that atmosphere of entire community repose which Sunday has traditionally brought and which, a legislature might reasonably believe, is necessary to the welfare of those who for ⊥**507** many generations have been accustomed to its recuperative effects.

The same considerations might also be deemed to justify the choice of Sunday as the single common day when labor ceases. For to many who do not regard it sacramentally, Sunday is nevertheless a day of special, long-established associations, whose particular temper makes it a haven that no other day could provide. The will of a majority of the community, reflected in the legislative process during scores of years, presumably prefers to take its leisure on Sunday. The spirit of any people expresses in goodly measure the heritage which links it to its past. Disruption of this heritage by a regulation which, like the unnatural labors of Claudius' shipwrights, does not divide the Sunday from the week, might prove a measure ill-designed to secure the desirable community repose for which Sunday legislation is designed. At all events, Maryland, Massachusetts and Pennsylvania, like thirty-one other States with similar regulations, could reasonably so find. Certainly, from failure to make a substitution for Sunday in securing a socially desirable day of surcease from subjection to labor and routine a purpose cannot be derived to establish or promote religion.

The question before the Court in these cases is not a new one. During a hundred and fifty years Sunday laws have been attacked in state and federal courts as disregarding constitutionally demanded Church-State separation, or infringing protected religious freedoms, or on the ground that they subserved no end within the legitimate compass of legislative power. One California court in 1858 held California's Sunday statute unconstitutional. **⊥508** That decision was overruled three years later. Every other appellate court that has considered the question has found the statutes supportable as civil regulations and **⊥509** not repugnant to religious freedom. These decisions are assailed as latter-day justifications upon specious civil grounds of legislation whose religious purposes were either overlooked or concealed by the judges who passed upon it. **⊥510** Of course, it is for this Court ultimately to determine whether federal constitutional guarantees are observed or undercut. But this does not mean that we are to be indifferent to the unanimous opinion of genera**⊥511**tions of judges who, in the conscientious discharge of obligations as solemn as our own, have sustained the Sunday laws as not inspired by religious purpose. The Court did not ignore that opinion in *Friedman* v. *New York; McGee* v. *North Carolina, Kidd* v. *Ohio;* and *Ullner* v. *Ohio*, dismissing for want of a substantial federal question appeals from state decisions sustaining Sunday laws which were obnoxious to the same objections urged in the present cases. I cannot ignore that consensus of view now. The statutes of Maryland, Massachusetts and Pennsylvania which we here examine are not constitutionally forbidden fusions of church and state.

V

⊥512 Appellees in the *Gallagher* case and appellants in the *Braunfeld* case contend that, as applied to them, Orthodox Jewish retailers and their Orthodox Jewish customers, the Massachusetts Lord's day statute and the Pennsylvania Sunday retail sales act violate the Due Process Clause of the Fourteenth Amendment because, in effect, the statutes deter the exercise and observance of their religion. The argument runs that by compelling the Sunday closing of retail stores and thus making unavailable for business and shopping uses one-seventh part of the week, these statutes force them either to give up the Sabbath observance—an essential part of their faith—or to forego advantages enjoyed by the non-Sabbatarian majority of the community. They point out, moreover, that because of the prevailing five-day working week of a large proportion of the population, Sunday is a day peculiarly profitable to retail sellers and peculiarly convenient to retail shoppers. The records in these cases support them in this.

The claim which these litigants urge assumes a number of aspects. First, they argue that any one-common-day-**⊥513**of-closing regulation which selected a day other than their Sabbath would be *ipso facto* unconstitutional in its application to them because of its effect in preferring persons who observe no Sabbath, therefore creating economic pressures which urge Sabbatarians to give up their usage. The creation of this pressure by the Sunday statutes, it is said, is not so necessary a means to the achievement of the ends of day-of-rest legislation as to justify its employment when weighed against the injury to Sabbatarian religion which it entails. Six-day-week regulation, with the closing day left to individual choice, is urged as a more reasonable alternative.

Second, they argue that even if legitimate state interests justify the enforcement against persons generally of a single common day of rest, the choice of Sunday as that day violates the rights of religious freedom of the Sabbatarian minority. By choosing a day upon which Sunday-observing Christians worship and abstain from labor, the statutes are said to discriminate between religions. The Sunday observer may practice his faith and yet work six days a week, while the observer of the Jewish Sabbath, his competitor, may work only during five days, to the latter's obvious disadvantage. Orthodox Jewish shoppers whose jobs occupy a five-day week have no week-end shopping day, while Sunday-observing Christians do. Leisure to attend Sunday services, and relative quiet throughout their duration, is assured by law, but no equivalent treatment is accorded to Friday evening and Saturday services. Sabbatarians feel that the power of the State is employed to coerce their observance of Sunday as a holy day; that the State accords a recognition to Sunday Christian doctrine which is withheld from Sabbatarian creeds. All of these prejudices could be avoided, it is argued, without impairing the effectiveness of common-day-of-rest regulation, either by fixing as the rest time some day which is held sacred by no sect, or by pro**⊥514**viding for a Sunday work ban from which Sabbatarians are excepted, on condition of their abstaining from labor on Saturday. Failure to adopt these alternatives in lieu of Sunday statutes applicable to Sabbatarians is said to constitute an unconstitutional choice of means.

Finally, it is urged that if, as means, these statutes are necessary to the goals which they seek to attain, nevertheless the goals themselves are not of sufficient value to society to justify the disadvantage which their attainment imposes upon the religious exercise of Sabbatarians.

The first of these contentions has already been discussed. The history of Sunday legislation convincingly demonstrates that Sunday statutes may serve other purposes than the provision merely of one day of physical stoppage in seven. These purposes fully justify common-day-of-rest statutes which choose Sunday as the day.

In urging that an exception in favor of those who observe some other day as sacred would not defeat the ends of Sunday legislation, and therefore that failure to provide such an exception is an unnecessary—hence an unconstitutional—burden on Sabbatarians, the *Gallagher* appellees and *Braunfeld* appellants point to such exceptions in twenty-one of the thirty-four jurisdictions which have statutes banning labor or employment or the selling of goods on Sunday. Actually, in less than half of these twenty-one States does the exemption extend to ⊥**515** sales activity as well as to labor. There are tenable reasons why a legislature might choose not to make such an exception. To whatever extent persons who come within the exception are present in a community, their activity would disturb the atmosphere of general repose and reintroduce into Sunday the business tempos of the week. Administration would be more difficult, with violations less evident and, in effect, two or more days to police ⊥**516** instead of one. If it is assumed that the retail demand for consumer items is approximately equivalent on Saturday and on Sunday, the Sabbatarian, in proportion as he is less numerous, and hence the competition less severe, might incur through the exception a competitive advantage over the non-Sabbatarian, who would then be in a position, presumably, to complain of discrimination against his religion. Employers who wished to avail themselves of the exception would have to employ only their co-religionists, and there might be introduced into private employment practices an element of religious differentiation which a legislature could regard as undesirable.

Finally, a relevant consideration which might cause a State's lawmakers to reject exception for observers of another day than Sunday is that administration of such a provision may require judicial inquiry into religious belief. A legislature could conclude that if all that is made requisite to qualify for the exemption is an abstinence from labor on some other day, there would be nothing to prevent an enterpriser from closing on his slowest business day, to take advantage of the whole of ⊥**517** the profitable week-end trade, thereby converting the Sunday labor ban, in effect, into a day-of-rest-in-seven statute, with choice of the day left to the individual. All of the state exempting statutes seem to reflect this consideration. Ten of them require that a person claiming exception "conscientiously" believe in the sanctity of another day or "conscientiously" observe another day as the Sabbath. Five demand that he keep another day as "holy time." Three allow the exemption only to members of a "religious" society observing another day, and a fourth provides for proof of membership in such a society by the certificate of a preacher or of any three adherents. In Illinois the claimant must observe some day as a "Sabbath," and in New Jersey he must prove that he devotes that day to religious exercises. Connecticut, one of the jurisdictions demanding conscientious belief, requires in addition that he who seeks the benefit of the exception file a notice of such belief with the prosecuting attorney.

⊥**518** Indicative of the practical administrative difficulties which may arise in attempts to effect, consistently with the purposes of Sunday closing legislation, an exception for persons conscientiously observing another day as Sabbath, are the provisions of § 53 of the British Shops Act, 1950, continuing in substance § 7 of the Shops (Sunday Trading Restriction) Act, 1936. These were the product of experience with earlier forms of exemptions which had proved unsatisfactory, and the new 1936 provisions were enacted only after the consideration and rejection of a number of proposed alternatives. They allow shops ⊥**519** which are registered under the section and which remain closed on Saturday to open for trade until 2 p.m. on Sunday. Applications for registration must contain a declaration that the shop occupier "conscientiously objects on religious grounds to carrying on trade or business on the Jewish Sabbath," and any person who, to procure registration, "knowingly or recklessly makes an untrue statement or untrue representation," is subject to fine and imprisonment. Whenever upon representations made to them the local authorities find reason to believe that a registered occupier is not a person of the Jewish religion or "that a conscientious objection on religious grounds . . . is not genuinely held," the authorities may furnish particulars of the case to a tribunal established after consultation with the London Committee of Deputies of the British Jews, which tribunal, if in their opinion the occupier is not a person of the Jewish religion or does not genuinely hold a conscientious objection to trade on the Jewish Sabbath, shall so report to the local authorities; and upon this report the occupier's registration is to be revoked. Surely, in light of the delicate ⊥**520** enforcement problems to which these provisions bear witness, the legislative choice of a blanket Sunday ban applicable to observers of all faiths cannot be held unreasonable. A legislature might in reason find that the alternative of exempting Sabbatarians would impede the effective operation of the Sunday statutes, produce harmful collateral effects, and entail, itself, a not inconsiderable intrusion into matters of religious faith. However preferable, personally, one might deem such an exception, I cannot find that the Constitution compels it.

It cannot, therefore, be said that Massachusetts and Pennsylvania have imposed gratuitous restrictions upon the Sunday activities of persons observing the Orthodox Jewish Sabbath in achieving the legitimate secular ends at which their Sunday statutes may aim. The remaining question is whether the importance to the public of those ends is sufficient to outweigh the restraint upon the religious exercise of Orthodox Jewish practicants which the restriction entails. The nature of the legislative purpose is the preservation of a traditional institution which assures to the community a time during which the mind and body are released from the demands and distractions of an increasingly mechanized and competition-driven society. The right to this ⊥**521** release has been claimed by workers and by small enterprises, especially by retail merchandisers, over centuries, and finds contemporary expression in legislation in three-quarters of the States. The nature of the injury which must be balanced against it is the economic disadvantage to the enterpriser, and the inconvenience to the consumer, which Sunday regulations impose upon those who choose to adhere to the Sabbatarian tenets of their faith.

These statutes do not make criminal, do not place under the onus of civil or criminal disability, any act which is itself prescribed by the duties of the Jewish or other religions. They do create an undeniable financial burden upon the observers of one of the fundamental tenets of certain religious creeds, a burden which does not fall equally upon other forms of observance. This was true of the tax which this Court held an unconstitutional infringement of the free exercise of religion in *Follett* v. *Town of McCormick.* But unlike the tax in *Follett,* the burden which the Sunday statutes impose is an incident of the only feasible means to achievement of their particular goal. And again unlike *Follett,* the measure of the burden is not determined by fixed legislative decree, beyond the power of the individual to alter. Upon persons who earn their livelihood by activities not prohibited on Sunday, and upon those whose jobs require only a five-day week, the burden is not considerable. Like the customers of Crown Kosher Super Market in the *Gallagher* case, they are inconvenienced in their shopping. This is hardly to be assessed as an injury of preponderant constitutional weight. The burden on retail sellers competing with Sunday-observing and non-observing retailers is considerably greater. But, without minimizing the fact of this disadvantage, the legislature may have concluded that its severity might be offset by the industry and commercial initiative of the individual merchant. More is demanded of him, admittedly, whether in the ⊥**522** form of additional labor or of material sacrifices, than is demanded of those who do not choose to keep his Sabbath. More would be demanded of him, of course, in a State in which there were no Sunday laws and in which his competitors chose—like "Two Guys From Harrison-Allentown"—to do business seven days a week. In view of the importance of the community interests which must be weighed in the balance, is the disadvantage wrought by the non-exempting Sunday statutes an impermissible imposition upon the Sabbatarian's religious freedom? Every court which has considered the question during a century and a half has concluded that it is not. This Court so concluded in *Friedman* v. *New York.* On the basis of the criteria for determining constitutionality, as opposed to what one might desire as a matter of legislative policy, a contrary conclusion cannot be reached.

VI

Two further grounds of unconstitutionality are urged in all these cases, based upon the selection in the challenged statutes of the activities included in, or excluded ⊥**523** from, the Sunday ban. First it is argued that, if the aim of the statutes is to secure a day of peace and repose, the laws of Massachusetts and Maryland, by their exceptions, and the retail sales act of Pennsylvania, by its enumeration of the articles whose sale is forbidden, operate so imperfectly in the service of this aim—show so little rational relation to it—that they must be accounted as arbitrary and therefore violative of due process. The extensive range of recreational and commercial Sunday activity permitted in these States is said to deprive the statutes of any reasonable basis. The distinctions drawn by the laws between what may be sold or done and what may not, it is claimed, are unsupported by reason. Second, these claimants argue that the same discriminations between items which may and may not be sold, and in some cases between the persons who may and those who may not sell identical items, deprive them of the equal protection of the laws.

Although these contentions require the Court to examine separately and with particularity the provisions of each of the three States' statutes which are attacked, the general considerations which govern these cases are the same. It is clear that in fashioning legislative remedies by fine distinctions to fit specific needs, "The range of the State's discretion is large." *Bain Peanut Co.* v. *Pinson.* This is especially so where, by the nature of its subject, regulation must take account of traditional and prevailing local customs. "The Constitution does not require things which are different in fact or opinion to be treated in law as though they were the same." *Tigner* v. *Texas.* "Evils in the same field may be of different dimensions and proportions, requiring different remedies. Or so the legislature may think. . . . Or the reform may take one step at a time, addressing itself to the phase of the ⊥**524** problem which seems most acute to the legislative mind. . . . The legislature may select one phase of one field and apply a remedy there, neglecting the others." *Williamson* v. *Lee Optical, Inc.*

Neither the Due Process nor the Equal Protection Clause demands logical tidiness. No finicky or exact conformity to abstract correlation is required of legislation. The Constitution is satisfied if a legislature responds to the practical living facts with which it deals. Through what precise points in a field of many competing pressures a legislature might most suitably have drawn its lines is not a question for judicial re-examination. It is enough to satisfy the Constitution that in drawing them the principle of reason has not been disregarded. And what degree of uniformity reason demands of a statute is, of course, a function of the complexity of the needs which the statute seeks to accommodate.

In the case of Sunday legislation, an extreme complexity of needs is evident. This is so, first, because one of the prime objectives of the legislation is the preservation of an atmosphere—a subtle desideratum, itself the product of a peculiar and changing set of local circumstances and local traditions. But in addition, in the achievement of that end, however formulated, numerous compromises must be made. Not all activity can halt on Sunday. Some of the very operations whose doings most contribute to the rush and clamor of the week must go on throughout that day as well, whether because life depends upon them, or because the cost of stopping and restarting them is simply too great, or because to be without their services would be more disruptive of peace than to have them to continue. Many activities have a double aspect: providing entertainment or recreation for some persons, they ⊥**525** entail labor and workday tedium for others. . . . ⊥**526** Moreover, the variation from activity to activity in the degree of disturbance which Sunday operation entails, and the similar variation in degrees of temptation to flout the law, and in degrees of ability to absorb and ignore various legal penalties, make exceedingly difficult the devising of effective, yet comprehensively fair, schemes of sanctions.

Early in the history of the Sunday laws there developed mechanisms which served to adapt their wide general prohibitions both to practical exigencies and to the evolving concerns and desires of the public. Where it was found that persons in certain activities tended with particular frequency to engage in violations, those activities were singled out for harsher punishment. On the other hand, practices found necessary or convenient to popular habits were specifically excepted from the ban. Under the basic English Sunday statute, 29 Charles II, c. 7, a wide general exception obtained for "Works of Necessity ⊥**527** and Charity"; this provision found its way into the American colonial laws, and has descended into all of their successors currently in force. The effect of the phrase has been to give the courts a wide range of discretion in determining exceptions. But reasonable men can and do differ as to what is "necessity." In every juris⊥**528**diction legislatures, presumably deeming themselves fitter tribunals for decisions of this sort than were courts, acted to resolve the question against, or in favor of, various particular activities. Some pursuits were expressly declared not works of necessity, or were specially banned. ⊥**529** Others were expressly permitted: series of exceptions, giving the laws resiliency in the course of cultural change, proliferated. Today, the general pattern in over half of the States and in England is similar. Broad general pro⊥**530**hibitions are qualified by numerous precise exemptions, often with provision for local variation within a State, and are frequently bolstered by special provisions more heavily penalizing named activities. The regulations of Maryland, Massachusetts and Pennsylvania are not atypical in this regard, although they are undoubtedly among the more complex of the statutory patterns.

The degree of explicitness of these provisions in so many jurisdictions demonstrates the intricacy of the adjustments which they are designed to make. . . . ⊥**531** Certainly, when relevant considerations of policy demand decisions and distinctions so fine, courts must accord to the legislature a wide range of power to classify and to delineate. It is true that, unlike their virtually unanimous attitude on the issue of religious freedom, state courts have not always sustained Sunday legislation against the charge of unconstitutional discrimination. Statutes and ordinances have been struck down as arbitrary or as violative of state constitutional prohibitions ⊥**532** of special legislation. A far greater number of courts, in similar classes of cases, have sustained the legislation. But the very diversity of judicial opinion as to what is rea⊥**533**sonable classification—like the conflicting views on what is such "necessity" as will justify Sunday operations—testifies that the question of inclusion with regard to Sunday bans is one where judgments rationally differ, and hence ⊥**534** where a State's determinations must be given every fair presumption of a reasonable support in fact. The restricted scope of this Court's review of state regulatory legislation under the Equal Protection Clause is of long ⊥**535** standing. The applicable principles are that a state statute may not be struck down as offensive of equal protection in its schemes of classification unless it is obviously arbitrary, and that, except in the case of a statute whose discriminations are so patently without reason that no conceivable situation of fact could be found to justify them, the claimant who challenges the statute bears the burden of affirmative demonstration that in the actual state of facts which surround its operation, its classifications lack rationality.

When these standards are applied, first, to the Maryland statute challenged in the *McGowan* case, appellants' claim under the Due Process and Equal Protection Clauses show themselves clearly untenable. Counsel contend that the Sunday sales prohibition, Md. Code Ann., 1957, Art. 27, § 521, is rendered arbitrary by its exception of retail sales of tobacco items and soft drinks, ⊥**536** ice and ice cream, confectionery, milk, bread, fruit, gasoline products, newspapers and periodicals, and of drugs and medical supplies by apothecaries—by the further exemption in Anne Arundel County, under § 509, of certain recreational activities and sales incidental to them—and by the permissibility under other state and local regulations of various amusements and public entertainments on Sunday, Sunday beer and liquor sales, and Sunday pinball machines and bingo. The short answer is that these kinds of commodity exceptions, and most of these exceptions for amusements and entertainments, can be found in the comprehensive Sunday statutes of England, Puerto Rico, a dozen American States, and many other countries having uniform-day-of-rest legislation. Surely unreason cannot be so widespread. The notion that, with these matters excepted, the Maryland statute lacks all rational foundation is baseless. The exceptions relate to products and services which a legislature could reasonably find necessary to the physical and mental health of the people or to their recreation and relaxation on a day of repose. Other sales activity and, under Art. 27, § 492, all other labor, are forbidden. That more or fewer activities than fall within the exceptions could with equal rationality have been excluded from the general ban does not make irrational the selection which has actually been made. There is presented in this record not a trace of evidence as to the habits and customs of the population of Maryland or of Anne Arundel County, nothing that suggests that the pattern of legislation which their representatives have devised is not reasonably related to local circumstances determining their ways of ⊥**537** life. Appellants have wholly failed to meet their burden of proof.

Counsel for McGowan urge that the allowance, limited to Anne Arundel County, of retail sales of merchandise customarily sold at bathing beaches, bathhouses, amusement parks and dancing saloons, violates the equal protection of the laws both by discriminating between Anne Arundel retailers and those in other counties, and by discriminating among classes of persons within Anne Arundel County who compete in sales of the same articles. Clearly appellants, who were convicted for selling within the county, would not ordinarily have standing to raise the issue of possible discrimination against out-of-county merchants; in any event, on this record, it is dubious that the contention was adequately raised below. Suffice to say, for purposes of the due process issue which appellants did raise, that the provision of different Sunday regulations for different regions of a State is not *ipso facto* arbitrary.

As for the asserted discrimination in favor of those who sell at the beach or the park articles not permitted to ⊥**538** be sold elsewhere, the answer must be that between such beach-side enterprisers and the general suburban merchandising store at which appellants are employed there is a reasonable line of demarcation. The reason of the exemption dictates the human logic of its scope. The legislature has found it desirable that persons seeking certain forms of recreation on Sunday have the convenience of purchasing on that day items which add enjoyment to the recreation and which, perhaps, could not or would not be provided for by a vacationer prior to the day of his Sunday outing. On the other hand, the policy of securing to the maximum possible number of distributive employees their Sunday off might reasonably preclude allowing every retail establishment in the county to open to serve this convenience. A tenable resolution, surely, is to permit these particular sales only on the premises where the items will be needed and used. The enforcement problem which could arise from permitting general merchandising outlets to open for the sale of these items alone, but not for the sale of thousands of other items at adjacent counters and shelves, might in itself justify the limitation of the exception to the group of on-the-premises merchants who are less likely to stock articles extraneous to the use of the enumerated amusement facilities.

The Massachusetts statute attacked in the *Gallagher* case contains a wider range of exceptions but, again, none that this record shows to be patently baseless and therefore constitutionally impermissible. The court below believed that reason was offended by such provisions as those which allow, apparently, digging for clams but not dredging for oysters, or which permit certain professional sports during the hours from 1:30 to 6:30 p.m. while restricting their amateur counterparts to 2 to 6, or which make lawful (as the court below read the statute) Sunday pushcart vending by conscientious Sabbatarians, but not ⊥**539** Sunday vending within a building. But the record below, on the basis of which a federal court has been asked to enjoin the enforcement of a state statute, contains no evidence concerning clam-digging or oyster-dredging, nothing to indicate that these two activities have anything more in common—requiring similar treatment—than that in each there is involved the pursuit of mollusca. There is nothing in the record concerning professional or amateur athletic events, and certainly nothing to support the conclusion that the problem of Sunday regulation of pushcarts is so similar to the problem of Sunday regulation of indoor markets as to require uniform treatment for both. These various differently treated situations may be different in fact, or they may not. A statute is not to be struck down on supposition.

It is true, as appellees there claim, that Crown Kosher Super Market may not sell on Sunday products which other retail establishments may sell on that day: bread (which may be sold during certain hours by innkeepers, common victuallers, confectioners and fruiterers, and, along with other bakery products, by bakers), confectionery, frozen desserts and dessert mix, and soda water (which may be sold by innkeepers, common victuallers, confectioners and fruiterers, and druggists), tobacco (which may be sold by innkeepers, common victuallers, druggists, and regular newsdealers), etc. (The sale of drugs and newspapers on Sunday is permitted generally.) But although Crown Kosher undoubtedly suffers an element of competition disadvantage from these provisions, the provisions themselves are not irrational. Their purpose, apparently, is to permit dealers specializing in certain products whose distribution on Sunday is regarded as necessary, to sell those products and also such other among the same group ⊥**540** of necessaries as are generally found sold together with the products in which they specialize, thus fostering the maximum dissemination of the permitted products with the minimum number of retail employees required to work to disseminate them. Shops such as newsdealers, druggists, and confectioners may in Massachusetts tend, for all we know, to be smaller, less noisy, more widely distributed so that access to them from residential areas entails less traveling, than is the case with other stores. They may tend to hire fewer employees. They may present, because they specialize in products whose sale is permitted, less of a policing problem than would general markets selling these and many other products. Again there is nothing in the record to support the conclusion that Massachusetts has failed to afford to the Crown Kosher Super Market treatment which is equivalent to that enjoyed by all other retailers of a class not rationally distinguishable from Crown. "The prohibition of the Equal Protection Clause goes no further than the invidious discrimination. We cannot say that that point has been reached here." *Williamson* v. *Lee Optical, Inc.*

Nor, on the record of the *McGinley* case, can any other conclusion be reached as to the 1959 Pennsylvania Sunday retail sales act. Appellants in this case argue that to punish by a fine of up to one hundred dollars per sale—or two hundred dollars per sale within one year after the first offense—the retail selling of some twenty enumerated broad categories of commodities, while punishing all other sales and laboring activity by the four-dollars per-Sunday ⊥**541** fine fixed by the earlier Lord's day statute, is arbitrary and violative of equal protection. But the court below found, and in this it is supported by the legislative history of the 1959 act, that the enactment providing severer penalties for these classes of sales was responsive to the appearance in the Commonwealth, only shortly before the act's passage, of a new kind of large-scale mercantile enterprise which, absorbing without difficulty a four-dollar-a-week fine, made a profitable business of persistent violation of the earlier statute. These new enterprises may have attracted a disturbing volume of Sunday traffic; they may have employed more retail salesmen, and under different conditions, than other kinds of businesses in the State; some of the legislators, apparently, so believed. The danger may have been apprehended that not only would these violations of long-standing State legislation continue, but that competition would force upon other enterprises which had for years closed on Sunday. Under this threat the 1959 statute was designed. It applies not only to the new merchandisers—if that were so, quite obviously, different constitutional problems would arise. Rather it singles out the area where a danger has been most evident, and within that area treats all business enterprises equally. That in so doing it may have drawn the line between the sale of a sofa cover, punished by a hundred-dollar fine, and the sale of an automobile seat cover, punished by a four dollar fine, is not sufficient to void the legislation. "[A] State may classify with reference to the evil to be prevented, and . . . if the class discriminated against is or reasonably might be considered to define those from whom the evil mainly is to be feared, it properly may be ⊥**542** picked out. A lack of abstract symmetry does not matter. The question is a practical one dependent upon experience. The demand for symmetry ignores the specific difference that experience is supposed to have shown to mark the class. It is not enough to invalidate the law that others may do the same thing and go unpunished, if, as a matter of fact, it is found that the danger is characteristic of the class named." Mr. *Justice* HOLMES, in *Patsone* v. *Pennsylvania*.

Even less should a legislature be required to hew the line of logical exactness where the statutory distinction challenged is merely one which sets apart offenses subject to penalties of differing degrees of severity, not one which divides the lawful from the unlawful. "Judgment on the deterrent effect of the various weapons in the armory of the law can lay little claim to scientific basis. Such judgment as yet is largely a prophecy based on meager and uninterpreted experience. . . .

". . . Moreover, the whole problem of deterrence is related to still wider considerations affecting the temper of the community in which law operates. The traditions of a society, the habits of obedience to law, the effectiveness of the law-enforcing agencies, are all peculiarly matters of time and place. They are thus matters within legislative competence." *Tigner* v. *Texas*. Appellants in *McGinley*, like appellants in the *McGowan* and appellees in the *Gallagher* cases, have had full opportunity to demonstrate the arbitrariness of the statute which they challenge. On this record they have entirely failed to satisfy the burden which they carry.

The *Braunfeld* case, however, comes here in a different posture. Appellants, plaintiffs below, allege in their ⊥**543** amended complaint that the 1959 Pennsylvania Sunday retail sales act is irrational and arbitrary. The three-judge court dismissed the amended complaint for failure to state a claim. Speaking for myself alone and not for Mr. *Justice* HARLAN on this point, I think that this was too summary a disposition. However difficult it may be for appellants to prove what they allege, they must be given an opportunity to do so if they choose to avail themselves of it, in view of the Court's decisions in this series of cases. I would remand No. 67 to the District Court.

. . . . . .

⊥**561** Mr. *Justice* DOUGLAS, dissenting.*

The question is not whether one day out of seven can be imposed by a State as a day of rest. The question is not whether Sunday can by force of custom and habit be retained as a day of rest. The question is whether a State can impose criminal sanctions on those who, unlike the Christian majority that makes up our society, worship on a different day or do not share the religious scruples of the majority.

If the "free exercise" of religion were subject to reasonable regulations, as it is under some constitutions, or if all

*NOTE: This opinion applies also to *Two Guys From Harrison-Allentown, Inc.*, v. *McGinley*, *Braunfeld et al.* v. *Brown*, and *Gallagher* v. *Crown Kosher Super Market, Inc.*

laws "respecting the establishment of religion" were not proscribed, I could understand how rational men, representing a predominantly Christian civilization, might think these Sunday laws did not unreasonably interfere with anyone's free exercise of religion and took no step toward a burdensome establishment of any religion.

But that is not the premise from which we start, as there is agreement that the fact that a State, and not the Federal Government, has promulgated these Sunday laws does not change the scope of the power asserted. For the classic view is that the First Amendment should be applied to the States with the same firmness as it is enforced against the Federal Government. ⊥**562** The most explicit statement perhaps was in *Board of Education* v. *Barnette:* "In weighing arguments of the parties it is important to distinguish between the due process clause of the Fourteenth Amendment as an instrument for transmitting the principles of the First Amendment and those cases in which it is applied for its own sake. The test of legislation which collides with the Fourteenth Amendment, because it also collides with the principles of the First, is much more definite than the test when only the Fourteenth is involved. Much of the vagueness of the due process clause disappears when the specific prohibitions of the First become its standard. The right of a State to regulate, for example, a public utility may well include, so far as the due process test is concerned, power to impose all of the restrictions which a legislature may have a 'rational basis' for adopting. But freedoms of speech and of press, of assembly, and of worship may not be infringed on such slender grounds. They are susceptible of restriction only to prevent grave and immediate danger to interests which the State may lawfully protect. It is important to note that while it is the Fourteenth Amendment which bears directly upon the State it is the more specific limiting principles of the First Amendment that finally govern this case."

With that as my starting point I do not see how a State can make protesting citizens refrain from doing innocent acts on Sunday because the doing of those acts offends sentiments of their Christian neighbors.

The institutions of our society are founded on the belief that there is an authority higher than the authority of the State; that there is a moral law which the State is powerless to alter; that the individual possesses rights, conferred by the Creator, which government must respect. ⊥**563** The Declaration of Independence stated the now familiar theme: "We hold these Truths to be self-evident, that all Men are created equal, that they are endowed by their Creator with certain unalienable Rights, that among these are Life, Liberty, and the Pursuit of Happiness."

And the body of the Constitution as well as the Bill of Rights enshrined those principles.

The Puritan influence helped shape our constitutional law and our common law as Dean Pound has said: The Puritan "put individual conscience and individual judgment in the first place." For these reasons we stated in *Zorach* v. *Clauson*, "We are a religious people whose institutions presuppose a Supreme Being."

But those who fashioned the First Amendment decided that if and when God is to be served, His service will not be motivated by coercive measures of government. "Congress shall make no law respecting an establishment of religion, or prohibiting the free exercise thereof"—such is the command of the First Amendment made applicable to the State by reason of the Due Process Clause of the Fourteenth. This means, as I understand it, that if a religious leaven is to be worked into the affairs of our people, it is to be done by individuals and groups, not by the Government. This necessarily means, *first*, that the dogma, creed, scruples, or practices of no religious group or sect are to be preferred over those of any others; *second*, that no one shall be interfered with by government for practicing the religion of his choice; *third*, that the State cannot compel one so to conduct himself as not to offend the religious scruples of another. The idea, as I understand it, was to limit the power of government to act in religious matters, ⊥**564** not to limit the freedom of religious men to act religiously nor to restrict the freedom of atheists or agnostics.

The First Amendment commands government to have no interest in theology or ritual; it admonishes government to be interested in allowing religious freedom to flourish—whether the result is to produce Catholics, Jews, or Protestants, or to turn the people toward the path of Buddha, or to end in a predominantly Moslem nation, or to produce in the long run atheists or agnostics. On matters of this kind government must be neutral. This freedom plainly includes freedom *from* religion with the right to believe, speak, write, publish and advocate antireligious programs. Certainly the "free exercise" clause does not require that everyone embrace the theology of some church or of some faith, or observe the religious practices of any majority or minority sect. The First Amendment by its "establishment" clause prevents, of course, the selection by government of an "official" church. Yet the ban plainly extends farther than that. We said in *Everson* v. *Board of Education* that it would be an "establishment" of a religion if the Government financed one church or several churches. For what better way to "establish" an institution than to find the fund that will support it? The "establishment" clause protects citizens also against any law which selects any religious custom, practice, or ritual, puts the force of government behind it, and fines, imprisons, or otherwise penalizes a person for not observing it. The Government plainly could not join forces with one religious group and decree a universal and symbolic circumcision. Nor could it require all children to be baptized or give tax exemptions only to those whose children were baptized.

Could it require a fast from sunrise to sunset throughout the Moslem month of Ramadan? I should think not. ⊥**565** Yet, why then can it make criminal the doing of other acts, as innocent as eating, during the day that Christians revere?

Sunday is a word heavily overlaid with connotations and traditions deriving from the Christian roots of our civilization that color all judgments concerning it. . . .

The issue of these cases would therefore be in better focus if we imagined that a state legislature, controlled by orthodox Jews and Seventh-Day Adventists, passed a law making it a crime to keep a shop open on Saturdays. Would a Baptist, Catholic, Methodist, or Presbyterian be compelled to obey that law or go to jail or pay a fine? Or suppose Moslems grew in political strength here and got a law through a state legislature making it a crime to keep a shop open on Fridays. Would the rest of us have to submit under the fear of criminal sanctions?

Dr. John Cogley recently summed up the dominance of the three-religion influence in our affairs: "For the foreseeable future, it seems, the United States is going to be a three-religion nation. At the present time all three are characteristically 'Amer⊥**566**ican,' some think flavorlessly so. For religion in America is almost uniformly 'respectable,' bourgeois, and prosperous. In the Protestant world the 'church' mentality has triumphed over the more venturesome spirit of the 'sect.' In the Catholic world, the mystical is muted in favor of booming organization and efficiently administered good works. And in the Jewish world the prophet is too frequently without honor, while the synagogue emphasis is focused on suburban togetherness. There are exceptions to these rules, of course; each of the religious communities continues to cast up its prophets, its rebels and radicals. But a Jeremiah, one fears, would be positively embarrassing to the present position of the Jews; a Francis of Assisi upsetting the complacency of American Catholics would be rudely dismissed as a fanatic; and a Kierkegaard, speaking with an American accent, would be considerably less welcome than Norman Vincent Peale in most Protestant pulpits."

This religious influence has extended far, far back of the First and Fourteenth Amendments. Every Sunday School student knows the Fourth Commandment:

"Remember the sabbath day to keep it holy.

"Six days shalt thou labour, and do all thy work:

"But the seventh day is the sabbath of the LORD thy God: in it thou shalt not do any work, thou, nor thy son, nor thy daughter, thy manservant, nor thy ⊥**567** maidservant, nor thy cattle, nor thy stranger that is within thy gates:

"For in six days the LORD made heaven and earth, the sea, and all that in them is, and rested the seventh day: wherefore the LORD blessed the sabbath day, and hallowed it." Exodus 20:8-11.

This religious mandate for observance of the Seventh-Day became, under Emperor Constantine, a mandate for observance of the First Day "in conformity with the practice of the Christian Church." This religious mandate has had a checkered history, but in general its command, enforced now by the ecclesiastical authorities, now by the civil authorities, and now by both, has held good down through the centuries. The general pattern of these laws in the United States was set in the eighteenth century and derives, most directly, from a seventeenth century English statute. Judicial comment on the ⊥**568** Sunday laws has always been a mixed bag. Some judges have asserted that the statutes have a "purely" civil aim, *i.e.*, limitation of work time and provision for a common and universal leisure. But other judges have recognized the religious significance of Sunday and that the laws existed to enforce the maintenance of that significance. In general, both threads of argument have continued to interweave in the case law on the subject. Prior to the time when the First Amendment was held applicable to the States by reason of the Due Process Clause of the Fourteenth, the Court at least by *obiter dictum* approved State Sunday laws on three occasions: *Soon Hing* v. *Crowley*; *Hennington* v. *Georgia*, *Petit* v. *Minnesota*. And in *Friedman* v. *New York*, the Court, by a divided vote, dismissed "for want of a substantial federal question" an appeal from a New York decision upholding the validity of a Sunday law against an attack based on the First Amendment.

The *Soon Hing*, *Hennington*, and *Petit* cases all rested on the police power of the State—the right to safeguard the health of the people by requiring the cessation of normal activities one day out of seven. The Court in the *Soon Hing* case rejected the idea that Sunday laws rested on the power of government "to legislate for the promotion of religious observances." The New York Court of Appeals in the *Friedman* case followed the reasoning of the earlier cases.

⊥**569** The Massachusetts Sunday law involved in one of these appeals was once characterized by the Massachusetts court as merely a civil regulation providing for a "fixed period of rest." *Commonwealth* v. *Has*. That decision was, according to the District Court in the *Gallagher* case, "an *ad hoc* improvisation" made "because of the realization that the Sunday law would be more vulnerable to constitutional attack under the state Constitution if the religious motivation of the statute were more explicitly avowed." Certainly prior to the *Has* case, the Massachusetts courts had indicated that the aim of the Sunday law was religious. After the *Has* case the Massachusetts court construed the Sunday law as a religious measure. In *Davis* v. *Somerville*, it was said: "Our Puritan ancestors intended that the day should be not merely a day of rest from labor, but also a day devoted to public and private worship and to religious meditation and repose, undisturbed by secular cares or amusements. They saw fit to enforce the observance of the day by penal legislation, and the statute regulations which they devised for that purpose have continued in force, without any substantial modification, to the present time."

In *Commonwealth* v. *White*, the court refused to liberalize its construction of an exception in its Sunday law for works of "necessity." That word, it said, "was originally inserted to secure the observance of the Lord's day in accordance with ⊥**570** the view of our ancestors, and it ever since has stood and still stands for the same purpose." In *Commonwealth* v. *McCarthy*, the court reiterated that the aim of the law was "to secure respect and reverence for the Lord's day."

The Pennsylvania Sunday laws before us in Nos. 36 and 67 have received the same construction. "Rest and quiet, on the Sabbath day, with the right and privilege of public and private worship, undisturbed by any mere worldly employment, are exactly what the statute was passed to protect." *Sparhawk* v. *Union Passenger R. Co.* A recent pronouncement by the Pennsylvania Supreme Court is found in *Commonwealth* v. *American Baseball Club.* "Christianity is part of the common law of Pennsylvania . . . and its people are christian people. Sunday is the holy day among christians."

The Maryland court, in sustaining the challenged law in No. 8, relied on *Judefind* v. *State* and *Levering* v. *Park Commissioner.* In the former the court said: "It is undoubtedly true that rest from secular employment on Sunday does have a tendency to foster and encourage the Christian religion—of all sects and denominations that observe that day—as rest from work and ordinary occupation enables many to engage in public worship who probably would not otherwise do so. But it would scarcely be asked of a Court, in what professes to be a Christian land, to declare a law unconstitutional because it requires rest from bodily labor on Sunday, (except works of necessity and charity,) and *thereby* promotes the **⊥571** cause of Christianity. If the Christian religion is, incidentally or otherwise, benefited or fostered by having this day of rest, as it undoubtedly is, there is all the more reason for the enforcement of laws that help to preserve it."

In the *Levering* case the court relied on the excerpt from the *Judefind* decision just quoted.

We have then in each of the four cases Sunday laws that find their source in Exodus, that were brought here by the Virginians and by the Puritans, and that are today maintained, construed, and justified because they respect the views of our dominant religious groups and provide a needed day of rest.

The history was accurately summarized a century ago by Chief Justice Terry of the Supreme Court of California in *Ex parte Newman:* "The truth is, however much it may be disguised, that this one day of rest is a purely religious idea. Derived from the Sabbatical institutions of the ancient Hebrew, it has been adopted into all the creeds of succeeding religious sects throughout the civilized world; and whether it be the Friday of the Mohammedan, the Saturday of the Israelite, or the Sunday of the Christian, it is alike fixed in the affections of its followers, beyond the power of eradication, and in most of the States of our Confederacy, the aid of the law to enforce its observance has been given under the pretence of a civil, municipal, or police regulation."

That case involved the validity of a Sunday law under a provision of the California Constitution guaranteeing the "free exercise" of religion. Justice Burnett stated why he concluded that the **⊥572** Sunday law, there sought to be enforced against a man selling clothing on Sunday, infringed California's constitution: "Had the act made Monday, instead of Sunday, a day of compulsory rest, the constitutional question would have been the same. The fact that the Christian *voluntarily* keeps holy the first day of the week, does not authorize the Legislature to make that observance *compulsory*. The Legislature can not compel the citizen to do that which the Constitution leaves him free to do or omit, at his election. The act violates as much the religious freedom of the Christian as of the Jew. Because the conscientious views of the Christian compel him to keep Sunday as a Sabbath, he has the right to object, when the Legislature invades his freedom of religious worship, and assumes the power to compel him to do that which he has right to omit if he pleases. The principle is the same, whether the act of the Legislature *compels* us to do that which we wish to do, or not to do. . . .

"Under the Constitution of this State, the Legislature can not pass any act, the legitimate effect of which is *forcibly* to establish any merely religious truth, or enforce any merely religious observances. The Legislature has no power over such a subject. When, therefore, the citizen is sought to be compelled by the Legislature to do any affirmative religious act, or to refrain from doing anything, because it violates simply a religious principle or observance, the act is unconstitutional."

The Court picks and chooses language from various decisions to bolster its conclusion that these Sunday laws in the modern setting are "civil regulations." No matter how much is written, no matter what is said, the parentage of these laws is the Fourth Commandment; and they **⊥573** serve and satisfy the religious predispositions of our Christian communities. After all, the labels a State places on its laws are not binding on us when we are confronted with a constitutional decision. We reach our own conclusion as to the character, effect, and practical operation of the regulation in determining its constitutionality.

It seems to me plain that by these laws the States compel one, under sanction of law, to refrain from work or recreation on Sunday because of the majority's religious views about that day. The State by law makes Sunday a symbol of respect or adherence. Refraining from work or recreation in deference to the majority's religious feelings about Sunday is within every person's choice. By what authority can government compel it?

Cases are put where acts that are immoral by our standards but not by the standards of other religious **⊥574** groups are made criminal. That category of cases, until today, has been a very restricted one confined to polygamy *(Reynolds* v. *United States)* and other extreme situations. The latest example is *Prince* v. *Massachusetts*, which upheld a statute making it criminal for a child under twelve to sell papers, periodicals, or merchandise on a street or in any public place. It was sustained in spite of the finding that the child thought it was her religious duty to perform the act. But that was a narrow holding which turned on the effect which street solicitation might have on the child-solicitor: "The state's authority over children's activities is broader than over like actions of adults. This is peculiarly true of public activities and in matters of employment. A democratic Society rests, for its continuance, upon the healthy, well-rounded growth of young people into full maturity as citizens, with all that implies. It may secure this against impeding restraints and dangers, within a broad range of selection. Among evils most appropriate for such action are the crippling effects of child employment, more especially in public places, and the possible harms arising from other activities subject to all the diverse influences of the street. It is too late now to doubt that legislation appropriately designed to reach such evils is within the state's police power, whether against the parent's claim to control of the child or one that religious scruples dictate contrary action."

None of the acts involved here implicates minors. None of the actions made constitutionally criminal today involves the doing of any act that any society has deemed to be immoral.

The conduct held constitutionally criminal today embraces the selling of pure, not impure, food; wholesome, **⊥575** not noxious articles. Adults, not minors, are involved. The innocent acts, now constitutionally classified as criminal, emphasize the drastic break we make with tradition.

These laws are sustained because, it is said, the First Amendment is concerned with religious convictions or opinion, not with conduct. But it is a strange Bill of Rights that makes it possible for the dominant religious group to bring the minority to heel because the minority, in the doing of acts which intrinsically are wholesome and not antisocial, does not defer to the majority's religious beliefs. Some have religious scruples against eating pork. Those scruples, no matter how bizarre they might seem to some, are within the ambit of the First Amendment. Is it possible that a majority of a state legislature having those religious scruples could make it criminal for the nonbeliever to sell pork? Some have religious scruples against slaughtering cattle. Could a state legislature, dominated by that group, make it criminal to run an abattoir?

The Court balances the need of the people for rest, recreation, late sleeping, family visiting and the like against the command of the First Amendment that no one need bow to the religious beliefs of another. There is in this realm no room for balancing. I see no place for it in the constitutional scheme. A legislature of Christians can no more make minorities conform to their weekly regime than a legislature of Moslems, or a legislature of Hindus. The religious regime of every group must be respected—unless it crosses the line of criminal conduct. But no one can be forced to come to a halt before it, or refrain from doing things that would offend it. That is my reading of the Establishment Clause and the Free Exercise Clause. Any other reading imports, I fear, an element common in other societies but foreign to us. . . .

⊥576 The State can, of course, require one day of rest a week: one day when every shop or factory is closed. Quite a few States make that requirement. Then the "day of rest" becomes purely and simply a health measure. But the Sunday laws operate differently. They force minorities to obey the majority's religious feelings of what is due and proper for a Christian community; they provide a coercive spur to the "weaker brethren," to those who are indifferent to the claims of a Sabbath through apathy or scruple. Can there be any doubt that Christians, now aligned vigorously in favor of these laws, would be as strongly opposed if they were prosecuted under a Moslem law that forbade them from engaging in secular activities on days that violated Moslem scruples?

There is an "establishment" of religion in the constitutional sense if any practice of any religious group has the sanction of law behind it. There is an interference with the "free exercise" of religion if what in conscience one **⊥577** can do or omit doing is required because of the religious scruples of the community. Hence I would declare each of those laws unconstitutional as applied to the complaining parties, whether or not they are members of a sect which observes as its Sabbath a day other than Sunday.

When these laws are applied to Orthodox Jews, as they are in No. 11 and in No. 67, or to Sabbatarians their vice is accentuated. If the Sunday laws are constitutional, kosher markets are on a five-day week. Thus those laws put an economic penalty on those who observe Saturday rather than Sunday as the Sabbath. For the economic pressures on these minorities, created by the fact that our communities are predominantly Sunday-minded, there is no recourse. When, however, the State uses its coercive powers—here the criminal law—to compel minorities to observe a second Sabbath, not their own, the State undertakes to aid and "prefer one religion over another"—contrary to the command of the Constitution.

In large measure the history of the religious clause of the First Amendment was a struggle to be free of economic sanctions for adherence to one's religion. A small tax was imposed in Virginia for religious education. Jefferson and Madison led the fight against the tax, Madison writing his famous Memorial and Remonstrance against that law. As a result, the tax measure was defeated and instead Virginia's famous "Bill for Religious Liberty," written by Jefferson, was enacted. That Act provided "That no man shall be compelled to frequent or support any religious worship, place, or ministry whatsoever, nor shall be enforced, restrained, molested, or burthened in his body or goods, nor shall other**⊥578**wise suffer on account of his religious opinions or belief. . . ."

The reverse side of an "establishment" is a burden on the "free exercise" of religion. Receipt of funds from the State benefits the established church directly; laying an extra tax on nonmembers benefits the established church indirectly. Certainly the present Sunday laws place Orthodox Jews and Sabbatarians under extra burdens because of their religious opinions or beliefs. Requiring them to abstain from their trade or business on Sunday reduces their work-week to five days, unless they violate their religious scruples. This places them at a competitive disadvantage and penalizes them for adhering to their religious beliefs.

"The sanction imposed by the state for observing a day other than Sunday as holy time is certainly more serious economically than the imposition of a license tax for preaching," which we struck down in *Murdock* v.

Pennsylvania and in *Follett* v. *McCormick*. The special protection which Sunday laws give the dominant religious groups and the penalty they place on minorities whose holy day is Saturday constitute, in my view, state interference with the "free exercise" of religion.

⊥**579** I dissent from applying criminal sanctions against any of these complainants since to do so implicates the States in religious matters contrary to the constitutional mandate. Reverend Allan C. Parker, Jr., Pastor of the ⊥**580** South Park Presbyterian Church, Seattle, Washington, has stated my views: "We forget that, though Sunday-worshiping Christians are in the majority in this country among religious people, we do not have the right to force our practice upon the minority. Only a Church which deems itself without error and intolerant of error can justify its intolerance of the minority.

"A Jewish friend of mine runs a small business establishment. Because my friend is a Jew his business is closed each Saturday. He respects my right to worship on Sunday and I respect his right to worship on Saturday. But there is a difference. As a Jew he closes his store voluntarily so that he will be able to worship his God in his fashion. Fine! But, as a Jew living under Christian inspired Sunday closing laws, he is required to close his store on Sunday so that I will be able to worship my God in my fashion.

"Around the corner from my church there is a small Seventh Day Baptist Church. I disagree with the Seventh Day Baptists on many points of doctrine. Among the tenets of their faith with which I disagree is the 'seventh day worship.' But they are good neighbors and fellow Christians, and while we disagree we respect one another. The good people of my congregation set aside their jobs on the first day of the week and gather in God's house for worship. Of course, it is easy for them to set aside their jobs since Sunday closing laws—inspired by the Church—keep them from their work. At the Seventh Day Baptist church the people set aside ⊥**581** their jobs on Saturday to worship God. This takes real sacrifice because Saturday is a good day for business. But that is not all—they are required by law to set aside their jobs on Sunday while more orthodox Christians worship.

". . . I do not believe that because I have set aside Sunday as a holy day I have the right to force all men to set aside that day also. Why should my faith be favored by the State over any other man's faith?"

With all deference, none of the opinions filed today in support of the Sunday laws has answered that question.

BRAUNFELD v. BROWN

366 U.S. 599
ON APPEAL FROM THE UNITED STATES DISTRICT COURT FOR THE EASTERN DISTRICT OF PENNSYLVANIA
Argued December 8, 1960 — Decided May 29, 1961

⊥**600** Mr. *Chief Justice WARREN* announced the judgment of the Court and an opinion in which Mr. *Justice BLACK*, Mr. *Justice CLARK*, and Mr. *Justice WHITTAKER* concur.

This case concerns the constitutional validity of the application to appellants of the Pennsylvania criminal statute, enacted in 1959, which proscribes the Sunday retail sale of certain enumerated commodities. Among the questions presented are whether the statute is a law ⊥**601** respecting an establishment of religion and whether the statute violates equal protection. Since both of these questions, in reference to this very statute, have already been answered in the negative, *Two Guys from Harrison-Allentown, Inc.*, v. *McGinley*, and since appellants present nothing new regarding them, they need not be considered here. Thus, the only question for consideration is whether the statute interferes with the free exercise of appellants' religion.

Appellants are merchants in Philadelphia who engage in the retail sale of clothing and home furnishings within the proscription of the statute in issue. Each of the appellants is a member of the Orthodox Jewish faith, which requires the closing of their places of business and a total abstention from all manner of work from nightfall each Friday until nightfall each Saturday. They instituted a suit in the court below seeking a permanent injunction against the enforcement of the 1959 statute. Their complaint, as amended, alleged that appellants had previously kept their places of business open on Sunday; that each of appellants had done a substantial amount of business on Sunday, compensating somewhat for their closing on Saturday; that Sunday closing will result in impairing the ability of all appellants to earn a livelihood and will render appellant Braunfeld unable to continue in his business, thereby losing his capital investment; that the statute is unconstitutional for the reasons stated above. . . .

Appellants contend that the enforcement against them of the Pennsylvania statute will prohibit the free exercise ⊥**602** of their religion because, due to the statute's compulsion to close on Sunday, appellants will suffer substantial economic loss, to the benefit of their non-Sabbatarian competitors, if appellants also continue their Sabbath observance by closing their businesses on Saturday; that this result will either compel appellants to give up their Sabbath observance, a basic tenet of the Orthodox Jewish faith, or will put appellants at a serious economic disadvantage if they continue to adhere to their Sabbath. Appellants also assert that the statute will operate so as to hinder the Orthodox Jewish faith in gaining new adherents. And the corollary to these arguments is that if the free exercise of appellants' religion is impeded, that religion is being subjected to discriminatory treatment by the State. . . .

⊥**603** Concededly, appellants and all other persons who wish to work on Sunday will be burdened economically by the State's day of rest mandate; and appellants point out that their religion requires them to refrain from work on Saturday as well. Our inquiry then is whether, in these circumstances, the First and Fourteenth Amendments forbid application of the Sunday Closing Law to appellants.

Certain aspects of religious exercise cannot, in any way, be restricted or burdened by either federal or state legislation. Compulsion by law of the acceptance of any creed or the practice of any form of worship is strictly forbidden. The freedom to hold religious beliefs and opinions is absolute. Thus, in *West Virginia State Board of Education* v. *Barnette* this Court held that state action compelling school children to salute the flag, on pain of expulsion from public school, was contrary to the First and Fourteenth Amendments when applied to those students whose religious beliefs forbade saluting a flag. But this is not the case at bar; the statute before us does not make criminal the holding of any religious belief or opinion, nor does it force anyone to embrace any religious belief or to say or believe anything in conflict with his religious tenets.

However, the freedom to act, even when the action is in accord with one's religious convictions, is not totally free from legislative restrictions. As pointed out in *Reynolds* v. *United States*, legislative power over mere opinion is forbidden but it may reach people's actions when they are found to be in violation of important social duties or subversive of good order, even when **⊥604** the actions are demanded by one's religion. . . .

And, in the *Barnette* case, the Court was careful to point out that "The freedom asserted by these appellees does not bring them into collision with rights asserted by any other individual. It is such conflicts which most frequently require intervention of the State to determine where the rights of one end and those of another begin. . . . It is . . . to be noted that the compulsory flag salute and **⊥605** pledge requires *affirmation of a belief* and an *attitude of mind*." (Emphasis added.)

Thus, in *Reynolds* v. *United States*, this Court upheld the polygamy conviction of a member of the Mormon faith despite the fact that an accepted doctrine of his church then imposed upon its male members the *duty* to practice polygamy. And, in *Prince* v. *Massachusetts* this Court upheld a statute making it a crime for a girl under eighteen years of age to sell any newspapers, periodicals or merchandise in public places despite the fact that a child of the Jehovah's Witnesses faith believed that it was her religious *duty* to perform this work.

It is to be noted that, in the two cases just mentioned, the religious practices themselves conflicted with the public interest. In such cases, to make accommodation between the religious action and an exercise of state authority is a particularly delicate task because resolution in favor of the State results in the choice to the individual of either abandoning his religious principle or facing criminal prosecution.

But, again, this is not the case before us because the statute at bar does not make unlawful any religious practices of appellants; the Sunday law simply regulates a secular activity and, as applied to appellants, operates so as to make the practice of their religious beliefs more expensive. Furthermore, the law's effect does not inconvenience all members of the Orthodox Jewish faith but only those who believe it necessary to work on Sunday. And even these are not faced with as serious a choice as forsaking their religious practices or subjecting themselves to criminal prosecution. Fully recognizing that the alter**⊥606**natives open to appellants and others similarly situated—retaining their present occupations and incurring economic disadvantage or engaging in some other commercial activity which does not call for either Saturday or Sunday labor—may well result in some financial sacrifice in order to observe their religious beliefs, still the option is wholly different than when the legislation attempts to make a religious practice itself unlawful.

To strike down, without the most critical scrutiny, legislation which imposes only an indirect burden on the exercise of religion, *i.e.*, legislation which does not make unlawful the religious practice itself, would radically restrict the operating latitude of the legislature. Statutes which tax income and limit the amount which may be deducted for religious contributions impose an indirect economic burden on the observance of the religion of the citizen whose religion requires him to donate a greater amount to his church; statutes which require the courts to be closed on Saturday and Sunday impose a similar indirect burden on the observance of the religion of the trial lawyer whose religion requires him to rest on a weekday. The list of legislation of this nature is nearly limitless.

Needless to say, when entering the area of religious freedom, we must be fully cognizant of the particular protection that the Constitution has accorded it. Abhorrence of religious persecution and intolerance is a basic part of our heritage. But we are a cosmopolitan nation made up of people of almost every conceivable religious preference. These denominations number almost three hundred. Consequently, it cannot be expected, much less required, that legislators enact no law regulating conduct that may in some way result in an economic disadvantage to some religious sects and not to others because of the special practices of the various religions. We do not believe that such an effect is an absolute test **⊥607** for determining whether the legislation violates the freedom of religion protected by the First Amendment.

Of course, to hold unassailable all legislation regulating conduct which imposes solely an indirect burden on the observance of religion would be a gross oversimplification. If the purpose or effect of a law is to impede the observance of one or all religions or is to discriminate invidiously between religions, that law is constitutionally invalid even though the burden may be characterized as being only indirect. But if the State regulates conduct by enacting a general law within its power, the purpose and effect of which is to advance the State's secular goals, the statute is valid despite its indirect burden on religious observance unless the State may accomplish its purpose by means which do not impose such a burden.

As we pointed out in *McGowan* v. *Maryland*, we cannot find a State without power to provide a weekly respite from all labor and, at the same time, to set one day of the week apart from the others as a day of rest, repose, recreation and tranquillity—a day when the hectic tempo of everyday existence ceases and a more pleasant atmosphere is created, a day which all members of the family and community have the opportunity to spend and enjoy together, a day on which people may visit friends and relatives who are not available during working days, a day when the weekly laborer may best regenerate himself. This is particularly true in this day and age of increasing state concern with public welfare legislation.

⊥608 Also, in *McGowan*, we examined several suggested alternative means by which it was argued that the State might accomplish its secular goals without even remotely or incidentally affecting religious freedom. We found there that a State might well find that those alternatives would not accomplish bringing about a general day of rest. We need not examine them again here.

However, appellants advance yet another means at the State's disposal which they would find unobjectionable. They contend that the State should cut an exception from the Sunday labor proscription for those people who, because of religious conviction, observe a day of rest other than Sunday. By such regulation, appellants contend, the economic disadvantages imposed by the present system would be removed and the State's interest in having all people rest one day would be satisfied.

A number of States provide such an exemption, and this may well be the wiser solution to the problem. But our concern is not with the wisdom of legislation but with its constitutional limitation. Thus, reason and experience teach that to permit the exemption might well undermine the State's goal of providing a day that, as best possible, eliminates the atmosphere of commercial noise and activity. Although not dispositive of the issue, enforcement problems would be more difficult since there would be two or more days to police rather than one and it would be more difficult to observe whether violations were occurring.

Additional problems might also be presented by a regulation of this sort. To allow only people who rest on a day other than Sunday to keep their businesses open on that day might well provide these people with an economic advantage over their competitors who must **⊥609** remain closed on that day; this might cause the Sunday-observers to complain that their religions are being discriminated against. With this competitive advantage existing, there could well be the temptation for some, in order to keep their businesses open on Sunday, to assert that they have religious convictions which compel them to close their businesses on what had formerly been their least profitable day. This might make necessary a state-conducted inquiry into the sincerity of the individual's religious beliefs, a practice which a State might believe would itself run afoul of the spirit of constitutionally protected religious guarantees. Finally, in order to keep the disruption of the day at a minimum, exempted employers would probably have to hire employees who themselves qualified for the exemption because of their own religious beliefs, a practice which a State might feel to be opposed to its general policy prohibiting religious discrimination in hiring. For all of these reasons, we cannot say that the Pennsylvania statute before us is invalid, either on its face or as applied.

Mr. *Justice* HARLAN concurs in the judgment. Mr. *Justice* BRENNAN and Mr. *Justice* STEWART concur in **⊥610** our disposition of appellants' claims under the Establishment Clause and the Equal Protection Clause. Mr. *Justice* FRANKFURTER and Mr. *Justice* HARLAN have rejected appellants' claim under the Free Exercise Clause in a separate opinion.

Accordingly, the decision is *Affirmed*.

Mr. *Justice* BRENNAN, concurring and dissenting.

I agree with *The* CHIEF JUSTICE that there is no merit in appellants' establishment and equal-protection claims. I dissent, however, as to the claim that Pennsylvania has prohibited the free exercise of appellants' religion.

The Court has demonstrated the public need for a weekly surcease from worldly labor, and set forth the considerations of convenience which have led the Commonwealth of Pennsylvania to fix Sunday as the time for that respite. I would approach this case differently, from the point of view of the individuals whose liberty is—concededly—curtailed by these enactments. For the values of the First Amendment, as embodied in the Fourteenth, look primarily towards the preservation of personal liberty, rather than towards the fulfillment of collective goals.

The appellants are small retail merchants, faithful practitioners of the Orthodox Jewish faith. They allege—and the allegation must be taken as true, since the case comes to us on a motion to dismiss the complaint—that ". . . one who does not observe the Sabbath [by refraining from labor] . . . cannot be an Orthodox Jew." **⊥611** In appellants' business area Friday night and Saturday are busy times; yet appellants, true to their faith, close during the Jewish Sabbath, and make up some, but not all, of the business thus lost by opening on Sunday. "Each of the plaintiffs," the complaint continues, "does a substantial amount of business on Sundays, and the ability of the plaintiffs to earn a livelihood will be greatly impaired by closing their business establishment on Sundays." Consequences even more drastic are alleged: "Plaintiff, Abraham Braunfeld, will be unable to continue in his business if he may not stay open on Sunday and he will thereby lose his capital investment." In other words, the issue in this case—and we do not understand either appellees or the Court to contend otherwise—is whether a State may put an individual to a choice between his business and his religion. The Court today holds that it may. But I dissent, believing that such a law prohibits the free exercise of religion.

The first question to be resolved, however, is somewhat broader than the facts of this case. That question concerns the appropriate standard of constitutional adjudication in cases in which a statute is assertedly in conflict with the First Amendment, whether that limitation applies of its own force, or as absorbed through the less definite words of the Fourteenth Amendment. The Court in such cases is not confined to the narrow inquiry whether the challenged law is rationally related to some legitimate legislative end. Nor is the case decided by a finding that the State's interest is substantial and important, as well as rationally justifiable. This canon of adjudication was clearly stated by Mr. *Justice* JACKSON, speaking for the Court in *West Virginia State Board of Education* v. *Barnette:*

"In weighing arguments of the parties it is important to distinguish between the due process clause of the Fourteenth Amendment as an instrument for ⊥**612** transmitting the principles of the First Amendment and those cases in which it is applied for its own sake. The test of legislation which collides with the Fourteenth Amendment, because it also collides with the principles of the First, is much more definite than the test when only the Fourteenth is involved. Much of the vagueness of the due process clause disappears when the specific prohibitions of the First become its standard. The right of a State to regulate, for example, a public utility may well include, so far as the due process test is concerned, power to impose all of the restrictions which a legislature may have a 'rational basis' for adopting. But freedoms of speech and of press, of assembly, and of worship may not be infringed on such slender grounds. They are susceptible of restriction only to prevent grave and immediate danger to interests which the State may lawfully protect. It is important to note that while it is the Fourteenth Amendment which bears directly upon the State it is the more specific limiting principles of the First Amendment that finally govern this case."

This exacting standard has been consistently applied by this Court as the test of legislation under all cases of the First Amendment, not only those specifically dealing with freedom of speech and of the press. For religious freedom—the freedom to believe and to practice strange and, it may be, foreign creeds—has classically been one of the highest values of our society. Even the most concentrated and fully articulated attack on this high standard has seemingly admitted its validity in principle, while ⊥**613** deploring some incidental phraseology. The honored place of religious freedom in our constitutional hierarchy, suggested long ago by the argument of counsel in *Permoli* v. *Municipality No. 1 of the City of New Orleans* and foreshadowed by a prescient footnote in *United States* v. *Carolene Products Co.* must now be taken to be settled. Or at least so it appeared until today. For in this case the Court seems to say, without so much as a deferential nod towards that high place which we have accorded religious freedom in the past, that any substantial state interest will justify encroachments on religious practice, at least if those encroachments are cloaked in the guise of some nonreligious public purpose.

Admittedly, these laws do not compel overt affirmation of a repugnant belief, as in *Barnette*, nor do they prohibit outright any of appellants' religious practices, as did the federal law upheld in *Reynolds* v. *United States* cited by the Court. That is, the laws do not say that appellants must work on Saturday. But their effect is that appellants may not simultaneously practice their religion and their trade, without being hampered by a substantial competitive disadvantage. Their effect is that no one may at one and the same time be an Orthodox Jew and compete effectively with his Sunday-observing fellow tradesmen. This clog upon the exercise of religion, this state-imposed burden on Orthodox Judaism, has exactly the same economic effect as a tax levied upon the sale of religious literature. And yet, such a tax, when applied in the form of an excise or license fee, was held invalid in *Follett* v. *Town of McCormick*. All this the Court, as I read its opinion, concedes.

What, then, is the compelling state interest which impels the Commonwealth of Pennsylvania to impede ⊥**614** appellants' freedom of worship? What overbalancing need is so weighty in the constitutional scale that it justifies this substantial, though indirect, limitation of appellants' freedom? It is not the desire to stamp out a practice deeply abhorred by society, such as polygamy, as in *Reynolds*, for the custom of resting one day a week is universally honored, as the Court has amply shown. Nor is it the State's traditional protection of children, as in *Prince* v. *Massachusetts* for appellants are reasoning and fully autonomous adults. It is not even the interest in seeing that everyone rests one day a week, for appellants' religion requires that they take such a rest. It is the mere convenience of having everyone rest on the same day. It is to defend this interest that the Court holds that a State need not follow the alternative route of granting an exemption for those who in good faith observe a day of rest other than Sunday.

It is true, I suppose, that the granting of such an exemption would make Sundays a little noisier, and the task of police and prosecutor a little more difficult. It is also true that a majority—21—of the 34 States which have general Sunday regulations have exemptions of this kind. We are not told that those States are significantly noisier, or that their police are significantly more burdened, than ⊥**615** Pennsylvania's. Even England, not under the compulsion of a written constitution, but simply influenced by considerations of fairness, has such an exemption for some activities. The Court conjures up several difficulties with such a system which seem to me more fanciful than real. Non-Sunday observers might get an unfair advantage, it is said. A similar contention against the draft exemption for conscientious objectors (another example of the exemption technique) was rejected with the observation that "its unsoundness is too apparent to require" discussion.

Selective Draft Law Cases. However widespread the complaint, it is legally baseless, and the State's reliance upon it cannot withstand a First Amendment claim. We are told that an official inquiry into the good faith with which religious beliefs are held might be itself unconstitutional. But this Court indicated otherwise in *United States* v. *Ballard*. Such an inquiry is no more an infringement of religious freedom than the requirement imposed by the Court itself in *McGowan* v. *Maryland*, decided this day, that a plaintiff show that his good-faith religious beliefs are hampered before he acquires standing to attack a statute under the Free Exercise Clause of the First Amendment. Finally, I find the Court's mention of a problem under state anti-discrimination statutes almost chimerical. Most such statutes provide that hiring may be made on a religious basis if religion is a *bona fide* occupational qualification. It happens, moreover, that Pennsylvania's statute has such a provision.

In fine, the Court, in my view, has exalted administrative convenience to a constitutional level high enough to ⊥**616** justify making one religion economically disadvantageous. The Court would justify this result on the ground that the effect on religion, though substantial, is indirect. The Court forgets, I think, a warning uttered during the congressional discussion of the First Amendment itself: ". . . the rights of conscience are, in their nature, of peculiar delicacy, and will little bear the gentlest touch of governmental hand. . . ."

I would reverse this judgment and remand for a trial of appellants' allegations, limited to the free-exercise-of-religion issue.

Mr. *Justice* STEWART, dissenting.

I agree with substantially all that Mr. *Justice* BRENNAN has written. Pennsylvania has passed a law which compels an Orthodox Jew to choose between his religious faith and his economic survival. That is a cruel choice. It is a choice which I think no State can constitutionally demand. For me this is not something that can be swept under the rug and forgotten in the interest of enforced Sunday togetherness. I think the impact of this law upon these appellants grossly violates their constitutional right to the free exercise of their religion.

ESTATE OF THORNTON v. CALDOR, INC.

472 U.S. 703

ON WRIT OF CERTIORARI TO THE SUPREME COURT OF CONNECTICUT

Argued November 7, 1984 — Decided June 26, 1985

⊥**704** *Chief Justice* BURGER delivered the opinion of the Court.

We granted certiorari to decide whether a state statute that provides employees with the absolute right not to work ⊥**705** on their chosen Sabbath violates the Establishment Clause of the First Amendment.

I

In early 1975, petitioner's decedent Donald E. Thornton began working for respondent Caldor, Inc., a chain of New England retail stores; he managed the men's and boys' clothing department in respondent's Waterbury, Connecticut, store. At that time, respondent's Connecticut stores were closed on Sundays pursuant to state law. Conn. Gen. Stat. §§ 53—300 to 53—303 (1958).

In 1977, following the state legislature's revision of the Sunday-closing laws, respondent opened its Connecticut stores for Sunday business. In order to handle the expanded store hours, respondent required its managerial employees to work every third or fourth Sunday. Thornton, a Presbyterian who observed Sunday as his Sabbath, initially ⊥**706** complied with respondent's demand and worked a total of 31 Sundays in 1977 and 1978. In October 1978, Thornton was transferred to a management position in respondent's Torrington store; he continued to work on Sundays during the first part of 1979. In November 1979, however, Thornton informed respondent that he would no longer work on Sundays because he observed that day as his Sabbath; he invoked the protection of Conn. Gen. Stat. § 53—303e(b) (Supp. 1962-1984), which provides: "No person who states that a particular day of the week is observed as his Sabbath may be required by his employer to work on such day. An employee's refusal to work on his Sabbath shall not constitute grounds for his dismissal."

Thornton rejected respondent's offer either to transfer him to a management job in a Massachusetts store that was closed on Sundays, or to transfer him to a nonsupervisory position in the Torrington store at a lower salary. In March 1980, respondent transferred Thornton to a clerical position in the Torrington store; Thornton resigned two days later ⊥**707** and filed a grievance with the State Board of Mediation and Arbitration alleging that he was discharged from his manager's position in violation of Conn. Gen. Stat. § 53—303e(b).

Respondent defended its action on the ground that Thornton had not been "discharged" within the meaning of the statute; respondent also urged the Board to find that the statute violated Article 7 of the Connecticut Constitution as well as the Establishment Clause of the First Amendment. After holding an evidentiary hearing the Board evaluated the sincerity of Thornton's claim and concluded it was based on a sincere religious conviction; it issued a formal decision sustaining Thornton's grievance. The Board framed the statutory issue as follows, "[i]f a discharge for refusal to work Sunday hours occurred and Sunday was the Grievant's Sabbath . . . ," § 53—303e(b) would be violated; the Board held that respondent had violated the statute by "discharg[ing] Mr. Thornton as a management employee for refusing to work . . . [on] Thornton's . . . Sabbath." The Board ordered respondent to reinstate Thornton with back pay and compensation for lost fringe benefits. The Superior Court, in affirming that ruling, concluded that the statute did not offend the Establishment Clause.

The Supreme Court of Connecticut reversed, holding the statute did not have a "clear secular purpose." By authorizing each employee to designate his own Sabbath as a day off, the statute evinced the "unmistakable purpose . . . [of] allow[ing] those persons who wish to worship on a particular day the freedom to do so." The court then held that the "primary effect" of the statute was to advance **⊥708** religion because the statute "confers its 'benefit' on an explicitly religious basis. Only those employees who designate a Sabbath are entitled not to work on that particular day, and may not be penalized for so doing." The court noted that the statute required the State Mediation Board to decide which religious activities may be characterized as an "observance of Sabbath" in order to assess employees' sincerity, and concluded that this type of inquiry is "exactly the type of 'comprehensive, discriminating and continuing state surveillance' . . . which creates excessive governmental entanglements between church and state." We granted certiorari. We affirm.

II

Under the Religion Clauses, Government must guard against activity that impinges on religious freedom, and must take pains not to compel people to act in the name of any religion. In setting the appropriate boundaries in Establishment Clause cases, the Court has frequently relied on our holding in *Lemon* for guidance, and we do so here. To pass constitutional muster under *Lemon* a statute must not only have a secular purpose and not foster excessive entanglement of government with religion, its primary effect must not advance or inhibit religion.

The Connecticut statute challenged here guarantees every employee, who "states that a particular day of the week is observed as his Sabbath," the right not to work on his chosen day. The State has thus decreed that those who observe a Sabbath any day of the week as a matter of religious conviction must be relieved of the duty to work on that day, no matter what burden or **⊥709** inconvenience this imposes on the employer or fellow workers. The statute arms Sabbath observers with an absolute and unqualified right not to work on whatever day they designate as their Sabbath.

In essence, the Connecticut statute imposes on employers and employees an absolute duty to conform their business practices to the particular religious practices of the employee by enforcing observance of the Sabbath the employee unilaterally designates. The State thus commands that Sabbath religious concerns automatically control over all secular interests at the workplace; the statute takes no account of the convenience or interests of the employer or those of other employees who do not observe a Sabbath. The employer and others must adjust their affairs to the command of the State whenever the statute is invoked by an employee.

There is no exception under the statute for special circumstances, such as the Friday Sabbath observer employed in an occupation with a Monday through Friday schedule—a school teacher, for example; the statute provides for no special consideration if a high percentage of an employer's workforce asserts rights to the same Sabbath. Moreover, there is no exception when honoring the dictates of Sabbath observers **⊥710** would cause the employer substantial economic burdens or when the employer's compliance would require the imposition of significant burdens on other employees required to work in place of the Sabbath observers. Finally, the statute allows for no consideration as to whether the employer has made reasonable accommodation proposals.

This unyielding weighting in favor of Sabbath observers over all other interests contravenes a fundamental principle of the Religion Clauses, so well articulated by Judge Learned Hand: "The First Amendment . . . gives no one the right to insist that in pursuit of their own interests others must conform their conduct to his own religious necessities." *Otten* v. *Baltimore & Ohio R. Co.* As such, the statute goes beyond having an incidental or remote effect of advancing religion. The statute has a primary effect that impermissibly advances a particular religious practice.

III

We hold that the Connecticut statute, which provides Sabbath observers with an absolute and unqualified right not to **⊥711** work on their Sabbath, violates the Establishment Clause of the First Amendment. Accordingly, the judgment of the Supreme Court of Connecticut is affirmed.

Affirmed.

Justice REHNQUIST dissents.

Justice O'CONNOR, with whom *Justice* MARSHALL joins, concurring.

The court applies the test enunciated in *Lemon* v. *Kurtzman*, and concludes that Conn. Gen. Stat. § 53—303e(b) has a primary effect that impermissibly advances religion. I agree, and I join the Court's opinion and judgment. In my view, the Connecticut Sabbath law has an impermissible effect because it conveys a message of endorsement of the Sabbath observance.

All employees, regardless of their religious orientation, would value the benefit which the statute bestows on Sabbath observers—the right to select the day of the week in which to refrain from labor. Yet Connecticut requires private employers to confer this valued and desirable benefit only on those employees who adhere to a particular religious belief. The statute singles out Sabbath observers for special and, as the Court concludes, absolute protection without according similar accommodation to ethical and religious beliefs and practices of other private employees. There can be little doubt that an objective observer or the public at large would perceive this statutory scheme precisely as the Court does today. The message conveyed is one of endorsement of a particular religious belief, to the detriment of those who do not share it. As such, the Connecticut statute has the effect of advancing religion, and cannot withstand Establishment Clause scrutiny.

I do not read the Court's opinion as suggesting that the religious accommodation provisions of Title VII of the Civil Rights Act are similarly invalid. These provisions preclude employment discrimination based on a person's reli⊥**712**gion and require private employers to reasonably accommodate the religious practices of employees unless to do so would cause undue hardship to the employer's business. 42 U.S.C. § 2000e(j) and 2000e—2(a)(1). Like the Connecticut Sabbath law, Title VII attempts to lift a burden on religious practice that is imposed by *private* employers, and hence it is not the sort of accommodation statute specifically contemplated by the Free Exercise Clause. The provisions of Title VII must therefore manifest a valid secular purpose and effect to be valid under the Establishment Clause. In my view, a statute outlawing employment discrimination based on race, color, religion, sex, or national origin has the valid secular purpose of assuring employment opportunity to all groups in our pluralistic society. Since Title VII calls for reasonable rather than absolute accommodation and extends that requirement to all religious beliefs and practices rather than protecting only the Sabbath observance, I believe an objective observer would perceive it as an anti-discrimination law rather than an endorsement of religion or a particular religious practice.

RELIGION AND LABOR RELATIONS

In recent years religious spokesmen have frequently expressed grave concern with respect to what they consider to be excessive intrusion by government into the affairs of religious organizations and their agencies. As the comment and cases in this book indicate, this intervention has taken many forms: use of the taxing power to aid or disadvantage religious groups, requirement of submission of voluminous forms and reports, regulation of religious fund-raising activities, even infiltration of church groups by government agents in an effort to destroy the sanctuary movement.

Some few cases have reached the Supreme Court with respect to government intervention in what, broadly viewed, might be designated religion and labor relations. They raised in various ways the question of the part that government may play in the regulation of religious organizations and those who work for them.

NATIONAL LABOR RELATIONS BOARD v. THE CATHOLIC BISHOP OF CHICAGO (1979) concerned unionization of lay teachers in schools controlled by the Catholic church. When unions sought to represent lay teachers in schools involved in this litigation, the NLRB ordered representation elections. Catholic school authorities insisted that the NLRB lacked jurisdiction to intervene in the dispute. For the NLRB to claim otherwise, they argued, would impermissibly entangle a government agency in religious matters. When elections were held and the parochial schools refused to bargain with unions chosen by lay teachers, the NLRB found the schools guilty of unfair labor practices. Subsequently, these schools challenged the NLRB order to bargain. In resulting litigation, a federal court of appeals found in favor of the Catholic schools. The Seventh Circuit Court of Appeals, on constitutional grounds, held that the National Labor Relations Act violated the First Amendment's religion clauses when applied to parochial school teachers.

The Supreme Court, on appeal, also recognized that NLRB jurisdiction over parochial schools would raise difficult constitutional questions, but there was a legitimate prior question as to whether that jurisdiction existed. Traditionally, the Court has insisted that an act of Congress ought not be construed to violate the Constitution if statutory construction will suffice; thus, the Court examined the legislative history of the National Labor Relations Act. Careful analysis convinced five justices that Congress had not intended church-operated schools to be covered by the statute. Consequently, they ruled that the NLRB did not have authority to order Catholic schools to bargain with unions representing lay teachers. By dealing with this case at the statutory level the Court was able to avoid the more difficult question of whether the NLRB's action amounted to excessive governmental entanglement forbidden by the Establishment Clause.

From 1978 to 1980, the Supreme Court heard three more NLRB cases with titles that suggest church-state controversies, but which were not decided on that basis. In *National Labor Relations Board* v. *Baptist Hospital* and *Beth Israel Hospital* v. *National Labor Relations Board,* the Court ruled that the NLRB is empowered to issue rules governing places where hospital employees may solicit coworkers on behalf of labor organizations. Such places include gift shops, employee cafeterias, and the first-floor waiting rooms. However, the Court ruled that the NLRB could not compel hospitals to permit solicitation in areas where patients would be affected, such as corridors and waiting rooms on floors where patients are cared for.

Although *Baptist Hospital* and *Beth Israel Hospital* involved work rules in institutions related to religious organizations, this litigation had nothing to do with First Amendment issues. A similar case is that of *National Labor Relations Board* v. *Yeshiva University.* Here, faculty members were seeking to unionize and to bargain with the Jewish university, which refused to bargain. The Court agreed with university administrators that all full-time Yeshiva faculty members could be classified as "managerial employees" and were not covered by the NLRA; thus, the university could not be compelled to bargain under NLRB rules.

In 1980 a variation of the situation in *Catholic Bishop* was involved in *National Labor Relations Board* v. *Bishop Ford Central Catholic High School.* There a Catholic high school was governed by lay trustees of an independent corporation, although the Christian mission of the school was obvious. When the NLRB claimed authority over labor disputes at the school, a federal court of appeals held that, notwithstanding the governing structure, the school carried out its services as a "church operated" agency, and therefore, as the Court had held in *Catholic Bishop,* was not subject to the authority of the NLRB. The Supreme Court let the lower court decision stand without opinion.

Three years later the United States District Court for the Southern District of New York heard a case which arose when the Lay Faculty Association, representing 343 lay teachers employed by the Catholic High School Association, filed charges with the New York State Labor Relations Board alleging unfair labor practices by the association. The Catholic High School Association sought a declaratory judgment from the Court that the State Labor Relations Board's assertion of jurisdiction over it constituted both a burden on its free exercise of religion and an excessive entanglement of church and state under the Establishment Clause.

District Judge Lasker found no basic differences in the fact situation here and that of the *Catholic Bishop* case except that the labor board here was a state rather than federal agency and that the New York statute was unquestionably intended to cover parochial school–lay teacher labor relations. Both parties agreed to the religious character of the schools and that they were "church-operated" as the term was used in *Catholic Bishop.* The constitutional issue was therefore clear.

The district judge found it unnecessary to determine whether the act violated the Free Exercise Clause. In light of the clear violation of the Establishment Clause the type and extent of state scrutiny required to monitor lay faculty employment conditions would inevitably result in excessive entanglement between church and state. The Constitution, said Judge Lasker, "does limit the kind and degree of state scrutiny of religious practices." The teachers' union appealed to the Court of Appeals for the Second Circuit, which examined both the free exercise and establishment issues, and by a two-to-one vote reversed the lower court's decision. It held that the indirect and incidental burden imposed on religion by the government's intervention was justified by a compelling state interest in collective bargaining. With respect to the constraints of the Establishment Clause, the court failed to find a degree of government surveillance sufficient to justify a charge of administrative entanglement. The primary goal of government in collective bargaining is to bring the parties to the bargaining table and then leave them to work out their problems. The fact that the board would necessarily be precluded by the First Amendment from looking into asserted religious motives does not preclude its exercise of jurisdiction. By limiting the board to the protection of teachers from unlawful discharge for nonreligiously motivated causes, the court had satisfactorily accommodated the interests of church and state. Using the analogy of keeping the camel's nose out of the tent, the majority opinion held that the accommodation "firmly tethers the State Board's jurisdiction outside the constitutional tent that protects the Association's First Amendment rights."[1] The Supreme Court may at a later time have an opportunity to examine this assessment.

In the mid-1970s, officials of church-related colleges and universities complained bitterly about oppressive, time-consuming federal regulations and reports. Several federal agencies undertook to require church-related agencies and institutions, even including theological seminaries, to report employment and admissions statistics by race, sex and religion, even though they received no government funds. Two examples gained notoriety in the early 1980s. In *Mississippi College* v. *Equal Employment Opportunity Commission,* the college, owned and operated by the Mississippi Baptist Convention, resisted the government agency's command to supply personnel data. A female part-time instructor, not a Baptist, was passed over for a position when the college hired a male Baptist instead. She filed a grievance with EEOC, claiming discrimination. EEOC requested detailed information on Mississippi College's hiring practices to determine if the college had violated the female's rights. College authorities refused to supply the information, claiming that the government's demand for information promoted entanglement of government with religion and violated the college's religious freedom to prefer Baptist instructors. The Fifth Court of Appeals, reversing the lower court, found against Mississippi College. The Supreme Court allowed that decision to stand.

The other example involves Southwestern Baptist Theological seminary in Fort Worth, Texas. Under EEOC regulations, all institutions of higher learning with fifteen or more employees are required to file form EEO-6, which requests data on the compensation, tenure, race, sex, and national origin of employees. Beginning in 1975, the seminary refused to file

[1] *Catholic High School Association of the Archdiocese of New York* v. *Culvert* 753 F.2d 1161, 1169 (1985).

the form on the grounds that the presumed jurisdiction of EEOC over the seminary violated the religion clauses of the First Amendment. EEOC sued the seminary to compel compliance. The federal district court ruled in favor of the seminary, saying that EEOC did not have jurisdiction over the school, a wholly religious entity. The Court of Appeals for the Fifth Circuit agreed in 1981 that the seminary has the status of a church and consequently those who teach or have supervision of teaching are ministers. It ruled that EEOC data does not have to be reported on them, but nonteaching personnel (support people and administrators) are not ministers, according to the Court of Appeals, and are subject to EEOC jurisdiction. (*Southwestern Baptist Theological Seminary* v. *Equal Employment Opportunity Commission*.) The seminary, which represented all six Southern Baptist seminaries in the litigation, disagreed with this opinion and early in 1982 asked the Supreme Court to consider the case, but the Court denied review.

In 1977 the Secretary of Labor brought an action in the United States District Court for the Western District of Arkansas against the Tony and Susan Alamo Foundation, a nonprofit religious corporation which operated a number of commercial businesses ranging from hog farms and candy production to retail clothing and motels. These businesses were staffed primarily by "associates," most of whom were former drug addicts, derelicts, or criminals receiving as pay in-kind benefits such as food, clothing, shelter, and medical benefits rather than cash. In the suit the associates asserted that they considered themselves to be volunteers working "only for religious and evangelical reasons."

The suit alleged violations by the foundation of the minimum wage, overtime, and recordkeeping provisions of the Fair Labor Standards Act. The district court held the foundation to be an enterprise, though nonprofit in nature, "engaged in ordinary commercial activities in competition with other commercial businesses." The associates were "employees" within the meaning of the FLSA, although receiving wages in another form than cash, and the foundation was therefore subject to the Act.

The court denied the claim that application of the Act to the foundation violated the Free Exercise and Establishment Clauses. The Eighth Court of Appeals subsequently also rejected the claim; the Supreme Court granted certiorari, and, after hearing, affirmed the decisions of the lower courts, *Alamo Foundation* v. *Secretary of Labor* (1985).

Justice White delivered the opinion for a unanimous Court. He agreed with the court of appeals that it was difficult to conclude that the extensive commercial enterprise of the foundation was "nothing but a religious liturgy engaged in bringing good news to a pagan world," and said that "by entering the economic arena and trafficking in the marketplace, the foundation has subjected itself to the standards Congress has prescribed for the benefit of employees" (471 U.S. 290, 294). The mixture of religious motivations with commercial objectives does not justify the payment of substandard wages nor alter the effect of a business on interstate commerce. The Fair Labor Standards Act does not expressly or by implication grant exemption to commercial activities carried on by religious organizations, and has been consistently so interpreted by the Secretary of Labor.

Justice White did not find that inclusion in the program actually burdened the free exercise of the religious rights of the claimants or resulted in excessive government entanglement in the affairs of the religious foundation. The recordkeeping requirements particularly objected to by the foundation as fostering excessive entanglement applied only to the foundation's commercial activities and would have no effect on evangelical activities. The Establishment Clause, he noted, does not exempt religious organizations from such governmental actions as fire inspections and zoning and building laws, and the FLSA's recordkeeping requirements, "while perhaps more burdensome in terms of paperwork, are not significantly more intrusive into religious affairs."

In 1972 Congress amended Section 702 of the Civil Rights Act of 1964 to exempt religious organizations from Title VII's prohibition against discrimination in employment on the basis of religion. In 1987 in CHURCH OF JESUS CHRIST OF LATTER-DAY SAINTS v. AMOS the Court was confronted with the question of whether application of that exemption to secular nonprofit activities of religious organizations violated the Establishment Clause.

The issue was first brought to the United States District Court for the District of Utah by a Mr. Mayson who, after working at the Deseret Gymnasium, a nonprofit organization owned and operated by the Corporation of the Presiding Bishop of The Church of Jesus Christ of Latter-day Saints, was dismissed in 1981 because he had not qualified for a "temple recommend." A recommend is a certificate issued to those who meet the standards of the Church and as members of the Church are eligible to attend its temples.

Mayson and others brought suit in the district court claiming that Section 702, if interpreted to allow religious employers to discriminate on religious grounds in hiring for nonreligious jobs, violated the Establishment Clause. The district court found, as Mayson contended, that the activity in which he worked was nonreligious. It then utilized the *Lemon* test and held that Section 702 was unconstitutional as applied to secular activities because it had the primary effect of advancing religion. The section of the statute, the court said, impermissibly sponsored religious organizations by granting them an "exclusive authorization to engage in conduct which can directly and immediately advance religious tenets and practices."

Appeal was taken to the Supreme Court, which ruled unanimously that Section 702, as amended, did not violate the Establishment Clause. Justice White, writing for the Court, agreed that religious organizations were better able to advance their purposes after passage of the 1972 exemption amendment, but many laws upheld by the Court in past decisions had given special consideration to religious groups. "A law is not unconstitutional," he wrote, "simply because it *allows* churches to advance religion, which is their very purpose. For a law to have forbidden 'effects' under *Lemon,* it must be fair to say that the *government itself* has advanced religion through its own activities and influence" (483 U.S. 331, 337). He found the statute in question to meet the challenge of all three prongs of the *Lemon* test. Quoting from *Walz,* he said, "There is ample room under the Establishment Clause for 'benevolent neutrality' which will permit religious exercise to exist without sponsorship and without interference."

He refused to accept the argument that the law violated equal protection principles by allowing religious employers greater freedom to discriminate than secular employers, and therefore should be judged under the "strict scrutiny" test rather than *Lemon.* He dismissed the contention saying, "In cases such as these, where a statute is neutral on its face and motivated by a permissible purpose of limiting governmental interference with the exercise of religion, we see no justification for applying strict scrutiny to a statute that passes the *Lemon* test" (483 U.S. 338, 339). The section in question legitimately sought to limit interference by government with efforts of religious groups to "define and carry out their religious missions."

Justice Brennan, joined by Justice Marshall, concurred in the judgment, but emphasized the danger to the religious liberty of employees and prospective employees posed by the exemption. Ideally, religious organizations should be able to discriminate *only* with regard to religious activities. However, he recognized another obvious danger of government interference and entanglement should agents of government seek to distinguish religious and secular activities.

Justice O'Connor also wrote a concurring opinion with which Justice Blackmun agreed. As she had in earlier cases, she questioned the use of the *Lemon* test in Establishment Clause litigation. She expressed her preference for the simpler test of "whether government's purpose is to endorse religion and whether the statute actually conveys a message of endorsement." She saw this statute as a legitimate accommodation of religion rather than an endorsement. Justice Blackmun joined her in letting it be known that they understood that the question of constitutionality of the application of the exemption to for-profit activities of religious organizations was not involved here and remained open.

As can be seen, the Court has, with respect to questions concerning labor and religion, avoided constitutional issues where possible, and has been resistant to government intervention except where the religious organization involved is rather clearly engaged in commercial activities in competition with other commercial businesses and the challenged government regulations impose a minimum burden. This is a relatively new area of law; tension and controversy will likely continue to increase as government regulation becomes ever more pervasive.

NATIONAL LABOR RELATIONS BOARD v. THE CATHOLIC BISHOP OF CHICAGO

440 U.S. 490
ON WRIT OF CERTIORARI TO THE UNITED STATES COURT OF APPEALS FOR THE SEVENTH CIRCUIT
Argued October 30, 1978 — Decided March 21, 1979

⊥491 Mr. *Chief Justice BURGER* delivered the opinion of the Court.

This case arises out of the National Labor Relations Board's exercise of jurisdiction over lay faculty members at two groups of Catholic high schools. We granted certiorari to consider two questions: (a) Whether teachers in schools operated by a church to teach both religious and secular subjects are within the jurisdiction granted by the National Labor Relations Act; and (b) if the Act authorizes such jurisdiction, does its exercise violate the guarantees of the Religion Clauses of the First Amendment?

⊥492 I

One group of schools is operated by the Catholic Bishop of Chicago, a corporation sole; the other group is operated by the Diocese of Fort Wayne-South Bend, Inc. The group operated by the Catholic Bishop of Chicago consists of two schools, Quigley North and Quigley South. Those schools are termed "minor seminaries" because of their role in educating high school students who may become priests. At one time, only students who manifested a positive and confirmed desire to be priests were admitted to the Quigley schools. In 1970, the requirement was changed so that students admitted to these schools need not show a definite inclination toward the priesthood. Now the students need only be recommended by their parish priest as having a potential for the priesthood or for Christian leadership. The schools continue to provide special religious instruction not offered in other Catholic secondary schools. The Quigley schools also offer essentially the same college-preparatory curriculum as public secondary schools.

Their students participate in a variety of extracurricular activities which include secular as well as religious events. The schools are recognized by the State and accredited by a regional educational organization.

The Diocese of Fort Wayne-South Bend, Inc., has five high schools. Unlike the Quigley schools, the special recom⊥**493**mendation of a priest is not a prerequisite for admission. Like the Quigley schools, however, these high schools seek to provide a traditional secular education but oriented to the tenets of the Roman Catholic faith; religious training is also mandatory. These schools are similarly certified by the State.

In 1974 and 1975, separate representation petitions were filed with the Board by interested union organizations for both the Quigley and the Fort Wayne-South Bend schools; representation was sought only for lay teachers. The schools challenged the assertion of jurisdiction on two grounds: (a) that they do not fall within the Board's discretionary jurisdictional criteria; and (b) that the Religion Clauses of the First Amendment preclude the Board's jurisdiction. The Board rejected the jurisdictional arguments on the basis of its decision in *Roman Catholic Archdiocese of Baltimore*. There the Board explained that its policy was to decline jurisdiction over religiously sponsored organizations "only when they are completely religious, not just religiously associated." Because neither group of schools was found to fall within the Board's "completely religious" category, the Board ordered elections. *Catholic Bishop of Chicago*.

⊥**494** In the Board-supervised election at the Quigley schools, the Quigley Education Alliance, a union affiliated with the Illinois Education Association, prevailed and was certified as the exclusive bargaining representative for 46 lay teachers. In the Diocese of Fort Wayne-South Bend, the Community Alliance for Teachers of Catholic High Schools, a similar union organization, prevailed and was certified as the representative for the approximately 180 lay teachers. Notwithstanding the Board's order, the schools declined to recognize the unions or to bargain. The unions filed unfair labor practice complaints with the Board under §§ 8(a)(1) and (5) of the National Labor Relations Act, 29 U.S.C. §§ 158(a)(1) and (5). The schools opposed the General Counsel's motion for summary judgment, again challenging the Board's exercise of jurisdiction over religious schools on both statutory and constitutional grounds.

The Board reviewed the record of previous proceedings and concluded that all of the arguments had been raised or could have been raised in those earlier proceedings. Since the arguments had been rejected previously, the Board granted summary judgment, holding that it had properly exercised its statutory discretion in asserting jurisdiction over these schools. The Board concluded that the schools had violated the Act and ordered that they cease their unfair labor practices and that they bargain collectively with the unions. *Catholic* ⊥**495** *Bishop of Chicago; Diocese of Fort Wayne-South Bend, Inc.*

II

The schools challenged the Board's orders in petitions to the Court of Appeals for the Seventh Circuit. That court denied enforcement of the Board's orders. The court considered the Board's actions in relation to its discretion in choosing to extend its jurisdiction only to religiously affiliated schools that were not "completely religious." It concluded that the Board had not properly exercised its discretion, because the Board's distinction between "completely religious" and "merely religiously associated" failed to provide a workable guide for the exercise of discretion:

"We find the standard itself to be a simplistic black or white, purported rule containing no borderline demarcation of where 'completely religious' takes over or, on the other hand, ceases. In our opinion the dichotomous 'completely religious—merely religiously associated' standard provides no workable guide to the exercise of discretion. The determination that an institution is so completely a religious entity as to exclude any viable secular components obviously implicates very sensitive questions of faith and tradition. See, *e.g.* [*Wisconsin* v.] *Yoder*."

The Court of Appeals recognized that the rejection of the Board's policy as to church-operated schools meant that the Board would extend its jurisdiction to all church-operated ⊥**496** schools. The court therefore turned to the question of whether the Board could exercise that jurisdiction, consistent with constitutional limitations. It concluded that both the Free Exercise Clause and the Establishment Clause of the First Amendment foreclosed the Board's jurisdiction. It reasoned that from the initial act of certifying a union as the bargaining agent for lay teachers the Board's action would impinge upon the freedom of church authorities to shape and direct teaching in accord with the requirements of their religion. It analyzed the Board's action in this way: "At some point, factual inquiry by courts or agencies into such matters [separating secular from religious training] would almost necessary raise First Amendment problems. If history demonstrates, as it does, that Roman Catholics founded an alternative school system for essentially religious reasons and continued to maintain them as an 'integral part of the religious mission of the Catholic Church,' *Lemon* v. *Kurtzman*, courts and agencies would be hard pressed to take official or judicial notice that these purposes were undermined or eviscerated by the determination to offer such secular subjects as mathematics, physics, chemistry, and English literature."

The court distinguished local regulations which required fire inspections or state laws mandating attendance, reasoning that they did not "have the clear inhibiting potential upon the relationship between teachers and employers with which the present Board order is directly concerned." The court held that interference with management prerogatives, found acceptable in an ordinary commercial setting, was not acceptable in an area protected by the First Amendment. "The real difficulty is found in the chilling aspect that the requirement of bargaining will impose on the exercise of the bishops' control of the religious mission of the schools."

III

⊥**497** The Board's assertion of jurisdiction over private schools is, as we noted earlier, a relatively recent development. Indeed, in 1951 the Board indicated that it would not exercise jurisdiction over nonprofit, educational institutions because to do so would not effectuate the purposes of the Act. *Trustees of Columbia University in the City of New York.* In 1970, however, the Board pointed to what it saw as an increased involvement in commerce by educational institutions and concluded that this required a different position on jurisdiction. In *Cornell University*, the Board overruled its *Columbia University* decision. *Cornell University* was followed by the assertion of jurisdiction over nonprofit, private secondary schools. *Shattuck School.* The Board now asserts jurisdiction over all private, nonprofit, educational institutions with gross annual revenues that meet its jurisdictional requirements whether they are secular or religious. See, *e.g.*, *Academia San Jorge* (advisory opinion stating that Board would not assert jurisdiction over Catholic educational institution which did not meet jurisdictional standards); *Windsor School, Inc.* (declining jurisdiction where private, proprietary school did not meet jurisdictional amounts).

The broad assertion of jurisdiction has not gone unchallenged. But the Board has rejected the contention that the Religion Clauses of the First Amendment bar the extension of its jurisdiction to church-operated schools. Where the Board has declined to exercise jurisdiction, it has done so only on the grounds of the employer's minimal impact on commerce. Thus, in *Association of Hebrew Teachers of Metropolitan Detroit*, the Board did not assert jurisdiction over the Association which offered ⊥**498** courses in Jewish culture in after-school classes, a nursery school, and a college. The Board termed the Association an "isolated instance of [an] atypical employer." It explained: "Whether an employer falls within a given 'class' of enterprise depends upon those of its activities which are predominant and give the employing enterprise its character. . . . [The] fact that an employer's activity . . . is dedicated to a sectarian religious purpose is not a sufficient reason for the Board to refrain from asserting jurisdiction." In the same year the Board asserted jurisdiction over an Association chartered by the State of New York to operate diocesan high schools. *Henry M. Hald High School Assn.* It rejected the argument that its assertion of jurisdiction would produce excessive governmental entanglement with religion. In the Board's view, the Association had chosen to entangle itself with the secular world when it decided to hire lay teachers.

When it ordered an election for the lay professional employees at five parochial high schools in Baltimore in 1975, the Board reiterated its belief that exercise of its jurisdiction is not contrary to the First Amendment: "[T]he Board's policy in the past has been to decline jurisdiction over similar institutions only when they are completely religious, not just religiously associated, and the Archdiocese concedes that instruction is not limited to religious subjects. That the Archdiocese seeks to provide an education based on Christian principles does not lead to a contrary conclusion. Most religiously associated institutions seek to operate in conformity with ⊥**499** their religious tenets." *Roman Catholic Archdiocese of Baltimore.*

The Board also rejected the First Amendment claims in *Cardinal Timothy Manning, Roman Catholic Archbishop of the Archdiocese of Los Angeles*: "Regulation of labor relations does not violate the First Amendment when it involves a *minimal intrusion* on religious conduct and is necessary to obtain [the Act's] objective." (Emphasis added.)

The Board thus recognizes that its assertion of jurisdiction over teachers in religious schools constitutes some degree of intrusion into the administration of the affairs of church-operated schools. Implicit in the Board's distinction between schools that are "completely religious" and those "religiously associated" is also an acknowledgment of some degree of entanglement. Because that distinction was measured by a school's involvement with commerce, however, and not by its religious association, it is clear that the Board never envisioned any sort of religious litmus test for determining when to assert jurisdiction. Nevertheless, by expressing its traditional jurisdictional standards in First Amendment terms, the Board has plainly recognized that intrusion into this area could run afoul of the Religion Clauses and hence preclude jurisdiction on constitutional grounds.

IV

That there are constitutional limitations on the Board's actions has been repeatedly recognized by this Court even while acknowledging the broad scope of the grant of jurisdiction. The First Amendment, of course, is a limitation on the power of Congress. Thus, if we were to conclude that the Act granted the challenged jurisdiction over these teachers we would be required to decide whether that was constitutionally permissible under the Religion Clauses of the First Amendment.

⊥**500** Although the respondents press their claims under the Religion Clauses, the question we consider first is whether Congress intended the Board to have jurisdiction over teachers in church-operated schools. In a number of cases the Court has heeded the essence of Mr. *Chief Justice* MARSHALL's admonition in *Murray* v. *The Charming Betsy*, by holding that an Act of Congress ought not be construed to violate the Constitution if any other possible construction remains available. Moreover, the Court has followed this policy in the interpretation of the Act now before us and related statutes.

In *Machinists* v. *Street*, for example, the Court considered claims that serious First Amendment questions would arise if the Railway Labor Act were construed to allow compulsory union dues to be used to support political candidates or causes not approved by some members. The Court looked to the language of the Act and the legislative history and concluded that they did not permit union dues to be used for such political purposes, thus avoiding "serious doubt of [the Act's] constitutionality."

Similarly in *McCulloch* v. *Sociedad Nacional de Marineros de Honduras*, a case involving the Board's assertion of jurisdiction over foreign seamen, the Court declined to read the National Labor Relations Act so as to give rise to a serious question of separation of powers which in turn would have implicated sensitive issues of the authority of the Executive over relations with foreign nations. The international implications of the case led the Court to describe it as involving "public questions particularly high in the scale of our national interest." Because of those questions the Court held that before sanctioning the Board's exercise of jurisdiction "'there must be present the affirmative intention of the Congress clearly expressed'" (quoting *Benz* v. *Compania Naviera Hidalgo*).

⊥501 The values enshrined in the First Amendment plainly rank high "in the scale of our national values." In keeping with the Court's prudential policy it is incumbent on us to determine whether the Board's exercise of its jurisdiction here would give rise to serious constitutional questions. If so, we must first identify "the affirmative intention of the Congress clearly expressed" before concluding that the Act grants jurisdiction.

V

In recent decisions involving aid to parochial schools we have recognized the critical and unique role of the teacher in fulfilling the mission of a church-operated school. What was said of the schools in *Lemon* v. *Kurtzman* is true of the schools in this case: "Religious authority necessarily pervades the school system." The key role played by teachers in such a school system has been the predicate for our conclusions that governmental aid channeled through teachers creates an impermissible risk of excessive governmental entanglement in the affairs of the church-operated schools. For example, in *Lemon* we wrote: "In terms of potential for involving some aspect of faith or morals *in secular subjects*, a textbook's content is ascertainable, but a teacher's handling of a subject is not. We cannot ignore the danger that a teacher under religious control and discipline poses to the separation of the religious from the purely secular aspects of pre-college education. The conflict of functions inheres in the situation." (Emphasis added.)

Only recently we again noted the importance of the teacher's function in a church school: "Whether the subject is 'remedial reading,' 'advanced reading,' or simply 'reading,' a teacher remains a teacher, and the danger that religious doctrine will become intertwined with secular instruction persists." *Meek* v. *Pittenger*. Cf. **⊥502** *Wolman* v. *Walter*. Good intentions by government—or third parties—can surely no more avoid entanglement with the religious mission of the school in the setting of mandatory collective bargaining than in the well-motivated legislative efforts consented to by the church-operated schools which we found unacceptable in *Lemon*, *Meek*, and *Wolman*.

The Board argues that it can avoid excessive entanglement since it will resolve only factual issues such as whether an anti-union animus motivated an employer's action. But at this stage of our consideration we are not compelled to determine whether the entanglement is excessive as we would were we considering the constitutional issue. Rather, we make a narrow inquiry whether the exercise of the Board's jurisdiction presents a significant risk that the First Amendment will be infringed.

Moreover, it is already clear that the Board's actions will go beyond resolving factual issues. The Court of Appeals' opinion refers to charges of unfair labor practices filed against religious schools. The court observed that in those cases the schools had responded that their challenged actions were mandated by their religious creeds. The resolution of such charges by the Board, in many instances, will necessarily involve inquiry into the good faith of the position asserted by the clergy-administrators and its relationship to the school's religious mission. It is not only the conclusions that may be reached by the Board which may impinge on rights guaranteed by the Religion Clauses, but also the very process of inquiry leading to findings and conclusions.

The Board's exercise of jurisdiction will have at least one other impact on church-operated schools. The Board will be called upon to decide what are "terms and conditions of **⊥503** employment" and therefore mandatory subjects of bargaining. Although the Board has not interpreted that phrase as it relates to educational institutions, similar state provisions provide insight into the effect of mandatory bargaining. The Oregon Court of Appeals noted that "nearly everything that goes on in the schools affects teachers and is therefore arguably a 'condition of employment.'" *Springfield Education Assn.* v. *Springfield School Dist. No. 19*.

The Pennsylvania Supreme Court aptly summarized the effect of mandatory bargaining when it observed that the "introduction of a concept of mandatory collective bargaining, regardless of how narrowly the scope of negotiation is defined, necessarily represents an encroachment upon the former autonomous position of management." *Pennsylvania Labor Relations Board* v. *State College Area School DST*. Inevitably the Board's inquiry will implicate sensitive issues that open the door to conflicts between clergy-administrators and the Board, or conflicts with negotiators for unions. What we said in *Lemon* applies as well here: "[p]arochial schools involve substantial religious activity and purpose.

"The substantial religious character of these church-related schools gives rise to entangling church-state relationships of the kind the Religion Clauses sought to avoid."

Mr. Justice DOUGLAS emphasized this in his concurring opinion in *Lemon*, noting "the admitted and obvious fact that the *raison d'être* of parochial schools is the propagation of a religious faith."

⊥**504** The church-teacher relationship in a church-operated school differs from the employment relationship in a public or other nonreligious school. We see no escape from conflicts flowing from the Board's exercise of jurisdiction over teachers in church-operated schools and the consequent serious First Amendment questions that would follow. We therefore turn to an examination of the National Labor Relations Act to decide whether it must be read to confer jurisdiction that would in turn require a decision on the constitutional claims raised by respondents.

VI

There is no clear expression of an affirmative intention of Congress that teachers in church-operated schools should be covered by the Act. Admittedly, Congress defined the Board's jurisdiction in very broad terms; we must therefore examine the legislative history of the Act to determine whether Congress contemplated that the grant of jurisdiction would include teachers in such schools.

In enacting the National Labor Relations Act in 1935, Congress sought to protect the right of American workers to bargain collectively. The concern that was repeated throughout the debates was the need to assure workers the right to organize to counterbalance the collective activities of employers which had been authorized by the National Industrial Recovery Act. But congressional attention focused on employment in private industry and on industrial recovery.

Our examination of the statute and its legislative history indicates that Congress simply gave no consideration to church-operated schools. It is not without significance, however, that the Senate Committee on Education and Labor chose a college professor's dispute with the college as an example of ⊥**505** employer-employee relations *not* covered by the Act.

Congress' next major consideration of the jurisdiction of the Board came during the passage of the Labor Management Relations Act of 1947—the Taft-Hartley Act. In that Act Congress amended the definition of "employer" in § 2 of the original Act to exclude nonprofit hospitals. There was some discussion of the scope of the Board's jurisdiction but the consensus was that nonprofit institutions in general did not fall within the Board's jurisdiction because they did not affect commerce.

The most recent significant amendment to the Act was passed in 1974, removing the exemption of nonprofit hospitals. The Board relies upon that amendment as showing that Congress approved the Board's exercise of jurisdiction over church-operated ⊥**506** schools. A close examination of that legislative history, however, reveals nothing to indicate an affirmative intention that such schools be within the Board's jurisdiction. Since the Board did not assert jurisdiction over teachers in a church-operated school until after the 1974 amendment, nothing in the history of the amendment can be read as reflecting Congress' tacit approval of the Board's action.

During the debate there were expressions of concern about the effect of the bill on employees of religious hospitals whose religious beliefs would not permit them to join a union. The result of those concerns was an amendment which reflects congressional sensitivity to First Amendment guarantees: "Any employee of a health care institution who is a member of and adheres to established and traditional tenets or teachings of a bona fide religion, body, or sect which has historically held conscientious objections to joining or facially supporting labor organizations shall not be required to join or financially support any labor organization as a condition of employment; except that such employee may be required, in lieu of periodic dues and initiation fees, to pay sums equal to such dues and initiation fees to a nonreligious charitable fund exempt from taxation under section 501(c)(3) of title 26, chosen by such employee from a list of at least three such funds, designated in a contract between such institution and a labor organization, or if the contract fails to designate such funds, then to any such fund chosen by the employee."

The absence of an "affirmative intention of the Congress clearly expressed" fortifies our conclusion that Congress did not contemplate that the Board would require church-operated schools to grant recognition to unions as bargaining agents for their teachers.

The Board relies heavily upon *Associated Press* v. *NLRB*. ⊥**507** There the Court held that the First Amendment was no bar to the application of the Act to the Associated Press, an organization engaged in collecting information and news throughout the world and distributing it to its members. Perceiving nothing to suggest that application of the Act would infringe First Amendment guarantees of press freedoms, the Court sustained Board jurisdiction. Here, on the contrary, the record affords abundant evidence that the Board's exercise of jurisdiction over teachers in church-operated schools would implicate the guarantees of the Religion Clauses.

Accordingly, in the absence of a clear expression of Congress' intent to bring teachers in church-operated schools within the jurisdiction of the Board, we decline to construe the Act in a manner that could in turn call upon the Court to resolve difficult and sensitive questions arising out of the guarantees of the First Amendment Religion Clauses.

Affirmed.

⊥**508** Mr. *Justice* BRENNAN, with whom Mr. *Justice* WHITE, Mr. *Justice* MARSHALL, and Mr. *Justice* BLACKMUN join, dissenting.

The Court today holds that coverage of the National Labor Relations Act does not extend to lay teachers employed by church-operated schools. That construction is plainly wrong in light of the Act's language, its legislative history, and this Court's precedents. It is justified solely on the basis of a canon of statutory construction seemingly invented by the Court for the purpose of deciding this case. I dissent.

I

The general principle of construing statutes to avoid unnecessary constitutional decisions is a well-settled and salutary ⊥**509** one. The governing canon, however, is not that expressed by the Court today. The Court requires that there be a "clear expression of an affirmative intention of Congress" before it will bring within the coverage of a broadly worded regulatory statute certain persons whose coverage might raise constitutional questions. But those familiar with the legislative process know that explicit expressions of congressional intent in such broadly inclusive statutes are not commonplace. Thus, by strictly or loosely applying its requirement, the Court can virtually remake congressional enactments. This flouts Mr. *Chief Justice* TAFT's admonition "that amendment may not be substituted for construction, and that a court may not exercise legislative functions to save [a] law from conflict with constitutional limitation." *Yu Cong Eng* v. *Trinidad.*

⊥**510** The settled canon for construing statutes wherein constitutional questions may lurk was stated in *Machinists* v. *Street,* cited by the Court: "'When the validity of an act of the Congress is drawn in question, and even if a serious doubt of constitutionality is raised, it is a cardinal principle that this Court will first ascertain whether a construction of the statute is *fairly possible* by which the question may be avoided.' *Crowell* v. *Benson*" (emphasis added).

This limitation to constructions that are "fairly possible," and "reasonable," see *Yu Cong Eng* v. *Trinidad,* acts as a ⊥**511** brake against wholesale judicial dismemberment of congressional enactments. It confines the judiciary to its proper role in construing statutes, which is to interpret them so as to give effect to congressional intention. The Court's new "affirmative expression" rule releases that brake.

II

The interpretation of the National Labor Relations Act announced by the Court today is not "fairly possible." The Act's wording, its legislative history, and the Court's own precedents leave "the intention of the Congress . . . revealed too distinctly to permit us to ignore it because of mere misgivings as to power." *Moore Ice Cream Co.* v. *Rose*. Section 2(2) of the Act, 29 U.S.C. § 152(2), defines "employer" as ". . . any person acting as an agent of an employer, directly or indirectly, but *shall not include* the United States or any wholly owned Government corporation, or any Federal Reserve Bank, or any State or political subdivision thereof, or any person subject to the Railway Labor Act, as amended from time to time, or any labor organization (other than when acting as an employer), or anyone acting in the capacity of officer or agent of such labor organization." (Emphasis added.)

Thus, the Act covers all employers not within the eight express exceptions. The Court today substitutes amendment for construction to insert one more exception—for church-operated schools. This is a particularly transparent violation of the judicial role: The legislative history reveals that Congress itself considered and rejected a very similar amendment.

The pertinent legislative history of the NLRA begins with the Wagner Act of 1935, 49 Stat. 449. Section 2(2) of that Act, identical in all relevant respects to the current section, excluded from its coverage neither church-operated schools ⊥**512** nor any other private nonprofit organization. Accordingly, in applying that Act, the National Labor Relations Board did not recognize an exception for nonprofit employers, even when religiously associated. An argument for an implied nonprofit exemption was rejected because the design of the Act was as clear then as it is now: "[N]either charitable institutions nor their employees are exempted from operation of the Act by its terms, although certain other employers and employees are exempted." *Central Dispensary & Emergency Hospital*. Both the lower courts and this Court concurred in the Board's construction.

The Hartley bill, which passed the House of Representa⊥**513**tives in 1947, would have provided the exception the Court today writes into the statute: "The term 'employer' . . . shall not include . . . any corporation, community chest, fund, or foundation organized and operated exclusively for *religious*, charitable, scientific, literary, or *educational* purposes, . . . no part of the net earnings of which inures to the benefit of any private shareholder or individual. . . ." (Emphasis added.)

But the proposed exception was not enacted. The bill reported by the Senate Committee on Labor and Public Welfare did not contain the Hartley exception. Instead, the Senate proposed an exception limited to nonprofit hospitals, and passed the bill in that form. The Senate version was accepted by the House in conference, thus limiting the exception ⊥**514** for nonprofit employers to nonprofit hospitals.

Even that limited exemption was ultimately repealed in 1974. In doing so, Congress confirmed the view of the Act expressed here: that it was intended to cover all employers—including nonprofit employers—unless expressly excluded, and that the 1947 amendment excluded only nonprofit hospitals. ⊥**515** Moreover, it is significant that in considering the 1974 amendments, the Senate expressly rejected an amendment proposed by Senator Ervin that was analogous to the one the

Court today creates—an amendment to exempt nonprofit hospitals operated by religious groups. Senator Cranston, floor manager of the Senate Committee bill and primary opponent of the proposed religious exception, explained: "[S]uch an exception for religiously affiliated hospitals would seriously erode *the existing national policy which holds religiously affiliated institutions generally such as* proprietary nursing homes, residential communities, and *educational facilities to the same standards as their nonsectarian counterparts*." (Emphasis added.)

⊥**516** In construing the Board's jurisdiction to exclude church-operated schools, therefore, the Court today is faithful to neither the statute's language nor its history. Moreover, it is also untrue to its own precedents. "This Court has consistently declared that in passing the National Labor Relations Act, Congress intended to and did vest in the Board the fullest *jurisdictional* breadth constitutionally permissible under the commerce Clause." *NLRB* v. *Reliance Fuel Oil Corp.* (emphasis in original). As long as an employer is within the reach of Congress' power under the Commerce Clause—and no one doubts that respondents are—the Court has held him to be covered by the Act regardless of the nature of his activity. Indeed, *Associated Press* v. *NLRB* construed the Act to ⊥**517** cover editorial employees of a nonprofit news-gathering organization despite a claim—precisely parallel to that made here—that their inclusion rendered the Act in violation of the First Amendment. Today's opinion is simply unable to explain the grounds that distinguish that case from this one.

Thus, the available authority indicates that Congress intended to include—not exclude—lay teachers of church-operated schools. The Court does not counter this with evidence that Congress *did* intend an exception it never stated. Instead, despite the legislative history to the contrary, it construes the Act as excluding lay teachers only because Congress did not state explicitly that they were covered. In Mr. *Justice CARDOZO's* words, this presses "avoidance of a ⊥**518** difficulty . . . to the point of disingenuous evasion." *Moore Ice Cream Co.* v. *Rose*.

III

Under my view that the NLRA includes within its coverage lay teachers employed by church-operated schools, the constitutional questions presented would have to be reached. I do not now do so only because the Court does not. I repeat for emphasis, however, that while the resolution of the constitutional question is not without difficulty, it is irresponsible to avoid it by a cavalier exercise in statutory interpretation which succeeds only in defying congressional intent. A statute is not "a nose of wax to be changed from that which the plain language imports. . . ." *Yu Cong Eng* v. *Trinidad*.

CHURCH OF JESUS CHRIST OF LATTER-DAY SAINTS v. AMOS

483 U.S. 327
ON APPEAL FROM THE UNITED STATES DISTRICT COURT FOR THE DISTRICT OF UTAH
Argued March 31, 1987 — Decided June 24, 1987

⊥**329** *Justice WHITE* delivered the opinion of the Court.

Section 702 of the Civil Rights Act of 1964, 78 Stat. 255, as amended, 42 U.S.C. § 2000e-1, exempts religious organizations from Title VII's prohibition against discrimination in employment on the basis of religion. The question pre⊥**330**sented is whether applying the § 702 exemption to the secular nonprofit activities of religious organizations violates the Establishment Clause of the First Amendment. The District Court held that it does, and these cases are here on direct appeal pursuant to 28 U.S.C. § 1252. We reverse.

I

The Deseret Gymnasium (Gymnasium) in Salt Lake City, Utah, is a nonprofit facility, open to the public, run by the Corporation of the Presiding Bishop of The Church of Jesus Christ of Latter-day Saints (CPB), and the Corporation of the President of The Church of Jesus Christ of Latter-day Saints (COP). The CPB and the COP are religious entities associated with The Church of Jesus Christ of Latter-day Saints (Church), an unincorporated religious association sometimes called the Mormon or LDS Church.

Appellee Mayson worked at the Gymnasium for some 16 years as an assistant building engineer and then as building engineer. He was discharged in 1981 because he failed to qualify for a temple recommend, that is, a certificate that he is a member of the Church and eligible to attend its temples.

⊥**331** Mayson and others purporting to represent a class of plaintiffs brought an action against the CPB and the COP alleging, among other things, discrimination on the basis of religion in violation of § 702 of the Civil Rights Act of 1964, 42 U.S.C. § 2000e-2. The defendants moved to dismiss this claim on the ground that § 702 shields them from liability. The plaintiffs contended that if construed to allow religious employers to discriminate on religious grounds in hiring for nonreligious jobs, § 702 violates the Establishment Clause.

The District Court first considered whether the facts of these cases require a decision on the plaintiffs' constitutional argument. Starting from the premise that the religious activities of religious employers can permissibly be exempted under § 702, the court developed a three-part test to determine whether an activity is religious. Applying this test to ⊥**332** Mayson's situation, the court found: first, that the Gymnasium is intimately connected to the Church financially and in matters of management; second, that there is no clear connection between the primary function which the Gymnasium performs and the religious beliefs and tenets of the Mormon Church or church administration; and third, that none of Mayson's duties at the Gymnasium are "even tangentially related to any conceivable religious belief or ritual of the Mormon Church or church administration." The court concluded that Mayson's case involves nonreligious activity.

The court next considered the plaintiffs' constitutional challenge to § 702. Applying the three-part test set out in *Lemon* v. *Kurtzman*, the court first held that § 702 has the permissible secular purpose of "assuring that the government remains neutral and does not meddle in religious affairs by interfering with the decision-making process in religions. . . ." ⊥**333** The court concluded, however, that § 702 fails the second part of the *Lemon* test because the provision has the primary effect of advancing religion. Among the considerations mentioned by the court were: that § 702 singles out religious entities for a benefit, rather than benefiting a broad grouping of which religious organizations are only a part; that § 702 is not supported by long historical tradition; and that § 702 burdens the free exercise rights of employees of religious institutions who work in nonreligious jobs. Finding that § 702 impermissibly sponsors religious organizations by granting them "an exclusive authorization to engage in conduct which can directly and immediately advance religious tenets and practices," the court declared the statute unconstitutional as applied to secular activity. The court entered summary judgment in favor of Mayson pursuant to Federal Rule of Civil Procedure 54(b) and ordered him reinstated with backpay. Subsequently, the court vacated its judg⊥**334**ment so that the United States could intervene to defend the constitutionality of § 702. After further briefing and argument the court affirmed its prior determination and reentered a final judgment for Mayson.

II

"This Court has long recognized that the government may (and sometimes must) accommodate religious practices and that it may do so without violating the Establishment Clause." *Hobbie* v. *Unemployment Appeals Comm'n of Fla.* It is well established, too, that "[t]he limits of permissible state accommodation to religion are by no means coextensive with the noninterference mandated by the Free Exercise Clause." *Walz* v. *Tax Comm'n*. There is ample room under the Establishment Clause for "benevolent neutrality which will permit religious exercise to exist without sponsorship and without interference." At some point, accommodation may devolve into "an unlawful ⊥**335** fostering of religion," *Hobbie*, but these are not such cases, in our view.

The private appellants contend that we should not apply the three-part *Lemon* approach, which is assertedly unsuited to judging the constitutionality of exemption statutes such as § 702. The argument is that an exemption statute will always have the effect of advancing religion and hence be invalid under the second (effects) part of the *Lemon* test, a result claimed to be inconsistent with cases such as *Walz* v. *Tax Comm'n*, which upheld property tax exemptions for religious organizations. The first two of the three *Lemon* factors, however, were directly taken from pre-*Walz* decisions and *Walz* did not purport to depart from prior Establishment Clause cases, except by adding a consideration that became the third element of the *Lemon* test. In any event, we need not reexamine *Lemon* as applied in this context, for the exemption involved here is in no way questionable under the *Lemon* analysis.

Lemon requires first that the law at issue serve a "secular legislative purpose." This does not mean that the law's purpose must be unrelated to religion—that would amount to a requirement "that the government show a callous indifference to religious groups," *Zorach* v. *Clauson*, and the Establishment Clause has never been so interpreted. Rather, *Lemon*'s "purpose" requirement aims at preventing the relevant governmental decisionmaker—in this case, Congress—from abandoning neutrality and acting with the intent of promoting a particular point of view in religious matters.

Under the *Lemon* analysis, it is a permissible legislative purpose to alleviate significant governmental interference with the ability of religious organizations to define and carry out their religious missions. Appellees argue that there is no such purpose here because § 702 provided adequate protection for religious employers prior to the 1972 amendment, ⊥**336** when it exempted only the religious activities of such employers from the statutory ban on religious discrimination. We may assume for the sake of argument that the pre-1972 exemption was adequate in the sense that the Free Exercise Clause required no more. Nonetheless, it is a significant burden on a religious organization to require it, on pain of substantial liability, to predict which of its activities a secular court will consider religious. The line is hardly a bright one, and an organization might understandably be concerned that a judge would not understand its religious tenets and sense of mission. Fear of potential liability might affect the way an organization carried out what it understood to be its religious mission.

After a detailed examination of the legislative history of the 1972 amendment, the District Court concluded that Congress' purpose was to minimize governmental "interfer[ence] with the decision-making process in religions." We agree with the District Court that this purpose does not violate the Establishment Clause.

The second requirement under *Lemon* is that the law in question have "a principal or primary effect . . . that neither advances nor inhibits religion." Undoubtedly, religious organizations are better able now to advance their purposes than they were prior to the 1972 amendment to § 702. But religious groups have been better able to advance their purposes on account of many laws that have passed constitutional muster: for example, the property tax exemption at issue in *Walz* v. *Tax Comm'n* or the loans of school books to school children, including parochial school students, upheld in *Board of Education* v. *Allen*. **⊥337** A law is not unconstitutional simply because it *allows* churches to advance religion, which is their very purpose. For a law to have forbidden "effects" under *Lemon*, it must be fair to say that the *government itself* has advanced religion through its own activities and influence. As the Court observed in *Walz*, "[F]or the men who wrote the religion Clauses of the First Amendment the 'establishment' of a religion connoted sponsorship, financial support, and active involvement of the sovereign in religious activity."

The District Court appeared to fear that sustaining the exemption would permit churches with financial resources impermissibly to extend their influence and propagate their faith by entering the commercial, profit-making world. The cases before us, however, involve a nonprofit activity instituted over 75 years ago in the hope that "all who assemble here, and who come for the benefit of their health, and for physical blessings, [may] feel that they are in a house dedicated to the Lord." Dedicatory Prayer for the Gymnasium. These cases therefore do not implicate the apparent concerns of the District Court. Moreover, we find no persuasive evidence in the record before us that the Church's ability to propagate its religious doctrine through the Gymnasium is any greater now than it was prior to the passage of the Civil Rights Act in 1964. In such circumstances, we do not see how any advancement of religion achieved by the Gymnasium can be fairly attributed to the Government, as opposed to the Church.

⊥338 We find unpersuasive the District Court's reliance on the fact that § 702 singles out religious entities for a benefit. Although the Court has given weight to this consideration in its past decisions, it has never indicated that statutes that give special consideration to religious groups are *per se* invalid. That would run contrary to the teaching of our cases that there is ample room for accommodation of religion under the Establishment Clause. Where, as here, government acts with the proper purpose of lifting a regulation that burdens the exercise of religion, we see no reason to require that the exemption come packaged with benefits to secular entities.

We are also unpersuaded by the District Court's reliance on the argument that § 702 is unsupported by long historical tradition. There was simply no need to consider the scope of the § 702 exemption until the 1964 Civil Rights Act was passed, and the fact that Congress concluded after eight years that the original exemption was unnecessarily narrow is a decision entitled to deference, not suspicion.

Appellees argue that § 702 offends equal protection principles by giving less protection to the employees of religious employers than to the employees of secular employers. Appellees rely on *Larson* v. *Valente*, **⊥339** for the proposition that a law drawing distinctions on religious grounds must be strictly scrutinized. But *Larson* indicates that laws discriminating *among* religions are subject to strict scrutiny and that laws "affording a uniform benefit to *all* religions" should be analyzed under *Lemon*. In a case such as this, where a statute is neutral on its face and motivated by a permissible purpose of limiting governmental interference with the exercise of religion, we see no justification for applying strict scrutiny to a statute that passes the *Lemon* test. The proper inquiry is whether Congress has chosen a rational classification to further a legitimate end. We have already indicated that Congress acted with a legitimate purpose in expanding the § 702 exemption to cover all activities of religious employers. To dispose of appellees' equal protection argument, it suffices to hold—as we now do—that as applied to the nonprofit activities of religious employers, § 702 is rationally related to the legitimate purpose of alleviating significant governmental interference with the ability of religious organizations to define and carry out their religious missions.

It cannot be seriously contended that § 702 impermissibly entangles church and state; the statute effectuates a more complete separation of the two and avoids the kind of intrusive inquiry into religious belief that the District Court engaged in in this case. The statute easily passes muster under the third part of the *Lemon* test.

⊥340 The judgment of the District Court is reversed, and the cases are remanded for further proceedings consistent with this opinion.

It is so ordered.

Justice BRENNAN, with whom *Justice* MARSHALL joins, concurring in the judgment.

I write separately to emphasize that my concurrence in the judgment rests on the fact that these cases involve a challenge to the application of § 702's categorical exemption to the activities of a *nonprofit* organization. I believe that the particular character of nonprofit activity makes inappropriate a case-by-case determination whether its nature is religious or secular.

These cases present a confrontation between the rights of religious organizations and those of individuals. Any exemption from Title VII's proscription on religious discrimination necessarily has the effect of burdening the religious liberty of prospective and current employees. An exemption says that a person may be put to the choice of either conforming to certain religious tenets or losing a job opportunity, a promotion, or, as in this case, employment itself. **⊥341** The potential for coercion created by such a provision is in serious tension with our commitment to individual freedom of conscience in matters of religious belief.

At the same time, religious organizations have an interest in autonomy in ordering their internal affairs, so that they may be free to:

"select their own leaders, define their own doctrines, resolve their own disputes, and run their own institutions. Religion includes important communal elements for most believers. They exercise their religion through religious organizations, and these organizations must be protected by the [Free Exercise] [C]lause." Laycock, Toward a General Theory of the Religion Clauses: The ⊥**342** Case of Church Labor Relations, and the Right to Church Autonomy, 81 Colum. L. Rev. 1373, 1389 (1981). See also *Serbian Eastern Orthodox Diocese* v. *Milivojevich* (church has interest in effecting binding resolution of internal governance disputes); *Kedroff* v. *Saint Nicholas Cathedral* (state statute purporting to transfer administrative control from one church authority to another violates Free Exercise Clause). For many individuals, religious activity derives meaning in large measure from participation in a larger religious community. Such a community represents an ongoing tradition of shared beliefs, an organic entity not reducible to a mere aggregation of individuals. Determining that certain activities are in furtherance of an organization's religious mission, and that only those committed to that mission should conduct them, is thus a means by which a religious community defines itself. Solicitude for a church's ability to do so reflects the idea that furtherance of the autonomy of religious organizations often furthers individual religious freedom as well.

The authority to engage in this process of self-definition inevitably involves what we normally regard as infringement on free exercise rights, since a religious organization is able to condition employment in certain activities on subscription to particular religious tenets. We are willing to countenance the imposition of such a condition because we deem it vital that, if certain activities constitute part of a religious community's practice, then a religious organization should be able to ⊥**343** require that only members of its community perform those activities. This rationale suggests that, ideally, religious organizations should be able to discriminate on the basis of religion *only* with respect to religious activities, so that a determination should be made in each case whether an activity is religious or secular. This is because the infringement on religious liberty that results from conditioning performance of *secular* activity upon religious belief cannot be defended as necessary for the community's self-definition. Furthermore, the authorization of discrimination in such circumstances is not an accommodation that simply enables a church to gain members by the normal means of prescribing the terms of membership for those who seek to participate in furthering the mission of the community. Rather, it puts at the disposal of religion the added advantages of economic leverage in the secular realm. As a result, the authorization of religious discrimination with respect to nonreligious activities goes beyond reasonable accommodation, and has the effect of furthering religion in violation of the Establishment Clause.

What makes the application of a religious-secular distinction difficult is that the character of an activity is not self-evident. As a result, determining whether an activity is religious or secular requires a searching case-by-case analysis. This results in considerable ongoing government entanglement in religious affairs. Furthermore, this prospect of government intrusion raises concern that a religious organization may be chilled in its free exercise activity. While a church may regard the conduct of certain functions as integral to its mission, a court may disagree. A religious organization therefore would have an incentive to characterize as religious only those activities about which there likely would be no dispute, even if it genuinely believed that religious commitment was important in performing other tasks as well. As a result, the community's process ⊥**344** of self-definition would be shaped in part by the prospects of litigation. A case-by-case analysis for all activities therefore would both produce excessive government entanglement with religion and create the danger of chilling religious activity.

The risk of chilling religious organizations is most likely to arise with respect to *nonprofit* activities. The fact that an operation is not organized as a profit-making commercial enterprise makes colorable a claim that it is not purely secular in orientation. In contrast to a for-profit corporation, a nonprofit organization must utilize its earnings to finance the continued provision of the goods or services it furnishes, and may not distribute any surplus to the owners. This makes plausible a church's contention that an entity is not operated simply in order to generate revenues for the church, but that the activities themselves are infused with a religious purpose. Furthermore, unlike for-profit corporations, nonprofits historically have been organized specifically to provide certain community services, not simply to engage in commerce. Churches often regard the provision of such services as a means of fulfilling religious duty and of providing an example of the way of life a church seems to foster.

⊥**345** Nonprofit activities therefore are most likely to present cases in which characterization of the activity as religious or secular will be a close question. If there is a danger that a religious organization will be deterred from classifying as religious those activities it actually regards as religious, it is likely to be in this domain. This substantial potential for chilling religious activity makes inappropriate a case-by-case determination of the character of a nonprofit organization, and justifies a categorical exemption for nonprofit activities. Such an exemption demarcates a sphere of deference with respect to those activities most likely to be religious. It permits infringement on employee free exercise rights in those stances in which discrimination is most likely to reflect a religious community's self-definition. While not every nonprofit activity may be operated for religious purposes, the likelihood that many are makes a categorical rule a suitable means to avoid chilling the exercise of religion.

Sensitivity to individual religious freedom dictates that religious discrimination be permitted only with respect to employment in religious activities. Concern for the autonomy of religious organizations demands that we avoid the entanglement and the chill on religious expression that a case-by-case determination would produce. We cannot escape the fact that these aims are in tension. Because of the nature of nonprofit activities, I believe that a categorical exemption for ⊥**346** such enterprises appropriately balances these competing concerns. As a result, I concur in the Court's judgment that the nonprofit Deseret Gymnasium may avail itself of an automatic exemption from Title VII's proscription on religious discrimination.

Justice BLACKMUN, concurring in the judgment. Essentially for the reasons set forth in *Justice* O'CONNOR's opinion, particularly the third and final paragraphs thereof, I too, concur in the judgment of the Court. I fully agree that the distinction drawn by the Court seems "to obscure far more than to enlighten," as *Justice* O'CONNOR states and that, surely, the "question of the constitutionality of the § 702 exemption as applied to for-profit activities of religious organizations remains open."

Justice O'CONNOR, concurring in the judgment.

Although I agree with the judgment of the Court, I write separately to note that this action once again illustrates certain difficulties inherent in the Court's use of the test articulated in *Lemon* v. *Kurtzman*. See *Wallace* v. *Jaffree* (O'Connor, J., concurring in judgment); *Lynch* v. *Donnelly* (O'Connor, J., concurring). As a result of this problematic analysis, while the holding of the opinion for the Court extends only to nonprofit organizations, its reasoning fails to acknowledge that the amended § 702, 42 U.S.C. § 2000e-1, raises different questions as it is applied to profit and nonprofit organizations.

In *Wallace* v. *Jaffree*, I noted a tension in the Court's use of the *Lemon* test to evaluate an Establishment Clause challenge to government efforts to accommodate the free exercise of religion:

"On the one hand, a rigid application of the *Lemon* test would invalidate legislation exempting religious observers from generally applicable government obligations. ⊥**347** By definition, such legislation has a religious purpose and effect in promoting the free exercise of religion. On the other hand, judicial deference to all legislation that purports to facilitate the free exercise of religion would completely vitiate the Establishment Clause. Any statute pertaining to religion can be viewed as an 'accommodation' of free exercise rights."

In my view, the opinion for the Court leans toward the second of the two unacceptable options described above. While acknowledging that "[u]ndoubtedly, religious organizations are better able now to advance their purposes than they were prior to the 1972 amendment to § 702," the Court seems to suggest that the "effects" prong of the *Lemon* test is not at all implicated as long as the government action can be characterized as "allowing" religious organizations to advance religion, in contrast to government action directly advancing religion. This distinction seems to me to obscure far more than to enlighten. Almost any government benefit to religion could be characterized as simply "allowing" a religion to better advance itself, unless perhaps it involved actual proselytization by government agents. In nearly every case of a government benefit to religion, the religious mission would not be advanced if the religion did not take advantage of the benefit; even a direct financial subsidy to a religious organization would not advance religion if for some reason the organization failed to make any use of the funds. It is for this same reason that there is little significance to the Court's observation that it was the Church rather than the government that penalized Mayson's refusal to adhere to Church doctrine. The Church had the power to put Mayson to a choice of qualifying for a temple recommend or losing his job because *the government* had lifted from religious organizations the general regulatory burden imposed by § 702.

⊥**348** The necessary first step in evaluating an Establishment Clause challenge to a government action lifting from religious organizations a generally applicable regulatory burden is to recognize that such government action *does* have the effect of advancing religion. The necessary second step is to separate those benefits to religion that constitutionally accommodate the free exercise of religion from those that provide unjustifiable awards of assistance to religious organizations. As I have suggested in earlier opinions, the inquiry framed by the *Lemon* test should be "whether government's purpose is to endorse religion and whether the statute actually conveys a message of endorsement." *Wallace*. To ascertain whether the statute conveys a message of endorsement, the relevant issue is how it would be perceived by an objective observer, acquainted with the text, legislative history, and implementation of the statute. Of course, in order to perceive the government action as a permissible accommodation of religion, there must in fact be an identifiable burden *on the exercise of religion* that can be said to be lifted by the government action. The determination of whether the objective observer will perceive an endorsement of religion "is not a question of simple historical fact. Although evidentiary submissions may help answer it, the question is, like the question whether racial or sex-based classifications communicate an invidious message, in large part a legal question to be answered on the basis of judicial interpretation of social facts." *Lynch* v. *Donnelly*.

The above framework, I believe, helps clarify why the amended § 702 raises different questions as it is applied to nonprofit and for-profit organizations. As *Justice* BRENNAN observes in his concurrence, "The fact that an operation is not organized as a profitmaking commercial enterprise makes colorable a claim that it is not purely secular in orientation" (opinion concurring in judgment). These cases involve a government decision to lift from a non⊥**349**profit activity of a religious organization the burden of demonstrating that the particular nonprofit activity is religious as well as the burden of refraining from discriminating on the basis of religion. Because there is a probability that a nonprofit activity of a religious organization will itself be involved in the organization's religious mission, in my view the objective observer should perceive the government action as an accommodation of the exercise of religion rather than as a government endorsement of religion.

It is not clear, however, that activities conducted by religious organizations solely as profit-making enterprises will be as likely to be directly involved in the religious mission of the organization. While I express no opinion on the issue, I emphasize that under the holding of the Court, and under my view of the appropriate Establishment Clause analysis, the question of the constitutionality of the § 702 exemption as applied to for-profit activities of religious organizations remains open.

RELIGIOUS INSTITUTION FUNCTIONING AS A GOVERNMENT AGENCY

A city is a complex organism made up of a variety of components which may be summarized under the headings "residential," "commercial," and "charitable," the latter category containing such institutions as schools, churches, synagogues, hospitals, and museums. It is understandable that those in the residential and charitable categories desire to be protected from the bustle and commotion of the commercial (although not to have businesses so far away as to be inconvenient), so cities have zoning laws designed to protect the public health, safety, tranquility, morals, and general welfare of the community. Because religious institutions are in the charitable category, it sometimes happens that the creation or enforcement of zoning laws take on First Amendment dimensions.

An example is the case of *Incorporated Village of Roslyn Harbor* v. *Jewish Reconstruction Synagogue.* A small congregation of Jews purchased a residence to use as a synagogue. The zoning law required that religious institutions be 100 feet from the property line. The residence purchased was only twenty-nine feet from the line. Although there was enough room on the lot for a structure to be in compliance with the zoning requirements, the congregation did not have the funds either to build a new structure or to move the house currently on the lot. The congregation petitioned the city for an exception, but some of the nearby residents objected. In litigation, New York's highest court ruled in favor of the synagogue, holding that to enforce strictly the ordinance against a congregation financially unable to achieve compliance was a denial of its free exercise of religion. The United States Supreme Court refused to hear the case.[1]

In *Lakewood, Ohio, Congregation of Jehovah's Witnesses* v. *City of Lakewood*, the religious group did not fare so well. A city zoning ordinance excluded church buildings in nearly ninety percent of a residential area. A congregation of Jehovah's Witnesses wanted to build a Kingdom Hall but was unable to do so because the allowable ten percent of land in the area already had church buildings. The Witnesses claimed that the law did not have a direct relation to public health, safety, or welfare. The city replied that the Kingdom Hall would be disruptive in the neighborhood because of the members' coming and going during the several meetings they had each week. The zoning board had the power to make exceptions, but refused to do so. In litigation, federal courts at both levels upheld the board's right to refuse. They rejected the congregation's argument that the ordinance prevented its free exercise of religion. The building of a church building is not a religious act. The ordinance did not prevent the Witnesses from worshiping, it just prevented their worshiping in a particular building. The city's interest in orderly residential areas was a justifiable burden on the group's religious exercise because it was so indirect. The Supreme Court allowed the decision to stand.[2]

In these cases the Supreme Court denied certiorari. The Court has historically given legislatures and zoning boards wide latitude to create zoning boundaries and to grant or withhold exceptions, so long as all interested parties are given adequate notice and the opportunity to request exceptions or express grievances. This reluctance to hear zoning cases included even those with First Amendment dimensions. An exception to that generalization, however, was LARKIN v. GRENDEL'S DEN (1982), perhaps because of the unusual facts of the case.

Massachusetts had a statute which prohibited the sale of alcoholic beverages within 500 feet of a school or a church if the governing body of the school or church filed a written objection to the application for a liquor license. In Cambridge a restaurant known as Grendel's Den applied for an alcoholic beverage license. It was located within ten feet of the Holy Cross Armenian Catholic Parish. The church, as it was allowed to do under the law, objected to the application (apparently because Grendel's Den was so close to the church and probably also because there were 25 other liquor licensees within 500 feet of the church).

[1] See *City of Evanston* v. *Lubavitch Chabad House of Illinois*, a similar case with an identical result.

[2] The material covered in this and the preceding paragraph is derived from Leo Pfeffer, *Religion, State, and the Burger Court* (Buffalo, NY: Prometheus Books, 1984), pp. 282–86.

After seeking administrative relief, with no success, the restaurant sued in federal court, claiming, among other things, that the law violated the Establishment Clause. Both levels of federal courts agreed that the statute was unconstitutional on establishment grounds. The Supreme Court affirmed that ruling.

Chief Justice Burger, writing for himself and seven others, agreed that the statute had a secular purpose: to protect spiritual, cultural, and educational institutions from the noise and possible disturbances associated with liquor outlets. In short, there was nothing wrong with zoning statutes which insulated churches from businesses selling alcoholic beverages. They could do so either by having an absolute ban on liquor outlets within a prescribed distance from churches, schools, etc., or by having a procedure by which those objecting to being close to liquor outlets could be heard. The problem with this particular statute was that it was the church itself which was permitted to veto a liquor application. Because the church assumed a role normally residing in a governmental agency, the statute failed the other two parts of the *Lemon* test. The statute had no provisions requiring that a church give reasons that caused it to act as it did; it was standardless. In this circumstance, churches could employ the law for religious goals, e.g., "favoring liquor licenses for members of that congregation or adherents of that faith." There was no evidence that had been done in this case, but the potential was there. Also, the appearance of cooperation between a church and the zoning commission provided a symbolic benefit to religion in the minds of many. The cumulative effect was that the statute had a primary effect which advanced religion.

Furthermore, the arrangement which gave the churches the potential for advancing their religion under protection of law, i.e., that churches were granted veto power, also created excessive entanglement between church and state. It "enmeshe[d] churches in the exercise of substantial governmental powers" and created the danger of political fragmentation and divisiveness along religious lines. "Ordinary human experience and a long line of cases teach that few entanglements could be more offensive to the spirit of the Constitution" (459 U.S. 116, 127).

Justice Rehnquist, in dissent, called this a silly case. Apparently the other Justices did not think so. Silly or not, what is its significance? After all, footnote seven said that it applied to no zoning statute other than that in Massachusetts. Also, it had a very narrow factual basis. But it at least signals states that they may not exercise their power under the Twenty-first Amendment in a way which infringes on the Establishment Clause.[3] From time to time in Establishment Clause cases, the Justices have debated the weight to be given to the "political divisiveness" dimension of the entanglement portion of the three-part test. Never has it been used alone to decide a case. Chief Justice Burger did not use it in such a way here, but he gave it such visibility that many thought it would have to be taken seriously so long as the *Lemon* test remained viable. Of course, in the late 1980s and the 1990s, as recounted in the essay in this book entitled "The Establishment of Religion," the test increasingly has been subject to philosophical challenge and practical neglect in deciding cases by the more conservative Justices. Finally, and this is its main point, *Larkin* notifies legislatures that religious institutions may never serve in a governmental capacity.

It was this meaning upon which the Court drew as precedent in deciding KIRYAS JOEL SCHOOL DISTRICT v. GRUMET (1994). In New York State, the Village of Kiryas Joel is populated entirely by Hasidic Jews of the Satmar group (or, as they would say it, the Satmar "court").[4] Consistent with the Satmar desire to remain distinctive and as distant from the corrupting secular world as possible, the Hasidim created parochial schools for their children. However, these schools did not provide the specialized instruction necessary for children with handicaps or learning disabilities. After some experimentation with the special education programs in public schools of neighboring communities, in which the Hasidic children felt terribly alienated, it was decided that it was necessary to have separate schools for them. In 1989 the state legislature passed a law which created a public school district for Kiryas Joel, fully recognizing that all the members of the school board for the district would be of the same religion. It was this which caused the New York State School Boards Association and some individuals to file suit, claiming that the Kiryas Joel public school district was an establishment of religion. When the Supreme Court granted certiorari, the plaintiffs had won in all three levels of New York courts.

After he rehearsed the facts of the case, Justice Souter, for the Court, immediately got to the heart of the case. He pointed out that the religion clauses of the First Amendment demand that government in its acts favors neither one religion over others nor believers over nonbelievers. Then he said:

> Chapter 748, the statute creating the Kiryas Joel Village School District, departs from this constitutional command by delegating

[3]The opinion makes this point in footnote five. The Twenty-first Amendment, ratified in 1933, repeals the Eighteenth and asserts that each state shall have administration over the transportation or importation of liquor into the state. Massachusetts had argued in this litigation that that amendment justified the statute under consideration.

[4]For an excellent, though more sociological than theological, description of Hasidism, see Jerome R. Mintz, *Hasidic People: A Place in the New World* (Cambridge: Harvard University Press, 1992).

> the State's discretionary authority over public schools to a group defined by its character as a religious community, in a legal and historical context that gives no assurance that governmental power has been or will be exercised neutrally (114 S.Ct. 2481, 2487).

That statement encapsulates the majority opinion.

In declaring the school district unconstitutional because it assigned governmental functions to a religious body, the opinion relied upon *Larkin*. That case held that a governmental unit may not cede its civic authority to a religious group to the end that the group thus essentially becomes a governing body. That is what happened in the creation of the Kiryas Joel School District. The state legislature chose a group according to a religious criterion and, by the creation of the district, gave it governmental authority.

That the religious group given governmental authority was the qualified voters of the community, rather than, say, the officers of a worshipping congregation, made no difference. The point was that the state legislature well knew that the village was exclusively populated by Hasidic Jews and, regardless of the implications of that fact for how the public school district would be governed, created the school district anyway. The result was the unconstitutional creation of a public governmental body based on a religious criterion. The legislature singled out a particular religious entity for special treatment, contrary to what the Establishment Clause permits.

In a somewhat less clearly argued section of the opinion, Justice Souter stated another reason why the Kiryas Joel School District was unconstitutional: because the legislative act did not inspire confidence that the legislature would, in the future, act in a religiously neutral way. That is, given that the legislature had shown religious favoritism to Kiryas Joel, who was to know whether the legislature would be so solicitous of other discrete religious groups in the future? Assuming that the creation of the Hasidic school district was constitutional, which it was not, there was no way to predict that the legislature would act in a nondiscriminatory way in the future if other religious groups had needs subject to legislative relief. The creation of the Kiryas Joel School District established a precedent which was fraught with possibilities of future discrimination. It was proper to forestall such results by preventing the beginning.

In a concurring opinion, Justice Stevens, joined by Justices Blackmun and Ginsburg, fully agreed with Justice Souter's reasoning, but added another reason to hold New York's plan unconstitutional. The creation of the public school district assisted the Hasidim in segregating themselves from the rest of society. The effect of that was to "cement the attachment of young adherents to a particular faith" (114 S.Ct. 2481, 2495). Action with such a result goes beyond mere accommodation of religion; it is promotion of religion and thus is not permitted by the Establishment Clause.

Justice O'Connor concurred in part and in the judgment. Although she thought it was very clear that government may accommodate religion, the accommodation had to be neutral in regard to religion. It could not be accomplished on the basis of preference of a particular sect. That was the flaw in this case; New York had accorded the Satmar Hasidim favorable treatment. She also agreed with the majority, in somewhat clearer language than Justice Souter's, that the uncertainty of legislative action required the invalidation of the law.

> The legislature may well be acting without any favoritism, so that if another group came to ask for a similar district, the group might get in on the same terms as the Satmars. But the nature of the legislative process makes it impossible to be sure of this. A legislature, unlike the judiciary or many administrative decisionmakers, has no obligation to respond to any group's requests. A group petitioning for a law may never get a definite response, or may get a "no" based not on the merits but on the press of other business or the lack of an influential sponsor. Such a legislative refusal to act would not normally be reviewable by a court. Under these circumstances, it seems dangerous to validate what appears to me to be a clear religious preference (114 S.Ct. 2481, 2498).

Justice Kennedy concurred in the judgment of the Court. He believed that the New York legislature had acted unconstitutionally in creating the public school district on the basis of religious faith. But he took strong exception to the unpredictability of legislative action rationale of Justices Souter and O'Connor. He argued that such reasoning inverted the usual presumption of the constitutionality of a legislative act and assumed the New York legislature was guilty of action based on religious identity until it proved itself innocent.

Justice Kennedy agreed with the view expressed by Justice O'Connor that SCHOOL DISTRICT OF GRAND RAPIDS v. BALL (1985) and AGUILAR v. FELTON (1985) should be revisited by the Court. Those cases had held that public school teachers could not be employed to offer courses in parochial school settings. That was precisely the arrangement in Kiryas Joel at one point; public school teachers came to the village's parochial schools to offer special education to the handicapped students. It was only after *Ball* and *Aguilar* that the New York legislature felt the need to create the public school district at issue in this case. Although Justice Kennedy was not quite so emphatic as Justice O'Connor, both thought the results of *Ball* and *Aguilar* should be reexamined, if the proper case should come along.

Justice Scalia, joined by Chief Justice Rehnquist and Justice Thomas, wrote a comprehensive dissent. He argued, first, that the Court had misapplied *Larkin.* That case had forbidden the state to cede political power to *a church,* whereas the New York legislature had created the public school district for the *members of a church* (actually Jews, but called a "church" here to maintain the parallelism of Justice Scalia's argument and, in fact, his very words at 114 S.Ct. 2507). The latter situation should not be invalidated by a case holding the former.

Next, Justice Scalia disputed the majority's holding that because the school district's boundaries were coterminous with the village's and that the population of the village was exclusively Satmar Hasidim, the school district was created using religious criteria. His view was that the district was created for demonstrably handicapped children who all happened to be of the same religion. The district was created to accommodate their handicaps, not their religion. He also made a distinction between the theology of the Hasidim and the cultural characteristics of their community, arguing that it was the latter which prevented the Hasidic parents from sending their handicapped children to neighboring public schools, not their theology. He did not seem to see any connection between the theology of the Hasidim and their "cultural characteristics." He summarized these points thusly:

> Entirely secular reasons (zoning for the village, cultural alienation of students for the school district) produced a political unit whose members happened to share the same religion. There is no evidence (indeed, no plausible suspicion) of the legislature's desire to favor the Satmar religion, as opposed to meeting distinctive secular needs or desires of citizens who happened to be Satmars (114 S.Ct. 2481, 2511; emphasis in original).

Next, Justice Scalia criticized the Court's view, supported by Justice O'Connor but disputed by Justice Kennedy, that the New York law was unconstitutional because the legislature might not treat another request by a religious group for accommodation in the same fashion and this lack of legislative action was unreviewable by courts.

> What I attack is the Court's imposition of novel "up front" procedural requirements on state legislatures. Making law (and making exceptions) one case at a time, whether through adjudication or through highly particularized rulemaking or legislation, violates, ex ante, no principle of fairness, equal protection, or neutrality, simply because it does not announce in advance how all future cases (and all future exceptions) will be disposed of (114 S.Ct. 2481, 2514).

He called such a procedure astounding, unique in jurisprudence and, although this is not his wording, just plain dumb.

Justice Scalia concluded his dissent with brief rebuttals of each of the concurring opinions.

LARKIN v. GRENDEL'S DEN

459 U.S. 116

ON APPEAL FROM THE UNITED STATES COURT OF APPEALS FOR THE FIRST CIRCUIT

Argued October 4, 1982 — Decided December 13, 1982

⊥**117** *Chief Justice BURGER* delivered the opinion of the Court.

The question presented by this appeal is whether a Massachusetts statute, which vests in the governing bodies of churches and schools the power effectively to veto applications for liquor licenses within a five hundred foot radius of the church or school, violates the Establishment Clause of the First Amendment or the Due Process Clause of the Fourteenth Amendment.

I

A

Appellee operates a restaurant located in the Harvard Square area of Cambridge, Massachusetts. The Holy Cross Armenian Catholic Parish is located adjacent to the restaurant; the back walls of the two buildings are ten feet apart. In 1977, appellee applied to the Cambridge License Commission for approval of an alcoholic beverages license for the restaurant.

Section 16C of Chapter 138 of the Massachusetts General Laws provides: "Premises . . . located within a radius of five hundred feet of a church or school shall not be licensed for the sale of alcoholic beverages if the governing body of such church or school files written objection thereto."

⊥**118** Holy Cross Church objected to appellee's application, expressing concern over "having so many licenses *so* near" (emphasis in original). The License Commission voted to deny the application, citing only the objection of Holy Cross Church and noting that the church "is within 10 feet of the proposed location."

On appeal, the Massachusetts Alcoholic Beverages Control Commission upheld the License Commission's action. The Beverages Control Commission found that "the church's objection under Section 16C was the only basis on which the [license] was denied."

Appellee then sued the License Commission and the Beverages Control Commission in United States District Court. Relief was sought on the grounds that § 16C, on its face and as applied, violated the Equal Protection and Due Process Clauses of the Fourteenth Amendment, the Establishment Clause of the First Amendment, and the Sherman Act.

The suit was voluntarily continued pending the decision of the Massachusetts Supreme Judicial Court in a similar challenge to § 16C, *Arno* v. *Alcoholic Beverages Control*

Commission. In *Arno*, the Massachusetts court characterized § 16C as delegating a ⊥**119** "veto power" to the specified institutions, but upheld the statute against Due Process and Establishment Clause challenges. Thereafter, the District Court denied appellants' motion to dismiss.

On the parties' cross-motion for summary judgment, the District Court declined to follow the Massachusetts Supreme Judicial Court's decision in *Arno*. The District Court held that § 16C violated the Due Process Clause and the Establishment Clause and held § 16C void on its face. The District Court rejected appellee's equal protection arguments, but held that the state's actions were not immune from antitrust review under the doctrine of *Parker* v. *Brown*. It certified the judgment to the First Circuit Court of Appeals pursuant to 28 U.S.C. § 1292, and the Court of Appeals accepted certification.

A panel of the First Circuit, in a divided opinion, reversed the District Court on the Due Process and Establishment Clause arguments, but affirmed its antitrust analysis.

Appellee's motion for rehearing *en banc* was granted and the *en banc* court, in a divided opinion, affirmed the District Court's judgment on Establishment Clause grounds without reaching the due process or antitrust claims.

B

The Court of Appeals noted that appellee does not contend that § 16C lacks a secular purpose, and turned to the question of "whether the law 'has the *direct* and *immediate* effect of advancing religion' as contrasted with 'only a *remote* and *incidental* effect advantageous to religious institutions,'" (emphasis in original), quoting *Committee for Public Education* v. *Nyquist*. The court concluded that § 16C confers a direct and substantial ⊥**120** benefit upon religions by "the grant of a veto power over liquor sales in roughly one million square feet . . . of what may be a city's most commercially valuable sites."

The court acknowledged that § 16C "extends its benefit beyond churches to schools," but concluded that the inclusion of schools "does not dilute [the statute's] forbidden religious classification," since § 16C does not "encompass all who are otherwise similarly situated to churches in all respects except dedication to 'divine worship.'" In the view of the Court of Appeals, this "explicit religious discrimination," provided an additional basis for its holding that § 16C violates the Establishment Clause.

The court found nothing in the Twenty-First Amendment to alter its conclusion, and affirmed the District Court's holding that § 16C is facially unconstitutional under the Establishment Clause of the First Amendment.

We noted probable jurisdiction and we affirm.

II

A

Appellants contend that the State may, without impinging on the Establishment Clause of the First Amendment, enforce what it describes as a "zoning" law in order to shield schools and places of divine worship from the presence nearby of liquor dispensing establishments. It is also contended that a zone of protection around churches and schools is essential to protect diverse centers of spiritual, educational and cultural enrichment. It is to that end that the State has vested in the governing bodies of all schools, public or private, and all churches, the power to prevent the issu⊥**121**ance of liquor licenses for any premises within 500 feet of their institutions.

Plainly schools and churches have a valid interest in being insulated from certain kinds of commercial establishments, including those dispensing liquor. Zoning laws have long been employed to this end, and there can be little doubt about the power of a state to regulate the environment in the vicinity of schools, churches, hospitals and the like by exercise of reasonable zoning laws.

We have upheld reasonable zoning ordinances regulating the location of so-called "adult" theaters, see *Young* v. *American Mini Theaters, Inc.*; and in *Grayned* v. *City of Rockford* we recognized the legitimate governmental interest in protecting the environment around certain institutions when we sustained an ordinance prohibiting willfully making, on grounds adjacent to a school, noises which are disturbing to the good order of the school sessions.

The zoning function is traditionally a governmental task requiring the "balancing [of] numerous competing considerations," and courts should properly "refrain from reviewing the merits of [such] decisions, absent a showing of arbitrariness or irrationality." *Village of Arlington Heights* v. *Metropolitan Housing Development Corp*. Given the broad powers of states under the Twenty-First Amendment, judicial deference to the legislative exercise of zoning powers by a city council or other legislative zoning body is especially appropriate in the area of liquor ⊥**122** regulation.

However, § 16C is not simply a legislative exercise of zoning power. As the Massachusetts Supreme Judicial Court concluded, § 16C delegates to private, nongovernmental entities power to veto certain liquor license applications, *Arno* v. *Alcoholic Beverages Control Commission*. This is a power ordinarily vested in agencies of government. See, *e.g.*, *California* v. *LaRue*, commenting that a "state agency . . . is itself the repository of the State's power under the Twenty-First Amendment." We need not decide whether, or upon what conditions, such power may ever be delegated to nongovernmental entities; here, of two classes of institutions to which the legislature has delegated this important decision-making power, one is secular, but one is religious. Under these circumstances, the deference normally due a legislative zoning judgment is not merited.

B

The purposes of the First Amendment guarantees relating to religion were twofold: to foreclose state interferences with the practice of religious faiths, and to foreclose the establishment of a state religion familiar in other Eighteenth Century systems. Religion and government, each insulated from the other, could then coexist. Jefferson's idea of a "wall," ⊥**123** was a useful figurative illustration to emphasize the concept of separateness. Some limited and incidental entanglement between church and state authority is inevitable in a complex modern society, but the concept of a "wall" of separation is a useful signpost. Here that "wall" is substantially breached by vesting discretionary governmental powers in religious bodies.

This Court has consistently held that a statute must satisfy three criteria to pass muster under the Establishment Clause: "First the statute must have a secular legislative purpose; second, its principal or primary effect must be one that neither advances nor inhibits religion . . . ; finally, the statute must not foster 'an excessive government entanglement with religion.'" *Lemon* v. *Kurtzman*. Independent of the first of those criteria, the statute, by delegating a governmental power to religious institutions, inescapably implicates the Establishment Clause.

The purpose of § 16C, as described by the District Court, is to "protec[t] spiritual, cultural, and educational centers from the 'hurly-burly' associated with liquor outlets." There can be little doubt that this embraces valid secular legislative purposes. However, these valid ⊥**124** secular objectives can be readily accomplished by other means—either through an absolute legislative ban on liquor outlets within reasonable prescribed distances from churches, schools, hospital and like institutions, or by ensuring a hearing for the views of affected institutions at licensing proceedings where, without question, such views would be entitled to substantial weight.

⊥**125** Appellants argue that § 16C has only a remote and incidental effect on the advancement of religion. The highest court in Massachusetts, however, has construed the statute as conferring upon churches a veto power over governmental licensing authority. Section 16C gives churches the right to determine whether a particular applicant will be granted a liquor license, or even which one of several competing applicants will receive a license.

The churches' power under the statute is standardless, calling for no reasons, findings, or reasoned conclusions. That power may therefore be used by churches to promote goals beyond insulating the church from undesirable neighbors; it could be employed for explicitly religious goals, for example, favoring liquor licenses for members of that congregation or adherents of that faith. We can assume that churches would act in good faith in their exercise of the statutory power, yet § 16C does not by its terms require that churches' power be used in a religiously neutral way. "[T]he potential for conflict inheres in the situation," *Levitt* v. *Committee for Public Education*; and appellants have not suggested any "effective means of guaranteeing" that the delegated power "will be used exclusively for secular, neutral, and nonideological purposes." *Committee for Public Education* v. *Nyquist*. In addition, the mere appearance of a joint exercise of legislative authority by Church and State provides a significant symbolic benefit to ⊥**126** religion in the minds of some by reason of the power conferred. It does not strain our prior holdings to say that the statute can be seen as having a "primary" and "principal" effect of advancing religion.

Turning to the third phase of the inquiry called for by *Lemon* v. *Kurtzman*, we see that we have not previously had occasion to consider the entanglement implications of a statute vesting significant governmental authority in churches. This statute enmeshes churches in the exercise of substantial governmental powers contrary to our consistent interpretation of the Establishment Clause; "[t]he objective is to prevent, as far as possible, the intrusion of either [Church or State] into the precincts of the other." *Lemon* v. *Kurtzman*. We went on in that case to state: "Under our system the choice has been made that government is to be entirely excluded from the area of religious instruction *and churches excluded from the affairs of government*. The Constitution decrees that religion must be a private matter for the individual, the family, and the institutions of private choice, and that while some involvement and entanglement are inevitable, lines must be drawn." (emphasis added.)

Our contemporary views do no more than reflect views approved by the Court more than a century ago: "The structure of our government has, for the preservation of civil liberty, rescued the temporal institutions from religious interference. On the other hand, it has secured religious liberty from the invasion of the civil authority." *Watson* v. *Jones*.

As these and other cases make clear, the core rationale underlying the Establishment Clause is preventing "a fusion of governmental and religious functions." *Abington School Dis*⊥**127***trict* v. *Schempp*. The Framers did not set up a system of government in which important, discretionary governmental powers would be delegated to or shared with religious institutions.

Section 16C substitutes the unilateral and absolute power of a church for the reasoned decisionmaking of a public legislative body acting on evidence and guided by standards, on issues with significant economic and political implications. The challenged statute thus enmeshes churches in the processes of government and creates the danger of "[p]olitical fragmentation and divisiveness along religious lines." *Lemon* v. *Kurtzman*. Ordinary human experience and a long line of cases teach that few entanglements could be more offensive to the spirit of the Constitution.

The judgment of the Court of Appeals is affirmed.

So ordered.

Justice REHNQUIST, dissenting.

Dissenting opinions in previous cases have commented that "great" cases, like "hard" cases, make bad law. ⊥**128** Today's opinion suggests that a third class of cases—silly cases—also make bad law. The Court wrenches from the decision of the Massachusetts Supreme Judicial Court the word "veto," and rests its conclusion on this single term. The aim of this effort is to prove that a quite sensible Massachusetts liquor zoning law is apparently some sort of sinister religious attack on secular government reminiscent of St. Bartholomew's Night. Being unpersuaded, I dissent.

In its original form, § 16C imposed a flat ban on the grant of alcoholic beverages licenses to any establishment located within 500 feet of a church or a school. This statute represented a legislative determination that worship and liquor sales are generally not compatible uses of land. The majority concedes, as I believe it must, that "an absolute legislative ban on liquor outlets within reasonable prescribed distances from churches, schools, hospitals, and like institutions," would be valid.

Over time, the legislature found that it could meet its goal of protecting people engaged in religious activities from liquor-related disruption with a less absolute prohibition. Rather than set out elaborate formulae or require an administrative agency to make findings of fact, the legislature settled on the simple expedient of asking churches to object if a proposed liquor outlet would disturb them. Thus, under the present version of § 16C, a liquor outlet within 500 feet of a church or school can be licensed unless the affected institution objects. The flat ban, which the majority concedes is valid, is more protective of churches and more restrictive of liquor sales than the present § 16C.

The evolving treatment of the grant of liquor licenses to outlets located within 500 feet of a church or a school seems to me to be the sort of legislative refinement that we should encourage, not forbid in the name of the First Amendment. If a particular church or a particular school located within the ⊥**129** 500-foot radius chooses not to object, the state has quite sensibly concluded that there is no reason to prohibit the issuance of the license. Nothing in the Court's opinion persuades me why the more rigid prohibition would be constitutional, but the more flexible not.

The Court rings in the metaphor of the "wall between church and state," and the "three part test" developed in *Walz* v. *Tax Commission*, to justify its result. However, by its frequent reference to the statutory provision as a "veto," the Court indicates a belief that § 16C effectively constitutes churches as third houses of the Massachusetts legislature. Surely we do not need a three part test to decide whether the grant of actual legislative power to churches is within the proscription of the Establishment Clause of the First and Fourteenth Amendments. The question in this case is not whether such a statute would be unconstitutional, but whether § 16C is such a statute. The Court in effect answers this question in the first sentence of its opinion without any discussion or statement of reasons. I do not think the question is so trivial that it may be answered by simply affixing a label to the statutory provision.

Section 16C does not sponsor or subsidize any religious group or activity. It does not encourage, much less compel, anyone to participate in religious activities or to support religious institutions. To say that it "advances" religion is to strain at the meaning of that word.

The Court states that § 16C "advances" religion because there is no guarantee that objections will be made "in a religiously neutral way." It is difficult to understand what the Court means by this. The concededly legitimate purpose of the statute is to protect citizens engaging in religious and educational activities from the incompatible activities of liquor outlets and their patrons. The only way to decide whether these activities are incompatible with one another in the case of a church is to ask whether the activities of liquor outlets and their patrons may interfere with religious ⊥**130** activity; this question cannot, in any meaningful sense, be "religiously neutral." In this sense, the flat ban of the original § 16C is no different from the present version. Whether the ban is unconditional or may be invoked only at the behest of a particular church, it is not "religiously neutral" so long as it enables a church to defeat the issuance of a liquor license when a similarly situated bank could not do the same. The state does not, in my opinion, "advance" religion by making provision for those who wish to engage in religious activities, as well as those who wish to engage in educational activities, to be unmolested by activities at a neighboring bar or tavern that have historically been thought incompatible.

The Court is apparently concerned for fear that churches might object to the issuance of a license for "explicitly religious reasons," such as "favoring liquor licenses for members of that congregation or adherents of that faith." If a church were to seek to advance the interests of its members in this way, there would be an occasion to determine whether it had violated any right of an unsuccessful applicant for a liquor license. But our ability to discern a risk of such abuse does not render § 16C violative of the Establishment Clause. The state can constitutionally protect churches from liquor for the same reasons it can protect them from fire and other harm.

The heavy First Amendment artillery that the Court fires at this sensible and unobjectionable Massachusetts statute is both unnecessary and unavailing. I would reverse the judgment of the Court of Appeals.

BOARD OF EDUCATION OF KIRYAS JOEL VILLAGE SCHOOL DISTRICT v. LOUIS GRUMET ET AL.

114 S.Ct. 2481
ON WRIT OF CERTIORARI TO THE COURT OF APPEALS OF NEW YORK
Argued March 30, 1994 — Decided June 27, 1994

⊥**2484** *Justice* SOUTER delivered the opinion of the Court.

The Village of Kiryas Joel in Orange County, New York, is a religious enclave of Satmar Hasidim, practitioners of a strict form of Judaism. The village fell within the Monroe-Woodbury Central School District until a special state statute passed in 1989 carved out a separate district, following village lines, to serve this distinctive population. 1989 N. Y. Laws, ch. 748. The question is whether the Act creating the separate school district violates the Establishment Clause of the First Amendment, binding on the States through the Fourteenth Amendment. Because this unusual act is tantamount to an allocation of political power on a religious criterion and neither presupposes nor requires governmental impartiality toward religion, we hold that it violates the prohibition against establishment.

⊥2485 I

The Satmar Hasidic sect takes its name from the town near the Hungarian and Romanian border where, in the early years of this century, Grand Rebbe Joel Teitelbaum molded the group into a distinct community. After World War II and the destruction of much of European Jewry, the Grand Rebbe and most of his surviving followers moved to the Williamsburg section of Brooklyn, New York. Then, 20 years ago, the Satmars purchased an approved but undeveloped subdivision in the town of Monroe and began assembling the community that has since become the Village of Kiryas Joel. When a zoning dispute arose in the course of settlement, the Satmars presented the Town Board of Monroe with a petition to form a new village within the town, a right that New York's Village Law gives almost any group of residents who satisfy certain procedural niceties. Neighbors who did not wish to secede with the Satmars objected strenuously, and after arduous negotiations the proposed boundaries of the Village of Kiryas Joel were drawn to include just the 320 acres owned and inhabited entirely by Satmars. The village, incorporated in 1977, has a population of about 8,500 today. Rabbi Aaron Teitelbaum, eldest son of the current Grand Rebbe, serves as the village rov (chief rabbi) and rosh yeshivah (chief authority in the parochial schools).

The residents of Kiryas Joel are vigorously religious people who make few concessions to the modern world and go to great lengths to avoid assimilation into it. They interpret the Torah strictly; segregate the sexes outside the home; speak Yiddish as their primary language; eschew television, radio, and English-language publications; and dress in distinctive ways that include headcoverings and special garments for boys and modest dresses for girls. Children are educated in private religious schools, most boys at the United Talmudic Academy where they receive a thorough grounding in the Torah and limited exposure to secular subjects, and most girls at Bais Rochel, an affiliated school with a curriculum designed to prepare girls for their roles as wives and mothers.

These schools do not, however, offer any distinctive services to handicapped children, who are entitled under state and federal law to special education services even when enrolled in private schools. Individuals with Disabilities Education Act, 20 U. S. C. §1400 *et seq.* (1988 ed. and Supp. IV); N. Y. Educ. Law, Art. 89 (McKinney 1981 and Supp. 1994). Starting in 1984 the Monroe-Woodbury Central School District provided such services for the children of Kiryas Joel at an annex to Bais Rochel, but a year later ended that arrangement in response to our decisions in *Aguilar* v. *Felton* and *School Dist. of Grand Rapids* v. *Ball*. Children from Kiryas Joel who needed special education (including the deaf, the mentally retarded, and others suffering from a range of physical, mental, or emotional disorders) were then forced to attend public schools outside the village, which their families found highly unsatisfactory. Parents of most of these children withdrew them from the Monroe-Woodbury secular schools, citing "the panic, fear and trauma [the children] suffered in leaving their own community and being with people whose ways were so different," and some sought administrative review of the public-school placements. *Board of Ed. of Monroe-Woodbury Central School Dist.* v. *Wieder*.

Monroe-Woodbury, for its part, sought a declaratory judgment in state court that New York law barred the district from providing special education services outside the district's regular public schools. The New York Court of Appeals disagreed, holding that state law left Monroe-Woodbury free to establish a separate school in the village because it gives educational authori-⊥2486ties broad discretion in fashioning an appropriate program. The court added, however, that the Satmars' constitutional right to exercise their religion freely did not require a separate school, since the parents had alleged emotional trauma, not inconsistency with religious practice or doctrine, as the reason for seeking separate treatment.

By 1989, only one child from Kiryas Joel was attending Monroe-Woodbury's public schools; the village's other handicapped children received privately funded special services or went without. It was then that the New York Legislature passed the statute at issue in this litigation, which provided that the Village of Kiryas Joel "is constituted a separate school district, . . . and shall have and enjoy all the powers and duties of a union free school district. . . ." 1989 N. Y. Laws, ch. 748. The statute thus empowered a locally elected board of education to take such action as opening schools and closing them, hiring teachers, prescribing textbooks, establishing disciplinary rules, and raising property taxes to fund operations. N. Y. Educ. Law §1709 (McKinney 1988). In signing the bill into law, Governor Cuomo recognized that the residents of the new school district were "all members of the same religious sect," but said that the bill was "a good faith effort to solve th[e] unique problem" associated with providing special education services to handicapped children in the village.

Although it enjoys plenary legal authority over the elementary and secondary education of all school-aged children in the village, the Kiryas Joel Village School

District currently runs only a special education program for handicapped children. The other village children have stayed in their parochial schools, relying on the new school district only for transportation, remedial education, and health and welfare services. If any child without handicap in Kiryas Joel were to seek a public-school education, the district would pay tuition to send the child into Monroe-Woodbury or another school district nearby. Under like arrangements, several of the neighboring districts send their handicapped Hasidic children into Kiryas Joel, so that two thirds of the full-time students in the village's public school come from outside. In all, the new district serves just over 40 full-time students, and two or three times that many parochial school students on a part-time basis.

Several months before the new district began operations, the New York State School Boards Association and respondents Grumet and Hawk brought this action against the State Education Department and various state officials, challenging Chapter 748 under the national and state constitutions as an unconstitutional establishment of religion. The State Supreme Court for Albany County allowed the Kiryas Joel Village ⊥**2487** School District and the Monroe-Woodbury Central School District to intervene as parties defendant and accepted the parties' stipulation discontinuing the action against the original state defendants, although the Attorney General of New York continued to appear to defend the constitutionality of the statute. On cross-motions for summary judgment, the trial court ruled for the plaintiffs (respondents here), finding that the statute failed all three prongs of the test in *Lemon* v. *Kurtzman* and was thus unconstitutional under both the National and State Constitutions. *Grumet* v. *New York State Ed. Dept.*

A divided Appellate Division affirmed on the ground that Chapter 748 had the primary effect of advancing religion, in violation of both constitutions and the state Court of Appeals affirmed on the federal question, while expressly reserving the state constitutional issue. Judge Smith wrote for the court in concluding that because both the district's public school population and its school board would be exclusively Hasidic, the statute created a "symbolic union of church and state" that was "likely to be perceived by the Satmarer Hasidim as an endorsement of their religious choices, or by nonadherents as a disapproval" of their own. As a result, said the majority, the statute's primary effect was an impermissible advancement of religious belief. In a concurring opinion, Judge Hancock found the effect purposeful, so that the statute violated the first as well as the second prong of *Lemon*. Chief Judge Kaye took a different tack, applying the strict scrutiny we have prescribed for statutes singling out a particular religion for special privileges or burdens; she found Chapter 748 invalid as an unnecessarily broad response to a narrow problem, since it creates a full school district instead of simply prescribing a local school for the village's handicapped children. In dissent, Judge Bellacosa objected that the new district was created to enable the village's handicapped children to receive a secular, public-school education; that this was, indeed, its primary effect; and that any attenuated benefit to religion was a reasonable accommodation of both religious and cultural differences.

We stayed the mandate of the Court of Appeals and granted certiorari.

II

"A proper respect for both the Free Exercise and the Establishment Clauses compels the State to pursue a course of 'neutrality' toward religion," *Committee for Public Ed. & Religious Liberty* v. *Nyquist*, favoring neither one religion over others nor religious adherents collectively over nonadherents. Chapter 748, the statute creating the Kiryas Joel Village School District, departs from this constitutional command by delegating the State's discretionary authority over public schools to a group defined by its character as a religious community, in a legal and historical context that gives no assurance that governmental power has been or will be exercised neutrally.

Larkin v. *Grendel's Den, Inc.* provides an instructive comparison with the litigation before us. There, the Court was requested to strike down a Massachusetts statute granting religious bodies veto power over applications for liquor licenses. Under the statute, the governing body of any church, synagogue, or school located within 500 feet of an applicant's premises could, simply by submitting written objection, prevent the Alcohol Beverage Control Commission from issuing a license. ⊥**2488** In spite of the State's valid interest in protecting churches, schools, and like institutions from "'the hurly-burly' associated with liquor outlets," the Court found that in two respects the statute violated "the wholesome 'neutrality' of which this Court's cases speak," *School Dist. of Abington* v. *Schempp*. The Act brought about a "'fusion of governmental and religious functions'" by delegating "important, discretionary governmental powers" to religious bodies, thus impermissibly entangling government and religion (quoting *Abington School Dist.* v. *Schempp*). And it lacked "any 'effective means of guaranteeing' that the delegated power '[would] be used exclusively for secular, neutral, and nonideological purposes,'" (quoting *Committee for Public Ed. & Religious Liberty* v. *Nyquist*); this, along with the "significant symbolic benefit to religion" associated with "the mere appearance of a joint exercise of legislative authority by Church and State," led the Court to conclude that the statute had a "'primary' and 'principal' effect of advancing religion." Comparable constitutional problems inhere in the statute before us.

A

Larkin presented an example of united civic and religious authority, an establishment rarely found in such straightforward form in modern America and a violation of "the core rationale underlying the Establishment Clause." See also *Allegheny County* v. *American Civil Liberties Union, Greater Pittsburgh Chapter* (Establishment Clause prevents delegating governmental power to religious group); *id.* (Kennedy, J., concurring in judgment in part and dissenting in part) (same); *Everson* v. *Board of Ed. of Ewing* (Establishment Clause prevents State from "participat[ing] in the affairs of any religious organizations or groups and *vice versa*"); *Torcaso* v. *Watkins* (same).

The Establishment Clause problem presented by Chapter 748 is more subtle, but it resembles the issue raised in *Larkin* to the extent that the earlier case teaches that a State may not delegate its civic authority to a group chosen according to a religious criterion. Authority over public schools belongs to the State, N.Y. Const., Art. XI, §1 (McKinney 1987), and cannot be delegated to a local school district defined by the State in order to grant political control to a religious group. What makes this litigation different from *Larkin* is the delegation here of civic power to the "qualified voters of the village of Kiryas Joel," 1989 N. Y. Laws, ch. 748, as distinct from a religious leader such as the village rov, or an institution of religious government like the formally constituted parish council in *Larkin*. In light of the circumstances of this case, however, this distinction turns out to lack constitutional significance.

It is, first, not dispositive that the recipients of state power in this case are a group of religious individuals united by common doctrine, not the group's leaders or officers. Although some school district franchise is common to all voters, the State's manipulation of the franchise for this district limited it to Satmars, giving the sect exclusive control of the political subdivision. In the circumstances of this case, the difference between thus vesting state power in the members of a religious group as such instead of the officers of its sectarian organization is one of form, not substance. It is true that ⊥**2489** religious people (or groups of religious people) cannot be denied the opportunity to exercise the rights of citizens simply because of their religious affiliations or commitments, for such a disability would violate the right to religious free exercise, see *McDaniel* v. *Paty*, which the First Amendment guarantees as certainly as it bars any establishment. But *McDaniel*, which held that a religious individual could not, because of his religious activities, be denied the right to hold political office, is not in point here. That individuals who happen to be religious may hold public office does not mean that a state may deliberately delegate discretionary power to an individual, institution, or community on the ground of religious identity. If New York were to delegate civic authority to "the Grand Rebbe," *Larkin* would obviously require invalidation (even though under *McDaniel* the Grand Rebbe may run for, and serve on his local school board), and the same is true if New York delegates political authority by reference to religious belief. Where "fusion" is an issue, the difference lies in the distinction between a government's purposeful delegation on the basis of religion and a delegation on principles neutral to religion, to individuals whose religious identities are incidental to their receipt of civic authority.

Of course, Chapter 748 delegates power not by express reference to the religious belief of the Satmar community, but to residents of the "territory of the village of Kiryas Joel." 1989 N. Y. Laws, ch. 748. Thus the second (and arguably more important) distinction between this case and *Larkin* is the identification here of the group to exercise civil authority in terms not expressly religious. But our analysis does not end with the text of the statute at issue, and the context here persuades us that Chapter 748 effectively identifies these recipients of governmental authority by reference to doctrinal adherence, even though it does not do so expressly. We find this to be the better view of the facts because of the way the boundary lines of the school district divide residents according to religious affiliation, under the terms of an unusual and special legislative act.

It is undisputed that those who negotiated the village boundaries when applying the general village incorporation statute drew them so as to exclude all but Satmars, and that the New York Legislature was well aware that the village remained exclusively Satmar in 1989 when it adopted Chapter 748. The significance of this fact to the state legislature is indicated by the further fact that carving out the village school district ran counter to customary districting practices in the State. Indeed, the trend in New York is not toward dividing school districts but toward consolidating them. The thousands of small common school districts laid out in the early 19th century have been combined and recombined, first into union free school districts and then into larger central school districts, until only a tenth as many remain today. Univ. of State of N. Y. and State Education Dept., School District Reorganization, Law Pamphlet 14, pp. 8–12 (1962) (hereinafter Law Pamphlet). Most of these cover several towns, many of them cross county boundaries, and only one remains precisely coterminous with an incorporated village. The object of the State's practice of consolidation is the creation of districts large enough to provide a comprehensive education at affordable cost, which is thought to require at least 500 pupils for a combined junior-senior high school. ⊥**2490** The Kiryas Joel Village School District, in contrast, has only 13 local, full-time students in all (even including out-of-area and part-time students leaves the number under 200), and in offering only special education and remedial programs it makes no pretense to be a full-service district.

The origin of the district in a special act of the legislature, rather than the State's general laws governing school district reorganization, is likewise anomalous. Although the legislature has established some 20 existing school districts by special act, all but one of these are districts in name only, having been designed to be run by private organizations serving institutionalized children. They have neither tax bases nor student populations of their own but serve children placed by other school districts or public agencies. Law Pamphlet, at 18 ("These districts are school districts only by way of a legal fiction"). The one school district petitioners point to that was formed by special act of the legislature to serve a whole community, as this one was, is a district formed for a new town, much larger and more heterogeneous than this village, being built on land that straddled two existing districts. Thus the Kiryas Joel Village School District is exceptional to the point of singularity, as the only district coming to our notice that the legislature carved from a single existing district to serve local residents. Clearly this district "cannot be seen as the fulfillment of [a village's] destiny as an independent governmental entity," *United States* v. *Scotland Neck Bd. of Ed.*, (Burger, C. J., concurring in result).

Because the district's creation ran uniquely counter to state practice, following the lines of a religious community where the customary and neutral principles would not have dictated the same result, we have good reasons to treat this district as the reflection of a religious criterion for identifying the recipients of civil authority. Not even the special needs of the children in this community can explain the legislature's unusual Act, for the State could have responded to the concerns of the Satmar parents without implicating the Establishment Clause, as we explain in some detail further on. We therefore find the legislature's Act to be substantially equivalent to defining a political subdivision and hence the qualification for its franchise by a religious test, resulting in a purposeful and forbidden "fusion of governmental and religious functions." *Larkin* v. *Grendel's Den*, 459 U.S., at 126 (internal quotation marks and citation omitted).*

⊥**2491** B

The fact that this school district was created by a special and unusual Act of the legislature also gives reason for concern whether the benefit received by the Satmar community is one that the legislature will provide equally to other religious (and nonreligious) groups. This is the second malady the *Larkin* Court identified in the law before it, the absence of an "effective means of guaranteeing" that governmental power will be and has been neutrally employed. But whereas in *Larkin* it was religious groups the Court thought might exercise civic power to advance the interests of religion (or religious adherents), here the threat to neutrality occurs at an antecedent stage.

The fundamental source of constitutional concern here is that the legislature itself may fail to exercise governmental authority in a religiously neutral way. The anomalously case-specific nature of the legislature's exercise of state authority in creating this district for a religious community leaves the Court without any direct way to review such state action for the purpose of safeguarding a principle at the heart of the Establishment Clause, that government should not prefer one religion to another, or religion to irreligion. Because the religious community of Kiryas Joel did not receive its new governmental authority simply as one of many communities eligible for equal treatment under a general law, we have no assurance that the next similarly situated group seeking a school district of its own will receive one; unlike an administrative agency's denial of an exemption from a generally applicable law, which "would be entitled to a judicial audience," *Olsen* v. *Drug Enforcement Admin.*, a legislature's failure to enact a special law is itself unreviewable. Nor can the historical context in this case furnish us with any reason to suppose that the Satmars are merely one in a series of communities receiving the benefit of special school district laws. Early on in the development of public education in New York, the State rejected highly localized school districts for New York City when they were promoted as a way to allow separate schooling for Roman Catholic children. And in more recent history, the special Act in this case stands alone.

The general principle that civil power must be exercised in a manner neutral to religion is one the *Larkin* Court recognized, although it did not discuss the specific possibility of legislative favoritism along religious lines because the statute before it delegated state authority to any religious group assembled near the premises of an applicant for a liquor license, as well as to a further category of institutions not identified by religion. But the principle is well grounded in our case law, as we have frequently relied explicitly on the general availability of any benefit provided religious groups or individuals in turning aside Establishment Clause challenges. In *Walz* v. *Tax Comm'n of New York City*, for example, the Court sustained a property tax exemption for religious properties in part because the State had "not singled out one particular church or religious group or even churches as such," but had exempted "a broad class of property owned by nonprofit, quasi-public corpora⊥**2492**tions." And *Bowen* v. *Kendrick* upheld a statute enlisting a "wide spectrum of organizations" in addressing adolescent sexuality because the law was "neutral with respect to the grantee's status as a sectarian or purely secular institution." See also *Texas Monthly, Inc.* v. *Bullock* (striking down sales tax exemption exclusively for religious publications); *id.*, at 14–15 (plurality opinion); *id.*, at 27–28 (Blackmun, J., concurring in judgment); *Estate of Thornton* v. *Caldor, Inc.* (O'Connor, J., concurring in judgment) (statute impermissibly "singles out Sabbath observers for special . . .

*Because it is the unusual circumstances of this district's creation that persuade us the State has employed a religious criterion for delegating political power, this conclusion does not imply that any political subdivision that is coterminous with the boundaries of a religiously homogeneous community suffers the same constitutional infirmity. The district in this case is distinguishable from one whose boundaries are derived according to neutral historical and geographic criteria, but whose population happens to comprise coreligionists.

protection without according similar accommodation to ethical and religious beliefs and practices of other private employees"); cf. *Witters* v. *Washington Dept. of Services for Blind* (Powell, J., concurring). Here the benefit flows only to a single sect, but aiding this single, small religious group causes no less a constitutional problem than would follow from aiding a sect with more members or religion as a whole, see *Larson* v. *Valente*, and we are forced to conclude that the State of New York has violated the Establishment Clause.

C

In finding that Chapter 748 violates the requirement of governmental neutrality by extending the benefit of a special franchise, we do not deny that the Constitution allows the state to accommodate religious needs by alleviating special burdens. Our cases leave no doubt that in commanding neutrality the Religion Clauses do not require the government to be oblivious to impositions that legitimate exercises of state power may place on religious belief and practice. Rather, there is "ample room under the Establishment Clause for 'benevolent neutrality which will permit religious exercise to exist without sponsorship and without interference,'" *Corporation of Presiding Bishop of Church of Jesus Christ of Later-day Saints* v. *Amos* (quoting *Walz* v. *Tax Comm'n*); "government may (and sometimes must) accommodate religious practices and . . . may do so without violating the Establishment Clause." *Hobbie* v. *Unemployment Appeals Comm'n of Fla.* The fact that Chapter 748 facilitates the practice of religion is not what renders it an unconstitutional establishment. Cf. *Lee* v. *Weisman* (Souter, J., concurring) ("That government must remain neutral in matters of religion does not foreclose it from ever taking religion into account"); *School Dist. of Abington* v. *Schempp* (Brennan, J., concurring) ("[H]ostility, not neutrality, would characterize the refusal to provide chaplains and places of worship for prisoners and soldiers cut off by the State from all civilian opportunities for public communion").

But accommodation is not a principle without limits, and what petitioners seek is an adjustment to the Satmars' religiously grounded preferences that our cases do not ⊥**2493** countenance. Prior decisions have allowed religious communities and institutions to pursue their own interests free from governmental interference, see *Corporation of Presiding Bishop* v. *Amos* (government may allow religious organizations to favor their own adherents in hiring, even for secular employment); *Zorach* v. *Clauson* (government may allow public schools to release students during the school day to receive off-site religious education), but we have never hinted that an otherwise unconstitutional delegation of political power to a religious group could be saved as a religious accommodation. Petitioners' proposed accommodation singles out a particular religious sect for special treatment, and whatever the limits of permissible legislative accommodations may be, compare *Texas Monthly, Inc.* v. *Bullock* (striking down law exempting only religious publications from taxation), with *Corporation of Presiding Bishop* v. *Amos* (upholding law exempting religious employers from Title VII), it is clear that neutrality as among religions must be honored.

This conclusion does not, however, bring the Satmar parents, the Monroe-Woodbury school district, or the State of New York to the end of the road in seeking ways to respond to the parents' concerns. Just as the Court in *Larkin* observed that the State's interest in protecting religious meeting places could be "readily accomplished by other means," there are several alternatives here for providing bilingual and bicultural special education to Satmar children. Such services can perfectly well be offered to village children through the Monroe-Woodbury Central School District. Since the Satmars do not claim that separatism is religiously mandated, their children may receive bilingual and bicultural instruction at a public school already run by the Monroe-Woodbury district. Or if the educationally appropriate offering by Monroe-Woodbury should turn out to be a separate program of bilingual and bicultural education at a neutral site near one of the village's parochial schools, this Court has already made it clear that no Establishment Clause difficulty would inhere in such a scheme, administered in accordance with neutral principles that would not necessarily confine special treatment to Satmars. See *Wolman* v. *Walter*.

To be sure, the parties disagree on whether the services Monroe-Woodbury actually provided in the late 1980's were appropriately tailored to the needs of Satmar children, but this dispute is of only limited relevance to the question whether such services could have been provided, had adjustments been made. As we understand New York law, parents who are dissatisfied with their handicapped child's program have recourse through administrative review proceedings (a process that appears not to have run its course prior to resort to Chapter 748, see *Board of Ed. of Monroe-Woodbury Central School Dist.* v. *Wieder*), and if the New York Legislature should remain dissatisfied with the responsiveness of the local school district, it could certainly enact general legislation tightening the mandate to school districts on matters of special education or bilingual and bicultural offerings.

III

Justice CARDOZO once cast the dissenter as "the gladiator making a last stand against the lions." B. Cardozo, Law and Literature 34 (1931). *Justice SCALIA's* dissent is certainly the work of a gladiator, but he thrusts at lions of his own imagining. We do not disable a religiously homogeneous group from exercising political power conferred on ⊥**2494** it without regard to religion. Unlike the states of Utah and New Mexico (which were laid out according to traditional political methodologies taking account of lines of latitude and longitude and topographical features, the reference line chosen for the Kiryas Joel Village School District was one purposely drawn to separate Satmars from non-Satmars. Nor do we impugn the motives of the New York Legislature, which no doubt intended to accommodate the Satmar community without violating the Establishment Clause; we simply refuse to ignore that the method it chose is one that aids a particular religious community, as such (Assembly sponsor thrice describes the Act's beneficiaries as the "Hasidic" children or community), rather than all groups similarly interested in separate schooling. The dissent protests it is novel to insist "up front" that a statute not tailor its benefits to apply only to one religious group, but if this were so, *Texas Monthly, Inc.* would have turned out differently (plurality opinion); *id.* (Blackmun, J., concurring in judgment), and language in *Walz* v. *Tax Comm'n of New York City* and *Bowen* v. *Kendrick*, purporting to rely on the breadth of the statutory schemes would have been mere surplusage. Indeed, under the dissent's theory, if New York were to pass a law providing school buses only for children attending Christian day schools, we would be constrained to uphold the statute against Establishment Clause attack until faced by a request from a non-Christian family for equal treatment under the patently unequal law. Cf. *Everson* v. *Board of Ed. of Ewing* (upholding school bus service provided all pupils). And to end on the point with which *Justice* SCALIA begins, the license he takes in suggesting that the Court holds the Satmar sect to be New York's established church, is only one symptom of his inability to accept the fact that this Court has long held that the First Amendment reaches more than classic, 18th century establishments. See *Torcaso* v. *Watkins*.

Our job, of course would be easier if the dissent's position had prevailed with the Framers and with this Court over the years. An Establishment Clause diminished to the dimensions acceptable to *Justice* SCALIA could be enforced by a few simple rules, and our docket would never see cases requiring the application of a principle like neutrality toward religion as well as among religious sects. But that would be as blind to history as to precedent, and the difference between *Justice* SCALIA and the Court accordingly turns on the Court's recognition that the Establishment Clause does comprehend such a principle and obligates courts to exercise the judgment necessary to apply it.

In this case we are clearly constrained to conclude that the statute before us fails the test of neutrality. It delegates a power this Court has said "ranks at the very apex of the function of a State," *Wisconsin* v. *Yoder*, to an electorate defined by common religious belief and practice, in a manner that fails to foreclose religious favoritism. It therefore crosses the line from permissible accommodation to impermissible establishment. The judgment of the Court of Appeals of the State of New York is accordingly

Affirmed.

Justice BLACKMUN, concurring.

For the reasons stated by *Justice* SOUTER and *Justice* STEVENS, whose opinions I join, I agree that the New York statute under review violates the Establishment Clause of the First Amendment. I write separately only to note my disagreement with any suggestion that today's decision signals a departure from the principles described in *Lemon* v. *Kurtzman*. The opinion of the Court (and of the plurality with respect to Part II-A) relies upon sever⊥**2495**al decisions, including *Larkin* v. *Grendel's Den, Inc.*, that explicitly rested on the criteria set forth in *Lemon*. Indeed, the two principles on which the opinion bases its conclusion that the legislative act is constitutionally invalid essentially are the second and third *Lemon* criteria. See *Larkin* (finding "a fusion of governmental and religious functions" under *Lemon*'s "entanglement" prong); *id.* (finding a lack of any "effective means of guaranteeing" that governmental power will be neutrally employed under *Lemon*'s "principal or primary effect" prong).

I have no quarrel with the observation of *Justice* O'CONNOR, that the application of constitutional principles, including those articulated in *Lemon*, must be sensitive to particular contexts. But I remain convinced of the general validity of the basic principles stated in *Lemon*, which have guided this Court's Establishment Clause decisions in over 30 cases.

Justice STEVENS, with whom *Justice* BLACKMUN and *Justice* GINSBURG join, concurring.

New York created a special school district for the members of the Satmar religious sect in response to parental concern that children suffered "panic, fear and trauma" when "leaving their own community and being with people whose ways were so different." To meet those concerns, the State could have taken steps to alleviate the children's fear by teaching their schoolmates to be tolerant and respectful of Satmar customs. Action of that kind would raise no constitutional concerns and would further the strong public interest in promoting diversity and understanding in the public schools.

Instead, the State responded with a solution that affirmatively supports a religious sect's interest in segregating itself and preventing its children from associating with their neighbors. The isolation of these children, while it may protect them from "panic, fear and trauma," also unquestionably increased the likelihood that they would remain within the fold, faithful adherents of their parents' religious faith. By creating a school district that is specifically intended to shield children from contact with others who have "different ways," the State provided official support to cement the attachment of young adherents to a particular faith. It is telling, in this regard, that two thirds of the school's full-time students are Hasidic handicapped children from *outside* the village; the Kiryas Joel school thus serves a population far wider than the village—one defined less by geography than by religion.

Affirmative state action in aid of segregation of this character is unlike the evenhanded distribution of a public benefit or service, a "release time" program for public school students involving no public premises or funds, or a decision to grant an exemption from a burdensome general rule. It is, I believe, fairly characterized as establishing, rather than merely accommodating, religion. For this reason, as well as the reasons set out in *Justice SOUTER's* opinion, I am persuaded that the New York law at issue in these cases violates the Establishment Clause of the First Amendment.

Justice O'CONNOR, concurring in part and concurring in the judgment.

I

The question at the heart of this case is: What may the government do, consistently with the Establishment Clause, to accommodate people's religious beliefs? The history of the Satmars in Orange County is especially instructive on this, because they have been involved in at least three accommodation problems, of which this case is only the most recent.

The first problem related to zoning law, and arose shortly after the Satmars moved to the town of Monroe in the early 1970's. **⊥2496** Though the area in which they lived was zoned for single-family homes, the Satmars subdivided their houses into several apartments, apparently in part because of their traditionally close-knit extended family groups. The Satmars also used basements of some of their buildings as schools and synagogues, which according to the town was also a zoning violation. Fortunately for the Satmars, New York state law had a way of accommodating their concerns. New York allows virtually any group of residents to incorporate their own village, with broad powers of self-government. The Satmars followed this course, incorporating their community as the village of Kiryas Joel, and their zoning problems, at least, were solved.

The Satmars' next need for accommodation arose in the mid-1980's. Satmar education is pervasively religious, and is provided through entirely private schooling. But though the Satmars could afford to educate most of their children, educating the handicapped is a difficult and expensive business. Moreover, it is a business that the government generally funds, with tax moneys that come from the Satmars as well as from everyone else. In 1984, therefore, the Monroe-Woodbury Central School District began providing handicapped education services to the Satmar children at an annex to the Satmar religious school. The curriculum and the environment of the services were entirely secular. They were the same sort of services available to handicapped students at secular public and private schools throughout the country.

In 1985, however, we held that publicly funded classes on religious school premises violate the Establishment Clause. *School Dist. of Grand Rapids* v. *Ball*; *Aguilar* v. *Felton*. Based on these decisions, the Monroe-Woodbury Central School District stopped providing services at the Kiryas Joel site, and required the Satmar children to attend public schools outside the village. This, however, was not a satisfactory arrangement for the Satmars, in part because the Satmar children had a hard time dealing with immersion in the non-Satmar world. By 1989, only one handicapped Kiryas Joel child was going to the public school—the others were getting either privately-funded services or no special education at all. Though the Satmars tried to reach some other arrangement with the Monroe-Woodbury School District, the problem was not resolved.

In response to these difficulties came the third accommodation. In 1989 the New York Legislature passed a statute to create a special school district covering only the village of Kiryas Joel. This school district could, of course, only operate secular schools, and the Satmars therefore wanted to use it only to provide education for the handicapped. But because the district provides this education in the village, Satmar children could take advantage of the district's services without encountering the problems they faced when they were sent out to Monroe-Woodbury schools. It is the constitutionality of the law creating this district that we are now called on to decide.

II

The three situations outlined above shed light on an important aspect of accommodation under the First Amendment: Religious needs can be accommodated through laws that are neutral with regard to religion. The Satmars' living arrangements were accommodated by their right—a right shared with all other communities, religious or not, throughout New York—to incorporate themselves as a village. From 1984 to 1985, the Satmar handicapped children's educational needs were accommodated by special education programs like those available to all handicapped children, religious or not. Other examples of such accommodations abound: The Constitution itself, for instance, accommodates the religious desires of those who were opposed to oaths by allowing any officeholder—of any religion, or none—to take either an oath of office or an affirmation. Art. **⊥2497** II, §1, cl. 8; Art. VI, cl. 3; see also Amdt. 4. Likewise, the selective service laws provide exemptions for conscientious objectors whether or not the objection is based on religious beliefs. *Welsh* v. *United States* (Harlan, J., concurring in result).

We have time and again held that the government generally may not treat people differently based on the God or gods they worship, or don't worship. "The clearest command of the Establishment Clause is that one religious denomination cannot be officially preferred over another." *Larson* v. *Valente*. "Just as we subject to the most exacting scrutiny laws that make classifications based on race . . . so too we strictly scrutinize governmental classifications based on religion." *Employment Div., Dept. of Human Resources of Ore.* v. *Smith*. "[T]he Establishment Clause prohibits government from abandoning secular purposes . . . to favor the adherents of any sect or religious organization." *Gillette* v. *United States*. "Neither [the State nor the Federal Governments] can constitutionally pass laws or impose requirements which aid all religions as against non-believers, and neither can aid those religions based on a belief in the existence of God as against those religions founded on different beliefs." *Torcaso* v. *Watkins*. See also *Texas Monthly, Inc.* v. *Bullock* (plurality opinion); *id.* (Blackmun, J., concurring in judgment); *Welsh*, (Harlan, J., concurring); *Walz* v. *Tax Comm'n of New York City* (opinion of Harlan, J.).

This emphasis on equal treatment is, I think, an eminently sound approach. In my view, the Religion Clauses—the Free Exercise Clause, the Establishment Clause, the Religious Test Clause, Art. VI, cl. 3, and the Equal Protection Clause as applied to religion—all speak with one voice on this point: Absent the most unusual circumstances, one's religion ought not affect one's legal rights or duties or benefits. As I have previously noted, "the Establishment Clause is infringed when the government makes adherence to religion relevant to a person's standing in the political community." *Wallace* v. *Jaffree* (O'Connor, J., concurring in judgment).

That the government is acting to accommodate religion should generally not change this analysis. What makes accommodation permissible, even praiseworthy, is not that the government is making life easier for some particular religious group as such. Rather, it is that the government is accommodating a deeply held belief. Accommodations may thus justify treating those who share this belief differently from those who do not; but they do not justify discriminations based on sect. A state law prohibiting the consumption of alcohol may exempt sacramental wines, but it may not exempt sacramental wine use by Catholics but not by Jews. A draft law may exempt conscientious objectors, but it may not exempt conscientious objectors whose objections are based on theistic belief (such as Quakers) as opposed to nontheistic belief (such as Buddhists) or atheistic belief. See *Welsh* (Harlan, J., concurring in result); see also *id.* (reaching this result on statutory interpretation grounds); *United States* v. *Seeger* (same). The Constitution permits "*nondiscriminatory* religious-practice exemption[s]," *Smith* (emphasis added), not sectarian ones.

III

I join Parts I, II-B, II-C, and III of the Court's opinion because I think this law, rather than being a general accommodation, singles out a particular religious group for ⊥**2498** favorable treatment. The Court's analysis of the history of this law and of the surrounding statutory scheme persuades me of this.

On its face, this statute benefits one group—the residents of Kiryas Joel. Because this benefit was given to this group based on its religion, it seems proper to treat it as a legislatively drawn religious classification. I realize this is a close question, because the Satmars may be the only group who currently need this particular accommodation. The legislature may well be acting without any favoritism, so that if another group came to ask for a similar district, the group might get it on the same terms as the Satmars. But the nature of the legislative process makes it impossible to be sure of this. A legislature, unlike the judiciary or many administrative decisionmakers, has no obligation to respond to any group's requests. A group petitioning for a law may never get a definite response, or may get a "no" based not on the merits but on the press of other business or the lack of an influential sponsor. Such a legislative refusal to act would not normally be reviewable by a court. Under these circumstances, it seems dangerous to validate what appears to me a clear religious preference.

Our invalidation of this statute in no way means that the Satmars' needs cannot be accommodated. There is nothing improper about a legislative intention to accommodate a religious group, so long as it is implemented through generally applicable legislation. New York may, for instance, allow all villages to operate their own school districts. If it does not want to act so broadly, it may set forth neutral criteria that a village must meet to have a school district of its own; these criteria can then be applied by a state agency, and the decision would then be reviewable by the judiciary. A district created under a generally applicable scheme would be acceptable even though it coincides with a village which was consciously created by its voters as an enclave for their religious group. I do not think the Court's opinion holds the contrary.

I also think there is one other accommodation that would be entirely permissible: the 1984 scheme, which was discontinued because of our decision in *Aguilar*. The Religion Clauses prohibit the government from favoring religion, but they provide no warrant for discriminating *against* religion. All handicapped children are entitled by law to government-funded special education. See, *e.g.*, Individuals with Disabilities Education Act, 20 U. S. C. §1400 *et seq*. If the government provides this education on-site at public schools and at nonsectarian private schools, it is only fair that it provide it on-site at sectarian schools as well.

I thought this to be true in *Aguilar* (O'Connor, J., dissenting), and I still believe it today. The Establishment Clause does not demand hostility to religion, religious ideas, religious people, or religious schools. Cf. *Lamb's Chapel* v. *Center Moriches Union Free School Dist.* It is the Court's insistence on disfavoring religion in *Aguilar* that led New York to favor it here. The Court should, in a proper case, be prepared to reconsider *Aguilar*, in order to bring our Establishment Clause jurisprudence back to what I think is the proper track—government impartiality, not animosity, towards religion.

IV

One aspect of the Court's opinion in this case is worth noting: Like the opinions in two recent cases, *Lee* v. *Weisman*; *Zobrest* v. *Catalina Foothills School Dist.*, and the case I think is most relevant to this one, *Larson* v. *Valente*, the Court's opinion does not focus on the Establishment Clause test we set forth in *Lemon* v. *Kurtzman*.

It is always appealing to look for a single test, a Grand Unified Theory that would ⊥**2499** resolve all the cases that may arise under a particular clause. There is, after all, only one Establishment Clause, one Free Speech Clause, one Fourth Amendment, one Equal Protection Clause.

But the same constitutional principle may operate very differently in different contexts. We have, for instance, no one Free Speech Clause test. We have different tests for content-based speech restrictions, for content-neutral speech restrictions, for restrictions imposed by the government acting as employer, for restrictions in nonpublic fora, and so on. This simply reflects the necessary recognition that the interests relevant to the Free Speech Clause inquiry—personal liberty, an informed citizenry, government efficiency, public order, and so on—are present in different degrees in each context.

And setting forth a unitary test for a broad set of cases may sometimes do more harm than good. Any test that must deal with widely disparate situations risks being so vague as to be useless. I suppose one can say that the general test for all free speech cases is "a regulation is valid if the interests asserted by the government are stronger than the interests of the speaker and the listeners," but this would hardly be a serviceable formulation. Similarly, *Lemon* has, with some justification, been criticized on this score.

Moreover, shoehorning new problems into a test that does not reflect the special concerns raised by those problems tends to deform the language of the test. Relatively simple phrases like "primary effect . . . that neither advances nor inhibits religion" and "entanglement," *Lemon*, acquire more and more complicated definitions which stray ever further from their literal meaning. Distinctions are drawn between statutes whose effect is to advance religion and statutes whose effect is to allow religious organizations to advance religion. See, *e.g.*, *Corporation of Presiding Bishop of Church of Jesus Christ of Latter-day Saints* v. *Amos* (O'Connor, J., concurring in judgment) (discussing this point). Assertions are made that authorizing churches to veto liquor sales in surrounding areas "can be seen as having a 'primary' and 'principal' effect of advancing religion." *Larkin* v. *Grendel's Den, Inc.* "Entanglement" is discovered in public employers monitoring the performance of public employees—surely a proper enough function—on parochial school premises, and in the public employees cooperating with the school on class scheduling and other administrative details. *Aguilar* v. *Felton*. Alternatives to *Lemon* suffer from a similar failing when they lead us to find "coercive pressure" to pray when a school asks listeners—with no threat of legal sanctions—to stand or remain silent during a graduation prayer. *Lee* v. *Weisman*. Some of the results and perhaps even some of the reasoning in these cases may have been right. I joined two of the cases cited above, *Larkin* and *Lee*, and continue to believe they were correctly decided. But I think it is more useful to recognize the relevant concerns in each case on their own terms, rather than trying to squeeze them into language that does not really apply to them.

Finally, another danger to keep in mind is that the bad test may drive out the good. Rather than taking the opportunity to derive narrower, more precise tests from the case law, courts tend to continually try to patch up the broad test, making it more and more amorphous and distorted. This, I am afraid, has happened with *Lemon*.

Experience proves that the Establishment Clause, like the Free Speech Clause, cannot easily be reduced to a single test. There are different categories of Establishment Clause cases, which may call for different approaches. Some cases, like this one, involve government actions targeted at particular in⊥**2500**dividuals or groups, imposing special duties or giving special benefits. Cases involving government speech on religious topics, see, *e.g.*, *Lee* v. *Weisman*; *Allegheny County* v. *American Civil Liberties Union Greater Pittsburgh Chapter*; *Lynch* v. *Donnelly*; *Stone* v. *Graham*, seem to me to fall into a different category and to require an analysis focusing on whether the speech endorses or disapproves of religion, rather than on whether the government action is neutral with regard to religion. See *Allegheny County* (O'Connor, J., concurring in part and concurring in judgment).

Another category encompasses cases in which the government must make decisions about matters of religious doctrine and religious law. See *Serbian Eastern Orthodox Diocese* v. *Milivojevich* (which also did not apply *Lemon*). These cases, which often arise in the application of otherwise neutral property or contract principles to religious institutions, involve complicated questions not present in other situations. See, *e.g.*, *id.* (looking at some aspects of religious law to determine the structure of the church, but refusing to look further into religious law to resolve the ultimate dispute). Government delegations of power to religious bodies may make up yet another category. As *Larkin* itself suggested, government impartiality towards religion may not be enough in such situations: A law that bars all alcohol sales within some distance of a church, school, or hospital may be valid, but an equally evenhanded law that gives each institution discretionary power over the sales may not be. Of course, there may well be additional categories, or more opportune places to draw the lines between the categories.

As the Court's opinion today shows, the slide away from *Lemon*'s unitary approach is well under way. A return to *Lemon*, even if possible, would likely be futile, regardless of where one stands on the substantive Establishment Clause questions. I think a less unitary approach provides a better structure for analysis. If each test covers a narrower and more homogeneous area, the tests may be more precise and therefore easier to apply. There may be more opportunity to pay attention to the specific nuances of each area. There might also be, I hope, more consensus on each of the narrow tests than there has been on a broad test. And abandoning the *Lemon* framework need not mean abandoning some of the insights that the test reflected, nor the insights of the cases that applied it.

Perhaps eventually under this structure we may indeed distill a unified, or at least a more unified, Establishment Clause test from the cases. Cf. *Clark* v. *Community for Creative Non-Violence* (uniting two strands of Free Speech Clause doctrine). But it seems to me that the case law will better be able to evolve towards this if it is freed from the *Lemon* test's rigid influence. The hard questions would, of course, still have to be asked; but they will be asked within a more carefully tailored and less distorted framework.

* * *

For the reasons stated, I would affirm the judgment of the Court of Appeals of the State of New York.

Justice KENNEDY, concurring in the judgment.

The Court's ruling that the Kiryas Joel Village School District violates the Establishment Clause is in my view correct, but my reservations about what the Court's reasoning implies for religious accommodations in general are sufficient to require a separate writing. As the Court recognizes, a legislative accommodation that discriminates among religions may become an establishment of religion. But the Court's opinion can be interpreted to say that an accommodation for ⊥**2501** a particular religious group is invalid because of the risk that the legislature will not grant the same accommodation to another religious group suffering some similar burden. This rationale seems to me without grounding in our precedents and a needless restriction upon the legislature's ability to respond to the unique problems of a particular religious group. The real vice of the school district, in my estimation, is that New York created it by drawing political boundaries on the basis of religion. I would decide the issue we confront upon this narrower theory, though in accord with many of the Court's general observations about the State's actions in this case.

I

This is not a case in which the government has granted a benefit to a general class of recipients of which religious groups are just one part. It is rather a case in which the government seeks to alleviate a specific burden on the religious practices of a particular religious group. I agree that a religious accommodation demands careful scrutiny to ensure that it does not so burden nonadherents or discriminate against other religions as to become an establishment. I disagree, however, with the suggestion that the Kiryas Joel Village School District contravenes these basic constitutional commands. But for the forbidden manner in which the New York Legislature sought to go about it, the State's attempt to accommodate the special needs of the handicapped Satmar children would have been valid.

"Government policies of accommodation, acknowledgment, and support for religion are an accepted part of our political and cultural heritage." *Allegheny County* v. *Greater Pittsburgh ACLU* (Kennedy, J., concurring in judgment in part and dissenting in part). Before the Revolution, colonial governments made a frequent practice of exempting religious objectors from general laws. See McConnell, The Origins and Historical Understanding of Free Exercise of Religion, 103 Harv. L. Rev. 1409, 1466–1473 (1990) (recounting colonial exemptions from oath requirements, compulsory military service, religious assessments, and other general legislation). As early as 1691, for instance, New York allowed Quakers to testify by affirmation rather than oath in civil court cases. T. Curry, The First Freedoms: Church and State in America to the Passage of the First Amendment 64 (1986). Later, during the American Revolution, the Continental Congress exempted religious objectors from military conscription. Resolution of July 18, 1775, reprinted in 2 Journals of the Continental Congress 187, 189 (1905) ("As there are some people, who, from religious principles, cannot bear arms in any case, this Congress intend no violence to their consciences . . ."). And since the framing of the Constitution, this Court has approved legislative accommodations for a variety of religious practices. See, *e.g.*, *Selective Draft Law Cases* (military draft exemption for religious objectors); *Zorach* v. *Clausen* (New York City program permitting public school children to leave school for one hour a week for religious observance and instruction); *Gillette* v. *United States* (military draft exemption for religious objectors); *Corporation of Presiding Bishop of Church of Jesus Christ of Latter-day Saints* v. *Amos* (exemption of religious organizations from Title VII's prohibition of religious discrimination); *Employment Div., Dept. of Human Resources of Ore.* v. *Smith* (exemption from drug laws for sacramental peyote use) (dicta).

⊥**2502** New York's object in creating the Kiryas Joel Village School District—to accommodate the religious practices of the handicapped Satmar children—is validated by the principles that emerge from these precedents. First, by creating the district, New York sought to alleviate a specific and identifiable burden on the Satmars' religious practice. The Satmars' way of life, which springs out of their strict religious beliefs, conflicts in many respects with mainstream American culture. They do not watch television or listen to radio; they speak Yiddish in their homes and do not read

English-language publications; and they have a distinctive hairstyle and dress. Attending the Monroe-Woodbury public schools, where they were exposed to much different ways of life, caused the handicapped Satmar children understandable anxiety and distress. New York was entitled to relieve these significant burdens, even though mainstream public schooling does not conflict with any specific tenet of the Satmars' religious faith. The Title VII exemption upheld in *Corporation of Presiding Bishop*, for example, covers religious groups who may not believe themselves obliged to employ co-religionists in every instance. See also *Walz* v. *Tax Comm'n of New York* ("The limits of permissible state accommodation to religion are by no means co-extensive with the noninterference mandated by the Free Exercise Clause"); accord, *Smith* (legislatures may grant accommodations even when courts may not).

Second, by creating the district, New York did not impose or increase any burden on non-Satmars, compared to the burden it lifted from the Satmars, that might disqualify the District as a genuine accommodation. In *Gillette*, the Court upheld a military draft exemption, even though the burden on those without religious objection to war (the increased chance of being drafted and forced to risk one's life in battle) was substantial. And in *Corporation of Presiding Bishop*, the Court upheld the Title VII exemption even though it permitted employment discrimination against nonpractitioners of the religious organization's faith. There is a point, to be sure, at which an accommodation may impose a burden on nonadherents so great that it becomes an establishment. See, *e.g.*, *Estate of Thornton* v. *Caldor, Inc.* (invalidating mandatory Sabbath day off because it provided "no exception when honoring the dictates of Sabbath observers would cause the employer substantial economic burdens or when the employer's compliance would require the imposition of significant burdens on other employees required to work in place of the Sabbath observers"). This case has not been argued, however, on the theory that non-Satmars suffer any special burdens from the existence of the Kiryas Joel Village School District.

Third, the creation of the school district to alleviate the special burdens born by the handicapped Satmar children cannot be said, for that reason alone, to favor the Satmar religion to the exclusion of any other. "The clearest command of the Establishment Clause," of course, "is that one religious denomination cannot be officially preferred over another." *Larson* v. *Valente*. I disagree, however, with the Court's conclusion that the school district breaches this command. The Court insists that religious favoritism is a danger here, because the "anomalously case-specific nature of the legislature's exercise of state authority in creating this district for a religious community leaves the Court without any direct way to review such state action" to ensure interdenominational neutrality. "Because the religious community of Kiryas Joel did not receive its new governmental authority simply as one of many communities eligible for equal treatment under a general law," the Court maintains, "we have no assurance that the next similarly situated group seeking a school district of its own will receive one; . . . a legislature's failure to ⊥**2503** enact a special law is itself unreviewable."

This reasoning reverses the usual presumption that a statute is constitutional and, in essence, adjudges the New York Legislature guilty until it proves itself innocent. No party has adduced any evidence that the legislature has denied another religious community like the Satmars its own school district under analogous circumstances. The legislature, like the judiciary, is sworn to uphold the Constitution, and we have no reason to presume that the New York Legislature would not grant the same accommodation in a similar future case. The fact that New York singled out the Satmars for this special treatment indicates nothing other than the uniqueness of the handicapped Satmar children's plight. It is normal for legislatures to respond to problems as they arise—no less so when the issue is religious accommodation. Most accommodations cover particular religious practices. See, *e.g.*, 21 CFR §1307.31 (1993) ("The listing of peyote as a controlled substance . . . does not apply to the nondrug use of peyote in bona fide religious ceremonies of the Native American Church"); 25 CFR §11.87H (1993) ("[I]t shall not be unlawful for any member of the Native American Church to transport into Navajo country, buy, sell, possess, or use peyote in any form in connection with the religious practices, sacraments or services of the Native American Church"); Dept. of Air Force, Reg. 35–10, ¶2–28(b)(2) (Apr. 1989) ("Religious head coverings are authorized for wear while in uniform when military headgear is not authorized. . . . Religious head coverings may be worn underneath military headgear if they do not interfere with the proper wearing, functioning, or appearance of the prescribed headgear . . . . For example, Jewish yarmulkes meet this requirement if they do not exceed 6 inches in diameter"); National Prohibition Act, §3, 41 Stat. 308 ("Liquor for nonbeverage purposes and wine for sacramental purposes may be manufactured, purchased, sold, bartered, transported, imported, exported, delivered, furnished and possessed"), repealed by Liquor Law Repeal and Enforcement Act, §1, 49 Stat. 872. They do not thereby become invalid.

Nor is it true that New York's failure to accommodate another religious community facing similar burdens would be insulated from challenge in the courts. The burdened community could sue the State of New York, contending that New York's discriminatory treatment of the two religious communities violated the Establishment Clause. To resolve this claim, the court would have only to determine whether the community does indeed bear the same burden on its religious practice as did the Satmars in Kiryas Joel. See *Olsen* v. *Drug Enforcement Admin.* (rejecting claim that the members of the Ethiopian Zion Coptic Church were entitled to an exemption from the marijuana laws on the same terms as the peyote exemption for the Native American Church). While a finding of discrimination would then raise a difficult question of relief, compare *Olsen* ("Faced with the choice between invalidation and extension of any controlled-substances religious exemption, which would the political branches choose? It would take a court bolder than this one to predict . . . that extension, not invalidation, would be the probable choice"), with *Califano* v. *Westcott* (curing gender discrimination in the AFDC program by extending benefits to children of unemployed mothers instead of denying benefits to children of unemployed fathers), the discrimination itself would not be beyond judicial remedy.

II

The Kiryas Joel Village School District thus does not suffer any of the typical infirmities that might invalidate an attempted legislative accommodation. In the ordinary case, the fact that New York has chosen to accommodate the burdens unique to one religious group would raise no constitutional problems. Without further evidence that New York has denied the same accommodation to religious ⊥**2504** groups bearing similar burdens, we could not presume from the particularity of the accommodation that the New York Legislature acted with discriminatory intent.

This particularity takes on a different cast, however, when the accommodation requires the government to draw political or electoral boundaries. "The principle that government may accommodate the free exercise of religion does not supersede the fundamental limitations imposed by the Establishment Clause," *Lee* v. *Weisman*, and in my view one such fundamental limitation is that government may not use religion as a criterion to draw political or electoral lines. Whether or not the purpose is accommodation and whether or not the government provides similar gerrymanders to people of all religious faiths, the Establishment Clause forbids the government to use religion as a line-drawing criterion. In this respect, the Establishment Clause mirrors the Equal Protection Clause. Just as the government may not segregate people on account of their race, so too it may not segregate on the basis of religion. The danger of stigma and stirred animosities is no less acute for religious line-drawing than for racial. Justice Douglas put it well in a statement this Court quoted with approval just last Term: "When racial or religious lines are drawn by the State, the multiracial, multireligious communities that our Constitution seeks to weld together as one become separatist; antagonisms that relate to race or to religion rather than to political issues are generated; communities seek not the best representative but the best racial or religious partisan. Since that system is at war with the democratic ideal, it should find no footing here." *Wright* v. *Rockefeller* (Douglas, J., dissenting) (quoted in *Shaw* v. *Reno*). I agree with the Court insofar as it invalidates the school district for being drawn along religious lines. As the plurality observes, the New York Legislature knew that everyone within the village was Satmar when it drew the school district along the village lines, and it determined who was to be included in the district by imposing, in effect, a religious test. There is no serious question that the legislature configured the school district, with purpose and precision, along a religious line. This explicit religious gerrymandering violates the First Amendment Establishment Clause.

It is important to recognize the limits of this principle. We do not confront the constitutionality of the Kiryas Joel Village itself, and the formation of the village appears to differ from the formation of the school district in one critical respect. As the Court notes, the village was formed pursuant to a religion-neutral self-incorporation scheme. Under New York law, a territory with at least 500 residents and not more than five square miles may be incorporated upon petition by at least 20 percent of the voting residents of that territory or by the owners of more than 50 percent of the territory's real property. N. Y. Village Law §§2–200, 2–202 (McKinney 1973 and Supp. 1994). Aside from ensuring that the petition complies with certain procedural requirements, the supervisor of the town in which the territory is located has no discretion to reject the petition. §2–206; see Decision on Sufficiency of Petition, in App. 8, 14 ("[T]he hollow provisions of the Village Law . . . allow me only to review the procedural niceties of the petition itself"). The residents of the town then vote upon the incorporation petition in a special election. N. Y. Village Law §2–212 (McKinney 1973). By contrast, the Kiryas Joel Village School District was created by state legislation. The State of New York had complete discretion not to enact it. The State thus had a direct hand in accomplishing the religious segregation.

As the plurality indicates, the Establishment Clause does not invalidate a town or a state "whose boundaries are derived according to neutral historical and geographic crite⊥**2505**ria, but whose population happens to comprise coreligionists." People who share a common religious belief or lifestyle may live together without sacrificing the basic rights of self-governance that all American citizens enjoy, so long as they do not use those rights to establish their religious faith. Religion flourishes in community, and the Establishment Clause must not be construed as some sort of homogenizing solvent that forces unconventional religious groups to choose between assimilating to mainstream American culture or losing their political rights. There is more than a fine line, however, between the voluntary association that leads to a political community comprised of people who share a common religious faith, and the forced separation that occurs when the government draws explicit political boundaries on the basis of peoples' faith. In creating the Kiryas Joel Village School District, New York crossed that line, and so we must hold the district invalid.

III

This is an unusual case, for it is rare to see a State exert such documented care to carve out territory for people of a particular religious faith. It is also unusual in that the problem to which the Kiryas Joel Village School District was addressed is attributable in no small measure to what I believe were unfortunate rulings by this Court.

Before 1985, the handicapped Satmar children of Kiryas Joel attended the private religious schools within the village that the other Satmar children attended. Because their handicaps were in some cases acute (ranging from mental retardation and deafness to spina bifida and cerebral palsy), the State of New York provided public funds for special education of these children at annexes to the religious schools. Then came the companion cases of *School Dist. of Grand Rapids* v. *Ball* and *Aguilar* v. *Felton*. In *Grand Rapids*, the Court invalidated a program in which public school teachers would offer supplemental classes at private schools, including religious schools, at the end of the regular school day. And in *Aguilar*, the Court invalidated New York City's use of Title I funding to pay the salaries of public school teachers who taught educationally deprived children of low-income families at parochial schools in the city. After these cases, the Monroe-Woodbury School District suspended its special education program at the Kiryas Joel religious schools, and the Kiryas Joel parents were forced to enroll their handicapped children at the Monroe-Woodbury public schools in order for the children to receive special education. The ensuing difficulties, as the Court recounts, led to the creation of the Kiryas Joel Village School District.

The decisions in *Grand Rapids* and *Aguilar* may have been erroneous. In light of the case before us, and in the interest of sound elaboration of constitutional doctrine, it may be necessary for us to reconsider them at a later date. A neutral aid scheme, available to religious and nonreligious alike, is the preferable way to address problems such as the Satmar handicapped children have suffered. See *Witters* (Powell, J., concurring). But for *Grand Rapids* and *Aguilar*, the Satmars would have had no need to seek special accommodations or their own school district. Our decisions led them to choose that unfortunate course, with the deficiencies I have described.

One misjudgment is no excuse, however, for compounding it with another. We must confront this case as it comes before us, without bending rules to free the Satmars from a predicament into which we put them. The Establishment Clause forbids the government to draw political boundaries on the basis of religious faith. For this reason, I concur in the judgment of the Court.

Justice SCALIA, with whom *The* CHIEF JUSTICE and *Justice* THOMAS join, dissenting.

The Court today finds that the Powers That Be, up in Albany, have conspired to ⊥**2506** effect an establishment of the Satmar Hasidim. I do not know who would be more surprised at this discovery: the Founders of our Nation or Grand Rebbe Joel Teitelbaum, founder of the Satmar. The Grand Rebbe would be astounded to learn that after escaping brutal persecution and coming to America with the modest hope of religious toleration for their ascetic form of Judaism, the Satmar had become so powerful, so closely allied with Mammon, as to have become an "establishment" of the Empire State. And the Founding Fathers would be astonished to find that the Establishment Clause—which they designed "to insure that no one powerful sect or combination of sects could use political or governmental power to punish dissenters," *Zorach* v. *Clauson* (Black, J., dissenting)—has been employed to prohibit characteristically and admirably American accommodation of the religious practices (or more precisely, cultural peculiarities) of a tiny minority sect. *I*, however, am *not* surprised. Once this Court has abandoned text and history as guides, nothing prevents it from calling religious toleration the establishment of religion.

I

Unlike most of our Establishment Clause cases involving education, these cases involve no public funding, however slight or indirect, to private religious schools. They do not involve private schools at all. The school under scrutiny is a public school specifically designed to provide a public secular education to handicapped students. The superintendent of the school, who is not Hasidic, is a 20-year veteran of the New York City public school system, with expertise in the area of bilingual, bicultural, special education. The teachers and therapists at the school all live outside the village of Kiryas Joel. While the village's private schools are profoundly religious and strictly segregated by sex, classes at the public school are co-ed and the curriculum secular. The school building has the bland appearance of a public school, unadorned by religious symbols or markings; and the school complies with the laws and regulations governing all other New York State public schools. There is no suggestion, moreover, that this public school has gone too far in making special adjustments to the religious needs of its students. Cf. *Zorach* v. *Clauson* (approving a program permitting early release of public school students to attend religious instruction). In sum, these cases involve only public aid to a school that is public as can be. The only thing distinctive about the school is that all the students share the same religion.

None of our cases has ever suggested that there is anything wrong with that. In fact, the Court has specifically *approved* the education of students of a single religion on a neutral site adjacent to a private religious school. See *Wolman* v. *Walter*. In that case, the Court rejected the argument that "any program that isolates the sectarian pupils is impermissible," and held that, "[t]he fact that a unit on a neutral site on occasion may serve only sectarian pupils does not provoke [constitutional] concerns." And just last Term, the Court held that the State could permit public employees to assist students in a Catholic school. See *Zobrest* v. *Catalina Foothills School Dist.* (sign-language translator for deaf student). If a State can furnish services to a group of sectarian students on a neutral site adjacent to a private religious school, or even *within* such a school, how can there be any defect in educating those same students in a public school? As the Court noted in *Wolman*, the constitutional dangers of establishment arise "from the nature of the institution, not from the nature of the pupils." There is no danger in educating religious students in a public school.

For these very good reasons, *Justice SOUTER's* opinion does not focus upon the school, but rather upon the school district ⊥**2507** and the New York Legislature that created it. His arguments, though sometimes intermingled, are two: that reposing governmental power in the Kiryas Joel School District is the same as reposing governmental power in a religious group; and that in enacting the statute creating the district, the New York State Legislature was discriminating on the basis of religion, *i.e.*, favoring the Satmar Hasidim over others. I shall discuss these arguments in turn.

II

For his thesis that New York has unconstitutionally conferred governmental authority upon the Satmar sect, *Justice SOUTER* relies extensively, and virtually exclusively, upon *Larkin* v. *Grendel's Den, Inc. Justice SOUTER* believes that the present case "resembles" *Grendel's Den* because that case "teaches that a state may not delegate its civic authority *to a group chosen according to a religious criterion*," (emphasis added). That misdescribes both what that case taught (which is that a state may not delegate its civil authority *to a church*), and what this case involves (which is a group chosen according to cultural characteristics). The statute at issue there gave churches veto power over the State's authority to grant a liquor license to establishments in the vicinity of the church. The Court had little difficulty finding the statute unconstitutional. "The Framers did not set up a system of government in which important, discretionary governmental powers would be delegated to or shared with religious institutions."

Justice SOUTER concedes that *Grendel's Den* "presented an example of united civic and religious authority, an establishment rarely found in such straightforward form in modern America." The uniqueness of the case stemmed from the grant of governmental power directly to a religious institution, and the Court's opinion focused on that fact, remarking that the transfer of authority was to "churches" (10 times), the "governing body of churches" (twice), "religious institutions" (twice) and "religious bodies" (once). Astonishingly, however, *Justice SOUTER* dismisses the difference between a transfer of government power to citizens who share a common religion as opposed to "the officers of its sectarian organization"—the critical factor that made *Grendel's Den* unique and "rar[e]"—as being "one of form, not substance."

Justice SOUTER's steamrolling of the difference between civil authority held by a church, and civil authority held by members of a church, is breathtaking. To accept it, one must believe that large portions of the civil authority exercised during most of our history were unconstitutional, and that much more of it than merely the Kiryas Joel School District is unconstitutional today. The history of the populating of North America is in no small measure the story of groups of people sharing a common religious and cultural heritage striking out to form their own communities. It is preposterous to suggest that the civil institutions of these communities, separate from their churches, were constitutionally suspect. And if they were, surely *Justice SOUTER* cannot mean that the inclusion of one or two nonbelievers in the community would have been enough to eliminate the constitutional vice. If the conferral of governmental power upon a religious institution *as such* (rather than upon American citizens who belong to the religious institution) is not the test of *Grendel's Den* invalidity, there is no reason why giving power to a body that is overwhelmingly dominated by the members of one sect would not suffice to invoke the Establishment Clause. That might have made the entire States of Utah and New Mexico unconstitutional at the time of their admission to the Union, and would undoubt⊥**2508**edly make many units of local government unconstitutional today.

Justice SOUTER's position boils down to the quite novel proposition that any group of citizens (say, the residents of Kiryas Joel) can be invested with political power, but not if they all belong to the same religion. Of course such *disfavoring* of religion is positively antagonistic to the purposes of the Religion Clauses, and we have rejected it before. In *McDaniel* v. *Paty*, we invalidated a state constitutional amendment that would have permitted all persons to participate in political conventions, except ministers. We adopted James Madison's view that the State could not "'punis[h] a religious profession with the privation of a civil right.'" *Id.*, at 626 (opinion of Burger, C. J.), quoting 5 Writings of James Madison 288 (G. Hunt ed. 1904). Or as Justice Brennan put it in his opinion concurring in judgment: "Religionists no less than members of any other group enjoy the full measure of protection afforded speech, association, and political activity generally." I see no reason why it is any less pernicious to deprive a group rather than an individual of its rights simply because of its religious beliefs.

Perhaps appreciating the startling implications for our constitutional jurisprudence of collapsing the distinction between religious institutions and their members, *Justice SOUTER* tries to limit his "unconstitutional conferral of civil authority" holding by pointing out several features supposedly unique to the present case: that the "boundary lines of the school district divide residents *according to* religious affiliation" (emphasis added); that the school district was created by "a special act of the legislature," and that the formation of the school district ran counter to the legislature's trend of consolidating districts in recent years. Assuming all these points to be true (and they are not), they would certainly bear upon whether the legislature had an impermissible religious motivation in creating the district (which is *Justice SOUTER's next* point, in the discussion of which I shall reply to these arguments). But they have nothing to do with whether conferral of power upon a group of citizens can be the conferral of power upon a religious institution. It can not. Or if it can, our Establishment Clause jurisprudence has been transformed.

III

I turn, next, to *Justice SOUTER's* second justification for finding an establishment of religion: his facile conclusion that the New York Legislature's creation of the Kiryas Joel School District was religiously motivated. But in the Land of the Free, democratically adopted laws are not so easily impeached by unelected judges. To establish the unconstitutionality of a facially neutral law on the mere basis of its asserted religiously preferential (or discriminatory) effects—or at least to establish it in conformity with our precedents—*Justice SOUTER* "must be able to show the absence of a neutral, secular basis" for the law. *Gillette* v. *United States*; see also ⊥**2509** *Arlington Heights* v. *Metropolitan Housing Development Corp.* (facially race-neutral laws can be invalidated on the basis of their effects only if "unexplainable on grounds other than race").

There is of course no possible doubt of a secular basis here. The New York Legislature faced a unique problem in Kiryas Joel: a community in which all the non-handicapped children attend private schools, and the physically and mentally disabled children who attend public school suffer the additional handicap of cultural distinctiveness. It would be troublesome enough if these peculiarly dressed, handicapped students were sent to the next town, accompanied by their similarly clad but unimpaired classmates. But all the unimpaired children of Kiryas Joel attend private school. The handicapped children suffered sufficient emotional trauma from their predicament that their parents kept them home from school. Surely the legislature could target this problem, and provide a public education for these students, in the same way it addressed, *by a similar law*, the unique needs of children institutionalized in a hospital. See *e.g.*, 1970 N. Y. Laws, ch. 843 (authorizing a union free school district for the area owned by Blythedale Children's Hospital).

Since the obvious presence of a neutral, secular basis renders the asserted preferential effect of this law inadequate to invalidate it, *Justice SOUTER* is required to come forward with direct evidence that religious preference was the objective. His case could scarcely be weaker. It consists, briefly, of this: The People of New York created the Kiryas Joel Village School District in order to further the Satmar religion, rather than for any proper secular purpose, because (1) they created the district in an extraordinary manner—by special Act of the legislature, rather than under the State's general laws governing school-district reorganization; (2) the creation of the district ran counter to a State trend towards consolidation of school districts; and (3) the District includes only adherents of the Satmar religion. On this indictment, no jury would convict.

One difficulty with the first point is that it is not true. There was really nothing so "special" about the formation of a school district by an Act of the New York Legislature. The State has created both large school districts, see *e.g.*, 1972 N. Y. Laws, ch. 928 (creating the Gananda School District out of land previously in two other districts), and small specialized school districts for institutionalized children, see *e.g.*, 1972 N. Y. Laws, ch. 559 (creating a union free school district for the area owned by Abbott House), through these special Acts. But in any event all that the first point proves, and the second point as well (countering the trend toward consolidation), is that New York regarded Kiryas Joel as a special case, requiring special measures. I should think it *obvious* that it did, and obvious that it *should have*. But even if the New York Legislature had never before created a school district by special statute (which is not true), and even if it had done nothing but consolidate school districts for over a century (which is not true), how ⊥**2510** could the departure from those past practices possibly demonstrate that the legislature had religious favoritism in mind? It could not. To be sure, when there is no special treatment there is no possibility of religious favoritism; but it is not logical to suggest that when there *is* special treatment there is *proof* of religious favoritism.

Justice SOUTER's case against the statute comes down to nothing more, therefore, than his third point: the fact that all the residents of the Kiryas Joel Village School District are Satmars. But all its residents also wear unusual dress, have unusual civic customs, and have not much to do with people who are culturally different from them. (The Court recognizes that "the Satmars prefer to live together 'to facilitate individual religious observance and maintain social, cultural and religious values,' but that it is not 'against their religion' to interact with others." On what basis does *Justice SOUTER* conclude that it is the theological distinctiveness rather than the cultural distinctiveness that was the basis for New York State's decision? The normal assumption would be that it was the latter, since it was not theology but dress, language, and cultural alienation that posed the educational problem for the children. *Justice SOUTER* not only does not adopt the logical assumption, he does not even give the New York Legislature the benefit of the doubt. The following is the level of his analysis:

"Not even the special needs of the children in this community can explain the legislature's unusual Act, for the State could have responded to the concerns of the Satmar parents [by other means]." In other words, we know the legislature must have been motivated by the desire to favor the Satmar Hasidim religion, because it *could* have met the needs of these children by a method that did not place the Satmar Hasidim in a separate school district. This is not a rational argument proving religious favoritism; it is rather a novel Establishment Clause principle to the effect that no secular objective may be pursued by a means that might also be used for religious favoritism if some other means is available.

I have little doubt that *Justice SOUTER* would laud this humanitarian legislation if all of the distinctiveness of the students of Kiryas Joel were attributable to the fact that their parents were nonreligious commune-dwellers, or American Indians, or gypsies. The creation of a special, one-culture school district for the benefit of those children would pose no problem. The neutrality demanded by the Religion Clauses requires the same indulgence towards cultural characteristics that *are* accompanied by religious belief. "The Establishment Clause does not license government to treat religion and those who teach or practice it, simply by virtue of their status as such, as . . . subject to unique disabilities." *McDaniel* v. *Paty* (Brennan, J., concurring in judgment).

Even if *Justice SOUTER* could successfully establish that the cultural distinctiveness of the Kiryas Joel students (which is the problem the New York Legislature addressed) was an *essential part* of their religious belief rather than merely an *accompaniment* of their religious belief, that would not discharge his heavy burden. In order to invalidate a facially neutral law, *Justice SOUTER* would have to show not only that legislators were aware that religion caused the problems addressed, but also that the legislature's proposed solution was motivated by a desire to disadvantage or benefit a religious group (*i.e.* to disadvantage or benefit them *because of their religion*). For example, if the city of Hialeah, knowing of the potential health problems raised by the Santeria religious practice of animal sacrifice, were to provide by ordinance a special, more frequent, municipal garbage collection for the carcasses of dead animals, we would not strike the ordinance down just because the city council was aware that a religious practice produced the problem the ordinance addressed. See *Church of Lukumi Babalu Aye, Inc.* v. *Hialeah*. Here a facially neutral statute ⊥**2511** extends an educational benefit to the one area where it was not effectively distributed. Whether or not the reason for the ineffective distribution had anything to do with religion, it is a remarkable stretch to say that the Act was motivated by a desire to favor or disfavor a particular religious group. The proper analogy to Chapter 748 is not the Court's hypothetical law providing school buses only to Christian students, but a law providing extra buses to rural school districts (which happen to be predominantly Southern Baptist).

At various times *Justice SOUTER* intimates, though he does not precisely say, that the boundaries of the school district were intentionally drawn on the basis of religion. He refers, for example, to "[t]he State's manipulation of the franchise for this district . . . , giving the sect exclusive control of the political subdivision," implying that the "giving" of political power to the religious sect was the object of the "manipulation." There is no evidence of that. The special district was created to meet the special educational needs of distinctive handicapped children, and the geographical boundaries selected for that district were (quite logically) those that already existed for the village. It sometimes appears as though the shady "manipulation" *Justice SOUTER* has in mind is that which occurred when the village was formed, so that the drawing of its boundaries infected the coterminous boundaries of the district. He says, for example, that "[i]t is undisputed that those who negotiated the village boundaries when applying the general village incorporation statute drew them so as to exclude all but Satmars." It is indeed. But non-Satmars were excluded, not (as he intimates) because of their religion, but—as *Justice O'CONNOR* clearly describes—because of their lack of desire for the high-density zoning that Satmars favored. It was a classic drawing of lines on the basis of communality of *secular governmental desires*, not communality of religion. What happened in the creation of the village is in fact precisely what happened in the creation of the school district, so that the former cannot possibly infect the latter, as *Justice SOUTER* tries to suggest. Entirely secular reasons (zoning for the village, cultural alienation of students for the school district) produced a political unit whose members happened to share the same religion. There is *no* evidence (indeed, no plausible suspicion) of the legislature's desire to favor the Satmar religion, as opposed to meeting distinctive secular needs or desires of citizens who happened to be Satmars. If there were, *Justice SOUTER* would say so; instead, he must merely insinuate.

IV

But even if Chapter 748 were intended to create a special arrangement for the Satmars *because of* their religion (not including, as I have shown in Part I, any conferral of governmental power upon a religious entity), it would be a permissible accommodation. "This Court has long recognized that the government may (and sometimes must) accommodate religious practices and that it may do so without violating the Establishment Clause." *Hobbie* v. *Unemployment Appeals Comm'n of Fla.*. Moreover, "there is ample room for accommodation of religion under the Establishment Clause," *Corporation for Presiding Bishop of Church of Jesus of Latter-day Saints* v. *Amos*, and for "play in the joints productive of a benevolent neutrality which will permit religious exercise to exist without sponsorship and without interference," *Walz* v. *Tax Comm'n of N. Y. City*. Accommodation is permissible, moreover, even when the statute deals specifically with religion, see, *e.g.*, *Zorach* v. *Clauson*, and even when accommodation is not commanded by the Free Exercise Clause, see, *e.g.*, *Walz*.

When a legislature acts to accommodate religion, particularly a minority sect, "it fol⊥**2512**lows the best of our traditions." *Zorach*. The Constitution itself contains an accommodation of sorts. Article VI, cl. 3, prescribes that executive, legislative and judicial officers of the Federal and State Governments shall bind themselves to support the Constitution "by Oath or Affirmation." Although members of the most populous religions found no difficulty in swearing an oath to God, Quakers, Moravians, and Mennonites refused to take oaths based on Matthew 5:34's injunction "swear not at all." The option of affirmation was added to accommodate these minority religions and enable their members to serve in government. Congress, from its earliest sessions, passed laws accommodating religion by refunding duties paid by specific churches upon the importation of plates for the printing of Bibles, see 6 Stat. 116 (1813), vestments, 6 Stat. 346 (1816), and bells, 6 Stat. 675 (1836). Congress also exempted church property from the tax assessments it levied on residents of the District of Columbia; and all 50 States have had similar laws. See *Walz*.

This Court has also long acknowledged the permissibility of legislative accommodation. In one of our early Establishment Clause cases, we upheld New York City's early release program, which allowed students to be released from public school during school hours to attend religious instruction or devotional exercises. See *Zorach*. We determined that the early release program "accommodates the public service to . . . spiritual needs," and noted that finding it unconstitutional would "show a callous indifference to religious groups." In *Walz*, we upheld a property tax exemption for religious organizations, observing that it was part of a salutary tradition of "permissible state accommodation to religion." And in *Presiding Bishop* we upheld a section of the Civil Rights Act of 1964 exempting religious groups from the antidiscrimination provisions of Title VII. We concluded that it was "a permissible legislative purpose to alleviate significant governmental interference with the ability of religious organizations to define and carry out their religious missions." In today's opinion, however, the Court seems uncomfortable with this aspect of our constitutional tradition. Although it acknowledges the concept of accommodation, it quickly points out that it is "not a principle without limits" and then gives reasons why the present case exceeds those limits, reasons which simply do not hold water. "[W]e have never hinted," the Court says, "that an otherwise unconstitutional delegation of political power to a religious group could be saved as a religious accommodation." Putting aside the circularity inherent in referring to a delegation as "otherwise unconstitutional" when its constitutionality turns on whether there is an accommodation, if this statement is true, it is only because we have never hinted that delegation of political power to citizens who share a particular religion could be unconstitutional. This is simply a replay of the argument we rejected in Part II.

The second and last reason the Court finds accommodation impermissible is, astoundingly, the mere risk that the State will not offer accommodation to a similar group in the future, and that neutrality will therefore not be preserved. Returning to the ill fitted crutch of *Grendel's Den*, the Court suggests that by acting through this special statute the New York Legislature has eliminated any "'effective means of guaranteeing' that governmental power will be and has been neutrally employed." How misleading. That language in *Grendel's Den* was an expression of concern *not* (as the context in which it is quoted suggests) about the courts' ability to assure the legislature's future neutrality, but about the legislature's ability to assure the neutrality of the churches to which it had transferred ⊥**2513** legislative power. That concern is inapposite here; there is no doubt about the legislature's capacity to control what transpires in a public school.

At bottom, the Court's "no guarantee of neutrality" argument is an assertion of *this Court's* inability to control the New York Legislature's future denial of comparable accommodation. We have "no assurance," the Court says, "that the next similarly situated group seeking a school district of its own will receive one," since "a legislature's failure to enact a special law is . . . unreviewable." See also (O'Connor, J., concurring in part and concurring in judgment). That is true only in the technical (and irrelevant) sense that the later group denied an accommodation may need to challenge the grant of the first accommodation in light of the later denial, rather than challenging the denial directly. But one way or another, "even if [an administrative agency is] not empowered or obliged to act, [a litigant] would be entitled to a judicial audience. Ultimately the courts cannot escape the obligation to address [a] plea that the exemption [sought] is mandated by the first amendment's religion clauses." *Olsen* v. *Drug Enforcement Admin.*

The Court's demand for "up front" assurances of a neutral system is at war with both traditional accommodation doctrine and the judicial role. As we have described, Congress's earliest accommodations exempted duties paid by specific churches on particular items. See, *e.g.*, 6 Stat. 346 (1816) (exempting vestments imported by "bishop of Bardstown"). Moreover, most efforts at accommodation seek to solve a problem that applies to members of only one or a few religions. Not every religion uses wine in its sacraments, but that does not make an exemption from Prohibition for sacramental wine-use impermissible, accord, *Church of Lukumi Babalu Aye, Inc.* v. *Hialeah* (Souter, J., concurring in judgment), nor does it require the State granting such an exemption to explain in advance how it will treat every other claim for dispensation from its controlled-substances laws.

Likewise, not every religion uses peyote in its services, but we have suggested that legislation which exempts the sacramental use of peyote from generally applicable drug laws is not only permissible, but desirable, see *Employment Div., Ore. Dept. of Human Resources* v. *Smith*, without any suggestion that some "up front" legislative guarantee of equal treatment for sacramental substances used by other sects must be provided. The record is clear that the necessary guarantee can and will be provided, after the fact, *by the courts*. See, *e.g.*, *Olsen* v. *Drug Enforcement Admin.* (rejecting claim that peyote exemption requires marijuana exemption for Ethiopian Zion Coptic Church); *Olsen* v. *Iowa* (same); *Kennedy* v. *Bureau of Narcotics and Dangerous Drugs* (accepting claim that peyote exemption for Native American Church requires peyote exemption for other religions that use that substance in their sacraments).

⊥2514 Contrary to the Court's suggestion, I do not think that the Establishment Clause prohibits formally established "state" churches and nothing more. I have always believed, and all my opinions are consistent with the view, that the Establishment Clause prohibits the favoring of one religion over others. In this respect, it is the Court that attacks lions of straw. What I attack is the Court's imposition of novel "up front" procedural requirements on state legislatures. Making law (and making exceptions) one case at a time, whether through adjudication or through highly particularized rulemaking or legislation, violates, *ex ante*, no principle of fairness, equal protection, or neutrality, simply because it does not announce in advance how all future cases (and all future exceptions) will be disposed of. If it did, the manner of proceeding of this Court itself would be unconstitutional. It is presumptuous for this Court to impose—*out of nowhere*—an unheard-of prohibition against proceeding in this manner upon the Legislature of New York State. I never heard of such a principle, nor has anyone else, nor will it ever be heard of again. Unlike what the New York Legislature has done, this *is* a special rule to govern only the Satmar Hasidim.

V

A few words in response to the separate concurrences: *Justice STEVENS* adopts, for these cases, a rationale that is almost without limit. The separate Kiryas Joel school district is problematic in his view because "[t]he isolation of these children, while it may protect them from 'panic, fear and trauma,' also unquestionably increased the likelihood that they would remain within the fold, faithful adherents of their parents' religious faith." So much for family values. If the Constitution forbids any state action that incidentally helps parents to raise their children in their own religious faith, it would invalidate a release program permitting public school children to attend the religious-instruction program of their parents' choice, of the sort we approved in *Zorach*, indeed, it would invalidate state laws according parents physical control over their children, at least insofar as that is used to take the little fellows to church or synagogue. *Justice STEVENS'* statement is less a legal analysis than a manifesto of secularism. It surpasses mere rejection of accommodation, and announces a positive hostility to religion—which, unlike all other noncriminal values, the state must not assist parents in transmitting to their offspring.

Justice KENNEDY's "political-line-drawing" approach founders on its own terms. He concedes that the Constitution does not prevent people who share a faith from forming their own villages and towns, and suggests that the formation of the village of Kiryas Joel was free from defect. He also notes that States are free to draw political lines on the basis of history and geography. I do not see, then, how a school district drawn to mirror the boundaries of an existing village (an existing geographic line), which itself is not infirm, can violate the Constitution. Thus, while *Justice KENNEDY* purports to share my criticism (Part IV) of the Court's unprecedented insistence that the New York Legislature make its accommodations only by general legislation, his own approach is little different. He says the village is constitutional because it was formed (albeit by members of a single religious sect) under a general New York law; but he finds the school district unconstitutional because it was the product of a specific enactment. In the end, his analysis is no different from the Court's.

Justice KENNEDY expresses the view that *School Dist. of Grand Rapids* v. *Ball* **⊥2515** and *Aguilar* v. *Felton*—the cases that created the need for the Kiryas Joel legislation by holding unconstitutional state provision of supplemental educational services in sectarian schools—"may have been erroneous," and he suggests that "it may be necessary for us to reconsider them at a later date." *Justice O'CONNOR* goes even further and expresses the view that *Aguilar* should be overruled. I heartily agree that these cases, so hostile to our national tradition of accommodation, should be overruled at the earliest opportunity; but meanwhile, today's opinion causes us to lose still further ground, and in the same anti-accommodationist direction.

Finally, *Justice O'CONNOR* observes that the Court's opinion does not focus on the so-called *Lemon* test and she urges that that test be abandoned, at least as a "unitary approach" to all Establishment Clause claims. I have previously documented the Court's convenient relationship with *Lemon*, which it cites only when useful, see *Lamb's Chapel* v. *Center Moriches Union Free School Dist.* (Scalia, J., concurring in judgment), and I no longer take any comfort in the Court's failure to rely on it in any particular case, as I once mistakenly did, see *Lee* v. *Weisman* (Scalia, J., dissenting). But the Court's snub of *Lemon* today (it receives only two "see also" citations, in the course of the opinion's description of *Grendel's Den*) is particularly noteworthy because all three courts below (who are not free to ignore Supreme Court precedent at will) relied on it, and the parties (also bound by our case law) dedicated over 80 pages of briefing to the application and continued vitality of the *Lemon* test. In addition to the other sound reasons for abandoning *Lemon*, see *e.g.*, *Edwards* v. *Aguillard* (Scalia, J., dissenting); *Wallace* v. *Jaffree* (Rehnquist, J., dissenting), it seems quite inefficient for this Court, which in reaching its decisions relies heavily on the briefing of the parties and, to a lesser extent, the opinions of lower courts, to mislead lower courts and parties about the relevance of the *Lemon* test. Compare *ante* (ignoring *Lemon* despite lower courts' reliance) with *Lamb's Chapel* (applying *Lemon* despite failure of lower court to mention it).

Unlike *Justice* O'CONNOR, however, I would not replace *Lemon* with nothing, and let the case law "evolve" into a series of situation-specific rules (government speech on religious topics, government benefits to particular groups, *etc.*) unconstrained by any "rigid influence." The problem with (and the allure of) *Lemon* has not been that it is "rigid," but rather that in many applications it has been utterly meaningless, validating whatever result the Court would desire. See *Lamb's Chapel* (Scalia, J., concurring in judgment); *Wallace* (Rehnquist, J., dissenting). To replace *Lemon* with nothing is simply to announce that we are now so bold that we no longer feel the need even to pretend that our haphazard course of Establishment Clause decisions is governed by any principle. The foremost principle I would apply is fidelity to the longstanding traditions of our people, which surely provide the diversity of treatment that *Justice* O'CONNOR seeks, but do not leave us to our own devices.

* * *

The Court's decision today is astounding. Chapter 748 involves no public aid to private schools and does not mention religion. In order to invalidate it, the Court casts aside, on the flimsiest of evidence, the strong presumption of validity that attaches to facially neutral laws, and invalidates the present accommodation because it does not trust New York to be as accommodating toward other religions (presumably those less powerful ⊥**2516** than the Satmar Hasidim) in the future. This is unprecedented—except that it continues, and takes to new extremes, a recent tendency in the opinions of this Court to turn the Establishment Clause into a repealer of our Nation's tradition of religious toleration. I dissent.

UNEQUAL GOVERNMENT TREATMENT OF RELIGIOUS GROUPS

Those in the media who report on religion and even scholars of religion frequently refer to "mainstream" or "mainline" religious groups. By these terms they refer to such denominations as Methodists, Baptists, Catholics, Episcopalians, Lutherans, etc. But the very terminology implies that there are other groups which are not "mainline," but rather are smaller, perhaps marginal in vitality, perhaps questionable in their theology (at least, from a "mainstream" point of view), and sometimes are led by people who are perceived (again, by the "mainstream") to be cunning and dishonest. In short, these nonmainline religious groups are regarded, in the best light, as curiosities and, in the worst, as unsavory and even dangerous.[1] These groups are frequently called "sects" or "cults" and, while these terms are acceptable and useful in the vocabulary of the sociologist of religion, in popular parlance they usually mean "strange," "weird," and, to say the very least, "unpopular."[2]

In times when fear of such groups has been intense, it has not been unusual for governments, often through their taxing power, to try to curb, if not destroy, these unpopular religions. The groups have sometimes responded with litigation, claiming that the government has violated their free exercise of religion. The Jehovah's Witnesses were the principal unpopular group in the 1930s and 1940s and governments singled them out for restrictive legislation: unequal treatment. This produced a great body of case law, much of which is reproduced elsewhere in this book. With the new wave of hysteria over cults in the 1970s and 1980s, unequal treatment of religions has come up in the courts again. Although there are many lower court cases, the Supreme Court had dealt with only one at the time of this writing, and it was decided on establishment grounds, rather than free exercise.[3] That case is LARSON v. VALENTE (1982).

[1]See J. Gordon Melton, *The Encyclopedia of American Religions* (Wilmington, NC: McGrath Publishing Co., 1978), 2 vols., for a listing and description of the over 1,200 religious bodies in this country, including between 500 and 600 "alternative religions," another name for the kind of groups described here.

[2]See Ronald B. Flowers, *Religion in Strange Times: The 1960s and 1970s* (Macon, GA: Mercer University Press, 1984), especially pp. 85-111 for a popular exposition of what sects and cults are, set in the context of the latest anxiety about such groups in this country. For information on the theology and structure of such groups see J. Gordon Melton, *Encyclopedic Handbook of Cults in America* and *Biographical Dictionary of American Cult and Sect Leaders*, both published by Garland Publishing Company of New York, 1986.

[3]The recent literature on cults and even on their legal problems is voluminous; some of it is included in the bibliography in this book. A good overview, aimed particularly at the legal issues, is Leo Pfeffer, *Religion, State, and the Burger Court* (Buffalo, NY: Prometheus Books, 1984), pp. 201-34. See also Thomas Robbins, William C. Shepherd, and James McBride, eds., *Cults, Culture, and the Law: Perspectives on New Religious Movements* (Chico, CA: Scholars Press, 1985).

The thing which most bothered people about cults was not their theology; in fact even those who were very concerned about cults usually came to know the theology of the group only after they had already formed their opposition to it. The two things about the most unpopular cults which elicited opposition were the way they won converts and the way they raised revenue. In terms of the former, cults were frequently accused of "brainwashing," "mind control," and/or "instant hypnotism."[4] In terms of the latter, both Hare Krishna and the Unification Church (the "Moonies") were singled out for criticism. Although members of Hare Krishna from time to time did solicit funds in other public places, they came to be identified in the popular mind with attempting to sell books and solicit donations in airports. Members of the Unification Church (the official name of which is The Holy Spirit Association for the Unification of World Christianity) frequented airports, shopping centers, street corners, and other public places to sell things (frequently flowers and/or candy) and to ask for contributions. They were often persistent in their efforts and some people found them annoying. That was compounded by the popular perception that the church members/sales people, mostly young people of late high school or college age, were essentially enslaved in this activity (they had been brainwashed, according to popular lore), working long hours under adverse conditions, and that the revenue went primarily to the personal fortune of the founder and leader of the group, Rev. Sun Myung Moon. It was these perceptions, whether or not they were true (they probably were greatly overstated), which forms the background of *Larson.*

In 1961 Minnesota adopted its Charitable Solicitation Act, designed to protect the public from fraudulent collections of funds. It required charitable organizations to register with the state's Department of Commerce before they could solicit contributions. Thereafter the registered organizations had to submit annual reports of receipts, expenditures for management, fund raising, and public education, and descriptions of transfers of property or funds out of state. If a report showed that a group had spent more than thirty percent of its income for administrative costs, its registry would be canceled and it could no longer solicit contributions within the state. Religious groups were exempt from the requirement. In 1978, however, apparently because of a growing concern about the type of fund raising done by cults, described above, Minnesota changed its law by adding a fifty percent rule. Simply stated, the amended law said that if a religious group received more than half of its revenue from its own membership, it would continue to be exempt from the Solicitation Act. But if a group received less than half of its revenue from its own membership, i.e., if more than half its contributions came from the general public, such as people in airports or shopping centers, it would have to register and file the financial disclosure forms. Almost immediately after the amendment, the Minnesota Department of Commerce wrote to the Unification Church saying that it was now required to register.

The Church initiated litigation, claiming that the fifty percent rule, among other things, denied its members religious freedom and that it discriminated between religious organizations, contrary to the Establishment Clause. When the case reached the Supreme Court, the courts below had ruled, with some slight exceptions, that the law was in violation of the Establishment Clause. The Court affirmed.

On the question of standing, which the appeals court had questioned, Minnesota now claimed that the Unification Church was not a religious organization and thus would not be exempt from statutory requirements even if the fifty percent rule were declared unconstitutional. Justice Brennan, writing for the Court, disagreed, saying that the fifty percent rule applied only to religious organizations. When Minnesota requested the Church's registration, it must have assumed that the Church was a religious organization. Furthermore, application of the Act to the Church would cause it injury by means of its filing requirements. For both of these reasons, the Church had standing to sue.

On the merits of the case, the Court began with the assumption that the Establishment Clause commands that one denomination cannot be officially preferred over another. Since the Act seemed to apply to religious groups unequally, it was subject to strict scrutiny by the Court. Clearly Minnesota had a significant interest in protecting its citizens from fraudulent charitable organizations. But unless the statute at bar was "closely fitted" to accomplishing that purpose, it would be declared unconstitutional.

Minnesota made three arguments for the legitimacy of its law: (1) members of a religious body can and will exercise supervision over its solicitation activities when more than fifty percent of its contributions come from members; (2) following from the first, membership control is an adequate safeguard against improper solicitations of the public by the organization; and (3) the need for public disclosure of solicitation revenues and procedures rises in proportion with the percentage of nonmember contributions. The Court found all three arguments lacking. In regard to the first, there simply was nothing in the record to support the idea that members of the group are more attentive to the supervision of its solicitation when they contributed more than half. The existence of the Act itself contradicted the second: the state passed the legislation because of the belief

[4]This issue is discussed in chapter four of this book.

that charitable organizations soliciting from the public cannot be relied upon to regulate themselves. Simple mathematics showed the third argument to be wrong. In short, the fifty percent rule treated religious groups differently, which was contrary to the Establishment Clause. Consequently, the Unification Church could not be compelled to register and report under that provision of the statute.[5]

This case was decided without using the three-part *Lemon* test. However, the opinion was written by Justice Brennan, who believed in the enduring applicability of the test.[6] But in this case the test was not applicable, he said, because the *Lemon* test is designed "to apply to laws affording a uniform benefit to *all* religion and not to laws "that discriminate *among* religions" like the case at bar. But if the test *were* to be applied, it was clear to him that the fifty percent rule would fail the entanglement prong because it discriminated between denominations and thus ran the risk of politicizing religion.

The four dissenters did not address the constitutional issue of the case, but simply argued that the lower court's decision in favor of the Unification Church should be set aside on essentially technical grounds, e.g., the Church's lack of standing to sue.

LARSON v. VALENTE

456 U.S. 228
ON APPEAL FROM THE UNITED STATES
COURT OF APPEALS FOR THE EIGHTH CIRCUIT
Argued December 9, 1981 — Decided April 21, 1982

⊥**230** *Justice* BRENNAN delivered the opinion of the Court.

The principal question presented by this appeal is whether a Minnesota statute, imposing certain registration and reporting requirements upon only those religious organizations that solicit more than fifty per cent of their funds from nonmembers, discriminates against such organizations in violation of the Establishment Clause of the First Amendment.

I

Appellants are John R. Larson, Commissioner of Securities, and Warren Spannaus, Attorney General, of the State of Minnesota. They are, by virtue of their offices, responsible for the implementation and enforcement of the Minnesota Charitable Solicitation Act, Minn. Stat. §§ 309.50-309.61 (1969 and Supp. 1982). This Act, in effect since 1961, provides for a system of registration and disclosure respecting ⊥**231** charitable organizations, and is designed to protect the contributing public and charitable beneficiaries against fraudulent practices in the solicitation of contributions for purportedly charitable purposes. A charitable organization subject to the Act must register with the Minnesota Department of Commerce before it may solicit contributions within the State. With certain specified exceptions, all charitable organizations registering under § 309.52 must file an extensive annual report with the Department, detailing, *inter alia,* their total receipts and income from all sources, their cost of management, fundraising, and public education, and their transfers of property or funds out of the State, along with a description of the recipients and purposes of those transfers. The Department is authorized by the Act to deny or withdraw the registration of any charitable organization if the Department finds that it would be in "the public interest" to do so and if the organization is found to have engaged in fraudulent, deceptive, or dishonest practices. Further, a charitable organization is deemed ineligible to maintain its registration under the Act if it expends or agrees to expend an "unreasonable amount" for management, general, and fundraising costs, with those costs being presumed unreasonable if they exceed thirty per cent of the organization's total income and revenue.

From 1961 until 1978, all "religious organizations" were exempted from the requirements of the Act. But effective March 29, 1978, the Minnesota Legislature amended the Act so as to include a "fifty per cent rule" in the exemption provision covering religious organizations. This fifty per cent rule provided that only those religious organizations that received more than half of their total con⊥**232**tributions from members or affiliated organizations would remain exempt from the registration and reporting requirement of the Act.

Shortly after the enactment of § 309.515, subd. 1(b), the Department notified appellee Holy Spirit Association for the Unification of World Christianity (Unification Church) that it was required to register under the Act because of the newly enacted provision. Appellees Valente, Barber, Haft, and Korman, claiming to be followers of the tenets of the Unifica⊥**233**tion Church, responded by bringing the present action in the United States District Court for the District of Minnesota. Appellees sought a declaration that the Act, on its face and as applied to them through § 309.151, subd. 1(b)'s fifty per cent rule, constituted an abridgment of their First Amendment rights of expression and free exercise of religion, as well as a denial of their right to equal protection of the laws, guaranteed by the Fourteenth Amendment; appellees also sought ⊥**234** temporary and permanent injunctive relief. Appellee Unification Church was later joined as a plaintiff by stipulation of the parties, and the action was transferred to a United States Magistrate.

---

[5]In a footnote the Court said that there might be other ways in which Minnesota could protect its citizens from fraudulent solicitation by religious groups. It just could not do it by statutorily treating them differently.

[6]In MARSH v. CHAMBERS, decided the year after *Larson*, the test was not even mentioned in the opinion. Justice Brennan, writing in dissent, referred to the test as "our settled doctrine" and chided the Court for not using it.

After obtaining a preliminary injunction, appellees moved for summary judgment. Appellees' evidentiary support for this motion included a "declaration" of appellee Haft, which described in some detail the origin, "religious principles," and practices of the Unification Church. The declaration stated that among the activities emphasized by the Church were "door-to-door and public-place proselytizing and solicitation of funds to support the Church," and that the application of the Act to the Church through § 309.515, subd. 1(b)'s fifty percent rule would deny its members their "religious freedom." Appellees also argued that by discriminating among religious organizations, § 309.515, subd. 1(b)'s fifty per cent rule violated the Establishment Clause.

Appellants replied that the Act did not infringe appellees' freedom to exercise their religious beliefs. Appellants sought to distinguish the present case from *Murdock* v. *Pennsylvania,* where this Court invalidated a municipal ordinance that had required the licensing of Jehovah's Witnesses who solicited donations in exchange for ⊥**235** religious literature, by arguing that unlike the activities of the petitioners in *Murdock*, appellees' solicitations bore no substantial relationship to any religious expression, and that they were therefore outside the protection of the First Amendment. Appellants also contended that the Act did not violate the Establishment Clause. Finally, appellants argued that appellees were not entitled to challenge the Act until they had demonstrated that the Unification Church was a religion and that its fundraising activities were a religious practice.

The Magistrate determined, however, that it was not necessary for him to resolve the questions of whether the Unification Church was a religion, and whether appellees' activities were religiously motivated, in order to reach the merits of appellees' claims. Rather he found that the "overbreadth" doctrine gave appellees standing to challenge the Act's constitutionality. On the merits, the Magistrate held that the Act was facially unconstitutional with respect to religious organizations, and was therefore entirely void as to such organizations, because § 309.515, subd. 1(b)'s fifty per cent rule failed the second of the three Establishment Clause "tests" set forth by this Court in *Lemon* v. *Kurtzman*. The Magistrate also held on due ⊥**236** process grounds that certain provisions of the Act were unconstitutional as applied to any groups or persons claiming the religious-organization exemption from the Act. The Magistrate therefore recommended, *inter alia,* that appellees be granted the declarative and permanent injunctive relief that they had sought—namely, a declaration that the Act was unconstitutional as applied to religious organizations and their members, and an injunction against enforcement of the Act as to any religious organization. Accepting these recommendations, the District Court entered summary judgment in favor of appellees on these issues.

On appeal, the United States Court of Appeals for the Eighth Circuit affirmed in part and reversed in part. On the issue of standing, the Court of Appeals affirmed the District Court's application of the overbreadth doctrine, citing *Village of Schaumburg* v. *Citizens for Better Environment* for ⊥**237** the proposition that "a litigant whose own activities are unprotected may nevertheless challenge a statute by showing that it substantially abridges the First Amendment rights of other parties not before the court." On the merits, the Court of Appeals affirmed the District Court's holding that the "inexplicable religious classification" embodied in the fifty per cent rule of § 309.515, subd. 1(b), violated the Establishment Clause. Applying the Minnesota rule of severability, the Court of Appeals also held that § 309.515, subd. 1(b), as a whole should not be stricken from the Act, but that the fifty per cent rule should be stricken from § 309.515, subd. 1(b). But the court disagreed with the District Court's conclusion that appellees and others should enjoy the religious organization exemption from the Act merely by claiming to be such organizations: The court held that proof of religious-organization status was required in order to gain the exemption, and left the question of appellees' status "open . . . for further development." The Court of Appeals accordingly vacated the judgment of the District Court and remanded the action for entry of a modified injunction and for further appropriate proceedings. We noted probable jurisdiction.

⊥**238** II

Appellants argue that appellees are not entitled to be heard on their Establishment Clause claims. Their rationale for this argument has shifted, however, as this litigation has progressed. Appellant's position in the courts below was that the Unification Church was not a religion, and more importantly that appellees' solicitations were not connected with any religious purpose. From these premises appellants concluded that appellees were not entitled to raise their Establishment Clause claims until they had demonstrated that their activities were within the protection of that Clause. The courts below rejected this conclusion, instead applying the overbreadth doctrine in order to allow appellees to raise their Establishment Clause claims. In this Court, appellants have taken an entirely new tack. They now argue that the Unification Church is not a "religious organization" within the meaning of Minnesota Charitable Solicitation Act, and that the Church therefore would not be entitled to an exemption under § 309.515, subd. l(b), even if the fifty per cent rule were declared unconstitutional. From this new premise appellants conclude that the courts below erred in invalidating § 309.515, subd. 1(b)'s fifty per cent rule without first requiring appellees to demonstrate that they would have been able to maintain their exempt status but for that rule, and thus that its adoption had caused them injury in fact. We have considered both of appellants' rationales, and hold that neither of them has merit.

"The essence of the standing inquiry is whether the parties seeking to invoke the court's jurisdiction have 'alleged such a personal stake in the outcome of the controversy as to assure ⊥**239** that concrete adverseness which sharpens the presentation of issues upon which the court so largely depends for illumination of difficult constitutional questions.'" *Duke Power Co.* v. *Carolina Environmental Study Group*, quoting *Baker* v. *Carr*. This requirement of a "personal stake" must consist of "a 'distinct and palpable injury . . .' to the plaintiff," *Duke Power Co.*, quoting *Warth* v. *Seldin*, and "a 'fairly traceable' causal connection between the claimed injury and the challenged conduct," *Duke Power Co.*, quoting *Arlington Heights* v. *Metropolitan Housing Dev. Corp.* Application of these constitutional standards to the record before us and the factual findings of the District Court convince us that the Art. III requirements for standing are plainly met by appellees.

Appellants argue in this Court that the Unification Church is not a "religious organization" within the meaning of the Act, and therefore that appellees cannot demonstrate injury in fact. We note at the outset, however, that in the years before 1978 the Act contained a general exemption provision for all religious organizations, and that during those years the Unification Church was not required by the State to register and report under the Act. It was only in 1978, shortly after the addition of the fifty per cent rule to the religious-organization exemption, that the State first attempted to impose the requirements of the Act upon the Unification Church. And when the State made this attempt, it deliberately chose to do so in express and exclusive reliance upon the newly enacted fifty per cent rule of § 309.515, subd. 1(b). The present suit was initiated by appellees in direct response to that attempt by the State to force the Church's registration. It is thus plain that appellants' ⊥**240** stated rationale for the application of the Act to appellees was that § 309.515, subd. 1(b), did apply to the Unification Church. But § 309.515, subd. 1(b), by its terms applies only to religious organizations. It follows, therefore, that an essential premise of the State's attempt to require the Unification Church to register under the Act by virtue of the fifty per cent rule in § 309.515, subd. 1(b), is that the Church is a religious organization. It is logically untenable for the State to take the position that the Church is not such an organization, because that position destroys an essential premise of the exercise of statutory authority at issue in this suit.

In the courts below, the State joined issue precisely on the premise that the fifty per cent rule of § 309.515, subd. 1(b), was sufficient authority in itself to compel appellees' registration. The adoption of that premise precluded the position ⊥**241** that the Church is not a religious organization. And it remains entirely clear that if we were to uphold the constitutionality of the fifty per cent rule, the State would without more, insist upon the Church's registration. In this Court, the State has changed its position, and purports to find independent bases for denying the Church an exemption from the Act. Considering the development of this case in the courts below, and recognizing the premise inherent in the State's attempt to apply the fifty per cent rule to appellees, we do not think that the State's change of position renders the controversy between these parties any less concrete. The fact that appellants chose to apply § 309.515, subd. 1(b), and its fifty per cent rule as the sole statutory authority requiring the Church to register under the Act compels the conclusion that, at least for purposes of this suit challenging that State application, the Church is indeed a religious organization within the meaning of the Act.

With respect to the question of injury in fact, we again take as the starting point of our analysis the fact that the State attempted to use § 309.515, subd. 1(b)'s fifty per cent rule in order to compel the Unification Church to register and report under the Act. That attempted use of the fifty per cent rule as the State's instrument of compulsion necessarily gives appellees standing to challenge the constitutional validity of the rule. The threatened application of § 309.515, subd. 1(b), and its fifty per cent rule to the Church surely amounts to a distinct and palpable injury to appellees: It disables them from soliciting contributions in the State of Minnesota unless the Church complies with registration and reporting requirements that are hardly *de minimis*. Just as surely, there is a fairly traceable causal connection between the claimed injury and the challenged conduct—here, between the claimed disabling and the threatened application of § 309.515, subd. 1(b), and its fifty per cent rule.

⊥**242** Of course, the Church cannot be assured of a continued religious-organization exemption even in the absence of the fifty per cent rule. Appellees have not yet shown an entitlement to the entirety of the broad injunctive relief that they sought in the District Court—namely, a permanent injunction barring the State from subjecting the Church to the registration and reporting requirements of the Act. But that fact by no means detracts from the palpability of the particular and discrete injury caused to appellees by the State's threatened application of § 309.515, subd. 1(b)'s fifty per cent rule. The Church may indeed be compelled, ultimately, to register under the Act on some ground other than the fifty per cent rule, and while this fact does affect the nature of the relief that can properly be granted to appellees on the present record, it does not deprive this Court of jurisdiction to hear the present case. In sum, contrary to appellants' suggestion, appellees have clearly demonstrated injury in fact.

Justice REHNQUIST's dissent attacks appellees' Art. III standing by arguing that appellees "have failed to show that a favorable decision of this Court will redress the injuries of which they complain." This argument follows naturally from the dissent's premise that the only meaningful relief that can be given to appellees is a total exemption from the requirements of the Act. But the argument, like the premise, is incorrect. This litigation began after the State attempted to compel the Church to register and report under the Act solely on the authority of § 309.515, subd. 1(b)'s fifty per cent rule. If that rule is declared unconstitutional, as appellees have requested, then the Church cannot be required to register and report under the Act by virtue of that rule. Since that rule was the sole basis for the State's attempt to compel registration that gave **⊥243** rise to the present suit, a discrete injury of which appellees now complain will indeed be completely redressed by a favorable decision of this Court.

Furthermore, if the fifty per cent rule of § 309.515, subd. 1(b), is declared unconstitutional, then the Church cannot be compelled to register and report under the Act unless the Church is determined not to be a religious organization. And as the Court of Appeals below observed: "[A] considerable burden is on the state, in questioning a claim of a religious nature. Strict or narrow construction of a statutory exemption for religious organizations is not favored. *Washington Ethical Society* v. *District of Columbia*." At the very least, then, a declaration that § 309.515, subd. 1(b)'s fifty per cent rule is unconstitutional would put the State to the task of demonstrating that the Unification Church is not a religious organization within the meaning of the Act—and such a task is surely more burdensome than that of demonstrating that the Church's proportion of nonmember contributions exceeds fifty per cent. Thus appellees will be given substantial and meaningful relief by a favorable decision of this Court.

⊥244 Since we conclude that appellees have established Art. III standing, we turn to the merits of the case.

III

A

The clearest command of the Establishment Clause is that one religious denomination cannot be officially preferred over another. Before the Revolution, religious establishments of differing denominations were common throughout the Colonies. But the Revolutionary generation emphatically disclaimed that European legacy, and "applied the logic of secular liberty to the condition of religion and the churches." If Parliament had lacked the authority to tax unrepresented colonists, then by the same token the newly independent States should be powerless to tax their citizens for the support of a denomination to which they did not belong. The **⊥245** force of this reasoning led to the abolition of most denominational establishments at the state level by the 1780's, and led ultimately to the inclusion of the Establishment Clause in the First Amendment in 1791.

This constitutional prohibition of denominational preferences is inextricably connected with the continuing vitality of the Free Exercise Clause. Madison once noted: "Security for civil rights must be the same as that for religious rights. It consists in the one case in the multiplicity of interests and in the other in the multiplicity of sects." Madison's vision—freedom for all religion being guaranteed by free competition between religions—naturally assumed that every denomination would be equally at liberty to exercise and propagate its beliefs. But such equality would be impossible in an atmosphere of official denominational preference. Free exercise thus can be guaranteed only when legislators—and voters—are required to accord to their own religions the very same treatment given to small, new, or unpopular denominations. As *Justice* JACKSON noted in another context, "there is no more effective practical guaranty against arbitrary and unreasonable government than to require that the principles of law which officials would impose upon a minority **⊥246** must be imposed generally." *Railway Express Agency, Inc.* v. *New York* (concurring opinion).

Since *Everson* v. *Board of Education* this Court has adhered to the principle, clearly manifested in the history and logic of the Establishment Clause, that no State can "pass laws which aid one religion" or that "prefer one religion over another." This principle of denominational neutrality has been restated on many occasions. In *Zorach* v. *Clauson*, we said that "[t]he government must be neutral when it comes to competition between sects." In *Epperson* v. *Arkansas*, we stated unambiguously: "The First Amendment mandates governmental neutrality between religion and religion, . . . The State may not adopt programs or practices . . . which 'aid or oppose' any religion. . . . This prohibition is absolute." And *Justice* GOLDBERG cogently articulated the relationship between the Establishment Clause and Free Exercise Clause when he said that "[t]he fullest realization of true religious liberty requires that government . . . effect no favoritism among sects . . . and that it work deterrence of no religious belief." *Abington School District*. In short, when we are presented with a state law granting a denominational preference, our precedents demand that we treat the law as suspect and that we apply strict scrutiny in adjudging its constitutionality.

B

The fifty per cent rule of § 309.515, subd. 1(b), clearly grants denominational preference of the sort consistently and firmly deprecated in our precedents. Consequently, **⊥247** that rule must be invalidated unless it is justified by a compelling governmental interest, cf *Widmar* v. *Vincent*, and unless it is closely fitted to further that interest, *Murdock* v. *Pennsylvania*. With that standard of review in mind, we turn to an examination of the governmental interest asserted by appellants.

⊥248 Appellants assert, and we acknowledge, that the State of Minnesota has a significant interest in protecting its citizens from abusive practices in the solicitation of funds for charity, and that this interest retains importance when the solicitation is conducted by a religious organization. We thus agree with the Court of

Appeals that the Act, "viewed as a whole, has a valid secular purpose," and we will therefore assume, *arguendo*, that the Act generally is addressed to a sufficiently "compelling" governmental interest. But our inquiry must focus more narrowly, upon the distinctions drawn by § 309.515, subd. 1(b), itself: Appellants must demonstrate that the challenged fifty per cent rule is closely fitted to further the interest that it assertedly serves.

Appellants argue that § 309.515, subd. 1(b)'s distinction between contributions solicited from members and from nonmembers is eminently sensible. They urge that members are reasonably assumed to have significant control over the solicitation of contributions from themselves to their organization, and over the expenditure of the funds that they contribute, as well. Further, appellants note that as a matter of Minnesota law, members of organizations have greater access than nonmembers to the financial records of the organization. Appellants conclude: "Where the safeguards of membership funding do not exist, the need for public disclosure is obvious. . . .

". . . As public contributions increase as a percentage of total contributions, the need for public disclosure increases. . . . The particular point at which public disclosure should be required . . . is a determination for the legislature. In this case, the Act's 'majority' distinction is a compelling point, since it is at this point that the organization becomes predominantly public-funded."

We reject the argument, for it wholly fails to justify the only aspect of § 309.515, subd. 1(b), under attack—the selective fifty per cent rule. Appellants' argument is based on three distinct premises: that members of a religious organiza⊥**249**tion can and will exercise supervision and control over the organization's solicitation activities when membership contributions exceed fifty per cent; that membership control, assuming its existence, is an adequate safeguard against abusive solicitations of the public by the organization; and that the need for public disclosure rises in proportion with the *percentage* of nonmember contributions. Acceptance of all three of these premises is necessary to appellants' conclusion, but we find no substantial support for any of them in the record.

Regarding the first premise, there is simply nothing suggested that would justify the assumption that a religious organization will be supervised and controlled by its members simply because they contribute more than half of the organization's solicited income. Even were we able to accept appellants' doubtful assumption that members will *supervise* their religious organization under such circumstances, the record before us is wholly barren of support for appellants' further assumption that members will effectively *control* the organization if they contribute more than half of its solicited income. Appellants have offered no evidence whatever that members of religious organizations exempted ⊥**250** by § 309.515, subd. 1(b)'s fifty per cent rule in fact control their organizations. Indeed, the legislative history of § 309.515, subd. 1(b), indicated precisely to the contrary. In short, the first premise of appellants' argument has no merit.

Nor do appellants offer any stronger justification for their second premise—that membership control is an adequate safeguard against abusive solicitations of the public by the organization. This premise runs directly contrary to the central thesis of the entire Minnesota charitable solicitations Act—namely, that charitable organizations soliciting contributions from the public cannot be relied upon to regulate themselves, and that state regulation is accordingly necessary. Appellants offer nothing to suggest why religious organizations should be treated any differently in this respect. And even if we were to assume that the members of religious organizations have some incentive, absent in nonreligious organizations, to protect the interests of nonmembers solicited by the organization, appellants' premise would still ⊥**251** fail to justify the fifty per cent rule: Appellants offer no reason why the members of religious organizations exempted under § 309.515, subd. 1(b)'s fifty per cent rule should have any *greater* incentive to protect nonmembers than the members of nonexempted religious organizations have. Thus we also reject appellants' second premise as without merit.

Finally, we find appellants' third premise—that the need for public disclosure rises in proportion with the percentage of nonmember contributions—also without merit. The flaw in appellants' reasoning here may be illustrated by the following example. Church A raises $10 million, 20 per cent from nonmembers. Church B raises $50,000, 60 per cent from nonmembers. Appellants would argue that although the public contributed $2 million to Church A and only $30,000 to Church B, there is less need for public disclosure with respect to Church A than with respect to Church B. We disagree; the need for public disclosure more plausibly rises in proportion with the *absolute amount*, rather than with the *percentage*, of nonmember contributions. The State of Minnesota has itself adopted this view elsewhere in § 309.515: With qualifications not relevant here, charitable organizations that receive annual nonmember contributions of less than $10,000 are exempted from the registration and reporting requirements of the Act.

We accordingly conclude that appellants have failed to demonstrate that the fifty per cent rule in § 309.515, subd. 1(b), is "closely fitted" to further a "compelling governmental interest."

C

In *Lemon* v. *Kurtzman*, we announced three "tests" that a statute must pass in order to avoid the prohibition of the Establishment Clause. ⊥**252** "First, the statute must have a secular legislative purpose; second, its principal or primary effect must be one that neither advances nor inhibits religion, *Board of Education* v.

Allen; finally, the statute must not foster 'an excessive governmental entanglement with religion.' *Walz* v. *Tax Comm'n*"

As our citations of *Board of Education* v. *Allen* and *Walz* v. *Tax Comm'n* indicated, the *Lemon* v. *Kurtzman* "test" are intended to apply to laws affording a uniform benefit to *all* religions, and not to provisions, like § 309.515, subd. 1(b)'s fifty per cent rule, that discriminate *among* religions. Although application of the *Lemon* tests is not necessary to the disposition of the case before us, those tests do reflect the same concerns that warranted the application of strict scrutiny to § 309.515, subd. 1(b)'s fifty per cent rule. The Court of Appeals found that rule to be invalid under the first two *Lemon* tests. We view the third of those tests as most directly implicated in the present case. *Justice* HARLAN well described the problems of entanglement in his separate opinion in *Walz*, where he observed that governmental involvement in programs concerning religion "may be so direct or in such degree as to engender a risk of politicizing religion. . . . [R]eligious groups inevitably represent certain points of view and not infrequently assert them in the political arena, as evidenced by the continuing debate respecting birth control and abortion laws. Yet history cautions that political fragmentation on sectarian lines must be guarded ⊥**253** against. . . . [G]overnment participation in certain programs, whose very nature is apt to entangle the state in details of administration and planning, may escalate to the point of inviting undue fragmentation."

The Minnesota statute challenged here is illustrative of this danger. By their "very nature," the distinctions drawn by § 309.515, subd. 1(b), and its fifty per cent rule "engender a risk of politicizing religion"—a risk, indeed, that has already been substantially realized.

It is plain that the principal effect of the fifty per cent rule in § 309.515, subd. 1(b), is to impose the registration and reporting requirements of the Act on some religious organizations but not on others. It is also plain that, as the Court of Appeals noted, "[t]he benefit conferred [by exemption] constitutes a substantial advantage; the burden of compliance with the Act is certainly not *de minimis*." We do not suggest that the burdens of compliance with the Act would be intrinsically impermissible if they were imposed evenhandedly. But this statute does not operate evenhandedly, nor was it designed to do so: The fifty per ⊥**254** cent rule of § 309.515, subd. 1(b), effects the *selective* legislative imposition of burdens and advantages upon particular denominations. The "risk of politicizing religion" that inheres in such legislation is obvious, and indeed is confirmed by the provision's legislative history. For the history of § 309.515, subd. 1(b)'s fifty per cent rule demonstrates that the provision was drafted with the explicit intention of including particular religious denominations and excluding others. For example, the second sentence of an early draft of § 309.515, subd. 1(b), read: "A religious society or organization which solicits from its religious affiliates who are qualified under this subdivision and who are represented in a body or convention *that elects and controls the governing board of the religious society or organization* is exempt from the requirements of . . . Sections 309.52 and 309.53." The legislative history discloses that the legislators perceived that the italicized language would bring a Roman Catholic Archdiocese within the Act, that the legislators did not want the amendment to have that effect and that an amendment deleting the italicized clause was passed in committee for the sole purpose of exempting the Archdiocese from the provisions of the Act. On the other hand, there were certain religious organizations that the legislators did not want to exempt from the Act. One State Senator explained that the fifty per cent rule was "an attempt to deal with the religious organizations which are soliciting on the street and soliciting by direct mail, but who are not substantial religious institutions in . . . our state." Another Senator said, "what you're trying to get at here is the people that are running around airports and running around streets and soliciting people and you're trying to remove them from the exemption that normally applies to religious organizations." Still another Senator, who ap⊥**255**parently had mixed feelings about the proposed provision, stated, "I'm not sure why we're so hot to regulate the Moonies anyway."

In short, the fifty per cent rule's capacity—indeed, its express design—to burden or favor selected religious denominations led the Minnesota Legislature to discuss the characteristics of various sects with a view towards "religious gerrymandering," *Gillette* v. *United States*. As *The* CHIEF JUSTICE stated in *Lemon*: "This kind of state inspection and evaluation of the religious content of a religious organization is fraught with the sort of entanglement that the Constitution forbids. It is a relationship pregnant with dangers of excessive government direction . . . of churches."

IV

In sum, we conclude that the fifty per cent rule of § 309.515, subd. 1(b), is not closely fitted to the furtherance of any compelling governmental interest asserted by appellants, and that the provision therefore violates the Establishment Clause. Indeed, we think that § 309.515, subd. 1(b)'s fifty per cent rule sets up precisely the sort of official denominational preference that the Framers of the First Amendment forbade. Accordingly, we hold that appellees cannot be compelled to register and report under the Act on the strength of that provision.

The judgment of the Court of Appeals is *Affirmed*.

⊥**256** *Justice* STEVENS, concurring.

As the Court points out, invalidation of the 50-percent rule would require the State to shoulder the considerable burden of demonstrating that the Unification Church is not a religious organization if the State persists in its attempt to require the Church to register and file financial statements. The burden is considerable because the record already establishes a prima facie case that the Church is a religious organization, and because a strict construction of a statutory exemption for religious organizations is disfavored and may give rise to constitutional questions. *Justice REHNQUIST* therefore is plainly wrong when he asserts in dissent that "invalidation of the fifty percent rule will have absolutely no effect on the Association's obligation to register and report as a *charitable organization* under the Act." (emphasis in original) The 50-percent rule has caused appellees a significant injury in fact because it has ⊥**257** substituted a simple method of imposing registration and reporting requirements for a more burdensome and less certain method of accomplishing that result. I therefore agree with the Court's conclusion that the appellees have standing to challenge the 50-percent rule in this case.

The more difficult question for me is whether the Court's policy of avoiding the premature adjudication of constitutional issues counsels postponement of any decision on the validity of the 50-percent rule until after the Unification Church's status as a religious organization within the meaning of the Minnesota statute is finally resolved. My difficulty stems from the fact that the trial and resolution of the statutory issue will certainly generate additional constitutional questions. Therefore, it is clear that at least one decision of constitutional moment is inevitable. Under these circumstances, it seems to me that reaching the merits is consistent with our "policy of strict necessity in disposing of constitutional issues," *Rescue Army* v. *Municipal Court*. ⊥**258** Moreover, a resolution of the question that has been fully considered by the District Court and by the Court of Appeals and that has been fully briefed and argued in this Court is surely consistent with the orderly administration of justice.

I agree with the Court's resolution of the Establishment Clause issue. Accordingly, I join the Court's opinion.

Justice WHITE, with whom *Justice REHNQUIST* joins, dissenting.

I concur in the dissent of *Justice REHNQUIST* with respect to standing. I also dissent on the merits.

I

It will be helpful first to indicate what occurred in the lower courts and what the Court now proposes to do. Based on two reports of a Magistrate, the District Court held unconstitutional the Minnesota limitation denying an exemption to religious organizations receiving less than 50 percent of their funding from their own members. The Magistrate recommended this action on the ground that the limitation could not pass muster under the second criterion set down in *Lemon* v. *Kurtzman* for identifying an unconstitutional establishment of religion—that the principal or primary effect of the statute is one that neither enhances nor inhibits religion. The 50-percent limitation failed this test because it subjected some churches to far more rigorous requirements than others, the effect being to "severely inhibit plaintiff's religious activities." This created a preference offensive to the Establishment Clause. The Magistrate relied on the inhibiting effect of the 50-percent rule without ref⊥**259**erence to whether or not it was the principal or primary effect of the limitation. In any event, the Magistrate recommended, and the District Court agreed, that the exemption from registration be extended to all religious organizations.

The Court of Appeals agreed with the District Court that the 50-percent rule violated the Establishment Clause. Its ruling, however, was on the ground that the limitation failed to satisfy the first *Lemon* criterion—that the statute have a secular rather than a religious purpose. The court conceded that the Act as a whole had the valid secular purpose of preventing fraudulent or deceptive practices in the solicitation of funds in the name of charity. The court also thought freeing certain organizations from regulation served a valid purpose because for those organizations public disclosure of funding would not significantly enhance the availability of information to contributors. Patriotic and fraternal societies that limit solicitation to voting members and certain charitable organizations that do not solicit in excess of $10,000 annually from the public fell into this category. But the court found no sound secular legislative purpose for the 50-percent limitation with respect to religious organizations because it "appears to be designed to shield favored sects, while continuing to burden other sects." The challenged provision, the Court of Appeals said, "expressly separates two classes of religious organizations and makes the separation for no valid secular purpose that has been suggested by defendants. Inexplicable disparate treatment will not generally be attributed to accident; it seems much more likely that at some stage of the legislative process special solicitude for particular religious organizations affected the choice of statutory language. The resulting discrimination is constitutionally invidious." The Court of Appeals went on to say that if it were necessary to apply the second part of the *Lemon* test, the provision would also fail to survive that examination because it advantaged some organizations and disadvantaged others.

⊥**260** In this Court, the case is given still another treatment. The *Lemon* v. *Kurtzman* tests are put aside because they are applicable only to laws affording uniform benefit to all religions, not to provisions that discriminate among religions. Rather, in cases of denominational preference, the Court says that "our precedents demand that we treat the law as suspect and that we apply strict scrutiny in adjudging its constitutionality." The Court then invalidates the challenged limitation.

It does so by first declaring that the 50-percent rule makes explicit and deliberate distinctions between different religious organizations. The State's submission that the 50-percent limitation is a law based on secular criteria which happens not to have an identical effect on all religious organizations is rejected. The Court then holds that the challenged rule is not closely fitted to serve any compelling state interest and rejects each of the reasons submitted by the State to demonstrate that the distinction between contributions solicited from members and from nonmembers is a sensible one. Among others, the Court rejects the proposition that membership control is an adequate safeguard against deceptive solicitations of the public. The ultimate conclusion is that the exemption provision violates the Establishment Clause.

II

I have several difficulties with this disposition of the case. First, the Court employs a legal standard wholly different from that applied in the courts below. The premise for the Court's standard is that the challenged provision is a deliberate and explicit legislative preference for some religious denominations over others. But there was no such finding in the District Court. That court proceeded under the second *Lemon* test and then relied only on the disparate impact of the provision. There was no finding of a discriminatory or preferential legislative purpose. If this case is to be judged by a standard not employed by the courts below and if the ⊥**261** new standard involves factual issues or even mixed questions of law and fact that have not been addressed by the District Court, the Court should not itself purport to make these factual determinations. It should remand to the District Court.

In this respect, it is no answer to say that the Court of Appeals appeared to find, although rather tentatively, that the state legislature had acted out of intentional denominational preferences. That court was no more entitled to supply the missing factual predicate for a different legal standard than is this Court. It is worth noting that none of the Court of Appeals' judges on the panel in this case is a resident of Minnesota.

Second, apparently realizing its lack of competence to judge the purposes of the Minnesota Legislature other than by the words it used, the Court disposes in a footnote of the State's claim that the 50-percent rule is a neutral, secular criterion that has disparate impact among religious organizations. The limitation, it is said, "is not simply a facially neutral statute" but one that makes "explicit and deliberate distinctions between different religious organizations." The rule itself, however, names no churches or denominations that are entitled to or denied the exemption. It neither qualifies nor disqualifies a church based on the kind or variety of its religious belief. Some religions will qualify and some will not, but this depends on the source of their contributions, not on their brand of religion.

To say that the rule on its face represents an explicit and deliberate preference for some religious beliefs over others is not credible. The Court offers no support for this assertion other than to agree with the Court of Appeals that the limitation might burden the less well organized denominations. This conclusion, itself, is a product of assumption and speculation. It is contrary to what the State insists is readily evident from a list of those charitable organizations that have registered under the Act and of those that are exempt. It is claimed that both categories include not only well-established, but also not so well-estab⊥**262**lished, organizations. The Court appears to concede that the Minnesota law at issue does not constitute an establishment of religion merely because it has a disparate impact. An intentional preference must be expressed. To find that intention on the face of the provision at issue here seems to me to be patently wrong.

Third, I cannot join the Court's easy rejection of the State's submission that a valid secular purpose justifies basing the exemption on the percentage of external funding. Like the Court of Appeals, the majority accepts the prevention of fraudulent solicitation as a valid, even compelling, secular interest. Hence, charities, including religious organizations, may be required to register if the State chooses to insist. But here the State has excused those classes of charities it thought had adequate substitute safeguards or for some other reason had reduced the risk which is being guarded against. Among those exempted are various patriotic and fraternal organizations that depend only on their members for contributions. The Court of Appeals did not question the validity of this exemption because of the built-in safeguards of membership funding. The Court of Appeals, however, would not extend the same reasoning to permit the State to exempt religious organizations receiving more than half of their contributions from their members while denying exemption to those who rely on the public to a greater extent. This Court, preferring its own judgment of the realities of fundraising by religious organizations to that of the state legislature, also rejects the State's submission that organizations depending on their members for more than half of their funds do not pose the same degree of danger as other religious organizations. In the course of doing so, the Court expressly disagrees with the notion that members in general can be relied upon to control their organizations.

⊥**263** I do not share the Court's view of our omniscience. The State has the same interest in requiring registration by organizations soliciting most of their funds from the public as it would have in requiring any charitable organization to register, including a religious organization, if it wants to solicit funds. And if the State determines that its interest in preventing fraud does not extend to those who do not raise a majority of their funds from the public, its interest in imposing the requirement on others is not thereby reduced in the least. Furthermore, as the State suggests, the legislature thought it made good sense, and the courts, including this one, should not so readily disagree.

Fourth, and finally, the Court agrees with the Court of Appeals and the District Court that the exemption must be extended to all religious organizations. The Court of Appeals noted that the exemption provision, so construed, could be said to prefer religious organizations over nonreligious organizations and hence amount to an establishment of religion. Nevertheless, the Court of Appeals did not further address the question, and the Court says nothing of it now. Arguably, however, there is a more evident secular reason for exempting religious organizations who rely on their members to a great extent than there is to exempt all religious organizations, including those who raise all or nearly all of their funds from the public.

Without an adequate factual basis, the majority concludes that the provision in question deliberately prefers some religious denominations to others. Without an adequate factual basis, it rejects the justification offered by the State. It reaches its conclusions by applying a legal standard different from that considered by either of the courts below.

I would reverse the judgment of the Court of Appeals.

⊥**264** *Justice REHNQUIST*, with whom *The CHIEF JUSTICE*, *Justice WHITE*, and *Justice O'CONNOR* join, dissenting.

From the earliest days of the Republic it has been recognized that "[t]his Court is without power to give advisory opinions. *Hayburn's Case*." The logical corollary of this limitation has been the Court's "long . . . considered practice not to decide abstract, hypothetical or contingent questions, or to decide any constitutional question in advance of the necessity for its decision." Such fundamental principles notwithstanding, the Court today delivers what is at best an advisory constitutional pronouncement. The advisory character of the pronouncement is all but conceded by the Court itself, when it acknowledges in the closing footnote of its opinion that appellees must still "prove that the Unification Church is a religious organization within the meaning of the Act" before they can avail themselves of the Court's extension of the exemption contained in the Minnesota statute. Because I find the Court's standing analysis wholly unconvincing, I respectfully dissent.

I

Part II of the Court's opinion concluded that appellees have standing to challenge § 309.515, subd. 1(b), of the Minnesota Charitable Solicitation Act (Act), because they have "plainly met" the case-or-controversy requirements of Art. III. This conclusion is wrong. Its error can best be demonstrated by first reviewing three factual aspects of the case which are either misstated or disregarded in the Court's opinion.

First, the Act applies to appellees not by virtue of the "fifty percent rule," but by virtue of § 309.52. That provision requires "charitable organizations" to register with the Securities and Real Estate Division of the Minnesota Department of Commerce. The Holy Spirit Association for the ⊥**265** Unification of World Christianity (Association) constitutes such a "charitable organization" because it "engages in or purports to engage in solicitation" for a "religious . . . purpose." Only after an organization is brought within the coverage of the Act by § 309.52 does the question of exemption arise. The exemption provided by the fifty percent rule of § 309.515, subd. 1(b), one of several exemptions within the Act, applies only to "religious organizations." Thus, unless the Association is a "religious organization" within the meaning of the Act, the fifty percent rule has absolutely nothing to do with the Association's duty to register and report as a "charitable organization" soliciting funds in Minnesota. This more-than-semantic distinction apparently is misunderstood by the Court, for it repeatedly asserts that the Association is required to register "under the Act *by virtue of* the fifty percent rule of § 309.515, subd. 1(b)."

Second, the State's effort to enforce the Act against the Association was based on the Association's status as a "charitable organization" within the meaning of § 309.52. The State initially sought registration from the Association by letter: "From the nature of your solicitation it appears that [the Association] must complete a Charitable Organization Registration Statement and submit it to the Minnesota Department of Commerce." ⊥**266** When the Association failed to register within the allotted time, the State commenced "routine enforcement procedures" by filing a complaint in Minnesota state court. The complaint alleges that "charitable organizations" are required by § 309.52 to register with the State, that the Association comes within the § 309.50, subd. 4, definition of "charitable organizations," and that "[t]he [Association] has failed to file a registration statement and financial information with the Minnesota Department of Commerce, resulting in a violation of Minn. Stat. § 309.52." This complaint, which never once mentions the fifty percent rule of § 309.515, subd. 1(b), nor characterizes the Association as a "religious organization," is still pending in Minnesota District Court, having been stayed by stipulation of the parties to this lawsuit. Because today's decision does nothing to impair the statutory basis of the complaint, or the State's reason for filing it, the State may proceed with its enforcement action before the ink on this Court's judgment is dry.

⊥**267** Third, appellees have never proved, and the lower courts have never found, that the Association is a "religious organization" for purposes of the fifty percent rule. The District Court expressly declined to make such a finding—"This court is not presently in a position to rule whether the [Association] is, in fact, a religious organization within the Act," and the Court of Appeals was content to decide the case despite the presence of this "'unresolved factual dispute concerning the true character of [appellees'] organization,'" (quoting *Village of Schaumburg* v. *Citizens for Better Environment*). The absence of such a finding is significant, for it is by no means clear that the Association would constitute a "religious organization" for purposes of the § 309.515, subd. 1(b), exemption. The appellees' assertion in the District Court that their actions were religious was "directly contradict[ed]" by a "heavy testimonial barrage against the [Association's] claim that it is a religion."

⊥268 II

The Court's opinion recognizes that the proper standing of appellees in this case is a constitutional prerequisite to the exercise of our Art. III power. To invoke that power, appellees must satisfy Art. III's case-or-controversy requirement by showing that they have a personal stake in the outcome of the controversy, consisting of a distinct and palpable injury. See also *Glad***⊥269***stone, Realtors* v. *Village of Bellwood; Duke Power Co.* v. *Carolina Environmental Study Group*. I do not disagree with the Court's conclusion that the threatened application of the Act to appellees constitutes injury in fact.

But injury in fact is not the only requirement of Art. III. The appellees must also show that their injury "fairly can be traced to the challenged action of the defendant." *Simon* v. *Eastern Kentucky Welfare Rights Org*. The Court purports to find such causation by use of the following sophism: "there is a fairly traceable causal connection between the claimed injury and the challenged conduct—here, between the claimed disabling and the threatened application of § 309.515, subd. 1(b), and its fifty per cent rule."

As was demonstrated above, that statute and the State require the Association to register because it is a "charitable organization" under § 309.52, not because of the fifty percent requirement contained in the exemption for religious organizations. Indeed, at this point in the litigation the fifty percent rule is entirely inapplicable to appellees because they have not shown that the Association is a "religious organization." Therefore, any injury to appellees resulting from the registration and reporting requirements is *caused* by § 309.52, not, as the Court concludes, by "the . . . threatened application of § 309.515, subd. 1(b)'s fifty per cent rule." Having failed to establish that the fifty percent rule is causally connected to their injury, appellees at this point lack standing to challenge it.

The error of the Court's analysis is even more clearly demonstrated by a closely related and equally essential requirement of Art. III. In addition to demonstrating an injury which is caused by the challenged provision, appellees must show "that the exercise of the Court's remedial powers would redress the claimed injuries." *Duke Power Co.* v. *Carolina Environmental Study Group*. The importance **⊥270** of redressability, an aspect of standing which has been recognized repeatedly by this Court, is of constitutional dimension: "[W]hen a plaintiff's standing is brought into issue the relevant inquiry is whether, assuming justiciability of the claim, the plaintiff has shown an injury to himself that is likely to be redressed by a favorable decision. Absent such a showing, exercise of its power by a federal court would be gratuitous and thus inconsistent with the Art. III limitation." *Simon* v. *Eastern Kentucky Welfare Rights Org*.

Appellees have failed to show that a favorable decision of this Court will redress the injuries of which they complain. By affirming the decision of the Court of Appeals, the Court today extends the exemption of § 309.515, subd. 1(b), to all "religious organizations" soliciting funds in Minnesota. But because appellees have not shown that the Association is a "religious organization" under that provision, they have not shown that they will be entitled to this newly expanded exemption. This uncertainty is expressly recognized by the Court: **⊥271** "We agree with the Court of Appeals that appellees and others claiming the benefits of the religious-organization exemption should not automatically enjoy those benefits. Rather, in order to receive them, appellees may be required by the State to prove that the Unification Church is a religious organization within the meaning of the Act." If the appellees fail in this proof—a distinct possibility given the State's "heavy testimonial barrage against [the Association's] claim that it is a religion,"—this court will have rendered a purely advisory opinion. In so doing, it will have struck down a state statute at the behest of a party without standing, contrary to the undeviating teaching of the cases previously cited. Those cases, I believe, require remand for a determination of whether the Association is a "religious organization" as that term is used in the Minnesota statute.

III

There can be no doubt about the impropriety of the Court's action this day. "If there is one doctrine more deeply rooted than any other in the process of constitutional adjudication, it is that we ought not to pass on questions of constitutionality . . . unless such adjudication is unavoidable." *Spector Motor* **⊥272** *Service, Inc.* v. *McLaughlin*. Nowhere does this doctrine have more force than in cases such as this one, where the defect is a possible lack of Art. III jurisdiction due to want of standing on the part of the party which seeks the adjudication. "Considerations of propriety, as well as long-established practice, demand that we refrain from passing upon the constitutionality of [legislative Acts] unless obliged to do so in the proper performance of our judicial function, when the question is raised by a party whose interests entitle him to raise it." *Blair* v. *United States*, quoted in *Ashwander* v. *TVA*. (Brandeis, J., concurring). The existence of injury in fact does not alone suffice to establish such an interest. "The necessity that the plaintiff who seeks to invoke judicial power stand to profit in some personal interest remains an Art. III requirement. A federal court cannot ignore this requirement without overstepping its assigned role in our system of adjudicating only actual cases and controversies." *Simon* v. *Eastern Kentucky Welfare Rights Org.*

IV

In sum, the Court errs when it finds that appellees have standing to challenge the constitutionality of § 309.515, subd. 1(b). Although injured to be sure, appellees have not demonstrated that their injury was caused by the fifty percent rule or will be redressed by its invalidation. This is not to say that appellees can never prove causation or redressability, only that they have not done so at this point. The case should be remanded to permit such proof. Until such time as the requirements of Art. III clearly have been satisfied, this Court should refrain from rendering significant constitutional decisions.

LEGISLATIVE CHAPLAINS

Although the case included in this anthology of Supreme Court opinions has to do with the constitutionality of chaplains for legislatures, the topic has broader dimensions. This is because chaplains also serve in other government institutions, notably the military, prisons, and hospitals. Because chaplains are clergy whose salary is paid by the government, the church-state question, of course, is whether the maintenance of chaplains is a violation of the Establishment Clause; is it an instance of government supporting and advancing religion?

In terms of the military, prisons, and government hospitals, it is commonly understood that these kinds of chaplaincies are constitutional because of their peculiar location. Persons in the military, for example, are compelled by the government (even if they have voluntarily enlisted) to be in an environment other than their normal one. Those who are religious are not able to practice their religion as they normally would. Consequently, government, which requires them to be in their new location, has an obligation to provide them an opportunity to practice their religion. So, even though the providing of chaplains with government funds might appear to violate the Establishment Clause, the Free Exercise Clause requires government to supply the opportunity for religious behavior, thus justifying the "violation." (Of course, those in government hospitals, unlike those in the military or prison, are not in their abnormal environment because of government action. But because they are in a context in which the free exercise of religion is limited, government provides chaplaincy services.)

The Supreme Court has not heard a case on the constitutionality of the institutional chaplaincy, but the concept is illustrated by the case of *Katcoff* v. *Marsh*.The plaintiffs were two law school students who, as taxpayers, sued to declare the Army chaplaincy program unconstitutional as a violation of the Establishment Clause. The federal district court found that they had standing, because they were attacking an action of Congress under the Taxing and Spending Clause of Article I of the Constitution (to tax and spend "to provide for the common Defense") and because they were asserting a specific constitutional limitation on Congress' power to tax and spend (the Establishment Clause), as they are required to do under FLAST v. COHEN and VALLEY FORGE CHRISTIAN COLLEGE v. AMERICANS UNITED FOR SEPARATION OF CHURCH AND STATE. On the merits of the case, the plaintiffs argued that it was unconstitutional for the government to finance the chaplaincy and that the way for the military to retain the benefits that it claimed were inherent in the chaplaincy program would be for the chaplains to be civilians, selected and financed by various denominations. The military claimed the chaplaincy proffered the benefits of the maintenance of good morale among military personnel and securing their right to exercise freely their religious preferences. The court found in favor of the military, citing the need for judicial deference to military judgment and that the chaplaincy program is not "a real threat to the Establishment Clause."

On appeal, the court of appeals affirmed the lower court in its deference to the judgment of Congress and the military in military matters and agreed with the concept that affording personnel the opportunity to worship prevented the chaplain program from being unconstitutional. The court stated the concept well:

> Since the program meets the requirement of voluntariness by leaving the practice of religion solely to the individual soldier, who is free to worship or not as he chooses without fear of any discipline or stigma, it might be viewed as not proscribed by the Establishment Clause. Indeed, if the Army prevented soldiers from worshipping in their own communities by removing them to areas where religious leaders of their persuasion and facilities were not available it could be accused of violating the Establishment Clause unless it provided them with a chaplaincy since its conduct would amount to inhibiting religion. . . . Unless the Army provided a chaplaincy it would deprive the soldier of his right under the Establishment Clause not to have religion inhibited and of his right under the Free Exercise Clause to practice his freely chosen religion (755 F.2d. 223, 231-32, 234, emphasis in original).

Katcoff was not sent forward to the Supreme Court. This was probably because the trial court commented that the case had the flavor of being "more the grist of a moot court competition than a case or controversy to occupy the energies of a federal court." Furthermore, the appeals court, referring to plaintiffs' suggestion of a civilian chaplaincy financed by various denominations, said "plaintiffs' proposal is so inherently impractical as to border on the frivolous" and, at another place, called it a "will-o'-the-wisp" proposal. (The likelihood of appeal was also diminished by the Supreme Court's 1986 reaffirmation of the necessity of judicial deference to military judgment on how to run the military in GOLDMAN v. WEINBERGER.) The case does have the value, however, of eliciting clear expositions of the traditional argument for the constitutionality of chaplaincy programs in the military (and state prisons and hospitals).[1]

The reference to the voluntary nature of religious worship under the ministrations of a military chaplain are reminiscent of an earlier case, *Anderson* v. *Laird.* The controversy here was over compulsory chapel or church attendance at the United States Army, Navy, and Air Force Academies. The plaintiffs, cadets and midshipmen, claimed that required attendance at religious exercises violated both the Establishment and Free Exercise Clauses. The military argued that the requirement was not for the purpose of promoting religion or encouraging participation in worship, although a cadet was free to worship. Rather, the purpose of chapel attendance was to teach the officers-in-training the role and function of religion in the lives of others. Since these cadets someday would be in command over others, often in stressful situations, it was important that they be aware of the significance of religion in people's lives. What better place to learn that than in the worship context, where religion was in action? So the sole reason for the requirement was to provide the opportunities for cadets to observe others in worship, a legitimate and important part of their military training.

The federal district court noted the tradition of judicial deference to military judgment in things military and agreed with the rationale just described, which meant that the requirement had a secular purpose and not a primary effect which advanced religion. Consequently, the compulsory chapel attendance was constitutional.

The Court of Appeals for the District of Columbia Circuit reversed in a *per curiam* decision. However, two judges felt the need to comment. The essence of the comments was that while military judgment demands judicial respect, those under military discipline are not deprived of all constitutional rights. This becomes apparent in the case of compulsory religious activity. Forced worship was one of the evils the Framers of the Constitution opposed and so it has been throughout American history. The military cannot make it otherwise, especially on such specious grounds as a distinction between "worship" and "attendance" (the military had argued that "the requirement to attend is not a requirement to worship"). The service academies' requirements were clearly unconstitutional, since they had a religious purpose, had the primary effect of advancing religion (providing a captive audience for worship), and violated the Free Exercise Clause as well. The Supreme Court refused to hear the case, allowing this judgment to stand.

The question of chaplains in legislatures is somewhat more difficult, since it cannot be claimed by defenders of the practice that legislators are entitled to chaplains because they are denied religious freedom by their service in the legislature. The traditional method of attack has been taxpayers challenging the constitutionality of the expenditure of government funds for the maintenance of legislative chaplains. A significant case of this type was *Elliott* v. *White* (1928). The plaintiff claimed that the expenditure of federal funds to maintain chaplains in the United States House of Representatives, Senate, Army, and Navy was a violation of the Establishment Clause and sought an injunction to prohibit the Treasurer of the United States from spending such funds. Although plaintiff claimed to sue as a citizen, not as a taxpayer, the Court of Appeals for the District of Columbia denied standing under the doctrine of *Frothingham* v. *Mellon* (see the discussion of standing above) and dismissed the challenge against the legislative chaplains.

When, in 1981, a similar challenge was launched in *Murray* v. *Morton,* a federal district court again denied plaintiff standing, asserting that *Elliott* v. *White* had not been superseded by *Flast* v. *Cohen.* (*Valley Forge* had not yet been decided.) The court did comment, in passing, that if a Senator or Representative filed suit, a court might hold that such a plaintiff's standing would not be denied by the *Elliott* precedent. On appeal, the case was argued before the entire Court of Appeals for the District of Columbia. Between the argument and the decision, the Supreme Court handed down MARSH v. CHAMBERS, so when the appeals court did decide the case, it did not mention standing at all, but simply said that *Marsh* made it obvious that a challenge to the public funding of congressional chaplains had no validity.

What was this *Marsh* case? It was a challenge against the public funding of a chaplain in the legislature of Nebraska, brought by a member of the legislature. The challenge was three-fold: (1) the state funding of a chaplain promoted religion and

[1]Discussion of some cases about religion in prisons, involving the Free Exercise Clause, may be found in chapter four.

thus violated the Establishment Clause; (2) the fact that Nebraska had employed a chaplain of one denomination (Presbyterian) for sixteen years impermissibly preferred one religion over others; and (3) the fact that the chaplain's prayers usually had a Judeo-Christian content resulted in preference of one religion over others.

A federal district court found that the existence of a chaplain and the saying of prayers in the legislature were constitutional, but the state's paying for such services was not. The court of appeals took a broader approach and found that the chaplain program failed all three parts of the Establishment Clause test.

The Supreme Court reversed that judgment. Chief Justice Burger, writing for himself and five other justices, pointed to the fact that at the federal level and in most of the states, there was a long tradition of legislative chaplains. Most specifically, the First Congress, following the precedent established by the Continental Congress, "adopted the policy of selecting a chaplain to open each session with prayer." The Congress passed a law authorizing the payment of such chaplains from government funds. Just three days later, these same legislators finalized the wording of the First Amendment. The inescapable conclusion from this is that the Framers of the Constitution must not have seen any inconsistency between the government-paid chaplain program and the concept of separation of church and state. Neither did the Court.

> In light of the unambiguous and unbroken history of more than 200 years, there can be no doubt that the practice of opening legislative sessions with prayer has become part of the fabric of our society. To invoke Divine guidance on a public body entrusted with making laws is not, in these circumstances, an "establishment" of religion or a step toward establishment; it is simply a tolerable acknowledgment of beliefs widely held among the people of this country (463 U.S. 783, 792).

In terms of the specific challenges to the Nebraska chaplain, none of them invalidated the program. The fact that only one chaplain had been appointed for sixteen years merely shows that the legislature was satisfied with his work, not because he was of a particular denomination. Paying the chaplain with state funds is not unconstitutional. Again, look to the precedent of the Framers of the Constitution. The practice has a long history; in Nebraska, over 100 years. The content of the prayers, in this case predominantly Judeo-Christian, is not relevant to constitutionality so long as they are not used to inculcate any particular religion or to proselytize anyone. There was no evidence of that in this case.

In *Marsh* the Court did not use the three-part *Lemon* test to reach its decision. Rather, it relied exclusively on an argument from history. This was a great concern to strict separationists, because they knew that more often than not the use of the test had led the Court to maintain what Jefferson had called the "wall of separation" between church and state. They were afraid that if the Court abandoned its use of the test, it might also take a more "accommodationist" view of the relation between church and state, as, indeed, it had done in this case.[2]

That the *Lemon* test had not been used was unacceptable to Justice Brennan, who wrote a dissent in which Justice Marshall joined. It was clear to him that "our settled doctrine" should have been employed. If it had been, the legislative chaplaincy would have failed all three parts for the following reasons:

> Legislative prayer clearly violates the principles of neutrality and separation that are embedded within the Establishment Clause. It is contrary to the fundamental message of *Engel* and *Schempp*. It intrudes on the right to conscience by forcing some legislators either to participate in a "prayer opportunity," with which they are in basic disagreement, or to make their disagreement a matter of public comment by declining to participate. It forces all residents of the State to support a religious exercise that may be contrary to their own beliefs. It requires the State to commit itself on fundamental theological issues. It has the potential of degrading religion by allowing a religious call to worship to be intermeshed with a secular call to order. And it injects religion into the political sphere by creating the potential that each and every selection of a chaplain, or consideration of a particular prayer, or even reconsideration of the practice itself, will provoke a political battle along religious lines and ultimately alienate some religiously identified group of citizens (463 U.S. 783, 808).

Because *Marsh* found the practice of having legislative chaplains to be constitutional, any subsequent attacks on the concept would have to take a

[2]The fears of separationists seemed to be realized in *Katkoff* v. *Marsh*, a challenge to the military chaplaincy described above. The district court decision mentioned the *Lemon* test, but, citing the precedent of *Marsh*, specifically declined to use it, using rather the test of "whether the Program is 'a real threat to the Establishment Clause,'" quoting *Marsh*. It found the chaplaincy constitutional. At the appeal level, the court commented that the chaplaincy program in the military would clearly fail all three parts of the Establishment Clause test. However, establishment cases should not be considered in a vacuum. Here the chaplaincy program related not only to the Establishment Clause, but also to the War Power Clause of Article 1, § 8 of the Constitution and to the Free Exercise Clause. These dimensions were enough to save the chaplaincy. The court did not cite *Marsh* exactly at that point, but earlier had pointed out that *Marsh* had shown that it was possible to decide an establishment case without using the test.

narrower and more novel approach. In late 1985 *Kurtz* v. *Kennickell* represented such a tactic. A taxpayer sued the Public Printer, the Secretary of the Treasury, and the Treasurer of the United States, seeking to prevent the publication of the annual compilation of the prayers offered by the chaplains of the Senate and House of Representatives (although the House ceased such publication in 1978). The federal district court, after finding that the plaintiff successfully negotiated the barriers of *Flast* and *Valley Forge* and thus had standing, set the case aside pending a discussion in the Senate Committee on Rules and Administration, which was poised on the brink of a reconsideration of the policy of publishing the prayers of the Senate Chaplain.[3]

MARSH v. CHAMBERS

463 U.S. 783
ON WRIT OF CERTIORARI TO THE UNITED STATES COURT OF APPEALS FOR THE EIGHTH CIRCUIT
Argued April 20, 1983 — Decided July 5, 1983

⊥784 *Chief Justice BURGER* delivered the opinion of the Court.

The question presented is whether the Nebraska Legislature's practice of opening each legislative day with a prayer by a chaplain paid by the State violates the Establishment Clause of the First Amendment.

I

The Nebraska Legislature begins each of its sessions with a prayer offered by a chaplain who is chosen biennially by the Executive Board of the Legislative Council and paid out of **⊥785** public funds. Robert E. Palmer, a Presbyterian minister, has served as chaplain since 1965 at a salary of $319.75 per month for each month the legislature is in session.

Ernest Chambers is a member of the Nebraska Legislature and a taxpayer of Nebraska. Claiming that the Nebraska Legislature's chaplaincy practice violates the Establishment Clause of the First Amendment, he brought this action under 42 U.S.C. § 1983, seeking to enjoin enforcement of the practice. After denying a motion to dismiss on the ground of legislative immunity, the District Court held that the Establishment Clause was not breached by the prayers, but was violated by paying the chaplain from public funds. It therefore enjoined the Legislature from using public funds to pay the chaplain; it declined to enjoin the policy of beginning sessions with prayers. Cross-appeals were taken.

The Court of Appeals for the Eighth Circuit rejected arguments that the case should be dismissed on Tenth Amendment, legislative immunity, standing or federalism grounds. On the merits of the chaplaincy issue, the court refused to treat respondent's challenges as separable issues as the District Court had done. Instead, the Court of Appeals assessed the practice as a whole because "[p]arsing out [the] **⊥786** elements" would lead to "an incongruous result."

Applying the three-part test of *Lemon* v. *Kurtzman*, the court held that the chaplaincy practice violated all three elements of the test: the purpose and primary effect of selecting the same minister for 16 years and publishing his prayers was to promote a particular religious expression; use of state money for compensation and publication led to entanglement. Accordingly, the Court of Appeals modified the District Court's injunction and prohibited the State from engaging in any aspect of its established chaplaincy practice.

We granted certiorari limited to the challenge to the practice of opening sessions with prayers by a State-employed clergyman and we reverse.

II

The opening of sessions of legislative and other deliberative public bodies with prayer is deeply embedded in the history and tradition of this country. From colonial times through the founding of the Republic and ever since, the practice of legislative prayer has coexisted with the principles of disestablishment and religious freedom. In the very courtrooms in which the United States District Judge and later three Circuit Judges heard and decided this case, the proceedings opened with an announcement that concluded, "God save the United States and this Honorable Court." The same invocation occurs at all sessions of this Court.

⊥787 The tradition in many of the colonies was, of course, linked to an established church, but the Continental Congress, beginning in 1774, adopted the traditional procedure of opening its sessions with a prayer offered by a paid chaplain. Although prayers were not offered during the Constitutional Convention, the First Congress, as one of **⊥788** its early items of business, adopted the policy of selecting a chaplain to open each session with prayer. Thus, on April 7, 1789, the Senate appointed a committee "to take under consideration the manner of electing Chaplains." On April 9, 1789, a similar committee was appointed by the House of Representatives. On April 25, 1789, the Senate elected its first chaplain; the House followed suit on May 1, 1789. A statute providing for the payment of these chaplains was enacted into law on Sept. 22, 1789.

On Sept. 25, 1789, three days after Congress authorized the appointment of paid chaplains, final agreement was reached on the language of the Bill of Rights. Clearly the men who wrote the First Amendment Religion Clause did not view paid legislative chaplains and opening prayers as a violation of that Amendment, for the practice of opening sessions with prayer has con-

[3] "Periodic Printing of the Chaplain's Prayers," *Congressional Record—Senate* 131 (October 29, 1985): S14277.

tinued without interruption ever since that early session of Congress. It has also been followed con⊥**789**sistently in most of the states, including Nebraska, where the institution of opening legislative sessions with prayer was adopted even before the State attained statehood.

⊥**790** Standing alone, historical patterns cannot justify contemporary violations of constitutional guarantees, but there is far more here than simply historical patterns. In this context, historical evidence sheds light not only on what the draftsmen intended the Establishment Clause to mean, but also on how they thought that Clause applied to the practice authorized by the First Congress—their actions reveal their intent. An act "passed by the first Congress assembled under the Constitution, many of whose members had taken part in framing that instrument, . . . is contemporaneous and weighty evidence of its true meaning" *Wisconsin* v. *Pelican Ins. Co.*

In *Walz* v. *Tax Comm'n* we considered the weight to be accorded to history: "It is obviously correct that no one acquires a vested or protected right in violation of the Constitution by long use, even when that span of time covers our entire national existence and indeed predates it. Yet an unbroken practice . . . is not something to be lightly cast aside." No more is Nebraska's practice of over a century, consistent with two centuries of national practice, to be cast aside. It can hardly be thought that in the same week Members of the First Congress voted to appoint and to pay a Chaplain for each House and also voted to approve the draft of the First Amendment for submission to the States, they intended the Establishment Clause of the Amendment to forbid what they had just declared acceptable. In applying the First Amendment to the states through the Fourteenth Amendment, *Cantwell* v. *Connecticut*, it would be incongruous to interpret that Clause as imposing more strin⊥**791**gent First Amendment limits on the States than the draftsmen imposed on the Federal Government.

This unique history leads us to accept the interpretation of the First Amendment draftsmen who saw no real threat to the Establishment Clause arising from a practice of prayer similar to that now challenged. We conclude that legislative prayer presents no more potential for establishment than the provision of school transportation, *Everson* v. *Board of Education*, beneficial grants for higher education, *Tilton* v. *Richardson*, or tax exemptions for religious organizations, *Walz*.

Respondent cites *Justice BRENNAN's* concurring opinion in *Abington School Dist.* v. *Schempp* and argues that we should not rely too heavily on "the advice of the Founding Fathers" because the messages of history often tend to be ambiguous and not relevant to a society far more heterogeneous than that of the Framers. Respondent also points out that John Jay and John Rutledge opposed the motion to begin the first session of the Continental Congress with prayer.

We do not agree that evidence of opposition to a measure weakens the force of the historical argument; indeed it infuses it with power by demonstrating that the subject was considered carefully and the action not taken thoughtlessly, by force of long tradition and without regard to the problems posed by a pluralistic society. Jay and Rutledge specifically grounded their objection on the fact that the delegates to the Congress "were so divided in religious sentiments . . . that [they] could not join in the same act of worship." Their ob⊥**792**jection was met by Samuel Adams, who stated that "he was no bigot, and could hear a prayer from a gentleman of piety and virtue. who was at the same time a friend to his country."

This interchange emphasizes that the delegates did not consider opening prayers as a proselytizing activity or as symbolically placing the government's "official seal of approval on one religious view." Rather, the Founding Fathers looked at invocations as "conduct whose . . . effect . . . harmonize[d] with the tenets of some or all religions." *McGowan* v. *Maryland*. The Establishment Clause does not always bar a state from regulating conduct simply because it "harmonizes with religious canons." *Id.* Here, the individual claiming injury by the practice is an adult, presumably not readily susceptible to "religious indoctrination," or peer pressure.

In light of the unambiguous and unbroken history of more than 200 years, there can be no doubt that the practice of opening legislative sessions with prayer has become part of the fabric of our society. To invoke Divine guidance on a public body entrusted with making the laws is not, in these circumstances, an "establishment" of religion or a step toward establishment; it is simply a tolerable acknowledgement of beliefs widely held among the people of this country. As *Justice DOUGLAS* observed, "[w]e are a religious people whose institutions presuppose a Supreme Being." *Zorach* v. *Clauson*.

III

We turn then to the question of whether any features of the Nebraska practice violate the Establishment Clause. ⊥**793** Beyond the bare fact that a prayer is offered, three points have been made: first, that a clergyman of only one denomination—Presbyterian—has been selected for 16 years; second, that the chaplain is paid at public expense; and third, that the prayers are in the Judeo-Christian tradition. Weighed against the historical background, these factors do not serve to invalidate Nebraska's practice.

The Court of Appeals was concerned that Palmer's long tenure has the effect of giving preference to his religious views. We, no more than Members of the Congresses of this century, can perceive any suggestion that choosing a clergyman of one denomination advances the beliefs of a particular church. To the contrary, the evidence indicates that Palmer was reappointed because his performance and personal qualities were acceptable to the body appointing him. Palmer was not the only clergyman heard by the Legislature; guest chaplains have officiated at the request of various legislators and as substitutes during Palmer's absences. Absent proof that the chaplain's reappointment stemmed from an impermissible motive, we con⊥**794**clude that his long tenure does not in itself conflict with the Establishment Clause.

Nor is the compensation of the chaplain from public funds a reason to invalidate the Nebraska Legislature's chaplaincy; remuneration is grounded in historic practice initiated, as we noted earlier, by the same Congress that adopted the Establishment Clause of the First Amendment. The Continental Congress paid its chaplain, as did some of the states. Currently, many state legislatures and the United States Congress provide compensation for their chaplains. Nebraska has paid its chaplain for well over a century. The content of the prayer is not of concern to judges where, as here, there is no indication that the prayer opportunity has been exploited to proselytize or advance any one, ⊥**795** or to disparage any other, faith or belief. That being so, it is not for us to embark on a sensitive evaluation or to parse the content of a particular prayer.

We do not doubt the sincerity of those, who like respondent, believe that to have prayer in this context risks the beginning of the establishment the Founding Fathers feared. But this concern is not well founded, for as *Justice* GOLDBERG aptly observed in his concurring opinion in *Abington:* "It is of course true that great consequences can grow from small beginnings, but the measure of constitutional adjudication is the ability and willingness to distinguish between real threat and mere shadow." The unbroken practice for two centuries in the National Congress, for more than a century in Nebraska and in many other states, gives abundant assurance that there is no real threat "while this Court sits," *Panhandle Oil Co.* v. *Mississippi ex rel. Knox* (Holmes, J., dissenting).

The judgment of the Court of Appeals is *Reversed.*

Justice BRENNAN, with whom *Justice* MARSHALL joins, dissenting.

The Court today has written a narrow and, on the whole, careful opinion. In effect, the Court holds that officially sponsored legislative prayer, primarily on account of its "unique history," is generally exempted from the First Amendment's prohibition against "the establishment of religion." The Court's opinion is consistent with dictum in at least one of our prior decisions, and its limited rationale should pose little threat to the overall fate of the Establishment Clause. Moreover, disagreement with the Court ⊥**796** requires that I confront the fact that some twenty years ago, in a concurring opinion in one of the cases striking down official prayer and ceremonial Bible reading in the public schools, I came very close to endorsing essentially the result reached by the Court today. Nevertheless, after much reflection, I have come to the conclusion that I was wrong then and that the Court is wrong today. I now believe that the practice of official invocational prayer, as it exists in Nebraska and most other State Legislatures, is unconstitutional. It is contrary to the doctrine as well as the underlying purposes of the Establishment Clause, and it is not saved either by its history or by any of the other considerations suggested in the Court's opinion.

I respectfully dissent.

I

The Court makes no pretense of subjecting Nebraska's practice of legislative prayer to any of the formal "tests" that have traditionally structured our inquiry under the Establishment Clause. That it fails to do so is, in a sense, a good thing, for it simply confirms that the Court is carving out an exception to the Establishment Clause rather than reshaping Establishment Clause doctrine to accommodate legislative prayer. For my purposes, however, I must begin by demonstrating what should be obvious: that, if the Court were to judge legislative prayer through the unsentimental eye of our settled doctrine, it would have to strike it down as a clear violation of the Establishment Clause.

The most commonly cited formulation of prevailing Establishment Clause doctrine is found in *Lemon* v. *Kurtzman:* ⊥**797** "Every analysis in this area must begin with consideration of the cumulative criteria developed by the Court over many years. Three such tests may be gleaned from our cases. First, the statute [at issue] must have a secular legislative purpose; second, its principal or primary effect must be one that neither advances nor inhibits religion; finally, the statute must not foster 'an excessive government entanglement with religion.'"

That the "purpose" of legislative prayer is preeminently religious rather than secular seems to me to be self-evident. "To invoke Divine guidance on a public body entrusted with making the laws," is nothing but a religious act. Moreover, whatever secular functions legislative prayer might play—formally opening the legislative session, getting the members of the body to quiet down, and imbuing them with a sense of seriousness and high purpose—could so plainly be performed in a purely nonreligious fashion that to claim a secular purpose for the prayer is an insult to the per⊥**798**fectly honorable individuals who instituted and continue the practice.

The "primary effect" of legislative prayer is also clearly religious. As we said in the context of officially sponsored prayers in the public schools, "prescribing a particular form of religious worship," even if the individuals involved have the choice not to participate, places "indirect coercive pressure upon religious minorities to conform to the prevailing officially approved religion. . . ." *Engel* v. *Vitale*. More importantly, invocations in Nebraska's legislative halls explicitly link religious beliefs and observance to the power and prestige of the State. "[T]he mere appearance of a joint exercise of legislative authority by Church and State provides a significant symbolic benefit to religion in the minds of some by reason of the power conferred." *Larkin* v. *Grendel's Den*.

Finally, there can be no doubt that the practice of legislative prayer leads to excessive "entanglement" between the State and religion. *Lemon* pointed out that "entanglement" can take two forms: First, a state statute or program might involve the state impermissibly in monitoring and overseeing ⊥**799** religious affairs. In the case of legislative prayer, the process of choosing a "suitable" chaplain, whether on a permanent or rotating basis, and insuring that the chaplain limits himself or herself to "suitable" prayers, involves precisely the sort of supervision that agencies of government should if at all possible avoid.

Second, excessive "entanglement" might arise out of "the divisive political potential" of a state statute or program. "Ordinarily political debate and division, however vigorous or even partisan, are normal and healthy manifestations of our democratic system of government, but political division along religious lines was one of the principal evils against which the First Amendment was intended to protect. The political divisiveness of such conflict is a threat to the normal political process." *Lemon*. In this case, this second aspect of entanglement is also clear. The controversy between Senator Chambers and his colleagues, which had reached the stage of difficulty and rancor long before this lawsuit was brought, has split the Nebraska ⊥**800** Legislature precisely on issues of religion and religious conformity. The record in this case also reports a series of instances, involving legislators other than Senator Chambers, in which invocations by Reverend Palmer and others led to controversy along religious lines. And in general, the history of legislative prayer has been far more eventful—and divisive—than a hasty reading of the Court's opinion might indicate.

In sum, I have no doubt that, if any group of law students were asked to apply the principles of *Lemon* to the question ⊥**801** of legislative prayer, they would nearly unanimously find the practice to be unconstitutional.

II

The path of formal doctrine, however, can only imperfectly capture the nature and importance of the issues at stake in this case. A more adequate analysis must therefore take ⊥**802** into account the underlying function of the Establishment Clause, and the forces that have shaped its doctrine.

A

Most of the provisions of the Bill of Rights, even if they are not generally enforceable in the absence of state action, nevertheless arise out of moral intuitions applicable to individuals as well as governments. The Establishment Clause, however, is quite different. It is, to its core, nothing less and nothing more than a statement about the proper role of *government* in the society that we have shaped for ourselves in this land.

The Establishment Clause embodies a judgment, born of a long and turbulent history, that, in our society, religion "must be a private matter for the individual, and family, and the institutions of private choice. . . ." *Lemon* v. *Kurtzman*. "Government in our democracy, state and national, must be neutral in matters of religious theory, doctrine, and practice. It may not be hostile to any religion or to the advocacy of no-religion; and it may not aid, foster, or promote one religion or religious theory against another or even against the militant opposite. The First Amendment mandates governmental neutrality between religion and nonreligion." *Epperson* v. *Arkansas*. "In the words of Jefferson, the clause against establishment of religion by law was intended to erect 'a wall of separation between church and state.'" *Everson* v. *Board of Education*.

⊥**803** The principles of "separation" and "neutrality" implicit in the Establishment Clause serve many purposes. Four of these are particularly relevant here.

The first, which is most closely related to the more general conceptions of liberty found in the remainder of the First Amendment, is to guarantee the individual right to conscience. The right to conscience, in the religious sphere, is not only implicated when the government engages in direct or indirect coercion. It is also implicated when the government requires individuals to support the practices of a faith with which they do not agree. "[T]o compel a man to furnish contributions of money for the propagation of [religious] opinions which he disbelieves, is sinful and tyrannical; . . . even . . . forcing him to support this or that teacher of his own religious persuasion, is depriving him of the comfortable liberty of giving his contributions to the particular pastor, whose morals he should make his pattern. . . ." *Everson* v. *Board of Education*.

The second purpose of separation and neutrality is to keep the state from interfering in the essential autonomy of religious life, either by taking upon itself the decision of reli⊥**804**gious issues, or by unduly involving itself in the supervision of religious institutions or officials.

The third purpose of separation and neutrality is to prevent the trivialization and degradation of religion by too close an attachment to the organs of government. The Establishment Clause "stands as an expression of principle on the part of the Founders of our Constitution that religion is too personal, too sacred, too holy to permit its 'unhallowed perversion' by a civil magistrate." *Engel* v. *Vitale*, quoting the Memorial and Remonstrance.

⊥**805** Finally, the principles of separation and neutrality help assure that essentially religious issues, precisely because of their importance and sensitivity, not become the occasion for battle in the political arena. With regard to most issues, the Government may be influenced by partisan argument and may act as a partisan itself. In each case, there will be winners and losers in the political battle, and the losers' most common recourse is the right to dissent and the right to fight the battle again another day. With regard to matters that are essentially religious, however, the Establishment Clause seeks that there should be no political battles, and that no American should at any point feel alien⊥**806**ated from his government because that government has declared or acted upon some "official" or "authorized" point of view on a matter of religion.

B

The imperatives of separation and neutrality are not limited to the relationship of government to religious institutions or denominations, but extend as well to the relationship of government to religious beliefs and practices. In *Torcaso* v. *Watkins*, for example, we struck down a state provision requiring a religious oath as a qualification to hold office, not only because it violated principles of free exercise of religion, but also because it violated the principles of non-establishment of religion. And, of course, in the pair of cases that hang over this one like a reproachful set of parents, we held that official prayer and prescribed Bible reading in the public schools represent a serious encroachment on the Establishment Clause. As we said in *Engel*, "[i]t is neither sacrilegious nor anti-religious to say that each separate government in this country should stay out of the business of writing or sanctioning official prayers and leave that purely religious function to the people themselves and to those the people choose to look to for religious guidance."

Nor should it be thought that this view of the Establishment Clause is a recent concoction of an overreaching judi⊥**807**ciary. Even before the First Amendment was written, the Framers of the Constitution broke with the practices of the Articles of Confederation and many state constitutions, and did not invoke the name of God in the document. This "omission of a reference to the Deity was not inadvertent; nor did it remain unnoticed." Moreover, Thomas Jefferson and Andrew Jackson, during their respective terms as President, both refused on Establishment Clause grounds to declare national days of thanksgiving or fasting. And James Madison, writing subsequent to his own Presidency on essentially the very issue we face today, stated: "Is the appointment of Chaplains to the two Houses of Congress consistent with the Constitution, and with the pure principle of religious freedom?

"In strictness, the answer on both points must be in the negative. The Constitution of the U.S. forbids everything like an establishment of a national religion. The law appointing Chaplains establishes a religious worship for the national representatives, to be performed by Ministers of religion, elected by a majority of⊥**808** them; and these are to be paid out of the national taxes. Does not this involve the principle of a national establishment, applicable to a provision for a religious worship for the Constituent as well as of the representative Body, approved by the majority, and conducted by Ministers of religion paid by the entire nation." Fleet, Madison's "Detached Memoranda," 3 Wm. & Mary Quarterly 534, 588 (1946).

C

Legislative prayer clearly violates the principles of neutrality and separation that are embedded within the Establishment Clause. It is contrary to the fundamental message of *Engel* and *Schempp*. It intrudes on the right to conscience by forcing some legislators either to participate in a "prayer opportunity," with which they are in basic disagreement, or to make their disagreement a matter of public comment by declining to participate. It forces all residents of the State to support a religious exercise that may be contrary to their own beliefs. It requires the State to commit itself on fundamental theological issues. It has the potential for degrading religion by allowing a religious call to worship to be intermeshed with a secular call to order. And it injects religion into the political sphere by creating the potential that each and every selection of a chaplain, or consideration of a particular prayer, or even reconsideration of the practice itself, will provoke a political battle along religious lines and ultimately alienate some religiously identified group of citizens.

⊥**809** D

One response to the foregoing account, of course, is that "neutrality" and "separation" do not exhaust the full meaning of the Establishment Clause as it has developed in our cases. It is indeed true that there are certain tensions inherent in the First Amendment itself, or inherent in the role of religion and religious belief in any free society, that have shaped the doctrine of the Establishment Clause, and required us to deviate from an absolute adherence to separation and neutrality. Nevertheless, these considerations, although very important, are also quite specific, and where none of them is present, the Establishment Clause gives us no warrant simply to look the other way and treat an unconstitutional practice as if it were constitutional. Because the Court occasionally suggests that some of these considerations might apply here, it becomes important that I briefly identify the most prominent of them and explain why they do not in fact have any relevance to legislative prayer.

(1)

A number of our cases have recognized that religious institutions and religious practices may, in certain contexts, receive the benefit of government programs and policies generally available, on the basis of some secular criterion, to a wide class of similarly situated nonreligious beneficiaries, and the precise cataloguing of those contexts is not necessarily an easy task. I need not tarry long here, however, because the provision for a daily official invocation by a nonmember officer of ⊥**810** a legislative body could by no stretch of the imagination appear anywhere in that catalogue.

(2)

Conversely, our cases have recognized that religion can encompass a broad, if not total, spectrum of concerns, overlapping considerably with the range of secular concerns, and that not every governmental act which coincides with or conflicts with a particular religious belief is for that reason an establishment of religion. The Court seems to suggest at one point that the practices of legislative prayer may be excused on this ground, but I cannot really believe that it takes this position seriously. The practice of legislative prayer is nothing like the statutes we considered in *McGowan* and *Harris* v. *McRae;* prayer is not merely "conduct whose . . . effect . . . harmonizes with the tenets of some or all religions," prayer is fundamentally and necessarily religious. "It is prayer which distinguishes religious phenomena from all those which resemble them or lie near to them, from the moral sense, for example, or aesthetic feeling." *Engel.*

(3)

We have also recognized that Government cannot, without adopting a decidedly *anti*-religious point of view, be forbid⊥**811**den to recognize the religious beliefs and practices of the American people as an aspect of our history and culture. Certainly, bona fide classes in comparative religion can be offered in the public schools. And certainly, the text of Abraham Lincoln's Second Inaugural Address which is inscribed on a wall of the Lincoln Memorial need not be purged of its profound theological content. The practice of offering invocations at legislative sessions cannot, however, simply be dismissed as "a tolerable *acknowledgment of beliefs* widely held among the people of this country." "Prayer is religion *in act.*" "Praying means to take hold of a word, the end, so to speak, of a line that leads to God." Reverend Palmer and other members of the clergy who offer invocations at legislative sessions are not museum pieces, put on display once a day for the edification of the legislature. Rather, they are engaged by the legislature to lead it—as a body—in an act of religious worship. If upholding the practice requires denial of this fact, I suspect that many supporters of legislative prayer would feel that they had been handed a pyrrhic victory.

(4)

Our cases have recognized that the purposes of the Establishment Clause can sometimes conflict. For example, in *Walz* v. *Tax Commissioner*, we upheld tax exemptions for religious institutions in part because subjecting those institutions to taxation might foster serious administrative entanglement. Here, however, no ⊥**812** such tension exists; the State can vindicate *all* the purposes of the Establishment Clause by abolishing legislative prayer.

(5)

Finally, our cases recognize that, in one important respect, the Constitution is *not* neutral on the subject of religion: Under the Free Exercise Clause, religiously motivated claims of conscience may give rise to constitutional rights that other strongly-held beliefs do not. Moreover, even when the government is not compelled to do so by the Free Exercise Clause, it may to some extent act to facilitate the opportunities of individuals to practice their religion. This is not, however, a case in which a State is accommodating individual religious interests. We are not faced here with the right of the legislature to allow its members to offer prayers during the course of ⊥**813** general legislative debate. We are certainly not faced with the right of legislators to form voluntary groups for prayer or worship. We are not even faced with the right of the state to employ members of the clergy to minister to the private religious needs of individual legislators. Rather, we are faced here with the regularized practice of conducting official prayers, on behalf of the entire legislature, as part of the order of business constituting the formal opening of every single session of the legislative term. If this is Free Exercise, the Establishment Clause has no meaning whatsoever.

III

With the exception of the few lapses I have already noted, each of which is commendably qualified so as to be limited to the facts of this case, the Court says almost nothing contrary to the above analysis. Instead, it holds that "the practice of opening legislative sessions with prayer has become part of the fabric of our society," and chooses not to interfere. I sympathize with the Court's reluctance to strike down a practice so prevalent and so ingrained as legislative prayer. I am, however, unconvinced by the Court's arguments, and cannot shake my conviction that legislative prayer violates both the letter and the spirit of the Establishment Clause.

A

The Court's main argument for carving out an exception sustaining legislative prayer is historical. The Court cannot—and does not—purport to find a pattern of "undeviating acceptance," *Walz*, of legislative prayer. It also disclaims exclusive reliance on the mere longevity of legislative prayer. The Court does, however, point out that, only three days before the First Congress reached agreement on the final wording of the Bill of Rights, it authorized the appointment of paid chaplains for ⊥**814** its own proceedings, and the Court argues that in light of this "unique history," the actions of Congress reveal its intent as to the meaning of the Establishment Clause. I agree that historical practice is "of considerable import in the interpretation of abstract constitutional language," *Walz*. This is a case, however, in which—absent the Court's invocation of history—there would be no question that the practice at issue was unconstitutional. And despite the surface appeal of the Court's argument, there are at least three reasons why specific historical practice should not in this case override that clear constitutional imperative.

First, it is significant that the Court's historical argument does not rely on the legislative history of the

Establishment Clause itself. Indeed, that formal history is profoundly unilluminating on this and most other subjects. Rather, the Court assumes that the Framers of the Establishment Clause would not have themselves authorized a practice that they thought violated the guarantees contained in the clause. This assumption, however, is questionable. Legislators, influenced by the passions and exigencies of the moment, the pressure of constituents and colleagues, and the press of business, do not always pass sober constitutional judgment on every piece of legislation they enact, and this **⊥815** must be assumed to be as true of the members of the First Congress as any other. Indeed, the fact that James Madison, who voted for the bill authorizing the payment of the first congressional chaplains, later expressed the view that the practice was unconstitutional, is instructive on precisely this point. Madison's later views may not have represented so much a change of *mind* as a change of *role*, from a member of Congress engaged in the hurley-burley of legislative activity to a detached observer engaged in unpressured reflection. Since the latter role is precisely the one with which this Court is charged, I am not at all sure that Madison's later writings should be any less influential in our deliberations than his earlier vote.

Second, the Court's analysis treats the First Amendment simply as an Act of Congress, as to whose meaning the intent of Congress is the single touchstone. Both the Constitution and its amendments, however, became supreme law only by virtue of their ratification by the States, and the understanding of the States should be as relevant to our analysis as the understanding of Congress. This observation is especially compelling in consid**⊥816**ering the meaning of the Bill of Rights. The first 10 Amendments were not enacted because the members of the First Congress came up with a bright idea one morning; rather, their enactment was forced upon Congress by a number of the States as a condition for their ratification of the original Constitution. To treat any practice authorized by the First Congress as presumptively consistent with the Bill of Rights is therefore somewhat akin to treating any action of a party to a contract as presumptively consistent with the terms of the contract. The latter proposition, if it were accepted, would of course resolve many of the heretofore perplexing issues in contract law.

Finally, and most importantly, the argument tendered by the Court is misguided because the Constitution is not a static document whose meaning of every detail is fixed for all time by the life experience of the Framers. We have recognized in a wide variety of constitutional contexts that the practices that were in place at the time any particular guarantee was enacted into the Constitution do not necessarily fix forever the meaning of that guarantee. To be truly faithful to the Framers, "our use of the history of their time must limit itself to broad purposes, not specific practices." *Abington School Dist.* v. *Schempp*. Our primary task must be to translate "the majestic generalities of the Bill of Rights, conceived as part of the pattern of liberal government in the eighteenth century, into concrete restraints on officials dealing with the **⊥817** problems of the twentieth century. . . ." *West Virginia State Bd. of Education* v. *Barnette*.

The inherent adaptability of the Constitution and its amendments is particularly important with respect to the Establishment Clause. "[O]ur religious composition makes us a vastly more diverse people than were our forefathers. . . . In the face of such profound changes, practices which may have been objectionable to no one in the time of Jefferson and Madison may today be highly offensive to many persons, the deeply devout and the nonbelievers alike." *Schempp*. President John Adams issued during his Presidency a number of official proclamations calling on all Americans to engage in Christian prayer. *Justice STORY*, in his treatise on the Constitution, contended that the "real object" of the First Amendment "was, not to countenance, much less to advance Mahometanism, Judaism, or infidelity, by prostrating Christianity; but to exclude all rivalry among Christian sects. . . ." Whatever deference Adams' actions and Story's views might once have deserved in this Court, the Establishment Clause must now be read in a very different light. Similarly, the members of the First Congress should be treated, not as sacred figures whose every action must be emulated, but as the authors of a document meant to last for the ages. Indeed, a proper respect for the Framers themselves forbids us to give so static and lifeless a meaning to their work. To my mind, the Court's focus here on a narrow piece of history is, in a fundamental sense, a betrayal of the lessons of history.

⊥818B

Of course, the Court does not rely entirely on the practice of the First Congress in order to validate legislative prayer. There is another theme which, although implicit, also pervades the Court's opinion. It is exemplified by the Court's comparison of legislative prayer with formulaic recitation of "God save the United States and this Honorable Court." It is also exemplified by the Court's apparent conclusion that legislative prayer is, at worst, a "mere shadow" on the Establishment Clause rather than a "real threat" to it. Simply put, the Court seems to regard legislative prayer as at most a *de minimis* violation, somehow unworthy of our attention. I frankly do not know what should be the proper disposition of features of our public life such as "God save the United States and this Honorable Court," "In God We Trust," "One Nation Under God," and the like. I might well adhere to the view expressed in *Schempp* that such mottos are consistent with the Establishment Clause, not because their import is *de minimis*, but because they have lost any true religious significance. Legislative invocations, however, are very different.

First of all, as *Justice STEVENS'* dissent so effectively highlights, legislative prayer, unlike mottos with fixed wordings, can easily turn narrowly and obviously sectarian. I agree with the Court that the federal judiciary should not sit as a board of censors on individual prayers, but to my mind the better way of avoiding that task is by striking down all official legislative invocations.

⊥**819** More fundamentally, however, *any* practice of legislative prayer, even if it might look "nonsectarian" to nine Justices of the Supreme Court,. will inevitably and continuously involve the state in one or another religious debate. Prayer is serious business—serious theological business—and it is not a mere "acknowledgment of beliefs widely held among the people of this country" for the State to immerse itself in that business. Some religious individuals or groups find it theologically problematic to engage in joint religious exercises predominantly influenced by faiths not their own. Some might object even to the attempt to fashion a "non-sectarian" prayer. Some would find it impossible to participate in any "prayer opportunity" marked by ⊥**820** Trinitarian references. Some would find a prayer *not* invoking the name of Christ to represent a flawed view of the relationship between human beings and God. Some might find any petitionary prayer to be improper. Some might find any prayer that lacked a petitionary element to be deficient. Some might be troubled by what they consider shallow public prayer, or non-spontaneous prayer, or prayer without adequate spiritual preparation or concentration. Some might, of course, have *theological* objections to any prayer sponsored by an organ of government. Some ⊥**821** might object on theological grounds to the level of political neutrality generally expected of government-sponsored invocational prayer. And some might object on theological grounds to the Court's requirement, that prayer, even though religious, not be proselytizing. If these problems arose in the context of a religious objection to some otherwise decidedly secular activity, then whatever remedy there is would have to be found in the Free Exercise Clause. But, in this case, we are faced with potential religious objections to an activity at the very center of religious life, and it is simply beyond the competence of government, and inconsistent with our conceptions of liberty, for the state to take upon itself the role of ecclesiastical arbiter.

IV

The argument is made occasionally that a strict separation of religion and state robs the nation of its spiritual identity. I believe quite the contrary. It may be true that individuals cannot be "neutral" on the question of religion. But the judgment of the Establishment Clause is that neutrality by the organs of *government* on questions of religion is both possible and imperative. Alexis de Tocqueville wrote the following concerning his travels through this land in the early 1830s: "The religious atmosphere of the country was the first thing that struck me on arrival in the United States. . . .

"In France I had seen the spirits of religion and of freedom almost always marching in opposite directions. In America I found them intimately linked together in joint reign over the same land.

⊥**822** "My longing to understand the reason for this phenomenon increased daily.

"To find this out, I questioned the faithful of all communions; I particularly sought the society of clergymen, who are the depositaries of the various creeds and have a personal interest in their survival. . . . I expressed my astonishment and revealed my doubts to each of them; I found that they all agreed with each other except about details; all thought that the main reason for the quiet sway of religion over the country was the complete separation of church and state. I have no hesitation in stating that throughout my stay in America I met nobody, lay or cleric, who did not agree about that." *Democracy in America*, 295. More recent history has only confirmed de Tocqueville's observations. If the Court had struck down legislative prayer today, it would likely have stimulated a furious reaction. But it would also, I am convinced, have invigorated both the "spirit of religion" and the "spirit of freedom."

I respectfully dissent.

Justice STEVENS, dissenting.

In a democratically elected legislature, the religious beliefs of the chaplain tend to reflect the faith of the majority of the ⊥**823** lawmakers' constituents. Prayers may be said by a Catholic priest in the Massachusetts Legislature and by a Presbyterian minister in the Nebraska Legislature, but I would not expect to find a Jehovah's Witness or a disciple of Mary Baker Eddy or the Reverend Moon serving as the official chaplain in any state legislature. Regardless of the motivation of the majority that exercises the power to appoint the chaplain, it seems plain to me that the designation of a member of one religious faith to serve as the sole official chaplain of a state legislature for a period of 16 years constitutes the preference of one faith over another in violation of the Establishment Clause of the First Amendment.

The Court declines to "embark on a sensitive evaluation or to parse the content of a particular prayer." Perhaps it does so because it would be unable to explain away the clearly sectarian content of some of the prayers given by Nebraska's chaplain. Or perhaps the Court is unwilling to ⊥**824** acknowledge that the tenure of the chaplain must inevitably be conditioned on the acceptability of that content to the silent majority.

I would affirm the judgment of the Court of Appeals.

RELIGIOUS SYMBOLS ON PUBLIC PROPERTY

A recurring question in church-state relations has been whether government may finance or sponsor religious symbols. The Christmas season has spawned the bulk of these controversies because communities across the country routinely supported nativity scenes.[1] Over the years a multitude of cases has been tried over whether such sponsorship is a violation of the Establishment Clause, i.e., is it a way of government's promoting a particular religion at the expense of others? Courts have answered both "yes" and "no." Until 1983 the Supreme Court had consistently avoided the dispute by simply denying appeals from decisions of the state and lower federal courts. But in that year the Court finally granted certiorari to such a case coming from Pawtucket, Rhode Island, and handed down its decision in LYNCH v. DONNELLY, 5 March 1984.

The case involved an elaborate 40,000 square-foot exhibit erected each Christmas for forty years by the city in cooperation with the downtown retail merchants' association in a park that was owned by a nonprofit organization. In addition to a live Santa Claus, a Santa Claus house, a wishing well, a banner reading "Seasons Greetings," and assorted reindeer, elves, and other figures, the display included a crèche complete with Mary, Joseph, the child Jesus, and other figures that ordinarily constitute the nativity scene. Various Pawtucket residents and members of the Rhode Island affiliate of the American Civil Liberties Union challenged inclusion of the crèche in the display, and a United States district court held that the city's action violated the Establishment Clause in that the city had "tried to endorse and promulgate religious beliefs" thus bestowing "more than a remote and incidental benefit on Christianity." The decision was affirmed by a divided Court of Appeals for the First Circuit, but by a five-to-four decision the Supreme Court reversed the lower courts.

In the majority opinion Chief Justice Burger acknowledged the desirability of preventing undue intrusion by either church or state into the "precincts of the other," called attention to Thomas Jefferson's wall of separation, and tested the action of the city of Pawtucket against the three-part test prescribed in LEMON v. KURTZMAN. However, he restated his often-expressed belief that total separation is not possible and maintained that the Court had consistently "declined to take a rigid, absolutist view of the Establishment Clause." He granted that the wall of separation was a "useful figure of speech" but insisted that the "metaphor itself is not a wholly accurate description of the practical aspects of the relationship that in fact exists between church and state."

Emphasizing that the Constitution mandates government accommodation of religions with hostility toward none, he cited the many instances in the country's history that evidenced official governmental recognition of the role of religion in American life. He agreed that the Court had in recent years often used the three-part *Lemon* test in ascertaining the line of separation, but the members of the Court had, he said, "repeatedly emphasized our unwillingness to be confined to any single test or criterion in this sensitive area." He then proceeded to find a secular purpose in Pawtucket's inclusion of the "passive" crèche as part of its traditional holiday display, no primary effect of advancing religion in violation of the Establishment Clause, since the nativity scene simply contributed to the festive character of the holiday season, and no entanglement of religion and the state or undue divisiveness resulting from the ownership and use of the crèche by the city.

Justice O'Connor wrote a concurring opinion to suggest, as she put it, "a clarification of our Establishment Clause doctrine." The "*Lemon* test," she said, quoting from MUELLER v. ALLEN, "provides 'no more than [a] helpful guidepost' in dealing with Establishment Clause challenges." She then read that test as "focusing on the evils of government endorsement or disapproval of religion" and held that inclusion of the crèche in the larger display had the secular purpose of celebration of a public holiday by use of its "traditional symbols." Pawtucket did not intend, by inclusion of the nativity scene, to "endorse the Christian beliefs represented by the crèche."

Justice Brennan, joined in dissent by Justices Marshall, Blackmun, and Stevens, sought to narrow the scope of the decision. Although he saw the Pawtucket action as an "impermissible endorsement of a particular faith," he emphasized that the majority opinion had not spoken to the question of public displays on public property of distinctively religious symbols standing alone, removed from the context of the particular holiday setting with the inclusion of secular figures. Brennan saw some cause for encouragement in the fact that the Court had at least returned to acknowledgement of the *Lemon* test after ignoring it in MARSH v. CHAMBERS, but he observed that the Court's "less than vigorous application of the *Lemon* test suggests that its commitment to those standards may only be superficial." He agreed that no single formula could resolve all Establishment Clause problems, but he obviously resented the majority's insistence that the test set forth in *Lemon* was simply "one path that may be followed or not at the Court's option."

Justice Blackmun, joined by Justice Stevens, also wrote a dissent. He, too, would have used the *Lemon* test to invalidate the Pawtucket display. In

[1]There have been controversies over government sponsorship and/or erection of other religious symbols, e.g., crosses, the lowering of the American flag to half-staff on Good Friday, and city seals which display religious symbols. Discussion of such issues may be found in Leo Pfeffer, *Religion, State, and the Burger Court* (Buffalo, NY: Prometheus Books, 1984), pp. 127-36; and Joseph Conn, "With This, We Conquer," *Church and State* 38 (March 1985): 9-10.

addition, he complained bitterly about the trivialization of religion inherent in the arrangement:

> The crèche has been relegated to the role of a neutral harbinger of the holiday season, useful for commercial purposes, but devoid of any inherent meaning and incapable of enhancing the religious tenor of a display of which it is an integral part. The city has its victory—but it is a Pyrrhic one indeed. . . . Surely, this is a misuse of a sacred symbol (465 U.S. 668, 727).

The Supreme Court had another opportunity to speak to the question of nativity scenes during its 1984-85 term in *Board of Trustees of the Village of Scarsdale* v. *McCreary*. In Scarsdale, New York, a crèche committee had for twenty-four years placed a nativity scene in a public park. In 1981 the city refused permission because some had argued that the Christmas display favored Christianity over other religions. The crèche committee initiated legal proceedings. A federal district court ruled that the display did violate the Establishment Clause and upheld the city's denial. A court of appeals reversed. Citing the recently decided *Lynch*, the court ruled that the city could not deny the committee the opportunity to display the nativity scene on public land. Many were pleased that the Supreme Court agreed to hear the case because they thought that it would clarify the *Lynch* opinion. In *McCreary* the nativity scene was not part of a larger Christmas display with secular holiday symbols such as Santa Claus, as in *Lynch*; it stood alone. Many believed that *McCreary* might be decided differently from *Lynch*. That both views were argued on the Court is shown by the fact that the decision was handed down as a four-to-four deadlock, Justice Powell not having participated in the case. A tie vote allows the ruling of the lower court to stand, so the village was required to permit the nativity scene to be erected. But such an opinion also is not broadly applicable and does not establish any legal precedent, so the issue of the standing-alone nativity scene was left unanswered.

That situation was changed with ALLEGHENY COUNTY v. ACLU OF PITTSBURGH (1989). This case was made complex in that two religious symbols were at issue. One was a nativity scene that stood on the grand staircase of the Allegheny County Courthouse, a very noticeable and public part of that building. Although the crèche had some plants and small evergreen trees around, there were no other figures, either religious or seasonal. It was a standing-alone nativity scene. Above it was an angel bearing a banner with the words "Gloria in Excelcis Deo!" There was also a sign: "This Display Donated by the Holy Name Society."

The other display was a block away at a building jointly owned by the city and county. There was displayed an 18-foot Chanukah menorah, donated by a group of Lubavitcher Hasidic Jews. Alongside the menorah was a 45-foot Christmas tree. At the foot of the tree was a sign bearing the mayor's name and a text in praise of liberty. The Pittsburgh chapter of the ACLU and some local residents sued, seeking a permanent injunction forbidding the displays because they violated the Establishment Clause.

Justice Blackmun, applying the Clause for the Court, utilized the terminology set forth by Justice O'Connor's concurrence in *Lynch*.

> Whether the key word is "endorsement," "favoritism," or "promotion," the essential principle remains the same. The Establishment Clause, at the very least, prohibits government from appearing to take a position on questions of religious belief or from "making adherence to a religion relevant in any way to a person's standing in the political community" (492 U.S. 573, 593-594).

Under this rubric the Court found the standing-alone nativity scene unconstitutional. Unlike the crèche in *Lynch*, there was nothing to detract from its religious message. That it stood on the central staircase of the county courthouse communicated a message of government approval and support.

> Thus, by permitting the display of the crèche in this particular physical setting, the county sends an unmistakable message that it supports and promotes the Christian praise to God that is the crèche's religious message. . . . [B]y prohibiting government endorsement of religion, the Establishment Clause prohibits precisely what occurred here: the government's lending its support to the communication of a religious organization's religious message. . . . The display of the crèche in this context, therefore, must be permanently enjoined (492 U.S. 573, 601-602).

When the Court turned to the question of the menorah, it reached a different conclusion. Justice Blackmun acknowledged that the menorah is a Jewish religious symbol. But he also said that it is a symbol of a holiday which has secular dimensions, as well, like the Christmas tree. To have the two in juxtaposition is to recognize that they represent two holidays, not one. If the city celebrated two religious holidays with these symbols, it still violated the Establishment Clause. But, if it celebrates them as secular holidays, then the Clause is not violated. Blackmun concluded that the two symbols together, along with the sign in praise of freedom, showed that the city did not want to endorse either religion, but "rather simply recognizes that both Christmas and Chanukah are part of the same winter-holiday season, which has attained secular status in our society" (492 U.S. 573, 616). The Christmas tree is far less a religious symbol than the menorah. In the display in question, the tree was the predominant element—it was 45 feet tall, the menorah only 18.

> In the shadow of the tree, the menorah is readily understood as simply a recognition that Christmas is not the only traditional way of observing the winter-holiday season. In these circumstances, then, the combination of the tree and the menorah communicates, not a simultaneous endorsement of both Christian and Jewish faith, but instead, a secular celebration of Christmas coupled with an acknowledgement of Chanukah as a contemporaneous alternative tradition. . . . [F]or purposes of the Establishment Clause, the city's overall display must be understood as conveying the city's secular recognition of different traditions for celebrating the winter-holiday season (492 U.S. 573, 617, 620).

(Although five justices joined Blackmun in the result he reached in this case, none completely agreed with his reasoning.) Consequently, standing-alone religious symbols on public property are unconstitutional, but those in a context that can be interpreted as seasonal or cultural are not.

Justice Kennedy, joined by Justices Rehnquist, White, and Scalia, wrote a blistering dissent which illustrated the tensions in the Court over the proper way to interpret the Establishment Clause. He blasted the "endorsement" language of interpreting the Clause as being so broad as to be unworkable. Its flaw is that it does not allow sufficient government accommodation of religion. In order to accomplish the desired accommodation, Kennedy was willing to adopt the test of history. With certain narrow exceptions, whatever cooperation or sanction government has given religion for a long time is acceptable under the Establishment Clause. In order to achieve that broad accommodation and reject the endorsement test, Kennedy narrowed the scope of the Establishment Clause prohibition of government aid to religion to coercion. Direct government benefits to religion and coercion to religious observance are all that are forbidden. Government support of religious symbols falls outside those boundaries and is acceptable.

In the October 1991 term, in an *amicus curiae* brief on LEE v. WEISMAN, the Justice Department urged the Court to adopt Justice Kennedy's "coercion test" as its hermeneutical principal in Establishment Clause cases. It turned out that Justice Kennedy wrote the Court's opinion in that case. He applied a variation of his coercion test, psychological coercion. He argued that dissenting students, such as Jewish students hearing Christian prayers, surrounded by classmates and their loved ones, would be under psychological pressure to participate in spite of their objection to the prayer. That is psychological coercion and enough to trigger Establishment Clause protection.

Not all the Justices were happy with that holding: Justice Scalia was outraged. He wrote:

> The Court presumably would separate graduation invocations and benedictions from other instances of public "preservation and transmission of religious beliefs" on the ground that they involve "psychological coercion." I find it a sufficient embarrassment that our Establishment Clause jurisprudence regarding holiday displays, see *Allegheny County* v. *Greater Pittsburgh ACLU*, has come to "requir[e] scrutiny more commonly associated with interior decorators than with the judiciary." *American Jewish Congress* v. *Chicago* (Easterbrook, J., dissenting). But interior decorating is a rock-hard science compared to psychology practiced by amateurs (505 U.S. 577, 636).

The coercion test, at least as it was articulated by Justice Kennedy in *Allegheny*, has never been adopted as a means of interpreting the Establishment Clause.

The issue in CAPITOL SQUARE REVIEW BOARD v. PINETTE (1995) was a variation on the theme of ROSENBERGER v. UNIVERSITY OF VIRGINIA: does the Establishment Clause bar a state from allowing a private group to communicate religious themes on public property? Capitol Square is an area around the Statehouse in Columbus, Ohio. For years it had been an open public forum, available to all to communicate messages of various sorts provided they were willing to meet the state's time, place, and manner restrictions. In 1993 the Ku Klux Klan petitioned to erect a cross in the square, a request denied by the Capitol Square Review Board, which had responsibility for administering the area. The Board's rationale was that a cross was religious expression and thus was prohibited by the Establishment Clause of the First Amendment. Vincent Pinette, the leader of the Ohio Klan, sued in federal district court and received an affirmative judgment. The Board then allowed the Klan to erect its cross, but appealed to the Court of Appeals for the Sixth Circuit, which affirmed the lower court. The Supreme Court granted certiorari and affirmed the lower courts, Justice Scalia for the majority.

Justice Scalia did not seem to think that this was a difficult case. Capitol Square had a long history of being a traditional public forum, open to virtually all comers to communicate a wide variety of messages, even in unattended displays. It was clear that the speech at issue here was that of a private group, it was not the government's speech. As did the *Rosenberger* Court (the two decisions were handed down the same day), Justice Scalia relied on Justice O'Connor's *dictum* in BOARD OF EDUCATION v. MERGENS: "[T]here is a crucial difference between *government* speech endorsing religion, which the

Establishment Clause forbids, and *private* speech endorsing religion, which the Free Speech and Free Exercise Clauses protect" (emphasis in original) 496 U.S. 226, 250. The case at bar was of the latter sort. Furthermore, the Court was able to cite precedent in holding that when the government merely accommodates religious speech as part of an open forum, as in WIDMAR v. VINCENT and LAMB'S CHAPEL v. CENTER MORICHES SCHOOL DISTRICT, it is not government endorsement of religion and not prohibited by the Establishment Clause.

> Religious expression cannot violate the Establishment Clause where it (1) is purely private and (2) occurs in a traditional or designated public forum, publicly announced and open to all on equal terms. Those conditions are satisfied here, and therefore the State may not bar respondents' cross from Capitol Square (115 S. Ct. 2440, 2450).

In the process of reaching the decision, Justice Scalia did not mention the *Lemon* test and, if anything, dismissed as less than useful the "endorsement" test used in recent years for interpreting the Establishment Clause. Public forum analysis and the concept of neutral accommodation of private speech was enough to decide the case. At one point, in dismissing the views expressed in Justice Stevens' dissent and Justice Souter's and Justice O'Connor's concurrences, he asserted that they would relegate religious speech to the same less-protected status as commercial speech and pornography. Then he declared:

> It will be a sad day when this Court casts piety in with pornography, and finds the First Amendment more hospitable to private expletives than to private prayers. This would be merely bizarre were religious speech simply as protected by the Constitution as other forms of speech; but it is outright perverse when one considers that private religious expression receives *preferential* treatment under the Free Exercise Clause (emphasis in original) (115 S. Ct. 2440, 2449).

It is decidedly ironic that Justice Scalia could rhapsodize about the Free Exercise Clause's giving preferred treatment to religion here when he marginalized and essentially declared the Clause irrelevant in EMPLOYMENT DIVISION OF OREGON v. SMITH.

Justice Stevens wrote a dissent which argued that the "endorsement" concept of interpreting Establishment Clause issues cannot be as easily swept aside as the plurality opinion contended. The Klan's cross, left unattended as a clearly religious symbol, surely understood as such by all but the most unenlightened observers, close to the seat of state government, had the effect of conveying state endorsement of religion. No amount of public forum analysis can deny that the cross was a religious symbol, put there to counteract another religious symbol, and the fact that the Review Board approved those symbols showed that they had state endorsement, if not its imprimatur.

> Just as the Constitution recognizes the State's interest in preventing its property from being used as a conduit for ideas it does not wish to give the appearance of ratifying, the Establishment Clause prohibits government from allowing, and thus endorsing, unattended displays that take a position on a religious issue. If the State allows such stationary displays in front of the seat of government, viewers will reasonably assume that it approves of them. A reasonable observer would likely infer endorsement from the location of the cross erected by the Klan in this case. . . . When the message is religious in character, it is a message the State can neither send nor reinforce without violating the Establishment Clause (115 S. Ct. 2440, 2469).

LYNCH v. DONNELLY

465 U.S. 668
ON WRIT OF CERTIORARI TO THE UNITED STATES COURT
OF APPEALS FOR THE FIRST CIRCUIT
Argued October 4, 1983 — Decided March 5, 1984

⊥**670** *Chief Justice BURGER* delivered the opinion of the Court.

We granted certiorari to decide whether the Establishment Clause of the First Amendment prohibits a municipality ⊥**671** from including a crèche, or Nativity scene, in its annual Christmas display.

I

Each year, in cooperation with the downtown retail merchants' association, the City of Pawtucket, Rhode Island, erects a Christmas display as part of its observance of the Christmas holiday season. The display is situated in a park owned by a nonprofit organization and located in the heart of the shopping district. The display is essentially like those to be found in hundreds of towns or cities across the Nation—often on public grounds—during the Christmas season. The Pawtucket display comprises many of the figures and decorations traditionally associated with Christmas, including, among other things, a Santa Claus house, reindeer pulling Santa's sleigh, candy-striped poles, a Christmas tree, carolers, cutout figures representing such characters as a clown, an elephant, and a teddy bear, hundreds of colored lights, a large banner that reads "SEASONS GREETINGS," and the crèche at issue here. All components of this display are owned by the City.

The crèche, which has been included in the display for 40 or more years, consists of the traditional figures, including the Infant Jesus, Mary and Joseph, angels, shepherds, kings, and animals, all ranging in heights from 5" to 5'. In 1973, when the present crèche was acquired, it cost the City $1,365; it now is valued at $200. The erection and dismantling of the crèche cost the City about $20 per year; nominal expenses are incurred in lighting the crèche. No money has been expended on its maintenance for the past 10 years.

Respondents, Pawtucket residents and individual members of the Rhode Island affiliate of the American Civil Liberties Union, and the affiliate itself, brought this action in the United States District Court for Rhode Island, challenging the City's inclusion of the crèche in the annual display. The District Court held that the City's inclusion of the crèche in the annual display violates the Establishment Clause, which is binding on the states through the ^**672** Fourteenth Amendment. The District Court found that, by including the crèche in the Christmas display, the City has "tried to endorse and promulgate religious beliefs," and that "erection of the crèche has the real and substantial effect of affiliating the City with the Christian beliefs that the crèche represents." This "appearance of official sponsorship," it believed, "confers more than a remote and incidental benefit on Christianity." Last, although the court acknowledged the absence of administrative entanglement, it found that excessive entanglement has been fostered as a result of the political divisiveness of including the crèche in the celebration. The City was permanently enjoined from including the crèche in the display.

A divided panel of the Court of Appeals for the First Circuit affirmed. We granted certiorari, and we reverse.

II

A

This Court has explained that the purpose of the Establishment and Free Exercise Clauses of the First Amendment is "to prevent, as far as possible, the intrusion of either [the church or the state] into the precincts of the other." *Lemon* v. *Kurtzman*. At the same time, however, the Court has recognized that "total separation is not possible in an absolute sense. Some relationship between government and religious organizations is inevitable." *Ibid.* In every Establishment Clause case, we must reconcile the inescapable tension between the objective of preventing unnecessary intrusion of either the church or the state upon the other, and the reality that, as the Court has so often noted, total separation of the two is not possible.

^**673** The Court has sometimes described the Religion Clauses as erecting a "wall" between church and state. The concept of a "wall" of separation is a useful figure of speech probably deriving from views of Thomas Jefferson. The metaphor has served as a reminder that the Establishment Clause forbids an established church or anything approaching it. But the metaphor itself is not a wholly accurate description of the practical aspects of the relationship that in fact exists between church and state.

No significant segment of our society and no institution within it can exist in a vacuum or in total or absolute isolation from all the other parts, much less from government. "It has never been thought either possible or desirable to enforce a regime of total separation. . . ." *Committee for Public Education & Religious Liberty* v. *Nyquist*. Nor does the Constitution require complete separation of church and state; it affirmatively mandates accommodation, not merely tolerance, of all religions, and forbids hostility toward any. Anything less would require the "callous indifference" we have said was never intended by the Establishment Clause. Indeed, we have observed, such hostility would bring us into "war with our national tradition as embodied in the First Amendment's guaranty of the free exercise of religion." *McCollum*.

B

The Court's interpretation of the Establishment Clause has comported with what history reveals was the contemporaneous understanding of its guarantees. A significant example ^**674** of the contemporaneous understanding of that Clause is found in the events of the first week of the First Session of the First Congress in 1789. In the very week that Congress approved the Establishment Clause as part of the Bill of Rights for submission to the states, it enacted legislation providing for paid chaplains for the House and Senate. In *Marsh* v. *Chambers*, we noted that seventeen Members of that First Congress had been Delegates to the Constitutional Convention where freedom of speech, press and religion and antagonism toward an established church were subjects of frequent discussion. We saw no conflict with the Establishment Clause when Nebraska employed members of the clergy as official Legislative Chaplains to give opening prayers at sessions of the state legislature.

The interpretation of the Establishment Clause by Congress in 1789 takes on special significance in light of the Court's emphasis that the First Congress "was a Congress whose constitutional decisions have always been regarded, as they should be regarded, as of the greatest weight in the interpretation of that fundamental instrument" *Myers* v. *United States*.

It is clear that neither the seventeen draftsmen of the Constitution who were Members of the First Congress, nor the Congress of 1789, saw any establishment problem in the employment of congressional Chaplains to offer daily prayers in the Congress, a practice that has continued for nearly two centuries. It would be difficult to identify a more striking example of the accommodation of religious belief intended by the Framers.

C

There is an unbroken history of official acknowledgment by all three branches of government of the role of religion in American life from at least 1789. Seldom in our opinions was this more affirmatively expressed than in *Justice DOUGLAS'* opinion for the Court validating a program allowing release of ^**675** public school students from classes to attend off-campus religious exercises. Rejecting a claim that the program violated the Establishment Clause, the Court asserted pointedly: "We are a religious people whose institutions presuppose a Supreme Being." *Zorach* v. *Clauson*.

Our history is replete with official references to the value and invocation of Divine guidance in deliberations and pronouncements of the Founding Fathers and contemporary leaders. Beginning in the early colonial period long before Independence, a day of Thanksgiving was celebrated as a religious holiday to give thanks for the bounties of Nature as gifts from God. President Washington and his successors proclaimed Thanksgiving, with all its religious overtones, a day of national celebration and Congress made it a National Holiday more than a century ago. That holiday has not lost its theme of expressing thanks for Divine aid any more than has Christmas lost its religious significance.

^**676** Executive Orders and other official announcements of Presidents and of the Congress have proclaimed both Christmas and Thanksgiving National Holidays in religious terms. And, by Acts of Congress, it has long been the practice that federal employees are released from duties on these National Holidays, while being paid from the same public revenues that provide the compensation of the Chaplains of the Senate and the House and the military services. Thus, it is clear that Government has long recognized—indeed it has subsidized—holidays with religious significance.

Other examples of reference to our religious heritage are found in the statutorily prescribed national motto "In God We Trust," which Congress and the President mandated for our currency, and in the language "One nation under God," as part of the Pledge of Allegiance to the American flag. That pledge is recited by thousands of public school children—and adults—every year.

Art galleries supported by public revenues display religious paintings of the 15th and 16th centuries, predominantly inspired by one religious faith. The National Gallery in ^**677** Washington, maintained with Government support, for example, has long exhibited masterpieces with religious messages, notably the Last Supper, and paintings depicting the Birth of Christ, the Crucifixion, and the Resurrection, among many others with explicit Christian themes and messages. The very chamber in which oral arguments on this case were heard is decorated with a notable and permanent—not seasonal—symbol of religion: Moses with Ten Commandments. Congress has long provided chapels in the Capitol for religious worship and meditation.

There are countless other illustrations of the Government's acknowledgment of our religious heritage and governmental sponsorship of graphic manifestations of that heritage. Congress has directed the President to proclaim a National Day of Prayer each year "on which [day] the people of the United States may turn to God in prayer and meditation at churches, in groups, and as individuals." Our Presidents have repeatedly issued such Proclamations. Presidential Proclamations and messages have also been issued to commemorate Jewish Heritage Week, and the Jewish High Holy Days. One cannot look at even this brief resume without finding that our history is pervaded by expressions of religious beliefs such as are found in *Zorach*. Equally pervasive is the evidence of accommodation of all faiths and all forms of religious expression, and hostility toward none. Through this accommoda^**678**tion, as *Justice DOUGLAS* observed, governmental action has "follow[ed] the best of our traditions" and "respect[ed] the religious nature of our people."

III

This history may help explain why the Court consistently has declined to take a rigid, absolutist view of the Establishment Clause. We have refused "to construe the Religion Clauses with a literalness that would underline the ultimate constitutional objective *as illuminated by history*." *Walz* v. *Tax Commission*. In our modern, complex society, whose traditions and constitutional underpinnings rest on and encourage diversity and pluralism in all areas, an absolutist approach in applying the Establishment Clause is simplistic and has been uniformly rejected by the Court.

Rather than mechanically invalidating all governmental conduct or statutes that confer benefits or give special recognition to religion in general or to one faith—as an absolutist approach would dictate—the Court has scrutinized challenged legislation or official conduct to determine whether, in reality, it establishes a religion or religious faith, or tends to do so. Joseph Story wrote a century and a half ago:

"The real object of the [First] Amendment was . . . to prevent any national ecclesiastical establishment, which should give to an hierarchy the exclusive patronage of the national government." 3 Story, Commentaries on the Constitution of the United States 728 (1833).

In each case, the inquiry calls for line drawing; no fixed, *per se* rule can be framed. The Establishment Clause like the Due Process Clauses is not a precise, detailed provision in a legal code capable of ready application. The purpose of the Establishment Clause "was to state an objective, not to write a statute." *Walz*. The line between permissible relationships and those barred by the Clause can no ^**679** more be straight and unwavering than due process can be defined in a single stroke or phrase or test. The Clause erects a "blurred, indistinct, and variable barrier depending on all the circumstances of a particular relationship." *Lemon*.

In the line-drawing process we have often found it useful to inquire whether the challenged law or conduct has a secular purpose, whether its principal or primary effect is to advance or inhibit religion, and whether it creates an excessive entanglement of government with religion. But, we have repeatedly emphasized our unwillingness to be confined to any single test or criterion in this sensitive area. In two cases, the Court did not even apply the *Lemon* "test." We did not, for example, consider that analysis relevant in *Marsh*. Nor did we find *Lemon* useful in *Larson* v. *Valente*, where there was substantial evidence of overt discrimination against a particular church.

In this case, the focus of our inquiry must be on the crèche in the context of the Christmas season. In *Stone*, for example, we invalidated a state statute requiring the posting of a copy of the Ten Commandments on public classroom walls. But the Court carefully pointed out that the Commandments were posted purely as a religious admonition, not "integrated into the school curriculum, where the Bible may constitutionally be used in an appropriate study of history, civilization, ethics, comparative religion or the like." Similarly, in *Abington*, although the Court struck down the practices in two States requiring daily Bible readings in public schools, it specifically noted that nothing in the Court's holding was intended to "indicat[e] that such study of the Bible or of religion, when presented objectively as part of a secular program of education, may not be effected consist⊥**680**ently with the First Amendment." Focus exclusively on the religious component of any activity would inevitably lead to its invalidation under the Establishment Clause.

The Court has invalidated legislation or governmental action on the ground that a secular purpose was lacking, but only when it has concluded there was no question that the statute or activity was motivated wholly by religious considerations. Even where the benefits to religion were substantial, as in *Everson*, *Board of Education* v. *Allen*, *Walz*, and *Tilton*, we saw a secular purpose and no conflict with the Establishment Clause.

The District Court inferred from the religious nature of the crèche that the City has no secular purpose for the display. In so doing, it rejected the City's claim that its reasons for including the crèche are essentially the same as its reasons for sponsoring the display as a whole. The District Court plainly erred by focusing almost exclusively on the crèche. When viewed in the proper context of the Christmas Holiday season, it is apparent that, on this record, there is insufficient evidence to establish that the inclusion of the crèche is a purposeful or surreptitious effort to express some kind of subtle governmental advocacy of a particular religious message. In a pluralistic society a variety of motives and purposes are implicated. The City, like the Congresses and Presidents, however, has principally taken note of a significant historical religious event long celebrated in the Western World. The crèche in the display depicts the historical origins of this traditional event long recognized as a National Holiday.

⊥**681** The narrow question is whether there is a secular purpose for Pawtucket's display of the crèche. The display is sponsored by the City to celebrate the Holiday and to depict the origins of that Holiday. These are legitimate secular purposes. The District Court's inference, drawn from the religious nature of the crèche, that the City has no secular purpose was, on this record, clearly erroneous.

The District Court found that the primary effect of including the crèche is to confer a substantial and impermissible benefit on religion in general and on the Christian faith in particular. Comparisons of the relative benefits to religion of different forms of governmental support are elusive and difficult to make. But to conclude that the primary effect of including the crèche is to advance religion in violation of the Establishment Clause would require that we view it as more beneficial to and more an endorsement of religion, for example, than expenditure of large sums of public money for textbooks supplied throughout the country to students attending church-sponsored schools, expenditure of public funds for transportation of ⊥**682** students to church-sponsored schools, federal grants for college building of church-sponsored institutions of higher education combining secular and religious education, noncategorical grants to church-sponsored colleges and universities, and the tax exemptions for church properties sanctioned in *Walz*. It would also require that we view it as more of an endorsement of religion that the Sunday Closing Laws upheld in *McGowan* v. *Maryland*, the release time program for religious training in *Zorach*, and the legislative prayers upheld in *Marsh*.

We are unable to discern a greater aid to religion deriving from inclusion of the crèche than from these benefits and endorsements previously held not violative of the Establishment Clause. What was said about the legislative prayers in *Marsh*, and implied about the Sunday Closing Laws in *McGowan* is true of the City's inclusion of the crèche: its "reason or effect merely happen to coincide or harmonize with the tenets of some . . . religions."

This case differs significantly from *Larkin* v. *Grendel's Den*, and *McCollum*, where religion was sub⊥**683**stantially aided. In *Grendel's Den*, important governmental power—a licensing veto authority—had been vested in churches. In *McCollum*, government had made religious instruction available in public school classrooms; the State had not only used the public school buildings for the teaching of religion, it had "afford[ed] sectarian groups an invaluable aid . . . [by] provid[ing] pupils for their religious classes through use of the State's compulsory public school machinery." No comparable benefit to religion is discernible here.

The dissent asserts some observers may perceive that the City has aligned itself with the Christian faith by including a Christian symbol in its display and that this serves to advance religion. We can assume, *arguendo*, that the display advances religion in a sense; but our precedents plainly contemplate that on occasion some advancement of religion will result from governmental action. The Court has made it abundantly clear, however, that "not every law that confers an 'indirect,' 'remote,' or 'incidental' benefit upon [religion] is, for that reason alone, constitutionally invalid." *Nyquist*. Here, whatever benefit to one faith or religion or to all religions, is indirect, remote and incidental; display of the crèche is no more an advancement or endorsement of religion than the Congressional and Executive recognition of the origins of the Holiday itself as "Christ's Mass," or the exhibition of literally hundreds of religious paintings in governmentally supported museums.

The District Court found that there had been no administrative entanglement between religion and state resulting from the City's ownership and use of the crèche. But it went on to hold that some political divisiveness was engendered by this litigation. Coupled with its finding of an impermissible sectarian purpose and effect, this persuaded the court that there was "excessive entanglement." The Court of Appeals expressly declined to ⊥**684** accept the District Court's finding that inclusion of the crèche has caused political divisiveness along religious lines, and noted that this Court has never held that political divisiveness alone was sufficient to invalidate government conduct.

Entanglement is a question of kind and degree. In this case, however, there is no reason to disturb the District Court's finding on the absence of administrative entanglement. There is no evidence of contact with church authorities concerning the content or design of the exhibit prior to or since Pawtucket's purchase of the crèche. No expenditures for maintenance of the crèche have been necessary; and since the City owns the crèche, now valued at $200, the tangible material it contributes is *de minimis*. In many respects the display requires far less ongoing, day-to-day interaction between church and state than religious paintings in public galleries. There is nothing here, of course, like the "comprehensive, discriminating, and continuing state surveillance" or the "enduring entanglement" present in *Lemon*.

The Court of Appeals correctly observed that this Court has not held that political divisiveness alone can serve to invalidate otherwise permissible conduct. And we decline to so hold today. This case does not involve a direct subsidy to church-sponsored schools or colleges, or other religious institutions, and hence no inquiry into potential political divisiveness is even called for. In any event, apart from this litigation there is no evidence of political friction or divisiveness over the crèche in the 40-year history of Pawtucket's Christmas celebration. The District Court stated that the inclusion of the crèche for the 40 years has been "marked by no apparent dissension" and that the display has had a "calm history." Curiously, it went on to hold that the political divisiveness engendered by this lawsuit was evidence of excessive entanglement. A litigant cannot, by the very act of commencing a lawsuit, however, create the ap⊥**685**pearance of divisiveness and then exploit it as evidence of entanglement.

We are satisfied that the City has a secular purpose for including the crèche, that the City has not impermissibly advanced religion, and that including the crèche does not create excessive entanglement between religion and government.

IV

Justice BRENNAN describes the crèche as a "recreation of an event that lies at the heart of Christian faith." The crèche, like a painting, is passive; admittedly it is a reminder of the origins of Christmas. Even the traditional, purely secular displays extant at Christmas, with or without a crèche, would inevitably recall the religious nature of the Holiday. The display engenders a friendly community spirit of good will in keeping with the season. The crèche may well have special meaning to those whose faith includes the celebration of religious masses, but none who sense the origins of the Christmas celebration would fail to be aware of its religious implications. That the display brings people into the central city, and serves commercial interests and benefits merchants and their employees, does not, as the dissent points out, determine the character of the display. That a prayer invoking Divine guidance in Congress is preceded and followed by debate and partisan conflict over taxes, budgets, national defense, and myriad mundane subjects, for example, has never been thought to demean or taint the sacredness of the invocation.

Of course the crèche is identified with one religious faith but no more so than the examples we have set out from prior cases in which we found no conflict with the Establishment ⊥**686** Clause. It would be ironic, however, if the inclusion of a single symbol of a particular historic religious event, as part of a celebration acknowledged in the Western World for 20 centuries, and in this country by the people, by the Executive Branch, by the Congress, and the courts for two centuries, would so "taint" the City's exhibit as to render it violative of the Establishment Clause. To forbid the use of this one passive symbol—the crèche—at the very time people are taking note of the season with Christmas hymns and carols in public schools and other public places, and while the Congress and Legislatures open sessions with prayers by paid chaplains would be a stilted over-reaction contrary to our history and to our holdings. If the presence of the crèche in this display violates the Establishment Clause, a host of other forms of taking official note of Christmas, and of our religious heritage, are equally offensive to the Constitution.

The Court has acknowledged that the "fears and political problems" that gave rise to the Religion Clauses in the 18th century are of far less concern today. We are unable to perceive the Archbishop of Canterbury, the Vicar of Rome, or other powerful religious leaders behind every public acknowledgement of the religious heritage long officially recognized by the three constitutional branches of government. Any notion that these symbols pose a real danger of establishment of a state church is farfetched indeed.

V

That this Court has been alert to the constitutionally expressed opposition to the establishment of religion is shown in numerous holdings striking down statutes or programs as violative of the Establishment Clause. ⊥**687** The most recent example of this careful scrutiny is found in the case invalidating a municipal ordinance granting to a church a virtual veto power over the licensing of liquor establishments near the church. *Grendel's Den*. Taken together these cases abundantly demonstrate the Court's concern to protect the genuine objectives of the Establishment Clause. It is far too late in the day to impose a crabbed reading of the Clause on the country.

VI

We hold that, notwithstanding the religious significance of the crèche, the City of Pawtucket has not violated the Establishment Clause of the First Amendment. Accordingly, the judgment of the Court of Appeals is reversed.

It is so ordered.

Justice O'CONNOR, concurring.

I concur in the opinion of the Court. I write separately to suggest a clarification of our Establishment Clause doctrine. The suggested approach leads to the same result in this case as that taken by the Court, and the Court's opinion, as I read it, is consistent with my analysis.

I

The Establishment Clause prohibits government from making adherence to a religion relevant in any way to a person's standing in the political community. Government can run afoul of that prohibition in two principal ways. One is ex⊥**688**cessive entanglement with religious institutions, which may interfere with the independence of the institutions, give the institutions access to government or governmental powers not fully shared by nonadherents of the religion, and foster the creation of political constituencies defined along religious lines. The second and more direct infringement is government endorsement or disapproval of religion. Endorsement sends a message to nonadherents that they are outsiders, not full members of the political community, and an accompanying message to adherents that they are insiders, favored members of the political community. Disapproval sends the opposite message.

Our prior cases have used the three-part test articulated in *Lemon* v. *Kurtzman*, as a guide to detecting these two forms of unconstitutional government action. It has never been entirely clear, however, ⊥**689** how the three parts of the test relate to the principles enshrined in the Establishment Clause. Focusing on institutional entanglement and on endorsement or disapproval of religion clarifies the *Lemon* test as an analytical device.

II

In this case, as even the District Court found, there is no institutional entanglement. Nevertheless, the appellees contend that the political divisiveness caused by Pawtucket's display of its crèche violates the excessive-entanglement prong of the *Lemon* test. The Court's opinion follows the suggestion in *Mueller* v. *Allen*, and concludes that "no inquiry into potential political divisiveness is even called for" in this case. In my view, political divisiveness along religious lines should not be an independent test of constitutionality.

Although several of our cases have discussed political divisiveness under the entanglement prong of *Lemon*, we have never relied on divisiveness as an independent ground for holding a government practice unconstitutional. Guessing the potential for political divisiveness inherent in a government practice is simply too speculative an enterprise, in part because the existence of the litigation, as this case illustrates, itself may affect the political response to the government practice. Political divisiveness is admittedly an evil addressed by the Establishment Clause. Its existence may be evidence that institutional entanglement is excessive or that a government practice is perceived as an endorsement of religion. But the constitutional inquiry should focus ultimately on the character of the government activity that might cause such divisiveness, not on the divisiveness itself. The entanglement prong of the *Lemon* test is properly limited to institutional entanglement.

⊥**690** III

The central issue in this case is whether Pawtucket has endorsed Christianity by its display of the crèche. To answer that question, we must examine both what Pawtucket intended to communicate in displaying the crèche and what message the City's display actually conveyed. The purpose and effect prongs of the *Lemon* test represent these two aspects of the meaning of the City's action.

The meaning of a statement to its audience depends both on the intention of the speaker and on the "objective" meaning of the statement in the community. Some listeners need not rely solely on the words themselves in discerning the speaker's intent: they can judge the intent by, for example, examining the context of the statement or asking questions of the speaker. Other listeners do not have or will not seek access to such evidence of intent. They will rely instead on the words themselves; for them the message actually conveyed may be something not actually intended. If the audience is large, as it always is when government "speaks" by word or deed, some portion of the audience will inevitably receive a message determined by the "objective" content of the statement, and some portion will inevitably receive the intended message. Examination of both the subjective and the objective components of the message communicated by a government action is therefore necessary to determine whether the action carries a forbidden meaning.

The purpose prong of the *Lemon* test asks whether government's actual purpose is to endorse or disapprove of religion. The effect prong asks whether, irrespective of government's actual purpose, the practice under review in fact conveys a message of endorsement or disapproval. An affirmative answer to either question should render the challenged practice invalid.

A

The purpose prong of the *Lemon* test requires that a government activity have a secular purpose. That requirement ⊥**691** is not satisfied, however, by the mere existence of some secular purpose, however dominated by religious purposes. In *Stone* v. *Graham*, for example, the Court held that posting copies of the Ten Commandments in schools violated the purpose prong of the *Lemon* test, yet the State plainly had some secular objectives, such as instilling most of the values of the Ten Commandments and illustrating their connection to our legal system. The proper inquiry under the purpose prong of *Lemon*, I submit, is whether the government intends to convey a message of endorsement or disapproval of religion.

Applying that formulation to this case, I would find that Pawtucket did not intend to convey any message of endorsement of Christianity or disapproval of non-Christian religions. The evident purpose of including the crèche in the larger display was not promotion of the religious content of the crèche but celebration of the public holiday through its traditional symbols. Celebration of public holidays, which have cultural significance even if they also have religious aspects, is a legitimate secular purpose.

The District Court's finding that the display of the crèche had no secular purpose was based on erroneous reasoning. The District Court believed that it should ascertain the City's purpose in displaying the crèche separate and apart from the general purpose in setting up the display. It also found that, because the tradition-celebrating purpose was suspect in the court's eyes, the City's use of an unarguably religious symbol "raises an inference" of intent to endorse. When viewed in light of correct legal principles, the District Court's finding of unlawful purpose was clearly erroneous.

B

Focusing on the evil of government endorsement or disapproval of religion makes clear that the effect prong of the *Lemon* test is properly interpreted not to require invalidation of a government practice merely because it in fact causes, ⊥**692** even as a primary effect, advancement or inhibition of religion. The laws upheld in *Walz* v. *Tax Commission* (tax exemption for religious, educational, and charitable organizations), in *McGowan* v. *Maryland* (mandatory Sunday closing law), and in *Zorach* v. *Clauson* (released time from school for off-campus religious instruction), had such effects, but they did not violate the Establishment Clause. What is crucial is that a government practice not have the effect of communicating a message of government endorsement or disapproval of religion. It is only practices having the effect, whether intentionally or unintentionally, that make religion relevant, in reality or public perception, to status in the political community.

Pawtucket's display of its crèche, I believe, does not communicate a message that the government intends to endorse the Christian beliefs represented by the crèche. Although the religious and indeed sectarian significance of the crèche as the district court found, is not neutralized by the setting, the overall holiday setting changes what viewers may fairly understand to be the purpose of the display—as a typical museum setting, though not neutralizing the religious content of a religious painting, negates any message of endorsement of the content. The display celebrates a public holiday, and no one contends that declaration of that holiday is understood to be an endorsement of religion. The holiday itself has very strong secular components and traditions. Government celebration of the holiday, which is extremely common, generally is not understood to endorse the religious content of the holiday, just as government celebration of Thanksgiving is not so understood. The crèche is a traditional symbol of the holiday that is very commonly displayed along with purely secular symbols, as it was in Pawtucket.

These features combine to make the government's display of the crèche in this particular physical setting no more an endorsement of the religion than such governmental "acknowl⊥**693**edgments" of religion as legislative prayers of the type approved in *Marsh* v. *Chambers*, government declaration of Thanksgiving as a public holiday, printing of "In God We Trust" on coins, and opening court sessions with "God save the United States and this honorable court." Those government acknowledgments of religion serve, in the only ways reasonably possible in our culture, the legitimate secular purposes of solemnizing public occasions, expressing confidence in the future, and encouraging the recognition of what is worthy of appreciation in society. For that reason, and because of their history and ubiquity, those practices are not understood as conveying government approval of particular religious beliefs. The display of the crèche likewise serves a secular purpose—celebration of a public holiday with traditional symbols. It cannot fairly be understood to convey a message of government endorsement of religion. It is significant in this regard that the crèche display apparently caused no political divisiveness prior to the filing of this lawsuit, although Pawtucket had incorporated the crèche in its annual Christmas display for some years. For these reasons, I conclude that Pawtucket's display of the crèche does not have the effect of communicating endorsement of Christianity.

The District Court's subsidiary findings on the effect test are consistent with this conclusion. The court found as facts that the crèche has a religious content, that it would not be seen as an insignificant part of the display, that its religious content is not neutralized by the setting, that the display is celebratory and not instructional, and that the city did not seek to counteract any possible religious message. These findings do not imply that the crèche communicates government approval of Christianity. The District Court also found, however, that the government was understood to place its imprimatur on the religious content of the crèche. But whether a government activity communicates endorsement of religion is not a question of simple historical fact. ⊥**694** Although evidentiary submissions may help answer it, the question is, like the question whether racial or sex-based classifications communicate an invidious message, in large part a legal question to be answered on the basis of judicial interpretation of social facts. The District Court's conclusion concerning the effect of Pawtucket's display of its crèche was in error as a matter of law.

IV

Every government practice must be judged in its unique circumstances to determine whether it constitutes an endorsement or disapproval of religion. In making that determination, courts must keep in mind both the fundamental place held by the Establishment Clause in our constitutional scheme and the myriad, subtle ways in which Establishment Clause values can be eroded. Government practices that purport to celebrate or acknowledge events with religious significance must be subjected to careful judicial scrutiny.

The City of Pawtucket is alleged to have violated the Establishment Clause by endorsing the Christian beliefs represented by the crèche included in its Christmas display. Giving the challenged practice the careful scrutiny it deserves, I cannot say that the particular crèche display at issue in this case was intended to endorse or had the effect of endorsing Christianity. I agree with the Court that the judgment below must be reversed.

Justice BRENNAN, with whom *Justice* MARSHALL, *Justice* BLACKMUN and *Justice* STEVENS join, dissenting.

The principles announced in the compact phrases of the Religion Clauses have, as the Court today reminds us, proven difficult to apply. Faced with that uncertainty, the Court properly looks for guidance to the settled test announced in *Lemon* v. *Kurtzman*, for assessing whether a challenged governmental practice involves an impermissible step toward the establishment of religion. Applying that test to this case, the ⊥**695** Court reaches an essentially narrow result which turns largely upon the particular holiday context in which the City of Pawtucket's nativity scene appeared. The Court's decision implicitly leaves open questions concerning the constitutionality of the public display on public property of a crèche standing alone, or the public display of other distinctively religious symbols such as a cross. Despite the narrow contours of the Court's opinion, our precedents in my view compel the holding that Pawtucket's inclusion of a life-sized display depicting the biblical description of the birth of Christ as part of its annual Christmas celebration is unconstitutional. Nothing in the history of such practices or the setting in which the City's crèche is presented obscures or diminishes the plain fact that Pawtucket's action amounts to an impermissible governmental endorsement of a particular faith.

I

Last Term, I expressed the hope that the Court's decision in *Marsh* v. *Chambers* would prove to be only a single, aberrant departure from our settled method ⊥**696** of analyzing Establishment Clause cases. That the Court today returns to the settled analysis of our prior cases gratifies that hope. At the same time the Court's less than vigorous application of the *Lemon* test suggests that its commitment to those standards may only be superficial. After reviewing the Court's opinion, I am convinced that this case appears hard not because the principles of decision are obscure, but because the Christmas holiday seems so familiar and agreeable. Although the ⊥**697** Court's reluctance to disturb a community's chosen method of celebrating such an agreeable holiday is understandable, that cannot justify the Court's departure from controlling precedent. In my view, Pawtucket's maintenance and display at public expense of a symbol as distinctively sectarian as a crèche simply cannot be squared with our prior cases. And it is plainly contrary to the purposes and values of the Establishment Clause to pretend, as the Court does, that the otherwise secular setting of Pawtucket's nativity scene dilutes in some fashion the crèche's singular religiosity, or that the City's annual display reflects nothing more than an "acknowledgment" of our shared national heritage. Neither the character of the Christmas holiday itself, nor our heritage of religious expression supports this result. Indeed, our remarkable and precious religious diversity as a nation which the Establishment Clause seeks to protect, runs directly counter to today's decision.

A

As we have sought to meet new problems arising under the Establishment Clause, our decisions, with few exceptions, have demanded that a challenged governmental practice satisfy the following criteria: "First, the [practice] must have a secular legislative purpose; second, its principal or primary effect must be one that neither advances nor inhibits religion; finally, [it] must not foster 'an excessive government entanglement with religion.'" *Lemon* v. *Kurtzman*.

⊥**698** This well-defined three-part test expresses the essential concerns animating the Establishment Clause. Thus, the test is designed to ensure that the organs of government remain strictly separate and apart from religious affairs, for "a union of government and religion tends to destroy government and degrade religion." *Engel* v. *Vitale*. And it seeks to guarantee that government maintains a position of neutrality with respect to religion and neither advances nor inhibits the promulgation and practice of religious beliefs. *Everson* v. *Board of Education*. ("Neither [a State nor the Federal Government] can pass laws which aid one religion, aid all religions, or prefer one religion over another"). In this regard, we must be alert in our examination of any challenged practice not only for an official establishment of religion, but also for those other evils at which the Clause was aimed—"sponsorship, financial support, and active involvement of the sovereign in religious activity." *Committee for Public Education* v. *Nyquist*.

Applying the three-part test to Pawtucket's crèche, I am persuaded that the City's inclusion of the crèche in its Christmas display simply does not reflect a "clearly secular purpose." *Nyquist*. Unlike the typical case in which the record reveals some contemporaneous expression of a clear purpose to advance religion, or, conversely, a clear secular purpose, ⊥**699** here we have no explicit statement of purpose by Pawtucket's municipal government accompanying its decision to purchase, display and maintain the crèche. Governmental purpose may nevertheless be inferred. For instance, in *Stone* v. *Graham*, this Court found, despite the state's avowed purpose of reminding school children of the secular application of the commands of the Decalogue, that the "preeminent purpose for posting the Ten Commandments on schoolroom walls is plainly religious in nature." In the present case, the City claims that its purposes were exclusively secular. Pawtucket sought, according to this view, only to participate in the celebration of a national holiday and to attract people to the downtown area in order to promote preChristmas retail sales and to help engender the spirit of goodwill and neighborliness commonly associated with the Christmas season.

Despite these assertions, two compelling aspects of this case indicate that our generally prudent "reluctance to attribute unconstitutional motives" to a governmental body, *Mueller* v. *Allen*, should be overcome. First, as was true in *Larkin* v. *Grendel's Den*, all of Pawtucket's "valid secular objectives can be readily accomplished by other means." Plainly, the City's interest in celebrating the holiday and in promoting both retail sales and goodwill are fully served by the elaborate display of Santa Claus, reindeer, and wishing wells that are already a part of Pawtucket's annual Christ⊥**700** mas display. More importantly, the nativity scene, unlike every other element of the Hodgson Park display, reflects a sectarian exclusivity that the avowed purposes of celebrating the holiday season and promoting retail commerce simply do not encompass. To be found constitutional, Pawtucket's seasonal celebration must at least be non-denominational and not serve to promote religion. The inclusion of a distinctively religious element like the crèche, however, demonstrates that a narrower sectarian purpose lay behind the decision to include a nativity scene. That the crèche retained this religious character for the people and municipal government of Pawtucket is suggested by the Mayor's testimony at trial in which he stated that for him, as well as others in the City, the effort to eliminate the nativity scene from Pawtucket's Christmas celebration "is a step towards establishing another religion, non-religion that it may be." Plainly, the City and its leaders understood that the inclusion of the crèche in its display would serve the wholly religious purpose ⊥**701** of "keep[ing] 'Christ in Christmas.'" From this record, therefore, it is impossible to say with the kind of confidence that was possible in *McGowan* v. *Maryland*, that a wholly secular goal predominates.

The "primary effect" of including a nativity scene in the City's display is, as the District Court found, to place the government's imprimatur of approval on the particular religious beliefs exemplified by the crèche. Those who believe in the message of the nativity receive the unique and exclusive benefit of public recognition and approval of their views. For many, the City's decision to include the crèche as part of its extensive and costly efforts to celebrate Christmas can only mean that the prestige of the government has been conferred on the beliefs associated with the crèche, thereby providing "a significant symbolic benefit to religion. . . ." *Larkin* v. *Grendel's Den*. The effect on minority religious groups, as well as on those who may reject all religion, is to convey the message that their views are not similarly worthy of public recognition nor entitled to public support. It was precisely this sort of religious chauvinism that the Establishment Clause was intended forever to prohibit. In this case, as in *Engel* v. *Vitale*, "[w]hen the power, prestige and financial support of government is placed behind ⊥**702** a particular religious belief, the indirect coercive pressure upon religious minorities to conform to the prevailing officially approved religion is plain." Our decision in *Widmar* v. *Vincent* rests upon the same principle. There the Court noted that a state university policy of "equal access" for both secular and religious groups would "not confer any imprimatur of State approval" on the religious groups permitted to use the facilities because "a broad spectrum of groups" would be served and there was no evidence that religious groups would dominate the forum. Here, by contrast, Pawtucket itself owns the crèche and instead of extending similar attention to a "broad spectrum" of religious and secular groups, it has singled out Christianity for special treatment.

Finally, it is evident that Pawtucket's inclusion of a crèche as part of its annual Christmas display does pose a significant threat of fostering "excessive entanglement." As the Court notes, the District Court found no administrative entanglement in this case, primarily because the City had been able to administer the annual display without extensive consultation with religious officials. Of course, there is no reason to disturb that finding, but it is worth noting that after today's decision, administrative entanglements may well develop. Jews and other non-Christian groups, prompted perhaps by the Mayor's remark that he will include a Menorah in future displays, can be expected to press government for inclusion of their symbols, and faced with such requests, government will have to become involved in accommodating the various demands. Cf. *Committee for Public Education* v. *Nyquist* ("competing efforts [by religious groups] to gain and maintain the support of government" may "occasio[n] considerable civil strife"). More importantly, although no political divisiveness was apparent in Pawtucket ⊥**703** prior to the filing of respondents' lawsuit, that act, as the District Court found, unleashed powerful emotional reactions which divided the City along religious lines. The fact that calm had prevailed prior to this suit does not immediately suggest the absence of any division on the point for, as the District Court observed, the quiescence of those opposed to the crèche may have reflected nothing more than their sense of futility in opposing the majority. Of course, the Court is correct to note that we have never held that the potential for divisiveness alone is sufficient to invalidate a challenged governmental practice; we have, nevertheless, repeatedly emphasized that "too close a proximity" between religious and civil authorities, may represent a "warning signal" that the values embodied in the Establishment Clause are at risk. *Committee for Public Education* v. *Nyquist*. Furthermore, the Court should not blind itself to the fact that because com⊥**704**munities differ in religious composition, the controversy over whether local governments may adopt religious symbols will continue to fester. In many communities, non-Christian groups can be expected to combat practices similar to Pawtucket's; this will be so especially in areas where there are substantial non-Christian minorities.

In sum, considering the District Court's careful findings of fact under the three-part analysis called for by our prior cases, I have no difficulty concluding that Pawtucket's display of the crèche is unconstitutional.

⊥**705** B

The Court advances two principal arguments to support its conclusion that the Pawtucket crèche satisfies the *Lemon* test. Neither is persuasive.

First. The Court, by focusing on the holiday "context" in which the nativity scene appeared, seeks to explain away the clear religious import of the crèche as both a symbol of Christian beliefs and a symbol of the City's support for those beliefs. Thus, although the Court concedes that the City's inclusion of the nativity scene plainly serves "to depict the origins" of Christmas as a "significant historical religious event," and that the crèche "is identified with one religious faith," we are nevertheless expected to believe that Pawtucket's use of the crèche does not signal the City's support for the sectarian symbolism that the nativity scene evokes. The effect of the crèche, of course, must be gauged not only by its inherent re⊥**706**ligious significance but also by the overall setting in which it appears. But it blinks reality to claim, as the Court does, that by including such a distinctively religious object as the crèche in its Christmas display, Pawtucket has done no more than make use of a "traditional" symbol of the holiday, and has thereby purged the crèche of its religious content and conferred only an "incidental and indirect" benefit on religion.

The court's struggle to ignore the clear religious effect of the crèche seems to me misguided for several reasons. In the first place, the City has positioned the crèche in a central and highly visible location within the Hodgson Park display. The District Court's findings in this regard are unambiguous:

"Despite the small amount of ground covered by the crèche, viewers would not regard the crèche as an insignificant part of the display. It is an almost life sized tableau marked off by a white picket fence. Furthermore, its location lends the crèche significance. The crèche faces the Roosevelt Avenue bus stops and access stairs where the bulk of the display is placed. Moreover, the crèche is near two of the most enticing parts of the display for children— Santa's house and the talking wishing well. Although the Court recognizes that one cannot see the crèche from all possible vantage points, it is clear from the City's own photos that people standing at the two bus shelters and looking down at the display will see the crèche centrally and prominently positioned." 525 F. Supp., at 1176-1177.

Moreover, the City has done nothing to disclaim government approval of the religious significance of the crèche, to suggest that the crèche represents only one religious symbol among many others that might be included in a seasonal display truly aimed at providing a wide catalogue of ethnic and religious celebrations, or to disassociate itself from the religious content of the crèche. In *Abington School Dist*. v. *Schempp* we noted that reading aloud ⊥**707** from the Bible would be a permissible schoolroom exercise only if it was "presented objectively as part of a secular program of education" that would remove any message of governmental endorsement of religion. Similarly, when the Court of Appeals for the District of Columbia approved the inclusion of a crèche as part of a national "Pageant of Peace" on federal parkland adjacent to the White House, it did so on the express condition that the government would erect "explanatory plaques" disclaiming any sponsorship of religious beliefs associated with the crèche. *Allen* v. *Morton*. In this case, by contrast, Pawtucket has made no effort whatever to provide a similar cautionary message.

Third, we have consistently acknowledged that an otherwise secular setting alone does not suffice to justify a governmental practice that has the effect of aiding religion. In *Hunt* v. *McNair*, for instance, we observed that "aid may normally be thought to have a primary effect of advancing religion . . . when it [supports] a specifically religious activity in an otherwise secular setting." The demonstrably secular context of public education, therefore, did not save the challenged practice of school prayer in *Engel* or in *Schempp*. Similarly, in *Tilton* v. *Richardson*, despite the generally secular thrust of the financing legislation under review, the Court unanimously struck down that aspect of the program which permitted church-related institutions eventually to assume total control over the use of buildings constructed with federal aid.

⊥**708** Finally, and most importantly, even in the context of Pawtucket's seasonal celebration, the crèche retains a specifically Christian religious meaning. I refuse to accept the notion implicit in today's decision that non-Christians would find that the religious content of the crèche is eliminated by the fact that it appears as part of the City's otherwise secular celebration of the Christmas holiday. The nativity scene is clearly distinct in its purpose and effect from the rest of the Hodgson Park display for the simple reason that it is the only one rooted in a biblical account of Christ's birth. It is the chief symbol of the characteristically Christian belief that a divine Savior was brought into the world and that the purpose of this miraculous birth was to illuminate a path toward salvation and redemption. For Christians, that path is exclusive, precious and holy. But for those who do not share these beliefs, the symbolic re-enactment of the birth of a divine being who has been miraculously incarnated as a man stands as a dramatic reminder of their differences with Christian faith. When government appears to sponsor such reli⊥**709** giously inspired views, we cannot say that the practice is "so separate and so indisputably marked off from the religious function, that [it] may fairly be viewed as reflect[ing] a neutral posture toward religious institutions." *Nyquist*. To be excluded on religious grounds by one's elected government is an insult and an injury that, until today, could not be countenanced by the Establishment Clause.

Second. The Court also attempts to justify the crèche by entertaining a beguilingly simple, yet faulty syllogism. The Court begins by noting that government may recognize Christmas day as a public holiday; the Court then asserts that the crèche is nothing more than a traditional element of Christmas celebrations; and it concludes that the inclusion of a crèche as part of a government's annual Christmas celebration is constitutionally permissible. The Court apparently believes that once it finds that the designation of Christmas as a public holiday is constitutionally acceptable, it is then free to conclude that virtually every form of governmental association with the celebration of the holiday is also constitutional. The vice of this dangerously superficial argument is that it overlooks the fact that the Christmas holiday in our national culture contains both secular and sectarian elements. To say that government may recognize the holiday's traditional, secular elements of ⊥**710** gift-giving, public festivities and community spirit, does not mean that government may indiscriminately embrace the distinctively sectarian aspects of the holiday. Indeed, in its eagerness to approve the crèche, the Court has advanced a rationale so simplistic that it would appear to allow the Mayor of Pawtucket to participate in the celebration of a Christmas mass, since this would be just another unobjectionable way for the City to "celebrate the holiday." As is demonstrated below, the Court's logic is fundamentally flawed both because it obscures the reason why public designation of Christmas day as a holiday is constitutionally acceptable, and blurs the distinction between the secular aspects of Christmas and its distinctively religious character, as exemplified by the crèche.

When government decides to recognize Christmas day as a public holiday, it does no more than accommodate the calendar of public activities to the plain fact that many Americans will expect on that day to spend time visiting with their families, attending religious services, and perhaps enjoying some respite from pre-holiday activities. The Free Exercise Clause, of course, does not necessarily compel the government to provide this accommodation, but neither is the Establishment Clause offended by such a step. Because it is clear that the celebration of Christmas has both secular and sectarian elements, it may well be that by taking note of the holiday, the government is simply seeking to serve the same kinds of wholly secular goals—for instance, promoting goodwill and a common day of rest—that were found to justify Sunday Closing laws in *McGowan*. If public officials go further and participate in the *secular* celebration ⊥**711** of Christmas—by, for example, decorating public places with such secular images as wreaths, garlands or Santa Claus figures—they move closer to the limits of their constitutional power but nevertheless remain within the boundaries set by the Establishment Clause. But when those officials participate in or appear to endorse the distinctively religious elements of this otherwise secular event, they encroach upon First Amendment freedoms. For it is at that point that the government brings to the forefront the theological content of the holiday, and places the prestige, power and financial support of a civil authority in the service of a particular faith.

The inclusion of a crèche in Pawtucket's otherwise secular celebration of Christmas clearly violates these principles. Unlike such secular figures as Santa Claus, reindeer and carolers, a nativity scene represents far more than a mere "traditional" symbol of Christmas.

The essence of the crèche's symbolic purpose and effect is to prompt the observer to experience a sense of simple awe and wonder appropriate to the contemplation of one of the central elements of Christian dogma—that God sent His son into the world to be a Messiah. Contrary to the Court's suggestion, the crèche is far from a mere representation of a "particular historic religious event." It is, instead, best understood as a mystical re-creation of an event that lies at the heart of Christian faith. To suggest, as the Court does, ⊥**712** that such a symbol is merely "traditional" and therefore no different from Santa's house or reindeer is not only offensive to those for whom the crèche has profound significance, but insulting to those who insist for religious or personal reasons that the story of Christ is in no sense a part of "history" nor an unavoidable element of our national "heritage."

For these reasons, the crèche in this context simply cannot be viewed as playing the same role that an ordinary museum display does. The Court seems to assume that forbidding Pawtucket from displaying a crèche would be tantamount to forbidding a state college from including the Bible or Milton's Paradise Lost in a course on English literature. But in those cases the religiously-inspired materials are being considered solely as literature. The purpose is plainly not to single out the particular religious beliefs that may have inspired the authors, but to see in these writings the outlines of a larger imaginative universe shared with other forms of literary expression. The same may be said of a course devoted to the study of art; when the course turns to Gothic architecture, the emphasis is not on the religious beliefs which the cathedrals exalt, but rather upon the "aesthetic consequences of [such religious] thought."

⊥**713** In this case, by contrast, the crèche plays no comparable secular role. Unlike the poetry of Paradise Lost which students in a literature course will seek to appreciate primarily for aesthetic or historical reasons, the angels, shepherds, Magi and infant of Pawtucket's nativity scene can only be viewed as symbols of a particular set of religious beliefs. It would be another matter if the crèche were displayed in a museum setting, in the company of other religiously-inspired artifacts, as an example, among many, of the symbolic representation of religious myths. In that setting, we would have objective guarantees that the crèche could not suggest that a particular faith had been singled out for public favor and recognition. The effect of Pawtucket's crèche, however, is not confined by any of these limiting attributes. In the absence of any other religious symbols or of any neutral disclaimer, the inescapable effect of the crèche will be to remind the average observer of the religious roots of the celebration he is witnessing and to call to mind the scriptural message that the nativity symbolizes. The fact that Pawtucket has gone to the trouble of making such an elaborate public celebration and of including a crèche in that otherwise secular setting inevitably serves to reinforce the sense that the City means to express solidarity with the Christian message of the crèche and to dismiss other faiths as unworthy of similar attention and support.

II

Although the Court's relaxed application of the *Lemon* test to Pawtucket's crèche is regrettable, it is at least understandable and properly limited to the particular facts of this case. The Court's opinion, however, also sounds a broader ⊥**714** and more troubling theme. Involving the celebration of Thanksgiving as a public holiday, the legend "In God We Trust" on our coins, and the proclamation "God save the United States and this Honorable Court" at the opening of judicial sessions, the Court asserts, without explanation, that Pawtucket's inclusion of a crèche in its annual Christmas display poses no more of threat to Establishment Clause values than these other official "acknowledgments" of religion.

Intuition tells us that some official "acknowledgment" is inevitable in a religious society if government is not to adopt a stilted indifference to the religious life of the people. It is equally true, however, that if government is to remain scrupulously neutral in matters of religious conscience, as our Constitution requires, then it must avoid those overly broad acknowledgments of religious practices that may imply governmental favoritism toward one set of religious beliefs. This does not mean, of course, that public officials may not take account, when necessary, of the separate existence and significance of the religious institutions and practices in the society they govern. Should government choose to incorporate some arguably religious element into its public ceremonies, that acknowledgment must be impartial; it must not tend to promote one faith or handicap another; and it should not sponsor religion generally over non-religion. Thus, in a series of decisions concerned with such acknowledgments, we have repeatedly held that any active form of public acknowledgment of religion indicating sponsorship or endorsement is forbidden. E.g., *Stone* v. *Graham* (posting of Ten Commandments in schoolroom); *Epperson* v. *Arkansas* (prohibition on teaching principles of Darwinian evolution); *Abington School Dist.* v. *Schempp* (mandatory Bible-reading at beginning of ⊥**715** school day); *Engel* v. *Vitale* (mandatory reading of state-composed prayer); *Illinois ex rel. McCollum* v. *Board of Education* (use of public-school facilities for religious instruction).

Despite this body of case law, the Court has never comprehensively addressed the extent to which government may acknowledge religion by, for example, incorporating religious references into public ceremonies and proclamations, and I do not presume to offer a comprehensive approach. Nevertheless, it appears from our prior decisions that at least three principles—tracing the narrow channels which government acknowledgments must follow to satisfy the Establishment Clause—may be identified. First, although the government may not be compelled to do so by the Free Exercise Clause, it may, consistently with the Establishment Clause, act to accommodate to some extent the opportunities of individuals to practice their religion. That is the essential meaning, I submit, of this Court's decision in *Zorach* v. *Clauson*, finding that government does not violate the Establishment Clause when it simply chooses to "close its doors or suspend its operations as to those who want to repair to their religious sanctuary for worship or instruction." And for me that principle would justify government's decision to declare December 25th a public holiday.

Second, our cases recognize that while a particular governmental practice may have derived from religious motivations and retain certain religious connotations, it is nonetheless permissible for the government to pursue the practice when it is continued today solely for secular reasons. As this Court noted with reference to Sunday Closing Laws in *McGowan* v. *Maryland*, the mere fact that a governmental practice coincides to some extent with certain religious beliefs does not render it unconstitutional. Thanksgiving Day, in my view, fits easily within this princi⊥**716**ple, for despite its religious antecedents, the current practice of celebrating Thanksgiving is unquestionably secular and patriotic. We all may gather with our families on that day to give thanks both for personal and national good fortune, but we are free, given the secular character of the holiday, to address that gratitude either to a divine beneficence or to such mundane sources as good luck or the country's abundant natural wealth.

Finally, we have noted that government cannot be completely prohibited from recognizing in its public actions the religious beliefs and practices of the American people as an aspect of our national history and culture. While I remain uncertain about these questions, I would suggest that such practices as the designation of "In God We Trust" as our national motto, or the references to God contained in the Pledge of Allegiance can best be understood, in Dean Rostow's apt phrase, as a form of "ceremonial deism," protected from Establishment Clause scrutiny chiefly because they have lost through rote repetition any significant religious content. ⊥**717** Moreover, these references are uniquely suited to serve such wholly secular purposes as solemnizing public occasions, or inspiring commitment to meet some national challenge in a manner that simply could not be fully served in our culture if government were limited to purely non-religious phrases. The practices by which the government has long acknowledged religion are therefore probably necessary to serve certain secular functions, and that necessity, coupled with their long history, gives those practices an essentially secular meaning.

The crèche fits none of these categories. Inclusion of the crèche is not necessary to accommodate individual religious expression. This is plainly not a case in which individual residents of Pawtucket have claimed the right to place a crèche as part of a wholly private display on public land. Nor is the inclusion of the crèche necessary to serve wholly secular goals; it is clear that the City's secular purposes of celebrating the Christmas holiday and promoting retail commerce can be fully served without the crèche. And the crèche, because of its unique association with Christianity, is clearly more sectarian than those references to God that we accept in ceremonial phrases or in other contexts that assure neutrality. The religious works on display at the National Gallery, Presidential references to God during an Inaugural Address, or the national motto present no risk of establishing religion. To be sure, our understanding of these expressions may begin in contemplation of some religious element, but it does not end there. Their message is dominantly secular. In contrast, the message of the crèche begins and ends with reverence for a particular image of the divine.

By insisting that such a distinctively sectarian message is merely an unobjectionable part of our "religious heritage," the Court takes a long step backwards ⊥**718** to the days when *Justice BREWER* could arrogantly declare for the Court that "this is a Christian nation." *Church of Holy Trinity* v. *United States*. Those days, I had thought, were forever put behind us by the Court's decision in *Engel* v. *Vitale* in which we rejected a similar argument advanced by the State of New York that its Regent's Prayer was simply an acceptable part of our "spiritual heritage."

III

The American historical experience concerning the public celebration of Christmas, if carefully examined, provides no support for the Court's decision. The opening sections of the Court's opinion, while seeking to rely on historical evidence, do no more than recognize the obvious: because of the strong religious currents that run through our history, an inflexible or absolutistic enforcement of the Establishment Clause would be both imprudent and impossible. This observation is at once uncontroversial and unilluminating. Simply enumerating the various ways in which the Federal Government has recognized the vital role religion plays in our society does nothing to help decide the question presented in this case.

Indeed, the Court's approach suggests a fundamental misapprehension of the proper uses of history in constitutional interpretation. Certainly, our decisions reflect the fact that an awareness of historical practice often can provide a useful guide in interpreting the abstract language of the Establishment Clause. But historical acceptance of a particular practice alone is never sufficient to justify a challenged governmental action, since, as the Court has rightly observed, "no one acquires a vested or protected right in violation of the Constitution by long use, even when that span of time covers our entire national existence and indeed predates it." *Walz*.

⊥719 Attention to the details of history should not blind us to the cardinal purposes of the Establishment Clause, nor limit our central inquiry in these cases—whether the challenged practices "threaten those consequences which the Framers deeply feared." *Abington School Dist.* v. *Schempp*. In recognition of this fact, the Court has, until today, consistently limited its historical inquiry to the particular practice under review.

In *McGowan*, for instance, the Court carefully canvassed the entire history of Sunday Closing laws from the Colonial period up to modern times. On the basis of this analysis, we concluded that while such laws were rooted in religious motivations, the current purpose was to serve the wholly secular goal of providing a uniform day of rest for all citizens. Our inquiry in *Walz* was similarly confined to the special history of the practice under review. There the Court found a pattern of "undeviating acceptance" over the entire course of the Nation's history of according property exemptions to religious organizations, a pattern which supported our finding that the practice did not violate the Religion Clauses. Finally, where direct inquiry into the Framer's intent reveals that the First Amendment was not understood to prohibit a particular practice, we have found such an understanding compelling. Thus, in *Marsh* v. *Chambers*, after marshalling the historical evidence which indicated that the First Congress had authorized the appointment of paid chaplains for its own proceedings only three days before it reached agreement on the final wording of the Bill of Rights, the Court concluded on the basis of this "unique history" that the modern-day practice of opening legislative sessions with prayer was constitutional.

Although invoking these decisions in support of its result, the Court wholly fails to discuss the history of the public celebration of Christmas or the use of publicly-displayed nativity scene. The Court, instead, simply asserts, without any historical analysis or support whatsoever, that the now familiar **⊥720** celebration of Christmas springs from an unbroken history of acknowledgement "by the people, by the Executive Branch, by the Congress, and the courts for two centuries. . . ." The Court's complete failure to offer any explanation of its assertion is perhaps understandable, however, because the historical record points in precisely the opposite direction. Two features of this history are worth noting. First, at the time of the adoption of the Constitution and the Bill of Rights, there was no settled pattern of celebrating Christmas, either as a purely religious holiday or as a public event. Second, the historical evidence, such as it is, offers no uniform pattern of widespread acceptance of the holiday and indeed suggests that the development of Christmas as a public holiday is a comparatively recent phenomenon.

The intent of the Framers with respect to the public display of nativity scenes is virtually impossible to discern primarily because the widespread celebration of Christmas did not emerge in its present form until well into the nineteenth century. Carrying a well-defined Puritan hostility to the celebration of Christ's birth with them to the New World, the founders of the Massachusetts Bay Colony pursued a vigilant policy of opposition to any public celebration of the holiday. **⊥721** To the Puritans, the celebration of Christmas represented a "Popish" practice lacking any foundation in Scripture. This opposition took legal form in 1659 when the Massachusetts Colony made the observance of Christmas day, "by abstinence from labor, feasting or any other way," an offense punishable by fine. Although the Colony eventually repealed this ban in 1681, the Puritan objection remained firm.

During the eighteenth century, sectarian division over the celebration of the holiday continued. As increasing numbers of members of the Anglican and the Dutch and German Reformed churches arrived, the practice of celebrating Christmas as a purely religious holiday grew. But denominational differences continued to dictate differences in attitude toward the holiday. American Anglicans, who carried with them the Church of England's acceptance of the holiday, Roman Catholics, and various German groups all made the celebration of Christmas a vital part of their religious life. By contrast, many nonconforming Protestant groups, including the Presbyterians, Congregationalists, Baptists and Methodists, continued to regard the holiday with suspicion and antagonism well into the nineteenth century. This pattern of sec**⊥722**tarian division concerning the holiday suggests that for the Framers of the Establishment Clause, who were acutely sensitive to such sectarian controversies, no single view of how government should approach the celebration of Christmas would be possible.

Many of the same religious sects that were devotedly opposed to the celebration of Christmas on purely religious grounds, were also some of the most vocal and dedicated foes of established religions in the period just prior to the Revolutionary War. The Puritans, and later the Presbyterians, Baptists and Methodists, generally associated the celebration of Christmas with the elaborate and, in their view, sacrilegious celebration of the holiday by the Church of England, and also with, for them, the more sinister theology of "Popery." In the eyes of these dissenting religious sects, therefore, the groups most closely associated with estab**⊥723**lished religion—the Churches of England and of Rome—were also most closely linked to the profane practice of publicly celebrating Christmas. For those who authored the Bill of Rights, it seems reasonable to suppose that the public celebration of Christmas would have been regarded as at least a sensitive matter, if not deeply controversial. As we have repeatedly observed, the Religion Clauses were intended to ensure a benign regime of competitive disorder among all denominations, so that each sect was free to vie against the others for the allegiance of its followers without state interference. The historical record, contrary to the Court's uninformed assumption, suggests that at the very least conflicting views toward the celebration of Christmas were an important element of that competition at the time of the adoption of the Constitution.

Furthermore, unlike the religious tax exemptions upheld in *Walz*, the public display of nativity scenes as part of governmental celebrations of Christmas does not come to us supported by an unbroken history of widespread acceptance. It was not until 1836 that a State first granted legal recognition to Christmas as a public holiday. This was followed in the period between 1845 and 1865, by twenty-eight jurisdictions which included Christmas day as a legal holiday. Congress did not follow the States' lead until 1870 when it established December 25th, along with the Fourth of July, New Year's Day, and Thanksgiving, as a legal holiday in the District of Columbia. This pattern of legal recognition tells us only that ⊥**724** public acceptance of the holiday was gradual and that the practice—in stark contrast to the record presented in either *Walz* or *Marsh*—did not take on the character of a widely recognized holiday until the middle of the nineteenth century.

The historical evidence with respect to public financing and support for governmental displays of nativity scenes is even more difficult to gauge. What is known suggests that German immigrants who settled in Pennsylvania early in the eighteenth century, presumably drawing upon European traditions, were probably the first to introduce nativity scenes to the American celebration of Christmas. It also appears likely that this practice expanded as more Roman Catholic immigrants settled during the nineteenth century. From these modest beginnings, the familiar crèche scene developed and gained widespread acceptance, much less official endorsement, until the twentieth century.

In sum, there is no evidence whatsoever that the Framers would have expressly approved a Federal celebration of the Christmas holiday including public displays of a nativity ⊥**725** scene; accordingly, the Court's repeated invocation of the decision in *Marsh*, is not only baffling, it is utterly irrelevant. Nor is there any suggestion that publicly financed and supported displays of Christmas crèches are supported by a record of widespread, undeviating acceptance that extends throughout our history. Therefore, our prior decisions which relied upon concrete, specific historical evidence to support a particular practice simply have no bearing on the question presented in this case. Contrary to today's careless decision, those prior cases have all recognized that the "illumination" provided by history must always be focused on the particular practice at issue in a given case. Without that guiding principle and the intellectual discipline it imposes, the Court is at sea, free to select random elements of America's varied history solely to suit the views of five Members of this Court.

IV

Under our constitutional scheme, the role of safeguarding our "religious heritage" and of promoting religious beliefs is reserved as the exclusive prerogative of our nation's churches, religious institutions and spiritual leaders. Because the Framers of the Establishment Clause understood that "religion is too personal, too sacred, too holy to permit its 'unhallowed perversion' by civil [authorities]," *Engel* v. *Vitale*, the clause demands that government play no role in this effort. The Court today brushes aside these concerns by insisting that Pawtucket has done nothing more than include a "traditional" symbol of Christmas in its celebration of this national holiday, thereby muting the religious content of the crèche. But the City's action should be recognized for what it is: a coercive, though perhaps small, step toward establishing the sectarian preferences of the majority at the expense of the minority, accomplished by placing public facilities and funds in support of the religious symbolism and theological tidings that the ⊥**726** crèche conveys. As *Justice FRANKFURTER*, writing in *McGowan* v. *Maryland*, observed, the Establishment Clause "withdr[aws] from the sphere of legitimate legislative concern and competence a specific, but comprehensive area of human conduct: man's belief or disbelief in the verity of some transcendental idea and man's expression in action of that belief or disbelief." That the Constitution sets this realm of thought and feeling apart from the pressures and antagonisms of government is one of its supreme achievements. Regrettably, the Court today tarnishes that achievement.

I dissent.

Justice BLACKMUN, with whom *Justice STEVENS* joins, dissenting.

As *Justice BRENNAN* points out, the logic of the Court's decision in *Lemon* v. *Kurtzman* compels an affirmance here. If that case and its guidelines mean anything, the presence of Pawtucket's crèche in a municipally sponsored display must be held to be a violation of the First Amendment.

Not only does the Court's resolution of this controversy make light of our precedents, but also, ironically, the majority does an injustice to the crèche and the message it manifests. While certain persons, including the Mayor of Pawtucket, undertook a crusade to "keep Christ in Christmas," the Court today has declared that presence virtually irrelevant. The majority urges that the display, "with or without a crèche," "recall[s] the religious nature of the Holiday," and "engenders a friendly community spirit of good will in keeping with the season." Before the District Court, an expert witness for the city made ⊥**727** a similar, though perhaps more candid, point, stating that Pawtucket's display invites people "to participate in the Christmas spirit, brotherhood, peace, and let loose with their money." The crèche has been relegated to the role of a neutral harbinger of the holiday season, useful for commercial purposes, but devoid of any inherent meaning and incapable of enhancing the religious tenor of a display of which it is an integral part. The city has its victory—but it is a Pyrrhic one indeed.

The import of the Court's decision is to encourage use of the crèche in a municipally sponsored display, a setting where Christians feel constrained in acknowledging its symbolic meaning and non-Christians feel alienated by its presence. Surely, this is a misuse of a sacred symbol. Because I cannot join the Court in denying either the force of our precedents or the sacred message that is at the core of the crèche, I dissent and join *Justice BRENNAN'S* opinion.

COUNTY OF ALLEGHENY v. AMERICAN CIVIL LIBERTIES UNION GREATER PITTSBURGH CHAPTER

492 U.S. 573

ON WRITS OF CERTIORARI TO THE UNITED STATES COURT OF APPEALS FOR THE THIRD CIRCUIT

Argued February 22, 1989 — Decided July 3, 1989

⊥**578** *Justice BLACKMUN* announced the judgment of the Court and delivered the opinion of the Court with respect to Parts III-A, IV, and V, an opinion with respect to Parts I and II, in which *Justice O'CONNOR* and *Justice STEVENS* join, an opinion with respect to Part III-B, in which *Justice STEVENS* joins, and an opinion with respect to Part VI.

This litigation concerns the constitutionality of two recurring holiday displays located on public property in downtown Pittsburgh. The first is a crèche placed on the Grand Staircase of the Allegheny County Courthouse. The second is a Chanukah menorah placed just outside the City-County Building, next to a Christmas tree and a sign saluting liberty. The Court of Appeals for the Third Circuit ruled that each display violates the Establishment Clause of the First Amendment because each has the impermissible effect of endorsing re⊥**579**ligion. We agree that the crèche display has that unconstitutional effect but reverse the Court of Appeals' judgment regarding the menorah display.

I

A

The County Courthouse is owned by Allegheny County and is its seat of government. It houses the offices of the County Commissioners, Controller, Treasurer, Sheriff, and Clerk of Court. Civil and criminal trials are held there. The "main," "most beautiful," and "most public" part of the courthouse is its Grand Staircase, set into one arch and surrounded by others, with arched windows serving as a backdrop.

Since 1981, the county has permitted the Holy Name Society, a Roman Catholic group, to display a crèche in the County Courthouse during the Christmas holiday season. Christmas, we note perhaps needlessly, is the holiday when Christians celebrate the birth of Jesus of Nazareth, whom they believe to be the Messiah. Western churches have celebrated Christmas Day on December 25 since the fourth century. As observed in this Nation, Christmas has a secular as well as a religious dimension.

⊥**580** The crèche in the County Courthouse, like other crèches, is a visual representation of the scene in the manger in Bethlehem shortly after the birth of Jesus, as described in the Gospels of Luke and Matthew. The crèche includes figures of the infant Jesus, Mary, Joseph, farm animals, shepherds, and wise men, all placed in or before a wooden representation of a manger, which has at its crest an angel bearing a banner that proclaims "Gloria in Excelsis Deo!" During the 1986-1987 holiday season, the crèche was on display on the Grand Staircase from November 26 to January 9. It had a wooden fence on three sides and bore a plaque stating: "This Display Donated by the Holy Name Society." Sometime during the week of December 2, the county placed red and white poinsettia plants around the fence. The county also placed a small evergreen tree, decorated with a red bow, behind each of the two endposts of the fence. These trees stood alongside the manger backdrop, and were slightly shorter than it was. The angel thus was at the apex of the crèche display. Altogether, the crèche, the fence, the poinsettias, and the trees occupied a substantial amount of space on the Grand Staircase. No figures of Santa Claus or other decora⊥**581**tions appeared on the Grand Staircase. Cf. *Lynch* v. *Donnelly*.

The county uses the crèche as the setting for its annual Christmas-carol program. During the 1986 season, the county invited high school choirs and other musical groups to perform during weekday lunch hours from December 3 through December 23. The county dedicated this program to world peace and to the families of prisoners-of-war and of persons missing-in-action in Southeast Asia.

Near the Grand Staircase is an area of the County Courthouse known as the "gallery forum" used for art and other cultural exhibits. The crèche, with its fence-and-floral frame, however, was distinct and not connected with any exhibit in the gallery forum. In addition, various departments and offices within the County Courthouse had their own Christmas decorations, but these also are not visible from the Grand Staircase.

B

The City-County Building is separate and a block removed from the County Courthouse and, as the name implies, is jointly owned by the city of Pittsburgh and

Allegheny County. The city's portion of the building houses the city's principal offices, including the Mayor's. The city is responsible for the building's Grant Street entrance which has three rounded arches supported by columns.

For a number of years, the city has had a large Christmas tree under the middle arch outside the Grant Street entrance. Following this practice, city employees on Novem⊥**582**ber 17, 1986, erected a 45-foot tree under the middle arch and decorated it with lights and ornaments. A few days later, the city placed at the foot of the tree a sign bearing the Mayor's name and entitled "Salute to Liberty." Beneath the title, the sign stated:

"During this holiday season, the City of Pittsburgh salutes liberty. Let these festive lights remind us that we are the keepers of the flame of liberty and our legacy of freedom."

At least since 1982, the city has expanded its Grant Street holiday display to include a symbolic representation of Chanukah, an 8-day Jewish holiday that begins on the 25th day of the Jewish lunar month of Kislev. The 25th of Kislev usually occurs in December, and thus Chanukah is the annual Jewish holiday that falls closest to Christmas Day each year. In 1986, Chanukah began at sundown on December 26.

According to Jewish tradition, on the 25th of Kislev in 164 B.C.E. (before the common era), the Maccabees rededicated the Temple of Jerusalem after recapturing it from the Greeks, or, more accurately, from the Greek-influenced Seleucid Empire, in the course of a political rebellion. ⊥**583** Chanukah is the holiday which celebrates that event. The early history of the celebration of Chanukah is unclear; it appears that the holiday's central ritual—the lighting of lamps—was well established long before a single explanation of that ritual took hold.

The Talmud explains the lamp-lighting ritual as a commemoration of an event that occurred during the rededication of the Temple. The Temple housed a seven-branch menorah, which was to be kept burning continuously. When the Maccabees rededicated the Temple, they had only enough oil to last for one day. But, according to the Talmud, the oil miraculously lasted for eight days (the length of time it took to obtain additional oil). To celebrate and publicly proclaim this miracle, the Talmud prescribes that it is a mitzvah (i.e., a religious deed or commandment), for Jews to place a lamp with eight lights just outside the entrance to their homes during the eight days of Chanukah. ⊥**584** Where practicality or safety from persecution so requires the lamp may be placed in a window or inside the home. The Talmud also ordains certain blessings to be recited each night of Chanukah before lighting the lamp. One such benediction has been translated into English as "We are blessing God who has sanctified us and commanded us with mitzvot and has told us to light the candles of Hanukkah."

Although Jewish law does not contain any rule regarding the shape or substance of a Chanukah lamp (or "hanukkiyyah"), it became customary to evoke the memory of the Temple menorah. The Temple menorah was of a tree-and-branch design; it had a central candlestick with six branches. In contrast, a Chanukah menorah of tree-and-branch design has eight branches—one for each day of the holiday—plus a ninth to hold the shamash (an extra candle used to light the other eight). Also in contrast to the Temple menorah, the Chanukah menorah is not a sanctified object; it need not be treated with special care.

⊥**585** Lighting the menorah is the primary tradition associated with Chanukah, but the holiday is marked by other traditions as well. One custom among some Jews is to give children Chanukah gelt, or money. Another is for the children to gamble their gelt using a dreidel, a top with four sides. Each of the four sides contains a Hebrew letter; together the four letters abbreviate a phrase that refers to the Chanukah miracle.

Chanukah, like Christmas, is a cultural event as well as a religious holiday. Indeed, the Chanukah story always has had a political or national as well as a religious dimension: it tells of national heroism in addition to divine intervention. Also, Chanukah, like Christmas, is a winter holiday; according to some historians, it was associated in ancient times with the winter solstice. Just as some Americans celebrate Christmas without regard to its religious significance, some nonreligious American Jews celebrate Chanukah as an expression of ethnic identity, and "as a cultural or national event, rather than as a specifically religious event."

⊥**586** The cultural significance of Chanukah varies with the setting in which the holiday is celebrated. In contemporary Israel, the nationalist and military aspects of the Chanukah story receive special emphasis. In this country, the tradition of giving Chanukah gelt has taken on greater importance because of the temporal proximity of Chanukah to Christmas. Indeed, some have suggested that the proximity of Christmas accounts for the social prominence of Chanukah in this country. Whatever the reason, Chanukah is observed by American Jews to an extent greater than its religious im⊥**587**portance would indicate: in the hierarchy of Jewish holidays, Chanukah ranks fairly low in religious significance. This socially heightened status of Chanukah reflects its cultural or secular dimension.

On December 22 of the 1986 holiday season, the city placed at the Grant Street entrance to the City-County Building an 18-foot Chanukah menorah of an abstract tree-and-branch design. The menorah was placed next to the city's 45-foot Christmas tree, against one of the columns that supports the arch into which the tree was set. The menorah is owned by Chabad, a Jewish group, but is stored, erected, and removed each year by the city. The tree, the sign, and the menorah were all removed on January 13.

II

This litigation began on December 10, 1986, when respondents, the Greater Pittsburgh Chapter of the American Civil Liberties Union and seven local residents, filed suit against the county and the city, seeking permanently to enjoin the county from displaying the crèche in the County Courthouse and the city from displaying the menorah in front of the City- ⊥588 County Building. Respondents claim that the displays of the crèche and the menorah each violate the Establishment Clause of the First Amendment, made applicable to state governments by the Fourteenth Amendment. Chabad was permitted to intervene to defend the display of its menorah.

On May 8, 1987, the District court denied respondent's request for a permanent injunction. Relying on *Lynch* v. *Donnelly*, the court stated that "the crèche was but part of the holiday decoration of the stairwell and a foreground for the highschool choirs which entertained each day at noon." Regarding the menorah, the court concluded that "it was but an insignificant part of another holiday display." The court also found that "the displays had a secular purpose" and "did not create an excessive entanglement of government with religion."

Respondents appealed, and a divided panel of the Court of Appeals reversed. Distinguishing *Lynch* v. *Donnelly*, the panel majority determined that the crèche and the menorah must be understood as endorsing Christianity and Judaism. The court observed: "Each display was located at or in a public building devoted ⊥589to core functions of government." The court also stated: "Further, while the menorah was placed near a Christmas tree, neither the crèche nor the menorah can reasonably be deemed to have been subsumed by a larger display of non-religious items." Because the impermissible effect of endorsing religion was sufficient basis for holding each display to be in violation of the Establishment Clause under *Lemon* v. *Kurtzman*, the Court of Appeals did not consider whether either one had an impermissible purpose or resulted in an unconstitutional entanglement between government and religion.

The dissenting judge stated that the crèche, "accompanied by poinsettia plants and evergreens, does not violate the Establishment Clause simply because plastic Santa Clauses or reindeer are absent." As to the menorah, he asserted: "Including a reference to Chanukah did no more than broaden the commemoration of the holiday season and stress the notion of sharing its joy."

Rehearing en banc was denied by a 6-5 vote. The county, the city, and Chabad each filed a petition for certiorari. We granted all three petitions.

III

A

This Nation is heir to a history and tradition of religious diversity that dates from the settlement of the North American continent. Sectarian differences among various Christian denominations were central to the origins of our Republic. Since then, adherents of religions too numerous to name have made the United States their home, as have those whose beliefs expressly exclude religion.

Precisely because of the religious diversity that is our national heritage, the Founders added to the Constitution a Bill of Rights, the very first words of which declare: "Congress shall make no law respecting an establishment of religion, ⊥590 or prohibiting the free exercise thereof. . . ." Perhaps in the early days of the Republic these words were understood to protect only the diversity within Christianity, but today they are recognized as guaranteeing religious liberty and equality to "the infidel, the atheist, or the adherent of a non-Christian faith such as Islam or Judaism." *Wallace* v. *Jaffree*. It is settled law that no government official in this Nation may violate these fundamental constitutional rights regarding matters of conscience.

In the course of adjudicating specific cases, this Court has come to understand the Establishment Clause to mean that government may not promote or affiliate itself with any religious doctrine or organization, may not discriminate among persons on the basis of their religious beliefs and practices, ⊥591 may not delegate a governmental power to a religious institution, and may not involve itself too deeply in such an institution's affairs. Although "the myriad, subtle ways in which Establishment Clause values can be eroded," *Lynch* v. *Donnelly*, are not susceptible to a single verbal formulation, this Court has attempted to encapsulate the essential precepts of the Establishment Clause. Thus, in *Everson* v. *Board of Education*, the court gave this often-repeated summary:

"The 'establishment of religion' clause of the First Amendment means at least this: Neither a state nor the Federal Government can set up a church. Neither can pass laws which aid one religion, aid all religions, or prefer one religion over another. Neither can force nor influence a person to go to or remain away from church against his will or force him to profess a belief or disbelief in any religion. No person can be punished for entertaining or professing religious beliefs or disbeliefs, for church attendance or non-attendance. No tax in any amount, large or small, can be levied to support any religious activities or institutions, whatever they may be called, or whatever form they may adopt to teach or practice religion. Neither a state nor the Federal Government can, openly or secretly, participate in the affairs of any religious organizations or groups and *vice versa.*"

⊥592 In *Lemon* v. *Kurtzman*, the Court sought to refine these principles by focusing on three "tests" for determining whether a government practice violates the Establishment Clause. Under the *Lemon* analysis, a statute or practice which touches upon religion, if it is to be permissible under the Establishment Clause, must have a secular purpose; it must neither advance nor inhibit religion in its principal or primary effect; and it must not foster an excessive entanglement with religion. This trilogy of tests has been applied regularly in the Court's later Establishment Clause cases.

Our subsequent decisions further have refined the definition of governmental action that unconstitutionally advances religion. In recent years, we have paid particularly close attention to whether the challenged governmental practice either has the purpose or effect of "endorsing" religion, a concern that has long had a place in our Establishment Clause jurisprudence. Thus, in *Wallace* v. *Jaffree*, the Court held unconstitutional Alabama's moment-of-silence statute because it was "enacted . . . for the sole purpose of expressing the State's endorsement of prayer activities." The Court similarly invalidated Louisiana's "Creationism Act" because it "endorses religion" in its purpose. *Edwards* v. *Aguillard*. And the educational ⊥**593** program in *School District of Grand Rapids* v. *Ball* was held to violate the Establishment Clause because of its "endorsement" effect. See also *Texas Monthly, Inc.* v. *Bullock* (plurality opinion) (tax exemption limited to religious periodicals "effectively endorses religious belief").

Of course, the word "endorsement" is not self-defining. Rather, it derives its meaning from other words that this Court has found useful over the years in interpreting the Establishment Clause. Thus, it has been noted that the prohibition against governmental endorsement of religion "preclude[s] government from conveying or attempting to convey a message that religion or a particular religious belief is *favored* or *preferred*." *Wallace* v. *Jaffree* (O'Connor, J., concurring in judgment) (emphasis added). Accord, *Texas Monthly, Inc.* v. *Bullock* (separate opinion concurring in the judgment) (reaffirming that "government may not favor religious belief over disbelief" or adopt a "preference for the dissemination of religious ideas"); *Edwards* v. *Aguillard* ("preference" for particular religious beliefs constitutes an endorsement of religion); *Abington School District* v. *Schempp* (Goldberg, J., concurring) ("The fullest realization of true religious liberty requires that government . . . effect no favoritism among sects or between religion and nonreligion"). Moreover, the term "endorsement" is closely linked to the term "promotion," *Lynch* v. *Donnelly* (O'Connor, J., concurring), and this Court long since has held that government "may not . . . promote one religion or religious theory against another or even against the militant opposite." *Epperson* v. *Arkansas*. See also *Wallace* v. *Jaffree* (using the concepts of endorsement, promotion, and favoritism interchangeably).

Whether the key word is "endorsement," "favoritism," or "promotion," the essential principle remains the same. The ⊥**594** Establishment Clause, at the very least, prohibits government from appearing to take a position on questions of religious belief or from "making adherence to a religion relevant in any way to a person's standing in the political community." *Lynch* v. *Donnelly* (O'Connor, J., concurring).

B

We have had occasion in the past to apply Establishment Clause principles to the government's display of objects with religious significance. In *Stone* v. *Graham*, we held that the display of a copy of the Ten Commandments on the walls of public classrooms violates the Establishment Clause. Closer to the facts of this litigation is *Lynch* v. *Donnelly*, in which we considered whether the city of Pawtucket, R.I., had violated the Establishment Clause by including a crèche in its annual Christmas display, located in a private park within the downtown shopping district. By a 5-4 decision in that difficult case, the Court upheld inclusion of the crèche in the Pawtucket display, holding, *inter alia*, that the inclusion of the crèche did not have the impermissible effect of advancing or promoting religion.

The rationale of the majority opinion in *Lynch* is none too clear: the opinion contains two strands, neither of which provides guidance for decision in subsequent cases. First, the opinion states that the inclusion of the crèche in the display was "no more an advancement or endorsement of religion" than other "endorsements" this Court has approved in the past—but the opinion offers no discernible measure for distinguishing between permissible and impermissible endorsements. Second, the opinion observes that any benefit the government's display of the crèche gave to religion was no more than "indirect, remote, and incidental"—without saying how or why.

⊥**595** Although *Justice O'CONNOR* joined the majority opinion in *Lynch*, she wrote a concurrence that differs in significant respects from the majority opinion. The main difference is that the concurrence provides a sound analytical framework for evaluating governmental use of religious symbols.

First and foremost, the concurrence squarely rejects any notion that this Court will tolerate some government endorsement of religion. Rather, the concurrence recognizes any endorsement of religion as "invalid," because it "sends a message to nonadherents that they are outsiders, not full members of the political community, and an accompanying message to adherents that they are insiders, favored members of the political community."

Second, the concurrence articulates a method for determining whether the government's use of an object with religious meaning has the effect of endorsing religion. The effect of the display depends upon the message that the government's practice communicates: the question is "what viewers may fairly understand to be the purpose of the display." That inquiry, of necessity, turns upon the context in which the contested object appears: "a typical museum setting, though not neutralizing the religious content of a religious painting, negates any message of endorsement of that content." The concurrence thus emphasizes that the constitutionality of the crèche in that case depended upon its "particular physical setting," and further observes: "Every government practice must be judged in its unique circumstances to determine whether it [endorses] religion."

⊥**596** The concurrence applied this mode of analysis to the Pawtucket crèche, seen in the context of that city's holiday celebration as a whole. In addition to the crèche, the city's display contained: a Santa Claus House with a live Santa distributing candy; reindeer pulling Santa's sleigh; a live 40-foot Christmas tree strung with lights; statues of carolers in old-fashioned dress; candy-striped poles; a "talking" wishing well; a large banner proclaiming "SEASONS GREETINGS"; a miniature "village" with several houses and a church; and various "cut-out" figures, including those of a clown, a dancing elephant, a robot, and a teddy bear. The concurrence concluded that both because the crèche is "a traditional symbol" of Christmas, a holiday with strong secular elements, and because the crèche was "displayed along with purely secular symbols," the crèche's setting "changes what viewers may fairly understand to be the purpose of the display" and "negates any message of endorsement" of "the Christian beliefs represented by the crèche."

The four *Lynch* dissenters agreed with the concurrence that the controlling question was "whether Pawtucket ha[d] run afoul of the Establishment Clause by endorsing religion through its display of the crèche." (Brennan, J., dissenting). The dissenters also agreed with the ⊥**597** general proposition that the context in which the government uses a religious symbol is relevant for determining the answer to that question. They simply reached a different answer: the dissenters concluded that the other elements of the Pawtucket display did not negate the endorsement of Christian faith caused by the presence of the crèche. They viewed the inclusion of the crèche in the city's overall display as placing "the government's imprimatur of approval on the particular religious beliefs exemplified by the crèche." Thus, they stated: "The effect on minority religious groups, as well as on those who may reject all religion, is to convey the message that their views are not similarly worthy of public recognition nor entitled to public support."

Thus, despite divergence at the bottom line, the five Justices in concurrence and dissent in *Lynch* agreed upon the relevant constitutional principles: the government's use of religious symbolism is unconstitutional if it has the effect of endorsing religious beliefs, and the effect of the government's use of religious symbolism depends upon its context. These general principles are sound, and have been adopted by the Court in subsequent cases. Since *Lynch*, the Court has made clear that, when evaluating the effect of government conduct under the Establishment Clause, we must ascertain whether "the challenged governmental action is sufficiently likely to be perceived by adherents of the controlling denominations as an endorsement, and by the nonadherents as a disapproval, of their individual religious choices." *Grand Rapids*. Accordingly, our present task is to determine whether the display of the crèche and the menorah, in their respective "particular physical settings," has the effect of endorsing or disapproving religious beliefs.

⊥**598** IV

We turn first to the county's crèche display. There is no doubt, of course, that the crèche itself is capable of communicating a religious message. Indeed, the crèche in this lawsuit uses words, as well as the picture of the nativity scene, to make its religious meaning unmistakably clear. "Glory to God in the Highest!" says the angel in the crèche—Glory to God because of the birth of Jesus. This praise to God in Christian terms is indisputably religious—indeed sectarian—just as it is when said in the Gospel or in a church service.

Under the Court's holding in *Lynch*, the effect of a crèche display turns on its setting. Here, unlike in *Lynch*, nothing in the context of the display detracts from the crèche's religious message. The *Lynch* display comprised a series of figures and objects, each group of which had its own focal point. Santa's house and his reindeer were objects of attention separate from the crèche, and had their specific visual story to tell. Similarly, whatever a "talking" wishing well may be, it obviously was a center of attention separate from the crèche. Here, in contrast, the crèche stands alone: it is the single element of the display on the Grand Staircase.

⊥**599** The floral decoration surrounding the crèche cannot be viewed as somehow equivalent to the secular symbols in the overall *Lynch* display. The floral frame, like all good frames, serves only to draw one's attention to the message inside the frame. The floral decoration surrounding the crèche contributes to, rather than detracts from, the endorsement of religion conveyed by the crèche. It is as if the county had allowed the Holy Name Society to display a cross on the Grand Staircase at Easter, and the county had surrounded the cross with Easter lilies. The county could not say that surrounding the cross with traditional flowers of the season would negate the endorsement of Christianity conveyed by the cross on the Grand Staircase. Its contention that the traditional Christmas greens negate the endorsement effect of the crèche fares no better.

Nor does the fact that the crèche was the setting for the county's annual Christmas carol-program diminish its religious meaning. First, the carol program in 1986 lasted only from December 3 to December 23 and occupied at most two hours a day. The effect of the crèche on those who viewed it when the choirs were not singing—the vast majority of the time—cannot be negated by the presence of the choir program. Second, because some of the carols performed at the site of the crèche were religious in nature, those carols were more likely to augment the religious quality of the scene than to secularize it.

Furthermore, the crèche sits on the Grand Staircase, the "main" and "most beautiful part" of the building that is the seat of county government. No viewer could reasonably think that it occupies this location without the ⊥**600** support and approval of the government. Thus, by permitting the "display of the crèche in this particular physical setting," *Lynch* (O'Connor, J., concurring), the county sends an unmistakable message that it supports and promotes the Christian praise to God that is the crèche's religious message.

The fact that the crèche bears a sign disclosing its ownership by a Roman Catholic organization does not alter this conclusion. On the contrary, the sign simply demonstrates that the government is endorsing the religious message of that organization, rather than communicating a message of its own. But the Establishment Clause does not limit only the religious content of the government's own communications. It also prohibits the government's support and promotion of religious communications by religious organizations. See, *e.g.*, *Texas Monthly* (government support of the distribution of religious messages by religious organizations violates the Establishment Clause). Indeed, the very concept of "endorsement" con⊥**601**veys the sense of promoting someone else's message. Thus, by prohibiting government endorsement of religion, the Establishment Clause prohibits precisely what occurred here: the government's lending its support to the communication of a religious organization's religious message.

Finally, the county argues that it is sufficient to validate the display of the crèche on the Grand Staircase that the display celebrates Christmas, and Christmas is a national holiday. This argument obviously proves too much. It would allow the celebration of the Eucharist inside a courthouse on Christmas Eve. While the county may have doubts about the constitutional status of celebrating the Eucharist inside the courthouse under the government's auspices, this Court does not. The government may acknowledge Christmas as a cultural phenomenon, but under the First Amendment it may not observe it as a Christian holy day by suggesting that people praise God for the birth of Jesus.

In sum, *Lynch* teaches that government may celebrate Christmas in some manner and form, but not in a way that endorses Christian doctrine. Here, Allegheny County has transgressed this line. It has chosen to celebrate Christmas in a way that has the effect of endorsing a patently Christian message: Glory to God for the birth of Jesus Christ. Under *Lynch*, and the rest of our cases, nothing more is required to ⊥**602** demonstrate a violation of the Establishment Clause. The display of the crèche in this context, therefore, must be permanently enjoined.

V

Justice KENNEDY and the three Justices who join him would find the display of the crèche consistent with the Establishment Clause. He argues that this conclusion necessarily follows from the Court's decision in *Marsh* v. *Chambers*, which sustained the constitutionality of legislative prayer. He also asserts that the crèche, even in this setting, poses "no realistic risk" of "represent[ing] an effort to proselytize," having repudiated the Court's endorsement inquiry in favor of a "proselytization" approach. The court's analysis of the crèche, he contends, "reflects an unjustified hostility toward religion."

Justice KENNEDY's reasons for permitting the crèche on the Grand Staircase and his condemnation of the Court's reasons for deciding otherwise are so far-reaching in their implications that they require a response in some depth.

A

In *Marsh*, the Court relied specifically on the fact that Congress authorized legislative prayer at the same time that it produced the Bill of Rights. *Justice KENNEDY*, however, argues that *Marsh* legitimates all "practices with no greater potential for an establishment of religion" than those "accepted traditions dating back to the Founding." Otherwise, the Justice asserts, such practices as our national motto ("In God We Trust") and our Pledge of Allegiance (with the phrase "under God," added in 1954, Pub. L. 396, 68 Stat. 249) are in danger of invalidity.

Our previous opinions have considered in dicta the motto and the pledge, characterizing them as consistent with the proposition that government may not communicate an en⊥**603**dorsement of religious belief *Lynch* (O'Connor, J., concurring); (Brennan, J., dissenting). We need not return to the subject of "ceremonial deism," because there is an obvious distinction between crèche displays and references to God in the motto and the pledge. However history may affect the constitutionality of nonsectarian references to religion by the government, history cannot legitimate practices that demonstrate the government's allegiance to a particular sect or creed.

Indeed, in *Marsh* itself, the Court recognized that not even the "unique history" of legislative prayer, can justify contemporary legislative prayers that have the effect of affiliating the government with any one specific faith or belief. The legislative prayers involved in *Marsh* did not violate this principle because the particular chaplain had "removed all references to Christ." Thus, *Marsh* plainly does not stand for the sweeping proposition *Justice KENNEDY* apparently would ascribe to it, namely, that all accepted practices 200 years old and their equivalents are constitutional today. Nor can *Marsh*, given its facts and its reasoning, compel the conclusion that the display of the crèche involved in this lawsuit is constitutional. Although *Justice KENNEDY* says that he "cannot comprehend" how the crèche display could be invalid after *Marsh*, surely he is able to distinguish between a specifically Christian symbol, like a crèche, and more general religious references, like the legislative prayers in *Marsh*.

⊥**604** *Justice KENNEDY*'s reading of *Marsh* would gut the core of the Establishment Clause, as this Court understands it. The history of this Nation, it is perhaps sad to say, contains numerous examples of official acts that endorsed Christianity specifically. See M. Borden, Jews, Turks, and Infidels (1984). Some of these examples date back to the Founding of the Republic, but this heritage of official discrimination ⊥605 against non-Christians has no place in the jurisprudence of the Establishment Clause. Whatever else the Establishment Clause may mean (and we have held it to mean no official preference even for religion over nonreligion, see, *e.g.*, *Texas Monthly*), it certainly means at the very least that government may not demonstrate a preference for one particular sect or creed (including a preference for Christianity over other religions). "The clearest command of the Establishment Clause is that one religious denomination cannot be officially preferred over another." *Larson* v. *Valente*. There have been breaches of this command throughout this Nation's history, but they cannot diminish in any way the force of the command.

B

Although *Justice KENNEDY's* misreading of *Marsh* is predicated on a failure to recognize the bedrock Establishment Clause principle that, regardless of history, government may not demonstrate a preference for a particular faith, even he is forced to acknowledge that some instances of such favoritism are constitutionally intolerable. He concedes also that the term "endorsement" long has been another way of defining a forbidden "preference" for ⊥606 a particular sect, but he would repudiate the Court's endorsement inquiry as a "jurisprudence of minutiae," because it examines the particular contexts in which the government employs religious symbols.

This label, of course, could be tagged on many areas of constitutional adjudication. For example, in determining whether the Fourth Amendment requires a warrant and probable cause before the government may conduct a particular search or seizure, "we have not hesitated to balance the governmental and privacy interests to asses the practicality of the warrant and probable cause requirements *in the particular context*," *Skinner* v. *Railway Labor Executives' Assn.* (emphasis added), an inquiry that "'depends on all the circumstances surrounding the search or seizure and the nature of the search or seizure itself,'" quoting *United States* v. *Montoya de Hernandez;* see also *National Treasury Employees Union* v. *Von Raab* (repeating the principle that the applicability of the warrant requirement turns on "the particular context" of the search at issue). It is perhaps unfortunate, but nonetheless inevitable, that the broad language of many clauses within the Bill of Rights must be translated into adjudicatory principles that realize their full meaning only after their application to a series of concrete cases.

Indeed, not even under *Justice KENNEDY's* preferred approach can the Establishment Clause be transformed into an exception to this rule. The Justice would substitute the term "proselytization" for "endorsement," but his "proselytization" test suffers from the same "defect," if one must call it that, of requiring close factual analysis. *Justice KENNEDY* "ha[s] no doubt, for example, that the [Establishment] Clause would forbid a city to permit the permanent erection of a large Latin cross on the roof of city hall . . . because such an obtrusive year-round religious dis⊥607play would place the government's weight behind an obvious effort to proselytize on behalf of a particular religion." He also suggests that a city would demonstrate an unconstitutional preference for Christianity if it displayed a Christian symbol during every major Christian holiday but did not display the religious symbols of other faiths during other religious holidays. But, for *Justice KENNEDY*, would it be enough of a preference for Christianity if that city each year displayed a crèche for 40 days during the Christmas season and a cross for 40 days during Lent (and never the symbols of other religions)? If so, then what if there were no cross but the 40-day crèche display contained a sign exhorting the city's citizens "to offer up their devotions to God their Creator, and his Son Jesus Christ, the Redeemer of the world"?

The point of these rhetorical questions is obvious. In order to define precisely what government could and could not do under *Justice KENNEDY's* "proselytization" test, the Court would have to decide a series of cases with particular fact patterns that fall along the spectrum of government references to religion (from the permanent display of a cross atop city hall to a passing reference to divine Providence in an official address). If one wished to be "uncharitable" to *Justice KENNEDY*, one could say that his methodology requires counting the number of days during which the government displays Christian symbols and subtracting from this the number of days during which non-Christian symbols are displayed, divided by the number of different non-Christian religions represented in these displays, and then somehow factoring into this equation the prominence of the display's location and the degree to which each symbol possesses an inherently proselytizing quality. *Justice KENNEDY*, of course, could defend his position by pointing to the inevitably fact-specific nature of the question whether a particular governmental practice signals the government's ⊥608 unconstitutional preference for a specific religious faith. But because *Justice KENNEDY's* formulation of this essential Establishment Clause inquiry is no less fact-intensive than the "endorsement" formulation adopted by the Court, *Justice KENNEDY* should be wary of accusing the Court's formulation as "using little more than intuition and a tape measure," lest he finds his own formulation convicted on an identical charge.

Indeed, perhaps the only real distinction between *Justice KENNEDY's* "proselytization" test and the Court's "endorsement" inquiry is a burden of "unmistakable" clarity that *Justice KENNEDY* apparently would require of government favoritism for specific sects in order to hold the favoritism in violation of the Establishment Clause. The question whether a particular practice "would place the government's weight behind an obvious effort to proselytize for a particular religion," is much the same as whether the practice demonstrates the government's support, promotion, or "endorsement" of the particular creed of a particular sect—except to the extent that it requires an "obvious" allegiance between the government and the sect.

Our cases, however, impose no such burden on demonstrating that the government has favored a particular sect or creed. On the contrary, we have expressly required "strict ⊥**609** scrutiny" of practices suggesting "a denominational preference," *Larson* v. *Valente*,. in keeping with "'the unwavering vigilance that the Constitution requires'" against any violation of the Establishment Clause. *Bowen* v. *Kendrick* (O'Connor, J., concurring); see also *Lynch* (O'Connor, J., concurring) ("the myriad, the subtle ways in which Establishment Clause values can be eroded" necessitates "careful judicial scrutiny" of "[g]overnment practices that purport to celebrate or acknowledge events with religious significance"). Thus, when all is said and done, *Justice KENNEDY's* effort to abandon the "endorsement" inquiry in favor of his "proselytization" test seems nothing more than an attempt to lower considerably the level of scrutiny in Establishment Clause cases. We choose, however, to adhere to the vigilance the Court has managed to maintain thus far, and to the endorsement inquiry that reflects our vigilance.

⊥**610** C

Although *Justice KENNEDY* repeatedly accuses the Court of harboring a "latent hostility" or "callous indifference" toward religion, nothing could be further from the truth, and the accusations could be said to be as offensive as they are absurd. *Justice KENNEDY* apparently has misperceived a respect for religious pluralism, a respect commanded by the Constitution, as hostility or indifference to religion. No misperception could be more antithetical to the values embodied in the Establishment Clause.

Justice KENNEDY's accusations are shot from a weapon triggered by the following proposition: if government may celebrate the secular aspects of Christmas, then it must be allowed to celebrate the religious aspects as well because, otherwise, the government would be discriminating against citizens who celebrate Christmas as a religious, and not just a secular, holiday. This proposition, however, is flawed at its foundation. The government does not discriminate against any citizen on the basis of the citizen's religious faith if the government is secular in its functions and operations. On the contrary, the Constitution mandates that the government remain secular, rather than affiliating itself with religious beliefs or institutions, precisely in order to avoid discriminating among citizens on the basis of their religious faiths.

A secular state, it must be remembered, is not the same as an atheistic or antireligious state. A secular state establishes neither atheism nor religion as its official creed. *Justice KENNEDY* thus has it exactly backwards when he says that enforcing the Constitution's requirement that govern⊥**611**ment remain secular is a prescription of orthodoxy. It follows directly from the Constitution's proscription against government affiliation with religious beliefs or institutions that there is no orthodoxy on religious matters in the secular state. Although *Justice KENNEDY* accuses the Court of an "Orwellian rewriting of history," perhaps it is *Justice KENNEDY* himself who has slipped into a form of Orwellian newspeak when he equates the constitutional command of secular government with a prescribed orthodoxy.

To be sure, in a pluralistic society there may be some would-be theocrats, who wish that their religion were an established creed, and some of them perhaps may be even audacious enough to claim that the lack of established religion discriminates against their preferences. But this claim gets no relief, for it contradicts the fundamental premise of the Establishment Clause itself. The antidiscrimination principle inherent in the Establishment Clause necessarily means that would-be discriminators on the basis of religion cannot prevail.

For this reason, the claim that prohibiting government from celebrating Christmas as a religious holiday discriminates against Christians in favor of nonadherents must fail. Celebrating Christmas as a religious, as opposed to a secular, holiday, necessarily entails professing, proclaiming, or believing that Jesus of Nazareth, born in a manger in Bethlehem, is the Christ, the Messiah. If the government celebrates Christmas as a religious holiday (for example by issuing an official proclamation saying: "We rejoice in the glory of Christ's birth!"), it means that the government really is declaring Jesus to be the Messiah, a specifically Christian belief. In contrast, confining the government's own celebration of Christmas to the holiday's secular aspects does not favor the religious beliefs of non-Christians over those of Christians. Rather, it simply permits the government to acknowledge the holiday without expressing an allegiance to ⊥**612** Christian beliefs, an allegiance that would truly favor Christians over non-Christians. To be sure, some Christians may wish to see the government proclaim its allegiance to Christianity in a religious celebration of Christmas, but the Constitution does not permit the gratification of that desire, which would contradict the "'logic of secular liberty"' it is the purpose of the Establishment Clause to protect. See *Larson* v. *Valente*, quoting B. Bailyn, The Ideological Origins of the American Revolution 265 (1967).

Of course, not all religious celebrations of Christmas located on government property violate the Establishment Clause. It obviously is not unconstitutional, for example, for a group of parishioners from a local church to go caroling through a city park on any Sunday in Advent or for a Christian club at a public university to sing carols during their Christmas meeting. The reason is that activities of this nature do not demonstrate the government's allegiance to, or endorsement of, the Christian faith.

Equally obvious, however, is the proposition that not all proclamations of Christian faith located on government property are permitted by the Establishment Clause just because they occur during the Christmas holiday season, as the example of a Mass in the courthouse surely illustrates. And once the judgment has been made that a particular proclamation of Christian belief, when disseminated from a particular location on government property, has the effect of demonstrating the government's endorsement of Christian faith, then it necessarily follows that the practice must be enjoined to protect the constitutional rights of those citizens who follow some creed other than Christianity. It is thus incontrovertible that the Court's decision today, premised on the determination that the crèche display on the Grand Staircase demon⊥**613**strates the county's endorsement of Christianity, does not represent a hostility or indifference to religion but, instead, the respect for religious diversity that the Constitution requires.

VI

The display of the Chanukah menorah in front of the City-County Building may well present a closer constitutional question. The menorah, one must recognize, is a religious symbol: it serves to commemorate the miracle of the oil as described in the Talmud. But the menorah's message is not exclusively religious. The menorah is the primary visual ⊥**614** symbol for a holiday that, like Christmas, has both religious and secular dimensions.

Moreover, the menorah here stands next to a Christmas tree and a sign saluting liberty. While no challenge has been made here to the display of the tree and the sign, their presence is obviously relevant in determining the effect of the menorah's display. The necessary result of placing a menorah next to a Christmas tree is to create an "overall holiday setting" that represents both Christmas and Chanukah—two holidays, not one.

The mere fact that Pittsburgh displays symbols of both Christmas and Chanukah does not end the constitutional inquiry. If the city celebrates both Christmas and Chanukah as religious holidays, then it violates the Establishment Clause. ⊥**615** The simultaneous endorsement of Judaism and Christianity is no less constitutionally infirm than the endorsement of Christianity alone.

Conversely, if the city celebrates both Christmas and Chanukah as secular holidays, then its conduct is beyond the reach of the Establishment Clause. Because government may celebrate Christmas as a secular holiday, it follows that government may also acknowledge Chanukah as a secular holiday. Simply put, it would be a form of discrimination against Jews to allow Pittsburgh to celebrate Christmas as a cultural tradition while simultaneously disallowing the city's acknowledgement of Chanukah as a contemporaneous cultural tradition.

⊥**616** Accordingly, the relevant question for Establishment Clause purposes is whether the combined display of the tree, the sign, and the menorah has the effect of endorsing both Christian and Jewish faiths, or rather simply recognizes that both Christmas and Chanukah are part of the same winter-holiday season, which has attained a secular status in our society. Of the two interpretations of this particular display, the latter seems far more plausible and is also in line with *Lynch*.

The Christmas tree, unlike the menorah, is not itself a religious symbol. Although Christmas trees once carried religious connotations, today they typify the secular celebration of Christmas. See *ACLU of Illinois* v. *City of St. Charles*, L. Tribe, American Constitutional Law 1295 (2d ed. 1988) (Tribe). Numerous Americans place ⊥**617** Christmas trees in their homes without subscribing to Christian religious beliefs, and when the city's tree stands alone in front of the City-County Building, it is not considered an endorsement of Christian faith. Indeed, a 40-foot Christmas tree was one of the objects that validated the crèche in *Lynch*. The widely accepted view of the Christmas tree as the preeminent secular symbol of the Christmas holiday season serves to emphasize the secular component of the message communicated by other elements of an accompanying holiday display, including the Chanukah menorah.

The tree, moreover, is clearly the predominant element in the city's display. The 45-foot tree occupies the central position beneath the middle archway in front of the Grant Street entrance to the City-County Building; the 18-foot menorah is positioned to one side. Given this configuration, it is much more sensible to interpret the meaning of the menorah in light of the tree, rather than vice versa. In the shadow of the tree, the menorah is readily understood as simply a recognition that Christmas is not the only traditional way of observing the winter-holiday season. In these circumstances, then, the combination of the tree and the menorah communicates, not a simultaneous endorsement of both Christian ⊥**618** and Jewish faith, but instead, a secular celebration of Christmas coupled with an acknowledgment of Chanukah as a contemporaneous alternative tradition.

Although the city has used a symbol with religious meaning as its representation of Chanukah, this is not a case in which the city has reasonable alternatives that are less religious in nature. It is difficult to imagine a predominantly secular symbol of Chanukah that the city could place next to its Christmas tree. An 18-foot dreidel would look out of place, and might be interpreted by some as mocking the celebration of Chanukah. The absence of a more secular alternative symbol is itself part of the context in which the city's actions must be judged in determining the likely effect of its use of the menorah. Where the government's secular message can be conveyed by two symbols, only one of which carries religious meaning, an observer reasonably might infer from the fact that the government has chosen to use the religious symbol that the government means to promote religious faith. See *Abington School District* v. *Schempp* (Brennan, J., concurring) (Establishment Clause forbids use of religious means to serve secular ends when secular means suffice); see also Tribe, at 1285. But where, as here, no such choice has been made, this inference of endorsement is not present.

⊥**619** The mayor's sign further diminishes the possibility that the tree and the menorah will be interpreted as a dual endorsement of Christianity and Judaism. The sign states that during the holiday season the city salutes liberty. Moreover, the sign draws upon the theme of light, common to both Chanukah and Christmas as winter festivals, and links that theme with the Nation's legacy of freedom, which allows an American to celebrate the holiday season in whatever way he wishes, religiously or otherwise. While no sign can disclaim an overwhelming message of endorsement, see *Stone* v. *Graham*, an "explanatory plaque" may confirm that in particular contexts the government's association with a religious symbol does not represent the government's sponsorship of religious beliefs. Here, the Mayor's sign serves to confirm what the context already reveals: that the display of the menorah is not an endorsement of religious faith but simply a recognition of cultural diversity.

⊥**620** Given all these considerations, it is not "sufficiently likely" that the residents of Pittsburgh will perceive the combined display of the tree, the sign, and the menorah as an "endorsement" or "disapproval . . . of their individual religious choices." *Grand Rapids*. While an adjudication of the display's effect must take into account the perspective of one who is neither Christian nor Jewish, as well as those who adhere to either of these religions, the constitutionality of its effect must also be judged according to the standard of a "reasonable observer." See *Witters* v. *Washington Dept. of Services for the Blind* (O'Connor, J., concurring in part and concurring in judgment); see also Tribe, at 1296 (challenged government practices should be judged "from the perspective of a 'reasonable nonadherent'"). When measured against this standard, the menorah need not be excluded from this particular display. The Christmas tree alone in the Pittsburgh location does not endorse Christian belief; and, on the facts before us, the addition of the menorah "cannot be fairly understood to" result in the simultaneous endorsement of Christian and Jewish faiths. On the contrary, for purposes of the Establishment Clause, the city's overall display must be understood as conveying the city's secular recognition of different traditions for celebrating the winter-holiday season.

The conclusion here that, in this particular context, the menorah's display does not have an effect of endorsing reli⊥**621**gious faith does not foreclose the possibility that the display of the menorah might violate either the "purpose" or "entanglement" prong of the *Lemon* analysis. These issues were not addressed by the Court of Appeals and may be considered by that court on remand.

VII

Lynch v. *Donnelly* confirms, and in no way repudiates, the longstanding constitutional principle that government may not engage in a practice that has the effect of promoting or endorsing religious beliefs. The display of the crèche in the County Courthouse has this unconstitutional effect. The display of the menorah in front of the City-County Building, however, does not have this effect, given its "particular physical setting."

The judgment of the Court of Appeals is affirmed in part and reversed in part, and the cases are remanded for further proceedings.

It is so ordered.

. . . . .

⊥**623** *Justice* O'CONNOR, with whom *Justice* BRENNAN and *Justice* STEVENS join as to Part II, concurring in part and concurring in the judgment.

I

Judicial review of government action under the Establishment Clause is a delicate task. The Court has avoided drawing lines which entirely sweep away all government recognition and acknowledgment of the role of religion in the lives of our citizens for to do so would exhibit not neutrality but hostility to religion. Instead the courts have made case-specific examinations of the challenged government action and have attempted to do so with the aid of the standards described by *Justice* BLACKMUN in Part III-A of the Court's opinion. Unfortunately, even the development of articulable standards and guidelines has not always resulted in agreement among the Members of this Court on the results in individual cases. And so it is again today.

The constitutionality of the two displays at issue in this case turns on how we interpret and apply the holding in *Lynch* v. *Donnelly*, in which we rejected an Establishment Clause challenge to the city of Pawtucket's inclusion of a crèche in its annual Christmas holiday display. The seasonal display reviewed in *Lynch* was located in a privately-owned park in the heart of the shopping district. In addition to the crèche, the display included "a Santa Claus house, reindeer pulling Santa's sleigh, candy-striped poles, a Christmas tree, carolers, cut-out figures representing such characters as a clown, an elephant, and a teddy bear, hundreds of colored lights, [and] a large banner that rea[d] 'SEASONS GREETINGS.'" The city owned all the components of the display. Setting up and dismantling the crèche cost the city about $20 a year, and nominal expenses were incurred in lighting the crèche.

The *Lynch* Court began its analysis by stating that Establishment Clause cases call for careful line-drawing: "no fixed, *per se* rule can be framed." Although de⊥**624**claring that it was not willing to be confined to any single test, the Court essentially applied the *Lemon* test, asking "whether the challenged law or conduct has a secular purpose, whether its principal or primary effect is to advance or inhibit religion, and whether it creates an excessive entanglement of government with religion" (citing *Lemon* v. *Kurtzman*). In reversing the lower court's decision, which held that inclusion of the crèche in the holiday display violated the Establishment Clause, the Court stressed that the lower court erred in "focusing almost exclusively on the crèche." "In so doing, it rejected the city's claim that its reasons for including the crèche are essentially the same as its reasons for sponsoring the display as a whole." When viewed in the "context of the Christmas Holiday season," the Court reasoned, there was insufficient evidence to suggest that *inclusion* of the crèche as *part* of the holiday display was an effort to advocate a particular religious message. The Court concluded that Pawtucket had a secular purpose for including the crèche in its Christmas holiday display, namely, "to depict the origins of that Holiday."

The Court also concluded that inclusion of the crèche in the display did not have the primary effect of advancing religion. "[D]isplay of the crèche is no more an advancement or endorsement of religion than the Congressional and Executive recognition of the origins of the Holiday itself as 'Christ's Mass,' or the exhibition of literally hundreds of religious paintings in governmentally supported museums." Finally, the Court found no excessive entanglement between religion and government. There was "no evidence of contact with church authorities concerning the content or design of the exhibit prior to or since Pawtucket's purchase of the crèche."

I joined the majority opinion in *Lynch* because, as I read that opinion, it was consistent with the analysis set forth in my separate concurrence, which stressed that "[e]very gov⊥**625**ernment practice must be judged in its *unique circumstances* to determine whether it constitutes an endorsement or disapproval of religion" (emphasis added). Indeed, by referring repeatedly to "inclusion of the crèche" in the larger holiday display, the *Lynch* majority recognized that the crèche had to be viewed in light of the total display of which it was a part. Moreover, I joined the Court's discussion in Part II of *Lynch* concerning government acknowledgments of religion in American life because, in my view, acknowledgments such as the legislative prayers upheld in *Marsh* v. *Chambers*, and the printing of "In God We Trust" on our coins serve the secular purposes of "solemnizing public occasions, expressing confidence in the future, and encouraging the recognition of what is worthy of appreciation in society." *Lynch*. Because they serve such secular purposes and because of their "history and ubiquity," such government acknowledgments of religion are not understood as conveying an endorsement of particular religious beliefs. At the same time, it is clear the "[g]overnment practices that purport to celebrate or acknowledge events with religious significance must be subjected to careful judicial scrutiny."

In my concurrence in *Lynch*, I suggested a clarification of our Establishment Clause doctrine to reinforce the concept that the Establishment Clause "prohibits government from making adherence to a religion relevant in any way to a person's standing in the political community." The government violates this prohibition if it endorses or disapproves of religion. "Endorsement sends a message to nonadherents that they are outsiders, not full members of the political community, and an accompanying message to adherents that they are insiders, favored members of the political community." Disapproval of religion conveys the opposite message. Thus, in my view, the central issue in *Lynch* was whether the city of Pawtucket had ⊥**626** endorsed Christianity by displaying a crèche as part of a larger exhibit of traditional secular symbols of the Christmas holiday season.

In *Lynch*, I concluded that the city's display of a crèche in its larger holiday exhibit in a private park in the commercial district had neither the purpose nor the effect of conveying a message of government endorsement of Christianity or disapproval of other religions. The purpose of including the crèche in the larger display was to celebrate the public holiday through its traditional symbols, not to promote the religious content of the crèche. Nor, in my view, did Pawtucket's display of the crèche along with secular symbols of the Christmas holiday objectively convey a message of endorsement of Christianity.

For the reasons stated in Part IV of the Court's opinion in this case, I agree that the crèche displayed on the Grand Staircase of the Allegheny County Courthouse, the seat of county government, conveys a message to nonadherents of Christianity that they are not full members of the political community, and a corresponding message to Christians that they are favored members of the political community. In contrast to the crèche in *Lynch*, which was displayed in a private park in the city's commercial district as part of a broader display of traditional secular symbols of the holiday season, this crèche stands alone in the County Courthouse. The display of religious symbols in public areas of core government buildings runs a special risk of "mak[ing] religion relevant, in reality or public perception, to status in the political community." *Lynch*. See also *American Jewish Congress v. City of Chicago* ("[b]ecause City Hall is so plainly under government ownership and control every display and activity in the building is implicitly marked with the stamp of government approval. The presence of a nativity scene in the lobby, therefore, inevitably creates a clear and strong impression that the local government tacitly endorses ⊥**627** Christianity"). The Court correctly concludes that placement of the central religious symbol of the Christmas holiday season at the Allegheny County Courthouse has the unconstitutional effect of conveying a government endorsement of Christianity.

II

In his separate opinion, *Justice KENNEDY* asserts that the endorsement test "is flawed in its fundamentals and unworkable in practice." In my view, neither criticism is persuasive. As a theoretical matter, the endorsement test captures the essential command of the Establishment Clause, namely, that government must not make a person's religious beliefs relevant to their standing in the political community by conveying a message "that religion or a particular religious belief is favored or preferred." *Wallace* v. *Jaffree*, *Grand Rapids School District* v. *Ball*. See also Beschle, The Conservative as Liberal: The Religion Clauses, Liberal Neutrality, and the Approach of Justice O'Connor, 62 Notre Dame L. Rev. 151 (1987); Note, Developments in the Law—Religion and the State, 100 Harv. L. Rev. 1606. 1647 (1987). We live in a pluralistic society. Our citizens come from diverse religious traditions or adhere to no particular religious beliefs at all. If government is to be neutral in matters of religion, rather than showing either favoritism or disapproval towards citizens based on their personal religious choices, government cannot endorse the religious practices and beliefs of some citizens without sending a clear message to nonadherents that they are outsiders or less than full members of the political community.

An Establishment Clause standard that prohibits only "coercive" practices or overt efforts at government proselytization, but fails to take account of the numerous more subtle ways that government can show favor- ⊥**628**itism to particular beliefs or convey a message of disapproval to others, would not, in my view, adequately protect the religious liberty or respect the religious diversity of the members of our pluralistic political community. Thus, this Court has never relied on coercion alone as the touchstone of Establishment Clause analysis. See, *e.g.*, *Committee for Public Education* v. *Nyquist*. ("[W]hile proof of coercion might provide a basis for a claim under the Free Exercise Clause, it [is] not a necessary element of any claim under the Establishment Clause"); *Engel* v. *Vitale*. To require a showing of coercion, even indirect coercion, as an essential element of an Establishment Clause violation would make the Free Exercise Clause a redundancy. See *Abington School District v. Schempp* ("The distinction between the two clauses is apparent—a violation of the Free Exercise Clause is predicated on coercion while the Establishment Clause violation need not be so attended"). See also Laycock, "Nonpreferential" Aid to Religion: A False Claim About Original Intent, 27 Wm. & Mary L. Rev. 875, 922 (1986) ("If coercion is also an element of the establishment clause, establishment adds nothing to free exercise"). Moreover, as even *Justice KENNEDY* recognizes, any Establishment Clause test limited to "*direct* coercion" clearly would fail to account for forms of "[s]ymbolic recognition or accommodation of religious faith" that may violate the Establishment Clause.

I continue to believe that the endorsement test asks the right question about governmental practices challenged on Establishment Clause grounds, including challenged practices involving the display of religious symbols. Moreover, commentators in the scholarly literature have found merit in the approach. See, *e.g.*, Beschle, at 174; Comment, *Lemon* Reconstituted: Justice O'Connor's Proposed Modification of the *Lemon* Test for Establishment Clause Violations, 1986 B. Y. U. L. Rev. 465; Marshall, "We Know It When We ⊥**629** See It": The Supreme Court and Establishment, 59 S. Cal. L. Rev. 495 (1986); Note, Developments in the Law at 1647. I also remain convinced that the endorsement test is capable of consistent application. Indeed, it is notable that the three Circuit courts which have considered challenges to the display of a crèche standing alone at city hall have each concluded, relying in part on endorsement analysis, that such a practice sends a message to nonadherents of Christianity that they are outsiders in the political community. See *American Jewish Congress* v. *City of Chicago*, *ACLU* v. *Birmingham*. See also *Friedman* v. *Board of County Commissioners of Bernalillo County* (county seal including Latin cross and Spanish motto translated as "With This We Conquer," conveys a message of endorsement of Christianity). To be sure, the endorsement test depends on a sensitivity to the unique circumstances and context of a particular challenged practice and, like any test that is sensitive to context, it may not always yield results with unanimous agreement at the margins. But that is true of many standards in constitutional law, and even the modified coercion test offered by *Justice KENNEDY* involves judgment and hard choices at the margin. He admits as much by acknowledging that the permanent display of a Latin cross at city hall would violate the Establishment Clause, as would the display of symbols of Christian holidays alone. Would the display of a Latin cross for six months have such an unconstitutional effect, or the display of the symbols of most Christian holidays and one Jewish holiday? Would the Christmas-time display of a crèche inside a courtroom be "coercive" if subpoenaed witnesses had no opportunity to "turn their backs" and walk away? Would displaying a crèche in front of a public school violate the Establishment Clause under *Justice KENNEDY's* test? ⊥**630** We cannot avoid the obligation to draw lines, often close and difficult lines, in deciding Establishment Clause cases, and that is not a problem unique to the endorsement test.

Justice KENNEDY submits that the endorsement test is inconsistent with our precedents and traditions because, in his words, if it were "applied without artificial exceptions for historical practice," it would invalidate many traditional practices recognizing the role of religion in our society. This criticism shortchanges both the endorsement test itself and my explanation of the reason why certain longstanding government acknowledgments of religion do not, under that test, convey a message of endorsement. Practices such as legislative prayers or opening Court sessions with "God save the United States and this honorable Court," serve the secular purposes of "solemnizing public occasions," and "expressing confidence in the future," *Lynch* (concurring opinion). These examples of ceremonial deism do not survive Establishment Clause scrutiny simply by virtue of their historical longevity alone. Historical acceptance of a practice does not in itself validate that practice under the Establishment Clause if the practice violates the values protected by that Clause, just as historical acceptance of racial or gender based discrimination does not immunize such practices from scrutiny under the 14th Amendment. As we recognized in *Walz* v. *Tax Comm'n of New York City*, "no one acquires a vested or protected right in violation of the Constitution by long use, even when that span of time covers our entire national existence and indeed predates it."

Under the endorsement test, the "history and ubiquity" of a practice is relevant not because it creates an "artificial exception" from that test. On the contrary, the "history and ubiquity" of a practice is relevant because it provides part of the context in which a reasonable observer evaluates whether a challenged governmental practice conveys a message of endorsement of religion. It is the combination of the **⊥631** longstanding existence of practices such as opening legislative sessions with legislative prayers or opening Court sessions with "God save the United States and this honorable Court," as well as their nonsectarian nature, that lead me to the conclusion that those particular practices, despite their religious roots, do not convey a message of endorsement of particular religious beliefs. See *Lynch* (concurring opinion); Note, Developments in the Law, 100 Harv. L. Rev., at 1652-1654. Similarly, the celebration of Thanksgiving as a public holiday, despite its religious origins, is now generally understood as a celebration of patriotic values rather than particular religious beliefs. The question under endorsement analysis, in short, is whether a reasonable observer would view such longstanding practices as a disapproval of their particular religious choices, in light of the fact that they serve a secular purpose rather than a sectarian one and have largely lost their religious significance over time. See L. Tribe, American Constitutional Law 1294-1296 (2d ed. 1988). Although the endorsement test requires careful and often difficult line-drawing and is highly context-specific, no alternative test has been suggested that captures the essential mandate of the Establishment Clause as well as the endorsement test does, and it warrants continued application and refinement.

Contrary to *Justice KENNEDY's* assertions, neither the endorsement test nor its application in this case reflect "an unjustified hostility toward religion." Instead, the endorsement standard recognizes that the religious liberty so precious to the citizens who make up our diverse country is protected, not impeded, when government avoids endorsing religion or favoring particular beliefs over others. Clearly, the government can *acknowledge* the role of religion in our society in numerous ways that do not amount to an endorsement. Moreover, the government can *accommodate* religion by lifting government-imposed burdens on religion. **⊥632** Indeed, the Free Exercise Clause may mandate that it do so in particular cases. In cases involving the lifting of government burdens on the free exercise of religion, a reasonable observer would take into account the values underlying the Free Exercise Clause in assessing whether the challenged practice conveyed a message of endorsement. By "build[ing] on the concerns at the core of nonestablishment doctrine and recogniz[ing] the role of accommodations in furthering free exercise," the endorsement test "provides a standard capable of consistent application and avoids the criticism levelled against the *Lemon* test." Rostain, Permissible Accommodations of Religion; Reconsidering the New York *Get* Statute, 96 Yale L. J. 1147, 1159-1160 (1987). The case before the Court today, however, does not involve lifting a governmental burden on the free exercise of religion. By repeatedly using the terms "acknowledgment" of religion and "accommodation" of religion interchangeably, however, *Justice KENNEDY* obscures the fact that the displays at issue in this case were not placed at city hall in order to remove a government-imposed burden on the free exercise of religion. Christians remain free to display their crèches at their homes and churches. Allegheny County has neither placed nor removed a governmental burden on the free exercise of religion but rather, for the reasons stated in Part IV of the Court's opinion, has conveyed a message of governmental endorsement of Christian beliefs. This the Establishment Clause does not permit.

III

For reasons which differ somewhat from those set forth in Part VI of *Justice BLACKMUN's* opinion, I also conclude that the city of Pittsburgh's combined holiday display of a Chanukah menorah, a Christmas tree, and a sign saluting liberty does not have the effect of conveying an endorsement of religion. I agree with *Justice BLACKMUN* **⊥633** that the Christmas tree, whatever its origins, is not regarded today as a religious symbol. Although Christmas is a public holiday that has both religious and secular aspects, the Christmas tree is widely viewed as a secular symbol of the holiday, in contrast to the crèche, which depicts the holiday's religious dimensions. A Christmas tree displayed in front of city hall, in my view, cannot fairly be understood as conveying government endorsement of Christianity. Although *Justice BLACKMUN's* opinion acknowledges that a Christmas tree alone conveys no endorsement of Christian beliefs, it formulates the question posed by Pittsburgh's combined display of the tree and the menorah as whether the display "has the effect of endorsing both Christian and Jewish faiths, or rather simply recognizes that both Christmas and Chanukah are part of the same winter-holiday season, which has attained a secular status in our society."

That formulation of the question disregards the fact that the Christmas tree is a predominantly secular symbol and, more significantly, obscures the religious nature of the menorah and the holiday of Chanukah. The opinion is correct to recognize that the religious holiday of Chanukah has historical and cultural as well as religious dimensions, and that there may be certain "secular aspects" to the holiday. But that is not to conclude, however, as *Justice BLACKMUN* seems to do, that

Chanukah has become a "secular holiday" in our society. The Easter holiday celebrated by Christians may be accompanied by certain "secular aspects" such as Easter bunnies and Easter egg hunts; but it is nevertheless a religious holiday. Similarly, Chanukah is a religious holiday with strong historical components particularly important to the Jewish people. Moreover, the menorah is the central religious symbol and ritual object of that religious holiday. Under *Justice BLACKMUN's* view, however, the menorah "has been relegated to the role of a neutral harbinger of the holiday season," *Lynch* ⊥**634** (Blackmun, J., dissenting), almost devoid of any religious significance. In my view, the relevant question for Establishment Clause purposes is whether the city of Pittsburgh's display of the menorah, the religious symbol of a religious holiday, next to a Christmas tree and a sign saluting liberty sends a message of government endorsement of Judaism or whether it sends a message of pluralism and freedom to choose one's own beliefs.

In characterizing the message conveyed by this display as either a "double endorsement" or a secular acknowledgment of the winter holiday season, the opinion states that "[i]t is distinctly implausible to view the combined display of the tree, the sign, and the menorah as endorsing Jewish faith alone." That statement, however, seems to suggest that it would be implausible for the city to endorse a faith adhered to by a minority of the citizenry. Regardless of the plausibility of a putative governmental purpose, the more important inquiry here is whether the governmental display of a minority faith's religious symbol could ever reasonably be understood to convey a message of endorsement of that faith. A menorah standing alone at city hall may well send such a message to nonadherents, just as in this case the crèche standing alone at the Allegheny County Courthouse sends a message of governmental endorsement of Christianity, whatever the county's purpose in authorizing the display may have been. Thus, the question here is whether Pittsburgh's holiday display conveys a message of endorsement of Judaism, when the menorah is the only religious symbol in the combined display and when the opinion acknowledges that the tree cannot reasonably be understood to convey an endorsement of Christianity. One need not characterize Chanukah as a "secular holiday" or strain to argue that the menorah has a "secular dimension," in order to conclude that the city of Pittsburgh's combined display does not convey a message of endorsement of Judaism or of religion in general.

⊥**635** In setting up its holiday display, which included the lighted tree and the menorah, the city of Pittsburgh stressed the theme of liberty and pluralism by accompanying the exhibit with a sign bearing the following message: "During this holiday season, the City of Pittsburgh salutes liberty. Let these festive lights remind us that we are the keepers of the flame of liberty and our legacy of freedom." This sign indicates that the city intended to convey its own distinctive message of pluralism and freedom. By accompanying its display of a Christmas tree—a secular symbol of the Christmas holiday season—with a salute to liberty, and by adding a religious symbol from a Jewish holiday also celebrated at roughly the same time of year, I conclude that the city did not endorse Judaism or religion in general, but rather conveyed a message of pluralism and freedom of belief during the holiday season. "Although the religious and indeed the sectarian significance" of the menorah "is not neutralized by the setting," *Lynch* (concurring opinion), this particular physical setting "changes what viewers may fairly understand to be the purpose of the display—as a typical museum setting, though not neutralizing the religious content of a religious painting, negates any message of endorsement of that content."

The message of pluralism conveyed by the city's combined holiday display is not a message that endorses religion over nonreligion. Just as government may not favor particular religious beliefs over others, "government may not favor religious belief over disbelief." *Texas Monthly Inc.* v. *Bullock*. Here, by displaying a secular symbol of the Christmas holiday season rather than a religious one, the city acknowledged a public holiday celebrated by both religious and nonreligious citizens alike, and it did so without endorsing Christian beliefs. A reasonable observer would, in my view, appreciate that the com⊥**636**bined display is an effort to acknowledge the cultural diversity of our country and to convey tolerance of different choices in matters of religious belief or nonbelief by recognizing that the winter holiday season is celebrated in diverse ways by our citizens. In short, in the holiday context, this combined display in its particular physical setting conveys neither an endorsement of Judaism or Christianity nor disapproval of alternative beliefs, and thus does not have the impermissible effect of "mak[ing] religion relevant, in reality or public perception, to status in the political community." *Lynch* (concurring opinion).

My conclusion does not depend on whether or not the city had "a more secular alternative symbol" of Chanukah, just as the Court's decision in *Lynch* clearly did not turn on whether the city of Pawtucket could have conveyed its tribute to the Christmas holiday season by using a "less religious" alternative to the crèche symbol in its display of traditional holiday symbols. See *Lynch* ("*Justice BRENNAN* argues that the city's objectives could have been achieved without including the crèche in the display. True or not, that is irrelevant. The question is whether the display of the crèche violates the Establishment Clause"). In my view, *Justice BLACKMUN's* new rule, that an inference of endorsement arises every time government uses a symbol with religious meaning if a "more secular alternative" is available, is too blunt an instrument for Establishment Clause analysis, which depends on sensitivity to the context and circumstances presented by each case. Indeed, the opinion appears to recognize the importance of this contextual sensitivity by creating an exception to its new rule in the very case announcing it; the opinion acknowledges that "a purely secular symbol" of Chanukah is available, namely, a dreidel or four-sided top, but rejects the use of such a symbol because it "might be interpreted by some as mocking the celebration of Chanukah." This recognition that the more *religious* ⊥**637** alternative may, depending on the circumstances, convey a message that is least likely to implicate Establishment Clause concerns is an excellent example of the need to focus on the specific practice in question in its particular physical setting and context in determining whether government has conveyed or attempted to convey a message that religion or a particular religious belief is favored or preferred.

In sum, I conclude that the city of Pittsburgh's combined holiday display had neither the purpose nor the effect of endorsing religion, but that Allegheny County's crèche display had such an effect. Accordingly, I join Parts I, II, III-A, IV, V, and VII of the Court's opinion, and concur in the judgment.

Justice BRENNAN, with whom *Justice* MARSHALL and *Justice* STEVENS join, concurring in part and dissenting in part.

I have previously explained at some length my views on the relationship between the Establishment Clause and government-sponsored celebrations of the Christmas holiday. I continue to believe that the display of an object that "retains a specifically Christian [or other] religious meaning," is incompatible with the separation of church and state demanded by our Constitution. I therefore agree with the Court that Allegheny County's display of a crèche at the county courthouse signals an endorsement of the Christian faith in violation of the Establishment Clause, and join Parts III- A, IV, and V of the Court's opinion. I cannot agree, however, that the city's display of a 45-foot Christmas tree and an 18-foot Chanukah menorah at the entrance to the building housing the Mayor's office shows no favoritism towards Christianity, Judaism, or both. Indeed, I should have thought that the answer as to the first display supplied the answer to the second.

According to the Court, the crèche display sends a message endorsing Christianity because the crèche itself bears a ⊥**638** religious meaning, because an angel in the display carries a banner declaring "Glory to God in the highest!," and because the floral decorations surrounding the crèche highlighted it rather than secularized it. The display of a Christmas tree and Chanukah menorah, in contrast, is said to show no endorsement of a particular faith or faiths, or of religion in general, because the Christmas tree is a secular symbol which brings out the secular elements of the menorah. And, *Justice* BLACKMUN concludes, even though the menorah has religious aspects, its display reveals no endorsement of religion because no other symbol could have been used to represent the secular aspects of the holiday of Chanukah without mocking its celebration. Rather than endorsing religion, therefore, the display merely demonstrates that "Christmas is not the only traditional way of observing the winter-holiday season," and confirms our "cultural diversity."

Thus, the decision as to the menorah rests on three premises: the Christmas tree is a secular symbol; Chanukah is a holiday with secular dimensions, symbolized by the menorah; and the government may promote pluralism by sponsoring or condoning displays having strong religious associations on its property. None of these is sound.

I

The first step toward *Justice* BLACKMUN's conclusion is the claim that, despite its religious origins, the Christmas tree is a secular symbol. He explains:

"The Christmas tree, unlike the menorah, is not itself a religious symbol. Although Christmas trees once carried religious connotations, today they typify the secular celebration of Christmas. Numerous Americans place Christmas trees in their homes without subscribing to Christian religious beliefs, and when the city's tree stands alone in front of the City-County Building, it is not considered an endorsement of Christian faith. In- ⊥**639**deed, a 40-foot Christmas tree was one of the objects that validated the crèche in *Lynch*. The widely accepted view of the Christmas tree as the preeminent secular symbol of the Christmas holiday season serves to emphasize the secular component of the message communicated by other elements of an accompanying holiday display, including the Chanukah menorah."

Justice O'CONNOR accepts this view of the Christmas tree because, "whatever its origins, [it] is not viewed today as a religious symbol. Although Christmas is a public holiday that has both religious and secular aspects, the Christmas tree is widely viewed as a secular symbol of the holiday, in contrast to the crèche which depicts the holiday's religious dimensions."

Thus, while acknowledging the religious origins of the Christmas tree, *Justices* BLACKMUN and O'CONNOR dismiss their significance. In my view, this attempt to take the "Christmas" out of the Christmas tree is unconvincing. That the tree may, without controversy, be deemed a secular symbol if found alone, does not mean that it will be so seen when combined with other symbols or objects. Indeed, *Justice* BLACKMUN admits that "the tree is capable of taking on a religious significance if it is decorated with religious symbols."

The notion that the Christmas tree is necessarily secular is, indeed, so shaky that, despite superficial acceptance of the idea, *Justice* O'CONNOR does not really take it seriously. While conceding that the "menorah standing alone at city hall may well send" a message of endorsement of the Jewish faith, she nevertheless concludes: "By accompanying its display of a Christmas tree—a secular symbol of the Christmas holiday season—with a salute to liberty, and by adding a religious symbol from a Jewish holiday also celebrated at roughly the same time of year, I conclude that the city did not endorse Judaism or religion in general, but rather conveyed a mes⊥**640**sage of pluralism and freedom of belief during the holiday season." But the "pluralism" to which *Justice* O'CONNOR refers is *religious* pluralism, and the "freedom of belief" she emphasizes is freedom of *religious* belief. The display of the tree and the menorah will symbolize such pluralism and freedom only if more than one religion is represented; if only Judaism is represented, the scene is about Judaism, not about pluralism. Thus, the pluralistic message *Justice* O'CONNOR stresses *depends* on the tree's possessing some religious significance.

In asserting that the Christmas tree, regardless of its surroundings, is a purely secular symbol, *Justices BLACKMUN* and *O'CONNOR* ignore the precept they otherwise so enthusiastically embrace: that context is all-important in determining the message conveyed by particular objects. See (Blackmun, J.) (relevant question is "whether the ⊥**641** display of the crèche and the menorah, in their respective 'particular physical settings,' has the effect of endorsing or disapproving religious beliefs") (quoting *Grand Rapids School Dist.* v. *Ball*), (O'Connor, J.) ("'[E]very government practice must be judged in its *unique circumstances* to determine whether it constitutes an endorsement or disapproval of religion'") (quoting *Lynch* v. *Donnelly* (O'Connor, J., concurring)); (O'Connor, J.) ("Establishment Clause analysis . . . depends on sensitivity to the context and circumstances presented by each case"); (emphasizing "the need to focus on the specific practice in question in its particular physical setting and context"). In analyzing the symbolic character of the Christmas tree, both *Justices BLACKMUN* and *O'CONNOR* abandon this contextual inquiry. In doing so, they go badly astray.

Positioned as it was, the Christmas tree's religious significance was bound to come to the fore. Situated next to the menorah—which *Justice BLACKMUN* acknowledges, is "a symbol with religious meaning," and indeed, is "the central religious symbol and ritual object of" Chanukah (O'Connor, J.)—the Christmas tree's religious dimension could not be overlooked by observers of the display. Even though the tree alone may be deemed predominantly secular, it can hardly be so characterized when placed next to such a forthrightly religious symbol. Consider a poster featuring a star of David, a statue of Buddha, a Christmas tree, a mosque, and a drawing of Krishna. There can be no doubt that, when found in such company, the tree serves as an unabashedly religious symbol.

Justice BLACKMUN believes that it is the tree that changes the message of the menorah, rather than the menorah that alters our view of the tree. After the abrupt dismissal of the suggestion that the flora surrounding the crèche might have diluted the religious character of the display at City Hall, his quick conclusion that ⊥**642** the Christmas tree had a secularizing effect on the menorah is surprising. The distinguishing characteristic, it appears, is the size of the tree. The tree, we are told, is much taller—$2^1/2$ times taller, in fact—than the menorah, and is located directly under one of the building's archways, whereas the menorah "is positioned to one side . . . [i]n the shadow of the tree."

As a factual matter, it seems to me that the sight of an 18-foot menorah would be far more eye-catching than that of a rather conventionally sized Christmas tree. It also seems to me likely that the symbol with the more singular message will predominate over one lacking such a clear meaning. Given the homogenized message that *Justice BLACKMUN* associates with the Christmas tree, I would expect that the menorah, with concededly religious character, would tend to dominate the tree. And, though *Justice BLACKMUN* shunts the point to a footnote at the end of his opinion, it is highly relevant that the menorah was lit during a religious ceremony complete with traditional religious blessings. I do not comprehend how the failure to challenge separately this portion of the city's festivities precludes us from considering it in assessing the message sent by the display as a whole. With such an openly religious introduction, it is most likely that the religious aspects of the menorah would be front and center in this display.

I would not, however, presume to say that my interpretation of the tree's significance is the "correct" one, or the one shared by most visitors to the City-County Building. I do not know how we can decide whether it was the tree that stripped the religious connotations from the menorah, or the menorah that laid bare the religious origins of the tree. Both are reasonable interpretations of the scene the city presented, and thus both, I think, should satisfy *Justice BLACKMUN's* requirement that the display "be judged according to the standard of a 'reasonable observer.'" I ⊥**643** shudder to think that the only "reasonable observer" is one who shares the particular views on perspective, spacing, and accent expressed in *Justice BLACKMUN's* opinion, thus making analysis under the Establishment Clause look more like an exam in Art 101 than an inquiry into constitutional law.

II

The second premise on which today's decision rests is the notion that Chanukah is a partly secular holiday, for which the menorah can serve as a secular symbol. It is no surprise and no anomaly that Chanukah has historical and societal roots that range beyond the purely religious. I would venture that most, if not all, major religious holidays have beginnings and enjoy histories studded with figures, events, and practices that are not strictly religious. It does not seem to me that the mere fact that Chanukah shares this kind of background makes it a secular holiday in any meaningful sense. The menorah is indisputably a religious symbol, used ritually in a celebration that has deep religious significance. That, in my view, is all that need be said. Whatever secular practices the holiday of Chanukah has taken on in its contemporary observances are beside the point.

Indeed, at the very outset of his discussion of the menorah display, *Justice BLACKMUN* recognizes that the menorah is a religious symbol. That should have been the end of the case. But, as did the Court in *Lynch*, *Justice BLACKMUN*, "by focusing on the holiday 'context' in which the [menorah] appeared, seeks to explain away the clear religious import of the [menorah] . . ." (Brennan, J., dissenting). By the end of the opinion, the menorah has become but a coequal symbol, with the Christmas tree, of "the winter holiday season." Pittsburgh's secularization of an inherently religious symbol, aided and abetted here by *Justice BLACKMUN's* opinion, recalls the effort in *Lynch* to render the crèche a secular symbol. As I said then: "To suggest, as the Court does, that such a symbol ⊥**644** is merely 'traditional' and therefore no different from Santa's house or reindeer is not only offensive to those for whom the crèche has profound significance, but insulting to those who insist for religious or personal reasons that the story of Christ is in no sense a part of 'history' nor an unavoidable element of our national 'heritage.'" As *Justice O'CONNOR* rightly observes, *Justice BLACKMUN* "obscures the religious nature of the menorah and the holiday of Chanukah."

I cannot, in short, accept the effort to transform an emblem of religious faith into the innocuous "symbol for a holiday that . . . has both religious and secular dimensions" (Blackmun, J.).

III

Justice BLACKMUN, in his acceptance of the city's message of "diversity," and, even more so, *Justice O'CONNOR*, in her approval of the "message of pluralism and freedom to choose one's own beliefs," appear to believe that, where seasonal displays are concerned, more is better. Whereas a display might be constitutionally problematic if it showcased the holiday of just one religion, those problems vaporize as soon as more than one religion is included. I know of no principle under the Establishment Clause, however, that permits us to conclude that governmental promotion of religion is acceptable so long as one religion is not favored. We have, on the contrary, interpreted that Clause to require neutrality, not just among religions, but between religion and nonreligion. See, e.g., *Everson* v. *Board of Education*, *Wallace* v. *Jaffree*.

Nor do I discern the theory under which the government is permitted to appropriate particular holidays and religious objects to its own use in celebrating "pluralism." The message of the sign announcing a "Salute to Liberty" is not religious, but patriotic; the government's use of a religion to promote its ⊥**645** own cause is undoubtedly offensive to those whose religious beliefs are not bound up with their attitude toward the Nation.

The uncritical acceptance of a message of religious pluralism also ignores the extent to which even that message may offend. Many religious faiths are hostile to each other, and indeed, refuse even to participate in ecumenical services designed to demonstrate the very pluralism *Justices BLACKMUN* and *O'CONNOR* extol. To lump the ritual objects and holidays of religions together without regard to their attitudes toward such inclusiveness, or to decide which religions should be excluded because of the possibility of offense, is not a benign or beneficent celebration of pluralism: it is instead an interference in religious matters precluded by the Establishment Clause.

The government-sponsored display of the menorah alongside a Christmas tree also works a distortion of the Jewish religious calendar. As *Justice BLACKMUN* acknowledges, "the proximity of Christmas [may] accoun[t] for the social prominence of Chanukah in this country." It is the proximity of Christmas that undoubtedly accounts for the city's decision to participate in the celebration of Chanukah, rather than the far more significant Jewish holidays of Rosh Hashanah and Yom Kippur. Contrary to the impression the city and *Justices BLACKMUN* and *O'CONNOR* seem to create, with their emphasis on "the winter-holiday season," December is not the holiday season for Judaism. Thus, the city's erection alongside the Christmas tree of the symbol of a relatively minor Jewish religious holiday, far from conveying "the city's secular recognition of different traditions for celebrating the winter-holiday season," (Blackmun, J.), or "a message of pluralism and freedom of belief," (O'Connor, J.), has the effect of promoting a Christianized version of Judaism. The holiday calendar they appear willing to accept revolves exclusively around a Christian holiday. And those religions that have ⊥**646** no holiday at all during the period between Thanksgiving and New Year's Day will not benefit, even in a second-class manner, from the city's once-a-year tribute to "liberty" and "freedom of belief." This is not "pluralism" as I understand it.

Justice STEVENS, with whom *Justice BRENNAN* and *JUSTICE MARSHALL* join, concurring in part and dissenting in part.

Governmental recognition of not one but two religions distinguishes this case from our prior Establishment Clause cases. It is, therefore, appropriate to reexamine the text and context of the Clause to determine its impact on this novel situation.

Relations between church and state at the end of the 1780's fell into two quite different categories. In several European countries, one national religion, such as the Church of England in Great Britain, was established. The established church typically was supported by tax revenues, by laws conferring privileges only upon members, and sometimes by violent persecution of nonadherents. In contrast, although several American Colonies had assessed taxes to support one chosen faith, none of the newly United States subsidized a single religion. Some States had repealed establishment laws altogether, while others had replaced single establishments with laws providing for nondiscriminatory support of more than one religion.

⊥**647** It is against this historical backdrop that James Madison, then a Representative from Virginia, rose to the floor of the First Congress on June 8, 1789, and proposed a number of amendments to the Constitution, including the following:

"The civil rights of none shall be abridged on account of religious belief or worship, *nor shall any national religion be established*, nor shall the full and equal rights of conscience be in any manner, or on any pretext, infringed." 1 Annals of Cong. 434 (1789) (emphasis added).

Congressional debate produced several reformulations of the underscored language. One Member suggested the words "Congress shall make no laws *touching religion*" (emphasis added), soon amended to "Congress shall make no law *establishing religion*" (emphasis added). After further alteration, this passage became one of the Religion Clauses to the First Amendment. Ratified in 1791, they state that "Congress shall make no law *respecting an establishment of religion*, or prohibiting the free exercise thereof," (emphasis added).

By its terms the initial draft of the Establishment Clause would have prohibited only the national established church that prevailed in England; multiple establishments, such as existed in six States, would have been permitted. But even ⊥**648** in those States and even among members of the established churches, there was widespread opposition to multiple establishments because of the social divisions they caused. Perhaps in response to this opposition, subsequent drafts broadened the scope of the Establishment Clause from "any national religion" to "religion," a word understood primarily to mean "[v]irtue, as founded upon reverence of God, and expectation of future rewards and punishments," and only secondarily "[a] system of divine faith and worship, as opposite to others." S. Johnson, A Dictionary of the English Language (7th ed. 1785); accord T. Sheridan, A Complete Dictionary of the English Language (6th ed. 1796). Cf. *Frazee* v. *Illinois Dept. of Employment Security* (construing "religion" protected by Free Ex⊥**649**ercise Clause to include "sincerely held religious belief" apart from "membership in an organized religious denomination"). Plainly, the Clause as ratified proscribes federal legislation establishing a number of religions as well as a single national church.

Similarly expanded was the relationship between government and religion that was to be disallowed. Whereas earlier drafts had barred only laws "establishing" or "touching" religion, the final text interdicts all laws "respecting an establishment of religion." This phrase forbids even a partial establishment, *Lemon* v. *Kurtzman*, *Engel* v. *Vitale*, not only of a particular sect in favor of others, but also of religion in preference to nonreligion, *Wallace* v. *Jaffree*. It is also significant that the final draft contains the word "respecting." Like "touching," "respecting" means concerning, or with reference to. But it also means with respect—that is, "reverence," "good-will," "regard"—to. Taking into account this richer meaning, the Establishment Clause, in banning laws that concern religion, especially prohibits those that pay homage to religion.

Treatment of a symbol of a particular tradition demonstrates one's attitude toward that tradition. Cf.*Texas* v. *Johnson*. Thus the prominent display of religious symbols on government property falls within the compass of the First Amendment, even though interference with personal choices about supporting a church, by means of governmental tithing, was the primary concern in 1791. See *Walz* v. *Tax Comm'n*. Whether the vice in such a display is ⊥**650** characterized as "coercion," (Kennedy, J., concurring in judgment in part and dissenting in part), or "endorsement," (O'Connor, J., concurring in part and concurring in judgment), or merely as state action with the purpose and effect of providing support for specific faiths, cf. *Lemon*, it is common ground that this symbolic governmental speech "respecting an establishment of religion" may violate the Constitution. Cf. *Jaffree*, *Lynch* v. *Donnelly*.

In my opinion the Establishment Clause should be construed to create a strong presumption against the display of religious symbols on public property. There is always a ⊥**651** risk that such symbols will offend nonmembers of the faith being advertised as well as adherents who consider the particular advertisement disrespectful. Some devout Christians believe that the crèche should be placed only in reverential settings, such as a church or perhaps a private home; they do not countenance its use as an aid to commercialization of Christ's birthday. Cf. *Lynch* (Blackmun, J., dissenting). In this very case, members of the Jewish faith firmly opposed the use to which the menorah was put by the particular sect that sponsored the display at Pittsburgh's City-County Building. Even though "[p]assersby who disagree with the message conveyed by these displays are free to ignore them, or even turn their backs," (Kennedy, J., concurring in judgment in part and dissenting in part), displays of this kind inevitably have a greater tendency to emphasize sincere and deeply felt differences among individuals than to achieve an ecumenical goal. The Establishment Clause does not allow public bodies to foment such disagreement.

⊥**652** Application of a strong presumption against the public use of religious symbols scarcely will "require a relentless extirpation of all contact between government and religion," (Kennedy, J., concurring in judgment in part and dissenting in part), for it will prohibit a display only when its message, evaluated in the context in which it is presented, is nonsecular. For example, a carving of Moses holding the Ten Commandments, if that is the only adornment on a courtroom wall, conveys an equivocal message, perhaps of respect for Judaism, for religion in general, or for law. The addition of carvrings depicting Confucius and Mohammed may honor religion, or particular religions, to an extent that the First Amendment does not tolerate any more than it does "the permanent erection of a large Latin cross on the roof of city hall" (Kennedy, J., concurring in judgment in part and dissenting in part). Placement of secular figures such as Caesar Augustus, William Blackstone, Napoleon Bonaparte, and John Marshall alongside these three religious leaders, however, signals respect not ⊥**653** for great proselytizers but for great lawgivers. It would be absurd to exclude such a fitting message from a courtroom, as it would to exclude religious paintings by Italian Renaissance masters from a public museum. Cf. *Lynch* (Brennan, J., dissenting). Far from "border[ing] on latent hostility toward religion," (Kennedy, J., concurring in judgment in part and dissenting in part), this careful consideration of context gives due regard to religious and nonreligious members of our society.

Thus I find wholly unpersuasive *Justice KENNEDY's* attempts to belittle the importance of the obvious differences between the display of the crèche in this case and that in *Lynch* v. *Donnelly*. Even if I had not dissented from the Court's conclusion that the crèche in *Lynch* was constitutional, I would conclude that Allegheny County's unambiguous exposition of a sacred symbol inside its courthouse promoted Christianity to a degree ⊥**654** that violated the Establishment Clause. Accordingly, I concur in the Court's judgment regarding the crèche for substantially the same reasons discussed in *Justice BRENNAN's* dissent, which I join, as well as Part IV of *Justice BLACKMUN's* opinion and Part I of *Justice O'CONNOR's* opinion.

I cannot agree with the Court's conclusion that the display at Pittsburgh's City-County Building was constitutional. Standing alone in front of a governmental headquarters, a lighted, 45-foot evergreen tree might convey holiday greetings linked too tenuously to Christianity to have constitutional moment. Juxtaposition of this tree with an 18-foot menorah does not make the latter secular, as *Justice BLACKMUN* contends. Rather, the presence of the Chanukah menorah, unquestionably a religious symbol, gives religious significance to the Christmas tree. The overall display thus manifests governmental approval of the Jewish and Christian religions. Cf. *Jaffree* (quoting *Lynch* (O'Connor, J., con⊥**655**curring)). Although it conceivably might be interpreted as sending "a message of pluralism and freedom to choose one's own beliefs," (O'Connor, J., concurring in part and concurring in judgment); accord (opinion of Blackmun, J.), the message is not sufficiently clear to overcome the strong presumption that the display, respecting two religions to the exclusion of all others, is the very kind of double establishment that the First Amendment was designed to outlaw. I would, therefore, affirm the judgment of the Court of Appeals in its entirety.

Justice KENNEDY, with whom *The CHIEF JUSTICE*, *Justice WHITE*, and *Justice SCALIA* join, concurring in the judgment in part and dissenting in part.

The majority holds that the County of Allegheny violated the Establishment Clause by displaying a crèche in the county courthouse, because the "principal or primary effect" of the display is to advance religion within the meaning of *Lemon* v. *Kurtzman*. This view of the Establishment Clause reflects an unjustified hostility toward religion, a hostility inconsistent with our history and our precedents, and I dissent from this holding. The crèche display is constitutional, and, for the same reasons, the display of a menorah by the city of Pittsburgh is permissible as well. On this latter point, I concur in the result, but not the reasoning, of Part VI of *Justice BLACKMUN's* opinion.

I

In keeping with the usual fashion of recent years, the majority applies the *Lemon* test to judge the constitutionality of the holiday displays here in question. I am content for present purposes to remain within the *Lemon* framework, but do not wish to be seen as advocating, let alone adopting, that test as our primary guide in this difficult area. Persuasive criticism of *Lemon* has emerged. See *Edwards* v. *Aguillard* (Scalia, J., dissenting); ⊥**656** *Aguilar* v. *Felton* (O'Connor, J., dissenting); *Wallace* v. *Jaffree* (Rehnquist, J., dissenting); *Roemer* v. *Maryland Bd. of Public Works* (1976) (White, J., concurring in judgment). Our cases often question its utility in providing concrete answers to Establishment Clause questions, calling it but a "'helpful sign pos[t]'" or "'guidelin[e]'" to assist our deliberations rather than a comprehensive test. *Mueller* v. *Allen* (quoting *Hunt* v. *McNair*); *Committee for Public Education* v. *Nyquist* (quoting *Tilton* v. *Richardson*); see *Lynch* v. *Donnelly* ("we have repeatedly emphasized our unwillingness to be confined to any single test or criterion in this sensitive area"). Substantial revision of our Establishment Clause doctrine may be in order; but it is unnecessary to undertake that task today, for even the *Lemon* test, when applied with proper sensitivity to our traditions and our case law, supports the conclusion that both the crèche and the menorah are permissible displays in the context of the holiday season.

The only *Lemon* factor implicated in this case directs us to inquire whether the "principal or primary effect" of the challenged government practice is "one that neither advances nor inhibits religion." The requirement of neutrality inherent in that formulation has sometimes been stated in categorical terms. For example, in *Everson* v. *Board of Education*, the first case in our modern Establishment Clause jurisprudence, *Justice BLACK* wrote that the Clause forbids laws "which aid one religion, aid all religions, or prefer one religion over another." We have stated that government "must be neutral in matters of religious theory, doctrine, and practice" and "may not aid, foster, or promote one religion or religious theory against another or even against the ⊥**657** militant opposite." *Epperson* v. *Arkansas*. And we have spoken of a prohibition against conferring an "'imprimatur of state approval'" on religion, *Mueller* v. *Allen* (quoting *Wid-*

mar v. *Vincent)*, or "favor[ing] the adherents of any sect or religious organization." *Gillette* v. *United States*.

These statements must not give the impression of a formalism that does not exist. Taken to its logical extreme, some of the language quoted above would require a relentless extirpation of all contact between government and religion. But that is not the history or the purpose of the Establishment Clause. Government policies of accommodation, acknowledgment, and support for religion are an accepted part of our political and cultural heritage. As *Chief Justice BURGER* wrote for the Court in *Walz* v. *Tax Comm'n*, we must be careful to avoid "[t]he hazards of placing too much weight on a few words or phrases of the Court," and so we have "declined to construe the Religion Clauses with a literalness that would undermine the ultimate constitutional objective as illuminated by history."

Rather than requiring government to avoid any action that acknowledges or aids religion, the Establishment Clause permits government some latitude in recognizing and accommodating the central role religion plays in our society. *Lynch* v. *Donnelly*, *Walz* v. *Tax Comm'n*. Any approach less sensitive to our heritage would border on latent hostility toward religion, as it would require government in all its multifaceted roles to acknowledge only the secular, to the exclusion and so to the detriment of the religious. A categorical approach would install federal courts as jealous guardians of an absolute "wall of separation," sending a clear message of disapproval. In this century, as the modern administrative state expands to touch the lives of its citizens in such diverse ways and redi⊥**658**rects their financial choices through programs of its own, it is difficult to maintain the fiction that requiring government to avoid all assistance to religion can in fairness be viewed as serving the goal of neutrality.

Our cases reflect this understanding. In *Zorach* v. *Clauson*, for example, we permitted New York City's public school system to accommodate the religious preferences of its students by giving them the option of staying in school or leaving to attend religious classes for part of the day. *Justice DOUGLAS* wrote for the Court:

"When the state encourages religious instruction . . . it follows the best of our traditions. For it then respects the religious nature of our people and accommodates the public service to their spiritual needs. To hold that it may not would be to find in the Constitution a requirement that the government show a callous indifference to religious groups. That would be preferring those who believe in no religion over those who do believe."

Nothing in the First Amendment compelled New York City to establish the release-time policy in *Zorach*, but the fact that the policy served to aid religion, and in particular those sects that offer religious education to the young, did not invalidate the accommodation. Likewise, we have upheld government programs supplying textbooks to students in parochial schools, *Board of Education* v. *Allen*, providing grants to church-sponsored universities and colleges, *Roemer* v. *Maryland Bd. of Public Works*, *Tilton* v. *Richardson*, and exempting churches from the obligation to pay taxes, *Walz* v. *Tax Comm'n*. These programs all have the effect of providing substantial benefits to particular religions, see, e.g., *Tilton* (grants to church-sponsored educational institutions "surely aid" those institutions), but they are nonetheless permissible. See *Lynch* v. *Donnelly*, *McGowan* v. ⊥**659** *Maryland*, *Illinois ex rel. McCollum* v. *Board of Education*. As *Justice GOLDBERG* wrote *in Abington School District* v. *Schempp:*

"It is said, and I agree, that the attitude of government toward religion must be one of neutrality. But untutored devotion to the concept of neutrality can lead to invocation or approval of results which partake not simply of that noninterference and noninvolvement with the religious which the Constitution commands, but of a brooding and pervasive devotion to the secular and a passive, or even active, hostility to the religious. Such results are not only not compelled by the Constitution, but, it seems to me, are prohibited by it.

"Neither government nor this Court can or should ignore the significance of the fact that a vast portion of our people believe in and worship God and that many of our legal, political and personal values derive historically from religious teachings. Government must inevitably take cognizance of the existence of religion . . ." (Goldberg, J., concurring, joined by Harlan, J.).

The ability of the organized community to recognize and accommodate religion in a society with a pervasive public sector requires diligent observance of the border between accommodation and establishment. Our cases disclose two limiting principles: government may not coerce anyone to support or participate in any religion or its exercise; and it may not, in the guise of avoiding hostility or callous indifference, give direct benefits to religion in such a degree that it in fact "establishes a [state] religion or religious faith, or tends to do so." *Lynch* v. *Donnelly*. These two principles, while distinct, are not unrelated, for it would be difficult indeed to establish a religion without some measure of more or less subtle coercion, be it in the form of taxation to supply the substantial benefits that would sustain ⊥**660** a state-established faith, direct compulsion to observance, or governmental exhortation to religiosity that amounts in fact to proselytizing.

It is no surprise that without exception we have invalidated actions that further the interests of religion through the coercive power of government. Forbidden involvements include compelling or coercing participation or attendance at a religious activity, see *Engel* v. *Vitale*, *McGowan* v. *Maryland* (discussing *McCollum* v. *Board of Education)*, requiring religious oaths to obtain government office or benefits, *Torcaso* v. *Watkins*, or delegating government power to religious groups, *Larkin* v. *Grendel's Den, Inc*. The freedom to worship as one pleases without government interference or oppression is the great object of both the Establishment and the Free

Exercise Clauses. Barring all attempts to aid religion through government coercion goes far toward attainment of this object. See *McGowan* v. *Maryland*, quoting 1 Annals of Congress 730 (1789) (James Madison, who proposed the First Amendment in Congress, "'apprehended the meaning of the [Religion Clauses] to be, that Congress should not establish a religion, and enforce the legal observation of it by law, nor compel men to worship God in any manner contrary to their conscience'"); *Cantwell* v. *Connecticut* (the Religion Clauses "forestal[l] compulsion by law of the acceptance of any creed or the practice of any form of worship").

As *Justice BLACKMUN* observes, some of our recent cases reject the view that coercion is the sole touchstone of an Establishment Clause violation. See *Engel* v. *Vitale* (dictum) (rejecting, without citation of authority, proposition that coercion is required to demonstrate an Establishment Clause violation); *Abington School District* v. *Schempp; Nyquist*. That may be true if by "coercion" is meant **⊥661** *direct* coercion in the classic sense of an establishment of religion that the Framers knew. But coercion need not be a direct tax in aid of religion or a test oath. Symbolic recognition or accommodation of religious faith may violate the Clause in an extreme case. I doubt not, for example, that the Clause forbids a city to permit the permanent erection of a large Latin cross on the roof of city hall. This is not because government speech about religion is *per se* suspect, as the majority would have it, but because such an obtrusive year-round religious display would place the government's weight behind an obvious effort to proselytize on behalf of a particular religion. Cf. *Friedman* v. *Board of County Comm'rs of Bernalillo County* (en banc) (Latin cross on official county seal); *American Civil Liberties Union of Georgia* v. *Rabun County Chamber of Commerce, Inc.* (cross erected in public park); *Lowe* v. *Eugene* (same). Speech may coerce in some circumstances, but this does not justify a ban on all government recognition of religion. As *Chief Justice BURGER* wrote for the Court in *Walz*:

"The general principle deducible from the First Amendment and all that has been said by the Court is this: that we will not tolerate either governmentally established religion or governmental interference with religion. Short of those expressly proscribed governmental acts there is room for play in the joints productive of a benevolent neutrality which will permit religious exercise to exist **⊥662** without sponsorship and without interference."

This is most evident where the government's act of recognition or accommodation is passive and symbolic, for in that instance any intangible benefit to religion is unlikely to present a realistic risk of establishment. Absent coercion, the risk of infringement of religious liberty by passive or symbolic accommodation is minimal. Our cases reflect this reality by requiring a showing that the symbolic recognition or accommodation advances religion to such a degree that it actually "establishes a religion or religious faith, or tends to do so." *Lynch*.

In determining whether there exists an establishment, or a tendency toward one, we refer to the other types of church-state contacts that have existed unchallenged throughout our history, or that have been found permissible in our caselaw. In *Lynch*, for example, we upheld the city of Pawtucket's holiday display of a crèche, despite the fact that "the display advance[d] religion in a sense." We held that the crèche conferred no greater benefit on religion than did governmental support for religious education, legislative chaplains, "recognition of the origins of the [Christmas] Holiday itself as 'Christ's Mass,'" or many other forms of symbolic or tangible governmental assistance to religious faiths that are ensconced in the safety of national tradition. And in *Marsh* v. *Chambers*, we found that Nebraska's practice of employing a legislative chaplain did not violate the Establishment Clause, because "legislative prayer presents no more potential for establishment than the provision of school transportation, beneficial grants for higher education, or tax exemptions for religious organizations." Non-coercive government action within the realm of flexible accommodation or passive acknowledgment of existing symbols does not violate the Establishment Clause unless it benefits religion in a way **⊥663** more direct and more substantial than practices that are accepted in our national heritage.

II

These principles are not difficult to apply to the facts of the case before us. In permitting the displays on government property of the menorah and the crèche, the city and county sought to do no more than "celebrate the season," and to acknowledge, along with many of their citizens, the historical background and the religious as well as secular nature of the Chanukah and Christmas holidays. This interest falls well within the tradition of government accommodation and acknowledgment of religion that has marked our history from the beginning. It cannot be disputed that government, if it chooses, may participate in sharing with its citizens the joy of the holiday season, by declaring public holidays, installing or permitting festive displays, sponsoring celebrations and parades, and providing holiday vacations for its employees. All levels of our government do precisely that. As we said in *Lynch*, "Government has long recognized—indeed it has subsidized—holidays with religious significance."

If government is to participate in its citizen's celebration of a holiday that contains both a secular and a religious component, enforced recognition of only the secular aspect would **⊥664** signify the callous indifference toward religious faith that our cases and traditions do not require; for by commemorating the holiday only as it is celebrated by nonadherents, the government would be refusing to acknowledge the plain fact, and the historical reality, that many of its citizens celebrate its religious aspects as well. Judicial invalidation of government's attempts to recognize the religious underpinnings of the holiday would signal not neutrality but a pervasive intent to insulate government from all things religious. The Religion Clauses do not require government to acknowledge these holidays or their religious component; but our strong tradition of government accommodation and acknowledgment permits government to do so. See *Lynch* v. *Donnelly*, *Zorach* v. *Clauson*, *Abington School District* v. *Schempp* (Goldberg, J., concurring).

There is no suggestion here that the government's power to coerce has been used to further the interests of Christianity or Judaism in any way. No one was compelled to observe or participate in any religious ceremony or activity. Neither the city nor the county contributed significant amounts of tax money to serve the cause of one religious faith. The crèche and the menorah are purely passive symbols of religious holidays. Passersby who disagree with the message conveyed by these displays are free to ignore them, or even to turn their backs, just as they are free to do when they disagree with any other form of government speech.

There is no realistic risk that the crèche or the menorah represent an effort to proselytize or are otherwise the first step down the road to an establishment of religion. *Lynch* ⊥**665** is dispositive of this claim with respect to the crèche, and I find no reason for reaching a different result with respect to the menorah. Both are the traditional symbols of religious holidays that over time have acquired a secular component. Without ambiguity, *Lynch* instructs that "the focus of our inquiry must be on the [religious symbol] in the context of the [holiday] season." In that context, religious displays that serve "to celebrate the Holiday and to depict the origins of that Holiday" give rise to no Establishment Clause concern. If Congress and the state legislatures do not run afoul of the Establishment Clause when they begin each day with a state-sponsored prayer for divine guidance offered by a chaplain whose salary is paid at government expense, I cannot comprehend how a menorah or a crèche, displayed in the limited context of the holiday season, can be invalid.

Respondents say that the religious displays involved here are distinguishable from the crèche in *Lynch* because they are located on government property and are not surrounded ⊥**666** by the candy canes, reindeer, and other holiday paraphernalia that were a part of the display in *Lynch*. Nothing in *Chief Justice BURGER's* opinion for the Court in *Lynch* provides support for these purported distinctions. After describing the facts, the *Lynch* opinion makes no mention of either of these factors. It concentrates instead on the significance of the crèche as part of the entire holiday season. Indeed, it is clear that the Court did not view the secular aspects of the display as somehow subduing the religious message conveyed by the crèche, for the majority expressly rejected the dissenters' suggestion that it sought "'to explain away the clear religious import of the crèche'" or had "equated the crèche with a Santa's house or reindeer." Crucial to the Court's conclusion was not the number, prominence, or type of secular items contained in the holiday display but the simple fact that, when displayed by government during the Christmas season, a crèche presents no realistic danger of moving government down the forbidden road toward an establishment of religion. Whether the crèche be surrounded by poinsettias, talking wishing wells, or carolers, the conclusion remains the same, for the relevant context is not the items in the display itself but the season as a whole.

The fact that the crèche and menorah are both located on government property, even at the very seat of government, is likewise inconsequential. In the first place, the *Lynch* Court did not rely on the fact that the setting for Pawtucket's display was a privately owned park, and it is difficult to suggest that anyone could have failed to receive a message of government sponsorship after observing Santa Claus ride the city fire engine to the park to join with the Mayor of Pawtucket in inaugurating the holiday season by turning on the lights of the city-owned display. Indeed, the District Court in *Lynch* found that "people might reasonably mistake ⊥**667** the Park for public property," and rejected as "frivolous" the suggestion that the display was not directly associated with the city.

Our cases do not suggest, moreover, that the use of public property necessarily converts otherwise permissible government conduct into an Establishment Clause violation. To the contrary, in some circumstances the First Amendment may *require* that government property be available for use by religious groups, see *Widmar* v. *Vincent*, *Fowler* v. *Rhode Island*, *Niemotko* v. *Maryland*, and even where not required, such use has long been permitted. The prayer approved in *Marsh* v. *Chambers*, for example, was conducted in the legislative chamber of the State of Nebraska, surely the single place most likely to be thought the center of state authority.

Nor can I comprehend why it should be that placement of a government-owned crèche on private land is lawful while placement of a privately owned crèche on public land is not. If anything, I should have thought government ownership of a religious symbol presented the more difficult question under the Establishment Clause, but as *Lynch* resolved that question to sustain the government action, the sponsorship here ought to be all the easier to sustain. In short, nothing about the religious displays here distinguishes them in any meaningful way from the crèche we permitted in *Lynch*.

If *Lynch* is still good law—and until today it was—the judgment below cannot stand. I accept and indeed approve both the holding and the reasoning of *Chief Justice BURGER's* opinion in *Lynch*, and so I must dissent from the judgment that the crèche is unconstitutional. On the same reasoning, I agree that the menorah display is constitutional.

⊥**668** III

The majority invalidates display of the crèche, not because it disagrees with the interpretation of *Lynch* applied above, but because it chooses to discard the reasoning of the *Lynch* majority opinion in favor of *Justice O'CONNOR's* concurring opinion in that case. It has never been my understanding that a concurring opinion "suggest[ing] a clarification of our . . . doctrine," *Lynch* (O'Connor, J., concurring), could take precedence over an opinion joined in its entirety by five Members of the Court. As a general rule, the principle of *stare decisis* directs us to adhere not only to the holdings of our prior cases, but also to their explications of the governing rules of law. Since the majority does not state its intent to overrule *Lynch* I find its refusal to apply the reasoning of that decision quite confusing.

Even if *Lynch* did not control, I would not commit this Court to the test applied by the majority today. The notion that cases arising under the Establishment Clause should be decided by an inquiry into whether a "'reasonable observer'" may "'fairly understand'" government action to "'sen[d] a message to nonadherents that they are outsiders, not full members of the political community,'" is a recent, and in my view most unwelcome, addition to our tangled Establishment Clause jurisprudence. Although a scattering of our cases have used "endorsement" as, another word for "preference" or "imprimatur," the endorsement test applied by the majority had its genesis in *Justice O'CONNOR's* concurring opinion in *Lynch*. See also *Corporation of the Presiding Bishop* v. *Amos* (O'Connor, J., concurring in judgment); *Estate of Thornton* v. *Caldor, Inc.* (O'Connor, J., concurring); *Wal***⊥669***lace* v. *Jaffree* (O'Connor, J., concurring in judgment). The endorsement test has been criticized by some scholars in the field, see, *e.g.*, Smith, Symbols, Perceptions, and Doctrinal Illusions: Establishment Neutrality and the "No Endorsement" Test, 86 Mich. L. Rev. 266 (1987); Tushnet, The Constitution of Religion, 18 Conn. L. Rev. 701, 711-712 (1986). Only one opinion for the Court has purported to apply it in full, see *School Dist. of Grand Rapids* v. *Ball*, but the majority's opinion in this case suggests that this novel theory is fast becoming a permanent accretion to the law. See also *Texas Monthly Inc.*, v. *Bullock* (opinion of Brennan, J.). For the reasons expressed below, I submit that the endorsement test is flawed in its fundamentals and unworkable in practice. The uncritical adoption of this standard is every bit as troubling as the bizarre result it produces in the case before us.

A

I take it as settled law that, whatever standard the Court applies to Establishment Clause claims, it must at least suggest results consistent with our precedents and the historical practices that, by tradition, have informed our First Amendment jurisprudence. It is true that, for reasons quite unrelated to the First Amendment, displays commemorating religious holidays were not commonplace in 1791. See generally J. Barnett, The American Christmas: A Study in National Culture 2-11 (1954). But the relevance of history is not confined to the inquiry into whether the challenged practice itself is a part of our accepted traditions dating back to the Founding.

Our decision in *Marsh* v. *Chambers* illustrates this proposition. The dissent in that case sought to characterize the decision as "carving out an exception to the Establishment **⊥670** Clause rather than reshaping Establishment Clause doctrine to accommodate legislative prayer," (Brennan, J., dissenting), but the majority rejected the suggestion that "historical patterns ca[n] justify contemporary violations of constitutional guarantees." *Marsh* stands for the proposition, not that specific practices common in 1791 are an exception to the otherwise broad sweep of the Establishment Clause, but rather that the meaning of the Clause is to be determined by reference to historical practices and understandings. Whatever test we choose to apply must permit not only legitimate practices two centuries old but also any other practices with no greater potential for an establishment of religion. See *Committee for Public Education* v. *Nyquist* (Rehnquist, J., dissenting in part). The First Amendment is a rule, not a digest or compendium. A test for implementing the protections of the Establishment Clause that, if applied with consistency, would invalidate longstanding traditions cannot be a proper reading of the Clause.

If the endorsement test, applied without artificial exceptions for historical practice, reached results consistent with history, my objections to it would have less force. But, as I understand that test, the touchstone of an Establishment Clause violation is whether nonadherents would be made to feel like "outsiders" by government recognition or accommodation of religion. Few of our traditional practices recognizing the part religion plays in our society can withstand scrutiny under a faithful application of this formula.

⊥671 Some examples suffice to make plain my concerns. Since the Founding of our Republic, American Presidents have issued Thanksgiving Proclamations establishing a national day of celebration and prayer. The first such proclamation was issued by President Washington at the request of the First Congress, and "recommend[ed] and assign[ed]" a day "to be devoted by the people of these States to the service of that great and glorious Being who is the beneficent author of all the good that was, that is, or that will be," so that "we may then unite in most humbly offering our prayers and supplications to the great Lord and Ruler of Nations, and beseech Him to . . . promote the knowledge and practice of true religion and virtue. . . ." 1 J. Richardson, A Compilation of Messages and Papers of the Presidents, 1789-1897, p. 64 (1899). Most of President Washington's successors have followed suit, and the forthrightly religious nature of these proclamations has not waned with the years. President Franklin D. Roosevelt went so far as to "suggest a nationwide reading of the Holy Scriptures during the period from Thanksgiving Day to Christmas" so that "we may bear more earnest witness to our gratitude to Almighty God." Presidential Proclamation No. 2629, 58 Stat. 1160. It requires little imagination to conclude that these proclamations would cause nonadherents to feel excluded, yet they have been a part of our national heritage from the beginning.

⊥672 The Executive has not been the only Branch of our Government to recognize the central role of religion in our society. The fact that this Court opens its sessions with the request that "God save the United States and this honorable Court" has been noted elsewhere. See *Lynch*. The Legislature has gone much further, not only employing legislative chaplains, see 2 U.S.C. § 61d, but also setting aside a special prayer room in the Capitol for use by Members of the House and Senate. The room is decorated with a large stained glass panel that depicts President Washington kneeling in prayer; around him is etched the first verse of the 16th Psalm: "Preserve me, O God, for in Thee do I put my trust." Beneath the panel is a rostrum on which a Bible is placed; next to the rostrum is an American Flag. See We the People: The Story of the United States Capitol 122 (1978). Some endorsement is inherent in these reasonable accommodations, yet the Establishment Clause does not forbid them.

The United States Code itself contains religious references that would be suspect under the endorsement test. Congress has directed the President to "set aside and proclaim a suitable day each year . . . as a National Day of Prayer, on which the people of the United States may turn to God in prayer and meditation at churches, in groups, and as individuals." 36 U.S.C. § 169h. This statute does not require anyone to pray, of course, but it is a straightforward endorsement of the concept of "turn[ing] to God in prayer." Also by statute, the Pledge of Allegiance to the Flag describes the United States as "one Nation under God." 36 U.S.C. § 172. **⊥673** To be sure, no one is obligated to recite this phrase, see *West Virginia State Board of Education* v. *Barnette*, but it borders on sophistry to suggest that the "'reasonable'" atheist would not feel less than a "'full membe[r] of the political community'" every time his fellow Americans recited, as part of their expression of patriotism and love for country, a phrase he believed to be false. Likewise, our national motto, "In God we trust," 36 U.S.C. § 186, which is prominently engraved in the wall above the Speaker's dias in the Chamber of the House of Representatives and is reproduced on every coin minted and every dollar printed by the Federal Government, 31 U.S.C. §§ 5112(d)(1), 5114(b), must have the same effect.

If the intent of the Establishment Clause is to protect individuals from mere feelings of exclusion, then legislative prayer cannot escape invalidation. It has been argued that "[these] government acknowledgments of religion serve, in the only ways reasonably possible in our culture, the legitimate secular purposes of solemnizing public occasions, expressing confidence in the future, and encouraging the recognition of what is worthy of appreciation in society." *Lynch* (O'Connor, J., concurring). I fail to see why prayer is the only way to convey these messages; appeals to patriotism, moments of silence, and any number of other approaches would be as effective, were the only purposes at issue the ones described by the *Lynch* concurrence. Nor is it clear to me why "encouraging the recognition of what is worthy of appreciation in society" can be characterized as a purely secular purpose, if it can be achieved only through religious prayer. No doubt prayer is "worthy of appreciation," but that is most assuredly not because it is secular. Even accepting the secular-solemnization explanation at face value, moreover, it seems incredible to suggest that the average observer of legislative prayer who either believes in no religion or whose faith rejects the concept of God would not receive the clear message that his faith is out of step with the politi**⊥674**cal norm. Either the endorsement test must invalidate scores of traditional practices recognizing the place religion holds in our culture, or it must be twisted and stretched to avoid inconsistency with practices we know to have been permitted in the past, while condemning similar practices with no greater endorsement effect simply by reason of their lack of historical antecedent. Neither result is acceptable.

B

In addition to disregarding precedent and historical fact, the majority's approach to government use of religious symbolism threatens to trivialize constitutional adjudication. By mischaracterizing the Court's opinion in *Lynch* as an endorsement-in-context test, the majority embraces a jurisprudence of minutiae. A reviewing court must consider whether the city has included Santas, talking wishing wells, reindeer, or other secular symbols as "a center of attention separate from the crèche." After determining whether these centers of attention are sufficiently "separate" that each "had their specific visual story to tell," the court must then measure their proximity to the crèche. A community that wishes to construct a constitutional display must also **⊥675** take care to avoid floral frames or other devices that might insulate the crèche from the sanitizing effect of the secular portions of the display. The majority also notes the presence of evergreens near the crèche that are identical to two small evergreens placed near official county signs. After today's decision, municipal greenery must be used with care.

Another important factor will be the prominence of the setting in which the display is placed. In this case, the Grand Staircase of the county courthouse proved too resplendent. Indeed, the Court finds that this location itself conveyed an "unmistakable message that [the county] supports and promotes the Christian praise to God that is the crèche's religious message."

My description of the majority's test, though perhaps uncharitable, is intended to illustrate the inevitable difficulties with its application. This test could provide workable guidance to the lower courts, if ever, only after this Court has decided a long series of holiday display cases, using little more than intuition and a tape measure. Deciding cases on ⊥**676** the basis of such an unguided examination of marginalia is irreconcilable with the imperative of applying neutral principles in constitutional adjudication. "It would be appalling to conduct litigation under the Establishment Clause as if it were a trademark case, with experts testifying about whether one display is really like another, and witnesses testifying they were offended—but would have been less so were the crèche five feet closer to the jumbo candy cane." *American Jewish Congress* v. *Chicago* (Easterbrook, J., dissenting).

Justice BLACKMUN employs in many respects a similar analysis with respect to the menorah, principally discussing its proximity to the Christmas tree and whether "it is . . . more sensible to interpret the menorah in light of the tree, rather than vice versa." (O'Connor, J., concurring in part and concurring in judgment) (concluding that combination of tree, menorah, and salute to liberty conveys no message of endorsement to reasonable observers). *Justice BLACKMUN* goes further, however, and in upholding the menorah as an acknowledgment of a holiday with secular aspects emphasizes the city's lack of "reasonable alternatives that are less religious in nature." This least-religious-means test presents several difficulties. First, it creates an internal inconsistency in *Justice BLACKMUN's* opinion. *Justice BLACKMUN* earlier suggests that the display of a crèche is sometimes constitutional. But it is obvious that there are innumerable secular symbols of Christmas, and that there will always be a more secular alternative available in place of a crèche. Second, the test as applied by *Justice BLACKMUN* is unworkable, for it requires not only that the Court engage in the unfamiliar task of deciding whether a particular alterna⊥**677**tive symbol is more or less religious, but also whether the alternative would "look out of place." Third, although *Justice BLACKMUN* purports not to be overruling *Lynch*, the more-secular-alternative test contradicts that decision, as it comes not from the Court's opinion, nor even from the concurrence, but from the dissent. See (Brennan, J., dissenting). The Court in *Lynch* noted that the dissent "argues that the city's objectives could have been achieved without including the crèche in the display." "True or false," we said, "that is irrelevant."

The result the court reaches in this case is perhaps the clearest illustration of the unwisdom of the endorsement test. Although *Justice O'CONNOR* disavows *Justice BLACKMUN's* suggestion that the minority or majority status of a religion is relevant to the question whether government recognition constitutes a forbidden endorsement (O'Connor, J., concurring in part and concurring in judgment), the very nature of the endorsement test, with its emphasis on the feelings of the objective observer, easily lends itself to this type of inquiry. If there be such a person as the "reasonable observer," I am quite certain that he or she will take away a salient message from our holding in this case: the Supreme Court of the United States has concluded that the First Amendment creates classes of religion based on the relative numbers of their adherents. Those religions enjoying the largest following must be consigned to the status of least-favored faiths so as to avoid any possible risk of offending members of minority religions. I would be the first to admit that many questions arising under the Establishment Clause do not admit of easy answers, but whatever the Clause requires, it is not the result reached by the Court today.

IV

The approach adopted by the majority contradicts important values embodied in the Clause. Obsessive, implacable resistance to all but the most carefully scripted and secu⊥**678**larized forms of accommodation requires this Court to act as a censor, issuing national decrees as to what is orthodox and what is not. What is orthodox, in this context, means what is secular; the only Christmas the State can acknowledge is one in which references to religion have been held to a minimum. The Court thus lends its assistance to an Orwellian rewriting of history as many understand it. I can conceive of no judicial function more antithetical to the First Amendment.

A further contradiction arises from the majority's approach, for the Court also assumes the difficult and inappropriate task of saying what every religious symbol means. Before studying this case, I had not known the full history of the menorah, and I suspect the same was true of my colleagues. More important, this history was, and is, likely unknown to the vast majority of people of all faiths who saw the symbol displayed in Pittsburgh. Even if the majority is quite right about the history of the menorah, it hardly follows that this same history informed the observer's view of the symbol and reason for its presence. This Court is illequipped to sit as a national theology board, and I question both the wisdom and the constitutionality of its doing so. Indeed, were I required to choose between the approach taken by the majority and a strict separationist view, I would have to respect the consistency of the latter.

The case before us is admittedly a troubling one. It must be conceded that, however neutral the purpose of the city and the county, the eager proselytizer may seek to use these symbols for his own ends. The urge to use them to teach or to taunt is always present. It is also true that some devout adherents of Judaism or Christianity may be as offended by the holiday display as are nonbelievers, if not more so. To place these religious symbols in a common hallway or sidewalk, where they may be ignored or even insulted, must be distasteful to many who cherish their meaning.

⊥**679** For these reasons, I might have voted against installation of these particular displays were I a local legislative official. But we have no jurisdiction over matters of taste within the realm of constitutionally permissible discretion. Our role is enforcement of a written Constitution. In my view, the principles of the Establishment Clause and our Nation's historic traditions of diversity and pluralism allow communities to make reasonable judgments respecting the accommodation or acknowledgment of holidays with both cultural and religious aspects. No constitutional violation occurs when they do so by displaying a symbol of the holiday's religious origins.

I dissent.

CAPITOL SQUARE REVIEW AND ADVISORY BOARD v. VINCENT J. PINETTE, DONNIE A. CARR and KNIGHTS OF THE KU KLUX KLAN

115 S. Ct. 2440
ON WRIT OF CERTIORARI TO THE
UNITED STATES COURT OF APPEALS FOR THE SIXTH CIRCUIT
Argued April 26, 1995 — Decided June 29, 1995

⊥**2444** *Justice SCALIA* announced the judgment of the Court and delivered the opinion of the Court with respect to Parts I, II, and III, and an opinion with respect to Part IV, in which *The CHIEF JUSTICE*, *Justice KENNEDY* and *Justice THOMAS* join.

The Establishment Clause of the First Amendment, made binding upon the States through the Fourteenth Amendment, provides that government "shall make no law respecting an establishment of religion." The question in this case is whether a State violates the Establishment Clause when, pursuant to a religiously neutral state policy, it permits a private party to display an unattended religious symbol in a traditional public forum located next to its seat of government.

I

Capitol Square is a 10-acre, state-owned plaza surrounding the Statehouse in Columbus, Ohio. For over a century the square has been used for public speeches, gatherings, and festivals advocating and celebrating a variety of causes, both secular and religious. Ohio Admin. Code Ann. § 128-4-02(A) (1994) makes the square available "for use by the public . . . for free discussion of public questions, or for activities of a broad public purpose," and Ohio Rev. Code Ann. § 105.41 (1994), gives the Capitol Square Review and Advisory Board responsibility for regulating public access. To use the square, a group must simply fill out an official application form and meet several criteria, which concern primarily safety, sanitation, and non-interference with other uses of the square, and which are neutral as to the speech content of the proposed event. Ohio Admin. Code § 128-4-02 (1994).

It has been the Board's policy "to allow a broad range of speakers and other gatherings of people to conduct events on the Capitol Square." Such diverse groups as homosexual rights organizations, the Ku Klux Klan and the United Way have held rallies. The Board has also permitted a variety of unattended dis⊥**2445**plays on Capitol Square: a State-sponsored lighted tree during the Christmas season, a privately-sponsored menorah during Chanukah, a display showing the progress of a United Way fundraising campaign, and booths and exhibits during an arts festival. Although there was some dispute in this litigation regarding the frequency of unattended displays, the District Court found, with ample justification, that there was no policy against them. 844 F. Supp. 1182, 1184 (SD Ohio 1993).

In November 1993, after reversing an initial decision to ban unattended holiday displays from the square during December 1993, the Board authorized the State to put up its annual Christmas tree. On November 29, 1993, the Board granted a rabbi's application to erect a menorah. That same day, the Board received an application from respondent Donnie Carr, an officer of the Ohio Ku Klux Klan, to place a cross on the square from December 8, 1993, to December 24, 1993. The Board denied that application on December 3, informing the Klan by letter that the decision to deny "was made upon the advice of counsel, in a good faith attempt to comply with the Ohio and United States Constitutions, as they have been interpreted in relevant decisions by the Federal and State Courts."

Two weeks later, having been unsuccessful in its effort to obtain administrative relief from the Board's decision, the Ohio Klan, through its leader Vincent Pinette, filed the present suit in the United States District Court for the Southern District of Ohio, seeking an injunction requiring the Board to issue the requested permit. The Board defended on the ground that the permit would violate the Establishment Clause. The District Court determined that Capitol Square was a traditional public forum open to all without any policy against free-standing displays; that the Klan's cross was entirely private expression entitled to full First Amendment protection; and that the Board had failed to show that the display of the cross could reasonably be construed as endorsement of Christianity by the State. The District Court issued the injunction and, after the Board's application for an emergency stay was denied (Stevens, J., in chambers), the Board permitted the Klan to erect its cross. The Board then received, and granted, several additional applications to erect crosses on Capitol Square during December 1993 and January 1994.

On appeal by the Board, the United States Court of Appeals for the Sixth Circuit affirmed the District Court's judgment. 30 F. 3d 675 (1994). That decision agrees with a ruling by the Eleventh Circuit, *Chabad-Lubavitch* v. *Miller*, but disagrees with decisions of the Second and Fourth Circuits, *Chabad-Lubavitch* v. *Burlington*, *Kaplan* v. *Burlington*, *Smith* v. *County of Albemarle*. We granted certiorari.

II

First, a preliminary matter: Respondents contend that we should treat this as a case in which freedom of speech (the Klan's right to present the message of the cross display) was denied because of the State's disagreement with that message's political content, rather than because of the State's desire to distance itself from sectarian religion. They suggest in their merits brief and in their oral argument that Ohio's genuine reason for disallowing the display was disapproval of the political views of the Ku Klux Klan. Whatever the fact may be, the case was not presented and decided that way. The record facts before us and the opinions below address only the Establishment Clause issue; that is the question upon which we granted certiorari; and that is the sole question before us to decide.

⊥2446 Respondents' religious display in Capitol Square was private expression. Our precedent establishes that private religious speech, far from being a First Amendment orphan, is as fully protected under the Free Speech Clause as secular private expression. *Lamb's Chapel* v. *Center Moriches Union Free School Dist.*; *Board of Ed. of Westside Community Schools (Dist. 66)* v. *Mergens*; *Widmar* v. *Vincent*; *Heffron* v. *International Soc. for Krishna Consciousness, Inc.* Indeed, in Anglo-American history, at least, government suppression of speech has so commonly been directed *precisely* at religious speech that a free-speech clause without religion would be *Hamlet* without the prince. Accordingly, we have not excluded from free-speech protections religious proselytizing, *Heffron*, or even acts of worship, *Widmar*. Petitioners do not dispute that respondents, in displaying their cross, were engaging in constitutionally protected expression. They do contend that the constitutional protection does not extend to the length of permitting that expression to be made on Capitol Square.

It is undeniable, of course, that speech which is constitutionally protected against state suppression is not thereby accorded a guaranteed forum on all property owned by the State. *Postal Service* v. *Council of Greenburgh Civic Assns.*; *Perry Ed. Assn.* v. *Perry Local Educators' Assn.* The right to use government property for one's private expression depends upon whether the property has by law or tradition been given the status of a public forum, or rather has been reserved for specific official uses. *Cornelius* v. *NAACP Legal Defense & Ed. Fund, Inc.* If the former, a State's right to limit protected expressive activity is sharply circumscribed: it may impose reasonable, content-neutral time, place and manner restrictions (a ban on all unattended displays, which did not exist here, might be one such), but it may regulate expressive *content* only if such a restriction is necessary, and narrowly drawn, to serve a compelling state interest. *Perry Ed. Assn.* These strict standards apply here, since the District Court and the Court of Appeals found that Capitol Square was a traditional public forum. 844 F. Supp., at 1184; 30 F. 3d, at 678.

Petitioners do not claim that their denial of respondents' application was based upon a content-neutral time, place, or manner restriction. To the contrary, they concede—indeed it is the essence of their case—that the Board rejected the display precisely because its content was religious. Petitioners advance a single justification for closing Capitol Square to respondents' cross: the State's interest in avoiding official endorsement of Christianity, as required by the Establishment Clause.

III

There is no doubt that compliance with the Establishment Clause is a state interest sufficiently compelling to justify content-based restrictions on speech. Whether that interest is implicated here, however, is a different question. And we do not write on a blank slate in answering it. We have twice previously addressed the combination of private religious expression, a forum available for public use, content-based regulation, and a State's interest in complying with the Establishment Clause. Both times, we have struck down the restriction on religious content. *Lamb's Chapel*; *Widmar*.

In *Lamb's Chapel*, a school district allowed private groups to use school facilities during off-hours for a variety of civic, social and recreational purposes, excluding, however, religious purposes. We held that even if school property during off-hours was not a public forum, the school district violated an **⊥2447** applicant's free-speech rights by denying it use of the facilities solely because of the religious viewpoint of the program it wished to present. We rejected the district's compelling-state-interest Establishment Clause defense (the same made here) because the school property was open to a wide variety of uses, the district was not directly sponsoring the religious group's activity, and "any benefit to religion or to the Church would have been no more than incidental." The *Lamb's Chapel* reasoning applies *a fortiori* here, where the property at issue is not a school but a full-fledged public forum.

Lamb's Chapel followed naturally from our decision in *Widmar*, in which we examined a public university's exclusion of student religious groups from facilities available to other student groups. There also we addressed official discrimination against groups who wished to use a "generally open forum" for religious speech. And there also the State claimed that its compelling interest in complying with the Establishment Clause justified the content-based restriction. We rejected the defense because the forum created by the State was open to a broad spectrum of groups and would provide only incidental benefit to religion. We stated categorically that "an open forum in a public university does not confer any imprimatur of state approval on religious sects or practices."

Quite obviously, the factors that we considered determinative in *Lamb's Chapel* and *Widmar* exist here as well. The State did not sponsor respondents' expression, the expression was made on government property that had been opened to the public for speech, and permission was requested through the same application process and on the same terms required of other private groups.

IV

Petitioners argue that one feature of the present case distinguishes it from *Lamb's Chapel* and *Widmar:* the forum's proximity to the seat of government, which, they contend, may produce the perception that the cross bears the State's approval. They urge us to apply the so-called "endorsement test," see, *e.g., Allegheny County* v. *American Civil Liberties Union, Greater Pittsburgh Chapter; Lynch* v. *Donnelly,* and to find that, because an observer might mistake private expression for officially endorsed religious expression, the State's content-based restriction is constitutional.

We must note, to begin with, that it is not really an "endorsement test" of any sort, much less the "endorsement test" which appears in our more recent Establishment Clause jurisprudence, that petitioners urge upon us. "Endorsement" connotes an expression or demonstration of approval or support. The New Shorter Oxford English Dictionary 818 (1993); Webster's New Dictionary 845 (2d ed. 1950). Our cases have accordingly equated "endorsement" with "promotion" or "favoritism." We find it peculiar to say that government "promotes" or "favors" a religious display by giving it the same access to a public forum that all other displays enjoy. And as a matter of Establishment Clause jurisprudence, we have consistently held that it is no violation for government to enact neutral policies that happen to benefit religion. See, *e.g., Bowen* v. *Kendrick; Witters* v. *Washington Dept. of Services for Blind; Mueller* v. *Allen; McGowan* v. *Maryland.* Where we have tested for endorsement of religion, the subject of the test was either expression *by the government itself, Lynch,* or else government action alleged to *discriminate in favor* of private religious expression or activity, *Board of Ed. of Kiryas Joel Village School Dist.* v. *Grumet, Allegheny County.* The test petitioners propose, which would attribute to ⊥**2448** a neutrally behaving government *private* religious expression, has no antecedent in our jurisprudence, and would better be called a "transferred endorsement" test.

Petitioners rely heavily on *Allegheny County* and *Lynch,* but each is easily distinguished. In *Allegheny County* we held that the display of a privately-sponsored crèche on the "Grand Staircase" of the Allegheny County Courthouse violated the Establishment Clause. That staircase was not, however, open to all on an equal basis, so the County was *favoring* sectarian religious expression ("[t]he Grand Staircase does not appear to be the kind of location in which all were free to place their displays"). We expressly distinguished that site from the kind of public forum at issue here, and made clear that if the staircase were available to all on the same terms, "the presence of the crèche in that location for over six weeks would then *not* serve to associate the government with the crèche" (emphasis added). In *Lynch* we held that a city's display of a crèche did not violate the Establishment Clause because, in context, the display did not endorse religion. The opinion does assume, as petitioners contend, that the *government's* use of religious symbols is unconstitutional if it effectively endorses sectarian religious belief. But the case neither holds nor even remotely assumes that the government's neutral treatment of *private* religious expression can be unconstitutional.

Petitioners argue that absence of perceived endorsement was material in *Lamb's Chapel* and *Widmar.* We did state in *Lamb's Chapel* that there was "no realistic danger that the community would think that the District was endorsing religion or any particular creed." But that conclusion was not the result of empirical investigation; it followed directly, we thought, from the fact that the forum was open and the religious activity privately sponsored. It is significant that we referred only to what would be thought by "the community"—not by outsiders or individual members of the community uninformed about the school's practice. Surely some of the latter, hearing of religious ceremonies on school premises, and not knowing of the premises' availability and use for all sorts of other private activities, *might* leap to the erroneous conclusion of state endorsement. But, we in effect said, given an open forum and private sponsorship, erroneous conclusions do not count. So also in *Widmar.* Once we determined that the benefit to religious groups from the public forum was incidental and shared by other groups, we categorically rejected the State's Establishment Clause defense.

What distinguishes *Allegheny County* and the dictum in *Lynch* from *Widmar* and *Lamb's Chapel* is the difference between government speech and private speech. "[T]here is a crucial difference between *government* speech endorsing religion, which the Establishment Clause forbids, and *private* speech endorsing religion, which the Free Speech and Free Exercise Clauses protect." *Mergens.* Petitioners assert, in effect, that that distinction disappears when the private speech is conducted too close to the symbols of government. But that, of course, must be merely a subpart of a more general principle: that the distinction disappears whenever private speech can be mistaken for government speech. That proposition cannot be accepted, at least where, as here, the government has not fostered or encouraged the mistake.

Of course, giving sectarian religious speech preferential access to a forum close to the seat of government (or anywhere else for ⊥**2449** that matter) would violate the Establishment Clause (as well as the Free Speech Clause, since it would involve content discrimination). And one can conceive of a case in which a governmental entity manipulates its administration of a public forum close to the seat of government (or within a government building) in such a manner that only certain religious groups take advantage of it, creating an impression of endorsement *that is in fact accurate*. But those situations, which involve governmental *favoritism*, do not exist here. Capitol Square is a genuinely public forum, is known to be a public forum, and has been widely used as a public forum for many, many years. Private religious speech cannot be subject to veto by those who see favoritism where there is none.

The contrary view, most strongly espoused by *Justice* STEVENS, but endorsed by *Justice* SOUTER and *Justice* O'CONNOR as well, exiles private religious speech to a realm of less-protected expression heretofore inhabited only by sexually explicit displays and commercial speech. *Young* v. *American Mini Theatres, Inc.*; *Central Hudson Gas & Electric Corp.* v. *Public Serv. Comm'n of N.Y.* It will be a sad day when this Court casts piety in with pornography, and finds the First Amendment more hospitable to private expletives, see *Cohen* v. *California*, than to private prayers. This would be merely bizarre were religious speech simply *as* protected by the Constitution as other forms of private speech; but it is outright perverse when one considers that private religious expression receives *preferential* treatment under the Free Exercise Clause. It is no answer to say that the Establishment Clause tempers religious speech. By its terms that Clause applies only to the words and acts of *government*. It was never meant, and has never been read by this Court, to serve as an impediment to purely *private* religious speech connected to the State only through its occurrence in a public forum.

Since petitioners' "transferred endorsement" principle cannot possibly be restricted to squares in front of state capitols, the Establishment Clause regime that it would usher in is most unappealing. To require (and permit) access by a religious group in *Lamb's Chapel*, it was sufficient that the group's activity was not in fact government sponsored, that the event was open to the public, and that the benefit of the facilities was shared by various organizations. Petitioners' rule would require school districts adopting similar policies in the future to guess whether some undetermined critical mass of the community might nonetheless perceive the district to be advocating a religious viewpoint. Similarly, state universities would be forced to reassess our statement that "an open forum in a public university does not confer any imprimatur of state approval on religious sects or practices." *Widmar*. Whether it does would henceforth depend upon immediate appearances. Policy makers would find themselves in a vise between the Establishment Clause on one side and the Free Speech and Free Exercise Clauses on the other. Every proposed act of private, religious expression in a public forum would force officials to weigh a host of imponderables. How close to government is too close? What kind of building, and in what context, symbolizes state authority? If the State guessed wrong in one direction, it would be guilty of an Establishment Clause violation; if in the other, it would be liable for suppressing free exercise or free speech (a risk not run when the State restrains only its *own* expression).

The "transferred endorsement" test would also disrupt the settled principle that policies providing incidental benefits to religion do not contravene the Establishment Clause. That principle is the basis for the constitutionality of a broad range of laws, not merely those that implicate free-speech issues, see, *e.g.*, *Witters*; *Mueller*. It has radical implications for our public policy to suggest that neutral laws are invalid whenever hypothetical observers may—*even reason*⊥**2450***ably*—confuse an incidental benefit to religion with state endorsement.

If Ohio is concerned about misperceptions, nothing prevents it from requiring all private displays in the Square to be identified as such. That would be a content-neutral "manner" restriction which is assuredly constitutional. See *Clark* v. *Community for Creative Non-Violence*. But the State may not, on the claim of misperception of official endorsement, ban all private religious speech from the public square, or discriminate against it by requiring religious speech alone to disclaim public sponsorship.

. . . . .

Religious expression cannot violate the Establishment Clause where it (1) is purely private and (2) occurs in a traditional or designated public forum, publicly announced and open to all on equal terms. Those conditions are satisfied here, and therefore the State may not bar respondents' cross from Capitol Square.

The judgment of the Court of Appeals is
affirmed.

Justice THOMAS, concurring.

I join the Court's conclusion that petitioner's exclusion of the Ku Klux Klan's cross cannot be justified on Establishment Clause grounds. But the fact that the legal issue before us involves the Establishment Clause should not lead anyone to think that a cross erected by the Ku Klux Klan is a purely religious symbol. The erection of such a cross is a political act, not a Christian one.

There is little doubt that the Klan's main objective is to establish a racist white government in the United States. In Klan ceremony, the cross is a symbol of white supremacy and a tool for the intimidation and harassment of racial minorities, Catholics, Jews, Communists, and any other groups hated by the Klan. The cross is associated with the Klan not because of religious worship, but because of the Klan's practice of cross-burning. Cross-burning was entirely unknown to the early Ku Klux Klan, which ⊥**2451** emerged in some Southern States during Reconstruction. W. Wade, The Fiery Cross: The Ku Klux Klan in America 146 (1987). The practice appears to have been the product of Thomas Dixon, whose book The Clansman formed the story for the movie, The Birth of a Nation. See M. Newton & J. Newton, The Ku Klux Klan: An Encyclopedia 145-146 (1991). In the book, cross-burning is borrowed from an "old Scottish rite" (Dixon apparently believed that the members of the Reconstruction Ku Klux Klan were the "reincarnated souls of the Clansmen of Old Scotland") that the Klan uses to celebrate the execution of a former slave. T. Dixon, The Clansman: An Historical Romance of the Ku Klux Klan 324-326 (1905). Although the cross took on some religious significance in the 1920's when the Klan became connected with certain southern white clergy, by the postwar period it had reverted to its original function as an instrument of intimidation. Wade.

To be sure, the cross appears to serve as a religious symbol of Christianity for some Klan members. The hymn "The Old Rugged Cross" is sometimes played during cross-burnings. See W. Moore, A Sheet and a Cross: A Symbolic Analysis of the Ku Klux Klan 287-288 (Ph.D. dissertation, Tulane University, 1975). But to the extent that the Klan had a message to communicate in Capitol Square, it was primarily a political one. During his testimony before the District Court, the leader of the local Klan testified that the cross was seen "as a symbol of freedom, as a symbol of trying to unite our people." The Klan chapter wished to erect the cross because it was also "a symbol of freedom from tyranny," and because it "was also incorporated in the confederate battle flag." Of course, the cross also had some religious connotation; the Klan leader linked the cross to what he claimed was one of the central purposes of the Klan: "to establish a Christian government in America." But surely this message was both political and religious in nature.

Although the Klan might have sought to convey a message with some religious component, I think that the Klan had a primarily nonreligious purpose in erecting the cross. The Klan simply has appropriated one of the most sacred of religious symbols as a symbol of hate. In my mind, this suggests that this case may not have truly involved the Establishment Clause, although I agree with the Court's disposition because of the manner in which the case has come before us. In the end, there may be much less here than meets the eye.

Justice O'CONNOR, with whom *Justice* SOUTER and *Justice* BREYER join, concurring in part and concurring in the judgment.

I join Parts I, II, and III of the Court's opinion and concur in the judgment. Despite the messages of bigotry and racism that may be conveyed along with religious connotations by the display of a Ku Klux Klan cross, see (Thomas, J., concurring), at bottom this case must be understood as it has been presented to us—as a case about private religious expression and whether the State's relationship to it violates the Establishment Clause. In my view, "the endorsement test asks the right question about governmental practices challenged on Establishment Clause grounds, including challenged practices involving the display of religious symbols," *Allegheny County* v. *American Civil Liberties Union, Greater Pittsburgh Chapter* (O'Connor, J., concurring in part and concurring in judgment), even where a neutral state policy toward private religious speech in a public forum is at issue. Accordingly, I see no necessity to carve out, as the plurality opinion would today, an exception to the endorsement test for the public forum context.

For the reasons given by *Justice* SOUTER, whose opinion I also join, I conclude on the facts of this case that there is "no realistic danger that the community would think that the [State] was endorsing religion or any particular creed," *Lamb's Chapel* v. *Center Moriches Union Free School Dist.*, by granting respondents a permit to erect their temporary cross on Capitol Square. I write separately, however, to em⊥**2452**phasize that, because it seeks to identify those situations in which government makes "'adherence to a religion relevant . . . to a person's standing in the political community,'" *Allegheny* (quoting *Lynch* v. *Donnelly* (O'Connor, J., concurring)), the endorsement test necessarily focuses upon the perception of a reasonable, informed observer.

I

"In recent years, we have paid particularly close attention [in Establishment Clause cases] to whether the challenged governmental practice either has the purpose or effect of 'endorsing' religion, a concern that has long had a place in our Establishment Clause jurisprudence." *Allegheny*. See also *Lamb's Chapel*; *School Dist. of Grand Rapids* v. *Ball* (asking "whether the symbolic union of church and state effected by the challenged governmental action is sufficiently likely to be perceived by adherents of the controlling denominations as an endorsement, and by the nonadherents as a disapproval, of their individual religious choices"). A government statement "'that religion or a particular religious belief is favored or preferred,'" *Allegheny* (quoting *Wallace* v. *Jaffree* (O'Connor, J., concurring in judgment)), violates the prohibition against establishment of religion because such "[e]ndorsement sends a message to nonadherents that they are outsiders, not full members of the political community, and an accompanying message to adherents that they are insiders, favored members of the political community," *Lynch* (O'Connor, J., concurring). Although "[e]xperience proves that the Establishment Clause . . . cannot easily be reduced to a single test," *Board of Ed. of Kiryas Joel Village School Dist.* v. *Grumet* (O'Connor, J., concurring in part and concurring in judgment), the endorsement inquiry captures the fundamental requirement of the Establishment Clause when courts are called upon to evaluate the constitutionality of religious symbols on public property.

While the plurality would limit application of the endorsement test to "expression *by the government itself*, . . . or else government action alleged to *discriminate in favor* of private religious expression or activity," I believe that an impermissible message of endorsement can be sent in a variety of contexts, not all of which involve direct government speech or outright favoritism. It is true that neither *Allegheny* nor *Lynch*, our two prior religious display cases, involved the same combination of private religious speech and a public forum that we have before us today. Nonetheless, as *Justice SOUTER* aptly demonstrates, we have on several occasions employed an endorsement perspective in Establishment Clause cases where private religious conduct has intersected with a neutral governmental policy providing some benefit in a manner that parallels the instant case. Thus, while I join the discussion of *Lamb's Chapel* and *Widmar* v. *Vincent*, in Part III of the Court's opinion, I do so with full recognition that the factors the Court properly identifies ultimately led in each case to the conclusion that there was no endorsement of religion by the State.

There is, as the plurality notes, "a crucial difference between *government* speech endorsing religion, which the Establishment Clause forbids, and *private* speech endorsing religion, which the Free Speech and Free Exercise Clauses protect." ⊥**2453** *Board of Ed. of Westside Community Schools (Dist. 66)* v. *Mergens*. But the quoted statement was made while applying the endorsement test itself; indeed, the sentence upon which the plurality relies was followed immediately by the conclusion that "secondary school students are mature enough and are likely to understand that a school does not endorse or support student speech that it merely permits on a nondiscriminatory basis." Thus, as I read the decisions *Justice SOUTER* carefully surveys, our prior cases do not imply that the endorsement test has no place where private religious speech in a public forum is at issue. Moreover, numerous lower courts (including the Court of Appeals in this case) have applied the endorsement test in precisely the context before us today. See, *e.g.*, *Chabad-Lubavitch of Georgia* v. *Miller; Kreisner* v. *San Diego; Americans United for Separation of Church and State* v. *Grand Rapids; Doe* v. *Small;* cf. *Smith* v. *County of Albemarle; Kaplan* v. *Burlington*. Given this background, I see no necessity to draw new lines where "[r]eligious expression . . . (1) is purely private and (2) occurs in a traditional or designated public forum."

None of this is to suggest that I would be likely to come to a different result from the plurality where truly private speech is allowed on equal terms in a vigorous public forum that the government has administered properly. That the religious display at issue here was erected by a private group in a public square available "for use by the public . . . for free discussion of public questions, or for activities of a broad public purpose," Ohio Admin. Code Ann. § 128-4-02(A) (1994), certainly informs the Establishment Clause inquiry under the endorsement test. Indeed, many of the factors the plurality identifies are some of those I would consider important in deciding cases like this one where religious speakers seek access to public spaces: "The State did not sponsor respondents' expression, the expression was made on government property that had been opened to the public for speech, and permission was requested through the same application process and on the same terms required of other groups." And, as I read the plurality opinion, a case is not governed by its proposed *per se* rule where such circumstances are otherwise—that is, where preferential placement of a religious symbol in a public space or government manipulation of the forum is involved.

To the plurality's consideration of the open nature of the forum and the private ownership of the display, however, I would add the presence of a sign disclaiming government sponsorship or endorsement on the Klan cross, which would make the State's role clear to the community. This factor is important because, as *Justice SOUTER* makes clear, certain aspects of the cross display in this case arguably intimate government approval of respondents' private religious message—particularly that the cross is an especially potent sectarian symbol which stood unattended in close proximity to official government buildings. In context, a disclaimer helps remove doubt about State approval of respondents' religious message. Cf. *Widmar* ("In light of the large number of groups meeting on campus, however, we doubt students could draw any reasonable inference of University support from the mere fact of a campus meeting place. The University's student handbook already notes that the University's name will not 'be identified in any way with the aims, policies, programs, products, or opinions of any organization or its members'"). On these facts, then, "the message [of inclusion] is one of neutrality rather than endorsement." *Mergens*.

Our agreement as to the outcome of this case, however, cannot mask the fact that I part company with the plurality on a funda⊥**2454**mental point: I disagree that "[i]t has radical implications for our public policy to suggest that neutral laws are invalid whenever hypothetical observers may—*even reasonably*—confuse an incidental benefit to religion with State endorsement." On the contrary, when the reasonable observer would view a government practice as endorsing religion, I believe that it is our *duty* to hold the practice invalid. The plurality today takes an exceedingly narrow view of the Establishment Clause that is out of step both with the Court's prior cases and with well-established notions of what the Constitution requires. The Clause is more than a negative prohibition against certain narrowly defined forms of government favoritism; it also imposes affirmative obligations that may require a State, in some situations, to take steps to avoid being perceived as supporting or endorsing a private religious message. That is, the Establishment Clause forbids a State from hiding behind the application of formally neutral criteria and remaining studiously oblivious to the effects of its actions. Governmental intent cannot control, and not all state policies are permissible under the Religion Clauses simply because they are neutral in form.

Where the government's operation of a public forum has the effect of endorsing religion, even if the governmental actor neither intends nor actively encourages that result, see *Lynch* (O'Connor, J., concurring), the Establishment Clause is violated. This is so not because of "'transferred endorsement,'" or mistaken attribution of private speech to the State, but because the State's own actions (operating the forum in a particular manner and permitting the religious expression to take place therein), and their relationship to the private speech at issue, *actually convey* a message of endorsement. At some point, for example, a private religious group may so dominate a public forum that a formal policy of equal access is transformed into a demonstration of approval. Cf. *Mergens* (concluding that there was no danger of an Establishment Clause violation in a public university's allowing access by student religious groups to facilities available to others "[a]t least in the absence of empirical evidence that religious groups will dominate [the school's] open forum"). Other circumstances may produce the same effect—whether because of the fortuity of geography, the nature of the particular public space, or the character of the religious speech at issue, among others. Our Establishment Clause jurisprudence should remain flexible enough to handle such situations when they arise.

In the end, I would recognize that the Establishment Clause inquiry cannot be distilled into a fixed, *per se* rule. Thus, "[e]very government practice must be judged in its unique circumstances to determine whether it constitutes an endorsement or disapproval of religion." *Lynch* (O'Connor, J., concurring). And this question cannot be answered in the abstract, but instead requires courts to examine the history and administration of a particular practice to determine whether it operates as such an endorsement. I continue to believe that government practices relating to speech on religious topics "must be subjected to careful judicial scrutiny," *ibid.*, and that the endorsement test supplies an appropriate standard for that inquiry.

II

Conducting the review of government action required by the Establishment Clause is always a sensitive matter. Unfortunately, as I noted in *Allegheny*, "even the development of articulable standards and guidelines has not always resulted in agreement among the Members of this Court on the results in individual cases." Today, *Justice STEVENS* reaches a different conclusion regarding whether the Board's decision to allow respondents' display on Capitol Square constituted an impermissible endorsement of the cross' religious message. Yet I believe it is important to note that we have not simply arrived at divergent results after conducting the same analysis. Our fundamental point of departure, it appears, concerns the knowledge that is properly attributed to the test's "reasonable observer [who] evaluates whether a ⊥**2455** challenged governmental practice conveys a message of endorsement of religion." *Id.* (O'Connor, J., concurring in part and concurring in judgment). In my view, proper application of the endorsement test requires that the reasonable observer be deemed more informed than the casual passerby postulated by the dissent.

Because an Establishment Clause violation must be moored in government action of some sort, and because our concern is with the political community writ large, see *Allegheny* (O'Connor, J., concurring in part and concurring in judgment); *Lynch*, the endorsement inquiry is not about the perceptions of particular individuals or saving isolated nonadherents from the discomfort of viewing symbols of a faith to which they do not subscribe. Indeed, to avoid "entirely sweep[ing] away all government recognition and acknowledgment of the role of religion in the lives of our citizens," *Allegheny* (O'Connor, J., concurring in part and concurring in judgment), our Establishment Clause jurisprudence must seek to identify the point at which the government becomes responsible, whether due to favoritism toward or disregard for the evident effect of religious speech, for the injection of religion into the political life of the citizenry.

I therefore disagree that the endorsement test should focus on the actual perception of individual observers, who naturally have differing degrees of knowledge. Under such an approach, a religious display is necessarily precluded so long as some passersby would perceive a governmental endorsement thereof. In my view, however, the endorsement test creates a more collective standard to gauge "the 'objective' meaning of the [government's] statement in the community," *Lynch* (O'Connor, J., concurring). In this respect, the applicable observer is similar to the "reasonable person" in tort law, who "is not to be identified with any ordinary individual, who might occasionally do unreasonable things" but is "rather a personification of a community ideal of reasonable behavior, determined by the [collective] social judgment." W. Keeton et al., Prosser and Keeton on The Law of Torts 175 (5th ed. 1984). Thus, "we do not ask whether there is *any* person who could find an endorsement of religion, whether *some* people may be offended by the display, or whether *some* reasonable person *might* think [the State] endorses religion." *Americans United* v. *Grand Rapids*. Saying that the endorsement inquiry should be conducted from the perspective of a hypothetical observer who is presumed to possess a certain level of information that all citizens might not share neither chooses the perceptions of the majority over those of a "reasonable nonadherent," cf. L. Tribe, American Constitutional Law 1293 (2d ed. 1988), nor invites disregard for the values the Establishment Clause was intended to protect. It simply recognizes the fundamental difficulty inherent in focusing on actual people: there is always *someone* who, with a particular quantum of knowledge, reasonably might perceive a particular action as an endorsement of religion. A State has not made religion relevant to standing in the political community simply because a particular viewer of a display might feel uncomfortable.

It is for this reason that the reasonable observer in the endorsement inquiry must be deemed aware of the history and context of the community and forum in which the religious display appears. As I explained in *Allegheny*, "the 'history and ubiquity' of a practice is relevant because it provides part of the context in which a reasonable observer evaluates whether a challenged governmental practice conveys a message of endorsement of religion." Nor can the knowledge attributed to the reasonable observer be limited to the information gleaned simply from viewing the challenged display. Today's proponents of the endorsement test all agree that we should attribute to the observer knowledge that the cross is a religious symbol, that Capitol Square is owned by the State, and that the large building nearby is the seat of state government. In my view, our hypothetical observer also should know the general histo⊥**2456**ry of the place in which the cross is displayed. Indeed, the fact that Capitol Square is a public park that has been used over time by private speakers of various types is as much a part of the display's context as its proximity to the Ohio Statehouse. Cf. *Allegheny* (noting that "[t]he Grand Staircase does not appear to be the kind of location in which all were free to place their displays for weeks at a time . . . "). This approach does not require us to assume an "'ultra-reasonable observer' who understands the vagaries of this Court's First Amendment jurisprudence," (Stevens, J., dissenting). An informed member of the community will know how the public space in question has been used in the past—and it is that fact, not that the space may meet the legal definition of a public forum, which is relevant to the endorsement inquiry.

The dissent's property-based argument fails to give sufficient weight to the fact that the cross at issue here was displayed in a forum traditionally open to the public. "The very fact that a sign is installed on public property," the dissent suggests, "implies official approval of its message." While this may be the case where a government building and its immediate curtilage are involved, it is not necessarily so with respect to those "places which by long tradition or by government fiat have been devoted to assembly and debate, . . . [particularly] streets and parks which 'have immemorially been held in trust for the use of the public and, time out of mind, have been used for purposes of assembly, communicating thoughts between citizens, and discussing public questions.'" *Perry Ed. Assn.* v. *Perry Local Educators' Assn.* (quoting *Hague* v. *Committee for Industrial Organization*). To the extent there is a presumption that "structures on government property—and, in particular, in front of buildings plainly identified with the State—imply state approval of their message," (Stevens, J., dissenting), that presumption can be rebutted where the property at issue is a forum historically available for private expression. The reasonable observer would recognize the distinction between speech the government supports and speech that it merely allows in a place that traditionally has been open to a range of private speakers accompanied, if necessary, by an appropriate disclaimer.

In this case, I believe, the reasonable observer would view the Klan's cross display fully aware that Capitol Square is a public space in which a multiplicity of groups, both secular and religious, engage in expressive conduct. It is precisely this type of knowledge that we presumed in *Lamb's Chapel* and in *Mergens*. Moreover, this observer would certainly be able to read and understand an adequate disclaimer, which the Klan had informed the State it would include in the display at the time it applied for the permit (Souter, J., concurring in part and concurring in judgment), and the content of which the Board could have defined as it deemed necessary as a condition of granting the Klan's application. Cf. *American Civil Liberties Union* v. *Wilkinson*. On the facts of this case, therefore, I conclude that the reasonable observer would not interpret the State's tolerance of the Klan's private religious display in Capitol Square as an endorsement of religion.

III

"To be sure, the endorsement test depends on a sensitivity to the unique circumstances and context of a particular challenged practice and, like any test that is sensitive to context, it may not always yield results with unanimous agreement at the margins." *Allegheny* (O'Connor, J., concurring in part and concurring in judgment). In my view, however, this flexibility is a virtue and not a vice; "courts must keep in mind both the fundamental place held by the Establishment Clause in our constitutional scheme and the myriad, subtle ways in which Establishment Clause values can be eroded," *Lynch* ⊥**2457** (O'Connor, J., concurring).

I agree that "compliance with the Establishment Clause is a state interest sufficiently compelling to justify content-based restrictions on speech." The Establishment Clause "prohibits government from appearing to take a position on questions of religious belief or from 'making adherence to a religion relevant in any way to a person's standing in the political community.'" *Allegheny* (quoting *Lynch* (O'Connor, J., concurring)). Because I believe that, under the circumstances at issue here, allowing the Klan cross, along with an adequate disclaimer, to be displayed on Capitol Square presents no danger of doing so, I conclude that the State has not presented a compelling justification for denying respondents their permit.

Justice SOUTER, with whom *Justice* O'CONNOR and *Justice* BREYER join, concurring in part and concurring in the judgment.

I concur in Parts I, II, and III of the Court's opinion. I also want to note specifically my agreement with the

Court's suggestion that the State of Ohio could ban all unattended private displays in Capitol Square if it so desired. The fact that the Capitol lawn has been the site of public protests and gatherings, and is the location of any number of the government's own unattended displays, such as statues, does not disable the State from closing the square to all privately owned, unattended structures. A government entity may ban posters on publicly owned utility poles to eliminate visual clutter, *City Council of Los Angeles* v. *Taxpayers for Vincent,* and may bar camping as part of a demonstration in certain public parks, *Clark* v. *Community for Creative Non-Violence*. It may similarly adopt a content-neutral policy prohibiting private individuals and groups from erecting unattended displays in forums around public buildings. See also *Ward* v. *Rock Against Racism* ("[E]ven in a public forum the government may impose reasonable restrictions on the time, place, or manner of protected speech, provided [that] the restrictions 'are justified without reference to the content of the regulated speech, that they are narrowly tailored to serve a significant governmental interest, and that they leave open ample alternative channels for communication of the information,'" quoting *Clark*, at 293).

Otherwise, however, I limit my concurrence to the judgment. Although I agree in the end that, in the circumstances of this case, petitioners erred in denying the Klan's application for a permit to erect a cross on Capitol Square, my analysis of the Establishment Clause issue differs from *Justice SCALIA's*, and I vote to affirm in large part because of the possibility of affixing a sign to the cross adequately disclaiming any government sponsorship or endorsement of it.

The plurality's opinion declines to apply the endorsement test to the Board's action, in favor of a *per se* rule: religious expression cannot violate the Establishment Clause where it (1) is private and (2) occurs in a public forum, even if a reasonable observer would see the expression as indicating state endorsement. This *per se* rule would be an exception to the endorsement test, not previously recognized and out of square with our precedents.

I

My disagreement with the plurality on the law may receive some focus from attention to a matter of straight fact that we see alike: in some circumstances an intelligent observer may mistake private, unattended religious displays in a public forum for government speech endorsing religion. See *ante* (acknowledging that "hypothetical observers may—*even reasonably*—confuse an incidental benefit to religion with state endorsement") (emphasis in original); see also *ante* (noting that an observer might be "misled" by the presence of the cross in **⊥2458** Capitol Square if the disclaimer was of insufficient size or if the observer failed to enquire whether the State had sponsored the cross). The Klan concedes this possibility as well, saying that, in its view, "on a different set of facts, the government might be found guilty of violating the endorsement test by permitting a private religious display in a public forum."

An observer need not be "obtuse," *Doe* v. *Small* (Easterbrook, J., concurring), to presume that an unattended display on government land in a place of prominence in front of a government building either belongs to the government, represents government speech, or enjoys its location because of government endorsement of its message. Capitol Square, for example, is the site of a number of unattended displays owned or sponsored by the government, some permanent (statues), some temporary (such as the Christmas tree and a "Seasons Greetings" banner), and some in between (flags, which are, presumably, taken down and put up from time to time). Given the domination of the square by the government's own displays, one would not be a dimwit as a matter of law to think that an unattended religious display there was endorsed by the government, even though the square has also been the site of three privately sponsored, unattended displays over the years (a menorah, a United Way "thermometer," and some artisans' booths left overnight during an arts festival), cf. *Allegheny County* v. *American Civil Liberties Union, Greater Pittsburgh Chapter* ("Even if the Grand Staircase occasionally was used for displays other than the crèche . . . it remains true that any display located there fairly may be understood to express views that receive the support and endorsement of the government"), and even though the square meets the legal definition of a public forum and has been used "[f]or over a century" as the site of "speeches, gatherings, and festivals." When an individual speaks in a public forum, it is reasonable for an observer to attribute the speech, first and foremost, to the speaker, while an unattended display (and any message it conveys) can naturally be viewed as belonging to the owner of the land on which it stands.

In sum, I do not understand that I am at odds with the plurality when I assume that in some circumstances an intelligent observer would reasonably perceive private religious expression in a public forum to imply the government's endorsement of religion. My disagreement with the plurality is simply that I would attribute these perceptions of the intelligent observer to the reasonable observer of Establishment Clause analysis under our precedents, where I believe that such reasonable perceptions matter.

II

In *Allegheny County*, the Court alluded to two elements of the analytical framework supplied by *Lemon* v. *Kurtzman* by asking "whether the challenged governmental practice either has the purpose or effect of 'endorsing' religion." We said that "the prohibition against governmental endorsement of religion 'preclude[s] government from conveying or attempting to convey a message that religion or a particular religious belief is favored or preferred,'" quoting *Wallace* v. *Jaffree* (O'Connor, J., concurring in judgment) (emphasis omitted), and held that "[t]he Establishment Clause, at the very least, prohibits government from appearing to take a position on questions of religious belief."

Allegheny County's endorsement test cannot be dismissed, as *Justice SCALIA* suggests, as applying only to situations in which there is an allegation that the Establishment Clause has been violated through "expression by the government itself" or "government action . . . discriminat[ing] in favor of private religious expression" (emphasis omitted). Such a distinction would, in all but a handful of cases, make meaningless the "effect-of-endorsing" part of *Allegheny County's* test. Effects matter to the Estab⊥**2459**lishment Clause, and one, principal way that we assess them is by asking whether the practice in question creates the appearance of endorsement to the reasonable observer. If a reasonable observer would perceive a religious display in a government forum as government speech endorsing religion, then the display has made "religion relevant, in . . . public perception, to status in the political community" (O'Connor, J., concurring). Unless we are to retreat entirely to government intent and abandon consideration of effects, it makes no sense to recognize a public perception of endorsement as a harm only in that subclass of cases in which the government owns the display. Indeed, the Court stated in *Allegheny County* that "once the judgment has been made that a particular proclamation of Christian belief, when disseminated from a particular location on government property, has the effect of demonstrating the government's endorsement of Christian faith, then it necessarily follows that the practice must be enjoined." Notably, we did not say that it was only a "particular government proclamation" that could have such an unconstitutional effect, nor does the passage imply anything of the kind.

The significance of the fact that the Court in *Allegheny County* did not intend to lay down a *per se* rule in the way suggested by the plurality today has been confirmed by subsequent cases. In *Board of Ed. of Westside Community Schools (Dist. 66)* v. *Mergens*, six Justices applied the endorsement test to decide whether the Establishment Clause would be violated by a public high school's application of the Equal Access Act, Pub. L. 98-377, 98 Stat. 1302, 20 U. S. C. §§ 4071-4074, to allow students to form a religious club having the same access to meeting facilities as other "noncurricular" groups organized by students. A plurality of four Justices concluded that such an equal access policy "does not convey a message of state approval or endorsement of the particular religion" espoused by the student religious group (O'Connor, J., joined by Rehnquist, C. J., and White and Blackmun, JJ.). Two others concurred in the judgment in order "to emphasize the steps [the school] must take to avoid appearing to endorse the [religious] club's goals" (opinion of Marshall, J., joined by Brennan, J.); see also *id.* ("If public schools are perceived as conferring the *imprimatur* of the State on religious doctrine or practice as a result of such a policy, the nominally 'neutral' character of the policy will not save it from running afoul of the Establishment Clause") (emphasis in original).

What is important is that, even though *Mergens* involved private religious speech in a nondiscriminatory "'limited open forum,'" a majority of the Court reached the conclusion in the case not by applying an irrebuttable presumption, as the plurality does today, but by making a contextual judgment taking account of the circumstances of the specific case. Cf. *Allegheny County* (O'Connor, J., concurring in part and concurring in judgment) ("[T]he endorsement test depends on a sensitivity to the unique circumstances and context of a particular challenged practice"); *Lynch* (O'Connor, J., concurring) ("Every government practice must be judged in its unique circumstances to determine whether it constitutes an endorsement or disapproval of religion"). The *Mergens* plurality considered the nature of the likely ⊥**2460** audience ("[S]econdary school students are mature enough . . . to understand that a school does not endorse or support student speech that it merely permits on a nondiscriminatory basis"); the details of the particular forum (noting "the broad spectrum of officially recognized student clubs" at the school, and the students' freedom "to initiate and organize additional student clubs"); the presumptively secular nature of most student organizations ("'[I]n the absence of empirical evidence that religious groups will dominate [the] . . . open forum, . . . the advancement of religion would not be the forum's "primary effect,"'" quoting *Widmar* v. *Vincent;* and the school's specific action or inaction that would disassociate itself from any religious message ("[N]o school officials actively participate" in the religious group's activities). The plurality, moreover, expressly relied on the fact that the school could issue a disclaimer specific to the religious group, concluding that "[t]o the extent a school makes clear that its recognition of [a religious student group] is not an endorsement . . . students will reasonably understand that the . . . recognition of the club evinces neutrality toward, rather than endorsement of, religious speech." See also *id.* (Marshall, J., concurring in judgment) (noting importance of schools "taking whatever further steps are necessary to make clear that their recognition of a religious club does not reflect their endorsement of the views of the club's participants").

Similarly, in *Lamb's Chapel* v. *Center Moriches Union Free School Dist.*, we held that an evangelical church, wanting to use public school property to show a series of films about child-rearing with a religious perspective, could not be refused access to the premises under a policy that would open the school to other groups showing similar films from a non-religious perspective. In reaching this conclusion, we expressly concluded that the policy would "not have the principal or primary effect of advancing or inhibiting religion." Again we looked to the specific circumstances of the private religious speech and the public forum: the film would not be shown during school hours or be sponsored by the school, it would be open to the public, and the forum had been used "repeatedly" by "a wide variety" of other private speakers. "Under these circumstances," we concluded, "there would have been no realistic danger that the community would think that the [school] was endorsing religion." We thus expressly looked to the endorsement effects of the private religious speech at issue, notwithstanding the fact that there was no allegation that the Establishment Clause had been violated through active "expression by the government itself" or affirmative "government action . . . discriminat[ing] in favor of private religious expression" (emphasis omitted). Indeed, the issue of whether the private religious speech in a government forum had the effect of advancing religion was central, rather than irrelevant, to our Establishment Clause enquiry. This is why I agree with the Court that "[t]he *Lamb's Chapel* reasoning applies *a fortiori* here."

Widmar v. *Vincent* is not to the contrary. Although *Widmar* was decided before our adoption of the endorsement test in *Allegheny County*, its reasoning fits with such a test and not with the *per se* rule announced today. There, in determining whether it would violate the Establishment Clause to allow private religious speech in a "generally open forum" at a university, the Court looked to the *Lemon* test and focused on the "effects" prong in reaching a contextual judgment. It was relevant that university students "should be able to appreciate that the University's policy is one of neutrality toward religion," that students were unlikely, as a matter of fact, to "draw any reasonable inference of University support from the mere fact of a campus meeting place," and that the University's student handbook carried a disclaimer that the Uni⊥**2461**versity should not "'be identified in any way with the . . . opinions of any [student] organization.'" "In this context," and in the "absence of empirical evidence that religious groups [would] dominate [the] open forum," the Court found that the forum at issue did not "confer any imprimatur of state approval on religious sects or practices."

Even if precedent and practice were otherwise, however, and there were an open question about applying the endorsement test to private speech in public forums, I would apply it in preference to the plurality's view, which creates a serious loophole in the protection provided by the endorsement test. In *Justice SCALIA's* view, as I understand it, the Establishment Clause is violated in a public forum only when the government itself intentionally endorses religion or willfully "foster[s]" a misperception of endorsement in the forum, or when it "manipulates" the public forum "in such a manner that only certain religious groups take advantage of it." If the list of forbidden acts is truly this short, then governmental bodies and officials are left with generous scope to encourage a multiplicity of religious speakers to erect displays in public forums. As long as the governmental entity does not "manipulat[e]" the forum in such a way as to exclude all other speech, the plurality's opinion would seem to invite such government encouragement, even when the result will be the domination of the forum by religious displays and religious speakers. By allowing government to encourage what it can not do on its own, the proposed *per se* rule would tempt a public body to contract out its establishment of religion, by encouraging the private enterprise of the religious to exhibit what the government could not display itself.

Something of the sort, in fact, may have happened here. Immediately after the District Court issued the injunction ordering petitioners to grant the Klan's permit, a local church council applied for a permit, apparently for the purpose of overwhelming the Klan's cross with other crosses. The council proposed to invite all local churches to erect crosses, and the Board granted "blanket permission" for "all churches friendly to or affiliated with" the council to do so. The end result was that a part of the square was strewn with crosses and while the effect in this case may have provided more embarrassment than suspicion of endorsement, the opportunity for the latter is clear.

III

As for the specifics of this case, one must admit that a number of facts known to the Board, or reasonably anticipated, weighed in favor of upholding its denial of the permit. For example, the Latin cross the Klan sought to erect is the principal symbol of Christianity around the world, and display of the cross alone could not reasonably be taken to have any secular point. It was displayed immediately in front of the Ohio Statehouse, with the government's flags flying nearby, and the government's statues close at hand. For much of the time the cross was supposed to stand on the square, it would have been the only private display on the public plot (the menorah's permit expired several days before the cross actually went up). There was nothing else on the Statehouse lawn that would have suggested a forum open to any and all private, unattended religious displays.

Based on these and other factors, the Board was understandably concerned about a possible Establishment Clause violation if it had granted the permit. But a flat denial of the Klan's application was not the Board's only option to protect against an appearance of endorsement, and the Board was required to find its most "narrowly drawn" alternative. *Perry Ed. Assn.* v. *Perry Local Educators' Assn.* Either of two possibilities would have been better suited to this situation. In support of the Klan's application, its representative stated in a letter to the Board that the cross would be accompanied by a disclaimer, legible "from a distance," explaining that the cross was erected by private individuals ⊥**2462** "without government support." The letter said that "the contents of the sign" were "open to negotiation." The Board, then, could have granted the application subject to the condition that the Klan attach a disclaimer sufficiently large and clear to preclude any reasonable inference that the cross was there to "demonstrat[e] the government's allegiance to, or endorsement of, Christian faith." *Allegheny County*. In the alternative, the Board could have instituted a policy of restricting all private, unattended displays to one area of the square, with a permanent sign marking the area as a forum for private speech carrying no endorsement from the State.

With such alternatives available, the Board cannot claim that its flat denial was a narrowly tailored response to the Klan's permit application and thus cannot rely on that denial as necessary to ensure that the State did not "appea[r] to take a position on questions of religious belief." For these reasons, I concur in the judgment.

. . . . .

⊥**2464** *Justice* STEVENS, dissenting.

The Establishment Clause should be construed to create a strong presumption against the installation of unattended religious symbols on public property. Although the State of Ohio has allowed Capitol Square, the area around the seat of its government, to be used as a public forum, and although it has occasionally allowed private groups to erect other sectarian displays there, neither fact provides a sufficient basis for rebutting that presumption. On the contrary, the sequence of sectarian displays disclosed by the record in this case illustrates the importance ⊥**2465** of rebuilding the "wall of separation between church and State" that Jefferson envisioned.

I

At issue in this case is an unadorned Latin cross, which the Ku Klux Klan placed, and left unattended, on the lawn in front of the Ohio State Capitol. The Court decides this case on the assumption that the cross was a religious symbol. I agree with that assumption notwithstanding the hybrid character of this particular object. The record indicates that the "Grand Titan of the Knights of the Ku Klux Klan for the Realm of Ohio" applied for a permit to place a cross in front of the State Capitol because "the Jews" were placing a "symbol for the Jewish belief" in the Square.* Some observers, unaware of who had sponsored the cross, or unfamiliar with the history of the Klan and its reaction to the menorah, might interpret the Klan's cross as an inspirational symbol of the crucifixion and resurrection of Jesus Christ. More knowledgeable observers might regard it, given the context, as an anti-Semitic symbol of bigotry and disrespect for a particular religious sect. Under the first interpretation, the cross is plainly a religious symbol. Under the second, an icon of intolerance expressing an anti-clerical message should also be treated as a religious symbol because the Establishment Clause must prohibit official sponsorship of irreligious as well as religious messages. This principle is no less binding if the anti-religious message is also a bigoted message. See *United States* v. *Ballard* (government lacks power to judge truth of religious beliefs); *Watson* v. *Jones* ("The law knows no heresy, and is committed to the support of no dogma, the establishment of no sect").

Thus, while this unattended, freestanding wooden cross was unquestionably a religious symbol, observers may well have received completely different messages from that symbol. Some might have perceived it as a message of love, others as a message of hate, still others as a message of exclusion—a Statehouse sign calling powerfully to mind their outsider status. In any event, it was a message that the State of Ohio may not communicate to its citizens without violating the Establishment Clause.

II

The plurality does not disagree with the proposition that the State may not espouse a religious message. It concludes, however, that the State has not sent such a message; it has merely allowed others to do so on its property. Thus, the State has provided an "incidental benefit" to religion by allowing private parties access to a traditional public forum. In my judgment, neither precedent nor respect for the values protected by the Establishment Clause justifies that conclusion.

The Establishment Clause, "at the very least, prohibits government from appearing to take a position on questions of religious belief or from 'making adherence to a religion relevant in any way to a person's standing in the political community.'" *County of Allegheny* v. *American Civil Liberties Un*⊥**2466***ion, Greater Pittsburgh Chapter*, quoting *Lynch* v. *Donnelly* (O'Connor, J., concurring). At least when religious symbols are involved, the question of whether the state is "appearing to take a position" is best judged from the standpoint of a "reasonable observer." It is especially important to take account of the perspective of a reasonable observer who may not share the particular religious belief it expresses. A paramount purpose of the Establishment Clause is to protect such a person from being made to feel like an outsider in matters of faith, and a stranger in the political community. If a reasonable person could perceive a government endorsement of religion from a private display, then the State may not allow its property to be used as a forum for that display. No less stringent rule can adequately protect non-adherents from a well-grounded perception that their sovereign supports a faith to which they do not subscribe.

In determining whether the State's maintenance of the Klan's cross in front of the Statehouse conveyed a

*The "Grand Titan" apparently was referring to a menorah that a private group placed in the Square during the season of Chanukah. The Klan found the menorah offensive. The Klan's cross, in turn, offended a number of observers. It was vandalized the day after it was erected, and a local church group applied for, and was granted, permission to display its own crosses around the Klan's to protest the latter's presence.

forbidden message of endorsement, we should be mindful of the power of a symbol standing alone and unexplained. Even on private property, signs and symbols are generally understood to express the owner's views. The location of the sign is a significant component of the message it conveys. "Displaying a sign from one's own residence often carries a message quite distinct from placing the same sign someplace else, or conveying the same text or picture by other means. Precisely because of their location, such signs provide information about the identity of the 'speaker.' As an early and eminent student of rhetoric observed, the identity of the speaker is an important component of many attempts to persuade. A sign advocating 'Peace in the Gulf' in the front lawn of a retired general or decorated war veteran may provoke a different reaction than the same sign in a 10-year-old child's bedroom window or the same message on a bumper sticker of a passing automobile. An espousal of socialism may carry different implications when displayed on the grounds of a stately mansion than when pasted on a factory wall or an ambulatory sandwich board." *City of Ladue* v. *Gilleo*. Like other speakers, a person who places a sign on her own property has the autonomy to choose the content of her own message. Cf. *McIntyre* v. *Ohio Elections Comm'n*. Thus, the location of a stationary, unattended sign generally is both a component of its message and an implicit endorsement of that message by the party with the power to decide whether it may be ⊥**2467** conveyed from that location.

So it is with signs and symbols left to speak for themselves on public property. The very fact that a sign is installed on public property implies official recognition and reinforcement of its message. That implication is especially strong when the sign stands in front of the seat of the government itself. The "reasonable observer" of any symbol placed unattended in front of any capitol in the world will normally assume that the sovereign—which is not only the owner of that parcel of real estate but also the lawgiver for the surrounding territory—has sponsored and facilitated its message.

That the State may have granted a variety of groups permission to engage in uncensored expressive activities in front of the capitol building does not, in my opinion, qualify or contradict the normal inference of endorsement that the reasonable observer would draw from the unattended, freestanding sign or symbol. Indeed, parades and demonstrations at or near the seat of government are often exercises of the right of the people to petition their government for a redress of grievances—exercises in which the government is the recipient of the message rather than the messenger. Even when a demonstration or parade is not directed against government policy, but merely has made use of a particularly visible forum in order to reach as wide an audience as possible, there usually can be no mistake about the identity of the messengers as persons other than the State. But when a statue or some other free-standing, silent, unattended, immoveable structure—regardless of its particular message—appears on the lawn of the Capitol building, the reasonable observer must identify the State either as the messenger, or, at the very least, as one who has endorsed the message. Contrast, in this light, the image of the cross standing alone and unattended and the image the observer would take away were a hooded Klansman holding, or standing next to, the very same cross.

This Court has never held that a private party has a right to place an unattended object in a public forum. Today the Court correctly recognizes that a State may impose a ban on all private unattended displays in such a forum. This is true despite the fact that our cases have condemned a number of laws that foreclose an entire medium of expression, even in places where free speech is otherwise allowed. The First Amendment affords protection to a ⊥**2468** basic liberty: "the freedom of speech" that an individual may exercise when using the public streets and parks. *Hague* v. *Committee for Industrial Organization* (opinion of Roberts, J.). The Amendment, however, does not destroy all property rights. In particular, it does not empower individuals to erect structures of any kind on public property. *City Council of Los Angeles* v. *Taxpayers for Vincent;* see also *Clark* v. *Community for Creative Non-Violence*. Thus our cases protecting the individual's freedom to engage in communicative conduct on public property (whether by speaking, parading, handbilling, waving a flag, or carrying a banner), *e.g.*, *Lovell* v. *Griffin*, or to send messages from her own property by placing a sign in the window of her home, *City of Ladue* v. *Gilleo*, do not establish the right to implant a physical structure (whether a campaign poster, a burning cross, or a statue of Elvis Presley) on public property. I think the latter "right," which creates a far greater intrusion on government property and interferes with the Government's ability to differentiate its own message from those of public individuals, does not exist.

Because structures on government property—and, in particular, in front of buildings plainly identified with the state—imply state approval of their message, the Government must have considerable leeway, outside of the religious arena, to choose what kinds of displays it will allow and what kinds it will not. Although the First Amendment requires the Government to allow leafletting or demonstrating outside its buildings, the state has greater power to exclude unattended symbols when they convey a type of message with which the state does not wish to be identified. I think it obvious, for example, that Ohio could prohibit certain categories of signs or symbols in Capitol Square—erotic exhibits, commercial advertising, and perhaps campaign posters as well—without violating the Free Speech Clause. Moreover, our "public forum" cases do not foreclose public entities from enforcing prohibitions against all unattended displays in public parks, or possibly even limiting the use of such displays to the communication of non-controversial messages. Such a limitation ⊥**2469** would not inhibit any of the traditional forms of expression that have been given full constitutional protection in public fora.

The State's general power to restrict the types of unattended displays does not alone suffice to decide this case, because Ohio did not profess to be exercising any such authority. Instead, the Capitol Square Review Board denied a permit for the cross because it believed the Establishment Clause required as much, and we cannot know whether the Board would have denied the permit on other grounds. Accordingly, we must evaluate the State's rationale on its own terms. But in this case, the endorsement inquiry under the Establishment Clause follows from the State's power to exclude unattended private displays from public property. Just as the Constitution recognizes the State's interest in preventing its property from being used as a conduit for ideas it does not wish to give the appearance of ratifying, the Establishment Clause prohibits government from allowing, and thus endorsing, unattended displays that take a position on a religious issue. If the State allows such stationary displays in front of its seat of government, viewers will reasonably assume that it approves of them. A reasonable observer would likely infer endorsement from the location of the cross erected by the Klan in this case. Even if the disclaimer at the foot of the cross (which stated that the cross was placed there by a private organization) were legible, that inference would remain, because a property owner's decision to allow a third party to place a sign on her property conveys the same message of endorsement as if she had erected it herself.

When the message is religious in character, it is a message the state can neither send nor reinforce without violating the Establishment Clause. Accordingly, I would hold that the Constitution generally forbids the placement of a symbol of a religious character in, on, or before a seat of government.

III

The Court correctly acknowledges that the state's duty to avoid a violation of the Establishment Clause can justify a content-based restriction on speech or expression, even when that restriction would otherwise be prohibited by the Free Speech Clause. The plurality asserts, however, that government cannot be perceived to be endorsing a religious display when it merely accords that display "the same access to a public forum that all other displays enjoy." I find this argument unpersuasive.

The existence of a "public forum" in itself cannot dispel the message of endorsement. A contrary argument would assume an "ultra-reasonable observer" who understands the vagaries of this Court's First Amendment jurisprudence. I think it presumptuous to consider such knowledge a precondition of Establishment Clause protection. Many (probably most) reasonable people do not know the difference between a "public forum," a "limited public forum," and a "non-public forum." They *do* know the difference between a state capitol and a church. Reasonable people have differing degrees of knowledge; that does not make them "'obtuse'" (quoting *Doe* v. *Small* (Easterbrook, J., concurring)); **⊥2470** nor does it make them unworthy of constitutional protection. It merely makes them human. For a religious display to violate the Establishment Clause, I think it is enough that *some* reasonable observers would attribute a religious message to the State.

The plurality appears to rely on the history of this particular public forum—specifically, it emphasizes that Ohio has in the past allowed three other private unattended displays. Even if the State could not reasonably have been understood to endorse the prior displays, I would not find this argument convincing, because it assumes that all reasonable viewers know all about the history of Capitol Square—a highly unlikely supposition. But the plurality's argument fails on its own terms, because each of the three previous displays conveyed the same message of approval and endorsement that this one does.

Most significant, of course, is the menorah that stood in Capitol Square during Chanukah. The display of that religious symbol should be governed by the same rule as the display of the cross. In my opinion, both displays are equally objectionable. Moreover, the fact that the State has placed its stamp of approval on two different religions instead of one only compounds the constitutional violation. The Establishment Clause does not merely prohibit the State from favoring one religious sect over others. It also proscribes state action supporting the establishment of a number of religions, as well as the official endorsement of religion in preference to nonreligion. The State's prior approval of the pro-religious message conveyed by the menorah is fully consistent with its endorsement of one of the messages conveyed by the cross: "The State of Ohio favors religion over irreligion." This message is incompatible with the principles embodied by our Establishment Clause.

The record identifies two other examples of freestanding displays that the State previously permitted in Capitol Square: a "United Way Campaign 'thermometer,'" and "craftsmen's booths and displays erected during an Arts Festival." Both of those examples confirm the proposition that a reasonable observer should infer official approval of the message conveyed by a structure erected in front of the **⊥2471** Statehouse. Surely the thermometer suggested that the State was encouraging passersby to contribute to the United Way. It seems equally clear that the State was endorsing the creativity of artisans and craftsmen by permitting their booths to occupy a part of the Square. Nothing about either of those freestanding displays contradicts the normal inference that the State has endorsed whatever message might be conveyed by permitting an unattended symbol to adorn the Capitol grounds. Accordingly, the fact that the menorah, and later the cross, stood in an area available "'for free discussion of public questions, or for activities of a broad public purpose,'" Ohio Rev. Code Ann. § 105.41 (1994), is fully consistent with the conclusion that the State sponsored those religious symbols. They, like the thermometer and the booths, were displayed in a context that connotes state approval.

This case is therefore readily distinguishable from *Widmar* v. *Vincent* and *Lamb's Chapel* v. *Center Moriches Union Free School Dist.* In both of those cases, as we made perfectly clear, there was no danger of incorrect identification of the speakers and no basis for inferring that their messages had been endorsed by any public entity. As we explained in the later case: "Under these circumstances, as in *Widmar*, there would have been no realistic danger that the community would think that the District was endorsing religion or any particular creed, and any benefit to religion or to the Church would have been no more than incidental. As in *Widmar*, permitting District property to be used to exhibit the film involved in this case would not have been an establishment of religion under the three-part test articulated in *Lemon* v. *Kurtzman:* The challenged governmental action has a secular purpose, does not have the principal or primary effect of advancing or inhibiting religion, and does not foster an excessive entanglement with religion."

In contrast, the installation of the religious symbols in Capitol Square quite obviously did "have the principal or primary effect of advancing or inhibiting religion"; indeed, no other effect is even suggested by the record. The primary difference is that in this case we are dealing with a *visual display*—a symbol readily associated with a religion, in a venue readily associated with the State. This clear image of endorsement was lacking in *Widmar* and *Lamb's Chapel*, in which the issue was access to government facilities. Moreover, there was no question in those cases of an unattended display; private speakers, who could be distinguished from the state, were present. Endorsement might still be present in an access case if, for example, the religious group sought the use of the roof of a public building for an obviously religious ceremony, where many onlookers might witness that ceremony and connect it to the State. But no such facts were alleged in *Widmar* or *Lamb's Chapel*. The religious practices in those cases were simply less obtrusive, and less likely to send a message of endorsement, than the eye-catching symbolism at issue in this case.

The battle over the Klan cross underscores the power of such symbolism. The menorah prompted the Klan to seek permission to erect an anti-Semitic symbol, which in turn not only prompted vandalism but also motivated other sects to seek permission to place their own symbols in the Square. These facts illustrate the potential for insidious entanglement that flows from state-endorsed proselytizing. There is no reason to believe that a menorah placed in front of a synagogue would have motivated any reaction from the Klan, or that a Klan cross placed on a Klansman's front lawn would have produced the same reaction as one that enjoyed the apparent imprimatur of the State of Ohio. ⊥**2472** Nor is there any reason to believe the placement of the displays in Capitol Square had any purpose other than to connect the State—though perhaps against its will—to the religious or anti-religious beliefs of those who placed them there. The cause of the conflict is the State's apparent approval of a religious or anti-religious message. Our Constitution wisely seeks to minimize such strife by forbidding state-endorsed religious activity.

IV

Conspicuously absent from the plurality's opinion is any mention of the values served by the Establishment Clause. It therefore seems appropriate to repeat a portion of a Court opinion authored by *Justice BLACK* who, more than any other Justice in the Court's history, espoused a literal interpretation of constitutional text:

"A large proportion of the early settlers of this country came here from Europe to escape the bondage of laws which compelled them to support and attend government-favored churches. The centuries immediately before and contemporaneous with the colonization of America had been filled with turmoil, civil strife, and persecutions, generated in large part by established sects determined to maintain their absolute political and religious supremacy. With the power of government supporting them, at various times and places, Catholics had persecuted Protestants, Protestants had persecuted Catholics, Protestant sects had persecuted other Protestant sects, Catholics of one shade of belief had persecuted Catholics of another shade of belief, and all of these had from time to time persecuted Jews. In efforts to force loyalty to whatever religious group happened to be on top and in league with the government of a particular time and place, men and women had been fined, cast in jail, cruelly tortured, and killed. Among the offenses for which these punishments had been inflicted were such things as speaking disrespectfully of the views of ministers of government-established churches, non-attendance at those churches, expressions of non-belief in their doctrines, and failure to pay taxes and tithes to support them.

"These practices of the old world were transplanted to and began to thrive in the soil of the new America. The very charters granted by the English Crown to the individuals and companies designated to make the laws which would control the destinies of the colonials authorized these individuals and companies to erect religious establishments which all, whether believers or non-believers, would be required to support and attend. An exercise of this authority was accompanied by a repetition of many of the old-world practices and persecutions. Catholics found themselves hounded and proscribed because of their faith; Quakers who followed their conscience went to jail; Baptists were peculiarly obnoxious to certain dominant Protestant sects; men and women of ⊥**2473** varied faiths who happened to be in a minority in a particular locality were persecuted because they steadfastly persisted in worshipping God only as their own consciences dictated. And all of these dissenters were compelled to pay tithes and taxes to support government-sponsored churches whose ministers preached inflammatory sermons designed to strengthen and consolidate the established faith by generating a burning hatred against dissenters.

. . . . .

"The 'establishment of religion' clause of the First Amendment means at least this: Neither a state nor the Federal Government can set up a church. Neither can pass laws which aid one religion, aid all religions, or prefer one religion over another. Neither can force nor influence a person to go to or to remain away from church against his will or force him to profess a belief or disbelief in any religion. . . . Neither a state nor the Federal Government can, openly or secretly, participate in the affairs of any religious organizations or groups and *vice versa*. In the words of Jefferson, the clause against establishment of religion by law was intended to erect 'a wall of separation between church and State.'" *Everson* v. *Board of Ed. of Ewing*.

In his eloquent dissent in that same case, *Justice JACKSON* succinctly explained—"that the effect of the religious freedom Amendment to our Constitution was to take every form of propagation of religion out of the realm of things which could directly or indirectly be made public business. . . . It was intended not only to keep the states' hands out of religion, but to keep religion's hands off the state, and, above all, to keep bitter religious controversy out of public life. . . ." *Id.*

The wrestling over the Klan cross in Capitol Square is far removed from the persecution that motivated William Penn to set sail for America, and the issue resolved in *Everson* is quite different from the controversy over symbols that gave rise to this litigation. Nevertheless the views expressed by both the majority and the dissenters in that landmark case counsel caution before approving the order of a federal judge commanding a State to authorize the placement of free-standing religious symbols in front of the seat of its government. The Court's decision today is unprecedented. It entangles two sovereigns in the propagation of religion, and it disserves the principle of tolerance that underlies the prohibition against state action "respecting an establishment of religion."

I respectfully dissent.

⊥**2474** *Justice* GINSBURG, dissenting.

We confront here, as *Justices* O'CONNOR and SOUTER point out, a large Latin cross that stood alone and unattended in close proximity to Ohio's Statehouse. Near the stationary cross were the government's flags and the government's statues. No human speaker was present to disassociate the religious symbol from the State. No other private display was in sight. No plainly visible sign informed the public that the cross belonged to the Klan and that Ohio's government did not endorse the display's message.

If the aim of the Establishment Clause is genuinely to uncouple government from church, see *Everson* v. *Board of Ed. of Ew*⊥**2475***ing*, a State may not permit, and a court may not order, a display of this character. Cf. Sullivan, Religion and Liberal Democracy, 59 U. Chi. L. Rev. 195, 197-214 (1992) (negative bar against establishment of religion implies affirmative establishment of secular public order). *Justice* SOUTER, in the final paragraphs of his opinion, suggests two arrangements that might have distanced the State from "the principal symbol of Christianity around the world,": a sufficiently large and clear disclaimer, or an area reserved for unattended displays carrying no endorsement from the State, a space plainly and permanently so marked. Neither arrangement is even arguably present in this case. The District Court's order did not mandate a disclaimer. And the disclaimer the Klan appended to the foot of the cross* was unsturdy: it did not identify the Klan as sponsor; it failed to state unequivocally that Ohio did not endorse the display's message; and it was not shown to be legible from a distance. The relief ordered by the District Court thus violated the Establishment Clause.

Whether a court order allowing display of a cross, but demanding a sturdier disclaimer, could withstand Establishment Clause analysis is a question more difficult than the one this case poses. I would reserve that question for another day and case. But I would not let the prospect of what might have been permissible control today's decision on the constitutionality of the display the District Court's order in fact authorized.

GOVERNMENT AID TO RELIGIOUS INSTITUTIONS OR VOCATIONS

One of the first Establishment Clause cases to be considered by the Supreme Court was BRADFIELD v. ROBERTS (1899). It raised the issue of whether the federal government could financially support the operation of a hospital operated by an order of Roman Catholic nuns. The hospital was in the District of Columbia. It had received an appropriation from Congress of $30,000 for the construction of two buildings. The plaintiff, challenging the act as a citizen, taxpayer, and resident of the District of Columbia, charged that the plan violated

*The disclaimer stated: "[T]his cross was erected by private individuals without government support for the purpose of expressing respect for the holiday season and to assert the right of all religious views to be expressed on an equal basis on public property."

the no-establishment principle for the obvious reason that government money supported a religious society's medical facility.

Writing for a unanimous Court, Justice Peckham brushed aside the problem of standing presented by a taxpayer suit. He almost as easily dealt with the substantive Establishment Clause issue. He did so by essentially declaring it to be a nonissue. The expenditure of government money for the Catholic hospital was not a violation because the religious affiliation of its operators was immaterial and irrelevant to what it did. The hospital was a secular corporation dedicated to providing secular services to the ill. Given that, there was no establishment problem.

> Whether the individuals who compose the corporation under its charter happen to be all Roman Catholics, or all Methodists, or Presbyterians, or Unitarians, or members of any other religious organization, or of no organization at all, is of not the slightest consequence with reference to the law of its incorporation, nor can the individual beliefs upon religious matters of the various incorporators be inquired into. Nor is it material that the hospital may be conducted under the auspices of the Roman Catholic Church. . . . The act of Congress, however, shows there is nothing sectarian in the corporation, and "the specific and limited object of its creation" is the opening and keeping a hospital in the city of Washington for the care of such sick and invalid persons as may place themselves under the treatment and care of the corporation (175 U.S. 291, 298, 299-300).

Given that *Bradfield* glossed over the establishment issue, it can still be said that EVERSON v. BOARD OF EDUCATION (1947) was the first Establishment Clause decision rendered by the Court.

In 1986 the Court was called upon to decide whether a state may provide financial aid to an individual who is preparing for a religious vocation in WITTERS v. WASHINGTON DEPARTMENT OF SERVICES FOR THE BLIND. Larry Witters, who suffered from a degenerative eye condition, applied for aid from the Washington State Commission for the Blind. The Commission had the mandate, under state law, to provide special education and/or assistance in training for professional life for persons with visual handicaps. Witters thus was eligible to receive state financial assistance. The problem was that he was enrolled in a private Christian college in order to prepare for a career in the ministry. Because of that, the Commission denied Witters aid, pursuant to the provisions in the State Constitution that forbade the use of any public funds for supporting or assisting in religious instruction.

After Witters exhausted all administrative remedies, with no success, he filed suit in state court to obtain the funds to which he felt he was entitled under state law. The court also denied him aid, holding that the State Constitution would not allow it. When he appealed to the State Supreme Court, he got the same answer, with one difference. The Washington Supreme Court decided the case, not on the basis of the Washington Constitution, but on the Establishment Clause of the United States Constitution. Relying on the "primary effect" test the court said that for Witters to receive state rehabilitation funds and apply them to education for the ministry would have the impermissible primary effect of advancing religion.

The United States Supreme Court, in a unanimous verdict, reversed that judgment. It found that the state program of aid to the handicapped clearly had a secular purpose: it was designed solely to aid a particular category of persons, not defined by religion, to be able to take their place in society as productive citizens. When it came to the second prong of the Establishment Clause test, the Court disagreed with the court below. Using language that has a "child benefit" sound, Justice Marshall for the Court noted that under the Washington program the money is paid directly to the student who then transfers it to the educational institution of his or her choice. Consequently, if any of the state money goes to a religious school, it is because the student chose to spend it there, not because of any state action. This being true, it is clear that there is no financial incentive for the student to undertake religious education: the amount of money made available is the same regardless of the type of school chosen. Furthermore, there was no reason to think that even if Witters were to be allowed to use the state money for ministerial training that a significant amount of the aggregate money Washington spent on educational aid for the handicapped would be used for religious education. Consequently:

> On the facts we have set out, it does not seem appropriate to view any aid ultimately flowing to the Inland Empire School of the Bible as resulting from a *state* action sponsoring or subsidizing religion. Nor does the mere circumstance that petitioner has chosen to use neutrally available state aid to help pay for his religious education confer any message of state endorsement of religion (474 U.S. 481, 488-489).

The Court chose not to consider the case on entanglement grounds because that test had not been argued in the courts below. It should also be noted, however, that the Court did not judge the case against Washington constitutional provisions, but rather sent the case back to the Washington Supreme Court for consideration on those grounds.

But at least the program was not unconstitutional as measured against the United States Constitution.[1]

The Court said that the free choice of the recipient of state money about how to use that money insulated the state from the charge of aid to religion. If that sounds similar to the language used in MUELLER v. ALLEN (the tax credit for assistance in paying parochial school tuition is triggered by the decision of the parent to send a child to private or parochial school, not by any state action), it did to some members of the Court as well. Justices Powell and O'Connor chided the Court for failing to cite *Mueller* as a precedent for the concept as it was used in *Witters* and alerted jurists that it should be thought of as support for the idea that

> state programs that are wholly neutral in offering educational assistance to a class defined without reference to religion do not violate the second part of the *Lemon* v. *Kurtzman* test, because any aid to religion results from the private choices of individual beneficiaries (Powell, J., concurring; 474 U.S. 481, 490-491).

In 1988, in BOWEN v. KENDRICK, the Court was compelled to deal with the issue of government aid to religious institutions, centering on the emotion-laden issues of abortion and the sexual activity of teenagers. In 1981 Congress had passed the Adolescent Family Life Act (AFLA) as a response to the health, economic, and social disruptions that frequently result from pregnancy and childbirth in the case of unmarried adults. The AFLA was designed, in part, to preclude some of those problems by preventing the behavior that produced them. The act was to provide: "care services"—services for the provision of care to pregnant adolescents and adolescent parents; and "prevention services"—which would encourage adolescents to refrain from sexual relations.

> These services include pregnancy testing and maternity counseling, adoption counseling and referral services, prenatal and postnatal health care, nutritional information, counseling, child care, mental health services, and perhaps most importantly for present purposes, "educational services relating to family life and problems associated with adolescent premarital sexual relations" (487 U.S. 589, 594, quoting 42 U.S.C. § 300z-1(a)(4)).

The reason that these laudable goals became the cause for litigation is that the AFLA sought to implement these services through grants to public and private agencies. Among the latter could be religion-based care providers. Because legislators recognized the complexity of the problems of teenage pregnancy, Congress specifically authorized that among grantees receiving money could be religious organizations. Congress also put some limitations on the funds. Although there were some narrow exceptions, in general grantees were not to provide family planning services, were not to provide abortions or abortion counseling or referral, and were not to advocate or encourage abortion. In the years before the case reached the Supreme Court a number of grants had been awarded to organizations related to religious denominations.

Suit was filed in a federal district court in 1983, challenging the constitutionality of the AFLA under the Establishment Clause. Plaintiffs were federal taxpayers, clergy, and the American Jewish Congress. They alleged that the act was unconstitutional both on its face and in its application. The District Court agreed with the plaintiffs, finding the act unconstitutional primarily because it facially violated the "primary effect" prong of the *Lemon* test. The AFLA required grantees to show how religious organizations would be involved in the provision of the services, it allowed for a direct role of such organizations in educating and counseling teenagers, and it permitted these organizations to teach on issues that involve religious doctrine.

The court also found the act unconstitutional in its application. That is, funds had actually gone to religious organizations, "pervasively sectarian" organizations, which did what the AFLA authorized. So, both on its face and as applied, the act had the impermissible primary effect of advancing religion. The court also found the AFLA wanting on the "entanglement" prong of the three-part test in that it would require extensive monitoring to insure that religion was not advanced by religiously oriented grantees.

On this record, the Supreme Court, in an opinion by Chief Justice Rehnquist, reversed the District Court. Like the District Court, Rehnquist dealt with the law on its face and as applied. In terms of the former, he concluded that the law had a secular purpose and hastened on to the primary effect test. To the argument that the AFLA violated the test because it explicitly recognized that religious organizations have a role to play in educating and counseling young people on matters of sexuality, Justice Rehnquist said that it just was not true. He asserted that no previous case had held that Congress may not recognize that religious institutions can contribute to the solving of secular societal problems. In this instance, if there was any advancement of religion in the law, it was only incidental and remote. Furthermore, the act did not focus only on religious institutions, but also re-

[1] In 1989 the Washington Supreme Court denied Witters the aid on the basis of the Washington State Constitution, which states, in pertinent part: "No public money or property shall be appropriated for or applied to any religious worship, exercise or instruction, or the support of any religious establishment. . . ." *Witters* v. *Washington Commission for the Blind.*

quired grantees to show how "charitable organizations, voluntary associations, and other groups in the private sector" would contribute to the education and counseling enterprise. To Rehnquist, this showed that the AFLA steered "a course of neutrality among religions, and between religion and nonreligion" (487 U.S. 589, 607).

A second objection to the facial provisions of the AFLA was that it allowed religious institutions to receive and utilize federal funds. But the Court again affirmed the counter argument that all types of public and private organizations were recipients of funds, not just religious. That act illustrates neutrality in terms of potential receipt of government funds. Furthermore, citing *Bradfield* v. *Roberts* (1899), Rehnquist argued that religious institutions are certainly able to receive government funds for publicly sponsored public welfare programs, so long as they are not "pervasively sectarian."

> [T]he contention that there is a substantial risk of [pervasively sectarian] institutions receiving direct aid is undercut by the AFLA's facially neutral grant requirements, the wide spectrum of public and private organizations which are capable of meeting the AFLA's requirements, and the fact that, of the eligible religious institutions, many will not deserve the label of "pervasively sectarian." . . . [W]e do not think the possibility that AFLA grants may go to religious institutions that can be considered "pervasively sectarian" is sufficient to conclude that no grants whatsoever can be given under the statute to religious organizations (487 U.S. 589, 610-611).

To the argument that the religion-based AFLA grantees advanced religion by providing educational and counseling services, or by teaching things that are of significant importance to religious doctrine, the Court responded that the fact that religious doctrine happened to correspond with the goals that the government sought to accomplish through the AFLA did not invalidate the program. The District Court had used as a reason for declaring the AFLA unconstitutional under the effects test the claim that the law created a symbolic link between government and religion. Justice Rehnquist essentially dismissed the argument, saying that whatever symbolic link was created between church and state was not sufficient to invalidate the statute. Finally, plaintiffs had argued that the act was invalid because it did not specifically forbid the spending of government funds for religious purposes. The majority responded that it had never been required that the statute must explicitly forbid such expenditures. Furthermore, there were sufficient reporting requirements and supervision to assure that government funds would not be used for impermissible purposes.

Of course, that provision raised the possibility of invalidating the act because it caused excessive entanglement between church and state. Rehnquist retreated to the former holding that the AFLA grantees are not likely to be pervasively sectarian and, consequently, whatever monitoring was necessary would not result in government intrusion into the day-by-day operation of religious institutions. This was enough to avoid crossing the line into impermissible excessive entanglement.

For all these reasons, the ALFA was not facially invalid in relation to the Establishment Clause. What about the application of the act? The District Court had ruled that the implementation of the AFLA was unconstitutional because federal funds, in several circumstances, had been given to pervasively sectarian institutions. The Supreme Court held that the lower court's procedure was flawed enough that it could not rule on the "as applied" dimension of the case. The District Court did not identify which grantees it was referring to and did not give specificities as to what would make an organization pervasively sectarian. Consequently, the Supreme Court remanded the case for further determination of how the statute was being administered.[2]

A vigorous dissent was written by Justice Blackmun, joined by Justices Brennan, Marshall, and Stevens. The thrust of it was that the AFLA clearly violates the primary effect test of the Establishment Clause. Far from being rescued from violation by the concept that there was simple correspondence between the interests of government and religious organizations on the multiple questions of sexuality, Blackmun argued that religious groups were included in the statute because of their views on morality.

> The AFLA, unlike any statute this Court has upheld, pays for teachers and counselors, employed by and subject to the direction of religious authorities, to educate impressionable young minds on issues of religious moment. . . . There is . . . a fundamental difference between government's employing religion because of its unique appeal to a higher authority and the transcendental nature of its message, and government's enlisting the aid of religiously committed individuals or organizations without regard to their sectarian motivation (487 U.S. 589, 638, 641).

The dissent also pointed to the amount of entanglement necessary "to prevent subsidizing the advancement of religion with AFLA funds" (487 U.S. 589, 649). For that reason also, the law was clearly unconstitutional.

[2]At the time of this writing, there is no information on the status or outcome of that remand.

BRADFIELD v. ROBERTS

175 U.S. 291
ON APPEAL FROM THE COURT OF APPEALS
OF THE DISTRICT OF COLUMBIA
Argued October 27, 1899 — Decided December 4, 1899

⊥291 Statement by *Mr. Justice PECKHAM.*

⊥292 This is a suit in equity, brought by the appellant to enjoin the defendant from paying any moneys to the directors of Providence Hospital, in the city of Washington, under an agreement entered into between the commissioners of the District of Columbia and the directors of the hospital, by virtue of the authority of an act of Congress, because of the alleged invalidity of the agreement for the reasons stated in the bill of complaint. In that bill complainant represents that he is a citizen and taxpayer of the United States and a resident of the District of Columbia, that the defendant is the Treasurei of the United States, and the object of the suit is to enjoin him from paying to or on account of Providence Hospital, in the city of Washington, District of Columbia, any moneys belonging to the United States, by virtue of a contract between the surgeon general of the army and the directors of that hospital, or by virtue of an agreement between the commissioners of the District of Columbia and such directors, under the authority of an appropriation contained in the sundry civil appropriation bill for the District of Columbia, approved June 4, 1897.

Complainant further alleged in his bill:

"That the said Providence Hospital is a private eleemosynary corporation, and that to the best of complainant's knowledge and belief it is composed of members of a monastic order or sisterhood of the Roman Catholic Church, and is conducted under the auspices of said church; that the title to its property is vested in the 'Sisters of Charity of Emmitsburg, Maryland;' that it was incorporated by a special act of Congress approved April 8, 1864, whereby, in addition to the usual powers of bodies corporate and politic, it was invested specially with 'full power and all the rights of opening and keeping a hospital in the city of Washington for the care of such sick and invalid persons as may place themselves under the treatment and care of said corporation.'

"That in view of the sectarian character of said Providence Hospital and the specific and limited object of its creation, the said contract between the same and the surgeon general of the army and also the said agreement between the same and **⊥293** the commissioners of the District of Columbia are unauthorized by law, and, moreover, involve a principle and a precedent for the appropriation of the funds of the United States for the use and support of religious societies, contrary to the article of the Constitution which declares that Congress shall make no law respecting a religious establishment, and also a precedent for giving to religious societies a legal agency in carrying into effect a public and civil duty which would, if once established, speedily obliterate the essential distinction between civil and religious functions. . . .

⊥295 *Mr. Justice PECKHAM*, after stating the facts, delivered the opinion of the court:

Passing the various objections made to the maintenance of this suit on account of an alleged defect of parties, and also in regard to the character in which the complainant sues, merely that of a citizen and taxpayer of the United States and a resident of the District of Columbia, we come to the main question as to the validity of the agreement between the commissioners of the District and the directors of the hospital, founded upon the appropriation contained in the act of Congress, the contention being that the agreement if carried out would result in an appropriation by Congress of money to a religious society, thereby violating the constitutional provision which forbids Congress from passing any law respecting an establishment of religion.

The appropriation is to be found in the general appropriation act for the government of the District of Columbia, approved March 3, 1897, 29 Stat. at L. 665, 679, chap. 387. It reads: "For two isolating buildings, to be constructed, in the discretion of the commissioners of the District of Columbia, on the grounds of two hospitals, and to be operated as a part of such hospitals, thirty thousand dollars." Acting under the **⊥296** authority of this appropriation the commissioners entered into the agreement in question.

As the bill alleges that Providence Hospital was incorporated by an act of Congress approved April 8, 1864 (13 Stat. at L. 43, chap. 50), and assumes to give some of its provisions, the act thus referred to is substantially made a part of the bill.

The act shows that the individuals named therein and their successors in office were incorporated under the name of "The Directors of Providence Hospital," with power to **⊥297** receive, hold, and convey personal and real property, as provided in its 1st section. By the 2d section the corporation was granted "full power and all the rights of opening and keeping a hospital in the city of Washington for the care of such sick and invalid persons as may place themselves under the treatment and care of the said corporation." The 3d section gave it full power to make such by-laws, rules, and regulations that might be necessary for the general accomplishment of the objects of the hospital, not inconsistent with the laws in force in the District of Columbia. Nothing is said about religion or about the religious faith of the incorporators of this institution in the act of incorporation. It is simply the ordinary case of the incorporation of a hospital for the purposes for which such an institution is generally conducted. It is claimed that the allegation in the complainant's bill, that the said "Providence Hospital is a private eleemosynary corporation, and that to the best of complainant's knowledge and belief it is composed of members of a monastic order or sisterhood of the Roman Catholic Church, and is conducted under the auspices of said church; that the title to its property is vested in the Sisters of Charity of Emmitsburg, Maryland," renders the agreement void for the reason therein stated, which is that Congress has no power to make "a law respecting a religious establishment," a phrase which is not synonymous with that used in the Constitution, which prohibits the passage of a law "respecting an establishment of religion."

If we were to assume, for the purpose of this question only, that under this appropriation an agreement with a religious corporation of the tenor of this agreement would be invalid, as resulting indirectly in the passage of an act respecting an establishment of religion, we are unable to see that the complainant in his bill shows that the corporation is of the kind described, but on the contrary he has clearly shown that it is not.

The above-mentioned allegations in the complainant's bill do not change the legal character of the corporation or render it on that account a religious or sectarian body. Assuming ⊥**298** that the hospital is a private eleemosynary corporation, the fact that its members, according to the belief of the complainant, are members of a monastic order or sisterhood of the Roman Catholic Church, and the further fact that the hospital is conducted under the auspices of said church, are wholly immaterial, as is also the allegation regarding the title to its property. The statute provides as to its property and makes no provision for its being held by anyone other than itself. The facts above stated do not in the least change the legal character of the hospital, or make a religious corporation out of a purely secular one as constituted by the law of its being. Whether the individuals who compose the corporation under its charter happen to be all Roman Catholics, or all Methodists, or Presbyterians, or Unitarians, or members of any other religious organization, or of no organization at all, is of not the slightest consequence with reference to the law of its incorporation, nor can the individual beliefs upon religious matters of the various incorporators be inquired into. Nor is it material that the hospital may be conducted under the auspices of the Roman Catholic Church. To be conducted under the auspices is to be conducted under the influence or patronage of that church. The meaning of the allegation is that the church exercises great and perhaps controlling influence over the management of the hospital. It must, however, be managed pursuant to the law of its being. That the influence of any particular church may be powerful over the members of a nonsectarian and secular corporation, incorporated for a certain defined purpose and with clearly stated powers, is surely not sufficient to convert such a corporation into a religious or sectarian body. That fact does not alter the legal character of the corporation, which is incorporated under an act of Congress, and its powers, duties, and character are to be solely measured by the charter under which it alone has any legal existence. There is no allegation that its hospital work is confined to members of that church or that in its management the hospital has been conducted so as to violate its charter in the smallest degree. It is simply the case of a secular corporation being managed by people ⊥**299** who hold to the doctrines of the Roman Catholic Church, but who nevertheless are managing the corporation according to the law under which it exists. The charter itself does not limit the exercise of its corporate powers to the members of any particular religious denomination, but, on the contrary, those powers are to be exercised in favor of anyone seeking the ministrations of that kind of an institution. All that can be said of the corporation itself is that it has been incorporated by an act of Congress, and for its legal powers and duties that act must be exclusively referred to. As stated in the opinion of the court of appeals, this corporation "is not declared the trustee of any church or religious society. Its property is to be acquired in its own name and for its own purposes; that property and its business are to be managed in its own way, subject to no visitation, supervision, or control by any ecclesiastical authority whatever, but only to that of the government which created it. In respect, then, of its creation, organization, management, and ownership of property it is an ordinary private corporation whose rights are determinable by the law of the land, and the religious opinions of whose members are not subjects of inquiry."

It is not contended that Congress has no power in the District to appropriate money for the purpose expressed in the appropriation, and it is not doubted that it has power to authorize the commissioners of the District of Columbia to enter into a contract with the trustees of an incorporated hospital for the purposes mentioned in the agreement in this case, and the only objection set up is the alleged "sectarian character of the hospital and the specific and limited object of its creation."

The other allegations in complainant's bill are simply statements of his opinion in regard to the results necessarily flowing from the appropriation in question when connected with the agreement mentioned.

The act of Congress, however, shows there is nothing sectarian in the corporation, and "the specific and limited object of its creation" is the opening and keeping a hospital in the city of Washington for the care of such sick and invalid persons as ⊥**300** may place themselves under the treatment and care of the corporation. To make the agreement was within the discretion of the commissioners, and was a fair exercise thereof.

The right reserved in the third section of the charter to amend, alter, or repeal the act leaves full power in Congress to remedy any abuse of the charter privileges.

Without adverting to any other objections to the maintenance of this suit, it is plain that complainant wholly fails to set forth a cause of action, and the bill was properly dismissed by the Court of Appeals, and its decree will therefore be

affirmed.

WITTERS v. WASHINGTON DEPARTMENT OF SERVICES FOR THE BLIND

474 U.S. 481

ON WRIT OF CERTIORARI TO THE SUPREME COURT OF WASHINGTON

Argued November 6, 1985 — Decided January 27, 1986

⊥**482** *Justice MARSHALL* delivered the opinion of the Court.

The Washington Supreme Court ruled that the First Amendment precludes the State of Washington from extending assistance under a state vocational rehabilitation assistance program to a blind person studying at a Christian college and seeking to become a pastor, missionary, or youth director. Finding no such federal constitutional barrier on the record presented to us, we reverse and remand.

⊥483 I

Petitioner Larry Witters applied in 1979 to the Washington Commission for the Blind for vocational rehabilitation services pursuant to Wash. Rev. Code § 74.16.181 (1981). That statute authorized the Commission, *inter alia*, to "[p]rovide for special education and/or training in the professions, business or trades" so as to "assist visually handicapped persons to overcome vocational handicaps and to obtain the maximum degree of self-support and self-care." Petitioner, suffering from a progressive eye condition, was eligible for vocational rehabilitation assistance under the terms of the statute. He was at the time attending Inland Empire School of the Bible, a private Christian college in Spokane, Washington, and studying Bible, ethics, speech, and church administration in order to equip himself for a career as a pastor, missionary, or youth director.

The Commission denied petitioner aid. It relied on an earlier determination embodied in a Commission policy statement that "[t]he Washington State constitution forbids the use of public funds to assist an individual in the pursuit of a career or degree in theology or related areas," and on its conclusion that petitioner's training was "religious **⊥484** instruction" subject to that ban. That was affirmed by a state hearings examiner, who held that the Commission was precluded from funding petitioner's training "in light of the State Constitution's prohibition against the state directly or indirectly supporting a religion." The hearings examiner cited Wash. Const. Art. I, § 11, providing in part that "no public money or property shall be appropriated for or applied to any religious worship, exercise or instruction, or the support of any religious establishment," and Wash. Const., Art. IX, § 4, providing that "[a]ll schools maintained or supported wholly or in part by the public funds shall be forever free from sectarian control or influence." That ruling in turn, was upheld on internal administrative appeal.

Petitioner then instituted an action in state superior court for review of the administrative decision; the court affirmed on the same state-law grounds cited by the agency. The State Supreme Court affirmed as well. The Supreme Court, however, declined to ground its ruling on the Washington Constitution. Instead, it explicitly reserved judgment on the state constitutional issue and chose to base its ruling on the Establishment Clause of the Federal Constitution. The court stated "The Supreme Court has developed a 3-part test for determining the constitutionality of state aid under the establishment clause of the First Amendment. 'First, the statute must have a secular legislative purpose; second, its principal or primary effect must be one that neither advances nor inhibits religion . . .; finally, the statute must not foster "an excessive government entanglement with religion."' *Lemon* v. *Kurtzman*. To withstand attack under the establishment clause, the challenged state action **⊥485** must satisfy each of the three criteria." *Witters* v. *Commission for the Blind*.

The Washington court had no difficulty finding the "secular purpose" prong of that test satisfied. Applying the second prong, however, that of "principal or primary effect," the court held that "provision of financial assistance by the State to enable someone to become a pastor, missionary, or church youth director clearly has the primary effect of advancing religion." The court, therefore held that provision of aid to petitioner would contravene the Federal Constitution. In light of that ruling, the court saw no need to reach the "entanglement" prong; it stated that the record was in any case inadequate for such an inquiry.

We granted certiorari, and we now reverse.

II

The Establishment Clause of the First Amendment has consistently presented this Court with difficult questions of interpretation and application. We acknowledge in *Lemon* v. *Kurtzman*, that "we can only dimly perceive the lines of demarcation in this extraordinarily sensitive area of constitutional law." Nonetheless, the Court's opinions in this area have at least clarified "the broad contours of our inquiry," *Committee for Public Education* v. *Nyquist*, and are sufficient to dispose of this case.

We are guided, as was the court below, by the three-part test set out by this Court in *Lemon*. Our analysis relating to the first prong of that test is simple: all parties concede the unmistakably secular purpose of the Washington program. That program was designed to promote the well-being of the visually handicapped through the provision of vocational rehabilita**⊥486**tion services, and no more than a minuscule amount of the aid awarded under the program is likely to flow to religious education. No party suggests that the State's "actual purpose" in creating the program was to endorse religion, *Wallace* v. *Jaffree*, or that the secular purpose articulated by the legislature is merely "sham." *Wallace*.

The answer to the question posed by the second prong of the *Lemon* test is more difficult. We conclude, however, that extension of aid to petitioner is not barred on that ground either. It is well-settled that the Establishment Clause is not violated every time money previously in the possession of a State is conveyed to a religious institution. For example, a State may issue a paycheck to one of its em**⊥487**ployees, who may then donate all or part of that paycheck to a religious institution, all without constitutional barrier; and the State may do so even knowing that the employee so intends to dispose of his salary. It is equally well-settled, on the other hand, that the State may not grant aid to a religious school, whether cash or in-kind, where the effect of the aid is "that of a direct subsidy to the religious school" from the State. *Grand Rapids School District* v. *Ball.* Aid may have that effect even though it takes the form of aid to students or parents. The question presented is whether, on the facts as they appear in the record before us, extension of aid to petitioner and the use of that aid by petitioner to support his religious education is a permissible transfer similar to the hypothetical salary donation described above, or is an impermissible "direct subsidy."

Certain aspects of Washington's program are central to our inquiry. As far as the record shows, vocational assistance provided under the Washington program is paid directly to the student, who transmits it to the educational institution of his or her choice. Any aid provided under Washington's program that ultimately flows to religious institutions does so only as a result of the genuinely independent and private choices of aid recipients. Washington's program is "made available generally without regard to the sectarian-nonsectarian, or public-nonpublic nature of the institution benefited," *Committee for Public Education* ⊥**488** v. *Nyquist*, and is in no way skewed towards religion. It is not one of "the ingenious plans for channeling state aid to sectarian schools that periodically reach this Court." It creates no financial incentive for students to undertake sectarian education. It does not tend to provide greater or broader benefits for recipients who apply their aid to religious education, nor are the full benefits of the program limited, in large part or in whole, to students at sectarian institutions. On the contrary, aid recipients have full opportunity to expend vocational rehabilitation aid on wholly secular education, and as a practical matter have rather greater prospects to do so. Aid recipients' choices are made among a huge variety of possible careers, of which only a small handful are sectarian. In this case, the fact that aid goes to individuals means that the decision to support religious education is made by the individual, not by the State.

Further, and importantly, nothing in the record indicated that, if petitioner succeeds, any significant portion of the aid expended under the Washington program as a whole will end up flowing to religious education. The function of the Washington program is hardly "to provide desired financial support for nonpublic, sectarian institutions." *Nyquist.* The program, providing vocational assistance to the visually handicapped, does not seem well-suited to serve as the vehicle for such a subsidy. No evidence has been presented indicating that any other person has ever sought to finance religious education or activity pursuant to the State's program. The combination of these factors, we think, makes the link between the state and the school petitioner wishes to attend a highly attenuated one.

On the facts we have set out, it does not seem appropriate to view any aid ultimately flowing to the Inland Empire School of the Bible as resulting from a *state* action sponsoring or subsidizing religion. Nor does the mere circumstance ⊥**489** that petitioner has chosen to use neutrally available state aid to help pay for his religious education confer any message of state endorsement of religion. Thus, while *amici* supporting respondent are correct in pointing out that aid to a religious institution unrestricted in its potential uses, if properly attributable to the State, is "clearly prohibited under the Establishment Clause," *Grand Rapids*, because it may subsidize the religious functions of that institution, that observation is not apposite to this case. On the facts present here, we think the Washington program works no state support of religion prohibited by the Establishment Clause.

III

We therefore reject the claim that, on the record presented, extension of aid under Washington's vocational rehabilitation program to finance petitioner's training at a Christian college to become a pastor, missionary, or youth director would advance religion in a manner inconsistent with the Establishment Clause of the First Amendment. On remand, the state court is of course free to consider the applicability of the "far stricter" dictates of the Washington state constitution, see *Witters* v. *Commission for the Blind*. It may also choose to reopen the factual record in order to consider the arguments made by respondent. We decline petitioner's invitation to leapfrog consideration of those issues by holding that the Free Exercise Clause *requires* Washington to extend vocational rehabilitation aid to petitioner regardless of what the state constitution commands or further factual development reveals, and we ex⊥**490**press no opinion on the matter.

The judgment of the Washington Supreme Court is reversed, and the case is remanded for further proceeding not inconsistent with this opinion.

It is so ordered.

Justice WHITE, concurring.

I remain convinced that the Court's decision finding constitutional violations where a state provides aid to private schools or their students misconstrue the Establishment Clause and disserve the public interest. Even under the cases in which I was in dissent, however, I agree with the Court that the Washington Supreme Court erred in this case. Hence, I join the Court's opinion and judgment. At the same time, I agree with most of *Justice POWELL's* concurring opinion with respect to the relevance of *Mueller* v. *Allen*, to this case.

Justice POWELL, with whom *The CHIEF JUSTICE* and *Justice REHNQUIST* join, concurring.

The Court's omission of *Mueller* v. *Allen* from its analysis may mislead courts and litigants by suggesting that *Mueller* is somehow inapplicable to cases such as this one. I write separately to emphasize that *Mueller* strongly supports the result we reach today.

As the Court states, the central question in this case is whether Washington's provision of aid to handicapped students has the "principal or primary effect" of advancing religion. *Lemon* v. *Kurtzman*. *Mueller* makes the answer clear: state programs that are wholly ⊥**491** neutral in offering educational assistance to a class defined without reference to religion do not violate the second part of the *Lemon* v. *Kurtzman* test, because any aid to religion results from the private choices of individual beneficiaries. Thus, in *Mueller*, we sustained a tax deduction for certain educational expenses, even though the great majority of beneficiaries were parents of children attending sectarian schools. We noted the state's traditionally broad taxing authority, but the decision rested principally on two other factors. First, the deduction was equally available to parents of public school children and parents of children attending private schools. Second, any benefit to religion resulted from the "numerous, private choices of individual parents of school-age children." *Mueller*.

The state program at issue here provides aid to handicapped students when their studies are likely to lead to employment. Aid does not depend on whether the student wishes to attend a public university or a private college, nor does it turn on whether the student seeks training for a religious or a secular career. It follows that under *Mueller* the state's program does not have the "principal or primary effect" of advancing religion.

⊥**492** The Washington Supreme Court reached a different conclusion because it found that the program had the practical effect of aiding religion *in this particular case*. In effect, the court analyzed the cases as if the Washington legislature had passed a private bill that awarded respondent free tuition to pursue religious studies.

Such an analysis conflicts with both common sense and established precedent. Nowhere in *Mueller* did we analyze the effect of Minnesota's tax deduction on the parents who were parties to the case; rather, we looked to the nature and consequences of the program *viewed as a whole*. The same is true of our evaluation of the tuition reimbursement programs at issue in *Nyquist*, and *Sloan* v. *Lemon*. This is the appropriate perspective for this case as well. Viewed in the proper light, the Washington program easily satisfies the second prong of the *Lemon* test.

I agree, for the reasons stated by the Court, that the State's program has a secular purpose, and that no entanglement challenge is properly raised on this record. I therefore join the Court's judgment. On the understanding that nothing we do today lessens the authority of our decision in *Mueller*, I join the Court's opinion as well.

⊥**493** *Justice O'CONNOR*, concurring in the judgment and concurring in part.

I join Parts I and III of the Court's opinion, and concur in the judgment. I also agree with the Court that both the purpose and effect of Washington's program of aid to handicapped students are secular. As *Justice POWELL's* separate opinion persuasively argues, the Court's opinion in *Mueller* v. *Allen* makes clear that "state programs that are wholly neutral in offering educational assistance to a class defined without reference to religion do not violate the second part of the *Lemon* v. *Kurtzman* test, because any aid to religion results from the private decisions of beneficiaries." The aid to religion at issue here is the result of petitioner's private choice. No reasonable observer is likely to draw from the facts before us an inference that the state itself is endorsing a religious practice or belief.

BOWEN v. KENDRICK

487 U.S. 589
ON APPEAL FROM THE UNITED STATES DISTRICT COURT FOR THE DISTRICT OF COLUMBIA
Argued March 30, 1988 — Decided June 29, 1988

⊥**593** *Chief Justice REHNQUIST* delivered the opinion of the Court.

This case involves a challenge to a federal grant program that provides funding for services relating to adolescent sexuality and pregnancy. Considering the federal statute both "on its face" and "as applied," the District Court ruled that the statute violated the Establishment Clause of the First Amendment insofar as it provided for the involvement of religious organizations in the federally funded programs. We conclude, however, that the statute is not unconstitutional on its face, and that a determination of whether any of the grants made pursuant to the statute violate the Establishment Clause requires further proceedings in the District Court.

I

The Adolescent Family Life Act (AFLA or Act), Pub. L. 97-35, 95 Stat. 578, codified at 42 U.S.C. § 300z *et seq.*(1982 ed. and Supp. III), was passed by Congress in 1981 in response to the "severe adverse health, social, and economic consequences" that often follow pregnancy and childbirth among unmarried adolescents. Like its predecessor, the Adolescent Health Services and Pregnancy Prevention and Care Act of 1978, Pub. L. 95-626, Tit. VI, 92 Stat. 3595-3601 (Title VI), the AFLA is essentially a scheme for providing grants to public or nonprofit private organizations or agencies "for services and research in the area of premarital adolescent sexual relations and pregnancy." S. Rep. No. 97-161, 1 (1981) (hereinafter Senate Report). These grants are intended to serve several purposes, including the promotion of "self discipline and other prudent approaches to the problem of adolescent premarital sexual relations," § 300z(b)(1), the promotion of adoption as an alternative for adolescent parents, § 300z(b)(2), the ⊥**594** establishment of new approaches to the delivery of care services for pregnant adolescents, § 300z(b)(3), and the support of research and demonstration projects "concerning the societal causes and consequences of adolescent premarital sexual relations, contraceptive use, pregnancy, and child rearing," § 300z(b)(4).

In pertinent part, grant recipients are to provide two types of services: "care services," for the provision of care to pregnant adolescents and adolescent parents, §300z-1(a)(7), and "prevention services," for the prevention of adolescent sexual relations, § 300z-1(a)(8). While the AFLA leaves it up to the Secretary of Health and Human Services (the Secretary) to define exactly what types of services a grantee must provide, see §§ 300z-1(a)(7) (8), 300z-1(b), the statute contains a listing of "necessary services" that may be funded. These services include pregnancy testing and maternity counseling, adoption counseling and referral services, prenatal and postnatal health care, nutritional information, counseling, child care, mental health services, and perhaps most importantly for present purposes, "educational services relating to family life and problems associated with adolescent premarital sexual relations," § 300z-1(a)(4).

⊥**595** In drawing up the AFLA and determining what services to provide under the Act, Congress was well aware that "the problems of adolescent premarital sex relations, pregnancy, and parenthood are multiple and complex." § 300z(a) (8)(A). Indeed, Congress expressly recognized that legislative or governmental action alone would be insufficient:

"[S]uch problems are best approached through a variety of integrated and essential services provided to adolescents and their families by other family members, religious and charitable organizations, voluntary associations, and other groups in the private sector as well as services provided by publicly sponsored initiatives" § 300z(a)(8)(B). ⊥**596** Accordingly, the AFLA expressly states that federally provided services in this area should promote the involvement of parents, and should "emphasize the provision of support by other family members, religious and charitable organizations, voluntary associations, and other groups." § 300z(a)(10)(C). The AFLA implements this goal by providing in § 300z-2 that demonstration projects funded by the government "shall use such methods as will strengthen the capacity of families to deal with the sexual behavior, pregnancy, or parenthood of adolescents and to make use of support systems such as other family members, friends, religious and charitable organizations, and voluntary associations." In addition, AFLA requires grant applicants, among other things, to describe how they will, "as appropriate in the provision of services[,] involve families of adolescents[, and] involve religious and charitable organizations, voluntary associations, and other groups in the private sector as well as services provided by publicly sponsored initiatives." § 300z-5(a)(21). This broad-based involvement of groups outside of the government was intended by Congress to "establish better coordination, integration, and linkages" among existing programs in the community, § 300z(b)(3) (1982 ed., Supp. III), to aid in the development of "strong family values and close family ties," § 300z(a)(10)(A), and to "help adolescents and their families deal with complex issues of adolescent premarital sexual relations and the consequences of such relations." § 300z(a)(10)(C).

In line with its purposes, the AFLA also imposes limitations on the use of funds by grantees. First, the AFLA expressly states that no funds provided for demonstration projects under the statute may be used for family planning services (other than counseling and referral services) unless appropriate family planning services are not otherwise available in the community. § 300z-3(b)(1). Second, the AFLA restricts the awarding of grants to "programs or projects ⊥**597** which do not provide abortions or abortion counseling or referral," except that the program may provide referral for abortion counseling if the adolescent and her parents request such referral. § 300z-10(a). Finally, the AFLA states that "grants may be made only to projects or programs which do not advocate, promote, or encourage abortion." § 300z-10(a).

Since 1981, when the AFLA was adopted, the Secretary has received 1,088 grant applications and awarded 141 grants. Funding has gone to a wide variety of recipients, including state and local health agencies, private hospitals, community health associations, privately-operated health care centers, and community and charitable organizations. It is undisputed that a number of grantees or subgrantees were organizations with institutional ties to religious denominations.

In 1983, this lawsuit against the Secretary was filed in the United States District Court for the District of Columbia by appellees, a group of federal taxpayers, clergymen, and the American Jewish Congress. Seeking both declaratory and injunctive relief, appellees challenged the constitutionality of the AFLA on the grounds that on its face and as applied the statute violates the religion clauses of the First Amendment. Following cross-motions for summary judgment, the ⊥**598** District Court held for appellees and declared that the AFLA was invalid both on its face and as applied "insofar as religious organizations are involved in carrying out the programs and purposes of the Act."

The court first found that under *Flast* v. *Cohen*, appellees had standing to challenge the statute both on its face and as applied. Turning to the merits, the District Court applied the three-part test for Establishment Clause cases set forth in *Lemon* v. *Kurtzman*. The court concluded that the AFLA has a valid secular purpose: the prevention of social and economic injury caused by teenage pregnancy and premarital sexual relations. In the court's view, however, the AFLA does not survive the second prong of the *Lemon* test because it has the "direct and immediate" effect of advancing religion insofar as it expressly requires grant applicants to describe how they will involve religious organizations in the provision of services. § 300z-5(a)(21)(B). The statute also permits religious organizations to be grantees and "envisions a direct role for those organizations in the education and counseling components of AFLA grants." As written, the AFLA makes it possible for religiously affiliated grantees to teach adolescents on issues that can be considered "fundamental elements of religious doctrine." The ⊥**599** AFLA does all this without imposing any restriction whatsoever against the teaching of "religion *qua* religion" or the inculcation of religious beliefs in federally funded programs. As the District Court put it, "[t]o presume that AFLA counselors from religious organizations can put their beliefs aside when counseling an adolescent on matters that are part of religious doctrine is simply unrealistic."

The District Court then concluded that the statute as applied also runs afoul of the *Lemon* effects test. The evidence presented by appellees revealed that AFLA grants had gone to various organizations that were affiliated with religious denominations and that had corporate requirements that the organizations abide by religious doctrines. Other AFLA grantees were not explicitly affiliated with organized religions, but were "religiously inspired and dedicated to teaching the dogma that inspired them." In the District Court's view, the record clearly established that the AFLA, as it has been administered by the Secretary, has in fact directly advanced religion, provided funding for institutions that were "pervasively sectarian," or allowed federal funds to be used for education and counseling that "amounts to the teaching of religion." As to the entanglement prong of *Lemon*, the court ruled that because AFLA funds are used largely for counseling and teaching, it would require overly intrusive monitoring or oversight to ensure that religion is not advanced by religiously affiliated AFLA grantees. Indeed, the court felt that "it is impossible to comprehend entanglement more extensive and continuous ⊥**600** than that necessitated by the AFLA."

In a separate order, filed August 13, 1987, the District Court ruled that the "constitutionally infirm language of the AFLA, namely its references to 'religious organizations,'" is severable from the Act pursuant to *Alaska Airlines, Inc.* v. *Brock*. The court also denied the Secretary's Fed. Rule Civ. Proc. 59(e) motion to clarify what the court meant by "religious organizations" for purposes of determining the scope of its injunction. On the same day that this order was entered, appellants docketed their appeal on the merits directly with this Court pursuant to 28 U.S.C. §1252. A separate appeal from the District Court's August 13 order was also docketed, as was a cross-appeal by appellees on the severability issue. On November 9, 1987, we noted probable jurisdiction in all three appeals and consolidated the cases for argument.

II

The District Court in this case held the AFLA unconstitutional both on its face and as applied. Few of our cases in the Establishment Clause area have explicitly distinguished between facial challenges to a statute and attacks on the statute as applied. Several cases have clearly involved challenges to a statute "on its face." For example, in *Edwards* v. *Aguillard*, we considered the validity of the Louisiana "Creationism Act," finding the Act "facially invalid." Indeed, in that case it was clear that only a facial challenge could have been considered, as the Act had not been implemented. Other cases, as well, have considered the validity of statutes without the benefit of a record as to how the statute had actually been applied. ⊥**601** See *Wolman* v. *Walter*, *Committee for Public Education & Religious Liberty* v. *Nyquist*.

In other cases we have, in the course of determining the constitutionality of a statute, referred not only to the language of the statute but to the manner in which it had been administered in practice. *Levitt* v. *Committee for Public Education & Religious Liberty*, *Meek* v. *Pittenger*. In several cases we have expressly recognized that an otherwise valid statute authorizing grants might be challenged on the grounds that the award of a grant in a particular case would be impermissible. *Hunt* v. *McNair* involved a challenge to a South Carolina statute that provided for the issuance of revenue bonds to assist "institutions of higher learning" in constructing new facilities. The plaintiffs in that case did not contest the validity of the statute as a whole, but contended only that a statutory grant to a religiously affiliated college would be invalid. In *Tilton* v. *Richardson* the Court reviewed a federal statute authorizing construction grants to colleges exclusively for secular educational purposes. We rejected the contention that the statute was invalid "on its face" and "as applied" to the four church-related colleges that were named as defendants in the case. However, we did leave open the possibility that the statute might authorize grants which could be invalid, stating that "[i]ndividual projects can be properly evaluated if and when challenges arise with respect to particular recipients and some evidence is then presented to show that the institution does in fact possess" sectarian characteristics that might make a grant of aid to the institution constitutionally impermissible. See also *Roemer* v. *Maryland Public Works Board* (upholding a similar statute authorizing grants to colleges against ⊥**602** a "facial" attack and pretermitting the question of whether "particular applications may result in unconstitutional use of funds"). There is, then, precedent in this area of constitutional law for distinguishing between the validity of the statute on its face and its validity in particular applications. Although the Court's opinions have not even adverted to (to say nothing of explicitly delineated) the consequences of this distinction between "on its face" and "as applied" in this context, we think they do justify the District Court's approach in separating the two issues as it did here.

This said, we turn to consider whether the District Court was correct in concluding that the AFLA was unconstitutional on its face. As in previous cases involving facial challenges on Establishment Clause grounds, *e.g.*, *Edwards* v. *Aguillard*, *Mueller* v. *Allen*, we assess the constitutionality of an enactment by reference to the three factors first articulated in *Lemon* v. *Kurtzman*. Under the *Lemon* standard, which guides "[t]he general nature of our inquiry in this area," *Mueller* v. *Allen*, a court may invalidate a statute only if it is motivated wholly by an impermissible purpose, *Lynch* v. *Donnelly*, *Stone* v. *Graham*, if its primary effect is the advancement of religion, *Estate of Thornton* v. *Caldor, Inc.*, or if it requires excessive entanglement between church and state, *Walz* v. *Tax Comm'n*. We consider each of these factors in turn.

As we see it, it is clear from the face of the statute that the AFLA was motivated primarily, if not entirely, by a legitimate secular purpose—the elimination or reduction of social and economic problems caused by teenage sexuality, pregnancy, and parenthood. Appellees cannot, and do not, dispute that, on the whole, religious concerns were not the sole motivation ⊥**603** behind the Act, nor can it be said that the AFLA lacks a legitimate secular purpose. In the court below, however, appellees argued that the *real* purpose of the AFLA could only be understood in reference to the AFLA's predecessor, Title VI. Appellees contended that Congress had an impermissible purpose in adopting the AFLA because it specifically amended Title VI to increase the role of religious organizations in the programs sponsored by the Act. In particular, they pointed to the fact that the AFLA, unlike Title VI, requires grant applicants to describe how they will involve religious organizations in the programs funded by the AFLA.

The District Court rejected this argument, however, reasoning that even if it is assumed that the AFLA was motivated in part by improper concerns, the parts of the statute to which appellees object were also motivated by other, entirely legitimate secular concerns. We agree with this conclusion. As the District Court correctly pointed out, Congress amended Title VI in a number of ways, most importantly for present purposes by attempting to enlist the aid of not only "religious organizations," but also "family members . . . , charitable organizations, voluntary associations, and other groups in the private sector," in addressing the problems associated with adolescent sexuality. § 300z(a)(8)(B); see also §§ 300z-5(a)(21)(A), (B). Compare Title VI, § 601(a)(5) ("the problems of adolescent [sexuality] . . . are best approached through a variety of integrated and essential services"). Congress' decision to amend the statute in this way reflects the entirely appropriate aim of increasing broad-based community involvement "in helping adolescent boys and girls understand the implications of premarital sexual relations, pregnancy, and parenthood." In adopting the AFLA, Congress expressly intended to expand the services already authorized by Title VI, to insure the increased participation of parents in education ⊥**604** and support services, to increase the flexibility of the programs, and to spark the development of new, innovative services. These are all legitimate secular goals that are furthered by the AFLA's additions to Title VI, including the challenged provisions that refer to religious organizations. There simply is no evidence that Congress' "actual purpose" in passing the AFLA was one of "endorsing religion." Nor are we in a position to doubt that Congress' expressed purposes are "sincere and not a sham."

As usual in Establishment Clause cases, the more difficult question is whether the primary effect of the challenged statute is impermissible. Before we address this question, however, it is useful to review again just what the AFLA sets out to do. Simply stated, it authorizes grants to institutions that are capable of providing certain care and prevention services to adolescents. Because of the complexity of the problems that Congress sought to remedy, potential grantees are required to describe how they will involve other organizations, including religious organizations, in the programs funded by the federal grants. There is no requirement in the Act that grantees be affiliated with any religious denomination, although the Act clearly does not rule out grants to religious organizations. The services to be pro⊥**605**vided under the AFLA are not religious in character, nor has there been any suggestion that religious institutions or organizations with religious ties are uniquely well qualified to carry out those services. Certainly it is true that a substantial part of the services listed as "necessary services" under the Act involve some sort of education or counseling, but there is nothing inherently religious about these activities and appellees do not contend that, by themselves, the AFLA's "necessary services" somehow have the primary effect of advancing religion. Finally, it is clear that the AFLA takes a particular approach toward dealing with adolescent sexuality and pregnancy—for example, two of its stated purposes are to "promote self discipline and other prudent approaches to the problem of adolescent premarital sexual relations," § 300z(b)(1), and to "promote adoption as an alternative," § 300z(b)(2)—but again, that approach is not inherently religious, although it may coincide with the approach taken by certain religions.

Given this statutory framework, there are two ways in which the statute, considered "on its face," might be said to have the impermissible primary effect of advancing religion. First, it can be argued that the AFLA advances religion by expressly recognizing that "religious organizations have a role to play" in addressing the problems associated with teen⊥**606**age sexuality. In this view, even if no religious institution receives aid or funding pursuant to the AFLA, the statute is invalid under the Establishment Clause because, among other things, it expressly enlists the involvement of religiously affiliated organizations in the federally subsidized programs, it endorses religious solutions to the problems addressed by the Act, or it creates symbolic ties between church and state. Secondly, it can be argued that the AFLA is invalid on its face because it allows religiously affiliated organizations to participate as grantees or subgrantees in AFLA programs. From this standpoint, the Act is invalid because it authorizes direct federal funding of religious organizations which, given the AFLA's educational function and the fact that the AFLA's "viewpoint" may coincide with the grantee's "viewpoint" on sexual matters, will result unavoidably in the impermissible "inculcation" of religious beliefs in the context of a federally funded program.

We consider the former objection first. As noted previously, the AFLA expressly mentions the role of religious organizations in four places. It states (1) that the problems of teenage sexuality are "best approached through a variety of integrated and essential services provided to adolescents and their families by[, among others,] religious organizations," § 300z(a)(8)(B), (2) that federally subsidized services "should emphasize the provision of support by[, among others,] religious organizations," § 300z(a)(10)(C) (3) that AFLA programs "shall use such methods as will strengthen the capacity of families . . . to make use of support systems such as . . . religious . . . organizations," § 300-2(a), and (4) that grant applicants shall describe how they will involve religious organizations, among other groups, in the provision of services under the Act. § 300z-5(a)(21)(A).

Putting aside for the moment the possible role of religious organizations as grantees, these provisions of the statute reflect at most Congress' considered judgment that religious organizations can help solve the problems to which the ⊥**607** AFLA is addressed. Nothing in our previous cases prevents Congress from making such a judgment or from recognizing the important part that religion or religious organizations may play in resolving certain secular problems. Particularly when, as Congress found, "prevention of adolescent sexual activity and adolescent pregnancy depends primarily upon developing strong family values and close family ties," § 300z(a)(10)(A), it seems quite sensible for Congress to recognize that religious organizations can influence values and can have some influence on family life, including parents' relations with their adolescent children. To the extent that this Congressional recognition has any effect of advancing religion, the effect is at most "incidental and remote." In addition, although the AFLA does require potential grantees to describe how they will involve religious organizations in the provision of services under the Act, it also requires grantees to describe the involvement of "charitable organizations, voluntary associations, and other groups in the private sector," § 300z-5(a)(21)(B). In our view, this reflects the statute's successful maintenance of "a course of neutrality among religions, and between religion and nonreligion," *Grand Rapids School District* v. *Ball*.

⊥**608** This brings us to the second grounds for objecting to the AFLA: the fact that it allows religious institutions to participate as recipients of federal funds. The AFLA defines an "eligible grant recipient" as a "public or nonprofit private organization or agency" which demonstrates the capability of providing the requisite services, § 300z-1(a)(3). As this provision would indicate, a fairly wide spectrum of organizations is eligible to apply for and receive funding under the Act, and nothing on the face of the Act suggests the AFLA is anything but neutral with respect to the grantee's status as a sectarian or purely secular institution. See Senate Report, at 16 ("Religious affiliation is not a criterion for selection as a grantee . . ."). In this regard, then, the AFLA is similar to other statutes that this Court has upheld against Establishment Clause challenges in the past. In *Roemer* v. *Maryland Board of Public Works*, for example, we upheld a Maryland statute that provided annual subsidies directly to qualifying colleges and universities in the State, including religiously affiliated institutions. As the plurality stated, "religious institutions need not be quarantined from public benefits that are neutrally available to all." Similarly, in *Tilton* v. *Richardson*, we approved the federal Higher Educational Facilities Act, which was intended by Congress to provide construction grants to "all colleges and universities regardless of any affiliation with or sponsorship by a religious body." And in *Hunt* v. *McNair*, we rejected a challenge to a South Carolina statute that made certain benefits "available to all institutions of higher education in South Carolina, whether or not having a religious affiliation." In other cases involving indirect ⊥**609** grants of state aid to religious institutions, we have found it important that the aid is made available regardless of whether it will ultimately flow to a secular or sectarian institution. See, *e.g.*, *Witters* v. *Washington Dept. of Services for the Blind*, *Mueller* v. *Allen*, *Everson* v. *Board of Education*, *Walz* v. *Tax Comm'n*.

We note in addition that this Court has never held that religious institutions are disabled by the First Amendment from participating in publicly sponsored social welfare programs. To the contrary, in *Bradfield* v. *Roberts*, the Court upheld an agreement between the Commissioners of the District of Columbia and a religiously affiliated hospital whereby the Federal Government would pay for the construction of a new building on the grounds of the hospital. In effect, the Court refused to hold that the mere fact that the hospital was "conducted under the auspices of the Roman Catholic Church" was sufficient to alter the purely secular legal character of the corporation, particularly in the absence of any allegation that the hospital discriminated on the basis of religion or operated in any way inconsistent with its secular charter. In the Court's view, the giving of federal aid to the hospital was entirely consistent with the Establishment Clause, and the fact that the hospital was religiously affiliated was "wholly immaterial." The propriety of this holding, and the long history of cooperation and interdependency between governments and charitable or religious organizations is reflected in the legislative history of the AFLA. See S. Rep. No. 98-496, 10 (1984) ("Charitable organizations with religious affiliations historically have provided social services with the support of their communities and without controversy").

Of course, even when the challenged statute appears to be neutral on its face, we have always been careful to ensure that direct government aid to religiously affiliated institutions does not have the primary effect of advancing religion. ⊥**610** One way in which direct government aid might have that effect is if the aid flows to institutions that are "pervasively sectarian." We stated in *Hunt* that

"[a]id normally may be thought to have a primary effect of advancing religion when it flows to an institution in which religion is so pervasive that a substantial portion of its functions are subsumed in the religious mission. . . ." The reason for this is that there is a risk that direct government funding, even if it is designated for specific secular purposes, may nonetheless advance the pervasively sectarian institution's "religious mission." Accordingly, a relevant factor in deciding whether a particular statute on its face can be said to have the improper effect of advancing religion is the determination of whether, and to what extent, the statute directs government aid to pervasively sectarian institutions. In *Grand Rapids School District*, for example, the Court began its "effects" inquiry with "a consideration of the nature of the institutions in which the [challenged] programs operate."

In this case, nothing on the face of the AFLA indicates that a significant proportion of the federal funds will be disbursed to "pervasively sectarian" institutions. Indeed, the contention that there is a substantial risk of such institutions receiving direct aid is undercut by the AFLA's facially neutral grant requirements, the wide spectrum of public and private organizations which are capable of meeting the AFLA's requirements, and the fact that, of the eligible religious institutions, many will not deserve the label of "pervasively sectarian." This is not a case like *Grand Rapids*, where the ⊥**611** challenged aid flowed almost entirely to parochial schools. In that case the state's "Shared Time" program was directed specifically at providing certain classes for nonpublic schools, and 40 of 41 of the schools that actually participated in the program were found to be "pervasively sectarian." Instead, this case more closely resembles *Tilton* and *Roemer*, where it was foreseeable that some proportion of the recipients of government aid would be religiously affiliated, but that only a small portion of these, if any, could be considered "pervasively sectarian." In those cases we upheld the challenged statutes on their face and as applied to the institutions named in the complaints, but left open the consequences which would ensue if they allowed federal aid to go to institutions that were in fact pervasively sectarian. As in *Tilton* and *Roemer*, we do not think the possibility that AFLA grants may go to religious institutions that can be considered "pervasively sectarian" is sufficient to conclude that no grants whatsoever can be given under the statute to religious organizations. We think that the District Court was wrong in concluding otherwise.

Nor do we agree with the District Court that the AFLA necessarily has the effect of advancing religion because the religiously affiliated AFLA grantees will be providing educational and counseling services to adolescents. Of course, we have said that the Establishment Clause does "prohibit government-financed or government-sponsored indoctrination into the beliefs of a particular religious faith," *Grand* ⊥**612** *Rapids*, and we have accordingly struck down programs that entail an unacceptable risk that government funding would be used to "advance the religious mission" of the religious institution receiving aid. But nothing in our prior cases warrants the presumption adopted by the District Court that religiously affiliated AFLA grantees are not capable of carrying out their functions under the AFLA in a lawful, secular manner. Only in the contest of aid to "pervasively sectarian" institutions have we invalidated an aid program on the grounds that there was a "substantial" risk that aid to these religious institutions would, knowingly or unknowingly, result in religious indoctrination. In contrast, when the aid is to flow to religiously affiliated institutions that were not pervasively sectarian, as in *Roemer*, we refused to presume that it would be used in a way that would have the primary effect of advancing religion. *Roemer* ("We must assume that the colleges . . . will exercise their delegated control over use of the funds in compliance with the statutory, and therefore the constitutional, mandate"). We think that the type of presumption that the District Court applied in this case is simply unwarranted. As we stated in *Roemer* "It has not been the Court's practice, in considering facial challenges to statutes of this kind, to strike them down in anticipation that particular applications may result in unconstitutional use of funds."

We also disagree with the District Court's conclusion that the AFLA is invalid because it authorizes "teaching" by religious grant recipients on "matters [that] are fundamental elements of religious doctrine," such as the harm of premarital sex and the reasons for choosing adoption over abortion. On an issue as sensitive and important as teenage sexuality, it is not surprising that the government's secular concerns would either coincide or conflict ⊥**613** with those of religious institutions. But the possibility or even the likelihood that some of the religious institutions who receive AFLA funding will agree with the message that Congress intended to deliver to adolescents through the AFLA is insufficient to warrant a finding that the statute on its face has the primary effect of advancing religion. Nor does the alignment of the statute and the religious views of the grantees run afoul of our proscription against "fund[ing] a specifically religious activity in an otherwise substantially secular setting." *Hunt*. The facially neutral projects authorized by the AFLA—including pregnancy testing, adoption counseling and referral services, prenatal and postnatal care, educational services, residential care, child care, consumer education, etc.—are not themselves "specifically religious activities," and they are not converted into such activities by the fact that they are carried out by organizations with religious affiliations.

As yet another reason for invalidating parts of the AFLA, the District Court found that the involvement of religious organizations in the Act has the impermissible effect of creating a "crucial symbolic link" between government and religion. If we were to adopt the District Court's reasoning, it could be argued that any time a government aid program provides funding to religious organizations in an area in which the organization also has an interest, an impermissible "symbolic link" could be created, no matter whether the aid was to be used solely for secular purposes. This would jeopardize government aid to religiously affiliated hospitals, for example, on the ground that patients would perceive a "symbolic link" between the hospital—part of whose "religious mission" might be to save lives—and whatever government entity is subsidizing the purely secular medical services provided to the patient. We decline to adopt the ⊥**614** District Court's reasoning and conclude that, in this case, whatever "symbolic link" might in fact be created by the AFLA's disbursement of funds to religious institutions is not sufficient to justify striking down the statute on its face.

A final argument that has been advanced for striking down the AFLA on "effects" grounds is the fact that the statute lacks an express provision preventing the use of federal funds for religious purposes. Clearly, if there were such a provision in this statute, it would be easier to conclude that the statute on its face could not be said to have the primary effect of advancing religion, but we have never stated that a *statutory* restriction is constitutionally required. The closest we came to such a holding was in *Tilton*, where we struck down a provision of the statute that would have eliminated government sanctions for violating the statute's restrictions on religious uses of funds after 20 years. The reason we did so, however, was because the 20-year limit on sanctions created a risk that the religious institution would, after the 20 years were up, act as if there were no longer any constitutional or statutory limitations on its use of the federally funded building. This aspect of the decision in *Tilton* was thus intended to indicate that the constitutional limitations on use of federal funds, as embodied in the statutory restriction, could not simply "expire" at some point during the economic life of the benefit that the grantee received from the government. In this case, although there is no express statutory limitation on religious use of funds, there is also no intimation in the statute that at some point, or for some grantees, religious uses are permitted. To the contrary, the 1984 Senate Report on the AFLA states that "the use of Adolescent Family Life Act funds to ⊥**615** promote religion, or to teach the religious doctrines of a particular sect, is contrary to the intent of this legislation." S. Rep. No. 98-496, p. 10 (1984). We note in addition that the AFLA requires each grantee to undergo evaluations of the services it provides, § 300z-6(b)(1), and also requires grantees to "make such reports concerning its use of Federal funds as the Secretary may require," § 300z-5(c). The application requirements of the Act, as well, require potential grantees to disclose in detail exactly what services they intend to provide and how they will be provided. § 300z-6(a). These provisions, taken together, create a mechanism whereby the Secretary can police the grants that are given out under the Act to ensure that federal funds are not used for impermissible purposes. Unlike some other grant programs, in which aid might be given out in one-time grants without ongoing supervision by the government, the programs established under the authority of the AFLA can be monitored to determine whether the funds are, in effect, being used by the grantees in such a way as to advance religion. Given this statutory scheme, we do not think that the absence of an express limitation on the use of federal funds for religious purposes means that the statute, on its face, has the primary effect of advancing religion.

This, of course, brings us to the third prong of the *Lemon* Establishment Clause "test"—the question whether the AFLA leads to "'an excessive government entanglement with religion.'" *Lemon*. There is no doubt that the monitoring of AFLA grants is necessary if the Secretary is to ensure that public money is to be spent in the way that Congress intended and in a way that comports with the Establishment Clause. Accordingly, this case presents us with yet another "Catch-22" argument: the very supervision of the aid to assure that it does not further religion renders the statute invalid. ⊥**616** For this and other reasons, the "entanglement" prong of the *Lemon* test has been much criticized over the years. Most of the cases in which the Court has divided over the "entanglement" part of the *Lemon* test have involved aid to parochial schools; in *Aguilar* v. *Felton*, for example, the Court's finding of excessive entanglement rested in large part on the undisputed fact that the elementary and secondary schools receiving aid were "pervasively sectarian" and had "'as a substantial purpose the inculcation of religious values.'" In *Aguilar*, the Court feared that an adequate level of supervision would require extensive and permanent on-site monitoring, and would threaten both the "freedom of religious belief of those who [were] not adherents of that denomination" and the "freedom of . . . the adherents of the denomination."

Here, by contrast, there is no reason to assume that the religious organizations which may receive grants are "pervasively sectarian" in the same sense as the Court has held parochial schools to be. There is accordingly no reason to fear that the less intensive monitoring involved here will cause the Government to intrude unduly in the day-to-day operation of the religiously affiliated AFLA grantees. Unquestionably, the Secretary will review the programs set up and run by the AFLA grantees, and undoubtedly this will involve a review of, for example, the educational materials that a ⊥**617** grantee proposes to use. The Secretary may also wish to have government employees visit the clinics or offices where AFLA programs are being carried out to see whether they are in fact being administered in accordance with statutory and constitutional requirements. But in our view, this type of grant monitoring does not amount to "excessive entanglement," at least in the context of a statute authorizing grants to religiously affiliated organizations that are not necessarily "pervasively sectarian."

In sum, in this somewhat lengthy discussion of the validity of the AFLA on its face, we have concluded that the statute has a valid secular purpose, does not have the primary effect of advancing religion, and does not create an excessive entanglement of church and state. We note, as is proper given the traditional presumption in favor of the constitutionality of statutes enacted by Congress, that our conclusion that the statute does not violate the Establishment Clause is consistent with the conclusion Congress reached in the course of its deliberations on the AFLA. As the Senate Committee Report states:

"In the committee's view, provisions for the involvement of religious organizations [in the AFLA] do not violate the constitutional separation between church and state. Recognizing the limitations of Government in dealing with a problem that has complex moral and social dimensions, the committee believes that promoting the involvement of religious organizations in the solution to ⊥**618** these problems is neither inappropriate or illegal."

For the foregoing reasons we conclude that the AFLA does not violate the Establishment Clause "on its face."

III

We turn now to consider whether the District Court correctly ruled that the AFLA was unconstitutional as applied. Our first task in this regard is to consider whether appellees had standing to raise this claim. In *Flast* v. *Cohen* we held that federal taxpayers have standing to raise Establishment Clause claims against exercises of congressional power under the taxing and spending power of Art. I, § 8, of the Constitution. Although we have considered the problem of standing and Article III limitations on federal jurisdiction many times since then, we have consistently adhered to *Flast* and the narrow exception it created to the general rule against taxpayer standing established in *Frothingham* v. *Mellon*. Accordingly, in this case there is no dispute that appellees have standing to raise their challenge to the AFLA on its face. What is disputed, however, is whether appellees also have standing to challenge the statute as applied. The answer to this question turns on our decision in *Valley Forge Christian College* v. *Americans United for Separation of Church and State, Inc.* In *Valley Forge*, we ruled that taxpayers did not have standing to challenge a decision by the Secretary of Health, Education, and Welfare (HEW) to dispose of certain property pursuant to the Federal Property and Administrative Services Act of 1949, 63 Stat. 77, as amended, 40 U.S.C. § 471 *et seq.* We rejected the taxpayers' claim of standing for two reasons: first, because "the source of their complaint is not a congressional action, but a decision by HEW to transfer a parcel of federal property," and second, because "the property transfer about which [the taxpayers] complain was not an exercise of ⊥**619** authority conferred by the Taxing and Spending Clause of Art. I, §8." Appellants now contend that appellees' standing in this case is deficient for the former reason; they argue that a challenge to the AFLA "as applied" is really a challenge to executive action, not to an exercise of congressional authority under the Taxing and Spending Clause. We do not think, however, that appellees' claim that AFLA funds are being used improperly by individual grantees is any less a challenge to congressional taxing and spending power simply because the funding authorized by Congress has flowed through and been administered by the Secretary. Indeed, *Flast* itself was a suit against the Secretary of HEW, who had been given the authority under the challenged statute to administer the spending program that Congress had created. In subsequent cases, most notably *Tilton*, we have not questioned the standing of taxpayer plaintiffs to raise Establishment Clause challenges, even when their claims raised questions about the administratively made grants. This is not a case like *Valley Forge*, where the challenge was to an exercise of executive authority pursuant to the Property Clause of Art. IV, § 3, or *Schlesinger* v. *Reservists Committee to Stop the War*, where the plaintiffs challenged the executive decision to allow Members of Congress to maintain their status as officers of the Armed Forces Reserve. Nor is this, as we stated in *Flast*, a challenge to "an incidental expenditure of tax funds in the administration of an essentially regulatory statute." The AFLA is at heart a program of disbursement of funds pursuant to Con⊥**620**gress' taxing and spending powers, and appellees' claims call into question how the funds authorized by Congress are being disbursed pursuant to the AFLA's statutory mandate. In this case there is thus a sufficient nexus between the taxpayer's standing as a taxpayer and the congressional exercise of taxing and spending power, notwithstanding the role the Secretary plays in administering the statute.

On the merits of the "as applied" challenge, it seems to us that the District Court did not follow the proper approach in assessing appellees' claim that the Secretary is making grants under the Act that violate the Establishment Clause of the First Amendment. Although the District Court stated several times that AFLA aid had been given to religious organizations that were "pervasively sectarian," it did not identify which grantees it was referring to, nor did it discuss with any particularity the aspects of those organizations which in its view warranted classification as "pervasively sectarian." The District Court did identify certain instances in which it felt AFLA funds were used for constitutionally improper purposes, but in our view the court did not adequately design its remedy to address the specific problems it found in the Secretary's administration of the statute. Accordingly, although there is no dispute that the record contains evidence of specific incidents of impermissible behavior by AFLA grantees, we feel that this case should be remanded to the District ⊥**621** Court for consideration of the evidence presented by appellees insofar as it sheds light on the manner in which the statute is presently being administered. It is the latter inquiry to which the Court must direct itself on remand.

In particular, it will be open to appellees on remand to show that AFLA aid is flowing to grantees that can be considered "pervasively sectarian" religious institutions, such as we have held parochial schools to be. As our previous discussion has indicated, and as *Tilton*, *Hunt*, and *Roemer* make clear, it is not enough to show that the recipient of a challenged grant is affiliated with a religious institution or that it is "religiously inspired."

The District Court should also consider on remand whether in particular cases AFLA aid has been used to fund "specifically religious activit[ies] in an otherwise substantially secular setting." *Hunt*. In *Hunt*, for example, we deemed it important that the conditions on which the aid was granted were sufficient to preclude the possibility that funds would be used for the construction of a building used for religious purposes. Here it would be relevant to determine, for example, whether the Secretary has permitted AFLA grantees to use materials that have an explicitly religious content or are designed to inculcate the views of a particular religious faith. As we have pointed out in our previous discussion, evidence that the views espoused on questions such as premarital sex, abortion, and the like happen to coincide with the religious views of the AFLA grantee would not be sufficient to show that the grant funds are being used in such a way as to have a primary effect of advancing religion.

If the District Court concludes on the evidence presented that grants are being made by the Secretary in violation of the Establishment Clause, it should then turn to the question of the appropriate remedy. We deal here with a funding statute with respect to which Congress has expressed the view that the use of funds by grantees to promote religion, ⊥**622** or to teach religious doctrines of a particular sect, would be contrary to the intent of the statute. The Secretary has promulgated a series of conditions to each grant, including a prohibition against teaching or promoting religion. While these strictures may not be coterminous with the requirements of the Establishment Clause, they make it very likely that any particular grant which would violate the Establishment Clause would also violate the statute and the grant conditions imposed by the Secretary. Should the court conclude that the Secretary has wrongfully approved certain AFLA grants, an appropriate remedy would require the Secretary to withdraw such approval.

IV

We conclude, first, that the District Court erred in holding that the AFLA is invalid on its face, and second, that the court should consider on remand whether particular AFLA grants have had the primary effect of advancing religion. Should the court conclude that the Secretary's current practice does allow such grants, it should devise a remedy to insure that grants awarded by the Secretary comply with the constitution and the statute. The judgment of the District Court is accordingly

Reversed.

Justice O'CONNOR, concurring.

This case raises somewhat unusual questions involving a facially valid statute that appears to have been administered in a way that led to violations of the Establishment Clause. I agree with the Court's resolution of those questions, and I join its opinion. I write separately, however, to explain why I do not believe that the Court's approach reflects any tolerance for the kind of improper administration that seems to have occurred in the government program at issue here.

The dissent says, and I fully agree, that "[p]ublic funds may not be used to advance the religious message." ⊥**623** As the Court notes, "there is no dispute that the record contains evidence of specific incidents of impermissible behavior by AFLA grantees." Because the District Court employed an analytical framework that did not require a detailed discussion of the voluminous record, the extent of this impermissible behavior and the degree to which it is attributable to poor administration by the Executive Branch is somewhat less clear. In this circumstance, two points deserve to be emphasized. First, any use of public funds to promote religious doctrines violates the Establishment Clause. Second, *extensive* violations—if they can be proved in this case—will be highly relevant in shaping an appropriate remedy that ends such abuses. For that reason, appellees may yet prevail on remand, and I do not believe that the Court's approach entails a relaxation of "the unwavering vigilance that the Constitution requires against any law 'respecting an establishment of religion.'"

The need for detailed factual findings by the District Court stems in part from the delicacy of the task given to the Executive Branch by the Adolescent Family Life Act (AFLA). Government has a strong and legitimate secular interest in encouraging sexual restraint among young people. At the same time, as the dissent rightly points out, "[t]here is a very real and important difference between running a soup kitchen or a hospital, and counseling pregnant teenagers on how to make the difficult decisions facing them." Using religious organizations to advance the secular goals of the AFLA, without thereby permitting religious indoctrination, is inevitably more difficult than in other projects, such as ministering to the poor and the sick. I nonetheless agree with the Court that the partnership between governmental and religious institutions contemplated by the AFLA need not result in constitutional violations, despite an undeniably greater risk than is present in cooperative undertakings that involve less sensitive objectives. If the District Court ⊥**624** finds on remand that grants are being made in violation of the Establishment Clause, an appropriate remedy would take into account the history of the program's administration as well as the extent of any continuing constitutional violations.

Justice KENNEDY, with whom *Justice* SCALIA joins, concurring.

I join the Court's opinion, and write this separate concurrence to discuss one feature of the proceedings on remand. The Court states that "it will be open to appellees on remand to show that AFLA aid is flowing to grantees that can be considered 'pervasively sectarian' religious institutions, such as we have held parochial schools to be." In my view, such a showing will not alone be enough, in an as-applied challenge, to make out a violation of the Establishment Clause.

Though I am not confident that the term "pervasively sectarian" is a well-founded juridical category, I recognize the thrust of our previous decisions that a statute which provides for exclusive or disproportionate funding to pervasively sectarian institutions may impermissibly advance religion and as such be invalid on its face. We hold today, however, that the neutrality of the grant requirements and the diversity of the organizations described in the statute before us foreclose the argument that it is disproportionately tied to pervasively sectarian groups. Having held that the statute is not facially invalid, the only purpose of further inquiring whether any particular grantee institution is pervasively sectarian is as a preliminary step to demonstrating that the funds are in fact being used to further religion. In sum, where, as in this case, a statute provides that the benefits of a program are to be distributed in a neutral fashion to religious and non-religious applicants alike, and the program withstands a facial challenge, it is not unconstitutional as applied solely by reason of the religious character of a specific recipient. The question in an as-applied challenge is not **⊥625** whether the entity is of a religious character, but how it spends its grant.

Justice BLACKMUN, with whom *Justice* BRENNAN, *Justice* MARSHALL, and *Justice* STEVENS join, dissenting.

In 1981, Congress enacted the Adolescent Family Life Act (AFLA), 95 Stat. 578, 42 U.S.C. § 300z *et seq.* (1982 ed. and Supp. III), thereby "involv[ing] families[,] . . . religious and charitable organizations, voluntary associations, and other groups," § 300z-5(a)(21), in a broad-scale effort to alleviate some of the problems associated with teenage pregnancy. It is unclear whether Congress ever envisioned that public funds would pay for a program during a session of which parents and teenagers would be instructed:

"You want to know the church teachings on sexuality.... You are the church. You people sitting here are the body of Christ. The teachings of you and the things you value are, in fact, the values of the Catholic Church."

Or of curricula that taught:

"The Church has always taught that the marriage act, or intercourse, seals the union of husband and wife (and is a representation of their union on all levels). Christ commits Himself to us when we come to ask for the sacrament of marriage. We ask Him to be active in our life. God is love. We ask Him to share His love in ours, and God procreates with us, He enters into our physical union with Him, and we begin new life."

Or the teaching of a method of family planning described on the grant application as "not only a method of birth regulation but also a philosophy of procreation," and promoted as helping "spouses who are striving . . . to transform their married life into testimony[,] . . . to cultivate their matrimonial spirituality[, and] to make themselves better in**⊥626**struments in God's plan," and as "facilitat[ing] the evangelization of homes."

Whatever Congress had in mind, however, it enacted a statute that facilitated and, indeed, encouraged the use of public funds for such instruction, by giving religious groups a central pedagogical and counseling role without imposing any restraints on the sectarian quality of the participation. As the record developed thus far in this litigation makes all too clear, federal tax dollars appropriated for AFLA purposes have been used, with Government approval, to support religious teaching. Today the majority upholds the facial validity of this statute and remands the case to the District Court for further proceedings concerning appellees' challenge to the manner in which the statute has been applied. Because I am firmly convinced that our cases require invalidating this statutory scheme, I dissent.

I

The District Court, troubled by the lack of express guidance from this Court as to the appropriate manner in which to examine Establishment Clause challenges to an entire statute as well as to specific instances of its implementation, reluctantly proceeded to analyze the AFLA both "on its face" and "as applied." Thereafter, on cross-motions for summary judgment supported by an extensive record of undisputed facts, the District Court applied the three-pronged analysis of *Lemon* v. *Kurtzman* and declared the AFLA unconstitutional both facially and as applied. The majority acknowledges that this Court in some cases has passed on the facial validity of a legislative enactment and in others limited its analysis to the particular applications at issue; yet, while confirming that the District Court was justified in analyzing the AFLA both ways, the Court fails to elaborate on the consequences that flow from the analytical division.

⊥627 While the distinction is sometimes useful in constitutional litigation, the majority misuses it here to divide and conquer appellees' challenge. By designating appellees' broad attack on the statute as a "facial" challenge, the majority justifies divorcing its analysis from the extensive record developed in the District Court, and thereby strips the challenge of much of its force and renders the evaluation of the *Lemon* "effects" prong particularly sterile and meaningless. By characterizing appellees' objections to the real-world operation of the AFLA an "as-applied" challenge, the Court risks misdirecting the litigants and the lower courts toward piecemeal litigation continuing indefinitely throughout the life of the AFLA. In my view, a more effective way to review Establishment Clause challenges is to look to the type of re**⊥628**lief prayed for by the plaintiffs, and the force of the arguments and supporting evidence they marshal. Whether we denominate a challenge that focuses on the systematically unconstitutional operation of a statute a "facial" challenge—because it goes to the statute as a whole—or an "as-applied" challenge—because we rely on real-world events—the Court should not blind itself to the facts revealed by the undisputed record.

As is evident from the parties' arguments, the record compiled below, and the decision of the District Court, this case has been litigated primarily as a broad challenge to the statutory scheme as a whole, not just to the awarding of grants to a few individual applicants. The thousands of pages of depositions, affidavits, and documentary evidence were not intended to demonstrate merely that particular grantees should not receive further funding. Indeed, because of the 5-year grant cycle, some of the original grantees are no longer AFLA participants. This record was designed to show that the AFLA had been interpreted and implemented by the Government in a manner that was clearly unconstitutional, and appellees sought declaratory and injunctive relief as to the entire statute.

⊥629 In discussing appellees' as-applied challenge, the District Court recognized that their objections went further than the validity of the particular grants under review:

"The undisputed record before the Court transforms the inherent conflicts between the AFLA and the Constitution into reality. . . . While the Court will not engage in an exhaustive recitation of the record, references to representative portions of the record reveal the extent to which the AFLA has in fact 'directly and immediately' advanced religion, funded 'pervasively sectarian' institutions, or permitted the use of federal tax dollars for education and counseling that amounts to the teaching of religion."

The majority declines to accept the District Court's characterization of the record, yet fails to renew it independently, relying instead on its assumptions and casual observations about the character of the grantees and potential grantees. **⊥630** In doing so, the Court neglects its responsibilities under the Establishment Clause and gives uncharacteristically short shrift to the District Court's understanding of the facts.

II

Before proceeding to apply *Lemon's* three-part analysis to the AFLA, I pause to note a particular flaw in the majority's method. A central premise of the majority opinion seems to be that the primary means of ascertaining whether a statute that appears to be neutral on its face in fact has the effect of advancing religion is to determine whether aid flows to "pervasively sectarian" institutions. This misplaced focus leads the majority to ignore the substantial body of case law the Court has developed in analyzing programs providing direct aid to parochial schools, **⊥631** and to rely almost exclusively on the few cases in which the Court has upheld the supplying of aid to private colleges, including religiously affiliated institutions.

"Pervasively sectarian," a vaguely defined term of art, has its roots in this Court's recognition that Government must not engage in detailed supervision of the inner workings of religious institutions, and the Court's sensible distaste for the "picture of state inspectors prowling the halls of parochial schools and auditing classroom instruction," *Lemon* v. *Kurtzman*. Under the "effects" prong of the *Lemon* test, the Court has used one variant or another of the pervasively sectarian concept to explain why any but the most indirect forms of government aid to such institutions would necessarily have the effect of advancing religion. For example, in *Meek* v. *Pittenger*, the Court explained

"[I]t would simply ignore reality to attempt to separate secular educational functions from the predominantly religious role performed by many of Pennsylvania's church-related elementary and secondary schools and to then characterize Act 195 as channeling aid to the secular without providing direct aid to the sectarian."

The majority first skews the Establishment Clause analysis by adopting a cramped view of what constitutes a pervasively sectarian institution. Perhaps because most of the Court's decisions in this area have come in the context of aid to parochial schools, which traditionally have been characterized as pervasively sectarian, the majority seems to equate the characterization with the institution. In support of that **⊥632** illusion, the majority relies heavily on three cases in which the Court has upheld direct government funding to liberal arts colleges with some religious affiliation, noting that such colleges were not "pervasively sectarian." But the happenstance that the few cases in which direct-aid statutes have been upheld have concerned religiously affiliated liberal arts colleges no more suggests that only parochial schools should be considered "pervasively sectarian," than it suggests that the only religiously affiliated institutions that may ever receive direct government finding are private liberal arts colleges. In fact, the cases on which the majority relies have stressed that the institutions' "*predominant* higher education mission is to provide their students with a *secular* education." *Tilton* v. *Richardson* (emphasis added). In sharp contrast, the District Court here concluded that AFLA grantees and participants included "organizations with institutional ties to religious denominations *and corporate requirements that the organizations abide by and not contradict religious doctrines*. In addition, other recipients of AFLA funds, while not explicitly affiliated with a religious denomination, are religiously inspired *and dedicated to teaching the dogma that inspired them*" (emphasis **⊥633**added). On a continuum of "sectarianism" running from parochial schools at one end to the colleges funded by the statutes upheld in *Tilton*, *Hunt*, and *Roemer* at the other, the AFLA grantees described by the District Court clearly are much closer to the former than to the latter.

More importantly, the majority also errs in suggesting that the inapplicability of the label is generally dispositive. While a plurality of the Court has framed the inquiry as "whether an institution is so 'pervasively sectarian' that it may receive no direct state aid of any kind," *Roemer* v. *Maryland Public Works Board*, the Court never has treated the absence of such a finding as a license to disregard the potential for impermissible fostering of religion. The characterization of an institution as "pervasively sectarian" allows us to eschew further inquiry into the use that will be made of direct government aid. In that sense, it is a sufficient, but not a necessary, basis for a finding that a challenged program creates an unacceptable Establishment Clause risk. The label thus serves in some cases as a proxy for a more detailed analysis of the institution, the nature of the aid, and the manner in which the aid may be used.

The voluminous record compiled by the parties and reviewed by the District Court illustrates the manner in which the AFLA has been interpreted and implemented by the agency responsible for the aid program, and eliminates whatever need there might be to speculate about what kind of institutions *might* receive funds and how they *might* be selected; the record explains the nature of the activities funded with government money, as well as the content of the educational programs and materials developed and disseminated. There is no basis for ignoring the volumes of depositions, pleadings, and undisputed facts reviewed by the District Court simply because the recipients of the government funds may not in every sense resemble parochial schools.

⊥634 III

As is often the case, it is the effect of the statute, rather than its purpose, that creates Establishment Clause problems. Because I have no meaningful disagreement with the majority's discussion of the AFLA's essentially secular purpose, and because I find the statute's effect of advancing religion dispositive, I turn to that issue directly.

A

The majority's holding that the AFLA is not unconstitutional on its face marks a sharp departure from our precedents. While aid programs providing nonmonetary, verifiably secular aid have been upheld notwithstanding the indirect effect they might have on the allocation of an institution's own funds for religious activities, direct cash subsidies have always required much closer scrutiny into the expected and potential uses of the funds, and much greater guarantees that the funds would not be used inconsistently with the Establishment Clause. Parts of the AFLA prescribing various forms of outreach, education and counseling services specifically authorize the expenditure of funds in ways previously held unconstitutional. For example, the Court has upheld the use of public funds to support a parochial school's purchase of secular textbooks already approved for use in public school, see *Wolman* v. *Walter*, *Meek* v. *Pittenger*, or its grading and administering of state-prepared tests, *Committee for Public Education & Religious Liberty* v. *Regan*. When the books, teaching materials, or examinations were to **⊥635** be selected or designed by the private schools themselves, however, the Court consistently has held that such government aid risked advancing religion impermissibly. The teaching materials that may be purchased, developed, or disseminated with AFLA funding are in no way restricted to those already selected and approved for use in secular contests.

Notwithstanding the fact that government funds are paying for religious organizations to teach and counsel impressionable adolescents on a highly sensitive subject of considerable religious significance, often on the premises of a church or parochial school and without any effort to remove religious symbols from the sites, the majority concludes that the AFLA is not facially invalid. The majority acknowledges the constitutional proscription on **⊥636** government-sponsored religious indoctrination but, on the basis of little more than an indefensible assumption that AFLA recipients are not pervasively sectarian and consequently are presumed likely to comply with statutory and constitutional mandates, dismisses as insubstantial the risk that indoctrination will enter counseling. Similarly, the majority rejects the District Court's conclusion that the subject matter renders the risk of indoctrination unacceptable, and does so, it says, because "the likelihood that some of the religious institutions who receive AFLA funding will agree with the message that Congress intended to deliver to adolescents through the AFLA" does not amount to the advancement of religion. I do not think the statute can be so easily and conveniently saved.

(1)

The District Court concluded that asking religious organizations to teach and counsel youngsters on matters of deep religious significance, yet expect them to refrain from making reference to religion is both foolhardy and unconstitutional. The majority's rejection of this view is illustrative of its doctrinal misstep in relying so heavily on the college-funding cases. The District Court reasoned:

"To presume that AFLA counselors from religious organizations can put their beliefs aside when counseling an adolescent on matters that are part of religious doctrine is simply unrealistic. . . . Even if it were possible, government would tread impermissibly on religious liberty merely by suggesting that religious organizations instruct *on doctrinal matters* without any conscious or unconscious reference to that doctrine. Moreover, the statutory scheme is fraught with the possibility that religious beliefs might infuse instruction and never be detected by the impressionable and unlearned adolescent to whom the instruction is directed" (emphasis in original). **⊥637** The majority rejects the District Court's assumptions as unwarranted outside the context of a pervasively sectarian institution. In doing so, the majority places inordinate weight on the nature of the institution receiving the funds, and ignores altogether the targets of the funded message and the nature of its content.

I find it nothing less than remarkable that the majority relies on statements expressing confidence that administrators of religiously affiliated liberal arts colleges would not breach statutory proscriptions and use government funds earmarked "for secular purposes only," to finance theological instruction or religious worship, in order to reject a challenge based on the risk of indoctrination inherent in "educational services relating to family life and problems associated with adolescent premarital sexual relations," or "outreach services to families of adolescents to discourage sexual relations among unemancipated minors." §§ 300z-l(a)(4)(G), (O). The two situations are simply not comparable.

⊥**638** The AFLA, unlike any statute this Court has upheld, pays for teachers and counselors, employed by and subject to the direction of religious authorities, to educate impressionable young minds on issues of religious moment. Time and again we have recognized the difficulties inherent in asking even the best-intentioned individuals in such positions to make "a total separation between secular teaching and religious doctrine." *Lemon* v. *Kurtzman*. Where the targeted audience is composed of children, of course, the Court's insistence on adequate safeguards has always been greatest. In those cases in which funding of colleges with religious affiliations has been upheld, the Court has relied on the assumption that "college students are less impressionable and less susceptible to religious indoctrination. . . . The skepticism of the college student is not an inconsiderable barrier to any attempt or tendency to subvert the congressional objectives and limitations" (footnote omitted). *Tilton* v. *Richardson*. See also *Widmar* v. *Vincent* ("University students are, of course, young adults. They are less impressionable than younger students and should be able to appreciate that the University's policy is one of neutrality toward religion").

(2)

By observing that the alignment of the statute and the religious views of the grantees do not render the AFLA a statute which funds "specifically religious activity," the majority ⊥**639** makes light of the religious significance in the counseling provided by some grantees. Yet this is a dimension that Congress specifically sought to capture by enlisting the aid of religious organizations in battling the problems associated with teenage pregnancy. Whereas there may be secular values promoted by the AFLA, including the encouragement of adoption and premarital chastity and the discouragement of abortion, it can hardly be doubted that when promoted in theological terms by religious figures, those values take on a religious nature. Not surprisingly, the record is replete with observations to that effect. It ⊥**640** should be undeniable by now that religious dogma may not be employed by government even to accomplish laudable secular purposes such as "the promotion of moral values, the contradiction to the materialistic trends of our times, the perpetuation of our institutions and the teaching of literature." *Abington School District* v. *Schempp* (holding unconstitutional daily reading of Bible verses and recitation of the Lord's Prayer in public schools); *Stone* v. *Graham* (holding unconstitutional posting of Ten Commandments despite notation explaining secular application thereof).

It is true, of course, that the Court has recognized that the Constitution does not prohibit the government from supporting secular social-welfare services solely because they are provided by a religiously affiliated organization. But such recognition has been closely tied to the nature of the subsidized social service: "the State may send a ⊥**641** cleric, indeed even a clerical order, to perform *a wholly secular task*" (emphasis added). *Roemer* v. *Maryland Public Works Board*. There is a very real and important difference between running a soup kitchen or a hospital, and counseling pregnant teenagers on how to make the difficult decisions facing them. The risk of advancing religion at public expense, and of creating an appearance that the government is endorsing the medium and the message, is much greater when the religious organization is directly engaged in pedagogy, with the express intent of shaping belief and changing behavior, than where it is neutrally dispensing medication, food, or shelter.

There is also, of course, a fundamental difference between government's employing religion *because* of its unique appeal to a higher authority and the transcendental nature of its message, and government's enlisting the aid of religiously committed individuals or organizations without regard to their sectarian motivation. In the latter circumstance, religion plays little or no role; it merely explains why the individual or organization has chosen to get involved in the publicly funded program. In the former, religion is at the core of the subsidized activity, and it affects the manner in which the "service" is dispensed. For some religious organizations ⊥**642** the answer to a teenager's question "Why shouldn't I have a abortion?" or "Why shouldn't I use barrier contraceptives?" will undoubtedly be different from an answer based solely on secular considerations. Public funds may not be used to endorse the religious message.

B

The problems inherent in a statutory scheme specifically designed to involve religious organizations in a government-funded pedagogical program are compounded by the lack of any statutory restrictions on the use of federal tax dollars to promote religion. Conscious of the remarkable omission from the AFLA of any restriction whatsoever on the use of public funds for sectarian purposes, the Court disingenuously argues that we have "never stated that a *statutory* restriction is constitutionally required." In *Tilton* v. *Richardson*, this Court upheld a statute providing grants and loans to colleges for the construction of academic facilities because it "expressly prohibit[ed] their use for religious instruction, training, or worship . . . and the record show[ed] that some church-related institutions ha[d] been required to disgorge benefits for failure to obey" the restriction, but severed and struck a provision of the statute that permitted the restriction to lapse after 20 years. The *Tilton* Court noted that the statute required applicants to ⊥**643** provide assurances only that use of the funded facility would be limited to secular purpose for the initial 20-year period, and that this limitation, "obviously opens the facility to use for any purpose at the end of that period." Because they expired after 20 years, "the statute's enforcement provisions [were] inadequate to ensure that the impact of the federal aid will not advance religion."

The majority interprets *Tilton* "to indicate that the constitutional limitations on use of federal funds, as embodied in the statutory restriction, could not simply 'expire'" after 20 years, but concludes that the absence of a statutory restriction in the AFLA is not troubling, because "there is also no intimation in the statute that at some point, or for some grantees religious uses are permitted." Although there is something to the notion that the lifting of a preexisting restriction may be more likely to be perceived as native authorization than would the absence of any restriction at all, there was in *Tilton* no provision that stated that after 20 years facilities built under the aid program could be converted into chapels. What there was in *Tilton* was an express *statutory* provision, which lapsed, leaving no restrictions; it was that vacuum that the Court found constitutionally impermissible. In the AFLA, by way of contrast, there is a vacuum right from the start.

⊥**644** If *Tilton* were indeed the only indication that cash-grant programs must include prohibitions on the use of public funds to advance or endorse religion, one might argue more plausibly that ordinary reporting requirements, in conjunction with some presumption that government agencies administer federal programs in a constitutional fashion, might suffice to ⊥**645** protect a statute against facial challenge. That, however, is simply not the case. In *Committee for Public Education & Religious Liberty* v. *Regan*, for example, the Court upheld a state program whereby private schools were reimbursed for the actual cost of administering state-required tests. The statute specifically required that no payments be made for religious instruction and incorporated an extensive auditing system. The Court warned, however: "Of course, under the relevant cases the outcome would likely be different were there no effective means for insuring that the cash reimbursements would cover only secular services." In this regard, the *Regan* Court merely echoed and reaffirmed what was already well established. In *Committee for Public Education & Religious Liberty* v. *Nyquist*, the Court explained:

"Nothing in the statute, for instance, bars a qualifying school from paying out of state funds the salaries of employees who maintain the school chapel, or the cost of renovating classrooms in which religion is taught, or the cost of heating and lighting those same facilities. *Absent appropriate restrictions* on expenditures for these and similar purposes, *it simply cannot be denied* that this section has a primary effect that advances religion in that it subsidizes directly the religious activities of sectarian elementary and secondary schools" (emphasis added). ⊥**646** See *id.* ("In the absence of an effective means of guaranteeing that the state aid derived from public funds will be used exclusively for secular, neutral, and nonideological purposes, it is clear from our cases that direct aid in whatever form is invalid"); *Lemon* v. *Kurtzman* ("The history of government grants of a continuing cash subsidy indicates that such programs have almost always been accompanied by varying measures of control and surveillance").

Despite the glaring omission of a restriction on the use of funds for religious purposes, the Court attempts to resurrect the AFLA by noting a legislative intent not to promote religion, and observing that various reporting provisions of the statute "create a mechanism whereby the Secretary can police the grants." However effective this "mechanism" might prove to be in enforcing clear statutory directives, it is of no help where, as here, no restrictions are found on the face of the statute, and the Secretary has not promulgated any by regulation. Indeed, the only restriction ⊥**647** on the use of AFLA funds for religious purposes is found in the Secretary's "Notice of Grant Award" sent to grantees, which specifies that public funds may not be used to "teach or promote religion," and apparently even that clause was not inserted until after this litigation was underway. Furthermore, the "enforcement" of the limitation on sectarian use of AFLA funds, such as it is, lacks any bite. There is no procedure pursuant to which funds used to promote religion must be refunded to the Government, as there was, for example, in *Tilton* v. *Richardson*.

Indeed, nothing in the AFLA precludes the funding of even "pervasively sectarian" organizations, whose work by definition cannot be segregated into religious and secular categories. And, unlike a pre-enforcement challenge, where there is no record to review, or a limited challenge to a specific grant, where the Court is reluctant to invalidate a statute "in anticipation that particular applications may result in unconstitutional use of funds," *Roemer* v. *Maryland Public Works Board*, in this litigation the District Court expressly found that funds have gone to pervasively sectarian institutions and tax dollars have been used for the teaching of religion. Moreover, appellees have specifically called into question the manner in which the grant program was administered and grantees were selected. These objections cannot responsibly be answered by reliance on the Secretary's enforcement mechanism.

⊥**648** C

By placing unsupportable weight on the "pervasively sectarian" label, and recharacterizing appellees' objections to the statute, the Court attempts to create an illusion of consistency between our prior cases and its present ruling that the AFLA is not facially invalid. But the Court ignores the unwavering vigilance that the Constitution requires against any law "respecting an establishment of religion," which, as we have recognized time and again, calls for fundamentally conservative decisionmaking: our cases do not require a plaintiff to demonstrate that a government action *necessarily* promotes religion, but simply that it creates such a substantial risk. See, *e.g.*, *Grand Rapids School District* v. *Ball* (observing a "substantial risk that, overtly or subtly, the religious message . . . will infuse the supposedly secular classes"); *Committee for Public Education & Religious Liberty* v. *Regan* (describing as "minimal" the chance that religious bias would enter the process of grading state-drafted tests in secular subjects, given "complete" state safeguards); *Wolman* v. *Walter* (noting "unacceptable risk of fostering of religion" as "an inevitable byproduct" of teacher-accompanied field trips); *Meek* v. *Pittenger* (finding "potential for impermissible fostering of religion"); *Levitt* v. *Committee for Public Education & Religious Liberty* (finding dispositive "the substantial risk that . . . examinations, prepared by teachers under the authority of religious institutions, will be drafted with an eye, unconsciously or otherwise, to inculcate students in the religious precepts of the sponsoring church"); *Lemon* v. *Kurtzman* (finding "potential for impermissible fostering of religion"). Given the nature of the subsidized activity, the lack of adequate safeguards, and the chronicle of past experience with this statute, there is no room for doubt that the AFLA creates a substantial risk of impermissible fostering of religion.

⊥649 IV

While it is evident that the AFLA does not pass muster under *Lemon's* "effects" prong, the unconstitutionality of the statute becomes even more apparent when we consider the unprecedented degree of entanglement between Church and State required to prevent subsidizing the advancement of religion with AFLA funds. The majority's brief discussion of *Lemon's* "entanglement" prong is limited to (a) criticizing it as a "Catch-22," and (b) concluding that because there is "no reason to assume that the religious organizations which may receive grants are 'pervasively sectarian' in the same sense as the Court has held parochial schools to be," there is no need to be concerned about the degree of monitoring which will be necessary to ensure compliance with the AFLA and the Establishment Clause. As to the former, although the majority is certainly correct that the Court's entanglement analysis has been criticized in the separate writings of some members of the Court, the question whether a government program leads to "'an excessive government entanglement with religion'" nevertheless is and remains a part of the applicable constitutional inquiry. *Lemon* v. *Kurtzman*. I accept the majority's conclusion that "[t]here is no doubt that the monitoring of AFLA grants is necessary . . . to ensure that public money to be spent . . . in a way that comports with the Establishment Clause," but disagree with its easy characterization of entanglement analysis as a "Catch-22." To the extent any metaphor is helpful, I would be more inclined to characterize the Court's excessive entanglement decisions as concluding that to implement the required monitoring, we would have to kill the patient to cure what ailed him.

⊥650 As to the Court's conclusion that our precedents do not indicate that the Secretary's monitoring will have to be exceedingly intensive or entangling, because the grant recipients are not sufficiently like parochial schools, I must disagree. As discussed above, the majority's excessive reliance on the distinction between the Court's parochial-school-aid cases and college-funding cases is unwarranted. *Lemon*, *Meek*, and *Aguilar* cannot be so conveniently dismissed solely because the majority declines to assume that the "pervasively sectarian" label can be applied here.

To determine whether a statute fosters excessive entanglement, a court must look at three factors: 1) the character and purpose of the institutions benefitted; 2) the nature of the aid; and 3) the nature of the relationship between the government and the religious organization. Thus, in *Lemon*, it was not solely the fact that teachers performed their duties within the four walls of the parochial school that rendered monitoring difficult and, in the end, unconstitutional. It seems inherent in the pedagogical function that there will be disagreements about what is or is not "religious" and which will require an intolerable degree of government intrusion and censorship.

"What would appear to some to be essential to good citizenship might well for others border on or constitute instruction in religion. . . . Unlike a book, a teacher cannot be inspected once so as to determine the extent and intent of his or her personal beliefs and subjective acceptance of the limitations imposed by the First Amendment." See also *New York* v. *Cathedral Academy* (noting that the State "would have to undertake a search **⊥651** for religious meaning in every classroom examination. . . . The prospect of church and state litigating in court about what does or does not have religious meaning touches the very core of the constitutional guarantee against religious establishment").

In *Roemer*, *Tilton*, and *Hunt*, the Court relied on "the ability of the State to identity and subsidize separate secular functions carried out at the school, *without on-the-site inspections being necessary to prevent diversion of the funds to sectarian purposes*," *Roemer* v. *Maryland Public Works Board* (emphasis added), and on the fact that one-time grants require "no continuing financial relationships or dependencies, no annual audits, and no government analysis of an institution's expenditures on secular as distinguished from religious activities." *Tilton* v. *Richardson*. AFLA grants, of course, are not simply onetime construction grants. As the majority readily acknowledges, the Secretary will have to "review the programs set up and run by the AFLA grantees[, including] a review of, for example, the educational materials that a grantee proposes to use." And, as the majority intimates, monitoring the use of AFLA funds will undoubtedly require more than the "minimal" inspection "necessary to ascertain that the facilities are devoted to secular education," *Tilton*. Since teachers and counselors, unlike buildings, "are not necessarily religiously neutral, greater governmental surveillance would be required to guarantee that state salary aid would not in fact subsidize religious instruction."

V

The AFLA, without a doubt, endorses religion. Because of its expressed solicitude for the participation of religious organizations in all AFLA programs in one form or another, the statute creates a symbolic and real partnership between the clergy and the fisc in addressing a problem with substan⊥**652**tial religious overtones. Given the delicate subject matter and the impressionable audience, the risk that the AFLA will convey a message of Government endorsement of religion is overwhelming. The statutory language and the extensive record established in the District Court make clear that the problem lies in the statute and its systematically unconstitutional operation, and not merely in isolated instances of misapplication. I therefore would find the statute unconstitutional without remanding to the District Court. I trust, however, that after all its labors thus far, the District Court will not grow weary prematurely and read into the Court's decision a suggestion that the AFLA has been constitutionally implemented by the Government, for the majority deliberately eschews any review of the facts. After such further ⊥**653** proceedings as are now to be deemed appropriate, and after the District Court enters findings of fact on the basis of the testimony and documents entered into evidence, it may well decide, as I would today, that the AFLA as a whole indeed has been unconstitutionally applied.

LARRY ZOBREST v. CATALINA FOOTHILLS SCHOOL DISTRICT

509 U.S. 1

ON WRIT OF CERTIORARI TO THE UNITED STATES COURT OF APPEALS FOR THE NINTH CIRCUIT

Argued February 24, 1993 — Decided June 18, 1993

⊥**3** *Chief Justice REHNQUIST* delivered the opinion of the Court.

Petitioner James Zobrest, who has been deaf since birth, asked respondent school district to provide a sign-language interpreter to accompany him to classes at a Roman Catholic high school in Tucson, Arizona, pursuant to the Individuals with Disabilities Education Act (IDEA), 20 U. S. C. § 1400 *et seq.*, and its Arizona counterpart, Ariz. Rev. Stat. Ann. § 15–761 *et seq.* (1991 and Supp. 1992). The United States Court of Appeals for the Ninth Circuit decided, however, that provision of such a publicly employed interpreter would violate the Establishment Clause of the First Amendment. We hold that the Establishment Clause does not bar the school district from providing the requested interpreter.

⊥**4** James Zobrest attended grades one through five in a school for the deaf, and grades six through eight in a public school operated by respondent. While he attended public school, respondent furnished him with a sign-language interpreter. For religious reasons, James' parents (also petitioners here) enrolled him for the ninth grade in Salpointe Catholic High School, a sectarian institution. When petitioners requested that respondent supply James with an interpreter at Salpointe, respondent referred the matter to the County Attorney, who concluded that providing an interpreter on the school's premises would violate the United States Constitution. Pursuant to Ariz. Rev. Stat. Ann. § 15–253(B) (1991), the question next was referred to the Arizona Attorney General, who concurred in the County Attorney's opinion. Respondent accordingly declined to provide the requested interpreter.

Petitioners then instituted this action in the United States District Court for the District of Arizona under 20 U. S. C. § 1415(e)(4)(A), which grants the district courts jurisdiction over disputes regarding the services due disabled children under the IDEA. Petitioners asserted that the IDEA and the Free Exercise Clause of the First Amendment require respondent to provide James with an interpreter at Salpointe, and that the Establishment Clause does not bar such relief. The complaint sought a preliminary injunction and "such other and further relief as the Court deems just and proper." The District Court denied petitioners' ⊥**5** request for a preliminary injunction, finding that the provision of an interpreter at Salpointe would likely offend the Establishment Clause. The court thereafter granted respondent summary judgment, on the ground that "[t]he interpreter would act as a conduit for the religious inculcation of James—thereby, promoting James' religious development at government expense." "That kind of entanglement of church and state," the District Court concluded, "is not allowed."

The Court of Appeals affirmed by a divided vote, 963 F. 2d 1190 (CA9 1992), applying the three-part test announced in *Lemon* v. *Kurtzman*. It first found that the IDEA has a clear secular purpose: "'to assist States and Localities to provide for the education of all handicapped children.'" Turning to the second prong of the *Lemon* inquiry, though, the Court of Appeals determined that the IDEA, if applied as petitioners proposed, would have the primary effect of advancing religion and thus would run afoul of the Establishment Clause. "By placing its employee in the sectarian school," the Court of Appeals reasoned, "the government would create the appearance that it was a 'joint sponsor' of the school's activities." This, the court held, would create the "symbolic union of government and religion" found impermissible in *School Dist. of Grand Rapids* v. *Ball*. In contrast, the dissenting judge argued that "[g]eneral welfare programs neutrally available to all children," such as the IDEA, pass constitutional muster, "because their benefits diffuse over the entire population." ⊥**6** We granted certiorari and now reverse.

Respondent has raised in its brief in opposition to certiorari and in isolated passages in its brief on the merits several issues unrelated to the Establishment Clause question. Respondent first argues that 34 CFR §76.532(a)(1), a regulation promulgated under the IDEA, precludes it from using federal funds to provide an interpreter to James at Salpointe. In the alternative, respondent claims that even if there is no affirmative bar to the relief, it is not *required* by statute or regulation to furnish interpreters to students at sectarian schools. And respondent adds that providing such ⊥7 a service would offend Art. II, § 12, of the Arizona Constitution.

It is a familiar principle of our jurisprudence that federal courts will not pass on the constitutionality of an Act of Congress if a construction of the Act is fairly possible by which the constitutional question can be avoided. See, *e.g.*, *United States* v. *Locke* and cases cited therein. In *Locke*, a case coming here by appeal under 28 U.S.C. § 1252 (1982 ed.), we said that such an appeal "brings before this Court not merely the constitutional question decided below, but the entire case." "The entire case," we explained, "includes nonconstitutional questions actually decided by the lower court as well as nonconstitutional grounds presented to, but not passed on, by the lower court." Therefore, in that case, we turned "first to the nonconstitutional questions pressed below."

Here, in contrast to *Locke*, and other cases applying the prudential rule of avoiding constitutional questions, only First Amendment questions were pressed in the Court of Appeals. In the opening paragraph of its opinion, the Court of Appeals noted that petitioners' appeal raised only First Amendment issues:

"The Zobrests appeal the district court's ruling that provision of a state-paid sign language interpreter to James Zobrest while he attends a sectarian high school would violate the Establishment Clause. The Zobrests also argue that denial of such assistance violates the Free Exercise Clause." 963 F. 2d, at 1191.

Respondent did not urge any statutory grounds for affirmance upon the Court of Appeals, and thus the Court of Appeals decided only the federal constitutional claims raised by petitioners. In the District Court, too, the parties chose to ⊥8 litigate the case on the federal constitutional issues alone. "Both parties' motions for summary judgment raised only federal constitutional issues." Accordingly, the District Court's order granting respondent summary judgment addressed only the Establishment Clause question.

Given this posture of the case, we think the prudential rule of avoiding constitutional questions has no application. The fact that there may be buried in the record a nonconstitutional ground for decision is not by itself enough to invoke this rule. "Where issues are neither raised before nor considered by the Court of Appeals, this Court will not ordinarily consider them." *Adickes* v. *S. H. Kress & Co.* We therefore turn to the merits of the constitutional claim.

We have never said that "religious institutions are disabled by the First Amendment from participating in publicly sponsored social welfare programs." *Bowen* v. *Kendrick*. For if the Establishment Clause did bar religious groups from receiving general government benefits, then "a church could not be protected by the police and fire departments, or have its public sidewalk kept in repair." *Widmar* v. *Vincent*. Given that a contrary rule would lead to such absurd results, we have consistently held that government programs that neutrally provide benefits to a broad class of citizens defined without reference to religion are not readily subject to an Establishment Clause challenge just because sectarian institutions may also receive an attenuated financial benefit. Nowhere have we stated this principle more clearly than in *Mueller* v. *Allen* and *Witters* v. *Washington Dept. of Services for Blind*, two cases dealing specifically ⊥9 with government programs offering general educational assistance.

In *Mueller*, we rejected an Establishment Clause challenge to a Minnesota law allowing taxpayers to deduct certain educational expenses in computing their state income tax, even though the vast majority of those deductions (perhaps over 90%) went to parents whose children attended sectarian schools. Two factors, aside from States' traditionally broad taxing authority, informed our decision. We noted that the law "permits *all* parents—whether their children attend public school or private—to deduct their children's educational expenses" (emphasis in original). See also *Widmar* ("The provision of benefits to so broad a spectrum of groups is an important index of secular effect"); *Board of Ed. of Westside Community Schools (Dist. 66)* v. *Mergens* (same). We also pointed out that under Minnesota's scheme, public funds become available to sectarian schools "only as a result of numerous private choices of individual parents of school-age children," thus distinguishing *Mueller* from our other cases involving "the direct transmission of assistance from the State to the schools themselves."

Witters was premised on virtually identical reasoning. In that case, we upheld against an Establishment Clause challenge the State of Washington's extension of vocational assistance, as part of a general state program, to a blind person studying at a private Christian college to become a pastor, missionary, or youth director. Looking at the statute as a whole, we observed that "[a]ny aid provided under Washington's program that ultimately flows to religious institutions does so only as a result of the genuinely independent and private choices of aid recipients." The program, we said, "creates no financial incentive for students ⊥10 to undertake sectarian education." We also remarked that, much like the law in *Mueller*, "Washington's program is 'made available generally without regard to the sectarian-nonsectarian, or public-nonpublic nature of the institution benefited.'" *Witters* (quoting *Committee for Public Education and Religious Liberty* v. *Nyquist*). In light of these factors, we held that Washington's program—even as applied to a student who sought state assistance so that he could become a pastor—would not advance religion in a manner inconsistent with the Establishment Clause.

That same reasoning applies with equal force here. The service at issue in this case is part of a general government program that distributes benefits neutrally to any child qualifying as "handicapped" under the IDEA, without regard to the "sectarian-nonsectarian, or public-nonpublic nature" of the school the child attends. By according parents freedom to select a school of their choice, the statute ensures that a government-paid interpreter will be present in a sectarian school only as a result of the private decision of individual parents. In other words, because the IDEA creates no financial incentive for parents to choose a sectarian school, an interpreter's presence there cannot be attributed to state decisionmaking. Viewed against the backdrop of *Mueller* and *Witters*, then, the Court of Appeals erred in its decision. When the government offers a neutral service on the premises of a sectarian school as part of a general program that "is in no way skewed towards religion," *Witters*, it follows under our prior decisions that provision of that service does not offend the Establishment Clause. See *Wolman* v. *Walter*. Indeed, this is an even easier case than *Mueller* and *Witters* in the sense that, under the IDEA, no funds traceable to the government ever find their way into sectarian schools' coffers. The only indirect economic benefit a sectarian school might receive by dint of the IDEA is the handicapped child's tuition—and that is, ⊥**11** of course, assuming that the school makes a profit on each student; that, without an IDEA interpreter, the child would have gone to school elsewhere; and that the school, then, would have been unable to fill that child's spot.

Respondent contends, however, that this case differs from *Mueller* and *Witters*, in that petitioners seek to have a public employee physically present in a sectarian school to assist in James' religious education. In light of this distinction, respondent argues that this case more closely resembles *Meek* v. *Pittenger* and *School Dist. of Grand Rapids* v. *Ball*. In *Meek*, we struck down a statute that, *inter alia*, provided "massive aid" to private schools—more than 75% of which were church related—through a direct loan of teaching material and equipment. The material and equipment covered by the statute included maps, charts, and tape recorders. According to respondent, if the government could not place a tape recorder in a sectarian school in *Meek*, then it surely cannot place an interpreter in Salpointe. The statute in *Meek* also authorized state-paid personnel to furnish "auxiliary services"—which included remedial and accelerated instruction and guidance counseling—on the premises of religious schools. We determined that this part of the statute offended the First Amendment as well. *Ball* similarly involved two public programs that provided services on private school premises; there, public employees taught classes to students in private school classrooms. We found that those programs likewise violated the Constitution, relying largely on *Meek*. According to respondent, if the government could not provide educational services on the premises of sectarian schools in *Meek* and *Ball*, then it surely cannot provide James with an interpreter on the premises of Salpointe.

⊥**12** Respondent's reliance on *Meek* and *Ball* is misplaced for two reasons. First, the programs in *Meek* and *Ball*—through direct grants of government aid—relieved sectarian schools of costs they otherwise would have borne in educating their students. See *Witters* ("[T]he State may not grant aid to a religious school, whether cash or in kind, where the effect of the aid is 'that of a direct subsidy to the religious school' from the State") (quoting *Ball*). For example, the religious schools in *Meek* received teaching material and equipment from the State, relieving them of an otherwise necessary cost of performing their educational function. "Substantial aid to the educational function of such schools," we explained, "necessarily results in aid to the sectarian school enterprise as a whole," and therefore brings about "the direct and substantial advancement of religious activity." So, too, was the case in *Ball:* The programs challenged there, which provided teachers in addition to instructional equipment and material, "in effect subsidize[d] the religious functions of the parochial schools by taking over a substantial portion of their responsibility for teaching secular subjects." "This kind of direct aid," we determined, "is indistinguishable from the provision of a direct cash subsidy to the religious school." The extension of aid to petitioners, however, does not amount to "an impermissible 'direct subsidy'" of Salpointe. For Salpointe is not relieved of an expense that it otherwise would have assumed in educating its students. And, as we noted above, any attenuated financial benefit that parochial schools do ultimately receive from the IDEA is attributable to "the private choices of individual parents." *Mueller*. Handicapped children, not sectarian schools, are the primary beneficiaries of the IDEA; to the extent sectarian schools benefit at all from the IDEA, they are only incidental beneficiaries. Thus, the function of the IDEA is hardly "'to provide desired financial ⊥**13** support for nonpublic, sectarian institutions.'" *Id.* (quoting *Nyquist*).

Second, the task of a sign-language interpreter seems to us quite different from that of a teacher or guidance counselor. Notwithstanding the Court of Appeals' intimations to the contrary, the Establishment Clause lays down no absolute bar to the placing of a public employee in a sectarian school. Such a flat rule, smacking of antiquated notions of "taint," would indeed exalt form over substance. Nothing in this record suggests that a sign-language interpreter would do more than accurately interpret whatever material is presented to the class as a whole. In fact, ethical guidelines require interpreters to "transmit everything that is said in exactly the same way it was intended." James' parents have chosen of their own free will to place him in a pervasively sectarian environment. The sign-language interpreter they have requested will neither add to nor subtract from that environment, and hence the provision of such assistance is not barred by the Establishment Clause.

The IDEA creates a neutral government program dispensing aid not to schools but to individual handicapped children. If a handicapped child chooses to enroll in a sectarian school, ⊥**14** we hold that the Establishment Clause does not prevent the school district from furnishing him with a sign-language interpreter there in order to facilitate his education. The judgment of the Court of Appeals is therefore

Reversed.

Justice BLACKMUN, with whom *Justice* SOUTER joins, and with whom *Justice* STEVENS and *Justice* O'CONNOR join as to Part I, dissenting.

Today, the Court unnecessarily addresses an important constitutional issue, disregarding longstanding principles of constitutional adjudication. In so doing, the Court holds that placement in a parochial school classroom of a public employee whose duty consists of relaying religious messages does not violate the Establishment Clause of the First Amendment. I disagree both with the Court's decision to reach this question and with its disposition on the merits. I therefore dissent.

I

"If there is one doctrine more deeply rooted than any other in the process of constitutional adjudication, it is that we ought not to pass on questions of constitutionality . . . unless such adjudication is unavoidable." *Specter Motor Service, Inc.,* v. *McLaughlin.* See *Brockett* v. *Spokane Arcades, Inc.*; *Ashwander* v. *TVA* (Brandeis, J., concurring); *Liverpool, New York and Philadelphia S.S. Co.* v. *Commissioners of Emigration.* This is a "fundamental rule of judicial restraint," *Three Affiliated Tribes of Fort Berthold Reservation* v. *Wold Engineering, P.C.*, which has received the sanction of time and experience. It has been described as a "corollary" to the Article III case or controversy requirement, see *Rescue Army* v. *Municipal Court of Los Angeles*, and is grounded in basic ⊥**15** principles regarding the institution of judicial review and this Court's proper role in our federal system.

Respondent School District makes two arguments that could provide grounds for affirmance, rendering consideration of the constitutional question unnecessary. First, respondent maintains that the Individuals with Disabilities Education Act (IDEA), 20 U. S. C. § 1400 *et seq.*, does not require it to furnish petitioner with an interpreter at any private school so long as special education services are made available at a public school. The United States endorses this interpretation of the statute, explaining that "the IDEA itself does not establish an individual entitlement to services for students placed in private schools at their parents' option." Brief for United States as *Amicus Curiae* 13. And several courts have reached the same conclusion. See, *e.g.*, *Goodall* v. *Stafford County School Bd.*; *McNair* v. *Cardimone*, aff'd *sub nom.* *McNair* v. *Oak Hills Local School Dist.*; *Work* v. *McKenzie*. Second, respondent contends that 34 CFR § 76.532(a)(1) (1992), a regulation promulgated under the IDEA, which forbids the use of federal funds to pay for "[r]eligious worship, instruction, or proselytization," prohibits provision of a sign-language interpreter at a sectarian school. The United States asserts that this regulation does not preclude the relief petitioners seek, but at least one federal court has concluded otherwise. See *Goodall*. This Court could easily refrain from deciding the constitutional claim by vacating and remanding the case for consideration of the statutory and regulatory issues. Indeed, the majority's decision does not eliminate the need to resolve these remaining questions. For, regardless of the Court's views on the Establishment Clause, petitioners will not obtain what they seek if the federal stat⊥**16**ute does not require or the federal regulations prohibit provision of a sign-language interpreter in a sectarian school.

The majority does not deny the existence of these alternative grounds, nor does it dispute the venerable principle that constitutional questions should be avoided when there are nonconstitutional grounds for a decision in the case. Instead, in its zeal to address the constitutional question, the majority casts aside this "time-honored canon of constitutional adjudication," *Specter Motor Service*, with the cursory observation that "the prudential rule of avoiding constitutional questions has no application" in light of the "posture" of this case. Because the parties chose not to litigate the federal statutory issues in the District Court and in the Court of Appeals, the majority blithely proceeds to the merits of their constitutional claim.

But the majority's statements are a *non sequitur*. From the rule against deciding issues not raised or considered below, it does not follow that the Court should consider constitutional issues needlessly. The obligation to avoid unnecessary adjudication of constitutional questions does not depend upon the parties' litigation strategy, but rather is a "self-imposed limitation on the exercise of this Court's jurisdiction [that] has an importance to the institution that transcends the significance of particular controversies." *City of Mesquite* v. *Aladdin's Castle, Inc.* It is a rule whose aim is to protect not parties but the law and the adjudicatory process. Indeed, just a few days ago, we expressed concern that "litigants, by agreeing on the legal issue presented, [could] extract the opinion of a court ⊥**17** on hypothetical Acts of Congress or dubious constitutional principles, an opinion that would be difficult to characterize as anything but advisory." *National Bank of Oregon* v. *Independent Insurance Agents of America, Inc.* See *United States* v. *CIO* (Frankfurter, J., concurring).

That the federal statutory and regulatory issues have not been properly briefed or argued does not justify the Court's decision to reach the constitutional claim. The very posture of this case should have alerted the courts that the parties were seeking what amounts to an advisory opinion. After the Arizona Attorney General concluded that provision of a sign-language interpreter would violate the Federal and State Constitutions, the parties bypassed the federal statutes and regulations and proceeded directly to litigate the constitutional issue. Under such circumstances, the weighty nonconstitutional questions that were left unresolved are hardly to be described as "buried in the record." When federal and state law questions similarly remained open in *Wheeler* v. *Barrera*, this Court refused to pass upon the scope or constitutionality of a federal statute that might have required publicly employed teachers to provide remedial instruction on the premises of sectarian schools. Prudence counsels that the Court follow a similar practice here by vacating and remanding this case for consideration of the nonconstitutional questions, rather than proceeding directly to the merits of the constitutional claim. See *Youakim* v. *Miller* (vacating and remanding for consideration of statutory issues not presented to or considered by lower court); *Escambia County* v. *McMillan* (vacating and remanding for lower court to consider statutory issue parties had not briefed and Court of Appeals had not passed upon); *Edward J. DeBartolo Corp.* v. *NLRB* (vacating and remanding for consideration of statutory question).

⊥**18** II

Despite my disagreement with the majority's decision to reach the constitutional question, its arguments on the merits deserve a response. Until now, the Court never has authorized a public employee to participate directly in religious indoctrination. Yet that is the consequence of today's decision.

Let us be clear about exactly what is going on here. The parties have stipulated to the following facts. Petitioner requested the State to supply him with a sign-language interpreter at Salpointe High School, a private Roman Catholic school operated by the Carmelite Order of the Catholic Church. Salpointe is a "pervasively religious" institution where "[t]he two functions of secular education and advancement of religious values or beliefs are inextricably intertwined." Salpointe's overriding "objective" is to "instill a sense of Christian values." Its "distinguishing purpose" is "the inculcation in its students of the faith and morals of the Roman Catholic Church." Religion is a required subject at Salpointe, and Catholic students are "strongly encouraged" to attend daily Mass each morning. Salpointe's teachers must sign a Faculty Employment Agreement which requires them to promote the relationship among the religious, the academic, and the extracurricular. They are encouraged to do so by "assist[ing] students in experiencing how the presence of God is manifest in nature, human history, in the struggles for economic and political justice, and other secular areas of the curriculum." The Agreement also sets forth detailed rules of ⊥**19** conduct teachers must follow in order to advance the school's Christian mission.

At Salpointe, where the secular and the sectarian are "inextricably intertwined," governmental assistance to the educational function of the school necessarily entails governmental participation in the school's inculcation of religion. A state-employed sign-language interpreter would be required to communicate the material covered in religion class, the nominally secular subjects that are taught from a religious perspective, and the daily Masses at which Salpointe encourages attendance for Catholic students. In an environment so pervaded by discussions of the divine, the interpreter's every gesture would be infused with religious significance. Indeed, petitioners willingly concede this point: "That the interpreter conveys religious messages is a given in the case." By this concession, petitioners would seem to surrender their constitutional claim.

The majority attempts to elude the impact of the record by offering three reasons why this sort of aid to petitioners survives Establishment Clause scrutiny. First, the majority observes that provision of a sign-language interpreter ⊥**20** occurs as "part of a general government program that distributes benefits neutrally to any child qualifying as 'handicapped' under the IDEA, without regard to the 'sectarian-nonsectarian, or public-nonpublic' nature of the school the child attends." Second, the majority finds significant the fact that aid is provided to pupils and their parents, rather than directly to sectarian schools. As a result, "'[a]ny aid . . . that ultimately flows to religious institutions does so only as a result of the genuinely independent and private choices of aid recipients.'" And, finally, the majority opines that "the task of a sign-language interpreter seems to us quite different from that of a teacher or guidance counselor."

But the majority's arguments are unavailing. As to the first two, even a general welfare program may have specific applications that are constitutionally forbidden under the Establishment Clause. See *Bowen* v. *Kendrick* (holding that Adolescent Family Life Act on its face did not violate the Establishment Clause, but remanding for examination of the constitutionality of particular applications). For example, a general program granting remedial assistance to disadvantaged schoolchildren attending public and private, secular and sectarian schools alike would clearly offend the Establishment Clause insofar as it authorized the provision of teachers. See *Aguilar* v. *Felton; Grand Rapids School District* v. *Ball; Meek* v. *Pittenger*. Such a program would not be saved simply because it supplied teachers to secular as well as sectarian schools. Nor would the fact that teachers were furnished to pupils and their parents, rather than directly to sectarian schools, immunize such a program from Establishment Clause scrutiny. See *Witters* ("Aid may have [unconstitutional] effect even though it takes the form of aid to students ⊥**21** or parents"); *Wolman* v. *Walter* (it would "exalt form over substance if this distinction [between equipment loaned to the pupil or his parent and equipment loaned directly to the school] were found to justify a . . . different" result); *Grand Rapids* (rejecting "fiction that a . . . program could be saved by masking it as aid to individual students"). The majority's decision must turn, then, upon the distinction between a teacher and a sign-language interpreter.

"Although Establishment Clause jurisprudence is characterized by few absolutes," at a minimum "the Clause does absolutely prohibit government-financed or government-sponsored indoctrination into the beliefs of a particular religious faith." *Grand Rapids*. See *Bowen* v.

Kendrick (O'Connor, J., concurring) ("*[A]ny* use of public funds to promote religious doctrines violates the Establishment Clause") (emphasis in original); *Meek* ("'The State must be certain, given the Religion Clauses, that subsidized teachers do not inculcate religion,'" quoting *Lemon* v. *Kurtzman*); *Levitt* v. *Committee for Public Education and Religious Liberty* ("[T]he State is constitutionally compelled to assure that the state-supported activity is not being used for religious indoctrination"). In keeping with this restriction, our cases consistently have rejected the provision by government of any resource capable of advancing a school's religious mission. Although the Court generally has permitted the provision of "secular and nonideological services unrelated to the primary, religion-oriented educational function of the sectarian school," *Meek*, it has always proscribed the provision of benefits that afford even "the opportunity for the transmission of sectarian views," *Wolman*.

Thus, the Court has upheld the use of public school buses to transport children to and from school, *Everson* v. *Board of Education*, while striking down the ⊥**22** employment of publicly funded buses for field trips controlled by parochial school teachers, *Wolman*. Similarly, the Court has permitted the provision of secular textbooks whose content is immutable and can be ascertained in advance, *Board of Education* v. *Allen*, while prohibiting the provision of any instructional materials or equipment that could be used to convey a religious message, such as slide projectors, tape recorders, record players, and the like, *Wolman*. State-paid speech and hearing therapists have been allowed to administer diagnostic testing on the premises of parochial schools, *Wolman*, whereas state-paid remedial teachers and counselors have not been authorized to offer their services because of the risk that they may inculcate religious beliefs, *Meek*.

These distinctions perhaps are somewhat fine, but "'lines must be drawn.'" *Grand Rapids*. And our cases make clear that government crosses the boundary when it furnishes the medium for communication of a religious message. If petitioners receive the relief they seek, it is beyond question that a state-employed sign-language interpreter would serve as the conduit for petitioner's religious education, thereby assisting Salpointe in its mission of religious indoctrination. But the Establishment Clause is violated when a sectarian school enlists "the machinery of the State to enforce a religious orthodoxy." *Lee* v. *Weisman*.

Witters and *Mueller* v. *Allen* are not to the contrary. Those cases dealt with the payment of cash or a tax deduction, where governmental involvement ended with the disbursement of funds or lessening of tax. This case, on the other hand, involves ongoing, daily, and intimate governmental participation in the teaching and propagation of religious doctrine. When government dispenses public funds to individuals who employ them to finance private choices, it is difficult to argue that government ⊥**23** is actually endorsing religion. But the graphic symbol of the concert of church and state that results when a public employee or instrumentality mouths a religious message is likely to "enlis[t]—at least in the eyes of impressionable youngsters—the powers of government to the support of the religious denomination operating the school." *Grand Rapids*. And the union of church and state in pursuit of a common enterprise is likely to place the imprimatur of governmental approval upon the favored religion, conveying a message of exclusion to all those who do not adhere to its tenets.

Moreover, this distinction between the provision of funds and the provision of a human being is not merely one of form. It goes to the heart of the principles animating the Establishment Clause. As *Amicus* Council on Religious Freedom points out, the provision of a state-paid sign-language interpreter may pose serious problems for the church as well as for the state. Many sectarian schools impose religiously based rules of conduct, as Salpointe has in this case. A traditional Hindu school would be likely to instruct its students and staff to dress modestly, avoiding any display of their bodies. And an orthodox Jewish yeshiva might well forbid all but kosher food upon its premises. To require public employees to obey such rules would impermissibly threaten individual liberty, but to fail to do so might endanger religious autonomy. For such reasons, it long has been feared that "a union of government and religion tends to destroy government and to degrade religion." *Engel* v. *Vitale*. The Establishment Clause was designed to avert exactly this sort of conflict.

III

The Establishment Clause "rests upon the premise that both religion and government can best work to achieve their lofty aims if each is left free from the other within its respective sphere." *McCollum* v. *Board of Education*. ⊥**24** To this end, our cases have strived to "chart a course that preserve[s] the autonomy and freedom of religious bodies while avoiding any semblance of established religion." *Walz* v. *Tax Commission*. I would not stray, as the Court does today, from the course set by nearly five decades of Establishment Clause jurisprudence. Accordingly, I dissent.

Justice O'CONNOR, with whom *Justice* STEVENS joins, dissenting.

I join Part I of *Justice* BLACKMUN'S dissent. In my view, the Court should vacate and remand this case for consideration of the various threshold problems, statutory and regulatory, that may moot the constitutional question urged upon us by the parties. "It is a fundamental rule of judicial restraint . . . that this Court will not reach constitutional questions in advance of the necessity of deciding them." *Three Affiliated Tribes of Fort Berthold Reservation* v. *Wold Engineering, P. C.* That "fundamental rule" suffices to dispose of the case before us, whatever the proper answer to the decidedly hypothetical issue addressed by the Court. I therefore refrain from addressing it myself. See *Rust* v. *Sullivan* (O'Connor, J., dissenting).

RELIGION AND PUBLIC EDUCATION

Public education, as it is understood today, developed out of a philosophy of education that existed during the colonial period of American history. The school was thought of as an arm of the church and its curriculum was permeated with religion. Nevertheless, not all the colonies had exactly the same attitudes about education; hence they implemented their educational philosophies in different ways. In the southern colonies, for example, there was virtually no general program of education in the seventeenth century. One reason for this was that in these colonies the established church, the Church of England, was liturgically (ritualistically) oriented and thus the least Bible-centered of all Protestant groups. Consequently, there was no religious compulsion for widespread literacy. Primarily as the result of the eighteenth century revival known as the Great Awakening, an interest in literacy for Bible reading did develop throughout the colonies, and education in the south became what education had been in the New England and middle colonies since the early seventeenth century.

In the middle colonies, schools were started early in the colonial period. The general pattern was for them to be founded, financed, and operated by the local church and clergy. There appears to have been little relationship between these schools and civil government, but the vast majority of the schools were inseparably linked with churches and had religion as a major part of their curricula.

In New England, schools were supported by a general tax collected by the civil government. However, due to a strong Congregationalist establishment in each of the colonies (except Rhode Island), the schools had definite religious dimensions. The religious character of these schools is illustrated by Massachusetts Bay's legislation passed in 1647 to create its township school system. "It being one chief product of that old deluder, Satan, to keep men from the knowledge of the Scriptures," the law stipulated "that learning may not be buried in the graves of our fathers in the church and commonwealth, the Lord assisting our endeavors . . ." schools were to be established in every township in the colony. It was necessary to educate people so that they could read their Bibles and discern God's will in it.[1]

But the schools were not destined to maintain their religious character. As a result of several factors, schools in the national period ceased to be controlled by sponsoring churches and became less obviously sectarian in their teaching. One of these factors was that many of the states had written into their constitutions provisions for religious liberty and nonestablishment comparable to that in the national Constitution, thus eliminating the possibility of state-supported, church-related schools. Furthermore, since there were so many different religious groups with such diverse theologies, it became clear to some that if education were allowed to remain under church sponsorship, it would be eternally fragmented and would participate in the competition, and sometimes hostility, that existed among the denominations. There was also the rationalistic distaste for sectarian religion which was widespread at the end of the eighteenth and the beginning of the nineteenth centuries. Rationalists believed that historically religion had worked to keep people in ignorance. They did not anticipate that religion would reverse itself and provide the enlightened education which was needed in the new nation.

But perhaps the strongest reason for removal of education from control of the churches was that a democracy required an educated citizenry. Particularly for those with rationalist leanings, although others understood this as well, the basis for government by the consent of the governed was rational and humane debate about the affairs of government. In a nation as diverse as this one, it would be necessary for the various opinions of individuals and groups to be expressed in civic dialogue in order that democratic government might function. Such dialogue would require a literate citizenry. This requirement that people participate intelligently in political debate and decisions suggested the need for universal schooling. Thus, if there were really to be separation of church and state, if the educational process were to be insulated from sectarian strife, and if this entire process were so necessary for the civil state to function, then education ought to be undertaken by the civil state. Consequently, the new nation moved toward the creation of a new institution, the common school sponsored by the different states in the union. Furthermore, this school was to be secular, totally avoiding teaching the tenets of sectarian religion.

Public schools, however, did not become totally secular. In the minds of those in the public school movement, the schools were not only to educate people so that they could participate in political debate, but also they were to train Americans to be moral, law-abiding citizens. In the process of instilling morality, religion was reintroduced into the schools. Advocates of the public schools, most of whom were rationalists, believed that the essence of Christianity lay in its moral principles. They ar-

---

[1]Leo Pfeffer, *Church, State, and Freedom*, rev. ed. (Boston: Beacon Press, 1967), pp. 321-24.

gued that if the public schools were to make people more fit for citizenship by instilling civic morality, then one could do no better than to teach the moral precepts of Christianity. To allow sectarian religion to intrude into the public schools would be divisive and would take up the students' time with irrelevant and meaningless issues. Thus the public schools were to be secular. But to make education secular was to exclude *only* sectarian particularities, *not* the *essence of religion.* Many were insistent on the necessity of including within the public school curriculum those items in which all Christians believed and upon which they all agreed, i.e., belief in the existence of God and the moral order. In short, in the nineteenth century the developing public schools included a definite religious dimension, what might be called a "lowest common denominator Christianity," or, as it turned out, a "lowest common denominator Protestantism."

In the light of these trends, one is not surprised at Professor Sidney Mead's conclusion that Americans, in the absence of an established church, adopted the public school as their established church. The schools took over the function which had always been assigned to the establishment in other countries, namely, making citizens moral.[2]

Although most Protestant religious leaders agreed that public schools should teach values or morality to promote good citizenship, in the early part of the twentieth century many of them became concerned that not enough was being done to teach the theological content of the Christian faith. There was a growing concern that American children were religiously illiterate, that the public schools were unable to do any more to correct that problem, and that the Sunday schools were not doing enough. Part of the problem was that the public schools commanded so much of the students' time and the Sunday schools so little. Was there a way the public school could be made to cooperate with the church in the religious education of children without reintroducing sectarian strife? An arrangement termed "released time" was devised to fill this need and was inaugurated in Gary, Indiana, in 1914. With the consent of parents, students could be released from the public schools for specified periods of time each week in order to go to churches or synagogues (since by this time Protestants had to take the existence of Catholics and Jews seriously) for instruction in their own faith, returning to the school at the end of the instruction to resume their normal study.

In 1940 the "Gary plan" was inaugurated in Champaign, Illinois. A rather significant alteration in the plan was that the religious classes were held in public school buildings. For a specified time each week, religious teachers would come into the classrooms to teach their particular religion. Students who desired religious instruction were assigned classes which were religiously homogeneous; nonparticipants were relocated to do some other school task or to bide their time until the religious instruction was ended.

Mrs. Vashti McCollum, whose son was a nonparticipant, challenged the plan in court. She claimed that it was a violation of the Establishment Clause, which by this time had been applied to the states by EVERSON v. BOARD OF EDUCATION (1947).[3] In the 1948 case of McCOLLUM v. BOARD OF EDUCATION, the Supreme Court agreed with that contention. Writing for the majority, Justice Black stated that released time aided religious groups in spreading their faiths through improper use of the tax-established and tax-supported public school system. Moreover, the state's compulsory school attendance laws were used to enable the teachers of religion to gain a captive audience. "This," he wrote, "is not separation of Church and State."

The released time issue was not dead, however. In 1952, in ZORACH v. CLAUSON, the Court considered a New York law that provided for the release of children who had parental permission to attend religious classes off the public school campus. The location of instruction was the only essential difference between the plans in New York and Champaign. In a majority opinion written by Justice Douglas, the Court upheld the constitutionality of New York's released time statute. Calling attention to the fact that religion has always played a large role in the life of the American people, Justice Douglas argued that by allowing children to be released for religious instruction the public schools were doing nothing more than adjusting their schedules to the religious interests of their constituents. Far from being a violation of the Establishment Clause, such a plan was following the best of our national traditions. To do any less would show governmental hostility to religion, which would be unconstitutional.

Three separate, vigorous dissenting opinions were written by Justices Black, Frankfurter, and Jackson.

[2]Sidney E. Mead, *The Lively Experiment: The Shaping of Christianity in America* (New York: Harper and Row, 1963), pp. 66-68. An extremely helpful history of the relationship between religion and the public schools is Robert Michaelsen, *Piety in the Public School: Trends and Issues in the Relationship Between Religion and the Public School in the United States* (New York: The Macmillan Company, 1970). See also Michaelsen's article "The Public School and 'America's Two Religions,'" *Journal of Church and State* 8 (Autumn 1966): 380-400. An equally valuable, more recent, book is Warren A. Nord, *Religion and American Education: Rethinking a National Dilemma* (Chapel Hill: University of North Carolina Press, 1995).

[3]Cf. Vashti McCollum, *One Woman's Fight* (Boston: Beacon Press, 1951, reissued, Madison, WI: Freedom From Religion Foundation, 1993).

The thrust of the dissents was that the location of religion classes was irrelevant. As long as school was in session for nonparticipants in religious instruction, the roll was checked, and truancy was forbidden, state machinery was still operating to provide a captive audience for the teaching of religion. The dissents in the *Zorach* case were among the most barbed that have been written in church-state cases until the late 1980s and the 1990s.

The expectation of many Americans that public schools should have some religious quality came to the surface forcefully in the prayer and Bible reading cases. The first of these was ENGEL v. VITALE, decided in 1962. The Board of Regents of New York's public schools composed a prayer and urged local school districts to cause it to be said by their pupils at the beginning of each school day. About 10 per cent of the school districts in New York complied with the recommendation, including the one in New Hyde Park, the defendant in this case. The regents had written the prayer as a part of their broad program of moral and spiritual training in the schools, an attempt to combat communism and juvenile delinquency. Knowing that the prayer could not be sectarian, they wrote one which would be denominationally neutral (although some critics called it a perfect example of the "public school religion" referred to earlier in this essay, what was also called by some a "to whom it may concern prayer").

Writing for a majority of eight, Justice Black pointed out that the New York program was clearly unconstitutional, in spite of the fact that the prayer showed no denominational preference and that students who did not want to participate could be excused. Enactment of the law was a violation of the Establishment Clause, whether or not compulsion could be shown:

> . . . we think that the constitutional prohibition against laws respecting an establishment of religion must at least mean that in this country it is not part of the business of government to compose official prayers for any group of the American people to recite as a part of a religious program carried on by government. . . . The New York laws officially prescribing the Regents' prayer are inconsistent both with the purposes of the Establishment Clause and with the Establishment Clause itself (370 U.S. 421, 425, 433).

A storm of protest erupted after the *Engel* decision. The Court had taken God out of the classroom; it had secularized the public schools. Some even suggested the schools had been made open prey to communism! In spite of the uproar, in 1963 the Court agreed to hear two other cases in this sensitive area. The first, ABINGTON TOWNSHIP SCHOOL DISTRICT v. SCHEMPP, involved a Pennsylvania law providing that at least ten verses of the Bible should be read at the beginning of each school day in each public school in the state. Reading was to be without comment and students could request to be excused. The other case, *Murray* v. *Curlett*, was a challenge to a Maryland law that provided for reading, without comment, of a chapter of the Bible and/or recitation of the Lord's Prayer as a part of the opening exercises in the state's public schools. These two cases were decided together under the *Schempp* title. As noted above, in the essay on the Establishment ot Religion, in this case the Court set forth the "secular purpose" and "primary effect" tests for interpreting the Establishment Clause. Applied to the cases at bar, the tests invalidated the devotional exercises in public schools. Clearly, the law required religious exercises that did not have a secular purpose but did have the primary effect of advancing religion. Consequently, the exercises were unconstitutional. *Engel* had held that state-written prayers for public school use were unconstitutional. *Schempp* went beyond that to say that required recitation of the Lord's Prayer or any other prayer was a violation of the Establishment Clause, as was the devotional reading of the Bible.

Although virtually unnoticed by the press and the general public at the time, the Court did suggest that academic teaching of religion in a nondevotional or a nonevangelistic way and as a part of the public schools' regular secular program of instruction was not only constitutional but was actually a good idea. In more recent years educators have developed strategies and curricular materials to accomplish that goal.

The issue of what could be taught in a public school classroom was presented in the strange case of EPPERSON v. ARKANSAS. In 1928 Arkansas had passed a law that prohibited teaching evolution in public schools. In 1965 the school administration of Little Rock adopted a biology textbook that contained the theory of evolution. A tenth-grade biology teacher, Mrs. Susan Epperson, was faced with a dilemma. The school board had adopted the book, but if she should teach it and the law were enforced, she would be guilty of a criminal offense and subject to dismissal. Consequently, she initiated litigation to invalidate the law. Mrs. Epperson was joined by a parent who had two sons attending the school in which she taught.

When the case reached the Supreme Court, the "monkey law" was found to be unconstitutional because of failure to pass the "secular purpose" test. It was clear to the Court that the law was enacted in order to impose upon the school curriculum a particular theological viewpoint of the nature of human beings.

Strangely, this case did not present the kind of controversy which is normally assumed to be necessary for plaintiffs to have standing to sue. The

Arkansas law had never been enforced and there was no indication that it would be. By the time the case reached the Supreme Court, it was not known whether Mrs. Epperson was still teaching in Little Rock (she was not), whether the two students were still subject to the biology course in question, or even whether they were still in school. The case was virtually an abstract question. But the Court accepted it, apparently to say finally and definitively what had been held in *McCollum, Engel,* and *Schempp*, but deviated from slightly in *Zorach:* the Establishment Clause insists that public schools must be secular both in their curricula and related programs. (The question of the teaching of evolution in public schools was resurrected in the early 1980s, the issue being whether "creation science" should be given "balanced treatment" with evolution. See the commentary on EDWARDS v. AGUILLARD below.)

The year *Epperson* was decided, 1968, fairly accurately marks the end of the radical 1960s and the beginning of a public trend toward conservatism. As this tendency toward religious, political, and cultural conservatism gained momentum, public schools came under increasing scrutiny and criticism. The charge was frequently made that public schools had lost both their quality in teaching academic subjects and their ability to impart morality and values. Critics of the schools saw much evidence of these failures in rising crime rates, increasing unemployment, the general lack of morality in society, and lack of discipline and respect for authority in the schools themselves, not to mention the fact that many students graduating from high school were hardly literate. Some critics, and they were many as the "Christian Right" gained momentum and visibility, went so far as to say that all the troubles of society were attributable to the fact that the Supreme Court's prayer decisions of 1962 and 1963 had taken religion and morality out of the schools. Further, they contended that those decisions had initiated a trend toward secularism in America. Consequently, efforts were made to reverse the results and effects of those decisions.

One effort to that end was the law passed by Kentucky in 1978 which mandated that a copy of the Ten Commandments, 16 x 20 inches and of durable material, be posted in every public school classroom in the state. At the bottom of each of these posters was to be printed a disclaimer of any religious intent or meaning. Nevertheless, each poster was to point out that the Ten Commandments were integral to the secular legal code of the western world, including the United States. To further protect the plan from being rejected by the judiciary, the statute provided that the posters should be purchased by funds coming from private, voluntary contributions. The project was directed and pushed through the legislature by the Lexington Heritage Foundation, which apparently intended to be the solicitor and conduit of private contributions that would support the act.

The law was challenged in court by William Stone, an attorney for the Kentucky Civil Liberties Union, and others. They contended that it violated both the Establishment and Free Exercise Clauses. (Graham, the defendant, was the state Superintendent of Public Instruction.) The state trial court found the act to be constitutional in that its purpose was secular and that it neither advanced nor inhibited religion. The state Supreme Court upheld the trial court ruling.

Without having heard oral arguments, the U.S. Supreme Court decided this case by means of an unsigned opinion. It disagreed with the Kentucky courts. Going no farther than the first part of its Establishment Clause test, the Court held that the statute did not have a secular purpose. The purpose of the statute was plainly religious: to promote the moral concepts espoused by the Judaeo-Christian tradition. The fact that the state said that the statute had a secular purpose, articulated by the disclaimer on the posters, did not necessarily mean this was true. That the Ten Commandments contain admonitions on worshipping and showing proper respect for the deity prevents them from being only secular law. Support of the program by voluntary contributions was irrelevant because the very posting of the commandments under the auspices of a state statute constituted, in itself, a violation of the Establishment Clause. As one might suspect, there was considerable disagreement with this decision in Kentucky and across the nation among religious conservatives.

One of the most visible efforts to put religion back into the public schools was to restore prayer, to circumvent the *Engel* and *Schempp* decisions. From 1963 on there had been attempts to amend the Constitution to permit voluntary, nondenominational prayer in the schools—efforts that had never been successful. Given that lack of success (although Ronald Reagan and George Bush, throughout their presidencies, continued to support the idea), another strategy was proposed, primarily under the leadership of Senator Jesse Helms of North Carolina. Senator Helms repeatedly introduced legislation to remove questions of prayer in the public schools from the jurisdiction of the federal courts. The idea gained some popularity with the advent of the Reagan administration, but lost momentum after Mr. Reagan's first attorney general argued against it.[4] In the meantime, there were many instances of schools going ahead with prayer and devotional exercises as if *Engel* and *Schempp* had never been handed down. Consequently, there were many cases in the lower courts having to do with prayer in the public schools.

---

[4] "Attorney General Speaks Out on Court Stripping," *Congressional Record—Senate* (May 6, 1982): S4726-4730.

Finally, the Supreme Court accepted WALLACE v. JAFFREE (1986). When it became clear that the Court was not inclined to change its rulings banning compulsory or state-prepared prayers in the public schools, many state legislatures or local school boards introduced a "minute of silence" at the beginning of each school day. Alabama was one of those states. In 1978 a statute provided for a minute of silence "for meditation." In 1981 the words "or voluntary prayer" were added to the law. At that point litigation was initiated, challenging the revised law as a violation of the Establishment Clause. The Court declared the revised law to be unconstitutional. It was clear that when the legislature added the new words it intended to characterize prayer as a favored practice, a violation of the secular purpose prong of the three-part test. Although there was some negative reaction from the religious and political right wing that this was just one more example of the Court's anti-religious bias, the decision did not prohibit prayer. Two concurring opinions and the majority opinion itself asserted that a mere moment of silence during the school day would be appropriate and that it *could* be used for voluntary prayer.

Another way to insert religion into public schools was the subject of *Bender* v. *Williamsport Area School District* (1986). High school students, who had formed a religious club, "Petros," had been prohibited from meeting during the regularly scheduled activity hour before the beginning of curricular offerings, even though a wide variety of other student clubs routinely met during that time. The students sued, claiming a denial of free speech and the free exercise of religion. The school board defended in the belief that to allow the students to meet on school property would be government sponsorship of religion, a violation of the Establishment Clause.

In 1981 the Supreme Court had dealt with a similar issue at the university level, WIDMAR v. VINCENT. There the Court applied a concept called a "limited public forum," i.e., the university makes facilities available to a wide variety of student groups to meet and discuss whatever is on their minds. This open forum is "limited" because it is confined to the students of the institution and their invited guests, not the general public. Relying on this concept from *Widmar*, the District Court in *Bender* held that "Petros" had the right to meet as a part of the limited open forum the high school provided for other student groups. The fact that the school did not create any special conditions for the religious club or even encourage it to meet (it was entirely student-initiated), showed that the school had a secular purpose in creating the forum and that to allow "Petros" to meet as one among many student groups and equal with them all showed that the practice did not have the primary effect of promoting religion or creating excessive entanglement between the school and religion. In addition, to deny only "Petros" the right to meet discriminated against speech with religious content, a violation of students' free speech rights.

When *Bender* reached the Supreme Court, it was not decided on the merits, but rather on a standing issue. The way the case was originally framed, an *individual* member of the Williamsport School Board, rather than the Board as a whole, did not have standing to appeal the decision of the District Court in the Court of Appeals. Consequently, the Court vacated the ruling of the Court of Appeals (which had denied the students the right to meet) and reinstated the decision of the District Court, in effect upholding the right of students to meet at noncurricular hours of the school day for even prayer and worship, so long as the meeting was a part of a regular program of meetings by student organizations on a variety of academic and nonacademic subjects. In 1984 the Equal Access Act became law (20 U.S.C. §§4071-4074). Although the Act is much longer, the following excerpt contains its essence:

> It shall be unlawful for any public secondary school which receives Federal financial assistance and which has a limited open forum to deny equal access or a fair opportunity to, or discriminate against, any students who wish to conduct a meeting within that limited open forum on the basis of the religious, political, philosophical, or other content of the speech at such meetings.

By means of this law, Congress essentially formalized the District Court's 1983 decision in *Bender*. Since the Supreme Court did not decide the case on the merits (1986), it did not even allude to the constitutionality of the Equal Access Act.

However, the Court addressed that question in BOARD OF EDUCATION v. MERGENS (1990). Westside High School in Omaha received a request from students for permission to start a religious club which would meet in noninstructional time. Permission was denied on the basis that such a club would violate the Establishment Clause. The students sued, claiming that the school board had violated the Equal Access Act. The Supreme Court agreed with that contention.

The Court approached the case in terms of both statutory provisions and constitutionality. The statutory interpretation hinged on the question of what does "noncurriculum related" mean. The Equal Access Act, borrowing from *Widmar*, had defined a "limited open forum" as existing when a school gave students the opportunity to meet as clubs in school facilities when the subject matter of the club was not related to the school's curriculum. The Board of Education claimed that it had not created a limited open forum because all the clubs it allowed on campus were curriculum related—so the religious club could be denied under the Equal Access Act. It accomplished this by saying that a club which had even the remotest relationship with something which was taught in the school was curriculum related. The Court rejected that definition. Rather, the Court held that unless a club was *directly* related to a curricular subject, it was "noncurriculum related." In the light of that definition, the Board of Education had impermissibly denied the student religious club access to school facilities.

The Board of Education also contended that the Equal Access Act violated the Establishment Clause in that it compelled the public school with a limited open forum to incorporate religious activities into the school's program and give state sanction or legitimization to religion. The Court disagreed. Congress's purpose was to prevent discrimination against religious speech in the public schools. Because the Act granted equal access to both secular *and* religious speech, its purpose was not to endorse or disapprove religion. The Act did not have the effect of advancing religion because it merely protected student religious speech, rather than promoting government religious speech. High school students are mature enough to know the difference. Furthermore, under the mechanism of the Act, religious clubs would be only one of a variety of types of clubs, thus demonstrating that the school was not promoting or endorsing religion. Finally, the Court held that the merely custodial presence of school faculty at the religious club meetings did not foster excessive entanglement between government and religion.

Four justices chose not to join in the totality of the Court's opinion, but concurred in the judgment. Justice Stevens was the lone dissenter. He argued that the Court had misapplied the precedent in *Widmar* in that it had defined "noncurriculum related" much too broadly. *Widmar* declared that there was a "limited open forum" when the university allowed controversial or advocacy groups to use its facilities. That is all the Court should have required of the public schools in the case at bar. Just because the school allows clubs which are not directly related to its curriculum, it should not be forced to allow all other clubs to meet in its facilities, if "they do not break either the laws or the furniture"[5] (496 U.S. 228, 288). Justice Stevens was particularly concerned that the overbroad definition of the Court might compel schools to accommodate groups which were not suitable for the public school environment. The Court's interpretation of the Act put school officials in a difficult dilemma:

> If a high school administration continues to believe that it is sound policy to exclude controversial groups, such as political clubs, the Ku Klux Klan, and perhaps gay rights advocacy groups, from its facilities, it now must also close its doors to traditional extracurricular activities that are noncontroversial but not directly related to any course being offered at the school (496 U.S. 228, 290).

In 1991 the Court accepted LEE v. WEISMAN, a case about prayers at the commencement exercises of public middle and high schools. The facts were simple. A principal of a middle school in Providence, Rhode Island, had asked a rabbi to offer an invocation and a benediction at commencement exercises. He had also given him a set of guidelines for prayers at public occasions, guidelines which had the approval of public school officials. The prayers were challenged by a family on the grounds that they violated the Establishment Clause.

The decision was eagerly anticipated, although with foreboding by separationists, because it was expected to be an indicator of the Court's view of the Establishment Clause. The Bush Administration had urged the Court to abandon the *Lemon* three-part test and to adopt the much more accommodationist "coercion standard" set forth by Justice Kennedy in his dissent in ALLEGHENY COUNTY v. ACLU OF PITTSBURGH. Separationists were delighted and accommodationists were dismayed when Justice Kennedy himself wrote the majority opinion and declined to do that.

The Court held that not only had the school officials impermissibly exercised some control over the content of the prayers and the selection of the one offering them, but that the context of the commencement exercises exerted some coercion on those who attended to participate in the prayers. To be sure, attendance at commencement was voluntary—yet it was not, given that commencement is a once-in-a-lifetime event of great importance to a young person.

> There can be no doubt that for many, if not most, of the students at graduation, the act of standing or remaining silent was an expression of participation in the Rabbi's prayer. That was the very point of the religious exercise. It is of little comfort to a dissenter, then, to be told that for her the act of standing or remaining in silence signifies mere respect, rather than participation. What matters is that, given our social conventions, a reasonable dissenter in this milieu could believe that the group exercise signified her own participation or approval of it. . . . [W]e think the State may not, consistent with the Establishment Clause, place primary and secondary school children in this position (505 U.S. 577, 593).

Consequently, although prayers at a commencement exercise is not the same as prayers in a class-

[5]The phrase was coined by Rep. Barney Frank, who spoke in support of the Bill on the House floor. Cf. 130 *Cong. Rec.* 20933 (1984).

room, the Court, relying on the precedents of *Engel* and *Schempp*, maintained a separationist view of the Establishment Clause, at least on this issue.

Justices Blackmun and Souter wrote supportive concurring opinions, but Justice Scalia, joined by Justices Rehnquist, White, and Thomas, wrote a sharp dissent. He harkened back to Justice Kennedy's dissent in *Allegheny* and recalled its principle that religious practices with long history should be given great deference by the Court. He argued that prayers at commencement exercises should be declared constitutional on that basis alone. He also scoffed at what he called the "psychological coercion" test employed by the majority—that it was not really coercion and should not have been the basis for striking down the commencement prayers.

> The narrow context of the present case involves a community's celebration of one of the milestones in its young citizens' lives; and it is a bold step for this Court to seek to banish from that occasion, and from thousands of similar celebrations throughout the land, the expression of gratitude to God that a majority of the community wishes to make. The issue before us today is not the abstract philosophical question whether the alternative of frustrating this desire of a religious majority is to be preferred over the alternative of imposing "psychological coercion," or a feeling of exclusion, upon nonbelievers. Rather the question is *whether a mandatory choice in favor of the former has been imposed by the United States Constitution.* As the age-old practices of our people show, the answer to that question is not at all in doubt (Emphasis in original; 505 U.S. 577, 645-46).

One wonders why Justice Scalia was so interested in the viability of religion in this case when he dealt it such a sharp blow to the groin in EMPLOYMENT DIVISION OF OREGON v. SMITH.

LAMB'S CHAPEL v. CENTER MORICHES UNION FREE SCHOOL DISTRICT (1993) did not involve any question of religion in public school curricula or even public school students. Rather, it dealt with the issue of the use of public school facilities by religious groups in noninstructional time. It was ultimately decided more nearly on free speech grounds than on religious considerations. The case involved denial by a school district of its facilities after school hours to Lamb's Chapel, an evangelical church, which wanted to use a school building to show a film series. The six-part film series, open to the public without cost, featured a nationally recognized psychologist who urged a return to "traditional Christian family values." The pastor of Lamb's Chapel agreed that the film was religious, that its showing had a religious purpose. The school district based its denial on a New York law authorizing local school boards to establish reasonable regulations for use of school property when the facilities were not in use by the school. On the basis of this law, the school district adopted rules allowing only two of the ten state-authorized uses, and specifically stated that "[t]he school premises shall not be used by any groups for religious purposes." To allow its facilities to be used for religious purposes, the school district argued, would violate the Establishment Clause.

Lamb's Chapel brought suit. Both the District Court and the Court of Appeals for the Second Circuit found in favor of the school district's denial of use of its facilities by Lamb's Chapel. Those courts held the school property to be a "limited public forum," where the school district's denial of use need be only "reasonable and viewpoint neutral." The Court of Appeals held the rule to be viewpoint neutral because it had been and would be applied to deny all uses of the school property for religious purposes.

Writing for the Court, Justice White noted the wide variety of organizations which had been permitted to use the property after hours; he also found no danger that the community would believe the school district to be endorsing any religion or creed. Any benefit to religion or to Lamb's Chapel would have been "no more than incidental." Permission to use the school property would not constitute establishment of religion as measured by the three-prong test set forth in LEMON v. KURTZMAN. Nor was there reasonable danger that allowing use of the facilities by a "radical" church to proselytize might lead to public unrest or violence. In reversing the judgment of the Court of Appeals, Justice White said the Court was being consistent with the line of cases in which it deals with free speech. The First Amendment forbids the government to regulate speech in ways that favor some viewpoints or ideas at the expense of others.

Justice Scalia, joined by Justice Thomas, concurred in the judgment but failed to accept most of the reasoning. He took his stand with the many critics of the test in stating that he would refuse to apply *Lemon*. He also disagreed with the Court's use of the "endorsement of religion" concept.

Justice Kennedy, concurring in part in a brief opinion, agreed with the judgment. Like Justice Scalia, Justice Kennedy thought the case should have been decided on the basis of free speech, without consideration of the Establishment Clause or of endorsement of religion.

In ROSENBERGER v. UNIVERSITY OF VIRGINIA (1995) the Court confronted the question of whether the Establishment Clause was a sufficient cause for the University to deny student funds to a student-run religious newspaper. The University collected a mandatory fee from each student. The money was to support various student activities which would enhance their educational experiences.

Part of a university's mission is to stimulate intellectual discussion. At the University of Virginia, student activity funds were used to that end by funding the printing of student newspapers. However, the University's guidelines prohibited the funding of explicitly religious newspapers. When the student editors of *Wide Awake*, a newspaper with a Christian character, were denied funding under that policy, they sued, claiming denial of free speech and free exercise of religion, among other things.

The Court, Justice Kennedy for the majority, found in favor of the student publication. By giving official approval to appropriate student groups and, especially, by supporting some of the groups with student activity funds, the University had created a limited public forum. A university, virtually by definition, is a public forum, given that such an institution typically fosters the vigorous discussion of a wide variety of topics of intellectual and social importance. The public forum is limited, however, because it is not routinely open to the general public, but is primarily for the student body of the institution. The administration of the limited public forum in a state university is subject to the freedom of speech guaranteed by the First Amendment.

Justice Kennedy began by explaining that free speech principles may be summarized with this general principle: "It is axiomatic that the government may not regulate speech based on its substantive content or the message it conveys" (115 S.Ct. 2510, 2516). However, government is not powerless to regulate speech. It may forbid speech in a limited public forum if it determines that the speech is not appropriate for the purpose for which the forum was created. This is called "content discrimination." Government may discriminate on the basis of content if it can show that it is outside the parameters of the nature of the limited forum. If, however, government approves of a subject matter as appropriate to the forum and then forbids speech about a specific viewpoint within that subject, it has violated the free speech principle. This "viewpoint discrimination" is routinely impermissible under the free speech right.

> Thus, in determining whether the State is acting to preserve the limits of the forum it has created so that the exclusion of a class of speech is legitimate, we have observed a distinction between, on the one hand, content discrimination, which may be permissible if it preserves the purposes of that limited forum, and, on the other hand, viewpoint discrimination, which is presumed impermissible when directed against speech otherwise within the forum's limitations (115 S.Ct. 2510, 2517).

In this case, the University of Virginia had inflicted impermissible viewpoint discrimination on *Wide Awake*. A category of approved student groups which were eligible to apply for funding from student activity fees was "student news, information, opinion, entertainment, or academic communications media groups." However, the policy excluded from eligibility for funding papers that "primarily promotes or manifests a particular belie[f] in or about a deity or an ultimate reality" (115 S.Ct. 2510, 2514, 2513). It was under this exclusion that *Wide Awake* was denied payments to its printing contractor. The Court found this to be viewpoint discrimination.

However, the University had argued that this exclusion was legitimate, in fact, required of it by the Establishment Clause. It was forbidden, under the no establishment principle, to fund specifically religious student publications so as not to give government aid and sanction to religion. Indeed, the Court of Appeals for the Fourth Circuit had held that the University's policy of funding student publications but not religious publications was discriminatory under the Free Speech Clause, but that the discrimination here was justified by the Establishment Clause, by the state's compelling interest to maintain the separation of church and state.

The Court disagreed with that contention and found that the University's viewpoint discrimination was not justified by the no establishment principle. The theme of Justice Kennedy's rationale was neutrality: that the Court has historically upheld government programs of aid to religion if that aid was neutrally granted.

> We have held that the guarantee of neutrality is respected, not offended, when the government, following neutral criteria and evenhanded policies, extends benefits to recipients whose ideologies and viewpoints, including religious ones, are broad and diverse (115 S.Ct. 2510, 2521).

The University's program of funding student organizations is neutral toward religion; it was not created to advance religion or a particular religious cause. Its sole purpose was to create a limited open forum and encourage student activities and speech, all consistent with the University's mission of education.

> Much like the arrangement in *Widmar*, the money goes to a special fund from which any group of students with [University approved] status can draw for purposes consistent with the University's educational mission; and to the extent the student is interested in speech, withdrawal is permitted to cover the whole spectrum of speech, whether it manifests a religious view, an antireligious view, or neither (115 S.Ct. 2510, 2522).

Given that *Wide Awake* applied for funding simply as a student newspaper, rather than a religious organization, the neutrality inherent in the Establishment Clause should have allowed it to be funded, rather than being an excuse to deny funding.

Justice Kennedy argued that other dimensions of Establishment Clause neutrality were the fact that the money involved was student activity fees, albeit required as a result of enrollment in the state university, rather than a tax. Furthermore, the money did not go to the newspaper itself, but rather was to pay its printing bill, i.e., to a third-party contractor. Finally, government neutrality was maintained by the distinction first articulated in BOARD OF EDUCATION v. MERGENS, that there is a difference between *government* speech endorsing religion, forbidden by the Establishment Clause, and *private* speech endorsing religion, which the government must permit under the Free Speech and Free Exercise Clauses. It was the latter circumstance here, given that the University made it clear that approved student groups were not organically or structurally related to the school. Given that no favoritism was shown to religious private speech, the Establishment Clause was not violated. The Court concluded:

> To obey the Establishment Clause, it was not necessary for the University to deny eligibility to student publications because of their viewpoint. The neutrality commanded of the State by the separate Clauses of the First Amendment was compromised by the University's course of action. . . . There is no Establishment Clause violation in the University's honoring its duties under the Free Speech Clause (115 S.Ct. 2510, 2524-2525).

Justice Souter, joined by Justices Stevens, Ginsburg, and Breyer, wrote a long and vigorous dissent. He began by pointing out that *Wide Awake* was not just a newspaper with a "religious viewpoint," as the majority mistakenly claimed, but was characterized by aggressive, explicit Christian evangelism. Under the rubric that the Establishment Clause prohibits state money from supporting preaching, he claimed that what the majority had allowed was impermissible. Why had the Court approved of this plan to subsidize the publication of *Wide Awake*? Because of its theory of evenhandedness, i.e., that the money was designed to facilitate freedom of speech, regardless of what that speech was (if it fit the purposes of the limited open forum, in this case, the University's educational mission). But, Justice Souter argued, evenhandedness is a threshold issue for Establishment Clause interpretation and is not dispositive. What is dispositive is the effect of the legislation or program. If the effect is to support and sanction religious proselytization, as it did here, it is a violation of the Establishment Clause, no matter how evenhandedly the aid is applied. There are two general rules, which the Court recognized but did not apply:

> [T]hat whenever affirmative government aid ultimately benefits religion, the Establishment Clause requires some justification beyond evenhandedness on the government's part; and that direct public funding of core sectarian activities, even if accomplished pursuant to an evenhanded program, would be entirely inconsistent with the Establishment Clause and would strike at the very heart of the Clause's protection (115 S.Ct. 2510, 2540).

Furthermore, the student activities fee, collected as it is by the state university as a mandatory assessment, is a tax, contrary to the Court's denial that it is. In this case, it was impermissibly used to support sectarian activity. Finally, the fact that the money was transmitted to a third party, a print shop, did not save the program. There are ways of impermissibly aiding religious groups other than direct payments to them. One way Justice Souter answered the Court's position was the *reductio ad absurdum* argument that if it were true that the Establishment Clause banned only direct payments to religious groups, as the Court seemed to say, then the State could hand out credit cards to religious entities and pay their monthly indebtedness to their creditors, so long as it could be done in an evenhanded way.

McCOLLUM v. BOARD OF EDUCATION

333 U.S. 203
ON APPEAL FROM THE SUPREME COURT OF ILLINOIS
Argued December 8, 1947 — Decided March 8, 1948

⊥**204** Mr. *Justice BLACK* delivered the opinion of the Court.

This case relates to the power of a state to utilize its tax-supported public school system in aid of religious ⊥**205** instruction insofar as that power may be restricted by the First and Fourteenth Amendments to the Federal Constitution.

The appellant, Vashti McCollum, began this action for mandamus against the Champaign Board of Education in the Circuit Court of Champaign County, Illinois. Her asserted interest was that of a resident and taxpayer of Champaign and of a parent whose child was then enrolled in the Champaign public schools. Illinois has a compulsory education law which, with exceptions, requires parents to send their children, aged seven to sixteen, to its tax-supported public schools where the children are to remain in attendance during the hours when the schools are regularly in session. Parents who violate this law commit a misdemeanor punishable by fine unless the children attend private or parochial schools which meet educational standards fixed by the State. District boards of education are given general supervisory powers over the use of the public school buildings within the school districts.

Appellant's petition for mandamus alleged that religious teachers, employed by private religious groups, were permitted to come weekly into the school buildings during the regular hours set apart for secular teaching, and then and there for a period of thirty minutes substitute their religious teaching for the secular education provided under the compulsory education law. The petitioner charged that this joint public-school religious-group program violated the First and Fourteenth Amendments to the United States Constitution. The prayer of her petition was that the Board of Education be ordered to "adopt and enforce rules and regulations prohibiting all instruction in and teaching of religious education in all public schools in Champaign School District Number 71, . . . and in all public school houses and buildings in said district when occupied by public schools."

⊥**206** The board first moved to dismiss the petition on the ground that under Illinois law appellant had no standing to maintain the action. This motion was denied. An answer was then filed, which admitted that regular weekly religious instruction was given during school hours to those pupils whose parents consented and that those pupils were released temporarily from their regular secular classes for the limited purpose of attending the religious classes. The answer denied that this coordinated program of religious instruction violated the State or Federal Constitution. Much evidence was heard, findings of fact were made, after which the petition for mandamus was denied on the ground that the school's religious instruction program violated neither the federal nor state constitutional provisions invoked by the appellant. On appeal the State Supreme Court affirmed. Appellant appealed to this Court and we noted probable jurisdiction on June 2, 1947.

The appellees press a motion to dismiss the appeal on several grounds, the first of which is that the judgment of the State Supreme Court does not draw in question the "validity of a statute of any State" as required by 28 U.S.C. § 344 (a). This contention rests on the admitted fact that the challenged program of religious instruction was not expressly authorized by statute. But the State Supreme Court has sustained the validity of the program on the ground that the Illinois statutes granted the board authority to establish such a program. This holding is sufficient to show that the validity of an Illinois statute was drawn in question within the meaning of 28 U.S.C. § 344 (a). A second ground for the motion to dismiss is that the appellant lacks standing to maintain the action, a ground which is also without merit. ⊥**207** A third ground for the motion is that the appellant failed properly to present in the State Supreme Court her challenge that the state program violated the Federal Constitution. But in view of the express rulings of both state courts on this question the argument cannot be successfully maintained. The motion to dismiss the appeal is denied.

Although there are disputes between the parties as to various inferences that may or may not properly be drawn from the evidence concerning the religious program, the following facts are shown by the record without dispute. In 1940 interested members of the Jewish, Roman Catholic, and a few of the Protestant faiths formed a voluntary association called the Champaign Council on Religious Education. They obtained permission from the Board of Education to offer classes in religious instruction to public school pupils in grades four to nine inclusive. Classes were made up of pupils whose parents signed printed cards requesting that their children be permitted to attend; they were held weekly, thirty minutes for ⊥**208** the lower grades, forty-five minutes for the higher. The council employed the religious teachers at no expense to the school authorities, but the instructors were subject to the approval and supervision of the superintendent of schools. The classes were taught in three ⊥**209** separate religious groups by Protestant teachers, Catholic priests, and a Jewish rabbi, although for the past several years there have apparently been no classes instructed in the Jewish religion. Classes were conducted in the regular classrooms of the school building. Students who did not choose to take the religious instruction were not released from public school duties; they were required to leave their classrooms and go to some other place in the school building for pursuit of their secular studies. On the other hand, students who were released from secular study for the religious instructions were required to be present at the religious classes. Reports of their presence or absence were to be made to their secular teachers.

The foregoing facts, without reference to others that appear in the record, show the use of tax-supported property for religious instruction and the close cooperation between the school authorities and the religious council in promoting religious education. The operation of the State's compulsory education system thus assists and is integrated with the program of religious instruction carried on by separate religious sects. Pupils compelled by law to go to school for secular education are released ⊥**210** in part from their legal duty upon the condition that they attend the religious classes. This is beyond all question a utilization of the tax-established and tax-supported public school system to aid religious groups to spread their faith. And it falls squarely under the ban of the First Amendment (made applicable to the States by the Fourteenth) as we interpreted it in *Everson* v. *Board of Education*. . . . ⊥**211** The majority in the *Everson* case, and the minority agreed that the First Amendment's language, properly interpreted, had erected a wall of separation between Church and State. They disagreed as to the facts shown by the record and as to the proper application of the First Amendment's language to those facts.

Recognizing that the Illinois program is barred by the First and Fourteenth Amendments if we adhere to the views expressed both by the majority and the minority in the *Everson* case, counsel for the respondents challenge those views as dicta and urge that we reconsider and repudiate them. They argue that historically the First Amendment was intended to forbid only government preference of one religion over another, not an impartial governmental assistance of all religions. In addition they ask that we distinguish or overrule our holding in the *Everson* case that the Fourteenth Amendment made the "establishment of religion" clause of the First Amendment applicable as a prohibition against the States. After giving full consideration to the arguments presented we are unable to accept either of these contentions.

To hold that a state cannot consistently with the First and Fourteenth Amendments utilize its public school system to aid any or all religious faiths or in the dissemination of their doctrines and ideals does not, as counsel urge, manifest a governmental hostility to religion or religious teachings. A manifestation of such hostility would be at war with our national tradition as embodied in the First Amendment's guaranty of the free ⊥**212** exercise of religion. For the First Amendment rests upon the premise that both religion and government can best work to achieve their lofty aims if each is left free from the other within its respective sphere. Or, as we said in the *Everson* case, the First Amendment has erected a wall between Church and State which must be kept high and impregnable.

Here not only are the State's tax-supported public school buildings used for the dissemination of religious doctrines. The State also affords sectarian groups an invaluable aid in that it helps to provide pupils for their religious classes through use of the State's compulsory public school machinery. This is not separation of Church and State.

The cause is reversed and remanded to the State Supreme Court for proceedings not inconsistent with this opinion.

Reversed and remanded.

Mr. *Justice FRANKFURTER* delivered the following opinion, in which Mr. *Justice JACKSON*, Mr. *Justice RUTLEDGE* and Mr. *Justice BURTON* join.*

We dissented in *Everson* v. *Board of Education*, because in our view the Constitutional principle requiring separation of Church and State compelled invalidation of the ordinance sustained by the majority. Illinois has here authorized the commingling of sectarian with secular instruction in the public schools. The Constitution of the United States forbids this.

This case, in the light of the *Everson* decision, demonstrates anew that the mere formulation of a relevant Constitutional principle is the beginning of the solution of a problem, not its answer. This is so because the mean⊥**213**ing of a spacious conception like that of the separation of Church from State is unfolded as appeal is made to the principle from case to case. We are all agreed that the First and the Fourteenth Amendments have a secular reach far more penetrating in the conduct of Government than merely to forbid an "established church." But agreement, in the abstract, that the First Amendment was designed to erect a "wall of separation between church and State," does not preclude a clash of views as to what the wall separates. Involved is not only the Constitutional principle but the implications of judicial review in its enforcement. Accommodation of legislative freedom and Constitutional limitations upon that freedom cannot be achieved by a mere phrase. We cannot illuminatingly apply the "wall-of-separation" metaphor until we have considered the relevant history of religious education in America, the place of the "released time" movement in that history, and its precise manifestation in the case before us.

To understand the particular program now before us as a conscientious attempt to accommodate the allowable functions of Government and the special concerns of the Church within the framework of our Constitution and with due regard to the kind of society for which it was designed, we must put this Champaign program of 1940 in its historic setting. Traditionally, organized education in the Western world was Church education. It could hardly be otherwise when the education of children was primarily study of the Word and the ways of God. Even in the Protestant countries, where there was a less close identification of Church and State, the basis of education was largely the Bible, and its chief purpose inculcation of piety. To the extent that the State intervened, it used its authority to further aims of the Church.

The emigrants who came to these shores brought this view of education with them. Colonial schools certainly ⊥**214** started with a religious orientation. When the common problems of the early settlers of the Massachusetts Bay Colony revealed the need for common schools, the object was the defeat of "one chief project of that old deluder, Satan, to keep men from the knowledge of the Scriptures." The Laws and Liberties of Massachusetts, 1648 edition.

The evolution of colonial education, largely in the service of religion, into the public school system of today is the story of changing conceptions regarding the American democratic society, of the functions of State-maintained education in such a society, and of the role therein of the free exercise of religion by the people. The modern public school derived from a philosophy of freedom reflected in the First Amendment. It is appropriate to recall that the Remonstrance of James Madison, an event basic in the history of religious liberty, was called forth by a proposal which involved support to religious education. As the momentum for popular education increased and in turn evoked strong claims for State support of religious education, contests not unlike that which in Virginia had produced Madison's Remonstrance appeared in various forms in other States. New York and Massachusetts provide famous chapters in the history that established dissociation of religious teaching from State-maintained schools. In New York, the rise of the common schools led, despite fierce sectarian opposition, to the barring of tax funds to church schools, and later to any school in which sectarian doctrine was ⊥**215**

*Mr. Justice RUTLEDGE and Mr. Justice BURTON concurred also in the Court's opinion.

taught. In Massachusetts, largely through the efforts of Horace Mann, all sectarian teachings were barred from the common school to save it from being rent by denominational conflict. The upshot of these controversies, often long and fierce, is fairly summarized by saying that long before the Fourteenth Amendment subjected the States to new limitations, the prohibition of furtherance by the State of religious instruction became the guiding principle, in law and feeling, of the American people. In sustaining Stephen Girard's will, this Court referred to the inevitable conflicts engendered by matters "connected with religious polity" and particularly "in a country composed of such a variety of religious sects as our country." *Vidal* v. *Girard's Executors*. That was more than one hundred years ago.

Separation in the field of education, then, was not imposed upon unwilling States by force of superior law. In this respect the Fourteenth Amendment merely reflected a principle then dominant in our national life. To the extent that the Constitution thus made it binding upon the States, the basis of the restriction is the whole experience of our people. Zealous watchfulness against fusion of secular and religious activities by Government itself, through any of its instruments but especially through its educational agencies, was the democratic response of the American community to the particular needs of a young and growing nation, unique in the composition of its ⊥**216** people. A totally different situation elsewhere, as illustrated for instance by the English provisions for religious education in State-maintained schools, only serves to illustrate that free societies are not cast in one mould. Different institutions evolve from different historic circumstances.

It is pertinent to remind that the establishment of this principle of Separation in the field of education was not due to any decline in the religious beliefs of the people. Horace Mann was a devout Christian, and the deep religious feeling of James Madison is stamped upon the Remonstrance. The secular public school did not imply indifference to the basic role of religion in the life of the people, nor rejection of religious education as a means of fostering it. The claims of religion were not minimized by refusing to make the public schools agencies for their assertion. The nonsectarian or secular public school was the means of reconciling freedom in general with religious freedom. The sharp confinement of the public schools to secular education was a recognition of the need of a democratic society to educate its children, insofar as the State undertook to do so, in an atmosphere free from pressures in a realm in which pressures are most resisted and where conflicts are most easily and most bitterly engendered. Designed to serve as perhaps the most powerful agency for promoting cohesion among a heterogeneous democratic people, the public school must keep scrupu⊥**217**lously free from entanglement in the strife of sects. The preservation of the community from divisive conflicts, of Government from irreconcilable pressures by religious groups, of religion from censorship and coercion however subtly exercised, requires strict confinement of the State to instruction other than religious, leaving to the individual's church and home, indoctrination in the faith of his choice.

This development of the public school as a symbol of our secular unity was not a sudden achievement nor attained without violent conflict. While in small communities of comparatively homogeneous religious beliefs, the need for absolute separation presented no urgencies, elsewhere the growth of the secular school encountered the resistance of feeling strongly engaged against it. But the inevitability of such attempts is the very reason for Constitutional provisions primarily concerned with the protection of minority groups. And such sects are shifting groups, varying from time to time, and place to place, thus representing in their totality the common interest of the nation.

Enough has been said to indicate that we are dealing not with a full-blown principle, nor one having the definiteness of a surveyor's metes and bounds. But by 1875 the separation of public education from Church entanglements, of the State from the teaching of religion, was firmly established in the consciousness of the nation. In ⊥**218** that year President Grant made his famous remarks to the Convention of the Army of the Tennessee: "Encourage free schools, and resolve that not one dollar appropriated for their support shall be appropriated to the support of any sectarian schools. Resolve that neither the State nor nation, nor both combined, shall support institutions of learning other than those sufficient to afford every child growing up in the land the opportunity of a good common-school education, unmixed with sectarian, pagan, or atheistical dogmas. Leave the matter of religion to the family altar, the church, and the private school, supported entirely by private contributions. Keep the church and the state forever separate." "The President's Speech at Des Moines," 22 *Catholic World* 433, 434-35 (1876).

So strong was this conviction, that rather than rest on the comprehensive prohibitions of the First and Fourteenth Amendments, President Grant urged that there be written into the United States Constitution particular elaborations, including a specific prohibition against the use of public funds for sectarian education, such as had ⊥**219** been written into many State constitutions. By 1894, in urging the adoption of such a provision in the New York Constitution, Elihu Root was able to summarize a century of the nation's history: "It is not a question of religion, or of creed, or of party; it is a question of declaring and maintaining the great American principle of eternal separation between Church and State." Root, Addresses on Government and Citizenship, 137, 140. The extent to which ⊥**220** this principle was deemed a presupposition of our Constitutional system is strikingly illustrated by the fact that every State admitted into the Union since 1876 was compelled by Congress to write into its constitution a requirement that it maintain a school system "free from sectarian control."

Prohibition of the commingling of sectarian and secular instruction in the public school is of course only half the story. A religious people was naturally concerned about the part of the child's education entrusted "to the family altar, the church, and the private school." The promotion of religious education took many forms. Laboring under financial difficulties and exercising only persuasive authority, various denominations felt handicapped in their task of religious education. Abortive **⊥221** attempts were therefore frequently made to obtain public funds for religious schools. But the major efforts of religious inculcation were a recognition of the principle of Separation by the establishment of church schools privately supported. Parochial schools were maintained by various denominations. These, however, were often beset by serious handicaps, financial and otherwise, so that the religious aims which they represented found other directions. There were experiments with vacation schools, with Saturday as well as Sunday schools. They all fell short of their purpose. It was urged that by appearing to make religion a one-day-a-week matter, the **⊥222** Sunday school, which acquired national acceptance, tended to relegate the child's religious education, and thereby his religion, to a minor role not unlike the enforced piano lesson.

Out of these inadequate efforts evolved the weekday church school, held on one or more afternoons a week after the close of the public school. But children continued to be children; they wanted to play when school was out, particularly when other children were free to do so. Church leaders decided that if the week-day church school was to succeed, a way had to be found to give the child his religious education during what the child conceived to be his "business hours."

The initiation of the movement may fairly be attributed to Dr. George U. Wenner. The underlying assumption of his proposal, made at the Interfaith Conference on Federation held in New York City in 1905, was that the public school unduly monopolized the child's time and that the churches were entitled to their share of it. This, the schools should "release." Accordingly, the Federation, citing the example of the Third Republic of France, urged that upon the request of their parents **⊥223** children be excused from public school on Wednesday afternoon, so that the churches could provide "Sunday school on Wednesday." This was to be carried out on church premises under church authority. Those not desiring to attend church schools would continue their normal classes. Lest these public school classes unfairly compete with the church education, it was requested that the school authorities refrain from scheduling courses or activities of compelling interest or importance.

The proposal aroused considerable opposition and it took another decade for a "released time" scheme to become part of a public school system. Gary, Indiana, inaugurated the movement. At a time when industrial **⊥224** expansion strained the communal facilities of the city, Superintendent of Schools Wirt suggested a fuller use of the school buildings. Building on theories which had become more or less current, he also urged that education was more than instruction in a classroom. The school was only one of several educational agencies. The library, the playground, the home, the church, all have their function in the child's proper unfolding. Accordingly, Wirt's plan sought to rotate the schedules of the children during the school-day so that some were in class, others were in the library, still others in the playground. And some, he suggested to the leading ministers of the City, might be released to attend religious classes if the churches of the City cooperated and provided them. They did, in 1914, and thus was "released time" begun. The religious teaching was held on church premises and the public schools had no hand in the conduct of these church schools. They did not supervise the choice of instructors or the subject matter taught. Nor did they assume responsibility for the attendance, conduct or achievement of the child in a church school; and he received no credit for it. The period of attendance in the religious schools would otherwise have been a play period for the child, with the result that the arrangement did not cut into public school instruction or truly affect the activities or feelings of the children who did not attend the church schools.

From such a beginning "released time" has attained substantial proportions. In 1914-15, under the Gary program, 619 pupils left the public schools for the church schools during one period a week. According to responsible figures almost 2,000,000 in some 2,200 communities **⊥225** participated in "released time" programs during 1947. A movement of such scope indicates the importance of the problem to which the "released time" programs are directed. But to the extent that aspects of these programs are open to Constitutional objection, the more extensively the movement operates, the more ominous the breaches in the wall of separation.

Of course, "released time" as a generalized conception, undefined by differentiating particularities, is not an issue for Constitutional adjudication. Local programs differ from each other in many and crucial respects. Some "released time" classes are under separate denominational auspices, others are conducted jointly by several denominations, often embracing all the religious affiliations of a community. Some classes in religion teach a limited sectarianism; others emphasize democracy, unity and spiritual values not anchored in a particular creed. Insofar as these are manifestations merely of the free exercise of religion, they are quite outside the scope of judicial concern, except insofar as the Court may be called upon to protect the right of religious freedom. It is only when challenge is made to the share that the public schools have in the execution of a particular "released time" program that close judicial scrutiny is demanded of the exact relation between the religious instruction and the public educational system in the specific situation before the Court.

⊥226 The substantial differences among arrangements lumped together as "released time" emphasize the importance of detailed analysis of the facts to which the Constitutional test of Separation is to be applied. How does "released time" operate in Champaign? Public school teachers distribute to their pupils cards supplied by church groups, so that the parents may indicate whether they desire religious instruction for their children. For those desiring it, religious classes are conducted in the regular classrooms of the public schools by teachers of religion paid by the churches and appointed by them, but, as the State court found, "subject to the approval and supervision of the superintendent." The courses do not profess to give secular instruction in subjects concerning religion. Their candid purpose is sectarian teaching. While a child can go to any of the religious classes offered, a particular sect wishing a teacher for its devotees requires the permission of the school superintendent "who in turn will determine whether or not it is practical for said group to teach in said school **⊥227** system." If no provision is made for religious instruction in the particular faith of a child, or if for other reasons the child is not enrolled in any of the offered classes, he is required to attend a regular school class, or a study period during which he is often left to his own devices. Reports of attendance in the religious classes are submitted by the religious instructor to the school authorities, and the child who fails to attend is presumably deemed a truant.

Religious education so conducted on school time and property is patently woven into the working scheme of the school. The Champaign arrangement thus presents powerful elements of inherent pressure by the school system in the interest of religious sects. The fact that this power has not been used to discriminate is beside the point. Separation is a requirement to abstain from fusing functions of Government and of religious sects, not merely to treat them all equally. That a child is offered an alternative may reduce the constraint; it does not eliminate the operation of influence by the school in matters sacred to conscience and outside the school's domain. The law of imitation operates, and nonconformity is not an outstanding characteristic of children. The result is an obvious pressure upon children to attend. Again, while the Champaign school population represents only a fraction of the more than two hundred and fifty sects of the nation, not even all the practicing sects in Champaign are willing or able to provide religious instruction. The children belonging to these non-participating sects will thus have inculcated in them a feeling of separatism when the school should be the training ground for habits of community, or they will have religious instruction in a faith which is not that of **⊥228** their parents. As a result, the public school system of Champaign actively furthers inculcation in the religious tenets of some faiths, and in the process sharpens the consciousness of religious differences at least among some of the children committed to its care. These are consequences not amenable to statistics. But they are precisely the consequences against which the Constitution was directed when it prohibited the Government common to all from becoming embroiled, however innocently, in the destructive religious conflicts of which the history of even this country records some dark pages.

Mention should not be omitted that the integration of religious instruction within the school system as practiced in Champaign is supported by arguments drawn from educational theories as diverse as those derived from Catholic conceptions and from the writings of John Dewey. Movements like "released time" are seldom **⊥229** single in origin or aim. Nor can the intrusion of religious instruction into the public school system of Champaign be minimized by saying that it absorbs less than an hour a week; in fact, that affords evidence of **⊥230** a design constitutionally objectionable. If it were merely a question of enabling a child to obtain religious instruction with a receptive mind, the thirty or forty-five minutes could readily be found on Saturday or Sunday. If that were all, Champaign might have drawn upon the French system, known in its American manifestation as "dismissed time," whereby one school day is shortened to allow all children to go where they please, leaving those who so desire to go to a religious school. The momentum of the whole school atmosphere and school planning is presumably put behind religious instruction, as given in Champaign, precisely in order to secure for the religious **⊥231** instruction such momentum and planning. To speak of "released time" as being only half or three quarters of an hour is to draw a thread from a fabric.

We do not consider, as indeed we could not, school programs not before us which, though colloquially characterized as "released time," present situations differing in aspects that may well be constitutionally crucial. Different forms which "released time" has taken during more than thirty years of growth include programs which, like that before us, could not withstand the test of the Constitution; others may be found unexceptionable. We do not now attempt to weigh in the Constitutional scale every separate detail or various combination of factors which may establish a valid "released time" program. We find that the basic Constitutional principle of absolute Separation was violated when the State of Illinois, speaking through its Supreme Court, sustained the school authorities of Champaign in sponsoring and effectively furthering religious beliefs by its educational arrangement.

Separation means separation, not something less. Jefferson's metaphor in describing the relation between Church and State speaks of a "wall of separation," not of a fine line easily overstepped. The public school is at once the symbol of our democracy and the most pervasive means for promoting our common destiny. In no activity of the State is it more vital to keep out divisive forces than in its schools, to avoid confusing, not to say fusing, what the Constitution sought to keep strictly apart. "The great American principle of eternal separation"—Elihu Root's phrase bears repetition—is one of the vital reliances of our Constitutional system for assuring unities among our people stronger than our diversities. It is the Court's duty to enforce this principle in its full integrity.

⊥**232** We renew our conviction that "we have staked the very existence of our country on the faith that complete separation between the state and religion is best for the state and best for religion." *Everson* v. *Board of Education.* If nowhere else, in the relation between Church and State, "good fences make good neighbors."

Mr. *Justice* JACKSON, concurring.

I join the opinion of Mr. *Justice* FRANKFURTER, and concur in the result reached by the Court, but with these reservations: I think it is doubtful whether the facts of this case establish jurisdiction in this Court, but in any event that we should place some bounds on the demands for interference with local schools that we are empowered or willing to entertain. I make these reservations a matter of record in view of the number of litigations likely to be started as a result of this decision.

A Federal Court may interfere with local school authorities only when they invade either a personal liberty or a property right protected by the Federal Constitution. Ordinarily this will come about in either of two ways:

First. When a person is required to submit to some religious rite or instruction or is deprived or threatened with deprivation of his freedom for resisting such unconstitutional requirement. We may then set him free or enjoin his prosecution. Typical of such cases was *West Virginia State Board of Education* v. *Barnette.* There penalties were threatened against both parent and child for refusal of the latter to perform a compulsory ritual which offended his convictions. We intervened to shield them against the penalty. But here, complainant's son may join religious classes if he chooses and if his parents so request, or he may stay out of them. The complaint is that when others join and he does not, it sets him apart as a dissenter, which is humiliating. ⊥**233** Even admitting this to be true, it may be doubted whether the Constitution which, of course, protects the right to dissent, can be construed also to protect one from the embarrassment that always attends nonconformity, whether in religion, politics, behavior or dress. Since no legal compulsion is applied to complainant's son himself and no penalty is imposed or threatened from which we may relieve him, we can hardly base jurisdiction on this ground.

Second. Where a complainant is deprived of property by being taxed for unconstitutional purposes, such as directly or indirectly to support a religious establishment. We can protect a taxpayer against such a levy. This was the *Everson Case*, as I saw it then and see it now. It was complained in that case that the school treasurer drew a check on public funds to reimburse parents for a child's bus fare if he went to a Catholic parochial school or a public school, but not if he went to any other private or denominational school. Reference to the record in that case will show that the School District was not operating busses, so it was not a question of allowing Catholic children to ride publicly owned busses along with others, in the interests of their safety, health or morals. The child had to travel to and from parochial school on commercial busses like other paying passengers and all other school children, and he was exposed to the same dangers. If it could, in fairness, have been said that the expenditure was a measure for the protection of the safety, health or morals of youngsters, it would not merely have been constitutional to grant it; it would have been unconstitutional to refuse it to any child merely because he was a Catholic. But in the *Everson Case* there was a direct, substantial and measurable burden on the complainant as a taxpayer to raise funds that were used to subsidize transportation to parochial schools. Hence, we ⊥**234** had jurisdiction to examine the constitutionality of the levy and to protect against it if a majority had agreed that the subsidy for transportation was unconstitutional.

In this case, however, any cost of this plan to the taxpayers is incalculable and negligible. It can be argued, perhaps, that religious classes add some wear and tear on public buildings and that they should be charged with some expense for heat and light, even though the sessions devoted to religious instruction do not add to the length of the school day. But the cost is neither substantial nor measurable, and no one seriously can say that the complainant's tax bill has been proved to be increased because of this plan. I think it is doubtful whether the taxpayer in this case has shown any substantial property injury.

If, however, jurisdiction is found to exist, it is important that we circumscribe our decision with some care. What is asked is not a defensive use of judicial power to set aside a tax levy or reverse a conviction, or to enjoin threats of prosecution or taxation. The relief demanded in this case is the extraordinary writ of mandamus to tell the local Board of Education what it must do. The prayer for relief is that a writ issue against the Board of Education "ordering it to immediately adopt and enforce rules and regulations prohibiting all instruction in and teaching of religious education in all public schools . . . and in all public school houses and buildings in said district when occupied by public schools." The plaintiff, as she has every right to be, is an avowed atheist. What she has asked of the courts is that they not only end the "released time" plan but also ban every form of teaching which suggests or recognizes that there is a God. She would ban all teaching of the Scriptures. She especially mentions as an example of invasion of her rights "having pupils learn and recite such statements as, 'The Lord is my Shepherd, I shall not want.'" And she objects to teaching that the King James version of the Bible "is ⊥**235** called the Christian's Guide Book, the Holy Writ and the Word of God," and many other similar matters. This Court is directing the Illinois courts generally to sustain plaintiff's complaint without exception of any of these grounds of complaint, without discriminating between them and without laying down any standards to define the limits of the effect of our decision.

To me, the sweep and detail of these complaints is a danger signal which warns of the kind of local controversy we will be required to arbitrate if we do not place appropriate limitation on our decision and exact strict compliance with jurisdictional requirements. Authorities list 256 separate and substantial religious bodies to exist in the continental United States. Each of them, through the suit of some discontented but unpenalized and untaxed representative, has as good a right as this plaintiff to demand that the courts compel the schools to sift out of their teaching everything inconsistent with its doctrines. If we are to eliminate everything that is objectionable to any of these warring sects or inconsistent with any of their doctrines, we will leave public education in shreds. Nothing but educational confusion and a discrediting of the public school system can result from subjecting it to constant law suits.

While we may and should end such formal and explicit instruction as the Champaign plan and can at all times prohibit teaching of creed and catechism and ceremonial and can forbid forthright proselyting in the schools, I think it remains to be demonstrated whether it is possible, even if desirable, to comply with such demands as plaintiff's completely to isolate and cast out of secular education all that some people may reasonably regard as religious instruction. Perhaps subjects such as mathematics, physics or chemistry are, or can be, completely secularized. But it would not seem practical to teach either practice or appreciation of the arts if we are to forbid ex⊥**236**posure of youth to any religious influences. Music without sacred music, architecture minus the cathedral, or painting without the scriptural themes would be eccentric and incomplete, even from a secular point of view. Yet the inspirational appeal of religion in these guises is often stronger than in forthright sermon. Even such a "science" as biology raises the issue between evolution and creation as an explanation of our presence on this planet. Certainly a course in English literature that omitted the Bible and other powerful uses of our mother tongue for religious ends would be pretty barren. And I should suppose it is a proper, if not an indispensable, part of preparation for a worldly life to know the roles that religion and religions have played in the tragic story of mankind. The fact is that, for good or for ill, nearly everything in our culture worth transmitting, everything which gives meaning to life, is saturated with religious influences, derived from paganism, Judaism, Christianity—both Catholic and Protestant—and other faiths accepted by a large part of the world's peoples. One can hardly respect a system of education that would leave the student wholly ignorant of the currents of religious thought that move the world society for a part in which he is being prepared.

But how one can teach, with satisfaction or even with justice to all faiths, such subjects as the story of the Reformation, the Inquisition, or even the New England effort to found "a Church without a Bishop and a State without a King," is more than I know. It is too much to expect that mortals will teach subjects about which their contemporaries have passionate controversies with the detachment they may summon to teaching about remote subjects such as Confucius or Mohammed. When instruction turns to proselyting and imparting knowledge becomes evangelism is, except in the crudest cases, a subtle inquiry.

⊥**237** The opinions in this case show that public educational authorities have evolved a considerable variety of practices in dealing with the religious problem. Neighborhoods differ in racial, religious and cultural compositions. It must be expected that they will adopt different customs which will give emphasis to different values and will induce different experiments. And it must be expected that, no matter what practice prevails, there will be many discontented and possibly belligerent minorities. We must leave some flexibility to meet local conditions, some chance to progress by trial and error. While I agree that the religious classes involved here go beyond permissible limits, I also think the complaint demands more than plaintiff is entitled to have granted. So far as I can see this Court does not tell the State court where it may stop, nor does it set up any standards by which the State court may determine that question for itself.

The task of separating the secular from the religious in education is one of magnitude, intricacy and delicacy. To lay down a sweeping constitutional doctrine as demanded by complainant and apparently approved by the Court, applicable alike to all school boards of the nation, "to immediately adopt and enforce rules and regulations prohibiting all instruction in and teaching of religious education in all public schools," is to decree a uniform, rigid and, if we are consistent, an unchanging standard for countless school boards representing and serving highly localized groups which not only differ from each other but which themselves from time to time change attitudes. It seems to me that to do so is to allow zeal for our own ideas of what is good in public instruction to induce us to accept the role of a super board of education for every school district in the nation.

It is idle to pretend that this task is one for which we can find in the Constitution one word to help us as judges to decide where the secular ends and the sectarian ⊥**238** begins in education. Nor can we find guidance in any other legal source. It is a matter on which we can find no law but our own prepossessions. If with no surer legal guidance we are to take up and decide every variation of this controversy, raised by persons not subject to penalty or tax but who are dissatisfied with the way schools are dealing with the problem, we are likely to have much business of the sort. And, more importantly, we are likely to make the legal "wall of separation between church and state" as winding as the famous serpentine wall designed by Mr. Jefferson for the University he founded.

Mr. *Justice* REED, dissenting.

The decisions reversing the judgment of the Supreme Court of Illinois interpret the prohibition of the First Amendment against the establishment of religion, made effective as to the states by the Fourteenth Amendment, to forbid pupils of the public schools electing, with the approval of their parents, courses in religious education. The courses are given, under the school laws of Illinois as approved by the Supreme Court of that state, by lay or clerical teachers supplied and directed by an interdenominational, local council of religious education. The classes are held in the respective school buildings of the pupils at study or released time periods so as to avoid conflict with recitations. The teachers and supplies are paid for by the interdenominational group. As I am **⊥239** convinced that this interpretation of the First Amendment is erroneous, I feel impelled to express the reasons for my disagreement. By directing attention to the many instances of close association of church and state in American society and by recalling that many of these relations are so much a part of our tradition and culture that they are accepted without more, this dissent may help in an appraisal of the meaning of the clause of the First Amendment concerning the establishment of religion and of the reasons which lead to the approval or disapproval of the judgment below.

The reasons for the reversal of the Illinois judgment, as they appear in the respective opinions, may be summarized by the following excerpts. The opinion of the Court, after stating the facts, says: "The foregoing facts, without reference to others that appear in the record, show the use of tax-supported property for religious instruction and the close cooperation between the school authorities and the religious council in promoting religious education. . . . And it falls squarely under the ban of the First Amendment (made applicable to the States by the Fourteenth) as we interpreted it in *Everson* v. *Board of Education*." Another opinion phrases it thus: "We do not now attempt to weigh in the Constitutional scale every separate detail or various combination of factors which may establish a valid 'released time' program. We find that the basic Constitutional principle of absolute separation was violated when the State of Illinois, speaking through its Supreme Court, sustained the school authorities of Champaign in sponsoring and effectively furthering religious beliefs by its educational arrangement." These expressions in the decisions seem to **⊥240** leave open for further litigation variations from the Champaign plan. Actually, however, future cases must run the gantlet not only of the judgment entered but of the accompanying words of the opinions. I find it difficult to extract from the opinions any conclusion as to what it is in the Champaign plan that is unconstitutional. Is it the use of school buildings for religious instruction; the release of pupils by the schools for religious instruction during school hours; the so-called assistance by teachers in handing out the request cards to pupils, in keeping lists of them for release and records of their attendance; or the action of the principals in arranging an opportunity for the classes and the appearance of the Council's instructors? None of the reversing opinions say whether the purpose of the Champaign plan for religious instruction during school hours is unconstitutional or whether it is some ingredient used in or omitted from the formula that makes the plan unconstitutional.

From the tenor of the opinions I conclude that their teachings are that any use of a pupil's school time, whether that use is on or off the school grounds, with the necessary school regulations to facilitate attendance, falls under the ban. I reach this conclusion notwithstanding one sentence of indefinite meaning in the second opinion: "We do not consider, as indeed we could not, school programs not before us which, though colloquially characterized as 'released time', present situations differing in aspects that may well be constitutionally crucial." The use of the words "cooperation," "fusion," "complete hands-off," "integrate" and "integrated" to describe the relations between the school and the Council in the plan evidences this. So does the interpretation of the word "aid." The criticized "momentum of the whole school atmosphere," "feeling of separatism," engendered in the non-participat**⊥241**ing sects, "obvious pressure . . . attend," and "divisiveness" lead to the stated conclusion. From the holding and the language of the opinions, I can only deduce that religious instruction of public school children during school hours is prohibited. The history of American education is against such an interpretation of the First Amendment.

The opinions do not say in words that the condemned practice of religious education is a law respecting an establishment of religion contrary to the First Amendment. The practice is accepted as a state law by all. I take it that when the opinion of the Court says that "The operation of the state's compulsory education system thus assists and is integrated with the program of religious instruction carried on by separate religious sects" and concludes "This is beyond all question a utilization of the tax-established and tax-supported public school system to aid religious groups to spread their faith," the intention of its author is to rule that this practice is a law "respecting an establishment of religion." That was the basis of *Everson* v. *Board of Education*. It seems obvious that the action of the School Board in permitting religious education in certain grades of the schools by all faiths did not prohibit the free exercise of religion. Even assuming that certain children who did not elect to take instruction are embarrassed to remain outside of the classes, one can hardly speak of that embarrassment as a prohibition against the free exercise of religion. As no issue of prohibition upon the free exercise of religion is before us, we need only examine the School Board's action to see if it constitutes an establishment of religion.

The facts, as stated in the reversing opinions, are adequately set out if we interpret the abstract words used in the light of the concrete incidents of the record. It is **⊥242** correct to say that the parents "consented" to the religious instruction of the children, if we understand "consent" to mean the signing of a card. It is correct to say that "instructors were subject to the approval and supervision of the superintendent of schools," if it is understood that there were no definitive written rules and that the practice was as is shown in the excerpts from the findings below. The substance of the ⊥**243** religious education course is determined by the members of the various churches on the council, not by the superintendent. The evidence and findings set out in the two preceding notes convince me that the "approval and supervision" referred to above are not of the teachers and the course of studies but of the orderly presentation of the courses to those students who may elect the instruction. The teaching largely covered Biblical incidents. The religious teachers and their teachings, in every real sense, ⊥**244** were financed and regulated by the Council of Religious Education, not the School Board.

The phrase "an establishment of religion" may have been intended by Congress to be aimed only at a state church. When the First Amendment was pending in Congress in substantially its present form, "Mr. Madison said, he apprehended the meaning of the words to be, that Congress should not establish a religion, and enforce the legal observation of it by law, nor compel men to worship God in any manner contrary to their conscience." Passing years, however, have brought about acceptance of a broader meaning, although never until today, I believe, has this Court widened its interpretation to any such degree as holding that recognition of the interest of our nation in religion, through the granting, to qualified representatives of the principal faiths, of opportunity to present religion as an optional, extracurricular subject during released school time in public school buildings, was equivalent to an establishment of religion. A reading of the general statements of eminent statesmen of former days, referred to in the opinions in this case and in *Everson* v. *Board of Education*, will show that circumstances such as those in this case were far from the minds of the authors. The words and spirit of those statements may be wholeheartedly accepted without in the least impugning the judgment of the State of Illinois.

⊥**245** Mr. Jefferson, as one of the founders of the University of Virginia, a school which from its establishment in 1819 has been wholly governed, managed and controlled by the State of Virginia, was faced with the same problem that is before this Court today: the question of the constitutional limitation upon religious education in public schools. In his annual report as Rector, to the President and Directors of the Literary Fund, dated October 7, 1822, approved by the Visitors of the University of whom Mr. Madison was one, Mr. Jefferson set forth his views at some length. These suggestions of Mr. Jefferson were ⊥**246** adopted and ch. II, § 1, of the Regulations of the University of October 4, 1824, provided that: "Should the religious sects of this State, or any of them, according to the invitation held out to them, establish within, or adjacent to, the precincts of the University, schools for instruction in the religion of their sect, the students of the University will be free, and expected to attend religious worship at the establishment of their respective sects, in the morning, and in time to meet their school in the University at its stated hour."

⊥**247** Thus, the "wall of separation between church and State" that Mr. Jefferson built at the University which he founded did not exclude religious education from that school. The difference between the generality of his statements on the separation of church and state and the specificity of his conclusions on education are considerable. A rule of law should not be drawn from a figure of speech.

Mr. Madison's *Memorial and Remonstrance against Religious Assessments*, relied upon by the dissenting Justices in *Everson*, is not applicable here. Mr. Madison was one of the principal opponents in the Virginia General Assembly of *A Bill Establishing a Provision for Teachers of the Christian Religion*. The monies raised by the taxing section of that bill were to be appropriated "by the Vestries, Elders, or Directors of each religious society, . . . to a provision for a Minister or Teacher ⊥**248** of the Gospel of their denomination, or the providing places of divine worship, and to none other use whatsoever. . . ." The conclusive legislative struggle over this act took place in the fall of 1785, before the adoption of the Bill of Rights. The *Remonstrance* had been issued before the General Assembly convened and was instrumental in the final defeat of the act, which died in committee. Throughout the *Remonstrance* Mr. Madison speaks of the "establishment" sought to be effected by the act. It is clear from its historical setting and its language that the *Remonstrance* was a protest against an effort by Virginia to support Christian sects by taxation. Issues similar to those raised by the instant case were not discussed. Thus, Mr. Madison's approval of Mr. Jefferson's report as Rector gives, in my opinion, a clearer indication of his views on the constitutionality of religious education in public schools than his general statements on a different subject.

This Court summarized the amendment's accepted reach into the religious field, as I understand its scope, in *Everson* v. *Board of Education*. The Court's opinion quotes the gist of the Court's reasoning in *Everson*. I agree, as there stated, that none of our governmental entities can "set up a church." I agree that they cannot "aid" all or any religions or prefer one "over another." But "aid" must be understood as a purposeful assistance directly to the church itself or to some religious group or organization doing religious work of such a character that it may fairly be said to be performing ecclesiastical functions. "Prefer" must give an advantage to one "over another." I agree that pupils cannot, "be released in part from their legal duty" of school attendance upon condition that they attend religious classes. But as Illinois has held that it is within the discretion of the School Board to permit absence from school for religious instruc⊥**249**tion no legal duty of school attendance is violated. If the sentence in the Court's opinion, concerning the pupils' release from legal duty, is intended to mean that the Constitution forbids a school to excuse a pupil from secular control during school hours to attend voluntarily a class in religious education, whether in or out of school buildings, I disagree. Of course, no tax can be levied to support organizations intended "to teach or practice religion." I agree too that the state cannot influence one toward religion against his will or punish him for his beliefs. Champaign's religious education course does none of these things.

It seems clear to me that the "aid" referred to by the Court in the *Everson* case could not have been those incidental advantages that religious bodies, with other groups similarly situated, obtain as a byproduct of organized society. This explains the well-known fact that all churches receive "aid" from government in the form of freedom from taxation. The *Everson* decision itself justified the transportation of children to church schools by New Jersey for safety reasons. It accords with *Cochran* v. *Louisiana State Board of Education*, where this Court upheld a free textbook statute of Louisiana against a charge that it aided private schools on the ground that the books were for the education of the children, not to aid religious schools. Likewise the National School Lunch Act aids all school children attending tax-exempt schools. In *Bradfield* v. *Roberts*, this Court held proper the payment of money by the Federal Government to build an addition to a hospital, chartered by individuals who were members of a Roman Catholic sisterhood, and operated under the auspices of the Roman Catholic Church. This was done over the objection that it aided the establish⊥**250**ment of religion. While obviously in these instances the respective churches, in a certain sense, were aided, this Court has never held that such "aid" was in violation of the First and Fourteenth Amendment.

Well-recognized and long-established practices support the validity of the Illinois statute here in question. That statute, as construed in this case, is comparable to those in many states. All differ to some extent. New York may be taken as a fair example. In many states the pro⊥**251**gram is under the supervision of a religious council composed of delegates who are themselves communicants of various faiths. As is shown by *Bradfield* v. *Roberts*, the fact that the members of the council have religious affiliations is not significant. In some, instruc⊥**252**tion is given outside of the school buildings; in others, within these buildings. Metropolitan centers like New York usually would have available quarters convenient to schools. Unless smaller cities and rural communities use the school building at times that do not interfere with recitations, they may be compelled to give up religious education. I understand that pupils not taking religious education usually are given other work of a secular nature within the schools. Since all these states use the facilities of the schools to aid the religious education to some extent, their desire to permit religious education to school children is thwarted by this Court's judgment. Under it, as I understand its language, children cannot be released or dismissed from school to attend classes in religion while other children must remain to pursue secular education. Teachers cannot keep the records as to which pupils are to be dismissed and which retained. To do so is said to be an "aid" in establishing religion; the use of public money for religion.

Cases running into the scores have been in the state courts of last resort that involved religion and the schools. Except where the exercises with religious significance partook of the ceremonial practice of sects or groups, their ⊥**253** constitutionality has been generally upheld. Illinois itself promptly struck down as violative of its own constitution required exercises partaking of a religious ceremony. *People ex rel. Ring* v. *Board of Education*. In that case compulsory religious exercises—a reading from the King James Bible, the Lord's Prayer and the singing of hymns—were forbidden as "worship services." In this case, the Supreme Court of Illinois pointed out that in the *Ring* case, the activities in the school were ceremonial and compulsory; in this, voluntary and educational.

The practices of the federal government offer many examples of this kind of "aid" by the state to religion. The Congress of the United States has a chaplain for each House who daily invokes divine blessings and guidance for ⊥**254** the proceedings. The armed forces have commissioned chaplains from early days. They conduct the public services in accordance with the liturgical requirements of their respective faiths, ashore and afloat, employing for the purpose property belonging to the United States and dedicated to the services of religion. Under the Servicemen's Readjustment Act of 1944, eligible veterans may receive training at government expense for the ministry in denominational schools. The schools of the District of Columbia have opening exercises which "include a reading from the Bible without note or comment, and the Lord's prayer."

In the United States Naval Academy and the United States Military Academy, schools wholly supported and completely controlled by the federal government, there are a number of religious activities. Chaplains are attached to both schools. Attendance at church services on Sunday is compulsory at both the Military and Naval Academies. At West Point the Protestant services are ⊥**255** held in the Cadet Chapel, the Catholic in the Catholic Chapel, and the Jewish in the Old Cadet Chapel; at Annapolis only Protestant services are held on the reservation, midshipmen of other religious persuasions attend the churches of the city of Annapolis. These facts indicate that both schools since their earliest beginnings have maintained and enforced a pattern of participation in formal worship.

With the general statements in the opinions concerning the constitutional requirement that the nation and the states, by virtue of the First and Fourteenth Amendments, may "make no law respecting an establishment of religion," I am in agreement. But, in the light of the meaning given to those words by the precedents, customs, and practices which I have detailed above, I cannot agree with the Court's conclusion that when pupils compelled by law to go to school for secular education are released from school so as to attend the religious classes, churches are unconstitutionally aided. Whatever may be the wisdom of the arrangement as to the use of the school buildings made with the Champaign Council of Religious Education, it is clear to me that past practice shows such cooperation between the schools and a nonecclesiastical body is not forbidden by the First Amendment. When actual church services have always been permitted on government property, the mere use of the school buildings by a non-sectarian group for religious education ought not to be condemned as an establishment of religion. For a nonsectarian organization to give the type of instruction here offered cannot be said to violate our rule as to the establishment of religion by the state. The prohibition of enactments respecting the establishment of religion do **⊥256** not bar every friendly gesture between church and state. It is not an absolute prohibition against every conceivable situation where the two may work together, any more than the other provisions of the First Amendment—free speech, free press—are absolutes. If abuses occur, such as the use of the instruction hour for sectarian purposes, I have no doubt, in view of the *Ring* case, that Illinois will promptly correct them. If they are of a kind that tend to the establishment of a church or interfere with the free exercise of religion, this Court is open for a review of any erroneous decision. This Court cannot be too cautious in upsetting practices embedded in our society by many years of experience. A state is entitled to have great leeway in its legislation when dealing with the important social problems of its population. A definite violation of legislative limits must be established. The Constitution should not be stretched to forbid national customs in the way courts act to reach arrangements to avoid federal taxation. Devotion to the great principle of religious liberty should not lead us into a rigid interpretation of the constitutional guarantee that conflicts with accepted habits of our people. This is an instance where, for me, the history of past practices is determinative of the meaning of a constitutional clause, not a decorous introduction to the study of its text. The judgment should be affirmed.

ZORACH v. CLAUSON

343 U.S. 306
ON APPEAL FROM THE COURT OF APPEALS OF NEW YORK
Argued January 31-February 1, 1952 — Decided April 28, 1952

⊥308 Mr. *Justice DOUGLAS* delivered the opinion of the Court.

New York City has a program which permits its public schools to release students during the school day so that they may leave the school buildings and school grounds and go to religious centers for religious instruction or devotional exercises. A student is released on written request of his parents. Those not released stay in the classrooms. The churches make weekly reports to the schools, sending a list of children who have been released from public school but who have not reported for religious instruction.

This "released time" program involves neither religious instruction in public school classrooms nor the expendi- **⊥309** ture of public funds. All costs, including the application blanks, are paid by the religious organizations. The case is therefore unlike *McCollum* v. *Board of Education*, which involved a "released time" program from Illinois. In that case the classrooms were turned over to religious instructors. We accordingly held that the program violated the First Amendment which (by reason of the Fourteenth Amendment) prohibits the states from establishing religion or prohibiting its free exercise.

Appellants, who are taxpayers and residents of New York City and whose children attend its public schools, challenge the present law, contending it is in essence not different from the one involved in the *McCollum* case. Their argument, stated elaborately in various ways, reduces itself to this: the weight and influence of the school is put behind a program for religious instruction; public school teachers police it, keeping tab on students who are released; the classroom activities come to a halt while the students who are released for religious instruction are on leave; the school is a crutch on which the churches are leaning for support in their religious training; without the cooperation of the schools this "released time" program, **⊥310** like the one in the *McCollum* case, would be futile and ineffective. The New York Court of Appeals sustained the law against this claim of unconstitutionality. The case is here on appeal. . . .

[O]ur problem reduces itself to whether New York by this system has either prohibited the "free exercise" of religion or has made a law "respecting an establishment of religion" within the meaning of the First Amendment.

⊥311 It takes obtuse reasoning to inject any issue of the "free exercise" of religion into the present case. No one is forced to go to the religious classroom and no religious exercise or instruction is brought to the classrooms of the public schools. A student need not take religious instruction. He is left to his own desires as to the manner or time of his religious devotions, if any.

There is a suggestion that the system involves the use of coercion to get public school students into religious classrooms. There is no evidence in the record before us that supports that conclusion. The present record indeed tells us that the school authorities are neutral in this regard and do no more than release students whose parents so request. . . . Hence we put aside that claim of coercion **⊥312** both as respects the "free exercise" of religion and "an establishment of religion" within the meaning of the First Amendment.

Moreover, apart from that claim of coercion, we do not see how New York by this type of "released time" program has made a law respecting an establishment of religion within the meaning of the First Amendment. There is much talk of the separation of Church and State in the history of the Bill of Rights and in the decisions clustering around the First Amendment. There cannot be the slightest doubt that the First Amendment reflects the philosophy that Church and State should be separated. And so far as interference with the "free exercise" of religion and an "establishment" of religion are concerned, the separation must be complete and unequivocal. The First Amendment within the scope of its coverage permits no exception; the prohibition is absolute. The First Amendment, however, does not say that in every and all respects there shall be a separation of Church and State. Rather, it studiously defines the manner, the specific ways, in which there shall be no concert or union or dependency one on the other. That is the common sense of the matter. Otherwise the state and religion would be aliens to each other—hostile, suspicious, and even unfriendly. Churches could not be required to pay even property taxes. Municipalities would not be permitted to render police or fire protection to religious groups. Policemen who helped parishioners into their places of worship would violate the Constitution. Prayers in our legislative halls; the ap⊥**313**peals to the Almighty in the messages of the Chief Executive; the proclamations making Thanksgiving Day a holiday; "so help me God" in our courtroom oaths—these and all other references to the Almighty that run through our laws, our public rituals, our ceremonies would be flouting the First Amendment. A fastidious atheist or agnostic could even object to the supplication with which the Court opens each session: "God save the United States and this Honorable Court."

We would have to press the concept of separation of Church and State to these extremes to condemn the present law on constitutional grounds. The nullification of this law would have wide and profound effects. A Catholic student applies to his teacher for permission to leave the school during hours on a Holy Day of Obligation to attend a mass. A Jewish student asks his teacher for permission to be excused for Yom Kippur. A Protestant wants the afternoon off for a family baptismal ceremony. In each case the teacher requires parental consent in writing. In each case the teacher, in order to make sure the student is not a truant, goes further and requires a report from the priest, the rabbi, or the minister. The teacher in other words cooperates in a religious program to the extent of making it possible for her students to participate in it. Whether she does it occasionally for a few students, regularly for one, or pursuant to a systematized program designed to further the religious needs of all the students does not alter the character of the act.

We are a religious people whose institutions presuppose a Supreme Being. We guarantee the freedom to worship as one chooses. We make room for as wide a variety of beliefs and creeds as the spiritual needs of man deem necessary. We sponsor an attitude on the part of government that shows no partiality to any one group and that lets each flourish according to the zeal of its adherents and the appeal of its dogma. When the state ⊥**314** encourages religious instruction or cooperates with religious authorities by adjusting the schedule of public events to sectarian needs, it follows the best of our traditions. For it then respects the religious nature of our people and accommodates the public service to their spiritual needs. To hold that it may not would be to find in the Constitution a requirement that the government show a callous indifference to religious groups. That would be preferring those who believe in no religion over those who do believe. Government may not finance religious groups nor undertake religious instruction nor blend secular and sectarian education nor use secular institutions to force one or some religion on any person. But we find no constitutional requirement which makes it necessary for government to be hostile to religion and to throw its weight against efforts to widen the effective scope of religious influence. The government must be neutral when it comes to competition between sects. It may not thrust any sect on any person. It may not make a religious observance compulsory. It may not coerce anyone to attend church, to observe a religious holiday, or to take religious instruction. But it can close its doors or suspend its operations as to those who want to repair to their religious sanctuary for worship or instruction. No more than that is undertaken here. . . .

⊥**315** In the *McCollum* case the classrooms were used for religious instruction and the force of the public school was used to promote that instruction. Here, as we have said, the public schools do no more than accommodate their schedules to a program of outside religious instruction. We follow the *McCollum* case. But we cannot expand it to cover the present released time program unless separation of Church and State means that public institutions can make no adjustments of their schedules to accommodate the religious needs of the people. We cannot read into the Bill of Rights such a philosophy of hostility to religion.

Affirmed.

Mr. *Justice* BLACK, dissenting.

Illinois ex rel. McCollum v. *Board of Education* held invalid as an "establishment of religion" an Illinois system under which school children, compelled by law to go to public schools, were freed from some hours of required school work on condition that they attend special religious classes held in the school buildings. Although the classes were taught by sectarian ⊥**316** teachers neither employed nor paid by the state, the state did use its power to further the program by releasing some of the children from regular class work, insisting that those released attend the religious classes, and requiring that those who remained behind do some kind of academic work while the others received their religious training. We said this about the Illinois system: "Pupils compelled by law to go to school for secular education are released in part from their legal duty upon the condition that they attend the religious classes. This is beyond all question a utilization of the tax-established and tax-supported public school system to aid religious groups to spread their faith. And it falls squarely under the ban of the First Amendment. . . ." *McCollum* v. *Board of Education*.

I see no significant difference between the invalid Illinois system and that of New York here sustained. Except for the use of the school buildings in Illinois, there is no difference between the systems which I consider even worthy of mention. In the New York program, as in that of Illinois, the school authorities release some of the children on the condition that they attend the religious classes, get reports on whether they attend, and hold the other children in the school building until the religious hour is over. As we attempted to make categorically clear, the *McCollum* decision would have been the same if the religious classes had not been held in the school buildings. We said: "Here *not only* are the State's tax-supported public school buildings used for the dissemination of religious doctrines. The State *also* affords sectarian groups an invaluable aid in that it helps to provide pupils for their religious classes through use of the State's compulsory public school machinery. *This* is **⊥317** not separation of Church and State." (Emphasis supplied.)

McCollum thus held that Illinois could not constitutionally manipulate the compelled classroom hours of its compulsory school machinery so as to channel children into sectarian classes. Yet that is exactly what the Court holds New York can do. . . .

In dissenting today, I mean to do more than give routine approval to our *McCollum* decision. I mean also to reaffirm my faith in the **⊥318** fundamental philosophy expressed in *McCollum* and *Everson* v. *Board of Education*. That reaffirmance can be brief because of the exhaustive opinions in those recent cases.

Difficulty of decision in the hypothetical situations mentioned by the Court, but not now before us, should not confuse the issues in this case. Here the sole question is whether New York can use its compulsory education laws to help religious sects get attendants presumably too unenthusiastic to go unless moved to do so by the pressure of this state machinery. That this is the plan, purpose, design and consequence of the New York program cannot be denied. The state thus makes religious sects beneficiaries of its power to compel children to attend secular schools. Any use of such coercive power by the state to help or hinder some religious sects or to prefer all religious sects over nonbelievers or vice versa is just what I think the First Amendment forbids. In considering whether a state has entered this forbidden field the question is not whether it has entered too far but whether it has entered at all. New York is manipulating its compulsory education laws to help religious sects get pupils. This is not separation but combination of Church and State.

The Court's validation of the New York system rests in part on its statement that Americans are "a religious people whose institutions presuppose a Supreme Being." This was at least as true when the First Amendment was adopted; and it was just as true when eight Justices of this Court invalidated the released time system in *McCollum* on the premise that a state can no more "aid all religions" than it can aid one. It was precisely because Eighteenth **⊥319** Century Americans were a religious people divided into many fighting sects that we were given the constitutional mandate to keep Church and State completely separate. Colonial history had already shown that, here as elsewhere zealous sectarians entrusted with governmental power to further their causes would sometimes torture, maim and kill those they branded "heretics," "atheists" or "agnostics." The First Amendment was therefore to insure that no one powerful sect or combination of sects could use political or governmental power to punish dissenters whom they could not convert to their faith. Now as then, it is only by wholly isolating the state from the religious sphere and compelling it to be completely neutral, that the freedom of each and every denomination and of all nonbelievers can be maintained. It is this neutrality the Court abandons today when it treats New York's coercive system as a program which *merely* "encourages religious instruction or cooperates with religious authorities." The abandonment is all the more dangerous to liberty because of the Court's legal exaltation of the orthodox and its derogation of unbelievers.

Under our system of religious freedom, people have gone to their religious sanctuaries not because they feared the law but because they loved their God. The choice of all has been as free as the choice of those who answered the call to worship moved only by the music of the old Sunday morning church bells. The spiritual mind of man has thus been free to believe, disbelieve, or doubt, without repression, great or small, by the heavy **⊥320** hand of government. Statutes authorizing such repression have been stricken. Before today, our judicial opinions have refrained from drawing invidious distinctions between those who believe in no religion and those who do believe. The First Amendment has lost much if the religious follower and the atheist are no longer to be judicially regarded as entitled to equal justice under law.

State help to religion injects political and party prejudices into a holy field. It too often substitutes force for prayer, hate for love, and persecution for persuasion. Government should not be allowed, under cover of the soft euphemism of "co-operation," to steal into the sacred area of religious choice.

Mr. *Justice* FRANKFURTER, dissenting.

By way of emphasizing my agreement with Mr. *Justice* JACKSON's dissent, I add a few words.

The Court tells us that in the maintenance of its public schools, "[The State government] can close its doors or suspend its operations" so that its citizens may be free for religious devotions or instruction. If that were the issue, it would not rise to the dignity of a constitutional controversy. Of course, a State may provide that the classes in its schools shall be dismissed, for any reason, or no reason, on fixed days, or for special occasions. The essence of this case is that the school system did not "close its doors", and did not "suspend its operations." There is all the difference in the world between letting the children out of school and letting some of them out of school into religious classes. If every one is free to make what use he will of time wholly unconnected from schooling required by law—those who wish sectarian instruction devoting it to that purpose, those who have ethical instruction at home, to that, those who study music, to that—then of course there is no conflict with the Fourteenth Amendment.

⊥**321** The pith of the case is that formalized religious instruction is substituted for other school activity which those who do not participate in the released time program are compelled to attend. The school system is very much in operation during this kind of released time. If its doors are closed, they are closed upon those students who do not attend the religious instruction, in order to keep them within the school. That is the very thing which raises the constitutional issue. It is not met by disregarding it. Failure to discuss this issue does not take it out of the case.

Again, the Court relies upon the absence from the record of evidence of coercion in the operation of the system. "If in fact coercion were used," according to the Court, "if it were established that any one or more teachers were using their office to persuade or force students to take the religious instruction, a wholly different case would be presented." Thus, "coercion" in the abstract is acknowledged to be fatal. But the Court disregards the fact that as the case comes to us, there could be no proof of coercion, for the appellants were not allowed to make proof of it. . . .

⊥**322** The result in the *McCollum* case was based on principles that received unanimous acceptance by this Court, barring only a single vote. I agree with Mr. *Justice* BLACK that those principles are disregarded ⊥**323** in reaching the result in this case. Happily they are not disavowed by the Court. From this I draw the hope that in future variations of the problem which are bound to come here, these principles may again be honored in the observance.

The deeply divisive controversy aroused by the attempts to secure public school pupils for sectarian instruction would promptly end if the advocates of such instruction were content to have the school "close its doors or suspend its operations"—that is, dismiss classes in their entirety, without discrimination—instead of seeking to use the public schools as the instrument for securing attendance at denominational classes. The unwillingness of the promoters of this movement to dispense with such use of the public schools betrays a surprising want of confidence in the inherent power of the various faiths to draw children to outside sectarian classes—an attitude that hardly reflects the faith of the greatest religious spirits.

Mr. *Justice* JACKSON, dissenting.

This released time program is founded upon a use of the State's power of coercion, which, for me, determines its unconstitutionality. Stripped to its essentials, the plan has two stages: first, that the State compel each student to yield a large part of his time for public secu⊥**324**lar education; and, second, that some of it be "released" to him on condition that he devote it to sectarian religious purposes.

No one suggests that the Constitution would permit the State directly to require this "released" time to be spent "under the control of a duly constituted religious body." This program accomplishes that forbidden result by indirection. If public education were taking so much of the pupils' time as to injure the public or the students' welfare by encroaching upon their religious opportunity, simply shortening everyone's school day would facilitate voluntary and optional attendance at Church classes. But that suggestion is rejected upon the ground that if they are made free many students will not go to the Church. Hence, they must be deprived of freedom for this period, with Church attendance put to them as one of the two permissible ways of using it.

The greater effectiveness of this system over voluntary attendance after school hours is due to the truant officer who, if the youngster fails to go to the Church school, dogs him back to the public schoolroom. Here schooling is more or less suspended during the "released time" so the nonreligious attendants will not forge ahead of the churchgoing absentees. But it serves as a temporary jail for a pupil who will not go to Church. It takes more subtlety of mind than I possess to deny that this is governmental constraint in support of religion. It is as unconstitutional, in my view, when exerted by indirection as when exercised forthrightly.

As one whose children, as a matter of free choice, have been sent to privately supported Church schools, I may challenge the Court's suggestion that opposition to this plan can only be antireligious, atheistic, or agnostic. My evangelistic brethren confuse an objection to compulsion with an objection to religion. It is possible to hold a faith with enough confidence to believe that what should be ⊥**325** rendered to God does not need to be decided and collected by Caesar.

The day that this country ceases to be free for irreligion it will cease to be free for religion—except for the sect that can win political power. The same epithetical jurisprudence used by the Court today to beat down those who oppose pressuring children into some religion can devise as good epithets tomorrow against those who object to pressuring them into a favored religion. And, after all, if we concede to the State power and wisdom to single out "duly constituted religious" bodies as exclusive alternatives for compulsory secular instruction, it would be logical to also uphold the power and wisdom to choose the true faith among those "duly constituted." We start down a rough road when we begin to mix compulsory public education with compulsory godliness.

A number of Justices just short of a majority of the majority that promulgates today's passionate dialectics joined in answering them in *Illinois ex rel. McCollum* v. *Board of Education*. The distinction attempted between that case and this is trivial, almost to the point of cynicism, magnifying its nonessential details and disparaging compulsion which was the underlying reason for invalidity. A reading of the Court's opinion in that case along with its opinion in this case will show such difference of overtones and undertones as to make clear that the *McCollum* case has passed like a storm in a teacup. The wall which the Court was professing to erect between Church and State has become even more warped and twisted than I expected. Today's judgment will be more interesting to students of psychology and of the judicial processes than to students of constitutional law.

ENGEL v. VITALE

370 U.S. 421
ON CERTIORARI TO THE COURT OF APPEALS OF NEW YORK
Argued April 3, 1962 — Decided June 25, 1962

⊥**422** Mr. *Justice BLACK* delivered the opinion of the Court.

The respondent Board of Education of Union Free School District No. 9, New Hyde Park, New York, acting in its official capacity under state law, directed the School District's principal to cause the following prayer to be said aloud by each class in the presence of a teacher at the beginning of each school day: "Almighty God, we acknowledge our dependence upon Thee, and we beg Thy blessings upon us, our parents, our teachers and our Country."

This daily procedure was adopted on the recommendation of the State Board of Regents, a governmental agency created by the State Constitution to which the New York Legislature has granted broad supervisory, executive, and ⊥**423** legislative powers over the State's public school system. These state officials composed the prayer which they recommended and published as a part of their "Statement on Moral and Spiritual Training in the Schools," saying "We believe that this Statement will be subscribed to by all men and women of good will, and we call upon all of them to aid in giving life to our program."

Shortly after the practice of reciting the Regents' prayer was adopted by the School District, the parents of ten pupils brought this action in a New York State Court insisting that use of this official prayer in the public schools was contrary to the beliefs, religions, or religious practices of both themselves and their children. Among other things, these parents challenged the constitutionality of both the state law authorizing the School District to direct the use of prayer in public schools and the School District's regulation ordering the recitation of this particular prayer on the ground that these actions of official governmental agencies violate that part of the First Amendment of the Federal Constitution which commands that "Congress shall make no law respecting an establishment of religion"—a command which was "made applicable to the State of New York by the Fourteenth Amendment of the said Constitution." The New York Court of Appeals, over the dissents of Judges Dye and Fuld, sustained an order of the lower state courts which had upheld the power of New York to use the Regent's prayer as a part of the daily procedures of its public schools so long as the schools did not compel any pupil to join in the prayer over his or his parents' objection. ⊥**424** We granted certiorari to review this important decision involving rights protected by the First and Fourteenth Amendments.

We think that by using its public school system to encourage recitation of the Regents' prayer, the State of New York has adopted a practice wholly inconsistent with the Establishment Clause. There can, of course, be no doubt that New York's program of daily classroom invocation of God's blessing as prescribed in the Regents' prayer is a religious activity. It is a solemn avowal of divine faith and supplication for the blessings of the Almighty. The nature of such a prayer has always been ⊥**425** religious, none of the respondents has denied this and the trial court expressly so found: "The religious nature of prayer was recognized by Jefferson and has been concurred in by theological writers, the United States Supreme Court and State courts and administrative officials, including New York's Commissioner of Education. A committee of the New York Legislature has agreed.

"The Board of Regents as *amicus curiae*, the respondents and intervenors all concede the religious nature of prayer, but seek to distinguish this prayer because it is based on our spiritual heritage. . . ."

The petitioners contend among other things that the state laws requiring or permitting use of the Regents' prayer must be struck down as a violation of the Establishment Clause because that prayer was composed by governmental officials as a part of a governmental program to further religious beliefs. For this reason, petitioners argue, the State's use of the Regents' prayer in its public school system breaches the constitutional wall of separation between Church and State. We agree with that contention since we think that the constitutional prohibition against laws respecting an establishment of religion must at least mean that in this country it is no part of the business of government to compose official prayers for any group of the American people to recite as a part of a religious program carried on by government.

It is a matter of history that this very practice of establishing governmentally composed prayers for religious services was one of the reasons which caused many of our early colonists to leave England and seek religious freedom in America. The Book of Common Prayer, ⊥**426** which was created under governmental direction and which was approved by Acts of Parliament in 1548 and 1549, set out in minute detail the accepted form and content of prayer and other religious ceremonies to be used in the established, tax-supported Church of England. The controversies over the Book and what should be its content repeatedly threatened to disrupt the peace of that country as the accepted forms of prayer in the established church changed with the views of the particular ruler that happened to be in control at the time. Powerful groups representing some of the varying religious views of the people struggled among themselves to impress their particular views upon the Government and ⊥**427** obtain amendments of the Book more suitable to their respective notions of how religious services should be conducted in order that the official religious establishment would advance their particular religious beliefs. Other groups, lacking the necessary political power to influence the Government on the matter, decided to leave England and its established church and seek freedom in America from England's governmentally ordained and supported religion.

It is an unfortunate fact of history that when some of the very groups which had most strenuously opposed the established Church of England found themselves sufficiently in control of colonial governments in this country to write their own prayers into law, they passed laws making their own religion the official religion of their respective colonies. Indeed, as late as the time of the Revolu⊥**428**tionary War, there were established churches in at least eight of the thirteen former colonies and established religions in at least four of the other five. But the successful Revolution against English political domination was shortly followed by intense opposition to the practice of establishing religion by law. This opposition crystallized rapidly into an effective political force in Virginia where the minority religious groups such as Presbyterians, Lutherans, Quakers and Baptists had gained such strength that the adherents to the established Episcopal Church were actually a minority themselves. In 1785-1786, those opposed to the established Church, led by James Madison and Thomas Jefferson, who, though themselves not members of any of these dissenting religious groups, opposed all religious establishments by law on grounds of principle, obtained the enactment of the famous "Virginia Bill for Religious Liberty" by which all religious groups were placed on an equal footing so far as the State was concerned. Similar though less far-reaching ⊥**429** legislation was being considered and passed in other States.

By the time of the adoption of the Constitution, our history shows that there was a widespread awareness among many Americans of the dangers of a union of Church and State. These people knew, some of them from bitter personal experience, that one of the greatest dangers to the freedom of the individual to worship in his own way lay in the Government's placing its official stamp of approval upon one particular kind of prayer or one particular form of religious services. They knew the anguish, hardship and bitter strife that could come when zealous religious groups struggled with one another to obtain the Government's stamp of approval from each King, Queen, or Protector that came to temporary power. The Constitution was intended to avert a part of this danger by leaving the government of this country in the hands of the people rather than in the hands of any monarch. But this safeguard was not enough. Our Founders were no more willing to let the content of their prayers and their privilege of praying whenever they pleased be influenced by the ballot box than they were to let these vital matters of personal conscience depend upon the succession of monarchs. The First Amendment was added to the Constitution to stand as a guarantee that neither the power nor the prestige of Federal Government would be used to control, support or influence the kinds of prayer the American people can say— ⊥**430** that the people's religions must not be subjected to the pressures of government for change each time a new political administration is elected to office. Under that Amendment's prohibition against governmental establishment of religion, as reinforced by the provisions of the Fourteenth Amendment, government in this country, be it state or federal, is without power to prescribe by law any particular form of prayer which is to be used as an official prayer in carrying on any program of governmentally sponsored religious activity.

There can be no doubt that New York's state prayer program officially establishes the religious beliefs embodied in the Regents' prayer. The respondents' argument to the contrary, which is largely based upon the contention that the Regents' prayer is "non-denominational" and the fact that the program, as modified and approved by state courts, does not require all pupils to recite the prayer but permits those who wish to do so to remain silent or be excused from the room, ignores the essential nature of the program's constitutional defects. Neither the fact that the prayer may be denominationally neutral nor the fact that its observance on the part of the students is voluntary can serve to free it from the limitations of the Establishment Clause, as it might from the Free Exercise Clause, of the First Amendment, both of which are operative against the States by virtue of the Fourteenth Amendment. Although these two clauses may in certain instances overlap, they forbid two quite different kinds of governmental encroachment upon religious freedom. The Establishment Clause, unlike the Free Exercise Clause, does not depend upon any showing of direct governmental compulsion and is violated by the enactment of laws which establish an official religion whether those laws operate directly to coerce nonobserving individuals or not. This is not to say, of course, that ⊥**431** laws officially prescribing a particular form of religious worship do not involve coercion of such individuals. When the power, prestige and financial support of government is placed behind a particular religious belief, the indirect coercive pressure upon religious minorities to conform to the prevailing officially approved religion is plain. But the purposes underlying the Establishment Clause go much further than that. Its first and most immediate purpose rested on the belief that a union of government and religion tends to destroy government and to degrade religion. The history of governmentally established religion, both in England and in this country, showed that whenever government had allied itself with one particular form of religion, the inevitable result had been that it had incurred the hatred, disrespect and even contempt of those who held contrary beliefs. That same history showed that many people had lost their respect for any religion that had relied upon the support of government to spread its faith. The Establishment Clause **⊥432** thus stands as an expression of principle on the part of the Founders of our Constitution that religion is too personal, too sacred, too holy, to permit its "unhallowed perversion" by a civil magistrate. Another purpose of the Establishment Clause rested upon an awareness of the historical fact that governmentally established religions and religious persecutions go hand in hand. The Founders knew that only a few years after the Book of Common Prayer became the only accepted form of religious services in the established Church of England, an Act of Uniformity was passed to compel all Englishmen to attend those services and to make it a criminal offense to conduct or attend religious gatherings of any other kind—a law **⊥433** which was consistently flouted by dissenting religious groups in England and which contributed to widespread persecutions of people like John Bunyan who persisted in holding "unlawful [religious] meetings . . . to the great disturbance and distraction of the good subjects of this kingdom. . . ." And they knew that similar persecutions had received the sanction of law in several of the colonies in this country soon after the establishment of official religions in those colonies. It was in large part to get completely away from this sort of systematic religious persecution that the Founders brought into being our Nation, our Constitution, and our Bill of Rights with its prohibition against any governmental establishment of religion. The New York laws officially prescribing the Regents' prayer are inconsistent both with the purposes of the Establishment Clause and with the Establishment Clause itself.

It has been argued that to apply the Constitution in such a way as to prohibit state laws respecting an **⊥434** establishment of religious services in public schools is to indicate a hostility toward religion or toward prayer. Nothing, of course, could be more wrong. The history of man is inseparable from the history of religion. And perhaps it is not too much to say that since the beginning of that history many people have devoutly believed that "More things are wrought by prayer than this world dreams of." It was doubtless largely due to men who believed this that there grew up a sentiment that caused men to leave the cross-currents of officially established state religions and religious persecution in Europe and come to this country filled with the hope that they could find a place in which they could pray when they pleased to the God of their faith in the language they chose. And there were men of this same faith in the **⊥435** power of prayer who led the fight for adoption of our Constitution and also for our Bill of Rights with the very guarantees of religious freedom that forbid the sort of governmental activity which New York has attempted here. These men knew that the First Amendment, which tried to put an end to governmental control of religion and of prayer, was not written to destroy either. They knew rather that it was written to quiet well-justified fears which nearly all of them felt arising out of an awareness that governments of the past had shackled men's tongues to make them speak only the religious thoughts that government wanted them to speak and to pray only to the God that government wanted them to pray to. It is neither sacrilegious nor anti-religious to say that each separate government in this country should stay out of the business of writing or sanctioning official prayers and leave that purely religious function to the people themselves and to those the people choose to look to for religious guidance.

⊥436 It is true that New York's establishment of its Regents' prayer as an officially approved religious doctrine of that State does not amount to a total establishment of one particular religious sect to the exclusion of all others—that, indeed, the governmental endorsement of that prayer seems relatively insignificant when compared to the governmental encroachments upon religion which were commonplace 200 years ago. To those who may subscribe to the view that because the Regents' official prayer is so brief and general there can be no danger to religious freedom in its governmental establishment, however, it may be appropriate to say in the words of James Madison, the author of the First Amendment: "[I]t is proper to take alarm at the first experiment on our liberties. . . . Who does not see that the same authority which can establish Christianity, in exclusion of all other Religions, may establish with the same ease any particular sect of Christians, in exclusion of all other Sects? That the same authority which can force a citizen to contribute three pence only of his property for the support of any one establishment, may force him to conform to any other establishment in all cases whatsoever?"

The judgment of the Court of Appeals of New York is reversed and the cause remanded for further proceedings not inconsistent with this opinion.

Reversed and remanded.

Mr. *Justice* FRANKFURTER took no part in the decision of this case.

Mr. *Justice* WHITE took no part in the consideration or decision of this case.

⊥**437** *Mr. Justice DOUGLAS*, concurring.

It is customary in deciding a constitutional question to treat it in its narrowest form. Yet at times the setting of the question gives it a form and content which no abstract treatment could give. The point for decision is whether the Government can constitutionally finance a religious exercise. Our system at the federal and state levels is presently honeycombed with such financing. Nevertheless, I think it is an unconstitutional undertaking whatever form it takes.

First, a word as to what this case does not involve.

⊥**438** Plainly, our Bill of Rights would not permit a State or Federal Government to adopt an official prayer and penalize anyone who would not utter it. This, however, is not the case, for there is no element of compulsion or coercion in New York's regulation requiring that public schools be opened each day with the following prayer: "Almighty God, we acknowledge our dependence upon Thee, and we beg Thy blessings upon us, our parents, our teachers and our Country."

The prayer is said upon the commencement of the school day, immediately following the pledge of allegiance to the flag. The prayer is said aloud in the presence of a teacher, who either leads the recitation or selects a student to do so. No student, however, is compelled to take part. The respondents have adopted a regulation which provides that "Neither teachers nor any school authority shall comment on participation or nonparticipation . . . nor suggest or request that any posture or language be used or dress be worn or be not used or not worn." Provision is also made for excusing children, upon written request of a parent or guardian, from the saying of the prayer or from the room in which the prayer is said. A letter implementing and explaining this regulation has been sent to each taxpayer and parent in the school district. As I read this regulation, a child is free to stand or not stand, to recite or not recite, without fear of reprisal or even comment by the teacher or any other school official.

In short, the only one who need utter the prayer is the teacher, and no teacher is complaining of it. Students can stand mute or even leave the classroom, if they desire.

⊥**439** *McCollum* v. *Board of Education* does not decide this case. It involved the use of public school facilities for religious education of students. Students either had to attend religious instruction or "go to some other place in the school building for pursuit of their secular studies. . . . Reports of their presence or absence were to be made to their secular teachers." The influence of the teaching staff was therefore brought to bear on the student body, to support the instilling of religious principles. In the present case, school facilities are used to say the prayer and the teaching staff is employed to lead the pupils in it. There is, however, no effort at indoctrination and no attempt at exposition. Prayers of course may be so long and of such a character as to amount to an attempt at the religious instruction that was denied the public schools by the *McCollum* case. But New York's prayer is of a character that does not involve any element of proselytizing as in the *McCollum* case.

The question presented by this case is therefore an extremely narrow one. It is whether New York oversteps the bounds when it finances a religious exercise.

What New York does on the opening of its public schools is what we do when we open court. Our Crier has from the beginning announced the convening of the Court and then added "God save the United States and this Honorable Court." That utterance is a supplication, a prayer in which we, the judges, are free to join, but which we need not recite any more than the students need recite the New York prayer.

What New York does on the opening of its public schools is what each House of Congress does at the open⊥**440**ing of each day's business. . . .

⊥**441** In New York the teacher who leads in prayer is on the public payroll; and the time she takes seems minuscule as compared with the salaries appropriated by state legislatures and Congress for chaplains to conduct prayers in the legislative halls. Only a bare fraction of the teacher's time is given to reciting this short 22-word prayer, about the same amount of time that our Crier spends announcing the opening of our sessions and offering a prayer for this Court. Yet for me the principle is the same, no matter how briefly the prayer is said, for in each of the instances given the person praying is a public official on the public payroll, performing a religious exercise in a governmental institution. It is said that the ⊥**442** element of coercion is inherent in the giving of this prayer. If that is true here, it is also true of the prayer with which this Court is convened, and of those that open the Congress. Few adults, let alone children, would leave our courtroom or the Senate or the House while those prayers are being given. Every such audience is in a sense a "captive" audience.

At the same time I cannot say that to authorize this prayer is to establish a religion in the strictly historic meaning of those words. A religion is not established in the usual sense merely by letting those who choose to do so say the prayer that the public school teacher leads. Yet once government finances a religious exercise it inserts a divisive influence into our communities. The New York Court said that the prayer given does not conform to all of the tenets of the Jewish, Unitarian, and Ethical Culture groups. One of the petitioners is an agnostic.

"We are a religious people whose institutions presuppose a Supreme Being." *Zorach* v. *Clauson*. Under our Bill of Rights free play is given for ⊥**443** making religion an active force in our lives. But "if a religious leaven is to be worked into the affairs of our people, it is to be done by individuals and groups, not by the Government." *McGowan* v. *Maryland*. By reason of the First Amendment government is commanded "to have no interest in theology or ritual," for on those matters "government must be neutral." The First Amendment leaves the Government in a position not of hostility to religion but of neutrality.

The philosophy is that the atheist or agnostic—the nonbeliever—is entitled to go his own way. The philosophy is that if government interferes in matters spiritual, it will be a divisive force. The First Amendment teaches that a government neutral in the field of religion better serves all religious interests.

My problem today would be uncomplicated but for *Everson* v. *Board of Education*, which allowed taxpayers' money to be used to pay "the bus fares of parochial school pupils as a part of a general program under which" the fares of pupils attending public and other schools were also paid. The *Everson* case seems in retrospect to be out of line with the First Amendment. Its result is appealing, as it allows aid to be given to needy children. Yet by the same token, public funds could be used to satisfy other needs of children in parochial schools—lunches, books, and tuition being obvious examples. Mr. *Justice RUTLEDGE* stated in dissent what I think is durable First Amendment philosophy: "The reasons underlying the Amendment's policy have not vanished with time or diminished in force. ⊥**444** Now as when it was adopted the price of religious freedom is double. It is that the church and religion shall live both within and upon that freedom. There cannot be freedom of religion, safeguarded by the state, and intervention by the church or its agencies in the state's domain or dependency on its largesse. The great condition of religious liberty is that it be maintained free from sustenance, as also from other interferences, by the state. For when it comes to rest upon that secular foundation it vanishes with the resting. Public money devoted to payment of religious costs, educational or other, brings the quest for more. It brings too the struggle of sect against sect for the larger share or for any. Here one by numbers alone will benefit most, there another. That is precisely the history of societies which have had an established religion and dissident groups. It is the very thing Jefferson and Madison experienced and sought to guard against, whether in its blunt or in its more screened forms. The end of such strife cannot be other than to destroy the cherished liberty. The dominating group will achieve the dominant benefit; or all will embroil the state in their dissensions."

What New York does with this prayer is a break with that tradition. I therefore join the Court in reversing the judgment below.

Mr. *Justice STEWART*, dissenting.

A local school board in New York has provided that those pupils who wish to do so may join in a brief prayer at the beginning of each school day, acknowledging their dependence upon God and asking His blessing upon them ⊥**445** and upon their parents, their teachers, and their country. The Court today decides that in permitting this brief nondenominational prayer the school board has violated the Constitution of the United States. I think this decision is wrong.

The Court does not hold, nor could it, that New York has interfered with the free exercise of anybody's religion. For the state courts have made clear that those who object to reciting the prayer must be entirely free of any compulsion to do so, including any "embarrassments and pressures." But the Court says that in permitting school children to say this simple prayer, the New York authorities have established "an official religion."

With all respect, I think the Court has misapplied a great constitutional principle. I cannot see how an "official religion" is established by letting those who want to say a prayer say it. On the contrary, I think that to deny the wish of these school children to join in reciting this prayer is to deny them the opportunity of sharing in the spiritual heritage of our Nation.

The Court's historical review of the quarrels over the Book of Common Prayer in England throws no light for me on the issue before us in this case. England had then and has now an established church. Equally unenlightening, I think, is the history of the early establishment and later rejection of an official church in our own States. For we deal here not with the establishment of a state church, which would, of course, be constitutionally impermissible, but with whether school children who want to begin their day by joining in prayer must be prohibited from doing so. Moreover, I think that the Court's task, in this as in all areas of constitutional adjudication, is not responsibly aided by the uncritical invocation of metaphors like the "wall of separation," a phrase nowhere to ⊥**446** be found in the Constitution. What is relevant to the issue here is not the history of an established church in sixteenth century England or in eighteenth century America, but the history of the religious traditions of our people, reflected in countless practices of the institutions and officials of our government.

At the opening of each day's Session of this Court we stand, while one of our officials invokes the protection of God. Since the days of John Marshall our Crier has said, "God save the United States and this Honorable Court." Both the Senate and the House of Representatives open their daily Sessions with prayer. Each of our Presidents, from George Washington to John F. Kennedy, has upon assuming his Office asked the protection and help of God. . . .

⊥**449** The Court today says that the state and federal governments are without constitutional power to prescribe any particular form of words to be recited by any group of the American people on any subject touching religion. One of the stanzas of "The Star-Spangled Banner," made our National Anthem by Act of Congress in 1931, contains these verses:

"Blest with victory and peace, may the heav'n rescued land

Praise the Pow'r that hath made and preserved us a nation!

Then conquer we must, when our cause it is just,

And this be our motto 'In God is our Trust.'"

In 1954 Congress added a phrase to the Pledge of Allegiance to the Flag so that it now contains the words "one Nation *under God,* indivisible, with liberty and justice for all." In 1952 Congress enacted legislation calling upon the President each year to proclaim a National Day of Prayer. Since 1865 the words "IN GOD WE TRUST" have been impressed on our coins.

⊥**450** Countless similar examples could be listed, but there is no need to belabor the obvious. It was all summed up by this Court just ten years ago in a single sentence: "We are a religious people whose institutions presuppose a Supreme Being." *Zorach* v. *Clauson*.

I do not believe that this Court, or the Congress, or the President has by the actions and practices I have mentioned established an "official religion" in violation of the Constitution. And I do not believe the State of New York has done so in this case. What each has done has been to recognize and to follow the deeply entrenched and highly cherished spiritual traditions of our Nation—traditions which come down to us from those who almost two hundred years ago avowed their "firm Reliance on the Protection of divine Providence" when they proclaimed the freedom and independence of this brave new world.

I dissent.

ABINGTON TOWNSHIP SCHOOL DISTRICT v. SCHEMPP (No. 142)

ON APPEAL FROM THE UNITED STATES DISTRICT COURT FOR THE EASTERN DISTRICT OF PENNSYLVANIA

MURRAY v. CURLETT (No. 119)

ON WRIT OF CERTIORARI TO THE COURT OF APPEALS OF MARYLAND

374 U.S. 203
Argued February 27-28, 1963 — Decided June 17, 1963

⊥**205** Mr. *Justice* CLARK delivered the opinion of the Court.

Once again we are called upon to consider the scope of the provision of the First Amendment to the United States Constitution which declares that "Congress shall make no law respecting an establishment of religion, or prohibiting the free exercise thereof. . . ." These companion cases present the issues in the context of state action requiring that schools begin each day with readings from the Bible. While raising the basic questions under slightly different factual situations, the cases permit of joint treatment. In light of the history of the First Amendment and of our cases interpreting and applying its requirements, we hold that the practices at issue and the laws requiring them are unconstitutional under the Establishment Clause, as applied to the States through the Fourteenth Amendment.

I

The Facts in Each Case: No. 142. The Commonwealth of Pennsylvania by law, requires that "At least ten verses from the Holy Bible shall be read, without comment, at the opening of each public school on each school day. Any child shall be excused from such Bible reading, or attending such Bible reading, upon the written request of his parent or guardian." The Schempp family, husband and wife and two of their three children, brought suit to enjoin enforcement of the statute, contending that their rights under the Fourteenth Amendment to the Constitution of the United States are, have been, and will continue to be violated unless this statute be declared unconstitutional as violative of these provisions of the First Amendment. They sought to enjoin the appellant school district, wherein the Schempp children attend school, and its officers and the ⊥**206** Superintendent of Public Instruction of the Commonwealth from continuing to conduct such readings and recitation of the Lord's Prayer in the public schools of the district pursuant to the statute. A three-judge statutory District Court for the Eastern District of Pennsylvania held that the statute is violative of the Establishment Clause of the First Amendment as applied to the States by the Due Process Clause of the Fourteenth Amendment and directed that appropriate injunctive relief issue. On appeal by the District, its officials and the Superintendent, we noted probable jurisdiction.

The appellees Edward Lewis Schempp, his wife Sidney, and their children, Roger and Donna, are of the Unitarian faith and are members of the Unitarian Church in Germantown, Philadelphia, Pennsylvania, where they, as well as another son, Ellory, regularly attend religious services. The latter was originally a party but having graduated from the school system *pendente lite* was voluntarily dismissed from the action. The other children attend the Abington Senior High School, which is a public school operated by appellant district.

On each school day at the Abington Senior High School between 8:15 and 8:30 a.m., while the pupils are attending their home rooms or advisory sections, opening exer⊥**207**cises are conducted pursuant to the statute. The exercises are broadcast into each room in the school building through an intercommunications system and are conducted under the supervision of a teacher by students attending the school's radio and television workshop. Selected students from this course gather each morning in the school's workshop studio for the exercises, which include readings by one of the students of 10 verses of the Holy Bible, broadcast to each room in the building. This is followed by the recitation of the Lord's Prayer, likewise over the intercommunications system, but also by the students in the various classrooms, who are asked to stand and join in repeating the prayer in unison. The exercises are closed with the flag salute and such pertinent announcements as are of interest to the students. Participation in the opening exercises, as directed by the statute, is voluntary. The student reading the verses from the Bible may select the passages and read from any version he chooses, although the only copies furnished by the school are the King James version, copies of which were circulated to each teacher by the school district.

During the period in which the exercises have been conducted the King James, the Douay and the Revised Standard versions of the Bible have been used, as well as the Jewish Holy Scriptures. There are no prefatory statements, no questions asked or solicited, no comments or explanations made and no interpretations given at or during the exercises. The students and parents are advised that the student may absent himself from the classroom or, should he elect to remain, not participate in the exercises.

It appears from the record that in schools not having an intercommunications system the Bible reading and the recitation of the Lord's Prayer were conducted by the **⊥208** home-room teacher, who chose the text of the verses and read them herself or had students read them in rotation or by volunteers. This was followed by a standing recitation of the Lord's Prayer, together with the Pledge of Allegiance to the Flag by the class in unison and a closing announcement of routine school items of interest.

At the first trial Edward Schempp and the children testified as to specific religious doctrines purveyed by a literal reading of the Bible "which were contrary to the religious beliefs which they held and to their familial teaching." The children testified that all of the doctrines to which they referred were read to them at various times as part of the exercises. Edward Schempp testified at the second trial that he had considered having Roger and Donna excused from attendance at the exercises but decided against it for several reasons, including his belief that the children's relationships with their teachers and classmates would be adversely affected.

⊥209 Expert testimony was introduced by both appellants and appellees at the first trial, which testimony was summarized by the trial court as follows: "Dr. Solomon Grayzel testified that there were marked differences between the Jewish Holy Scriptures and the Christian Holy Bible, the most obvious of which was the absence of the New Testament in the Jewish Holy Scriptures. Dr. Grayzel testified that portions of the New Testament were offensive to Jewish tradition and that, from the standpoint of Jewish faith, the concept of Jesus Christ as the Son of God was 'practically blasphemous.' He cited instances in the New Testament which, assertedly, were not only sectarian in nature but tended to bring the Jews into ridicule or scorn. Dr. Grayzel gave as his expert opinion that such material from the New Testament could be explained to Jewish children in such a way as to do no harm to them. But if portions of the New Testament were read without explanation, they could be, and in his specific experience with children Dr. Grayzel observed, had been, psychologically harmful to the child and had caused a divisive force within the social media of the school.

"Dr. Grayzel also testified that there was significant difference in attitude with regard to the respective Books of the Jewish and Christian Religions in that Judaism attaches no special significance to the reading of the Bible *per se* and that the Jewish Holy Scriptures are source materials to be studied. But Dr. Grayzel did state that many portions of the New, **⊥210** as well as of the Old, Testament contained passages of great literary and moral value.

"Dr. Luther A. Weigle, an expert witness for the defense, testified in some detail as to the reasons for and the methods employed in developing the King James and the Revised Standard Versions of the Bible. On direct examination, Dr. Weigle stated that the Bible was non-sectarian. He later stated that the phrase 'non-sectarian' meant to him non-sectarian within the Christian faiths. Dr. Weigle stated that his definition of the Holy Bible would include the Jewish Holy Scriptures, but also stated that the 'Holy Bible' would not be complete without the New Testament. He stated that the New Testament 'conveyed the message of Christians.' In his opinion, reading of the Holy Scriptures to the exclusion of the New Testament would be a sectarian practice. Dr. Weigle stated that the Bible was of great moral, historical and literary value. This is conceded by all the parties and is also the view of the court."

The trial court, in striking down the practices and the statute requiring them, made specific findings of fact that the children's attendance at Abington Senior High School is compulsory and that the practice of reading 10 verses from the Bible is also compelled by law. It also found that: "The reading of the verses, even without comment, possesses a devotional and religious character and constitutes in effect a religious observance. The devotional and religious nature of the morning exercises is made all the more apparent by the fact that the Bible reading is followed immediately by a recital in unison by the pupils of the Lord's Prayer. The fact that some pupils, or theoretically all pupils, might be excused from attendance at the exercises **⊥211** does not mitigate the obligatory nature of the ceremony for . . . Section 1516 . . . unequivocally requires the exercises to be held every school day in every school in the Commonwealth. The exercises are held in the school buildings and perforce are conducted by and under the authority of the local school authorities and during school sessions. Since the statute requires the reading of the 'Holy Bible,' a Christian document, the practice . . . prefers the Christian religion. The record demonstrates that it was the intention of . . . the Commonwealth . . . to introduce a religious ceremony into the public schools of the Commonwealth."

No. 119. In 1905 the Board of School Commissioners of Baltimore City adopted a rule pursuant to Art. 77, § 202 of the Annotated Code of Maryland. The rule provided for the holding of opening exercises in the schools of the city, consisting primarily of the "reading, without comment, of a chapter in the Holy Bible and/or the use of the Lord's Prayer." The petitioners, Mrs. Madalyn Murray and her son, William J. Murray III, are both professed atheists. Following unsuccessful attempts to have the respondent school board rescind the rule, this suit was filed for mandamus to compel its rescission and cancellation. It was alleged that William was a student in a public school of the city and Mrs. Murray, his mother, was a taxpayer therein; that it was the practice under the rule to have a reading on each school morning from the King James version of the Bible; that at petitioners' insistence the rule was amended to permit children to ⊥**212** be excused from the exercise on request of the parent and that William had been excused pursuant thereto; that nevertheless the rule as amended was in violation of the petitioners' rights "to freedom of religion under the First and Fourteenth Amendments" and in violation of "the principle of separation between church and state, contained therein. . . ." The petition particularized the petitioners' atheistic beliefs and stated that the rule, as practiced, violated their rights "in that it threatens their religious liberty by placing a premium on belief as against non-belief and subjects their freedom of conscience to the rule of the majority; it pronounces belief in God as the source of all moral and spiritual values, equating these values with religious values, and thereby renders sinister, alien and suspect the beliefs and ideals of your Petitioners, promoting doubt and question of their morality, good citizenship and good faith."

The respondents demurred and the trial court, recognizing that the demurrer admitted all facts well pleaded, sustained it without leave to amend. The Maryland Court of Appeals affirmed, the majority of four justices holding the exercise not in violation of the First and Fourteenth Amendments, with three justices dissenting. We granted certiorari.

II

It is true that religion has been closely identified with our history and government. As we said in *Engel* v. *Vitale*, "The history of man is inseparable from the history of religion. And . . . since ⊥**213** the beginning of that history many people have devoutly believed that "More things are wrought by prayer than this world dreams of." In *Zorach* v. *Clauson* we gave specific recognition to the proposition that "[w]e are a religious people whose institutions presuppose a Supreme Being." The fact that the Founding Fathers believed devotedly that there was a God and that the unalienable rights of man were rooted in Him is clearly evidenced in their writings, from the Mayflower Compact to the Constitution itself. This background is evidenced today in our public life through the continuance in our oaths of office from the Presidency to the Alderman of the final supplication, "So help me God." Likewise each House of the Congress provides through its Chaplain an opening prayer, and the sessions of this Court are declared open by the crier in a short ceremony, the final phrase of which invokes the grace of God. Again, there are such manifestations in our military forces, where those of our citizens who are under the restrictions of military service wish to engage in voluntary worship. Indeed, only last year an official survey of the country indicated that 64% of our people have church membership, while less than 3% profess no religion whatever. It can be truly said, therefore, that today, as in the beginning, our national life reflects a religious people who, in the words of Madison, are "earnestly praying, as . . . in duty bound, that the Supreme Lawgiver of the Universe . . . guide them into every measure which may be worthy of his [blessing. . . .]" Memorial and Remonstrance Against Religious Assessments.

⊥**214** This is not to say, however, that religion has been so identified with our history and government that religious freedom is not likewise as strongly imbedded in our public and private life. Nothing but the most telling of personal experiences in religious persecution suffered by our forebears, could have planted our belief in liberty of religious opinion any more deeply in our heritage. It is true that this liberty frequently was not realized by the colonists, but this is readily accountable by their close ties to the Mother Country. However, the views of Madison and Jefferson, preceded by Roger Williams, came to be incorporated not only in the Federal Constitution but likewise in those of most of our States. This freedom to worship was indispensable in a country whose people came from the four quarters of the earth and brought with them a diversity of religious opinion. Today authorities list 83 separate religious bodies, each with membership exceeding 50,000, existing among our people, as well as innumerable smaller groups.

III

Almost a hundred years ago in *Minor* v. *Board of Education of Cincinnati*, Judge Alphonso Taft, father ⊥**215** of the revered Chief Justice, in an unpublished opinion stated the ideal of our people as to religious freedom as one of "absolute equality before the law, of all religious opinions and sects. . . .

"The government is neutral, and, while protecting all, it prefers none, and it *disparages* none."

Before examining this "neutral" position in which the Establishment and Free Exercise Clauses of the First Amendment place our Government it is well that we discuss the reach of the Amendment under the cases of this Court.

First, this Court has decisively settled that the First Amendment's mandate that "Congress shall make no law respecting an establishment of religion, or prohibiting the free exercise thereof" has been made wholly applicable to the States by the Fourteenth Amendment. Twenty-three years ago in *Cantwell* v. *Connecticut*, this Court, through *Mr. Justice* ROBERTS, said "The fundamental concept of liberty embodied in that [Fourteenth] Amendment embraces the liberties guaranteed by the First Amendment. The First Amendment declares that Congress shall make no law respecting an establishment of religion or prohibiting the free exercise thereof. The Fourteenth Amend-⊥**216**ment has rendered the legislatures of the states as incompetent as Congress to enact such laws. . . ."

In a series of cases since *Cantwell* the Court has repeatedly reaffirmed that doctrine, and we do so now.

Second, this Court has rejected unequivocally the contention that the Establishment Clause forbids only governmental preference of one religion over another. Almost 20 years ago in *Everson*, the Court said that "[n]either a state nor the Federal Government can set up a church. Neither can pass laws which aid one religion, aid all religions, or prefer one religion over another." And Mr. *Justice JACKSON*, dissenting, agreed: "There is no answer to the proposition . . . that the effect of the religious freedom Amendment to our Constitution was to take every form of propagation of religion out of the realm of things which could directly or indirectly be made public business and thereby be supported in whole or in part at taxpayers' expense. . . . This freedom was first in the Bill of Rights because it was first in the forefathers' minds; it was set forth in absolute terms, and its strength is its rigidity."

⊥217 Further, Mr. *Justice RUTLEDGE*, joined by *Justices FRANKFURTER, JACKSON* and *BURTON*, declared: "The [First] Amendment's purpose was not to strike merely at the official establishment of a single sect, creed or religion, outlawing only a formal relation such as had prevailed in England and some of the colonies. Necessarily it was to uproot all such relationships. But the object was broader than separating church and state in this narrow sense. It was to create a complete and permanent separation of the spheres of religious activity and civil authority by comprehensively forbidding every form of public aid or support for religion."

The same conclusion has been firmly maintained ever since that time and we reaffirm it now.

While none of the parties to either of these cases has questioned these basic conclusions of the Court, both of which have been long established, recognized and consistently reaffirmed, others continue to question their history, logic and efficacy. Such contentions, in the light of the consistent interpretation in cases of this Court, seem entirely untenable and of value only as academic exercises.

IV

The interrelationship of the Establishment and the Free Exercise Clauses was first touched upon by Mr. *Justice ROBERTS* for the Court in *Cantwell* v. *Connecticut*, where it was said that their "inhibition of legislation" had "a double aspect. On the one hand, it forestalls compulsion by law of the acceptance of any creed or the practice of any form of worship. Freedom of **⊥218** conscience and freedom to adhere to such religious organization or form of worship as the individual may choose cannot be restricted by law. On the other hand, it safeguards the free exercise of the chosen form of religion. Thus the Amendment embraces two concepts,—freedom to believe and freedom to act. The first is absolute but, in the nature of things, the second cannot be."

A half dozen years later in *Everson* v. *Board of Education*, this Court, through Mr. *Justice BLACK*, stated that the "scope of the First Amendment . . . was designed forever to suppress" the establishment of religion or the prohibition of the free exercise thereof. In short, the Court held that the Amendment "requires the state to be a neutral in its relations with groups of religious believers and nonbelievers; it does not require the state to be their adversary. State power is no more to be used so as to handicap religions than it is to favor them."

And Mr. *Justice JACKSON*, in dissent, declared that public schools are organized "on the premise that secular education can be isolated from all religious teaching so that the school can inculcate all needed temporal knowledge and also maintain a strict and lofty neutrality as to religion. The assumption is that after the individual has been instructed in worldly wisdom he will be better fitted to choose his religion."

Moreover, all of the four dissenters, speaking through Mr. *Justice RUTLEDGE*, agreed that "Our constitutional policy . . . does not deny the value or the necessity for religious training, teaching or observance. Rather it secures their free exercise. But to that end it does deny that the state can undertake or sustain them in any form or degree. For this **⊥219** reason the sphere of religious activity, as distinguished from the secular intellectual liberties, has been given the twofold protection and, as the state cannot forbid, neither can it perform or aid in performing the religious function. The dual prohibition makes that function altogether private."

Only one year later the Court was asked to reconsider and repudiate the doctrine of these cases in *McCollum* v. *Board of Education*. It was argued that "historically the First Amendment was intended to forbid only government preference of one religion over another. . . . In addition they ask that we distinguish or overrule our holding in the *Everson* case that the Fourteenth Amendment made the 'establishment of religion' clause of the First Amendment applicable as a prohibition against the States." The Court, with Mr. *Justice REED* alone dissenting, was unable to "accept either of these contentions." Mr. *Justice FRANKFURTER*, joined by *Justices JACKSON, RUTLEDGE* and *BURTON*, wrote a very comprehensive and scholarly concurrence in which he said that "[s]eparation is a requirement to abstain from fusing functions of Government and of religious sects, not merely to treat them all equally." Continuing, he stated that: "the Constitution . . . prohibited the Government common to all from becoming embroiled, however innocently, in the destructive religious conflicts of which the history of even this country records some dark pages."

In 1952 in *Zorach* v. *Clauson*, Mr. *Justice DOUGLAS* for the Court reiterated: "There cannot be the slightest doubt that the First Amendment reflects the philosophy that Church and State should be separated. And so far as interference with the 'free exercise' of religion and an **⊥220** 'establishment' of religion are concerned, the separation must be complete and unequivocal. The First Amendment within the scope of its coverage permits no exception; the prohibition is absolute. The First Amendment, however, does not say that in every and all respects there shall be a separation of Church and State.

Rather, it studiously defines the manner, the specific ways, in which there shall be no concert or union or dependency one on the other. That is the common sense of the matter."

And then in 1961 in *McGowan* v. *Maryland* and in *Torcaso* v. *Watkins* each of these cases was discussed and approved. *Chief Justice WARREN* in *McGowan*, for a unanimous Court on this point, said: "But, the First Amendment, in its final form, did not simply bar a congressional enactment *establishing a church;* it forbade all laws *respecting an establishment of religion*. Thus, this Court has given the Amendment a 'broad interpretation . . . in the light of its history and the evils it was designed forever to suppress. . . .'"

And Mr. *Justice BLACK* for the Court in *Torcaso*, without dissent but with *Justices FRANKFURTER* and HARLAN concurring in the result, used this language: "We repeat and again reaffirm that neither a State nor the Federal Government can constitutionally force a person 'to profess a belief or disbelief in any religion.' Neither can constitutionally pass laws or impose requirements which aid all religions as against nonbelievers, and neither can aid those religions based on a belief in the existence of God as against those religions founded on different beliefs."

Finally, in *Engel* v. *Vitale*, only last year, these principles were so universally recognized that the Court, with⊥**221**out the citation of a single case and over the sole dissent of Mr. *Justice STEWART*, reaffirmed them. The Court found the 22-word prayer used in "New York's program of daily classroom invocation of God's blessings as prescribed in the Regents' prayer . . . [to be] a religious activity." It held that "it is no part of the business of government to compose official prayers for any group of the American people to recite as a part of a religious program carried on by government." In discussing the reach of the Establishment and Free Exercise Clauses of the First Amendment the Court said "Although these two clauses may in certain instances overlap, they forbid two quite different kinds of governmental encroachment upon religious freedom. The Establishment Clause, unlike the Free Exercise Clause, does not depend upon any showing of direct governmental compulsion and is violated by the enactment of laws which establish an official religion whether those laws operate directly to coerce non-observing individuals or not. This is not to say, of course, that laws officially prescribing a particular form of religious worship do not involve coercion of such individuals. When the power, prestige and financial support of government is placed behind a particular religious belief, the indirect coercive pressure upon religious minorities to conform to the prevailing officially approved religion is plain."

And in further elaboration the Court found that the "first and most immediate purpose [of the Establishment Clause] rested on the belief that a union of government and religion tends to destroy government and to degrade religion." When government, the Court said, allies itself with one particular form of religion, the ⊥**222** inevitable result is that it incurs "the hatred, disrespect and even contempt of those who held contrary beliefs."

V

The wholesome "neutrality" of which this Court's cases speak thus stems from a recognition of the teachings of history that powerful sects or groups might bring about a fusion of governmental and religious functions or a concert or dependency of one upon the other to the end that official support of the State or Federal Government would be placed behind the tenets of one or of all orthodoxies. This the Establishment Clause prohibits. And a further reason for neutrality is found in the Free Exercise Clause, which recognizes the value of religious training, teaching and observance and, more particularly, the right of every person to freely choose his own course with reference thereto, free of any compulsion from the state. This the Free Exercise Clause guarantees. Thus, as we have seen, the two clauses may overlap. As we have indicated, the Establishment Clause has been directly considered by this Court eight times in the past score of years and, with only one Justice dissenting on the point, it has consistently held that the clause withdrew all legislative power respecting religious belief or the expression thereof. The test may be stated as follows: what are the purpose and the primary effect of the enactment? If either is the advancement or inhibition of religion then the enactment exceeds the scope of legislative power as circumscribed by the Constitution. That is to say that to withstand the strictures of the Establishment Clause there must be a secular legislative purpose and a primary effect that neither advances nor inhibits religion. The Free Exercise Clause, likewise considered many times here, withdraws from legislative power, state and federal, the exertion of any restraint on the free exer⊥**223**cise of religion. Its purpose is to secure religious liberty in the individual by prohibiting any invasions thereof by civil authority. Hence it is necessary in a free exercise case for one to show the coercive effect of the enactment as it operates against him in the practice of his religion. The distinction between the two clauses is apparent—a violation of the Free Exercise Clause is predicated on coercion while the Establishment Clause violation need not be so attended.

Applying the Establishment Clause principles to the cases at bar we find that the States are requiring the selection and reading at the opening of the school day of verses from the Holy Bible and the recitation of the Lord's Prayer by the students in unison. These exercises are prescribed as part of the curricular activities of students who are required by law to attend school. They are held in the school buildings under the supervision and with the participation of teachers employed in those schools. None of these factors, other than compulsory school attendance, was present in the program upheld in *Zorach* v. *Clauson*. The trial court in No. 142 has found that such an opening exercise is a religious ceremony and was intended by the

State to be so. We agree with the trial court's finding as to the religious character of the exercises. Given that finding, the exercises and the law requiring them are in violation of the Establishment Clause.

There is no such specific finding as to the religious character of the exercises in No. 119, and the State contends (as does the State in No. 142) that the program is an effort to extend its benefits to all public school children without regard to their religious belief. Included within its secular purposes, it says, are the promotion of moral values, the contradiction to the materialistic trends of our times, the perpetuation of our institutions and the teaching of literature. The case came up ⊥**224** on demurrer, of course, to a petition which alleged that the uniform practice under the rule had been to read from the King James version of the Bible and that the exercise was sectarian. The short answer, therefore, is that the religious character of the exercise was admitted by the State. But even if its purpose is not strictly religious, it is sought to be accomplished through readings, without comment, from the Bible. Surely the place of the Bible as an instrument of religion cannot be gainsaid, and the State's recognition of the pervading religious character of the ceremony is evident from the rule's specific permission of the alternative use of the Catholic Douay version as well as the recent amendment permitting nonattendance at the exercises. None of these factors is consistent with the contention that the Bible is here used either as an instrument for nonreligious moral inspiration or as a reference for the teaching of secular subjects.

The conclusion follows that in both cases the laws require religious exercises and such exercises are being conducted in direct violation of the rights of the appellees and petitioners. Nor are these required exercises mitigated by the fact that individual students may absent ⊥**225** themselves upon a parental request, for that fact furnishes no defense to a claim of unconstitutionality under the Establishment Clause. Further, it is no defense to urge that the religious practices here may be relatively minor encroachments on the First Amendment. The breach of neutrality that is today a trickling stream may all too soon become a raging torrent and, in the words of Madison, "it is proper to take alarm at the first experiment on our liberties."

It is insisted that unless these religious exercises are permitted a "religion of secularism" is established in the schools. We agree of course that the State may not establish a "religion of secularism" in the sense of affirmatively opposing or showing hostility to religion, thus "preferring those who believe in no religion over those who do believe." *Zorach* v. *Clauson*. We do not agree, however, that this decision in any sense has that effect. In addition, it might well be said that one's education is not complete without a study of comparative religion or the history of religion and its relationship to the advancement of civilization. It certainly may be said that the Bible is worthy of study for its literary and historic qualities. Nothing we have said here indicates that such study of the Bible or of religion, when presented objectively as part of a secular program of education, may not be effected consistently with the First Amendment. But the exercises here do not fall into those categories. They are religious exercises, required by the States in violation of the command of the First Amendment that the Government maintain strict neutrality, neither aiding nor opposing religion.

Finally, we cannot accept that the concept of neutrality, which does not permit a State to require a religious exercise even with the consent of the majority of those ⊥**226** affected, collides with the majority's right to free exercise of religion. While the Free Exercise Clause clearly prohibits the use of state action to deny the rights of free exercise to anyone, it has never meant that a majority could use the machinery of the State to practice its beliefs. Such a contention was effectively answered by Mr. *Justice* JACKSON for the Court in *West Virginia Board of Education* v. *Barnette*: "The very purpose of a Bill of Rights was to withdraw certain subjects from the vicissitudes of political controversy, to place them beyond the reach of majorities and officials and to establish them as legal principles to be applied by the courts. One's right to . . . freedom of worship . . . and other fundamental rights may not be submitted to vote; they depend on the outcome of no elections."

The place of religion in our society is an exalted one, achieved through a long tradition of reliance on the home, the church and the inviolable citadel of the individual heart and mind. We have come to recognize through bitter experience that it is not within the power of government to invade that citadel, whether its purpose or effect be to aid or oppose, to advance or retard. In the relationship between man and religion, the State is firmly committed to a position of neutrality. Though the application of that rule requires interpretation of a delicate sort, the rule itself is clearly and concisely stated in the words of the First Amendment. Applying that rule to the facts of these cases, we affirm the judgment in No. 142. ⊥**227** In No. 119, the judgment is reversed and the cause remanded to the Maryland Court of Appeals for further proceedings consistent with this opinion.

It is so ordered.

Mr. *Justice* DOUGLAS, concurring. I join the opinion of the Court and add a few words in explanation.

While the Free Exercise Clause of the First Amendment is written in terms of what the State may not require of the individual, the Establishment Clause, serving the same goal of individual religious freedom, is written in different terms.

Establishment of a religion can be achieved in several ways. The church and state can be one; the church may control the state or the state may control the church; or the relationship may take one of several possible forms of a working arrangement between the two bodies. Under all of these arrangements the church typically has a place in the state's budget, and church law usually governs such matters as baptism, marriage, divorce and separation, at least for its members and sometimes for the entire body politic. Education, too, is usually high on the priority ⊥**228** list of church interests. In the past schools were often made the exclusive responsibility of the church. Today in some state-church countries the state runs the public schools, but compulsory religious exercises are often required of some or all students. . . .

The vice of all such arrangements under the Establishment Clause is that the state is lending its assistance to a church's efforts to gain and keep adherents. Under the First Amendment it is strictly a matter for the individual and his church as to what church he will belong to and how much support, in the way of belief, time, activity or money, he will give to it. "This pure Religious Liberty" "declared . . . [all forms of church-state relationships] and their fundamental idea to be oppressions of conscience and abridgments of that liberty which God and nature had conferred on every living soul."

In these cases we have no coercive religious exercise aimed at making the students conform. The prayers announced are not compulsory, though some may think they have that indirect effect because the nonconformist student may be induced to participate for fear of being called an "oddball." But that coercion, if it be present, ⊥**229** has not been shown; so the vices of the present regimes are different.

These regimes violate the Establishment Clause in two different ways. In each case the State is conducting a religious exercise; and, as the Court holds, that cannot be done without violating the "neutrality" required of the State by the balance of power between individual, church and state that has been struck by the First Amendment. But the Establishment Clause is not limited to precluding the State itself from conducting religious exercises. It also forbids the State to employ its facilities or funds in a way that gives any church, or all churches, greater strength in our society than it would have by relying on its members alone. Thus, the present regimes must fall under that clause for the additional reason that public funds, though small in amount, are being used to promote a religious exercise. Through the mechanism of the State, all of the people are being required to finance a religious exercise that only some of the people want and that violates the sensibilities of others.

The most effective way to establish any institution is to finance it, and this truth is reflected in the appeals by church groups for public funds to finance their religious schools. Financing a church either in its strictly religious activities or in its other activities is equally unconstitutional, as I understand the Establishment Clause. Budgets for one activity may be technically separable from budgets for others. But the institution is an inseparable whole, a living organism, which is strengthened in proselytizing when it is strengthened in any department by contributions from other than its own members.

⊥**230** Such contributions may not be made by the State even in a minor degree without violating the Establishment Clause. It is not the amount of public funds expended; as this case illustrates, it is the use to which public funds are put that is controlling. For the First Amendment does not say that some forms of establishment are allowed; it says that "no law respecting an establishment of religion" shall be made. What may not be done directly may not be done indirectly lest the Establishment Clause become a mockery.

Mr. Justice BRENNAN, concurring.

Almost a century and a half ago, John Marshall, in M'*Culloch* v. *Maryland*, enjoined ". . . we must never forget, that it is *a constitution* we are expounding." The Court's historic duty to expound the meaning of the Constitution has encountered few issues more intricate or more demanding than that of the relationship between religion and the public schools. Since undoubtedly we are "a religious people whose institutions presuppose a Supreme Being," *Zorach* v. *Clauson*, deep feelings are aroused when aspects of that relationship are claimed to violate the injunction of the First Amendment that government may make "no law respecting an establishment of religion, or prohibiting the free exercise thereof. . . ." Americans regard the public schools as a most vital civic institution for the preservation of a democratic system of government. It is therefore understandable that the constitutional prohibitions encounter their severest test when they are sought to be applied in the school classroom. Nevertheless it is this Court's inescapable duty to declare whether exercises in the public schools of the States, such as those of Pennsylvania and Maryland questioned here, are involvements of religion in public institutions of a kind which offends the First and Fourteenth Amendments.

⊥**231** When John Locke ventured in 1689, "I esteem it above all things necessary to distinguish exactly the business of civil government from that of religion and to settle the just bounds that lie between the one and the other," he anticipated the necessity which would be thought by the Framers to require adoption of a First Amendment, but not the difficulty that would be experienced in defining those "just bounds." The fact is that the line which separates the secular from the sectarian in American life is elusive. The difficulty of defining the boundary with precision inheres in a paradox central to our scheme of liberty. While our institutions reflect a firm conviction that we are a religious people, those institutions by solemn constitutional injunction may not officially involve religion in such a way as to prefer, discriminate against, or oppress, a particular sect or religion. Equally the Constitution enjoins those involvements of religious with secular institutions which (a) serve the essentially religious activities of religious institutions; (b) employ the organs of government for essentially religious purposes; or (c) use essentially religious means to serve governmental ends where secular means would suffice. The constitutional mandate expresses a deliberate and considered judgment that such matters are to be left to the conscience of the citizen, and declares as a basic postulate of the relation between the citizen and his government that "the rights of conscience are, in their nature, of peculiar delicacy, and will little bear the gentlest touch of governmental hand. . . ."

I join fully in the opinion and the judgment of the Court. I see no escape from the conclusion that the exer⊥**232**cises called in question in these two cases violate the constitutional mandate. The reasons we gave only last Term in *Engel* v. *Vitale* for finding in the New York Regents' prayer an impermissible establishment of religion, compel the same judgment of the practices at bar. The involvement of the secular with the religious is no less intimate here; and it is constitutionally irrelevant that the State has not composed the material for the inspirational exercises presently involved. It should be unnecessary to observe that our holding does not declare that the First Amendment manifests hostility to the practice or teaching of religion, but only applies prohibitions incorporated in the Bill of Rights in recognition of historic needs shared by Church and State alike. While it is my view that not every involvement of religion in public life is unconstitutional, I consider the exercises at bar a form of involvement which clearly violates the Establishment Clause.

The importance of the issue and the deep conviction with which views on both sides are held seem to me to justify detailing at some length my reasons for joining the Court's judgment and opinion.

I

The First Amendment forbids both the abridgment of the free exercise of religion and the enactment of laws "respecting an establishment of religion." The two clauses, although distinct in their objectives and their applicability, emerged together from a common panorama of history. The inclusion of both restraints upon the power of Congress to legislate concerning religious matters shows unmistakably that the Framers of the First Amendment were not content to rest the protection of religious liberty exclusively upon either clause. "In assuring the free exercise of religion," Mr. *Justice FRANKFURTER* has said, ⊥**233** "the Framers of the First Amendment were sensitive to the then recent history of those persecutions and impositions of civil disability with which sectarian majorities in virtually all of the Colonies had visited deviation in the matter of conscience. This protection of unpopular creeds, however, was not to be the full extent of the Amendment's guarantee of freedom from governmental intrusion in matters of faith. The battle in Virginia, hardly four years won, where James Madison had led the forces of disestablishment in successful opposition to Patrick Henry's proposed Assessment Bill levying a general tax for the support of Christian teachers, was a vital and compelling memory in 1789." *McGowan* v. *Maryland*.

It is true that the Framers' immediate concern was to prevent the setting up of an official federal church of the kind which England and some of the Colonies had long supported. But nothing in the text of the Establishment Clause supports the view that the prevention of the setting up of an official church was meant to be the full extent of the prohibitions against official involvements in religion. It has rightly been said: "If the framers of the Amendment meant to prohibit Congress merely from the establishment of a 'church,' one may properly wonder why they didn't so state. That the words *church* and *religion* were regarded as synonymous seems highly improbable, particularly in view of the fact that the contemporary state constitutional provisions dealing with the subject of establishment used definite phrases such as 'religious sect,' 'sect,' or 'denomination.' . . . With such specific wording in contemporary state constitutions, why was not a similar wording adopted for the First Amendment if its framers intended to prohibit nothing more than what the States were pro⊥**234**hibiting?" Lardner, How Far Does the Constitution Separate Church and State? 45 Am. Pol. Sci. Rev. 110, 112 (1951).

Plainly, the Establishment Clause, in the contemplation of the Framers, "did not limit the constitutional proscription to any particular, dated form of state-supported theological venture." "What Virginia had long practiced, and what Madison, Jefferson and others fought to end, was the extension of civil government's support to religion in a manner which made the two in some degree interdependent, and thus threatened the freedom of each. The purpose of the Establishment Clause was to assure that the national legislature would not exert its power in the service of any purely religious end; that it would not, as Virginia and virtually all of the Colonies had done, make of religion, as religion, an object of legislation. . . . The Establishment Clause withdrew from the sphere of legitimate legislative concern and competence a specific, but comprehensive, area of human conduct: man's belief or disbelief in the verity of some transcendental idea and man's expression in action of that belief or disbelief." *McGowan* v. *Maryland*.

In sum, the history which our prior decisions have summoned to aid interpretation of the Establishment Clause permits little doubt that its prohibition was designed comprehensively to prevent those official involvements of religion which would tend to foster or discourage religious worship or belief.

But an awareness of history and an appreciation of the aims of the Founding Fathers do not always resolve concrete problems. The specific question before us has, for example, aroused vigorous dispute whether the architects of the First Amendment—James Madison and Thomas Jefferson particularly—understood the prohibition against any "law respecting an establishment of ⊥**235** religion" to reach devotional exercises in the public schools. It may be that Jefferson and Madison would have held such exercises to be permissible—although even in Jefferson's case serious doubt is suggested by his admonition against "putting the Bible and Testament into the hands of the children at an age when their judgments are not sufficiently matured for religious inquiries. . . ." But **⊥236** I doubt that their view, even if perfectly clear one way or the other, would supply a dispositive answer to the question presented by these cases. A more fruitful inquiry, it seems to me, is whether the practices here challenged threaten those consequences which the Framers deeply feared; whether, in short, they tend to promote that type of interdependence between religion and state which the First Amendment was designed to prevent. Our task is to translate "the majestic generalities of the Bill of Rights, conceived as part of the pattern of liberal government in the eighteenth century, into concrete restraints on officials **⊥237** dealing with the problems of the twentieth century. . . ." *West Virginia State Board of Education* v. *Barnette*.

A too literal quest for the advice of the Founding Fathers upon the issues of these cases seems to me futile and misdirected for several reasons: First, on our precise problem the historical record is at best ambiguous, and statements can readily be found to support either side of the proposition. The ambiguity of history is understandable if we recall the nature of the problems uppermost in the thinking of the statesmen who fashioned the religious guarantees; they were concerned with far more flagrant intrusions of government into the realm of religion than any that our century has witnessed. While it is clear to me that the Framers meant the Establishment Clause to prohibit more than the creation of an established federal church such as existed in England, I have no doubt that, in their preoccupation with the imminent question of established churches, they gave no dis**⊥238**tinct consideration to the particular question whether the clause also forbade devotional exercises in public institutions.

Second, the structure of American education has greatly changed since the First Amendment was adopted. In the context of our modern emphasis upon public education available to all citizens, any views of the eighteenth century as to whether the exercises at bar are an "establishment" offer little aid to decision. Education, as the Framers knew it, was in the main confined to private schools more often than not under strictly sectarian supervision. Only gradually did control of education pass largely to public officials. It would, therefore, **⊥239** hardly be significant if the fact was that the nearly universal devotional exercises in the schools of the young Republic did not provoke criticism; even today religious ceremonies in church-supported private schools are constitutionally unobjectionable.

⊥240 Third, our religious composition makes us a vastly more diverse people than were our forefathers. They knew differences chiefly among Protestant sects. Today the Nation is far more heterogeneous religiously, including as it does substantial minorities not only of Catholics and Jews but as well of those who worship according to no version of the Bible and those who worship no God at all. **⊥241** In the face of such profound changes, practices which may have been objectionable to no one in the time of Jefferson and Madison may today be highly offensive to many persons, the deeply devout and the nonbelievers alike.

Whatever Jefferson or Madison would have thought of Bible reading or the recital of the Lord's Prayer in what few public schools existed in their day, our use of the history of their time must limit itself to broad purposes, not specific practices. By such a standard, I am persuaded, as is the Court, that the devotional exercises carried on in the Baltimore and Abington schools offend the First Amendment because they sufficiently threaten in our day those substantive evils the fear of which called forth the Establishment Clause of the First Amendment. It is "*a constitution* we are expounding," and our interpretation of the First Amendment must necessarily be responsive to the much more highly charged nature of religious questions in contemporary society.

Fourth, the American experiment in free public education available to all children has been guided in large measure by the dramatic evolution of the religious diversity among the population which our public schools serve. The interaction of these two important forces in our national life has placed in bold relief certain positive values in the consistent application to public institutions generally, and public schools particularly, of the constitutional decree against official involvements of religion which might produce the evils the Framers meant the Establishment Clause to forestall. The public schools are supported entirely, in most communities, by public funds—funds exacted not only from parents, nor alone from those who hold particular religious views, nor indeed from those who subscribe to any creed at all. It is implicit in the history and character of American public education that the public schools serve a uniquely **⊥242** public function: the training of American citizens in an atmosphere free of parochial, divisive, or separatist influences of any sort—an atmosphere in which children may assimilate a heritage common to all American groups and religions. This is a heritage neither theistic nor atheistic, but simply civic and patriotic.

Attendance at the public schools has never been compulsory; parents remain morally and constitutionally free to choose the academic environment in which they wish their children to be educated. The relationship of the Establishment Clause of the First Amendment to the public school system is preeminently that of reserving such a choice to the individual parent, rather than vesting it in the majority of voters of each State or school district. The choice which is thus preserved is between a public secular education with its uniquely democratic values, and some form of private or sectarian education, which offers values of its own. In my judgment the First Amendment forbids the State to inhibit that freedom of choice by diminishing the attractiveness of either alternative either by restricting the liberty of the private schools to inculcate whatever values they wish, or by jeopardizing the freedom of the public schools from private or sectarian pressures. The choice between these very different forms of education is one—very much like the choice of whether or not to worship—which our Constitution leaves to the individual parent. It is no proper function of the state or local government to influence or restrict that election. The lesson of history—drawn more from the experiences of other countries than from our own—is that a system of free public education forfeits its unique contribution to the growth of democratic citizenship when that choice ceases to be freely available to each parent.

II

⊥**243** The exposition by this Court of the religious guarantees of the First Amendment has consistently reflected and reaffirmed the concerns which impelled the Framers to write those guarantees into the Constitution. It would be neither possible nor appropriate to review here the entire course of our decisions on religious questions. There emerge from those decisions, however, three principles of particular relevance to the issue presented by the cases at bar, and some attention to those decisions is therefore appropriate.

First. One line of decisions derives from contests for control of a church property or other internal ecclesiastical disputes. This line has settled the proposition that in order to give effect to the First Amendment's purpose of requiring on the part of all organs of government a strict neutrality toward theological questions, courts should not undertake to decide such questions. These principles were first expounded in the case of *Watson* v. *Jones*, which declared that judicial intervention in such a controversy would open up "the whole subject of the doctrinal theology, the usages and customs, the written laws, and fundamental organization of every religious denomination. . . ." Courts above all must be neutral, for "[t]he law knows no heresy, and is committed to the support of no dogma, the establishment of no sect." This principle has re⊥**244**cently been reaffirmed in *Kedroff* v. *St. Nicholas Cathedral*, and *Kreshik* v. *St. Nicholas Cathedral*.

The mandate of judicial neutrality in theological controversies met its severest test in *United States* v. *Ballard*. That decision put in sharp relief certain principles which bear directly upon the questions presented in these cases. Ballard was indicted for fraudulent use of the mails in the dissemination of religious literature. He requested that the trial court submit to the jury the question of the truthfulness of the religious views he championed. The requested charge was refused, and we upheld that refusal, reasoning that the First Amendment foreclosed any judicial inquiry into the truth or falsity of the defendant's religious beliefs. We said: "Man's relation to his God was made no concern of the state. He was granted the right to worship as he pleased and to answer to no man for the verity of his religious views." "Men may believe what they cannot ⊥**245** prove. They may not be put to the proof of their religious doctrines or beliefs. . . . Many take their gospel from the New Testament. But it would hardly be supposed that they could be tried before a jury charged with the duty of determining whether those teachings contained false representations."

The dilemma presented by the case was severe. While the alleged truthfulness of *nonreligious* publications could ordinarily have been submitted to the jury, Ballard was deprived of that defense only because the First Amendment forbids governmental inquiry into the verity of *religious* beliefs. In dissent Mr. *Justice JACKSON* expressed the concern that under this construction of the First Amendment "[p]rosecutions of this character easily could degenerate into religious persecution." The case shows how elusive is the line which enforces the Amendment's injunction of strict neutrality, while manifesting no official hostility toward religion—a line which must be considered in the cases now before us. Some might view the result of the *Ballard* case as a manifestation of hostility—in that the conviction stood because the defense could not be raised. To others it ⊥**246** might represent merely strict adherence to the principle of neutrality already expounded in the cases involving doctrinal disputes. Inevitably, insistence upon neutrality, vital as it surely is for untrammeled religious liberty, may appear to border upon religious hostility. But in the long view the independence of both church and state in their respective spheres will be better served by close adherence to the neutrality principle. If the choice is often difficult, the difficulty is endemic to issues implicating the religious guarantees of the First Amendment. Freedom of religion will be seriously jeopardized if we admit exceptions for no better reason than the difficulty of delineating hostility from neutrality in the closest cases.

Second. It is only recently that our decisions have dealt with the question whether issues arising under the Establishment Clause may be isolated from problems implicating the Free Exercise Clause. *Everson* v. *Board of Education* is in my view the first of our decisions which treats a problem of asserted unconstitutional involvement as raising questions purely under the Establishment Clause. A scrutiny of several earlier decisions said by some to have etched the contours of the clause shows that such cases neither raised nor decided any constitutional issues under the First Amendment. *Bradfield* v. *Roberts*, for example, involved challenges to a federal grant to a hospital administered by a Roman Catholic order. The Court rejected the claim for lack of evidence that any sectarian influence changed its character as a secular institution chartered as such by the Congress. . . .

⊥**248** [Another] case in this group is *Cochran* v. *Louisiana State Board*, which involved a challenge to a state statute providing public funds to support a loan of free textbooks to pupils of both public and private schools. The constitutional issues in this Court extended no further than the claim that this program amounted to a taking of private property for nonpublic use. The Court rejected the claim on the ground that no private use of property was involved; ". . . we can not doubt that the taxing power of the State is exerted for a public purpose." The case therefore raised no issue under the First Amendment.

In *Pierce* v. *Society of Sisters*, a Catholic parochial school and a private but nonsectarian military academy challenged a state law requiring all children between certain ages to attend the public schools. This Court held the law invalid as an arbitrary and unreasonable interference both with the rights of the schools and with the liberty of the parents of the children who attended them. The due process guarantee of the Fourteenth Amendment "excludes any general power of the State to standardize its children by forcing them to accept instruction from public teachers only." While one of the plaintiffs was indeed a parochial school, the case obviously decided no First Amendment question but recognized only the constitutional right to establish and patronize private schools—including parochial schools—which meet the state's reasonable minimum curricular requirements.

⊥249 *Third*. It is true, as the Court says, that the "two clauses [Establishment and Free Exercise] may overlap." Because of the overlap, however, our decisions under the Free Exercise Clause bear considerable relevance to the problem now before us, and should be briefly reviewed. The early free exercise cases generally involved the objections of religious minorities to the application to them of general nonreligious legislation governing conduct. *Reynolds* v. *United States* involved the claim that a belief in the sanctity of plural marriage precluded the conviction of members of a particular sect under nondiscriminatory legislation against such marriage. The Court rejected the claim, saying "Laws are made for the government of actions, and while they cannot interfere with mere religious beliefs and opinions, they may with practices. . . . Can a man excuse his practices to the contrary because of his religious belief? To permit this would be to make the professed doctrines of religious belief superior to the law of the land, and in effect to permit every citizen to become a law unto himself. Government could exist only in name under such circumstances."

⊥250 *Davis* v. *Beason* similarly involved the claim that the First Amendment insulated from civil punishment certain practices inspired or motivated by religious beliefs. The claim was easily rejected: "It was never intended or supposed that the amendment could be invoked as a protection against legislation for the punishment of acts inimical to the peace, good order and morals of society."

But we must not confuse the issue of governmental power to regulate or prohibit conduct *motivated by religious beliefs* with the quite different problem of governmental authority to compel behavior *offensive to religious principles*. In *Hamilton* v. *Regents of the University of California*, the question was that of the power of a State to compel students at the State University to participate in military training instruction against their religious convictions. The validity of the statute was sustained against claims based upon the First Amendment. But the decision rested on a very narrow principle: since there was neither a constitutional right nor a legal obligation to attend the State University, the obligation to participate in military training courses, **⊥251** reflecting a legitimate state interest, might properly be imposed upon those who chose to attend. Although the rights protected by the First and Fourteenth Amendments were presumed to include "the right to entertain the beliefs, to adhere to the principles and to teach the doctrines on which these students base their objections to the order prescribing military training," those Amendments were construed not to free such students from the military training obligations if they chose to attend the University. *Justices BRANDEIS, CARDOZO* and *STONE*, concurring separately, agreed that the requirement infringed no constitutionally protected liberties. They added, however, that the case presented no question under the Establishment Clause. The military instruction program was not an establishment since it in no way involved "instruction in the practice or tenets of a religion." Since the only question was one of free exercise, they concluded, like the majority, that the strong state interest in training a citizen militia justified the restraints imposed, at least so long as attendance at the University was voluntary.

Hamilton has not been overruled, although *United States* v. *Schwimmer* and *United States* v. *Macintosh*, upon which the Court in *Hamilton* relied, have since been overruled by *Girouard* v. *United States*. But if *Hamilton* retains any vitality with respect to higher education, we recognized its inapplicability to cognate questions in the public primary and secondary schools when we held in *West Virginia Board of Education* v. *Barnette* that a State had no power to expel from public schools students who refused on religious grounds to comply with a daily flag **⊥252** salute requirement. Of course, such a requirement was no more a law "respecting an establishment of religion" than the California law compelling the college students to take military training. The *Barnette* plaintiffs, moreover, did not ask that the whole exercise be enjoined, but only that an excuse or exemption be provided for those students whose religious beliefs forbade them to participate in the ceremony. The key to the holding that such a requirement abridged rights of free exercise lay in the fact that attendance at school was not voluntary but compulsory. The Court said "This issue is not prejudiced by the Court's previous holding that where a State, without compelling attendance, extends college facilities to pupils who voluntarily enroll, it may prescribe military training as part of the course without offense to the Constitution. . . . *Hamilton* v. *Regents*. In the present case attendance is not optional."

The *Barnette* decision made another significant point. The Court held that the State must make participation in the exercise voluntary for all students and not alone for those who found participation obnoxious on religious grounds. In short, there was simply no need to "inquire whether nonconformist beliefs will exempt from the duty to salute" because the Court found no state "power to make the salute a legal duty."

The distinctions between *Hamilton* and *Barnette* are, I think, crucial to the resolution of the cases before us. The different results of those cases are attributable only in part to a difference in the strength of the particular state interests which the respective statutes were designed to serve. Far more significant is the fact that *Hamilton* dealt with the voluntary attendance at college of young adults, while *Barnette* involved the compelled attendance **⊥253** of young children at elementary and secondary schools. This distinction warrants a difference in constitutional results. And it is with the involuntary attendance of young school children that we are exclusively concerned in the cases now before the Court.

III

No one questions that the Framers of the First Amendment intended to restrict exclusively the powers of the Federal Government. Whatever limitations that Amendment now imposes upon the States derive from the Fourteenth Amendment. The process of absorption of the religious guarantees of the First Amendment as protections against the States under the Fourteenth Amendment began with the Free Exercise Clause. In 1923 the Court held that the protections of the Fourteenth included at least a person's freedom "to worship God according to the dictates of his own conscience. . . ." *Meyer* v. *Nebraska*. *Cantwell* v. *Connecticut* completed in 1940 the process of absorption **⊥254** of the Free Exercise Clause and recognized its dual aspect: the Court affirmed freedom of belief as an absolute liberty, but recognized that conduct, while it may also be comprehended by the Free Exercise Clause, "remains subject to regulation for the protection of society." This was a distinction already drawn by *Reynolds* v. *United States*. From the beginning this Court has recognized that while government may regulate the behavioral manifestations of religious beliefs, it may not interfere at all with the beliefs themselves.

The absorption of the Establishment Clause has, however, come later and by a route less easily charted. It has been suggested, with some support in history, that absorption of the First Amendment's ban against congressional legislation "respecting an establishment of religion" is conceptually impossible because the Framers meant the Establishment Clause also to foreclose any attempt by Congress to disestablish the existing official state churches. Whether or not such was the understanding of the Framers and whether such a purpose would have inhibited the absorption of the Establishment Clause at the threshold of the Nineteenth Century are questions not dispositive of our present inquiry. For it is **⊥255** clear on the record of history that the last of the formal state establishments was dissolved more than three decades before the Fourteenth Amendment was ratified, and thus the problem of protecting official state churches from federal encroachments could hardly have been any concern of those who framed the post-Civil War Amendments. Any such objective of the First Amendment, having become historical anachronism by 1868, cannot be thought to have deterred the absorption of the Establishment Clause to any greater degree than it would, for example, have deterred the absorption of the Free Exercise Clause. That no organ of the Federal Government possessed in 1791 any power to restrain the interference of the States in religious matters is indisputable. It is equally plain, on the other hand, that the Fourteenth Amendment created a panoply of new federal rights for the protection of citizens of the various States. And among those rights was freedom from such state governmental involvement in the affairs of religion as the Establishment Clause had originally foreclosed on the part of Congress.

⊥256 It has also been suggested that the "liberty" guaranteed by the Fourteenth Amendment logically cannot absorb the Establishment Clause because that clause is not one of the provisions of the Bill of Rights which in terms protects a "freedom" of the individual. The fallacy in this contention, I think, is that it underestimates the role of the Establishment Clause as a co-guarantor, with the Free Exercise Clause, of religious liberty. The Framers did not entrust the liberty of religious beliefs to either clause alone. The Free Exercise Clause "was not to be the full extent of the Amendment's guarantee of freedom from governmental intrusion in matters of faith." *McGowan* v. *Maryland*.

Finally, it has been contended that absorption of the Establishment Clause is precluded by the absence of any intention on the part of the Framers of the Fourteenth Amendment to circumscribe the residual powers of the States to aid religious activities and institutions in ways which fell short of formal establishments. That argument relies in part upon the express terms of the **⊥257** abortive Blaine Amendment—proposed several years after the adoption of the Fourteenth Amendment—which would have added to the First Amendment a provision that "[n]o State shall make any law respecting an establishment of religion. . . ." Such a restriction would have been superfluous, it is said, if the Fourteenth Amendment had already made the Establishment Clause binding upon the States.

The argument proves too much, for the Fourteenth Amendment's protection of the free exercise of religion can hardly be questioned; yet the Blaine Amendment would also have added an explicit protection against state laws abridging that liberty. Even if we assume that the draftsmen of the Fourteenth Amendment saw no immediate connection between its protections against state action infringing personal liberty and the guarantees of the First Amendment, it is certainly too late in the day to suggest that their assumed inattention to the question dilutes the force of these constitutional guarantees in their application to the States. It is enough to conclude **⊥258** that the religious liberty embodied in the Fourteenth Amendment would not be viable if the Constitution were interpreted to forbid only establishments ordained by Congress.

⊥259 The issue of what particular activities the Establishment Clause forbids the States to undertake is our more immediate concern. In *Everson* v. *Board of Education*, a careful study of the relevant history led the Court to the view, consistently recognized in decisions since

Everson, that the Establishment Clause embodied the Framers' conclusion that government and religion have discrete interests which are mutually best served when each avoids too close a proximity to the other. It is not only the nonbeliever who fears the injection of sectarian doctrines and controversies into the civil polity, but in as high degree it is the devout believer who fears the secularization of a creed which becomes too deeply involved with and dependent upon the government. **⊥260** It has rightly been said of the history of the Establishment Clause that "our tradition of civil liberty rests not only on the secularism of a Thomas Jefferson but also on the fervent sectarianism . . . of a Roger Williams." Freund, The Supreme Court of the United States (1961), 84.

Our decisions on questions of religious education or exercises in the public schools have consistently reflected this dual aspect of the Establishment Clause. *Engel* v. *Vitale* unmistakably has its roots in three earlier cases which, on cognate issues, shaped the contours of the Establishment Clause. First, in *Everson* the Court held that reimbursement by the town of parents for the cost of transporting their children by public carrier to parochial (as well as public and private nonsectarian) schools did not offend the Establishment Clause. Such reimbursement, by easing the financial burden upon Catholic parents, may indirectly have fostered the operation of the Catholic schools, and may thereby indirectly have facilitated the teaching of Catholic principles, thus serving ultimately a religious goal. But this form of governmental assistance was difficult to distinguish from myriad other incidental if not insignificant government benefits enjoyed by religious institutions—fire and police protection, tax exemptions, and the pavement of streets and sidewalks, for example. "The State contributes no money to the schools. It does not support them. Its legislation, as applied, does no more than provide a general program to help parents get their children, regardless of their religion, safely and expeditiously to and from **⊥261** accredited schools." Yet even this form of assistance was thought by four Justices of the *Everson* Court to be barred by the Establishment Clause because too perilously close to that public support of religion forbidden by the First Amendment.

The other two cases, *Illinois ex rel. McCollum* v. *Board of Education* and *Zorach* v. *Clauson*, can best be considered together. Both involved programs of released time for religious instruction of public school students. I reject the suggestion that *Zorach* overruled *McCollum* in silence. The distinction which the Court drew in *Zorach* between the two cases is, in my view, faithful to the function of the Establishment Clause.

I should first note, however, that *McCollum* and *Zorach* do not seem to me distinguishable in terms of the free exercise claims advanced in both cases. The nonparticipant in the *McCollum* program was given secular instruction in a separate room during the times his classmates had religious lessons; the nonparticipant in any *Zorach* program also received secular instruction, while his classmates repaired to a place outside the school for religious instruction.

The crucial difference, I think, was that the *McCollum* program offended the Establishment Clause while the *Zorach* program did not. This was not, in my view, because of the difference in public expenditures involved. True, the *McCollum* program involved the regular use of school facilities, classrooms, heat and light and time from the regular school day—even though the actual **⊥262** incremental cost may have been negligible. All religious instruction under the *Zorach* program, by contrast, was carried on entirely off the school premises, and the teacher's part was simply to facilitate the children's release to the churches. The deeper difference was that the *McCollum* program placed the religious instructor in the public school classroom in precisely the position of authority held by the regular teachers of secular subjects, while the *Zorach* program did not. The *McCollum* pro**⊥263**gram, in lending to the support of sectarian instruction all the authority of the governmentally operated public school system, brought government and religion into that proximity which the Establishment Clause forbids. To be sure, a religious teacher presumably commands substantial respect and merits attention in his own right. But the Constitution does not permit that prestige and capacity for influence to be augmented by investiture of all the symbols of authority at the command of the lay teacher for the enhancement of secular instruction.

More recent decisions have further etched the contours of Establishment. In the *Sunday Law Cases*, we found in state laws compelling a uniform day of rest from worldly labor no violation of the Establishment Clause. The basic **⊥264** ground of our decision was that, granted the Sunday Laws were first enacted for religious ends, they were continued in force for reasons wholly secular, namely, to provide a universal day of rest and ensure the health and tranquillity of the community. In other words, government may originally have decreed a Sunday day of rest for the impermissible purpose of supporting religion but abandoned that purpose and retained the laws for the permissible purpose of furthering overwhelmingly secular ends.

Such was the evolution of the contours of the Establishment Clause before *Engel* v. *Vitale*. There, a year ago, we held that the daily recital of the state-composed Regents' Prayer constituted an establishment of religion because, although the prayer itself revealed no *sectarian* content or purpose, its nature and meaning were quite clearly *religious*. New York, in authorizing its recitation, had not maintained that distance between the public and the religious sectors commanded by the Establishment Clause when it placed the "power, prestige and financial support of government" behind the prayer. In *Engel*, as in *McCollum*, it did not matter that the amount of time and expense allocated to the daily recitation was small so long as the exercise itself was manifestly religious. Nor did it matter that few children had complained of the practice, for the measure of the seriousness of a breach of the Establishment Clause has never been thought to be the number of people who complain of it.

We also held two Terms ago in *Torcaso* v. *Watkins*, that a State may not constitutionally require an applicant for the office of Notary Public to swear or affirm that he believes in God. The problem of that case was strikingly similar to the issue presented 18 years before in the flag salute case, *West Virginia Board of Education* v. *Barnette*. In neither case was there any claim of establishment of religion, but only of infringement of **⊥265** the individual's religious liberty—in the one case, that of the nonbeliever who could not attest to a belief in God; in the other, that of the child whose creed forbade him to salute the flag. But *Torcaso* added a new element not present in *Barnette*. The Maryland test oath involved an attempt to employ essentially religious (albeit nonsectarian) means to achieve a secular goal to which the means bore no reasonable relationship. No one doubted the State's interest in the integrity of its Notaries Public, but that interest did not warrant the screening of applicants by means of a religious test. The *Sunday Law Cases* were different in that respect. Even if Sunday Laws retain certain religious vestiges, they are enforced today for essentially secular objectives which cannot be effectively achieved in modern society except by designating Sunday as the universal day of rest. The Court's opinions cited very substantial problems in selecting or enforcing an alternative day of rest. But the teaching of both *Torcaso* and the *Sunday Law Cases* is that government may not employ religious means to serve secular interests, however legitimate they may be, at least without the clearest demonstration that nonreligious means will not suffice.

IV

⊥266 I turn now to the cases before us. The religious nature of the exercises here challenged seems plain. Unless *Engel* v. *Vitale* is to be overruled, or we are to engage in wholly disingenuous distinction, we cannot sus**⊥267**tain these practices. Daily recital of the Lord's Prayer and the reading of passages of Scripture are quite as clearly breaches of the command of the Establishment Clause as was the daily use of the rather bland Regents' Prayer in the New York public schools. Indeed, I would suppose that, if anything, the Lord's Prayer and the Holy Bible are more clearly sectarian, and the present violations of the First Amendment consequently more serious. But the religious exercises challenged in these cases have a long history. And almost from the beginning, Bible reading and daily prayer in the schools have been the subject of debate, criticism by educators and other public officials, and proscription by courts and legislative councils. At the outset, then, we must carefully canvass both aspects of this history.

The use of prayers and Bible readings at the opening of the school day long antedates the founding of our Republic. The Rules of the New Haven Hopkins Grammar School required in 1684 "[t]hat the Scholars being **⊥268** called together, the Mr. shall every morning begin his work with a short prayer for a blessing on his Laboures and their learning. . . ." More rigorous was the provision in a 1682 contract with a Dutch schoolmaster in Flatbush, New York: "When the school begins, one of the children shall read the morning prayer, as it stands in the catechism, and close with the prayer before dinner; in the afternoon it shall begin with the prayer after dinner, and end with the evening prayer. The evening school shall begin with the Lord's prayer, and close by singing a psalm."

After the Revolution, the new States uniformly continued these long-established practices in the private and the few public grammar schools. The school committee of Boston in 1789 for example, required the city's several schoolmasters "daily to commence the duties of their office by prayer and reading a portion of the Sacred Scriptures. . . ." That requirement was mirrored throughout the original States, and exemplified the universal practice well into the nineteenth century. As the free public schools gradually supplanted the private academies and sectarian schools between 1800 and 1850, morning devotional exercises were retained with few alterations. Indeed, public pressures upon school administrators in many parts of the country would hardly have condoned abandonment of practices to which a century or more of private religious education had accustomed the American people. The controversy centered, in **⊥269** fact, principally about the elimination of plainly sectarian practices and textbooks, and led to the eventual substitution of nonsectarian, though still religious, exercises and materials.

Statutory provision for daily religious exercises is, however, of quite recent origin. At the turn of this century, there was but one State—Massachusetts—which had a law making morning prayer or Bible reading obligatory. Statutes elsewhere either permitted such practices or simply left the question to local option. It was not until after 1910 that 11 more States, within a few years, joined Massachusetts in making one or both exercises compulsory. The Pennsylvania law with which we are **⊥270** concerned in the *Schempp* case, for example, took effect in 1913; and even the Rule of the Baltimore School Board involved in the *Murray* case dates only from 1905. In no State has there ever been a constitutional or statutory prohibition against the recital of prayers or the reading of Scripture, although a number of States have outlawed these practices by judicial decision or administrative order. What is noteworthy about the panoply of state and local regulations from which these cases emerge is the relative recency of the statutory codification of practices which have ancient roots, and the rather small number of States which have ever prescribed compulsory religious exercises in the public schools.

The purposes underlying the adoption and perpetuation of these practices are somewhat complex. It is beyond question that the religious benefits and values realized from daily prayer and Bible reading have usually been considered paramount, and sufficient to justify the continuation of such practices. To Horace Mann, embroiled in an intense controversy over the role of sectarian instruction and textbooks in the Boston public schools, there was little question that the regular use of the Bible—which he thought essentially nonsectarian—would bear fruit in the spiritual enlightenment of his pupils. A contemporary of Mann's, the Commissioner of Education of a neighboring State, expressed a view which many enlightened educators of that day shared: "As a textbook of morals the Bible is pre-eminent, and should have a prominent place in our schools, ⊥**271** either as a reading book or as a source of appeal and instruction. Sectarianism, indeed, should not be countenanced in the schools; but the Bible is not sectarian. . . . The Scriptures should at least be read at the opening of the school, if no more. Prayer may also be offered with the happiest effects."

Wisconsin's Superintendent of Public Instruction, writing a few years later in 1858, reflected the attitude of his eastern colleagues, in that he regarded "with special favor the use of the Bible in public schools, as pre-eminently first in importance among text-books for teaching the noblest principles of virtue, morality, patriotism, and good order—love and reverence for God—charity and good will to man."

Such statements reveal the understanding of educators that the daily religious exercises in the schools served broader goals than compelling formal worship of God or fostering church attendance. The religious aims of the educators who adopted and retained such exercises were comprehensive, and in many cases quite devoid of sectarian bias—but the crucial fact is that they were nonetheless religious. While it has been suggested that daily prayer and reading of Scripture now serve secular goals as well, there can be no doubt that the origins of these practices were unambiguously religious, even where the educator's aim was not to win adherents to a particular creed or faith.

Almost from the beginning religious exercises in the public schools have been the subject of intense criticism, vigorous debate, and judicial or administrative prohibition. Significantly, educators and school boards ⊥**272** early entertained doubts about both the legality and the soundness of opening the school day with compulsory prayer or Bible reading. Particularly in the large Eastern cities, where immigration had exposed the public schools to religious diversities and conflicts unknown to the homogeneous academies of the eighteenth century, local authorities found it necessary even before the Civil War to seek an accommodation. In 1843, the Philadelphia School Board adopted the following resolutions:

"RESOLVED, that no children be required to attend or unite in the reading of the Bible in the Public Schools, whose parents are conscientiously opposed thereto:

"RESOLVED, that those children whose parents conscientiously prefer and desire any particular version of the Bible, without note or comment, be furnished with same."

A decade later, the Superintendent of Schools of New York State issued an even bolder decree that prayers could no longer be required as part of public school activities, and that where the King James Bible was read, Catholic students could not be compelled to attend. This type of accommodation was not restricted to the East Coast; the Cincinnati Board of Education resolved in 1869 that "religious instruction and the reading of religious books, including the Holy Bible, are prohibited in the common schools of Cincinnati, it being the true object and intent of this rule to allow the children of the parents of all sects and opinions, in matters of faith and worship, ⊥**273** to enjoy alike the benefit of the common-school fund." The Board repealed at the same time an earlier regulation which had required the singing of hymns and psalms to accompany the Bible reading at the start of the school day. And in 1889, one commentator ventured the view that "[t]here is not enough to be gained from Bible reading to justify the quarrel that has been raised over it."

Thus a great deal of controversy over religion in the public schools had preceded the debate over the Blaine Amendment, precipitated by President Grant's insistence that matters of religion should be left "to the family altar, the church, and the private school, supported entirely by private contributions." There was ample precedent, too, for Theodore Roosevelt's declaration that in the interest of "absolutely nonsectarian public schools" it was "not our business to have the Protestant Bible or the Catholic Vulgate or the Talmud read in those schools." The same principle appeared in the message of an Ohio Governor who vetoed a compulsory Bible-reading bill in 1925: "It is my belief that religious teaching in our homes, Sunday schools, churches, by the good ⊥**274** mothers, fathers, and ministers of Ohio is far preferable to compulsory teaching of religion by the state. The spirit of our federal and state constitutions from the beginning . . . [has] been to leave religious instruction to the discretion of parents."

The same theme has recurred in the opinions of the Attorneys General of several States holding religious exercises or instruction to be in violation of the state or federal constitutional command of separation of church and state. Thus the basic principle upon which our decision last year in *Engel* v. *Vitale* necessarily rested, and which we reaffirm today, can hardly be thought to be radical or novel.

Particularly relevant for our purposes are the decisions of the state courts on questions of religion in the public schools. Those decisions, while not, of course, authoritative in this Court, serve nevertheless to define the problem before us and to guide our inquiry. With the growth of religious diversity and the rise of vigorous dissent it was inevitable that the courts would be called upon to enjoin religious practices in the public schools which offended certain sects and groups. The earliest of such decisions declined to review the propriety of actions taken by school authorities, so long as those actions were within ⊥**275** the purview of the administrators' powers. Thus, where the local school board *required* religious exercises, the courts would not enjoin them, and where, as in at least one case, the school officials *forbade* devotional practices, the court refused on similar grounds to overrule that decision. Thus, whichever way the early cases came up, the governing principle of nearly complete deference to administrative discretion effectively foreclosed any consideration of constitutional questions.

The last quarter of the nineteenth century found the courts beginning to question the constitutionality of public school religious exercises. The legal context was still, of course, that of the state constitutions, since the First Amendment had not yet been held applicable to state action. And the state constitutional prohibitions against church-state cooperation or governmental aid to religion were generally less rigorous than the Establishment Clause of the First Amendment. It is therefore remarkable that the courts of a half dozen States found compulsory religious exercises in the public schools in violation of their respective state constitutions. These **⊥276** courts attributed much significance to the clearly religious origins and content of the challenged practices, and to the impossibility of avoiding sectarian controversy in their conduct. The Illinois Supreme Court expressed in 1910 the principles which characterized these decisions: "The public school is supported by the taxes which each citizen, regardless of his religion or his lack of it, is compelled to pay. The school, like the government, is simply a civil institution. It is secular, and not religious, in its purposes. The truths of the Bible are the truths of religion, which do not come within the province of the public school. . . . No one denies that they should be taught to the youth of the State. The constitution and the law do not interfere with such teaching, but they do banish theological polemics from the schools and the school districts. This is done, not from any hostility to religion, but because it is no part of the duty of the State to teach religion,—to take the money of all and apply it to teaching the children of all the religion of a part, only. Instruction in religion must be voluntary." *Ring* v. *Board of Education*.

The Supreme Court of South Dakota, in banning devotional exercises from the public schools of that State, also cautioned that "[t]he state as an educator must keep out of this field, and especially is this true in the common schools, where the child is immature, without fixed religious convictions. . . ." *Finger* v. *Weedman*.

⊥277 Even those state courts which have sustained devotional exercises under state law have usually recognized the primarily religious character of prayers and Bible readings. If such practices were not for that reason unconstitutional, it was necessarily because the state constitution forbade only public expenditures for *sectarian* instruction, or for activities which made the schoolhouse a "place of worship," but said nothing about the subtler question of laws "respecting an establishment of religion." Thus the panorama of history permits no **⊥278** other conclusion than that daily prayers and Bible readings in the public schools have always been designed to be, and have been regarded as, essentially religious exercises. Unlike the Sunday closing laws, these exercises appear neither to have been divorced from their religious origins nor deprived of their centrally religious character by the passage of time. On this distinction alone we might well rest a constitutional decision. But three further contentions have been pressed in the argument of these cases. These contentions deserve careful consideration, for if the position of the school authorities were correct in respect to any of them, we would be misapplying the principles of *Engel* v. *Vitale*.

A

First, it is argued that however clearly religious may have been the origins and early nature of daily prayer and Bible reading, these practices today serve so clearly secular educational purposes that their religious attributes may be overlooked. I do not doubt, for example, that morning devotional exercises may foster better discipline in the classroom, and elevate the spiritual level on which the school day opens. The Pennsylvania Superintendent of Public Instruction, testifying by deposition in the *Schempp* case, offered his view that daily Bible reading "places upon the children or those hearing the reading of this, and the atmosphere which goes on in the reading . . . one of the last vestiges of moral value **⊥279** that we have left in our school system." The exercise thus affords, the Superintendent concluded, "a strong contradiction to the materialistic trends of our time." Baltimore's Superintendent of Schools expressed a similar view of the practices challenged in the *Murray* case, to the effect that "[t]he acknowledgement of the existence of God as symbolized in the opening exercises establishes a discipline tone which tends to cause each individual pupil to constrain his overt acts and to consequently conform to accepted standards of behavior during his attendance at school." These views are by no means novel.

It is not the business of this Court to gainsay the judgments of experts on matters of pedagogy. Such decisions must be left to the discretion of those administrators charged with the supervision of the Nation's public schools. The limited province of the courts is to determine whether the means which the educators have chosen to achieve legitimate pedagogical ends infringe the constitutional freedoms of the First Amendment. The secular purposes which devotional exercises are said to serve fall into two categories—those which depend upon an immediately religious experience shared by the participating children; and those which appear sufficiently divorced from the religious content of the devotional material that they can be served equally by nonreligious **⊥280** materials. With respect to the first objective, much has been written about the moral and spiritual values of infusing some religious influence or instruction into the public school classroom. To the extent that only *religious* materials will serve this purpose, it seems to me that the purpose as well as the means is so plainly religious that the exercise is necessarily forbidden by the Establishment Clause. The fact that purely secular benefits may eventually result does not seem to me to justify the exercises, for similar indirect nonreligious benefits could no doubt have been claimed for the released time program invalidated in *McCollum*.

The second justification assumes that religious exercises at the start of the school day may directly serve solely secular ends—for example, by fostering harmony and tolerance among the pupils, enhancing the authority of the teacher, and inspiring better discipline. To the extent that such benefits result not from the content of the readings and recitation, but simply from the holding of such a solemn exercise at the opening assembly or the first class of the day, it would seem that less sensitive materials might equally well serve the same purpose. I have previously suggested that *Torcaso* and the *Sunday Law Cases* forbid the use of religious means to achieve sec- **⊥281** ular ends where nonreligious means will suffice. That principle is readily applied to these cases. It has not been shown that readings from the speeches and messages of great Americans, for example, or from the documents of our heritage of liberty, daily recitation of the Pledge of Allegiance, or even the observance of a moment of reverent silence at the opening of class, may not adequately serve the solely secular purposes of the devotional activities without jeopardizing either the religious liberties of any members of the community or the proper degree of separation between the spheres of religion and government. Such substitutes would, I think, be unsatisfactory or inadequate only to the extent that the present activities do in fact serve religious goals. While I do not question the judgment of experienced educators that the challenged practices may well achieve valuable secular ends, it seems to me that the State acts unconstitutionally if it either sets about to attain even indirectly religious ends by religious means, or if it uses religious means to serve secular ends where secular means would suffice.

B

Second, it is argued that the particular practices involved in the two cases before us are unobjectionable **⊥282** because they prefer no particular sect or sects at the expense of others. Both the Baltimore and Abington procedures permit, for example, the reading of any of several versions of the Bible, and this flexibility is said to ensure neutrality sufficiently to avoid the constitutional prohibition. One answer, which might be dispositive, is that any version of the Bible is inherently sectarian, else there would be no need to offer a system of rotation or alternation of versions in the first place, that is, to allow different sectarian versions to be used on different days. The sectarian character of the Holy Bible has been at the core of the whole controversy over religious practices in the public schools throughout its long and often bitter history. To **⊥283** vary the version as the Abington and Baltimore schools have done may well be less offensive than to read from the King James version every day, as once was the practice. But the result even of this relatively benign procedure is that majority sects are preferred in approximate proportion to their representation in the community and in the student body, while the smaller sects suffer commensurate discrimination. So long as the subject matter of the exercise is sectarian in character, these consequences cannot be avoided.

The argument contains, however, a more basic flaw. There are persons in every community—often deeply devout—to whom any version of the Judaeo-Christian Bible is offensive. There are others whose reverence for the Holy Scriptures demands private study or reflection and to whom public reading or recitation is sacrilegious, as one of the expert witnesses at the trial of the *Schempp* case explained. To such persons it is not the fact of using the Bible in the public schools, nor the content of any particular version, that is offensive, but only the manner in **⊥284** which it is used. For such persons, the anathema of public communion is even more pronounced when prayer is involved. Many deeply devout persons have always regarded prayer as a necessarily private experience. One Protestant group recently commented, for example: "When one thinks of prayer as sincere outreach of a **⊥285** human soul to the Creator, 'required prayer' becomes an absurdity." There is a similar problem with respect to comment upon the passages of Scripture which are to be read. Most present statutes forbid comment, and this practice accords with the views of many religious groups as to the manner in which the Bible should be read. However, as a recent survey discloses, scriptural passages read without comment frequently convey no message to the younger children in the school. Thus there has developed a practice in some schools of bridging the gap between faith and understanding by means of "definitions," even where "comment" is forbidden by statute. The present practice therefore poses a difficult dilemma: While Bible reading is almost universally required to be without comment, since only by such a prohibition can sectarian interpretation be excluded from the classroom, **⊥286** the rule breaks down at the point at which rudimentary definitions of Biblical terms are necessary for comprehension if the exercise is to be meaningful at all.

It has been suggested that a tentative solution to these problems may lie in the fashioning of a "common core" of theology tolerable to all creeds but preferential to none. But as one commentator has recently observed, "[h]istory is not encouraging to" those who hope to fashion a "common denominator of religion detached from its manifestation in any organized church." Sutherland, Establishment According to *Engel*, 76 Harv. L. Rev. 25, 51 (1962). Thus, the notion of a "common core" litany or supplication offends many deeply devout worshippers who do not find clearly sectarian practices objectionable. Father Gustave Weigel has recently expressed **⊥287** a widely shared view: "The moral code held by each separate religious community can reductively be unified, but the consistent particular believer wants no such reduction." And, as the American Council on Education warned several years ago, "The notion of a common core suggests a watering down of the several faiths to the point where common essentials appear. This might easily lead to a new sect—a public school sect—which would take its place alongside the existing faiths and compete with them." *Engel* is surely authority that nonsectarian religious practices, equally with sectarian exercises, violate the Establishment Clause. Moreover, even if the Establishment Clause were oblivious to nonsectarian religious practices, I think it quite likely that the "common core" approach would be sufficiently objectionable to many groups to be foreclosed by the prohibitions of the Free Exercise Clause.

C

A third element which is said to absolve the practices involved in these cases from the ban of the religious guarantees of the Constitution is the provision to excuse or exempt students who wish not to participate. Insofar as these practices are claimed to violate the Establishment ⊥**288** Clause, I find the answer which the District Court gave after our remand of *Schempp* to be altogether dispositive: "The fact that some pupils, or theoretically all pupils, might be excused from attendance at the exercises does not mitigate the obligatory nature of the ceremony. . . . The exercises are held in the school buildings and perforce are conducted by and under the authority of the local school authorities and during school sessions. Since the statute requires the reading of the 'Holy Bible,' a Christian document, the practice, as we said in our first opinion, prefers the Christian religion. The record demonstrates that it was the intention of the General Assembly of the Commonwealth of Pennsylvania to introduce a religious ceremony into the public schools of the Commonwealth."

Thus the short, and to me sufficient, answer is that the availability of excusal or exemption simply has no relevance to the establishment question, if it is once found that these practices are essentially religious exercises designed at least in part to achieve religious aims through the use of public school facilities during the school day.

The more difficult question, however, is whether the availability of excusal for the dissenting child serves to refute challenges to these practices under the Free Exercise Clause. While it is enough to decide these cases to dispose of the establishment questions, questions of free exercise are so inextricably interwoven into the history and present status of these practices as to justify disposition of this second aspect of the excusal issue. The answer is that the excusal procedure itself necessarily operates in such a way as to infringe the rights of free exercise of those children who wish to be excused. We have held in *Barnette* and *Torcaso*, respectively, that a State may require neither public school students nor candidates ⊥**289** for an office of public trust to profess beliefs offensive to religious principles. By the same token the State could not constitutionally require a student to profess publicly his disbelief as the prerequisite to the exercise of his constitutional right of abstention. And apart from *Torcaso* and *Barnette*, I think *Speiser* v. *Randall* suggests a further answer. We held there that a State may not condition the grant of a tax exemption upon the willingness of those entitled to the exemption to affirm their loyalty to the Government, even though the exemption was itself a matter of grace rather than of constitutional right. We concluded that to impose upon the eligible taxpayers the affirmative burden of proving their loyalty impermissibly jeopardized the freedom to engage in constitutionally protected activities close to the area to which the loyalty oath related. *Speiser* v. *Randall* seems to me to dispose of two aspects of the excusal or exemption procedure now before us. First, by requiring what is tantamount in the eyes of teachers and schoolmates to a profession of disbelief, or at least of nonconformity, the procedure may well deter those children who do not wish to participate for any reason based upon the dictates of conscience from exercising an indisputably constitutional right to be excused. Thus the excusal ⊥**290** provision in its operation subjects them to a cruel dilemma. In consequence, even devout children may well avoid claiming their right and simply continue to participate in exercises distasteful to them because of an understandable reluctance to be stigmatized as atheists or nonconformists simply on the basis of their request.

Such reluctance to seek exemption seems all the more likely in view of the fact that children are disinclined at this age to step out of line or to flout "peer group norms." Such is the widely held view of experts who have studied the behaviors and attitudes of children. This is also ⊥**291** the basis of Mr. *Justice FRANKFURTER's* answer to a similar contention made in the *McCollum* case: "That a child is offered an alternative may reduce the constraint; it does not eliminate the operation of influence by the school in matters sacred to conscience and outside the school's domain. The law of imitation operates, and nonconformity is not an ⊥**292** outstanding characteristic of children. The result is an obvious pressure upon children to attend. . . ."

⊥**293** *Speiser* v. *Randall* also suggests the answer to a further argument based on the excusal procedure. It has been suggested by the School Board, in *Schempp*, that we ought not pass upon the appellees' constitutional challenge at least until the children have availed themselves of the excusal procedure and found it inadequate to redress their grievances. Were the right to be excused not itself of constitutional stature, I might have some doubt about this issue. But we held in *Speiser* that the constitutional vice of the loyalty oath procedure discharged any obligation to seek the exemption before challenging the constitutionality of the conditions upon which it might have been denied. Similarly, we have held that one need not apply for a permit to distribute constitutionally protected literature, *Lovell* v. *Griffin*, or to deliver a speech, *Thomas* v. *Collins*, before he may attack the constitutionality of a licensing system of which the defect is patent. Insofar as these cases implicate only questions of establishment, it seems to me that the availability of an excuse is constitutionally irrelevant. Moreover, the excusal procedure seems to me to operate in such a way as to discourage the free exercise of religion on the part of those who might wish to utilize it, thereby rendering it unconstitutional in an additional and quite distinct respect.

To summarize my views concerning the merits of these two cases: The history, the purpose and the operation of the daily prayer recital and Bible reading leave no doubt that these practices standing by themselves constitute an impermissible breach of the Establishment Clause. Such devotional exercises may well serve legitimate nonreligious purposes. To the extent, however, that such pur⊥**294**poses are really without religious significance, it has never been demonstrated that secular means would not suffice. Indeed, I would suggest that patriotic or other nonreligious materials might provide adequate substitutes—inadequate only to the extent that the purposes now served are indeed directly or indirectly religious. Under such circumstances, the States may not employ religious means to reach a secular goal unless secular means are wholly unavailing. I therefore agree with the Court that the judgment in *Schempp* must be affirmed, and that in *Murray* must be reversed.

V

These considerations bring me to a final contention of the school officials in these cases: that the invalidation of the exercises at bar permits this Court no alternative but to declare unconstitutional every vestige, however slight, of cooperation or accommodation between religion and government. I cannot accept that contention. While it is not, of course, appropriate for this Court to decide questions not presently before it, I venture to suggest that religious exercises in the public schools present a unique problem. For not every involvement of religion in public life violates the Establishment Clause. Our decision in these cases does not clearly forecast anything about the constitutionality of other types of interdependence between religious and other public institutions.

Specifically, I believe that the line we must draw between the permissible and the impermissible is one which accords with history and faithfully reflects the understanding of the Founding Fathers. It is a line which the Court has consistently sought to mark in its decisions expounding the religious guarantees of the First Amendment. What the Framers meant to foreclose, and what our decisions under the Establishment Clause have for⊥**295**bidden, are those involvements of religious with secular institutions which (a) serve the essentially religious activities of religious institutions; (b) employ the organs of government for essentially religious purposes; or (c) use essentially religious means to serve governmental ends, where secular means would suffice. When the secular and religious institutions become involved in such a manner, there inhere in the relationship precisely those dangers—as much to church as to state—which the Framers feared would subvert religious liberty and the strength of a system of secular government. On the other hand, there may be myriad forms of involvements of government with religion which do not import such dangers and therefore should not, in my judgment, be deemed to violate the Establishment Clause. Nothing in the Constitution compels the organs of government to be blind to what everyone else perceives—that religious differences among Americans have important and pervasive implications for our society. Likewise nothing in the Establishment Clause forbids the application of legislation having purely secular ends in such a way as to alleviate burdens upon the free exercise of an individual's religious beliefs. Surely the Framers would never have understood that such a construction sanctions that involvement which violates the Establishment Clause. Such a conclusion can be reached, I would suggest, only by using the words of the First Amendment to defeat its very purpose.

The line between permissible and impermissible forms of involvement between government and religion has already been considered by the lower federal and state courts. I think a brief survey of certain of these forms of accommodation will reveal that the First Amendment commands not official hostility toward religion, but only a strict neutrality in matters of religion. Moreover, it may serve to suggest that the scope of our holding today ⊥**296** is to be measured by the special circumstances under which these cases have arisen, and by the particular dangers to church and state which religious exercises in the public schools present. It may be helpful for purposes of analysis to group these other practices and forms of accommodation into several rough categories.

A. *The Conflict Between Establishment and Free Exercise.*—There are certain practices, conceivably violative of the Establishment Clause, the striking down of which might seriously interfere with certain religious liberties also protected by the First Amendment. Provisions for churches and chaplains at military establishments for those in the armed services may afford one such example. ⊥**297** The like provision by state and federal governments for chaplains in penal institutions may afford another example. It is argued that such provisions may be assumed to contravene the Establishment Clause, yet be sustained on constitutional grounds as necessary to secure to the members of the Armed Forces and prisoners those rights of worship guaranteed under the Free Exercise Clause. Since government has deprived such persons of the oppor⊥**298**tunity to practice their faith at places of their choice, the argument runs, government may, in order to avoid infringing the free exercise guarantees, provide substitutes where it requires such persons to be. Such a principle might support, for example, the constitutionality of draft exemptions for ministers and divinity students; of the excusal of children from school on their respective religious holidays; and of the allowance by government of temporary use of public buildings by religious organizations when their own churches have become unavailable because of a disaster or emergency.

Such activities and practices seem distinguishable from the sponsorship of daily Bible reading and prayer recital.

For one thing, there is no element of coercion present in the appointment of military or prison chaplains; the soldier or convict who declines the opportunities for worship would not ordinarily subject himself to the suspicion or obloquy of his peers. Of special significance to this distinction is the fact that we are here usually deal⊥**299**ing with adults, not with impressionable children as in the public schools. Moreover, the school exercises are not designed to provide the pupils with general opportunities for worship denied them by the legal obligation to attend school. The student's compelled presence in school for five days a week in no way renders the regular religious facilities of the community less accessible to him than they are to others. The situation of the school child is therefore plainly unlike that of the isolated soldier or the prisoner.

The State must be steadfastly neutral in all matters of faith, and neither favor nor inhibit religion. In my view, government cannot sponsor religious exercises in the public schools without jeopardizing that neutrality. On the other hand, hostility, not neutrality, would characterize the refusal to provide chaplains and places of worship for prisoners and soldiers cut off by the State from all civilian opportunities for public communion, the withholding of draft exemptions for ministers and conscientious objectors, or the denial of the temporary use of an empty public building to a congregation whose place of worship has been destroyed by fire or flood. I do not say that government must provide chaplains or draft exemptions, or that the courts should intercede if it fails to do so.

B. *Establishment and Exercises in Legislative Bodies*.—The saying of invocational prayers in legislative chambers, state or federal, and the appointment of legislative chaplains, might well represent no involvements of the kind prohibited by the Establishment Clause. Legislators, federal and state, are mature adults who may presumably absent themselves from such public and cere⊥**300**monial exercises without incurring any penalty, direct or indirect. It may also be sufficient that, at least in the case of the Congress, Art. I, § 5, of the Constitution makes each House the monitor of the "Rules of its Proceedings" so that it is at least arguable whether such matters present "political questions" the resolution of which is exclusively confided to Congress. Finally, there is the difficult question of who may be heard to challenge such practices.

C. *Non-Devotional Use of the Bible in the Public Schools*.—The holding of the Court today plainly does not foreclose teaching about the Holy Scriptures or about the differences between religious sects in classes in literature or history. Indeed, whether or not the Bible is involved, it would be impossible to teach meaningfully many subjects in the social sciences or the humanities without some mention of religion. To what extent, and at what points in the curriculum, religious materials should be cited are matters which the courts ought to entrust very largely to the experienced officials who superintend our Nation's public schools. They are experts in such matters, and we are not. We should heed Mr. *Justice JACKSON's* caveat that any attempt by this Court to announce curricular standards would be "to decree a uniform, rigid and, if we are consistent, an unchanging standard for countless school boards represent⊥**301**ing and serving highly localized groups which not only differ from each other but which themselves from time to time change attitudes." *Illinois ex rel. McCollum* v. *Board of Education*.

We do not, however, in my view usurp the jurisdiction of school administrators by holding as we do today that morning devotional exercises in any form are constitutionally invalid. But there is no occasion now to go further and anticipate problems we cannot judge with the material now before us. Any attempt to impose rigid limits upon the mention of God or references to the Bible in the classroom would be fraught with dangers. If it should sometime hereafter be shown that in fact religion can play no part in the teaching of a given subject without resurrecting the ghost of the practices we strike down today, it will then be time enough to consider questions we must now defer.

D. *Uniform Tax Exemptions Incidentally Available to Religious Institutions*.—Nothing we hold today questions the propriety of certain tax deductions or exemptions which incidentally benefit churches and religious institutions, along with many secular charities and nonprofit organizations. If religious institutions benefit, it is in spite of rather than because of their religious character. For religious institutions simply share benefits which government makes generally available to educational, charitable, and eleemosynary groups. There is no indication that taxing authorities have used such benefits in any way to subsidize worship or foster belief in God. And as ⊥**302** among religious beneficiaries, the tax exemption or deduction can be truly nondiscriminatory, available on equal terms to small as well as large religious bodies, to popular and unpopular sects, and to those organizations which reject as well as those which accept a belief in God.

E. *Religious Considerations in Public Welfare Programs*.—Since government may not support or directly aid religious *activities* without violating the Establishment Clause, there might be some doubt whether nondiscriminatory programs of governmental aid may constitutionally include *individuals* who become eligible wholly or partially for religious reasons. For example, it might be suggested that where a State provides unemployment compensation generally to those who are unable to find suitable work, it may not extend such benefits to persons who are unemployed by reason of religious beliefs or practices without thereby establishing the religion to which those persons belong. Therefore, the argument runs, the State may avoid an establishment only by singling out and excluding such persons on the ground that religious beliefs or practices have made them potential beneficiaries. Such a construction would, it seems to me, require government to impose religious discriminations and disabilities, thereby jeopardizing the free exercise of religion, in order to avoid what is thought to constitute an establishment.

The inescapable flaw in the argument, I suggest, is its quite unrealistic view of the aims of the Establishment Clause. The Framers were not concerned with the effects of certain incidental aids to individual worshippers which come about as byproducts of general and nondiscriminatory welfare programs. If such benefits serve to make ⊥**303** easier or less expensive the practice of a particular creed, or of all religions, it can hardly be said that the purpose of the program is in any way religious, or that the consequence of its nondiscriminatory application is to create the forbidden degree of interdependence between secular and sectarian institutions. I cannot therefore accept the suggestion, which seems to me implicit in the argument outlined here, that every judicial or administrative construction which is designed to prevent a public welfare program from abridging the free exercise of religious beliefs, is for that reason *ipso facto* an establishment of religion.

F. *Activities Which, Though Religious in Origin, Have Ceased to Have Religious Meaning*.—As we noted in our *Sunday Law* decisions, nearly every criminal law on the books can be traced to some religious principle or inspiration. But that does not make the present enforcement of the criminal law in any sense an establishment of religion, simply because it accords with widely held religious principles. As we said in *McGowan* v. *Maryland*, "the 'Establishment' Clause does not ban federal or state regulation of conduct whose reason or effect merely happens to coincide or harmonize with the tenets of some or all religions." This rationale suggests that the use of the motto "In God We Trust" on currency, on documents and public buildings and the like may not offend the clause. It is not that the use of those four words can be dismissed as "de minimis"—for I suspect there would be intense opposition to the abandonment of that motto. The truth is that we have simply interwoven the motto so deeply into the fabric of our civil polity that its present use may well not present that type of involvement which the First Amendment prohibits.

This general principle might also serve to insulate the various patriotic exercises and activities used in the public schools and elsewhere which, whatever may have been ⊥**304** their origins, no longer have a religious purpose or meaning. The reference to divinity in the revised pledge of allegiance, for example, may merely recognize the historical fact that our Nation was believed to have been founded "under God." Thus reciting the pledge may be no more of a religious exercise than the reading aloud of Lincoln's Gettysburg Address, which contains an allusion to the same historical fact.

The principles which we reaffirm and apply today can hardly be thought novel or radical. They are, in truth, as old as the Republic itself, and have always been as integral a part of the First Amendment as the very words of that charter of religious liberty. No less applicable today than they were when first pronounced a century ago, one year after the very first court decision involving religious exercises in the public schools, are the words of a distinguished Chief Justice of the Commonwealth of Pennsylvania, Jeremiah S. Black: "The manifest object of the men who framed the institutions of this country, was to have a *State without religion*, and a *Church without politics*—that is to say, they meant that one should never be used as an engine for any purpose of the other, and that no man's rights in one should be tested by his opinions about the other. As the Church takes no note of men's political differences, so the State looks with equal eye on all the modes of religious faith. . . . Our fathers seem to have been perfectly sincere in their belief that the members of the Church would be more patriotic, and the citizens of the State more religious, by keeping their respective functions entirely separate." Essay on Religious Liberty, in Black, ed., Essays and Speeches of Jeremiah S. Black, (1886), 53.

⊥**305** Mr. *Justice* GOLDBERG, with whom Mr. *Justice* HARLAN joins, concurring.

As is apparent from the opinions filed today, delineation of the constitutionally permissible relationship between religion and government is a most difficult and sensitive task, calling for the careful exercise of both judicial and public judgment and restraint. The considerations which lead the Court today to interdict the clearly religious practices, presented in these cases are to me wholly compelling; I have no doubt as to the propriety of the decision and therefore join the opinion and judgment of the Court. The singular sensitivity and concern which surround both the legal and practical judgments involved impel me, however, to add a few words in further explication, while at the same time avoiding repetition of the carefully and ably framed examination of history and authority by my Brethren.

The First Amendment's guarantees, as applied to the States through the Fourteenth Amendment, foreclose not only laws "respecting an establishment of religion" but also those "prohibiting the free exercise thereof." These two proscriptions are to be read together, and in light of the single end which they are designed to serve. The basic purpose of the religion clause of the First Amendment is to promote and assure the fullest possible scope of religious liberty and tolerance for all and to nurture the conditions which secure the best hope of attainment of that end.

The fullest realization of true religious liberty requires that government neither engage in nor compel religious practices, that it effect no favoritism among sects or between religion and nonreligion, and that it work deterrence of no religious belief. But devotion even to these simply stated objectives presents no easy course, for the unavoidable accommodations necessary to achieve the ⊥**306** maximum enjoyment of each and all of them are often difficult of discernment. There is for me no simple and clear measure which by precise application can readily and invariably demark the permissible from the impermissible.

It is said, and I agree, that the attitude of government toward religion must be one of neutrality. But untutored devotion to the concept of neutrality can lead to invocation or approval of results which partake not simply of that noninterference and noninvolvement with the religious which the Constitution commands, but of a brooding and pervasive devotion to the secular and a passive, or even active, hostility to the religious. Such results are not only not compelled by the Constitution, but, it seems to me, are prohibited by it.

Neither government nor this Court can or should ignore the significance of the fact that a vast portion of our people believe in and worship God and that many of our legal, political and personal values derive historically from religious teachings. Government must inevitably take cognizance of the existence of religion and, indeed, under certain circumstances the First Amendment may require that it do so. And it seems clear to me from the opinions in the present and past cases that the Court would recognize the propriety of providing military chaplains and of the teaching *about* religion, as distinguished from the teaching *of* religion, in the public schools. The examples could readily be multiplied, for both the required and the permissible accommodations between state and church frame the relation as one free of hostility or favor and productive of religious and political harmony, but without undue involvement of one in the concerns or practices of the other. To be sure, the judgment in each case is a delicate one, but it must be made if we are to do loyal service as judges to the ultimate First Amendment objective of religious liberty.

⊥**307** The practices here involved do not fall within any sensible or acceptable concept of compelled or permitted accommodation and involve the state so significantly and directly in the realm of the sectarian as to give rise to those very divisive influences and inhibitions of freedom which both religion clauses of the First Amendment preclude. The state has ordained and has utilized its facilities to engage in unmistakably religious exercises—the devotional reading and recitation of the Holy Bible—in a manner having substantial and significant import and impact. That it has selected, rather than written, a particular devotional liturgy seems to me without constitutional import. The pervasive religiosity and direct governmental involvement inhering in the prescription of prayer and Bible reading in the public schools, during and as part of the curricular day, involving young impressionable children whose school attendance is statutorily compelled, and utilizing the prestige, power, and influence of school administration, staff, and authority, cannot realistically be termed simply accommodation, and must fall within the interdiction of the First Amendment. I find nothing in the opinion of the Court which says more than this. And, of course, today's decision does not mean that all incidents of government which import of the religious are therefore and without more banned by the strictures of the Establishment Clause. As the Court declared only last Term in *Engel* v. *Vitale:* "There is of course nothing in the decision reached here that is inconsistent with the fact that school children and others are officially encouraged to express love for our country by reciting historical documents such as the Declaration of Independence which contain references to the Deity or by singing officially espoused anthems which include the composer's professions of faith in a Supreme Being, or ⊥**308** with the fact that there are many manifestations in our public life of belief in God. Such patriotic or ceremonial occasions bear no true resemblance to the unquestioned religious exercise that the State . . . has sponsored in this instance."

The First Amendment does not prohibit practices which by any realistic measure create none of the dangers which it is designed to prevent and which do not so directly or substantially involve the state in religious exercises or in the favoring of religion as to have meaningful and practical impact. It is of course true that great consequences can grow from small beginnings, but the measure of constitutional adjudication is the ability and willingness to distinguish between real threat and mere shadow.

Mr. *Justice* STEWART, dissenting.

I think the records in the two cases before us are so fundamentally deficient as to make impossible an informed or responsible determination of the constitutional issues presented. Specifically, I cannot agree that on these records we can say that the Establishment Clause has necessarily been violated. But I think there exist serious questions under both that provision and the Free Exercise Clause—insofar as each is imbedded in the Fourteenth Amendment—which require the remand of these cases for the taking of additional evidence.

I

The First Amendment declares that "Congress shall make no law respecting an establishment of religion, or prohibiting the free exercise thereof. . . ." It is, I ⊥**309** think, a fallacious oversimplification to regard these two provisions as establishing a single constitutional standard of "separation of church and state," which can be mechanically applied in every case to delineate the required boundaries between government and religion. We err in the first place if we do not recognize, as a matter of history and as a matter of the imperatives of our free society, that religion and government must necessarily interact in countless ways. Secondly, the fact is that while in many contexts the Establishment Clause and the Free Exercise Clause fully complement each other, there are areas in which a doctrinaire reading of the Establishment Clause leads to irreconcilable conflict with the Free Exercise Clause.

A single obvious example should suffice to make the point. Spending federal funds to employ chaplains for the armed forces might be said to violate the Establishment Clause. Yet a lonely soldier stationed at some faraway outpost could surely complain that a government which did not provide him the opportunity for pastoral guidance was affirmatively prohibiting the free exercise of his religion. And such examples could readily be multiplied. The short of the matter is simply that the two relevant clauses of the First Amendment cannot accurately be reflected in a sterile metaphor which by its very nature may distort rather than illumine the problems involved in a particular case.

II

As a matter of history, the First Amendment was adopted solely as a limitation upon the newly created National Government. The events leading to its adoption strongly suggest that the Establishment Clause was primarily an attempt to insure that Congress not only would be powerless to establish a national church, but ⊥**310** would also be unable to interfere with existing state establishments. Each State was left free to go its own way and pursue its own policy with respect to religion. Thus Virginia from the beginning pursued a policy of disestablishmentarianism. Massachusetts, by contrast, had an established church until well into the nineteenth century.

So matters stood until the adoption of the Fourteenth Amendment, or more accurately, until this Court's decision in *Cantwell* v. *Connecticut*, in 1940. In that case the Court said "The First Amendment declares that Congress shall make no law respecting an establishment of religion or prohibiting the free exercise thereof. The Fourteenth Amendment has rendered the legislatures of the states as incompetent as Congress to enact such laws."

I accept without question that the liberty guaranteed by the Fourteenth Amendment against impairment by the States embraces in full the right of free exercise of religion protected by the First Amendment, and I yield to no one in my conception of the breadth of that freedom. I accept too the proposition that the Fourteenth Amendment has somehow absorbed the Establishment Clause, although it is not without irony that a constitutional provision evidently designed to leave the States free to go their own way should now have become a restriction upon their autonomy. But I cannot agree with what seems to me the insensitive definition of the Establishment Clause contained in the Court's opinion, nor with the different but, I think, equally mechanistic definitions contained in the separate opinions which have been filed.

III

⊥**311** Since the *Cantwell* pronouncement in 1940, this Court has only twice held invalid state laws on the ground that they were laws "respecting an establishment of religion" in violation of the Fourteenth Amendment: *McCollum* v. *Board of Education; Engel* v. *Vitale*. On the other hand, the Court has upheld against such a challenge laws establishing Sunday as a compulsory day of rest, and a law authorizing reimbursement from public funds for the transportation of parochial school pupils.

Unlike other First Amendment guarantees, there is an inherent limitation upon the applicability of the Establishment Clause's ban on state support to religion. That limitation was succinctly put in *Everson* v. *Board of Education*. "State power is no more to be used so as to handicap religions than it is to favor them." And in a later case, this Court recognized that the limitation was one which was itself compelled by the free exercise guarantee. "To hold that a state cannot consistently with the First and Fourteenth Amendments utilize its public school system to aid any or all religious faiths or sects in the dissemination of their doctrines and ideals does not . . . manifest a governmental hostility to religion or religious teachings. A manifestation of such hostility would be at war with our national tradition as embodied in the First Amendment's guaranty of the free ⊥**312** exercise of religion." *McCollum* v. *Board of Education*.

That the central value embodied in the First Amendment—and, more particularly, in the guarantee of "liberty" contained in the Fourteenth—is the safeguarding of an individual's right to free exercise of his religion has been consistently recognized. Thus, in the case of *Hamilton* v. *Regents*, Mr. *Justice* CARDOZO, concurring, assumed that it was ". . . *the religious liberty* protected by the First Amendment against invasion by the nation [which] is protected by the Fourteenth Amendment against invasion by the states." And in *Cantwell* v. *Connecticut* the purpose of those guarantees was described in the following terms: "On the one hand, it forestalls compulsion by law of the acceptance of any creed or the practice of any form of worship. Freedom of conscience and freedom to adhere to such religious organization or form of worship as the individual may choose cannot be restricted by law. On the other hand, it safeguards the free exercise of the chosen form of religion."

It is this concept of constitutional protection embodied in our decisions which makes the cases before us such difficult ones for me. For there is involved in these cases a substantial free exercise claim on the part of those who affirmatively desire to have their children's school day open with the reading of passages from the Bible.

It has become accepted that the decision in *Pierce* v. *Society of Sisters*, upholding the right of parents to send their children to nonpublic schools, was ultimately based upon the recognition of the validity of the free exercise claim involved in that situation. It might be argued here that parents who wanted their children to be exposed to religious influences in school could, under *Pierce*, send their children to private or parochial ⊥**313** schools. But the consideration which renders this contention too facile to be determinative has already been recognized by the Court: "Freedom of speech, freedom of the press, freedom of religion are available to all, not merely to those who can pay their own way." *Murdock* v. *Pennsylvania*.

It might also be argued that parents who want their children exposed to religious influences can adequately fulfill that wish off school property and outside school time. With all its surface persuasiveness, however, this argument seriously misconceives the basic constitutional justification for permitting the exercises at issue in these cases. For a compulsory state educational system so structures a child's life that if religious exercises are held to be an impermissible activity in schools, religion is placed at an artificial and state-created disadvantage. Viewed in this light, permission of such exercises for those who want them is necessary if the schools are truly to be neutral in the matter of religion. And a refusal to permit religious exercises thus is seen, not as the realization of state neutrality, but rather as the establishment of a religion of secularism, or at the least, as government support of the beliefs of those who think that religious exercises should be conducted only in private.

What seems to me to be of paramount importance, then, is recognition of the fact that the claim advanced here in favor of Bible reading is sufficiently substantial to make simple reference to the constitutional phrase "establishment of religion" as inadequate an analysis of the cases before us as the ritualistic invocation of the nonconstitutional phrase "separation of church and state." What these cases compel, rather, is an analysis of just what the "neutrality" is which is required by the interplay of the Establishment and Free Exercise Clauses of the First Amendment, as imbedded in the Fourteenth.

IV

⊥**314** Our decisions make clear that there is no constitutional bar to the use of government property for religious purposes. On the contrary, this Court has consistently held that the discriminatory barring of religious groups from public property is itself a violation of First and Fourteenth Amendment guarantees. A different standard has been applied to public school property, because of the coercive effect which the use by religious sects of a compulsory school system would necessarily have upon the children involved. But insofar as the *McCollum* decision rests on the Establishment rather than the Free Exercise Clause, it is clear that its effect is limited to religious instruction—to government support of proselytizing activities of religious sects by throwing the weight of secular authority behind the dissemination of religious tenets.

The dangers both to government and to religion inherent in official support of instruction in the tenets of various religious sects are absent in the present cases, which involve only a reading from the Bible unaccompanied by comments which might otherwise constitute instruction. Indeed, since, from all that appears in either record, any teacher who does not wish to do so is free not to participate, it cannot even be contended that some ⊥**315** infinitesimal part of the salaries paid by the State are made contingent upon the performance of a religious function.

In the absence of evidence that the legislature or school board intended to prohibit local schools from substituting a different set of readings where parents requested such a change, we should not assume that the provisions before us—as actually administered—may not be construed simply as authorizing religious exercises, nor that the designations may not be treated simply as indications of the promulgating body's view as to the community's preference. We are under a duty to interpret these provisions so as to render them constitutional if reasonably possible. In the *Schempp* case there is evidence which indicates that variations were in fact permitted by the very school there involved, and that further variations were not introduced only because of the absence of requests from parents. And in the *Murray* case the Baltimore rule itself contains a provision permitting another version of the Bible to be substituted for the King James version.

If the provisions are not so construed, I think that their validity under the Establishment Clause would be extremely doubtful, because of the designation of a particular religious book and a denominational prayer. But since, even if the provisions are construed as I believe they must be, I think that the cases before us must be remanded for further evidence on other issues—thus affording the plaintiffs an opportunity to prove that local variations are not in fact permitted—I shall for the bal⊥**316**ance of this dissenting opinion treat the provisions before us as making the variety and content of the exercises, as well as a choice as to their implementation, matters which ultimately reflect the consensus of each local school community. In the absence of coercion upon those who do not wish to participate—because they hold less strong beliefs, or no beliefs at all—such provisions cannot, in my view, be held to represent the type of support of religion barred by the Establishment Clause. For the only support which such rules provide for religion is the withholding of state hostility—a simple acknowledgment on the part of secular authorities that the Constitution does not require extirpation of all expression of religious belief.

V

I have said that these provisions authorizing religious exercises are properly to be regarded as measures making possible the free exercise of religion. But it is important to stress that, strictly speaking, what is at issue here is a privilege rather than a right. In other words, the question presented is not whether exercises such as those at issue here are constitutionally compelled, but rather whether they are constitutionally invalid. And that issue, in my view, turns on the question of coercion.

It is clear that the dangers of coercion involved in the holding of religious exercises in a schoolroom differ qualitatively from those presented by the use of similar exercises or affirmations in ceremonies attended by adults. Even as to children, however, the duty laid upon government in connection with religious exercises in the public schools is that of refraining from so structuring the school environment as to put any kind of pressure on a child to participate in those exercises; it is not that of providing an atmosphere in which children are kept scrupulously insulated from any awareness that some of their fellows

⊥**317** may want to open the school day with prayer, or of the fact that there exist in our pluralistic society differences of religious belief.

These are not, it must be stressed, cases like *Brown* v. *Board of Education*, in which this Court held that, in the sphere of public education, the Fourteenth Amendment's guarantee of equal protection of the laws required that race not be treated as a relevant factor. A segregated school system is not invalid because its operation is coercive; it is invalid simply because our Constitution presupposes that men are created equal, and that therefore racial differences cannot provide a valid basis for governmental action. Accommodation of religious differences on the part of the State, however, is not only permitted but required by that same Constitution.

The governmental neutrality which the First and Fourteenth Amendments require in the cases before us, in other words, is the extension of evenhanded treatment to all who believe, doubt, or disbelieve—a refusal on the part of the State to weight the scales of private choice. In these cases, therefore, what is involved is not state action based on impermissible categories, but rather an attempt by the State to accommodate those differences which the existence in our society of a variety of religious beliefs makes inevitable. The Constitution requires that such efforts be struck down only if they are proven to entail the use of the secular authority of government to coerce a preference among such beliefs.

It may well be, as has been argued to us, that even the supposed benefits to be derived from noncoercive religious exercises in public schools are incommensurate with the administrative problems which they would create. The choice involved, however, is one for each local community and its school board, and not for this Court. For, as I have said, religious exercises are not constitutionally invalid if they simply reflect differences which exist in the ⊥**318** society from which the school draws its pupils. They become constitutionally invalid only if their administration places the sanction of secular authority behind one or more particular religious or irreligious beliefs.

To be specific, it seems to me clear that certain types of exercises would permit situations in which no possibility of coercion on the part of secular officials could be claimed to exist. Thus, if such exercises were held either before or after the official school day, or if the school schedule were such that participation were merely one among a number of desirable alternatives, it could hardly be contended that the exercises did anything more than to provide an opportunity for the voluntary expression of religious belief. On the other hand, a law which provided for religious exercises during the school day and which contained no excusal provision would obviously be unconstitutionally coercive upon those who did not wish to participate. And even under a law containing an excusal provision, if the exercises were held during the school day, and no equally desirable alternative were provided by the school authorities, the likelihood that children might be under at least some psychological compulsion to participate would be great. In a case such as the latter, however, I think we would err if we *assumed* such coercion in the absence of any evidence.

VI

⊥**319** Viewed in this light, it seems to me clear that the records in both of the cases before us are wholly inadequate to support an informed or responsible decision. Both cases involve provisions which explicitly permit any student who wishes, to be excused from participation in the exercises. There is no evidence in either case as to whether there would exist any coercion of any kind upon a student who did not want to participate. No evidence at all was adduced in the *Murray case*, because it was decided upon a demurrer. All that we have in that case, therefore, is the conclusory language of a pleading. While such conclusory allegations are acceptable for procedural purposes, I think that the nature of the constitutional problem involved here clearly demands that no decision be made except upon evidence. In the *Schempp* case the record shows no more than a subjective prophecy by a parent of what he thought would happen if a request were made to be excused from participation in the exercises under the amended statute. No such request was ever made, and there is no evidence whatever as to what might or would actually happen, nor of what administrative arrangements the school actually might or could make to free from pressure of any kind those who do not want to participate in the exercises. There were no District Court findings on this issue, since the case under the amended statute was decided exclusively on Establishment Clause grounds.

What our Constitution indispensably protects is the freedom of each of us, be he Jew or Agnostic, Christian or ⊥**320** Atheist, Buddhist or Freethinker, to believe or disbelieve, to worship or not worship, to pray or keep silent, according to his own conscience, uncoerced and unrestrained by government. It is conceivable that these school boards, or even all school boards, might eventually find it impossible to administer a system of religious exercises during school hours in such a way as to meet this constitutional standard—in such a way as completely to free from any kind of official coercion those who do not affirmatively want to participate. But I think we must not assume that school boards so lack the qualities of inventiveness and good will as to make impossible the achievement of that goal.

I would remand both cases for further hearings.

EPPERSON v. ARKANSAS

393 U.S. 97

ON APPEAL FROM THE SUPREME COURT OF ARKANSAS

Argued October 16, 1968 — Decided November 12, 1968

⊥**98** Mr. *Justice FORTAS* delivered the opinion of the Court.

I

This appeal challenges the constitutionality of the "anti-evolution" statute which the State of Arkansas adopted in 1928 to prohibit the teaching in its public schools and universities of the theory that man evolved from other species of life. The statute was a product of the upsurge of "fundamentalist" religious fervor of the twenties. The Arkansas statute was an adaptation of the famous Tennessee "monkey law" which that State adopted in 1925. The constitutionality of the Tennessee law was upheld by the Tennessee Supreme Court in the celebrated *Scopes* case of 1927.

The Arkansas law makes it unlawful for a teacher in any state-sponsored school or university "to teach the ⊥**99** theory or doctrine that mankind ascended or descended from a lower order of animals," or "to adopt or use in any such institution a textbook that teaches" this theory. Violation is a misdemeanor and subjects the violator to dismissal from his position.

The present case concerns the teaching of biology in a high school in Little Rock. According to the testimony, until the events here in litigation, the official textbook furnished for the high school biology course did not have a section on the Darwinian Theory. Then, for the academic year 1965-1966, the school administration, on recommendation of the teachers of biology in the school system, adopted and prescribed a textbook which contained a chapter setting forth "the theory about the origin . . . of man from a lower form of animal."

⊥**100** Susan Epperson, a young woman who graduated from Arkansas' school system and then obtained her master's degree in zoology at the University of Illinois, was employed by the Little Rock school system in the fall of 1964 to teach 10th grade biology at Central High School. At the start of the next academic year, 1965, she was confronted by the new textbook (which one surmises from the record was not unwelcome to her). She faced at least a literal dilemma because she was supposed to use the new textbook for classroom instruction and presumably to teach the statutorily condemned chapter; but to do so would be a criminal offense and subject her to dismissal.

She instituted the present action in the Chancery Court of the State, seeking a declaration that the Arkansas statute is void and enjoining the State and the defendant officials of the Little Rock school system from dismissing her for violation of the statute's provisions.

The Chancery Court held that the statute violated the Fourteenth Amendment to the United States Constitution. The court noted that this Amendment encompasses the prohibitions upon state interference with freedom of speech and thought which are contained in the First Amendment. Accordingly, it held that the challenged statute is unconstitutional because, in violation of the First Amendment, it "tends to hinder the quest for knowledge, restrict the freedom to learn, and restrain the freedom to teach." In this perspective, the Act, ⊥**101** it held, was an unconstitutional and void restraint upon the freedom of speech guaranteed by the Constitution.

On appeal, the Supreme Court of Arkansas reversed. Its two-sentence opinion is set forth in the margin.* It sustained the statute as an exercise of the State's power to specify the curriculum in public schools. It did not address itself to the competing constitutional considerations.

Appeal was duly prosecuted to this Court. Only Arkansas and Mississippi have such "anti-evolution" or "monkey" laws on their books. There is no record of any prosecutions in Arkan⊥**102**sas under its statute. It is possible that the statute is presently more of a curiosity than a vital fact of life in these States. Nevertheless, the present case was brought, the appeal as of right is properly here, and it is our duty to decide the issues presented.

II

At the outset, it is urged upon us that the challenged statute is vague and uncertain and therefore within the condemnation of the Due Process Clause of the Fourteenth Amendment. The contention that the Act is vague and uncertain is supported by language in the brief opinion of Arkansas' Supreme Court. . . .

⊥**103** In any event, we do not rest our decision upon the asserted vagueness of the statute. On either interpretation of its language, Arkansas' statute cannot stand. It is of no moment whether the law is deemed to prohibit mention of Darwin's theory, or to forbid any or all of the infinite varieties of communication embraced within the term "teaching." Under either interpretation, the law must be stricken because of its conflict with the constitutional prohibition of state laws respecting an establishment of religion or prohibiting the free exercise thereof. The overriding fact is that Arkansas' law selects from the body of knowledge a particular segment which it proscribes for the sole reason that it is deemed to conflict with a particular religious doctrine; that is, with a particular interpretation of the Book of Genesis by a particular religious group.

III

The antecedents of today's decision are many and unmistakable. They are rooted in the foundation soil of our Nation. They are fundamental to freedom.

Government in our democracy, state and national, must be neutral in matters of religious theory, doctrine, ⊥**104** and practice. It may not be hostile to any religion or to the

*"Per Curiam. Upon the principal issue, that of constitutionality, the court holds that Initiated Measure No. 1 of 1928 is a valid exercise of the state's power to specify the curriculum in its public schools. The court expresses no opinion on the question whether the Act prohibits any explanation of the theory of evolution or merely prohibits teaching that the theory is true; the answer not being necessary to a decision in the case, and the issue not having been raised.

"The decree is reversed and the cause dismissed."

advocacy of no-religion; and it may not aid, foster, or promote one religion or religious theory against another or even against the militant opposite. The First Amendment mandates governmental neutrality between religion and religion, and between religion and nonreligion.

As early as 1872, this Court said "The law knows no heresy, and is committed to the support of no dogma, the establishment of no sect." *Watson* v. *Jones*. This has been the interpretation of the great First Amendment which this Court has applied in the many and subtle problems which the ferment of our national life has presented for decision within the Amendment's broad command.

Judicial interposition in the operation of the public school system of the Nation raises problems requiring care and restraint. Our courts, however, have not failed to apply the First Amendment's mandate in our educational system where essential to safeguard the fundamental values of freedom of speech and inquiry and of belief. By and large, public education in our Nation is committed to the control of state and local authorities. Courts do not and cannot intervene in the resolution of conflicts which arise in the daily operation of school systems and which do not directly and sharply implicate basic constitutional values. On the other hand, "[t]he vigilant protection of constitutional freedoms is nowhere more vital than in the community of American schools," *Shelton* v. *Tucker*. As this ⊥**105** Court said in *Keyishian* v. *Board of Regents*, the First Amendment "does not tolerate laws that cast a pall of orthodoxy over the classroom. . . ."

⊥**106** There is and can be no doubt that the First Amendment does not permit the State to require that teaching and learning must be tailored to the principles or prohibitions of any religious sect or dogma. In *Everson* v. *Board of Education*, this Court, in upholding a state law to provide free bus service to school children, including those attending parochial schools, said: "Neither [a State nor the Federal Government] can pass laws which aid one religion, aid all religions, or prefer one religion over another."

At the following Term of Court, in *McCollum* v. *Board of Education*, the Court held that Illinois could not release pupils from class to attend classes of instruction in the school buildings in the religion of their choice. This, it said, would involve the State in using tax-supported property for religious purposes, thereby breaching the "wall of separation" which, according to Jefferson, the First Amendment was intended to erect between church and state. While study of religions and of the Bible from a literary and historic viewpoint, presented objectively as part of a secular program of education, need not collide with the First Amendment's prohibition, the State may not adopt programs or practices in its public schools or colleges which "aid or oppose" any religion. This prohibition is absolute. It forbids alike the preference of a religious doctrine or the prohibition ⊥**107** of theory which is deemed antagonistic to a particular dogma. As Mr. Justice CLARK stated in *Joseph Burstyn, Inc.* v. *Wilson*, "the state has no legitimate interest in protecting any or all religions from views distasteful to them. . . ." The test was stated as follows in *Abirigton School District* v. *Schempp*: "[W]hat are the purpose and the primary effect of the enactment? If either is the advancement or inhibition of religion then the enactment exceeds the scope of legislative power as circumscribed by the Constitution."

These precedents inevitably determine the result in the present case. The State's undoubted right to prescribe the curriculum for its public schools does not carry with it the right to prohibit, on pain of criminal penalty, the teaching of a scientific theory or doctrine where that prohibition is based upon reasons that violate the First Amendment. It is much too late to argue that the State may impose upon the teachers in its schools any conditions that it chooses, however restrictive they may be of constitutional guarantees.

In the present case, there can be no doubt that Arkansas has sought to prevent its teachers from discussing the theory of evolution because it is contrary to the belief of some that the Book of Genesis must be the exclusive source of doctrine as to the origin of man. No suggestion has been made that Arkansas' law may be justified by considerations of state policy other than the religious views of some of its citizens. It is clear ⊥**108** that fundamentalist sectarian conviction was and is the law's reason for existence. Its antecedent, Tennessee's "monkey law," candidly stated its purpose: to make it unlawful "to teach any theory that denies the story of the Divine Creation of man as taught in the Bible, and to teach instead that man has descended from a ⊥**109** lower order of animals." Perhaps the sensational publicity attendant upon the *Scopes* trial induced Arkansas to adopt less explicit language. It eliminated Tennessee's reference to "the story of the Divine Creation of man" as taught in the Bible, but there is no doubt that the motivation for the law was the same: to suppress the teaching of a theory which, it was thought, "denied" the divine creation of man.

Arkansas' law cannot be defended as an act of religious neutrality. Arkansas did not seek to excise from the curricula of its schools and universities all discussion of the origin of man. The law's effort was confined to an attempt to blot out a particular theory because of its supposed conflict with the Biblical account, literally read. Plainly, the law is contrary to the mandate of the First, and in violation of the Fourteenth, Amendment to the Constitution.

The judgment of the Supreme Court of Arkansas is *Reversed*.

Mr. *Justice* BLACK, concurring.

I am by no means sure that this case presents a genuine justiciable case or controversy. Although Arkansas Initiated Act No. 1, the statute alleged to be unconstitutional, was passed by the voters of Arkansas in 1928, we are informed that there has never been even a single attempt by the State to enforce it. And the pallid, unenthusiastic, even apologetic defense of the Act presented by the State in this Court indicates that the State would make no attempt to enforce the law ⊥**110** should it remain on the books for the next century. Now, nearly 40 years after the law has slumbered on the books as though dead, a teacher alleging fear that the state might arouse from its lethargy and try to punish her has asked for a declaratory judgment holding the law unconstitutional. She was subsequently joined by a parent who alleged his interest in seeing that his two then school-age sons "be informed of all scientific theories and hypotheses. . . ." But whether this Arkansas teacher is still a teacher, fearful of punishment under the Act, we do not know. It may be, as has been published in the daily press, that she has long since given up her job as a teacher and moved to a distant city, thereby escaping the dangers she had imagined might befall her under this lifeless Arkansas Act. And there is not one iota of concrete evidence to show that the parent-intervenor's sons have not been or will not be taught about evolution. The textbook adopted for use in biology classes in Little Rock includes an entire chapter dealing with evolution. There is no evidence that this chapter is not being freely taught in the schools that use the textbook and no evidence that the intervenor's sons, who were 15 and 17 years old when this suit was brought three years ago, are still in high school or yet to take biology. Unfortunately, however, the State's languid interest in the case has not prompted it to keep this Court informed concerning facts that might easily justify dismissal of this alleged lawsuit as moot or as lacking the qualities of a genuine case or controversy.

Notwithstanding my own doubts as to whether the case presents a justiciable controversy, the Court brushes aside these doubts and leaps headlong into the middle of the very broad problems involved in federal intrusion into state powers to decide what subjects and schoolbooks it may wish to use in teaching state pupils. While I hesitate to enter into the consideration and deci⊥**111** sion of such sensitive state-federal relationships, I reluctantly acquiesce. But, agreeing to consider this as a genuine case or controversy, I cannot agree to thrust the Federal Government's long arm the least bit further into state school curriculums than decision of this particular case requires. And the Court, in order to invalidate the Arkansas law as a violation of the First Amendment, has been compelled to give the State's law a broader meaning than the State Supreme Court was willing to give it. . . .

⊥**112** It seems to me that in this situation the statute is too vague for us to strike it down on any ground but that: vagueness. Under this statute as construed by the Arkansas Supreme Court, a teacher cannot know whether he is forbidden to mention Darwin's theory at all or only free to discuss it as long as he refrains from contending that it is true. It is an established rule that a statute which leaves an ordinary man so doubtful about its meaning that he cannot know when he has violated it denies him the first essential of due process. Holding the statute too vague to enforce would not only follow longstanding constitutional precedents but it would avoid having this Court take unto itself the duty of a State's highest court to interpret and mark the boundaries of the State's laws. And, more important, it would not place this Court in the unenviable position of violating the principle of leaving the States absolutely free to choose their own curriculums for their own schools so long as their action does not palpably conflict with a clear constitutional command.

The Court, not content to strike down this Arkansas Act on the unchallengeable ground of its plain vagueness, chooses rather to invalidate it as a violation of the Establishment of Religion Clause of the First Amendment. I would not decide this case on such a sweeping ground for the following reasons, among others.

1. In the first place I find it difficult to agree with the Court's statement that "there can be no doubt that Arkansas has sought to prevent its teachers from discussing the theory of evolution because it is contrary to the belief of some that the Book of Genesis must be the exclusive source of doctrine as to the origin of man." It may be instead that the people's motive was merely that it would be best to remove this contro⊥**113**versial subject from its schools; there is no reason I can imagine why a State is without power to withdraw from its curriculum any subject deemed too emotional and controversial for its public schools. And this Court has consistently held that it is not for us to invalidate a statute because of our views that the "motives" behind its passage were improper; it is simply too difficult to determine what those motives were.

2. A second question that arises for me is whether this Court's decision forbidding a State to exclude the subject of evolution from its schools infringes the religious freedom of those who consider evolution an anti-religious doctrine. If the theory is considered anti-religious, as the Court indicates, how can the State be bound by the Federal Constitution to permit its teachers to advocate such an "anti-religious" doctrine to schoolchildren? The very cases cited by the Court as supporting its conclusion hold that the State must be neutral, not favoring one religious or anti-religious view over another. The Darwinian theory is said to challenge the Bible's story of creation; so too have some of those who believe in the Bible, along with many others, challenged the Darwinian theory. Since there is no indication that the literal Biblical doctrine of the origin of man is included in the curriculum of Arkansas schools, does not the removal of the subject of evolution leave the State in a neutral position toward these supposedly competing religious and anti-religious doctrines? Unless this Court is prepared simply to write off as pure nonsense the views of those who consider evolution an anti-religious doctrine, then this issue presents problems under the Establishment Clause far more troublesome than are discussed in the Court's opinion.

3. I am also not ready to hold that a person hired to teach school children takes with him into the classroom

a constitutional right to teach sociological, economic, ⊥**114** political, or religious subjects that the school's managers do not want discussed. This Court has said that the rights of free speech "while fundamental in our democratic society, still do not mean that everyone with opinions or beliefs to express may address a group at any public place and at any time." I question whether it is absolutely certain, as the Court's opinion indicates, that "academic freedom" permits a teacher to breach his contractual agreement to teach only the subjects designated by the school authorities who hired him.

Certainly the Darwinian theory, precisely like the Genesis story of the creation of man, is not above challenge. In fact the Darwinian theory has not merely been criticized by religionists but by scientists, and perhaps no scientist would be willing to take an oath and swear that everything announced in the Darwinian theory is unquestionably true. The Court, it seems to me, makes a serious mistake in bypassing the plain, unconstitutional vagueness of this statute in order to reach out and decide this troublesome, to me, First Amendment question. However wise this Court may be or may become hereafter, it is doubtful that, sitting in Washington, it can successfully supervise and censor the curriculum of every public school in every hamlet and city in the United States. I doubt that our wisdom is so nearly infallible.

I would either strike down the Arkansas Act as too vague to enforce, or remand to the State Supreme Court for clarification of its holding and opinion.

Mr. *Justice* HARLAN, concurring.

I think it deplorable that this case should have come to us with such an opaque opinion by the State's highest court. With all respect, that court's handling of the ⊥**115** case savors of a studied effort to avoid coming to grips with this anachronistic statute and "to pass the buck" to this Court. This sort of temporizing does not make for healthy operations between the state and federal judiciaries. Despite these observations, I am in agreement with this Court's opinion that, the constitutional claims having been properly raised and necessarily decided below, resolution of the matter by us cannot properly be avoided.

I concur in so much of the Court's opinion as holds that the Arkansas statute constitutes an "establishment of religion" forbidden to the States by the Fourteenth Amendment. I do not understand, however, why the Court finds it necessary to explore at length appellants' contentions that the statute is unconstitutionally vague and that it interferes with free speech, only to conclude that these issues need not be decided in this case. In the process of not deciding them, the Court obscures its otherwise straightforward holding, and opens its opinion to possible implications from which I am constrained to disassociate myself.

Mr. *Justice* STEWART, concurring in the result.

The States are most assuredly free "to choose their own curriculums for their own schools." A State is en⊥**116**tirely free, for example, to decide that the only foreign language to be taught in its public school system shall be Spanish. But would a State be constitutionally free to punish a teacher for letting his students know that other languages are also spoken in the world? I think not.

It is one thing for a State to determine that "the subject of higher mathematics, or astronomy, or biology" shall or shall not be included in its public school curriculum. It is quite another thing for a State to make it a criminal offense for a public school teacher so much as to mention the very existence of an entire system of respected human thought. That kind of criminal law, I think, would clearly impinge upon the guarantees of free communication contained in the First Amendment, and made applicable to the States by the Fourteenth.

The Arkansas Supreme Court has said that the statute before us may or may not be just such a law. The result, as Mr. *Justice* BLACK points out, is that "a teacher cannot know whether he is forbidden to mention Darwin's theory at all." Since I believe that no State could constitutionally forbid a teacher "to mention Darwin's theory at all," and since Arkansas may, or may not, have done just that, I conclude that the statute before us is so vague as to be invalid under the Fourteenth Amendment.

STONE v. GRAHAM

449 U.S. 39
ON WRIT OF CERTIORARI TO THE SUPREME COURT OF
THE STATE OF KENTUCKY
Without Argument Decided November 17, 1980

⊥**39** *PER CURIAM.*

A Kentucky statute requires the posting of a copy of the Ten Commandments, purchased with private contributions, on the wall of each public classroom in the State. Peti⊥**40**tioners, claiming that this statute violates the Establishment and Free Exercise Clauses of the First Amendment, sought an injunction against its enforcement. The state trial court upheld the statute, finding that its "avowed purpose" was "secular and not religious," and that the statute would "neither advance nor inhibit any religion or religious group" nor involve the State excessively in religious matters. The Supreme Court of the Commonwealth of Kentucky affirmed by an equally divided court. *Stone* v. *Graham*. We reverse.

This Court has announced a three-part test for determining whether a challenged state statute is permissible under the Establishment Clause of the United States Constitution: "First, the statute must have a secular legislative purpose; second, its principal or primary effect must be one that neither advances nor inhibits religion . . . ; finally the statute must not foster 'an excessive government entanglement with religion.'" *Lemon* v. *Kurtzman*.

If a statute violates any of these three principles, it must be ⊥41 struck down under the Establishment Clause. We conclude that Kentucky's statute requiring the posting of the Ten Commandments in public schoolrooms had no secular legislative purpose, and is therefore unconstitutional.

The Commonwealth insists that the statute in question serves a secular legislative purpose, observing that the legislature required the following notation in small print at the bottom of each display of the Ten Commandments: "The secular application of the Ten Commandments is clearly seen in its adoption as the fundamental legal code of Western Civilization and the Common Law of the United States."

The trial court found the "avowed" purpose of the statute to be secular, even as it labeled the statutory declaration "self-serving." Under this Court's rulings, however, such an "avowed" secular purpose is not sufficient to avoid conflict with the First Amendment. In *Abington School District* v. *Schempp* this Court held unconstitutional the daily reading of Bible verses and the Lord's Prayer in the public schools, despite the school district's assertion of such secular purposes as "the promotion of moral values, the contradiction to the materialistic trends of our times, the perpetuation of our institutions and the teaching of literature."

The pre-eminent purpose for posting the Ten Commandments on schoolroom walls is plainly religious in nature. The Ten Commandments is undeniably a sacred text in the Jewish and Christian faiths, and no legislative recitation of a supposed secular purpose can blind us to that fact. The Commandments do not confine themselves to arguably secular matters, such as honoring one's parents, killing or murder, ⊥42 adultery, stealing, false witness, and covetousness. Rather, the first part of the Commandments concerns the religious duties of believers: worshipping the Lord God alone, avoiding idolatry, not using the Lord's name in vain, and observing the sabbath day.

This is not a case in which the Ten Commandments are integrated into the school curriculum, where the Bible may constitutionally be used in an appropriate study of history, civilization, ethics, comparative religion, or the like. *Abington School District* v. *Schempp*. Posting of religious texts on the wall serves no such educational function. If the posted copies of the Ten Commandments are to have any effect at all, it will be to induce the school children to read, meditate upon, perhaps to venerate and obey, the Commandments. However desirable this might be as a matter of private devotion, it is not a permissible state objective under the Establishment Clause.

It does not matter that the posted copies of the Ten Commandments are financed by voluntary private contributions, for the mere posting of the copies under the auspices of the legislature provides the "official support of the State . . . Government" that the Establishment Clause prohibits. Nor is it significant that the Bible verses involved in this case are merely posted on the wall, rather than read aloud as in *Schempp* and *Engel*, for "it is no defense to urge that the religious practices here may be relatively minor encroachments on the First Amendment." *Abington School District* v. *Schempp*. We conclude that Ky. Rev. ⊥43 Stat. § 158.178 (1980) violates the first part of the *Lemon* v. *Kurtzman* test and thus the Establishment Clause of the Constitution.

The petition for a writ of certiorari is granted and the judgment below is reversed.

The CHIEF JUSTICE and *Justice BLACKMUN* dissent. They would grant certiorari and give this case plenary consideration.

Justice STEWART dissents from this summary reversal of the courts of Kentucky, which, so far as appears, applied wholly correct constitutional criteria in reaching their decisions.

Justice REHNQUIST, dissenting.

With no support beyond its own *ipse dixit*, the Court concludes that the Kentucky statute involved in this case "has *no* secular legislative purpose," (emphasis supplied), and that "[t]he pre-eminent purpose for posting the Ten Commandments on schoolroom walls is plainly religious in nature." This even though, as the trial court found, "[t]he General Assembly thought the statute had a secular legislative purpose and specifically said so." The Court's summary rejection of a secular purpose articulated by the legislature and confirmed by the state court is without precedent in Establishment Clause jurisprudence. This Court regularly looks to legislative articulations of a statute's purpose in Establishment Clause cases ⊥44 and accords such pronouncements the deference they are due. See, *e.g.*, *Committee for Public Education* v. *Nyquist*, ("we need touch only briefly on the requirement of a 'secular legislative purpose.' As the recitation of legislative purposes appended to New York's law indicates, each measure is adequately supported by legitimate, nonsectarian state interests"); *Lemon* v. *Kurtzman*, ("the statutes themselves clearly state they are intended to enhance the quality of the secular education"); *Sloan* v. *Lemon*; *Board of Education* v. *Allen*. See also *Florey* v. *Sioux Falls School District* (upholding rules permitting public school Christmas observances with religious elements as promoting the articulated secular purpose of "advanc[ing] the student's knowledge and appreciation of the role that our religious heritage has played in the social, cultural and historical development of civilization"). The fact that the asserted secular purpose may overlap with what some may see as a religious objective does not render it unconstitutional. As this Court stated in *McGowan* v. *Maryland*, in upholding the validity of Sunday closing laws, "the present purpose and effect of most of [these laws] is to provide a uniform day of rest for all citizens; the fact that this day is Sunday, a day of particular significance for the dominant Christian sects, does not bar the state from achieving its secular goals."

Abington School District v. *Schempp*, repeatedly cited by the Court, is not to the contrary. No statutory findings of secular purpose supported the challenged enactments in that case. In one of the two cases considered in *Abington School District* the trial court had determined that the challenged exercises were intended by the State to be religious exercises. A contrary finding is presented here. In the other case no specific finding had been ⊥**45** made, and "the religious character of the exercise was admitted by the State."

The Court rejects the secular purpose articulated by the State because the Decalogue "is undeniably a sacred text." It is equally undeniable, however, as the elected representatives of Kentucky determined, that the Ten Commandments have had a significant impact on the development of secular legal codes of the western world. The trial court concluded that evidence submitted substantiated this determination. See also *Anderson* v. *Salt Lake City Corp*. (upholding construction on public land of monument inscribed with Ten Commandments because they have "substantial secular attributes"). Certainly the State was permitted to conclude that a document with such secular significance should be placed before its students, with an appropriate statement of the document's secular import. ("It does not seem reasonable to require removal of a passive monument, involving no compulsion, because its accepted precepts, as a foundation for law, reflect the religious nature of an ancient era.") See also *Opinion of the Justices* (upholding placement of plaques with the motto "In God We Trust" in public schools).

The Establishment Clause does not require that the public sector be insulated from all things which may have a religious ⊥**46** significance or origin. This Court has recognized that "religion has been closely identified with our history and government," *Abington School District*, and that "[t]he history of man is inseparable from the history of religion," *Engel* v. *Vitale*. Kentucky has decided to make students aware of this fact by demonstrating the secular impact of the Ten Commandments. The words of Mr. *Justice JACKSON*, concurring in *McCollum* v. *Board of Education*, merit quotation at length: "I think it remains to be demonstrated whether it is possible, even if desirable, to comply with such demands as plaintiff's completely to isolate and cast out of secular education all that some people may reasonably regard as religious instruction. Perhaps subjects such as mathematics, physics or chemistry are, or can be, completely secularized. But it would not seem practical to teach either practice or appreciation of the arts if we are to forbid exposure of youth to any religious influences. Music without sacred music, architecture minus the cathedral, or painting without the scriptural themes would be eccentric and incomplete, even from a secular point of view. . . . I should suppose it is a proper, if not an indispensable, part of preparation for a worldly life to know the roles that religion and religions have played in the tragic story of mankind. The fact is that, for good or for ill, nearly everything in our culture worth transmitting, everything which gives meaning to life, is saturated with religious influences, derived from paganism, Judaism, Christianity—both Catholic and Protestant—and other faiths accepted by a large part of the world's peoples. One can hardly respect the system of education that would leave the student wholly ignorant of the currents of religious thought that move the world society for a part in which he is being prepared."

⊥**47** I therefore dissent from what I cannot refrain from describing as a cavalier summary reversal, without benefit of oral argument or briefs on the merits, of the highest court of Kentucky.

WALLACE v. JAFFREE

472 U.S. 38
ON APPEAL FROM THE UNITED STATES
COURT OF APPEALS
FOR THE ELEVENTH CIRCUIT
Argued December 4, 1984 — Decided June 4, 1985

⊥**40** *Justice STEVENS* delivered the opinion of the Court.

At an early stage of this litigation, the constitutionality of three Alabama statutes was questioned: (1) § 16-1-20, enacted in 1978, which authorized a one-minute period of silence in all public schools "for meditation"; (2) § 16-1-20.1, enacted in 1981, which authorized a period of silence "for meditation or voluntary prayer"; and (3) § 16-1-20.2, enacted in 1982, which authorized teachers to lead "willing students" in a prescribed prayer to "Almighty God . . . the Creator and Supreme Judge of the world." ⊥**41**

At the preliminary injunction stage of this case, the District Court distinguished § 16-1-20 from the other two statutes. It then held that there was "nothing wrong" with § 16-1-20, but that §§ 16-1-20.1 and 16-1-20.2 were both invalid because the sole purpose of both was "an effort on the part of the State of Alabama to encourage a religious activity." After the trial on the merits, the District Court did not change its interpretation of these two statutes, but held that they were constitutional because, in its opinion, Alabama has the power to establish a state religion if it chooses to do so.

The Court of Appeals agreed with the District Court's initial interpretation of the purpose of both §§ 16-1-20.1 and 16-1-20.2, and held them both unconstitutional. We have already affirmed the Court of Appeals' holding with respect to § 16-1-20.2. 466 U.S. 924 (1984). Moreover, appellees have not questioned the holding that § 16-1-20 is valid. Thus, the narrow question for decision is whether § 16-1-20.1, which authorizes a period of silence for "meditation or voluntary prayer," is a ⊥**42** law respecting the establishment of religion within the meaning of the First Amendment.

I

Appellee Ishmael Jaffree is a resident of Mobile County, Alabama. On May 28, 1982, he filed a complaint on behalf of three of his minor children; two of them were second-grade students and the third was then in kindergarten. The complaint named members of the Mobile County School Board, various school officials, and the minor plaintiffs' three teachers as defendants. The complaint alleged that the appellees brought the action "seeking principally a declaratory judgment and an injunction restraining the Defendants and each of them from maintaining or allowing the maintenance of regular religious prayer services or other forms of religious observances in the Mobile County Public Schools in violation of the First Amendment as made applicable to states by the Fourteenth Amendment to the United States Constitution." The complaint further alleged that two of the children had been subjected to various acts of religious indoctrination "from the beginning of the school year in September, 1981"; that the defendant teachers had "on a daily basis" led their classes in saying certain prayers in unison; that the minor children were exposed to ostracism from their peer group class members if they did not participate; and that Ishmael Jaffree had repeatedly but unsuccessfully requested that the devotional services be stopped. The original complaint made no reference to any Alabama statute. **⊥43**

On June 4, 1982, appellees filed an amended complaint seeking class certification, and on June 30, 1982, they filed a second amended complaint naming the Governor of Alabama and various State officials as additional defendants. In that amendment the appellees challenged the constitutionality of three Alabama statutes: §§ 16-1-20, 16-1-20.1, 16-1-20.2.

On August 2, 1982, the District Court held an evidentiary hearing on appellees' motion for a preliminary injunction. At that hearing, State Senator Donald G. Holmes testified that he was the "prime sponsor" of the bill that was enacted in 1981 as § 161-20.1. He explained that the bill was an "effort to return voluntary prayer to our public schools . . . it is a beginning and a step in the right direction." Apart from the purpose to return voluntary prayer to public school, Senator Holmes unequivocally testified that he had "no other purpose in mind." A week after the hearing, the District Court entered a preliminary injunction. The court held that appellees were likely to prevail on the merits because the enactment of §§ 16-1-20.1 and 16-1-20.2 did not reflect a clearly secular purpose. **⊥44**

In November 1982, the District Court held a four-day trial on the merits. The evidence related primarily to the 1981-1982 academic year—the year after the enactment of § 16-1-20.1 and prior to the enactment of § 16-1-20.2. The District Court found that during that academic year each of the minor plaintiffs' teachers had led classes in prayer activities, even after being informed of appellees' objections to these activities.

In its lengthy conclusions of law, the District Court reviewed a number of opinions of this Court interpreting **⊥45** the Establishment Clause of the First Amendment, and then embarked on a fresh examination of the question whether the First Amendment imposes any barrier to the establishment of an official religion by the State of Alabama. After reviewing at length what it perceived to be newly discovered historical evidence, the District Court concluded that "the establishment clause of the first amendment to the United States Constitution does not prohibit the state from establishing a religion." 554 F. Supp. 1104 at 1128 (1983). In a separate opinion, the District Court dismissed appellees' challenge to the three Alabama statutes because of a failure to state any claim for which relief could be granted. The court's dismissal of this challenge was also based on its conclusion that the Establishment Clause did not bar the States from establishing a religion. 554 F. Supp. 1130 (1983) **⊥46**

The Court of Appeals consolidated the two cases; not surprisingly, it reversed. The Court of Appeals noted that this Court had considered and had rejected the historical argu**⊥47**ments that the District Court found persuasive, and that the District Court had misapplied the doctrine of *stare decisis*. The Court of Appeals then held that the teachers' religious activities violated the Establishment Clause of the First Amendment. With respect to § 16-1-20.1 and § 16-1-20.2, the Court of Appeals stated that "both statutes advance and encourage religious activities." The Court of Appeals then quoted with approval the District Court's finding that § 16-1-20.1, and § 16-1-20.2, were efforts "'to encourage a religious activity. Even though these statutes are permissive in form, it is nevertheless state involvement respecting an establishment of religion.'" Thus, the Court of Appeals concluded that both statutes were "specifically the type which the Supreme Court addressed in *Engel* v. *Vitale*." 705 F. Supp. 1526 at 1535 (1983) **⊥48**

A suggestion for rehearing *en banc* was denied over the dissent of four judges who expressed the opinion that the full court should reconsider the panel decision insofar as it held § 16-1-20.1 unconstitutional. When this Court noted probable jurisdiction, it limited argument to the question that those four judges thought worthy of reconsideration. The judgment of the Court of Appeals with respect to the other issues presented by the appeals was affirmed.

II

Our unanimous affirmance of the Court of Appeals' judgment concerning § 16-1-20.2 makes it unnecessary to comment at length on the District Court's remarkable conclusion that the Federal Constitution imposes no obstacle to Alabama's establishment of a state religion. Before analyzing the precise issue that is presented to us, it is nevertheless appropriate to recall how firmly embedded in our constitutional jurisprudence is the proposition that the several States have no greater power to restrain the individual freedoms ⊥49 protected by the First Amendment than does the Congress of the United States.

As is plain from its text, the First Amendment was adopted to curtail the power of Congress to interfere with the individual's freedom to believe, to worship, and to express himself in accordance with the dictates of his own conscience. Until the Fourteenth Amendment was added to the Constitution, the First Amendment's restraints on the exercise of federal power simply did not apply to the States. But when the Constitution was amended to prohibit any State from depriving any person of liberty without due process of law, that Amendment imposed the same substantive limitations on the States' power to legislate that the First Amendment had always imposed on the Congress' power. The Court has confirmed and endorsed this elementary proposition of law time and time again. ⊥50

Writing for a unanimous Court in *Cantwell* v. *Connecticut*, *Justice ROBERTS* explained: " . . . We hold that the statute, as construed and applied to the appellants, deprives them of their liberty without due process of law in contravention of the Fourteenth Amendment. The fundamental concept of liberty embodied in that Amendment embraces the liberties guaranteed by the First Amendment. The First Amendment declares that Congress shall make no law respecting an establishment of religion or prohibiting the free exercise thereof. The Fourteenth Amendment has rendered the legislatures of the states as incompetent as Congress to enact such law. The constitutional inhibition of legislation on the subject of religion has a double aspect. On the one hand, it forestalls compulsion by law of the acceptance of any creed or the practice of any form of worship. Freedom of conscience and freedom to adhere to such religious organization or form of worship as the individual may choose cannot be restricted by law. On the other hand, it safeguards the free exercise of the chosen form of religion."

Cantwell, of course, is but one case in which the Court has identified the individual's freedom of conscience as the central liberty that unifies the various clauses in the First Amendment. Enlarging on this theme, *The CHIEF JUSTICE* recently wrote: ⊥51 "We begin with the proposition that the right of freedom of thought protected by the First Amendment against state action includes both the right to speak freely and the right to refrain from speaking at all. A system which secures the right to proselytize religious, political, and ideological causes must also guarantee the concomitant right to decline to foster such concepts. The right to speak and the right to refrain from speaking are complementary components of the broader concept of 'individual freedom of mind.'

"The Court in *Barnette* was faced with a state statute which required public school students to participate in daily ceremonies by honoring the flag both with words and traditional salute gestures. In overruling its prior decision in *Minersville District* v. *Gobitis*, the Court held that 'a ceremony so touching matters of opinion and political attitude may [not] be imposed upon the individual by official authority under powers committed to any political organization under our Constitution.' Compelling the affirmative act of a flag salute involved a more serious infringement upon personal liberties than the passive act of carrying the state motto on a license plate, but the difference is essentially one of degree. Here, as in *Barnette*, we are faced with a state measure which forces an individual, as part of his daily life—indeed constantly while his automobile is in public view—to be an ⊥52 instrument for fostering public adherence to an ideological point of view he finds unacceptable. In doing so, the State 'invades the sphere of intellect and spirit which it is the purpose of the First Amendment to our Constitution to reserve from all official control.'" *Wooley* v. *Maynard*.

Just as the right to speak and the right to refrain from speaking are complementary components of a broader concept of individual freedom of mind, so also the individual's freedom to choose his own creed is the counterpart of his right to refrain from accepting the creed established by the majority. At one time it was thought that this right merely proscribed the preference of one Christian sect over another, but would not require equal respect for the conscience of the infidel, the atheist, or the adherent of a non-Christian faith such as Mohammedism or Judaism. But when the underlying principle has been examined in the crucible of litigation, the ⊥53 Court has unambiguously concluded that the individual freedom of conscience protected by the First Amendment embraces the right to select any religious faith or none at all. This conclusion derives support not only from the interest in respecting the individual's freedom of conscience, but also from the conviction that religious beliefs worthy of respect are the product of free and voluntary choice by the faithful, ⊥54 and from recognition of the fact that the political interest in forestalling intolerance extends beyond intolerance among Christian sects—or even intolerance among "religions"—to encompass intolerance of the disbeliever and the uncertain. ⊥55 As *Justice JACKSON* eloquently stated in *Board of Education* v. *Barnette:* "If there is any fixed star in our constitutional constellation, it is that no official, high or petty, can prescribe what shall be orthodox in politics, nationalism, religion, or other matters of opinion or force citizens to confess by word or act their faith therein." The State of Alabama, no less than the Congress of the United States, must respect that basic truth.

III

When the Court has been called upon to construe the breadth of the Establishment Clause, it has examined the criteria developed over a period of many years. Thus, in *Lemon* v. *Kurtzman*, we wrote: "Every analysis in this area must begin with consideration of the cumulative criteria developed by the Court over many years. Three such tests may be gleaned from our cases. First, the statute must have a secular legislative purpose; second, its principal or primary effect must be one that neither advances nor inhibits religion; finally, the statute must not foster 'an excessive ⊥56 government entanglement with religion.'" It is the first of these three criteria that is most plainly implicated by this case. As the District Court correctly recognized, no consideration of the second or third criteria is necessary if a statute does not have a clearly secular purpose. For even though a statute that is motivated in part by a religious purpose may satisfy the first criterion, the First Amendment requires that a statute must be invalidated if it is entirely motivated by a purpose to advance religion.

In applying the purpose test, it is appropriate to ask "whether government's actual purpose is to endorse or disapprove of religion." *Lynch* v. *Donnelly*. In this case, the answer to that question is dispositive. For the record not only provides us with an unambiguous affirmative answer, but it also reveals that the enactment of § 16-1-20.1 was not motivated by any clearly secular purpose—indeed, the statute had *no* secular purpose.

IV

The sponsor of the bill that became § 16-1-20.1, Senator Donald Holmes, inserted into the legislative record—appar⊥57ently without dissent—a statement indicating that the legislation was an "effort to return voluntary prayer" to the public schools. Later Senator Holmes confirmed this purpose before the District Court. In response to the question whether he had any purpose for the legislation other than returning voluntary prayer to public schools, he stated, "No, I did not have no other purpose in mind." The State did not present evidence of any secular purpose. ⊥58

The unrebutted evidence of legislative intent contained in the legislative record and in the testimony of the sponsor of § 16-1-20.1 is confirmed by a consideration of the relationship between this statute and the two other measures that were considered in this case. The District Court found that the 1981 statute and its 1982 sequel had a common, nonsecular purpose. The wholly religious character of the later enactment is plainly evident from its text. When the differences between § 16-1-20.1 and its 1978 predecessor, § 16-1-20, are examined, it is equally clear that the 1981 statute has the same wholly religious character.

There are only three textual differences between § 16-1-20.1 and § 16-1-20: (1) the earlier statute applies only to grades one through six, whereas § 16-1-20.1 applies to all grades; (2) the earlier statute uses the word "shall" whereas § 16-1-20.1 uses the word "may"; (3) the earlier statute refers ⊥59 only to "meditation" whereas § 16-1-20.1 refers to "meditation or voluntary prayer." The first difference is of no relevance in this litigation because the minor appellees were in kindergarten or second grade during the 1981-1982 academic year. The second difference would also have no impact on this litigation because the mandatory language of § 16-1-20 continued to apply to grades one through six. Thus, the only significant textual difference is the addition of the words "or voluntary prayer."

The legislative intent to return prayer to the public schools is, of course, quite different from merely protecting every student's right to engage in voluntary prayer during an appropriate moment of silence during the school day. The 1978 statute already protected that right, containing nothing that prevented any student from engaging in voluntary prayer during a silent minute of meditation. Appellants have not identified any secular purpose that was not fully served by § 16-1-20 before the enactment of § 16-1-20.1. Thus, only two conclusions are consistent with the text of § 16-1-20.1: (1) the statute was enacted to convey a message of State endorsement and promotion of prayer; or (2) the statute was enacted for no purpose. No one suggests that the statute was nothing but a meaningless or irrational act.

We must, therefore, conclude that the Alabama Legislature intended to change existing law and that it was moti⊥60vated by the same purpose that the Governor's Answer to the Second Amended Complaint expressly admitted; that the statement inserted in the legislative history revealed; and that Senator Holmes' testimony frankly described. The Legislature enacted § 16-1-20.1 despite the existence of § 16-1-20 for the sole purpose of expressing the State's endorsement of prayer activities for one minute at the beginning of each school day. The addition of "or voluntary prayer" indicates that the State intended to characterize prayer as a favored practice. Such an endorsement is not consistent with the established principle that the Government must pursue a course of complete neutrality toward religion.

The importance of that principle does not permit us to treat this as an inconsequential case involving nothing more than a few words of symbolic speech on behalf of the political majority. For whenever the State itself speaks on a religious ⊥61 subject, one of the questions that we must ask is "whether the Government intends to convey a message of endorsement or disapproval of religion." *Lynch* v. *Donnelly*. The well-supported concurrent findings of the District Court and the Court of Appeals—that § 161-20.1 was intended to convey a message of State approval of prayer activities in the public schools—make it unnecessary, and indeed inappropriate, to evaluate the practical significance of the addition of the words "or voluntary prayer" to the statute. Keeping in mind, as we must, "both the fundamental place held by the Establishment Clause in our constitutional scheme and the myriad, subtle ways in which Establishment Clause values can be eroded," *Id.* we conclude that § 16-1-20.1 violates the First Amendment.

The judgment of the Court of Appeals is affirmed.

It is so ordered. ⊥62

Justice POWELL, concurring.

I concur in the Court's opinion and judgment that Ala. Code § 16-1-20.1 violates the Establishment Clause of the First Amendment. My concurrence is prompted by Alabama's persistence in attempting to institute state-sponsored prayer in the public schools by enacting three successive statutes. I agree fully with *Justice O'CONNOR's* assertion that some moment-of-silence statutes may be constitutional, a suggestion set forth in the Court's opinion as well. ⊥**63**

I write separately to express additional views and to respond to criticism of the three-pronged *Lemon* test. *Lemon* v. *Kurtzman* identifies standards that have proven useful in analyzing case after case both in our decisions and in those of other courts. It is the only coherent test a majority of the Court has ever adopted. Only once since our decision in *Lemon,* have we addressed an Establishment Clause issue without resort to its three-pronged test. See *Marsh* v. *Chambers*. *Lemon* has not been overruled or its test modified. Yet, continued criticism of it could encourage other courts to feel free to decide Establishment Clause cases on an *ad hoc* basis. ⊥**64**

The first inquiry under *Lemon* is whether the challenged statute has a "secular legislative purpose." As *Justice O'CONNOR* recognizes, this secular purpose must be "sincere"; a law will not pass constitutional muster if the secular purpose articulated by the legislature is merely a "sham." In *Stone* v. *Graham*, for example, we held that a statute requiring the posting of the Ten Commandments in public schools violated the Establishment Clause, even though the Kentucky legislature asserted that its goal was educational. We have not interpreted the first prong of *Lemon*, however, as requiring that a statute have "exclusively secular" objectives. If such a requirement existed, much conduct and legislation approved by this Court in the past would have been invalidated. ⊥**65**

The record before us, however, makes clear that Alabama's purpose was solely religious in character. Senator Donald Holmes, the sponsor of the bill that became Alabama Code § 16-1-20.1, freely acknowledged that the purpose of this statute was "to return voluntary prayer" to the public schools. I agree with *Justice O'CONNOR* that a single legislator's statement, particularly if made following enactment, is not necessarily sufficient to establish purpose. But, as noted in the Court's opinion, the religious purpose of § 16-1-20.1 is manifested in other evidence, including the sequence and history of the three Alabama statutes.

I also consider it of critical importance that neither the District Court nor the Court of Appeals found a secular purpose, while both agreed that the purpose was to advance religion. In its first opinion (enjoining the enforcement of § 16-1-20.1 pending a hearing on the merits), the District Court said that the statute did "not reflect a clearly secular purpose." Instead, the District Court found that the enactment of the statute was an "effort on the part of the State of Alabama to encourage a religious activity." The Court of Appeals likewise applied the *Lemon* test and found "a lack of secular purpose on the part of the Alabama legislature." ⊥**66** It held that the objective of § 16-1-20.1 was the "advancement of religion." When both courts below are unable to discern an arguably valid secular purpose, this Court normally should hesitate to find one.

I would vote to uphold the Alabama statute if it also had a clear secular purpose. Nothing in the record before us, however, identifies a clear secular purpose, and the State also has failed to identify any non-religious reason for the statute's enactment. Under these circumstances, the Court is required by our precedents to hold that the statute fails the first prong of the *Lemon* test and therefore violates the Establishment Clause.

Although we do not reach the other two prongs of the *Lemon* test, I note that the "effect" of a straightforward moment-of-silence statute is unlikely to "advance or inhibit religion." Nor would such a statute "foster 'an excessive government entanglement with religion.'" *Lemon* ⊥**67** v. *Kurtzman*.

I join the opinion and judgment of the Court.

Justice O'CONNOR, concurring in the judgment.

Nothing in the United States Constitution as interpreted by this Court or in the laws of the State of Alabama prohibits public school students from voluntarily praying at any time before, during, or after the school day. Alabama has facilitated voluntary silent prayers of students who are so inclined by enacting Ala. Code § 16-1-20, which provides a moment of silence in appellees' schools each day. The parties to these proceedings concede the validity of this enactment. At issue in these appeals is the constitutional validity of an additional and subsequent Alabama statute, Ala. Code § 16-1-20.1, which both the District Court and the Court of Appeals concluded was enacted solely to officially encourage prayer during the moment of silence. I agree with the judgment of the Court that, in light of the findings of the Courts below and the history of its enactment, § 16-1-20.1 of the Alabama Code violates the Establishment Clause of the First Amendment. In my view, there can be little doubt that the purpose and likely effect of this subsequent enactment is to endorse and sponsor voluntary prayer in the public schools. I write separately to identify the peculiar features of the Alabama law that render it invalid, and to explain why moment of silence laws in other States do not necessarily manifest the same infirmity. I also write to explain why neither history nor the Free Exercise Clause of the First Amendment validate the Alabama law struck down by the Court today.

I

The religion clauses of the First Amendment, coupled with the Fourteenth Amendment's guaranty of ordered liberty, preclude both the Nation and the States from making any law respecting an establishment of religion or prohibiting ⊥**68** the free exercise thereof. Although a distinct jurisprudence has enveloped each of these clauses, their common purpose is to secure religious liberty. On these principles the Court has been and remains unanimous.

As this case once again demonstrates, however, "it is far easier to agree on the purpose that underlies the First Amendment's Establishment and Free Exercise Clauses than to obtain agreement on the standards that should govern their application." *Walz* v. *Tax Comm'n*. It once appeared that the Court had developed a workable standard by which to identify impermissible government establishments of religion. Under the now familiar *Lemon* test, statutes must have both a secular legislative purpose and a principal or primary effect that neither advances nor inhibits religion, and in addition they must not foster excessive government entanglement with religion. Despite its initial promise, the *Lemon* test has proven problematic. The required inquiry into "entanglement" has been modified and questioned, see *Mueller* v. *Allen*, and in one case we have upheld state action against an Establishment Clause challenge without applying the *Lemon* test at all, *Marsh* v. *Chambers*. The author of *Lemon* himself apparently questions the test's general applicability. See *Lynch* v. *Donnelly*. *Justice REHNQUIST* today suggests that we abandon *Lemon* entirely, and in the process limit the reach of the Establishment Clause to state discrimination between sects and government designation of a particular church as a "state" or "national" one.

Perhaps because I am new to the struggle, I am not ready to abandon all aspects of the *Lemon* test. I do believe, however, that the standards announced in *Lemon* should be ⊥**69** reexamined and refined in order to make them more useful in achieving the underlying purpose of the First Amendment. We must strive to do more than erect a constitutional "signpost," *Hunt* v. *McNair*, to be followed or ignored in a particular case as our predilections may dictate. Instead, our goal should be "to frame a principle for constitutional adjudication that is not only grounded in the history and language of the first amendment, but one that is also capable of consistent application to the relevant problems." Choper, Religion in the Public Schools: A Proposed Constitutional Standard, 47 Minn. L. Rev. 329, 332-333 (1963) (footnotes omitted). Last Term, I proposed a refinement of the *Lemon* test with this goal in mind, *Lynch* v. *Donnelly*.

The *Lynch* concurrence suggested that the religious liberty protected by the Establishment Clause is infringed when the government makes adherence to religion relevant to a person's standing in the political community. Direct government action endorsing religion or a particular religious practice is invalid under this approach because it "sends a message to nonadherents that they are outsiders, not full members of the political community, and an accompanying message to adherents that they are insiders, favored members of the political community." Under this view, *Lemon's* inquiry as to the purpose and effect of a statute requires courts to examine whether government's purpose is to endorse religion and whether the statute actually conveys a message of endorsement.

The endorsement test is useful because of the analytic content it gives to the *Lemon*-mandated inquiry into legislative purpose and effect. In this country, church and state must necessarily operate within the same community. Because of this coexistence, it is inevitable that the secular interests of Government and the religious interests of various sects and their adherents will frequently intersect, conflict, and combine. A statute that ostensibly promotes a secular interest ⊥**70** often has an incidental or even a primary effect of helping or hindering a sectarian belief. Chaos would ensue if every such statute were invalid under the Establishment Clause. For example, the State could not criminalize murder for fear that it would thereby promote the Biblical command against killing. The task for the Court is to sort out those statutes and government practices whose purpose and effect go against the grain of religious liberty protected by the First Amendment.

The endorsement test does not preclude government from acknowledging religion or from taking religion into account in making law and policy. It does preclude government from conveying or attempting to convey a message that religion or a particular religious belief is favored or preferred. Such an endorsement infringes the religious liberty of the nonadherent, for "[w]hen the power, prestige and financial support of government is placed behind a particular religious belief, the indirect coercive pressure upon religious minorities to conform to the prevailing officially approved religion is plain." *Engel* v. *Vitale*. At issue today is whether state moment of silence statutes in general, and Alabama's moment of silence statute in particular, embody an impermissible endorsement of prayer in public schools.

A

Twenty-five states permit or require public school teachers to have students observe a moment of silence in their classrooms. A few statutes provide that the moment of silence ⊥**71** is for the purpose of meditation alone. The typical statute however, calls for a moment of silence at the beginning of the school day during which students may meditate, pray, or reflect on the activities of the day. Federal trial courts have divided on the constitutionality of these moment of silence laws. Relying on this Court's decisions disapproving vocal prayer and Bible reading in the public schools, see *Abington School District* v. *Schempp*, *Engel* v. *Vitale*, the courts that have struck down the moment of silence statutes generally conclude that their purpose and effect is to encourage prayer in public schools.

The *Engel* and *Abington* decisions are not dispositive on the constitutionality of moment of silence laws. In those ⊥**72** cases, public school teachers and students led their classes in devotional exercises. In *Engel*, a New

York statute required teachers to lead their classes in a vocal prayer. The Court concluded that "it is no part of the business of government to compose official prayers for any group of the American people to recite as part of a religious program carried on by the government." In *Abington*, the Court addressed Pennsylvania and Maryland statutes that authorized morning Bible readings in public schools. The Court reviewed the purpose and effect of the statutes, concluded that they required religious exercises, and therefore found them to violate the Establishment Clause. Under all of these statutes, a student who did not share the religious beliefs expressed in the course of the exercise was left with the choice of participating, thereby compromising the nonadherent's belief, or withdrawing, thereby calling attention to his or her nonconformity. The decisions acknowledged the coercion implicit under the statutory schemes, but they expressly turned only on the fact that the government was sponsoring a manifestly religious exercise.

A state sponsored moment of silence in the public schools is different from state sponsored vocal prayer or Bible reading. First, a moment of silence is not inherently religious. Silence, unlike prayer or Bible reading, need not be associated with a religious exercise. Second, a pupil who participates in a moment of silence need not compromise his or her beliefs. During a moment of silence, a student who objects to prayer is left to his or her own thoughts, and is not compelled to listen to the prayers or thoughts of others. For these simple reasons, a moment of silence statute does not stand or fall under the Establishment Clause according to how the Court regards vocal prayer or Bible reading. Scholars and at least one member of this Court have recognized the distinction and suggested that a moment of silence in public schools would be constitutional. See *Abington* (Brennan, J., concurring) ("[T]he observance of a mo⊥**73**ment of reverent silence at the opening of class" may serve "the solely secular purposes of the devotional activities without jeopardizing either the religious liberties of any members of the community or the proper degree of separation between the spheres of religion and government"); L. Tribe, American Constitutional Law § 14-6, p. 829 (1978); P. Freund, The Legal Issue, in Religion and the Public Schools 23 (1966); Choper, 47 Minn. L. Rev. at 371; Kauper, Prayer, Public Schools, and the Supreme Court, 61 Mich. L. Rev. 1031, 1041 (1963). As a general matter, I agree. It is difficult to discern a serious threat to religious liberty from a room of silent, thoughtful school children.

By mandating a moment of silence, a State does not necessarily endorse any activity that might occur during the period. Even if a statute specifies that a student may choose to pray silently during a quiet moment, the State has not thereby encouraged prayer over other specified alternatives. Nonetheless, it is also possible that a moment of silence statute, either as drafted or as actually implemented, could effectively favor the child who prays over the child who does not. For example, the message of endorsement would seem inescapable if the teacher exhorts children to use the designated time to pray. Similarly, the face of the statute or its legislative history may clearly establish that it seeks to encourage or promote voluntary prayer over other alternatives, rather than merely provide a quiet moment that may be dedicated to prayer by those so inclined. The crucial question is whether the State has conveyed or attempted to convey the message that children should use the moment of silence for prayer. ⊥**74** This question cannot be answered in the abstract, but instead requires courts to examine the history, language, and administration of a particular statute to determine whether it operates as an endorsement of religion.

Before reviewing Alabama's moment of silence law to determine whether it endorses prayer, some general observations on the proper scope of the inquiry are in order. First, the inquiry into the purpose of the legislature in enacting a moment of silence law should be deferential and limited. In determining whether the government intends a moment of silence statute to convey a message of endorsement or disapproval of religion, a court has no license to psychoanalyze the legislators. If a legislature expresses a plausible secular purpose for a moment of silence statute in either the text or the legislative history, or if the statute disclaims an intent to encourage prayer over alternatives during a moment of silence, then courts should gener⊥**75**ally defer to that stated intent. It is particularly troublesome to denigrate an expressed secular purpose due to post-enactment testimony by particular legislators or by interested persons who witnessed the drafting of the statute. Even if the text and official history of a statute express no secular purpose, the statute should be held to have an improper purpose only if it is beyond purview that endorsement of religion or a religious belief "was and is the law's reason for existence." *Epperson* v. *Arkansas*. Since there is arguably a secular pedagogical value to a moment of silence in public schools, courts should find an improper purpose behind such a statute only if the statute on its face, in its official legislative history, or in its interpretation by a responsible administrative agency suggests it has the primary purpose of endorsing prayer.

Justice REHNQUIST suggests that this sort of deferential inquiry into legislative purpose "means little," because "it only requires the legislature to express any secular purpose and omit all sectarian references." It is not a trivial matter, however, to require that the legislature manifest a secular purpose and omit all sectarian endorsement from its laws. That requirement is precisely tailored to the Establishment Clause's purpose of assuring that Government not intentionally endorse religion or a religious practice. It is of course possible that a legislature will enunciate a sham secular purpose for a statute. I have little doubt that our courts are capable of distinguishing a sham secular purpose from a sincere one, or that the *Lemon* inquiry into the effect of an enactment would help decide those close cases where the validity of an expressed secular purpose is in doubt. While the secular purpose requirement alone may rarely be determinative in striking down a statute, it nevertheless serves an important function. It reminds government that ⊥76 when it acts it should do so without endorsing a particular religious belief or practice that all citizens do not share. In this sense the secular purpose requirement is squarely based in the text of the Establishment Clause it helps to enforce.

Second, the *Lynch* concurrence suggested that the effect of a moment of silence law is not entirely a question of fact: "[W]hether a government activity communicates endorsement of religion is not a question of simple historical fact. Although evidentiary submissions may help answer it, the question is, like the question whether racial or sex-based classifications communicate an invidious message, in large part a legal question to be answered on the basis of judicial interpretation of social facts." The relevant issue is whether an objective observer, acquainted with the text, legislative history, and implementation of the statute, would perceive it as a state endorsement of prayer in public schools. A moment of silence law that is clearly drafted and implemented so as to permit prayer, meditation, and reflection within the prescribed period, without endorsing one alternative over the others, should pass this test.

B

The analysis above suggests that moment of silence laws in many States should pass Establishment Clause scrutiny because they do not favor the child who chooses to pray during a moment of silence over the child who chooses to medi⊥77tate or reflect. Alabama Code § 16-1-20.1 does not stand on the same footing. However deferentially one examines its text and legislative history, however objectively one views the message attempted to be conveyed to the public, the conclusion is unavoidable that the purpose of the statute is to endorse prayer in public schools. I accordingly agree with the Court of Appeals that the Alabama statute has a purpose which is in violation of the Establishment Clause, and cannot be upheld.

In finding that the purpose of Alabama Code § 161-20.1 is to endorse voluntary prayer during a moment of silence, the Court relies on testimony elicited from State Senator Donald G. Holmes during a preliminary injunction hearing. Senator Holmes testified that the sole purpose of the statute was to return voluntary prayer to the public schools. For the reasons expressed above, I would give little, if any, weight to this sort of evidence of legislative intent. Nevertheless, the text of the statute in light of its official legislative history leaves little doubt that the purpose of this statute corresponds to the purpose expressed by Senator Holmes at the preliminary injunction hearing.

First, it is notable that Alabama already had a moment of silence statute before it enacted § 16-1-20.1. Appellees do not challenge this statute—indeed, they concede its validity. The only significant addition made by Alabama Code § 16-1-20.1 is to specify expressly that voluntary prayer is one of the authorized activities during a moment of silence. Any doubt as to the legislative purpose of that addition is removed by the official legislative history. The sole purpose reflected in the official history is "to return voluntary prayer to our public schools." Nor does anything in the legislative history contradict an intent to encourage children to choose prayer over other alternatives during the moment of silence. Given this legislative history, it is not surprising that the State of Alabama conceded in the ⊥78 courts below that the purpose of the statute was to make prayer part of daily classroom activity, and that both the District Court and the Court of Appeals concluded that the law's purpose was to encourage religious activity. In light of the legislative history and the findings of the courts below, I agree with the Court that the State intended Alabama Code § 16-1-20.1 to convey a message that prayer was the endorsed activity during the state-prescribed moment of silence. While it is therefore unnecessary also to determine the effect of the statute, it also seems likely that the message actually conveyed to objective observers by Alabama Code § 16-1-20.1 is approval of the child who selects prayer over other alternatives during a moment of silence.

Given this evidence in the record, candor requires us to admit that this Alabama statute was intended to convey a message of state encouragement and endorsement of religion. In *Walz* v. *Tax Comm'n*, the Court stated that the religion clauses of the First Amendment are flexible enough to "permit religious exercise to exist without sponsorship and without interference." Alabama Code § 16-1-20.1 does more than permit prayer to occur during a moment of silence "without interference." It ⊥79 endorses the decision to pray during a moment of silence, and accordingly sponsors a religious exercise. For that reason, I concur in the judgment of the Court.

II

In his dissenting opinion, *Justice REHNQUIST* reviews the text and history of the First Amendment religion clauses. His opinion suggests that a long line of this Court's decisions are inconsistent with the intent of the drafters of the Bill of Rights. He urges the Court to correct the historical inaccuracies in its past decisions by embracing a far more restricted interpretation that presumably would permit vocal group prayer in public schools.

The United States, in an *amicus* brief, suggests a less sweeping modification of Establishment Clause principles. In the Federal Government's view, a state sponsored moment of silence is merely an "accommodation" of the desire of some public school children to practice their religion by praying silently. Such an accommodation is contemplated by the First Amendment's guaranty that the Government will not prohibit the free exercise of religion. Because the moment of silence implicates free exercise values, the United States suggests that the *Lemon*-mandated inquiry into purpose and effect should be modified.

There is an element of truth and much helpful analysis in each of these suggestions. Particularly when we are interpreting the Constitution, "a page of history is worth a volume of logic." *New York Trust Co.* v. *Eisner*. Whatever the provision of the Constitution that is at issue, I continue to believe that "fidelity to the notion of *constitutional*—as opposed to purely judicial—limits on governmental action requires us to impose a heavy burden on those who claim that practices accepted when [the provision] was ⊥**80** adopted are now constitutionally impermissible." *Tennessee* v. *Garner*. The Court properly looked to history in upholding legislative prayer, *Marsh* v. *Chambers*, property tax exemptions for houses of worship, *Walz* v. *Tax Comm'n*, and Sunday closing laws, *McGowan* v. *Maryland*. As *Justice HOLMES* once observed, "[i]f a thing has been practiced for two hundred years by common consent, it will need a strong case for the Fourteenth Amendment to affect it." *Jackman* v. *Rosenbaum Co.*

Justice REHNQUIST does not assert, however, that the drafters of the First Amendment expressed a preference for prayer in public schools, or that the practice of prayer in public schools enjoyed uninterrupted government endorsement from the time of enactment of the Bill of Rights to the present era. The simple truth is that free public education was virtually non-existent in the late eighteenth century. Since there then existed few government-run schools, it is unlikely that the persons who drafted the First Amendment, or the state legislators who ratified it, anticipated the problems of interaction of church and state in the public schools. Even at the time of adoption of the Fourteenth Amendment, education in Southern States was still primarily in private hands, and the movement toward free public schools supported by general taxation had not taken hold.

This uncertainty as to the intent of the Framers of the Bill of Rights does not mean we should ignore history for guidance on the role of religion in public education. The Court has not done so. ⊥**81** When the intent of the Framers is unclear, I believe we must employ both history and reason in our analysis. The primary issue raised by *Justice REHNQUIST*'s dissent is whether the historical fact that our Presidents have long called for public prayers of Thanks should be dispositive on the constitutionality of prayer in public schools. I think not. At the very least, Presidential proclamations are distinguishable from school prayer in that they are received in a noncoercive setting and are primarily directed at adults, who presumably are not readily susceptible to unwilling religious indoctrination. This Court's decisions have recognized a distinction when government sponsored religious exercises are directed at impressionable children who are required to attend school, for then government endorsement is much more likely to result in coerced religious beliefs. Although history provides a touchstone for constitutional problems, the Establishment Clause concern for religious liberty is dispositive here.

The element of truth in the United States' arguments, I believe, lies in the suggestion that Establishment Clause analysis must comport with the mandate of the Free Exercise Clause that government make no law prohibiting the free exercise of religion. ⊥**82** Our cases have interpreted the Free Exercise Clause to compel the Government to exempt persons from some generally applicable government requirements so as to permit those persons to freely exercise their religion. Even where the Free Exercise Clause does not compel the Government to grant an exemption, the Court has suggested that the Government in some circumstances may voluntarily choose to exempt religious observers without violating the Establishment Clause. See, *e.g.*, *Gillette* v. *United States*; *Braunfeld* v. *Brown*. The challenge posed by the United States' argument is how to define the proper Establishment Clause limits on voluntary government efforts to facilitate the free exercise of religion. On the one hand, a rigid application of the *Lemon* test would invalidate legislation exempting religious observers from generally applicable government obligations. By definition, such legislation has a religious purpose and effect in promoting the free exercise of religion. On the other hand, judicial deference to all legislation that purports to facilitate the free exercise of religion would completely vitiate the Establishment Clause. Any statute pertaining to religion can be viewed as an "accommodation" of free exercise rights. Indeed, the statute at issue in *Lemon*, which provided salary supplements, textbooks, and instructional materials to Pennsylvania parochial schools, can be viewed as an accommodation of the religious beliefs of parents who choose to send their children to religious schools.

It is obvious that either of the two Religion Clauses, "if expanded to a logical extreme, would tend to clash with the other." *Walz*. The Court has long exacerbated the conflict by calling for government "neutrality" toward religion. It is difficult to square any notion of "complete neutrality," with the mandate of the Free Exercise Clause that government must sometimes exempt a religious observer from an otherwise generally applicable obligation. A government that confers a benefit on an explicitly religious basis is not ⊥**83** neutral toward religion.

The solution to the conflict between the religion clauses lies not in "neutrality," but rather in identifying workable limits to the Government's license to promote the free exercise of religion. The text of the Free Exercise Clause speaks of laws that prohibit the free exercise of religion. On its face, the Clause is directed at government interference with free exercise. Given that concern, one can plausibly assert that government pursues free exercise clause values when it lifts a government imposed burden on the free exercise of religion. If a statute falls within this category, then the standard Establishment Clause test should be modified accordingly. It is disingenuous to look for a purely secular purpose when the manifest objective of a statute is to facilitate the free exercise of religion by lifting a government-imposed burden. Instead, the Court should simply acknowledge that the religious purpose of such a statute is legitimated by the Free Exercise Clause. I would also go further. In assessing the effect of such a statute—that is, in determining whether the statute conveys the message of endorsement of religion or a particular religious belief—courts should assume that the "objective observer," is acquainted with the Free Exercise Clause and the values it promotes. Thus individual perceptions or resentment that a religious observer is exempted from a particular government requirement, would be entitled to little weight if the Free Exercise Clause strongly supported the exemption.

While this "accommodation" analysis would help reconcile our Free Exercise and Establishment Clause standards, it would not save Alabama's moment of silence law. If we assume that the religious activity that Alabama seeks to protect is silent prayer, then it is difficult to discern any state-imposed burden on that activity that is lifted by Alabama Code § 16-1-20.1. No law prevents a student who is so inclined from praying silently in public schools. ⊥**84** Moreover, state law already provided a moment of silence to these appellees irrespective of Alabama Code § 16-1-20.1. Of course, the State might argue that § 16-1-20.1 protects not silent prayer, but rather group silent prayer under State sponsorship. Phrased in these terms, the burden lifted by the statute is not one imposed by the State of Alabama, but by the Establishment Clause as interpreted in *Engel* and *Abington*. In my view, it is beyond the authority of the State of Alabama to remove burdens imposed by the Constitution itself. I conclude that the Alabama statute at issue today lifts no state-imposed burden on the free exercise of religion, and accordingly cannot properly be viewed as an accommodation statute.

III

The Court does not hold that the Establishment Clause is so hostile to religion that it precludes the States from affording schoolchildren an opportunity for voluntary silent prayer. To the contrary, the moment of silence statutes of many States should satisfy the Establishment Clause standard we have here applied. The Court holds only that Alabama has intentionally crossed the line between creating a quiet moment during which those so inclined may pray, and affirmatively endorsing the particular religious practice of prayer. This line may be a fine one, but our precedents and the principles of religious liberty require that we draw it. In my view, the judgment of the Court of Appeals must be affirmed.

Chief Justice BURGER, dissenting.

Some who trouble to read the opinions in this case will find it ironic—perhaps even bizarre—that on the very day we heard arguments in this case, the Court's session opened with an invocation for Divine protection. Across the park a few hundred yards away, the House of Representatives and ⊥**85** the Senate regularly open each session with a prayer. These legislative prayers are not just one minute in duration, but are extended, thoughtful invocations and prayers for Divine guidance. They are given, as they have been since 1789, by clergy appointed as official Chaplains and paid from the Treasury of the United States. Congress has also provided chapels in the Capitol, at public expense, where Members and others may pause for prayer, meditation—or a moment of silence.

Inevitably some wag is bound to say that the Court's holding today reflects a belief that the historic practice of the Congress and this Court is justified because members of the Judiciary and Congress are more in need of Divine guidance than are schoolchildren. Still others will say that all this controversy is "much ado about nothing," since no power on earth—including this Court and Congress—can stop any teacher from opening the school day with a moment of silence for pupils to meditate, to plan their day—or to pray if they voluntarily elect to do so.

I make several points about today's curious holding.

(a) It makes no sense to say that Alabama has "endorsed prayer" by merely enacting a new statute "to specify expressly that voluntary prayer is *one* of the authorized activities during a moment of silence." (O'Connor, J., concurring in the judgment) (emphasis added). To suggest that a moment-of-silence statute that includes the word "prayer" unconstitutionally endorses religion, while one that simply provides for a moment of silence does not, manifests not neutrality but hostility toward religion. For decades our opinions have stated that hostility toward any religion or toward all religions is as much forbidden by the Constitution as is an official establishment of religion. The Alabama legislature has no more "endorsed" religion than a state or the Congress does when it provides for legislative chaplains, or than this Court does when it opens each session with an invocation to ⊥**86** God. Today's decision recalls the observation of *Justice* GOLDBERG: "[U]ntutored devotion to the concept of neutrality can lead to invocation or approval of results which partake not simply of that noninterference and noninvolvement with the religious which the Constitution commands, but of a brooding and pervasive dedication to the secular and a passive, or even active, hostility to the religious. Such results are not only not compelled by the Constitution but, it seems to me, are prohibited by it." *School District* v. *Schempp*.

(b) The inexplicable aspect of the foregoing opinions, however, is what they advance as support for the holding concerning the purpose of the Alabama legislature. Rather than determining legislative purpose from the fact of the statute as a whole, the opinions rely on three factors in concluding that the Alabama legislature had a "wholly religious" purpose for enacting the statute under review, Ala. Code § 16-1-20.1: (i) statements of the statute's sponsor, (ii) admissions in Governor James' Answer to the Second Amended Complaint, and (iii) the difference between § 16-1-20.1 and its predecessor statute.

Curiously, the opinions do not mention that all of the sponsor's statements relied upon—including the statement "inserted" into the Senate Journal—were made after the legislature had passed the statute; indeed, the testimony that the Court finds critical was given well over a year after the statute was enacted. As even the appellees concede, there is not a shred of evidence that ⊥**87** the legislature as a whole shared the sponsor's motive or that a majority in either house was even aware of the sponsor's view of the bill when it was passed. The sole relevance of the sponsor's statement, therefore, is that they reflect the personal, subjective motives of a single legislator. No case in the 195-year history of this Court supports the disconcerting idea that postenactment statements by individual legislators are relevant in determining the constitutionality of legislation.

Even if an individual legislator's after-the-fact statements could rationally be considered relevant, all of the opinions fail to mention that the sponsor also testified that one of his purposes in drafting and sponsoring the moment-of-silence bill was to clear up a widespread misunderstanding that a schoolchild is legally *prohibited* from engaging in silent, individual prayer once he steps inside a public school building. That testimony is at least as important as the statements the Court relies upon, and surely that testimony manifests a permissible purpose.

The Court also relies on the admissions of Governor James' Answer to the Second Amended Complaint. Strangely, however, the Court neglects to mention that there was no trial bearing on the constitutionality of the Alabama statutes; trial became unnecessary when the District Court held that the Establishment Clause does not apply to the states. The absence of a trial on the issue of the constitutionality of § 16-1-20.1 is significant because the Answer filed by the State Board and Superintendent of Education did not make the same admissions that the Governor's Answer made. The Court cannot know whether, if this case had been tried, those state officials would have offered evidence to contravene appellees' allegations concerning legislative purpose. Thus, it is completely inappropriate to accord any relevance to the admissions in the Governor's Answer. ⊥**88**

The several preceding opinions conclude that the principal difference between § 16-1-20.1 and its predecessor statute proves that the sole purpose behind the inclusion of the phase "or voluntary prayer" in § 16-1-20.1 was to endorse and promote prayer. This reasoning is simply a subtle way of focusing exclusively on the religious component of the statute rather than examining the statute as a whole. Such logic—if it can be called that—would lead the Court to hold, for example, that a state may enact a statute that provides reimbursement for bus transportation to the parents of all schoolchildren, but may not add parents of parochial school students to an existing program providing reimbursement for parents of public school students. Congress amended the statutory Pledge of Allegiance 31 years ago to add the words "under God." Do the several opinions in support of the judgment today render the Pledge unconstitutional? That would be the consequence of their method of focusing on the difference between § 16-1-20.1 and its predecessor statute rather than examining § 16-1-20.1 as a whole. Any such holding would of course make a mockery of our decisionmaking in Establishment Clause cases. And even were the Court's method correct, the inclusion of the words "or voluntary prayer" in § 16-1-20.1 is wholly consistent with the clearly permissible purpose of clarifying that silent, voluntary prayer is not *forbidden* in the public school building. ⊥**89**

(c) The Court's extended treatment of the "test" of *Lemon* v. *Kurtzman* suggests a naive preoccupation with an easy, bright-line approach for addressing constitutional issues. We have repeatedly cautioned that *Lemon* did not establish a rigid caliper capable of resolving every Establishment Clause issue, but that it sought only to provide "signposts." "In each [Establishment Clause] case, the inquiry calls for line drawing; no fixed, *per se* rule can be framed." *Lynch* v. *Donnelly*. In any event, our responsibility is not to apply tidy formulas by rote; our duty is to determine whether the statute or practice at issue is a step toward establishing a state religion. Given today's decision, however, perhaps it is understandable that the opinions in support of the judgment all but ignore the Establishment Clause itself and the concerns that underlie it.

(d) The notion that the Alabama statute is a step toward creating an established church borders on, if it does not trespass into, the ridiculous. The statute does not remotely threaten religious liberty; it affirmatively furthers the values of religious freedom and tolerance that the Establishment Clause was designed to protect. Without pressuring those who do not wish to pray, the statute simply creates an opportunity to think, to plan, or to pray if one wishes—as Congress does by providing chaplains and chapels. It accommodates the purely private, voluntary religious choices of the individual pupils who wish to pray while at the same time creating a time for nonreligious reflection for those who do not choose to pray. The statute also provides a meaningful opportunity for schoolchildren to appreciate the absolute constitutional right of each individual to worship and believe as the individual wishes. The statute "endorses" only the view that the religious observances of others should be tolerated and, ⊥**90** where possible, accommodated. If the government may not accommodate religious needs when it does so in a wholly neutral and noncoercive manner, the "benevolent neutrality" that we have long considered the correct constitutional standard will quickly translate into the "callous indifference" that the Court has consistently held the Establishment Clause does not require.

The Court today has ignored the wise admonition of *Justice* GOLDBERG that "the measure of constitutional adjudication is the ability and willingness to distinguish between real threat and mere shadow." *School District* v. *Schempp*. The innocuous statute that the Court strikes down does not even rise to the level of "mere shadow." *Justice* O'CONNOR paradoxically acknowledges, "It is difficult to discern a serious threat to religious liberty from a room of silent, thoughtful schoolchildren." I would add to that, "even if they choose to pray."

The mountains have labored and brought forth a mouse.

Justice WHITE, dissenting.

For the most part agreeing with the opinion of *The* CHIEF JUSTICE, I dissent from the Court's judgment invalidating Alabama Code § 16-1-20.1. Because I do, it is apparent that in my view the First Amendment does not proscribe either (1) statutes authorizing or requiring in so many words a moment of silence before classes begin or (2) a statute that provides, when it is initially passed, for a moment of silence for meditation or prayer. As I read the filed opin⊥**91**ions, a majority of the Court would approve statutes that provide for a moment of silence but did not mention prayer. But if a student asked whether he could pray during that moment, it is difficult to believe that the teacher could not answer in the affirmative. If that is the case, I would not invalidate a statute that at the outset provided the legislative answer to the question "May I pray?" This is so even if the Alabama statute is infirm, which I do not believe it is, because of its peculiar legislative history.

I appreciate *Justice* REHNQUIST's explication of the history of the religion clauses of the First Amendment. Against that history, it would be quite understandable if we undertook to reassess our cases dealing with these clauses, particularly those dealing with the Establishment Clause. Of course, I have been out of step with many of the Court's decisions dealing with this subject matter, and it is thus not surprising that I would support a basic reconsideration of our precedents.

Justice REHNQUIST, dissenting.

Thirty-eight years ago this Court, in *Everson* v. *Board of Education*, summarized its exegesis of Establishment Clause doctrine thus: "In the words of Jefferson, the clause against establishment of religion by law was intended to erect 'a wall of separation between church and State.' *Reynolds* v. *United States*." This language from *Reynolds*, a case involving the Free Exercise Clause of the First Amendment rather than the Establishment Clause, quoted from Thomas Jefferson's letter to the Danbury Baptist Association the phrase "I contemplate with sovereign reverence that act of the whole American people which declared that their legislature should 'make no law respecting an establishment of religion, or prohibiting the free exercise thereof,' thus building a wall of separation ⊥**92** between church and State." 3 Writings of Thomas Jefferson 113 (H. Washington ed. 1861).

It is impossible to build sound constitutional doctrine upon a mistaken understanding of constitutional history, but unfortunately the Establishment Clause has been expressly freighted with Jefferson's misleading metaphor for nearly forty years. Thomas Jefferson was of course in France at the time the constitutional amendments known as the Bill of Rights were passed by Congress and ratified by the states. His letter to the Danbury Baptist Association was a short note of courtesy, written fourteen years after the amendments were passed by Congress. He would seem to any detached observer as a less than ideal source of contemporary history as to the meaning of the Religion Clauses of the First Amendment.

Jefferson's fellow Virginian James Madison, with whom he was joined in the battle for the enactment of the Virginia Statute of Religious Liberty of 1786, did play as large a part as anyone in the drafting of the Bill of Rights. He had two advantages over Jefferson in this regard: he was present in the United States, and he was a leading member of the First Congress. But when we turn to the record of the proceedings in the First Congress leading up to the adoption of the Establishment Clause of the Constitution, including Madison's significant contributions thereto, we see a far different picture of its purpose than the highly simplified "wall of separation between church and State."

During the debates in the thirteen colonies over ratification of the Constitution, one of the arguments frequently used by opponents of ratification was that without a Bill of Rights guaranteeing individual liberty the new general government carried with it a potential for tyranny. The typical response to this argument on the part of those who favored ratification was that the general gov⊥**93**ernment established by the Constitution had only delegated powers, and that these delegated powers were so limited that the government would have no occasion to violate individual liberties. This response satisfied some, but not others, and of the eleven colonies which ratified the Constitution by early 1789, five proposed one or another amendments guaranteeing individual liberty. Three—New Hampshire, New York, and Virginia—included in one form or another a declaration of religious freedom. Rhode Island and North Carolina flatly refused to ratify the Constitution in the absence of amendments in the nature of a Bill of Rights. Virginia and North Carolina proposed identical guarantees of religious freedom: "[A]ll men have an equal, natural and unalienable right to the free exercise of religion, according to the dictates of conscience, and that no particular religious sect or society ought to be favored or established, by law, in preference to others." J. Elliot, Debates on the Federal Constitution 1891; vol. 3 at 659; 4 at 244.

On June 8, 1789, James Madison rose in the House of Representatives and "reminded the House that this was the day that he had heretofore named for bringing forward amendments to the Constitution." 1 Annals of Cong. 424. Madison's subsequent remarks in urging the House to adopt his drafts of the proposed amendments were less those of a dedicated advocate of the wisdom of such measures than those of a prudent statesman seeking the enactment of meas⊥**94**ures sought by a number of his fellow citizens which could surely do no harm and might do a great deal of good. He said, *inter alia:* "It appears to me that this House is bound by every motive of prudence, not to let the first session pass over without proposing to the State Legislatures, some things to be incorporated into the Constitution, that will render it as acceptable to the whole people of the United States, as it has been found acceptable to a majority of them. I wish, among other reasons why something should be done, that those who had been friendly to the adoption of this Constitution may have the opportunity of proving to those who were opposed to it that they were as sincerely devoted to liberty and a Republican Government, as those who charged them with wishing the adoption of this Constitution in order to lay the foundation of an aristocracy or despotism. It will be a desirable thing to extinguish from the bosom of every member of the community, any apprehensions that there are those among his countrymen who wish to deprive them of the liberty for which they valiantly fought and honorably bled. And if there are amendments desired of such a nature as will not injure the Constitution, and they can be ingrafted so as to give satisfaction to the doubting part of our fellow-citizens, the friends of the Federal Government will evince that spirit of deference and concession for which they have hitherto been distinguished." *Id.* at 431-432.

The language Madison proposed for what ultimately became the Religion Clauses of the First Amendment was this: "The civil rights of none shall be abridged on account of religious belief or worship, nor shall any national religion be established, nor shall the full and equal rights of conscience be in any manner, or on any pretext, infringed." *Id.* at 434. ⊥**95** On the same day that Madison proposed them, the amendments which formed the basis for the Bill of Rights were referred by the House to a committee of the whole, and after several weeks' delay were then referred to a Select Committee consisting of Madison and ten others. The Committee revised Madison's proposal regarding the establishment of religion to read: "[N]o religion shall be established by law, nor shall the equal rights of conscience be infringed." *Id.* at 729.

The Committee's proposed revisions were debated in the House on August 15, 1789. The entire debate on the Religion Clauses is contained in two full columns of the "Annals," and does not seem particularly illuminating. Representative Peter Sylvester of New York expressed his dislike for the revised version, because it might have a tendency "to abolish religion altogether." Representative John Vining suggested that the two parts of the sentence be transposed; Representative Elbridge Gerry thought the language should be changed to read "that no religious doctrine shall be established by law." Roger Sherman of Connecticut had the traditional reason for opposing provisions of a Bill of Rights—that Congress had no delegated authority to "make religious establishments"—and therefore he opposed the adoption of the amendment. Representative Daniel Carroll of Maryland thought it desirable to adopt the words proposed, saying "[h]e would not contend with gentlemen about the phraseology, his object was to secure the substance in such a manner as to satisfy the wishes of the honest part of the community."

Madison then spoke, and said that "he apprehended the meaning of the words to be, that Congress should not establish a religion, and enforce the legal observation of it by law, nor compel men to worship God in any manner contrary to their conscience." *Id.*, at 730. He said that some of the state conventions had thought that Congress might rely on ⊥**96** the "necessary and proper" clause to infringe the rights of conscience or to establish a national religion, and "to prevent these effects he presumed the amendment was intended, and he thought it as well expressed as the nature of the language would admit." *Ibid.*

Representative Benjamin Huntington then expressed the view that the Committee's language might "be taken in such latitude as to be extremely hurtful to the cause of religion. He understood the amendment to mean what had been expressed by the gentleman from Virginia; but others might find it convenient to put another construction upon it." Huntington, from Connecticut, was concerned that in the New England states, where state established religions were the rule rather than the exception, the federal courts might not be able to entertain claims based upon an obligation under the bylaws of a religious organization to contribute to the support of a minister or the building of a place of worship. He hoped that "the amendment would be made in such a way as to secure the rights of conscience, and a free exercise of the rights of religion, but not to patronize those who professed no religion at all." *Id.*, at 730-731.

Madison responded that the insertion of the word "national" before the word "religion" in the Committee version should satisfy the minds of those who had criticized the language. "He believed that the people feared one sect might obtain a pre-eminence, or two combine together, and establish a religion to which they would compel others to conform. He thought that if the word 'national' was introduced, it would point the amendment directly to the object it was intended to prevent." *Id.*, at 731. Representative Samuel Livermore expressed himself as dissatisfied with Madison's proposed amendment, and thought it would be better if the Committee language were altered to read that "Congress shall make no laws touching religion, or infringing the rights of conscience." *Ibid.*

Representative Gerry spoke in opposition to the use of the word "national" because of strong feelings expressed during ⊥**97** the ratification debates that a federal government, not a national government, was created by the

Constitution. Madison thereby withdrew his proposal but insisted that his reference to a "national religion" only referred to a national establishment and did not mean that the government was a national one. The question was taken on Representative Livermore's motion, which passed by a vote of 31 for and 20 against. *Ibid.*

The following week, without any apparent debate, the House voted to alter the language of the Religion Clause to read "Congress shall make no law establishing religion, or to prevent the free exercise thereof, or to infringe the rights of conscience." *Id.* at 766. The floor debates in the Senate were secret, and therefore not reported in the Annals. The Senate on September 3, 1789 considered several different forms of the Religion Amendment, and reported this language back to the House: "Congress shall make no law establishing articles of faith or a mode of worship, or prohibiting the free exercise of religion." C. Antieau, A. Downey, & E. Roberts, Freedom From Federal Establishment 130 (1964).

The House refused to accept the Senate's changes in the Bill of Rights and asked for a conference; the version which emerged from the conference was that which ultimately found its way into the Constitution as a part of the First Amendment. "Congress shall make no law respecting an establishment of religion, or prohibiting the free exercise thereof." The House and the Senate both accepted this language on successive days, and the amendment was proposed in this form.

On the basis of the record of these proceedings in the House of Representatives, James Madison was undoubtedly the most important architect among the members of the ⊥**98** House of the amendments which became the Bill of Rights, but it was James Madison speaking as an advocate of sensible legislative compromise, not as an advocate of incorporating the Virginia Statute of Religious Liberty into the United States Constitution. During the ratification debate in the Virginia Convention, Madison had actually opposed the idea of any Bill of Rights. His sponsorship of the amendments in the House was obviously not that of a zealous believer in the necessity of the Religion Clauses, but of one who felt it might do some good, could do no harm, and would satisfy those who had ratified the Constitution on the condition that Congress propose a Bill of Rights. His original language "nor shall any national religion be established" obviously does not conform to the "wall of separation" between church and State idea which latter day commentators have ascribed to him. His explanation on the floor of the meaning of his language—"that Congress should not establish a religion, and enforce the legal observation of it by law" is of the same ilk. When he replied to Huntington in the debate over the proposal which came from the Select Committee of the House, he urged that the language "no religion shall be established by law" should be amended by inserting the word "national" in front of the word "religion."

It seems indisputable from these glimpses of Madison's thinking, as reflected by actions on the floor of the House in 1789, that he saw the amendment as designed to prohibit the establishment of a national religion, and perhaps to prevent discrimination among sects. He did not see it as requiring neutrality on the part of government between religion and irreligion. Thus the Court's opinion in *Everson*—while correct in bracketing Madison and Jefferson together in their exertions in their home state leading to the enactment of the ⊥**99** Virginia Statute of Religious Liberty—is totally incorrect in suggesting that Madison carried these views onto the floor of the United States House of Representatives when he proposed the language which would ultimately become the Bill of Rights.

The repetition of this error in the Court's opinion in *McCollum* v. *Board of Education* and *Engel* v. *Vitale*, does not make it any sounder historically. Finally, in *Abington School District* v. *Schempp*, the Court made the truly remarkable statement that "the views of Madison and Jefferson preceded by Roger Williams came to be incorporated not only in the Federal Constitution but likewise in those of most of our States." On the basis of what evidence we have, this statement is demonstrably incorrect as a matter of history. And its repetition in varying forms in succeeding opinions of the Court can give it no more authority than it possesses as a matter of fact; *stare decisis* may bind courts as to matters of law, but it cannot bind them as to matters of history.

None of the other Members of Congress who spoke during the August 15th debate expressed the slightest indication that they thought the language before them from the Select Committee, or the evil to be aimed at, would require that the Government be absolutely neutral as between religion and irreligion. The evil to be aimed at, so far as those who spoke were concerned, appears to have been the establishment of a national church, and perhaps the preference of one religious sect over another, but it was definitely not concern about whether the Government might aid all religions evenhandedly. If one were to follow the advice of *Justice* BRENNAN, concurring in *Abington School District* v. *Schempp*, and construe the Amendment in the light of what par⊥**100**ticular "practices . . . challenged threaten those consequences which the Framers deeply feared; whether, in short, they tend to promote that type of interdependence between religion and state which the First Amendment was designed to prevent," one would have to say that the First Amendment Establishment Clause should be read no more broadly than to prevent the establishment of a national religion or the governmental preference of one religious sect over another.

The actions of the First Congress, which reenacted the Northwest Ordinance for the governance of the Northwest Territory in 1789, confirm the view that Congress did not mean that the Government should be neutral between religion and irreligion. The House of Representatives took up the Northwest Ordinance on the same day as Madison introduced his proposed amendments which became the Bill of Rights; while at that time the

Federal Government was of course not bound by draft amendments to the Constitution which had not yet been proposed by Congress, say nothing of ratified by the States, it seems highly unlikely that the House of Representatives would simultaneously consider proposed amendments to the Constitution and enact an important piece of territorial legislation which conflicted with the intent of those proposals. The Northwest Ordinance reenacted the Northwest Ordinance of 1787 and provided that "[r]eligion, morality, and knowledge, being necessary to good government and the happiness of mankind, schools and the means of education shall forever be encouraged." Land grants for schools in the Northwest Territory were not limited to public schools. It was not until 1845 that Congress limited land grants in the new States and Territories to nonsectarian schools.

On the day after the House of Representatives voted to adopt the form of the First Amendment Religion Clause which was ultimately proposed and ratified, Representative ⊥**101** Elias Boudinot proposed a resolution asking President George Washington to issue a Thanksgiving Day proclamation. Boudinot said he "could not think of letting the session pass over without offering an opportunity to all the citizens of the United States of joining with one voice, in returning to Almighty God their sincere thanks for the many blessings he had poured down upon them." 1 Annals of Cong. 914 (1789). Representative Aedanas Burke objected to the resolution because he did not like "this mimicking of European customs"; Representative Thomas Tucker objected that whether or not the people had reason to be satisfied with the Constitution was something that the states knew better than the Congress, and in any event "it is a religious matter, and, as such, is proscribed to us." *Id.*, at 915. Representative Sherman supported the resolution "not only as a laudable one in itself, but as warranted by a number of precedents in Holy Writ: for instance, the solemn thanksgivings and rejoicings which took place in the time of Solomon, after the building of the temple, was a case in point. This example, he thought, worthy of Christian imitation on the present occasion. . . ." *Ibid.*

Boudinot's resolution was carried in the affirmative on September 25, 1789. Boudinot and Sherman, who favored the Thanksgiving proclamation, voted in favor of the adoption of the proposed amendments to the Constitution, including the Religion Clause; Tucker, who opposed the Thanksgiving proclamation, voted against the adoption of the amendments which became the Bill of Rights.

Within two weeks of this action by the House, George Washington responded to the Joint Resolution which by now had been changed to include the language that the President "recommend to the people of the United States a day of public thanksgiving and prayer, to be observed by acknowledging with grateful hearts the many and signal favors of Almighty God, especially by affording them an opportunity peaceably to establish a form of government for their safety and happiness." 1 J. Richardson, Messages and Papers of ⊥**102** the Presidents, 1789-1897, p. 64 (1897). The Presidential proclamation was couched in these words: "Now, therefore, I do recommend and assign Thursday, the 26th day of November next, to be devoted by the people of these States to the service of that great and glorious Being who is the beneficent author of all the good that was, that is, or that will be; that we may then all unite in rendering unto Him our sincere and humble thanks for His kind care and protection of the people of this country previous to their becoming a nation; for the signal and manifold mercies and the favorable interpositions of His providence in the course and conclusion of the late war; for the great degree of tranquility, union, and plenty which we have since enjoyed; for the peaceable and rational manner in which we have been enabled to establish constitutions of government for our safety and happiness, and particularly the national one now lately instituted; for the civil and religious liberty with which we are blessed, and the means we have of acquiring and diffusing useful knowledge; and in general, for all the great and various favors which He has been pleased to confer upon us.

"And also that we may then unite in most humbly offering our prayers and supplications to the great Lord and Ruler of Nations, and beseech Him to pardon our national and other transgressions; to enable us all, whether in public or private stations, to perform our several and relative duties properly and punctually; to render our National Government a blessing to all the people by constantly being a Government of wise, just, and constitutional laws, discreetly and faithfully executed and obeyed; to protect and guide all sovereigns and nations (especially such as have shown kindness to us), and to bless them with good governments, peace, and concord; to promote the knowledge and practice of true religion and virtue, and the increase of science among them and ⊥**103** us; and, generally, to grant unto all mankind such a degree of temporal prosperity as He alone knows to be best." *Ibid.*

George Washington, John Adams, and James Madison all issued Thanksgiving proclamations; Thomas Jefferson did not, saying: "Fasting and prayer are religious exercises; the enjoining them an act of discipline. Every religious society has a right to determine for itself the times for these exercises, and the objects proper for them, according to their own particular tenets; and this right can never be safer than in their own hands, where the Constitution had deposited it." 11 Writings of Thomas Jefferson 429 (A. Lipscomb ed. 1904).

As the United States moved from the 18th into the 19th century, Congress appropriated time and again public moneys in support of sectarian Indian education carried on by religious organizations. Typical of these was Jefferson's treaty with the Kaskaskia Indians, which provided annual cash support for the Tribe's Roman Catholic priest and church. It was not until 1897, when aid to sectarian edu⊥**104**cation for Indians had reached

$500,000 annually, that Congress decided thereafter to cease appropriating money for education in sectarian schools. This history shows the fallacy of the notion found in *Everson* that "no tax in any amount" may be levied for religious activities in any form.

Joseph Story, a member of this Court from 1811 to 1845, and during much of that time a professor at the Harvard Law School, published by far the most comprehensive treatise on the United States Constitution that had then appeared. Volume 2 of Story's Commentaries on the Constitution of the United States 630-632 (5th ed. 1891) discussed the meaning of the Establishment Clause of the First Amendment this way: "Probably at the time of the adoption of the Constitution and of the amendment to it now under consideration [First Amendment], the general if not the universal sentiment in America was, that Christianity ought to receive encouragement from the State so far as was not incompatible with the private rights of conscience and the freedom of religious worship. An attempt to level all religions, and to make it a matter of state policy to hold all in utter indifference, would have created universal disapprobation, if not universal indignation.

. . . . .

"The real object of the [First] [A]mendment was not to countenance, much less to advance, Mahometanism, or Judaism, or infidelity, by prostrating Christianity; but to exclude all rivalry among Christian sects, and to prevent ⊥**105** any national ecclesiastical establishment which should give to a hierarchy the exclusive patronage of the national government. It thus cut off the means of religious persecution (the vice and pest of former ages), and of the subversion of the rights of conscience in matters of religion, which had been trampled upon almost from the days of the Apostles to the present age. . . ."

Thomas Cooley's eminence as a legal authority rivaled that of Story. Cooley stated in his treatise entitled Constitutional Limitations that aid to a particular religious sect was prohibited by the United States Constitution, but he went on to say: "But while thus careful to establish, protect, and defend religious freedom and equality, the American constitutions contain no provisions which prohibit the authorities from such solemn recognition of a superintending Providence in public transactions and exercises as the general religious sentiment of mankind inspires, and as seems meet and proper in finite and dependent beings. Whatever may be the shades of religious belief, all must acknowledge the fitness of recognizing in important human affairs the superintending care and control of the Great Governor of the Universe, and of acknowledging with thanksgiving his boundless favors, or bowing in contrition when visited with the penalties of his broken laws. No principle of constitutional law is violated when thanksgiving or fast days are appointed; when chaplains are designated for the army and navy; when legislative sessions are opened with prayer or the reading of the Scriptures, or when religious teaching is encouraged by a general exemption of the houses of religious worship from taxation for the support of State government. Undoubtedly the spirit of the Constitution will require, in all these cases, that care be taken to avoid discrimination ⊥**106** in favor of or against any one religious denomination or sect; but the power to do any of these things does not become unconstitutional simply because of its susceptibility to abuse. . . ." *Id.*, at 470-471. Cooley added that, "[t]his public recognition of religious worship, however, is not based entirely, perhaps not even mainly, upon a sense of what is due to the Supreme Being himself as the author of all good and of all law; but the same reasons of state policy which induce the government to aid institutions of charity and seminaries of instruction will incline it also to foster religious worship and religious institutions, as conservators of the public morals and valuable, if not indispensable, assistants to the preservation of the public order." *Id.*, at 470.

It would seem from this evidence that the Establishment Clause of the First Amendment had acquired a well-accepted meaning: it forbade establishment of a national religion, and forbade preference among religious sects or denominations. Indeed, the first American dictionary defined the word "establishment" as "the act of establishing, founding, ratifying or ordainin(g,") such as in "[t]he episcopal form of religion so called, in England." 1 N. Webster, American Dictionary of the English Language (1st ed. 1828). The Establishment Clause did not require government neutrality between religion and irreligion nor did it prohibit the federal government from providing non-discriminatory aid to religion. There is simply no historical foundation for the proposition that the Framers intended to build the "wall of separation" that was constitutionalized in *Everson*.

Notwithstanding the absence of an historical basis for this theory of rigid separation, the wall idea might well have served as a useful albeit misguided analytical concept, had it led this Court to unified and principled results in Establishment Clause cases. The opposite, unfortunately, has been ⊥**107** true; in the 38 years since *Everson* our Establishment Clause cases have been neither principled nor unified. Our recent opinions, many of them hopelessly divided pluralities, have with embarrassing candor conceded that the "wall of separation" is merely a "blurred, indistinct, and variable barrier," which "is not wholly accurate" and can only be "dimly perceived." *Lemon* v. *Kurtzman*.

Whether due to its lack of historical support or its practical unworkability, the *Everson* "wall" has proven all but useless as a guide to sound constitutional adjudication. It illustrates only too well the wisdom of Benjamin Cardozo's observation that "[m]etaphors in law are to be narrowly watched, for starting as devices to liberate thought, they end often by enslaving it." *Berkey* v. *Third Avenue R. Co.*

But the greatest injury of the "wall" notion is its mischievous diversion of judges from the actual intentions of the drafters of the Bill of Rights. The "crucible of litigation," is well adapted to adjudicating factual disputes on the basis of testimony presented in court, but no amount of repetition of historical errors in judicial opinions can make the errors true. The "wall of separation between church and State" is a metaphor based on bad history, a metaphor which has proved useless as a guide to judging. It should be frankly and explicitly abandoned. ⊥**108**

The Court has more recently attempted to add some mortar to *Everson's* wall through the three-part test of *Lemon* v. *Kurtzman*, which served at first to offer a more useful test for purposes of the Establishment Clause than did the "wall" metaphor. Generally stated, the *Lemon* test proscribes state action that has a sectarian purpose or effect, or causes an impermissible governmental entanglement with religion.

Lemon cited *Board of Education* v. *Allen* as the source of the "purpose" and "effect" prongs of the three-part test. The *Allen* opinion explains, however, how it inherited the purpose and effect elements from *Schempp* and *Everson*, both of which contain the historical errors described above. Thus the purpose and effect prongs have the same historical deficiencies as the wall concept itself: they are in no way based on either the language or intent of the drafters.

The secular purpose prong has proven mercurial in application because it has never been fully defined, and we have never fully stated how the test is to operate. If the purpose prong is intended to void those aids to sectarian institutions accompanied by a stated legislative purpose to aid religion, the prong will condemn nothing so long as the legislature utters a secular purpose and says nothing about aiding religion. Thus the constitutionality of a statute may depend upon what the legislators put into the legislative history and, more importantly, what they leave out. The purpose prong means little if it only requires the legislature to express any secular purpose and omit all sectarian references, because legislators might do just that. Faced with a valid legislative secular purpose, we could not properly ignore that purpose without a factual basis for doing so.

However, if the purpose prong is aimed to void all statutes enacted with the intent to aid sectarian institutions, whether stated or not, then most statutes providing any aid, such as ⊥**109** textbooks or bus rides for sectarian school children, will fail because one of the purposes behind every statute, whether stated or not, is to aid the target of its largesse. In other words, if the purpose prong requires an absence of *any* intent to aid sectarian institutions, whether or not expressed, few state laws in this area could pass the test, and we would be required to void some state aids to religion which we have already upheld.

The entanglement prong of the *Lemon* test came from *Walz* v. *Tax Commission*. *Walz* involved a constitutional challenge to New York's time-honored practice of providing state property tax exemptions to church property used in worship. The *Walz* opinion refused to "undermine the ultimate constitutional objective [of the Establishment Clause] as illuminated by history," and upheld the tax exemption. The Court examined the historical relationship between the state and church when church property was in issue, and determined that the challenged tax exemption did not so entangle New York with the Church as to cause an intrusion or interference with religion. Interferences with religion should arguably be dealt with under the Free Exercise Clause, but the entanglement inquiry in *Walz* was consistent with that case's broad survey of the relationship between state taxation and religious property.

We have not always followed *Walz's* reflective inquiry into entanglement, however. One of the difficulties with the entanglement prong is that, when divorced from the logic of *Walz* it creates an "insoluble paradox" in school aid cases: we have required aid to parochial schools to be closely watched lest it be put to sectarian use, yet this close supervision itself will create an entanglement. For example, in *Wolman*, the Court in part struck the State's nondiscriminatory provision of buses for parochial school field trips because the state supervision ⊥**110** of sectarian officials in charge of field trips would be too onerous. This type of self-defeating result is certainly not required to ensure that States do not establish religion.

The entanglement test as applied in cases like *Wolman* also ignores the myriad state administrative regulations properly placed upon sectarian institutions such as curriculum, attendance, and certification requirements for sectarian schools, or fire and safety regulations for churches. Avoiding entanglement between church and State may be an important consideration in a case like *Walz*, but if the entanglement prong were applied to all state and church relations in the automatic manner in which it has been applied to school aid cases, the State could hardly require anything of church-related institutions as a condition for receipt of financial assistance.

These difficulties arise because the *Lemon* test has no more grounding in the history of the First Amendment than does the wall theory upon which it rests. The three-part test represents a determined effort to craft a workable rule from an historically faulty doctrine; but the rule can only be as sound as the doctrine it attempts to service. The three-part test has simply not provided adequate standards for deciding Establishment Clause cases, as this Court has slowly come to realize. Even worse, the *Lemon* test has caused this Court to fracture into unworkable plurality opinions, depending upon how each of the three factors applies to a certain state action. The results from our school services cases show the difficulty we have encountered in making the *Lemon* test yield principled results.

For example, a State may lend to parochial school children geography textbooks that contain maps of the United States, but the State may not lend maps of the United States for use in geography class. A State may lend textbooks on American colonial history, but it may not lend a film on ⊥**111** George Washington, or a film projector to show it in history class. A State may lend classroom workbooks, but may not lend workbooks in which the parochial school children write, thus rendering them nonreusable. A State may pay for bus transportation to religious schools but may not pay for bus transportation from the parochial school to the public zoo or natural history museum for a field trip. A State may pay for diagnostic services conducted in the parochial school but therapeutic services must be given in a different building; speech and hearing "services" conducted by the State inside the sectarian school are forbidden, but the State may conduct speech and hearing diagnostic testing inside the sectarian school. Exceptional parochial school students may receive counseling, but it must take place outside of the parochial school, such as in a trailer parked down the street. A State may give cash to a parochial school to pay for the administration of State-written tests and state-ordered reporting services, but it may not provide funds for teacher-prepared tests on secular subjects. Religious instruction may not be given in public school, but the public school may release students during the day for religion classes elsewhere, and may enforce attendance at those classes with its truancy laws.

These results violate the historically sound principle "that the Establishment Clause does not forbid governments . . . to [provide] general welfare under which benefits are distributed to private individuals, even though many of those indi⊥**112**viduals may elect to use those benefits in ways that 'aid' religious instruction or worship." *Committee for Public Education* v. *Nyquist*. It is not surprising in the light of this record that our most recent opinions have expressed doubt on the usefulness of the *Lemon* test.

Although the test initially provided helpful assistance, *e.g.*, *Tilton* v. *Richardson*, we soon began describing the test as only a "guideline," *Committee for Public Education* v. *Nyquist*, and lately we have described it as "no more than [a] useful signpos[t]." *Mueller* v. *Allen*. We have noted that the *Lemon* test is "not easily applied," *Meek*, and as *Justice WHITE* noted in *Committee for Public Education* v. *Regan*, under the *Lemon* test we have "sacrifice[d] clarity and predictability for flexibility." In *Lynch* we reiterated that the *Lemon* test has never been binding on the Court, and we cited two cases where we had declined to apply it.

If a constitutional theory has no basis in the history of the amendment it seeks to interpret, is difficult to apply and yields unprincipled results, I see little use in it. The "crucible of litigation," has produced only consistent unpredictability, and today's effort is just a continuation of "the sisyphean task of trying to patch together the 'blurred, indistinct and variable barrier' described in *Lemon* v. *Kurtzman*." *Regan* (Stevens, J. dissenting). We have done much straining since 1947, but still we admit that we can only "dimly perceive" the *Everson* wall. Our perception has been clouded not by the Constitution but by the mists of an unnecessary metaphor. ⊥**113**

The true meaning of the Establishment Clause can only be seen in its history. As drafters of our Bill of Rights, the Framers inscribed the principles that control today. Any deviation from their intentions frustrates the permanence of that Charter and will only lead to the type of unprincipled decisionmaking that has plagued our Establishment Clause cases since *Everson*.

The Framers intended the Establishment Clause to prohibit the designation of any church as a "national" one. The Clause was also designed to stop the Federal Government from asserting a preference for one religious denomination or sect over others. Given the "incorporation" of the Establishment Clause as against the States via the Fourteenth Amendment in *Everson*, States are prohibited as well from establishing a religion or discriminating between sects. As its history abundantly shows, however, nothing in the Establishment Clause requires government to be strictly neutral between religion and irreligion, nor does that Clause prohibit Congress or the States from pursuing legitimate secular ends through nondiscriminatory sectarian means.

The Court strikes down the Alabama statute in *Wallace* v. *Jaffree* because the State wished to "endorse prayer as a favored practice." It would come as much of a shock to those who drafted the Bill of Rights as it will to a large number of thoughtful Americans today to learn that the Constitution, as construed by the majority, prohibits the Alabama Legislature from "endorsing" prayer. George Washington himself, at the request of the very Congress which passed the Bill of Rights, proclaimed a day of "public thanksgiving and prayer, to be observed by acknowledging with grateful hearts the many and signal favors of Almighty God." History must judge whether it was the father of his country in 1789, or a majority of the Court today, which has strayed from the meaning of the Establishment Clause.

The State surely has a secular interest in regulating the manner in which public schools are conducted. Nothing in ⊥**114** the Establishment Clause of the First Amendment, properly understood, prohibits any such generalized "endorsement" of prayer. I would therefore reverse the judgment of the Court of Appeals in *Wallace* v. *Jaffree*.

EDWARDS v. AGUILLARD

482 U.S. 578
ON APPEAL FROM THE UNITED STATES COURT OF APPEALS FOR THE FIFTH CIRCUIT
Argued December 10, 1986 — Decided June 19, 1987

⊥**580** *Justice BRENNAN* delivered the opinion of the Court.

The question for decision is whether Louisiana's "Balanced Treatment for Creation-Science and Evolution-Science in Public School Instruction" Act (Creationism Act), La. Rev. Stat. Ann. §§ 17:286.1-17:286.7 (West 1982), is facially in⊥**581**valid as violative of the Establishment Clause of the First Amendment.

I

The Creationism Act forbids the teaching of the theory of evolution in public schools unless accompanied by instruction in "creation science." No school is required to teach evolution or creation science. If either is taught, however, the other must also be taught. The theories of evolution and creation science are statutorily defined as "the scientific evidences for [creation or evolution] and inferences from those scientific evidences." §§ 17.286.3(2) and (3).

Appellees, who include parents of children attending Louisiana public schools, Louisiana teachers, and religious leaders challenged the constitutionality of the Act in District Court, seeking an injunction and declaratory relief. Appellants, Louisiana officials charged with implementing the Act, defended on the ground that the purpose of the Act is to protect a legitimate secular interest, namely, academic freedom. Appellees attacked the Act as facially invalid because ⊥**582** it violated the Establishment Clause and made a motion for summary judgment. The District Court granted the motion. The court held that there can be no valid secular reason for prohibiting the teaching of evolution, a theory historically opposed by some religious denominations. The court further concluded that "the teaching of 'creation-science' and 'creationism,' as contemplated by the statute, involves teaching 'tailored to the principles' of a particular religious sect or group of sects." The District Court therefore held that the Creationism Act violated the Establishment Clause either because it prohibited the teaching of evolution or because it required the teaching of creation science with the purpose of advancing a particular religious doctrine.

The Court of Appeals affirmed. The court observed that the statute's avowed purpose of protecting academic freedom was inconsistent with requiring, upon risk of sanction, the teaching of creation science whenever evolution is taught. The court found that the Louisiana Legislature's actual intent was "to discredit evolution by counterbalancing its teaching at every turn with the teaching of creationism, a religious belief." Because the Creationism Act was thus a law furthering a particular religious belief, the Court of Appeals held that the Act violated the Establishment Clause. A suggestion for rehearing en banc was denied over a dissent. We noted probable jurisdiction, and now affirm.

II

The Establishment Clause forbids the enactment of any law "respecting an establishment of religion." The Court ⊥**583** has applied a three-pronged test to determine whether legislation comports with the Establishment Clause. First, the legislature must have adopted the law with a secular purpose. Second, the statute's principal or primary effect must be one that neither advances nor inhibits religion. Third, the statute must not result in an excessive entanglement of government with religion. State action violates the Establishment Clause if it fails to satisfy any of these prongs.

In this case, the Court must determine whether the Establishment Clause was violated in the special context of the public elementary and secondary school system. States and local school boards are generally afforded considerable discretion in operating public schools. "At the same time . . . we have necessarily recognized that the discretion of the States and local school boards in matters of education must be exercised in a manner that comports with the transcendent imperatives of the First Amendment." *Board of Education, Island Trees Union Free School Dist. No. 26* v. *Pico*.

The Court has been particularly vigilant in monitoring compliance with the Establishment Clause in elementary and ⊥**584** secondary schools. Families entrust public schools with the education of their children, but condition their trust on the understanding that the classroom will not purposely be used to advance religious views that may conflict with the private beliefs of the student and his or her family. Students in such institutions are impressionable and their attendance is involuntary. The State exerts great authority and coercive power through mandatory attendance requirements, and because of the students' emulation of teachers as role models and the children's susceptibility to peer pressure. Furthermore, "[t]he public school is at once the symbol of our democracy and the most pervasive means for promoting our common destiny. In no activity of the State is it more vital to keep out divisive forces than in its schools. . . ." *McCollum* v. *Board of Education*.

Consequently, the Court has been required often to invalidate statutes which advance religion in public elementary and secondary schools. See *e.g.*, *Grand Rapids School Dist.* v. *Ball* (school district's use of religious school teachers in public schools); *Wallace* v. *Jaffree* (Alabama statute authorizing moment of silence for school prayer); *Stone* v. ⊥**585** *Graham* (posting copy of Ten Commandments on public classroom wall); *Epperson* v. *Arkansas* (statute forbidding teaching of evolution); *Abington School Dist.* v. *Schempp* (daily reading of Bible); *Engel* v. *Vitale* (recitation of "denominationally neutral" prayer).

Therefore, in employing the three-pronged *Lemon* test, we must do so mindful of the particular concerns that arise in the context of public elementary and secondary schools. We now turn to the evaluation of the Act under the *Lemon* test.

III

Lemon's first prong focuses on the purpose that animated adoption of the Act. "The purpose prong of the *Lemon* test asks whether government's actual purpose is to endorse or disapprove of religion." *Lynch* v. *Donnelly*. A governmental intention to promote religion is clear when the State enacts a law to serve a religious purpose.

This intention may be evidenced by promotion of religion in general, see *Wallace* v. *Jaffree* (Establishment Clause protects individual freedom of conscience "to select any religious faith or none at all"); or by advancement of a particular religious belief, *e.g.*, *Stone* v. *Graham* (invalidating requirement to post Ten Commandments, which are "undeniably a sacred text in the Jewish and Christian faiths"); *Epperson* v. *Arkansas* (holding that banning the teaching of evolution in public schools violates the First Amendment since "teaching and learning" must not "be tailored to the principles or prohibitions of any religious sect or dogma"). If the law was enacted for the purpose of endorsing religion, "no consideration of the second or third criteria [of *Lemon*] is necessary." *Wallace* v. *Jaffree*. In this case, appellants have identified no clear secular purpose for the Louisiana Act.

⊥586 True, the Act's stated purpose is to protect academic freedom. This phrase might, in common parlance, be understood as referring to enhancing the freedom of teachers to teach what they will. The Court of Appeals, however, correctly concluded that the Act was not designed to further that goal. We find no merit in the State's argument that the "legislature may not [have] use[d] the terms 'academic freedom' in the correct legal sense. They might have [had] in mind, instead, a basic concept of fairness; teaching all of the evidence." Even if "academic freedom" is read to mean "teaching all of the evidence" with respect to the origin of human beings, the Act does not further this purpose. The goal of providing a more comprehensive science curriculum is not furthered either by outlawing the teaching of evolution or by requiring the teaching of creation science.

A

While the Court is normally deferential to a State's articulation of a secular purpose, it is required that the statement **⊥587** of such purpose be sincere and not a sham. As *Justice O'CONNOR* stated in *Wallace:* "It is not a trivial matter, however, to require that the legislature manifest a secular purpose and omit all sectarian endorsements from its laws. That requirement is precisely tailored to the Establishment Clause's purpose of assuring that Government not intentionally endorse religion or a religious practice."

It is clear from the legislative history that the purpose of the legislative sponsor, Senator Bill Keith, was to narrow the science curriculum. During the legislative hearings, Senator Keith stated: "My preference would be that neither [creationism nor evolution] be taught." Such a ban on teaching does not promote—indeed, it undermines—the provision of a comprehensive scientific education.

It is equally clear that requiring schools to teach creation science with evolution does not advance academic freedom. The Act does not grant teachers a flexibility that they did not already possess to supplant the present science curriculum with the presentation of theories, besides evolution, about the origin of life. Indeed, the Court of Appeals found that no law prohibited Louisiana public school teachers from teaching any scientific theory. As the president of the Louisiana Science Teachers Association testified, "[a]ny scientific concept that's based on established fact can be included in our curriculum already, and no legislation allowing this is necessary." The Act provides Louisiana schoolteachers with no new authority. Thus the stated purpose is not furthered by it.

The Alabama statute held unconstitutional in *Wallace* v. *Jaffree*, is analogous. In *Wallace*, the State characterized its new law as one designed to provide a 1-minute period for meditation. We rejected that stated purpose as in**⊥588**sufficient, because a previously adopted Alabama law already provided for such a 1-minute period. Thus, in this case, as in *Wallace*, "[a]ppellants have not identified any secular purpose that was not fully served by [existing state law] before the enactment of [the statute in question]."

Furthermore, the goal of basic "fairness" is hardly furthered by the Act's discriminatory preference for the teaching of creation science and against the teaching of evolution. While requiring that curriculum guides be developed for creation science, the Act says nothing of comparable guides for evolution. Similarly, resource services are supplied for creation science but not for evolution. Only "creation scientists" can serve on the panel that supplies the resource services. The Act forbids school boards to discriminate against anyone who "chooses to be a creation-scientist" or to teach "creationism," but fails to protect those who choose to teach evolution or any other noncreation science theory, or who refuse to teach creation science.

If the Louisiana Legislature's purpose was solely to maximize the comprehensiveness and effectiveness of science instruction, it would have encouraged the teaching of all scientific theories about the origins of humankind. But under **⊥589** the Act's requirements, teachers who were once free to teach any and all facets of this subject are now unable to do so. Moreover, the Act fails even to ensure that creation science will be taught, but instead requires the teaching of this theory only when the theory of evolution is taught. Thus we agree with the Court of Appeals' conclusion that the Act does not serve to protect academic freedom, but has the distinctly different purpose of discrediting "evolution by counterbalancing its teaching at every turn with the teaching of creationism. . . ."

B

Stone v. *Graham* invalidated the State's requirement that the Ten Commandments be posted in public classrooms. "The Ten Commandments are undeniably a sacred text in the Jewish and Christian faiths, and no legislative recitation of a supposed secular purpose can blind us to that fact." As a result, the contention that the law was designed to provide instruction on a "fundamental legal code" was "not sufficient to avoid conflict with the First Amendment." Similarly *Abington School Dist.* v. *Schempp* held unconstitutional a statute "requiring the selection and reading at the opening of the school day of verses from the Holy Bible and the recitation of the Lord's Prayer by the students in unison," despite the proffer of such secular purposes as the "promotion of moral values, the con⊥**590**tradiction to the materialistic trends of our times, the perpetuation of our institutions and the teaching of literature."

As in *Stone* and *Abington*, we need not be blind in this case to the legislature's preeminent religious purpose in enacting this statute. There is a historic and contemporaneous link between the teachings of certain religious denominations and the teaching of evolution. It was this link that concerned the Court in *Epperson* v. *Arkansas*, which also involved a facial challenge to a statute regulating the teaching of evolution. In that case, the Court reviewed an Arkansas statute that made it unlawful for an instructor to teach evolution or to use a textbook that referred to this scientific theory. Although the Arkansas antievolution law did not explicitly state its predominate religious purpose, the Court could not ignore that "[t]he statute was a product of the upsurge of 'fundamentalist' religious fervor" that has long viewed this particular scientific theory as contradicting the literal interpretation of the Bible. After reviewing the history of antievolution statutes, the Court determined that "there can be no doubt that the motivation for the [Arkansas] law was the same [as other antievolution statutes]: to suppress the teaching of a theory which, it was thought, 'denied' the divine creation of man." The Court found that there can be no legitimate ⊥**591** state interest in protecting particular religions from scientific views "distasteful to them," and concluded "that the First Amendment does not permit the State to require that teaching and learning must be tailored to the principles or prohibitions of any religious sect or dogma."

These same historic and contemporaneous antagonisms between the teachings of certain religious denominations and the teaching of evolution are present in this case. The preeminent purpose of the Louisiana Legislature was clearly to advance the religious viewpoint that a supernatural being created humankind. The term "creation science" was defined as embracing this particular religious doctrine by those responsible for the passage of the Creationism Act. Senator Keith's leading expert on creation science, Edward Boudreaux, testified at the legislative hearings that the theory of creation science included belief in the existence of a supernatural creator (noting that "creation scientists" point to high probability that life was "created by an intelligent mind"). Senator Keith also cited testimony from other experts to support the creation-science view that "a creator [was] responsible for the universe and everything in it." The legislative history ⊥**592** therefore reveals that the term "creation science," as contemplated by the legislature that adopted this Act, embodies the religious belief that a supernatural creator was responsible for the creation of humankind.

Furthermore, it is not happenstance that the legislature required the teaching of a theory that coincided with this religious view. The legislative history documents that the Act's primary purpose was to change the science curriculum of public schools in order to provide persuasive advantage to a particular religious doctrine that rejects the factual basis of evolution in its entirety. The sponsor of the Creationism Act, Senator Keith, explained during the legislative hearings that his disdain for the theory of evolution resulted from the support that evolution supplied to views contrary to his own religious beliefs. According to Senator Keith, the theory of evolution was consonant with the "cardinal principle[s] of religious humanism, secular humanism, theological liberalism, aetheistism [*sic*]." The state senator repeatedly stated that scientific evidence supporting his religious views should be included in the public school curriculum to redress the fact that the theory of evolution incidentally coincided with what he characterized as religious beliefs antithetical to his own. ⊥**593** The legislation therefore sought to alter the science curriculum to reflect endorsement of a religious view that is antagonistic to the theory of evolution.

In this case, the purpose of the Creationism Act was to restructure the science curriculum to conform with a particular religious viewpoint. Out of many possible science subjects taught in the public schools, the legislature chose to affect the teaching of the one scientific theory that historically has been opposed by certain religious sects. As in *Epperson*, the legislature passed the Act to give preference to those religious groups which have as one of their tenets the creation of humankind by a divine creator. The "overriding fact" that confronted the Court in *Epperson* was "that Arkansas' law selects from the body of knowledge a particular segment which it proscribes for the sole reason that it is deemed to conflict with . . . a particular interpretation of the Book of Genesis by a particular religious group." Similarly, the Creationism Act is designed *either* to promote the theory of creation science which embodies a particular religious tenet by requiring that creation science be taught whenever evolution is taught *or* to prohibit the teaching of a scientific theory disfavored by certain religious sects by forbidding the teaching of evolution when creation science is not also taught. The Establishment Clause, however, "forbids *alike* the preference of a religious doctrine or the prohibition of theory which is deemed antagonistic to a particular dogma" (emphasis added). Because the primary purpose of the Creationism Act is to advance a particular religious belief, the Act endorses religion in violation of the First Amendment.

We do not imply that a legislature could never require that scientific critiques of prevailing scientific theories be taught. Indeed, the Court acknowledged in *Stone* that its decision ⊥**594** forbidding the posting of the Ten Commandments did not mean that no use could ever be made of the Ten Commandments, or that the Ten Commandments played an exclusively religious role in the history of Western Civilization. In a similar way, teaching a variety of scientific theories about the origins of humankind to schoolchildren might be validly done with the clear secular intent of enhancing the effectiveness of science instruction. But because the primary purpose of the Creationism Act is to endorse a particular religious doctrine, the Act furthers religion in violation of the Establishment Clause.

IV

Appellants contend that genuine issues of material fact remain in dispute, and therefore the District Court erred in granting summary judgment. Federal Rule of Civil Procedure 56(c) provides that summary judgment "shall be rendered forthwith if the pleadings, depositions, answers to interrogatories, and admissions on file, together with the affidavits, if any, show that there is no genuine issue as to any material fact and that the moving party is entitled to a judgment as a matter of law." A court's finding of improper purpose behind a statute is appropriately determined by the statute on its face, its legislative history, or its interpretation by a responsible administrative agency. The plain meaning of the statute's words, enlightened by their context and the contemporaneous legislative history, can control the determination of legislative purpose. ⊥**595** Moreover, in determining the legislative purpose of a statute, the Court has also considered the historical context of the statute, and the specific sequence of events leading to passage of the statute.

In this case, appellees' motion for summary judgment rested on the plain language of the Creationism Act, the legislative history and historical context of the Act, the specific sequence of events leading to the passage of the Act, the State Board's report on a survey of school superintendents, and the correspondence between the Act's legislative sponsor and its key witnesses. Appellants contend that affidavits made by two scientists, two theologians, and an education administrator raise a genuine issue of material fact and that summary judgment was therefore barred. The affidavits define creation science as "origin through abrupt appearance in complex form" and allege that such a viewpoint constitutes a true scientific theory.

We agree with the lower courts that these affidavits do not raise a genuine issue of material fact. The existence of "uncontroverted affidavits" does not bar summary judgment. Moreover, the postenactment testimony of outside experts is of little use in determining the Louisiana Legislature's purpose in enacting this statute. The Louisiana Legislature did hear and rely on scientific experts in passing the bill, but none of the persons making the affidavits produced by the ap⊥**596**pellants participated in or contributed to the enactment of the law or its implementation. The District Court, in its discretion, properly concluded that a Monday-morning "battle of the experts" over possible technical meanings of terms in the statute would not illuminate the contemporaneous purpose of the Louisiana Legislature when it made the law. We therefore conclude that the District Court did not err in finding that appellants failed to raise a genuine issue of material fact, and in granting summary judgment.

V

The Louisiana Creationism Act advances a religious doctrine by requiring either the banishment of the theory of evolution from public school classrooms or the presentation of a religious viewpoint that rejects evolution in its entirety. ⊥**597** The Act violates the Establishment Clause of the First Amendment because it seeks to employ the symbolic and financial support of government to achieve a religious purpose. The judgment of the Court of Appeals therefore is

Affirmed.

Justice POWELL, with whom *Justice* O'CONNOR joins, concurring.

I write separately to note certain aspects of the legislative history, and to emphasize that nothing in the Court's opinion diminishes the traditionally broad discretion accorded state and local school officials in the selection of the public school curriculum.

The Court consistently has applied the three-pronged test of *Lemon* v. *Kurtzman* to determine whether a particular state action violates the Establishment Clause of the Constitution. See, *e.g.*, *Grand Rapids School . Dist.* v. *Ball* ("We have particularly relied on *Lemon* in every case involving the sensitive relationship between government and religion in the education of our children"). The first requirement of the *Lemon* test is that the challenged statute have a "secular legislative purpose." If no valid secular purpose can be identified, then the statute violates the Establishment Clause.

A

"The starting point in every case involving construction of a statute is the language itself." *Blue Chip Stamps* v. *Manor Drug Stores*. ⊥**598** The Balanced Treatment for Creation-Science and Evolution-Science Act (Act or Balanced Treatment Act), La. Rev. Stat. Ann. §17:286.1 *et seq.* (West 1982), provides in part:

"[P]ublic schools within [the] state shall give balanced treatment to creation-science and to evolution-science. Balanced treatment of these two models shall be given in classroom lectures taken as a whole for each course, in textbook materials taken as a whole for each course, in library materials taken as a whole for the sciences and taken as a whole for the humanities, and in other educational programs in public schools, to the extent that such lectures, textbooks, library materials, or educational programs deal in any way with the subject of the origin of man, life, the earth, or the universe. When creation or evolution is taught, each shall be taught as a theory, rather than as proven scientific fact." § 17:286.4(A). "Balanced treatment" means "providing whatever information and instruction in both creation and evolution models the classroom teacher determines is necessary and appropriate to provide insight into both theories in view of the textbooks and other instructional materials available for use in his classroom." § 17:286.3(1). "Creation-science" is defined as "the scientific evidences for creation and inferences from those scientific evidences." § 17:286.3(2). "Evolution-science" means "the scientific evidences for evolution and inferences from those scientific evidences." § 17:286.3(3).

Although the Act requires the teaching of the scientific evidences of both creation and evolution whenever either is taught, it does not define either term. "A fundamental canon of statutory construction is that, unless otherwise defined, words will be interpreted as taking their ordinary, contemporary, common meaning." *Perrin* v. *United States*. The "doctrine or theory of creation" is commonly defined as "holding that matter, the various forms of life, and the world were created by a transcendent God out ⊥**599** of nothing." Webster's Third New International Dictionary 532 unabridged (1981). "Evolution" is defined as "the theory that the various types of animals and plants have their origin in other preexisting types, the distinguishable differences being due to modifications in successive generations." Thus, the Balanced Treatment Act mandates that public schools present the scientific evidence to support a theory of divine creation whenever they present the scientific evidence to support the theory of evolution. "[C]oncepts concerning God or a supreme being of some sort are manifestly religious. . . . These concepts do not shed that religiosity merely because they are presented as a philosophy or as a science." *Malnak* v. *Yogi*. From the face of the statute, a purpose to advance a religious belief is apparent.

A religious purpose alone is not enough to invalidate an act of a state legislature. The religious purpose must predominate. The Act contains a statement of purpose: to "protec[t] academic freedom." § 17:286.2. This statement is puzzling. Of course, the "academic freedom" of teachers to present information in public schools, and students to receive it, is broad. But it necessarily is circumscribed by the Establishment Clause. "Academic freedom" does not encompass the right of a legislature to structure the public school curriculum in order to advance a particular religious belief. Nevertheless, I read this statement in the Act as rendering the purpose of the statute at least ambiguous. Accordingly, I proceed to review the legislative history of the Act.

B

In June 1980, Senator Bill Keith introduced Senate Bill 956 in the Louisiana Legislature. The stated purpose of the bill ⊥**600** was to "assure academic freedom by requiring the teaching of the theory of creation ex nihilo in all public schools where the theory of evolution is taught." The bill defined the "theory of creation ex nihilo" as "the belief that the origin of the elements, the galaxy, the solar system, of life, of all the species of plants and animals, the origin of man, and the origin of all things and their processes and relationships were created ex nihilo and fixed by God." This theory was referred to by Senator Keith as "scientific creationism."

While a Senate committee was studying scientific creationism, Senator Keith introduced a second draft of the bill requiring balanced treatment of "evolution-science" and "creation-science." Although the Keith bill prohibited "instruction in any religious doctrine or materials," it defined "creation-science" to include

"the scientific evidences and related inferences that indicate (a) sudden creation of the universe, energy, and life from nothing, (b) the insufficiency of mutation and natural selection in bringing about development of all living kinds from a single organism; (c) changes only within fixed limits or originally created kinds of plants and animals; (d) separate ancestry for man and apes; (e) explanation of the earth's geology by catastrophism, including the occurrence of a worldwide flood; and (f) a ⊥**601** relatively recent inception of the earth and living kinds."

Significantly, the model Act on which the Keith bill relied was also the basis for a similar statute in Arkansas. See *McLean* v. *Arkansas Board of Education*. The District Court in *McLean* carefully examined this model Act, particularly the section defining creation science, and concluded that "[b]oth [its] concepts and wording . . . convey an inescapable religiosity." The court found that "[t]he ideas of [this section] are not merely similar to the literal interpretation of Genesis; they are identical and parallel to no other story of creation."

The complaint in *McLean* was filed on May 27, 1981. On May 28, the Louisiana Senate committee amended the Keith bill to delete the illustrative list of scientific evidences. According to the legislator who proposed the amendment, it was "not intended to try to gut [the bill] in any way, or defeat the purpose [for] which Senator Keith introduced [it]," and was not viewed as working "any violence to the bill." Instead, the concern was "whether this should be an all inclusive list."

The legislature then held hearings on the amended bill that became the Balanced Treatment Act under review. The principal creation scientist to testify in support of the Act was Dr. Edward Boudreaux. He did not elaborate on the nature of creation science except to indicate that the "scientific evidences" of the theory are "the objective information of science [that] point[s] to conditions of a creator." He further testified that the recognized creation scientists in the United States, who "numbe[r] something like a thousand [and] who hold doctorate and masters degrees in all areas of science," are affiliated with either or both the Institute for Creation Research and the Creation Research Society. Information on both of these organizations is part of the legislative history, ⊥**602** and a review of their goals and activities sheds light on the nature of creation science as it was presented to, and understood by, the Louisiana Legislature.

The Institute for Creation Research is an affiliate of the Christian Heritage College in San Diego, California. The Institute was established to address the "urgent need for our nation to return to belief in a personal, omnipotent Creator, who has a purpose for His creation and to whom all people must eventually give account." A goal of the Institute is "a revival of belief in special creation as the true explanation of the origin of the world." Therefore, the Institute currently is working on the "development of new methods for teaching scientific creationism in public schools." The Creation Research Society (CRS) is located in Ann Arbor, Michigan. A member must subscribe to the following statement of belief: "The Bible is the written word of God, and because it is inspired throughout, all of its assertions are historically and scientifically true." To study creation science at the CRS, a member must accept "that the account of origins in Genesis is a factual presentation of simple historical truth."

⊥**603** C

When, as here, "both courts below are unable to discern an arguably valid secular purpose, this Court normally should hesitate to find one." *Wallace* v. *Jaffree*. My examination of the language and the legislative history of the Balanced Treatment Act confirms that the intent of the Louisiana Legislature was to promote a particular religious belief. The legislative history of the Arkansas statute prohibiting the teaching of evolution examined in *Epperson* v. *Arkansas* was strikingly similar to the legislative history of the Balanced Treatment Act. In *Epperson*, the Court found:

"It is clear that fundamentalist sectarian conviction was and is the law's reason for existence. Its antecedent, Tennessee's 'monkey law,' candidly stated its purpose: to make it unlawful 'to teach any theory that denies the story of the Divine Creation of man as taught in the Bible, and to teach instead that man has descended from a lower order of animals.' Perhaps the sensational publicity attendant upon the *Scopes* trial induced Arkansas to adopt less explicit language. It eliminated Tennessee's reference to 'the story of the Divine creation of man' as taught in the Bible, but there is no doubt that the motivation for the law was the same: to suppress the teaching of a theory which, it was thought, 'denied' the divine creation of man."

Here, it is clear that religious belief is the Balanced Treatment Act's "reason for existence." The tenets of creation science parallel the Genesis story of creation, and this is a ⊥**604** religious belief. "[N]o legislative recitation of a supposed secular purpose can blind us to that fact." *Stone* v. *Graham*. Although the Act as finally enacted does not contain explicit reference to its religious purpose, there is no indication in the legislative history that the deletion of "creation ex nihilo" and the four primary tenets of the theory was intended to alter the purpose of teaching creation science. Instead, the statements of purpose of the sources of creation science in the United States make clear that their purpose is to promote a religious belief. I find no persuasive evidence in the legislative history that the legislature's purpose was any different. The fact that the Louisiana Legislature purported to add information to the school curriculum rather than detract from it as in *Epperson* does not affect my analysis. Both legislatures acted with the unconstitutional purpose of structuring the public school curriculum to make it compatible with a particular religious belief: the "divine creation of man."

That the statute is limited to the scientific evidences supporting the theory does not render its purpose secular. In reaching its conclusion that the Act is unconstitutional, the Court of Appeals "[did] not deny that the underpinnings of creationism may be supported by scientific evidence." And there is no need to do so. Whatever the academic merit of particular subjects or theories, the Establishment Clause limits the discretion of state officials to pick and choose among them for the purpose of promoting a particular religious belief. The language of the statute and its legislative history convince me that the Louisiana Legislature exercised its discretion for this purpose in this case.

⊥**605** II

Even though I find Louisiana's Balanced Treatment Act unconstitutional, I adhere to the view "that the States and locally elected school boards should have the responsibility for determining the educational policy of the public schools." *Board of Education, Island Trees Union Free School Dist., No. 26* v. *Pico*. A decision respecting the subject matter to be taught in public schools does not violate the Establishment Clause simply because the material to be taught "'happens to coincide or harmonize with the tenets of some or all religions.'" *Harris* v. *McRae*. In the context of a challenge under the Establishment Clause, interference with the decisions of these authorities is warranted only when the purpose for their decisions is clearly religious.

The history of the Religion Clauses of the First Amendment has been chronicled by this Court in detail. Therefore, only a brief review at this point may be appropriate. The early settlers came to this country from Europe to escape religious persecution that took the form of forced support of state-established churches. The new Americans thus reacted strongly when they perceived the same type of religious intolerance emerging in this country. The reaction in Virginia, the home of many of the Founding Fathers, is instructive. George Mason's draft of the Virginia Declaration of Rights was adopted by the House of Burgesses in 1776. Because of James Madison's influence, the Declaration of Rights embodied the guarantee of *free exercise* of religion, as opposed to *toleration*.

Eight years later, a provision prohibiting the establishment of religion became a part of Virginia law when James Madison's Memorial and Remonstrance against Re⊥**606**ligious Assessments, written in response to a proposal that all Virginia citizens be taxed to support the teaching of the Christian religion, spurred the legislature to consider and adopt Thomas Jefferson's Bill for Establishing Religious Freedom. Both the guarantees of free exercise and against the establishment of religion were then incorporated into the Federal Bill of Rights by its drafter, James Madison.

While the "meaning and scope of the First Amendment" must be read "in light of its history and the evils it was designed forever to suppress," *Everson* v. *Board of Education*, this Court has also recognized that "this Nation's history has not been one of entirely sanitized separation between Church and State." *Committee for Public Education & Religious Liberty* v. *Nyquist*. "The fact that the Founding Fathers believed devotedly that there was a God and that the unalienable rights of man were rooted in Him is clearly evidenced in their writings, from the Mayflower Compact to the Constitution itself." *Abington School District* v. *Schempp*. The Court properly has noted "an unbroken history of official acknowledgment . . . of the role of religion in American life," *Lynch* v. *Donnelly*, and has recognized that these references to "our religious heritage" are constitutionally acceptable.

As a matter of history, schoolchildren can and should properly be informed of all aspects of this Nation's religious heritage. I would see no constitutional problem if schoolchildren were taught the nature of the Founding Father's religious beliefs and how these beliefs affected the attitudes ⊥**607** of the times and the structure of our government. Courses in comparative religion of course are customary and constitutionally appropriate. In fact, since religion permeates our history, a familiarity with the nature of religious beliefs is necessary to understand many historical as well as contemporary events. In addition, it is worth noting that the Estab⊥**608**lishment Clause does not prohibit *per se* the educational use of religious documents in public school education. Although this Court has recognized that the Bible is "an instrument of religion," *Abington School District* v. *Schempp*, it also has made clear that the Bible "may constitutionally be used in an appropriate study of history, civilization, ethics, comparative religion, or the like." *Stone* v. *Graham*. The book is, in fact, "the world's all-time best seller" with undoubted literary and historic value apart from its religious content. The Establishment Clause is properly understood to prohibit the use of the Bible and other religious documents in public school education only when the purpose of the use is to advance a particular religious belief.

III

In sum, I find that the language and the legislative history of the Balanced Treatment Act unquestionably demonstrate that its purpose is to advance a particular religious belief. Although the discretion of state and local authorities over public school curricula is broad, "the First Amendment does not permit the State to require that teaching and learning must be tailored to the principles or prohibitions of any religious sect or dogma." *Epperson* v. *Arkansas*. Accordingly, I concur in the opinion of the Court and its judgment that the Balanced Treatment Act violates the Establishment Clause of the Constitution.

Justice WHITE, concurring in the judgment.

As it comes to us, this is not a difficult case. Based on the historical setting and plain language of the Act both courts construed the statutory words "creation science" to refer to a religious belief, which the Act required to be taught if evolu⊥**609**tion was taught. In other words, the teaching of evolution was conditioned on the teaching of a religious belief. Both courts concluded that the state legislature's primary purpose was to advance religion and that the statute was therefore unconstitutional under the Establishment Clause.

We usually defer to courts of appeals on the meaning of a state statute, especially when a district court has the same view. Of course, we have the power to disagree, and the lower courts in a particular case may be plainly wrong. But if the meaning ascribed to a state statute by a court of appeals is a rational construction of the statute, we normally accept it. *Brockett* v. *Spokane Arcades*. We do so because we believe "that district courts and courts of appeals are better schooled in and more able to interpret the laws of their respective States." *Brockett* v. *Spokane Arcades*. *Brockett* also indicates that the usual rule applies in First Amendment cases.

Here, the District Judge, relying on the terms of the Act, discerned its purpose to be the furtherance of a religious belief, and a panel of the Court of Appeals agreed. Of those four judges, two are Louisianians. I would accept this view of the statute. Even if as an original matter I might have arrived at a different conclusion based on a reading of the statute and the record before us, I cannot say that the two courts below are so plainly wrong that they should be reversed. Rehearing en banc was denied by an 8-7 vote, the dissenters expressing their disagreement with the panel decision. The disagreement, however, was over the construction of the Louisiana statute, particularly the assessment of its purpose, and offers no justification for departing from the usual rule counseling against *de novo* constructions of state statutes.

⊥**610** If the Court of Appeals' construction is to be accepted, so is its conclusion that under our prior cases the Balanced Treatment Act is unconstitutional because its primary purpose is to further a religious belief by imposing certain requirements on the school curriculum. Unless, therefore, we are to reconsider the Court's decisions interpreting the Establishment Clause, I agree that the judgment of the Court of Appeals must be affirmed.

Justice SCALIA, with whom *The* CHIEF JUSTICE joins, dissenting.

Even if I agreed with the questionable premise that legislation can be invalidated under the Establishment Clause on the basis of its motivation alone, without regard to its effects, I would still find no justification for today's decision. The Louisiana legislators who passed the "Balanced Treatment for Creation-Science and Evolution-Science Act," each of whom had sworn to support the Constitution, were well aware of the potential Establishment Clause problems and considered that aspect of the legislation with great care. After seven hearings and several months of study, resulting in substantial revision of the original proposal, they approved the Act overwhelmingly and specifically articulated the secular purpose they meant it to serve. Although the record contains abundant evidence of the sincerity of that purpose (the only issue pertinent to this case), the Court today holds, essentially on the basis of "its visceral knowledge regarding what *must* have motivated the legislators" (emphasis added), that the members of the Louisiana Legislature knowingly violated their oaths and then lied about it. I dissent. Had requirements of the Balanced Treatment Act that ⊥**611** are not apparent on its face been clarified by an interpretation of the Louisiana Supreme Court, or by the manner of its implementation, the Act might well be found unconstitutional; but the question of its constitutionality cannot rightly be disposed of on the gallop, by impugning the motives of its supporters.

I

This case arrives here in the following posture: The Louisiana Supreme Court has never been given an opportunity to interpret the Balanced Treatment Act, State officials have never attempted to implement it, and it has never been the subject of a full evidentiary hearing. We can only guess at its meaning. We know that it forbids instruction in either "creation-science" or "evolution-science" without instruction in the other, but the parties are sharply divided over what creation science consists of. Appellants insist that it is a collection of educationally valuable scientific data that has been censored from classrooms by an embarrassed scientific establishment. Appellees insist it is not science at all but thinly veiled religious doctrine. Both interpretations of the intended meaning of that phrase find considerable support in the legislative history.

At least at this stage in the litigation, it is plain to me that we must accept appellants' view of what the statute means. To begin with, the statute itself *defines* "creation-science" as "the *scientific evidences* for creation and inferences from those *scientific evidences*." § 17:286.3(2) (emphasis added). If, however, that definition is not thought sufficiently helpful, the means by which the Louisiana Supreme Court will give the term more precise content is quite clear—and again, at this stage in the litigation, favors the appellants' view. "Creation science" is unquestionably a "term of art," and thus, under Louisiana law, is "to be interpreted according to [its] received meaning and acceptation with the learned in the art, trade or profession to which [it] refer[s]." La. Civ. ⊥**612** Code Ann., Art. 15 (West 1952). The only evidence in the record of the "received meaning and acceptation" of "creation science" is found in five affidavits filed by appellants. In those affidavits, two scientists, a philosopher, a theologian, and an educator, all of whom claim extensive knowledge of creation science, swear that it is essentially a collection of scientific data supporting the theory that the physical universe and life within it appeared suddenly and have not changed substantially since appearing. These experts insist that creation science is a strictly scientific concept that can be presented without religious reference. At this point, then, we must assume that the Balanced Treatment Act does *not* require the presentation of religious doctrine.

Nothing in today's opinion is plainly to the contrary, but what the statute means and what it requires are of rather little concern to the Court. Like the Court of Appeals, the Court finds it necessary to consider only the motives of the legislators who supported the Balanced Treatment Act. After examining the statute, its legislative history, and its historical and social context, the Court holds that the Louisiana Legislature acted without "a secular legislative purpose" and that the Act therefore fails the "purpose" prong of the three-part test set forth in *Lemon* v. *Kurtzman*. As I explain below, ⊥**613** I doubt whether that "purpose" requirement of *Lemon* is a proper interpretation of the Constitution; but even if it were, I could not agree with the Court's assessment that the requirement was not satisfied here.

This Court has said little about the first component of the *Lemon* test. Almost invariably, we have effortlessly discovered a secular purpose for measures challenged under the Establishment Clause, typically devoting no more than a sentence or two to the matter.

Nevertheless, a few principles have emerged from our cases, principles which should, but to an unfortunately large extent do not, guide the Court's application of *Lemon* today. It is clear, first of all, that regardless of what "legislative purpose" may mean in other contexts, for the purpose of the *Lemon* test it means the "actual" motives of those responsible for the challenged action. The Court recognizes this, as it has in the past, see, *e.g.*, *Witters* v. *Washington Dept. of Services for Blind*, *Wallace* v. ⊥**614** *Jaffree*. Thus, if those legislators who supported the Balanced Treatment Act *in fact* acted with a "sincere" secular purpose, the Act survives the first component of the *Lemon* test, regardless of whether that purpose is likely to be achieved by the provisions they enacted.

Our cases have also confirmed that when the *Lemon* Court referred to "a secular . . . purpose," it meant "*a* secular purpose." The author of *Lemon*, writing for the Court, has said that invalidation under the purpose prong is appropriate when "there [is] *no question* that the statute or activity was motivated *wholly* by religious considerations." *Lynch* v. *Donnelly* (emphasis added); *Wallace* v. *Jaffree* ("[T]he First Amendment requires that a statute must be invalidated if it is *entirely* motivated by a purpose to advance religion") (emphasis added; footnote omitted). In all three cases in which we struck down laws under the Establishment Clause for lack of a secular purpose, we found that the legislature's sole motive was to promote religion. See *Wallace* v. *Jaffree*, *Stone* v. *Graham*, *Epperson* v. *Arkansas*, see also *Lynch* v. *Donnelly* (describing *Stone* and *Epperson* as cases in which we invalidated laws "motivated wholly by religious considerations"). Thus, the majority's invalidation of the Balanced Treatment Act is defensible only if the record indicates that the Louisiana Legislature had *no* secular purpose.

It is important to stress that the purpose forbidden by *Lemon* is the purpose to "advance religion." *Witters* v. *Washington Dept. of Services for Blind* ("endorse religion"); *Wallace* v. *Jaffree* ("advance religion"); *ibid.* ("endorse . . . religion"); *Committee for Public Education & Religious Liberty* v. *Nyquist* ("'advancing' . . . religion"); *Levitt* v. *Committee for* ⊥**615** *Public Education & Religious Liberty* ("advancing religion"); *Walz* v. *Tax Comm'n of New York City* ("establishing, sponsoring, or supporting religion"); *Board of Education* v. *Allen* ("'advancement or inhibition of religion'") (quoting *Abington School Dist.* v. *Schempp*). Our cases in no way imply that the Establishment Clause forbids legislators merely to act upon their religious convictions. We surely would not strike down a law providing money to feed the hungry or shelter the homeless if it could be demonstrated that, but for the religious beliefs of the legislators, the funds would not have been approved. Also, political activism by the religiously motivated is part of our heritage. Notwithstanding the majority's implication to the contrary, we do not presume that the sole purpose of a law is to advance religion merely because it was supported strongly by organized religions or by adherents of particular faiths. To do so would deprive religious men and women of their right to participate in the political process. Today's religious activism may give us the Balanced Treatment Act, but yesterday's resulted in the abolition of slavery, and tomorrow's may bring relief for famine victims.

Similarly, we will not presume that a law's purpose is to advance religion merely because it "'happens to coincide or harmonize with the tenets of some or all religions,'" *Harris* v. *McRae*, or because it benefits religion, even substantially. We have, for example, turned back Establishment Clause challenges to restrictions on abortion funding, *Harris* v. *McRae*. And to Sunday closing laws, *McGowan* v. *Maryland*, despite the fact that both "agre[e] with the dictates of [some] Judaeo-Christian religions." "In many instances, the Congress or state legislatures conclude that the general welfare of soci⊥**616**ety, wholly apart from any religious considerations, demands such regulation." On many past occasions we have had no difficulty finding a secular purpose for governmental action far more likely to advance religion than the Balanced Treatment Act. See, *e.g.*, *Mueller* v. *Allen* (tax deduction for expenses of religious education); *Wolman* v. *Walter* (aid to religious schools); *Meek* v. *Pittenger* (same); *Committee for Public Education & Religious Liberty* v. *Nyquist* (same); *Lemon* v. *Kurtzman* (same); *Walz* v. *Tax Comm'n of New York City* (tax exemption for church property); *Board of Education* v. *Allen* (textbook loans to students in religious schools). Thus, the fact that creation science coincides with the beliefs of certain religions, a fact upon which the majority relies heavily, does not itself justify invalidation of the Act.

Finally, our cases indicate that even certain kinds of governmental actions undertaken with the specific intention of improving the position of religion do not "advance religion" as that term is used in *Lemon*. Rather, we have said that in at least two circumstances government *must* act to advance religion, and that in a third it *may* do so.

First, since we have consistently described the Establishment Clause as forbidding not only state action motivated by the desire to *advance* religion, but also that intended to "disapprove," "inhibit," or evince "hostility" toward religion, and since we have said that governmental "neutrality" toward religion is the preeminent goal of the First Amendment, ⊥**617** a State which discovers that its employees are inhibiting religion must take steps to prevent them from doing so, even though its purpose would clearly be to advance religion. Thus, if the Louisiana Legislature sincerely believed that the State's science teachers were being hostile to religion, our cases indicate that it could act to eliminate that hostility without running afoul of *Lemon's* purpose test.

Second, we have held that intentional governmental advancement of religion is sometimes required by the Free Exercise Clause. For example, in *Hobbie* v. *Unemployment Appeals Comm'n of Fla.*, *Thomas* v. *Review Bd, Indiana Employment Security Div.*, *Wisconsin* v. *Yoder, and Sherbert* v. *Verner*, we held that in some circumstances States must accommodate the beliefs of religious citizens by exempting them from generally applicable regulations. We have not yet come close to reconciling *Lemon* and our Free Exercise cases, and typically we do not really try. It is clear, however, that members of the Louisiana Legislature were not impermissibly motivated for purposes of the *Lemon* test if they believed that approval of the Balanced Treatment Act was *required* by the Free Exercise Clause.

We have also held that in some circumstances government may act to accommodate religion, even if that action is not required by the First Amendment. It is well established that "[t]he limits of permissible state accommodation to religion are by no means coextensive with the noninterference mandated by the Free Exercise Clause." *Walz* v. *Tax Comm'n.* ⊥**618** We have implied that voluntary governmental accommodation of religion is not only permissible, but desirable. Thus, few would contend that Title VII of the Civil Rights Act of 1964, which both forbids religious discrimination by private-sector employers, 78 Stat. 255, 42 U.S.C. § 2000e-2(a)(1), and requires them reasonably to accommodate the religious practices of their employees, § 2000e(j), violates the Establishment Clause, even though its "purpose" is, of course, to advance religion, and even though it is almost certainly not required by the Free Exercise Clause. While we have warned that at some point, accommodation may devolve into "an unlawful fostering of religion," *Hobbie* v. *Unemployment Appeals Comm'n of Fla.*, we have not suggested precisely (or even roughly) where that point might be. It is possible, then, that even if the sole motive of those voting for the Balanced Treatment Act was to advance religion, and its passage vas not actually required, or even believed to be required, by either the Free Exercise or Establishment Clauses, the Act would nonetheless survive scrutiny under *Lemon's* purpose test.

One final observation about the application of that test: Although the Court's opinion gives no hint of it, in the past we have repeatedly affirmed "our reluctance to attribute unconstitutional motives to the States." *Mueller* v. *Allen*. We "presume that legislatures act in a constitutional manner." *Illinois* v. *Krull*. Whenever we are called upon to judge the constitutionality of an act of a state legislature, "we must have 'due regard to the fact that this Court is not exercising a primary judgment but is sitting in judgment **⊥619** upon those who also have taken the oath to observe the Constitution and who have the responsibility for carrying on government.'" *Rostker* v. *Goldberg*. This is particularly true, we have said, where the legislature has specifically considered the question of a law's constitutionality.

With the foregoing in mind, I now turn to the purposes underlying adoption of the Balanced Treatment Act.

II

A

We have relatively little information upon which to judge the motives of those who supported the Act. About the only direct evidence is the statute itself and transcripts of the seven committee hearings at which it was considered. Unfortunately, several of those hearings were sparsely attended, and the legislators who were present revealed little about their motives. We have no committee reports, no floor debates, no remarks inserted into the legislative history, no statement from the Governor, and no postenactment statements or testimony from the bill's sponsor or any other legislators. Nevertheless, there is ample evidence that the majority is wrong in holding that the Balanced Treatment Act is without secular purpose.

At the outset, it is important to note that the Balanced Treatment Act did not fly through the Louisiana Legislature on wings of fundamentalist religious fervor—which would be unlikely, in any event, since only a small minority of the State's citizens belong to fundamentalist religious denominations. See B. Quinn, H. Anderson, M. Bradley, P. Goetting, & P. Shriver, Churches and Church Membership in the United States 16 (1982). The Act had its genesis (so to speak) in legislation introduced by Senator Bill Keith in June **⊥620** 1980. After two hearings before the Senate Committee on Education, Senator Keith asked that his bill be referred to a study commission composed of members of both Houses of the Louisiana Legislature. He expressed hope that the joint committee would give the bill careful consideration and determine whether his arguments were "legitimate." The committee met twice during the interim, heard testimony (both for and against the bill) from several witnesses, and received staff reports. Senator Keith introduced his bill again when the legislature reconvened. The Senate Committee on Education held two more hearings and approved the bill after substantially amending it (in part over Senator Keith's objection). After approval by the full Senate, the bill was referred to the House Committee on Education. That committee conducted a lengthy hearing, adopted further amendments, and sent the bill on to the full House, where it received favorable consideration. The Senate concurred in the House amendments and on July 20, 1981, the Governor signed the bill into law.

Senator Keith's statements before the various committees that considered the bill hardly reflect the confidence of a man preaching to the converted. He asked his colleagues to "keep an open mind" and not to be "biased" by misleading characterizations of creation science. He also urged them to "look at this subject on its merits and not on some preconceived idea." Senator Keith's reception was not especially warm. Over his strenuous objection, the Senate Committee on Education voted 5-1 to amend his bill to deprive it of any force; as amended, the bill merely gave teachers *permission* to balance the teaching of creation science or evolution with the other. The House Committee restored the "mandatory" language to the bill by a vote of only 6-5, and both the full House (by vote of 52-35), and full Senate (23-15), had to repel further efforts to gut the bill.

⊥621 The legislators understood that Senator Keith's bill involved a "unique" subject, and they were repeatedly made aware of its potential constitutional problems. Although the Establishment Clause, including its secular purpose requirement, was of substantial concern to the legislators, they eventually voted overwhelmingly in favor of the Balanced Treatment Act: The House approved it 71-19 (with 15 members absent), the Senate 26-12 (with all members present). The legislators specifically designated the protection of "academic freedom" as the purpose of the Act. We cannot accurately assess whether this purpose is a "sham," until we first examine the evidence presented to the legislature far more carefully than the Court has done.

Before summarizing the testimony of Senator Keith and his supporters, I wish to make clear that I by no means intend to endorse its accuracy. But my views (and the views of this Court) about creation science and evolution are (or should be) beside the point. Our task is not to judge the debate about teaching the origins of life, but to ascertain what the members of the Louisiana Legislature believed. The vast majority of them voted to approve a bill which explicitly stated a secular purpose;

what is crucial is not their *wisdom* in believing that purpose would be achieved by the bill, but their *sincerity* in believing it would be.

Most of the testimony in support of Senator Keith's bill came from the Senator himself and from scientists and educators he presented, many of whom enjoyed academic credentials that may have been regarded as quite impressive by members of the Louisiana Legislature. To a substantial extent, their testimony was devoted to lengthy, and, to the layman, seemingly expert scientific expositions on the origin ⊥**622** of life. These scientific lectures touched upon, *inter alia*, biology, paleontology, genetics, astronomy, astrophysics, probability analysis, and biochemistry. The witnesses repeatedly assured committee members that "hundreds and hundreds" of highly respected, internationally renowned scientists believed in creation science and would support their testimony.

Senator Keith and his witnesses testified essentially as set forth in the following numbered paragraphs:

(1) There are two and only two scientific explanations for the beginning of life—evolution and creation science. Both are bona fide "sciences." Both posit a theory of the origin of life and subject that theory to empirical testing. Evolution posits that life arose out of inanimate chemical compounds and has gradually evolved over millions of years. Creation science posits that all life forms now on earth appeared suddenly and relatively recently and have changed little. Since there are only two possible explanations of the origin of life, any evidence that tends to disprove the theory of evolution necessarily tends to prove the theory of creation science, and vice versa. For example, the abrupt appearance in the fossil record of complex life, and the extreme rar⊥**623**ity of transitional life forms in that record, are evidence for creation science.

(2) The body of scientific evidence supporting creation science is as strong as that supporting evolution. In fact, it may be *stronger*. The evidence for evolution is far less compelling than we have been led to believe. Evolution is not a scientific "fact," since it cannot actually be observed in a laboratory. Rather, evolution is merely a scientific theory or "guess." It is a very bad guess at that. The scientific problems with evolution are so serious that it could accurately be termed a "myth."

(3) Creation science is educationally valuable. Students exposed to it better understand the current state of scientific evidence about the origin of life. Those students even have a better understanding of evolution. Creation science can and should be presented to children without any religious content.

(4) Although creation science is educationally valuable and strictly scientific, it is now being censored from or misrepresented in the public schools. ⊥**624** Evolution, in turn, is misrepresented as an absolute truth. Teachers have been brainwashed by an entrenched scientific establishment composed almost exclusively of scientists to whom evolution is like a "religion." These scientists discriminate against creation scientists so as to prevent evolution's weaknesses from being exposed.

(5) The censorship of creation science has at least two harmful effects. First, it deprives students of knowledge of one of the two scientific explanations for the origin of life and leads them to believe that evolution is proven fact; thus, their education suffers and they are wrongly taught that science has proved their religious beliefs false. Second, it violates the Establishment Clause. The United States Supreme Court has held that secular humanism is a religion (referring to *Torcaso* v. *Watkins*). Belief in evolution is a central tenet of that religion. Thus, by censoring creation science and instructing students that evolution is fact, public school teachers are *now* advancing religion in violation of the Establishment Clause.

⊥**625** Senator Keith repeatedly and vehemently denied that his purpose was to advance a particular religious doctrine. At the outset of the first hearing on the legislation, he testified: "We are not going to say today that you should have some kind of religious instructions in our schools. . . . We are not talking about religion today. . . . I am not proposing that we take the Bible in each science class and read the first chapter of Genesis." At a later hearing, Senator Keith stressed: "[T]o . . . teach religion and disguise it as creationism . . . is not my intent. My intent is to see to it that our textbooks are not censored." He made many similar statements throughout the hearings.

We have no way of knowing, of course, how many legislators believed the testimony of Senator Keith and his witnesses. But in the absence of evidence to the contrary, we ⊥**626** have to assume that many of them did. Given that assumption, the Court today plainly errs in holding that the Louisiana Legislature passed the Balanced Treatment Act for exclusively religious purposes.

B

Even with nothing more than this legislative history to go on, I think it would be extraordinary to invalidate the Balanced Treatment Act for lack of a valid secular purpose. Striking down a law approved by the democratically elected representatives of the people is no minor matter. "The cardinal principle of statutory construction is to save and not to destroy. We have repeatedly held that as between two possible interpretations of a statute, by one of which it would be unconstitutional and by the other valid, our plain duty is to adopt that which will save the act." *NLRB* v. *Jones & Laughlin Steel Corp.* So, too, it seems to me, with discerning statutory purpose. Even if the legislative history were silent or ambiguous about the existence of a secular purpose—and here it is not—the statute should survive *Lemon's* purpose test. But even more validation than mere legislative history is present here. The Louisiana Legislature explicitly set forth its secular purpose ⊥**627** ("protecting academic freedom") in the very text of the Act. La. Rev. Stat. § 17:286.2 (West 1982). We have in the past repeatedly relied upon or deferred to such expressions.

The Court seeks to evade the force of this expression of purpose by stubbornly misinterpreting it, and then finding that the provisions of the Act do not advance that misinterpreted purpose, thereby showing it to be a sham. The Court first surmises that "academic freedom" means "enhancing the freedom of teachers to teach what they will,"—even though "academic freedom" in that sense has little scope in the structured elementary and secondary curriculums with which the Act is concerned. Alternatively, the Court suggests that it might mean "maximiz[ing] the comprehensiveness and effectiveness of science instruction,"—though that is an exceedingly strange interpretation of the words, and one that is refuted on the very face of the statute. Had the Court devoted to this central question of the meaning of the legislatively expressed purpose a small fraction of the research into legislative history that produced its quotations of religiously motivated statements by individual legislators, it would have discerned quite readily what "academic freedom" meant: *students'* freedom from *indoctrination*. The legislature wanted to ensure that students would be free to decide for themselves how life began, based upon a fair and balanced presentation of the scientific evidence—that is, to protect "the right of each [student] voluntarily to determine what to believe (and what not to believe) free of any coercive pressures from the State." *Grand* ⊥**628** *Rapids School District* v. *Ball*. The legislature did not care *whether* the topic of origins was taught; it simply wished to ensure that *when* the topic was taught, students would receive "'all of the evidence.'"

As originally introduced, the "purpose" section of the Balanced Treatment Act read: "This Chapter is enacted for the purposes of protecting academic freedom . . . *of students* . . . and assisting *students* in their search for truth" (emphasis added). Among the proposed findings of fact contained in the original version of the bill was the following: "Public school instruction in only evolution-science . . . *violates the principle of academic freedom because it denies students a choice between scientific models and instead indoctrinates them in evolution science alone*" (emphasis added). Senator Keith unquestionably understood "academic freedom" to mean "freedom from indoctrination" (purpose of bill is "to protect academic freedom by providing student choice"); (purpose of bill is to protect "academic freedom" by giving students a "choice" rather than subjecting them to "indoctrination on origins").

If one adopts the obviously intended meaning of the statutory term "academic freedom," there is no basis whatever for concluding that the purpose they express is a "sham."⊥**629** To the contrary, the Act pursues that purpose plainly and consistently. It requires that, whenever the subject of origins is covered, evolution be "taught as a theory, rather than as proven scientific fact" and that scientific evidence inconsistent with the theory of evolution (viz., "creation science") be taught as well. Living up to its title of "*Balanced Treatment* for Creation-Science and Evolution-Science Act," it treats the teaching of creation the same way. It does *not* mandate instruction in creation science, *forbids* teachers to present creation science "as proven scientific fact," and *bans* the teaching of creation science unless the theory is (to use the Court's terminology) "discredit[ed] '. . . at every turn'" with the teaching of evolution. It surpasses understanding how the Court can see in this a purpose "to restructure the science curriculum to conform with a particular religious viewpoint," "to provide a persuasive advantage to a particular religious doctrine," "to promote the theory of creation science which embodies a particular religious tenet," and "to endorse a particular religious doctrine."

The Act's reference to "creation" is not convincing evidence of religious purpose. The Act defines creation science as "*scientific evidenc[e]*" (emphasis added), and Senator Keith and his witnesses repeatedly stressed that the subject can and should be presented without religious content. We have no basis on the record to conclude that creation science need be anything other than a collection of scientific data supporting the theory that life abruptly appeared on earth. Creation science, its proponents insist, no more must explain *whence* life came than evolution must explain whence came the inanimate materials from which it says life evolved. But even if that were not so, to posit a past creator is not to posit the eternal and personal God who is the object of religious veneration. ⊥**630** Indeed, it is not even to posit the "*unmoved* mover" hypothesized by Aristotle and other notably nonfundamentalist philosophers. Senator Keith suggested this when he referred to "a creator *however you define a creator*" (emphasis added).

The Court cites three provisions of the Act which, it argues, demonstrate a "discriminatory preference for the teaching of creation science" and no interest in "academic freedom." First, the Act prohibits discrimination only against creation scientists and those who teach creation science. Second, the Act requires local school boards to develop and provide to science teachers "a curriculum guide on presentation of creation-science." Finally, the Act requires the Governor to designate seven creation scientists who shall, upon request, assist local school boards in developing the curriculum guides. But none of these provisions casts doubt upon the sincerity of the legislators' articulated purpose of "academic freedom"—unless, of course, one gives that term the obviously erroneous meanings preferred by the Court. The Louisiana legislators had been told repeatedly that creation scientists were scorned by most educators and scientists, who themselves had an almost religious faith in evolution. It is hardly surprising, then, that in seeking to achieve a balanced, "nonindoctrinating" curriculum, the legislators protected from discrimination only those teachers whom they thought were *suffering* from discrimination. (Also, the legislators were undoubtedly aware of *Epperson* v. *Arkansas*, and thus could quite reasonably have concluded that discrimination against evolutionists was already prohibited.) The two provisions respecting the development of curriculum guides are also consistent with "academic freedom" as the Louisiana Legislature understood the term. Witnesses had informed the legislators that, because of the hostility of most scientists and educators to creation science, the topic had been censored from or badly misrepresented in elementary ⊥631 and secondary school texts. In light of the unavailability of works on creation science suitable for classroom use (a fact appellees concede), and the existence of ample materials on evolution, it was entirely reasonable for the legislature to conclude that science teachers attempting to implement the Act would need a curriculum guide on creation science, but not on evolution, and that those charged with developing the guide would need an easily accessible group of creation scientists. Thus, the provisions of the Act of so much concern to the Court *support* the conclusion that the legislature acted to advance "academic freedom."

The legislative history gives ample evidence of the sincerity of the Balanced Treatment Act's articulated purpose. Witness after witness urged the legislators to support the Act so that students would not be "indoctrinated" but would instead be free to decide for themselves, based upon a fair presentation of the scientific evidence, about the origin of life. See, *e.g.*, (Sunderland) ("all that we are advocating" is presenting "scientific data" to students and "letting [them] make up their own mind[s]"); (Sunderland) (Students are now being "indoctrinated" in evolution through the use of "censored school books. . . . All that we are asking for is [the] open unbiased education in the classroom . . . your students deserve"); (Morris) ("A student cannot [make an intelligent decision about the origin of life] unless he is well informed about both [evolution and creation science]"); (Sanderford) ("We are asking very simply [that] . . . creationism [be presented] alongside . . . evolution and let people make their own mind[s] up"); (Young) (the bill would require teachers to live up to their "obligation to present all theories" and thereby enable "students to make judgments themselves"); (Boudreaux) ("Our intention is truth and as a scientist, I am interested in truth"); (Boudreaux) ("[W]e [teachers] are guilty of a lot of ⊥632 brainwashing. . . . We have a duty to . . . [present the] truth" to students "at all levels from gradeschool on through the college level"); (Kalivoda) ("This [hearing] is being held I think to determine whether children will benefit from freedom of information or if they will be handicapped educationally by having little or no information about creation"); (Kalivoda) ("I am not interested in teaching religion in schools. . . . I am interested in the truth and [students] having the opportunity to hear more than one side"); (Reiboldt) ("The students have a right to know there is an alternate creationist point of view. They have a right to know the scientific evidences which suppor[t] that alternative"); (Young statement) (passage of the bill will ensure that "communication of scientific ideas and discoveries may be unhindered"); (Moms) ("[A]re we going to allow [students] to look at evolution, to look at creationism, and to let one or the other stand or fall on its own merits, or will we by failing to pass this bill . . . deny students an opportunity to hear another viewpoint?"); (Young) ("We want to give the children here in this state an equal opportunity to see both sides of the theories"). Senator Keith expressed similar views.

Legislators other than Senator Keith made only a few statements providing insight into their motives, but those statements cast no doubt upon the sincerity of the Act's articulated purpose. The legislators were concerned primarily about the manner in which the subject of origins was presented in Louisiana schools specifically, about whether scientifically valuable information was being censored and students misled about evolution. Representatives Cain, Jenkins, and F. Thompson seemed impressed by the scientific evidence presented in support of creation science. At the first study commission hearing, Senator Picard and Representative M. Thompson ques⊥633tioned Senator Keith about Louisiana teachers' treatment of evolution and creation science. At the close of the hearing, Representative M. Thompson told the audience:

"We as members of the committee will also receive from the staff information of what is currently being taught in the Louisiana public schools. We really want to see [it]. I . . . have no idea in what manner [biology] is presented and in what manner the creationist theories [are] excluded in the public school[s]. We want to look at what the status of the situation is." Legislators made other comments suggesting a concern about censorship and misrepresentation of scientific information.

It is undoubtedly true that what prompted the legislature to direct its attention to the misrepresentation of evolution in the schools (rather than the inaccurate presentation of other topics) was its awareness of the tension between evolution and the religious beliefs of many children. But even appellees concede that a valid secular purpose is not rendered impermissible simply because its pursuit is prompted by concern for religious sensitivities. If a history teacher falsely told her students that the bones of Jesus Christ had been discovered, or a physics teacher that the Shroud of Turin had been conclusively established to be inexplicable on the basis of natural causes, I cannot believe (despite the majority's implication to the contrary) that legislators or school board members would be constitutionally prohibited from taking corrective action, simply because that action was prompted by concern for the religious beliefs of the misinstructed students.

In sum, even if one concedes, for the sake of argument, that a majority of the Louisiana Legislature voted for the Balanced Treatment Act partly in order to foster (rather ⊥634 than merely eliminate discrimination against) Christian fundamentalist beliefs, our cases establish that that alone would not suffice to invalidate the Act, so long as there was a genuine secular purpose as well. We have, moreover, no adequate basis for disbelieving the secular purpose set forth in the Act itself, or for concluding that it is a sham enacted to conceal the legislators' violation of their oaths of office. I am astonished by the Court's unprecedented readiness to reach such a conclusion, which I can only attribute to an intellectual predisposition created by the facts and the legend of *Scopes* v. *State*—an instinctive reaction that any governmentally imposed requirements bearing upon the teaching of evolution must be a manifestation of Christian fundamentalist repression. In this case, however, it seems to me the Court's position is the repressive one. The people of Louisiana, including those who are Christian fundamentalists, are quite entitled, as a secular matter, to have whatever scientific evidence there may be against evolution presented in their schools, just as Mr. Scopes was entitled to present whatever scientific evidence there was for it. Perhaps what the Louisiana Legislature has done is unconstitutional because there is no such evidence, and the scheme they have established will amount to no more than a presentation of the Book of Genesis. But we cannot say that on the evidence before us in this summary judgment context, which includes ample uncontradicted testimony that "creation science" is a body of scientific knowledge rather than revealed belief. *Infinitely less* can we say (or should we say) that the scientific evidence for evolution is so conclusive that no one could be gullible enough to believe that there is any real scientific evidence to the contrary, so that the legislation's stated purpose must be a lie. Yet that illiberal judgment, that *Scopes*-in-reverse, is ultimately the basis on which the Court's facile rejection of the Louisiana Legislature's purpose must rest.

⊥**635** Since the existence of secular purpose is so entirely clear, and thus dispositive, I will not go on to discuss the fact that, even if the Louisiana Legislature's purpose were exclusively to advance religion, some of the well-established exceptions to the impermissibility of that purpose might be applicable—the validating intent to eliminate a perceived discrimination against a particular religion, to facilitate its free exercise, or to accommodate it. I am not in any case enamored of those amorphous exceptions, since I think them no more than unpredictable correctives to what is (as the next Part of this opinion will discuss) a fundamentally unsound rule. It is surprising, however, that the Court does not address these exceptions, since the context of the legislature's action gives some reason to believe they may be applicable.

⊥**636** Because I believe that the Balanced Treatment Act had a secular purpose, which is all the first component of the *Lemon* test requires, I would reverse the judgment of the Court of Appeals and remand for further consideration.

III

I have to this point assumed the validity of the *Lemon* "purpose" test. In fact, however, I think the pessimistic evaluation that *The CHIEF JUSTICE* made of the totality of *Lemon* is particularly applicable to the "purpose" prong: it is "a constitutional theory [that] has no basis in the history of the amendment it seeks to interpret, is difficult to apply and yields unprincipled results. . . ." *Wallace* v. *Jaffree*.

Our cases interpreting and applying the purpose test have made such a maze of the Establishment Clause that even the most conscientious governmental officials can only guess what motives will be held unconstitutional. We have said essentially the following: Government may not act with the purpose of advancing religion, except when forced to do so by the Free Exercise Clause (which is now and then); or when eliminating existing governmental hostility to religion (which exists sometimes); or even when merely accommodating governmentally uninhibited religious practices, except that at some point (it is unclear where) intentional accommodation results in the fostering of religion, which is of course unconstitutional.

But the difficulty of knowing what vitiating purpose one is looking for is as nothing compared with the difficulty of knowing how or where to find it. For while it is possible to discern the objective "purpose" of a statute (i. e., the public good at which its provisions appear to be directed), or even the formal motivation for a statute where that is explicitly set forth (as it was, to no avail, here), discerning the subjective motivation of those enacting the statute is, to be honest, almost always an impossible task. The number of possible ⊥**637** motivations, to begin with, is not binary, or indeed even finite. In the present case, for example, a particular legislator need not have voted for the Act either because he wanted to foster religion or because he wanted to improve education. He may have thought the bill would provide jobs for his district, or may have wanted to make amends with a faction of his party he had alienated on another vote, or he may have been a close friend of the bill's sponsor, or he may have been repaying a favor he owed the majority leader, or he may have hoped the Governor would appreciate his vote and make a fund raising appearance for him, or he may have been pressured to vote for a bill he disliked by a wealthy contributor or by a flood of constituent mail, or he may have been seeking favorable publicity, or he may have been reluctant to hurt the feelings of a loyal staff member who worked on the bill, or he may have been settling an old score with a legislator who opposed the bill, or he may have been mad at his wife who opposed the bill, or he may have been intoxicated and utterly *un*motivated when the vote was called, or he may have accidentally voted "yes" instead of "no," or, of course, he may have had (and very likely did have) a combination of some of the above and many other motivations. To look for *the sole purpose* of even a single legislator is probably to look for something that does not exist.

Putting that problem aside, however, where ought we to look for the individual legislator's purpose? We cannot of course assume that every member present (if, as is unlikely, we know who or even how many they were) agreed with the motivation expressed in a particular legislator's preenactment floor or committee statement. Quite obviously, "[w]hat motivates one legislator to make a speech about a statute is not necessarily what motivates scores of others to enact it." *United States* v. *O'Brien*. Can we assume, then, that they all agree with the motivation expressed in the staff-prepared committee reports they might have read—even though we are unwilling to **⊥638** assume that they agreed with the motivation expressed in the very statute that they voted for? Should we consider postenactment floor statements? Or postenactment testimony from legislators, obtained expressly for the lawsuit? Should we consider media reports on the realities of the legislative bargaining? All of these sources, of course, are eminently manipulable. Legislative histories can be contrived and sanitized, favorable media coverage orchestrated, and postenactment recollections conveniently distorted. Perhaps most valuable of all would be more objective indications—for example, evidence regarding the individual legislators' religious affiliations. And if that, why not evidence regarding the fervor or tepidity of their beliefs?

Having achieved, through these simple means, an assessment of what individual legislators intended, we must still confront the question (yet to be addressed in any of our cases) how *many* of them must have the invalidating intent. If a state senate approves a bill by vote of 26 to 25, and only one of the 26 intended solely to advance religion, is the law unconstitutional? What if 13 of the 26 had that intent? What if 3 of the 26 had the impermissible intent, but 3 of the 25 voting against the bill were motivated by religious hostility or were simply attempting to "balance" the votes of their impermissibly motivated colleagues? Or is it possible that the intent of the bill's sponsor is alone enough to invalidate it—on a theory, perhaps, that even though everyone else's intent was pure, what they produced was the fruit of a forbidden tree?

Because there are no good answers to these questions, this Court has recognized from *Chief Justice Marshall*, see *Fletcher* v. *Peck*, to *Chief Justice* WARREN, *United States* v. *O'Brien*, that determining the subjective intent of legislators is a perilous enterprise. It is perilous, I might note, not just for the judges who will very likely reach the wrong result, **⊥639** but also for the legislators who find that they must assess the validity of proposed legislation—and risk the condemnation of having voted for an unconstitutional measure—not on the basis of what the legislation contains, nor even on the basis of what they themselves intend, but on the basis of what *others* have in mind.

Given the many hazards involved in assessing the subjective intent of governmental decisionmakers, the first prong of *Lemon* is defensible, I think, only if the text of the Establishment Clause demands it. That is surely not the case. The Clause states that "Congress shall make no law respecting an establishment of religion." One could argue, I suppose, that any time Congress acts with the *intent* of advancing religion, it has enacted a "law respecting an establishment of religion"; but far from being an unavoidable reading, it is quite an unnatural one. I doubt, for example, that the Clayton Act, 38 Stat. 730, as amended, 15 U.S.C. § 12 *et seq.*, could reasonably be described as a "law respecting an establishment of religion" if bizarre new historical evidence revealed that it lacked a secular purpose, even though it has no discernible nonsecular effect. It is, in short, far from an inevitable reading of the Establishment Clause that it forbids all governmental action intended to advance religion; and if not inevitable, any reading with such untoward consequences must be wrong.

In the past we have attempted to justify our embarrassing Establishment Clause jurisprudence on the ground that it **⊥640** "sacrifices clarity and predictability for flexibility." *Committee for Public Education & Religious Liberty* v. *Regan*. One commentator has aptly characterized this as "a euphemism . . . for . . . the absence of any principled rationale." I think it time that we sacrifice some "flexibility" for "clarity and predictability." Abandoning *Lemon's* purpose test—a test which exacerbates the tension between the Free Exercise and Establishment Clauses, has no basis in the language or history of the Amendment, and, as today's decision shows, has wonderfully flexible consequences—would be a good place to start.

BOARD OF EDUCATION OF THE WESTSIDE COMMUNITY SCHOOLS v. MERGENS

496 U.S. 226

ON WRIT OF CERTIORARI TO THE UNITED STATES COURT OF APPEALS FOR THE EIGHTH CIRCUIT

Argued January 9, 1990 — Decided June 4, 1990

⊥231 *Justice* O'CONNOR delivered the opinion of the Court except as to Part III.

This case requires us to decide whether the Equal Access Act, 98 Stat. 1302, 20 U.S.C. §§ 4071-4074, prohibits Westside High School from denying a student religious group permission to meet on school premises during noninstructional time, and if so, whether the Act, so construed, violates the Establishment Clause of the First Amendment.

I

Respondents are current and former students at Westside High School, a public secondary school in Omaha, Nebraska. At the time this suit was filed, the school enrolled about 1,450 students and included grades 10 to 12; in the 1987-1988 school year, ninth graders were added. Westside High School is part of the Westside Community School system, an independent public school district. Petitioners are the Board of Education of Westside Community Schools (District 66); Wayne W. Meier, the president of the school board; James E. Findley, the principal of Westside High School; Kenneth K. Hanson, the superintendent of schools for the school district; and James A. Tangdell, the assistant superintendent of schools for the school district.

Students at Westside High School are permitted to join various student groups and clubs, all of which meet after school hours on school premises. The students may choose from approximately 30 recognized groups on a voluntary basis. A list of student groups, together with a brief description of each provided by the school, appears in the Appendix to this opinion.

School Board Policy 5610 concerning "Student Clubs and Organizations" recognizes these student clubs as a "vital part of the total education program as a means of developing citizenship, wholesome attitudes, good human relations, knowledge and skills." Board Policy 5610 also provides that each club shall have faculty sponsorship and that ⊥**232** "clubs and organizations shall not be sponsored by any political or religious organization, or by any organization which denies membership on the basis of race, color, creed, sex or political belief." Board Policy 6180 on "Recognition of Religious Beliefs and Customs" requires that "[s]tudents adhering to a specific set of religious beliefs or holding to little or no belief shall be alike respected." In addition, Board Policy 5450 recognizes its students' "Freedom of Expression," consistent with the authority of the Board.

There is no written school board policy concerning the formation of student clubs. Rather, students wishing to form a club present their request to a school official who determines whether the proposed club's goals and objectives are consistent with school board policies and with the school district's "Mission and Goals"—a broadly worked "blueprint" that expresses the district's commitment to teaching academic, physical, civic, and personal skills and values.

In January 1985, respondent Bridget Mergens met with Westside's principal, Dr. Findley, and requested permission to form a Christian club at the school. The proposed club would have the same privileges and meet on the same terms and conditions as other Westside student groups, except that the proposed club would not have a faculty sponsor. According to the students' testimony at trial, the club's purpose would have been, among other things, to permit the students to read and discuss the Bible, to have fellowship, and to pray together. Membership would have been voluntary and open to all students regardless of religious affiliation.

Findley denied the request, as did associate superintendent Tangdell. In February 1985, Findley and Tangdell informed Mergens that they had discussed the matter with superintendent Hanson and that he had agreed that her request should be denied. The school officials explained that school policy required all student clubs to have a faculty sponsor, ⊥**233** which the proposed religious club would not or could not have, and that a religious club at the school would violate the Establishment Clause. In March 1985, Mergens appealed the denial of her request to the Board of Education, but the Board voted to uphold the denial.

Respondents, by and through their parents as next friends, then brought this suit in the United States District Court for the District of Nebraska seeking declaratory and injunctive relief. They alleged that petitioners' refusal to permit the proposed club to meet at Westside violated the Equal Access Act, 20 U.S.C. §§ 4071-4074, which prohibits public secondary schools that receive federal financial assistance and that maintain a "limited open forum" from denying "equal access" to students who wish to meet within the forum on the basis of the content of the speech at such meetings, § 4071(a). Respondents further alleged that petitioners' actions denied them their First and Fourteenth Amendment rights to freedom of speech, association, and the free exercise of religion. Petitioners responded that the Equal Access Act did not apply to Westside and that, if the Act did apply, it violated the Establishment Clause of the First Amendment and was therefore unconstitutional. The United States intervened in the action pursuant to 28 U.S.C. § 2403 to defend the constitutionality of the Act.

The District Court entered judgment for petitioners. The court held that the Act did not apply in this case because Westside did not have a "limited open forum" as defined by the Act—all of Westside's student clubs, the court concluded, were curriculum-related and tied to the educational function of the school. The court rejected respondents' constitutional claims, reasoning that Westside did not have a limited public forum as set forth in *Widmar* v. *Vincent*, and that Westside's denial of respondents' request was reasonably related to legitimate pedagogical concerns.

⊥**234** The United States Court of Appeals for the Eighth Circuit reversed. The Court of Appeals held that the District Court erred in concluding that all the existing student clubs at Westside were curriculum-related. The Court of Appeals noted that the "broad interpretation" advanced by the Westside school officials "would make the [Equal Access Act] meaningless" and would allow any school to "arbitrarily deny access to school facilities to any unfavored student club on the basis of its speech content," which was "exactly the result that Congress sought to prohibit by enacting the [Act]." The Court of Appeals instead found that "[m]any of the student clubs at WHS, including the chess club, are noncurriculum-related." Accordingly, because it found that Westside maintained a limited open forum under the Act, the Court of Appeals concluded that the Act applied to "forbi[d] discrimination against [respondents'] proposed club on the basis of its religious content."

The Court of Appeals then rejected petitioners' contention that the Act violated the Establishment Clause. Noting that the Act extended the decision in *Widmar* v. *Vincent* to public secondary schools, the Court of Appeals concluded that "[a]ny constitutional attack on the [Act] must therefore be predicated on the difference between secondary school students and university students." Because "Congress considered the difference in the maturity level of secondary students and university students before passing the [Act]," the Court of Appeals held, on the basis of Congress' fact-finding, that the Act did not violate the Establishment Clause.

We granted certiorari and now affirm.

II

A

In *Widmar* v. *Vincent* we invalidated, on free speech grounds, a state university regulation that prohibited ⊥**235** student use of school facilities "'for purposes of religious worship or religious teaching.'" In doing so, we held that an "equal access" policy would not violate the Establishment Clause under our decision in *Lemon* v. *Kurtzman*. In particular, we held that such a policy would have a secular purpose, would not have the primary effect of advancing religion, and would not result in excessive entanglement between government and religion. We noted, however, that "[u]niversity students are, of course, young adults. They are less impressionable than younger students and should be able to appreciate that the University's policy is one of neutrality toward religion."

In 1984, Congress extended the reasoning of *Widmar* to public secondary schools. Under the Equal Access Act, a public secondary school with a "limited open forum" is prohibited from discriminating against students who wish to conduct a meeting within that forum on the basis of the "religious, political, philosophical, or other content of the speech at such meetings." 20 U.S.C. §§ 4071(a) and (b). Specifically, the Act provides:

"It shall be unlawful for any public secondary school which receives Federal financial assistance and which has a limited open forum to deny equal access or a fair opportunity to, or discriminate against, any students who wish to conduct a meeting within that limited open forum on the basis of the religious, political, philosophical, or other content of the speech at such meetings." 20 U.S.C. § 4071(a). A "limited open forum" exists whenever a public secondary school "grants an offering to or opportunity for one or more noncurriculum related student groups to meet on school premises during noninstructional time." § 4071(b). "Meeting" is defined to include "those activities of student groups which are permitted under a school's limited open forum and are not directly related to the school curriculum." § 4072(3). ⊥**236** "Noninstructional time" is defined to mean "time set aside by the school before actual classroom instruction begins or after actual classroom instruction ends." § 4072(4). Thus, even if a public secondary school allows only one "noncurriculum related student group" to meet, the Act's obligations are triggered and the school may not deny other clubs, on the basis of the content of their speech, equal access to meet on school premises during noninstructional time.

The Act further specifies that "[s]chools shall be deemed to offer a fair opportunity to students who wish to conduct a meeting within its limited open forum" if the school uniformly provides that the meetings are voluntary and student-initiated; are not sponsored by the school, the government, or its agents or employees; do not materially and substantially interfere with the orderly conduct of educational activities within the school; and are not directed, controlled, conducted, or regularly attended by "nonschool persons." §§ 4071(c)(1) (2) (4), and (5). "Sponsorship" is defined to mean "the act of promoting, leading or participating in a meeting. The assignment of a teacher, administrator or other school employee to a meeting for custodial purposes does not constitute sponsorship of the meeting." § 4072(2). If the meetings are religious, employees or agents of the school or government may attend only in a "nonparticipatory capacity." § 4071(c)(3). Moreover, a State may not influence the form of any religious activity, require any person to participate in such activity, or compel any school agent or employee to attend a meeting if the content of the speech at the meeting is contrary to that person's beliefs. §§ 4071(d) (1) (2), and (3).

Finally, the Act does not "authorize the United States to deny or withhold Federal financial assistance to any school," § 4071(e), or "limit the authority of the school, its agents or employees, to maintain order and discipline on school premises, to protect the well-being of students and faculty, and to ⊥**237** assure that attendance of students at the meetings is voluntary," § 4071(f).

B

The parties agree that Westside High School receives federal financial assistance and is a public secondary school within the meaning of the Act. The Act's obligation to grant equal access to student groups is therefore triggered if Westside maintains a "limited open forum"—*i.e.*, if it permits one or more "noncurriculum related student groups" to meet on campus before or after classes.

Unfortunately, the Act does not define the crucial phrase "noncurriculum related student group." Our immediate task is therefore one of statutory interpretation. We begin, of course, with the language of the statute. The common meaning of the term "curriculum" is "the whole body of courses offered by an educational institution or one of its branches." Webster's Third New International Dictionary 557 (1976); see also Black's Law Dictionary 345 (5th ed. 1979) ("The set of studies or courses for a particular period, designated by a school or branch of a school"). Any sensible interpretation of "noncurriculum related student group" must therefore be anchored in the notion that such student groups are those that are not related to the body of courses offered by the school. The difficult question is the degree of "unrelatedness to the curriculum" required for a group to be considered "noncurriculum related."

The Act's definition of the sort of "meeting[s]" that must be accommodated under the statute, § 4071(a), sheds some light on this question. "[T]he term 'meeting' includes those activities of student groups which are . . . not *directly related* to the school curriculum." § 4072(3) (emphasis added). Con⊥**238**gress' use of the phrase "directly related" implies that student groups directly related to the subject matter of courses offered by the school do not fall within the "noncurriculum related" category and would therefore be considered "curriculum related."

The logic of the Act also supports this view, namely, that a curriculum-related student group is one that has more than just a tangential or attenuated relationship to courses offered by the school. Because the purpose of granting equal access is to prohibit discrimination between religious or political clubs on the one hand and other noncurriculum-related student groups on the other, the Act is premised on the notion that a religious or political club is itself likely to be a noncurriculum-related student group. It follows, then, that a student group that is "curriculum related" must at least have a more direct relationship to the curriculum than a religious or political club would have.

Although the phrase "noncurriculum related student group" nevertheless remains sufficiently ambiguous that we might normally resort to legislative history, we find the legislative history on this issue less than helpful. Because the bill that led to the Act was extensively rewritten in a series of multilateral negotiations after it was passed by the House and reported out of committee by the Senate, the committee reports shed no light on the language actually adopted. During congressional debate on the subject, legislators referred to a number of different definitions, and thus both petitioners and respondents can cite to legislative history favoring their interpretation of the phrase. Compare 130 Cong. Rec. 19223 (1984) (statement of Sen. Hatfield) (curriculum-related clubs are those that are "really a kind of extension of the classroom"), with *ibid.* (statement of Sen. Hatfield) (in response to question whether school districts would have full authority to decide what was curriculum-related, "[w]e in no way seek to limit that discretion").

⊥**239** We think it significant, however, that the Act, which was passed by wide, bipartisan majorities in both the House and the Senate, reflects at least some consensus on a broad legislative purpose. The committee reports indicate that the Act was intended to address perceived widespread discrimination against religious speech in public schools, see H. R. Rep. No. 98-710, p. 4 (1984); S. Rep. No. 98-357, pp. 10-11 (1984), and, as the language of the Act indicates, its sponsors contemplated that the Act would do more than merely validate the status quo. The committee reports also show that the Act was enacted in part in response to two federal appellate court decisions holding that student religious groups could not, consistent with the Establishment Clause, meet on school premises during noninstructional time. A broad reading of the Act would be consistent with the view of those who sought to end discrimination by allowing students to meet and discuss religion before and after classes.

In light of this legislative purpose, we think that the term "noncurriculum related student group" is best interpreted broadly to mean any student group that does not *directly* relate to the body of courses offered by the school. In our view, a student group directly relates to a school's curriculum if the subject matter of the group is actually taught, or will soon be taught, in a regularly offered course; if the subject matter of the group concerns the body of courses as a whole; if participation in the group is required for a particular course; or if participation in the group results in academic ⊥**240** credit. We think this limited definition of groups that directly relate to the curriculum is a commonsense interpretation of the Act that is consistent with Congress' intent to provide a low threshold for triggering the Act's requirements.

For example, a French club would directly relate to the curriculum if a school taught French in a regularly offered course or planned to teach the subject in the near future. A school's student government would generally relate directly to the curriculum to the extent that it addresses concerns, solicits opinions, and formulates proposals pertaining to the body of courses offered by the school. If participation in a school's band or orchestra were required for the band or orchestra classes, or resulted in academic credit, then those groups would also directly relate to the curriculum. The existence of such groups at a school would not trigger the Act's obligations.

On the other hand, unless a school could show that groups such as a chess club, a stamp collecting club, or a community service club fell within our description of groups that directly relate to the curriculum, such groups would be "noncurriculum related student groups" for purposes of the Act. The existence of such groups would create a "limited open forum" under the Act and would prohibit the school from denying equal access to any other student group on the basis of the content of that group's speech. Whether a specific student group is a "noncurriculum related student group" will therefore depend on a particular school's curriculum, but such determinations would be subject to factual findings well within the competence of trial courts to make.

Petitioners contend that our reading of the Act unduly hinders local control over schools and school activities, but we think that schools and school districts nevertheless retain a significant measure of authority over the type of officially recognized activities in which their students participate. ⊥**241** First, schools and school districts maintain their traditional latitude to determine appropriate subjects of instruction. To the extent that a school chooses to structure its course offerings and existing student groups to avoid the Act's obligations, that result is not prohibited by the Act. On matters of statutory interpretation, "[o]ur task is to apply the text, not to improve on it." Second, the Act expressly does not limit a school's authority to prohibit meetings that would "materially and substantially interfere with the orderly conduct of educational activities within the school." The Act also preserves the authority of the school, its agents or employees, to maintain order and discipline on school premises, to protect the well-being of students and faculty, and to assure that attendance of students at meetings is voluntary." § 4071(f). Finally, because the Act applies only to public secondary schools that receive federal financial assistance, § 4071(a), a school district seeking to escape the statute's obligations could simply forgo federal funding. Although we do not doubt that in some cases this may be an unrealistic option, Congress clearly sought to prohibit schools from discriminating on the basis of the content of a student group's speech, and that obligation is the price a federally funded school must pay if it opens its facilities to noncurriculum-related student groups.

The dissent suggests that "an extracurricular student organization is 'noncurriculum related' if it has as its purpose (or as part of its purpose) the advocacy of partisan theological, political, or ethical views." (Act is triggered only if school permits "controversial" or "distasteful" groups to use its facilities); ("noncurriculum" subjects are those that "'cannot properly be included in a public school curriculum'"). This interpretation of the Act, we are told, is mandated by Congress' intention to ⊥**242** "track our own Free Speech Clause jurisprudence," by incorporating rating *Widmar's* notion of a "limited public forum" into the language of the Act.

This suggestion is flawed for at least two reasons. First, the Act itself neither uses the phrase "limited public forum" nor so much as hints that that doctrine is somehow "incorporated" into the words of the statute. The operative language of the statute, 20 U.S.C. § 4071(a), of course, refers to a "limited open forum," a term that is specifically defined in the next subsection, § 4071(b). Congress was presumably aware that "limited public forum," as used by the Court is a term of art, and had it intended to import that concept into the Act, one would suppose that it would have done so explicitly. Indeed, Congress' deliberate choice to use a different term—and to define that term—can only mean that it intended to establish a standard different from the one established by our free speech cases. To paraphrase the dissent, "[i]f Congress really intended to [incorporate] *Widmar* for reasons of administrative clarity, Congress kept its intent well hidden, both in the statute and in the debates preceding its passage."

Second, and more significant, the dissent's reliance on the legislative history to support its interpretation of the Act shows just how treacherous that task can be. The dissent appears to agree with our view that the legislative history of the Act, even if relevant, is highly unreliable, yet the interpretation it suggests rests solely on a few passing, general references by legislators to our decision in *Widmar*. We think that reliance on legislative history is hazardous at best, but where "'not even the sponsors of the bill ⊥**243** knew what it meant,'" such reliance cannot form a reasonable basis on which to interpret the text of a statute. For example, the dissent appears to place great reliance on a comment by Senator Levin that the Act extends the rule in *Widmar* to secondary schools, but Senator Levin's understanding of the "rule," expressed in the same breath as the statement on which the dissent relies, fails to support the dissent's reading of the Act. See 130 Cong. Rec. 19236 (1984) ("The pending amendment will allow students equal access to secondary schools student-initiated religious meetings before and after school where the school *generally* allows groups of secondary school students to meet during those times") (emphasis added). Moreover, a number of Senators, during the same debate, warned that some of the views stated did not reflect their own views. ("I am troubled with the legislative history that you are making here") (statement of Sen. Chiles); ("[T]here have been a number of statements made on the floor today which may be construed as legislative history modifying what my understanding was or what anyone's understanding might be of this bill") (statement of Sen. Denton). The only thing that can be said with any confidence is that *some* Senators may have thought that the obligation of the Act would be triggered only when a school permits advocacy groups to meet on school premises during noninstructional time. That conclusion, of course, cannot bear the weight the dissent places on it.

C

The parties in this case focus their dispute on 10 of Westside's approximately 30 voluntary student clubs: Interact (a service club related to Rotary International); Chess; Subsurfers (a club for students interested in scuba diving); National Honor Society; Photography; Welcome to Westside (a club to introduce new students to the ⊥**244** school); Future Business Leaders of America; Zonta (the female counterpart to Interact); Student Advisory Board (student government); and Student Forum (student government). Petitioners contend that all of these student activities are curriculum-related because they further the goals of particular aspects of the school's curriculum. Welcome to Westside, for example, helps "further the School's overall goal of developing effective citizens by requiring student members to contribute to their fellow students." The student government clubs "advance the goals of the School's political science classes by providing an understanding and appreciation of government processes." Subsurfers furthers "one of the essential goals of the Physical Education Department—enabling students to develop lifelong recreational interests." Chess "supplement[s] math and science courses because it enhances students' ability to engage in critical thought processes." Participation in Interact and Zonta "promotes effective citizenship, a critical goal of the WHS curriculum, specifically the Social Studies Department."

To the extent that petitioners contend that "curriculum related" means anything remotely related to abstract educational goals, however, we reject that argument. To define "curriculum related" in a way that results in almost no schools having limited open fora, or in a way that permits schools to evade the Act by strategically describing existing student groups, would render the Act merely hortatory. See 130 Cong. Rec. 19222 (1984) (statement of Sen. Leahy) ("[A] limited open forum should be triggered by what a school does, not by what it says"). As the court below explained:

"Allowing such a broad interpretation of 'curriculum-related' would make the [Act] meaningless. A school's administration could simply declare that it maintains a closed forum and choose which student clubs it wanted to allow by tying the purposes of those student clubs to ⊥**245** some broadly defined educational goal. At the same time the administration could arbitrarily deny access to school facilities to any unfavored student club on the basis of its speech content. This is exactly the result that Congress sought to prohibit by enacting the [Act]. A public secondary school cannot simply declare that it maintains a closed forum and then discriminate against a particular student group on the basis of the content of the speech of that group." See also *Garnett* v. *Renton School Dist. No. 403* ("Complete deference [to the school district] would render the Act meaningless because school boards could circumvent the Act's requirements simply by asserting that all student groups are curriculum related").

Rather, we think it clear that Westside's existing student groups include one or more "noncurriculum related student groups." Although Westside's physical education classes apparently include swimming, counsel stated at oral argument that scuba diving is not taught in any regularly offered course at the school. Based on Westside's own description of the group, Subsurfers does not directly relate to the curriculum as a whole in the same way that a student government or similar group might. Moreover, participation in Subsurfers is not required by any course at the school and does not result in extra academic credit. Thus, Subsurfers is a "noncurriculum related student group" for purposes of the Act. Similarly, although math teachers at Westside have encouraged their students to play chess, chess is not taught in any regularly offered course at the school, and participation in the Chess Club is not required for any class and does not result in extra credit for any class. The Chess Club is therefore another "noncurriculum related student group" at ⊥**246** Westside. Moreover, Westside's principal acknowledged at trial that the Peer Advocates program—a service group that works with special education classes—does not directly relate to any courses offered by the school and is not required by any courses offered by the school. Peer Advocates would therefore also fit within our description of a "noncurriculum related student group." The record therefore supports a finding that Westside has maintained a limited open forum under the Act.

Although our definition of "noncurriculum related student activities" looks to a school's actual practice rather than its stated policy, we note that our conclusion is also supported by the school's own description of its student activities. As reprinted in the Appendix to this opinion, the school states that Band "is included in our regular curriculum"; Choir "is a course offered as part of the curriculum"; Distributive Education "is an extension of the Distributive Education class"; International Club is "developed through our foreign language classes"; Latin Club is "designed for those students who are taking Latin as a foreign language"; Student Publications "includes classes offered in preparation of the yearbook (Shield) and the student newspaper (Lance)"; Dramatics "is an extension of a regular academic class"; and Orchestra "is an extension of our regular curriculum." These descriptions constitute persuasive evidence that these student clubs directly relate to the curriculum. By inference however, the fact that the descriptions of student activities such as Subsurfers and chess do not include such references strongly suggests that those clubs do not, by the school's own admission, directly relate to the curriculum. We therefore conclude that Westside permits "one or more noncurriculum related student groups to meet on school premises during noninstructional time." Because Westside maintains a "limited open forum" under the Act, it is prohibited from ⊥**247** discriminating, based on the content of the students' speech, against students who wish to meet on school premises during noninstructional time.

The remaining statutory question is whether petitioners' denial of respondents' request to form a religious group constitutes a denial of "equal access" to the school's limited open forum. Although the school apparently permits respondents to meet informally after school, respondents seek equal access in the form of official recognition by the school. Official recognition allows student clubs to be part of the student activities program and carries with it access to the school newspaper, bulletin boards, the public address system, and the annual Club Fair. Given that the Act explicitly prohibits denial of "equal access . . . to . . . any students who wish to conduct a meeting within [the school's] limited open forum" on the basis of the religious content of the speech at such meetings, we hold that Westside's denial of respondents' request to form a Christian club denies them "equal access" under the Act.

Because we rest our conclusion on statutory ground, we need not decide—and therefore express no opinion on—whether the First Amendment requires the same result.

III

Petitioners contend that even if Westside has created a limited open forum within the meaning of the Act, its denial of official recognition to the proposed Christian club must nevertheless stand because the Act violates the Establishment Clause of the First Amendment, as applied to the States through the Fourteenth Amendment. Specifically, petitioners maintain that because the school's recognized student activities are an integral part of its educational mission, official recognition of respondents' proposed club would effectively incorporate religious activities into the school's official program, endorse participation in the religious club, and pro-⊥**248**vide the club with an official platform to proselytize other students.

We disagree. In *Widmar*, we applied the three-part *Lemon* test to hold that an "equal access" policy, at the university level, does not violate the Establishment Clause. We concluded that "an open-forum policy, including nondiscrimination against religious speech, would have a secular purpose," and would in fact *avoid* entanglement with religion. We also found that although incidental benefits accrued to religious groups who used university facilities, this result did not amount to an establishment of religion. First, we stated that a university's forum does not "confer any imprimatur of state approval on religious sects or practices." Indeed, the message is one of neutrality rather than endorsement; if a State refused to let religious groups use facilities open to others, then it would demonstrate not neutrality but hostility toward religion. "The Establishment Clause does not license government to treat religion and those who teach or practice it, simply by virtue of their status as such, as subversive of American ideals and therefore subject to unique disabilities." *McDaniel* v. *Paty* (Brennan, J. concurring in judgment). Second, we noted that "[t]he [University's] provision of benefits to [a] broad . . . spectrum of groups"—both nonreligious and religious speakers—was "an important index of secular effect."

We think the logic of *Widmar* applies with equal force to the Equal Access Act. As an initial matter, the Act's prohibition of discrimination on the basis of "political, philosophical, or other" speech as well as religious speech is a sufficient basis for meeting the secular purpose prong of the *Lemon* test. ⊥**249** Congress' avowed purpose—to prevent discrimination against religious and other types of speech—is undeniably secular. Even if some legislators were motivated by a conviction that religious speech in particular was valuable and worthy of protection, that alone would not invalidate the Act, because what is relevant is the legislative *purpose* of the statute, not the possibly religious *motives* of the legislators who enacted the law. Because the Act on its face grants equal access to both secular and religious speech, we think it clear that the Act's purpose was not to "'endorse or disapprove of religion,'" *Wallace* v. *Jaffree* (1985) (quoting *Lynch* v. *Donnelly* (O'Connor, J., concurring)).

Petitioners' principal contention is that the Act has the primary effect of advancing religion. Specifically, petitioners urge that, because the student religious meetings are held under school aegis, and because the state's compulsory attendance laws bring the students together (and thereby provide a ready-made audience for student evangelists), an objective observer in the position of a secondary school student will perceive official school support for such religious meetings.

⊥**250** We disagree. First, although we have invalidated the use of public funds to pay for teaching state-required subjects at parochial schools, in part because of the risk of creating "a crucial symbolic link between government and religion, thereby enlisting—at least in the eyes of impressionable youngsters—the powers of government to the support of the religious denomination operating the school," *Grand Rapids School Dist.* v. *Ball*, there is crucial difference between *government* speech endorsing religion, which the Establishment Clause forbids, and *private* speech endorsing religion, which the Free Speech and Free Exercise Clauses protect. We think that secondary school students are mature enough and are likely to understand that a school does not endorse or support student speech that it merely permits on a nondiscriminatory basis. The proposition that schools do not endorse everything they fail to censor is not complicated. "[P]articularly in this age of massive media information . . . the few years difference in age between high school and college students [does not] justif[y] departing from *Widmar*." *Bender* v. *Williamsport Area School District* (Powell, J., dissenting).

Indeed, we note that Congress specifically rejected the argument that high school students are likely to confuse an equal access policy with state sponsorship of religion. See S. Rep. No. 98-357, p. 8 (1984); at 35 ("[S]tudents below the college level are capable of distinguishing between State-initiated, school sponsored, or teacher-led religious ⊥**251** speech on the one hand and student-initiated, student-led religious speech on the other"). Given the deference due "the duly enacted and carefully considered decision of a coequal and representative branch of our Government," we do not lightly second-guess such legislative judgments, particularly where the judgments are based in part on empirical determinations.

Second, we note that the Act expressly limits participation by school officials at meetings of student religious groups, §§ 4071(c) (2) and (3), and that any such meetings must be held during "noninstructional time," § 4071(b). The Act therefore avoids the problems of "the students' emulation of teachers as role models" and "mandatory attendance requirements." To be sure, the possibility of *student* peer pressure remains, but there is little if any risk of official state endorsement or coercion where no formal classroom activities are involved and no school officials actively participate. Moreover, petitioners' fear of a mistaken inference of endorsement is largely self-imposed, because the school itself has control over any impressions it gives its students. To the extent a school makes clear that its recognition of respondents' proposed club is not an endorsement of the views of the club's participants, students will reasonably understand that the school's official recognition of the club evinces neutrality toward, rather than endorsement of, religious speech.

⊥**252** Third, the broad spectrum of officially recognized student clubs at Westside, and the fact that Westside students are free to initiate and organize additional student clubs, counteract any possible message of official endorsement of or preference for religion or a particular religious belief. Although a school may not itself lead or direct a religious club, a school that permits a student-initiated and student-led religious club to meet after school, just as it permits any other student group to do, does not convey a message of state approval or endorsement of the particular religion. Under the Act, a school with a limited open forum may not lawfully deny access to a Jewish students' club, a Young Democrats club, or a philosophy club devoted to the study of Nietzsche. To the extent that a religious club is merely one of many different student-initiated voluntary clubs, students should perceive no message of government endorsement of religion. Thus, we conclude that the Act does not, at least on its face and as applied to Westside, have the primary effect of advancing religion.

Petitioners' final argument is that by complying with the Act's requirement, the school risks excessive entanglement between government and religion. The proposed club, petitioners urge, would be required to have a faculty sponsor who would be charged with actively directing the activities of the group, guiding its leaders, and ensuring balance in the presentation of controversial ideas. Petitioners claim that this influence over the club's religious program would entangle the government in day-to-day surveillance of religion of the type forbidden by the Establishment Clause.

⊥253 Under the Act, however, faculty monitors may not participate in any religious meetings, and nonschool person may not direct, control, or regularly attend activities of student groups. §§ 4071(c)(3) and (5). Moreover, the Act prohibits school "sponsorship" of any religious meetings, § 4071(c)(2), which means that school officials may not promote, lead, or participate in any such meeting, § 4072(2). Although the Act permits "[t]he assignment of a teacher, administrator, or other school employee to the meeting for custodial purposes," such custodial oversight of the student-initiated religious group, merely to ensure order and good behavior, does not impermissibly entangle government in the day-to-day surveillance or administration of religious activities. Indeed, as the Court noted in *Widmar*, a denial of equal access to religious speech might well create greater entanglement problems in the form of invasive monitoring to prevent religious speech at meetings at which such speech might occur.

Accordingly, we hold that the Equal Access Act does not on its face contravene the Establishment Clause. Because we hold that petitioners have violated the Act, we do not decide respondents' claims under the Free Speech and the Free Exercise Clauses. For the foregoing reasons, the judgment of the Court of Appeals is affirmed.

It is so ordered.

. . . . .

⊥258 *Justice KENNEDY*, with whom *Justice SCALIA* joins, concurring in part and concurring in the judgment.

The Court's interpretation of the statutory term "noncurriculum related groups" is proper and correct, in my view, and I join Parts I and II of the Court's opinion. I further agree that the Act does not violate the Establishment Clause, and so I concur in the judgment; but my view of the analytic premise that controls the establishment question differs from that employed by the plurality. I write to explain **⊥259** why I cannot join all that is said in Part III of *Justice O'CONNOR's* opinion.

I

A brief initial comment on the statutory issue is in order. The student clubs recognized by Westside school officials are a far cry from the groups given official recognition by university officials in *Widmar* v. *Vincent*. As *Justice STEVENS* points out in dissent, one of the consequences of the statute, as we now interpret it, is that clubs of a most controversial character might have access to the student life of high schools that in the past have given official recognition only to clubs of a more conventional kind.

It must be apparent to all that the Act has made a matter once left to the discretion of local school officials the subject of comprehensive regulation by federal law. This decision, however, was for Congress to make, subject to constitutional limitations. Congress having decided in favor of legislative intervention, it faced the task of formulating general statutory standards against the background protection of the Free Speech Clause, as well as the Establishment and Free Exercise Clauses. Given the complexities of our own jurisprudence in these areas, there is no doubt that the congressional task was a difficult one. While I can not pretend that the language Congress used in the Act is free from ambiguity in some of its vital provisions, the Court's interpretation of the phrase "noncurriculum related" seems to me to be the most rational and indeed the most plausible interpretation available, given the words and structure of the Act and the constitutional implications of the subject it addresses.

There is one structural feature of the statute that should be noted. The opinion of the Court states that "[i]f the meetings are religious, employees or agents of the school or government may attend only in a 'nonparticipatory capacity.'" This is based upon a provision in the Act in which nonparticipation is one **⊥260** of several statutory criteria that a school must meet in order to "be deemed to offer a fair opportunity to students who wish to conduct a meeting within its limited open forum." § 4071(c). It is not altogether clear, however, whether satisfaction of these criteria is the sole means of meeting the statutory requirement that schools with noncurriculum related student groups provide a "fair opportunity" to religious clubs. § 4071(a). Although we need not answer it today, left open is the question whether school officials may prove that they are in compliance with the statute without satisfying all of the criteria in § 4071(c). But in the matter before us, the school has not attempted to comply with the statute through any means, and we have only to determine whether it is possible for the statute to be implemented in a constitutional manner.

II

I agree with the plurality that a school complying with the statute by satisfying the criteria in § 4071(c) does not violate the Establishment Clause. The accommodation of religion mandated by the Act is a neutral one, and in the context of this case it suffices to inquire whether the Act violates either one of two principles. The first is that the government cannot "give direct benefits to religion in such a degree that it in fact 'establishes a [state] religion or religious faith, or tends to do so.'" Any incidental benefits that accompany official recognition of a religious club under the criteria set forth in the § 4071(c) do not lead to the establishment of religion under this standard. The second principle controlling the case now before us, in my view, is that the government cannot coerce any student to participate in a religious activity. The Act is consistent with this stan⊥**261**dard as well. Nothing on the face of the Act or in the facts of the case as here presented demonstrates that enforcement of the statute will result in the coercion of any student to participate in a religious activity. The Act does not authorize school authorities to require, or even to encourage, students to become members of a religious club or to attend a club's meetings, see §§ 4071(c)(d), 4072(2); the meetings take place while school is not in session, see §§ 4071(b), 4072(4); and the Act does not compel any school employee to participate in, or to attend, a club's meetings or activities, see §§ 4071(c)(d)(4).

The plurality uses a different test, one which asks whether school officials, by complying with the Act, have endorsed religion. It is true that when government gives impermissible assistance to a religion it can be said to have "endorsed" religion; but endorsement cannot be the test. The word endorsement has insufficient content to be dispositive. And for reasons I have explained elsewhere, its literal application may result in neutrality in name but hostility in fact when the question is the government's proper relation to those who express some religious preference.

I should think it inevitable that a public high school "endorses" a religious club, in a common-sense use of the term, if the club happens to be one of many activities that the school permits students to choose in order to further the development of their intellect and character in an extracurricular setting. But no constitutional violation occurs if the school's action is based upon a recognition of the fact that membership in a religious club is one of many permissible ways for a student to further his or her own personal enrichment. The inquiry with respect to coercion must be whether the government imposes pressure upon a student to participate in a religious activity. This inquiry, of course, must be undertaken with sensitivity to the special circumstances that exist in a secondary school where the line between voluntary and ⊥**262** coerced participation may be difficult to draw. No such coercion, however, has been shown to exist as a necessary result of this statute, either on its face or as respondents seek to invoke it on the facts of this case.

For these reasons, I join Parts I and II of the Court's opinion, and concur in the judgment.

Justice MARSHALL, with whom *Justice* BRENNAN joins, concurring in the judgment.

I agree with the majority that "noncurriculum" must be construed broadly to "prohibit schools from discriminating on the basis of the content of a student group's speech." As the majority demonstrates, such a construction "is consistent with Congress' intent to provide a low threshold for triggering the Act's requirements." In addition, to the extent that Congress intended the Act to track this Court's free speech jurisprudence, as the dissent argues, the majority's construction is faithful to our commitment to nondiscriminatory access to open forum in public schools. When a school allows student-initiated clubs not directly tied to the school's curriculum to use school facilities, it has "created a forum generally open to student groups" and is therefore constitutionally prohibited from enforcing a "content-based exclusion" of other student speech. In this respect, the Act as construed by the majority simply codifies in statute what is already constitutionally mandated: schools may not discriminate among student-initiated groups that seek access to school facilities for expressive purposes not directly related to the school's curriculum.

The Act's low threshold for triggering equal access, however, raises serious Establishment Clause concerns where secondary schools with fora that differ substantially from the forum in *Widmar* are required to grant access to student religious groups. Indeed, as applied in the present case, the Act mandates a religious group's access to a forum that is dedicated to promoting fundamental values and citizenship as ⊥**263** defined by the school. The Establishment Clause does not forbid the operation of the Act in such circumstances, but it does require schools to change their relationship to their forum so as to disassociate themselves effectively from religious clubs' speech. Thus, although I agree with the plurality that the Act as applied to Westside *could* withstand Establishment Clause scrutiny (O'Connor, J., joined by Rehnquist, C.J., and White and Blackmun, JJ.), I write separately to emphasize the steps Westside must take to avoid appearing to endorse the Christian Club's goals. The plurality's Establishment Clause analysis pays inadequate attention to the differences between this case and *Widmar* and dismisses too lightly the distinctive pressures created by Westside's highly structured environment.

I

A

This case involves the intersection of two First Amendment guarantees—the Free Speech Clause and the

Establishment Clause. We have long regarded free and open debate over matters of controversy as necessary to the functioning of our constitutional system. That the Constitution requires toleration of speech over its suppression is no less true in our Nation's schools.

But the Constitution also demands that the State not take action that has the primary effect of advancing religion. ⊥**264** The introduction of religious speech into the public schools reveals the tension between these two constitutional commitments, because the failure of a school to stand apart from religious speech can convey a message that the school endorses rather than merely tolerates that speech. Recognizing the potential dangers of school-endorsed religious practice, we have shown particular "vigilan[ce] in monitoring compliance with the Establishment Clause in elementary and secondary schools." *Edwards* v. *Aguillard*. This vigilance must extend to our monitoring of the actual effects of an "equal access" policy. If public schools are perceived as conferring the imprimatur of the State on religious doctrine or practice as a result of such a policy, the nominally "neutral" character of the policy will not save it from running afoul of the Establishment Clause.

B

We addressed at length the potential conflict between toleration and endorsement of religious speech in *Widmar*. There, a religious study group sought the same access to university facilities that the university afforded to over 100 ⊥**265** officially recognized student groups, including many political organizations. In those circumstances, we concluded that granting religious organizations similar access to the public forum would have neither the purpose nor the primary effect of advancing religion. The plurality suggests that our conclusion in *Widmar* controls this case. But the plurality fails to recognize that the wide-open and independent character of the student forum in *Widmar* differs substantially from the forum at Westside.

Westside currently does not recognize any student club that advocates a controversial viewpoint. Indeed, the clubs at Westside that trigger the Act involve scuba diving, chess, and counseling for special education students. As a matter of school policy, Westside encourages student participation in clubs based on a broad conception of its educational mission. That mission comports with the Court's acknowledgment "that public schools are vitally important 'in the preparation of individuals for participation as citizens,' and as vehicles for 'inculcating fundamental values necessary to the maintenance of a democratic political system.'" Given the nature and function of student clubs at Westside, the school makes no effort to disassociate itself from the activities and goals of its student clubs.

The entry of religious clubs into such a realm poses a real danger that those clubs will be viewed as part of the school's effort to inculcate fundamental values. The school's message with respect to its existing clubs is not one of toleration but one of endorsement. As the majority concedes, the program is part of the "district's commitment to teaching academic, physical, civic, and personal skills and values." But although a school may permissibly encourage its students to become well-rounded as student-athletes, student-musicians, and student-tutors, the Constitution for⊥**266**bids schools to encourage students to become well-rounded as student worshippers. Neutrality toward religion, as required by the Constitution, is not advanced by requiring a school that endorses the goals of some noncontroversial secular organizations to endorse the goals of religious organizations as well.

The fact that the Act, when triggered, provides access to political as well as religious speech does not ameliorate the potential threat of endorsement. The breadth of beneficiaries under the Act does suggest that the Act may satisfy the "secular purpose" requirement of the Establishment Clause inquiry we identified in *Lemon*. But the crucial question is how the Act affects each school. If a school already houses numerous ideological organizations, then the addition of a religion club will most likely not violate the Establishment Clause because the risk that students will erroneously attribute the views of the religion club to the school is minimal. To the extent a school tolerates speech by a wide range of ideological clubs, students cannot reasonably understand the school to endorse all of the groups' divergent and contradictory views. But if the religion club is the sole advocacy-oriented group in the forum, or one of a very limited number, and the school continues to promote its student-club program as instrumental to citizenship, then the school's failure to disassociate itself from the religious activity will reasonably be understood as an endorsement of that activity. That political and other advocacy-oriented groups are permitted to participate in a forum that, through school support and encouragement, is devoted to fostering a student's civic identity does not ameliorate the appearance of school endorsement unless the invitation is accepted and the forum is transformed into a forum like that in *Widmar*.

For this reason, the plurality's reliance on *Widmar* is misplaced. The University of Missouri took concrete steps to ensure "that the University's name will not 'be identified in ⊥**267** any way with the aims, policies, programs, products, or opinions of any organization or its members,'" (quoting University of Missouri student handbook). Westside, in contrast, explicitly promotes its student clubs "as a vital part of the total education program [and] as a means of developing citizenship." And while the University of Missouri recognized such clubs as the Young Socialist Alliance and the Young Democrats, Westside has recognized no such political clubs.

The different approaches to student clubs embodied in these policies reflect a significant difference, for Establishment Clause purposes, between the respective roles that Westside High School and the University of Missouri attempt to play in their students' lives. To the extent that a school emphasizes the autonomy of its students, as does the University of Missouri, there is a corresponding decrease in the likelihood that student speech will be regarded as school speech. Conversely, where a school such as Westside regards its student clubs as a mechanism for defining and transmitting fundamental values, the inclusion of a religious club in the school's program will almost certainly signal school endorsement of the religious practice.

Thus, the underlying difference between this case and *Widmar* is not that college and high school students have varying capacities to perceive the subtle differences between toleration and endorsement, but rather that the University of Missouri and Westside actually choose to define their respective missions in different ways. That high schools tend to emphasize student autonomy less than universities may suggest that high school administrators tend to perceive a difference in the maturity of secondary and university students. But the school's behavior, not the purported immaturity of high school students, is dispositive. If Westside stood apart from its club program and expressed the view, endorsed by Congress through its passage of the Act, that high school stu⊥**268**dents are capable of engaging in wide-ranging discussion of sensitive and controversial speech, the inclusion of religious groups in Westside's forum would confirm the school's commitment to nondiscrimination. Here, though, the Act requires the school to permit religious speech in a forum explicitly designed to advance the school's interest in shaping the character of its students.

The comprehensiveness of the access afforded by the Act further highlights the Establishment Clause dangers posed by the Act's application to forum such as Westside's. The Court holds that "[o]fficial recognition allows student clubs to be part of the student activities program and carries with it access to the school newspaper, bulletin boards, the public address system, and the annual Club Fair." Students would be alerted to the meetings of the religion club over the public address system; they would see religion club material posted on the official school bulletin board and club notices in the school newspaper; they would be recruited to join the religion club at the school sponsored Club Fair. If a school has a variety of ideological clubs, as in *Widmar*, I agree with the plurality that a student is likely to understand that "a school does not endorse or support student speech that it merely permits on a nondiscriminatory basis." When a school has a religion club but no other political or ideological organizations, however, that relatively fine distinction may be lost.

Moreover, in the absence of a truly robust forum that includes the participation of more than one advocacy-oriented group, the presence of a religious club could provide a fertile ground for peer pressure, especially if the club commanded support from a substantial portion of the student body. Indeed, it is precisely in a school without such a forum that intolerance for different religious and other views would be most dangerous and that a student who does not share the religious beliefs of his classmates would perceive "that religion or a particular religious belief is favored or preferred." ⊥**269** *Wallace* v. *Jaffree* (O'Connor J., concurring in judgment) .

The plurality concedes that there is a "possibility of *student* peer pressure," but maintains that this does not amount to "official state endorsement." This dismissal is too facile. We must remain sensitive, especially in the public schools, to "the numerous more subtle ways that government can show favoritism to particular beliefs or convey a message of disapproval to others." When the government, through mandatory attendance laws, brings students together in a highly controlled environment every day for the better part of their waking hours and regulates virtually every aspect of their existence during that time, we should not be so quick to dismiss the problem of peer pressure as if the school environment had nothing to do with creating and fostering it. The State has structured an environment in which students holding mainstream views may be able to coerce adherents of minority religions to attend club meetings or to adhere to club beliefs. Thus, the State cannot disclaim its responsibility for those resulting pressures.

II

Given these substantial risks posed by the inclusion of the proposed Christian Club within Westside's present forum, Westside must redefine its relationship to its club program. The plurality recognizes that such redefinition is necessary to avoid the risk of endorsement and construes the Act accordingly. The plurality holds that the Act "limits participation by school officials at meetings of student religious groups," (citing § 4071(c)(2) and (3)), and requires religious club meetings to be held during noninstructional time. It also holds that schools may not sponsor any religious meetings. Fi⊥**270**nally, and perhaps most importantly, the plurality states that schools bear the responsibility for taking whatever further steps are necessary to make clear that their recognition of a religious club does not reflect the endorsement of the views of the club's participants.

Westside thus must do more than merely prohibit faculty members from actively participating in the Christian Club's meetings. It must fully disassociate itself from the Club's religious speech and avoid appearing to sponsor or endorse the Club's goals. It could, for example, entirely discontinue encouraging student participation in clubs and clarify that the clubs are not instrumentally related to the school's overall mission. Or, if the school sought to continue its general endorsement of those student clubs that did not engage in controversial speech, it could do so if it also affirmatively disclaimed any endorsement of the Christian Club.

III

The inclusion of the Christian Club in the type of forum presently established at Westside, without more, will not assure government neutrality toward religion. Rather, because the school endorses the extracurricular program as part of its educational mission, the inclusion of the Christian Club in that program will convey to students the school-sanctioned message that involvement in religion develops "citizenship, wholesome attitudes, good human relations, knowledge and skills." We need not question the value of that message to affirm that it is not the place of schools to issue it. Accordingly, schools such as Westside must be responsive not only to the broad term of the Act's coverage, but also to this Court's mandate that they effectively disassociate themselves from the religious speech that now may become commonplace in their facilities.

Justice STEVENS, dissenting.

The dictionary is a necessary, and sometimes sufficient, aid to the judge confronted with the task of construing an opaque ⊥**271** act of Congress. In a case like this, however, I believe we must probe more deeply to avoid a patently bizarre result. Can Congress really have intended to issue an order to every public high school in the nation stating, in substance, that if you sponsor a chess club, a scuba diving club, or a French club—without having formal classes in those subjects—you must also open your doors to every religious, political, or social organization no matter how controversial or distasteful its views may be? I think not. A fair review of the legislative history of the Equal Access Act (Act), 98 Stat. 1302, 20 U.S.C. §§ 4071-4074, discloses that Congress intended to recognize a much narrower forum than the Court has legislated into existence today.

I

The Act's basic design is easily summarized: when a public high school has a "limited open forum," it must not deny any student group access to that forum on the basis of the religious, political, philosophical or other content of the speech of the group. Although the consequences of having a limited open forum are thus quite clear, the definition of such a forum is less so. Nevertheless, there is considerable agreement about how this difficulty must be resolved. The Court correctly identifies three useful guides to Congress' intent. First, the text of the statute says that a school creates a limited open forum if it allows meetings on school premises by "noncurriculum related student groups," a concept that is ambiguous at best. Second, because this concept is ambiguous, the statute must be interpreted by reference to its general purpose, as revealed by its overall structure and by the legislative history. Third, the Act's legislative history reveals that Congress intended to guarantee student religious groups access to high school forum comparable to the college forum involved in ⊥**272** *Widmar* v. *Vincent*. All of this is common ground, shared by the parties and by every Court of Appeals to have construed the Act.

A fourth agreement would seem to follow from these three. If "noncurriculum related" is an ambiguous term, and if it must therefore be interpreted in light of Congressional purpose, and if the purpose of Congress was to ensure that the rule of *Widmar* applied to high schools as it did to colleges, then the incidence of the Act in this case should depend upon whether, in light of *Widmar*, Westside would have to permit the Christian student group to meet if Westside were a college. The characteristics of the college forum in *Widmar* should thus provide a useful background for interpreting the meaning of the undefined term "noncurriculum related student groups." But this step the Court does not take, and it is accordingly here that I part company with it.

Our decision in *Widmar* encompassed two constitutional holdings. First, we interpreted the Free Speech Clause of the First Amendment to determine whether the University of Missouri at Kansas City had, by its own policies, abdicated discretion that it would otherwise have to make content-based discriminations among student groups seeking to meet on its campus. We agreed that it had. Next, we interpreted the Establishment Clause of the First Amendment to determine whether the University was prohibited from permitting student-initiated religious groups to participate in that forum. We agreed that it was ⊥**273** not.

To extend *Widmar* to high schools, then, would require us to pose two questions. We would first ask whether a high school had established a forum comparable under our Free Speech Clause jurisprudence to that which existed in *Widmar*. Only if this question were answered affirmatively would we then need to test the constitutionality of the Act by asking whether the Establishment Clause has different consequences when applied to a high school's open forum than when applied to a college's. I believe that in this case the first question must instead be answered in the negative, and that this answer ultimately proves dispositive under the Act just as it would were only constitutional considerations in play.

The forum at Westside is considerably different from that which existed at the University of Missouri. In *Widmar*, we held that the Universal had created "a generally open forum." Over 100 officially recognized student groups routinely participated in that forum. They included groups whose activities not only were unrelated to any specific courses, but also were of a kind that a state university could not properly sponsor or endorse. Thus, for example, they included such political organizations as the Young Socialist Alliance, the Women's Union, and the Young Democrats. The University permitted use of its facilities for speakers advocating transcendental meditation and humanism. Since the University had allowed such organizations and speakers the use of campus facilities, we concluded that the University could not discriminate against a religious group on the basis of the content of its speech. The forum established by the state university accommodated participating groups that were "noncurriculum related" not only because they did not mirror the school's classroom instruction, but also because they advocated ⊥274 controversial positions that a state university's obligation of neutrality prevented it from endorsing.

The Court's opinion in *Widmar* left open the question whether its holding would apply to a public high school that had established a similar public forum. That question has now been answered in the affirmative by the District Court, the Court of Appeals, and by this Court. I agree with that answer. Before the question was answered judicially, Congress decided to answer it legislatively in order to preclude continued unconstitutional discrimination against high school students interested in religious speech. According to Senator Hatfield, a cosponsor of the Act, "All [it] does is merely to try to protect, as I say, a right that is guaranteed under the Constitution that is being denied certain students." 130 Cong. Rec. 19218 (1984). As the Court of Appeals correctly recognized, the Act codified the decision in *Widmar*, "extending its holding to secondary public schools." What the Court of Appeals failed to recognize, however, is the critical difference between the university forum in *Widmar* and the high school forum involved in this case. None of the clubs at the high school is even arguably controversial or partisan.

⊥275 Nor would it be wise to ignore this difference. High school students may be adult enough to distinguish between those organizations that are sponsored by the school and those which lack school sponsorship even though they participate in a forum that the school does sponsor. But high school students are also young enough that open fora may be less suitable for them than for college students. The need to decide whether to risk treating students as adults too soon, or alternatively to risk treating them as children too long, is an enduring problem for all educators. The youth of these students, whether described in terms of "impressionability" or "maturity," may be irrelevant to our application of the constitutional restrictions that limit educational discretion in the public schools, but it surely is not irrelevant to our interpretation of the educational policies that have been adopted. We would do no honor to Westside's administrators or the Congress by assuming that either treated casually the differences between high school and college students when formulating the policy and the statute at issue here.

⊥276 For these reasons, I believe that the distinctions between Westside's program and the University of Missouri's program suggest what is the best understanding of the Act: an extracurricular student organization is "noncurriculum related" if it has as its purpose (or as part of its purpose) the advocacy of partisan theological, political, or ethical views. A school that admits at least one such club has apparently made the judgment that students are better off if the student community is permitted to, and perhaps even encouraged to, compete along ideological lines. This pedagogical strategy may be defensible or even desirable. But it is wrong to presume that Congress endorsed that strategy—and dictated its nationwide adoption—simply because it approved the application of *Widmar* to high schools. And it seems absurd to presume that Westside has invoked the same strategy by recognizing clubs like Swimming Team and Subsurfers which, though they may not correspond directly to anything in Westside's course offerings, are no more controversial than a grilled cheese sandwich.

Accordingly, as I would construe the Act, a high school could properly sponsor a French club, a chess club, or a scuba diving club simply because their activities are fully consistent with the school's curricular mission. It would not matter whether formal courses in any of those subjects—or indirectly related subjects—were being offered as long as faculty encouragement of student participation in such groups could be consistent with both the school's obligation of neutrality and its legitimate pedagogical concerns. Nothing in *Widmar* implies that the existence of a French club, for example, would create a constitutional obligation to allow student members of the Ku Klux Klan or the Communist Party to ⊥277 have access to school facilities. More importantly, nothing in that case suggests that the constitutional issue should turn on whether French is being taught in a formal course while the club is functioning.

Conversely, if a high school decides to allow political groups to use its facilities, it plainly cannot discriminate among controversial groups because it agrees with the positions of some and disagrees with the ideas advocated by others. Again, the fact that the history of the Republican Party might be taught in a political science course could not justify a decision to allow the young Republicans to form a club while denying Communists, white supremacists, or Christian Scientists the same privilege. In my judgment, the political activities of the young Republicans are "noncurriculum related" for reasons that have nothing to do with the content of the political science course. The statutory definition of what is "noncurriculum related" should depend on the constitutional concern that motivated our decision in *Widmar*.

In this case, the district judge reviewed each of the clubs in the high school program and found that they are all "tied to the educational function of the institution." He correctly concluded that this club system "differs dramatically from those found to create an open forum policy in *Widmar* and *Bender*." I agree ⊥278 with his conclusion that, under a proper interpretation of the Act, this dramatic difference requires a different result.

As I have already indicated, the majority, although it agrees that Congress intended by this Act to endorse the application of *Widmar* to high schools, does not compare this case to *Widmar*. Instead, the Court argues from two other propositions: first, that Congress intended to prohibit discrimination against religious groups; and, second, that the statute must not be construed in a fashion that would allow school boards to circumvent its reach by definitional fiat. I am in complete agreement with both of these principles. I do not, however, believe that either yields the conclusion which the majority adopts.

First, as the majority correctly observes, Congress intended the Act to prohibit schools from excluding—or believing that they were legally obliged to exclude—religious student groups solely because the groups were religious. Congress was clearly concerned with two lines of decisions in the Courts of Appeals: one line prohibiting schools that wished to admit student-initiated religious groups from doing so, and a second line allowing schools to exclude religious groups solely because of Establishment Clause concerns. These cases, however, involve only schools which either desire to recognize religious student groups, or **⊥279** schools which, like the University of Missouri at Kansas City, purport to exclude religious groups from a forum that is otherwise conceded to be open. It is obvious that Congress need go no further than our *Widmar* decision to redress this problem, and equally obvious that the majority's expansive reading of "noncurriculum related" is irrelevant to the Congressional objective of ending discrimination against religious student groups.

Second, the majority is surely correct that a "'limited open forum should be triggered by what a school does, not by what it says'" quoting 130 Cong. Rec. 19222 (1984) (statement of Sen. Leahy). If, however, it is the recognition of advocacy groups that signals the creation of such a forum, I see no danger that school administrators will be able to manipulate the Act to defeat Congressional intent. Indeed, it seems to me that it is the majority's own test that is suspect on this score. It would appear that the school could alter the "noncurriculum related" status of Subsurfers simply by, for example, including one day of scuba instruction in its swimming classes, or by requiring **⊥280** physical education teachers to urge student participation in the club, or even by soliciting regular comments from the club about how the school could better accommodate the club's interest within coursework. This may be what the school does rather than what it says, but the "doing" is mere bureaucratic procedure unrelated to the substance of the forum or the speech it encompasses.

Not only is the Court's preferred construction subject to manipulation, but it also is exceptionally difficult to apply even in the absence of deliberate evasion. For example, the Court believes that Westside's swim team is "directly related" to the curriculum, but the scuba diving club is not. The Court's analysis makes every high school football program a borderline case, for while many schools teach football in physical education classes, they usually teach touch football or flag football, and the varsity team usually plays tackle football. Tackle football involves more equipment and greater risk, and so arguably stands in the same relation to touch football as scuba diving does to swimming. Likewise, it would appear that high school administrators might reasonably have difficulty figuring out whether a cheerleading squad or pep club might trigger the Act's application. The answer, I suppose, might depend upon how strongly students were encouraged to support the football team. Obviously, every test will produce some hard cases, but the Court's test seems to produce nothing but hard cases.

⊥281 For all of these reasons, the argument for construing "noncurriculum related" by recourse to the facts of *Widmar*, and so by reference to the existence of advocacy groups, seems to me overwhelming. It provides a test that is both more simple and more easily administered than what the majority has crafted. Indeed, the only plausible answer to this construction of the statute is that it could easily be achieved without reference to the exotic concept of "noncurriculum related" organizations. This point was made at length on the Senate floor by Senator Gorton. Senator Hatfield answered that the term had been recommended to him by lawyers, apparently in an effort to capture the distinctions important to the judiciary's construction of the Free Speech Clause.

⊥282 Congress may sometimes, however, have a clear intent with respect to the whole of a statute even when it muddles the definition of a particular part, just as, in other cases, the intent behind a particular provision may be clear though the more comprehensive purpose of the statute is obscure. In this case, Congress' general intent is—as Senator Gorton certainly understood—a necessary guide to the Act's more particular terms. In answer to this strategy, the Court points out that references to *Widmar* must be considered in context. That is surely so. But when this is done it becomes immediately clear that those references are neither "few" nor "passing" nor even "general," they are instead the sheet anchors holding fast a debate that would otherwise be swept away in a gale of confused utterances.

⊥283 We might wish, along with Senator Gorton, that Congress had chosen a better term to effectuate its purposes. But our own efforts to articulate "public forum" analysis have not, in my opinion, been altogether satisfactory. Lawyers and legislators seeking to capture our distinctions in legislative terminology should be forgiven if they occasionally stumble. Certainly **⊥284** we should not hold Congress to a standard of precision we ourselves are sometimes unable to obtain. "Our duty is to ask what Congress intended, and not to assay whether Congress might have stated that intent more naturally, more artfully, or more pithily" *Sullivan* v. *Everhart* (Stevens, J., dissenting).

II

My construction of the Act makes it unnecessary to reach the Establishment Clause question that the plurality decides. It is nevertheless appropriate to point out that the question is much more difficult than the plurality assumes. **⊥285** The plurality focuses upon whether the Act might run afoul of the Establishment Clause because of the danger that some students will mistakenly believe that the student-initiated religious clubs are sponsored by the school. I believe that the **⊥286** plurality's construction of the statute obliges it to answer a further question: whether the Act violates the Establishment Clause by authorizing religious organizations to meet on high school grounds even when the high school's teachers and administrators deem it unwise to admit controversial or partisan organizations of any kind.

Under the plurality's interpretation of the Act, Congress has imposed a difficult choice on public high schools receiving federal financial assistance. If such a school continues to allow students to participate in such familiar and innocuous activities as a school chess or scuba diving club, it must also allow religious groups to make use of school facilities. In⊥**287**deed, it is hard to see how a cheerleading squad or a pep club, among the most common student groups in American high schools, could avoid being "noncurriculum related" under the majority's test. The Act, as construed by the majority, comes perilously close to an outright command to allow organized prayer, and perhaps the kind of religious ceremonies involved in *Widmar*, on school premises.

We have always treated with special sensitivity the Establishment Clause problems that result when religious observances are moved into the public schools. "The public school is at once the symbol of our democracy and the most pervasive means for promoting our common destiny. In no activity of the State is it more vital to keep out divisive forces than in its schools . . ." *Illinois ex rel. McCollum Board of Education, School Dist. No. 71*, (Frankfurter, J., concurring). As the plurality recognizes, student-initiated religious groups may exert a considerable degree of pressure even without official school sponsorship." The law of imitation operates, and nonconformity is not an outstanding characteristic of children." *Id.*, (Frankfurter, J., concurring). Testimony in this case indicated that one purpose of the proposed Bible Club was to convert students to Christianity. The influence that could result is the product not only of the Equal Access Act and student-initiated speech, but also of the compulsory attendance laws, which we have long recognized to be of special constitutional importance in this context. Moreover, the speech allowed is not simply the individual expression of personal conscience, as was the case in *Tinker* v. *Des Moines Independent Community School Dist.* or *West Virginia State Bd. of Ed.* v. *Barnette*, but is instead the collective statement of an organiza⊥**288**tion—a "student club," with powers and responsibilities defined by that status—that would not exist absent the state's intervention.

I tend to agree with the plurality that the Constitution does not forbid a local school district, or Congress, from bringing organized religion into the schools so long as all groups, religious or not, are welcomed equally if "they do not break either the laws or the furniture." That Congress has such authority, however, does not mean that the concerns underlying the Establishment Clause are irrelevant when, and if, that authority is exercised. Certainly we should not rush to embrace the conclusion that Congress swept aside these concerns by the hurried passage of clumsily drafted legislation.

⊥**289** There is an additional reason, also grounded in constitutional structure, why the Court's rendering of the Act is unsatisfying: so construed, the Act alters considerably the balance between state and federal authority over education, a balance long respected by both Congress and this Court. The traditional allocation of responsibility makes sense for pedagogical, political, and ethical reasons. We have, of course, sometimes found it necessary to limit local control over schools in order to protect the constitutional integrity of public education. "That [Boards of Education] are educating ⊥**290** the young for citizenship is reason for scrupulous protection of Constitutional freedoms of the individual, if we are not to strangle the free mind at its source and teach youth to discount important principles of our government as mere platitudes." *West Virginia Bd. of Educ.* v. *Barnette*. Congress may make similar judgments, and has sometimes done so, finding it necessary to regulate public education in order to achieve important national goals.

The Court's construction of this Act, however, leads to a sweeping intrusion by the federal government into the operation of our public schools, and does so despite the absence of any indication that Congress intended to divest local school districts of their power to shape the educational environment. If a high school administration continues to believe that it is sound policy to exclude controversial groups, such as political clubs, the Ku Klux Klan, and perhaps gay rights advocacy groups, from its facilities, it now must also close its doors to traditional extracurricular activities that are non-controversial but not directly related to any course being offered at the school. Congress made frequent reference to the primacy of local control in public education, and the legislative history of the Act is thus inconsistent with the Court's rigid definition of "noncurriculum related groups." In⊥**291**deed, the very fact that Congress omitted any definition in the statute itself is persuasive evidence of an intent to allow local officials broad discretion in deciding whether or not to create limited public forum. I see no reason—and no evidence of congressional intent—to constrain that discretion any more narrowly than our holding in *Widmar* requires.

III

Against all these arguments the Court interposes Noah Webster's famous dictionary. It is a massive tome but no match for the weight the Court would put upon it. The Court relies heavily on the dictionary's definition of "curriculum." That word, of course, is not the Act's; moreover, the word "noncurriculum" is not in the dictionary. Neither Webster nor Congress has authorized us to assume that "noncurriculum" is a precise antonym of the word "curriculum." "Nonplus," for example, does not mean "minus" and it would be incorrect to assume that a "nonentity" is not an "entity" at all. Purely as a matter of defining a newly-coined word, the term "noncurriculum" could fairly be construed to describe either the subjects that are "not a part of the current curriculum" or the subjects that "cannot properly be included in a public school curriculum." Either of those definitions is perfectly "sensible" because both describe subjects "that are not related to the body of courses offered by the school." When one considers the basic purpose of the Act, and its unquestioned linkage to our decision in *Widmar*, the latter definition surely is the more "sensible."

I respectfully dissent.

ROBERT E. LEE v. DANIEL WEISMAN

505 U.S. 577
ON WRIT OF CERTIORARI TO THE UNITED STATES COURT OF APPEALS FOR THE FIRST CIRCUIT
Argued November 6, 1991 — Decided June 24, 1992

⊥**580** *Justice KENNEDY* delivered the opinion of the Court.

School principals in the public school system of the city of Providence, Rhode Island, are permitted to invite members of the clergy to offer invocation and benediction prayers as part of the formal graduation ceremonies for middle schools and for high schools. The question before us is whether including clerical members who offer prayers as part of the official school graduation ceremony is consistent with the Religion Clauses of the First Amendment, provisions the Fourteenth Amendment makes applicable with full force to the States and their school districts.

⊥**581** I

A

Deborah Weisman graduated from Nathan Bishop Middle School, a public school in Providence, at a formal ceremony in June 1989. She was about 14 years old. For many years it has been the policy of the Providence School Committee and the Superintendent of Schools to permit principals to invite members of the clergy to give invocations and benedictions at middle school and high school graduations. Many, but not all, of the principals elected to include prayers as part of the graduation ceremonies. Acting for himself and his daughter, Deborah's father, Daniel Weisman, objected to any prayers at Deborah's middle school graduation, but to no avail. The school principal, petitioner Robert E. Lee, invited a rabbi to deliver prayers at the graduation exercises for Deborah's class. Rabbi Leslie Gutterman, of the Temple Beth El in Providence, accepted.

It has been the custom of Providence school officials to provide invited clergy with a pamphlet entitled "Guidelines for Civic Occasions," prepared by the National Conference of Christians and Jews. The Guidelines recommend that public prayers at nonsectarian civic ceremonies be composed with "inclusiveness and sensitivity," though they acknowledge that "[p]rayer of any kind may be inappropriate on some civic occasions." The principal gave Rabbi Gutterman the pamphlet before the graduation and advised him the invocation and benediction should be nonsectarian.

Rabbi Gutterman's prayers were as follows:

"INVOCATION.

"God of the Free, Hope of the Brave:

"For the legacy of America where diversity is celebrated and the rights of minorities are protected, we ⊥**582** thank You. May these young men and women grow up to enrich it.

"For the liberty of America, we thank You. May these new graduates grow up to guard it.

"For the political process of America in which all its citizens may participate, for its court system where all may seek justice we thank You. May those we honor this morning always turn to it in trust.

"For the destiny of America we thank You. May the graduates of Nathan Bishop Middle School so live that they might help to share it.

"May our aspirations for our country and for these young people, who are our hope for the future, be richly fulfilled. AMEN."

"BENEDICTION

"O God, we are grateful to You for having endowed us with the capacity for learning which we have celebrated on this joyous commencement.

"Happy families give thanks for seeing their children achieve an important milestone. Send Your blessings upon the teachers and administrators who helped prepare them.

"The graduates now need strength and guidance for the future, help them to understand that we are not complete with academic knowledge alone. We must each strive to fulfill what You require of us all: To do justly, to love mercy, to walk humbly.

"We give thanks to You, Lord, for keeping us alive, sustaining us and allowing us to reach this special, happy occasion. AMEN."

⊥**583** The record in this case is sparse in many respects, and we are unfamiliar with any fixed custom or practice at middle school graduations, referred to by the school district as "promotional exercises." We are not so constrained with reference to high schools, however. High school graduations are such an integral part of American cultural life that we can with confidence describe their customary features, confirmed by aspects of the record and by the parties' representations at oral argument. In the Providence school system, most high school graduation ceremonies are conducted away from the school, while most middle school ceremonies are held on school premises. Classical High School, which Deborah now attends, has conducted its graduation ceremonies on school premises. The parties stipulate that attendance at graduation ceremonies is voluntary. The graduating students enter as a group in a processional, subject to the direction of teachers and school officials, and sit together, apart from their families. We assume the clergy's participation in any high school graduation exercise would be about what it was at Deborah's middle school ceremony. There the students stood for the Pledge of Allegiance and remained standing during the Rabbi's prayers. Even on the assumption that there was a respectful moment of silence both before and after the prayers, the Rabbi's two presentations must not have extended much beyond a minute each, if that. We do not know whether he remained on stage during the whole ceremony, or whether the students received individual diplomas on stage, or if he helped to congratulate them.

The school board (and the United States, which supports it as *amicus curiae*) argued that these short prayers and others like them at graduation exercises are of profound meaning to many students and parents throughout this country who consider that due respect and acknowledgment for divine guidance and for the deepest spiritual aspirations of ⊥**584** our people ought to be expressed at an event as important in life as a graduation. We assume this to be so in addressing the difficult case now before us, for the significance of the prayers lies also at the heart of Daniel and Deborah Weisman's case.

B

Deborah's graduation was held on the premises of Nathan Bishop Middle School on June 29, 1989. Four days before the ceremony, Daniel Weisman, in his individual capacity as a Providence taxpayer and as next friend of Deborah, sought a temporary restraining order in the United States District Court for the District of Rhode Island to prohibit school officials from including an invocation or benediction in the graduation ceremony. The court denied the motion for lack of adequate time to consider it. Deborah and her family attended the graduation, where the prayers were recited. In July 1989, Daniel Weisman filed an amended complaint seeking a permanent injunction barring petitioners, various officials of the Providence public schools, from inviting the clergy to deliver invocations and benedictions at future graduations. We find it unnecessary to address Daniel Weisman's taxpayer standing, for a live and justiciable controversy is before us. Deborah Weisman is enrolled as a student at Classical High School in Providence and from the record it appears likely, if not certain, that an invocation and benediction will be conducted at her high school graduation.

The case was submitted on stipulated facts. The District Court held that petitioners' practice of including invocations and benedictions in public school graduations violated the Establishment Clause of the First Amendment, and it enjoined petitioners from continuing the practice. The court applied the three-part Establishment Clause test set forth in *Lemon* v. *Kurtzman*. Under that test as described in our past cases, to satisfy the Establishment Clause a governmen⊥**585**tal practice must (1) reflect a clearly secular purpose; (2) have a primary effect that neither advances nor inhibits religion; and (3) avoid excessive government entanglement with religion. The District Court held that petitioners' actions violated the second part of the test, and so did not address either the first or the third. The court decided, based on its reading of our precedents, that the effects test of *Lemon* is violated whenever government action "creates an identification of the state with a religion, or with religion in general," or when "the effect of the governmental action is to endorse one religion over another, or to endorse religion in general." The court determined that the practice of including invocations and benedictions, even so-called nonsectarian ones, in public school graduations creates an identification of governmental power with religious practice, endorses religion, and violates the Establishment Clause. In so holding the court expressed the determination not to follow *Stein* v. *Plainwell Community Schools*, in which the Court of Appeals for the Sixth Circuit, relying on our decision in *Marsh* v. *Chambers*, held that benedictions and invocations at public school graduations are not always unconstitutional. In *Marsh* we upheld the constitutionality of the Nebraska State Legislature's practice of opening each of its sessions with a prayer offered by a chaplain paid out of public funds. The District Court in this case disagreed with the Sixth Circuit's reasoning because it believed that *Marsh* was a narrow decision, "limited to the unique situation of legislative prayer," and did not have any relevance to school prayer cases.

On appeal, the United States Court of Appeals for the First Circuit affirmed. The majority opinion by Judge Torruella adopted the opinion of the District Court. Judge Bownes joined the majority, but wrote a separate concurring opinion in which he decided that the ⊥**586** practices challenged here violated all three parts of the *Lemon* test. Judge Bownes went on to agree with the District Court that *Marsh* had no application to school prayer cases and that the *Stein* decision was flawed. He concluded by suggesting that under Establishment Clause rules no prayer, even one excluding any mention of the Deity, could be offered at a public school graduation ceremony. Judge Campbell dissented, on the basis of *Marsh* and *Stein*. He reasoned that if the prayers delivered were nonsectarian, and if school officials ensured that persons representing a variety of beliefs and ethical systems were invited to present invocations and benedictions, there was no violation of the Establishment Clause. We granted certiorari and now affirm.

II

These dominant facts mark and control the confines of our decision: State officials direct the performance of a formal religious exercise at promotional and graduation ceremonies for secondary schools. Even for those students who object to the religious exercise, their attendance and participation in the state-sponsored religious activity are in a fair and real sense obligatory, though the school district does not require attendance as a condition for receipt of the diploma.

This case does not require us to revisit the difficult questions dividing us in recent cases, questions of the definition and full scope of the principles governing the extent of permitted accommodation by the State for the religious beliefs and practices of many of its citizens. See *Allegheny County* v. *Greater Pittsburgh ACLU; Wallace* v. *Jaffree; Lynch* v. *Donnelly*. For without reference to those principles in other contexts, the controlling precedents as they relate to prayer and religious exercise in primary and secondary public schools compel the holding here that the policy of the city of Providence is an ⊥**587** unconstitutional one. We can decide the case without reconsidering the general constitutional framework by which public schools' efforts to accommodate religion are measured. Thus we do not accept the invitation of petitioners and *amicus* the United States to reconsider our decision in *Lemon* v. *Kurtzman*. The government involvement with religious activity in this case is pervasive, to the point of creating a state-sponsored and state-directed religious exercise in a public school. Conducting this formal religious observance conflicts with settled rules pertaining to prayer exercises for students, and that suffices to determine the question before us.

The principle that government may accommodate the free exercise of religion does not supersede the fundamental limitations imposed by the Establishment Clause. It is beyond dispute that, at a minimum, the Constitution guarantees that government may not coerce anyone to support or participate in religion or its exercise, or otherwise act in a way which "establishes a [state] religion or religious faith, or tends to do so." *Lynch*. The State's involvement in the school prayers challenged today violates these central principles.

That involvement is as troubling as it is undenied. A school official, the principal, decided that an invocation and a benediction should be given; this is a choice attributable to the State, and from a constitutional perspective it is as if a state statute decreed that the prayers must occur. The principal chose the religious participant, here a rabbi, and that choice is also attributable to the State. The reason for the choice of a rabbi is not disclosed by the record, but the potential for divisiveness over the choice of a particular member of the clergy to conduct the ceremony is apparent.

Divisiveness, of course, can attend any state decision respecting religions, and neither its existence nor its potential ⊥**588** necessarily invalidates the State's attempt to accommodate religion in all cases. The potential for divisiveness is of particular relevance here though, because it centers around an overt religious exercise in a secondary school environment where, as we discuss below, subtle coercive pressures exist and where the student had no real alternative which would have allowed her to avoid the fact or appearance of participation.

The State's role did not end with the decision to include a prayer and with the choice of clergyman. Principal Lee provided Rabbi Gutterman with a copy of the "Guidelines for Civic Occasions," and advised him that his prayers should be nonsectarian. Through these means the principal directed and controlled the content of the prayer. Even if the only sanction for ignoring the instructions were that the rabbi would not be invited back, we think no religious representative who valued his or her continued reputation and effectiveness in the community would incur the State's displeasure in this regard. It is a cornerstone principle of our Establishment Clause jurisprudence that "it is no part of the business of government to compose official prayers for any group of the American people to recite as a part of a religious program carried on by government," *Engel* v. *Vitale*, and that is what the school officials attempted to do.

Petitioners argue, and we find nothing in the case to refute it, that the directions for the content of the prayers were a good-faith attempt by the school to ensure that the sectarianism which is so often the flashpoint for religious animosity be removed from the graduation ceremony. The concern is understandable, as a prayer which uses ideas or images identified with a particular religion may foster a different sort of sectarian rivalry than an invocation or benediction in terms more neutral. The school's explanation, however, does not resolve the dilemma caused by its participation. The question is not the good faith of the school in attempting to make ⊥**589** the prayer acceptable to most persons, but the legitimacy of its undertaking that enterprise at all when the object is to produce a prayer to be used in a formal religious exercise which students, for all practical purposes, are obligated to attend.

We are asked to recognize the existence of a practice of nonsectarian prayer, prayer within the embrace of what is known as the Judeo-Christian tradition, prayer which is more acceptable than one which, for example, makes explicit references to the God of Israel, or to Jesus Christ, or to a patron saint. There may be some support, as an empirical observation, for the statement of the Court of Appeals for the Sixth Circuit, picked up by Judge Campbell's dissent in the Court of Appeals in this case, that there has emerged in this country a civic religion, one which is tolerated when sectarian exercises are not. If common ground can be defined which permits once conflicting faiths to express the shared conviction that there is an ethic and a morality which transcend human invention, the sense of community and purpose sought by all decent societies might be advanced. But though the First Amendment does not allow the government to stifle prayers which aspire to these ends, neither does it permit the government to undertake that task for itself.

The First Amendment's Religion Clauses mean that religious beliefs and religious expression are too precious to be either proscribed or prescribed by the State. The design of the Constitution is that preservation and transmission of religious beliefs and worship is a responsibility and a choice committed to the private sphere, which itself is promised freedom to pursue that mission. It must not be forgotten then, that while concern must be given to define the protection granted to an objector or a dissenting nonbeliever, these same Clauses exist to protect religion from government in⊥**590**terference. James Madison, the principal author of the Bill of Rights, did not rest his opposition to a religious establishment on the sole ground of its effect on the minority. A principal ground for his view was: "[E]xperience witnesseth that ecclesiastical establishments, instead of maintaining the purity and efficacy of Religion, have had a contrary operation." Memorial and Remonstrance Against Religious Assessments (1785).

These concerns have particular application in the case of school officials, whose effort to monitor prayer will be perceived by the students as inducing a participation they might otherwise reject. Though the efforts of the school officials in this case to find common ground appear to have been a good-faith attempt to recognize the common aspects of religion and not the divisive ones, our precedents do not permit school officials to assist in composing prayers as an incident to a formal exercise for their students. *Engel* v. *Vitale*. And these same precedents caution us to measure the idea of a civic religion against the central meaning of the Religion Clauses of the First Amendment, which is that all creeds must be tolerated and none favored. The suggestion that government may establish an official or civic religion as a means of avoiding the establishment of a religion with more specific creeds strikes us as a contradiction that cannot be accepted.

The degree of school involvement here made it clear that the graduation prayers bore the imprint of the State and thus put school-age children who objected in an untenable position. We turn our attention now to consider the position of the students, both those who desired the prayer and she who did not.

To endure the speech of false ideas or offensive content and then to counter it is part of learning how to live in a pluralistic society, a society which insists upon open discourse towards the end of a tolerant citizenry. And toler⊥**591**ance presupposes some mutuality of obligation. It is argued that our constitutional vision of a free society requires confidence in our own ability to accept or reject ideas of which we do not approve, and that prayer at a high school graduation does nothing more than offer a choice. By the time they are seniors, high school students no doubt have been required to attend classes and assemblies and to complete assignments exposing them to ideas they find distasteful or immoral or absurd or all of these. Against this background, students may consider it an odd measure of justice to be subjected during the course of their educations to ideas deemed offensive and irreligious, but to be denied a brief, formal prayer ceremony that the school offers in return. This argument cannot prevail, however. It overlooks a fundamental dynamic of the Constitution.

The First Amendment protects speech and religion by quite different mechanisms. Speech is protected by insuring its full expression even when the government participates, for the very object of some of our most important speech is to persuade the government to adopt an idea as its own. *Meese* v. *Keene;* see also *Keller* v. *State Bar of California; Abood* v. *Detroit Board of Education*. The method for protecting freedom of worship and freedom of conscience in religious matters is quite the reverse. In religious debate or expression the government is not a prime participant, for the Framers deemed religious establishment antithetical to the freedom of all. The Free Exercise Clause embraces a freedom of conscience and worship that has close parallels in the speech provisions of the First Amendment, but the Establishment Clause is a specific prohibition on forms of state intervention in religious affairs with no precise counterpart in the speech provisions. *Buckley* v. *Valeo*. The explanation lies in the lesson of history that was and is the inspiration for the Establishment Clause, the lesson that in ⊥**592** the hands of government what might begin as a tolerant expression of religious views may end in a policy to indoctrinate and coerce. A state-created orthodoxy puts at grave risk that freedom of belief and conscience which are the sole assurance that religious faith is real, not imposed.

The lessons of the First Amendment are as urgent in the modern world as in the 18th Century when it was written. One timeless lesson is that if citizens are subjected to state-sponsored religious exercises, the State disavows its own duty to guard and respect that sphere of inviolable conscience and belief which is the mark of a free people. To compromise that principle today would be to deny our own tradition and forfeit our standing to urge others to secure the protections of that tradition for themselves.

As we have observed before, there are heightened concerns with protecting freedom of conscience from subtle coercive pressure in the elementary and secondary public schools. Our decisions in *Engel* v. *Vitale* and *Abington School District* recognize, among other things, that prayer exercises in public schools carry a particular risk of indirect coercion. The concern may not be limited to the context of schools, but it is most pronounced there. What to most believers may seem nothing more than a reasonable request that the nonbeliever respect their religious practices, in a school context may appear to the non-believer or dissenter to be an attempt to employ the machinery of the State to enforce a religious orthodoxy.

⊥**593** We need not look beyond the circumstances of this case to see the phenomenon at work. The undeniable fact is that the school district's supervision and control of a high school graduation ceremony places public pressure, as well as peer pressure, on attending students to stand as a group or, at least, maintain respectful silence during the Invocation and Benediction. This pressure, though subtle and indirect, can be as real as any overt compulsion. Of course, in our culture standing or remaining silent can signify adherence to a view or simple respect for the views of others. And no doubt some persons who have no desire to join a prayer have little objection to standing as a sign of respect for those who do. But for the dissenter of high school age, who has a reasonable perception that she is being forced by the State to pray in a manner her conscience will not allow, the injury is no less real. There can be no doubt that for many, if not most, of the students at the graduation, the act of standing or remaining silent was an expression of participation in the Rabbi's prayer. That was the very point of the religious exercise. It is of little comfort to a dissenter, then, to be told that for her the act of standing or remaining in silence signifies mere respect, rather than participation. What matters is that, given our social conventions, a reasonable dissenter in this milieu could believe that the group exercise signified her own participation or approval of it.

Finding no violation under these circumstances would place objectors in the dilemma of participating, with all that implies, or protesting. We do not address whether that choice is acceptable if the affected citizens are mature adults, but we think the State may not, consistent with the Establishment Clause, place primary and secondary school children in this position. Research in psychology supports the common assumption that adolescents are often susceptible to pressure from their peers towards conformity, and that the influence is strongest in matters of social convention. Brittain, Adolescent Choices and Parent-Peer Cross-Pressures, **⊥594** 28 Am. Sociological Rev. 385 (June 1963); Clasen & Brown, The Multidimensionality of Peer Pressure in Adolescence, 14 J. of Youth and Adolescence 451 (Dec. 1985); Brown, Clasen, & Eicher, Perceptions of Peer Pressure, Peer Conformity Dispositions, and Self-Reported Behavior Among Adolescents, 22 Developmental Psychology 521 (July 1986). To recognize that the choice imposed by the State constitutes an unacceptable constraint only acknowledges that the government may no more use social pressure to enforce orthodoxy than it may use more direct means.

The injury caused by the government's action, and the reason why Daniel and Deborah Weisman object to it, is that the State, in a school setting, in effect required participation in a religious exercise. It is, we concede, a brief exercise during which the individual can concentrate on joining its message, meditate on her own religion, or let her mind wander. But the embarrassment and the intrusion of the religious exercise cannot be refuted by arguing that these prayers, and similar ones to be said in the future, are of a *de minimis* character. To do so would be an affront to the Rabbi who offered them and to all those for whom the prayers were an essential and profound recognition of divine authority. And for the same reason, we think that the intrusion is greater than the two minutes or so of time consumed for prayers like these. Assuming, as we must, that the prayers were offensive to the student and the parent who now object, the intrusion was both real and, in the context of a secondary school, a violation of the objectors' rights. That the intrusion was in the course of promulgating religion that sought to be civic or nonsectarian rather than pertaining to one sect does not lessen the offense or isolation to the objectors. At best it narrows their number, at worst increases their sense of isolation and affront.

There was a stipulation in the District Court that attendance at graduation and promotional ceremonies is voluntary. Petitioners and **⊥595** the United States, as *amicus*, made this a center point of the case, arguing that the option of not attending the graduation excuses any inducement or coercion in the ceremony itself. The argument lacks all persuasion. Law reaches past formalism. And to say a teenage student has a real choice not to attend her high school graduation is formalistic in the extreme. True, Deborah could elect not to attend commencement without renouncing her diploma; but we shall not allow the case to turn on this point. Everyone knows that in our society and in our culture high school graduation is one of life's most significant occasions. A school rule which excuses attendance is beside the point. Attendance may not be required by official decree, yet it is apparent that a student is not free to absent herself from the graduation exercise in any real sense of the term "voluntary," for absence would require forfeiture of those intangible benefits which have motivated the student through youth and all her high school years. Graduation is a time for family and those closest to the student to celebrate success and express mutual wishes of gratitude and respect, all to the end of impressing upon the young person the role that it is his or her right and duty to assume in the community and all of its diverse parts.

The importance of the event is the point the school district and the United States rely upon to argue that a formal prayer ought to be permitted, but it becomes one of the principal reasons why their argument must fail. Their contention, one of considerable force were it not for the constitutional constraints applied to state action, is that the prayers are an essential part of these ceremonies because for many persons an occasion of this significance lacks meaning if there is no recognition, however brief, that human achievements cannot be understood apart from their spiritual essence. We think the Government's position that this interest suffices to force students to choose between compliance or forfeiture demonstrates fundamental inconsistency in its argumentation. It fails to acknowledge that what for many of **⊥596** Deborah's classmates and their parents was a spiritual imperative was for Daniel and Deborah Weisman religious conformance compelled by the State. While in some societies the wishes of the majority might prevail, the Establishment Clause of the First Amendment is addressed to this contingency and rejects the balance urged upon us. The Constitution forbids the State to exact religious conformity from a student as the price of attending her own high school graduation. This is the calculus the Constitution commands.

The Government's argument gives insufficient recognition to the real conflict of conscience faced by the young student. The essence of the Government's position is that with regard to a civic, social occasion of this importance it is the objector, not the majority, who must take unilateral and private action to avoid compromising religious scruples, here by electing to miss the graduation exercise. This turns conventional First Amendment analysis on its head. It is a tenet of the First Amendment that the State cannot require one of its citizens to forfeit his or her rights and benefits as the price of resisting conformance to state-sponsored religious practice. To say that a student must remain apart from the ceremony at the opening invocation and closing benediction is to risk compelling conformity in an environment analogous to the classroom setting, where we have said the risk of compulsion is especially high. Just as in *Engel* v. *Vitale*, and *Abington School District* v. *Schempp*, we found that provisions within the challenged legislation permitting a student to be voluntarily excused from attendance or participation in the daily prayers did not shield those practices from invalidation, the fact that attendance at the graduation ceremonies is voluntary in a legal sense does not save the religious exercise.

Inherent differences between the public school system and a session of a State Legislature distinguish this case from *Marsh* v. *Chambers*. The considera⊥**597**tions we have raised in objection to the invocation and benediction are in many respects similar to the arguments we considered in *Marsh*. But there are also obvious differences. The atmosphere at the opening of a session of a state legislature where adults are free to enter and leave with little comment and for any number of reasons cannot compare with the constraining potential of the one school event most important for the student to attend. The influence and force of a formal exercise in a school graduation are far greater than the prayer exercise we condoned in *Marsh*. The *Marsh* majority in fact gave specific recognition to this distinction and placed particular reliance on it in upholding the prayers at issue there. Today's case is different. At a high school graduation, teachers and principals must and do retain a high degree of control over the precise contents of the program, the speeches, the timing, the movements, the dress, and the decorum of the students. In this atmosphere the state-imposed character of an invocation and benediction by clergy selected by the school combine to make the prayer a state-sanctioned religious exercise in which the student was left with no alternative but to submit. This is different from *Marsh* and suffices to make the religious exercise a First Amendment violation. Our Establishment Clause jurisprudence remains a delicate and fact-sensitive one, and we cannot accept the parallel relied upon by petitioners and the United States between the facts of *Marsh* and the case now before us. Our decisions in *Engel* v. *Vitale* and *Abington School District* v. *Schempp* require us to distinguish the public school context.

We do not hold that every state action implicating religion is invalid if one or a few citizens find it offensive. People may take offense at all manner of religious as well as nonreligious messages, but offense alone does not in every case show a violation. We know too that sometimes to endure ⊥**598** social isolation or even anger may be the price of conscience or nonconformity. But, by any reading of our cases, the conformity required of the student in this case was too high an exaction to withstand the test of the Establishment Clause. The prayer exercises in this case are especially improper because the State has in every practical sense compelled attendance and participation in an explicit religious exercise at an event of singular importance to every student, one the objecting student had no real alternative to avoid.

Our jurisprudence in this area is of necessity one of line-drawing, of determining at what point a dissenter's rights of religious freedom are infringed by the State.

"The First Amendment does not prohibit practices which by any realistic measure create none of the dangers which it is designed to prevent and which do not so directly or substantially involve the state in religious exercises or in the favoring of religion as to have meaningful and practical impact. It is of course true that great consequences can grow from small beginnings, but the measure of constitutional adjudication is the ability and willingness to distinguish between real threat and mere shadow." *Abington School District* v. *Schempp*.

Our society would be less than true to its heritage if it lacked abiding concern for the values of its young people, and we acknowledge the profound belief of adherents to many faiths that there must be a place in the student's life for precepts of a morality higher even than the law we today enforce. We express no hostility to those aspirations, nor would our oath permit us to do so. A relentless and all-pervasive attempt to exclude religion from every aspect of public life could itself become inconsistent with the Constitution. We recognize that, at graduation time and throughout the course of the educational process, there will ⊥**599** be instances when religious values, religious practices, and religious persons will have some interaction with the public schools and their students. But these matters, often questions of accommodation of religion, are not before us. The sole question presented is whether a religious exercise may be conducted at a graduation ceremony in circumstances where, as we have found, young graduates who object are induced to conform. No holding by this Court suggests that a school can persuade or compel a student to participate in a religious exercise. That is being done here, and it is forbidden by the Establishment Clause of the First Amendment.

For the reasons we have stated, the judgment of the Court of Appeals is

Affirmed.

Justice BLACKMUN, with whom *Justice* STEVENS and *Justice* O'CONNOR join, concurring.

Nearly half a century of review and refinement of Establishment Clause jurisprudence has distilled one clear understanding: Government may neither promote nor affiliate itself with any religious doctrine or organization, nor may it obtrude itself in the internal affairs of any religious institution. The application of these principles to the present case mandates the decision reached today by the Court.

I

This Court first reviewed a challenge to state law under the Establishment Clause in *Everson* v. *Board of Education*. Relying on the history of the ⊥**600** Clause, and the Court's prior analysis, *Justice BLACK* outlined the considerations that have become the touchstone of Establishment Clause jurisprudence: Neither a State nor the Federal Government can pass laws which aid one religion, aid all religions, or prefer one religion over another. Neither a State nor the Federal Government, openly or secretly, can participate in the affairs of any religious organization and vice versa. "In the words of Jefferson, the clause ⊥**601** against establishment of religion by law was intended to erect 'a wall of separation between church and State.'" *Everson*. The dissenters agreed: "The Amendment's purpose . . . was to create a complete and permanent separation of the spheres of religious activity and civil authority by comprehensively forbidding every form of public aid or support for religion." (Rutledge, J., dissenting, joined by Frankfurter, Jackson, and Burton, JJ.).

In *Engel* v. *Vitale*, the Court considered for the first time the constitutionality of prayer in a public school. Students said aloud a short prayer selected by the State Board of Regents: "Almighty God, we acknowledge our dependence upon Thee, and we beg Thy blessings upon us, our parents, our teachers and our Country." *Justice BLACK*, writing for the Court, again made clear that the First Amendment forbids the use of the power or prestige of the government to control, support, or influence the religious beliefs and practices of the American people. Although the prayer was "denominationally neutral" and "its observance on the part of the students [was] voluntary," the Court found that it violated this essential precept of the Establishment Clause.

A year later, the Court again invalidated government-sponsored prayer in public schools in *Abington School District* v. *Schempp*. In *Schempp*, the school day for Baltimore, Maryland, and Abington Township, Pennsylvania, students began with a reading from the Bible, or a recitation of the Lord's Prayer, or both. After a thorough review of the Court's prior Establishment Clause cases, the Court concluded:

⊥**602** "[T]he Establishment Clause has been directly considered by this Court eight times in the past score of years and, with only one Justice dissenting on the point, it has consistently held that the clause withdrew all legislative power respecting religious belief or the expression thereof. The test may be stated as follows: what are the purpose and the primary effect of the enactment? If either is the advancement or inhibition of religion, then the enactment exceeds the scope of legislative power as circumscribed by the Constitution." Because the schools' opening exercises were government-sponsored religious ceremonies, the Court found that the primary effect was the advancement of religion and held, therefore, that the activity violated the Establishment Clause."

Five years later, the next time the Court considered whether religious activity in public schools violated the Establishment Clause, it reiterated the principle that government "may not aid, foster, or promote one religion or religious theory against another or even against the militant opposite." *Epperson* v. *Arkansas*. "'If [the purpose or primary effect] is the advancement or inhibition of religion then the enactment exceeds the scope of legislative power as circumscribed by the Constitution.'" *Id*. Finding that the Arkansas law aided religion by preventing the teaching of evolution, the Court invalidated it.

In 1971, *Chief Justice BURGER* reviewed the Court's past decisions and found: "Three . . . tests may be gleaned from our cases." *Lemon* v. *Kurtzman*. In order for a statute to survive an Establishment Clause challenge, "[f]irst, the statute must have a secular legislative purpose; second, its principal or primary effect must be one that neither advances nor inhibits religion; finally the statute must not foster an excessive government entanglement with ⊥**603** religion." *Id*. After *Lemon*, the Court continued to rely on these basic principles in resolving Establishment Clause disputes.

Application of these principles to the facts of this case is straightforward. There can be "no doubt" that the "invocation of God's blessings" delivered at Nathan Bishop Middle School "is a religious activity." *Engel*. In the words of *Engel*, the Rabbi's prayer "is a solemn avowal of divine faith and supplication for the blessings of the Almighty. The nature of such a prayer has always been religious." The question then is whether the government has "plac[ed] its official stamp of approval" on the prayer. As the Court ably demonstrates, when the government "compose[s] official prayers," selects the member of the clergy to deliver the prayer, has the prayer delivered at a public school event that is planned, supervised and given by school officials, and pres⊥**604**sures students to attend and participate in the prayer, there can be no doubt that the government is advancing and promoting religion.* As our prior decisions teach us, it is this that the Constitution prohibits.

II

I join the Court's opinion today because I find nothing in it inconsistent with the essential precepts of the Establishment Clause developed in our precedents. The

*In this case, the religious message it promotes is specifically Judeo-Christian. The phrase in the benediction: "We must each strive to fulfill what you require of us all, to do justly, to love mercy, to walk humbly" obviously was taken from the Book of the Prophet Micah, ch. 6, v. 8.

Court holds that the graduation prayer is unconstitutional because the State "in effect required participation in a religious exercise." Although our precedents make clear that proof of government coercion is not necessary to prove an Establishment Clause violation, it is sufficient. Government pressure to participate in a religious activity is an obvious indication that the government is endorsing or promoting religion.

But it is not enough that the government restrain from compelling religious practices: it must not engage in them either. The Court repeatedly has recognized that a violation of the Establishment Clause is not predicated on coercion. See, *e.g.*, *Wallace* v. *Jaffree* (O'Connor, J., concurring in judgment) ("The decisions [in *Engel* and *Schempp*] acknowledged the coercion implicit under the statutory schemes, but they expressly turned only on the fact that the government was sponsoring a manifestly religious exercise" (citation omitted)); *Comm. for Public Ed.* v. *Nyquist* ("[P]roof of coercion . . . [is] not a necessary element of any claim under the Establishment Clause"). The Establishment Clause proscribes public schools from "conveying or attempting to con⊥**605**vey a message that religion or a particular religious belief is *favored* or *preferred*," *County of Allegheny* v. *ACLU* (internal quotations omitted) (emphasis in original), even if the schools do not actually "impos[e] pressure upon a student to participate in a religious activity." *Westside Community Bd. of Ed.* v. *Mergens* (Kennedy, J., concurring).

The scope of the Establishment Clause's prohibitions developed in our case law derives from the Clause's purposes. The First Amendment encompasses two distinct guarantees—the government shall make no law respecting an establishment of religion or prohibiting the free exercise thereof—both with the common purpose of securing religious liberty. Through vigorous enforcement of both clauses, we "promote and assure the fullest possible scope of religious liberty and tolerance for all and . . . nurture the conditions which secure the best hope of attainment of that end." *Schempp* (Goldberg, J., concurring).

There is no doubt that attempts to aid religion through government coercion jeopardize freedom of conscience. Even subtle pressure diminishes the right of each individual to choose voluntarily what to believe. Representative Carroll explained during congressional debate over the Estab⊥**606**lishment Clause: "[T]he rights of conscience are, in their nature, of peculiar delicacy, and will little bear the gentlest touch of governmental hand." I Annals of Cong. 757 (August 15, 1789).

Our decisions have gone beyond prohibiting coercion, however, because the Court has recognized that "the fullest possible scope of religious liberty," *Schempp* (Goldberg, J., concurring), entails more than freedom from coercion. The Establishment Clause protects religious liberty on a grand scale; it is a social compact that guarantees for generations a democracy and a strong religious community—both essential to safeguarding religious liberty. "Our fathers seem to have been perfectly sincere in their belief that the members of the Church would be more patriotic, and the citizens of the State more religious, by keeping their respective functions entirely separate." Religious Liberty, in Essays and Speeches of Jeremiah S. Black 53 (C. Black ed. 1885) (Chief Justice of the Commonwealth of Pennsylvania).

The mixing of government and religion can be a threat to free government, even if no one is forced to participate. When the government puts its imprimatur on a particular religion, it conveys a message of exclusion to all those who do not adhere to the favored beliefs. A government cannot ⊥**607** be premised on the belief that all persons are created equal when it asserts that God prefers some. Only "[a]nguish, hardship and bitter strife" result "when zealous religious groups struggl[e] with one another to obtain the Government's stamp of approval." *Engel*. Such a struggle can "strain a political system to the breaking point." *Walz* v. *Tax Commission* (opinion of Harlan, J.).

When the government arrogates to itself a role in religious affairs, it abandons its obligation as guarantor of democracy. Democracy requires the nourishment of dialogue and dissent, while religious faith puts its trust in an ultimate divine authority above all human deliberation. When the government appropriates religious truth, it "transforms rational debate into theological decree." Nuechterlein, Note, The Free Exercise Boundaries of Permissible Accommodation Under the Establishment Clause, 99 Yale L.J. 1127, 1131 (1990). Those who disagree no longer are questioning the policy judgment of the elected but the rules of a higher authority who is beyond reproach.

⊥**608** Madison warned that government officials who would use religious authority to pursue secular ends "exceed the commission from which they derive their authority and are Tyrants. The People who submit to it are governed by laws made neither by themselves, nor by an authority derived from them, and are slaves." Memorial and Remonstrance against Religious Assessments (1785). Democratic government will not last long when proclamation replaces persuasion as the medium of political exchange.

Likewise, we have recognized that "[r]eligion flourishes in greater purity, without than with the aid of Gov[ernment]." *Id.* To "make room for as wide a variety of beliefs and creeds as the spiritual needs of man deem necessary," *Zorach* v. *Clauson*, the government must not align itself with any one of them. When the government favors a particular religion or sect, the disadvantage to all others is obvious, but even the favored religion may fear being "taint[ed] . . . with a corrosive secularism." *Grand Rapids School Dist.* v. *Ball*. The favored religion may be compromised as political figures reshape the religion's beliefs for their own purposes; it may be reformed as government largesse brings government regulation. Keeping religion in the hands of private groups minimizes state intrusion on religious choice and best enables each religion to "flourish according to the ⊥**609** zeal of its adherents and the appeal of its dogma." *Zorach*.

It is these understandings and fears that underlie our Establishment Clause jurisprudence. We have believed that religious freedom cannot exist in the absence of a free democratic government, and that such a government cannot endure when there is fusion between religion and the political regime. We have believed that religious freedom cannot thrive in the absence of a vibrant religious community and that such a community cannot prosper when it is bound to the secular. And we have believed that these were the animating principles behind the adoption of the Establishment Clause. To that end, our cases have prohibited government endorsement of religion, its sponsorship, and active involvement in religion, whether or not citizens were coerced to conform.

I remain convinced that our jurisprudence is not misguided, and that it requires the decision reached by the Court today. Accordingly, I join the Court in affirming the judgment of the Court of Appeals.

Justice SOUTER, with whom *Justice* STEVENS and *Justice* O'CONNOR join, concurring.

I join the whole of the Court's opinion, and fully agree that prayers at public school graduation ceremonies indirectly coerce religious observance. I write separately nonetheless on two issues of Establishment Clause analysis that underlie my independent resolution of this case: whether the Clause applies to governmental practices that do not favor one religion or denomination over others, and whether state coercion of religious conformity, over and above state endorsement of religious exercise or belief, is a necessary element of an Establishment Clause violation.

I

Forty-five years ago, this Court announced a basic principle of constitutional law from which it has not strayed: the ⊥**610** Establishment Clause forbids not only state practices that "aid one religion . . . or prefer one religion over another," but also those that "aid all religions." *Everson* v. *Board of Education of Ewing*. Today we reaffirm that principle, holding that the Establishment Clause forbids state-sponsored prayers in public school settings no matter how nondenominational the prayers may be. In barring the State from sponsoring generically Theistic prayers where it could not sponsor sectarian ones, we hold true to a line of precedent from which there is no adequate historical case to depart.

A

Since *Everson*, we have consistently held the Clause applicable no less to governmental acts favoring religion generally than to acts favoring one religion over others. Thus, in *Engel* v. *Vitale*, we held that the public schools may not subject their students to readings of any prayer, however "denominationally neutral." More recently, in *Wallace* v. *Jaffree*, we held that an Alabama moment-of-silence statute passed for the sole purpose of "returning voluntary prayer to public schools," violated the Establishment Clause even though it did not encourage students to pray to any particular deity. We said that "when the underlying principle has been examined in the crucible of litigation, the Court has unambiguously concluded that the individual freedom of conscience protected by the First Amendment embraces the right to select any religious faith or none at all." This conclusion, we held,

"derives support not only from the interest in respecting the individual's freedom of conscience, but also from the conviction that religious beliefs worthy of respect are the product of free and voluntary choice by the faithful, ⊥**611** and from recognition of the fact that the political interest in forestalling intolerance extends beyond intolerance among Christian sects—or even intolerance among 'religions'—to encompass intolerance of the disbeliever and the uncertain."

Likewise, in *Texas Monthly, Inc.* v. *Bullock*, we struck down a state tax exemption benefiting only religious periodicals; even though the statute in question worked no discrimination among sects, a majority of the Court found that its preference for religious publications over all other kinds "effectively endorses religious belief." See *id.* (Blackmun, J., concurring in judgment) ("A statutory preference for the dissemination of religious ideas offends our most basic understanding of what the Establishment Clause is all about and hence is constitutionally intolerable"). And in *Torcaso* v. *Watkins*, we struck down a provision of the Maryland Constitution requiring public officials to declare a "'belief in the existence of God,'" reasoning that, under the Religion Clauses of the First Amendment, "neither a State nor the Federal Government . . . can constitutionally pass laws or impose requirements which aid all religions as against non-believers. . . ." See also *Epperson* v. *Arkansas* ("The First Amendment mandates governmental neutrality between religion and religion, and between religion and nonreligion"); *School Dist. of Abington* v. *Schempp* ("this Court has rejected unequivocally the contention that the Establishment Clause forbids only governmental preference of one religion over another"); *id.* (Stewart, J., dissenting) (the Clause applies "to each of us, be he Jew or Agnostic, Christian or Atheist, Buddhist or Freethinker").

Such is the settled law. Here, as elsewhere, we should stick to it absent some compelling reason to discard it.

⊥**612** B

Some have challenged this precedent by reading the Establishment Clause to permit "nonpreferential" state promotion of religion. The challengers argue that, as originally understood by the Framers, "[t]he Establishment Clause did not require government neutrality between religion and irreligion nor did it prohibit the Federal Government from providing nondiscriminatory aid to religion." *Wallace* (Rehnquist, J., dissenting); see also R. Cord, Separation of Church and State: Historical Fact and Current Fiction (1988). While a case has been made for this position, it is not so convincing as to warrant reconsideration of our settled law; indeed, I find in the history of the Clause's textual development a more powerful argument supporting the Court's jurisprudence following *Everson*.

When James Madison arrived at the First Congress with a series of proposals to amend the National Constitution, one of the provisions read that "[t]he civil rights of none shall be abridged on account of religious belief or worship, nor shall any national religion be established, nor shall the full and equal rights of conscience be in any manner, or on any pretext, infringed." 1 Annals of Cong. 434 (1789). Madison's language did not last long. It was sent to a Select Committee of the House, which, without explanation, changed it to read that "no religion shall be established by law, nor shall the equal rights of conscience be infringed." *Id.*, at 729. Thence the proposal went to the Committee of the Whole, which was in turn dissatisfied with the Select Committee's language and adopted an alternative proposed by Samuel Livermore of New Hampshire: "Congress shall make no laws touching religion, or infringing the rights of conscience." See *id.*, at 731. Livermore's proposal would have forbidden laws having anything to do with religion and was thus not **⊥613** only far broader than Madison's version, but broader even than the scope of the Establishment Clause as we now understand it.

The House rewrote the amendment once more before sending it to the Senate, this time adopting, without recorded debate, language derived from a proposal by Fisher Ames of Massachusetts: "Congress shall make no law establishing Religion, or prohibiting the free exercise thereof, nor shall the rights of conscience be infringed." 1 Documentary History of the First Federal Congress of the United States of America 136 (Senate Journal) (L. de Pauw ed. 1972); see 1 Annals of Cong. 765 (1789). Perhaps, on further reflection, the Representatives had thought Livermore's proposal too expansive, or perhaps, as one historian has suggested, they had simply worried that his language would not "satisfy the demands of those who wanted something said specifically against establishments of religion." L. Levy, The Establishment Clause 81 (1986) (hereinafter Levy). We do not know; what we do know is that the House rejected the Select Committee's version, which arguably ensured only that "no religion" enjoyed an official preference over others, and deliberately chose instead a prohibition extending to laws establishing "religion" in general.

The sequence of the Senate's treatment of this House proposal, and the House's response to the Senate, confirm that the Framers meant the Establishment Clause's prohibition to encompass nonpreferential aid to religion. In September 1789, the Senate considered a number of provisions that would have permitted such aid, and ultimately it adopted one of them. First, it briefly entertained this language: "Congress shall make no law establishing One Religious Sect or Society in preference to others, nor shall the rights of conscience be infringed." 1 Documentary History, at 151 **⊥614** (Senate Journal). After rejecting two minor amendments to that proposal, the Senate dropped it altogether and chose a provision identical to the House's proposal, but without the clause protecting the "rights of conscience." With no record of the Senate debates, we cannot know what prompted these changes, but the record does tell us that, six days later, the Senate went half circle and adopted its narrowest language yet: "Congress shall make no law establishing articles of faith or a mode of worship, or prohibiting the free exercise of religion." *Id.*, at 166. The Senate sent this proposal to the House along with its versions of the other constitutional amendments proposed.

Though it accepted much of the Senate's work on the Bill of Rights, the House rejected the Senate's version of the Establishment Clause and called for a joint conference committee, to which the Senate agreed. The House conferees ultimately won out, persuading the Senate to accept this as the final text of the Religion Clauses: "Congress shall make no law respecting an establishment of religion, or prohibiting the free exercise thereof." What is remarkable is that, unlike the earliest House drafts or the final Senate proposal, the prevailing language is not limited to laws respecting an establishment of "a religion," "a national religion," "one religious sect," or specific "articles of faith." The Framers re**⊥615**peatedly considered and deliberately rejected such narrow language and instead extended their prohibition to state support for "religion" in general.

Implicit in their choice is the distinction between preferential and nonpreferential establishments, which the weight of evidence suggests the Framers appreciated. See, *e.g.*, Laycock, "Nonpreferential" Aid to Religion: A False Claim About Original Intent, 27 Wm. & Mary L. Rev. 875 (hereinafter Laycock, "Nonpreferential" Aid) 902-906; Levy 91-119. But cf. T. Curry, The First Freedoms 208-222 (1986). Of particular note, the Framers were vividly familiar with efforts in the colonies and, later, the States to impose general, nondenominational assessments and other incidents of ostensibly ecumenical establishments. The Virginia Statute for Religious Freedom, written by Jefferson and sponsored by Madison, captured the separationist response to such measures. Condemning all establishments, however nonpreferentialist, the Statute broadly guaranteed that "no man shall be compelled to frequent or support any religious worship, place, or ministry whatsoever," including his own. Act for Establishing Religious Freedom (1785), in 5 The Founders' Constitution 84, 85 (P. Kurland & R. Lerner eds. 1987). Forcing a citizen to support even his own church would, among other things, deny "the ministry those temporary rewards, which proceeding from an approbation of their personal conduct, are an additional incitement to earnest and unremitting labours for the instruction of mankind." *Id.* In general, Madison later added, "religion & Govt. will both exist in greater purity, the less they are mixed together."

Letter from J. Madison to E. Livingston, 10 July 1822, in 5 The Founders' Constitution, at 105, 106.

What we thus know of the Framers' experience underscores the observation of one prominent commentator, that confining the Establishment Clause to a prohibition on preferential aid "requires a premise that the Framers were extraordinarily bad drafters—that they believed one thing but adopted language that said something substantially different, and that they did so after repeatedly attending to the ⊥**616** choice of language." Laycock, "Nonpreferential" Aid 882-883; see also *Allegheny County* v. *American Civil Liberties Union, Greater Pittsburgh Chapter* (opinion of Stevens, J.). We must presume, since there is no conclusive evidence to the contrary, that the Framers embraced the significance of their textual judgment. Thus, on balance, history neither contradicts nor warrants reconsideration of the settled principle that the Establishment Clause forbids support for religion in general no less than support for one religion or some.

C

While these considerations are, for me, sufficient to reject the nonpreferentialist position, one further concern animates my judgment. In many contexts, including this one, nonpreferentialism requires some distinction between "sectarian" religious practices and those that would be, by some measure, ecumenical enough to pass Establishment Clause muster. Simply by requiring the enquiry, non-preferentialists invite the courts to engage in comparative theology. I can hardly imagine a subject less amenable to the compe⊥**617**tence of the federal judiciary, or more deliberately to be avoided where possible.

This case is nicely in point. Since the nonpreferentiality of a prayer must be judged by its text, *Justice BLACKMUN* pertinently observes, *ante*, at 604, n. *, that Rabbi Gutterman drew his exhortation "[t]o do justly, to love mercy, to walk humbly" straight from the King James version of Micah, ch. 6, v. 8. At some undefinable point, the similarities between a state-sponsored prayer and the sacred text of a specific religion would so closely identify the former with the latter that even a nonpreferentialist would have to concede a breach of the Establishment Clause. And even if Micah's thought is sufficiently generic for most believers, it still embodies a straightforwardly Theistic premise, and so does the Rabbi's prayer. Many Americans who consider themselves religious are not Theistic; some, like several of the Framers, are Deists who would question Rabbi Gutterman's plea for divine advancement of the country's political and moral good. Thus, a non-preferentialist who would condemn subjecting public school graduates to, say, the Anglican liturgy would still need to explain why the government's preference for Theistic over non-Theistic religion is constitutional.

Nor does it solve the problem to say that the State should promote a "diversity" of religious views; that position would necessarily compel the government and, inevitably, the courts to make wholly inappropriate judgments about the number of religions the State should sponsor and the relative frequency with which it should sponsor each. In fact, the prospect would be even worse than that. As Madison observed in criticizing religious presidential proclamations, the practice of sponsoring religious messages tends, over time, "to narrow the recommendation to the standard of the predominant sect." Madison's "Detached Memoranda," 3 Wm. & Mary Q. 534, 561 (E. Fleet ed. 1946) (hereinafter Madison's "Detached Memoranda"). We have not changed much since the days of Madison, and the judiciary should not ⊥**618** willingly enter the political arena to battle the centripetal force leading from religious pluralism to official preference for the faith with the most votes.

II

Petitioners rest most of their argument on a theory that, whether or not the Establishment Clause permits extensive nonsectarian support for religion, it does not forbid the state to sponsor affirmations of religious belief that coerce neither support for religion nor participation in religious observance. I appreciate the force of some of the arguments supporting a "coercion" analysis of the Clause. See generally *Allegheny County* (opinion of Kennedy, J.); McConnell, Coercion: The Lost Element of Establishment, 27 Wm. & Mary L. Rev. 933 (1986). But we could not adopt that reading without abandoning our settled law, a course that, in my view, the text of the Clause would not readily permit. Nor does the extratextual evidence of original meaning stand so unequivocally at odds with the textual premise inherent in existing precedent that we should fundamentally reconsider our course.

A

Over the years, this Court has declared the invalidity of many noncoercive state laws and practices conveying a message of religious endorsement. For example, in *Allegheny County*, we forbade the prominent display of a nativity scene on public property; without contesting the dissent's observation that the crèche coerced no one into accepting or supporting whatever message it proclaimed, five Members of the Court found its display unconstitutional as a state endorsement of Christianity. Likewise, in *Wallace* v. *Jaffree*, we struck down a state law requiring a moment of silence in public classrooms not because the statute coerced students to participate in prayer (for it did not), but because the manner of ⊥**619** its enactment "convey[ed] a message of state approval of prayer activities in the public schools." Cf. *Engel* v. *Vitale* ("When the power, prestige and financial support of government is placed behind a particular religious belief, the indirect coercive pressure upon religious minorities to conform to the prevailing officially approved religion is plain. But the purposes underlying the Establishment Clause go much further than that").

In *Epperson* v. *Arkansas*, we invalidated a state law that barred the teaching of Darwin's theory of evolution because, even though the statute obviously did not coerce anyone to support religion or participate in any religious practice, it was enacted for a singularly religious purpose. See also *Edwards* v. *Aguillard* (statute requiring instruction in "creation science" "endorses religion in violation of the First Amendment"). And in *School Dist. of Grand Rapids* v. *Ball*, we invalidated a program whereby the State sent public school teachers to parochial schools to instruct students on ostensibly nonreligious matters; while the scheme clearly did not coerce anyone to receive or subsidize religious instruction, we held it invalid because, among other things, "[t]he symbolic union of church and state inherent in the [program] threatens to convey a message of state support for religion to students and to the general public." See also *Texas Monthly, Inc.* v. *Bullock* (plurality opinion) (tax exemption benefiting only religious publications "effectively endorses religious belief"); (Blackmun, J., concurring in judgment) (exemption unconstitutional because State "engaged in preferential support for the communication of religious messages").

Our precedents may not always have drawn perfectly straight lines. They simply cannot, however, support the position that a showing of coercion is necessary to a successful Establishment Clause claim.

⊥620 B

Like the provisions about "due" process and "unreasonable" searches and seizures, the constitutional language forbidding laws "respecting an establishment of religion" is not pellucid. But virtually everyone acknowledges that the Clause bans more than formal establishments of religion in the traditional sense, that is, massive state support for religion through, among other means, comprehensive schemes of taxation. This much follows from the Framers' explicit rejection of simpler provisions prohibiting either the establishment of a religion or laws "establishing religion" in favor of the broader ban on laws "respecting an establishment of religion."

While some argue that the Framers added the word "respecting" simply to foreclose federal interference with State establishments of religion, see, *e.g.*, Amar, The Bill of Rights as a Constitution, 100 Yale L. J. 1131, 1157 (1991), the language sweeps more broadly than that. In Madison's words, the Clause in its final form forbids "everything like" a national religious establishment, see Madison's "Detached Memoranda" 558, and, after incorporation, it forbids "everything like" a State religious establishment. The sweep is broad enough that Madison himself characterized congressional provisions for legislative and military chaplains as unconstitutional "establishments." Madison's "Detached Memoranda" 558-559.

⊥621 While petitioners insist that the prohibition extends only to the "coercive" features and incidents of establishment, they cannot easily square that claim with the constitutional text. The First Amendment forbids not just laws "respecting an establishment of religion," but also those "prohibiting the free exercise thereof." Yet laws that coerce non-adherents to "support or participate in any religion or its exercise," *Allegheny County* (opinion of Kennedy, J.), would virtually by definition violate their right to religious free exercise. See *Employment Div., Dept. of Human Resources of Ore.* v. *Smith* (under Free Exercise Clause, "government may not compel affirmation of religious belief"), citing *Torcaso* v. *Watkins;* see also J. Madison, Memorial and Remonstrance Against Religious Assessments (1785) (compelling support for religious establishments violates "free exercise of Religion"), quoted in 5 The Founders' Constitution, at 82, 84. Thus, a literal application of the coercion test would render the Establishment Clause a virtual nullity, as petitioners' counsel essentially conceded at oral argument.

Our cases presuppose as much; as we said in *School Dist. of Abington*, "[t]he distinction between the two clauses is apparent—a violation of the Free Exercise Clause is predicated on coercion while the Establishment Clause violation need not be so attended." See also Laycock, "Nonpreferential" Aid 922 ("If coercion is . . . an element of the establishment clause, establishment adds nothing to free exercise"). While one may argue that the Framers meant the Establishment Clause simply to ornament the First Amendment, cf. T. Curry, The First Freedoms 216-217 (1986), that must be a reading of last resort. Without compelling evidence to the contrary, we should presume that the Framers meant the Clause to stand for something more than petitioners attribute to it.

⊥622 C

Petitioners argue from the political setting in which the Establishment Clause was framed, and from the Framers' own political practices following ratification, that government may constitutionally endorse religion so long as it does not coerce religious conformity. The setting and the practices warrant canvassing, but while they yield some evidence for petitioners' argument, they do not reveal the degree of consensus in early constitutional thought that would raise a threat to *stare decisis* by challenging the presumption that the Establishment Clause adds something to the Free Exercise Clause that follows it.

The Framers adopted the Religion Clauses in response to a long tradition of coercive state support for religion, particularly in the form of tax assessments, but their special antipathy to religious coercion did not exhaust their hostility to the features and incidents of establishment. Indeed, Jefferson and Madison opposed any political appropriation of religion and, even when challenging the hated assessments, they did not always temper their rhetoric with distinctions between coercive and noncoercive state action. When, for example, Madison criticized Virginia's general assessment bill, he invoked principles antithetical to all state efforts to promote religion. An assessment, he wrote, is improper not simply because it forces people to donate "three pence" to religion, but, more broadly, because "it is itself a signal of persecution. It degrades from the equal rank of Citizens all those whose opinions in Religion do not bend to those of the Legislative authority." J. Madison, Memorial and Remonstrance Against Religious Assessments (1785), in 5 The Founders' Constitution, at 83. Madison saw that, even without the tax collector's participation, an official endorsement of religion can impair religious liberty.

Petitioners contend that because the early Presidents included religious messages in their inaugural and Thanksgiving Day addresses, the Framers could not have meant the ⊥**623** Establishment Clause to forbid noncoercive state endorsement of religion. The argument ignores the fact, however, that Americans today find such proclamations less controversial than did the founding generation, whose published thoughts on the matter belie petitioners' claim. President Jefferson, for example, steadfastly refused to issue Thanksgiving proclamations of any kind, in part because he thought they violated the Religion Clauses. Letter from Thomas Jefferson to Rev. S. Miller (Jan. 23, 1808), in 5 The Founders' Constitution, at 98. In explaining his views to the Reverend Samuel Miller, Jefferson effectively anticipated, and rejected, petitioners' position:

"[I]t is only proposed that I should recommend, not prescribe a day of fasting & prayer. That is, that I should *indirectly* assume to the U. S. an authority over religious exercises which the Constitution has directly precluded from them. It must be meant too that this recommendation is to carry some authority, and to be sanctioned by some penalty on those who disregard it; not indeed of fine and imprisonment, but of some degree of proscription perhaps in public opinion" (emphasis in original). By condemning such noncoercive state practices that, in "recommending" the majority faith, demean religious dissenters "in public opinion," Jefferson necessarily condemned what, in modern terms, we call official endorsement of religion. He accordingly construed the Establishment Clause to forbid not simply state coercion, but also state endorsement, of religious belief and observance. And if he opposed ⊥**624** impersonal presidential addresses for inflicting "proscription in public opinion," all the more would he have condemned less diffuse expressions of official endorsement.

During his first three years in office, James Madison also refused to call for days of thanksgiving and prayer, though later, amid the political turmoil of the War of 1812, he did so on four separate occasions. See Madison's "Detached Memoranda," 562, and n. 54. Upon retirement, in an essay condemning as an unconstitutional "establishment" the use of public money to support congressional and military chaplains, *id.*, he concluded that "[r]eligious procla⊥**625**mations by the Executive recommending thanksgivings & fasts are shoots from the same root with the legislative acts reviewed. Altho' recommendations only, they imply a religious agency, making no part of the trust delegated to political rulers." *Id.*, at 560. Explaining that "[t]he members of a Govt . . . can in no sense, be regarded as possessing an advisory trust from their Constituents in their religious capacities," *ibid.*, he further observed that the state necessarily freights all of its religious messages with political ones: "the idea of policy [is] associated with religion, whatever be the mode or the occasion, when a function of the latter is assumed by those in power." *Id.*, at 562.

Madison's failure to keep pace with his principles in the face of congressional pressure cannot erase the principles. He admitted to backsliding, and explained that he had made the content of his wartime proclamations inconsequential enough to mitigate much of their impropriety. See *ibid.*; see also Letter from J. Madison to E. Livingston (July 10, 1822), in 5 The Founders' Constitution, at 105. While his writings suggest mild variations in his interpretation of the Establishment Clause, Madison was no different in that respect from the rest of his political generation. That he expressed so much doubt about the constitutionality of religious proclamations, however, suggests a brand of separationism stronger even than that embodied in our traditional jurisprudence. So too does his characterization of public subsidies for legislative and military chaplains as unconstitutional "establishments," for the federal courts, however expansive their general view of the Establishment Clause, have upheld both practices.

⊥**626** To be sure, the leaders of the young Republic engaged in some of the practices that separationists like Jefferson and Madison criticized. The First Congress did hire institutional chaplains, see *Marsh* v. *Chambers*, and Presidents Washington and Adams unapologetically marked days of "public thanksgiving and prayer," see R. Cord, Separation of Church and State 53 (1988). Yet in the face of the separationist dissent, those practices prove, at best, that the Framers simply did not share a common understanding of the Establishment Clause, and, at worst, that they, like other politicians, could raise constitutional ideals one day and turn their backs on them the next. "Indeed, by 1787 the provisions of the state bills of rights had become what Madison called mere 'paper parchments'—expressions of the most laudable sentiments, observed as much in the breach as in practice." Kurland, The Origins of the Religion Clauses of the Constitution, 27 Wm. & Mary L. Rev. 839, 852 (1986) (footnote omitted). Sometimes the National Constitution fared no better. Ten years after proposing the First Amendment, Congress passed the Alien and Sedition Acts, measures patently unconstitutional by modern standards. If the early Congress's political actions were determinative, and not merely relevant, evidence of constitutional meaning, we would have to gut our current First Amendment doctrine to make room for political censorship.

While we may be unable to know for certain what the Framers meant by the Clause, we do know that, around the time of its ratification, a respectable body of opinion supported a considerably broader reading than petitioners urge upon us. This consistency with the textual considerations is enough to preclude fundamentally reexamining our settled law, and I am accordingly left with the task of considering whether the state practice at issue here violates our traditional understanding of the Clause's proscriptions.

⊥**627** III

While the Establishment Clause's concept of neutrality is not self-revealing, our recent cases have invested it with specific content: the state may not favor or endorse either religion generally over non-religion or one religion over others. See, *e.g.*, *Allegheny County; Texas Monthly* (plurality opinion); *id.* (Blackmun, J., concurring in judgment); *Edwards* v. *Aguillard; School Dist. of Grand Rapids; Wallace* v. *Jaffree;* see also Laycock, Formal, Substantive, and Disaggregated Neutrality Toward Religion, 39 De Paul L. Rev. 993 (1990). This principle against favoritism and endorsement has become the foundation of Establishment Clause jurisprudence, ensuring that religious belief is irrelevant to every citizen's standing in the political community, see *Allegheny County;* J. Madison, Memorial and Remonstrance Against Religious Assessments (1785), in 5 The Founders' Constitution, at 82-83, and protecting religion from the demeaning effects of any governmental embrace, see *id.*, at 83. Now, as in the early Republic, "religion & Govt. will both exist in greater purity, the less they are mixed together." Letter from J. Madison to E. Livingston (10 July 1822), in 5 The Founders' Constitution, at 106. Our aspiration to religious liberty, embodied in the First Amendment, permits no other standard.

A

That government must remain neutral in matters of religion does not foreclose it from ever taking religion into account. The State may "accommodate" the free exercise of religion by relieving people from generally applicable rules that interfere with their religious callings. See, *e.g.*, *Corporation of Presiding Bishop of Church of Jesus Christ of Latter-Day Saints* v. *Amos;* see also *Sherbert* v. *Verner*. Contrary to the ⊥**628** views of some, such accommodation does not necessarily signify an official endorsement of religious observance over disbelief.

In everyday life, we routinely accommodate religious beliefs that we do not share. A Christian inviting an Orthodox Jew to lunch might take pains to choose a kosher restaurant; an atheist in a hurry might yield the right of way to an Amish man steering a horse-drawn carriage. In so acting, we express respect for, but not endorsement of, the fundamental values of others. We act without expressing a position on the theological merit of those values or of religious belief in general, and no one perceives us to have taken such a position.

The government may act likewise. Most religions encourage devotional practices that are at once crucial to the lives of believers and idiosyncratic in the eyes of nonadherents. By definition, secular rules of general application are drawn from the nonadherent's vantage and, consequently, fail to take such practices into account. Yet when enforcement of such rules cuts across religious sensibilities, as it often does, it puts those affected to the choice of taking sides between God and government. In such circumstances, accommodating religion reveals nothing beyond a recognition that general rules can unnecessarily offend the religious conscience when they offend the conscience of secular society not at all. Thus, in freeing the Native American Church from federal laws forbidding peyote use, see Drug Enforcement Administration Miscellaneous Exemptions, 21 C. F. R. ⊥**629** § 1307.31 (1991), the government conveys no endorsement of peyote rituals, the Church, or religion as such; it simply respects the centrality of peyote to the lives of certain Americans. See Note, The Free Exercise Boundaries of Permissible Accommodation Under the Establishment Clause, 99 Yale L. J. 1127, 1135-1136 (1990).

B

Whatever else may define the scope of accommodation permissible under the Establishment Clause, one requirement is clear: accommodation must lift a discernible burden on the free exercise of religion. Concern for the position of religious individuals in the modern regulatory state cannot justify official solicitude for a religious practice unburdened by general rules; such gratuitous largesse would effectively favor religion over disbelief. By these lights one easily sees that, in sponsoring the graduation prayers at issue here, the State has crossed the line from permissible accommodation to unconstitutional establishment.

Religious students cannot complain that omitting prayers from their graduation ceremony would, in any realistic sense, "burden" their spiritual callings. To be sure, many of them invest this rite of passage with spiritual significance, but they may express their religious feelings about it before and after the ceremony. They may even organize a privately sponsored baccalaureate if they desire the company of likeminded students. Because they accordingly have no need for the machinery of the State to affirm their beliefs, the ⊥**630** government's sponsorship of prayer at the graduation ceremony is most reasonably understood as an official endorsement of religion and, in this instance, of Theistic religion. One may fairly say, as one commentator has suggested, that the government brought prayer into the ceremony "precisely because some people want a symbolic affirmation that government approves and endorses their religion, and because many of the people who want this affirmation place little or no value on the costs to religious minorities." Laycock, Summary and Synthesis: The Crisis in Religious Liberty, 60 Geo. Wash. L. Rev. 841, 844 (1992).

Petitioners would deflect this conclusion by arguing that graduation prayers are no different from presidential religious proclamations and similar official "acknowledgments" of religion in public life. But religious invocations in Thanksgiving Day addresses and the like, rarely noticed, ignored without effort, conveyed over an impersonal medium, and directed at no one in particular, inhabit a pallid zone worlds apart from official prayers delivered to a captive audience of public school students and their families. Madison himself respected the difference between the trivial and the serious in constitutional practice. Realizing that his con⊥**631**temporaries were unlikely to take the Establishment Clause seriously enough to forgo a legislative chaplainship, he suggested that "[r]ather than let this step beyond the landmarks of power have the effect of a legitimate precedent, it will be better to apply to it the legal aphorism de minimis non curat lex. . . ." Madison's "Detached Memoranda" 559; see also Letter from J. Madison to E. Livingston, 10 July 1822, in 5 The Founders' Constitution, at 105. But that logic permits no winking at the practice in question here. When public school officials, armed with the State's authority, convey an endorsement of religion to their students, they strike near the core of the Establishment Clause. However "ceremonial" their messages may be, they are flatly unconstitutional.

Justice SCALIA, with whom *The* CHIEF JUSTICE, *Justice* WHITE, and *Justice* THOMAS join, dissenting.

Three Terms ago, I joined an opinion recognizing that the Establishment Clause must be construed in light of the "[g]overnment policies of accommodation, acknowledgment, and support for religion [that] are an accepted part of our political and cultural heritage." That opinion affirmed that "the meaning of the Clause is to be determined by reference to historical practices and understandings." It said that "[a] test for implementing the protections of the Establishment Clause that, if applied with consistency, would invalidate longstanding traditions cannot be a proper reading of the Clause." *Allegheny County* v. *Greater Pittsburgh ACLU* (Kennedy, J., concurring in judgment in part and dissenting in part).

These views of course prevent me from joining today's opinion, which is conspicuously bereft of any reference to history. In holding that the Establishment Clause prohibits invocations and benedictions at public-school graduation ceremonies, the Court—with nary a mention that it is doing ⊥**632** so—lays waste a tradition that is as old as public-school graduation ceremonies themselves, and that is a component of an even more longstanding American tradition of nonsectarian prayer to God at public celebrations generally. As its instrument of destruction, the bulldozer of its social engineering, the Court invents a boundless, and boundlessly manipulable, test of psychological coercion, which promises to do for the Establishment Clause what the Durham rule did for the insanity defense. See *Durham* v. *United States*. Today's opinion shows more forcefully than volumes of argumentation why our Nation's protection, that fortress which is our Constitution, cannot possibly rest upon the changeable philosophical predilections of the Justices of this Court, but must have deep foundations in the historic practices of our people.

I

Justice HOLMES' aphorism that "a page of history is worth a volume of logic," *New York Trust Co.* v. *Eisner*, applies with particular force to our Establishment Clause jurisprudence. As we have recognized, our interpretation of the Establishment Clause should "compor[t] with what history reveals was the contemporaneous understanding of its guarantees." *Lynch* v. *Donnelly*. "[T]he line we must draw between the permissible and the impermissible is one which accords with history and faithfully reflects the understanding of the Founding Fathers." *Abington School District* v. *Schempp* (Brennan, J., concurring). "[H]istorical evidence sheds light not only on what the draftsmen intended the Establishment Clause to mean, but also on how they thought that Clause applied" to contemporaneous practices. *Marsh* v. *Chambers*. Thus, "[t]he existence from the beginning of the Nation's life of a practice, [while] not conclusive of its constitutionality . . . , is a fact of considerable import in the interpretation" of the ⊥**633** Establishment Clause. *Walz* v. *Tax Comm'n of New York City* (Brennan, J., concurring).

The history and tradition of our Nation are replete with public ceremonies featuring prayers of thanksgiving and petition. Illustrations of this point have been amply provided in our prior opinions, see, *e.g.*, *Lynch*, *Marsh*; see also *Wallace* v. *Jaffree* (Rehnquist, J., dissenting); *Engel* v. *Vitale* (Stewart, J., dissenting), but since the Court is so oblivious to our history as to suggest that the Constitution restricts "preservation and transmission of religious beliefs . . . to the private sphere," it appears necessary to provide another brief account.

From our Nation's origin, prayer has been a prominent part of governmental ceremonies and proclamations. The Declaration of Independence, the document marking our birth as a separate people, "appeal[ed] to the Supreme Judge of the world for the rectitude of our intentions" and avowed "a firm reliance on the protection of divine Providence." In his first inaugural address, after swearing his oath of office on a Bible, George Washington deliberately made a prayer a part of his first official act as President:

"it would be peculiarly improper to omit in this first official act my fervent supplications to that Almighty Being who rules over the universe, who presides in the councils of nations, and whose providential aids can supply every human defect, that His benediction may consecrate to the liberties and happiness of the people of the United States a Government instituted by themselves for these essential purposes." Inaugural Addresses of the Presidents of the United States 2 (1989).

Such supplications have been a characteristic feature of inaugural addresses ever since. Thomas Jefferson, for example, ⊥**634** prayed in his first inaugural address: "may that Infinite Power which rules the destinies of the universe lead our councils to what is best, and give them a favorable issue for your peace and prosperity." *Id.*, at 17. In his second inaugural address, Jefferson acknowledged his need for divine guidance and invited his audience to join his prayer:

"I shall need, too, the favor of that Being in whose hands we are, who led our fathers, as Israel of old, from their native land and planted them in a country flowing with all the necessaries and comforts of life; who has covered our infancy with His providence and our riper years with His wisdom and power, and to whose goodness I ask you to join in supplications with me that He will so enlighten the minds of your servants, guide their councils, and prosper their measures that whatsoever they do shall result in your good, and shall secure to you the peace, friendship, and approbation of all nations." *Id.*, at 22-23.

Similarly, James Madison, in his first inaugural address, placed his confidence

"in the guardianship and guidance of that Almighty Being whose power regulates the destiny of nations, whose blessings have been so conspicuously dispensed to this rising Republic, and to whom we are bound to address our devout gratitude for the past, as well as our fervent supplications and best hopes for the future." *Id.*, at 28.

Most recently, President Bush, continuing the tradition established by President Washington, asked those attending his inauguration to bow their heads, and made a prayer his first official act as President. *Id.*, at 346.

Our national celebration of Thanksgiving likewise dates back to President Washington. As we recounted in *Lynch*,

⊥**635** "The day after the First Amendment was proposed, Congress urged President Washington to proclaim 'a day of public thanksgiving and prayer, to be observed by acknowledging with grateful hearts the many and signal favours of Almighty God.' President Washington proclaimed November 26, 1789, a day of thanksgiving to 'offe[r] our prayers and supplications to the Great Lord and Ruler of Nations, and beseech him to pardon our national and other transgressions. . . .'"

This tradition of Thanksgiving Proclamations—with their religious theme of prayerful gratitude to God—has been adhered to by almost every President.

The other two branches of the Federal Government also have a long-established practice of prayer at public events. As we detailed in *Marsh*, Congressional sessions have opened with a chaplain's prayer ever since the First Congress. And this Court's own sessions have opened with the invocation "God save the United States and this Honorable Court" since the days of *Chief Justice* MARSHALL.

In addition to this general tradition of prayer at public ceremonies, there exists a more specific tradition of invocations and benedictions at public-school graduation exercises. By one account, the first public-high-school graduation ceremony took place in Connecticut in July 1868—the very month, as it happens, that the Fourteenth Amendment (the vehicle by which the Establishment Clause has been applied against the States) was ratified—when "15 seniors from the Norwich Free Academy marched in their best Sunday suits and dresses into a church hall and waited through majestic music and long prayers." Brodinsky, Commencement Rites Obsolete? Not At All, A 10-Week Study Shows, Updat⊥**636**ing School Board Policies, Vol. 10, p. 3 (Apr. 1979). As the Court obliquely acknowledges in describing the "customary features" of high school graduations, and as respondents do not contest, the invocation and benediction have long been recognized to be "as traditional as any other parts of the [school] graduation program and are widely established." H. McKown, Commencement Activities 56 (1931); see also Brodinsky, at 5.

II

The Court presumably would separate graduation invocations and benedictions from other instances of public "preservation and transmission of religious beliefs" on the ground that they involve "psychological coercion." I find it a sufficient embarrassment that our Establishment Clause jurisprudence regarding holiday displays, see *Allegheny County* v. *Greater Pittsburgh ACLU*, has come to "requir[e] scrutiny more commonly associated with interior decorators than with the judiciary." *American Jewish Congress* v. *Chicago* (Easterbrook, J., dissenting). But interior decorating is a rock-hard science compared to psychology practiced by amateurs. A few citations of "[r]esearch in psychology" that have no particular bearing upon the precise issue here, cannot disguise the fact that the Court has gone beyond the realm where judges know what they are doing. The Court's argument that state officials have "coerced" students to take part in the invocation and benediction at graduation ceremonies is, not to put too fine a point on it, incoherent.

The Court identifies two "dominant facts" that it says dictate its ruling that invocations and benedictions at public-school graduation ceremonies violate the Establishment Clause. Neither of them is in any relevant sense true.

⊥**637** A

The Court declares that students' "attendance and participation in the [invocation and benediction] are in a fair and real sense obligatory." But what exactly is this "fair and real sense"? According to the Court, students at graduation who want "to avoid the fact or appearance of participation," in the invocation and benediction are *psychologically* obligated by "public pressure, as well as peer pressure, . . . to stand as a group or, at least, maintain respectful silence" during those prayers. This assertion—*the very linchpin of the Court's opinion*—is almost as intriguing for what it does not say as for what it says. It does not say, for example, that students are psychologically coerced to bow their heads, place their hands in a Dürer-like prayer position, pay attention to the prayers, utter "Amen," or in fact pray. (Perhaps further intensive psychological research remains to be done on these matters.) It claims only that students are psychologically coerced "to stand . . . *or*, at least, maintain respectful silence" (emphasis added). Both halves of this disjunctive (*both* of which must amount to the fact or appearance of participation in prayer if the Court's analysis is to survive on its own terms) merit particular attention.

To begin with the latter: The Court's notion that a student who simply *sits* in "respectful silence" during the invocation and benediction (when all others are standing) has somehow joined—or would somehow be perceived as having joined—in the prayers is nothing short of ludicrous. We indeed live in a vulgar age. But surely "our social conventions" have not coarsened to the point that anyone who does not stand on his chair and shout obscenities can reasonably be deemed to have assented to everything said in his presence. Since the Court does not dispute that students exposed to prayer at graduation ceremonies retain (despite "subtle coercive pressures,") the free will to sit, there is absolutely no basis for the Court's ⊥**638** decision. It is fanciful enough to say that "a reasonable dissenter," standing head erect in a class of bowed heads, "could believe that the group exercise signified her own participation or approval of it." It is beyond the absurd to say that she could entertain such a belief while pointedly declining to rise.

But let us assume the very worst, that the non-participating graduate is "subtly coerced" . . . to stand! Even that half of the disjunctive does not remotely establish a "participation" (or an "appearance of participation") in a religious exercise. The Court acknowledges that "in our culture standing . . . can signify adherence to a view or simple respect for the views of others." (Much more often the latter than the former, I think, except perhaps in the proverbial town meeting, where one votes by standing.) But if it is a permissible inference that one who is standing is doing so simply out of respect for the prayers of others that are in progress, then how can it possibly be said that a "reasonable dissenter . . . could believe that the group exercise signified her own participation or approval"? Quite obviously, it cannot. I may add, moreover, that maintaining respect for the religious observances of others is a fundamental civic virtue that government (including the public schools) can and should cultivate—so that even if it were the case that the displaying of such respect might be mistaken for taking part in the prayer, I would deny that the dissenter's interest in avoiding *even the false appearance of participation* constitutionally trumps the government's interest in fostering respect for religion generally.

The opinion manifests that the Court itself has not given careful consideration to its test of psychological coercion. For if it had, how could it observe, with no hint of concern or disapproval, that students stood for the Pledge of Allegiance, which immediately preceded Rabbi Gutterman's invocation? The government can, of course, no more coerce political orthodoxy than religious orthodoxy. *West* ⊥**639** *Virginia Board of Education* v. *Barnette*. Moreover, since the Pledge of Allegiance has been revised since *Barnette* to include the phrase "under God," recital of the Pledge would appear to raise the same Establishment Clause issue as the invocation and benediction. If students were psychologically coerced to remain standing during the invocation, they must also have been psychologically coerced, moments before, to stand for (and thereby, in the Court's view, take part in or appear to take part in) the Pledge. Must the Pledge therefore be barred from the public schools (both from graduation ceremonies and from the classroom)? In *Barnette* we held that a public-school student could not be compelled to *recite* the Pledge; we did not even hint that she could not be compelled to observe respectful silence—indeed, even to *stand* in respectful silence—when those who wished to recite it did so. Logically, that ought to be the next project for the Court's bulldozer.

I also find it odd that the Court concludes that high school graduates may not be subjected to this supposed psychological coercion, yet refrains from addressing whether "mature adults" may. I had thought that the reason graduation from high school is regarded as so significant an event is that it is generally associated with transition from adolescence to young adulthood. Many graduating seniors, of course, are old enough to vote. Why, then, does the Court treat them as though they were first-graders? Will we soon have a jurisprudence that distinguishes between mature and immature adults?

B

The other "dominant fac[t]" identified by the Court is that "[s]tate officials direct the performance of a formal religious exercise" at school graduation ceremonies. "Direct[ing] the performance of a formal religious exercise" has a sound of liturgy to it, summoning up images of the principal directing acolytes where to carry the cross, or showing the rabbi where to unroll the Torah. A Court professing to be ⊥**640** engaged in a "delicate and fact-sensitive" line-drawing, would better describe what it means as "prescribing the content of an invocation and benediction." But even that would be false. All the record shows is that principals of the Providence public schools, acting within their delegated authority, have invited clergy to deliver invocations and benedictions at graduations; and that Principal Lee invited Rabbi Gutterman, provided him a two-page flyer, prepared by the National Conference of Christians and Jews, giving general advice on inclusive prayer for civic occasions, and advised him that his prayers at graduation should be nonsectarian. How these facts can fairly be transformed into the charges that Principal Lee "directed and controlled the content of [Rabbi Gutterman's] prayer," that school officials "monitor prayer," and attempted to "'compose official prayers,'" and that the "government involvement with religious activity in this case is pervasive," is difficult to fathom. The Court identifies nothing in the record remotely suggesting that school officials have ever drafted, edited, screened or censored graduation prayers, or that Rabbi Gutterman was a mouthpiece of the school officials.

These distortions of the record are, of course, not harmless error: without them the Court's solemn assertion that the school officials could reasonably be perceived to be "enforc[ing] a religious orthodoxy," would ring as hollow as it ought.

III

The deeper flaw in the Court's opinion does not lie in its wrong answer to the question whether there was state-induced "peer-pressure" coercion; it lies, rather, in the Court's making violation of the Establishment Clause hinge on such a precious question. The coercion that was a hallmark of historical establishments of religion was coercion of religious orthodoxy and of financial support *by force of law and threat of penalty*. Typically, attendance at the state ⊥**641** church was required; only clergy of the official church could lawfully perform sacraments; and dissenters, if tolerated, faced an array of civil disabilities. L. Levy, The Establishment Clause 4 (1986). Thus, for example, in the colony of Virginia, where the Church of England had been established, ministers were required by law to conform to the doctrine and rites of the Church of England; and all persons were required to attend church and observe the Sabbath, were tithed for the public support of Anglican ministers, and were taxed for the costs of building and repairing churches.

The Establishment Clause was adopted to prohibit such an establishment of religion at the federal level (and to protect state establishments of religion from federal interference). I will further acknowledge for the sake of argument that, as some scholars have argued, by 1790 the term "establishment" had acquired an additional meaning—"financial support of religion generally, by public taxation"—that reflected the development of "general or multiple" establishments, not limited to a single church. But that would still be an establishment coerced *by force of law*. And I will further concede that our constitutional tradition, from the Declaration of Independence and the first inaugural address of Washington, quoted earlier, down to the present day, has, with a few aberrations, see *Holy Trinity Church* v. *United States*, ruled out of order government-sponsored endorsement of religion—even when no legal coercion is present, and indeed even when no ersatz, "peer-pressure" psycho-coercion is present—where the endorsement is sectarian, in the sense of specifying details upon which men and women who believe in a benevolent, omnipotent Creator and Ruler of the world, are known to differ (for example, the divinity of Christ). But there is simply no support for the proposition that the officially sponsored nondenominational invocation and benediction read by Rabbi Gutterman—with no one legally coerced to recite ⊥**642** them—violated the Constitution of the United States. To the contrary, they are so characteristically American they could have come from the pen of George Washington or Abraham Lincoln himself.

Thus, while I have no quarrel with the Court's general proposition that the Establishment Clause "guarantees that government may not coerce anyone to support or participate in religion or its exercise," I see no warrant for expanding the concept of coercion beyond acts backed by threat of penalty—a brand of coercion that, happily, is readily discernible to those of us who have made a career of reading the disciples of Blackstone rather than of Freud. The Framers were indeed opposed to coercion of religious worship by the National Government; but, as their own sponsorship of nonsectarian prayer in public events demonstrates, they understood that "[s]peech is not coercive; the listener may do as he likes." *American Jewish Congress* v. *Chicago* (Easterbrook, J., dissenting).

This historical discussion places in revealing perspective the Court's extravagant claim that the State has "for all practical purposes," and "in every practical sense," compelled students to participate in prayers at graduation. Beyond the fact, stipulated to by the parties, that attendance at graduation is voluntary, there is nothing in the record to indicate that failure of attending students to take part in the invocation or benediction was subject to any penalty or discipline. Contrast this with, for example, the facts of *Barnette*: Schoolchildren were required by law to recite the Pledge of Allegiance; failure to do so resulted in expulsion, threatened the expelled child with the prospect of being sent to a reformatory for criminally inclined juveniles, and subjected his parents to prosecution (and incarceration) for causing delinquency. To characterize the "subtle coercive pressures," allegedly present here as the "practical" equiva⊥**643**lent of the legal sanctions in *Barnette* is . . . well, let me just say it is not a "delicate and fact-sensitive" analysis.

The Court relies on our "school prayer" cases, *Engel* v. *Vitale*, and *Abington School District* v. *Schempp*. But whatever the merit of those cases, they do not support, much less compel, the Court's psycho-journey. In the first place, *Engel* and *Schempp* do not constitute an exception to the rule, distilled from historical practice, that public ceremonies may include prayer, rather, they simply do not fall within the scope of the rule (for the obvious reason that school instruction is not a public ceremony). Second, we have made clear our understanding that school prayer occurs within a framework in which legal coercion to attend school (*i.e.*, coercion under threat of penalty) provides the ultimate backdrop. In *Schempp*, for example, we emphasized that the prayers were "prescribed as part of the curricular activities of students who are *required by law* to attend school" (emphasis added).

Engel's suggestion that the school-prayer program at issue there—which permitted students "to remain silent or be excused from the room"—involved "indirect coercive pressure," should be understood against this backdrop of legal coercion. The question whether the opt-out procedure in *Engel* sufficed to dispel the coercion resulting from the mandatory attendance requirement is quite different from the question whether forbidden coercion exists in an environment *utterly devoid of legal compulsion*. And finally, our school-prayer cases turn in part on the fact that the classroom is inherently an instructional setting, and daily prayer there—where parents are not present to counter "the students' emulation of teachers as role models and the children's susceptibility to peer pressure," *Edwards* v. *Aguillard*—might be thought to raise special concerns regarding state interference with the liberty of parents to direct the religious upbringing of their children: "Families entrust pub⊥**644**lic schools with the education of their children, but condition their trust on the understanding that the classroom will not purposely be used to advance religious views that may conflict with the private beliefs of the student and his or her family." *Ibid.*; see *Pierce* v. *Society of Sisters*. Voluntary prayer at graduation—a one-time ceremony at which parents, friends and relatives are present—can hardly be thought to raise the same concerns.

IV

Our religion-clause jurisprudence has become bedeviled (so to speak) by reliance on formulaic abstractions that are not derived from, but positively conflict with, our long-accepted constitutional traditions. Foremost among these has been the so-called *Lemon* test, which has received well-earned criticism from many members of this Court. The Court today demonstrates the irrelevance of *Lemon* by essentially ignoring it, and the interment of that case may be the one happy byproduct of the Court's otherwise lamentable decision. Unfortunately, however, the Court has replaced *Lemon* with its psycho-coercion test, which suffers the double disability of having no roots whatever in our people's historic practice, and being as infinitely expandable as the reasons for psychotherapy itself.

Another happy aspect of the case is that it is only a jurisprudential disaster and not a practical one. Given the odd basis for the Court's decision, invocations and benedictions will be able to be given at public-school graduations next ⊥**645** June, as they have for the past century and a half, so long as school authorities make clear that anyone who abstains from screaming in protest does not necessarily participate in the prayers. All that is seemingly needed is an announcement, or perhaps a written insertion at the beginning of the graduation Program, to the effect that, while all are asked to rise for the invocation and benediction, none is compelled to join in them, nor will be assumed, by rising, to have done so. That obvious fact recited, the graduates and their parents may proceed to thank God, as Americans have always done, for the blessings He has generously bestowed on them and on their country.

. . . . .

The reader has been told much in this case about the personal interest of Mr. Weisman and his daughter, and very little about the personal interests on the other side. They are not inconsequential. Church and state would not be such a difficult subject if religion were, as the Court apparently thinks it to be, some purely personal avocation that can be indulged entirely in secret, like pornography, in the privacy of one's room. For most believers it is not that, and has never been. Religious men and women of almost all denominations have felt it necessary to acknowledge and beseech the blessing of God as a people, and not just as individuals, because they believe in the "protection of divine Providence," as the Declaration of Independence put it, not just for individuals but for societies; because they believe God to be, as Washington's first Thanksgiving Proclamation put it, the "Great Lord and Ruler of Nations." One can believe in the effectiveness of such public worship, or one can deprecate and deride it. But the long-standing American tradition of prayer at official ceremonies displays with unmistakable clarity that the Establishment Clause does not forbid the government to accommodate it.

The narrow context of the present case involves a community's celebration of one of the milestones in its young citi⊥**646**zens' lives, and it is a bold step for this Court to seek to banish from that occasion, and from thousands of similar celebrations throughout this land, the expression of gratitude to God that a majority of the community wishes to make. The issue before us today is not the abstract philosophical question whether the alternative of frustrating this desire of a religious majority is to be preferred over the alternative of imposing "psychological coercion," or a feeling of exclusion, upon nonbelievers. Rather, the question is *whether a mandatory choice in favor of the former has been imposed by the United States Constitution*. As the age-old practices of our people show, the answer to that question is not at all in doubt.

I must add one final observation: The founders of our Republic knew the fearsome potential of sectarian religious belief to generate civil dissension and civil strife. And they also knew that nothing, absolutely nothing, is so inclined to foster among religious believers of various faiths a toleration—no, an affection—for one another than voluntarily joining in prayer together, to the God whom they all worship and seek. Needless to say, no one should be compelled to do that, but it is a shame to deprive our public culture of the opportunity, and indeed the encouragement, for people to do it voluntarily. The Baptist or Catholic who heard and joined in the simple and inspiring prayers of Rabbi Gutterman on this official and patriotic occasion was inoculated from religious bigotry and prejudice in a manner that can not be replicated. To deprive our society of that important unifying mechanism, in order to spare the nonbeliever what seems to me the minimal inconvenience of standing or even sitting in respectful nonparticipation, is as senseless in policy as it is unsupported in law.

For the foregoing reasons, I dissent.

LAMB'S CHAPEL v. CENTER MORICHES UNION FREE SCHOOL DISTRICT

508 U.S. 384

ON WRIT OF CERTIORARI TO THE UNITED STATES COURT OF APPEALS FOR THE SECOND CIRCUIT

Argued February 24, 1993 — Decided June 7, 1993

⊥**386** *Justice WHITE* delivered the opinion of the Court.

Section 414 of the New York Education Law (McKinney 1988 and Supp. 1993), authorizes local school boards to adopt reasonable regulations for the use of school property for 10 specified purposes when the property is not in use for school purposes. Among the permitted uses is the holding of "social, civic and recreational meetings and entertainments, and other uses pertaining to the welfare of the community; but such meetings, entertainment and uses shall be non-exclusive and open to the general public." § 414(c). The list of permitted uses does not include meetings for religious purposes, and a New York appellate court in *Trietley* v. *Board of Ed. of Buffalo*, ruled that local boards could not allow student bible clubs to meet ⊥**387** on school property because "[r]eligious purposes are not included in the enumerated purposes for which a school may be used under section 414." In *Deeper Life Christian Fellowship, Inc.* v. *Sobol* the Court of Appeals for the Second Circuit accepted *Trietley* as an authoritative interpretation of state law. Furthermore, the Attorney General of New York supports *Trietley* as an appropriate approach to deciding this case.

Pursuant to § 414's empowerment of local school districts, the Board of Center Moriches Union Free School District (District) has issued rules and regulations with respect to the use of school property when not in use for school purposes. The rules allow only 2 of the 10 purposes authorized by § 414: social, civic, or recreational uses (Rule 10) and use by political organizations if secured in compliance with § 414 (Rule 8). Rule 7, however, consistent with the judicial interpretation of state law, provides that "[t]he school premises shall not be used by any group for religious purposes."

The issue in this case is whether, against this background of state law, it violates the Free Speech Clause of the First Amendment, made applicable to the States by the Fourteenth Amendment, to deny a church access to school premises to exhibit for public viewing and for assertedly religious purposes, a film dealing with family and child-rearing issues faced by parents today.

I

Petitioners (Church) are Lamb's Chapel, an evangelical church in the community of Center Moriches, and its pastor John Steigerwald. Twice the Church applied to the District for permission to use school facilities to show a six-part film series containing lectures by Doctor James Dobson. A bro⊥**388**chure provided on request of the District identified Dr. Dobson as a licensed psychologist, former associate clinical professor of pediatrics at the University of Southern California, best-selling author, and radio commentator. The brochure stated that the film series would discuss Dr. Dobson's views on the undermining influences of the media that could only be counterbalanced by returning to traditional, Christian family values instilled at an early stage. The brochure went on to describe the contents of each of the six parts of the series. The District denied the first application, saying ⊥**389** that "[t]his film does appear to be church related and therefore your request must be refused." The second application for permission to use school premises for showing the film, which described it as a "Family oriented movie—from the Christian perspective," was denied using identical language.

The Church brought suit in District Court, challenging the denial as a violation of the Freedom of Speech and Assembly Clauses, the Free Exercise Clause, and the Establishment Clause of the First Amendment, as well as the Equal Protection Clause of the Fourteenth Amendment. As to each cause of action, the Church alleged that the actions were undertaken under color of state law, in violation of 42 U. S. C. § 1983. The District Court granted summary judgment for respondents, rejecting all of the Church's claims. With respect to the free-speech claim under the First Amendment, the District Court characterized the District's facilities as a "limited public forum." The court noted that the enumerated purposes for which § 414 allowed access to school facilities did not include religious worship or instruction, that Rule 7 explicitly proscribes using school facilities for religious purposes, and that the Church had conceded that its showing of the film would be for religious purposes. The District Court stated that once a limited public forum is opened to a particular type of speech, selectively denying access to other activities of the same genre is forbidden. Noting that the District had not opened its facilities to orga⊥**390**nizations similar to Lamb's Chapel for religious purposes, the District Court held that the denial in this case was viewpoint neutral and, hence, not a violation of the Freedom of Speech Clause. The District Court also rejected the assertion by the Church that denying its application demonstrated a hostility to religion and advancement of nonreligion not justified under the Establishment of Religion Clause of the First Amendment.

The Court of Appeals affirmed the judgment of the District Court "in all respects." *Lamb's Chapel* v. *Center Moriches Union Free School Dist.* It held that the school property, when not in use for school purposes, was neither a traditional nor a designated public forum; rather, it was a limited public forum open only for designated purposes, a classification that "allows it to remain nonpublic except as to specified uses." The court observed that exclusions in such a forum need only be reasonable and viewpoint neutral, and ruled that denying access to the Church for the purpose of showing its film did not violate this standard. Because the holding below was questionable under our decisions, we granted the petition for certiorari, which in principal part challenged the holding below as contrary to the Free Speech Clause of the First Amendment.

II

There is no question that the District, like the private owner of property, may legally preserve the property under its control for the use to which it is dedicated. *Cornelius* v. *NAACP Legal Defense and Ed. Fund, Inc.*; *Perry Ed. Assn.* v. *Perry Local Educators' Assn.* ⊥**391** It is also common ground that the District need not have permitted after-hours use of its property for any of the uses permitted by § 414 of the state education law. The District, however, did open its property for 2 of the 10 uses permitted by § 414. The Church argued below that because under Rule 10 of the rules issued by the District, school property could be used for "social, civic, and recreational" purposes, the District had opened its property for such a wide variety of communicative purposes that restrictions on communicative uses of the property were subject to the same constitutional limitations as restrictions in traditional public fora such as parks and sidewalks. Hence, its view was that subject-matter or speaker exclusions on District property were required to be justified by a compelling state interest and to be narrowly drawn to achieve that end. See *Perry*, *Cornelius*. Both the District Court and the Court of Appeals rejected this submission, which is also presented to this Court. The argument has considerable force, for the District's property is heavily used by a wide variety of private organizations, including some that presented a "close question," which the Court of Appeals resolved in the District's favor, as to whether the District had in fact already opened its property for religious uses. We need ⊥**392** not rule on this issue, however, for even if the courts below were correct in this respect—and we shall assume for present purposes that they were—the judgment below must be reversed.

With respect to public property that is not a designated public forum open for indiscriminate public use for communicative purposes, we have said that "[c]ontrol over access to a nonpublic forum can be based on subject matter and speaker identity so long as the distinctions drawn are reasonable in ⊥**393** light of the purpose served by the forum and are viewpoint neutral." *Cornelius*, citing *Perry Education Assn.* The Court of Appeals appeared to recognize that the total ban on using District property for religious purposes could survive First Amendment challenge only if excluding this category of speech was reasonable and viewpoint neutral. The court's conclusion in this case was that Rule 7 met this test. We cannot agree with this holding, for Rule 7 was unconstitutionally applied in this case.

The Court of Appeals thought that the application of Rule 7 in this case was viewpoint neutral because it had been and would be applied in the same way to all uses of school property for religious purposes. That all religions and all uses for religious purposes are treated alike under Rule 7, however, does not answer the critical question whether it discriminates on the basis of viewpoint to permit school property to be used for the presentation of all views about family issues and child-rearing except those dealing with the subject matter from a religious standpoint.

There is no suggestion from the courts below or from the District or the State that a lecture or film about child-rearing and family values would not be a use for social or civic purposes otherwise permitted by Rule 10. That subject matter is not one that the District has placed off limits to any and all speakers. Nor is there any indication in the record before us that the application to exhibit the particular film involved here was or would have been denied for any reason other than the fact that the presentation would have ⊥**394** been from a religious perspective. In our view, denial on that basis was plainly invalid under our holding in *Cornelius*, that "[a]lthough a speaker may be excluded from a nonpublic forum if he wishes to address a topic not encompassed within the purpose of the forum . . . or if he is not a member of the class of speakers for whose special benefit the forum was created . . . the government violates the First Amendment when it denies access to a speaker solely to suppress the point of view he espouses on an otherwise includible subject."

The film involved here no doubt dealt with a subject otherwise permissible under Rule 10, and its exhibition was denied solely because the film dealt with the subject from a religious standpoint. The principle that has emerged from our cases "is that the First Amendment forbids the government to regulate speech in ways that favor some viewpoints or ideas at the expense of others." *City Council of Los Angeles* v. *Taxpayers for Vincent*. That principle applies in the circumstances of this case; as Judge Posner said for the Seventh Circuit Court of Appeals, to discriminate "against a particular point of view . . . would . . . flunk the test . . . [of] *Cornelius*, provided that the defendants have no defense based on the establishment clause." *May* v. *Evansville-Vanderburgh School Corp*.

The District, as a respondent, would save its judgment below on the ground that to permit its property to be used for religious purposes would be an establishment of religion forbidden by the First Amendment. This Court suggested in *Widmar* v. *Vincent*, that the interest of the State in avoiding an Establishment Clause violation "may be [a] compelling" one justifying an abridgment of free speech otherwise protected by the First Amendment; but the Court went on to hold that permitting use of Univer⊥**395**sity property for religious purposes under the open access policy involved there would not be incompatible with the Court's Establishment Clause cases.

We have no more trouble than did the *Widmar* Court in disposing of the claimed defense on the ground that the posited fears of an Establishment Clause violation are unfounded. The showing of this film would not have been during school hours, would not have been sponsored by the school, and would have been open to the public, not just to church members. The District property had repeatedly been used by a wide variety of private organizations. Under these circumstances, as in *Widmar*, there would have been no realistic danger that the community would think that the District was endorsing religion or any particular creed, and any benefit to religion or to the Church would have been no more than incidental. As in *Widmar*, permitting District property to be used to exhibit the film involved in this case would not have been an establishment of religion under the three-part test articulated in *Lemon* v. *Kurtzman:* The challenged governmental action has a secular purpose, does not have the principal or primary effect of advancing or inhibiting religion, and does not foster an excessive entanglement with religion.

The District also submits that it justifiably denied use of its property to a "radical" church for the purpose of proselytizing, since to do so would lead to threats of public unrest and even violence. ⊥**396** There is nothing in the record to support such a justification, which in any event would be difficult to defend as a reason to deny the presentation of a religious point of view about a subject the District otherwise makes open to discussion on District property.

We note that the Attorney General for the State of New York, a respondent here, does not rely on either the Establishment Clause or possible danger to the public peace in supporting the judgment below. Rather, he submits that the exclusion is justified because the purpose of the access rules is to promote the interests of the public in general rather than sectarian or other private interests. In light of the variety of the uses of District property that have been permitted under Rule 10, this approach has its difficulties. This is particularly so since Rule 10 states that District property may be used for social, civic, or recreational use "only if it can be nonexclusive and open to all residents of the school district that form a homogeneous group deemed relevant to the event." At least arguably, the Rule does not require that permitted uses need be open to the public at large. However that may be, this was not the basis of the judgment that we are reviewing. The Court of Appeals, as we understand it, ruled that because the District had the power to permit or exclude certain subject matters, it was entitled to deny use for any religious purpose, including the purpose in this case. The Attorney General also defends this as a permissible subject-matter exclusion rather than a denial based on viewpoint, a submission that we have already rejected.

The Attorney General also argues that there is no express finding below that the Church's application would have been granted absent the religious connection. This fact is beside the point for the purposes of this opinion, which is concerned with the validity of the stated reason for denying the ⊥**397** Church's application, namely, that the film sought to be shown "appeared to be church related."

For the reasons stated in this opinion, the judgment of the Court of Appeals is

Reversed.

Justice KENNEDY, concurring in part and concurring in the judgment.

Given the issues presented as well as the apparent unanimity of our conclusion that this overt, viewpoint-based discrimination contradicts the Speech Clause of the First Amendment and that there has been no substantial showing of a potential Establishment Clause violation, I agree with *Justice* SCALIA that the Court's citation of *Lemon* v. *Kurtzman* is unsettling and unnecessary. The same can be said of the Court's use of the phrase "endorsing religion," which, as I have indicated elsewhere, cannot suffice as a rule of decision consistent with our precedents and our traditions in this part of our jurisprudence. See *Allegheny County* v. *American Civil Liberties Union, Greater Pittsburgh Chapter* (Kennedy, J., concurring in judgment in part and dissenting in part). With these observations, I concur in part and concur in the judgment.

Justice SCALIA, with whom *Justice* THOMAS joins, concurring in the judgment.

I join the Court's conclusion that the District's refusal to allow use of school facilities for petitioners' film viewing, while generally opening the schools for community activities, violates petitioners' First Amendment free-speech rights (as does N. Y. Educ. Law § 414 (McKinney 1988 and Supp. 1993), to the extent it compelled the District's denial). I also agree with the Court that allowing Lamb's Chapel to use school facilities poses "no realistic danger" of a violation of the Establishment Clause, ⊥**398** but I cannot accept most of its reasoning in this regard. The Court explains that the showing of petitioners' film on school property after school hours would not cause the community to "think that the District was endorsing religion or any particular creed," and further notes that access to school property would not violate the three-part test articulated in *Lemon* v. *Kurtzman*.

As to the Court's invocation of the *Lemon* test: Like some ghoul in a late-night horror movie that repeatedly sits up in its grave and shuffles abroad, after being repeatedly killed and buried, *Lemon* stalks our Establishment Clause jurisprudence once again, frightening the little children and school attorneys of Center Moriches Union Free School District. Its most recent burial, only last Term, was, to be sure, not fully six-feet under: our decision in *Lee* v. *Weisman*, conspicuously avoided using the supposed "test" but also declined the invitation to repudiate it. Over the years, however, no fewer than five of the currently sitting Justices have, in their own opinions, personally driven pencils through the creature's heart (the author of today's opinion repeatedly), and a sixth has joined an opinion doing so. See, *e.g.*, *Weisman* (Scalia, J., joined by, *inter alios*, Thomas, J., dissenting); *Allegheny County* v. *American Civil Liberties Union, Greater Pittsburgh Chapter* (Kennedy, J., concurring in judgment in part and dissenting in part); *Corporation of Presiding Bishop of Church of Jesus Christ of Latter-day Saints* v. *Amos* (O'Connor, J., concurring); *Wallace* v. *Jaffree* (Rehnquist, J., dissenting), (White, J., dissenting); *School Dist. of Grand Rapids* v. *Ball* (White, J., dissenting); *Widmar* v. *Vincent* (White, J., dissenting); *New York* v. *Cathedral Academy* ⊥**399** (White, J., dissenting); *Roemer* v. *Maryland Bd. of Public Works* (White, J., concurring in judgment); *Committee for Public Education & Religious Liberty* v. *Nyquist* (White, J., dissenting).

The secret of the *Lemon* test's survival, I think, is that it is so easy to kill. It is there to scare us (and our audience) when we wish it to do so, but we can command it to return to the tomb at will. See, *e.g.*, *Lynch* v. *Donnelly* (noting instances in which Court has not applied *Lemon* test). When we wish to strike down a practice it forbids, we invoke it, see, *e.g.*, *Aguilar* v. *Felton* (striking down state remedial education program administered in part in parochial schools); when we wish to uphold a practice it forbids, we ignore it entirely, see *Marsh* v. *Chambers* (upholding state legislative chaplains). Sometimes, we take a middle course, calling its three prongs "no more than helpful signposts," *Hunt* v. *McNair*. Such a docile and useful monster is worth keeping around, at least in a somnolent state; one never knows when one might need him.

For my part, I agree with the long list of constitutional scholars who have criticized *Lemon* and bemoaned the strange Establishment Clause geometry of crooked lines and wavering shapes its intermittent use has produced. See, *e.g.*, Choper, The Establishment Clause and Aid to Parochial Schools—An Update, 75 Cal. L. Rev. 5 (1987); Marshall, "We Know It When We See It": The Supreme Court and Establishment, 59 S. Cal. L. Rev. 495 (1986); McConnell, Accommodation of Religion, 1985 S. Ct. Rev. 1; Kurland, The Religion Clauses and the Burger Court, 34 Cath. U. L. Rev. 1 (1984); R. Cord, Separation of Church and State (1982); Choper, The Religion Clauses of the First Amendment: Reconciling the Conflict, 41 U. Pitt. L. Rev. 673 (1980). I will decline to apply *Lemon*—whether it vali⊥**400**dates or invalidates the government action in question—and therefore cannot join the opinion of the Court today.

I cannot join for yet another reason: the Court's statement that the proposed use of the school's facilities is constitutional because (among other things) it would not signal endorsement of religion in general. What a strange notion, that a Constitution which *itself* gives "religion in general" preferential treatment (I refer to the Free Exercise Clause) forbids endorsement of religion in general. The Attorney General of New York not only agrees with that strange notion, he has an explanation for it: "Religious advocacy," he writes, "serves the community only in the eyes of its adherents and yields a benefit only to those who already believe." That was *not* the view of those who adopted our Constitution, who believed that the public virtues inculcated by religion are a public good. It suffices to point out that during the summer of 1789, when it was in the process of drafting the First Amendment, Congress enacted the famous Northwest Territory Ordinance of 1789, Article III of which provides, "Religion, morality, and knowledge, *being necessary to good government and the happiness of mankind*, schools and the means of education shall forever be encouraged." 1 Stat. 52 (emphasis added). Unsurprisingly, then, indifference to "religion in general" is *not* what our cases, both old and recent, demand. See, *e.g.*, *Zorach* v. *Clauson* ("When the state encourages reli⊥**401**gious instruction or cooperates with religious authorities by adjusting the schedule of public events to sectarian needs, it follows the best of our traditions"); *Walz* v. *Tax Comm'n of New York City* (upholding property tax exemption for church property); *Lynch* (the Constitution "affirmatively mandates accommodation, not merely tolerance, of all religions. . . . Anything less would require the 'callous indifference' we have said was never intended"); *id.*, ("our precedents plainly contemplate that on occasion some advancement of religion will result from governmental action"); *Marsh*, *Presiding Bishop* (exemption for religious organizations from certain provisions of Civil Rights Act).

. . . . .

For the reasons given by the Court, I agree that the Free Speech Clause of the First Amendment forbids what respondents have done here. As for the asserted Establishment Clause justification, I would hold, simply and clearly, that giving Lamb's Chapel nondiscriminatory access to school facilities cannot violate that provision because it does not signify state or local embrace of a particular religious sect.

RONALD W. ROSENBERGER v. RECTOR and VISITORS OF THE UNIVERSITY OF VIRGINIA

115 S. Ct. 2510
ON WRIT OF CERTIORARI TO THE UNITED STATES COURT OF APPEALS FOR THE FOURTH CIRCUIT
Argued March 1, 1995 — Decided June 29, 1995

⊥**2513** *Justice KENNEDY* delivered the opinion of the Court.

The University of Virginia, an instrumentality of the Commonwealth for which it is named and thus bound by the First and Fourteenth Amendments, authorizes the payment of outside contractors for the printing costs of a variety of student publications. It withheld any authorization for payments on behalf of petitioners for the sole reason that their student paper "primarily promotes or manifests a particular belie[f] in or about a deity or an ultimate reality." That the paper did promote or manifest views within the defined exclusion seems plain enough. The challenge is to the University's regulation and its denial of authorization, the case raising issues under the Speech and Establishment Clauses of the First Amendment.

⊥2514 I

The public corporation we refer to as the "University" is denominated by state law as "the Rector and Visitors of the University of Virginia," Va. Code Ann. § 23-69 (1993), and it is responsible for governing the school, see §§ 23-69 to 23-80. Founded by Thomas Jefferson in 1819, and ranked by him, together with the authorship of the Declaration of Independence and of the Virginia Act for Religious Freedom, Va. Code Ann. § 57-1, as one of his proudest achievements, the University is among the Nation's oldest and most respected seats of higher learning. It has more than 11,000 undergraduate students, and 6,000 graduate and professional students. An understanding of the case requires a somewhat detailed description of the program the University created to support extracurricular student activities on its campus.

Before a student group is eligible to submit bills from its outside contractors for payment by the fund described below, it must become a "Contracted Independent Organization" (CIO). CIO status is available to any group the majority of whose members are students, whose managing officers are full-time students, and that complies with certain procedural requirements. A CIO must file its constitution with the University; must pledge not to discriminate in its membership; and must include in dealings with third parties and in all written materials a disclaimer, stating that the CIO is independent of the University and that the University is not responsible for the CIO. CIOs enjoy access to University facilities, including meeting rooms and computer terminals. A standard agreement signed between each CIO and the University provides that the benefits and opportunities afforded to CIOs "should not be misinterpreted as meaning that those organizations are part of or controlled by the University, that the University is responsible for the organizations' contracts or other acts or omissions, or that the University approves of the organizations' goals or activities."

All CIOs may exist and operate at the University, but some are also entitled to apply for funds from the Student Activities Fund (SAF). Established and governed by University Guidelines, the purpose of the SAF is to support a broad range of extracurricular student activities that "are related to the educational purpose of the University." The SAF is based on the University's "recogni[tion] that the availability of a wide range of opportunities" for its students "tends to enhance the University environment." The Guidelines require that it be administered "in a manner consistent with the educational purpose of the University as well as with state and federal law." The SAF receives its money from a mandatory fee of $14 per semester assessed to each full-time student. The Student Council, elected by the students, has the initial authority to disburse the funds, but its actions are subject to review by a faculty body chaired by a designee of the Vice President for Student Affairs.

Some, but not all, CIOs may submit disbursement requests to the SAF. The Guidelines recognize 11 categories of student groups that may seek payment to third-party contractors because they "are related to the educational purpose of the University of Virginia." One of these is "student news, information, opinion, entertainment, or academic communications media groups." The Guidelines also specify, however, that the costs of certain activities of CIOs that are otherwise eligible for funding will not be reimbursed by the SAF. The student activities which are excluded from SAF support are religious activities, philanthropic contributions and activities, political activities, activities that would jeopardize the University's tax-exempt status, those which involve payment of honoraria or similar fees, or social entertainment or related expenses. The prohibition on "political activities" is defined so that it is limited to electioneering and lobbying. The Guidelines provide that "[t]hese restrictions on funding political activities are not intended to preclude funding of any otherwise eligible student organization which . . . espouses particular positions or ideological viewpoints, including those that may be **⊥2515** unpopular or are not generally accepted." A "religious activity," by contrast, is defined as any activity that "primarily promotes or manifests a particular belie[f] in or about a deity or an ultimate reality."

The Guidelines prescribe these criteria for determining the amounts of third-party disbursements that will be allowed on behalf of each eligible student organization: the size of the group, its financial self-sufficiency, and the University-wide benefit of its activities. If an organization seeks SAF support, it must submit its bills to the Student Council, which pays the organization's creditors upon determining that the expenses are appropriate. No direct payments are made to the student groups. During the 1990–1991 academic year, 343 student groups qualified as CIOs. One hundred thirty-five of them applied for support from the SAF, and 118 received funding. Fifteen of the groups were funded as "student news, information, opinion, entertainment, or academic communications media groups."

Petitioners' organization, Wide Awake Productions (WAP), qualified as a CIO. Formed by petitioner Ronald Rosenberger and other undergraduates in 1990,

WAP was established "[t]o publish a magazine of philosophical and religious expression," "[t]o facilitate discussion which fosters an atmosphere of sensitivity to and tolerance of Christian viewpoints," and "[t]o provide a unifying focus for Christians of multicultural backgrounds." WAP publishes Wide Awake: A Christian Perspective at the University of Virginia. The paper's Christian viewpoint was evident from the first issue, in which its editors wrote that the journal "offers a Christian perspective on both personal and community issues, especially those relevant to college students at the University of Virginia." The editors committed the paper to a two-fold mission: "to challenge Christians to live, in word and deed, according to the faith they proclaim and to encourage students to consider what a personal relationship with Jesus Christ means." The first issue had articles about racism, crisis pregnancy, stress, prayer, C. S. Lewis' ideas about evil and free will, and reviews of religious music. In the next two issues, Wide Awake featured stories about homosexuality, Christian missionary work, and eating disorders, as well as music reviews and interviews with University professors. Each page of Wide Awake, and the end of each article or review, is marked by a cross. The advertisements carried in Wide Awake also reveal the Christian perspective of the journal. For the most part, the advertisers are churches, centers for Christian study, or Christian bookstores. By June 1992, WAP had distributed about 5,000 copies of Wide Awake to University students, free of charge.

WAP had acquired CIO status soon after it was organized. This is an important consideration in this case, for had it been a "religious organization," WAP would not have been accorded CIO status. As defined by the Guidelines, a "religious organization" is "an organization whose purpose is to practice a devotion to an acknowledged ultimate reality or deity." At no stage in this controversy has the University contended that WAP is such an organization.

A few months after being given CIO status, WAP requested the SAF to pay its printer $5,862 for the costs of printing its newspaper. The Appropriations Committee of the Student Council denied WAP's request on the ground that Wide Awake was a "religious activity" within the meaning of the Guidelines, *i.e.*, that the newspaper "promote[d] or manifest[ed] a particular belie[f] in or about a deity or an ultimate reality." It made its determination after examining the first issue. WAP appealed the denial to the full Student Council, contending that WAP met all the applicable Guidelines and that denial of SAF support on the basis of the magazine's religious perspective violated the Constitution. The appeal was denied without further comment, and WAP appealed to the next level, the Student Activities Committee. In a letter signed by the Dean of Students, the committee sustained the denial of funding.

Having no further recourse within the University structure, WAP, Wide Awake, and three of its editors and members filed suit in ⊥**2516** the United States District Court for the Western District of Virginia, challenging the SAF's action as violative of Rev. Stat. § 1979, 42 U. S. C. § 1983. They alleged that refusal to authorize payment of the printing costs of the publication, solely on the basis of its religious editorial viewpoint, violated their rights to freedom of speech and press, to the free exercise of religion, and to equal protection of the law. They relied also upon Article I of the Virginia Constitution and the Virginia Act for Religious Freedom, Va. Code Ann. §§ 57-1, 57-2 (1986 and Supp. 1994), but did not pursue those theories on appeal. The suit sought damages for the costs of printing the paper, injunctive and declaratory relief, and attorney's fees.

On cross-motions for summary judgment, the District Court ruled for the University, holding that denial of SAF support was not an impermissible content or viewpoint discrimination against petitioners' speech, and that the University's Establishment Clause concern over its "religious activities" was a sufficient justification for denying payment to third-party contractors. The court did not issue a definitive ruling on whether reimbursement, had it been made here, would or would not have violated the Establishment Clause. 795 F. Supp. 175, 181-182 (WD Va. 1992).

The United States Court of Appeals for the Fourth Circuit, in disagreement with the District Court, held that the Guidelines did discriminate on the basis of content. It ruled that, while the State need not underwrite speech, there was a presumptive violation of the Speech Clause when viewpoint discrimination was invoked to deny third-party payment otherwise available to CIOs. 18 F. 3d 269, 279-281 (1994). The Court of Appeals affirmed the judgment of the District Court nonetheless, concluding that the discrimination by the University was justified by the "compelling interest in maintaining strict separation of church and state."

II

It is axiomatic that the government may not regulate speech based on its substantive content or the message it conveys. *Police Dept. of Chicago* v. *Mosley*. Other principles follow from this precept. In the realm of private speech or expression, government regulation may not favor one speaker over another. *City Council of Los Angeles* v. *Taxpayers for Vincent*. Discrimination against speech because of its message is presumed to be unconstitutional. See *Turner Broadcasting System, Inc.* v. *FCC*. These rules informed our determination that the government offends the First Amendment when it imposes financial burdens on certain speakers based on the content of their expression. *Simon & Schuster, Inc.* v. *Members of N. Y. State Crime Victims Bd.* When the government targets not subject matter but particular views taken by speakers on a subject, the violation of the First Amendment is all the more blatant. See *R. A. V.* v. *St. Paul*. Viewpoint discrimination is thus an egregious form of content discrimination. The government must abstain from regulating speech when the specific motivating ideology or the opinion or perspective of the speaker is the rationale for the restriction. See *Perry Ed. Assn.* v. *Perry Local Educators' Assn.*

These principles provide the framework forbidding the State from exercising viewpoint discrimination, even when the limited public forum is one of its own creation. In a case involving a school district's provision of school facilities for private uses, we declared that "[t]here is no question that the District, like the private owner of property, may legally preserve the property under its control for the use to which it is dedicated." *Lamb's Chapel* v. *Center Moriches Union Free School Dist.* The necessities of confining a forum to the limited and legitimate purposes for which it was created may justify the State in reserving it for certain groups or for the discussion **⊥2517** of certain topics. See, *e.g.*, *Cornelius* v. *NAACP Legal Defense & Ed. Fund, Inc.*; *Perry Ed. Assn.* Once it has opened a limited forum, however, the State must respect the lawful boundaries it has itself set. The State may not exclude speech where its distinction is not "reasonable in light of the purpose served by the forum," *Cornelius*, nor may it discriminate against speech on the basis of its viewpoint, *Lamb's Chapel.* Thus, in determining whether the State is acting to preserve the limits of the forum it has created so that the exclusion of a class of speech is legitimate, we have observed a distinction between, on the one hand, content discrimination, which may be permissible if it preserves the purposes of that limited forum, and, on the other hand, viewpoint discrimination, which is presumed impermissible when directed against speech otherwise within the forum's limitations. See *Perry Ed. Assn.*

The SAF is a forum more in a metaphysical than in a spatial or geographic sense, but the same principles are applicable. See, *e.g.*, *Perry Ed. Assn.* (forum analysis of a school mail system); *Cornelius* (forum analysis of charitable contribution program). The most recent and most apposite case is our decision in *Lamb's Chapel.* There, a school district had opened school facilities for use after school hours by community groups for a wide variety of social, civic, and recreational purposes. The district, however, had enacted a formal policy against opening facilities to groups for religious purposes. Invoking its policy, the district rejected a request from a group desiring to show a film series addressing various child-rearing questions from a "Christian perspective." There was no indication in the record in *Lamb's Chapel* that the request to use the school facilities was "denied for any reason other than the fact that the presentation would have been from a religious perspective." Our conclusion was unanimous: "[I]t discriminates on the basis of viewpoint to permit school property to be used for the presentation of all views about family issues and child-rearing except those dealing with the subject matter from a religious standpoint."

The University does acknowledge (as it must in light of our precedents) that "ideologically driven attempts to suppress a particular point of view are presumptively unconstitutional in funding, as in other contexts," but insists that this case does not present that issue because the Guidelines draw lines based on content, not viewpoint. As we have noted, discrimination against one set of views or ideas is but a subset or particular instance of the more general phenomenon of content discrimination. See, *e.g.*, *R. A. V.* And, it must be acknowledged, the distinction is not a precise one. It is, in a sense, something of an understatement to speak of religious thought and discussion as just a viewpoint, as distinct from a comprehensive body of thought. The nature of our origins and destiny and their dependence upon the existence of a divine being have been subjects of philosophic inquiry throughout human history. We conclude, nonetheless, that here, as in *Lamb's Chapel*, viewpoint discrimination is the proper way to interpret the University's objections to Wide Awake. By the very terms of the SAF prohibition, the University does not exclude religion as a subject matter but selects for disfavored treatment those student journalistic efforts with religious editorial viewpoints. Religion may be a vast area of inquiry, but it also provides, as it did here, a specific premise, a perspective, a standpoint from which a variety of subjects may be discussed and considered. The prohibited perspective, not the general subject matter, resulted in the refusal to make third-party payments, for the subjects discussed were **⊥2518** otherwise within the approved category of publications.

The dissent's assertion that no viewpoint discrimination occurs because the Guidelines discriminate against an entire class of viewpoints reflects an insupportable assumption that all debate is bipolar and that anti-religious speech is the only response to religious speech. Our understanding of the complex and multifaceted nature of public discourse has not embraced such a contrived description of the marketplace of ideas. If the topic of debate is, for example, racism, then exclusion of several views on that problem is just as offensive to the First Amendment as exclusion of only one. It is as objectionable to exclude both a theistic and an atheistic perspective on the debate as it is to exclude one, the other, or yet another political, economic, or social viewpoint. The dissent's declaration that debate is not skewed so long as multiple voices are silenced is simply wrong; the debate is skewed in multiple ways.

The University's denial of WAP's request for third-party payments in the present case is based upon viewpoint discrimination not unlike the discrimination the school district relied upon in *Lamb's Chapel* and that we found invalid. The church group in *Lamb's Chapel* would have been qualified as a social or civic organization, save for its religious purposes. Furthermore, just as the school district in *Lamb's Chapel* pointed to nothing but the religious views of the group as the rationale for excluding its message, so in this case the University justifies its denial of SAF participation to WAP on the ground that the contents of Wide Awake reveal an avowed religious perspective. It bears only passing mention that the dissent's attempt to distinguish *Lamb's Chapel* is entirely without support in the law. Relying on the transcript of oral argument, the dissent seems to argue that we found viewpoint discrimination in that case because the government excluded Christian, but not atheistic, viewpoints from being expressed in the forum there. The Court relied on no such distinction in holding that discriminating against religious speech was discriminating on the basis of viewpoint. There is no indication in the opinion of the Court (which, unlike an advocate's statements at oral argument, is the law) that exclusion or inclusion of other religious or antireligious voices from that forum had any bearing on its decision.

The University tries to escape the consequences of our holding in *Lamb's Chapel* by urging that this case involves the provision of funds rather than access to facilities. The University begins with the unremarkable proposition that the State must have substantial discretion in determining how to allocate scarce resources to accomplish its educational mission. Citing our decisions in *Rust* v. *Sullivan*, *Regan* v. *Taxation with Representation of Wash.*, and *Widmar* v. *Vincent*, the University argues that content-based funding decisions are both inevitable and lawful. Were the reasoning of *Lamb's Chapel* to apply to funding decisions as well as to those involving access to facilities, it is urged, its holding "would become a judicial juggernaut, constitutionalizing the ubiquitous content-based decisions that schools, colleges, and other government entities routinely make in the allocation of public funds."

To this end the University relies on our assurance in *Widmar* v. *Vincent*. There, in the course of striking down a public university's exclusion of religious groups from use of school facilities made available to all other student groups, we stated: "Nor do we question the right of the University to make academic judgments as to how best to allocate scarce resources." The quoted language in *Widmar* was but a proper recognition of the principle that when the State is the speaker, it may make content-based choices. When the University determines the content of the education it provides, it is the University speaking, and we have permitted the government to regulate the content of what is or is not expressed when it is the speaker or when it enlists private entities to convey its own message. In the same vein, in *Rust* v. *Sulli*⊥**2519***van* we upheld the government's prohibition on abortion-related advice applicable to recipients of federal funds for family planning counseling. There, the government did not create a program to encourage private speech but instead used private speakers to transmit specific information pertaining to its own program. We recognized that when the government appropriates public funds to promote a particular policy of its own it is entitled to say what it wishes. When the government disburses public funds to private entities to convey a governmental message, it may take legitimate and appropriate steps to ensure that its message is neither garbled nor distorted by the grantee.

It does not follow, however, and we did not suggest in *Widmar*, that viewpoint-based restrictions are proper when the University does not itself speak or subsidize transmittal of a message it favors but instead expends funds to encourage a diversity of views from private speakers. A holding that the University may not discriminate based on the viewpoint of private persons whose speech it facilitates does not restrict the University's own speech, which is controlled by different principles. See, *e.g.*, *Board of Ed. of Westside Community Schools (Dist. 66)* v. *Mergens*; *Hazelwood School Dist.* v. *Kuhlmeier*. For that reason, the University's reliance on *Regan* v. *Taxation with Representation of Wash.* is inapposite as well. *Regan* involved a challenge to Congress' choice to grant tax deductions for contributions made to veterans' groups engaged in lobbying, while denying that favorable status to other charities which pursued lobbying efforts. Although acknowledging that the Government is not required to subsidize the exercise of fundamental rights, we reaffirmed the requirement of viewpoint neutrality in the Government's provision of financial benefits by observing that "[t]he case would be different if Congress were to discriminate invidiously in its subsidies in such a way as to 'ai[m] at the suppression of dangerous ideas'" (quoting *Cammarano* v. *United States*, in turn quoting *Speiser* v. *Randall*). *Regan* relied on a distinction based on preferential treatment of certain speakers—veterans organizations—and not a distinction based on the content or messages of those groups' speech. The University's regulation now before us, however, has a speech-based restriction as its sole rationale and operative principle.

The distinction between the University's own favored message and the private speech of students is evident in the case before us. The University itself has taken steps to ensure the distinction in the agreement each CIO must sign. The University declares that the student groups eligible for SAF support are not the University's agents, are not subject to its control, and are not its responsibility. Having offered to pay the third-party contractors on behalf of private speakers who convey their own messages, the University may not silence the expression of selected viewpoints.

The University urges that, from a constitutional standpoint, funding of speech differs from provision of access to facilities because money is scarce and physical facilities are not. Beyond the fact that in any given case this proposition might not be true as an empirical matter, the underlying premise that the University could discriminate based on viewpoint if demand for space exceeded its availability is wrong as well. The government cannot justify viewpoint discrimination among private speakers on the economic fact of scarcity. Had the meeting rooms in *Lamb's Chapel* been scarce, had the demand been greater than the supply, our decision would have been no different. It would have been incumbent on the State, of course, to ration or allocate the scarce resources on some acceptable neutral principle; but nothing in our decision indicated that scarcity would give the State the right to ⊥**2520** exercise viewpoint discrimination that is otherwise impermissible.

Vital First Amendment speech principles are at stake here. The first danger to liberty lies in granting the State the power to examine publications to determine whether or not they are based on some ultimate idea and if so for the State to classify them. The second, and corollary, danger is to speech from the chilling of individual thought and expression. That danger is especially real in the University setting, where the State acts against a background and tradition of thought and experiment that is at the center of our intellectual and philosophic tradition. In ancient Athens, and, as Europe entered into a new period of intellectual awakening, in places like Bologna, Oxford, and Paris, universities began as voluntary and spontaneous assemblages or concourses for students to speak and to write and to learn. The quality and creative power of student intellectual life to this day remains a vital measure of a school's influence and attainment. For the University, by regulation, to cast disapproval on particular viewpoints of its students risks the suppression of free speech and creative inquiry in one of the vital centers for the nation's intellectual life, its college and university campuses.

The Guideline invoked by the University to deny third-party contractor payments on behalf of WAP effects a sweeping restriction on student thought and student inquiry in the context of University sponsored publications. The prohibition on funding on behalf of publications that "primarily promot[e] or manifes[t] a particular belie[f] in or about a deity or an ultimate reality," in its ordinary and commonsense meaning, has a vast potential reach. The term "promotes" as used here would comprehend any writing advocating a philosophic position that rests upon a belief in a deity or ultimate reality. See Webster's Third New International Dictionary 1815 (1961) (defining "promote" as "to contribute to the growth, enlargement, or prosperity of: further, encourage"). And the term "manifests" would bring within the scope of the prohibition any writing that is explicable as resting upon a premise which presupposes the existence of a deity or ultimate reality. See *id.*, at 1375 (defining "manifest" as "to show plainly: make palpably evident or certain by showing or displaying"). Were the prohibition applied with much vigor at all, it would bar funding of essays by hypothetical student contributors named Plato, Spinoza, and Descartes. And if the regulation covers, as the University says it does, those student journalistic efforts which primarily manifest or promote a belief that there is no deity and no ultimate reality, then undergraduates named Karl Marx, Bertrand Russell, and Jean-Paul Sartre would likewise have some of their major essays excluded from student publications. If any manifestation of beliefs in first principles disqualifies the writing, as seems to be the case, it is indeed difficult to name renowned thinkers whose writings would be accepted, save perhaps for articles disclaiming all connection to their ultimate philosophy. Plato could contrive perhaps to submit an acceptable essay on making pasta or peanut butter cookies, provided he did not point out their (necessary) imperfections.

Based on the principles we have discussed, we hold that the regulation invoked to deny SAF support, both in its terms and in its application to these petitioners, is a denial of their right of free speech guaranteed by the First Amendment. It remains to be considered whether the violation following from the University's action is excused by the necessity of complying with the Constitution's prohibition against state establishment of religion. We turn to that question.

III

Before its brief on the merits in this Court, the University had argued at all stages of the litigation that inclusion of WAP's contractors in SAF funding authorization would violate the Establishment Clause. Indeed, that is ⊥**2521** the ground on which the University prevailed in the Court of Appeals. We granted certiorari on this question: "Whether the Establishment Clause compels a state university to exclude an otherwise eligible student publication from participation in the student activities fund, solely on the basis of its religious viewpoint, where such exclusion would violate the Speech and Press Clauses if the viewpoint of the publication were nonreligious." The University now seems to have abandoned this position, contending that "[t]he fundamental objection to petitioners' argument is not that it implicates the Establishment Clause but that it would defeat the ability of public education at all levels to control the use of public funds." That the University itself no longer presses the Establishment Clause claim is some indication that it lacks force; but as the Court of Appeals rested its judgment on the point and our dissenting colleagues would find it determinative, it must be addressed.

The Court of Appeals ruled that withholding SAF support from Wide Awake contravened the Speech Clause of the First Amendment, but proceeded to hold that the University's action was justified by the necessity of avoiding a violation of the Establishment Clause, an interest it found compelling. Recognizing that this Court has regularly "sanctioned awards of direct nonmonetary benefits to religious groups where the government has created open fora to which all similarly situated organizations are invited," the Fourth Circuit asserted that direct monetary subsidization of religious organizations and projects is "a beast of an entirely different color." The court declared that the Establishment Clause would not permit the use of public funds to support "'a specifically religious activity in an otherwise substantially secular setting.'" It reasoned that because Wide Awake is "a journal pervasively devoted to the discussion and advancement of an avowedly Christian theological and personal philosophy," the University's provision of SAF funds for its publication would "send an unmistakably clear signal that the University of Virginia supports

Christian values and wishes to promote the wide promulgation of such values." If there is to be assurance that the Establishment Clause retains its force in guarding against those governmental actions it was intended to prohibit, we must in each case inquire first into the purpose and object of the governmental action in question and then into the practical details of the program's operation. Before turning to these matters, however, we can set forth certain general principles that must bear upon our determination.

A central lesson of our decisions is that a significant factor in upholding governmental programs in the face of Establishment Clause attack is their neutrality towards religion. We have decided a series of cases addressing the receipt of government benefits where religion or religious views are implicated in some degree. The first case in our modern Establishment Clause jurisprudence was *Everson* v. *Board of Ed. of Ewing*. There we cautioned that in enforcing the prohibition against laws respecting establishment of religion, we must "be sure that we do not inadvertently prohibit [the government] from extending its general state law benefits to all its citizens without regard to their religious belief." We have held that the guarantee of neutrality is respected, not offended, when the government, following neutral criteria and evenhanded policies, extends benefits to recipients whose ideologies and viewpoints, including religious ones, are broad and diverse. See *Board of Ed. of Kiryas Joel Village School Dist.* v. *Grumet*, (Souter, J.) ("[T]he principle is well grounded in our case law [and] we have frequently relied explicitly on the general availability of any benefit provided religious groups or individuals in turning aside Establishment Clause challenges"); *Witters* v. *Washington Dept. of Services for Blind;* **⊥2522** *Mueller* v. *Allen; Widmar*. More than once have we rejected the position that the Establishment Clause even justifies, much less requires, a refusal to extend free speech rights to religious speakers who participate in broad-reaching government programs neutral in design. See *Lamb's Chapel; Mergens; Widmar*.

The governmental program here is neutral toward religion. There is no suggestion that the University created it to advance religion or adopted some ingenious device with the purpose of aiding a religious cause. The object of the SAF is to open a forum for speech and to support various student enterprises, including the publication of newspapers, in recognition of the diversity and creativity of student life. The University's SAF Guidelines have a separate classification for, and do not make third-party payments on behalf of, "religious organizations," which are those "whose purpose is to practice a devotion to an acknowledged ultimate reality or deity." The category of support here is for "student news, information, opinion, entertainment, or academic communications media groups," of which Wide Awake was 1 of 15 in the 1990 school year. WAP did not seek a subsidy because of its Christian editorial viewpoint; it sought funding as a student journal, which it was.

The neutrality of the program distinguishes the student fees from a tax levied for the direct support of a church or group of churches. A tax of that sort, of course, would run contrary to Establishment Clause concerns dating from the earliest days of the Republic. The apprehensions of our predecessors involved the levying of taxes upon the public for the sole and exclusive purpose of establishing and supporting specific sects. The exaction here, by contrast, is a student activity fee designed to reflect the reality that student life in its many dimensions includes the necessity of wide-ranging speech and inquiry and that student expression is an integral part of the University's educational mission. The fee is mandatory, and we do not have before us the question whether an objecting student has the First Amendment right to demand a pro rata return to the extent the fee is expended for speech to which he or she does not subscribe. We must treat it, then, as an exaction upon the students. But the $14 paid each semester by the students is not a general tax designed to raise revenue for the University. See *United States* v. *Butler* ("A tax, in the general understanding of the term, and as used in the Constitution, signifies an exaction for the support of the Government"); see also *Head Money Cases*. The SAF cannot be used for unlimited purposes, much less the illegitimate purpose of supporting one religion. Much like the arrangement in *Widmar*, the money goes to a special fund from which any group of students with CIO status can draw for purposes consistent with the University's educational mission; and to the extent the student is interested in speech, withdrawal is permitted to cover the whole spectrum of speech, whether it manifests a religious view, an antireligious view, or neither. Our decision, then, cannot be read as addressing an expenditure from a general tax fund. Here, the disbursements from the fund go to private contractors for the cost of printing that which is protected under the Speech Clause of the First Amendment. This is a far cry from a general public assessment designed and effected to provide financial support for a church.

Government neutrality is apparent in the State's overall scheme in a further meaningful respect. The program respects the critical difference "between *government* speech endorsing religion, which the Establishment Clause forbids, and *private* speech endorsing religion, which the Free Speech and Free Exercise Clauses protect." *Mergens* **⊥2523** (opinion of O'Connor, J.). In this case, "the government has not willfully fostered or encouraged" any mistaken impression that the student newspapers speak for the University. *Capitol Square Review and Advisory Bd.* v. *Pinette*. The University has taken pains to disassociate itself from the private speech involved in this case. The Court of Appeals' apparent concern that Wide Awake's religious orientation would be attributed to the University is not a plausible fear, and there is no real likelihood that the speech in question is being either endorsed or coerced by the State.

The Court of Appeals (and the dissent) are correct to extract from our decisions the principle that we have recognized special Establishment Clause dangers where the government makes direct money payments to sectarian institutions, citing *Roemer* v. *Board of Pub. Works of Md.*; *Bowen* v. *Kendrick*; *Hunt* v. *McNair*; *Tilton*; *Board of Ed. of Central School Dist. No. 1* v. *Allen*. The error is not in identifying the principle but in believing that it controls this case. Even assuming that WAP is no different from a church and that its speech is the same as the religious exercises conducted in *Widmar* (two points much in doubt), the Court of Appeals decided a case that was, in essence, not before it, and the dissent would have us do the same. We do not confront a case where, even under a neutral program that includes nonsectarian recipients, the government is making direct money payments to an institution or group that is engaged in religious activity. Neither the Court of Appeals nor the dissent, we believe, takes sufficient cognizance of the undisputed fact that no public funds flow directly to WAP's coffers.

It does not violate the Establishment Clause for a public university to grant access to its facilities on a religion-neutral basis to a wide spectrum of student groups, including groups which use meeting rooms for sectarian activities, accompanied by some devotional exercises. This is so even where the upkeep, maintenance, and repair of the facilities attributed to those uses is paid from a student activities fund to which students are required to contribute. The government usually acts by spending money. Even the provision of a meeting room, as in *Mergens* and *Widmar*, involved governmental expenditure, if only in the form of electricity and heating or cooling costs. The error made by the Court of Appeals, as well as by the dissent, lies in focusing on the money that is undoubtedly expended by the government, rather than on the nature of the benefit received by the recipient. If the expenditure of governmental funds is prohibited whenever those funds pay for a service that is, pursuant to a religion-neutral program, used by a group for sectarian purposes, then *Widmar*, *Mergens*, and *Lamb's Chapel* would have to be overruled. Given our holdings in these cases, it follows that a public university may maintain its own computer facility and give student groups access to that facility, including the use of the printers, on a religion neutral, say first-come-first-served, basis. If a religious student organization obtained access on that religion-neutral basis and used a computer to compose or a printer or copy machine to print speech with a religious content or viewpoint, the State's action in providing the group with access would no more violate the Establishment Clause than would giving those groups access to an assembly hall. ⊥**2524** There is no difference in logic or principle, and no difference of constitutional significance, between a school using its funds to operate a facility to which students have access, and a school paying a third-party contractor to operate the facility on its behalf. The latter occurs here. The University provides printing services to a broad spectrum of student newspapers qualified as CIOs by reason of their officers and membership. Any benefit to religion is incidental to the government's provision of secular services for secular purposes on a religion-neutral basis. Printing is a routine, secular, and recurring attribute of student life.

By paying outside printers, the University in fact attains a further degree of separation from the student publication, for it avoids the duties of supervision, escapes the costs of upkeep, repair, and replacement attributable to student use, and has a clear record of costs. As a result, and as in *Widmar*, the University can charge the SAF, and not the taxpayers as a whole, for the discrete activity in question. It would be formalistic for us to say that the University must forfeit these advantages and provide the services itself in order to comply with the Establishment Clause. It is, of course, true that if the State pays a church's bills it is subsidizing it, and we must guard against this abuse. That is not a danger here, based on the considerations we have advanced and for the additional reason that the student publication is not a religious institution, at least in the usual sense of that term as used in our case law, and it is not a religious organization as used in the University's own regulations. It is instead a publication involved in a pure forum for the expression of ideas, ideas that would be both incomplete and chilled were the Constitution to be interpreted to require that state officials and courts scan the publication to ferret out views that principally manifest a belief in a divine being.

Were the dissent's view to become law, it would require the University, in order to avoid a constitutional violation, to scrutinize the content of student speech, lest the expression in question—speech otherwise protected by the Constitution—contain too great a religious content. The dissent, in fact, anticipates such censorship as "crucial" in distinguishing between "works characterized by the evangelism of Wide Awake and writing that merely happens to express views that a given religion might approve." That eventuality raises the specter of governmental censorship, to ensure that all student writings and publications meet some baseline standard of secular orthodoxy. To impose that standard on student speech at a university is to imperil the very sources of free speech and expression. As we recognized in *Widmar*, official censorship would be far more inconsistent with the Establishment Clause's dictates than would governmental provision of secular printing services on a religion-blind basis.

"[T]he dissent fails to establish that the distinction [between 'religious' speech and speech 'about' religion] has intelligible content. There is no indication when 'singing hymns, reading scripture, and teaching biblical principles' cease to be 'singing, teaching, and reading'—all apparently forms of 'speech,' despite their religious subject matter—and become unprotected 'worship.' . . .

"[E]ven if the distinction drew an arguably principled line, it is highly doubtful that it would lie within the judicial competence to administer. Merely to draw the distinction would require the university—and ultimately the courts—to inquire into the significance of words and practices to different religious faiths, and in varying circumstances by the same faith. Such inquiries would tend inevitably to entangle the State with religion in a manner forbidden by our cases."

. . . . .

To obey the Establishment Clause, it was not necessary for the University to deny eligibility to student publications because of their viewpoint. The neutrality commanded of the State by the separate Clauses of the First Amendment was compromised by ⊥**2525** the University's course of action. The viewpoint discrimination inherent in the University's regulation required public officials to scan and interpret student publications to discern their underlying philosophic assumptions respecting religious theory and belief. That course of action was a denial of the right of free speech and would risk fostering a pervasive bias or hostility to religion, which could undermine the very neutrality the Establishment Clause requires. There is no Establishment Clause violation in the University's honoring its duties under the Free Speech Clause.

The judgment of the Court of Appeals must be, and is, reversed.

It is so ordered.

Justice O'CONNOR, concurring.

"We have time and again held that the government generally may not treat people differently based on the God or gods they worship, or don't worship." *Board of Ed. of Kiryas Joel Village School Dist.* v. *Grumet* (O'Connor, J., concurring in part and concurring in judgment). This insistence on government neutrality toward religion explains why we have held that schools may not discriminate against religious groups by denying them equal access to facilities that the schools make available to all. See *Lamb's Chapel* v. *Center Moriches Union Free School Dist.*; *Widmar* v. *Vincent*. Withholding access would leave an impermissible perception that religious activities are disfavored: "the message is one of neutrality rather than endorsement; if a State refused to let religious groups use facilities open to others, then it would demonstrate not neutrality but hostility toward religion." *Board of Ed. of Westside Community Schools (Dist. 66)* v. *Mergens*. "The Religion Clauses prohibit the government from favoring religion, but they provide no warrant for discriminating *against* religion." *Kiryas Joel* (O'Connor, J.). Neutrality, in both form and effect, is one hallmark of the Establishment Clause.

As *Justice* SOUTER demonstrates, however, there exists another axiom in the history and precedent of the Establishment Clause. "Public funds may not be used to endorse the religious message." *Bowen* v. *Kendrick* (Blackmun, J., dissenting); see also *id.* (O'Connor, J., concurring). Our cases have permitted some government funding of secular functions performed by sectarian organizations. See, *e.g.*, *id.* (funding for sex education); *Roemer* v. *Board of Pub. Works of Md.* (cash grant to colleges not to be used for "sectarian purposes"); *Bradfield* v. *Roberts* (funding of health care for indigent patients). These decisions, however, provide no precedent for the use of public funds to finance religious activities.

This case lies at the intersection of the principle of government neutrality and the prohibition on state funding of religious activities. It is clear that the University has established a generally applicable program to encourage the free exchange of ideas by its students, an expressive marketplace that includes some 15 student publications with predictably divergent viewpoints. It is equally clear that petitioners' viewpoint is religious and that publication of Wide Awake is a religious activity, under both the University's regulation and a fair reading of our precedents. Not to finance Wide Awake, according to petitioners, violates the principle of neutrality by sending a message of hostility toward religion. To finance Wide Awake, argues the University, violates the prohibition on direct state funding of religious activities.

When two bedrock principles so conflict, understandably neither can provide the definitive answer. Reliance on categorical platitudes is unavailing. Resolution instead depends on the hard task of judging—sifting through the details and determining whether ⊥**2526** the challenged program offends the Establishment Clause. Such judgment requires courts to draw lines, sometimes quite fine, based on the particular facts of each case. See *Lee* v. *Weisman* ("Our jurisprudence in this area is of necessity one of line-drawing"). As *Justice* HOLMES observed in a different context: "Neither are we troubled by the question where to draw the line. That is the question in pretty much everything worth arguing in the law. Day and night, youth and age are only types." *Irwin* v. *Gavit*.

In *Witters* v. *Washington Dept. of Services for Blind*, for example, we unanimously held that the State may, through a generally applicable financial aid program, pay a blind student's tuition at a sectarian theological institution. The Court so held, however, only after emphasizing that "vocational assistance provided under the Washington program is paid directly to the student, who transmits it to the educational institution of his or her choice." The benefit to religion under the program, therefore, is akin to a public servant contributing her government paycheck to the church. We thus resolved the conflict between the neutrality principle and the funding prohibition, not by permitting one to trump the other, but by relying on the elements of choice peculiar to the facts of that case: "The aid to religion at issue here is the result of petitioner's private choice. No reasonable observer is likely to draw from the facts before us an inference that the State itself is endorsing a religious practice or belief." (O'Connor, J., concurring in part and concurring in judgment).

The need for careful judgment and fine distinctions presents itself even in extreme cases. *Everson* v. *Board of Ed. of Ewing* provided perhaps the strongest exposition of the no-funding principle: "No tax in any amount, large or small, can be levied to support any religious activities or institutions, whatever they may be called, or whatever form they may adopt to teach or practice religion." Yet the Court approved the use of public funds, in a general program, to reimburse parents for their children's bus fares to attend Catholic schools. Although some would cynically dismiss the Court's disposition as inconsistent with its protestations (Jackson, J., dissenting) ("the most fitting precedent is that of Julia who, according to Byron's reports, 'whispering "I will ne'er consent,"—consented'"), the decision reflected the need to rely on careful judgment—not simple categories—when two principles, of equal historical and jurisprudential pedigree, come into unavoidable conflict.

So it is in this case. The nature of the dispute does not admit of categorical answers, nor should any be inferred from the Court's decision today. Instead, certain considerations specific to the program at issue lead me to conclude that by providing the same assistance to Wide Awake that it does to other publications, the University would not be endorsing the magazine's religious perspective.

First, the student organizations, at the University's insistence, remain strictly independent of the University. The University's agreement with the Contracted Independent Organizations (CIO)—*i.e.*, student groups—provides:

"The University is a Virginia public corporation and the CIO is not part of that corporation, but rather exists and operates independently of the University. . . . The parties understand and agree that this Agreement is the only source of any control the University may have over the CIO or its activities. . . ."

And the agreement requires that student organizations include in every letter, contract, publication, or other written materials the following disclaimer:

⊥2527 "Although this organization has members who are University of Virginia students (faculty) (employees), the organization is independent of the corporation which is the University and which is not responsible for the organization's contracts, acts or omissions."

Any reader of Wide Awake would be on notice of the publication's independence from the University.

Second, financial assistance is distributed in a manner that ensures its use only for permissible purposes. A student organization seeking assistance must submit disbursement requests; if approved, the funds are paid directly to the third-party vendor and do not pass through the organization's coffers. This safeguard accompanying the University's financial assistance, when provided to a publication with a religious viewpoint such as Wide Awake, ensures that the funds are used only to further the University's purpose in maintaining a free and robust marketplace of ideas, from whatever perspective. This feature also makes this case analogous to a school providing equal access to a generally available printing press (or other physical facilities), and unlike a block grant to religious organizations.

Third, assistance is provided to the religious publication in a context that makes improbable any perception of government endorsement of the religious message. Wide Awake does not exist in a vacuum. It competes with 15 other magazines and newspapers for advertising and readership. The widely divergent viewpoints of these many purveyors of opinion, all supported on an equal basis by the University, significantly diminishes the danger that the message of any one publication is perceived as endorsed by the University. Besides the general news publications, for example, the University has provided support to The Yellow Journal, a humor magazine that has targeted Christianity as a subject of satire, and Al-Salam, a publication to "promote a better understanding of Islam to the University Community." Given this wide array of non-religious, anti-religious and competing religious viewpoints in the forum supported by the University, any perception that the University endorses one particular viewpoint would be illogical. This is not the harder case where religious speech threatens to dominate the forum. Cf. *Capitol Square Review and Advisory Bd.* v. *Pinette* (O'Connor, J., concurring in part and concurring in judgment); *Mergens*.

Finally, although the question is not presented here, I note the possibility that the student fee is susceptible to a Free Speech Clause challenge by an objecting student that she should not be compelled to pay for speech with which she disagrees. There currently exists a split in the lower courts as to whether such a challenge would be successful. Compare *Hays County Guardian* v. *Supple; Kania* v. *Fordham; Good* v. *Associated Students of Univ. of Wash.* with *Smith* v. *Regents of Univ. of Cal.* While the Court does not resolve the question here, the existence of such an opt-out possibility not available to citizens generally provides a potential basis for distinguishing proceeds of the student fees in this case from proceeds of the general assessments in support of religion that lie at the core of the prohibition against religious funding, and from government funds generally. Unlike monies dispensed from state or federal treasuries, the Student Activities Fund is collected from students who themselves administer the fund and select qualifying recipients only **⊥2528** from among those who originally paid the fee. The government neither pays into nor draws from this common pool, and a fee of this sort appears conducive to granting individual students proportional refunds. The Student Activities Fund, then, represents not government resources, whether derived from tax revenue, sales of assets, or otherwise, but a fund that simply belongs to the students.

The Court's decision today therefore neither trumpets the supremacy of the neutrality principle nor signals the demise of the funding prohibition in Establishment Clause jurisprudence. As I observed last Term, "[e]xperience proves that the Establishment Clause, like the Free Speech Clause, cannot easily be reduced to a single test."

Kiryas Joel (O'Connor, J., concurring in part and concurring in judgment). When bedrock principles collide, they test the limits of categorical obstinacy and expose the flaws and dangers of a Grand Unified Theory that may turn out to be neither grand nor unified. The Court today does only what courts must do in many Establishment Clause cases—focus on specific features of a particular government action to ensure that it does not violate the Constitution. By withholding from Wide Awake assistance that the University provides generally to all other student publications, the University has discriminated on the basis of the magazine's religious viewpoint in violation of the Free Speech Clause. And particular features of the University's program—such as the explicit disclaimer, the disbursement of funds directly to third-party vendors, the vigorous nature of the forum at issue, and the possibility for objecting students to opt out—convince me that providing such assistance in this case would not carry the danger of impermissible use of public funds to endorse Wide Awake's religious message.

Subject to these comments, I join the opinion of the Court.

Justice THOMAS, concurring.

I agree with the Court's opinion and join it in full, but I write separately to express my disagreement with the historical analysis put forward by the dissent. Although the dissent starts down the right path in consulting the original meaning of the Establishment Clause, its misleading application of history yields a principle that is inconsistent with our Nation's long tradition of allowing religious adherents to participate on equal terms in neutral government programs.

Even assuming that the Virginia debate on the so-called "Assessment Controversy" was indicative of the principles embodied in the Establishment Clause, this incident hardly compels the dissent's conclusion that government must actively discriminate against religion. The dissent's historical discussion glosses over the fundamental characteristic of the Virginia assessment bill that sparked the controversy: The assessment was to be imposed for the support of clergy in the performance of their function of teaching religion. Thus, the "Bill Establishing a Provision for Teachers of the Christian Religion" provided for the collection of a specific tax, the proceeds of which were to be appropriated "by the Vestries, Elders, or Directors of each religious society . . . to a provision for a Minister or Teacher of the Gospel of their denomination, or the providing places of divine worship, and to none other use whatsoever."

⊥2529 James Madison's Memorial and Remonstrance Against Religious Assessments (hereinafter Madison's Remonstrance) must be understood in this context. Contrary to the dissent's suggestion, Madison's objection to the assessment bill did not rest on the premise that religious entities may never participate on equal terms in neutral government programs. Nor did Madison embrace the argument that forms the linchpin of the dissent: that monetary subsidies are constitutionally different from other neutral benefits programs. Instead, Madison's comments are more consistent with the neutrality principle that the dissent inexplicably discards. According to Madison, the Virginia assessment was flawed because it "violate[d] that equality which ought to be the basis of every law." Madison's Remonstrance ¶4. The assessment violated the "equality" principle not because it allowed religious groups to participate in a generally available government program, but because the bill singled out religious entities for special benefits. See *ibid.* (arguing that the assessment violated the equality principle "by subjecting some to peculiar burdens" and "by granting to others peculiar exemptions").

Legal commentators have disagreed about the historical lesson to take from the Assessment Controversy. For some, the experience in Virginia is consistent with the view that the Framers saw the Establishment Clause simply as a prohibition on governmental preferences for some religious faiths over others. See R. Cord, Separation of Church and State: Historical Fact and Current Fiction 20-23 (1982); Smith, Getting Off on the Wrong Foot and Back on Again: A Reexamination of the History of the Framing of the Religion Clauses of the First Amendment and a Critique of the *Reynolds* and *Everson* Decisions, 20 Wake Forest L. Rev. 569, 590-591 (1984). Other commentators have rejected this view, concluding that the Establishment Clause forbids not only government preferences for some religious sects over others, but also government preferences for religion over irreligion. See, *e.g.*, Laycock, "Nonpreferential" Aid to Religion: A False Claim About Original Intent, 27 Wm. & Mary L. Rev. 875, 875 (1986).

I find much to commend the former view. Madison's focus on the preferential nature of the assessment was not restricted to the fourth paragraph of the Remonstrance discussed above. The funding provided by the Virginia assessment was to be extended only to Christian sects, and the Remonstrance seized on this defect:

"Who does not see that the same authority which can establish Christianity, in exclusion of all other Religions, may establish with the same ease any particular sect of Christians, in exclusion of all other Sects." Madison's Remonstrance ¶3.

In addition to the third and fourth paragraphs of the Remonstrance, "Madison's sev**⊥2530**enth, ninth, eleventh, and twelfth arguments all speak, in some way, to the same intolerance, bigotry, unenlightenment, and persecution that had generally resulted from previous exclusive religious establishments." Cord, at 21. The conclusion that Madison saw the principle of nonestablishment as barring governmental preferences for *particular* religious faiths seems especially clear in light of statements he made in the more-relevant context of the House debates on the First Amendment. See *Wallace* v. *Jaffree* (Rehnquist, J., dissenting) (Madison's views "as reflected by actions on the floor of the House in 1789, [indicate] that he saw the

[First] Amendment as designed to prohibit the establishment of a national religion, and perhaps to prevent discrimination among sects," but not "as requiring neutrality on the part of government between religion and irreligion"). Moreover, even if more extreme notions of the separation of church and state can be attributed to Madison, many of them clearly stem from "arguments reflecting the concepts of natural law, natural rights, and the social contract between government and a civil society," Cord, at 22, rather than the principle of nonestablishment in the Constitution. In any event, the views of one man do not establish the original understanding of the First Amendment.

But resolution of this debate is not necessary to decide this case. Under any understanding of the Assessment Controversy, the history cited by the dissent cannot support the conclusion that the Establishment Clause "categorically condemn[s] state programs directly aiding religious activity" when that aid is part of a neutral program available to a wide array of beneficiaries. Even if Madison believed that the principle of nonestablishment of religion precluded government financial support for religion *per se* (in the sense of government benefits specifically targeting religion), there is no indication that at the time of the framing he took the dissent's extreme view that the government must discriminate against religious adherents by excluding them from more generally available financial subsidies.

In fact, Madison's own early legislative proposals cut against the dissent's suggestion. In 1776, when Virginia's Revolutionary Convention was drafting its Declaration of Rights, Madison prepared an amendment that would have disestablished the Anglican Church. This amendment (which went too far for the Convention and was not adopted) is not nearly as sweeping as the dissent's version of disestablishment; Madison merely wanted the Convention to declare that "no man or class of men ought, on account of religion[,] to be invested with *peculiar* emoluments or privileges . . . ." Madison's Amendments to the Declaration of Rights (May 29–June 12, 1776), in 1 Papers of James Madison 174 (W. Hutchinson & W. Rachal eds. 1962) (emphasis added). Likewise, Madison's Remonstrance stressed that "just government" is "best supported by protecting every citizen in the enjoyment of his Religion with the same equal hand which protects his person and his property; by neither invading the equal rights of any Sect, nor suffering any Sect to invade those of another." Madison's Remonstrance ¶8; cf. *Terrett* v. *Taylor* (holding that the Virginia constitution did not prevent the government from "aiding the votaries of every sect to . . . perform their own religious duties," or from "establishing funds for the support of ministers, for public charities, for the endowment of churches, or for the sepulture of the dead").

⊥**2531** Stripped of its flawed historical premise, the dissent's argument is reduced to the claim that our Establishment Clause jurisprudence permits neutrality in the context of access to government *facilities* but requires discrimination in access to government *funds*. The dissent purports to locate the prohibition against "direct public funding" at the "heart" of the Establishment Clause, but this conclusion fails to confront historical examples of funding that date back to the time of the founding. To take but one famous example, both Houses of the First Congress elected chaplains, see S. Jour., 1st Cong., 1st Sess., 10 (1820 ed.); H. R. Jour., 1st Cong., 1st Sess., 26 (1826 ed.), and that Congress enacted legislation providing for an annual salary of $500 to be paid out of the Treasury, see Act of Sept. 22, 1789, ch. 17, § 4, 1 Stat. 70, 71. Madison himself was a member of the committee that recommended the chaplain system in the House. See H. R. Jour., at 11-12; 1 Annals of Cong. 891 (1789); Cord, at 25. This same system of "direct public funding" of congressional chaplains has "continued without interruption ever since that early session of Congress." *Marsh* v. *Chambers*.

The historical evidence of government support for religious entities through property tax exemptions is also overwhelming. As the dissent concedes, property tax exemptions for religious bodies "have been in place for over 200 years without disruption to the interests represented by the Establishment Clause." In my view, the dissent's acceptance of this tradition puts to rest the notion that the Establishment Clause bars monetary aid to religious groups even when the aid is equally available to other groups. A tax exemption in many cases is economically and functionally indistinguishable from a direct monetary subsidy. In ⊥**2532** one instance, the government relieves religious entities (along with others) of a generally applicable tax; in the other, it relieves religious entities (along with others) of some or all of the burden of that tax by returning it in the form of a cash subsidy. Whether the benefit is provided at the front or back end of the taxation process, the financial aid to religious groups is undeniable. The analysis under the Establishment Clause must also be the same: "Few concepts are more deeply embedded in the fabric of our national life, beginning with pre-Revolutionary colonial times, than for the government to exercise at the very least this kind of benevolent neutrality toward churches and religious exercise. . . ." *Walz*.

Consistent application of the dissent's "no-aid" principle would require that "'a church could not be protected by the police and fire departments, or have its public sidewalk kept in repair.'" *Zobrest* v. *Catalina Foothills School Dist.* (quoting *Widmar* v. *Vincent*). The dissent admits that "evenhandedness may become important to ensuring that religious interests are not inhibited." Surely the dissent must concede, however, that the same result should obtain whether the government provides the populace with fire protection by reimbursing the costs of smoke detectors and overhead sprinkler systems or by establishing a public fire department. If churches may benefit on equal terms with other groups in the latter program—that is, if a public fire department may extinguish fires at churches—then they may also benefit on equal terms in the former program.

Though our Establishment Clause jurisprudence is in hopeless disarray, this case provides an opportunity to reaffirm one basic principle that has enjoyed an uncharacteristic degree of consensus: The Clause does not compel the exclusion of religious groups from government benefits programs that are generally available to a broad class of participants. See *Lamb's Chapel* v. *Center Moriches Union Free School Dist.*; *Zobrest*; *Board of Ed. of Westside Community Schools (Dist. 66)* v. *Mergens*; *Texas Monthly, Inc.* v. *Bullock*; *Witters* v. *Washington Dept. of Services for Blind*; *Mueller* v. *Allen*; *Widmar*. Under the dissent's view, however, the University of Virginia may provide neutral access to the University's own printing press, but it may not provide the same service when the press is owned by a third party. Not surprisingly, the dissent offers no logical justification for this conclusion, and none is evident in the text or original meaning of the First Amendment.

If the Establishment Clause is offended when religious adherents benefit from neutral programs such as the University of Virginia's Student Activities Fund, it must also ⊥**2533** be offended when they receive the same benefits in the form of in-kind subsidies. The constitutional demands of the Establishment Clause may be judged against either a baseline of "neutrality" or a baseline of "no aid to religion," but the appropriate baseline surely cannot depend on the fortuitous circumstances surrounding the *form* of aid. The contrary rule would lead to absurd results that would jettison centuries of practice respecting the right of religious adherents to participate on neutral terms in a wide variety of government-funded programs.

Our Nation's tradition of allowing religious adherents to participate in evenhanded government programs is hardly limited to the class of "essential public benefits" identified by the dissent. A broader tradition can be traced at least as far back as the First Congress, which ratified the Northwest Ordinance of 1787. See Act of Aug. 7, 1789, ch. 8, 1 Stat. 50. Article III of that famous enactment of the Confederation Congress had provided: "Religion, morality, and knowledge . . . being necessary to good government and the happiness of mankind, schools and the means of learning shall forever be encouraged." *Id.*, at 52, n. (a). Congress subsequently set aside federal lands in the Northwest Territory and other territories for the use of schools. See, *e.g.*, Act of Mar. 3, 1803, ch. 21, § 1, 2 Stat. 225-226; Act of Mar. 26, 1804, ch. 35, § 5, 2 Stat. 279; Act of Feb. 15, 1811, ch. 14, § 10, 2 Stat. 621; Act of Apr. 18, 1818, ch. 67, § 6, 3 Stat. 430; Act of Apr. 20, 1818, ch. 126, § 2, 3 Stat. 467. Many of the schools that enjoyed the benefits of these land grants undoubtedly were church-affiliated sectarian institutions as there was no requirement that the schools be "public." See C. Antieau, A. Downey, & E. Roberts, Freedom From Federal Establishment, Formation and Early History of the First Amendment Religion Clauses 163 (1964). Nevertheless, early Congresses found no problem with the provision of such neutral benefits. See also *id.*, at 174 (noting that "almost universally[,] Americans from 1789 to 1825 accepted and practiced governmental aid to religion and religiously oriented educational institutions").

Numerous other government benefits traditionally have been available to religious adherents on neutral terms. Several examples may be found in the work of early Congresses, including copyright protection for "the author and authors of any map, chart, book or books," Act of May 31, 1790, ch. 15, § 1, 1 Stat. 124, 124, and a privilege allowing "every printer of newspapers [to] send one paper to each and every other printer of newspapers within the United States, free of postage," Act of Feb. 20, 1792, ch. 7, § 21, 1 Stat. 232, 238. Neither of these laws made any exclusion for the numerous authors or printers who manifested a belief in or about a deity.

Thus, history provides an answer for the constitutional question posed by this case, but it is not the one given by the dissent. The dissent identifies no evidence that the Framers intended to disable religious entities from participating on neutral terms in evenhanded government programs. The evidence that does exist points in the opposite direction and provides ample support for today's decision.

Justice SOUTER, with whom *Justice* STEVENS, *Justice* GINSBURG and *Justice* BREYER join, dissenting.

The Court today, for the first time, approves direct funding of core religious activities by an arm of the State. It does so, however, only after erroneous treatment of some familiar principles of law implementing the First Amendment's Establishment and Speech Clauses, and by viewing the very funds in question as beyond the reach of the Establishment Clause's funding restrictions as such. Because there is no warrant for distinguishing among public funding sources for purposes of applying the First Amendment's prohibition of religious establishment, I would hold that the University's refusal to support petitioners' religious activities is compelled by the Establishment Clause. I would therefore affirm.

I

The central question in this case is whether a grant from the Student Activities Fund to pay Wide Awake's printing expenses ⊥**2534** would violate the Establishment Clause. Although the Court does not dwell on the details of Wide Awake's message, it recognizes something sufficiently religious in the publication to demand Establishment Clause scrutiny. Although the Court places great stress on the eligibility of secular as well as religious activities for grants from the Student Activities Fund, it recognizes that such evenhanded availability is not by itself enough to satisfy constitutional requirements for any aid scheme that results in a benefit to religion. Something more is necessary to justify any religious aid. Some members of the Court, at least, may think the funding permissible on a view that it is indirect, since the money goes to Wide Awake's printer, not through Wide Awake's own checking account. The Court's principal reliance, however, is on an argument that providing religion with economically valuable services is permissible on the theory that services are economically indistinguishable from religious access to governmental speech forums, which sometimes is permissible. But this reasoning would commit the Court to approving direct religious aid beyond anything justifiable for the sake of access to speaking forums. The Court implicitly recognizes this in its further attempt to circumvent the clear bar to direct governmental aid to religion. Different members of the Court seek to avoid this bar in different ways. The opinion of the Court makes the novel assumption that only direct aid financed with tax revenue is barred, and draws the erroneous conclusion that the involuntary Student Activities Fee is not a tax. I do not read *Justice O'CONNOR's* opinion as sharing that assumption; she places this Student Activities Fund in a category of student funding enterprises from which religious activities in public universities may benefit, so long as there is no consequent endorsement of religion. The resulting decision is in unmistakable tension with the accepted law that the Court continues to avow.

A

The Court's difficulties will be all the more clear after a closer look at Wide Awake than the majority opinion affords. The character of the magazine is candidly disclosed on the opening page of the first issue, where the editor-in-chief announces Wide Awake's mission in a letter to the readership signed, "Love in Christ": it is "to challenge Christians to live, in word and deed, according to the faith they proclaim and to encourage students to consider what a personal relationship with Jesus Christ means." The masthead of every issue bears St. Paul's exhortation, that "[t]he hour has come for you to awake from your slumber, because our salvation is nearer now than when we first believed. Romans 13:11."

Each issue of Wide Awake contained in the record makes good on the editor's promise and echoes the Apostle's call to accept salvation:

"The only way to salvation through Him is by confessing and repenting of sin. It is the Christian's duty to make sinners aware of their need for salvation. Thus, Christians must confront and condemn sin, or else they fail in their duty of love." Mourad & Prince, A Love/Hate Relationship, November/December 1990, p. 3.

"When you get to the final gate, the Lord will be handing out boarding passes, and He will examine your ticket. If, in your lifetime, you did not request a seat on His Friendly Skies Flyer by trusting Him and asking Him to be your pilot, then you will not be on His list of reserved seats (and the Lord will know you not). You will not be able to buy a ticket then; no amount of money or desire will do the trick. You will be met by your chosen pilot and flown straight to Hell on an express jet (without air conditioning or toilets, of course)." Ace, The Plane Truth, *id.*, at 3.

"'Go into all the world and preach the good news to all creation.' (Mark 16:15) The Great Commission is the prime-directive for our lives as Christians. . . ." Liu, Christianity and the Five-legged Stool, September/October 1991, p. 3.

"The Spirit provides access to an intimate relationship with the Lord of the Universe, awakens our minds to comprehend spiritual truth and empowers us to serve as effective ambassadors for the Lord Jesus ⊥**2535** in our earthly lives." Buterbaugh, A Spiritual Advantage, March/April 1991, p. 21.

There is no need to quote further from articles of like tenor, but one could examine such other examples as religious poetry, see Macpherson, I Have Started Searching for Angels, November/December 1990, p. 18; religious textual analysis and commentary, see Buterbaugh, Colossians 1:1-14: Abundant Life, *id.*, at 20; Buterbaugh, John 14-16: A Spiritual Advantage, March/April, pp. 20-21; and instruction on religious practice, see Early, Thanksgiving and Prayer, November/December 1990, p. 21 (providing readers with suggested prayers and posing contemplative questions about biblical texts); Early, Hope and Spirit, March/April 1991, p. 21 (similar).

Even featured essays on facially secular topics become platforms from which to call readers to fulfill the tenets of Christianity in their lives. Although a piece on racism has some general discussion on the subject, it proceeds beyond even the analysis and interpretation of biblical texts to conclude with the counsel to take action because that is the Christian thing to do:

"God calls us to take the risks of voluntarily stepping out of our comfort zones and to take joy in the whole richness of our inheritance in the body of Christ. We must take the love we receive from God and share it with all peoples of the world.

"Racism is a disease of the heart, soul, and mind, and only when it is extirpated from the individual consciousness and replaced with the love and peace of God will true personal and communal healing begin." Liu, et al., "Eracing" Mistakes, November/December 1990, p. 14.

The same progression occurs in an article on eating disorders, which begins with descriptions of anorexia and bulimia and ends with this religious message:

"As thinking people who profess a belief in God, we must grasp firmly the truth, the reality of who we are because of Christ. Christ is the Bread of Life (John 6:35). Through Him, we are full. He alone can provide the ultimate source of spiritual fulfillment which permeates the emotional, psychological, and physical dimensions of our lives." Ferguson & Lassiter, From Calorie to Calvary, September/October 1991, p. 14.

This writing is no merely descriptive examination of religious doctrine or even of ideal Christian practice in confronting life's social and personal problems. Nor is it merely the expression of editorial opinion that incidentally coincides with Christian ethics and reflects a Christian view of human obligation. It is straightforward exhortation to enter into a relationship with God as revealed in Jesus Christ, and to satisfy a series of moral obligations derived from the teachings of Jesus Christ. These are not the words of "student news, information, opinion, entertainment, or academic communicatio[n] . . ." (in the language of the University's funding criterion), but the words of "challenge [to] Christians to live, in word and deed, according to the faith they proclaim and . . . to consider what a personal relationship with Jesus Christ means" (in the language of Wide Awake's founder). The subject is not the discourse of the scholar's study or the seminar room, but of the evangelist's mission station and the pulpit. It is nothing other than the preaching of the word, which (along with the sacraments) is what most branches of Christianity offer those called to the religious life.

Using public funds for the direct subsidization of preaching the word is categorically forbidden under the Establishment Clause, and if the Clause was meant to accomplish nothing else, it was meant to bar this use of public money. Evidence on the subject antedates even the Bill of Rights itself, as may be seen in the writings of Madison, whose authority on questions about the meaning of the Establishment Clause is well settled. Four years before the First Congress proposed the First Amendment, Madison gave his opinion on the legitimacy of using public funds for religious purposes, in the Memorial ⊥**2536** and Remonstrance Against Religious Assessments, which played the central role in ensuring the defeat of the Virginia tax assessment bill in 1786 and framed the debate upon which the Religion Clauses stand:

"Who does not see that . . . the same authority which can force a citizen to contribute three pence only of his property for the support of any one establishment, may force him to conform to any other establishment in all cases whatsoever?" James Madison, Memorial and Remonstrance Against Religious Assessments ¶3 (hereinafter Madison's Remonstrance).

Madison wrote against a background in which nearly every Colony had exacted a tax for church support, the practice having become "so commonplace as to shock the freedom-loving colonials into a feeling of abhorrence." *Everson*. Madison's Remonstrance captured the colonists' "conviction that individual religious liberty could be achieved best under a government which was stripped of all power to tax, to support, or otherwise to assist any or all religions, or to interfere with the beliefs of any religious individual or group." *Ibid.** Their senti-

**Justice THOMAS* suggests that Madison would have approved of the assessment bill if only it had satisfied the principle of evenhandedness. Nowhere in the Remonstrance, however, did Madison advance the view that Virginia should be able to provide financial support for religion as part of a generally available subsidy program. Indeed, while *Justice THOMAS* claims that the "funding provided by the Virginia assessment was to be extended only to Christian sects," it is clear that the bill was more general in scope than this. While the bill, which is reprinted in *Everson* v. *Board of Ed. of Ewing*, provided that each taxpayer could designate a religious society to which he wanted his levy paid, id., at 73, it would also have allowed a taxpayer to refuse to appropriate his levy to any religious society, in which case the legislature was to use these unappropriated sums to fund "seminaries of learning." *Id.* (contrary to *Justice THOMAS*'s unsupported assertion, this portion of the bill was no less obligatory than any other). While some of these seminaries undoubtedly would have been religious in character, others would not have been, as a seminary was generally understood at the time to be "any school, academy, college or university, in which young persons are instructed in the several branches of learning which may qualify them for their future employments." N. Webster, An American Dictionary of the English Language (1st ed. 1828); see also 14 The Oxford English Dictionary 956 (2d ed. 1989). Not surprisingly, then, scholars have generally agreed that the bill would have provided funding for nonreligious schools. See, *e.g.*, Laycock, "Nonpreferential" Aid to Religion: A False Claim About Original Intent, 27 Wm. & Mary L. Rev. 875, 897 (1986) ("Any taxpayer could refuse to designate a church, with undesignated church taxes going to a fund for schools. . . . The bill used the phrase 'seminaries of learning,' which almost certainly meant schools generally and not just schools for the training of ministers"); T. Buckley, Church and State in Revolutionary Virginia, 1776–1787, p. 133 (1977) ("The assessment had been carefully drafted to permit those who preferred to support education rather than religion to do so"); T. Curry, The First Freedoms 141 (1986) ("[T]hose taxes not designated for any specific denomination [were] allocated to education"). It is beside the point that "there was no system of public education in Virginia until several decades after the assessment bill was proposed" (Thomas, J., concurring); because the bill was never passed, the funds that it would have made available for secular, public schools never materialized. The fact that the bill, if passed, would have funded secular as well as religious instruction did nothing to soften Madison's opposition to it.

Nor is it fair to argue that Madison opposed the bill only because it treated religious groups unequally. In various paragraphs of the Remonstrance, Madison did complain about the bill's peculiar burdens and exemptions, but to identify this factor as the sole point of Madison's opposition to the bill is unfaithful to the Remonstrance's text. Madison strongly inveighed against the proposed aid for religion for a host of reasons (the Remonstrance numbers 15 paragraphs, each containing at least one point in opposition), and crucial here is the fact that many of those reasons would have applied whether or not the state aid was being distributed equally among sects, and whether or not the aid was going to those sects in the context of an evenhanded government program. See, *e.g.*, Madison's Remonstrance ¶1 ("[I]n matters of Religion, no man's right is abridged by the institution of Civil Society, and . . . Religion is wholly exempt from its cognizance"); ¶6 (arguing that State support of religion "is a contradiction to the Christian Religion itself; for every page of it disavows a dependence on the powers of this world"); ¶7 ("[E]xperience witnesseth that ecclesiastical establishments, instead of maintaining the purity and efficacy of Religion, have had a contrary operation"). Madison's objections were supplemented by numerous other petitions in opposition to the bill that likewise do not suggest that the lack of evenhandedness was its dispositive flaw. L. Levy, The Establishment Clause 63–67 (2d ed. 1994). For example, the petition that received the largest number of signatories was motivated by the view that religion should only be supported voluntarily. Indeed, Madison's Remonstrance did not argue for a bill distributing aid to all sects and religions on an equal basis, and the outgrowth of the Remonstrance and the defeat of the Virginia assessment was not such a bill; rather, it was the Virginia Bill for Establishing Religious Freedom, which, as discussed in the text, proscribed the use of tax dollars for religious purposes.

ment as expressed by Madison in Virginia, led not only ⊥**2537** to the defeat of Virginia's tax assessment bill, but also directly to passage of the Virginia Bill for Establishing Religious Freedom, written by Thomas Jefferson. That bill's preamble declared that "to compel a man to furnish contributions of money for the propagation of opinions which he disbelieves, is sinful and tyrannical," Jefferson, A Bill for Establishing Religious Freedom, reprinted in 5 The Founder's Constitution 84–85 (P. Kurland & R. Lerner eds. 1987), and its text provided "[t]hat no man shall be compelled to frequent or support any religious worship, place, or ministry whatsoever . . . ," *ibid.* See generally *Everson,* at 13. We have "previously recognized that the provisions of the First Amendment, in the drafting and adoption of which Madison and Jefferson played such leading roles, had the same objective and were intended to provide the same protection against governmental intrusion on religious liberty as the Virginia statute." *Ibid.*; see also Laycock, "Nonpreferential" Aid to Religion: A False Claim About Original Intent, 27 Wm. & Mary L. Rev. 875, 921, 923 (1986) ("[I]f the debates of the 1780's support any proposition, it is that the Framers opposed government financial support for religion. . . . They did not substitute small taxes for large taxes; three pence was as bad as any larger sum. The principle was what mattered. With respect to money, religion was to be wholly voluntary. Churches either would support themselves or they would not, but the government would neither help nor interfere") (footnote omitted); T. Curry, The First Freedoms 217 (1986) (At the time of the framing of the Bill of Rights, "[t]he belief that government assistance to religion, especially in the form of taxes, violated religious liberty had a long history"); J. Choper, Securing Religious Liberty 16 (1995) ("There is broad consensus that a central threat to the religious freedom of individuals and groups—indeed, in the judgment of many the most serious infringement upon religious liberty—is posed by forcing them to pay taxes in support of a religious establishment or religious activities").**

⊥**2538** The principle against direct funding with public money is patently violated by the contested use of today's student activity fee. Like today's taxes generally, the fee is Madison's threepence. The University exercises the power of the State to compel a student to pay it, and the use of any part of it for the direct support of religious activity thus strikes at what we have repeatedly held to be the heart of the prohibition on establishment. *Everson* ("The 'establishment of religion clause' . . . means at least this. . . . No tax in any amount, large or small, can be levied to support any religious activities or institutions, whatever they may be called, or whatever form they may adopt to teach or practice religion"); see *School Dist. of Grand Rapids* v. *Ball* ("Although Establishment Clause jurisprudence is characterized by few absolutes, the Clause does absolutely prohibit government-financed or government-sponsored indoctrination into the beliefs of a particular religious faith"); *Committee for Public Education* v. *Nyquist* ("In the absence of an effective means of guaran-

---

In attempting to recast Madison's opposition as having principally been targeted against "governmental preferences for *particular* religious faiths," (emphasis in original), *Justice THOMAS* wishes to wage a battle that was lost long ago, for "this Court has rejected unequivocally the contention that the Establishment Clause forbids only governmental preference of one religion over another," *School Dist. of Abington* v. *Schempp*; see also *Texas Monthly, Inc.* v. *Bullock*; id. (Blackmun, J., concurring in judgment); *Wallace* v. *Jaffree*; *Torcaso* v. *Watkins*; *Engel* v. *Vitale*; *Everson*; see generally *Lee* v. *Weisman* (Souter, J., concurring).

***Justice THOMAS* attempts to cast doubt on this accepted version of Establishment Clause history by reference to historical facts that are largely inapposite. As I have said elsewhere, individual Acts of Congress, especially when they are few and far between, scarcely serve as an authoritative guide to the meaning of the religion clauses, for "like other politicians, [members of the early Congresses] could raise constitutional ideals one day and turn their backs on them the next. [For example,] . . . [t]en years after proposing the First Amendment, Congress passed the Alien and Sedition Acts, measures patently unconstitutional by modern standards. If the early Congress's political actions were determinative, and not merely relevant, evidence of constitutional meaning, we would have to gut our current First Amendment doctrine to make room for political censorship." *Lee* v. *Weisman* (concurring opinion). The legislation cited by *Justice THOMAS,* including the Northwest Ordinance, is no more dispositive than the Alien and Sedition Acts in interpreting the First Amendment. Even less persuasive, then, are citations to constitutionally untested Acts dating from the mid-19th century, for without some rather innovative argument, they cannot be offered as providing an authoritative gloss on the Framers' intent.

Justice THOMAS's references to Madison's actions as a legislator also provide little support for his cause. *Justice THOMAS* seeks to draw a significant lesson out of the fact that, in seeking to disestablish the Anglican Church in Virginia in 1776, Madison did not inveigh against state funding of religious activities. That was not the task at hand, however. Madison was acting with the specific goal of eliminating the special privileges enjoyed by Virginia Anglicans, and he made no effort to lay out the broader views of church and state that came to bear in his drafting of the First Amendment some 13 years later. That Madison did not speak in more expansive terms than necessary in 1776 was hardly surprising for, as it was, his proposal was defeated by the Virginia Convention as having gone too far.

Similarly, the invocation of Madison's tenure on the congressional committee that approved funding for legislative chaplains provides no support for more general principles that run counter to settled Establishment Clause jurisprudence. As I have previously pointed out, Madison, upon retirement, "insisted that 'it was not with my approbation, that the deviation from [the immunity of religion from civil jurisdiction] took place in Congs., when they appointed Chaplains, to be paid from the Natl. Treasury.'" *Lee,* quoting Letter from J. Madison to E. Livingston (July 10, 1822), in 5 The Founders' Constitution, at 105. And when we turned our attention to deciding whether funding of legislative chaplains posed an establishment problem, we did not address the practice as one instance of a larger class of permissible government funding of religious activities. Instead, *Marsh* v. *Chambers,* explicitly relied on the singular, 200-year pedigree of legislative chaplains, noting that "[t]his unique history" justified carving out an exception for the specific practice in question. Given that the decision upholding this practice was expressly limited to its facts, then, it would stand the Establishment Clause on its head to extract from it a broad rule permitting the funding of religious activities.

teeing that the state aid derived from public funds will be used exclusively for secular, neutral, and nonideological purposes, it is clear from our cases that direct aid in whatever form is invalid"); *id.* ("Primary among those evils" against which the Establishment Clause guards "have been sponsorship, financial support, and active involvement of the sovereign in religious activity"); see also *Lee* v. *Weisman* (Scalia, J., dissenting) ("The coercion that was a hallmark of historical establishments of religion was coercion of religious orthodoxy and of financial support by force of law and threat of penalty"); cf. *Flast* v. *Cohen* (holding that taxpayers have an adequate stake in the outcome of Establishment Clause litigation to satisfy Article III standing requirements, af⊥**2539**ter stating that "[o]ur history vividly illustrates that one of the specific evils feared by those who drafted the Establishment Clause and fought for its adoption was that the taxing and spending power would be used to favor one religion over another or to support religion in general").

The Court, accordingly, has never before upheld direct state funding of the sort of proselytizing published in Wide Awake and, in fact, has categorically condemned state programs directly aiding religious activity, *School Dist.* v. *Ball* (striking programs providing secular instruction to nonpublic school students on nonpublic school premises because they are "indistinguishable from the provision of a direct cash subsidy to the religious school that is most clearly prohibited under the Establishment Clause"); *Wolman* v. *Walter* (striking field trip aid program because it constituted "an impermissible direct aid to sectarian education"); *Meek* v. *Pittenger* (striking material and equipment loan program to nonpublic schools because of the inability to "channe[l] aid to the secular without providing direct aid to the sectarian"); *Committee for Public Education* v. *Nyquist* (striking aid to nonpublic schools for maintenance and repair of facilities because "[n]o attempt is made to restrict payments to those expenditures related to the upkeep of facilities used exclusively for secular purposes"); *Levitt* v. *Committee for Public Ed. & Religious Liberty* (striking aid to nonpublic schools for state-mandated tests because the state had failed to "assure that the state-supported activity is not being used for religious indoctrination"); *Tilton* v. *Richardson* (striking as insufficient a 20-year limit on prohibition for religious use in federal construction program for university facilities because unrestricted use even after 20 years "is in effect a contribution of some value to a religious body").

Even when the Court has upheld aid to an institution performing both secular and sectarian functions, it has always made a searching enquiry to ensure that the institution kept the secular activities separate from its sectarian ones, with any direct aid flowing only to the former and never the latter. *Bowen* v. *Kendrick* (upholding grant program for services related to premarital adolescent sexual relations on ground that funds cannot be "used by the grantees in such a way as to advance religion"); *Roemer* v. *Board of Pub. Works of Md.* (upholding general aid program restricting uses of funds to secular activities only); *Hunt* v. *McNair* (upholding general revenue bond program excluding from participation facilities used for religious purposes); *Tilton* v. *Richardson* (upholding general aid program for construction of academic facilities as "[t]here is no evidence that religion seeps into the use of any of these facilities"); see *Board of Ed. of Central School Dist No. 1* v. *Allen* (upholding textbook loan program limited to secular books requested by individual students for secular educational purposes).

Reasonable minds may differ over whether the Court reached the correct result in each of these cases, but their common principle has never been questioned or repudiated. "Although Establishment Clause jurisprudence is characterized by few absolutes, the Clause does absolutely prohibit government-financed . . . indoctrination into the beliefs of a particular religious faith." *School Dist.* v. *Ball.*

B

Why does the Court not apply this clear law to these clear facts and conclude, as I do, that the funding scheme here is a clear con⊥**2540**stitutional violation? The answer must be in part that the Court fails to confront the evidence set out in the preceding section. Throughout its opinion, the Court refers uninformatively to Wide Awake's "Christian viewpoint," or its "religious perspective," and in distinguishing funding of Wide Awake from the funding of a church, the Court maintains that "[Wide Awake] is not a religious institution, at least in the usual sense." The Court does not quote the magazine's adoption of Saint Paul's exhortation to awaken to the nearness of salvation, or any of its articles enjoining readers to accept Jesus Christ, or the religious verses, or the religious textual analyses, or the suggested prayers. And so it is easy for the Court to lose sight of what the University students and the Court of Appeals found so obvious, and to blanch the patently and frankly evangelistic character of the magazine by unrevealing allusions to religious points of view.

Nevertheless, even without the encumbrance of detail from Wide Awake's actual pages, the Court finds something sufficiently religious about the magazine to require examination under the Establishment Clause, and one may therefore ask why the unequivocal prohibition on direct funding does not lead the Court to conclude that funding would be unconstitutional. The answer is that the Court focuses on a subsidiary body of law, which it correctly states but ultimately misapplies. That subsidiary body of law accounts for the Court's substantial attention to the fact that the University's funding scheme is "neutral," in the formal sense that it makes funds available on an evenhanded basis to secular and sectarian applicants alike. While this is indeed true and relevant under our cases, it does not alone satisfy the requirements of the Establishment Clause, as the Court recognizes when it says that evenhandedness is only a "significant factor" in certain Establishment Clause analysis, not a dispositive one. See also (O'Connor, J., concurring) ("Neutrality, in both form and effect, is one hallmark of the Establishment Clause"); *Capitol Square Review and Advisory Board* v. *Pinette* (O'Connor, J., concurring in part and concurring in the judgment) ("the Establishment Clause forbids a State from hiding behind the application of formally neutral criteria and remaining studiously oblivious to the effects of its actions. . . . [N]ot all State policies are permissible under the Religion Clauses simply because they are neutral in form"). This recognition reflects the Court's appreciation of two general rules: that whenever affirmative government aid ultimately benefits religion, the Establishment Clause requires some justification beyond evenhandedness on the government's part; and that direct public funding of core sectarian activities, even if accomplished pursuant to an evenhanded program, would be entirely inconsistent with the Establishment Clause and would strike at the very heart of the Clause's protection. See *ante* ("We do not confront a case where, even under a neutral program that includes nonsectarian recipients, the government is making direct money payments to an institution or group that is engaged in religious activity"); see also (O'Connor, J., concurring) ("[Our] decisions . . . provide no precedent for the use of public funds to finance religious activities").

In order to understand how the Court thus begins with sound rules but ends with an unsound result, it is necessary to explore those rules in greater detail than the Court does. As the foregoing quotations from the Court's opinion indicate, the relationship between the prohibition on direct aid and the requirement of evenhandedness when affirmative government aid does result in some benefit to religion reflects the relationship between basic rule and marginal criterion. **⊥2541** At the heart of the Establishment Clause stands the prohibition against direct public funding, but that prohibition does not answer the questions that occur at the margins of the Clause's application. Is any government activity that provides any incidental benefit to religion likewise unconstitutional? Would it be wrong to put out fires in burning churches, wrong to pay the bus fares of students on the way to parochial schools, wrong to allow a grantee of special education funds to spend them at a religious college? These are the questions that call for drawing lines, and it is in drawing them that evenhandedness becomes important. However the Court may in the past have phrased its line-drawing test, the question whether such benefits are provided on an evenhanded basis has been relevant, for the question addresses one aspect of the issue whether a law is truly neutral with respect to religion (that is, whether the law either "advance[s] [or] inhibit[s] religion," *Allegheny County* v. *Greater Pittsburgh Chapter, American Civil Liberties Union.* In *Widmar* v. *Vincent*, for example, we noted that "[t]he provision of benefits to [a] broad . . . spectrum of [religious and nonreligious] groups is an important index of secular effect." In the doubtful cases (those not involving direct public funding), where there is initially room for argument about a law's effect, evenhandedness serves to weed out those laws that impermissibly advance religion by channelling aid to it exclusively. Evenhandedness is therefore a prerequisite to further enquiry into the constitutionality of a doubtful law, but evenhandedness goes no further. It does not guarantee success under Establishment Clause scrutiny.

Three cases permitting indirect aid to religion, *Mueller* v. *Allen, Witters* v. *Washington Dept. of Services for Blind*, and *Zobrest* v. *Catalina Foothills School Dist.* are among the latest of those to illustrate this relevance of evenhandedness when advancement is not so obvious as to be patently unconstitutional. Each case involved a program in which benefits given to individuals on a religion-neutral basis ultimately were used by the individuals, in one way or another, to support religious institutions. In each, the fact that aid was distributed generally and on a neutral basis was a necessary condition for upholding the program at issue. But the significance of evenhandedness stopped there. We did not, in any of these cases, hold that satisfying the condition was sufficient, or dispositive. Even more importantly, we never held that evenhandedness might be sufficient to render direct aid to religion constitutional. Quite the contrary. Critical to our decisions in these cases was the fact that the aid was indirect; it reached religious institutions "only as a result of the genuinely independent and private choices of aid recipients," *Witters*. In noting and relying on this particular feature of each of the programs at issue, we in fact reaffirmed the core prohibition on direct funding of religious ac**⊥2542**tivities. Thus, our holdings in these cases were little more than extensions of the unremarkable proposition that "a State may issue a paycheck to one of its employees, who may then donate all or part of that paycheck to a religious institution, all without constitutional barrier. . . ." *Witters*. Such "attenuated financial benefit[s], ultimately controlled by the private choices of individual[s]," we have found, are simply not within the contemplation of the Establishment Clause's broad prohibition. *Mueller*.

Evenhandedness as one element of a permissibly attenuated benefit is, of course, a far cry from evenhandedness as a sufficient condition of constitutionality for direct financial support of religious proselytization, and our cases have unsurprisingly repudiated any such attempt to cut the Establishment Clause down to a mere prohibition against unequal direct aid. See, *e.g.*, *Tilton* v. *Richardson* (striking portion of general aid program providing grants for construction of college and university facilities to the extent program made possible the use of funds for sectarian activities); *Wolman* v. *Walter* (striking funding of field trips for nonpublic school students, such as are "provided to public **⊥2543** school students in the district," because of unacceptable danger that state funds would be used to foster religion). And nowhere has the Court's adherence to the preeminence of the no-direct-funding principle over the principle of evenhandedness been as clear as in *Bowen* v. *Kendrick*.

Bowen involved consideration of the Adolescent Family Life Act (AFLA), a federal grant program providing funds to institutions for counseling and educational services related to adolescent sexuality and pregnancy. At the time of the litigation, 141 grants had been awarded under the AFLA to a broad array of both secular and religiously affiliated institutions. In an Establishment Clause challenge to the Act brought by taxpayers and other interested parties, the District Court resolved the case on a pre-trial motion for summary judgment, holding the AFLA program unconstitutional both on its face and also insofar as religious institutions were involved in receiving grants under the Act. When this Court reversed on the issue of facial constitutionality under the Establishment Clause, we said that there was "no intimation in the statute that at some point, or for some grantees, religious uses are permitted." On the contrary, after looking at the legislative history and applicable regulations, we found safeguards adequate to ensure that grants would not be "used by . . . grantees in such a way as to advance religion."

With respect to the claim that the program was unconstitutional as applied, we remanded the case to the District Court "for consideration of the evidence presented by appellees insofar as it sheds light on the manner in which the statute is presently being administered." Specifically, we told the District Court, on remand, to "consider . . . whether in particular cases AFLA aid has been used to fund 'specifically religious activit[ies] in an otherwise substantially secular setting.'" *Ibid.*, quoting *Hunt* v. *McNair*. In giving additional guidance to the District Court, we suggested that application of the Act would be unconstitutional if it turned out that aid recipients were using materials "that have an explicitly religious content or are designed to inculcate the views of a particular religious faith." At no point in our opinion did we suggest that the breadth of potential recipients, or distribution on an evenhanded basis, could have justified the use of federal funds for religious activities, a position that would have made no sense after we had pegged the Act's facial constitutionality to our conclusion that advancement of religion was not inevitable. *Justice* O'CONNOR's separate opinion in the case underscored just this point: "I fully agree . . . that '[p]ublic funds may not be used to endorse the religious message.' [(Blackmun, J., dissenting)]. . . . *[A]ny* use of public funds to promote religious doctrines violates the Establishment Clause." (emphasis in original).

Bowen was no sport; its pedigree was the line of *Everson* v. *Board of Ed.*, *Board of Ed.* v. *Allen*, *Tilton* v. *Richardson*, *Hunt* v. *McNair*, and *Roemer* v. *Board of Pub. Works of Md.* Each of these cases involved a general aid program that provided benefits to a broad array of secular and sectarian institutions on an evenhanded basis, but in none of them was that fact dispositive. The plurality opinion in *Roemer* made this point exactly:

"The Court has taken the view that a secular purpose and a facial neutrality may not be enough, if in fact the State is lending direct support to a religious activity. The State may not, for example, pay for what is actually a religious education, even though it purports to be paying for a secular one, and even though it makes its aid available to secular and religious institutions alike" (opinion of Blackmun, J.).

Instead, the central enquiry in each of these general aid cases, as in *Bowen*, was whether **⊥2544** secular activities could be separated from the sectarian ones sufficiently to ensure that aid would flow to the secular alone.

Witters, *Mueller*, and *Zobrest* expressly preserve the standard thus exhibited so often. Each of these cases explicitly distinguished the indirect aid in issue from contrasting examples in the line of cases striking down direct aid, and each thereby expressly preserved the core constitutional principle that direct aid to religion is impermissible. See *Zobrest* (distinguishing *Meek* v. *Pittenger* and *School Dist.* v. *Ball*, and noting that "'[t]he state may not grant aid to a religious school, whether cash or in kind, where the effect of the aid is that of a direct subsidy to the religious school'") (quoting *Witters*); see also *ibid.*; *Mueller*. It appears that the University perfectly understood the primacy of the no-direct-funding rule over the evenhandedness principle when it drew the line short of funding "any activity which primarily promotes or manifests a particular belief(s) in or about a deity or an ultimate reality."

C

Since conformity with the marginal or limiting principle of evenhandedness is insufficient of itself to demonstrate the constitutionality of providing a government benefit that reaches religion, the Court must identify some further element in the funding scheme that does demonstrate its permissibility. For one reason or another, the Court's chosen element appears to be the fact that under the University's Guidelines, funds are sent to the printer chosen by Wide Awake, rather than to Wide Awake itself.

1

If the Court's suggestion is that this feature of the funding program brings this case into line with *Witters*, *Mueller*, and *Zobrest*, the Court has misread those cases, which turned on the fact that the choice to benefit religion was made by a non-religious third party standing between the government and a religious institution. **⊥2545** Here there is no third party standing between the government and the ultimate religious beneficiary to break the circuit by its independent discretion to put state money to religious use. The printer, of course, has no option to take the money and use it to print a secular journal instead of Wide Awake. It only gets the money because of its contract to print a message of religious evangelism at the direction of Wide Awake, and it will receive payment only for doing precisely that. The formalism of distinguishing between payment to Wide Awake so it can pay an approved bill and payment of the approved bill itself cannot be the basis of a decision of Constitutional law. If this indeed were a critical distinction, the Constitution would permit a State to pay all the bills of any religious institution; in fact, despite the Court's purported adherence to the no-direct-funding principle, the State could simply hand out credit cards to religious institutions and honor the monthly statements (so long as someone could devise an evenhanded umbrella to cover the whole scheme). *Witters* and the other cases cannot be distinguished out of existence this way.

2

It is more probable, however, that the Court's reference to the printer goes to a different attempt to justify the payment. On this purported justification, the payment to the printer is significant only as the last step in an argument resting on the assumption that a public university may give a religious group the use of any of its equipment or facilities so long as secular groups are likewise eligible. The Court starts with the cases of *Widmar* v. *Vincent*, *Board of Ed. of Westside Community Schools* v. *Mergens*, and *Lamb's Chapel* v. *Center Moriches Union Free School Dist.*, in which religious groups were held to be entitled to access for speaking in government buildings open generally for that purpose. The Court reasons that the availability of a forum has economic value (the government built and maintained the building, while the speakers saved the rent for a hall); and that economically there is no difference between the University's provision of the value of the room and the value, say, of the University's printing equipment; and that therefore the University must be able to provide the use of the latter. Since it may do that, the argument goes, it would be unduly formalistic to draw the line at paying for an outside printer, who simply does what the magazine's publishers could have done with the University's own printing equipment.

The argument is as unsound as it is simple, and the first of its troubles emerges from an examination of the cases relied upon to support it. The common factual thread running through *Widmar*, *Mergens*, and *Lamb's Chapel*, is that a governmental institution created a limited forum for the use of students in a school or college, or for the public at large, but sought to exclude speakers with religious messages. See generally *Perry Ed. Assn.* v. *Perry Local Educators' Assn.* (forum analysis). In each case the restriction was struck down either as an impermissible attempt to regulate the content of speech in an open forum (as in *Widmar* and *Mergens*) or to suppress a particular religious viewpoint (as in *Lamb's Chapel*). In each case, to be sure, the religious speaker's use of the room passed muster as an incident of a plan to facilitate speech generally for a secular purpose, entailing neither secular entanglement with religion nor risk that the religious speech would be taken to be the speech ⊥**2546** of the government or that the government's endorsement of a religious message would be inferred. But each case drew ultimately on unexceptionable Speech Clause doctrine treating the evangelist, the Salvation Army, the millennialist or the Hare Krishna like any other speaker in a public forum. It was the preservation of free speech on the model of the street corner that supplied the justification going beyond the requirement of evenhandedness.

The Court's claim of support from these forum-access cases is ruled out by the very scope of their holdings. While they do indeed allow a limited benefit to religious speakers, they rest on the recognition that all speakers are entitled to use the street corner (even though the State paves the roads and provides police protection to everyone on the street) and on the analogy between the public street corner and open classroom space. Thus, the Court found it significant that the classroom speakers would engage in traditional speech activities in these forums, too, even though the rooms (like street corners) require some incidental state spending to maintain them. The analogy breaks down entirely, however, if the cases are read more broadly than the Court wrote them, to cover more than forums for literal speaking. There is no traditional street corner printing provided by the government on equal terms to all comers, and the forum cases cannot be lifted to a higher plane of generalization without admitting that new economic benefits are being extended directly to religion in clear violation of the principle barring direct aid. The argument from economic equivalence thus breaks down on recognizing that the direct state aid it would support is not mitigated by the street corner analogy in the service of free speech. Absent that, the rule against direct aid stands as a bar to printing services as well as printers.

3

It must, indeed, be a recognition of just this point that leads the Court to take a third tack, not in coming up with yet a third attempt at justification within the rules of existing case law, but in recasting the scope of the Establishment Clause in ways that make further affirmative justification unnecessary. *Justice O'CONNOR* makes a comprehensive analysis of the manner in which the activity fee is assessed and distributed. She concludes that the funding differs so sharply from religious funding out of governmental treasuries generally that it falls outside Establishment Clause's purview in the absence of a message of religious endorsement (which she finds not to be present). The opinion of the Court concludes more expansively that the activity fee is not a tax, and then proceeds to find the aid permissible on the legal assumption that the bar against direct aid applies only to aid derived from tax revenue. I have already indicated why it is fanciful to treat the fee as anything but a tax (noting mandatory nature of the fee), and will not repeat the point again. The novelty of the assumption that the direct aid bar only extends to aid derived from taxation, however, requires some response.

Although it was a taxation scheme that moved Madison to write in the first instance, the Court has never held that government resources obtained without taxation could be used for direct religious support, and our cases on direct government aid have frequently spoken in terms in no way limited to tax revenues. *E.g.*, *School Dist.* v. *Ball* ("Although Establishment Clause jurisprudence is characterized by few absolutes, the Clause does absolutely prohibit government-financed or government-sponsored indoctrination into the beliefs of a particular religious faith"); *Nyquist* ("In the absence of an effective means of guaranteeing that the state aid derived from public funds will be used exclusively for secular, neutral, and nonideological purposes, it is clear from our cases that direct aid in whatever form is invalid"); *id.* ("Primary among those evils" against which the Establishment Clause guards "have been sponsorship, financial support, and active involvement of the sovereign in religious activity") (citations and internal quotation marks omitted); see also T. Curry, The First Freedoms 217 (1986) (At the time ⊥**2547** of the framing of the Bill of Rights, "[t]he belief that government assistance to religion, especially in the form of taxes, violated religious liberty had a long history").

Allowing non-tax funds to be spent on religion would, in fact, fly in the face of clear principle. Leaving entirely aside the question whether public non-tax revenues could ever be used to finance religion without violating the endorsement test, see *Allegheny County* v. *American Civil Liberties Union*, any such use of them would ignore one of the dual objectives of the Establishment Clause, which was meant not only to protect individuals and their republics from the destructive consequences of mixing government and religion, but to protect religion from a corrupting dependence on support from the Government. *Engel* v. *Vitale* (the Establishment Clause's "first and most immediate purpose rested on the belief that a union of government and religion tends to destroy government and to degrade religion"); *Everson* (Rutledge, J., dissenting) ("The great condition of religious liberty is that it be maintained free from sustenance, as also from other interferences, by the state. For when it comes to rest upon that secular foundation it vanishes with the resting") (citing Madison's Remonstrance ¶¶7, 8); *School Dist. of Abington* v. *Schempp* (Brennan, J., concurring) ("It is not only the nonbeliever who fears the injection of sectarian doctrines and controversies into the civil polity, but in as high degree it is the devout believer who fears the secularization of a creed which becomes too deeply involved with and dependent upon the government"); Jefferson, A Bill for Establishing Religious Freedom, reprinted in 5 The Founder's Constitution, at 84-85. Since the corrupting effect of government support does not turn on whether the Government's own money comes from taxation or gift or the sale of public lands, the Establishment Clause could hardly relax its vigilance simply because tax revenue was not implicated. Accordingly, in the absence of a forthright disavowal, one can only assume that the Court does not mean to eliminate one half of the Establishment Clause's justification.

D

Nothing in the Court's opinion would lead me to end this enquiry into the application of the Establishment Clause any differently from the way I began it. The Court is ordering an instrumentality of the State to support religious evangelism with direct funding. This is a flat violation of the Establishment Clause.

II

Given the dispositive effect of the Establishment Clause's bar to funding the magazine, there should be no need to decide whether in the absence of this bar the University would violate the Free Speech Clause by limiting funding as it has done. *Widmar* (university's compliance with its Establishment Clause obligations can be a compelling interest justifying speech restriction). But the Court's speech analysis may have independent application, and its flaws should not pass unremarked.

The Court acknowledges the necessity for a university to make judgments based on the content of what may be said or taught when it decides, in the absence of unlimited amounts of money or other resources, how to honor its educational responsibilities. *Widmar;* cf. *Perry* (subject matter and speaker identity distinctions "are inherent and inescapable in the process of limiting a nonpublic forum to activities compatible with the intended purpose of the property"). Nor does the Court generally question that in allocating public funds a state university enjoys spacious discretion. Cf. *Rust* v. *Sullivan* ("[W]hen the government appropriates public funds to establish a program it is entitled to define the limits of that program"); *Regan* v. *Taxation* ⊥**2548** *with Representation of Wash.* (upholding government subsidization decision partial to one class of speaker). Accordingly, the Court recognizes that the relevant enquiry in this case is not merely whether the University bases its funding decisions on the subject matter of student speech; if there is an infirmity in the basis for the University's funding decision, it must be that the University is impermissibly distinguishing among competing viewpoints, citing, *inter alia*, *Perry;* see also *Lamb's Chapel* (subject matter distinctions permissible in controlling access to limited public forum if reasonable and viewpoint neutral); *Cornelius* v. *NAACP Legal Defense & Ed. Fund, Inc.* (similar); *Regan.*

The issue whether a distinction is based on viewpoint does not turn simply on whether a government regulation happens to be applied to a speaker who seeks to advance a particular viewpoint; the issue, of course, turns on whether the burden on speech is explained by reference to viewpoint. See *Cornelius* ("[T]he government violates the First Amendment when it denies access to a speaker solely to suppress the point of view he espouses on an otherwise includible subject"). As when deciding whether a speech restriction is content-based or content-neutral, "[t]he government's purpose is the controlling consideration." *Ward* v. *Rock Against Racism;* see also *ibid.* (content neutrality turns on, *inter alia*, whether a speech restriction is "justified without reference to the content of the regulated speech"). So, for example, a city that enforces its excessive noise ordinance by pulling the plug on a rock band using a forbidden amplification system is not guilty of viewpoint discrimination simply because the band wishes to use that equipment to espouse antiracist views. Nor does a municipality's decision to prohibit political advertising on bus placards amount to viewpoint discrimination when in the course of applying this policy it denies space to a person who wishes to speak in favor of a particular political candidate.

Accordingly, the prohibition on viewpoint discrimination serves that important purpose of the Free Speech Clause, which is to bar the government from skewing public debate. Other things being equal, viewpoint discrimination occurs when government allows one message while prohibiting the messages of ⊥**2549** those who can reasonably be expected to respond. See *First Nat. Bank of Boston* v. *Bellotti* ("Especially where . . . the legislature's suppression of speech suggests an attempt to give one side of a debatable public question an advantage in expressing its views to the people, the First Amendment is plainly offended"); *Madison Joint School Dist. No.* 8 v. *Wisconsin Employment Relations Comm'n* ("To permit one side of a debatable public question to have a monopoly in expressing its views . . . is the antithesis of constitutional guarantees"); *United States* v. *Kokinda* (viewpoint discrimination involves an "inten[t] to discourage one viewpoint and advance another"). It is precisely this element of taking sides in a public debate that identifies viewpoint discrimination and makes it the most pernicious of all distinctions based on content. Thus, if government assists those espousing one point of view, neutrality requires it to assist those espousing opposing points of view, as well.

There is no viewpoint discrimination in the University's application of its Guidelines to deny funding to Wide Awake. Under those Guidelines, a "religious activit[y]," which is not eligible for funding, is "an activity which primarily promotes or manifests a particular belief(s) in or about a deity or an ultimate reality." It is clear that this is the basis on which Wide Awake Productions was denied funding. Letter from Student Council to Ronald W. Rosenberger. ("In reviewing the request by Wide Awake Productions, the Appropriations Committee determined your organization's request could not be funded as it is a religious activity"). The discussion of Wide Awake's content shows beyond any question that it "primarily promotes or manifests a particular belief(s) in or about a deity . . . ," in the very specific sense that its manifest function is to call students to repentance, to commitment to Jesus Christ, and to particular moral action because of its Christian character.

If the Guidelines were written or applied so as to limit only such Christian advocacy and no other evangelical efforts that might compete with it, the discrimination would be based on viewpoint. But that is not what the regulation authorizes; it applies to Muslim and Jewish and Buddhist advocacy as well as to Christian. And since it limits funding to activities promoting or manifesting a particular belief not only "in" but "about" a deity or ultimate reality, it applies to agnostics and atheists as well as it does to deists and theists (as the University maintained at oral argument and as the Court recognizes). The Guidelines, and their application to Wide Awake, thus do not skew debate by funding one position but not its competitors. As understood by their application to Wide Awake, they simply deny funding for hortatory speech that "primarily promotes or manifests" any view on the merits of religion; they deny funding for the entire subject matter of religious apologetics.

The Court, of course, reads the Guidelines differently, but while I believe the Court is wrong in construing their breadth, the important point is that even on the Court's own construction the Guidelines impose no viewpoint discrimination. In attempting to demonstrate the potentially chilling effect such funding restrictions might have on learning in our nation's universities, the Court describes the Guidelines as "a sweeping restriction on student thought and student inquiry," disentitling a vast array of topics to funding. As the Court reads the Guidelines to exclude "any writing that is explicable as resting upon a premise which presupposes the existence of a deity or ultimate reality," as well as "those student journalistic efforts which primarily manifest or promote a belief that there is no deity and no ultimate reality," the Court concludes that the major works of writers from Descartes to Sartre would be barred from the funding forum. The Court goes so far as to suggest that the Guidelines, properly interpreted, tolerate nothing much more ⊥**2550** than essays on "making pasta or peanut butter cookies . . . ."

Now, the regulation is not so categorically broad as the Court protests. The Court reads the word "primarily" ("primarily promotes or manifests a particular belief(s) in or about a deity or an ultimate reality") right out of the Guidelines, whereas it is obviously crucial in distinguishing between works characterized by the evangelism of Wide Awake and writing that merely happens to express views that a given religion might approve, or simply descriptive writing informing a reader about the position of a given religion. But, as I said, that is not the important point. Even if the Court were indeed correct about the funding restriction's categorical breadth, the stringency of the restriction would most certainly not work any impermissible viewpoint discrimination under any prior understanding of that species of content discrimination. If a University wished to fund no speech beyond the subjects of pasta and cookie preparation, it surely would not be discriminating on the basis of someone's viewpoint, at least absent some controversial claim that pasta and cookies did not exist. The upshot would be an instructional universe without higher education, but not a universe where one viewpoint was enriched above its competitors.

The Guidelines are thus substantially different from the access restriction considered in *Lamb's Chapel*, the case upon which the Court heavily relies in finding a viewpoint distinction here. *Lamb's Chapel* addressed a school board's regulation prohibiting the after-hours use of school premises "by any group for religious purposes," even though the forum otherwise was open for a variety of social, civic, and recreational purposes. "Religious" was understood to refer to the viewpoint of a believer, and the regulation did not purport to deny access to any speaker wishing to express a non-religious or expressly antireligious point of view on any subject. ("The issue in this case is whether . . . it violates the Free Speech Clause of the First Amendment . . . to deny a church access to school premises to exhibit for public viewing and for assertedly religious purposes, a film dealing with family and child-rearing issues").

With this understanding, it was unremarkable that in *Lamb's Chapel* we unanimously determined that the access restriction, as applied to a speaker wishing to discuss family values from a Christian perspective, impermissibly distinguished between speakers on the basis of viewpoint. Equally obvious is the distinction between that case and this one, where the regulation is being applied, not to deny funding for those who discuss issues in general from a religious viewpoint, but to those engaged in promoting or opposing religious conversion and religious observances as such. If this amounts to viewpoint discrimination, the Court has all but eviscerated the line between viewpoint and content.

⊥2551 To put the point another way, the Court's decision equating a categorical exclusion of both sides of the religious debate with viewpoint discrimination suggests the Court has concluded that primarily religious and antireligious speech, grouped together, always provides an opposing (and not merely a related) viewpoint to any speech about any secular topic. Thus, the Court's reasoning requires a university that funds private publications about any primarily nonreligious topic also to fund publications primarily espousing adherence to or rejection of religion. But a university's decision to fund a magazine about racism, and not to fund publications aimed at urging repentance before God does not skew the debate either about racism or the desirability of religious conversion. The Court's contrary holding amounts to a significant reformulation of our viewpoint discrimination precedents and will significantly expand access to limited-access forums. See *Greer* v. *Spock* (upholding regulation prohibiting political speeches on military base); *Cornelius* (exclusion from fundraising drive of political activity or advocacy groups is facially viewpoint neutral despite inclusion of charitable, health and welfare agencies); *Perry* (ability of teachers' bargaining representative to use internal school mail system does not require that access be provided to "any other citizen's group or community organization with a message for school personnel"); *Lehman* v. *Shaker Heights* (exclusion of political messages from forum permissible despite ability of nonpolitical speakers to use the forum).

III

Since I cannot see the future I cannot tell whether today's decision portends much more than making a shambles out of student activity fees in public colleges. Still, my apprehension is whetted by *Chief Justice BURGER's* warning in *Lemon* v. *Kurtzman*: "in constitutional adjudication some steps, which when taken were thought to approach 'the verge,' have become the platform for yet further steps. A certain momentum develops in constitutional theory and it can be a 'downhill thrust' easily set in motion but difficult to retard or stop."

I respectfully dissent.

GOVERNMENT AID TO CHURCH-RELATED SCHOOLS

The development of parochial schools in this country is closely related to the history of immigration. Beginning about 1830 vast numbers of immigrants began to come to this country from northern and western Europe; later, particularly after 1865, they came from southern and eastern Europe. Many of these immigrants were Roman Catholics. In an attempt to incorporate these immigrants into the church and simultaneously to try to educate the children born to American Catholic parents, the Roman Catholic Church began a massive effort to create Catholic schools. In 1790 there were not any Catholic educational institutions in this country, but by 1840 there were more than two hundred schools, about half of them being west of the Allegheny Mountains. For several reasons the Catholics did not rely on the developing public school system to educate their children.

Traditionally, Catholics had insisted that the education of children should be performed by the home, the church, and the church school. They did not believe that education provided by a secular state would fit the Catholic philosophy of education. The bishop of Trenton went so far as to say that "the idea that the state has a right to teach . . . is not a Christian idea. It is a pagan one."[1] Most Catholics could not conceive of the state's replacing the home and the church as the principal educative agents.[2]

---

[1]Quoted in Neil G. McCluskey, *Catholic Education in America* (New York: Teachers College, Columbia University, 1964), p. 11.

[2]Throughout the history of the Catholic church in the United States, however, about one half of the Catholic children have attended public schools, probably because of economic necessity.

They believed that education without religion was, at best, stilted and truncated and, at worst, dangerous. The leadership of the church contended that education must include religion in order to give a sense of morality to children.

As noted in an earlier essay, public schools attempted to teach morality through the teaching of religion. Why did Catholics think that they had to have their own schools? Because they saw that the religion which was taught in the public schools was a kind of "religion in general" with Protestant overtones. Consequently, when the bishops of the American Catholic church met in 1884, they insisted that a school be built next to every Catholic church within two years of that date and that all Catholic parents send their children to one of those schools unless a bishop gave special permission to do otherwise. Although neither school building nor attendance ever reached those goals, Catholics have continued to be serious about their schools.

Catholics were not the only ones who established parochial schools. Many Jewish congregations did, too, for the obvious reason that they could not accept the religious content of the public schools. Some Protestant groups began parochial schools because the public schools were not Protestant enough for them.[3]

The Catholic church's efforts to create parochial schools intensified the anti-Catholicism which was rampant in the nineteenth and early part of the twentieth centuries. Many viewed the public schools as a means to unify the American population. If children of immigrants would attend the public schools with the children of native Americans, then their differences would disappear, they would become Americanized, and American society would become more homogeneous. The fact that Catholics had their own schools showed that they wanted to be different, which was regarded as un-American.[4]

During and just after World War I, this anti-Catholicism was combined with nationalism to form a direct attack upon foreignness and non-public schools. Right after America entered the war, a number of states passed laws forbidding the teaching of foreign languages, especially German. Among these states was Nebraska, which, in 1919, passed a law providing that no foreign language could be taught in any school in the state unless the student had completed the eighth grade. In *Meyer* v. *Nebraska* (1923) the U.S. Supreme Court held that such laws violated the Due Process Clause of the Fourteenth Amendment because they withdrew from teachers the liberty to teach and from parents the liberty to employ teachers to instruct their children.

Oregon's legislature, in 1922, passed a similar but broader law that required all able-bodied and teachable students to attend public school. The law was challenged by a private military academy and by a school operated by the Society of the Sisters of the Holy Name of Jesus and Mary. Again, because the First Amendment had not yet been applied to the states, the basis of the challenge was the Fourteenth Amendment. In the 1925 decision of PIERCE v. SOCIETY OF SISTERS, the Court, recalling the *Meyer* case, held that the Oregon law impermissibly denied private and parochial schools the right to do business and interfered with the liberty of parents to educate their children as they chose. This case is often called the "Magna Carta" of parochial schools.

Now that it was clear that parochial schools had the right to exist, the Catholic church continued its efforts to obtain state aid for its schools, an effort which had been started as early as 1840 by Bishop John Hughes of New York. Legal questions growing out of such aid first came to the Court in the 1930 case of COCHRAN v. LOUISIANA STATE BOARD OF EDUCATION. Louisiana's legislature had enacted a statute providing for the purchase of secular textbooks for use by school children, including those enrolled in parochial schools. The law was challenged on the basis that the Fourteenth Amendment forbids states from depriving persons of their property without due process of law. The use of tax money to provide books for parochial schools, it was argued, amounted to the use of the money for a private, rather than public, purpose; thus, the statute was unconstitutional. The Court did not agree, arguing that the beneficiaries of the program were not the parochial schools but the children of the state, some of whom happened to be enrolled in parochial schools. This case introduced the "child benefit theory" into consideration of whether and how to provide state aid to church-related schools. Supporters of parochial schools were greatly encouraged by the ruling, although the relation of this theory to the First Amendment was not clear.

Seventeen years passed before another case concerning aid to parochial schools came before the Court. In EVERSON v. BOARD OF EDUCATION (1947), Justice Black's separationist rhetoric notwithstanding, the Court approved of providing bus fares for children enrolled in church schools. The opinion stated that the state-supported bus rides were part of the state's public welfare program; even though the program helped children to attend church schools, aid to the schools them-

[3]For a survey of the history of church-related schools in this country, as well as some of the contemporary problems confronting such schools, see James C. Carper and Thomas C. Hunt, eds., *Religious Schooling in America* (Birmingham, AL: Religious Education Press, 1984).

[4]An expression of this attitude toward the public schools, without the anti-Catholicism, may be seen in Mr. Justice Frankfurter's majority opinion in MINERSVILLE SCHOOL DISTRICT v. GOBITIS and his dissenting opinion in WEST VIRGINIA BOARD OF EDUCATION v. BARNETTE.

selves was indirect and thus permissible. This language had a "child benefit" ring; furthermore, it was based on the Court's interpretation of the Establishment Clause. The decision suggested to proponents of state aid to church-related schools that a wide range of aid programs could become a reality. At the time, however, these proponents did not know that the limit of permissible aid which the Court would allow would not be expanded for the next thirty years.

Still later, advocates of state aid to church-related schools, primarily Catholics, were given more cause for optimism with the passage of the Elementary and Secondary Education Act of 1965. This act of Congress included a section which allowed federal funds to be used for aiding schools populated by educationally deprived children from low-income families, even though the schools were church-related. This surely would be a great supplement to book lending and bus transportation programs.

In 1968 the Court decided BOARD OF EDUCATION v. ALLEN. The case reaffirmed the constitutionality of loans of secular textbooks to children in parochial schools. This time the Court used "child benefit" language and affirmed that the program had a secular purpose and did nothing to advance or inhibit religion. Justice White, the author of the opinion, assumed that one could easily distinguish between secular and religious education imparted in a parochial school. He seemed to say that virtually any kind of state aid could be provided to the secular side of the school.

Also decided in 1968 was FLAST v. COHEN, in which the Court allowed taxpayer suits on First Amendment questions to be filed in federal courts. Two years later WALZ v. TAX COMMISSION was decided, adding the "excessive entanglement" test to the "secular purpose" and "primary effect" tests for interpreting the Establishment Clause. These decisions of 1968 and 1970 were to play a major role in reversing what seemed to be a pro-accommodationist trend in decisions concerning aid to church-related schools.

In 1968 the Pennsylvania legislature enacted a law authorizing action whereby the state "purchased educational services" from church-related schools. That is, Pennsylvania paid parochial schools for teaching specified secular subjects: mathematics, modern foreign languages, physical sciences, and physical education. To guarantee the secularity of the courses, all instructional material had to be approved by the state superintendent of public instruction.

A year later Rhode Island adopted a plan whereby teachers of secular subjects in parochial schools that served students from the lower end of the socioeconomic scale would receive from the state 15 percent of their annual salary. Taxpayers in both states filed suits in federal courts. In 1971 the Supreme Court considered the Rhode Island plan in *Early* v. *DiCenso* and the Pennsylvania law in LEMON v. KURTZMAN. The two cases were decided together under the latter title. Writing for a majority of eight, Chief Justice Burger found both programs to be in violation of the Establishment Clause because they fostered excessive entanglement between church and state. In each case, state aid was to be given only to the secular side of the parochial school's program. Burger declared that continual government surveillance would be required to guarantee that teachers receiving salary supplements were not teaching religion and that services purchased were really free from religious content. Such interaction between church schools and civil authority was not the separation that the Establishment Clause was designed to guarantee.

Still, the issue of providing aid to parochial schools was far from settled. Even before the *Lemon* decision, New York had enacted legislation to provide aid of a different type, some of which might be called "parent benefit." Pennsylvania also enacted new legislation immediately after *Lemon*. Challenges to all these programs made their way to the Supreme Court by means of taxpayers' suits in federal courts. Several decisions were handed down on 25 June 1973, a disastrous day from the viewpoint of those who favor state aid to church-related schools.

In COMMITTEE FOR PUBLIC EDUCATION AND RELIGIOUS LIBERTY (PEARL) v. NYQUIST, the Court considered a comprehensive New York plan to aid church-related schools. The first section of the law provided for direct money grants to nonpublic schools serving a high concentration of pupils from low-income families. State money was to be used for maintenance and repair of facilities and equipment in order to insure the students' health, welfare, and safety. The amount of money would depend on the age of the facility but could not be more than 50 percent of the cost for equivalent services in the public schools. The second section of the act provided for tuition reimbursement to parents who had children in nonpublic elementary or secondary schools, if the parents' annual taxable income was less than $5,000. The third section of the law provided aid for parents whose annual taxable income was between $5,000 and $25,000. In filing a state income tax return, a parent was allowed to deduct a stipulated sum from his/her adjusted gross income for each child attending a nonpublic school. The amount of the deduction was unrelated to the amount of tuition actually paid and decreased as the amount of taxable income increased.

In a decision written by Justice Powell, the Court found all three of the programs unconstitutional because they failed the "primary effect" test. In the maintenance and repair section of the act, no provision was made to restrict payments to expenditures for the upkeep of facilities used exclusively for secular purposes; thus, the effect of the plan was to subsidize and advance the religious mission of sectarian schools. The fact that tuition reimbursements were made directly to parents did not mitigate the fact that the effect of the aid was clearly to provide financial support for sectarian institutions. The Court was convinced that the state sought to relieve parents' financial burden sufficiently to assure that they would continue to have the option of sending their children to church-related schools. Although the method of the third section of the act was different from the second, it also provided the parent "the same form of encouragement and reward for sending his children to nonpublic schools" 413 U.S. 756, 791.

On the same day the *Nyquist* decision was announced, the Court also struck down a Pennsylvania plan of tuition reimbursement that was virtually identical with that in section two of the New York plan. In *Sloan* v. *Lemon* (1973) the Court said that tuition reimbursement in Pennsylvania suffered from the same infirmity as in New York: the primary effect was to advance religion.

On that fateful day the Court struck down still another New York attempt to aid church-related schools, the purchase of mandated services. New York required all accredited schools to give examinations to students and to keep records on both students and teachers. It was contended that if the state paid for such expenses in the public schools, it ought to do the same for nonpublic schools. But the program paid for teacher-prepared tests as well as state-standardized tests, and therein lay a problem. In *Levitt* v. *Committee for Public Education and Religious Liberty (PEARL)* (1973), the Court argued that testing was a part of the teaching process, and, because the state had no way to determine if the teacher-prepared tests were entirely free from religious instruction, the program was an impermissible aid to religion.

In 1974, in *Wheeler* v. *Barrera,* the Court ruled that a state receiving funds under Title I of the Elementary and Secondary Education Act must provide "comparable but not identical" services to disadvantaged students attending both public and nonpublic schools. This must be done even though the state's constitution prohibits any aid to church-related schools, as in the case of Missouri. A state may refuse to make comparable services available to disadvantaged children in nonpublic schools, but by doing so, Title I funds would be forfeited.

In MEEK v. PITTENGER (1975), the Court struck down still other attempts by Pennsylvania to provide aid to its church-related schools. At issue was another comprehensive law which provided for the loan of textbooks to church school students and the loan of instructional equipment (projectors, recorders, laboratory apparatus) and materials (periodicals, photographs, maps, films) directly to the schools. In addition, Pennsylvania provided "auxiliary services": remedial teaching, psychological and therapeutic services, guidance, counseling, and testing by state-paid personnel who came to the premises of parochial schools.

In an opinion written by Justice Stewart, the Court found the loan of the textbooks to be permissible under the doctrine of the *Allen* case. But all other aspects of the law were found to violate the Establishment Clause. The loan of instructional equipment and materials had the primary effect of advancing the religious mission of the schools. Provision of "auxiliary services," because it involved the activity of public school teachers, fostered excessive entanglement between state and church because of the continual surveillance required to insure that religion was not taught.

The cumulative effect of all the decisions from *Lemon* through *Meek* was to dash accommodationists' hopes of providing new means for aiding church-related schools. As each of these cases was decided, the number and intensity of the dissenters increased (e.g., Chief Justice Burger's reference to "the crabbed attitude" of the Court in *Meek*). At the same time, many Catholic responses escalated in criticism of the Court until, after the *Meek* decision, John T. Cicco, superintendent of Catholic schools in the Pittsburgh diocese, could say: "I don't believe the Court would give Catholics anything, no matter what they would come up with."[5]

Some will argue that the Court responded to such criticism in its decision in WOLMAN v. WALTER (1977). More likely, the Court was acknowledging that the Ohio statute which was the basis for the case had been carefully written to avoid the objections the Court had found in *Meek.* For whatever reason, *Wolman* approved of a number of ways states could financially aid church-related schools: the news media described the decision as an "instruction manual" for legislatures. In a decision written by Justice Blackmun, the Court again approved of textbook loans to parochial school students. Approval was given to state-financed academic testing of students, using standardized tests, thus avoiding the objection, raised in *Levitt,* to the possibility of religious content in teacher-prepared tests. The justices approved of state-subsidized speech, hearing, and psychological diagnostic services administered in parochial schools by public school employees. However, the sole purpose of the services must be to determine a student's deficiency or need for assistance. Therapeutic services such as guid-

[5]"Parochiaid Defeated Again," *Church and State* 28 (July-August 1975): 7.

ance counseling, speech help, or remedial reading would be allowed, so long as the services were performed away from the "pervasively sectarian atmosphere of the church-related school," thus distinguishing the Ohio plan from that disallowed in *Meek*.

However, the Court did not give blanket approval to the Ohio plan. It declared unconstitutional the state's supplying of projectors, maps and globes, and other instructional equipment because they were not actually loaned to parents and pupils, despite Ohio's protestations to the contrary. Finally, the Court struck down state financing of instructional field trips because they would be under the direction of religious schools and could easily be transformed into religious education.

In arriving at its decision, the Court claimed that it applied its three-part test consistently with its previous opinions, although seven of the justices disagreed with that claim enough to write dissents on one or more of the parts of Ohio's school plan. Consequently, *Wolman* is a very complicated case.

Although the impulse to establish parochial schools was over a century old, the 1970s and 1980s saw a rapid increase in parochial educational activity. One reason was the alleged secularization and incompetence of the public schools, already noted; another was a protest against judicially commanded desegregation of public schools, in most cases implemented by busing. Although the accusation that proliferating private and parochial schools in this time were "segregation academies" was perhaps too broadly made, nonetheless, there was some truth to it.

A major question for the sponsors of the new private and church-related schools was whether or not any state or federal money could be used to help finance them. Many believed that *Wolman* was a definitive case, i.e., that it had set the limits once and for all. However, because its strict separationism was not to the liking of many supporters of church-related schools, various governmental agencies continued to devise plans to try to give public aid to the schools. Because such plans were routinely challenged by separationists, the Court ruled on several cases. One of these, *New York* v. *Cathedral Academy,* goes back to a much earlier set of cases. In 1973 the Court handed down a decision in *Levitt* v. *Committee for Public Education and Religious Liberty* (PEARL) in which it invalidated state financing of the grading of teacher-prepared tests on the grounds that such tests might have religious content. In that case the Court affirmed an injunction of a federal district court forbidding payments to parochial schools in New York, including payments for expenses the schools had already incurred in the last one-half of the 1971-1972 school year. In 1972 the New York legislature had passed a law which allowed the state to pay the schools for expenses already incurred in the program banned by the district court.

There was some precedent for New York's action. When the Court invalidated some state payments to parochial schools in Rhode Island and Pennsylvania in *Lemon,* Pennsylvania had not yet paid all the money due to the parochial schools for services they had already performed. In a dispute over whether the state could fulfill the remainder of its contract with the schools, the Court ruled, in a case designated *Lemon II,* that it could. That is, even though the program had been declared unconstitutional, the Court permitted the remaining payments under the concept of fairness and equity because the schools had been led to believe, while the program was still in effect, that they would be paid for those services.

When a dispute arose over whether New York could finish its contracted payments for testing services in the parochial schools, invalidated in *Levitt, Lemon II* was cited as precedent. In *Cathedral Academy,* however, payments were not allowed because the Court declared that the situation was different from *Lemon II.* According to this finding, when the district court imposed the original injunction it had specifically enjoined payments for amounts "heretofore or hereafter expended." Consequently, for New York to try to fulfill the remainder of its obligation to the parochial schools, under the concept of equity, it had to go against the express language of the district court. The Supreme Court held that to be impermissible.

Even as this litigation was in progress, the New York legislature drafted a new bill to pay for state-mandated services in the parochial schools. This time, however, the legislature restricted payments to grading of state-prepared examinations, which naturally concerned only secular subjects. (There were other parts to the plan, such as reporting pupil attendance and other educational data, but preparation and grading of exams were at the heart of the case.) This law was attacked by a group of strict separationists who contended that it made no difference who prepared and graded the tests. As long as the new law still provided for state funds to go to parochial schools, the separationists argued, it was unconstitutional under the Establishment Clause. After some complex legal transactions, the case finally reached the Supreme Court under the title COMMITTEE FOR PUBLIC EDUCATION AND RELIGIOUS FREEDOM v. REGAN.

While *Regan* was making its way to the Court, the *Wolman* case had been decided. Included in the array of programs for which Ohio had been willing to pay parochial schools was one which provided payment for the administration of state-prepared standardized tests (the same ones used in the public schools) and scoring of same by state employees. The Court had been convinced that, under such circumstances, no danger existed that the tests could be used to teach religion. Consequently, the program was upheld.

A majority of five saw enough similarity between the testing program in *Wolman* and the one being considered in *Regan* to find the latter constitutional. Only state-prepared standardized tests were paid for by state money; thus the law was constitutional. That the money was paid directly to the parochial schools and that the tests were graded by parochial school personnel rather than state personnel were not deemed to be significant problems by the majority. Dissenting justices would have invalidated the law under the Establishment Clause.

In MUELLER v. ALLEN (1983) the Court again addressed the question as to whether a state can provide financial aid through tax deductions to parents who send their children to parochial schools. A decade before, in *Nyquist,* income tax deductions to partially pay a student's tuition to parochial school had been declared unconstitutional because they had the primary effect of advancing religion. That is, by providing the tax advantage, the state provided parents an incentive to send their children to church-related schools, thereby furthering the schools' religious mission. *Mueller* grew out of a challenge to a Minnesota law which provided financial assistance, through state income tax deductions, for "tuition, textbooks, and transportation" of dependents attending elementary or secondary schools. The deduction was available to all parents who had children in school, whether the schools were private, church-related, *or public.* That factual difference from *Nyquist* made the decision come out differently. Justice Rehnquist, who had dissented in *Nyquist,* wrote for the Court that (1) the plan had the secular purpose of providing for a well-educated citizenry, because the exemption could finance educational expenses at either public or parochial schools; (2) it did not have the primary effect of advancing religion, since the aid did not flow to religious schools exclusively (which had the effect of leaving *Nyquist* intact: a law aiding only parochial schools would still be unconstitutional); and (3) it did not create excessive entanglement between church and state, since the act which triggered the tax deduction to the parent was the decision of the parent without any interaction with a state official. The law did provide that state officials would have to choose which textbooks could qualify for the deduction (the state could not pay for religion books). But this was not a problem since the Court had approved a virtually identical procedure many years before in BOARD OF EDUCATION v. ALLEN.

Four dissenters argued that the across-the-board feature of the plan was a fiction, since only under the most unusual circumstances did public schools charge any tuition. It was clear that parents who send their children to church-related schools were the primary (almost the only) beneficiaries of the tax reduction plan, so that it was not materially different from that declared unconstitutional in *Nyquist.* The majority was not persuaded. For them, the law was neutral on its face and its constitutionality should not be set aside on the basis of annual statistical reports. Justice Powell, the author of *Nyquist,* joined the majority. Thus was the way opened for other states, and perhaps the federal government, to provide tuition assistance for parents to send their children to private and church-related schools.

In 1985 the Court decided on still other ways to provide government aid to religious schools in GRAND RAPIDS SCHOOL DISTRICT v. BALL and AGUILAR v. FELTON, handed down the same day. These cases involved the employment of public school teachers to teach secular subjects in parochial schools on a part-time basis. The Court had dealt with a similar plan indirectly in 1974 when it had affirmed a district court's invalidation of a plan for public school teachers to teach remedial reading and mathematics for nonpublic school pupils in *Public Funds for Public Schools* v. *Marburger.* But it was not until these two cases that such plans were given full review.

Grand Rapids involved two programs, Shared Time and Community Education. The former offered classes intended to supplement "core curriculum" courses required by the state: art, music, physical education, and "remedial" and "enrichment" reading and mathematics. The Shared Time teachers were full-time public school employees, although some of them had taught in parochial schools. The Community Education program offered classes after the regular school day in voluntary courses including, but not limited to, arts and crafts, gymnastics, yearbook production, newspaper, chess, and nature appreciation. The teachers were generally parochial school teachers hired, on a part-time basis, by the public schools to teach these supplementary courses. The offerings of both programs were taught in parochial school rooms, which, during the times of these particular classes, had to be devoid of any religious symbols. In addition, a sign had to be posted designating the room as a public school classroom.

Felton involved a program virtually identical to the Shared Time dimension of *Grand Rapids.* The teachers were public school teachers hired to present traditional academic subjects in parochial school classrooms. They were directed to avoid teaching religion, to avoid involvement in religious activities normally occurring in the parochial school room, and to minimize contact with parochial school personnel. Supervision procedures were created to try to guarantee the requisite level of secularity. The program under consideration in *Felton* was aimed at educationally deprived children from low-income families and was federally financed under Title I of the Elementary and Secondary Education Act of 1965. The program in *Grand Rapids,* on the other hand, was state financed and aimed at students (and even adults, in the Community Education program) from all economic classes.

In each case, the Court declared the school aid program to be unconstitutional. The plan in *Grand Rapids* was found to have the primary effect of advancing religion in three ways: (1) the state-paid teachers, working in a sectarian environment, might indoctrinate students in religion, (2) the fact of state-paid teachers working in parochial schools symbolically conveys the message of state support of religion, and (3) the programs effectively subsidize religion by assuming a portion of the parochial school's responsibility for teaching secular subjects. In *Felton* the defect was excessive entanglement. To guarantee that no religion was taught required an impermissible amount of surveillance by state personnel. Furthermore, state and parochial school officials had to regularly meet together to plan and to solve problems. There was also frequent contact between the regular parochial school teachers and the state-paid teachers.

Both decisions were five-to-four (although Justices Burger and O'Connor did agree to the unconstitutionality of the Community Education part of *Grand Rapids).* The dissenters criticized the majority for impugning the integrity of teachers hired to work in the parochial schools, especially since the record of the programs showed no evidence of indoctrination. They faulted the zealous application of the *Lemon* test, especially the "excessive entanglement" portion. Finally, in *Felton,* they called attention to the human cost of the decision, since the remedial and enrichment teaching denied was for educationally deprived children from low-income families.

During the latter part of the period in which the Court was handing down its most separationist decisions on state aid to elementary and secondary church-related schools, it also heard some cases on state aid to church-related colleges. Because the conditions were somewhat different in institutions of higher education, so were the decisions.

Title I of the Higher Education Facilities Act of 1963 provided federal construction grants for college building and facilities, but it specified that funds were not to be used to construct any building in which sectarian instruction or religious worship took place. The government maintained an interest in the federally financed buildings for twenty years. After that period, colleges could use the building for any purpose; they no longer had to be used for only secular educational activities.

The law was implemented at four church-related colleges in Connecticut and was challenged in federal court by some taxpayers from that state who claimed that it was unconstitutional. The Court dealt with their complaint in TILTON v. RICHARDSON (1971). Chief Justice Burger wrote the opinion of the Court. He said that the provision whereby federally financed buildings could be used for religious purposes after twenty years was a violation of the Establishment Clause, but that, in general, building grants for church-related colleges were not unconstitutional. The key distinctions between colleges and secondary and elementary schools are that the former do not have as their primary goal the inculcation of the doctrine of the sponsoring church, that college students are less impressionable than younger students, and that college teachers are guided by their own internal scholarly disciplines and seek to stimulate critical thinking by their students. Consequently, the building grants do not have the effect of advancing religion. In addition, because colleges and their teachers are more "objective" in their approach to religion and because the federal monies are used to construct buildings, which are non-ideological by nature, it is not necessary for government to maintain a continual surveillance to guarantee that the funds are put to secular use. Consequently, the law does not have the effect of creating excessive entanglement between state and church.

There were four dissenters in *Tilton* who felt that the distinctions between colleges and lower level schools were oversimplified and that the college grants ought to be found unconstitutional on the precedent of *Lemon.*

Two years later, on that important 25 June 1973, when the Court announced so many decisions on government aid to church-related schools, it also handed down *Hunt* v. *McNair,* a college case similar to *Tilton.* The South Carolina legislature had created an agency to issue bonds, the proceeds of which were to be used to finance college facilities. Facilities so financed could not be used for religious worship or instruction. The bonds were to be paid off from tuition and other income of the college. Actually, no state money was involved in the program. The only state aid was the creation of an instrumentality through which institutions could borrow money at a lower rate of interest because of the tax-exempt nature of the state agency. A South Carolina taxpayer challenged the arrangement, as implemented at a Baptist college, as a violation of the Establishment Clause.

In a six-to-three decision, the Court held that the law was constitutional. Relying heavily on *Tilton's* description of a church-related college and the teaching done there, the Court found that the law had a secular purpose and that it did not advance the religious mission of the sponsoring church. In reference to the third test, because religious indoctrination was not a major goal of the college and since the form of aid (buildings) was not one that lent itself to abuse, only modest policing was necessary. In addition, it was clear that the state agency did not participate in a significant way in the management of the college's facilities. Consequently, the program did not foster excessive entanglement between church and state.

In the case of ROEMER v. BOARD OF PUBLIC WORKS (1976), the Court dealt with a program of aid to church-related colleges that was not limited to construction and maintenance of buildings. In 1971 a Maryland statute was enacted which authorized the payment of state funds to any accredited private college so long as it met certain academic criteria, refrained from awarding "only seminarian or theological degrees," and did not utilize the funds for sectarian purposes. Otherwise, the institutions could use the state funds as they chose. Each time a college applied to the Board of Public Works, the Maryland agency administering the program, the school's chief executive officer was required to file an affidavit stating that the funds would not be used in a sectarian way and describing the nonsectarian use to which they would be put. At the end of the year, the chief executive officer was required to file another affidavit stating that the funds had not been used for sectarian purposes. Four Maryland taxpayers filed suit in federal court, claiming that this virtually unrestricted use of state money by church-related colleges was a violation of the Establishment Clause.

Justice Blackmun, writing for the Court, found that the legislation clearly had a secular purpose. The program passed the primary effect test because the church-related colleges were not "pervasively sectarian"; and, because of the requirement placed upon the colleges of certifying that the funds had been used for secular purposes, it was clear that the aid went to the "secular side" of the college, rather than to support religious activity. The fact of such certification did not raise entanglement between church and state to an excessive level, since only rarely would on-campus inspections be required and, if conducted, they would be brief and no more extensive than those inspections already made to determine accreditation. Four dissenters were incredulous that the program was held not to advance the religious mission of the colleges. Justice Stevens also pointedly remarked that the existence of state funds caused church-related colleges to compromise the level of their religiosity in order to get the money.

In the decade 1976-1986 the Court decided only one church-state case at the college level, WIDMAR v. VINCENT, which did not confront the issue of state aid to church-related colleges. But in that same decade the Court did pass judgment on a type of state aid which included church colleges. During the 1970s a number of states created plans to give financial assistance to college students. Tennessee was one of those states. Actually, Tennessee legislated two such plans. The first was challenged in court and declared unconstitutional on establishment grounds. Before appeal was considered, the state modified the statute and then repealed it in its entirety and replaced it with another law. The second law provided that a student desiring aid initiated the process by submitting an application along with a financial disclosure form. If the information showed a student had financial need and was indeed enrolled in a college or university, he or she was sent a certificate showing the amount of state money to which he or she was entitled. The money could be spent by the student at any type of institution of higher learning; public, private, or church-related. The maximum amount which could be allocated to each student at the time of the litigation was the total of tuition and fees at the college of the student's choice or $1,200, whichever was less. However, the money did not have to be spent on tuition and fees. It could be used, and sometimes was, for other educational expenses such as books, room rent, health care, and transportation. There was clear evidence that some students utilizing the state's aid attended schools which were church-related and sometimes pervasively religious.

The program was challenged in a federal district court as being in violation of the Establishment Clause: *Americans United for Separation of Church and State* v. *Blanton* (1977). The court ruled that the plan was constitutional. Because the money went to the student, who could spend the money at any accredited college or university in the state, it was clear that the state did not intend to aid any particular religion or religious school and, as the program was implemented, it did not, especially because the money did not have to go to the school for tuition and fees, but could be spent for related educational expenses. What was essentially a "child benefit" plan did not violate the Establishment Clause. That judgment was affirmed without a hearing by the Supreme Court.

In summary, decisions of the Supreme Court indicate that certain kinds of state aid may be made available to parochial schools: bus transportation, textbook loans, and services for the educational health and welfare of the student, so long as it is manifestly clear that the performance of these services is absolutely secular. This secularity requirement is easily seen by comparing *Meek* and *Wolman.* Because the parochial school is an arm of the church and its principal purpose is the instruction of children in the church's doctrine and the advancement of its religious mission, any other forms of aid which would contribute to this cause have been declared unconstitutional. As a result of *Mueller,* government aid may be given to church-related schools by means of tuition supplements through tax deductions for parents sending children to such schools, provided that the deductions are available to parents of children going to any kind of school, i.e., the tax deductions must be applicable to educational expenses across the board. On the other hand, when it comes to the financing of particular educational activities within parochial schools, the negative decisions in *Grand Rapids* and *Felton* mean that *Wolman* still sets the boundaries of what is permissible. However, the Court recognizes that a college or university may be church-related without being sectarian or having as its primary purpose the advancement of the religious mission of the sponsoring church. This is the case primarily because of the greater sophistication of college students and the more objective nature of college-level teaching in accordance with the canons of academic freedom. Even though both *Tilton* and *Roemer* were decided by the slimmest of margins, five-to-four, while *Hunt* was a six-to-three decision, that distinction between precollegiate schools and colleges persists to the present.

PIERCE v. SOCIETY OF THE SISTERS OF THE HOLY NAMES OF JESUS AND MARY

268 U.S. 510
ON APPEAL FROM THE DISTRICT COURT OF THE UNITED STATES FOR THE DISTRICT OF OREGON
Argued March 16 and 17, 1925 — Decided June 1, 1925

⊥**529** Mr. *Justice* McREYNOLDS delivered the opinion of the court.

These appeals are from decrees, based upon undenied allegations, which granted preliminary orders restraining ⊥**530** appellants from threatening or attempting to enforce the Compulsory Education Act adopted November 7, 1922, under the initiative provision of her Constitution by the voters of Oregon. They present the same points of law; there are no controverted questions of fact. Rights said to be guaranteed by the Federal Constitution were specially set up, and appropriate prayers asked for their protection.

The challenged act, effective September 1, 1926, requires every parent, guardian, or other person having control or charge or custody of a child between eight and sixteen years to send him "to a public school for the period of time a public school shall be held during the current year" in the district where the child resides; and failure so to do is declared a misdemeanor. There are ⊥**531** exemptions—not specially important here—for children who are not normal, or who have completed the eighth grade, or whose parents or private teachers reside at considerable distances from any public school, or who hold special permits from the county superintendent. The manifest purpose is to compel general attendance at public schools by normal children, between eight and sixteen, who have not completed the eighth grade. And without doubt enforcement of the statute would seriously impair, perhaps destroy, the profitable features of appellees' business, and greatly diminish the value of their property.

Appellee the Society of Sisters is an Oregon corporation, organized in 1880, with power to care for orphans, educate and instruct the youth, establish and maintain academies or schools, and acquire necessary real and per⊥**532**sonal property. It has long devoted its property and effort to the secular and religious education and care of children, and has acquired the valuable good will of many parents and guardians. It conducts interdependent primary and high schools and junior colleges, and maintains orphanages for the custody and control of children between eight and sixteen. In its primary schools many children between those ages are taught the subjects usually pursued in Oregon public schools during the first eight years. Systematic religious instruction and moral training according to the tenets of the Roman Catholic Church are also regularly provided. All courses of study, both temporal and religious, contemplate continuity of training under appellee's charge; the primary schools are essential to the system and the most profitable. It owns valuable buildings, especially constructed and equipped for school purposes. The business is remunerative—the annual income from primary schools exceeds $30,000—and the successful conduct of this requires long-time contracts with teachers and parents. The Compulsory Education Act of 1922 has already caused the withdrawal from its schools of children who would otherwise continue, and their income has steadily declined. The appellants, public officers, have proclaimed their purpose strictly to enforce the statute.

After setting out the above facts, the Society's bill alleges that the enactment conflicts with the right of parents to choose schools where their children will receive appropriate mental and religious training, the right of the child to influence the parents' choice of a school, the right of schools and teachers therein to engage in a useful business or profession, and is accordingly repugnant to the Constitution and void. And, further, that unless enforcement of the measure is enjoined, the corporation's business and property will suffer irreparable injury.

Appellee Hill Military Academy is a private corporation organized in 1908 under the laws of Oregon, engaged ⊥**533** in owning, operating, and conducting for profit an elementary, college preparatory, and military training school for boys between the ages of five and twenty-one years. The average attendance is one hundred, and the annual fees received for each student amount to some $800. The elementary department is divided into eight grades, as in the public schools; the college preparatory department has four grades, similar to those of the public high schools; the courses of study conform to the requirements of the state board of education. Military instruction and training are also given, under the supervision of an Army officer. It owns considerable real and personal property, some useful only for school purposes. The business and incident good will are very valuable. In order to conduct its affairs longtime contracts must be made for supplies, equipment, teachers, and pupils. Appellants, law officers of the state and county, have publicly announced that the Act of November 7, 1922, is valid, and have declared their intention to enforce it. By reason of the statute and threat of enforcement, appellee's business is being destroyed and its property depreciated, parents and guardians are refusing to make contracts for the future instruction of their sons, and some are being withdrawn.

The Academy's bill states the foregoing facts and then alleges that the challenged act contravenes the corporation's rights guaranteed by the Fourteenth Amendment, and that unless appellants are restrained from proclaiming its validity and threatening to enforce it, irreparable injury will result. The prayer is for an appropriate injunction.

No answer was interposed in either cause, and after proper notices they were heard by three judges on motions for preliminary injunctions upon the specifically alleged facts. The court ruled that the Fourteenth Amendment guaranteed appellees against the ⊥**534** deprivation of their property without due process of law consequent upon the unlawful interference by appellants with the free choice of patrons, present and prospective. It declared the right to conduct schools was property, and that parents and guardians, as a part of their liberty, might direct the education of children by selecting reputable teachers and places. Also, the appellees' schools were not unfit or harmful to the public, and that enforcement of the challenged statute would unlawfully deprive them of patronage, and thereby destroy appellee's business and property. Finally, that the threats to enforce the act would continue to cause irreparable injury; and the suits were not premature.

No question is raised concerning the power of the state reasonably to regulate all schools, to inspect, supervise, and examine them, their teachers and pupils; to require that all children of proper age attend some school, that teachers shall be of good moral character and patriotic disposition, that certain studies plainly essential to good citizenship must be taught, and that nothing be taught which is manifestly inimical to the public welfare.

The inevitable practical result of enforcing the act under consideration would be destruction of appellees' primary schools, and perhaps all other private primary schools for normal children within the state of Oregon. Appellees are engaged in a kind of undertaking not inherently harmful, but long regarded as useful and meritorious. Certainly there is nothing in the present records to indicate that they have failed to discharge their obligations to patrons, students, or the state. And there are no peculiar circumstances or present emergencies which demand extraordinary measures relative to primary education.

Under the doctrine of *Meyer* v. *Nebraska* we think it entirely plain that the Act of 1922 unreasonably interferes with the liberty of parents and guardians to direct the upbringing and education of chil⊥**535**dren under their control. As often heretofore pointed out, rights guaranteed by the Constitution may not be abridged by legislation which has no reasonable relation to some purpose within the competency of the state. The fundamental theory of liberty upon which all governments in this Union repose excludes any general power of the state to standardize its children by forcing them to accept instruction from public teachers only. The child is not the mere creature of the state; those who nurture him and direct his destiny have the right, coupled with the high duty, to recognize and prepare him for additional obligations.

Appellees are corporations, and therefore, it is said, they cannot claim for themselves the liberty which the Fourteenth Amendment guarantees. Accepted in the proper sense, this is true. But they have business and property for which they claim protection. These are threatened with destruction through the unwarranted compulsion which appellants are exercising over present and prospective patrons of their schools. And this court has gone very far to protect against loss threatened by such action.

The courts of the state have not construed the act, and we must determine its meaning for ourselves. Evidently it was expected to have general application, and cannot be construed as though merely intended to amend the charters of certain private corporations, as in *Berea College* v. *Kentucky*. No argument in favor of such view has been advanced.

Generally it is entirely true, as urged by counsel, that no person in any business has such an interest in possible customers as to enable him to restrain exercise of proper power of the state upon the ground that he will be de⊥**536**prived of patronage. But the injunctions here sought are not against the exercise of any *proper* power. Appellees asked protection against arbitrary, unreasonable, and unlawful interference with their patrons, and the consequent destruction of their business and property. Their interest is clear and immediate, within the rule approved in *Truax* v. *Raich*, *Truax* v. *Corrigan*, and *Terrace* v. *Thompson* and many other cases where injunctions have issued to protect business enterprises against interference with the freedom of patrons or customers.

The suits were not premature. The injury to appellees was present and very real, not a mere possibility in the remote future. If no relief had been possible prior to the effective date of the act, the injury would have become irreparable. Prevention of impending injury by unlawful action is a well-recognized function of courts of equity.

The decrees below are *affirmed*.

COCHRAN v. LOUISIANA STATE BOARD OF EDUCATION

281 U.S. 370

ON APPEAL FROM THE SUPREME COURT OF THE STATE OF LOUISIANA

Argued April 15, 1930 — Decided April 28, 1930

⊥**373** Mr. *Chief Justice HUGHES* delivered the opinion of the Court.

The appellants, as citizens and taxpayers of the state of Louisiana, brought this suit to restrain the State Board of Education and other state officials from expending any part of the severance tax fund in purchasing school books and in supplying them free of cost to the school children of the state, under Acts No. 100 and No. 143 of 1928, upon the ground that the legislation violated specified provisions of the Constitution of the state and also section 4 of article 4 and the Fourteenth Amendment of the Federal Constitution. The Supreme Court of the state affirmed the judgment of the trial court which refused to issue an injunction.

⊥374 Act No. 100 of 1928 provided that the severance tax fund of the state, after allowing funds and appropriations as required by the state Constitution, should be devoted "first, to supplying school books to the school children of the State." The Board of Education was directed to provide "school books for school children free of cost to such children." Act No. 143 of 1928 made appropriations in accordance with the above provisions.

The Supreme Court of the state, following its decision in *Borden* v. *Louisiana State Board of Education*, held that these acts were not repugnant to either the state or the Federal Constitution.

No substantial Federal question is presented under section 4 of article 4 of the Federal Constitution guaranteeing to every state a republican form of government, as questions arising under this provision are political, not judicial, in character.

The contention of the appellant under the Fourteenth Amendment is that taxation for the purchase of school books constituted a taking of private property for a private purpose. The purpose is said to be to aid private, religious, sectarian, and other schools not embraced in the public educational system of the state by furnishing textbooks free to the children attending such private schools. The operation and effect of the legislation in question were described by the Supreme Court of the state as follows: "One may scan the acts in vain to ascertain where any money is appropriated for the purchase of school books for the use of any church, private, sectarian, or even public school. The appropriations were made for the specific purpose of purchasing school books for the use of the school children of the state, free of cost to them. **⊥375** It was for their benefit and the resulting benefit to the state that the appropriations were made. True, these children attend some school, public or private, the latter, sectarian or nonsectarian, and that the books are to be furnished them for their use, free of cost, whichever they attend. The schools, however, are not the beneficiaries of these appropriations. They obtain nothing from them, nor are they relieved of a single obligation, because of them. The school children and the state alone are the beneficiaries. It is also true that the sectarian schools, which some of the children attend, instruct their pupils in religion, and books are used for that purpose, but one may search diligently the acts, though without result, in an effort to find anything to the effect that it is the purpose of the state to furnish religious books for the use of such children. . . . What the statutes contemplate is that the same books that are furnished children attending public schools shall be furnished children attending private schools. This is the only practical way of interpreting and executing the statutes, and this is what the state board of education is doing. Among these books, naturally, none is to be expected, adapted to religious instruction." The court also stated, although the point is not of importance in relation to the Federal question, that it was "only the use of the books that is granted to the children, or, in other words, the books are lent to them."

Viewing the statute as having the effect thus attributed to it, we cannot doubt that the taxing power of the state is exerted for a public purpose. The legislation does not segregate private schools, or their pupils, as its beneficiaries or attempt to interfere with any matters of exclusively private concern. Its interest is education, broadly; its method, comprehensive. Individual interests are aided only as the common interest is safeguarded.

Judgment *affirmed*.

EVERSON v. BOARD OF EDUCATION OF EWING TOWNSHIP

330 U.S. 1
ON APPEAL FROM THE COURT OF ERRORS AND APPEALS OF NEW JERSEY
Argued November 20, 1946 — Decided February 10, 1947

⊥3 Mr. *Justice BLACK* delivered the opinion of the Court.

A New Jersey statute authorizes its local school districts to make rules and contracts for the transportation of children to and from schools. The appellee, a township board of education, acting pursuant to this statute, authorized reimbursement to parents of money expended by them for the bus transportation of their children on regular busses operated by the public transportation system. Part of this money was for the payment of transportation of some children in the community to Catholic parochial schools. These church schools give their students, in addition to secular education, regular religious instruction conforming to the religious tenets and modes of worship of the Catholic Faith. The superintendent of these schools is a Catholic priest.

The appellant, in his capacity as a district taxpayer, filed suit in a state court challenging the right of the Board to reimburse parents of parochial school students. He **⊥4** contended that the statute and the resolution passed pursuant to it violated both the State and the Federal Constitutions. That court held that the legislature was without power to authorize such payment under the state constitution. The New Jersey Court of Errors and Appeals reversed, holding that neither the statute nor the resolution passed pursuant to it was in conflict with the State constitution or the provisions of the Federal Constitution in issue. The case is here on appeal.

Since there has been no attack on the statute on the ground that a part of its language excludes children attending private schools operated for profit from enjoying State payment for their transportation, we need not consider this exclusionary language; it has no relevancy to any constitutional question here presented. Furthermore, if the exclusion clause had been properly challenged, we do not know whether New Jersey's highest court would construe its statutes as precluding payment of the school ⊥**5** transportation of any group of pupils, even those of a private school run for profit. Consequently, we put to one side the question as to the validity of the statute against the claim that it does not authorize payment for the transportation generally of school children in New Jersey.

The only contention here is that the state statute and the resolution, insofar as they authorized reimbursement to parents of children attending parochial schools, violate the Federal Constitution in these two respects, which to some extent overlap. *First.* They authorize the State to take by taxation the private property of some and bestow it upon others, to be used for their own private ⊥**6** purposes. This, it is alleged, violates the due process clause of the Fourteenth Amendment. *Second.* The statute and the resolution forced inhabitants to pay taxes to help support and maintain schools which are dedicated to, and which regularly teach, the Catholic Faith. This is alleged to be a use of state power to support church schools contrary to the prohibition of the First Amendment which the Fourteenth Amendment made applicable to the states.

First. The due process argument that the state law taxes some people to help others carry out their private purposes is framed in two phases. The first phase is that a state cannot tax A to reimburse B for the cost of transporting his children to church schools. This is said to violate the due process clause because the children are sent to these church schools to satisfy the personal desires of their parents, rather than the public's interest in the general education of all children. This argument, if valid, would apply equally to prohibit state payment for the transportation of children to any non-public school, whether operated by a church or any other non-government individual or group. But, the New Jersey legislature has decided that a public purpose will be served by using tax-raised funds to pay the bus fares of all school children, including those who attend parochial schools. The New Jersey Court of Errors and Appeals has reached the same conclusion. The fact that a state law, passed to satisfy a public need, coincides with the personal desires of the individuals most directly affected is certainly an inadequate reason for us to say that a legislature has erroneously appraised the public need.

It is true that this Court has, in rare instances, struck down state statutes on the ground that the purpose for which tax-raised funds were to be expended was not a public one. But the Court has also pointed out that this far-reaching authority must be exercised with the most extreme caution. Otherwise, a state's power to legislate for the public welfare might be seriously curtailed, a power which is a primary reason for the existence of states. Changing local conditions create new local problems which may lead a state's people and its local authorities to believe that laws authorizing new types of public services are necessary to promote the general well-being ⊥**7** of the people. The Fourteenth Amendment did not strip the states of their power to meet problems previously left for individual solution.

It is much too late to argue that legislation intended to facilitate the opportunity of children to get a secular education serves no public purpose. The same thing is no less true of legislation to reimburse needy parents, or all parents, for payment of the fares of their children so that they can ride in public busses to and from schools rather than run the risk of traffic and other hazards incident to walking or "hitchhiking." Nor does it follow that a law has a private rather than a public purpose because it provides that tax-raised funds will be paid to reimburse individuals on account of money spent by them in a way which furthers a public program. Subsidies and loans to individuals such as farmers and homeowners, and to privately owned transportation systems, as well as many other kinds of businesses, have been commonplace practices in our state and national history.

Insofar as the second phase of the due process argument may differ from the first, it is by suggesting that taxation for transportation of children to church schools constitutes support of a religion by the State. But if the law is invalid for this reason, it is because it violates the First Amendment's prohibition against the establishment of religion ⊥**8** by law. This is the exact question raised by appellant's second contention, to consideration of which we now turn.

Second. The New Jersey statute is challenged as a "law respecting an establishment of religion." The First Amendment, as made applicable to the states by the Fourteenth, commands that a "state shall make no law respecting an establishment of religion, or prohibiting the free exercise thereof. . . ." These words of the First Amendment reflected in the minds of early Americans a vivid mental picture of conditions and practices which they fervently wished to stamp out in order to preserve liberty for themselves and for their posterity. Doubtless their goal has not been entirely reached; but so far has the Nation moved toward it that the expression "law respecting an establishment of religion," probably does not so vividly remind present-day Americans of the evils, fears, and political problems that caused that expression to be written into our Bill of Rights. Whether this New Jersey law is one respecting an "establishment of religion" requires an understanding of the meaning of that language, particularly with respect to the imposition of taxes. Once again, therefore, it is not inappropriate briefly to review the background and environment of the period in which that constitutional language was fashioned and adopted.

A large proportion of the early settlers of this country came here from Europe to escape the bondage of laws which compelled them to support and attend government-favored churches. The centuries immediately before and contemporaneous with the colonization of America had been filled with turmoil, civil strife, and persecutions, generated in large part by established sects determined to ⊥**9** maintain their absolute political and religious supremacy. With the power of government supporting them, at various times and places, Catholics had persecuted Protestants, Protestants had persecuted Catholics, Protestant sects had persecuted other Protestant sects, Catholics of one shade of belief had persecuted Catholics of another shade of belief, and all of these had from time to time persecuted Jews. In efforts to force loyalty to whatever religious group happened to be on top and in league with the government of a particular time and place, men and women had been fined, cast in jail, cruelly tortured, and killed. Among the offenses for which these punishments had been inflicted were such things as speaking disrespectfully of the views of ministers of government-established churches, non-attendance at those churches, expressions of non-belief in their doctrines, and failure to pay taxes and tithes to support them.

These practices of the old world were transplanted to and began to thrive in the soil of the new America. The very charters granted by the English Crown to the individuals and companies designated to make the laws which would control the destinies of the colonials authorized these individuals and companies to erect religious establishments which all, whether believers or nonbelievers, would be required to support and attend. An exercise of ⊥**10** this authority was accompanied by a repetition of many of the old-world practices and persecutions. Catholics found themselves hounded and proscribed because of their faith; Quakers who followed their conscience went to jail; Baptists were peculiarly obnoxious to certain dominant Protestant sects; men and women of varied faiths who happened to be in a minority in a particular locality were persecuted because they steadfastly persisted in worshipping God only as their own consciences dictated. And all of these dissenters were compelled to pay tithes and taxes to support government-sponsored churches whose ministers preached inflammatory sermons designed to strengthen and consolidate the established faith by generating a burning hatred against dissenters.

⊥**11** These practices became so commonplace as to shock the freedom-loving colonials into a feeling of abhorrence. The imposition of taxes to pay ministers' salaries and to build and maintain churches and church property aroused their indignation. It was these feelings which found expression in the First Amendment. No one locality and no one group throughout the Colonies can rightly be given entire credit for having aroused the sentiment that culminated in adoption of the Bill of Rights' provisions embracing religious liberty. But Virginia, where the established church had achieved a dominant influence in political affairs and where many excesses attracted wide public attention, provided a great stimulus and able leadership for the movement. The people there, as elsewhere, reached the conviction that individual religious liberty could be achieved best under a government which was stripped of all power to tax, to support, or otherwise to assist any or all religions, or to interfere with the beliefs of any religious individual or group.

The movement toward this end reached its dramatic climax in Virginia in 1785-86 when the Virginia legislative body was about to renew Virginia's tax levy for the support of the established church. Thomas Jeffer⊥**12**son and James Madison led the fight against this tax. Madison wrote his great Memorial and Remonstrance against the law. In it, he eloquently argued that a true religion did not need the support of law; that no person, either believer or non-believer, should be taxed to support a religious institution of any kind; that the best interest of a society required that the minds of men always be wholly free; and that cruel persecutions were the inevitable result of government-established religions. Madison's Remonstrance received strong support throughout Virginia and the Assembly postponed consideration of the proposed tax measure until its next session. When the proposal came up for consideration at that session, it not only died in committee, but the Assembly enacted the famous "Virginia Bill for Religious Liberty" originally written by Thomas Jefferson. The preamble to that Bill stated among other things that "Almighty God hath created the mind free; that all attempts to influence it by temporal punishments or burthens, or by civil incapacitations, tend only to beget habits of hypocrisy and meanness, and are ⊥**13** a departure from the plan of the Holy author of our religion, who being Lord both of body and mind, yet chose not to propagate it by coercions on either . . . ; that to compel a man to furnish contributions of money for the propagation of opinions which he disbelieves, is sinful and tyrannical; that even the forcing him to support this or that teacher of his own religious persuasion, is depriving him of the comfortable liberty of giving his contributions to the particular pastor, whose morals he would make his pattern. . . ."

And the statute itself enacted "That no man shall be compelled to frequent or support any religious worship, place, or ministry whatsoever, nor shall be enforced, restrained, molested, or burthened in his body or goods, nor shall otherwise suffer on account of his religious opinions or belief. . . ."

This Court has previously recognized that the provisions of the First Amendment, in the drafting and adoption of which Madison and Jefferson played such leading roles, had the same objective and were intended to provide the same protection against governmental intrusion on religious liberty as the Virginia statute. Prior to the adoption of the Fourteenth Amendment, the First Amendment did not apply as a restraint against the states. Most of them did soon provide similar constitutional protections ⊥**14** for religious liberty. But some states persisted for about half a century in imposing restraints upon the free exercise of religion and in discriminating against particular religious groups. In recent years, so far as the provision against the establishment of a religion is concerned, the question has most frequently arisen in connection with proposed state aid to church schools and efforts to carry on religious teachings in the public schools in accordance with the tenets of a particular sect. Some churches have either sought or accepted state financial support for their schools. Here again the efforts to obtain state aid or acceptance of it have not been limited to any one particular faith. The state courts, in the main, have remained faithful to the language of their own constitutional provisions designed to protect religious freedom and to separate religions and governments. Their decisions, however, show the difficulty in drawing the line between tax legislation which provides funds for the welfare of the general public and that which is designed to support institutions which teach religion.

The meaning and scope of the First Amendment, preventing establishment of religion or prohibiting the free exercise thereof, in the light of its history and the evils it ⊥**15** was designed forever to suppress, have been several times elaborated by the decisions of this Court prior to the application of the First Amendment to the states by the Fourteenth. The broad meaning given the Amendment by these earlier cases has been accepted by this Court in its decisions concerning an individual's religious freedom rendered since the Fourteenth Amendment was interpreted to make the prohibitions of the First applicable to state action abridging religious freedom. There is every reason to give the same application and broad interpretation to the "establishment of religion" clause. The interrelation of these complementary clauses was well summarized in a statement of the Court of Appeals of South Carolina, quoted with approval by this Court in *Watson* v. *Jones*: "The structure of our government has, for the preservation of civil liberty, rescued the temporal institutions from religious interference. On the other hand, it has secured religious liberty from the invasion of the civil authority."

The "establishment of religion" clause of the First Amendment means at least this: Neither a state nor the Federal Government can set up a church. Neither can pass laws which aid one religion, aid all religions, or prefer one religion over another. Neither can force nor influence a person to go to or to remain away from church against his will or force him to profess a belief or disbelief in any religion. No person can be punished for entertain⊥**16**ing or professing religious beliefs or disbeliefs, for church attendance or non-attendance. No tax in any amount, large or small, can be levied to support any religious activities or institutions, whatever they may be called, or whatever form they may adopt to teach or practice religion. Neither a state nor the Federal Government can, openly or secretly, participate in the affairs of any religious organizations or groups and *vice versa*. In the words of Jefferson, the clause against establishment of religion by law was intended to erect "a wall of separation between church and State."

We must consider the New Jersey statute in accordance with the foregoing limitations imposed by the First Amendment. But we must not strike that state statute down if it is within the State's constitutional power even though it approaches the verge of that power. New Jersey cannot consistently with the "establishment of religion" clause of the First Amendment contribute tax-raised funds to the support of an institution which teaches the tenets and faith of any church. On the other hand, other language of the amendment commands that New Jersey cannot hamper its citizens in the free exercise of their own religion. Consequently, it cannot exclude individual Catholics, Lutherans, Mohammedans, Baptists, Jews, Methodists, Nonbelievers, Presbyterians, or the members of any other faith, *because of their faith, or lack of it*, from receiving the benefits of public welfare legislation. While we do not mean to intimate that a state could not provide transportation only to children attending public schools, we must be careful, in protecting the citizens of New Jersey against state-established churches, to be sure that we do not inadvertently prohibit New Jersey from extending its general state law benefits to all its citizens without regard to their religious belief.

⊥**17** Measured by these standards, we cannot say that the First Amendment prohibits New Jersey from spending tax-raised funds to pay the bus fares of parochial school pupils as a part of a general program under which it pays the fares of pupils attending public and other schools. It is undoubtedly true that children are helped to get to church schools. There is even a possibility that some of the children might not be sent to the church schools if the parents were compelled to pay their children's bus fares out of their own pockets when transportation to a public school would have been paid for by the State. The same possibility exists where the state requires a local transit company to provide reduced fares to school children including those attending parochial schools, or where a municipally owned transportation system undertakes to carry all school children free of charge. Moreover, state-paid policemen, detailed to protect children going to and from church schools from the very real hazards of traffic, would serve much the same purpose and accomplish much the same result as state provisions intended to guarantee free transportation of a kind which the state deems to be best for the school children's welfare. And parents might refuse to risk their children to the serious danger of traffic accidents going to and from parochial schools, the approaches to which were not protected by policemen. Similarly, parents might be reluctant to permit their children to attend schools which the state had cut off from such general government services as ordinary police and fire protection, connections for sewage disposal, public ⊥**18** highways and sidewalks. Of course, cutting off church schools from these services, so separate and so indisputably marked off from the religious function, would make it far more difficult for the schools to operate. But such is obviously not the purpose of the First Amendment. That Amendment requires the state to be a neutral in its relations with groups of religious believers and non-believers; it does not require the state to be their adversary. State power is no more to be used so as to handicap religions than it is to favor them.

This Court has said that parents may, in the discharge of their duty under state compulsory education laws, send their children to a religious rather than a public school if the school meets the secular educational requirements which the state has power to impose. It appears that these parochial schools meet New Jersey's requirements. The State contributes no money to the schools. It does not support them. Its legislation, as applied, does no more than provide a general program to help parents get their children, regardless of their religion, safely and expeditiously to and from accredited schools.

The First Amendment has erected a wall between church and state. That wall must be kept high and impregnable. We could not approve the slightest breach. New Jersey has not breached it here.

Affirmed.

Mr. *Justice* JACKSON, dissenting.

I find myself, contrary to first impressions, unable to join in this decision. I have a sympathy, though it is not ideological, with Catholic citizens who are compelled by law to pay taxes for public schools, and also feel constrained by conscience and discipline to support other schools for their own children. Such relief to them as ⊥**19** this case involves is not in itself a serious burden to taxpayers and I had assumed it to be as little serious in principle. Study of this case convinces me otherwise. The Court's opinion marshals every argument in favor of state aid and puts the case in its most favorable light, but much of its reasoning confirms my conclusions that there are no good grounds upon which to support the present legislation. In fact, the undertones of the opinion, advocating complete and uncompromising separation of Church from State, seem utterly discordant with its conclusion yielding support to their commingling in educational matters. The case which irresistibly comes to mind as the most fitting precedent is that of Julia who, according to Byron's reports, "whispering 'I will ne'er consent,'—consented."

I

The Court sustains this legislation by assuming two deviations from the facts of this particular case; first, it assumes a state of facts the record does not support, and secondly, it refuses to consider facts which are inescapable on the record.

The Court concludes that this "legislation, as applied, does no more than provide a general program to help parents get their children, regardless of their religion, safely and expeditiously to and from accredited schools," and it draws a comparison between "state provisions intended to guarantee free transportation" for school children with services such as police and fire protection, and implies that we are here dealing with "laws authorizing new types of public services. . . ." This hypothesis permeates the opinion. The facts will not bear that construction.

The Township of Ewing is not furnishing transportation to the children in any form; it is not operating school busses itself or contracting for their operation; and it is not performing any public service of any kind with this ⊥**20** taxpayer's money. All school children are left to ride as ordinary paying passengers on the regular busses operated by the public transportation system. What the Township does, and what the taxpayer complains of, is at stated intervals to reimburse parents for the fares paid, provided the children attend either public schools or Catholic Church schools. This expenditure of tax funds has no possible effect on the child's safety or expedition in transit. As passengers on the public busses they travel as fast and no faster, and are as safe and no safer, since their parents are reimbursed as before.

In addition to thus assuming a type of service that does not exist, the Court also insists that we must close our eyes to a discrimination which does exist. The resolution which authorizes disbursement of this taxpayer's money limits reimbursement to those who attend public schools and Catholic schools. That is the way the Act is applied to this taxpayer.

The New Jersey Act in question makes the character of the school, not the needs of the children, determine the eligibility of parents to reimbursement. The Act permits payment for transportation to parochial schools or public schools but prohibits it to private schools operated in whole or in part for profit. Children often are sent to private schools because their parents feel that they require more individual instruction than public schools can provide, or because they are backward or defective and need special attention. If all children of the state were objects of impartial solicitude, no reason is obvious for denying transportation reimbursement to students of this class, for these often are as needy and as worthy as those who go to public or parochial schools. Refusal to reimburse those who attend such schools is understandable only in the light of a purpose to aid the schools, because the state might well abstain from aiding a profit-making private enterprise. Thus, under the Act ⊥**21** and resolution brought to us by this case, children are classified according to the schools they attend and are to be aided if they attend the public schools or private Catholic schools, and they are not allowed to be aided if they attend private secular schools or private religious schools of other faiths.

Of course, this case is not one of a Baptist or a Jew or an Episcopalian or a pupil of a private school complaining of discrimination. It is one of a taxpayer urging that he is being taxed for an unconstitutional purpose. I think he is entitled to have us consider the Act just as it is written. The statement by the New Jersey court that it holds the Legislature may authorize use of local funds "for the transportation of pupils to any school," in view of the other constitutional views expressed, is not a holding that this Act authorizes transportation of *all* pupils to *all* schools. As applied to this taxpayer by the action he complains of, certainly the Act does not authorize reimbursement to those who choose any alternative to the public school except Catholic Church schools.

If we are to decide this case on the facts before us, our question is simply this: Is it constitutional to tax this complainant to pay the cost of carrying pupils to Church schools of one specified denomination?

II

Whether the taxpayer constitutionally can be made to contribute aid to parents of students because of their attendance at parochial schools depends upon the nature of those schools and their relation to the Church. The Constitution says nothing of education. It lays no obligation on the states to provide schools and does not undertake to regulate state systems of education if they see fit to maintain them. But they cannot, through school policy any more than through other means, invade rights secured **⊥22** to citizens by the Constitution of the United States. One of our basic rights is to be free of taxation to support a transgression of the constitutional command that the authorities "shall make no law respecting an establishment of religion, or prohibiting the free exercise thereof. . . ."

The function of the Church school is a subject on which this record is meager. It shows only that the schools are under superintendence of a priest and that "religion is taught as part of the curriculum." But we know that such schools are parochial only in name—they, in fact, represent a world-wide and age-old policy of the Roman Catholic Church. . . .

⊥23 It is no exaggeration to say that the whole historic conflict in temporal policy between the Catholic Church and non-Catholics comes to a focus in their respective school policies. The Roman Catholic Church, counseled by experience in many ages and many lands and with all sorts and conditions of men, takes what, from the viewpoint of its own progress and the success of its mission, is a wise estimate of the importance of education to religion. It does not leave the individual to pick up religion by chance. It relies on early and indelible indoctrination in the faith and order of the Church by the word and example of persons consecrated to the task.

Our public school, if not a product of Protestantism, at least is more consistent with it than with the Catholic culture and scheme of values. It is a relatively recent development dating from about 1840. It is organized on **⊥24** the premise that secular education can be isolated from all religious teaching so that the school can inculcate all needed temporal knowledge and also maintain a strict and lofty neutrality as to religion. The assumption is that after the individual has been instructed in worldly wisdom he will be better fitted to choose his religion. Whether such a disjunction is possible, and if possible whether it is wise, are questions I need not try to answer.

I should be surprised if any Catholic would deny that the parochial school is a vital, if not the most vital, part of the Roman Catholic Church. If put to the choice, that venerable institution, I should expect, would forego its whole service for mature persons before it would give up education of the young, and it would be a wise choice. Its growth and cohesion, discipline and loyalty, spring from its schools. Catholic education is the rock on which the whole structure rests, and to render tax aid to its Church school is indistinguishable to me from rendering the same aid to the Church itself.

III

It is of no importance in this situation whether the beneficiary of this expenditure of tax-raised funds is primarily the parochial school and incidentally the pupil, or whether the aid is directly bestowed on the pupil with indirect benefits to the school. The state cannot maintain a Church and it can no more tax its citizens to furnish free carriage to those who attend a Church. The prohibition against establishment of religion cannot be circumvented by a subsidy, bonus or reimbursement of expense to individuals for receiving religious instruction and indoctrination.

The Court, however, compares this to other subsidies and loans to individuals and says, "Nor does it follow that a law has a private rather than a public purpose because **⊥25** it provides that tax-raised funds will be paid to reimburse individuals on account of money spent by them in a way which furthers a public program." Of course, the state may pay out tax-raised funds to relieve pauperism, but it may not under our Constitution do so to induce or reward piety. It may spend funds to secure old age against want, but it may not spend funds to secure religion against skepticism. It may compensate individuals for loss of employment, but it cannot compensate them for adherence to a creed.

It seems to me that the basic fallacy in the Court's reasoning, which accounts for its failure to apply the principles it avows, is in ignoring the essentially religious test by which beneficiaries of this expenditure are selected. A policeman protects a Catholic, of course—but not because he is a Catholic; it is because he is a man and a member of our society. The fireman protects the Church school—but not because it is a Church school; it is because it is property, part of the assets of our society. Neither the fireman nor the policeman has to ask before he renders aid "Is this man or building identified with the Catholic Church?" But before these school authorities draw a check to reimburse for a student's fare they must ask just that question, and if the school is a Catholic one they may render aid because it is such, while if it is of any other faith or is run for profit, the help must be withheld. To consider the converse of the Court's reasoning will best disclose its fallacy. That there is no parallel between police and fire protection and this plan of reimbursement is apparent from the incongruity of the limitation of this Act if applied to police and fire service. Could we sustain an Act that said the police shall protect pupils on the way to or from public schools and Catholic schools but not ⊥26 while going to and coming from other schools, and firemen shall extinguish a blaze in public or Catholic school buildings but shall not put out a blaze in Protestant Church schools or private schools operated for profit? That is the true analogy to the case we have before us and I should think it pretty plain that such a scheme would not be valid.

The Court's holding is that this taxpayer has no grievance because the state has decided to make the reimbursement a public purpose and therefore we are bound to regard it as such. I agree that this Court has left, and always should leave to each state, great latitude in deciding for itself, in the light of its own conditions, what shall be public purposes in its scheme of things. It may socialize utilities and economic enterprises and make taxpayers' business out of what conventionally had been private business. It may make public business of individual welfare, health, education, entertainment or security. But it cannot make public business of religious worship or instruction, or of attendance at religious institutions of any character. There is no answer to the proposition, more fully expounded by Mr. *Justice* RUTLEDGE, that the effect of the religious freedom Amendment to our Constitution was to take every form of propagation of religion out of the realm of things which could directly or indirectly be made public business and thereby be supported in whole or in part at taxpayers' expense. That is a difference which the Constitution sets up between religion and almost every other subject matter of legislation, a difference which goes to the very root of religious freedom and which the Court is overlooking today. This freedom was first in the Bill of Rights because it was first in the forefathers' minds; it was set forth in absolute terms, and its strength is its rigidity. It was intended not only to keep the states' hands out of religion, but to ⊥27 keep religion's hands off the state, and, above all, to keep bitter religious controversy out of public life by denying to every denomination any advantage from getting control of public policy or the public purse. Those great ends I cannot but think are immeasurably compromised by today's decision.

This policy of our Federal Constitution has never been wholly pleasing to most religious groups. They all are quick to invoke its protections; they all are irked when they feel its restraints. This Court has gone a long way, if not an unreasonable way, to hold that public business of such paramount importance as maintenance of public order, protection of the privacy of the home, and taxation may not be pursued by a state in a way that even indirectly will interfere with religious proselyting.

But we cannot have it both ways. Religious teaching cannot be a private affair when the state seeks to impose regulations which infringe on it indirectly, and a public affair when it comes to taxing citizens of one faith to aid another, or those of no faith to aid all. If these principles seem harsh in prohibiting aid to Catholic education, it must not be forgotten that it is the same Constitution that alone assures Catholics the right to maintain these schools at all when predominant local sentiment would forbid them. Nor should I think that those who have done so well without this aid would want to see this separation between Church and State broken down. If the state may aid these religious schools, it may therefore regulate them. Many groups have sought aid from tax funds only to find that it carried political controls with it. Indeed this Court has ⊥28 declared that "It is hardly lack of due process for the Government to regulate that which it subsidizes." *Wickard* v. *Filburn*.

But in any event, the great purposes of the Constitution do not depend on the approval or convenience of those they restrain. I cannot read the history of the struggle to separate political from ecclesiastical affairs, well summarized in the opinion of Mr. *Justice* RUTLEDGE in which I generally concur, without a conviction that the Court today is unconsciously giving the clock's hands a backward turn.

Mr. *Justice* FRANKFURTER joins in this opinion.

Mr. *Justice* RUTLEDGE, with whom Mr. *Justice* FRANKFURTER, Mr. *Justice* JACKSON and Mr. *Justice* BURTON agree, dissenting. . . .

⊥29 This case forces us to determine squarely for the first time what was "an establishment of religion" in the First Amendment's conception; and by that measure to decide whether New Jersey's action violates its command. The facts may be stated shortly, to give setting and color to the constitutional problem.

By statute New Jersey has authorized local boards of education to provide for the transportation of children "to and from school other than a public school" except one ⊥30 operated for profit wholly or in part, over established public school routes, or by other means when the child lives "remote from any school." The school board of Ewing Township has provided by resolution for "the transportation of pupils of Ewing to the Trenton and Pennington High Schools and Catholic Schools by way of public carrier. . . ."

Named parents have paid the cost of public conveyance of their children from their homes in Ewing to three public high schools and four parochial schools outside the district. Semiannually the Board has reimbursed the parents from public school funds raised by general taxation. Religion is taught as part of the curriculum in each ⊥31 of the four private schools, as appears affirmatively by the testimony of the superintendent of parochial schools in the Diocese of Trenton.

The Court of Errors and Appeals of New Jersey, reversing the Supreme Court's decision, has held the Ewing board's action not in contravention of the state constitution or statutes or of the Federal Constitution. We have to consider only whether this ruling accords with the prohibition of the First Amendment implied in the due process clause of the Fourteenth.

I

Not simply an established church, but any law respecting an establishment of religion is forbidden. The Amendment was broadly but not loosely phrased. It is the compact and exact summation of its author's views formed during his long struggle for religious freedom. In Madison's own words characterizing Jefferson's Bill for Establishing Religious Freedom, the guaranty he put in our national charter, like the bill he piloted through the Virginia Assembly, was "a Model of technical precision, and perspicuous brevity." Madison could not have confused "church" and "religion," or "an established church" and "an establishment of religion."

The Amendment's purpose was not to strike merely at the official establishment of a single sect, creed or religion, outlawing only a formal relation such as had prevailed in England and some of the colonies. Necessarily it was to uproot all such relationships. But the object was broader than separating church and state in this narrow sense. It was to create a complete and permanent separation of the ⊥**32** spheres of religious activity and civil authority by comprehensively forbidding every form of public aid or support for religion. In proof the Amendment's wording and history unite with this Court's consistent utterances whenever attention has been fixed directly upon the question.

"Religion" appears only once in the Amendment. But the word governs two prohibitions and governs them alike. It does not have two meanings, one narrow to forbid "an establishment" and another, much broader, for securing "the free exercise thereof." "Thereof" brings down "religion" with its entire and exact content, no more and no less, from the first into the second guaranty, so that Congress and now the states are as broadly restricted concerning the one as they are regarding the other.

No one would claim today that the Amendment is constricted, in "prohibiting the free exercise" of religion, to securing the free exercise of some formal or creedal observance, of one sect or of many. It secures all forms of religious expression, creedal, sectarian or nonsectarian, wherever and however taking place, except conduct which trenches upon the like freedoms of others or clearly and presently endangers the community's good order and security. For the protective purposes of this phase of the basic freedom, street preaching, oral or by distribution of ⊥**33** literature, has been given "the same high estate under the First Amendment as . . . worship in the churches and preaching from the pulpits." And on this basis parents have been held entitled to send their children to private, religious schools. Accordingly, daily religious education commingled with secular is "religion" within the guaranty's comprehensive scope. So are religious training and teaching in whatever form. The word connotes the broadest content, determined not by the form or formality of the teaching or where it occurs, but by its essential nature regardless of those details. "Religion" has the same broad significance in the twin prohibition concerning "an establishment." The Amendment was not duplicitous. "Religion" and "establishment" were not used in any formal or technical sense. The prohibition broadly forbids state support, financial or other, of religion in any guise, form or degree. It outlaws all use of public funds for religious purposes.

II

No provision of the Constitution is more closely tied to or given content by its generating history than the religious clause of the First Amendment. It is at once the refined product and the terse summation of that history. The history includes not only Madison's authorship and the proceedings before the First Congress, but also the long and intensive struggle for religious freedom in America, more especially in Virginia, of which the Amend⊥**34**ment was the direct culmination. In the documents of the times, particularly of Madison, who was leader in the Virginia struggle before he became the Amendment's sponsor, but also in the writings of Jefferson and others and in the issues which engendered them is to be found irrefutable confirmation of the Amendment's sweeping content.

For Madison, as also for Jefferson, religious freedom was the crux of the struggle for freedom in general. Madison was coauthor with George Mason of the religious clause in Virginia's great Declaration of Rights of 1776. He is credited with changing it from a mere statement of the principle of tolerance to the first official legislative pronouncement that freedom of conscience and religion are inherent rights of the individual. He sought also to have the Declara⊥**35**tion expressly condemn the existing Virginia establishment. But the forces supporting it were then too strong.

Accordingly Madison yielded on this phase but not for long. At once he resumed the fight, continuing it before succeeding legislative sessions. As a member of the General Assembly in 1779 he threw his full weight behind Jefferson's historic Bill for Establishing Religious Freedom. That bill was a prime phase of Jefferson's broad program of democratic reform undertaken on his return from the Continental Congress in 1776 and submitted for the General Assembly's consideration in 1779 as his proposed revised Virginia code. With Jefferson's departure for Europe in 1784, Madison became the Bill's prime ⊥**36** sponsor. Enactment failed in successive legislatures from its introduction in June, 1779, until its adoption in January, 1786. But during all this time the fight for religious freedom moved forward in Virginia on various fronts with growing intensity. Madison led throughout, against Patrick Henry's powerful opposing leadership until Henry was elected governor in November, 1784.

The climax came in the legislative struggle of 1784-1785 over the Assessment Bill. This was nothing more nor less than a taxing measure for the support of religion, designed to revive the payment of tithes suspended since 1777. So long as it singled out a particular sect for preference it incurred the active and general hostility of dissentient groups. It was broadened to include them, with the result that some subsided temporarily in their opposition. As altered, the bill gave to each taxpayer the privilege of designating which church should receive his share of the tax. In default of designation the legislature applied it to pious uses. But what is of the utmost significance here, "in ⊥**37** its final form the bill left the taxpayer the option of giving his tax to education."

Madison was unyielding at all times, opposing with all his vigor the general and nondiscriminatory as he had the earlier particular and discriminatory assessments proposed. The modified Assessment Bill passed second reading in December, 1784, and was all but enacted. Madison and his followers, however, maneuvered deferment of final consideration until November, 1785. And before the Assembly reconvened in the fall he issued his historic Memorial and Remonstrance.

This is Madison's complete, though not his only, interpretation of religious liberty. It is a broadside attack upon all forms of "establishment" of religion, both general and particular, nondiscriminatory or selective. Reflecting not only the many legislative conflicts over the Assessment Bill and the Bill for Establishing Religious Freedom but also, for example, the struggles for religious incorporations and the continued maintenance of the glebes, the Remonstrance is at once the most concise and the most accurate statement of the views of the First Amendment's author concerning what is "an establishment of religion. . . ."

⊥**38** The Remonstrance, stirring up a storm of popular protest, killed the Assessment Bill. It collapsed in committee shortly before Christmas, 1785. With this, the way was cleared at last for enactment of Jefferson's Bill for Establishing Religious Freedom. Madison promptly drove it through in January of 1786, seven years from the time it was first introduced. This dual victory substantially ended the fight over establishments, settling the issue against them.

The next year Madison became a member of the Constitutional Convention. Its work done, he fought valiantly to secure the ratification of its great product in Virginia as elsewhere, and nowhere else more effectively. Madison was certain in his own mind that under the Constitution "there is not a shadow of right in the general government to intermeddle with religion" and that "this subject is, for the honor of America, perfectly free and ⊥**39** unshackled. The government has no jurisdiction over it. . . ." Nevertheless he pledged that he would work for a Bill of Rights, including a specific guaranty of religious freedom, and Virginia, with other states, ratified the Constitution on this assurance.

Ratification thus accomplished, Madison was sent to the first Congress. There he went at once about performing his pledge to establish freedom for the nation as he had done in Virginia. Within a little more than three years from his legislative victory at home he had proposed and secured the submission and ratification of the First Amendment as the first article of our Bill of Rights.

All the great instruments of the Virginia struggle for religious liberty thus became warp and woof of our constitutional tradition, not simply by the course of history, but by the common unifying force of Madison's life, thought and sponsorship. He epitomized the whole of that tradition in the Amendment's compact, but nonetheless comprehensive, phrasing.

As the Remonstrance discloses throughout, Madison opposed every form and degree of official relation between religion and civil authority. For him religion was a wholly private matter beyond the scope of civil power ⊥**40** either to restrain or to support. Denial or abridgment of religious freedom was a violation of rights both of conscience and of natural equality. State aid was no less obnoxious or destructive to freedom and to religion itself than other forms of state interference. "Establishment" and "free exercise" were corrective and coextensive ideas, representing only different facets of the single great and fundamental freedom. The Remonstrance, following the Virginia statute's example, referred to the history of religious conflicts and the effects of all sorts of establishments, current and historical, to suppress religion's free exercise. With Jefferson, Madison believed that to tolerate any fragment of establishment would be by so much to perpetuate restraint upon that freedom. Hence he sought to tear out the institution not partially but root and branch, and to bar its return forever.

In no phase was he more unrelentingly absolute than in opposing state support or aid by taxation. Not even "three pence" contribution was thus to be exacted from any citizen for such a purpose.

⊥**41** Tithes had been the lifeblood of establishment before and after other compulsions disappeared. Madison and his coworkers made no exceptions or abridgments to the complete separation they created. Their objection was not to small tithes. It was to any tithes whatsoever. "If it were lawful to impose a small tax for religion, the admission would pave the way for oppressive levies." Not the amount but "the principle of assessment was wrong." And the principle was as much to prevent "the interference of law in religion" as to restrain religious intervention in political matters. In this field the authors of our freedom would not tolerate "the first experiment on our liberties" or "wait till usurped power had strengthened itself by exercise, and entangled the question in precedents." Nor should we.

In view of this history no further proof is needed that the Amendment forbids any appropriation, large or small, from public funds to aid or support any and all religious exercises. But if more were called for, the debates in the First Congress and this Court's consistent expressions, whenever it has touched on the matter directly, supply it.

⊥**42** By contrast with the Virginia history, the congressional debates on consideration of the Amendment reveal only sparse discussion, reflecting the fact that the essential issues had been settled. Indeed the matter had become so well understood as to have been taken for granted in all but formal phrasing. Hence, the only enlightening reference shows concern, not to preserve any power to use public funds in aid of religion, but to prevent the Amendment from outlawing private gifts inadvertently by virtue of the breadth of its wording. . . .

⊥**44** III

Compulsory attendance upon religious exercises went out early in the process of separating church and state, together with forced observance of religious forms and ceremonies. Test oaths and religious qualification for office followed later. These things none devoted to our great tradition of religious liberty would think of bringing back. Hence today, apart from efforts to inject religious training or exercises and sectarian issues into the public schools, the only serious surviving threat to maintaining that complete and permanent separation of religion and civil power which the First Amendment commands is through use of the taxing power to support religion, religious establishments, or establishments having a religious foundation whatever their form or special religious function.

Does New Jersey's action furnish support for religion by use of the taxing power? Certainly it does, if the test remains undiluted as Jefferson and Madison made it, that money taken by taxation from one is not to be used or given to support another's religious training or belief, or indeed one's own. Today as then the furnishing of "con⊥**45**tributions of money for the propagation of opinions which he disbelieves" is the forbidden exaction; and the prohibition is absolute for whatever measure brings that consequence and whatever amount may be sought or given to that end.

The funds used here were raised by taxation. The Court does not dispute, nor could it, that their use does in fact give aid and encouragement to religious instruction. It only concludes that this aid is not "support" in law. But Madison and Jefferson were concerned with aid and support in fact, not as a legal conclusion "entangled in precedents." Here parents pay money to send their children to parochial schools and funds raised by taxation are used to reimburse them. This not only helps the children get to school and the parents to send them. It aids them in a substantial way to get the very thing which they are sent to the particular school to secure, namely, religious training and teaching.

Believers of all faiths, and others who do not express their feeling toward ultimate issues of existence in any creedal form, pay the New Jersey tax. When the money so raised is used to pay for transportation to religious schools, the Catholic taxpayer to the extent of his proportionate share pays for the transportation of Lutheran, Jewish and otherwise religiously affiliated children to receive their non-Catholic religious instruction. Their parents likewise pay proportionately for the transportation of Catholic children to receive Catholic instruction. Each ⊥**46** thus contributes to "the propagation of opinions which he disbelieves" in so far as their religions differ, as do others who accept no creed without regard to those differences. Each thus pays taxes also to support the teaching of his own religion, an exaction equally forbidden since it denies "the comfortable liberty" of giving one's contribution to the particular agency of instruction he approves.

New Jersey's action therefore exactly fits the type of exaction and the kind of evil at which Madison and Jefferson struck. Under the test they framed it cannot be said that the cost of transportation is no part of the cost of education or of the religious instruction given. That it is a substantial and a necessary element is shown most plainly by the continuing and increasing demand for the state to assume it. Nor is there pretense that it relates only to the secular instruction given in religious schools or that any attempt is or could be made toward allocating proportional shares as between the secular and the religious instruction. It is precisely because the instruction is religious and relates to a particular faith, whether one or another, that parents send their children to religious schools under the *Pierce* doctrine. And the very purpose of the state's contribution is to defray the cost of conveying the pupil to the place where he will receive not simply secular, but also and primarily religious, teaching and guidance.

Indeed the view is sincerely avowed by many of various faiths, that the basic purpose of all education is or should be religious, that the secular cannot be and should not be separated from the religious phase and emphasis. Hence, ⊥**47** the inadequacy of public or secular education and the necessity for sending the child to a school where religion is taught. But whatever may be the philosophy or its justification, there is undeniably an admixture of religious with secular teaching in all such institutions. That is the very reason for their being. Certainly for purposes of constitutionality we cannot contradict the whole basis of the ethical and educational convictions of people who believe in religious schooling.

Yet this very admixture is what was disestablished when the First Amendment forbade "an establishment of religion." Commingling the religious with the secular teaching does not divest the whole of its religious permeation and emphasis or make them of minor part, if proportion were material. Indeed, on any other view, the constitutional prohibition always could be brought to naught by adding a modicum of the secular.

An appropriation from the public treasury to pay the cost of transportation to Sunday school, to weekday special classes at the church or parish house, or to the meetings of various young people's religious societies, such as the Y.M.C.A., the Y.W.C.A., the Y.M.H.A., the Epworth League, could not withstand the constitutional attack.

This would be true, whether or not secular activities were mixed with the religious. If such an appropriation could not stand, then it is hard to see how one becomes valid for the same things upon the more extended scale of daily instruction. Surely constitutionality does not turn on where or how often the mixed teaching occurs.

Finally, transportation, where it is needed, is as essential to education as any other element. Its cost is as much a part of the total expense, except at times in amount, as the cost of textbooks, of school lunches, of athletic equipment, of writing and other materials; indeed of all other ⊥**48** items composing the total burden. Now as always the core of the educational process is the teacher-pupil relationship. Without this the richest equipment and facilities would go for naught. But the proverbial Mark Hopkins conception no longer suffices for the country's requirements. Without buildings, without equipment, without library, textbooks and other materials, and without transportation to bring teacher and pupil together in such an effective teaching environment, there can be not even the skeleton of what our times require. Hardly can it be maintained that transportation is the least essential of these items, or that it does not in fact aid, encourage, sustain and support, just as they do, the very process which is its purpose to accomplish. No less essential is it, or the payment of its cost, than the very teaching in the classroom or payment of the teacher's sustenance. Many types of equipment, now considered essential, better could be done without.

For me, therefore, the feat is impossible to select so indispensable an item from the composite of total costs, and characterize it as not aiding, contributing to, promoting or sustaining the propagation of beliefs which it is the very end of all to bring about. Unless this can be maintained, and the Court does not maintain it, the aid thus given is outlawed. Payment of transportation is no more, nor is it any the less essential to education, whether religious or secular, than payment for tuitions, for teachers' salaries, for buildings, equipment and necessary materials. Nor is it any the less directly related, in a school giving religious instruction, to the primary religious objective all those essential items of cost are intended to achieve. No rational line can be drawn between payment for such larger, but not more necessary, items and payment for transportation. The only line that can be drawn is one between more dollars and less. Certainly in this ⊥**49** realm such a line can be no valid constitutional measure. Now, as in Madison's time, not the amount but the principle of assessment is wrong.

IV

But we are told that the New Jersey statute is valid in its present application because the appropriation is for a public, not a private purpose, namely, the promotion of education, and the majority accept this idea in the conclusion that all we have here is "public welfare legislation." If that is true and the Amendment's force can be thus destroyed, what has been said becomes all the more pertinent. For then there could be no possible objection to more extensive support of religious education by New Jersey.

If the fact alone be determinative that religious schools are engaged in education, thus promoting the general and individual welfare, together with the legislature's decision that the payment of public moneys for their aid makes their work a public function, then I can see no possible basis, except one of dubious legislative policy, for the state's refusal to make full appropriation for support of private, religious schools, just as is done for public ⊥**50** instruction. There could not be, on that basis, valid constitutional objection.

Of course paying the cost of transportation promotes the general cause of education and the welfare of the individual. So does paying all other items of educational expense. And obviously, as the majority say, it is much too late to urge that legislation designed to facilitate the opportunities of children to secure a secular education serves no public purpose. Our nationwide system of public education rests on the contrary view, as do all grants in aid of education, public or private, which is not religious in character.

These things are beside the real question. They have no possible materiality except to obscure the all-pervading, inescapable issue. Stripped of its religious phase, the case presents no substantial federal question. The public function argument, by casting the issue in terms of promoting the general cause of education and the welfare of the individual, ignores the religious factor and its essential connection with the transportation, thereby leaving out the only vital element in the case. So of course do the "public welfare" and "social legislation" ideas, for they come to the same thing.

⊥**51** We have here then one substantial issue, not two. To say that New Jersey's appropriation and her use of the power of taxation for raising the funds appropriated are not for public purposes but are for private ends, is to say that they are for the support of religion and religious teaching. Conversely, to say that they are for public purposes is to say that they are not for religious ones.

This is precisely for the reason that education which includes religious training and teaching, and its support, have been made matters of private right and function, not public, by the very terms of the First Amendment. That is the effect not only in its guaranty of religion's free exercise, but also in the prohibition of establishments. It was on this basis of the private character of the function of religious education that this Court held parents entitled to send their children to private, religious schools. Now it declares in effect that the appropriation of public funds to defray part of the cost of attending those schools is for a public purpose. If so, I do not understand why the state cannot go farther or why this case approaches the verge of its power.

In truth this view contradicts the whole purpose and effect of the First Amendment as heretofore conceived. The "public function"—"public welfare"—"social legislation" argument seeks, in Madison's words, to "employ Religion [that is, here, religious education] as an engine of Civil policy." It is of one piece with the Assessment Bill's preamble, although with the vital difference that it wholly ignores what that preamble explicitly states.

⊥52 Our constitutional policy is exactly the opposite. It does not deny the value or the necessity for religious training, teaching or observance. Rather it secures their free exercise. But to that end it does deny that the state can undertake or sustain them in any form or degree. For this reason the sphere of religious activity, as distinguished from the secular intellectual liberties, has been given the twofold protection and, as the state cannot forbid, neither can it perform or aid in performing the religious function. The dual prohibition makes that function altogether private. It cannot be made a public one by legislative act. This was the very heart of Madison's Remonstrance, as it is of the Amendment itself.

It is not because religious teaching does not promote the public or the individual's welfare, but because neither is furthered when the state promotes religious education, that the Constitution forbids it to do so. Both legislatures and courts are bound by that distinction. In failure to observe it lies the fallacy of the "public function"—"social legislation" argument, a fallacy facilitated by easy transference of the argument's basing from due process unrelated to any religious aspect to the First Amendment.

By no declaration that a gift of public money to religious uses will promote the general or individual welfare, or the cause of education generally, can legislative bodies overcome the Amendment's bar. Nor may the courts sustain their attempts to do so by finding such consequences for appropriations which in fact give aid to or promote religious uses. Legislatures are free to make, ⊥53 and courts to sustain, appropriations only when it can be found that in fact they do not aid, promote, encourage or sustain religious teaching or observances, be the amount large or small. No such finding has been or could be made in this case. The Amendment has removed this form of promoting the public welfare from legislative and judicial competence to make a public function. It is exclusively a private affair.

The reasons underlying the Amendment's policy have not vanished with time or diminished in force. Now as when it was adopted the price of religious freedom is double. It is that the church and religion shall live both within and upon that freedom. There cannot be freedom of religion, safeguarded by the state, and intervention by the church or its agencies in the state's domain or dependency on its largesse. The great condition of religious liberty is that it be maintained free from sustenance, as also from other interferences, by the state. For when it comes to rest upon that secular foundation it vanishes with the resting. Public money devoted to payment of religious costs, educational or other, brings the quest for more. It brings too the struggle of sect against sect for the larger share or for any. Here one by numbers alone will benefit most, there another. That is precisely the history of societies which have had an established religion and dissident ⊥54 groups. It is the very thing Jefferson and Madison experienced and sought to guard against, whether in its blunt or in its more screened forms. The end of such strife cannot be other than to destroy the cherished liberty. The dominating group will achieve the dominant benefit; or all will embroil the state in their dissensions.

Exactly such conflicts have centered of late around providing transportation to religious schools from public funds. The issue and the dissension work typically, in Madison's phrase, to "destroy that moderation and harmony which the forbearance of our laws to intermeddle with Religion, has produced amongst its several sects." This occurs, as he well knew, over measures ⊥55 at the very threshold of departure from the principle.

In these conflicts wherever success has been obtained it has been upon the contention that by providing the transportation the general cause of education, the general welfare, and the welfare of the individual will be forwarded; hence that the matter lies within the realm of public function, for legislative determination. State courts have divided upon the issue, some taking the view that only the individual, others that the institution receives the benefit. A few have recognized that this dichotomy is false, that both in fact are aided.

⊥56 The majority here does not accept in terms any of those views. But neither does it deny that the individual or the school, or indeed both, are benefited directly and substantially. To do so would cut the ground from under the public function—social legislation thesis. On the contrary, the opinion concedes that the children are aided by being helped to get to the religious schooling. By converse necessary implication as well as by the absence of express denial, it must be taken to concede also that the school is helped to reach the child with its religious teaching. The religious enterprise is common to both, as is the interest in having transportation for its religious purposes provided.

Notwithstanding the recognition that this two-way aid is given and the absence of any denial that religious teaching is thus furthered, the Court concludes that the aid so given is not "support" of religion. It is rather only support of education as such, without reference to its religious content, and thus becomes public welfare legislation. To this elision of the religious element from the case is added gloss in two respects, one that the aid extended partakes of the nature of a safety measure, the other that failure to provide it would make the state unneutral in religious matters, discriminating against or hampering such children concerning public benefits all others receive.

⊥57 As will be noted, the one gloss is contradicted by the facts of record and the other is of whole cloth with the "public function" argument's excision of the religious factor. But most important is that this approach, if valid, supplies a ready method for nullifying the Amendment's guaranty, not only for this case and others involving small grants in aid for religious education, but equally for larger ones. The only thing needed will be for the Court again to transplant the "public welfare—public function" view from its proper nonreligious due process bearing to First Amendment application, holding that religious education is not "supported" though it may be aided by the appropriation, and that the cause of education generally is furthered by helping the pupil to secure that type of training.

This is not therefore just a little case over bus fares. In paraphrase of Madison, distant as it may be in its present form from a complete establishment of religion, it differs from it only in degree; and is the first step in that direction. Today as in his time "the same authority which can force a citizen to contribute three pence only . . . for the support of any one [religious] establishment, may force him" to pay more; or "to conform to any other establishment in all cases whatsoever." And now, as then, "either . . . we must say, that the will of the Legislature is the only measure of their authority; and that in the plenitude of this authority, they may sweep away all our fundamental rights; or, that they are bound to leave this particular right untouched and sacred."

The realm of religious training and belief remains, as the Amendment made it, the kingdom of the individual **⊥58** man and his God. It should be kept inviolately private, not "entangled . . . in precedents" or confounded with what legislatures legitimately may take over into the public domain.

V

No one conscious of religious values can be unsympathetic toward the burden which our constitutional separation puts on parents who desire religious instruction mixed with secular for their children. They pay taxes for others' children's education, at the same time the added cost of instruction for their own. Nor can one happily see benefits denied to children which others receive, because in conscience they or their parents for them desire a different kind of training others do not demand.

But if those feelings should prevail, there would be an end to our historic constitutional policy and command. No more unjust or discriminatory in fact is it to deny attendants at religious schools the cost of their transportation than it is to deny them tuitions, sustenance for their teachers, or any other educational expense which others receive at public cost. Hardship in fact there is which none can blink. But, for assuring to those who undergo it the greater, the most comprehensive freedom, it is one written by design and firm intent into our basic law.

Of course discrimination in the legal sense does not exist. The child attending the religious school has the same right as any other to attend the public school. But he foregoes exercising it because the same guaranty which assures this freedom forbids the public school or any agency of the **⊥59** state to give or aid him in securing the religious instruction he seeks.

Were he to accept the common school, he would be the first to protest the teaching there of any creed or faith not his own. And it is precisely for the reason that their atmosphere is wholly secular that children are not sent to public schools under the *Pierce* doctrine. But that is a constitutional necessity, because we have staked the very existence of our country on the faith that complete separation between the state and religion is best for the state and best for religion.

That policy necessarily entails hardship upon persons who forego the right to educational advantages the state can supply in order to secure others it is precluded from giving. Indeed this may hamper the parent and the child forced by conscience to that choice. But it does not make the state unneutral to withhold what the Constitution forbids it to give. On the contrary it is only by observing the prohibition rigidly that the state can maintain its neutrality and avoid partisanship in the dissensions inevitable when sect opposes sect over demands for public moneys to further religious education, teaching or training in any form or degree, directly or indirectly. Like St. Paul's freedom, religious liberty with a great price must be bought. And for those who exercise it most fully, by insisting upon religious education for their children mixed with secular, by the terms of our Constitution the price is greater than for others.

The problem then cannot be cast in terms of legal discrimination or its absence. This would be true, even though the state in giving aid should treat all religious instruction alike. Thus, if the present statute and its application were shown to apply equally to all religious schools **⊥60** of whatever faith, yet in the light of our tradition it could not stand. For then the adherent of one creed still would pay for the support of another, the childless taxpayer with others more fortunate. Then too there would seem to be no bar to making appropriations for transportation and other expenses of children attending public or other secular schools, after hours in separate places and classes for their exclusively religious instruction. The person who embraces no creed also would be forced to pay for teaching what he does not believe. Again, it was the furnishing of "contributions of money for the propagation of opinions which he disbelieves" that the fathers outlawed. That consequence and effect are not removed by multiplying to all-inclusiveness the sects for which support is exacted. The Constitution requires, not comprehensive identification of state with religion, but complete separation.

VI

Short treatment will dispose of what remains. Whatever might be said of some other application of New Jersey's statute, the one made here has no semblance of bearing as a safety measure or, indeed, for securing expeditious conveyance. The transportation supplied is by public conveyance, subject to all the hazards and delays of the highway and the streets incurred by the public generally in going about its multifarious business.

Nor is the case comparable to one of furnishing fire or police protection, or access to public highways. These things are matters of common right, part of the general ⊥**61** need for safety. Certainly the fire department must not stand idly by while the church burns. Nor is this reason why the state should pay the expense of transportation or other items of the cost of religious education. . . .

I have chosen to place my dissent upon the broad ground I think decisive, though strictly speaking the case might be decided on narrower issues. The New Jersey statute might be held invalid on its face for the exclusion of chil⊥**62**dren who attend private, profit-making schools. I cannot assume, as does the majority, that the New Jersey courts would write off this explicit limitation from the statute. Moreover, the resolution by which the statute was applied expressly limits its benefits to students of public and Catholic schools. There is no showing that there are no other private or religious schools in this populous district. I do not think it can be assumed there were none. But in the view I have taken, it is unnecessary to limit grounding to these matters.

⊥**63** Two great drives are constantly in motion to abridge, in the name of education, the complete division of religion and civil authority which our forefathers made. One is to introduce religious education and observances into the public schools. The other, to obtain public funds for the aid and support of various private religious schools. In my opinion both avenues were closed by the Constitution. Neither should be opened by this Court. The matter is not one of quantity, to be measured by the amount of money expended. Now as in Madison's day it is one of principle, to keep separate the separate spheres as the First Amendment drew them; to prevent the first experiment upon our liberties; and to keep the question from becoming entangled in corrosive precedents. We should not be less strict to keep strong and untarnished the one side of the shield of religious freedom than we have been of the other.

The judgment should be reversed.

BOARD OF EDUCATION v. ALLEN

392 U.S. 236
ON APPEAL FROM THE COURT OF APPEALS OF NEW YORK
Argued April 22, 1968 — Decided June 10, 1968

⊥**238** Mr. *Justice WHITE* delivered the opinion of the Court.

A law of the State of New York requires local public school authorities to lend textbooks free of charge to all students in grades seven through 12; students attending private schools are included. This case presents the question whether this statute is a "law respecting an establishment of religion, or prohibiting the free exercise thereof," and so in conflict with the First and Fourteenth Amendments to the Constitution, because it authorizes the loan of textbooks to students attending parochial schools. We hold that the law is not in violation of the Constitution. . . .

⊥**239** The books now loaned are "textbooks which are designated for use in any public, elementary or secondary schools of the state or are approved by any boards of education," and which—according to a 1966 amendment—"a pupil is required to use as a text for a semester or more in a particular class in the school he legally attends."

⊥**240** Appellant Board of Education of Central School District No. 1 in Rensselaer and Columbia Counties, brought suit in the New York courts against appellee James Allen. The complaint alleged that § 701 violated both the State and Federal Constitutions; that if appellants, in reliance on their interpretation of the Constitution, failed to lend books to parochial school students within their counties appellee Allen would remove appellants from office; and that to prevent this, appellants were complying with the law and submitting to their constituents a school budget including funds for books to be lent to parochial school pupils. Appellants therefore sought a declaration that § 701 was invalid, an order barring appellee Allen from removing appellants from office for failing to comply with it, and another order restraining him from apportioning state funds to school districts for the purchase of textbooks to be lent to parochial students. . . .

⊥**241** *Everson* v. *Board of Education* is the case decided by this Court that is most nearly in ⊥**242** point for today's problem. New Jersey reimbursed parents for expenses incurred in busing their children to parochial schools. The Court stated that the Establishment Clause bars a State from passing "laws which aid one religion, aid all religions, or prefer one religion over another," and bars too any "tax in any amount, large or small . . . levied to support any religious activities or institutions, whatever they may be called, or whatever form they may adopt to teach or practice religion." Nevertheless, said the Court, the Establishment Clause does not prevent a State from extending the benefits of state laws to all citizens without regard for their religious affiliation and does not prohibit "New Jersey from spending tax-raised funds to pay the bus fares of parochial school pupils as a part of a general program under which it pays the fares of pupils attending public and other schools." The statute was held to be valid even though one of its results was that "children are helped to get to church schools" and "some of the children might not be sent to the church schools if the parents were compelled to pay their children's bus fares out of their own pockets." As with public provision of police and fire protection, sewage facilities, and streets and sidewalks, payment of bus fares was of some value to the religious school, but was nevertheless not such support of a religious institution as to be a prohibited establishment of religion within the meaning of the First Amendment.

Everson and later cases have shown that the line between state neutrality to religion and state support of religion is not easy to locate. "The constitutional standard is the separation of Church and State. The problem, like many problems in constitutional law, is one of degree." Based ⊥**243** on *Everson*, *Zorach*, *McGowan*, and other cases, *Abington School District* v. *Schempp* fashioned a test subscribed to by eight Justices for distinguishing between forbidden involvements of the State with religion and those contacts which the Establishment Clause permits: "The test may be stated as follows: what are the purpose and the primary effect of the enactment? If either is the advancement or inhibition of religion then the enactment exceeds the scope of legislative power as circumscribed by the Constitution. That is to say that to withstand the strictures of the Establishment Clause there must be a secular legislative purpose and a primary effect that neither advances nor inhibits religion. *Everson* v. *Board of Education*. . . ."

This test is not easy to apply, but the citation of *Everson* by the *Schempp* Court to support its general standard made clear how the *Schempp* rule would be applied to the facts of *Everson*. The statute upheld in *Everson* would be considered a law having "a secular legislative purpose and a primary effect that neither advances nor inhibits religion." We reach the same result with respect to the New York law requiring school books to be loaned free of charge to all students in specified grades. The express purpose of § 701 was stated by the New York Legislature to be furtherance of the educational opportunities available to the young. Appellants have shown us nothing about the necessary effects of the statute that is contrary to its stated purpose. The law merely makes available to all children the benefits of a general program to lend school books free of charge. Books are fur⊥**244** nished at the request of the pupil and ownership remains, at least technically, in the State. Thus no funds or books are furnished to parochial schools, and the financial benefit is to parents and children, not to schools. Perhaps free books make it more likely that some children choose to attend a sectarian school, but that was true of the state-paid bus fares in *Everson* and does not alone demonstrate an unconstitutional degree of support for a religious institution.

Of course books are different from buses. Most bus rides have no inherent religious significance, while religious books are common. However, the language of § 701 does not authorize the loan of religious books, and the State claims no right to distribute religious literature. Although the books loaned are those required by the parochial school for use in specific courses, each book ⊥**245** loaned must be approved by the public school authorities; only secular books may receive approval. The law was construed by the Court of Appeals of New York as "merely making available secular textbooks at the request of the individual student" and the record contains no suggestion that religious books have been loaned. Absent evidence, we cannot assume that school authorities, who constantly face the same problem in selecting textbooks for use in the public schools, are unable to distinguish between secular and religious books or that they will not honestly discharge their duties under the law. In judging the validity of the statute on this record we must proceed on the assumption that books loaned to students are books that are not unsuitable for use in the public schools because of religious content.

The major reason offered by appellants for distinguishing free textbooks from free bus fares is that books, but not buses, are critical to the teaching process, and in a sectarian school that process is employed to teach religion. However this Court has long recognized that religious schools pursue two goals, religious instruction and secular education. In the leading case of *Pierce* v. *Society of Sisters* the Court held that although it would not question Oregon's power to compel school attendance or require that the attendance be at an institution meeting State-imposed requirements as to quality and nature of curriculum, Oregon had not shown that its interest in secular education required that all children attend publicly operated schools. A premise of this holding was the view that the State's interest in education would be served sufficiently by reliance on the secular teaching that accompanied religious training in the schools maintained by the Society of Sisters. Since *Pierce*, a substantial body of case law has confirmed the power of the States to insist that attendance at private schools, if it is to satisfy state compulsory-attendance ⊥**246** laws, be at institutions which provide minimum hours of instruction, employ teachers of specified training, and cover prescribed subjects of instruction. Indeed, the State's interest in assuring that these standards are being met has been considered a sufficient reason for refusing to accept instruction at home as compliance with com⊥**247**pulsory education statutes. These cases were a sensible corollary of *Pierce* v. *Society of Sisters:* if the State must satisfy its interest in secular education through the instrument of private schools, it has a proper interest in the manner in which those schools perform their secular educational function. Another corollary was *Cochran* v. *Louisiana State Board of Education* where appellants said that a statute requiring school books to be furnished without charge to all students, whether they attended public or private schools, did not serve a "public purpose," and so offended the Fourteenth Amendment. Speaking through *Chief Justice HUGHES*, the Court summarized as follows its conclusion that Louisiana's interest in the secular education being provided by private schools made provision of textbooks to students in those schools a properly public concern: "[The State's] interest is education, broadly; its method, comprehensive. Individual interests are aided only as the common interest is safeguarded."

Underlying these cases, and underlying also the legislative judgments that have preceded the court decisions, has been a recognition that private education has played and is playing a significant and valuable role in raising national levels of knowledge, competence, and experience. . . .

⊥**248** Against this background of judgment and experience, unchallenged in the meager record before us in this case, we cannot agree with appellants either that all teaching in a sectarian school is religious or that the processes of secular and religious training are so intertwined that secular textbooks furnished to students by the public are in fact instrumental in the teaching of religion. This case comes to us after summary judgment entered on the pleadings. Nothing in this record supports the proposition that all textbooks, whether they deal with mathematics, physics, foreign languages, history, or literature, are used by the parochial schools to teach religion. No evidence has been offered about particular schools, particular courses, particular teachers, or particular books. We are unable to hold, based solely on judicial notice, that this statute results in unconstitutional involvement of the State with religious instruction or that § 701, for this or the other reasons urged, is a law respecting the establishment of religion within the meaning of the First Amendment.

Appellants also contend that § 701 offends the Free Exercise Clause of the First Amendment. However, "it is necessary in a free exercise case for one to show the ⊥**249** coercive effect of the enactment as it operates against him in the practice of his religion," *Abington School District* v. *Schempp*, and appellants have not contended that the New York law in any way coerces them as individuals in the practice of their religion.

The judgment is affirmed.

Mr. *Justice* HARLAN, concurring.

Although I join the opinion and judgment of the Court, I wish to emphasize certain of the principles which I believe to be central to the determination of this case, and which I think are implicit in the Court's decision.

The attitude of government toward religion must, as this Court has frequently observed, be one of neutrality. Neutrality is, however, a coat of many colors. It requires that "government neither engage in nor compel religious practices, that it effect no favoritism among sects or between religion and nonreligion, and that it work deterrence of no religious belief" *Abington School District* v. *Schempp*. Realization of these objectives entails "no simple and clear measure," *id.*, by which this or any case may readily be decided, but these objectives do suggest the principles which I believe to be applicable in the present circumstances. I would hold that where the contested governmental activity is calculated to achieve nonreligious purposes otherwise within the competence of the State, and where the activity does not involve the State "so significantly and directly in the realm of the sectarian as to give rise to . . . divisive influences and inhibitions of freedom," *id.*, it is not forbidden by the religious clauses of the First Amendment.

⊥**250** In my opinion, § 701 of the Education Law of New York does not employ religion as its standard for action or inaction, and is not otherwise inconsistent with these principles.

Mr. *Justice* BLACK, dissenting.

The Court here affirms a judgment of the New York Court of Appeals which sustained the constitutionality of a New York law providing state tax-raised funds to supply school books for use by pupils in schools owned and operated by religious sects. I believe the New York law held valid is a flat, flagrant, open violation of the First and Fourteenth Amendments which together forbid Congress or state legislatures to enact any law "respecting an establishment of religion." For that reason I would reverse the New York Court of Appeals' judgment. . . .

⊥**251** The *Everson* and *McCollum* cases plainly interpret the First and Fourteenth Amendments as protecting the taxpayers of a State from being compelled to pay taxes to their government to support the agencies of private religious organizations the taxpayers oppose. To authorize a State to tax its residents for such church purposes is to put the State squarely in the religious activities of certain religious groups that happen to be strong enough politically to write their own religious preferences and prejudices into the laws. This links state and churches together in controlling the lives and destinies of our citizenship—a citizenship composed of people of myriad religious faiths, some of them bitterly hostile to and completely intolerant of the others. It was to escape laws precisely like this that a large part of the Nation's early immigrants fled to this country. It was also to escape such laws and such consequences that the First Amendment was written in language strong and clear barring passage of any law "respecting an establishment of religion."

It is true, of course, that the New York law does not as yet formally adopt or establish a state religion. But it takes a great stride in that direction and coming events cast their shadows before them. The same powerful sectarian religious propagandists who have succeeded in securing passage of the present law to help religious schools carry on their sectarian religious purposes can and doubtless will continue their propaganda, looking toward complete domination and supremacy of their particular brand of religion. And it nearly always is ⊥**252** by insidious approaches that the citadels of liberty are more successfully attacked.

I know of no prior opinion of this Court upon which the majority here can rightfully rely to support its holding this New York law constitutional. In saying this, I am not unmindful of the fact that the New York Court of Appeals purported to follow *Everson* v. *Board of Education*, in which this Court, in an opinion written by me, upheld a New Jersey law authorizing reimbursement to parents for the transportation of children attending sectarian schools. That law did not attempt to deny the benefit of its general terms to children of any faith going to any legally authorized school. Thus, it was treated in the same way as a general law paying the streetcar fare *of all school children*, or a law providing midday lunches for all children or all school children, or a law to provide police protection for children going to and from school, or general laws to provide police and fire protection for buildings, including, of course, churches and church school buildings as well as others.

As my *Brother DOUGLAS* so forcefully shows, in an argument with which I fully agree, upholding a State's power to pay bus or streetcar fares for school children cannot provide support for the validity of a state law using tax-raised funds to buy school books for a religious school. The First Amendment's bar to establishment of religion must preclude a State from using funds levied from all of its citizens to purchase books for use by sectarian schools, which, although "secular," realistically will in some way inevitably tend to propagate the religious views of the favored sect. Books are the most essential tool of education since they contain the resources of knowledge which the educational process is designed to exploit. In this sense it is not difficult **⊥253** to distinguish books, which are the heart of any school, from bus fares, which provide a convenient and helpful general public service. With respect to the former, state financial support actively and directly assists the teaching and propagation of sectarian religious viewpoints in clear conflict with the First Amendment's establishment bar; with respect to the latter, the State merely provides a general and nondiscriminatory service in no way related to substantive religious views and beliefs.

This New York law, it may be said by some, makes but a small inroad and does not amount to complete state establishment of religion. But that is no excuse for upholding it. It requires no prophet to foresee that on the argument used to support this law others could be upheld providing for state or federal government funds to buy property on which to erect religious school buildings or to erect the buildings themselves, to pay the salaries of the religious school teachers, and finally to have the sectarian religious groups cease to rely on voluntary contributions of members of their sects while waiting for the Government to pick up all the bills for the religious schools. Arguments made in favor of this New York law point squarely in this direction, namely, that the fact that government has not heretofore aided religious schools with tax-raised funds amounts to a discrimination against those schools and against religion. . . .

I still subscribe to the belief that tax-raised funds cannot constitutionally be used to support religious schools, buy their school books, erect their buildings, pay their **⊥254** teachers, or pay any other of their maintenance expenses, even to the extent of one penny. The First Amendment's prohibition against governmental establishment of religion was written on the assumption that state aid to religion and religious schools generates discord, disharmony, hatred, and strife among our people, and that any government that supplies such aids is to that extent a tyranny. And I still believe that the only way to protect minority religious groups from majority groups in this country is to keep the wall of separation between church and state high and impregnable as the First and Fourteenth Amendments provide. The Court's affirmance here bodes nothing but evil to religious peace in this country.

Mr. Justice DOUGLAS, dissenting.

We have for review a statute which authorizes New York State to supply textbooks to students in parochial as well as in public schools. The New York Court of Appeals sustained the law on the grounds that it involves only "secular textbooks" and that that type of aid falls within *Everson* v. *Board of Education*, where a divided Court upheld a state law which made bus service available to students in parochial schools as well as to students in public schools.

The statute on its face empowers each parochial school to determine for itself which textbooks will be eligible for loans to its students, for the Act provides that the **⊥255** only text which the State may provide is "a book which a pupil is required to use as a text for a semester or more in a particular class in the school he legally attends." This initial and crucial selection is undoubtedly made by the parochial school's principal or its individual instructors, who are, in the case of Roman Catholic schools, normally priests or nuns.

The next step under the Act is an "individual request" for an eligible textbook, but the State Education Department has ruled that a pupil may make his request to the local public board of education through a "private school official." Local boards have accordingly provided for those requests to be made by the individual or "by groups or classes." And forms for textbook requisitions to be filled out by the head of the private school are provided.

The role of the local public school board is to decide whether to veto the selection made by the parochial school. This is done by determining first whether the text has been or should be "approved" for use in public schools and second whether the text is "secular," "nonreligious," or "nonsectarian." The local boards ap**⊥256** parently have broad discretion in exercising this veto power.

Thus the statutory system provides that the parochial school will ask for the books that it wants. Can there be the slightest doubt that the head of the parochial school will select the book or books that best promote its sectarian creed?

If the board of education supinely submits by approving and supplying the sectarian or sectarian-oriented textbooks, the struggle to keep church and state separate has been lost. If the board resists, then the battle line between church and state will have been drawn and the contest will be on to keep the school board independent or to put it under church domination and control.

⊥257 Whatever may be said of *Everson*, there is nothing ideological about a bus. There is nothing ideological about a school lunch, or a public nurse, or a scholarship. The constitutionality of such public aid to students in parochial schools turns on considerations not present in this textbook case. The textbook goes to the very heart of education in a parochial school. It is the chief, although not solitary, instrumentality for propagating a particular religious creed or faith. How can we possibly approve such state aid to a religion? A parochial school textbook may contain many, many more seeds of creed and dogma than a prayer. Yet we struck down in *Engel* v. *Vitale* an official New York prayer for its public schools, even though it was not plainly denominational. For we emphasized the violence done the Establishment Clause when the power was given religious-political groups "to write their own prayers into law." That risk is compounded here by giving parochial schools the initiative in selecting the textbooks they desire to be furnished at public expense.

Judge Van Voorhis, joined by Chief Judge Fuld and Judge Breitel dissenting below, said that the difficulty with the textbook **⊥258** loan program "is that there is no reliable standard by which secular and religious textbooks can be distinguished from each other." The New York Legislature felt that science was a non-sectarian subject. Does this mean that any general science textbook intended for use in grades 7-12 may be provided by the State to parochial school students? May John M. Scott's Adventures in Science (1963) be supplied under the textbook loan program? This book teaches embryology in the following manner:

"To you an animal usually means a mammal, such as a cat, dog, squirrel, or guinea pig. The new animal or embryo develops inside the body of the mother until birth. The fertilized egg becomes an embryo or developing animal. Many cell divisions take place. In time some cells become muscle cells, others nerve cells or blood cells, and organs such as eyes, stomach, and intestine are formed.

"The body of a human being grows in the same way, but it is much more remarkable than that of any animal, for the embryo has a human soul infused into the body by God. Human parents are partners with God in creation. They have very great powers and great responsibilities, for through their cooperation with God souls are born for heaven." (At 618-619.)

Comparative economics would seem to be a nonsectarian subject. Will New York, then, provide Arthur J. Hughes' general history text, Man in Time (1964), to **⊥259** this manner: "Capitalism is an economic system based on man's right to private property and on his freedom to use that property in producing goods which will earn him a just profit on his investment. Man's right to private property stems from the Natural Law implanted in him by God. It is as much a part of man's nature as the will to self-preservation." (At 560.)

"The broadest definition of socialism is government ownership of all the means of production and distribution in a country. . . . Many, but by no means all, Socialists in the nineteenth century believed that crime and vice existed because poverty existed, and if poverty were eliminated, then crime and vice would disappear. While it is true that poor surroundings are usually unhealthy climates for high moral training, still, man has the free will to check himself. Many Socialists, however, denied free will and said that man was a creation of his environment. . . . If Socialists do not deny Christ's message, they often ignore it. Christ showed us by His life that this earth is a testing ground to prepare man for eternal happiness. Man's interests should be in this direction at least part of the time and not always directed toward a futile quest for material goods." (At 561-564.)

Mr. Justice JACKSON said, ". . . I should suppose it is a proper, if not an indispensable, part of preparation for a **⊥260** worldly life to know the roles that religion and religions have played in the tragic story of mankind." *McCollum* v. *Board of Education*. Yet, as he inquired, what emphasis should one give who teaches the Reformation, the Inquisition, or the early effort in New England to establish "'a Church without a Bishop and a State without a King?'" What books should be chosen for those subjects?

Even where the treatment given to a particular topic in a school textbook is not blatantly sectarian, it will necessarily have certain shadings that will lead a parochial school to prefer one text over another.

The Crusades, for example, may be taught as a Christian undertaking to "save the Holy Land" from the Moslem Turks who "became a threat to Christianity and its holy places," which "they did not treat . . . with respect" **⊥261** (H. Wilson, F. Wilson, B. Erb & E. Clucas, Out of the Past 284 (1954)), or as essentially a series of wars born out of political and materialistic motives (see G. Leinwand, The Pageant of World History 136-137 (1965)).

Is the dawn of man to be explained in the words, "God created man and made man master of the earth" (P. Furlong, The Old World and America 5 (1937)), or in the language of evolution (see T. Wallbank, Man's Story 32-35 (1961))?

Is the slaughter of the Aztecs by Cortes and his entourage to be lamented for its destruction of a New World culture (see J. Caughey, J. Franklin, & E. May, Land of the Free 27-28 (1965)), or forgiven because the Spaniards "carried the true Faith" to a barbaric people who practiced human sacrifice (see P. Furlong, Sr. Margaret, & D. Sharkey, America Yesterday 17, 34 (1963))?

Is Franco's revolution in Spain to be taught as a crusade against anti-Catholic forces (see R. Hoffman, G. Vincitorio, & M. Swift, Man and His History 666-667 (1958)) or as an effort by reactionary elements to regain control of that country (see G. Leinwand, The Pageant of World History, *supra*, at 512)? Is the expansion of **⊥262** communism in select areas of the world a manifestation of the forces of Evil campaigning against the forces of Good? See A. Hughes, Man in Time, *supra*, at 565-568, 666-669, 735-748.

It will be often difficult, as *Mr. Justice JACKSON* said, to say "where the secular ends and the sectarian begins in education." But certain it is that once the so-called "secular" textbook is the prize to be won by that religious faith which selects the book, the battle will be on for those positions of control. Judge Van Voorhis expressed the fear that in the end the state might dominate the church. Others fear that one sectarian group, gaining control of the state agencies which approve the "secular" textbooks, will use their control to disseminate ideas most congenial to their faith. It must be remembered that the very existence of the religious school—whether Catholic or Mormon, Presbyterian or Episcopalian—is to provide an education oriented to the dogma of the particular faith. . . .

⊥264 The challenged New York law leaves to the Board of Regents, local boards of education, trustees, and other school authorities the supervision of the textbook program.

⊥265 The Board of Regents (together with the Commissioner of Education) has powers of censorship over all textbooks that contain statements seditious in character, or evince disloyalty to the United States or are favorable to any nation with which we are at war. Those powers can cut a wide swath in many areas of education that involve the ideological element.

In general textbooks are approved for distribution by "boards of education, trustees or such body or officer as perform the functions of such boards. . . ." These school boards are generally elected, though in a few cities they are appointed. Where there are trustees, they are elected. And superintendents who advise on textbook selection are appointed by the board of education or the trustees.

The initiative to select and requisition "the books desired" is with the parochial school. Powerful religious-political pressures will therefore be on the state agencies to provide the books that are desired.

These then are the battlegrounds where control of textbook distribution will be won or lost. Now that "secular" textbooks will pour into religious schools, we can rest assured that a contest will be on to provide those books for religious schools which the dominant religious group concludes best reflect the theocentric or other philosophy of the particular church.

⊥266 The stakes are now extremely high just as they were in the school prayer cases—to obtain approval of what is "proper." For the "proper" books will radiate the "correct" religious view not only in the parochial school but in the public school as well.

Even if I am wrong in that basic premise, we still should not affirm the judgment below. Judge Van Voorhis, dissenting in the New York Court of Appeals, thought that the result of tying parochial school textbooks to public funds would be to put nonsectarian books into religious schools, which in the long view would tend towards state domination of the church. That would, indeed, be the result if the school boards did not succumb to "sectarian" pressure or control. So, however the case be viewed—whether sectarian groups win control of school boards or do not gain such control—the principle of separation of church and state, inherent in the Establishment Clause of the First Amendment, is violated by what we today approve.

What Madison wrote in his famous Memorial and Remonstrance against Religious Assessments is highly pertinent here: "Who does not see that the same authority which can establish Christianity, in exclusion of all other Religions, may establish with the same ease any particular sect of Christians, in exclusion of all other Sects? That the same authority which can force a citizen to contribute three pence only of his property for the support of any one establishment, may force him to conform to any other establishment in all cases whatsoever?"

. . . . .

⊥269 Mr. *Justice* FORTAS, dissenting.

The majority opinion of the Court upholds the New York statute by ignoring a vital aspect of it. Public funds are used to buy, for students in sectarian schools, textbooks which are selected and prescribed by the sec**⊥270**tarian schools themselves. As my *Brother* DOUGLAS points out, despite the transparent camouflage that the books are furnished to students, the reality is that they are selected and their use is prescribed by the sectarian authorities. The child must use the prescribed book. He cannot use a different book prescribed for use in the public schools. The State cannot choose the book to be used. It is true that the public school boards must "approve" the book selected by the sectarian authorities; but this has no real significance. The purpose of these provisions is to hold out promise that the books will be "secular," but the fact remains that the books are chosen by and for the sectarian schools.

It is misleading to say, as the majority opinion does, that the New York "law merely makes available to all children the benefits of a general program to lend school books free of charge." This is not a "general" program. It is a specific program to use state **⊥271** funds to buy books prescribed by sectarian schools which, in New York, are primarily Catholic, Jewish, and Lutheran sponsored schools. It could be called a "general" program only if the school books made available to all children were precisely the same—the books selected for and used in the public schools. But this program is not one in which all children are treated alike, regardless of where they go to school. This program, in its unconstitutional features, is hand-tailored to satisfy the specific needs of sectarian schools. Children attending such schools are given *special* books—books selected by the sectarian authorities. How can this be other than the use of public money to aid those sectarian establishments?

It is also beside the point, in my opinion, to "assume," as the majority opinion does, that "books loaned to students are books that are not unsuitable for use in the public schools because of religious content." The point is that the books furnished to students of sectarian schools are selected by the religious authorities and are prescribed by them.

This case is not within the principle of *Everson* v. *Board of Education*. Apart from the differences between textbooks and bus rides, the present statute does not call for extending to children attending sectarian schools the same service or facility extended to children in public schools. This statute calls for furnishing special, separate, larly chosen by religious sects or their representatives for use in their sectarian schools. This is the infirmity, in my opinion. This is the feature that makes it impossible, in my view, to reach any conclusion other than that this statute is an unconstitutional use of public funds to support an establishment of religion.

This is the feature of the present statute that makes it totally inaccurate to suggest, as the majority does **⊥272** here, that furnishing these specially selected books for use in sectarian schools is like "public provision of police and fire protection, sewage facilities, and streets and sidewalks." These are furnished to all alike. They are not selected on the basis of specification by a religious sect. And patrons of any one sect do not receive services or facilities different from those accorded members of other religions or agnostics or even atheists.

I would reverse the judgment below.

LEMON v. KURTZMAN

403 U.S. 602
ON APPEAL FROM THE UNITED STATES DISTRICT COURT FOR THE EASTERN DISTRICT OF PENNSYLVANIA
Argued March 3, 1971 — Decided June 28, 1971

⊥606 *Mr. Chief Justice BURGER* delivered the opinion of the Court.

These two appeals raise questions as to Pennsylvania and Rhode Island statutes providing state aid to church-related elementary and secondary schools. Both statutes are challenged as violative of the Establishment and Free Exercise Clauses of the First Amendment and the Due Process Clause of the Fourteenth Amendment.

Pennsylvania has adopted a statutory program that provides financial support to nonpublic elementary and **⊥607** secondary schools by way of reimbursement for the cost of teachers' salaries, textbooks, and instructional materials in specified secular subjects. Rhode Island has adopted a statute under which the State pays directly to teachers in nonpublic elementary schools a supplement of 15% of their annual salary. Under each statute state aid has been given to church-related educational institutions. We hold that both statutes are unconstitutional.

I

The Rhode Island Statute

The Rhode Island Salary Supplement Act was enacted in 1969. It rests on the legislative finding that the quality of education available in nonpublic elementary schools has been jeopardized by the rapidly rising salaries needed to attract competent and dedicated teachers. The Act authorizes state officials to supplement the salaries of teachers of secular subjects in nonpublic elementary schools by paying directly to a teacher an amount not in excess of 15% of his current annual salary. As supplemented, however, a nonpublic school teacher's salary cannot exceed the maximum paid to teachers in the State's public schools, and the recipient must be certified by the state board of education in substantially the same manner as public school teachers.

In order to be eligible for the Rhode Island salary supplement, the recipient must teach in a nonpublic school at which the average per-pupil expenditure on secular education is less than the average in the State's public schools during a specified period. Appellant State Commissioner of Education also requires eligible schools to submit financial data. If this information indicates a per-pupil expenditure in excess of the statutory limita**⊥608**tion, the records of the school in question must be examined in order to assess how much of the expenditure is attributable to secular education and how much to religious activity.

The Act also requires that teachers eligible for salary supplements must teach only those subjects that are offered in the State's public schools. They must use "only teaching materials which are used in the public schools." Finally, any teacher applying for a salary supplement must first agree in writing "not to teach a course in religion for so long as or during such time as he or she receives any salary supplements" under the Act.

Appellees are citizens and taxpayers of Rhode Island. They brought this suit to have the Rhode Island Salary Supplement Act declared unconstitutional and its operation enjoined on the ground that it violates the Establishment and Free Exercise Clauses of the First Amendment. Appellants are state officials charged with administration of the Act, teachers eligible for salary supplements under the Act, and parents of children in church-related elementary schools whose teachers would receive state salary assistance.

A three-judge federal court was convened. It found that Rhode Island's nonpublic elementary schools accommodated approximately 25% of the State's pupils. About 95% of these pupils attended schools affiliated with the Roman Catholic church. To date some 250 teachers have applied for benefits under the Act. All of them are employed by Roman Catholic schools.

⊥609 The court held a hearing at which extensive evidence was introduced concerning the nature of the secular instruction offered in the Roman Catholic schools whose teachers would be eligible for salary assistance under the Act. Although the court found that concern for religious values does not necessarily affect the content of secular subjects, it also found that the parochial school system was "an integral part of the religious mission of the Catholic Church."

The District Court concluded that the Act violated the Establishment Clause, holding that it fostered "excessive entanglement" between government and religion. In addition two judges thought that the Act had the impermissible effect of giving "significant aid to a religious enterprise." We affirm.

The Pennsylvania Statute

Pennsylvania has adopted a program that has some but not all of the features of the Rhode Island program.

The Pennsylvania Nonpublic Elementary and Secondary Education Act was passed in 1968 in response to a crisis that the Pennsylvania Legislature found existed in the State's nonpublic schools due to rapidly rising costs. The statute affirmatively reflects the legislative conclusion that the State's educational goals could appropriately be fulfilled by government support of "those purely secular educational objectives achieved through nonpublic education. . . ."

The statute authorizes appellee state Superintendent of Public Instruction to "purchase" specified "secular education services" from nonpublic schools. Under the "contracts" authorized by the statute, the State directly reimburses nonpublic schools solely for their actual expenditures for teachers' salaries, textbooks, and instructional materials. A school seeking reimbursement must ⊥**610** maintain prescribed accounting procedures that identify the "separate" cost of the "secular educational service." These accounts are subject to state audit. The funds for this program were originally derived from a new tax on horse and harness racing, but the Act is now financed by a portion of the state tax on cigarettes.

There are several significant statutory restrictions on state aid. Reimbursement is limited to courses "presented in the curricula of the public schools." It is further limited "solely" to courses in the following "secular" subjects: mathematics, modern foreign languages, physical science, and physical education. Textbooks and instructional materials included in the program must be approved by the state Superintendent of Public Instruction. Finally, the statute prohibits reimbursement for any course that contains "any subject matter expressing religious teaching, or the morals or forms of worship of any sect."

The Act went into effect on July 1, 1968, and the first reimbursement payments to schools were made on September 2, 1969. It appears that some $5 million has been expended annually under the Act. The State has now entered into contracts with some 1,181 nonpublic elementary and secondary schools with a student population of some 535,215 pupils—more than 20% of the total number of students in the State. More than 96% of these pupils attend church-related schools, and most of these schools are affiliated with the Roman Catholic church.

Appellants brought this action in the District Court to challenge the constitutionality of the Pennsylvania statute. The organizational plaintiffs-appellants are associations of persons resident in Pennsylvania declaring ⊥**611** belief in the separation of church and state; individual plaintiffs-appellants are citizens and taxpayers of Pennsylvania. Appellant Lemon, in addition to being a citizen and a taxpayer, is a parent of a child attending public school in Pennsylvania. Lemon also alleges that he purchased a ticket at a race track and thus had paid the specific tax that supports the expenditures under the Act. Appellees are state officials who have the responsibility for administering the Act. In addition seven church-related schools are defendants-appellees.

A three-judge federal court was convened. The District Court held that the individual plaintiffs-appellants had standing to challenge the Act. The organizational plaintiffs-appellants were denied standing under *Flast* v. *Cohen*.

The court granted appellees' motion to dismiss the complaint for failure to state a claim for relief. It held that the Act violated neither the Establishment nor the Free Exercise Clause, Chief Judge Hastie dissenting. We reverse.

II

In *Everson* v. *Board of Education* this Court upheld a state statute that reimbursed the parents of parochial school children for bus transportation ⊥**612** expenses. There Mr. *Justice* BLACK, writing for the majority, suggested that the decision carried to "the verge" of forbidden territory under the Religion Clauses. Candor compels acknowledgment, moreover, that we can only dimly perceive the lines of demarcation in this extraordinarily sensitive area of constitutional law.

The language of the Religion Clauses of the First Amendment is at best opaque, particularly when compared with other portions of the Amendment. Its authors did not simply prohibit the establishment of a state church or a state religion, an area history shows they regarded as very important and fraught with great dangers. Instead they commanded that there should be "no law *respecting* an establishment of religion." A law may be one "respecting" the forbidden objective while falling short of its total realization. A law "respecting" the proscribed result, that is, the establishment of religion, is not always easily identifiable as one violative of the Clause. A given law might not *establish* a state religion but nevertheless be one "respecting" that end in the sense of being a step that could lead to such establishment and hence offend the First Amendment.

In the absence of precisely stated constitutional prohibitions, we must draw lines with reference to the three main evils against which the Establishment Clause was intended to afford protection: "sponsorship, financial support, and active involvement of the sovereign in religious activity." *Walz* v. *Tax Commission*.

Every analysis in this area must begin with consideration of the cumulative criteria developed by the Court over many years. Three such tests may be gleaned from our cases. First, the statute must have a secular legislative purpose; second, its principal or primary effect must be one that neither advances nor inhibits religion; ⊥**613** finally, the statute must not foster "an excessive government entanglement with religion." *Walz*.

Inquiry into the legislative purposes of the Pennsylvania and Rhode Island statutes affords no basis for a conclusion that the legislative intent was to advance religion. On the contrary, the statutes themselves clearly state that they are intended to enhance the quality of the secular education in all schools covered by the compulsory attendance laws. There is no reason to believe the legislatures meant anything else. A State always has a legitimate concern for maintaining minimum standards in all schools it allows to operate. As in *Allen*, we find nothing here that undermines the stated legislative intent; it must therefore be accorded appropriate deference.

In *Allen* the Court acknowledged that secular and religious teaching were not necessarily so intertwined that secular textbooks furnished to students by the State were in fact instrumental in the teaching of religion. The legislatures of Rhode Island and Pennsylvania have concluded that secular and religious education are identifiable and separable. In the abstract we have no quarrel with this conclusion.

The two legislatures, however, have also recognized that church-related elementary and secondary schools have a significant religious mission and that a substantial portion of their activities is religiously oriented. They have therefore sought to create statutory restrictions designed to guarantee the separation between secular and religious educational functions and to ensure that State financial aid supports only the former. All these provisions are precautions taken in candid recognition that these programs approached, even if they did not intrude upon, the forbidden areas under the Religion Clauses. We need not decide whether these legislative precautions restrict the principal or primary effect of the programs to the point where they do not offend the Religion ⊥**614** Clauses, for we conclude that the cumulative impact of the entire relationship arising under the statutes in each State involves excessive entanglement between government and religion.

III

In *Walz* v. *Tax Commission* the Court upheld state tax exemptions for real property owned by religious organizations and used for religious worship. That holding, however, tended to confine rather than enlarge the area of permissible state involvement with religious institutions by calling for close scrutiny of the degree of entanglement involved in the relationship. The objective is to prevent, as far as possible, the intrusion of either into the precincts of the other.

Our prior holdings do not call for total separation between church and state; total separation is not possible in an absolute sense. Some relationship between government and religious organizations is inevitable. Fire inspections, building and zoning regulations, and state requirements under compulsory school-attendance laws are examples of necessary and permissible contacts. Indeed, under the statutory exemption before us in *Walz*, the State had a continuing burden to ascertain that the exempt property was in fact being used for religious worship. Judicial caveats against entanglement must recognize that the line of separation, far from being a "wall," is a blurred, indistinct, and variable barrier depending on all the circumstances of a particular relationship.

This is not to suggest, however, that we are to engage in a legalistic minuet in which precise rules and forms must govern. A true minuet is a matter of pure form and style, the observance of which is itself the substantive end. Here we examine the form of the relationship for the light that it casts on the substance.

⊥**615** In order to determine whether the government entanglement with religion is excessive, we must examine the character and purposes of the institutions that are benefited, the nature of the aid that the State provides, and the resulting relationship between the government and the religious authority. Mr. *Justice HARLAN*, in a separate opinion in *Walz*, echoed the classic warning as to "programs, whose very nature is apt to entangle the state in details of administration. . . ." Here we find that both statutes foster an impermissible degree of entanglement.

(a) *Rhode Island program*

The District Court made extensive findings on the grave potential for excessive entanglement that inheres in the religious character and purpose of the Roman Catholic elementary schools of Rhode Island, to date the sole beneficiaries of the Rhode Island Salary Supplement Act.

The church schools involved in the program are located close to parish churches. This understandably permits convenient access for religious exercises since instruction in faith and morals is part of the total educational process. The school buildings contain identifying religious symbols such as crosses on the exterior and crucifixes, and religious paintings and statues either in the classrooms or hallways. Although only approximately 30 minutes a day are devoted to direct religious instruction, there are religiously oriented extracurricular activities. Approximately two-thirds of the teachers in these schools are nuns of various religious orders. Their dedicated efforts provide an atmosphere in which religious instruction and religious vocations are natural and proper parts of life in such schools. Indeed, as the District Court found, the role of teaching nuns in enhancing the religious atmosphere has led the parochial school au⊥**616**thorities to attempt to maintain a one-to-one ratio between nuns and lay teachers in all schools rather than to permit some to be staffed almost entirely by lay teachers.

On the basis of these findings the District Court concluded that the parochial schools constituted "an integral part of the religious mission of the Catholic Church." The various characteristics of the schools make them "a powerful vehicle for transmitting the Catholic faith to the next generation." This process of inculcating religious doctrine is, of course, enhanced by the impressionable age of the pupils, in primary schools particularly. In short, parochial schools involve substantial religious activity and purpose.

The substantial religious character of these church-related schools gives rise to entangling church-state relationships of the kind the Religion Clauses sought to avoid. Although the District Court found that concern for religious values did not inevitably or necessarily intrude into the content of secular subjects, the considerable religious activities of these schools led the legislature to provide for careful governmental controls and surveillance by state authorities in order to ensure that state aid supports only secular education.

The dangers and corresponding entanglements are enhanced by the particular form of aid that the Rhode Island Act provides. Our decisions from *Everson* to *Allen* have permitted the States to provide church-related schools with secular, neutral, or nonideological services, facilities, or materials. Bus transportation, school lunches, public health services, and secular textbooks supplied in common to all students were not ⊥**617** thought to offend the Establishment Clause. We note that the dissenters in *Allen* seemed chiefly concerned with the pragmatic difficulties involved in ensuring the truly secular content of the textbooks provided at state expense.

In *Allen* the Court refused to make assumptions, on a meager record, about the religious content of the textbooks that the State would be asked to provide. We cannot, however, refuse here to recognize that teachers have a substantially different ideological character from books. In terms of potential for involving some aspect of faith or morals in secular subjects, a textbook's content is ascertainable, but a teacher's handling of a subject is not. We cannot ignore the danger that a teacher under religious control and discipline poses to the separation of the religious from the purely secular aspects of pre-college education. The conflict of functions inheres in the situation.

In our view the record shows these dangers are present to a substantial degree. The Rhode Island Roman Catholic elementary schools are under the general supervision of the Bishop of Providence and his appointed representative, the Diocesan Superintendent of Schools. In most cases, each individual parish, however, assumes the ultimate financial responsibility for the school, with the parish priest authorizing the allocation of parish funds. With only two exceptions, school principals are nuns appointed either by the Superintendent or the Mother Provincial of the order whose members staff the school. By 1969 lay teachers constituted more than a third of all teachers in the parochial elementary schools, and their number is growing. They are first interviewed by the superintendent's office and then by the school principal. The contracts are signed by the parish priest, and he retains some discretion in negotiating salary levels. Religious authority necessarily pervades the school system.

⊥**618** The schools are governed by the standards set forth in a "Handbook of School Regulations," which has the force of synodal law in the diocese. It emphasizes the role and importance of the teacher in public schools: "The prime factor for the success or the failure of the school is the spirit and personality, as well as the professional competency, of the teacher. . . ." The Handbook also states that: "Religious formation is not confined to formal courses; nor is it restricted to a single subject area." Finally, the Handbook advises teachers to stimulate interest in religious vocations and missionary work. Given the mission of the church school, these instructions are consistent and logical.

Several teachers testified, however, that they did not inject religion into their secular classes. And the District Court found that religious values did not necessarily affect the content of the secular instruction. But what has been recounted suggests the potential if not actual hazards of this form of state aid. The teacher is employed by a religious organization, subject to the direction and discipline of religious authorities, and works in a system dedicated to rearing children in a particular faith. These controls are not lessened by the fact that most of the lay teachers are of the Catholic faith. Inevitably some of a teacher's responsibilities hover on the border between secular and religious orientation.

We need not and do not assume that teachers in parochial schools will be guilty of bad faith or any conscious design to evade the limitations imposed by the statute and the First Amendment. We simply recognize that a dedicated religious person, teaching in a school affiliated with his or her faith and operated to inculcate its tenets, will inevitably experience great difficulty in remaining religiously neutral. Doctrines and faith are not inculcated or advanced by neutrals. With the best of intentions such a teacher would find it hard to make ⊥**619** a total separation between secular teaching and religious doctrine. What would appear to some to be essential to good citizenship might well for others border on or constitute instruction in religion. Further difficulties are inherent in the combination of religious discipline and the possibility of disagreement between teacher and religious authorities over the meaning of the statutory restrictions.

We do not assume, however, that parochial school teachers will be unsuccessful in their attempts to segregate their religious beliefs from their secular educational responsibilities. But the potential for impermissible fostering of religion is present. The Rhode Island Legislature has not, and could not, provide state aid on the basis of a mere assumption that secular teachers under religious discipline can avoid conflicts. The State must be certain, given the Religion Clauses, that subsidized teachers do not inculcate religion—indeed the State here has undertaken to do so. To ensure that no trespass occurs, the State has therefore carefully conditioned its aid with pervasive restrictions. An eligible recipient must teach only those courses that are offered in the public schools and use only those tests and materials that are found in the public schools. In addition the teacher must not engage in teaching any course in religion.

A comprehensive, discriminating, and continuing state surveillance will inevitably be required to ensure that these restrictions are obeyed and the First Amendment otherwise respected. Unlike a book, a teacher cannot be inspected once so as to determine the extent and intent of his or her personal beliefs and subjective acceptance of the limitations imposed by the First Amendment. These prophylactic contacts will involve excessive and enduring entanglement between state and church.

⊥620 There is another area of entanglement in the Rhode Island program that gives concern. The statute excludes teachers employed by nonpublic schools whose average per-pupil expenditures on secular education equal or exceed the comparable figures for public schools. In the event that the total expenditures of an otherwise eligible school exceed this norm, the program requires the government to examine the school's records in order to determine how much of the total expenditures is attributable to secular education and how much to religious activity. This kind of state inspection and evaluation of the religious content of a religious organization is fraught with the sort of entanglement that the Constitution forbids. It is a relationship pregnant with dangers of excessive government direction of church schools and hence of churches. The Court noted "the hazards of government supporting churches" in *Walz* v. *Tax Commission* and we cannot ignore here the danger that pervasive modern governmental power will ultimately intrude on religion and thus conflict with the Religion Clauses.

(b) *Pennsylvania program*

The Pennsylvania statute also provides state aid to church-related schools for teachers' salaries. The complaint describes an educational system that is very similar to the one existing in Rhode Island. According to the allegations, the church-related elementary and secondary schools are controlled by religious organizations, have the purpose of propagating and promoting a particular religious faith, and conduct their operations to fulfill that purpose. Since this complaint was dismissed for failure to state a claim for relief, we must accept these allegations as true for purposes of our review.

As we noted earlier, the very restrictions and surveillance necessary to ensure that teachers play a strictly nonideological role give rise to entanglements between **⊥621** church and state. The Pennsylvania statute, like that of Rhode Island, fosters this kind of relationship. Reimbursement is not only limited to courses offered in the public schools and materials approved by state officials, but the statute excludes "any subject matter expressing religious teaching, or the morals or forms of worship of any sect." In addition, schools seeking reimbursement must maintain accounting procedures that require the State to establish the cost of the secular as distinguished from the religious instruction.

The Pennsylvania statute, moreover, has the further defect of providing state financial aid directly to the church-related school. This factor distinguishes both *Everson* and *Allen*, for in both those cases the Court was careful to point out that state aid was provided to the student and his parents—not to the church-related school. In *Walz* v. *Tax Commission* the Court warned of the dangers of direct payments to religious organizations:

"Obviously a direct money subsidy would be a relationship pregnant with involvement and, as with most governmental grant programs, could encompass sustained and detailed administrative relationships for enforcement of statutory or administrative standards. . . ."

The history of government grants of a continuing cash subsidy indicates that such programs have almost always been accompanied by varying measures of control and surveillance. The government cash grants before us now provide no basis for predicting that comprehensive measures of surveillance and controls will not follow. In particular the government's post-audit power to inspect and evaluate a church-related school's financial records and to determine which expenditures are religious and **⊥622** which are secular creates an intimate and continuing relationship between church and state.

IV

A broader base of entanglement of yet a different character is presented by the divisive political potential of these state programs. In a community where such a large number of pupils are served by church-related schools, it can be assumed that state assistance will entail considerable political activity. Partisans of parochial schools, understandably concerned with rising costs and sincerely dedicated to both the religious and secular educational missions of their schools, will inevitably champion this cause and promote political action to achieve their goals. Those who oppose state aid, whether for constitutional, religious, or fiscal reasons, will inevitably respond and employ all of the usual political campaign techniques to prevail. Candidates will be forced to declare and voters to choose. It would be unrealistic to ignore the fact that many people confronted with issues of this kind will find their votes aligned with their faith.

Ordinarily political debate and division, however vigorous or even partisan, are normal and healthy manifestations of our democratic system of government, but political division along religious lines was one of the principal evils against which the First Amendment was intended to protect. The potential divisiveness of such conflict is a threat to the normal political process. To have States or communities divide on the issues presented by state aid to parochial schools would tend to confuse **⊥623** and obscure other issues of great urgency. We have an expanding array of vexing issues, local and national, domestic and international, to debate and divide on. It conflicts with our whole history and tradition to permit questions of the Religion Clauses to assume such importance in our legislatures and in our elections that they could divert attention from the myriad issues and problems that confront every level of government. The highways of church and state relationships are not likely to be one-way streets, and the Constitution's authors sought to protect religious worship from the pervasive power of government. The history of many countries attests to the hazards of religion's intruding into the political arena or of political power intruding into the legitimate and free exercise of religious belief.

Of course, as the Court noted in *Walz*, "[a]dherents of particular faiths and individual churches frequently take strong positions on public issues." We could not expect otherwise, for religious values pervade the fabric of our national life. But in *Walz* we dealt with a status under state tax laws for the benefit of all religious groups. Here we are confronted with successive and very likely permanent annual appropriations that benefit relatively few religious groups. Political fragmentation and divisiveness on religious lines are thus likely to be intensified.

The potential for political divisiveness related to religious belief and practice is aggravated in these two statutory programs by the need for continuing annual appropriations and the likelihood of larger and larger demands as costs and populations grow. The Rhode Island District Court found that the parochial school system's "monumental and deepening financial crisis" would "inescapably" require larger annual appropriations subsidizing greater percentages of the salaries of lay teachers. Although no facts have been developed in this respect ⊥**624** in the Pennsylvania case, it appears that such pressures for expanding aid have already required the state legislature to include a portion of the state revenues from cigarette taxes in the program.

V

In *Walz* it was argued that a tax exemption for places of religious worship would prove to be the first step in an inevitable progression leading to the establishment of state churches and state religion. That claim could not stand up against more than 200 years of virtually universal practice imbedded in our colonial experience and continuing into the present.

The progression argument, however, is more persuasive here. We have no long history of state aid to church-related educational institutions comparable to 200 years of tax exemption for churches. Indeed, the state programs before us today represent something of an innovation. We have already noted that modern governmental programs have self-perpetuating and self-expanding propensities. These internal pressures are only enhanced when the schemes involve institutions whose legitimate needs are growing and whose interests have substantial political support. Nor can we fail to see that in constitutional adjudication some steps, which when taken were thought to approach "the verge," have become the platform for yet further steps. A certain momentum develops in constitutional theory and it can be a "downhill thrust" easily set in motion but difficult to retard or stop. Development by momentum is not invariably bad; indeed, it is the way the common law has grown, but it is a force to be recognized and reckoned with. The dangers are increased by the difficulty of perceiving in advance exactly where the "verge" of the precipice lies. As well as constituting an independent evil against which the Religion Clauses were intended to protect, involve⊥**625**ment or entanglement between government and religion serves as a warning signal.

Finally, nothing we have said can be construed to disparage the role of church-related elementary and secondary schools in our national life. Their contribution has been and is enormous. Nor do we ignore their economic plight in a period of rising costs and expanding need. Taxpayers generally have been spared vast sums by the maintenance of these educational institutions by religious organizations, largely by gifts of faithful adherents.

The merit and benefits of these schools, however, are not the issue before us in these cases. The sole question is whether state aid to these schools can be squared with the dictates of the Religion Clauses. Under our system the choice has been made that government is to be entirely excluded from the area of religious instruction and churches excluded from the affairs of government. The Constitution decrees that religion must be a private matter for the individual, the family, and the institutions of private choice, and that while some involvement and entanglement are inevitable, lines must be drawn.

The judgment of the Rhode Island District Court in No. 569 and No. 570 is affirmed. The judgment of the Pennsylvania District Court in No. 89 is reversed, and the case is remanded for further proceedings consistent with this opinion.

Mr. *Justice* MARSHALL took no part in the consideration or decision of [*Lemon* v. *Kurtzman*].

Mr. *Justice* DOUGLAS, whom Mr. *Justice* BLACK joins, concurring.

While I join the opinion of the Court, I have expressed at some length my views as to the rationale of today's decision in these three cases. . . .

⊥**627** In *Walz* v. *Tax Commission* the Court in approving a tax exemption for church property said: "Determining that the legislative purpose of tax exemption is not aimed at establishing, sponsoring, or supporting religion does not end the inquiry, however. We must also be sure that the end result—the effect—is not an excessive government entanglement with religion."

There is in my view such an entanglement here. The surveillance or supervision of the States needed to police grants involved in these three cases, if performed, puts a public investigator into every classroom and entails a pervasive monitoring of these church agencies by the secular authorities. Yet if that surveillance or supervision does not occur the zeal of religious proselytizers promises to carry the day and make a shambles of the Establishment Clause. Moreover, when taxpayers of ⊥**628** many faiths are required to contribute money for the propagation of one faith, the Free Exercise Clause is infringed.

The analysis of the constitutional objections to these two state systems of grants to parochial or sectarian schools must start with the admitted and obvious fact that the *raison d'être* of parochial schools is the propagation of a religious faith. They also teach secular subjects; but they came into existence in this country because

Protestant groups were perverting the public schools by using them to propagate their faith. The Catholics naturally rebelled. If schools were to be used to propagate a particular creed or religion, then Catholic ideals should also be served. Hence the advent of parochial schools.

By 1840 there were 200 Catholic parish schools in the United States. By 1964 there were 60 times as many. Today 57% of the 9,000 Catholic parishes in the country have their church schools. "[E]very diocesan chancery has its school department, and enjoys a primacy of status." The parish schools indeed consume 40% to 65% of the parish's total income. The parish is so "school centered" "[t]he school almost becomes the very reason for being."

Early in the 19th century the Protestants obtained control of the New York school system and used it to promote reading and teaching of the Scriptures as revealed in the King James version of the Bible. The contests **⊥629** between Protestants and Catholics, often erupting into violence including the burning of Catholic churches, are a twice-told tale; the Know-Nothing Party, which included in its platform "daily Bible reading in the schools," carried three States in 1854—Massachusetts, Pennsylvania, and Delaware. Parochial schools grew, but not Catholic schools alone. Other dissenting sects established their own schools—Lutherans, Methodists, Presbyterians, and others. But the major force in shaping the pattern of education in this country was the conflict between Protestants and Catholics. The Catholics logically argued that a public school was sectarian when it taught the King James version of the Bible. They therefore wanted it removed from the public schools; and in time they tried to get public funds for their own parochial schools.

The constitutional right of dissenters to substitute their parochial schools for public schools was sustained by the Court in *Pierce* v. *Society of Sisters*.

The story of conflict and dissension is long and well known. The result was a state of so-called equilibrium where religious instruction was eliminated from public schools and the use of public funds to support religious schools was deemed to be banned.

But the hydraulic pressures created by political forces and by economic stress were great and they began to **⊥630** change the situation. Laws were passed—state and federal—that dispensed public funds to sustain religious schools and the plea was always in the educational frame of reference: education in all sectors was needed, from languages to calculus to nuclear physics. And it was forcefully argued that a linguist or mathematician or physicist trained in religious schools was just as competent as one trained in secular schools.

And so we have gradually edged into a situation where vast amounts of public funds are supplied each year to sectarian schools.

And the argument is made that the private parochial school system takes about $9 billion a year off the back of government—as if that were enough to justify violating the Establishment Clause.

While the evolution of the public school system in this country marked an escape from denominational control and was therefore admirable as seen through the eyes of those who think like Madison and Jefferson, it has disadvantages. The main one is that a state system may attempt to mold all students alike according to the views of the dominant group and to discourage the emergence of individual idiosyncrasies.

Sectarian education, however, does not remedy that condition. The advantages of sectarian education relate solely to religious or doctrinal matters. They give the **⊥631** church the opportunity to indoctrinate its creed delicately and indirectly, or massively through doctrinal courses.

Many nations follow that course; Moslem nations teach the Koran in their schools; Sweden vests its elementary education in the parish; Newfoundland puts its school system under three superintendents—one from the Church of England, one from the Catholic church, one from the United Church. In Ireland the public schools are under denominational managership—Catholic, Episcopalian, Presbyterian, and Hebrew.

England puts sectarian schools under the umbrella of its school system. It finances sectarian education; it exerts control by prescribing standards; it requires some free scholarships; it provides nondenominational membership on the board of directors.

The British system is, in other words, one of surveillance over sectarian schools. We too have surveillance over sectarian schools but only to the extent of making sure that minimum educational standards are met, *viz.*, competent teachers, accreditation of the school for diplomas, the number of hours of work and credits allowed, and so on.

But we have never faced, until recently, the problem of policing sectarian schools. Any surveillance to date has been minor and has related only to the consistently unchallenged matters of accreditation of the sectarian school in the State's school system.

The Rhode Island Act allows a supplementary salary to a teacher in a sectarian school if he or she "does not teach a course in religion."

⊥632 The Pennsylvania Act provides for state financing of instruction in mathematics, modern foreign languages, physical science, and physical education, provided that the instruction in those courses "shall not include any subject matter expressing religious teaching, or the morals or forms of worship of any sect."

Public financial support of parochial schools puts those schools under disabilities with which they were not previously burdened. For, as we held in *Cooper* v. *Aaron*, governmental activities relating to schools "must be exercised consistently with federal constitutional requirements." There we were concerned with equal protection; here we are faced with issues of Establishment of religion and its Free Exercise as those concepts are used in the First Amendment.

Where the governmental activity is the financing of the private school, the various limitations or restraints imposed by the Constitution on state governments come into play. Thus, Arkansas, as part of its attempt to avoid the consequences of *Brown* v. *Board of Education*, withdrew its financial support from some public schools and sent the funds instead to private schools. That state action was held to violate the Equal Protection Clause. Louisiana tried a like tactic and it too was invalidated. Whatever might be the result in case of grants to students, it is clear that once ⊥**633** one of the States finances a private school, it is duty-bound to make certain that the school stays within secular bounds and does not use the public funds to promote sectarian causes.

The government may, of course, finance a hospital though it is run by a religious order, provided it is open to people of all races and creeds. The government itself could enter the hospital business; and it would, of course, make no difference if its agents who ran its hospitals were Catholics, Methodists, agnostics, or whatnot. For the hospital is not indulging in religious instruction or guidance or indoctrination. As Mr. *Justice JACKSON* said in *Everson* v. *Board of Education*: "[Each State has] great latitude in deciding for itself, in the light of its own conditions, what shall be public purposes in its scheme of things. It may socialize utilities and economic enterprises and make taxpayers' business out of what conventionally had been private business. It may make public business of individual welfare, health, education, entertainment or security. But it cannot make public business of religious worship or instruction, or of attendance at religious institutions of any character."

The reason is that given by Madison in his Remonstrance: "[T]he same authority which can force a citizen to contribute three pence only of his property for ⊥**634** the support of any one establishment, may force him to conform to any other establishment. . . ."

When Madison in his Remonstrance attacked a taxing measure to support religious activities, he advanced a series of reasons for opposing it. One that is extremely relevant here was phrased as follows: "[I]t will destroy that moderation and harmony which the forbearance of our laws to intermeddle with Religion, has produced amongst its several sects." Intermeddling, to use Madison's word, or "entanglement," to use what was said in *Walz*, has two aspects. The intrusion of government into religious schools through grants, supervision, or surveillance may result in establishment of religion in the constitutional sense when what the State does enthrones a particular sect for overt or subtle propagation of its faith. Those activities of the State may also intrude on the Free Exercise Clause by depriving a teacher, under threats of reprisals, of the right to give sectarian construction or interpretation of, say, history and literature, or to use the teaching of such subjects to inculcate a religious creed or dogma.

Under these laws there will be vast governmental suppression, surveillance, or meddling in church affairs. As I indicated in *Tilton* v. *Richardson*, decided this day, school prayers, the daily routine of parochial schools, must go if our decision in *Engel* v. *Vitale* is honored. If it is not honored, then the state has established a religious sect. Elimination of prayers is only part of the problem. The curriculum presents subtle and difficult problems. The constitutional mandate can in part be carried out by censoring the curricula. What is palpably a sectarian course can be marked for ⊥**635** deletion. But the problem only starts there. Sectarian instruction, in which, of course, a State may not indulge, can take place in a course on Shakespeare or in one on mathematics. No matter what the curriculum offers, the question is, what is *taught?* We deal not with evil teachers but with zealous ones who may use any opportunity to indoctrinate a class.

It is well known that everything taught in most parochial schools is taught with the ultimate goal of religious education in mind. Rev. Joseph H. Fichter, S.J., stated in Parochial School: A Sociological Study: "It is a commonplace observation that in the parochial school religion permeates the whole curriculum, and is not confined to a single half-hour period of the day. Even arithmetic can be used as an instrument of pious thoughts, as in the case of the teacher who gave this problem to her class: 'If it takes forty thousand priests and a hundred and forty thousand sisters to care for forty million Catholics in the United States, how many more priests and sisters will be needed to convert and care for the hundred million non-Catholics in the United States?'"

One can imagine what a religious zealot, as contrasted to a civil libertarian, can do with the Ref⊥**636**ormation or with the Inquisition. Much history can be given the gloss of a particular religion. I would think that policing these grants to detect sectarian instruction would be insufferable to religious partisans and would breed division and dissension between church and state.

This problem looms large where the church controls the hiring and firing of teachers: "[I]n the public school the selection of a faculty and the administration of the school usually rests with a school board which is subject to election and recall by the voters, but in the parochial school the selection of a faculty and the administration of the school is in the hands of the bishop alone, and usually is administered through the local priest. If a faculty member in the public school believes that he has been treated unjustly in being disciplined or dismissed, he can seek redress through the civil court and he is guaranteed a hearing. But if a faculty member in a parochial school is disciplined or dismissed he has no recourse whatsoever. The word of the bishop or priest is final, even without explanation if he so chooses. The tax payers have a voice in the way their money is used in the public school, but the people who support a parochial school have no voice at all in such affairs." L. Boettner, Roman Catholicism 375 (1962).

Board of Education v. *Allen* dealt only with textbooks. Even so, some had difficulty giving approval. Yet books can be easily examined independently of other aspects of the teaching process. In the present cases we deal with the totality of instruction destined to be sectarian, at least in part, if the religious character of the school is to be maintained. A school which operates to commingle religion with other instruction plainly cannot completely secularize its instruction. ⊥637 Parochial schools, in large measure, do not accept the assumption that secular subjects should be unrelated to religious teaching.

Lemon involves a state statute that prescribes that courses in mathematics, modern foreign languages, physical science, and physical education "shall not include any subject matter expressing religious teaching, or the morals or forms of worship of any sect." The subtleties involved in applying this standard are obvious. It places the State astride a sectarian school and gives it power to dictate what is or is not secular, what is or is not religious. I can think of no more disrupting influence apt to promote rancor and ill-will between church and state than this kind of surveillance and control. They are the very opposite of the "moderation and harmony" between church and state which Madison thought was the aim and purpose of the Establishment Clause.

The *DiCenso* cases have all the vices which are in *Lemon*, because the supplementary salary payable to the teacher is conditioned on his or her not teaching "a course in religion."

Moreover, the *DiCenso* cases reveal another, but related, knotty problem presented when church and state launch one of these educational programs. The Bishop of Rhode Island has a Handbook of School Regulations for the Diocese of Providence.

The school board supervises "the education, both spiritual and secular, in the parochial schools and diocesan high schools."

The superintendent is an agent of the bishop and he interprets and makes "effective state and diocesan educational directives."

⊥638 The pastors visit the schools and "give their assistance in promoting spiritual and intellectual discipline."

Community supervisors "assist the teacher in the problems of instruction" and these duties are:

"I. To become well enough acquainted with the teachers of their communities so as to be able to advise the community superiors on matters of placement and reassignment.

"II. To act as liaison between the provincialate and the religious teacher in the school.

"III. To cooperate with the superintendent by studying the diocesan school regulations and to encourage the teachers of their community to observe these regulations.

"IV. To avoid giving any orders or directions to the teachers of their community that may be in conflict with diocesan regulations or policy regarding curriculum, testing, textbooks, method, or administrative matters.

"V. To refer questions concerning school administration beyond the scope of their own authority to the proper diocesan school authorities, namely, the superintendent of schools or the pastor."

The length of the school day includes Mass: "A full day session for Catholic schools at the elementary level consists of five and one-half hours, exclusive of lunch and Mass, but inclusive of recess for pupils in grades 1-3."

A course of study or syllabus prescribed for an elementary or secondary school is "mandatory."

⊥639 Religious instruction is provided as follows:

"A. Systematic religious instructions must be provided in all schools of the diocese.

"B. Modern catechetics requires a teacher with unusual aptitudes, specialized training, and such unction of the spirit that his words possess the force of a personal call. He should be so filled with his subject that he can freely improvize in discussion, dramatization, drawing, song, and prayer. A teacher so gifted and so permeated by the message of the Gospel is rare. Perhaps no teacher in a given school attains that ideal. But some teachers come nearer it than others. If our pupils are to hear the Good News so that their minds are enlightened and their hearts respond to the love of God and His Christ, if they are to be formed into vital, twentieth-century Christians, they should receive their religious instructions only from the very best teachers.

"C. Inasmuch as the textbooks employed in religious instruction above the fifth grade require a high degree of catechetical preparation, religion should be a departmentalized subject in grade six through twelve."

Religious activities are provided, through observance of specified holy days and participation in Mass.

"Religious formation" is not restricted to courses but is achieved "through the example of the faculty, the tone of the school . . . and religious activities."

No unauthorized priest may address the students.

"Retreats and days of recollection form an integral part of our religious program in the Catholic schools."

Religious factors are used in the selection of students: "Although wealth should never serve as a criterion for accepting a pupil into a Catholic school, all other ⊥640 things being equal, it would seem fair to give preference to a child whose parents support the parish. Regular use of the budget, rather than the size of the contributions, would appear equitable. It indicates whether parents regularly attend Mass."

These are only highlights of the handbook. But they indicate how pervasive is the religious control over the school and how remote this type of school is from the secular school. Public funds supporting that structure are used to perpetuate a doctrine and creed in innumerable and in pervasive ways. Those who man these schools are good people, zealous people, dedicated people. But they are dedicated to ideas that the Framers of our Constitution placed beyond the reach of government.

If the government closed its eyes to the manner in which these grants are actually used it would be allowing public funds to promote sectarian education. If it did not close its eyes but undertook the surveillance needed, it would, I fear, intermeddle in parochial affairs in a way that would breed only rancor and dissension.

We have announced over and over again that the use of taxpayers' money to support parochial schools violates the First Amendment, applicable to the States by virtue of the Fourteenth.

We said in unequivocal words in *Everson* v. *Board of Education*, "No tax in any amount, large or small, can be levied to support any religious activities or institutions, whatever they may be called, or whatever form they may adopt to teach or practice religion." We reiterated the same idea in *Zorach* v. *Clauson*, and in *McGowan* v. *Maryland*, and in *Torcaso* v. *Watkins*. We repeated the same idea in *McCollum* v. *Board of Education* and added that a State's ⊥**641** tax-supported public schools could not be used "for the dissemination of religious doctrines" nor could a State provide the church "pupils for their religious classes through use of the State's compulsory public school machinery."

Yet in spite of this long and consistent history there are those who have the courage to announce that a State may nonetheless finance the *secular* part of a sectarian school's educational program. That, however, makes a grave constitutional decision turn merely on cost accounting and bookkeeping entries. A history class, a literature class, or a science class in a parochial school is not a separate institute; it is part of the organic whole which the State subsidizes. The funds are used in these cases to pay or help pay the salaries of teachers in parochial schools; and the presence of teachers is critical to the essential purpose of the parochial school, *viz.*, to advance the religious endeavors of the particular church. It matters not that the teacher receiving taxpayers' money only teaches religion a fraction of the time. Nor does it matter that he or she teaches no religion. The school is an organism living on one budget. What the taxpayers give for salaries of those who teach only the humanities or science without any trace of proselytizing enables the school to use all of its own funds for religious training. As Judge Coffin said, we would be blind to realities if we let "sophisticated bookkeeping" sanction "almost total subsidy of a religious institution by assigning the bulk of the institution's expenses to 'secular' activities." And sophisticated attempts to avoid the Constitution are just as invalid as simple-minded ones.

In my view the taxpayers' forced contribution to the parochial schools in the ⊥**642** present cases violates the First Amendment.

Mr. *Justice* MARSHALL, who took no part in the consideration or decision of No. 89, while intimating no view as to the continuing vitality of *Everson* v. *Board of Education*, concurs in Mr. *Justice* DOUGLAS' opinion covering Nos. 569 and 570.

Mr. *Justice* BRENNAN.*

I agree that the judgments in Nos. 569 and 570 must be affirmed. In my view the judgment in No. 89 must be reversed outright. I dissent in No. 153 insofar as the plurality opinion and the opinion of my *Brother WHITE* sustain the constitutionality, as applied to sectarian institutions, of the Federal Higher Education Facilities Act of 1963. In my view that Act is unconstitutional insofar as it authorizes grants of federal tax monies to sectarian institutions, but is unconstitutional only to that extent. I therefore think that our remand of the case should be limited to the direction of a hearing to determine whether the four institutional appellees here are sectarian institutions.

I continue to adhere to the view that to give concrete meaning to the Establishment Clause "the line we must draw between the permissible and the impermissible is one which accords with history and faithfully reflects the understanding of the Founding Fathers. It is a line which the Court has consistently sought to mark in its decisions expounding the religious guarantees of the First ⊥**643** Amendment. What the Framers meant to foreclose, and what our decisions under the Establishment Clause have forbidden, are those involvements of religious with secular institutions which (a) serve the essentially religious activities of religious institutions; (b) employ the organs of government for essentially religious purposes; or (c) use essentially religious means to serve governmental ends, where secular means would suffice. When the secular and religious institutions become involved in such a manner, there inhere in the relationship precisely those dangers—as much to church as to state—which the Framers feared would subvert religious liberty and the strength of a system of secular government." *Abington School District* v. *Schempp*.

The common feature of all three statutes before us is the provision of a direct subsidy from public funds for activities carried on by sectarian educational institutions. We have sustained the reimbursement of parents for bus fares of students under a scheme applicable to both public and nonpublic schools, *Everson* v. *Board of Education*. We have also sustained the loan of textbooks in secular subjects to students of both public and nonpublic schools, *Board of Education* v. *Allen*.

The statutory schemes before us, however, have features not present in either the *Everson* or *Allen* schemes. For example, the reimbursement or the loan of books ended government involvement in *Everson* and *Allen*. In contrast each of the schemes here exacts a promise in some form that the subsidy will not be used to finance ⊥**644** courses in religious subjects—promises that must be and are policed to assure compliance. Again, although the federal subsidy, similar to the *Everson* and *Allen* subsidies, is available to both public and nonpublic colleges and universities, the Rhode Island and Pennsylvania subsidies are restricted to nonpublic schools, and for practical purposes to Roman Catholic parochial schools. These and other features I shall mention mean for me that *Everson* and *Allen* do not control these cases. Rather, the history of public subsidy of sectarian schools, and the purposes and operation of these particular statutes must be examined to determine whether the statutes breach the Establishment Clause.

*This opinion also applies to No. 153, *Tilton* v. *Richardson*.

I

⊥**645** In sharp contrast to the "undeviating acceptance given religious tax exemptions from our earliest days as a Nation," subsidy of sectarian educational institutions became embroiled in bitter controversies very soon after the Nation was formed. Public education was, of course, virtually nonexistent when the Constitution was adopted. Colonial Massachusetts in 1647 had directed towns to establish schools, Benjamin Franklin in 1749 proposed a Philadelphia Academy, and Jefferson labored to establish a public school system in Virginia. But these were the exceptions. Education in the Colonies was overwhelmingly a private enterprise, usually carried on as a denominational activity by the dominant Protestant sects. In point of fact, government generally looked to the church to provide education, and often contributed support through donations of land and money.

Nor was there substantial change in the years immediately following ratification of the Constitution and the Bill of Rights. Schools continued to be local and, in the main, denominational institutions. But the demand for public education soon emerged. The evolution of the struggle in New York City is illustrative. In 1786, the first New York State Legislature ordered that one section in each township be set aside for the "gospel and schools." With no public schools, various private agencies and churches operated "charity schools" for the poor of New ⊥**646** York City and received money from the state common school fund. The forerunner of the city's public schools was organized in 1805 when DeWitt Clinton founded "The Society for Establishment of a Free School in the City of New York for the Education of such poor Children as do not belong to or are not provided for by any Religious Society." The State and city aided the society, and it built many schools. Gradually, however, competition and bickering among the Free School Society and the various church schools developed over the apportionment of state school funds. As a result, in 1825, the legislature transferred to the city council the responsibility for distributing New York City's share of the state funds. The council stopped funding religious societies which operated 16 sectarian schools but continued supporting schools connected with the Protestant Orphan Asylum Society. Thereafter, in 1831, the Catholic Orphan Asylum Society demanded and received public funds to operate its schools but a request of Methodists for funds for the same purpose was denied. Nine years later, the Catholics enlarged their request for public monies to include all parochial schools, contending that the council was subsidizing sectarian books and instruction of the Public School Society, which Clinton's Free School Society had become. The city's Scotch Presbyterian and Jewish communities immediately followed with requests for funds to finance their schools. Although the Public School Society undertook to revise its texts to meet the objections, in 1842, the state legislature closed the bitter controversy by enacting a law that established a City Board of Education to set up free public schools, prohibited the distribution of public funds to sectarian schools, and prohibited the teaching of sectarian doctrine in any public school.

The Nation's rapidly developing religious heterogeneity, the tide of Jacksonian democracy, and growing ⊥**647** urbanization soon led to widespread demands throughout the States for secular public education. At the same time strong opposition developed to use of the States' taxing powers to support private sectarian schools. Although the controversy over religious exercises in the public schools continued into this century, the opponents of subsidy to sectarian schools had largely won their fight by 1900. In fact, after 1840, no efforts of sectarian schools to obtain a share of public school funds succeeded. Between 1840 and 1875, 19 States added provisions to their constitutions prohibiting the use of public school funds to aid sectarian schools, and by 1900, 16 more States had added similar provisions. In fact, no State admitted to the Union after 1858, except West Virginia, omitted such provision from its first constitution. Today fewer than a half-dozen States omit such provisions from their constitutions. ⊥**648** And in 1897, Congress included in its appropriation act for the District of Columbia a statement declaring it "to be the policy of the Government of the United States to make no appropriation of money or property for the purpose of founding, maintaining, or aiding by payment for services, expenses, or otherwise, any church or religious denomination, or any institution or society which is under sectarian or ecclesiastical control."

Thus for more than a century, the consensus, enforced by legislatures and courts with substantial consistency, has been that public subsidy of sectarian schools constitutes an impermissible involvement of secular with ⊥**649** religious institutions. If this history is not itself compelling against the validity of the three subsidy statutes, in the sense we found in *Walz* that "undeviating acceptance" was highly significant in favor of the validity of religious tax exemption, other forms of governmental involvement that each of the three statutes requires tip the scales in my view against the validity of each of them. These are involvements that threaten "dangers—as much to church as to state—which the Framers feared would subvert religious liberty and the strength of a system of secular government." *Schempp*.

"[G]overnment and religion have discrete interests which are mutually best served when each avoids too close a proximity to the other. It is not only the nonbeliever who fears the injection of sectarian doctrines and controversies into the civil polity, but in as high degree it is the devout believer who fears the secularization of a creed which becomes too deeply involved with and dependent upon the government." All three of these statutes require "too close a proximity" of government to the subsidized sectarian institutions and in my view create real dangers of "the secularization of a creed."

⊥650 II

The Rhode Island statute requires Roman Catholic teachers to surrender their right to teach religion courses and to promise not to "inject" religious teaching into their secular courses. This has led at least one teacher to stop praying with his classes, a concrete testimonial to the self-censorship that inevitably accompanies state regulation of delicate First Amendment freedoms. Both the Rhode Island and Pennsylvania statutes prescribe extensive standardization of the content of secular courses, and of the teaching materials and textbooks to be used in teaching the courses. And the regulations to implement those requirements necessarily require policing of instruction in the schools. The picture of state inspectors prowling the halls of parochial schools and auditing classroom instruction surely raises more than an imagined specter of governmental "secularization of a creed."

The same dangers attend the federal subsidy even if less obviously. The Federal Government exacts a promise that no "sectarian instruction" or "religious worship" will take place in a subsidized building. The Office of Education polices the promise. In one instance federal ⊥651 officials demanded that a college cease teaching a course entitled "The History of Methodism" in a federally assisted building, although the Establishment Clause "plainly does not foreclose teaching *about* the Holy Scriptures or about the differences between religious sects in classes in literature or history." *Schempp*. These examples illustrate the complete incompatibility of such surveillance with the restraints barring interference with religious freedom.

Policing the content of courses, the specific textbooks used, and indeed the words of teachers is far different from the legitimate policing carried on under state compulsory attendance laws or laws regulating minimum levels of educational achievement. Government's legitimate interest in ensuring certain minimum skill levels and the acquisition of certain knowledge does not carry with it power to prescribe what shall not be taught, or what methods of instruction shall be used, or what opinions the teacher may offer in the course of teaching.

Moreover, when a sectarian institution accepts state financial aid it becomes obligated under the Equal Protection Clause of the Fourteenth Amendment not to discriminate in admissions policies and faculty selection. ⊥652 The District Court in the Rhode Island case pinpointed the dilemma: "Applying these standards to parochial schools might well restrict their ability to discriminate in admissions policies and in the hiring and firing of teachers. At some point the school becomes 'public' for more purposes than the Church could wish. At that point, the Church may justifiably feel that its victory on the Establishment Clause has meant abandonment of the Free Exercise Clause."

III

In any event, I do not believe that elimination of these aspects of "too close a proximity" would save these three statutes. I expressed the view in *Walz* that "[g]eneral subsidies of religious activities would, of course, constitute impermissible state involvement with religion." I do not think the subsidies under these statutes fall outside "[g]eneral subsidies of religious activities" merely because they are restricted to support of the teaching of secular subjects. In *Walz*, the passive aspect of the benefits conferred by a tax exemption, particularly since cessation of the exemptions might easily lead to impermissible involvements and conflicts, led me to conclude that exemptions were consistent with the First Amendment values. However, I contrasted direct government subsidies: "Tax exemptions and general subsidies, however, are qualitatively different. Though both provide economic assistance, they do so in fundamentally different ways. A subsidy involves the direct transfer of public monies to the subsidized enterprise and uses resources exacted from taxpayers as a whole. An exemption, on the other hand, involves no such ⊥653 transfer. It assists the exempted enterprise only passively, by relieving a privately funded venture of the burden of paying taxes. In other words, '[i]n the case of direct subsidy, the state forcibly diverts the income of both believers and non-believers to churches,' while '[i]n the case of an exemption, the state merely refrains from diverting to its own uses income independently generated by the churches through voluntary contributions.' Thus, 'the symbolism of tax exemption is significant as a manifestation that organized religion is not expected to support the state; by the same token the state is not expected to support the church.'"

Pennsylvania, Rhode Island, and the Federal Government argue strenuously that the government monies in all these cases are not "[g]eneral subsidies of religious activities" because they are paid specifically and solely for the secular education that the sectarian institutions provide.

Before turning to the decisions of this Court on which this argument is based, it is important to recall again the history of subsidies to sectarian schools. ⊥654 The universality of state constitutional provisions forbidding such grants, as well as the weight of judicial authority disapproving such aid as a violation of our tradition of separation of church and state, reflects a time-tested judgment that such grants do indeed constitute impermissible aid to religion. The recurrent argument, consistently rejected in the past, has been that government grants to sectarian schools ought not be viewed as impermissible subsidies "because [the schools] relieve the State of a burden, which it would otherwise be itself required to bear. . . . they will render a service to the state by performing for it its duty of educating the children of the people." *Cook County* v. *Chicago Industrial School*.

Nonetheless, it is argued once again in these cases that sectarian schools and universities perform two separable functions. First, they provide secular education, and second, they teach the tenets of a particular sect. Since the State has determined that the secular education provided in sectarian schools serves the legitimate state interest in the education of its citizens, it is contended that state aid solely to the secular education function does not involve the State in aid to religion. *Pierce* v. *Society of Sisters* and *Board of Education* v. *Allen* are relied on as support for the argument.

Our opinion in *Allen* recognized that sectarian schools provide both a secular and a sectarian education: "[T]his Court has long recognized that religious schools pursue two goals, religious instruction and secular education. In the leading case of *Pierce* v. *Society of Sisters*, the Court held that . . . Oregon had not shown that its interest in secular education required that all children attend publicly operated schools. A premise of this ⊥**655** holding was the view that the State's interest in education would be served sufficiently by reliance on the secular teaching that accompanied religious training in the schools maintained by the Society of Sisters.

. . . . .

"[T]he continued willingness to rely on private school systems, including parochial systems, strongly suggests that a wide segment of informed opinion, legislative and otherwise, has found that those schools do an acceptable job of providing secular education to their students. This judgment is further evidence that parochial schools are performing, in addition to their sectarian function, the task of secular education." *Board of Education* v. *Allen*.

But I do not read *Pierce* or *Allen* as supporting the proposition that public subsidy of a sectarian institution's secular training is permissible state involvement. I read them as supporting the proposition that as an identifiable set of skills and an identifiable quantum of knowledge, secular education may be effectively provided either in the religious context of parochial schools, or outside the context of religion in public schools. The State's interest in secular education may be defined broadly as an interest in ensuring that all children within its boundaries acquire a minimum level of competency in certain skills, such as reading, writing, and arithmetic, as well as a minimum amount of information and knowledge in certain subjects such as history, geography, science, literature, and law. Without such skills and knowledge, an individual will be at a severe disadvantage both in participating in democratic self-government and in earning a living in a modern industrial economy. But the State has no proper interest in prescribing the precise forum in which such skills and knowlege are learned since acquisition of this ⊥**656** secular education is neither incompatible with religious learning, nor is it inconsistent with or inimical to religious precepts.

When the same secular educational process occurs in both public and sectarian schools, *Allen* held that the State could provide secular textbooks for use in that process to students in both public and sectarian schools. Of course, the State could not provide textbooks giving religious instruction. But since the textbooks involved in *Allen* would, at least in theory, be limited to secular education, no aid to sectarian instruction was involved.

More important, since the textbooks in *Allen* had been previously provided by the parents, and not the schools, no aid to the institution was involved. Rather, as in the case of the bus transportation in *Everson*, the general program of providing all children in the State with free secular textbooks assisted all parents in schooling their children. And as in *Everson*, there was undoubtedly the possibility that some parents might not have been able to exercise their constitutional right to send their children to parochial school if the parents were compelled themselves to pay for textbooks. However, as my *Brother* BLACK wrote for the Court in *Everson*, "[C]utting off church schools from these [general] services, so separate and so indisputably marked off from the religious function, would make it far more difficult for the schools to operate. But such is obviously not the purpose of the First Amendment. That Amendment requires the state to be a neutral in its relations with groups of religious believers and nonbelievers; it does not require the state to be their adversary. State power is no more to be used so as to handicap religions than it is to favor them."

⊥**657** *Allen*, in my view, simply sustained a statute in which the State was "neutral in its relations with groups of religious believers and non-believers." The only context in which the Court in *Allen* employed the distinction between secular and religious in a parochial school was to reach its conclusion that the textbooks that the State was providing could and would be secular. The present cases, however, involve direct subsidies of tax monies to the schools themselves and we cannot blink the fact that the secular education those schools provide goes hand in hand with the religious mission that is the only reason for the schools' existence. Within the institution, the two are inextricably intertwined.

The District Court in the *DiCenso* case found that all the varied aspects of the parochial school's program—the nature of its faculty, its supervision, decor, program, extra-curricular activities, assemblies, courses, etc.—produced an "intangible 'religious atmosphere,'" since the "diocesan school system is an integral part of the religious mission of the Catholic Church" and "a powerful vehicle for transmitting the Catholic faith to the next generation." Quality teaching in secular subjects is an integral part of this religious enterprise. "Good secular teaching is as essential to the religious mission of the parochial schools as a roof for the school or desks for the classrooms." That teaching cannot be separated from the environment in which it occurs, for its integration with the religious mission is both the theory and the strength of the religious school.

The common ingredient of the three prongs of the test ⊥**658** set forth at the outset of this opinion is whether the statutes involve government in the "essentially religious activities" of religious institutions. My analysis of the operation, purposes, and effects of these statutes leads me inescapably to the conclusion that they do impermissibly involve the States and the Federal Government with the "essentially religious activities" of sectarian educational institutions. More specifically, for the reasons stated, I think each government uses "essentially religious means to serve governmental ends, where secular means would suffice." This Nation long ago committed itself to primary reliance upon publicly supported public education to serve its important goals in secular education. Our religious diversity gave strong impetus to that commitment. . . .

⊥**659** I conclude that, in using sectarian institutions to further goals in secular education, the three statutes do violence to the principle that "government may not employ religious means to serve secular interests, however legitimate they may be, at least without the clearest demonstration that nonreligious means will not suffice." *Schempp*.

IV

The plurality's treatment of the issues in *Tilton*, No. 153, diverges so substantially from my own that I add these further comments. I believe that the Establishment Clause forbids the Federal Government to provide funds to sectarian universities in which the propagation and advancement of a particular religion are a function or purpose of the institution. Since the District Court made no findings whether the four institutional appellees here are sectarian, I would remand the case to the District Court with directions to determine whether the institutional appellees are "sectarian" institutions.

I reach this conclusion for the reasons I have stated: the necessarily deep involvement of government in the religious activities of such an institution through the policing of restrictions, and the fact that subsidies of tax monies directly to a sectarian institution necessarily aid the proselytizing function of the institution. The plurality argues that neither of these dangers is present.

At the risk of repetition, I emphasize that a sectarian university is the equivalent in the realm of higher education of the Catholic elementary schools in Rhode Island; it is an educational institution in which the propagation ⊥**660** and advancement of a particular religion are a primary function of the institution. I do not believe that construction grants to such a sectarian institution are permissible. The reason is not that religion "permeates" the secular education that is provided. Rather, it is that the secular education is provided within the environment of religion; the institution is dedicated to two goals, secular education and religious instruction. When aid flows directly to the institution, both functions benefit. The plurality would examine only the activities that occur within the federally assisted building and ignore the religious nature of the school of which it is a part. The "religious enterprise" aided by the construction grants involves the maintenance of an educational environment—which includes high-quality, purely secular educational courses—within which religious instruction occurs in a variety of ways.

The plurality also argues that no impermissible entanglement exists here. My *Brother WHITE* cogently comments upon that argument: "Why the federal program in the *Tilton* case is not embroiled in the same difficulties [as the Rhode Island program] is never adequately explained." I do not see any significant difference in the Federal Government's telling the sectarian university not to teach any nonsecular subjects in a certain building, and Rhode Island's telling the Catholic school teacher not to teach religion. The vice is the creation through subsidy of a relationship in which the government polices the teaching practices of a religious school or university. The plurality suggests that the facts that college students are less impressionable and that college courses are less susceptible to religious permeation may lessen the need for federal policing. But the record shows that such policing has occurred and occurred in a heavy-handed way. Given the dangers of self-censorship in such a situation, I cannot agree that the dangers of ⊥**661** entanglement are insubstantial. Finally, the plurality suggests that the "nonideological" nature of a building, as contrasted with a teacher, reduces the need for policing. But the Federal Government imposes restrictions on every class taught in the federally assisted building. It is therefore not the "nonideological" building that is policed; rather, it is the courses given there and the teachers who teach them. Thus, the policing is precisely the same as under the state statutes, and that is what offends the Constitution.

V

I, therefore, agree that the two state statutes that focus primarily on providing public funds to sectarian schools are unconstitutional. However, the federal statute in No. 153 is a general program of construction grants to all colleges and universities, including sectarian institutions. Since I believe the statute's extension of eligibility to sectarian institutions is severable from the broad general program authorized, I would hold the Higher Education Facilities Act unconstitutional only insofar as it authorized grants of federal tax monies to sectarian institutions—institutions that have a purpose or function to propagate or advance a particular religion. Therefore, if the District Court determines that any of the four institutional appellees here are "sectarian," that court, in my view, should enjoin the other appellees from making grants to it.

Mr. *Justice WHITE*, concurring in the judgments in No. 153 and No. 89 and dissenting in Nos. 569 and 570.

It is our good fortune that the States of this country long ago recognized that instruction of the young and old ranks high on the scale of proper governmental func⊥**662**tions and not only undertook secular education as a public responsibility but also required compulsory attendance at school by their young. Having recognized the value of educated citizens and assumed the task of educating them, the States now before us assert a right to provide for the secular education of children whether they attend public schools or choose to enter private institutions, even when those institutions are church-related. The Federal Government also asserts that it is entitled, where requested, to contribute to the cost of secular education by furnishing buildings and facilities to all institutions of higher learning, public and private alike. Both the United States and the States urge that if parents choose to have their children receive instruction in the required secular subjects in a school where religion is also taught and a religious atmosphere may prevail, part or all of the cost of such secular instruction may be paid for by government grants to the religious institution conducting the school and seeking the grant. Those who challenge this position would bar official contributions to secular education where the family prefers the parochial to both the public and nonsectarian private school.

The issue is fairly joined. It is precisely the kind of issue the Constitution contemplates this Court must ultimately decide. This is true although neither affirmance nor reversal of any of these cases follows automatically from the spare language of the First Amendment, from its history, or from the cases of this Court construing it and even though reasonable men can very easily and sensibly differ over the import of that language.

But, while the decision of the Court is legitimate, it is surely quite wrong in overturning the Pennsylvania and Rhode Island statutes on the ground that they amount to an establishment of religion forbidden by the First Amendment.

⊥**663** No one in these cases questions the constitutional right of parents to satisfy their state-imposed obligation to educate their children by sending them to private schools, sectarian or otherwise, as long as those schools meet minimum standards established for secular instruction. The States are not only permitted, but required by the Constitution, to free students attending private schools from any public school attendance obligation. The States may also furnish transportation for students and books for teaching secular subjects to students attending parochial and other private as well as public schools; we have also upheld arrangements whereby students are released from public school classes so that they may attend religious instruction. Outside the field of education, we have upheld Sunday closing laws, state and federal laws exempting church property and church activity from taxation, and governmental grants to religious organizations for the purpose of financing improvements in the facilities of hospitals managed and controlled by religious orders.

Our prior cases have recognized the dual role of parochial schools in American society: they perform both religious and secular functions. Our cases also recognize that legislation having a secular purpose and extending governmental assistance to sectarian schools in the performance of their secular functions does not constitute "law[s] respecting an establishment of religion" forbidden by the First Amendment merely because a secular program may incidentally benefit a church in fulfilling its religious mis⊥**664**sion. That religion may indirectly benefit from governmental aid to the secular activities of churches does not convert that aid into an impermissible establishment of religion.

This much the Court squarely holds in the *Tilton* case, where it also expressly rejects the notion that payments made directly to a religious institution are, without more, forbidden by the First Amendment. In *Tilton*, the Court decides that the Federal Government may finance the separate function of secular education carried on in a parochial setting. It reaches this result although sectarian institutions undeniably will obtain substantial benefit from federal aid; without federal funding to provide adequate facilities for secular education, the student bodies of those institutions might remain stationary or even decrease in size and the institutions might ultimately have to close their doors.

It is enough for me that the States and the Federal Government are financing a separable secular function of overriding importance in order to sustain the legislation here challenged. That religion and private interests other than education may substantially benefit does not convert these laws into impermissible establishments of religion.

It is unnecessary, therefore, to urge that the Free Exercise Clause of the First Amendment at least permits government in some respects to modify and mold its secular programs out of express concerns for free-exercise values. . . . ⊥**665** The Establishment Clause, however, coexists in the First Amendment with the Free Exercise Clause and the latter is surely relevant in cases such as these. Where a state program seeks to ensure the proper education of its young, in private as well as public schools, free exercise considerations at least counsel against refusing support for students attending parochial schools simply because in that setting they are also being instructed in the tenets of the faith they are constitutionally free to practice.

I would sustain both the federal and the Rhode Island programs at issue in these cases, and I therefore concur in the judgment in No. 163 and dissent from the judgments in Nos. 569 and 570. Although I would also reject the facial challenge to the Pennsylvania statute, I concur in the judgment in No. 89 for the reasons given below.

The Court strikes down the Rhode Island statute on its face. No fault is found with the secular purpose of the program; there is no suggestion that the purpose of the program was aid to religion disguised in secular attire. Nor does the Court find that the primary effect of the program is to aid religion rather than to implement secular goals. The Court nevertheless finds ⊥**666** that impermissible "entanglement" will result from administration of the program. The reasoning is a curious and mystifying blend, but a critical factor appears to be an unwillingness to accept the District Court's express findings that on the evidence before it none of the teachers here involved mixed religious and secular instruction. Rather, the District Court struck down the Rhode Island statute because it concluded that activities outside the secular classroom would probably have a religious content and that support for religious education therefore necessarily resulted from the financial aid to the secular programs, since that aid generally strengthened the parochial schools and increased the number of their students.

In view of the decision in *Tilton*, however, where these same factors were found insufficient to invalidate the federal plan, the Court is forced to other considerations. Accepting the District Court's observation in *DiCenso* that education is an integral part of the religious mission of the Catholic church—an observation that should neither surprise nor alarm anyone, especially judges who have already approved substantial aid to parochial schools in various forms—the majority then interposes findings and conclusions that the District Court expressly abjured, namely, that nuns, clerics, and dedicated Catholic laymen unavoidably pose a grave risk in that they might not be able to put aside their religion in the secular classroom. Although stopping short of considering them untrustworthy, the Court concludes that for them the difficulties of avoiding teaching religion along with secular subjects would pose intolerable risks and would in any event entail an unacceptable enforcement regime. Thus, the potential for impermissible fostering of religion in secular classrooms—an untested assumption of the Court—paradoxically renders unacceptable the State's efforts at insuring that secular teachers under religious discipline successfully avoid conflicts between the religious mission **⊥667** of the school and the secular purpose of the State's education program.

The difficulty with this is twofold. In the first place, it is contrary to the evidence and the District Court's findings in *DiCenso*. The Court points to nothing in this record indicating that any participating teacher had inserted religion into his secular teaching or had had any difficulty in avoiding doing so. The testimony of the teachers was quite the contrary. The District Court expressly found that "[t]his concern for religious values does not necessarily affect the content of secular subjects in diocesan schools. On the contrary, several teachers testified at trial that they did not inject religion into their secular classes, and one teacher deposed that he taught exactly as he had while employed in a public school. This testimony gains added credibility from the fact that several of the teachers were non-Catholics. Moreover, because of the restrictions of Rhode Island's textbook loan law . . . and the explicit requirement of the Salary Supplement Act, teaching materials used by applicants for aid must be approved for use in the public schools." *DiCenso* v. *Robinson*. Elsewhere, the District Court reiterated that the defect of the Rhode Island statute was "not that religious doctrine overtly intrudes into all instruction," but factors aside from secular courses plus the fact that good secular teaching was itself essential for implementing the religious mission of the parochial school.

Secondly, the Court accepts the model for the Catholic elementary and secondary schools that was rejected for the Catholic universities or colleges in the *Tilton* case. There it was urged that the Catholic condition of higher learning was an integral part of the religious mission of the church and that these institutions did everything they could to foster the faith. The Court's response was that on the record before it none of **⊥668** the involved institutions was shown to have complied with the model and that it would not purport to pass on cases not before it. Here, however, the Court strikes down this Rhode Island statute based primarily on its own model and its own suppositions and unsupported views of what is likely to happen in Rhode Island parochial school classrooms, although on this record there is no indication that entanglement difficulties will accompany the salary supplement program.

The Court thus creates an insoluble paradox for the State and the parochial schools. The State cannot finance secular instruction if it permits religion to be taught in the same classroom; but if it exacts a promise that religion not be so taught—a promise the school and its teachers are quite willing and on this record able to give—and enforces it, it is then entangled in the "no entanglement" aspect of the Court's Establishment Clause jurisprudence.

Why the federal program in the *Tilton* case is not embroiled in the same difficulties is never adequately explained. Surely the notion that college students are more mature and resistant to indoctrination is a make-weight, for in *Tilton* there is careful note of the federal condition on funding and the enforcement mechanism available. If religious teaching in federally financed buildings was permitted, the powers of resistance of college students would in no way save the federal scheme. Nor can I imagine the basis for finding college clerics more reliable in keeping promises than their counterparts in elementary and secondary schools—particularly those in the Rhode Island case, since within five years the majority of teachers in Rhode Island parochial schools will be lay persons, many of them non-Catholic.

Both the District Court and this Court in *DiCenso* have seized on the Rhode Island formula for supplementing **⊥669** teachers' salaries since it requires the State to verify the amount of school money spent for secular as distinguished from religious purposes. Only teachers in those schools having per-pupil expenditures for secular subjects below the state average qualify under the system, an aspect of the state scheme which is said to provoke serious "entanglement." But this is also a slender reed on which to strike down this law, for as the District Court found, only once since the inception of the program has it been necessary to segregate expenditures in this manner.

The District Court also focused on the recurring nature of payments by the State of Rhode Island; salaries must be supplemented and money appropriated every year and hence the opportunity for controversy and friction over state aid to religious schools will constantly remain before the State. The Court in *DiCenso* adopts this theme, and makes much of the fact that under the federal scheme the grant to a religious institution is a one-time matter. But this argument is without real force. It is apparent that federal interest in any grant will be a continuing one since the conditions attached to the grant must be enforced. More important, the federal grant program is an ongoing one. The same grant will not be repeated, but new ones to the same or different schools will be made year after year. Thus the same potential for recurring political controversy accompanies the federal program. Rhode Island may have the problem of appropriating money each year to supplement the salaries of teachers, but the United States must each year seek financing for the new grants it desires to make and must supervise the ones already on the record.

With respect to Pennsylvania, the Court, accepting as true the factual allegations of the complaint, as it must for purposes of a motion to dismiss, would reverse the dismissal of the complaint and invalidate the legislation. **⊥670** The critical allegations, as paraphrased by the Court, are that "the church-related elementary and secondary schools are controlled by religious organizations, have the purpose of propagating and promoting a particular religious faith, and conduct their operations to fulfill that purpose." From these allegations the Court concludes that forbidden entanglements would follow from enforcing compliance with the secular purpose for which the state money is being paid.

I disagree. There is no specific allegation in the complaint that sectarian teaching does or would invade secular classes supported by state funds. That the schools are operated to promote a particular religion is quite consistent with the view that secular teaching devoid of religious instruction can successfully be maintained, for good secular instruction is, as Judge Coffin wrote for the District Court in the Rhode Island case, essential to the success of the religious mission of the parochial school. I would no more here than in the Rhode Island case substitute presumption for proof that religion is or would be taught in state-financed secular courses or assume that enforcement measures would be so extensive as to border on a free exercise violation. We should not forget that the Pennsylvania statute does not compel church schools to accept state funds. I cannot hold that the First Amendment forbids an agreement between the school and the State that the state funds would be used only to teach secular subjects. . . .

TILTON v. RICHARDSON

403 U.S. 672

ON APPEAL FROM THE UNITED STATES DISTRICT COURT FOR THE DISTRICT OF CONNECTICUT

Argued March 2-3, 1971 — Decided June 28, 1971

⊥674 Mr. *Chief Justice BURGER* announced the judgment of the Court and an opinion in which Mr. *Justice HARLAN*, Mr. *Justice STEWART*, and Mr. *Justice BLACKMUN* join.

This appeal presents important constitutional questions as to federal aid for church-related colleges and universities under Title I of the Higher Education Facilities Act of 1963, which provides construction grants for buildings and facilities used **⊥675** exclusively for secular educational purposes. We must determine first whether the Act authorizes aid to such church-related institutions, and, if so, whether the Act violates either the Establishment or Free Exercise Clauses of the First Amendment.

I

The Higher Education Facilities Act was passed in 1963 in response to a strong nationwide demand for the expansion of college and university facilities to meet the sharply rising number of young people demanding higher education. The Act authorizes federal grants and loans to "institutions of higher education" for the construction of a wide variety of "academic facilities." But § 751 (a) (2) expressly excludes "any facility used or to be used for sectarian instruction or as a place for religious worship, or . . . any facility which . . . is used or to be used primarily in connection with any part of the program of a school or department of divinity. . . ."

The Act is administered by the United States Commissioner of Education. He advises colleges and universities applying for funds that under the Act no part of the project may be used for sectarian instruction, religious worship, or the programs of a divinity school. The Commissioner requires applicants to provide assurances that these restrictions will be respected. The United States retains a 20-year interest in any facility constructed with Title I funds. If, during this period, the recipient violates the statutory conditions, the United States is entitled to recover an amount equal to the proportion of its present value that the federal grant bore to the original cost of the facility. During the 20-year period, the statutory restrictions are enforced by the Office of Education primarily by way of on-site inspections.

⊥676 Appellants are citizens and taxpayers of the United States and residents of Connecticut. They brought this suit for injunctive relief against the officials who administer the Act. Four church-related colleges and universities in Connecticut receiving federal construction grants under Title I were also named as defendants. Federal funds were used for five projects at these four institutions: (1) a library building at Sacred Heart University; (2) a music, drama, and arts building at Annhurst College; (3) a science building at Fairfield University; (4) a library building at Fairfield; and (6) a language laboratory at Albertus Magnus College.

A three-judge federal court was convened. Appellants attempted to show that the four recipient institutions were "sectarian" by introducing evidence of their relations with religious authorities, the content of their curricula, and other indicia of their religious character. The sponsorship of these institutions by religious organizations is not disputed. Appellee colleges introduced testimony that they had fully complied with the statutory conditions and that their religious affiliation in no way interfered with the performance of their secular educational functions. The District Court ruled that Title I authorized grants to church-related colleges and universities. It also sustained the constitutionality of the Act, finding that it had neither the purpose nor the effect of promoting religion. We noted probable jurisdiction.

II

We are satisfied that Congress intended the Act to include all colleges and universities regardless of any affiliation with or sponsorship by a religious body. Congress defined "institutions of higher education," which are eligible to receive aid under the Act, in broad and **⊥677** inclusive terms. Certain institutions, for example, institutions that are neither public nor nonprofit, are expressly excluded, and the Act expressly prohibits use of the facilities for religious purposes. But the Act makes no reference to religious affiliation or nonaffiliation. Under these circumstances "institutions of higher education" must be taken to include church-related colleges and universities.

This interpretation is fully supported by the legislative history. Although there was extensive debate on the wisdom and constitutionality of aid to institutions affiliated with religious organizations, Congress clearly included them in the program. The sponsors of the Act so stated and amendments aimed at the exclusion of church-related institutions were defeated.

III

Numerous cases considered by the Court have noted the internal tension in the First Amendment between the Establishment Clause and the Free Exercise Clause. *Walz* v. *Tax Comm'n* is the most recent decision seeking to define the boundaries of the neutral area between these two provisions within which the legislature may legitimately act. There, as in other decisions, the Court treated the three main concerns against which the Establishment Clause sought to protect: "sponsorship, financial support, and active involvement of the sovereign in religious activity."

Every analysis must begin with the candid acknowledgment that there is no single constitutional caliper that can be used to measure the precise degree to which these three factors are present or absent. Instead, our **⊥678** analysis in this area must begin with a consideration of the cumulative criteria developed over many years and applying to a wide range of governmental action challenged as violative of the Establishment Clause.

There are always risks in treating criteria discussed by the Court from time to time as "tests" in any limiting sense of that term. Constitutional adjudication does not lend itself to the absolutes of the physical sciences or mathematics. The standards should rather be viewed as guidelines with which to identify instances in which the objectives of the Religion Clauses have been impaired. And, as we have noted in *Lemon* v. *Kurtzman* and *Earley* v. *DiCenso*, candor compels the acknowledgment that we can only dimly perceive the boundaries of permissible government activity in this sensitive area of constitutional adjudication.

Against this background we consider four questions: First, does the Act reflect a secular legislative purpose? Second, is the primary effect of the Act to advance or inhibit religion? Third, does the administration of the Act foster an excessive government entanglement with religion? Fourth, does the implementation of the Act inhibit the free exercise of religion?

(a)

The stated legislative purpose appears in the preamble where Congress found and declared that "the security and welfare of the United States require that this and future generations of American youth be assured ample opportunity for the fullest development of their intellectual capacities, and that this opportunity will be jeopardized unless the Nation's colleges and universities are encouraged and assisted in their efforts to accommodate rapidly growing numbers of youth who aspire to a higher education."

⊥679 This expresses a legitimate secular objective entirely appropriate for governmental action.

The simplistic argument that every form of financial aid to church-sponsored activity violates the Religion Clauses was rejected long ago in *Bradfield* v. *Roberts*. There a federal construction grant to a hospital operated by a religious order was upheld. Here the Act is challenged on the ground that its primary effect is to aid the religious purposes of church-related colleges and universities. Construction grants surely aid these institutions in the sense that the construction of buildings will assist them to perform their various functions. But bus transportation, textbooks, and tax exemptions all gave aid in the sense that religious bodies would otherwise have been forced to find other sources from which to finance these services. Yet all of these forms of governmental assistance have been upheld. The crucial question is not whether some benefit accrues to a religious institution as a consequence of the legislative program, but whether its principal or primary effect advances religion.

A possibility always exists, of course, that the legitimate objectives of any law or legislative program may be subverted by conscious design or law enforcement. There is nothing new in this argument. But judicial concern about these possibilities cannot, standing alone, warrant striking down a statute as unconstitutional.

The Act itself was carefully drafted to ensure that the federally subsidized facilities would be devoted to the secular and not the religious function of the recipient institutions. It authorizes grants and loans only for academic facilities that will be used for defined secular purposes and expressly prohibits their use for religious ⊥680 instruction, training, or worship. These restrictions have been enforced in the Act's actual administration, and the record shows that some church-related institutions have been required to disgorge benefits for failure to obey them.

Finally, this record fully supports the findings of the District Court that none of the four church-related institutions in this case has violated the statutory restrictions. The institutions presented evidence that there had been no religious services or worship in the federally financed facilities, that there are no religious symbols or plaques in or on them, and that they had been used solely for nonreligious purposes. On this record, therefore, these buildings are indistinguishable from a typical state university facility. Appellants presented no evidence to the contrary.

Appellants instead rely on the argument that government may not subsidize any activities of an institution of higher learning that in some of its programs teaches religious doctrines. This argument rests on *Everson* where the majority stated that the Establishment Clause barred any "tax . . . levied to support any religious . . . institutions . . . whatever form they may adopt to teach or practice religion." In *Allen*, however, it was recognized that the Court had fashioned criteria under which an analysis of a statute's purpose and effect was determinative as to whether religion was being advanced by government action.

Under this concept appellants' position depends on the validity of the proposition that religion so permeates the secular education provided by church-related colleges and universities that their religious and secular educational functions are in fact inseparable. The argument that government grants would thus inevitably advance ⊥681 religion did not escape the notice of Congress. It was carefully and thoughtfully debated, but was found unpersuasive. It was also considered by this Court in *Allen*. There the Court refused to assume that religiosity in parochial elementary and secondary schools necessarily permeates the secular education that they provide.

This record, similarly, provides no basis for any such assumption here. Two of the five federally financed buildings involved in this case are libraries. The District Court found that no classes had been conducted in either of these facilities and that no restrictions were imposed by the institutions on the books that they acquired. There is no evidence to the contrary. The third building was a language laboratory at Albertus Magnus College. The evidence showed that this facility was used solely to assist students with their pronunciation in modern foreign languages—a use which would seem peculiarly unrelated and unadaptable to religious indoctrination. Federal grants were also used to build a science building at Fairfield University and a music, drama, and arts building at Annhurst College.

There is no evidence that religion seeps into the use of any of these facilities. Indeed, the parties stipulated in the District Court that courses at these institutions are taught according to the academic requirements intrinsic to the subject matter and the individual teacher's concept of professional standards. Although appellants introduced several institutional documents that stated certain religious restrictions on what could be taught, other evidence showed that these restrictions were not in fact enforced and that the schools were characterized by an atmosphere of academic freedom rather than religious indoctrination. All four institutions, for example, subscribe to the 1940 Statement of Principles on Aca- ⊥682 demic Freedom and Tenure endorsed by the American Association of University Professors and the Association of American Colleges.

Rather than focus on the four defendant colleges and universities involved in this case, however, appellants seek to shift our attention to a "composite profile" that they have constructed of the "typical sectarian" institution of higher education. We are told that such a "composite" institution imposes religious restrictions on admissions, requires attendance at religious activities, compels obedience to the doctrines and dogmas of the faith, requires instruction in theology and doctrine, and does everything it can to propagate a particular religion. Perhaps some church-related schools fit the pattern that appellants describe. Indeed, some colleges have been declared ineligible for aid by the authorities that administer the Act. But appellants do not contend that these four institutions fall within this category. Individual projects can be properly evaluated if and when challenges arise with respect to particular recipients and some evidence is then presented to show that the institution does in fact possess these characteristics. We cannot, however, strike down an Act of Congress on the basis of a hypothetical "profile."

(b)

Although we reject appellants' broad constitutional arguments we do perceive an aspect in which the statute's enforcement provisions are inadequate to ensure that the impact of the federal aid will not advance religion. If a recipient institution violates any of the statutory restrictions on the use of a federally financed facility, § 754 (b) (2) permits the Government to recover an amount equal to the proportion of the facility's present value that the federal grant bore to its original cost.

⊥683 This remedy, however, is available to the Government only if the statutory conditions are violated "within twenty years after completion of construction." This 20-year period is termed by the statute as "the period of Federal interest" and reflects Congress' finding that after 20 years "the public benefit accruing to the United States" from the use of the federally financed facility "will equal or exceed in value" the amount of the federal grant.

Under § 754 (b) (2), therefore, a recipient institution's obligation not to use the facility for sectarian instruction or religious worship would appear to expire at the end of 20 years. We note, for example, that under § 718 (b) (7) (C), an institution applying for a federal grant is only required to provide assurances that the facility will not be used for sectarian instruction or religious worship "during at least the period of the Federal interest therein (as defined in section 754 of this title)."

Limiting the prohibition for religious use of the structure to 20 years obviously opens the facility to use for any purpose at the end of that period. It cannot be assumed that a substantial structure has no value after that period and hence the unrestricted use of a valuable property is in effect a contribution of some value to a religious body. Congress did not base the 20-year provision on any contrary conclusion. If, at the end of 20 years, the building is, for example, converted into a chapel or otherwise used to promote religious interests, the original federal grant will in part have the effect of advancing religion.

To this extent the Act therefore trespasses on the Religion Clauses. The restrictive obligations of a recipient institution under § 751 (a) (2) cannot, compatibly with the Religion Clauses, expire while the building has substantial value. This circumstance does not require us to ⊥**684** invalidate the entire Act, however. . . .

We have found nothing in the statute or its objectives intimating that Congress considered the 20-year provision essential to the statutory program as a whole. In view of the broad and important goals that Congress intended this legislation to serve, there is no basis for assuming that the Act would have failed of passage without this provision; nor will its excision impair either the operation or administration of the Act in any significant respect.

IV

We next turn to the question of whether excessive entanglement characterize the relationship between government and church under the Act. Our decision today in ⊥**685** *Lemon* v. *Kurtzman* and *Robinson* v. *DiCenso* has discussed and applied this independent measure of constitutionality under the Religion Clause. There we concluded that excessive entanglements between government and religion were fostered by Pennsylvania and Rhode Island statutory programs under which state aid was provided to parochial elementary and secondary schools. Here, however, three factors substantially diminish the extent and the potential danger of the entanglement.

In *DiCenso* the District Court found that the parochial schools in Rhode Island were "an integral part of the religious mission of the Catholic Church." There, the record fully supported the conclusion that the inculcation of religious values was a substantial if not the dominant purpose of the institutions. The Pennsylvania case was decided on the pleadings, and hence we accepted as true the allegations that the parochial schools in that State shared the same characteristics.

Appellants' complaint here contains similar allegations. But they were denied by the answers, and there was extensive evidence introduced on the subject. Although the District Court made no findings with respect to the religious character of the four institutions of higher learning, we are not required to accept the allegations as true under these circumstances, particularly where, as here, appellants themselves do not contend that these four institutions are "sectarian."

There are generally significant differences between the religious aspects of church-related institutions of higher learning and parochial elementary and secondary schools. The "affirmative if not dominant policy" of the instruction in pre-college church schools is "to assure future ⊥**686** adherents to a particular faith by having control of their total education at an early age." *Walz* v. *Tax Comm'n*. There is substance to the contention that college students are less impressionable and less susceptible to religious indoctrination. Common observation would seem to support that view, and Congress may well have entertained it. The skepticism of the college student is not an inconsiderable barrier to any attempt or tendency to subvert the congressional objectives and limitations. Furthermore, by their very nature, college and postgraduate courses tend to limit the opportunities for sectarian influence by virtue of their own internal disciplines. Many church-related colleges and universities are characterized by a high degree of academic freedom and seek to evoke free and critical responses from their students.

The record here would not support a conclusion that any of these four institutions departed from this general pattern. All four schools are governed by Catholic religious organizations, and the faculties and student bodies at each are predominantly Catholic. Nevertheless, the evidence shows that non-Catholics were admitted as students and given faculty appointments. Not one of these four institutions requires its students to attend religious services. Although all four schools require their students to take theology courses, the parties stipulated that these courses are taught according to the academic requirements of the subject matter and the teacher's concept of professional standards. The parties also stipulated that the courses covered a range of human religious ⊥**687** experiences and are not limited to courses about the Roman Catholic religion. The schools introduced evidence that they made no attempt to indoctrinate students or to proselytize. Indeed, some of the required theology courses at Albertus Magnus and Sacred Heart are taught by rabbis. Finally, as we have noted, these four schools subscribe to a well-established set of principles of academic freedom, and nothing in this record shows that these principles are not in fact followed. In short, the evidence shows institutions with admittedly religious functions but whose predominant higher education mission is to provide their students with a secular education.

Since religious indoctrination is not a substantial purpose or activity of these church-related colleges and universities, there is less likelihood than in primary and secondary schools that religion will permeate the area of secular education. This reduces the risk that government aid will in fact serve to support religious activities. Correspondingly, the necessity for intensive government surveillance is diminished and the resulting entanglements between government and religion lessened. Such inspection as may be necessary to ascertain that the facilities are devoted to secular education is minimal and indeed hardly more than the inspections that States impose over all private schools within the reach of compulsory education laws.

The entanglement between church and state is also lessened here by the nonideological character of the aid that the Government provides. Our cases from *Everson* to *Allen* have permitted church-related schools to receive government aid in the form of secular, neutral, or nonideological services, facilities, or materials that are supplied to all students regardless of the affiliation of the school that they attend. In *Lemon* and *DiCenso*, however, the state programs subsidized teachers, either directly or indirectly. Since teachers are not necessarily **⊥688** religiously neutral, greater governmental surveillance would be required to guarantee that state salary aid would not in fact subsidize religious instruction. There we found the resulting entanglement excessive. Here, on the other hand, the Government provides facilities that are themselves religiously neutral. The risks of Government aid to religion and the corresponding need for surveillance are therefore reduced.

Finally, government entanglements with religion are reduced by the circumstance that, unlike the direct and continuing payments under the Pennsylvania program, and all the incidents of regulation and surveillance, the Government aid here is a one-time, single-purpose construction grant. There are no continuing financial relationships or dependencies, no annual audits, and no government analysis of an institution's expenditures on secular as distinguished from religious activities. Inspection as to use is a minimal contact.

No one of these three factors standing alone is necessarily controlling; cumulatively all of them shape a narrow and limited relationship with government which involves fewer and less significant contacts than the two state schemes before us in *Lemon* and *DiCenso*. The relationship therefore has less potential for realizing the substantive evils against which the Religion Clauses were intended to protect.

We think that cumulatively these three factors also substantially lessen the potential for divisive religious fragmentation in the political arena. This conclusion is admittedly difficult to document, but neither have appellants pointed to any continuing religious aggravation on this matter in the political processes. Possibly this can be explained by the character and diversity of the recipient colleges and universities and the absence of any intimate continuing relationship or dependency between government and religiously affiliated institutions. The **⊥689** potential for divisiveness inherent in the essentially local problems of primary and secondary schools is significantly less with respect to a college or university whose student constituency is not local but diverse and widely dispersed.

V

Finally, we must consider whether the implementation of the Act inhibits the free exercise of religion in violation of the First Amendment. Appellants claim that the Free Exercise Clause is violated because they are compelled to pay taxes, the proceeds of which in part finance grants under the Act. Appellants, however, are unable to identify any coercion directed at the practice or exercise of their religious beliefs. Their share of the cost of the grants under the Act is not fundamentally distinguishable from the impact of the tax exemption sustained in *Walz* or the provision of textbooks upheld in *Allen*.

We conclude that the Act does not violate the Religion Clauses of the First Amendment except that part of § 754 (b) (2) providing a 20-year limitation on the religious use restrictions contained in § 751 (a) (2). We remand to the District Court with directions to enter a judgment consistent with this opinion.

Vacated and remanded.

Mr. *Justice* DOUGLAS, with whom Mr. *Justice* BLACK and Mr. *Justice* MARSHALL concur, dissenting in part.

The correct constitutional principle for this case was stated by President Kennedy in 1961 when questioned as **⊥690** to his policy respecting aid to private and parochial schools: "[T]he Constitution clearly prohibits aid to the school, to parochial schools. I don't think there is any doubt of that.

"The Everson case, which is probably the most celebrated case, provided only by a 5 to 4 decision was it possible for a local community to provide bus rides to nonpublic school children. But all through the majority and minority statements on that particular question there was a very clear prohibition against aid to the school direct. The Supreme Court made its decision in the Everson case by determining that the aid was to the child, not to the school. Aid to the school is—there isn't any room for debate on that subject. It is prohibited by the Constitution, and the Supreme Court has made that very clear. And therefore there would be no possibility of our recommending it."

Taxpayer appellants brought this suit challenging the validity of certain expenditures, made by the Department of Health, Education, and Welfare, for the construction of (1) a library at Sacred Heart University, (2) a music, drama, and arts building at Annhurst College, (3) a library and a science building at Fairfield University, and (4) a laboratory at Albertus Magnus College. The complaint alleged that all of these institutions were controlled by religious orders and the Roman Catholic Diocese of Bridgeport, Conn., and that if the funds for construction were authorized by Title I of the

Higher Education Facilities Act of 1963, then that statute was unconstitutional because it violated the ⊥691 Establishment Clause. A three-judge District Court was convened and rejected appellants' claims.

Title I of the Higher Education Facilities Act of 1963 authorizes grants and loans up to 50% of the cost for the construction of undergraduate academic facilities in both public and private colleges and universities. A project is eligible if construction will result "in an urgently needed substantial expansion of the institution's student enrollment capacity, capacity to provide needed health care to students or personnel of the institution, or capacity to carry out extension and continuing education programs on the campus of such institution." The Commissioner of Education is authorized to prescribe basic criteria and is instructed to "give special consideration to expansion of undergraduate enrollment capacity."

Academic facilities are "structures suitable for use as classrooms, laboratories, libraries, and related facilities necessary or appropriate for instruction of students, or for research . . . programs." Specifically excluded are facilities "used or to be used for sectarian instruction or as a place for religious worship" or any facilities used "primarily in connection with any part of the program of a school or department of divinity." The United States retains a 20-year interest in the facilities and should a facility be used other than as an academic facility then the United States is entitled to recover an amount equal to the proportion of present value which the federal grant bore to the original cost of the facility. According to a stipulation entered below, during the 20 years the Office of Education attempts to insure that facilities are used in the manner required by the Act primarily by on-site inspections. At the end of the 20-year period the federal interest in the facility ceases and ⊥692 the college may use it as it pleases.

The public purpose in secular education is, to be sure, furthered by the program. Yet the sectarian purpose is aided by making the parochial school system viable. The purpose is to increase "student enrollment" and the students obviously aimed at are those of the particular faith now financed by taxpayers' money. Parochial schools are not beamed at agnostics, atheists, or those of a competing sect. The more sophisticated institutions may admit minorities; but the dominant religious character is not changed.

The reversion of the facility to the parochial school at the end of 20 years is an outright grant, measurable by the present discounted worth of the facility. A gift of taxpayers' funds in that amount would plainly be unconstitutional. The Court properly bars it even though disguised in the form of a reversionary interest.

But the invalidation of this one clause cannot cure the constitutional infirmities of the statute as a whole. The Federal Government is giving religious schools a block grant to build certain facilities. The fact that money is ⊥693 given once at the beginning of a program rather than apportioned annually as in *Lemon* and *DiCenso* is without constitutional significance. The First Amendment bars establishment of a religion. And as I noted today in *Lemon* and *DiCenso*, this bar has been consistently interpreted from *Everson* v. *Board of Education*, through *Torcaso* v. *Watkins*, as meaning: "No tax in any amount, large or small, can be levied to support any religious activities or institutions, whatever they may be called, or whatever form they may adopt to teach or practice religion." Thus it is hardly impressive that rather than giving a smaller amount of money annually over a long period of years, Congress instead gives a large amount all at once. The plurality's distinction is in effect that small violations of the First Amendment over a period of years are unconstitutional while a huge violation occurring only once is *de minimis*. I cannot agree with such sophistry.

What I have said in *Lemon* and in the *DiCenso* cases decided today is relevant here. The facilities financed by taxpayers' funds are not to be used for "sectarian" purposes. Religious teaching and secular teaching are so enmeshed in parochial schools that only the strictest supervision and surveillance would insure compliance with the condition. Parochial schools may require religious exercises, even in the classroom. A parochial school operates on one budget. Money not spent for one purpose becomes available for other purposes. Thus the fact that there are no religious observances in federally financed facilities is not controlling because required religious observances will take place in other buildings. Our decision in *Engel* v. *Vitale* held that a requirement of a prayer in public schools violated the Establishment Clause. Once these schools become federally funded they become bound by federal standards ⊥694 and accordingly adherence to *Engel* would require an end to required religious exercises. That kind of surveillance and control will certainly be obnoxious to the church authorities and if done will radically change the character of the parochial school. Yet if that surveillance is not searching and continuous, this federal financing is obnoxious under the Establishment and Free Exercise Clauses for the reasons stated in the companion cases.

In other words, surveillance creates an entanglement of government and religion which the First Amendment was designed to avoid. Yet after today's decision there will be a requirement of surveillance which will last for the useful life of the building and as we have previously noted, "[it] is hardly lack of due process for the Government to regulate that which it subsidizes." *Wickard* v. *Filburn*. The price of the subsidy under the Act is violation of the Free Exercise Clause. Could a course in the History of Methodism be taught in a federally financed building? Would a religiously slanted version of the Reformation or Quebec politics under Duplessis be permissible? How can the Government know what is taught in the federally financed building without a continuous auditing of classroom instruction? Yet both the Free Exercise Clause and academic freedom are violated when the Government agent must be present to determine whether the course content is satisfactory.

As I said in the *Lemon* and *DiCenso* cases, a parochial school is a unitary institution with subtle blending of sectarian and secular instruction. Thus the practices of religious schools are in no way affected by the minimal requirement that the government financed facility may ⊥**695** not "be used for sectarian instruction or as a place of religious worship." Money saved from one item in the budget is free to be used elsewhere. By conducting religious services in another building, the school has—rent free—a building for nonsectarian use. This is not called Establishment simply because the government retains a continuing interest in the building for its useful life, even though the religious schools need never pay a cent for the use of the building.

Much is made of the need for public aid to church schools in light of their pressing fiscal problems. Dr. Eugene C. Blake of the Presbyterian Church, however, wrote in 1959: "When one remembers that churches pay no inheritance tax (churches do not die), that churches may own and operate business and be exempt from the 52 percent corporate income tax, and that real property used for church purposes (which in some states are most generously construed) is tax exempt, it is not unreasonable to prophesy that with reasonably prudent management, the churches ought to be able to control the whole economy of the nation within the predictable future. That the growing wealth and property of the churches was partially responsible for revolutionary expropriations of church property in England in the sixteenth century, in France in the eighteenth century, in Italy in the nineteenth century, and in Mexico, Russia, Czechoslovakia and Hungary (to name a few examples) in the twentieth century, seems self-evident. A government with mounting tax problems cannot be expected to keep its hands off the wealth of a rich church forever. That such a revolution is always ⊥**696** accompanied by anticlericalism and atheism should not be surprising."

The mounting wealth of the churches makes ironic their incessant demands on the public treasury. I said in my dissent in *Walz* v. *Tax Comm'n*: "The religiously used real estate of the churches today constitutes a vast domain. Their assets total over $141 billion and their annual income at least $22 billion. And the extent to which they are feeding from the public trough in a variety of forms is alarming."

It is almost unbelievable that we have made the radical departure from Madison's Remonstrance memorialized in today's decision.

⊥**697** I dissent not because of any lack of respect for parochial schools but out of a feeling of despair that the respect which through history has been accorded the First Amendment is this day lost.

It should be remembered that in this case we deal with federal grants and with the command that "Congress shall make no law respecting an establishment of religion, or prohibiting the free exercise thereof." The million-dollar grants sustained today put Madison's miserable "three pence" to shame. But he even thought, as I do, that even a small amount coming out of the pocket of taxpayers and going into the coffers of a church was not in keeping with our constitutional idea.

I would reverse the judgment below.

COMMITTEE FOR PUBLIC EDUCATION & RELIGIOUS LIBERTY v. NYQUIST

413 U.S. 756
ON APPEAL FROM THE UNITED STATES DISTRICT COURT FOR THE SOUTHERN DISTRICT OF NEW YORK
Argued April 16, 1973 — Decided June 25, 1973

⊥**759** Mr. *Justice POWELL* delivered the opinion of the Court.

This case raises a challenge under the Establishment Clause of the First Amendment to the constitutionality of a recently enacted New York law which provides financial assistance, in several ways, to nonpublic elementary and secondary schools in that State. The case involves an intertwining of societal and constitutional issues of the greatest importance.

⊥**760** James Madison, in his Memorial and Remonstrance Against Religious Assessments, admonished that a "prudent jealousy" for religious freedoms required that they never become "entangled . . . in precedents." His strongly held convictions, coupled with those of Thomas Jefferson and others among the Founders, are reflected in the first Clauses of the First Amendment of the Bill of Rights, which state that "Congress shall make no law respecting an establishment of religion, or prohibiting the free exercise thereof." Yet, despite Madison's admonition and the "sweep of the absolute prohibition" of the Clauses, this Nation's history has not been one of entirely sanitized separation between Church and State. It has never been thought either possible or desirable to enforce a regime of total separation, and as a consequence cases arising under these Clauses have presented some of the most perplexing questions to come before this Court. Those cases have occasioned thorough and ⊥**761** thoughtful scholarship by several of this Court's most respected former Justices, including *Justices BLACK, FRANKFURTER, HARLAN, JACKSON, RUTLEDGE*, and *Chief Justice WARREN*.

As a result of these decisions and opinions, it may no longer be said that the Religion Clauses are free of "entangling" precedents. Neither, however, may it be said that Jefferson's metaphoric "wall of separation" between Church and State has become "as winding as the famous serpentine wall" he designed for the University of Virginia. *McCollum* v. *Board of Education* (Jackson, J., separate opinion). Indeed, the controlling constitutional standards have become firmly rooted and the broad contours of our inquiry are now well defined. Our task, therefore, is to assess New York's several forms of aid in the light of principles already delineated.

I

In May 1972, the Governor of New York signed into law several amendments to the State's Education and Tax Laws. The first five sections of these amendments established three distinct financial aid programs for non⊥**762**public elementary and secondary schools. Almost immediately after the signing of these measures a complaint was filed in the United States District Court for the Southern District of New York challenging each of the three forms of aid as violative of the Establishment Clause. The plaintiffs were an unincorporated association, known as the Committee for Public Education and Religious Liberty (PEARL), and several individuals who were residents and taxpayers in New York, some of whom had children attending public schools. Named as defendants were the State Commissioner of Education, the Comptroller, and the Commissioner of Taxation and Finance. Motions to intervene on behalf of defendants were granted to a group of parents with children enrolled in nonpublic schools, and to the Majority Leader and President pro tem of the New York State Senate. By consent of the parties, a three-judge court was convened pursuant to 28 U.S.C. §§ 2281 and 2283, and the case was decided without an evidentiary hearing. Because the questions before the District Court were resolved on the basis of the pleadings, that court's decision turned on the constitutionality of each provision on its face.

The first section of the challenged enactment, entitled "Health and Safety Grants for Nonpublic School Children," provides for direct money grants from the State to "qualifying" nonpublic schools to be used for the "maintenance and repair of . . . school facilities and equipment to ensure the health, welfare and safety of enrolled pupils." A "qualifying" school is any non⊥**763**public, nonprofit elementary or secondary school which "has been designated during the [immediately preceding] year as serving a high concentration of pupils from low-income families for purposes of Title IV of the Federal Higher Education Act of 1965." Such schools are entitled to receive a grant of $30 per pupil per year, or $40 per pupil per year if the facilities are more than 25 years old. Each school is required to submit to the Commissioner of Education an audited statement of its expenditures for maintenance and repair during the preceding year, and its grant may not exceed the total of such expenses. The Commissioner is also required to ascertain the average per-pupil cost for equivalent maintenance and repair services in the public schools, and in no event may the grant to nonpublic qualifying schools exceed 50% of that figure.

"Maintenance and repair" is defined by the statute to include "the provision of heat, light, water, ventilation and sanitary facilities, cleaning, janitorial and custodial services; snow removal; necessary upkeep and renovation of buildings, grounds and equipment; fire and accident protection; and such other items as the commissioner may deem necessary to ensure the health, welfare and safety of enrolled pupils." This section is prefaced by a series of legislative findings which shed light on the State's purpose in enacting the law. These findings conclude that the State "has a primary responsibility to ensure the health, welfare and safety of children attending . . . nonpublic schools"; that the "fiscal crisis in nonpublic education . . . has caused a diminution of proper maintenance and repair programs, threatening the health, welfare and safety of nonpublic school children" ⊥**764** in low-income urban areas; and that "a healthy and safe school environment" contributes "to the stability of urban neighborhoods." For these reasons, the statute declares that "the state has the right to make grants for maintenance and repair expenditures which are clearly secular, neutral and nonideological in nature."

The remainder of the challenged legislation—§§ 2 through 5—is a single package captioned the "Elementary and Secondary Education Opportunity Program." It is composed, essentially, of two parts, a tuition grant program and a tax benefit program. Section 2 establishes a limited plan providing tuition reimbursements to parents of children attending elementary or secondary nonpublic schools. To qualify under this section the parent must have an annual taxable income of less than $6,000. The amount of reimbursement is limited to $60 for each grade school child and $100 for each high school child. Each parent is required, however, to submit to the Commissioner of Education a verified statement containing a receipted tuition bill, and the amount of state reimbursement may not exceed 50% of that figure. No restrictions are imposed on the use of the funds by the reimbursed parents.

This section, like § 1, is prefaced by a series of legislative findings designed to explain the impetus for the State's action. Expressing a dedication to the "vitality of our pluralistic society," the findings state that a "healthy competitive and diverse alternative to public education is not only desirable but indeed vital to a state and nation that have continually reaffirmed the value of individual differences." The findings further emphasize that the ⊥**765** right to select among alternative educational systems "is diminished or even denied to children of lower-income families, whose parents, of all groups, have the least options in determining where their children are to be educated." Turning to the public schools, the findings state that any "precipitous decline in the number of nonpublic school pupils would cause a massive increase in public school enrollment and costs," an increase that would "aggravate an already serious fiscal crisis in public education" and would "seriously jeopardize the quality education for all children." Based on these premises, the statute asserts the State's right to relieve the financial burden of parents who send their children to nonpublic schools through this tuition reimbursement program. Repeating the declaration contained in § 1, the findings conclude that "such assistance is clearly secular, neutral and nonideological."

The remainder of the "Elementary and Secondary Education Opportunity Program," contained in §§ 3, 4, and

5 of the challenged law, is designed to provide a form of tax relief to those who fail to qualify for tuition reimbursement. Under these sections parents may subtract from their adjusted gross income for state income tax purposes a designated amount for each dependent for whom they have paid at least $50 in nonpublic school tuition. If the taxpayer's adjusted gross income is less than $9,000 he may subtract $1,000 for each of as many as three dependents. As the taxpayer's income rises, the amount he may subtract diminishes. Thus, if a taxpayer has adjusted gross income of $15,000, he may subtract only $400 per dependent, and if his income is **⊥766** $25,000 or more, no deduction is allowed. The amount of the deduction is not dependent upon how much the taxpayer actually paid for nonpublic school tuition, and is given in addition to any deductions to which the taxpayer may be entitled for other religious or charitable contributions. As indicated in the memorandum from the Majority Leader and President pro tem of the Senate, submitted to each New York legislator during consideration of the bill, the actual tax benefits under these provisions were carefully calculated in advance. Thus, comparable tax **⊥767** benefits pick up at approximately the point at which tuition reimbursement benefits leave off.

While the scheme of the enactment indicates that the purposes underlying the promulgation of the tuition reimbursement program should be regarded as pertinent as well to these tax law sections, § 3 does contain an additional series of legislative findings. Those findings may be summarized as follows: (i) contributions to religious, charitable and educational institutions are already deductible from gross income; (ii) nonpublic educational institutions are accorded tax exempt status; (iii) such institutions provide educations for children attending them and also serve to relieve the public school systems of the burden of providing for their education; and, therefore, (iv) the "legislature . . . finds and determines that similar modifications . . . should also be provided to parents for tuition paid to nonpublic elementary and secondary schools on behalf of their dependents."

Although no record was developed in this case, a number of pertinent generalizations may be made about the nonpublic schools which would benefit from these enactments. The District Court, relying on findings in a similar case recently decided by the same court, adopted a profile of these sectarian, nonpublic schools similar to the one suggested in the plaintiffs' complaint. Qualifying institutions, under all three segments of the enactment, could be ones that: "(a) impose religious restrictions on admissions; (b) require attendance of pupils at religious activities; (c) require obedience by students to the doctrines and dogmas of a particular faith; (d) require pupils to attend instruction in the theology or doc**⊥768**trine of a particular faith; (e) are an integral part of the religious mission of the church sponsoring it; (f) have as a substantial purpose the inculcation of religious values; (g) impose religious restrictions on faculty appointments; and (h) impose religious restrictions on what or how the faculty may teach." 350 F. Supp., at 663.

Of course, the characteristics of individual schools may vary widely from that profile. Some 700,000 to 800,000 students, constituting almost 20% of the State's entire elementary and secondary school population, attend over 2,000 nonpublic schools, approximately 85% of which are church-affiliated. And while "all or practically all" of the 280 schools entitled to receive "maintenance and repair" grants "are related to the Roman Catholic Church and teach Catholic religious doctrine to some degree," institutions qualifying under the remainder of the statute include a substantial number of Jewish, Lutheran, Episcopal, Seventh Day Adventist, and other church-affiliated schools.

Plaintiffs argued below that because of the substantially religious character of the intended beneficiaries, each of the State's three enactments offended the Establishment Clause. The District Court, in an opinion carefully canvassing this Court's recent precedents, held **⊥769** unanimously that § 1 (maintenance and repair grants) and § 2 (tuition reimbursement grants) were invalid. As to the income tax provisions of §§ 3, 4, and 5, however, a majority of the District Court, over the dissent of Circuit Judge Hays, held that the Establishment Clause had not been violated. Finding the provisions of the law severable, it enjoined permanently any further implementation of §§ 1 and 2 but declared the remainder of the law independently enforceable. The plaintiffs appealed directly to this Court, challenging the District Court's adverse decision as to the third segment of the statute. The defendant state officials have appealed so much of the court's decision as invalidates the first and second portions of the 1972 law, the intervenor Majority Leader and President pro tem of the Senate also appeals from those aspects of the lower court's opinion, and the intervening parents of nonpublic school children have appealed only from the decision as to § 2. This Court noted probable jurisdiction over each appeal and ordered the cases consolidated for oral argument. Thus, the constitutionality of each of New York's recently promulgated aid provisions is squarely before us. We affirm the District Court insofar as it struck down §§ 1 and 2 and reverse its determination regarding §§ 3, 4, and 5.

⊥770II

The history of the Establishment Clause has been recounted frequently and need not be repeated here. See *Everson* v. *Board of Education* (Black, J., opinion of the Court), (Rutledge, J., dissenting); *McCollum* v. *Board* **⊥771** *of Education* (Frankfurter, J., separate opinion); *McGowan* v. *Maryland; Engel* v. *Vitale*. It is enough to note that it is now firmly established that a law may be one "respecting the establishment of religion" even though its consequence is not to promote a "state religion," *Lemon* v. *Kurtzman*, and even though it does not aid one religion more than another but merely benefits all religions alike. *Everson* v. *Board of Education*. It is equally well established, however, that not every law that confers an "indirect," "remote," or "incidental" benefit upon religious institutions is, for that reason alone, constitutionally invalid. ⊥**772** What our cases require is careful examination of any law challenged on establishment grounds with a view to ascertaining whether it furthers any of the evils against which that Clause protects. Primary among those evils have been "sponsorship, financial support, and active involvement in the sovereign in religious activity." *Walz* v. *Tax Commission*.

Most of the cases coming to this Court raising Establishment Clause questions have involved the relationship between religion and education. Among these religion-education precedents, two general categories of cases may be identified: those dealing with religious activities within the public schools, and those involving public aid in varying forms to sectarian educational institutions. While the New York legislation places this case in the latter category, its resolution requires consideration not only of the several aid-to-sectarian-education cases but also of our other education precedents and of several important non-education cases. For the now well defined three-part test that has emerged from our decisions is a product of considerations derived from the full sweep of the Establishment Clause cases. Taken together ⊥**773** these decisions dictate that to pass muster under the Establishment Clause the law in question, first, must reflect a clearly secular legislative purpose, *e.g.*, *Epperson* v. *Arkansas*; second, must have a primary effect that neither advances nor inhibits religion, *e.g.*, McGowan v. *Maryland; School District of Abington Township* v. *Schempp;* and, third, must avoid excessive government entanglement with religion, *e.g.*, *Walz* v. *Tax Comm'n*.

In applying these criteria to the three distinct forms of aid involved in this case, we need touch only briefly on the requirement of a "secular legislative purpose." As the recitation of legislative purposes appended to New York's law indicates, each measure is adequately supported by legitimate, nonsectarian state interests. We do not question the propriety, and fully secular content, of New York's interest in preserving a healthy and safe educational environment for all of its school children. And we do not doubt—indeed, we fully recognize—the validity of the State's interests in promoting pluralism and diversity among its public and nonpublic schools. Nor do we hesitate to acknowledge the reality of its concern for an already overburdened public school system that might suffer in the event that a significant percentage of children presently attending nonpublic schools should abandon those schools in favor of the public schools.

⊥**774** But the propriety of a legislature's purposes may not immunize from further scrutiny a law which either has a primary effect that advances religion, or which fosters excessive entanglements between Church and State. Accordingly, we must weigh each of the three aid provisions challenged here against these criteria of effect and entanglement.

A

The "maintenance and repair" provisions of § 1 authorize direct payments to nonpublic schools, virtually all of which are Roman Catholic schools in low income areas. The grants, totaling \$30 or \$40 per pupil depending on the age of the institution, are given largely without restriction on usage. So long as expenditures do not exceed 50% of comparable expenses in the public school system, it is possible for a sectarian elementary or secondary school to finance its entire "maintenance and repair" budget from state tax-raised funds. No attempt is made to restrict payments to those expenditures related to the upkeep of facilities used exclusively for secular purposes, nor do we think it possible within the context of these religion-oriented institutions to impose such restrictions. Nothing in the statute, for instance, bars a qualifying school from paying out of state funds the salary of employees who maintain the school chapel, or the cost of renovating classrooms in which religion is taught, or the cost of heating and lighting those same facilities. Absent appropriate restrictions on expenditures for these and similar purposes, it simply cannot be denied that this section has a primary effect that advances religion in that it subsidizes directly the religious activities of sectarian elementary and secondary schools.

The state officials nevertheless argue that these expenditures for "maintenance and repair" are similar to other financial expenditures approved by this Court. ⊥**775** Primarily they rely on *Everson* v. *Board of Education*, *Board of Education* v. *Allen*, and *Tilton* v. *Richardson*. In each of those cases it is true that the Court approved a form of financial assistance which conferred undeniable benefits upon private, sectarian schools. But a close examination of those cases illuminates their distinguishing characteristics. In *Everson*, the Court, in a five-to-four decision, approved a program of reimbursements to parents of public as well as parochial school children for bus fares paid in connection with transportation to and from school, a program which the Court characterized as approaching the "verge" of impermissible state aid. In *Allen*, decided some 20 years later, the Court upheld a New York law authorizing the provision of *secular* textbooks for all children in grades seven through 12 attending public and nonpublic schools. Finally, in *Tilton*, the Court upheld federal grants of funds for the construction of facilities to be used for clearly *secular* purposes by public and nonpublic institutions of higher learning.

These cases simply recognize that sectarian schools perform secular, educative functions as well as religious functions, and that some forms of aid may be channeled to the secular without providing direct aid to the sectarian. But the channel is a narrow one, as the above cases illustrate. Of course, it is true in each case that the provision of such neutral, nonideological aid, assisting only the secular functions of sectarian schools, served indirectly and incidentally to promote the religious function by rendering it more likely that children would attend sectarian schools and by freeing the budgets of those schools for use in other non-secular areas. But an indirect and incidental effect beneficial to religious institutions has never been thought a sufficient defect to warrant the invalidation of a state law. In *McGowan* v. *Maryland*, ⊥**776** Sunday Closing Laws were sustained even though one of their undeniable effects was to render it somewhat more likely that citizens would respect religious institutions and even attend religious services. Also, in *Walz* v. *Tax Commission*, property tax exemptions for church property were held not violative of the Establishment Clause despite the fact that such exemptions relieved churches of a financial burden.

Tilton draws the line most clearly. While a bare majority was there persuaded, for the reasons stated in the plurality opinion and in Mr. *Justice WHITE's* concurrence, that carefully limited construction grants to colleges and universities could be sustained, the Court was unanimous in its rejection of one clause of the federal statute in question. Under that clause, the Government was entitled to recover a portion of its grant to a sectarian institution in the event that the constructed facility was used to advance religion by, for instance, converting the building to a chapel or otherwise allowing it to be used to promote religious interests. But because the statute provided that the condition would expire at the end of 20 years, the facilities would thereafter be available for use by the institution for any sectarian purpose. In striking down this provision, the plurality opinion emphasized that "[l]imiting the prohibition for religious use of the structure to 20 years obviously opens the facility to use for any purpose at the end of that period." And in that event, "the original federal grant will in part have the effect of advancing religion." If tax-raised funds may not be granted to institutions of higher learning where the possibility exists that those funds will be used to construct a facility utilized for sectarian activities 20 years hence, *a fortiori* they ⊥**777** may not be distributed to elementary and secondary sectarian schools for the maintenance and repair of facilities without any limitations on their use. If the State may not erect buildings in which religious activities are to take place, it may not maintain such buildings or renovate them when they fall into disrepair.

It might be argued, however, that while the New York "maintenance and repair" grants lack specifically articulated secular restrictions, the statute does provide a sort of statistical guarantee of separation by limiting grants to 50% of the amount expended for comparable services in the public schools. The legislature's supposition might have been that at least 50% of the ordinary public school maintenance and repair budget would be devoted to purely secular facility upkeep in sectarian schools. The shortest answer to this argument is that the statute itself allows, as a ceiling, grants satisfying the entire "amount of expenditures for maintenance and repair of such school" providing only that it is neither more than $30 or $40 per pupil nor more than 50% of the comparable ⊥**778** public school expenditures. Quite apart from the language of the statute, our cases make clear that a mere statistical judgment will not suffice as a guarantee that state funds will not be used to finance religious education. In *Earley* v. *DiCenso*, the companion case to *Lemon* v. *Kurtzman*, the Court struck down a Rhode Island law authorizing salary supplements to teachers of secular subjects. The grants were not to exceed 15% of any teacher's annual salary. Although the law was invalidated on entanglement grounds, the Court made clear that the State could not have avoided violating the Establishment Clause by merely assuming that its teachers would succeed in segregating "their religious beliefs from their secular educational responsibilities."

"The Rhode Island Legislature has not, *and could not*, provide state aid on the basis of a mere assumption that secular teachers under religious discipline ⊥**779** can avoid conflicts. The State *must be certain*, *given the Religion Clauses*, that subsidized teachers do not inculcate religion. . . ." (Emphasis supplied.)

Nor could the State of Rhode Island have prevailed by simply relying on the assumption that, whatever a secular teacher's inabilities to refrain from mixing the religious with the secular, he would surely devote at least 15% of his efforts to purely secular education, thus exhausting the state grant. It takes little imagination to perceive the extent to which States might openly subsidize parochial schools under such a loose standard of scrutiny.

What we have said demonstrates that New York's maintenance and repair provisions violate the Establishment Clause because their effect, inevitably, is to subsidize and advance the religious mission of sectarian ⊥**780** schools. We have no occasion, therefore, to consider the further question whether those provisions as presently written would also fail to survive scrutiny under the administrative entanglement aspect of the three-part test because assuring the secular use of all funds requires too intrusive and continuing a relationship between Church and State, *Lemon* v. *Kurtzman*.

B

New York's tuition reimbursement program also fails the "effect" test, for much the same reasons that govern its maintenance and repair grants. The state program is designed to allow direct, unrestricted grants of $50 to $100 per child (but no more than 50% of tuition actually paid) as reimbursement to parents in low-income brackets who send their children to nonpublic schools. To qualify, a parent must have earned less than $5,000 in taxable income and must present a receipted tuition bill from a nonpublic school, the bulk of which are concededly sectarian in orientation.

There can be no question that these grants could not, consistently with the Establishment Clause, be given directly to sectarian schools, since they would suffer from the same deficiency that renders invalid the grants for maintenance and repair. In the absence of an effective means of guaranteeing that the state aid derived from public funds will be used exclusively for secular, neutral, and nonideological purposes, it is clear from our cases that direct aid in whatever form is invalid. As Mr. *Justice BLACK* put it quite simply in *Everson:* "No tax in any amount, large or small, can be levied to support any religious activities or institutions, whatever they may be called, or whatever form they may adopt to teach or practice religion."

⊥781 The controlling question here, then, is whether the fact that the grants are delivered to parents rather than schools is of such significance as to compel a contrary result. The State and intervenor-appellees rely on *Everson* and *Allen* for their claim that grants to parents, unlike grants to institutions, respect the "wall of separation" required by the Constitution. It is true that in those cases the Court upheld laws that provided benefits to children attending religious schools and to their parents: As noted above, in *Everson* parents were reimbursed for bus fares paid to send children to parochial schools, and in *Allen* textbooks were loaned directly to the children. But those decisions made clear that, far from providing a *per se* immunity from examination of the substance of the State's program, the fact that aid is disbursed to parents rather than to the schools is only one among many factors to be considered.

In *Everson*, the Court found the bus fare program analogous to the provision of services such as police and fire protection, sewage disposal, highways, and sidewalks for parochial schools. Such services, **⊥782** provided in common to all citizens, are "so separate and so indisputably marked off from the religious function," that they may fairly be viewed as reflections of a neutral posture toward religious institutions. *Allen* is founded upon a similar principle. The Court there repeatedly emphasized that upon the record in that case there was no indication that textbooks would be provided for anything other than purely secular courses. "Of course books are different from buses. Most bus rides have no inherent religious significance, while religious books are common. However, the language of [the law under consideration] does not authorize the loan of religious books, and the State claims no right to distribute religious literature. . . . Absent evidence, we cannot assume that school authorities . . . are unable to distinguish between secular and religious books or that they will not honestly discharge their duties under the law."

⊥783 The tuition grants here are subject to no such restrictions. There has been no endeavor "to guarantee the separation between secular and religious educational functions and to ensure that State financial aid supports only the former." *Lemon* v. *Kurtzman*. Indeed, it is precisely the function of New York's law to provide assistance to private schools, the great majority of which are sectarian. By reimbursing parents for a portion of their tuition bill, the State seeks to relieve their financial burdens sufficiently to assure that they continue to have the option to send their children to religion-oriented schools. And while the other purposes for that aid—to perpetuate a pluralistic educational environment and to protect the fiscal integrity of overburdened public schools—are certainly unexceptionable, the effect of the aid is unmistakably to provide desired financial support for nonpublic, sectarian institutions.

⊥784 Mr. *Justice BLACK*, dissenting in *Allen*, warned that "[i]t requires no prophet to foresee that on the argument used to support this law others could be up-**⊥785**held providing for state or federal government funds to buy property on which to erect religious school buildings or to erect the buildings themselves, to pay the salaries of the religious school teachers, and finally to have the sectarian religious groups cease to rely on voluntary contributions of members of their sects while waiting for the government to pick up all the bills for the religious schools."

His fears regarding religious buildings and religious teachers have not come to pass, *Tilton* v. *Richardson; Lemon* v. *Kurtzman*, and insofar as tuition grants constitute a means of "pick[ing] up . . . the bills for the religious schools," neither has his greatest fear materialized. But the ingenious plans for channeling state aid to sectarian schools that periodically reach this Court abundantly support the wisdom of *Mr. Justice BLACK's* prophecy.

Although we think it clear, for the reasons above stated, that New York's tuition grant program fares no better under the "effect" test than its maintenance and repair program, in view of the novelty of the question we will address briefly the subsidiary arguments made by the state officials and intervenors in its defense.

First, it has been suggested that it is of controlling significance that New York's program calls for *reimbursement* for tuition already paid rather than for direct contributions which are merely routed through the parents to the schools, in advance of or in lieu of payment **⊥786** by the parents. The parent is not a mere conduit, we are told, but is absolutely free to spend the money he receives in any manner he wishes. There is no element of coercion attached to the reimbursement, and no assurance that the money will eventually end up in the hands of religious schools. The absence of any element of coercion, however, is irrelevant to questions arising under the Establishment Clause. In *School District of Abington Township* v. *Schempp* it was contended that Bible recitations in public schools did not violate the Establishment Clause because participation in such exercises was not coerced. The Court rejected that argument, noting that while proof of coercion might provide a basis for a claim under the Free Exercise Clause, it was not a necessary element of any claim under the Establishment Clause. *Mr. Justice BRENNAN's* concurring views reiterated the Court's conclusion: "Thus the short, and for me sufficient, answer is that the availability of excusal or exemption simply has no relevance to the establishment question, if it is once found that these practices are essentially religious exercises designed at least in part to achieve religious aims. . . ." [*Abington* v. *Schempp*].

A similar inquiry governs here: if the grants are offered as an incentive to parents to send their children to sectarian schools by making unrestricted cash payments to them, the Establishment Clause is violated whether or not the actual dollars given eventually find their way into the sectarian institutions. Whether the grant is labeled a reimbursement, a reward or a subsidy, its substantive impact is still the same. In sum, we agree with ⊥**787** the conclusion of the District Court that "[w]hether he gets it during the current year, or as reimbursement for the past year, is of no constitutional importance."

Second, the Majority Leader and President pro tem of the State Senate argues that it is significant here that the tuition reimbursement grants pay only a portion of the tuition bill, and an even smaller portion of the religious school's total expenses. The New York statute limits its reimbursement to 50% of any parent's actual outlay. Additionally, intervenor estimates that only 30% of the total cost of nonpublic education is covered by tuition payments, with the remaining coming from "voluntary contributions, endowments and the like." On the basis of these two statistics, appellee reasons that the "maximum tuition reimbursement by the State is thus only 15% of the educational costs in the nonpublic schools." And, "since compulsory education laws of the State, by necessity require significantly more than 15% of school time to be devoted to teaching secular courses," the New York statute provides "a statistical guarantee of neutrality." It should readily be seen that this is simply another variant of the argument we have rejected as to maintenance and repair costs and it can fare no better here. Obviously, if accepted, this argument would provide the foundation for massive, direct subsidization of sectarian elementary and secondary schools. Our cases, however, have long since foreclosed ⊥**788** the notion that mere statistical assurances will suffice to sail between the Scylla and Charybdis of "effect" and "entanglement."

Finally, the State argues that its program of tuition grants should survive scrutiny because it is designed to promote the free exercise of religion. The State notes that only "low-income parents" are aided by this law, and without state assistance their right to have their children educated in a religious environment "is diminished or even denied." It is true, of course, that this Court has long recognized and maintained the right to choose nonpublic over public education. *Pierce* v. *Society of Sisters*. It is also true that a state law interfering with a parent's right to have his child educated in a sectarian school would run afoul of the Free Exercise Clause. But this Court repeatedly has recognized that tension inevitably exists between the Free Exercise and the Establishment Clauses and that it may often not be possible to promote the former without offending the latter. As a result of this tension, our cases require the State to maintain an attitude of "neutrality," neither "advancing" nor "inhibiting" religion. In its attempt to enhance the opportunities of the poor to choose between public and nonpublic education, the State has taken a step which can only be regarded as one "advancing" religion. However great our sympathy, *Everson* v. *Board of Education* (Jackson, J., dissenting), for the burdens experienced by those who must pay public school taxes at the same time that they support other schools because ⊥**789** of the constraints of "conscience and discipline," and notwithstanding the "high social importance" of the State's purposes, *Wisconsin* v. *Yoder*, neither may justify an eroding of the limitations of the Establishment Clause now firmly emplanted.

C

Sections 3, 4, and 5 establish a system for providing income tax benefits to parents of children attending New York's nonpublic schools. In this Court, the parties have engaged in a considerable debate over what label best fits the New York law. Appellants insist that the law is, in effect, one establishing a system of tax "credits." The State and the intervenors reject that characterization and would label it, instead, a system of income tax "modifications." The Solicitor General, in an *amicus curiae* brief filed in this Court, has referred throughout to the New York law as one authorizing tax "deductions." The District Court majority found that the aid was "in effect a tax *credit*" (emphasis in original). Because of the peculiar nature of the benefit allowed, it is difficult to adopt any single traditional label lifted from the law of income taxation. It is, at least in its form, a tax deduction since it is an amount subtracted from adjusted gross income, prior to computation of the tax due. Its effect, as the District Court concluded, is more like that of a tax credit since the deduction is not related to the amount actually spent for tuition and is apparently designed to yield a predetermined amount of tax "forgiveness" in exchange for performing a specific act which the State desires to encourage—the usual attribute of a tax credit. We see no reason to select one label over the other, as the constitutionality of this hybrid benefit does not turn in any event on the label we accord it. As *Mr. Chief Justice BURGER's* opinion for the Court in *Lemon* v. *Kurtzman* notes, constitu⊥**790**tional analysis is not a "legalistic minuet in which precise rules and forms govern." Instead we must "examine the form of the relationship for the light that it casts on the substance."

These sections allow parents of children attending nonpublic elementary and secondary schools to subtract from adjusted gross income a specified amount if they do not receive a tuition reimbursement under § 2, and if they have an adjusted gross income of less than $25,000. The amount of the deduction is unrelated to the amount of money actually expended by any parent on tuition, but is calculated on the basis of a formula contained in the statute. The formula is apparently the product of a legislative attempt to assure that each family would receive a carefully estimated net benefit, and that the tax benefit would be comparable to, and compatible with, the tuition grant for lower income families. Thus, a parent who earns less than $5,000 is entitled to a tuition reimbursement of $50 if he has one child attending an elementary, nonpublic school, while a parent who earns more (but less than $9,000) is entitled to have a precisely equal amount taken off his tax bill. Additionally, a taxpayer's benefit under these sections is unrelated to, and not reduced by, any deductions to which he may be entitled for charitable contributions to religious institutions.

In practical terms there would appear to be little difference, for purposes of determining whether such aid has the effect of advancing religion, between the tax ⊥**791** benefit allowed here and the tuition grant allowed under § 2. The qualifying parent under either program receives the same form of encouragement and reward for sending his children to nonpublic schools. The only difference is that one parent receives an actual cash payment while the other is allowed to reduce by an arbitrary amount the sum he would otherwise be obliged to pay over to the State. We see no answer to Judge Hays' dissenting statement below that "[i]n both instances the money involved represents a charge made upon the state for the purpose of religious education."

Appellees defend the tax portion of New York's legislative package on two grounds. First, they contend that it is of controlling significance that the grants or credits are directed to the parents rather than to the schools. This is the same argument made in support of the tuition reimbursements and rests on the same reading of the same precedents of this Court, primarily *Everson* and *Allen*. Our treatment of this issue in Part IIB is applicable here and requires rejection of this claim. Second, appellees place their strongest reliance on *Walz* in which New York's property tax exemption for religious organizations was upheld. We think that *Walz* provides no support for appellees' position. Indeed, its rationale plainly compels the conclusion that New York's tax package violates the Establishment Clause.

⊥**792** Tax exemptions for church property enjoyed an apparently universal approval in this country both before and after the adoption of the First Amendment. The Court in *Walz* surveyed the history of tax exemptions and found that each of the 50 States has long provided for tax exemptions for places of worship, that Congress has exempted religious organizations from taxation for over three-quarters of a century, and that congressional enactments in 1802, 1813, and 1870 specifically exempted church property from taxation. In sum, the Court concluded that "[f]ew concepts are more deeply embedded in the fabric of our national life, beginning with pre-Revolutionary colonial times, than for the government to exercise at the very least this kind of benevolent neutrality toward churches and religious exercise generally." We know of no historical precedent for New York's recently promulgated tax relief program. Indeed, it seems clear that tax benefits for parents whose children attend parochial schools are a recent innovation, occasioned by the growing financial plight of such nonpublic institutions and designed, albeit unsuccessfully, to tailor state aid in a manner not incompatible with the recent decisions of this Court.

But historical acceptance without more would not alone have sufficed, as "no one acquires a vested or protected right in violation of the Constitution by long use." *Walz* v. *Tax Commission*. It was the reason underlying that long history of tolerance of tax exemptions for religion that proved controlling. A proper respect for both the Free Exercise and the Establishment Clauses compels the State ⊥**793** to pursue a course of "neutrality" towards religion. Yet governments have not always pursued such a course, and oppression has taken many forms, one of which has been taxation of religion. Thus, if taxation was regarded as a form of "hostility" toward religion, "exemption constitute[d] a reasonable and balanced attempt to guard against those dangers." Special tax benefits, however, cannot be squared with the principle of neutrality established by the decisions of this Court. To the contrary, insofar as such benefits render assistance to parents who send their children to sectarian schools, their purpose and inevitable effect are to aid and advance those religious institutions.

Apart from its historical foundations, *Walz* is a product of the same dilemma and inherent tension found in most government-aid-to-religion controversies. To be sure, the exemption of church property from taxation conferred a benefit, albeit an indirect and incidental one. Yet that "aid" was a product not of any purpose to support or to subsidize, but of a fiscal relationship designed to minimize involvement and entanglement between Church and State. "The exemption," the Court emphasized, "tends to complement and reinforce the desired separation insulating each from the other." Furthermore, "[e]llimination of the exemption would tend to expand the involvement of government by giving rise to tax valuation of church property, tax liens, tax foreclosures, and the direct confrontations and conflicts that follow in the train of those legal processes." The granting of the tax benefits under the New York statute, unlike the extension of an exemption, would tend to increase rather than limit the involvement between Church and State.

One further difference between tax exemptions for church property and tax benefits for parents should be ⊥**794** noted. The exemption challenged in *Walz* was not restricted to a class composed exclusively or even predominantly of religious institutions. Instead the exemption covered all property devoted to religious, educational or charitable purposes. As the parties here must concede, tax reductions authorized by this law flow primarily to the parents of children attending sectarian, nonpublic schools. Without intimating whether this factor alone might have controlling significance in another context in some future case, it should be apparent that in terms of the potential divisiveness of any legislative measure the narrowness of the benefited class would be an important factor.

In conclusion, we find the *Walz* analogy unpersuasive, and in light of the practical similarity between New

York's tax and tuition reimbursement programs, we hold that neither form of aid is sufficiently restricted to assure that it will not have the impermissible effect of advancing the sectarian activities of religious schools.

III

Because we have found that the challenged sections have the impermissible effect of advancing religion, we need not consider whether such aid would result in entanglement of the State with religion in the sense of "[a] comprehensive, discriminating, and continuing surveillance." *Lemon* v. *Kurtzman*. But the importance of the competing societal interests implicated in this case prompts us to make the further observation that, apart from any specific entanglement of the State in particular religious programs, assistance of the sort here involved carries grave potential for entanglement in the broader sense of continuing political strife over aid to religion.

⊥**795** Few would question most of the legislative findings supporting this statute. We recognized in *Board of Education* v. *Allen* that "private education has played and is playing a significant and valuable role in raising levels of knowledge, competency, and experience," and certainly private parochial schools have contributed importantly to this role. Moreover, the tailoring of the New York statute to channel the aid provided primarily to afford low-income families the option of determining where their children are to be educated is most appealing. There is no doubt that the private schools are confronted with increasingly grave fiscal problems, that resolving these problems by increasing tuition charges forces parents to turn to the public schools, and that this in turn—as the present legislation recognizes—exacerbates the problems of public education at the same time that it weakens support for the parochial schools.

These, in briefest summary, are the underlying reasons for the New York legislation and for similar legislation in other States. They are substantial reasons. Yet they must be weighed against the relevant provisions and purposes of the First Amendment, which safeguard the separation of Church from State and which have been regarded from the beginning as among the most cherished features of our constitutional system.

One factor of recurring significance in this weighing process is the potentially divisive political effect of an aid program. As Mr. *Justice* BLACK's opinion in *Everson* ⊥**796** v. *Board of Education* emphasizes, competition among religious sects for political and religious supremacy has occasioned considerable civil strife, "generated in large part" by competing efforts to gain or maintain the support of government. As Mr. *Justice HARLAN* put it, "[w]hat is at stake as a matter of policy in Establishment Clause cases is preventing that kind and degree of government involvement in religious life that, as history teaches us, is apt to lead to strife and frequently strain a political system to the breaking point." *Walz* v. *Tax Commission* (concurring opinion).

The Court recently addressed this issue specifically and fully in *Lemon* v. *Kurtzman*. After describing the political activity and bitter differences likely to result from the state programs there involved, the Court said: "The potential for political divisiveness related to religious belief and practice is aggravated in these two statutory programs by the need for continuing annual appropriations and the likelihood of larger and larger demands as costs and population grow."

The language of the Court applies with peculiar force to the New York statute now before us. Section 1 (grants for maintenance) and § 2 (tuition grants) will require continuing annual appropriations. Sections 3, 4, and 5 (income tax relief) will not necessarily require ⊥**797** annual re-examination, but the pressure for frequent enlargement of the relief is predictable. All three of these programs start out at modest levels: the maintenance grant is not to exceed $40 per pupil per year in approved schools; the tuition grant provides parents not more than $50 a year for each child in the first eight grades and $100 for each child in the high school grades; and the tax benefit, though more difficult to compute, is equally modest. But we know from long experience with both Federal and State Governments that aid programs of any kind tend to become entrenched, to escalate in cost, and to generate their own aggressive constituencies. And the larger the class of recipients, the greater the pressure for accelerated increases. Moreover, the State itself, concededly anxious to avoid assuming the burden of educating children now in private and parochial schools, has a strong motivation for increasing this aid as public school costs rise and population increases. In this situation, where the underlying issue is the deeply emotional one of Church-State relationships, the potential for serious divisive political consequences needs no elaboration. And while the prospect of such divisive⊥**798**ness may not alone warrant the invalidation of state laws that otherwise survive the careful scrutiny required by the decisions of this Court, it is certainly a "warning signal" not to be ignored.

Our examination of New York's aid provisions, in light of all relevant considerations, compels the judgment that each, as written, has a "primary effect that advances religion" and offends the constitutional prohibition against laws "respecting the establishment of religion." We therefore affirm the three-judge court's holding as to §§ 1 and 2, and reverse as to §§ 3, 4, and 5.

It is so ordered.

Mr. *Chief Justice* BURGER, joined in part by Mr. *Justice* WHITE, and joined by Mr. *Justice* REHNQUIST, concurring in part and dissenting in part.

I join in that part of the Court's opinion in *Committee for Public Education and Religious Liberty* v. *Nyquist*, which holds the New York "maintenance and repair" provision unconstitutional under the Establishment Clause because it is a direct aid to religion. I disagree, however, with the Court's decisions in *Nyquist* and in *Sloan* v. *Lemon* to strike down the New York and Pennsylvania tuition grant programs and the New York tax relief provisions. I believe the Court's decisions on those statutory provisions ignore the teachings of *Everson* v. *Board of Education* ⊥**799** and *Board of Education* v. *Allen* and fail to observe what I thought the Court had held in *Walz* v. *Tax Comm'n*. I therefore dissent as to those aspects of the two holdings.

While there is no straight line running through our decisions interpreting the Establishment and Free Exercise Clauses of the First Amendment, our cases do, it seems to me, lay down one solid, basic principle: that the Establishment Clause does not forbid governments, state or federal, from enacting a program of general welfare under which benefits are distributed to private individuals, even though many of those individuals may elect to use those benefits in ways that "aid" religious instruction or worship. Thus, in *Everson* the Court held that a New Jersey township could reimburse all parents of school-age children for bus fares paid in transporting their children to school. *Justice* BLACK's opinion for the Court stated that the New Jersey "legislation, as applied, does no more than provide a general program to *help parents* get their children, regardless of their religion, safely and expeditiously to and from accredited schools." (Emphasis added).

Twenty-one years later, in *Board of Education* v. *Allen*, the Court again upheld a state program that provided for direct aid to the parents of all school children including those in private schools. The statute there required "local public school authorities to lend textbooks free of charge to all students in grades seven through 12; students attending private schools [were] included." Recognizing that *Everson* was the case "most nearly in point," the *Allen* Court interpreted *Everson* as holding that "the Establishment ⊥**800** Clause does not prevent a state from extending the benefits of state laws to all citizens without regard to their religious affiliation. . . ." Applying that principle to the statute before it, the *Allen* Court stated ". . . Appellants have shown us nothing about the necessary effects of the statute that is contrary to its stated purpose. The law merely *makes available to all children* the benefits of a general program to lend school books free of charge. Books are furnished at the request of the pupil and ownership remains, at least technically, in the State. *Thus no funds or books are furnished to parochial schools, and the financial benefit is to the parents and children, not to schools*." (Emphasis added).

The Court's opinions in both *Everson* and *Allen* recognized that the statutory programs at issue there may well have facilitated the decision of many parents to send their children to religious schools. Indeed, the Court in both cases specifically acknowledged that some children might not obtain religious instruction but for the benefits provided by the State. Notwithstanding, the Court held that such an indirect or incidental "benefit" to the religious institutions that sponsored parochial schools was not conclusive indicia of a "law respecting an establishment of religion."

⊥**801** One other especially pertinent decision should be noted. In *Quick Bear* v. *Leupp*, the Court considered the question whether government aid to individuals who choose to use the benefits for sectarian purposes contravenes the Establishment Clause. There the Federal Government had set aside certain trust and treaty funds for the educational benefit of the members of the Sioux Indian Tribe. When some beneficiaries elected to attend religious schools, and the Government entered into payment contracts with the sectarian institutions, suit was brought to enjoin the disbursement of public money to those schools. Speaking of the constitutionality of such a program, the Court said: "But we cannot concede the proposition that Indians cannot be allowed to use their own money to educate their children in the schools of their own choice because the Government is necessarily undenominational, as it cannot make any law respecting an establishment of religion or prohibiting the free exercise thereof."

The essence of all these decisions, I suggest, is that government aid to individuals generally stands on an entirely different footing from direct aid to religious institutions. I say "generally" because it is obviously possible to conjure hypothetical statutes that constitute either a subterfuge for direct aid to religious institutions or a discriminatory enactment favoring religious over nonreligious activities. Thus, a State could not enact a statute providing for a $10 gratuity to everyone who attended religious services weekly. Such a law would plainly be governmental sponsorship of religious activities; no statutory preamble expressing purely sec⊥**802**ular legislative motives would be persuasive. But at least where the state law is genuinely directed at enhancing the freedom of individuals to exercise a recognized right, even one involving both secular and religious consequences as is true of the right of parents to send their children to private schools, see *Pierce* v. *Society of Sisters*, then the Establishment Clause no longer has a prohibitive effect.

This fundamental principle which I see running through our prior decisions in this difficult and sensitive field of law, and which I believe governs the present cases, is premised more on experience and history than on logic. It is admittedly difficult to articulate the reasons why a State should be permitted to reimburse parents of private-school children—partially at least—to take into account the State's enormous savings in not having to provide schools for those children, when a State is not allowed to pay the same benefit directly to sectarian schools on a per-pupil basis. In either case, the private individual makes the ultimate decision that may indirectly benefit church sponsored schools; to that extent the state involvement with religion is substantially attenuated. The answer, I believe, lies in the experienced judgment of various members of this Court over the years that the balance between the policies of free exercise and establishment of religion tips in favor of the former when the legislation moves away from direct aid to religious institutions and takes on the character of general aid to individual families. This judgment reflects the caution with which we scrutinize any effort to give official support to religion and the tolerance with which we treat general welfare legislation. But, whatever its ⊥**803** basis, that principle is established in our cases, from the early case of *Quick Bear* to the more recent holdings in *Everson* and *Allen*, and it ought to be followed here.

The tuition grant and tax relief programs now before us are, in my view, indistinguishable in principle, purpose and effect from the statutes in *Everson* and *Allen*. In the instant cases as in *Everson* and *Allen* the States have merely attempted to equalize the costs incurred by parents in obtaining an education for their children. The only discernible difference between the programs in *Everson* and *Allen* and these cases is in the method of the distribution of benefits: here the particular benefits of the Pennsylvania and New York statutes are given only to parents of private school children, while in *Everson* and *Allen* the statutory benefits were made available to parents of both public and private school children. But to regard that difference as constitutionally meaningful is to exalt form over substance. It is beyond dispute that the parents of public school children in New York and Pennsylvania presently receive the "benefit" of having their children educated totally at state expense; the statutes enacted in those States and at issue here merely attempt to equalize that "benefit" by giving to parents of private school children, in the form of dollars or tax deductions, what the parents of public school children receive in kind. It is no more than simple equity to grant partial relief to parents who support the public schools they do not use.

The Court appears to distinguish the Pennsylvania and New York statutes from *Everson* and *Allen* on the ground that here the state aid is not apportioned between the religious and secular activities of the sectarian schools attended by some recipients, while in *Everson* and *Allen* the state aid was purely secular in nature. But that distinction has not been followed in the past, see *Quick Bear* v. *Leupp*, and is not likely to be considered ⊥**804** controlling in the future. There are at present many forms of government assistance to individuals that can be used to serve religious ends, such as social security benefits or "G.I. Bill" payments, which are not subject to nonreligious use restrictions. Yet, I certainly doubt that today's majority would hold those statutes unconstitutional under the Establishment Clause.

Since I am unable to discern in the Court's analysis of *Everson* and *Allen* any neutral principle to explain the result reached in these cases, I fear that the Court has in reality followed the unsupportable approach of measuring the "effect" of a law by the percentage of the recipients who choose to use the money for religious, rather than secular, education. Indeed, in discussing the New York tax credit provisions, the Court's opinion argues that "the tax reductions authorized by this law flow primarily to the parents of children attending sectarian, nonpublic schools." While the opinion refrains from "intimating whether this factor alone might have controlling significance in another context in some future case," similar references to this factor elsewhere in the Court's opinion suggest that it has been given considerable weight. Thus, the Court observes as to the New York tuition grant program: "Indeed, it is precisely the function of New York's law to provide assistance to private schools, *the great majority of which are sectarian*." (Emphasis added.)

With all due respect, I submit that such a consideration is irrelevant to a constitutional determination of the "effect" of a statute. For purposes of constitutional adjudication of that issue, it should make no difference whether 5%, 20%, or 80% of the beneficiaries of an educational program of general application elect to utilize their benefits for religious purposes. The "primary effect" branch of our three-pronged test was never, at least to my understanding, intended to vary with the ⊥**805** *number* of churches benefitted by a statute under which state aid is distributed to private citizens.

Such a consideration, it is true, might be relevant in ascertaining whether the *primary legislative purpose* was to advance the cause of religion. But the Court has, and I think correctly, summarily dismissed the contention that either New York or Pennsylvania had an improper purpose in enacting these laws. The Court fully recognizes that the legislatures of New York and Pennsylvania have a legitimate interest in "promoting pluralism and diversity among . . . public and nonpublic schools," in assisting those who reduce the State's expenses in providing public education, and in protecting the already overburdened public school system against a massive influx of private school children. And in light of this Court's recognition of these secular legislative purposes, I fail to see any acceptable resolution to these cases except one favoring constitutionality.

I would therefore uphold these New York and Pennsylvania statutes. However sincere our collective protestations of the debt owed by the public generally to the parochial school systems, the wholesome diversity they engender will not survive on expressions of good will.

Mr. *Justice* WHITE joins this opinion insofar as it relates to the New York and Pennsylvania tuition grant statutes and the New York tax relief statute.

. . . . .

⊥**813** Mr. *Justice* WHITE, joined in part by *The* CHIEF JUSTICE and Mr. *Justice* REHNQUIST, dissenting.

Each of the States regards the education of its young to be a critical matter, so much so that it compels school attendance and provides an educational system at public expense. Any otherwise qualified child is entitled to a free elementary and secondary school education, or at least an education that costs him very little as compared with its cost to the State.

This Court has held, however, that the Due Process Clause of the Constitu⊥**814**tion entitles parents to send their children to nonpublic schools, secular or sectarian, if those schools are sufficiently competent to educate the child in the necessary secular subjects. *Pierce* v. *Society of Sisters*. About 10% of the Nation's children, approximately 5.2 million students, now take this option and are not being educated in public schools at public expense. Under state law these children have a right to a free public education and it would not appear unreasonable if the State, relieved of the expense of educating a child in the public school, contributed to the expense of his education elsewhere. The parents of such children pay taxes, including school taxes. They could receive in return a free education in the public schools. They prefer to send their children, as they have the right to do, to nonpublic schools that furnish the satisfactory equivalent of a public school education but also offer subjects or other assumed advantages not available in public schools. Constitutional considerations aside, it would be understandable if a State gave such parents a call on the public treasury up to the amount it would have cost the State to educate the child in public school, or to put it another way, up to the amount the parents save the State by not sending their children to public school.

In light of the Free Exercise Clause of the First Amendment, this would seem particularly the case where the parent desires his child to attend a school that offers not only secular subjects but religious training as well. A State should put no unnecessary obstacles in the way of religious training for the young. "When the State encourages religious instruction . . . it follows the best of our traditions." *Zorach* v. *Clauson; Walz* v. *Tax Commission*. Positing an obligation on the State to educate its children, which every State acknowledges, it should be wholly acceptable for the State to contribute ⊥**815** to the secular education of children going to sectarian schools rather than to insist that if parents want to provide their children with religious as well as secular education, the State will refuse to contribute anything to their secular training.

Historically the States of the Union have not furnished public aid for education in private schools. But in the last few years, as private education, particularly the parochial school system, has encountered financial difficulties, with many schools being closed and many more apparently headed in that direction, there has developed a variety of programs seeking to extend at least some aid to private educational institutions. Some States have provided only fringe benefits or auxiliary services. Others attempted more extensive efforts to keep the private school system alive. Some made direct arrangements with private and parochial schools for the purchase of secular educational services furnished by those schools. Others provided tuition grants to parents sending their children to private schools, permitted dual enrollments or shared time arrangements or extended substantial tax benefits in some form.

⊥**816** The dimensions of the situations are not difficult to outline. The 5.2 million private elementary and secondary school students in 1972 attended some 3,200 nonsectarian private schools and some 18,000 schools that are church related. Twelve thousand of the latter were Roman Catholic schools and enrolled 4.37 million pupils or 83% of the total nonpublic school membership. Sixty-⊥**817**two percent of nonpublic school students are concentrated in eight industrialized, urbanized States: New York, Pennsylvania, Illinois, California, Ohio, New Jersey, Michigan, and Massachusetts. Eighty-three percent of the nonpublic school enrollment is to be found in large metropolitan areas. Nearly one out of five students in each of the Nation's largest cities are enrolled in nonpublic schools.

Nonpublic school enrollment has dropped at the rate of 6% per year for the past five years. Since 1965 nonpublic school enrollment has dropped 23%; the public schools show an increase of 12%. Projected to 1980, it is estimated that seven States (the eight mentioned in the text less Massachusetts) will lose 1,416,122 nonpublic school students. Whatever the reasons, there has been, and there probably will be, a movement to the public schools, with the prospect of substantial increases ⊥**818** in public school budgets that are already under intense attack and with the States and cities that are primarily involved already facing severe financial crises. It is this prospect that has prompted some of these States to attempt, by a variety of devices, to save or slow the demise of the nonpublic school system, an educational resource that could deliver quality education at a cost to the public substantially below the per pupil cost of the public schools.

⊥**819** There are, then, the most profound reasons, in addition to those normally attending the question of the constitutionality of a state statute, for this Court to proceed with the utmost care in deciding these cases. It should not, absent a clear mandate in the Constitution, invalidate these New York and Pennsylvania statutes and thereby not only scuttle state efforts to hold off serious financial problems in their public schools but ⊥**820** also make it more difficult, if not impossible, for parents to follow the dictates of their conscience and seek a religious as well as secular education for their children.

I am quite unreconciled to the Court's decision in *Lemon* v. *Kurtzman*. I thought then, and I think now, that the Court's conclusion there was not required by the First Amendment and is contrary to the long range interests of the country. I therefore have little difficulty in accepting the New York maintenance grant, which does not and could not, by its terms, approach the actual repair and maintenance cost incurred in connection with the secular education services performed for the State in parochial schools. But accepting *Lemon* and the invalidation of the New York maintenance grant, I would, with *The CHIEF JUSTICE* and *Mr. Justice REHNQUIST*, sustain the New York and Pennsylvania tuition grant statutes and the New York tax credit provisions.

No one contends that he can discern from the sparse language of the Establishment Clause that a State is forbidden to aid religion in any manner whatsoever or, if it does not mean that, what kind of or how much aid is permissible. And one cannot seriously believe that the history of the First Amendment furnishes unequivocal answers to many of the fundamental issues of church-state relations. In the end the courts have fashioned answers to these questions as best they can, the language of the Constitution and its history having left them a wide range of choice among many alternatives. But decision has been unavoidable; and, in choosing, the courts necessarily have carved out what they deemed to be the most desirable national policy governing various aspects of church-state relationships.

The course of these decisions has made it clear that the First Amendment does not bar all state aid to religion, of whatever kind or extent. States do, and ⊥**821** they may, furnish churches and parochial schools with police and fire protection as well as water and sewage facilities. Also, "all of the 50 States provide for tax exemption of places of worship, most of them doing so by constitutional guarantee." *Walz* v. *Tax Commission*. This is a multimillion-dollar benefit to religious institutions, but a benefit that this Court has held is wholly consistent with the First Amendment. Bus transportation may be furnished to students attending parochial schools as well as to those going to public schools. So too the State may furnish school books to such students, although in doing so they "relieve[d] those churches of an enormous aggregate cost for those books." *Walz*. A State may also become the owner of the property of a church-sponsored college and lease it back to the college, all with the purpose and effect of permitting revenue bonds issued in connection with the college's operation to be tax exempt and working a lower rate of interest and substantial savings to the sectarian institution. *Hunt* v. *McNair*.

The Court thus has not barred all aid to religion or to religious institutions. Rather, it has attempted to devise a formula that would help identify the kind and degree of aid that is permitted or forbidden by the Establishment Clause. Until 1970, the test for compliance with the Clause was whether there "was a secular legislative purpose and primary effect that neither advances nor inhibits religion . . ."; given a secular purpose, what is "the primary effect of the enactment?" *Abington School District* v. *Schempp*; *Board of Education* v. *Allen*. In 1970, a third element surfaced—whether there is "an ⊥**822** excessive government entanglement with religion." *Walz* v. *Tax Commission*. That element was not fatal to real property tax exemptions for church property but proved to be the crucial element in *Lemon* v. *Kurtzman* where the Court struck down the efforts by the States of Pennsylvania and Rhode Island to stave off financial disaster for their parochial school systems, the saving of which each of these States deemed important to the public interest. In accordance with one formula or the other, the laws in question furnished part of the cost incurred by private schools in furnishing secular education to substantial segments of the children in those States. Conceding a valid secular purpose and not reaching the question of primary effect, the Court concluded that the laws excessively, and therefore fatally, entangled the State with religion. What appeared to be an insoluble dilemma for the States, however, proved no insuperable barrier to the Federal Government in aiding sectarian institutions of higher learning by direct grants for specified facilities, *Tilton* v. *Richardson*. And *Hunt* v. *McNair*, decided this day, evidences the difficulty in perceiving when the State's involvement with religion passes the peril point.

But whatever may be the weight and contours of entanglement as a separate constitutional criterion, it is of remote relevance in the case before us with respect to the validity of tuition grants or tax credits involving or requiring no relationships whatsoever between the State and any church or any church school. So also the Court concedes the State's genuine secular purpose underlying these statutes. It therefore necessarily arrives at the remaining consideration in the three-fold test which is apparently accepted from prior cases: Whether the law in question has "a primary effect that neither advances nor inhibits religion." *Abington School District* v. *Schempp*. While purporting to ⊥**823** accept the standard stated in this manner, the Court strikes down the New York maintenance law, and for the same reason invalidates the tuition grants, because its "effect, inevitably, is to subsidize and advance the religious mission of sectarian schools." But the test is one of "primary" effect, not *any* effect. The Court makes no attempt at that ultimate judgment necessarily entailed by the standard heretofore fashioned in our cases. Indeed, the Court merely invokes the statement in *Everson* v. *Board of Education* that no tax can be levied "to support any religious activities. . . ." But admittedly there was no tax levied here for the *purpose* of supporting religious activities; and the Court appears to accept those cases, including *Tilton*, that inevitably involved aid of some sort or in some amount to the religious activities of parochial schools. In those cases the judgment was that as long as the aid to the school could fairly be characterized as supporting the secular educational functions of the school, whatever support to religion resulted from this direct, *Tilton* v. *Richardson*, or indirect, *Everson* v. *School District*; *Board of Education* v. *Allen*; *Walz* v. *Tax Commission*; *Hunt* v. *McNair*, contribution to the school's overall budget was not violative of the primary effect test nor of the Establishment Clause.

There is no doubt here that Pennsylvania and New York have sought in the challenged laws to keep their parochial schools system alive and capable of providing adequate secular education to substantial numbers of students. This purpose satisfies the Court, even though to rescue schools that would otherwise fail will inevitably enable those schools to continue whatever religious functions they perform. By the same token, it seems to me, preserving the secular functions of these schools is the overriding consequence of these laws and the resulting, ⊥824 but incidental, benefit to religion should not invalidate them.

At the very least I would not strike down these statutes on their face. The Court's opinion emphasizes a particular kind of parochial school, one restricted to students of particular religious beliefs and conditioning attendance on religious study. Concededly, there are many parochial schools that do not impose such restrictions. Where they do not, it is even more difficult for me to understand why the primary effect of these statutes is to advance religion. I do not think it is and therefore dissent from the Court's judgment invalidating the challenged New York and Pennsylvania statutes.

The CHIEF JUSTICE and Mr. *Justice* REHNQUIST join this opinion insofar as it relates to the New York and Pennsylvania tuition grant statutes and the New York tax credit statute.

[Mr. Justice Rehnquist wrote an opinion, in which the Chief Justice and Mr. Justice White concurred, dissenting in part.]

MEEK v. PITTENGER

421 U.S. 349
ON APPEAL FROM THE UNITED STATES DISTRICT COURT FOR THE EASTERN DISTRICT OF PENNSYLVANIA
Argued February 19, 1975 — Decided May 19, 1975

⊥351 Mr. *Justice* STEWART announced the judgment of the Court and delivered the opinion of the Court (Parts I, II, IV, and V), together with an opinion (Part III), in which Mr. *Justice* BLACKMUN and Mr. *Justice* POWELL, joined.

This case requires us to determine once again whether a state law providing assistance to nonpublic, church-related, elementary and secondary schools is constitutional under the Establishment Clause of the First Amendment, made applicable to the States by the Fourteenth Amendment.

I

With the stated purpose of assuring that every school child in the Commonwealth will equitably share in the benefits of auxiliary services, textbooks, and instructional **⊥352** material provided free of charge to children attending public schools, the Pennsylvania General Assembly in 1972 added Acts 194 and 195 to the Pennsylvania Public School Code of 1949.

Act 194 authorizes the Commonwealth to provide "auxiliary services" to all children enrolled in nonpublic elementary and secondary schools meeting Pennsylvania's compulsory attendance requirements. "Auxiliary serv**⊥353**ices" include counseling, testing, and psychological services, speech and hearing therapy, teaching and related services for exceptional children, for remedial students, and for the educationally disadvantaged, "and such other secular, neutral, nonideological services as are of benefit to nonpublic school children and are presently or hereafter provided for public schoolchildren of the Commonwealth." Act 194 specifies that the teaching and services are to be provided in the nonpublic schools themselves by personnel drawn from the appropriate "intermediate unit," part of the public school system of the Commonwealth established to provide special services to local school districts.

Act 195 authorizes the State Secretary of Education, either directly or through the intermediate units, to lend textbooks without charge to children attending nonpublic elementary and secondary schools that meet the Common**⊥354**wealth's compulsory attendance requirements. The books that may be lent are limited to those "which are acceptable for use in any public, elementary, or secondary school of the Commonwealth."

Act 195 also authorizes the Secretary of Education, pursuant to requests from the appropriate nonpublic school officials, to lend directly to the nonpublic schools "instructional materials and equipment, useful to the education" of nonpublic school children. "Instructional **⊥355** materials" are defined to include periodicals, photographs, maps, charts, sound recordings, films, "or any other printed and published materials of a similar nature." "Instructional equipment," as defined by the Act, includes projection equipment, recording equipment, and laboratory equipment.

On February 7, 1973, three individuals and four organizations filed a complaint in the District Court for the **⊥356** Eastern District of Pennsylvania challenging the constitutionality of Act 194 and Act 195, and requesting an injunction prohibiting the expenditure of any funds under either statute. The complaint alleged that each Act "is a law respecting an establishment of religion in violation of the First Amendment" because each Act "authorizes and directs payments to or use of books, materials and equipment in schools which (1) are controlled by churches or religious organizations, (2) have as their purpose the teaching, propagation and promotion of a particular religious faith, (3) conduct their operations, curriculums and programs to fulfill that purpose, (4) impose religious restrictions on admissions, (5) require attendance at instruction in theology and religious doctrine, (6) require attendance at or participation in religious worship, (7) are an integral part of the religious mission of the sponsoring church, (8) have as a substantial or dominant purpose the inculcation of religious values, (9) impose religious restrictions on faculty appointments, and (10) impose religious restrictions on what the faculty may teach." The Secretary of Education and the Treasurer of the Commonwealth were named as the defendants.

⊥**357** A three-judge court was convened. After an evidentiary hearing, the court entered its final judgment. In that judgment the court unanimously upheld the constitutionality of the textbook loan program authorized by Act 195. By a divided vote the court also upheld the constitutionality of Act 194's provision of auxiliary services to children in nonpublic elementary and secondary schools and Act 195's authorization of loans of instructional material directly to nonpublic elementary and secondary schools. The court unanimously invalidated that portion of Act 195 authorizing the expenditure of Commonwealth funds for the purchase of instructional equipment for loan to nonpublic schools, but only to the extent that the provision allowed the loan of equipment "which from its nature can be diverted to religious purposes." The court gave as examples projection and recording equipment. By a vote of 2-1, the court upheld this provision of Act 195 insofar as it authorizes the loan of instructional equipment that cannot be readily diverted to religious uses.

Except with respect to that provision of Act 195 which permits loan of instructional equipment capable of diversion, therefore, the plaintiffs' request for preliminary and final injunctive relief was denied. The plaintiffs (hereinafter the appellants) appealed directly to this Court. We noted probable jurisdiction.

II

⊥**358** In judging the constitutionality of the various forms of assistance authorized by Acts 194 and 195, the District Court applied the three-part test that has been clearly stated, if not easily applied, by this Court in recent Establishment Clause cases. First, the statute must have a secular legislative purpose. Second, it must have a "primary effect" that neither advances nor inhibits religion. Third, the statute and its administration must avoid excessive government entanglement with religion.

These tests constitute a convenient, accurate distillation of this Court's efforts over the past decades to evaluate a wide range of governmental action challenged as violative of the constitutional prohibition against laws "respecting an establishment of religion," and thus provide the proper framework of analysis for the issues presented in the case before us. It is well to emphasize, ⊥**359** however, that the tests must not be viewed as setting the precise limits to the necessary constitutional inquiry, but serve only as guidelines with which to identify instances in which the objectives of the Establishment Clause have been impaired.

Primary among the evils against which the Establishment Clause protects "have been sponsorship, financial support, and active involvement of the sovereign in religious activities." The Court has broadly stated that "[n]o tax in any amount, large or small, can be levied to support any religious activities or institutions, whatever they may be called, or whatever form they may adopt to teach or practice religion." But it is clear that not all legislative programs that provide indirect or incidental benefit to a religious institution are prohibited by the Constitution. "The problem, like many problems in constitutional law, is one of degree."

III

The District Court held that the textbook loan provisions of Act 195 are constitutionally indistinguishable from the New York textbook loan program upheld in *Board of Education* v. *Allen*. We agree.

Approval of New York's textbook loan program in the *Allen* case was based primarily on this Court's earlier decision in *Everson* v. *Board of Education*, holding that the constitutional prohibition against laws "respect⊥**360**ing an establishment of religion" did not prevent "New Jersey from spending tax-raised funds to pay the bus fares of parochial school pupils as a part of a general program under which it pays the fares of pupils attending public and other schools." Similarly, the Court in *Allen* found that the New York textbook law "merely makes available to all children the benefits of a general program to lend school books free of charge. Books are furnished at the request of the pupil and ownership remains, at least technically, in the State. Thus no funds or books are furnished to parochial schools, and the financial benefit is to parents and children, not to schools." The Court conceded that provision of free textbooks might make it "more likely that some children choose to attend a sectarian school, but that was true of the state-paid bus fares in *Everson* and does not alone demonstrate an unconstitutional degree of support for a religious institution."

Like the New York program, the textbook provisions of Act 195 extend to all schoolchildren the benefits of Pennsylvania's well-established policy of lending textbooks free of charge to elementary and secondary school students. ⊥**361** As in *Allen*, Act 195 provides that the textbooks are to be lent directly to the student, not to the nonpublic school itself although, again as in *Allen*, the administrative practice is to have student requests for the books filed initially with the nonpublic school and to have the school authorities prepare collective summaries of these requests which they forward to the appropriate public officials. Thus, the financial benefit of Pennsylvania's textbook program, like New York's, is to parents and children, not to the nonpublic schools.

Under New York law the books that could be lent were limited to textbooks "which are designated for use in any public, elementary or secondary schools of the state or are approved by any boards of education, trustees, or other school authorities." The law was construed by the New York Court of Appeals to apply solely to secular textbooks. Act 195 similarly limits the books that may be lent to "textbooks which are acceptable for use in any public, elementary, or secondary school of the Commonwealth." Moreover, the record in the case ⊥**362** before us, like the record in *Allen*, contains no suggestion that religious textbooks will be lent or that the books provided will be used for anything other than purely secular purposes.

In sum, the textbook loan provisions of Act 195 are in every material respect identical to the loan program approved in *Allen*. Pennsylvania, like New York, "merely makes available to all children the benefits of a general program to lend school books free of charge." As such, those provisions of Act 195 do not offend the constitutional prohibition against laws "respecting an establishment of religion."

IV

Although textbooks are lent only to students, Act 195 authorizes the loan of instructional material and equip- ⊥363 ment directly to qualifying nonpublic elementary and secondary schools in the Commonwealth. The appellants assert that such direct aid to Pennsylvania's nonpublic schools, including church-related institutions, constitutes an impermissible establishment of religion.

Act 195 is accompanied by legislative findings that the welfare of the Commonwealth requires that present and future generations of schoolchildren be assured ample opportunity to develop their intellectual capacities. Act 195 is intended to further that objective by extending the benefits of free educational aids to every schoolchild in the Commonwealth, including nonpublic school students who comprise approximately one quarter of the schoolchildren in Pennsylvania. We accept the legitimacy of this secular legislative purpose. But we agree with the appellants that the direct loan of instructional material and equipment has the unconstitutional primary effect of advancing religion because of the predominantly religious character of the schools benefiting from the Act.

The only requirement imposed on nonpublic schools to qualify for loans of instructional material and equipment is that they satisfy the Commonwealth's compulsory attendance law by providing, in the English language, the subjects and activities prescribed by the standards of the State Board of Education. Commonwealth officials, as a matter of ⊥364 state policy, do not inquire into the religious characteristics, if any, of the nonpublic schools requesting aid pursuant to Act 195. The Coordinator of Nonpublic School Services, the chief administrator of Acts 194 and 195, testified that a school would not be barred from receiving loans of instructional material and equipment even though its dominant purpose was the inculcation of religious values, even if it imposed religious restrictions on admissions or on faculty appointments, and even if it required attendance at classes in theology or at religious services. In fact, of the 1,320 nonpublic schools in Pennsylvania that comply with the requirements of the compulsory attendance law and thus qualify for aid under Act 195, more than 75% are church-related or religiously affiliated educational institutions. Thus, the primary beneficiaries of Act 195's instructional material and equipment loan provisions, like the beneficiaries of the "secular educational services" reimbursement program considered in *Lemon* v. *Kurtzman*, and the parent tuition reimbursement plan considered in *Sloan* v. *Lemon*, are nonpublic schools with a predominant sectarian character.

It is, of course, true that as part of general legislation made available to all students, a State may include church-related schools in programs providing bus transportation, school lunches, and public health facilities—secular and nonideological services unrelated to the primary, religious-oriented educational function of the sectarian school. The indirect and incidental benefits to church-related schools from those programs do not offend the constitutional prohibition against establish- ⊥365 ment of religion. But the massive aid provided the church-related nonpublic schools of Pennsylvania by Act 195 is neither indirect nor incidental.

For the 1972-1973 school year the Commonwealth authorized just under $12 million of direct aid to the predominantly church-related nonpublic schools of Pennsylvania through the loan of instructional material and equipment pursuant to Act 195. To be sure, the material and equipment that are the subjects of the loan—maps, charts, and laboratory equipment, for example—are "self-polic[ing], in that starting as secular, nonideological and neutral, they will not change in use." But faced with the substantial amounts of direct support authorized by Act 195, it would simply ignore reality to attempt to separate secular educational functions from the predominantly religious role performed by many of Pennsylvania's church-related elementary and secondary schools and to then characterize Act 195 as channeling aid to the secular without providing direct aid to the sectarian. Even ⊥366 though earmarked for secular purposes, "when it flows to an institution in which religion is so pervasive that a substantial portion of its functions are subsumed in the religious mission," state aid has the impermissible primary effect of advancing religion. *Hunt* v. *McNair*.

The church-related elementary and secondary schools that are the primary beneficiaries of Act 195's instructional material and equipment loans typify such religion-pervasive institutions. The very purpose of many of those schools is to provide an integrated secular and religious education; the teaching process is, to a large extent, devoted to the inculcation of religious values and belief. Substantial aid to the educational function of such schools, accordingly, necessarily results in aid to the sectarian school enterprise as a whole. "[T]he secular education those schools provide goes hand in hand with the religious mission that is the only reason for the schools' existence. Within the institution, the two are inextricably intertwined." *Lemon* v. *Kurtzman*. For this reason, Act 195's direct aid to Pennsylvania's predominantly church-related, nonpublic elementary and secondary schools, even though ostensibly limited to wholly neutral, secular instructional material and equipment, inescapably results in the direct and substantial advancement of religious activity and thus constitutes an impermissible establishment of religion.

V

⊥367 Unlike Act 195, which provides only for the loan of teaching material and equipment, Act 194 authorizes the Secretary of Education, through the intermediate units, to supply professional staff, as well as supportive materials, equipment, and personnel, to the nonpublic schools of the Commonwealth. The "auxiliary services" authorized by Act 194—remedial and accelerated instruction, guidance counseling and testing, speech and hearing services—are provided directly to nonpublic schoolchildren with the appropriate special need. But the services are provided only on the nonpublic school premises, and only when "requested by nonpublic school representatives."

The legislative findings accompanying Act 194 are virtually identical to those in Act 195: Act 194 is intended to assure full development of the intellectual capacities of the children of Pennsylvania by extending the bene⊥368fits of free auxiliary services to all students in the Commonwealth. The appellants concede the validity of this secular legislative purpose. Nonetheless, they argue that Act 194 constitutes an impermissible establishment of religion because the auxiliary services are provided on the premises of predominantly church-related schools.

In rejecting the appellants' argument, the District Court emphasized that "auxiliary services" are provided directly to the children involved and are expressly limited to those services which are secular, neutral, and nonideological. The court also noted that the instruction and counseling in question served only to supplement the basic, normal educational offerings of the qualifying nonpublic schools. Any benefits to church-related schools that may result from the provision of such services, the District Court concluded, are merely incidental and indirect, and thus not impermissible. The court also held that no continuing supervision of the personnel providing auxiliary services would be necessary to establish that Act 194's secular limitations were observed or to guarantee that a member of the auxiliary services staff had not "succumb[ed] to sectarianization of his or her professional work."

⊥369 We need not decide whether substantial state expenditures to enrich the curricula of church-related elementary and secondary schools, like the expenditure of state funds to support the basic educational program of those schools, necessarily results in the direct and substantial advancement of religious activity. For decisions of this Court make clear that the District Court erred in relying entirely on the good faith and professionalism of the secular teachers and counselors functioning in church-related schools to ensure that a strictly nonideological posture is maintained.

In *Earley* v. *DiCenso*, a companion case to *Lemon* v. *Kurtzman*, the Court invalidated a Rhode Island statute authorizing salary supplements for teachers of secular subjects in nonpublic schools. The Court expressly rejected the proposition, relied upon by the District Court in the case before us, that it was sufficient for the State to assume that teachers in church-related schools would succeed in segregating their religious beliefs from the secular educational duties. "We need not and do not assume that teachers in parochial schools will be guilty of bad faith or any conscious design to evade the limitations imposed by the statute and the First Amendment. . . .

"But the potential for impermissible fostering of religion is present. . . . The State must be certain, given the Religion Clauses, that subsidized teachers do not inculcate religion. . . .

⊥370 "A comprehensive, discriminating, and continuing state surveillance will inevitably be required to ensure that these restrictions are obeyed and the First Amendment otherwise respected. . . ."

The prophylactic contacts required to ensure that teachers play a strictly nonideological role, the Court held, necessarily give rise to a constitutionally intolerable degree of entanglement between church and state. The same excessive entanglement would be required for Pennsylvania to be "certain," as it must be, that Act 194 personnel do not advance the religious mission of the church-related schools in which they serve.

That Act 194 authorizes state-funding of teachers only for remedial and exceptional students, and not for normal students participating in the core curriculum, does not distinguish this case from *Earley* v. *DiCenso* and *Lemon* v. *Kurtzman*. Whether the subject is "remedial reading," "advanced reading," or simply "reading," a teacher remains a teacher, and the danger that religious doctrine will become intertwined with secular instruction persists. The likelihood of inadvertent fostering of re⊥371ligion may be less in a remedial arithmetic class than in a medieval history seminar, but a diminished probability of impermissible conduct is not sufficient: "The State must be certain, given the Religion Clauses, that subsidized teachers do not inculcate religion." And a state-subsidized guidance counselor is surely as likely as a state-subsidized chemistry teacher to fail on occasion to separate religious instruction and the advancement of religious beliefs from his secular educational responsibilities.

The fact that the teachers and counselors providing auxiliary services are employees of the public intermediate unit, rather than of the church-related schools in which they work, does not substantially eliminate the need for continuing surveillance. To be sure, auxiliary services personnel, because not employed by the nonpublic schools, are not directly subject to the discipline of a religious authority. But they are performing important educational services in schools in which education is an integral part of the dominant sectarian mission and in which an atmosphere dedicated to the advancement of religious belief is constantly maintained. ⊥372 The potential for impermissible fostering of religion under these circumstances, although somewhat reduced, is nonetheless present. To be certain that auxiliary teachers remain religiously neutral, as the Constitution demands, the State would have to impose limitations on the activities of auxiliary personnel and then engage in some form of continuing surveillance to ensure that those restrictions were being followed.

In addition, Act 194, like the statutes considered in *Lemon* v. *Kurtzman* and *Committee for Public Education & Religious Liberty* v. *Nyquist*, creates a serious potential for divisive conflict over the issue of aid to religion—"entanglement in the broader sense of continuing political strife." *Committee for Public Education & Religious Liberty* v. *Nyquist*. The recurrent nature of the appropriation process guarantees annual reconsideration of Act 194 and the prospect of repeated confrontation between proponents and opponents of the auxiliary services program. The Act thus provides successive opportunities for political fragmentation and division along religious lines, one of the principal evils against which the Establishment Clause was intended to protect. This potential for political entanglement, together with the administrative entanglement which would be necessary to ensure that auxiliary services personnel remain strictly neutral and nonideological when functioning in church-related schools, compels the conclusion that Act 194 violates the constitutional prohibition against laws "respecting an establishment of religion."

⊥**373** The judgment of the District Court as to Act 194 is reversed; its judgment as to the textbook provisions of Act 195 is affirmed, but as to that Act's other provisions now before us its judgment is reversed.

It is so ordered.

Mr. *Justice* BRENNAN, with whom Mr. *Justice* DOUGLAS and Mr. *Justice* MARSHALL join, concurring and dissenting.

I join in the reversal of the District Court's judgment insofar as that judgment upheld the constitutionality of Act 194 and the provisions of Act 195 respecting instructional materials and equipment, but dissent from Part III and the affirmance of the judgment upholding the constitutionality of the textbook provisions of Act 195.

A three-factor test by which to determine the compatibility with the Establishment Clause of state subsidies of sectarian educational institutions has evolved over 50 years of this Court's stewardship in the field. The law in question must, first, reflect a clearly secular legislative purpose, second, have a primary effect that neither ⊥**374** advances nor inhibits religion, and, third, avoid excessive government entanglement with religion. But four years ago, the Court, albeit without express recognition of the fact, added a significant fourth factor to the test: "A broader basis of entanglement of yet a different character is presented by the divisive political potential of these state programs." *Lemon* v. *Kurtzman*. The evaluation of this factor in determining compatibility of a state subsidy law with the Establishment Clause is essential, said the Court, because: "In a community where . . . a large number of pupils are served by church-related schools, it can be assumed that state assistance will entail considerable political activity. Partisans of parochial schools, understandably concerned with rising costs and sincerely dedicated to both the religious and secular educational missions of their schools, will inevitably champion this cause and promote political action to achieve their goals. Those who oppose state aid, whether for constitutional, religious, or fiscal reasons, will inevitably respond and employ all the usual political techniques to prevail. Candidates will be forced to declare and voters to choose. It would be unrealistic to ignore the fact that many people confronted with issues of this kind will find their votes aligned with their faith.

"Ordinary political debate and division, however vigorous or even partisan, are normal and healthy manifestations of our democratic system of government, *but political division along religious lines was one of the principal evils against which the First Amendment was intended to protect*. . . . The potential divisiveness of such conflict is a threat to the normal political process. . . . It conflicts with our whole history and tradition to permit questions of ⊥**375** the Religion Clauses to assume such importance in our legislatures and in our elections that they could divert attention from the myriad issues and problems that confront every level of government. . . .

". . . *Here we are confronted with successive and very likely permanent annual appropriations that benefit relatively few religious groups. Political fragmentation and divisiveness on religious lines are thus likely to be intensified.*

"*The potential for political divisiveness related to religious belief and practice is aggravated . . . by the need for continuing annual appropriations and the likelihood of larger and larger demands as costs and populations grow. . . .*" (Emphasis added.)

This factor was key in *Kurtzman's* determination that Pennsylvania and Rhode Island statutes providing state aid to church-related elementary and secondary schools violated the Establishment Clause. The Pennsylvania statute provided financial support by way of reimbursement for the cost of teachers' salaries, textbooks, and instructional materials in specified secular subjects. The Rhode Island statute provided a program under which the State paid directly to teachers in nonpublic schools a supplement of 15% of their annual salary.

Committee for Public Education v. *Nyquist*, decided two years later, emphasized the importance to be attached by judges to this fourth factor: "One factor of recurring significance in this weighing process is the potentially divisive political effect of an aid program." The Court held that the factor applied "with peculiar force to the New York statute now before us." That statute created three aid programs. The first provided for direct money grants to be used for maintenance and ⊥**376** repair of facilities to ensure the students' welfare, health, and safety. The second established a tuition reimbursement plan for parents of children attending nonpublic elementary schools. The third provided tax relief for parents not qualifying for tuition reimbursements. Stating that "while the prospect of [political] divisiveness may not alone warrant the invalidation of state laws that otherwise survive the careful scrutiny required by the decisions of this Court, it is certainly a 'warning signal' not to be ignored," the Court held that "in light of all relevant considerations," each of the New York programs had a "'primary effect that advances religion' and offends the constitutional prohibition against laws 'respecting an establishment of religion.'"

The Court today also relies on the factor of divisive political potential but only as support for its holding that Act 194 is an unconstitutional law "respecting an establishment of religion," stating: "In addition, Act 194, like the statutes considered in *[Kurtzman* and *Nyquist]* creates a serious potential for divisive conflict over the issue of aid to religion— 'entanglement in the broader sense of political strife.' . . . The recurrent nature of the appropriation process guarantees annual reconsideration of Act 194 and the prospect of repeated confrontation between proponents and opponents of the auxiliary services program. The Act thus provides successive opportunities for political fragmentation and division along religious lines, one of the principal evils against which the Establishment Clause was intended to protect."

Contrary to the plain and explicit teaching of *Kurtzman* and *Nyquist*, however, and inconsistently with its own treatment of Act 194, the Court, in considering ⊥**377** the constitutionality of Act 195 says not a single word about the political divisiveness factor in Part III of the opinion upholding the textbook loan program created by that Act, and makes only a passing footnote reference to the factor, without evaluation of its bearing on the result, in holding that Act 195's program for loans of instructional materials and equipment constitutes Act 195 in that respect "direct aid to Pennsylvania's predominantly church-related, nonpublic elementary and secondary schools, even though ostensibly limited to wholly neutral, secular instructional material and equipment, [that] inescapably results in the direct and substantial advancement of religious activity . . . and thus constitutes an impermissible establishment of religion."

I recognize that the plurality was on the horns of a dilemma. The plurality notes that the total 1972-1973 appropriation under Act 195 was $16,660,000, of which $4,670,000 was appropriated to finance the textbook program. The plurality notes further that "aid programs like Act 195 . . . are dependent on continuing annual appropriations . . . which generate increasing demands as costs and population grow . . . ," and, indeed, that the total Act 195 appropriation was increased $900,000 to $17,560,000 for the 1973-1974 school year. Plainly then, as in *Nyquist*, the political divisiveness factor applies "with peculiar force to the . . . statute now before us." But to comply with *Nyquist*, as is required, the plurality obviously must attach determinative weight to the factor as respects both the textbook loan and instructional materials and equipment loan provisions, since both are inextricably intertwined in Act 195. For in light of the massive appropriations in⊥**378**volved, the plurality would be hard put to explain how the factor weighs determinatively against the validity of the instructional materials loan provisions, and not also against the validity of the textbook loan provisions. The plurality therefore would extricate itself from the horns of the dilemma by simply ignoring the factor in the weighing process.

But however much this evasion may be tolerable in the case of the instructional materials loan provisions, since these are invalidated on other grounds, responsibility for evaluating the weight to be accorded the factor cannot be evaded, in the case of the textbook loan provisions, by reliance, as the plurality does, upon its agreement with the District Court that the textbook loan program is indistinguishable from the New York textbook loan program upheld in *Board of Education* v. *Allen*. For *Allen*, which I joined, was decided before *Kurtzman* ordained that the political divisiveness factor must be involved in the weighing process, and understandably neither the parties to *Allen* nor the Court addressed that factor in that case. But whether or not *Allen* can withstand overruling in light of *Kurtzman* and *Nyquist*, which I question, it is clear that *Kurtzman*—which, I repeat, applied the factor to a Pennsylvania program that included reimbursement for the cost of textbooks—requires that the Court weigh the factor in the instant case. Further, giving the factor the weight that *Kurtzman* and *Nyquist* require, compels, in my view ⊥**379** the conclusion that the textbook loan program of Act 195, equally with the program for loan of instructional materials and equipment, violates the Establishment Clause. The plurality's answer is that a difference in result is justified because Act 195 distinguishes between recipients of the loans: textbooks are lent to students, while instructional material and equipment are lent directly to the schools. That answer will not withstand analysis.

First, it is pure fantasy to treat the textbook program as a loan to students. It is true that, like the New York statute in *Allen*, Act 195 in terms talks of loans by the State of acceptable secular textbooks directly to students attending nonpublic schools. But even the plurality acknowledges that "the administrative practice is to have student requests for the books filed initially with the nonpublic school and to have the school authorities prepare collective summaries of these requests which they forward to the appropriate public officials. . . ." Further, "the nonpublic schools are permitted to store on their premises the textbooks being lent to students." Even if these practices were also followed under the New York statute, the regulations implementing Act 195 make clear, as the record in *Allen* did not, that the nonpublic school in Pennsylvania is something more than a conduit between the State and pupil. The Commonwealth has promulgated "Guidelines for the Administration of Acts 194 and 195" to implement the statutes. These regulations, unlike those upheld in *Allen*, constitute a much more intrusive and detailed involvement of the State and its processes into the administration of nonpublic schools. The whole business is handled by the schools and public authorities and neither parents nor students have a say. The guidelines make crystal clear that the nonpublic school, not its pupils, is the motivating force behind the textbook ⊥380 loan, and that virtually the entire loan transaction is to be, and is in fact, conducted between officials of the nonpublic school, on the one hand, and officers of the state, on the other.

For example, § 4.3 of the Guidelines requires that on or before March 1 of each year, an official of each nonpublic school submit to the Pennsylvania Department of Education a loan request for the desired textbooks. The requests must be submitted on standardized forms "distributed by the Department of Education . . . to each nonpublic school or the appropriate chief administrator." Section 4.6 of the Guidelines provides that the "[t]extbooks requested will be shipped directly to the appropriate nonpublic school." Thus, although in terms the form provided by the Commonwealth for parents of nonpublic school students states that the parents of these pupils request the loan of textbooks directly from the State, the form is not returnable to the State, but to the nonpublic school, which tabulates the requests and submits its total to the State. Then, after the submission by the nonpublic school is approved by the appropriate state official, the books are transported not to the children whose parents ostensibly made the request, but directly to the nonpublic school, where they are physically retained when not in use in the classroom.

Indeed, the Guidelines make no attempt to mask the true nature of the loan transaction. In explicit words § 4.10 describes the transaction: "Textbooks *loaned to the nonpublic schools:* (a) shall be maintained on an inventory by the nonpublic school." (Emphasis added.) Section 4.11 provides: "It is presumed that textbooks on *loan to nonpublic schools* after a period of time will be lost, missing, obsolete or worn out. This information should be communicated to the Department of Education. After a period of six years, textbooks shall be ⊥381 declared unserviceable and the disposal of such shall be at the discretion of the Secretary of Education." (Emphasis added.) Thus, the loan of the texts is treated by the regulations as what it in fact is: a loan from the State directly to the nonpublic school. Finally, § 4.12 completely removes any possible doubt. It provides: "The nonpublic school or the agency which it is a member shall be responsible for maintaining files on future certificates of requests from parents of children for all textbook materials loaned to them under this Act. The file must be open to inspection for the appropriate authority. A letter certifying the certificates on file shall accompany all loan requests."

Plainly, then, whatever may have been the case under the New York statute sustained in *Allen*, the loan ostensibly to students is, under Act 195, a loan in fact to the schools. In this regard, it should be observed that sophisticated attempts to avoid the Constitution are just as invalid as simple-minded ones.

Second, in any event, *Allen* itself made clear that, far from providing a *per se* immunity from examination of the substance of the State's program, even if the fact were, and it is not, that textbooks are loaned to the children rather than to the schools, that is only one among the factors to be weighed in determining the compatibility of the program with the Establishment Clause. And, clearly, in the context of application of the factor of political divisiveness, it is wholly irrelevant whether the loan is to the children or to the school. A divisive political potential exists because aid programs, like Act 195, are dependent on continuing ⊥382 annual appropriations, and Act 195's textbook loan program, even if we accepted it as a form of loans to students, involves increasingly massive sums now approaching $5,000,000 annually. It would blind reality to treat massive aid to nonpublic schools, under the guise of loans to the students, as not creating "a serious potential for divisive conflict over the issue of aid to religion." The focus of the textbook loan program in terms of massive financial support for religious schools that creates the potential divisiveness is no less real than it is in the case of Act 195's instructional materials provisions and Act 194's invalidated program for auxiliary services. Act 195 is intended solely as a financial aid program to relieve the desperate financial plight of nonpublic, primarily parochial, schools. The plurality suggests that it is immaterial that Act 195 has that cast, in contrast with New York's statute in *Allen* which authorized loans to students attending both public and nonpublic schools. On the contrary, Act 195's limitation of its financial support to aid to nonpublic school children exacerbates the potential for political divisive⊥383ness. "In this situation, where the underlying issue is the deeply emotional one of Church-State relationships, the potential for seriously divisive political consequences needs no elaboration." *Committee for Public Education* v. *Nyquist*.

Finally, the textbook loan provisions of Act 195, even if ostensibly limiting loans to nonpublic school children, violate the Establishment Clause for reasons independent of the political divisiveness factor. As I have said, unlike the New York statute in *Allen* which extended assistance to all students, whether attending public or nonpublic schools, Act 195 extends textbook assistance only to a special class of students, children who attend nonpublic schools which are, as the plurality notes, primarily religiously oriented. The Act in that respect contains the same fatal defect as the New York statute held violative of the Establishment Clause in *Public Funds* v. *Marburger*. The statute there involved was N. J. Stat. Ann. § 18A:58-63 which furnished state aid, in amounts up to $10 for elementary school students and up to $20 for high school students, to the parents of nonpublic school students as reimbursement for the cost of ⊥384 "secular, non-ideological textbooks, instructional materials and supplies." We affirmed the holding of the three-judge court that "because the language of [the statute] limits the assistance provided therein only to parents of children who attend nonpublic, predominately religiously affiliated schools and not to parents of all school children, we are satisfied that its primary effect is to advance religion and that it is thereby unconstitutional." *Marburger* thus establishes that the plurality's reliance today upon *Allen* is clearly misplaced.

Indeed, that reliance is also misplaced in light of its own holding today invalidating the provisions of Act 195 respecting the loan of instructional materials and equipment. I have no doubt that such materials and equipment are tools that substantially enhance the quality of the secular education provided by the religiously oriented schools. But surely the heart tools of that education are the textbooks that are prescribed for use and kept at the schools, albeit formally at the request of the students. Thus, what the Court says of the instructional materials and equipment, may be said perhaps even more accurately of the textbooks: "But faced with the substantial amounts of direct support authorized by Act 195, it would simply ignore reality to attempt to separate secular educational functions from the predominantly religious role performed by many of Pennsylvania's church-related elementary and secondary schools and to then characterize Act 195 as channeling aid to the secular without providing direct aid to the sectarian. Even though earmarked for secular purposes, 'when it flows to an institution in which religion is so pervasive that a substantial portion of its functions are subsumed in the religious mission,' state aid has the impermissible primary effect of advancing religion."

In sum, I join the Court's opinion as to Parts I, II, IV, **⊥385** and V, except that I would go further in Part IV and rest the invalidation of the provisions of Act 195 for loans of instructional materials and equipment also upon the political divisiveness factor. I dissent from part III.

Mr. *Chief Justice* BURGER, concurring in the judgment in part and dissenting in part.

I agree with the Court only insofar as it affirms the judgment of the District Court. My limited agreement with the Court as to this action leads me, however, to agree generally with the views expressed by Mr. *Justice* REHNQUIST and Mr. *Justice* WHITE in regard to the other programs under review. I especially find it difficult to accept the Court's extravagant suggestion of potential entanglement which it finds in the "auxiliary services" program of Pa. Stat. 194. Here, the Court's holding, it seems to me, goes beyond any prior holdings of this Court and, indeed, conflicts with our holdings in *Board of Education* v. *Allen* and *Lemon* v. *Kurtzman*. There is absolutely no support in this record or, for that matter, in ordinary human experience to support the concern some see with respect to the "dangers" lurking in extending common, nonsectarian tools of the education process—especially remedial tools—to students in private schools. As I noted in my separate opinion in *Committee for Public Education* v. *Nyquist*, the "fundamental principle which I see running through our prior decisions in this difficult and sensitive field of law . . . is premised more on experience and history than on logic." Certainly, there is no basis in "experience and history" to conclude that a State's attempt to provide—through the services of its own state-selected professionals—the remedial assistance necessary for all its children poses the same potential for **⊥386** unnecessary administrative entanglement or divisive political confrontation which concerned the Court in *Lemon* v. *Kurtzman*. Indeed, I see at least as much potential for divisive political debate in opposition to the crabbed attitude the Court shows in this case.

If the consequence of the Court's holding operated only to penalize *institutions* with a religious affiliation, the result would be grievous enough; nothing in the Religion Clauses of the First Amendment permits governmental power to discriminate *against* or affirmatively stifle religions or religious activity. But this holding does more: it penalizes *children*—children who have the misfortune to have to cope with the learning process under extraordinarily heavy physical and psychological burdens, for the most part congenital. This penalty strikes them not because of any act of theirs but because of their parents' choice of religious exercise. This, as Mr. *Justice* REHNQUIST effectively demonstrates, totally turns its back on what Mr. *Justice* DOUGLAS wrote for the Court in *Zorach* v. *Clauson*, particularly that: "When the state encourages religious instruction or cooperates with religious authorities by adjusting the schedule of public events to sectarian needs, it follows the best of our traditions. For it then respects the religious nature of our people and accommodates the public service to the spiritual needs."

To hold, as the Court now does, that the Constitution permits the States to give special assistance to some of its children whose handicaps prevent their deriving the benefit normally anticipated from the education required to become a productive member of society and, at the same time, to deny those benefits to other children *only because* they attend a Lutheran, Catholic or other church-**⊥387**sponsored school does not simply tilt the Constitution against religion; it literally turns the Religion Clause on its head. As Mr. *Justice* DOUGLAS said for the Court in *Zorach*, this is ". . . to find in the Constitution a requirement that the government show a callous indifference to religious groups. That would be preferring those who believe in no religion over those who do believe."

The melancholy consequence of what the Court does today is to force the parent to choose between the "free exercise" of a religious belief by opting for a sectarian education for his child or to forego the opportunity for his child to learn to cope with—or overcome—serious congenital learning handicaps, through remedial assistance financed by his taxes. Affluent parents, by employing private teaching specialists, will be able to cope with this denial of equal protection, which is, for me, a gross violation of Fourteenth Amendment rights, but all others will be forced to make a choice between their judgment as to their children's spiritual needs and their temporal need for special remedial learning assistance. One can only hope that, at some future date, the Court will come to a more enlightened and tolerant view of the First Amendment's guarantee of free exercise of religion, thus eliminating the denial of equal protection to children in church-sponsored schools, and take a more realistic view that carefully limited aid to children is not a step toward establishing a state religion—at least while this Court sits.

Mr. *Justice* REHNQUIST, with whom Mr. *Justice* WHITE joins, concurring in the judgment in part and dissenting in part.

Substantially for the reasons set forth in my dissent and those of *The* CHIEF JUSTICE and Mr. *Justice* ⊥**388** WHITE in *Committee for Public Education & Religious Liberty* v. *Nyquist*, and *Sloan* v. *Lemon*, I would affirm the judgment of the District Court.

Two Acts of the Pennsylvania Legislature are under attack in this case. Act 195 includes a program that provides for the loan of textbooks free of charge to elementary and secondary school students attending nonpublic schools, just as other provisions of Pennsylvania law provide similar benefits to children attending public schools. I agree with the Court that this program is constitutionally indistinguishable from the New York textbook loan program upheld in *Board of Education* v. *Allen* and on the authority of that case I join the judgment of the Court insofar as it upholds the textbook loan program.

The Court strikes down other provisions of Act 195 dealing with instructional materials and equipment because it finds that they have "the unconstitutional primary effect of advancing religion because of the predominantly religious character of the schools benefiting from the Act." This apparently follows from the high percentage of nonpublic schools that are "church-related or religiously affiliated educational institutions." The Court ⊥**389** thus again appears to follow "the unsupportable approach of measuring the 'effect' of a law by the percentage of" sectarian schools benefited. I find that approach to the "primary effect" branch of our three-pronged test no more satisfactory in the context of this instructional materials and equipment program than it was in the context of the tuition reimbursement and tax relief programs involved in *Nyquist* and *Sloan*.

One need look no further than to the majority opinion for a demonstration of the arbitrariness of the percentage approach to primary effect. In determining the constitutionality of the textbook loan program established by Act 195, the Court views the program in the context of the State's "well-established policy of lending textbooks free of charge to elementary and secondary school students." But when it comes time to consider the same Act's instructional materials and equipment program, which is not alleged to make available to private schools any materials and equipment that are not provided to public schools, the majority strikes down this program because more than 75% of the nonpublic schools are church-related or religiously affiliated.

If the number of sectarian schools were measured as a percentage of all schools, public and private, then no doubt the majority would conclude that the primary effect of the instructional materials and equipment program is not to advance religion. One looks in vain, ⊥**390** however, for an explanation of the majority's selection of the number of private schools as the denominator in its instructional materials and equipment calculations. The only apparent explanation might be that Act 195 applies only to private schools while different legislation provides equipment and materials to public schools. But surely this is not a satisfactory explanation, for the plurality tells us, in connection with its discussion of the textbook loan program, which is administered to the public schools through the same statutory provision that provides equipment and materials to the public schools, that "it is of no constitutional significance whether the general program is codified in one statute or two." We are left then with no explanation for the arbitrary course chosen.

The failure of the majority to justify the differing approaches to textbooks and instructional materials and equipment in the above respect is symptomatic of its failure even to attempt to distinguish the Pennsylvania textbook loan program, which it upholds, from the Pennsylvania instructional materials and equipment loan program, which it finds unconstitutional. One might expect that the distinction lies either in the nature of the tangible items being loaned or in the manner in which the programs are operated. But the majority concedes that "the material and equipment that are the subjects of the loan—maps, charts, and laboratory equipment, for example—are 'self-polic[ing], in that starting as secular, nonideo⊥**391**logical and neutral, they will not change in use.'" Nor can the fact that the school is the bailee be regarded as constitutionally determinative. In the textbook loan program upheld in *Allen*, the private schools were responsible for transmitting the book requests to the Board of Education and were permitted to store the loaned books on their premises. I fail to see how the instructional materials and equipment program can be distinguished in any significant respect. Under both programs "ownership remains, at least technically, in the State." Once it is conceded that no danger of diversion exists, it is difficult to articulate any principled basis upon which to distinguish the two Act 195 programs.

The Court eschews its primary effect analysis in striking down Act 194, and relies instead upon the proposition that the Act "give[s] rise to a constitutionally intolerable degree of entanglement between church and state." Acknowledging that Act 194 authorizes state financing "of teachers only for remedial and exceptional students, and not for normal students participating in the core curriculum," the Court nonetheless finds this case indistinguishable from *Lemon* v. *Kurtzman* and companion cases, in which salary supplement programs for core curriculum teachers were found unconstitutional. "[A] state-subsidized guidance counselor is surely as likely as a state-subsidized chemistry teacher to fail on occasion to separate religious instruction and the advancement of religious bodies from his secular educational responsibilities."

I find this portion of the Court's opinion deficient as ⊥**392** a matter of process and insupportable as a matter of law. The burden of proof ordinarily rests upon the plaintiff, but the Court's conclusion that the dangers presented by a state-subsidized guidance counselor are the same as those presented by a state-subsidized chemistry teacher is apparently no more than an *ex cathedra* pronouncement on the part of the Court, if one may use that term in a case such as this, since the District Court found the facts to be exactly the opposite—after consideration of stipulations of fact and an evidentiary hearing. "The Commonwealth, recognizing the logistical realities, provided for traveling therapists rather than traveling pupils. There is no evidence whatsoever that the presence of the therapists in the schools will involve them in the religious missions of the schools. . . . The notion that by setting foot inside a sectarian school a professional therapist or counselor will succumb to sectarianization of his or her professional work is not supported by any evidence."

The propensity of the Court to disregard findings of fact by district courts in Establishment Clause cases is at variance with the established division of responsibilities between trial and appellate courts in the federal system.

As a matter of constitutional law, the holding by the majority that this case is controlled by *Lemon* v. *Kurtzman* marks a significant *sub silentio* extension of that 1971 decision. In that case the Court struck down the Rhode Island salary supplement program, under which teachers employed by nonpublic schools could qualify for additional salary payments from the State in order to bring their salaries ⊥**393** more closely in line with the prevailing scale in public schools, and a Pennsylvania program authorizing direct reimbursement to nonpublic schools; in order to qualify, the teachers could teach only subjects that were offered in the public schools. The premise supporting the Court's conclusion that these programs "involve[d] excessive entanglement between government and religion" is found at 403 U.S., at 617: "We cannot ignore the danger that a teacher *under religious control and discipline* poses to the separation of the religious from the purely secular aspects of precollege education. The conflict of functions inheres in the situation." (Emphasis added.)

The auxiliary services program established by Act 194 differs from the programs struck down in *Lemon* in two important respects. First the opportunities for religious instruction through the auxiliary services program are greatly reduced because of the considerably more limited reach of the Act. Unlike the core curriculum instruction provided in the *Lemon* programs, "auxiliary services" are defined in Act 194 to embrace a narrow range of services: "'Auxiliary services' means guidance, counseling and testing services; psychological services; services for exceptional children; remedial and therapeutic services; speech and hearing services; services for the improvement of the educational disadvantaged (such as, but not limited to, teaching English as a second language), and such other secular, neutral, nonideological services as are of benefit to nonpublic school children and are presently or hereafter provided for public school children of the Commonwealth."

Even if the distinction between these services and core curricula is thought to be matter of degree, the sec⊥**394**ond distinction between the programs involved in *Lemon* and Act 194 is a difference in kind. Act 194 provides that these auxiliary services shall be provided by personnel of the public school system. Since the danger of entanglement articulated in *Lemon* flowed from the susceptibility of parochial school teachers to "religious control and discipline," I would have assumed that exorcisation of that constitutional "evil" would lead to a different constitutional result. The Court does not contend that the public school employees who would administer the auxiliary services are subject to "religious control and discipline." In fact the Court concedes that "auxiliary services personnel, because not employed by the nonpublic schools, are not directly subject to the discipline of a religious authority." The decision of the Court that Act 194 is unconstitutional rests ultimately upon the unsubstantiated factual proposition that "[t]he potential for impermissible fostering of religion under these circumstances, although somewhat reduced, is nonetheless present." "The test [of entanglement] is inescapably one of degree," *Walz* v. *Tax Commission*, but if the Court is free to ignore the record, then appellees are left to wonder, with good reason, whether the possibility of meeting the entanglement test is now anything more than "a promise to the ear to be broken to the hope, a teasing illusion like a munificent bequest in a pauper's will." *Edwards* v. *California*.

I remain convinced of the correctness of Mr. *Justice* ⊥**395** *WHITE*'s statement in his dissenting opinion in *Committee for Public Education & Religious Liberty* v. *Nyquist*: "Positing an obligation on the State to educate its children, which every State acknowledges, it should be wholly acceptable for the State to contribute to the secular education of children going to sectarian schools rather than to insist that if parents want to provide their children with religious as well as secular education, the State will refuse to contribute anything to their secular training."

I am disturbed as much by the overtones of the Court's opinion as by its actual holding. The Court apparently believes that the Establishment Clause of the First Amendment not only mandates religious neutrality on the part of government but also requires that this Court go further and throw its weight on the side of those who believe that our society as a whole should be a purely secular one. Nothing in the First Amendment or in the cases interpreting it requires such an extreme approach to this difficult question, and "[a]ny interpretation of [the Establishment Clause] and constitutional values it serves must also take account of the free exercise clause and the values it serves." As Mr. *Justice DOUGLAS* wrote for the Court in *Zorach* v. *Clauson*: "We are a religious people whose institutions presuppose a Supreme Being. We guarantee the freedom to worship as one chooses. We make room for as wide a variety of beliefs and creeds as the spiritual needs of man deem necessary. We sponsor an attitude on the part of government that shows no partiality to any one group and that lets each flourish according to the zeal of its adherents and ⊥**396** the appeal of its dogma. When the state encourages religious instruction or cooperates with religious authorities by adjusting the schedule of public events to sectarian needs, it follows the best of our traditions. For it then respects the religious nature of our people and accommodates the public service to their spiritual needs. To hold that it may not would be to find in the Constitution a requirement that the government show a callous indifference to religious groups. That would be preferring those who believe in no religion over those who do believe. Government may not finance religious groups nor undertake religious instruction nor blend secular and sectarian education nor use secular institutions to force one or some religion on any person. But we find no constitutional requirement which makes it necessary for government to be hostile to religion and to throw its weight against efforts to widen the effective scope of religious influence."

Except insofar as the Court upholds the textbook loan program, I respectfully dissent.

ROEMER v. BOARD OF PUBLIC WORKS OF MARYLAND

426 U.S. 736
ON APPEAL FROM THE UNITED STATES DISTRICT COURT
FOR THE DISTRICT OF MARYLAND
Argued February 23, 1976 — Decided June 21, 1976

⊥**739** Mr. *Justice BLACKMUN* announced the judgment of the Court and delivered an opinion in which *The CHIEF JUSTICE* and Mr. *Justice POWELL* joined.

We are asked once again to police the constitutional boundary between church and state. Maryland, this time, is the alleged trespasser. It has enacted a statute which, as amended, provides for annual non-categorical grants to private colleges, among them religiously affiliated institutions, subject only to the restrictions that the funds not be used for "sectarian purposes." A three-judge District Court, by a divided vote, refused to enjoin the operation of the statute, and a direct appeal has been taken to this Court.

I

⊥**740** The challenged grant program was instituted by Laws of 1971 and is now embodied in Md. Ann. Code, Art. 77A, §§ 65-69 (1975). It provides fundings for "any private institution of higher learning within the State of Maryland," provided the institution is accredited by the State Department of Education, was established in Maryland prior to July 1, 1970, maintains one or more "associate of arts or baccalaureate degree" programs, and refrains from awarding "only seminarian or theological degrees." The aid is in the form of an annual fiscal year subsidy to qualifying colleges and universities. The formula by which each institution's entitlement is computed has been changed several times and is not independently at issue here. It now provides for a qualifying institution to receive, for each full-time student (excluding students enrolled in seminarian or theological academic programs), an amount equal to 15% of the State's per full-time pupil appropriation for a student in the state college system. As first enacted, the grants were completely unrestricted. They remain non-categorical in nature, and a recipient institution may put them to whatever use it prefers, with but one exception. In 1972, following this Court's decisions in *Lemon* v. *Kurtzman*, *(Lemon I)*, and *Tilton* v. *Richardson*, § 68A was added to the statute by Laws of 1972. It provides: "None of the moneys payable under this subtitle ⊥**741** shall be utilized by the institutions for sectarian purposes."

The administration of the grant program is entrusted to the State's Board of Public Works "assisted by the Maryland Council for Higher Education." These bodies are to adopt "criteria and procedures . . . for the implementation and administration of the aid program." They are specifically authorized to adopt "criteria and procedures" governing the method of application for grants and of their disbursement, the verification of degrees conferred, and the "submission of reports or data concerning the utilization of these moneys by [the aided] institutions." Primary responsibility for the program rests with the Council for Higher Education, an appointed commission which antedates the aid program, which has numerous other responsibilities in the educational field, and which has derived from these a "considerable expertise as to the character and functions of the various private colleges and universities in the State."

The Council performs what the District Court described as a "two-step screening process" to insure compliance with the statutory restrictions on the grants. First, it determines whether an institution applying for aid is eligible at all, or is one "awarding primarily theo- ⊥**742**logical or seminary degrees." Several applicants have been disqualified at this stage of the process. Second, the Council requires that those institutions that are eligible for funds not put them to any sectarian use. An application must be accompanied by an affidavit of the institution's chief executive officer stating that the funds will not be used for sectarian purposes, and by a description of the specific nonsectarian uses that are planned. These may be changed only after written notice to the Council. By the end of the fiscal year the institution must file a "Utilization of Funds Report" describing and itemizing the use of the funds. The chief executive officer must certify the report and also file his own "Post-expenditure Affidavit," stating that the funds have not been put to sectarian uses. The recipient institution is further required to segregate state funds in a "special revenue account" and to identify aided non-sectarian expenditures separately in its budget. It must retain "sufficient documentation of the State funds expended to permit verification by the Council that funds were not spent for sectarian purposes." Any question of sectarian ⊥**743** use that may arise is to be resolved by the Council, if possible, on the basis of information submitted to it by the institution and without actual examination of its books. Failing that, a "verification or audit" may be undertaken. The District Court found that the audit would be "quick and non-judgmental," taking one day or less.

In 1971, $1.7 million was disbursed to 17 private institutions in Maryland. The disbursements were under the statute as originally enacted, and were therefore not subject to § 68A's specific prohibition on sectarian use. Of the 17 institutions, five were church related, and these received $525,000 of the $1.7 million. A total of $1.8 million was to be awarded to 18 institutions in 1972, the second year of the grant program; of this amount, $603,000 was to go to church-related institutions. Before disbursement, however, this suit, challenging the grants as in violation of the Establishment Clause of the First Amendment, was filed. The $603,000 was placed in escrow and was so held until after the entry of the District Court's judgment on October 21, 1974. These and subsequent awards, therefore, are ⊥**744** subject to § 68A and to the Council's procedures for insuring compliance therewith.

Plaintiffs in this suit, appellants here, are four individual Maryland citizens and taxpayers. Their complaint sought a declaration of the statute's invalidity, an order enjoining payments under it to church-affiliated institutions, and a declaration that the State was entitled to recover from such institutions any amounts already disbursed. In addition to the responsible state officials, plaintiff-appellants joined as defendants the five institutions they claimed were constitutionally ineligible for this form of aid: Western Maryland College, College of Notre Dame, Mount Saint Mary's College, Saint Joseph College, and Loyola College. Of these, the last four are affiliated with the Roman Catholic Church; Western Maryland, was a Methodist affiliate. The District Court ruled with respect to all five. Western Maryland, however, has since been dismissed as a defendant-appellee. We are concerned, therefore, only with the four Roman Catholic affiliates.

After carefully assessing the role that the Catholic Church plays in the lives of these institutions, a matter to which we return in greater detail below, and applying the ⊥**745** three-part requirement of *Lemon I*, that state aid such as this have a secular purpose, a primary effect other than the advancement of religion, and no tendency to entangle the State excessively in church affairs, the District Court ruled that the amended statute was constitutional and was not to be enjoined. The court considered the original, unamended statute to have been unconstitutional under *Lemon I*, but it refused to order a refund of amounts theretofore paid out, reasoning that any refund was barred by the decision in *Lemon* v. *Kurtzman (Lemon II)*. The District Court therefore denied all relief. This appeal followed. We noted probable jurisdiction.

II

A system of government that makes itself felt as pervasively as ours could hardly be expected never to cross paths with the church. In fact, our State and Federal Governments impose certain burdens upon, and impart certain benefits to, virtually all our activities, and religious activity is not an exception. The Court has enforced a scrupulous neutrality by the State, as ⊥**746** among religions, and also as between religious and other activities, but a hermetic separation of the two is an impossibility it has never required. It long has been established, for example, that the State may send a cleric, indeed even a clerical order, to perform a wholly secular task. In *Bradfield* v. *Roberts*, the Court upheld the extension of public aid to a corporation which, although composed entirely of members of a Roman Catholic sisterhood acting "under the auspices of said church," was limited by its corporate charter to the secular purpose of operating a charitable hospital.

And religious institutions need not be quarantined from public benefits that are neutrally available to all. The Court has permitted the State to supply transportation for children to and from church-related as well as public schools. *Everson* v. *Board of Education*. It has done the same with respect to secular textbooks loaned by the State on equal terms to students attending both public and church-related elementary schools. *Board of Education* v. *Allen*. Since it had not been shown in *Allen* that the secular textbooks would be put to other than secular purposes, the Court concluded that, as in *Everson*, the State was merely "extending the benefits of state laws to all citizens." Just as *Bradfield* dispels any notion that a religious person can never be in the State's pay for a secular purpose, ⊥**747** *Everson* and *Allen* put to rest any argument that the State may never act in such a way that has the incidental effect of facilitating religious activity. The Court has not been blind to the fact that in aiding a religious institution to perform a secular task, the State frees the institution's resources to be put to sectarian ends. If this were impermissible, however, a church could not be protected by the police and fire departments, or have its public sidewalk kept in repair. The Court never has held that religious activities must be discriminated against in this way.

Neutrality is what is required. The State must confine itself to secular objectives, and neither advance nor impede religious activity. Of course, that principle is more easily stated than applied. The Court has taken the view that a secular purpose and a facial neutrality may not be enough, if in fact the State is lending direct support to a religious activity. The State may not, for example, pay for what is actually a religious education, even though it purports to be paying for a secular one, and even though it makes its aid available to secular and religious institutions alike. The Court also has taken the view that the State's efforts to perform a secular task, and at the same time avoid aiding in the performance of a religious one, may not lead it into such an intimate relationship with religious authority that it appears either to be sponsoring or to be exces⊥**748**sively interfering with that authority. In *Lemon I* as noted above, the Court distilled these concerns into a three-prong test, resting in part on prior case law, for the constitutionality of statutes affording state aid to church-related schools: "First, the statute must have a secular legislative purpose; second, its principal or primary effect must be one that neither advances nor inhibits religion . . .; finally, the statute must not foster 'an excessive government entanglement with religion.'"

At issue in *Lemon I* were two state-aid plans, a Rhode Island program to grant a 15% supplement to the salaries of private, church-related school teachers teaching secular courses, and a Pennsylvania program to reimburse private church-related schools for the entire cost of secular courses also offered in public schools. Both failed the third part of the test, that of "excessive government entanglement." This part the Court held in turn required a consideration of three factors: (1) the character and purposes of the benefited institutions, (2) the nature of the aid provided, and (3) the resulting relationship between the State and the religious authority. As to the first of these, in reviewing the Rhode Island program, the Court found that the aided schools, elementary and secondary, were characterized by "substantial religious activity and purpose." They were located near parish churches. Religious instruction was considered "part of the total ⊥**749** educational process." Religious symbols and religious activities abounded. Two-thirds of the teachers were nuns, and their operation of the schools was regarded as an "'integral part of the religious mission of the Catholic Church.'" The schooling came at an impressionable age. The form of aid also cut against the programs. Unlike the textbooks in *Allen* and the bus transportation in *Everson*, the services of the state-supported teachers could not be counted on to be purely secular. They were bound to mix religious teachings with secular ones, not by conscious design, perhaps, but because the mixture was inevitable when teachers (themselves usually Catholics) were "employed by a religious organization, subject to the direction and discipline of religious authorities, and work[ed] in a system dedicated to rearing children in a particular faith." The State's efforts to supervise and control the teaching of religion in supposedly secular classes would therefore inevitably entangle it excessively in religious affairs. The Pennsylvania program similarly foundered.

The Court also pointed to another kind of church-state entanglement threatened by the Rhode Island and Pennsylvania programs, namely, their "divisive political potential." They represented "successive and very likely permanent annual appropriations that benefit relatively few religious groups." Political factions, supporting and opposing the programs, were bound to divide along religious lines. This was "one of the principal evils against which the First Amendment was intended to protect." It was stressed that the political divisiveness of the programs was "aggravated . . . by the need for continuing annual appropriations."

⊥**750** In *Tilton* v. *Richardson*, a companion case to *Lemon I*, the Court reached the contrary result. The aid challenged in *Tilton* was in the form of federal grants for the construction of academic facilities at private colleges, some of them church related, with the restriction that the facilities not be used for any sectarian purpose. Applying *Lemon I's* three-part test, the Court found the purpose of the federal aid program there under consideration to be secular. Its primary effect was not the advancement of religion, for sectarian use of the facilities was prohibited. Enforcement of this prohibition was made possible by the fact that religion did not so permeate the defendant colleges that their religious and secular functions were inseparable. On the contrary, there was no evidence that religious activities took place in the funded facilities. Courses at the colleges were "taught according to the academic requirements intrinsic to the subject matter," and "an atmosphere of academic freedom rather than religious indoctrination" was maintained.

Turning to the problem of excessive entanglement, the Court first stressed the character of the aided institutions. It pointed to several general differences between college and precollege education: college students are less susceptible to religious indoctrination; college courses tend to entail an internal discipline that inherently limits the opportunities for sectarian influence; and a high degree of academic freedom tends to prevail at the college level. It found no evidence that the col⊥**751**leges in *Tilton* varied from this pattern. Though controlled and largely populated by Roman Catholics, the colleges were not restricted to adherents of that faith. No religious services were required to be attended. Theology courses were mandatory, but they were taught in academic fashion, and with treatment of beliefs other than Roman Catholicism. There were no attempts to proselytise among students, and principles of academic freedom prevailed. With colleges of this character, there was little risk that religion would seep into the teaching of secular subjects, and the state surveillance necessary to separate the two, therefore, was diminished. The Court next looked to the type of aid provided, and found it to be neutral or nonideological in nature. Like the textbooks and bus transportation in *Allen* and *Everson*, but unlike the teachers services in *Lemon I*, physical facilities were capable of being restricted to secular purposes. Moreover, the construction grant was a one-shot affair, not involving annual audits and appropriations.

As for political divisiveness, no "continuing religious aggravation" over the program had been shown, and the

Court reasoned that this might be because of the lack of continuity in the church-state relationship, the character and diversity of the colleges, and the fact that they served a dispersed student constituency rather than a local one. "Cumulatively," all these considerations persuaded the Court that church-state entanglement was not excessive.

In *Hunt* v. *McNair* the challenged aid was also for the construction of secular college facilities, the state plan being one to finance the construction by revenue bonds issued through the medium of a state authority. In effect, the college serviced and repaid the bonds, but at the lower cost resulting from the tax-free status of the interest payments. The Court upheld the program on reasoning analogous to that in ⊥**752** *Tilton*. In applying the second of the *Lemon I* test's three parts, that concerning "primary effect," the following refinement was added: "Aid normally may be thought to have a primary effect of advancing religion when it flows to an institution in which religion is so pervasive that a substantial portion of its functions are subsumed in the religious mission or when it funds a specifically religious activity in an otherwise substantially secular setting."

Although the college which *Hunt* concerned was subject to substantial control by its sponsoring Baptist Church, it was found to be similar to the colleges in *Tilton* and not "pervasively sectarian." As in *Tilton*, state aid went to secular facilities only, and thus not to any "specifically religious activity."

Committee for Public Education & Religious Liberty v. *Nyquist* followed in *Lemon I's* wake much as *Hunt* followed in *Tilton's*. The aid in *Nyquist* was to elementary and secondary schools which, the District Court found, generally conformed to a "profile" of a sectarian or substantially religious school. The state aid took three forms: direct subsidies for the maintenance and repair of buildings; reimbursement of parents for a percentage of tuition paid; and certain tax benefits for parents. All three forms of aid were found to have an impermissible primary effect. The mainte⊥**753**nance and repair subsidies, being unrestricted, could be used for the upkeep of a chapel or classrooms used for religious instruction. The reimbursements and tax benefits to parents could likewise be used to support wholly religious activities.

In *Levitt* v. *Committee for Public Education* the Court also invalidated a program for public aid to church-affiliated schools. The grants, which were to elementary and secondary schools in New York, were in the form of reimbursements for the schools' testing and recordkeeping expenses. The schools met the same sectarian profile as did those in *Nyquist*, at least in some cases. There was therefore "substantial risk" that the state-funded tests would be "drafted with an eye, unconsciously or otherwise, to inculcate students in the religious precepts of the sponsoring church."

Last Term, in *Meek* v. *Pittenger*, the Court ruled yet again on a state-aid program for church-related elementary and secondary schools. On the authority of *Allen*, it upheld a Pennsylvania program for lending textbooks to private school students. It found, however, that *Lemon I* required the invalidation of two other forms of aid to the private schools. The first was the loan of instructional materials and equipment. Like the textbooks, these were secular and nonideological in nature. Unlike the textbooks, however, they were loaned directly to the schools. The schools, similar to those in *Lemon I*, were ones in which "the teaching process is, to a large extent, devoted to the inculcation of religious values and belief." Aid flowing directly to such "religion-pervasive institutions" had the primary effect of advancing religion. The other form of aid was the provision of "auxiliary" educational serv⊥**754**ices: remedial instruction, counseling and testing, and speech and hearing therapy. These also were intended to be neutral and nonideological, and in fact were to be provided by public school teachers. Still, there was danger that the teachers, in such a sectarian setting would allow religion to seep into their instruction. To attempt to prevent this from happening would excessively entangle the State in church affairs. The Court referred again to the danger of political divisiveness, heightened, as it had been in *Lemon I* and *Nyquist*, by the necessity of annual legislative reconsideration of the aid appropriation.

So the slate we write on is anything but clean. Instead, there is little room for further refinement of the principles governing public aid to church-affiliated private schools. Our purpose is not to unsettle those principles, so recently reaffirmed, or to expand upon them substantially, but merely to insure that they are faithfully applied in this case.

III

The first part of *Lemon I's* three-part test is not in issue; appellants do not challenge the District Court's finding that the purpose of Maryland's aid program is the secular one of supporting private higher education generally, as an economic alternative to a wholly public system. The focus of the debate is on the second and third parts, those concerning the primary effect of ad⊥**755** vancing religion, and excessive church-state entanglement. We consider them in the same order.

A

While entanglement is essentially a procedural problem, the primary effect question is the substantive one of what private educational activities, by whatever procedure, may be supported by state funds. *Hunt* requires (1) that no state aid at all go to institutions that are so "pervasively sectarian" that secular activities cannot be separated from sectarian ones, and (2) that if secular activities *can* be separated out, they alone may be funded.

(1) The District Court's finding in this case was that the appellee colleges are not "pervasively sectarian." This conclusion it supported with a number of subsidiary findings concerning the role of religion on these campuses:

(a) Despite their formal affiliation with the Roman Catholic Church, the colleges are "characterized by a high degree of institutional autonomy." None of the four receives funds from, or makes reports to, the Catholic Church. The Church is represented on their governing boards, but, as with Mount Saint Mary's, "no instance of entry of Church considerations into college decisions was shown."

(b) The colleges employ Roman Catholic chaplains and hold Roman Catholic religious exercises on campus. Attendance at such is not required; the encouragement of spiritual development is only "one secondary objective" of each college; and "at none of these institutions does this encouragement go beyond providing the opportunities or occasions for religious experience." It was the District Court's general finding that "religious indoctrination is not a substantial purpose or activity of any of these defendants."

(c) ⊥**756** Mandatory religion or theology courses are taught at each of the colleges, primarily by Roman Catholic clerics, but these only supplement a curriculum covering "the spectritum of a liberal arts program." Nontheology courses are taught in an "atmosphere of intellectual freedom" and without "religious pressures." Each college subscribes to, and abides by, the 1940 Statement of Principles on Academic Freedom of the American Association of University Professors.

(d) Some classes are begun with prayer. The percentage of classes in which this is done varies with the college, from a "miniscule" percentage at Loyola and Mount Saint Mary's, to a majority at Saint Joseph. There is no "actual college policy" of encouraging the practice. "It is treated as a facet of the instructor's academic freedom." Classroom prayers were therefore regarded by the District Court as "peripheral to the subject of religious permeation," as were the facts that some instructors wear clerical garb and some classrooms have religious symbols. The court concluded "None of these facts impairs the clear and con⊥**757**vincing evidence that courses at each defendant are taught 'according to the academic requirements intrinsic to the subject matter and the individual teacher's concept of professional standards' [citing *Tilton* v. *Richardson*]."

In support of this finding the court relied on the fact that a Maryland education department group had monitored the teacher education program at Saint Joseph College, where classroom prayer is most prevalent, and had seen "no evidence of religion entering any elements of that program."

(e) The District Court found that, apart from the theology departments, faculty hiring decisions are not made on a religious basis. At two of the colleges, Notre Dame and Mount Saint Mary's, no inquiry at all is made into an applicant's religion. Religious preference is to be noted on Loyola's application form, but the purpose is to allow full appreciation of the applicant's background. Loyola also attempts to employ each year two members of a particular religious order which once staffed a college recently merged into Loyola. Budgetary considerations lead the colleges generally to favor members of religious orders, who often receive less than full salary. Still, the District Court found that "academic quality" was the principal hiring criterion, and that any "hiring bias," or "effort by any defendant to stock its faculty with members of a particular religious group," would have been noticed by other faculty members, who had never been heard to complain.

(f) The great majority of students at each of the colleges are Roman Catholic, but the District Court concluded from a "thorough analysis of the student ad⊥**758**mission and recruiting criteria" that the student bodies "are chosen without regard to religion."

We cannot say that the foregoing findings as to the role of religion in particular aspects of the colleges are clearly erroneous. Appellants ask us to set those findings aside in certain respects. Not surprisingly, they have gleaned from this record of thousands of pages, compiled during several weeks of trial, occasional evidence of a more sectarian character than the District Court ascribes to the colleges. It is not our place, however, to reappraise the evidence, unless it plainly fails to support the findings of the trier of facts. That is certainly not the case here, and it would make no difference even if we were to second-guess the District Court in certain particulars. To answer the question whether an institution is so "pervasively sectarian" that it may receive no direct state aid of any kind, it is necessary to paint a general picture of the institution, composed of many elements. The general picture that the District Court has painted of the appellee institutions is similar in almost all respects to that of the church-affiliated colleges considered in *Tilton* and *Hunt*. We ⊥**759** find no constitutionally significant distinction between them, at least for purposes of the "pervasive sectarianism" test.

(2) Having found that the appellee institutions are not, "so permeated by religion that the secular side cannot be separated from the sectarian," the District Court proceeded to the next question posed by *Hunt*: whether aid in fact was extended only to "the secular side." This requirement the court regarded as satisfied by the statutory prohibition against sectarian use, and by the administrative enforcement of that prohibition through the Council for Higher Education. We agree. *Hunt* requires only that state funds not be used to support "specifically religious activity." It is clear that fund uses exist that meet this require⊥**760**ment. We have no occasion to elaborate further on what is and is not a "specifically religious activity," for no particular use of the state funds is set out in this statute. Funds are put to the use of the college's choice, provided it is not a sectarian use, of which the college must satisfy the Council. If the question is whether the statute sought to be enjoined authorizes state funds for "specifically religious activity," that question fairly answers itself. The statute in terms forbids the use of funds for "sectarian purposes," and this prohibition appears to be at least as broad as *Hunt's* prohibition of the public funding of "specifically religious activity." We

must assume that the colleges, and the Council, will exercise their delegated control over use of the funds in compliance with the statutory, and therefore the constitutional, mandate. It is to be expected that they will give a wide berth to "specifically religious activity," and thus minimize constitutional questions. ⊥**761** Should such questions arise, the courts will consider them. It has not been the Court's practice, in considering facial challenges to statutes of this kind, to strike them down in anticipation that particular applications may result in unconstitutional use of funds.

B

If the foregoing answer to the "primary effect" ques⊥**762**tion seems easy, it serves to make the "excessive entanglement" problem more difficult. The statute itself clearly denies the use of public funds for "sectarian purposes." It seeks to avert such use, however, through a process of annual interchange—proposal and approval, expenditure and review—between the colleges and the Council. In answering the question whether this will be an "excessively entangling" relationship, we must consider the several relevant factors identified in prior decisions:

(1) First is the character of the aided institutions. This has been fully described above. As the District Court found, the colleges perform "essentially secular educational functions" that are distinct and separable from religious activity. This finding, which is a prerequisite under the "pervasive sectarianism" test to any state aid at all, is also important for purposes of the entanglement test because it means that secular activities, for the most, can be taken at face value. There is no danger, or at least only a substantially reduced danger, that an ostensibly secular activity—the study of biology, the learning of a foreign language, an athletic event—will actually be infused with religious content or significance. The need for close surveillance of purportedly secular activities is correspondingly reduced. Thus the District Court found that in this case "there is no necessity for state officials to investigate the conduct of particular classes of educational programs to determine whether a school is attempting to indoctrinate its students under the guise of secular education." We cannot say the District Court erred in this judgment or gave it undue significance. The Court took precisely the same view with respect to the aid extended to the very similar institutions in *Tilton*.

⊥**763** (2) As for the form of aid, we have already noted that no particular use of state funds is before us in this case. The *process* by which aid is disbursed, and a use for it chosen, are before us. We address this as a matter of the "resulting relationship" of secular and religious authority.

(3) As noted, the funding process is an annual one. The subsidies are paid out each year, and they can be put to annually varying uses. The colleges propose particular uses for the Council's approval, and, following expenditure, they report to the Council on the use to which the funds have been put.

The District Court's view was that in the light of the character of the aided institutions, and the resulting absence of any need "to investigate the conduct of particular classes," the annual nature of the subsidy was not fatal. In fact, an annual, ongoing relationship had existed in *Tilton*, where the Government retained the right to inspect subsidized buildings for sectarian use, and the ongoing church-state involvement had been even greater in *Hunt*, where the State was actually the lessor of the subsidized facilities, retaining extensive powers to regulate their use.

We agree with the District Court that "excessive entanglement" does not necessarily result from the fact that the subsidy is an annual one. It is true that the Court favored the "one-time, single purpose" construction grants in *Tilton* because they entailed "no continuing financial relationships or dependencies, no annual audits, and no government analysis of an institution's expenditures." The present aid program cannot claim these aspects. But if the question is whether this case is more like *Lemon I* or more like *Tilton*—and surely that is the ⊥**764** fundamental question before us—the answer must be that it is more like *Tilton*.

Tilton is distinguishable only by the form of aid. We cannot discount the distinction entirely, but neither can we regard it as decisive. As the District Court pointed out, ongoing, annual supervision of college facilities was explicitly foreseen in *Tilton*, and even more so in *Hunt*. *Tilton* and *Hunt* would be totally indistinguishable, at least in terms of annual supervision, if funds were used under the present statute to build or maintain physical facilities devoted to secular use. The present statute contemplates annual decisions by the Council as to what is a "sectarian purpose," but, as we have noted, the secular and sectarian activities of the colleges are easily separated. Occasional audits are possible here, but we must accept the District Court's finding that they would be "quick and non-judgmental." They and the other contacts between the Council and the colleges are not likely to be any more entangling than the inspections and audits incident to the normal process of the colleges' accreditations by the State.

While the form-of-aid distinctions of *Tilton* are thus of questionable importance, the character-of-institution distinctions of *Lemon I* are most impressive. To reiterate a few of the relevant points: the elementary and secondary schooling in *Lemon* came at an impressionable age; the aided schools were "under the general supervision" of the Roman Catholic diocese; each had a local Catholic parish that assumed "ultimate financial responsibility" for it; the principals of the schools were usually appointed by church authorities; religion "pervade[d] the school system"; teachers were specifically instructed by the "Handbook of School Regula⊥**765**tions" that "[r]eligious formation is not confined to formal courses; nor is it restricted to a single subject area." These things made impossible what is crucial to a nonentangling aid program: the ability of the State to identify and subsidize separate secular functions carried out at the school, without on-the-site inspections being necessary to prevent diversion of the funds to sectarian purposes. The District Court gave primary importance to this consideration, and we cannot say it erred.

(4) As for political divisiveness, the District Court recognized that the annual nature of the subsidy, along with its promise of an increasing demand for state funds as the colleges' dependency grew, aggravated the danger of "[p]olitical fragmentation . . . on religious lines." *Lemon I.* Nonetheless, the District Court found that the program "does not create a substantial danger of political entanglement." Several reasons were given. As was stated in *Tilton*, the danger of political divisiveness is "substantially less" when the aided institution is not an elementary or secondary school, but a college, "whose student constituency is not local but diverse and widely dispersed." Furthermore, political divisiveness is diminished by the fact that the aid is extended to private colleges generally, more than two thirds of which have no religious affiliation; this is in sharp contrast to *Nyquist*, for example, where 95% of the aided schools were Roman Catholic parochial schools. Finally, the substantial autonomy of the colleges was thought to mitigate political divisiveness, in that controversies surrounding the aid program are not likely to involve the Catholic Church itself, or even the religious character of the schools, but only their "fiscal responsi⊥**766**bility and educational requirements."

The District Court's reasoning seems to us entirely sound. Once again, appellants urge that this case is controlled by previous cases in which the form of aid was similar (*Lemon I; Nyquist, Levitt*), rather than those in which the character of the aided institution was the same (*Tilton, Hunt*). We disagree. Though indisputably relevant, the annual nature of the aid cannot be dispositive. On the one hand, the Court has *struck down* a "permanent," nonannual tax exemption, reasoning that "the pressure for frequent enlargement of the relief is predictable," as it always is. *Committee for Public Education & Religious Liberty* v. *Nyquist*. On the other hand, in *Tilton* it has upheld a program for "one-time, single-purpose" construction grants, despite the fact that such grants would, in fact, be "annual," at least insofar as new grants would be annually applied for. Our holdings are better reconciled in terms of the character of the aided institutions, found to be so dissimilar as between those considered in *Tilton* and *Hunt*, on the one hand, and those considered in *Lemon I*, *Nyquist*, and *Levitt*, on the other.

There is no exact science in gauging the entanglement of church and state. The wording of the test, which speaks of "*excessive* entanglement," itself makes that clear. The relevant factors we have identified are to be considered "cumulatively" in judging the degree of entanglement. They may cut different ways, as certainly they do here. In reaching the conclusion that it did, the District Court gave dominant importance to the character of the aided institutions and to its finding that they are capable of separating secular and religious functions. For the rea⊥**767**sons stated above, we cannot say that the emphasis was misplaced or the finding erroneous.

The judgment of the District Court is affirmed.

It is so ordered.

Mr. *Justice* WHITE, with whom Mr. *Justice* REHNQUIST joins, concurring in the judgment.

While I join in the judgment of the Court, I am unable to concur in the plurality opinion substantially for the reasons set forth in my opinions in *Lemon* v. ⊥**768** *Kurtzman (Lemon I)*, and *Committee for Public Education* v. *Nyquist*. I am no more reconciled now to *Lemon I* than I was when it was decided. The threefold test of *Lemon I* imposes unnecessary, and, as I believe today's plurality opinion demonstrates, superfluous tests for establishing "when the State's involvement with religion passes the peril point" for First Amendment purposes. *Nyquist*.

"It is enough for me that the [State is] financing a separable secular function of overriding importance in order to sustain the legislation here challenged." *Lemon I*. As long as there is a secular legislative purpose, and as long as the primary effect of the legislation is neither to advance nor inhibit religion, I see no reason—particularly in light of the "sparse language of the Establishment Clause," *Nyquist*—to take the constitutional inquiry further. However, since 1970, the Court has added a third element to the inquiry: whether there is "an excessive government entanglement with religion." *Walz* v. *Tax Commission*. I have never understood the constitutional foundation for this added element; it is at once both insolubly paradoxical, ⊥**769** and—as the Court has conceded from the outset—a "blurred, indistinct and variable barrier." *Lemon I*. It is not clear that the "weight and contours of entanglement as a separate constitutional criterion," *Nyquist*, are any more settled now than when they first surfaced. Today's plurality opinion leaves the impression that the criterion really may not be "separate" at all. In affirming the District Court's conclusion that the legislation here does not create an "excessive entanglement" of church and state, the plurality emphasizes with approval that "the District Court gave dominant importance to the character of the aided institutions and to its finding that they are capable of separating secular and religious functions." Yet these are the same factors upon which the plurality focus in concluding that the Maryland legislation satisfies the first part of the *Lemon I* test: that on the record the "appellee colleges are not 'pervasively sectarian,'" and that the aid at issue was capable of, and is in fact, extended only to "the secular side" of the appellee colleges' operations. It is unclear to me how the first and third parts of the *Lemon I* test are substantially different. The "excessive entanglement" test appears no less "curious and mystifying" than when it was first announced. *Lemon I*.

I see no reason to indulge in the redundant exercise of evaluating the same facts and findings under a different label. No one in this case challenges the District ⊥**770** Court's finding that the purpose of the legislation here is secular. And I do not disagree with the plurality that the primary effect of the aid program is not advancement of religion. That is enough in my view to sustain the aid programs against constitutional challenge, and I would say no more.

Mr. *Justice* BRENNAN, with whom Mr. *Justice* MARSHALL joins, dissenting.

I agree with Judge Bryan, dissenting from the judgment under review, that the Maryland Act "*in these instances* does in truth offend the Constitution by its provisions of funds, in that it exposes State money for use in advancing religion, no matter the vigilance to avoid it." Each of the institutions is a church-affiliated or church-related body. The subsidiary findings concerning the role of religion on each of the campuses, summarized by the plurality opinion, conclusively establish that fact. In that circumstance, I agree with Judge Bryan that "[o]f telling decisiveness here is the payment of the grants directly to the colleges unmarked in purpose. . . . Presently the Act is simply a blunderbuss discharge of public funds to a church-affiliated or church-related college." In other words, the Act provides for payment of general subsidies to religious institutions from public funds and I have heretofore expressed my view that "[g]eneral subsidies of religious activities would, of course, constitute impermissible state involvement with religion." *Walz* v. *Tax Commission*. This is because general subsidies "tend to promote that type of interdependence between religion and state which the First Amendment was designed to prevent." *Abington School District* v. ⊥**771** *Schempp*. "What the Framers meant to foreclose, and what our decisions under the Establishment Clause have forbidden, are those involvements of religions with secular institutions which . . . serve the essentially religious activities of religious institutions. *Id.*

The history of the bitter controversies over public subsidy of sectarian educational institutions that began soon after the Nation was formed is recited in my separate opinion in *Lemon* v. *Kurtzman (Lemon I)*. My reasons for concluding in *Lemon I* that all three statutes there before us impermissibly provided a direct subsidy from public funds for activities carried on by sectarian educational institutions also support my agreement with Judge Bryan in this case "than an injunction should issue as prayed in the complaint, stopping future payments under the Maryland Act to the [appellee] colleges." I said in *Lemon I*: "I believe that the Establishment Clause forbids . . . Government to provide funds to sectarian universities in which the propagation and advancement of a particular religion are a function or purpose of the institution. . . .

"I reach this conclusion for [these] reasons . . . : the necessarily deep involvement of government in the religious activities of such an institution through the policing of restrictions, and the fact that subsidies of tax monies directly to a sectarian institution necessarily aid the proselytizing function of the institution. . . .

"I do not believe that [direct] grants to such a sectarian institution are permissible. The reason is not that religion 'permeates' the secular education that is provided. Rather, it is that the secular edu⊥**772**cation is provided within the environment of religion; the institution is dedicated to two goals, secular education *and* religious instruction. When aid flows directly to the institution, both functions benefit." (Emphasis in original.)

The discrete interests of government and religion are mutually best served when each avoids too close a proximity to the other. "It is not only the non-believer who fears the injection of sectarian doctrines and controversies into the civil polity, but in as high degree it is the devout believer who fears the secularization of a creed which becomes too deeply involved with and dependent upon the government." *Abington School Dist.* v. *Schempp*. The Maryland Act requires "too close a proximity" of government to the subsidized sectarian institutions and in my view creates real dangers of the "secularization of a creed." *Ibid.*; *Lemon I*.

Unlike Judge Bryan, I would also reverse the District Court's denial of appellants' motion that the appellee institutions be required to refund all payments made to them. I adhere to the views expressed in Mr. *Justice* DOUGLAS' dissent, which I joined, in *Lemon* v. *Kurtzman (Lemon II)*: "There is as much a violation of the Establishment Clause of the First Amendment whether the payment from public funds to sectarian schools involves last year, the current year or next year. . . .

"Whether the grant is for . . . last year or at the present time, taxpayers are forced to contribute to sectarian schools a part of their tax dollars."

I would reverse the judgment of the District Court and remand with directions to enter a new judgment per⊥**773**manently enjoining the Board of Public Works of the State of Maryland from implementing the Maryland Act, and requiring the appellee institutions to refund all payments made to them pursuant to the Act.

Mr. *Justice* STEWART, dissenting.

In my view, the decisive differences between this case and *Tilton* v. *Richardson* lie in the nature of the theology courses that are a compulsory part of the curriculum at each of the appellee institutions and the type of governmental assistance provided to these church-affiliated colleges. In *Tilton* the Court emphasized that the theology courses were taught as academic subjects. "Although all four schools require their students to take theology courses, the parties stipulated that these courses are taught according to academic requirements of the subject matter and the teacher's concept of professional standards. The parties also stipulated that the courses covered a range of human religious experiences and are not limited to courses about the Roman Catholic religion. The schools introduced evidence that they made no attempt to indoctrinate students or to proselytize. Indeed, some of the required theology courses at Albertus Magnus and Sacred Heart are taught by rabbis."

Here, by contrast, the District Court was unable to find that the compulsory religion courses were taught as an academic discipline.

"[T]he hiring patterns for religion or theology departments are a special case and present a unique problem. All five defendants staff their religion or theology departments chiefly with clerics of the affiliated church. At two defendants, Western ⊥774 Maryland and Mt. St. Mary's, *all* members of the religion or theology faculty are clerics. The problem presented by the make-up of these departments is obvious. Recognition of the academic freedom of these instructors does not necessarily lead to a conclusion that courses in the religion or theology departments at the five defendants have no overtones of indoctrination.

. . . . .

"The theology and religion courses of each defendant must be viewed in the light of that shared objective [of encouraging spiritual development of the students]. While most of the defendants do not offer majors in religion or theology, each maintains a vigorous religion or theology department. The primary concern of these departments, either admittedly or by the obvious thrust of the courses, is Christianity. As already noted, the departments are staffed almost entirely with clergy of the affiliated church. At each of the defendants, certain of these courses are required.

". . . [A] department staffed mainly by clerics of the affiliated church and geared toward a limited array of the possible theology or religion courses affords a congenial means of furthering the secondary objective of fostering religious experience." (Emphasis in the original.)

In the light of these findings, I cannot agree with the Court's assertion that there is "no constitutionally significant distinction" between the colleges in *Tilton* and those in the present case. The findings in *Tilton* clearly established that the federal building construction grants benefited academic institutions that made no attempt to inculcate the religious beliefs of the affiliated church. In the present case, by contrast, ⊥775 the compulsory theology courses may be "devoted to deepening religious experiences in the particular faith rather than to teaching theology as an academic discipline." In view of this salient characteristic of the appellee institutions and the noncategorical grants provided to them by the State of Maryland, I agree with the conclusion of the dissenting member of the three-judge court that the challenged Act "*in these instances* does in truth offend the Constitution by its provisions of funds, in that it exposes State money for use in advancing religion, no matter the vigilance to avoid it." (Emphasis in original.)

For the reasons stated, and those expressed by Mr. *Justice* BRENNAN and Mr. *Justice* STEVENS, I dissent from the judgment and opinion of the Court and the plurality's opinion.

Mr. *Justice* STEVENS, dissenting.

My views are substantially those expressed by Mr. *Justice* BRENNAN. However, I would add emphasis to the pernicious tendency of a state subsidy to tempt religious schools to compromise their religious mission without wholly abandoning it. The disease of entanglement may infect a law discouraging wholesome religious activity as well as a law encouraging the propagation of a given faith.

WOLMAN v. WALTER

433 U.S. 229
ON APPEAL FROM THE UNITED STATES DISTRICT COURT
FOR THE SOUTHERN DISTRICT OF OHIO
Argued April 25, 1977 — Decided June 24, 1977

⊥232 Mr. *Justice* BLACKMUN delivered the opinion of the Court (Parts I, V, VI, VII, and VIII), together with an opinion (Parts II, III, and IV), in which *The* CHIEF JUSTICE, Mr. *Justice* STEWART, and Mr. *Justice* POWELL joined.

This is still another case presenting the recurrent issue of the limitations imposed by the Establishment Clause of the First Amendment, made applicable to the States by the Fourteenth Amendment, on state aid to pupils in church-related elementary and secondary schools. Appellants are citizens and taxpayers of Ohio. They challenge all but one of the provisions of Ohio ⊥233 Rev. Code § 3317.06 (Supp. 1976) which authorize various forms of aid. The appellees are the State Superintendent of Public Instruction, the State Treasurer, the State Auditor, the Board of Education of the City School District of Columbus, Ohio, and, at their request, certain representative potential beneficiaries of the statutory program. A three-judge court was convened. It held the statute constitutional in all respects. We noted probable jurisdiction.

I

Section 3317.06 was enacted after this Court's May 1975 decision in *Meek* v. *Pittenger*, and obviously is an attempt to conform to the teachings of that decision.*

*At the time *Meek* was decided, an appeal was pending before us from a District Court judgment holding constitutional the predecessor Ohio statute providing for aid to nonpublic schools. *Wolman* v. *Essex*. This Court vacated that judgment and remanded the case for further consideration in light of *Meek*.

On remand, the District Court entered a consent order, dated November 17, 1975, declaring the predecessor statute, which by then had been repealed, violative of the First and Fourteenth Amendments, but reserving decision on the constitutionality of the successor legislation. Appellants, who were plaintiffs in the original suit, then shifted their challenge to the present, successor statute.

The state appellees so acknowledged at oral argument. In broad outline, the statute authorizes the State to provide nonpublic school pupils with books, instructional materials and equipment, standardized testing and scoring, diagnostic services, therapeutic services, and field trip transportation.

The initial biennial appropriation by the Ohio Legislature for implementation of the statute was the sum of $88,800,000. ⊥**234** Funds so appropriated are paid to the State's public school districts and are then expended by them. All disbursements made with respect to nonpublic schools have their equivalents in disbursements for public schools, and the amount expended per pupil in nonpublic schools may not exceed the amount expended per pupil in the public schools.

The parties stipulated that during the 1974-75 school year there were 720 chartered nonpublic schools in Ohio. Of these, all but 29 were sectarian. More than 96% of the nonpublic enrollment attended sectarian schools, and more than 92% attended Catholic schools. It was also stipulated that, if they were called, officials of representative Catholic schools would testify that such schools operate under the general supervision of the Bishop of their Diocese; that most principals are members of a religious order within the Catholic Church; that a little less than one-third of the teachers are members of such religious orders; that "in all probability a majority of the teachers are members of the Catholic faith"; and that many of the rooms and hallways in these schools are decorated with a Christian symbol. All such schools teach the secular subjects required to meet the State's minimum standards. The state-mandated five hour day is expanded to include, usually, one-half hour of religious instruction. Pupils who are not members of the Catholic faith are not required to attend religious classes or to participate in religious exercises or activities, and no teacher is required to teach religious doctrine as a part of the secular courses taught in the schools.

The parties also stipulated that nonpublic school officials, if called, would testify that none of the schools covered by the statute discriminate in the admission of pupils or in the hiring ⊥**235** of teachers on the basis of race, creed, color, or national origin.

The District Court concluded: "Although the stipulations of the parties evidence several significant points of distinction, the character of these schools is substantially comparable to that of the schools involved in *Lemon* v. *Kurtzman*."

II

The mode of analysis for Establishment Clause questions is defined by the three-part test that has emerged from the ⊥**236** Court's decisions. In order to pass muster, a statute must have a secular legislative purpose, must have a principal or primary effect that neither advances nor inhibits religion, and must not foster an excessive government entanglement with religion.

In the present case we have no difficulty with the first prong of this three-part test. We are satisfied that the challenged statute reflects Ohio's legitimate interest in protecting the health of its youth and in providing a fertile educational environment for all the school children of the State. As is usual in our cases, the analytical difficulty has to do with the effect and entanglement criteria.

We have acknowledged before, and we do so again here, that the wall of separation that must be maintained between church and state "is a blurred, indistinct, and variable barrier depending on all the circumstances of a particular relationship." *Lemon*. Nonetheless, the Court's numerous precedents "have become firmly rooted," *Nyquist*, and now provide substantial guidance. We therefore turn to the task of applying the rules derived from our decisions to the respective provisions of the statute at issue.

III
Textbooks

Section 3317.06 authorizes the expenditure of funds:

"(A) To purchase such secular textbooks as have been approved by the superintendent of public instruction for ⊥**237** use in public schools in the state and to loan such textbooks to pupils attending nonpublic schools within the district or to their parents. Such loans shall be based upon individual requests submitted by such nonpublic school pupils or parents. Such requests shall be submitted to the local public school district in which the nonpublic school is located. Such individual requests for the loan of textbooks shall, for administrative convenience, be submitted by the nonpublic school pupil or his parent to the nonpublic school which shall prepare and submit collective summaries of the individual requests to the local public school district. As used in this section, 'textbook' means any book or book substitute which a pupil uses as a text or text substitute in a particular class or program in the school he regularly attends."

The parties' stipulations reflect operation of the textbook program in accord with the dictates of the statute. In addition, it was stipulated: "The secular textbooks used in nonpublic schools will be the same as the textbooks used in the public schools of the state. Common suppliers will be used to supply books to both public and nonpublic school pupils.

"Textbooks, including book substitutes, provided under this Act shall be limited to books, reusable workbooks, or manuals, whether bound or in looseleaf form, intended for use as a principal source of study material for a given class or group of students, a copy of which is expected to be available for the individual use of each pupil in such class or group."

This system for the loan of textbooks to individual students bears a striking resemblance to the systems approved in *Board of Education* v. *Allen* and in ⊥**238** *Meek* v. *Pittenger*. Indeed, the only distinction offered by appellants is that the challenged statute defines "textbook" as "any book or book substitute." Appellants argue that a "book substitute" might include auxiliary equipment and materials that, they assert, may not constitutionally be loaned. See Part VII. We find this argument untenable in light of the statute's separate treatment of instructional materials and equipment in its subsections (B) and (C), and in light of the stipulation defining textbooks as "limited to books, reusable workbooks, or manuals." Appellants claim that the stipulation shows only the intent of the Department of Education, and that the statute is so vague as to fail to insure against sectarian abuse of the assistance programs, citing *Meek* and *Lemon*. We find no grounds, however, to doubt the Board of Education's reading of the statute, or to fear that the Board is using the stipulations as a subterfuge. As read, the statute provides the same protections against abuse as were provided in the textbook programs under consideration in *Allen* and in *Meek*.

In the alternative, appellants urge that we overrule *Allen* and *Meek*. This we decline to do. Accordingly, we conclude that § 3317.06 (A) is constitutional.

IV
Testing and Scoring

Section 3317.06 authorizes expenditure of funds:

"(J) To supply for use by pupils attending nonpublic schools within the district such standardized tests and **⊥239** scoring services as are in use in the public schools of the state."

These tests "are used to measure the progress of students in secular subjects." Nonpublic school personnel are not involved in either the drafting or scoring of the tests. The statute does not authorize any payment to nonpublic school personnel for the costs of administering the tests.

In *Levitt* v. *Committee for Public Education* this Court invalidated a New York statutory scheme for reimbursement of church-sponsored schools for the expenses of teacher-prepared testing. The reason behind that decision was straightforward. The system was held unconstitutional because "no means are available, to assure that internally prepared tests are free of religious instruction."

⊥240 There is no question that the State has a substantial and legitimate interest in insuring that its youth receive an adequate secular education. The State may require that schools that are utilized to fulfill the State's compulsory education requirement meet certain standards of instruction, and may examine both teachers and pupils to ensure that the State's legitimate interest is being fulfilled. Under the section at issue, the State provides both the schools and the school district with the means of ensuring that the minimum standards are met. The nonpublic school does not control the content of the test or its result. This serves to prevent the use of the test as a part of religious teaching, and thus avoids that kind of direct aid to religion found present in *Levitt*. Similarly, the inability of the school to control the test eliminates the need for the supervision that gives rise to **⊥241** excessive entanglement. We therefore agree with the District Court's conclusion that § 3317.06 (J) is constitutional.

V
Diagnostic Services

Section 3317.06 authorizes expenditures of funds:

"(D) To provide speech and hearing diagnostic services to pupils attending nonpublic schools within the district. Such service shall be provided in the nonpublic school attended by the pupil receiving the service.

. . . . .

"(F) To provide diagnostic psychological services to pupils attending nonpublic schools within the district. Such services shall be provided in the school attended by the pupil receiving the service."

It will be observed that these speech and hearing and psychological diagnostic services are to be provided within the nonpublic school. It is stipulated, however, the personnel (with the exception of physicians) who perform the services are employees of the local board of education; that physicians may be hired on a contract basis; that the purpose of these services is to determine the pupil's deficiency or need of assistance; and that treatment of any defect so found would take place off the nonpublic school premises.

Appellants assert that the funding of these services is constitutionally impermissible. They argue that the speech and **⊥242** hearing staff might engage in unrestricted conversation with the pupil and, on occasion, might fail to separate religious instruction from secular responsibilities. They further assert that the communication between the psychological diagnostician and the pupil will provide an impermissible opportunity for the intrusion of religious influence.

The District Court found these dangers so insubstantial as not to render the statute unconstitutional. We agree. This Court's decisions contain a common thread to the effect that the provision of health services to all school children—public and nonpublic—does not have the primary effect of aiding religion. In *Lemon* v. *Kurtzman*, the Court stated: "Our decisions from *Everson* to *Allen* have permitted the States to provide church-related schools with secular, neutral, or nonideological services, facilities, or materials. Bus transportation, school lunches, *public health services*, and secular textbooks supplied in common to all students were not thought to offend the Establishment Clause." (Emphasis added.)

See also *Meek* v. *Pittenger*. Indeed, appellants recognize this fact in not challenging subsection (E) of the statute that authorizes publicly funded physician, nursing, dental, and optometric services in nonpublic schools. We perceive no basis for drawing a different conclusion with respect to diagnostic speech and hearing services and diagnostic psychological services.

In *Meek* the Court did hold unconstitutional a portion of a Pennsylvania statute at issue there that authorized certain ⊥**243** auxiliary services—"remedial and accelerated instruction, guidance counseling and testing, speech and hearing services"—on nonpublic school premises. The Court noted that the teacher or guidance counselor might "fail on occasion to separate religious instruction and the advancement of religious beliefs from his secular educational responsibilities." The Court was of the view that the publicly employed teacher or guidance counselor might depart from religious neutrality because he was "performing important educational services in schools in which education is an integral part of the dominant sectarian mission and in which an atmosphere dedicated to the advancement of religious belief is constantly maintained." The statute was held unconstitutional on entanglement grounds, namely, that in order to insure that the auxiliary teachers and guidance counselors remained neutral, the State would have to engage in continuing surveillance on the school premises. See also *Public Funds for Public Schools* v. *Marburger*. The Court in *Meek* explicitly stated, however, that the provision of diagnostic speech and hearing services by Pennsylvania seemed "to fall within that class of general welfare services for children that may be provided by the State regardless of the incidental benefit that accrues to church-related schools." ⊥**244** The provision of such services was invalidated only because it was found unseverable from the unconstitutional portions of the statute.

The reason for considering diagnostic services to be different from teaching or counseling is readily apparent. First, diagnostic services, unlike teaching or counseling, have little or no educational content and are not closely associated with the educational mission of the nonpublic school. Accordingly, any pressure on the public diagnostician to allow the intrusion of sectarian views is greatly reduced. Second, the diagnostician has only limited contact with the child, and that contact involves chiefly the use of objective and professional testing methods to detect students in need of treatment. The nature of the relationship between the diagnostician and the pupil does not provide the same opportunity for the transmission of sectarian views as attends the relationship between teacher and student or that between counselor and student.

We conclude that providing diagnostic services on the nonpublic school premises will not create an impermissible risk of the fostering of ideological views. It follows that there is no need for excessive surveillance, and there will not be impermissible entanglement. We therefore hold that §§ 3317.06 (D) and (F) are constitutional.

VI
Therapeutic Services

Sections 3317.06 (G), (H), (I), and (K) authorize expenditures of funds for certain therapeutic, guidance, and remedial services for students who have been identified as having a need for specialized attention. Personnel providing the serv⊥**245**ices must be employees of the local board of education or under contract with the State Department of Health. The services are to be performed only in public schools, in public centers, or in mobile units located off the nonpublic school premises. The parties have stipulated: "The determination as to whether these programs would be offered in the public school, public center, or mobile unit will depend on the distance between the public and nonpublic school, the safety factors involved in travel, and the adequacy of accommodations in public schools and public centers."

⊥**246** Appellants concede that the provision of remedial, therapeutic, and guidance services in public schools, public centers, or mobile units is constitutional if both public and nonpublic school students are served simultaneously. Their challenge is limited to the situation where a facility is used to service only nonpublic school students. They argue that any program that isolates the sectarian pupils is impermissible because the public employee providing the service might tailor his approach to reflect and reinforce the ideological view of the sectarian school attended by the children. Such action by the employee, it is claimed, renders direct aid to the sectarian institution. Appellants express particular concern over mobile units because they perceive a danger that such a unit might operate merely as an annex of the school or schools it services.

At the outset, we note that in its present posture the case does not properly present any issue concerning the use of a public facility as an adjunct of a sectarian educational enterprise. The District Court construed the statute, as do we, to authorize services only on sites that are "neither physically ⊥**247** nor educationally involved with the functions of the nonpublic school." Thus, the services are to be offered under circumstances that reflect their religious neutrality.

We recognize that, unlike the diagnostician, the therapist may establish a relationship with the pupil in which there might be opportunities to transmit ideological views. In *Meek* the Court acknowledged the danger that publicly employed personnel who provide services analogous to those at issue here might transmit religious instruction and advance religious beliefs in their activities. But, as discussed in Part V, the Court emphasized that this danger arose from the fact that the services were performed in the pervasively sectarian atmosphere of the church-related school. The danger existed there not because the public employee was likely deliberately to subvert his task to the service of religion, but rather because the pressures of the environment might alter his behavior from its normal course. So long as these types of services are offered at truly religiously neutral locations, the danger perceived in *Meek* does not arise.

The fact that a unit on a neutral site on occasion may serve only sectarian pupils does not provoke the same concerns that troubled the Court in *Meek*. The influence on a therapist's behavior that is exerted by the fact that he serves a sectarian pupil is qualitatively different from the influence of the pervasive atmosphere of a religious institution. The dangers ⊥**248** perceived in *Meek* arose from the nature of the institution, not from the nature of the pupils.

Accordingly, we hold that providing therapeutic and remedial services at a neutral site off the premises of the nonpublic schools will not have the impermissible effect of advancing religion. Neither will there be any excessive entanglement arising from supervision of public employees to insure that they maintain a neutral stance. It can hardly be said that the supervision of public employees performing public functions on public property creates an excessive entanglement between church and state. Sections 3317.06 (G), (H), (I), and (K) are constitutional.

VII
Instructional Materials and Equipment

Sections 3317.06 (B) and (C) authorize expenditures of funds for the purchase and loan to pupils or their parents upon individual request of instructional materials and instructional equipment of the kind in use in the public schools within the district and which is "incapable of diversion to religious use." Section 3717.06 also provides that the materials and equipment may be stored on the premises of a nonpublic school and that publicly hired personnel who ⊥**249** administer the lending program may perform their services upon the nonpublic school premises when necessary "for efficient implementation of the lending program."

Although the exact nature of the material and equipment is not clearly revealed, the parties have stipulated: "It is expected that materials and equipment loaned to pupils or parents under the new law will be similar to such former materials and equipment except that to the extent that the law requires that materials and equipment capable of diversion to religious issues will not be supplied." Equipment provided under the predecessor statute, invalidated as set forth in n. 1, *supra*, included projectors, tape recorders, record players, maps and globes, science kits, weather forecasting charts, and the like. The District Court found the new statute, as now limited, constitutional because the Court could not distinguish the loan of materials and equipment from the textbook provisions upheld in *Meek* and in *Allen*.

In *Meek*, however, the Court considered the constitutional validity of a direct loan to nonpublic schools of instructional material and equipment, and, despite the apparent secular nature of the goods, held the loan impermissible. Mr. *Justice STEWART*, in writing for the Court, stated: "The very purpose of many of those schools is to provide an integrated secular and religious education; the teach⊥**250**ing process is, to a large extent, devoted to the inculcation of religious values and belief. See *Lemon* v. *Kurtzman*. Substantial aid to the educational function of such schools, accordingly, necessarily results in aid to the sectarian school enterprise as a whole. '[T]he secular education those schools provide goes hand in hand with the religious mission that is the only reason for the schools' existence. Within the institution, the two are inextricably intertwined.'"

Thus, even though the loan ostensibly was limited to neutral and secular instructional material and equipment, it inescapably had the primary effect of providing a direct and substantial advancement of the sectarian enterprise.

Appellees seek to avoid *Meek* by emphasizing that it involved a program of direct loans to nonpublic schools. In contrast, the material and equipment at issue under the Ohio statute are loaned to the pupil or his parent. In our view, however, it would exalt form over substance if this distinction were found to justify a result different from that in *Meek*. Before *Meek* was decided by this Court, Ohio authorized the loan of material and equipment directly to the nonpublic schools. Then, in light of *Meek*, the state legislature decided to channel the goods through the parents and pupils. Despite the technical change in legal bailee, the program in substance is the same as before: the equipment is substantially the same; it will receive the same use by the students; and it may still be stored and distributed on the nonpublic school premises. In view of the impossibility of separating the secular education function from the sectarian, the state aid inevitably flows in part in support of the religious role of the schools.

Indeed, this conclusion is compelled by the Court's prior consideration of an analogous issue in *Committee for Public Education* v. *Nyquist*. There the Court considered, among others, a tuition reimbursement program ⊥**251** whereby New York gave low income parents who sent their children to nonpublic schools a direct and unrestricted cash grant of $50 to $100 per child (but no more than 50% of tuition actually paid). The State attempted to justify the program, as Ohio does here, on the basis that the aid flowed to the parents rather than to the church-related schools. The Court observed, however, that, unlike the bus program in *Everson* v. *Board of Education* and the book program in *Allen*, there "has been no endeavor 'to guarantee the separation between secular and religious educational functions and to insure that State financial aid supports only the former,'" quoting *Lemon* v. *Kurtzman*. The Court thus found that the grant program served to establish religion. If a grant in cash to parents is impermissible, we fail to see how a grant in kind of goods furthering the religious enterprise can fare any better. Accordingly, we hold §§ 3317.06 (B) and (C) to be unconstitutional.

VIII
Field Trips

⊥**252** Section 3317.06 also authorizes expenditures of funds:

"(L) To provide such field trip transportation and services to nonpublic school students as are provided to public school students in the district. School districts may contract with commercial transportation companies for such transportation service if school district busses are unavailable."

There is no restriction on the timing of field trips; the only restriction on number lies in the parallel the statute draws to field trips provided to public school students in the district. The parties have stipulated that the trips "would consist of visits to governmental, industrial, cultural, and scientific centers designed to enrich the secular studies of students." ⊥**253** The choice of destination, however, will be made by the nonpublic school teacher from a wide range of locations.

The District Court held this feature to be constitutionally indistinguishable from that with which the Court was concerned in *Everson* v. *Board of Education*. We do not agree. In *Everson* the Court approved a system under which a New Jersey board of education reimbursed parents for the cost of sending their children to and from school, public or parochial, by public carrier. The Court analogized the reimbursement to situations where a municipal common carrier is ordered to carry all school children at a reduced rate, or where the police force is ordered to protect all children on their way to and from school. The critical factors in these examples, as in the *Everson* reimbursement system, are that the school has no control over the expenditure of the funds and the effect of the expenditure is unrelated to the content of the education provided. Thus, the bus fare program in *Everson* passed constitutional muster because the school did not determine how often the pupil traveled between home and school—every child must make one round trip every day—and because the travel was unrelated to any aspect of the curriculum.

The Ohio situation is in sharp contrast. First, the nonpublic school controls the timing of the trips and, within a certain range, their frequency and destinations. Thus, the schools, rather than the children, truly are the recipients of the service and, as this Court has recognized, this fact alone may be sufficient to invalidate the program as impermissible direct aid. See *Lemon* v. *Kurtzman*. Second, although a trip may be to a location that would be of interest to those in public schools, it is the individual teacher who makes a field trip meaningful. The experience begins with the study and discussion of the place to be visited; it continues on location with the teacher pointing out items of interest and stimulating the imagination; and it ends with a ⊥**254** discussion of the experience. The field trips are an integral part of the educational experience, and where the teacher works within and for a sectarian institution, an unacceptable risk of fostering of religion is an inevitable byproduct. In *Lemon* the Court stated: "We need not and do not assume that teachers in parochial schools will be guilty of bad faith or any conscious decision to evade the limitations imposed by the statute and the First Amendment. We simply recognize that a dedicated religious person, teaching in a school affiliated with his or her faith and operated to inculcate its tenets, will inevitably experience great difficulty in remaining religiously neutral."

Funding of field trips, therefore, must be treated as was the funding of maps and charts in *Meek* v. *Pittenger*, the funding of buildings and tuition in *Committee for Public Education* v. *Nyquist*, and the funding of teacher-prepared tests in *Levitt* v. *Committee for Public Education*; it must be declared an impermissible direct aid to sectarian education.

Moreover, the public school authorities will be unable adequately to insure secular use of the field trip funds without close supervision of the nonpublic teachers. This would create excessive entanglement: "A comprehensive, discriminating, and continuing state surveillance will inevitably be required to insure that these restrictions are obeyed and the First Amendment otherwise respected. Unlike a book, a teacher cannot be inspected once so as to determine the extent and intent of his or her personal beliefs and subjective acceptance of the limitations imposed by the First Amendment. These prophylactic contacts will involve excessive and enduring entanglement between church and state." *Lemon* v. *Kurtzman*.

⊥**255** We hold § 3317.06 (L) to be unconstitutional.

IX

In summary, we hold constitutional those portions of the Ohio statute authorizing the State to provide nonpublic school pupils with books, standardized testing and scoring, diagnostic services, and therapeutic and remedial services. We hold unconstitutional those portions relating to instructional materials and equipment and field trip services.

The judgment of the District Court is therefore affirmed in part and reversed in part.

It is so ordered.

The CHIEF JUSTICE dissents from Parts VII and VIII of the Court's opinion.

For the reasons stated in Mr. *Justice* REHNQUIST's separate opinion in *Meek* v. *Pittenger* and Mr. *Justice* WHITE's dissenting opinion in *Committee for Public Education* v. *Nyquist*, Mr. *Justice* WHITE and Mr. *Justice* REHNQUIST concur in the judgment with respect to textbooks, testing, and scoring, and diagnostic and therapeutic services (Parts III, IV, V and VI of the opinion) and dissent from the judgment with respect to instructional materials and equipment and field trips (Parts VII and VIII of the opinion).

Mr. *Justice* BRENNAN, concurring and dissenting

I join Parts I, VII, and VIII of the Court's opinion, and the reversal of the District Court's judgment insofar as that judgment upheld the constitutionality of §§ 3317.06(B), (C), and (L).

I dissent however from Parts II, III, IV, V, and VI of the opinion and the affirm⊥256ance of the District Court's judgment insofar as it sustained the constitutionality of §§ 3317.06 (A), (D), (F), (G), (H), (I), (J), and (K). The Court holds that Ohio has managed in these respects to fashion a statute that avoids an effect or entanglement condemned by the Establishment Clause. But "The [First] Amendment nullifies sophisticated as well as simple-minded . . ." attempts to avoid its prohibitions, *Lane* v. *Wilson*, and, in any event, ingenuity in draftsmanship cannot obscure the fact that this subsidy to sectarian schools amounts to $88,800,000 (less now the sums appropriated to finance §§ 3317.06 (B) and (C) which today are invalidated) just for the initial biennium. The Court nowhere evaluates this factor in determining the compatibility of the statute with the Establishment Clause, as that Clause requires, *Everson* v. *Board of Education*. Its evaluation, even after deduction of the amount appropriated to finance §§ 3317.06 (B) and (C), compels in my view the conclusion that a divisive political potential of unusual magnitude inheres in the Ohio program. This suffices without more to require the conclusion that the Ohio statute in its entirety offends the First Amendment's prohibition against laws "respecting an establishment of religion." *Meek* v. *Pittenger*, (Brennan, J., concurring); *Lemon* v. *Kurtzman*, (Douglas, J., concurring); *Everson* v. *Board of Education*.

Mr. *Justice* MARSHALL, concurring and dissenting.

I join Parts I, V, VII, and VIII of the Court's opinion. For the reasons stated below, however, I am unable to join the remainder of the Court's opinion or its judgment upholding the constitutionality of §§ 3317.06 (A), (G), (H), (I), (J), and (K).

The Court upholds the textbook loan provision, § 3317.06 (A), on the precedent of *Board of Education* v. *Allen*. **⊥257** It also recognizes, however, that there is "a tension" between *Allen* and the reasoning of the Court in *Meek* v. *Pittenger*. I would resolve that tension by overruling *Allen*. I am now convinced that *Allen* is largely responsible for reducing the "high and impregnable" wall between church and state erected by the First Amendment, *Everson* v. *Board of Education*, to "a blurred, indistinct, and variable barrier" incapable of performing its vital functions of protecting both church and state.

In *Allen*, we upheld a textbook loan program on the assumption that the sectarian school's twin functions of religious instruction and secular education were separable. In *Meek*, we flatly rejected that assumption as a basis for allowing a State to loan secular teaching materials and equipment to such schools: "The very purpose of many of those schools is to provide an integrated secular and religious education; the teaching process is, to a large extent, devoted to the inculcation of religious values and belief. . . . Substantial aid to the educational function of such schools, accordingly, necessarily results in aid to the sectarian school enterprise as a whole. '[T]he secular education those schools provide goes hand in hand with the religious mission that is the only reason for the schools' existence. Within the institution, the two are inextricably intertwined.' *Lemon* v. *Kurtzman* (opinion of Brennan, J.)."

Thus, although *Meek* upheld a textbook loan program on the strength of *Allen*, it left the rationale of *Allen* undamaged only if there is a constitutionally significant difference between a loan of pedagogical materials directly to a sectarian school and a loan of those materials to students for use in sectarian **⊥258** schools. As the Court convincingly demonstrates, there is no such difference.

Allen has also been undercut by our recognition in *Lemon* that "the divisive political potential" of programs of aid to sectarian schools is one of the dangers of entanglement of church and state that the First Amendment was intended to forestall. We were concerned in *Lemon* with the danger that the need for annual appropriations of larger and larger sums would lead to "[p]olitical fragmentation and divisiveness on religious lines." This danger exists whether the appropriations are made to fund textbooks, other instructional supplies, or, as in *Lemon*, teachers' salaries. As Mr. *Justice* BRENNAN has noted, *Allen* did not consider the significance of the potential for political divisiveness inherent in programs of aid to sectarian schools. *Meek* v. *Pittenger* (separate opinion).

It is, of course, unquestionable that textbooks are central to the educational process. Under the rationale of *Meek*, therefore, they should not be provided by the State to sectarian schools because "[s]ubstantial aid to the educational function of such schools . . . necessarily results in aid to the sectarian school enterprise as a whole." It is **⊥259** also unquestionable that the cost of textbooks is certain to be substantial. Under the rationale of *Lemon*, therefore, they should not be provided because of the dangers of political "divisiveness on religious lines." I would, accordingly, overrule *Board of Education* v. *Allen* and hold unconstitutional § 3317.06(A).

By overruling *Allen*, we would free ourselves to draw a line between acceptable and unacceptable forms of aid that would be both capable of consistent application and responsive to the concerns discussed above. That line, I believe, should be placed between general welfare programs that serve children in sectarian schools because the schools happen to be a convenient place to reach the programs' target populations and programs of educational assistance. General welfare programs, in contrast to programs of educational assistance, do not provide "[s]ubstantial aid to the educational function" of schools, whether secular or sectarian, and therefore do not provide the kind of assistance to the religious **⊥260** mission of sectarian schools we found impermissible in *Meek*. Moreover, because general welfare programs do not assist the sectarian functions of denominational schools, there is no reason to expect that political disputes over the merits of those programs will divide the public along religious lines.

In addition to § 3317.06 (A), which authorizes the textbook loan program, paragraphs (B), (C), and (L), held unconstitutional by the Court, clearly fall on the wrong side of the constitutional line I propose. Those paragraphs authorize, respectively, the loan of instructional materials and equipment and the provision of transportation for school field trips. There can be no contention that these programs provide anything other than educational assistance.

I also agree with the Court that the services authorized by paragraphs (D), (F) and (G) are constitutionally permissible. Those services are speech and hearing diagnosis, psychological diagnosis and psychological and speech and hearing therapy. Like the medical, nursing, dental, and optometric services authorized by paragraph (E) and not challenged by appellants, these services promote the children's health and well-being, and have only an indirect and remote impact on their educational progress.

The Court upholds paragraphs (H), (I), and (K), which it groups with paragraph (G), under the rubric of "therapeutic services." I cannot agree that the services **⊥261** authorized by these three paragraphs should be treated like the psychological services provided by paragraph (G). Paragraph (H) authorizes the provision of guidance and counseling services. The parties stipulated that the functions to be performed by the guidance and counseling personnel would include assisting students in "developing meaningful educational and career goals," and "planning school programs of study." In addition, these personnel will discuss with parents "their children's a) educational progress and needs, b) course selections, c) educational and vocational opportunities and plans, and d) study skills." The counselors will also collect and organize information for use by parents, teachers, and students. This description makes clear that paragraph (H) authorizes services that would directly support the educational programs of sectarian schools. It is, therefore, in violation of the First Amendment.

Paragraphs (I) and (K) provide remedial services and programs for disabled children. The stipulation of the parties indicates that these paragraphs will fund specialized teachers who will both provide instruction themselves and create instructional plans for use in the students' regular classrooms. These "therapeutic services" are clearly intended to aid the sectarian schools to improve the performance of their students in the classroom. I would not treat them as if they were programs of physical or psychological therapy.

Finally, the Court upholds paragraph (J), which provides standardized tests and scoring services, on the ground that these tests are clearly nonideological and that the State has an interest in assuring that the education received by sectarian school students meets minimum standards. I do not question the legitimacy of this interest, and if Ohio required students to obtain specified scores on certain tests before being promoted or graduated, I would agree that it could administer those tests to sectarian school students to ensure that its standards were being met. The record indicates, however, only that the tests **⊥262** "are used to measure the progress of students in secular subjects." It contains no indication that the measurements are taken to assure compliance with state standards rather than for internal administrative purposes of the schools. To the extent that the testing is done to serve the purposes of the sectarian schools rather than the State, I would hold that its provision by the State violates the First Amendment.

Mr. *Justice POWELL*, concurring in part and dissenting in part.

Our decisions in this troubling area draw lines that often must seem arbitrary. No doubt we could achieve greater analytical tidiness if we were to accept the broadest implications of the observation in *Meek* v. *Pittenger*, that "[s]ubstantial aid to the educational function of [sectarian] schools . . . necessarily results in aid to the sectarian enterprise as a whole." If we took that course, it would become impossible to sustain state aid of any kind—even if the aid is wholly secular in character and is supplied to the pupils rather than the institutions. *Meek* itself would have to be overruled, along with *Board of Education* v. *Allen*, and even perhaps *Everson* v. *Board of Education*. The persistent desire of a number of States to find proper means of helping sectarian education to survive would be doomed. This Court has not yet thought that such a harsh result is required by the Establishment Clause. Certainly few would consider it in the public interest. Parochial schools, quite apart from their sectarian purpose, have provided an educational alternative for millions of young Americans; they often afford wholesome competition with our public schools; and in some States they relieve substantially the tax burden incident to the operation of public schools. The State has, moreover, a legitimate interest in facilitating education of the highest quality for all children within its boundaries, whatever school their parents have chosen for them.

⊥263 It is important to keep these issues in perspective. At this point in the 20th century we are quite far removed from the dangers that prompted the Framers to include the Establishment Clause in the Bill of Rights. The risk of significant religious or denominational control over our democratic processes—or even of deep political division along religious lines—is remote, and when viewed against the positive contributions of sectarian schools, any such risk seems entirely tolerable in light of the continuing oversight of this Court. Our decisions have sought to establish principles that preserve the cherished safeguard of the Establishment Clause without resort to blind absolutism. If this endeavor means a loss of some analytical tidiness, then that too is entirely tolerable. Most of the Court's decision today follows in this tradition, and I join Parts I through VI of its opinion.

With respect to Part VII, I concur only in the judgment. I am not persuaded, nor did *Meek* hold, that all loans of secular instructional material and equipment "inescapably [have] the primary effect of providing a direct and substantial advancement of the sectarian enterprise." If that were the case, then *Meek* surely would have overruled *Allen*. Instead the Court reaffirmed *Allen*, thereby necessarily holding that at least some such loans of materials helpful in the educational process are permissible—so long as the aid is incapable of diversion to religious uses, cf. *Committee for Public Education* v. *Nyquist*, and so long as the materials are lent to the individual students or their parents and not to the sectarian institutions. Here the statute is expressly limited to materials incapable of diversion. Therefore the relevant question is whether the materials are such that they are "furnished for the use of *individual* students and at their request." *Allen* (emphasis added).

The Ohio statute includes some materials such as wall maps, ⊥**264** charts and other classroom paraphernalia for which the concept of a loan to individuals is a transparent fiction. A loan of these items is indistinguishable from forbidden "direct aid" to the sectarian institution itself, whoever the technical bailee. Since the provision makes no attempt to separate these instructional materials from others meaningfully lent to individuals, I agree with the Court that it cannot be sustained under our precedents. But I would find no constitutional defect in a properly limited provision lending to the individuals themselves only appropriate instructional materials and equipment similar to that customarily used in public schools.

I dissent as to Part VIII, concerning field trip transportation. The Court writes as though the statute funded the salary of the teacher who takes the students on the outing. In fact only the bus and driver are provided for the limited purpose of physical movement between the school and the secular destination of the field trip. As I find this aid indistinguishable in principle from that upheld in *Everson*, I would sustain the District Court's judgment approving this part of the Ohio statute.

Mr. *Justice STEVENS*, concurring in part and dissenting in part.

The distinction between the religious and secular is a fundamental one. To quote from Clarence Darrow's argument in the *Scopes* case: "The realm of religion . . . is where knowledge leaves off, and where faith begins, and it never has needed the arm of the State for support, and wherever it has received it, it has harmed both the public and the religion that it would pretend to serve."

⊥**265** The line drawn by the Establishment Clause of the First Amendment must also have a fundamental character. It should not differentiate between direct and indirect subsidies, or between instructional materials like globes and maps on the one hand and instructional materials like textbooks on the other. For that reason, rather than the three-part test described in Part II of the Court's opinion, I would adhere to the test enunciated for the Court by Mr. *Justice BLACK*: "No tax in any amount, large or small, can be levied to support any religious activities or institutions, whatever they may be called, or whatever form they may adopt to teach or practice religion." *Everson* v. *Board of Education*.

Under that test, a state subsidy of sectarian schools is invalid regardless of the form it takes. The financing of buildings, field trips, instructional materials, educational tests, and school books are all equally invalid. For all give aid to the school's educational mission, which at heart is religious. On the other hand, I am not prepared to exclude the possibility ⊥**266** that some parts of the statute before us may be administered in a constitutional manner. The State can plainly provide public health services to children attending nonpublic schools. The diagnostic and therapeutic services described in Parts V and VI of the Court's opinion may fall into this category. Although I have some misgivings on this point, I am not prepared to hold this part of the statute invalid on its face.

This Court's efforts to improve on the *Everson* test have not proved successful. "Corrosive precedents" have left us without firm principles on which to decide these cases. As this case demonstrates, the States have been encouraged to search for new ways of achieving forbidden ends. See *Committee for Public Education* v. *Nyquist*. What should be a "high and impregnable" wall between church and state, has been reduced to a "blurred, indistinct, and variable barrier." The result has been, as Clarence Darrow predicted, harm to "both the public and the religion that [this aid] would pretend to serve."

Accordingly, I dissent from Parts II, III, and IV of the Court's opinion.

COMMITTEE FOR PUBLIC EDUCATION AND RELIGIOUS LIBERTY v. REGAN

444 U.S. 646
ON APPEAL FROM THE UNITED STATES DISTRICT COURT FOR THE SOUTHERN DISTRICT OF NEW YORK
Argued November 27, 1979 — Decided February 20, 1980

⊥**648** Mr. *Justice WHITE* delivered the opinion of the Court.

The issue in this case is the constitutionality under the First and Fourteenth Amendments of the United States Constitution of a New York statute authorizing the use of public funds to reimburse church-sponsored and secular nonpublic schools for performing various testing and reporting services mandated by state law. The District Court sustained the statute. We noted probable jurisdiction and now affirm the District Court's judgment.

I

In 1970 the New York Legislature appropriated public funds to reimburse both church-sponsored and secular nonpublic schools for performing various services mandated by the State. The most expensive of these services was the "administration, grading and the compiling and reporting of the results of tests and examinations." Covered tests included both state-prepared examinations and the more common and traditional teacher-prepared tests. Although the legislature stipulated that "[n]othing contained in this act shall be construed to authorize the making of any payment under this act for religious ⊥**649** worship or instruction," the statute did not provide for any state audit of school financial records that would ensure that public funds were used only for secular purposes.

In *Levitt* v. *Committee for Public Education, (Levitt I)*, the Court struck down this enactment as violative of the Establishment Clause. The majority focused its concern on the statute's reimbursement of funds spent by schools on traditional teacher-prepared tests. The Court was troubled that, "despite the obviously integral role of such testing in the total teaching process, no attempt is made under the statute, and no means are available, to assure that internally prepared tests are free of religious instruction." It was not assumed that nonpublic school teachers would attempt in bad faith to evade constitutional requirements. Rather, the Court simply observed that "the potential for conflict 'inheres in the situation,' and because of that the State is constitutionally compelled to assure that the state-supported activity is not being used for religious indoctrination." *Lemon* v. *Kurtzman*. Because the State failed to provide the required assurance, the challenged statute was deemed to constitute an impermissible aid to religion.

The Court distinguished its earlier holdings in *Everson* v. *Board of Education* and *Board of Education* v. *Allen* on grounds that the state aid upheld in those cases, in the form of bus rides and loaned secular textbooks for sectarian schoolchildren, was "of a substantially different character" from that presented in *Levitt I*. Teacher-prepared tests were deemed by the Court to be an integral part of the teaching process. But so obviously are textbooks an integral part of the teaching ⊥**650** process. The crucial feature that distinguished tests, according to the Court, was that, "'[i]n terms of potential for involving some aspect of faith or morals in secular subjects, a textbook's content is ascertainable, but a teacher's handling of a subject is not.'" *Lemon* v. *Kurtzman*. Thus the inherent teacher discretion in devising, presenting, and grading traditional tests, together with the failure of the legislature to provide for a method of auditing to ensure that public funds would be spent exclusively on secular services, disabled the enactment from withstanding constitutional scrutiny.

Almost immediately the New York Legislature attempted to eliminate these defects from its statutory scheme. A new statute was enacted in 1974, and it directed New York's Com⊥**651**missioner of Education to apportion and to pay to nonpublic schools the actual costs incurred as a result of compliance with certain state-mandated requirements, including "the requirements of the state's pupil evaluation program, ⊥**652** the basic educational data system, regents examinations, the statewide evaluation plan, the uniform procedure for public attendance reporting, and other similar state prepared examinations and reporting procedures." New York Laws 1974, ch. 507, § 3.

Of signal interest and importance in light of *Levitt I*, the new scheme does not reimburse nonpublic schools for the preparation, administration, or grading of teacher-prepared tests. Further, the 1974 statute, unlike the 1970 version struck down in *Levitt I*, provides a means by which payments of state funds are audited, thus ensuring that only the actual costs incurred in providing the covered secular services are reimbursed out of state funds.

Although the new statutory scheme was tailored to comport with the reasoning in *Levitt I*, the District Court invalidated the enactment with respect to both the tests and the reporting procedure, *Committee for Public Education and Religious Liberty* v. *Levitt (Levitt II)*. The District Court understood the decision in *Meek* v. *Pittenger* to require this result. In *Meek*, decided after *Levitt I*, this Court held unconstitutional two Pennsylvania statutes insofar as they provided auxiliary services and instructional material and equipment apart from textbooks to nonpublic schools in the State, most of which were sectarian. The Court ruled that in "religion-pervasive" institutions, secular and religious education are so "inextricably intertwined" that "[s]ubstantial aid to the educational function of such schools . . . necessarily results in aid for the sectarian school enterprise as a whole" and hence amounts to a forbidden establishment of religion.

Levitt II was appealed to this Court. We vacated the District Court's judgment and remanded the case in light of our decision in *Wolman* v. *Walter*. On ⊥**653** remand the District Court ruled that under *Wolman* "state aid may be extended to [a sectarian] school's educational activities if it can be shown with a high degree of certainty that the aid will only have secular value of legitimate interest to the State and does not present any appreciable risk of being used to aid transmission of religious views." Applying this "more flexible concept," the District Court concluded that New York's statutory scheme of reimbursement did not violate the Establishment Clause.

Our jurisdiction to review the District Court's judgment lies under 28 U.S.C. § 1253.

II

Under the precedents of this Court a legislative enactment does not contravene the Establishment Clause if it has a secular legislative purpose, if its principal or primary effect neither advances nor inhibits religion, and if it does not foster an excessive government entanglement with religion.

In *Wolman* v. *Walter* this Court reviewed and sustained in relevant part an Ohio statutory scheme that authorized, *inter alia*, the expenditure of state funds "[to] supply for use by pupils attending nonpublic schools within the district such standardized tests and scoring services as are in use in the public schools of the state."

We held that this provision, which was aimed at providing the young with an adequate secular education, reflected a secular state purpose. As the opinion of Mr. *Justice BLACKMUN* stated, "[t]he State may require that schools that are utilized to fulfill the State's compulsory-education requirement meet certain standards of instruction, . . . and may examine both ⊥**654** teachers and pupils to ensure that the State's legitimate interest is being fulfilled." *Wolman* v. *Walter*. See *Levitt I*; *Lemon* v. *Kurtzman*. Mr. *Justice BLACKMUN* further explained that under the Ohio provision the nonpublic school did not control the content of the test or its result. This "serves to prevent the use of the test as a part of religious teaching, and thus avoids that kind of direct aid to religion found present in *Levitt [I]*." *Wolman* v. *Walter*. The provision of testing services hence did not have the primary effect of aiding religion. It was also decided that "the inability of the school to control the test eliminates the need for the supervision that gives rise to excessive entanglement." We thus concluded that the Ohio statute, insofar as it concerned examinations, passed our Establishment Clause tests.

III

We agree with the District Court that *Wolman* v. *Walter* controls this case. Although the Ohio statute under review in *Wolman* and the New York statute before us here are not identical, the differences are not of constitutional dimension. Addressing first the testing provisions, we note that here, as in *Wolman*, there is clearly a secular purpose behind the legislative enactment: "To provide educational opportunity of a quality which will prepare [New York] citizens for the challenges of American life in the last decades of the twentieth century." Also like the Ohio statute, the New York plan calls for tests that are prepared by the State and administered on the premises by nonpublic school personnel. The nonpublic school thus has no control whatsoever over the content of the tests. The Ohio tests, however, were graded by the State; here there are three types of tests involved, one graded by the State and the other two by nonpublic school personnel, with the costs of the grading service, as well as the cost of administering all three ⊥**655** tests, being reimbursed by the State. In view of the nature of the tests, the District Court found that the grading of the examinations by nonpublic school employees afforded no control to the school over the outcome of any of the tests.

The District Court explained that the State-prepared tests are primarily of three types: pupil evaluation program (PEP) tests, comprehensive ("end-of-the-course") achievement tests, and Regents Scholarship and College Qualifications Tests (RSCQT). Each of the tests addresses a secular academic subject; none deals with religious subject matter. The RSCQT examinations are graded by State Education Department personnel, and the District Court correctly concluded that "the risk of [RSCQT examinations] being used for religious purposes through grading is non-existent." The PEP tests, administered universally in grades three and six and optionally in grade nine, are graded by nonpublic school employees, but they "consist entirely of objective, multiple-choice questions, which can be graded by machine and, even if graded by hand, afford the schools no more control over the results than if the tests were graded by the State." The comprehensive tests, based on state courses of study for use in grades nine through twelve, are also graded on the premises by school employees, but "consist ⊥**656** largely or entirely of objective questions with multiple-choice answers." Even though some of the comprehensive tests may include an essay question or two, the District Court found that the chance that grading the answers to state-drafted questions in secular subjects could or would be used to gauge a student's grasp of religious ideas was "minimal," especially in light of the "complete" state procedures designed to guard against serious inconsistencies in grading and any misuse of essay questions. These procedures include the submission of completed and graded comprehensive tests to the State Department of Education for review off the school premises.

We see no reason to differ with the factual or legal characterization of the testing procedure arrived at by the District Court. As in *Wolman* v. *Walter*, "[t]he nonpublic school does not control the content of the test or its result"; and here, as in *Wolman*, this factor "serves to prevent the use of the test as a part of religious teaching," thus avoiding the kind of direct aid forbidden by the Court's prior cases. The District Court was correct in concluding that there was no substantial risk that the examinations could be used for religious educational purposes.

The District Court was also correct in its characterization of the recordkeeping and reporting services for which the State reimburses the nonpublic school. Under the New York law, "[e]ach year, private schools must submit to the State a Basic Educational Data System (BEDS) report. This report contains information regarding the student body, faculty, support staff, physical facilities, and curriculum of each school. Schools are also required to submit annually a report showing the attendance record of each minor who is a student at the school." Although recordkeeping is related to the educational program, the District Court characterized it and the reporting function as "ministerial [and] lacking in ideological content or use." ⊥**657** These tasks are not part of the teaching process and cannot "be used to foster an ideological outlook." Reimbursement for the costs of so complying with state law, therefore, has primarily a secular, rather than a religious, purpose and effect.

IV

The New York statute, unlike the Ohio statute at issue in *Wolman*, provides for direct cash reimbursement to the nonpublic school for administering the state-prescribed examinations and for grading two of them. We agree with the District Court that such reimbursement does not invalidate the New York statute. If the State furnished state-prepared tests, thereby relieving the nonpublic schools of the expense of preparing their own examinations, but left the grading of the tests to the schools, and if the grading procedures could be used to further the religious mission of the school, serious Establishment Clause problems would be posed under the Court's cases, for by furnishing the tests it might be concluded that the State was directly aiding religious education. But as we have already concluded, grading the secular tests furnished by the State in this case is a function that has a secular purpose and primarily a secular effect. This conclusion is not changed simply because the State pays the school for perform⊥**658**ing the grading function. As the District Court observed, "[p]utting aside the question of whether direct financial aid can be administered without excessive entanglement by the State in the affairs of a sectarian institution, there does not appear to be any reason why payments to sectarian schools to cover the cost of specified activities would have the impermissible effect of advancing religion if the same activities performed by sectarian school personnel without reimbursement but with State-furnished materials have no such effect."

A contrary view would insist on drawing a constitutional distinction between paying the nonpublic school to do the grading and paying state employees or some independent service to perform that task, even though the grading function is the same regardless of who performs it and would not have the primary effect of aiding religion whether or not performed by nonpublic school personnel. In either event, the nonpublic school is being relieved of the cost of grading state-required, state-furnished examinations. We decline to embrace a formalistic dichotomy that bears so little relationship either to common sense or to the realities of school finance. None of our cases requires us to invalidate these reimbursements simply because they involve payments in cash. The Court "has not accepted the recurrent argument that all aid is forbidden because aid to one aspect of an institution frees it to spend its other resources on religious ends." *Hunt* v. *McNair*. Because the recordkeeping and ⊥**659** reporting functions also have neither a religious purpose nor a primarily religious effect, we reach the same results with respect to the reimbursements for these services.

Of course, under the relevant cases the outcome would likely be different were there no effective means for insuring that the cash reimbursements would cover only secular services. See *Levitt I; Committee for Public Education* v. *Nyquist; Lemon* v. *Kurtzman*. But here, as we shall see, the New York law provides ample safeguards against excessive or misdirected reimbursement.

V

The District Court recognized that "[w]here a state is required in determining what aid, if any, may be extended to a sectarian school, to monitor the day-to-day activities of the teaching staff, to engage in onerous, direct oversight, or to make on-site judgments from time to time as to whether different school activities are religious in character, the risk of entanglement is too great to permit governmental involvement." After examining the New York statute and its operation, however, the District Court concluded that "[t]he activities subsidized under the Statute here at issue . . . do not pose any substantial risk of such entanglement."

The District Court described the process of reimbursement: "Schools which seek reimbursement must 'maintain a separate account or system of accounts for the expenses incurred in rendering' the reimbursable services, and they must submit to the N.Y. State Commissioner of Education an application for reimbursement with additional reports and documents prescribed by the Commissioner. . . . Reimbursable costs include proportionate shares of the teachers' salaries and fringe benefits attrib⊥**660**utable to administration of the examinations and reporting of State-required data on pupil attendance and performance, plus the cost of supplies and other contractual expenditures such as data processing services. Applications for reimbursement cannot be approved until the Commissioner audits vouchers or other documents submitted by the schools to substantiate their claims. . . . The Statute further provides that the State Department of Audit and Control shall from time to time inspect the accounts of recipient schools in order to verify the cost to the schools of rendering the reimbursable services. If the audit reveals that a school has received an amount in excess of its actual costs, the excess must be returned to the State immediately. . . ."

We agree with the District Court that "[t]he services for which the private schools would be reimbursed are discrete and clearly identifiable." The reimbursement process, furthermore, is straightforward and susceptible to the routinization that characterizes most reimbursement schemes. On its face, therefore, the New York plan suggests no excessive entanglement, and we are not prepared to read into the plan as an inevitability the bad faith ⊥**661** upon which any future excessive entanglement would be predicated.

VI

It is urged that the District Court judgment is unsupportable under *Meek* v. *Pittenger*, which is said to have held that any aid to even secular educational functions of a sectarian school is forbidden, or more broadly still, that any aid to a sectarian school is suspect since its religious teaching is so pervasively intermixed with each and every one of its activities. The difficulty with this position is that a majority of the Court, including the author of *Meek* v. *Pittenger*, upheld in *Wolman* a state statute under which the State, by preparing and grading tests in secular subjects, relieved sectarian schools of the cost of these functions, functions that they otherwise would have had to perform themselves and that were intimately connected with the educational processes. Yet the *Wolman* opinion at no point suggested that this holding was inconsistent with the decision in *Meek*. Unless the majority in *Wolman* was silently disavowing *Meek*, in whole or in part, that case was simply not understood by this Court to stand for the broad proposition urged by appellants and espoused by the District Court in *Levitt II*.

That *Meek* was understood more narrowly was suggested by Mr. *Justice POWELL* in his separate opinion in *Wolman:* "I am not persuaded," he said, "nor did *Meek* hold, that all loans ⊥**662** of secular instructional material and equipment" inescapably have the effect of direct advancement of religion. And obviously the testing services furnished by the State in *Wolman* were approved on the premise that those services did not and could not have the primary effect of advancing the sectarian aims of the nonpublic schools. With these indicators before it, the District Court properly put the two cases together and sustained the reimbursements involved here because it had been shown with sufficient clarity that they would serve the State's legitimate secular ends without any appreciable risk of being used to transmit or teach religious views.

This is not to say that this case, any more than past cases, will furnish a litmus-paper test to distinguish permissible from impermissible aid to religiously oriented schools. But Establishment Clause cases are not easy; they stir deep feelings; and we are divided among ourselves, perhaps reflecting the different views on this subject of the people of this country. What is certain is that our decisions have tended to avoid categorical imperatives and absolutist approaches at either end of the range of possible outcomes. This course sacrifices clarity and predictability for flexibility, but this promises to be the case until the continuing interaction between the courts and the States—the former charged with interpreting and upholding the Constitution and the latter seeking to provide education for their youth—produces a single, more encompassing construction of the Establishment Clause.

The judgment of the District Court is
Affirmed.

Mr. *Justice* BLACKMUN, with whom Mr. *Justice* BRENNAN and Mr. *Justice* MARSHALL join, dissenting.

The Court in this case, I fear, takes a long step backwards in the inevitable controversy that emerges when a state legislature continues to insist on providing public aid to parochial schools.

⊥**663** I thought that the Court's judgments in *Meek* v. *Pittenger* and in *Wolman* v. *Walter* (which the Court concedes is the controlling authority here), at last had fixed the line between that which is constitutionally appropriate public aid and that which is not. The line necessarily was not a straight one. It could not be, when this Court, on the one hand, in *Everson* v. *Board of Education*, by a 5-4 vote, decided that there was no barrier under the First and Fourteenth Amendments to parental reimbursement of the cost of fares for the transportation of children attending parochial schools, and in *Board of Education* v. *Allen*, by a 6-3 vote, ruled that New York's lending of approved textbooks to students in private secondary schools was not violative of those Amendments, and yet, on the other hand, in *Lemon* v. *Kurtzman*, struck down, as violative of the Religion Clauses, statutes that, respectively, would have supplemented nonpublic school teachers' salaries and would have authorized the "purchase" of certain "secular educational services" from nonpublic schools, and also in *Levitt* v. *Committee for Public Education (Levitt I)*, struck down New York's previous attempt to reimburse nonpublic schools for the expenses of tests and examinations. See also *Committee for Public Education* v. *Nyquist*, where the Court nullified New York's financial aid programs for "maintenance and repair" of facilities and equipment, a tuition reimbursement plan, and tax relief for parents who did not qualify for tuition reimbursement, and *Sloan* v. *Lemon*, where the Court ruled invalid a state plan for parental reimbursement of a portion of nonpublic school tuition expenses. And see *Roemer* v. *Maryland Public Works Bd.*

But, I repeat, the line, wavering though it may be, was indeed drawn in *Meek* and in *Wolman*, albeit with different ⊥**664** combinations of Justices, those who perceive no barrier under the First and Fourteenth Amendments and who would rule in favor of almost any aid a state legislature saw fit to provide, on the one hand, and those who perceive a broad barrier and would rule against aid of almost any kind, on the other hand, in turn joining Justices in the center on these issues to make order and a consensus out of the earlier decisions. Now, some of those who joined in *Lemon*, *Levitt I*, *Meek*, and *Wolman* in invalidating, depart and validate. I am able to attribute this defection only to a concern about the continuing and emotional controversy and to a persuasion that a good-faith attempt on the part of a state legislature is worth a nod of approval.

I

In order properly to analyze the amended school aid plan that the New York Legislature produced in response to its defeat in *Levitt*, it is imperative, it seems to me, to examine the statute's operational details with great precision and with fewer generalities than the Court does today. One should do more than give a passing glance at selected provisions of the statute, and one should not ignore the considerations that prompted the three-judge District Court initially and *unanimously* to hold New York's revised plan to be unconstitutional, *Committee for Public Education and Religious Liberty* v. *Levitt*, *(Levitt II)* and that prompted Judge Ward, in his persuasive dissent in *Levitt III*, *Committee for Public Education and Religious Liberty* v. *Levitt*, after our remand, to differ so vigorously with his two colleagues who meanwhile changed their minds, mistakenly in my view.

II

The Court and all three judges of the District Court are correct, of course, in recognizing that the "mode of analysis for Establishment ⊥665 Clause questions is defined by the three-part test that has emerged from the Court's decisions." *Wolman* v. *Walter* (plurality opinion). To pass constitutional muster under this test, the New York statute now challenged, Chapter 507, 1974 N.Y. Laws, as amended, "must have a secular legislative purpose, must have a principal or primary effect that neither advances nor inhibits religion, and must not foster excessive government entanglement with religion."

I have no trouble in agreeing with the Court that Chapter 507 manifests a clear secular purpose. I therefore would evaluate Chapter 507 under the two remaining inquiries of the three-part test.

In deciding whether Chapter 507 has an impermissible primary effect of advancing religion, or whether it fosters excessive government entanglement with sectarian affairs, one must keep in focus the nature of the assistance prescribed by the New York statute. The District Court found that $8-10 million annually would be expended under Chapter 507, with the great majority of these funds going to sectarian schools to pay for personnel costs associated with attendance reporting. The court found that such payments would amount to from 1% to 5.4% of the personnel budget of an individual religious school receiving assistance under Chapter 507. Moreover, Chapter 507 provides direct cash payments by the State of New York to religious schools, as opposed to providing services or providing cash payments to third parties who have rendered services. And the money paid sectarian schools under Chapter 507 is designated to reimburse costs that are incurred by religious schools in order to meet basic state testing and reporting requirements, costs that would have been incurred regardless of the availability of reimbursement from the State.

This direct financial assistance provided by Chapter 507 differs significantly from the types of state aid to religious schools approved by the Court in *Wolman* v. *Walter*. For ⊥666 example, in *Wolman* the Court approved that portion of the Ohio statute that provided to religious schools the standardized tests and scoring services furnished to public schools. But, unlike New York's Chapter 507, Ohio's statute provided only the tests themselves and scoring by employees of neutral testing organizations. It did not authorize direct financial aid of any type to religious schools.

Similarly, the other forms of assistance upheld in *Wolman* did not involve direct cash assistance. Rather, the Court approved the State's providing sectarian school students therapeutic, remedial, and guidance programs administered by public employees on public property. It also approved certain public health services furnished by public employees to religious school pupils, even though administered in part on the sectarian premises, on the basis of its recognition in a number of cases, see, *e.g.*, *Meek* v. *Pittenger*, that provision of health services to all school children does not advance religion so as to contravene the Establishment Clause. And it upheld the lending by Ohio of textbooks to pupils under the "unique presumption" created by *Board of Education* v. *Allen* and reaffirmed since that time. *E.g.*, *Meek* v. *Pittenger*.

It is clear, however, that none of the programs upheld in *Wolman* provided direct financial support to sectarian schools. At the very least, then, the Court's holding today goes further in approving state assistance to sectarian schools than the Court had gone in past decisions. But beyond merely failing to approve the type of direct financial aid at issue in this case, *Wolman* reaffirmed the finding of the Court in *Meek* v. *Pittenger* that *direct* aid to the educational function of religious schools necessarily advances the sectarian enterprise as a whole. ⊥667 Thus, the Court in *Wolman* invalidated Ohio's practice of loaning instructional materials directly to sectarian schools, "even though the loan ostensibly was limited to neutral and secular instructional material and equipment, [because] it inescapably had the primary effect of providing a direct and substantial advancement of the sectarian enterprise." In the same vein, the Court disapproved Ohio's provision of fieldtrip transportation directly to religious schools as impermissible direct aid that, because of the pervasively religious nature of the schools involved, furthered the religious goals of the schools, and that also required government surveillance of expenditures to such a degree as to foster entanglement of the State in religion.

Wolman thus re-enforces the conclusion that substantial direct financial aid to a religious school, even though ostensibly for secular purposes, runs the great risk of furthering the religious mission of the school as a whole because that religious mission so pervades the functioning of the school. The Court specifically recognized this in *Meek*: "[F]aced with the substantial amounts of direct support authorized by [the statute at issue], it would simply ignore reality to attempt to separate secular educational functions from the predominantly religious role performed by many . . . church-related elementary and secondary schools and to then characterize [the statute] as channeling aid to the secular without providing direct aid to the sectarian. Even though earmarked for secular purposes, 'when it flows to an institution in which religion is so pervasive that a substantial portion of its functions are subsumed in the religious mission,' state aid has the impermissible primary effect of advancing religion. *Hunt* v. *McNair*."

⊥668 Under the principles announced in these decided cases, I am compelled to conclude that Chapter 507, by providing substantial financial assistance directly to sectarian schools, has a primary effect of advancing religion. The vast majority of the schools aided under Chapter 507 typify the religious-pervasive institution the very purpose of which is to provide an integrated secular and sectarian education. The aid provided by Chapter

507 goes primarily to reimburse such schools for personnel costs incurred in complying with state reporting and testing requirements, costs that must be incurred if the school is to be accredited to provide a combined sectarian-secular education to school-age pupils. To continue to function as religious schools, sectarian schools thus are required to incur the costs outlined in § 3 of Chapter 507, or else lose accreditation by the State of New York. These reporting and testing requirements would be met by the schools whether reimbursement were available or not. As such, the attendance, informational, and testing expenses compensated by Chapter 507 are essential to the overall educational functioning of sectarian schools in New York in the same way instruction in secular subjects is essential. Therefore, just as direct aid for ostensibly secular purposes by provision of instructional materials or direct financial subsidy is forbidden by the Establishment Clause, so direct aid for the performance of recordkeeping and testing activities that are an essential part of the sectarian school's functioning also is interdicted. The Court stated in *Meek*, and reaffirmed in *Wolman*: "The very purpose of many [religious] schools is to provide an integrated secular and religious education; the teaching process is, to a large extent, devoted to the inculcation of religious values and belief. See *Lemon* v. *Kurtzman*. Substantial aid to the educational function of such schools, accordingly, necessarily results in aid to the sectarian school enterprise as **⊥669** a whole. '[T]he secular education those schools provide goes hand in hand with the religious mission that is the only reason for the schools' existence. Within the institution, the two are inextricably intertwined.'"

It is also true that the keeping of pupil attendance records is essential to the religious mission of sectarian schools. To ensure that the school is fulfilling its religious mission properly, it is necessary to provide a way to determine whether pupils are attending the sectarian classes required of them. Accordingly, Chapter 507 not only advances religion by aiding the educational mission of the sectarian school as a whole; it also subsidizes directly the religious mission of such schools. Chapter 507 makes no attempt, and none is possible, to separate the portion of the overall expense of attendance-taking attributable to the desire to ensure that students are attending religious instruction from that portion attributable to the desire to ensure that state attendance laws are complied with. This type of direct aid the Establishment Clause does not permit.

I thus would hold that the aid provided by Chapter 507 constitutes a direct subsidy of the operating costs of the sectarian school that aids the school as a whole, and that the statute therefore directly advances religion in violation of the Establishment Clause of the First Amendment.

III

Beyond this, Chapter 507 also fosters government entanglement with religion to an impermissible extent. Unlike *Wolman*, under Chapter 507 sectarian employees are compensated by the State for grading examinations. In some cases, such grading requires the teacher to exercise subjective judgment. For the State properly to ensure that judgment is **⊥670** not exercised to inculcate religion, a "comprehensive, discriminating, and continuing state surveillance will inevitably be required." *Lemon* v. *Kurtzman*.

Moreover, Chapter 507 provides for continuing reimbursement with regard to examinations in which the questions may vary from year to year, and for examinations that may be offered in the future. This will require the State continually to evaluate the examinations to ensure that reimbursement for expenses incurred in connection with their administration and grading will not offend the First Amendment. This, too, fosters impermissible government involvement in sectarian affairs, since it is likely to lead to continuing adjudication of disputes between the State and others as to whether certain questions or new examinations present such opportunities for the advancement of religion that reimbursement for administering and grading them should not be permitted. Cf. *New York* v. *Cathedral Academy*.

Finally, entanglement also is fostered by the system of reimbursement for personnel expenses. The State must make sure that it reimburses sectarian schools only for those personnel costs attributable to the sectarian employees' secular activities described in § 3 of Chapter 507. It is difficult to see how the State adequately may discover whether the time for which reimbursement is made available was devoted only to secular activities without some type of ongoing surveillance of the sectarian employees and religious schools at issue. It is this type of extensive entanglement that the Establishment Clause forbids. I fail to see, and I am uncomfortable with, the so-called "ample safeguards" upon which the Court and the District Court's majority, *Levitt III*, are content to rest so assured.

I therefore conclude that Chapter 507 has a primary effect of advancing religion and also fosters excessive government entanglement with religion. The statute, consequently, is unconstitutional under the Establishment Clause, **⊥671** at least to the extent it provides reimbursement directly to sectarian nonpublic schools.

I would reverse the judgment of the District Court.

Mr. *Justice* STEVENS, dissenting.

Although I agree with Mr. *Justice* BLACKMUN's demonstration of why today's holding is not compelled by precedent, my vote also rests on a more fundamental disagreement with the Court. The Court's approval of a direct subsidy to sectarian schools to reimburse them for staff time spent in taking attendance and grading standardized tests is but another in a long line of cases making largely ad hoc decisions about what payments may or may not be constitutionally made to nonpublic schools. In groping for a rationale to support today's decision, the Court has taken a position that could equally be used to support a subsidy to pay for staff time attributable to conducting fire drills or even for constructing and maintaining fireproof premises in which to conduct class. Though such subsidies might represent expedient fiscal policy, I firmly believe they would violate the Establishment Clause of the First Amendment.

The Court's adoption of such a position confirms my view, expressed in *Wolman* v. *Walter* (Stevens, J., dissenting), and *Roemer* v. *Board of Public Works* (Stevens, J., dissenting), that the entire enterprise of trying to justify various types of subsidies to nonpublic schools should be abandoned. Rather than continuing with the sisyphean task of trying to patch together the "blurred, indistinct, and variable barrier" described in *Lemon* v. *Kurtzman*, I would resurrect the "high and impregnable" wall between church and state constructed by the Framers of the First Amendment. See *Everson* v. *Board of Education*.

MUELLER v. ALLEN

463 U.S. 388
ON WRIT OF CERTIORARI
TO THE UNITED STATES COURT OF APPEALS
FOR THE EIGHTH CIRCUIT
Argued April 18, 1983 — Decided June 29, 1983

⊥390 *Justice REHNQUIST* delivered the opinion of the Court.

Minnesota allows taxpayers, in computing their state income tax, to deduct certain expenses incurred in providing for the education of their children. Minn. Stat. §290.09, subd. 22 (1982). The United States Court of Appeals for the Eighth Circuit held that the Establishment Clause of the First and Fourteenth Amendments was not offended by this arrangement. Because this question was reserved in *Committee for Public Education* v. *Nyquist*, and bec**⊥391**ause of a conflict between the decision of the Court of Appeals for the Eighth Circuit and that of the Court of Appeals for the First Circuit in *Rhode Island Federation of Teachers* v. *Norberg*, we granted certiorari. We now affirm.

Minnesota, like every other state, provides its citizens with free elementary and secondary schooling. It seems to be agreed that about 820,000 students attended this school system in the most recent school year. During the same year, approximately 91,000 elementary and secondary students attended some 500 privately supported schools located in Minnesota, and about 95% of these students attended schools considering themselves to be sectarian.

Minnesota, by a law originally enacted in 1955 and revised in 1976 and again in 1978, permits state taxpayers to claim a deduction from gross income for certain expenses incurred in educating their children. The deduction is limited to actual expenses incurred for the "tuition, textbooks and transportation" of dependents attending elementary or secondary schools. A deduction may not exceed $500 per dependent in grades K through six and $700 per dependent in grades seven through twelve.

⊥392 Petitioners—certain Minnesota taxpayers—sued in the United States District court for the District of Minnesota claiming that § 290.09, subd. 22, violated the Establishment Clause by providing financial assistance to sectarian institutions. They named as respondents the Commissioner of the Department of Revenue of Minnesota and several parents who took advantage of the tax deduction for expenses incurred in sending their children to parochial schools. The District Court granted respondent's motion for summary judgment, holding that the statute was "neutral on its face and in its application and does not have a primary effect of either advancing or inhibiting religion." 514 F. Supp. 998. On appeal, the Court of Appeals affirmed, concluding that the Minnesota statute substantially benefited a "broad class of Minnesota citizens."

Today's case is no exception to our oft-repeated statement that the Establishment Clause presents especially difficult questions of interpretation and application. It is easy enough to quote the few words comprising that clause—"Congress shall make no law respecting an establishment of **⊥393** religion." It is not at all easy, however, to apply this Court's various decisions construing the Clause to governmental programs of financial assistance to sectarian schools and the parents of children attending those schools. Indeed, in many of these decisions "we have expressly or implicitly acknowledged that 'we can only dimly perceive the lines of demarcation in this extraordinarily sensitive area of constitutional law.'" *Lemon* v. *Kurtzman*.

One fixed principle in this field is our consistent rejection of the argument that "any program which in some manner aids an institution with a religious affiliation" violates the Establishment Clause. *Hunt* v. *McNair*. For example, it is now well-established that a state may reimburse parents for expenses incurred in transporting their children to school, *Everson* v. *Board of Education*, and that it may loan secular textbooks to all schoolchildren within the state, *Board of Education* v. *Allen*.

Notwithstanding the repeated approval given programs such as those in *Allen* and *Everson*, our decisions also have struck down arrangements resembling, in many respects, these forms of assistance. In this case we **⊥394** are asked to decide whether Minnesota's tax deduction bears greater resemblance to those types of assistance to parochial schools we have approved, or to those we have struck down. Petitioners place particular reliance on our decision in *Committee for Public Education* v. *Nyquist*, where we held invalid a New York statute providing public funds for the maintenance and repair of the physical facilities of private schools and granting thinly disguised "tax benefits," actually amounting to tuition grants, to the parents of children attending private schools. As explained below, we conclude that § 290.09, subd. 22, bears less resemblance to the arrangement struck down in *Nyquist* than it does to assistance programs upheld in our prior decisions and those discussed with approval in *Nyquist*.

The general nature of our inquiry in this area has been guided, since the decision in *Lemon* v. *Kurtzman*, by the "three-part" test laid down in that case: "First, the statute must have a secular legislative purpose; second, its principal or primary effect must be one that neither advances nor inhibits religion . . . ; finally, the statute must not foster 'an excessive government entanglement with religion.'" *Id.* While this principle is well settled, our cases have also emphasized that it provides "no more than [a] helpful signpost" in dealing with Establishment Clause challenges. *Hunt* v. *McNair*. With this caveat in mind, we turn to the specific challenges raised against § 290.09, subd. 22, under the *Lemon* framework.

Little time need be spent on the question of whether the Minnesota tax deduction has a secular purpose. Under our prior decisions, governmental assistance programs have consistently survived this inquiry even when they have run afoul of other aspects of the *Lemon* framework. This reflects, at least in part, our reluctance to attribute unconstitutional motives to the states, particularly when a plausible secular purpose ⊥**395** for the state's program may be discerned from the face of the statute.

A state's decision to defray the cost of educational expenses incurred by parents—regardless of the type of schools their children attend—evidences a purpose that is both secular and understandable. An educated populace is essential to the political and economic health of any community, and a state's efforts to assist parents in meeting the rising cost of educational expenses plainly serves this secular purpose of ensuring that the state's citizenry is well-educated. Similarly, Minnesota, like other states, could conclude that there is a strong public interest in assuring the continued financial health of private schools, both sectarian and non-sectarian. By educating a substantial number of students such schools relieve public schools of a correspondingly great burden—to the benefit of all taxpayers. In addition, private schools may serve as a benchmark for public schools, in a manner analogous to the "TVA yardstick" for private power companies. As *Justice POWELL* has remarked: "Parochial schools, quite apart from their sectarian purpose, have provided an educational alternative for millions of young Americans; they often afford wholesome competition with our public schools; and in some States they relieve substantially the tax burden incident to the operation of public schools. The State has, moreover, a legitimate interest in facilitating education of the highest quality for all children within its boundaries, whatever school their parents have chosen for them." *Wolman* v. *Walter*. All these justifications are readily available to support § 290.09, subd. 22, and each is sufficient to satisfy the secular purpose inquiry of *Lemon*.

⊥**396** We turn therefore to the more difficult but related question whether the Minnesota statute has "the primary effect of advancing the sectarian aims of the nonpublic schools." In concluding that it does not, we find several features of the Minnesota tax deduction particularly significant. First, an essential feature of Minnesota's arrangement is the fact that § 290.09, subd. 22, is only one among many deductions—such as those for medical expenses and charitable contributions—available under the Minnesota tax laws. Our decisions consistently have recognized that traditionally "[l]egislatures have especially broad latitude in creating classifications and distinctions in tax statutes," *Reagan* v. *Taxation with Representation*, in part because the "familiarity with local conditions" enjoyed by legislators especially enables them to "achieve an equitable distribution of the tax burden." *Madden* v. *Kentucky*. Under our prior decisions, the Minnesota legislature's judgment that a deduction for educational expenses fairly equalizes the tax burden of its citizens and encourages desirable expenditures for educational purposes is entitled to substantial deference.

⊥**397** Other characteristics of § 290.09, subd. 22, argue equally strongly for the provision's constitutionality. Most importantly, the deduction is available for educational expenses incurred by *all* parents, including those whose children attend non-sectarian private schools or sectarian private schools. Just as in *Widmar* v. *Vincent*, where we concluded that the state's provision of a forum neutrally "open to a broad class of nonreligious as well as religious speakers" does not "confer any imprimatur of State approval," so here: "the provision of benefits to so broad a spectrum of groups is an important index of secular effect."

⊥**398** In this respect, as well as others, this case is vitally different from the scheme struck down in *Nyquist*. There, public assistance amounting to tuition grants, was provided only to parents of children in *nonpublic* schools. This fact had considerable bearing on our decision striking down the New York statute at issue; we explicitly distinguished both *Allen* and *Everson* on the grounds that "In both cases the class of beneficiaries included *all* schoolchildren, those in public as well as those in private schools." Moreover, we intimated that "public assistance (e.g., scholarships) made available generally without regard to the sectarian-nonsectarian or public-nonpublic nature of the institution benefited," might not offend the Establishment Clause. We think the tax deduction adopted by Minnesota is more similar to this latter type of program than it is to the arrangement struck down in *Nyquist*. Unlike the assistance at issue in *Nyquist*, § 290.09, subd. 22, permits *all* parents—whether their children attend public school or private—to deduct their childrens' educational expenses. As *Widmar* and our other decisions indicate, a program, like § 290.09, subd. 22, that neutrally pro⊥**399**vides state assistance to a broad spectrum of citizens is not readily subject to challenge under the Establishment Clause.

We also agree with the Court of Appeals that, by channeling whatever assistance it may provide to parochial schools through individual parents, Minnesota has reduced the Establishment Clause objections to which its action is subject. It is true, of course, that financial assistance provided to parents ultimately has an economic effect comparable to that of aid given directly to the schools attended by their children. It is also true, however, that under Minnesota's arrangement public funds become available only as a result of numerous, private choices of individual parents of school-age children.

For these reasons, we recognized in *Nyquist* that the means by which state assistance flows to private schools is of some importance: we said that "the fact that aid is disbursed to parents rather than to . . . schools" is a material consideration in Establishment Clause analysis, albeit "only one among many to be considered." *Nyquist.* It is noteworthy that all but one of our recent cases invalidating state aid to parochial schools have involved the direct transmission of assistance from the state to the schools themselves. The exception, of course, was *Nyquist,* which, as discussed previously, is distinguishable from this case on other grounds. Where, as here, aid to parochial schools is available only as a result of decisions of individual parents no "imprimatur of State approval," *Widmar,* can be deemed to have been conferred on any particular religion, or on religion generally.

We find it useful, in the light of the foregoing characteristics of § 290.09, subd. 22, to compare the attenuated financial benefits flowing to parochial schools from the section to the evils against which the Establishment Clause was designed to protect. These dangers are well-described by our statement that "what is at stake as a matter of policy [in Establishment Clause cases] is preventing that kind and degree of government involvement in religious life that, as history ⊥**400** teaches us, is apt to lead to strife and frequently strain a political system to the breaking point." *Walz* v. *Tax Comm'n.* It is important, however, to "keep these issues in perspective": "At this point in the 20th century we are quite far removed from the dangers that prompted the Framers to include the Establishment Clause in the Bill of Rights. The risk of significant religious or denominational control over our democratic processes—or even of deep political division along religious lines—is remote, and when viewed against the positive contributions of sectarian schools, any such risk seems entirely tolerable in light of the continuing oversight of this Court." *Wolman.* The Establishment Clause of course extends beyond prohibition of a state church or payment of state funds to one or more churches. We do not think, however, that its prohibition extends to the type of tax deduction established by Minnesota. The historic purposes of the Clause simply do not encompass the sort of attenuated financial benefit, ultimately controlled by the private choices of individual parents, that eventually flows to parochial schools from the neutrally available tax benefit at issue in this case.

Petitioners argue that, notwithstanding the facial neutrality of § 290.09, subd. 22, in application the statute primarily benefits religious institutions. Petitioners rely, as they did ⊥**401** below, on a statistical analysis of the type of persons claiming the tax deduction. They contend that most parents of public school children incur no tuition expenses, and that other expenses deductible under § 290.09, subd. 22, are negligible in value; moreover, they claim that 96% of the children in private schools in 1978-1979 attended religiously-affiliated institutions. Because of all this, they reason, the bulk of deductions taken under § 290.09, subd. 22, will be claimed by parents of children in sectarian schools. Respondents reply that petitioners have failed to consider the impact of deductions for items such as transportation, summer school tuition, tuition paid by parents whose children attended schools outside the school districts in which they resided, rental or purchase costs for a variety of equipment, and tuition for certain types of instruction not ordinarily provided in public schools.

We need not consider these contentions in detail. We would be loath to adopt a rule grounding the constitutionality of a facially neutral law on annual reports reciting the extent to which various classes of private citizens claimed benefits under the law. Such an approach would scarcely provide the certainty that this field stands in need of, nor can we perceive principled standards by which such statistical evidence might be evaluated. Moreover, the fact that private persons fail in a particular year to claim the tax relief to which they are entitled—under a facially neutral statute—should be of little importance in determining the constitutionality of the statute permitting such relief.

Finally, private educational institutions, and parents paying for their children to attend these schools, make special contributions to the areas in which they operate. "Parochial ⊥**402** schools, quite apart from their sectarian purpose, have provided an educational alternative for millions of young Americans; they often afford wholesome competition with our public schools; and in some States they relieve substantially the tax burden incident to the operation of public schools." *Wolman.* If parents of children in private schools choose to take especial advantage of the relief provided by § 290.09, subd. 22, it is no doubt due to the fact that they bear a particularly great financial burden in educating their children. More fundamentally, whatever unequal effect may be attributed to the statutory classification can fairly be regarded as a rough return for the benefits, discussed above, provided to the state and all taxpayers by parents sending their children to parochial schools. In the light of all this, we believe it wiser to decline to engage in the type of empirical inquiry into those persons benefited by state law which petitioners urge.

Thus, we hold that the Minnesota tax deduction for educational expenses satisfies the primary effect inquiry of our Establishment Clause cases.

⊥**403** Turning to the third part of the *Lemon* inquiry, we have no difficulty in concluding that the Minnesota statute does not "excessively entangle" the state in religion. The only plausible source of the "comprehensive, discriminating, and continuing state surveillance" necessary to run afoul of this standard would lie in the fact that state officials must determine whether particular textbooks qualify for a deduction. In making this decision, state officials must disallow deductions taken from "instructional books and materials used in the teaching of religious tenets, doctrines or worship, the purpose of which is to inculcate such tenets, doctrines or worship." §

290.09, subd. 22, Making decisions such as this does not differ substantially from making the types of decisions approved in earlier opinions of this Court. In *Board of Education* v. *Allen*, for example, the Court upheld the loan of secular textbooks to parents or children attending nonpublic schools; though state officials were required to determine whether particular books were or were not secular, the system was held not to violate the Establishment Clause. The same result follows in this case.

⊥**404** For the foregoing reasons, the judgment of the Court of Appeals is *Affirmed*.

Justice MARSHALL, with whom *Justice* BRENNAN, *Justice* BLACKMUN and *Justice* STEVENS join, dissenting.

The Establishment Clause of the First Amendment prohibits a State from subsidizing religious education, whether it does so directly or indirectly. In my view, this principle of neutrality forbids not only the tax benefits struck down in *Committee for Public Education* v. *Nyquist*, but any tax benefit, including the tax deduction at issue here, which subsidizes tuition payments to sectarian schools. I also believe that the Establishment Clause prohibits the tax deductions that Minnesota authorizes for the cost of books and other instructional materials used for sectarian purposes.

I

The majority today does not question the continuing vitality of this Court's decision in *Nyquist*. That decision established that a State may not support religious education either through direct grants to parochial schools or through financial aid to parents of parochial school students. *Nyquist* also established that financial aid to parents of students attending parochial schools is no more permissible if it is provided in the form of a tax credit than if provided in the form of cash payments. Notwithstanding these accepted prin⊥**405**ciples, the Court today upholds a statute that provides a tax deduction for the tuition charged by religious schools. The Court concludes that the Minnesota statute is "vitally different" from the New York statute at issue in *Nyquist*. As demonstrated below, there is no significant difference between the two schemes. The Minnesota tax statute violates the Establishment Clause for precisely the same reason as the statute struck down in *Nyquist:* it has a direct and immediate effect of advancing religion.

A

In calculating their net income for state income tax purposes, Minnesota residents are permitted to deduct the cost of their children's tuition, subject to a ceiling of $500 or $700 per child. By taking this deduction, a taxpayer reduces his tax bill by a sum equal to the amount of tuition multiplied by his rate of tax. Although this tax benefit is available to any parents whose children attend schools which charge tuition, the vast majority of the taxpayers who are eligible to receive the benefit are parents whose children attend religious schools. In the 1978-1979 school year, 90,000 students were enrolled in nonpublic schools charging tuition; over 95% of those students attended sectarian schools. Although the statute also allows a deduction for the tuition expenses of children attending public schools, Minnesota public schools are generally prohibited by law from charging tuition. Public schools may assess tuition charges only for students accepted from outside the district. In the 1978-1979 school year, only 79 public school students fell into this category. The parents of the remaining 815,000 students who attended public schools were ineligible to receive this tax benefit.

Like the law involved in *Nyquist*, the Minnesota law can be said to serve a secular purpose: promoting pluralism and diversity among the State's public and nonpublic schools. But the Establishment Clause requires more than that legislation have a secular purpose. "[T]he ⊥**406** propriety of a legislature's purposes may not immunize from further scrutiny a law which . . . has a primary effect that advances religion." *Nyquist*. Moreover, even if one "'primary' effect [is] to promote some legitimate end under the State's police power," the legislation is not "immune from further examination to ascertain whether it also has the direct and immediate effect of advancing religion." *Id*.

As we recognized in *Nyquist*, direct government subsidization of parochial school tuition is impermissible because "the effect of the aid is unmistakably to provide desired financial support for nonpublic, sectarian institutions." *Id*., "[A]id to the educational function of [parochial] schools . . . necessarily results in aid to the sectarian enterprise as a whole" because "[t]he very purpose of those schools is to provide an integrated secular and religious education." *Meek* v. *Pittenger*. For this reason, aid to sectarian schools must be restricted to ensure that it may not be used to further the religious mission of those schools. While "services such as police and fire protection, sewage disposal, highways, and sidewalks," may be provided to parochial schools in common with other institutions, because this type of assistance is clearly "'marked off from the religious function'" of those schools, *Everson* v. *Board of Education*, unrestricted financial assistance, such as grants for the maintenance and construction of parochial schools, may not be ⊥**407** provided. *Nyquist*. "In the absence of an effective means of guaranteeing that the state aid derived from public funds will be used exclusively for secular, neutral, and nonideological purposes, it is clear from our cases that direct aid in whatever form is invalid." *Id*.

Indirect assistance in the form of financial aid to parents for tuition payments is similarly impermissible because it is not "subject to . . . restrictions" which "'guarantee the separation between secular and religious educational functions and . . . ensure that State financial aid supports only the former.'" *Id*. By ensuring that parents will be reimbursed for tuition payments they make, the Minnesota statute requires that taxpayers in general pay for the cost of parochial education and extends a financial "incentive to parents to send their children to sectarian schools." *Nyquist*. As was true of the law struck down in *Nyquist*, "it is precisely the function of [Minnesota's] law to provide assistance to private schools, the great majority of which are sectarian. By reimbursing parents for a portion of their tuition bill, the State seeks to relieve their financial burdens sufficiently to assure that they continue to have the option to send their children to religion-oriented schools. And while the other purposes for that aid—to perpetuate a pluralistic educational environment and to protect the fiscal integrity of overburdened public schools—are certainly unexceptional, the effect of the aid is unmistakably to provide desired financial support for nonpublic, sectarian institutions." *Id.*

That parents receive a reduction of their tax liability, rather than a direct reimbursement, is of no greater significance here than it was in *Nyquist*. "[F]or purposes of determining whether such aid has the effect of advancing religion," **⊥408** it makes no difference whether the qualifying "parent receives an actual cash payment [or] is allowed to reduce . . . the sum he would otherwise be obliged to pay over to the State." *Id.* It is equally irrelevant whether a reduction in taxes takes the form of a tax "credit," a tax "modification," or a tax "deduction." *Id.* What is of controlling significance is not the form but the "substantive impact" of the financial aid. *Id.* "[I]nsofar as such benefits render assistance to parents who send their children to *sectarian* schools, their purpose and inevitable effect are to aid and advance those religious institutions." *Nyquist*.

B

The majority attempts to distinguish *Nyquist* by pointing to two differences between the Minnesota tuition-assistance program and the program struck down in *Nyquist*. Neither of these distinctions can withstand scrutiny.

1

The majority first attempts to distinguish *Nyquist* on the ground that Minnesota makes all parents eligible to deduct up to $500 or $700 for each dependent, whereas the New York law allowed a deduction only for parents whose children attended nonpublic schools. Although Minnesota taxpayers who send their children to local public schools may not deduct tuition expenses because they incur none, they may deduct other expenses, such as the cost of gym clothes, pencils, and notebooks, which are shared by all parents of school-age children. This, in the majority's view, distinguishes the Minnesota scheme from the law at issue in *Nyquist*.

That the Minnesota statute makes some small benefit available to all parents cannot alter the fact that the most substantial benefit provided by the statute is available only to those parents who send their children to schools that charge tuition. It is simply undeniable that the single largest expense that may be deducted under the Minnesota statute is tuition. The statute is little more than a subsidy of tuition mas**⊥409**querading as a subsidy of general educational expenses. The other deductible expenses are *de minimis* in comparison to tuition expenses.

Contrary to the majority's suggestion, the bulk of the tax benefits afforded by the Minnesota scheme are enjoyed by parents of parochial school children not because parents of public school children fail to claim deductions to which they are entitled, but because the latter are simply *unable* to claim the largest tax deduction that Minnesota authorizes. Fewer than 100 of more than 900,000 school-age children in Minnesota attend public schools that charge a general tuition. Of the total number of taxpayers who are eligible for the tuition deduction, approximately 96% send their children to religious schools. Parents who send their children to free public schools are simply ineligible to obtain the full benefit of the deduction except in the unlikely event that they buy $700 worth of pencils, notebooks, and bus rides for their school-age children. Yet parents who pay at least $700 in tuition to nonpublic, sectarian schools can claim the full deduction even if they incur no other educational expenses.

That this deduction has a primary effect of promoting religion can easily be determined without any resort to the type of "statistical evidence" that the majority fears would lead to constitutional uncertainty. The only factual inquiry necessary is the same as that employed in *Nyquist* **⊥410** and *Sloan* v. *Lemon*: whether the deduction permitted for tuition expenses primarily benefits those who send their children to religious schools. In *Nyquist* we unequivocally rejected any suggestion that, in determining the effect of the New York statute, this Court should look exclusively to what the statute on its face purports to do and ignore the actual operation of the challenged provision. In determining the effect of the New York statute, we emphasized that "virtually all" of the schools receiving direct grants for maintenance and repair were Roman Catholic schools, that reimbursements were given to parents "who send their children to nonpublic schools, the bulk of which are concededly sectarian in orientation," *id.*, that "it is precisely the function of New York's law to provide assistance to private schools, the great majority of which are sectarian," *id.* and that "tax reductions authorized by this law flow primarily to the parents of children attending sectarian, nonpublic schools." *Id.* Similarly, in *Sloan* v. *Lemon*, we considered important to our "consider[ation of] the new law's effect . . . [that] 'more than 90% of the children attending nonpublic schools in the Commonwealth of Pennsylvania are enrolled in schools that are controlled by religious institutions or that have the purpose of propagating and promoting religious faith.'"

⊥411 In this case, it is undisputed that well over 90% of the children attending tuition-charging schools in Minnesota are enrolled in sectarian schools. History and experience likewise instruct us that any generally available financial assistance for elementary and secondary school tuition expenses mainly will further religious education because the majority of the schools which charge tuition are sectarian. Because Minnesota, like every other State, is committed to providing free public education, tax assistance for tuition payments inevitably redounds to the benefit of nonpublic sectarian schools and parents who send their children to those schools.

2

The majority also asserts that the Minnesota statute is distinguishable from the statute struck down in *Nyquist* in another respect: the tax benefit available under Minnesota law is a "genuine tax deduction," whereas the New York law provided a benefit which, while nominally a deduction, also had features of a "tax credit." Under the Minnesota law, the amount of the tax benefit varies directly with the amount of the expenditure. Under the New York law, the amount of deduction was not dependent upon the amount actually paid for tuition but was a predetermined amount which depended on the tax bracket of each taxpayer. The deduction was designed to yield roughly the same amount of tax "forgiveness" for each taxpayer.

This is a distinction without a difference. Our prior decisions have rejected the relevance of the majority's formalistic distinction between tax deductions and the tax benefit at issue in *Nyquist*. ⊥**412** The deduction afforded by Minnesota law was "designed to yield a [tax benefit] in exchange for performing a specific act which the State desires to encourage." *Nyquist*. Like the tax benefit held impermissible in *Nyquist* the tax deduction at issue here concededly was designed to "encourag[e] desirable expenditures for educational purposes." Of equal importance, as the majority also concedes, the "economic consequence" of these programs is the same, for in each case the "financial assistance provided to parents ultimately has an economic effect comparable to that of aid given directly to the schools." It was precisely the substantive impact of the financial support, and not its particular form, that rendered the program in *Nyquist* and *Sloan* ⊥**413** v. *Lemon* unconstitutional.

C

The majority incorrectly asserts that Minnesota's tax deduction for tuition expenses "bears less resemblance to the arrangement struck down in *Nyquist* than it does to assistance programs upheld in our prior decisions and discussed with approval in *Nyquist*." One might as well say that a tangerine bears less resemblance to an orange than to an apple. The two cases relied on by the majority, *Board of Education* v. *Allen*, and *Everson* v. *Board of Education*, are inapposite today for precisely the same reasons that they were inapposite in *Nyquist*.

We distinguished these cases in *Nyquist* and again in *Sloan* v. *Lemon*. Financial assistance for tuition payments has a consequence that "is quite unlike the sort of 'indirect' and 'incidental' benefits that flowed to sectarian schools from programs aiding all parents by supplying bus transportation and secular textbooks for their children. *Such benefits were carefully restricted to the purely secular side of church-affiliated institutions* and provided no special aid for those who had chosen to support religious schools. Yet such aid approached the 'verge' of the constitutionally impermissible." *Sloan* v. *Lemon*. As previously noted, the Minnesota tuition tax deduction is not available to *all* parents, but only to parents whose children attend schools that charge tuition, which are comprised almost entirely of sectarian schools. More importantly, the assistance that flows to parochial schools as a result of the tax benefit is not restricted, and cannot be restricted, to the secular functions of those schools.

⊥**414** II

In my view, Minnesota's tax deduction for the cost of textbooks and other instructional materials is also constitutionally infirm. The majority is simply mistaken in concluding that a tax deduction, unlike a tax credit or a direct grant to parents, promotes religious education in a manner that is only "attenuated." A tax deduction has a primary effect that advances religion if it is provided to offset expenditures which are not restricted to the secular activities of parochial schools.

The instructional materials which are subsidized by the Minnesota tax deduction plainly may be used to inculcate religious values and belief. In *Meek* v. *Pittenger*, we held that even the use of "wholly neutral, secular instructional material and equipment" by church-related schools contributes to religious instruction because "'[t]he secular education those schools provide goes hand in hand with the religious mission that is the only reason for the schools' existence.'" In *Wolman* v. *Walter*, we concluded that precisely the same impermissible effect results when the instructional materials are loaned to the pupil or his parent, rather than directly to the schools. We stated that "it would exalt form over substance if this distinction were found to justify a result different from that in *Meek*." It follows that a tax deduction to offset the cost of purchasing instructional materials for use in sectarian schools, like a loan of such materials to parents, "necessarily results in aid to the sectarian school enterprise as a whole" and is therefore a "substantial advancement of religious activity" that "constitutes an impermissible establishment of religion." *Ibid.*

There is no reason to treat Minnesota's tax deduction for textbooks any differently. Secular textbooks, like other secular instructional materials, contribute to the religious mission of the parochial school that use those books. Although this Court upheld the loan of secular textbooks to religious ⊥**415** schools in *Board of Education* v. *Allen*, the Court believed at that time that it lacked sufficient experience to determine "based solely on judicial notice" that "the processes of secular and religious training are so intertwined that secular textbooks furnished to students by the public [will always be] instrumental in the teaching of religion." This basis for distinguishing secular instructional materials and secular textbooks is simply untenable, and is inconsistent with many of our more recent decisions concerning state aid to parochial schools.

In any event, the Court's assumption in *Allen* that the textbooks at issue there might be used only for secular education was based on the fact that those very books had been chosen by the State for use in the public schools. In contrast, the Minnesota statute does not limit the tax deduction to those books which the State has approved for use in public schools. Rather, it permits a deduction for books that are chosen by the parochial schools themselves. Indeed, under the Minnesota statutory scheme, textbooks chosen by parochial schools but not used by public schools are likely to be precisely the ones purchased by parents for their children's use. Like the law upheld in *Board of Education* v. *Allen*, Minn. Stat. §§ 123.932 and 123.933 (1982) authorize the state board of education to provide textbooks used in public schools to nonpublic school students. Parents have little reason to purchase textbooks that can be borrowed under this provision.

⊥**416** III

There can be little doubt that the State of Minnesota intended to provide, and has provided, "[s]ubstantial aid to the educational function of [church-related] schools," and that the tax deduction for tuition and other educational expenses "necessarily results in aid to the sectarian school enterprise as a whole." *Meek* v. *Pittenger*. It is beside the point that the State may have legitimate secular reasons for providing such aid. In focusing upon the contributions made by church-related schools, the majority has lost sight of the issue before us in this case. "The sole question is whether state aid to these schools can be squared with the dictates of the Religion Clauses. Under our system the choice has been made that government is to be entirely excluded from the area of religious instruction. . . . The Constitution decrees that religion must be a private matter for the individual, the family, and the institutions of private choice, and that while some involvement and entanglement are inevitable, lines must be drawn." *Lemon* v. *Kurtzman*.

In my view, the lines drawn in *Nyquist* were drawn on a reasoned basis with appropriate regard for the principles of neutrality embodied by the Establishment Clause. I do not believe that the same can be said of the lines drawn by the majority today. For the first time, the Court has upheld financial support for religious schools without any reason at all to assume that the support will be restricted to the secular functions of those schools and will not be used to support reli⊥**417**gious instruction. This result is flatly at odds with the fundamental principle that a State may provide no financial support whatsoever to promote religion. As the Court stated in *Everson*, "No tax in any amount, large or small, can be levied to support any religious activities or institutions, whatever they may be called, or whatever form they may adopt to teach or practice religion."

I dissent.

AGUILAR v. FELTON

473 U.S. 402
ON APPEAL FROM THE UNITED STATES COURT OF APPEALS FOR THE SECOND CIRCUIT
Argued December 5, 1984 — Decided July 1, 1985

⊥**404** *Justice* BRENNAN delivered the opinion of the Court.

The City of New York uses federal funds to pay the salaries of public employees who teach in parochial schools. In this companion case to *School District of Grand Rapids* v. *Ball*, we determine whether this practice violates the Establishment Clause of the First Amendment.

I

A

The program at issue in this case, originally enacted as Title I of the Elementary and Secondary Education Act of 1965, authorizes the Secretary of Education to distribute financial assistance to local educational institutions to meet the needs of educationally deprived children from low-income families. The funds are to be appropriated in accordance with programs proposed by local educational agencies and approved by state educational agencies. 20 U.S.C. ⊥**405** § 3805(a). "To the extent consistent with the number of educationally deprived children in the school district of the local educational agency who are enrolled in private elementary and secondary schools, such agency shall make provisions for including special educational services and arrangements . . . in which such children can participate." § 3806(a). The proposed programs must also meet the following statutory requirements: the children involved in the program must be educationally deprived, § 3804(a), the children must reside in areas comprising a high concentration of low-income families, § 3805(b), and the programs must sup⊥**406**plement, not supplant, programs that would exist absent funding under Title I. § 3807(b).

Since 1966, the City of New York has provided instructional services funded by Title I to parochial school students on the premises of parochial schools. Of those students eligible to receive funds in 1981-1982, 13.2% were enrolled in private schools. Of that group, 84% were enrolled in schools affiliated with the Roman Catholic Archdiocese of New York and the Diocese of Brooklyn and 8% were enrolled in Hebrew day schools. With respect to the religious atmosphere of these schools, the Court of Appeals concluded that "the picture that emerges is of a system in which religious considerations play a key role in the selection of students and teachers, and which has as its substantial purpose the inculcation of religious values."

The programs conducted at these schools include remedial reading, reading skills, remedial mathematics, English as a second language, and guidance services. These programs are carried out by regular employees of the public schools (teachers, guidance counselors, psychologists, psychiatrists and social workers) who have volunteered to teach in the parochial schools. The amount of time that each professional spends in the parochial school is determined by the number of students in the particular program and the needs of these students.

The City's Bureau of Nonpublic School Reimbursement makes teacher assignments, and the instructors are super⊥**407**vised by field personnel, who attempt to pay at least one unannounced visit per month. The field supervisors, in turn, report to program coordinators, who also pay occasional unannounced supervisory visits to monitor Title I classes in the parochial schools. The professionals involved in the program are directed to avoid involvement with religious activities that are conducted within the private schools and to bar religious materials in their classrooms. All material and equipment used in the programs funded under Title I are supplied by the Government and are used only in those programs. The professional personnel are solely responsible for the selection of the students. Additionally, the professionals are informed that contact with private school personnel should be kept to a minimum. Finally, the administrators of the parochial schools are required to clear the classrooms used by the public school personnel of all religious symbols.

B

In 1978, six taxpayers commenced this action in the District Court for the Eastern District of New York, alleging that the Title I program administered by the City of New York violates the Establishment Clause. These taxpayers, appellees in today's case, sought to enjoin the further distribution of funds to programs involving instruction on the premises of parochial schools. Initially the case was held for the outcome of *National Coalition for Public Education and Religious Liberty* v. *Harris*, ("PEARL"), which involved an identical challenge to the Title I program. When the District Court in PEARL affirmed the constitutionality of the Title I program, and this Court dismissed the appeal for want of jurisdiction, the challenge of the present appellees was renewed. The District Court granted the appellants' motion for summary judgment based upon the evidentiary record developed in PEARL.

⊥**408** A unanimous panel of the Court of Appeals for the Second Circuit reversed, holding that "[t]he Establishment Clause, as it has been interpreted by the Supreme Court in *Public Funds for Public Schools* v. *Marburger*, *Meek* v. *Pittenger*, and *Wolman* v. *Walter*, constitutes an insurmountable barrier to the use of federal funds to send public school teachers and other professionals into religious schools to carry on instruction, remedial or otherwise, or to provide clinical and guidance services of the sort at issue here." 739 F. 2d, at 49-50. We postponed probable jurisdiction. We conclude that jurisdiction by appeal does not properly lie. Treating the papers as a petition for a writ of certiorari, we grant the petition and now affirm the judgment below.

II

In *School District of the City of Grand Rapids* v. *Ball*, the Court has today held unconstitutional under the Establishment Clause two remedial and enhancement programs operated by the Grand Rapids Public School District, in which ⊥**409** classes were provided to private school children at public expense in classrooms located in and leased from the local private schools. The New York programs challenged in this case are very similar to the programs we examined in *Ball*. In both cases, publicly funded instructors teach classes composed exclusively of private school students in private school buildings. In both cases, an overwhelming number of the participating private schools are religiously affiliated. In both cases, the publicly funded programs provide not only professional personnel, but also all materials and supplies necessary for the operation of the programs. Finally, the instructors in both cases are told that they are public school employees under the sole control of the public school system.

The appellants attempt to distinguish this case on the ground that the City of New York, unlike the Grand Rapids Public School District, has adopted a system for monitoring the religious content of publicly funded Title I classes in the religious schools. At best, the supervision in this case would assist in preventing the Title I program from being used, intentionally or unwittingly, to inculcate the religious beliefs of the surrounding parochial school. But appellants' argument fails in any event, because the supervisory system established by the City of New York inevitably results in the excessive entanglement of church and state, an Establishment Clause concern distinct from that addressed by the effects doctrine. Even where state aid to parochial institutions does not have the primary effect of advancing religion, the provision of such aid may nonetheless violate the Establishment Clause owing to the nature of the interaction of church and state in the administration of that aid.

The principle that the state should not become too closely entangled with the church in the administration of assistance is rooted in two concerns. When the state becomes enmeshed with a given denomination in matters of religious significance, the freedom of religious belief of those who are not adherents of that denomination suffers, even when the ⊥**410** governmental purpose underlying the involvement is largely secular. In addition, the freedom of even the adherents of the denomination is limited by the governmental intrusion into sacred matters. "[T]he First Amendment rests upon the premise that both religion and government can best work to achieve their lofty aims if each is left free from the other within its respective sphere." *McCollum* v. *Board of Education*.

In *Lemon* v. *Kurtzman*, the Court held that the supervision necessary to ensure that teachers in parochial schools were not conveying religious messages to their students would constitute the excessive entanglement of church and state: "A comprehensive, discriminating, and continuing state surveillance will inevitably be required to ensure that these restrictions are obeyed and the First Amendment otherwise respected. Unlike a book, a teacher cannot be inspected once so as to determine the extent and intent of his or her personal beliefs and subjective acceptance of the limitations imposed by the First Amendment. These prophylactic contacts will involve excessive and enduring entanglement between state and church." Similarly, in *Meek* v. *Pittenger*, we invalidated a state program that offered, *inter alia*, guidance, testing, remedial and therapeutic services performed by public employees on the premises of the parochial schools. As in *Lemon*, we observed that though a comprehensive system of supervision might conceivably prevent teachers from having the primary effect of advancing religion, such a system would inevitably lead to an unconstitutional administrative entanglement between church and state. "The prophylactic contacts required to ensure that teachers play a strictly nonideological role, the Court held [in *Lemon*], necessarily give rise to a constitution⊥**411**ally intolerable degree of entanglement between church and state. The same excessive entanglement would be required for Pennsylvania to be 'certain,' as it must be, that . . . personnel do not advance the religious mission of the church-related schools in which they serve."

In *Roemer* v. *Maryland Public Works Board*, the Court sustained state programs of aid to religiously affiliated institutions of higher learning. The state allowed the grants to be used for any nonsectarian purpose. The Court upheld the grants on the ground that the institutions were not "'pervasively sectarian,'" and therefore a system of supervision was unnecessary to ensure that the grants were not being used to effect a religious end. In so holding, the Court identified "what is crucial to a nonentangling aid program: the ability of the State to identify and subsidize separate secular functions carried out at the school, without on-the-site inspections being necessary to prevent diversion of the funds to sectarian purposes." Similarly, in *Tilton* v. *Richardson*, the Court upheld one-time grants to sectarian institutions because ongoing supervision was not required. See also *Hunt* v. *McNair*.

As the Court of Appeals recognized, the elementary and secondary schools here are far different from the colleges at issue in *Roemer*, *Hunt*, and *Tilton*. Unlike the colleges, which were found not to be "pervasively sectarian," many of the schools involved in this case are the same sectarian schools which had "'as a substantial purpose the inculcation of religious values'" in *Committee for Public Education* v. *Nyquist*. Moreover, our holding in *Meek* invalidating instructional services much like those at issue in this case rested ⊥**412** on the ground that the publicly funded teachers were "performing important educational services in schools in which education is an integral part of the dominant sectarian mission and in which an atmosphere dedicated to the advancement of religious belief is constantly maintained." The court below found that the schools involved in this case were "well within this characterization." Unlike the schools in *Roemer*, many of the schools here receive funds and report back to their affiliated church, require attendance at church religious exercises, begin the school day or class period with prayer, and grant preference in admission to members of the sponsoring denominations. In addition, the Catholic schools at issue here, which constitute the vast majority of the aided schools, are under the general supervision and control of the local parish.

The critical elements of the entanglement proscribed in *Lemon* and *Meek* are thus present in this case. First, as noted above, the aid is provided in a pervasively sectarian environment. Second, because assistance is provided in the form of teachers, ongoing inspection is required to ensure the absence of a religious message. In short, the scope and duration of New York's Title I ⊥**413** program would require a permanent and pervasive State presence in the sectarian schools receiving aid.

This pervasive monitoring by public authorities in the sectarian schools infringes precisely those Establishment Clause values at the root of the prohibition of excessive entanglement. Agents of the State must visit and inspect the religious school regularly, alert for the subtle or overt presence of religious matter in Title I classes. Cf. *Lemon* v. *Kurtzman* ("What would appear to some to be essential to good citizenship might well for others border on or constitute instruction in religion"). In addition, the religious school must obey these same agents when they make determinations as to what is and what is not a "religious symbol" and thus off limits in a Title I classroom. In short, the religious school, which has as a primary purpose the advancement and preservation of a particular religion must endure the ongoing presence of state personnel whose primary purpose is to monitor teachers and students in an attempt to guard against the infiltration of religious thought.

The administrative cooperation that is required to maintain the educational program at issue here entangles Church and State in still another way that infringes interests at the heart of the Establishment Clause. Administrative personnel of the public and parochial school systems must work together in resolving matters related to schedules, classroom assignments, problems that arise in the implementation of the program, requests for additional services, and the dissemination of information regarding the program. Furthermore, the program necessitates "frequent contacts between the regular and the remedial teachers (or other professionals), in which each side reports on individual student needs, problems encountered, and results achieved."

We have long recognized that underlying the Establishment Clause is "the objective . . . to prevent, as far as possible, the intrusion of either [Church or State] into the precincts of the other." *Lemon* v. *Kurtzman*. ⊥**414** Although "[s]eparation in this context cannot mean absence of all contact," *Walz* v. *Tax Commission*, the detailed monitoring and close administrative contact required to maintain New York's Title I program can only produce "a kind of continuing day-to-day relationship which the policy of neutrality seeks to minimize." The numerous judgments that must be made by agents of the state concern matters that may be subtle and controversial, yet may be of deep religious significance to the controlling denominations. As government agents must make these judgments, the dangers of political divisiveness along religious lines increase. At the same time, "[t]he picture of state inspectors prowling the halls of parochial schools and auditing classroom instruction surely raised more than an imagined specter of governmental 'secularization of a creed.'" *Lemon* v. *Kurtzman*.

III

Despite the well-intentioned efforts taken by the City of New York, the program remains constitutionally flawed owing to the nature of the aid, to the institution receiving the aid, and to the constitutional principles that they implicate—that neither the State nor Federal Government shall promote or hinder a particular faith or faith generally through the advancement of benefits or through the excessive entanglement of church and state in the administration of those benefits.

Affirmed.

Justice POWELL, concurring.

I concur in the Court's opinions and judgments today in this case and in *Grand Rapids School District* v. *Ball* holding that the aid to parochial schools involved in those cases violates the Establishment Clause of the First ⊥**415** Amendment. I write to emphasize additional reasons why precedents of this Court require us to invalidate these two educational programs that concededly have "done so much good and little, if any, detectable harm." The Court has previously recognized the important role of parochial schools: "Parochial schools, quite apart from their sectarian purpose, have provided an educational alternative for millions of young Americans; they often afford wholesome competition with our public schools; and in some States they relieve substantially the tax burden incident to the operation of public schools. The State has, moreover, a legitimate interest in facilitating education of the highest quality for all children within its boundaries, whatever school their parents have chosen for them" *Mueller* v. *Allen* (quoting *Wolman* v. *Walter*). Regrettably, however, the Title I and Grand Rapids programs do not survive the scrutiny required by our Establishment Clause cases.

I agree with the Court that in this case the Establishment Clause is violated because there is too great a risk of government entanglement in the administration of the religious schools; the same is true in *Ball*. As beneficial as the Title I program appears to be in accomplishing its secular goal of supplementing the education of deprived children, its elaborate structure, the participation of public school teachers, and the government surveillance required to ensure that public funds are used for secular purposes inevitably present a serious risk of excessive entanglement. Our cases have noted that "'[t]he State must be *certain*, given the Religion Clauses, that subsidized teachers do not inculcate religion.'" *Meek* v. *Pittenger* (emphasis added) (quoting *Lemon* v. *Kurtzman*). ⊥**416** This is true whether the subsidized teachers are religious school teachers, as in *Lemon*, or public school teachers teaching secular subjects to parochial school children at the parochial schools. Judge Friendly, writing for the unanimous Court of Appeals, agreed with this assessment of our cases. He correctly observed that the structure of the Title I program required the active and extensive surveillance that the City has provided, and, "under *Meek*, this very surveillance constitutes excessive entanglement even if it has succeeded in preventing the fostering of religion."

This risk of entanglement is compounded by the additional risk of political divisiveness stemming from the aid to religion at issue here. I do not suggest that at this point in our history the Title I program or similar parochial aid plans could result in the establishment of a state religion. There likewise is small chance that these programs would result in significant religious or denominational control over our democratic processes. Nonetheless, there remains a considerable risk of continuing political strife over the propriety of direct aid to religious schools and the proper allocation of limited governmental resources. As this Court has repeatedly recognized, there is a likelihood whenever direct governmental aid is extended to some groups that there will be competition and strife among them and others to gain, maintain, or increase the financial support of government. In states such as New York that have large and varied sectarian populations, one can be assured that politics will enter into any state decision to aid parochial schools. Public schools, as well as private schools, are under increasing financial pressure to meet real and perceived needs. Thus, any proposal to extend direct governmental ⊥**417** aid to parochial schools alone is likely to spark political disagreement from taxpayers who support the public schools, as well as from nonrecipient sectarian groups, who may fear that needed funds are being diverted from them. In short, aid to parochial schools of the sort at issue here potentially leads to "that kind and degree of government involvement in religious life that, as history teaches us, is apt to lead to strife and frequently strain a political system to the breaking point." *Walz* v. *Tax Commission*. Although the Court's opinion does not discuss it at length, the potential for such divisiveness is a strong additional reason for holding that the Title I and Grand Rapids programs are invalid on entanglement grounds.

The Title I program at issue in this case also would be invalid under the "effects" prong of the test adopted in *Lemon* v. *Kurtzman*. As has been discussed thoroughly in *Ball*, with respect to the Grand Rapids programs, the type of aid provided in New York by the Title I program amounts to a state subsidy of the parochial schools by relieving those schools of the duty to provide the remedial and supplemental education their children require. This is not the type of "indirect and incidental effect beneficial to [the] religious institutions" that we suggested in *Nyquist* would survive Establishment Clause scrutiny. Rather, by directly assuming part of the parochial schools' education function, the effect of the Title I aid is "inevitably . . . to subsidize and advance the religious mission of [the] sectarian schools," even though the program provides that only secular subjects will ⊥**418** be taught. As in *Meek* v. *Pittenger*, the secular education these schools provide goes "'hand in hand'" with the religious mission that is the reason for the schools' existence. Because of the predominantly religious nature of the schools, the substantial aid provided by the Title I program "inescapably results in the direct and substantial advancement of religious activity."

I recognize the difficult dilemma in which governments are placed by the interaction of the "effects" and entanglement prongs of the *Lemon* test. Our decisions require governments extending aid to parochial schools to tread an extremely narrow line between being certain that the "principal or primary effect" of the aid is not to advance religion, and avoiding excessive entanglement. Nonetheless, the Court has never foreclosed the possibility that some types of aid to parochial schools could be valid under the Establishment Clause. Our cases have upheld evenhanded secular assistance to both parochial and public school children in some areas. I do not read the Court's opinion as precluding these types of indirect aid to parochial schools. In the cases cited, the assistance programs made funds available equally to public and nonpublic schools without entanglement. The constitutional defect in the Title I program, as indicated above, is that it provides a direct financial subsidy to be administered in significant part by public school teachers within parochial schools—resulting in both the advancement of religion and forbidden entanglement. If, for example, Congress could fashion a program of evenhanded financial assistance to both public and private schools that could ⊥**419** be administered, without governmental supervision in the private schools, so as to prevent the diversion of the aid from secular purposes, we would be presented with a different question.

I join the opinions and judgments of the Court.

Chief Justice BURGER, dissenting.

Under the guise of protecting Americans from the evils of an Established Church such as those of the Eighteenth Century and earlier times, today's decision will deny countless schoolchildren desperately needed remedial teaching services funded under Title I. The program at issue covers remedial reading, reading skills, remedial mathematics, English as a second language, and assistance for children needing special help in the learning process. The "remedial reading" portion of this program, for example, reaches children who suffer from dyslexia, a disease known to be difficult to diagnose and treat. Many of these children now will not receive the special training they need, simply because their parents desire that they attend religiously affiliated schools.

What is disconcerting about the result reached today is that, in the face of the human cost entailed by this decision, the Court does not even attempt to identify any threat to religious liberty posed by the operation of Title I. I share *Justice WHITE's* concern that the Court's obsession with the criteria identified in *Lemon* v. *Kurtzman* has led to results that are "contrary to the long-range interests of the country." As I wrote in *Wallace* v. *Jaffree*, "our responsibility is not to apply tidy formulas by rote; our duty is to determine whether the statute or practice at issue is a step toward establishing a state religion." Federal programs designed to prevent a generation of children from growing up without being able to read effectively are not remotely steps in that direction. It borders on paranoia to perceive the Archbishop of Canterbury or the Bishop of ⊥**420** Rome lurking behind programs that are just as vital to the nation's schoolchildren as textbooks, transportation to and from school, and school nursing services.

On the merits of this case, I dissent for the reasons stated in my separate opinion in *Meek* v. *Pittenger*. We have frequently recognized that some interaction between church and state is unavoidable, and that an attempt to eliminate all contact between the two would be both futile and undesirable. *Justice* DOUGLAS, writing for the Court in *Zorach* v. *Clauson*, stated: "The First Amendment . . . does not say that in every and all respects there shall be a separation of Church and State. . . . Otherwise the state and religion would be aliens to each other—hostile, suspicious, and even unfriendly." The Court today fails to demonstrate how the interaction occasioned by the program at issue presents any threat to the values underlying the Establishment Clause.

I cannot join in striking down a program that, in the words of the Court of Appeals, "has done so much good and little, if any, detectable harm." The notion that denying these services to students in religious schools is a neutral act to protect us from an Established Church has no support in logic, experience, or history. Rather than showing the neutrality the Court boasts of, it exhibits nothing less than hostility toward religion and the children who attend church-sponsored schools.

Justice WHITE, dissenting.

As evidenced by my dissenting opinions in *Lemon* v. *Kurtzman* and *Committee for Public Education* v. *Nyquist*, I have long disagreed with the Court's interpretation and application of the Establishment Clause in the context of state aid to private schools. For the reasons stated in those dissents, I am firmly of the belief that the Court's decisions in these cases, like its decisions in *Lemon* and *Nyquist*, are "not required by the First Amendment and [are] contrary to the long-range interests of the country." For those same reasons, I am satisfied that what the States have sought to do in these cases is well within their authority and is not forbidden by the Establishment Clause. Hence, I dissent and would reverse the judgment in each of these cases.

Justice REHNQUIST, dissenting.

I dissent for the reasons stated in my dissenting opinion in *Wallace* v. *Jaffree*. In *Aguilar* v. *Felton* the Court takes advantage of the "Catch-22" paradox of its own creation, ⊥**421** whereby aid must be supervised to ensure no entanglement but the supervision itself is held to cause an entanglement. The Court in *Aguilar* strikes down nondiscriminatory nonsectarian aid to educationally deprived children from low-income families. The Establishment Clause does not prohibit such sorely needed assistance; we have indeed travelled far afield from the concerns which prompted the adoption of the First Amendment when we rely on gossamer abstractions to invalidate a law which obviously meets an entirely secular need. I would reverse.

Justice O'CONNOR, with whom *Justice* REHNQUIST joins as to Parts II and III, dissenting.

Today the Court affirms the holding of the Court of Appeals that public schoolteachers can offer remedial instruction to disadvantaged students who attend religious schools "only if such instruction . . . [is] afforded at a neutral site off the premises of the religious school." This holding rests on the theory, enunciated in Part V of the Court's opinion in *Meek* v. *Pittenger*, that public schoolteachers who set foot on parochial school premises are likely to bring religion into their classes, and that the supervision necessary to prevent religious teaching would unduly entangle church and state. Even if this theory were valid in the abstract, it cannot validly be applied to New York City's 19-year-old Title I program. The Court greatly exaggerates the degree of supervision necessary to prevent public school teachers from inculcating religion, and thereby demonstrates the flaws of a test that condemns benign cooperation between church and state. I would uphold Congress' efforts to afford remedial instruction to disadvantaged schoolchildren in both public and parochial schools.

I

As in *Wallace* v. *Jaffree* and *Thornton* v. *Caldor, Inc.*, the Court in this litigation adheres to the three-part Establishment Clause ⊥**422** test enunciated in *Lemon* v. *Kurtzman*. To survive the *Lemon* test, a statute must have both a secular legislative purpose and a principal or primary effect that neither advances nor inhibits religion. Under *Lemon* and its progeny, direct state aid to parochial schools that has the purpose or effect of furthering the religious mission of the schools is unconstitutional. I agree with that principle. According to the Court, however, the New York Title I program is defective not because of any improper purpose or effect, but rather because it fails the third part of the *Lemon* test: the Title I program allegedly fosters excessive government entanglement with religion. I disagree with the court's analysis of entanglement and I question the utility of entanglement as a separate Establishment Clause standard in most cases. Before discussing entanglement, however, it is worthwhile to explore the purpose and effect of the New York Title I program in greater depth than does the majority opinion.

The purpose of Title I is to provide special educational assistance to disadvantaged children who would not otherwise receive it. Congress recognized that poor academic performance by disadvantaged children is part of the cycle of poverty. Congress sought to break the cycle by providing classes in remedial reading, mathematics, and English to disadvantaged children in parochial as well as public schools, for public schools enjoy no monopoly on education in low income areas. Congress permitted remedial instruction by public school teachers on parochial school premises only if such instruction is "not normally provided by the nonpublic school" and would "contribute particularly to meeting the special educational needs of educationally deprived children."

⊥**423** After reviewing the text of the statute and its legislative history, the District Court concluded that Title I serves a secular purpose of aiding needy children regardless of where they attend school. The Court of Appeals did not dispute this finding, and no party in this Court contends that the purpose of the statute or of the New York City Title I program is to advance or endorse religion. Indeed, the record demonstrates that New York City public schoolteachers offer Title I classes on the premises of parochial schools solely because alternative means to reach the disadvantaged parochial school students—such as instruction for parochial school students at the nearest public school, either after or during regular school hours—were unsuccessful. As the Court of Appeals acknowledged, New York City "could reasonably have regarded [Title I instruction on parochial school premises] as the most effective way to carry out the purposes of the Act." Whether one looks to the face of the statute or to its implementation, the Title I program is undeniably animated by a legitimate secular purpose.

The Court's discussion of the effect of the New York City Title I program is even more perfunctory than its analysis of the program's purpose. The Court's opinion today in *Grand Rapids School Dist.* v. *Ball*, which strikes down a Grand Rapids scheme that the Court asserts is very similar to the New York program, identifies three ways in which public instruction on parochial school premises may have the impermissible effect of advancing religion. First, "state-paid instructors, influenced by the pervasively sectarian nature of the religious schools in which they work, may ⊥**424** subtly or overtly indoctrinate the students in particular religious tenets at public expense." Second, "state-provided instruction in the religious school buildings threatens to convey a message of state support for religion to students and to the general public." Third, "the programs in effect subsidize the religious functions of the parochial schools by taking over a substantial portion of their responsibility for teaching secular subjects." While addressing the effect of the Grand Rapids program at such length, the Court overlooks the effect of Title I in New York City.

One need not delve too deeply in the record to understand why the Court does not belabor the effect of the Title I program. The abstract theories explaining why on-premises instruction might possibly advance religion dissolve in the face of experience in New York. As the District Court found in 1980: "New York City has been providing Title I services in nonpublic schools for fourteen years. The evidence presented in this action includes: extensive background information on Title I; an in-depth description of New York City's program; a detailed review of Title I rules and regulations and the ways in which they are enforced; and the testimony and affidavits of federal officials, state officers, school administrators, Title I teachers and supervisors, and parents of children receiving Title I services. The evidence establishes that the result feared in other cases has not materialized in the City's Title I program. The presumption—that the 'religious mission' will be advanced by providing educational services on parochial school premises—is not supported by the facts of this case." *National Coalition for Public Education and Religious Liberty* v. *Harris*. Indeed, in 19 years there has never been a single incident in which a Title I instructor "subtly or overtly" attempted to "indoctrinate the students in particular religious tenets at public expense."

⊥**425** Common sense suggests a plausible explanation for this unblemished record. New York City's public Title I instructors are professional educators who can and do follow instructions not to inculcate religion in their classes. They are unlikely to be influenced by the sectarian nature of the parochial schools where they teach, not only because they are carefully supervised by public officials, but also because the vast majority of them visit several different schools each week and are not of the same religion as their parochial students. In light of the ample record, an objective observer of the implementation of the Title I program in New York would hardly view it as endorsing the tenets of the participating parochial schools. To the contrary, the actual and perceived effect of the program is precisely the effect intended by Congress: impoverished school children are being helped to overcome learning deficits, improving their test scores, and receiving a significant boost in their struggle to obtain both a thorough education and the opportunities that flow from it.

The only type of impermissible effect that arguably could carry over from the *Grand Rapids* decision to this litigation, then, is the effect of subsidizing "the religious functions of the parochial schools by taking over a substantial portion of their responsibility for teaching secular subjects." That effect is tenuous, however, in light of the statutory directive that Title I funds may be used only to provide services that otherwise would not be available to the participating students. The Secretary of Education has vigorously enforced the requirement that Title I funds supplement rather than supplant the services of local education agencies.

⊥**426** Even if we were to assume that Title I remedial classes in New York may have duplicated to some extent instruction parochial schools would have offered in the absence of Title I, the Court's delineation of this third type of effect proscribed by the Establishment Clause would be seriously flawed. Our Establishment Clause decisions have not barred remedial assistance to parochial school children, but rather remedial assistance *on the premises of the parochial school*. Under *Wolman* v. *Walter*, the New York City classes prohibited by the Court today would have survived Establishment Clause scrutiny if they had been offered in a neutral setting off the property of the private school. Yet it is difficult to understand why a remedial reading class offered on parochial school premises is any more likely to supplant the secular course offerings of the parochial school than the same class offered in a portable classroom next door to the school. Unless *Wolman* was wrongly decided, the defect in the Title I program cannot lie in the risk that it will supplant secular course offerings.

II

Recognizing the weakness of any claim of an improper purpose or effect, the Court today relies entirely on the entanglement prong of *Lemon* to invalidate the New York City Title I program. The Court holds that the occasional presence of peripatetic public school teachers on parochial school grounds threatens undue entanglement of church and state because (1) the remedial instruction is afforded in a pervasively sectarian environment; (2) ongoing supervision is required to assure that the public schoolteachers do not attempt to inculcate religion; (3) the administrative personnel of the parochial and public school systems must work together in resolving administrative and scheduling problems; and (4) the instruction is likely to result in political divisiveness over the propriety of direct aid.

⊥**427** This analysis of entanglement, I acknowledge, finds support in some of this Court's precedents. In *Meek* v. *Pittenger* the Court asserted that it could not rely "on the good faith and professionalism of the secular teachers and counselors functioning in church related schools to ensure that a strictly nonideological posture is maintained." Because "a teacher remains a teacher," the Court stated, there remains a risk that teachers will intertwine religious doctrine with secular instruction. The continuing state surveillance necessary to prevent this from occurring would produce undue entanglement of church and state. The Court's opinion in *Meek* further asserted that public instruction on parochial school premises creates a serious risk of divisive political conflict over the issue of aid to religion. *Meek's* analysis of entanglement was reaffirmed in *Wolman* two Terms later.

I would accord these decisions the appropriate deference commanded by the doctrine of *stare decisis* if I could discern logical support for their analysis. But experience has demonstrated that the analysis in Part V of the *Meek* opinion is flawed. At the time *Meek* was decided, thoughtful dissents pointed out the absence of any record support for the notion that public school teachers would attempt to inculcate religion simply because they temporarily occupied a parochial school classroom, or that such instruction would produce political divisiveness. Experience has given greater force to the arguments of the dissenting opinions in *Meek*. It is not intuitively obvious that a dedicated public school teacher will tend to disobey instructions and commence proselytizing students at public expense merely because the classroom is within a parochial school. *Meek* is correct in asserting that a teacher of remedial reading "remains a teacher," but surely it is significant that the teacher involved is a professional, full-time public school employee who is unaccustomed to bringing religion into the classroom. ⊥**428** Given that not a single incident of religious indoctrination has been identified as occurring in the thousands of classes offered in Grand Rapids and New York over the past two decades, it is time to acknowledge that the risk identified in *Meek* was greatly exaggerated.

Just as the risk that public school teachers in parochial classrooms will inculcate religion has been exaggerated, so has the degree of supervision required to manage that risk. In this respect the New York Title I program is instructive. What supervision has been necessary in New York to enable public school teachers to help disadvantaged children for 19 years without once proselytizing? Public officials have prepared careful instructions warning public school teachers of their exclusively secular mission, and have required Title I teachers to study and observe them. Under the rules, Title I teachers are not accountable to parochial or private school officials; they have sole responsibility for selecting the students who participate in their class, must administer their own tests for determining eligibility, cannot engage in team teaching or cooperative activities with parochial school teachers, must make sure that all materials and equipment they use are not otherwise used by the parochial school, and must not participate in religious activities in the schools or introduce any religious matter into their teaching. To ensure compliance with the rules, a field supervisor and a program coordinator, who are full-time public school employees, make unannounced visits to each teacher's classroom at least once a month.

The Court concludes that this degree of supervision of public school employees by other public school employees constitutes excessive entanglement of church and state. I cannot agree. The supervision that occurs in New York's Title I program does not differ significantly from the supervision any public school teacher receives, regardless of the location of the classroom. *Justice POWELL* suggests that the required supervision is extensive because the State must be ⊥**429** *certain* that public school teachers do not inculcate religion. That reasoning would require us to close our public schools, for there is always some chance that a public school teacher will bring religion into the classroom, regardless of its location. Even if I remained confident of the usefulness of entanglement as an Establishment Clause test, I would conclude that New York's efforts to prevent religious indoctrination in Title I classes have been adequate and have not caused excessive institutional entanglement of church and state.

The Court's reliance on the potential for political divisiveness as evidence of undue entanglement is also unpersuasive. There is little record support for the proposition that New York's admirable Title I program has ignited any controversy other than this litigation. In *Mueller* v. *Allen*, the Court cautioned that the "elusive inquiry" into political divisiveness should be confined to a narrow category of parochial aid cases. The concurring opinion in *Lynch* v. *Donnelly*, went further, suggesting that Establishment Clause analysis should focus solely on the character of the government activity that might cause political divisiveness, and that "the entanglement prong of the *Lemon* test is properly limited to institutional entanglement."

I adhere to the doubts about the entanglement test that were expressed in *Lynch*. It is curious indeed to base our interpretation of the Constitution on speculation as to the likelihood of a phenomenon which the parties may create merely by prosecuting a lawsuit. My reservations about the entanglement test, however, have come to encompass its institutional aspects as well. As *Justice REHNQUIST* has pointed out, many of the inconsistencies in our Establishment Clause decisions can be ascribed to our insistence that parochial aid programs with a valid purpose and effect may still be invalid by virtue of undue entanglement. ⊥**430** For example, we permit a State to pay for bus transportation to a parochial school, but preclude States from providing buses for parochial school field trips, on the theory such trips involve excessive state supervision of the parochial officials who lead them. To a great extent, the anomalous results in our Establishment Clause cases are "attributable to [the] 'entanglement' prong." Choper, The Religion Clauses of the First Amendment: Reconciling the Conflict, 41 U. Pitt. L. Rev. 673, 681 (1980).

Pervasive institutional involvement of church and state may remain relevant in deciding the *effect* of a statute which is alleged to violate the Establishment Clause, but state efforts to ensure that public resources are used only for nonsectarian ends should not in themselves serve to invalidate an otherwise valid statute. The

State requires sectarian organizations to cooperate on a whole range of matters without thereby advancing religion or giving the impression that the government endorses religion. If a statute lacks a purpose or effect of advancing or endorsing religion, I would not invalidate it merely because it requires some ongoing cooperation between church and state or some state supervision to ensure that state funds do not advance religion.

III

Today's ruling does not spell the end of the Title I program of remedial education for disadvantaged children. Children attending public schools may still obtain the benefits of the program. Impoverished children who attend parochial schools may also continue to benefit from Title I programs offered off the premises of their schools—possibly in portable ⊥**431** classrooms just over the edge of school property. The only disadvantaged children who lose under the Court's holding are those in cities where it is not economically and logistically feasible to provide public facilities for remedial education adjacent to the parochial school. But this subset is significant, for it includes more than 20,000 New York City schoolchildren and uncounted others elsewhere in the country.

For these children, the Court's decision is tragic. The Court deprives them of a program that offers a meaningful chance at success in life, and it does so on the untenable theory that public school teachers (most of whom are of different faiths than their students) are likely to start teaching religion merely because they have walked across the threshold of a parochial school. I reject this theory and the analysis in *Meek* v. *Pittenger* on which it is based. I cannot close my eyes to the fact that, over almost two decades, New York's public schoolteachers have helped thousands of impoverished parochial schoolchildren to overcome educational disadvantages without once attempting to inculcate religion. Their praiseworthy efforts have not eroded and do not threaten the religious liberty assured by the Establishment Clause. The contrary judgment of the Court of Appeals should be reversed.

I respectfully dissent.

SCHOOL DISTRICT OF THE CITY OF GRAND RAPIDS v. BALL

473 U.S. 373
ON WRIT OF CERTIORARI TO THE UNITED STATES COURT OF APPEALS FOR THE SIXTH CIRCUIT
Argued December 5, 1984 — Decided July 1, 1985

⊥**375** *Justice* BRENNAN delivered the opinion of the court.

The School District of Grand Rapids, Michigan, adopted two programs in which classes for nonpublic school students are financed by the public school system, taught by teachers hired by the public school system, and conducted in "leased" classrooms in the nonpublic schools. Most of the nonpublic schools involved in the programs are sectarian religious schools. This case raises the question whether these programs impermissibly involve the government in the support of sectarian religious activities and thus violate the Establishment Clause of the First Amendment.

I

A

At issue in this case are the Community Education and Shared Time programs offered in the nonpublic schools of Grand Rapids, Michigan. These programs, first instituted in the 1976-1977 school year, provide classes to nonpublic school students at public expense in classrooms located in and leased from the local nonpublic schools.

The Shared Time program offers classes during the regular school day that are intended to be supplementary to the "core curriculum" courses that the State of Michigan requires as a part of an accredited school program. Among the subjects offered are "remedial" and "enrichment" mathematics, "remedial" and "enrichment" reading, art, music, and physical education. A typical nonpublic school student attends these classes for one or two class periods per week; approximately "ten percent of any given nonpublic school student's time during the academic year would consist of Shared Time instruction." Although Shared Time itself is a program offered only in the nonpublic schools, there was testimony that the courses included in that program are offered, albeit perhaps in a somewhat different form, in the ⊥**376** public schools as well. All of the classes that are the subject of this case are taught in elementary schools, with the exception of Math Topics, a remedial math course taught in the secondary schools.

The Shared Time teachers are full-time employees of the public schools, who often move from classroom to classroom during the course of the school day. A "significant portion" of the teachers (approximately 10%) "previously taught in nonpublic schools, and many of those had been assigned to the same nonpublic school where they were previously employed." The School District of Grand Rapids hires Shared Time teachers in accordance with its ordinary hiring procedures. The public school system apparently provides all of the supplies, materials, and equipment used in connection with Shared Time instruction.

The Community Education Program is offered throughout the Grand Rapids community in schools and on other sites, for children as well as adults. The classes at issue here are taught in the nonpublic elementary schools and commence at the conclusion of the regular school day. Among the courses offered are Arts and Crafts, Home Economics, Spanish, Gymnastics, Yearbook Production, Christmas Arts and Crafts, Drama, Newspaper, Humanities, Chess, Model ⊥**377** Building, and Nature Appreciation. The District Court found that "[a]lthough certain Community Education courses offered at nonpublic school sites are not offered at the public schools on a Community Education basis, all Community Education programs are otherwise available at the public schools, usually as a part of their more extensive regular curriculum."

Community Education teachers are part-time public school employees. Community Education courses are completely voluntary and are offered only if 12 or more students enroll. Because a well-known teacher is necessary to attract the requisite number of students, the School District accords a preference in hiring to instructors already teaching within the school. Thus, "virtually every Community Education course conducted on facilities leased from nonpublic schools has an instructor otherwise employed full time by the same nonpublic school."

Both programs are administered similarly. The Director of the program, a public school employee, sends packets of course listings to the participating nonpublic schools before the school year begins. The nonpublic school administrators then decide which courses they want to offer. The Director works out an academic schedule for each school, taking into account, *inter alia*, the varying religious holidays celebrated by the schools of different denominations.

Nonpublic school administrators decide which classrooms will be used for the programs, and the Director then inspects the facilities and consults with Shared Time teachers to make sure the facilities are satisfactory. The public school system pays the nonpublic schools for the use of the necessary classroom space by entering into "leases" at the rate of $6 per classroom per week. The "leases," however, contain no mention of the particular room, space, or facility leased and teachers' rooms, libraries, lavatories, and similar facilities are made available at no additional charge. ⊥**378** Each room used in the programs has to be free of any crucifix, religious symbol, or artifact, although such religious symbols can be present in the adjoining hallways, corridors, and other facilities used in connection with the program. During the time that a given classroom is being used in the programs, the teacher is required to post a sign stating that it is a "public school classroom." The signs read as follows: "GRAND RAPIDS PUBLIC SCHOOLS' ROOM. THIS ROOM HAS BEEN LEASED BY THE GRAND RAPIDS PUBLIC SCHOOL DISTRICT, FOR THE PURPOSE OF CONDUCTING PUBLIC SCHOOL EDUCATIONAL PROGRAMS. THE ACTIVITY IN THIS ROOM IS CONTROLLED SOLELY BY THE GRAND RAPIDS PUBLIC SCHOOL DISTRICT." However, there are no signs posted outside the school buildings indicating that public school courses are conducted inside or that the facilities are being used as a public school annex.

Although petitioners label the Shared Time and Community Education students as "part-time public school students," the students attending Shared Time and Community Education courses in facilities leased from a nonpublic school are the same students who attend that particular school otherwise. There is no evidence that any public school student has ever attended a Shared Time or Community Education class in a nonpublic school.

The District Court found that "[t]hough Defendants claim the Shared Time program is available to all students, the record is abundantly clear that only nonpublic school students wearing the cloak of a 'public school student' can enroll in it." The District Court noted that "[w]hereas public school students are assembled at the public facility nearest to their residence, students in religious schools are assembled on the basis of religion without any consideration of residence or school district boundaries." Thus, "beneficiaries are wholly designated on the basis of religion," and these "public school" classes, in contrast to ordinary public ⊥**379** school classes which are largely neighborhood-based, are as segregated by religion as are the schools at which they are offered.

Forty of the forty-one schools at which the programs operate are sectarian in character. The schools of course vary from one another, but substantial evidence suggests that they share deep religious purposes. For instance, the Parent Handbook of one Catholic school states the goals of Catholic education as "[a] God oriented environment which *permeates* the total educational program," "[a] Christian atmosphere which guides and encourages participation in the church's commitment to social justice," and "[a] continuous development of knowledge of the Catholic faith, its traditions, teachings and theology." A policy statement of the Christian schools similarly proclaims that "it is not sufficient that the teachings of Christianity be a separate subject in the curriculum, but *the Word of God must be an all-pervading force in the educational program*." These Christian schools require all parents seeking to enroll their children either to subscribe to a particular doctrinal statement or to agree to have their children taught according to the doctrinal statement. The District Court found that the schools are "pervasively sectarian," and concluded "without hesitation that the purposes of these schools is to advance their particular religions," and that "a substantial portion of their functions are subsumed in the religious mission."

⊥**380** B

Respondents are six taxpayers who filed suit against the School District of Grand Rapids and a number of state officials. They charged that the Shared Time and Community Education programs violated the Establishment Clause of the First Amendment of the Constitution, made applicable to the States through the Fourteenth Amendment. After an 8-day bench trial, the District Court entered a judgment on the merits on behalf of respondents and enjoined further operation of the programs.

Applying the familiar three-part purpose, effect, and entanglement test set out in *Lemon* v. *Kurtzman*, the court held that, although the purpose of the programs was secular, their effect was "distinctly impermissible."

The court relied in particular on the fact that the programs at issue involved publicly provided instructional services that served nonpublic school students segregated largely by religion on nonpublic school premises. The court also noted that the programs conferred "direct benefits, both financial and otherwise, to the sectarian institutions." Finally, the court found that the programs necessarily entailed an unacceptable level of entanglement, both political and administrative, between the ⊥**381** public school systems and the sectarian schools. Petitioners appealed the judgment of the District Court to the Court of Appeals for the Sixth Circuit. A divided panel of the Court of Appeals affirmed. We granted certiorari and now affirm.

II

A

The First Amendment's guarantee that "Congress shall make no law respecting an establishment of religion," as our cases demonstrate, is more than a pledge that no single religion will be designated as a state religion. It is also more than a mere injunction that governmental programs discriminating among religions are unconstitutional. The Establishment Clause instead primarily proscribes "sponsorship, financial support, and active involvement of the sovereign in religious activity." *Nyquist*. As *Justice BLACK*, writing for the Court in *Everson* v. *Board of Education*, stated: "Neither [a State nor the Federal Government] can pass laws which aid one religion, aid all religions, or prefer one religion over another. . . . No tax in any amount, large or small, can be levied to support any religious activities or institutions, whatever they may be called, or whatever form they may adopt to teach or practice religion."

Since *Everson* made clear that the guarantees of the Establishment Clause apply to the States, we have often grappled with the problem of state aid to nonpublic, religious schools. In all of these cases, our goal has been to give meaning to the sparse language and broad purposes of the ⊥**382** Clause, while not unduly infringing on the ability of the States to provide for the welfare of their people in accordance with their own particular circumstances. Providing for the education of schoolchildren is surely a praiseworthy purpose. But our cases have consistently recognized that even such a praiseworthy, secular purpose cannot validate government aid to parochial schools when the aid has the effect of promoting a single religion or religion generally or when the aid unduly entangles the government in matters religious. For just as religion throughout history has provided spiritual comfort, guidance, and inspiration to many, it can also serve powerfully to divide societies and to exclude those whose beliefs are not in accord with particular religions or sects that have from time to time achieved dominance. The solution to this problem adopted by the Framers and consistently recognized by this Court is jealously to guard the right of every individual to worship according to the dictates of conscience while requiring the government to maintain a course of neutrality among religions, and between religion and non-religion. Only in this way can we "make room for as wide a variety of beliefs and creeds as the spiritual needs of man deem necessary" and "sponsor an attitude on the part of government that shows no partiality to any one group and lets each flourish according to the zeal of its adherents and the appeal of its dogma." *Zorach* v. *Clauson*.

We have noted that the three-part test first articulated in *Lemon* v. *Kurtzman* guides "[t]he general nature of our inquiry in this area," *Mueller* v. *Allen:* "Every analysis in this area must begin with consideration of the cumulative criteria developed by the Court over many years. Three such tests may be gleaned from our cases. First, the statute must have a secular legislative purpose; second, its principal or primary ⊥**383** effect must be one that neither advances nor inhibits religion, finally, the statute must not foster 'an excessive government entanglement with religion.'" *Lemon* v. *Kurtzman*. These tests "must not be viewed as setting the precise limits to the necessary constitutional inquiry, but serve only as guidelines with which to identify instances in which the objectives of the Establishment Clause have been impaired." *Meek* v. *Pittenger*. We have particularly relied on *Lemon* in every case involving the sensitive relationship between government and religion in the education of our children. The government's activities in this area can have a magnified impact on impressionable young minds, and the occasional rivalry of parallel public and private school systems offers an all-too-ready opportunity for divisive rifts along religious lines in the body politic. The *Lemon* test concentrates attention on the issues—purposes, effect, entanglement—that determined whether a particular state action is an improper "law respecting an establishment of religion." We therefore reaffirm that state action alleged to violate the Establishment Clause should be measured against the *Lemon* criteria.

As has often been true in school aid cases, there is no dispute as to the first test. Both the District Court and the Court of Appeals found that the purpose of the Community Education and Shared Time programs was "manifestly secular." We find no reason to disagree with this holding, and therefore go on to consider whether the primary or principal effect of the challenged programs is to advance or inhibit religion.

⊥**384** B

Our inquiry must begin with a consideration of the nature of the institutions in which the programs operate. Of the 41 private schools where these "part-time public schools" have operated, 40 are identifiably religious schools. It is true that each school may not share all of the characteristics of religious schools as articulated, for example, in the complaint in *Meek* v. *Pittenger*. The District Court found, however, that "[b]ased upon the massive testimony and exhibits, the conclusion is inescapable that the religious institutions receiving instructional services from the public schools are sectarian in the sense that a substantial portion of their functions are subsumed in the religious mission." At the religious schools here—as at the sectarian schools that have been the subject of our past cases—"the secular education those schools provide goes hand in hand with the religious mission that is the only reason for the schools' existence. Within that institution, the two are inextricably intertwined." *Lemon* v. *Kurtzman*. ⊥**385**

Given that 40 of the 41 schools in this case are thus "pervasively sectarian," the challenged public-school programs operating in the religious schools may impermissibly advance religion in three different ways. First, the teachers participating in the programs may become involved in intentionally or inadvertently inculcating particular religious tenets or beliefs. Second, the programs may provide a crucial symbolic link between government and religion, thereby enlisting—at least in the eyes of impressionable youngsters—the powers of government to the support of the religious denomination operating the school. Third, the programs may have the effect of directly promoting religion by impermissibly providing a subsidy to the primary religious mission of the institutions affected.

(1)

Although Establishment Clause jurisprudence is characterized by few absolutes, the Clause does absolutely prohibit government-financed or government-sponsored indoctrination into the beliefs of a particular religious faith. Such indoctrination, if permitted to occur, would have devastating effects on the right of each individual voluntarily to determine what to believe (and what not to believe) free of any coercive pressures from the State, while at the same time tainting the resulting religious beliefs with a corrosive secularism. ⊥**386**

In *Meek* v. *Pittenger*, the Court invalidated a statute providing for the loan of state-paid professional staff—including teachers—to nonpublic schools to provide remedial and accelerated instruction, guidance counseling and testing, and other services on the premises of the nonpublic schools. Such a program, if not subjected to a "comprehensive, discriminating, and continuing state surveillance," *Lemon* v. *Kurtzman*, would entail an unacceptable risk that the state-sponsored instructional personnel would "advance the religious mission of the church-related schools, in which they serve." *Meek*. Even though the teachers were paid by the State, "[t]he potential for impermissible fostering of religion under these circumstances, although somewhat reduced, is nonetheless present." The program in *Meek*, if not sufficiently monitored, would simply have entailed too great a risk of state-sponsored indoctrination.

The programs before us today share the defect that we identified in *Meek*. With respect to the Community Education Program, the District Court found that "virtually every Community Education course conducted on facilities leased from nonpublic schools has an instructor otherwise employed full time by the same nonpublic school." These instructors, many of whom no doubt teach in the religious schools precisely because they are adherents of the controlling denomination and want to serve their religious community zealously, are expected during the regular school day to inculcate their students with the tenets and beliefs of their particular religious faiths. Yet the premise of the program is that those instructors can put aside their religious convictions and engage in entirely secular Community Education instruction as soon as the school day is over. Moreover, they are expected to do so before the same religious-school students and in the same religious-school classrooms that they employed to advance religious purposes ⊥**387** during the "official" school day. Nonetheless, as petitioners themselves asserted, Community Education classes are not specifically monitored for religious content.

We do not question that the dedicated and professional religious school teachers employed by the Community Education program will attempt in good faith to perform their secular mission conscientiously. Nonetheless, there is a substantial risk that, overtly or subtly, the religious message they are expected to convey during the regular school day will infuse the supposedly secular classes they teach after school. The danger arises "not because the public employee [is] likely deliberately to subvert his task to the service of religion, but rather because the pressures of the environment might alter his behavior from its normal course." *Wolman* v. *Walter*. "The conflict of functions inheres in the situation." *Lemon* v. *Kurtzman*.

The Shared Time program, though structured somewhat differently, nonetheless also poses a substantial risk of state-sponsored indoctrination. The most important difference between the programs is that most of the instructors in the Shared Time program are full-time teachers hired by the public schools. Moreover, although "virtually every" Community Education instructor is a full-time religious school teacher, only "[a] significant portion" of the Shared Time instructors previously worked in the religious schools. Nonetheless, as with the Community Education program, no attempt is made to monitor the Shared Time courses for religious content. ⊥**388**

Thus despite these differences between the two programs, our holding in *Meek* controls the inquiry with respect to Shared Time, as well as Community Education. Shared Time instructors are teaching academic subjects in religious schools in courses virtually indistinguishable from the other courses offered during the regular religious-school day. The teachers in this program, even more than their Community Education colleagues, are "performing important educational services in schools in which education is an integral part of the dominant sectarian mission and in which an atmosphere dedicated to the advancement of religious belief is constantly maintained." *Meek* v. *Pittenger*. Teachers in such an atmosphere may well subtly (or overtly) conform their instruction to the environment in which they teach, while students will perceive the instruction provided in the context of the dominantly religious message of the institution, thus reinforcing the indoctrinating effect. As we stated in *Meek*, "[w]hether the subject is 'remedial reading,' 'advanced reading,' or simply 'reading,' a teacher remains a teacher, and the danger that religious doctrine will become intertwined with secular instruction persists." Unlike types of aid that the Court has upheld, such as state-created standardized tests, *Committee for Public Education* v. *Regan*, or diagnostic services, *Wolman* v. *Walter*, there is a "substantial risk" that programs operating in this environment would "be used for religious educational purposes." *Committee for Public Education* v. *Regan*.

The Court of Appeals of course recognized that respondents adduced no evidence of specific incidents of religious indoctrination in this case. But the absence of proof of specific incidents is not dispositive. When conducting a supposedly secular class in the pervasively sectarian environment of a religious school, a teacher may knowingly or unwillingly tailor the content of the course to fit the school's announced goals. If so, there is no reason to believe **⊥389** that this kind of ideological influence would be detected or reported by students, by their parents, or by the school system itself. The students are presumably attending religious schools precisely in order to receive religious instruction. After spending the balance of their school day in classes heavily influenced by a religious perspective, they would have little motivation or ability to discern improper ideological content that may creep into a Shared Time or Community Education course. Neither their parents nor the parochial schools would have cause to complain if the effect of the publicly-supported instruction were to advance the schools' sectarian mission. And the public school system itself has no incentive to detect or report any specific incidents or improper state-sponsored indoctrination. Thus, the lack of evidence of specific incidents of indoctrination is of little significance.

(2)

Our cases have recognized that the Establishment Clause guards against more than direct, state-funded efforts to indoctrinate youngsters in specific religious beliefs. Government promotes religion as effectively when it fosters a close identification of its powers and responsibilities with those of any—or all—religious denominations as when it attempts to inculcate specific religious doctrines. If this identification conveys a message of government endorsement or disapproval of religion, a core purpose of the Establishment Clause is violated. As we stated in *Larkin* v. *Grendel's Den, Inc.*: "[T]he mere appearance of a joint exercise of legislative authority by Church and State provides a significant symbolic benefit to **⊥390** religion in the minds of some by reason of the power conferred."

It follows that an important concern of the effects test is whether the symbolic union of church and state effected by the challenged governmental action is sufficiently likely to be perceived by adherents of the controlling denominations as an endorsement, and by the nonadherents as a disapproval, of their individual religious choices. The inquiry into this kind of effect must be conducted with particular care when many of the citizens perceiving the governmental message are children in their formative years. The symbolism of a union between church and state is most likely to influence children of tender years, whose experience is limited and whose beliefs consequently are the function of environment as much as of free and voluntary choice.

Our school-aid cases have recognized a sensitivity to the symbolic impact of the union of church and state. Grappling with problems in many ways parallel to those we face today, *McCollum* v. *Board of Education* held that a public school may not permit part-time religious instruction on its premises as a part of the school program, even if participation in that instruction is entirely voluntary and even if the instruction itself is conducted only by nonpublic-school personnel. Yet in *Zorach* v. *Clauson*, **⊥391** the Court held that a similar program conducted off the premises of the public school passed constitutional muster. The difference in symbolic impact helps to explain the difference between the cases. The symbolic connection of church and state in the *McCollum* program presented the students with a graphic symbol of the "concert or union or dependency" of church and state. This very symbolic union was conspicuously absent in the *Zorach* program.

In the programs challenged in this case, the religious school students spend their typical school day moving between religious-school and "public-school" classes. Both types of classes take place in the same religious-school building and both are largely composed of students who are adherents of the same denomination. In this environment, the students would be unlikely to discern the crucial difference between the religious-school classes and the "public-school" classes, even if the latter were successfully kept free of religious indoctrination. As one commentator has written: "This pervasive [religious] atmosphere makes on the young student's mind a lasting imprint that the holy and transcendental should be central to all facets of life. It increases respect for the church as an institution to guide one's total life adjustments and undoubtedly helps stimulate interest in religious vocations. . . . In short, the parochial school's total operation serves to fulfill both secular and religious functions concurrently, and the two cannot be completely separated. Support of any part of its activity entails some support of the disqualifying religious function of molding the religious personality **⊥392** of the young student." Gianella, Religious Liberty, Nonestablishment and Doctrinal Development: Part II. The Nonestablishment Principle, 81 Harv. L. Rev. 513, 574 (1968). Consequently, even the student who notices the "public school" sign temporarily posted would have before him a powerful symbol of state endorsement and encouragement of the religious beliefs taught in the same class at some other time during the day.

As Judge Friendly, writing for the Second Circuit in the companion case to the case at bar, stated: "Under the City's plan public school teachers are, so far as appearance is concerned, a regular adjunct of the religious school. They pace the same halls, use classrooms in the same building, teach the same students, and confer with the teachers hired by the religious school, many of them members of religious orders. The religious school appears to the public as a joint enterprise staffed with some teachers paid by its religious sponsor and others by the public." *Felton* v. *Secretary, United States Dept. of Ed.* This effect—the symbolic union of government and religion in one sectarian enterprise—is an impermissible effect under the Establishment Clause.

(3)

In *Everson* v. *Board of Education*, the Court stated that "[no] tax in any amount, large or small, can be levied to support any religious activities or institutions, whatever they may be called, or whatever form they may adopt to teach or practice religion." With but one exception, our subsequent cases have struck down attempts by States to make payments out of public tax dollars ⊥**393** directly to primary or secondary religious educational institutions.

Aside from cash payments, the Court has distinguished between two categories of programs in which public funds are used to finance secular activities that religious schools would otherwise fund from their own resources. In the first category, the Court has noted that it is "well established . . . that not every law that confers an 'indirect,' 'remote,' or 'incidental' benefit upon religious institutions is, for that reason alone, constitutionally invalid." *Committee for Public Education* v. *Nyquist*. In such "indirect" aid cases, the government has used primarily secular means to accomplish a primarily secular end, and no "primary effect" of advancing religion has thus been found. On this rationale, the Court has upheld programs providing for loans of secular textbooks to nonpublic school students, and programs providing bus transportation for nonpublic school children.

In the second category of cases, the Court has relied on the Establishment Clause prohibition of forms of aid that provide "direct and substantial advancement of the sectarian enterprise." *Wolman* v. *Walter*. In such "direct ⊥**394** aid" cases, the government, although acting for a secular purpose, has done so by directly supporting a religious institution. Under this rationale, the Court has struck down state schemes providing for tuition grants and tax benefits for parents whose children attend religious school, and programs providing for "loan" of instructional materials to be used in religious schools. In *Sloan* and *Nyquist*, the aid was formally given to parents and not directly to the religious schools, while in *Wolman* and *Meek*, the aid was in-kind assistance rather than the direct contribution of public funds. Nonetheless, these differences in form were insufficient to save programs whose effect was indistinguishable from that of a direct subsidy to the religious school.

Thus, the Court has never accepted the mere possibility of subsidization, as the above cases demonstrate, as sufficient to invalidate an aid program. On the other hand, this effect is not wholly unimportant for Establishment Clause purposes. If it were, the public schools could gradually take on themselves the entire responsibility for teaching secular subjects on religious school premises. The question in each case must be whether the effect of the proffered aid is "direct and substantial," *Committee for Public Education* v. *Nyquist*, or indirect and incidental. "The problem, like many problems in constitutional law, is one of degree." *Zorach* v. *Clauson*. ⊥**395**

We have noted in the past that the religious school has dual functions, providing its students with a secular education while it promotes a particular religious perspective. In *Meek* and *Wolman*, we held unconstitutional state programs providing for loans of instructional equipment and materials to religious schools, on the ground that the programs advanced the "primary, religion-oriented educational function of the sectarian school." *Meek*. The programs challenged here, which provide teachers in addition to the instructional equipment and materials, have a similar—and forbidden—effect of advancing religion. This kind of direct aid to the educational function of the religious school is indistinguishable from the provision of a direct cash subsidy to the religious school that is most clearly prohibited under the Establishment Clause.

Petitioners claim that the aid here, like the textbooks in *Allen*, flows primarily to the students, not to the religious schools. Of course, all aid to religious schools ultimately "flows to" the students, and petitioners' argument if accepted would validate all forms of nonideological aid to religious schools, including those explicitly rejected in our prior cases. Yet in *Meek*, we held unconstitutional the loan of instructional materials to religious schools and in *Wolman*, we rejected the fiction that a similar program could be saved by masking it as aid to individual students. ⊥**396** It follows *a fortiori* that the aid here, which includes not only instructional materials but also the provision of instructional services by teachers in the parochial school building, "inescapably [has] the primary effect of providing a direct and substantial advancement of the sectarian enterprise." Where, as here, no meaningful distinction can be made between aid to the student and aid to the school, "the concept of a loan to individuals is a transparent fiction." *Wolman* v. *Walter*.

Petitioners also argue that this "subsidy" effect is not significant in this case, because the Community Education and Shared Time programs supplemented the curriculum with courses not previously offered in the religious schools and not required by school rule or state regulation. Of course, this fails to distinguish the programs here from those found unconstitutional in *Meek*.

As in *Meek*, we do not find that this feature of the program is controlling. First, there is no way of knowing whether the religious schools would have offered some or all of these courses if the public school system had not offered them first. The distinction between courses that "supplement" and those that "supplant" the regular curriculum is therefore not nearly as clear as petitioners allege. Second, although the precise courses offered in these programs may have been new to the participating religious schools, their general subject matter—reading, math, etc.—was surely a part of the curriculum in the past, and the concerns of the Establishment Clause may thus be triggered despite the "supplemental" nature of the courses. Third, and most important, petitioners' argument would permit the public schools gradually to take over the entire secular curriculum of the religious school, for the latter could surely discontinue existing courses so that they might be replaced a year or two later by a Community Education or Shared Time course with the same content. The average ⊥**397** religious school student, for instance, now spends 10 percent of the school day in Shared Time classes. But there is no principled basis on which this Court can impose a limit on the percentage of the religious-school day that can be subsidized by the public school. To let the genie out of the bottle in this case would be to permit ever larger segments of the religious school curriculum to be turned over to the public school system, thus violating the cardinal principle that the State may not in effect become the prime supporter of the religious school system.

III

We conclude that the challenged programs have the effect of promoting religion in three ways. The state-paid instructors, influenced by the pervasively sectarian nature of the religious school in which they work, may subtly or overtly indoctrinate the students in particular religious tenets at public expense. The symbolic union of church and state inherent in the provision of secular, state-provided instruction in the religious school buildings threatens to convey a message of state support for religion to students and to the general public. Finally, the programs in effect subsidize the religious functions of the parochial schools by taking over a substantial portion of their responsibility for teaching secular subjects. For these reasons, the conclusion is inescapable that the Community Education and Shared Time programs have the "primary or principal" effect of advancing religion, and therefore violate the dictates of the Establishment Clause of the First Amendment.

Nonpublic schools have played an important role in the development of American education, and we have long recog⊥**398**nized that parents and their children have the right to choose between public schools and available sectarian alternatives. As *The CHIEF JUSTICE* noted in *Lemon* v. *Kurtzman*, "nothing we have said can be construed to disparage the role of church-related elementary and secondary schools in our national life. Their contribution has been and is enormous." But the Establishment Clause "rest[s] on the belief that a union of government and religion tends to destroy government and to degrade religion." *Engel* v. *Vitale*. Therefore, "[t]he Constitution decrees that religion must be a private matter for the individual, the family, and the institutions of private choice, and that while some involvement and entanglement are inevitable, lines must be drawn." *Lemon* v. *Kurtzman*. Because "the controlling constitutional standards have become firmly rooted and the broad contours of our inquiry are now well defined," *Committee for Public Education* v. *Nyquist*, the position of those lines has now become quite clear and requires affirmance of the Court of Appeals.

It is so ordered.

Chief Justice BURGER, concurring in the judgment in part and dissenting in part.

I agree with the Court that, under our decisions in *Lemon* v. *Kurtzman*, and *Earley* v. *DiCenso*, the Grand Rapids Community Education program violates the Establishment Clause. As to the Shared Time program, I dissent for the reasons stated in my dissenting opinion in *Aguilar* v. *Felton*.

Justice O'CONNOR, concurring in the judgment in part and dissenting in part.

For the reasons stated in my dissenting opinion in *Aguilar* v. *Felton*, I dissent from the Court's holding that the Grand Rapids Shared Time program impermissibly ⊥**399** advances religion. Like the New York Title I program, the Grand Rapids Shared Time program employs full-time public school teachers who offer supplemental instruction to parochial school children on the premises of religious schools. Nothing in the record indicates that Shared Time instructors have attempted to proselytize their students. I see no reason why public school teachers in Grand Rapids are any more likely than their counterparts in New York to disobey their instructions.

The Court relies on the District Court's finding that a "significant portion of the Shared Time instructors previously taught in nonpublic schools, and many of these had been assigned to the same nonpublic school where they were previously employed." In fact, only 13 Shared Time instructors have ever been employed by any parochial school, and only a fraction of those 13 now work in a parochial school where they were previously employed. The experience of these few teachers does not significantly increase the risk that the perceived or actual effect of the Shared Time program will be to inculcate religion at public expense. I would uphold the Shared Time program.

I agree with the Court, however, that the Community Education program violates the Establishment Clause. The record indicates that Community Education courses in the parochial schools are overwhelmingly taught by instructors who are current full-time employees of the parochial school. The teachers offer secular subjects to the same parochial school students who attend their regular parochial school classes. In addition, the supervisors of the Community Education program in the parochial schools are by and large the principals of the very schools where the classes are offered. When full-time parochial school teachers receive public funds to teach secular courses to their parochial school students ⊥**400** under parochial school supervision, I agree that the program has the perceived and actual effect of advancing the religious aims of the church-related schools. This is particularly the case where, as here, religion pervades the curriculum and the teachers are accustomed to bring religion to play in everything they teach. I concur in the judgment of the Court that the Community Education program violates the Establishment Clause.

Justice WHITE, dissenting.

As evidenced by my dissenting opinions in *Lemon* v. *Kurtzman* and *Committee for Public Education* v. *Nyquist*, I have long disagreed with the Court's interpretation and application of the Establishment Clause in the context of state aid to private schools. For the reasons stated in those dissents, I am firmly of the belief that the Court's decisions in these cases, like its decisions in *Lemon* and *Nyquist*, are "not required by the First Amendment and [are] contrary to the long-range interests of the country." For those same reasons, I am satisfied that what the States have sought to do in these cases is well within their authority and is not forbidden by the Establishment Clause. Hence, I dissent and would reverse the judgment in each of these cases.

Justice REHNQUIST, dissenting.

I dissent for the reasons stated in my dissenting opinion in *Wallace* v. *Jaffree*. In *Grand Rapids*, the Court relies heavily on the principles of *Everson* and *McCollum*, but de⊥**401**clines to discuss the faulty "wall" premise upon which those cases rest. In doing so the Court blinds itself to the first 150 years' history of the Establishment Clause.

The Court today attempts to give content to the "effects" prong of the *Lemon* test by holding that a "symbolic link between government and religion" creates an impermissible effect. But one wonders how the teaching of "Math Topics," "Spanish," and "Gymnastics," which is struck down today, creates a greater "symbolic link" than the municipal crèche upheld in *Lynch* v. *Donnelley* or the legislative chaplain upheld in *Marsh* v. *Chambers*.

A most unfortunate result of *Grand Rapids* is that to support its holding the Court, despite its disclaimers, impugns the integrity of public school teachers. Contrary to the law and the teachers' promises, they are assumed to be eager inculcators of religious dogma requiring, in the Court's words, "ongoing supervision." Not one instance of attempted religious inculcation exists in the records of the school aid cases decided today, even though both the Grand Rapids and New York programs have been in operation for a number of years. I would reverse.

3 GOVERNMENT INTERVENTION IN CHURCH CONTROVERSIES

Clearly, the purpose of the First Amendment is to prevent domination of the state by the church or domination of the church by the state. Their co-existence, however, makes inevitable some degree of involvement in the internal affairs of each on the part of the other. One area in which the state has been drawn into church affairs—either by its own volition or at the invitation of church members—is that of disputes within churches.

While state courts have always disclaimed the right or intent to deal with purely ecclesiastical disputes, they have frequently accepted jurisdiction of cases involving church conflicts and schisms, particularly where property rights are involved. There is a line of cases from the nineteenth century having to do with communitarian groups.[1] There were a large number of these groups, which can be generally described as seeking to create ideal societies based on religious principles: religiously based utopias. A central feature of many of these groups was collectivism, based on the pattern of the New Testament church. Acts 2:44-45 says of the early Christians: "And all who believed were together and had all things in common; and they sold their possessions and goods and distributed them to all, as any had need." Many nineteenth-century groups required, as a condition of membership, that persons joining sell their goods and give the proceeds to the common treasury of the community. Sometimes controversies arose, however, and frequently those who wanted to leave the community wanted to claim for his or her own the amount originally contributed to the community, if not a larger share of its wealth. Sometimes they brought legal proceedings against the communities to obtain their goals, thus leaving in their wake a series of Supreme Court opinions. Generally these litigants were unsuccessful, given the Court's reluctance to interfere in disputes which had doctrinal content or overtones, discussed more fully below.

Often the attempt to regain money from the communities was based on a charge such as that the community's founder and/or current administrators were guilty of fraud or some other unacceptable behavior, that the members of the community were the unwilling victims of these unscrupulous persons. Dean M. Kelley describes these cases as the precursors of the more recent "anti-cult" cases, in which similar charges of malfeasance have been leveled at the leadership of "alternative religions."[2]

The first of these cases to reach the Supreme Court was *Goesele* v. *Bimeler*, which grew out of a

[1]These cases were brought to our attention by the eminent church-state scholar Dean M. Kelley. They will be discussed in Volume One of his multivolume *The Law of Church and State in America: Historical Survey and Analysis* (Westport, CT: Greenwood Press, forthcoming).

[2]See *Ibid.*, Vol 1. Of many examples of such proceedings, perhaps one of the most well-publicized was the attempt of the State of California, motivated by the complaints of disgruntled former members, to place the World-Wide Church of God in receivership and put the administration of the church under the control of the state. That episode is documented, perhaps not with the greatest objectivity but apparently factually accurately, in Stanley R. Rader, *Against the Gates of Hell: The Threat to Religious Freedom in America* (New York: Everest House, 1980).

dispute over the property of a community known as Zoar, in Ohio. Originating in Germany, this pietistic community had a faith and style of life similar to the Quakers. Because their environment was not hospitable to their faith, in 1816 they migrated to America, under the leadership of Joseph Michael Bäumler, later known as Bimeler. They named their community Zoar because it was a refuge from evil, just as the Old Testament Zoar had been an asylum from the wickedness of Sodom.[3] One source[4] argues that, in spite of its Biblical name, unlike most groups of this sort, Zoar's communitarianism was not based on religious principles. Rather it was forced on the residents by their poverty; they decided that common ownership of wealth and property would be more equitable for all in times of hardship. So, in 1819, the majority of the community voted to adopt the communistic life-style. However, that the preamble of the agreement they collectively signed contained the clause "that the members of the society have, *in a spirit of Christian love*, agreed to unite in a communion of property, according to the rules and regulations specified,"[5] casts some doubt on that purely secularist interpretation. Some fifteen years later the group's fortunes improved considerably with a contract to help build the Ohio Canal. This gave capital to invest in other projects and this, along with their industriousness and frugality, led to financial comfort for the community.

Joseph Bimeler died in 1853 and, deprived of his leadership and inspiration, the community went into a period of decline. Finally, in 1898, the residents voted to divide the property among themselves and dissolve the community.[6] However, during the times of prosperity, shortly before Bimeler's death, an attempt was made to wrest some of the group's wealth from it by means of the law, *Goesele* v. *Bimeler*. The plaintiff was a descendent of one Johannes Goesele, who had signed the group's compact to become a communitarian kind of society, which stipulated that none of the signees had any individual rights to the wealth of the community, nor could they transmit any of it to their heirs. Consequently, the Court held that descendent plaintiff had no grounds to claim ownership to any part of the wealth of the community.

Apparently the plaintiff argued that the contract was void because Bimeler was guilty of some fraud, as one of the three trustees designated by the compact to manage the affairs of the community. Plaintiff had obtained depositions from several disaffected former members of the community who testified that Bimeler was a scoundrel who had mismanaged the affairs of the community. But the Court rehearsed the history of the community in America and concluded that Bimeler had, in fact, been honest, trustworthy, and a careful and inventive steward of the community's assets. The Court concluded that an injustice had been done to Bimeler's character, that there was no evidence of plaintiff's accusations, and that the community's property, held in a communitarian way, should remain intact.

This case is the first of several in which the Court was unwilling to find for disaffected former members of religious organizations who tried to attack the integrity of the group by bringing accusations of one sort or another against the leadership.

In 1856 the Court decided BAKER v. NACHTRIEB, a case involving property disputes in a religious community variously known as Economy, Harmony, or the Rappites. The migration of the followers of George Rapp from Germany to America in 1803-04 actually antedated that of the inhabitants of Zoar, described above. But in character, the two communities were very similar. Most pertinent here, both communities believed in holding property and all other assets in common.[7] The case, as it came before the Court, is another example of a disgruntled member trying to regain what he had contributed to the common wealth of the society. Like other such claims before and since, he attempted to charge the leader of the group with mismanagement, malfeasance, and corruption. But the Court, in an opinion written by Justice John A. Campbell, took seriously that the plaintiff, at the time he left the society, had signed a document acknowledging that he had voluntarily left and that George Rapp had given him $200.00 although, under the rules of the society, he did not have to do so. The Court found this to be evidence contrary to the allegation of corruption on the part of Rapp and disallowed this attempt to penetrate the society's contract and take some of its property.

Although the attempt of the plaintiff did not involve a frontal attack on the group's doctrine, it did challenge the written agreement of the group to hold all things in common, which was based on a biblical precedent (which the society held to be a command). The decision demonstrates that the Court was willing to protect the viability of a "different" religious group's style of life against what it held to be inaccurate attacks on the character of the leadership of the group. This is a precedent which needs to be remembered by some lower courts in the latter part of the twentieth century as they hear "anti-cult" cases.

The Harmony society came under attack again in 1887 in SPEIDEL V. HENRICI. Again, the attempt was to gain a portion of the assets of the society by

[3]See Genesis 19, especially verses 22-23.

[4]Alice Felt Tyler, *Freedom's Ferment: Phases of American Social History from the Colonial Period to the Outbreak of the Civil War* (New York: Harper and Row, 1944, 1962), 129.

[5]14 Howard 589, 604 (emphasis added).

[6]Tyler, *Freedom's Ferment*, 128-130.

[7]Cf. Tyler, *Freedom's Ferment*, pp. 121-125.

a descendent of one of the original settlers. This time the attack detailed the doctrines of the group: its belief in the coming end of time, its precept of holding all things in common, its belief in religiously motivated celibacy, its practices of disciplining members who somehow backslid from strict obedience of the rules of the society. The allegation was not so much that such doctrines were wrong, but that George Rapp did not believe them: deception and fraud! Furthermore, Rapp ruled over the group with absolute authority, dominating his followers both physically and mentally. Although the words are not used, the allegation is a foreshadowing of the accusations of "brainwashing" and "mind control" made against the leaders of alternative religions in recent times.

Justice Horace Gray, writing for the Court, was able to deal with the case easily, without getting into the thorny problems of doctrine and alleged mental, if not physical, captivity of the members of the society. The case had become moot. After all, George Rapp had died in 1847 and the plaintiff had withdrawn voluntarily from the society more than 50 years before filing the suit attempting to obtain some of the considerable resources of the society. The allegations of the plaintiff were too stale at the time of litigation and consequently the Court refused to decide in his favor.

In *Schwartz* v. *Duss* (1902) the Court was invited one last time to rule on an attempt by some to obtain some of the assets of the Harmony society. This time the allegation was that the trustees at the time were not pursuing the original purposes of the charter of the society. It appears that now that there were very few members of the society (most had died without being replaced by new converts), the trustees had conveyed many of the assets of the society to a holding company and had used some of the property for their own purposes. However, the Court, based on the evidence and consistent rulings below, essentially ruled that the plaintiffs had no right to the remaining assets of the society and could not challenge the conveyance of any of the assets to the holding company because they had no legal interest in the matter. This was because none of the plaintiffs were ever members of the society and they had no stake in the disposition of the society's assets as descendants of members because the original compact specifically declared that all members gave up individual rights to property and gave no rights to heirs or other representatives. Again, the Court recognized the autonomy of a religious group to manage its affairs and protect them from subsequent attacks from disgruntled members or descendants thereof.[8]

[8]The final days of the Harmony society are described in Yaacov Oved, *Two Hundred Years of American Communes* (New Brunswick, NJ: Transaction Books, 1988), 80-81.

In 1914 the Court decided a case in which a monastic order sued to retain the assets of a former monk, now deceased, ORDER OF ST. BENEDICT v. STEINHAUSER. The Benedictines were founded in the sixth century by Benedict of Nursia, Italy. It is an order in which members normally stay in the house where they are assigned, a monastic community. Occasionally, an abbot will assign a monk to labor in charitable or parish work out in "the world." That was the case with Father Augustin Wirth of St. Mary's Abbey in New Jersey. He worked in several parishes, with the permission of the Abbot, and died, in 1901, while serving as priest in a parish in Minnesota.

In addition to parish duties, Father Wirth wrote a number of books, from which he received royalties. When he died, the executor of his estate, one Albert Steinhauser, took possession of the assets derived from the sales of the books. When the Order filed suit, claiming ownership of the assets, Steinhauser cross-sued, claiming that the Order had no legitimate claim and, if it did, such a claim was contrary to public policy.

Justice Charles Evans Hughes, for the Court, found in favor of the Order. It was clear that the constitution of the St. Mary's Abbey of New Jersey, like Benedictine houses historically, required that the property and earnings of members of the Order be given over to the possession of the Order. Individual members should possess no more for their individual support than allowed by the Abbot. That situation could be changed if one left the Order, which one could do voluntarily. The Court found that Father Wirth had not left the Order, but rather remained under its authority until he died. Apparently the Abbot allowed him to retain the royalties from his publications, but they were not to be used for his own purposes. Rather they were to be used for charitable purposes mutually agreeable to Father Wirth and his Abbot. Consequently, given that Father Wirth and his use of the proceeds from his books were continually under the supervision of the Order, the Court ruled that the Order had a legitimate claim on the decedent's estate.

The Court made short work of Steinhauser's second point, that the Abbey's continued possession of Father Wirth's assets was against public policy. The legislature of New Jersey had incorporated the Order of St. Benedict of New Jersey in 1868. As part of that process, the Order was empowered to write by-laws which included the concepts of perpetual membership and the ownership of members' assets mentioned above. Given this explicit incorporation by the state legislature, the features of the Order's ownership of Father Wirth's assets complained of by executor Steinhauser were not against public policy. Indeed, they were specifically sanctioned by the state.

The Court buttressed its opinion by citing a number of precedent cases, including some mentioned in this survey. Dean Kelley, commenting on these citations, makes a fitting conclusion to this set of cases.

> Rather than leaving the matter there, the court went on to link this holding with [previous like decisions], cementing a firm recognition by the courts over a century of the rights of religious bodies to choose for themselves unconventional forms of organization and operation that—so long as voluntary—would not be disturbed by civil law.[9]

Frequently, however, in the adjudication of property disputes, doctrinal issues cannot be completely avoided because they are often the cause of division. In cases of that sort, in order to keep the doctrinal involvement to a minimum, the courts generally follow a rule which places churches in two categories: "congregational" and "hierarchical." For example, in disputes between factions of a local Congregational or Baptist church, majority decision of the autonomous congregation will ordinarily be accepted by the courts. The church polity of the Roman Catholic, Episcopal, and Presbyterian churches is such, however, that the members of a local church are under the control of a larger hierarchical church body with respect to doctrine and procedure. There, the courts will follow the decision of the proper institutional authority in the hierarchical structure.[10]

State courts have not, however, always been content to apply this self-restraining rule. Particularly in cases involving congregationally governed churches, they have sometimes felt that the momentary majority faction within the church has departed from the fundamental doctrines on which the church was founded to the extent that the minority group has greater entitlement to the property. Obviously, the ascertainment of the original doctrines and the nature and extent of the departure from those beliefs represents a substantial state intervention into doctrinal issues.[11]

The United States Supreme Court was confronted with an internal church dispute for the first time in 1872 in WATSON v. JONES. This litigation arose when the Walnut Street Presbyterian Church of Louisville, Kentucky, suffered a split in 1866 after the General Assembly of the Presbyterian Church in the U.S.A. issued instructions that persons who had voluntarily aided the rebellion or believed in slavery as a divine institution could not be received as church members until they agreed "to repent and forsake these sins." Although the General Assembly held the loyal faction to be the "true" Walnut Street Church, the Kentucky Supreme Court found in favor of the nonloyal group. Because members of the church lived in Indiana as well as Kentucky, the United States Circuit Court accepted jurisdiction on grounds of diverse citizenship and decided in favor of the loyal group. The case eventually reached the Supreme Court.

Justice Miller, speaking for the Court, rejected the use of the "departure-from-doctrine" guideline for federal courts. Because the Presbyterian Church had a hierarchical policy, and because the General Assembly was the highest church body, he held that it was binding on the Court to accept as final the findings of the assembly. Miller expressed the opinion that ecclesiastical agencies are more competent than civil court judges in an area such as this. Further and more importantly, he declared that federal courts must refrain from consideration of religious doctrine and practice because "[t]he law knows no heresy, and is committed to the support of no dogma, the establishment of no sect." Although the *Watson* decision, as a rule of federal common law, was not binding on state courts, Justice Brennan was to say in 1969 that its language had a "clear constitutional ring." Its words, taken at face value, left no role for federal courts to review the determination of the appropriate church body.

Not until 1929 did the Court have occasion to return to the issue. In that year, in *Gonzales* v. *Archbishop,* the Court forcefully reiterated the *Watson* ruling as it accepted without question a decision of the Roman Catholic archbishop of the Philippines concerning a chaplain's appointment. However, Justice Brandeis in the majority opinion weakened the doctrine when he suggested that civil courts might give "marginal" review to decisions of church authorities to ascertain if there had been "fraud, col-

---

[9]Kelley, *The Law of Church and State in America*, Vol. 1, (forthcoming).

[10]Judges have found, however, that it is often not a simple task to determine the polity of a church body. Church organizations do not necessarily fit neatly into either designation, and a limited amount of judicial intervention cannot be avoided in seeking to ascertain the proper category. In 1983 the Fourth District Court of Illinois found that there was such conflicting evidence as to the polity of the Lutheran Church-Missouri Synod that it could not constitutionally make the detailed inquiry that was necessary to determine the polity of the synod because such an investigation would in itself be an unconstitutional inquiry. (*Grace Evangelical Lutheran Church of River Forest* v. *Lutheran Church-Missouri Synod*) [1983]. The U.S. Supreme Court denied certiorari the next year.

[11]An explanation of the "departure from doctrine" standard is found in Paul G. Kauper's "Church Autonomy and the First Amendment: The Presbyterian Church Case," in *Church and State: Supreme Court and the First Amendment*, ed. Philip B. Kurland (Chicago: University of Chicago Press, 1975), 69-76.

lusion, or arbitrariness" on the part of the ecclesiastical agency.

In 1952 in KEDROFF v. SAINT NICHOLAS CATHEDRAL, the Court converted its decision in *Watson,* as now qualified by Brandeis's suggestion in *Gonzales,* into a constitutional rule of law. Because by that time both religion clauses of the First Amendment had been applied to the states by incorporation, the case had particular significance for state courts. In *Kedroff,* the Court invalidated a New York statute designed to free the Russian Orthodox Church in America from Moscow's control and to give it title to Saint Nicholas Cathedral and other assets of the church in the United States. The Court held that the First Amendment prevented the legislature from determining which group was to control the cathedral. The decision of the Patriarch of Moscow, the appropriate hierarchical authority, was entitled to enforcement.

Because the New York Court of Appeals had earlier upheld the legislative act, the Supreme Court remanded the case for appropriate action. When the Court of Appeals undertook to reassert its original support of the independent churches, the Supreme Court reversed this judicial action in *Kreshik* v. *Saint Nicholas Cathedral* (1960), thus refusing to permit the judiciary to do what the legislature could not.

Notwithstanding Supreme Court decisions warning against judicial interpretation of religious doctrines in property disputes, state courts continued to resort to the "departure-from-doctrine" standard. Such had been the situation in PRESBYTERIAN CHURCH IN THE UNITED STATES v. MARY ELIZABETH BLUE HULL MEMORIAL PRESBYTERIAN CHURCH (1969). Here the dispute, which had caused two Georgia congregations to withdraw from the general church, was social and political as well as religious. The local congregations contended that they were entitled to keep the church property after the break. The General Assembly, they contended, had departed from doctrine and practice not only by the ordination of women and the use of literature which taught alien "neo-orthodoxy" but also by membership in the National Council of Churches of Christ and by the issuance of pronouncements on the Vietnam conflict. A jury decided that the General Assembly had indeed substantially departed from doctrine and could not therefore deprive the local churches of their property. The Supreme Court of Georgia affirmed this verdict, and the United States Supreme Court agreed to review on First Amendment grounds.

Written by Justice Brennan, the majority opinion reversed the Georgia court and categorically ruled out further use of the departure-from-doctrine standard in subsequent state court proceedings. The majority opinion agreed that a civil court is a proper forum for the settlement of property disputes, but held that the *Watson* rule means that courts may not interpret and weigh church doctrine as they resolve the disputes. Interpretation of religious tenets is reserved to the appropriate church authority. The Court further suggested that certain recognized "neutral principles of law" developed for settlement of secular property disputes could be applied to church disputes. The "neutral principles of law" concept was affirmed and further delineated the following year in *Maryland and Virginia Eldership of the Churches of God* v. *The Church of God at Sharpsburg* (1970). Here, a *per curiam* opinion of the Court upheld the procedure followed by the Maryland Court of Appeals in settling a church property dispute by reliance upon such neutral principles as provisions of state laws governing the holding of property by religious corporations, language in deeds conveying the property to the local churches, the charters of the religious corporations, and appropriate provisions of the constitution of the General Eldership.

Justice Brennan, joined by Douglas and Marshall, wrote a concurring opinion in which he summed up three approaches that states might use in resolving church property disputes: the *Watson* hierarchical-congregational policy approach; the "neutral principles of law" doctrine; and the passage of special laws governing church property arrangements "in a manner that precludes state interference in doctrine."

In spite of the clear mandate against judicial interpretation of religious dogma, the qualification found in the *Gonzales* case (i.e., permitting marginal review of the decision of the ecclesiastical authority as to "fraud, collusion, and arbitrariness") survived even the Presbyterian Church case. It was to the *Gonzales* qualification of *Watson* that the Supreme Court addressed itself in 1976 in SERBIAN EASTERN ORTHODOX DIOCESE FOR THE UNITED STATES AND CANADA v. MILIVOJEVICH. Here, by a seven-to-two vote, the Court overturned a ruling by the Illinois Supreme Court that the decision of the Mother Church of the Serbian Orthodox Church in Belgrade, Yugoslavia, had been "arbitrary" when thirteen years earlier it had suspended and defrocked Bishop Milivojevich. The Illinois court had ordered the bishop's reinstatement after a review of the action of the Mother Church had convinced the court that the prescribed church procedure had not been followed. Justice Brennan, for the majority, asserted that this detailed review, "under the umbrella of arbitrariness," had far exceeded the "minimal" review allowed civil courts. By substituting its interpretation of doctrine for that of the appropriate church authority, the Illinois court had violated the First and Fourteenth Amendments despite its contention that it had applied neutral principles of law. This narrowing of the "arbitrariness" rule further evidenced the increasing unwillingness of the Supreme Court to sustain encroachments of civil authorities upon matters of ecclesiastical custom or law.

However, to some who read the majority opinion, the Court seemed to be negating or severely restricting the neutral principles approach. In conflicting state court decisions that followed, some judges apparently were convinced that they must inevitably defer to the findings of the highest church tribunal of the church polity. Others believed that the church tribunal was the final authority only if the dispute could not be resolved through neutral principles of law relying on "objective, well-established concepts of trust and property law" such as the examination of state statutes, deeds, and local church charters, as well as the provisions of the general church constitution.

In 1979, in JONES v. WOLF (1979), the Court was again confronted with a dispute over ownership of church property in a hierarchical structure after a schism had occurred in the Vineville Presbyterian Church in Macon, Georgia. Making an apparent effort to give guidance to civil courts and also to allow them greater latitude in resolving church property controversies, Justice Blackmun, writing for the Court, expressly approved the neutral principles approach. He wrote:

> The primary advantages of the neutral-principles approach are that it is completely secular in operation, and yet flexible enough to accommodate all forms of religious organization and polity. The method relies exclusively on objective, well-established concepts of trust and property law familiar to lawyers and judges. It thereby promises to free civil courts completely from entanglement in questions of religious doctrine, polity, and practice (443 U.S. 595, 603).

He admitted that this approach is not free of difficulty, and accepted the doctrine of judicial deference to the highest internal authority of a hierarchical polity as an acceptable alternative. Sternly warning against judicial inquiry into religious doctrine and practice, Blackmun emphasized once again the limited role of civil courts in church disputes.[12]

Joined by Chief Justice Burger and Justices Stewart and White, Justice Powell dissented. He argued for the rule of compulsory deference to the "authoritative resolution of the dispute within the church itself."[13]

Although disappointed litigants in intrachurch disputes have continued to appeal to the Supreme Court for redress from lower court decisions, that body has not since *Wolf* accepted a case for oral hearing and decision. In 1984, in addition to the *Grace Evangelical Lutheran Church* case commented on earlier, the Court refused certiorari in an Ohio property dispute between a local A.M.E. congregation and the Mother Church *(Board of Trustees of the Allen Chapel A.M.E. Church* v. *Grogans).*

During its 1985-1986 session, the Court refused to hear appeals from decisions involving disputes within a Church of Christ congregation in Florida and a Baptist church in Chesapeake, Virginia.[14]

However, in the Virginia case, which concerned removal of a pastor, Justice Marshall, joined by Justice Brennan, dissented from the denial of certiorari maintaining that the excessive involvement of the trial court in settling the dispute warranted review by the Court. The lower court had, Marshall complained, "imposed its own view of proper procedures on the congregation's decision-making," and had engaged in action which "threatens to erode the First Amendment's prohibitions against entanglement between religious and secular authority. . . ." (475 U.S. 1148, 1149).

Another area in which the Court has encountered great difficulty is that of "defining" religion, and in recent years it has evidenced a strong desire to abandon the effort altogether. The Court's first and classic definition of religion was that undertaken by Justice Field in DAVIS v. BEASON (1890). Broad as it was, Field's definition was not extensive enough to encompass the practice of polygamy as a religious tenet.

State and federal courts have since been required to define religion in connection with such varied issues as conscientious objection to war,[15] tax exemp-

[12]A similar suggestion was made by the Supreme Court in what was actually the first church-state case to come before it, *Terrett* v. *Taylor* (1815). The Virginia Legislature in 1801 had rescinded a 1776 statute that had confirmed to the Episcopal Church the property it held. Relying on the "maxims of eternal justice," rather than any specific provision of the Constitution, the Court voided the rescinding act. Church property, Justice Story held for the Court, enjoys the same protection as property of non-religious corporations.

[13]An excellent discussion of *Jones* v. *Wolf* and the entire problem of civil adjudication of church property disputes is found in Arlin M. Adams and William R. Hanlon, "*Jones* v. *Wolf*: Church Autonomy and the Religion Clauses of the First Amendment," *University of Pennsylvania Law Review* 128 (June 1980): 1291-1339.

[14]*Black* v. *Wyche* (1986) and *Little* v. *First Baptist Church, Crestwood* (1986).

[15]In the area of conscientious objection to war, the definition of religion, or "religious training and belief," came to be particularly important. See the discussion of such cases as UNITED STATES v. SEEGER (1965) and WELSH v. UNITED STATES (1970) at a later point. Two helpful articles which specifically deal with the definition of religion in American constitutional law are, Timothy L. Hall, "The Sacred and the Profane: A First Amendment Definition of Religion," *Texas Law Review* 61(August 1982): 139-73, and Terry L. Slye, "Rendering Unto Caesar: Defining 'Religion' for Purposes of Administering

tion for religious organizations, the alleged use of religious claims to defraud, and the religious rights to be accorded Black Muslims, Buddhists, members of the Church of the New Song, and other minority religious groups when they are in prison.[16]

Undoubtedly, one of the most unusual cases ever to reach the Supreme Court was UNITED STATES v. BALLARD (1944). This case involved the "I Am" movement, founded by Guy and Edna Ballard and their son Donald. The organizers of the movement were charged in a federal district court with having used the mails to defraud by representing that they could by virtue of supernatural powers, heal diseases and other ailments or injuries. All together, eighteen misrepresentations were listed in the twelve counts against them. The trial judge instructed members of the jury that they should not decide whether the religious claims made by the defendants were actually true but only whether the Ballards *believed* them to be true.

Justice Douglas, for the majority, upheld the action of the judge of the lower court. Determination of the truth of religious allegations, Douglas said, was beyond the power of any agency of the secular state even though those beliefs "might seem incredible, if not preposterous, to most people." He quoted with approval the Court's words in *Watson* v. *Jones:* "The law knows no heresy, and is committed to the support of no dogma, the establishment of no sect." Thus, the only issue for secular courts to determine was whether asserted religious belief was sincerely held.

Justice Jackson, in dissent, would have gone even further by also withholding from the jury the question of whether the Ballards believed their religious claims to be true; he would have dismissed the charges completely and "have done with this business of judicially examining other people's faiths." The Court majority was not at the time willing to support it, but the Jackson position has been reflected in the Court's later reluctance to define religion, its refusal to insist on traditional definitions, and its greater tolerance toward "self definition," if the beliefs of a group are "sincere and meaningful" to them. In 1953 Justice Douglas said for the majority in *Fowler* v. *Rhode Island:* "it is no business of courts to say that what is a religious practice or activity for one group is not religion under the protection of the First Amendment" (345 U.S. 67, 70).

Almost two decades later Chief Justice Burger in WISCONSIN v. YODER cautioned in less libertarian and conceivably ominous words that "the very concept of ordered liberty precludes allowing every person to make his own standards on matters of conduct in which society as a whole has important interests" (406 U.S. 205, 215-216). Again, in THOMAS v. REVIEW BOARD OF INDIANA EMPLOYMENT SECURITY DIVISION, he observed that "Only beliefs rooted in religion are protected by the Free Exercise Clause," and speculated that "One can, of course, imagine an asserted claim so bizarre, so clearly nonreligious in motivation, as not to be entitled to protection under the Free Exercise Clause . . ." (450 U.S. 707, 714, 715). Yet in that same 1981 case the Chief Justice essentially restated the philosophy expressed in *Ballard* when he said, "religious beliefs need not be acceptable, logical, consistent, or comprehensible to others in order to merit First Amendment protection."

Religion-Based Tax Exemptions," *Harvard Journal of Law and Public Policy* 6 (Summer 1983): 219-94.

[16]Problems have arisen with some regularity within prisons concerning religious dietary requests and other prisoner demands considered by them to be mandated by their religious beliefs. For example, in early 1996 the Court refused to consider an appeal from a military court ruling against a former soldier who contended that his free exercise of religion guarantee had been violated while he was in jail awaiting military trial. The prisoner contended that his constitutional rights had been violated when he was refused access to the *Book of Shadows*, the "Wiccan Bible." The jailer denied access because the Wiccan religion "was not a recognized religious practice in the state of North Carolina." Later the military court spoke of Wicca as "a pagan religion not unlike the Druid faith, believing in the sacredness of nature." *Phillips* v. *United States.*

BAKER v. NACHTRIEB

19 Howard 126 (60 U.S. 126)
ON APPEAL FROM THE CIRCUIT COURT FOR THE WESTERN DISTRICT OF PENNSYLVANIA
Argued December 5, 1856 — Decided December 16, 1856

⊥**126** Mr. *Justice* CAMPBELL delivered the opinion of the court.

The appellee, who describes himself as a member in the common and joint stock association for mutual benefit and advantage, and for the mutual acquisition and enjoyment of property, called the "Harmony Society," filed a bill in the Circuit Court against the appellants as the trustees and managers of its business and estate. The object of the bill is to obtain for the plaintiff a decree for the amount of the share to which he is entitled in the property of the Society, or compensation for his labor and service during the time he was a member.

In 1819, he became associated with George Rapp and others, in the Harmony Society in Indiana, and remained with them there, or at Economy, in Beaver County, Pennsylvania, till 1846. He devoted his time, skill, attention and care during that period to the increase of the wealth and the promotion of the interest of the Society.

⊥**127** These facts are admitted in the pleadings of either party.

The bill avers, that in 1846, the plaintiff being then 48 years old, and worn out with years and labor for said

Association, was wrongfully and unjustly excluded from it, and deprived of any share in its property, benefits or advantages, by the combination and covin of George Rapp and his associates; that at the time of his exclusion he was entitled to a large sum of money, which those persons unjustly and illegally appropriated to their own use; that George Rapp was the leader and trustee of the Association, invested with the title to its property; and that, since his death, the defendants have acquired the control and management of its business and affairs and the possession of its effects. The plaintiff calls for the production of the Articles of Association, which from time to time have regulated this Society, and prays for an account and distribution of its property, or a compensation for his labor.

The defendants produce a series of articles, by which the Association has been governed since its organization in 1805.

They admit that from small beginnings the Society have become independent in their circumstances, being the owners of lands ample for the supply of their subsistence, warm and comfortable houses for the members and engines and machinery to diminish and cheapen their labors. They affirm that the plaintiff participated in all the individual, social and religious benefits which were enjoyed by his fellows, under their contract, until he became possessed by a spirit of discontent and disaffection, a short time before his membership terminated. They deny that the plaintiff was wrongfully excluded from the Association, or deprived of a share or participation in the property and effects, by the combination or covin of George Rapp and his associates; but assert, that voluntarily, and of his own accord, he separated himself from the Society. They deny that he had a title to any compensation for labor and service while he was a member, other than that which was expended for his support, maintenance and instruction, and that which he derived during the time from the spiritual and social advantages he enjoyed. To support this averment, they epitomize the history of the Harmony Society, and the agreements which, from time to time, have been the basis of its organization.

The Society was composed at first of Germans, who emigrated to the United States in 1805, under the leadership of George Rapp. The members were associated and combined by the common belief that the government of the patriarchal age, united to the community of property, adopted in the days of the Apostles, would conduce to promote their temporal and ⊥**128** eternal happiness. The founders of the Society surrendered up their property to the Association for the common benefit. The Society was settled originally in Pennsylvania, was removed in 1814 and 1815 to Indiana, and again in 1825 to Economy, in Pennsylvania.

The organic law of the Society, in regard to their property, is contained in sections of the Articles of Association, adopted in 1827 by the associates, of whom the plaintiff was one. They are as follows: "All the property of the Society, real, personal and mixed, in law or equity, and howsoever contributed and acquired, shall be deemed, now and forever, joint and indivisible stock; each individual is to be considered to have finally and irrevocably parted with all his former contributions, whether in land, goods, money or labor, and the same rule shall apply to all future contributions whatever they may be.

"Should any individual withdraw from the Society, or depart this life, neither he, in the one case, nor his representatives in the latter, shall be entitled to demand an account of said contributions, whether in land, goods, money or labor; or to claim anything from the Society as matter of right. But it shall be left altogether to the discretion of the Superintendent to decide whether any, and, if any, what allowance shall be made to such member, or his representatives, as a donation."

The defendants, admitting, as we have seen, that the plaintiff, until 1846, was a contented member of the Association, answer and say, that during that year he became disaffected; used violent threats against the associates; made repeated declarations of his intentions to leave the Society, and in that year fulfilled his design by a voluntary withdrawal and separation from the Society, receiving at the same time from George Rapp $200 as a donation. They exhibit as a part of the answer, a writing, signed by the plaintiff, to the following effect:

"To-day I have withdrawn myself from the Harmony Society, and ceased to be a member thereof; I have also received of George Rapp two hundred dollars as a donation, agreeably to contract.

Joshua Nachtrieb.

Economy, June 18, 1846."

This statement of the pleadings shows that no issue was made in them upon the merit of the doctrines, social or religious, which form the basis of this Association; nor any question in reference to the religious instruction and ministration, or the domestic economy or physical discipline which their leader and the other managers have adopted and enforced. ⊥**129** Nor do they suggest any inquiry into the condition of the members, and whether they have experienced hardship, oppression, or undue mortification, from the ambition, avarice, or fanaticism of their guides and administrators.

The bill depends on the averments, that the plaintiff approved the constitution of the Society; submitted to its government; obeyed its regulations, and prized the advantage of being a member. The burden of his complaint is, that he was wrongfully, and without any fault or consent on his part, deprived of his station through the combination of the leader and his assistants. And the defendants concede the character the plaintiff claims for himself; they concede that the plaintiff was an approved and blameless member of the Association, and was entitled to whatever its constitution and order provided for the temporal good or the eternal felicity of the members, and assert that he enjoyed them until he became disaffected and repining, and finally surrendered to a spirit of discontent, which moved him to abandon his condition and privileges. As an evidence of this, they produce a writing, signed by him, in which he acknowledges a voluntary secession from the Society, and claims that the case has arisen to authorize him to make an appeal to the bounty of the Superintendent, and that the Superintendent has answered that appeal by a donation. The value of this writing is now to be considered. The power of the Superintendent to subtract from the otherwise "joint and indivisible stock" of the Society a portion for the individual use of a seceding member, depends upon the concession that the member has withdrawn voluntarily. He cannot supply one who is the victim of covin or combination. The evidence shows that the mind of the plaintiff, in June, 1846, was disquieted in consequence of his connection with the Association, and that he contemplated a change in his condition; that he made inquiries upon the expediency of a removal from Economy, and made some preparations for his departure; that the leader of the Society, suspecting his discontent, and discovering some deviation by him from the rules of the Society, rebuked him with harshness, and menaced him with a sentence of expulsion. Some of the witnesses testify to such a sentence, while the testimony of others reduces the expressions to an admonition and menace. But two days after the occurrence of the last of these scenes, and before any removal had taken place, the writing in the record was executed by him, embodying his decision to leave the Society, and to accept the bounty the constitution permitted the Superintendent to bestow. This writing would have much probative force, if we were simply to treat it as an admission of the statements it contains, when ⊥**130** considered in connection with other evidence in the record. But, we think, this writing is something more than an admission, and stands in a different light from an ordinary receipt. The writing must be treated as the contract of dissolution, between the plaintiff and the Society, of their mutual obligations and engagements to each other. No evidence of prior declarations or antecedent conduct is admissible to contradict or to vary it.

It was prepared to preserve the remembrance of what the parties had prescribed to themselves to do, and expresses their intention in their own language; that such was its object, is corroborated by the fact that for three years there is no evidence of a contrary sentiment. Treating this writing as an instrument of evidence of this class, it is clear that the bill has not made a case in which its validity can be impeached. To enable the plaintiff to show that the rule of the leader (Rapp), instead of being patriarchal, was austere, oppressive, or tyrannical, his discipline vexatious and cruel; his instructions fanatical, and, upon occasions, impious; his system repugnant to public order, and the domestic happiness of its members; his management of their revenues and estate rapacious, selfish, or dishonest; and that the condition of his subjects was servile, ignorant and degraded, so that none of them were responsible for their contracts or engagements to him, from a defect of capacity and freedom, as has been attempted by him in the testimony collected in this cause, it was a necessary prerequisite that his bill should have been so framed as to exhibit such aspects of the internal arrangements and social and religious economy of the Association. This was not done; and for this cause the evidence cannot be considered. The authorities cited from the decisions of this court are decisive. *Very* v. *Levy*; *Patton* v. *Taylor*; *Crockett* v. *Lee*.

Decree reversed—Bill dismissed.

SPEIDEL v. HENRICI

120 U.S. 377

ON APPEAL FROM THE CIRCUIT COURT FOR THE WESTERN DISTRICT OF PENNSYLVANIA

Argued December 14, 1886 — Decided March 7, 1887

⊥**385** Mr. *Justice* GRAY delivered the opinion of the court.

This bill was filed against the Trustees of the Harmony Society, an unincorporated association of persons living together as a community, by a former member of the Society, claiming a share in property in the hands of the Trustees.

The bill is sought to be maintained on the ground that the trust was not a charity, in the legal sense, and the members of the Society were equitable tenants in common of the property held in trust. The learned counsel for the appellants differ in their views of the trust; the one insisting that it was unlawful because founded in fraud and against public policy, and should therefore be dissolved; and the other contending that it was a lawful and continuing trust. We have not found it necessary to consider which of these is the sound view, because we are of opinion that the plaintiff did not show himself to be entitled to invoke the interposition of a court of equity. . . .

⊥**387** Independently of any statute of limitations, courts of equity uniformly decline to assist a person who has slept upon his rights and shows no excuse for his laches in asserting them. . . .

The allegations of this bill, so far as they are material to the defense of laches, are in substance as follows:

⊥**388** The Harmony Society is a voluntary association, formed in 1805 by the plaintiff's parents and other heads of families, who had emigrated from Germany under the leadership of one Rapp, and become subject to his control in both spiritual and temporal affairs. In that year Rapp, for the purpose of acquiring absolute dominion over their means and mode of living, falsely and fraudulently represented to them that they could not be saved from eternal damnation, except by renouncing the plan of a separate home for each family, yielding up all their possessions, as had been done by the early Christians, and laying them at the feet of Rapp as their apostle, to be put into a common fund of the Society, and thenceforth living as a community under his control, receiving in return only the necessaries of life; and they, induced by and relying on his false and fraudulent representations, immediately yielded up all their possessions to the common fund of the Society, and placed the fund in his keeping as their trustee, and thenceforth lived as a community or common household, submitted themselves and their families to do for the community such work as he directed, allowed the avails thereof to form part of the common fund, and relinquished to him and his successors in the leadership of the community the management of the trust fund and the control of their own persons and those of their wives and children, and received only the necessaries of life in return. Rapp received and accepted the trust fund, and all the accretions to it by the work of the inhabitants of the community or otherwise, not as his own, but in trust for the members of those families and the contributors to the fund, and for their common benefit; and always, up to his death in 1847, recognized and acknowledged said trust, and disclaimed any greater interest in the fund than that of any other contributor, and any other right to its management and control than by virtue of his leadership of the community. In 1807 Rapp obliged his followers to abjure matrimony, and thenceforth did not permit them to marry in the community, and compelled anyone about to marry to leave it. The plaintiff was born in the community in 1807, and was reared in and as a part of it, under Rapp's teachings and ⊥**389** control, and faithfully worked for it from the age of twelve to the age of twenty-four years, and allowed the avails of his work to become part of the common fund, and received in return nothing but the necessaries of life, which were of far less value than the avails of his work; and in 1831, being about to marry, had to leave and did leave the community. The trust fund so received and accepted by Rapp, with its profits, interest and accretions, now amounts to $8,000,000, and yields an annual income of $200,000, and is held by the defendants on the same trust on which Rapp held it in his lifetime; and neither Rapp nor the defendants ever rendered any account to the plaintiff or to the beneficiaries of the fund, although the plaintiff, before bringing this suit in May, 1882, demanded of the defendants an account and a settlement of his share.

The trust on which Rapp, and the defendants as his successors, held the common fund of the Harmony Society, is described in one place in the bill as "for the members of said families and the contributors of said fund, and for their common benefit," that is to say, as is clearly explained by what goes before, in trust for their common benefit as a community, living together in the community, working for the community, subject to the regulations of the community, and supported by the community. This was the "said trust" which, as the bill afterwards alleges, Rapp, up to his death, and his successors, until the bringing of this suit, "always recognized and acknowledged." The constant avowal of the Trustees, that they held the trust fund upon such a trust, is wholly inconsistent with and adverse to the claim of the plaintiff that they held the fund in trust for the benefit of the same persons as individuals, though withdrawn from the community, living by themselves, and taking no part in its work.

The plaintiff, upon his own showing, withdrew from the community in 1831, and never returned to it, and for more than fifty years, took no step to demand an account of the Trustees, or to follow up the rights which he claimed in this bill.

If he ever had any rights, he could not assert ⊥**390** them after such a delay; not on the ground of an express and lawful trust, because the express trust stated in the bill, and constantly avowed by the Trustees during this long period, was wholly inconsistent with any trust which would sustain his claim; not on the ground that the express trust stated in the bill was unlawful and void, and therefore the Trustees held the trust fund for the benefit of all the contributors in proportion to the amounts of their contributions, because that would be an implied or resulting trust, and barred by lapse of time. In any aspect of the case, therefore, if it was not strictly within the Statute of Limitations, yet the plaintiff showed so little vigilance and so great laches that the circuit court rightly held that he was not entitled to relief in equity.

Decree affirmed.

WATSON v. JONES

13 Wallace 679 (80 U. S. 679)
⊥**680** ON APPEAL FROM THE CIRCUIT COURT OF THE UNITED STATES FOR THE DISTRICT OF KENTUCKY
Argued March 10, 1871 — Decided April 15, 1872

[Editor's note: The following is a condensation of the facts of the case, as given in 13 Wallace.] ⊥**690** From the commencement of the late war of insurrection to its close, the General Assembly of the Presbyterian Church at its annual meetings expressed, in declaratory statements ⊥**691** or resolutions, its sense of the obligation of all good citizens to support the Federal Government in that struggle; and when, by the Proclamation of President Lincoln, emancipation of the slaves of the States in insurrection was announced, that body also expressed views favorable to emancipation, and adverse to the institution of slavery. At its meeting in Pittsburg, in May, 1865, instructions were given to the Presbyteries, the Board of Missions, and to the sessions of the Churches, that when any persons from the Southern States should make application for employment as missionaries, or for admission as members or ministers of churches, inquiry should be made as to their sentiments in regard to loyalty to the government, and on the subject of slavery; and if it was found that they had been guilty of voluntarily aiding the war of the rebellion, or held the doctrine announced by the large body of the churches in the insurrectionary States, which had organized a new General Assembly, that "the system of negro slavery in the South is a divine institution, and that it is the peculiar mission of the Southern Church to conserve that institution" they should be required to repent and forsake these sins before they could be received.

In the month of September, thereafter, the Presbytery of Louisville, under whose immediate jurisdiction was the Walnut Street Church, adopted and published in pamphlet form, what is called "a declaration and testimony against the erroneous and heretical doctrines and practices which have obtained and been propagated in the Presbyterian Church of the United States during the last five years." This declaration denounced, in the severest terms, the action of the General Assembly in the matters we have just mentioned, declared their intention to refuse to be governed by that action, and invited the cooperation of all the members of the Presbyterian Church who shared these sentiments of the declaration, in a conceded resistance to what they called the usurpation of authority by the Assembly.

The General Assembly of 1866 denounced the declaration and testimony, and declared that every Pres⊥**692**bytery which refused to obey its order should be *ipso facto* dissolved and called to answer before the next General Assembly, giving the Louisville Presbytery an opportunity for repentance and conformity. The Louisville Presbytery divided, and the adherence of the declaration and testimony sought and obtained admission in 1868, into "The Presbyterian Church of the Confederate States" of which we have already spoken, as having several years previously withdrawn from the General Assembly of the United States, and set up a new organization.

In January, 1866, the congregation of the Walnut Street Church became divided, . . . each claiming to constitute the Church, although the issue as to membership was not distinctly made in the chancery suit of *Avery* v. *Watson*. Both parties at this time recognized the same superior church judicatories.

On the 19th June, 1866, the Synod of Kentucky became divided, the opposing parties in each claiming to constitute respectively the true Presbytery and the true Synod; each meanwhile recognizing and claiming to adhere to the same General Assembly. Of these contesting bodies, the appellants adhered to one; the appellees to another.

On the 1st of June, 1867, the Presbytery and Synod recognized by the appellants, were declared by the General Assembly to be "in no sense the true and lawful Synod and Presbytery, in connection with and under the care and authority of the General Assembly of the Presbyterian Church in the United States of America;" and were permanently excluded from connection with or representation in the Assembly; by the same resolution the Synod and Presbytery adhered to by appellees were declared to be the true and lawful Presbytery of Louisville, and Synod of Kentucky.

⊥**693** The Synod of Kentucky thus excluded by a resolution adopted the 28th June, 1867, declared "That, in its future action, it will be governed by this recognized sundering of all its relation to the aforesaid revolutionary body (the General Assembly) by the acts of that body itself." The Presbytery took substantially the same action.

In this final severance of Presbytery and Synod from the General Assembly, the appellants and appellees continued to adhere to both bodies at first recognized by them respectively. . . . The reader will now readily perceive, if he have not done so before, how in the earliest stages of this controversy it was found that a majority of the members of the Walnut Street Church concurred with the action of the General Assembly, while Watson and Gault, as ruling elders, and Fulton and Farley as trustees, constituting in each case a majority of the Session and of the trustees, with Mr. McElroy, the pastor, sympathized with the party of the declaration and testimony of the Louisville Presbytery. And how this led to efforts by each party to exclude the other from participation in the session of the Church and the use of the property ⊥**694** . . .

The division and separation finally extended to the Presbytery of Louisville and the Synod of Kentucky. It is now complete and apparently irreconcilable, and we are called upon to declare the beneficial uses of the church property in this condition of total separation between the members of what was once a united and harmonious congregation of the Presbyterian Church. . . .

⊥**713** Mr. *Justice MILLER* now delivered the opinion of the court:

This case belongs to a class, happily rare in our courts, in which one of the parties to a controversy, essentially ecclesiastical, resorts to the judicial tribunals of the State for the maintenance of rights which the Church has refused to acknowledge, or found itself unable to protect. Much as such dissensions among the members of a religious society should ⊥**714** be regretted, a regret which is increased when passing from the control of the judicial and legislative bodies of the entire organization to which the society belongs, an appeal is made to the secular authority; the courts when so called on must perform their functions as in other cases.

Religious organizations come before us in the same attitude as other voluntary associations for benevolent or charitable purposes, and their rights of property, or of contract, are equally under the protection of the law, and the actions of their members subject to its restraints. Conscious as we may be of the excited feeling engendered by this controversy, and of the extent to which it has agitated the intelligent and pious body of Christians in whose bosom it originated, we enter upon its consideration with the satisfaction of knowing that the principles on which we are to decide so much of it as is proper for our decision, are those applicable alike to all of its class, and that our duty is the simple one of applying those principles to the facts before us. . . .

⊥**722** The questions which have come before the civil courts concerning the rights to property held by ecclesiastical bodies, may, so far as we have been able to examine them, be profitably classified under three general heads, which of course do not include cases governed by considerations applicable to a church established and supported by law as the religion of the State.

1. The first of these is when the property which is the subject of controversy has been, by the deed or will of the donor, or other instrument by which the property is held, by the express terms of the instrument devoted to the teaching, support or spread of some specific form of religious doctrine or belief.

2. The second is when the property is held by a religious congregation which, by the nature of its organization, is strictly independent of other ecclesiastical associations, and so far as church government is concerned, owes no fealty or obligation to any higher authority.

3. The third is where the religious congregation or ecclesiastical body holding the property is but a subordinate member of some general church organization in which there are superior ecclesiastical tribunals with a general and ultimate power of control more or less complete in some su⊥**723**preme judicatory over the whole membership of that general organization.

In regard to the first of these classes it seems hardly to admit of a rational doubt that an individual or an association of individuals may dedicate property by way of trust to the purpose of sustaining, supporting and propagating definite religious doctrines or principles, providing that in doing so they violate no law of morality, and give to the instrument by which their purpose is evidenced, the formalities which the laws require. And it would seem also to be the obvious duty of the court, in a case properly made, to see that the property so dedicated is not diverted from the trust which is thus attached to its use. So long as there are persons qualified within the meaning of the original dedication, and who are also willing to teach the doctrines or principles prescribed in the act of dedication, and so long as there is any one so interested in the execution of the trust as to have a standing in court, it must be that they can prevent the diversion of the property or fund to other and different uses. This is the general doctrine of courts of equity as to charities, and it seems equally applicable to ecclesiastical matters.

In such case, if the trust is confided to a religious congregation of the independent or congregational form of church government, it is not in the power of the majority of that congregation, however preponderant, by reason of a change of views on religious subjects, to carry the property so confided to them to the support of new and conflicting doctrine. A pious man building and dedicating a house of worship to the sole and exclusive use of those who believe in the doctrine of the Holy Trinity, and placing it under the control of a congregation which at the time holds the same belief, has a right to expect that the law will prevent that property from being used as a means of support and dissemination of the Unitarian doctrine, and as a place of Unitarian worship. Nor is the principle varied when the organization to which the trust is confided is of the second or associated form of church government. The protection which the law ⊥**724** throws around the trust is the same. And though the task may be a delicate one and a difficult one, it will be the duty of the court in such cases, when the doctrine to be taught or the form of worship to be used is definitely and clearly laid down, to inquire whether the party accused of violating the trust is holding or teaching a different doctrine, or using a form of worship which is so far variant as to defeat the declared objects of the trust. In the leading case on this subject, in the English courts, of the *Attorney-General* v. *Pearson*, Lord Eldon said: "I agree with the defendants that the religious belief of the parties is irrelevant to the matters in dispute, except so far as the King's Court is called upon to execute the trust." That was a case in which the trust deed declared the house which was erected under it, was for the worship and service of God. And though we may not be satisfied with the very artificial and elaborate argument by which the Chancellor arrives at the conclusion, that because any other view of the nature of the Godhead than the Trinitarian view was heresy by the laws of England, and any one giving expression to the Unitarian view was liable to be severely punished for heresy by the secular courts, at the time the deed was made, that the trust was, therefore, for Trinitarian worship, we may still accept the statement that the court has the right to enforce a trust clearly defined on such a subject. . . .

The second class of cases which we have described has reference to the case of a church of a strictly congregational or independent organization, governed solely within itself, either by a majority of its members or by such other local organism as it may have instituted for the purpose of ecclesiastical government; and to property held by such a church, either by way of purchase or donation, with no other specific ⊥**725** trust attached to it in the hands of the church than that it is for the use of that congregation as a religious society.

In such cases, where there is a schism which leads to a separation into distinct and conflicting bodies, the rights of such bodies to the use of the property must be determined by the ordinary principles which govern voluntary associations. If the principle of government in such cases is that the majority rules, then the numerical majority of members must control the right to the use of the property. If there be within the congregation officers in whom are vested the powers of such control, then those who adhere to the acknowledged organism by which the body is governed are entitled to the use of the property. The minority in choosing to separate themselves into a distinct body, and refusing to recognize the authority of the governing body, can claim no rights in the property from the fact that they had once been members of the Church or congregation. This ruling admits of no inquiry into the existing religious opinions of those who comprise the legal or regular organization; for, if such was permitted, a very small minority, without any officers of the church among them, might be found to be the only faithful supporters of the religious dogmas of the founders of the Church. There being no such trust imposed upon the property when purchased or given, the court will not imply one for the purpose of expelling from its use those who by regular succession and order constitute the Church, because they may have changed in some respect their views of religious truth. . . .

The case of *Smith* v. *Nelson* asserts this doctrine in a case where a legacy was left to the Associate Congregation of Ryegate, the interest whereof was to be annually paid to their minister forever. In that case, though the Ryegate ⊥**726** congregation was one of a number of Presbyterian churches connected with the general Presbyterian body at large, the court held that the only inquiry was whether the society still exists, and whether they have a minister chosen and appointed by the majority and regularly ordained over the society, agreeably to the usage of that denomination. And though we may be of opinion that the doctrine of that case needs modification, so far as it discusses the relation of the Ryegate congregation to the other judicatories of the body to which it belongs, it certainly lays down the principle correctly if that congregation was to be treated as an independent one.

But the third of these classes of cases is the one which is oftenest found in the courts, and which, with reference to the number and difficulty of the questions involved, and to other considerations, is every way the most important.

It is the case of property acquired in any of the usual modes for the general use of a religious congregation which is itself part of a large and general organization of some religious denomination, with which it is more or less intimately connected by religious views and ecclesiastical government.

The case before us is one of this class, growing out of a schism which has divided the congregation and its officers, and the presbytery and synod, and which appeals to the courts to determine the right to the use of the property so acquired. Here is no case of property devoted forever by the instrument which conveyed it, or by any specific declaration of its owner, to the support of any special religious dogmas, or any peculiar form of worship, but of property purchased for the use of a religious congregation, and so long as any existing religious congregation can be ascertained to be that congregation, or its regular and legitimate successor, it is entitled to the use of the property. In the case of an independent congregation we have pointed out how this identity, or succession, is to be ascertained but in cases of this character we are bound to look at the fact that the local congregation is itself but a member of a much ⊥**727** larger and more important religious organization, and is under its government and control, and is bound by its orders and judgments. There are in the Presbyterian system of ecclesiastical government, in regular succession, the Presbytery over the session or local church, the Synod over the Presbytery, and the General Assembly over all. These are called, in the language of the church organs, "judicatories," and they entertain appeals from the decisions of those below, and prescribe corrective measures in other cases.

In this class of cases we think the rule of action which should govern the civil courts, founded in a broad and sound view of the relations of church and state under our system of laws, and supported by a preponderating weight of judicial authority is, that, whenever the questions of discipline or of faith or ecclesiastical rule, custom or law have been decided by the highest of these church judicatories to which the matter has been carried, the legal tribunals must accept such decisions as final, and as binding on them, in their application to the case before them.

We concede at the outset that the doctrine of the English courts is otherwise. In the case of *The Attorney-General* v. *Pearson*, the proposition is laid down by Lord Eldon, and sustained by the peers, that it is the duty of the court in such cases to inquire and decide for itself, not only what was the nature and power of these church judicatories, but what is the true standard of faith in the church organization, and which of the contending parties before the court holds to this standard. And in the subsequent case of *Craigdallie* v. *Aikman* the same learned judge expresses in strong terms his chagrin that the Court of Sessions of Scotland, from which the case had been appealed, had failed to find on this latter subject, so that he could rest the case on religious belief, but had declared that in this matter there was no difference between the parties. And we can very well understand how the Lord Chancellor of England, who is, in his office, in a large sense, the head and representative of ⊥**728** the Established Church, who controls very largely the church patronage, and whose judicial decision may be, and not unfrequently is, invoked in cases of heresy and ecclesiastical contumacy, should feel, even in dealing with a dissenting church, but little delicacy in grappling with the most abstruse problems of theological controversy, or in construing the instruments which those churches have adopted as their rules of government, or inquiring into their customs and usages. The dissenting church in England is not a free church in the sense in which we apply the term in this country, and it was much less free in Lord Eldon's time than now. Laws then existed upon the statute book hampering the free exercise of religious belief and worship in many most oppressive forms, and although Protestant dissenters were less burdened than Catholics and Jews, there did not exist that full, entire and practical freedom for all forms of religious belief and practice which lies at the foundation of our political principles. . . .

In this country the full and free right to entertain any religious belief, to practice any religious principle, and to teach any religious doctrine which does not violate the laws of morality and property, and which does not infringe personal rights, is conceded to all. The law knows no heresy, and is committed to the support of no dogma, the establishment of no sect. The right to organize voluntary religious associations to assist in the expression and dissemination of⊥**729** any religious doctrine, and to create tribunals for the decision of controverted questions of faith within the association, and for the ecclesiastical government of all the individual members, congregations and officers within the general association, is unquestioned. All who unite themselves to such a body do so with an implied consent to this government, and are bound to submit to it. But it would be a vain consent and would lead to the total subversion of such religious bodies, if any one aggrieved by one of their decisions could appeal to the secular courts and have them reversed. It is of the essence of these religious unions, and of their right to establish tribunals for the decision of questions arising among themselves, that those decisions should be binding in all cases of ecclesiastical cognizance, subject only to such appeals as the organism itself provides for.

Nor do we see that justice would be likely to be promoted by submitting those decisions to review in the ordinary judicial tribunals. Each of these large and influential bodies (to mention no others, let reference be had to the Protestant Episcopal, the Methodist Episcopal, and the Presbyterian churches) has a body of constitutional and ecclesiastical law of its own, to be found in their written organic laws, their books of discipline, in their collections of precedents, in their usage and customs, which as to each constitute a system of ecclesiastical law and religious faith that tasks the ablest minds to become familiar with. It is not to be supposed that the judges of the civil courts can be as competent in the ecclesiastical law and religious faith of all these bodies as the ablest men in each are in reference to their own. It would therefore be an appeal from the more learned tribunal in the law which should decide the case, to one which is less so.

We have said that these views are supported by the preponderant weight of authority in this country, and for the reasons which we have given, we do not think the doctrines of the English Chancery Court on this subject should have with us the influence which we would cheerfully accord to it on others. . . .

⊥**730** One of the most careful and well considered judgments on the subject is that of the Court of Appeals of South Carolina, delivered by Chancellor Johnson in the case of *Harmon* v. *Dreher*. The case turned upon certain rights in the use of the church property claimed by the minister notwithstanding his expulsion from the synod as one of its members. "He stands," says the Chancellor, "convicted of the offenses alleged against him, by the sentence of the spiritual body of which he was a voluntary member, and whose proceedings he had bound himself to abide. It belongs not to the civil power to enter into or review the proceedings of a spiritual court. The structure of our government has, for the preservation of civil liberty, rescued the temporal institutions from religious interference. On the other hand, it has secured religious liberty from the invasion of the civil authority. The judgments, therefore, of ⊥**731** religious associations, bearing on their own members, are not examinable here, and I am not to inquire whether the doctrines attributed to Mr. Dreher were held by him, or whether if held were anti-Lutheran; or whether his conduct was or was not in accordance with the duty he owed to the synod or to his denomination. . . . When a civil right depends upon an ecclesiastical matter, it is the civil court and not the ecclesiastical which is to decide. But the civil tribunal tries the civil right, and no more, taking the ecclesiastical decisions out of which the civil right arises, as it finds them." The principle is re-affirmed by the same court in the *John's Island Church* case. . . .

⊥**732** In the case of *Watson* v. *Farris*, which was a case growing out of the schism in the Presbyterian Church in Missouri in regard to this same declaration and testimony and the action of the General Assembly, that court held that whether a case was regularly or irregularly before the Assembly was a question which the Assembly had the right to determine for itself, and no civil court could reverse, modify, or impair its action in a matter of merely ecclesiastic concern.

We cannot better close this review of the authorities than in the language of the Supreme Court of Pennsylvania, in the case of *The German Reformed Church* v. *Seibert*: "The decisions of ecclesiastical courts, like every other judicial tribunal, are final, as they are the best judges of what constitutes an offense against the word of God and the discipline of the Church. Any other than those courts must be incompetent judges of matters of faith, discipline and doctrine; and civil courts, if they should be so unwise as to attempt to supervise their judgments on matters which come within their jurisdiction, would only involve themselves in a sea of uncertainty and doubt which would do anything but improve either religion or good morals."

In the subsequent case of *McGinnis* v. *Watson*, this principle is again applied and supported by a more elaborate argument.

The Court of Appeals of Kentucky, in the case of *Watson* v. *Avery* before referred to, while admitting the general principle here laid down, maintains that when a decision of an ecclesiastical tribunal is set up in the civil courts, it is always open to inquiry whether the tribunal acted within its jurisdiction, and if it did not, its decision could not be conclusive.

There is, perhaps, no word in legal terminology so frequently used as the word "jurisdiction," so capable of use in a general and vague sense, and which is used so often by men learned in the law without a due regard to precision in its application. As regards its use in the matters we have ⊥**733** been discussing, it may very well be conceded that if the General Assembly of the Presbyterian Church should undertake to try one of its members for murder, and punish him with death or imprisonment, its sentence would be of no validity in a civil court or anywhere else. Or if it should at the instance of one of its members entertain jurisdiction as between him and another member as to their individual right to property, real or personal, the right in no sense depending on ecclesiastical questions, its decision would be utterly disregarded by any civil court where it might be set up. And it might be said in a certain general sense very justly, that it was because the General Assembly had no jurisdiction of the case. Illustrations of this character could be multiplied in which the proposition of the Kentucky court would be strictly applicable.

But it is a very different thing where a subject-matter of dispute, strictly and purely ecclesiastical in its character—a matter over which the civil courts exercise no jurisdiction—a matter which concerns theological controversy, church discipline, ecclesiastical government, or the conformity of the members of the church to the standard of morals required of them—becomes the subject of its action. It may be said here, also, that no jurisdiction has been conferred on the tribunal to try the particular case before it, or that, in its judgment, it exceeds the powers conferred upon it, or that the laws of the church do not authorize the particular form of proceeding adopted; and, in a sense often used in the courts, all of those may be said to be questions of jurisdiction. But it is easy to see that if the civil courts are to inquire into all these matters, the whole subject of the doctrinal theology, the usages and customs, the written laws, and fundamental organization of every religious denomination may, and must, be examined into with minuteness and care, for they would become, in almost every case, the *criteria* by which the validity of the ecclesiastical decree would be determined in the civil court. This principle would deprive these bodies of the right of construing their own church laws, would open the way to all the evils which we ⊥**734** have depicted as attendant upon the doctrine of Lord Eldon, and would, in effect, transfer to the civil courts where property rights were concerned the decision of all ecclesiastical questions.

And this is precisely what the Court of Appeals of Kentucky did in the case of *Watson* v. *Avery*. Under cover of inquiries into the jurisdiction of the synod and presbytery over the congregation, and of the General Assembly over all, it went into an elaborate examination of the principles of Presbyterian church government, and ended by overruling the decision of the highest judicatory of that church in the United States, both on the jurisdiction and the merits; and, substituting its own judgment for that of the ecclesiastical court, decided that ruling elders, declared to be such by that tribunal, are not such, and must not be recognized by the congregation, though four-fifths of its members believe in the judgment of the Assembly and desired to conform to its decree.

But we need pursue this subject no further. Whatever may have been the case before the Kentucky court, the appellants in the case presented to us have separated themselves wholly from the church organization to which they belonged when this controversy commenced. They now deny its authority, denounce its action, and refuse to abide by its judgments. They have first erected themselves into a new organization, and have since joined themselves to another totally different, if not hostile, to the one to which they belonged when the difficulty first began. Under any of the decisions which we have examined, the appellants, in their present position, have no right to the property, or to the use of it, which is the subject of this suit.

The novelty of the questions presented to this court for the first time, their intrinsic importance and far-reaching influence, and the knowledge that the schism in which the case originated has divided the Presbyterian churches throughout Kentucky and Missouri, have seemed to us to justify the careful and laborious examination and discussion which we ⊥**735** have made of the principles which should govern the case. For the same reasons we have held it under advisement for a year; not uninfluenced by the hope, that since the civil commotion, which evidently lay at the foundation of the trouble, has passed away, that charity, which is so large an element in the faith of both parties, and which, by one of the apostles of that religion, is said to be the greatest of all the Christian virtues, would have brought about a reconciliation. But we have been disappointed. It is not for us to determine or apportion the moral responsibility which attaches to the parties of this result. We can only pronounce the judgment of the law as applicable to the case presented to us, and that requires us to affirm the decree of the Circuit Court as it stands.

DECREE AFFIRMED.

ORDER OF ST. BENEDICT v. STEINHAUSER

234 U.S. 640

ON WRIT OF CERTIORARI TO THE CIRCUIT COURT OF APPEALS FOR THE EIGHTH CIRCUIT

Argued March 11, 1914 — Decided June 22, 1914

⊥**641** Mr. *Justice HUGHES* delivered the opinion of the court.

This suit was brought by the Order of St. Benedict of New Jersey, a corporation of that state, to establish its title to personal property left by Augustin Wirth, deceased, a member of the Order, who died at Springfield, Minnesota, in December, 1901. The defendant Albert Steinhauser as administrator of the estate of the decedent, holding letters from the probate court of Brown county, Minnesota, filed a cross bill asserting ownership in his representative capacity, and praying discovery and account with respect to whatever part of the estate had come into the complainant's possession. The circuit court entered a decree dismissing the cross bill and granting the relief sought by the complainant's bill. 179 Fed. 137. The circuit court of appeals reversed this decree, directing the dismissal of the original bill and the granting of the prayer of the cross bill. 194 Fed. 289. Certiorari was allowed.

The monastic brotherhood known as the Order of St. Benedict was established by St. Benedict in the early part of the sixth century at Subiaco, Italy, whence it spread over western Europe. It was brought to the United States in 1846. The members of the brotherhood follow what is known as "the rule of St. Benedict," a collection ⊥**642** of mandates essentially unchanged from the beginning. The vows are those of obedience, stability, chastity, and poverty.

We are not concerned in the present case with any question of ecclesiastical requirement or monastic discipline. The question is solely one of civil rights. The claim in suit rests upon the constitution of the complainant corporation, and the obligations inherent in membership.

The Order of St. Benedict of New Jersey was incorporated in 1868 by special act of the legislature of that state. The incorporators were described as "being a society of religious men, living in community, and devoted to charitable works and the education of youth." The corporation was empowered to hold property and to make by-laws for the government of the Order, provided that these should not be repugnant to the Constitution of the United States or of the state of New Jersey, that the clear yearly income of the real estate should not exceed a sum stated, and that no one should remain an incorporator "except regular members of said religious society living in community, and governed by the laws thereof." Under this charter the Order adopted a constitution, among the provisions of which are the following:

"Section 11. Membership is lost at once:

"1. By being dismissed according to the disciplinary statutes of the Order of St. Benedict of New Jersey, approved of by Pope Pius IX. for the American Cassinese Congregation of Benedictines.

"2. By voluntary leaving the Order for any purpose whatsoever.

"3. By joining any other order or secret society, or any other religious denominations.

"Section 12. Since the Order of St. Benedict of New Jersey is solely a charitable institution, the real estate of said order and the individual earnings of its members are and must be considered as common property of the ⊥**643** Order of St. Benedict of New Jersey, from which the members of said Order derive their support, and the balance of which income and property should serve for the following up and carrying out of the charitable objects of the Order.

"It is therefore agreed upon by all the members of the said Order of St. Benedict of New Jersey that no member can or will claim at any time or under any circumstances more than their decent support for the time for which they are members of the Charter of the Order of St. Benedict of New Jersey, and no further.

"And moreover, that each member individually pledges himself to have all property which he now holds or hereafter may hold in his own name conveyed as soon as possible to the legal title of the Order of St. Benedict of New Jersey."

Augustin Wirth was born in Bavaria in 1828. He came to this country in 1851; and, in the next year, he took the solemn vows of the Order at St. Vincent's Abbey in Pennsylvania, and was ordained to the priesthood. For a few years he had charge of a church at Greenburgh, Pennsylvania, near St. Vincent's, and in 1857 he went to Kansas, where he established a college and a church which afterwards became an abbey. He continued his work in Kansas until 1868, and then was sent to Minnesota, where he remained until 1875. He then resumed his pastorate at Greenburgh, Pennsylvania, and later had charge of a parish at Elizabeth, New Jersey, until 1887. It is evident that while in Kansas he had joined the monastery of St. Benedict there established, and in 1887, with the permission of both Abbots, he transferred his stability to St. Mary's Abbey in Newark, New Jersey, the home of the complainant, the New Jersey Order, of which he thus became a member. He remained continuously at this Abbey for about two years, until 1889; he was in ill health and was taken care of by the Order. He was then sent to a church in Wilmington, Delaware, and after a few ⊥**644** months he returned to his pastorate in Elizabeth, New Jersey, in which he continued until 1897. After traveling for some time in Europe for his health, visiting Rome and various monasteries, he took a parish, in 1898, at Springfield, Minnesota, with the requisite permission *ad tempus* from the Abbot of St. Mary's; and there he remained until his death. At the request of the New Jersey Abbot he was buried in the cemetery of the Benedictine Order in Minnesota. The circuit court found that his membership in the complainant Order continued to the last, and this finding was not disturbed by the circuit court of appeals. We regard the fact as satisfactorily established. His absence from the Abbey when engaged in pastoral work was upon the consent of the Abbot, and he was subject to recall at any time.

Father Wirth published many works on religious subjects. He obtained copyrights for his books, and made his contract with the publishers, in the name of "Augustine Wirth, O. S. B." The property here in question consists chiefly of the proceeds received from sales of these books (including notes and mortgages in which they had been invested), credits on account of sales made before and after his death, and the copyrights. He received the royalties personally during his lifetime; and after his death, until October 17, 1906 (when suit was brought against the publishers by the administrator), the accruing royalties were paid to the complainant. The New Jersey Order also, through the Abbot of St. John's Abbey in Minnesota, collected certain sums on outstanding notes held by the decedent, and paid therefrom the decedent's debts.

It is clear that, according to the principles of the complainant's organization, Father Wirth was not entitled to retain for his own benefit either the moneys which he received for his services in the various churches with which he was connected, or those which he derived from ⊥**645** the sale of his books. By the explicit provision of the constitution of the complainant (§ 12), it was a necessary consequence of his continued membership, that his gains—from whatever source—belonged to it, and that, as against the complainant, he could not assert title to the property which he received. The claim of the Order, based upon this conception of its rights, is resisted upon the grounds, (1) that the decedent had the permission of the Abbot to retain, as his own property, the proceeds of the sales of his books, and (2) that the obligation sought to be enforced by the complainant is void as being against public policy.

1. While there was evidence that Father Wirth was required to account to the Abbot for the salary and perquisites received in his church work, it appeared that the income from his books was treated in a different manner. This income he was allowed to retain and use. When he joined the complainant, in 1887, he did not make a transfer of any property to the Order, although already he had some property as a result of his literary labors. The evidence showed that he made loans and investments; and from the moneys in his hands, he paid his personal expenses, including his outlays on his visit to Europe. Because of his going to Rome without leave, and his expenditures on this trip, he was admonished by the Abbot Primate, O. S. B., who had already written to the Abbot of St. Mary's that Father Wirth should be required to account. But no such account was given, and it would seem that such disagreements as arose between the decedent and his ecclesiastical superiors in this country related to church moneys, and not to the proceeds of book sales. The circuit court of appeals, disagreeing with the finding of the circuit court, concluded that Father Wirth was permitted by the Abbot of St. Vincent's, and by the complainant's Abbot, to retain these proceeds as his own property.

⊥646 It is undisputed that the decedent did have a special permission with respect to the use of this income. Originally given by the Abbot of St. Vincent's, it was continued by the Abbot of St. Mary's. It was given in recognition of the fact that his literary work was in addition to the duties which he was normally required to perform. But, as we think, the conclusion of the court below does not give proper weight to the testimony as to the nature and scope of the privilege thus accorded. It was explicitly testified by the Abbot that Father Wirth was permitted to keep the moneys in question, not as his own, but to have their use for charitable purposes with the permission of his superiors. It was this permission which was originally given and which the complainant's Abbot renewed. This testimony was not controverted, and, in view of the constitution of the Order, we find no ground for treating the permission as being of a different character. It is said that it does not appear how the decedent, while in Minnesota, for example, could have expended the money for the charitable purposes of the Order in New Jersey. But the purposes of this Order were broadly charitable and religious; the decedent prosecuted his educational and religious work with the Abbot's consent, and the use of these moneys for charitable purposes, wherever he was located for the time, might well be in furtherance of the objects of the Order. It may have been the concession of a special privilege to permit the decedent to act directly in the distribution of the moneys which he had earned by his additional labors, instead of turning them over to the head of the Order, but we cannot say that it was a permission without restriction, or one which essentially altered his relation to the Order and his fundamental duty while he remained a member of it.

On the contrary, we agree with the circuit court, not only in its finding of fact that the permission was limited as stated, but also in its holding that, in view of the basic **⊥647** law of the organization, there is no warrant for the conclusion that the Abbot had any authority to allow Father Wirth to assert an independent title, or to hold the property as absolutely his own. It is said that the "Rule of St. Benedict" recognizes the right of the member of the Order to keep whatever the Abbot permits him to have. But this plainly refers to the necessities of life, and not to accumulations in direct antagonism to the principles of the society. Whatever indulgence may have been shown to the decedent with respect to the submission of appropriate accounts, it cannot be said that while his membership continued he had, or could have, the privilege of accumulating an individual estate for his own benefit and free from his obligations to the Order. This could not but be regarded as violative of the constitution of the complainant, and beyond the competency of its official head to grant.

2. We are thus brought to the question whether the requirement, which lies at the foundation of this suit, is void as against public policy; that is, whether, by reason of repugnance to the essential principles of our institutions, the obligation, though voluntarily assumed, and the trust arising from it, cannot be enforced. In support of this view, it seems to be premised that a member of the Order can be absolved from his vows only by the action of the Head of the Church; and that unless the requisite dispensation is thus obtained the member is bound for life in temporal, as well as in spiritual, affairs. This, it is said, is the necessary import of testimony given by the Abbot. It is thus assumed that the vows in connection with the "Rule" bind the member in complete servitude to the Order for life, or until the Head of the Church absolves him from his obligations; and it is concluded that an agreement for such a surrender, being opposed to individual liberty and to the inherent right of every person to acquire and hold property, is unenforceable in the civil **⊥648** courts, and cannot form the basis for an equitable title in the complainant.

This argument, we think, disregards the explicit provision of the complainant's constitution as to voluntary withdrawal. It overlooks the distinction between civil and ecclesiastical rights and duties; between the Order of St. Benedict of New Jersey, a corporation of that state, and the monastic brotherhood subject to church authority; between the obligation imposed by the corporate organization and religious vows. As we have said, the question here is not one of canon law or ecclesiastical polity. The requirement of complainant's constitution must be read according to its terms, and its validity must be thus determined. Granted that it is to be examined in the light of that to which it refers, still, obligations which are inconsistent with its express provisions cannot be imported into it. This constitution, as already stated, definitely provides: "Membership is lost at once:—2. By voluntary leaving the Order for any purpose whatsoever" (§ 11.) This language cannot be taken to mean other than what it distinctly says. So far as the corporation, and the civil rights and obligations incident to membership therein, are concerned, it leaves no doubt that the member may voluntarily leave the Order at any time. His membership in the corporation, and the obligation he assumes, are subject to that condition. If he severs his connection with the corporation, it cannot be heard to claim any property he may subsequently acquire. His obligation runs with his membership, and the latter may be terminated at will.

With this privilege of withdrawal expressly recognized, we are unable to say that the agreement expressed in § 12 of the complainant's constitution, that the gains and acquisitions of members shall belong to the corporation, must be condemned. These go to the corporation in exchange for the privileges of membership, and ⊥**649** to further the common purpose to which the members are devoted. No constitutional right is invaded and no statutory restriction is transgressed. The legislature of New Jersey, which, subject to constitutional inhibition, is the arbiter of the public policy of that state, granted the charter by special act to the Benedictine Society of "religious men living in community," and it cannot be said that the constitution adopted by the Order was repugnant to the charter provisions, or exceeded the authority plainly intended to be conferred. It would seem to be clear that the obligation assumed, instead of being opposed to the public policy of the state where it was created, was directly sanctioned.

The validity of agreements providing for community ownership with renunciation of individual rights of property during the continuance of membership in the community, where there is freedom to withdraw, has repeatedly been affirmed. The case of *Goesele* v. *Bimeler*, related to a religious society called Separatists. By an agreement made in 1819, the members of the society agreed to unite in a "communion of property." They renounced "all individual ownership of property, present or future, real or personal." Amendatory articles of like import were signed in 1824. As to these agreements, the court said: "The articles of 1819 and 1824 are objected to as not constituting a contract which a court of equity would enforce. . . . What is there in either of these articles that is contrary to good morals, or that is opposed to the policy of the laws? An association of individuals is formed under a religious influence, who are in a destitute condition, having little to rely on for their support but their industry; and they agree to labor in common for the good of the society, and a comfortable maintenance for each individual; and whatever shall be acquired beyond this shall go to the common stock. This contract provides for every member of the ⊥**650** community, in sickness and in health, and under whatsoever misfortune may occur. . . . By disclaiming all individual ownership of the property acquired by their labor, for the benefits secured by the articles, the members give durability to the fund accumulated, and to the benevolent purposes to which it is applied. No legal objection is perceived to such a partnership." (Pp. 606, 607.) In *Schwartz* v. *Duss*, the controversy related to the property of the Harmony Society, a community in Pennsylvania. It was said that the cardinal principle of the society was "self-abnegation" which was manifested "not only by submission to a religious head, but by a community instead of individual ownership of property, and the dedication of their labor to the society." It had been held by the supreme court of Pennsylvania that the agreements constituting the community were not offensive to the public policy of that state (*Schriber* v. *Rapp*), and, as to this, it was said by this court: "The supreme court observed that the point made against the articles as being against public policy was attended with no difficulty, and *Chief Justice* GIBSON said for the court: 'An association for the purposes expressed is prohibited neither by statute nor the common law.'" (Id. p. 26.) In *Burt* v. *Oneida Community*, in describing the character of that society, the court of appeals of New York said that its main purpose was the "propagandism of certain communistic views as to the acquisition and enjoyment of property" and "the endeavor to put into practical operation an economic and industrial scheme which should embody and illustrate the doctrines which they held and inculcated." "Necessarily" said the court, "the basic proposition of such a community was the absolute and complete surrender of the separate and individual rights of property of the persons entering it; the abandonment of all purely selfish pursuits, and the investiture of the title to their ⊥**651** property and the fruits of their industry in the common body, from which they could not afterwards be severed or withdrawn except by unanimous consent. It was fashioned according to the pentecostal ideal, that all who believed should be together and have all things common. It was intended to be in fact, as they frequently styled themselves, but a single family upon a large scale, with only one purse, where self was to be abjured and the general good alone considered." The court, viewing it solely as a business undertaking, held that the organization "was not prohibited by any statute, or in contravention of any law regulating the possession, ownership, or tenure of property."

It is said that in these cases, the contracts had been fully performed, and that the effort was made either to partition or distribute the property of the society, or to recover the value of property which had been actually conveyed, or services which had been rendered to it. But the validity of the agreements there in question, against the objection based upon public policy, was distinctly recognized.

In the present case, there was no infringement of Father Wirth's liberty or right to property. He did not withdraw from the Order. He had agreed, by accepting membership under the complainant's constitution, that his individual earnings and acquisitions, like those of other members, should go into the common fund, and, except as required for the maintenance of the members, should be used in carrying out the charitable objects of the Order. It is not unlikely that the copyrights upon his books derived their commercial value largely, if not altogether, from his membership. Certainly, the equitable ownership of these copyrights, by virtue of his obligation, vested in the complainant, ⊥**652** and the moneys in question when received became in equity its property and were subject to its disposition. As to both, Father Wirth stood in the position of a trustee.

The further objection that the claim is barred by the statute of limitations was held by the circuit court to be untenable, and we agree with that view. The applicable limitation is six years (Minn. Rev. Laws 1905, § 4076), and the bill was filed within six years after Father Wirth's death. There is no such clear evidence of repudiation of the trust as would warrant the conclusion that the statute began to run at an earlier date.

The decree of the Circuit Court of Appeals is reversed and that of the Circuit Court is affirmed.

It is so ordered.

UNITED STATES v. BALLARD

322 U.S. 78

ON WRIT OF CERTIORARI TO THE UNITED STATES CIRCUIT COURT OF APPEALS FOR THE NINTH CIRCUIT

Argued March 3 and 6, 1944 — Decided April 24, 1944

⊥**79** Mr. *Justice DOUGLAS* delivered the opinion of the Court:

Respondents were indicted and convicted for using, and conspiring to use, the mails to defraud. The indictment was in twelve counts. It charged a scheme to defraud by organizing and promoting the I Am movement through the use of the mails. The charge was that certain designated corporations were formed, literature distributed and sold, funds solicited, and memberships in the I Am movement sought "by means of false and fraudulent representations, pretenses and promises." The false representations charged were eighteen in number. It is sufficient at this point to say that they covered respondents' alleged religious doctrines or beliefs. They were all set forth in the first count. The following are representative:

that Guy W. Ballard, now deceased, alias Saint Germain, Jesus, George Washington, and Godfre Ray King, had been selected and thereby designated by the alleged "ascertained masters," Saint Germain, as a divine messenger, and that the words of "ascended masters" and the words of the alleged divine entity, Saint Germain, would be transmitted to mankind through the medium of the said Guy W. Ballard;

that Guy W. Ballard, during his lifetime, and Edna W. Ballard, and Donald Ballard, by reason of their alleged high spiritual attainments and righteous conduct, had been selected as divine messengers through which the words of the alleged "ascended masters," in⊥**80**cluding the alleged Saint Germain, would be communicated to mankind under the teachings commonly known as the "I Am" movement;

that Guy W. Ballard, during his lifetime, and Edna W. Ballard and Donald Ballard had, by reason of supernatural attainments, the power to heal persons of ailments and diseases and to make well persons afflicted with any diseases, injuries, or ailments, and did falsely represent to persons intended to be defrauded that the three designated persons had the ability and power to cure persons of those diseases normally classified as curable and also of diseases which are ordinarily classified by the medical profession as being incurable diseases; and did further represent that the three designated persons had in fact cured either by the activity of one, either, or all of said persons, hundreds of persons afflicted with diseases and ailments.

Each of the representations enumerated in the indictment was followed by the charge that respondents "well knew" it was false. After enumerating the eighteen misrepresentations the indictment also alleged:

At the time of making all of the afore-alleged representations by the defendants, and each of them, the defendants, and each of them, well knew that all of said aforementioned representations were false and untrue and were made with the intention on the part of the defendants, and each of them, to cheat, wrong, and defraud persons intended to be defrauded, and to obtain from persons intended to be defrauded by the defendants, money, property, and other things of value and to convert the same to the use and the benefit of the defendants, and each of them.

The indictment contained twelve counts, one of which charged a conspiracy to defraud. The first count set forth all of the eighteen representations, as we have said. Each of the other counts incorporated and realleged all of them and added no additional ones. There was a demurrer and a motion to quash each of which asserted among other things that the indictment attacked the religious beliefs ⊥**81** of respondents and sought to restrict the free exercise of their religion in violation of the Constitution of the United States. These motions were denied by the District Court. Early in the trial, however, objections were raised to the admission of certain evidence concerning respondents' religious beliefs. The court conferred with counsel in absence of the jury and with the acquiescence of counsel for the United States and for respondents confined the issues on this phase of the case to the question of the good faith of respondents. At the request of counsel for both sides the court advised the jury of that action in the following language:

Now gentlemen, here is the issue in this case:

First, the defendants in this case made certain representations of belief in a divinity and in a supernatural power. Some of the teachings of the defendants, representations, might seem extremely improbable to a great many people. For instance, the appearance of Jesus to dictate some of the works that we have had introduced in evidence, as testified to here at the opening transcription, or shaking hands with Jesus, to some people that might seem highly improbable. I point that out as one of the many statements.

Whether that is true or not is not the concern of this Court and is not the concern of the jury—and they are going to be told so in their instructions. As far as this Court sees the issue, it is immaterial what these defendants preached or wrote or taught in their classes. They are not going to be permitted to speculate on the actuality of the happening of those incidents. Now, I think I have made that as clear as I can. Therefore, the religious beliefs of these defendants cannot be an issue in this court.

The issue is: Did these defendants honestly and in good faith believe those things? If they did, they should be acquitted. I cannot make it any clearer than that.

If these defendants did not believe those things, they did not believe that Jesus came down and dic⊥**82**tated, or that Saint Germain came down and dictated, did not believe the things that they wrote, the things that they preached, but used the mail for the purpose of getting money, the jury should find them guilty. Therefore, gentlemen, religion cannot come into this case.

The District Court reiterated that admonition in the charge to the jury and made it abundantly clear. The following portion of the charge is typical:

The question of the defendants' good faith is the cardinal question in this case. You are not to be concerned with the religious belief of the defendants, or any of them. The jury will be called upon to pass on the question of whether or not the defendants honestly and in good faith believed the representations which are set forth in the indictment, and honestly and in good faith believed that the benefits which they represented would flow from their belief to those who embraced and followed their teachings, or whether these representations were mere pretenses without honest belief on the part of the defendants or any of them, and, were the representations made for the purpose of procuring money, and were the mails used for this purpose.

As we have said, counsel for the defense acquiesced in this treatment of the matter, made no objection to it during the trial, and indeed treated it without protest as the law of the case throughout the proceedings prior to the verdict. Respondents did not change their position before the District Court after verdict and contend that the truth or verity of their religious doctrines or beliefs should have been submitted to the jury. In their motion for new trial they did contend, however, that the withdrawal of these issues from the jury was error because it was in effect an amendment of the indictment. That was also one of their specifications of errors on appeal. And other errors urged on appeal included the overruling of the demurrer to the indictment and the motion to quash, and the ⊥**83** disallowance of proof of the truth of respondents' religious doctrines or beliefs.

The Circuit Court of Appeals reversed the judgment of conviction and granted a new trial, one judge dissenting. In its view the restriction of the issue in question to that of good faith was error. Its reason was that the scheme to defraud alleged in the indictment was that respondents made the eighteen alleged false representations; and that to prove that defendants devised the scheme described in the indictment "it was necessary to prove that they schemed to make some, at least, of the [eighteen] representations . . . and that some, at least, of the representations which they schemed to make were false." One judge thought that the ruling of the District Court was also error because it was "as prejudicial to the issue of honest belief as to the issue of purposeful misrepresentation."

The case is here on a petition for a writ of certiorari which we granted because of the importance of the question presented.

The United States contends that the District Court withdrew from the jury's consideration only the truth or falsity of those representations which related to religious concepts or beliefs and that there were representations charged in the indictment which fell within a different category. The argument is that this latter group of ⊥**84** representations was submitted to the jury, that they were adequate to constitute an offense under the Act, and that they were supported by the requisite evidence. . . .

A careful reading of the whole charge leads us to agree with the Circuit Court of Appeals on this phase of the case that the only issue submitted to the jury was the question as stated by the District Court, of respondents' "belief in their representations and promises."

The United States contends that respondents acquiesced in the withdrawal from the jury of the truth of their reli⊥**85**gious doctrines or beliefs and that their consent bars them from insisting on a different course once that one turned out to be unsuccessful. Reliance for that position is sought in *Johnson* v. *United States*. That case stands for the proposition that, apart from situations involving an unfair trial, an appellate court will not grant a new trial to a defendant on the ground of improper introduction of evidence or improper comment by the prosecutor, where the defendant acquiesced in that course and made no objection to it. In fairness to respondents that principle cannot be applied here. The real objection of respondents is not that the truth of their religious doctrines or beliefs should have been submitted to the jury. Their demurrer and motion to quash made clear their position that that issue should be withheld from the jury on the basis of the First Amendment. Moreover, their position at all times was and still is that the court should have gone the whole way and withheld from the jury both that issue and the issue of their good faith. Their demurrer and motion to quash asked for dismissal of the entire indictment. Their argument that the truth of their religious doctrines or beliefs should have gone to the jury when the question of their good faith was submitted was and is merely an alternative argument. They never forsook their position that the indictment should have been dismissed and that none of it was good. Moreover, respondents' motion for new trial challenged the propriety of the action of the District Court in withdrawing from the jury the issue of the truth of their religious doctrines or beliefs without also withdrawing the question of their good faith. So we conclude that the rule of *Johnson* v. *United States* does not prevent respondents from reasserting now that no part of the indictment should have been submitted to the jury.

As we have noted, the Circuit Court of Appeals held that the question of the truth of the representations concerning ⊥**86** respondents' religious doctrines or beliefs should have been submitted to the jury. And it remanded the case for a new trial. It may be that the Circuit Court of Appeals took that action because it did not think that the indictment could be properly construed as charging a scheme to defraud by means other than misrepresentations of respondents' religious doctrines or beliefs. Or that court may have concluded that the withdrawal of the issue of the truth of those religious doctrines or beliefs was unwarranted because it resulted in a substantial change in the character of the crime charged. But on whichever basis that court rested its actions, we do not agree that the truth or verity of respondents' religious doctrines or beliefs should have been submitted to the jury. Whatever this particular indictment might require, the First Amendment precludes such a course, as the United States seem to concede. "The law knows no heresy, and is committed to the support of no dogma, the establishment of no sect." *Watson* v. *Jones*. The First Amendment has a dual aspect. It not only "forestalls compulsion by law of the acceptance of any creed or the practice of any form of worship" but also "safeguards the free exercise of the chosen form of religion." *Cantwell* v. *Connecticut*. "Thus the Amendment embraces two concepts,—freedom to believe and freedom to act. The first is absolute but, in the nature of things, the second cannot be." Freedom of thought, which includes freedom of religious belief, is basic in a society of free men. *West Virginia State Bd. of Edu.* v. *Barnette*. It embraces the right to maintain theories of life and of death and of the hereafter which are rank heresy to followers of the orthodox faiths. Heresy trials are foreign to our Constitution. Men may believe what they cannot prove. They may not be put to the proof of their religious doctrines or beliefs. Religious experiences which are as real as life to some may be incomprehensible to others. ⊥**87** Yet the fact that they may be beyond the ken of mortals does not mean that they can be made suspect before the law. Many take their gospel from the New Testament. But it would hardly be supposed that they could be tried before a jury charged with the duty of determining whether those teachings contained false representations. The miracles of the New Testament, the Divinity of Christ, life after death, the power of prayer are deep in the religious convictions of many. If one could be sent to jail because a jury in a hostile environment found those teachings false, little indeed would be left of religious freedom. The Fathers of the Constitution were not unaware of the varied and extreme views of religious sects, of the violence of disagreement among them, and of the lack of any one religious creed on which all men would agree. They fashioned a charter of government which envisaged the widest possible toleration of conflicting views. Man's relation to his God was made no concern of the state. He was granted the right to worship as he pleased and to answer to no man for the verity of his religious views. The religious views espoused by respondents might seem incredible, if not preposterous, to most people. But if those doctrines are subject to trial before a jury charged with finding their truth or falsity, then the same can be done with the religious beliefs of any sect. When the triers of fact undertake that task, they enter a forbidden domain. The First Amendment does not select any one group or any one type of religion for preferred treatment. It puts them all in that position. "With man's relations to his Maker and the obligations he may think they impose, and the manner in which an expression shall be made by him of his belief on those subjects, no interference can be permitted, provided always the laws of society, designed to secure its peace and prosperity, and the morals of its people, are not interfered with."⊥**88** So we conclude that the District Court ruled properly when it withheld from the jury all questions concerning the truth or falsity of the religious beliefs or doctrines of respondents. . . .

The judgment is reversed and the cause is remanded to the Circuit Court of Appeals for further proceedings in conformity to this opinion.

Reversed.

Mr. *Chief Justice* STONE, dissenting:

I am not prepared to say that the constitutional guaranty of freedom of religion affords immunity from criminal prosecution for the fraudulent procurement of money by false statements as to one's religious experiences, ⊥**89** more than it renders polygamy or libel immune from criminal prosecution. I cannot say that freedom of thought and worship includes freedom to procure money by making knowingly false statements about one's religious experiences. To go no further, if it were shown that a defendant in this case had asserted as a part of the alleged fraudulent scheme, that he had physically shaken hands with St. Germain in San Francisco on a day named, or that, as the indictment here alleges, by the exertion of his spiritual power he "had in fact cured . . . hundreds of persons afflicted with diseases and ailments," I should not doubt that it would be open to the Government to submit to the jury proof that he had never been in San Francisco and that no such cures had ever been effected. In any event I see no occasion for making any pronouncement on this subject in the present case.

The indictment charges respondents' use of the mails to defraud and a conspiracy to commit that offense by false statements of their religious experiences which had not in fact occurred. But it also charged that representations were "falsely and fraudulently" made, that respondents "well knew" that these representations were untrue, and that they were made by respondents with the intent to cheat and defraud those to whom they were made. With the assent of the prosecution and the defense the trial judge withdrew from the consideration of the jury the question whether the alleged religious experiences had in fact occurred, but submitted to the jury the single issue whether petitioners honestly believed that they had occurred, with the instruction that if the jury did not so find, then it should return a verdict of guilty. On this ⊥**90** issue the jury, on ample evidence that respondents were without belief in the statements which they had made to their victims, found a verdict of guilty. The state of one's mind is a fact as capable of fraudulent misrepresentation as is one's physical condition or the state of his bodily health. There are no exceptions to the charge and no contention that the trial court rejected any relevant evidence which petitioners sought to offer. Since the indictment and the evidence support the conviction, it is irrelevant whether the religious experiences alleged did or did not in fact occur or whether that issue could or could not, for constitutional reasons, have been rightly submitted to the jury. Certainly none of respondents' constitutional rights are violated if they are prosecuted for the fraudulent procurement of money by false representations as to their beliefs, religious or otherwise.

Obviously if the question whether the religious experiences in fact occurred could not constitutionally have been submitted to the jury the court rightly withdrew it. If it could have been submitted I know of no reason why the parties could not, with the advice of counsel, assent to its withdrawal from the jury. And where, as here, the indictment charges two sets of false statements, each independently sufficient to sustain the conviction, I cannot accept respondents' contention that the withdrawal of one set and the submission of the other to the jury amounted to an amendment of the indictment. . . .

⊥**92** On the issue submitted to the jury in this case it properly rendered a verdict of guilty. As no legally sufficient reason for disturbing it appears, I think the judgment below should be reversed and that of the District Court reinstated.

Mr. Justice ROBERTS and *Mr. Justice* FRANKFURTER join in this opinion.

Mr. Justice JACKSON, dissenting:

I should say the defendants have done just that for which they are indicted. If I might agree to their conviction without creating a precedent, I cheerfully would do so. I can see in their teachings nothing but humbug, untainted by any trace of truth. But that does not dispose of the constitutional question whether misrepresentation of religious experience or belief is prosecutable; it rather emphasizes the danger of such prosecutions.

The Ballard family claimed miraculous communication with the spirit world and supernatural power to heal the sick. They were brought to trial for mail fraud on an indictment which charged that their representations were false and that they "well knew" they were false. The trial judge, obviously troubled, ruled that the court could not try whether the statements were untrue, but could inquire whether the defendants knew them to be untrue; and, if so, they could be convicted.

I find it difficult to reconcile this conclusion with our traditional religious freedoms.

In the first place, as a matter of either practice or philosophy I do not see how we can separate an issue as to what is believed from considerations as to what is believable. The most convincing proof that one believes his statements is to show that they have been true in his expe⊥**93**rience. Likewise, that one knowingly falsified is best proved by showing that what he said happened never did happen. How can the Government prove these persons knew something to be false which it cannot prove to be false? If we try religious sincerity severed from religious verity, we isolate the dispute from the very considerations which in common experience provide its most reliable answer.

In the second place, any inquiry into intellectual honesty in religion raises profound psychological problems. William James, who wrote on these matters as a scientist, reminds us that it is not theology and ceremonies which keep religion going. Its vitality is in the religious experiences of many people. "If you ask what these experiences are, they are conversations with the unseen, voices and visions, responses to prayer, changes of heart, deliverances from fear, inflowings of help, assurances of support, whenever certain persons set their own internal attitude in certain appropriate ways." If religious liberty includes, as it must, the right to communicate such experiences to others, it seems to me an impossible task for juries to separate fancied ones from real ones, dreams from happenings, and hallucinations from true clairvoyance. Such experiences, like some tones and colors, have existence for one, but none at all for another. They cannot be verified to the minds of those whose field of consciousness does not include religious insight. When one comes to trial which turns on any aspect of religious belief or representation, unbelievers among his judges are likely not to understand and are almost certain not to believe him.

And then I do not know what degree of skepticism or disbelief in a religious representation amounts to actionable fraud. James points out that "Faith means belief ⊥**94** in something concerning which doubt is still theoretically possible." Belief in what one may demonstrate to the senses is not faith. All schools of religious thought make enormous assumptions, generally on the basis of revelations authenticated by some sign or miracle. The appeal in such matters is to a very different plane of credulity than is invoked by representations of secular fact in commerce. Some who profess belief in the Bible read literally what others read as allegory or metaphor, as they read Aesop's fables. Religious symbolism is even used by some with the same mental reservations one has in teaching of Santa Claus or Uncle Sam or Easter bunnies or dispassionate judges. It is hard in matters so mystical to say how literally one is bound to believe the doctrine he teaches and even more difficult to say how far it is reliance upon a teacher's literal belief which induces followers to give him money.

There appear to be persons—let us hope not many—who find refreshment and courage in the teachings of the "I Am" cult. If the members of the sect get comfort from the celestial guidance of their "Saint Germain," however doubtful it seems to me, it is hard to say that they do not get what they pay for. Scores of sects flourish in this country by teaching what to me are queer notions. It is plain that there is wide variety in American religious taste. The Ballards are not alone in catering to it with a pretty dubious product.

The chief wrong which false prophets do to their following is not financial. The collections aggregate a tempting total, but individual payments are not ruinous. I doubt if the vigilance of the law is equal to making money stick by overcredulous people. But the real harm is on the mental and spiritual plane. There are those who hunger and thirst after higher values which they feel wanting in ⊥95 their humdrum lives. They live in mental confusion or moral anarchy and seek vaguely for truth and beauty and moral support. When they are deluded and then disillusioned, cynicism and confusion follow. The wrong of these things, as I see it, is not in the money the victims part with half so much as in the mental and spiritual poison they get. But that is precisely the thing the Constitution put beyond the reach of the prosecutor, for the price of freedom of religion or of speech or of the press is that we must put up with, and even pay for, a good deal of rubbish.

Prosecutions of this character easily could degenerate into religious persecution. I do not doubt that religious leaders may be convicted of fraud for making false representations on matters other than faith or experience, as for example if one represents that funds are being used to construct a church when in fact they are being used for personal purposes. But that is not this case, which reaches into wholly dangerous ground. When does less than full belief in a professed credo become actionable fraud if one is soliciting gifts or legacies? Such inquiries may discomfort orthodox as well as unconventional religious teachers, for even the most regular of them are sometimes accused of taking their orthodoxy with a grain of salt.

I would dismiss the indictment and have done with this business of judicially examining other people's faiths.

KEDROFF v. SAINT NICHOLAS CATHEDRAL

344 U.S. 94
ON APPEAL FROM THE COURT OF APPEALS OF NEW YORK
Argued February 1, 1952 — Reargued October 14, 1952
Decided November 24, 1952

⊥95 Mr. *Justice REED* delivered the opinion of the Court.

The right to the use and occupancy of a church in the city of New York is in dispute.

The right to such use is claimed by appellee, a corporation created in 1925 by an act of the Legislature of New York for the purpose of acquiring a cathedral for the Russian Orthodox Church in North America as a central place of worship and residence of the ruling archbishop "in accordance with the doctrine, discipline and worship of the Holy Apostolic Catholic Church of Eastern Confession as taught by the holy scriptures, holy tradition, seven ecumenical councils and holy fathers of that church."

The corporate right is sought to be enforced so that the head of the American churches, religiously affiliated with the Russian Orthodox Church, may occupy the ⊥96 Cathedral. At the present time that head is the Metropolitan of All America and Canada, the Archbishop of New York, Leonty, who like his predecessors was elected to his ecclesiastical office by a sobor of the American churches.

That claimed right of the corporation to use and occupancy for the archbishop chosen by the American churches is opposed by appellants who are in possession. Benjamin Fedchenkoff bases his right on an appointment in 1934 by the Supreme Church Authority of the Russian Orthodox Church, to wit, the Patriarch *locum tenens* of Moscow and all Russia and its Holy Synod, as Archbishop of the Archdiocese of North America and the Aleutian Islands. The other defendant-appellant is a priest of the Russian Orthodox Church, also acknowledging the spiritual and administrative control of the Moscow hierarchy.

Determination of the right to use and occupy Saint Nicholas depends upon whether the appointment of Ben⊥97jamin by the Patriarch or the election of the Archbishop for North America by the convention of the American churches validly selects the ruling hierarch for the American churches. The Court of Appeals of New York, reversing the lower court, determined that the prelate appointed by the Moscow ecclesiastical authorities was not entitled to the Cathedral and directed the entry of a judgment that appellee corporation be reinvested with the possession and administration of the temporalities of St. Nicholas Cathedral. This determination was made on the authority of Article 5-C of the Religious Corporations Law of New York against appellants' contention that this New York statute, as construed, violated the Fourteenth Amendment to the Constitution of the United States.

Because of the constitutional questions thus generally involved, we noted probable jurisdiction, and, after argument and submission of the case last term, ordered reargument and requested counsel to include a discussion of whether the judgment might be sustained on state grounds. . . .

Article 5-C was added to the Religious Corporations Law of New York in 1945 and provided both for the incorporation and administration of Russian Orthodox churches. Clarifying amendments were added in 1948. ⊥**98** The purpose of the article was to bring all the New York churches, formerly subject to the administrative jurisdiction of the Most Sacred Governing Synod in Moscow or the Patriarch of Moscow, into an administratively autonomous metropolitan district. That district was North American in area, created pursuant to resolutions adopted at a sobor held at Detroit in 1924. This declared autonomy was made effective by a further legislative requirement that all the churches formerly administratively subject to the Moscow synod and patri⊥**99**archate should for the future be governed by the ecclesiastical body and hierarchy of the American metropolitan district. The foregoing analysis follows the interpretation of this article by the Court of Appeals of New York, an interpretation binding upon us. ⊥**100**

Article 5-C is challenged as invalid under the constitutional prohibition against interference with the exercise of religion. The appellants' contention, of course, is based on the theory that the principles of the First Amendment are made applicable to the states by the Fourteenth.

The Russian Orthodox Church is an autocephalous member of the Eastern Orthodox Greek Catholic Church. It sprang from the Church of Constantinople in the Tenth Century. The schism of 1054 A.D. split the Universal Church into those of the East and the West. Gradually self-government was assumed by the Russian Church until in the Sixteenth Century its autonomy was recognized and a Patriarch of Moscow appeared. For the next one hun⊥**101**dred years the development of the church kept pace with the growth of power of the Czars but it increasingly became a part of the civil government—a state church. Throughout that period it also remained a hierarchical church with a Patriarch at its head, governed by the conventions or sobors called by him. However, from the time of Peter the Great until 1917 no sobor was held. No patriarch ruled or was chosen. During that time the church was governed by a Holy Synod, a group of ecclesiastics with a Chief Procurator representative of the government as a member.

Late in the Eighteenth Century the Russian Church entered the missionary field in the Aleutian Islands and Alaska. From there churches spread slowly down the Pacific Coast and later, with the Slavic immigration, to our eastern cities, particularly to Detroit, Cleveland, Chicago, Pittsburgh and New York. The character of the administrative unit changed with the years as is indicated by the changes in its name. In 1904 when a diocese of North America was created its first archbishop, Tikhon, shortly thereafter established himself in his seat at Saint Nicholas Cathedral. His appointment came from the Holy Synod of Russia as did those of his successors in order Platon and Evdokim. Under those appointments the successive archbishops occupied the Cathedral and residence of Saint Nicholas under the administrative authority of the Holy Synod.

In 1917 Archbishop Evdokim returned to Russia permanently. Early that year an All Russian Sobor was held, the first since Peter the Great. It occurred during the interlude of political freedom following the fall of the Czar. A patriarch was elected and installed—Tikhon who had been the first American Archbishop. Uncertainties as to the succession to and administration of the American archbishopric made their appearance following this sobor and were largely induced ⊥**102** by the almost contemporaneous political disturbances which culminated swiftly in the Bolshevik Revolution of 1917. The Russian Orthodox Church was drawn into this maelstrom. After a few years the Patriarch was imprisoned. There were suggestions of his counterrevolutionary activity. Church power was transferred, partly through a sobor considered by many as non-canonical to a Supreme Church Council. The declared reforms were said to have resulted in a "Living Church" or sometimes in a "Renovated Church." Circumstances and pressures changed. Patriarch Tikhon was released from prison and died in 1925. He named three bishops as *locum tenens* for the patriarchal throne. It was one of these, Sergius, who in 1933 appointed the appellant Benjamin as Archbishop. The Church was registered as a religious organization under Soviet law in 1927. Thereafter the Russian Church and the Russian State approached if not a reconciliation at least an adjustment which eventuated by 1943 in the election of Sergius, one of the bishops named as *locum tenens* by Tikhon, to the Patriarchate. The Living or Renovated Church, whether deemed a reformed, a schismatic or a new church, apparently withered away. After Sergius' death a new patriarch of the Russian Orthodox Church, Alexi, was chosen Patriarch in 1945 at Moscow at a sobor recognized by all parties to this litigation as a true sobor held in accordance with the church canons.

The Russian upheaval caused repercussions in the North American Diocese. That Diocese at the time of the Soviet Revolution recognized the spiritual and ad⊥**103**ministrative control of Moscow. White Russians, both lay and clerical, found asylum in America from the revolutionary conflicts, strengthening the feeling of abhorrence of the secular attitude of the new Russian Government. The church members already here, immigrants and native-born, while habituated to look to Moscow for religious direction, were accustomed to our theory of separation between church and state. The Russian turmoil, the restraints on religious activities and the evolution of a new ecclesiastical hierarchy in the form of the "Living Church," deemed noncanonical or schismatic by most churchmen, made very difficult Russian administration of the American diocese. Furthermore, Patriarch Tikhon, on November 20, 1920, issued Decision No. 362 relating to church administration for troublesome times. This granted a large measure of autonomy, when the Russian ruling authority was unable to function, subject to "confirmation later to the Central Church Authority when it is reestablished." Naturally the growing number of American-born members of the Russian Church did not cling to a hierarchy identified with their country of remote origin with the same national feeling that moved their immigrant ancestors. These facts and forces generated in America a separatist movement.

That movement brought about the arrangements at the Detroit Sobor of 1924 for a temporary American administration of the church on account of the disturbances in Russia. This was followed by the declarations of autonomy of the successive sobors since that date, a spate ⊥**104** of litigation concerning control of the various churches and occupancy of ecclesiastical positions, the New York legislation and this controversy. . . .

⊥**105** From those circumstances it seems clear that the Russian Orthodox Church was, until the Russian Revolution, an hierarchical church with unquestioned paramount jurisdiction in the governing body in Russia over the American Metropolitanate. Nothing indicates that either the Sacred Synod or the succeeding Patriarchs ⊥**106** relinquished that authority or recognized the autonomy of the American church. The Court of Appeals decision proceeds, we understand, upon the same assumption. That court did consider "whether there exists in Moscow at the present time a true central organization of the Russian Orthodox Church capable of functioning as the head of a free international religious body." It concluded that this aspect of the controversy had not been sufficiently developed to justify a judgment upon that ground.

The Religious Corporations Law.—The New York Court of Appeals depended for its judgment, refusing recognition to Archbishop Benjamin, the appointee of the Moscow Hierarchy of the Russian Orthodox Church, upon Article 5-C of the Religious Corporations Law. Certainly a legislature is ⊥**107** free to act upon such information as it may have as to the necessity for legislation. But an enactment by a legislature cannot validate action which the Constitution prohibits, and we think that the statute here in question passes the constitutional limits. We conclude that Article 5-C undertook by its terms to transfer the control of the New York churches of the Russian Orthodox religion from the central governing hierarchy of the Russian Orthodox Church, the Patriarch of Moscow and the Holy Synod, to the governing authorities of the Russian Church in America, a church organization limited to the diocese of North America and the Aleutian Islands. This transfer takes place by virtue of the statute. Such a law violates the Fourteenth Amendment. It prohibits in this country the free exercise of religion. Legislation that regulates church administration, the operation of the churches, the appointment of clergy, by requiring conformity to church statutes "adopted at a general conven⊥**108**tion (sobor) held in the City of New York on or about or between October fifth to eighth, nineteen hundred thirty-seven, and any amendments thereto," prohibits the free exercise of religion. Although this statute requires the New York churches to "in all other respects conform to, maintain and follow the faith, doctrine, ritual, communion, discipline, canon law, traditions and usages of the Eastern Confession (Eastern Orthodox or Greek Catholic Church)," their conformity is by legislative fiat and subject to legislative will. Should the state assert power to change the statute requiring conformity to ancient faith and doctrine to one establishing a different doctrine, the invalidity would be unmistakable.

Although § 5 of the Religious Corporations Law had long controlled religious corporations, the Court of Appeals held that its rule was not based on any constitutional requirement or prohibition. Since certain events of which the Court took judicial notice indicated to it that the Russian Government exercised control over the cen⊥**109**tral church authorities and that the American church acted to protect its pulpits and faith from such influences, the Court of Appeals felt that the Legislature's reasonable belief in such conditions justified the State in enacting a law to free the American group from infiltration of such atheistic or subversive influences.

This legislation, Art 5-C, in the view of the Court of Appeals, gave the use of the churches to the Russian Church in America on the theory that this church would most faithfully carry out the purposes of the religious trust. Thus dangers of political use of church pulpits would be minimized. Legislative power to punish subversive action cannot be doubted. If such action should be actually attempted by a cleric, neither his robe nor his pulpit would be a defense. But in this case no problem ⊥**110** of punishment for the violation of law arises. There is no charge of subversive or hostile action by any ecclesiastic. Here there is a transfer by statute of control over churches. This violates our rule of separation between church and state. That conclusion results from the purpose, meaning and effect of the New York legislation stated above, considered in the light of the history and decisions considered below.

Hierarchical churches may be defined as those organized as a body with other churches having similar faith and doctrine with a common ruling convocation or ecclesiastical head. . . .

⊥**115** This controversy concerning the right to use St. Nicholas Cathedral is strictly a matter of ecclesiastical government, the power of the Supreme Church Authority of the Russian Orthodox Church to appoint the ruling hierarch of the archdiocese of North America. No one disputes that such power did lie in that Authority prior to the Russian Revolution.

Watson v. *Jones*, although it contains a reference to the relations of church and state under our system of laws, was decided without depending upon prohibition of state interference with the free exercise of religion. It was decided in 1871, before judicial recognition of the coercive power of the Fourteenth Amendment to protect the limitations of the First Amendment against state action. . . . ⊥**116** The opinion radiates, however, a spirit of freedom for religious organizations, an independence from secular control or manipulation, in short, power to decide for themselves, free from state interference, matters of church government as well as those of faith and doctrine. Freedom to select the clergy, where no improper methods of choice are proven, we think, must now be said to have federal constitutional protection as a part of the free exercise of religion against state interference. ⊥**117**

Legislative Power.—The Court of Appeals of New York recognized, generally, the soundness of the philosophy of ecclesiastical control of church administration and polity but concluded that the exercise of that control was not free from legislative interference. That Court presented forcefully the argument supporting legislative power to act on its own knowledge of "the Soviet attitude toward things religious." It was said: "The Legislature realized that the North American church, in order to be free of Soviet interference in its affairs, had declared its temporary administrative autonomy in 1924, pursuant to the ukase of 1920, while retaining full *spiritual* communion with the patriarchate, and that there was a real danger that those properties and temporalities long enjoyed and used by the Russian Orthodox Church worshippers in this State would be taken from them by the representatives of the patriarchate. . . ." ⊥**119**

In upholding the validity of Article 5-C, the New York Court of Appeals apparently assumes Article 5-C does nothing more than permit the trustees of the Cathedral to use it for services consistent with the desires of the members of the Russian Church in America. Its reach goes far beyond that point. By fiat it displaces one church administrator with another. It passes the control of matters strictly ecclesiastical from one church authority to another. It thus intrudes for the benefit of one segment of a church the power of the state into the forbidden area of religious freedom contrary to the principles of the First Amendment. . . . New York's Article 5-C directly prohibits the free exercise of an ecclesiastical right, the Church's choice of its hierarchy. . . . ⊥**120**

The record before us shows no schism over faith or doctrine between the Russian Church in America and the Russian Orthodox Church. It shows administrative control of the North American Diocese by the Supreme Church Authority of the Russian Orthodox Church, including the appointment of the ruling hierarch in North America from the foundation of the diocese until the Russian Revolution. We find nothing that indicates a relinquishment of this power by the Russian Orthodox Church.

Ours is a government which by the law of its being allows no statute, state or national, that prohibits the free exercise of religion. There are occasions when civil courts must draw lines between the responsibilities of church and state for the disposition or use of property. Even in those cases when the property right follows as an incident from decisions of the church custom or law on ecclesiastical ⊥**121** issues, the church rule controls. This under our Constitution necessarily follows in order that there may be free exercise of religion.

The decree of the Court of Appeals of New York must be reversed, and the case remanded to that court for such further action as it deems proper and not in contravention of this opinion.

It is so ordered.

Mr. *Justice FRANKFURTER*, concurring.

Let me put to one side the question whether in our day a legislature could, consistently with due process, displace the judicial process and decide a particular controversy affecting property so as to decree that A not B owns it or is entitled to its possession. Obviously a legislature would not have that power merely because the property belongs to a church.

In any event, this proceeding rests on a claim which cannot be determined without intervention by the State in a religious conflict. St. Nicholas Cathedral is not just a piece of real estate. It is no more that than is St. Patrick's Cathedral or the Cathedral of St. John the Divine. A cathedral is the seat and center of ecclesiastical authority. St. Nicholas Cathedral is an archiepiscopal see of one of the great religious organizations. What is at stake here is the power to exercise religious authority. That is the essence of this controversy. It is that even though the religious authority becomes manifest and is exerted through authority over the Cathedral as the outward symbol of a religious faith. ⊥**122**

The judiciary has heeded, naturally enough, the menace to a society like ours of attempting to settle such religious struggles by state action. And so, when courts are called upon to adjudicate disputes which, though generated by conflicts of faith, may fairly be isolated as controversies over property and therefore within judicial competence, the authority of courts is in strict subordination to the ecclesiastical law of a particular church prior to a schism. This very limited right of resort to courts for determination of claims, civil in their nature, between rival parties among the communicants of a religious faith is merely one aspect of the duty of courts to enforce the rights of members in an association, temporal or religious, according to the laws of that association.

Legislatures have no such obligation to adjudicate and no such power. Assuredly they have none to settle conflicts of religious authority and none to define religious obedience. These aspects of spiritual differences constitute the heart of this controversy. The New York legislature decreed that one party to the dispute and not the other should control the common center of devotion. In doing so the legislature effectively authorized one party to give religious direction not only to its adherents but also to its opponents.

The arguments by which New York seeks to justify this inroad into the realm of faith are echoes of past attempts at secular intervention in religious conflicts. It is said that an impressive majority both of the laity and of the priesthood of the old local church now adhere to the party whose candidate New York enthroned, as it were, as Archbishop. Be that as it may, it is not a function of civil government under our constitutional system to assure rule to any religious body by a counting of heads. ⊥**123** Our Constitution does assure that anyone is free to worship according to his conscience. A legislature is not free to vest in a schismatic head the means of acting under the authority of his old church, by affording him the religious power which the use and occupancy of St. Nicholas Cathedral make possible.

Again, it is argued that New York may protect itself from dangers attributed to submission by the mother church in Moscow to political authority. To reject this claim one does not have to indulge in the tendency of lawyers to carry arguments to the extreme of empty formal logic. Scattered throughout the country there are religious bodies with ties to various countries of a world in tension—tension due in part to shifting political affiliation and orientation. The consideration which permeates the court's opinion below would give each State the right to assess the circumstances in the foreign political entanglements of its religious bodies that make for danger to the State, and the power, resting on plausible legislative findings, to divest such bodies of spiritual authority and of the temporal property which symbolizes it.

Memory is short but it cannot be forgotten that in the State of New York there was strong feeling against the Tsarist regime at a time when the Russian Church was governed by a Procurator of the Tsar. And when Mussolini exacted the Lateran Agreement, argument was not wanting by those friendly to her claims that the Church of Rome was subjecting herself to political authority. The fear, perhaps not wholly groundless, that the loyalty of its citizens might be diluted by their adherence to a ⊥**124** church entangled in antagonistic political interests, reappears in history as the ground for interference by civil government with religious attachments. Such fear readily leads to persecution of religious beliefs deemed dangerous to ruling political authority. It was on this basis, after all, that Bismarck sought to detach German Catholics from Rome by a series of laws not too different in purport from that before us today. The long, unedifying history of the contest between the secular state and the church is replete with instances of attempts by civil gov⊥**125**ernment to exert pressure upon religious authority. Religious leaders have often made gestures of accommodation to such pressures. History also indicates that the vitality of great world religions survived such efforts. In any event, under our Constitution it is not open to the governments of this Union to reinforce the loyalty of their citizens by deciding who is the true exponent of their religion.

Finally, we are told that the present Moscow Patriarchate is not the true superior church of the American communicants. The vicissitudes of war and revolution which have beset the Moscow Patriarchate since 1917 are said to have resulted in a discontinuity which divests the present Patriarch of his authority over the American church. Both parties to the present controversy agree that the present Patriarch is the legitimately chosen holder of his office, and the account of the proceedings and pronouncements of the American schismatic group so indicate. Even were there doubt about this it is hard to see by what warrant the New York Legislature is free to substitute its own judgment as to the validity of Patriarch Alexi's claim and to disregard acknowledgment of the present Patriarch by his coequals in the Eastern Confession, the Patriarchs of Constantinople, Alexandria, Antioch, and Jerusalem, and by religious leaders throughout the world, including the present Archbishop of York. ⊥**126**

These considerations undermine the validity of the New York legislation in that it enters the domain of religious control barred to the States by the Fourteenth Amendment.

Mr. *Justice* BLACK agrees with this opinion on the basis of his view that the Fourteenth Amendment makes the First Amendment applicable to the States.

Mr. *Justice* DOUGLAS, while concurring in the opinion of the Court, also joins this opinion.

Mr. *Justice* JACKSON, dissenting. . . .

⊥**127** I greatly oversimplify the history of this controversy to indicate its nature rather than to prove its merits. This Cathedral was incorporated and built in the era of the Czar, under the regime of a state-ridden church in a church-ridden state. The Bolshevik Revolution may have freed the state from the grip of the church, but it did not free the church from the grip of the state. It only brought to the top a new master for a captive and submissive ecclesiastical establishment. By 1945, the Moscow patriarchy had been reformed and manned under the Soviet regime and it sought to re-establish in other countries its prerevolutionary control of church property and its sway over the minds of the religious. As the Court's opinion points out, it demanded of the Russian Church in America, among other things, that it abstain "from political activities against the U.S.S.R." The American Cathedral group, along with others, refused submission to the representative of the Moscow Patriarch, whom it regarded as an arm of the Soviet Government. Thus, we have an ostensible religious schism with decided political overtones.

If the Fourteenth Amendment is to be interpreted to leave anything to the courts of a state to decide without our interference, I should suppose it would be claims to ownership or possession of real estate within its borders and the vexing technical questions pertaining to the creation, interpretation, termination, and enforcement of uses and trusts, even though they are for religious and charitable purposes. This controversy, I believe, is a matter for settlement by state law and not within the proper province of this Court. . . .

I. . . .

⊥**128** Nothing in New York law required this denomination to incorporate its Cathedral. The Religious Corporations Law of the State expressly recognizes unincorporated churches and undertakes no regulation of them or their affairs. But this denomination wanted the advantages of a corporate charter for its Cathedral, to obtain immunity from personal liability and other benefits. This statute does not interfere with religious freedom but furthers it. If they elect to come under it, the statute makes separate provision for each of many denominations with corporate controls appropriate to its own ecclesiastical order. When it sought the privilege of incorporation under the New York law applicable to its denomination, it seems to me that this Cathedral and all connected with its temporal affairs were submitted to New York law. . . . ⊥**129**

What has been done here, as I see it, is to exercise this reserved power which permits the State to alter corporate controls in response to the lessons of experience. Of course, the power is not unlimited and could be so exercised as to deprive one of property without due process of law. But, I do not think we can say that a legislative application of a principle so well established in our common law as the *cy-pres* doctrine is beyond the powers reserved by the New York Constitution.

II

The Court holds, however, that the State cannot exercise its reserved power to control this property without invading religious freedom, because it is a Cathedral and devoted to religious uses. I forbear discussion of the extent to which restraints imposed upon Congress by the First Amendment are transferred against the State by the Fourteenth Amendment beyond saying that I consider that the same differences which apply to freedom of speech and press are applicable to questions of freedom of religion and of separation of church and state.

It is important to observe what New York has not done in this case. It has not held that Benjamin may not act as Archbishop or be revered as such by all who will follow him. It has not held that he may not have a Cathedral. ⊥**130** Indeed, I think New York would agree that no one is more in need of spiritual guidance than the Soviet faction. It has only held that this cleric may not have a particular Cathedral which, under New York law, belongs to others. It has not interfered with his or anyone's exercise of his religion. New York has not outlawed the Soviet-controlled sect nor forbidden it to exercise its authority or teach its dogma in any place whatsoever except on this piece of property owned and rightfully possessed by the Cathedral Corporation.

The fact that property is dedicated to a religious use cannot, in my opinion, justify the Court in sublimating an issue over property rights into one of deprivation of religious liberty which alone would bring in the religious guaranties of the First Amendment. I assume no one would pretend that the State cannot decide a claim of trespass, larceny, conversion, bailment or contract, where the property involved is that of a religious corporation or is put to religious use, without invading the principle of religious liberty.

Of course, possession of the property will help either side that obtains it to maintain its prestige and to continue or extend its sway over the minds and souls of the devout. So would possession of a bank account, an income-producing office building, or any other valuable property. But if both claimants are religious corporations or personalities, can not the State decide the issues that arise over ownership and possession without invading the religious freedom of one or the other of the parties?

Thus, if the American group, which owns the title to the Cathedral, had by force barred Benjamin from entering it physically, would the Court say it was an interference with religious freedom to entertain and decide his ejectment action? If state courts are to decide such controversies at all instead of leaving them to be settled by a show of force, is it constitutional to decide for only ⊥**131** one side of the controversy and unconstitutional to decide for the other? In either case, the religious freedom of one side or the other is impaired if the temporal goods they need are withheld or taken from them.

As I have earlier pointed out, the Soviet Ecclesiast's claim, denial of which is said to be constitutional error, is not that this New York property is impressed with a trust by virtue of New York law. The claim is that it is impressed with a trust by virtue of the rules of the Russian Orthodox Church. This Court so holds.

I shall not undertake to wallow through the complex, obscure and fragmentary details of secular and ecclesiastical history, theology, and canon law in which this case is smothered. To me, whatever the canon law is found to be and whoever is the rightful head of the Moscow patriarchate, I do not think New York law must yield to the authority of a foreign and unfriendly state masquerading as a spiritual institution.

I have supposed that a State of this Union was entirely free to make its own law, independently of any foreign-made law, except as the Full Faith and Credit Clause of the Constitution might require deference to the law of a sister state or the Supremacy Clause require submission to federal law. I do not see how one can spell out of the principles of separation of church and state a doctrine that a state submit property rights to settlement by canon law. If there is any relevant inference to be drawn, I should think it would be to the contrary, though I see no obstacle to the state allowing ecclesiastical law to

PRESBYTERIAN CHURCH IN THE UNITED STATES v. MARY ELIZABETH BLUE HULL MEMORIAL PRESBYTERIAN CHURCH

393 U.S. 440
ON WRIT OF CERTIORARI TO THE SUPREME COURT OF GEORGIA
Argued December 9 and 10, 1968 — Decided January 27, 1969

⊥**441** Mr. *Justice BRENNAN* delivered the opinion of the Court.

This is a church property dispute which arose when two local churches withdrew from a hierarchical general church organization. Under Georgia law the right to the property previously used by the local churches was made to turn on a civil court jury decision as to whether the general church abandoned or departed from the tenets of faith and practice it held at the time the local churches affiliated with it. The question presented is whether the restraints of the First Amendment, as applied to the States through the Fourteenth Amendment, permit a civil court to award church property on the basis of the interpretation and significance the civil court assigns to aspects of church doctrine.

Petitioner, Presbyterian Church in the United States, is an association of local Presbyterian churches governed ⊥**442** by a hierarchical structure of tribunals which consists of, in ascending order, (1) the Church Session, composed of the Elders of the local church; (2) the Presbytery, composed of several churches in a geographical area; (3) the Synod, generally composed of all Presbyteries within a State; and (4) the General Assembly, the highest governing body.

A dispute arose between petitioner, the general church, and two local churches in Savannah, Georgia—the respondents, Hull Memorial Presbyterian Church and Eastern Heights Presbyterian Church—over control of the properties used until then by the local churches. In 1966, the membership of the local churches, in the belief that certain actions and pronouncements of the general church were violations of that organization's constitution and departures from the doctrine and practice in force at the time of affiliation, voted to withdraw from the general church and to reconstitute the local churches as an autonomous Presbyterian organization. The ministers of the two churches renounced the general church's ⊥**443** jurisdiction and authority over them, as did all but two of the ruling elders. In response, the general church, through the Presbytery of Savannah, established an Administrative Commission to seek a conciliation. The dissident local churchmen remained steadfast; consequently, the Commission acknowledged the withdrawal of the local leadership and proceeded to take over the local churches' property on behalf of the general church until new local leadership could be appointed.

The local churchmen made no effort to appeal the Commission's action to higher church tribunals—the Synod of Georgia or the General Assembly. Instead, the churches filed separate suits in the Superior Court of Chatham County to enjoin the general church from trespassing on the disputed property, title to which was in the local churches. The cases were consolidated for trial. The general church moved to dismiss the actions and cross-claimed for injunctive relief in its own behalf on the ground that civil courts were without power to determine whether the general church had departed from its tenets of faith and practice. The motion to dismiss was denied, and the case was submitted to the jury on the theory that Georgia law implies a trust of local church property for the benefit of the general church on the sole condition that the general church adhere to its tenets of faith and practice existing at the time of affiliation by the local churches. Thus, the jury was instructed to determine whether the actions of the general church "amount to a fundamental or substantial abandonment of the original tenets and doctrines of the [general ⊥**444** church], so that the new tenets and doctrines are utterly variant from the purposes for which the [general church] was founded." The jury returned a verdict for the local churches, and the trial judge thereupon declared that the implied trust had terminated and enjoined the general church from interfering with the use of the property in question. The Supreme Court of Georgia affirmed. We granted certiorari to consider the First Amendment questions raised.*

We reverse. ⊥**445**

It is of course true that the State has a legitimate interest in resolving property disputes, and that a civil court is a proper forum for that resolution. Special problems arise, however, when these disputes implicate controversies over church doctrince and practice. The approach of this Court in such cases was originally developed in *Watson* v. *Jones*, a pre-*Erie* v. *Thompkins* diversity decision decided before the application of the First Amendment to the States but nonetheless informed by First

*We reject the contention of respondent local churches that no First Amendment issues were raised or decided in the state courts. Petitioner's answer and cross-claim in each case included an express allegation that the action of respondents in appropriating the church property to their use was "in violation of the laws of Georgia, *the United States of America*, and the Southern Presbyterian Church." (Italics supplied.) At trial petitioner's counsel objected to the admission of all testimony "pertaining to [the] alleged deviation from the faith and practice of the Presbyterian Church in the United States" because that question was "exclusively within the right of the Presbyterian Church in the United States through its proper judicial body to determine." On appeal, petitioner again contended "that questions of an ecclesiastical nature concerning whether or not a church has abandoned its tenents [sic] and doctrines or some of them, are exclusively within the jurisdiction of the church courts and should not be submitted to a jury for determination as this would destroy the doctrine of separation of church and state." Petitioner thus clearly raised claims under the First Amendment as applied to the States by the Fourteenth Amendment. *Kedroff* v. *St. Nicholas* Cathedral. . . .

Amendment considerations. There, as here, civil courts were asked to resolve a property dispute between a national Presbyterian organization and local churches of that organization. There, as here, the disputes arose out of a controversy over church doctrine. There, as here, the Court was asked to decree the termination of an implied trust because of departures from doctrine by the national organization. The *Watson* Court refused, pointing out that it was wholly inconsistent with the American concept of the re⊥**446**lationship between church and state to permit civil courts to determine ecclesiastical questions. . . . ⊥**447** The logic of this language leaves the civil courts *no* role in determining ecclesiastical questions in the process of resolving property disputes.

Later cases, however, also decided on nonconstitutional grounds, recognized that there might be some circumstances in which marginal civil court review of ecclesiastical determinations would be appropriate. The scope of this review was delineated in *Gonzalez* v. *Archbishop*. There, Gonzalez claimed the right to be appointed to a chaplaincy in the Roman Catholic Church under a will which provided that a member of his family receive that appointment. The Roman Catholic Archbishop of Manila, Philippine Islands, refused to appoint Gonzalez on the ground that he did not satisfy the qualifications established by Canon Law for that office. Gonzalez brought suit in the Court of First Instance of Manila for a judgment directing the Archbishop, among other things, to appoint him chaplain. The trial court entered such an order, but the Supreme Court of the Philippine Islands reversed and "absolved the Archbishop from the complaint." This Court affirmed. Mr. *Justice BRANDEIS*, speaking for the Court, defined the civil court role in the following words: "In the absence of fraud, collusion, or arbitrariness, the decisions of the proper church tribunals on matters purely ecclesiastical, although affecting civil rights, are accepted in litigation before the secular courts as conclusive, because the parties in interest made them so by contract or otherwise."

In *Kedroff* v. *St. Nicholas Cathedral*, the Court converted the principle of *Watson* as qualified by *Gonzalez* into a Constitutional rule. . . . ⊥**449**

Thus, the First Amendment severely circumscribes the role that civil courts may play in resolving church property disputes. It is obvious, however, that not every civil court decision as to property claimed by a religious organization jeopardizes values protected by the First Amendment. Civil courts do not inhibit free exercise of religion merely by opening their doors to disputes involving church property. And there are neutral principles of law, developed for use in all property disputes, which can be applied without "establishing" churches to which property is awarded. But First Amendment values are plainly jeopardized when church property litigation is made to turn on the resolution by civil courts of controversies over religious doctrine and practice. If civil courts undertake to resolve such controversies in order to adjudicate the property dispute, the hazards are ever present of inhibiting the free development of religious doctrine and of implicating secular interests in matters of purely ecclesiastical concern. Because of these hazards, the First Amendment enjoins the employment of organs of government for essentially religious purposes, *Abington* v. *Schempp*; the Amendment therefore commands civil courts to decide church property disputes without resolving underlying controversies over religious doctrine. Hence, States, religious organizations and individuals must structure relationships involving church property so as not to require the civil courts to resolve ecclesiastical questions.

The Georgia courts have violated the command of the First Amendment. The departure-from-doctrine element of the implied trust theory which they applied ⊥**450** requires the civil judiciary to determine whether actions of the general church constitute such a "substantial departure" from the tenets of faith and practice existing at the time of the local churches' affiliation that the trust in favor of the general church must be declared to have terminated. This determination has two parts. The civil court must first decide whether the challenged actions of the general church depart substantially from prior doctrine. In reaching such a decision, the court must of necessity make its own interpretation of the meaning of church doctrines. If the court should decide that a substantial departure has occurred, it must then go on to determine whether the issue on which the general church has departed holds a place of such importance in the traditional theology as to require that the trust be terminated. A civil court can make this determination only after assessing the relative significance to the religion of the tenets from which departure was found. Thus, the departure-from-doctrine element of the Georgia implied trust theory requires the civil court to determine matters at the very core of a religion—the interpretation of particular church doctrines and the importance of those doctrines to the religion. Plainly, the First Amendment forbids civil courts from playing such a role.

Since the Georgia courts on remand may undertake to determine whether petitioner is entitled to relief on its cross-claims, we find it appropriate to remark that the departure-from-doctrine element of Georgia's implied trust theory can play *no* role in any future judicial proceedings. The departure-from-doctrine approach is not susceptible of the marginal judicial involvement contemplated in *Gonzalez*. In *Gonzalez*, Gonzalez' rights under a will ⊥**451** turned on a church decision, the Archbishop's, as to church law, the qualifications for the chaplaincy. It was the archbishopric, not the civil courts, which had the task of analyzing and interpreting church law in order to determine the validity of Gonzalez' claim to a chaplaincy. Thus, the civil courts could adjudicate the rights under the will without interpreting or weighing church doctrine but simply by engaging in the narrowest kind of review of a specific church decision—*i.e.*, whether that decision resulted from fraud, collusion, or arbitrariness. Such review does not inject the civil courts into substantive ecclesiastical matters. In contrast, under Georgia's departure-from-doctrine approach, it is not possible for the civil courts to play so limited a role. Under this approach, property rights do not turn on a church decision as to church doctrine. The standard of departure-from-doctrine, though it calls for resolution of ecclesiastical questions, is a creation of state, not church law. Nothing in the record suggests that this state standard has been interpreted and applied in a decision of the general church. Any decisions which have been made by the general church about the local churches' withdrawal have at most a tangential relationship to the state-fashioned departure-from-doctrine standard. A determination whether such decisions are fraudulent, collusive, or arbitrary would therefore not answer the questions posed by the state standard. To reach those questions would require the civil courts to engage in the forbidden process of interpreting and weighing church doctrine. Even if the general church had attempted to apply the state standard, the civil courts could not review and enforce the church decision without violating the Constitution. The First Amendment prohibits a State from employing religious organizations as an arm of the civil judiciary to perform the function of interpreting and applying state standards. ⊥**452** Thus, a civil court may no more review a church decision applying a state departure-from-doctrine standard than it may apply that standard itself.

The judgment of the Supreme Court of Georgia is reversed, and the case is remanded for further proceedings not inconsistent with this opinion.

It is so ordered.

SERBIAN EASTERN ORTHODOX DIOCESE FOR THE UNITED STATES OF AMERICA AND CANADA v. MILIVOJEVICH

426 U.S. 696

ON WRIT OF CERTIORARI TO THE SUPREME COURT OF ILLINOIS

Argued March 22, 1976 — Decided June 21, 1976

⊥**697** Mr. *Justice* BRENNAN delivered the opinion of the Court.

In 1963, the Holy Assembly of Bishops and the Holy Synod of the Serbian Orthodox Church (Mother Church) ⊥**698** suspended and ultimately removed respondent Dionisije Milivojevich (Dionisije) as Bishop of the American-Canadian Diocese of that Church, and appointed petitioner Bishop Firmilian Ocokoljich (Firmilian) as Administrator of the Diocese, which the Mother Church then reorganized into three Dioceses. In 1964 the Holy Assembly and Holy Synod defrocked Dionisije as a Bishop and cleric of the Mother Church. In this civil action brought by Dionisije and the other respondents in Illinois Circuit Court, the Supreme Court of Illinois held that the proceedings of the Mother Church respecting Dionisije were procedurally and substantively defective under the internal regulations of the Mother Church and were therefore arbitrary and invalid. The State Supreme Court also invalidated the Diocesan reorganization into three Dioceses. We granted certiorari to determine whether the actions of the Illinois Supreme Court constituted improper judicial interference with decisions of the highest authorities of a hierarchial church in violation of the First and Fourteenth Amendments. We hold that the inquiries made by the Illinois Supreme Court into matters of ecclesiastical cognizance and polity and the court's actions pursuant thereto contravened the First and Fourteenth Amendments. We therefore reverse.

I

The basic dispute is over control of the Serbian Eastern Orthodox Diocese for the United States of America and Canada (American-Canadian Diocese), its property and assets. Petitioners are Bishops Firmilian Ocokoljich, Gregory Udicki, and Sava Vukovich, and the Serbian Eastern ⊥**699** Orthodox Diocese for the United States of America and Canada (the religious body in this country). Respondents are Bishop Dionisije Milivojevich, the Serbian Orthodox Monastery of St. Sava, and the Serbian Eastern Orthodox Diocese for the United States of America and Canada, an Illinois religious corporation. A proper perspective of the relationship of these parties and the nature of this dispute requires some background discussion.

The Serbian Orthodox Church, one of the 14 autocephalous, hierarchical churches which came into existence following the schism of the universal Christian church in 1054, is an episcopal church whose Seat is the Patriarchate in Belgrade, Yugoslavia. Its highest legislative, judicial, ecclesiastical, and administrative authority resides in the Holy Assembly of Bishops, a body composed of all Diocesan Bishops presided over by a Bishop designated by the Assembly to be Patriarch. The Church's highest executive body, the Holy Synod of Bishops, is composed of the Patriarch and four Diocesan Bishops selected by the Holy Assembly. The Holy Synod and the Holy Assembly have the exclusive power to remove, suspend, defrock, or appoint Diocesan Bishops. The Mother Church is governed according to the Holy Scriptures, Holy Tradition, Rules of the Ecumenical Councils, the Holy Apostles, the Holy Faiths of the Church, the Mother Church Constitution adopted in 1931, and a "penal code" adopted in 1962. These sources of law are sometimes ambiguous and seemingly inconsistent. Pertinent provisions of the Mother Church Constitution provide that the Church's "main administrative division is composed of dioceses, both in regard to church hierarchial and church administrative aspect," Art. 12, and that "[d]ecisions of establishing, naming liquidating, reorganizing, and the seat of the dioceses, and establishing or eliminating of position of vicar bish⊥**700**ops, is decided upon by the [Holy Assembly], in agreement with the patriarchal Council," Art. 16.

During the late 19th century, migrants to North America of Serbian descent formed autonomous religious congregations throughout this country and Canada. These congregations were then under the jurisdiction of the Russian Orthodox Church, but that Church was unable to care for their needs and the congregations sought permission to bring themselves under the jurisdiction of the Serbian Orthodox Church.

In 1913 and 1916, Serbian priests and laymen organized a Serbian Orthodox Church in North America. The 32 Serbian Orthodox congregations were divided into 4 presbyteries, each presided over by a Bishop's Aide, and constitutions were adopted. In 1917, the Russian Orthodox Church commissioned a Serbian priest, Father Mardary, to organize an independent Serbian Diocese in America. Four years later, as a result of Father Mardary's efforts, the Holy Assembly of Bishops of the Mother Church created the Eastern Orthodox Diocese for the United States of America and Canada and designated a Serbian Bishop to complete the formal organization of a diocese. From that time until 1963, each bishop who governed the American-Canadian Diocese was a Yugoslav citizen appointed by the Mother Church without consultation with Diocesan officials.

In 1927, Father Mardary called a Church National Assembly embracing all of the known Serbian Orthodox congregations in the United States. The assembly drafted and adopted the constitution of the Serbian Orthodox Diocese for the United States of America and Canada, and submitted the constitution to the Mother Church for approval. The Holy Assembly made changes to provide for appointment of the Diocesan Bishop by the Holy Assembly and to require Holy As⊥**701**sembly approval for any amendments to the constitution, and with these changes approved the constitution. The American-Canadian Diocese was the only diocese of the Mother Church with its own constitution.

Article 1 of the constitution provides that the American-Canadian Diocese "is considered ecclesiastically-judicially as an organic part of the Serbian Patriarchate in the Kingdom of Yugoslavia," and Art. 2 provides that all "statutes and rules which regulate the ecclesiastical-canonical authority and position of the Serbian Orthodox Church in the Kingdom of Yugoslavia are also compulsory for the" American-Canadian Diocese. Article 3 states that the "jurisdiction of the . . . Diocese . . . includes the entire political territory of the United States of America and Canada, which as such by its geographical location enjoys full administrative freedom and accordingly, it can independently regulate and rule the activities of its church, school and other diocesan institutions and all funds and beneficiencies, through its organs. . . ." Article 9 provides that the Bishop of the Diocese "is appointed by the Holy Assembly of Bishops of the Serbian Patriarchate"; various provisions of the constitution accord that Bishop extensive powers both over religious matters and with respect to control of Diocesan property. The constitution also provides for such Diocesan organs as a Diocesan National Assembly, which exercises considerable legislative and administrative authority within the Diocese.

In 1927, Father Mardary also organized a not-for-profit corporation, the Serbian Eastern Orthodox Council for the United States and Canada, under the laws of Illinois. The corporation was to hold title to 30 acres of land in Libertyville, Ill., that Father Mardary had personally purchased in 1924. The charter of that corporation was allowed to lapse, and Father Mardary organized ⊥**702** another Illinois not-for-profit corporation, respondent Serbian Eastern Orthodox Diocese for the United States and Canada, under Illinois laws governing incorporation of hierarchial religious organizations. In 1945, respondent not-for-profit monastery corporation, the Monastery of St. Sava, was organized under these same Illinois laws, and title to the Libertyville property was transferred to it. Similar secular property-holding corporations were subsequently organized in New York, California, and Pennsylvania.

Respondent Bishop Dionisije Milivojevich was elected Bishop of the American-Canadian Diocese by the Holy Assembly of Bishops in 1931. He became a controversial figure; during the years before 1963, the Holy Assembly received numerous complaints challenging his fitness to serve as Bishop and his administration of the Diocese.

During his tenure, however, the Diocese grew so substantially that Dionisije requested that the Patriarch and Holy Assembly appoint bishops to assist him but to serve under his supervision. Eventually, the Diocese sought its elevation by the Holy Assembly to the rank of Metropolia, that South America be added to the Diocese, and that several assistant bishops be appointed under Dionisije. Dionisije specifically recommended that petitioners Firmilian Ocokoljich and Gregory Udicki, and one Stefan Lastavica be named assistant bishops. A delegation from the Diocese was sent to the May 1962 meeting of the Holy Assembly in Belgrade to urge adoption of these reorganization proposals, and on June 12, 1962, the Holy Synod appointed a delegation to visit the United States and study the proposals. The delegation was also directed to confer with Dionisije concerning the complaints made against him and his administration over the years.

The delegation remained in the United States for three ⊥**703** months, visiting parishes throughout the Diocese and discussing both the reorganization proposals and the complaints against Dionisije. After completion of its survey, the delegation suggested to the Holy Synod the assignment of vicar bishops to the Diocese and recommended that a commission be appointed to conduct a thorough investigation into the complaints against Dionisije. However, the Holy Assembly on May 10, 1963, instead recommended that the Holy Synod institute disciplinary proceedings against Dionisije. The Holy Synod thereupon met immediately and suspended Dionisije pending investigation and disposition of the complaints. The Holy Synod appointed petitioner

Firmilian, Dionisije's chief episcopal deputy since 1955 and one of Dionisije's candidates for assistant bishop, as Administrator of the Diocese pending completion of the proceedings.

The Holy Assembly thereafter reconvened and, acting under Art. 16 of the constitution of the Mother Church, reorganized the American-Canadian Diocese into three new dioceses—the Middle Western, the Western, and the Eastern—whose boundaries were roughly those of the episcopal districts previously created by Dionisije. The final fixing of boundaries for the new dioceses and all other organizational and administrative matters were left to be determined by the officials of the old American-Canadian Diocese. Dionisije was appointed Bishop of the Middle Western Diocese and, seven days later, petitioners Achimandrites Firmilian and Gregory, and Stefan were appointed temporary administrators for the new dioceses.

⊥**704** Dionisije's immediate reaction to these decisions of the Mother Church was to refuse to accept the reorganization on the ground that it contravened the administrative autonomy of the Diocese guaranteed by the Diocesan constitution, and to refuse to accept his suspension on the ground that it was not effectuated in compliance with the constitution and laws of the Mother Church. On May 25, 1963, he prepared and mailed a circular to all American-Canadian parishes stating his refusal to recognize these actions, and on May 27 he issued a press release stating his refusal to recognize his suspension and his intent to litigate it in the civil courts. This refusal to recognize the Diocesan reorganization and his suspension as Bishop was again stated by Dionisije in a circular issued on June 3 and addressed to the Patriarch, the Holy Assembly, the Holy Synod, all clergy, congregations, Diocesan committees, and all Serbians in North America. He also continued to officiate as Bishop, refusing to turn administration of the Diocese over to Firmilian; in a May 30 letter to Firmilian, Dionisije repeated this refusal, asserted that he no longer recognized the decisions of the Holy Assembly and Holy Synod, and charged those bodies with being "communistic."

The Diocesan Council met on June 6, and Dionisije reaffirmed his refusal to turn over administration of the Diocese to Firmilian; he also announced that he had discharged two of his vicars general because of their loyalty to the Mother Church. The Council resolved at the meeting to advise the Holy Synod that the proposal to reorganize the Diocese into three dioceses would be submitted to the Diocesan National Assembly in August for acceptance or rejection. The Council also requested that the Holy Assembly promptly send a committee to investigate the complaints against Dionisije.

On June 13, the Holy Synod appointed such a commis-⊥**705**sion, composed of two Bishops and the Secretary of the Holy Synod. On July 5, the commission met with Dionisije, who reiterated his refusal to recognize his suspension or the diocesan reorganization, and who demanded all accusations in writing. The commission refused to give Dionisije the written accusations on the ground that defiance of decisions of higher church authorities itself established wrongful conduct, and advised him that the Holy Synod would appoint a Bishop as court prosecutor to prepare an indictment against him.

On the basis of the commission's report and recommendations, which recited Dionisije's refusal to accept the decisions of the Holy Synod and Holy Assembly and his refusal to recognize the court of the Holy Synod or its competence to try him, the Holy Assembly met on July 27, 1963, and voted to remove Dionisije as Bishop. The minutes of the Holy Assembly meeting and the Patriarch's letter to Dionisije informing him of the Holy Assembly's actions made clear that the removal was based solely on his acts of defiance subsequent to his May 10, 1963, suspension, and his violation of his oath and loss of certain qualifications for Bishop under Art. 104 of the constitution of the Mother Church.

The Diocesan National Assembly, with Dionisije presiding despite his removal, met in August 1963 and issued a resolution repudiating the division of the Diocese into three dioceses and demanding a revocation by the Mother Church of the decisions concerning that division. When the Holy Assembly refused to reconsider, the Diocesan National Assembly in November 1963 declared the Diocese completely autonomous and reinstated the provisions of the diocesan constitution that provided for election of the Bishop of the Diocese itself and for amendments without the approval of the Holy Assembly.

Meanwhile, the Holy Synod in October 1963 for-⊥**706**warded to Dionisije a formal written indictment based on the charges of canonical misconduct. In November 1963, Dionisije responded with a demand for the verified reports and complaints referred to in the indictment and for a six-month extension to answer the indictment. The Holy Assembly granted a 30-day extension in which to answer, but declined to furnish verified charges on the grounds that they were described in the indictment that additional details would be evidentiary in nature, and that there was no legal or canonical basis for forwarding such material to an accused Bishop.

Dionisije returned the indictment in January, refusing to answer without the verified charges, denouncing the Holy Assembly and Holy Synod as schismatic and pro-Communist, and asserting that the Mother Church was proceeding in violation of its penal code and constitution.

The Holy Synod, on February 25, 1964, declared that it could not proceed further without Dionisije and referred the matter to the Holy Assembly, which tried Dionisije as a default case on March 5, 1964, because of his refusal to participate. The indictment was also amended at that time to include charges based on Dionisije's acts of rebellion such as those committed at the November meeting of the National Assembly which had declared the Diocese separate from the Mother Church. Considering the original and amended indictments, the Holy Assembly unanimously found Dionisije guilty of all charges and divested him of his episcopal and monastic ranks.

Even before the Holy Assembly had removed Dionisije as Bishop, he had commenced what eventually became his protracted litigation, now carried on for almost 13 years. Acting upon the threat contained in his May 27, 1963, press release, Dionisije filed suit in ⊥**707** the Circuit Court of Lake County, Ill., on July 26, 1963, seeking to enjoin petitioners from interfering with the assets of respondent corporations and to have himself declared the true Diocesan Bishop. Petitioners countered with a separate complaint, which was consolidated with the original action, seeking declaratory relief that Dionisije had been removed as Bishop of the Diocese and that the Diocese had been properly reorganized into three dioceses, and injunctive relief granting petitioner Bishops control of the reorganized dioceses and their property. After the trial court granted summary judgment for respondents and dismissed petitioners, counter-complaint, the Illinois Appellate Court reversed and remanded for a hearing on the merits.

Following a lengthy trial, the trial court filed an unreported Memorandum Opinion and entered a Final Decree which concluded that "no substantial evidence was produced . . . that fraud, collusion or arbitrariness existed in any of the actions or decisions preliminary to or during the final proceedings of the decision to defrock Bishop Dionisije made by the highest Hierarchical bodies of the Mother Church;" that the property held by respondent corporations is held in trust for all members of the American-Canadian Diocese; that it was "improper and beyond the power of the Mother Church to take its action in dividing the whole American Diocese into three new Dioceses, changing its boundaries, and in appointing new bishops for ⊥**708** said so-called new Dioceses;" and that "Firmilian was validly appointed by the Holy Episcopal Synod as temporary Administrator of the whole American-Canadian Diocese in place of the defrocked Bishop Dionisije."

On appeal, the Supreme Court of Illinois affirmed in part and reversed in part, essentially holding that Dionisije's removal and defrockment must be set aside as "arbitrary" because the proceedings resulting in those actions were not conducted according to the Illinois Supreme Court's interpretation of the Church's constitution and penal code, and that the diocesan reorganization was invalid because it was beyond the scope of the Mother Church's authority to effectuate such changes without Diocesan approval. Although the court denied rehearing, it amended its original opinion to hold that, although Dionisije had been properly suspended, that suspension terminated by operation of church law when he was not validly tried within one year to his indictment. Thus, the court purported in effect to reinstate Dionisije as Diocesan Bishop.

II

The fallacy fatal to the judgment of the Illinois Supreme Court is that it rests upon an impermissible rejection of the decisions of the highest ecclesiastical tribunals of this hierarchial church upon the issues in dispute, and impermissibly substitutes its own inquiry into church polity and resolutions based thereon of those disputes. Consistently with the First and Fourteenth Amendments "[c]ivil courts do not inquire whether the relevant [hierarchial] church governing body has power under religious law . . . [to decide such disputes]. . . . Such a determination . . . frequently necessitates the interpretation of ambiguous religious law and usage. ⊥**709** To permit civil courts to probe deeply enough into the allocation of power within a [hierarchial] church so as to decide . . . religious law . . . [governing church polity] . . . would violate the First Amendment in much the same manner as civil determination of religious doctrine." *Md. and Va. Churches* v. *Sharpsburg Church*. For where resolution of the disputes cannot be made without extensive inquiry by civil courts into religious law and polity, the First and Fourteenth Amendments mandate that civil courts shall not disturb the decisions of the highest ecclesiastical tribunal within a church of hierarchial polity, but must accept such decisions as binding on them, in their application to the religious issues of doctrine or polity before them.

Resolution of the religious disputes at issue here affects the control of church property in addition to the structure and administration of the American-Canadian Diocese. This is because the Diocesan Bishop controls respondent Monastery of St. Sava and is the principal officer of respondent property holding corporations. Resolution of the religious dispute over Dionisije's defrockment therefore determines control of the property. Thus, this case essentially involves not a church property dispute but a religious dispute the resolution of which under our cases is for ecclesiastical and not civil tribunals. Even when rival church factions seek resolution of a church property dispute in the civil courts there is substantial danger that the State will become entangled in essentially religious controversies or intervene on behalf of groups espousing particular doctrinal beliefs. Because of this danger, "the First Amendment severely circumscribes the role that civil courts may play in resolving church property disputes." *Presbyterian Church* v. *Hull Church*. "First Amend⊥**710**ment values are plainly jeopardized when church property litigation is made to turn on the resolution by civil courts of controversies over religious doctrine and practice. If civil courts undertake to resolve such controversies in order to adjudicate the property dispute, the hazards are ever present in inhibiting the free development of religious doctrine and of implicating secular interests in matters of purely ecclesiastical concern. . . . [T]he [First] Amendment therefore commands civil courts to decide church property disputes without resolving underlying controversies over religious doctrine." This principle applies with equal force to church disputes over church polity and church administration.

The principles limiting the role of civil courts in the resolution of religious controversies that incidentally affect civil rights were initially fashioned in *Watson* v.

Jones, a diversity case decided before the First Amendment had been rendered applicable to the States through the Fourteenth Amendment. With respect to hierarchical churches, *Watson* held that "the rule of action which should govern the civil courts . . . is, that, whenever the questions of discipline, or of faith, or ecclesiastical rule, custom, or law have been decided by the highest of these church judicatories to which the matter has been carried, the legal tribunals must accept such decisions as final, and as binding on them, in their application to the case before them."

In language having "a clear constitutional ring," *Presbyterian Church* v. *Hull Church*, *Watson* reasoned:

"The law knows no heresy, and is committed to the ⊥711 support of no dogma, the establishment of no sect. The right to organize voluntary religious associations to assist in the expression and dissemination of any religious doctrine, and to create tribunals for the decision of controverted questions of faith within the association, and for the ecclesiastical government of all the individual members, congregations, and officers within the general association, is unquestioned. All who unite themselves to such a body do so with an implied consent to this government, and are bound to submit to it. But it would be a vain consent and would lead to the total subversion of such religious bodies, if any one aggrieved by one of their decisions could appeal to the secular courts and have them reversed. *It is of the essence of these religious groups, and of their right to establish tribunals for the decision of questions arising among themselves, that those decisions should be binding in all cases of ecclesiastical cognizance, subject only to such appeals as the organism itself provides for*" (emphasis supplied).

Gonzalez v. *Archbishop* applied this principle in a case involving dispute over entitlement to certain income under a will that turned upon an ecclesiastical determination as to whether an individual would be appointed to a chaplaincy in the Roman Catholic Church. The Court, speaking through *Mr. Justice BRANDEIS*, observed:

"Because the appointment [to the chaplaincy] is a canonical act, it is the function of the church authorities to determine what the essential qualifications of a chaplain are and whether the candidate possesses them. In the absence of fraud, collusion, or arbitrariness, the decisions of the proper church ⊥712 tribunals on matters purely ecclesiastical, although affecting civil rights, are accepted in litigation before the secular courts as conclusive, because the parties in interest made them so by contract or otherwise.

Thus, although *Watson* had left civil courts no role to play in reviewing ecclesiastical decisions during the course of resolving church property disputes, *Gonzalez* first adverted to the possibility of "marginal civil court review," *Presbyterian Church* v. *Hull Church*, in cases challenging decisions of ecclesiastical tribunals as products of "fraud, collusion, or arbitrariness." However, since there was "not even a suggestion that [the Archbishop] exercised his authority [in making the chaplaincy decision] arbitrarily," the suggested "fraud, collusion, or arbitrariness" exception to the *Watson* rule was dictum only. And although references to the suggested exception appear in opinions in cases decided since the *Watson* rule has been held to be mandated by the First Amendment, no decision of this Court has given concrete content to or applied the "exception." However, it was the predicate for the Illinois Supreme Court's decision in this case, and we therefore turn to the question whether reliance upon it in the circumstances of this case was consistent with the prohibition of the First and Fourteenth Amendments against rejection of the decisions of the Mother Church upon the religious disputes in issue.

The conclusion of the Illinois Supreme Court that the decisions of the Mother Church were "arbitrary" was grounded upon an inquiry that persuaded the Illinois Su⊥713preme Court that the Mother Church had not followed its own laws and procedures in arriving at those decisions. We have concluded that whether or not there is room for "marginal civil court review" under the narrow rubrics of "fraud" or "collusion" when church tribunals act in bad faith for secular purposes, no "arbitrariness" exception—in the sense of an inquiry whether the decisions of the highest ecclesiastical tribunal of a hierarchical church complied with church laws and regulations—is consistent with the constitutional mandate that civil courts are bound to accept the decisions of the highest judicatories of a religious organization of hierarchical polity on matters of discipline, faith, internal organization, or ecclesiastical rule, custom or law. For civil courts to analyze whether the ecclesiastical actions of a church judicatory are in that sense "arbitrary" must inherently entail inquiry into the procedures that canon or ecclesiastical law supposedly require the church adjudicatory to follow, or else into the substantive criteria by which they are supposedly to decide the ecclesiastical question. But this is exactly the inquiry that the First Amendment prohibits; recognition of such an exception would undermine the general rule that religious controversies are not the proper subject of civil court inquiry, and that a civil court must accept the ecclesiastical decisions of church tribunals as it finds them. *Watson* itself requires our conclusion in its rejection of the analogous argument that ecclesiastical decisions of the highest church judicatories need only be accepted if the subject matter of the dispute is within their "jurisdiction."

"But it is a very different thing where a subject-matter of dispute, strictly and purely ecclesiastical in its character,—a matter over which the civil courts ⊥714 exercise no jurisdiction,—*a matter which concerns theological controversy, church discipline, ecclesiastical government, or the conformity of the members of the church to the standard of morals required of them*,—becomes the subject of its action. It may be said here, also, that no jurisdiction has been conferred on the tribunal to try the particular case before it, or that, in its judgment, it exceeds the powers conferred upon it, or that the laws of the church do not authorize the particular form of proceeding adopted; and, in a sense often used in the courts, all of those may be said to be quotations of jurisdiction. But it is easy to see that *if the civil courts are to inquire into all these matters, the whole subject of the doctrinal theology, the usages and customs, the written laws, and fundamental organization of every religious denomination may, and must, be examined into with minuteness and care, for they would become, in almost every case, the* criteria *by which the validity of the ecclesiastical decree would be determined in the civil court. This principle would deprive these bodies of the right of construing their own church laws,* would open the way to all the evils which we have depicted as attendant upon the doctrine of Lord Eldon, *and would, in effect, transfer to the civil courts where property rights were concerned the decision of all ecclesiastical questions.*" (Emphasis supplied.)

Indeed, it is the essence of religious faith that ecclesiastical decisions are reached and are to be accepted as matters of faith whether or not rational or measurable by ⊥**715** objective criteria. Constitutional concepts of due process, involving secular notions of "fundamental fairness" or impermissible objectives, are therefore hardly relevant to such matters of ecclesiastical cognizance.

The constitutional evils that attend upon any "arbitrariness" exception in the sense applied by the Illinois Supreme Court to justify civil court review of ecclesiastical decisions of final church tribunals are manifest in the instant case. The Supreme Court of Illinois recognized that all parties agree that the Serbian Orthodox Church is a hierarchical church, and that the sole power to appoint and remove Bishops of the Church resides in its highest ranking organs, the Holy Assembly and the Holy Synod. Indeed, final authority with respect to the ⊥**716** promulgation and interpretation of all matters of church discipline and internal organization rests with the Holy Assembly. . . . ⊥**717** Nor is there any dispute that questions of church discipline and the composition of the church hierarchy are at the core of ecclesiastical concern; the Bishop of a church is clearly one of the central figures in such a hierarchy and the embodiment of the church within his diocese, and the Mother Church constitution states that [h]e is, according to the church canonical regulations, chief representative and guiding leader of all spiritual life and church order in the diocese." Article 13.

Yet having recognized that the Serbian Eastern Church is hierarchical and that the decisions to suspend and ⊥**718** defrock respondent Dionisije were made by the religious bodies in whose sole discretion the authority to make those ecclesiastical decisions was vested, the Supreme Court of Illinois nevertheless invalidated the decision to defrock Dionisije on the ground that it was "arbitrary" because a "detailed review of the evidence discloses that the proceedings resulting in Bishop Dionisije's removal and defrockment were not in accordance with the prescribed procedure of the constitution and the penal code of the Serbian Orthodox Church." Not only was this "detailed review" impermissible under the First and Fourteenth Amendments, but in reaching this conclusion, the court evaluated conflicting testimony concerning internal church procedures and rejected the interpretations of relevant procedural provisions by the Mother Church's highest tribunals. The court also failed to take cognizance of the fact that the church judicatories were also guided by other sources of law, such as canon law, which are admittedly not always consistent, and it rejected the testimony of petitioners' five expert witnesses that church procedures were properly followed, denigrating the testimony of one witness as contradictory and discounting that of another on the ground that it was "premised upon an assumption which did not consider the penal code," even though there was some question whether that code even applied to discipline of Bishops. The court ⊥**719** accepted, on the other hand, the testimony of respondents' sole expert witness that the Church's procedures had been contravened in various specifics. We need not, and under the First Amendment cannot, demonstrate the propriety or impropriety of each of Dionisije's procedural claims, but we can note that the state court even rejected petitioners' contention that Dionisije's failure to participate in the proceedings undermined all procedural contentions because Arts. 66 and 70 of the penal code specify that if a person charged with a violation fails to participate or answer the indictment, the allegations are admitted and due process will be concluded without his participation; the court merely asserted that "application of this provision . . . must be viewed from the perspective that Bishop Dionisije refused to participate because he maintained that the proceedings against him were in violation of the constitution and the penal code of the Serbian Orthodox Church." The court found no support in any church dogma for this judicial rewriting of church law, and compounded further the error of this intrusion into a religious thicket by declaring that although Dionisije had, even under the court's analysis, been properly suspended and replaced by Firmilian as temporary administrator, he must be reinstated as Bishop because church law mandated a trial on ecclesiastical charges within one year of the indictment. Yet the only reason more time than that had expired was due to Dionisije's decision to resort to the civil courts for redress without attempting to vindicate himself by pursuing available ⊥**720** remedies within the church. Indeed, the Illinois Supreme Court overlooked the clear substantive canonical violations for which the church disciplined Dionisije, violations based on Dionisije's conceded open defiance and rebellion against the church hierarchy immediately after the Holy Assembly's decision to suspend him (a decision which even the Illinois courts deemed to be proper) and Dionisije's decision to litigate the Mother Church's authority in the civil courts rather than participate in the disciplinary proceedings before the Holy Synod and the Holy Assembly. Instead, the Illinois Supreme Court would sanction this circumvention of the tribunals set up to resolve internal church disputes and has ordered the Mother Church to reinstate as Bishop one who espoused views regarded by the church hierarchy to be schismatic and which the proper church tribunals have already determined merit severe sanctions. In short, under the guise of "minimal" review under the umbrella of "arbitrariness," the Illinois Supreme Court has unconstitutionally undertaken the resolution of quintessentially religious controversies whose resolution the First Amendment commits exclusively to the highest ecclesiastical tribunals of this hierarchical church. And although the Diocesan Bishop controls respondent Monastery of St. Sava and is the principal officer of respondent property-holding corporations, the civil courts must accept that consequence as the incidental effect of an ecclesiastical determination that is not subject to judicial abrogation, having been reached by the final church judicatory in which authority to make the decision resides.

III

Similar considerations inform our resolution of the second question we must address—the constitutionality of the Supreme Court of Illinois' holding that the Mother Church's reorganization of the American-Canadian Dio⊥**721**cese into three Dioceses was invalid because it was "in clear and palpable excess of its own jurisdiction." Essentially, the court premised this determination on its view that the early history of the Diocese "manifested a clear intention to retain independence and autonomy in its administrative affairs while at the same time becoming ecclesiastically and judicially an organic part of the Serbian Orthodox Church," and its interpretation of the constitution of the American-Canadian Diocese as confirming this intention. It also interpreted the constitution of the Serbian Orthodox Church, which was adopted after the Diocesan constitution, in a manner consistent with this conclusion.

This conclusion was not, however, explicitly based on the "fraud, collusion, or arbitrariness" exception. Rather the Illinois Supreme Court relied on purported "neutral principles" for resolving property disputes which would "not entangle this court in the determination of theological or doctrinal matters." Nevertheless the Supreme Court of Illinois substituted its interpretation of the Diocesan and Mother Church constitutions for that of the highest ecclesiastical tribunals in which church law vests authority to make that interpretation. This the First and Fourteenth Amendments forbid.

We will not delve into the various church constitutional provisions relevant to this conclusion, for that would repeat the error of the Illinois Supreme Court. It suffices to note that the reorganization of the Diocese involves a matter of internal church government, an issue at the core of ecclesiastical affairs; Arts. 57 and 64 of the Mother Church constitution commit such questions of church polity to the final province of the Holy Assembly. *Kedroff* v. *St. Nicholas Cathedral* stated that religious freedom encompasses the ⊥**722** "power [of religious bodies] to decide for themselves, free from state interference, matters of church government as well as those of faith and doctrine." The subordination of the Diocese to the Mother Church in such matters, which are not only "administrative," but also "hierarchical," was provided, and the power of the Holy Assembly to reorganize the Diocese is expressed in the Mother Church constitution. Contrary to the interpretation of the Illinois court, the church judicatories interpreted the provisions of the Diocesan constitution not to interdict or govern this action, but only to relate to the day-to-day administration of Diocesan property. ⊥**723** The constitutional provisions of the American-Canadian Diocese were not so express that the civil courts could enforce them without engaging in a searching and therefore impermissible inquiry into church polity. See *Md. and Va. Churches* v. *Sharpsburg Church*.

The control of Diocesan property may be little affected by the changes; respondents' allegation that the reorganization was a fraudulent subterfuge to divert Diocesan property from its intended beneficiaries has been rejected by the Illinois courts. Formal title to the property remains in respondent property-holding corporations, to be held in trust for all members of the new Dioceses. The boundaries of the reorganized Dioceses generally conform to the episcopal districts which the American-Canadian Diocese had already employed for its internal government, and the appointed administrators of the new Dioceses were the same individuals nominated by Dionisije as assistant bishops to govern similar divisions under him. Indeed, even the Illinois courts' rationale that the reorganization would effectuate an abrogation of the Diocesan constitution has no support in the record, which establishes rather that the details of the reorganization and any decisions pertaining to a distribution of ⊥**724** the property among the three Dioceses were expressly left for the Diocesan National Assembly to determine. In response to inquiries from the Diocese, the Holy Assembly assured Bishop Firmilian:

"1. That all the rights of the former American-Canadian Diocese, as they relate to the autonomy in the administrative sense, remain unchanged. The only exception is the forming of three dioceses and

"2. That the Constitution of the former American-Canadian Diocese remains the same and that the Dioceses in America and Canada will not, in an administrative sense, the management *(or direction)* of the properties be managed *(or directed)* in the same manner as those in Yugoslavia."

As a practical matter the effect of the reorganization is a tripling of the Diocesan representational strength in the Holy Assembly and a decentralization of hierarchical authority to permit closer attention to the needs of individual congregations within each of the new Dioceses, a result which Dionisije and Diocesan representatives had already concluded was necessary. Whether corporate bylaws or other documents governing the individual property-holding corporations may affect any desired disposition of the Diocesan property is a question not before us.

IV

In short, the First and Fourteenth Amendments permit hierarchical religious organizations to establish their own rules and regulations for internal discipline and government, and to create tribunals for adjudicating disputes over these matters. When this choice is exercised and ecclesiastical tribunals are created to decide disputes over ⊥**725** the government and direction of subordinate bodies, the Constitution requires that civil courts accept their decisions as binding upon them.

Reversed.

The CHIEF JUSTICE concurs in the judgment.

Mr. *Justice WHITE*, concurring.

Major predicates for the Court's opinion are that the Serbian Orthodox Church is a hierarchical church and the American and Canadian diocese, involved here, is part of that church. These basic issues are for the courts' ultimate decision, and the fact that church authorities may render their opinions on them does not foreclose the courts from coming to their independent judgment. I do not understand the Court's opinion to suggest otherwise and join the views expressed therein.

Mr. *Justice REHNQUIST*, with whom Mr. *Justice STEVENS* joins, dissenting.

The Court's opinion, while long on the ecclesiastical history of the Serbian Orthodox Church, is somewhat short on the procedural history of this case. A casual reader of some of the passages in the Court's opinion could easily gain the impression that the State of Illinois had commenced a proceeding designed to brand Bishop Firmilian as a heretic, with appropriate pains and penalties. But the state trial judge in the Circuit Court of Lake County was not the Bishop of Beauvais, trying Joan of Arc for heresy; the jurisdiction of his court was invoked by petitioners themselves, who sought an injunction establishing their control over property of the American-Canadian Diocese of the church located in Lake County.

The jurisdiction of that court having been invoked ⊥**726** for such a purpose by both petitioners and respondents, contesting claimants to diocesan authority, it was entitled to ask if the real bishop of the American-Canadian diocese would please stand up. The protracted proceedings in the Illinois courts were devoted to the ascertainment of who that individual was, a question which the Illinois courts sought to answer by application of the canon law of the church, just as they would have attempted to decide a similar dispute among the members of any other voluntary association. The Illinois courts did not in the remotest sense inject their doctrinal preference into the dispute. They were forced to decide between two competing sets of claimants to church office in order that they might resolve a dispute over real property located within the State. Each of the claimants had requested them to decide the issue. Unless the First Amendment requires control of disputed church property to be awarded solely on the basis of ecclesiastical paper title, I can find no constitutional infirmity in the judgment of the Supreme Court of Illinois.

Unless civil courts are to be wholly divested of authority to resolve conflicting claims to real property owned by a hierarchical church, and such claims are to be resolved by brute force, civil courts must of necessity make some factual inquiry even under the rules the Court purports to apply in this case. We are told that "a civil court must accept the ecclesiastical decisions of church tribunals as it finds them." But even this rule requires that proof be made as to what these decisions are, and if proofs on that issue conflict the civil court will inevitably have to choose one over the other. In so choosing, if the choice is to be a rational one, reasons must be adduced as to why one proffered decision is to prevail over another. Such reasons will ⊥**727** obviously be based on the canon law by which the disputants have agreed to bind themselves, but they must also represent a preference for one view of that law over another.

If civil courts, consistently with the First Amendment may do that much, the question arises why they may not do what the Illinois courts did here regarding the defrockment of Bishop Dionisije, and conclude, on the basis of testimony from experts on the canon law at issue, that the decision of the religious tribunal involved was rendered in violation of its own stated rules of procedure. Suppose the Holy Assembly in this case had a membership of 100; its rules provided that a bishop could be defrocked by a majority vote of any session at which a quorum was present, and also provided that a quorum was not to be less than 40. Would a decision of the Holy Assembly attended by 30 members, 16 of whom voted to defrock Bishop Dionisije, be binding on civil courts in a dispute such as this? The hypothetical example is a clearer case than the one involved here, but the principle is the same. If the civil courts are to be bound by any sheet of parchment bearing the ecclesiastical seal and purporting to be a decree of a church court, they can easily be converted into handmaidens of arbitrary lawlessness.

The cases upon which the Court relies are not a uniform line of authorities leading inexorably to reversal of the Illinois judgment. On the contrary, they embody two distinct doctrines which have quite separate origins. The first is a common-law doctrine regarding the appropriate roles for civil courts called upon to adjudicate church property disputes—a doctrine which found general application in federal courts prior to *Erie R. Co.* v. *Tompkins*, but which has never had any application to our review of a state-court ⊥**728** decision. The other is derived from the First Amendment to the Federal Constitution, and is of course applicable to this case; it, however, lends no more support to the Court's decision than does the common-law doctrine.

The first decision of this Court regarding the role of civil courts in adjudicating church property disputes was *Watson* v. *Jones*. There the Court canvassed the American authorities and concluded that where people had chosen to organize themselves into voluntary religious associations, and had agreed to be bound by the decisions of the hierarchy created to govern such associations, the civil courts could not be availed of to hear appeals from otherwise final decisions of such hierarchical authorities. The bases from which this principle was derived clearly had no constitutional dimension; there was not the slightest suggestion that the First Amendment or any other provision of the Constitution was relevant to the decision in that case. Instead the Court was merely recognizing and applying general rules as to the limited role which civil courts must have in settling private intraorganizational disputes. While those rules, and the reasons behind them, may seem especially relevant to intrachurch disputes, adherence or nonadherence to such principles was certainly not thought to present any First Amendment issues. For as the Court in *Watson* observed:

"Religious organizations come before us in the same attitude as other voluntary associations for benevolent or charitable purposes, and their rights of property, or of contract, are equally under the protection of the law, and the actions of their members subject to its restraints."

The Court's equation of religious bodies with other private voluntary associations makes it clear that the prin⊥**729**ciples discussed in that case were not dependent upon those embodied in the First Amendment.

A year later *Watson's* observations about the roles of civil courts were followed in *Bouldin* v. *Alexander*, where the Court held that the appointed trustees of the property of a congregational church "cannot be removed from their trusteeship by a minority of the church society or meeting, without warning, and acting without charges, without citation or trial, and in direct contravention of the church rules."

Again, there was nothing to suggest that this was based upon anything but commonsense rules for deciding an intraorganizational dispute; in an organization which has provided for majority rule through certain procedures, a minority's attempt to usurp that rule and those procedures need be given no effect by civil courts.

In *Gonzalez* v. *Archbishop*, the Court again recognized the principles underlying *Watson* in upholding a decision of the Supreme Court of the Philippine Islands that the petitioner was not entitled to the chaplaincy which he claimed because the decision as to whether he possessed the necessary qualifications for that post was one committed to the appropriate church authorities. In dicta which the Court today conveniently truncates, Mr. *Justice BRANDEIS* observed:

"In the absence of fraud, collusion, or arbitrariness, the decisions of the proper church tribunals on matters purely ecclesiastical, although affecting civil rights, are accepted in litigation before the secular courts as conclusive, *because the parties in interest made them so by contract or otherwise. Under like circumstances, effect is given in the courts to the determinations of the judicatory bodies estab*⊥**730***lished by clubs and civil associations*" (emphasis supplied).

Gonzalez clearly has no more relevance to the meaning of the First Amendment than do its two predecessors.

The year 1952 was the first occasion on which this Court examined what limits the First and Fourth Amendments might place upon the ability of the States to entertain and resolve disputes over church property. In *Kedroff* v. *St. Nicholas Cathedral*, the Court reversed a decision of the New York Court of Appeals which had upheld a statute awarding control of the New York property of the Russian Orthodox Church to an American group seeking to terminate its relationships with the hierarchical Mother Church in Russia. The New York Legislature had concluded that the communist government of Russia was actually in control of the Mother Church and that "the Moscow patriarchate was no longer capable of functioning as a true religious body, but had become a tool of the Soviet Government primarily designed to implement its foreign policy," and the New York Court of Appeals sustained the statute against the constitutional attack. This Court, however, held the statute was a violation of the Free Exercise Clause, noting that it [b]y fiat . . . displaces one church administrator with another. It passes the control of matters strictly ecclesiastical from one church authority to another. It thus intrudes for the benefit of one segment of a church the power of the state into the forbidden area of religious freedom contrary to the principles of the First Amendment."

On remand from the decision in *Kedroff*, the New York Court of Appeals again held that the American ⊥**731** group was entitled to the church property at issue. This time relying upon the common law of the State, the Court of Appeals ruled that the Moscow Patriarchate was so dominated by the secular government of Russia that his appointee could not validly occupy the Church's property. On appeal, this Court reversed summarily, noting in its *per curiam* that "the decision now under review rests on the same premises which were found to have underlain the enactment of the statute struck down in *Kedroff*."

Nine years later, in *Presbyterian Church in the United States v. Mary Elizabeth Blue Hull Memorial Presbyterian Church*, the Court held that Georgia's common law, which implied a trust upon local church property for the benefit of the general church only on the condition that the general church adhere to its tenets of faith and practice existing at the time of affiliation by the local churches, was inconsistent with the First and Fourteenth Amendments and therefore could not be utilized to resolve church property disputes. The Georgia law was held impermissible because "[u]nder [the Georgia] approach, property rights do not turn on a church decision as to church doctrine. The standard of departure-from-doctrine, though it calls for resolution of ecclesiastical questions, is a creation of state, not church, law."

Finally, in *Maryland & Virginia Eldership of the Churches of God v. Church of God at Sharpsburg, Inc.*, the Court considered an appeal from a judgment of the Court of Appeals of Maryland upholding the dismissal of two actions brought by the Eldership seeking to prevent two of its local churches from withdrawing from that general religious association. The Eldership had also claimed the rights to select the ⊥**732** clergy and to control the property of the two local churches, but the Maryland courts, relying "upon provisions of the state statutory law governing the holding of property by religious corporations, upon language in the deeds conveying the properties in question to the local church corporations, upon the terms of the charters of the corporations, *and upon provisions in the constitution of the General Eldership pertinent to the ownership and control of church property*," (emphasis supplied), concluded that the Eldership had no right to invoke the State's authority to compel their local churches to remain within the fold or to succeed to control of their property. This Court dismissed the Eldership's contention that this judgment violated the First Amendment for want of a substantial federal question.

Despite the Court's failure to do so, it does not seem very difficult to derive the operative constitutional principle from this line of decisions. As should be clear from even this cursory study, *Watson*, *Bouldin*, and *Gonzalez* have no direct relevance to the question before us today: ⊥**733** whether the First Amendment, as made applicable to the States by the Fourteenth, prohibits Illinois from permitting its civil courts to settle religious property disputes in the manner presented to us on this record. I think it equally clear that the only cases which are relevant to that question— *Kedroff*, *Kreshik*, *Blue Hull*, and *Md. & Va. Churches*—require that this question be answered in the negative. The rule of those cases, one which seems fairly implicit in the history of our First Amendment, is that the government may not displace the free religious choices of its citizens by placing its weight behind a particular religious belief, tenet, or sect. That is what New York attempted to do in *Kedroff* and *Kreshik*, albeit perhaps for nonreligious reasons, and the Court refused to permit it. In *Blue Hull*, the State transgressed the line drawn by the First Amendment when it applied a state-created rule of law based upon "departure from doctrine" to prevent the national hierarchy of the Presbyterian Church in the United States from seeking to reclaim possession and use of two local churches. When the Georgia courts themselves required an examination into whether there had been a departure from the doctrine of the church in order to apply this state-created rule, they went beyond mere application of neutral principles of law to such a dispute.

There is nothing in this record to indicate that the Illinois courts have been instruments of any such impermissible intrusion by the State on one side or the other of a religious dispute. There is nothing in the Supreme Court of Illinois' opinion indicating that it placed its thumb on the scale in favor of the respondents. Instead that opinion appears to be precisely what it pur⊥**734**ports to be: an application of neutral principles of law consistent with the decisions of this Court. Indeed, petitioners make absolutely no claim to the contrary. They agree that the Illinois courts should have decided the issues which they presented; but they contend that in doing so those courts should have deferred entirely to the representations of the announced representatives of the Mother Church. Such blind deference, however, is counselled neither by logic nor by the First Amendment. To make available the coercive powers of civil courts to rubber-stamp ecclesiastical decisions of hierarchical religious associations, when such deference is not accorded similar acts of secular voluntary associations, would, in avoiding the Free Exercise problems petitioners envision, itself create far more serious problems under the Establishment Clause.

In any event the Court's decision in *Md. & Va. Churches* demonstrates that petitioners' position in this regard is untenable. And as I read that decision, it seems to me to compel affirmance of at least that portion of the Illinois court's decision which denied petitioners' request for the aid of the civil courts in enforcing its desire to divide the American-Canadian diocese. I see no distinction between the Illinois courts' refusal to place their weight behind the representatives of the Serbian Mother Church who sought to prevent portions of their American congregation from splitting off from that body and the Maryland courts' refusal to do the same thing for the Eldership of the Church of God. The Court today expressly eschews any explanation for its failure to follow *Md & Va. Churches*, contenting itself with this conclusory statement:

"The constitutional provisions of the American-Canadian Diocese were not so express that the civil ⊥**735** courts could enforce them without engaging in a searching and therefore impermissible inquiry into church polity."

But comparison of the relevant discussions by the state tribunals regarding their consideration of church documents makes this claimed distinction seem quite specious.

In conclusion, while there may be a number of good arguments that civil courts of a State should, as a matter of the wisest use of their authority, avoid adjudicating religious disputes to the maximum extent possible, they obviously cannot avoid all such adjudications. And while common-law principles like those discussed in *Watson*, *Bouldin*, and *Gonzalez* may offer some sound principles for those occasions when such adjudications are required, they are certainly not rules to which state courts are required to adhere by virtue of the Fourteenth Amendment. The principles which that Amendment, through its incorporation of the First, *does* enjoin upon the state courts—that they remain neutral on matters of religious doctrine—have not been transgressed by the Supreme Court of Illinois.

JONES v. WOLF

443 U.S. 595
ON WRIT OF CERTIORARI TO THE SUPREME COURT OF THE STATE OF GEORGIA
Argued January 16, 1979 — Decided July 2, 1979

⊥597 Mr. *Justice BLACKMUN* delivered the opinion of the Court.

This case involves a dispute over the ownership of church property following a schism in a local church affiliated with a hierarchical church organization. The question for decision is whether civil courts, consistent with the First and Fourteenth Amendments to the Constitution, may resolve the dispute on the basis of "neutral principles of law," or whether they must defer to the resolution of an authoritative tribunal of the hierarchical church.

I

The Vineville Presbyterian Church of Macon, Ga., was organized in 1904, and first incorporated in 1915. Its corporate charter lapsed in 1935, but was revived and renewed in 1939, and continues in effect at the present time.

The property at issue and on which the church is located was acquired in three transactions, and is evidenced by conveyances to the "Trustees of [or 'for'] Vineville Presbyterian Church and their successors in office," or simply to the "Vineville Presbyterian Church." The funds used to acquire the property were contributed entirely by local church members. Pursuant to resolutions adopted by the congregation, the church repeatedly has borrowed money on the property. This indebtedness is evidenced by security deeds variously issued in the name of the "Trustees of the Vineville Presbyterian Church."

In the same year it was organized, the Vineville church was established as a member church of the Augusta-Macon Presbytery of the Presbyterian Church in the United States (PCUS). The PCUS has a generally hierarchical or connec⊥598tional form of government, as contrasted with a congregational form. Under the polity of the PCUS, the government of the local church is committed to its Session in the first instance, but the actions of this assembly or "court" are subject to the review and control of the higher church courts, the Presbytery, Synod, and General Assembly, respectively. The powers and duties of each level of the hierarchy are set forth in the constitution of the PCUS, the Book of Church Order, which is part of the record in the present case.

On May 27, 1973, at a congregational meeting of the Vineville church attended by a quorum of its duly enrolled members, 164 of them, including the pastor, voted to separate from the PCUS. Ninety-four members opposed the resolution. The majority immediately informed the PCUS of the action, and then united with another denomination, the Presbyterian Church in America. Although the minority remained on the church rolls for three years, they ceased to participate in the affairs of the Vineville church and conducted their religious activities elsewhere.

In response to the schism within the Vineville congregation, the Augusta-Macon Presbytery appointed a commission to investigate the dispute and, if possible, to resolve it. The commission eventually issued a written ruling declaring that the minority faction constituted "the true congregation of Vineville Presbyterian Church," and withdrawing from the majority faction "all authority to exercise office derived from the [PCUS]." The majority took no part in the commission's inquiry, and did not appeal its ruling to a higher PCUS tribunal.

Representatives of the minority faction sought relief in federal court, but their complaint was dismissed for want of jurisdiction. *Lucas* v. *Hope*, cert. denied. They then brought this class action in state court, seeking declaratory and injunctive orders establishing their right to exclusive possession and use of the ⊥599 Vineville church property as a member congregation of the PCUS. The trial court, purporting to apply Georgia's "neutral principles of law" approach to church property disputes, granted judgment for the majority. The Supreme Court of Georgia, holding that the trial court had correctly stated and applied Georgia law, and rejecting the minority's challenge based on the First and Fourteenth Amendment, affirmed. We granted a writ of certiorari.

II

Georgia's approach to church property litigation has evolved in response to *Presbyterian Church* v. *Hull Church (Presbyterian Church I)*, rev'g *Presbyterian Church* v. *Eastern Heights Church*. That case was a property dispute between the PCUS and two local Georgia churches that had withdrawn from the PCUS. The Georgia Supreme Court resolved the controversy by applying a theory of implied trust, whereby the property of a local church affiliated with a hierarchical church organization was deemed to be held in trust for the general church, provided the general church had not "substantially abandoned" the tenets of faith and practice as they existed at the time of affiliation. This Court reversed, holding that Georgia would have to find some other way of resolving church property disputes that did not draw the state courts into religious controversies. The Court did not specify what that method should be, although it noted in passing that "there are neutral principles of law, developed for use in all property disputes, which can be applied without 'establishing' churches to which property is awarded." 393 U.S., at 449.

⊥600 On remand, the Georgia Supreme Court concluded that, without the departure-from-doctrine element, the implied trust theory would have to be abandoned in its entirety. *Presbyterian Church* v. *Eastern Heights Church (Presbyterian Church II)*. In its place, the court adopted what is now known as the "neutral principles of law" method for resolving church property disputes. The court examined the deeds to the properties, the state statutes dealing with implied trusts, Ga. Code §§ 108-106, 108-107, and the Book of Church Order, to determine whether there was any basis for a trust in favor of the general church. Finding nothing that would give rise to a trust in any of these documents, the court awarded the property on the basis of the legal title, which was in the local church, or in the names of trustees for the local church. Review was again sought in this Court, but was denied.

The neutral principles analysis was further refined by the Georgia Supreme Court in *Carnes* v. *Smith*. That case concerned a property dispute between The United Methodist Church and a local congregation that had withdrawn from that church. As in *Presbyterian Church II*, the court found no basis for a trust in favor of the general church in the deeds, the corporate charter, or the state statutes dealing with implied trusts. The court observed, however, that the constitution of The United Methodist Church, its Book of Discipline, contained an express trust provision in favor of the general church. On this basis, the church property was ⊥**601** awarded to the denominational church.

In the present case, the Georgia courts sought to apply the neutral principles analysis of *Presbyterian Church II* and *Carnes* to the facts presented by the Vineville church controversy. Here, as in those two earlier cases, the deeds conveyed the property to the local church. Here, as in the earlier cases, neither the state statutes dealing with implied trusts, nor the corporate charter of the Vineville church, indicated that the general church had any interest in the property. And here, as in *Presbyterian Church II*, but in contrast to *Carnes*, the provisions of the constitution of the general church, the Book of Church Order, concerning the ownership and control of property failed to reveal any language of trust in favor of the general church. The courts accordingly held that legal title to the property of the Vineville church was vested in the local congregation. Without further analysis or elaboration, they further decreed that the local congregation was represented by the majority faction, respondents herein.

⊥**602** III

The only question presented by this case is which faction of the formerly united Vineville congregation is entitled to possess and enjoy the property located at 2193 Vineville Avenue in Macon, Ga. There can be little doubt about the general authority of civil courts to resolve this question. The State has an obvious and legitimate interest in the peaceful resolution of property disputes, and in providing a civil forum where the ownership of church property can be determined conclusively.

It is also clear, however, that "the First Amendment severely circumscribes the role that civil courts may play in resolving church property disputes." Most importantly, the First Amendment prohibits civil courts from resolving church property disputes on the basis of religious doctrine and practice. *Serbian Orthodox Diocese* v. *Milivojevich; Md. & Va. Churches* v. *Sharpsburg Church, Presbyterian Church I*. As a corollary to this commandment, the Amendment requires that civil courts defer to the resolution of issues of religious doctrine or polity by the highest court of a hierarchical church organization. *Serbian Orthodox Diocese*, cf. *Watson* v. *Jones*. Subject to these limitations, however, the First Amendment does not dictate that a State must follow a particular method of resolving church property disputes. Indeed, "a State may adopt *any* one of various approaches for settling church property disputes so long as it involves no consideration of doctrinal matters, whether the ritual and liturgy of worship or the tenets of faith." *Md. & Va. Churches* (Brennan, J., concurring) (emphasis in original).

At least in general outline, we think the "neutral principles of law" approach is consistent with the foregoing constitutional principles. The neutral principles approach was ap⊥**603**proved in *Md. & Va. Churches*, an appeal from a judgment of the Court of Appeals of Maryland settling a local church property dispute on the basis of the language of the deeds, the terms of the local church charters, the state statutes governing the holding of church property, and the provisions in the constitution of the general church concerning the ownership and control of church property. Finding that this analysis entailed "no inquiry into religious doctrine," the Court dismissed the appeal for want of a substantial federal question. "Neutral principles of law" also received approving reference in *Presbyterian Church I*; in Mr. Justice BRENNAN's concurrence in *Md. &Va. Churches;* and in *Serbian Orthodox Diocese*.

The primary advantages of the neutral principles approach are that it is completely secular in operation, and yet flexible enough to accommodate all forms of religious organization and polity. The method relies exclusively on objective, well-established concepts of trust and property law familiar to lawyers and judges. It thereby promises to free civil courts completely from entanglement in questions of religious doctrine, polity, and practice. Furthermore, the neutral principles analysis shares the peculiar genius of private-law systems in general—flexibility in ordering private rights and obligations to reflect the intentions of the parties. Through appropriate reversionary clauses and trust provisions, religious societies can specify what is to happen to church property in the event of a particular contingency, or what religious body will determine the ownership in the event of a schism or doctrinal controversy. In this manner, a religious organization ⊥**604** can ensure that a dispute over the ownership of church property will be resolved in accord with the desires of the members.

This is not to say that the application of the neutral principles approach is wholly free of difficulty. The neutral principles method, at least as it has evolved in Georgia, requires a civil court to examine certain religious documents, such as a church constitution, for language of trust in favor of the general church. In undertaking such an examination, a civil court must take special care to scrutinize the document in purely secular terms, and not to rely on religious precepts in determining whether the document indicates that the parties have intended to create a trust. In addition, there may be cases where the deed, the corporate charter, or the constitution of the general church incorporates religious concepts in the provisions relating to the ownership of property. If in such a case the interpretation of the instruments of ownership would require the civil court to resolve a religious controversy, then the court must defer to the resolution of the doctrinal issue by the authoritative ecclesiastical body. *Serbian Orthodox Diocese*.

On balance, however, the promise of nonentanglement and neutrality inherent in the neutral principles approach more than compensates for what will be occasional problems in application. These problems, in addition, should be gradually eliminated as recognition is given to the obligation of "States, religious organizations, and individuals [to] structure relationships involving church property so as not to require the civil courts to resolve ecclesiastical questions." *Presbyterian Church I*. We therefore hold that a State is constitutionally entitled to adopt neutral principles of law as a means of adjudicating a church property dispute.

The dissent would require the States to abandon the neutral principles method, and instead would insist as a matter of constitutional law that whenever a dispute arises over the ⊥**605** ownership of church property, civil courts must defer to the "authoritative resolution of the dispute within the church itself." It would require, first, that civil courts review ecclesiastical doctrine and polity to determine where the church has "placed ultimate authority over the use of the church property." After answering this question, the courts would be required to "determine whether the dispute has been resolved within that structure of government and, if so, what decision has been made." They would then be required to enforce that decision. We cannot agree, however, that the First Amendment requires the States to adopt a rule of compulsory deference to religious authority in resolving church property disputes, even where no issue of doctrinal controversy is involved.

The dissent suggests that a rule of compulsory deference would somehow involve less entanglement of civil courts in matters of religious doctrine, practice, and administration. Under its approach, however, civil courts would always be required to examine the polity and administration of a church to determine which unit of government has ultimate control over church property. In some cases, this task would not prove to be difficult. But in others, the locus of control would be ambiguous, and "A careful examination of the constitutions of the general and local church, as well as other relevant documents, [would] be necessary to ascertain the form of governance adopted by the members of the religious association." In such cases, the suggested rule would appear to require "a searching and therefore impermissible inquiry into church polity." *Serbian Orthodox Diocese*. The neutral principles approach, in contrast, obviates entirely the need for an analysis or examination of ecclesiastical polity or doctrine in settling church property disputes.

The dissent also argues that a rule of compulsory deference is necessary in order to protect the free exercise rights "of ⊥**606** those who have formed the association and submitted themselves to its authority." This argument assumes that the neutral principles method would somehow frustrate the free exercise rights of the members of a religious association. Nothing could be further from the truth. The neutral principles approach cannot be said to "inhibit" the free exercise of religion, any more than do other neutral provisions of state law governing the manner in which churches own property, hire employees, or purchase goods. Under the neutral principles approach, the outcome of a church property dispute is not foreordained. At any time before the dispute erupts, the parties can ensure, if they so desire, that the faction loyal to the hierarchical church will retain the church property. They can modify the deeds or the corporate charter to include a right of reversion or trust in favor of the general church. Alternatively, the constitution of the general church can be made to recite an express trust in favor of the denominational church. The burden involved in taking such steps will be minimal. And the civil courts will be bound to give effect to the result indicated by the parties, provided it is embodied in some legally cognizable form.

IV

It remains to be determined whether the Georgia neutral principles analysis was constitutionally applied on the facts of this case. Although both the trial court and the Supreme Court of Georgia viewed the case as involving nothing more than an application of the principles developed in *Presbyterian Church II* and in *Carnes*, the present case contains a significant complicating factor absent in each of those earlier cases. *Presbyterian Church II* and *Carnes* each involved a ⊥**607** church property dispute between the general church and the entire local congregation. Here, the local congregation was itself divided between a majority of 164 members who sought to withdraw from the PCUS, and a minority of 94 members who wished to maintain the affiliation. Neither of the state courts alluded to this problem, however; each concluded without discussion or analysis that the title to the property was in the local church and that the local church was represented by the majority rather than the minority.

Petitioners earnestly submit that the question of which faction is the true representative of the Vineville church is an ecclesiastical question that cannot be answered by a civil court. At least, it is said, it cannot be answered by a civil court in a case involving a hierarchical church, like the PCUS, where a duly appointed church commission has determined which of the two factions represents the "true congregation." Respondents, in opposition, argue in effect that the Georgia courts did no more than apply the ordinary presumption that, absent some indication to the contrary, a voluntary religious association is represented by a majority of its members.

If in fact Georgia has adopted a presumptive rule of majority representation, defeasible upon a showing that the identity of the local church is to be determined by some other means, we think this would be consistent with both the neutral principles analysis and the First Amendment. Majority rule is generally employed in the governance of religious societies. See *Bouldin* v. *Alexander*. Furthermore, the majority faction generally can be identified without resolving any question of religious doctrine or polity. Certainly, there was no dispute in the present case about the identity of the duly enrolled members of the Vineville church when the dispute arose, or about the fact that a quorum was present, or about the final vote. Most importantly, any rule of majority representation can always be overcome, under the neutral principles approach, either by providing, in the corporate ⊥**608** charter or the constitution of the general church, that the identity of the local church is to be established in some other way, or by providing that the church property is held in trust for the general church and those who remain loyal to it. Indeed, the State may adopt any method of overcoming the majoritarian presumption, so long as the use of that method does not impair free exercise rights or entangle the civil courts in matters of religious controversy.

Neither the trial court nor the Supreme Court of Georgia, however, explicitly stated that it was adopting a presumptive rule of majority representation. Moreover, there are at least some indications that under Georgia law the process of identifying the faction that represents the Vineville church involves considerations of religious doctrine and polity. Georgia law requires that "church property be held according to the terms of the church government," and provides that a local church affiliated with a hierarchical religious association "is part of the whole body of the general church and is subject to the higher authority of the organization and its law and regulations." *Carnes* v. *Smith;* ⊥**609** see Ga. Code §§ 22-5507, 22-5508. All this may suggest that the identity of the "Vineville Presbyterian Church" named in the deeds must be determined according to terms of the Book of Church Order, which sets out the laws and regulations of churches affiliated with the PCUS. Such a determination, however, would appear to require a civil court to pass on questions of religious doctrine, and to usurp the function of the commission appointed by the Presbytery, which already has determined that petitioners represent the "true congregation" of the Vineville church. Therefore, if Georgia law provides that the identity of the Vineville church is to be determined according to the "laws and regulations" of the PCUS, then the First Amendment requires that the Georgia courts give deference to the presbyterial commission's determination of that church's identity.

This Court, of course, does not declare what the law of Georgia is. Since the grounds for the decision that respond⊥**610**ents represent the Vineville church remain unarticulated, the judgment of the Supreme Court of Georgia is vacated and the case is remanded for further proceedings not inconsistent with this opinion.

It is so ordered.

Mr. Justice POWELL, with whom *The* CHIEF JUSTICE, *Mr. Justice* STEWART, and *Mr. Justice* WHITE join, dissenting.

This case presents again a dispute among church members over the control of a local church's property. Although the Court appears to accept established principles that I have thought would resolve this case, it superimposes on these principles a new structure of rules that will make the decision of these cases by civil courts more difficult. The new analysis also is more likely to invite intrusion into church polity forbidden by the First Amendment.

I

The Court begins by stating that "[t]his case involves a dispute over the ownership of church property," suggesting that the concern is with legal or equitable ownership in the real property sense. But the ownership of the property of the Vineville church is not at issue. The deeds place title in the Vineville Presbyterian Church, or in trustees of that church, and none of the parties has questioned the validity of those deeds. The question actually presented is which of the factions within the local congregation has the right to control the actions of the titleholder, and thereby to control the use of the property, as the Court later acknowledges.

Since 1872 disputes over control of church property usually have been resolved under principles established by *Watson* v. *Jones*. Under the new and complex, two-stage analysis approved today, a court instead first must apply newly defined "neutral principles of law" to determine ⊥**611** whether property titled to the local church is held in trust for the general church organization with which the local church is affiliated. If it is, then the court will grant control of the property to the councils of the general church. If not, then control by the local congregation will be recognized. In the latter situation, if there is a schism in the local congregation, as in this case, the second stage of the new analysis becomes applicable. Again, the Court fragments the analysis into two substeps for the purpose of determining which of the factions should control the property.

As this new approach inevitably will increase the involvement of civil courts in church controversies, and as it departs from long-established precedents, I dissent.

A

The first stage in the "neutral principles of law" approach operates as a restrictive rule of evidence. A court

is required to examine the deeds to the church property, the charter of the local church (if there is one), the book of order or discipline of the general church organization, and the state statutes governing the holding of church property. The object of the inquiry, where the title to the property is in the local church, is "to determine whether there [is] any basis for a trust in favor of the general church." The court's investigation is to be "completely secular," "rel[ying] exclusively on objective, well-established concepts of trust and property law familiar to lawyers and judges." Thus, where religious documents such as church constitutions or books of order must be examined "for language of trust in favor of the general church," "a civil court must take special care to scrutinize the documents in purely secular terms, and not to rely on religious precepts in determining whether the document indicates that the parties have intended to create a trust." It follows that the civil courts using this analysis may consider the form of religious govern-
⊥612 ment adopted by the church members for the resolution of intrachurch disputes only if that policy has been stated, in express relation to church property, in the language of trust and property law.

One effect of the Court's evidentiary rule is to deny to the courts relevant evidence as to the religious polity—that is, the form of governance— adopted by the church members. The constitutional documents of churches tend to be drawn in terms of religious precepts. Attempting to read them "in purely secular terms" is more likely to promote confusion than understanding. Moreover, whenever religious polity has not been expressed in specific statements referring to the property **⊥613** of a church, there will be no evidence of that polity cognizable under the neutral-principles rule. Lacking such evidence, presumably a court will impose some rule of church government derived from state law. In the present case, for example, the general and unqualified authority of the Presbytery over the actions of the Vineville church had not been expressed in secular terms of control of its property. As a consequence, the Georgia courts could find no acceptable evidence of this authoritative relationship, and they imposed instead a congregational form of government determined from state law.

This limiting of the evidence relative to religious government cannot be justified on the ground that it "free[s] civil courts completely from entanglement in questions of religious doctrine, polity, and practice." For unless the body identified as authoritative under state law resolves the underlying dispute in accord with the decision of the church's own authority, the state court effectively will have reversed the decisions of doctrine and practice made in accordance with church law. The schism in the Vineville church, for example, resulted from disagreements among the church members over questions of doctrine and practice. Under the Book of Church Order, these questions were resolved authoritatively by the higher church courts, which then gave control of the local church to the faction loyal to that resolution. The Georgia courts, as a matter of state law, granted control to the schismatic faction, and thereby effectively reversed the doctrinal decision of the church courts. This indirect interference by the civil courts with the resolution of religious disputes within the church is no less proscribed by the First Amendment than is the direct decision of questions of doctrine and practice.

⊥614 When civil courts step in to resolve intrachurch disputes over control of church property, they will either support or overturn the authoritative resolution of the dispute within the church itself. The new analysis, under the attractive banner of "neutral principles," actually invites the civil courts to do the latter. The proper rule of decision, that I thought had been settled until today, requires a court to give effect in all cases to the decisions of the church government agreed upon by the members before the dispute arose.

B

The Court's basic neutral-principles approach, as a means of isolating decisions concerning church property from other decisions made within the church, relies on the concept of a trust of local church property in favor of the general church. Because of this central premise, the neutral-principles rule suffices to settle only disputes between the central councils of a church organization and a unanimous local congregation. Where, as here, the neutral-principles inquiry reveals no trust in favor of the general church, and the local congregation is split into factions, the basic question remains unresolved: which faction should have control of the local church?

⊥615 The Court acknowledges that the church law of the Presbyterian Church in the United States (PCUS), of which the Vineville church is a part, provides for the authoritative resolution of this question by the Presbytery. Indeed, the Court indicates that Georgia, consistently with the First Amendment, may adopt the *Watson* v. *Jones* rule of adherence to the resolution of the dispute according to church law—a rule that would necessitate reversal of the judgment for the respondents. But instead of requiring the state courts to take this approach, the Court approves as well an alternative rule of state law: the Georgia courts are said to be free to "adop[t] a presumptive rule of majority representation, defeasible upon a showing that the identity of the local church is to be determined by some other means." This showing may be made by proving that the church has provid[ed], in the corporate charter or the constitution of the general church, that the identity of the local church is to be established in some other way."

On its face, this rebuttable presumption also requires reversal of the state court's judgment in favor of the schismatic faction. The polity of the PCUS commits to the Presbytery the resolution of the dispute within the local church. Having shown this structure of church government for the determination of the identity of the local congregation, the petitioners have rebutted any presumption that this question has been left to a majority vote of the local congregation.

The Court nevertheless declines to order reversal. Rather than decide the case here in accordance with established First Amendment principles, the Court leaves open the possibility that the state courts might adopt some restrictive evidentiary rule that would render the petitioners' evidence inadequate to overcome the presumption of majority control. But, aside from a passing reference to the use of the neutral-principles approach developed earlier in its ⊥**616** opinion, the Court affords no guidance as to the constitutional limitations on such an evidentiary rule; the state courts, it says, are free to adopt any rule that is constitutional.

"Indeed, the state may adopt any method of overcoming the majoritarian presumption, so long as the use of that method does not impair free exercise rights or entangle the civil courts in matters of religious controversy."

In essence, the Court's instructions on remand therefore allow the state courts the choice of following the long-settled rule of *Watson* v. *Jones* or of adopting some other rule—unspecified by the Court—that the state courts view as consistent with the First Amendment. Not only questions of state law but also important issues of federal constitutional law thus are left to the state courts for their decision, and if they depart from *Watson* v. *Jones*, they will travel a course left totally uncharted by this Court.

II

Disputes among church members over the control of church property arise almost invariably out of disagreements regarding doctrine and practice. Because of the religious nature of these disputes, civil courts should decide them according to principles that do not interfere with the free exercise of religion in accordance with church polity and doctrine. *Serbian* ⊥**617** *Orthodox Diocese* v. *Milivojevich*, *Presbyterian Church* v. *Hull Church*, *Kedroff* v. *Saint Nicholas Cathedral;* (Frankfurter, J., concurring). See also *Kreshik* v. *Saint Nicholas Cathedral; Maryland & Va. Eldership* v. *Sharpsburg Church*, appeal dismissed for want of a substantial federal question. The only course that achieves this constitutional requirement is acceptance by civil courts of the decisions reached within the polity chosen by the church members themselves. The classic statement of this view is found in *Watson* v. *Jones*.

"The right to organize voluntary religious associations to assist in the expression and dissemination of any religious doctrine, and to create tribunals for the decision of controverted questions of faith, within the association, and for the ecclesiastical government of all the individual members, congregations, and officers within the general association, is unquestioned. All who unite themselves to such a body do so with an implied consent to this government, and are bound to submit to it. But it would be a vain consent and would lead to the total subversion of such religious bodies, if any one aggrieved by one of their decisions could appeal to the secular courts and have them reversed. It is of the essence of these religious ⊥**618** unions, and of their right to establish tribunals for the decision of questions arising among themselves, that those decisions should be binding in all cases of ecclesiastical cognizance, subject only to such appeals as the organism itself provides for."

Accordingly, in each case involving an intrachurch dispute—including disputes over church property— the civil court must focus directly on ascertaining, and then following, the decision made within the structure of church governance. By doing so, the court avoids two equally unacceptable departures from the genuine neutrality mandated by the First Amendment. First, it refrains from direct review and revision of decisions of the church on matters of religious doctrine and practice that underlie the church's determination of intrachurch controversies, including those that relate to control of church property. Equally important, by recognizing the authoritative resolution reached with the religious association, the civil court avoids interfering indirectly with the religious governance of those who have formed the association and submitted themselves to its authority. See *Watson* v. *Jones; Kedroff* v. *Saint Nicholas Cathedral*.

III

Until today, and under the foregoing authorities, the first question presented in a case involving an intrachurch dispute over church property was where within the religious associa⊥**619**tion the rules of polity, accepted by its members before the schism, had placed ultimate authority over the use of the church property. The courts, in answering this question have recognized two broad categories of church government. One is congregational, in which authority over questions of church doctrine, practice, and administration rests entirely in the local congregation or some body within it. In disputes over the control and use of the property of such a church, the civil courts enforce the authoritative resolution of the controversy within the local church itself. *Watson* v. *Jones*. The second is hierarchical, in which the local church is but an integral and subordinate part of a larger church and is under the authority of the general church. Since the decisions of the local congregation are subject to review by the tribunals of the church hierarchy, this Court has held that the civil courts must give effect to the duly made decisions of the highest body within the hierarchy that has considered the dispute. As we stated in *Serbian Orthodox Diocese* v. *Milivojevich*,

"[T]he First and Fourteenth Amendments permit hierarchical religious organizations to establish their own rules and regulations for internal discipline and government, and to create tribunals for adjudicating disputes over these matters. When this choice is exercised and ecclesiastical tribunals are created to decide disputes over the government and direction of subordinate bodies, the Constitution *requires* that civil courts accept their decisions as binding upon them."

A careful examination of the constitutions of the general ⊥**620** and local church, as well as other relevant documents, may be necessary to ascertain the form of governance adopted by the members of the religious association. But there is no reason to restrict the courts to statements of polity related directly to church property. For the constitutionally necessary limitations are imposed not on the evidence to be considered but instead on the object of the inquiry, which is both limited and clear: the civil court must determine whether the local church remains autonomous, so that its members have unreviewable authority to withdraw it (and its property) from the general church, or whether the local church is inseparably integrated into and subordinate to the general church.

IV

The principles developed in prior decisions thus afford clear guidance in the case before us. The Vineville church is presbyterian, a part of the PCUS. The presbyterian form of church government, adopted by the PCUS, is "a hierarchical structure of tribunals which consists of, in ascending order, (1) the Church Session, composed of the leaders of the local church; (2) the Presbytery, composed of several churches in a geographical area; (3) the Synod, generally composed of all Presbyteries within a State; and (4) the General Assembly, the highest governing body." *Presbyterian Church* v. *Hull* ⊥**621** *Church*. The Book of Church Order subjects the Session to "review and control" by the Presbytery in all matters, even authorizing the Presbytery to replace the leadership of the local congregation, to winnow its membership, and to take control of it. No provision of the Book of Church Order gives the Session the authority to withdraw the local church from the PCUS; similarly, no section exempts such a decision by the local church from review by the Presbytery. Thus, while many matters, including the management of the church property, are committed in the first instance to the Session and congregation of the local church, their actions are subject to review by the Presbytery. Here, the Presbytery exercised its authority over the local church, removing the dissidents from church office, asserting direct control over the government of the church, and recognizing the petitioners as the legitimate congregation and Session of the church. It is undisputed that under the established government of the Presbyterian church—accepted by the members of the church before the schism—the use and control of the church property have been determined authoritatively to be in the petitioners. Accordingly, under the principles I have thought were settled, there is no occasion for the further examination of the law of Georgia that the Court directs. On remand, the Georgia courts should be directed to enter judgment for the petitioners.

4 THE FREE EXERCISE OF RELIGION

It is easy to assert that the members of a free society ought to have the right of the free exercise of religion. It is considerably more difficult to define what such free exercise is and what, if any, are its limitations. The authors of the Bill of Rights codified the concept in the Free Exercise Clause, and the Supreme Court, in a series of cases down to the present, has wrestled with the questions of the meaning and limitations of free exercise. It is no wonder that this concept has been called a "lively experiment."[1]

As the newly independent Americans in the late eighteenth century contemplated the form this new nation would take, religion was a matter of considerable concern. A free society would not attempt to dictate religious belief for its citizens. There must be freedom of religious belief. But that would be a hollow freedom if the government (either state or national) said to its citizens: "You can believe what you want, so long as you do nothing about it." That is, freedom of belief is not complete without the freedom to put those beliefs into action, to let those beliefs make a difference in the lives of those who hold them. Consequently, the states and then the Constitutional Convention, in their respective constitutions, implemented the conviction that there ought to be religious freedom in the new nation.

There were essentially two views of the nature and scope of free exercise, that articulated by John Locke and Thomas Jefferson and that expounded by James Madison and most of the other major contributors to constitutional principles at both the state and national levels.[2] The Lockean-Jeffersonian view is that religion is confined only to matters spiritual and has no bearing on worldly matters. To be sure, the state should have nothing to do with spiritual matters, i.e., in theological beliefs or the rituals of worship, citizens should have free exercise in those matters. But, if religion (religious activity) should spill over into worldly affairs, the laws of the state must prevail. Religious freedom is defined from the perspective of the citizen's duty to the state. This is a belief/action distinction. Religious belief is protected from state interference, but religious behavior cannot be.

[1]Cf. Sidney E. Mead, *The Lively Experiment: The Shaping of Christianity in America* (New York: Harper and Row, 1963). The phrase was originally used by John Clarke, a contemporary of Roger Williams and an apologist for the religious liberty of Rhode Island. He used the phrase precisely on the point of the viability of a state with religious freedom: "yr petitioners have it much in their hearts . . . to hold forth a lively experiment, that a flourishing civill State may stand, yea, and best be maintain'd . . . with a full liberty in religious concernmts." Cf. Charles M. Andrews, *The Colonial Period of American History: Vol. II, The Settlements* (New Haven: Yale University Press, 1939), 42. The same phrase is used in the Charter of Rhode Island, July 8, 1663, to be found in Ebenezer Hazard, *Historical Collections; Consisting of State Papers, and Other Authentic Documents; Intended as Materials for an History of the United States of America*, Vol II, first published 1792-94, (Freeport, NY: Books for Libraries Press, reprint 1969), 613.

[2]A major source for this essay is the wonderfully comprehensive article by Michael W. McConnell, "The Origins and Historical Understanding of Free Exercise of Religion," *Harvard Law Review* 103 (May 1990): 1410-1517.

Madison's view of religious freedom is broader than Jefferson's, principally because Madison understood it as being derived from a duty to God. Madison wrote, in ¶ 1 of his *Memorial and Remonstrance* (see Appendix B):

> [W]e hold it for a fundamental and undeniable truth "that Religion or the duty which we owe to our Creator and the manner of discharging it, can be directed only by reason and conviction, not by force or violence." The Religion then of every man must be left to the conviction and conscience of every man; and it is the right of every man to exercise it as these may dictate. This right is in its nature an unalienable right. . . . It is the duty of every man to render to the Creator such homage and such only as he believes to be acceptable to him. This duty is precedent, both in order of time and in degree of obligation, to the claims of Civil Society. . . . We maintain therefore that in matters of Religion, no man's right is abridged by the institution of Civil Society and that Religion is wholly exempt from its cognizance.[3]

For Jefferson, freedom of religion meant freedom from sectarian religion. For Madison, freedom of religion meant the freedom to practice an active faith.[4] Because religious freedom is derived from a duty to God and because that takes precedent to the requirements of civil government, religious freedom is a broad, fundamental, inalienable right.[5]

Given that most of the state constitutions had included language which contained the broader, Madisonian, view of religious freedom, which they urged on the Constitutional Convention at the time of ratification, and that Madison himself was at the center of the formulation of the Bill of Rights, it is hardly surprising that the Free Exercise Clause of the First Amendment expressed the broader view. Professor McConnell argues convincingly that the language of the Free Exercise Clause affirmatively protects religiously motivated action by both individuals and corporate religious bodies, so that it actually sets religion aside for special treatment.[6]

Does that mean that "anything goes" if it is done in the name of religion? Is expansive governmentally granted religious freedom a license for any sort of behavior which the government has prevented itself from prohibiting? The question had come up early and had been answered in the negative. Jefferson's "Bill for Establishing Religious Freedom" (see Appendix A) says: "it is time enough for the rightful purposes of civil government for its officers to interfere when principles break out into overt acts against peace and good order." Several state constitutions contained similar language.[7] So it was commonly understood that government can prevent religious activity when that behavior is contrary to the public good. However, the Free Exercise Clause of the First Amendment contained no language expressing that principle. It was left to the courts to determine when religious activity spilled over its legitimate boundaries to become a danger to the public welfare.

---

[3]The quotation is from Article XVI of the Virginia Declaration of Rights, 1776.

[4]Another helpful way of expressing these different views of free exercise of religion is found in Douglas Laycock, "Free Exercise and the Religious Freedom Restoration Act," *Fordham Law Review* 62 (February 1994): 885-886.

[5]Another way to express the distinction between the two views of religious freedom is to speak of exemptions from generally applicable laws for religious behavior. Professor McConnell summarizes the disparate views:

> The debate over free exercise exemptions hinges on two different conceptions of the threat government poses to religious liberty. Under the no-exemption view, the free exercise clause exists solely to prevent the government from singling out religious practice for peculiar disability. The evil to be prevented is, in Judge Bork's words, "laws that directly and intentionally penalize religious observance." The remedy is to strike down the offending legislation and to treat religious institutions and practices the same way that comparable nonreligious institutions and practices are treated. Under the exemptions view, on the other hand, the free exercise clause protects religious practices against even the incidental or unintended effects of government action. The evil includes not only active hostility, but also majoritarian presuppositions, ignorance, and indifference. The remedy generally is to leave the government policy in place, but to carve out an exemption when the application of the policy impinges on religious practices without adequate justification. (p. 1418)

The issue of whether or not the Free Exercise Clause allows (demands) exemptions from generally applicable laws for religious behavior has become a very significant question in the history of litigation over the Clause.

[6]McConnell, "The Origins and Historical Understanding of Free Exercise of Religion," 1480-1500.

[7]Examples are the Constitution of New York (1777): "[T]he liberty of conscience, hereby granted, shall not be so construed as to excuse acts of licentiousness, or justify practices inconsistent with the peace or safety of this State" in 2 *Federal and State Constitutions*, Colonial Charters, and Other Organic Laws of the United States (B. Poore, 2d ed. 1878), 1338; the Maryland Declaration of Rights (1776):"[U]nless, under colour of religion, any man shall disturb the good order, peace or safety of the State, or shall infringe the laws of morality, or injure others, in their natural, civil, or religious rights" in 1 *Federal and State Constitutions*, 819; and the Massachusetts Constitution (1780): "[P]rovided that he doth not disturb the public peace or obstruct others in their religious worship "in 1 *Federal and State Constitutions*, 957.

Before reviewing the pertinent cases, however, it is important to notice again (see the essay "Introduction") that when the Bill of Rights was ratified in 1791, and for a long time thereafter, it was understood by all that it applied only to the federal government and not to the states. In fact, Madison attempted to draft a provision which would apply the Free Exercise Clause to the states, but to no avail. Apparently the view was that such a measure was unnecessary, both in deference to states' rights and in recognition that the various state constitutions had some form of provision for religious freedom already.[8]

The first Free Exercise Clause case to come before the Supreme Court was REYNOLDS v. UNITED STATES (1879), involving members of the Church of Jesus Christ of Latter-day Saints (Mormons). The issue was whether the religiously motivated practice of polygamy was protected by the Free Exercise Clause. Although apparently various states early had laws prohibiting bigamy, the federal government did not have such a statute until 1862. It is clear that the government adopted a policy of prohibiting plural marriage only when the Mormon church began to practice it.[9] Whatever one might think of polygamy, it is obvious that Mormons became the object of prohibitive government action when they began to assert it as a religious duty. The Court found against the Mormons. In a Jeffersonian approach to the question, the Court held that the generally applicable law against plural marriages was not entitled to an exception, even though the practitioner of polygamy claimed his behavior was based on theological principle. It is clear that the Justices believed that not only was polygamy contrary to the law, it was also harmful to the moral fiber of society, an "odious" practice.

In reaching its decision, the Court established a "belief/action" distinction.

> Congress was deprived of all legislative power over mere opinion, but was left free to reach actions which were in violation of social duties or subversive of good order. . . . Laws are made for the government of actions, and while they cannot interfere with mere religious belief and opinion, they may with practices (98 U.S. 145, 164, 166).

What is especially important about this distinction is that the Court left government officials wide discretion as to when to interfere with religious exercise. They had to show that the actions were "in violation of social duties or subversive of good order," but had wide latitude to define what actually constituted such subversion. The potential for government interference into religious activity was very great after *Reynolds*.

The law remained such until CANTWELL v. CONNECTICUT (1940), an extremely important free exercise case. The "landmark" nature of the case is for two reasons. First, *Cantwell* is the first time that the Free Exercise Clause was applied to the states by its incorporation into the Due Process Clause of the Fourteenth Amendment (see the essay "Introduction"). Henceforth, the Free Exercise Clause has applied to every level of government, not just the federal. Secondly, in *Cantwell* the Justices narrowed the "belief/action" distinction of *Reynolds*. To the accusation that Jehovah's Witnesses were guilty of incitement to riot and disturbing the peace by their sidewalk evangelism, the Court said "no." Religious activity such as that was subject to government interference only when it presented a "clear and present danger" to individuals or to the community.

> [T]he [First] Amendment embraces two concepts,—freedom to believe and freedom to act. The first is absolute but, in the nature of things, the second cannot be. Conduct remains subject to regulation for the protection of society. . . . In every case the power to regulate must be so exercised as not, in attaining a permissible end, unduly to infringe the protected freedom. . . . When clear and present danger of riot, disorder, interference with traffic upon the public streets, or other immediate threat to public safety, peace, or order, appears, the power of the state to prevent or punish is obvious. Equally obvious is it that a state may not unduly suppress the free communication of views, religious or other, under the guise of conserving desirable conditions (310 U.S. 296, 303, 304, 308).

The effect of *Cantwell* was to narrow the prerogative of government officials in determining when to interfere with religious activity. Whereas under the *Reynolds* rule the government had wide opportunity to interfere with religiously motivated activity, now it had the burden to show that such activity presented a "clear and present danger" to persons or the society before it could intervene. After *Cantwell*, religious freedom was the rule, government interference was the exception. *Cantwell* was an important case which greatly advanced the scope of religious freedom.

---

[8]McConnell, "The Origins and Historical Understanding of Free Exercise of Religion," 1484.

[9]See Gordon M. Bakken, "Reynolds v. United States," in Kermit L. Hall, ed., *The Oxford Companion to the Supreme Court of the United States* (New York: Oxford University Press, 1992), 734; Anson P. Stokes, *Church and State in the United States* (New York: Harper and Brothers, 1950), II: 275-285, III: 51-52. Of course, it is probably true that the federal government had not taken a stand on this issue prior to 1862 *because* state laws were regulating the marriage relationship. It was only when the Mormons began to practice polygamy in federally governed territories, outside the reach of any state's law, that the federal government passed the statute upon which the Supreme Court based its decisions.

So the law remained until 1963, when the Court decided SHERBERT v. VERNER, the first of several cases involving the denial of unemployment compensation to workers who quit their jobs because of religious reasons. A Seventh-day Adventist employee found that she could no longer work when her place of employment went to a six-day work week. Her religion required her to abstain from work on her Sabbath, Saturday. She was denied unemployment compensation because she had quit work which was available to her. Claiming that she was put to the choice of following her religion and not being able to work or receive unemployment benefits, or being available to work only by violating the precepts of her religion, Mrs. Sherbert sued. She claimed protection by the Free Exercise Clause. In finding in her favor, the Supreme Court formulated a test for adjudicating free exercise cases, the "*Sherbert* test" or the "compelling state interest test." This is a test which balances government interests in the public welfare against the constitutionally guaranteed right of individuals and/or groups to practice their religion. Although not in the words of the Court, the following formulation expresses well the operation and result of the test.

The test is best expressed in a series of questions:

1. *In the case before the court, has the government imposed a burden on the free exercise of the plaintiff's religion?* Related to that question are two auxiliary questions:
   (a) Does the religion demand the kind of behavior in question; and
   (b) Is the plaintiff engaged in good faith in that religion?
   If the answer to this set of inquiries is negative, the case is over and the plaintiff has lost. If the answer is affirmative, the consideration must go on to the second major question.
2. *Does a compelling state interest justify the burden placed on the exercise of religion?* The state's interest must be of the greatest importance to take precedence over the free exercise of an individual's religion.
   If the answer to this question is negative, the plaintiff has won the case. If the answer is affirmative, the inquiry goes to the third question.
3. *Does the state have an alternative way of achieving its goals rather than infringing on the free exercise of the individual's religion?* If the answer is negative, the state has won its case. If the answer is affirmative, the state must adopt the alternative method and cease its assault on the plaintiff's religious exercise; the plaintiff has won the case.

The "*Sherbert* test" continued to recognize that the government may intervene in religious activity, but it demanded that the government have an extremely good reason for doing so. If anything, it put a finer point on the "clear and present danger" test of *Cantwell,* for it placed a great burden on the government to show that it has a legitimate reason for interfering in religious behavior. This "compelling state interest" test is also known as the "strict scrutiny" standard.

> In contrast to ordinary scrutiny, where courts presume that the legislation or challenged governmental activity is constitutional and the plaintiff has the burden of showing a constitutional violation, strict scrutiny assumes that it is unconstitutional and the government has the burden of demonstrating its compelling interest. Courts must focus on government's purpose rather than merely on the effect of governmental action to determine the validity of a challenged law or regulation.[10]

The test showed great respect for the constitutionally guaranteed right of religious freedom. Religious freedom was clearly the rule; government interference was the exception.

FRAZEE v. ILLINOIS DEPARTMENT OF EMPLOYMENT SECURITY (1989) modified the "*Sherbert* test" in the way it was described above. Frazee refused to accept work on Sunday because of his religious belief that work on Sunday was wrong. But Illinois denied him unemployment compensation because he did not belong to a religious group which taught, as a matter of doctrine, what Frazee said he believed about Sunday work. The Supreme Court found in Frazee's favor. Religious behavior based on an individual's sincere religious beliefs is protected just as much by the Free Exercise Clause as that of those who act in response to some doctrine taught by a religious group. The result of *Frazee* was to remove auxiliary questions (a) and (b) in the formulation of the "*Sherbert* test" above.

The "*Sherbert* test" or "compelling state interest test" became the standard analytic tool for courts, both federal and state, after 1963.[11] Religious freedom was preserved in most of the cases in which it was challenged, although there were some exceptions.[12] That changed in 1990, when the Court handed down EMPLOYMENT DIVISION OF OREGON v. SMITH.

---

[10]Harold J. Spaeth, "Strict Scrutiny," in Hall, ed., *The Oxford Companion to the Supreme Court of the United States,* 845.

[11]Mitchell A. Tyner, "Is Religious Liberty a 'Luxury' We Can No Longer Afford?" *Liberty: A Magazine of Religious Freedom* (Sept.-Oct. 1990): 1, 4. Tyner pointed out that as of May 30, 1990, *Sherbert* had been cited in 546 federal cases and 393 state court cases, for a total of 939 citations in 27 years.

[12]See, e.g., GOLDMAN v. WEINBERGER (1986), BOWEN v. ROY (1986), O'LONE v. ESTATE OF SHABAZZ (1987), and LYNG v. NORTHWEST INDIAN CEMETERY PROTECTIVE ASSOCIATION (1988).

In *Smith*, the Court repudiated the strict scrutiny standard for interpreting the Free Exercise Clause. In an opinion written by Justice Antonin Scalia, the Court held that if the religious activity at bar was contrary to a generally applicable law, the compelling state interest test could not be applied. To be sure, legislation which was specifically designed to attack religious activity would not be valid under the Free Exercise Clause, but laws which were religion-neutral and applicable as part of general legislation were sustainable against the free exercise principle. That is, laws of general application were not subject to strict scrutiny and no exception could be granted in the name of protecting free exercise of religion. No matter how destructive such a law might be to religious activity, if it were a law of general application, there could be no exemptions based on free exercise of religion.

That was not all. Justice Scalia also wrote that the Free Exercise Clause *itself* could not be used as a defense against laws of general applicability *unless* it were used in tandem with other enumerated constitutional freedoms such as speech, peaceable assembly, or the press. This had the effect of marginalizing the Free Exercise Clause. No longer a discrete freedom with a "life of its own," it now had power only when it was used in combination with other constitutional principles.

The effect of *Smith* was to return Free Exercise Clause jurisprudence to the "belief/action" standard of REYNOLDS v. UNITED STATES. Whereas the Court had, in some of the Jehovah's Witnesses cases of the 1940s, called religious freedom a "preferred freedom,"[13] and, with the "*Sherbert* test," had shown considerable solicitude for religious freedom, with *Smith* it marginalized the concept and enormously broadened the possibility for government interference with, or even prohibition of, religious activity.

What is particularly interesting about the reasoning in and the result of *Smith* is that it was totally gratuitous on the part of Justice Scalia and his colleagues in the majority. Neither side in the litigation, either in briefs or oral argument, even mentioned, much less asked for, the abandoning of the strict scrutiny standard in free exercise cases or the marginalizing of the Clause. The issue came up nowhere in the record of the case. Apparently it had crossed no one's mind. Justice Scalia and his colleagues simply reached beyond the boundaries of the issues/concepts presented at bar to impose their free exercise judicial philosophy on all subsequent free exercise litigation. It was hardly the behavior one would expect from a collection of Justices who had been appointed by presidents who claimed to want to move away from a Court of judicial activism to a Court of judicial passivism.[14]

In 1993 the Court heard CHURCH OF THE LUKUMI BABALU AYE v. CITY OF HIALEAH. Many believed that this case would give the Court the opportunity to turn away from its disastrous decision in *Smith*, or at least to clarify it. It did neither. Even *Smith* had said that legislation which targets religion specifically in such a way that prohibits the free exercise of religion is unconstitutional. The Court found that the city of Hialeah had written just such legislation in its attempt to forbid the members of the Santeria religion from practicing animal sacrifice, a ceremony very important to their religion. Justice Kennedy found that because the city's legislation was narrowly drawn to forbid *only* the church's animal sacrifice and not the slaughtering of animals generally, it was in violation of the Free Exercise Clause, even under the *Smith* doctrine. So, *Babalu Aye* neither expanded nor contracted religious freedom.

Even before *Babalu Aye*, a group of religious groups under the leadership of some constitutional scholars began to search for a way to undo *Smith* through legislation. The Religious Freedom Restoration Act (RFRA) was born. As conversations proceeded, a remarkable coalition of religious and civil rights groups from all across the political and theological spectrum converged to urge Congress to pass legislation to restore the "compelling state interest test" as the accepted procedure for deciding free exercise cases.[15] The goal was to pass legislation

[13]Cf. JONES v. OPELIKA 315 U.S. 584, 608; MURDOCK v. PENNSYLVANIA 319 U.S. 105, 115; UNITED STATES v. BALLARD 331 U.S. 78, 87. It is true that in some of those quotes freedom of speech, press, and others are mentioned as preferred freedoms along with religion. But there is never even a hint that the others take precedence over religion or that freedom of religion receives life only because of its affiliation with the others.

[14]Justice Scalia was appointed by President Reagan, as was Justice Kennedy. Chief Justice Rehnquist was appointed to the Court by President Nixon and to the position of Chief Justice by President Reagan. Justice Stevens was appointed by President Ford and Justice White by President Kennedy. Justice O'Connor, who was appointed by President Reagan, joined in the judgment but excoriated her colleagues in the majority for abandoning the "compelling state interest test."

[15]Groups supporting the bill were: Agudath Israel of America, American Civil Liberties Union, American Conference on Religious Movements, American Humanist Association, American Jewish Committee, American Jewish Congress, American Muslim Council, Americans for Religious Liberty, Americans United for Separation of Church and State, Anti-Defamation League, Association for American Indian Affairs, Baptist Joint Committee on Public Affairs, Central Conference of American Rabbis, Christian Church (Disciples of Christ), Christian Legal Society, Christian Life Commission of the Southern Baptist Convention, Christian Science Committee on Publication, Church of the Brethren, Church of Jesus Christ of

which would mandate that the courts, including the Supreme Court, would once again employ strict scrutiny in deciding free exercise cases.

Can Congress legislate a *procedure* to be used in adjudication? The authority to enact RFRA and apply it to the federal judiciary was said to be found in the Necessary and Proper Clause of Article I, Section 8 of the Constitution.[16] The authority to apply RFRA to the states comes from Section 5 of the Fourteenth Amendment.[17] The latter is based on the premise, of course, that the Free Exercise Clause is made applicable to the states through the Due Process Clause (Section 1) of the Fourteenth Amendment;[18] the process of incorporation. In the words of the House Judiciary Committee:

> Pursuant to Section 5 of the Fourteenth Amendment and the Necessary and Proper Clause embodied in Article I, Section 8 of the Constitution, the legislative branch has been given the authority to provide statutory protection for a constitutional value when the Supreme Court has been unwilling to assert its authority.[19]

After extensive hearings in both houses of Congress, the Religious Freedom Restoration Act received virtually unanimous votes of approval in each house and was signed into law by President Clinton, November 16, 1993.[20] The scope and effect of RFRA is described well by two persons who were leaders in the legislative process:

> So Congress in 1993 did what the First Congress had done in 1789. It enacted a general principle of religious liberty, saying nothing about individual cases, and it authorized enforcement by the judiciary, leaving application of the principle to case-by-case determinations. . . . The Religious Freedom Restoration Act is the most important congressional action with respect to religion since the First Congress proposed the First Amendment. . . . RFRA increases the likelihood of success for religious claims, because government will find it far more difficult to justify restrictions on religious exercise under RFRA's compelling interest test than under *Smith*'s nondiscrimination standard. . . . RFRA is not a mere technical change from *Smith*. Rather, it restores a fundamentally different vision of human liberty. Religious believers acting on their faith are not suspicious characters seeking unprincipled special treatment. They are exercising a fundamental human right, and the American commitment is to let them exercise it unless there is an extraordinary reason to interfere—not a rational reason, or even a substantial reason, but a compelling reason. What is suspicious is not the believer practicing his faith, but the government seeking to stop him. RFRA can achieve its purpose only if the courts enforce this vision.[21]

However, since the passage of RFRA, there have been questions raised about its constitutionality. At the time this is being written, there are conflicting opinions from lower federal courts about whether RFRA is a proper act of Congress under Section 5 of the Fourteenth Amendment. In the case of *Flores v. City of Boerne*, a case involving a dispute over the designating of a church as a historical landmark, a federal district court found RFRA to be unconstitu-

Latter-day Saints, Church of Scientology International, Coalitions for America, Concerned Women for America, Episcopal Church, Evangelical Lutheran Church in America, Federation of Reconstructionist Congregations and Havurot, First Liberty Institute, Friends Committee on National Legislation, General Conference of Seventh-day Adventists, Guru Gobind Singh Foundation, Hadassah, Home School Legal Defense Association, House of Bishops of the Episcopal Church, International Institute for Religious Freedom, Mennonite Central Committee Washington Office, NA'AMAT USA, National Association of Evangelicals, National Council of Churches, National Council of Jewish Women, National Drug Strategy Network, National Federation of Temple Sisterhoods, National Jewish Commission on Law and Public Affairs, National Jewish Community Relations Advisory Council, National Sikh Center, Native American Church of North America, People For the American Way Action Fund, Presbyterian Church (USA) Social Justice and Peacemaking Unit, Rabbinical Council of America, Traditional Values Coalition, Union of American Hebrew Congregations, Union of Orthodox Jewish Congregations of America, Unitarian Universalist Association of Congregations, United Church of Christ Office for Church in Society, United Methodist Church Board of Church and Society, United States Catholic Conference (did not agree to support the bill until March 9, 1993).

"The Religious Freedom Restoration Act," newsletter of the Coalition for the Free Exercise of Religion, Washington, D.C., n.d., p. 4; "Fast Start: Early Action Good Sign for Religious Liberty Bill," *Report From the Capital* 48 (April 1993): 4-5.

[16]"The Congress shall have Power . . . [t]o make all Laws which shall be necessary and proper for carrying into Execution the foregoing Powers, and all other Powers vested by this Constitution in the Government of the United States, or in any Department or Officer thereof."

[17]"The Congress shall have power to enforce, by appropriate legislation, the provisions of this article."

[18]"[N]or shall any State deprive any person of life, liberty, or property, without due process of law."

[19]H.R. Rep. No. 103-88, 103d Cong., 1st Sess. 9 (1993).

[20]See Appendix C for the text of the act.

[21]Douglas Laycock and Oliver S. Thomas, "Interpreting the Religious Freedom Restoration Act," *Texas Law Review* 73 (December 1994): 221, 243, 244-245.

tional, although in a not very thoroughly argued opinion. The court correctly recognized that in RFRA Congress sought to overturn or deflect the Supreme Court's decision in *Smith*. But the Supreme Court itself, in *Marbury* v. *Madison,* had declared that it is the province of the judiciary to say what the law is. Under that doctrine, the *Boerne* court held that RFRA improperly invades the concept of the separation of powers by imposing on the functions of the judiciary. Consequently, RFRA is unconstitutional. Furthermore, the doctrine of *stare decisis* demands that *Smith* be the law to follow in free exercise litigation.

Other courts have addressed the same question and come to the opposite conclusion. Examples are *Belgard* v. *Hawaii* and *Sasnett* v. *Wisconsin Department of Corrections,* both cases involving the religious freedom rights of prisoners. In *Belgard,* citing *Katzenbach* v. *Morgan,* the court ruled that Congress can disagree with the Supreme Court on the scope of constitutional rights.

> *Morgan* gave Congress wide latitude to interpret the Constitution and expand a fundamental right pursuant to section 5 of the Fourteenth Amendment in an area where the Supreme Court had already spoken and afforded that right a narrower scope (883 F. Supp. 510, 515 (1995)).

Given that assumption, the court held RFRA to be within the proper function of Congress, not a violation of the separation of powers concept, and thus constitutional. The *Sasnett* court reached the same conclusion in an even more thoroughly argued opinion.

After all these decisions, the Fifth Circuit Court of Appeals reversed *Flores* v. *Boerne*. Whereas the trial court had declared RFRA unconstitutional, the Fifth Circuit, in a detailed opinion, declared that the passage of RFRA was within the legitimate roles of Congress. Beginning with a quote about Section 5 of the Fourteenth Amendment from the House Judiciary Committee in its debate over RFRA,[22] the court argued strongly that the section clearly gives Congress the authority to do what it did in passing RFRA.

> Congress' power under Section 5 is remedial. Congress' constitutional power to legislate pursuant to Section 5 is tied to Congress' superior ability to find and redress nascent or disguised violations of the Amendment. In short, "Congress may act only where a violation lurks." *E.E.O.C.* v. *Wyoming,* (Burger, C.J., dissenting).
>
> The United States offers three remedial justifications for RFRA: 1) RFRA deters governmental violations of the Free Exercise Clause; 2) RFRA prohibits laws that have the effect of impeding religious exercise; and, 3) RFRA protects the free exercise rights of adherents of minority religions (73 F. 3d 1359).

The court took up each of these in turn and found that each was a legitimate function of Section 5.

Like *Belgard* before it, the Appeals Court relied on *Katzenbach* v. *Morgan* for precedent.

> In *Katzenbach* v. *Morgan,* . . . the Court held that the inquiry into what is "appropriate legislation" under Section 5 is whether the statute "may be regarded as an enactment to enforce [the Fourteenth Amendment], whether it is 'plainly adapted to that end' and whether it is not prohibited by but is consistent with 'the letter and spirit of the constitution'" (73 F. 3d 1357).

The court found that RFRA meets each of these criteria and thus is constitutional.

Consequently, given the disagreements among the lower courts, it is likely that the Supreme Court itself will sometime deal with the question of the constitutionality of the Religious Freedom Restoration Act. In the interim, it seems that in the free exercise cases decided in the lower courts, more often than not religious freedom is being protected by the higher, pre-*Smith,* standard of review interjected by RFRA.

THE MORMON CASES

Both because of specific guarantees of the basic documents of national and state governments and the general spirit of liberality that has ordinarily prevailed in this country, the American people enjoy a great degree of religious freedom. At least 1550 religious bodies exist in the United States[1] and quite remarkable, sometimes even bizarre, activities have been countenanced as legitimate exercises of religion.

Broad though it is, however, religious freedom is not without limits. No freedom is absolute, and liberty can never be equated with license. The cherished right of the individual to free exercise of religion often conflicts with equally valued rights of other individuals and the interests of society. It is difficult, at best, to apply general constitutional principles to concrete problem situations; when these principles collide with one another, the difficulty is increased.

One of the primary functions and traditional powers of government is its authority to protect the health, safety, morals, and welfare of society. Exercise of this

[22]Cf. footnote 17 and accompanying text.

[1]J. Gordon Melton gives this figure in his extensive study of the various religious groups in the United States, *The Encyclopedia of American Religions* (Detroit: Gale Research Company, 2nd edition 1987; 2nd edition supplement).

"police power" has frequently created conflict between governmental authority and avowed religious rights of individuals and groups. Examples are not difficult to find. Compulsory vaccination of school children is required though opposed by some on religious grounds. Physical examinations before marriage or before admission to state universities are demanded even of those whose religion forbids such examination. Practice of medicine for a fee by an unlicensed physician is illegal though the practitioner claims to heal through prayer. Sabbatarians are often subjected to Sunday observance laws that result in economic loss as well as religious distress. Handling of poisonous snakes in a public place without reasonable care, even as a religious ritual, is forbidden.[2] Churches must comply with zoning ordinances and building codes thought necessary to protect the public.

Violations of statutory provisions in these and innumerable other areas result in prosecution of those who, on religious grounds, fail to comply with the law. Courts, as constitutional arbiters, are then called on to undertake the difficult, if not impossible, task of resolving the resulting conflict between religious claims and asserted societal interests. Members of recognized mainline churches seldom find it necessary to call on courts to protect their First Amendment rights. Members of "cults" and other new or unorthodox movements that have not yet gained public acceptance often feel that need acutely. Their doctrines and methods are viewed as "strange" by the public, and they are regarded with great distrust. They are too often subjected to discriminatory action by government as well as individuals.[3]

From their earliest creation, state courts have dealt with the issue of religious liberty in cases brought before them. But, because Congress enacted no such legislation and the states were long held not to be subject to the inhibitions of the First Amendment, no such cases reached the Supreme Court of the United States during its first hundred years, and only a few were heard by the Court until 1940. Since that time, however, a substantial body of federal constitutional law relating to freedom of religion has been developed. There has been an ever increasing opportunity for both federal and state courts to add to and refine this case law in recent years. In 1983, Frank Way and Barbara J. Burt reported that from 1946 to 1956 there were sixty-six state and federal cases in which free exercise claims were raised. In the ten years from 1970 to 1980 there were 384 such cases.[4]

Adherents of the Church of Jesus Christ of Latter-day Saints, better known as Mormons,[5] gave the Supreme Court its first opportunity to speak directly to the issue of religious liberty in litigation involving claims of its violation. The Mormons were subjected to both private and governmental harassment almost from the founding of their denomination by Joseph Smith in 1830. Most of Smith's followers migrated within a short time to the Midwest. After a few years in Ohio, they moved on to Jackson County, Missouri. There they were regarded with great suspicion by the other inhabitants of the area. This distrust stemmed in part from accounts of the eccentric religious beliefs and practices of the Mormons. However, it was likely also fostered by the group and their obvious growth and prosperity, which aroused fear on the part of some that they might eventually be dominated or dispossessed by the sect.

In 1834 a mob destroyed the printing shop of the community newspaper and committed other acts of violence. Appeals to the governor, President Andrew Jackson, and Congress proved futile. The Mormons then formed their own militia in 1838—an action that aggravated the situation still further. Subsequently the governor issued what came to be known as the "Boggs Exterminating Order," and seventeen Mormons were killed by state forces.

[2]As late as 1976, through denial of a petition for a writ of certiorari, in *Pack* v. *Tennessee ex rel. Swan*, the Supreme Court let stand action of the State of Tennessee in permanently enjoining a religious group, the Holiness Church of God in Jesus Name, of Newport, Tennessee, from handling or displaying dangerous and poisonous snakes or consuming strychnine or other similarly poisonous substances.

[3]Although the Supreme Court has rather consistently refused to hear appeals, members of such new and unorthodox religions as the Founding Church of Scientology, the Worldwide Church of God, the Unification Church, the Intentional Society for Krishna Consciousness, and Children of God have in recent years been heavily involved in litigation in lower courts. An excellent discussion of the tribulations of unpopular new religions is found in Chapter 7 of Leo Pfeffer's *Religion, State and the Supreme Court* (New York: Prometheus Books, 1984), pp. 201-34.

[4]"Religious Marginality and the Free Exercise Clause," *The American Political Science Review* 77 (September 1983): 652-65. The study also found a much higher success rate for the claims. The authors attribute the great increase in cases to several causes among which are greater involvement of rapidly proliferating "marginal religions" in litigation; increase in population availability of legal remedies under legislation such as Title VII of the Civil Rights Act of 1964, which was not available in earlier years; and the perception of a more favorable attitude on the part of the judges.

[5]Anthony A. Hoekema, *The Four Major Cults* (Grand Rapids: William B. Eerdmans Publishing Co., 1963) gives an excellent account of both the Mormon and Jehovah's Witnesses movements. Hoekema also discusses Christian Science and Seventh-day Adventism, which sometimes have been involved in religious rights litigations.

The members of the sect moved the next year to Illinois, where they established a large colony called Nauvoo; but again they were soon at odds with the residents of nearby communities. Armed conflict broke out in 1844, and the state militia was ordered to defeat and disarm the Nauvoo Legion. Joseph Smith and his brother were arrested and, while awaiting trial for treason, were murdered by a mob.

After Smith's death, a division occurred within the church, and the newly elected president, Brigham Young, led one faction on a long trek westward to the Great Salt Lake area. There they established the "State of Deseret," which became the Territory of Utah in 1850. Young served not only as president of the church in Utah but also as governor of the territory from 1850 to 1854.

Efforts of the church met with great economic as well as spiritual success in Utah, but its members soon came once again under great popular and governmental pressure. This time the primary cause of the conflict was polygamy, or "plural marriage." There had been rumors in Illinois that Joseph Smith and some of the other leaders of the community engaged in polygamy: he claimed to have received a "revelation" concerning the practice the year before his death. Not until 1852, however, did Brigham Young, who ultimately married twenty-seven women in all, proclaim polygamy to be an official tenet of the church.

Polygamy was probably never practiced by many members of the Mormon church. But the idea of plural marriage in any case was repugnant to most Americans, who saw it as posing a serious threat to the traditional concept of the monogamous family unit as the bulwark of a stable society. The great public outcry led Congress in 1862 to pass the Morrill Act in order "to punish and prevent the practice of polygamy in the Territories."

Among others, George Reynolds, private secretary to Brigham Young, was prosecuted and convicted under the statute. A territorial court rejected his contention that the law could not be constitutionally applied to a Mormon who practiced polygamy in the belief that it was a religious duty. Reynolds appealed to the Supreme Court, and in REYNOLDS v. UNITED STATES (1879) that body handed down its first decision directly concerning an alleged violation of religious freedom as guaranteed by the First Amendment.

Confronted for the first time with specific litigation requiring location of the constitutional line of demarcation between religious rights of the individual and regulatory power of the federal government, the Court found it necessary to formulate the first of several "tests" or standards that it has since developed and applied to reach decisions—or at least to rationalize its decisions. No one test has been exclusively or consistently applied, and it has sometimes seemed that the justices groped for arguments to justify their preconceived conclusions.

In unanimously sustaining the statute as applied to Reynolds, the Court, speaking through Chief Justice Waite, announced a rather simplistic and antilibertarian "action-belief" doctrine as its guiding standard. That is, the First Amendment makes *belief* absolute, but not action based on that belief. As the Chief Justice said, "Congress was deprived of all legislative power over mere opinion, but was left free to reach actions which were in violation of social duties or subversive of good order." Or as he phrased it at another point: "Laws are made for the government of actions, and while they cannot interfere with mere religious belief and opinions, they may with practices." Interestingly, one may note the use in the opinion of the *argumentum ad horrendum* where Waite suggested that a contrary decision of the Court might later be used to justify human sacrifice as a religious practice or the efforts of a wife to burn herself on the funeral pyre of her husband because she believes it to be her religious duty.

A dozen years later, in DAVIS v. BEASON, another unanimous Court extended the "belief-action" dichotomy to allow punishment for even the advocacy of belief or for the association with others who believe in polygamy. Davis, a Mormon but not a practicing polygamist, had been convicted of violating a statute of the Idaho Territory by taking falsely an oath required of a voter. The oath was to the effect that not only was he not a bigamist but also was not a member of any organization that taught or encouraged its members to practice polygamy and he did not teach or encourage anyone to commit such a crime "either as a religious duty or otherwise." Observing that "[c]rime is not the less odious because sanctioned by what any particular sect may designate as religion," Justice Field again denied that the First Amendment was ever intended to be "invoked as a protection against legislation for the punishment of acts inimical to the peace, good order and morals of society."

In *Church of Jesus Christ of Latter-day Saints* v. *United States*, another case decided in 1890, the Court upheld a federal statute revoking the charter of the Mormon Church and confiscating much of its property. These and other punitive actions taken against members of the church forced its president to issue an order in 1890 which renounced polygamous marriages and advised church members "to refrain from contracting any marriage forbidden by the law of the land."[6]

[6]Not all of the members of the church have followed this advice. Some Mormons have come in conflict with the law in more recent years and have fared no better in court than their forebears. In *Cleveland* v. *United States* (1946), the Supreme Court upheld the convictions of

Utah was admitted as a state in 1896 under a constitution forbidding polygamous or plural marriages.

During a period in which the American people were not yet sensitized to minority rights, these legislative acts and decisions of the Court occasioned no outburst of public indignation. In general, they were regarded as a triumph for the forces of morality in their battle for order and decency. The "belief-action" test, which gave an extraordinarily narrow definition of the constitutional guarantee of "free exercise of religion," has not been specifically overruled by the Court. However, it has never again been advanced as the sole standard used to arrive at a decision, and since 1970 has seldom been cited as controlling.[7]

REYNOLDS v. UNITED STATES

98 U.S. 145
IN ERROR TO THE SUPREME COURT OF THE TERRITORY OF UTAH
Motion Submitted February 13, 1878 — Decided February 18, 1878
Argued November 14, 15, 1878 — Redecided January 4, 1879

⊥**146** This is an indictment for bigamy under Section 5352, Revised Statutes, which, omitting its exceptions, is as follows:

"Every person having a husband or wife living, who marries another, whether married or single, in a Territory, or other place over which the United States have exclusive jurisdiction, is guilty of bigamy, and shall be punished by a fine of not more than $500, and by imprisonment for a term of not more than five years." . . .

⊥**153** Mr. *Chief Justice WAITE* delivered the opinion of the court:

The assignments of error, when grouped, present the following questions:

1. Was the indictment bad because found by a grand jury of less than sixteen persons?
2. Were the challenges of certain petit jurors by the accused improperly overruled?
3. Were the challenges of certain other jurors by the Government improperly sustained?
4. Was the testimony of Amelia Jane Schofield, given at a former trial for the same offense, but under another indictment, improperly admitted in evidence?
5. Should the accused have been acquitted if he married the second time, because he believed it to be his religious duty?
6. Did the court err in that part of the charge which directed the attention of the jury to the consequences of polygamy?

These questions will be considered in their order.

[Discussion of first four questions omitted] ⊥**161**

5. As to the defense of religious belief or duty.

On the trial, the plaintiff in error, the accused, proved that at the time of his alleged second marriage he was, and for many years before had been, a member of the Church of Jesus Christ of Latter-Day Saints, commonly called the Mormon Church, and a believer in its doctrines; that it was an accepted doctrine of that Church "That it was the duty of male members of said Church, circumstances permitting, to practice polygamy; . . . that this duty was enjoined by different books which the members of said Church believed to be of divine origin, and among others the Holy Bible, and also that the members of the Church believed that the practice of polygamy was directly enjoined upon the male members thereof by the Almighty God, in a revelation to Joseph Smith, the founder and prophet of said Church; that the failing or refusing to practice polygamy by such male members of said Church, when circumstances would admit, would be punished, and that the penalty for such failure and refusal would be damnation in the life to come." He also proved "That he had received permission from the recognized authorities in said Church to enter into polygamous marriage; . . . that Daniel H. Wells, one having authority in said Church to perform the marriage ceremony, married the said defendant on or about the time the crime is alleged to have been committed, to some woman by the name of Schofield, and that such marriage ceremony was performed under and pursuant to the doctrines of said Church."

Upon this proof he asked the court to instruct the jury that if they found from the evidence that he "was married as ⊥**162** charged (if he was married) in pursuance of and in conformity with what he believed at the time to

---

members of a fundamental Mormon sect for violation of the Mann "White Slave" Act when they transported their plural wives across state lines. The Court in 1955 let stand the decision of a Utah court which denied custody of their children to parents who taught them the now disavowed tenets concerning plural marriage (*In re Black*).

[7]Professor Laurence H. Tribe of Harvard University traces at considerable length the departure of the Court from the *Reynolds* belief-action doctrine, particularly subsequent to the pronouncement of new "tests" in *Sherbert* v. *Verner*, in *The Constitutional Protection of Individual Rights: Limits on Government Authority* (Mineola, N.Y.: The Foundation Press, Inc., 1978). Chapter 14 of this outstanding work is devoted to the topic "Rights of Religious Autonomy." Rodney K. Smith is highly critical of the Court's use of the belief-action dichotomy and the Jeffersonian concept of free exercise which permitted government to regulate beliefs when they resulted in acts against "peace and good order" in *Reynolds*, and is gratified by the abandonment of the test by today's Court. "Getting Off on the Wrong Foot and Back on Again: A Reexamination of the History of the Framing of the Religion Clauses of the First Amendment and a Critique of the *Reynolds* and *Everson* Decisions," *Wake Forest Law Review* 20 (Fall 1984): 569-642. Of course, all of this discussion may have been rendered moot by the Supreme Court's decision in EMPLOYMENT DIVISION OF OREGON v. SMITH.

be a religious duty, that the verdict must be 'not guilty.'" This request was refused, and the court did charge "That there must have been a criminal intent, but that if the defendant, under the influence of a religious belief that it was right—under an inspiration, if you please, that it was right—deliberately married a second time, having a first wife living, the want of consciousness of evil intent, the want of understanding on his part that he was committing a crime, did not excuse him; but the law inexorably in such case implies the criminal intent."

Upon this charge and refusal to charge the question is raised, whether religious belief can be accepted as a justification of an overt act made criminal by the law of the land. The inquiry is not as to the power of Congress to prescribe criminal laws for the Territories, but as to the guilt of one who knowingly violates a law which has been properly enacted, if he entertains a religious belief that the law is wrong.

Congress cannot pass a law for the government of the Territories which shall prohibit the free exercise of religion. The first amendment to the Constitution expressly forbids such legislation. Religious freedom is guaranteed everywhere throughout the United States, so far as congressional interference is concerned. The question to be determined is, whether the law now under consideration comes within this prohibition.

The word "religion" is not defined in the Constitution. We must go elsewhere, therefore, to ascertain its meaning, and nowhere more appropriately, we think, than to the history of the times in the midst of which the provision was adopted. The precise point of the inquiry is, what is the religious freedom which has been guaranteed?

Before the adoption of the Constitution, attempts were made in some of the Colonies and States to legislate not only in respect to the establishment of religion, but in respect to its doctrines and precepts as well. The people were taxed, against their will, for the support of religion, and sometimes for the support of particular sects to whose tenets they could not and did not subscribe. Punishments were prescribed for a failure to attend upon public worship, and sometimes for entertaining **⊥163** heretical opinions. The controversy upon this general subject was animated in many of the States, but seemed at last to culminate in Virginia. In 1784, the House of Delegates of that State having under consideration "A bill establishing provision for teachers of the Christian religion," postponed it until the next session, and directed that the bill should be published and distributed, and that the People be requested "to signify their opinion respecting the adoption of such a bill at the next session of the Assembly."

This brought out a determined opposition. Amongst others, Mr. Madison prepared a "Memorial and Remonstrance," which was widely circulated and signed, and in which he demonstrated that religion, or the duty we owe the Creator," was not within the cognizance of civil government. At the next session the proposed bill was not only defeated, but another, "for establishing religious freedom," drafted by Mr. Jefferson, was passed. In the preamble of this Act, religious freedom is defined; and after a recital "That to suffer the civil magistrate to intrude his powers into the field of opinion, and to restrain the profession or propagation of principles on supposition of their ill tendency, is a dangerous fallacy which at once destroys all religious liberty," it is declared "that it is time enough for the rightful purposes of civil government for its officers to interfere when principles break out into overt acts against peace and good order." In these two sentences is found the true distinction between what properly belongs to the Church and what to the State.

In a little more than a year after the passage of this statute the convention met which prepared the Constitution of the United States. Of this convention Mr. Jefferson was not a member, he being then absent as minister to France. As soon as he saw the draft of the Constitution proposed for adoption, he, in a letter to a friend, expressed his disappointment at the absence of an express declaration insuring the freedom of religion, but was willing to accept it as it was, trusting that the good sense and honest intentions of the people would bring about the necessary alterations. **⊥164** Five of the States, while adopting the Constitution, proposed amendments. Three, New Hampshire, New York and Virginia, included in one form or another a declaration of religious freedom in the changes they desired to have made, as did also North Carolina, where the convention at first declined to ratify the Constitution until the proposed amendments were acted upon. Accordingly, at the first session of the first Congress the amendment now under consideration was proposed with others by Mr. Madison. It met the views of the advocates of religious freedom, and was adopted. Mr. Jefferson afterwards, in reply to an address to him by a committee of the Danbury Baptist Association, took occasion to say: "Believing with you that religion is a matter which lies solely between man and his God; that he owes account to none other for his faith or his worship; that the legislative powers of the Government reach actions only, and not opinions, I contemplate with sovereign reverence that act of the whole American people which declared that their Legislature should 'make no law respecting an establishment of religion or prohibiting the free exercise thereof,' thus building a wall of separation between Church and State. Adhering to this expression of the Supreme will of the Nation in behalf of the rights of conscience, I shall see, with sincere satisfaction, the progress of those sentiments which tend to restore man to all his natural rights, convinced he has no natural right in opposition to his social duties." Coming as this does from an acknowledged leader of the advocates of the measure, it may be accepted almost as an authoritative declaration of the scope and effect of the amendment thus secured. Congress was deprived of all legislative power over mere opinion, but was left free to reach actions which were in violation of social duties or subversive of good order.

Polygamy has always been odious among the Northern and Western Nations of Europe and, until the establishment of the Mormon Church, was almost exclusively a feature of the life of Asiatic and African people. At common law, the second marriage was always void, and from the earliest history of England polygamy has been treated as an offense against society. After the establishment of the eccle⊥**165**siastical courts, and until the time of James I., it was punished through the instrumentality of those tribunals, not merely because ecclesiastical rights had been violated, but because upon the separation of the ecclesiastical courts from the civil, the ecclesiastical were supposed to be the most appropriate for the trial of matrimonial causes and offenses against the rights of marriage; just as they were for testamentary causes and the settlement of the estates of deceased persons.

By the Statute of 1 James I., ch. 11, the offense, if committed in England or Wales, was made punishable in the civil courts, and the penalty was death. As this statute was limited in its operation to England and Wales, it was at a very early period reenacted, generally with some modifications, in all the Colonies. In connection with the case we are now considering, it is a significant fact that on the 8th of December, 1788, after the passage of the Act establishing religious freedom, and after the convention of Virginia had recommended as an amendment to the Constitution of the United States the declaration in a Bill of Rights that "all men have an equal, natural and unalienable right to the free exercise of religion, according to the dictates of conscience," the Legislature of that State substantially enacted the Statute of James I., death penalty included, because as recited in the preamble, "It hath been doubted whether bigamy or polygamy be punishable by the laws of this Commonwealth." From that day to this we think it may safely be said there never has been a time in any State of the Union when polygamy has not been an offense against society, cognizable by the civil courts and punishable with more or less severity. In the face of all this evidence, it is impossible to believe that the constitutional guaranty of religious freedom was intended to prohibit legislation in respect to this most important feature of social life. Marriage, while from its very nature a sacred obligation, is, nevertheless, in most civilized nations, a civil contract, and usually regulated by law. Upon it society may be said to be built, and out of its fruits spring social relations and social obligations and duties, with which government is necessarily required to deal. In fact, according as monogamous or polygamous marriages are allowed, do we find the principles on which the government of ⊥**166** the people, to a greater or less extent, rests. Professor Lieber says: polygamy leads to the patriarchal principle, and which, when applied to large communities, fetters the people in stationary despotism, while that principle cannot long exist in connection with monogamy. Chancellor Kent observes that this remark is equally striking and profound. An exceptional colony of polygamists under an exceptional leadership may sometimes exist for a time without appearing to disturb the social condition of the people who surround it; but there cannot be a doubt that, unless restricted by some form of constitution, it is within the legitimate scope of the power of every civil government to determine whether polygamy or monogamy shall be the law of social life under its dominion.

In our opinion the statute immediately under consideration is within the legislative power of Congress. It is constitutional and valid as prescribing a rule of action for all those residing in the Territories, and in places over which the United States have exclusive control. This being so, the only question which remains is, whether those who make polygamy a part of their religion are excepted from the operation of the statute. If they are, then those who do not make polygamy a part of their religious belief may be found guilty and punished, while those who do must be acquitted and go free. This would be introducing a new element into criminal law. Laws are made for the government of actions, and while they cannot interfere with mere religious belief and opinions, they may with practices. Suppose one believed that human sacrifices were a necessary part of religious worship, would it be seriously contended that the civil government under which he lived could not interfere to prevent a sacrifice? Or if a wife religiously believed it was her duty to burn herself upon the funeral pile of her dead husband, would it be beyond the power of the civil government to prevent her carrying her belief into practice?

So here, as a law of the organization of society under the exclusive dominion of the United States, it is provided that plural marriages shall not be allowed. Can a man excuse his practices to the contrary because of his religious belief? ⊥**167** To permit this would be to make the professed doctrines of religious belief superior to the law of the land, and in effect to permit every citizen to become a law unto himself. Government could exist only in name under such circumstances.

A criminal intent is generally an element of crime, but every man is presumed to intend the necessary and legitimate consequences of what he knowingly does. Here the accused knew he had been once married, and that his first wife was living. He also knew that his second marriage was forbidden by law. When, therefore, he married the second time, he is presumed to have intended to break the law. And the breaking of the law is the crime. Every act necessary to constitute the crime was knowingly done, and the crime was, therefore, knowingly committed. Ignorance of a fact may sometimes be taken as evidence of a want of criminal intent, but not ignorance of the law. The only defense of the accused in this case is his belief that the law ought not to have been enacted. It matters not that his belief was a part of his professed religion; it was still belief, and belief only.

In *Regina* v. *Wagstaffe* the parents of a sick child, who omitted to call in medical attendance because of their religious belief that what they did for its cure would be effective, were held not to be guilty of manslaughter, while it was said the contrary would have been the result if the child had actually been starved to death by the parents, under the notion that it was their religious duty to abstain from giving it food. But when the offense consists of a positive act which is knowingly done, it would be dangerous to hold that the offender might escape punishment because he religiously believed the law which he had broken ought never to have been made. No case, we believe, can be found that has gone so far.

6. As to that part of the charge which directed the attention of the jury to the consequences of polygamy.

The passage complained of is as follows: "I think it not improper, in the discharge of your duties in this case, that you should consider what are to be the consequences to the innocent victims of this delusion. As this contest goes on, they multiply, ⊥**168** and there are pure-minded women and there are innocent children; innocent in a sense even beyond the degree of the innocence of childhood itself. These are to be the sufferers; and as jurors fail to do their duty, and as these cases come up in the Territory of Utah, just so do these victims multiply and spread themselves over the land."

While every appeal by the court to the passions or the prejudices of a jury should be promptly rebuked, and while it is the imperative duty of a reviewing court to take care that wrong is not done in this way, we see no just cause for complaint in this case. Congress, in 1862, saw fit to make bigamy a crime in the Territories. This was done because of the evil consequences that were supposed to flow from plural marriages. All the court did was to call the attention of the jury to the peculiar character of the crime for which the accused was on trial, and to remind them of the duty they had to perform. There was no appeal to the passions, no instigation of prejudice. Upon the showing made by the accused himself, he was guilty of a violation of the law under which he had been indicted: and the effort of the court seems to have been not to withdraw the minds of the jury from the issue to be tried, but to bring them to it; not to make them partial, but to keep them impartial.

Upon a careful consideration of the whole case, we are satisfied that no error was committed by the court below, *and the judgment is consequently affirmed.*

DAVIS v. BEASON

133 U.S. 333

ON APPEAL FROM THE THIRD JUDICIAL DISTRICT COURT OF THE TERRITORY OF IDAHO

Argued December 9, 10, 1889 — Decided February 3, 1890

⊥**334** Statement by Mr. *Justice FIELD:*

In April, 1889, the appellant, Samuel D. Davis, was indicted in the District Court of the Third Judicial District of the Territory of Idaho, in the County of Oneida, in connection with divers persons named, and divers other persons whose names were unknown to the grand jury, for a conspiracy to unlawfully pervert and obstruct the due administration of the laws of the Territory in this, that they would unlawfully procure themselves to be admitted to registration as electors of said County of Oneida for the general election then next to occur in that county, when they were not entitled to be admitted to such registration, by appearing before the respective registrars of the election precincts in which they resided, and taking the oath prescribed by the Statute of the State, in substance as follows: "I do swear (or affirm) that I am a male citizen of the United States of the age of twenty-one years (or will be on the 6th day of November, 1888); and that I have (or will have) actually resided in this Territory four months and in this county for thirty days next preceding the day of the next ensuing election; that I have never been convicted of treason, felony or bribery; and that I am not registered or entitled to vote at any other place in this Territory; and I do further swear that I am not a bigamist or polygamist; that I am not a member of any order, organization or association which teaches, advises, counsels or encourages its members, devotees or any other person to commit the crime of bigamy or polygamy, or any other crime defined by law as a duty arising or resulting from membership in such order, organization or association, or which practices bigamy, polygamy or plural or celestial marriage as a doctrinal right of such organization; that I do not and will not, publicly or privately, or in any manner whatever, teach, advise, counsel or encourage any person to commit the crime of bigamy or polygamy, or any other crime defined by law, either as a religious duty or otherwise; that I do regard the Constitution of the United States and the laws thereof and the laws of this Territory, as interpreted by the courts, as the supreme laws of the land, the teachings of any order, organization or association to the contrary notwithstanding, so help me God," when, in truth, each of the defendants was ⊥**335** a member of an order, organization and association, namely, the Church of Jesus Christ of Latter-Day Saints, commonly known as the Mormon Church, which they knew taught, advised, counseled and encouraged its members and devotees to commit the crimes of bigamy and polygamy as duties arising and resulting from membership in said order, organization and association, and which order, organization and association, as they all knew, practiced bigamy and polygamy and plural and celestial marriage as doctrinal rights of said organization; and that in pursuance of said conspiracy the said defendants went before the registrars of different precincts of the county (which are designated) and took and had administered to them respectively the oath aforesaid.

The defendants demurred to the indictment, and the demurrer being overruled they pleaded separately not guilty. On the trial which followed on the 12th of September, 1889, the jury found the defendant Samuel

D. Davis guilty as charged in the indictment. The defendant was thereupon sentenced to pay a fine of $500, and in default of its payment to be confined in the county jail of Oneida County for a term not exceeding 250 days, and was remanded to the custody of the sheriff until the judgment should be satisfied.

Soon afterwards, on the same day, the defendant applied to the court before which the trial was had, and obtained a writ of *habeas corpus*, alleging that he was imprisoned and restrained of his liberty by the sheriff of the county; that his imprisonment was by virtue of his conviction and the judgment mentioned and the warrant issued thereon; that such imprisonment was illegal; and that such illegality consisted in this: (1) that the facts in the indictment and record did not constitute a public offense, and the acts charged were not criminal or punishable under any statute or law of the territory; and (2) that so much of the statute of the territory as ⊥**336** provides that no person is entitled to register or vote at any election who is "a member of any order, organization or association which teaches, advises, counsels or encourages its members, devotees or any other person to commit the crime of bigamy or polygamy, or any other crime defined by law, as a duty arising or resulting from membership in such order, organization or association, or which practices bigamy or polygamy or plural or celestial marriage as a doctrinal rite of such organization," is a "law respecting an establishment of re⊥**337**ligion," in violation of the First Amendment of the Constitution, and void.

The court ordered the writ to issue, directed to the sheriff, returnable before it, at three o'clock in the afternoon of that day, commanding the sheriff to have the body of the defendant before the court at the hour designated, with the time and cause of his imprisonment, and to do and receive what should then be considered concerning him. On the return of the writ, the sheriff produced the body of the defendant and also the warrant of commitment under which he was held, and the record of the case showing his conviction for the conspiracy mentioned and the judgment thereon. To this return, the defendant, admitting the facts stated therein, excepted to their insufficiency to justify his detention. The court, holding that sufficient cause was not shown for the discharge of the defendant, ordered him to be remanded to the custody of the sheriff. From this judgment the defendant appealed to this court. . . .

⊥**341** Mr. *Justice FIELD* delivered the opinion of the court:

On this appeal our only inquiry is whether the District Court of the Territory had jurisdiction of the offense charged in the indictment of which the defendant was found guilty. If it had jurisdiction, we can go no farther. We cannot look into any alleged errors in its rulings on the trial of the defendant. The writ of *habeas corpus* cannot be turned into a writ of error to review the action of that court. Nor can we inquire whether the evidence established the fact alleged, that the defendant was a member of an order or organization known as the Mormon Church, called the Church of Jesus Christ of Latter-Day Saints, or the fact that the order or organization taught and counseled its members and devotees to commit the crimes of bigamy and polygamy as duties arising from membership therein. On this hearing we can only consider whether, these allegations being taken as true, an offense was committed of which the territorial court had jurisdiction to try the defendant. And on this point there can be no serious discussion or difference of opinion. Bigamy and polygamy are crimes by the laws of the civilized and Christian countries. They are crimes by the laws of the United States, and they are crimes by the laws of Idaho. They tend to destroy the purity of the marriage relation, to disturb the peace of families, to degrade woman and to debase man. Few crimes are more pernicious to the best interests of society and receive more general or more deserved punishment. To extend exemption from punishment for such crimes would be to shock the moral judgment of the community. To call their ⊥**342** advocacy a tenet of religion is to offend the common sense of mankind. If they are crimes, then to teach, advise and counsel their practice is to aid in their commission, and such teaching and counseling are themselves criminal and proper subjects of punishment, as aiding and abetting crime are in all other cases.

The term "religion" has reference to one's views of his relations to his Creator, and to the obligations they impose of reverence for his being and character, and of obedience to his will. It is often confounded with the *cultus* or form of worship of a particular sect, but is distinguishable from the latter. The First Amendment to the Constitution, in declaring that Congress shall make no law respecting the establishment of religion, or forbidding the free exercise thereof, was intended to allow everyone under the jurisdiction of the United States to entertain such notions respecting his relations to his Maker and the duties they impose as may be approved by his judgment and conscience, and to exhibit his sentiments in such form of worship as he may think proper, not injurious to the equal rights of others, and to prohibit legislation for the support of any religious tenets, or the modes of worship of any sect. The oppressive measures adopted, and the cruelties and punishments inflicted by the governments of Europe for many ages, to compel parties to conform in their religious beliefs and modes of worship to the views of the most numerous sect, and the folly of attempting in that way to control the mental operations of persons and enforce an outward conformity to a prescribed standard, led to the adoption of the Amendment in question. It was never intended or supposed that the Amendment could be invoked as a protection against legislation for the punishment of acts inimical to the peace, good order and morals of society. With man's relations to his Maker and the obligations he may think they impose, and the manner in which an expression shall be made by him of his belief on those subjects, no interference can be permitted, provided always the laws of society, designed to secure its peace and prosperity, and the morals of its people, are not interfered with. However free the exercise of religion may ⊥**343** be, it must be subordinate to the criminal laws of the country, passed with reference to actions regarded by general consent as properly the subjects of punitive legislation. There have been sects which denied as a part of their religious tenets that there should be any marriage tie, and advocated promiscuous intercourse of the sexes as prompted by the passions of their members. And history discloses the fact that the necessity of human sacrifices, on special occasions, has been a tenet of many sects. Should a sect of either of these kinds ever find its way into this country, swift punishment would follow the carrying into effect of its doctrines, and no heed would be given to the pretense that, as religious beliefs, their supporters could be protected in their exercise by the Constitution of the United States. Probably never before in the history of this country has it been seriously contended that the whole punitive power of the government, for acts recognized by the general consent of the Christian world in modern times as proper matters for prohibitory legislation, must be suspended in order that the tenets of a religious sect encouraging crime may be carried out without hindrance. . . .

⊥**345** It is assumed by counsel of the petitioner that, because no mode of worship can be established or religious tenets enforced in this country, therefore any form of worship may be followed and any tenets, however destructive of society, may be held and advocated, if asserted to be a part of the religious doctrines of those advocating and practicing them. But nothing is further from the truth. Whilst legislation for the establishment of a religion is forbidden, and its free exercise permitted, it does not follow that everything which may be so called can be tolerated. Crime is not the less odious because sanctioned by what any particular sect may designate as religion.

It only remains to refer to the laws which authorized the Legislature of the Territory of Idaho to prescribe the qualifications of voters and the oath they were required to take. The Revised Statutes provide that "the legislative power of every Territory shall extend to all rightful subjects of legislation not inconsistent with the Constitution and laws of the United States. But no law shall be passed interfering with the primary disposal of the soil; no tax shall be imposed upon the property of the United States; nor shall the lands or other property of nonresidents be taxed higher than the lands or other property of residents."

Under this general authority it would seem that the Territorial Legislature was authorized to prescribe any qualifications for voters calculated to secure obedience to its laws. But, in addition to the above law, section 1859 of the Revised Statutes ⊥**346** provides that "every male citizen above the age of twenty-one, including persons who have legally declared their intention to become citizens in any Territory hereafter organized, and who are actual residents of such Territory at the time of the organization thereof, shall be entitled to vote at the first election in such Territory, and to hold any office therein; subject, nevertheless, to the limitations specified in the next section," namely, that at all elections in any Territory subsequently organized by Congress, as well as at all elections in Territories already organized, the qualifications of voters and for holding office shall be such as may be prescribed by the Legislative Assembly of each Territory, subject, nevertheless, to the following restrictions:

First. That the right of suffrage and of holding office shall be exercised only by citizens of the United States above the age of twenty-one or persons above that age who have declared their intention to become such citizens;

Second. That the elective franchise or the right of holding office shall not be denied to any citizen on account of race, color or previous condition of servitude;

Third. That no soldier or sailor or other person in the army or navy, or attached to troops in the service of the United States, shall be allowed to vote unless he has made his permanent domicil in the Territory for six months; and,

Fourth. That no person belonging to the army or navy shall be elected to or hold a civil office or appointment in the Territory.

These limitations are the only ones placed upon the authority of Territorial Legislatures against granting the right of suffrage or of holding office. They have the power, therefore, to prescribe any reasonable qualifications of voters and for holding office not inconsistent with the above limitations. In our judgment, section 501 of the Revised Statutes of Idaho Territory, which provides that "no person under guardianship, *non compos mentis* or insane, nor any person convicted of treason, felony or bribery in this Territory, or in any other State or Territory in the Union, unless restored to civil rights; nor any person who is a bigamist or polygamist, or who teaches, advises, ⊥**347** counsels or encourages any person or persons to become bigamists or polygamists, or to commit any other crime defined by law, or to enter into what is known as plural or celestial marriage, or who is a member of any order, organization or association which teaches, advises, counsels or encourages its members or devotees or any other persons to commit the crime of bigamy or polygamy, or any other crime defined by law, either as a rite or ceremony of such order, organization or association, or otherwise, is permitted to vote at any election, or to hold any position or office of honor, trust or profit within this Territory," is not open to any constitutional or legal objection. With the exception of persons under guardianship or of unsound mind, it simply excludes from the privilege of voting, or of holding any office of honor, trust or profit, those who have been convicted of certain offenses, and those who advocate a practical resistance to the laws of the Territory and justify and approve the commission of crimes forbidden by it. The second subdivision of section 504 of the Revised Statutes of Idaho, requiring every person desiring to have his name registered as a voter to take an oath that he does not belong to an order that advises a disregard of the criminal law of the Territory, is not open to any valid legal objection to which our attention has been called.

The position that Congress has, by its Statute, covered the whole subject of punitive legislation against bigamy and polygamy, leaving nothing for territorial action on the subject, does not impress us as entitled to much weight. The Statute of Congress of March 22, 1882, amending a previous section of the Revised Statutes in reference to bigamy, declares "that no polygamist, bigamist or any person cohabiting with more than one woman, and no woman cohabiting with any of the persons described as aforesaid in this section, in any Territory or other place over which the United States have exclusive jurisdiction, shall be entitled to vote at any election held in any such Territory or other place, or be eligible for election or appointment to or be entitled to hold any office or place of public trust, honor or emolument in, under or for any such Territory or place, or under the United States."

⊥**348**This is a general law applicable to all Territories and other places under the exclusive jurisdiction of the United States. It does not purport to restrict the legislation of the Territories over kindred offenses or over the means for their ascertainment and prevention. The cases in which the legislation of Congress will supersede the legislation of a State or Territory, without specific provisions to that effect, are those in which the same matter is the subject of legislation by both. There the action of Congress may well be considered as covering the entire ground. But here there is nothing of this kind. The Act of Congress does not touch upon teaching, advising and counseling the practice of bigamy and polygamy, that is, upon aiding and abetting in the commission of those crimes, nor upon the mode adopted, by means of the oath required for registration, to prevent persons from being enabled by their votes to defeat the criminal laws of the country.

The judgment of the court below is therefore *Affirmed.*

THE JEHOVAH'S WITNESSES CASES

Almost fifty years passed before the Supreme Court again dealt directly with the issue of religious liberty. The Jehovah's Witnesses, who like the Mormons were subjected to much mistreatment before they ultimately attained "respectability," provided the opportunity for the Court to develop a significant body of federal case law on the subject. In the years since 1938, approximately eighty cases involving the sect have been carried to the Supreme Court. All individuals, as well as religious bodies, owe this sometimes intolerant and belligerent—but always tenacious—group a debt of gratitude for forcing the Court to wrestle with issues which it sometimes would surely have preferred to avoid. In the process of thinking and rethinking the issues raised in the continuing litigation, the Court has been forced to develop and refine new formulae giving not only greater clarity but also greater breadth to the meaning of the free exercise clause.

The Jehovah's Witnesses movement, which denies that it is a religion as such, was organized in the 1870s by Charles Taze Russell; the followers were known for years as "Russellites." In 1884 the Watch Tower Bible and Tract Society was incorporated. On his death in 1916 Russell's position was filled by Joseph F. Rutherford, who was president of the group when it first began to attract wide public attention in the 1930s due to rapid growth and an unorthodox attitude toward both organized government and religious organizations.

Witnesses ordinarily refuse to vote, hold office, perform jury or military duty, or to cooperate or compromise with various other government regulations. Their most spectacular brushes with the law and the public probably arose through refusal to salute the flag, regarded as a "graven image" to which Exodus 20:4-5 forbids obeisance. Their distinctive interpretation of Old Testament texts prohibiting the eating of blood causes them to refuse blood transfusions for themselves and family members.

Organized religions enjoy no more respect from the Witnesses than does government. Their frequently repeated slogans proclaim that religion is a "snare" and a "racket," and their strongest invectives are reserved for the Roman Catholic Church.

Though they maintain modest kingdom halls, Jehovah's Witnesses rely for membership primarily on direct evangelism which takes them to the street corners and from door to door where they distribute tracts, books, and their regular publications, *Awake!* and *Watchtower.* "Contributions" for the printed materials are accepted, but they are given free if a contribution is not offered.

Every baptized Witness is considered a minister, which explains the sect's insistent claim for deferment from compulsory military service. There are two principal classes of ministers: (1) "publishers," who "publish the glad tidings" on a part-time basis and (2) "pioneers," who do not hold a secular job but spend their entire time working for the sect. At least in the early years the movement attracted primarily the disadvantaged and the alienated, who ranked low in both income and education.

In view of these unconventional doctrines and aggressive proselytizing tactics, it is not surprising that as the number of converts to the movement increased, both the public and public officials reacted negatively. Frequently the reaction took the form of mob violence against members of the group. Community and state officials moved more "legally" to curb the Witnesses by enacting new ordinances or redirecting existing laws at Witness techniques. Licensing laws, permit requirements, tax measures, anti-littering laws, sound truck regulations, anti-peddling ordinances—all these and more were utilized.

The Witnesses were not intimidated by this harassment. They pressed forward with perseverance in their active personal evangelism. Though they hold government in low esteem, they have not been the least reluctant to turn to one of its agencies to sustain them when they needed it. Vigorously and persistently they have called on the courts to protect their constitutional rights; and when state courts have failed to do so, they have sought to avail themselves of the opportunity presented by recent developments in the incorporation movement to appeal their cases to the United States Supreme Court. The first appeal—which challenged the ordinance of a small Georgia town requiring written permission of the city manager prior to distribution of circulars, handbills, and other advertising or literature—was dismissed by the Court in 1937 for lack of a substantial federal question *(Coleman* v. *Griffen)*.

Attorneys for the Witnesses then prepared another legal attack on the same ordinance *(Lovell* v. *Griffen)*. This appeal was accepted and considered by the Court, not on the basis of religious liberty, but on the closely related First Amendment guarantee of free press, which had been incorporated a few years earlier. A unanimous Court held the ordinance void on its face: it gave the city manager no reasonable guideline to govern his exercise of authority. His unfettered power of censorship through prior restraint was so great as to constitute a clear violation of freedom of press. The Court observed that freedom to publish without freedom to circulate would be of little value.

At the next session of the Court a similar ordinance of Irvington, New Jersey, was invalidated by a seven-to-one vote *(Schneider* v. *Irvington)*. Since both these cases were decided on free press grounds, the Court did not need to determine whether there might be a difference of degree in the right to distribute religious pamphlets as opposed to literature containing other ideas, and hence no pressure to reconsider the test governing free exercise of religion announced in the Mormon cases.[1]

In 1940 came the landmark case of CANTWELL v. CONNECTICUT. Here, a Jehovah's Witness and his two sons were approaching persons on the streets of a predominantly Roman Catholic neighborhood of New Haven, Connecticut, asking permission to play for them a record entitled "Enemies," which contained a particularly vitriolic attack on the Roman Catholic Church. Although the listeners were incensed, no violence occurred. The father and sons were arrested, however, and eventually convicted of breach of the peace and of failure to obtain in advance a "certificate of approval" from the secretary of the Public Welfare Council. That official had the authority to withhold the permit if he was not satisfied that the cause represented by the applicant was a "religious one" or was a "bona fide object of charity and philanthropy and conforms to reasonable standards of efficiency and integrity."

Although the opinion written by Justice Roberts for a unanimous Court specified that nothing said in the opinion was "intended even remotely to imply that, under the cloak of religion, persons may, with impunity, commit frauds upon the public," it voided both the conviction of the Cantwells and the Connecticut statute.

The *Cantwell* decision has had great significance other than as a major victory for Jehovah's Witnesses. For the first time the Court specifically incorporated the Free Exercise Clause into the Fourteenth Amendment, thus applying it to the states. The Court also found it necessary in *Cantwell* to construct a doctrine for the determination of the limits of governmental control over religious freedom on a broader base than the "belief-action" test of the Mormon cases. Although the opinion pays its respects to this distinction, it clearly goes beyond: it warns that the power to regulate freedom to act must not be used in such a way as "unduly to infringe the protected freedom."

Justice Roberts also for the first time applied the liberal "clear and present danger" doctrine (first enunciated by Justice Holmes in the famous 1919 free speech case of *Schenck* v. *United States)* to the free exercise of religion. This requirement of a show-

[1]Even after the free exercise clause was incorporated, the Court sometimes avoided the religious issue. For example, in *Marin* v. *Struthers* (1943), another Jehovah's Witness case, the majority opinion relied on speech and press grounds alone to invalidate a city ordinance making it unlawful to knock on doors or ring doorbells to summon the occupants to the door to receive handbills or other literature. Nearly 50 years later, Justice Scalia, in EMPLOYMENT DIVISION OF OREGON v. SMITH (1990), argued: "The only decisions in which we have held that the First Amendment bars application of a neutral, generally applicable law to religiously motivated action have involved not the Free Exercise Clause alone, but the Free Exercise Clause in conjunction with other constitutional protections, such as freedom of speech and of the press, . . . or the right of parents, acknowledged in *Pierce* v. *Society of Sisters* to direct the education of their children, . . ." 494 U.S. 872, 881.

ing of clear and present danger to the public interest to justify state restraint of religion was to prove extremely significant, as the second flag salute case and others would show.

Some preliminary consideration was also given to a concept of "nondiscrimination" or "neutrality" when the opinion indicated that any classification using religion as a basis is invalid, whether the classification works to the advantage or disadvantage of a religious activity. The Court indicated that while a carefully drawn nondiscriminatory statute that incidentally infringes on religious groups or activities might be countenanced, a law drafted or applied specifically to disadvantage the activities of these groups is clearly unconstitutional.[2] Here, the standard was applied to the benefit of the Witnesses.

The same test sometimes worked to their detriment. In 1942 the Court, in JONES v. OPELIKA, used it to uphold a practice which posed an extremely serious threat to the economically deprived group: the requirement of the payment of a tax for the distribution of literature. By a five-to-four vote the Court found that the ordinance did not discriminate against religious or other types of literature. The tax fell on all salesmen alike, and the First Amendment does not "require a subsidy in the form of fiscal exemption."

Justice Murphy, in dissent, sought to tie the Free Exercise Clause to the "preferred freedoms" concept. The Court had used this phrase in some speech and press cases after 1938 to insist on a "more exacting judicial scrutiny" of First Amendment guarantees than that given other constitutional rights. Murphy went further, however; he would elevate freedom of religion to a plane above even the other First Amendment rights. Those engaged in the dissemination of all ideas and opinions should enjoy a favored position over purely commercial endeavors, but a still higher level is reached when religious doctrines are involved. Even dearer than free speech and free press, he argued, is the right of individuals to worship freely, and "to carry their message or their gospel to every living creature."

Largely because of the appointment of Wiley B. Rutledge to fill the vacancy created by Justice Byrnes's resignation, the "preferred freedoms" doctrine became majority opinion the next year when the Court, by another five-to-four vote, overruled *Opelika*[3] in MURDOCK v. PENNSYLVANIA. Writing for the new majority, Justice Douglas brushed aside the nondiscriminatory argument and clearly enunciated the preferred position of the First Amendment freedoms with a particular emphasis on religion as he sought to restore "to their high, constitutional position the liberties of itinerant evangelists who disseminate their religious beliefs and the tenets of their faith through distribution of literature."

Though some judges, such as Justice Frankfurter, who always referred to the concept as a "mischievous phrase," refused to accept the "preferred freedoms" test, it has often been adhered to implicitly, if not explicitly, and has been important in giving added dignity to religious rights. The next year the *Murdock* holding was extended in *Follett* v. *McCormick* to give tax immunity to a Jehovah's Witness whose sole source of income was the sale of religious books.

But the most dramatic public controversy involving Jehovah's Witnesses was incited by their refusal to permit their children to comply with the flag-salute requirement imposed by many public school boards. Such nonconformity is never popular; and as World War II approached with its mounting patriotic fervor, it became a highly emotional issue.

Children of members of the sect were frequently expelled as a result of refusal to participate in the flag salute. Their parents then came under legal pressures because of compulsory school attendance laws and were convicted in numerous state courts. At least three times between 1938 and 1940, the Witnesses appealed in vain to the Supreme Court for relief. In 1940, the year the Court heard the *Cantwell* case, it finally agreed to consider the flag-salute issue in MINERSVILLE SCHOOL DISTRICT v. GOBITIS. Contrary to the decision in *Cantwell,* the Court, with only Justice Stone in eloquent dissent, found against the Witnesses' claim of violation of their constitutional rights. Justice Frankfurter used the nondiscrimination test to emphasize that the flag-salute requirement was a general law applicable to all and was not intended to restrict religious beliefs. He stressed the relationship between symbolism and national unity. Religion is a "precious right," he agreed, but it is not absolute; and when, as here, it collides with national security, "reasonable accommodations" must be made in an effort to "reconcile two rights in order to prevent either from destroying the other."

Seldom does a Court that votes eight-to-one then reverse itself in the brief span of three years. Such did happen here for a variety of reasons. Two changes in personnel occurred, when Justices Jackson and Rutledge replaced Justices Hughes and

[2]This doctrine of "neutrality" has been proposed as the primary test for determining the limits of government with respect to both religion clauses by Professor Philip B. Kurland of the University of Chicago Law School. See *Religion and the Law: Of Church and State and the Supreme Court* (Chicago: Aldine Publishing Company, 1962).

[3]*Jones* v. *Opelika* was put back on the Court's docket in 1943. Because the issues were the same as those in *Murdock* v. *Pennsylvania*, they were argued together with that case. Hence, *Jones* v. *Opelika II* is merely a *per curiam* opinion explaining this fact.

McReynolds. The Court was also likely affected both by the severe criticism to which its decision was subjected by legal scholars and many religious leaders and by the wave of public violence against the Witnesses by persons who apparently assumed that the Court, in rejecting the claims of the Witnesses, had rejected the movement. In an unprecedented move, three members of the Court in effect invited a rehearing of the flag-salute issue. Dissenting in *Jones* v. *Opelika I,* Justices Black, Douglas, and Murphy, who surprisingly had been in the *Gobitis* majority two years before, recanted. They had come to believe that *Gobitis* as well as *Opelika I* had been "wrongly decided."

The opportunity for reversal came quickly. In WEST VIRGINIA STATE BOARD OF EDUCATION v. BARNETTE the Court, by a six-to-three vote, struck down a West Virginia requirement different in no significant way from that involved in the *Gobitis* case. Relying primarily on freedom of speech and press rather than of religion, Justice Jackson for the majority measured the peaceful nonparticipation on the part of the students against the "clear and present danger" test, which he here read to mean "grave and immediate danger," and found insufficient grounds for state restraint.[4]

After a rather inauspicious beginning, the Jehovah's Witnesses have forged, through their unflagging persistence, a quite remarkable record of judicial victories before the Supreme Court; and they have ultimately won the vast majority of the cases appealed to the high tribunal. Yet, in some few instances, the Court has denied their claims without later reversing itself. In 1941, in COX v. NEW HAMPSHIRE, the Court upheld as a reasonable police regulation a city's requirement that Witnesses, like other groups, give notice and obtain a permit before staging a parade or procession on the public streets. The next year, in *Chaplinsky* v. *New Hampshire,* the Court sustained the conviction of a Witness for cursing in strong terms a city marshal who interfered with his street-corner preaching. In the opinion for the Court, Justice Murphy who, though a Roman Catholic, ordinarily voted for the Witnesses, observed that he could not "conceive that cursing a public officer is the exercise of religion in any sense of the term." In 1944 the Court, recognizing the power of the state to protect children from physical harm or abuse even at the hands of religiously motivated parents or other relatives, upheld a state child labor law in PRINCE v. MASSACHUSETTS when applied to a nine-year-old girl who, in the company of her aunt, was distributing religious literature at night on a downtown street corner.

Prince v. *Massachusetts* has since been used by state courts as a precedent for state action ordering necessary blood transfusions for children of Jehovah's Witnesses when the parents refuse to agree to the transfusions. The Supreme Court has never considered the blood transfusion issue except as it has consistently denied certiorari from lower court decisions raising the point. The lower courts have regularly held that parents cannot on religious grounds deny their child a blood transfusion if such a transfusion is necessary to save the child's life. Court orders may be obtained authorizing the transfusion. Similar action may be taken with respect to a pregnant woman who refuses a transfusion. Courts also ordinarily hold that parents with minor children will not be allowed to endanger the future welfare of the children by refusing on religious grounds to submit to transfusion.

Competent adults without minor children pose a greater problem when they refuse transfusions on religious grounds. Although most appellate courts uphold court-ordered transfusions even in these instances, there has been at least one case in which an Illinois court ruled that a competent adult without minor children could not, over her religiously based protestations, be compelled to receive a transfusion.[5]

In *Neimotko* v. *Maryland* (1951) the Supreme Court struck down denial of a permit by a city council to Jehovah's Witnesses who sought use of a city park for religious services after having received "unsatisfactory responses" to questions with respect to their attitude toward flag salutes and military service and

[4] *Barnette* was the controlling precedent used in 1977 by a federal district court judge and the Court of Appeals for the Third Circuit in striking down a New Jersey statute requiring students to stand at "respectful attention" if they did not participate in the school's flag salute ceremony (*Lipp* v. *Norris*). See also *Goetz* v. *Ansell* (1973) and *Banks* v. *Board of Public Instruction of Dade County, Florida* (1970). The Supreme Court also used *Barnette* as a precedent for holding that New Hampshire could not punish a Jehovah's Witness couple for covering up the state motto "Live Free or Die" on their automobile license plates, a motto which they considered to be repugnant to their moral, religious, and political beliefs. Chief Justice Burger, for the majority of six, agreed that the requirement that the motto be displayed was a less serious violation of personal liberty than coerced flag salute but he viewed the difference as one only of degree. In both instances the individual was being forced to express "an ideological point of view" he could not accept. "The First Amendment," he wrote, "protects the right of individuals to hold a point of view different from the majority and to refuse to foster, in the way New Hampshire commands, an idea they find morally objectionable" (*Wooley* v. *Maynard,* 1977).

[5] *In re Brooks* (1965). Some of the leading state cases involving the blood transfusion issue are: *Jehovah's*

to their interpretation of the Bible. The Court unanimously held the denial violative of both freedom of speech and of equal protection of the laws.

Although the Jehovah's Witnesses have ceased to be the main focus of controversies involving religious liberty, justices of succeeding courts have frequently resorted to the tests applied and refined in cases occasioned by Witnesses. The quest for new judicial standards has continued as cases involving individuals and groups as diverse as conscientious objectors to war, Sabbatarians, Black Muslims[6] and the gentle Amish have made their way to the high court.

Two of these tests should be mentioned because together they seem to represent the present position of the Court: the "alternative means" test and the "compelling interest" rule. The "alternative means" test, although used earlier in free speech cases, was first advanced in connection with free exercise of religion in 1961 in BRAUNFELD v. BROWN, a case in which the majority opinion upheld the Sunday closing laws against claims of violation of religious rights of Orthodox Jewish merchants. But the potential of the test for expanding religious liberty was exhibited two years later in SHERBERT v. VERNER. There it was used to invalidate a state law denying unemployment compensation to a Seventh-day Adventist who could not obtain employment because of her refusal to work on Saturday. The rule forbids the state, as it seeks further to legitimate secular goals, to impose even an indirect burden on religious observances unless the state can show that there are no practicable less-restrictive "alternative means" by which the legislative purpose can be achieved. The Court found no effective alternative means available to the state in *Braunfeld;* it did in *Sherbert.* Exemption could be granted from the statute for refusal to work for religious reasons.

The second rule imposes upon the state the necessity of justifying infringement of religious rights by a showing of nothing less than a "compelling" state

---

Witnesses v. *King County Hospital* (1968), in which the Supreme Court affirmed in a *per curiam* opinion a lower court ruling upholding a Washington law which allowed children in need of blood transfusions to be declared wards of the state if their parents, on religious grounds, withheld permission; *Raleigh Fitkin-Paul Morgan Memorial Hospital* v. *Anderson* (1964), which involved a pregnant woman; *John F. Kennedy Memorial Hospital* v. *Heston* (1971), in which an unmarried childless woman refused a transfusion. Cf. Ronald B. Flowers, "Freedom of Religion Versus Civil Authority in Matters of Health," in "The Uneasy Boundary: Church and State," *The Annals of the American Academy of Political and Social Science,* ed. Dean M. Kelley 446 (November 1979): 156-59.

[6]The problems of conscientious objectors, Sabbatarians, and Amish are discussed in some detail at other points in the book. In recent years public and judicial controversies have sometimes arisen concerning the beliefs, activities, and ultimate goals of the Nation of Islam, or the Black Muslims, an aggressive black separatist religious group. Because of their strident demands for racial separation, members of this unconventional sect were sometimes considered racial extremists rather than a genuine religious group. In 1975, after the death of Elijah Muhammad, founder of the organization, his son Wallace took over the leadership of the group and made it less racist and much closer to classical Islam. His supporters began accepting white members, muted their militancy, and began working more nearly for the economic welfare of all poor people, not just blacks. The name of the group was changed to "American Muslim Mission" which was disbanded as a national organization in 1985 by Wallace who encouraged all its members to work with good Muslims everywhere. In 1978, Louis Farrakhan split with Muhammad over the revisions and reinstituted the Nation of Islam with much the same ideological stance that it had under Elijah Muhammad. For a good account of the various changes in the movement, see Lawrence H. Mamiga, "From Black Muslim to Bilalian: The Evolution of a Movement," *Journal for the Scientific Study of Religion* 21 (1982): 138-52.

Most litigation involving Black Muslims has developed from refusals of prison authorities to permit them to exercise their religious tenets to the same degree as prisoners of other religious persuasions. Some lower courts have sustained the denials on the basis of the recognized need for prison discipline and the possibility that the group's black supremacy arguments would tend to encourage challenges to the authority of white prison guards and officials. However, the lower court decisions have usually been reversed on appeal, particularly where rulings have been based on a summary determination that Black Muslims were not members of a bona fide religion.

In 1964 a Black Muslim case, *Cooper* v. *Pate,* was accepted by the U.S. Supreme Court. A federal district court in Illinois had rejected the claims of a Black Muslim prisoner that he had been discriminated against because of his religious beliefs by prison officials when they denied him the right to obtain his Qur'an and other Muslim literature, to have visits by Black Muslim ministers, and to attend religious services. A court of appeals affirmed the decision, but the Supreme Court in a brief *per curiam* opinion reversed the lower courts. The district court subsequently ruled that the challenged prison restrictions could be imposed only if a "clear and present danger to prison security" would result from the requested religious privileges. (Eight years later the Court in another *per curiam* opinion written in *Cruz* v. *Beto* extended the same free exercise rights to a Buddhist convict.) Other cases involving Black Muslim rights in prison are *Williford* v. *California* (1963), *Knuckles* v. *Prasse* (1971) and *Hutto* v. *Finney* (1978). Undoubtedly the most publicized Black Muslim case to reach the Supreme Court was that of world boxing champion Muhammad Ali who had been convicted for refusing to serve in the Vietnam War notwithstanding his claim of conscientious objector status. The conviction was set aside in a *per curiam* decision *(Cassius M. Clay Jr. (Muhammad Ali)* v. *United States* 1971). O'LONE v. SHABAZZ (1987) is discussed later.

interest that requires the encroachment. This rule was first advanced by the Court in *Sherbert.* It was given greater emphasis and clarity in 1972 in WISCONSIN v. YODER, in which the Court upheld the right of Amish parents to take their children from public school after the eighth grade. Chief Justice Burger, in the majority opinion, placed an even heavier burden of proof on the state than verbalized in *Sherbert,* when he emphasized that the "compelling state interest" means that "[o]nly those interests of the highest order, and those not otherwise served can overbalance the legitimate claim to the free exercise of religion" (406 U.S. 205, 215).

In 1986, in her dissenting opinion in GOLDMAN v. WEINBERGER, Justice O'Connor summed up her understanding of the tests applied by the present Court when she wrote:

> First, when the government attempts to deny a Free Exercise claim, it must show that an unusually important interest is at stake, whether that interest is denominated "compelling," "of the highest order," or "overriding." Second, the government must show that granting the requested exemption will do substantial harm to that interest, whether by showing that the means adopted is the "least restrictive" or "essential," or that the interest will not "otherwise be served" (475 U.S. 503, 530).

As had those previously used, these tests involved judicial balancing of the competing interests of religious freedom and the goals that the state was seeking to achieve by restricting that freedom. Both tilted the scale heavily in favor of religion. Applied together, as in WISCONSIN v. YODER, they gave an extremely wide latitude to actions based on religious belief, and accorded to the First Amendment commitment to free exercise of religion a position second to none in the scale of constitutional values. When restrained by state actions, practitioners of widely disparate religious beliefs and actions called upon the "compelling governmental interest" and "least restraint" tests. They did not always win their appeal, but the tests were applied.

As will be discussed at some length later, in EMPLOYMENT DIVISION, DEPARTMENT OF HUMAN RESOURCES OF OREGON v. SMITH (1990) the Court appeared to abandon the combined tests in considering claims based exclusively on free exercise grounds, except in a very limited category of cases. In *Smith,* Justice Scalia, for a majority of six, held the compelling interest test to be inapplicable to challenges of valid neutral criminal laws of general applicability that require or forbid acts contrary to claimants' religious beliefs. A state is free to provide nondiscriminatory exemption for a particular religious practice but is not constitutionally *required* to do so. Accommodation on religious grounds is properly left to the political process. Many close followers of the Court have expressed fears that *Smith* may signal a significant retreat of the Court from its role as champion of free exercise of religion, especially for members of unorthodox minority religions.

CANTWELL v. CONNECTICUT

310 U.S. 296
ON APPEAL AND WRIT OF CERTIORARI TO THE SUPREME COURT OF ERRORS OF THE STATE OF CONNECTICUT
Argued March 29, 1940 — Decided May 20, 1940

⊥**300** Mr. *Justice ROBERTS* delivered the opinion of the Court:

Newton Cantwell and his two sons, Jesse and Russell, members of a group known as Jehovah's Witnesses, and claiming to be ordained ministers, were arrested in New Haven, Connecticut, and each was charged by information in five counts, with statutory and common law offenses. After trial in the Court of Common Pleas of New Haven County each of them was convicted on the third count, which charged a violation of § 6294 of the General Statutes of Connecticut, and on the fifth count, which charged commission of the common law offense of inciting a breach of the peace. On appeal to the Supreme Court the conviction of all three on the third count was affirmed. The conviction of Jesse Cantwell, on the fifth count, was also affirmed, but the conviction of Newton and Russell on that count was reversed and a new trial ordered as to them.

By demurrers to the information, by requests for rulings of law at the trial, and by their assignments of error in the State Supreme Court, the appellants pressed the contention that the statute under which the third count was drawn was offensive to the due process clause of the Fourteenth Amendment because, on its face and as construed and applied, it denied them freedom of speech and prohibited their free exercise of religion. In like manner ⊥**301** they made the point that they could not be found guilty on the fifth count, without violation of the Amendment.

We have jurisdiction on appeal from the judgments on the third count, as there was drawn in question the validity of a state statute under the federal Constitution, and the decision was in favor of validity. Since the conviction on the fifth count was not based upon a statute, but presents a substantial question under the federal Constitution, we granted the writ of certiorari in respect of it.

The facts adduced to sustain the convictions on the third count follow. On the day of their arrest the appellants were engaged in going singly from house to house on Cassius Street in New Haven. They were individually equipped with a bag containing books and pamphlets on religious subjects, a portable phonograph and a set of records, each of which, when played, introduced, and was a description of, one of the books. Each appellant asked the person who responded to his call for permission to play one of the records. If permission was granted he asked the person to buy the book described and, upon refusal, he solicited such contribution towards the publication of the pamphlets as the listener was willing to make. If a contribution was received a pamphlet was delivered upon condition that it would be read.

Cassius Street is in a thickly populated neighborhood, where about ninety per cent of the residents are Roman Catholics. A phonograph record, describing a book entitled "Enemies," included an attack on the Catholic religion. None of the persons interviewed were members of Jehovah's Witnesses.

The statute under which the appellants were charged provides:

"No person shall solicit money, services, subscriptions or any valuable thing for any alleged religious, charitable ⊥**302** or philanthropic cause, from other than a member of the organization for whose benefit such person is soliciting or within the county in which such person or organization is located unless such cause shall have been approved by the secretary of the public welfare council. Upon application of any person in behalf of such cause, the secretary shall determine whether such cause is a religious one or is a bona fide object of charity or philanthropy and conforms to reasonable standards of efficiency and integrity, and, if he shall so find, shall approve the same and issue to the authority in charge a certificate to that effect. Such certificate may be revoked at any time. Any person violating any provision to this section shall be fined not more than one hundred dollars or imprisoned not more than thirty days or both."

The appellants claimed that their activities were not within the statute but consisted only of distribution of books, pamphlets, and periodicals. The State Supreme Court construed the finding of the trial court to be that "in addition to the sale of the books and the distribution of the pamphlets the defendants were also soliciting contributions or donations of money for an alleged religious cause, and thereby came within the purview of the statute." It overruled the contention that the Act, as applied to the appellants, offends the due process clause of the Fourteenth Amendment, because it abridges or denies religious freedom and liberty of speech and press. The court stated that it was the solicitation that brought the appellants within the sweep of the Act and not their other activities in the dissemination of literature. It declared the legislation constitutional as an effort by the State to protect the public against fraud and imposition in the solicitation of funds for what purported to be religious, charitable, or philanthropic causes.

The facts which were held to support the conviction of Jesse Cantwell on the fifth count were that he stopped ⊥**303** two men in the street, asked, and received, permission to play a phonograph record, and played the record "Enemies," which attacked the religion and church of the two men, who were Catholics. Both were incensed by the contents of the record and were tempted to strike Cantwell unless he went away. On being told to be on his way he left their presence. There was no evidence that he was personally offensive or entered into any argument with those he interviewed.

The court held that the charge was not assault or breach of the peace or threats on Cantwell's part, but invoking or inciting others to breach of the peace, and that the facts supported the conviction of that offense.

First. We hold that the statute, as construed and applied to the appellants, deprives them of their liberty without due process of law in contravention of the Fourteenth Amendment. The fundamental concept of liberty embodied in that Amendment embraces the liberties guaranteed by the First Amendment. The First Amendment declares that Congress shall make no law respecting an establishment of religion or prohibiting the free exercise thereof. The Fourteenth Amendment has rendered the legislatures of the states as incompetent as Congress to enact such laws. The constitutional inhibition of legislation on the subject of religion has a double aspect. On the one hand, it forestalls compulsion by law of the acceptance of any creed or the practice of any form of worship. Freedom of conscience and freedom to adhere to such religious organization or form of worship as the individual may choose cannot be restricted by law. On the other hand, it safeguards the free exercise of the chosen form of religion. Thus the Amendment embraces two concepts,—freedom to believe and freedom to act. The first is absolute but, in the nature of things, the ⊥**304** second cannot be. Conduct remains subject to regulation for the protection of society. The freedom to act must have appropriate definition to preserve the enforcement of that protection. In every case the power to regulate must be so exercised as not, in attaining a permissible end, unduly to infringe the protected freedom. No one would contest the proposition that a state may not, by statute, wholly deny the right to preach or to disseminate religious views. Plainly such a previous and absolute restraint would violate the terms of the guaranty. It is equally clear that a state may by general and non-discriminatory legislation regulate the times, the places, and the manner of soliciting upon its streets, and of holding meetings thereon; and may in other respects safeguard the peace, good order and comfort of the community, without unconstitutionally invading the liberties protected by the Fourteenth Amendment. The appellants are right in their insistence that the Act in question is not such a regulation. If a certificate is procured, solicitation is permitted without restraint but, in the absence of a certificate, solicitation is altogether prohibited.

The appellants urge that to require them to obtain a certificate as a condition of soliciting support for their views amounts to a prior restraint on the exercise of their religion within the meaning of the Constitution. The State insists that the Act, as construed by the Supreme Court of Connecticut, imposes no previous restraint upon the dissemination of religious views or teaching but merely safeguards against the perpetration of frauds under the cloak of religion. Conceding that this is so, the question remains whether the method adopted by Connecticut to ⊥**305** that end transgresses the liberty safeguarded by the Constitution.

The general regulation, in the public interest, of solicitation, which does not involve any religious test and does not unreasonably obstruct or delay the collection of funds, is not open to any constitutional objection, even though the collection be for a religious purpose. Such regulation would not constitute a prohibited previous restraint on the free exercise of religion or interpose an inadmissible obstacle to its exercise.

It will be noted, however, that the Act requires an application to the secretary of the public welfare council of the State; that he is empowered to determine whether the cause is a religious one, and that the issue of a certificate depends upon his affirmative action. If he finds that the cause is not that of religion, to solicit for it becomes a crime. He is not to issue a certificate as a matter of course. His decision to issue or refuse it involves appraisal of facts, the exercise of judgment, and the formation of an opinion. He is authorized to withhold his approval if he determines that the cause is not a religious one. Such a censorship of religion as the means of determining its right to survive is a denial of liberty protected by the First Amendment and included in the liberty which is within the protection of the Fourteenth.

The State asserts that if the licensing officer acts arbitrarily, capriciously, or corruptly, his action is subject to judicial correction. Counsel refer to the rule prevailing in Connecticut that the decision of a commission or an administrative official will be reviewed upon a claim that "it works material damage to individual or corporate rights, or invades or threatens such rights, or is so unreasonable as to justify judicial intervention, or is not consonant with justice, or that a legal duty has not ⊥**306** been performed." It is suggested that the statute is to be read as requiring the officer to issue a certificate unless the cause in question is clearly not a religious one; and that if he violates his duty his action will be corrected by a court.

To this suggestion there are several sufficient answers. The line between a discretionary and a ministerial act is not always easy to mark and the statute has not been construed by the State court to impose a mere ministerial duty on the secretary of the welfare council. Upon his decision as to the nature of the cause, the right to solicit depends. Moreover, the availability of a judicial remedy for abuses in the system of licensing still leaves that system one of previous restraint which, in the field of free speech and press, we have held inadmissible. A statute authorizing previous restraint upon the exercise of the guaranteed freedom by judicial decision after trial is as obnoxious to the Constitution as one providing for like restraint by administrative action.

Nothing we have said is intended even remotely to imply that, under the cloak of religion, persons may, with impunity, commit frauds upon the public. Certainly penal laws are available to punish such conduct. Even the exercise of religion may be at some slight inconvenience in order that the state may protect its citizens from injury. Without doubt a state may protect its citizens from fraudulent solicitation by requiring a stranger in the community, before permitting him publicly to solicit funds for any purpose, to establish his identity and his authority to act for the cause which he purports to represent. The state is likewise free to regulate the time ⊥**307** and manner of solicitation generally, in the interest of public safety, peace, comfort or convenience. But to condition the solicitation of aid for the perpetuation of religious views or systems upon a license, the grant of which rests in the exercise of a determination by state authority as to what is a religious cause, is to lay a forbidden burden upon the exercise of liberty protected by the Constitution.

Second. We hold that, in the circumstances disclosed, the conviction of Jesse Cantwell on the fifth count must be set aside. Decision as to the lawfulness of the conviction demands the weighing of two conflicting interests. The fundamental law declares the interest of the United States that the free exercise of religion be not prohibited and that freedom to communicate information and opinion be not abridged. The state of Connecticut has an obvious interest in the preservation and protection of peace and good order within her borders. We must determine whether the alleged protection of the State's interest, means to which end would, in the absence of limitation by the federal Constitution, lie wholly within the State's discretion, has been pressed, in this instance, to a point where it has come into fatal collision with the overriding interest protected by the federal compact.

Conviction on the fifth count was not pursuant to a statute evincing a legislative judgment that street discussion of religious affairs, because of its tendency to provoke disorder, should be regulated, or a judgment that the playing of a phonograph on the streets should in the interest of comfort or privacy be limited or prevented. Violation of an Act exhibiting such a legislative judgment and narrowly drawn to prevent the supposed evil, would pose a question differing from that we must here answer. Such a declaration of the State's policy ⊥**308** would weigh heavily in any challenge of the law as infringing constitutional limitations. Here, however, the judgment is based on a common law concept of the most general and undefined nature. The court below has held that the petitioner's conduct constituted the commission of an offense under the State law, and we accept this decision as binding upon us to that extent.

The offense known as breach of the peace embraces a great variety of conduct destroying or menacing public order and tranquillity. It includes not only violent acts but acts and words likely to produce violence in others. No one would have the hardihood to suggest that the principle of freedom of speech sanctions incitement to riot or that religious liberty connotes the privilege to exhort others to physical attack upon those belonging to another sect. When clear and present danger of riot, disorder, interference with traffic upon the public streets, or other immediate threat to public safety, peace, or order, appears, the power of the state to prevent or punish is obvious. Equally obvious is it that a state may not unduly suppress free communication of views, religious or other, under the guise of conserving desirable conditions. Here we have a situation analogous to a conviction under a statute sweeping in a great variety of conduct under a general and indefinite characterization, and leaving to the executive and judicial branches too wide a discretion in its application.

Having these considerations in mind, we note that Jesse Cantwell, on April 26, 1938, was upon a public street, where he had a right to be, and where he had a right peacefully to impart his views to others. There is no showing that his deportment was noisy, truculent, overbearing or offensive. He requested of two pedestrians permission to play to them a phonograph record. The permission was granted. It is not claimed that he **⊥309** intended to insult or affront the hearers by playing the record. It is plain that he wished only to interest them in his propaganda. The sound of the phonograph is not shown to have disturbed residents of the street, to have drawn a crowd, or to have impeded traffic. Thus far he had invaded no right or interest of the public or of the men accosted.

The record played by Cantwell embodies a general attack on all organized religious systems as instruments of Satan and injurious to man; it then singles out the Roman Catholic Church for strictures couched in terms which naturally would offend not only persons of that persuasion, but all others who respect the honestly held religious faith of their fellows. The hearers were in fact highly offended. One of them said he felt like hitting Cantwell and the other that he was tempted to throw Cantwell off the street. The one who testified he felt like hitting Cantwell said, in answer to the question "Did you do anything else or have any other reaction?" "No, sir, because he said he would take the victrola and he went." The other witness testified that he told Cantwell he had better get off the street before something happened to him and that was the end of the matter as Cantwell picked up his books and walked up the street.

Cantwell's conduct, in the view of the court below, considered apart from the effect of his communication upon his hearers, did not amount to a breach of the peace. One may, however, be guilty of the offense if he commit acts or make statements likely to provoke violence and disturbance of good order, even though no such eventuality be intended. Decisions to this effect are many, but examination discloses that, in practically all, the provocative language which was held to amount to a breach of the peace consisted of profane, indecent, or abusive remarks directed to the person of the hearer. Resort to epithets or **⊥310** personal abuse is not in any proper sense communication of information or opinion safeguarded by the Constitution, and its punishment as a criminal act would raise no question under that instrument.

We find in the instant case no assault or threatening of bodily harm, no truculent bearing, no intentional discourtesy, no personal abuse. On the contrary, we find only an effort to persuade a willing listener to buy a book or to contribute money in the interest of what Cantwell, however misguided others may think him, conceived to be true religion.

In the realm of religious faith, and in that of political belief, sharp differences arise. In both fields the tenets of one man may seem the rankest error to his neighbor. To persuade others to his own point of view, the pleader, as we know, at times, resorts to exaggeration, to vilification of men who have been, or are, prominent in church or state, and even to false statement. But the people of this nation have ordained in the light of history, that, in spite of the probability of excesses and abuses, these liberties are, in the long view, essential to enlightened opinion and right conduct on the part of the citizens of a democracy.

The essential characteristic of these liberties is, that under their shield many types of life, character, opinion and belief can develop unmolested and unobstructed. Nowhere is this shield more necessary than in our own country for a people composed of many races and of many creeds. There are limits to the exercise of these liberties. The danger in these times from the coercive activities of those who in the delusion of racial or religious conceit would incite violence and breaches of the peace in order to deprive others of their equal right to the exercise of their liberties, is emphasized by events familiar to all. These and other transgressions of those limits the states appropriately may punish. **⊥311**

Although the contents of the record not unnaturally aroused animosity, we think that, in the absence of a statute narrowly drawn to define and punish specific conduct as constituting a clear and present danger to a substantial interest of the State, the petitioner's communication, considered in the light of the constitutional guaranties, raised no such clear and present menace to public peace and order as to render him liable to conviction of the common law offense in question.

The judgment affirming the convictions on the third and fifth counts is reversed and the cause is remanded for further proceedings not inconsistent with this opinion.

Reversed.

JONES v. OPELIKA (No. 280)

ON WRIT OF CERTIORARI TO THE SUPREME COURT OF THE STATE OF ALABAMA

BOWDEN v. FORT SMITH (No. 314)

ON WRIT OF CERTIORARI TO THE SUPREME COURT OF THE STATE OF ARKANSAS

JOBIN v. ARIZONA (No. 966)

ON APPEAL FROM THE SUPREME COURT OF THE STATE OF ARIZONA
316 U.S. 584
Argued February 5 and April 30, 1942 — Decided June 8, 1942

⊥585 Mr. *Justice REED* delivered the opinion of the Court:

By writ of certiorari in Nos. 280 and 314 and by appeal in No. 966 we have before us the question of the constitu⊥586tionality of various city ordinances imposing the license taxes upon the sale of printed matter for nonpayment of which the appellant, Jobin, and the petitioners, Jones, Bowden and Sanders, all members of the organization known as Jehovah's Witnesses, were convicted.

No. 280

The City of Opelika, Alabama, filed a complaint in the Circuit Court of Lee County charging petitioner Jones with violation of its licensing ordinance by selling books without a license, by operating as a Book Agent without a license, and by operating as a transient agent, dealer or distributor of books without a license. The license fee for Book Agents (Bibles excepted) was $10 per annum, that for transient agents, dealers or distributors of books $5. ⊥587 Under § 1 of the ordinance all licenses were subject to revocation in the discretion of the City Commission, with or without notice. There is a clause providing for severance in case of invalidity of any section, condition or provision. Petitioner demurred, alleging that the ordinance, because of unlimited discretion in revocation and requirement of a license, was an unconstitutional encroachment upon freedom of the press. During the trial without a jury these contentions, with the added claim of interference with freedom of religion, were renewed at the end of the city's case, and at the close of all the evidence. The court overruled these motions, and found petitioner guilty on evidence that without a license he had been displaying pamphlets in his upraised hand and walking on a city street selling them two for five cents. The court excluded as irrelevant testimony designed to show that the petitioner was an ordained minister, and that his activities ⊥588 were in furtherance of his beliefs and the teachings of Jehovah's Witnesses. Once again by an unsuccessful motion for new trial the constitutional issues were raised. The Court of Appeals of Alabama reversed the conviction on appeal because it thought the unlimited discretion of the City Commission to revoke the licenses invalidated the ordinance. Without discussion of this point the Supreme Court of Alabama decided that non-discriminatory licensing of the sale of books or tracts was constitutional, reversed the Court of Appeals, and stayed execution pending certiorari. This Court, having granted certiorari, dismissed the writ for lack of a final judgment. The Court of Appeals thereupon entered a judgment sustaining the conviction, which was affirmed by the Alabama Supreme Court and is final. We therefore grant the petition for rehearing of the dismissal of the writ, and proceed with the consideration of the case.

No. 315

Petitioners Bowden and Sanders were arrested by police officers of Fort Smith, Arkansas, brought before the Municipal Court on charges of violation of City Ordinance No. 1172, and convicted. They appealed to the Sebastian Circuit Court, and there moved to dismiss on the ground that the ordinance was an unconstitutional restriction of freedom of religion and of the press, contrary to the Fourteenth Amendment. The circuit judge heard the case de novo without a jury on stipulated facts. The ordinance required a license "For each person peddling dry goods, notions, wearing apparel, household goods or other articles not herein or otherwise specifically mentioned $25 per month, $10 per week, $2.50 per day." ⊥589 The petitioners, in the exercise of their beliefs concerning their duty to preach the gospel, admitted going from house to house without a license, playing phonographic transcriptions of Bible lectures, and distributing books setting forth their views to the residents in return for a contribution of twenty-five cents per book. When persons desiring books were unable to contribute, the books were in some instances given away free. The circuit judge concluded as a matter of law that the books were "other articles" and that petitioners were guilty of peddling without a license. A motion for new trial was denied. On appeal the Supreme Court of Arkansas held the ordinance constitutional on the authority of its previous decision in *Cook* v. *Harrison* and affirmed the convictions. This Court denied certiorari, but later, because of the similarity of the issues presented to those in the Jobin Case, No. 966, vacated the denial of certiorari and issued a writ.

No. 966

The City of Casa Grande, Arizona, by ordinance made it a misdemeanor for any person to carry on any occupation or business specified without first procuring a license. ⊥590 Transient merchants, peddlers and street vendors were listed as subject to a quarterly license fee of $25.00, payable in advance. In the Superior Court of Pinal County Jobin was tried and convicted by a jury on a complaint charging that not having "a permanent place of business in the City," he there carried on the "business of peddling, vending, selling, offering for sale and soliciting the sale of ⊥591 goods, wares and merchandise, to wit: pamphlets, books and publications without first having procured a license," contrary to the ordinance. The evidence for the state showed that without a license the appellant called at two homes and a laundry and offered for sale and sold books and pamphlets of a religious nature. At one home, accompanied by his wife, he was refused admission, but was allowed by the girl who came to the door to play a portable phonograph on the porch. The girl purchased one of his stock of books, "Religion," for a quarter, and received a pamphlet free. During the conversation he stated that he was an ordained minister preaching the gospel and quoted passages from the Bible. At the second home the lady of the house allowed him and his wife to enter and play the phonograph, but she refused to buy either books or pamphlets. When departing the appellant left some literature on the table although informed by the lady that it would not be read and had better be given to someone else. At the laundry the appellant introduced himself as one of the Jehovah's Witnesses and discussed with the proprietor their work and religion generally. The proprietor bought the book "Religion" for a quarter but declined to buy others at the same price. He was given a pamphlet free. When arrested the appellant stated that he was "selling religious books and preaching the gospel of the kingdom," and that because of his religious beliefs he would not take out a license. A motion at the close of the evidence for a directed verdict of acquittal on the ground that the ordinance violated the Fourteenth Amendment was denied. The jury was instructed to acquit unless it found the defendant was selling books or pamphlets. It returned a verdict of guilty. On appeal the Supreme Court of Arizona held that the ordinance, an "ordinary occupational license tax ordinance," did not deny freedom of religion and of the press and affirmed the conviction. An appeal to this Court ⊥**592** was allowed under § 237 of the Judicial Code, 28, USCA §344.

The Opelika ordinance required book agents to pay $10.00 per annum, transient distributors of books (annual only) $5.00. The license fee in Casa Grande was $25 per quarter, that in Fort Smith ranged from $2.50 per day to $25 per month. All the fees were small, yet substantial. But the appellant and the petitioners, so far as the records disclose, advanced no claim and presented no proof in the courts below that these fees were invalid because so high as to make the cost of compliance a deterrent to the further distribution of their literature in those cities. Although petitioners in No. 314 contended that their enterprise was operated at a loss, there was no suggestion that they could not obtain from the same sources which now supply the funds to meet whatever deficit there may be sums sufficient to defray license fees also. The amount of the fees was not considered in the opinions below except for a bare statement by the Alabama court that the exaction was "reasonable," and neither the briefs nor the assignments of error in this Court have directed their attack specifically to that issue. Consequently there is not before us the question of the power to lay fees, objectionable in their effect because of their size, upon the constitutionally protected rights of free speech, press or the exercise of religion. If the size of the fees were to be considered, to reach a conclusion one would desire to know the estimated volume, the margin of profit, the solicitor's commission, the expense of policing and other pertinent facts of income and expense. In the circumstances we venture no opinion concerning the validity of license taxes if it were proved, or at least distinctly claimed, that the burden of the tax was a substantial clog upon activities of the sort here involved. The ⊥**593** sole constitutional question considered is whether a nondiscriminatory license fee, presumably appropriate in amount, may be imposed upon these activities.

We turn to the constitutional problem squarely presented by these ordinances. There are ethical principles of greater value to mankind than the guarantees of the Constitution, personal liberties which are beyond the power of government to impair. These principles and liberties belong to the mental and spiritual realm where the judgments and decrees of mundane courts are ineffective to direct the course of man. The rights of which our Constitution speaks have a more earthy quality. They are not absolutes to be exercised independently of other cherished privileges, protected by the same organic instrument. Conflicts in the exercise of rights arise and the conflicting forces seek adjustments in the courts, as do these parties, claiming on the one side the freedom of religion, speech and the press, guaranteed by the Fourteenth Amendment, and on the other the right to employ the sovereign power explicitly reserved to the State by the Tenth Amendment to ensure orderly living without which constitutional guarantees of civil liberties would be a mockery. Courts, no more than Constitutions, can intrude into the consciences of men or compel them to believe contrary to their faith or think contrary ⊥**594** to their convictions, but courts are competent to adjudge the acts men do under color of a constitutional right, such as that of freedom of speech or of the press or the free exercise of religion and to determine whether the claimed right is limited by other recognized powers, equally precious to mankind. So the mind and spirit of man remain forever free, while his actions rest subject to necessary accommodation to the competing needs of his fellows.

If all expression of religion or opinion, however, were subject to the discretion of authority, our unfettered dynamic thoughts or moral impulses might be made only colorless and sterile ideas. To give them life and force, the Constitution protects their use. No difference of view as to the importance of the freedoms of press or religion exist. They are "fundamental personal rights and liberties." *Schneider* v. *Irvington*. To proscribe the dissemination of doctrines or arguments which do not transgress military or moral limits is to destroy the principal bases of democracy,—knowledge and discussion. One man, with views contrary to the rest of his compatriots, is entitled to the privilege of expressing his ideas by speech or broadside to anyone willing to listen or to read. Too many settled beliefs have in time been rejected to justify this generation in refusing a hearing to its own dissentients. But that hearing may be limited by action of the proper legislative body to times, places and methods for the enlightenment of the community which, in view of existing social and economic conditions, are not at odds with the preservation of peace and good order.

This means that the proponents of ideas cannot determine entirely for themselves the time and place and manner for the diffusion of knowledge or for their evangelism, any more than the civil authorities may hamper or suppress the public dissemination of facts and prin⊥**595**ciples by the people. The ordinary requirements of civilized life compel this adjustment of interests. The task of reconcilement is made harder by the tendency to accept as dominant any contention supported by a claim of interference with the practice of religion or the spread of ideas. Believing as this nation has from the first that the freedoms of worship and expression are closely akin to the illimitable privileges of thought itself, any legislation affecting those freedoms is scrutinized to see that the interferences allowed are only those appropriate to the maintenance of a civilized society. The determination of what limitations may be permitted under such an abstract test rests with the legislative bodies, the courts, the executive and the people themselves guided by the experience of the past, the needs of revenue for law enforcement, the requirements and capacities of police protection, the dangers of disorder and other pertinent factors.

Upon the courts falls the duty of determining the validity of such enactments as may be challenged as unconstitutional by litigants. In dealing with these delicate adjustments this Court denies any place to administrative censorship of ideas or capricious approval of distributors. In *Lovell* v. *Griffin* the requirement of permission from the city manager invalidated the ordinance; in *Schneider* v. *Irvington*, that of a police officer. In the *Cantwell* Case, the secretary of the public welfare council was to determine whether the object of charitable solicitation was worthy. We held the requirement bad. Ordinances abso⊥**596**lutely prohibiting the exercise of the right to disseminate information are a fortiori, invalid.

The differences between censorship and complete prohibition, either of subject matter or the individuals participating, upon the one hand, and regulation of the conduct of individuals in the time, manner and place of their activities upon the other, are decisive. "One who is a martyr to a principle . . . does not prove by his martyrdom that he has kept within the law," said Mr. *Justice* CARDOZO concurring in *Hamilton* v. *University of California*, which held that conscientious objection to military training would not excuse a student, during his enrollment, from attending required courses in that science. There is to be noted, too, a distinction between nondiscriminatory regulation of operations which are incidental to the exercise of religion or the freedom of speech or the press and those which are imposed upon the religious rite itself or the unmixed dissemination of information. Casual reflection verifies the suggestion that both teachers and preachers need to receive support for themselves as well as alms and benefactions for charity and the spread of knowledge. But when, as in these cases, the practitioners of these noble callings choose to utilize the vending of their religious books and tracts as a source of funds, the financial aspects of their transactions need not be wholly disregarded. To subject any religious or didactic group to a reasonable fee for their money-making activities does not require a finding that the licensed acts are purely commercial. It is enough that money is earned by the sale ⊥**597** of articles. A book agent cannot escape a license requirement by a plea that it is a tax on knowledge. It would hardly be contended that the publication of newspapers is not subject to the usual government fiscal exactions or the obligations placed by statutes on other business. The Constitution draws no line between a payment from gross receipts or a net income tax and a suitably calculated occupational license. Commercial advertising cannot escape control by the simple expedient of printing matter of public interest on the same sheet or handbill. Nor does the fact that to the participants a formation in the streets is an "information march," and "one of their ways of worship," suffice to exempt such a procession from a city ordinance which, narrowly construed, required a license for such parade.

When proponents of religious or social theories use the ordinary commercial methods of sales of articles to raise propaganda funds, it is a natural and proper exercise of the power of the state to charge reasonable fees for the privilege of canvassing. Careful as we may and should be to protect the freedoms safeguarded by the Bill of Rights, it is difficult to see in such enactments a shadow of prohibition of the exercise of religion or of abridgement of the freedom of speech or the press. It is prohibition and unjustifiable abridgement which are interdicted, not taxation. Nor do we believe it can be fairly said that because such proper charges may be expanded into unjustifiable abridgements they are therefore invalid on their face. The freedoms claimed by those seeking relief here are guaranteed against abridgement by the Fourteenth Amendment. Its commands protect their rights. The legislative power of municipalities must yield when ⊥**598** abridgement is shown. If we were to assume, as is here argued, that the licensed activities involve religious rites, a different question would be presented. These are not taxes on free will offerings. But it is because we view these sales as partaking more of commercial than religious or educational transactions that we find the ordinances, as here presented, valid. A tax on religion or a tax on interstate commerce may alike be forbidden by the Constitution. It does not follow that licenses for selling Bibles or for manufacture of articles of general use, measured by extra-state sales, must fall. It may well be that the wisdom of American communities will persuade them to permit the poor and weak to draw support from the petty sales of religious books without contributing anything for the privilege of using the streets and conveniences of the municipality. Such an exemption, however, would be a voluntary, not a constitutionally enforced, contribution.

In the ordinances of Casa Grande and Fort Smith, we have no discretionary power in the public authorities to refuse a license to anyone desirous of selling religious literature. No censorship of the material which enters into the books or papers is authorized. No religious symbolism is involved such as was urged against the flag salute in *Minersville School Dist.* v. *Gobitis*. For us there is no occasion to apply here the principles taught by that opinion. Nothing more is asked from one group than from another which uses similar methods of propagation. We see nothing in the collection of a non-discriminatory license fee, uncontested in amount, from those selling books or papers, which abridges the freedoms of worship, speech or press to the claim that even small license charges, if valid, will impose upon the itinerant colporteur a crushing ag**⊥599**gregate, it is plain that if each single fee is, as we assume, commensurate with the activities licensed, then though the accumulation of fees from city to city may in time bulk large, he will have enjoyed a correlatively enlarged field of distribution. The First Amendment does not require a subsidy in the form of fiscal exemption.

Accordingly the challenge to the Fort Smith and Casa Grande ordinances fails.

There is an additional contention by petitioner as to the Opelika ordinance. It is urged that since the licenses were revocable, arbitrarily, by the local authorities, there can be no true freedom for petitioners in the dissemination of information because of the censorship upon their actions after the issuance of the license. But there has been neither application for nor revocation of a license. The complaint was bottomed on sales without a license. It was that charge against which petitioner claimed the protection of the Constitution. This issue he had standing to raise. From what has been said previously it follows that the objection to the unconstitutionality of requiring a license fails. There is no occasion, at this time, to pass on the validity of the revocation section, as it does not affect his present defense.

In *Lovell* v. *Griffin* we held invalid a statute which placed the grant of a license within the discretion of the licensing authority. By this discretion, the right to obtain a license was made an empty right. Therefore the formality of going through an application was naturally not deemed a prerequisite to insistence on a constitutional right. Here we have a very different situation. A license is required that may properly be required. The fact that such a license, if it were granted, may subse**⊥600**quently be revoked does not necessarily destroy the licensing ordinance. The hazard of such revocation is much too contingent for us now to declare the licensing provisions to be invalid. *Lovell* v. *Griffin* has, in effect, held that discretionary control in the general area of free speech is unconstitutional. Therefore, the hazard that the license properly granted would be improperly revoked is far too slight to justify declaring the valid part of the ordinance, which is alone now at issue, also unconstitutional.

The judgments in Nos. 280, 314 and 966 are *affirmed*.

Mr. *Chief Justice* STONE:

The First Amendment, which the Fourteenth makes applicable to the states, declares: "Congress shall make no law respecting an establishment of religion, or prohibiting the free exercise thereof; or abridging the freedom of speech, or of the press." I think that the ordinance in each of these cases is on its face a prohibited invasion of the freedoms thus guaranteed, and that the judgment in each should be reversed.

The ordinance in the Opelika case should be held invalid on two independent grounds. One is that the annual tax in addition to the 50 cent "issuance fee" which the ordinance imposes is an unconstitutional restriction on those freedoms, for reasons which will presently appear. The other is that the requirement of a license for dissemination of ideas, when as here the license is revocable at will without cause and in the unrestrained discretion of administrative officers, is likewise an unconstitutional restraint on those freedoms.

The sole condition which the Opelika ordinance prescribes for grant of the license is payment of the designated annual tax and issuance fee. The privilege thus purchased, for the period of a year, is forthwith revocable in the unrestrained and unreviewable discretion of the **⊥601** licensing commission without cause and without notice or opportunity for a hearing. The case presents in its baldest form the question whether the freedoms which the Constitution purports to safeguard can be completely subjected to uncontrolled administrative action. Only recently this Court was unanimous in holding void on its face the requirement of a license for the distribution of pamphlets which was to be issued in the sole discretion of a municipal officer. *Lovell v. Griffin*. The precise ground of our decision was that the ordinance made enjoyment of the freedom which the Constitution guarantees contingent upon the uncontrolled will of administrative officers. We declared:

"We think that the ordinance is invalid on its face. Whatever the motive which induced its adoption, its character is such that it strikes at the very foundation of the freedom of the press by subjecting it to license and censorship. The struggle for the freedom of the press was primarily directed against the power of the licensor. It was against that power that John Milton directed his assault by his 'Appeal for the Liberty of Unlicensed Printing.' And the liberty of the press became initially a right to publish '*without* a license what formerly could be published only *with* one.' While this freedom from previous restraint upon publication cannot be regarded as exhausting the guaranty of liberty, the prevention of that restraint was a leading purpose in the adoption of the constitutional provision."

That purpose cannot rightly be defeated by so transparent a subterfuge as the pronouncement that, while a license may not be required if its award is contingent upon the whim of an administrative officer, it may be if its retention and the enjoyment of the privilege which it purports to give are wholly contingent upon his whim. In either case enjoyment of the freedom is dependent upon the same contingency and the censorship is as effective ⊥**602** in one as in the other. Nor is any palliative afforded by the assertion that the defendant's failure to apply for a license deprives him of standing to challenge the ordinance because of its revocation provision, by the terms of which retention of the license and exercise of the privilege may be cut off at any time without cause.

Indeed, the present ordinance is a more callous disregard of the constitutional right than that exhibited in *Lovell* v. *Griffin*. There at least the defendant might have been given a license if he had applied for it. In any event he would not have been compelled to pay a money exaction for a license to exercise the privilege of free speech—a license which if granted in this case would have been wholly illusory. Here the defendant Jones was prohibited from distributing his pamphlets at all unless he paid in advance a year's tax for the exercise of the privilege and subjected himself to termination of the license without cause, notice or hearing, at the will of city officials. To say that he who is free to withhold at will the privilege of publication exercises a power of censorship prohibited by the Constitution, but that he who has unrestricted power to withdraw the privilege does not, would be to ignore history and deny the teachings of experience, as well as to perpetuate the evils at which the First Amendment was aimed.

It is of no significance that the defendant did not apply for a license. As this Court has often pointed out, when a licensing statute is on its face a lawful exercise of regulatory power, it will not be assumed that it will be unlawfully administered in advance of an actual denial of application for the license. But here it is the prohibition of publication, save at the uncontrolled will of public officials, which transgresses constitutional limitations and makes the ordinance void on its face. The Constitution can hardly be thought to deny to one subjected to the restraints of such an ordinance the right to attack its constitutionality, because he has not yielded to its demands. . . . ⊥**603**

In all three cases the question presented by the record and fully argued here and below is whether the ordinances—which as applied penalize the defendants for not having paid the flat fee taxes levied—violate the freedom of speech, press, and religion guaranteed by the First and Fourteenth Amendments. Defendants' challenge to the ordinances, naming them, is a challenge to the substantial taxes which they impose, in specified amounts, and not to some tax of a different or lesser amount which some other ordinance might levy. In their briefs here they argue, as upon the records they are entitled to do, that the taxes are an unconstitutional burden on the right of ⊥**604** free speech and free religion comparable to license taxes which the Court has often held to be an inadmissible burden on interstate commerce. They argue also that the cumulative effect of such taxes, in town after town throughout the country, would be destructive of freedom of the press for all persons except those financially able to distribute their literature without soliciting funds for the support of their cause.

While these are questions which have been studiously left unanswered by the opinion of the Court, it seems inescapable that an answer must be given before the convictions can be sustained. Decision of them cannot rightly be avoided now by asserting that the amount of the tax has not been put in issue; that the tax is "uncontested in amount" by the defendants, and can therefore be assumed by us to be "presumably appropriate," "reasonable," or "suitably calculated"; that it has not been proved that the burden of the tax is a substantial clog on the activities of the defendants, or that those who have defrayed the expense of their religious activities will not willingly defray the license taxes also. All these are considerations which would seem to be irrelevant to the question now before us—whether a flat tax, more than a nominal fee to defray the expenses of a regulatory license, can constitutionally be laid on a noncommercial, non-profit activity devoted exclusively to the dissemination of ideas, educational and religious in character, to those persons who consent to receive them.

Nor is the essential issue here disguised by the reiterated characterization of these exactions, not as taxes but as "fees"—a characterization to which the records lend no support. All these ordinances on their face purport to be an exercise of the municipality's taxing power. In none is there the slightest pretense by the taxing authority, or the slightest suggestion by the state court, that the "fee" is to defray expenses of the licensing system. The ⊥**605** amounts of the "fees," without more, demonstrate that such a contention is groundless. In No. 280, Opelika itself contends that the issue relates solely to its power to raise money for general revenue purposes, and the Supreme Court of Alabama referred to the levy as a "reasonable" "tax." The tax exacted by Opelika, on the face of the ordinance, is in addition to a 50 cent "issuance fee," which alone is presumably what the city deems adequate to defray the cost of administering the licensing system. Similarly in the Fort Smith and Casa Grande cases, the state courts sustained the ordinances as a tax, and nothing else. If this litigation has involved any controversy—and the state courts all seemed to think that it did—the controversy has been one solely relating to the power to tax, and not the power to collect a "fee" to support a licensing system which, as has already been indicated, has no regulatory purpose other than that involved in the raising of revenue.

This Court has often had occasion to point out that where the state may, as a regulatory measure, license activities which it is without constitutional authority to tax, it may charge a small or nominal fee sufficient to defray the expense of licensing, and similarly it may charge a reasonable fee for the use of its highways by interstate motor traffic which it cannot tax. But we are not concerned in these cases with a nominal fee for a regulatory license, which may be assumed for argument's sake to be valid. Here the licenses are not regulatory, save as the licenses conditioned upon payment of the tax may serve to restrain or suppress publication. None of the ordinances, if complied with, purports to or could control the time, place or manner of the distribution of the books and pamphlets concerned. None has any discernible relationship to the police ⊥**606** protection or the good order of the community. The only condition and purpose of the licenses under all three ordinances is suppression of the specified distributions of literature in default of the payment of a substantial tax fixed in amount and measured neither by the extent of the defendants' activities under the license nor the amounts which they receive for and devote to religious purposes in the exercise of the licensed privilege. Opelika exacts a license fee for book agents of $10 per annum and of $5 per annum for transient distributors of books, in addition to a 50 cent "issuance fee" on each license. The Supreme Court of Alabama found it unnecessary to determine whether both or only one of these taxes was payable by defendant Jones. The Fort Smith tax of $25 a month or $10 a week or $2.50 a day is substantial in amount for transient distributors of literature of the character here involved; the Opelika exaction is even more onerous when applied against one who may be in the city for only a day or two; and the tax of $25 per quarter exacted by the Casa Grande ordinance, adopted in a community having an adult population of less than 1,000 and applied to distributions of literature like the present, is prohibitive in effect.

In considering the effect of such a tax on the defendants' activities it is important to note that the state courts have applied levies obviously devised for the taxation of business employments—in the first case the "business or vocation" of "book agent"; in the second the business of peddling specified types of merchandise or "other articles"; in the third, the practice of the callings of "peddlers, transient merchants and vendors"—to activities which concededly are not ordinary business or commercial transactions. As appears by stipulation or undisputed testimony, the defendants are Jehovah's Witnesses, engaged in spreading their religious doctrines in conformity to the teachings of St. Matthew, Matt. 10:11-14 and ⊥**607** 24:14, by going from city to city, from village to village, and house to house, to proclaim them. After asking and receiving permission from the householder, they play to him phonograph records and tender to him books or pamphlets advocating their religious views. For the latter they ask payment of a nominal amount, two to five cents for the pamphlets and twenty-five cents for books, as a contribution to the religious cause which they seek to advance. But they distribute the pamphlets, and sometimes the books, gratis when the householder is unwilling or unable to pay for them. The literature is published for such distribution by non-profit charitable corporations organized by Jehovah's Witnesses. The funds collected are used for the support of the religious movement and no one derives a profit from the publication and distribution of the literature. In the *Opelika* case the defendant's activities were confined to distribution of literature and solicitation of funds in the public streets.

No one could doubt that taxation which may be freely laid upon activities not within the protection of the Bill of Rights could—when applied to the dissemination of ideas—be made the ready instrument for destruction of that right. Few would deny that a license tax laid specifically on the privilege of disseminating ideas would infringe the right of free speech. For one reason among others, if the state may tax the privilege it may fix the rate of tax and, through the tax, control or suppress the activity which it taxes. If the distribution of the literature had been carried on by the defendants without solicitation of funds, there plainly would have been no basis, either statutory or constitutional, for levying the tax. It is the collection of funds which has been seized upon to justify the extension, to the defendants' activities, of the tax laid upon business callings. But if we assume, despite our recent ⊥**608** decision in *Schneider* v. *Irvington*, that the essential character of these activities is in some measure altered by the collection of funds for the support of a religious undertaking, still it seems plain that the operation of the present flat tax is such as to abridge the privileges which the defendants here invoke.

It lends no support to the present tax to insist that its restraint on free speech and religion is nondiscriminatory because the same levy is made upon business callings carried on for profit, many of which involve no question of freedom of speech and religion and all of which involve commercial elements—lacking here—which for present purposes may be assumed to afford a basis for taxation apart from the exercise of freedom of speech and religion. The constitutional protection of the Bill of Rights is not to be evaded by classifying with business callings an activity whose sole purpose is the dissemination of ideas, and taxing it as business callings are taxed. The immunity which press and religion enjoy may sometimes be lost when they are united with other activities not immune. But here the only activities involved are the dissemination of ideas, educational and religious, and the collection of funds for the propagation of those ideas, which we have said is likewise the subject of constitutional protection.

The First Amendment is not confined to safeguarding freedom of speech and freedom of religion against discriminatory attempts to wipe them out. On the contrary, the Constitution, by virtue of the First and the Fourteenth Amendments, has put those freedoms in a preferred position. Their commands are not restricted to cases where the protected privilege is sought out for attack. They extend at least to every form of taxation which, because it is a condition of the exercise of the privilege, is capable of being used to control or suppress it.

⊥**609** Even were we to assume—what I do not concede—that there could be a lawful non-discriminatory license tax of a percentage of the gross receipts collected by churches and other religious orders in support of their religious work, we have no such tax here. The tax imposed by the ordinances in these cases is more burdensome and destructive of the activity taxed than any gross receipts tax. The tax is for a fixed amount, unrelated to the extent of the defendants' activities or the receipts derived from them. It is thus the type of flat tax which, when applied to interstate commerce, has repeatedly been deemed by this Court to be prohibited by the commerce clause. When applied as it is here to activities involving the exercise of religious freedom, its vice is emphasized in that it is levied and paid in advance of the activities save only as others may volunteer to pay the tax. It requires a sizable out-of-pocket expense by someone who may never succeed in raising a penny in his exercise of the privilege which is taxed.

The defendants' activities, if taxable at all, are taxable only because of the funds which they solicit. But that solicitation is for funds for religious purposes, and the present taxes are in no way gauged to the receipts. The taxes are insupportable either as a tax on the dissemination of ideas or as a tax on the collection of funds for religious purposes. For on its face a flat license tax restrains in advance the freedom taxed and tends inevitably to suppress its exercise. The First Amendment prohibits all laws abridging freedom of press and religion, not merely some laws or all except tax laws. It is true that the constitutional guaranties of freedom of press and religion, like the commerce clause, make no distinction between fixed-sum ⊥**610** taxes and other kinds. But that fact affords no excuse for courts, whose duty is to enforce those guaranties, to close their eyes to the characteristics of a tax which render it destructive of freedom of press and religion.

We may lay to one side the Court's suggestion that a tax otherwise unconstitutional is to be deemed valid unless it is shown that there are none who, for religion's sake, will come forward to pay the unlawful exaction. The defendants to whom the ordinances have been applied have not paid it and there is nothing in the Constitution to compel them to seek the charity of others to pay it before protesting the tax. It seems fairly obvious that if the present taxes, laid in small communities upon peripatetic religious propagandists, are to be sustained, a way has been found for the effective suppression of speech and press and religion despite constitutional guaranties. The very taxes now before us are better adapted to that end than were the stamp taxes which so successfully curtailed the dissemination of ideas by eighteenth century newspapers and pamphleteers, and which were a moving cause of the American Revolution. Vivid recollections of the effect of those taxes on the freedom of press survived to inspire the adoption of the First Amendment.

Freedom of press and religion, explicitly guaranteed by the Constitution, must at least be entitled to the same freedom from burdensome taxation which it has been thought that the more general phraseology of the commerce clause has extended to interstate commerce. Whatever doubts may be entertained as to this Court's function to relieve, unaided by Congressional legislation, from burdensome taxation under the commerce clause, ⊥**611** it cannot be thought that that function is wanting under the explicit guaranties of freedom of speech, press and religion. In any case the flat license tax can hardly become any the less burdensome or more permissible, when levied on activities within the protection extended by the First and Fourteenth Amendments both to the orderly communication of ideas, educational and religious, to persons willing to receive them, see *Cantwell* v. *Connecticut*, and to the practice of religion and the solicitation of funds in its support.

In its potency as a prior restraint on publication the flat license tax falls short only of outright censorship or suppression. The more humble and needy the cause, the more effective is the suppression.

Mr. *Justice* BLACK, Mr. *Justice* DOUGLAS and Mr. *Justice* MURPHY join in this opinion.

Mr. *Justice* MURPHY, with whom The CHIEF JUSTICE, Mr. *Justice* BLACK, and Mr. *Justice* DOUGLAS concur, dissenting:

When a statute is challenged as impinging on freedom of speech, freedom of the press, or freedom of worship, those historic privileges which are so essential to our political welfare and spiritual progress, it is the duty of this Court to subject such legislation to examination, in the light of the evidence adduced, to determine whether it is so drawn as not to impair the substance of those cherished freedoms in reaching its objective. Ordinances that may operate to restrict the circulation or dissemination of ideas on religious or other subjects should be framed with fastidious care and precise language to avoid undue encroachment on these fundamental liberties. And the protection of the Constitution must be extended to all, ⊥**612** not only to those whose views accord with prevailing thought but also to dissident minorities who energetically spread their beliefs. Being satisfied by the evidence that the ordinances in the cases now before us, as construed and applied in the state courts, impose a burden on the circulation and discussion of opinion and information in matters of religion, and therefore violate the petitioners' rights to freedom of speech, freedom of the press, and freedom of worship in contravention of the Fourteenth Amendment, I am obliged to dissent from the opinion of the Court.

It is not disputed that petitioners, Jehovah's Witnesses, were ordained ministers preaching the gospel, as they understood it, through the streets and from house to house, orally and by playing religious records with the consent of the householder, and by distributing books and pamphlets setting forth the tenets of their faith. It does not appear that their motives were commercial, but only that they were evangelizing their faith as they saw it. In No. 280 the trial court excluded as irrelevant petitioner's testimony that he was an ordained minister and that his activities on the streets of Opelika were in furtherance of his ministerial duties. The testimony of ten clergymen of Opelika that they distributed free religious literature in their churches, the cost of which was defrayed by voluntary contribution, and that they had never been forced to pay any license fee, was also excluded. It is admitted here that petitioner was a Jehovah's Witness and considered himself an ordained minister.

The Supreme Court of Arizona stated in No. 966 that appellant was "a regularly ordained minister of the denomination commonly known as Jehovah's Witnesses, . . . going from house to house in the city of Casa Grande preaching the gospel, as he understood it, by means of his ⊥**613** spoken word, by playing various records on a phonograph, with the approval of the householder, and by distributing printed books, pamphlets and tracts which set forth his views as to the meaning of the Bible. The method of distribution of these printed books, pamphlets and tracts was as follows: He first offered them for sale at various prices ranging from five to twenty-five cents each. If the householder did not desire to purchase any of them he then left a small leaflet summarizing some of the doctrines which he preached."

The facts were stipulated in No. 314. Each petitioner "claims to be an ordained minister of the gospel. . . . They do not engage in this work for any selfish reason but because they feel called upon to publish the news and preach the gospel of the Kingdom to all the world as a witness before the end comes. . . . They believe that the only effective way to preach is to go from house to house and make personal contact with the people and distribute to them books and pamphlets setting forth their views of Christianity." Petitioners "were going from house to house in the residential section within the city of Fort Smith . . . presenting to the residents of these houses various booklets, leaflets and periodicals setting forth their views of Christianity held by Jehovah's Witnesses." They solicited "a contribution of twenty-five cents for each book," but "these books in some instances are distributed free when the people wishing them are unable to contribute."

There is no suggestion in any of these three cases that petitioners were perpetrating a fraud, that they were demeaning themselves in any obnoxious manner, that their activities created any public disturbance or inconvenience, that private rights were contravened, or that the literature distributed was offensive to morals or created any "clear and present danger" to organized society.

The ordinance in each case is sought to be sustained as a system of non-discriminatory taxation of various busi⊥**614**nesses, professions and vocations, including the distribution of books for which contributions are asked, for the sole purpose of raising revenue. Any inclination to take the position that petitioners, who were proselytizing by distributing informative literature setting forth their religious tenets, and whose activities were wholly unrelated to any commercial purposes, were not within the purview of these occupational tax ordinances, is foreclosed by the decisions of the state courts below to the contrary. As so construed the ordinances in effect impose direct taxes on the dissemination of ideas and the distribution of literature, relating to and dealing with religious matters, for which a contribution is asked in an attempt to gain converts, because those were petitioners' activities. Such taxes have been held to violate the Fourteenth Amendment, and that should be the holding here.

FREEDOM OF SPEECH AND FREEDOM OF THE PRESS

In view of the recent decisions of this Court striking down acts which impair freedom ⊥**615** of speech and freedom of the press no elaboration on that subject is now necessary. We have "unequivocally held that the streets are proper places for the exercise of the freedom of communicating information and disseminating opinion and that, though the states and municipalities may appropriately regulate the privilege in the public interest, they may not unduly burden or proscribe its employment in these public thoroughfares." *Valentine* v. *Chrestensen*, decided April 13, 1942. And as the distribution of pamphlets to spread information and opinion on the streets and from house to house for non-commercial purposes is protected from the prior restraint of censorship, so should it be protected from the burden of taxation.

The opinion of the Court holds that the amount of the tax is not before us and that a "nondiscriminatory license fee, presumably appropriate in amount, may be imposed upon these activities." Both of these holdings must be rejected.

Where regulation or infringement of the liberty of discussion and the dissemination of information and opinion are involved, there are special reasons for testing the challenged statute on its face. That should be done here.

Consideration of the taxes leads to but one conclusion—that they prohibit or seriously hinder the distribution of petitioners' religious literature. The opinion of the Court admits that all the taxes are "substantial." The $25 quar⊥**616**terly tax of Casa Grande approaches prohibition. The 1940 population of that town was 1,545. With so few potential purchasers it would take a gifted evangelist, indeed, in view of the antagonism generally encountered by Jehovah's Witnesses, to sell enough tracts at prices ranging from five to twenty-five cents to gross enough to pay the tax. While the amount is actually lower in Opelika and may be lower in Fort Smith in that it is possible to get a license for a short period, and while the circle of purchasers is wider in those towns, these exactions also place a heavy hand on petitioners' activities. The petitioners should not be subjected to such tribute.

But whatever the amount, the taxes are in reality taxes upon the dissemination of religious ideas, a dissemination carried on by the distribution of religious literature for religious reasons alone and not for personal profit. As such they place a burden on freedom of speech, freedom of the press, and the exercise of religion even if the question of amount is laid aside. Liberty of circulation is the very life blood of a free press, and taxes on the circulation of ideas have a long history of misuse against freedom of thought. And taxes on circulation solely for the purpose of revenue were success⊥**617**fully resisted, prior to the adoption of the First Amendment, as interferences with freedom of the press. Surely all this was familiar knowledge to the framers of the Bill of Rights. We need not shut our eyes to the possibility that use may again be made of such taxes, either by discrimination in enforcement or otherwise, to suppress the unpalatable view of militant minorities such as Jehovah's Witnesses. As the evidence excluded in No. 280 tended to show, no attempt was made there to apply the ordinance to ministers functioning in a more orthodox manner than petitioner.

Other objectionable features in addition to the factor of historical misuse exist. There is the unfairness present in any system of flat fee taxation, bearing no relation to the ability to pay. And there is the cumulative burden of many such taxes throughout the municipalities of the land, as the number of recent cases involving such ordinances abundantly demonstrates. The activities of Jehovah's ⊥**618** Witnesses are widespread, and the aggregate effect of numerous exactions, no matter how small, can conceivably force them to choose between refraining from attempting to recoup part of the cost of their literature, or else paying out large sums in taxes. Either choice hinders and may even possibly put an end to their activities. There is no basis, other than a refusal to consider the characteristics of taxes such as these, for any assumption that such taxes are "commensurate with the activities licensed." Nor is there any assurance that "a correlatively enlarged field of distribution" will insure sufficient proceeds even to meet such exactions, let alone leaving any residue for the continuation of petitioners' evangelization.

Freedom of speech, freedom of the press, and freedom of religion all have a double aspect— freedom of thought and freedom of action. Freedom to think is absolute of its own nature; the most tyrannical government is powerless to control the inward workings of the mind. But even an aggressive mind is of no missionary value unless there is freedom of action, freedom to communicate its message to others by speech and writing. Since in any form of action there is a possibility of collision with the rights of others, there can be no doubt that this freedom to act is not absolute but qualified, being subject to regulation in the public interest which does not unduly infringe the right. However, there is no assertion here that the ordinances were regulatory, but if there were such a claim, they still should not be sustained. No abuses justifying regulation are advanced and the ordinances are not narrowly and precisely drawn to deal with actual, or even hypothetical evils, while at the same time preserving the substance of the right. ⊥**619** They impose a tax on the dissemination of information and opinion anywhere within the city limits, whether on the streets or from house to house. "As we have said, the streets are natural and proper places for the dissemination of information and opinion; and one is not to have the exercise of his liberty of expression in appropriate places abridged on the plea that it may be exercised elsewhere." *Schneider* v. *Irvington*. These taxes abridge that liberty.

It matters not that petitioners asked contributions for their literature. Freedom of speech and freedom of the press cannot and must not mean freedom only for those who can distribute their broadsides without charge. There may be others with messages more vital but purses less full, who must seek some reimbursement for their outlay or else forego passing on their ideas. The pamphlet, an historic weapon against oppression, is today the convenient vehicle of those with limited resources because newspaper space and radio time are expensive and the cost of establishing such enterprises great. If freedom of speech and freedom of the press are to have any concrete meaning, people seeking to distribute information and opinion, to the end only that others shall have the benefit thereof, should not be taxed for circulating such matter. It is unnecessary to consider now the validity of such taxes on commercial enterprises engaged in the dissemination of ideas. Petitioners were not engaged in a traffic for profit. While the courts below held their activities were covered by the ⊥**620** ordinances, it is clear that they were seeking only to further their religious convictions by preaching the gospel to others.

The exercise, without commercial motives, of freedom of speech, freedom of the press, or freedom of worship are not proper sources of taxation for general revenue purposes. In dealing with a permissible regulation of these freedoms and the fee charged in connection therewith, we emphasized the fact that the fee was not a revenue tax, but one to meet the expense incident to the administration of the Act and to the maintenance of public order, and stated only that, "There is nothing contrary to the Constitution in the charge of a fee limited to the purpose stated." *Cox* v. *New Hampshire*. The taxes here involved are ostensibly for revenue purposes; they are not regulatory fees. Respondents do not show that the instant activities of Jehovah's Witnesses create special problems causing a drain on the municipal coffers, or that these taxes are commensurate with any expenses entailed by the presence of the Witnesses. In the absence of such a showing I think no tax whatever can be levied on petitioners' activities in distributing their literature or disseminating their ideas. If the guaranties of freedom of speech and freedom of the press are to be preserved, municipalities should not be free to raise general revenue by taxes on the circulation of information and opinion in non-commercial causes; other sources can be found, the taxation of which will not choke off ideas. Taxes such as the instant ones violate petitioners' right to freedom of speech and freedom of the press, protected against state invasion by the Fourteenth Amendment. ⊥**621**

FREEDOM OF RELIGION

Under the foregoing discussion of freedom of speech and freedom of the press any person would be exempt from taxation upon the act of distributing information or opinion of any kind, whether political, scientific, or religious in character, when done solely in an effort to spread knowledge and ideas, with no thought of commercial gain. But there is another, and perhaps more precious reason why these ordinances cannot constitutionally apply to petitioners. Important as free speech and a free press are to a free government and a free citizenry, there is a right even more dear to many individuals—the right to worship their Maker according to their needs and the dictates of their souls and to carry their message or their gospel to every living creature. These ordinances infringe that right, which is also protected by the Fourteenth Amendment.

Petitioners were itinerant ministers going through the streets and from house to house in different communities, preaching the gospel by distributing booklets and pamphlets setting forth their views of the Bible and the tenets of their faith. While perhaps not so orthodox as the oral sermon, the use of religious books is an old, recognized and effective mode of worship and means of proselytizing. For this petitioners were taxed. The mind rebels at the thought that a minister of any of the old established churches could be made to pay fees to the community before entering the pulpit. These taxes on petitioners' efforts to preach the "news of the Kingdom" should be struck down because they burden petitioners' right to worship the Deity in their own fashion and to spread the gospel as they understand it. There is here no contention that their manner of worship gives rise to conduct which calls for regulation, and these ordinances are not aimed at any such practices.

One need only read the decisions of this and other courts in the past few years to see the unpopularity of Jehovah's Witnesses ⊥**622** and the difficulties put in their path because of their religious beliefs. An arresting parallel exists between the troubles of Jehovah's Witnesses and the struggles of various dissentient groups in the American colonies for religious liberty which culminated in the Virginia Statute for Religious Freedom, the Northwest Ordinance of 1787, and the First Amendment. In most of the colonies there was an established church, and the way of the dissenter was hard. All sects, including Quaker, Methodist, Baptist, Episcopalian, Separatist, Rogerine, and Catholic, suffered. Many of the non-conforming ministers were itinerants, and measures were adopted to curb their unwanted activities. The books of certain denominations were banned. Virginia and Connecticut had burdensome licensing requirements. Other states required oaths before one could preach which many ministers could not conscientiously take. ⊥**623** Research reveals no attempt to control or persecute by the more subtle means of taxing the function of preaching, or even any attempt to tap it as a source of revenue.

By applying these occupational taxes to petitioners' non-commercial activities, respondents now tax sincere efforts to spread religious beliefs, and a heavy burden falls upon a new set of itinerant zealots, the Witnesses. That burden should not be allowed to stand, especially if, as the excluded testimony in No. 280 indicates, the accepted clergymen of the town can take to their pulpits and distribute their literature without the impact of taxation. Liberty of conscience is too full of meaning for the individuals in this nation to permit taxation to prohibit or substantially impair the spread of religious ideas, even though they are controversial and run counter to the established notions of a community. If this Court is to err in evaluating claims that freedom of speech, freedom of the press, and freedom of religion have been invaded, far better that it err in being overprotective of these precious rights.

Mr. *Justice* BLACK, Mr. *Justice* DOUGLAS, Mr. *Justice* MURPHY:

The opinion of the Court sanctions a device which in our opinion suppresses or tends to suppress the free exercise of a religion practiced by a minority group. This is but another step in the direction which *Minersville School Dist.* v. *Gobitis* took against the same religious minority and is a logical extension of the principles upon which that decision rested. Since we joined in the opinion in the *Gobitis* Case, we think this is an ap⊥**624**propriate occasion to state that we now believe that it was also wrongly decided. Certainly our democratic form of government functioning under the historic Bill of Rights has a high responsibility to accommodate itself to the religious views of minorities however unpopular and unorthodox those views may be. The First Amendment does not put the right freely to exercise religion in a subordinate position. We fear, however, that the opinions in these and in the *Gobitis* Case do exactly that.

MURDOCK v. PENNSYLVANIA

319 U.S. 105
ON WRIT OF CERTIORARI TO THE SUPERIOR COURT OF THE COMMONWEALTH OF PENNSYLVANIA
Argued March 10 and 11, 1943 — Decided May 3, 1943

⊥**106** Mr. *Justice* DOUGLAS delivered the opinion of the Court:

The City of Jeannette, Pennsylvania, has an ordinance, some forty years old, which provides in part:

"That all persons canvassing for or soliciting within said Borough, orders for goods, paintings, pictures, wares, or merchandise of any kind, or persons delivering such articles under orders so obtained or solicited, shall be required to procure from the Burgess a license to transact said business and shall pay to the Treasurer of said Borough therefore the following sums according to the time for which said license shall be granted.

"For one day $1.50, for one week seven dollars ($7.00), for two weeks twelve dollars ($12.00), for three weeks twenty dollars ($20.00), provided that the provisions of this ordinance shall not apply to persons selling by sample to manufacturers or licensed merchants or dealers doing business in said Borough of Jeannette."

Petitioners are "Jehovah's Witnesses." They went about from door to door in the City of Jeannette distributing literature and soliciting people to "purchase" certain religious books and pamphlets, all published by the ⊥**107** Watch Tower Bible & Tract Society. The "price" of the books was twenty-five cents each, the "price" of the pamphlets five cents each. In connection with these activities petitioners used a phonograph on which they played a record expounding certain of their views on religion. None of them obtained a license under the ordinance. Before they were arrested each had made "sales" of books. There was evidence that it was their practice in making these solicitations to request a "contribution," of twenty-five cents each for the books and five cents each for the pamphlets but to accept lesser sums or even to donate the volumes in case an interested person was without funds. In the present case some donations of pamphlets were made when books were purchased. Petitioners were convicted and fined for violation of the ordinance. Their judgments of conviction were sustained by the Superior Court of Pennsylvania against their contention that the ordinance deprived them of the freedom of speech, press, and religion guaranteed by the First Amendment. Petitions for leave to appeal to the Supreme Court of Pennsylvania were denied. The cases are here on petitions for writs of certiorari which we granted along with the petitions for rehearing of *Jones* v. *Opelika* and its companion cases. ⊥**108**

The First Amendment, which the Fourteenth makes applicable to the states, declares that "Congress shall make no law respecting an establishment of religion, or prohibiting the free exercise thereof; or abridging the freedom of speech, or of the press. . . ." It could hardly be denied that a tax laid specifically on the exercise of those freedoms would be unconstitutional. Yet the license tax imposed by this ordinance is in substance just that.

Petitioners spread their interpretations of the Bible and their religious beliefs largely through the hand distribution of literature by full or part time workers. They claim to follow the example of Paul, teaching "publickly, and from house to house." Acts 20:20. They take literally the mandate of the Scriptures, "Go ye into all the world, and preach the gospel to every creature." Mark 16:15. In doing so they believe that they are obeying a commandment of God.

The hand distribution of religious tracts is an age-old form of missionary evangelism—as old as the history of printing presses. It has been a potent force in various religious movements down through the years. This form of evangelism is utilized today on a large scale by various religious sects whose colporteurs carry the Gospel to thou⊥**109**sands upon thousands of homes and seek through personal visitations to win adherents to their faith. It is more than preaching, it is more than distribution of religious literature. It is a combination of both. Its purpose is as evangelical as the revival meeting. This form of religious activity occupies the same high estate under the First Amendment as do worship in the churches and preaching from the pulpits. It has the same claim to protection as the more orthodox and conventional exercises of religion. It also has the same claim as the others to the guarantees of freedom of speech and freedom of the press.

The integrity of this conduct or behavior as a religious practice has not been challenged. Nor do we have presented any question as to the sincerity of petitioners in their religious beliefs and practices, however misguided they may be thought to be. Moreover, we do not intimate or suggest in respecting their sincerity that any conduct can be made a religious rite and by the zeal of the practitioners swept into the First Amendment. *Reynolds* v. ⊥**110** *United States* and *Davis* v. *Beason* denied any such claim to the practice of polygamy and bigamy. Other claims may well arise which deserve the same fate. We only hold that spreading one's religious beliefs or preaching the Gospel through distribution of religious literature and through personal visitations is an age-old type of evangelism with as high a claim to constitutional protection as the more orthodox types. The manner in which it is practiced at times gives rise to special problems with which the police power of the states is competent to deal. But that merely illustrates that the rights with which we are dealing are not absolutes. We are concerned, however, in these cases merely with one narrow issue. There is presented for decision no question whatsoever concerning punishment for any alleged unlawful acts during the solicitation. Nor is there involved here any question as to the validity of a registration system for colporteurs and other solicitors. The cases present a single issue—the constitutionality of an ordinance which as construed and applied requires religious colporteurs to pay a license tax as a condition to the pursuit of their activities.

The alleged justification for the exaction of this license tax is the fact that the religious literature is distributed with a solicitation of funds. Thus it was stated in *Jones* v. *Opelika* that when a religious sect uses "ordinary commercial methods of sales of articles to raise propaganda funds," it is proper for the state to charge "reasonable fees for the privilege of canvassing." Situations will arise where it will be difficult to determine whether a particular activity is religious or purely commercial. The distinction at times is vital. As we stated only the other day in *Jamison* v. *Texas*, "The state can prohibit the use of the streets for ⊥**111** the distribution of purely commercial leaflets, even though such leaflets may have 'a civic appeal, or a moral platitude' appended. *Valentine* v. *Chrestensen*. They may not prohibit the distribution of handbills in the pursuit of a clearly religious activity merely because the handbills invite the purchase of books for the improved understanding of the religion or because the handbills seek in a lawful fashion to promote the raising of funds for religious purposes." But the mere fact that the religious literature is "sold" by itinerant preachers rather than "donated" does not transform evangelism into a commercial enterprise. If it did, then the passing of the collection plate in church would make the church service a commercial project. The constitutional rights of those spreading their religious beliefs through the spoken and printed word are not to be gauged by standards governing retailers or wholesalers of books. The right to use the press for expressing one's views is not to be measured by the protection afforded commercial handbills. It should be remembered that the pamphlets of Thomas Paine were not distributed free of charge. It is plain that a religious organization needs funds to remain a going concern. But an itinerant evangelist however misguided or intolerant he may be, does not become a mere book agent by selling the Bible or religious tracts to help defray his expenses or to sustain him. Freedom of speech, freedom of the press, freedom of religion are available to all, not merely to those who can pay their own way. As we have said, the problem of drawing the line between a purely commercial activity and a religious one will at times be difficult. On this record it plainly cannot be said that petitioners were engaged in a commercial rather than a religious venture. It is a distortion of the facts of record to describe their activities as the occupation of selling books and pamphlets. And the Pennsylvania court did not rest the judgments of conviction on that basis, though it did find ⊥**112** that petitioners "sold" the literature. The Supreme Court of Iowa in *State* v. *Mead* described the selling activities of members of this same sect as "merely incidental and collateral" to their "main object which was to preach and publicize the doctrines of their order." That accurately summarizes the present record.

We do not mean to say that religious groups and the press are free from all financial burdens of government. We have here something quite different, for example, from a tax on the income of one who engages in religious activities or a tax on property used or employed in connection with those activities. It is one thing to impose a tax on the income or property of a preacher. It is quite another thing to exact a tax from him for the privilege of delivering a sermon. The tax imposed by the City of Jeannette is a flat license tax, the payment of which is a condition of the exercise of these constitutional privileges. The power to tax the exercise of a privilege is the power to control or suppress its enjoyment. Those who can tax the exercise of this religious practice can make its exercise so costly as to deprive it of the resources necessary for its maintenance. Those who can tax the privilege of engaging in this form of missionary evangelism can close its doors to all those who do not have a full purse. Spreading religious beliefs in this ancient and honorable manner would thus be denied the needy. Those who can deprive religious groups of their colporteurs can take from them a part of the vital power of the press which has survived from the Reformation.

It is contended, however, that the fact that the license tax can suppress or control this activity is unim⊥**113**portant if it does not do so. But that is to disregard the nature of this tax. It is a license tax—a flat tax imposed on the exercise of a privilege granted by the Bill of Rights. A state may not impose a charge for the enjoyment of a right granted by the Federal Constitution. Thus, it may not exact a license tax for the privilege of carrying on interstate commerce, although it may tax the property used in, or the income derived from, that commerce, so long as those taxes are not discriminatory. A license tax applied to activities guaranteed by the First Amendment would have the same destructive effect. It is true that the First Amendment, like the commerce clause, draws no distinction between license taxes, fixed sum taxes, and other kinds of taxes. But that is no reason why we should shut our eyes to the nature of the tax and its destructive influence. The power to impose a license tax on the exercise of these freedoms is indeed as potent as the power of censorship which this Court has repeatedly struck down. For that reason the dissenting opinions in *Jones* v. *Opelika* stressed the nature of this type of tax. In that case as in the present ones, we have something very different from a registration system under which those going from house to house are required to give their names, addresses and other marks of identification to the authorities. In all of these cases the issuance of the permit or license is dependent on the payment of a license tax. And the license tax is fixed in amount and unrelated to the scope of the activities of petitioners or to their realized revenues. It is not a nominal fee ⊥**114** imposed as a regulatory measure to defray the expenses of policing the activities in question. It is in no way apportioned. It is a flat license tax levied and collected as a condition to the pursuit of activities whose enjoyment is guaranteed by the First Amendment. Accordingly, it restrains in advance those constitutional liberties of press and religion and inevitably tends to suppress their exercise. That is almost uniformly recognized as the inherent vice and evil of this flat license tax. As stated by the Supreme Court of Illinois in a case involving this same sect and an ordinance similar to the present one, a person cannot be compelled "to purchase, through a license fee or a license tax, the privilege freely granted by the Constitution." *Blue Island* v. *Kozul*. So, it may not be said that proof is lacking that these license taxes either separately or cumulatively have restricted or are likely to restrict petitioners' religious activities. On their face they are a restriction of the free exercise of those freedoms which are protected by the First Amendment.

The taxes imposed by this ordinance can hardly help but be as severe and telling in their impact on the freedom ⊥**115** of the press and religion as the "taxes on knowledge" at which the First Amendment was partly aimed. They may indeed operate even more subtly. Itinerant evangelists moving throughout a state or from state to state would feel immediately the cumulative effect of such ordinances as they become fashionable. The way of the religious dissenter has long been hard. But if the formula of this type of ordinance is approved, a new device for the suppression of religious minorities will have been found. This method of disseminating religious beliefs can be crushed and closed out by the sheer weight of the toll or tribute which is exacted town by town, village by village. The spread of religious ideas through personal visitations by the literature ministry of numerous religious groups would be stopped.

The fact that the ordinance is "non-discriminatory" is immaterial. The protection afforded by the First Amendment is not so restricted. A license tax certainly does not acquire constitutional validity because it classifies the privileges protected by the First Amendment along with the wares and merchandise of hucksters and peddlers and treats them all alike. Such equality in treatment does not save the ordinance. Freedom of press, freedom of speech, freedom of religion are in a preferred position.

It is claimed, however, that the ultimate question in determining the constitutionality of this license tax is whether the state has given something for which it can ask a return. That principle has wide applicability. But it is quite irrelevant here. This tax is not a charge for the enjoyment of a privilege or benefit bestowed by the state. The privilege in question exists apart from state authority. It is guaranteed the people by the Federal Constitution.

Considerable emphasis is placed on the kind of literature which petitioners were distributing—its provocative, ⊥**116** abusive, and ill-mannered character and the assault which it makes on our established churches and the cherished faiths of many of us. But those considerations are not justification for the license tax which the ordinance imposes. Plainly a community may not suppress, or the state tax, the dissemination of views because they are unpopular, annoying or distasteful. If that device were ever sanctioned, there would have been forged a ready instrument for the suppression of the faith which any minority cherishes but which does not happen to be in favor. That would be a complete repudiation of the philosophy of the Bill of Rights.

Jehovah's Witnesses are not "above the law." But the present ordinance is not directed to the problems with which the police power of the state is free to deal. It does not cover, and petitioners are not charged with, breaches of the peace. They are pursuing their solicitations peacefully and quietly. Petitioners, moreover, are not charged with or prosecuted for the use of language which is obscene, abusive, or which incites retaliation. Nor do we have here, as we did in *Cox* v. *New Hampshire* and *Chaplinsky* v. *New Hampshire*, state regulation of the streets to protect and insure the safety, comfort, or convenience of the public. Furthermore, the present ordinance is not narrowly drawn to safeguard the people of the community in their homes against the evils of solicitations. As we have said, it is not merely a registration ordinance calling for an identification of the solicitors so as to give the authorities some basis for investigating strangers coming into the community. And the fee is not a nominal one, imposed as a regulatory measure and calculated to defray the expense of protecting those on the streets and at home against the abuses of solicitors. ⊥**117** Nor can the present ordinance survive if we assume that it has been construed to apply only to solicitation from house to house. The ordinance is not narrowly drawn to prevent or control abuses or evils arising from that activity. Rather, it sets aside the residential area as a prohibited zone, entry of which is denied petitioners unless the tax is paid. That restraint and one which is city wide in scope (*Jones* v. *Opelika*) are different only in degree. Each is an abridgment of freedom of press and a restraint on the free exercise of religion. They stand or fall together.

The judgment in *Jones* v. *Opelika* has this day been vacated. Freed from that controlling precedent, we can restore to their high, constitutional position the liberties of itinerant evangelists who disseminate their religious beliefs and the tenets of their faith through distribution of literature. The judgments are reversed and the causes are remanded to the Pennsylvania Superior Court for proceedings not inconsistent with this opinion.

Reversed.

The following dissenting opinions are applicable to *Jones* v. *Opelika* and *Murdock* v. *Pennsylvania*.

Mr. *Justice* REED, dissenting:

These cases present for solution the problem of the constitutionality of certain municipal ordinances levying a tax for the production of revenue on the sale of books ⊥**118** and pamphlets in the streets or from door to door. Decisions sustaining the particular ordinances were entered in the three cases first listed at the last term of this Court. In that opinion the ordinances were set out and the facts and issues stated. A rehearing has been granted. The present judgments vacate the old and invalidate the ordinances. The eight cases of this term involve canvassing from door to door only under similar ordinances, which are in the form stated in the Court's opinion. By a *per curiam* opinion of this day, the Court affirms its acceptance of the arguments presented by the dissent of last term in *Jones* v. *Opelika*. The Court states its position anew in the *Jeannette* Cases.

This dissent does not deal with an objection which theoretically could be made in each case, to wit, that the licenses are so excessive in amount as to be prohibitory.

This matter is not considered because that defense is not relied upon in the pleadings, the briefs or at the bar. No evidence is offered to show the amount is oppressive. An unequal tax, levied on the activities of distributors of informatory publications, would be a phase of discrimination against the freedom of speech, press or religion. Nor do we deal with discrimination against the petitioners, as individuals or as members of the group, calling themselves Jehovah's Witnesses. There is no contention in any of these cases that such discrimination is practiced in the application of the ordinances. Obviously an improper application by a city, which resulted in the arrest of Witnesses and failure to enforce the ordinance against other groups, such as the Adventists, would raise entirely distinct issues.

A further and important disclaimer must be made in order to focus attention sharply upon the constitutional issue. This dissent does not express, directly or by inference, any conclusion as to the constitutional rights of state or federal governments to place a privilege tax upon the ⊥**119** soliciting of a free-will contribution for religious purposes. Petitioners suggest that their books and pamphlets are not sold but are given either without price or in appreciation of the recipient's gift for the furtherance of the work of the Witnesses. The pittance sought, as well as the practice of leaving books with poor people without cost, gives strength to this argument. In our judgment, however, the plan of national distribution by the Watch Tower Bible & Tract Society, with its wholesale prices of five or twenty cents per copy for books, delivered to the public by the Witnesses at twenty-five cents per copy, justifies the characterization of the transaction as a sale by all the state courts. The evidence is conclusive that the Witnesses normally approach a prospect with an offer of a book for twenty-five cents. Sometimes, apparently rarely, a book is left with a prospect without payment. The *quid pro quo* is demanded. If the profit was greater, twenty cents or even one dollar, no difference in principle would emerge. The Witness sells books to raise money for propagandising his faith, just as other religious groups might sponsor bazaars or peddle tickets to church suppers, or sell Bibles or prayer books for the same object. However high the purpose or noble the aims of the Witness, the transaction has been found by the state courts to be a sale under their ordinances and, though our doubt was greater than it is, the state's conclusion would influence us to follow its determination. ⊥**120**

In the opinion in *Jones* v. *Opelika* on the former hearing, attention was called to the differentiation between these cases of taxation and those of forbidden censorship, prohibition, or discrimination. There is no occasion to repeat what has been written so recently as to the constitutional right to tax the money raising activities of religious or didactic groups. There are, however, other reasons, not fully developed in that opinion, that add to our conviction that the Constitution does not prohibit these general occupational taxes.

The real contention of the Witnesses is that there can be no taxation of the occupation of selling books and pamphlets because to do so would be contrary to the due process clause of the Fourteenth Amendment, which now is held to have drawn the contents of the First Amendment into the category of individual rights protected ⊥**121** from state deprivation. Since the publications teach a religion which conforms to our standards of legality, it is urged that these ordinances prohibit the free exercise of religion and abridge the freedom of speech and of the press. . . . Is subjection to non-discriminatory, nonexcessive taxation in the distribution of religious literature, a prohibition of the exercise of religion or an abridgment of the freedom of the press? ⊥**122**

Nothing has been brought to our attention which would lead to the conclusion that the contemporary advocates of the adoption of a Bill of Rights intended such an exemption. The words of the Amendment do not support such a construction. "Free" cannot be held to be without cost but rather its meaning must accord with the freedom guaranteed. "Free" means a privilege to print or pray without permission and without accounting to authority for one's actions. In the Constitutional Convention the proposal for a Bill of Rights of any kind received scant attention. In the course of the ratification of the Constitution, however, the absence of a Bill of Rights was used vigorously by the opponents of the new government. A number of the states suggested amendments. Where these suggestions have any bearing at all upon religion or free speech, they indicate nothing as to any feeling concerning taxation either of religious bodies or their evangelism. This was not because freedom of ⊥**123** religion or free speech was not understood. It was because the subjects were looked upon from standpoints entirely distinct from taxation.

The available evidence of Congressional action shows clearly that the draftsmen of the amendments had in mind the practice of religion and the right to be heard, rather than any abridgment or interference with either by taxa⊥**124**tion in any form. The amendments were proposed by ⊥**125** Mr. Madison. He was careful to explain to the Congress the meaning of the amendment on religion. The draft was commented upon by Mr. Madison when it read: "no religion shall be established by law, nor shall the equal rights of conscience be infringed."

He said that he apprehended the meaning of the words on religion to be that Congress should not establish a religion and enforce the legal observation of it by law, nor compel men to worship God in any manner contrary to their conscience. No such specific interpretation of the amendment on freedom of expression has been found in the debates. The clearest is probably from Mr. Benson who said that "The committee who framed this report proceeded on the principle that these rights belonged to the people; they conceived them to be inherent; and all that they mean to provide against was their being infringed by the Government."

There have been suggestions that the English taxes on newspapers, springing from the tax act of 10 Anne, c. 19,

§ CI, influenced the adoption of the First Amendment. ⊥126 These taxes were obnoxious but an examination of the sources of the suggestion is convincing that there is nothing to support it except the fact that the tax on newspapers was in existence in England and was disliked. The simple answer is that if there had been any purpose of Congress to prohibit any kind of taxes on the press, its knowledge of the abominated English taxes would have led it to ban them unequivocally.

It is only in recent years that the freedoms of the First Amendment have been recognized as among the fundamental personal rights protected by the Fourteenth Amendment from impairment by the states. Until then these liberties were not deemed to be guarded from state action by the Federal Constitution. The states placed ⊥127 restraints upon themselves in their own Constitutions in order to protect their people in the exercise of the freedoms of speech and of religion. Pennsylvania may be taken as a fair example. Its constitution reads:

"All men have a natural and indefeasible right to worship Almighty God according to the dictates of their own consciences; no man can of right be compelled to attend, erect or support any place of worship, or to maintain any ministry against his consent; no human authority can, in any case whatever, control or interfere with the rights of conscience and no preference shall ever be given by law to any religious establishments or modes of worship."

"No person who acknowledges the being of a God, and a future state of rewards and punishments shall, on account of his religious sentiments, be disqualified to hold any office or place of trust or profit under this Commonwealth."

"The printing press shall be free to every person who may undertake to examine the proceedings of the Legislature or any branch of government, and no law shall ever be made to restrain the right thereof. The free communication of thoughts and opinions is one of the invaluable rights of man, and every citizen may freely speak, write and print on any subject, being responsible for the abuse of that liberty. . . ."

It will be observed that there is no suggestion of freedom from taxation, and this statement is equally true of the other state constitutional provisions. It may be concluded that neither in the state or the federal constitutions was general taxation of church or press interdicted.

Is there anything in the decisions of this Court which indicates that church or press is free from the financial ⊥128 burdens of government? We find nothing. Religious societies depend for their exemptions from taxation upon state constitutions or general statutes, not upon the Federal Constitution. This Court has held that the chief purpose of the free press guarantee was to prevent previous restraints upon publication. In *Grosjean* v. *American Press Co.*, it was said that the predominant purpose was to preserve "an untrammeled press as a vital source of public information." In that case, a gross receipts tax on advertisements in papers with a circulation of more than twenty thousand copies per week was held invalid because "a deliberate and calculated device in the guise of a tax to limit the circulation. . . ." There was this further comment:

"It is not intended by anything we have said to suggest that the owners of newspapers are immune from any of the ordinary forms of taxation for support of the government. But this is not an ordinary form of tax, but one single in kind, with a long history of hostile misuse against the freedom of the press."

It may be said, however, that ours is a too narrow, technical and legalistic approach to the problem of state taxation of the activities of church and press; that we should look not to the expressed or historical meaning of the First Amendment but to the broad principles of free speech and free exercise of religion which pervade our national way of life. It may be that the Fourteenth Amendment guarantees these principles rather than the more definite concept expressed in the First Amendment. This would mean that as a Court, we should determine what sort of liberty it is that the due process clause of ⊥129 the Fourteenth Amendment guarantees against state restrictions on speech and church.

But whether we give content to the literal words of the First Amendment or to principles of the liberty of the press and the church, we conclude that cities or states may levy reasonable, non-discriminatory taxes on such activities as occurred in these cases. . . . ⊥130

It is urged that such a tax as this may be used readily to restrict the dissemination of ideas. This must be conceded but the possibility of misuse does not make a tax unconstitutional. No abuse is claimed here. The ordinances in some of these cases are the general occupation license type covering many businesses. In the *Jeannette* prosecutions, the ordinance involved lays the usual tax on canvassing or soliciting sales of goods, wares and merchandise. It was passed in 1898. Every power of taxation or regulation is capable of abuse. Each one, to some extent, prohibits the free exercise of religion and abridges the freedom of the press, but that is hardly a reason for denying the power. If the tax is used oppressively, the law will protect the victims of such action.

This decision forces a tax subsidy notwithstanding our accepted belief in the separation of church and state. Instead of all bearing equally the burdens of government, this Court now fastens upon the communities the entire cost of policing the sales of religious literature. That the burden may be heavy is shown by the record in the *Jeannette* Cases. There are only eight prosecutions but one hundred and four Witnesses solicited in Jeannette the day ⊥131 of the arrests. They had been requested by the authorities to await the outcome of a test case before continuing their canvassing. The distributors of religious literature, possibly of all informatory publications, become today privileged to carry on their occupations without contributing their share to the support of the government which provides the opportunity for the exercise of their liberties.

Nor do we think it can be said, properly, that these sales of religious books are religious exercises. The opinion of the Court in the *Jeannette* Cases emphasizes for the first time the argument that the sale of books and pamphlets is in itself a religious practice. The Court says the Witnesses "spread their interpretations of the Bible and their religious beliefs largely through the hand distribution of literature by full or part time workers." "The hand distribution of religious tracts is an age-old form of missionary evangelism—as old as the history of printing presses." "It is more than preaching, it is more than distribution of religious literature. It is a combination of both. Its purpose is as evangelical as the revival meeting. This form of religious activity occupies the same high estate under the First Amendment as do worship in the churches and preaching from the pulpits." "Those who can tax the exercise of this religious practice can make its exercise so costly as to deprive it of the resources necessary for its maintenance." "The judgment in *Jones* v. *Opelika* has this day been vacated. Freed from that controlling precedent, we can restore to their high, constitutional position the liberties of itinerant evangelists who disseminate their religious beliefs and the tenets of their faith through distribution of literature." The record shows that books entitled "Creation" and "Salvation," as well as Bibles, were offered for sale. We shall assume the first two publications, also, are religious books. Certainly there can be no dissent from the statement that ⊥**132** selling religious books is an age-old practice or that it is evangelism in the sense that the distributors hope the readers will be spiritually benefited. That does not carry us to the conviction, however, that when distribution of religious books is made at a price, the itinerant colporteur is performing a religious rite, is worshipping his Creator in his way. Many sects practice healing the sick as an evidence of their religious faith or maintain orphanages or homes for the aged or teach the young. These are, of course, in a sense, religious practices but hardly such examples of religious rites as are encompassed by the prohibition against the free exercise of religion.

And even if the distribution of religious books was a religious practice protected from regulation by the First Amendment, certainly the affixation of a price for the articles would destroy the sacred character of the transaction. The evangelist becomes also a book agent.

The rites which are protected by the First Amendment are in essence spiritual—prayer, mass, sermons, sacrament—not sales of religious goods. The card furnished each Witness to identify him as an ordained minister does not go so far as to say the sale is a rite. It states only that the Witnesses worship by exhibiting to people "the message of said gospel in printed form, such as the Bible, books, booklets and magazines and thus afford the people the opportunity of learning of God's gracious provision for them." On the back of the card appears:

"You may contribute twenty-five cents to the Lord's work and receive a copy of this beautiful book." The sale of these religious books has, we think, relation to their religious exercises, similar to the "information march," said by the Witnesses to be one of their "ways of worship" and by this Court to be subject to regulation by license in *Cox* v. *New Hampshire*.

The attempted analogy in the dissenting opinion in *Jones* v. *Opelika*, which now be⊥**133**comes the decision of this Court, between the forbidden burden of a state tax for the privilege of engaging in interstate commerce and a state tax on the privilege of engaging in the distribution of religious literature is wholly irrelevant. A state tax on the privilege of engaging in interstate commerce is held invalid because the regulation of commerce between the states has been delegated to the Federal Government. This grant includes the necessary means to carry the grant into effect and forbids state burdens without congressional consent. It is not the power to tax interstate commerce which is interdicted, but the exercise of that power by an unauthorized sovereign, the individual state. Although the fostering of commerce was one of the chief purposes for organizing the present Government, that commerce may be burdened with a tax by the United States. Commerce must pay its way. It is not exempt from any type of taxation if imposed by an authorized authority. The Court now holds that the First Amendment wholly exempts the church and press from a privilege tax, presumably by the national as well as the state governments.

The limitations of the Constitution are not maxims of social wisdom but definite controls on the legislative process. We are dealing with power, not its abuse. This late withdrawal of the power of taxation over the distribution activities of those covered by the First Amendment fixes what seems to us an unfortunate principle of tax exemption, capable of indefinite extension. We had thought that such an exemption required a clear and certain grant. This we do not find in the language of the First and Fourteenth Amendments. We are therefore of the opinion the judgments below should be affirmed.

⊥**134** Mr. *Justice* ROBERTS, Mr. *Justice* FRANKFURTER, and Mr. *Justice* JACKSON join in this dissent.

Mr. *Justice* FRANKFURTER, dissenting:

While I wholly agree with the views expressed by Mr. *Justice* REED, the controversy is of such a nature as to lead me to add a few words.

A tax can be a means for raising revenue, or a device for regulating conduct, or both. Challenge to the constitutional validity of a tax measure requires that it be analyzed and judged in all its aspects. We must therefore distinguish between the questions that are before us in these cases and those that are not. It is altogether incorrect to say that the question here is whether a state can limit the free exercise of religion by imposing burdensome taxes. As the opinion of my *Brother* REED demonstrates, we have not here the question whether the taxes imposed in these cases are in practical operation an unjustifiable curtailment upon the petitioners' undoubted right to communicate their views to others. No claim is made that the effect of these taxes, either separately or cumulatively, has been, or is likely to be, to restrict the petitioners' religious propaganda activities in any degree. Counsel expressly disclaim any such contention. They insist on absolute immunity from any kind of monetary exaction for their occupation. Their claim is that no tax, no matter how trifling, can constitutionally be laid upon the activity of distributing religious literature, regardless of the actual effect of the tax upon such activity. That is the only ground upon which these ordinances have been attacked, that is the only question raised in or decided by the state courts; and that is the only question presented to us. No complaint is made against the size of the taxes. If an appropriate claim, indicating that the taxes were oppressive in their effect upon the petition⊥**135**ers' activities, had been made, the issues here would be very different. No such claim has been made, and it would be gratuitous to consider its merits.

Nor have we occasion to consider whether these measures are invalid on the ground that they unjustly or unreasonably discriminate against the petitioners. Counsel do not claim, as indeed they could not, that these ordinances were intended to or have been applied to discriminate against religious groups generally or Jehovah's Witnesses particularly. No claim is made that the effect of the taxes is to hinder or restrict the activities of Jehovah's Witnesses while other religious groups, perhaps older or more prosperous, can carry on theirs. This question, too, is not before us.

It cannot be said that the petitioners are constitutionally exempt from taxation merely because they may be engaged in religious activities or because such activities may constitute an exercise of a constitutional right. It will hardly be contended, for example, that a tax upon the income of a clergyman would violate the Bill of Rights, even though the tax is ultimately borne by the members of his church. A clergyman, no less than a judge, is a citizen. And not only in time of war would neither willingly enjoy immunity from the obligations of citizenship. It is only fair that he also who preaches the word of God should share in the costs of the benefits provided by government to him as well as to the other members of the community. And so, no one would suggest that a clergyman who uses an automobile or the telephone in connection with his work thereby gains a constitutional exemption from taxes levied upon the use of automobiles or upon telephone calls. Equally alien is it to our constitutional system to suggest that the Constitution of the United States exempts church-held lands from state taxation. Plainly, a tax measure is not invalid under the federal Constitution merely because it falls upon persons engaged in activities of a religious nature. ⊥**136**

Nor can a tax be invalidated merely because it falls upon activities which constitute an exercise of a constitutional right. The First Amendment of course protects the right to publish a newspaper or a magazine or a book. But the crucial question is—how much protection does the Amendment give, and against what is the right protected? It is certainly true that the protection afforded the freedom of the press by the First Amendment does not include exemption from all taxation. A tax upon newspaper publishing is not invalid simply because it falls upon the exercise of a constitutional right. Such a tax might be invalid if it invidiously singled out newspaper publishing for bearing the burdens of taxation or imposed upon them in such ways as to encroach on the essential scope of a free press. If the Court could justifiably hold that the tax measures in these cases were vulnerable on that ground, I would unreservedly agree. But the Court has not done so, and indeed could not. . . . ⊥**137**

As I read the Court's opinion, it does not hold that the taxes in the cases before us in fact do hinder or restrict the petitioners in exercising their constitutional rights. It holds that "The power to tax the exercise of a privilege is the power to control or suppress its enjoyment." This assumes that because the taxing power exerted in *Magnano Co.* v. *Hamilton*, the well-known oleomargarine tax case, may have had the effect of "controlling" or "suppressing" the enjoyment of a privilege and still was sustained by this Court, and because all exertions of the taxing power may have that effect, if perchance a particular exercise of the taxing power does have that effect, it would have to be sustained under our ruling in the *Magnano Co.* Case.

The power to tax, like all powers of government, legislative, executive and judicial alike, can be abused or perverted. The power to tax is the power to destroy only in the sense that those who have power can misuse it. *Mr. Justice HOLMES* disposed of this smooth phrase as a constitutional basis for invalidating taxes when he wrote "The power to tax is not the power to destroy while this Court sits." *Panhandle Oil Co.* v. *Mississippi*. The fact that a power can be perverted does not mean that every exercise of the power is a perversion of the power. Thus, if a tax indirectly suppresses or controls the enjoyment of a constitutional privilege which a legislature cannot directly suppress or control, of course it is bad. But it is irrelevant that a tax can suppress or control if it does not. The Court holds that "Those who can tax the exercise of this religious practice can make its exercise so costly as to deprive it of resources necessary for its maintenance." But this is not the same as saying that "Those who do tax the exercise of this religious practice have made its exercise so costly as to deprive it of the resources necessary for its maintenance." ⊥**138**

The Court could not plausibly make such an assertion because the petitioners themselves disavow any claim that the taxes imposed in these cases impair their ability to exercise their constitutional rights. We cannot invalidate the tax measures before us simply because there may be others, not now before us, which are oppressive in their effect. The Court's opinion does not deny that the ordinances involved in these cases have in no way disabled the petitioners to engage in their religious activities. It holds only that "Those who can tax the privilege of engaging in this form of missionary evangelism can close its doors to all those who do not have a full purse." I quite agree with this statement as an abstract proposition. Those who possess the power to tax might wield it in tyrannical fashion. It does not follow, however, that every exercise of the power is an act of tyranny, or that government should be impotent because it might be tyrannical. The question before us now is whether these ordinances have deprived the petitioners of their constitutional rights, not whether some other ordinances not now before us might be enacted which might deprive them of such rights. To deny constitutional power to secular authority merely because of the possibility of its abuse is as valid as to deny the basis of spiritual authority because those in whom it is temporarily vested may misuse it. . . . ⊥**139**

It is strenuously urged that the Constitution denies a city the right to control the expression of men's minds and the right of men to win others to their views. But the Court is not divided on this proposition. No one disputes it. All members of the Court are equally familiar with the history that led to the adoption of the Bill of Rights and are equally zealous to enforce the constitutional protection of the free play of the human spirit. Escape from the real issue before us cannot be found in such generalities. The real issue here is not whether a city may charge for the dissemination of ideas but whether the states have power to require those who need additional facilities to help bear the cost of furnishing such facilities. Street hawkers make demands upon municipalities that involve the expenditure of dollars and cents, whether they hawk printed matter or other things. As the facts in these cases show, the cost of maintaining the peace, the additional demands upon governmental facilities for assuring security, involve outlays which have to be met. To say that the Constitution forbids the states to obtain the necessary revenue from the whole of a class that enjoys these benefits ⊥**140** and facilities, when in fact no discrimination is suggested as between purveyors of printed matter and purveyors of other things, and the exaction is not claimed to be actually burdensome, is to say that the Constitution requires not that the dissemination of ideas in the interest of religion shall be free but that it shall be subsidized by the state. Such a claim offends the most important of all aspects of religious freedom in this country, namely, that of the separation of church and state.

The ultimate question in determining the constitutionality of a tax measure is—has the state given something for which it can ask a return? There can be no doubt that these petitioners, like all who use the streets, have received the benefits of government. Peace is maintained, traffic is regulated, health is safeguarded—these are only some of the many incidents of municipal administration. To secure them costs money, and a state's source of money is its taxing power. There is nothing in the Constitution which exempts persons engaged in religious activities from sharing equally in the costs of benefits to all, including themselves, provided by government.

I cannot say, therefore, that in these cases the community has demanded a return for that which it did not give. Nor am I called upon to say that the state has demanded unjustifiably more than the value of what it gave, nor that its demand in fact cramps activities pursued to promote religious beliefs. No such claim was made at the bar, and there is no evidence in the records to substantiate any such claim if it had been made. Under these circumstances, therefore, I am of opinion that the ordinances in these cases must stand.

Mr. *Justice* JACKSON joins in this dissent.

MINERSVILLE SCHOOL DISTRICT v. GOBITIS

310 U.S. 586

ON WRIT OF CERTIORARI TO THE UNITED STATES CIRCUIT COURT OF APPEALS FOR THE THIRD CIRCUIT

Argued April 25, 1940 — Decided June 3, 1940

⊥**591** Mr. *Justice FRANKFURTER* delivered the opinion of the Court:

A grave responsibility confronts this Court whenever in course of litigation it must reconcile the conflicting claims of liberty and authority. But when the liberty invoked is liberty of conscience, and the authority is authority to safeguard the nation's fellowship, judicial conscience is put to its severest test. Of such a nature is the present controversy.

Lillian Gobitis, aged twelve, and her brother William, aged ten, were expelled from the public schools of Minersville, Pennsylvania, for refusing to salute the national flag as part of a daily school exercise. The local Board of Education required both teachers and pupils to participate in this ceremony. The ceremony is a familiar one. The right hand is placed on the breast and the following pledge recited in unison: "I pledge allegiance to my flag, and to the Republic for which it stands; one nation indivisible, with liberty and justice for all." While the words are spoken, teachers and pupils extend their right hands in salute to the flag. The Gobitis family are affiliated with "Jehovah's Witnesses," for whom the Bible as the Word of God is the supreme authority. The chil⊥**592**dren had been brought up conscientiously to believe that such a gesture of respect for the flag was forbidden by command of Scripture.

The Gobitis children were of an age for which Pennsylvania makes school attendance compulsory. Thus they were denied a free education, and their parents had to put them into private schools. To be relieved of the financial burden thereby entailed, their father on behalf of the children and in his own behalf, brought this suit. He sought to enjoin the authorities from continuing to exact participation in the flag-salute ceremony as a condition of his children's attendance at the Minersville school. After trial of the issues, Judge Maris gave relief in the District Court, on the basis of a thoughtful opinion, at a preliminary stage of the litigation; his decree was affirmed by the Circuit Court of Appeals. Since this decision ran counter to several *per curiam* dispositions of this Court, we granted certiorari to give the matter full reconsideration. By their able submissions, the Committee on the Bill of Rights of the American Bar Association and the American Civil Liberties Union, as friends of the Court, have helped us to our conclusion.

We must decide whether the requirement of participation in such a ceremony, exacted from a child who refuses ⊥**593** upon sincere religious grounds, infringes without due process of law the liberty guaranteed by the Fourteenth Amendment.

Centuries of strife over the erection of particular dogmas as exclusive or all-comprehending faiths led to the inclusion of a guarantee for religious freedom in the Bill of Rights. The First Amendment, and the Fourteenth through its absorption of the First, sought to guard against repetition of those bitter religious struggles by prohibiting the establishment of a state religion and by securing to every sect the free exercise of its faith. So pervasive is the acceptance of this precious right that its scope is brought into question, as here, only when the conscience of individuals collides with the felt necessities of society.

Certainly the affirmative pursuit of one's convictions about the ultimate mystery of the universe and man's relation to it is placed beyond the reach of law. Government may not interfere with organized or individual expression of belief or disbelief. Propagation of belief—or even of disbelief in the supernatural—is protected, whether in church or chapel, mosque or synagogue, tabernacle or meetinghouse. Likewise the Constitution assures generous immunity to the individual from imposition of penalties for offending, in the course of his own religious activities, the religious views of others, be they a minority or those who are dominant in government.

But the manifold character of man's relations may bring his conception of religious duty into conflict with the secular interests of his fellow-men. When does the constitutional guarantee compel exemption from doing what society thinks necessary for the promotion of some great common end, or from a penalty for conduct which appears dangerous to the general good? To state the ⊥**594** problem is to recall the truth that no single principle can answer all of life's complexities. The right to freedom of religious belief, however dissident and however obnoxious to the cherished beliefs of others—even of a majority—is itself the denial of an absolute. But to affirm that the freedom to follow conscience has itself no limits in the life of a society would deny that very plurality of principles which, as a matter of history, underlies protection of religious toleration. Our present task then, as so often the case with courts, is to reconcile two rights in order to prevent either from destroying the other. But, because in safeguarding conscience we are dealing with interests so subtle and so dear, every possible leeway should be given to the claims of religious faith.

In the judicial enforcement of religious freedom we are concerned with a historic concept. The religious liberty which the Constitution protects has never excluded legislation of general scope not directed against doctrinal loyalties of particular sects. Judicial nullification of legislation cannot be justified by attributing to the framers of the Bill of Rights views for which there is no historic warrant. Conscientious scruples have not, in the course of the long struggle for religious toleration, relieved the individual from obedience to a general law not aimed at the promotion or restriction of religious beliefs. The mere possession of religious convictions ⊥**595** which contradict the relevant concerns of a political society does not relieve the citizen from the discharge of political responsibilities. The necessity for this adjustment has again and again been recognized. In a number of situations the exertion of political authority has been sustained, while basic considerations of religious freedom have been left inviolate. In all these cases the general laws in question, upheld in their application to those who refused obedience from religious conviction, were manifestations of specific powers of government deemed by the legislature essential to secure and maintain that orderly, tranquil, and free society without which religious toleration itself is unattainable. Nor does the freedom of speech assured by Due Process move in a more absolute circle of immunity than that enjoyed by religious freedom. Even if it were assumed that freedom of speech goes beyond the historic concept of full opportunity to utter and to disseminate views, however heretical or offensive to dominant opinion, and includes freedom from conveying what may be deemed an implied but rejected affirmation, the question remains whether school children, like the Gobitis children, must be excused from conduct required of all the other children in the promotion of national cohesion. We are dealing with an interest inferior to none in the hierarchy of legal values. National unity is the basis of national security. To deny the legislature the right to select appropriate means for its attainment presents a totally different order of problem from that of the propriety of subordinating the possible ugliness of littered streets to the free expression of opinion through distribution of handbills. ⊥**596**

Situations like the present are phases of the profoundest problem confronting a democracy—the problem which Lincoln cast in memorable dilemma: "Must a government of necessity be too *strong* for the liberties of its people, or too *weak* to maintain its own existence?" No mere textual reading or logical talisman can solve the dilemma. And when the issue demands judicial determination, it is not the personal notion of judges of what wise adjustment requires which must prevail.

Unlike the instances we have cited, the case before us is not concerned with an exertion of legislative power for the promotion of some specific need or interest of secular society—the protection of the family, the promotion of health, the common defense, the raising of public revenues to defray the cost of government. But all these specific activities of government presuppose the existence of an organized political society. The ultimate foundation of a free society is the binding tie of cohesive sentiment. Such a sentiment is fostered by all those agencies of the mind and spirit which may serve to gather up the traditions of a people, transmit them from generation to generation, and thereby create that continuity of a treasured common life which constitutes a civilization. "We live by symbols." The flag is the symbol of our national unity, transcending all internal differences, however large, within the framework of the Constitution. This Court has had occasion to say that ". . . the flag is the symbol of the Nation's power, the emblem of freedom in its truest, best sense . . . it signifies government resting on the consent of the governed; liberty regulated by law; the protection of the weak against the strong; security against the exercise of arbitrary power; and absolute safety for free institutions against foreign aggression." *Halter* v. *Nebraska*. ⊥**597**

The case before us must be viewed as though the legislature of Pennsylvania had itself formally directed the flag-salute for the children of Minersville; had made no exemption for children whose parents were possessed of conscientious scruples like those of the Gobitis family; and had indicated its belief in the desirable ends to be secured by having its public school children share a common experience at those periods of development when their minds are supposedly receptive to its assimilation, by an exercise appropriate in time and place and setting, and one designed to evoke in them appreciation of the nation's hopes and dreams, its sufferings and sacrifices. The precise issue, then, for us to decide is whether the legislatures of the various states and the authorities in a thousand counties and school districts of this country are barred from determining the appropriateness of various means to evoke that unifying sentiment without which there can ultimately be no liberties, civil or religious. To stigmatize legislative judgment in providing for this universal gesture of respect for the symbol of our national life in the setting of the common school as a lawless inroad on that freedom of conscience which the Constitution protects, would amount to no less than the pronouncement of pedagogical and psychological dogma in a field where courts possess no marked and certainly no ⊥**598** controlling competence. The influences which help toward a common feeling for the common country are manifold. Some may seem harsh and others no doubt are foolish. Surely, however, the end is legitimate. And the effective means for its attainment are still so uncertain and so unauthenticated by science as to preclude us from putting the widely prevalent belief in flag-saluting beyond the pale of legislative power. It mocks reason and denies our whole history to find in the allowance of a requirement to salute our flag on fitting occasions the seeds of sanction for obeisance to a leader.

The wisdom of training children in patriotic impulses by those compulsions which necessarily pervade so much of the educational process is not for our independent judgment. Even were we convinced of the folly of such a measure, such belief would be no proof of its unconstitutionality. For ourselves, we might be tempted to say that the deepest patriotism is best engendered by giving unfettered scope to the most crochety beliefs. Perhaps it is best, even from the standpoint of those interests which ordinances like the one under review seek to promote, to give to the least popular sect leave from conformities like those here in issue. But the courtroom is not the arena for debating issues of educational policy. It is not our province to choose among competing considerations in the subtle process of securing effective loyalty to the traditional ideals of democracy, while respecting at the same time individual idiosyncracies among a people so diversified in racial origins and religious allegiances. So to hold would in effect make us the school board for the country. That authority has not been given to this Court, nor should we assume it.

We are dealing here with the formative period in the development of citizenship. Great diversity of psychological and ethical opinion exists among us concerning the best way to train children for their place in society. Be⊥**599**cause of these differences and because of reluctance to permit a single, iron-cast system of education to be imposed upon a nation compounded of so many strains, we have held that, even though public education is one of our most cherished democratic institutions, the Bill of Rights bars a state from compelling all children to attend the public schools. But it is a very different thing for this Court to exercise censorship over the conviction of legislatures that a particular program or exercise will best promote in the minds of children who attend the common schools an attachment to the institutions of their country.

What the school authorities are really asserting is the right to awaken in the child's mind considerations as to the significance of the flag contrary to those implanted by the parent. In such an attempt the state is normally at a disadvantage in competing with the parent's authority, so long—and this is the vital aspect of religious toleration—as parents are unmolested in their right to counteract by their own persuasiveness the wisdom and rightness of those loyalties which the state's educational system is seeking to promote. Except where the transgression of constitutional liberty is too plain for argument, personal freedom is best maintained—so long as the remedial channels of the democratic process remain open and unobstructed—when it is ingrained in a people's habits and not enforced against popular policy by the coercion of adjudicated law. That the flag-salute is an allowable portion of a school program for those who do not invoke conscientious scruples is surely not debatable. But for us to insist that, though the ceremony may be ⊥**600** required, exceptional immunity must be given to dissidents, is to maintain that there is no basis for a legislative judgment that such an exemption might introduce elements of difficulty into the school discipline, might cast doubts in the minds of the other children which would themselves weaken the effect of the exercise.

The preciousness of the family relation, the authority and independence which give dignity to parenthood, indeed the enjoyment of all freedom, presuppose the kind of ordered society which is summarized by our flag. A society which is dedicated to the preservation of these ultimate values of civilization may in self-protection utilize the educational process of inculcating those almost unconscious feelings which bind men together in a comprehending loyalty, whatever may be their lesser differences and difficulties. That is to say, the process may be utilized so long as men's right to believe as they please, to win others to their way of belief, and their right to assemble in their chosen places of worship for the devotional ceremonies of their faith, are all fully respected.

Judicial review, itself a limitation on popular government, is a fundamental part of our constitutional scheme. But to the legislature no less than to courts is committed the guardianship of deeply-cherished liberties. Where all the effective means of inducing political changes are left free from interference, education in the abandonment of foolish legislation is itself a training in liberty. To fight out the wise use of legislative authority in the forum of public opinion and before legislative assemblies rather than to transfer such a contest to the judicial arena, serves to vindicate the self-confidence of a free people.

Reversed.

⊥**601** Mr. *Justice* McREYNOLDS concurs in the result.

Mr. *Justice* STONE, dissenting:

I think the judgment below should be affirmed.

Two youths, now fifteen and sixteen years of age, are by the judgment of this Court held liable to expulsion from the public schools and to denial of all publicly supported educational privileges because of their refusal to yield to the compulsion of a law which commands their participation in a school ceremony contrary to their religious convictions. They and their father are citizens and have not exhibited by any action or statement of opinion, any disloyalty to the Government of the United States. They are ready and willing to obey all its laws which do not conflict with what they sincerely believe to be the higher commandments of God. It is not doubted that these convictions are religious, that they are genuine, or that the refusal to yield to the compulsion of the law is in good faith and with all sincerity. It would be a denial of their faith as well as the teachings of most religions to say that children of their age could not have religious convictions.

The law which is thus sustained is unique in the history of Anglo-American legislation. It does more than suppress freedom of speech and more than prohibit the free exercise of religion, which concededly are forbidden by the First Amendment and are violations of the liberty guaranteed by the Fourteenth. For by this law the state seeks to coerce these children to express a sentiment which, as they interpret it, they do not entertain, and which violates their deepest religious convictions. It is not denied that such compulsion is a prohibited infringement of personal liberty, freedom of speech and religion, guaranteed by the Bill of Rights, except in so far as it may be justified and supported as a proper exercise of the state's power over public education. Since the state, ⊥**602** in competition with parents, may through teaching in the public schools indoctrinate the minds of the young, it is said that in aid of its undertaking to inspire loyalty and devotion to constituted authority and the flag which symbolizes it, it may coerce the pupil to make affirmation contrary to his belief and in violation of his religious faith. And, finally, it is said that since the Minersville School Board and others are of the opinion that the country will be better served by conformity than by the observance of religious liberty which the Constitution prescribes, the courts are not free to pass judgment on the Board's choice.

Concededly the constitutional guaranties of personal liberty are not always absolutes. Government has a right to survive and powers conferred upon it are not necessarily set at naught by the express prohibitions of the Bill of Rights. It may make war and raise armies. To that end it may compel citizens to give military service and subject them to military training despite their religious objections. It may suppress religious practices dangerous to morals, and presumably those also which are inimical to public safety, health and good order. But it is a long step, and one which I am unable to take, to the position that government may, as a supposed educational measure and as a means of disciplining the young, compel public affirmations which violate their religious conscience.

The very fact that we have constitutional guaranties of civil liberties and the specificity of their command where freedom of speech and of religion are concerned require some accommodation of the powers which government normally exercises, when no question of civil liberty is involved, to the constitutional demand that those liberties be protected against the action of govern⊥**603**ment itself. The state concededly has power to require and control the education of its citizens, but it cannot by a general law compelling attendance at public schools preclude attendance at a private school adequate in its instruction, where the parent seeks to secure for the child the benefits of religious instruction not provided by the public school. And only recently we have held that the state's authority to control its public streets by generally applicable regulations is not an absolute to which free speech must yield, and cannot be made the medium of its suppression any more than can its authority to penalize littering of the streets by a general law be wed to suppress the distribution of handbills as a means of communicating ideas to their recipients.

In these cases it was pointed out that where there are competing demands of the interests of government and of liberty under the Constitution, and where the performance of governmental functions is brought into conflict with specific constitutional restrictions, there must, when that is possible, be reasonable accommodation between them so as to preserve the essentials of both and that it is the function of courts to determine whether such accommodation is reasonably possible. In the cases just mentioned the Court was of opinion that there were ways enough to secure the legitimate state end without infringing the asserted immunity, or that the inconvenience caused by the inability to secure that end satisfactorily through other means, did not outweigh freedom of speech or religion. So here, even if we believe that such compulsions will contribute to national unity, there are other ways to teach loyalty and patriotism which are the sources of national unity, than by compelling the pupil to affirm that which he does not believe and by ⊥604 commanding a form of affirmance which violates his religious convictions. Without recourse to such compulsion the state is free to compel attendance at school and require teaching by instruction and study of all in our history and in the structure and organization of our government, including the guaranties of civil liberty which tend to inspire patriotism and love of country. I cannot say that government here is deprived of any interest or function which it is entitled to maintain at the expense of the protection of civil liberties by requiring it to resort to the alternatives which do not coerce an affirmation of belief.

The guaranties of civil liberty are but guaranties of freedom of the human mind and spirit and of reasonable freedom and opportunity to express them. They presuppose the right of the individual to hold such opinions as he will and to give them reasonably free expression, and his freedom, and that of the state as well, to teach and persuade others by the communication of ideas. The very essence of the liberty which they guarantee is the freedom of the individual from compulsion as to what he shall think and what he shall say, at least where the compulsion is to bear false witness to his religion. If these guaranties are to have any meaning they must, I think, be deemed to withhold from the state any authority to compel belief for the expression of it where that expression violates religious convictions, whatever may be the legislative view of the desirability of such compulsion.

History teaches us that there have been but few infringements of personal liberty by the state which have not been justified, as they are here, in the name of righteousness and the public good, and few which have not been directed, as they are now, at politically helpless minorities. The framers were not unaware that under the system which they created most governmental cur- ⊥605 tailments of personal liberty would have the support of a legislative judgment that the public interest would be better served by its curtailment than by its constitutional protection. I cannot conceive that in prescribing, as limitations upon the powers of government, the freedom of the mind and spirit secured by the explicit guaranties of freedom of speech and religion, they intended or rightly could have left any latitude for a legislative judgment that the compulsory expression of belief which violates religious convictions would better serve the public interest than their protection. The Constitution may well elicit expressions of loyalty to it and to the government which it created, but it does not command such expressions or otherwise give any indication that compulsory expressions of loyalty play any such part in our scheme of government as to override the constitutional protection of freedom of speech and religion. And while such expressions of loyalty, when voluntarily given, may promote national unity, it is quite another matter to say that their compulsory expression by children in violation of their own and their parents' religious convictions can be regarded as playing so important a part in our national unity as to leave school boards free to exact it despite the constitutional guaranty of freedom of religion. The very terms of the Bill of Rights preclude, it seems to me, any reconciliation of such compulsions with the constitutional guaranties by a legislative declaration that they are more important to the public welfare than the Bill of Rights.

But even if this view be rejected and it is considered that there is some scope for the determination by legislatures whether the citizen shall be compelled to give public expression of such sentiments contrary to his religion, I am not persuaded that we should refrain from passing upon the legislative judgment "as long as the remedial ⊥606 channels of the democratic process remain open and unobstructed." This seems to me no more than the surrender of the constitutional protection of the liberty of small minorities to the popular will. We have previously pointed to the importance of a searching judicial inquiry into the legislative judgment in situations where prejudice against discrete and insular minorities may tend to curtail the operation of those political processes ordinarily to be relied on to protect minorities. And until now we have not hesitated similarly to scrutinize legislation restricting the civil liberty of racial and religious minorities although no political process was affected. Here we have such a small minority entertaining in good faith a religious belief, which is such a departure from the usual course of human conduct, that most persons are disposed to regard it with little toleration or concern. In such circumstances careful scrutiny of legislative efforts to secure conformity of belief and opinion by a compulsory affirmation of the desired belief, is especially needful if civil rights are to receive any protection. Tested by this standard, I am not prepared to say that the right of this small and helpless minority, including children having a strong religious conviction, whether they understand its nature or not, to refrain from an expression obnoxious to their religion, is to be overborne by the interest of the state in maintaining discipline in the schools.

The Constitution expresses more than the conviction of the people that democratic processes must be preserved at all costs. It is also an expression of faith and a command that freedom of mind and spirit must be preserved, which government must obey, if it is to adhere to that justice and moderation without which no free government can exist. For this reason it would seem that legislation which operates to repress the religious freedom of small minorities, which is admittedly within the scope of the protection of the Bill of Rights, must at least be subject to the same judicial scrutiny as legislation which we have recently held to infringe the constitutional liberty of religious and racial minonties.

With such scrutiny I cannot say that the inconveniences which may attend some sensible adjustment of school discipline in order that the religious convictions of these children may be spared, presents a problem so momentous or pressing as to outweigh the freedom from compulsory violation of religious faith which has been thought worthy of constitutional protection.

WEST VIRGINIA STATE BOARD OF EDUCATION v. BARNETTE

319 U.S. 624
ON APPEAL FROM THE DISTRICT COURT OF THE UNITED STATES FOR THE SOUTHERN DISTRICT OF WEST VIRGINIA
Argued March 11, 1943 — Decided June 14, 1943

⊥625 Mr. *Justice* JACKSON delivered the opinion of the Court:

Following the decision by this Court on June 3, 1940, in *Minersville School Dist.* v. *Gobitis*, the West Virginia legislature amended its statutes to require all schools therein to conduct courses of instruction in history, civics, and in the Constitutions of the United States and of the State "for the purpose of teaching, fostering and perpetuating the ideals, principles and spirit of Americanism, and increasing the knowledge of the organization and machinery of the government." Appel**⊥626**lant Board of Education was directed, with advice of the State Superintendent of Schools, to "prescribe the courses of study covering these subjects" for public schools. The Act made it the duty of private, parochial and denominational schools to prescribe courses of study "similar to those required for the public schools."

The Board of Education on January 9, 1942, adopted a resolution containing recitals taken largely from the Court's *Gobitis* opinion and ordering that the salute to the flag become "a regular part of the program of activities in the public schools," that all teachers and pupils "shall be required to participate in the salute honoring the Nation represented by the Flag; provided, however, that refusal to salute the Flag be regarded as an Act of insubordination, and shall be dealt with accordingly."

⊥627 The resolution originally required the "commonly accepted salute to the Flag" which it defined. Objections to the salute as "being too much like Hitler's" were raised by the Parent and Teachers Association, the Boy and Girl **⊥628** Scouts, the Red Cross, and the Federation of Women's Clubs. Some modification appears to have been made in deference to these objections, but no concession was made to Jehovah's Witnesses. What is now required is the "stiff-arm" salute, the saluter to keep the right hand raised with palm turned up while the following is repeated: "I pledge allegiance to the Flag of **⊥629** the United States of America and to the Republic for which it stands; one Nation, indivisible, with liberty and justice for all."

Failure to conform is "insubordination" dealt with by expulsion. Readmission is denied by statute until compliance. Meanwhile the expelled child is "unlawfully absent" and may be proceeded against as a delinquent. His parents or guardians are liable to prosecution, and if convicted are subject to fine not exceeding $50 and jail term not exceeding thirty days.

Appellees, citizens of the United States and of West Virginia, brought suit in the United States District Court for themselves and others similarly situated asking its injunction to restrain enforcement of these laws and regulations against Jehovah's Witnesses. The Witnesses are an unincorporated body teaching that the obligation imposed by law of God is superior to that of laws enacted by temporal government. Their religious beliefs include a literal version of Exodus, Chapter 20, verses 4 and 5, which says: "Thou shalt not make unto thee any graven image, or any likeness of anything that is in heaven above, or that is in the earth beneath, or that is in the water under the earth; thou shalt not bow down thyself to them, nor serve them." They consider that the flag is an "image" within this command. For this reason they refuse to salute it. **⊥630**

Children of this faith have been expelled from school and are threatened with exclusion for no other cause. Officials threaten to send them to reformatories maintained for criminally inclined juveniles. Parents of such children have been prosecuted and are threatened with prosecutions for causing delinquency.

The Board of Education moved to dismiss the complaint setting forth these facts and alleging that the law and regulations are an unconstitutional denial of religious freedom, and of freedom of speech, and are invalid under the "due process" and "equal protection" clauses of the Fourteenth Amendment to the Federal Constitution. The cause was submitted on the pleadings to a District Court of three judges. It restrained enforcement as to the plaintiffs and those of that class. The Board of Education brought the case here by direct appeal.

This case calls upon us to reconsider a precedent decision, as the Court throughout its history often has been required to do. Before turning to the *Gobitis* Case, however, it is desirable to notice certain characteristics by which this controversy is distinguished.

The freedom asserted by these appellees does not bring them into collision with rights asserted by any other individual. It is such conflicts which most frequently require intervention of the State to determine where the rights of one end and those of another begin. But the refusal of these persons to participate in the ceremony does not interfere with or deny rights of others to do so. Nor is there any question in this case that their behavior is peaceable and orderly. The sole conflict is between authority and rights of the individual. The State asserts power to condition access to public education on making a prescribed sign and profession and at the same time to coerce ⊥**631** attendance by punishing both parent and child. The latter stand on a right of self-determination in matters that touch individual opinion and personal attitude.

As the present *Chief Justice* said in dissent in the *Gobitis* Case, the State may "require teaching by instruction and study of all in our history and in the structure and organization of our government, including the guaranties of civil liberty, which tend to inspire patriotism and love of country." Here, however, we are dealing with a compulsion of students to declare a belief. They are not merely made acquainted with the flag salute so that they may be informed as to what it is or even what it means. The issue here is whether this slow and easily neglected route to aroused loyalties constitutionally may be short-cut by substituting a compulsory salute and slogan. This issue is not prejudiced by ⊥**632** the Court's previous holding that where a State, without compelling attendance, extends college facilities to pupils who voluntarily enroll, it may prescribe military training as part of the course without offense to the Constitution. It was held that those who take advantage of its opportunities may not on ground of conscience refuse compliance with such conditions. In the present case attendance is not optional. That case is also to be distinguished from the present one because, independently of college privileges or requirements, the State has power to raise militia and impose the duties of service therein upon its citizens.

There is no doubt that, in connection with the pledges, the flag salute is a form of utterance. Symbolism is a primitive but effective way of communicating ideas. The use of an emblem or flag to symbolize some system, idea, institution, or personality, is a short cut from mind to mind. Causes and nations, political parties, lodges and ecclesiastical groups seek to knit the loyalty of their followings to a flag or banner, a color or design. The State announces rank, function, and authority through crowns and maces, uniforms and black robes; the church speaks through the Cross, the Crucifix, the altar and shrine, and clerical raiment. Symbols of State often convey political ideas just as religious symbols come to convey theological ones. Associated with many of these symbols are appropriate gestures of acceptance or respect: a salute, a bowed or bared head, a bended knee. A person gets from a ⊥**633** symbol the meaning he puts into it, and what is one man's comfort and inspiration is another's jest and scorn.

Over a decade ago *Chief Justice* HUGHES led this Court in holding that the display of a red flag as a symbol of opposition by peaceful and legal means to organized government was protected by the free speech guaranties of the Constitution. Here it is the State that employs a flag as a symbol of adherence to government as presently organized. It requires the individual to communicate by word and sign his acceptance of the political ideas it thus bespeaks. Objection to the form of communication when coerced is an old one, well known to the framers of the Bill of Rights.

It is also to be noted that the compulsory flag salute and pledge requires affirmation of a belief and an attitude of mind. It is not clear whether the regulation contemplates that pupils forego any contrary convictions of their own and become unwilling converts to the prescribed ceremony or whether it will be acceptable if they simulate assent by words without belief and by a gesture barren of meaning. It is now a commonplace that censorship or suppression of expression of opinion is tolerated by our Constitution only when the expression presents a clear and present danger of action of a kind the State is empowered to prevent and punish. It would seem that involuntary affirmation could be commanded only on even more immediate and urgent grounds than silence. But here the power of com⊥**634**pulsion is invoked without any allegation that remaining passive during a flag salute ritual creates a clear and present danger that would justify an effort even to muffle expression. To sustain the compulsory flag salute we are required to say that a Bill of Rights which guards the individual's right to speak his own mind, left it open to public authorities to compel him to utter what is not in his mind.

Whether the First Amendment to the Constitution will permit officials to order observance of ritual of this nature does not depend upon whether as a voluntary exercise we would think it to be good, bad or merely innocuous. Any credo of nationalism is likely to include what some disapprove or to omit what others think essential, and to give off different overtones as it takes on different accents or interpretations. If official power exists to coerce acceptance of any patriotic creed, what it shall contain cannot be decided by courts, but must be largely discretionary with the ordaining authority, whose power to prescribe would no doubt include power to amend. Hence validity of the asserted power to force an American citizen publicly to profess any statement of belief or to engage in any ceremony of assent to one, presents questions of power that must be considered independently of any idea we may have as to the utility of the ceremony in question.

Nor does the issue as we see it turn on one's possession of particular religious views or the sincerity with which they are held. While religion supplies appellees' motive for enduring the discomforts of making the issue in this case, many citizens who do not share these religious views ⊥**635** hold such a compulsory rite to infringe constitutional liberty of the individual. It is not necessary to inquire whether nonconformist beliefs will exempt from the duty to salute unless we first find power to make the salute a legal duty.

The *Gobitis* decision, however, *assumed*, as did the argument in that case and in this, that power exists in the

State to impose the flag salute discipline upon school children in general. The Court only examined and rejected a claim based on religious beliefs of immunity from an unquestioned general rule. The question which underlies the ⊥**636** flag salute controversy is whether such a ceremony so touching matters of opinion and political attitude may be imposed upon the individual by official authority under powers committed to any political organization under our Constitution. We examine rather than assume existence of this power and, against this broader definition of issues in this case, re-examine specific grounds assigned for the *Gobitis* decision.

1. It was said that the flag-salute controversy confronted the Court with "the problem which Lincoln cast in memorable dilemma: 'Must a government of necessity be too *strong* for the liberties of its people, or too *weak* to maintain its own existence?'" and that the answer must be in favor of strength.

We think these issues may be examined free of pressure or restraint growing out of such considerations.

It may be doubted whether Mr. Lincoln would have thought that the strength of government to maintain itself would be impressively vindicated by our confirming power of the state to expel a handful of children from school. Such oversimplification, so handy in political debate, often lacks the precision necessary to postulates of judicial reasoning. If validly applied to this problem, the utterance cited would resolve every issue of power in favor of those in authority and would require us to override every liberty thought to weaken or delay execution of their policies.

Government of limited power need not be anemic government. Assurance that rights are secure tends to diminish fear and jealousy of strong government, and by making us feel safe to live under it makes for its better support. Without promise of a limiting Bill of Rights it is ⊥**637** doubtful if our Constitution could have mustered enough strength to enable its ratification. To enforce those rights today is not to choose weak government over strong government. It is only to adhere as a means of strength to individual freedom of mind in preference to officially disciplined uniformity for which history indicates a disappointing and disastrous end.

The subject now before us exemplifies this principle. Free public education, if faithful to the ideal of secular instruction and political neutrality, will not be partisan or enemy of any class, creed, party, or faction. If it is to impose any ideological discipline, however, each party or denomination must seek to control, or failing that, to weaken the influence of the educational system. Observance of the limitations of the Constitution will not weaken government in the field appropriate for its exercise.

2. It was also considered in the *Gobitis* Case that functions of educational officers in states, counties and school districts were such that to interfere with their authority "would in effect make us the school board for the country."

The Fourteenth Amendment, as now applied to the States, protects the citizen against the State itself and all of its creatures—Boards of Education not excepted. These have, of course, important, delicate, and highly discretionary functions, but none that they may not perform within the limits of the Bill of Rights. That they are educating the young for citizenship is reason for scrupulous protection of Constitutional freedoms of the individual, if we are not to strangle the free mind at its source and teach youth to discount important principles of our government as mere platitudes.

Such Boards are numerous and their territorial jurisdiction often small. But small and local authority may feel less sense of responsibility to the Constitution, and agencies of publicity may be less vigilant in calling it to ac⊥**638**count. The action of Congress in making flag observance voluntary and respecting the conscience of the objector in a matter so vital as raising the Army contrasts sharply with these local regulations in matters relatively trivial to the welfare of the nation. There are village tyrants as well as village Hampdens, but none who acts under color of law is beyond reach of the Constitution.

3. The *Gobitis* opinion reasoned that this is a field "where courts possess no marked and certainly no controlling competence," that it is committed to the legislatures as well as the courts to guard cherished liberties and that it is constitutionally appropriate to "fight out the wise use of legislative authority in the forum of public opinion and before legislative assemblies rather than to transfer such a contest to the judicial arena," since all the "effective means of inducing political changes are left free."

The very purpose of a Bill of Rights was to withdraw certain subjects from the vicissitudes of political controversy, to place them beyond the reach of majorities and officials and to establish them as legal principles to be applied by the courts. One's right to life, liberty, and property, to free speech, a free press, freedom of worship and assembly, and other fundamental rights may not be submitted to vote; they depend on the outcome of no elections. ⊥**639**

In weighing arguments of the parties it is important to distinguish between the due process clause of the Fourteenth Amendment as an instrument for transmitting the principles of the First Amendment and those cases in which it is applied for its own sake. The test of legislation which collides with the Fourteenth Amendment, because it also collides with the principles of the First, is much more definite than the test when only the Fourteenth is involved. Much of the vagueness of the due process clause disappears when the specific prohibitions of the First become its standard. The right of a State to regulate, for example, a public utility may well include, so far as the due process test is concerned, power to impose all of the restrictions which a legislature may have a "rational basis" for adopting. But freedoms of speech and of press, of assembly, and of worship may not be infringed on such slender grounds. They are susceptible of restriction only to prevent grave and immediate danger to interests which the state may lawfully protect. It is important to note that while it is the Fourteenth Amendment which bears directly upon the State it is the more specific limiting principles of the First Amendment that finally govern this case.

Nor does our duty to apply the Bill of Rights to assertions of official authority depend upon our possession of marked competence in the field where the invasion of rights occurs. True, the task of translating the majestic generalities of the Bill of Rights, conceived as part of the pattern of liberal government in the eighteenth century, into concrete restraints on officials dealing with the problems of the twentieth century, is one to disturb self-confidence. These principles grew in soil which also produced a philosophy that the individual was the center of society, that his liberty was attainable through mere absence of governmental restraints, and that government should be entrusted with few controls and only the mildest supervi⊥**640**sion over men's affairs. We must transplant these rights to a soil in which the laissez-faire concept or principle of non-interference has withered at least as to economic affairs, and social advancements are increasingly sought through closer integration of society and through expanded and strengthened governmental controls. These changed conditions often deprive precedents of reliability and cast us more than we would choose upon our own judgment. But we act in these matters not by authority of our competence but by force of our commissions. We cannot, because of modest estimates of our competence in such specialties as public education, withhold the judgment that history authenticates as the function of this Court when liberty is infringed.

4. Lastly, and this is the very heart of the *Gobitis* opinion, it reasons that "national unity is the basis of national security," that the authorities have "the right to select appropriate means for its attainment," and hence reaches the conclusion that such compulsory measures toward "national unity" are constitutional. Upon the verity of this assumption depends our answer in this case.

National unity as an end which officials may foster by persuasion and example is not in question. The problem is whether under our Constitution compulsion as here employed is a permissible means for its achievement.

Struggles to coerce uniformity of sentiment in support of some end thought essential to their time and country have been waged by many good as well as by evil men. Nationalism is a relatively recent phenomenon but at other times and places the ends have been racial or territorial security, support of a dynasty or regime, and particular plans for saving souls. As first and moderate methods to attain unity have failed, those bent on its accomplishment must resort to an ever increasing severity. ⊥**641** As governmental pressure toward unity becomes greater, so strife becomes more bitter as to whose unity it shall be. Probably no deeper division of our people could proceed from any provocation than from finding it necessary to choose what doctrine and whose program public educational officials shall compel youth to unite in embracing. Ultimate futility of such attempts to compel coherence is the lesson of every such effort from the Roman drive to stamp out Christianity as a disturber of its pagan unity, the Inquisition, as a means to religious and dynastic unity, the Siberian exiles as a means to Russian unity, down to the fast failing efforts of our present totalitarian enemies. Those who begin coercive elimination of dissent soon find themselves exterminating dissenters. Compulsory unification of opinion achieves only the unanimity of the graveyard.

It seems trite but necessary to say that the First Amendment to our Constitution was designed to avoid these ends by avoiding these beginnings. There is no mysticism in the American concept of the State or of the nature or origin of its authority. We set up government by consent of the governed, and the Bill of Rights denies those in power any legal opportunity to coerce that consent. Authority here is to be controlled by public opinion, not public opinion by authority.

The case is made difficult not because the principles of its decision are obscure but because the flag involved is our own. Nevertheless, we apply the limitations of the Constitution with no fear that freedom to be intellectually and spiritually diverse or even contrary will disintegrate the social organization. To believe that patriotism will not flourish if patriotic ceremonies are voluntary and spontaneous instead of a compulsory routine is to make an unflattering estimate of the appeal of our institutions to free minds. We can have intellectual individualism ⊥**642** and the rich cultural diversities that we owe to exceptional minds only at the price of occasional eccentricity and abnormal attitudes. When they are so harmless to others or to the State as those we deal with here, the price is not too great. But freedom to differ is not limited to things that do not matter much. That would be a mere shadow of freedom. The test of its substance is the right to differ as to things that touch the heart of the existing order.

If there is any fixed star in our constitutional constellation, it is that no official, high or petty, can prescribe what shall be orthodox in politics, nationalism, religion, or other matters of opinion or force citizens to confess by word or act their faith therein. If there are any circumstances which permit an exception, they do not now occur to us.

We think the action of the local authorities in compelling the flag salute and pledge transcends constitutional limitations on their power and invades the sphere of intellect and spirit which it is the purpose of the First Amendment to our Constitution to reserve from all official control.

The decision of this Court in *Minersville School Dist.* v. *Gobitis* and the holdings of those few *per curiam* decisions which preceded and foreshadowed it are overruled, and the judgment enjoining enforcement of the West Virginia Regulation is *Affirmed*.

Mr. *Justice* ROBERTS and Mr. *Justice* REED adhere to the views expressed by the Court in *Minersville School* ⊥**643** *Dist.* v. *Gobitis* and are of the opinion that the judgment below should be *reversed*.

Mr. *Justice* BLACK and Mr. *Justice* DOUGLAS, concurring:

We are substantially in agreement with the opinion just read, but since we originally joined with the Court in the *Gobitis* Case, it is appropriate that we make a brief statement of reasons for our change of view.

Reluctance to make the Federal Constitution a rigid bar against state regulation of conduct thought inimical to the public welfare was the controlling influence which moved us to consent to the *Gobitis* decision. Long reflection convinced us that although the principle is sound, its application in the particular case was wrong. We believe that the statute before us fails to accord full scope to the freedom of religion secured to the appellees by the First and Fourteenth Amendments.

The statute requires the appellees to participate in a ceremony aimed at inculcating respect for the flag and for this country. The Jehovah's Witnesses, without any desire to show disrespect for either the flag or the country, interpret the Bible as commanding, at the risk of God's displeasure, that they not go through the form of a pledge of allegiance to any flag. The devoutness of their belief is evidenced by their willingness to suffer persecution and punishment, rather than make the pledge.

No well ordered society can leave to the individuals an absolute right to make final decisions, unassailable by the State, as to everything they will or will not do. The First Amendment does not go so far. Religious faiths, honestly held, do not free individuals from responsibility to conduct themselves obediently to laws which are either imperatively necessary to protect society as a whole from grave ⊥**644** and pressingly imminent dangers or which, without any general prohibition, merely regulate time, place or manner of religious activity. Decision as to the constitutionality of particular laws which strike at the substance of religious tenets and practices must be made by this Court. The duty is a solemn one, and in meeting it we cannot say that a failure, because of religious scruples, to assume a particular physical position and to repeat the words of a patriotic formula creates a grave danger to the nation. Such a statutory exaction is a form of test oath, and the test oath has always been abhorrent in the United States.

Words uttered under coercion are proof of loyalty to nothing but self-interest. Love of country must spring from willing hearts and free minds, inspired by a fair administration of wise laws enacted by the people's elected representatives within the bounds of express constitutional prohibitions. These laws must, to be consistent with the First Amendment, permit the widest toleration of conflicting viewpoints consistent with a society of free men.

Neither our domestic tranquillity in peace nor our martial effort in war depend on compelling little children to participate in a ceremony which ends in nothing for them but a fear of spiritual condemnation. If, as we think, their fears are groundless, time and reason are the proper antidotes for their errors. The ceremonial, when enforced against conscientious objectors, more likely to defeat than to serve its high purpose, is a handy implement for disguised religious persecution. As such, it is inconsistent with our Constitution's plan and purpose.

Mr. *Justice* MURPHY, concurring;

I agree with the opinion of the Court and join in it.

The complaint challenges an order of the State Board of Education which requires teachers and pupils to participate in the prescribed salute to the flag. For refusal to conform with the requirement the State law prescribes ex⊥**645**pulsion. The offender is required by law to be treated as unlawfully absent from school and the parent or guardian is made liable to prosecution and punishment for such absence. Thus not only is the privilege of public education conditioned on compliance with the requirement, but noncompliance is virtually made unlawful. In effect compliance is compulsory and not optional. It is the claim of appellees that the regulation is invalid as a restriction on religious freedom and freedom of speech, secured to them against State infringement by the First and Fourteenth Amendments to the Constitution of the United States.

A reluctance to interfere with considered state action, the fact that the end sought is a desirable one, the emotion aroused by the flag as a symbol for which we have fought and are now fighting again,— all of these are understandable. But there is before us the right of freedom to believe, freedom to worship one's Maker according to the dictates of one's conscience, a right which the Constitution specifically shelters. Reflection has convinced me that as a judge I have no loftier duty or responsibility than to uphold that spiritual freedom to its farthest reaches.

The right of freedom of thought and of religion as guaranteed by the Constitution against State action includes both the right to speak freely and the right to refrain from speaking at all, except in so far as essential operations of government may require it for the preservation of an orderly society,—as in the case of compulsion to give evidence in court. Without wishing to disparage the purposes and intentions of those who hope to inculcate sentiments of loyalty and patriotism by requiring a declaration of allegiance as a feature of public education, or unduly belittle the benefits that may accrue therefrom, I am impelled to conclude that such a requirement is not essential to the maintenance of effective government and orderly society. To many it is deeply distasteful to join in a public chorus of affirmation of private belief. By some, in⊥**646**cluding the members of this sect, it is apparently regarded as incompatible with a primary religious obligation and therefore a restriction on religious freedom. Official compulsion to affirm what is contrary to one's religious beliefs is the antithesis of freedom of worship which, it is well to recall, was achieved in this country only after what Jefferson characterized as the "severest contests in which I have ever been engaged."

I am unable to agree that the benefits that may accrue to society from the compulsory flag salute are sufficiently definite and tangible to justify the invasion of freedom and privacy that is entailed or to compensate for a restraint on the freedom of the individual to be vocal or silent according to his conscience or personal inclination. The trenchant words in the preamble to the Virginia Statute for Religious Freedom remain unanswerable: ". . . all attempts to influence [the mind] by temporal punishments, or burdens, or by civil incapacitations, tend only to beget habits of hypocrisy and meanness, . . ." Any spark of love for country which may be generated in a child or his associates by forcing him to make what is to him an empty gesture and recite words wrung from him contrary to his religious beliefs is overshadowed by the desirability of preserving freedom of conscience to the full. It is in that freedom and the example of persuasion, not in force and compulsion, that the real unity of America lies.

Mr. *Justice* FRANKFURTER, dissenting:

One who belongs to the most vilified and persecuted minority in history is not likely to be insensible to the freedoms guaranteed by our Constitution. Were my purely personal attitude relevant I should wholeheartedly associate myself with the general libertarian views in the Court's opinion, representing as they do the thought and ⊥**647** action of a lifetime. But as judges we are neither Jew nor Gentile, neither Catholic nor agnostic. We owe equal attachment to the Constitution and are equally bound by our judicial obligations whether we derive our citizenship from the earliest or the latest immigrants to these shores. As a member of this Court I am not justified in writing my private notions of policy into the Constitution, no matter how deeply I may cherish them or how mischievous I may deem their disregard. The duty of a judge who must decide which of two claims before the Court shall prevail, that of a State to enact and enforce laws within its general competence or that of an individual to refuse obedience because of the demands of his conscience, is not that of the ordinary person. It can never be emphasized too much that one's own opinion about the wisdom or evil of a law should be excluded altogether when one is doing one's duty on the bench. The only opinion of our own even looking in that direction that is material is our opinion whether legislators could in reason have enacted such a law. In the light of all the circumstances, including the history of this question in this Court, it would require more daring than I possess to deny that reasonable legislators could have taken the action which is before us for review. Most unwillingly, therefore, I must differ from my brethren with regard to legislation like this. I cannot bring my mind to believe that the "liberty" secured by the Due Process Clause gives this Court authority to deny to the State of West Virginia the attainment of that which we all recognize as a legitimate legislative end, namely, the promotion of good citizenship, by employment of the means here chosen.

Not so long ago we were admonished that "the only check upon our own exercise of power is our own sense of self-restraint. For the removal of unwise laws from the statute books appeal lies not to the court but to the ballot and to the processes of democratic government." ⊥**648** *United States* v. *Butler* (dissent). We have been told that generalities do not decide concrete cases. But the intensity with which a general principle is held may determine a particular issue, and whether we put first things first may decide a specific controversy.

The admonition that judicial self-restraint alone limits arbitrary exercise of our authority is relevant every time we are asked to nullify legislation. The Constitution does not give us greater veto power when dealing with one phase of "liberty" than with another, or when dealing with grade school regulations than with college regulations that offend conscience, as was the case in *Hamilton* v. *University of California*. In neither situation is our function comparable to that of a legislature or are we free to act as though we were a super-legislature. Judicial self-restraint is equally necessary whenever an exercise of political or legislative power is challenged. There is no warrant in the constitutional basis of this Court's authority for attributing different roles to it depending upon the nature of the challenge to the legislation. Our power does not vary according to the particular provision of the Bill of Rights which is invoked. The right not to have property taken without just compensation has, so far as the scope of judicial power is concerned, the same constitutional dignity as the right to be protected against unreasonable searches and seizures, and the latter has no less claim than freedom of the press or freedom of speech or religious freedom. In no instance is this Court the primary protector of the particular liberty that is invoked. This Court has recognized, what hardly could be denied, that all the provisions of the first ten Amendments are "specific" prohibitions, *United States* v. *Carolene Products Co.* But each specific Amendment, in so far as embraced within the Fourteenth Amendment, must be equally respected, and the function of this ⊥**649** Court does not differ in passing on the constitutionality of legislation challenged under different Amendments. . . .

The framers of the federal Constitution might have chosen to assign an active share in the process of legislation to this Court. They had before them the well-known example of New York's Council of Revision, which had been functioning since 1777. After stating that "laws inconsistent with the spirit of this constitution, or with the public good, may be hastily and unadvisedly passed," the state constitution made the judges of New York part of the legislative process by providing that "all bills which have passed the senate and assembly shall, before they become laws," be presented to a Council of which the judges constituted a majority, "for their revisal and consideration." Art. 3, New York Constitution of 1777. Judges exercised this legislative function in New York⊥**650** for nearly fifty years. . . . But the framers of the Constitution denied such legislative powers to the federal judiciary. They chose instead to insulate the judiciary from the legislative function. They did not grant to this Court supervision over legislation.

The reason why from the beginning even the narrow judicial authority to nullify legislation has been viewed with a jealous eye is that it serves to prevent the full play of the democratic process. The fact that it may be an undemocratic aspect of our scheme of government does not call for its rejection or its disuse.

The precise scope of the question before us defines the limits of the constitutional power that is in issue. The State of West Virginia requires all pupils to share in the salute to the flag as part of school training in citizenship. The present action is one to enjoin the enforcement of this requirement by those in school attendance. We have not before us any attempt by the State to punish disobedient children or visit penal consequences on their parents. All that is in question is the right of the State to compel participation in this exercise by those who choose to attend the public schools.

We are not reviewing merely the action of a local school board. The flag salute requirement in this case comes before us with the full authority of the State of West Virginia. We are in fact passing judgment on "the power of the State as a whole." *Rippey* v. *Texas*. Practically we are passing upon the political power of each of the forty-eight states. Moreover, since the First Amendment has been read into the Fourteenth, our problem is precisely the same as it would be if we had before us an Act of Congress for the District of Columbia. To suggest that we are here con⊥**651**cerned with the heedless action of some village tyrants is to distort the augustness of the constitutional issue and the reach of the consequences of our decision.

Under our constitutional system the legislature is charged solely with civil concerns of society. If the avowed or intrinsic legislative purpose is either to promote or to discourage some religious community or creed, it is clearly within the constitutional restrictions imposed on legislatures and cannot stand. But it by no means follows that legislative power is wanting whenever a general non-discriminatory civil regulation in fact touches conscientious scruples or religious beliefs of an individual or a group. Regard for such scruples or beliefs undoubtedly presents one of the most reasonable claims for the exertion of legislative accommodation. It is, of course, beyond our power to rewrite the State's requirement, by providing exemptions for those who do not wish to participate in the flag salute or by making some other accommodations to meet their scruples. That wisdom might suggest the making of such accommodations and that school administration would not find it too difficult to make them and yet maintain the ceremony for those not refusing to conform, is outside our province to suggest. Tact, respect, and generosity toward variant views will always commend themselves to those charged with the duties of legislation so as to achieve a maximum of good will and to require a minimum of unwilling submission to a general law. But the real question is, who is to make such accommodations, the courts or the legislature?

This is no dry, technical matter. It cuts deep into one's conception of the democratic process—it concerns no less the practical differences between the means for making these accommodations that are open to courts and to legislatures. A court can only strike down. It can only say "This or that law is void." It cannot modify or qualify, it cannot make exceptions to a general require⊥**652**ment. And it strikes down not merely for a day. At least the finding of unconstitutionality ought not to have ephemeral significance unless the Constitution is to be reduced to the fugitive importance of mere legislation. When we are dealing with the Constitution of the United States, and more particularly with the great safeguards of the Bill of Rights, we are dealing with principles of liberty and justice "so rooted in the traditions and conscience of our people as to be ranked as fundamental"—something without which "a fair and enlightened system of justice would be impossible." *Palko* v. *Connecticut*. If the function of this Court is to be essentially no different from that of a legislature, if the considerations governing constitutional construction are to be substantially those that underlie legislation, then indeed judges should not have life tenure and they should be made directly responsible to the electorate. There have been many but unsuccessful proposals in the last sixty years to amend the Constitution to that end.

Conscientious scruples, all would admit, cannot stand against every legislative compulsion to do positive acts in conflict with such scruples. We have been told that such compulsions override religious scruples only as to major concerns of the state. But the determination of what is major and what is minor itself raises questions of policy. For the way in which men equally guided by reason appraise importance goes to the very heart of policy. Judges should be very diffident in setting their judgment against that of a state in determining what is and what is not a major concern, what means are appropriate to proper ends, and what is the total social cost in striking the balance of imponderables.

What one can say with assurance is that the history out of which grew constitutional provisions for religious equal⊥**653**ity and the writings of the great exponents of religious freedom—Jefferson, Madison, John Adams, Benjamin Franklin—are totally wanting in justification for a claim by dissidents of exceptional immunity from civic measures of general applicability, measures not in fact disguised assaults upon such dissident views. The great leaders of the American Revolution were determined to remove political support from every religious establishment. They put on an equality the different religious sects—Episcopalians, Presbyterians, Catholics, Baptists, Methodists, Quakers, Hugenots— which, as dissenters, had been under the heel of the various orthodoxies that prevailed in different colonies. So far as the state was concerned, there was to be neither orthodoxy nor heterodoxy. And so Jefferson and those who followed him wrote guaranties of religious freedom into our constitutions. Religious minorities as well as religious majorities were to be equal in the eyes of the political state. But Jefferson and the others also knew that minorities may disrupt society. It never would have occurred to them to write into the Constitution the subordination of the general civil authority of the state to sectarian scruples.

The constitutional protection of religious freedom terminated disabilities, it did not create new privileges. It gave religious equality, not civil immunity. Its essence is freedom from conformity to religious dogma, not freedom from conformity to law because of religious dogma. Religious loyalties may be exercised without hindrance from the state, not the state may not exercise that which except by leave of religious loyalties is within the domain of temporal power. Otherwise each individual could set up his own censor against obedience to laws conscientiously deemed for the public good by those whose business it is to make laws.

The prohibition against any religion establishment by the government placed denominations on an equal foot⊥**654**ing—it assured freedom from support by the government to any mode of worship and the freedom of individuals to support any mode of worship. Any person may therefore believe or disbelieve what he pleases. He may practice what he will in his own house of worship or publicly within the limits of public order. But the lawmaking authority is not circumscribed by the variety of religious beliefs, otherwise the constitutional guaranty would be not a protection of the free exercise of religion but a denial of the exercise of legislation.

The essence of the religious freedom guaranteed by our Constitution is therefore this: no religion shall either receive the state's support or incur its hostility. Religion is outside the sphere of political government. This does not mean that all matters on which religious organizations or beliefs may pronounce are outside the sphere of government. Were this so, instead of the separation of church and state, there would be the subordination of the state on any matter deemed within the sovereignty of the religious conscience. Much that is the concern of temporal authority affects the spiritual interests of men. But it is not enough to strike down a nondiscriminatory law that it may hurt or offend some dissident view. It would be too easy to cite numerous prohibitions and injunctions to which laws run counter if the variant interpretations of the Bible were made the tests of obedience to law. The validity of secular laws cannot be measured by their conformity to religious doctrines. It is only in a theocratic state that ecclesiastical doctrines measure legal right or wrong.

An act compelling profession of allegiance to a religion, no matter how subtly or tenuously promoted, is bad. But an act promoting good citizenship and national allegiance is within the domain of governmental authority and is therefore to be judged by the same considerations of power and of constitutionality as those involved in the many ⊥**655** claims of immunity from civil obedience because of religious scruples.

That claims are pressed on behalf of sincere religious convictions does not of itself establish their constitutional validity. Nor does waving the banner of religious freedom relieve us from examining into the power we are asked to deny the states. Otherwise the doctrine of separation of church and state, so cardinal in the history of this nation and for the liberty of our people, would mean not the disestablishment of a state church but the establishment of all churches and of all religious groups. . . .

Law is concerned with external behavior and not with the inner life of man. It rests in large measure upon compulsion. Socrates lives in history partly because he gave his life for the conviction that duty of obedience to secular law does not presuppose consent to its enactment or belief in its virtue. The consent upon which free government rests is the consent that comes from sharing in the process of making and unmaking laws. The state is not shut out from a domain because the individual conscience may deny the state's claim. The individual con⊥**656**science may profess what faith it chooses. It may affirm and promote that faith—in the language of the Constitution, it may "exercise" it freely—but it cannot thereby restrict community action through political organs in matters of community concern, so long as the action is not asserted in a discriminatory way either openly or by stealth. One may have the right to practice one's religion and at the same time owe the duty of formal obedience to laws that run counter to one's beliefs. Compelling belief implies denial of opportunity to combat it and to assert dissident views. Quite another matter is submission to conformity of action while denying its wisdom or virtue and with ample opportunity for seeking its change or abrogation. . . . ⊥**657**

Parents have the privilege of choosing which schools they wish their children to attend. And the question here is whether the state may make certain requirements that seem to it desirable or important for the proper education of those future citizens who go to schools maintained by the states, or whether the pupils in those schools may be relieved from those requirements if they run counter to the consciences of their parents. Not only have parents the right to send children to schools of their own choosing but the state has no right to bring such schools "under a strict governmental control" or give affirmative direction ⊥**658** concerning the intimate and essential details of such schools, intrust their control to public officers, and deny both owners and patrons reasonable choice and discretion in respect of teachers, curriculum, and textbooks." *Farrington* v. *Tokushige*. Why should not the state likewise have constitutional power to make reasonable provisions for the proper instruction of children in schools maintained by it?

When dealing with religious scruples we are dealing with an almost numberless variety of doctrines and beliefs entertained with equal sincerity by the particular groups for which they satisfy man's needs in his relation to the mysteries of the universe. There are in the United States more than 250 distinctive established religious denominations. In the state of Pennsylvania there are 120 of these, and in West Virginia as many as 65. But if religious scruples afford immunity from civic obedience to laws, they may be invoked by the religious beliefs of any individual even though he holds no membership in any sect or organized denomination. Certainly this Court cannot be called upon to determine what claims of conscience should be recognized and what should be rejected as satisfying the "religion" which the Constitution protects. That would indeed resurrect the very discriminatory treatment of religion which the Constitution sought forever to forbid. . . .

⊥661 We are told that a flag salute is a doubtful substitute for adequate understanding of our institutions. The states that require such a school exercise do not have to justify it as the only means for promoting good citizenship in children, but merely as one of diverse means for accomplishing a worthy end. We may deem it a foolish measure, but the point is that this Court is not the organ of government to resolve doubts as to whether it will fulfill its purpose. Only if there be no doubt that any rea**⊥662**sonable mind could entertain can we deny to the states the right to resolve doubts their way and not ours.

That which to the majority may seem essential for the welfare of the state may offend the consciences of a minority. But, so long as no inroads are made upon the actual exercise of religion by the minority, to deny the political power of the majority to enact laws concerned with civil matters, simply because they may offend the consciences of a minority, really means that the consciences of a minority are more sacred and more enshrined in the Constitution than the consciences of a majority.

We are told that symbolism is a dramatic but primitive way of communicating ideas. Symbolism is inescapable. Even the most sophisticated live by symbols. But it is not for this Court to make psychological judgments as to the effectiveness of a particular symbol in inculcating concededly indispensable feelings, particularly if the state happens to see fit to utilize the symbol that represents our heritage and our hopes. And surely only flippancy could be responsible for the suggestion that constitutional validity of a requirement to salute our flag implies equal validity of a requirement to salute a dictator. The significance of a symbol lies in what it represents. To reject the swastika does not imply rejection of the Cross. And so it bears repetition to say that it mocks reason and denies our whole history to find in the allowance of a requirement to salute our flag on fitting occasions the seeds of sanction for obeisance to a leader. To deny the power to employ educational symbols is to say that the state's educational system may not stimulate the imagination because this may lead to unwise stimulation.

The right of West Virginia to utilize the flag salute as part of its educational process is denied because, so it is argued, it cannot be justified as a means of meeting a "clear and present danger" to national unity. In passing it deserves to be noted that the four cases which unani**⊥663**mously sustained the power of states to utilize such an educational measure arose and were all decided before the present World War. But to measure the state's power to make such regulations as are here resisted by the imminence of national danger is wholly to misconceive the origin and purpose of the concept of "clear and present danger." To apply such a test is for the Court to assume, however unwittingly, a legislative responsibility that does not belong to it. To talk about "clear and present danger" as the touchstone of allowable educational policy by the states whenever school curricula may impinge upon the boundaries of individual conscience, is to take a felicitous phrase out of the context of the particular situation where it arose and for which it was adapted. Mr. *Justice HOLMES* used the phrase "clear and present danger" in a case involving mere speech as a means by which alone to accomplish sedition in time of war. By that phrase he meant merely to indicate that, in view of the protection given to utterance by the First Amendment, in order that mere utterance may not be proscribed, "the words used are used in such circumstances and are of such a nature as to create a clear and present danger that will bring about the substantive evils that Congress has a right to prevent." *Schenck* v. *United States*. The "substantive evils" about which he was speaking were inducement of insubordination in the military and naval forces of the United States and obstruction of enlistment while the country was at war. He was not enunciating a formal rule that there can be no restriction upon speech and, still less, no compulsion where conscience balks, unless imminent danger would thereby be wrought "to our institutions or our government."

The flag salute exercise has no kinship whatever to the oath tests so odious in history. For the oath test was one of the instruments for suppressing heretical beliefs. **⊥664** Saluting the flag suppresses no belief nor curbs it. Children and their parents may believe what they please, avow their belief and practice it. It is not even remotely suggested that the requirement for saluting the flag involves the slightest restriction against the fullest opportunity on the part both of the children and of their parents to disavow as publicly as they choose to do so the meaning that others attach to the gesture of salute. All channels of affirmative free expression are open to both children and parents. Had we before us any act of the state putting the slightest curbs upon such free expression, I should not lag behind any member of this Court in striking down such an invasion of the right to freedom of thought and freedom of speech protected by the Constitution. . . .

⊥670 Of course patriotism cannot be enforced by the flag salute. But neither can the liberal spirit be enforced by judicial invalidation of illiberal legislation. Our constant preoccupation with the constitutionality of legislation rather than with its wisdom tends to preoccupation of the American mind with a false value. The tendency of focusing attention on constitutionality is to make constitutionality synonymous with wisdom, to regard a law as all right if it is constitutional. Such an attitude is a great enemy of liberalism. Particularly in legislation affecting freedom of thought and freedom of speech much which should offend a free-spirited society is constitutional. Reliance for the most precious interests of civilization, therefore, must be found outside of their vindication in courts of law. Only a persistent positive translation of the faith of a free society into the convictions and habits and actions of a community is the ultimate reliance against unabated temptations to fetter the human spirit.

COX v. NEW HAMPSHIRE

312 U.S. 569
ON APPEAL FROM THE SUPREME COURT OF THE STATE OF NEW HAMPSHIRE
Argued March 7, 1941 — Decided March 31, 1941

⊥570 Mr. *Chief Justice* HUGHES delivered the opinion of the Court:

Appellants are five "Jehovah's Witnesses" who, with sixty-three others of the same persuasion, were convicted in the municipal court of Manchester, New Hampshire, for violation of a state statute prohibiting a "parade or ⊥571 procession" upon a public street without a special license.

Upon appeal, there was a trial *de novo* of these appellants before a jury in the Superior Court, the other defendants having agreed to abide by the final decision in that proceeding. Appellants were found guilty and the judgment of conviction was affirmed by the Supreme Court of the State.

By motions and exceptions, appellants raised the questions that the statute was invalid under the Fourteenth Amendment of the Constitution of the United States in that it deprived appellants of their rights of freedom of worship, freedom of speech and press, and freedom of assembly, vested unreasonable and unlimited arbitrary and discriminatory powers in the licensing authority, and was vague and indefinite. These contentions were overruled and the case comes here on appeal.

The statutory prohibition is as follows:

"No theatrical or dramatic representation shall be performed or exhibited, and no parade or procession upon any public street or way, and no open-air public meeting upon any ground abutting thereon, shall be permitted, unless a special license therefor shall first be obtained from the selectmen of the town, or from a licensing committee for cities hereinafter provided for."

⊥572 The facts, which are conceded by the appellants to be established by the evidence, are these: The sixty-eight defendants and twenty other persons met at a hall in the City of Manchester on the evening of Saturday, July 8, 1939, "for the purpose of engaging in an information march." The company was divided into four or five groups, each with about fifteen to twenty persons. Each group then proceeded to a different part of the business district of the city and there "would line up in single-file formation and then proceed to march along the sidewalk, 'single-file,' that is, following one another." Each of the defendants carried a small staff with a sign reading "Religion is a Snare and a Racket" and on the reverse "Serve God and Christ the King." Some of the marchers carried placards bearing the statement "Fascism or Freedom. Hear Judge Rutherford and Face the Facts." The marchers also handed out printed leaflets announcing a meeting to be held at a later time in the hall from which they had started, where a talk on government would be given to the public free of charge. Defendants did not apply for a permit and none was issued.

There was a dispute in the evidence as to the distance ⊥573 between the marchers. Defendants said that they were from fifteen to twenty feet apart. The State insists that the evidence clearly showed that the "marchers were as close together as it was possible for them to walk." Appellants concede that this dispute is not material to the questions presented. The recital of facts which prefaced the opinion of the state court thus summarizes the effect of the march: "Manchester had a population of over 75,000 in 1930, and there was testimony that on Saturday nights in an hour's time 26,000 persons passed one of the intersections where the defendants marched. The marchers interfered with the normal sidewalk travel, but no technical breach of the peace occurred. The march was a prearranged affair, and no permit for it was sought, although the defendants understood that under the statute one was required."

Appellants urge that each of the defendants was a minister ordained to preach the gospel in accordance with his belief and that the participation of these ministers in the march was for the purpose of disseminating information in the public interest and was one of their ways of worship.

The sole charge against appellants was that they were "taking part in a parade or procession" on public streets without a permit as the statute required. They were not prosecuted for distributing leaflets, or for conveying information by placards or otherwise, or for issuing invitations to a public meeting, or for holding a public meeting, or for maintaining or expressing religious beliefs. Their right to do any one of these things apart from engaging in a "parade or procession" upon a public street is not here involved and the question of the validity of a statute addressed to any other sort of conduct than that complained of is not before us.

There appears to be no ground for challenging the ruling of the state court that appellants were in fact ⊥574 engaged in a parade or procession upon the public streets. As the state court observed: "It was a march in formation, and its advertising and informatory purpose did not make it otherwise. . . . It is immaterial that its tactics were few and simple. It is enough that it proceeded in an ordered and close file as a collective body of persons on the city streets."

Civil liberties, as guaranteed by the Constitution, imply the existence of an organized society maintaining public order without which liberty itself would be lost in the excesses of unrestrained abuses. The authority of a municipality to impose regulations in order to assure the safety and convenience of the people in the use of public highways has never been regarded as inconsistent with civil liberties but rather as one of the means of safeguarding the good order upon which they ultimately depend. The control of travel on the streets of cities is the most familiar illustration of this recognition of social need. Where a restriction of the use of highways in that relation is designed to promote the public convenience in the interest of all, it cannot be disregarded by the attempted exercise of some civil right which in other circumstances would be entitled to protection. One would not be justified in ignoring the familiar red traffic light because he thought it his religious duty to disobey the municipal command or sought by that means to direct public attention to an announcement of his opinions. As regulation of the use of the streets for parades and processions is a traditional exercise of control by local government, the question in a particular case is whether that control is exerted so as not to deny or unwarrantedly abridge the right of assembly and the opportunities for the communication of thought and the discussion of public questions immemorially associated with resort to public places.

⊥575 In the instant case, we are aided by the opinion of the Supreme Court of the State which construed the statute and defined the limitations of the authority conferred for the granting of licenses for parades and processions. The court observed that if the clause of the Act requiring a license "for all open-air public meetings upon land contiguous to a highway" was invalid, that invalidity did not nullify the Act in its application to the other situations described. Recognizing the importance of the civil liberties invoked by appellants, the court thought it significant that the statute prescribed "no measures for controlling or suppressing the publication on the highways of facts and opinions, either by speech or by writing"; that communication "by the distribution of literature or by the display of placards and signs" was in no respect regulated by the statute; that the regulation with respect to parades and processions was applicable only "to organized formations of persons using the highways"; and that "the defendants, separately, or collectively in groups not constituting a parade or procession," were "under no contemplation of the Act." In this light, the court thought that interference with liberty of speech and writing seemed slight; that the distribution of pamphlets and folders by the groups "traveling in unorganized fashion" would have had as large a circulation, and that "signs carried by members of the groups not in marching formation would have been as conspicuous, as published by them while in parade or procession."

It was with this view of the limited objective of the statute that the state court considered and defined the duty of the licensing authority and the rights of the appellants to a license for their parade, with regard only to considerations of time, place and manner so as to **⊥576** conserve the public convenience. The obvious advantage of requiring application for a permit was noted as giving the public authorities notice in advance so as to afford opportunity for proper policing. And the court further observed that, in fixing time and place, the license served "to prevent confusion by overlapping parades or processions, to secure convenient use of the streets by other travelers, and to minimize the risk of disorder." But the court held that the licensing board was not vested with arbitrary power or an unfettered discretion; that its discretion must be exercised with "uniformity of method of treatment upon the facts of each application, free from improper or inappropriate considerations and from unfair discrimination"; that a "systematic, consistent and just order of treatment, with reference to the convenience of public use of the highways, is the statutory mandate." The defendants, said the court, "had a right, under the Act, to a license to march when, where and as they did, if after a required investigation it was found that the convenience of the public in the use of the streets would not thereby be unduly disturbed, upon such conditions or changes in time, place and manner as would avoid disturbance."

If a municipality has authority to control the use of its public streets for parades or processions, as it undoubtedly has, it cannot be denied authority to give consideration, without unfair discrimination, to time, place and manner in relation to the other proper uses of the streets. We find it impossible to say that the limited authority conferred by the licensing provisions of the statute in question as thus construed by the state court contravened any constitutional right.

There remains the question of license fees which, as the court said, had a permissible range from $300 to a nominal amount. The court construed the Act as requiring "a reasonable fixing of the amount of the fee." "The **⊥577** charge," said the court, "for a circus parade or a celebration procession of length, each drawing crowds of observers, would take into account the greater public expense of policing the spectacle, compared with the slight expense of a less expansive and attractive parade or procession, to which the charge would be adjusted." The fee was held to be not a revenue tax, but one to meet the expense incident to the administration of the Act and to the maintenance of public order in the matter licensed." There is nothing contrary to the Constitution in the charge of a fee limited to the purpose stated. The suggestion that a flat fee should have been charged fails to take account of the difficulty of framing a fair schedule to meet all circumstances, and we perceive no constitutional ground for denying to local governments that flexibility of adjustment of fees which in the light of varying conditions would tend to conserve rather than impair the liberty sought.

There is no evidence that the statute has been administered otherwise than in the fair and nondiscriminatory manner which the state court has construed it to require.

The decisions upon which appellants rely are not applicable. In *Lovell* v. *Griffin* the ordinance prohibited the distribution of literature of any kind at any time, at any place, and in any manner without a permit from the city manager, thus striking at the very foundation of the freedom of the press by subjecting it to license and censorship. In *Hague* v. *Committee for Industrial Organization*, the ordinance dealt with the exercise of the right of assembly for the purpose of communicating views; it did not make comfort or convenience in the use of streets the standard of official action but enabled the local official absolutely to refuse a permit on his mere opinion that such refusal would prevent "riots, disturbances or disorderly assemblage." The ordi⊥**578**nance thus created as the record disclosed, an instrument of arbitrary suppression of opinions on public questions. The court said that "uncontrolled official suppression of the privilege cannot be made a substitute for the duty to maintain order in connection with the exercise of the right." In *Schneider* v. *Irvington* the ordinance was directed at canvassing and banned unlicensed communication of any views, or the advocacy of any cause, from door to door, subject only to the power of a police officer to determine as a censor what literature might be distributed and who might distribute it. In *Cantwell* v. *Connecticut* the statute dealt with the solicitation of funds for religious causes and authorized an official to determine whether the cause was a religious one and to refuse a permit if he determined it was not, thus establishing a censorship of religion.

Nor is any question of peaceful picketing here involved, as in *Thornhill* v. *Alabama* and *Carlson* v. *California*. The statute, as the state court said, is not aimed at any restraint of freedom of speech, and there is no basis for an assumption that it would be applied so as to prevent peaceful picketing as described in the cases cited.

The argument as to freedom of worship is also beside the point. No interference with religious worship or the practice of religion in any proper sense is shown, but only the exercise of local control over the use of streets for parades and processions.

The judgment of the Supreme Court of New Hampshire is *affirmed*.

PRINCE v. MASSACHUSETTS

321 U.S. 158

APPEAL FROM THE SUPERIOR COURT OF MASSACHUSETTS, PLYMOUTH COUNTY

Argued December 14, 1943 — Decided January 31, 1944

⊥**159** Mr. *Justice RUTLEDGE* delivered the opinion of the Court.

The case brings for review another episode in the conflict between Jehovah's Witnesses and state authority. This time Sarah Prince appeals from convictions for violating Massachusetts' child labor laws, by acts said to be a rightful exercise of her religious convictions.

When the offenses were committed she was the aunt and custodian of Betty M. Simmons, a girl nine years of age. Originally there were three separate complaints. They ⊥**160** were, shortly, for (1) refusal to disclose Betty's identity and age to a public officer whose duty was to enforce the statutes; (2) furnishing her with magazines, knowing she was to sell them unlawfully, that is, on the street; and (3) as Betty's custodian, permitting her to work contrary to law. The complaints were made, respectively, pursuant to §§ 79, 80 and 81 of Chapter 149, Gen. Laws of Mass. The Supreme Judicial Court reversed the conviction under the first complaint on state grounds, but sustained the judgments founded in the other two. They present the only questions for our decision. These are whether §§ 80 and 81, as applied, contravene the Fourteenth Amendment by denying or abridging appellant's freedom of religion and by denying to her the equal protection of the laws.

Sections 80 and 81 form parts of Massachusetts' comprehensive child labor law. They provide methods for enforcing the prohibitions of § 69, which is as follows:

"No boy under twelve and no girl under eighteen shall sell, expose or offer for sale any newspapers, magazines, periodicals or any other articles of merchandise of any ⊥**161** description, or exercise the trade of bootblack or scavenger, or any other trade, in any street or public place."

Sections 80 and 81, so far as pertinent, read:

"Whoever furnishes or sells to any minor any article of any description with the knowledge that the minor intends to sell such article in violation of any provision of sections sixty-nine to seventy-three, inclusive, or after having received written notice to this effect from any officer charged with the enforcement thereof, or knowingly procures or encourages any minor to violate any provisions of said sections, shall be punished by a fine of not less than ten nor more than two hundred dollars or by imprisonment for not more than two months, or both." § 80.

"Any parent, guardian or custodian having a minor under his control who compels or permits such minor to work in violation of any provision of sections sixty to seventy-four, inclusive, . . . shall for the first offense be punished by a fine of not less than two nor more than ten dollars or by imprisonment for not more than five days, or both; . . ." § 81.

The story told by the evidence has become familiar. It hardly needs repeating, except to give setting to the variations introduced through the part played by a child of tender years. Mrs. Prince, living in Brockton, is the mother of two young sons. She also has legal custody of Betty Simmons, who lives with them. The children too are Jehovah's Witnesses and both Mrs. Prince and Betty testified they were ordained ministers. The former was accustomed to go each week on the streets of Brockton to distribute "Watchtower" and "Consolation," according to the usual plan. She had permitted the children to ⊥162 engage in this activity previously, and had been warned against doing so by the school attendance officer, Mr. Perkins. But, until December 18, 1941, she generally did not take them with her at night.

That evening, as Mrs. Prince was preparing to leave her home, the children asked to go. She at first refused. Childlike, they resorted to tears; and, motherlike, she yielded. Arriving downtown, Mrs. Prince permitted the children "to engage in the preaching work with her upon the sidewalks." That is, with specific reference to Betty, she and Mrs. Prince took positions about twenty feet apart near a street intersection. Betty held up in her hand, for passers-by to see, copies of "Watchtower" and "Consolation." From her shoulder hung the usual canvas magazine bag, on which was printed "Watchtower and Consolation 5 cents per copy." No one accepted a copy from Betty that evening and she received no money. Nor did her aunt. But on other occasions, Betty had received funds and given out copies.

Mrs. Prince and Betty remained until 8:45 p.m. A few minutes before this, Mr. Perkins approached Mrs. Prince. A discussion ensued. He inquired and she refused to give Betty's name. However, she stated the child attended the Shaw School. Mr. Perkins referred to his previous warnings and said he would allow five minutes for them to get off the street. Mrs. Prince admitted she supplied Betty with the magazines and said, "[N]either you nor anybody else can stop me . . . This child is exercising her God-given right and her constitutional right to preach the gospel, and no creature has a right to interfere with God's commands." However, Mrs. Prince and Betty departed. She remarked as she went, "I'm not going through this any more. We've been through it time and time again. I'm going home and put the little girl to bed." It may be added that testimony, by Betty, her aunt and others, was offered at the trials, and was ex⊥163cluded, to show that Betty believed it was her religious duty to perform this work and failure would bring condemnation "to everlasting destruction at Armageddon."

As the case reaches us, the questions are no longer open whether what the child did was a "sale" or an "offer to sell" within § 69 or was "work" within § 81. The state court's decision has foreclosed them adversely to appellant as a matter of state law. The only question remaining therefore is whether, as construed and applied, the statute is valid. Upon this the court said: "We think that freedom of the press and of religion is subject to incidental regulation to the slight degree involved in the prohibition of the selling of religious literature in streets and public places by boys under twelve and girls under eighteen, and in the further statutory provisions herein considered, which have been adopted as means of enforcing ⊥164 that prohibition."

Appellant does not stand on freedom of the press. Regarding it as secular, she concedes it may be restricted as Massachusetts has done. Hence, she rests squarely on freedom of religion under the First Amendment, applied by the Fourteenth to the states. She buttresses this foundation, however, with a claim of parental right as secured by the due process clause of the latter Amendment. These guaranties, she thinks, guard alike herself and the child in what they have done. Thus, two claimed liberties are at stake. One is the parent's, to bring up the child in the way he should go, which for appellant means to teach him the tenets and the practices of their faith. The other freedom is the child's, to observe these; and among them is "to preach the gospel . . . by public distribution" of "Watchtower" and "Consolation," in conformity with the scripture: "A little child shall lead them."

If by this position appellant seeks for freedom of conscience a broader protection than for freedom of the mind, it may be doubted that any of the great liberties insured by the First Article can be given higher place than the others. All have preferred position in our basic scheme. All are interwoven there together. Differences there are, in them and in the modes appropriate for their exercise. But they have unity in the charter's prime place because they have unity in their human sources and ⊥165 functionings. Heart and mind are not identical. Intuitive faith and reasoned judgment are not the same. Spirit is not always thought. But in the everyday business of living, secular or otherwise, these variant aspects of personality find inseparable expression in a thousand ways. They cannot be altogether parted in law more than in life.

To make accommodation between these freedoms and an exercise of state authority always is delicate. It hardly could be more so than in such a clash as this case presents. On one side is the obviously earnest claim for freedom of conscience and religious practice. With it is allied the parent's claim to authority in her own household and in the rearing of her children. The parent's conflict with the state over control of the child and his training is serious enough when only secular matters are concerned. It becomes the more so when an element of religious conviction enters. Against these sacred private interests, basic in a democracy, stand the interests of society to protect the welfare of children, and the state's assertion of authority to that end, made here in a manner conceded valid if only secular things were involved. The last is no mere corporate concern of official authority. It is the interest of youth itself, and of the whole community, that children be both safeguarded from abuses and given opportunities for growth into free and independent well-developed men and citizens. Between contrary pulls of such weight, the safest and most objective recourse is to the lines already marked out, not precisely but for guides, in narrowing the no man's land where this battle has gone on.

The rights of children to exercise their religion, and of parents to give them religious training and to encourage them in the practice of religious belief, as against preponderant sentiment and assertion of state power voicing it, have had recognition here, most recently in *West Virginia State Board of Education* v. *Barnette*. ⊥**166** Previously in *Pierce* v. *Society of Sisters*, this Court had sustained the parent's authority to provide religious with secular schooling, and the child's right to receive it, as against the state's requirement of attendance at public schools. And in *Meyer* v. *Nebraska*, children's rights to receive teaching in languages other than the nation's common tongue were guarded against the state's encroachment. It is cardinal with us that the custody, care and nurture of the child reside first in the parents, whose primary function and freedom include preparation for obligations the state can neither supply nor hinder. And it is in recognition of this that these decisions have respected the private realm of family life which the state cannot enter.

But the family itself is not beyond regulation in the public interest, as against a claim of religious liberty. And neither rights of religion nor rights of parenthood are beyond limitation. Acting to guard the general interest in youth's well being, the state as *parens patriae* may restrict the parent's control by requiring school attendance, regulating or prohibiting the child's labor and in many other ways. Its authority is not nullified merely because the parent grounds his claim to control the child's course of conduct on religion or conscience. Thus, he cannot claim freedom from compulsory vaccination for the child more than for himself on religious grounds. The right to practice religion freely does not include liberty to expose the community or the child ⊥**167** to communicable disease or the latter to ill health or death. The catalogue need not be lengthened. It is sufficient to show what indeed appellant hardly disputes, that the state has a wide range of power for limiting parental freedom and authority in things affecting the child's welfare; and that this includes, to some extent, matters of conscience and religious conviction.

But it is said the state cannot do so here. This, first, because when state action impinges upon a claimed religious freedom, it must fall unless shown to be necessary for or conducive to the child's protection against some clear and present danger and, it is added, there was no such showing here. The child's presence on the street, with her guardian, distributing or offering to distribute the magazine, it is urged, was in no way harmful to her, nor in any event more so than the presence of many other children at the same time and place, engaged in shopping and other activities not prohibited. Accordingly, in view of the preferred position the freedoms of the First Article occupy, the statute in its present application must fall. It cannot be sustained by any presumption of validity. And, finally, it is said, the statute is, as to children, an absolute prohibition, not merely a reasonable regulation, of the denounced activity.

Concededly a statute or ordinance identical in terms with § 69, except that it is applicable to adults or all persons generally, would be invalid. ⊥**168** But the mere fact a state could not wholly prohibit this form of adult activity, whether characterized locally as a "sale" or otherwise, does not mean it cannot do so for children. Such a conclusion granted would mean that a state could impose no greater limitation upon child labor than upon adult labor. Or, if an adult were free to enter dance halls, saloons, and disreputable places generally, in order to discharge his conceived religious duty to admonish or dissuade persons from frequenting such places, so would be a child with similar convictions and objectives, if not alone then in the parent's company, against the state's command.

The state's authority over children's activities is broader than over like actions of adults. This is peculiarly true of public activities and in matters of employment. A democratic society rests, for its continuance, upon the healthy, well-rounded growth of young people into full maturity as citizens, with all that implies. It may secure this against impeding restraints and dangers within a broad range of selection. Among evils most appropriate for such action are the crippling effects of child employment, more especially in public places, and the possible harms arising from other activities subject to all the diverse influences of the street. It is too late now to doubt ⊥**169** that legislation appropriately designed to reach such evils is within the state's police power, whether against the parent's claim to control of the child or one that religious scruples dictate contrary action.

It is true children have rights, in common with older people, in the primary use of highways. But even in such use streets afford dangers for them not affecting adults. And in other uses, whether in work or in other things, this difference may be magnified. This is so not only when children are unaccompanied but certainly to some extent when they are with their parents. What may be wholly permissible for adults therefore may not be so for children, either with or without their parents' presence.

Street preaching, whether oral or by handing out literature, is not the primary use of the highway, even for adults. While for them it cannot be wholly prohibited, it can be regulated within reasonable limits in accommodation to the primary and other incidental uses. But, for obvious reasons, notwithstanding appellant's contrary view, the validity of such a prohibition applied to children not accompanied by an older person hardly would seem open to question. The case reduces itself therefore to the question whether the presence of the child's guardian puts a limit to the state's power. That fact may lessen the likelihood that some evils the legislation seeks to avert will occur. But it cannot forestall all of them. The zealous though lawful exercise of the right to engage in propagandizing the community, whether in religious, political or other matters, may and at times does create situa⊥**170**tions difficult enough for adults to cope with and wholly inappropriate for children, especially of tender years, to face. Other harmful possibilities could be stated, of emotional excitement and psychological or physical injury. Parents may be free to become martyrs themselves. But it does not follow they are free, in identical circumstances, to make martyrs of their children before they have reached the age of full and legal discretion when they can make that choice for themselves. Massachusetts has determined that an absolute prohibition, though one limited to streets and public places and to the incidental uses proscribed, is necessary to accomplish its legitimate objectives. Its power to attain them is broad enough to reach these peripheral instances in which the parent's supervision may reduce but cannot eliminate entirely the ill effects of the prohibited conduct. We think that with reference to the public proclaiming of religion, upon the streets and in other similar public places, the power of the state to control the conduct of children reaches beyond the scope of its authority over adults, as is true in the case of other freedoms, and the rightful boundary of its power has not been crossed in this case.

In so ruling we dispose also of appellant's argument founded upon denial of equal protection. It falls with that based on denial of religious freedom, since in this instance the one is but another phrasing of the other. Shortly, the contention is that the street, for Jehovah's Witnesses and their children, is their church, since their conviction makes it so; and to deny them access to it for religious purposes as was done here has the same effect as excluding altar boys, youthful choristers, and other children from the edifices in which they practice their religious beliefs and worship. The argument hardly needs more than statement, after what has been said, to refute it. However Jehovah's Witnesses may conceive them, the public highways have not become their religious prop⊥**171**erty merely by their assertion. And there is no denial of equal protection in excluding their children from doing there what no other children may do.

Our ruling does not extend beyond the facts the case presents. We neither lay the foundation "for any [that is, every] state intervention in the indoctrination and participation of children in religion" which may be done "in the name of their health and welfare" nor give warrant for "every limitation on their religious training and activities." The religious training and indoctrination of children may be accomplished in many ways, some of which, as we have noted, have received constitutional protection through decisions of this Court. These and all others except the public proclaiming of religion on the streets, if this may be taken as either training or indoctrination of the proclaimer, remain unaffected by the decision.

The judgment is *Affirmed*.

Mr. *Justice* MURPHY, dissenting:

This attempt by the state of Massachusetts to prohibit a child from exercising her constitutional right to practice her religion on the public streets cannot, in my opinion, be sustained.

The record makes clear the basic fact that Betty Simmons, the nine-year old child in question, was engaged in a genuine religious, rather than commercial, activity. She was a member of Jehovah's Witnesses and had been taught the tenets of that sect by her guardian, the appellant. Such tenets included the duty of publicly distributing religious tracts on the street and from door to door. Pursuant to this religious duty and in the company of the appellant, Betty Simmons on the night of December 18, 1941, was standing on a public street corner and offering to distribute Jehovah's Witness literature to passers-by. There was no expectation of pecuniary profit to ⊥**172** herself or to appellant. It is undisputed, furthermore, that she did this of her own desire and with appellant's consent. She testified that she was motivated by her love of the Lord and that He commanded her to distribute this literature; this was, she declared, her way of worshipping God. She was occupied, in other words, in "an age-old form of missionary evangelism" with a purpose "as evangelical as the revival meeting." *Murdock* v. *Pennsylvania*.

Religious training and activity, whether performed by adult or child, are protected by the Fourteenth Amendment against interference by state action, except insofar as they violate reasonable regulations adopted for the protection of public health, morals and welfare. Our problem here is whether a state, under the guise of enforcing its child labor laws, can lawfully prohibit girls under the age of eighteen and boys under the age of twelve from practicing their religious faith insofar as it involves the distribution or sale of religious tracts on the public streets. No question of freedom of speech or freedom of press is present and we are not called upon to determine the permissible restraints on those rights. Nor are any truancy or curfew restrictions in issue. The statutes in question prohibit all children within the specified age limits from selling or offering to sell "any newspapers, magazines, periodicals or any other articles of merchandise of any description . . . in any street or public place." Criminal sanctions are imposed on the parents and guardians who compel or permit minors in their control to engage in the prohibited transactions. The state court has construed these statutes to cover the activities here involved, thereby imposing an indirect restraint through the parents and guardians on the free exercise by minors of their religious beliefs. This indirect restraint is no less effective than a direct one. A square conflict between the con⊥**173**stitutional guarantee of religious freedom and the state's legitimate interest in protecting the welfare of its children is thus presented.

As the opinion of the Court demonstrates, the power of the state lawfully to control the religious and other activities of children is greater than its power over similar activities of adults. But that fact is no more decisive of the issue posed by this case than is the obvious fact that the family itself is subject to reasonable regulation in the public interest. We are concerned solely with the reasonableness of this particular prohibition of religious activity by children.

In dealing with the validity of statutes which directly or indirectly infringe religious freedom and the right of parents to encourage their children in the practice of a religious belief, we are not aided by any strong presumption of the constitutionality of such legislation. On the contrary, the human freedoms enumerated in the First Amendment and carried over into the Fourteenth Amendment are to be presumed to be invulnerable and any attempt to sweep away those freedoms is prima facie invalid. It follows that any restriction or prohibition must be justified by those who deny that the freedoms have been unlawfully invaded. The burden was therefore on the state of Massachusetts to prove the reasonableness and necessity of prohibiting children from engaging in religious activity of the type involved in this case.

The burden in this instance, however, is not met by vague references to the reasonableness underlying child labor legislation in general. The great interest of the state in shielding minors from the evil vicissitudes of early life does not warrant every limitation on their religious training and activities. The reasonableness that justifies the prohibition of the ordinary distribution of literature in the public streets by children is not necessarily the rea⊥**174**sonableness that justifies such a drastic restriction when the distribution is part of their religious faith. If the right of a child to practice its religion in that manner is to be forbidden by constitutional means, there must be convincing proof that such a practice constitutes a grave and immediate danger to the state or to the health, morals or welfare of the child. The vital freedom of religion, which is "of the very essence of a scheme of ordered liberty," *Palko* v. *Connecticut*, cannot be erased by slender references to the state's power to restrict the more secular activities of children.

The state, in my opinion, has completely failed to sustain its burden of proving the existence of any grave or immediate danger to any interest which it may lawfully protect. There is no proof that Betty Simmons' mode of worship constituted a serious menace to the public. It was carried on in an orderly, lawful manner at a public street corner. And "one who is rightfully on a street which the state has left open to the public carries with him there as elsewhere the constitutional right to express his views in an orderly fashion. This right extends to the communication of ideas by handbills and literature as well as by the spoken word." *Jamison* v. *Texas*. The sidewalk, no less than the cathedral or the evangelist's tent, is a proper place, under the Constitution, for the orderly worship of God. Such use of the streets is as necessary to the Jehovah's Witnesses, the Salvation Army and others who practice religion without benefit of conventional shelters as is the use of the streets for purposes of passage.

It is claimed, however, that such activity was likely to affect adversely the health, morals and welfare of the child. Reference is made in the majority opinion to "the crippling effects of child employment, more especially in pub⊥**175**lic places, and the possible harms arising from other activities subject to all the diverse influences of the street." To the extent that they flow from participation in ordinary commercial activities, these harms are irrelevant to this case. And the bare possibility that such harms might emanate from distribution of religious literature is not, standing alone, sufficient justification for restricting freedom of conscience and religion. Nor can parents or guardians be subjected to criminal liability because of vague possibilities that their religious teachings might cause injury to the child. The evils must be grave, immediate, substantial. Yet there is not the slightest indication in this record, or in sources subject to judicial notice, that children engaged in distributing literature pursuant to their religious beliefs have been or are likely to be subject to any of the harmful "diverse influences of the street." Indeed, if probabilities are to be indulged in, the likelihood is that children engaged in serious religious endeavor are immune from such influences. Gambling, truancy, irregular eating and sleeping habits, and the more serious vices are not consistent with the high moral character ordinarily displayed by children fulfilling religious obligations. Moreover, Jehovah's Witness children invariably make their distributions in groups subject at all times to adult or parental control, as was done in this case. The dangers are thus exceedingly remote, to say the least. And the fact that the zealous exercise of the right to propagandize the community may result in violent or disorderly situations difficult for children to face is no excuse for prohibiting the exercise of that right.

No chapter in human history has been so largely written in terms of persecution and intolerance as the one dealing with religious freedom. From ancient times to the present day, the ingenuity of man has known no limits in its ability to forge weapons of oppression for use against ⊥**176** those who dare to express or practice unorthodox religious beliefs. And the Jehovah's Witnesses are living proof of the fact that even in this nation, conceived as it was in the ideals of freedom, the right to practice religion in unconventional ways is still far from secure. Theirs is a militant and unpopular faith, pursued with a fanatical zeal. They have suffered brutal beatings; their property has been destroyed; they have been harassed at every turn by the resurrection and enforcement of little used ordinances and statutes. To them, along with other present-day religious minorities, befalls the burden of testing our devotion to the ideals and constitutional guarantees of religious freedom. We should therefore hesitate before approving the application of a statute that might be used as another instrument of oppression. Religious freedom is too sacred a right to be restricted or prohibited in any degree without convincing proof that a legitimate interest of the state is in grave danger.

Mr. Justice JACKSON:

The novel feature of this decision is this: the Court holds that a state may apply child labor laws to restrict or prohibit an activity of which, as recently as last term, it held: "This form of religious activity occupies the same high estate under the First Amendment as do worship in the churches and preaching from the pulpits. It has the same claim to protection as the more orthodox and conventional exercises of religion." ". . . the mere fact that the religious literature is sold by itinerant preachers rather than 'donated' does not transform evangelism into a commercial enterprise. If it did, then the passing of the collection plate in church would make the church service a commercial project. The constitutional rights of those spreading their religious beliefs through the spoken ⊥**177** and printed word are not to be gauged by standards governing retailers or wholesalers of books." *Murdock* v. *Pennsylvania.*

It is difficult for me to believe that going upon the streets to accost the public is the same thing for application of public law as withdrawing to a private structure for religious worship. But if worship in the churches and the activity of Jehovah's Witnesses on the streets "occupy the same high estate" and have the "same claim to protection" it would seem that child labor laws may be applied to both if to either. If the *Murdock* doctrine stands along with today's decision, a foundation is laid for any state intervention in the indoctrination and participation of children in religion, provided it is done in the name of their health or welfare.

This case brings to the surface the real basis of disagreement among members of this Court in previous Jehovah's Witness cases. Our basic difference seems to be as to the method of establishing limitations which of necessity bound religious freedom.

My own view may be shortly put: I think the limits begin to operate whenever activities begin to affect or collide with liberties of others or of the public. Religious activities which concern only members of the faith are and ought to be free—as nearly absolutely free as anything can be. But beyond these, many religious denominations or sects engage in collateral and secular activities intended to obtain means from unbelievers to sustain the worshippers and their leaders. They raise money, not merely by passing the plate to those who voluntarily attend services or by contributions by their own people, but by solicitations and drives addressed to the public by holding public dinners and entertainments, by various kinds ⊥**178** of sales and Bingo games and lotteries. All such money-raising activities on a public scale are, I think, Caesar's affairs and may be regulated by the state so long as it does not discriminate against one because he is doing them for a religious purpose, and the regulation is not arbitrary and capricious, in violation of other provisions of the Constitution.

The Court in the *Murdock* case rejected this principle of separating immune religious activities from secular ones in declaring the disabilities which the Constitution imposed on local authorities. Instead, the Court now draws a line based on age that cuts across both true exercise of religion and auxiliary secular activities. I think this is not a correct principle for defining the activities immune from regulation on grounds of religion, and *Murdock* overrules the grounds on which I think affirmance should rest. I have no alternative but to dissent from the grounds of affirmance of a judgment which I think was rightly decided, and upon right grounds, by the Supreme Judicial Court of Massachusetts.

Mr. Justice ROBERTS *and Mr. Justice* FRANKFURTER join in this opinion.

CONSCIENTIOUS OBJECTION TO WAR

There is likely no more direct collision between the authority of government and the liberty of the individual than in the relationship of the state and the conscientious objector to war. Both legislative and judicial bodies have encountered great difficulty in seeking to reconcile the demands of national security and the preservation of individual liberty in this area. The problem is real in peacetime; it becomes acute in time of war or national emergency.[1]

Even in American colonial times, conscientious objection was a recognized problem. Quakers, Mennonites, and Brethren—having made pacifism a religious tenet—made up the great majority of such objectors. Although exceptions with regard to service in the militia were sometimes made on their behalf, colonial records are replete with instances of fines and imprisonments for refusal to bear arms.

During the American Revolution conscientious objectors suffered many inconveniences and some actual mistreatment at the hands of both individuals and government. Though there was no draft law at the time, public sentiment was such that pacifists were often considered traitors. In Pennsylvania, where the Quakers and Mennonites were most numerous, Benjamin Franklin, as a member of the Committee of Safety, interested himself the first year of the war in providing exemption from military service for the conscientious objector. The Pennsylvania Assembly responded by allowing exemption, provided an assessment of money approximating the expense and loss of time of those who served in the army was paid.

[1]For an excellent discussion of the problem of conscientious objection through the World War II period, see Mulford Q. Sibley and Philip E. Jacob, *Conscription of Conscience: The American State and the Conscientious Objector, 1940-1947* (Ithaca, New York: Cornell University Press, 1952). More recent developments, with a particular emphasis on "selective" conscientious objection, are recounted in Kent Greenawalt, "All or Nothing at All: The Defeat of Selective Conscientious Objection," in *Church and State: The Supreme Court and the First Amendment*, ed. Philip B. Kurland (Chicago: University of Chicago Press, 1975), pp. 168-231.

The Continental Congress in 1775 also took cognizance of the presence of conscientious objectors. That body acknowledged the position of the objectors by passing a resolution which read:

> As there are some people, who, from religious principles, cannot bear arms in any case, this Congress intend no violence to their consciences, but earnestly recommend it to them, to contribute liberally in this time of universal calamity, to the relief of their distressed brethren in the several colonies, and do all other services to their oppressed Country, which they can consistently with their religious principles.[2]

The United States Constitution as it was submitted to the states for ratification in 1787 contained no reference to the issue of conscientious objection. Three state ratifying conventions submitted proposals for amendments to exempt from military service those persons religiously opposed to bearing arms. Fear was expressed in Pennsylvania's convention that conscientious objectors might be coerced into military service. In the first Congress in 1789, James Madison proposed as part of a constitutional amendment a clause providing that "no person religiously scrupulous of bearing arms shall be compelled to render military service in person."[3] The proposal was not adopted, but several state constitutions did include provisions of this type. When the first militia law was passed by Congress in 1792, there was some discussion as to the advisability of providing exemptions for conscientious objectors; a decision was finally made to leave the matter to the states.

Since there was no national conscription during the War of 1812 or the Mexican War, no special problem existed with respect to conscientious objectors in those wars, although a certain amount of pressure was brought to bear by local opinion and militia laws enacted by state legislatures. With the Civil War, however, came compulsory military service in both North and South, and conscientious objection became a live issue. The Federal Conscription Act of 1864 allowed conscientious objectors who were members of religious denominations with articles of faith that prohibited the bearing of arms to pay a substitute or to accept noncombatant duties. In the Confederacy, at least until 1864, similar provisions were made for members of certain designated pacifist denominations.

No conscription law existed during the Spanish-American War, but when the United States entered World War I, Congress again resorted to compulsory military service. The Selective Draft Act, passed on 18 May 1917, subjected all male citizens between the ages of twenty-one and thirty years of age to duty for the period of the emergency. The act exempted regularly ordained ministers and theological students from the draft. It further provided exemption from combatant duty for members of "any well-recognized religious sect or organization at present organized and existing and whose existing creed or principles forbid its members to participate in war in any form."[4]

While such conscientious objectors were thus exempted from combatant duties, no provision was made for objectors outside these recognized groups until the War Department ordered that persons with "personal scruples against war" be treated as conscientious objectors. Neither were there provisions for those who might have scruples against noncombatant service, and several hundred persons were imprisoned for refusal to undertake such service.

The constitutionality of the Draft Act was soon contested in a federal district court by a conscientious objector who was prosecuted on refusal to register. Among other contentions, he charged establishment of religion under the First Amendment where exemption was granted to members of recognized churches without similar treatment for others of like belief who were not members of a recognized pacifist church. A similar argument was made with regard to the exemptions of ministers and theological students. The district court, however, upheld the constitutionality of the Selective Draft Act, saying that the law was not one respecting an establishment of religion as contemplated in the First Amendment (*United States* v. *Stephens*, 1917).

The Supreme Court unanimously upheld the Draft Act in January 1918. Chief Justice White, speaking for the Court, brushed aside the argument that the exemption of certain religious groups constituted an establishment of religion:

> We pass without anything but statement the proposition that an establishment of a religion or an interference with the free exercise thereof repugnant to the First Amendment resulted from the exemption clauses of the act . . . because we think its unsoundness is too apparent to require us to do more (*Arver* v. *United States* [Selective Draft Law Cases], 245 U.S. 366, 389).

After the termination of World War I, conscientious objection ceased to be a pressing issue insofar as

[2] *Journals of the Continental Congress, 1774-1789, May 10-September 20*, ed. Worthington C. Ford, 34 vols. (Washington: Government Printing Office, 1904-1937), vol. 2: 1775, p. 189.

[3] *The Debates and Proceedings in the Congress of the United States: With An Appendix, Containing Important State Papers and Public Documents, and All the Laws of a Public Nature; With a Copious Index*, comp. Joseph Gales, 42 vols. (Washington: Gales & Seaton, 1834-1856),1:451.

[4] Selective Draft Act, Ch. 15, 40 Stat. 76, 78 (1917).

selective service was concerned. A decade later, however, the Court was confronted with the problem of the right of an individual to reserve conscientious scruples against military service in connection with the oath of allegiance prescribed for aliens applying for naturalization. The Naturalization Act of 1906 required an applicant for citizenship to declare under oath that he would "support and defend the Constitution and laws of the United States against all enemies, foreign and domestic, and bear true faith and allegiance to the same."[5]

In 1927 forty-nine-year-old Madame Rosika Schwimmer, a native of Hungary and a well-known pacifist lecturer and writer, appeared before a federal district court to obtain her naturalization papers for American citizenship. One of a series of questions asked of all prospective citizens was the following: "If necessary, are you willing to take up arms in defense of this country?" This question had been inserted soon after World War I by the head of the Naturalization Service without any specific congressional authorization. Madame Schwimmer was willing to take the oath of allegiance without reservations, but in answer to the question, she stated that as an uncompromising pacifist she had no sense of nationalism and therefore would not personally take up arms, regardless of whether or not other women were compelled to do so.

Because of her refusal to answer the question affirmatively, the district court denied her application for naturalization. The circuit court reversed the district court, and the case went on certiorari to the Supreme Court, where by a six-to-three vote the Court held that her application should be denied (UNITED STATES v. SCHWIMMER).

Justice Butler spoke for the majority. He held that naturalized as well as native-born citizens owed the obligation of allegiance to the government. The burden was upon the applicant to prove that she had the qualifications specified in the statute. It is the duty of citizens to bear arms in defense of the country if the need should arise. Refusing to do so or holding and expressing opinions against this duty might serve to influence others to refuse to perform their obligations, and the safety of the country might be endangered. Religious scruples were not here involved because the applicant had no religion.

Justice Holmes, joined by Justice Brandeis, filed a strong dissent. He emphasized the fact that the applicant was a woman of superior intelligence and character. Because of her sex and age she would not have been called upon to bear arms. Though he personally disagreed with Madame Schwimmer's pacifist optimism with respect to the abolition of war, Holmes made a strong plea for "freedom for the thought that we hate," and comparing her philosophy to that of the Quakers, said that he "would suggest that the Quakers have done their share to make the country what it is, that many citizens agree with the applicant's belief, and that I had not supposed hitherto that we regretted our inability to expel them because they believe more than some of us do in the teaching of the Sermon on the Mount" (279 U.S. 644, 655 [1929]).

Two years later the Supreme Court again had occasion to interpret the Naturalization Act in a case which more directly involved a religious issue. Douglas C. Macintosh, Baptist professor at the Yale Divinity School and a chaplain with the Canadian Army during World War I, was denied naturalization because he refused to state in advance that he would fight in any war in which the country was involved. He qualified his answer by saying that he would take up arms only if he felt the war was morally justified; he was not willing to put allegiance to government before allegiance to the will of God.

By a five-to-four vote the Court upheld the denial of Macintosh's application (UNITED STATES v. MACINTOSH). Although the question again turned only on the interpretation of the naturalization statute, Justice Sutherland, in his opinion for the Court, went further than the majority opinion in *Schwimmer*. In what was in effect *obiter dictum*, he made it clear that concessions made to conscientious objectors were *privileges* conferred as a matter of grace by Congress and not constitutional rights. In dismissing the contention made by counsel for Macintosh that it was a constitutional principle that a citizen could not be forced to bear arms if he had conscientious scruples against doing so, Sutherland commented:

> This, if it means what it seems to say, is an astonishing statement. Of course, there is no such principle of the Constitution, fixed or otherwise. The conscientious objector is relieved from the obligation to bear arms in obedience to no constitutional provision, express or implied; but because, and only because, it has accorded with the policy of Congress thus to relieve him (183 U.S. 605, 623).

Chief Justice Hughes wrote a vigorous dissent in which Justices Holmes, Brandeis, and Stone joined. He pointed out that the question here involved was not whether Congress had the right to exact a promise to bear arms as a requisite for naturalization. Rather, the issue was whether Congress had exacted such a commitment. The words used were general; he did not believe that such a demand could be implied for it was "directly opposed to the spirit of our institutions and to the historic practice of the Congress."

Although the *Schwimmer* and *Macintosh* decisions were widely criticized, they remained law for fifteen

[5]Act of 29 June 1906, Ch. 3592, 34 Stat. 596, 598 (1906).

years. Their doctrine was utilized in 1934 to uphold suspension of several young men from the University of California at Los Angeles. As members of the Methodist Episcopal Church with conscientious scruples against military service, they refused to take the prescribed R.O.T.C. course in military science and tactics (HAMILTON v. REGENTS OF THE UNIVERSITY OF CALIFORNIA). Justice Butler denied that their suspension violated the Fourteenth Amendment as claimed: Government, federal and state, each in its own sphere owes a duty to the people within its jurisdiction to preserve itself in adequate strength to maintain peace and order and to insure the just enforcement of law. And every citizen owes the reciprocal duty, according to his capacity, to support and defend government against all enemies (293 U.S. 245, 262). As has been observed at an earlier point, Justice Cardozo's brief concurring opinion in *Hamilton* had great subsequent significance because there the assumption was first made that religious liberty as guaranteed in the First Amendment against the national government was protected by the Fourteenth Amendment against state action as well.

In 1945 the naturalization cases were again used as precedent by the Supreme Court in *In re Summers*, when it upheld denial of admission to the state bar to a conscientious objector. Although the applicant had expressed his willingness to take an oath to uphold the Constitution of Illinois, the Committee on Character and Fitness decided that his beliefs in nonviolence and his unwillingness to serve in the state militia would prevent his taking the requisite oath.

A year after the *Summers* decision, the Court reexamined the naturalization cases and came to the conclusion in GIROUARD v. UNITED STATES that they no longer stated the correct rule of law. Girouard, a Seventh-day Adventist, stated in his petition for naturalization that he was entirely willing to serve in any future war in a noncombatant capacity, but that he was forbidden by his conscience to bear arms. The United States District Court in Massachusetts admitted him to citizenship, but a court of appeals reversed the action on authority of the *Schwimmer* and *Macintosh* cases.

With Justice Douglas writing the opinion, the five-man Supreme Court majority held that in the absence of express language to the contrary, it was not to be assumed that Congress had intended to make a promise to bear arms a prerequisite to naturalization. The required oath did not specifically demand that aliens promise to bear arms, and Congress had not explicitly made the answering of the question with respect to willingness to bear arms a requirement for citizenship.

The bearing of arms, Justice Douglas said, is not the only way in which our institutions may be supported and defended. He pointed to such persons as civilian workers, Quakers, and nuclear physicists as examples of those who serve in as patriotic a way as those who enter military service. Although he agreed that the authority of government to provide for its defense is unchallenged, Justice Douglas concluded that

> The struggle for religious liberty has through the centuries been an effort to accommodate the demands of the State to the conscience of the individual. The victory for freedom of thought recorded in our Bill of Rights recognizes that in the domain of conscience there is a moral power higher than the State (328 U.S. 61, 68).

Notwithstanding Justice Douglas's broad statement, the *Girouard* decision was not based on constitutional issues, but on the interpretation of the intent of Congress in the naturalization statutes. It held only that if aliens are to be kept from American citizenship because of conscientious objection, it must be done by clear statutory enactment. The statutory ambiguity was largely removed by the Naturalization Act of 1952, which provided that a conscientious objector can take the oath and become a citizen if he can prove "by clear and convincing evidence to the satisfaction of the naturalization court that he is opposed to the bearing of arms in the Armed Forces of the United States by reason of religious training and belief."[6]

In 1940, for the first time in its history, the United States departed from its traditional policy of maintaining a peacetime army of volunteers only. The conscientious objector provision of the Selective Training and Service Act was broader than its 1917 predecessor. Rather than requiring membership in a "well-recognized" religious group, it exempted from combatant service any person "who, by reason of religious training and belief, is conscientiously opposed to participation in war in any form."[7] It also provided for assignment to "work of national importance" for those conscientiously opposed to noncombatant service.

Construction of the phrase "religious training and belief" soon presented local draft boards and ultimately federal courts with grave difficulties. The phrase received conflicting interpretations from different courts of appeal when political, philosophical, and ethical objectors contended that although their objection did not result from any formalized religious training or beliefs, it was based upon a moral conscience that was religious in nature.

[6]Immigration and Nationality Act, 66 Stat. 163, 258 (1952).

[7]54 Stat. 885, 889 (1940).

In 1948, Congress amended the statute to define the term "religious training and belief" to mean "an individual's belief in a relation to a Supreme Being involving duties superior to those arising from any human relation, but [not including] essentially political, sociological, or philosophical views or a merely personal moral code."[8]

This statutory language, found in section 6(j) of the act, was interpreted by the Supreme Court in 1965 in three cases decided under the title of UNITED STATES v. SEEGER. All three of the men involved were conscientious objectors who had been convicted in federal district courts for refusal to submit to induction after Selective Service officials had rejected their claims for exemption. None of the three had a traditional concept of God. Seeger, for example, said that he preferred to leave open the question of his belief in a Supreme Being, but that his "skepticism or disbelief in the existence of God" did "not necessarily mean lack of faith in anything whatsoever." His, he stated, was a "belief in and devotion to goodness and virtue for their own sakes, and a religious faith in a purely ethical creed."

The Second Court of Appeals had not only reversed the district court's conviction of Seeger, the appeals court held that section 6(j), insofar as it required a theistic belief, was unconstitutional as a preferment of religion to irreligion in violation of the First Amendment. Justice Clark, for a unanimous Supreme Court, avoided the constitutional question but gave an extremely broad construction to section 6(j) in upholding the right of exemption for Seeger and his fellow appellants. Congress, Clark held, had not intended to restrict the exemption for conscientious objectors only to those who believe in a traditional God. The expression "Supreme Being," rather than "God," had been employed by Congress "so as to embrace all religions" while excluding "essentially political, sociological, or philosophical views." The test of belief required by the act is "whether a given belief that is sincere and meaningful occupies a place in the life of its possessor parallel to that filled by the orthodox belief in God of one who clearly qualifies for the exemption" (380 U.S. 163, 166). The Court emphasized that each claimant had based his conscientious objection on a religious belief.

An irritated Congress responded to the Court's reading of section 6(j) by amending the governing act in 1967. The new act removed the Supreme Being clause while retaining the restrictive phrase which ruled out inclusion of "essentially political, sociological, or philosophical views, or a merely personal moral code" as "religious training and belief."[9]

[8]Selective Service Act of 1948, 62 Stat. 604, 613 (1948).

[9]Military Selective Service Act of 1967, 81 Stat. 100, 104 (1967); 50 U.S.C. App., Sec. 456(j) (1973).

In 1969 the new provision was held unconstitutional by several district judges as a violation of the Establishment Clause of the First Amendment. The leading case was *United States* v. *Sisson* heard in the U.S. District Court in Boston. Sisson, a "selective" conscientious objector to the Vietnam War, based his objection on philosophical and political grounds. Judge Wyzanski held section 6(j) unconstitutional on two counts. On the basis of the Free Exercise Clause, he held that "no statute can require combat service of a conscientious objector whose principles are either religious or akin thereto." On Establishment Clause grounds he ruled that section 6(j) "invalidly discriminates in favor of certain types of religious objectors to the prejudice of Sisson" (297 F. Supp 902, 906, D., Mass. [1969]). Judge Wyzanski summed up his complaint against the provisions concerning exemption, saying: "In short, in the Draft Act Congress unconstitutionally discriminated against atheists, agnostics, and men like Sisson who, whether they be religious or not, are motivated in their objection to the draft by profound moral convictions of their beings" (297 F. Supp. 902, 911).

The Supreme Court, for procedural reasons, refused to take the Sisson case on appeal; but the next year, in WELSH v. UNITED STATES, it did give consideration to some of the questions raised in that case. Elliott A. Welsh II, a Los Angeles commodities broker, answered affirmatively the question as to whether his objection to participation in war was based on "religious training and belief." But he struck out the word "religious" and said that his beliefs had been formed by reading in the fields of history and sociology. Although he had first said that his beliefs were nonreligious, he later wrote his appeal board that his beliefs were "certainly religious in the ethical sense of the word."

Justice Black, for four members of an eight-man Court, refused to distinguish Welsh's views from those of Seeger; but to uphold the exemption claim without voiding section 6(j), he had to stretch the construction of the terminology even more than in the Seeger case. Black maintained that the restrictive clause did not have to be read to exclude persons with strong beliefs about the foreign and domestic affairs of the nation, nor did it deny exemption to those whose beliefs were grounded in good part "in considerations of public policy." He concluded that section 6(j) "exempts from military service all those whose consciences, spurred by deeply held moral, ethical, or religious beliefs, would give them no rest or peace if they allowed themselves to become a part of an instrument of war" (398 U.S. 333, 344).

Justice Harlan wrote a concurring opinion in which he acknowledged that he had erred in joining the majority in *Seeger* where the Court had upheld an exemption claim not based on a theistic belief. He felt that the Court had already gone too far in distorting the legislative intent of the act, and he refused to subscribe to the "lobotomy" now performed in the *Welsh* decision. Harlan would have preferred to hold the section unconstitutional as violating the establishment clause by giving a preference to the "religious" and disadvantaging those who belong to religions that do not worship a Supreme Being. However, he accepted Justice Black's "test" as merely a "patchwork of judicial making" to cure the "defects of under-inclusion in section 6(j)" so that local draft boards could continue to administer the law.

As the unpopular war in Vietnam continued and opposition became more vocal, it was almost inevitable that the Court would eventually have to speak to the question of "selective" conscientious objection claims.[10] It did so in 1971 in the companion cases of GILLETTE v. UNITED STATES and NEGRE v. LARSEN. Gillette, a rock musician from Yonkers, New York, expressed his willingness to take part in a war of national defense or a peace-keeping war sponsored by the United Nations, but he refused to enter the armed forces while the country was engaged in an "unjust war" in Vietnam. He based his opposition on a "a humanistic approach to religion." Negre, a gardener from California who was already in the Army, said that as a devout Roman Catholic he had a religious duty to distinguish "just" and "unjust" wars and to refuse to participate in such an "unjust" war as that in which Americans were involved in Vietnam. He therefore sought a discharge from the Army.

Justice Marshall, writing for himself and seven other members of the Court, upheld the power of Congress to rule out "selective" conscientious objection by granting exemptions only to those persons "conscientiously opposed to participation in war in any form." He denied that the statutory requirement of opposition to all wars to justify exemption results in discrimination among religions in violation of the First Amendment. He stated further that restricting exemptions to those opposed to participation in all wars serves to minimize the entanglement of government in religion. It also reduces the possibility of discrimination involved in the weighing of individual claims concerning "just" and "unjust" wars. He found the purposes of section 6(j) to be "neutral" and "secular," as required by the First Amendment. Finally, he noted the government's interest in procuring manpower and concluded that any "incidental burdens" imposed on particular persons were "strictly justified by substantial governmental interests that relate directly to the very impacts questioned" (401 U.S. 437, 462). Justice Douglas, in lone dissent, condemned the statute as "a species of those which show an invidious discrimination in favor of religious persons and against others with like scruples" (401 U.S. 437, 468).

The Veteran's Readjustment Benefits Act of 1966 did not provide educational benefits for conscientious objectors who performed "alternative civilian service."[11] William Robison challenged that provision on behalf of himself and all others in a like situation as violative of both the Free Exercise Clause and the equal protection of the laws guarantee as applied to the federal government through the Due Process Clause of the Fifth Amendment. In *Johnson* v. *Robison* (1974) the Supreme Court, with only Justice Douglas dissenting, rejected both contentions.

Justice Brennan, for the majority, reasoned with respect to the Free Exercise Clause that if a conscientious objector could be imprisoned for refusal to serve in what he considered to be an unjust war, as the Court had held in *Gillette*, denial of educational benefits was only an "incidental" burden on Robison's free exercise of religion, if there was a burden at all. Speaking to the equal protection contention, he found the disruptions and disabilities caused military veterans and those who perform alternative services to be both quantitatively and qualitatively sufficiently different to constitute a rational basis for Congress's distinction as to privileges granted. Justice Douglas, in dissent, had no difficulty finding discrimination in the act and warned that "Where Government places a price on the free exercise of one's religious scruples it crosses the forbidden line" (415 U.S. 360, 390).

Later in the same year, in a *per curiam* opinion speaking principally to a very technical issue concerning the granting of injunctive relief, the Court in effect defeated an effort of the American Friends Service Committee and several of its conscientious objector employees to obtain a refund of that part of their withholding taxes used for military purposes. They contended that the withholding of taxes on salaries deprived them of their free exercise right to express their opposition on religious grounds to all wars through this form of protest. Justice Douglas was again the only dissenter (*U.S.* v. *American Friends Service Committee*, 1974). Controversy relating to the

[10]Actually, in 1955, the Supreme Court had been faced with a most unusual "selective" conscientious objector case in *Sicurella* v. *United States*. There, a Jehovah's Witness had been denied exemption because of his expressed willingness to fight in a "theocratic war" on the orders of Jehovah and to justify the use of force in defending "his ministry, Kingdom interest . . . and his fellow brethren." The Court, in reversing his conviction, expressed doubt that Witness doctrine contemplated a theocratic war, and even stronger doubt that "the yardstick of Congress includes within its measure such spiritual wars between the powers of good and evil where the Jehovah's Witnesses, if they participate, will do so without carnal weapons" (345 U.S. 385, 391).

[11]Title 38 U.S.C., Sec. 1652(a) (1).

draft subsided at the conclusion of the Vietnam conflict. Interest was revived, however, when, following the Soviet invasion of Afghanistan, President Carter asked for and received approval of Congress for resumption of draft registration at age eighteen. He also sought an amendment to the Military Selective Service Act to allow registration of women. After much debate, Congress failed to amend the act or to appropriate funds to register women. On 2 July 1980, President Carter issued a proclamation ordering the registration. In *Rostker* v. *Goldberg* (1981) the Supreme Court by a vote of six-to-three upheld the registration provision against the charge that the equal protection of the law clause as applied to the federal government by the Fifth Amendment was violated by requiring registration of males only.

Although opposition to registration never reached the level of widespread indignation occasioned by the draft in earlier years, dissent existed and a considerable number of young men refused to register. Congress's response was to pass legislation in 1983 making male college students between the ages of eighteen and twenty-six who had failed to register ineligible for federal financial aid. By a vote of seven-to-two the Court upheld the constitutionality of the statute in *Selective Service System* v. *Minnesota Public Interest Research Group* (1984).

To punish those young men who failed to register, the government adopted a "passive enforcement policy" whereby only those who reported themselves in some way as having violated the law or who were reported by others were prosecuted. There was no provision for exemption on religious grounds in the draft registration requirements, and the government was undoubtedly aware that the system would result primarily in prosecutions of religious and moral objectors and of those who objected vocally to registration.

A number of cases in which the passive enforcement policy had been used were heard at the district court level; two made their way to the Supreme Court. One, *Wayte* v. *U.S.* (1985), received a full hearing, and the Court by a seven-to-two vote failed to accept Wayte's argument that he was being selectively punished for his expression of ideas in violation of the First and Fifth Amendments. The nation, reasoned Mr. Powell for the majority, has a compelling interest to ensure its safety, and the enforcement policy "placed no more limitation on speech than was necessary to ensure registration for the national defense." On the basis of the *Wayte* ruling, the case of Mark Schmucker, a Mennonite who had written a letter stating that registration would violate his religious conscience, was remanded to the Court of Appeals for the Sixth Circuit from which the case had come on certiorari for further consideration (*U.S.* v. *Schmucker*, 1985).

In the absence of actual conscription, debate concerning exemption for conscientious objectors to war is today in abeyance. Should the nation again be forced to resort to a draft, however, both Congress and the Court can expect to be faced once more with difficult questions concerning not only the breadth of exemptions allowed but also the possibility of a constitutional *right* to conscientious objector exemptions. But because of the statutory revisions and the Court decisions of the last several decades, debate can begin at a much more advanced point than in 1917, when only members of "well-recognized" pacifist churches could claim the privilege of exemption from combatant duty.

UNITED STATES v. SCHWIMMER

279 U.S. 644
ON WRIT OF CERTIORARI TO THE UNITED STATES CIRCUIT COURT OF APPEALS FOR THE SEVENTH CIRCUIT
Argued April 12, 1929 — Decided May 27, 1929

⊥**646** Mr. *Justice BUTLER* delivered the opinion of the court:

Respondent filed a petition for naturalization in the District Court for the Northern District of Illinois. The court found her unable, without mental reservation, to take the prescribed oath of allegiance and not attached to the principles of the Constitution of the United States and not well disposed to the good order and happiness of the same; and it denied her application. The Circuit Court of Appeals reversed the decree and directed the district court to grant respondent's petition.

The Naturalization Act of June 16, 1906, requires:

"He [the applicant for naturalization] shall, before he is admitted to citizenship, declare on oath in open court . . . that he will support and defend the Constitution and laws of the United States against all enemies, foreign and domestic, and bear true faith and allegiance to the same." U.S.C. title 8, § 381.

"It shall be made to appear to the satisfaction of the court . . . that during that time [at least five years preceding the application] he has behaved as a man of good moral character, attached to the principles of the Constitution of the United States, and well disposed to the good order and happiness of the same. . . ." § 382.

Respondent was born in Hungary in 1877, and is a citizen of that country. She came to the United States in August, 1921, to visit and lecture, has resided in Illinois since the latter part of that month, declared her intention to become a citizen the following November, and filed petition for naturalization in September, 1926. On a preliminary form, she stated that she understood the prin⊥**647**ciples of and fully believed in our form of government and that she had read, and in becoming a citizen was willing to take, the oath of allegiance. Question 22 was this: "If necessary, are you willing to take up arms in defense of this country?" She answered: "I would not take up arms personally."

She testified that she did not want to remain subject to Hungary, found the United States nearest her ideals of a democratic republic, and that she could wholeheartedly take the oath of allegiance. She said: "I cannot see that a woman's refusal to take up arms is a contradiction to the oath of allegiance." For the fulfillment of the duty to support and defend the Constitution and laws, she had in mind other ways and means. She referred to her interest in civic life, to her wide reading and attendance at lectures and meetings, mentioned her knowledge of foreign languages and that she occasionally glanced through Hungarian, French, German, Dutch, Scandinavian, and Italian publications and said that she could imagine finding in meetings and publications attacks on the American form of government and she would conceive it her duty to uphold it against such attacks. She expressed steadfast opposition to any undemocratic form of government like proletariat, Fascist, white terror, or military dictatorships. "All my past work proves that I have always served democratic ideals and fought—though not with arms—against undemocratic institutions." She stated that before coming to this country she had defended American ideals and had defended America in 1924 during an international pacifist congress in Washington.

She also testified: "If . . . the United States can compel its women citizens to take up arms in the defense of the country—something that no other civilized government has ever attempted—I would not be able to comply with this requirement of American citizenship. In this **⊥648** case I would recognize the right of the government to deal with me as it is dealing with its male citizens who for conscientious reasons refuse to take up arms."

The district director of naturalization by letter called her attention to a statement made by her in private correspondence: "I am an uncompromising pacifist. . . . I have no sense of nationalism, only a cosmic consciousness of belonging to the human family." She answered that the statement in her petition demonstrated that she was an uncompromising pacifist. "Highly as I prize the privilege of American citizenship I could not compromise my way into it by giving an untrue answer to question 22, though for all practical purposes I might have done so, as even men of my age—I was forty-nine years old last September—are not called to take up arms. . . . That 'I have no nationalistic feeling' is evident from the fact that I wish to give up the nationality of my birth and to adopt a country which is based on principles and institutions more in harmony with my ideals. My 'cosmic consciousness of belonging to the human family' is shared by all those who believe that all human beings are the children of God."

And at the hearing she reiterated her ability and willingness to take the oath of allegiance without reservation and added: "I am willing to do everything that an American citizen has to do except fighting. If American women would be compelled to do that, I would not do that. I am an uncompromising pacifist. . . . I do not care how many other women fight, because I consider it a question of conscience. I am not willing to bear arms. In every other single way I am ready to follow the law and do everything that the law compels American citizens to do. That is why I can take the oath of allegiance, because, as far as I can find out, there is nothing that I could be compelled to do that I cannot do. . . . With reference to spreading propaganda among the women throughout **⊥649** the country about my being an uncompromising pacifist and not willing to fight, I am always ready to tell anyone who wants to hear it that I am an uncompromising pacifist and will not fight. In my writings and in my lectures I take up the question of war and pacifism if I am asked for that."

Except for eligibility to the Presidency, naturalized citizens stand on the same footing as do native-born citizens. All alike owe allegiance to the government, and the government owes to them the duty of protection. These are reciprocal obligations and each is a consideration for the other. But aliens can acquire such equality only by naturalization according to the uniform rules prescribed by the Congress. They have no natural right to become citizens, but only that which is by statute conferred upon them. Because of the great value of the privileges conferred by naturalization, the statutes prescribing qualifications and governing procedure for admission are to be construed with definite purpose to favor and support the government. And, in order to safeguard against admission of those who are unworthy or who for any reason fail to measure up to required standards, the law puts the burden upon every applicant to show by satisfactory evidence that he has the specified qualifications.

Every alien claiming citizenship is given the right to submit his petition and evidence in support of it. And, if the requisite facts are established, he is entitled as of right to admission. On applications for naturalization, the court's function is "to receive the testimony, to compare it with the law, and to judge on both law and fact." *Spratt* v. *Spratt*. We quite recently declared that: "Citizenship is a high privilege and when doubts exist concerning a grant of it, generally at least, **⊥650** they should be resolved in favor of the United States and against the claimant." *United States* v. *Manzi*. And when, upon a fair consideration of the evidence adduced upon an application for citizenship, doubt remains in the mind of the court as to any essential matter of fact, the United States is entitled to the benefit of such doubt and the application should be denied.

That it is the duty of citizens by force of arms to defend our government against all enemies whenever necessity arises is a fundamental principle of the Constitution.

The common defense was one of the purposes for which the people ordained and established the Constitution. It empowers Congress to provide for such defense, to declare war, to raise and support armies, to maintain a navy, to make rules for the government and regulation of the land and naval forces, to provide for organizing, arming and disciplining the militia, and for calling it forth to execute the laws of the Union, suppress insurrections and repel invasions; it makes the President commander in chief of the army and navy and of the militia of the several states when called into the service of the United States; it declares that, a well-regulated militia being necessary to the security of a free state, the right of the people to keep and bear arms shall not be infringed. We need not refer to the numerous statutes that contemplate defense of the United States, its Constitution, and laws by armed citizens. This court, in the *Selective Draft Law Cases* speaking through *Chief Justice WHITE*, said that "the very conception of a just government and its duty to the citizen includes the reciprocal obligation of the citizen to render military service in case of need. . . ."

Whatever tends to lessen the willingness of citizens to discharge their duty to bear arms in the country's defense detracts from the strength and safety of the government. ⊥**651** And their opinions and beliefs as well as their behavior indicating a disposition to hinder in the performance of that duty are subjects of inquiry under the statutory provisions governing naturalization and are of vital importance, for if all or a large number of citizens oppose such defense the "good order and happiness" of the United States cannot long endure. And it is evident that the views of applicants for naturalization in respect of such matters may not be disregarded. The influence of conscientious objectors against the use of military force in defense of the principles of our government is apt to be more detrimental than their mere refusal to bear arms. The fact that, by reason of sex, age or other cause, they may be unfit to serve, does not lessen their purpose or power to influence others. It is clear from her own statements that the declared opinions of respondent as to armed defense by citizens against enemies of the country were directly pertinent to the investigation of her application. . . .

The fact that she is an uncompromising pacifist with no sense of nation⊥**652**alism but only a cosmic sense of belonging to the human family justifies belief that she may be opposed to the use of military force as contemplated by our Constitution and laws. And her testimony clearly suggests that she is disposed to exert her power to influence others to such opposition.

A pacifist in the general sense of the word is one who seeks to maintain peace and to abolish war. Such purposes are in harmony with the Constitution and policy of our government. But the word is also used and understood to mean one who refuses or is unwilling for any purpose to bear arms because of conscientious considerations and who is disposed to encourage others in such refusal. And one who is without any sense of nationalism is not well bound or held by the ties of affection to any nation or government. Such persons are liable to be incapable of the attachment for and devotion to the principles of our Constitution that are required of aliens seeking naturalization.

It is shown by official records and everywhere well known that during the recent war there were found among those who described themselves as pacifists and conscientious objectors many citizens—though happily a minute part of all—who were unwilling to bear arms in that crisis and who refused to obey the laws of the United States and the lawful commands of its officers and encouraged such disobedience in others. Local boards found it necessary to issue a great number of noncombatant certificates, and several thousand who were called to camp made claim because of conscience for exemption from any form of military service. Several hundred were convicted and sentenced to imprisonment for offenses involving disobedience, desertion, propaganda and sedition. It is obvious that the acts of such offenders evidence a want of that attachment to the principles of the Constitution of which ⊥**653** the applicant is required to give affirmative evidence by the Naturalization Act.

The language used by respondent to describe her attitude in respect of the principles of the Constitution was vague and ambiguous; the burden was upon her to show what she meant and that her pacifism and lack of nationalistic sense did not oppose the principle that it is a duty of citizenship by force of arms when necessary to defend the country against all enemies, and that her opinions and beliefs would not prevent or impair the true faith and allegiance required by the act. She failed to do so. The district court was bound by the law to deny her application.

The decree of the Circuit Court of Appeals is reversed.
The decree of the District Court is affirmed.

Mr. *Justice HOLMES*, dissenting:

The applicant seems to be a woman of superior character and intelligence, obviously more than ordinarily desirable as a citizen of the United States. It is agreed that she is qualified for citizenship except so far as the views set forth in a statement of facts "may show that the applicant is not attached to the principles of the Constitution of the United States and well disposed to the good order and happiness of the same, and except in so far as the same may show that she cannot take the oath of allegiance without a mental reservation." The views referred to are an extreme opinion in favor of pacifism and a statement that she would not bear arms to defend the Constitution. So far as the adequacy of her oath is concerned, I hardly can see how that is affected by the statement, inasmuch as she is a woman over fifty years of age, and would not be allowed to bear arms if she wanted ⊥**654** to. And as to the opinion the whole examination of the applicant shows that she holds none of the now-dreaded creeds, but thoroughly believes in organized government and prefers that of the United States to any other in the world. Surely it cannot show lack of attachment to the principles of the Constitution that she thinks that it can be improved. I suppose that most intelligent people think that it might be. Her particular improvement looking to the abolition of war seems to me not materially different in its bearing on this case from a wish to establish cabinet government as in England, or a single house, or one term of seven years for the President. To touch a more burning question, only a judge mad with partisanship would exclude because the applicant thought that the 18th Amendment should be repealed.

Of course, the fear is that if a war came the applicant would exert activities such as were dealt with in *Schenck* v. *United States*. But that seems to me unfounded. Her position and motives are wholly different from those of Schenck. She is an optimist and states in strong and, I do not doubt, sincere words her belief that war will disappear and that the impending destiny of mankind is to unite in peaceful leagues. I do not share that optimism nor do I think that a philosophic view of the world would regard war as absurd. But most people who have known it regard it with horror, as a last resort, and, even if not yet ready for cosmopolitan efforts, would welcome any practicable combinations that would increase the power on the side of peace. The notion that the applicant's optimistic anticipations would make her a worse citizen is sufficiently answered by her examination, which seems to me a better argument for her admission than any that I can offer. Some of her answers might excite popular prejudice, but if there is any principle of the Constitution that more imperatively calls for attachment than any other it is the principle of free ⊥**655** thought—not free thought for those who agree with us but freedom for the thought that we hate. I think that we should adhere to that principle with regard to admission into, as well as to life within, this country. And, recurring to the opinion that bars this applicant's way, I would suggest that the Quakers have done their share to make the country what it is, that many citizens agree with the applicant's belief, and that I had not supposed hitherto that we regretted our inability to expel them because they believe more than some of us do in the teachings of the Sermon on the Mount.

Mr. *Justice BRANDEIS* concurs in this opinion.

Mr. *Justice SANFORD*, dissenting:

I agree, in substance, with the views expressed by the Circuit Court of Appeals, and think its decree should be affirmed.

UNITED STATES v. MACINTOSH

283 U.S. 605
ON WRIT OF CERTIORARI TO THE UNITED STATES CIRCUIT COURT OF APPEALS FOR THE SECOND CIRCUIT
Argued April 27, 1931 — Decided May 25, 1931

⊥**613** Mr. *Justice SUTHERLAND* delivered the opinion of the court:

The respondent was born in the Dominion of Canada. He came to the United States in 1916, and in 1925 declared his intention to become a citizen. His petition for naturalization was presented to the Federal District Court for Connecticut, and that court, after hearing and consideration, denied the application upon the ground that, since petitioner would not promise in advance to bear arms in defense of the United States unless he believed the war to be morally justified, he was not attached to the principles of the Constitution. The Circuit Court of Appeals reversed the decree and directed the district court to admit respondent to citizenship. . . .

⊥**615** Naturalization is a privilege, to be given, qualified or withheld as Congress may determine, and which the alien may claim as of right only upon compliance with the terms which Congress imposes. That Congress regarded the admission to citizenship as a serious matter is apparent from the conditions and precautions with which it carefully surrounded the subject. . . .

⊥**616** Why does the statute require examination of the applicant and witnesses in open court and under oath, and for what purpose is the government authorized to cross-examine concerning any matter *touching* or in any way *affecting* the right of naturalization? Clearly, it would seem, in order that the court and the government, whose power and duty in that respect these provisions take for granted, may discover whether the applicant is fitted for citizenship—and to that end, by actual inquiry, ascertain, among other things, whether he has intelligence and good character; whether his oath to support and defend the Constitution and laws of the United States, and to bear true faith and allegiance to the same, will be taken without mental reservation or purpose inconsistent therewith; whether his views are compatible with the obligations and duties of American citizenship; whether he will upon his own part observe the laws of the land; whether he is willing to support the government in time of war, as well as in time of peace, and to assist in the defense of the country, not to the extent or in the manner that he may choose, but to such extent and in such manner as he lawfully may be required to do. These, at least, are matters which are of the essence of the statutory requirements, and in respect of which the mind and conscience of the applicant ⊥**617** may be probed by pertinent inquiries, as fully as the court, in the exercise of a sound discretion, may conclude is necessary. . . .

The applicant had complied with all the formal requirements of the law, and his personal character and conduct were shown to be good in all respects. His right to naturalization turns altogether upon the effect to be given to certain answers and qualifying statements made in response to interrogatories propounded to him.

Upon the preliminary form for petition for naturalization, the following questions, among others, appear: "20. Have you read the following oath of allegiance? [which is then quoted]. Are you willing to take this oath in becoming a citizen?" "22. If necessary, are you willing to take up arms in defense of this country?" In response to the questions designated 20, he answered "Yes." In response to the question designated 22, he answered, "Yes; but I should want to be free to judge of the neces⊥**618**sity." By a written memorandum subsequently filed, he amplified these answers as follows:

"20 and 22. I am willing to do what I judge to be in the best interests of my country, but only in so far as I can believe that this is not going to be against the best interests of humanity in the long run. I do not undertake to support 'my country, right or wrong' in any dispute which may arise, and I am not willing to promise beforehand, and without knowing the cause for which my country may go to war, either that I will or that I will not 'take up arms in defense of this country,' however 'necessary' the war may seem to be to the government of the day.

It is only in a sense consistent with these statements that I am willing to promise to 'support and defend' the government of the United States 'against all enemies, foreign and domestic.' But, just because I am not certain that the language of questions 20 and 22 will bear the construction I should have to put upon it in order to be able to answer them in the affirmative, I have to say that I do not know that I can say 'Yes' in answer to these two questions."

Upon the hearing before the district court on the petition, he explained his position more in detail. He said that he was not a pacifist; that if allowed to interpret the oath for himself he would interpret it as not inconsistent with his position and would take it. He then proceeded to say that he would answer question 22 in the affirmative only on the understanding that he would have to believe that the war was morally justified before he would take up arms in it or give it his moral support. He was ready to give to the United States all the allegiance he ever had given or ever could give to any country, but he could not put allegiance to the government of any country before allegiance to the will of God. He did not anticipate engaging in any propaganda against the prosecution of a war which the ⊥**619** government had already declared and which it considered to be justified; but he preferred not to make any absolute promise at the time of the hearing, because of his ignorance of all the circumstances which might affect his judgment with reference to such a war. He did not question that the government under certain conditions could regulate and restrain the conduct of the individual citizen, even to the extent of imprisonment. He recognized the principle of the submission of the individual citizen to the opinion of the majority in a democratic country; but he did not believe in having his own moral problems solved for him by the majority. The position thus taken was the only one he could take consistently with his moral principles and with what he understood to be the moral principles of Christianity. He recognized, in short, the right of the government to restrain the freedom of the individual for the good of the social whole; but was convinced, on the other hand, that the individual citizen should have the right respectfully to withhold from the government military services (involving, as they probably would, the taking of human life), when his best moral judgment would compel him to do so. He was willing to support his country, even to the extent of bearing arms, if asked to do so by the government, in any war which he could regard as morally justified.

There is more to the same effect, but the foregoing is sufficient to make plain his position.

These statements of the applicant fairly disclose that he is unwilling to take the oath of allegiance, except with these important qualifications: That he will do what he judges to be in the best interests of the country only in so far as he believes it will not be against the best interests of humanity in the long run; that he will not assist in the defense of the country by force of arms or give any war his moral support unless he believes it to be morally justified, however necessary the war might ⊥**620** seem to the government of the day; that he will hold himself free to judge of the morality and necessity of the war, and, while he does not anticipate engaging in propaganda against the prosecution of a war declared and considered justified by the government, he prefers to make no promise even as to that; and that he is convinced that the individual citizen should have the right to withhold his military services when his best moral judgment impels him to do so. . . .

⊥**621** There are few finer or more exalted sentiments than that which finds expression in opposition to war. Peace is a sweet and holy thing, and war is a hateful and an abominable thing to be avoided by any sacrifice or concession that a free people can make. But thus far mankind has been unable to devise any method of indefinitely prolonging the one or of entirely abolishing the other, and, unfortunately, there is nothing which seems to afford ⊥**622** positive ground for thinking that the near future will witness the beginning of the reign of perpetual peace for which good men and women everywhere never cease to pray. The Constitution, therefore, wisely contemplating the ever present possibility of war, declares that one of its purposes is to "provide for the common defense." In express terms Congress is empowered "to declare war," which necessarily connotes the plenary power to wage war with all the force necessary to make it effective; and "to raise . . . armies," which necessarily connotes the like power to say who shall serve in them and in what way.

From its very nature the war power, when necessity calls for its exercise, tolerates no qualifications or limitations, unless found in the Constitution or in applicable principles of international law. In the words of John Quincy Adams, "This power is tremendous; it is strictly constitutional; but it breaks down every barrier so anxiously erected for the protection of liberty, property and of life."

To the end that war may not result in defeat, freedom of speech may, by act of Congress, be curtailed or denied so that the morale of the people and the spirit of the army may not be broken by seditious utterances; freedom of the press curtailed to preserve our military plans and movements from the knowledge of the enemy; deserters and spies put to death without indictment or trial by jury; ships and supplies requisitioned; property of alien enemies, theretofore under the protection of the Constitution, seized without process and converted to the public use without compensation and without due process of law in the ordinary sense of that term; prices of food and other necessities of life fixed or regulated; railways taken over and operated by the government; and other drastic powers, wholly inadmissible in time of peace, exercised to meet the emergencies of war.

⊥**623** These are but illustrations of the breadth of the power; and it necessarily results from their consideration that whether any citizen shall be exempt from serving in the armed forces of the nation in time of war is dependent upon the will of Congress and not upon the scruples of the individual, except as Congress provides. That body, thus far, has seen fit, by express enactment, to relieve from the obligation of armed service those persons who belong to the class known as conscientious objectors; and this policy is of such long standing that it is thought by some to be beyond the possibility of alteration. Indeed, it seems to be assumed in this case that the privilege is one that Congress itself is powerless to take away. Thus it is said in the carefully prepared brief of respondent:

"To demand from an alien who desires to be naturalized an unqualified promise to bear arms in every war that may be declared, despite the fact that he may have conscientious religious scruples against doing so in some hypothetical future war, would mean that such an alien would come into our citizenry on an unequal footing with the native born, and that he would be forced, as the price of citizenship, to forego a privilege enjoyed by others. That is the manifest result of the fixed principle of our Constitution, zealously guarded by our laws, that a citizen cannot be forced and need not bear arms in a war if he has conscientious religious scruples against doing so."

This, if it means what it seems to say, is an astonishing statement. Of course, there is no such principle of the Constitution, fixed or otherwise. The conscientious objector is relieved from the obligation to bear arms in obedience to no constitutional provision, express or implied; but because, and only because, it has accorded with the policy of Congress thus to relieve him. . . . ⊥**624** The privilege of the native-born conscientious objector to avoid bearing arms comes not from the Constitution, but from the acts of Congress. That body may grant or withhold the exemption as in its wisdom it sees fit; and if it be withheld, the native-born conscientious objector cannot successfully assert the privilege. No other conclusion is compatible with the well-nigh limitless extent of the war powers as above illustrated, which include, by necessary implication, the power, in the last extremity, to compel the armed service of any citizen in the land, without regard to his objections or his views in respect of the justice or morality of the particular war or of war in general. In *Jacobson* v. *Massachusetts* this Court, speaking of the liberties guaranteed to the individual by the 14th Amendment, said:

". . . and yet he may be compelled, by force if need be, against his will and without regard to his personal wishes or his pecuniary interests, or even his religious or political convictions, to take his place in the ranks of the army of his country and risk the chance of being shot down in its defense."

The applicant for naturalization here is unwilling to become a citizen with this understanding. He is unwilling to leave the question of his future military service to the wisdom of Congress where it belongs, and where every native-born or admitted citizen is obliged to leave it. In effect, he offers to take the oath of allegiance only with the qualification that the question whether the war is necessarily or morally justified must, so far as his support is concerned, be conclusively determined by reference to his opinion.

⊥**625** When he speaks of putting his allegiance to the will of God above his allegiance to the government, it is evident, in the light of his entire statement, that he means to make *his own interpretation* of the will of God the decisive test which shall conclude the government and stay its hand. We are a Christian people according to one another the equal right of religious freedom, and acknowledging with reverence the duty of obedience to the will of God. But, also, we are a nation with the duty to survive; a nation whose Constitution contemplates war as well as peace; whose government must go forward upon the assumption, and safely can proceed upon no other, that unqualified allegiance to the nation and submission and obedience to the laws of the land, as well those made for war as those made for peace, are not inconsistent with the will of God.

The applicant here rejects that view. He is unwilling to rely, as every native-born citizen is obliged to do, upon the probable continuance by Congress of the long established and approved practice of exempting the honest conscientious objector, while at the same time asserting his willingness to conform to whatever the future law constitutionally shall require of him; but discloses a present and fixed purpose to refuse to give his moral or armed support to any future war in which the country may be actually engaged, if, in his opinion, the war is not morally justified, the opinion of the nation as expressed by Congress to the contrary notwithstanding.

If the attitude of this claimant, as shown by his statements and the inferences properly to be deduced from them, be held immaterial to the question of his fitness for admission to citizenship, where shall the line be drawn? Upon what ground of distinction may we hereafter reject another applicant who shall express his willingness to re⊥**626**spect any particular principle of the Constitution or obey any future statute only upon the condition that he shall entertain the opinion that it is morally justified? The applicant's attitude, in effect, is a refusal to take the oath of allegiance except in an altered form. The qualifications upon which he insists, it is true, are made by parol and not by the way of written amendment to the oath; but the substance is the same.

It is not within the province of the courts to make bargains with those who seek naturalization. They must accept the grant and take the oath in accordance with the terms fixed by the law, or forego the privilege of citizenship. There is no middle choice. If one qualification of the oath be allowed, the door is opened for others, with utter confusion as the probable final result. As this court said in *United States* v. *Manzi:*

"Citizenship is a high privilege, and when doubts exist concerning a grant of it, generally at least, they should be resolved in favor of the United States and against the claimant."

The Naturalization Act is to be construed "with definite purpose to favor and support the government," and the United States is entitled to the benefit of any doubt which remains in the mind of the court as to any essential matter of fact. The burden was upon the applicant to show that his views were not opposed to "the principle that it is a duty of citizenship, by force of arms when necessary, to defend the country against all enemies, and that [his] opinions and beliefs would not prevent or impair the true faith and allegiance required by the act." *United States* v. *Schwimmer*. We are of opinion that he did not meet this requirement. The examiner and the court of first instance who heard and weighed the evidence and saw the applicant and witnesses so concluded. That conclusion, if we were in ⊥**627** doubt, would not be rejected except for good and persuasive reasons, which we are unable to find.

The decree of the Circuit Court of Appeals is reversed and that of the District Court is *affirmed*.

Mr. *Chief Justice HUGHES* dissenting:

I am unable to agree with the judgment in this case. It is important to note the precise question to be determined. It is solely one of law, as there is no controversy as to the facts. The question is not whether naturalization is a privilege to be granted or withheld. That it is such a privilege is undisputed. Nor, whether the Congress has the power to fix the conditions upon which the privilege is granted. That power is assumed. Nor, whether the Congress may in its discretion compel service in the army in time of war or punish the refusal to serve. That power is not here in dispute. Nor is the question one of the authority of Congress to exact a promise to bear arms as a condition of its grant of naturalization. That authority, for the present purpose, may also be assumed.

The question before the Court is the narrower one whether the Congress has exacted such a promise. That the Congress has not made such an express requirement is apparent. The question is whether that exaction is to be implied from certain general words which do not, as it seems to me, either literally or historically, demand the implication. I think that the requirement should not be implied, because such a construction is directly opposed to the spirit of our institutions and to the historic practice of the Congress. It must be conceded that departmental zeal may not be permitted to outrun the authority conferred by statute. If such a promise is to be demanded, contrary to principles which have been respected as fundamental, the Congress should exact it in unequivocal ⊥**628** terms, and we should not, by judicial decision, attempt to perform what, as I see it, is a legislative function.

In examining the requirements for naturalization, we find that the Congress has expressly laid down certain rules which concern the opinions and conduct of the applicant. Thus it is provided that no person shall be naturalized "who disbelieves in or who is opposed to organized government, or who is a member of or affiliated with any organization entertaining and teaching such disbelief in or opposition to organized government, or who advocates or teaches the duty, necessity, or propriety of the unlawful assaulting or killing of any officer or officers, either of specific individuals or of officers generally, of the government of the United States, or of any other organized government, because of his or their official character, or who is a polygamist." Act of June 29, 1906. The respondent, Douglas Clyde Macintosh, entertained none of these disqualifying opinions and had none of the associations or relations disapproved. Among the specific requirements as to beliefs, we find none to the effect that one shall not be naturalized if by reason of his religious convictions he is opposed to war or is unwilling to promise to bear arms. In view of the questions which have repeatedly been brought to the attention of the Congress in relation to such beliefs, and having regard to the action of the Congress when its decision was of immediate importance in the raising of armies, the omission of such an express requirement from the naturalization statute is highly significant.

Putting aside these specific requirements as fully satisfied, we come to the general conditions imposed by the statute. We find one as to good behavior during the specified period of residence preceding application. No applicant could appear to be more exemplary than Macintosh. A Canadian by birth, he first came to the United ⊥**629** States as a graduate student at the University of Chicago, and in 1907 he was ordained as a Baptist minister. In 1909 he began to teach in Yale University and is now a member of the faculty of the Divinity School, Chaplain of the Yale Graduate School, and Dwight Professor of Theology. After the outbreak of the Great War, he voluntarily sought appointment as a chaplain with the Canadian Army and as such saw service at the front. Returning to this country, he made public addresses in 1917 in support of the Allies. In 1918, he went again to France where he had charge of an American Y.M.C.A. hut at the front until the armistice, when he resumed his duties at Yale University. It seems to me that the applicant has shown himself in his behavior and character to be highly desirable as a citizen and, if such a man is to be excluded from naturalization, I think the disqualification should be found in unambiguous terms and not in an implication which shuts him out and gives admission to a host far less worthy.

The principal ground for exclusion appears to relate to the terms of the oath which the applicant must take. It should be observed that the respondent was willing to take the oath, and he so stated in his petition. But, in response to further inquiries, he explained that he was not willing "to promise beforehand" to take up arms, "without knowing the cause for which my country may go to war" and that "he would have to believe that the war was morally justified." He declared that "his first allegiance was to the will of God"; that he was ready to give to the United States "all the allegiance he ever had given or ever could give to any country, but that he could not put allegiance to the government of any country before allegiance to the will of God." The question then is whether the terms of the oath are to be taken as necessarily implying an assurance of willingness to bear arms, so that one whose conscientious convictions or belief of the su⊥**630**preme allegiance to the will of God will not permit him to make such an absolute promise, cannot take the oath and hence is disqualified for admission to citizenship.

The statutory provision as to the oath which is said to require this promise is this: "That he will support and defend the Constitution and laws of the United States against all enemies, foreign and domestic, and bear true faith and allegiance to the same." Act of June 29, 1906. That these general words have not been regarded as implying a promise to bear arms notwithstanding religious or conscientious scruples, or as requiring one to promise to put allegiance to temporal power above what is sincerely believed to be one's duty of obedience to God, is apparent, I think, from a consideration of their history. This oath does not stand alone. It is the same oath in substance that is required by act of Congress of civil officers generally (except the President, whose oath is prescribed by the Constitution). The Congress, in prescribing such an oath for civil officers, acts under Article 6, § 3, of the Constitution, which provides: "The Senators and Representatives before mentioned, and the Members of the Several Legislatures, and all executive and judicial Officers, both of the United States and of the several States, shall be bound by Oath or Affirmation, to support this Constitution; but no religious test shall ever be required as a Qualification to any Office or public Trust under the United States." The general oath of office, in the form which has been prescribed by the Congress for over sixty years, contains the provision "that I will support and defend the Constitution of the United States against all enemies, foreign and domestic; that I will bear true faith and allegiance to the same; that I take this obligation freely, without any mental reservation or purpose of evasion." (Rev. Stat. § 1757, U.S.C. title 5, §16.) It goes without ⊥**631** saying that it was not the intention of the Congress in framing the oath to impose any religious test. When we consider the history of the struggle for religious liberty, the large number of citizens of our country from the very beginning, who have been unwilling to sacrifice their religious convictions, and in particular, those who have been conscientiously opposed to war and who would not yield what they sincerely believed to be their allegiance to the will of God, I find it impossible to conclude that such persons are to be deemed disqualified for public office in this country because of the requirement of the oath which must be taken before they enter upon their duties. The terms of the promise "to support and defend the Constitution of the United States against all enemies, foreign and domestic," are not, I think, to be read as demanding any such result. There are other and most important methods of defense, even in time of war, apart from the personal bearing of arms. We have but to consider the defense given to our country in the late war, both in industry and in the field, by workers of all sorts, by engineers, nurses, doctors and chaplains, to realize that there is opportunity even at such a time for essential service in the activities of defense which do not require the overriding of such religious scruples. I think that the requirement of the oath of office should be read in the light of our regard from the beginning for freedom of conscience. While it has always been recognized that the supreme power of government may be exerted and disobedience to its commands may be punished, we know that with many of our worthy citizens it would be a most heart-searching question if they were asked whether they would promise to obey a law believed to be in conflict with religious duty. Many of their most honored exemplars in the past have been willing to suffer imprisonment or even death rather than to make such a promise. And we also know, in particular, that a promise to engage in ⊥**632** war by bearing arms, or thus to engage in a war believed to be unjust, would be contrary to the tenets of religious groups among our citizens who are of patriotic purpose and exemplary conduct. To conclude that the general oath of office is to be interpreted as disregarding the religious scruples of these citizens and as disqualifying them for office because they could not take the oath with such an interpretation would, I believe, be generally regarded as contrary not only to the specific intent of the Congress but as repugnant to the fundamental principle of representative government.

But the naturalization oath is in substantially the same terms as the oath of office to which I have referred. I find no ground for saying that these words are to be interpreted differently in the two cases. On the contrary, when the Congress reproduced the historic words of the oath of office in the naturalization oath, I should suppose that, according to familiar rules of interpretation, they should be deemed to carry the same significance.

The question of the proper interpretation of the oath is, as I have said, distinct from that of legislative policy in exacting military service. The latter is not dependent upon the former. But the long-established practice of excusing from military service those whose religious convictions oppose it confirms the view that the Congress in the terms of the oath did not intend to require a promise to give such service. The policy of granting exemptions in such cases has been followed from colonial times and is abundantly shown by the provisions of colonial and state statutes, of state constitutions, and of acts of Congress. . . .

⊥**633** Much has been said of the paramount duty to the state, a duty to be recognized, it is urged, even though it conflicts with convictions of duty to God. Undoubtedly that duty to the state exists within the domain of power, for government may enforce obedience to laws regardless of scruples. When one's belief collides with the power of the state, the latter is supreme within its sphere and submission or punishment follows. But, in the forum of conscience, duty to a moral power higher than the state has always been maintained. The reservation of that supreme obligation, as a matter of principle, would unquestionably be made by many of our conscientious and law-abiding citizens. The essence of religion is belief in a relation to God involving duties superior to those ⊥**634** arising from any human relation. As was stated by Mr. *Justice FIELD*, in *Davis* v. *Beason*: "The term 'religion' has reference to one's views of his relations to his Creator, and to the obligations they impose of reverence for his being and character, and of obedience to his will." One cannot speak of religious liberty, with proper appreciation of its essential and historic significance, without assuming the existence of a belief in supreme allegiance to the will of God. Professor Macintosh, when pressed by the inquiries put to him, stated what is axiomatic in religious doctrine. And, putting aside dogmas with their particular conceptions of deity, freedom of conscience itself implies respect for an innate conviction of paramount duty. The battle for religious liberty has been fought and won with respect to religious beliefs and practices, which are not in conflict with good order, upon the very ground of the supremacy of conscience within its proper field. What that field is, under our system of government, presents in part a question of constitutional law and also, in part, one of legislative policy in avoiding unnecessary clashes with the dictates of conscience. There is abundant room for enforcing the requisite authority of law as it is enacted and requires obedience, and for maintaining the conception of the supremacy of law as essential to orderly government without demanding that either citizens or applicants for citizenship shall assume by oath an obligation to regard allegiance to God as subordinate to allegiance to civil power. The attempt to exact such a promise, and thus to bind one's conscience by the taking of oaths or the submission to tests, has been the cause of many deplorable conflicts. The Congress has sought to avoid such conflicts in this country by respecting our happy tradition. In no sphere of legislation has the intention to prevent such clashes been more conspicuous than in relation to the bearing of arms. It would require strong evidence ⊥**635** that the Congress intended a reversal of its policy in prescribing the general terms of the naturalization oath. I find no such evidence.

Nor is there ground, in my opinion, for the exclusion of Professor Macintosh because his conscientious scruples have particular reference to wars believed to be unjust. There is nothing new in such an attitude. Among the most eminent statesmen here and abroad have been those who condemned the action of their country in entering into wars they thought to be unjustified. Agreements for the renunciation of war presuppose a preponderant public sentiment against wars of aggression. If, while recognizing the power of Congress, the mere holding of religious or conscientious scruples against all wars should not disqualify a citizen from holding office in this country, or an applicant otherwise qualified from being admitted to citizenship, there would seem to be no reason why a reservation of religious or conscientious objection to participation in wars believed to be unjust should constitute such a disqualification.

Apart from the terms of the oath, it is said that the respondent has failed to meet the requirement of "attachment to the principles of the Constitution." Here, again, is a general phrase which should be construed, not in opposition to, but in accord with, the theory and practice of our government in relation to freedom of conscience. What I have said as to the provisions of the oath I think applies equally to this phase of the case.

The judgment in *United States* v. *Schwimmer* stands upon the special facts of that case, but I do not regard it as requiring a reversal of the judgment here. I think that the judgment below should be affirmed.

Mr. *Justice HOLMES*, Mr. *Justice BRANDEIS* and Mr. *Justice STONE* concur in this opinion.

HAMILTON v. REGENTS OF THE UNIVERSITY OF CALIFORNIA

293 U.S. 245
ON APPEAL FROM THE SUPREME COURT OF THE STATE OF CALIFORNIA
Argued October 17 and 18, 1934 — Decided December 3, 1934

⊥**250** Mr. *Justice BUTLER* delivered the opinion of the Court.

This is an appeal under § 237 (a), Judicial Code, 28 U.S.C. § 344 (a), from a judgment of the highest court of California sustaining a state law that requires students at its university to take a course in military science and tactics the validity of which was by the appellants challenged as repugnant to the Constitution and laws of the United States.

The appellants are the above named minors and the fathers of each as his guardian *ad litem* and individually. They are taxpayers and citizens of the United States and of California. Appellees are the regents constituting a corporation created by the State to administer the university, its president and its provost. Appellants applied to the state supreme court for a writ of mandate compelling appellees to admit the minors into the university as students. So far as they are material to the questions presented here, the allegations of the petition are:

In October, 1933, each of these minors registered, became a student in the university and fully conformed to all its requirements other than that compelling him to take the course in military science and tactics in the Reserve Officers Training Corps which they assert to be an integral part of the military establishment of the United States and not connected in any way with the militia or military establishment of the State. The primary object of there establishing units of the training corps is to qualify students for appointment in the Officers Reserve ⊥**251** Corps. The courses in military training are those prescribed by the War Department. The regents require enrollment and participation of able-bodied male students who are citizens of the United States. These courses include instruction in rifle marksmanship, scouting and patrolling, drill and command, musketry, combat principles, and use of automatic rifles. Arms, equipment and uniforms for use of students in such courses are furnished by the War Department of the United States government.

These minors are members of the Methodist Episcopal Church and of the Epworth League and connected religious societies and organizations. For many years their fathers have been ordained ministers of that church. The Southern California Conference at its 1931 session adopted a resolution:

"With full appreciation of the heroic sacrifices of all those who have conscientiously and unselfishly served their country in times of war, but with the belief that the time has come in the unfolding light of the new day for the settlement of human conflicts by pacific means, and because we as Christians owe our first and supreme allegiance to Jesus Christ. Because the Methodist Episcopal Church in her General Conference of 1928 has declared: 'We renounce war as an instrument of national policy.' Because our nation led the nations of the world in signing the Paris Peace Pact, and the Constitution of the United States, Article 6, § 2, provides that: 'This Constitution and the laws of the United States which shall be made in pursuance thereof and all treaties made under authority of the United States shall be the Supreme Law of the Land.' Thus making the Paris Pact the supreme law of the land which declares: 'The high contracting parties agree that the settlement of all disputes or conflict—shall never be sought except by pacific means.' ⊥**252**

"Therefore we, the Southern California Conference, memorialize the General Conference which convenes in Atlantic City in May, 1932; to petition the United States Government to grant exemption from military service to such citizens who are members of the Methodist Episcopal Church, as conscientiously believe that participation in war is a denial of their supreme allegiance to Jesus Christ."

And in 1932 the General Conference of that Church adopted as a part of its tenets and discipline:

"We hold that our country is benefited by having as citizens those who unswervingly follow the dictates of their consciences. . . . Furthermore, we believe it to be the duty of the churches to give moral support to those individuals who hold conscientious scruples against participation in military training or military service. We petition the government of the United States to grant to members of the Methodist Episcopal Church who may be conscientious objectors to war the same exemption from military service as has long been granted to members of the Society of Friends and other similar religious organizations. Similarly we petition all educational institutions which require military training to excuse from such training any student belonging to the Methodist Episcopal Church who has conscientious scruples against it. We earnestly petition the government of the United States to cease to support financially all military training in civil educational institutions."

And the Southern California Conference at its 1933 session adopted the following:

"Reserve Officers' Training Corps—Recalling the action of the General Conference asking for exemption from military service for those members of our church to whom war and preparation for war is a violation of conscience, we request the authorities of our State Universities at Berkeley, Los Angeles and Tucson, to exempt Methodist students from the R.O.T.C. on the grounds of conscien⊥**253**tious objection, and we hereby pledge the moral and official backing of this Conference, seeking such exemption, provided that it be understood that no conscientious objector shall participate in the financial profits of war. The Secretary of the Conference is asked to send copies of this paragraph to the governing boards of these institutions."

Appellants as members of that church accept and feel themselves morally, religiously and conscientiously bound by its tenets and discipline as expressed in the quoted conference resolutions; each is a follower of the teachings of Jesus Christ; each accepts as a guide His teachings and those of the Bible and holds as a part of his religious and conscientious belief that war, training for war and military training are immoral, wrong and contrary to the letter and spirit of His teaching and the precepts of the Christian religion.

Therefore these students at the beginning of the fall term in 1933 petitioned the university for exemption from military training and participation in the activities of the training corps, upon the ground of their religious and conscientious objection to war and to military training. Their petition was denied. Thereupon, through that church's bishop in California, they and their fathers petitioned the regents that military training be made optional in order that conscientious and religious objectors to war, training for war and military training might not be confronted with the necessity of violating and forswearing their beliefs or being denied the right of education in the state university to which these minors are entitled under the constitution and laws of the State of California and of the United States.

The regents refused to make military training optional or to exempt these students. Then, because of their religious and conscientious objections, they declined to take the prescribed course and solely upon that ground the regents by formal notification suspended them from ⊥254 the university, but with leave to apply for readmission at any time conditioned upon their ability and willingness to comply with all applicable regulations of the university governing the matriculation and attendance of students. The university affords opportunity for education such as may not be had at any other institution in California except at a greater cost which these minors are not able to pay. And they, as appellees at the time of their suspension well knew, are willing to take as a substitute for military training such other courses as may be prescribed by the university. . . . ⊥259

The petition is not to be understood as showing that students required by the regents' order to take the prescribed course thereby serve in the army or in any sense become a part of the military establishment of the United States. Nor is the allegation that the courses are prescribed by the War Department to be taken literally. We take judicial notice of the long-established voluntary co-operation between federal and state authorities in respect of the military instruction given in the land grant colleges. The War Department has not been empowered ⊥260 to determine or in any manner to prescribe the military instruction in these institutions. The furnishing of officers, men and equipment conditioned upon the giving of courses and the imposing of discipline deemed appropriate, recommended or approved by the Department does not support the suggestion that the training is not exclusively prescribed and given under the authority of the State. The States are interested in the safety of the United States, the strength of its military forces and its readiness to defend them in war and against every attack of public enemies. Undoubtedly every State has authority to train its able-bodied male citizens of suitable age appropriately to develop fitness, should any such duty be laid upon them, to serve in the United States army or in state militia (always liable to be called forth by federal authority to execute the laws of the Union, suppress insurrection or repel invasion, Constitution, Art. I, § 8, cls. 12, 15 and 16) or as members of local constabulary forces, or as officers needed effectively to police the state. And, when made possible by the national government, the State in order more effectively to teach and train its citizens for these and like purposes may avail itself of the services of officers and equipment belonging to the military establishment of the United States. So long as its action is within retained powers and not inconsistent with any exertion of the authority of the national government and transgresses no right safeguarded to the citizen by the Federal Constitution, the State is the sole judge of the means to be employed and the amount of training to be exacted for the effective accomplishment of these ends.

⊥261 The clauses of the Fourteenth Amendment invoked by appellants declare: "No State shall make or enforce any law which shall abridge the privileges or immunities of citizens of the United States; nor shall any State deprive any person of life, liberty or property, without due process of law." Appellants' contentions are that the enforcement of the order prescribing instruction in military science and tactics abridges some privilege or immunity covered by the first clause and deprives of liberty safeguarded by the second. The "privileges and immunities" protected are only those that belong to citizens of the United States as distinguished from citizens of the States—those that arise from the Constitution and laws of the United States as contrasted with those that spring from other sources. Appellants assert—unquestionably in good faith—that all war, preparation for war and the training required by the university are repugnant to the tenets and discipline of their church, to their religion and to their consciences. The "privilege" of attending the university as a student comes not from federal sources but is given by the State. It is not within the asserted protection. The only "immunity" claimed by these students is freedom from obligation to comply with the rule prescribing military training. But that "immunity" cannot be regarded as not within, or as distinguishable from, the "liberty" of which they claim to have been deprived by the enforcement of the regents' order. If the regents' order is not repugnant to the due process clause, then it does not violate the privileges and immunities ⊥262 clause. Therefore we need only decide whether by state action the "liberty" of these students has been infringed.

There need be no attempt to enumerate or comprehensively to define what is included in the "liberty" protected by the due process clause. Undoubtedly it does include the right to entertain the beliefs, to adhere to the principles and to teach the doctrines on which these students base their objections to the order prescribing military training. The fact that they are able to pay their way in this university but not in any other institution in California is without significance upon any constitutional or other question here involved. California has not drafted or called them to attend the university. They are seeking education offered by the State and at the same time insisting that they be excluded from the prescribed course solely upon grounds of their religious beliefs and conscientious objections to war, preparation for war and military education. Taken on the basis of the facts alleged in the petition, appellants' contentions amount to no more than an assertion that the due process clause of the Fourteenth Amendment as a safeguard of "liberty" confers the right to be students in the state university free from obligation to take military training as one of the conditions of attendance.

Viewed in the light of our decisions that proposition must at once be put aside as untenable.

Government, federal and state, each in its own sphere owes a duty to the people within its jurisdiction to preserve itself in adequate strength to maintain peace and order and to assure the just enforcement of law. And every citizen owes the reciprocal duty, according to his capacity, to support and defend government against all **⊥263** enemies.

United States v. *Schwimmer* involved a petition for naturalization by one opposed to bearing arms in defense of country. Holding the applicant not entitled to citizenship we said: "That it is the duty of citizens by force of arms to defend our government against all enemies whenever necessity arises is a fundamental principle of the Constitution. . . . Whatever tends to lessen the willingness of citizens to discharge their duty to bear arms in the country's defense detracts from the strength and safety of the Government."

In *United States* v. *Macintosh*, a later naturalization case, the applicant was unwilling, because of conscientious objections, to take unqualifiedly the statutory oath of allegiance which contains this statement: "That he will support and defend the Constitution and laws of the United States against all enemies, foreign and domestic, and bear true faith and allegiance to the same." His petition stated that he was willing if necessary to take up arms in defense of this country, "but I should want to be free to judge of the necessity." In amplification he said: "I do not undertake to support 'my country, right or wrong' in any dispute which may arise, and I am not willing to promise beforehand, and without knowing the cause for which my country may go to war, either that I will or that I will not 'take up arms in defense of this country,' however 'necessary' the war may seem to be to the government of the day." The opinion of this Court quotes from petitioner's brief a statement to the effect that it is a "fixed principle of our Constitution, zealously guarded by our laws, that a citizen cannot be forced and need not bear arms in a war if he has conscientious religious scruples against doing so." And, referring to that part of the **⊥264** argument in behalf of the applicant this Court said "This, if it means what it seems to say, is an astonishing statement. Of course, there is no such principle of the Constitution, fixed or otherwise. The conscientious objector is relieved from the obligation to bear arms in obedience to no constitutional provision, express or implied; but because, and only because, it has accorded with the policy of Congress thus to relieve him. . . . The privilege of the native-born conscientious objector to avoid bearing arms comes not from the Constitution, but from the acts of Congress. That body may grant or withhold the exemption as in its wisdom it sees fit; and if it be withheld, the native-born conscientious objector cannot successfully assert the privilege. No other conclusion is compatible with the well-nigh limitless extent of the war powers as above illustrated, which include, by necessary implication, the power, in the last extremity, to compel the armed service of any citizen in the land, without regard to his objections or his views in respect of the justice or morality of the particular war or of war in general. In *Jacobson* v. *Massachusetts*, this Court [upholding a state compulsory vaccination law] speaking of the liberties guaranteed to the individual by the Fourteenth Amendment, said: '. . . and yet he may be compelled, by force if need be, against his will and without regard to his personal wishes or his pecuniary interests, or even his religious or political convictions, to take his place in the ranks of the army of his country and risk the chance of being shot down in its defense.'"

And see *University of Maryland* v. *Coale*, a case, similar to that now before us, decided against the contention of a student in the University of Maryland who on conscientious grounds objected to military training there required. His appeal to this Court was dismissed for the want of a substantial federal question. **⊥265**

Plainly there is no ground for the contention that the regents' order, requiring able-bodied male students under the age of twenty-four as a condition of their enrollment to take the prescribed instruction in military science and tactics, transgresses any constitutional right asserted by these appellants.

The contention that the regents' order is repugnant to the Briand-Kellogg Peace Pact requires little consideration. In that instrument the United States and the other high contracting parties declare that they condemn recourse to war for the solution of international controversies and renounce it as an instrument of national policy in their relations with one another and agree that the settlement or solution of all disputes or conflicts which may arise among them shall never be sought except by pacific means. Clearly there is no conflict between the regents' order and the provisions of this treaty.

Affirmed.

Mr. Justice CARDOZO.

Concurring in the opinion I wish to say an extra word.

I assume for present purposes that the religious liberty protected by the First Amendment against invasion by the nation is protected by the Fourteenth Amendment against invasion by the states.

Accepting that premise, I cannot find in the respondents' ordinance an obstruction by the state to "the free exercise" of religion as the phrase was understood by the founders of the nation, and by the generations that have followed. . . .

⊥266 Instruction in military science is not instruction in the practice or tenets of a religion. Neither directly nor indirectly is government establishing a state religion when it insists upon such training. Instruction in military science, unaccompanied here by any pledge of military service, is not an interference by the state with the free exercise of religion when the liberties of the constitution are read in the light of a century and a half of history during days of peace and war. . . .

From the beginnings of our history Quakers and other conscientious objectors have been exempted as an act of grace from military service, but the exemption, when granted, has been coupled with a condition, at least in many instances, that they supply the army with a substitute or with the money necessary to hire one. ⊥**267** For one opposed to force, the affront to conscience must be greater in furnishing men and money wherewith to wage a pending contest than in studying military science without the duty or the pledge of service. Never in our history has the notion been accepted, or even, it is believed, advanced, that acts thus indirectly related to service in the camp or field are so tied to the practice of religion as to be exempt, in law or in morals, from regulation by the state. On the contrary, the very lawmakers who were willing to give release from warlike acts had not thought that they were doing any⊥**268**thing inconsistent with the moral claims of an objector, still less with his constitutional immunities, in coupling the exemption with these collateral conditions.

Manifestly a different doctrine would carry us to lengths that have never yet been dreamed of. The conscientious objector, if his liberties were to be thus extended, might refuse to contribute taxes in furtherance of a war, whether for attack or for defense, or in furtherance of any other end condemned by his conscience as irreligious or immoral. The right of private judgment has never yet been so exalted above the powers and the compulsion of the agencies of government. One who is a martyr to a principle—which may turn out in the end to be a delusion or an error—does not prove by his martyrdom that he has kept within the law.

I am authorized to state that Mr. *Justice* BRANDEIS and Mr. *Justice* STONE join in this opinion.

GIROUARD v. UNITED STATES

328 U.S. 61
ON WRIT OF CERTIORARI TO THE UNITED STATES CIRCUIT COURT OF APPEALS FOR THE FIRST CIRCUIT
Argued March 4, 1946 — Decided April 22, 1946

⊥**61** Mr. *Justice* DOUGLAS delivered the opinion of the Court.

In 1943 petitioner, a native of Canada, filed his petition of naturalization in the District Court of Massachusetts. He stated in his application that he understood the prin⊥**62**ciples of the government of the United States, believed in its form of government, and was willing to take the oath of allegiance which reads as follows:

"I hereby declare, on oath, that I absolutely and entirely renounce and abjure all allegiance and fidelity to any foreign prince, potentate, state, or sovereignty of whom or which I have heretofore been a subject or citizen; that I will support and defend the Constitution and laws of the United States of America against all enemies, foreign and domestic; that I will bear true faith and allegiance to the same; and that I take this obligation freely without any mental reservation or purpose of evasion: So Help Me God."

To the question in the application "If necessary, are you willing to take up arms in defense of this country?" he replied, "No (Non-combatant) Seventh Day Adventist." He explained that answer before the examiner by saying "it is a purely religious matter with me, I have no political or personal reasons other than that." He did not claim before his Selective Service board exemption from all military service, but only from combatant military duty. At the hearing in the District Court petitioner testified that he was a member of the Seventh Day Adventist denomination, of whom approximately 10,000 were then serving in the armed forces of the United States as non-combatants, especially in the medical corps; and that he was willing to serve in the army but would not bear arms. The District Court admitted him to citizenship. The Circuit Court of Appeals reversed, one judge dissenting. It took that action on the authority of *United States* v. *Schwimmer*; *United States* v. *Macintosh*, and *United States* v. *Bland*, saying that the facts of the present case brought it squarely within the principles of those cases. The case is here on ⊥**63** a petition for a writ of certiorari which we granted so that those authorities might be reexamined.

The *Schwimmer*, *Macintosh* and *Bland* Cases involved, as does the present one, a question of statutory construction. At the time of those cases, Congress required an alien, before admission to citizenship, to declare on oath in open court that "he will support and defend the Constitution and laws of the United States against all enemies, foreign and domestic, and bear true faith and allegiance to the same." It also required the court to be satisfied that the alien had during the five year period immediately preceding the date of his application "behaved as a man of good moral character, attached to the principles of the Constitution of the United States, and well disposed to the good order and happiness of the same." Those provisions were reenacted into the present law in substantially the same form.

While there are some factual distinctions between this case and the *Schwimmer* and *Macintosh* Cases, the *Bland* Case on its facts is indistinguishable. But the principle emerging from the three cases obliterates any factual distinction among them. As we recognized in *Re Summers*, they stand for the same general rule—that an alien who refuses to bear arms will not be admitted to citizenship. As an original proposition, we could not agree with that rule. The fallacies underlying ⊥**64** it were, we think, demonstrated in the dissents of Mr. *Justice* HOLMES in the *Schwimmer* Case and of Mr. *Chief Justice* HUGHES in the *Macintosh* Case.

The oath required of aliens does not in terms require that they promise to bear arms. Nor has Congress expressly made any such finding a prerequisite to citizenship. To hold that it is required is to read it into the Act by implication. But we could not assume that Congress intended to make such an abrupt and radical departure from our traditions unless it spoke in unequivocal terms.

The bearing of arms, important as it is, is not the only way in which our institutions may be supported and defended, even in times of great peril. Total war in its modern form dramatizes as never before the great cooperative effort necessary for victory. The nuclear physicists who developed the atomic bomb, the worker at his lathe, the seaman on cargo vessels, construction battalions, nurses, engineers, litter bearers, doctors, chaplains—these, too, made essential contributions. And many of them made the supreme sacrifice. *Mr. Justice HOLMES* stated in the *Schwimmer* Case that "the Quakers have done their share to make the country what it is." And the annals of the recent war show that many whose religious scruples prevented them from bearing arms, nevertheless were unselfish participants in the war effort. Refusal to bear arms is not necessarily a sign of disloyalty or a lack of attachment to our institutions. One may serve his country faithfully and devotedly, though his religious scruples make it impossible for him to shoulder a rifle. Devotion to one's country can be as real and as enduring among non-combatants as among combatants. One may adhere to what he deems to be his obligation to God and yet assume all military risks to secure victory. The effort of war is indivisible; and those whose religious scruples prevent them from killing are no less patriots than those whose special traits or handicaps result in their ⊥**65** assignment to duties far behind the fighting front. Each is making the utmost contribution according to his capacity. The fact that his role may be limited by religious convictions rather than by physical characteristics has no necessary bearing on his attachment to his country or on his willingness to support and defend it to his utmost.

Petitioner's religious scruples would not disqualify him from becoming a member of Congress or holding other public offices. While Article 6, Clause 3 of the Constitution provides that such officials, both of the United States and the several States, "shall be bound by Oath or Affirmation, to support this Constitution," it significantly adds that "no religious Test shall ever be required as a Qualification to any Office or public Trust under the United States." The oath required is in no material respect different from that prescribed for aliens under the Nationality Act. It has long contained the provision "that I will support and defend the Constitution of the United States against all enemies, foreign and domestic; that I will bear true faith and allegiance to the same; that I take this obligation freely, without any mental reservation or purpose of evasion." As *Mr. Chief Justice HUGHES* stated in his dissent in the *Macintosh* Case, "the history of the struggle for religious liberty, the large number of citizens of our country from the very beginning, who have been unwilling to sacrifice their religious convictions, and in particular, those who have been conscientiously opposed to war and who would not yield what they sincerely believed to be their allegiance to the will of God"—these considerations make it impossible to conclude "that such persons are to be deemed disqualified for public office in this country because of the requirement of the oath which must be taken before they enter upon their duties."

There is not the slightest suggestion that Congress set a stricter standard for aliens seeking admission to citizen⊥**66**ship than it did for officials who make and enforce the laws of the nation and administer its affairs. It is hard to believe that one need forsake his religious scruples to become a citizen but not to sit in the high councils of state.

As *Mr. Chief Justice HUGHES* pointed out (*United States* v. *Macintosh*) religious scruples against bearing arms have been recognized by Congress in the various draft laws. This is true of the Selective Training and Service Act of 1940 as it was of earlier acts. He who is inducted into the armed services takes an oath which includes the provision "that I will bear true faith and allegiance to the United States of America; that I will serve them honestly and faithfully against all their enemies whomsoever." Congress has thus recognized that one may adequately discharge his obligations as a citizen by rendering non-combatant as well as combatant services. This respect by Congress over the years for the conscience of those having ⊥**67** religious scruples against bearing arms is cogent evidence of the meaning of the oath. It is recognition by Congress that even in time of war one may truly support and defend our institutions though he stops short of using weapons of war.

That construction of the naturalization oath received new support in 1942. In the Second War Powers Act, Congress relaxed certain of the requirements for aliens who served honorably in the armed forces of the United States during World War II and provided machinery to expedite their naturalization. Residence requirements were relaxed, educational tests were eliminated, and no fees were required. But no change in the oath was made; nor was any change made in the requirement that the alien be attached to the principles of the Constitution. Yet it is clear that these new provisions cover non-combatants as well as combatants. If petitioner had served as a non-⊥**68**combatant (as he was willing to do), he could have been admitted to citizenship by taking the identical oath which he is willing to take. Can it be that the oath means one thing to one who has served to the extent permitted by his religious scruples and another thing to one equally willing to serve but who has not had the opportunity? It is not enough to say that petitioner is not entitled to the benefits of the new Act since he did not serve in the armed forces. He is not seeking the benefits of the expedited procedure and the relaxed requirements. The oath which he must take is identical with the oath which both non-combatants and combatants must take. It would, indeed, be a strange construction to say that "support and defend the Constitution and laws of the United States of America against all enemies, foreign and domestic" demands something more from some than it does from others. That oath can hardly be adequate for one who is unwilling to bear arms because of religious scruples and yet exact from another a promise to bear arms despite religious scruples.

Mr. Justice HOLMES stated in the *Schwimmer* Case: "if there is any principle of the Constitution that more imperatively calls for attachment than any other it is the principle of free thought—not free thought for those who agree with us but freedom for the thought that we hate. I think that we should adhere to that principle with regard to admission into, as well as to life within this country." The struggle for religious liberty has through the centuries been an effort to accommodate the demands of the State to the conscience of the individual. The victory for freedom of thought recorded in our Bill of Rights recognizes that in the domain of conscience there is a moral power higher than the State. Throughout the ages men have suffered death rather than subordinate their allegiance to God to the authority of the State. Freedom of religion guaranteed by the First Amendment is the product of that struggle. As we **⊥69** recently stated in *United States* v. *Ballard*, "Freedom of thought, which includes freedom of religious belief, is basic in a society of free men. *West Virginia State Bd. of Edu.* v. *Barnette*." The test oath is abhorrent to our tradition. Over the years Congress has meticulously respected that tradition and even in time of war has sought to accommodate the military requirements to the religious scruples of the individual. We do not believe that Congress intended to reverse that policy when it came to draft the naturalization oath. Such an abrupt and radical departure from our traditions should not be implied. See *Schneiderman* v. *United States*. Cogent evidence would be necessary to convince us that Congress took that course.

We conclude that the *Schwimmer*, *Macintosh* and *Bland* Cases do not state the correct rule of law.

We are met, however, with the argument that even though those cases were wrongly decided, Congress has adopted the rule which they announced. The argument runs as follows: Many efforts were made to amend the law so as to change the rule announced by those cases; but in every instance the bill died in committee. Moreover, when the Nationality Act of 1940 was passed, Congress reenacted the oath in its pre-existing form, though at the same time it made extensive changes in the requirements and procedure for naturalization. From this it is argued that Congress adopted and reenacted the rule of the *Schwimmer*, *Macintosh*, and *Bland* Cases.

We stated in *Helvering* v. *Hallock* that "It would require very persuasive circumstances enveloping Congressional silence to debar this Court from reexamining its own doctrines." It is at best treacherous to find in Congressional silence alone the adoption of a controlling rule of law. We do not think under the circumstances of this legislative history that we can properly **⊥70** place on the shoulders of Congress the burden of the Court's own error. The history of the 1940 Act is at most equivocal. It contains no affirmative recognition of the rule of the *Schwimmer*, *Macintosh* and *Bland* Cases. The silence of Congress and its inaction are as consistent with a desire to leave the problem fluid as they are with an adoption by silence of the rule of those cases. But for us, it is enough to say that since the date of those cases Congress never acted affirmatively on this question but once and that was in 1942. At that time, as we have noted, Congress specifically granted naturalization privileges to non-combatants who like petitioner were prevented from bearing arms by their religious scruples. That was affirmative recognition that one could be attached to the principles of our government and could support and defend it even though his religious convictions prevented him from bearing arms. And, as we have said, we cannot believe that the oath was designed to exact something more from one person than from another. Thus the affirmative action taken by Congress in 1942 negatives any inference that otherwise might be drawn from its silence when it reenacted the oath in 1940.

Reversed.

Mr. Justice JACKSON took no part in the consideration or decision of this case.

Mr. Chief Justice STONE, dissenting.

I think the judgment should be affirmed, for the reason that the court below, in applying the controlling provisions of the naturalization statutes, correctly applied them as earlier construed by this Court, whose construction Congress has adopted and confirmed.

In three cases decided more than fifteen years ago, this Court denied citizenship to applicants for naturalization who had announced that they proposed to take the prescribed **⊥71** oath of allegiance with the reservation or qualification that they would not, as naturalized citizens, assist in the defense of this country by force of arms or give their moral support to the government in any war which they did not believe to be morally justified or in the best interests of the country. See *United States* v. *Schwimmer*; *United States* v. *Macintosh*; *United States* v. *Bland*.

In each of these cases this Court held that the applicant had failed to meet the conditions which Congress had made prerequisite to naturalization by § 4 of the Naturalization Act of June 29, 1906, the provisions of which, here relevant, were enacted in the Nationality Act of October 14, 1940. Section 4 of the Naturalization Act of 1906, paragraph "Third," provided that before the admission to citizenship the applicant should declare on oath in open court that "he will support and defend the Constitution and laws of the United States against all enemies, foreign and domestic, and bear true faith and allegiance to the same." And paragraph "Fourth" required that before admission it be made to appear "to the satisfaction of the court admitting any alien to citizenship" that at least for a period of five years immediately preceding his application the applicant "has behaved as a man of good moral character, attached to the principles of the Constitution of the United States, and well disposed to the good order and happiness of the same." In applying these provisions in the cases mentioned, this Court held only that an applicant who is unable to take the oath of allegiance without the reservations or qualifications insisted upon by the applicants in those cases manifests his want of attachment to the principles of the Constitution and his unwillingness to meet **⊥72** the requirements of the oath, that he will support and defend the Constitution of the United States and bear true faith and allegiance to the same, and so does not comply with the statutory conditions of his naturalization. No question of the constitutional power of Congress to withhold citizenship on these grounds was involved. That power was not doubted. See *Selective Draft Law Cases* (*Arver* v. *United States*); *Hamilton* v. *University of California*. The only question was of construction of the statute which Congress at all times has been free to amend if dissatisfied with the construction adopted by the Court.

With three other Justices of the Court I dissented in the *Macintosh* and *Bland* Cases, for reasons which the Court now adopts as ground for overruling them. Since this Court in three considered earlier opinions has rejected the construction of the statute for which the dissenting Justices contended, the question, which for me is decisive of the present case, is whether Congress has likewise rejected that construction by its subsequent legislative action, and has adopted and confirmed the Court's earlier construction of the statutes in question. A study of Congressional action taken with respect to proposals for amendment of the naturalization laws since the decision in the *Schwimmer* Case, leads me to conclude that Congress has adopted and confirmed this Court's earlier construction **⊥73** of the naturalization laws. For that reason alone I think that the judgment should be affirmed.

The construction of the naturalization statutes, adopted by this Court in the three cases mentioned, immediately became the target of an active, publicized legislative attack in Congress which persisted for a period of eleven years, until the adoption of the Nationality Act in 1940. Two days after the *Schwimmer* Case was decided, a bill was introduced in the House, H. R. 3547, 71st Cong, 1st Sess, to give the Naturalization Act a construction contrary to that which had been given to it by this Court and which, if adopted, would have made the applicants rejected by this Court in the *Schwimmer*, *Macintosh* and *Bland* Cases eligible for citizenship. This effort to establish by Congressional action that the construction which this Court had placed on the Naturalization Act was not one which Congress had adopted or intended, was renewed without success after the decision in the *Macintosh* and *Bland* Cases, and was continued for a period of about ten years. All of these measures were of substantially the same pattern as H. R. 297, 72d Cong. 1st Sess, introduced December 8, 1931, at the first session of Congress, after the decision in the *Macintosh* Case. It provided that no person otherwise qualified "shall be debarred from citizenship by reason of his or her religious views or philosophical opinions with respect to the lawfulness of war as a means of settling international disputes, but every alien admitted to citizenship shall be subject to the same obligations as the native-born citizen." H. R. 3547, 71st Cong. 1st Sess, **⊥74** introduced immediately after the decision in the *Schwimmer* Case, had contained a like provision, but with the omission of the last clause beginning "but every alien." Hearings were had before the House Committee on Immigration and Naturalization on both bills at which their proponents had stated clearly their purpose to set aside the interpretation placed on the oath of allegiance by the *Schwimmer* and *Macintosh* Cases. There was opposition on each occasion. Bills identical with H. R. 297 were introduced in three later Congresses. None of these bills were reported out of Committee. The other proposals, all of which failed of passage, had the same purpose and differed only in phraseology.

Thus, for six successive Congresses, over a period of more than a decade, there were continuously pending before Congress in one form or another proposals to overturn the rulings in the three Supreme Court decisions in question. Congress declined to adopt these proposals after full hearings and after speeches on the floor advocating the change. In the meantime the decisions of this Court had been followed in *Clarke's Case*; *Beale* v. *United States*; *Re Warkentin*. In *Beale* v. *United States*, the court pointed out that the proposed amendments affecting the provisions of the statutes relating to admission to citizenship had failed, saying: "We must conclude, therefore, that these statutory requirements as construed **⊥75** by the Supreme Court have congressional sanction and approval."

Any doubts that such were the purpose and will of Congress would seem to have been dissipated by the reenactment by Congress in 1940 of Paragraphs "Third" and "Fourth" of § 4 of the Naturalization Act of 1906, and by the incorporation in the Act of 1940 of the very form of oath which had been administratively prescribed for the applicants in the *Schwimmer*, *Macintosh* and *Bland* Cases.

The Nationality Act of 1940 was a comprehensive, slowly matured and carefully considered revision of the naturalization laws. The preparation of this measure was not only delegated to a Congressional Committee, but was considered by a committee of Cabinet members, one of whom was the Attorney General. Both were aware of our decisions in the *Schwimmer* and related cases and that no other question pertinent to the naturalization laws had been as persistently and continuously before Congress in the ten years following the decision in the *Schwimmer* Case. The modifications in the provisions of Paragraphs "Third" and "Fourth" of § 4 of the 1906 Act show conclusively the careful attention which was given to them.

⊥**76** In the face of this legislative history the "failure of Congress to alter the Act after it had been judicially construed, and the enactment by Congress of legislation which implicitly recognizes the judicial construction as effective, is persuasive of legislative recognition that the judicial construction is the correct one. This is the more so where, as here, the application of the statute . . . has brought forth sharply conflicting views both on the Court and in Congress, and where after the matter has been fully brought to the attention of the public and the Congress, the latter has not seen fit to change the statute." *Apex Hosiery Co.* v. *Leader*. It is the responsibility of Congress, in reenacting a statute, to make known its purpose in a controversial matter of interpretation of its former language, at least when the matter has, for over a decade, been persistently brought to its attention. In the light of this legislative history, it is abundantly clear that Congress has performed that duty. In any case it is not lightly to be implied that Congress has failed to perform it and has delegated to this Court the responsibility of giving new content to language deliberately readopted after this Court has construed it. For us to make such an assumption is to discourage, if not to deny, legislative responsibility. By thus adopting and confirming this Court's construction of what Congress had enacted in the Naturalization Act of 1906 Congress gave that construction the same legal significance as though it had written the very words into the Act of 1940.

The only remaining question is whether Congress repealed this construction by enactment of the 1942 amendments ⊥**77** of the Nationality Act. That Act extended special privileges to applicants for naturalization who were aliens and who have served in the armed forces of the United States in time of war, by dispensing with or modifying existing requirements, relating to declarations of intention, period of residence, education, and fees. It left unchanged the requirements that the applicant's behavior show his attachment to the principles of the Constitution and that he take the oath of allegiance. In adopting the 1942 amendments Congress did not have before it any question of the oath of allegiance with which it had been concerned when it adopted the 1940 Act. In 1942 it was concerned with the grant of special favors to those seeking naturalization who had worn the uniform and rendered military service in time of war and who could satisfy such naturalization requirements as had not been dispensed with by the amendments. In the case of those entitled to avail themselves of these privileges, Congress left it to the naturalization authorities, as in other cases, to determine whether, by their applications and their conduct in the military service, they satisfy the requirements for naturalization which have not been waived.

It is pointed out that one of the 1942 amendments, 8 USCA §1004, provided that the provisions of the amendment should not apply to "any conscientious objector who performed no military duty whatever or refused to wear the uniform." It is said that the implication of this provision is that conscientious objectors who rendered noncombatant service and wore the uniform were, under the 1942 amendments, to be admitted to citizenship. From this it is argued that since the 1942 amendments apply to those who have been in noncombatant, as well as combatant, military service, the amendment must be taken to include some who have rendered ⊥**78** noncombatant service who are also conscientious objectors and who would be admitted to citizenship under the 1942 amendments, even though they made the same reservations as to the oath of allegiance as did the applicants in the *Schwimmer*, *Macintosh* and *Bland* Cases. And it is said that although the 1942 amendments are not applicable to petitioner, who has not been in military service, the oath cannot mean one thing as to him and another as to those who have been in the noncombatant service.

To these suggestions there are two answers. One is that if the 1942 amendment be construed as including noncombatants who are also conscientious objectors, who are unwilling to take the oath without the reservations made by the applicants in the *Schwimmer*, *Macintosh* and *Bland* Cases, the only effect would be to exempt noncombatant conscientious objectors from the requirements of the oath, which had clearly been made applicable to all objectors, including petitioner, by the Nationality Act of 1940, and from which petitioner was not exempted by the 1942 amendments. If such is the construction of the 1942 Act, there is no constitutional or statutory obstacle to Congress' taking such action. Congress if it saw fit could have admitted to citizenship those who had rendered noncombatant service, with a modified oath or without any oath at all. Petitioner has not been so exempted.

Since petitioner was never in the military or naval forces of the United States, we need not decide whether the 1942 amendments authorized any different oath for those who had been in noncombatant service than for others. The amendments have been construed as requiring the same oath, without reservations, from conscientious objectors, as from others. *Re Nielsen*. Not all of those who rendered noncombatant service were conscientious objectors. Few were. There were others in the noncombatant service who had announced their conscientious ⊥**79** objections to combatant service, who may have waived or abandoned their objections. Such was the experience in the First World War. See "Statement Concerning the Treatment of Conscientious Objectors in the Army," prepared and punished by direction of the Secretary of War, June 18, 1919. All such could have taken the oath without the reservations made by the applicants in the *Schwimmer*, *Macintosh* and *Bland* Cases and would have been entitled to the benefits of the 1942 amendments, provided they had performed military duty and had not refused to wear the uniform. The fact that Congress recognized by indirection, in 8 USCA § 1004, that those who had appeared in the role of conscientious objectors, might become citizens by taking the oath of allegiance and establishing their attachment to the principles of the Constitution, does not show that Congress dispensed with the requirements of the oath as construed by this Court and plainly confirmed by Congress in the Nationality Act of 1940. There is no necessary inconsistency in this respect between the 1940 Act and the 1942 amendments. Without it repeal by implication is not favored. The amendments and their legislative history give no hint of any purpose of Congress to relax, at least for persons who had rendered no military service, the requirements of the oath of allegiance and proof of attachment to the Constitution as this Court had interpreted them and as the Nationality Act of 1940 plainly required them to be interpreted. It is not the function of this Court to disregard the will of Congress in the exercise of its constitutional power.

Mr. *Justice Reed* and Mr. *Justice Frankfurter* join in this opinion.

UNITED STATES v. SEEGER (No. 50)

ON WRIT OF CERTIORARI TO THE UNITED STATES CIRCUIT COURT OF APPEALS FOR THE SECOND CIRCUIT

UNITED STATES v. JAKOBSON (No. 51)

ON WRIT OF CERTIORARI TO THE UNITED STATES CIRCUIT COURT OF APPEALS FOR THE SECOND CIRCUIT

PETER v. UNITED STATES (No. 29)

ON WRIT OF CERTIORARI TO THE UNITED STATES CIRCUIT COURT OF APPEALS FOR THE NINTH CIRCUIT
380 U.S. 163
Argued November 16 and 17, 1964 — Decided March 8, 1965

⊥**164** Mr. *Justice CLARK* delivered the opinion of the Court.

These cases involve claims of conscientious objectors under § 6(j) of the Universal Military Training and Service Act, 50 USC App § 456(j) (1958 ed.), which exempts from combatant training and service in the armed forces of the United States those persons who by ⊥**165** reason of their religious training and belief are conscientiously opposed to participation in war in any form. The cases were consolidated for argument and we consider them together although each involves different facts and circumstances. The parties raise the basic question of the constitutionality of the section which defines the term "religious training and belief," as used in the Act, as "an individual's belief in a relation to a Supreme Being involving duties superior to those arising from any human relation, but [not including] essentially political, sociological, or philosophical views or a merely personal moral code." The constitutional attack is launched under the First Amendment's Establishment and Free Exercise Clauses and is twofold: (1) The section does not exempt nonreligious conscientious objectors; and (2) it discriminates between different forms of religious expression in violation of the Due Process Clause of the Fifth Amendment. . . . We granted certiorari in each of the cases because of their importance in the administration of the Act.

We have concluded that Congress, in using the expression "Supreme Being" rather than the designation "God," was merely clarifying the meaning of religious training and belief so as to embrace all religions and to exclude essentially political, sociological or philosophical views. We believe that under this construction, the test of belief ⊥**166** "in a relation to a Supreme Being" is whether a given belief that is sincere and meaningful occupies a place in the life of its possessor parallel to that filled by the orthodox belief in God of one who clearly qualifies for the exemption. Where such beliefs have parallel positions in the lives of their respective holders we cannot say that one is "in a relation to a Supreme Being" and the other is not. We have concluded that the beliefs of the objectors in these cases meet these criteria, and, accordingly, we affirm the judgments in Nos. 50 and 51 and reverse the judgment in No. 29.

THE FACTS IN THE CASES

No. 50: Seeger was convicted in the District Court for the Southern District of New York of having refused to submit to induction in the armed forces. He was originally classified 1-A in 1953 by his local board, but this classification was changed in 1955 to 2-S (student) and he remained in this status until 1958 when he was reclassified 1-A. He first claimed exemption as a conscientious objector in 1957 after successive annual renewals of his student classification. Although he did not adopt verbatim the printed Selective Service System form, he declared that he was conscientiously opposed to participation in war in any form by reason of his "religious" belief; that he preferred to leave the question as to his belief in a Supreme Being open, "rather than answer 'yes' or 'no'"; that his "skepticism or disbelief in the existence of God" did "not necessarily mean lack of faith in anything whatsoever"; that his was a "belief in and devotion to goodness and virtue for their own sakes, and a religious faith in a purely ethical creed." He cited such personages as Plato, Aristotle and Spinoza for support of his ethical belief in intellectual and moral integrity "without belief in God, except in the remotest sense." His belief was found to be sincere, hon⊥**167**est, and made in good faith; and his conscientious objection to be based upon individual training and belief, both of which included research in religious and cultural fields. Seeger's claim, however, was denied solely because it was not based upon a "belief in a relation to a Supreme Being" as required by § 6(j) of the Act. At trial Seeger's counsel admitted that Seeger's belief was not in relation to a

Supreme Being as commonly understood, but contended that he was entitled to the exemption because "under the present law Mr. Seeger's position would also include definitions of religion which have been stated more recently," and could be "accommodated" under the definition of religious training and belief in the Act. He was convicted and the Court of Appeals reversed, holding that the Supreme Being requirement of the section distinguished "between internally derived and externally compelled beliefs" and was, therefore, an "impermissible classification" under the Due Process Clause of the Fifth Amendment.

No. 51: Jakobson was also convicted in the Southern District of New York on a charge of refusing to submit to induction. On his appeal the Court of Appeals reversed on the ground that rejection of his claim may have rested on the factual finding, erroneously made, that he did not believe in a Supreme Being as required by § 6(j).

Jakobson was originally classified 1-A in 1953 and intermittently enjoyed a student classification until 1956. It was not until April 1958 that he made claim to noncombatant classification (1-A-O) as a conscientious objector. He stated on the Selective Service System form that he believed in a "Supreme Being" who was "Creator of Man" in the sense of being "ultimately responsible for the existence of" man and who was "the Supreme Reality" of which "the existence of man is the *result.*" (Emphasis in the original.) He explained that his reli⊥**168**gious and social thinking had developed after much meditation and thought. He had concluded that man must be "partly spiritual" and, therefore, "partly akin to the Supreme Reality"; and that his "most important religious law" was that "no man ought ever to wilfully sacrifice another man's life as a means to any other end. . . ." In December 1958 he requested a 1-O classification since he felt that participation in any form of military service would involve him in "too many situations and relationships that would be a strain on [his] conscience that [he felt he] must avoid." He submitted a long memorandum of "notes on religion" in which he defined religion as the "*sum and essence of one's basic attitudes to the fundamental problems of human existence,*" (emphasis in the original); he said that he believed in "Godness" which was "the Ultimate Cause for the fact of the Being of the Universe"; that to deny its existence would but deny the existence of the universe because "anything that Is, has an Ultimate Cause for its Being." There was a relationship to Godness, he stated, in two directions, i.e., "vertically, towards Godness directly," and "horizontally, toward Godness through Mankind and the World." He accepted the latter one. The Board classified him 1-A-O and Jakobson appealed. The hearing officer found that the claim was based upon a personal moral code and that he was not sincere in his claim. The Appeal Board classified him 1-A. It did not indicate upon what ground it based its decision, i.e., insincerity or a conclusion that his belief was only a personal moral code. The Court of Appeals reversed, finding that his claim came within the requirements of § 6(j). Because it could not determine whether the Appeal Board had found that Jakobson's beliefs failed to come within the statutory definition, or whether it had concluded that he lacked sincerity, it directed dismissal of the indictment. ⊥**169**

No. 29: Forest Britt Peter was convicted in the Northern District of California on a charge of refusing to submit to induction. In his Selective Service System form he stated that he was not a member of a religious sect or organization; he failed to execute section VII of the questionnaire but attached to it a quotation expressing opposition to war, in which he stated that he concurred. In a later form he hedged the question as to his belief in a Supreme Being by saying that it depended on the definition and he appended a statement that he felt it a violation of his moral code to take human life and that he considered this belief superior to his obligation to the state. As to whether his conviction was religious, he quoted with approval Reverend John Haynes Holmes' definition of religion as "the consciousness of some power manifest in nature which helps man in the ordering of his life in harmony with its demands . . . [; it] is the supreme expression of human nature; it is man thinking his highest, feeling his deepest, and living his best." The source of his conviction he attributed to reading and meditation "in our democratic American culture, with its values derived from the western religious and philosophical tradition." As to his belief in a Supreme Being, Peter stated that he supposed "you could call that a belief in the Supreme Being or God. These just do not happen to be the words I use." In 1959 he was classified 1-A, although there was no evidence in the record that he was not sincere in his beliefs. After his conviction for failure to report for induction the Court of Appeals, assuming arguendo that he was sincere, affirmed.

BACKGROUND OF § 6(J)

Chief Justice HUGHES, in his opinion in *United States* v. *Macintosh*, enunciated the rationale behind the long recognition of conscientious objec⊥**170**tion to participation in war accorded by Congress in our various conscription laws when he declared that "in the forum of conscience, duty to a moral power higher than the State has always been maintained." In a similar vein Harlan Fiske Stone, later Chief Justice, drew from the Nation's past when he declared that "both morals and sound policy require that the state should not violate the conscience of the individual. All our history gives confirmation to the view that liberty of conscience has a moral and social value which makes it worthy of preservation at the hands of the state. So deep in its significance and vital, indeed, is it to the integrity of man's moral and spiritual nature that nothing short of the self-preservation of the state should warrant its violation; and it may well be questioned whether the state which preserves its life by a settled policy of violation of the conscience of the individual will not in fact ultimately lose it by the process."

Governmental recognition of the moral dilemma posed for persons of certain religious faiths by the call to arms came early in the history of this country. Various methods of ameliorating their difficulty were adopted by the Colonies, and were later perpetuated in state statutes and constitutions. Thus by the time of the Civil War there existed a state pattern of exempting conscientious objectors on religious grounds. In the Federal Militia Act of 1862 control of conscription was left primarily in the States. However, General Order No. 99, issued by the Adjutant General pursuant to that Act, provided for striking from the conscription list those who were exempted by the States; it also established a commutation or substitution system fashioned from earlier state enactments. With the Federal Conscription Act of 1863, ⊥**171** which enacted the commutation and substitution provisions of General Order No. 99, the Federal Government occupied the field entirely, and in the 1864 Draft Act, it extended exemptions to those conscientious objectors who were members of religious denominations opposed to the bearing of arms and who were prohibited from doing so by the articles of faith of their denominations. In that same year the Confederacy exempted certain pacifist sects from military duty.

The need for conscription did not again arise until World War I. The Draft Act of 1917 afforded exemptions to conscientious objectors who were affiliated with a "well-recognized religious sect or organization [then] organized and existing and whose existing creed or principles [forbade] its members to participate in war in any form. . . ." The Act required that all persons be inducted into the armed services, but allowed the conscientious objectors to perform noncombatant service in capacities designated by the President of the United States. Although the 1917 Act excused religious objectors only, in December 1917, the Secretary of War instructed that "personal scruples against war" be considered as constituting "conscientious objection." This Act, including its conscientious objector provisions, was upheld against constitutional attack in the *Selective Draft Law* Cases.

In adopting the 1940 Selective Training and Service Act Congress broadened the exemption afforded in the 1917 Act by making it unnecessary to belong to a pacifist religious sect if the claimant's own opposition to war was based on "religious training and belief." Those found to be within the exemption were not ⊥**172** inducted into the armed services but were assigned to noncombatant service under the supervision of the Selective Service System. The Congress recognized that one might be religious without belonging to an organized church just as surely as minority members of a faith not opposed to war might through religious reading reach a conviction against participation in war. Indeed, the consensus of the witnesses appearing before the congressional committees was that individual belief—rather than membership in a church or sect—determined the duties that God imposed upon a person in his everyday conduct; and that "there is a higher loyalty than loyalty to this country, loyalty to God." Thus, while shifting the test from membership in such a church to one's individual belief the Congress nevertheless continued its historic practice of excusing from armed service those who believed that they owed an obligation, superior to that due the state, of not participating in war in any form.

Between 1940 and 1948 two courts of appeals held that the phrase "religious training and belief" did not include philosophical, social or political policy. *United States* v. *Kauten; Berman* v. *United States*. Then in 1948 the Congress amended the language of the statute and declared that "religious training and belief" was to be defined as "an individual's belief in a relation to a Supreme Being involving duties superior to those arising from any human relation, but [not including] essentially political, sociological, or philosophical views or a merely personal moral code." The only significant mention of ⊥**173** this change in the provision appears in the report of the Senate Armed Services Committee recommending adoption. It said simply this: "This section reenacts substantially the same provisions as were found in subsection 5(g) of the 1940 act. Exemption extends to anyone who, because of religious training and belief in his relation to a Supreme Being, is conscientiously opposed to combatant military service or to both combatant and non-combatant military service."

INTERPRETATION OF § 6(J)

1. The crux of the problem lies in the phrase "religious training and belief" which Congress has defined as "belief in a relation to a Supreme Being involving duties superior to those arising from any human relation." In assigning meaning to this statutory language we may narrow the inquiry by noting briefly those scruples expressly excepted from the definition. The section excludes those persons who, disavowing religious belief, decide on the basis of essentially political, sociological or economic considerations that war is wrong and that they will have no part of it. These judgments have historically been reserved for the Government, and in matters which can be said to fall within these areas the conviction of the individual has never been permitted to override that of the state. The statute further excludes those whose opposition to war stems from a "merely personal moral code," a phrase to which we shall have occasion to turn later in discussing the application of § 6(j) to these cases. We also pause to take note of what is not involved in this litigation. No party claims to be an atheist or attacks the statute on this ground. The question is not, therefore, one between theistic and atheistic beliefs. We do not deal with ⊥**174** or intimate any decision on that situation in these cases. Nor do the parties claim the monotheistic belief that there is but one God; what they claim (with the possible exception of Seeger who bases his po-

sition here not on factual but on purely constitutional grounds) is that they adhere to theism, which is the "Belief in the existence of a god or gods; . . . Belief in superhuman powers or spiritual agencies in one or many gods, as opposed to atheism." Our question, therefore, is the narrow one: Does the term "Supreme Being" as used in § 6(j) mean the orthodox God or the broader concept of a power or being, or a faith, "to which all else is subordinate or upon which all else is ultimately dependent"? Webster's New International Dictionary (Second Edition). In considering this question we resolve it solely in relation to the language of § 6(j) and not otherwise.

2. Few would quarrel, we think, with the proposition that in no field of human endeavor has the tool of language proved so inadequate in the communication of ideas as it has in dealing with the fundamental questions of man's predicament in life, in death or in final judgment and retribution. This fact makes the task of discerning the intent of Congress in using the phrase "Supreme Being" a complex one. Nor is it made the easier by the richness and variety of spiritual life in our country. Over 250 sects inhabit our land. Some believe in a purely personal God, some in a supernatural deity; others think of religion as a way of life envisioning as its ultimate goal the day when all men can live together in perfect understanding and peace. There are those who think of God as the depth of our being; others, such as the Buddhists, strive for a state of lasting rest through self-denial and inner purification; in Hindu philosophy, the Supreme Being **⊥175** is the transcendental reality which is truth, knowledge and bliss. Even those religious groups which have traditionally opposed war in every form have splintered into various denominations: from 1940 to 1947 there were four denominations using the name "Friends"; the "Church of the Brethren" was the official name of the oldest and largest church body of four denominations composed of those commonly called Brethren; and the "Mennonite Church" was the largest of 17 denominations, including the Amish and Hutterites, grouped as "Mennonite bodies" in the 1936 report on the Census of Religious Bodies. This vast panoply of beliefs reveals the magnitude of the problem which faced the Congress when it set about providing an exemption from armed service. It also emphasizes the care that Congress realized was necessary in the fashioning of an exemption which would be in keeping with its long-established policy of not picking and choosing among religious beliefs.

In spite of the elusive nature of the inquiry, we are not without certain guidelines. In amending the 1940 Act, Congress adopted almost intact the language of *Chief Justice HUGHES* in *United States* v. *Macintosh:*

"The essence of religion is belief in a relation to God involving duties superior to those arising from any human relation."

By comparing the statutory definition with those words, however, it becomes readily apparent that the Congress deliberately broadened them by substituting the phrase "Supreme Being" for the appellation "God." And in so doing it is also significant that Congress did not elaborate on the form or nature of this higher authority which it chose to designate as "Supreme Being." By so refraining it must have had in mind the admonitions of the **⊥176** Chief Justice when he said in the same opinion that even the word "God" had myriad meanings for men of faith:

"[P]utting aside dogmas with their particular conceptions of deity, freedom of conscience itself implies respect for an innate conviction of paramount duty. The battle for religious liberty has been fought and won with respect to religious beliefs and practices, which are not in conflict with good order, upon the very ground of the supremacy of conscience within its proper field."

Moreover, the Senate Report on the bill specifically states that § 6(j) was intended to re-enact "substantially the same provisions as were found" in the 1940 Act. That statute, of course, refers to "religious training and belief" without more. Admittedly, all of the parties here purport to base their objection on religious belief. It appears, therefore, that we need only look to this clear statement of congressional intent as set out in the report. Under the 1940 Act it was necessary only to have a conviction based upon religious training and belief; we believe that is all that is required here. Within that phrase would come all sincere religious beliefs which are based upon a power or being, or upon a faith, to which all else is subordinate or upon which all else is ultimately dependent. The test might be stated in these words: A sincere and meaningful belief which occupies in the life of its possessor a place parallel to that filled by the God of those admittedly qualifying for the exemption comes within the statutory definition. This construction avoids imputing to Congress an intent to classify different religious beliefs, exempting some and excluding others, and is in accord with the well-established congressional policy of equal treatment for those whose opposition to service is grounded in their religious tenets. **⊥177**

3. The Government takes the position that since *Berman* v. *United States* was cited in the Senate Report on the 1948 Act, Congress must have desired to adopt the *Berman* interpretation of what constitutes "religious belief." Such a claim, however, will not bear scrutiny. First, we think it clear that an explicit statement of congressional intent deserves more weight than the parenthetical citation of a case which might stand for a number of things. Congress specifically stated that it intended to re-enact substantially the same provisions as were found in the 1940 Act. Moreover, the history of that Act reveals no evidence of a desire to restrict the concept of religious belief. On the contrary, the Chairman of the House Military Affairs Committee which reported out the 1940 exemption provisions stated:

"We heard the conscientious objectors and all of their representatives that we could possibly hear, and, summing it all up, their whole objection to the bill, aside from their objection to compulsory military training, was based upon the right of conscientious objection and in most instances to the right of the ministerial students to continue in their studies, and we have provided ample protection for those classes and those groups."

During the House debate on the bill, Mr. Faddis of Pennsylvania made the following statement:

"We have made provision to take care of conscientious objectors. I am sure the committee has had all the sympathy in the world with those who appeared claiming to have religious scruples against rendering military service in its various degrees. Some appeared who had conscientious scruples against handling lethal weapons, but who had no ⊥**178** scruples against performing other duties which did not actually bring them into combat. Others appeared who claimed to have conscientious scruples against participating in any of the activities that would go along with the Army. The committee took all of these into consideration and has written a bill which, I believe, will take care of all the reasonable objections of this class of people." 86 Cong. Rec. 11418 (1940).

Thus the history of the Act belies the notion that it was to be restrictive in application and available only to those believing in a traditional God. . . . ⊥**179**

Section 6(j), then, is no more than a clarification of the 1940 provision involving only certain "technical amendments," to use the words of Senator Gurney. As such it continues the congressional policy of providing exemption from military service for those whose opposition ⊥**180** is based on grounds that can fairly be said to be "religious." To hold otherwise would not only fly in the face of Congress' entire action in the past; it would ignore the historic position of our country on this issue since its founding.

4. Moreover, we believe this construction embraces the ever-broadening understanding of the modern religious community. The eminent Protestant theologian, Dr. Paul Tillich, whose views the Government concedes would come within the statute, identifies God not as a projection "out there" or beyond the skies but as the ground of our very being. The Court of Appeals stated in No. 51 that Jakobson's views "parallel [those of] this eminent theologian rather strikingly." In his book, Systematic Theology, Dr. Tillich says:

"I have written of the God above the God of theism. . . . In such a state [of self-affirmation] the God of both religious and theological language disappears. But something remains, namely, the seriousness of that doubt in which meaning within meaninglessness is affirmed. The source of this affirmation of meaning within meaninglessness, of certitude within doubt, is not the God of traditional theism but the 'God above God,' the power of being, which works through those who have no name for it, not even the name God."⊥**181**

Another eminent cleric, the bishop of Woolwich, John A. T. Robinson, in his book, Honest To God (1963), states:

"The Bible speaks of a God 'up there.' No doubt its picture of a three-decker universe, of 'the heaven above, the earth beneath and the waters under the earth,' was once taken quite literally. . . ." "[Later] *in place of a God who is literally or physically 'up there' we have accepted, as part of our mental furniture, a God who is spiritually or metaphysically 'out there.'* . . . But now it seems there is no room for him, not merely in the inn, but in the entire universe: for there are no vacant places left. In reality, of course, our new view of the universe has made not the slightest difference. . . ."

"But the idea of a God spiritually or metaphysically 'out there' dies very much harder. Indeed, most people would be seriously disturbed by the thought that it should need to die at all. For it is their God, and they have nothing to put in its place. . . . Every one of us lives with some mental picture of a God 'out there,' a God who 'exists' above and beyond the world he made, a God 'to' whom we pray and to whom we 'go' when we die." "But the signs are that we are reaching the point at which the whole conception of a God 'out there,' which has served us so well since the collapse of the three-decker universe, is itself becoming more of a hindrance than a help." (Emphasis in original.)

The Schema of the recent Ecumenical Council included a most significant declaration on religion: ⊥**182**

"The community of all peoples is one. One is their origin, for God made the entire human race live on all the face of the earth. One, too, is their ultimate end, God. Men expect from the various religions answers to the riddles of the human condition: What is man? What is the meaning and purpose of our lives? What is the moral good and what is sin? What are death, judgment, and retribution after death?

. . . . .

"Ever since primordial days, numerous peoples have had a certain perception of that hidden power which hovers over the course of things and over the events that make up the lives of men; some have even come to know of a Supreme Being and Father. Religions in an advanced culture have been able to use more refined concepts and a more developed language in their struggle for an answer to man's religious questions.

. . . . .

"Nothing that is true and holy in these religions is scorned by the Catholic Church. Ceaselessly the Church proclaims Christ, 'the Way, the Truth, and the Life,' in whom God reconciled all things to Himself. The Church regards with sincere reverence those ways of action and of life, precepts and teachings which, although they differ from the ones she sets forth, reflect nonetheless a ray of that Truth which enlightens all men."

Dr. David Saville Muzzey, a leader in the Ethical Culture Movement, states in his book, Ethics As a Religion (1951), that "[e]verybody except the avowed atheists (and they are comparatively few) believes in some kind of God," and that "The proper question to ask, therefore, is **⊥183** not the futile one, Do you believe in God? but rather, What *kind* of God do you believe in?" Dr. Muzzey attempts to answer that question:

"Instead of positing a personal God, whose existence man can neither prove nor disprove, the ethical concept is founded on human experience. It is anthropocentric, not theocentric. Religion, for all the various definitions that have been given of it, must surely mean the devotion of man to the highest ideal that he can conceive. And that ideal is a community of spirits in which the latent moral potentialities of men shall have been elicited by their reciprocal endeavors to cultivate the best in their fellow men. What ultimate reality is we do not know; but we have the faith that it expresses itself in the human world as the power which inspires in men moral purpose."

"Thus the 'God' that we love is not the figure on the great white throne, but the perfect pattern, envisioned by faith, of humanity as it should be, purged of the evil elements which retard its progress toward 'the knowledge, love and practice of the right.'"

These are but a few of the views that comprise the broad spectrum of religious beliefs found among us. But they demonstrate very clearly the diverse manners in which beliefs, equally paramount in the lives of their possessors, may be articulated. They further reveal the difficulties inherent in placing too narrow a construction on the provisions of § 6(j) and thereby lend conclusive support to the construction which we today find that Congress intended.

5. We recognize the difficulties that have always faced the trier of fact in these cases. We hope that the test that we lay down proves less onerous. The examiner is fur**⊥184**nished a standard that permits consideration of criteria with which he has had considerable experience. While the applicant's words may differ, the test is simple of application. It is essentially an objective one, namely, does the claimed belief occupy the same place in the life of the objector as an orthodox belief in God holds in the life of one clearly qualified for exemption?

Moreover, it must be remembered that in resolving these exemption problems one deals with the beliefs of different individuals who will articulate them in a multitude of ways. In such an intensely personal area, of course, the claim of the registrant that his belief is an essential part of a religious faith must be given great weight. Recognition of this was implicit in this language, cited by the *Berman* court from *State* v. *Amana Society:*

"Surely a scheme of life designed to obviate [man's inhumanity to man], and by removing temptations, and all the allurements of ambition and avarice, to nurture the virtues of unselfishness, patience, love, and service, ought not to be denounced as not pertaining to religion *when its devotees regard it as an essential tenet of their religious faith.*"

The validity of what he believes cannot be questioned. Some theologians, and indeed some examiners, might be tempted to question the existence of the registrant's "Supreme Being" or the truth of his concepts. But these are inquiries foreclosed to Government. As Mr. *Justice* DOUGLAS stated in *United States* v. *Ballard:* "Men may believe what they cannot prove. They may not be put to the proof of their religious doctrines or beliefs. Religious experiences which are as real as life to some may be incomprehensible to others." Local **⊥185** boards and courts in this sense are not free to reject beliefs because they consider them "incomprehensible." Their task is to decide whether the beliefs professed by a registrant are sincerely held and whether they are, in his own scheme of things, religious.

But we hasten to emphasize that while the "truth" of a belief is not open to question, there remains the significant question whether it is "truly held." This is the threshold question of sincerity which must be resolved in every case. It is, of course, a question of fact—a prime consideration to the validity of every claim for exemption as a conscientious objector. The Act provides a comprehensive scheme for assisting the Appeal Boards in making this determination, placing at their service the facilities of the Department of Justice, including the Federal Bureau of Investigation and hearing officers. Finally, we would point out that in *Estep* v. *United States*, this Court held that:

"The provision making the decisions of the local boards 'final' means to us that Congress chose not to give administrative action under this Act the customary scope of judicial review which obtains under other statutes. It means that the courts are not to weigh the evidence to determine whether the classification made by the local boards was justified. The decisions of the local boards made in conformity with the regulations are final even though they may be erroneous. The question of jurisdiction of the local board is reached only if there is no basis in fact for the classification which it gave the registrant."

APPLICATION OF § 6(J) TO THE INSTANT CASES

As we noted earlier, the statutory definition excepts those registrants whose beliefs are based on a "merely personal moral code." The records in these cases, how**⊥186**ever, show that at no time did any one of the applicants suggest that his objection was based on a "merely personal moral code." Indeed at the outset each of them claimed in his application that his objection was based on a religious belief. We have construed the statutory definition broadly and it follows that any exception to it must be interpreted narrowly. The use by Congress of the words "merely personal" seems to us to restrict the exception to a moral code which is not only personal but which is the sole basis for the registrant's belief and is in no way related to a Supreme Being. It follows, therefore, that if the claimed religious beliefs of the respective registrants in these cases meet the test that we lay down then their objections cannot be based on a "merely personal" moral code.

In Seeger, No. 50, the Court of Appeals failed to find sufficient "externally compelled beliefs." However, it did find that "it would seem impossible to say with assurance that [Seeger] is not bowing to 'external commands' in virtually the same sense as is the objector who defers to the will of a supernatural power." Of course, as we have said, the statute does not distinguish between externally and internally derived beliefs. Such a determination would, as the Court of Appeals observed, prove impossible as a practical matter, and we have found that Congress intended no such distinction.

The Court of Appeals also found that there was no question of the applicant's sincerity. He was a product of a devout Roman Catholic home; he was a close student of Quaker beliefs from which he said "much of [his] thought is derived"; he approved of their opposition to war in any form; he devoted his spare hours to the Amer⊥**187**ican Friends Service Committee and was assigned to hospital duty.

In summary, Seeger professed "religious belief" and "religious faith." He did not disavow any belief "in a relation to a Supreme Being"; indeed he stated that "the cosmic order does, perhaps, suggest a creative intelligence." He decried the tremendous "spiritual" price man must pay for his willingness to destroy human life. In light of his beliefs and the unquestioned sincerity with which he held them, we think the Board, had it applied the test we propose today, would have granted him the exemption. We think it clear that the beliefs which prompted his objection occupy the same place in his life as the belief in a traditional deity holds in the lives of his friends, the Quakers. We are reminded once more of Dr. Tillich's thoughts:

"And if that word [God] has not much meaning for you, translate it, and speak of the depths of your life, of the source of your being, of your ultimate concern, *of what you take seriously without any reservation*. Perhaps, in order to do so, you must forget everything traditional that you have learned about God. . . ." Tillich, The Shaking of the Foundations 57 (1948). (Emphasis supplied.)

It may be that Seeger did not clearly demonstrate what his beliefs were with regard to the usual understanding of the term "Supreme Being." But as we have said Congress did not intend that to be the test. We therefore *affirm* the judgment in No. 50. . . ⊥**188**

Mr. Justice DOUGLAS, concurring.

If I read the statute differently from the Court, I would have difficulties. For then those who embraced one religious faith rather than another would be subject to penalties; and that kind of discrimination, as we held in *Sherbert* v. *Verner*, would violate the Free Exercise Clause of the First Amendment. It would also result in a denial of equal protection by preferring some religions over others—an invidious discrimination that would run afoul of the Due Process Clause of the Fifth Amendment.

The legislative history of this Act leaves much in the dark. But it is, in my opinion, not a tour de force if we construe the words "Supreme Being" to include the cosmos, as well as an anthropomorphic entity. If it is a tour de force so to hold, it is no more so than other instances where we have gone to extremes to construe an Act of Congress to save it from demise on constitutional grounds. In a more extreme case than the present one we said that the words of a statute may be strained "in the candid service of avoiding a serious constitutional doubt." *United States* v. *Rumely*. ⊥**189**

The words "a Supreme Being" have no narrow technical meaning in the field of religion. Long before the birth of our Judeo-Christian civilization the idea of God had taken hold in many forms. Mention of only two—Hinduism and Buddhism—illustrates the fluidity and evanescent scope of the concept. In the Hindu *religion* the Supreme Being is conceived in the forms of several cult Deities. The chief of these, which stands for the Hindu Triad, are Brahma, Vishnu and Siva. Another Deity, and the one most widely worshipped, is Sakti, the Mother Goddess, conceived as power, both destructive and creative. Though Hindu religion encompasses the worship of many Deities, it believes in only one single God, the eternally existent One Being with his manifold attributes and manifestations. This idea is expressed in Rigveda, the earliest sacred text of the Hindus, in verse 46 of a hymn attributed to the mythical seer Dirghatamas (Rigveda, I, 164):

"They call it Indra, Mitra, Varuna and Agni
And also heavenly beautiful Garutman:
The Real is One, though sages name it variously—
They call it Agni, Yama, Matarisvan."

Indian *philosophy*, which comprises several schools of thought, has advanced different theories of the nature of the Supreme Being. According to the Upanisads, Hindu sacred texts, the Supreme Being is described as the power which creates and sustains everything, and to which the created things return upon dissolution. The word which is commonly used in the Upanisads to indicate the Supreme Being is Brahman. Philosophically, the ⊥**190** Supreme Being is the transcendental Reality which is Truth, Knowledge, and Bliss. It is the source of the entire universe. In this aspect Brahman is Isvara, a personal Lord and Creator of the universe, an object of worship. But, in the view of one school of thought, that of Sankara, even this is an imperfect and limited conception of Brahman which must be transcended: to think of Brahman as the Creator of the material world is necessarily to form a concept infected with illusion, or maya—which is what the world really is, in highest truth. Ultimately, mystically, Brahman must be understood as without attributes, as neti neti (not this, not that).

Buddhism—whose advent marked the reform of Hinduism—continued somewhat the same concept. As stated by Nancy Wilson Ross, "God—if I may borrow that word for a moment—the universe, and man are one indissoluble existence, one total whole. Only THIS—capital THIS—is. Anything and everything that appears to us as an individual entity or phenomenon, whether it be a planet or an atom, a mouse or a man, is but a temporary manifestation of THIS in form; every activity that takes place, whether it be birth or death, loving or eating breakfast, is but a temporary manifestation of THIS in activity. When we look at things this way, naturally we cannot believe that each individual person has been endowed with a special and individual soul or self. Each one of us is but a cell, as it were, in the body of the Great Self, a cell that comes into being, performs its functions, and passes away, transformed into another manifestation. Though we have temporary individuality, that temporary, limited individuality is not either a true self or our true self. Our true self is the Great Self, our true body is the Body of Reality, or the Dharmakaya, to give it its technical Buddhist name." The World of Zen. ⊥**191**

Does a Buddhist believe in "God" or a "Supreme Being"? That, of course, depends on how one defines "God," as one eminent student of Buddhism has explained:

"It has often been suggested that Buddhism is an atheistic system of thought, and this assumption has given rise to quite a number of discussions. Some have claimed that since Buddhism knew no God, it could not be a religion; others that since Buddhism obviously was a religion which knew no God, the belief in God was not essential to religion. These discussions assumed that *God* is an unambiguous term, which is by no means the case." Conze, Buddhism.

Dr. Conze then says that if "God" is taken to mean a personal Creator of the universe, then the Buddhist has no interest in the concept. But if "God" means something like the state of oneness with God as described by some Christian mystics, then the Buddhist surely believes in "God," since this state is almost indistinguishable from the Buddhist concept of Nirvana, "the supreme Reality; . . . the eternal, hidden and incomprehensible Peace." And finally, if "God" means one of the many Deities in at least superficially polytheistic religion Hinduism, then Buddhism tolerates a belief in many Gods: "the Buddhists believe that a Faith can be kept alive only if it can be adapted to the mental habits of the average person. In consequence, we find that, in the earlier Scriptures, the deities of Brahmanism are taken for granted and that, later on, the Buddhists adopted the local Gods of any district to which they came."

When the present Act was adopted in 1948 we were a nation of Buddhists, Confucianists, and Taoists, as well as Christians. Hawaii, then a Territory, was indeed filled with Buddhists, Buddhism being "probably the major ⊥**192** faith, if Protestantism and Roman Catholicism are deemed different faiths." Stokes and Pfeffer, Church and State in the United States. Organized Buddhism first came to Hawaii in 1887 when Japanese laborers were brought to work on the plantations. There are now numerous Buddhist sects in Hawaii, and the temple of the Shin sect in Honolulu is said to have the largest congregation in the city. See Mulholland, Religion in Hawaii.

In the continental United States Buddhism is found "in real strength" in Utah, Arizona, Washington, Oregon, and California. "Most of the Buddhists in the United States are Japanese or Japanese Americans; however, there are 'English' departments in San Francisco, Los Angeles, and Tacoma." Mead, Handbook of Denominations. The Buddhist Churches of North America, organized in 1914 as the Buddhist Mission of North America and incorporated under the present name in 1942, represent the Jodo Shinshu Sect of Buddhism in this country. This sect is the only Buddhist group reporting information to the annual Yearbook of American Churches. In 1961, the latest year for which figures are available, this group alone had 55 churches and an inclusive membership of 60,000; it maintained 89 church schools with a total enrollment of 11,150. Yearbook of American Churches. According to one source, the total number of Buddhists of all sects in North America is 171,000. See World Almanac.

When the Congress spoke in the vague general terms of a Supreme Being I cannot, therefore, assume that it was so parochial as to use the words in the narrow sense urged on us. I would attribute tolerance and sophistication to the Congress, commensurate with the religious complexion of our communities. In sum, I agree with the Court that any person opposed to war on the basis of a sincere belief, which in his life fills the same place as a be⊥**193**lief in God fills in the life of an orthodox religionist, is entitled to exemption under the statute. None comes to us an avowedly irreligious person or as an atheist; one, as a sincere believer in "goodness and virtue for their own sakes." His questions and doubts on theological issues, and his wonder, are no more alien to the statutory standard than are the awe-inspired questions of a devout Buddhist.

WELSH v. UNITED STATES

398 U.S. 333

ON WRIT OF CERTIORARI TO THE UNITED STATES CIRCUIT COURT OF APPEALS FOR THE NINTH CIRCUIT

Argued January 20, 1970 — Decided June 15, 1970

⊥**335** Mr. *Justice BLACK* announced the judgment of the Court and delivered an opinion in which Mr. *Justice DOUGLAS*, Mr. *Justice BRENNAN*, and Mr. *Justice MARSHALL* join.

The petitioner, Elliott Ashton Welsh II, was convicted by a United States District Judge of refusing to submit to induction into the Armed Forces in violation of 50 USC App § 462(a), and was on June 1, 1966, sentenced to imprisonment for three years. One of petitioner's defenses to the prosecution was that § 6(j) of the Universal Military Training and Service Act exempted him from combat and noncombat service because he was "by reason of religious training and belief . . . conscientiously opposed to participation in war in any form."

After finding that there was no religious basis for petitioner's conscientious objector claim, the Court of Appeals, Judge Hamley dissenting, affirmed the conviction. We granted certiorari chiefly to review the contention that Welsh's conviction should be set aside on the basis of this Court's decision in *United States* v. *Seeger*. For the reasons to be stated, and without passing upon the constitutional arguments that have been raised, we vote to reverse this conviction because of its fundamental inconsistency with the *United States* v. *Seeger*.

The controlling facts in this case are strikingly similar to those in *Seeger*. Both Seeger and Welsh were brought up in religious homes and attended church in their childhood, but in neither case was this church one which taught its members not to engage in war at any time for **⊥336** any reason. Neither Seeger nor Welsh continued his childhood religious ties into his young manhood, and neither belonged to any religious group or adhered to the teaching of any organized religion during the period of his involvement with the Selective Service System. At the time of registration for the draft, neither had yet come to accept pacifist principles. Their views on war developed only in subsequent years, but when their ideas did fully mature both made application to their local draft boards for conscientious objector exemptions from military service under § 6(j) of the Universal Military Training and Service Act. That section then provided in part:

"Nothing contained in this title shall be construed to require any person to be subject to combatant training and service in the armed forces of the United States who, by reason of religious training and belief, is conscientiously opposed to participation in war in any form. Religious training and belief in this connection means an individual's belief in a relation to a Supreme Being involving duties superior to those arising from any human relation, but does not include essentially political, sociological, or philosophical news or a merely personal moral code."

In filling out their exemption applications both Seeger and Welsh were unable to sign the statement that, as printed in the Selective Service form, stated "I am, by reason of my religious training and belief, conscien**⊥337**tiously opposed to participation in war in any form." Seeger could sign only after striking the words "training and" and putting quotations marks around the word "religious." Welsh could sign only after striking the words "my religious training and." On those same applications, neither could definitely affirm or deny that he believed in a "Supreme Being," both stating that they preferred to leave the question open. But both Seeger and Welsh affirmed on those applications that they held deep conscientious scruples against taking part in wars where people were killed. Both strongly believed that killing in war was wrong, unethical, and immoral, and their consciences forbade them to take part in such an evil practice. Their objection to participating in war in any form could not be said to come from a "still, small voice of conscience"; rather, for them that voice was so loud and insistent that both men preferred to go to jail rather than serve in the Armed Forces. There was never any question about the sincerity and depth of Seeger's convictions as a conscientious objector, and the same is true of Welsh. In this regard the Court of Appeals noted, "[t]he government concedes that [Welsh's] beliefs are held with the strength of more traditional religious convictions." But in both cases the Selective Service System concluded that the beliefs of these men were in some sense insufficiently "religious" to qualify them for conscientious objector exemptions under the terms of § 6(j). Seeger's conscientious objector claim was denied "solely because it was not based upon a 'belief in a relation to a Supreme Being' as required by § 6(j) of the Act," *United States* v. *Seeger*, while Welsh was **⊥338** denied the exemption because his Appeal Board and the Department of Justice hearing officer "could find no religious basis for the registrant's beliefs, opinions and convictions." Both Seeger and Welsh subsequently refused to submit to induction into the military and both were convicted of that offense. . . . **⊥340**

In the case before us the Government seeks to distinguish our holding in *Seeger* on basically two grounds, **⊥341** both of which were relied upon by the Court of Appeals in affirming Welsh's conviction. First, it is stressed that Welsh was far more insistent and explicit than Seeger in denying that his views were religious. For example, in filling out their conscientious objector applications, Seeger put quotation marks around the word "religious," but Welsh struck the word "religious" entirely and later characterized his beliefs as having been formed "by reading in the fields of history and sociology." The Court of Appeals found that Welsh had "denied that his objection to war was premised on religious belief" and concluded that "[t]he Appeal Board was entitled to take him at his word." We think this attempt to distinguish *Seeger* fails for the reason that it places undue emphasis on the registrant's interpretation of his own beliefs. The Court's statement in *Seeger* that a registrant's characterization of his own belief as "religious" should carry great weight, does not imply that his declaration that his views are nonreligious should be treated similarly. When a registrant states that his objections to war are "religious," that information is highly relevant to the question of the function his beliefs have in his life. But very few registrants are fully aware of the broad scope of the word "religious" as used in § 6(j), and accordingly a registrant's statement that his beliefs are nonreligious is a highly unreliable guide for those charged with administering the exemption. Welsh himself presents a case in point. Although he originally characterized his beliefs as nonreligious, he later upon reflection wrote a long and thoughtful letter to his Appeal Board in which he declared that his beliefs were "certainly religious in the ethical sense of the word." He explained:

"I believe I mentioned taking of life as not being, for me, a religious wrong. Again, I assumed Mr. Brady (the Department of Justice hearing **⊥342** officer) was using the word 'religious' in the conventional sense, and, in order to be perfectly honest did not characterize my belief as 'religious.'"

The Government also seeks to distinguish *Seeger* on the ground that Welsh's views, unlike Seeger's, were "essentially political, sociological, or philosophical views or a merely personal moral code." As previously noted, the Government made the same argument about Seeger, and not without reason, for Seeger's views had a substantial political dimension. In this case, Welsh's conscientious objection to war was undeniably based in part on his perception of world politics. In a letter to his local board, he wrote:

"I can only act according to what I am and what I see. And I see that the military complex wastes both human and material resources, that it fosters disregard for (what I consider a paramount concern) human needs and ends; I see that the means we employ to 'defend' our 'way of life' profoundly change that way of life. I see that in our failure to recognize the political, social, and economic realities of the world, we, *as a nation*, fail our responsibility *as a nation*."

We certainly do not think that § 6(j)'s exclusion of those persons with "essentially political, sociological, or philosophical views or a merely personal moral code" should be read to exclude those who hold strong beliefs about our domestic and foreign affairs or even those whose conscientious objection to participation in all wars is founded to a substantial extent upon considerations of public policy. The two groups of registrants that obviously do fall within these exclusions from the exemption are those whose beliefs are not deeply held and those whose objection to war does not rest at all upon moral, ethical, or religious principle but instead rests solely upon **⊥343** considerations of policy, pragmatism, or expediency. In applying § 6(j)'s exclusion of those whose views are "essentially political, sociological, or philosophical" or of those who have a "merely personal moral code," it should be remembered that these exclusions are definitional and do not therefore restrict the category of persons who are conscientious objectors by "religious training and belief." Once the Selective Service System has taken the first step and determined under the standards set out here and in *Seeger* that the registrant is a "religious" conscientious objector, it follows that his views cannot be "essentially political, sociological, or philosophical." Nor can they be a "merely personal moral code."

Welsh stated that he "believe[d] the taking of life—anyone's life—to be morally wrong." In his original conscientious objector application he wrote the following:

"I believe that human life is valuable in and of itself; in its living; therefore I will not injure or kill another human being. This belief (and the corresponding 'duty' to abstain from violence toward another person) is not 'superior to those arising from any human relation.' On the contrary: *it is essential to every human relation*. I cannot, therefore, conscientiously comply with the Government's insistence that I assume duties which I feel are immoral and totally repugnant." Welsh elaborated his beliefs in later communications with Selective Service officials. On the basis of these beliefs and the conclusion of the Court of Appeals that he held them "with the strength of more traditional religious convictions," we think Welsh was clearly entitled to a conscientious objector exemption. Section **⊥344** 6(j) requires no more. That section exempts from military service all those whose consciences, spurred by deeply held moral, ethical, or religious beliefs, would give them no rest or peace if they allowed themselves to become a part of an instrument of war.

The judgment is Reversed.

Mr. *Justice* BLACKMUN took no part in the consideration or decision of this case.

Mr. *Justice* HARLAN, concurring in the result.

Candor requires me to say that I joined the Court's opinion in *United States* v. *Seeger* only with the gravest misgivings as to whether it was a legitimate exercise in statutory construction, and today's decision convinces me that in doing so I made a mistake which I should now acknowledge.

In *Seeger* the Court construed § 6(j) of the Universal Military Training and Service Act so as to sustain a conscientious objector claim not founded on a theistic belief.... **⊥345**

Today the prevailing opinion makes explicit its total elimination of the statutorily required religious content for a conscientious objector exemption. The prevailing opinion now says: "If an individual deeply and sincerely holds beliefs that are *purely ethical* or *moral* in source and content but that nevertheless impose upon him a duty of conscience to refrain from participating in any war at any time" (emphasis added), he qualifies for a § 6(j) exemption.

In my opinion, the liberties taken with the statute both in *Seeger* and today's decision cannot be justified in the name of the familiar doctrine of construing federal statutes in a manner that will avoid possible constitutional infirmities in them. There are limits to the permissible application of that doctrine, and, as I will undertake to show in this opinion, those limits were crossed in *Seeger*, and even more apparently have been exceeded in the present case. I therefore find myself unable to escape facing the constitutional issue that this case squarely presents: whether § 6(j) in limiting this draft exemption to those opposed to war in general because of theistic beliefs runs afoul of the religious clauses of the First Amendment. For reasons later appearing I believe it does, and on that basis I concur in the judgment reversing this conviction, and adopt the test announced by Mr. *Justice* BLACK, not as a matter of statutory construction, but as the touchstone for salvaging a congressional policy of long standing that would otherwise have to be nullified.

I. . . .

⊥**351** B

Against this legislative history it is a remarkable feat of judicial surgery to remove, as did *Seeger*, the theistic requirement of § 6(j). The prevailing opinion today, however, in the name of interpreting the will of Congress, has performed a lobotomy and completely transformed the statute by reading out of it any distinction between religiously acquired beliefs and those deriving from "essentially political, sociological, or philosophical views or a merely personal moral code. . . ."⊥**354**

Unless we are to assume an Alice-in-Wonderland world where words have no meaning, I think it fair to say that Congress' choice of language cannot fail to convey to the discerning reader the very policy choice that the prevailing opinion today completely obliterates: that between conventional religions that usually have an organized and formal structure and dogma and a cohesive group identity, even when nontheistic, and cults that represent schools of thought and in the usual case are without formal structure or are, at most, loose and informal associations of individuals who share common ethical, moral, or intellectual views.

II

When the plain thrust of a legislative enactment can only be circumvented by distortion to avert an inevitable constitutional collision, it is only by exalting form over substance that one can justify this veering off the path that has been plainly marked by the statute. Such a course betrays extreme skepticism as to constitutionality, and, in this instance, reflects a groping to preserve the conscientious objector exemption at all cost.

I cannot subscribe to a wholly emasculated construction of a statute to avoid facing a latent constitutional question, in purported fidelity to the salutary doctrine of avoiding unnecessary resolution of constitutional issues, a principle to which I fully adhere. . . . ⊥**356**

III

The constitutional question that must be faced in this case is whether a statute that defers to the individual's conscience only when his views emanate from adherence to theistic religious beliefs is within the power of Congress. Congress, of course, could, entirely consistently with the requirements of the Constitution, eliminate *all* exemptions for conscientious objectors. Such a course would be wholly "neutral" and, in my view, would not offend the Free Exercise Clause, for reasons set forth in my dissenting opinion in *Sherbert* v. *Verner*. . . . ⊥**357**

The "radius" of this legislation is the conscientiousness with which an individual opposes war in general, yet the statute, as I think it must be construed, excludes from its "scope" individuals motivated by teachings of non-theistic religions, and individuals guided by an inner ethical voice that bespeaks secular and not "religious" reflection. It not only accords a preference to the "religious" but also disadvantages adherents of religions that do not worship a Supreme Being. The constitutional infirmity cannot be cured, moreover, even by an impermissible construction that eliminates the theistic requirement and simply draws the line between religious and nonreligious. This in my view offends the Establishment Clause and is that kind of classification ⊥**358** that this Court has condemned. . . .

⊥**365** The policy of exempting religious conscientious objectors is one of longstanding tradition in this country and accords recognition to what is, in a diverse and "open" society, the important value of reconciling in⊥**366**dividuality of belief with practical exigencies whenever possible. It dates back to colonial times and has been perpetuated in state and federal conscription statutes. That it has been phrased in religious terms reflects, I assume, the fact that ethics and morals, while the concern of secular philosophy, have traditionally been matters taught by organized religion and that for most individuals spiritual and ethical nourishment is derived from that source. It further reflects, I would suppose, the assumption that beliefs emanating from a religious source are probably held with great intensity.

When a policy has roots so deeply embedded in history, there is a compelling reason for a court to hazard the necessary statutory repairs if they can be made within the administrative framework of the statute and without impairing other legislative goals, even though they entail, not simply eliminating an offending section, but rather building upon it. Thus I am prepared to accept the prevailing opinion's conscientious objector test, not as a reflection of congressional statutory intent but as patch⊥**367**work of judicial making that cures the defect of underinclusion in § 6(j) and can be administered by local boards in the usual course of business. Like the prevailing opinion, I also conclude that petitioner's beliefs are held with the required intensity and consequently vote to *reverse* the judgment of conviction.

Mr. Justice WHITE, with whom *The* CHIEF JUSTICE and Mr. *Justice* STEWART join, dissenting.

Whether or not *United States* v. *Seeger* accurately reflected the intent of Congress in providing draft exemptions for religious conscientious objectors to war, I cannot join today's construction of § 6(j) extending draft exemption to those who disclaim religious objections to war and whose views about war represent a purely personal code arising not from religious training and belief as the statute requires but from readings in philosophy, history, and sociology. Our obli⊥**368**gation in statutory construction cases is to enforce the will of Congress, not our own; and as Mr. *Justice* HARLAN has demonstrated, construing § 6(j) to include Welsh exempts from the draft a class of persons to whom Congress has expressly denied an exemption.

For me that conclusion should end this case. Even if Welsh is quite right in asserting that exempting religious believers is an establishment of religion forbidden by the First Amendment, he nevertheless remains one of those persons whom Congress took pains not to relieve from military duty. Whether or not § 6(j) is constitutional, Welsh had no First Amendment excuse for refusing to report for induction. If it is contrary to the express will of Congress to exempt Welsh, as I think it is, then there is no warrant for saving the religious exemption and the statute by redrafting it in this Court to include Welsh and all others like him. . . . ⊥**369**

If I am wrong in thinking that Welsh cannot benefit from invalidation of § 6(j) on Establishment Clause grounds, I would nevertheless affirm his conviction; for I cannot hold that Congress violated the Clause in exempting from the draft all those who oppose war by reason of religious training and belief. In exempting religious conscientious objectors, Congress was making one of two judgments, perhaps both. First, § 6(j) may represent a purely practical judgment that religious objectors, however admirable, would be of no more use in combat than many others unqualified for military service. Exemption was not extended to them to further religious belief or practice but to limit military service to those who were prepared to undertake the fighting that the armed services have to do. On this basis, the exemption has neither the primary purpose nor the effect of furthering religion. As *Mr. Justice FRANKFURTER*, joined by *Mr. Justice HARLAN*, said, in a separate opinion in the Sunday Closing Law Cases, an establishment contention "can prevail only if the absence of any substantial legislative purpose other than a religious one is made to appear."

Second, Congress may have granted the exemption because otherwise religious objectors would be forced into conduct that their religions forbid and because ⊥**370** in the view of Congress to deny the exemption would violate the Free Exercise Clause or at least raise grave problems in this respect. True, this Court has more than once stated its unwillingness to construe the First Amendment, standing alone, as requiring draft exemptions for religious believers. But this Court is not alone in being obliged to construe the Constitution in the course of its work; nor does it even approach having a monopoly on the wisdom and insight appropriate to the task. Legislative exemptions for those with religious convictions against war date from colonial days. As *Chief Justice HUGHES* explained in his dissent in *United States* v. *Macintosh*, the importance of giving immunity to those having conscientious scruples against bearing arms has consistently been emphasized in debates in Congress and such draft exemptions are "'indicative of the actual operation of the principles of the Constitution.'" However this Court might construe the First Amendment, Congress has regularly steered clear of free exercise problems by granting exemptions to those who conscientiously oppose war on religious grounds. . . . ⊥**371**

Congress has the power "To raise and support Armies" and "To make all Laws which shall be necessary and proper for carrying into Execution" that power. Art I, § 8. The power to raise armies must be exercised consistently with the First Amendment which, among other things, forbids laws prohibiting the free exercise of religion. It is surely essential therefore—surely "necessary and proper" —in enacting laws for the raising of armies to take account of the First Amendment and to avoid possible violations of the Free Exercise Clause. If this was the course Congress took, then just as in *Katzenbach* v. *Morgan* where we accepted the judgment of Congress as to what legislation was appropriate to enforce the Equal Protection Clause of the Fourteenth Amendment, here we should respect congressional judgment accommodating the Free Exercise Clause and the power to raise armies. This involves no surrender of the Court's function as ultimate arbiter in disputes over interpretation of the Constitution. But it was enough in *Katzenbach* "to perceive a basis upon which the Congress might resolve the conflict as it did," and plainly in the case before us there is an arguable basis for § 6(j) in the Free Exercise Clause since, without the exemption, the law would compel some members of the public to engage in combat ⊥**372** operations contrary to their religious convictions. Indeed, one federal court has recently held that to draft a man for combat service contrary to his conscientious beliefs would violate the First Amendment. *United States* v. *Sisson*. There being substantial roots in the Free Exercise Clause for § 6(j) I would not frustrate congressional will by construing the Establishment Clause to condition the exemption for religionists upon extending the exemption also to those who object to war on nonreligious grounds.

We have said that neither support nor hostility, but neutrality, is the goal of the religion clauses of the First Amendment. "Neutrality," however, is not self-defining. If it is "favoritism" and not "neutrality" to exempt religious believers from the draft, is it "neutrality" and not "inhibition" of religion to compel religious believers to fight when they have special reasons for not doing so, reasons to which the Constitution gives particular recognition? It cannot be ignored that the First Amendment itself contains a religious classification. The Amendment protects belief and speech, but as a general proposition, the free speech provisions stop short of immunizing conduct from official regulation. The Free Exercise Clause, however, has a deeper cut: it protects conduct as well as religious belief and speech. "[I]t safeguards the free exercise of the chosen form of religion. Thus the Amendment embraces two concepts,—freedom to believe and freedom to act. The first is absolute but, in the nature of things, the second cannot be." *Cantwell* v. *Connecticut*. Although socially harmful acts may as a rule be banned despite the Free Exercise Clause even where religiously motivated, there is an area of conduct that cannot be forbidden to religious practitioners but which may be forbidden to others. ⊥**373** We should thus not labor to find a violation of the Establishment Clause when free exercise values prompt Congress to relieve religious believers from the burdens of the law at least in those instances where the law is not merely prohibitory but commands the performance of military duties that are forbidden by a man's religion. . . .

The Establishment Clause as construed by this Court unquestionably has independent significance; its function is not wholly auxiliary to the Free Exercise Clause. ⊥**374** It bans some involvements of the State with religion that otherwise might be consistent with the Free Exercise Clause. But when in the rationally based judgment of Congress free exercise of religion calls for shielding religious objectors from compulsory combat duty, I am reluctant to frustrate the legislative will by striking down the statutory exemption because it does not also reach those to whom the Free Exercise Clause offers no protection whatsoever.

I would affirm the judgment below.

GILLETTE v. UNITED STATES (No. 85)

ON WRIT OF CERTIORARI TO THE UNITED STATES CIRCUIT COURT OF APPEALS FOR THE SECOND CIRCUIT

NEGRE v. LARSEN (No. 325)

ON WRIT OF CERTIORARI TO THE UNITED STATES CIRCUIT COURT OF APPEALS FOR THE NINTH CIRCUIT

401 U.S. 437

Argued December 9, 1970 — Decided March 8, 1971

⊥**439** Mr. *Justice MARSHALL* delivered the opinion of the Court.

These cases present the question whether conscientious objection to a particular war, rather than objection to war as such, relieves the objector from responsibilities of military training and service. Specifically, we are called upon to decide whether conscientious scruples relating to a particular conflict are within the purview of established provisions relieving conscientious objectors to war from military service. Both petitioners also invoke constitutional principles barring government interference with the exercise of religion and requiring governmental neutrality in matters of religion.

In No. 85, petitioner Gillette was convicted of wilful failure to report for induction into the armed forces. Gillette defended on the ground that he should have been ruled exempt from induction as a conscientious objector to war. In support of his unsuccessful request for classification as a conscientious objector, this petitioner had stated his willingness to participate in a war of national defense or a war sponsored by the United Nations as a peace-keeping measure, but declared his opposition to American military operations in Vietnam, which he characterized as "unjust." Petitioner concluded that he could not in conscience enter and serve in the armed forces during the period of the Vietnam conflict. Gillette's view of his duty to abstain from any involvement in a war seen as unjust is, in his words, "based on a humanist approach to religion," and his personal decision concerning military service was guided by fundamental principles of conscience and deeply held views about the purpose and obligation of human existence. ⊥**440**

The District Court determined that there was a basis in fact to support administrative denial of exemption in Gillette's case. The denial of exemption was upheld, and Gillette's defense to the criminal charge rejected, not because of doubt about the sincerity or the religious character of petitioner's objection to military service, but because his objection ran to a particular war. In affirming the conviction, the Court of Appeals concluded that Gillette's conscientious beliefs "were specifically directed against the war in Vietnam," while the relevant exemption provision of the Military Selective Service Act of 1967, "requires opposition 'to participation in war in any form.'"

In No. 325, petitioner Negre, after induction into the Army, completion of basic training, and receipt of orders for Vietnam duty, commenced proceedings looking to his discharge as a conscientious objector to war. Application for discharge was denied, and Negre sought judicial relief by habeas corpus. The District Court found a basis in fact for the Army's rejection of petitioner's application for discharge. Habeas relief was denied, and the denial was affirmed on appeal, because, in the language of the Court of Appeals, Negre "objects to the war in Vietnam, not to all wars," and therefore does "not qualify for separation [from the Army], as a conscientious objector." Again, no question is raised as to the sincerity or the religious quality of this petitioner's views. In line with religious counseling, and numerous religious texts, Negre, ⊥**441** a devout Catholic, believes that it is his duty as a faithful Catholic to discriminate between "just" and "unjust" wars, and to forswear participation in the latter. His assessment of the Vietnam conflict as an unjust war became clear in his mind after completion of infantry training, and Negre is now firmly of the view that any personal involvement in that war would contravene his conscience and "all that I had been taught in my religious training."

We granted certiorari in these cases in order to resolve vital issues concerning the exercise of congressional power to raise and support armies, as affected by the religious guarantees of the First Amendment. We affirm the judgments below in both cases.

I

Each petitioner claims a nonconstitutional right to be relieved of the duty of military service in virtue of his conscientious scruples. Both claims turn on the proper construction of § 6(j) of the Military Selective Service Act of 1967 which provides:

"Nothing contained in this title . . . shall be construed to require any person to be subject to combatant training and service in the armed forces of the United States who, by reason of religious training and belief, is conscientiously opposed to participation in war in any form." ⊥**442**

This language controls Gillette's claim to exemption, which was asserted administratively prior to the point of induction. Department of Defense Directive No. 1300.6 (May 10, 1968), prescribes that post-induction claims to conscientious objector status shall be honored, if valid, by the various branches of the armed forces. Section 6(j) of the Act, as construed by the courts, is incorporated by the various service regulations issued pursuant to the Directive, and thus the standards for measuring claims of in-service objectors, such as Negre, are the same as the statutory tests applicable in a pre-induction situation. ⊥**443**

For purposes of determining the statutory status of conscientious objection to a particular war, the focal language of § 6(j) is the phrase, "conscientiously opposed to participation in war in any form." This language, on a straightforward reading, can bear but one meaning; that conscientious scruples relating to war and military service must amount to conscientious opposition to participating personally in any war and all war.

A different result cannot be supported by reliance on the materials of legislative history. Petitioners and ⊥**444** *amici* point to no episode or pronouncement in the legislative history of § 6(j), or of predecessor provisions, that tends to overthrow the obvious interpretation of the words themselves. ⊥**445**

It is true that the legislative materials reveal a deep concern for the situation of conscientious objectors to war, who absent special status would be put to a hard choice between contravening imperatives of religion and conscience or suffering penalties. Moreover, there are clear indications that congressional reluctance to impose such a choice stems from a recognition of the value of conscientious action to the democratic community at large, and from respect for the general proposition that fundamental principles of conscience and religious duty may sometimes override the demands of the secular state. But there are countervailing considerations, which are also the concern of Congress, and the legislative materials simply do not support the view that Congress intended to recognize any conscientious claim whatever as a basis for relieving the claimant from the general responsibility or the various incidents of military service. The claim that is recognized by § 6(j) is a ⊥**446** claim of conscience running against war as such. This claim, not one involving opposition to a particular war only, was plainly the focus of congressional concern.

Finding little comfort in the wording or the legislative history of § 6(j), petitioners rely heavily on dicta in the decisional law dealing with objectors whose conscientious scruples ran against war as such, but who indicated certain reservations of an abstract nature. It is instructive that none of the cases relied upon embraces an interpretation of § 6(j) at variance with the construction we adopt today.

Sicurella v. *United States* presented the only previous occasion for this Court to focus on the "participation in war in any form" language of § 6(j). In *Sicurella* a Jehovah's Witness who opposed participation in secular wars was held to possess the requisite conscientious scruples concerning war, although he was not opposed to participation in a "theocratic war" commanded by Jehovah. The Court noted that the "theocratic war" reservation was highly abstract—no such war had occurred since biblical times, and none was contemplated. Congress, on the other hand, had in mind "real shooting wars," and Sicurella's abstract reservations did not undercut his conscientious opposition to participating in such wars. Plainly, *Sicurella* cannot be read to support the claims of those, like petitioners, ⊥**447** who for a variety of reasons consider one particular "real shooting war" to be unjust, and therefore oppose participation in that war. . . .

⊥448 II

Both petitioners argue that § 6(j), construed to cover only objectors to all war, violates the religious clauses of the First Amendment. The First Amendment provides that "Congress shall make no law respecting an establishment of religion, or prohibiting the free exercise thereof. . . ." Petitioners contend that Congress interferes with free exercise of religion by failing to relieve objectors to a particular war from military service, when the objection is religious or conscientious in nature. While the two religious clauses—pertaining to "free exercise" and ⊥**449** "establishment" of religion—overlap and interact in many ways, it is best to focus first on petitioners' other contention, that § 6(j) is a law respecting the establishment of religion. For despite free exercise overtones, the gist of the constitutional complaint is that § 6(j) impermissibly discriminates among types of religious belief and affiliation.

On the assumption that these petitioners' beliefs concerning war have roots that are "religious" in nature, within the meaning of the Amendment as well as this Court's decisions construing § 6(j), petitioners ask how their claims to relief from military service can be permitted to fail, while other "religious" claims are upheld by the Act. It is a fact that § 6(j), properly construed, has this effect. Yet we cannot conclude in mechanical fashion, or at all, that the section works an establishment of religion. . . . ⊥**450**

A

The critical weakness of petitioners' establishment claim arises from the fact that § 6(j), on its face, simply does not discriminate on the basis of religious affiliation or religious belief, apart of course from beliefs concerning war. The section says that anyone who is conscientiously opposed to all war shall be relieved of military service. The specified objection must have a grounding in "religious training and belief," but no par⊥**451**ticular sectarian affiliation or theological position is required. The Draft Act of 1917 extended relief only to those conscientious objectors affiliated with some "well-recognized religious sect or organization" whose principles forbade members' participation in war, but the attempt to focus on particular sects apparently broke down in administrative practice, *Welsh* v. *United States*, and the 1940 Selective Training and Service Act discarded all sectarian restriction. Thereafter Congress has framed the conscientious objector exemption in broad terms compatible with "its long-established policy of not picking and choosing among religious beliefs." *United States* v. *Seeger*.

Thus, there is no occasion to consider the claim that when Congress grants a benefit expressly to adherents of one *religion*, courts must either nullify the grant or somehow extend the benefit to cover all religions. For § 6(j) does not single out any religious organization or religious creed for special treatment. Rather petitioners' contention is that since Congress has recognized one sort of conscientious objection concerning war, whatever its religious basis, the Establishment Clause commands that another, different objection be carved out and protected by the courts.

Properly phrased, petitioners' contention is that the special statutory status accorded conscientious objection to all war, but not objection to a particular war, works **⊥452** a de facto discrimination among religions. This happens, say petitioners, because some religious faiths themselves distinguish between personal participation in "just" and in "unjust" wars, commending the former and forbidding the latter, and therefore adherents of some religious faiths—and individuals whose personal beliefs of a religious nature include the distinction—cannot object to all wars consistently with what is regarded as the true imperative of conscience. Of course, this contention of de facto religious discrimination, rendering § 6(j) fatally underinclusive, cannot simply be brushed aside. The question of governmental neutrality is not concluded by the observation that § 6(j) on its face makes no discrimination between religions, for the Establishment Clause forbids subtle departures from neutrality, "religious gerrymanders," as well as obvious abuses. . . .

For the reasons that follow, we believe that petitioners have failed to make the requisite showing with respect to § 6(j).

Section 6(j) serves a number of valid purposes having nothing to do with a design to foster or favor any sect, religion, or cluster of religions. There are considera**⊥453**tions of a pragmatic nature, such as the hopelessness of converting a sincere conscientious objector into an effective fighting man, but no doubt the section reflects as well the view that "in the forum of conscience, duty to a moral power higher than the State has always been maintained." *United States* v. *Macintosh*. We have noted that the legislative materials show congressional concern for the hard choice that conscription would impose on conscientious objectors to war, as well as respect for the value of conscientious action and for the principle of supremacy of conscience.

Naturally the considerations just mentioned are affirmative in character, going to support the existence of an exemption rather than its restriction specifically to persons who object to all war. The point is that these affirmative purposes are neutral in the sense of the Establishment Clause. Quite apart from the question whether the Free Exercise Clause might require some sort of exemption, it is hardly impermissible for Congress to attempt to accommodate free exercise values, in line with "our happy tradition" of "avoiding unnecessary clashes with the dictates of conscience." *United States* v. *Macintosh*. . . . **⊥454**

In the draft area for 30 years the exempting provision has focused on individual conscientious belief, not on sectarian affiliation. The relevant individual belief is simply objection to all war, not adherence to any extraneous theological viewpoint. And while the objection must have roots in conscience and personality that are "religious" in nature, this requirement has never been construed to elevate conventional piety or religiosity of any kind above the imperatives of a personal faith.

In this state of affairs it is impossible to say that § 6(j) intrudes upon "voluntarism," in religious life, or that the congressional purpose in enacting § 6(j) is to promote or foster those religious organizations that traditionally have taught the duty to abstain from participation in any war. A claimant, seeking judicial protection for his own conscientious beliefs, would be hard put to argue that § 6(j) encourages membership in putatively "favored" religious organizations, for the painful dilemma of the sincere conscientious objector arises precisely because he feels himself bound in conscience not to compromise his beliefs or affiliations.

B

We conclude not only that the affirmative purposes underlying § 6(j) are neutral and secular, but also that valid neutral reasons exist for limiting the exemption to objectors to all war, and that the section therefore cannot be said to reflect a religious preference.

⊥455 Apart from the Government's need for manpower, perhaps the central interest involved in the administration of conscription laws is the interest in maintaining a fair system for determining "who serves when not all serve." When the Government exacts so much, the importance of fair, evenhanded, and uniform decisionmaking is obviously intensified. The Government argues that the interest in fairness would be jeopardized by expansion of § 6(j) to include conscientious objection to a particular war. The contention is that the claim to relief on account of such objection is intrinsically a claim of uncertain dimensions, and that granting the claim in theory would involve a real danger of erratic or even discriminatory decisionmaking in administrative practice.

A virtually limitless variety of beliefs are subsumable under the rubric, "objection to a particular war." All the factors that might go into nonconscientious dissent from policy, also might appear as the concrete basis of an objection that has roots as well in conscience and religion. Indeed, over the realm of possible situations, opposition to a particular war may more likely be political and nonconscientious, than otherwise. The difficulties of sort⊥**456**ing the two, with a sure hand, are considerable. Moreover, the belief that a particular war at a particular time is unjust is by its nature changeable and subject to nullification by changing events. Since objection may fasten on any of an enormous number of variables, the claim is ultimately subjective, depending on the claimant's view of the facts in relation to his judgment that a given factor or congeries of factors colors the character of the war as a whole. In short, it is not at all obvious in theory what sorts of objections should be deemed sufficient to excuse an objector, and there is considerable force in the Government's contention that a program of excusing objectors to particular wars may be "impossible to conduct with any hope of reaching fair and consistent results. . . ."

For their part, petitioners make no attempt to provide a careful definition of the claim to exemption that they ask the courts to carve out and protect. They do not explain why objection to a particular conflict—much less an objection that focuses on a particular facet of a conflict—should excuse the objector from all military service whatever, even from military operations that are connected with the conflict at hand in remote or tenuous ways. They suggest no solution to the problems arising from the fact that altered circumstances may quickly render the objection to military service moot.

To view the problem of fairness and evenhanded decisionmaking, in the present context, as merely a commonplace chore of weeding out "spurious claims," is to minimize substantial difficulties of real concern to a responsible legislative body. For example, under the petitioners' unarticulated scheme for exemption, an objector's claim to exemption might be based on some feature of a current conflict that most would regard as incidental, ⊥**457** or might be predicated on a view of the facts that most would regard as mistaken. The particular complaint about the war may itself be "sincere," but it is difficult to know how to judge the "sincerity" of the objector's conclusion that the war in toto is unjust and that any personal involvement would contravene conscience and religion. . . . ⊥**460**

Of course, we do not suggest that Congress would have acted irrationally or unreasonably had it decided to exempt those who object to particular wars. Our analysis of the policies of § 6(j) is undertaken in order to determine the existence *vel non* of a neutral, secular justification for the lines Congress has drawn. We find that justifying reasons exist and therefore hold that the Establishment Clause is not violated.

⊥**461** III

Petitioners' remaining contention is that Congress interferes with the free exercise of religion by conscripting persons who oppose a particular war on grounds of conscience and religion. Strictly viewed, this complaint does not implicate problems of comparative treatment of different sorts of objectors, but rather may be examined in some isolation from the circumstance that Congress has chosen to exempt those who conscientiously object to all war. And our holding that § 6(j) comports with the Establishment Clause does not automatically settle the present issue. For despite a general harmony of purpose between the two religious clauses of the First Amendment, the Free Exercise Clause no doubt has a reach of its own.

Nonetheless, our analysis of § 6(j) for Establishment Clause purposes has revealed governmental interests of a kind and weight sufficient to justify under the Free Exercise Clause the impact of the conscription laws on those who object to particular wars. . . . ⊥**462**

The conscription laws, applied to such persons as to others, are not designed to interfere with any religious ritual or practice, and do not work a penalty against any theological position. The incidental burdens felt by persons in petitioners' position are strictly justified by substantial governmental interests that relate directly to the very impacts questioned. And more broadly, of course, there is the Government's interest in procuring the manpower necessary for military purposes, pursuant to the constitutional grant of power to Congress to raise and support armies.

⊥**463** IV

Since petitioners' statutory and constitutional claims to relief from military service are without merit, it follows that in Gillette's case (No. 85) there was a basis in fact to support administrative denial of exemption, and that in Negre's case (No. 325) there was a basis in fact to support the Army's denial of a discharge. Accordingly, the judgments below are

Affirmed.

Mr. *Justice* BLACK concurs in the Court's judgment and in Part I of the opinion of the Court.

Mr. *Justice* DOUGLAS, dissenting in *Gillette* v. *United States* (No. 85).

Gillette's objection is to combat service in the Vietnam war, not to wars in general, and the basis of his objection is his conscience. His objection does not put him into the statutory exemption which extends to one "who, by reason of religious training and belief, is conscientiously opposed to participation in war in any form."

He stated his views as follows:

"I object to any assignment in the United States Armed Forces while this unnecessary and unjust war is being waged, on the grounds of religious belief specifically 'Humanism.' This essentially means respect and love for man, faith in his inherent goodness and perfectability, and confidence in his capability to improve some of the pains of the human condition."

This position is substantially the same as that of Sisson in *United States* v. *Sisson* ⊥**464** where the District Court summarized the draftee's position as follows:

"Sisson's table of ultimate values is moral and ethical. It reflects quite as real, pervasive, durable, and commendable a marshalling of priorities as a formal religion. It is just as much a residue of culture, early training, and beliefs shared by companions and family. What another derives from the discipline of a church, Sisson derives from the discipline of conscience."

There is no doubt that the views of Gillette are sincere, genuine, and profound. The District Court in the present case faced squarely the issue presented in *Sisson* and being unable to distinguish the case on the facts, refused to follow *Sisson*.

The question, Can a conscientious objector, whether his objection be rooted in "religion" or in moral values, be required to kill? has never been answered by the Court. *Hamilton* v. *Regents*, did no more than hold that the Fourteenth Amendment did not require a State to make its university available to one who would not take military training. *United States* v. *Macintosh* denied naturalization to a person who "would not promise in advance to bear arms in defense of the United States unless he believed the war to be morally justified." The question of compelling a man to kill against his conscience was not squarely involved. Most of the talk in the majority opinion concerned "serving in the armed forces of the ⊥**465** Nation in time of war." Such service can, of course, take place in noncombatant roles. The ruling was that such service is "dependent upon the will of Congress and not upon the scruples of the individual, except as Congress provides." The dicta of the Court in the *Macintosh* case squint towards the denial of Gillette's claim, though as I have said, the issue was not squarely presented.

Yet if dicta are to be our guide, my choice is the dicta of *Chief Justice HUGHES* who, dissenting in *Macintosh*, spoke as well for *Justices HOLMES*, *BRANDEIS*, and *STONE*:

"Nor is there ground, in my opinion, for the exclusion of Professor Macintosh because his conscientious scruples have particular reference to wars believed to be unjust. There is nothing new in such an attitude. Among the most eminent statesmen here and abroad have been those who condemned the action of their country in entering into wars they thought to be unjustified. Agreements for the renunciation of war presuppose a preponderant public sentiment against wars of aggression. If, while recognizing the power of Congress, the mere holding of religious or conscientious scruples against all wars should not disqualify a citizen from holding office in this country, or an applicant otherwise qualified from being admitted to citizenship, there would seem to be no reason why a reservation of religious or conscientious objection to participation in wars believed to be unjust should constitute such a disqualification."

I think the Hughes view is the constitutional view. It is true that the First Amendment speaks of the free exercise of religion, not of the free exercise of conscience or belief. Yet conscience and belief are the main ingredients of First Amendment rights. They are the ⊥**466** bedrock of free speech as well as religion. . . .

⊥**468** The law as written is a species of those which show an invidious discrimination in favor of religious persons and against others with like scruples. . . . ⊥**469**

I had assumed that the welfare of the single human soul was the ultimate test of the vitality of the First Amendment.

This is an appropriate occasion to give content to our dictum in *Board of Education* v. *Barnette*: "[F]reedom to differ is not limited to things that do not matter much. . . . The test of its sub⊥**470**stance is the right to differ as to things that touch the heart of the existing order."

I would reverse this judgment.

Mr. Justice DOUGLAS, dissenting in *Negre* v. *Larsen* (No. 325).

I approach the facts of this case with some diffidence, as they involve doctrines of the Catholic Church in which I was not raised. But we have on one of petitioner's briefs an authoritative lay Catholic scholar, Dr. John T. Noonan, Jr., and from that brief I deduce the following:

Under the doctrines of the Catholic Church a person has a moral duty to take part in wars declared by his government so long as they comply with the tests of his church for just wars. Conversely, a Catholic has a moral duty not to participate in unjust wars. ⊥**471**

The Fifth Commandment, "Thou shalt not kill," provides a basis for the distinction between just and unjust wars. In the 16th century Francisco Victoria, Dominican master of the University of Salamanca and pioneer in international law, elaborated on the distinction. "If a subject is convinced of the injustice of a war, he ought not to serve in it, even on the command of his prince. This is clear, for no one can authorize the killing of an innocent person." He realized not all men had the information of the prince and his counsellors on the causes of a war, but where "the proofs and tokens of the injustice of the war may be such that ignorance would be no excuse even to the subjects" who are not normally informed, that ignorance will not be an excuse if they participate. Well over 400 years later, today, the Baltimore Catechism makes an exception to the Fifth Commandment for a "soldier fighting a just war."

No one can tell a Catholic that this or that war is either just or unjust. This is a personal decision that an individual must make on the basis of his own conscience after studying the facts. ⊥**472**

Like the distinction between just and unjust wars, the duty to obey conscience is not a new doctrine in the Catholic Church. When told to stop preaching by the Sanhedrin, to which they were subordinate by law, "Peter and the apostles answered and said, 'We must obey God rather than men.'" That duty has not changed. Pope Paul VI has expressed it as follows: "On his part, man perceives and acknowledges the imperatives of the divine law through the mediation of conscience. In all his activity a man is bound to follow his conscience, in order that he may come to God, the end and purpose of life."

While the fact that the ultimate determination of whether a war is unjust rests on individual conscience, the Church has provided guides. . . . ⊥**473**

Louis Negre is a devout Catholic. In 1951 when he was four, his family immigrated to this country from ⊥**474** France. He attended Catholic schools in Bakersfield, California, until graduation from high school. Then he attended Bakersfield Junior College for two years. Following that, he was inducted into the Army.

At the time of his induction he had his own convictions about the Vietnam war and the Army's goals in the war. He wanted, however, to be sure of his convictions. "I agreed to myself that before making any decision or taking any type of stand on the issue, I would permit myself to see and understand the Army's explanation of its reasons for violence in Vietnam. For, without getting an insight on the subject, it would be unfair for me to say anything, without really knowing the answer."

On completion of his advanced infantry training, "I knew that if I would permit myself to go to Vietnam I would be violating my own concepts of natural law and would be going against all that I had been taught in my religious training." Negre applied for a discharge as a conscientious objector. His application was denied. He then refused to comply with an order to proceed for shipment to Vietnam. A general court-martial followed, but he was acquitted. After that he filed this application for discharge as a conscientious objector. ⊥**475**

Negre is opposed under his religious training and beliefs to participation in any form in the war in Vietnam. His sincerity is not questioned. His application for a discharge, however, was denied because his religious training and beliefs led him to oppose only a particular war which according to his conscience was unjust.

For the reasons I have stated in my dissent in the *Gillette* case decided this day, I would reverse the judgment.

RELIGION AND THE RIGHT TO WORK

Although the right to work is not one of the enumerated rights guaranteed in the Constitution, the right to engage in a legitimate occupation for financial gain, free of unreasonable burden by government is undoubtedly considered an inalienable right by the American people. Historically, the courts have ordinarily found that guarantee in the due process and equal protection of the laws provisions of the Fifth and Fourteenth Amendments. Occasionally, however, the right to work has become legally involved with the religion clauses of the First Amendment. A substantial number of these cases have in recent years made their way to the Supreme Court.

Because they were decided primarily on the basis of Establishment Clause issues, the compulsory Sunday closing law cases decided by the Court in 1961 are discussed in Chapter 3. However, in two of the cases—BRAUNFELD v. BROWN and *Gallagher* v. *Crown Kosher Super Markets*—Orthodox Jewish merchants claimed that the laws of Pennsylvania and Massachusetts, by limiting their businesses to a five-day week, placed them at a great economic disadvantage in their competition with non-Sabbatarian storekeepers and placed an unreasonable burden on their free exercise of religion. The Court majority conceded that the laws did indeed impose an indirect burden on their religious rights, but maintained that the burden was not unreasonable and that there was no viable less-restrictive alternative means by which the states could accomplish their secular objectives. Justice Stewart, in dissent, insisted that a state could not constitutionally compel "an Orthodox Jew to choose between his religious faith and his economic survival."

SHERBERT v. VERNER, decided two years later, involved a similar yet different constitutional claim—that of an employee rather than a business owner—and one in which the Free Exercise Clause is primary rather than secondary. Mrs. Adell Sherbert joined the Seventh-day Adventist Church in 1957. At the time, she was employed at a textile mill in the Spartanburg, South Carolina, area. She experienced no conflict between her job and her new religion because the mill worked a five-day week, but in 1959 the mill changed to a six-day week for all three shifts. The sixth work day was Saturday. She refused to work on Saturday and was dismissed by her employer.

After her discharge, Mrs. Sherbert applied to three other textile mills for a five-day position, but none was available. At that point she applied to the state Employment Security Commission for unemployment compensation. In her application she stated her willingness to work in other mills, or even in other industries, as long as Saturday work was not involved. The request for unemployment compensation was denied and she sued.

Two South Carolina courts upheld the findings of the Employment Security Commission that Mrs. Sherbert's refusal to accept Saturday employment disqualified her for unemployment benefits as a worker who failed to accept "suitable work when offered . . . by the employment office or the employer." At no time during the court proceedings was there any question about the sincerity of her beliefs or that prohibition of Saturday work is a basic belief of the Seventh-day Adventist Church.

In a seven-to-two decision, the Supreme Court reversed the lower courts and ruled in favor of the Sabbatarian. The Court held that to disqualify the appellant for unemployment benefits only because she refused to work on Saturday, a decision based firmly on her religious beliefs, was to impose an unconstitutional burden upon the free exercise of her religion. Withholding of benefits forced the appellant to choose between following the teachings of her religion and not working or receiving benefits, or abandoning one of the precepts of her religion in order to accept work. For the government to compel such a choice was clearly a violation of the Free Exercise Clause. "To condition the availability of benefits upon this appellant's willingness to violate a cardinal principle of her religious faith," wrote Justice Brennan for the majority, "effectively penalizes the free exercise of her constitutional liberties. . . ." (374 U.S. 398, 406.)

The Court also denied that to decide in favor of the appellant was to "establish" the Seventh-day Adventist religion. To allow Sabbatarians to be the recipients of unemployment compensation along with Sunday worshippers merely reflects governmental neutrality in the area of religious differences.[1] Not to allow the benefits to Sabbatarians would show hostility to their religion.

Of interest is the fact that the two dissenters and even Justice Stewart, who concurred in the result of the decision, wrote that they believed this case was clearly inconsistent with the decision reached by the Court in *Braunfeld*. Indeed, they failed to see how *Braunfeld* could continue to stand in the light of this opinion. The injury suffered by Mr. Braunfeld when the Sunday closing law was upheld (i.e., having to close his business) was much greater than that which would have been suffered by Mrs. Sherbert if the Court had not found in her favor (i.e., losing twenty-two weeks of unemployment pay). In view of the expression of these doubts, it is rather surprising that the Sunday closing law dispute has not been taken to the Court again. This failure may be due to the fact that many Sunday laws have been repealed or modified and, except for sporadic holiday season efforts, existing laws have been largely ignored in more recent times by law enforcement officials; thus the weight of such laws is no longer so onerous to Sabbatarians.[2]

It has been said that, with the possible exception of WISCONSIN v. YODER, the *Sherbert* case broadens free exercise claims more than any other previous decision of the Supreme Court. In the Sunday closing law cases the Court argued that if the state's laws had only an indirect effect on the Sabbatarians' exercise of religion, there was no basis for challenge to the laws. In the Sherbert case, however, the Court said that even indirect inhibitions of religious exercise could be challenged under the Free Exercise Clause. Furthermore, in the *Braunfeld* and *Crown Kosher Market* cases the Sabbatarians asked only to be left alone, to be able to practice their religion without economic damage to themselves. In the *Sherbert* case the Sabbatarian demanded that the state pay her money when she refused to work for religious reasons, and the Court held that she was entitled to that money.[3] In this case, the Court indeed gave the Free Exercise Clause a broad interpretation.

As has been mentioned earlier, the "least restrictive alternative means" test advanced by the Court in *Braunfeld* and subsequently used in *Sherbert* to the appellant's benefit represented a significant development. *Sherbert*, in turn, established the requirement of showing of "compelling state interest" to justify even incidental infringement of religious rights. Combined for use as a judicial standard, the two concepts had great potential for an extremely broad reading of free exercise rights.

This interpretation gained statutory status in 1972 when the Civil Rights Act of 1964 was amended to provide that "it shall be an unlawful employment practice for an employer . . . to . . . discharge any individual, or otherwise to discriminate against any individual with respect to his compensation, terms, conditions or privileges of employment, because of such individual's . . . religion." The act also undertook to define religion as used in the revision, and incorporated a 1967 Equal Employment Opportunity Commission "guideline" for enforcement of the law when it provided:

> The term "religion" includes all aspects of religious observance and practice, as well as belief, unless an employer demonstrates that he is unable to reasonably accommodate to an employee's or prospective employee's religious observances or practice without undue hardship on the conduct of the employer's business [Title VII, 701(j) U.S.C., 2000C(j)].

The burden of proof with regard to undue hardship was placed on the employer.

This definition, together with the accompanying condition, was an effort to do by legislation what the Supreme Court had failed to do the year before because of a four-to-four deadlock in *Dewey* v. *Reynolds Metal Company*. In that case a federal Court of Appeals had upheld a company's refusal to accede to the demands of a Sabbatarian that the company make arrangements to accommodate his religious conviction. The evenly divided vote had the

[1]For an elaboration of this "neutrality" argument, see Wilber G. Katz, *Religion and American Constitutions* (Evanston, Ill.: Northwestern University Press, 1963), pp. 12-18, 97, 100, and the concurring opinion by Justice Brennan in ABINGTON SCHOOL DISTRICT v. SCHEMPP.

[2]Leo Pfeffer, *God, Caesar, and the Constitution: The Court as Referee of Church-State Confrontation* (Boston: Beacon Press, 1975), p. 333.

[3]*Ibid.*, p. 332. Pfeffer's entire section, pp. 300-37, is extremely helpful in understanding the issues this case raises.

effect of affirming the lower court's determination that existing law did not mandate the requested company action.

After the 1972 amendment, litigation quickly developed in an effort to determine the meaning of the requirement for reasonable accommodation of employee religious needs without undue hardship on the part of the company.[4] In late 1976, the Court considered the amended law in *Parker Seal Company* v. *Cummins*. Paul Cummins was a supervisor in the Berea, Kentucky, plant of the Parker Seal Company. A member of the Worldwide Church of God, a Sabbatarian group, Cummins refused to work on Saturday. For more than a year the company accommodated Cummins's Sabbatarianism, although other supervisors were compelled to work on Saturday. When resentment developed among the other supervisors, Cummins was fired. The Sixth U.S. Circuit Court of Appeals found that the company had not made sufficient effort to accommodate Cummins. In a *per curiam* decision which did not include a written opinion, another divided Court (four-to-four with Justice Stevens disqualifying himself) affirmed the lower court's opinion to the benefit of Cummins.

However, in June 1977, the full Court, in TRANS WORLD AIRLINES, INC. v. HARDISON, reversed the Eighth Circuit Court of Appeals which had found in favor of the Sabbatarian claims of another member of the same denomination. The Supreme Court refused to construe the 1972 statute as dictating that companies discriminate against some employees in order to satisfy the religious preferences of other employees. Justice Byron White, for the majority of seven, held that the law did not require the abandonment of neutral union seniority programs nor force employers to bear more than a minimal cost to accommodate workers who wished to have Saturday off for religious reasons. Justices Thurgood Marshall and William Brennan, in dissent, decried the undesirable impact on those Sabbatarians "who could be forced to live on welfare as the price they must pay for worshipping their God."

Four years later in THOMAS v. REVIEW BOARD OF INDIANA EMPLOYMENT SECURITY DIVISION, the Court was again asked to rule on denial of unemployment compensation, this time with respect to a Jehovah's Witness who quit his job with a machinery company after he was transferred from the department where he had been employed in working with steel products for industrial use to one that produced turrets for military tanks. Thomas maintained that his religious beliefs forbade working in the production of armaments, but he was denied unemployment benefits on the strength of a state law which mandated such denial of compensation to any person voluntarily leaving a job "without good cause [arising] in connection with [his] work."

The Indiana Supreme Court found no undue burden on Eddie Thomas's right to free exercise of religion. It further held that for the state to provide benefits under such circumstances would in effect constitute an establishment of religion. But the United States Supreme Court by a vote of eight-to-one, denied both findings. Chief Justice Burger ruled that "Where the state conditions receipt of an important benefit upon conduct proscribed by a religious faith, or where it denies such a benefit because of conduct mandated by religious belief, thereby putting substantial pressure on an adherent to modify his behavior and to violate his beliefs, a burden on religion exists" (450 U.S. 707, 717). The state, he explained, had not shown that this denial of benefits was the least restrictive means of achieving some compelling state interest. With respect to the establishment charge, he quoted from Sherbert in finding payment of benefits to reflect "nothing more than the governmental obligation of neutrality in the face of religious differences. . . ." Justice Rehnquist, in dissent, complained that the decision added "mud to the already muddied waters of First Amendment jurisprudence."

One week before adjournment of the 1985-86 session, the Court handed down a decision in a potentially highly significant case involving the balancing of religious rights on the part of a religiously affiliated school and a teacher's right to protection against sexual discrimination by that school. However, the decision of the Court in *Ohio Civil Rights Commission* v. *Dayton Christian Schools* was decided on highly technical grounds and postponed the ultimate resolution of many of the questions raised.

Dayton Christian Schools operated three schools as part of its religious mission. To assure the desired fundamentalist Christian commitment on the part of the board of directors and educational staff, all were required annually to sign a Statement of Faith of religious precepts. After working for five years as a teacher in the elementary school, Linda Hoskinson became pregnant and so informed the school officials. She also told them that she desired to keep teaching both during her pregnancy and in the following school year. She was, however, notified that her teaching contract would not be renewed because her teaching as a new parent would be in conflict with the school's philosophy that the mother should be in the home during the early years of child rearing.

On receipt of the notification, she consulted a lawyer who wrote a letter to the superintendent alleging the existence of discriminatory practices at the school. Shortly thereafter Mrs. Hoskinson was suspended effective immediately because she had

[4]See, for example, *Johnson* v. *United States Postal Service* (1974) and *United States* v. *City of Albuquerque* (1975).

violated the "biblical chain of command" for internal resolution of disputes which she had agreed in her contract to follow. The provision in her contract required that she "agree to follow the Biblical pattern of Matthew 18:15-17 and Galatians 6:1 and always give a good report (with) all differences . . . to be resolved by utilizing Biblical principles—always presenting a united front." In going to the attorney she had breached her contract.

The day after she was dismissed Mrs. Hoskinson filed a sex discrimination complaint with the Ohio Civil Rights Commission which, after preliminary investigation and failure to resolve the controversy by conciliation, notified the school that the commission would begin a hearing on the charge before an administrative hearing examiner. While the administrative proceedings were still pending, Dayton Christian Schools filed a suit in the United States District Court for the Southern District of Ohio, seeking an injunction to bar the administrative proceedings. Application of the Ohio Civil Rights Commission statutes to the employment practices of the schools based on sincerely held religious beliefs would, the suit contended, violate both the Free Exercise and Establishment Clauses.

That court refused to issue the injunction, holding that the state has a "compelling and overriding interest in eliminating sex discrimination in the employment setting" sufficient to justify "the slight infringement that may result in Plaintiff's free exercise rights." However, the Dayton Christian Schools appealed the district court's findings. The United States Court of Appeals for the Sixth Circuit reversed the decision, and ruled in favor of the school on free exercise and establishment grounds. The decision emphasized the potential for "highly intrusive" intervention and surveillance on the part of the commission in ruling on such matters as reinstatement and backpay, although these specific issues were not at the moment before the court.

By unanimous vote the Supreme Court reversed the decision of the court of appeals and remanded the case for further proceedings, but the Court split five-to-four as to the appropriateness of the action of the district court in taking jurisdiction over the suit in the first instance. Justice Rehnquist, for himself and four other justices, held that the district court should have abstained from adjudicating the case. He cited numerous precedents to the effect that, out of concern for comity and federalism, a federal court should not enjoin a pending proceeding in state courts or state administrative bodies except in the "very unusual situation that an injunction is necessary to prevent great and immediate irreparable injury." The elimination of sex discrimination is an important state interest, and mere investigation by the commission to ascertain the real reason for Mrs. Hoskinson's discharge would violate no constitutional rights. "Even religious schools," said Justice Rehnquist, "cannot claim to be wholly free from state regulation," and constitutional claims resulting from a final commission order could properly be raised in state court.

Justice Stevens wrote for Justices Brennan, Marshall, and Blackmun. He concurred in the judgment and agreed with the majority that investigation of the charges by the commission and the holding of a hearing on the charges were not prohibited by the First Amendment. He disagreed, however, with the majority's contention that the district court should have abstained from adjudicating the case, thereby possibly delaying or denying the school a hearing in federal court as to the constitutionality of any provisional administrative remedy which the commission might determine. Although the merits of Mrs. Hoskinson's case were not spoken to, the decision did appear to have considerable significance in the larger area of liability of religious schools to investigation and hearing proceedings by civil rights commissions under state antidiscrimination laws.[5] However, through the October 1995 term, the Court had not revisited the issue.

After the *Thomas* decision, lower courts kept the issues of Sabbatarians and job termination, unem-

[5]In 1985 a federal court of appeals affirmed a district court ruling that the Equal Employment Opportunity Commission had no jurisdiction under Title VII of the Civil Rights Act of 1964 with respect to alleged sexual discrimination in pastoral hiring. Carole Rayburn took her case to the EEOC and then to court when the Seventh-day Adventist Church in Takoma Park, Maryland, turned down her request for employment as an intern with assignment as an associate in pastoral care. The district court dismissed Rayburn's suit on the ground that government scrutiny of the hiring practices of the church would infringe on its freedom of religion.

Judge J. Harvie Williamson III of the Fourth Circuit Court of Appeals agreed that state scrutiny here would constitute both substantial infringement of free exercise of religion and impermissible entanglement. He argued that:

> The right to choose ministers without government restriction underlies that well being of the religious community . . . for perpetuation of a church's existence may depend upon those whom it selects to preach its values, teach its message, and interpret its doctrines both to its membership and the world at large (*Rayburn* v. *General Conference of Seventh-day Adventists*, 772 F.2d 1164, 1168).

He cautioned, however, that decisions of churches may be subject to Title VII scrutiny where the decision "does not involve the church's spiritual functions."

ployment compensation, reasonable accommodation, and undue hardship alive.[6] In April 1986 the United States Supreme Court accepted another case, HOBBIE v. UNEMPLOYMENT APPEALS COMMISSION OF FLORIDA, which involved a Seventh-day Adventist who was denied unemployment compensation benefits after being fired by her employer for refusing to work on her Sabbath. The decision was handed down 25 February 1987.

The difference between this and earlier cases was that Paula A. Hobbie was not a Seventh-day Adventist at the time she was employed. Converted two and one-half years thereafter, she informed her employer that she would not, for religious reasons, be able to continue to work at her place of employment, a jewelry store, on her Sabbath.

A temporary arrangement was made with her immediate supervisor that she would work other evenings and Sundays when she was scheduled to work on Friday evening or on Saturday. However, when the general manager heard of the arrangement he met with her and her minister and informed Hobbie that she could either work her scheduled shifts or resign. When she refused to accept either alternative, she was discharged.

Subsequently, she filed a claim for unemployment compensation, but her claim was disallowed by a Florida Bureau of Unemployment Compensation claims examiner. The state Appeals Commission upheld the denial of benefits because her refusal to work scheduled shifts constituted "misconduct connected with [her] work." The Fifth District Court of Florida affirmed the ruling.

By a vote of eight-to-one, with Justice Brennan writing for the majority and Justices Powell and Stevens concurring, the Supreme Court refused to make a distinction between this case and *Sherbert* and *Thomas*. Subjecting the situation here to the strict scrutiny test followed in those cases, the Court failed to find proof of a compelling state interest in denial of the benefits. The Court, therefore, held the disqualification of Hobbie from receipt of unemployment compensation benefits to violate the Free Exercise Clause of the First Amendment.

The Court refused to accept the argument that Hobbie's situation should be distinguished from that of the employees involved in *Sherbert* and *Thomas* because they had held their religious beliefs at the time they were employed; her beliefs had changed after she was hired. The change caused a conflict, Florida argued, between her faith and her job which had not existed at the time she was employed.

To accept the state's contention of non-entitlement, said Justice Brennan, would "single out the religious convert for different, less favorable treatment than that given an individual whose adherence to his or her faith precedes employment" (480 U.S. 136, 144). The timing of the conversion, he wrote, was "immaterial to our determination that her free exercise rights have been burdened." The "First Amendment protects the free exercise rights of employees who adopt religious beliefs or convert from one faith to another after they are hired" (480 U.S. 136,144). Chief Justice Rehnquist dissented, stating that he adhered to the views he had expressed in *Thomas*.

Yet another variation of the unemployment compensation issue was brought to the Supreme Court the next year in FRAZEE v. ILLINOIS DEPARTMENT OF EMPLOYMENT SECURITY. William A. Frazee was denied benefits because he refused the offer of a temporary job with Kelly Services that would have required him to work on Sunday. He said that as a Christian he could not do so. Denial of benefits was affirmed by a review board and two Illinois courts because, unlike the claimants in *Sherbert*, *Thomas*, and *Hobbie*, he was not a member of a particular religious sect or church. Nor did he maintain that his refusal resulted from a "tenet, belief, or teaching of an established religious body."

---

[6]See *Anderson* v. *General Dynamics Convair Aerospace Division* (1982) and *Turpen* v. *Missouri-Kansas-Texas Railroad Company* (1984). Two years before *Thomas* the Court refused to review a lower court's ruling that religious liberty similarly took precedence over the payment of union dues. (*International Association of Machinists and Aerospace Workers, AFL-CIO* v. *Anderson* [1979].) The Court in 1986 also granted certiorari in another case, *Ansonia Board of Education* v. *Philbrook* which raises the question of reasonable accommodation and undue hardship with respect to a teacher's right to use his/her personal leave for religious observances. Philbrook, a member of the Worldwide Church of God, found it necessary to be absent from school approximately six days each year. His contract with the school district entitled him to three days off with pay per year for religious observances, but forbade him to use any of his personal leave for that purpose. He offered two proposed accommodations which the board did not find acceptable.

Philbrook filed a complaint against the school and the teachers' union charging that the school's leave policy violated Title VII of the Civil Rights Act of 1964 and the Free Exercise Clause. The district court held that he had failed to prove religious discrimination. The Second Court of Appeals, however, found that he had established a prima facia case of discrimination under Title VII, and, reaching only the statutory question, reversed and remanded the decision of the district court.

Observing that "*Hardison* did not sound a death knell to the employer's duty to accommodate under Title VII," Judge Oakes said for the court, "Where the employer and the employee each propose a reasonable accommodation, Title VII requires the employer to accept the proposal the employee prefers unless that accommodation causes undue hardship on the employer's conduct of his business" (757 F.2d 476, 484). The appeals court did not accept the argument of the school board that accommodating Philbrook would constitute preferential treatment.

While agreeing that his personal professed religious belief was unquestionably sincere, the Illinois State Appellate Court held that belief alone was not sufficient cause for his refusal of Sunday employment.

Justice Byron White wrote for a unanimous Court. He agreed that "membership in an organized religious denomination, especially one with a specific tenet forbidding members to work on Sunday, would simplify the problem of identifying sincerely held religious beliefs." However, Frazee's refusal was based on a sincerely held religious belief and he could therefore seek protection under the Free Exercise Clause without claiming that he was acting in response to the tenets of a particular religious organization.

The Court's decisions in *Sherbert*, *Thomas*, and *Hobbie* had not turned on the fact that the claimants were complying with the doctrine of a particular religious body, but on the fact that each "had a sincere belief that religion required him or her to refrain from the work in question." It is true the Court had said in *Thomas* that "Only beliefs rooted in religion are protected by the Free Exercise Clause." But the State of Illinois and its courts had conceded the sincerity of Frazee's personal professed religious belief, and had failed to make a showing of any state interests compelling enough to override his "legitimate claim to the free exercise of religion."

Undoubtedly the most significant, controversial, and potentially damaging Supreme Court decision in recent years concerning the Free Exercise Clause was announced 17 April 1990. The specific holding of the Court in EMPLOYMENT DIVISION, DEPARTMENT OF HUMAN RESOURCES OF OREGON v. SMITH was not as surprising or alarming as was the fact that the Court abandoned the "compelling state interest" test it had mandated almost three decades earlier in *Sherbert* (1963). Justice Scalia, in the majority opinion, even went so far as to refer to the test as a "luxury" which the country could not afford.

Galen Black and Alfred Smith, members of the Native American Church—in one of the central ceremonies of that church—ingested a small amount of peyote for sacramental purposes. Both were employees of a private alcohol and drug prevention and rehabilitation nonprofit organization. When their employers discovered that Black and Smith had taken the drug, they were discharged. Subsequently their applications for unemployment compensation were denied by the state for work-related misconduct.

The denials were reversed by the State Court of Appeals on free exercise grounds and the Oregon Supreme Court affirmed on the basis of the *Sherbert* test, finding insufficient governmental interest to justify the burden imposed on the claimants' religious freedom. When the state appealed to the United States Supreme Court, the Court by a 5-to-3 vote remanded the case to the Oregon Supreme Court to determine whether sacramental use of peyote was illegal under that state's law (*Smith I*). The state court responded by holding that ingestion of peyote for religious reasons was not exempt from the state's prohibition against the use of illegal drugs. The court, however, then proceeded to invalidate the law as infringing the Free Exercise Clause. Oregon again successfully sought a writ of certiorari from the United States Supreme Court.

Dividing 6-to-3, the Court upheld the state's denial of unemployment compensation. In writing the majority opinion, Justice Scalia distinguished the present case from *Sherbert* and the other unemployment cases. He agreed that the Court had held that a state "could not condition the availability of unemployment insurance on an individual's willingness to forego conduct required by his religion." But, he said, the conduct involved in the earlier rulings was not, as here, prohibited by law. Citing *Torcaso*, *Ballard*, *Larson* v. *Valente*, and other free exercise cases, he conceded that government could not "compel affirmation of religious beliefs," "punish the expression of religious doctrines it believes to be false," "impose special disabilities on the basis of religious views or religious status," or "lend its power to one or the other side in controversies over religious authority or dogma." In the case now before the Court, however, the respondents went far beyond these restraints on the state to contend that the Constitution also forbids government to require any person to "observe a generally applicable law that requires (or forbids) the performance of an act that his religious belief forbids (or requires)." Disputing this contention, Justice Scalia stated: "We have never held that an individual's religious beliefs excuse him from compliance with an otherwise valid law prohibiting conduct that the State is free to regulate."

Referring to such cases as *Cantwell*, *Murdock*, and *Yoder*, which appear to refute this disclaimer, he said that each of these decisions also involved other constitutional guarantees such as freedom of speech or press. No governmental action had been invalidated on the basis of the *Sherbert* test outside the area of unemployment compensation denial cases; and in recent years, the Court, wrote Justice Scalia, had refrained from even applying the test except in that area.

He turned back to the Court's earliest excursion into the meaning of the Free Exercise Clause in *Reynolds* v. *United States* when it ruled that to exempt an individual from a law because it did not coincide with the person's religious beliefs would permit him to "become a law unto himself." Such an interpretation of the clause, Scalia said, "contradicts both constitutional tradition and common sense."

A state was free to establish a nondiscriminatory exemption based on religious practice, but such exemption was not constitutionally required. Justice Scalia agreed that minority groups would be disadvantaged but found this to be an "unavoidable consequence of democratic government," to be "preferred to a system in which each conscience is a law unto itself or in which judges weigh the social importance of all laws against the centrality of all religious beliefs."

In a concurring opinion equal in length to that of the majority, Justice O'Connor accepted the immediate result reached by the Court, but decried the departure from the compelling interest test as "incompatible with our Nation's fundamental commitment to individual religious liberty." In her eyes, the state's action could have been justified without the Court's strained, narrow reading of the Free Exercise Clause resulting in disavowal of a sound and consistent strict scrutiny standard. She challenged the majority's use of precedents such as *Cantwell*, *Yoder*, and *Roy* to support its unnecessary rejection of the test. "The compelling interest test," she stated,

> effectuates the First Amendment's command that religious liberty is an independent liberty, that it occupies a preferred position, and that the Court will not permit encroachments upon this liberty, whether direct or indirect, unless required by clear and compelling governmental interests 'of the highest order' (494 U.S. 872, 895).

Justice O'Connor expressed particular concern with two majority contentions: first, the suggestion that the burdening of minority religions was an "unavoidable consequence" of our democratic system and second, that exemption from generally applicable criminal laws was properly left to the political process. The very purpose of the First Amendment, as she viewed it, was "precisely to protect the rights of those whose religious practices are not shared by the majority and may be viewed with hostility."

Justice Blackmun, in dissent, joined by Brennan and Marshall, supported Justice O'Connor in her analysis and criticism of the rejection of the test. He would, however, have gone further and ruled against Oregon's denial of unemployment benefits. The American Indian Religious Freedom Act, the dissenters agreed, may not create rights enforceable against governmental action restricting religious freedom. . . ." But, they maintained, unless the Court applies the strict scrutiny standards to even the unorthodox claims of the Native Americans, "both the First Amendment and the stated policy of Congress will offer to Native Americans an unfulfilled and hollow promise."

There were those who supported the decision, but an imposing number of religious groups, constitutional scholars, and concerned individuals immediately expressed shock and dismay.[7] When the Court denied appeal for rehearing, these critics looked to Congress for relief. In response to their demands, legislation appropriately entitled "The Religious Freedom Restoration Act" was introduced into the 101st Congress to reestablish the "compelling governmental interest" and "least restrictive means" tests for free exercise cases. The act was reintroduced in the 102nd Congress, in January 1992 had over 120 co-sponsors, and was passed by the 103rd Congress in November 1993. It served to express strong congressional disapproval of the Court's severe diminution—if not abandonment—of the "compelling governmental interest" test, thus leaving the protection of minority beliefs and practices to the uncertain whims of the political process.

SHERBERT v. VERNER

374 U.S. 398

ON APPEAL FROM THE SUPREME COURT OF SOUTH CAROLINA

Argued April 24, 1963 — Decided June 17, 1963

⊥**399** Mr. *Justice BRENNAN* delivered the opinion of the Court.

Appellant, a member of the Seventh-day Adventist Church, was discharged by her South Carolina employer because she would not work on Saturday, the Sabbath Day of her faith. When she was unable to obtain other employment because from conscientious scruples she would not take Saturday work, she filed a claim for ⊥**400** unemployment compensation benefits under the South Carolina Unemployment Compensation Act. That law provides that, to be eligible for benefits, a claimant must be "able to work and . . . available for work"; and, fur⊥**401**ther, that a claimant is ineligible for benefits "[i]f . . . he has failed, without good cause . . . to accept available suitable work when offered him by the employment office or the employer. . . ." The appellee Employment Security Commission, in administrative proceedings

[7]An indication of the impact that *Smith* might have on subsequent litigation came just one week after that holding, in *Minnesota* v. *Hershberger*. With only Justices O'Connor and Stevens dissenting, the Court vacated the judgment of the Minnesota Supreme Court that members of the Old Order Amish were exempt from a state law which required them to place reflecting triangles on their buggies. The case was remanded to the Minnesota high court for further consideration in light of the *Smith* decision. That court recognized that *Smith* had, indeed, changed the ground rules for federal free exercise litigation and would require a decision against the Amish. But the court reached a decision consistent with its earlier one by applying the religion clauses of the state constitution, which enabled it to apply a balancing test similar to the *Sherbert* test. It accommodated Amish religious objections to state requirements [462 N.W.2d 393 (1990)]. Since *Smith*, lawyers are more frequently filing their clients' free exercise cases in state courts, which, in turn, are more frequently relying on the provisions on religion in their state constitutions.

under the statute, found that appellant's restriction upon her availability for Saturday work brought her within the provision disqualifying for benefits insured workers who fail, without good cause, to accept "suitable work when offered . . . by the employment office or the employer. . . ." The Commission's finding was sustained by the Court of Common Pleas for Spartanburg County. That court's judgment was in turn affirmed by the South Carolina Supreme Court, which rejected appellant's contention that, as applied to her, the disqualifying provisions of the South Carolina statute abridged her right to the free exercise of her religion secured under the Free Exercise Clause of the First Amendment through the Fourteenth Amendment. The State Supreme Court held specifically that appellant's ineligibility infringed no constitutional liberties because such a construction of the statute "places no restriction upon the appellant's freedom of religion nor does it in any way prevent her in the exercise of her right and freedom to observe her religious beliefs in accordance with the dictates of her conscience." We noted probable ⊥**402** jurisdiction of appellant's appeal. We reverse the judgment of the South Carolina Supreme Court and remand for further proceedings not inconsistent with this opinion.

I

The door of the Free Exercise Clause stands tightly closed against any governmental regulation of religious *beliefs* as such. Government may neither compel affirmation of a repugnant belief, nor penalize or discriminate against individuals or groups because they hold religious views abhorrent to the authorities; nor employ the taxing power to inhibit the dissemination of particular religious views. On the other hand, ⊥**403** the Court has rejected challenges under the Free Exercise Clause to governmental regulation of certain overt acts prompted by religious beliefs or principles, for "even when the action is in accord with one's religious convictions, [it] is not totally free from legislative restrictions." *Braunfeld* v. *Brown*. The conduct or actions so regulated have invariably posed some substantial threat to public safety, peace or order.

Plainly enough, appellant's conscientious objection to Saturday work constitutes no conduct prompted by religious principles of a kind within the reach of state legislation. If, therefore, the decision of the South Carolina Supreme Court is to withstand appellant's constitutional challenge, it must be either because her disqualification as a beneficiary represents no infringement by the State of her constitutional rights of free exercise, or because any incidental burden on the free exercise of appellant's religion may be justified by a "compelling state interest in the regulation of a subject within the State's constitutional power to regulate. . . ." *NAACP* v. *Button*.

II

We turn first to the question whether the disqualification for benefits imposes any burden on the free exercise of appellant's religion. We think it is clear that it does. In a sense the consequences of such a disqualification to religious principles and practices may be only an indirect result of welfare legislation within the State's general competence to enact; it is true that no criminal sanctions directly compel appellant to work a six-day week. But this is only the beginning, not the end, of our ⊥**404** inquiry. For "[i]f the purpose or effect of a law is to impede the observance of one or all religions or is to discriminate invidiously between religions, that law is constitutionally invalid even though the burden may be characterized as being only indirect." *Braunfeld* v. *Brown*. Here not only is it apparent that appellant's declared ineligibility for benefits derives solely from the practice of her religion, but the pressure upon her to forego that practice is unmistakable. The ruling forces her to choose between following the precepts of her religion and forfeiting benefits, on the one hand, and abandoning one of the precepts of her religion in order to accept work, on the other hand. Governmental imposition of such a choice puts the same kind of burden upon the free exercise of religion as would a fine imposed against appellant for her Saturday worship.

Nor may the South Carolina court's construction of the statute be saved from constitutional infirmity on the ground that unemployment compensation benefits are not appellant's "right" but merely a "privilege." It is too late in the day to doubt that the liberties of religion and expression may be infringed by the denial of or placing of conditions upon a benefit or privilege. . . . ⊥**406**

To condition the availability of benefits upon this appellant's willingness to violate a cardinal principle of her religious faith effectively penalizes the free exercise of her constitutional liberties.

Significantly South Carolina expressly saves the Sunday worshipper from having to make the kind of choice which we here hold infringes the Sabbatarian's religious liberty. When in times of "national emergency" the textile plants are authorized by the State Commissioner of Labor to operate on Sunday, "no employee shall be required to work on Sunday . . . who is conscientiously opposed to Sunday work; and if any employee should refuse to work on Sunday on account of conscientious . . . objections he or she shall not jeopardize his or her seniority by such refusal or be discriminated against in any other manner." No question of the disqualification of a Sunday worshipper for benefits is likely to arise, since we cannot suppose that an employer will discharge him in violation of this statute. The unconstitutionality of the disqualification of the Sabbatarian is thus compounded by the religious discrimination which South Carolina's general statutory scheme necessarily effects.

III

We must next consider whether some compelling state interest enforced in the eligibility provisions of the South

Carolina statute justifies the substantial infringement of appellant's First Amendment right. It is basic that no showing merely of a rational relationship to some colorable state interest would suffice; in this highly sensitive constitutional area, "[o]nly the gravest abuses, endangering paramount interests, give occasion for permissible limitation." *Thomas* v. *Collins*. ⊥**407** No such abuse or danger has been advanced in the present case. The appellees suggest no more than a possibility that the filing of fraudulent claims by unscrupulous claimants feigning religious objections to Saturday work might not only dilute the unemployment compensation fund but also hinder the scheduling by employers of necessary Saturday work. But that possibility is not apposite here because no such objection appears to have been made before the South Carolina Supreme Court, and we are unwilling to assess the importance of an asserted state interest without the views of the state court. Nor, if the contention had been made below, would the record appear to sustain it; there is no proof whatever to warrant such fears of malingering or deceit as those which the respondents now advance. Even if consideration of such evidence is not foreclosed by the prohibition against judicial inquiry into the truth or falsity of religious beliefs—a question as to which we intimate no view since it is not before us—it is highly doubtful whether such evidence would be sufficient to warrant a substantial infringement of religious liberties. For even if the possibility of spurious claims did threaten to dilute the fund and disrupt the scheduling of work, it would plainly be incumbent upon the appellees to demonstrate that no alternative forms of regulation would combat such abuses without infringing First Amendment rights. ⊥**408**

In these respects, then, the state interest asserted in the present case is wholly dissimilar to the interests which were found to justify the less direct burden upon religious practices in *Braunfeld* v. *Brown*. The Court recognized that the Sunday closing law which that decision sustained undoubtedly served "to make the practice of [the Orthodox Jewish merchants'] . . . religious beliefs more expensive." But the statute was nevertheless saved by a countervailing factor which finds no equivalent in the instant case—a strong state interest in providing one uniform day of rest for all workers. That secular objective could be achieved, the court found, only by declaring Sunday to be that day of rest. Requiring exemptions for Sabbatarians, while theoretically possible, appeared to present an administrative ⊥**409** problem of such magnitude, or to afford the exempted class so great a competitive advantage, that such a requirement would have rendered the entire statutory scheme unworkable. In the present case no such justifications underlie the determination of the state court that appellant's religion makes her ineligible to receive benefits.

IV

In holding as we do, plainly we are not fostering the "establishment" of the Seventh-day Adventist religion in South Carolina, for the extension of unemployment benefits to Sabbatarians in common with Sunday worshippers reflects nothing more than the governmental obligation of neutrality in the face of religious differences, and does not represent that involvement of religious with secular institutions which it is the object of the Establishment Clause to forestall. Nor does the recognition of the appellant's right to unemployment benefits under the state statute serve to abridge any other person's religious liberties. Nor do we, by our decision today, declare the existence of a constitutional right to unemployment benefits on the part ⊥**410** of all persons whose religious convictions are the cause of their unemployment. This is not a case in which an employee's religious convictions serve to make him a nonproductive member of society. Finally, nothing we say today constrains the States to adopt any particular form or scheme of unemployment compensation. Our holding today is only that South Carolina may not constitutionally apply the eligibility provisions so as to constrain a worker to abandon his religious convictions respecting the day of rest. This holding but reaffirms a principle that we announced a decade and a half ago, namely that no State may "exclude individual Catholics, Lutherans, Mohammedans, Baptists, Jews, Methodists, Non-believers, Presbyterians, or the members of any other faith, *because of their faith, or lack of it*, from receiving the benefits of public welfare legislation." *Everson* v. *Board of Education*.

In view of the result we have reached under the First and Fourteenth Amendments' guarantee of free exercise of religion, we have no occasion to consider appellant's claim that the denial of benefits also deprived her of the equal protection of the laws in violation of the Fourteenth Amendment.

The judgment of the South Carolina Supreme Court is reversed and the case is remanded for further proceedings not inconsistent with this opinion.

It is so ordered.

Mr. Justice DOUGLAS, concurring.

The case we have for decision seems to me to be of small dimensions, though profoundly important. The question is whether the South Carolina law which denies unemployment compensation to a Seventh-day Adventist, who, because of her religion, has declined to work on her Sabbath, is a law "prohibiting the free exercise" of religion as those words are used in the First Amendment. ⊥**411** It seems obvious to me that this law does run afoul of that clause.

Religious scruples of Moslems require them to attend a mosque on Friday and to pray five times daily. Religious scruples of a Sikh require him to carry a regular or a symbolic sword. Religious scruples of a Jehovah's Witness teach him to be a colporteur, going from door to door, from town to town, distributing his religious pamphlets. Religious scruples of a Quaker compel him to refrain from swearing and to affirm instead. Religious scruples of a Buddhist may require him to refrain from partaking of any flesh, even of fish.

The examples could be multiplied, including those of the Seventh-day Adventist whose Sabbath is Saturday and who is advised not to eat some meats.

These suffice, however, to show that many people hold beliefs alien to the majority of our society—beliefs that are protected by the First Amendment but which could easily be trod upon under the guise of "police" or "health" regulations reflecting the majority's views.

Some have thought that a majority of a community can, through state action, compel a minority to observe their particular religious scruples so long as the majority's rule can be said to perform some valid secular function. ⊥**412** That was the essence of the Court's decision in the Sunday Blue Law Cases, a ruling from which I then dissented and still dissent.

That ruling of the Court travels part of the distance that South Carolina asks us to go now. She asks us to hold that when it comes to a day of rest a Sabbatarian must conform with the scruples of the majority in order to obtain unemployment benefits.

The result turns not on the degree of injury, which may indeed be nonexistent by ordinary standards. The harm is the interference with the individual's scruples or conscience—an important area of privacy which the First Amendment fences off from government. The interference here is as plain as it is in Soviet Russia, where a churchgoer is given a second-class citizenship, resulting in harm though perhaps not in measurable damages.

This case is resolvable not in terms of what an individual can demand of government, but solely in terms of what government may not do to an individual in violation of his religious scruples. The fact that government cannot exact from me a surrender of one iota of my religious scruples does not, of course, mean that I can demand of government a sum of money, the better to exercise them. For the Free Exercise Clause is written in terms of what the government cannot do to the individual, not in terms of what the individual can exact from the government.

Those considerations, however, are not relevant here. If appellant is otherwise qualified for unemployment benefits, payments will be made to her not as a Seventh-day Adventist, but as an unemployed worker. Conceivably these payments will indirectly benefit her church, ⊥**413** but no more so than does the salary of any public employee. Thus, this case does not involve the problems of direct or indirect state assistance to a religious organization—matters relevant to the Establishment Clause, not in issue here.

Mr. *Justice* STEWART, concurring in the result.

Although fully agreeing with the result which the Court reaches in this case, I cannot join the Court's opinion. This case presents a double-barreled dilemma, which in all candor I think the Court's opinion has not succeeded in papering over. The dilemma ought to be resolved.

I

Twenty-three years ago in *Cantwell* v. *Connecticut* the Court said that both the Establishment Clause and the Free Exercise Clause of the First Amendment were made wholly applicable to the States by the Fourteenth Amendment. In the intervening years several cases involving claims of state abridgment of individual religious freedom have been decided here—most recently *Braunfeld* v. *Brown*, and *Torcaso* v. *Watkins*. During the same period "cases dealing with the specific problems arising under the 'Establishment' Clause which have reached this Court are few in number." The most recent are last Term's *Engel* v. *Vitale*, and this Term's *Schempp* and *Murray* cases.

I am convinced that no liberty is more essential to the continued vitality of the free society which our Constitution guarantees than is the religious liberty protected by the Free Exercise Clause explicit in the First Amendment and imbedded in the Fourteenth. And I regret that on ⊥**414** occasion, and specifically in *Braunfeld* v. *Brown*, the Court has shown what has seemed to me a distressing insensitivity to the appropriate demands of this constitutional guarantee. By contrast I think that the Court's approach to the Establishment Clause has on occasion, and specifically in *Engel, Schempp* and *Murray*, been not only insensitive, but positively wooden, and that the Court has accorded to the Establishment Clause a meaning which neither the words, the history, nor the intention of the authors of that specific constitutional provision even remotely suggests.

But my views as to the correctness of the Court's decisions in these cases are beside the point here. The point is that the decisions are on the books. And the result is that there are many situations where legitimate claims under the Free Exercise Clause will run into head-on collision with the Court's insensitive and sterile construction of the Establishment Clause. The controversy now before us is clearly such a case. Because the appellant refuses to accept available jobs which would require her to work on Saturdays, South Carolina has declined to pay unemployment compensation benefits to her. Her refusal to work on Saturdays is based on the tenets of her religious faith. The Court says that South Carolina cannot under these circumstances declare her to be not "available for work" within the meaning of its statute because to do so would violate her constitutional right to the free exercise of her religion.

Yet what this Court has said about the Establishment Clause must inevitably lead to a diametrically opposite result. If the appellant's refusal to work on Saturdays ⊥**415** were based on indolence, or on a compulsive desire to watch the Saturday television programs, no one would say that South Carolina could not hold that she was not "available for work" within the meaning of its statute. That being so, the Establishment Clause as construed by this Court not only *permits* but affirmatively *requires* South Carolina equally to deny the appellant's claim for unemployment compensation when her refusal to work on Saturdays is based upon her religious creed. For, as said in *Everson* v. *Board of Education*, the Establishment Clause bespeaks "a government . . . stripped of all power . . . to support, or otherwise to assist any or all religions . . .," and no State "can pass laws which aid one religion. . . ." In Mr. *Justice RUTLEDGE'S* words, adopted by the Court today in *Schempp*, the Establishment Clause forbids "every form of public aid or support for religion." In the words of the Court in *Engel* v. *Vitale*, reaffirmed today in the *Schempp* case, the Establishment Clause forbids the "financial support of government" to be "placed behind a particular religious belief."

To require South Carolina to so administer its laws as to pay public money to the appellant under the circumstances of this case is thus clearly to require the State to violate the Establishment Clause as construed by this Court. This poses no problem for me, because I think the Court's mechanistic concept of the Establishment Clause is historically unsound and constitutionally wrong. I think the process of constitutional decision in the area of the relationships between government and religion demands considerably more than the invocation of broad-brushed rhetoric of the kind I have quoted. And I think that the guarantee of religious liberty embodied in the Free Exercise Clause affirmatively requires government to create an atmosphere of hospitality and accommoda**⊥416**tion to individual belief or disbelief. In short, I think our Constitution commands the positive protection by government of religious freedom—not only for a minority, however small—not only for the majority, however large—but for each of us.

South Carolina would deny unemployment benefits to a mother unavailable for work on Saturdays because she was unable to get a babysitter. Thus, we do not have before us a situation where a State provides unemployment compensation generally, and singles out for disqualification only those persons who are unavailable for work on religious grounds. This is not, in short, a scheme which operates so as to discriminate against religion as such. But the Court nevertheless holds that the State must prefer a religious over a secular ground for being unavailable for work—that state financial support of the appellant's religion is constitutionally required to carry out "the governmental obligation of neutrality in the face of religious differences. . . ."

Yet in cases decided under the Establishment Clause the Court has decreed otherwise. It has decreed that government must blind itself to the differing religious beliefs and traditions of the people. With all respect, I think it is the Court's duty to face up to the dilemma posed by the conflict between the Free Exercise Clause of the Constitution and the Establishment Clause as interpreted by the Court. It is a duty, I submit, which we owe to the people, the States, and the Nation, and a duty which we owe to ourselves. For so long as the resounding but fallacious fundamentalist rhetoric of some of our Establishment Clause opinions remains on our books, to be disregarded at will as in the present case, **⊥417** or to be undiscriminatingly invoked as in the *Schempp* case, so long will the possibility of consistent and perceptive decision in this most difficult and delicate area of constitutional law be impeded and impaired. And so long, I fear, will the guarantee of true religious freedom in our pluralistic society be uncertain and insecure.

II

My second difference with the Court's opinion is that I cannot agree that today's decision can stand consistently with *Braunfeld* v. *Brown*. The Court says that there was a "less direct burden upon religious practices" in that case than in this. With all respect, I think the Court is mistaken, simply as a matter of fact. The *Braunfeld* case involved a state *criminal* statute. The undisputed effect of that statute, as pointed out by Mr. *Justice BRENNAN* in his dissenting opinion in that case, was that "'Plaintiff, Abraham Braunfeld, will be unable to continue in his business if he may not stay open on Sunday and he will thereby lose his capital investment.' In other words, the issue in this case—and we do not understand either appellees or the Court to contend otherwise—is whether a State may put an individual to a choice between his business and his religion."

The impact upon the appellant's religious freedom in the present case is considerably less onerous. We deal here not with a criminal statute, but with the particularized administration of South Carolina's Unemployment Compensation Act. Even upon the unlikely assumption that the appellant could not find suitable non-Saturday employment, the appellant at the worst would be denied **⊥418** a maximum of 22 weeks of compensation payments. I agree with the Court that the possibility of that denial is enough to infringe upon the appellant's constitutional right to the free exercise of her religion. But it is clear to me that in order to reach this conclusion the Court must explicitly reject the reasoning of *Braunfeld* v. *Brown*. I think the *Braunfeld* case was wrongly decided and should be overruled, and accordingly I concur in the result reached by the Court in the case before us.

Mr. *Justice HARLAN*, whom Mr. *Justice WHITE* joins, dissenting.

Today's decision is disturbing both in its rejection of existing precedent and in its implications for the future. The significance of the decision can best be understood after an examination of the state law applied in this case.

South Carolina's Unemployment Compensation Law was enacted in 1936 in response to the grave social and economic problems that arose during the depression of that period. As stated in the statute itself:

"Economic insecurity due to unemployment is a serious menace to health, morals and welfare of the people of this State; *involuntary unemployment* is therefore a subject of general interest and concern . . .; the achievement of social security requires protection against this greatest hazard of our economic life; this can be provided by encouraging the employers *to provide more stable employment and by the systematic accumulation of funds during periods of employment to provide benefits for periods of unemployment*, thus maintaining purchasing power and limiting the serious social consequences of poor relief assistance." (Emphasis added.) ⊥**419**

Thus the purpose of the legislature was to tide people over, and to avoid social and economic chaos, during periods when *work was unavailable*. But at the same time there was clearly no intent to provide relief for those who for purely personal reasons were or became *unavailable for work*. In accordance with this design, the legislature provided that "[a]n unemployed insured worker shall be eligible to receive benefits with respect to any week *only* if the Commission finds that . . . [h]e is able to work and is available for work. . . ." (Emphasis added.)

The South Carolina Supreme Court has uniformly applied this law in conformity with its clearly expressed purpose. It has consistently held that one is not "available for work" if his unemployment has resulted not from the inability of industry to provide a job but rather from personal circumstances, no matter how compelling. The reference to "involuntary unemployment" in the legislative statement of policy, whatever a sociologist, philosopher, or theologian might say, has been interpreted not to embrace such personal circumstances.

In the present case all that the state court has done is to apply these accepted principles. Since virtually all of the mills in the Spartanburg area were operating on a six-day week, the appellant was "unavailable for work," and thus ineligible for benefits, when personal considera⊥**420**tions prevented her from accepting employment on a full-time basis in the industry and locality in which she had worked. The fact that these personal considerations sprang from her religious convictions was wholly without relevance to the state court's application of the law. Thus in no proper sense can it be said that the State discriminated against the appellant on the basis of her religious beliefs or that she was denied benefits *because* she was a Seventh-day Adventist. She was denied benefits just as any other claimant would be denied benefits who was not "available for work" for personal reasons.

With this background, this Court's decision comes into clearer focus. What the Court is holding is that if the State chooses to condition unemployment compensation on the applicant's availability for work, it is constitutionally compelled to *carve out an exception*—and to provide benefits—for those whose unavailability is due to their religious convictions. Such a holding has particular significance in two respects. ⊥**421**

First, despite the Court's protestations to the contrary, the decision necessarily overrules *Braunfeld* v. *Brown*, which held that it did not offend the "Free Exercise" Clause of the Constitution for a State to forbid a Sabbatarian to do business on Sunday. The secular purpose of the statute before us today is even clearer than that involved in *Braunfeld*. And just as in *Braunfeld*—where exceptions to the Sunday closing laws for Sabbatarians would have been inconsistent with the purpose to achieve a uniform day of rest and would have required case-by-case inquiry into religious beliefs—so here, an exception to the rules of eligibility based on religious convictions would necessitate judicial examination of those convictions and would be at odds with the limited purpose of the statute to smooth out the economy during periods of industrial instability. Finally, the indirect financial burden of the present law is far less than that involved in *Braunfeld*. Forcing a store owner to close his business on Sunday may well have the effect of depriving him of a satisfactory livelihood if his religious convictions require him to close on Saturday as well. Here we are dealing only with temporary benefits, amounting to a fraction of regular weekly wages and running for not more than 22 weeks. Clearly, any differences between this case and *Braunfeld* cut against the present appellant. ⊥**422**

Second, the implications of the present decision are far more troublesome than its apparently narrow dimensions would indicate at first glance. The meaning of today's holding, as already noted, is that the State must furnish unemployment benefits to one who is unavailable for work if the unavailability stems from the exercise of religious convictions. The State, in other words, must *single out* for financial assistance those whose behavior is religiously motivated, even though it denies such assistance to others whose identical behavior (in this case, inability to work on Saturdays) is not religiously motivated.

It has been suggested that such singling out of religious conduct for special treatment may violate the constitutional limitations on state action. My own view, however, is that at least under the circumstances of this case it would be a permissible accommodation of religion for the State, if it *chose* to do so, to create an exception to its eligibility requirements for persons like the appellant. The constitutional obligation of "neutrality" is not so narrow a channel that the slightest deviation from an absolutely straight course leads to condemnation. There are too many instances in which no such course can be charted, too many areas in which the pervasive activities of the State justify some special provision for religion to prevent it from being submerged by an all-embracing secularism. The State violates its obligation of neutrality ⊥**423** when, for example, it mandates a daily religious exercise in its public schools, with all the attendant pressures on the school children that such an exercise entails. But there is, I believe, enough flexibility in the Constitution to permit a legislative judgment accommodating an unemployment compensation law to the exercise of religious beliefs such as appellant's.

For very much the same reasons, however, I cannot subscribe to the conclusion that the State is constitutionally *compelled* to carve out an exception to its general rule of eligibility in the present case. Those situations in which the Constitution may require special treatment on account of religion are, in my view, few and far between, and this view is amply supported by the course of constitutional litigation in this area. Such compulsion in the present case is particularly inappropriate in light of the indirect, remote, and insubstantial effect of the decision below on the exercise of appellant's religion and in light of the direct financial assistance to religion that today's decision requires.

For these reasons I respectfully dissent from the opinion and judgment of the Court.

TRANS WORLD AIRLINES, INC. v. HARDISON INTERNATIONAL ASSOCIATION OF MACHINISTS AND AEROSPACE WORKERS, AFL-CIO v. HARDISON

432 U.S. 63

ON WRITS OF CERTIORARI TO THE UNITED STATES COURT OF APPEALS FOR THE EIGHTH CIRCUIT

Argued March 30, 1977 — Decided June 16, 1977

⊥66 Mr. *Justice WHITE* delivered the opinion of the Court.

Section 703(a) (1) of the Civil Rights Act of 1964, Title VII, 42 U. S. C. § 2000e — 2(a) (1), makes it an unlawful employment practice for an employer to discriminate against an employee or a prospective employee on the basis of his or her religion. At the time of the events involved here, a guideline of the Equal Employment Opportunity Commission (EEOC), 29 CFR § 1605.1(b), required, as the Act itself now does, 42 U. S. C. § 2000e (j), that an employer, short of "undue hardship," make "reasonable accommodations" to the religious needs of its employees. The issue in this case is the extent of the employer's obligation under Title VII to accommodate an employee whose religious beliefs prohibit him from working on Saturdays.

I

We summarize briefly the facts found by the District Court.

Petitioner Trans World Airlines (TWA) operates a large maintenance and overhaul base in Kansas City, Mo. On June 5, 1967, respondent Larry G. Hardison was hired by TWA to work as a clerk in the Stores Department at its Kansas City base. Because of its essential role in the Kansas City operation, the Stores Department must operate 24 hours per day, 365 days per year, and whenever an employee's job in that department is not filled, an employee must be **⊥67** shifted from another department, or a supervisor must cover the job, even if the work in other areas may suffer.

Hardison, like other employees at the Kansas City base, was subject to a seniority system contained in a collective-bargaining agreement that TWA maintains with petitioner International Association of Machinists and Aerospace Workers (IAM). The seniority system is implemented by the union steward through a system of bidding by employees for particular shift assignments as they become available. The most senior employees have first choice for job and shift assignments, and the most junior employees are required to work when the union steward is unable to find enough people willing to work at a particular time or in a particular job to fill TWA's needs.

In the spring of 1968 Hardison began to study the religion known as the Worldwide Church of God. One of the tenets of that religion is that one must observe the Sabbath by refraining from performing any work from sunset on Friday until sunset on Saturday. The religion also proscribes work on certain specified religious holidays.

When Hardison informed Everett Kussman, the manager of the Stores Department, of his religious conviction regarding **⊥68** observance of the Sabbath, Kussman agreed that the union steward should seek a job swap for Hardison or a change of days off; that Hardison would have his religious holidays off whenever possible if Hardison agreed to work the traditional holidays when asked; and that Kussman would try to find Hardison another job that would be more compatible with his religious beliefs. The problem was temporarily solved when Hardison transferred to the 11 p.m.-7 a.m. shift. Working this shift permitted Hardison to observe his Sabbath.

The problem soon reappeared when Hardison bid for and received a transfer from Building 1, where he had been employed, to Building 2, where he would work the day shift. The two buildings had entirely separate seniority lists; and while in Building 1 Hardison had sufficient seniority to observe the Sabbath regularly, he was second from the bottom on the Building 2 seniority list.

In Building 2 Hardison was asked to work Saturdays when a fellow employee went on vacation. TWA agreed to permit the union to seek a change of work assignments for Hardison, but the union was not willing to violate the seniority provisions set out in the collective-bargaining contract, and Hardison had insufficient seniority to bid for a shift having Saturdays off.

A proposal that Hardison work only four days a week was rejected by the company. Hardison's job was essential, and on weekends he was the only available person on his shift to perform it. To leave the position empty would have impaired Supply Shop functions, which were critical to airline operations; to fill Hardison's position with a supervisor or an **⊥69** employee from another area would simply have undermanned another operation; and to employ someone not regularly assigned to work Saturdays would have required TWA to pay premium wages.

When an accommodation was not reached, Hardison refused to report for work on Saturdays. A transfer to the twilight shift proved unavailing since that schedule still required Hardison to work past sundown on Fridays. After a hearing, Hardison was discharged on grounds of insubordination for refusing to work during his designated shift.

Hardison, having first invoked the administrative remedy provided by Title VII, brought this action for injunctive relief in the United States District Court against TWA and IAM, claiming that his discharge by TWA constituted religious discrimination in violation of Title VII, 42 U. S. C. § 2000e — 2(a) (1). He also charged that the union had discriminated against him by failing to represent him adequately in his dispute with TWA and by depriving him of his right to exercise his religious beliefs. Hardison's claim of religious discrimination rested on 1967 EEOC guidelines requiring employers "to make reasonable accommodations to the religious needs of employees" whenever such accommodation would not work an "undue hardship," 29 CFR § 1605.1, 32 Fed. Reg. 10298 (1967), and on similar language adopted by Congress in the 1972 amendments to Title VII, 42 U. S. C. § 2000e (j).

After a bench trial, the District Court ruled in favor of the defendants. Turning first to the claim against the union, the District Court ruled that although the 1967 EEOC guidelines were applicable to unions, the union's duty to accommodate Hardison's belief did not require it to ignore its seniority system as Hardison appeared to claim. As for Hardison's **⊥70** claim against TWA, the District Court rejected at the outset TWA's contention that requiring it in any way to accommodate the religious needs of its employees would constitute an unconstitutional establishment of religion. As the District Court construed the Act, however, TWA had satisfied its "reasonable accommodation" obligations, and any further accommodation would have worked an undue hardship on the company.

The Eighth Circuit Court of Appeals reversed the judgment for TWA. It agreed with the District Court's constitutional ruling, but held that TWA had not satisfied its duty to accommodate. Because it did not appear that Hardison had attacked directly the judgment in favor of the union, the Court of Appeals affirmed that judgment without ruling on its substantive merits.

In separate petitions for certiorari TWA and IAM contended that adequate steps had been taken to accommodate Hardison's religious observances and that to construe the statute to require further efforts at accommodation would create an establishment of religion contrary to the First Amendment of the Constitution. TWA also contended that the Court of Appeals improperly ignored the District Court's findings of fact.

We granted both petitions for certiorari. Because we agree with petitioners that their conduct was not a violation of Title VII, we need not reach the other questions presented.

⊥71 II

The Court of Appeals found that TWA had committed an unlawful employment practice under § 703(a) (1) of the Act, 42 U. S. C. § 2000e-2(a) (1), which provides:

"(a) It shall be an unlawful employment practice for an employer—

"(1) to fail or refuse to hire or to discharge any individual, or otherwise to discriminate against any individual with respect to his compensation, terms, conditions, or privileges of employment, because of such individual's race, color, religion, sex, or national origin."

The emphasis of both the language and the legislative history of the statute is on eliminating discrimination in employment; similarly situated employees are not to be treated differently solely because they differ with respect to race, color, religion, sex, or national origin. This is true regardless of whether **⊥72** the discrimination is directed against majorities or minorities.

The prohibition against religious discrimination soon raised the question of whether it was impermissible under § 703(a) (1) to discharge or refuse to hire a person who for religious reasons refused to work during the employer's normal work-week. In 1966 an EEOC guideline dealing with this problem declared that an employer had an obligation under the statute, "to accommodate to the reasonable religious needs of employees . . . where such accommodation can be made without serious inconvenience to the conduct of the business."

In 1967 the EEOC amended its guidelines to require employers "to make reasonable accommodations to the religious needs of employees and prospective employees where such accommodation can be made without undue hardship on the conduct of the employer's business." The Commission did not suggest what sort of accommodations are "reasonable" or when hardship to an employer becomes "undue."

⊥73 This question—the extent of the required accommodation—remained unsettled when this Court affirmed by an equally divided Court the Sixth Circuit's decision in *Dewey* v. *Reynolds Metals Co*. The discharge of an employee who for religious reasons had refused to work on Sundays was there held by the Court of Appeals not to be an unlawful employment practice because the manner in which the employer allocated Sunday work assignments was discriminatory in neither its purpose nor effect; and consistent with the 1967 EEOC guidelines, the employer had made a reasonable accommodation of the employee's beliefs by giving him the opportunity to secure a replacement for his Sunday work.

In part "to resolve by legislation" some of the issues raised in *Dewey* (remarks of Sen. Randolph), Congress included the following definition of religion in its 1972 amendments to Title VII:

"The term 'religion' includes all aspects of religious observance and practice, as well as belief, unless an employer demonstrates that he is unable to reasonably accom⊥74modate to an employee's or prospective employee's religious observance or practice without undue hardship on the conduct of the employer's business." Title VII § 701(j), 42 U. S. C. § 2000e (j). The intent and effect of this definition was to make it an unlawful employment practice under § 703(a) (1) for an employer not to make reasonable accommodations, short of undue hardship, for the religious practices of his employees and prospective employees. But like the EEOC guidelines, the statute provides no guidance for determining the degree of accommodation that is required of an employer. The brief legislative history of § 701(j) is likewise of little assistance in this regard. The proponent of the measure, Senator Jennings ⊥75 Randolph, expressed his general desire "to assure that freedom from religious discrimination in the employment of workers is for all time guaranteed by law," but he made no attempt to define the precise circumstances under which the "reasonable accommodation" requirement would be applied.

In brief, the employer's statutory obligation to make reasonable accommodation for the religious observances of its employees, short of incurring an undue hardship, is clear, but the reach of that obligation has never been spelled out by Congress or by Commission guidelines. With this in mind, we turn to a consideration of whether TWA has met its obliga⊥76tion under Title VII to accommodate the religious observances of its employees.

III

The Court of Appeals held that TWA had not made reasonable efforts to accommodate Hardison's religious needs under the 1967 EEOC guidelines in effect at the time the relevant events occurred. In its view, TWA had rejected three reasonable alternatives, any one of which would have satisfied its obligation without undue hardship. First, within the framework of the seniority system, TWA could have permitted Hardison to work a four-day week, utilizing in his place a supervisor or another worker on duty elsewhere. That this would have caused other shop functions to suffer was insufficient to amount to undue hardship in the opinion of the Court of Appeals. Second—according to the Court of Appeals, also within the bounds of the collective-bargaining contract—the company could have filled Hardison's Saturday shift from other available personnel competent to do the job, of which the court said there were at least 200. That this would have involved premium overtime pay was not deemed an undue hardship. Third, TWA could have arranged a "swap between Hardison and another employee either for another shift or for the Sabbath days." In response to the assertion that this would have involved a breach of the senior⊥77ity provisions of the contract, the court noted that it had not been settled in the courts whether the required statutory accommodation to religious needs stopped short of transgressing seniority rules, but found it unnecessary to decide the issue because, as the Court of Appeals saw the record, TWA had not sought, and the union had therefore not declined to entertain, a possible variance from the seniority provisions of the collective-bargaining agreement. The company had simply left the entire matter to the union steward who the Court of Appeals said "likewise did nothing."

We disagree with the Court of Appeals in all relevant respects. It is our view that TWA made reasonable efforts to accommodate and that each of the Court of Appeals' suggested alternatives would have been an undue hardship within the meaning of the statute as construed by the EEOC guidelines.

A

It might be inferred from the Court of Appeals' opinion and from the brief of the EEOC in this Court that TWA's efforts to accommodate were no more than negligible. The findings of the District Court, supported by the record, are to the contrary. In summarizing its more detailed findings, the District Court observed: "TWA established as a matter of fact that it did take appropriate action to accommodate as required by Title VII. It held several meetings with plaintiff at which it attempted to find a solution to plaintiff's problems. It did accommodate plaintiff's observance of his special religious holidays. It authorized the union steward to search for someone who would swap shifts, which apparently was normal procedure."

It is also true that TWA itself attempted without success to find Hardison another job. The District Court's view was that TWA had done all that could reasonably be expected within the bounds of the seniority system.

⊥78 The Court of Appeals observed, however, that the possibility of a variance from the seniority system was never really posed to the union. This is contrary to the District Court's findings and to the record. The District Court found that when TWA first learned of Hardison's religious observances in April, 1968, it agreed to permit the union's steward to seek a swap of shifts or days off but that "the steward reported that he was unable to work out scheduling changes and that he understood no one was willing to swap days with plaintiff." Later, in March 1969, at a meeting held just two days before Hardison first failed to report for his Saturday shift, TWA again "offered to accommodate plaintiff's religious observance by agreeing to any trade of shifts that plaintiff and the union could work out. Any shift or change was impossible within the seniority framework and the union was not willing to violate the seniority provisions set out in the contract to make a shift or change." As the record shows, Hardison himself testified that Kussman was willing, but the union was not, to work out a shift or job trade with another employee.

We shall say more about the seniority system, but at this juncture it appears to us that the system itself represented a significant accommodation to the needs, both religious and secular, of all of TWA's employees. As will become apparent, the seniority system represents a neutral way of minimizing the number of occasions when an employee must work on a day that he would prefer to have off. Additionally, recognizing that weekend work schedules are the least popular, the company made further accommodation by reducing its work force to a bare minimum on those days.

B

We are also convinced, contrary to the Court of Appeals, that TWA cannot be faulted for having failed itself to work ⊥**79** out a shift or job swap for Hardison. Both the union and TWA had agreed to the seniority system; the union was unwilling to entertain a variance over the objections of men senior to Hardison; and for TWA to have arranged unilaterally for a swap would have amounted to a breach of the collective-bargaining agreement.

(1)

Hardison and the EEOC insist that the statutory obligation to accommodate religious needs takes precedence over both the collective-bargaining contract and the seniority rights of TWA's other employees. We agree that neither a collective-bargaining contract nor a seniority system may be employed to violate the statute, but we do not believe that the duty to accommodate requires TWA to take steps inconsistent with the otherwise valid agreement. Collective bargaining, aimed at effecting workable and enforceable agreements between management and labor, lies at the core of our national labor policy, and seniority provisions are universally included in these contracts. Without a clear and express indication from Congress, we cannot agree with Hardison and the EEOC that an agreed-upon seniority system must give way when necessary to accommodate religious observances. The issue is important and warrants some discussion.

⊥**80** Any employer who, like TWA, conducts an around-the-clock operation is presented with the choice of allocating work schedules either in accordance with the preferences of its employees or by involuntary assignment. Insofar as the varying shift preferences of its employees complement each other, TWA could meet its manpower needs through voluntary work scheduling. In the present case, for example, Hardison's supervisor foresaw little difficulty in giving Hardison his religious holidays off since they fell on days that most other employees preferred to work, while Hardison was willing to work on the traditional holidays that most other employees preferred to have off.

Whenever there are not enough employees who choose to work a particular shift, however, some employees must be assigned to that shift even though it is not their first choice. Such was evidently the case with regard to Saturday work; even though TWA cut back its weekend work force to a skeleton crew, not enough employees chose those days off to staff the Stores Department through voluntary scheduling. In these circumstances, TWA and IAM agreed to give first preference to employees who had worked in a particular department the longest.

Had TWA nevertheless circumvented the seniority system by relieving Hardison of Saturday work and ordering a senior employee to replace him, it would have denied the latter his shift preference so that Hardison could be given his. The senior employee would also have been deprived of his contractual rights under the collective-bargaining agreement.

It was essential to TWA's business to require Saturday and Sunday work from at least a few employees even though most employees preferred those days off. Allocating the burdens of weekend work was a matter for collective bargaining. In considering criteria to govern this allocation, TWA and the union had two alternatives: adopt a neutral system, such as seniority, a lottery, or rotating shifts; or allocate days off in ⊥**81** accordance with the religious needs of its employees. TWA would have had to adopt the latter in order to assure Hardison and others like him of getting the days off necessary for strict observance of their religion, but it could have done so only at the expense of others who had strong, but perhaps nonreligious reasons for not working on weekends. There were no volunteers to relieve Hardison on Saturdays, and to give Hardison Saturdays off, TWA would have had to deprive another employee of his shift preference at least in part because he did not adhere to a religion that observed the Saturday Sabbath.

Title VII does not contemplate such unequal treatment. The repeated, unequivocal emphasis of both the language and the legislative history of Title VII is on eliminating discrimination in employment, and such discrimination is proscribed when it is directed against majorities as well as minorities. Indeed, the foundation of Hardison's claim is that TWA and IAM engaged in religious *discrimination* in violation of § 703(a) (1) when they failed to arrange for him to have Saturdays off. It would be anomalous to conclude that by "reasonable accommodation" Congress meant that an employer must deny the shift and job preference of some employees, as well as deprive them of their contractual rights, in order to accommodate or prefer the religious needs of others, and we conclude that Title VII does not require an employer to go that far.

(2)

Our conclusion is supported by the fact that seniority systems are afforded special treatment under Title VII itself. Section 703(h) provides in pertinent part: "Notwithstanding any other provision of this sub-chapter, it shall not be an unlawful employment practice for an employer to apply different standards of compensation, or different terms, conditions, or privileges of em⊥**82**ployment pursuant to a bona fide seniority or merit system . . . provided that such differences are not the result of an intention to discriminate because of race, color, religion, sex, or national origin. . . ." "[T]he unmistakable purpose of § 703(h) was to make clear that the routine application of a bona fide seniority system would not be unlawful under Title VII." *International Brotherhood of Teamsters* v. *United States*. Section 703(h) is "a definitional provision; as with other provisions of § 703, subsection (h) delineates which employment practices are illegal and thereby prohibited and which are not." *Franks* v. *Bowman Transportation Co., Inc.* Thus, absent a discriminatory purpose, the operation of a seniority system cannot be an unlawful employment practice even if the system has some discriminatory consequences.

There has been no suggestion of discriminatory intent in this case. "The seniority system was not designed with the intention to discriminate against religion nor did it act to lock members of any religion into a pattern wherein their freedom to exercise their religion was limited. It was coincidental that in plaintiff's case the seniority system acted to compound his problems in exercising his religion." The Court of Appeals' conclusion that TWA was not limited by the terms of its seniority system was in substance nothing more than a ruling that operation of the seniority system was itself an unlawful employment practice even though no discriminatory purpose had been shown. That ruling is plainly inconsistent with the dictates of § 703(h), both on its face and as interpreted in the recent decisions of this Court.

⊥**83** As we have said, TWA was not required by Title VII to carve out a special exception to its seniority system in order to help Hardison to meet his religious obligations.

⊥84 C

The Court of Appeals also suggested that TWA could have permitted Hardison to work a four-day week if necessary in order to avoid working on his Sabbath. Recognizing that this might have left TWA short-handed on the one shift each week that Hardison did not work, the court still concluded that TWA would suffer no undue hardship if it were required to replace Hardison either with supervisory personnel or with qualified personnel from other departments. Alternatively, the Court of Appeals suggested that TWA could have replaced Hardison on his Saturday shift with other available employees through the payment of premium wages. Both of these alternatives would involve costs to TWA, either in the form of lost efficiency in other jobs or as higher wages.

To require TWA to bear more than a *de minimis* cost in order to give Hardison Saturdays off is an undue hardship. Like abandonment of the seniority system, to require TWA to bear additional costs when no such costs are incurred to give other employees the days off that they want would involve unequal treatment of employees on the basis of their religion. By suggesting that TWA should incur certain costs in order to give Hardison Saturdays off the Court of Appeals would in effect require TWA to finance an additional Saturday off and then to choose the employee who will enjoy it on the basis of his religious beliefs. While incurring extra costs to secure a replacement for Hardison might remove the necessity of compelling another employee to work involun⊥**85**tarily in Hardison's place, it would not change the fact that the privilege of having Saturdays off would be allocated according to religious beliefs.

As we have seen, the paramount concern of Congress in enacting Title VII was the elimination of discrimination in employment. In the absence of clear statutory language or legislative history to the contrary, we will not readily construe the statute to require an employer to discriminate against some employees in order to enable others to observe their Sabbath.

Reversed.

Mr. *Justice* MARSHALL, with whom Mr. *Justice* BRENNAN joins, dissenting.

One of the most intractable problems arising under Title VII of the Civil Rights Act of 1964 has been whether an employer is guilty of religious discrimination when he discharges an employee (or refuses to hire a job applicant) because of the employee's religious practices. Particularly troublesome has been the plight of adherents to minority faiths who do not observe the holy days on which most businesses are closed—Sundays, Christmas, and Easter—but who need time off for their own days of religious observance. The Equal Employment Opportunity Commission has grappled with this problem in two sets of regulations, and in a long line of decisions. Initially the Commission concluded that an employer was "free under Title VII to establish a normal workweek . . . generally applicable to all employees," and that an employee could not "demand any alteration in [his work schedule] to accommodate his religious needs." Eventually, however, the Commission changed its view and decided that employers must reasonably accommodate such requested schedule changes except where "undue hardship" would result—for example, "where the employee's needed work cannot be per⊥**86**formed by another employee of substantially similar qualifications during the period of absence." In amending Title VII in 1972 Congress confronted the same problem, and adopted the second position of the EEOC. Both before and after the 1972 amendment the lower courts have considered at length the circumstances in which employers must accommodate the religious practices of employees, reaching what the Court correctly describes as conflicting results. And on two occasions this Court has attempted to provide guidance to the lower courts, only to find ourselves evenly divided. *Parker Seal Co.* v. *Cummins; Dewey* v. *Reynolds Metals Co.*

Today's decision deals a fatal blow to all efforts under Title VII to accommodate work requirements to religious practices. The Court holds, in essence, that although the EEOC regulations and the Act state that an employer must make reasonable adjustments in his work demands to take account of religious observances, the regulation and Act do not ⊥**87** really mean what they say. An employer, the Court concludes, need not grant even the most minor special privilege to religious observers to enable them to follow their faith. As a question of social policy, this result is deeply troubling, for a society that truly values religious pluralism cannot compel adherents of minority religions to make the cruel choice of surrendering their religion or their job. And as a matter of law today's result is intolerable, for the Court adopts the very position that Congress expressly rejected in 1972, as if we were free to disregard congressional choices that a majority of this Court thinks unwise. I therefore dissent.

I

With respect to each of the proposed accommodations to respondent's religious observances that the Court discusses, it ultimately notes that the accommodation would have required "unequal treatment," in favor of the religious observer. That is quite true. But if an accommodation can be rejected simply because it involves preferential treatment, then the regulation and the statute, while brimming with "sound and fury," ultimately "signif[y] nothing."

The accommodation issue by definition arises only when a neutral rule of general applicability conflicts with the religious practices of a particular employee. In some of the reported cases, the rule in question has governed work attire; in other cases it has required attendance at some religious function; in still other instances, it has compelled membership in a union; and in the largest class of cases, it has concerned work schedules. What all these cases have in common is an employee who could comply with the rule only by violating what the employee views as a religious commandment. In each ⊥**88** instance, the question is whether the employee is to be exempt from the rule's demands. To do so will always result in a privilege being "allocated according to religious beliefs," unless the employer gratuitously decides to repeal the rule in toto. What the statute says, in plain words, is that such allocations are required unless "undue hardship" would result.

The point is perhaps best made by considering a not-altogether-hypothetical example. See EEOC Decision No. 71-779, 1973 CCH EEOC Decisions ¶ 6180 (Dec. 21, 1970). Assume that an employer requires all employees to wear a particular type of hat at work in order to make the employees readily identifiable to customers. Such a rule obviously does not, on its face, violate Title VII, and an employee who altered the uniform for reasons of taste could be discharged. But a very different question would be posed by the discharge of an employee who, for religious reasons, insisted on wearing, over her hair a tightly fitted scarf which was visible through the hat. In such a case the employer could accommodate this religious practice without undue hardship—or any hardship at all. Yet as I understand the Court's analysis—and nothing in the Court's response, is to the contrary—the accommodation would not be required because it would afford the privilege of wearing scarfs to a select few based on their religious beliefs. The employee thus would have to give up either the religious practice or the job. This, I submit, makes a mockery of the statute.

In reaching this result, the Court seems almost oblivious to the legislative history of the 1972 amendment to Title VII which is briefly recounted in the Court's opinion. That history is far more instructive than the Court allows. After the EEOC promulgated its second set of guidelines requiring reasonable accommodations unless undue hardship would result, at least two courts issued decisions questioning, whether the guidelines were consistent with Title VII. ⊥**89** These courts reasoned, in language strikingly similar to today's decision, that to excuse religious observers from neutral work rules would "discriminate against . . . other employees" and "constitute unequal administration of the collective-bargaining agreement." *Dewey* v. *Reynolds Metals Co.* They therefore refused to equate "religious discrimination with failure to accommodate." When Congress was reviewing Title VII in 1972, Senator Jennings Randolph informed the Congress of these decisions which, he said, had "clouded" the meaning of religious discrimination. 118 Cong. Rec. 706 (1972). He introduced an amendment, tracking the language of the EEOC regulation, to make clear that Title VII requires religious accommodation, even though unequal treatment would result. The primary purpose of the amendment, he explained, was to protect Saturday Sabbatarians like himself from employers who refuse "to hire or to continue in employment employees whose religious practices rigidly require them to abstain from work in the nature of hire on particular days." His amendment was unanimously approved by the Senate on a roll call vote, and was accepted by the Conference Committee, whose report was approved by both Houses. Yet the Court today, in rejecting any accommodation that involves preferential treatment, follows the *Dewey* decision in direct contravention of congressional intent.

The Court's interpretation of the statute, by effectively nullifying it, has the singular advantage of making consideration of petitioners' constitutional challenge unnecessary. The Court does not even rationalize its construction on this ground, however, nor could it, since "resort to an alternative construction to avoid deciding a constitutional question is appro⊥**90**priate only when such a course is 'fairly possible' or when the statute provides a 'fair alternative' construction." *Swain* v. *Pressley*.

Moreover, while important constitutional questions would be posed by interpreting the law to compel employers (or fellow employees) to incur substantial costs to aid the religious observer, not all accommodations are costly, and the constitutionality of the statute is not placed in serious doubt simply because it sometimes requires an exemption from a work rule. Indeed, this Court has repeatedly found no Establishment Clause problems in exempting religious observers from state-imposed duties, *e.g.*, *Wisconsin* v. *Yoder; Sherbert* v. *Verner; Zorach* v. *Clauson*, even when the exemption was in no way compelled by the Free Exercise Clause, *e.g.*, *Gillette* v. *United States; Welsh* v. *United States (White, J.*, dissenting); *Sherbert* v. *Verner (Harlan, J.*, dissenting); *Braunfeld* v. *Brown*, (dictum); *McGowan* v. *Maryland, (Frankfurter, J.*, concurring). If the State does not establish ⊥**91** religion over nonreligion by excusing religious practitioners from obligations owed the State, I do not see how the State can be said to establish religion by requiring employers to do the same with respect to obligations owed the employer. Thus, I think it beyond dispute that the Act does—and, consistently with the First Amendment, can—require employers to grant privileges to religious observers as part of the accommodation process.

II

Once it is determined that the duty to accommodate sometimes requires that an employee be exempted from an otherwise valid work requirement, the only remaining question is whether this is such a case: Did TWA prove that it exhausted all reasonable accommodations, and that the only remaining alternatives would have caused undue hardship on TWA's business? To pose the question is to answer it, for all that the District Court found TWA had done to accommodate respondent's Sabbath observance was that it "held several meetings with [respondent] . . . [and] authorized the union steward to search for someone who would swap shifts." *Hardison* v. *TWA*. To conclude that TWA, one of the largest air carriers in the Nation, would have suffered undue hardship had it done anything more defies both reason and common sense.

The Court implicitly assumes that the only means of accommodation open to TWA were to compel an unwilling employee to replace respondent; to pay premium wages to a voluntary substitute; or to employ one less person during ⊥**92** respondent's Sabbath shift. Based on this assumption, the Court seemingly finds that each alternative would have involved undue hardship not only because Hardison would have been given a special privilege, but also because either another employee would have been deprived of rights under the collective-bargaining agreement, or because "more than a *de minimis* cost" would have been imposed on TWA. But the Court's myopic view of the available options is not supported by either the District Court's findings or the evidence adduced at trial. Thus, the Court's conclusion cannot withstand analysis, even assuming that its rejection of the alternatives it does discuss is justifiable.

⊥**93** To begin with, the record simply does not support the Court's assertion, made without accompanying citations, that "[t]here were no volunteers to relieve Hardison on Saturdays." Everett Kussman, the manager of the department in which respondent worked, testified that he had made no effort to find volunteers, and the Union stipulated that its steward had not done so either. Thus, contrary to the Court's assumption, there may have been one or more employees who, for reasons of either sympathy or personal convenience, willingly would have substi⊥**94**tuted for respondent on Saturdays until respondent could either regain the non-Saturday shift he had held for the three preceding months or transfer back to his old department where he had sufficient seniority to avoid Saturday work. Alternatively, there may have been an employee who preferred respondent's Thursday-Monday daytime shift to his own; in fact, respondent testified that he had informed Kussman and the Union steward that the clerk on the Sunday-Thursday night shift (the "graveyard" shift) was dissatisfied with his hours. Thus, respondent's religious observance might have been accommodated by a simple trade of days or shifts without necessarily depriving any employee of his or her contractual rights and without ⊥**95** imposing significant costs on TWA. Of course it is also possible that no trade—or none consistent with the seniority system—could have been arranged. But the burden under the EEOC regulation is on TWA to establish that a reasonable accommodation was not possible. Because it failed either to explore the possibility of a voluntary trade or to assure that its delegate, the Union steward, did so, TWA was unable to meet its burden.

Nor was a voluntary trade the only option open to TWA that the Court ignores; to the contrary, at least two other options are apparent from the record. First, TWA could have paid overtime to a voluntary replacement for respondent—assuming that someone would have been willing to work Saturdays for premium pay—and passed on the cost to respondent. In fact, one accommodation Hardison suggested would have done just that by requiring Hardison to work overtime when needed at regular pay. Under this plan, the total overtime cost to the employer—and the total number of overtime hours available for other employees—would not have reflected Hardison's Sabbath absences. Alternatively, TWA could have transferred respondent back to his previous department where he had accumulated substantial seniority, as respondent also suggested. Admittedly, both options would have violated the collective-bargaining agreement; the former because the agreement required that employees working over forty hours per week receive premium pay, and the latter because the agreement prohibited employees from trans⊥**96**ferring departments more than once every six months. But neither accommodation would have deprived any other employee of rights under the contract or violated the seniority system in any way.

Plainly an employer cannot avoid his duty to accommodate by signing a contract that precludes all reasonable accommodations; even the Court appears to concede as much. Thus I do not believe it can be even seriously argued that TWA would have suffered "undue hardship" to its business had it required respondent to pay the extra costs of his replacement, or had it transferred respondent to his former department.

What makes this case most tragic, however, is not that respondent Hardison has been needlessly deprived of his livelihood simply because he chose to follow the dictates of his conscience. Nor is the tragedy of the case exhausted by the impact it will have on thousands of Americans like Hardison who could be forced to live on welfare as the price they must pay for ⊥**97** worshipping their God. The ultimate tragedy is that despite Congress' best efforts, one of this Nation's pillars of strength—our hospitality to religious diversity—has been seriously eroded. All Americans will be a little poorer until today's decision is erased. I respectfully dissent.

THOMAS v. REVIEW BOARD OF INDIANA EMPLOYMENT SECURITY DIVISION

450 U.S. 707
ON WRIT OF CERTIORARI TO THE SUPREME COURT OF THE STATE OF INDIANA
Argued October 7, 1980 — Decided April 6, 1981

⊥**709** *Chief Justice BURGER* delivered the opinion of the Court.

We granted certiorari to consider whether the State's denial of unemployment compensation benefits to the petitioner, a Jehovah's Witness who terminated his job because his religious beliefs forbade participation in the production of armaments, constituted a violation of his First Amendment right to free exercise of religion.

I

Thomas terminated his employment in the Blaw-Knox Foundry and Machinery Company when he was transferred from the roll foundry to a department that produced turrets for military tanks. He claimed his religious beliefs prevented him from participating in the production of war materials. The respondent Review Board denied him unemployment compensation benefits by applying disqualifying provisions of the Indiana Employment Security Act. ⊥**710**

Thomas, a Jehovah's Witness, was hired initially to work in the roll foundry at Blaw-Knox. The function of that department was to fabricate sheet steel for a variety of industrial uses. On his application form, he listed his membership in the Jehovah's Witnesses, and noted that his hobbies were Bible study and Bible reading. However, he placed no conditions on his employment; and, he did not describe his religious tenets in any detail on the form.

Approximately a year later, the roll foundry closed, and Blaw-Knox transferred Thomas to a department that fabricated turrets for military tanks. On his first day at this new job, Thomas realized that the work he was doing was weapons related. He checked the bulletin board where in-plant openings were listed, and discovered that all of the remaining departments at Blaw-Knox were engaged directly in the production of weapons. Since no transfer to another department would resolve his problem, he asked for a layoff. When that request was denied, he quit, asserting that he could not work on weapons without violating the principles of his religion. The record does not show that he was offered any non-weapons work by his employer, or that any such work was available.

Upon leaving Blaw-Knox, Thomas applied for unemployment compensation benefits under the Indiana Employment Security Act. At an administrative hearing where he was ⊥**711** not represented by counsel, he testified that he believed that contributing to the production of arms violated his religion. He said that when he realized that his work on the tank turret line involved producing weapons for war, he consulted another Blaw-Knox employee—a friend and fellow Jehovah's Witness. The friend advised him that working on weapons parts at Blaw-Knox was not "unscriptural." Thomas was not able to "rest with" this view, however. He concluded that his friend's view was based upon a less strict reading of Witness' principles than his own.

When asked at the hearing to explain what kind of work his religious convictions would permit, Thomas said that he would have no difficulty doing the type of work that he had done at the roll foundry. He testified that he could, in good conscience, engage indirectly in the production of materials that might be used ultimately to fabricate arms—for example, as an employee of a raw material supplier or of a roll foundry.

The hearing referee found that Thomas' religious beliefs specifically precluded him from producing or directly aiding in the manufacture of items used in warfare. He also found that Thomas had terminated his employment because of these religious convictions. The referee reported:

"Claimant continually searched for a transfer to another department which would not be so armament related, ⊥**712** however, this did not materialize, and prior to the date of his leaving, claimant requested a layoff, which was denied; and on November 6, 1975, *claimant did quit due to his religious convictions*."

The referee concluded nonetheless that Thomas' termination was not based upon a "good cause [arising] in connection with [his] work," as required by the Indiana unemployment compensation statute. Accordingly, he was held not entitled to benefits. The Review Board adopted the referee's findings and conclusions, and affirmed the denial of benefits.

The Indiana Court of Appeals, accepting the finding that Thomas terminated his employment "due to his religious convictions," reversed the decision of the Review Board, and held that § 22-4-15-1, as applied, improperly burdened Thomas' right to the free exercise of his religion. Accordingly, it ordered the Board to extend benefits to Thomas. *Thomas* v. *Review Board*.

The Supreme Court of Indiana, dividing 3-2, vacated the decision of the Court of Appeals, and denied Thomas benefits. *Thomas* v. *Review Board*. With reference to the Indiana unemployment compensation statute, the court said:

"It is not intended to facilitate changing employment or to provide relief for those who quit work voluntarily for personal reasons. Voluntary unemployment is not compensable under the purpose of the Act, which is to provide benefits for persons unemployed through no fault of their own.

"Good cause which justifies voluntary unemployment must ⊥**713** be job-related and objective in character."

The court held that Thomas had quit voluntarily for personal reasons, and therefore did not qualify for benefits.

In discussing the petitioner's free exercise claim, the court stated: "[A] personal philosophical choice rather than a religious choice, does not rise to the level of a first amendment claim." The court found the basis and the precise nature of Thomas' belief unclear—but it concluded that the belief was more "personal philosophical choice" than religious belief. Nonetheless, it held that, even assuming that Thomas quit for religious reasons, he would not be entitled to benefits: under Indiana law, a termination motivated by religion is not for "good cause" objectively related to the work.

The Indiana court concluded that denying Thomas benefits would create only an indirect burden on his free exercise right and that the burden was justified by the legitimate state interest in preserving the integrity of the insurance fund and maintaining a stable work force by encouraging workers not to leave their jobs for personal reasons.

Finally, the court held that awarding unemployment compensation benefits to a person who terminates employment voluntarily for religious reasons, while denying such benefits to persons who terminate for other personal but nonreligious reasons, would violate the Establishment Clause of the First Amendment.

The judgment under review must be examined in light of our prior decisions, particularly *Sherbert* v. *Verner*.

II

Only beliefs rooted in religion are protected by the Free Exercise Clause, which, by its terms, gives special protection to the exercise of religion. *Sherbert* v. *Verner*; *Wis*⊥**714***consin* v. *Yoder*. The determination of what is a "religious" belief or practice is more often than not a difficult and delicate task, as the division in the Indiana Supreme Court attests. However, the resolution of that question is not to turn upon a judicial perception of the particular belief or practice in question; religious beliefs need not be acceptable, logical, consistent, or comprehensible to others in order to merit First Amendment protection.

In support of his claim for benefits, Thomas testified:

"Q. And then when it comes to actually producing the tank itself, hammering it out; that you will not do. . . .

"A. That's right, that's right when . . . I'm daily faced with the knowledge that these are tanks. . . .

. . . . .

"A. I really could not, you know, conscientiously continue to work with armaments. It would be against all of the . . . religious principles that . . . I have come to learn. . . ."

Based upon this and other testimony, the referee held that Thomas "quit due to his religious convictions." The Review Board adopted that finding, and the finding is not challenged in this Court.

The Indiana Supreme Court apparently took a different view of the record. It concluded that "although the claimant's reasons for quitting were described as religious, it was unclear what his belief was, and what the religious basis of his belief was." In that court's view, Thomas had made a merely "personal philosophical choice rather than a religious choice." ⊥**715**

In reaching its conclusion, the Indiana court seems to have placed considerable reliance on the facts that Thomas was "struggling" with his beliefs and that he was not able to "articulate" his belief precisely. It noted, for example, that Thomas admitted before the referee that he would not object to "working for United States Steel or Inland Steel . . . produc[ing] the raw product necessary for the production of any kind of tank . . . [because I] would not be a direct party to whoever they shipped it to [and] would not be . . . chargeable in . . . conscience. . . ." *Thomas* v. *Review Board*.

The court found this position inconsistent with Thomas' stated opposition to participation in the production of armaments. But, Thomas' statements reveal no more than that he found work in the roll foundry sufficiently insulated from producing weapons of war. We see, therefore, that Thomas drew a line, and it is not for us to say that the line he drew was an unreasonable one. Courts should not undertake to dissect religious beliefs because the believer admits that he is "struggling" with his position or because his beliefs are not articulated with the clarity and precision that a more sophisticated person might employ.

The Indiana court also appears to have given significant weight to the fact that another Jehovah's Witness had no scruples about working on tank turrets; for that other Witness, at least, such work was "scripturally" acceptable. Intrafaith differences of that kind are not uncommon among followers of a particular creed, and the judicial process is singularly ill equipped to resolve such differences in relation to the Religion Clauses. One can, of course, imagine an asserted claim so bizarre, so clearly nonreligious in motivation, as not to be entitled to protection under the Free Exercise Clause; but that is not the case here, and the guarantee of free exercise is not limited to beliefs which are shared by all of the members ⊥**716** of a religious sect. Particularly in this sensitive area, it is not within the judicial function and judicial competence to inquire whether the petitioner or his fellow worker more correctly perceived the commands of their common faith. Courts are not arbiters of scriptural interpretation.

The narrow function of a reviewing court in this context is to determine whether there was an appropriate finding that petitioner terminated his work because of an honest conviction that such work was forbidden by his religion. Not surprisingly, the record before the referee and the Review Board was not made with an eye to the microscopic examination often exercised in appellate judicial review. However, judicial review is confined to the facts as found and conclusions drawn. On this record, it is clear that Thomas terminated his employment for religious reasons.

III

A

More than 30 years ago, the Court held that a person may not be compelled to choose between the exercise of a First Amendment right and participation in an otherwise available public program. A state may not "exclude individual Catholics, Lutherans, Mohammedans, Baptists, Jews, Methodists, Non-believers, Presbyterians, or the members of any other faith, because of their faith, or lack of it, from receiving the benefits of public welfare legislation." *Everson* v. *Board of Education*.

Later, in *Sherbert*, the Court examined South Carolina's attempt to deny unemployment compensation benefits to a Sabbatarian who declined to work on Saturday. In sustaining her right to receive benefits, the Court held:

"The ruling [disqualifying Mrs. Sherbert from benefits because of her refusal to work on Saturday in violation of her faith] forces her to choose between following the ⊥**717** precepts of her religion and forfeiting benefits, on the one hand, and abandoning one of the precepts of her religion in order to accept work, on the other hand. Governmental imposition of such a burden puts the same kind of burden upon the free exercise of religion as would a fine imposed against [her] for her Saturday worship."

The respondent Review Board argues, and the Indiana Supreme Court held, that the burden upon religion here is only the indirect consequence of public welfare legislation that the state clearly has authority to enact. "Neutral objective standards must be met to qualify for compensation." *Thomas* v. *Review Board* Indiana requires applicants for unemployment compensation to show that they left work for "good cause in connection with the work."

A similar argument was made and rejected in *Sherbert*, however. It is true that, as in *Sherbert*, the Indiana law does not *compel* a violation of conscience. But, "this is only the beginning, not the end, of our inquiry." In a variety of ways we have said that "a regulation neutral on its face may, in its application, nonetheless offend the constitutional requirement for governmental neutrality if it unduly burdens the free exercise of religion." *Wisconsin* v. *Yoder*. Cf. *Walz* v. *Tax Commissioner*.

Here, as in *Sherbert*, the employee was put to a choice between fidelity to religious belief or cessation of work; the coercive impact on Thomas is indistinguishable from *Sherbert*, where the Court held:

"[N]ot only is it apparent that appellant's declared ineligibility for benefits derives solely from the practices of her religion, but the pressure upon her to forego that practice is unmistakable."

Where the state conditions receipt of an important benefit upon conduct proscribed by a religious faith, or where it denies ⊥**718** such a benefit because of conduct mandated by religious belief, thereby putting substantial pressure on an adherent to modify his behavior and to violate his beliefs, a burden upon religion exists. While the compulsion may be indirect, the infringement upon free exercise is nonetheless substantial.

The State also contends that *Sherbert* is inapposite because, in that case, the employee was dismissed by the employer's action. But we see that Mrs. Sherbert was dismissed because she refused to work on Saturdays after the plant went to a six-day workweek. Had Thomas simply presented himself at the Blaw-Knox plant turret line but refused to perform any assigned work, it must be assumed that he, like Sherbert, would have been terminated by the employer's action, if no other work was available. In both cases, the termination flowed from the fact that the employment, once acceptable, became religiously objectionable because of changed conditions.

B

The mere fact that the petitioner's religious practice is burdened by a governmental program does not mean that an exemption accommodating his practice must be granted. The state may justify an inroad on religious liberty by showing that it is the least restrictive means of achieving some compelling state interest. However, it is still true that "[t]he essence of all that has been said and written on the subject is that only those interests of the highest order can overbalance legitimate claims to the free exercise of religion." *Wisconsin* v. *Yoder*.

The purposes urged to sustain the disqualifying provision of the Indiana unemployment compensation scheme are twofold: (1) to avoid the widespread unemployment and the consequent burden on the fund resulting if people were permitted to leave jobs for "personal" reasons; and (2) to ⊥**719** avoid a detailed probing by employers into job applicants' religious beliefs. These are by no means unimportant considerations. When the focus of the inquiry is properly narrowed, however, we must conclude that the interests advanced by the state do not justify the burden placed on free exercise of religion.

There is no evidence in the record to indicate that the number of people who find themselves in the predicament of choosing between benefits and religious beliefs is large enough to create "widespread unemployment," or even to seriously affect unemployment—and no such claim was advanced by the Review Board. Similarly, although detailed inquiry by employers into applicants' religious beliefs is undesirable, there is no evidence in the record to indicate that such inquiries will occur in Indiana, or that they have occurred in any of the states that extend benefits to people in the petitioner's position. Nor is there any reason to believe that the number of people terminating employment for religious reasons will be so great as to motivate employers to make such inquiries.

Neither of the interests advanced is sufficiently compelling to justify the burden upon Thomas' religious liberty. Accordingly, Thomas is entitled to receive benefits unless, as the state contends and the Indiana court held, such payment would violate the Establishment Clause.

IV

The respondent contends that to compel benefit payments to Thomas involves the state in fostering a religious faith. There is, in a sense, a "benefit" to Thomas deriving from his religious beliefs, but this manifests no more than the tension between the two Religion Clauses which the Court resolved in *Sherbert:*

"In holding as we do, plainly we are not fostering the 'establishment' of the Seventh-day Adventist religion ⊥**720** in South Carolina, for the extension of unemployment benefits to Sabbatarians in common with Sunday worshippers reflects nothing more than the governmental obligation of neutrality in the face of religious differences, and does not represent that involvement of religion with secular institutions which it is the object of the Establishment Clause to forestall." *Sherbert* v. *Verner*.

See also *Wisconsin* v. *Yoder; Walz* v. *Tax Commission of the City of New York; O'Hair* v. *Andrus*.

Unless we are prepared to overrule *Sherbert*, Thomas cannot be denied the benefits due him on the basis of the finding of the referee, the Review Board and the Indiana Court of Appeals that he terminated his employment because of his religious convictions.

Reversed.

Justice BLACKMUN joins parts I, II, and III of the Court's opinion. As to Part IV thereof, he concurs in the result.

Justice REHNQUIST, dissenting:

The Court today holds that the State of Indiana is constitutionally required to provide direct financial assistance to a person solely on the basis of his religious beliefs. Because I believe that the decision today adds mud to the already muddied waters of First Amendment jurisprudence, I dissent.

I

The Court correctly acknowledges that there is a "tension" between the Free Exercise and Establishment Clauses of the First Amendment of the United States Constitution. Although the relationship of the two clauses has been the subject of much commentary, the "tension" is a fairly recent ⊥**721** vintage, unknown at the time of the framing and adoption of the First Amendment. The causes of the tension, it seems to me, are three-fold. First, the growth of social welfare legislation during the latter part of the 20th century has greatly magnified the potential for conflict between the two clauses, since such legislation touches the individual at so many points in his life. Second, the decision by this Court that the First Amendment was "incorporated" into the Fourteenth Amendment and thereby made applicable against the States, *Stromberg* v. *California; Cantwell* v. *Connecticut*, similarly multiplied the number of instances in which the "tension" might arise. The third, and perhaps most important, cause of the tension is our overly expansive interpretation of *both* clauses. By broadly construing both clauses, the Court has constantly narrowed the channel between the Scylla and Charybdis through which any state or federal action must pass in order to survive constitutional scrutiny.

None of these developments could have been foreseen by those who framed and adopted the First Amendment. The First Amendment was adopted well before the growth of much social welfare legislation and at a time when the Federal Government was in a real sense considered a government of limited delegated powers. Indeed, the principal argument against adopting the Constitution *without* a "Bill of Rights" was not that such an enactment would be *undesirable*, but that it was *unnecessary* because of the limited nature of the Federal Government. So long as the government enacts little social welfare legislation, as was the case in 1791, there are few occasions in which the two clauses may conflict. Moreover, as originally enacted, the First Amendment applied only to the Federal Government, not the government of the States. *Barron* v. *Baltimore*. The Framers could hardly anticipate *Barron* being superseded by the "selective incorporation" doctrine adopted by the Court, a decision which greatly expanded the number of stat⊥**722**utes which would be subject to challenge under the First Amendment. Because those who drafted and adopted the First Amendment could not have foreseen either the growth of social welfare legislation or the incorporation of the First Amendment into the Fourteenth Amendment, we simply do not know how they would view the scope of the two clauses.

II

The decision today illustrates how far astray the Court has gone in interpreting the Free Exercise and Establishment Clauses of the First Amendment. Although the

Court holds that a State is constitutionally required to provide direct financial assistance to persons solely on the basis of their religious beliefs and recognizes the "tension" between the two clauses, it does little to help resolve that tension or to offer meaningful guidance to other courts which must decide cases like this on a day-by-day basis. Instead, it simply asserts that there is no Establishment Clause violation here and leaves tension between the two Religion Clauses to be resolved on a case-by-case basis. As suggested above, however, I believe that the "tension" is largely of this Court's own making, and would diminish almost to the vanishing point if the clauses were properly interpreted.

Just as it did in *Sherbert* v. *Verner*, the Court today reads the Free Exercise Clause more broadly than is warranted. As to the proper interpretation of the Free Exercise Clause, I would accept the decision of *Braunfeld* v. *Brown* and the dissent in *Sherbert*. In *Braunfeld*, we held that Sunday Closing laws do not violate the First Amendment rights of Sabbatarians. *Chief Justice WARREN* explained that the statute did not make unlawful any religious practices of appellants; it simply made the practice of their religious beliefs more expensive. We concluded that "to strike down, without the most critical scrutiny, legislation which imposes only an indirect burden on the exercise of religion, *i.e.*, legislation which does not ⊥**723** make unlawful the religious practice itself, would radically restrict the operating latitude of the legislature." Likewise in this case, it cannot be said that the State discriminated against Thomas on the basis of his religious beliefs or that he was denied benefits *because* he was a Jehovah's Witness. Where, as here, a State has enacted a general statute, the purpose and effect of which is to advance the State's secular goals, the Free Exercise Clause does not in my view require the State to conform that statute to the dictates of religious conscience of any group. As *Justice HARLAN* recognized in his dissent in *Sherbert* v. *Verner*, "Those situations in which the Constitution may require special treatment on account of religion are . . . few and far between." Like him I believe that although a State could choose to grant exemptions to religious persons from state unemployment regulations, a State is not constitutionally compelled to do so. ⊥**724**

The Court's treatment of the Establishment Clause issue is equally unsatisfying. Although today's decision requires a State to provide direct financial assistance to persons solely on the basis of their religious beliefs, the Court nonetheless blandly assures us, just as it did in *Sherbert*, that its decision "plainly" does not foster the "establishment" of religion. I would agree that the Establishment Clause, properly interpreted, would not be violated if Indiana volun⊥**725**tarily chose to grant unemployment benefits to those persons who left their jobs for religious reasons. But I also believe that the decision below is inconsistent with many of our prior Establishment Clause cases. Those cases, if faithfully applied, would require us to hold that such voluntary action by a State *did* violate the Establishment Clause.

Justice STEWART noted this point in his concurring opinion in *Sherbert*. He observed that decisions like *Sherbert*, and the one rendered today, squarely conflict with the more extreme language of many of our prior Establishment Clause cases. In *Everson* v. *Board of Education* the Court stated that the Establishment Clause bespeaks a "government . . . stripped of all power . . . to support, or otherwise to assist any or all religions . . .," and no State "can pass laws which aid one religion [or] all religions." In *Torcaso* v. *Watkins* the Court asserted that the government cannot "constitutionally pass laws or impose requirements which aid all religions as against non-believers." And in *School District of Abington Township* v. *Schempp* the Court adopted *Justice RUTLEDGE'S* words in *Everson* that the Establishment Clause forbids "every form of public aid or support for religion." See also *Engel* v. *Vitale*.

In recent years the Court has moved away from the mechanistic "no-aid-to-religion" approach to the Establishment Clause and has stated a three-part test to determine the constitutionality of governmental aid to religion. See *Lemon* v. *Kurtzman; Committee for Public Education & Religious Liberty* v. *Nyquist*. First, the statute must serve a secular legislative purpose. Second, it must have a "primary effect" that neither advances nor inhibits religion. And third, the State and its administration must avoid excessive entanglement with religion. *Walz* v. *Tax Commission*. ⊥**726**

It is not surprising that the Court today makes no attempt to apply those principles to the facts of this case. If Indiana were to legislate what the Court today requires—an unemployment compensation law which permitted benefits to be granted to those persons who quit their jobs for religious reasons—the statute would "plainly" violate the Establishment Clause as interpreted in such cases as *Lemon* and *Nyquist*. First, although the unemployment statute as a whole would be enacted to serve a secular legislative purpose, the proviso would clearly serve only a religious purpose. It would grant financial benefits for the sole purpose of accommodating religious beliefs. Second, there can be little doubt that the primary effect on the proviso would be to "advance" religion by facilitating the exercise of religious belief. Third, any statute including such a proviso would surely "entangle" the State in religion far more than the mere grant of tax exemptions, as in *Walz*, or the award of tuition grants and tax credits, as in *Nyquist*. By granting financial benefits to persons solely on the basis of their religious beliefs, the State must necessarily inquire whether the claimant's belief is "religious" and whether it is sincerely held. Otherwise any dissatisfied employee may leave his job without cause and claim that he did so because his own particular beliefs required it.

It is unclear from the Court's opinion whether it has temporarily retreated from its expansive view of the Establishment Clause, or wholly abandoned it. I would welcome the latter. Just as I think that *Justice HARLAN* in *Sherbert* correctly stated the proper approach to free exercise questions, I believe that *Justice STEWART*, dissenting in *School District* v. *Schempp*, accurately stated the reach of the Establishment Clause. He explained that the Establishment Clause is limited to "government support of proselytizing activities of religious sects by throwing the weight of secular authorities behind the dissemination of religious tenets." See *McCollum* v. *Board of Education*. (Reed, J., dissenting) ⊥**727** (impermissible aid is only "purposeful assistance directly to the church itself or to some religious group . . . performing ecclesiastical functions.") Conversely, governmental assistance which does not have the effect of "inducing" religious belief, but instead merely "accommodates" or implements an independent religious choice does not impermissibly involve the government in religious choices and therefore does not violate the Establishment Clause of the First Amendment. I would think that in this case, as in *Sherbert*, had the state voluntarily chosen to pay unemployment compensation benefits to persons who left their jobs for religious reasons, such aid would be constitutionally permissible because it redounds directly to the benefit of the individual. Accord, *Wolman* v. *Walter* (upholding various disbursements made to pupils in parochial schools).

In sum, my difficulty with today's decision is that it reads the Free Exercise Clause too broadly and it fails to squarely acknowledge that such a reading conflicts with many of our Establishment Clause cases. As such, the decision simply exacerbates the "tension" between the two clauses. If the Court were to construe the Free Exercise Clause as it did in *Braunfeld* and the Establishment Clause as *Justice STEWART* did in *Schempp*, the circumstances in which there would be a conflict between the two clauses would be few and far between. Although I heartily agree with the Court's tacit abandonment of much of our rhetoric about the Establishment Clause, I regret that the Court cannot see its way clear to restore what was surely intended to have been a greater degree of flexibility to the federal and state governments in legislating consistently with the Free Exercise Clause. Accordingly, I would affirm the judgment of the Indiana Supreme Court.

HOBBIE v. UNEMPLOYMENT APPEALS COMMISSION OF FLORIDA

480 U.S. 136
ON APPEAL FROM THE FLORIDA FIFTH DISTRICT COURT OF APPEALS
Argued December 10, 1986 — Decided February 25, 1987

⊥**137** *Justice BRENNAN* delivered the opinion of the Court.

Appellant's employer discharged her when she refused to work certain scheduled hours because of sincerely held religious convictions adopted after beginning employment. The question to be decided is whether Florida's denial of unemployment compensation benefits to appellant violates the Free Exercise Clause of the First Amendment of the Constitution, as applied to the States through the Fourteenth Amendment.

⊥**138** I

Lawton and Company (Lawton), a Florida jeweler, hired appellant Paula Hobbie in October 1981. She was employed by Lawton for 2 years, first as a trainee and then as assistant manager of a retail jewelry store. In April 1984, Hobbie informed her immediate supervisor that she was to be baptized into the Seventh-Day Adventist Church and that, for religious reasons, she would no longer be able to work on her Sabbath, from sundown on Friday to sundown on Saturday. The supervisor devised an arrangement with Hobbie: she agreed to work evenings and Sundays, and he agreed to substitute for her whenever she was scheduled to work on a Friday evening or a Saturday.

This arrangement continued until the general manager of Lawton learned of it in June 1984. At that time, after a meeting with Hobbie and her minister, the general manager informed appellant that she could either work her scheduled shifts or submit her resignation to the company. When Hobbie refused to do either, Lawton discharged her.

On June 4, 1984, appellant filed a claim for unemployment compensation with the Florida Department of Labor and Employment Security. Under Florida law, unemployment compensation benefits are available to persons who become "unemployed through no fault of their own." Lawton contested the payment of benefits on the ground that Hobbie was "disqualified for benefits" because she had been discharged for "misconduct connected with [her] work." ⊥**139** A claims examiner for the Bureau of Unemployment Compensation denied Hobbie's claim for benefits, and she appealed that determination. Following a hearing before a referee, the Unemployment Appeals Commission (Appeals Commission) affirmed the denial of benefits, agreeing that Hobbie's refusal to work scheduled shifts constituted "misconduct connected with [her] work."

Hobbie challenged the Appeals Commission's order in the Florida Fifth District Court of Appeal. On September 10, 1985, that court summarily affirmed the Appeals Commission. We postponed jurisdiction, and we now reverse.

II

Under our precedents, the Appeals Commission's disqualification of appellant from receipt of benefits violates the Free Exercise Clause of the First Amendment, applicable to the ⊥**140** States through the Fourteenth Amendment. *Sherbert* v. *Verner*. In *Sherbert* we considered South Carolina's denial of unemployment compensation benefits to a Sabbatarian who, like Hobbie, refused to work on Saturdays. The Court held that the State's disqualification of Sherbert "force[d] her to choose between following the precepts of her religion and forfeiting benefits, on the one hand, and abandoning one of the precepts of her religion in order to accept work, on the other hand. Governmental imposition of such a choice puts the same kind of burden upon the free exercise of religion as would a fine imposed against [her] for her Saturday worship."

We concluded that the State had imposed a burden upon Sherbert's free exercise rights that had not been justified by a compelling state interest.

In *Thomas*, too, the Court held that a State's denial of unemployment benefits unlawfully burdened an employee's right to free exercise of religion. Thomas, a Jehovah's Witness, held religious beliefs that forbade his participation in the production of armaments. He was forced to leave his job when the employer closed his department and transferred him to a division that fabricated turrets for tanks. Indiana then denied Thomas unemployment compensation benefits. The Court found that the employee had been "put to a choice between fidelity to religious belief or cessation of work" and that the coercive impact of the forfeiture of benefits in this situation was undeniable:

"'Not only is it apparent that appellant's declared ineligibility for benefits derives solely from the practice of ⊥**141** . . . religion, but the pressure upon [the employee] to forego that practice is unmistakable.'"

We see no meaningful distinction among the situations of Sherbert, Thomas, and Hobbie. We again affirm, as stated in *Thomas*:

"Where the state conditions receipt of an important benefit upon conduct proscribed by a religious faith, *or where it denies such a benefit because of conduct mandated by religious belief, thereby putting substantial pressure on an adherent to modify his behavior and to violate his beliefs*, a burden upon religion exists. While the compulsion may be indirect, the infringement upon free exercise is nonetheless substantial." (Emphasis added.)

Both *Sherbert* and *Thomas* held that such infringements must be subjected to strict scrutiny and could be justified only by proof by the State of a compelling interest. The Appeals Commission does not seriously contend that its denial of benefits can withstand strict scrutiny; rather it urges that we hold that its justification should be determined under the less rigorous standard articulated in *Chief Justice BURGER's* opinion in *Bowen* v. *Roy*: "[T]he Government meets its burden when it demonstrates that a challenged requirement for governmental benefits, neutral and uniform in its application, is a reasonable means of promoting a legitimate public interest." Five Justices expressly rejected this argument in *Roy*. We reject the argument again today. As *Justice O'CONNOR* pointed out in *Roy*, "[s]uch a test has no basis in precedent and relegates a serious First Amendment value to the barest level of minimal scrutiny that the Equal Protection ⊥**142** Clause already provides." ("[O]nly those interests of the highest order and those not otherwise served can over-balance legitimate claims to the free exercise of religion.")

The Appeals Commission also suggests two grounds upon which we might distinguish *Sherbert* and *Thomas* from the present case. First, the Appeals Commission points out that in *Sherbert* the employee was deemed completely ineligible for benefits under South Carolina's unemployment insurance scheme because she would not accept work that conflicted with her Sabbath. The Appeals Commission contends that, ⊥**143** under Florida law, Hobbie faces only a limited disqualification from receipt of benefits, and that once this fixed term has been served, she will again "be on an equal footing with all other workers, provided she avoids employment that conflicts with her religious beliefs." The Appeals Commission argues that such a disqualification provision is less coercive than the ineligibility determination in *Sherbert*, and that the burden it imposes on free exercise is therefore permissible.

This distinction is without substance. The immediate effects of ineligibility and disqualification are identical, and the disqualification penalty is substantial. Moreover, *Sherbert* was given controlling weight in *Thomas*, which involved a disqualification provision similar in all relevant respects to the statutory section implicated here.

The Appeals Commission also attempts to distinguish this case by arguing that, unlike the employees in *Sherbert* and *Thomas*, Hobbie was the "agent of change" and is therefore responsible for the consequences of the conflict between her job and her religious beliefs. In *Sherbert* and *Thomas*, the employees held their respective religious beliefs at the time of hire; subsequent changes in the conditions of employment made by *the employer* caused the conflict between work and belief. In this case, Hobbie's beliefs changed during the course of her employment, creating a conflict between job and faith that had not previously existed. The Appeals Commission contends that "it is . . . unfair for an employee to ⊥**144** adopt religious beliefs that conflict with existing employment and expect to continue the employment without compromising those beliefs" and that this "intentional disregard of the employer's interests . . . constitutes misconduct."

In effect, the Appeals Commission asks us to single out the religious convert for different, less favorable treatment than that given an individual whose adherence to his or her faith precedes employment. We decline to do so. The First Amendment protects the free exercise rights of employees who adopt religious beliefs or convert from one faith to another after they are hired. The timing of Hobbie's conversion is immaterial to our determination that her free exercise rights have been burdened; the salient inquiry under the Free Exercise Clause is the burden involved. In *Sherbert*, *Thomas*, and the present case, the employee was forced to choose between fidelity to religious belief and continued employment; the forfeiture of unemployment benefits for choosing the former over the latter brings unlawful coercion to bear on the employee's choice.

Finally, we reject the Appeals Commission's argument that the awarding of benefits to Hobbie would violate the Establishment Clause. This Court has long recognized that the government may (and sometimes must) accommodate religious practices and that it may do so without violating the ⊥**145** Establishment Clause. See, e.g., *Wisconsin* v. *Yoder* (judicial exemption of Amish children from compulsory attendance at high school); *Walz* v. *Tax Comm'n* (tax exemption for churches). As in *Sherbert*, the accommodation at issue here does not entangle the State in an unlawful fostering of religion:

"In holding as we do, plainly we are not fostering the 'establishment' of the Seventh-day Adventist religion in South Carolina, for the extension of unemployment benefits to Sabbatarians in common with Sunday worshipers reflects nothing more than the governmental obligation of neutrality in the face of religious differences, and does not represent the involvement of religious with secular institutions which it is the object of the Establishment Clause to forestall."

⊥**146** III

We conclude that Florida's refusal to award unemployment compensation benefits to appellant violated the Free Exercise Clause of the First Amendment. Here, as in *Sherbert* and *Thomas*, the State may not force an employee "to choose between following the precepts of her religion and forfeiting benefits, . . . and abandoning one of the precepts of her religion in order to accept work." The judgment of the Florida Fifth District Court of Appeal is therefore

Reversed.

Chief Justice REHNQUIST, dissenting. I adhere to the views I stated in dissent *in Thomas* v. *Review Bd. of Indiana Employment Security Div*. Accordingly, I would affirm.

Justice POWELL, concurring in the judgment.

The Court properly concludes that *Sherbert* v. *Verner*, and *Thomas* v. *Review Bd. of Indiana Employment Security Div.*, control the decision in this case. In both of those cases, the Court applied strict scrutiny analysis to a State's decision to deny unemployment benefits to an employee forced to leave a job because of his or her religious convictions. In each of these cases, the Court found that the State's action was not justified by a compelling interest and therefore violated the Free Exercise Clause of the First Amendment. The situation in this case is remarkably similar: The State denied Hobbie unemployment compensation, even though she was forced to leave her job because of sincerely held religious beliefs. As the Court recognizes, there is "no meaningful distinction among the situations of Sherbert, Thomas, and ⊥**147** Hobbie." Accordingly, the established analysis of *Sherbert* and *Thomas* should apply to this case.

This Court's decision last term in *Bowen* v. *Roy*, did nothing to undercut the applicability of *Sherbert* and *Thomas* to the present case. A plurality in *Roy* indicated that "some incidental neutral restraints on the free exercise of religion," such as the requirement that applicants for Social Security benefits use assigned numbers, need not be supported by a compelling justification. The plurality distinguished *Sherbert* and *Thomas* as cases where the statute at issue "created a mechanism for individualized exemptions." The plurality noted:

"If a [S]tate creates such a mechanism, its refusal to extend an exemption to an instance of religious hardship suggests a discriminatory intent. . . . In [*Sherbert* and *Thomas*], therefore, it was appropriate to require the State to demonstrate a compelling reason for denying the requested exemption."

Thus, the decision in *Roy* makes explicitly clear that its reasoning does not apply to the state conduct in this case.

The Court recognizes in a footnote that the reasoning of *Roy* does not apply to this case. Instead of relying on this distinction, however, the Court reaches out to reject the reasoning of *Roy in toto*. This strikes me as inappropriate and unnecessary. Given its context, the Court's rejection of *Roy's* reasoning is dictum. The proper approach in this case is to apply the established precedent of *Sherbert* and *Thomas*. Because the Court goes further, I concur only in the judgment.

Justice STEVENS, concurring in the judgment.

As the Court concludes, this case is controlled by *Sherbert* v. *Verner*, and *Thomas* v. *Review Bd. of Indiana Employment Security Div*. The State of Florida provides ⊥**148** unemployment benefits to those persons who become "unemployed through no fault of their own," Fla. Stat. § 443.021 (1985), but singles out the religiously motivated choice that subjected Paula Hobbie to dismissal as her fault and indeed as "misconduct connected with . . . work." § 443.101. The State thus regards her "religious claims less favorably than other claims," see *Bowen* v. *Roy* (Stevens, J., concurring in part and concurring in result). In such an instance, granting unemployment benefits is necessary to protect religious observers against unequal treatment. See *United States* v. *Lee* (Stevens, J., concurring in judgment). I also agree with the Court's explanation of why the two grounds upon which we might distinguish *Sherbert* and *Thomas* must be rejected. Accordingly, I concur in the judgment.

FRAZEE v. ILLINOIS DEPARTMENT OF EMPLOYMENT SECURITY

489 U.S. 829

ON APPEAL FROM THE APPELLATE COURT OF ILLINOIS, THIRD DISTRICT

Argued March 1, 1989 — Decided March 29, 1989

⊥**830** *Justice* WHITE delivered the opinion of the Court.

The Illinois Unemployment Insurance Act provides that "An individual shall be ineligible for benefits if he has failed, without good cause, either to apply for available, suitable work when so directed . . . or to accept suitable work when offered him. . . ." Ill. Rev. Stat., ch. 48, ¶ 433 (1986). In April 1984, William Frazee refused a temporary retail position offered him by Kelly Services because the job would have required him to work on Sunday. Frazee told Kelly that, as a Christian, he could not work on "the Lord's day." Frazee then applied to the Illinois Department of Employment Security for unemployment benefits claiming that there was good cause for his refusal to work on Sunday. His application was denied. Frazee appealed the denial of benefits to the Department of Employment Security's Board of Review which also denied his claim. The Board of Review stated: "When a refusal of work is based on religious convictions, the refusal must be based upon some tenets or dogma accepted by the individual of some church, sect, or denomination, and such a refusal based solely on an individual's personal belief is personal and noncompelling and does not render the work un⊥**831**suitable." The Board of review concluded that Frazee had refused an offer of suitable work without good cause. The Circuit Court of the Tenth Judicial Circuit of Illinois, Peoria County, affirmed, finding that the agency's decision was "not contrary to law nor against the manifest weight of the evidence," thereby rejecting Frazee's claim based on the Free Exercise Clause of the First Amendment.

Frazee's free exercise claim was again rejected by the Appellate Court of Illinois, Third District. The court characterized Frazee's refusal to work as resting on his "personal professed religious belief," and made it clear that it did "not question the sincerity of the plaintiff." It then engaged in a historical discussion of religious prohibitions against work on the Sabbath and, in particular, on Sunday. Nonetheless, the court distinguished *Sherbert* v. *Verner*, *Thomas* v. *Review Bd. of Indiana Employment Security Div.*, and *Hobbie* v. *Unemployment Compensation Appeals Comm'n of Florida*, from the facts of Frazee's case. Unlike the claimants in *Sherbert*, *Thomas*, and *Hobbie*, Frazee was not a member of an established religious sect or church, nor did he claim that his refusal to work resulted from a "tenet, belief or teaching of an established religious body." To the Illinois Court, Frazee's position that he was "a Christian" and as such felt it wrong to work on Sunday was not enough. For a Free Exercise Clause claim to succeed, said the Illinois Appellate Court, "[T]he injunction against Sunday labor must be found in a tenet or dogma of an established religious sect. [Frazee] does not profess to be a member of any such sect." The Illinois Supreme Court denied Frazee leave to appeal.

The mandatory appellate jurisdiction of this Court was invoked under 28 U.S.C. §1257(2), since the state court ⊥**832** rejected a challenge to the constitutionality of Illinois' statutory "good cause" requirement as applied in this case. We noted probable jurisdiction, and now reverse.

We have had more than one occasion before today to consider denials of unemployment compensation benefits to those who have refused work on the basis of their religious beliefs. In *Sherbert* v. *Verner*, the Court held that a State could not "constitutionally apply the eligibility provisions [of its unemployment compensation program] so as to constrain a worker to abandon his religious convictions respecting the day of rest." *Thomas* v. *Review Bd. of Indiana Employment Security Div.* also held that the State's refusal to award unemployment compensation benefits to one who terminated his job because his religious beliefs forbade participation in the production of armaments violated the First Amendment right to free exercise. Just two years ago, in *Hobbie* v. *Unemployment Appeals Comm'n of Florida*, Florida's denial of unemployment compensation benefits to an employee discharged for her refusal to work on her Sabbath because of religious convictions adopted subsequent to her employment was also declared to be a violation of the Free Exercise Clause. In each of these cases, the appellant was "forced to choose between fidelity to religious belief and . . . employment," and we found "the forfeiture of unemployment benefits for choosing the former over the latter brings unlawful coercion to bear on the employee's choice." In each of these cases, we concluded that the denial of unemployment compensation benefits violated the Free Exercise Clause of the First Amendment of the Constitution, as applied to the States through the Fourteenth Amendment.

It is true, as the Illinois court noted, that each of the claimants in those cases was a member of a particular religious sect, but none of those decisions turned on that consideration or on any tenet of the sect involved that forbade the work the ⊥**833** claimant refused to perform. Our judgments in those cases rested on the fact that each of the claimants had a sincere belief that religion required him or her to refrain from the work in question. Never did we suggest that unless a claimant belongs to a sect that forbids what his job requires, his belief, however sincere, must be deemed a purely personal preference rather than a religious belief. Indeed, in *Thomas*, there was disagreement among sect members as to whether their religion made it sinful to work in an armaments factory; but we considered this to be an irrelevant issue and hence rejected the State's submission that unless the religion involved formally forbade work on armaments, *Thomas*' belief did not qualify as a religious belief. Because *Thomas* unquestionably had a sincere belief that his religion prevented him from doing such work, he was entitled to invoke the protection of the Free Exercise Clause.

There is no doubt that "[o]nly beliefs rooted in religion are protected by the Free Exercise Clause." *Thomas*. Purely secular views do not suffice. Nor do we underestimate the difficulty of distinguishing between religious and secular convictions and in determining whether a professed belief is sincerely held. States are clearly entitled to assure themselves that there is an ample predicate for invoking the Free Exercise Clause. We do not face problems about sincerity or about the religious nature of

Frazee's convictions, however. The courts below did not question his sincerity, and the State concedes it. Furthermore, the Board of Review characterized Frazee's views as "religious convictions," and the Illinois Appellate Court referred to his refusal to work on Sunday as based on a "personal professed religious belief."

⊥834 Frazee asserted that he was a Christian, but did not claim to be a member of a particular Christian sect. It is also true that there are assorted Christian denominations that do not profess to be compelled by their religion to refuse Sunday work, but this does not diminish Frazee's protection flowing from the Free Exercise Clause. *Thomas* settled that much. Undoubtedly, membership in an organized religious denomination, especially one with a specific tenet forbidding members to work on Sunday, would simplify the problem of identifying sincerely held religious beliefs, but we reject the notion that to claim the protection of the Free Exercise Clause, one must be responding to the commands of a particular religious organization. Here Frazee's refusal was based on a sincerely held religious belief. Under our cases, he was entitled to invoke First Amendment protection.

The State does not appear to defend this aspect of the decision below. In its brief and at oral arguments, the State conceded that the Free Exercise Clause does not demand adherence to a tenet or dogma of an established religious sect. Instead, the State proposes its own test for identifying a "religious" belief, asserts that Frazee has not met such a test, and asks that we affirm on this basis. We decline to address this submission; for as the case comes to us, Frazee's conviction was recognized as religious but found to be inadequate ⊥835 because it was not claimed to represent a tenet of a religious organization of which he was a member. That ground for decision was clearly erroneous.

The State offers no justification for the burden that the denial of benefits places on Frazee's right to exercise his religion. The Illinois Appellate Court ascribed great significance to America's weekend way of life. The Illinois court asked: "What would Sunday be today if professional football, baseball, basketball and tennis were barred. Today Sunday is not only a day for religion, but for recreation and labor. Today the supermarkets are open, service stations dispense fuel, utilities continue to serve the people and factories continue to belch smoke and tangible products," concluding that "[i]f all Americans were to abstain from working on Sunday, chaos would result." We are unpersuaded, however, that there will be a mass movement away from Sunday employ if William Frazee succeeds in his claim.

As was the case in *Thomas* where there was "no evidence in the record to indicate that the number of people who find themselves in the predicament of choosing between benefits and religious beliefs is large enough to create 'widespread unemployment,' or even to seriously affect unemployment," *Thomas*, there is nothing before us in this case to suggest that Sunday shopping, or Sunday sporting, for that matter, will grind to a halt as a result of our decision today. And, as we have said in the past, there may exist state interests sufficiently compelling to override a legitimate claim to the free exercise of religion. No such interest has been presented here.

The judgment of the Appellate Court of Illinois for the Third District is therefore reversed and the case is remanded for further proceedings not inconsistent with this opinion.

It is so ordered.

EMPLOYMENT DIVISION, DEPARTMENT OF HUMAN RESOURCES OF OREGON v. SMITH

494 U.S. 872
ON WRIT OF CERTIORARI TO THE SUPREME COURT OF OREGON
Argued November 6, 1989 — Decided April 17, 1990

⊥874 *Justice* SCALIA delivered the opinion of the Court.

This case requires us to decide whether the Free Exercise Clause of the First Amendment permits the State of Oregon to include religiously inspired peyote use within the reach of its general criminal prohibition on use of that drug, and thus permits the State to deny unemployment benefits to persons dismissed from their jobs because of such religiously inspired use.

I

Oregon law prohibits the knowing or intentional possession of a "controlled substance" unless the substance has been prescribed by a medical practitioner. Ore. Rev. Stat. § 475.992(4) (1987). The law defines "controlled substance" as a drug classified in Schedules I through V of the Federal Controlled Substances Act, 21 U.S.C. §§ 811-812 (1982 ed. and Supp. V), as modified by the State Board of Pharmacy. Ore. Rev. Stat. § 475.005(6) (1987). Persons who violate this provision by possessing a controlled substance listed on Schedule I are "guilty of a Class B felony." § 475.992(4)(a). As compiled by the State Board of Pharmacy under its statutory authority, see Ore. Rev. Stat. § 475.035 (1987), Schedule I contains the drug peyote, a hallucinogen derived from the plant *Lophophorawilliamsii Lemaire*. Ore. Admin. Rule 855-80-021(3)(s) (1988).

Respondents Alfred Smith and Galen Black were fired from their jobs with a private drug rehabilitation organization because they ingested peyote for sacramental purposes at a ceremony of the Native American Church, of which both are members. When respondents applied to petitioner Employment Division for unemployment compensation, they were determined to be ineligible for benefits because they had been discharged for work-related "misconduct." The Oregon Court of Appeals reversed that determination, holding that the denial of benefits violated respondents' free exercise rights under the First Amendment.

⊥875 On appeal to the Oregon Supreme Court, petitioner argued that the denial of benefits was permissible because respondents' consumption of peyote was a crime under Oregon law. The Oregon Supreme Court reasoned, however, that the criminality of respondents' peyote use was irrelevant to resolution of their constitutional claim —since the purpose of the "misconduct" provision under which respondents had been disqualified was not to enforce the State's criminal laws but to preserve the financial integrity of the compensation fund, and since that purpose was inadequate to justify the burden that disqualification imposed on respondents' religious practice. Citing our decisions in *Sherbert* v. *Verner*; and *Thomas* v. *Review Board, Indiana Employment Security Div.*, the court concluded that respondents were entitled to payment of unemployment benefits. *Smith* v. *Employment Div., Dept. of Human Resources*. We granted certiorari.

Before this Court in 1987, petitioner continued to maintain that the illegality of respondents' peyote consumption was relevant to their constitutional claim. We agreed, concluding that "if a State has prohibited through its criminal laws certain kinds of religiously motivated conduct without violating the First Amendment, it certainly follows that it may impose the lesser burden of denying unemployment compensation benefits to persons who engage in that conduct." *Employment Div., Dept. of Human Resources of Oregon* v. *Smith*. We noted, however, that the Oregon Supreme Court had not decided whether respondents' sacramental use of peyote was in fact proscribed by Oregon's controlled substance law, and that this issue was a matter of dispute between the parties. Being "uncertain about the legality of the religious use of peyote in Oregon," we determined that it would not be "appropriate for us to decide whether the practice is protected by the Federal Constitution." Accordingly, we **⊥876** vacated the judgment of the Oregon Supreme Court and remanded for further proceedings. On remand, the Oregon Supreme Court held that respondents' religiously inspired use of peyote fell within the prohibition of the Oregon statute, which "makes no exception for the sacramental use" of the drug. It then considered whether that prohibition was valid under the Free Exercise Clause, and concluded that it was not. The court therefore reaffirmed its previous ruling that the State could not deny unemployment benefits to respondents for having engaged in that practice. We again granted certiorari.

II

Respondents' claim for relief rests on our decisions in *Sherbert* v. *Verner*, *Thomas* v. *Review Board, Indiana Employment Security Div.*, and *Hobbie* v. *Unemployment Appeals Comm'n of Florida*, in which we held that a State could not condition the availability of unemployment insurance on an individual's willingness to forgo conduct required by his religion. As we observed in *Smith I*, however, the conduct at issue in those cases was not prohibited by law. We held that distinction to be critical, for "if Oregon does prohibit the religious use of peyote, and if that prohibition is consistent with the Federal Constitution, there is no federal right to engage in that conduct in Oregon," and "the State is free to withhold unemployment compensation from respondents for engaging in work-related misconduct, despite its religious motivation." Now that the Oregon Supreme Court has confirmed that Oregon does prohibit the religious use of peyote, we proceed to consider whether that prohibition is permissible under the Free Exercise Clause.

A

The Free Exercise Clause of the First Amendment, which has been made applicable to the States by incorporation into **⊥877** the Fourteenth Amendment, provides that "Congress shall make no law respecting an establishment of religion, or *prohibiting the free exercise thereof. . . .*" U. S. Const. Am. I (emphasis added). The free exercise of religion means, first and foremost, the right to believe and profess whatever religious doctrine one desires. Thus, the First Amendment obviously excludes all "governmental regulation of religious *beliefs* as such." *Sherbert* v. *Verner*. The government may not compel affirmation of religious belief, punish the expression of religious doctrines it believes to be false, impose special disabilities on the basis of religious views or religious status, or lend its power to one or the other side in controversies over religious authority or dogma.

But the "exercise of religion" often involves not only belief and profession but the performance of (or abstention from) physical acts: assembling with others for a worship service, participating in sacramental use of bread and wine, proselytizing, abstaining from certain foods or certain modes of transportation. It would be true, we think (though no case of ours has involved the point), that a state would be "prohibiting the free exercise [of religion]" if it sought to ban such acts or abstentions only when they are engaged in for religious reasons, or only because of the religious belief that they display. It would doubtless be unconstitutional, for example, to ban the casting of "statues that are to be used **⊥878** for worship purposes," or to prohibit bowing down before a golden calf.

Respondents in the present case, however, seek to carry the meaning of "prohibiting the free exercise [of religion]" one large step further. They contend that their religious motivation for using peyote places them beyond the reach of a criminal law that is not specifically directed at their religious practice, and that is concededly constitutional as applied to those who use the drug for other reasons. They assert, in other words, that "prohibiting the free exercise [of religion]" includes requiring any individual to observe a generally applicable law that requires (or forbids) the performance of an act that his religious belief forbids (or requires). As a textual matter, we do not think the words must be given that meaning.

It is no more necessary to regard the collection of a general tax, for example, as "prohibiting the free exercise [of religion]" by those citizens who believe support of organized government to be sinful, than it is to regard the same tax as "abridging the freedom . . . of the press" of those publishing companies that must pay the tax as a condition of staying in business. It is a permissible reading of the text, in the one case as in the other, to say that if prohibiting the exercise of religion (or burdening the activity of printing) is not the object of the tax but merely the incidental effect of a generally applicable and otherwise valid provision, the First Amendment has not been offended.

Our decisions reveal that the latter reading is the correct one. We have never held that an individual's religious be⊥**879**liefs excuse him from compliance with an otherwise valid law prohibiting conduct that the State is free to regulate. On the contrary, the record of more than a century of our free exercise jurisprudence contradicts that proposition. As described succinctly by *Justice FRANKFURTER* in *Minersville School Dist. Bd. of Educ.* v. *Gobitis*, "Conscientious scruples have not, in the course of the long struggle for religious toleration, relieved the individual from obedience to a general law not aimed at the promotion or restriction of religious beliefs. The mere possession of religious convictions which contradict the relevant concerns of a political society does not relieve the citizen from the discharge of political responsibilities (footnote omitted)." We first had occasion to assert that principle in *Reynolds* v. *United States*, where we rejected the claim that criminal laws against polygamy could not be constitutionally applied to those whose religion commanded the practice. "Laws," we said, "are made for the government of actions, and while they cannot interfere with mere religious belief and opinions, they may with practices. . . . Can a man excuse his practices to the contrary because of his religious belief? To permit this would be to make the professed doctrines of religious belief superior to the law of the land, and in effect to permit every citizen to become a law unto himself."

Subsequent decisions have consistently held that the right of free exercise does not relieve an individual of the obligation to comply with a "valid and neutral law of general applicability on the ground that the law proscribes (or prescribes) conduct that his religion prescribes (or proscribes)." *United States* v. *Lee* (Stevens, J., concurring in judgment). In *Prince* v. *Massachusetts*, we held that a mother could be prosecuted under the child labor laws ⊥**880** for using her children to dispense literature in the streets, her religious motivation notwithstanding. We found no constitutional infirmity in "excluding [these children] from doing there what no other children may do." In *Braunfeld* v. *Brown* (plurality opinion), we upheld Sunday-closing laws against the claim that they burdened the religious practices of persons whose religions compelled them to refrain from work on other days. In *Gillette* v. *United States* we sustained the military selective service system against the claim that it violated free exercise by conscripting persons who opposed a particular war on religious grounds.

Our most recent decision involving a neutral, generally applicable regulatory law that compelled activity forbidden by an individual's religion was *United States* v. *Lee*. There, an Amish employer, on behalf of himself and his employees, sought exemption from collection and payment of Social Security taxes on the ground that the Amish faith prohibited participation in governmental support programs. We rejected the claim that an exemption was constitutionally required. There would be no way, we observed, to distinguish the Amish believer's objection to Social Security taxes from the religious objections that others might have to the collection or use of other taxes. "If, for example, a religious adherent believes war is a sin, and if a certain percentage of the federal budget can be identified as devoted to war-related activities, such individuals would have a similarly valid claim to be exempt from paying that percentage of the income tax. The tax system could not function if denominations were allowed to challenge the tax system because tax payments were spent in a manner that violates their religious belief." Cf. *Hernandez* v. *Commissioner* (rejecting free exercise challenge to payment of income taxes alleged to make religious activities more difficult).

⊥**881** The only decisions in which we have held that the First Amendment bars application of a neutral, generally applicable law to religiously motivated action have involved not the Free Exercise Clause alone, but the Free Exercise Clause in conjunction with other constitutional protections, such as freedom of speech and of the press, see *Cantwell* v. *Connecticut* (invalidating a licensing system for religious and charitable solicitations under which the administrator had discretion to deny a license to any cause he deemed nonreligious); *Murdock* v. *Pennsylvania* (invalidating a flat tax on solicitation as applied to the dissemination of religious ideas); *Follett* v. *McCormick* (same), or the right of parents, acknowledged in *Pierce* v. *Society of Sisters* to direct the education of their children, see *Wisconsin* v. *Yoder* (invalidating compulsory school-attendance laws as applied to Amish parents who refused on religious grounds to send their children to school). ⊥**882** Some of our cases prohibiting compelled expression, decided exclusively upon free speech grounds, have also involved freedom of religion, cf. *Wooley* v. *Maynard* (invalidating compelled display of a license plate slogan that offended individual religious beliefs); *West Virginia Board of Education* v. *Barnette* (invalidating compulsory flag salute statute challenged by religious objectors). And it is easy to envision a case in which a challenge on freedom of association grounds would likewise be reinforced by Free Exercise Clause concerns. Cf. *Roberts* v. *United States Jaycees* ("An individual's freedom to speak, to worship, and to petition the government for the redress of grievances could not be vigorously protected from interference by the State [if] a correlative freedom to engage in group effort toward those ends were not also guaranteed").

The present case does not present such a hybrid situation, but a free exercise claim unconnected with any communicative activity or parental right. Respondents urge us to hold, quite simply, that when otherwise prohibitable conduct is accompanied by religious convictions, not only the convictions but the conduct itself must be free from governmental regulation. We have never held that, and decline to do so now. There being no contention that Oregon's drug law represents an attempt to regulate religious beliefs, the communication of religious beliefs, or the raising of one's children in those beliefs, the rule to which we have adhered ever since *Reynolds* plainly controls. "Our cases do not at their farthest reach support the proposition that a stance of conscientious opposition relieves an objector from any colliding duty fixed by a democratic government." *Gillette* v. *United States*.

B

Respondents argue that even though exemption from generally applicable criminal laws need not automatically be extended to religiously motivated actors, at least the claim for a ⊥**883** religious exemption must be evaluated under the balancing test set forth in *Sherbert* v. *Verner*. Under the *Sherbert* test, governmental actions that substantially burden a religious practice must be justified by a compelling governmental interest, see also *Hernandez* v. *Commissioner*. Applying that test we have, on three occasions, invalidated state unemployment compensation rules that conditioned the availability of benefits upon an applicant's willingness to work under conditions forbidden by his religion. See *Sherbert* v. *Verner*, *Thomas* v. *Review Board, Indiana Employment Div.*, *Hobbie* v. *Unemployment Appeals Comm'n of Florida*. We have never invalidated any governmental action on the basis of the *Sherbert* test except the denial of unemployment compensation. Although we have sometimes purported to apply the *Sherbert* test in contexts other than that, we have always found the test satisfied, see *United States* v. *Lee*, *Gillette* v. *United States*. In recent years we have abstained from applying the *Sherbert* test (outside the unemployment compensation field) at all. In *Bowen* v. *Roy* we declined to apply *Sherbert* analysis to a federal statutory scheme that required benefit applicants and recipients to provide their Social Security numbers. The plaintiffs in that case asserted that it would violate their religious beliefs to obtain and provide a Social Security number for their daughter. We held the statute's application to the plaintiffs valid regardless of whether it was necessary to effectuate a compelling interest. In *Lyng* v. *Northwest Indian Cemetery Protective Assn.*, we declined to apply *Sherbert* analysis to the Government's logging and road construction activities on lands used for religious purposes by several Native American Tribes, even though it was undisputed that the activities "could have devastating effects on traditional Indian religious practices." ⊥**884** In *Goldman* v. *Weinberger*, we rejected application of the *Sherbert* test to military dress regulations that forbade the wearing of yarmulkes. In *O'Lone* v. *Estate of Shabazz*, we sustained, without mentioning the *Sherbert* test, a prison's refusal to excuse inmates from work requirements to attend worship services.

Even if we were inclined to breathe into *Sherbert* some life beyond the unemployment compensation field, we would not apply it to require exemptions from a generally applicable criminal law. The *Sherbert* test, it must be recalled, was developed in a context that lent itself to individualized governmental assessment of the reasons for the relevant conduct. As a plurality of the Court noted in *Roy*, a distinctive feature of unemployment compensation programs is that their eligibility criteria invite consideration of the particular circumstances behind an applicant's unemployment: "The statutory conditions [in *Sherbert* and *Thomas*] provided that a person was not eligible for unemployment compensation benefits if, 'without good cause,' he had quit work or refused available work. The 'good cause' standard created a mechanism for individualized exemptions." *Bowen* v. *Roy* (opinion of Burger, C. J., joined by Powell and Rehnquist, JJ.). See also *Sherbert* (reading state unemployment compensation law as allowing benefits for unemployment caused by at least some "personal reasons"). As the plurality pointed out in *Roy*, our decisions in the unemployment cases stand for the proposition that where the State has in place a system of individual exemptions, it may not refuse to extend that system to cases of "religious hardship" without compelling reason. Whether or not the decisions are that limited, they at least have nothing to do with an across-the-board criminal prohibition on a particular form of conduct. Although, as noted earlier, we have sometimes used the *Sherbert* test to analyze free exercise challenges to such laws, see *United States* v. ⊥**885** *Lee*, *Gillette* v. *United States*, we have never applied the test to invalidate one. We conclude today that the sounder approach, and the approach in accord with the vast majority of our precedents, is to hold the test inapplicable to such challenges. The government's ability to enforce generally applicable prohibitions of socially harmful conduct, like its ability to carry out other aspects of public policy, "cannot depend on measuring the effects of a governmental action on a religious objector's spiritual development." To make an individual's obligation to obey such a law contingent upon the law's coincidence with his religious beliefs, except where the State's interest is "compelling"—permitting him, by virtue of his beliefs, "to become a law unto himself," *Reynolds* v. *United States*—contradicts both constitutional tradition and common sense.

The "compelling government interest" requirement seems benign, because it is familiar from other fields. But using it as the standard that must be met before the government may accord different treatment on the basis of race, ⊥**886** or before the government may regulate the content of speech, is not remotely comparable to using it for the purpose asserted here. What it produces in those other fields—equality of treatment, and an unrestricted flow of contending speech—are constitutional norms; what it would produce here—a private right to ignore generally applicable laws—is a constitutional anomaly.

Nor is it possible to limit the impact of respondents' proposal by requiring a "compelling state interest" only when the conduct prohibited is "central" to the individual's religion. It is no ⊥**887** more appropriate for judges to determine the "centrality" of religious beliefs before applying a "compelling interest" test in the free exercise field, than it would be for them to determine the "importance" of ideas before applying the "compelling interest" test in the free speech field. What principle of law or logic can be brought to bear to contradict a believer's assertion that a particular act is "central" to his personal faith? Judging the centrality of different religious practices is akin to the unacceptable "business of evaluating the relative merits of differing religious claims." *United States* v. *Lee* (Stevens, J., concurring). As we reaffirmed only last Term, "[i]t is not within the judicial ken to question the centrality of particular beliefs or practices to a faith, or the validity of particular litigants' interpretation of those creeds." *Hernandez* v. *Commissioner*. Repeatedly and in many different contexts, we have warned that courts must not presume to determine the place of a particular belief in a religion or the plausibility of a religious claim.

⊥**888** If the "compelling interest" test is to be applied at all, then, it must be applied across the board, to all actions thought to be religiously commanded. Moreover, if "compelling interest" really means what it says (and watering it down here would subvert its rigor in the other fields where it is applied), many laws will not meet the test. Any society adopting such a system would be courting anarchy, but that danger increases in direct proportion to the society's diversity of religious beliefs, and its determination to coerce or suppress none of them. Precisely because "we are a cosmopolitan nation made up of people of almost every conceivable religious preference," *Braunfeld* v. *Brown*, and precisely because we value and protect that religious divergence, we cannot afford the luxury of deeming *presumptively invalid*, as applied to the religious objector, every regulation of conduct that does not protect an interest of the highest order. The rule respondents favor would open the prospect of constitutionally required religious exemptions from civic obligations of almost every conceivable kind—ranging from ⊥**889** compulsory military service, to the payment of taxes, to health and safety regulation such as manslaughter and child neglect laws, compulsory vaccination laws, drug laws, and traffic laws; to social welfare legislation such as minimum wage laws, child labor laws, animal cruelty laws, environmental protection laws, and laws providing for equality of opportunity for the races. The First Amendment's protection of religious liberty does not require this.

⊥**890** Values that are protected against government interference through enshrinement in the Bill of Rights are not thereby banished from the political process. Just as a society that believes in the negative protection accorded to the press by the First Amendment is likely to enact laws that affirmatively foster the dissemination of the printed word, so also a society that believes in the negative protection accorded religious belief can be expected to be solicitous of that value in its legislation as well. It is therefore not surprising that a number of States have made an exception to their drug laws for sacramental peyote use. See, *e.g.*, Ariz. Rev. Stat. Ann. § 13-3402(B)(1)-(3) (1989); Colo. Rev. Stat. § 12-22-317(3) (1985); N. M. Stat. Ann. § 30-31-6(D) (Supp. 1989). But to say that a nondiscriminatory religious-practice exemption is permitted, or even that it is desirable, is not to say that it is constitutionally required, and that the appropriate occasions for its creation can be discerned by the courts. It may fairly be said that leaving accommodation to the political process will place at a relative disadvantage those religious practices that are not widely engaged in; but that unavoidable consequence of democratic government must be preferred to a system in which each conscience is a law unto itself or in which judges weigh the social importance of all law against the centrality of all religious beliefs.

. . . . .

Because respondents' ingestion of peyote was prohibited under Oregon law, and because that prohibition is constitutional, Oregon may, consistent with the Free Exercise Clause, deny respondents unemployment compensation when their dismissal results from use of the drug. The decision of the Oregon Supreme Court is accordingly reversed.

It is so ordered.

⊥**891** *Justice* O'CONNOR, with whom *Justice* BRENNAN, *Justice* MARSHALL, and *Justice* BLACKMUN join as to Part I and II concurring in the judgment.

Although I agree with the result the Court reaches in this case, I cannot join its opinion. In my view, today's holding dramatically departs from well-settled First Amendment jurisprudence, appears unnecessary to resolve the question presented, and is incompatible with our Nation's fundamental commitment to individual religious liberty.

I

At the outset, I note that I agree with the Court's implicit determination that the constitutional question upon which we granted review—whether the Free Exercise Clause protects a person's religiously motivated use of peyote from the reach of a State's general criminal law prohibition—is properly presented in this case. As the Court recounts, respondents Alfred Smith and Galen Black were denied unemployment compensation benefits because their sacramental use of peyote constituted work-related "misconduct," not because they violated Oregon's general criminal prohibition against possession of peyote. We held, however, in *Employment Div., Dept. of Human Resources of Oregon* v. *Smith (Smith I)*, that whether a State may, consistent with federal law, deny unemployment compensation benefits to persons for their religious use of peyote depends on whether the State, as a matter of state law, has criminalized the underlying conduct. The Oregon Supreme Court, on remand from this Court, concluded that "the Oregon statute against possession of controlled substances, which include peyote, makes no exception for the sacramental use of peyote."

⊥892 Respondents contend that, because the Oregon Supreme Court declined to decide whether the Oregon Constitution prohibits criminal prosecution for the religious use of peyote, any ruling on the federal constitutional question would be premature. Respondents are of course correct that the Oregon Supreme Court may eventually decide that the Oregon Constitution requires the State to provide an exemption from its general criminal prohibition for the religious use of peyote. Such a decision would then reopen the question whether a State may nevertheless deny unemployment compensation benefits to claimants who are discharged for engaging in such conduct. As the case comes to us today, however, the Oregon Supreme Court has plainly ruled that Oregon's prohibition against possession of controlled substances does not contain an exemption for the religious use of peyote. In light of our decision in *Smith I*, which makes this finding a "necessary predicate to a correct evaluation of respondents' federal claim," the question presented and addressed is properly before the Court.

II

The Court today extracts from our long history of free exercise precedents the single categorical rule that "if prohibiting the exercise of religion . . . is . . . merely the incidental effect of a generally applicable and otherwise valid provision, the First Amendment has not been offended." Indeed, the Court holds that where the law is a generally applicable criminal prohibition, our usual free exercise jurisprudence does not even apply. To reach this sweeping result, however, the Court must not only give a strained reading of the First Amendment but must also disregard our consistent application of free exercise doctrine to cases involving generally applicable regulations that burden religious conduct.

⊥893 A

The Free Exercise Clause of the First Amendment commands that "Congress shall make no law . . . prohibiting the free exercise [of religion]." In *Cantwell* v. *Connecticut*, we held that this prohibition applies to the States by incorporation into the Fourteenth Amendment and that it categorically forbids government regulation of religious beliefs. As the Court recognizes, however, the "free *exercise*" of religion often, if not invariably, requires the performance of (or abstention from) certain acts. "[B]elief and action cannot be neatly confined in logic-tight compartments." *Wisconsin* v. *Yoder*. Because the First Amendment does not distinguish between religious belief and religious conduct, conduct motivated by sincere religious belief, like the belief itself, must therefore be at least presumptively protected by the Free Exercise Clause.

The Court today, however, interprets the Clause to permit the government to prohibit, without justification, conduct mandated by an individual's religious beliefs, so long as that prohibition is generally applicable. But a law that prohibits certain conduct—conduct that happens to be an act of worship for someone—manifestly does prohibit that person's free exercise of his religion. A person who is barred from engaging in religiously motivated conduct is barred from freely exercising his religion. Moreover, that person is barred from freely exercising his religion regardless of whether the law prohibits the conduct only when engaged in for religious reasons, only by members of that religion, or by all persons. It is difficult to deny that a law that prohib**⊥894**its religiously motivated conduct, even if the law is generally applicable, does not at least implicate First Amendment concerns.

The Court responds that generally applicable laws are "one large step" removed from laws aimed at specific religious practices. The First Amendment, however, does not distinguish between laws that are generally applicable and laws that target particular religious practices. Indeed, few States would be so naive as to enact a law directly prohibiting or burdening a religious practice as such. Our free exercise cases have all concerned generally applicable laws that had the effect of significantly burdening a religious practice. If the First Amendment is to have any vitality, it ought not be construed to cover only the extreme and hypothetical situation in which a State directly targets a religious practice. As we have noted in a slightly different context, "'[s]uch a test has no basis in precedent and relegates a serious First Amendment value to the barest level of minimum scrutiny that the Equal Protection Clause already provides.'" *Hobbie* v. *Unemployment Appeals Comm'n of Florida* (quoting *Bowen* v. *Roy*).

To say that a person's right to free exercise has been burdened, of course, does not mean that he has an absolute right to engage in the conduct. Under our established First Amendment jurisprudence, we have recognized that the freedom to act, unlike the freedom to believe, cannot be absolute. Instead, we have respected both the First Amendment's express textual mandate and the governmental interest in regulation of conduct by requiring the Government to justify any substantial burden on religiously motivated conduct by a compelling state interest and by means narrowly tailored to achieve that interest. **⊥895** The compelling interest test effectuates the First Amendment's command that religious liberty is an independent liberty, that it occupies a preferred position, and that the Court will not permit encroachments upon this liberty, whether direct or indirect, unless required by clear and compelling governmental interests "of the highest order," *Yoder*. "Only an especially important governmental interest pursued by narrowly tailored means can justify exacting a sacrifice of First Amendment freedoms as the price for an equal share of the rights, benefits, and privileges enjoyed by other citizens." *Roy* (opinion concurring in part and dissenting in part).

The Court attempts to support its narrow reading of the Clause by claiming that "[w]e have never held that an individual's religious beliefs excuse him from compliance with an otherwise valid law prohibiting conduct that the State is free to regulate." But as the Court later notes, as it must, in cases such as *Cantwell* and *Yoder* we have in fact interpreted the Free Exercise Clause to forbid application of a generally applicable prohibition to religiously motivated conduct. Indeed, in *Yoder* we expressly rejected the interpretation the Court now adopts:

"[O]ur decisions have rejected the idea that religiously grounded conduct is always outside the protection of the Free Exercise Clause. It is true that activities of individuals, even when religiously based, are often subject **⊥896** to regulation by the States in the exercise of their undoubted power to promote the health, safety, and general welfare, or the Federal Government in the exercise of its delegated powers. But to agree that religiously grounded conduct must often be subject to the broad police power of the State is not to deny that there are areas of conduct protected by the Free Exercise Clause of the First Amendment and thus beyond the power of the State to control, *even under regulations of general applicability*. . . .

". . . A regulation neutral on its face may, in its application, nonetheless offend the constitutional requirement for government neutrality if it unduly burdens the free exercise of religion" (emphasis added; citations omitted).

The Court endeavors to escape from our decisions in *Cantwell* and *Yoder* by labeling them "hybrid" decisions, but there is no denying that both cases expressly relied on the Free Exercise Clause and that we have consistently regarded those cases as part of the mainstream of our free exercise jurisprudence. Moreover, in each of the other cases cited by the Court to support its categorical rule, we rejected the particular constitutional claims before us only after carefully weighing the competing interests. . . . That we rejected the free exer**⊥897**cise claims in those cases hardly calls into question the applicability of First Amendment doctrine in the first place. Indeed, it is surely unusual to judge the vitality of a constitutional doctrine by looking to the win-loss record of the plaintiffs who happen to come before us.

B

Respondents, of course, do not contend that their conduct is automatically immune from all governmental regulation simply because it is motivated by their sincere religious beliefs. The Court's rejection of that argument might therefore be regarded as merely harmless dictum. Rather, respondents invoke our traditional compelling interest test to argue that the Free Exercise Clause requires the State to grant them a limited exemption from its general criminal prohibition against the possession of peyote. The Court today, however, denies them even the opportunity to make that argument, concluding that "the sounder approach, and the approach in accord with the vast majority of our precedents, is to hold the [compelling interest] test inapplicable to" challenges to general criminal prohibitions.

In my view, however, the essence of a free exercise claim is relief from a burden imposed by government on religious practices or beliefs, whether the burden is imposed directly through laws that prohibit or compel specific religious practices, or indirectly through laws that, in effect, make abandonment of one's own religion or conformity to the religious beliefs of others the price of an equal place in the civil community. As we explained in *Thomas*: "Where the state conditions receipt of an important benefit upon conduct proscribed by a religious faith, or where it denies such a benefit because of conduct mandated by religious belief, thereby putting substantial pressure on an adherent to modify his behavior and to violate his beliefs, a burden upon religion exists." **⊥898** A State that makes criminal an individual's religiously motivated conduct burdens that individual's free exercise of religion in the severest manner possible, for it "results in the choice to the individual of either abandoning his religious principle or facing criminal prosecution." *Braunfeld*. I would have thought it beyond argument that such laws implicate free exercise concerns.

Indeed, we have never distinguished between cases in which a State conditions receipt of a benefit on conduct prohibited by religious beliefs and cases in which a State affirmatively prohibits such conduct. The *Sherbert* compelling interest test applies in both kinds of cases. As I noted in *Bowen* v. *Roy*.

"The fact that the underlying dispute involves an award of benefits rather than an exaction of penalties does not grant the Government license to apply a different version of the Constitution. . . .

". . . The fact that appellees seek exemption from a precondition that the Government attaches to an award of benefits does not, therefore, generate a meaningful distinction between this case and one where appellees seek an exemption from the Government's imposition of penalties upon them" (opinion concurring in part and dissenting in part). I would reaffirm that principle today: a neutral criminal law prohibiting conduct that a State may legitimately regulate is, if anything, *more* burdensome than a neutral civil **⊥899** statute placing legitimate conditions on the award of a state benefit.

Legislatures, of course, have always been "left free to reach actions which were in violation of social duties or subversive of good order." Yet because of the close relationship between conduct and religious belief, "[i]n every case the power to regulate must be so exercised as not, in attaining a permissible end, unduly to infringe the protected freedom." *Cantwell.* Once it has been shown that a government regulation or criminal prohibition burdens the free exercise of religion, we have consistently asked the Government to demonstrate that unbending application of its regulation to the religious objector "is essential to accomplish an overriding governmental interest," *Lee*, or represents "the least restrictive means of achieving some compelling state interest," *Thomas*. To me, the sounder approach—the approach more consistent with our role as judges to decide each case on its individual merits—is to apply this test in each case to determine whether the burden on the specific plaintiffs before us is constitutionally significant and whether the particular criminal interest asserted by the State before us is compelling. Even if, as an empirical matter, a government's criminal laws might usually serve a compelling interest in health, safety, or public order, the First Amendment at least requires a case-by-case determination of the question, sensitive to the facts of each particular claim. Given the range of conduct that a State might legitimately make **⊥900** criminal, we cannot assume, merely because a law carries criminal sanctions and is generally applicable, that the First Amendment never requires the State to grant a limited exemption for religiously motivated conduct.

Moreover, we have not "rejected" or "declined to apply" the compelling interest test in our recent cases. Recent cases have instead affirmed that test as a fundamental part of our First Amendment doctrine. The cases cited by the Court signal no retreat from our consistent adherence to the compelling interest test. In both *Bowen* v. *Roy*, and *Lyng* v. *Northwest Indian Cemetery Protective Assn.*, for example, we expressly distinguished *Sherbert* on the ground that the First Amendment does not "require the Government *itself* to behave in ways that the individual believes will further his or her spiritual development. . . . The Free Exercise Clause simply cannot be understood to require the Government to conduct its own internal affairs in ways that comport with the religious beliefs of particular citizens." *Roy*, see *Lyng*. This distinction makes sense because "the Free Exercise Clause is written in terms of what the government cannot do to the individual, not in terms of what the individual can exact from the government." *Sherbert* (Douglas, J., concurring). Because the case *sub judice*, like the other cases in which we have applied *Sherbert*, plainly falls into the former category, I would apply those established precedents to the facts of this case.

Similarly, the other cases cited by the Court for the proposition that we have rejected application of the *Sherbert* test outside the unemployment compensation field are distinguishable because they arose in the narrow, specialized contexts in which we have not traditionally re**⊥901**quired the government to justify a burden on religious conduct by articulating a compelling interest. . . .

The Court today gives no convincing reason to depart from settled First Amendment jurisprudence. There is nothing talismanic about neutral laws of general applicability or general criminal prohibitions, for laws neutral toward religion can coerce a person to violate his religious conscience or intrude upon his religious duties just as effectively as laws aimed at religion. Although the Court suggests that the compelling interest test, as applied to generally applicable laws, would result in a "constitutional anomaly," the First Amendment unequivocally makes freedom of religion, like freedom from race discrimination and freedom of speech, a "constitutional nor[m]," not an "anomaly." Nor would application of our established free exercise doctrine to this case necessarily be incompatible with our equal protection cases. We have in any event recognized that the Free Exercise Clause protects values distinct from those protected by the Equal Protection Clause. As the language of the **⊥902** Clause itself makes clear, an individual's free exercise of religion is a preferred constitutional activity. A law that makes criminal such an activity therefore triggers constitutional concern—and heightened judicial scrutiny—even if it does not target the particular religious conduct at issue. Our free speech cases similarly recognize that neutral regulations that affect free speech values are subject to a balancing, rather than categorical, approach. The Court's parade of horribles not only fails as a reason for discarding the compelling interest test, it instead demonstrates just the opposite: that courts have been quite capable of applying our free exercise jurisprudence to strike sensible balances between religious liberty and competing state interests.

Finally, the Court today suggests that the disfavoring of minority religions is an "unavoidable consequence" under our system of government and that accommodation of such religions must be left to the political process. In my view, however, the First Amendment was enacted precisely to protect the rights of those whose religious practices are not shared by the majority and may be viewed with hostility. The history of our free exercise doctrine amply demonstrates the harsh impact majoritarian rule has had on unpopular or emerging religious groups such as the Jehovah's Witnesses and the Amish. Indeed, the words of *Justice JACKSON* in *West Virginia Board of Education* v. *Barnette* (overruling *Minersville School District* v. *Gobitis)*, are apt:

⊥903 "The very purpose of a Bill of Rights was to withdraw certain subjects from the vicissitudes of political controversy, to place them beyond the reach of majorities and officials and to establish them as legal principles to be applied by the courts. One's right to life, liberty, and property, to free speech, a free press, freedom of worship and assembly, and other fundamental rights may not be submitted to vote; they depend on the outcome of no elections." See also *United States* v. *Ballard* ("The Fathers of the Constitution were not unaware of the varied and extreme views of religious sects, of the violence of disagreement among them, and of the lack of any one religious creed on which all men would agree. They fashioned a charter of government which envisaged the widest possible toleration of conflicting views"). The compelling interest test reflects the First Amendment's mandate of preserving religious liberty to the fullest extent possible in a pluralistic society. For the Court to deem this command a "luxury," is to denigrate "[t]he very purpose of a Bill of Rights."

III

The Court's holding today not only misreads settled First Amendment precedent; it appears to be unnecessary to this case. I would reach the same result applying our established free exercise jurisprudence.

A

There is no dispute that Oregon's criminal prohibition of peyote places a severe burden on the ability of respondents to freely exercise their religion. Peyote is a sacrament of the Native American Church and is regarded as vital to respondents' ability to practice their religion. . . . ⊥**904** As we noted in *Smith I*, the Oregon Supreme Court concluded that "the Native American Church is a recognized religion, that peyote is a sacrament of that church, and that respondent's beliefs were sincerely held." Under Oregon law, as construed by that State's highest court, members of the Native American Church must choose between carrying out the ritual embodying their religious beliefs and avoidance of criminal prosecution. That choice is, in my view, more than sufficient to trigger First Amendment scrutiny.

There is also no dispute that Oregon has a significant interest in enforcing laws that control the possession and use of controlled substances by its citizens. Indeed, under federal law (incorporated by Oregon law in relevant part, see Ore. Rev. Stat. § 475.005(6) (1989)), peyote is specifically regulated as a Schedule I controlled substance, which means that Congress has found that it has a high potential for abuse, that there is no currently accepted medical use, and that there is a lack of accepted safety for use of the drug under medical supervision. See 21 U.S.C. § 812(b)(1). In light of our recent decisions holding that the governmental ⊥**905** interests in the collection of income tax, a comprehensive social security system, and military conscription, are compelling, respondents do not seriously dispute that Oregon has a compelling interest in prohibiting the possession of peyote by its citizens.

B

Thus, the critical question in this case is whether exempting respondents from the State's general criminal prohibition "will unduly interfere with fulfillment of the governmental interest." *Lee*; see also *Roy* "([T]he Government must accommodate a legitimate free exercise claim unless pursuing an especially important interest by narrowly tailored means"); *Yoder, Braunfeld.* Although the question is close, I would conclude that uniform application of Oregon's criminal prohibition is "essential to accomplish," *Lee*, its overriding interest in preventing the physical harm caused by the use of a Schedule I controlled substance. Oregon's criminal prohibition represents that State's judgment that the possession and use of controlled substances, even by only one person, is inherently harmful and dangerous. Because the health effects caused by the use of controlled substances exist regardless of the motivation of the user, the use of such substances, even for religious purposes, violates the very purpose of the laws that prohibit them. Moreover, in view of the societal interest in preventing trafficking in controlled substances, uniform application of the criminal prohibition at issue is essential to the effectiveness of Oregon's stated interest in preventing any possession of peyote.

⊥**906** For these reasons, I believe that granting a selective exemption in this case would seriously impair Oregon's compelling interest in prohibiting possession of peyote by its citizens. Under such circumstances, the Free Exercise Clause does not require the State to accommodate respondents' religiously motivated conduct. Unlike in *Yoder*, where we noted that "[t]he record strongly indicates that accommodating the religious objections of the Amish by forgoing one, or at most two, additional years of compulsory education will not impair the physical or mental health of the child, or result in an inability to be self-supporting or to discharge the duties and responsibilities of citizenship, or in any other way materially detract from the welfare of society," a religious exemption in this case would be incompatible with the State's interest in controlling use and possession of illegal drugs.

Respondents contend that any incompatibility is belied by the fact that the Federal Government and several States provide exemptions for the religious use of peyote, see 21 CFR § 1307.31 (1989); 307 Or., at 73, n. 2, 763 P. 2d, at 148, n. 2 (citing 11 state statutes that expressly exempt sacramental peyote use from criminal proscription). But other governments may surely choose to grant an exemption without Oregon, with its specific asserted interest in uniform application of its drug laws, being *required* to do so by the First Amendment. Respondents also note that the sacramental use of peyote is central to the tenets of the Native American Church, but I agree with the Court, that because "[i]t is not within the judicial ken to question the centrality of particular beliefs or practices to a faith," *Hernandez*, our determination of the constitutionality of Oregon's general criminal prohibition cannot, and should not, turn on the centrality of the particular ⊥**907** religious practice at issue. This does not mean, of course, that courts may not make factual findings as to whether a claimant holds a sincerely held religious belief that conflicts with, and thus is burdened by, the challenged law. The distinction between questions of centrality and questions of sincerity and burden is admittedly fine, but it is one that is an established part of our free exercise doctrine.

I would therefore adhere to our established free exercise jurisprudence and hold that the State in this case has a compelling interest in regulating peyote use by its citizens and that accommodating respondents' religiously motivated conduct "will unduly interfere with fulfillment of the governmental interest." *Lee*. Accordingly, I concur in the judgment of the Court.

Justice BLACKMUN, with whom *Justice* BRENNAN and *Justice* MARSHALL join, dissenting.

This Court over the years painstakingly has developed a consistent and exacting standard to test the constitutionality of a state statute that burdens the free exercise of religion. Such a statute may stand only if the law in general, and the State's refusal to allow a religious exemption in particular, are justified by a compelling interest that cannot be served by less restrictive means.

⊥908 Until today, I thought this was a settled and inviolate principle of this Court's First Amendment jurisprudence. The majority, however, perfunctorily dismisses it as a "constitutional anomaly." As carefully detailed in *Justice* O'CONNOR's concurring opinion, the majority is able to arrive at this view only by mischaracterizing this Court's precedents. The Court discards leading free exercise cases such as *Cantwell* v. *Connecticut* and *Wisconsin* v. *Yoder*. The Court views traditional free exercise analysis as somehow inapplicable to criminal prohibitions (as opposed to conditions on the receipt of benefits), and to state laws of general applicability (as opposed, presumably, to laws that expressly single out religious practices). The Court cites cases in which, due to various exceptional circumstances, we found strict scrutiny inapposite, to hint that the Court has repudiated that standard altogether. In short, it effectuates a wholesale overturning of settled law concerning the Religion Clauses of our Constitution. One hopes that the Court is aware of the consequences, and that its result is not a product of overreaction to the serious problems the country's drug crisis has generated.

This distorted view of our precedents leads the majority to conclude that strict scrutiny of a state law burdening the free exercise of religion is a "luxury" that a well-ordered society **⊥909** cannot afford, and that the repression of minority religions is an "unavoidable consequence of democratic government." I do not believe the Founders thought their dearly bought freedom from religious persecution a "luxury," but an essential element of liberty—and they could not have thought religious intolerance "unavoidable," for they drafted the Religion Clauses precisely in order to avoid that intolerance.

For these reasons, I agree with *Justice* O'CONNOR's analysis of the applicable free exercise doctrine, and I join parts I and II of her opinion. As she points out, "the critical question in this case is whether exempting respondents from the State's general criminal prohibition 'will unduly interfere with fulfillment of the governmental interest.'" I do disagree, however, with her specific answer to that question.

I

In weighing respondents' clear interest in the free exercise of their religion against Oregon's asserted interest in enforcing its drug laws, it is important to articulate in precise terms the state interest involved. It is not the State's broad interest **⊥910** in fighting the critical "war on drugs" that must be weighed against respondents' claim, but the State's narrow interest in refusing to make an exception for the religious, ceremonial use of peyote. See *Bowen* v. *Roy* ("This Court has consistently asked the Government to demonstrate that unbending application of its regulation to the religious objector 'is essential to accomplish an overriding governmental interest,'") quoting *Lee; Thomas* v. *Review Bd. of Indiana Employment Security Div*. ("focus of the inquiry" concerning State's asserted interest must be "properly narrowed"); *Yoder* ("Where fundamental claims of religious freedom are at stake," the Court will not accept a State's "sweeping claim" that its interest in compulsory education is compelling, despite the validity of this interest "in the generality of cases, we must searchingly examine the interests that the State seeks to promote . . . and the impediment to those objectives that would flow from recognizing the claimed Amish exception.") Failure to reduce the competing interests to the same plane of generality tends to distort the weighing process in the State's favor.

The State's interest in enforcing its prohibition, in order to be sufficiently compelling to outweigh a free exercise claim, **⊥911** cannot be merely abstract or symbolic. The State cannot plausibly assert that unbending application of a criminal prohibition is essential to fulfill any compelling interest, if it does not, in fact, attempt to enforce that prohibition. In this case, the State actually has not evinced any concrete interest in enforcing its drug laws against religious users of peyote. Oregon has never sought to prosecute respondents, and does not claim that it has made significant enforcement efforts against other religious users of peyote. The State's asserted interest thus amounts only to the symbolic preservation of an unenforced prohibition. But a government interest in "symbolism, even symbolism for so worthy a cause as the abolition of unlawful drugs," *Treasury Employees* v. *Von Raab* (Scalia, J., dissenting), cannot suffice to abrogate the constitutional rights of individuals.

Similarly, this Court's prior decisions have not allowed a government to rely on mere speculation about potential harms, but have demanded evidentiary support for a refusal to allow a religious exception. In this case, the State's justification for refusing to recognize an exception to its criminal laws for religious peyote use is entirely speculative.

The State proclaims an interest in protecting the health and safety of its citizens from the dangers of unlawful drugs. It offers, however, no evidence that the religious use of pey⊥**912**ote has ever harmed anyone. The factual findings of other courts cast doubt on the State's assumption that religious use of peyote is harmful. See *State* v. *Whittingham* ("the State failed to prove that the quantities of peyote used in the sacraments of the Native American Church are sufficiently harmful to the health and welfare of the participants so as to permit a legitimate intrusion under the State's police power"); *People* v. *Woody* ("as the Attorney General . . . admits, the opinion of scientists and other experts is 'that peyote . . . works no permanent deleterious injury to the Indian'").

The fact that peyote is classified as a Schedule I controlled substance does not, by itself, show that any and all uses of peyote, in any circumstance, are inherently harmful and dangerous. The Federal Government, which created the classifications of unlawful drugs from which Oregon's drug laws are derived, apparently does not find peyote so dangerous as to preclude an exemption for religious use. Moreover, ⊥**913** other Schedule I drugs have lawful uses.

The carefully circumscribed ritual context in which respondents used peyote is far removed from the irresponsible and unrestricted recreational use of unlawful drugs. The Native American Church's internal restrictions on, and supervision of, its members' use of peyote substantially obviate the State's health and safety concerns. . . .

⊥**914** Moreover, just as in *Yoder*, the values and interests of those seeking a religious exemption in this case are congruent, to a great degree, with those the State seeks to promote through its drug laws. Not only does the Church's doctrine forbid nonreligious use of peyote; it also generally advocates self-reliance, familial responsibility, and abstinence from alcohol. . . . ⊥**915** There is considerable evidence that the spiritual and social support provided by the Church has been effective in combatting the tragic effects of alcoholism on the Native American population. . . . Far from promoting the lawless and irresponsible use of drugs, Native American Church members' spiri⊥**916**tual code exemplifies values that Oregon's drug laws are presumably intended to foster.

The State also seeks to support its refusal to make an exception for religious use of peyote by invoking its interest in abolishing drug trafficking. There is however, practically no illegal traffic in peyote. Also, the availability of peyote for religious use, even if Oregon were to allow an exemption from its criminal laws, would still be strictly controlled by federal regulations, see 21 U.S.C. §§ 821-823 (registration requirements for distribution of controlled substances); 21 CFR § 1307.31 (1989) (distribution of peyote to Native American Church subject to registration requirements), and by the State of Texas, the only State in which peyote grows in significant quantities. See Texas Health & Safety Code, § 481.111 (1990); Texas Admin. Code, Tit. 37, pt. 1, ch. 13, Controlled Substances Regulations, §§ 13.35-13.41 (1989). Peyote simply is not a popular drug; its distribution for use in religious rituals has nothing to do with the vast and violent traffic in illegal narcotics that plagues this country.

Finally, the State argues that granting an exception for religious peyote use would erode its interest in the uniform, fair, and certain enforcement of its drug laws. The State fears that, if it grants an exemption for religious peyote use, a flood of other claims to religious exemptions will follow. It would then be placed in a dilemma, it says, between allowing a patchwork of exemptions that would hinder its law enforcement efforts, and risking a violation of the Establishment Clause by arbitrarily limiting its religious exemptions. This ⊥**917** argument, however, could be made in almost any free exercise case. . . . This Court, however, consistently has rejected similar arguments in past free exercise cases, and it should do so here as well. . . .

The State's apprehension of a flood of other religious claims is purely speculative. Almost half the States, and the Federal Government, have maintained an exemption for religious peyote use for many years, and apparently have not found themselves overwhelmed by claims to other religious exemptions. Allowing an exemption for religious peyote use ⊥**918** would not necessarily oblige the State to grant a similar exemption to other religious groups. The unusual circumstances that make the religious use of peyote compatible with the State's interests in health and safety and in preventing drug trafficking would not apply to other religious claims. Some religions, for example, might not restrict drug use to a limited ceremonial context, as does the Native American Church. Some religious claims involve drugs such as marijuana and heroin, in which there is significant illegal traffic, with its attendant greed and violence, so that it would be difficult to grant a religious exemption without seriously compromising law enforcement efforts. That the State might grant an exemption for religious peyote use, but deny other religious claims arising in different circumstances, would not violate the Establishment Clause. Though the State must treat all religions equally, and not favor one over another, this obligation is fulfilled by the uniform application of the "compelling interest" test to all free exercise claims, not by reaching uniform results as to all claims. A showing that religious peyote use does not unduly interfere with the State's interests is "one that probably few other religious groups or sects could make," *Yoder*, this does not mean that an exemption limited to peyote use is tantamount to an establishment of religion. . . . ⊥**919**

II

Finally, although I agree with *Justice* O'CONNOR that courts should refrain from delving into questions of whether, as a matter of religious doctrine, a particular practice is "central" to the religion, I do not think this means that the courts must turn a blind eye to the severe impact of a State's restrictions on the adherents of a minority religion. . . .

Respondents believe, and their sincerity has never been at issue, that the peyote plant embodies their deity, and eating it is an act of worship and communion. Without peyote, they could not enact the essential ritual of their religion. . . . ⊥920

If Oregon can constitutionally prosecute them for this act of worship, they, like the Amish, may be "forced to migrate to some other and more tolerant region." This potentially devastating impact must be viewed in light of the federal policy—reached in reaction to many years of religious persecution and intolerance—of protecting the religious freedom of Native Americans. See American Indian Religious Freedom Act, 92 Stat. 469, 42 U.S.C. § 1996 ("it shall be the policy of the United States to protect and preserve for American Indians their inherent right of freedom to believe, express, and exercise the traditional religions . . . , including but not limited to access to sites, use and possession of sacred objects, and the freedom to worship through ceremonials and traditional rites"). Congress recognized that certain substances, such as peyote, "have religious significance because they are sacred, they have power, they heal, they are necessary to the exercise of ⊥921 the rites of the religion, they are necessary to the cultural integrity of the tribe, and, therefore, religious survival." H.R. Rep. No. 95-1308, p. 2 (1978), U.S. Code Cong. & Admin. News 1978, pp. 1262, 1263.

The American Indian Religious Freedom Act, in itself, may not create rights enforceable against government action restricting religious freedom, but this Court must scrupulously apply its free exercise analysis to the religious claims of Native Americans, however unorthodox they may be. Otherwise, both the First Amendment and the stated policy of Congress will offer to Native Americans merely an unfulfilled and hollow promise.

III

For these reasons, I conclude that Oregon's interest in enforcing its drug laws against religious use of peyote is not sufficiently compelling to outweigh respondents' right to the free exercise of their religion. Since the State could not constitutionally enforce its criminal prohibition against respondents, the interests underlying the State's drug laws cannot justify its denial of unemployment benefits. Absent such justification, the State's regulatory interest in denying benefits for religiously motivated "misconduct" is indistinguishable from the state interest this Court has rejected in *Frazee*, *Hobbie*, *Thomas*, and *Sherbert*. The State of Oregon cannot, consistently with the Free Exercise Clause, deny respondents unemployment benefits.

I dissent.

RELIGION AND THE RIGHT TO WORSHIP

In 1993 the Court was confronted with a case in which a religious group's very right to worship was at issue. In CHURCH OF THE LUKUMI BABALU AYE v. CITY OF HIALEAH, the city of Hialeah, Florida, was charged with violation of the Free Exercise Clause. The free exercise violation of which it was accused struck at the heart of the worship practices of a congregation of the Santeria religion.

Santeria is an immigrant religion found principally among Cuban-Americans in South Florida and New York. One could have argued that the significance of this case was scanty, given that it was of immediate concern only to the members of this small, unorthodox movement. However, it was widely viewed by mainstream religious groups as a case of extreme importance in that it presented the Court with an opportunity to affirm, extend, clarify, or perhaps retreat from its controversial holding in EMPLOYMENT DIVISION OF OREGON v. SMITH (1990) about the methodology of interpreting the Free Exercise Clause.

In arriving at its decision, the Court reviewed four ordinances passed by the Hialeah City Council in 1987 shortly after the president of the Church of Lukumi Babalu Aye leased land in Hialeah and announced plans to set up a house of worship, a school, a cultural center, and a museum.

The Santeria religion originated in this hemisphere when hundreds of thousands of East Africans were brought to Cuba as slaves. Their native African religion soon absorbed many Roman Catholic concepts, resulting in the creation of Santeria, "the way of the saints." Exiles from the Cuban revolution brought this religion to the United States.

Residents of Hialeah were deeply concerned by the possibility of a Santeria church in their community. Most alarming to them was the fact that the church engaged in the sacrificing of animals—chickens, ducks, pigeons, guinea pigs, goats, sheep, and turtles. These sacrifices are performed at all birth, marriage, and death ceremonies, for the cure of the sick, upon the initiation of priests and new members, and at a yearly festival. Except after healing and death rites, the sacrificed animals are usually cooked and eaten.

At an emergency session in June 1987, the city council took notice of the residents' "great concern regarding the possibility of public ritualistic animal sacrifices." Such practice was "inconsistent with public morals, peace or safety." Florida's attorney general held that because religious animal sacrifice was contrary to state law, a city ordinance prohibiting such sacrifices would not be contrary to the law. The city council announced a policy "to oppose the ritualistic sacrifices of animals" and declared that any person or organization practicing animal sacrifice would be prosecuted. Subsequently, three more ordinances were enacted: these defined sacrifices and pointedly limited prohibition of sacrifice, as defined, to any individual or group that "kills, slaughters or sacrifices animals for any type of ritual, regardless of whether or not the flesh or blood of the animal is to be consumed." Numerous exemptions were granted.

The church soon filed a suit in federal district court which, in its pre-*Smith* ruling, applied the "compelling interest" test, balancing governmental and religious interests. Certain considerations outweighed the religious rights involved: health hazards, cruelty to animals, emotional damage to children witnessing the sacrifices, and respect for the zoning powers of the city. The effect of the ordinances on religious conduct, the court held, was "incidental to [their] secular purpose and effect."

In a very brief *per curiam* opinion, the Eleventh Court of Appeals affirmed the district court's opinion, holding that the ordinances were consistent with the Constitution. There was no need for the district court to refer to the *Smith* rule because the court had "employed an arguably stricter standard" than that required in *Smith*.

Writing for a unanimous Supreme Court, Justice Kennedy had no difficulty in finding the Hialeah ordinances unconstitutional. Even before giving a careful discussion of the Santeria religion and the actions of the city council, he wrote: "Our review confirms that the laws in question were enacted by officials who did not understand, failed to perceive, or chose to ignore the fact that their official actions violated the Nation's essential commitment to religious freedom." The enactments, he said, "had an impermissible object" and the "principle of general applicability was violated because the secular ends asserted in defense of the laws were pursued only with respect to conduct motivated by religious beliefs" (508 U.S. 520, 524). The judgment of the court of appeals was reversed; the ordinances were invalidated.

Justice Kennedy accepted the holding in *Smith* that even though a law had the incidental effect of burdening a religious practice, a compelling governmental interest did not have to be proved if the law was neutral and of general applicability. The terms "neutral" and "general applicability," Kennedy pointed out, are interrelated to the degree that if an action fails to satisfy one, it will almost certainly not satisfy the other. The action would then have to be judged by the compelling interest standard. "At a minimum," he said, "the protections of the Free Exercise Clause pertain if the law at issue discriminates against some or all religious beliefs or regulates or prohibits conduct because it is undertaken for religious reasons" (508 U.S. 520, 532).

The broadly drawn Hialeah ordinances clearly targeted members of the Santeria religion through the use of such words as "sacrifice" and "ritual." Statements at the city council meetings also made it clear that the objective of the ordinances was the suppression of the religious practices of the Santeria. If the ordinances could not meet the *Smith* test, certainly they would not survive the more rigorous scrutiny required by the compelling interest rule.

Justice Kennedy concluded his opinion for the Court with a trenchant statement that

> The Free Exercise Clause commits government itself to religious tolerance, and upon even slight suspicion that proposals for state intervention stem from animosity to religion or distrust of its practices, all officials must pause to remember their own high duty to the Constitution and to the rights it secures. . . . Legislators may not devise mechanisms, overt or disguised, designed to persecute or oppress a religion or its practices (508 U.S. 520, 547).

The finding of illegality of the Hialeah ordinances occasioned no dissent, but there were substantial differences among members of the Court as to Justice Kennedy's reasoning. Chief Justice Rehnquist and Justices Thomas, Scalia, and Souter joined part of the opinion, concurring in the judgment.

Justice Scalia, joined by the Chief Justice, wrote a separate opinion; Justice Blackmun, joined by Justice O'Connor, followed suit. Justice Scalia agreed with the opinion of the Court with respect to the overlap of the terms "neutrality" and "general applicability" but that, he thought, was of minor importance. He disagreed with Kennedy's procedure of examining legislative history: he would consider challenged legislation only on the basis of its stated terms. Scalia would not seek the subjective motives of the lawmakers.

Justice Blackmun restated his belief that *Smith* was incorrectly decided "because it ignored the value of religious freedom as an affirmative individual liberty and treated the Free Exercise Clause as no more than an antidiscrimination principle." He would require a showing by the state that legislation which "intentionally or unintentionally places a burden upon religiously motivated practice" meets the compelling interest test. Here the ordinances in question, far from use of the least restrictive means, were both overinclusive and underinclusive.

Justice Souter, in still a third "concurring in judgment" opinion, expressed strong doubt as to whether the rule established in *Smith* merits adherence. He viewed the new standard as not germane in this case and called on the Court to reexamine the *Smith* rule. A showing of formal neutrality and general applicability was insufficient. Neither precedent nor the historic background and text of the Free Exercise Clause justified the standard announced in *Smith*: "'neutral generally applicable' laws . . . have the unavoidable potential of putting the believer to a choice between God and government" (508 U.S. 520, 577).

CHURCH OF THE LUKUMI BABALU AYE v. CITY OF HIALEAH

508 U.S. 520
ON WRIT OF CERTIORARI TO THE UNITED STATES COURT OF APPEALS FOR THE ELEVENTH CIRCUIT
Argued November 4, 1992 — Decided June 11, 1993

⊥**523** *Justice KENNEDY* delivered the opinion of the Court, except as to Part II–A–2.*

The principle that government may not enact laws that suppress religious belief or practice is so well understood that few violations are recorded in our opinions. Cf. *McDaniel* v. *Paty; Fowler* v. *Rhode Island.* Concerned that this fundamental nonpersecution principle of the First Amendment was implicated here, however, we granted certiorari.

⊥**524** Our review confirms that the laws in question were enacted by officials who did not understand, failed to perceive, or chose to ignore the fact that their official actions violated the Nation's essential commitment to religious freedom. The challenged laws had an impermissible object; and in all events the principle of general applicability was violated because the secular ends asserted in defense of the laws were pursued only with respect to conduct motivated by religious beliefs. We invalidate the challenged enactments and reverse the judgment of the Court of Appeals.

I

A

This case involves practices of the Santeria religion, which originated in the nineteenth century. When hundreds of thousands of members of the Yoruba people were brought as slaves from eastern Africa to Cuba, their traditional African religion absorbed significant elements of Roman Catholicism. The resulting syncretion, or fusion, is Santeria, "the way of the saints." The Cuban Yoruba express their devotion to spirits, called *orishas*, through the iconography of Catholic saints, Catholic symbols are often present at Santeria rites, and Santeria devotees attend the Catholic sacraments. 723 F. Supp. 1467, 1469–1470 (SD Fla. 1989); 13 The Encyclopedia of Religion 66 (M. Eliade ed. 1987); 1 Encyclopedia of the American Religious Experience 183 (C. Lippy & P. Williams eds. 1988).

The Santeria faith teaches that every individual has a destiny from God, a destiny fulfilled with the aid and energy of the *orishas*. The basis of the Santeria religion is the nurture of a personal relation with the *orishas*, and one of the principal forms of devotion is an animal sacrifice. 13 The Encyclopedia of Religion, at 66. The sacrifice of animals as part of religious rituals has ancient roots. See generally 12 *id.*, at 554–556. Animal sacrifice is mentioned throughout the Old Testament, see 14 Encyclopaedia Judaica 600, 600–⊥**525** 605 (1971), and it played an important role in the practice of Judaism before destruction of the second Temple in Jerusalem, see *id.*, at 605–612. In modern Islam, there is an annual sacrifice commemorating Abraham's sacrifice of a ram in the stead of his son. See C. Glassé, The Concise Encyclopedia of Islam 178 (1989); 7 The Encyclopedia of Religion, at 456.

According to Santeria teaching, the *orishas* are powerful but not immortal. They depend for survival on the sacrifice. Sacrifices are performed at birth, marriage, and death rites, for the cure of the sick, for the initiation of new members and priests, and during an annual celebration. Animals sacrificed in Santeria rituals include chickens, pigeons, doves, ducks, guinea pigs, goats, sheep, and turtles. The animals are killed by the cutting of the carotid arteries in the neck. The sacrificed animal is cooked and eaten, except after healing and death rituals. See 723 F. Supp., at 1471–1472; 13 The Encyclopedia of Religion, at 66; M. González-Wippler, The Santería Experience 105 (1982).

Santeria adherents faced widespread persecution in Cuba, so the religion and its rituals were practiced in secret. The open practice of Santeria and its rites remains infrequent. See 723 F. Supp., at 1470; 13 The Encyclopedia of Religion, at 67; M. González-Wippler, Santería: The Religion 3–4 (1989). The religion was brought to this Nation most often by exiles from the Cuban revolution. The District Court estimated that there are at least 50,000 practitioners in South Florida today.

B

Petitioner Church of the Lukumi Babalu Aye, Inc. (Church), is a not-for-profit corporation organized under Florida law in 1973. The Church and its congregants practice the Santeria religion. The president of the Church is petitioner Ernesto Pichardo, who is also the Church's priest and holds the religious title of *Italero*, the second highest in the Santeria faith. In April 1987, the Church leased land in ⊥**526** the city of Hialeah, Florida, and announced plans to establish a house of worship as well as a school, cultural center, and museum. Pichardo indicated that the Church's goal was to bring the practice of the Santeria faith, including its ritual of animal sacrifice, into the open. The Church began the process of obtaining utility service and receiving the necessary licensing, inspection, and zoning approvals. Although the Church's efforts at obtaining the necessary licenses and permits were far from smooth, it appears that it received all needed approvals by early August 1987.

The prospect of a Santeria church in their midst was distressing to many members of the Hialeah community, and the announcement of the plans to open a Santeria

*The *CHIEF JUSTICE*, *Justice SCALIA*, and *Justice THOMAS* join all but Part II-A-2 of this opinion. *Justice WHITE* joins all but Part II-A of this opinion. *Justice SOUTER* joins only Parts I, III, and IV of this opinion.

church in Hialeah prompted the city council to hold an emergency public session on June 9, 1987. The resolutions and ordinances passed at that and later meetings are set forth in the appendix following this opinion.

A summary suffices here, beginning with the enactments passed at the June 9 meeting. First, the city council adopted Resolution 87–66, which noted the "concern" expressed by residents of the city "that certain religions may propose to engage in practices which are inconsistent with public morals, peace or safety," and declared that "[t]he City reiterates its commitment to a prohibition against any and all acts of any and all religious groups which are inconsistent with public morals, peace or safety." Next, the council approved an emergency ordinance, Ordinance 87–40, that incorporated in full, except as to penalty, Florida's animal cruelty laws. Fla. Stat. ch. 828 (1987). Among other things, the incorporated state law subjected to criminal punishment "[w]hoever . . . unnecessarily or cruelly . . . kills any animal." §828.12.

The city council desired to undertake further legislative action, but Florida law prohibited a municipality from enacting legislation relating to animal cruelty that conflicted with ⊥**527** state law. §828.27(4). To obtain clarification, Hialeah's city attorney requested an opinion from the attorney general of Florida as to whether §828.12 prohibited "a religious group from sacrificing an animal in a religious ritual or practice" and whether the city could enact ordinances "making religious animal sacrifice unlawful." The attorney general responded in mid-July. He concluded that the "ritual sacrifice of animals for purposes other than food consumption" was not a "necessary" killing and so was prohibited by §828.12. Fla. Op. Atty. Gen. 87–56, Annual Report of the Atty. Gen. 146, 147, 149 (1988). The attorney general appeared to define "unnecessary" as "done without any useful motive, in a spirit of wanton cruelty or for the mere pleasure of destruction without being in any sense beneficial or useful to the person killing the animal." He advised that religious animal sacrifice was against state law, so that a city ordinance prohibiting it would not be in conflict.

The city council responded at first with a hortatory enactment, Resolution 87–90, that noted its residents' "great concern regarding the possibility of public ritualistic animal sacrifices" and the state law prohibition. The resolution declared the city policy "to oppose the ritual sacrifices of animals" within Hialeah and announced that any person or organization practicing animal sacrifice "will be prosecuted."

In September 1987, the city council adopted three substantive ordinances addressing the issue of religious animal sacrifice. Ordinance 87–52 defined "sacrifice" as "to unnecessarily kill, torment, torture, or mutilate an animal in a public or private ritual or ceremony not for the primary purpose of food consumption," and prohibited owning or possessing an animal "intending to use such animal for food purposes." It restricted application of this prohibition, however, to any individual or group that "kills, slaughters or sacrifices animals for any type of ritual, regardless of whether or not the flesh or blood of the animal is to be consumed." The ordinance ⊥**528** contained an exemption for slaughtering by "licensed establishment[s]" of animals "specifically raised for food purposes." Declaring, moreover, that the city council "has determined that the sacrificing of animals within the city limits is contrary to the public health, safety, welfare and morals of the community," the city council adopted Ordinance 87–71. That ordinance defined sacrifice as had Ordinance 87–52, and then provided that "[i]t shall be unlawful for any person, persons, corporations or associations to sacrifice any animal within the corporate limits of the City of Hialeah, Florida." The final Ordinance, 87–72, defined "slaughter" as "the killing of animals for food" and prohibited slaughter outside of areas zoned for slaughterhouse use. The ordinance provided an exemption, however, for the slaughter or processing for sale of "small numbers of hogs and/or cattle per week in accordance with an exemption provided by state law." All ordinances and resolutions passed the city council by unanimous vote. Violations of each of the four ordinances were punishable by fines not exceeding $500 or imprisonment not exceeding 60 days, or both.

Following enactment of these ordinances, the Church and Pichardo filed this action pursuant to 42 U. S. C. §1983 in the United States District Court for the Southern District of Florida. Named as defendants were the city of Hialeah and its mayor and members of its city council in their individual capacities. Alleging violations of petitioners' rights under, *inter alia,* the Free Exercise Clause, the complaint sought a declaratory judgment and injunctive and monetary relief. The District Court granted summary judgment to the individual defendants, finding that they had absolute immunity for their legislative acts and that the ordinances and resolutions adopted by the council did not constitute an official policy of harassment, as alleged by petitioners. 688 F. Supp. 1522 (SD Fla. 1988).

After a 9-day bench trial on the remaining claims, the District Court ruled for the city, finding no violation of petition⊥**529**ers' rights under the Free Exercise Clause. 723 F. Supp. 1467 (SD Fla. 1989). (The court rejected as well petitioners' other claims, which are not at issue here.) Although acknowledging that "the ordinances are not religiously neutral," and that the city's concern about animal sacrifice was "prompted" by the establishment of the Church in the city, the District Court concluded that the purpose of the ordinances was not to exclude the Church from the city but to end the practice of animal sacrifice, for whatever reason practiced. The court also found that the ordinances did not target religious conduct "on their face," though it noted that in any event "specifically regulating [religious] conduct" does not violate the First Amendment "when [the conduct] is deemed inconsistent with public health and welfare." Thus, the court concluded that, at most, the ordinances' effect on petitioners' religious conduct was "incidental to [their] secular purpose and effect."

The District Court proceeded to determine whether the governmental interests underlying the ordinances were compelling and, if so, to balance the "governmental and religious interests." The court noted that "[t]his 'balance depends upon the cost to the government of altering its activity to allow the religious practice to continue unimpeded versus the cost to the religious interest imposed by the government activity.'" *Ibid.*, quoting *Grosz* v. *City of Miami Beach*. The court found four compelling interests. First, the court found that animal sacrifices present a substantial health risk, both to participants and the general public. According to the court, animals that are to be sacrificed are often kept in unsanitary conditions and are uninspected, and animal remains are found in public places. Second, the court found emotional injury to children who witness the sacrifice of animals. Third, the court found compelling the city's in⊥**530**terest in protecting animals from cruel and unnecessary killing. The court determined that the method of killing used in Santeria sacrifice was "unreliable and not humane, and that the animals, before being sacrificed, are often kept in conditions that produce a great deal of fear and stress in the animal." Fourth, the District Court found compelling the city's interest in restricting the slaughter or sacrifice of animals to areas zoned for slaughterhouse use. This legal determination was not accompanied by factual findings.

Balancing the competing governmental and religious interests, the District Court concluded the compelling governmental interests "fully justify the absolute prohibition on ritual sacrifice" accomplished by the ordinances. The court also concluded that an exception to the sacrifice prohibition for religious conduct would "'unduly interfere with fulfillment of the governmental interest'" because any more narrow restrictions—*e.g.*, regulation of disposal of animal carcasses—would be unenforceable as a result of the secret nature of the Santeria religion. A religious exemption from the city's ordinances, concluded the court, would defeat the city's compelling interests in enforcing the prohibition.

The Court of Appeals for the Eleventh Circuit affirmed in a one-paragraph *per curiam* opinion. Judgt. order reported at 936 F. 2d 586 (1991). Choosing not to rely on the District Court's recitation of a compelling interest in promoting the welfare of children, the Court of Appeals stated simply that it concluded the ordinances were consistent with the Constitution. It declined to address the effect of *Employment Div., Dept. of Human Resources of Oregon* v. *Smith*, decided after the District Court's opinion, because the District Court "employed an arguably stricter standard" than that applied in *Smith*.

⊥**531** II

The Free Exercise Clause of the First Amendment, which has been applied to the States through the Fourteenth Amendment, provides that "Congress shall make no law respecting an establishment of religion, or *prohibiting the free exercise thereof*. . . ." U. S. Const., Amdt. 1 (emphasis added). The city does not argue that Santeria is not a "religion" within the meaning of the First Amendment. Nor could it. Although the practice of animal sacrifice may seem abhorrent to some, "religious beliefs need not be acceptable, logical, consistent, or comprehensible to others in order to merit First Amendment protection." *Thomas* v. *Review Bd. of Indiana Employment Security Div.* Given the historical association between animal sacrifice and religious worship, petitioners' assertion that animal sacrifice is an integral part of their religion "cannot be deemed bizarre or incredible." *Frazee* v. *Illinois Dept. of Employment Security*. Neither the city nor the courts below, moreover, have questioned the sincerity of petitioners' professed desire to conduct animal sacrifices for religious reasons. We must consider petitioners' First Amendment claim.

In addressing the constitutional protection for free exercise of religion, our cases establish the general proposition that a law that is neutral and of general applicability need not be justified by a compelling governmental interest even if the law has the incidental effect of burdening a particular religious practice. *Employment Div., Dept. of Human Resources of Oregon* v. *Smith*. Neutrality and general applicability are interrelated, and, as becomes apparent in this case, failure to satisfy one requirement is a likely indication that the other has not been satisfied. A law failing to satisfy these requirements must be justified by a compelling governmental interest and must be narrowly tailored to advance ⊥**532** that interest. These ordinances fail to satisfy the *Smith* requirements. We begin by discussing neutrality.

A

In our Establishment Clause cases we have often stated the principle that the First Amendment forbids an official purpose to disapprove of a particular religion or of religion in general. See, *e.g.*, *Board of Ed. of Westside Community Schools (Dist. 66)* v. *Mergens*, (plurality opinion); *Grand Rapids School Dist.* v. *Ball*; *Wallace* v. *Jaffree*; *Epperson* v. *Arkansas*; *School Dist. of Abington* v. *Schempp*; *Everson* v. *Board of Ed. of Ewing*. These cases, however, for the most part have addressed governmental efforts to benefit religion or particular religions, and so have dealt with a question different, at least in its formulation and emphasis, from the issue here. Petitioners allege an attempt to disfavor their religion because of the religious ceremonies it commands, and the Free Exercise Clause is dispositive in our analysis.

At a minimum, the protections of the Free Exercise Clause pertain if the law at issue discriminates against some or all religious beliefs or regulates or prohibits conduct because it is undertaken for religious reasons. See, *e.g.*, *Braunfeld* v. *Brown*, (plurality opinion); *Fowler* v.

Rhode Island. Indeed, it was "historical instances of religious persecution and intolerance that gave concern to those who drafted the Free Exercise Clause." *Bowen* v. *Roy* (opinion of Burger, C. J.). See J. Story, Commentaries on the Constitution of the United States §§991–992 (abridged ed. 1833) (reprint 1987); T. Cooley, Constitutional Limitations 467 (1868) (reprint 1972); *McGowan* v. *Maryland* (opinion of Frankfurter, J.); *Douglas* v. *Jeannette* (Jackson, J., concurring in re⊥**533** sult); *Davis* v. *Beason*. These principles, though not often at issue in our Free Exercise Clause cases, have played a role in some. In *McDaniel* v. *Paty*, for example, we invalidated a State law that disqualified members of the clergy from holding certain public offices, because it "impose[d] special disabilities on the basis of . . . religious status," *Employment Div., Dept. of Human Resources of Oregon* v. *Smith*. On the same principle, in *Fowler* v. *Rhode Island*, we found that a municipal ordinance was applied in an unconstitutional manner when interpreted to prohibit preaching in a public park by a Jehovah's Witness but to permit preaching during the course of a Catholic mass or Protestant church service. See also *Niemotko* v. *Maryland*. Cf. *Larson* v. *Valente* (state statute that treated some religious denominations more favorably than others violated the Establishment Clause).

1

Although a law targeting religious beliefs as such is never permissible, *McDaniel* v. *Paty*, (plurality opinion); *Cantwell* v. *Connecticut*, if the object of a law is to infringe upon or restrict practices because of their religious motivation, the law is not neutral, see *Employment Div., Dept. of Human Resources of Oregon* v. *Smith;* and it is invalid unless it is justified by a compelling interest and is narrowly tailored to advance that interest. There are, of course, many ways of demonstrating that the object or purpose of a law is the suppression of religion or religious conduct. To determine the object of a law, we must begin with its text, for the minimum requirement of neutrality is that a law not discriminate on its face. A law lacks facial neutrality if it refers to a religious practice without a secular meaning discernable from the language or context. Petitioners contend that three of the ordinances fail this test of facial neutrality because they use the words ⊥**534** "sacrifice" and "ritual," words with strong religious connotations. We agree that these words are consistent with the claim of facial discrimination, but the argument is not conclusive. The words "sacrifice" and "ritual" have a religious origin, but current use admits also of secular meanings. See Webster's Third New International Dictionary 1961, 1996 (1971). See also 12 The Encyclopedia of Religion, at 556 ("[T]he word *sacrifice* ultimately became very much a secular term in common usage"). The ordinances, furthermore, define "sacrifice" in secular terms, without referring to religious practices.

We reject the contention advanced by the city, that our inquiry must end with the text of the laws at issue. Facial neutrality is not determinative. The Free Exercise Clause, like the Establishment Clause, extends beyond facial discrimination. The Clause "forbids subtle departures from neutrality," *Gillette* v. *United States*, and "covert suppression of particular religious beliefs," *Bowen* v. *Roy*, (opinion of Burger, C. J.). Official action that targets religious conduct for distinctive treatment cannot be shielded by mere compliance with the requirement of facial neutrality. The Free Exercise Clause protects against governmental hostility which is masked, as well as overt. "The Court must survey meticulously the circumstances of governmental categories to eliminate, as it were, religious gerrymanders." *Walz* v. *Tax Comm'n of New York City*, (Harlan, J., concurring).

The record in this case compels the conclusion that suppression of the central element of the Santeria worship service was the object of the ordinances. First, though use of the words "sacrifice" and "ritual" does not compel a finding of improper targeting of the Santeria religion, the choice of these words is support for our conclusion. There are further respects in which the text of the city council's enactments discloses the improper attempt to target Santeria. ⊥**535** Resolution 87–66, adopted June 9, 1987, recited that "residents and citizens of the City of Hialeah have expressed their concern that certain religions may propose to engage in practices which are inconsistent with public morals, peace or safety," and "reiterate[d]" the city's commitment to prohibit "any and all [such] acts of any and all religious groups." No one suggests, and on this record it cannot be maintained, that city officials had in mind a religion other than Santeria.

It becomes evident that these ordinances target Santeria sacrifice when the ordinances' operation is considered. Apart from the text, the effect of a law in its real operation is strong evidence of its object. To be sure, adverse impact will not always lead to a finding of impermissible targeting. For example, a social harm may have been a legitimate concern of government for reasons quite apart from discrimination. *McGowan* v. *Maryland*. See, *e.g.*, *Reynolds* v. *United States; Davis* v. *Beason*. See also Ely, Legislative and Administrative Motivation in Constitutional Law, 79 Yale L. J. 1205, 1319 (1970). The subject at hand does implicate, of course, multiple concerns unrelated to religious animosity, for example, the suffering or mistreatment visited upon the sacrificed animals, and health hazards from improper disposal. But the ordinances when considered together disclose an object remote from these legitimate concerns. The design of these laws accomplishes instead a "religious gerrymander," *Walz* v. *Tax Comm'n of New York City*, (Harlan, J., concurring), an impermissible attempt to target petitioners and their religious practices.

It is a necessary conclusion that almost the only conduct subject to Ordinances 87–40, 87–52, and 87–71 is the religious exercise of Santeria church members. The texts show that they were drafted in tandem to achieve this result. We begin with Ordinance 87–71. It prohibits the sacrifice of animals but defines sacrifice as "to unnecessarily kill . . . an animal in a public or private ritual or ceremony not for the ⊥**536** primary purpose of food consumption." The definition excludes almost all killings of animals except for religious sacrifice, and the primary purpose requirement narrows the proscribed category even further, in particular by exempting Kosher slaughter, see 723 F. Supp., at 1480. We need not discuss whether this differential treatment of two religions is itself an independent constitutional violation. It suffices to recite this feature of the law as support for our conclusion that Santeria alone was the exclusive legislative concern. The net result of the gerrymander is that few if any killings of animals are prohibited other than Santeria sacrifice, which is proscribed because it occurs during a ritual or ceremony and its primary purpose is to make an offering to the *orishas*, not food consumption. Indeed, careful drafting ensured that, although Santeria sacrifice is prohibited, killings that are no more necessary or humane in almost all other circumstances are unpunished.

Operating in similar fashion is Ordinance 87–52, which prohibits the "possess[ion], sacrifice, or slaughter" of an animal with the "inten[t] to use such animal for food purposes." This prohibition, extending to the keeping of an animal as well as the killing itself, applies if the animal is killed in "any type of ritual" and there is an intent to use the animal for food, whether or not it is in fact consumed for food. The ordinance exempts, however, "any licensed [food] establishment" with regard to "any animals which are specifically raised for food purposes," if the activity is permitted by zoning and other laws. This exception, too, seems intended to cover Kosher slaughter. Again, the burden of the ordinance, in practical terms, falls on Santeria adherents but almost no others: If the killing is—unlike most Santeria sacrifices—unaccompanied by the intent to use the animal for food, then it is not prohibited by Ordinance 87–52; if the killing is specifically for food but does not occur during the course of "any type of ritual," it again falls outside the prohibition; and if ⊥**537** the killing is for food and occurs during the course of a ritual, it is still exempted if it occurs in a properly zoned and licensed establishment and involves animals "specifically raised for food purposes." A pattern of exemptions parallels the pattern of narrow prohibitions. Each contributes to the gerrymander.

Ordinance 87–40 incorporates the Florida animal cruelty statute, Fla. Stat. § 828.12 (1987). Its prohibition is broad on its face, punishing "[w]hoever . . . unnecessarily . . . kills any animal." The city claims that this ordinance is the epitome of a neutral prohibition. The problem, however, is the interpretation given to the ordinance by respondent and the Florida attorney general. Killings for religious reasons are deemed unnecessary, whereas most other killings fall outside the prohibition. The city, on what seems to be a *per se* basis, deems hunting, slaughter of animals for food, eradication of insects and pests, and euthanasia as necessary. There is no indication in the record that respondent has concluded that hunting or fishing for sport is unnecessary. Indeed, one of the few reported Florida cases decided under §828.12 concludes that the use of live rabbits to train greyhounds is not unnecessary. See *Kiper* v. *State*. Further, because it requires an evaluation of the particular justification for the killing, this ordinance represents a system of "individualized governmental assessment of the reasons for the relevant conduct," *Employment Div., Dept. of Human Resources of Oregon* v. *Smith*. As we noted in *Smith*, in circumstances in which individualized exemptions from a general requirement are available, the government "may not refuse to extend that system to cases of 'religious hardship' without compelling reason." *Id.*, quoting *Bowen* v. *Roy* (opinion of Burger, C. J.). Respondent's application of the ordinance's test of necessity devalues religious reasons for killing by judging them to be of lesser import than nonre⊥**538**ligious reasons. Thus, religious practice is being singled out for discriminatory treatment.

We also find significant evidence of the ordinances' improper targeting of Santeria sacrifice in the fact that they proscribe more religious conduct than is necessary to achieve their stated ends. It is not unreasonable to infer, at least when there are no persuasive indications to the contrary, that a law which visits "gratuitous restrictions" on religious conduct, *McGowan* v. *Maryland*, (opinion of Frankfurter, J.), seeks not to effectuate the stated governmental interests, but to suppress the conduct because of its religious motivation.

The legitimate governmental interests in protecting the public health and preventing cruelty to animals could be addressed by restrictions stopping far short of a flat prohibition of all Santeria sacrificial practice. If improper disposal, not the sacrifice itself, is the harm to be prevented, the city could have imposed a general regulation on the disposal of organic garbage. It did not do so. Indeed, counsel for the city conceded at oral argument that, under the ordinances, Santeria sacrifices would be illegal even if they occurred in licensed, inspected, and zoned slaughterhouses. Thus, these broad ordinances prohibit Santeria sacrifice even when it does not threaten the city's ⊥**539** interest in the public health. The District Court accepted the argument that narrower regulation would be unenforceable because of the secrecy in the Santeria rituals and the lack of any central religious authority to require compliance with secular disposal regulations. See 723 F. Supp., at 1486–1487, and nn. 58–59. It is difficult to understand, however, how a prohibition of the sacrifices themselves, which occur in private, is enforceable if a ban on improper disposal, which occurs in public, is not. The neutrality of a law is suspect if First Amendment freedoms are curtailed to prevent isolated collateral harms not themselves prohibited by direct regulation. See, *e.g.*, *Schneider* v. *State*.

Under similar analysis, narrower regulation would achieve the city's interest in preventing cruelty to animals. With regard to the city's interest in ensuring the adequate care of animals, regulation of conditions and treatment, regardless of why an animal is kept, is the logical response to the city's concern, not a prohibition on possession for the purpose of sacrifice. The same is true for the city's interest in prohibiting cruel methods of killing. Under federal and Florida law and Ordinance 87–40, which incorporates Florida law in this regard, killing an animal by the "simultaneous and instantaneous severance of the carotid arteries with a sharp instrument"—the method used in Kosher slaughter—is approved as humane. See 7 U. S. C. § 1902(b); Fla. Stat. § 828.23(7)(b) (1991); Ordinance 87-40, § 1. The District Court found that, though Santeria sacrifice also results in severance of the carotid arteries, the method used during sacrifice is less reliable and therefore not humane. See 723 F. Supp., at 1472–1473. If the city has a real concern that other methods are less humane, however, the subject of the regulation should be the method of slaughter itself, not a religious classification that is said to bear some general relation to it.

Ordinance 87-72—unlike the three other ordinances—does appear to apply to substantial nonreligious conduct and ⊥**540** not to be overbroad. For our purposes here, however, the four substantive ordinances may be treated as a group for neutrality purposes. Ordinance 87-72 was passed the same day as Ordinance 87-71 and was enacted, as were the three others, in direct response to the opening of the Church. It would be implausible to suggest that the three other ordinances, but not Ordinance 87-72, had as their object the suppression of religion. We need not decide whether the Ordinance 87-72 could survive constitutional scrutiny if it existed separately; it must be invalidated because it functions, with the rest of the enactments in question, to suppress Santeria religious worship.

2

In determining if the object of a law is a neutral one under the Free Exercise Clause, we can also find guidance in our equal protection cases. As *Justice HARLAN* noted in the related context of the Establishment Clause, "[n]eutrality in its application requires an equal protection mode of analysis." *Walz* v. *Tax Comm'n of New York City*, (concurring opinion). Here, as in equal protection cases, we may determine the city council's object from both direct and circumstantial evidence. *Arlington Heights* v. *Metropolitan Housing Development Corp.* Relevant evidence includes, among other things, the historical background of the decision under challenge, the specific series of events leading to the enactment or official policy in question, as well as the legislative or administrative history, including contemporaneous statements made by members of the decisionmaking body. These objective factors bear on the question of discriminatory object. *Personnel Adm'r of Mass.* v. *Feeney*.

That the ordinances were enacted "'because of,' not merely 'in spite of,'" their suppression of Santeria religious practice, is revealed by the events preceding enactment of the ordinances. Although respondent claimed at oral argument ⊥**541** that it had experienced significant problems resulting from the sacrifice of animals within the city before the announced opening of the Church, the city council made no attempt to address the supposed problem before its meeting in June 1987, just weeks after the Church announced plans to open. The minutes and taped excerpts of the June 9 session, both of which are in the record, evidence significant hostility exhibited by residents, members of the city council, and other city officials toward the Santeria religion and its practice of animal sacrifice. The public crowd that attended the June 9 meetings interrupted statements by council members critical of Santeria with cheers and the brief comments of Pichardo with taunts. When Councilman Martinez, a supporter of the ordinances, stated that in prerevolution Cuba "people were put in jail for practicing this religion," the audience applauded.

Other statements by members of the city council were in a similar vein. For example, Councilman Martinez, after noting his belief that Santeria was outlawed in Cuba, questioned, "if we could not practice this [religion] in our homeland [Cuba], why bring it to this country?" Councilman Cardoso said that Santeria devotees at the Church "are in violation of everything this country stands for." Councilman Mejides indicated that he was "totally against the sacrificing of animals" and distinguished Kosher slaughter because it had a "real purpose." The "Bible says we are allowed to sacrifice an animal for consumption," he continued, "but for any other purposes, I don't believe that the Bible allows that." The president of the city council, Councilman Echevarria, asked, "What can we do to prevent the Church from opening?"

Various Hialeah city officials made comparable comments. The chaplain of the Hialeah Police Department told the city council that Santeria was a sin, "foolishness," "an abomination to the Lord," and the worship of "demons." He advised ⊥**542** the city council that "We need to be helping people and sharing with them the truth that is found in Jesus Christ." He concluded: "I would exhort you . . . not to permit this Church to exist." The city attorney commented that Resolution 87–66 indicated that "This community will not tolerate religious practices which are abhorrent to its citizens . . . ." Similar comments were made by the deputy city attorney. This history discloses the object of the ordinances to target animal sacrifice by Santeria worshippers because of its religious motivation.

3

In sum, the neutrality inquiry leads to one conclusion: The ordinances had as their object the suppression of religion. The pattern we have recited discloses animosity to Santeria adherents and their religious practices; the ordinances by their own terms target this religious exercise; the texts of the ordinances were gerrymandered with care to proscribe religious killings of animals but to exclude almost all secular killings; and the ordinances suppress much more religious conduct than is necessary in order to achieve the legitimate ends asserted in their defense. These ordinances are not neutral, and the court below committed clear error in failing to reach this conclusion.

B

We turn next to a second requirement of the Free Exercise Clause, the rule that laws burdening religious practice must be of general applicability. *Employment Div., Dept. of Human Resources of Oregon* v. *Smith.* All laws are selective to some extent, but categories of selection are of paramount concern when a law has the incidental effect of burdening religious practice. The Free Exercise Clause "protect[s] religious observers against unequal treatment," *Hobbie* v. *Unemployment Appeals Comm'n of Florida* (Stevens, J., concurring in judgment), and inequality results when a legislature decides that ⊥**543** the governmental interests it seeks to advance are worthy of being pursued only against conduct with a religious motivation.

The principle that government, in pursuit of legitimate interests, cannot in a selective manner impose burdens only on conduct motivated by religious belief is essential to the protection of the rights guaranteed by the Free Exercise Clause. The principle underlying the general applicability requirement has parallels in our First Amendment jurisprudence. See, *e.g.*, *Cohen* v. *Cowles Media Co.*; *University of Pennsylvania* v. *EEOC*; *Minneapolis Star & Tribune Co.* v. *Minnesota Comm'r of Revenue*; *Larson* v. *Valente*; *Presbyterian Church in United States* v. *Mary Elizabeth Blue Hull Memorial Presbyterian Church.* In this case we need not define with precision the standard used to evaluate whether a prohibition is of general application, for these ordinances fall well below the minimum standard necessary to protect First Amendment rights.

Respondent claims that Ordinances 87-40, 87-52, and 87-71 advance two interests: protecting the public health and preventing cruelty to animals. The ordinances are underinclusive for those ends. They fail to prohibit nonreligious conduct that endangers these interests in a similar or greater degree than Santeria sacrifice does. The underinclusion is substantial, not inconsequential. Despite the city's proffered interest in preventing cruelty to animals, the ordinances are drafted with care to forbid few killings but those occasioned by religious sacrifice. Many types of animal deaths or kills for nonreligious reasons are either not prohibited or approved by express provision. For example, fishing—which occurs in Hialeah, see A. Khedouri & F. Khedouri, South Florida Inside Out 57 (1991)—is legal. Extermination of mice and rats within a home is also permitted. Florida law incorporated by Ordinance 87–40 sanctions ⊥**544** euthanasia of "stray, neglected, abandoned, or unwanted animals," Fla. Stat. § 828.058 (1987); destruction of animals judicially removed from their owners "for humanitarian reasons" or when the animal "is of no commercial value," § 828.073(4)(c)(2); the infliction of pain or suffering "in the interest of medical science," § 828.02; the placing of poison in one's yard or enclosure, § 828.08; and the use of a live animal "to pursue or take wildlife or to participate in any hunting," § 828.122(6)(b), and "to hunt wild hogs," § 828.122(6)(e).

The city concedes that "neither the State of Florida nor the City has enacted a generally applicable ban on the killing of animals." It asserts, however, that animal sacrifice is "different" from the animal killings that are permitted by law. According to the city, it is "self-evident" that killing animals for food is "important"; the eradication of insects and pests is "obviously justified"; and the euthanasia of excess animals "makes sense." These *ipse dixits* do not explain why religion alone must bear the burden of the ordinances, when many of these secular killings fall within the city's interest in preventing the cruel treatment of animals.

The ordinances are also underinclusive with regard to the city's interest in public health, which is threatened by the disposal of animal carcasses in open public places and the consumption of uninspected meat. Neither interest is pursued by respondent with regard to conduct that is not motivated by religious conviction. The health risks posed by the improper disposal of animal carcasses are the same whether Santeria sacrifice or some nonreligious killing preceded it. The city does not, however, prohibit hunters from bringing their kill to their houses, nor does it regulate disposal after their activity. Despite substantial testimony at trial that the same public health hazards result from improper disposal of garbage by restaurants, ⊥**545** restaurants are outside the scope of the ordinances. Improper disposal is a general problem that causes substantial health risks, but which respondent addresses only when it results from religious exercise.

The ordinances are underinclusive as well with regard to the health risk posed by consumption of uninspected meat. Under the city's ordinances, hunters may eat their kill and fisherman may eat their catch without undergoing governmental inspection. Likewise, state law requires inspection of meat that is sold but exempts meat from animals raised for the use of the owner and "members of his household and nonpaying guests and employees." Fla. Stat. § 585.88(1)(a) (1991). The asserted interest in inspected meat is not pursued in contexts similar to that of religious animal sacrifice.

Ordinance 87-72, which prohibits the slaughter of animals outside of areas zoned for slaughterhouses, is underinclusive on its face. The ordinance includes an exemption for "any person, group, or organization" that "slaughters or processes for sale, small numbers of hogs and/or cattle per week in accordance with an exemption provided by state law." See Fla. Stat. § 828.24(3) (1991). Respondent has not explained why commercial operations that slaughter "small numbers" of hogs and cattle do not implicate its professed desire to prevent cruelty to animals and preserve the public health. Although the city has classified Santeria sacrifice as slaughter, subjecting it to this ordinance, it does not regulate other killings for food in like manner.

We conclude, in sum, that each of Hialeah's ordinances pursues the city's governmental interests only against conduct motivated by religious belief. The ordinances "ha[ve] every appearance of a prohibition that society is prepared to impose upon [Santeria worshippers] but not upon itself." *The Florida Star* v. *B. J. F.* (Scalia, J., concurring in part and concurring in judgment). This ⊥**546** precise evil is what the requirement of general applicability is designed to prevent.

III

A law burdening religious practice that is not neutral or not of general application must undergo the most rigorous of scrutiny. To satisfy the commands of the First Amendment, a law restrictive of religious practice must advance "'interests of the highest order'" and must be narrowly tailored in pursuit of those interests. *McDaniel* v. *Paty*, quoting *Wisconsin* v. *Yoder*. The compelling interest standard that we apply once a law fails to meet the *Smith* requirements is not "water[ed] . . . down" but "really means what it says." *Employment Div., Dept. of Human Resources of Oregon* v. *Smith*. A law that targets religious conduct for distinctive treatment or advances legitimate governmental interests only against conduct with a religious motivation will survive strict scrutiny only in rare cases. It follows from what we have already said that these ordinances cannot withstand this scrutiny.

First, even were the governmental interests compelling, the ordinances are not drawn in narrow terms to accomplish those interests. As we have discussed, all four ordinances are overbroad or underinclusive in substantial respects. The proffered objectives are not pursued with respect to analogous non-religious conduct, and those interests could be achieved by narrower ordinances that burdened religion to a far lesser degree. The absence of narrow tailoring suffices to establish the invalidity of the ordinances. See *Arkansas Writers' Project, Inc.* v. *Ragland*.

Respondent has not demonstrated, moreover, that, in the context of these ordinances, its governmental interests are compelling. Where government restricts only conduct protected by the First Amendment and fails to enact feasible ⊥**547** measures to restrict other conduct producing substantial harm or alleged harm of the same sort, the interest given in justification of the restriction is not compelling. It is established in our strict scrutiny jurisprudence that "a law cannot be regarded as protecting an interest 'of the highest order' . . . when it leaves appreciable damage to that supposedly vital interest unprohibited." *The Florida Star* v. *B. J. F.*, (Scalia, J., concurring in part and concurring in judgment). See *Simon & Schuster, Inc.* v. *Members of New York State Crime Victims Bd.* Cf. *The Florida Star* v. *B. J. F.*; *Smith* v. *Daily Mail Publishing Co.*, (Rehnquist, J., concurring in judgment). As we show above, the ordinances are underinclusive to a substantial extent with respect to each of the interests that respondent has asserted, and it is only conduct motivated by religious conviction that bears the weight of the governmental restrictions. There can be no serious claim that those interests justify the ordinances.

IV

The Free Exercise Clause commits government itself to religious tolerance, and upon even slight suspicion that proposals for state intervention stem from animosity to religion or distrust of its practices, all officials must pause to remember their own high duty to the Constitution and to the rights it secures. Those in office must be resolute in resisting importunate demands and must ensure that the sole reasons for imposing the burdens of law and regulation are secular. Legislators may not devise mechanisms, overt or disguised, designed to persecute or oppress a religion or its practices. The laws here in question were enacted contrary to these constitutional principles, and they are void.

Reversed.

. . . . .

⊥**557** *Justice* SCALIA, with whom *The* CHIEF JUSTICE joins, concurring in part and concurring in the judgment.

The Court analyzes the "neutrality" and the "general applicability" of the Hialeah ordinances in separate sections (Parts II–A and II–B, respectively), and allocates various invalidating factors to one or the other of those sections. If it were necessary to make a clear distinction between the two terms, I would draw a line somewhat different from the Court's. But I think it is not necessary, and would frankly acknowledge that the terms are not only "interrelated," but substantially overlap.

The terms "neutrality" and "general applicability" are not to be found within the First Amendment itself, of course, but are used in *Employment Div., Dept. of Human Resources of Oregon* v. *Smith*, and earlier cases to describe those characteristics which cause a law that prohibits an activity a particular individual wishes to engage in for religious reasons nonetheless not to constitute a "law . . . prohibiting the free exercise" of religion within the meaning of the First Amendment. In my view, the defect of lack of neutrality applies primarily to those laws that *by their terms* impose disabilities on the basis of religion (*e.g.*, a law excluding members of a certain sect from public benefits, cf. *McDaniel* v. *Paty*), see *Bowen* v. *Roy* (opinion of Burger, C. J.); whereas the defect of lack of general applicability applies primarily to those laws which, though neutral in their terms, through their design, construction, or enforcement target the practices of a particular religion for discriminatory treatment, see *Fowler* v. *Rhode Island*. But certainly a law that is not of general applicability (in the sense ⊥**558** I have described) can be considered "nonneutral"; and certainly no law that is nonneutral (in the relevant sense) can be thought to be of general applicability. Because I agree with most of the invalidating factors set forth in Part II of the Court's opinion, and because it seems to me a matter of no consequence under which rubric ("neutrality," Part II–A, or "general applicability," Part II–B) each invalidating factor is discussed, I join the judgment of the Court and all of its opinion except section 2 of Part II–A.

I do not join that section because it departs from the opinion's general focus on the object of the *laws* at issue to consider the subjective motivation of the *lawmakers*, *i.e.*, whether the Hialeah City Council actually *intended* to disfavor the religion of Santeria. As I have noted elsewhere, it is virtually impossible to determine the singular "motive" of a collective legislative body, see, *e.g.*, *Edwards* v. *Aguillard* (Scalia, J., dissenting), and this Court has a long tradition of refraining from such inquiries, see, *e.g.*, *Fletcher* v. *Peck* (Marshall, C. J.); *United States* v. *O'Brien*.

Perhaps there are contexts in which determination of legislative motive *must* be undertaken. See, *e.g.*, *United States* v. *Lovett*. But I do not think that is true of analysis under the First Amendment (or the Fourteenth, to the extent it incorporates the First). The First Amendment does not refer to the purposes for which legislators enact laws, but to the effects of the laws enacted: "Congress shall make no law . . . prohibiting the free exercise [of religion] . . . ." This does not put us in the business of invalidating laws by reason of the evil motives of their authors. Had the Hialeah City Council set out resolutely to suppress the practices of Santeria, but ineptly adopted ordinances that failed to do so, I do not see how those laws could be said to "prohibi[t] the free exercise" of ⊥**559** religion. Nor, in my view, does it matter that a legislature consists entirely of the pure-hearted, if the law it enacts in fact singles out a religious practice for special burdens. Had the ordinances here been passed with no motive on the part of any councilman except the ardent desire to prevent cruelty to animals (as might in fact have been the case), they would nonetheless be invalid.

Justice SOUTER, concurring in part and concurring in the judgment.

This case turns on a principle about which there is no disagreement, that the Free Exercise Clause bars government action aimed at suppressing religious belief or practice. The Court holds that Hialeah's animal-sacrifice laws violate that principle, and I concur in that holding without reservation.

Because prohibiting religious exercise is the object of the laws at hand, this case does not present the more difficult issue addressed in our last free-exercise case, *Employment Div., Dept. of Human Resources of Oregon* v. *Smith*, which announced the rule that a "neutral, generally applicable" law does not run afoul of the Free Exercise Clause even when it prohibits religious exercise in effect. The Court today refers to that rule in dicta, and despite my general agreement with the Court's opinion I do not join Part II, where the dicta appear, for I have doubts about whether the *Smith* rule merits adherence. I write separately to explain why the *Smith* rule is not germane to this case and to express my view that, in a case presenting the issue, the Court should reexamine the rule *Smith* declared.

I

According to *Smith*, if prohibiting the exercise of religion results from enforcing a "neutral, generally applicable" law, the Free Exercise Clause has not been offended. I call this the *Smith* rule to distinguish it from the noncontroversial principle, also expressed in *Smith* though ⊥**560** established long before, that the Free Exercise Clause is offended when prohibiting religious exercise results from a law that is not neutral or generally applicable. It is this noncontroversial principle, that the Free Exercise Clause requires neutrality and general applicability, that is at issue here. But before turning to the relationship of *Smith* to this case, it will help to get the terms in order, for the significance of the *Smith* rule is not only in its statement that the Free Exercise Clause requires no more than "neutrality" and "general applicability," but in its adoption of a particular, narrow conception of free-exercise neutrality.

That the Free Exercise Clause contains a "requirement for governmental neutrality," *Wisconsin* v. *Yoder*, is hardly a novel proposition; though the term does not appear in the First Amendment, our cases have used it as shorthand to describe, at least in part, what the Clause commands. See, *e.g.*, *Jimmy Swaggart Ministries* v. *Board of Equalization of California; Thomas* v. *Review Bd. of Indiana, Employment Security Div.*; *Yoder*; *Committee for Public Ed. & Religious Liberty* v. *Nyquist*; *School Dist. of Abington* v. *Schempp*; see also *McDaniel* v. *Paty* (plurality opinion) (invalidating a non-neutral law without using the term). Nor is there anything unusual about the notion that the Free Exercise Clause requires general applicability, though the Court, until today, has not used exactly that term in stating a reason for invalidation. See *Fowler* v. *Rhode Island*; cf. *Minneapolis Star & Tribune Co.* v. *Minnesota Comm'r of Revenue*; *Larson* v. *Valente*.

⊥**561** While general applicability is, for the most part, self-explanatory, free-exercise neutrality is not self-revealing. Cf. *Lee* v. *Weisman* (Souter, J., concurring) (considering Establishment Clause neutrality). A law that is religion neutral on its face or in its purpose may lack neutrality in its effect by forbidding something that religion requires or requiring something that religion forbids. Cf. McConnell & Posner, An Economic Approach to Issues of Religious Freedom, 56 U. Chi. L. Rev. 1, 35 (1989) ("a regulation is not neutral in an economic sense if, whatever its normal scope or its intentions, it arbitrarily imposes greater costs on religious than on comparable nonreligious activities"). A secular law, applicable to all, that prohibits consumption of alcohol, for example, will affect members of religions that require the use of wine differently from members of other religions and nonbelievers, disproportionately burdening the practice of, say, Catholicism or Judaism. Without an exemption for sacramental wine, Prohibition may fail the test of religion neutrality.

It does not necessarily follow from that observation, of course, that the First Amendment requires an exemption from Prohibition; that depends on the meaning of neutrality as the Free Exercise Clause embraces it. The point here is the unremarkable one that our common notion of neutrality is broad enough to cover not merely what might be called formal neutrality, which as a free-exercise requirement ⊥**562** would only bar laws with an object to discriminate against religion, but also what might be called substantive neutrality, which, in addition to demanding a secular object, would generally require government to accommodate religious differences by exempting religious practices from formally neutral laws. See generally Laycock, Formal, Substantive, and Disaggregated Neutrality Toward Religion, 39 DePaul L. Rev. 993 (1990). If the Free Exercise Clause secures only protection against deliberate discrimination, a formal requirement will exhaust the Clause's neutrality command; if the Free Exercise Clause, rather, safeguards a right to engage in religious activity free from unnecessary governmental interference, the Clause requires substantive, as well as formal, neutrality.

Though *Smith* used the term "neutrality" without a modifier, the rule it announced plainly assumes that free-exercise neutrality is of the formal sort. Distinguishing between laws whose "object" is to prohibit religious exercise and those that prohibit religious exercise as an "incidental effect," *Smith* placed only the former within the reaches of the Free Exercise Clause; the latter, laws that satisfy formal neutrality, *Smith* would subject to no free exercise scrutiny at all, even when they prohibit religious exercise in application. The four Justices who rejected the *Smith* rule, by contrast, read the Free Exercise Clause as embracing what I have termed substantive neutrality. The enforcement of a law "neutral on its face," they said, may "nonetheless offend [the Free Exercise Clause's] requirement ⊥**563** for government neutrality if it unduly burdens the free exercise of religion" (opinion of O'Connor, J., joined by Brennan, Marshall, and Blackmun, JJ.). The rule these Justices saw as flowing from free-exercise neutrality, in contrast to the *Smith* rule, "requir[es] the government to justify *any* substantial burden on religiously motivated conduct by a compelling state interest and by means narrowly tailored to achieve that interest." *Id.*, (emphasis supplied).

The proposition for which the *Smith* rule stands, then, is that formal neutrality, along with general applicability, are sufficient conditions for constitutionality under the Free Exercise Clause. That proposition is not at issue in this case, however, for Hialeah's animal-sacrifice ordinances are not neutral under any definition, any more than they are generally applicable. This case, rather, involves the noncontroversial principle repeated in *Smith*, that formal neutrality and general applicability are necessary conditions for free-exercise constitutionality. It is only "this fundamental nonpersecution principle of the First Amendment [that is] implicated here," and it is to that principle that the Court adverts when it holds that Hialeah's ordinances "fail to satisfy the *Smith* requirements." In applying that principle the Court does not tread on troublesome ground.

In considering, for example, whether Hialeah's animal-sacrifice laws violate free-exercise neutrality, the Court rightly observes that "[a]t a minimum, the protections of the Free Exercise Clause pertain if the law at issue discriminates against some or all religious beliefs or regulates or prohibits conduct because it is undertaken for religious reasons," and correctly finds Hialeah's laws to fail those standards. The question whether the protections of the Free Exercise Clause also pertain if the law at issue, though nondiscriminatory in its object, has the effect nonetheless of placing a burden on religious exercise is not before the Court ⊥**564** today, and the Court's intimations on the matter are therefore dicta.

The Court also rightly finds Hialeah's laws to fail the test of general applicability, and as the Court "need not define with precision the standard used to evaluate whether a prohibition is of general application, for these ordinances fall well below the minimum standard necessary to protect First Amendment rights," it need not discuss the rules that apply to prohibitions found to be generally applicable. The question whether "there are areas of conduct protected by the Free Exercise Clause of the First Amendment and thus beyond the power of the State to control, even under regulations of general applicability," *Yoder*, is not before the Court in this case, and, again, suggestions on that score are dicta.

II

In being so readily susceptible to resolution by applying the Free Exercise Clause's "fundamental nonpersecution principle," this is far from a representative free-exercise case. While, as the Court observes, the Hialeah City Council has provided a rare example of a law actually aimed at suppressing religious exercise, *Smith* was typical of our free-exercise cases, involving as it did a formally neutral, generally applicable law. The rule *Smith* announced, however, was decidedly untypical of the cases involving the same type of law. Because

Smith left those prior cases standing, we are left with a free-exercise jurisprudence in tension with itself, a tension that should be addressed, and that may legitimately be addressed, by reexamining the *Smith* rule in the next case that would turn upon its application.

A

In developing standards to judge the enforceability of formally neutral, generally applicable laws against the mandates of the Free Exercise Clause, the Court has addressed ⊥**565** the concepts of neutrality and general applicability by indicating, in language hard to read as not foreclosing the *Smith* rule, that the Free Exercise Clause embraces more than mere formal neutrality, and that formal neutrality and general applicability are not sufficient conditions for free-exercise constitutionality:

"In a variety of ways we have said that '[a] regulation neutral on its face may, in its application, nonetheless offend the constitutional requirement for governmental neutrality if it unduly burdens the free exercise of religion.'" *Thomas*, (quoting *Yoder*).

"[T]o agree that religiously grounded conduct must often be subject to the broad police power of the State is not to deny that there are areas of conduct protected by the Free Exercise Clause of the First Amendment and thus beyond the power of the State to control, even under regulations of general applicability."

Not long before the *Smith* decision, indeed, the Court specifically rejected the argument that "neutral and uniform" requirements for governmental benefits need satisfy only a reasonableness standard, in part because "[s]uch a test has no basis in precedent." *Hobbie* v. *Unemployment Appeals Comm'n of Florida*. Rather, we have said, "[o]ur cases have established that '[t]he free exercise inquiry asks whether government has placed a substantial burden on the observation of a central religious belief or practice and, if so, whether a compelling governmental interest justifies the burden.'" *Swaggart Ministries* (quoting *Hernandez* v. *Commissioner*).

Thus we have applied the same rigorous scrutiny to burdens on religious exercise resulting from the enforcement of formally neutral, generally applicable laws as we have applied to burdens caused by laws that single out religious ex⊥**566**ercise: "'only those interests of the highest order and those not otherwise served can overbalance legitimate claims to the free exercise of religion.'" *McDaniel* v. *Paty* (quoting *Yoder*). Compare *McDaniel* (applying that test to a law aimed at religious conduct) with *Yoder* (applying that test to a formally neutral, general law). Other cases in which the Court has applied heightened scrutiny to the enforcement of formally neutral, generally applicable laws that burden religious exercise include *Hernandez* v. *Commissioner*; *Frazee* v. *Illinois Dept. of Employment Security*; *Hobbie* v. *Unemployment Appeals Comm'n*; *Bob Jones University* v. *United States*; *United States* v. *Lee*; *Thomas*; *Sherbert* v. *Verner*; and *Cantwell* v. *Connecticut*.

Though *Smith* sought to distinguish the free-exercise cases in which the Court mandated exemptions from secular laws of general application, I am not persuaded. *Wisconsin* v. *Yoder*, and *Cantwell* v. *Connecticut*, according to *Smith*, were not true free-exercise cases but "hybrid[s]" involving "the Free Exercise Clause in conjunction with other constitutional protections, such as freedom of speech and of the press, or the right of parents . . . to direct the education of their children." *Smith*. Neither opinion, however, leaves any doubt that "fundamental claims of religious freedom [were] at stake." *Yoder*; see also *Cantwell*. ⊥**567** And the distinction *Smith* draws strikes me as ultimately untenable. If a hybrid claim is simply one in which another constitutional right is implicated, then the hybrid exception would probably be so vast as to swallow the *Smith* rule, and, indeed, the hybrid exception would cover the situation exemplified by *Smith*, since free speech and associational rights are certainly implicated in the peyote-smoking ritual. But if a hybrid claim is one in which a litigant would actually obtain an exemption from a formally neutral, generally applicable law under another constitutional provision, then there would have been no reason for the Court in what *Smith* calls the hybrid cases to have mentioned the Free Exercise Clause at all.

Smith sought to confine the remaining free-exercise exemption victories, which involved unemployment compensa⊥**568**tion systems, see *Frazee*; *Hobbie*; *Thomas*; and *Sherbert*, as "stand[ing] for the proposition that where the State has in place a system of individual exemptions, it may not refuse to extend that system to cases of 'religious hardship' without compelling reason." But prior to *Smith* the Court had already refused to accept that explanation of the unemployment compensation cases. See *Hobbie*; *Bowen* v. *Roy* (opinion of Blackmun, J.); *id.* (opinion of O'Connor, J., joined by Brennan and Marshall, JJ.); *id.* (White, J., dissenting). And, again, the distinction fails to exclude *Smith*: "If *Smith* is viewed as an unemployment compensation case, the distinction is obviously spurious. If *Smith* is viewed as a hypothetical criminal prosecution for peyote use, there would be an individual governmental assessment of the defendants' motives and actions in the form of a criminal trial." McConnell, Free Exercise Revisionism and the *Smith* Decision, 57 U. Chi. L. Rev. 1109, 1124 (1990). *Smith* also distinguished the unemployment compensation cases on the ground that they did not involve "an across-the-board criminal prohibition on a particular form of conduct." But even *Chief Justice BURGER'S* plurality opinion in *Bowen* v. *Roy*, on which *Smith* drew for its analysis of the unemployment compensation cases, would have applied its reasonableness test only to "denial of government benefits" and not to "governmental action or legislation that criminalizes religiously inspired activity or inescapably compels conduct that some find objectionable for religious reasons," *Bowen* v. *Roy* (opinion of Burger, C. J., joined by Powell and Rehnquist, JJ.); to the latter category of governmental action, it would have applied the test employed in *Yoder,* which involved an across-the-board criminal prohibition and which *Chief Justice* BURGER'S opinion treated as an ordinary free-⊥**569** exercise case. See *Bowen* v. *Roy; Yoder;* see also *McDaniel* v. *Paty* (noting cases in which courts considered claims for exemptions from general criminal prohibitions, cases the Court thought were "illustrative of the general nature of free-exercise protections and the delicate balancing required by our decisions in *Sherbert* and *Yoder,* when an important state interest is shown").

As for the cases on which *Smith* primarily relied as establishing the rule it embraced, *Reynolds* v. *United States* and *Minersville School Dist.* v. *Gobitis,* their subsequent treatment by the Court would seem to require rejection of the *Smith* rule. *Reynolds,* which in upholding the polygamy conviction of a Mormon stressed the evils it saw as associated with polygamy, ("polygamy leads to the patriarchal principle, and . . . fetters the people in stationary despotism"); has been read as consistent with the principle that religious conduct may be regulated by general or targeting law only if the conduct "pose[s] some substantial threat to public safety, peace or order." *Sherbert* v. *Verner;* see also *United States* v. *Lee; Bob Jones University; Yoder.* And *Gobitis,* after three Justices who originally joined the opinion renounced it for disregarding the government's constitutional obligation "to accommodate itself to the religious views of minorities," *Jones* v. *Opelika* (opinion of Black, Douglas, and Murphy, JJ.), was explicitly overruled in *West Virginia Board of Education* v. *Barnette;* see also *id.* (Black and Douglas, JJ., concurring).

Since holding in 1940 that the Free Exercise Clause applies to the States, see *Cantwell* v. *Connecticut,* the Court repeatedly has stated that the Clause sets strict limits on the government's power to burden religious exercise, whether it is a law's object to do so or its unantici-⊥**570**pated effect. *Smith* responded to these statements by suggesting that the Court did not really mean what it said, detecting in at least the most recent opinions a lack of commitment to the compelling-interest test in the context of formally neutral laws. But even if the Court's commitment were that pallid, it would argue only for moderating the language of the test, not for eliminating constitutional scrutiny altogether. In any event, I would have trouble concluding that the Court has not meant what it has said in more than a dozen cases over several decades, particularly when in the same period it repeatedly applied the compelling-interest test to require exemptions, even in a case decided the year before *Smith.* See *Frazee* v. *Illinois Dept. of Employment Security.* In sum, it seems to me difficult to escape the con⊥**571**clusion that, whatever *Smith*'s virtues, they do not include a comfortable fit with settled law.

B

The *Smith* rule, in my view, may be reexamined consistently with principles of *stare decisis.* To begin with, the *Smith* rule was not subject to "full-dress argument" prior to its announcement. *Mapp* v. *Ohio* (Harlan, J., dissenting). The State of Oregon in *Smith* contended that its refusal to exempt religious peyote use survived the strict scrutiny required by "settled free exercise principles," inasmuch as the State had "a compelling interest in regulating" the practice of peyote use and could not "accommodate the religious practice without compromis⊥**572**ing its interest." Respondents joined issue on the outcome of strict scrutiny on the facts before the Court and neither party squarely addressed the proposition the Court was to embrace, that the Free Exercise Clause was irrelevant to the dispute. Sound judicial decisionmaking requires "both a vigorous prosecution and a vigorous defense" of the issues in dispute, *Christiansburg Garment Co.* v. *EEOC,* and a constitutional rule announced *sua sponte* is entitled to less deference than one addressed on full briefing and argument. Cf. *Ladner* v. *United States* (declining to address "an important and complex" issue concerning the scope of collateral attack upon criminal sentences because it had received "only meagre argument" from the parties, and the Court thought it "should have the benefit of a full argument before dealing with the question").

The *Smith* rule's vitality as precedent is limited further by the seeming want of any need of it in resolving the question presented in that case. *Justice* O'CONNOR reached the same result as the majority by applying, as the parties had requested, "our established free exercise jurisprudence," and the majority never determined that the case could not be resolved on the narrower ground, going instead straight to the broader constitutional rule. But the Court's better practice, one supported by the same principles of restraint that underlie the rule of *stare decisis,* is not to " 'formulate a rule of constitutional law broader than is required by the precise facts to which it is to be applied.' " *Ashwander* v. *TVA* (Brandeis, J., concurring) (quoting *Liverpool, New York & Philadelphia S. S. Co.* v. *Commissioners of Emigration*). While I am not suggesting that the *Smith* Court lacked the power to announce its rule, I think a rule of law unnecessary to the outcome of a case, especially one not put ⊥**573** into play by the parties, approaches without more the sort of "*dicta* . . . which may be followed if sufficiently persuasive but which are not controlling." *Humphrey's Executor* v. *United States;* see also *Kastigar* v. *United States.*

I do not, of course, mean to imply that a broad constitutional rule announced without full briefing and argument necessarily lacks precedential weight. Over time, such a decision may become "part of the tissue of the law," *Radovich* v. *National Football League* (Frankfurter, J., dissenting), and may be subject to reliance in a way that new and unexpected decisions are not. *Smith,* however, is not such a case. By the same token, by pointing out *Smith*'s recent vintage I do not mean to suggest that novelty alone is enough to justify reconsideration. "*[S]tare decisis,*" as *Justice* FRANKFURTER wrote, "is a principle of policy and not a mechanical formula," *Helvering* v.

Hallock, and the decision whether to adhere to a prior decision, particularly a constitutional decision, is a complex and difficult one that does not lend itself to resolution by application of simple, categorical rules, but that must account for a variety of often competing considerations.

The considerations of full briefing, necessity, and novelty thus do not exhaust the legitimate reasons for reexamining prior decisions, or even for reexamining the *Smith* rule. One important further consideration warrants mention here, however, because it demands the reexamination I have in mind. *Smith* presents not the usual question of whether to follow a constitutional rule, but the question of which constitutional rule to follow, for *Smith* refrained from overruling prior free-exercise cases that contain a free-exercise rule fundamentally at odds with the rule *Smith* declared. *Smith*, indeed, announced its rule by relying squarely upon ⊥**574** the precedent of prior cases. ("Our decisions reveal that the . . . reading" of the Free Exercise Clause contained in the *Smith* rule "is the correct one"). Since that precedent is nonetheless at odds with the *Smith* rule, as I have discussed above, the result is an intolerable tension in free-exercise law which may be resolved, consistently with principles of *stare decisis*, in a case in which the tension is presented and its resolution pivotal.

While the tension on which I rely exists within the body of our extant case law, a rereading of that case law will not, of course, mark the limits of any enquiry directed to reexamining the *Smith* rule, which should be reviewed in light not only of the precedent on which it was rested but also of the text of the Free Exercise Clause and its origins. As for text, *Smith* did not assert that the plain language of the Free Exercise Clause compelled its rule, but only that the rule was "a permissible reading" of the Clause. Suffice it to say that a respectable argument may be made that the pre-*Smith* law comes closer to fulfilling the language of the Free Exercise Clause than the rule *Smith* announced. "[T]he Free Exercise Clause . . . , by its terms, gives special protection to the exercise of religion," *Thomas*, specifying an activity and then flatly protecting it against government prohibition. The Clause draws no distinction between laws whose object is to prohibit religious exercise and laws with that effect, on its face seemingly applying to both.

Nor did *Smith* consider the original meaning of the Free Exercise Clause, though overlooking the opportunity was no unique transgression. Save in a handful of passing remarks, the Court has not explored the history of the Clause since its early attempts in 1879 and 1890, see *Reynolds* v. *United States* and *Davis* v. *Beason*, attempts that recent scholarship makes clear were incomplete. See generally McConnell, The Origins and Historical Understanding of Free Exercise of Religion, ⊥**575** 103 Harv. L. Rev. 1409 (1990). The curious absence of history from our free-exercise decisions creates a stark contrast with our cases under the Establishment Clause, where historical analysis has been so prominent.

This is not the place to explore the history that a century of free-exercise opinions have overlooked, and it is enough to note that, when the opportunity to reexamine *Smith* presents itself, we may consider recent scholarship raising serious questions about the *Smith* rule's consonance with the original understanding and purpose of the Free Exercise Clause. See McConnell, The Origins and Historical Understanding of Free Exercise of Religion; Durham, Religious Liberty and the Call of Conscience, 42 DePaul L. Rev. 71, 79–85 (1992); see also Office of Legal Policy, U. S. Dept. of Justice, Report to the Attorney General, Religious Liberty under the Free Exercise Clause 38–42 (1986) (predating *Smith*). There appears to be a strong argument from the ⊥**576** Clause's development in the First Congress, from its origins in the post-Revolution state constitutions and pre-Revolution colonial charters, and from the philosophy of rights to which the Framers adhered, that the Clause was originally understood to preserve a right to engage in activities necessary to fulfill one's duty to one's God, unless those activities threatened the rights of others or the serious needs of the State. If, as this scholarship suggests, the Free Exercise Clause's original "purpose [was] to secure religious liberty in the individual by prohibiting any invasions thereof by civil authority," *School Dist. of Abington* v. *Schempp*, then there would be powerful reason to interpret the Clause to accord with its natural reading, as applying to all laws prohibiting religious exercise in fact, not just those aimed at its prohibition, and to hold the neutrality needed to implement such a purpose to be the substantive neutrality of our pre-*Smith* cases, not the formal neutrality sufficient for constitutionality under *Smith*.

⊥**577** The scholarship on the original understanding of the Free Exercise Clause is, to be sure, not uniform. See, *e.g.*, Hamburger, A Constitutional Right of Religious Exemption: An Historical Perspective, 60 Geo. Wash. L. Rev. 915 (1992); Bradley, Beguiled: Free Exercise Exemptions and the Siren Song of Liberalism, 20 Hofstra L. Rev. 245 (1991). And there are differences of opinion as to the weight appropriately accorded original meaning. But whether or not one considers the original designs of the Clause binding, the interpretive significance of those designs surely ranks in the hierarchy of issues to be explored in resolving the tension inherent in free-exercise law as it stands today.

III

The extent to which the Free Exercise Clause requires government to refrain from impeding religious exercise defines nothing less than the respective relationships in our constitutional democracy of the individual to government and to God. "Neutral, generally applicable" laws, drafted as they are from the perspective of the nonadherent, have the unavoidable potential of putting the believer to a choice between God and government. Our cases now present competing answers to the question when government, while pursuing secular ends, may compel disobedience to what one believes religion commands. The case before us is rightly decided without resolving the existing tension, which remains for another day when it may be squarely faced.

Justice BLACKMUN, with whom *Justice* O'CONNOR joins, concurring in the judgment.

The Court holds today that the city of Hialeah violated the First and Fourteenth Amendments when it passed a set of restrictive ordinances explicitly directed at petitioners' religious practice. With this holding I agree. I write separately to emphasize that the First Amendment's protection of religion extends beyond those rare occasions on which the government explicitly targets religion (or a particular reli⊥**578**gion) for disfavored treatment, as is done in this case. In my view, a statute that burdens the free exercise of religion "may stand only if the law in general, and the State's refusal to allow a religious exemption in particular, are justified by a compelling interest that cannot be served by less restrictive means." *Employment Div., Oregon Dept. of Human Resources* v. *Smith* (dissenting opinion). The Court, however, applies a different test. It applies the test announced in *Smith*, under which "a law that is neutral and of general applicability need not be justified by a compelling governmental interest even if the law has the incidental effect of burdening a particular religious practice." I continue to believe that *Smith* was wrongly decided, because it ignored the value of religious freedom as an affirmative individual liberty and treated the Free Exercise Clause as no more than an antidiscrimination principle. Thus, while I agree with the result the Court reaches in this case, I arrive at that result by a different route.

When the State enacts legislation that intentionally or unintentionally places a burden upon religiously motivated practice, it must justify that burden by "showing that it is the least restrictive means of achieving some compelling state interest." *Thomas* v. *Review Bd. of Indiana Employment Security Div.* A State may no more create an underinclusive statute, one that fails truly to promote its purported compelling interest, than it may create an overinclusive statute, one that encompasses more protected conduct than necessary to achieve its goal. In the latter circumstance, the broad scope of the statute is unnecessary to serve the interest, and the statute fails for that reason. In the former situation, the fact that allegedly harmful conduct falls outside the statute's scope belies a governmental assertion that it has genuinely pursued an interest "of the highest order." If the State's goal is important enough to prohibit religiously motivated activity, it ⊥**579** will not and must not stop at religiously motivated activity. Cf. *Zablocki* v. *Redhail* (invalidating certain restrictions on marriage as "grossly underinclusive with respect to [their] purpose"); *Supreme Court of New Hampshire* v. *Piper* (a rule excluding nonresidents from the bar of New Hampshire "is underinclusive . . . because it permits lawyers who move away from the State to retain their membership in the bar").

In this case, the ordinances at issue are both overinclusive and underinclusive in relation to the state interests they purportedly serve. They are overinclusive, as the majority correctly explains, because the "legitimate governmental interests in protecting the public health and preventing cruelty to animals could be addressed by restrictions stopping far short of a flat prohibition of all Santeria sacrificial practice." They are underinclusive as well, because "[d]espite the city's proffered interest in preventing cruelty to animals, the ordinances are drafted with care to forbid few killings but those occasioned by religious sacrifice." Moreover, the "ordinances are also underinclusive with regard to the city's interest in public health. . . ."

When a law discriminates against religion as such, as do the ordinances in this case, it automatically will fail strict scrutiny under *Sherbert* v. *Verner* (holding that governmental regulation that imposes a burden upon religious practice must be narrowly tailored to advance a compelling state interest). This is true because a law that targets religious practice for disfavored treatment both burdens the free exercise of religion and, by definition, is not precisely tailored to a compelling governmental interest.

Thus, unlike the majority, I do not believe that "[a] law burdening religious practice that is not neutral or not of general application must undergo the most rigorous of scrutiny." In my view, regulation that targets religion in this way, *ipso facto*, fails strict scrutiny. It is for this reason ⊥**580** that a statute that explicitly restricts religious practices violates the First Amendment. Otherwise, however, "[t]he First Amendment . . . does not distinguish between laws that are generally applicable and laws that target particular religious practices." *Smith* (opinion concurring in judgment).

It is only in the rare case that a state or local legislature will enact a law directly burdening religious practice as such. Because the respondent here does single out religion in this way, the present case is an easy one to decide.

A harder case would be presented if petitioners were requesting an exemption from a generally applicable anticruelty law. The result in the case before the Court today, and the fact that every Member of the Court concurs in that result, does not necessarily reflect this Court's views of the strength of a State's interest in prohibiting cruelty to animals. This case does not present, and I therefore decline to reach, the question whether the Free Exercise Clause would require a religious exemption from a law that sincerely pursued the goal of protecting animals from cruel treatment. The number of organizations that have filed *amicus* briefs on behalf of this interest, however, demonstrates that it is not a concern to be treated lightly.

RELIGIOUS TESTS FOR PUBLIC SERVICE OR BENEFITS

Although Article VI of the United States Constitution forbids religious tests for federal office, many states retained, and sometimes enforced, such tests. Several of the original state constitutions excluded from office or even disfranchised nonbelievers, Catholics, and Jews. Only Christians were eligible for the office of governor in Massachusetts and Maryland. The governor was required to be a Protestant in four other states. Similar requirements were often imposed on witnesses and jurors, and a number of states specifically banned ministers of the gospel from holding public office.

Delaware in 1792 became the first state to adopt a constitutional provision forbidding religious tests as a requirement for public office. Many other states followed suit; and even in those states where archaic constitutional requirements of oaths remained, they were largely ignored. Because there had been few attempts to enforce them, there was little governing case law. By 1946 the Supreme Court was able to say with confidence in *Girouard* v. *United States*: "The test oath is abhorrent to our tradition."

Fifteen years after this statement, the Court found it necessary to consider for the first time a religious test oath in TORCASO v. WATKINS. The case came to the Court from Maryland. In 1776 the state had adopted its first constitution, which guaranteed the right to hold public office to all who would subscribe to a "declaration of a belief in the Christian religion." In 1864 the constitution was revised to require either "a declaration of belief in the Christian religion," or the belief "in the existence of God, and in a future state of rewards and punishments."

The 1867 constitution kept only the requirement of "a declaration of belief in the existence of God." In 1922 the Maryland attorney general ruled that it was still mandatory that every state official be "required in some definite way" to declare his belief in the existence of God.

Almost forty years later Roy Torcaso was appointed to the minor state office of notary public. As an atheist, he refused to take the mandatory oath and was consequently denied his commission. Torcaso appealed to the state circuit court, claiming that the required oath violated the First and Fourteenth Amendments as well as Article VI of the original Constitution. The circuit court rejected his arguments, and the Maryland Court of Appeals affirmed the decision of the lower state court. Torcaso then took his case to the Supreme Court.

The unanimous Court used the First Amendment—by then applicable to the states—to invalidate Maryland's oath requirement as an invasion of the appellant's "freedom of belief and religion." Therefore, it did not have to consider the question raised by Torcaso of whether Article VI of the Constitution applied to state officers.

In his opinion, Justice Black denied that, as the Maryland Court of Appeals had assumed, the Court had in any way repudiated its strong position taken in EVERSON v. BOARD OF EDUCATION concerning limitations imposed by the Establishment Clause. He reaffirmed the *Everson* statement that neither a state nor the federal government could "force a person to profess a belief or disbelief in any religion."

The *Torcaso* decision is significant for several reasons. It denies categorically that religious tests for office can be imposed at any level of government. It holds that the First Amendment forbids different treatment by government of believers and nonbelievers, thus guaranteeing freedom of irreligion as well as religion. In *Torcaso*, the Court also accepted an expanded concept of religion. It emphasized that no distinction could be shown between "those religions based on a belief in the existence of God" and such nontheistic religions as Buddhism, Taoism, Ethical Culture, and Secular Humanism.[1]

Gradually the states repealed their constitutional bans on the holding of public officers by ministers. By 1975 only Tennessee retained the restrictive provision and that only as applied to service in the legislature. In 1976 the restriction was extended to candidates for the state constitutional convention to be held the next year. Paul A. McDaniel, the ordained minister of a Baptist church in Chattanooga, filed for election to the convention. Selma Cash Paty, an opposing candidate, brought suit seeking McDaniel's disqualification, but McDaniel was overwhelmingly elected. The state court in which the suit was filed found the provision to be violative of the First and Fourteenth Amendments, but the Supreme Court of Tennessee reversed the holding. According to that body, the disqualification did not place a burden on "religious action . . . [only] in the lawmaking

[1]In 1965 the Maryland Court of Appeals acted on the basis of the *Torcaso* holding to void a requirement that all jurors swear to a belief in God. The state court there accepted the contention of a Buddhist that exclusion of nonbelievers in God from the grand jury and the jury that had indicted and convicted him had violated his constitutional rights. *Schowgurow* v. *State* (1965).

One of the claims of the "New Christian Right," in its criticism of public schools and promotion of "Christian schools" is that the public schools are, as a matter of fact, teaching a religion: secular humanism. Frequently spokespersons for this view have cited *Torcaso*, pointing to the reference to secular humanism in footnote #11 of that decision as a confirmation of the claim that secular humanism is a religion. For a case argued and decided on that premise, cf. *Smith* v. *Board of School Commissioners of Mobile County* and, as commentary, Ronald B. Flowers, "They Got Our Attention Didn't They?: The Tennessee and Alabama Schoolbook Cases," *Religion and Public Education* 15 (Summer 1988): 262-285.

process of government—where religious action is absolutely prohibited by the establishment clause."

The United States Supreme Court, in McDANIEL v. PATY (1978), with Justice Blackmun not participating, unanimously invalidated the restriction. However, four separate opinions were written expressing at least three different rationales for voiding the law in question. Chief Justice Burger, joined by Justices Powell, Rehnquist, and Stevens, held the disqualification unconstitutional but sought to distinguish the ruling from that of *Torcaso*, where the Court had found a violation of freedom of religious *belief* to result from the religious oath required of office holders. Instead, this opinion emphasized denial of religious *action* by the Tennessee statute.

Justice Brennan, joined by Justice Marshall, concurred in the judgment, but Brennan contended that *Torcaso* governed and that both belief and exercise of that belief had been infringed. Justice Stewart also concurred that *Torcaso* governed, arguing that more than action was involved. But Stewart was apparently unwilling to join Brennan and Marshall in all their reasoning.

In his separate concurring opinion, Justice White relied not on the Free Exercise Clause of the First Amendment but rather on the Equal Protection Clause of the Fourteenth. While expressing understanding for the state's desire to maintain separation between church and state, White found this action both unnecessary to accomplish that purpose and unconstitutional. On equal protection grounds, he contended that the law discriminated against legislators because its restriction did not apply to officials of the other two branches.

Situations have sometimes arisen in which, although no formal religious test was imposed, individuals have been forced to decide between sacrificing a desire for a position or benefit from government and religious conviction. There, too, a substantial, though indirect, burden is imposed on free exercise of religion.

Chief Justice Burger recognized this burden when, in writing the majority opinion in 1981 in THOMAS v. REVIEW BOARD OF INDIANA EMPLOYMENT SECURITY DIVISION, he said that:

> Where the state conditions receipt of an important benefit upon conduct proscribed by a religious faith, or where it denies such a benefit because of conduct mandated by religious belief, thereby putting substantial pressure on an adherent to modify his behavior and violate his beliefs, a burden upon religion exists. While the compulsion may be indirect, the infringement upon free exercise is nonetheless substantial (450 U.S. 707, 717-18).

In 1986, a case involving a clear conflict between continued service in the military and adherence to a strongly held religious obligation was heard and decided by the Supreme Court. Civilian courts have traditionally exhibited great deference toward military regulations governing the conduct of service personnel. Different standards prevail in weighing constitutional rights of members of the military services, or even of civilians while on military enclaves, from those used by the courts for persons engaged in ordinary civilian pursuits. The Supreme Court has, for example, upheld the authority of a base commander to prohibit political speeches or demonstrations on a military base and the requirement that prior approval be obtained from the appropriate commander before distribution of leaflets or even petitions to members of Congress and the Secretary of Defense.[2] As the majority opinion of the Court observed in a highly publicized case arising from the Vietnam conflict, that body has consistently held that "the military is, by necessity, a specialized society separate from civilian society."[3]

Obviously, then, an individual entering military service can expect limitations on certain constitutional rights that he or she would take for granted as a civilian. Simcha Goldman, an Orthodox Jew and ordained rabbi serving as a clinical psychologist at the mental clinic at March Air Force Base, discovered in 1981 how limited his rights really were when he ran afoul of an Air Force regulation that forbade the wearing of headgear while indoors, except by on-duty security police. As a male Orthodox Jew, he felt a strong religious obligation to cover his head with a yarmulke indoors as well as out. He had worn the yarmulke indoors on duty at the hospital, covering it with his regulation service cap while outdoors, for four years without formal complaint.

Only after he apparently incurred the wrath of a military prosecutor by testifying as a defense witness in a court-martial was a complaint filed against Goldman for violation of the headgear regulation. He subsequently received a letter of reprimand from the hospital commander, together with a warning that failure to comply with the regulation could result in a court-martial. The commander also withdrew an earlier recommendation that Goldman's request to extend his active duty be approved, and replaced it with a negative recommendation.

Goldman contended that the headgear regulation infringed his First Amendment right to free exercise of his religious belief, and appealed to a federal district court. The district court permanently enjoined the Air Force from enforcing the regulation against him, but the Court of Appeals for the District of Columbia reversed the decision. The appellate court ruling went on writ of certiorari to the Supreme

[2]*Greer* v. *Spock* (1976); *Brown* v. *Glines* (1990); *Secretary of the Navy* v. *Huff* (1980).

[3]*Parker* v. *Levy* (1974).

Court, was argued in January 1986, and the Court's holding in GOLDMAN v. WEINBERGER was announced the following March.

By a five-to-four vote, with Justice Rehnquist writing for the majority, the Court upheld the regulation as applied to Goldman. Chief Justice Burger and Justices White, Powell, and Stevens joined in the opinion. A concurring opinion was written by Justice Stevens joined by White and Powell. Separate dissenting opinions were filed by Justices Brennan, Blackmun, and O'Connor. Justice Marshall joined Brennan and O'Connor in their dissents.

Justice Rehnquist's relatively brief opinion for the majority emphasized the ordinary high degree of judicial deference to military regulations, saying, "Our review of military regulations challenged on First Amendment grounds is far more deferential than constitutional reviews of similar laws or regulations designed for civilian society" (475 U.S. 503, 507). The Court, therefore, would not challenge the professional judgment of the Air Force that habits of discipline and unity essential to military discipline and morale were furthered by the outfitting of personnel in standardized uniforms for the "subordination of personal preferences and identities in favor of the overall group mission" (475 U.S. 503, 508). Although regulations against wearing of religious apparel might well be objectionable to Goldman and others, "the First Amendment does not require the military to accommodate such practices in the face of its view that they would detract from the uniformity sought by the dress regulations" (475 U.S. 503, 509-510).

Justice Brennan, in dissent, lamented that the Court had abdicated "its role as principal expositor of the Constitution and protector of individual liberties in favor of credulous deference to unsupported assertions of military necessity" (475 U.S. 503, 514). "The Court and the military services," he said, "have presented patriotic Orthodox Jews with a painful dilemma—the choice between fulfilling a religious obligation and serving their country. Should the draft be reinstated, compulsion will replace choice" (475 U.S. 503, 524). Justice Brennan concluded his dissent: ". . . we must hope that Congress will correct this wrong." In 1988 Congress responded to his appeal when it provided that "a member of the armed forces may wear an item of religious apparel while wearing the uniform of the member's armed force." An exception to this general rule could be made by the Secretary concerned if he should determine that "the wearing of the item would interfere with the performance of the member's military duties" or that the item of apparel was not "neat and conservative."[4]

The Supreme Court in 1985 passed up an opportunity to speak to the question of a state's denial of another important benefit—the privilege of driving a car in that state—because an applicant for a driver's license refused to comply with a requirement which she contended unconstitutionally burdened the free exercise of her religious beliefs.

Although she was not a member of an organized church, Frances J. Quaring refused on religious grounds to have her photograph taken and attached to her driver's license as required by Nebraska law. She maintained that the requirement imposed an excessive burden on her sincerely held religious belief that the Second Commandment expressly forbids the making of any graven images or likeness of anything in creation. A federal district court upheld her contention and enjoined state officials from refusing to issue her a license without the photograph.

The United States Court of Appeals for the Eighth Circuit upheld the issuance of the injunction against the state's claim that providing the exemption on religious grounds would create an impermissible establishment of religion. The court failed to find sufficient compelling state interest or undue administrative burden to justify the infringement of Quaring's religious liberty. The exemption mandated by the district court, the appellate court held, was a reasonable accommodation of religion and did not constitute an establishment of religion. The Supreme Court granted certiorari, but in a *per curiam* opinion announced that it affirmed the judgment of the Court of Appeals by an equally divided (four-to-four) vote.[5]

In the last weeks of the 1985-1986 session the Court heard and decided another case involving a choice between receiving a governmental benefit and adhering to a religious commitment. Stephen Roy, a Native American descended from the Abenaki Indian Tribe, refused to comply with the government's requirement that he furnish the Social Security numbers of the members of his family to state welfare agencies in order to receive benefits under the Aid to Families with Dependent Children and Food Stamp programs. Roy, his wife, and another five-year-old daughter had Social Security numbers, but he had recently decided that to obtain a Social Security number for his two-year-old daughter, Little Bird of the Snow, and allow the government to make routine use of that number would violate his religious beliefs as a Native American that control of one's life is essential to the attainment of spiritual purity and to "becoming a holy person." Uses of a number over which she had no control would "rob the spirit" of his daughter.[6]

[4]10 U.S.C. § 774 (1988).

[5]*Jensen* v. *Quaring* (1985); case below: *Quaring* v. *Peterson* (1984).

[6]Two years earlier the United States Court of Appeals for the Ninth Circuit had heard an appeal from the District Court for the Northern District of California ruling in which that court upheld denial of benefits under the Aid to Families and Dependent Children to a parent who refused to obtain a Social Security number for a child. He

The Pennsylvania Department of Public Welfare responded to Roy's refusal by stopping AFDC and medical benefits for the child and taking steps to reduce food stamps which the family was receiving. He filed suit in a federal district court, claiming the right of exemption from the requirement on free exercise grounds. After an extended hearing, the trial court agreed with his argument and enjoined the Secretary of Health and Human Services from using or disseminating the Social Security number which, as became evident during the trial, had already been issued to the child. Both federal and state officials were also enjoined from denying benefits until Little Bird of the Snow's sixteenth birthday due to refusal to provide a Social Security number.

In an extremely complex decision, the Court vacated the judgment of the trial court, but the justices spoke with a unique mix of opinions and votes. Chief Justice Burger, writing his final church-state majority opinion for the Court, divided the opinion into three parts. Seven of his colleagues joined in Parts I and II. Only Justice Powell and Rehnquist joined him in Part III. Justice Blackmun filed a separate opinion concurring in part, as did Justice Stevens. Justice O'Connor, joined by Justices Brennan and Marshall, filed an opinion concurring in part and dissenting in part; Justice White dissented alone. To make the decision even more confusing, Justices Blackmun and Stevens raised questions on mootness and ripeness grounds as to whether the issues involved should even be considered by the Court.

In Parts I and II of his opinion for the Court with which seven other justices agreed, Chief Justice Burger upheld the requirement of the Social Security number for eligibility for the benefits in question and the right of the government to make use of the account in the administration of the AFDC plan. He agreed that the Free Exercise Clause protects an individual against some forms of government compulsion, but it does not, he said, "afford an individual a right to dictate the conduct of the government's internal procedures."

With respect to Roy's claim of harm done to his daughter's spirit, Burger said:

> Never to our knowledge has the Court interpreted the First Amendment to require the Government itself to behave in ways that the individual believes will further his or her spiritual development or that of his or her family. The Free Exercise Clause simply cannot be understood to require the Government to conduct its own internal affairs in ways that comport with the religious beliefs of particular citizens. Just as the Government may not insist that appellees engage in any set form of religious observance, so appellees may not demand that the Government join in their chosen religious practices by refraining from using a number to identify their daughter (476 U.S. 693, 699-700).

It was Part III of the opinion that stirred debate among the justices, and for good reason. There the Chief Justice sought to advance a significantly less strenuous standard for determining the constitutionality of government interference with free exercise claims. He expressed his recognition of the importance of various government benefits today, but he sought to distinguish denial of those benefits by a "uniformly applicable statute neutral on its face" as being of a different and less intrusive nature than government action making religiously inspired activity illegal or compelling conduct found objectionable for religious reasons. This distinction, he argued, entitled the government to "wide latitude," and justified a less strict test than the "least restrictive means of accomplishing a compelling state interest" standard developed and applied in *Sherbert*, *Yoder*, and *Thomas*. Instead, he would say that in cases involving denial of government benefits the government could meet its burden of proof when it "demonstrates that a challenged requirement for government benefits, neutral and uniform in its application, is a reasonable means of promoting a legitimate public interest." A quite different standard, indeed.

The Free Exercise Clause, he said, did not mandate that Congress grant a special exemption from its religiously neutral statutory requirement to Roy. "Appellees," he said

> may not use the Free Exercise Clause to demand government benefits, but only on their own terms, particularly where that insistence works a demonstrable disadvantage to the Government in the administration of the programs. As the Court has recognized before, given the diversity of beliefs in our pluralistic society and the necessity of providing governments with sufficient operating latitude, some incidental neutral restraints on the free exercise of religion are inescapable (476 U.S. 693, 711-712).

Had the Chief Justice's more relaxed standard, expounded in Part III, prevailed with a majority of the Court, BOWEN v. ROY, which attracted almost no public attention when released, might well have become a landmark decision because of the significant weakening of the standard applied by the Court to governmental restraint of free exercise of religion. Only Justices Rehnquist and Powell joined the Chief Justice in that part of the opinion.

claimed the requirement infringed his religious belief that the Book of Revelation condemns the use of a universal number such as a Social Security number as the "mark of the beast," by means of which the Antichrist endeavors to control mankind. The court of appeals reversed and remanded the decision of the district court (*Callahan* v. *Woods*, 1984).

Justice O'Connor agreed that the government's stated goal for requiring the Social Security number as preventing fraud and abuse in the welfare system was "both laudable and compelling," and she joined Parts I and II of the opinion. However, she took the Chief Justice sharply to task in her "dissent in part" for his proposed departure from the least restrictive means-compelling state interest test. The test he proposed to substitute, she said, had "no basis in precedent and relegates a serious First Amendment value to the barest level of minimal scrutiny that the Equal Protection Clause already provides." She reviewed the precedents for the test which had prevailed in recent years and concluded that "Only an especially important governmental interest pursued by narrowly tailored means can justify exacting a sacrifice of First Amendment freedoms as the price for an equal share of the rights, benefits, and privileges enjoyed by other citizens" (476 U.S. 693, 728). Justice White dissented, stating simply that *Thomas* and *Sherbert* controlled the case at hand.

The problems of imprisoned Black Muslims seeking to carry out their religious practices have been discussed at an earlier point. The Supreme Court in 1987 by a vote of only five-to-four handed down a ruling in O'LONE v. ESTATE OF SHABAZZ which upheld restrictive prison rules applied to Islamic inmates. In doing so, Chief Justice Rehnquist, writing for the majority, agreed that prisoners do not forfeit all constitutional protection. He held, however, that constitutionally challenged prison regulations should be judged under a "reasonableness" test less restrictive than that ordinarily applied to alleged infringement of fundamental rights.

In *O'Lone*, officials at Leesburg State Prison in New Jersey had instituted regulations that prevented Islamic prisoners from attending Jumu'ah—the central service for Muslims—on Friday afternoons. The United States District Court found no constitutional violation, but the Court of Appeals disagreed and placed the burden on prison officials of disproving the availability of reasonable alternative approaches by means of which the Muslims' religious rights "can be accommodated without creating bona fide security problems."

When the case came before the Supreme Court, Chief Justice Rehnquist found this holding on the part of the Court of Appeals to be in error. He pointed out the various other religious ceremonies in which the Muslims were able to participate, also noting the problems that would be created with the inmates if they saw the establishment of special arrangements providing the Muslims a way to avoid heavy work details. He could see no easy alternatives to the policy mandated. Citing earlier holdings, he refused to substitute the judgment of the Court "for the determinations of those charged with the formidable task of running a prison."

Justice Brennan, joined by Justices Marshall, Blackmun, and Stevens, pointed out that the prison authorities had completely blocked Muslim participation in an essential and non-dangerous religious ceremony. They should therefore face the burden of demonstrating that the limitations imposed were "necessary to further an important government interest, and that these restrictions are no greater than necessary to achieve prison objectives." The facility, he pointed out, had arranged work details for Jewish inmates that allowed them to attend services on Saturday and for Christians to attend Sunday services. Demonstration of "reasonableness" was insufficient when an individual was being denied full "membership in a spiritual community."

The debate within the Court as to the appropriate test to apply when considering alleged government violation of the Free Exercise Clause continued in 1988 in LYNG v. NORTHWEST INDIAN CEMETERY ASSOCIATION. Involved in this case was the contention by both various individuals and organizations that Forest Service plans to construct a road and to allow timber harvesting in an area of national forest in northwest California violated the Free Exercise Clause.

The area in question had traditionally been used by certain Indian tribes for religious rites which required privacy and silence in a natural setting. A federal district court and a court of appeals had agreed that the proposed actions would have "severe adverse effects" on the religious practices of the Indians, and that the government had failed to show a compelling interest sufficient to justify the proposed construction and timber harvesting.

Justice O'Connor, writing the opinion for a majority of five, ruled against the contention that government must show a compelling state interest or the actions would constitute a violation of the Free Exercise Clause. Without denying the sincerity of the Indians or the severe adverse effects of the proposed state actions, she found the situation analogous to BOWEN v. ROY. In both instances, she said, the contention was that the government action would "interfere significantly with private persons' ability to pursue spiritual fulfillment according to their own religious beliefs." In neither case, she stated, were the parties involved *coerced* into violating their religious beliefs nor was their religious action penalized.

Quoting from *Sherbert*, she wrote: "For the Free Exercise Clause is written in terms of what the government cannot do to the individual, not in terms of what the individual can exact from the government." "Prohibit" was the crucial word in the First Amendment clause.

She agreed that indirect coercion or penalties placed upon free exercise of religion as well as clearcut prohibitions are subject to judicial scrutiny. This scrutiny, however, did not involve application of the compelling interest test to otherwise lawful actions, even though those actions may have "incidental effects" which "may make it more difficult to practice certain religions but which have no tendency to coerce individuals into acting contrary to their religious beliefs. . . ." Continuing, she asserted that "However much we might wish that it were otherwise, government simply could not operate if it were required to satisfy every citizen's religious needs and desires" (485 U.S. 439, 452).

Justice Brennan, joined by Justices Marshall and Blackmun, took the majority sternly to task for use of the "coercion" test rather than the "compelling state interest" standard which he insisted should be mandated. Brennan expressed his dismay at the majority's holding that a "federal land-use decision that promises to destroy an entire religion does not burden the practice of that faith in a manner recognized by the Free Exercise Clause." The majority, he said, had brushed aside the compelling interest requirement maintaining that the First Amendment forbids only "outright prohibitions, indirect coercion, and penalties on the free exercise of religion." Justice Kennedy abstained from participation.

TORCASO v. WATKINS

367 U.S. 488
ON APPEAL FROM THE COURT OF APPEALS OF MARYLAND
Argued April 24, 1961 — Decided June 19, 1961

⊥489 Mr. *Justice BLACK* delivered the opinion of the Court.

Article 37 of the Declaration of Rights of the Maryland Constitution provides: "[N]o religious test ought ever to be required as a qualification for any office of profit or trust in this State, other than a declaration of belief in the existence of God. . . ."

The appellant Torcaso was appointed to the office of Notary Public by the Governor of Maryland but was refused a commission to serve because he would not declare his belief in God. He then brought this action in a Maryland Circuit Court to compel issuance of his commission, charging that the State's requirement that he declare this belief violated "the First and Fourteenth Amendments to the Constitution of the United States. . . ."*

There is, and can be, no dispute about the purpose or effect of the Maryland Declaration of Rights requirement before us—it sets up a religious test which was designed to **⊥490** and, if valid, does bar every person who refuses to declare a belief in God from holding a public "office of profit or trust" in Maryland. The power and authority of the State of Maryland thus is put on the side of one particular sort of believers—those who are willing to say they believe in "the existence of God." It is true that there is much historical precedent for such laws. Indeed, it was largely to escape religious test oaths and declarations that a great many of the early colonists left Europe and came here hoping to worship in their own way. It soon developed, however, that many of those who had fled to escape religious test oaths turned out to be perfectly willing, when they had the power to do so, to force dissenters from their faith to take test oaths in conformity with that faith. This brought on a host of laws in the new Colonies imposing burdens and disabilities of various kinds upon varied beliefs depending largely upon what group happened to be politically strong enough to legislate in favor of its own beliefs. The effect of all this was the formal or practical "establishment" of particular religious faiths in most of the Colonies, with consequent burdens imposed on the free exercise of the faiths of non-favored believers.

There were, however, wise and farseeing men in the Colonies—too many to mention—who spoke out against test oaths and all the philosophy of intolerance behind them. . . .

*Appellant also claimed that the State's test oath requirement violates the provision of Art. VI of the Federal Constitution that "no religious Test shall ever be required as a Qualification to any Office or public Trust under the United States." Because we are reversing the judgment on other grounds, we find it unnecessary to consider appellant's contention that this provision applies to state as well as federal offices.

⊥**491** When our Constitution was adopted, the desire to put the people "securely beyond the reach" of religious test oaths brought about the inclusion in Article VI of that document of a provision that, "no religious Test shall ever be required as a Qualification to any Office or public Trust under the United States." Article VI supports the accuracy of our observation in *Girouard* v. *United States* that "[t]he test oath is abhorrent to our tradition." Not satisfied, however, with Article VI and other guarantees in the original Constitution, the First Congress proposed and the States very shortly thereafter ⊥**492** adopted our Bill of Rights, including the First Amendment. That Amendment broke new constitutional ground in the protection it sought to afford to freedom of religion, speech, press, petition and assembly. Since prior cases in this Court have thoroughly explored and documented the history behind the First Amendment, the reasons for it, and the scope of the religious freedom it protects, we need not cover that ground again. What was said in our prior cases we think controls our decision here.

In *Cantwell* v. *Connecticut* we said: "The First Amendment declares that Congress shall make no law respecting an establishment of religion or prohibiting the free exercise thereof. The Fourteenth Amendment has rendered the legislatures of the states as incompetent as Congress to enact such laws. . . . Thus the Amendment embraces two concepts,—freedom to believe and freedom to act. The first is absolute but, in the nature of things, the second cannot be."

Later we decided *Everson* v. *Board of Education* and said this: "The 'establishment of religion' clause of the First Amendment means at least this: Neither a state nor ⊥**493** the Federal Government can set up a church. Neither can pass laws which aid one religion, aid all religions, or prefer one religion over another. Neither can force nor influence a person to go to or to remain away from church against his will or force him to profess a belief or disbelief in any religion. No person can be punished for entertaining or professing religious beliefs or disbeliefs, for church attendance or non-attendance. No tax in any amount, large or small, can be levied to support any religious activities or institutions, whatever they may be called, or whatever form they may adopt to teach or practice religion. Neither a state nor the Federal Government can, openly or secretly, participate in the affairs of any religious organizations or groups and *vice versa*. In the words of Jefferson, the clause against establishment of religion by law was intended to erect 'a wall of separation between church and State.'"

While there were strong dissents in the *Everson* case, they did not challenge the Court's interpretation of the First Amendment's coverage as being too broad, but thought the Court was applying that interpretation too narrowly to the facts of that case. Not long afterward in *Illinois ex rel. McCollum* v. *Board of Education*, we were urged to repudiate as dicta the above-quoted *Everson* interpretation of the scope of the First Amendment's coverage. We declined to do this, but instead strongly reaffirmed what had been said in *Everson*, calling attention to the fact that both the majority and the minority in *Everson* had agreed on the principles declared in this part of the *Everson* opinion. And a concurring opinion in *McCollum*, written by Mr. *Justice FRANKFURTER* and joined by the other *Everson* dissenters, said this: "We are all agreed that the First and Fourteenth Amendments have a secular reach far more penetrat⊥**494**ing in the conduct of Government than merely to forbid an 'established church.' . . . We renew our conviction that 'we have staked the very existence of our country on the faith that complete separation between the state and religion is best for the state and best for religion.'"

The Maryland Court of Appeals thought, and it is argued here, that this Court's later holding and opinion in *Zorach* v. *Clauson* had in part repudiated the statement in the *Everson* opinion quoted above and previously reaffirmed in *McCollum*. But the Court's opinion in *Zorach* specifically stated: "We follow the *McCollum* case." Nothing decided or written in *Zorach* lends support to the idea that the Court there intended to open up the way for government, state or federal, to restore the historically and constitutionally discredited policy of probing religious beliefs by test oaths or limiting public offices to persons who have, or perhaps more properly profess to have, a belief in some particular kind of religious concept.

⊥**495** We repeat and again reaffirm that neither a State nor the Federal Government can constitutionally force a person "to profess a belief or disbelief in any religion." Neither can constitutionally pass laws or impose requirements which aid all religions as against nonbelievers, and neither can aid those religions based on a belief in the existence of God as against those religions founded on different beliefs.*

In upholding the State's religious test for public office the highest court of Maryland said: "The petitioner is not compelled to believe or disbelieve, under threat of punishment or other compulsion. True, unless he makes the declaration of belief he cannot hold public office in Maryland, but he is not compelled to hold office."

The fact, however, that a person is not compelled to hold public office cannot possibly be an excuse for barring him ⊥**496** from office by state-imposed criteria forbidden by the Constitution. This was settled by our holding in *Wieman* v. *Updegraff*. We there pointed out that whether or not "an abstract right to public employment exists," Congress could not pass a law providing "'. . . that no federal employee shall attend Mass or take any active part in missionary work.'"

This Maryland religious test for public office unconstitutionally invades the appellant's freedom of belief and religion and therefore cannot be enforced against him.

---

*Among religions in this country which do not teach what would generally be considered a belief in the existence of God are Buddhism, Taoism, Ethical Culture, Secular Humanism and others.

The judgment of the Court of Appeals of Maryland is accordingly reversed and the cause is remanded for further proceedings not inconsistent with this opinion.

Reversed and remanded.

Mr. *Justice* FRANKFURTER and Mr. *Justice* HARLAN concur in the result.

McDANIEL v. PATY

435 U.S. 618
ON APPEAL FROM THE SUPREME COURT OF THE STATE OF TENNESSEE
Argued December 5, 1977 — Decided April 19, 1978

⊥620 Mr. *Chief Justice* BURGER announced the judgment of the Court and delivered an opinion in which Mr. *Justice* POWELL, Mr. *Justice* REHNQUIST, and Mr. *Justice* STEVENS joined.

The question presented by this appeal is whether a Tennessee statute barring "Ministers of the Gospel, or priest[s] of any denomination whatever" from serving as delegates to the State's limited constitutional convention deprived appellant McDaniel, an ordained minister, of the right to the free exercise of religion guaranteed by the First Amendment and made applicable to the States by the Fourteenth Amendment. The First Amendment forbids laws "prohibiting the free exercise" of religion. **⊥621**

I

In its first constitution, in 1796, Tennessee disqualified ministers from serving as legislators.*

That disqualifying provision has continued unchanged since its adoption; it is now Art. IX, § 1 of the state constitution. The state legislature applied this provision to candidates for delegate to the State's 1977 limited constitutional convention when it enacted Chapter 848, Section 4 of the 1976 Tennessee Public Acts: "Any citizen of the state who can qualify for membership in the House of Representatives of the General Assembly may become a candidate for delegate to the convention. . . ."

McDaniel, an ordained minister of a Baptist Church in Chattanooga, Tenn., filed as a candidate for delegate to the constitutional convention. An opposing candidate, appellee Selma Cash Paty, sued in the Chancery Court for a declaratory judgment that McDaniel was disqualified to serve as a delegate and for a judgment striking his name from the ballot. Chancellor Franks of the Chancery Court held that § 4 of ch. 848 violated the First and Fourteenth Amendments to the Federal Constitution and declared McDaniel eligible for the office of delegate. Accordingly, McDaniel's name remained on the ballot and in the ensuing election he was elected by a vote almost equal to that of three opposing candidates.

After the election, the Tennessee Supreme Court reversed the Chancery Court, holding that the disqualification of clergy imposed no burden upon "religious belief" and restricted "religious action . . . [only] in the law making process of government—where religious action is absolutely prohibited by the establishment clause. . . ." **⊥622** The state interest in preventing the establishment of religion and in avoiding the divisiveness and tendency to channel political activity along religious lines, resulting from clergy participation in political affairs, were deemed by that court sufficiently weighty to justify the disqualification, notwithstanding the guarantee of the Free Exercise Clause.

We noted probable jurisdiction.

II

A

The disqualification of ministers from legislative office was a practice carried from England by seven of the original States; later six new States similarly excluded clergymen from some political offices. In England the practice of excluding clergy from the House of Commons was justified on a variety of grounds: to prevent dual office holding, that is, membership by a minister in both Parliament and Convocation; to insure that the priest or deacon devoted himself to his "sacred calling" rather than to "such mundane activities as were appropriate to a member of the House of Commons"; and to prevent ministers, who after 1533 were subject to the Crown's powers over the benefices of the clergy, from using membership in Commons to diminish its independence by increasing the influence of the King and the nobility.

The purpose of the several States in providing for disqualification was primarily to assure the success of a new political experiment, the separation of church and state. **⊥623** Prior to 1776, most of the 13 colonies had some form of an established, or government-sponsored, church. Even after ratification of the First Amendment, which prohibited the Federal Government from following such a course, some States continued pro-establishment provisions. Massachusetts, the last State to accept disestablishment, did so in 1833.

In light of this history and a widespread awareness during that period of undue and often dominant clerical influence in public and political affairs here, in England, and on the Continent, it is not surprising that strong views were held by some that one way to assure disestablishment was to keep clergymen out of public office. Indeed, some of the foremost political philosophers and statesmen of that period held such views regarding the clergy. Earlier, John Locke argued for confining the authority of the English clergy "within the bounds of the church, nor can it in any manner be extended to civil af-

---

*"Whereas ministers of the gospel are, by their profession, dedicated to God and the care of Souls, and ought not to be diverted from the great duties of their functions, therefore, no ministers of the gospel, or priest of any denomination whatever, shall be eligible to a seat in either House of the legislature." Tenn. Const, of 1796, Art. VIII, § 1.

fairs; because the church itself is a thing absolutely separate and distinct from the commonwealth." Thomas Jefferson initially advocated such a position in his 1783 draft of a constitution for Virginia. James Madison, however, disagreed and vigorously urged ⊥**624** the position which in our view accurately reflects the spirit and purpose of the Religion Clauses of the First Amendment. Madison's response to Jefferson's position was:

"Does not The exclusion of Ministers of the Gospel as such violate a fundamental principle of liberty by punishing a religious profession with the privation of a civil right? does it [not] violate another article of the plan itself which exempts religion from the cognizance of Civil power? does it not violate justice by at once taking away a right and prohibiting a compensation for it? does it not in fine violate impartiality by shutting the door against the Ministers of one Religion and leaving it open for those of every other."

Madison was not the only articulate opponent of clergy disqualification. When proposals were made earlier to prevent clergymen from holding public office, John Witherspoon, a Presbyterian minister, president of Princeton University, and the only clergyman to sign the Declaration of Independence, made a cogent protest and, with tongue in cheek, offered an amendment to a provision much like that challenged here:

"No clergyman, of any denomination, shall be capable of being elected a member of the Senate or House of Representatives, because (here insert the grounds of offensive disqualification, which I have been able to discover). Provided always, and it is the true intent and meaning of this part of the constitution, that if at any time he shall be completely deprived of the clerical character by those by whom he was invested with it, as by deposition for cursing and swearing, drunkenness or uncleanness, he shall then be fully restored to all the privileges of a free ⊥**625** citizen; his offense [of being a clergyman] shall no more be remembered against him; but he may be chosen either to the Senate or House of Representatives, and shall be treated with all the respect due to his *brethren*, the other members of Assembly."

As the value of the disestablishment experiment was perceived, 11 of the 13 States disqualifying the clergy from some types of public office gradually abandoned that limitation. New York, for example, took that step in 1846 after delegates to the State's constitutional convention argued that the exclusion of clergymen from the legislature was an "odious distinction." Only Maryland and Tennessee continued their clergy disqualification provisions into this century and, in 1974, a three-judge District Court held Maryland's provision violative of the First and Fourteenth Amendments' guarantees of the free exercise of religion. Today Tennessee remains the only State excluding ministers from certain public offices.

The essence of this aspect of our national history is that in all but a few States the selection or rejection of clergymen for public office soon came to be viewed as something safely left to the good sense and desires of the people.

B

This brief review of the history of clergy disqualification provisions also amply demonstrates, however, that, at least during the early segment of our national life, those provisions enjoyed the support of responsible American statesmen and were accepted as having a rational basis. Against this background we do not lightly invalidate a statute enacted pursuant to a provision of a state constitution which has been sustained by its highest court. The challenged provision came to the Tennessee Supreme Court clothed with the presumption of validity to which that court was bound to give deference.

⊥**626** However, the right to the free exercise of religion unquestionably encompasses the right to preach, proselyte, and perform other similar religious functions, or, in other words, to be a minister of the type McDaniel was found to be. *Murdock* v. *Pennsylvania*, *Cantwell* v. *Connecticut*. Tennessee also acknowledges the right of its adult citizens generally to seek and hold office as legislators or delegates to the state constitutional convention. Yet under the clergy disqualification provision, McDaniel can not exercise both rights simultaneously because the State has conditioned the exercise of one on the surrender of the other. Or, in James Madison's words, the State is "punishing a religious profession with the privation of a civil right." In so doing, Tennessee has encroached upon McDaniel's right to the free exercise of religion, "[T]o condition the availability of benefits [including access to the ballot] upon this appellant's willingness to violate a cardinal principle of [his] religious faith [by surrendering his religiously impelled ministry] effectively penalizes the free exercise of [his] constitutional liberties." *Sherbert* v. *Verner*.

If the Tennessee disqualification provision were viewed as depriving the clergy of a civil right solely because of their religious beliefs, our inquiry would be at an end. The Free Exercise Clause categorically forbids government from regulating, prohibiting or rewarding religious beliefs as such. *Sherbert* v. *Verner; Cantwell* v. *Connecticut*. In *Torcaso* v. *Watkins* the Court reviewed the Maryland constitutional requirement that all holders of "any office of profit or trust in this State" declare their belief in the existence of God. In striking down the Maryland requirement, the Court did not evaluate the interests assertedly justifying it but rather held that it violated freedom of religious belief.

In our view, however, *Torcaso* does not govern. By its ⊥**627** terms, the Tennessee disqualification operates against McDaniel because of his *status* as a "minister" or "priest." The meaning of those words is, of course, a question of state law. And although the question has not been examined extensively in state law sources, such authority as is available indicates that ministerial status is defined in terms of conduct and activity rather than in terms of belief. Because the Tennessee disqualification is directed primarily at status, acts and conduct it is unlike the requirement in *Torcaso*, which focused on *belief*.

Hence, the Free Exercise Clause's absolute prohibition of infringements on the "freedom to believe" is inapposite here.

This does not mean, of course, that the disqualification escapes judicial scrutiny or that McDaniel's activity does not enjoy significant First Amendment protection. The Court ⊥**628** recently declared in *Wisconsin* v. *Yoder*: "The essence of all that has been said and written on the subject is that only those interests of the highest order and those not otherwise served can overbalance legitimate claims to the free exercise of religion."

Tennessee asserts that its interest in preventing the establishment of a state religion is consistent with the Establishment Clause and thus of the highest order. The constitutional history of the several States reveals that generally the interest in preventing establishment prompted the adoption of clergy disqualification provisions; Tennessee does not appear to be an exception to this pattern. There is no occasion to inquire whether promoting such an interest is a permissible legislative goal, however, for Tennessee has failed to demonstrate that its views of the dangers of clergy participation in the political process have not lost whatever validity they may once have enjoyed. The essence of the rationale underlying the Tennessee restriction on ministers is that if elected to public office they will necessarily exercise ⊥**629** their powers and influence to promote the interests of one sect or thwart the interests of another thus pitting one against the others, contrary to the anti-establishment principle with its command of neutrality. See *Walz* v. *Tax Commission*. However widely that view may have been held in the 18th century by many, including enlightened statesmen of that day, the American experience provides no persuasive support for the fear that clergymen in public office will be less careful of anti-establishment interests or less faithful to their oaths of civil office than their unordained counterparts.

We hold that § 4 of ch. 848 violates McDaniel's First Amendment right to the free exercise of his religion made applicable to the States by the Fourteenth Amendment. Accordingly, the judgment of the Tennessee Supreme Court is reversed and the case is remanded to that court for further proceedings not inconsistent with this opinion.

Reversed and remanded.

Mr. *Justice* BLACKMUN took no part in the consideration or decision of this case.

Mr. *Justice* BRENNAN, with whom Mr. *Justice* MARSHALL joins, concurring in the judgment.

I would hold that § 4 of the legislative call to the Tennessee constitutional convention, to the extent that it incorporates ⊥**630** Art. IX, § 1, of the Tennessee Constitution, violates both the Free Exercise and Establishment Clauses of the First Amendment as applied to the States through the Fourteenth Amendment. I therefore concur in the reversal of the judgment of the Tennessee Supreme Court.

I

The Tennessee Supreme Court sustained Tennessee's exclusion on the ground that it "does not infringe upon religious belief or religious action within the protection of the free exercise clause[, and] that such indirect burden as may be imposed upon ministers and priests by excluding them from the lawmaking process of government is justified by the compelling state interest in maintaining the wall of separation between church and state." In reaching this conclusion, the state court relied on two interrelated propositions which are inconsistent with decisions of this Court. The first is that a distinction may be made between "religious belief or religious action" on the one hand, and the "career or calling" of the ministry on the other. The court stated that "[i]t is not religious belief, but the career or calling, by which one is identified as dedicated to the full time promotion of the religious objectives of a particular religious sect, that disqualifies." The second is that the disqualification provision does not interfere with the free exercise of religion because the practice of the ministry is left unimpaired; only candidacy for legislative office is proscribed.

⊥**631** The characterization of the exclusion as one burdening appellant's "career or calling" and not religious belief cannot withstand analysis. Clearly freedom of belief protected by the Free Exercise Clause embraces freedom to profess or practice that belief, even including doing so to earn a livelihood. One's religious belief surely does not cease to enjoy the protection of the First Amendment when held with such depth of sincerity as to impel one to join the ministry.

Whether or not the provision discriminates among religions (and I accept for purposes of discussion the State Supreme ⊥**632** Court's construction that it does not), it establishes a religious classification—involvement in protected religious activity—governing the eligibility for office which I believe is absolutely prohibited. The provision imposes a unique disability upon those who exhibit a defined level of intensity of involvement in protected religious activity. Such a classification as much imposes a test for office based on religious conviction as one based on denominational preference. A law which limits political participation to those who eschew prayer, public worship, or the ministry as much establishes a religious test as one which disqualifies Catholics, or Jews, or Protestants. *Wieman* v. *Updegraff*. Because the challenged provision establishes as a condition of office the willingness to eschew certain protected religious practices, *Torcaso* v. *Watkins* compels the conclusion that it violates the Free Exercise Clause. *Torcaso* struck down Maryland's requirement that an appointee to the office of Notary Public declare his belief in the existence of God expressly disavowing "the historically and constitutionally discredited policy of probing religious beliefs by test oaths or limiting public offices to persons who have, or perhaps more properly profess to have, a belief in some particular kind ⊥**633** of religious concept." That principle equally condemns the religious qualification for elective office imposed by Tennessee.

The second proposition—that the law does not interfere with free exercise because it does not directly prohibit religious activity, but merely conditions eligibility for office on its abandonment—is also squarely rejected by precedent. In *Sherbert* v. *Verner* a state statute disqualifying from unemployment compensation benefits persons unwilling to work on Saturdays was held to violate the Free Exercise Clause as applied to a Sabbatarian whose religious faith forbade Saturday work. That decision turned upon the fact that "[t]he ruling forces her to choose between following the precepts of her religion and forfeiting benefits, on the one hand, and abandoning one of the precepts of her religion in order to accept work, on the other hand. Governmental imposition of such a choice puts the same kind of burden upon the free exercise of religion as would a fine imposed against appellant for her Saturday worship." Similarly, in "prohibiting legislative service because of a person's leadership role in a religious faith," Tennessee's disqualification provision imposed an unconstitutional penalty upon appellant's exercise of his religious faith.

⊥**634** Nor can Tennessee's political exclusion be distinguished from *Sherbert's* welfare disqualification as the Tennessee court thought, by suggesting that the unemployment compensation involved in *Sherbert* was necessary to sustain life while participation in the Constitutional Convention is a voluntary activity not itself compelled by religious belief. *Torcaso* answers that contention. There we held that "[t]he fact . . . that a person is not compelled to hold public office cannot possibly be an excuse for barring him from office by state-imposed criteria forbidden by the Constitution."

The opinion of the Tennessee Supreme Court makes clear that the statute requires appellant's disqualification solely because he is a minister of a religious faith. If appellant were to renounce his ministry, presumably he could regain eligibility for elective office, but if he does not, he must forego an opportunity for political participation he otherwise would enjoy. *Sherbert* and *Torcaso* compel the conclusion that because the challenged provision requires appellant to purchase his right to engage in the ministry by sacrificing his candidacy it impairs the free exercise of his religion.

The plurality recognizes that *Torcaso* held "categorically forbid[den]," a provision disqualifying from political office on the basis of religious belief, but draws what I respectfully suggest is a sophistic distinction between that holding and Tennessee's disqualification provision. The purpose of the Tennessee provision is not to regulate activities associated with a ministry, such as dangerous snake-handling or human sacrifice, which the State validly could prohibit, but to bar from political office persons regarded as deeply committed to religious participation because of that participation—participation itself not regarded as harmful by the State and which therefore must be conceded to be protected. As the plurality recognizes, petitioner was disqualified because he "fill[ed] a 'leadership role in religion,' and . . . 'dedicated ⊥**635** [himself] to the full time *promotion* of the religious objectives of a particular religious sect.' (emphasis added)." According to the plurality, McDaniel could not be and was not in fact barred for *his* belief in religion, but was barred because of his commitment to persuade or lead others to accept that belief. I simply cannot fathom why the Free Exercise Clause "categorically forbids" hinging qualification for office on the act of declaring a belief in religion, but not on the act of discussing that belief with others. ⊥**636**

II

The State Supreme Court's justification of the prohibition, echoed here by the State, as intended to prevent those most intensely involved in religion from injecting sectarian goals and policies into the lawmaking process, and thus to avoid fomenting religious strife or the fusing of church with state affairs, itself raises the question whether the exclusion violates the Establishment Clause. As construed, the exclusion manifests patent hostility toward, not nonneutrality in respect of, religion, forces or influences a minister or priest to abandon his ministry as the price of public office, and in sum, has a primary effect which inhibits religion. See *Everson* v. *Board of Education; McCollum* v. *Board of Education; Torcaso* v. *Watkins; Lemon* v. *Kurtzman; Meek* v. *Pittenger*.

⊥**637** The fact that responsible statesmen of the day, including some of the United States Constitution's Framers, were attracted by the concept of clergy disqualification does not provide historical support for concluding that those provisions are harmonious with the Establishment Clause. Notwithstanding the presence of such provisions in seven state constitutions when the Constitution was being written, the Framers refused to follow suit. That the disqualification provisions contained in state constitutions contemporaneous with the United States Constitution and the Bill of Rights cannot furnish a guide concerning the understanding of the harmony of such provisions with the Establishment Clause is evident from the presence in state constitutions, side-by-side with disqualification clauses, of provisions which would have clearly contravened the First Amendment had it applied to the States, such as those creating an official church, and limiting political office to Protestants or theistic believers generally. In short, the regime of religious liberty embodied in state constitutions was very different from that established by the Constitution of the United States. When, with the adoption of the Fourteenth Amendment, the strictures of the First Amendment became wholly applicable to the States, see *Cantwell* v. *Connecticut; Everson* v. *Board of Education*, earlier conceptions of permissible state action with respect to religion—including those regarding clergy disqualification—were superseded.

Our decisions interpreting the Establishment Clause have aimed at maintaining erect the wall between church and state. ⊥**638** State governments, like the Federal Government, have been required to refrain from favoring the tenets or adherents of any religion or of religion over nonreligion, from insinuating themselves in ecclesiastical affairs or disputes, and from establishing programs which unnecessarily or excessively entangle government with religion. On the other hand, the Court's decisions have indicated that the limits of permissible governmental action with respect to religion under the Establishment Clause must reflect an appropriate accommodation of our heritage as a religious people whose freedom to develop and preach religious ideas and practices is protected by the Free Exercise Clause. Thus, we have rejected as unfaithful to our constitutionally protected tradition of religious liberty, any conception of the Religion Clauses as stating a "strict no-aid" theory or as stating a unitary principle, that "religion may not be used as a basis for classification for purposes of governmental action, whether that action be the conferring of rights or privileges or the imposition of duties or obliga⊥**639**tions." Such rigid conceptions of neutrality have been tempered by constructions upholding religious classifications where necessary to avoid "[a] manifestation of . . . hostility [toward religion] at war with our national tradition as embodied in the First Amendment's guaranty of the free exercise of religion." *McCollum* v. *Board of Education*. This understanding of the interrelationship of the Religion Clauses has permitted government to take religion into account when necessary to further secular purposes unrelated to the advancement of religion, and to exempt, when possible, from generally applicable governmental regulation individuals whose religious beliefs and practices would otherwise thereby be infringed, or to create without state involvement an atmosphere in which voluntary religious exercise may flourish.

Beyond these limited situations in which government may take cognizance of religion for purposes of accommodating our traditions of religious liberty, government may not use religion as a basis of classification for the imposition of duties, penalties, privileges or benefits. "State power is no more to be used so as to handicap religions, than it is to favor them." *Everson* v. *Board of Education*.

Tennessee nevertheless invokes the Establishment Clause to excuse the imposition of a civil disability upon those deemed ⊥**640** to be deeply involved in religion. In my view, that Clause will not permit, much less excuse or condone, the deprivation of religious liberty here involved.

Fundamental to the conception of religious liberty protected by the Religion Clauses is the idea that religious beliefs are a matter of voluntary choice by individuals and their associations, and that each sect is entitled to "flourish according to the zeal of its adherents and the appeal of its dogma." *Zorach* v. *Clauson*. Accordingly, religious ideas, no less than any other, may be the subject of debate which is "uninhibited, robust, and wide-open . . ." *New York Times Co.* v. *Sullivan*. Government may not interfere with efforts to proselyte or worship in public places. *Kunz* v. *New York*. It may not tax the dissemination of religious ideas. *Murdock* v. *Pennsylvania*. It may not seek to shield its citizens from those who would solicit them with their religious beliefs. *Martin* v. *City of Struthers*.

That public debate of religious ideas, like any other, may arouse emotion, may incite, may foment religious divisiveness and strife does not rob it of constitutional protection. *Cantwell* v. *Connecticut*; cf. *Terminiello* v. *Chicago*. The mere fact that a purpose of the Establishment Clause is to reduce or eliminate religious divisiveness or strife, does not place religious discussion, association, or political participation in a status less preferred than rights of discussion, association and political participation generally. "Adherents of particular faiths and individual churches frequently take strong positions on public ⊥**641** issues including . . . vigorous advocacy of legal or constitutional positions. Of course, churches as much as secular bodies and private citizens have that right." *Walz* v. *Tax Commission*.

The State's goal of preventing sectarian bickering and strife may not be accomplished by regulating religious speech and political association. The Establishment Clause does not license government to treat religion and those who teach or practice it, simply by virtue of their status as such, as subversive of American ideals and therefore subject to unique disabilities. Cf. *Wieman* v. *Updegraff*. Government may not inquire into the religious beliefs and motivations of officeholders—it may not remove them from office merely for making public statements regarding religion, nor question whether their legislative actions stem from religious conviction. Cf. *Bond* v. *Floyd*.

In short, government may not as a goal promote "safe-thinking" with respect to religion and fence out from political participation those, such as ministers, whom it regards as overinvolved in religion. Religionists no less than members of any other group enjoy the full measure of protection afforded speech, association and political activity generally. The Establishment Clause, properly understood, is a shield against any attempt by government to inhibit religion as it has done here; *Abington School District* v. *Schempp*. It may not be used as a sword to justify repression of religion or its adherents from any aspect of public life.

⊥**642** Our decisions under the Establishment Clause prevent government from supporting or involving itself in religion or from becoming drawn into ecclesiastical disputes. These prohibitions naturally tend, as they were designed to, to avoid channelling political activity along religious lines and to reduce any tendency toward religious divisiveness in society. Beyond enforcing these prohibitions, however, government may not go. The antidote which the Constitution provides against zealots who would inject sectarianism into the political process is to subject their ideas to refutation in the marketplace of ideas and their platforms to rejection at the polls. With these safeguards, it is unlikely that they will succeed in inducing government to act along religiously divisive lines, and, with judicial enforcement of the Establishment Clause, any measure of success they achieve must be short-lived, at best.

Mr. *Justice* STEWART, concurring in the judgment.

Like Mr. *Justice* BRENNAN, I believe that *Torcaso* v. *Watkins* controls this case. There, the Court held that Maryland's refusal to commission Torcaso as a Notary Public because he would not declare his belief in God violated the First Amendment, as incorporated by the Fourteenth. The offense against the First and Fourteenth Amendments lay not simply in requiring an oath, but in "limiting public offices to persons who have, or perhaps more properly profess to have, a belief in some particular kind of religious concept." As the Court noted, "The Fact . . . that a person is not compelled to hold public office cannot possibly be ⊥**643** an excuse for barring him from office by state-imposed criteria forbidden by the Constitution." Except for the fact that Tennessee bases its disqualification not on a person's statement of belief but on his decision to pursue a religious vocation as directed by his belief, that case is indistinguishable from this one—and that sole distinction is without constitutional consequence.

Mr. *Justice* WHITE, concurring in the judgment.

While I share the view of my Brothers that Tennessee's disqualification of ministers from serving as delegates to the State's constitutional convention is constitutionally impermissible, I disagree as to the basis for this invalidity. Rather than relying on the Free Exercise Clause, as do the other Members of the Court, I would hold Chapter 848, Section 4 of the 1976 Tennessee Public Acts unconstitutional under the Equal Protection Clause of the Fourteenth Amendment.

The plurality states that § 4 "has encroached upon McDaniel's right to the free exercise of religion," but fails to explain in what way McDaniel has been deterred in the observance of his religious beliefs. Certainly he has not felt compelled to abandon the ministry as a result of the challenged statute, nor has he been required to disavow any of his ⊥**644** religious beliefs. Because I am not persuaded that the Tennessee statute in any way interferes with McDaniel's ability to exercise his religion as he desires, I would not rest the decision on the Free Exercise Clause but instead would turn to McDaniel's argument that the statute denies him equal protection of the laws.

Our cases have recognized the importance of the right of an individual to seek elective office and accordingly have afforded careful scrutiny to state regulations burdening that right. In *Lubin* v. *Panish*, for example, we noted: "This legitimate state interest, however, must be achieved by a means that does not unfairly or unnecessarily burden either a minority party's or an individual candidate's equally important interest in the continued availability of political opportunity. The interests involved are not merely those of parties or individual candidates; the voters can assert their preferences only through candidates or parties or both and it is this broad interest that must be weighed in the balance. The right of a party or an individual to a place on a ballot is entitled to protection and is intertwined with the rights of voters."

Recognizing that "the rights of voters and the rights of candidates do not lend themselves to neat separation . . .," *Bullock* v. *Carter*, the Court has required States to provide substantial justification for any requirement that prevents a class of citizens from gaining ballot access and has held unconstitutional state laws requiring the payment of prohibitively large filing fees, requiring the payment of even moderate fees by indigent candidates, and ⊥**645** having the effect of excluding independent and minority party candidates from the ballot.

The restriction in this case, unlike the ones challenged in the previous cases, is absolute on its face: there is no way in which a Tennessee minister can qualify as a candidate for the State's constitutional convention. The State's asserted interest in this absolute disqualification is its desire to maintain the required separation between church and state. While the State recognizes that not all ministers would necessarily allow their religious commitments to interfere with their duties to the State and to their constituents, it asserts that the potential for such conflict is sufficiently great to justify § 4's candidacy disqualification.

Although the State's interest is a legitimate one, close scrutiny reveals that the challenged law is not "reasonably necessary to the accomplishment of . . ." that objective. *Bullock.* All 50 States are required by the First and Fourteenth Amendments to maintain a separation between church and state, and yet all of the States other than Tennessee are able to achieve this objective without burdening ministers' rights to candidacy. This suggests that the underlying assumption on which the Tennessee statute is based—that a minister's duty to the superiors of his church will interfere with his governmental service—is unfounded. Moreover, the rationale of the Tennessee statute is undermined by the fact that it is both underinclusive and overinclusive. While the State asserts an interest in keeping religious and governmental interests separate, the disqualification of ministers applies only to legislative positions, and not to executive and judicial offices. On the other hand, that statute's sweep is also overly broad, for it applies with equal force to those ministers whose religious beliefs would not prevent them from properly discharging their duties as constitutional convention delegates.

⊥**646** The facts of this case show that the voters of McDaniel's district desired to have him represent them at the limited constitutional convention. Because I conclude that the State's justification for frustrating the desires of these voters and for depriving McDaniel and all other ministers of the right to seek this position is insufficient, I would hold § 4 unconstitutional as a violation of the Equal Protection Clause.

GOLDMAN v. WEINBERGER

475 U.S. 503
ON WRIT OF CERTIORARI TO THE UNITED STATES COURT OF APPEALS FOR THE DISTRICT OF COLUMBIA CIRCUIT
Argued January 14, 1986 — Decided March 25, 1986

⊥**504** *Justice REHNQUIST* delivered the opinion of the Court.

Petitioner S. Simcha Goldman contends that the Free Exercise Clause of the First Amendment to the United States Constitution permits him to wear a yarmulke while in uniform, notwithstanding an Air Force regulation mandating uniform dress for Air Force personnel. The District Court for the District of Columbia permanently enjoined the Air Force from enforcing its regulation against petitioner and from penalizing him for wearing his yarmulke. The Court of Appeals for the District of Columbia Circuit reversed on the ground that the Air Force's strong interest in discipline justified the strict enforcement of its uniform dress requirements. We granted certiorari because of the importance of the question, and now affirm.

Petitioner Goldman is an Orthodox Jew and ordained rabbi. In 1973, he was accepted into the Armed Forces Health Professions Scholarship Program and placed on inactive reserve status in the Air Force while he studied clinical psychology at Loyola University of Chicago. During his three years in the scholarship program, he received a monthly stipend and an allowance for tuition, books, and fees. After completing his Ph.D. in psychology, petitioner ⊥**505** entered active service in the United States Air Force as a commissioned officer, in accordance with a requirement that participants in the scholarship program serve one year of active duty for each year of subsidized education. Petitioner was stationed at March Air Force Base in Riverside, California, and served as a clinical psychologist at the mental health clinic on the base.

Until 1981, petitioner was not prevented from wearing his yarmulke on the base. He avoided controversy by remaining close to his duty station in the health clinic and by wearing his service cap over the yarmulke when out of doors. But in April 1981, after he testified as a defense witness at a court-martial wearing his yarmulke but not his service cap, opposing counsel lodged a complaint with Colonel Joseph Gregory, the Hospital Commander, arguing that petitioner's practice of wearing his yarmulke was a violation of Air Force Regulation (AFR) 35-10. This regulation states in pertinent part that "[h]eadgear will not be worn . . . [w]hile indoors except by armed security police in the performance of their duties."

Colonel Gregory informed petitioner that wearing a yarmulke while on duty does indeed violate AFR 35-10, and ordered him not to violate this regulation outside the hospital. Although virtually all of petitioner's time on the base was spent in the hospital, he refused. Later, after petitioner's attorney protested to the Air Force General Counsel, Colonel Gregory revised his order to prohibit petitioner from wearing the yarmulke even in the hospital. Petitioner's request to report for duty in civilian clothing pending legal resolution of the issue was denied. The next day he received a formal letter of reprimand, and was warned that failure to obey AFR 35-10 could subject him to a court-martial. Colonel Gregory also withdrew a recommendation that petitioner's application to extend the term of his active service be approved, and substituted a negative recommendation.

⊥**506** Petitioner then sued respondent Secretary of Defense and others, claiming that the application of AFR 35-10 to prevent him from wearing his yarmulke infringed upon his First Amendment freedom to exercise his religious beliefs. The United States District Court for the District of Columbia preliminarily enjoined the enforcement of the regulation, 530 F. Supp. 12 (1981), and then after a full hearing permanently enjoined the Air Force from prohibiting petitioner from wearing a yarmulke while in uniform. Respondents appealed to the Court of Appeals for the District of Columbia Circuit, which reversed. As an initial matter, the Court of Appeals determined that the appropriate level of scrutiny of a military regulation that clashes with a constitutional right is neither strict scrutiny nor rational basis. Instead, it held that a military regulation must be examined to determine whether "legitimate military ends are sought to be achieved," and whether it is "designed to accommodate the individual right to an appropriate degree." Applying this test, the court concluded that "the Air Force's interest in uniformity renders the strict enforcement of its regulation permissible." The full Court of Appeals denied a petition for rehearing en banc, with three judges dissenting.

Petitioner argues that AFR 35-10, as applied to him, prohibits religiously motivated conduct and should therefore be analyzed under the standard enunciated in *Sherbert* v. *Verner*. But we have repeatedly held that "the military is, by necessity, a specialized society separate from civilian society." ⊥**507** *Parker* v. *Levy*. "[T]he military must insist upon a respect for duty and a discipline without counterpart in civilian life," *Schlesinger* v. *Councilman*, in order to prepare for and perform its vital role.

Our review of military regulations challenged on First Amendment grounds is far more deferential than constitutional review of similar laws or regulations designed for civilian society. The military need not encourage debate or tolerate protest to the extent that such tolerance is required of the civilian state by the First Amendment; to accomplish its mission the military must foster instinctive obedience, unity, commitment, and esprit de corps. The essence of military service "is the subordination of the desires and interests of the individual to the needs of the service." *Orloff* v. *Willoughby*.

These aspects of military life do not, of course, render entirely nugatory in the military context the guarantees of the First Amendment. But "within the military community there is simply not the same [individual] autonomy as there is in the larger civilian community." *Parker* v. *Levy*. In the context of the present case, when evaluating whether military needs justify a particular restriction on religiously motivated conduct, courts must give great deference to the professional judgment of military authorities concerning the relative importance of a particular military interest. Not only are courts "'ill-equipped to determine the impact upon discipline that any particular intrusion upon military authority might have,'" *Chappell* v. *Wallace*, ⊥**508** but the military authorities have been charged by the Executive and Legislative Branches with carrying out our Nation's military policy. "Judicial deference . . . is at its apogee when legislative action under the congressional authority to raise and support armies and make rules and regulations for their governance is challenged." *Rostker* v. *Goldberg*.

The considered professional judgment of the Air Force is that the traditional outfitting of personnel in standardized uniforms encourages the subordination of personal preferences and identities in favor of the overall group mission. Uniforms encourage a sense of hierarchical unity by tending to eliminate outward individual distinctions except for those of rank. The Air Force considers them as vital during peacetime as during war because its personnel must be ready to provide an effective defense on a moment's notice; the necessary habits of discipline and unity must be developed in advance of trouble. We have acknowledged that "[t]he inescapable demands of military procedures and orders must be virtually reflex with no time for debate or reflection." *Chappell* v. *Wallace*.

To this end, the Air Force promulgated AFR 35-10, a 190-page document, which states that "Air Force members will wear the Air Force uniform while performing their military duties, except when authorized to wear civilian clothes on duty." The rest of the document describes in minute detail all of the various items of apparel that must be worn as part of the Air Force uniform. It authorizes a few individualized options with respect to certain pieces of jewelry and hair style, but even these are subject to severe limitations. In general, authorized headgear may ⊥**509** be worn only out of doors. Indoors, "[h]eadgear [may] not be worn . . . except by armed security police in the performance of their duties." A narrow exception to this rule exists for headgear worn during indoor religious ceremonies. In addition, military commanders may in their discretion permit visible religious headgear and other such apparel in designated living quarters and nonvisible items generally.

Petitioner Goldman contends that the Free Exercise Clause of the First Amendment requires the Air Force to make an exception to its uniform dress requirements for religious apparel unless the accoutrements create a "clear danger" of undermining discipline and esprit de corps. He asserts that in general, visible but "unobtrusive" apparel will not create such a danger and must therefore be accommodated. He argues that the Air Force failed to prove that specific exception for his practice of wearing an unobtrusive yarmulke would threaten discipline. He contends that the Air Force's assertion to the contrary is mere *ipse dixit*, with no support from actual experience or a scientific study in the record, and is contradicted by expert testimony that religious exceptions to AFR 35-10 are in fact desirable and will increase morale by making the Air Force a more humane place.

But whether or not expert witnesses may feel that religious exceptions to AFR 35-10 are desirable is quite beside the point. The desirability of dress regulations in the military is decided by the appropriate military officials, and they are under no constitutional mandate to abandon their considered professional judgment. Quite obviously, to the extent the regulations do not permit the wearing of religious apparel such as a yarmulke, a practice described by petitioner as silent devotion akin to prayer, military life may be more objectionable for petitioner and probably others. But the First Amendment does not require the military to accommodate ⊥**510** such practices in the face of its view that they would detract from the uniformity sought by the dress regulations. The Air Force has drawn the line essentially between religious apparel which is visible and that which is not, and we hold that those portions of the regulations challenged here reasonably and evenhandedly regulate dress in the interest of the military's perceived need for uniformity. The First Amendment therefore does not prohibit them from being applied to petitioner even though their effect is to restrict the wearing of the headgear required by his religious beliefs.

The judgment of the Court of Appeals is
Affirmed.

Justice STEVENS, with whom *Justice* WHITE and *Justice* POWELL join, concurring.

Captain Goldman presents an especially attractive case for an exception from the uniform regulations that are applicable to all other Air Force personnel. His devotion to this faith is readily apparent. The yarmulke is a familiar and accepted sight. In addition to its religious significance for the wearer, the yarmulke may evoke the deepest respect and admiration—the symbol of a distinguished tradition and an ⊥**511** eloquent rebuke to the ugliness of anti-Semitism. Captain Goldman's military duties are performed in a setting in which a modest departure from the uniform regulation creates almost no danger of impairment of the Air Force's military mission. Moreover, on the record before us, there is reason to believe that the policy of strict enforcement against Captain Goldman had a retaliatory motive—he had worn his yarmulke while testifying on behalf of a defendant in a court-martial proceeding. Nevertheless, as the case has been argued, ⊥**512** I believe we must test the validity of the Air Force's rule not merely as it applies to Captain Goldman but also as it applies to all service personnel who have sincere religious beliefs that may conflict with one or more military commands.

Justice BRENNAN is unmoved by the Government's concern "that while a yarmulke might not seem obtrusive to a Jew, neither does a turban to a Sikh, a saffron robe to a Satchidananda Ashram-Integral Yogi, nor do dreadlocks to a Rastafarian." He correctly points out that "turbans, saffron robes, and dreadlocks are not before us in this case," and then suggests that other cases may be fairly decided by reference to a reasonable standard based on "functional utility, health and safety considerations, and the goal of a polished, professional appearance." As the Court has explained, this approach attaches no weight to the separate interest in uniformity itself. Because professionals in the military service attach great importance to that plausible interest, it is one that we must recognize as legitimate and rational even though personal experience or admiration for the performance of the "rag-tag band of soldiers" that won us our freedom in the revolutionary war might persuade us that the Government has exaggerated the importance of that interest.

The interest in uniformity, however, has a dimension that is of still greater importance for me. It is the interest in uniform treatment for the members of all religious faiths. The very strength of Captain Goldman's claim creates the danger that a similar claim on behalf of a Sikh or a Rastafarian might readily be dismissed as "so extreme, so unusual, or so faddish an image that public confidence in his ability to perform his duties will be destroyed." If exceptions from dress code regulations are to be granted on the basis of a multifactored test such as that proposed by *Justice* BRENNAN, inevitably the decisionmaker's evaluation of the charac⊥**513**ter and the sincerity of the requestor's faith—as well as the probable reaction of the majority to the favored treatment of a member of that faith—will play a critical part in the decision. For the difference between a turban or a dreadlock on the one hand, and a yarmulke on the other, is not merely a difference in "appearance"—it is also the difference between a Sikh or a Rastafarian, on the one hand, and an Orthodox Jew on the other. The Air Force has no business drawing distinctions between such persons when it is enforcing commands of universal application.

As the Court demonstrates, the rule that is challenged in this case is based on a neutral, completely objective standard—visibility. It was not motivated by hostility against, or any special respect for, any religious faith. An exception for yarmulkes would represent a fundamental departure from the true principle of uniformity that supports that rule. For that reason, I join the Court's opinion and its judgment.

Justice BRENNAN, with whom *Justice* MARSHALL joins, dissenting.

Simcha Goldman invokes this Court's protection of his First Amendment right to fulfill one of the traditional religious obligations of a male Orthodox Jew—to cover his head before an omnipresent God. The Court's response to Gold⊥**514**man's request is to abdicate its role as principal expositor of the Constitution and protector of individual liberties in favor of credulous deference to unsupported assertions of military necessity. I dissent.

I

In ruling that the paramount interests of the Air Force override Dr. Goldman's free exercise claim, the Court overlooks the sincere and serious nature of his constitutional claim. It suggests that the desirability of certain dress regulations, rather than a First Amendment right, is at issue. The Court declares that in selecting dress regulations, "military officials are under no constitutional mandate to abandon their considered professional judgment." If Dr. Goldman wanted to wear a hat to keep his head warm or to cover a bald spot I would join the majority. Mere personal preferences in dress are not constitutionally protected. The First Amendment, however, restrains the Government's ability to prevent an Orthodox Jewish serviceman from, or punish him for, wearing a yarmulke.

The Court also attempts, unsuccessfully, to minimize the burden that was placed on Dr. Goldman's rights. The fact that "the regulations don't permit the wearing of . . . a yarmulke," does not simply render military life for observant Orthodox Jews "objectionable." It sets up an almost absolute bar to the fulfillment of a religious duty. Dr. Goldman spent most of his time in uniform indoors, where the dress code forbade him even from covering his head with his service cap. Consequently, he was asked to violate the tenets of his faith virtually every minute of every work day.

II

A

Dr. Goldman has asserted a substantial First Amendment claim, which is entitled to meaningful review by this Court. ⊥**515** The Court, however, evades its responsibility by eliminating, in all but name only, judicial review of military regulations that interfere with the fundamental constitutional rights of service personnel.

Our cases have acknowledged that in order to protect our treasured liberties, the military must be able to command service members to sacrifice a great many of the individual freedoms they enjoyed in the civilian community and to endure certain limitations on the freedoms they retain. Notwithstanding this acknowledgment, we have steadfastly maintained that "'our citizens in uniform may not be stripped of basic rights simply because they have doffed their civilian clothes.'" *Chappell* v. *Wallace*. And, while we have hesitated, due to our lack of expertise concerning military affairs and our respect for the delegated authority of a coordinate branch, to strike down restrictions on individual liberties which could reasonably be justified as necessary to the military's vital function, we have never abdicated our obligation of judicial review.

Today the Court eschews its constitutionally mandated role. It adopts for review of military decisions affecting First Amendment rights a subrational-basis standard—absolute, uncritical "deference to the professional judgment of military authorities." If a branch of the military declares one of its rules sufficiently important to outweigh a service person's constitutional rights, it seems that the Court will accept that conclusion, no matter how absurd or unsupported it may be.

⊥**516** A deferential standard of review, however, need not, and should not, mean that the Court must credit arguments that defy common sense. When a military service burdens the free exercise rights of its members in the name of necessity, it must provide, as an initial matter and at a minimum, *credible* explanation of how the contested practice is likely to interfere with the proffered military interest. Unabashed *ipse dixit* cannot outweigh a constitutional right.

In the present case, the Air Force asserts that its interests in discipline and uniformity would be undermined by an exception to the dress code permitting observant male Orthodox Jews to wear yarmulkes. The Court simply restates these assertions without offering any explanation how the exception Dr. Goldman requests reasonably could interfere with the Air Force's interests. Had the Court given actual consideration to Goldman's claim, it would have been compelled to decide in his favor.

B

1

The Government maintains in its brief that discipline is jeopardized whenever exceptions to military regulations are granted. Service personnel must be trained to obey even the most arbitrary command reflexively. Non-Jewish personnel will perceive the wearing of a yarmulke by an Orthodox Jew as an unauthorized departure from the rules and will begin to question the principle of unswerving obedience. Thus shall our fighting forces slip down the treacherous slope ⊥**517** toward unkempt appearance, anarchy, and, ultimately, defeat at the hands of our enemies.

The contention that the discipline of the armed forces will be subverted if Orthodox Jews are allowed to wear yarmulkes with their uniforms surpasses belief. It lacks support in the record of this case and the Air Force offers no basis for it as a general proposition. While the perilous slope permits the services arbitrarily to refuse exceptions requested to satisfy mere personal preferences, before the Air Force may burden free exercise rights it must advance, at the *very least*, a rational reason for doing so.

Furthermore, the Air Force cannot logically defend the content of its rule by insisting that discipline depends upon absolute adherence to whatever rule is established. If, as General Usher admitted at trial, the dress code codified religious exemptions from the "no-headgear-indoors" regulation, then the wearing of a yarmulke would be sanctioned by the code and could not be considered an unauthorized deviation from the rules.

2

The Government also argues that the services have an important interest in uniform dress, because such dress establishes the preeminence of group identity, thus fostering esprit de corps and loyalty to the service that transcends individual bonds. In its brief, the Government characterizes the yarmulke as an assertion in individuality and as a badge of religious and ethnic identity, strongly suggesting that, as such, it could drive a wedge of divisiveness between members of the services.

First, the purported interests of the Air Force in complete uniformity of dress and in elimination of individuality or visible identification with any group other than itself are belied by the service's own regulations. The dress code expressly abjures the need for total uniformity:

⊥**518** "(1) The American public and its elected representatives draw certain conclusions on military effectiveness based on what they see; that is, the image the Air Force presents. The image must instill public confidence and leave no doubt that the service member lives by a common standard and responds to military order and discipline.

"(2) Appearance in uniform is an important part of this image. . . . Neither the Air Force nor the public expects absolute uniformity of appearance. Each member has the right, within limits, to express individuality through his or her appearance. However, the image of a disciplined service member who can be relied on to do his or her job excludes the extreme, the unusual, and the fad."

It cannot be seriously contended that a serviceman in a yarmulke presents so extreme, so unusual, or so faddish an image that public confidence in his ability to perform his duties will be destroyed. Under the Air Force's own standards, then, Dr. Goldman should have and could have been granted an exception to wear his yarmulke.

The dress code also allows men to wear up to three rings and one identification bracelet of "neat and conservative," but non-uniform, design. This jewelry is apparently permitted even if, as is often the case with rings, it associates the wearer with a denominational school or a religious or secular fraternal organization. If these emblems of religious, social, and ethnic identity are not deemed to be unacceptably divisive, the Air Force cannot rationally justify its bar against yarmulkes on that basis.

Moreover, the services allow, and rightly so, other manifestations of religious diversity. It is clear to all service personnel that some members attend Jewish services, some ⊥**519** Christian, some Islamic, and some yet other religious services. Barracks mates see Mormons wearing temple garments, Orthodox Jews wearing tzitzit, and Catholics wearing crosses and scapulars. That they come from different faiths and ethnic backgrounds is not a secret that can or should be kept from them.

I find totally implausible the suggestion that the overarching group identity of the Air Force would be threatened if Orthodox Jews were allowed to wear yarmulkes with their uniforms. To the contrary, a yarmulke worn with a United States military uniform is an eloquent reminder that the shared and proud identity of United States serviceman embraces and unites religious and ethnic pluralism.

Finally, the Air Force argues that while Dr. Goldman describes his yarmulke as an "unobtrusive" addition to his uniform, obtrusiveness is a purely relative, standardless judgment. The Government notes that while a yarmulke might not seem obtrusive to a Jew, neither does a turban to a Sikh, a saffron robe to a Satchidananda Ashram-Integral Yogi, nor do dreadlocks to a Rastafarian. If the Court were to require the Air Force to permit yarmulkes, the service must also allow all of these other forms of dress and grooming.

The Government dangles before the Court a classic parade of horribles, the specter of a brightly-colored, "rag-tag band of soldiers." Although turbans, saffron robes, and dreadlocks are not before us in this case and must each be evaluated against the reasons a service branch offers for prohibiting personnel from wearing them while in uniform, a reviewing court could legitimately give deference to dress and grooming rules that have a *reasoned* basis in, for example, functional utility, health and safety considerations, and the goal of a polished, professional appearance. AFR 35-10, ¶ 1-12a and 1-12a(1) (1978) ⊥**520** (identifying neatness, cleanliness, safety, and military image as the four elements of the dress code's "high standard of dress and personal appearance"). It is the lack of any reasoned basis for prohibiting yarmulkes that is so striking here.

Furthermore, contrary to its intimations, the Air Force has available to it a familiar standard for determining whether a particular style of yarmulke is consistent with a polished, professional military appearance—the "neat and conservative" standard by which the service judges jewelry. No rational reason exists why yarmulkes cannot be judged by the same criterion. Indeed, at argument Dr. Goldman declared himself willing to wear whatever style and color yarmulke the Air Force believes best comports with its uniform.

3

Department of Defense directive 1300.17 (June 18, 1985) grants commanding officers the discretion to permit service personnel to wear religious items and apparel that are not visible with the uniform, such as crosses, temple garments, and scapulars. *Justice* STEVENS favors this "visibility test" because he believes that it does not involve the Air Force in drawing distinctions among faiths. He rejects functional utility, health, and safety considerations, and similar grounds as criteria for religious exceptions to the dress code, because he fears that these standards will allow some service persons to satisfy their religious dress and grooming obligations, while preventing others from fulfilling theirs. But, the visible/not visible standard has that same effect. Furthermore, it restricts the free exercise rights of a larger number of service persons. The visibility test permits "only" individuals whose outer garments and grooming are indistinguishable from those of mainstream Christians to fulfill their religious duties. In my view, the ⊥**521** Constitution requires the selection of criteria that permit the greatest possible number of persons to practice their faiths freely.

Implicit in *Justice STEVENS'* concurrence, and in the Government's arguments, is what might be characterized as a fairness concern. It would be unfair to allow Orthodox Jews to wear yarmulkes, while prohibiting members of other minority faiths with visible dress and grooming requirements from wearing their saffron robes, dreadlocks, turbans, and so forth. While I appreciate and share this concern for the feelings and the free exercise rights of members of these other faiths, I am baffled by this formulation of the problem. What puzzles me is the implication that a neutral standard that could result in the disparate treatment of Orthodox Jews and, for example, Sikhs is *more* troublesome or unfair than the existing neutral standard that does result in the different treatment of Christians, on the one hand, and Orthodox Jews and Sikhs on the other. *Both* standards are constitutionally suspect; before either can be sustained, it must be shown to be a narrowly tailored means of promoting important military interests.

I am also perplexed by the related notion that for purposes of constitutional analysis religious faiths may be divided into two categories—those with visible dress and grooming requirements and those without. This dual category approach seems to incorporate an assumption that fairness, the First Amendment, and, perhaps, Equal Protection, require all faiths belonging to the same category to be treated alike, but permit a faith in one category to be treated differently from a faith belonging to the other category. The practical effect of this categorization is that, under the guise of neutrality and evenhandedness, majority religions are favored over distinctive minority faiths. This dual category analysis is fundamentally flawed and leads to a result that the First Amendment was intended to prevent. Under the Constitution there is only *one* relevant category—*all* faiths. Bur⊥**522**dens placed on the free exercise rights of members of one faith must be justified independently of burdens placed on the rights of members of another religion. It is not enough to say that Jews cannot wear yarmulkes simply because Rastafarians might not be able to wear dreadlocks.

Unless the visible/not visible standard for evaluating requests for religious exceptions to the dress code promotes a significant military interest, it is constitutionally impermissible. *Justice STEVENS* believes that this standard advances an interest in the "uniform treatment" of all religions. As I have shown, that uniformity is illusory, unless uniformity means uniformly accommodating majority religious practices and uniformly rejecting distinctive minority practices. But, more directly, Government agencies are not free to define their own interests in uniform treatment of different faiths. That function has been assigned to the First Amendment. The First Amendment requires that burdens on free exercise rights be justified by independent and important interests that promote the function of the agency. The only independent military interest furthered by the visibility standard is uniformity of dress. And, that interest, as I demonstrated in Part II B §2, *supra*, does not support a prohibition against yarmulkes.

The Air Force has failed utterly to furnish a credible explanation why an exception to the dress code permitting Orthodox Jews to wear neat and conservative yarmulkes while in uniform is likely to interfere with its interest in discipline and uniformity. We cannot "distort the Constitution to approve all that the military may deem expedient." *Korematsu* v. *United States* (Jackson, J., dissenting). Under any meaningful level of judicial review, Simcha Goldman should prevail.

⊥**523** III

Through our Bill of Rights, we pledged ourselves to attain a level of human freedom and dignity that had no parallel in history. Our constitutional commitment to religious freedom and acceptance of religious pluralism is one of our greatest achievements in that noble endeavor. Almost 200 years after the First Amendment was drafted, tolerance and respect for all religions still set us apart from most other countries and draws to our shores refugees from religious persecution from around the world.

Guardianship of this precious liberty is not the exclusive domain of federal courts. It is the responsibility as well of the States and of the other branches of the Federal Government. Our military services have a distinguished record of providing for many of the religious needs of their personnel. But that they have satisfied much of their constitutional obligation does not remove their actions from judicial scrutiny. Our Nation has preserved freedom of religion, not through trusting to the good faith of individual agencies of government alone, but through the constitutionally mandated vigilant oversight and checking authority of the judiciary.

It is not the province of the federal courts to second-guess the professional judgments of the military services, but we are bound by the Constitution to assure ourselves that there exists a rational foundation for assertions of military necessity when they interfere with the free exercise of religion. "The concept of military necessity is seductively broad," and military decisionmakers themselves are as likely to succumb to its allure as are the courts and the general public. Definitions of necessity are influenced by decisionmakers' experiences and values. As a consequence, in pluralistic societies such as ours, institutions dominated by a majority are inevitably, if inadvertently, insensitive to the needs and values of minorities when these needs and values differ from those ⊥**524** of the majority. The military, with its strong ethic of conformity and unquestioning obedience, may be particularly impervious to minority needs and values. A critical function of the Religion Clauses of the First Amendment is to protect the rights of members of minority religions against quiet erosion by majoritarian social institutions that dismiss minority beliefs and practices as unimportant, because unfamiliar. It is the constitutional role of this Court to ensure that this purpose of the First Amendment be realized.

The Court and the military services have presented patriotic Orthodox Jews with a painful dilemma—the choice between fulfilling a religious obligation and serving their country. Should the draft be reinstated, compulsion will replace choice. Although the pain the services inflict on Orthodox Jewish servicemen is clearly the result of insensitivity rather than design, it is unworthy of our military because it is unnecessary. The Court and the military have refused these servicemen their constitutional rights; we must hope that Congress will correct this wrong.

Justice BLACKMUN, dissenting.

I would reverse the judgment of the Court of Appeals, but for reasons somewhat different from those respectively enunciated by *Justice BRENNAN* and *Justice O'CONNOR*. I feel that the Air Force is justified in considering not only the costs of allowing Captain Goldman to cover his head indoors, but also the cumulative costs of accommodating constitutionally indistinguishable requests for religious exemptions. Because, however, the Government has failed to make any ⊥**525** meaningful showing that either set of costs is significant, I dissent from the Court's rejection of Goldman's claim.

The Government concedes that Goldman wears his yarmulke out of sincere religious conviction. For Goldman, as for many other Jews, "a yarmulke is an expression of respect for God . . . intended to keep the wearer aware of God's presence." If the Free Exercise Clause of the First Amendment means anything, it must mean that an individual's desire to follow his or her faith is not simply another personal preference, to be accommodated by government when convenience allows. Indeed, this Court has read the Clause, I believe correctly, to require that "only those interests of the highest order and those not otherwise served can overbalance legitimate claims to the free exercise of religion." *Wisconsin* v. *Yoder*. In general, government "may justify an inroad on religious liberty only by showing that it is the least restrictive means of achieving some compelling state interest." *Thomas* v. *Review Board of Indiana Employment Security Div*. The clear import of *Sherbert*, *Yoder*, and *Thomas* is that this showing must be made even when the inroad results from the "evenhanded" application of a facially neutral requirement. "Rules are rules" is not by itself a sufficient justification for infringing religious liberty.

Nor may free exercise rights be compromised simply because the military says they must be. To be sure, application of the First Amendment to members of the armed services must take into account "the different character of the military community and of the military mission." *Parker* v. *Levy*. As *Justice BRENNAN* and *Justice O'CONNOR* point out, however, military personnel do not forfeit their constitutional rights as a price of enlistment. Except as otherwise required by "interests of the highest order," soldiers as well as civilians are entitled to follow the dictates of their faiths.

⊥526 In my view, this case does not require us to determine the extent to which the ordinary test for inroads on religious freedom must be modified in the military context, because the Air Force has failed to produce even a minimally credible explanation for its refusal to allow Goldman to keep his head covered indoors. I agree with the Court that deference is due the considered judgment of military professionals that, as a general matter, standardized dress serves to promote discipline and esprit de corps. But Goldman's modest supplement to the Air Force uniform clearly poses by itself no threat to the Nation's military readiness. Indeed, the District Court specifically found that Goldman has worn a yarmulke on base for years without any adverse effect on his performance, any disruption of operations at the base, or any complaints from other personnel.

The Air Force argues that it has no way of distinguishing fairly between Goldman's request for an exemption and the potential requests of others whose religious practices may conflict with the appearance code, perhaps in more conspicuous ways. In theory, this argument makes some sense. Like any rules prescribing a uniform, the Air Force dress code is by nature arbitrary; few of its requirements could be defended on purely functional grounds. Particularly for personnel such as Goldman who serve in noncombat roles, variations from the prescribed attire frequently will interfere with no military goals other than those served by uniformity itself. There thus may be no basis on which to distinguish some variations from others, aside from the degree to which they detract from the overall image of the service, a criterion that raises special constitutional problems when applied to religious practices. To allow noncombat personnel to wear yarmulkes but not turbans or dreadlocks because the latter seem more obtrusive—or, as *Justice BRENNAN* suggests, less "polished" and "professional,"—would be to discriminate in favor of this country's more established, **⊥527** mainstream religions, the practices of which are more familiar to the average observer. Not only would conventional faiths receive special treatment under such an approach; they would receive special treatment precisely "because" they are conventional. In general, I see no constitutional difficulty in distinguishing between religious practices based on how difficult it would be to accommodate them, but favoritism based on how unobtrusive a practice appears to the majority could create serious problems of equal protection and religious establishment, problems the Air Force clearly has a strong interest in avoiding by drawing an objective line at visibility.

The problem with this argument, it seems to me, is not doctrinal but empirical. The Air Force simply has not shown any reason to fear that a significant number of enlisted personnel and officers would request religious exemptions that could not be denied on neutral grounds such as safety, let alone that granting these requests would noticeably impair the overall image of the service. The Air Force contends that the potential for such disruption was demonstrated at trial through the introduction of an Army publication discussing the beliefs and practices of a variety of religious denominations, some of which have traditions or requirements involving attire. See Department of the Army Pamphlet No. 165-13-1, Religious Requirements and Practices of Certain Selected Groups: A Handbook Supplement for Chaplains (1980). But that publication provides no indication whatsoever as to how many soldiers belong to the denominations it describes, or as to how many are likely to seek religious exemptions from the dress code.

In these circumstances, deference seems unwarranted. Reasoned military judgments, of course, are entitled to respect, but the military has failed to show that this particular judgment with respect to Captain Goldman is a reasoned one. If, in the future, the Air Force is besieged with requests for **⊥528** religious exemptions from the dress code, and those requests cannot be distinguished on functional grounds from Goldman's, the service may be able to argue credibly that circumstances warrant a flat rule against any visible religious apparel. That, however, would be a case different from the one at hand.

Justice O'CONNOR, with whom *Justice* MARSHALL joins, dissenting.

The issue posed in this case is whether, consistent with the Free Exercise Clause of the First Amendment, the Air Force may prohibit Captain Goldman, an Orthodox Jewish psychologist, from wearing a yarmulke while he is in uniform on duty inside a military hospital.

The Court rejects Captain Goldman's claim without even the slightest attempt to weigh his asserted right to the free exercise of his religion against the interest of the Air Force in uniformity of dress within the military hospital. No test for Free Exercise claims in the military context is even articulated, much less applied. It is entirely sufficient for the Court if the military perceives a need for uniformity.

Justice STEVENS acknowledges that "Captain Goldman's military duties are performed in a setting in which a modest departure from the uniform regulation creates almost no danger of impairment of the Air Force's military mission." Nevertheless, *Justice* STEVENS is persuaded that a governmental regulation based on *any* "neutral, completely objective standard," will survive a free exercise challenge.

In contrast, *Justice BRENNAN* recognizes that the Court "overlooks the sincere and serious nature of [the] constitutional claim." He properly notes that, even with respect to military rules and regulations, the courts have a duty to weigh sincere First Amendment claims of its members against the necessity of the particular application of the rule. But *Justice BRENNAN* applies no particular test or standard to determine such claims.

⊥**529** *Justice BLACKMUN* focuses on the particular ways in which the military may pursue its interest in uniformity, but nonetheless declines "to determine the extent to which the ordinary test for inroads on religious freedom must be modified in the military context."

I believe that the Court should attempt to articulate and apply an appropriate standard for a free exercise claim in the military context, and should examine Captain Goldman's claim in light of that standard.

Like the Court today in this case involving the military, the Court in the past has had some difficulty, even in the civilian context, in articulating a clear standard for evaluating free exercise claims that result from the application of general state laws burdening religious conduct. In *Sherbert* v. *Verner*, and *Thomas* v. *Review Board*, the Court required the States to demonstrate that their challenged policies were "the least restrictive means of achieving some compelling state interest" in order to deprive claimants of unemployment benefits when the refusal to work was based on sincere religious beliefs. In *Wisconsin* v. *Yoder*, the Court noted that "only those interests of the highest order and those not otherwise served can overbalance legitimate claims to the free exercise of religion" in deciding that the Amish were exempt from a State's requirement that children attend school through the age of 16. In *United States* v. *Lee*, the Court stated that "[t]he State may justify a limitation on religious liberty by showing that it is essential to accomplish an overriding governmental interest," and held that the Amish could not exempt themselves from the Social Security system on religious grounds.

⊥**530**These tests, though similar, are not identical. One can, however, glean at least two consistent themes from this Court's precedents. First, when the government attempts to deny a free exercise claim, it must show that an unusually important interest is at stake, whether that interest is denominated "compelling," "of the highest order," or "overriding." Second, the government must show that granting the requested exemption will do substantial harm to that interest, whether by showing that the means adopted is the "least restrictive" or "essential," or that the interest will not "otherwise be served." These two requirements are entirely sensible in the context of the assertion of a free exercise claim. First, because the government is attempting to override an interest specifically protected by the Bill of Rights, the government must show that the opposing interest it asserts is of especial importance before there is any chance that its claim can prevail. Second, since the Bill of Rights is expressly designed to protect the individual against the aggregated and sometimes intolerant powers of the state, the government must show that the interest asserted will in fact be substantially harmed by granting the type of exemption requested by the individual.

There is no reason why these general principles should not apply in the military, as well as the civilian, context. As this Court has stated unanimously, "'our citizens in uniform may not be stripped of basic rights simply because they have doffed their civilian clothes.'" *Chappell* v. *Wallace*. Furthermore, the test that one can glean from this Court's decisions in the civilian context is sufficiently flexible to take into account the special importance of defending our Nation with⊥**531**out abandoning completely the freedoms that make it worth defending.

The first question that the Court should face here, therefore, is whether the interest that the Government asserts against the religiously based claim of the individual is of unusual importance. It is perfectly appropriate at this step of the analysis to take account of the special role of the military. The mission of our armed services is to protect our Nation from those who would destroy all our freedoms. I agree that, in order to fulfill that mission, the military is entitled to take some freedoms from its members. As the Court notes, the military "'must insist upon a respect for duty and a discipline without counterpart in civilian life.'" The need for military discipline and esprit de corps is unquestionably an especially important governmental interest.

But the mere presence of such an interest cannot, as the majority implicitly believes, end the analysis of whether a refusal by the Government to honor the free exercise of an individual's religion is constitutionally acceptable. A citizen pursuing even the most noble cause must remain within the bounds of the law. So, too, the Government may, even in pursuing its most compelling interests, be subject to specific restraints in doing so. The second question in the analysis of a free exercise claim under this Court's precedents must also be reached here: will granting an exemption of the type requested by the individual do substantial harm to the especially important governmental interest?

I have no doubt that there are many instances in which the unique fragility of military discipline and esprit de corps necessitates rigidity by the Government when similar rigidity to preserve an assertedly analogous interest would not pass constitutional muster in the civilian sphere. ⊥**532** Nonetheless, as *Justice BRENNAN* persuasively argues, the Government can present no sufficiently convincing proof in this case to support an assertion that granting an exemption of the type requested here would do substantial harm to military discipline and esprit de corps.

First, the Government's asserted need for absolute uniformity is contradicted by the Government's own exceptions to its rule. As *Justice BRENNAN* notes, an Air Force dress code in force at the time of Captain

Goldman's service states: "Neither the Air Force nor the public expects absolute uniformity of appearance. Each member has the right, within limits, to express individuality through his or her appearance. However, the image of a disciplined service member who can be relied on to do his or her job excludes the extreme, the unusual, and the fad." Furthermore, the Government does not assert, and could not plausibly argue, that petitioner's decision to wear his yarmulke while indoors at the hospital presents a threat to health or safety. And finally, the District Court found as fact that in this particular case, far from creating discontent or indiscipline in the hospital where Captain Goldman worked, "[f]rom September 1977 to May 7, 1981, *no objection* was raised to Goldman's wearing of his yarmulke while in uniform."

In the rare instances where the military has not consistently or plausibly justified its asserted need for rigidity of enforcement, and where the individual seeking the exemption establishes that the assertion by the military of a threat to discipline or esprit de corps is in his or her case completely unfounded, I would hold that the Government's policy of uniformity must yield to the individual's assertion of the right of free exercise of religion. On the facts of this case, therefore, ⊥**533** I would require the Government to accommodate the sincere religious belief of Captain Goldman. Napoleon may have been correct to assert that, in the military sphere, morale is to all other factors as three is to one, but contradicted assertions of necessity by the military do not on the scales of justice bear a similarly disproportionate weight to sincere religious beliefs of the individual.

I respectfully dissent.

BOWEN v. ROY

476 U.S. 693
ON APPEAL FROM THE UNITED STATES DISTRICT COURT FOR THE MIDDLE DISTRICT OF PENNSYLVANIA
Argued January 14, 1986 — Decided June 11, 1986

⊥**695** *Chief Justice BURGER* announced the judgment of the Court and delivered the opinion of the Court with respect to Parts I and II, and an opinion with respect to Part III, in which *Justice POWELL* and *Justice REHNQUIST* join.

The question presented is whether the Free Exercise Clause of the First Amendment compels the government to accommodate a religiously-based objection to the statutory requirements that a Social Security number be provided by an applicant seeking to receive certain welfare benefits and that the States use these numbers in administering the benefit programs.

I

Appellees Stephen J. Roy and Karen Miller applied for and received benefits under the Aid to Families with Dependent Children program and the Food Stamp program. They refused to comply, however, with the requirement, contained in 42 U.S.C. § 602(a)(25) and 7 U.S.C. § 2025(e), that participants in these programs furnish their state welfare agencies with the Social Security numbers of the members of their household as a condition of receiving benefits. Appellees contended that obtaining a Social Security number for their two-year-old daughter, Little Bird of the Snow, would violate their Native American religious beliefs. The Pennsylvania Department of Public Welfare thereafter terminated AFDC and medical benefits payable to appellees on the child's behalf and instituted proceedings to reduce the level of food stamps that appellees' household was receiving. Appellees then filed this action against the Secretary of the Pennsylvania Department of Public Welfare, the Secretary of Health and Human Services, and the Secretary of Agriculture, arguing that the Free Exercise Clause entitled them to an exemption from the Social Security number requirement. In their com⊥**696**plaint, appellees stated that "[t]he sole basis" for the denial of welfare benefits was "Mr. Roy's refusal to obtain a Social Security Number for Little Bird of the Snow," and thus requested injunctive relief, damages, and benefits. In the statement of "undisputed facts," the parties agreed that Little Bird of the Snow did not have a Social Security number.

At trial, Roy testified that he had recently developed a religious objection to obtaining a Social Security number for Little Bird of the Snow. Roy is a Native American descended from the Abenaki Tribe, and he asserts a religious belief that control over one's life is essential to spiritual purity and indispensable to "becoming a holy person." Based on recent conversations with an Abenaki chief, Roy believes that technology is "robbing the spirit of man." In order to prepare his daughter for greater spiritual power, therefore, Roy testified to his belief that he must keep her person and spirit unique and that the uniqueness of the Social Security number as an identifier, coupled with the other uses of the number over which she has no control, will serve to "rob the spirit" of his daughter and prevent her from attaining greater spiritual power.

For purposes of determining the breadth of Roy's religious concerns, the trial judge raised the possibility of using the phonetics of his daughter's name to derive a Social Security number. Although Roy saw "a lot of good" in this suggestion, he stated it would violate his religious beliefs because the special number still would apply uniquely and identify her. Roy also testified that his religious objection would not be satisfied even if the Social Security Administration appended the daughter's full tribal name to her Social Security number.

⊥**697** In Roy's own testimony, he emphasized the evil that would flow simply from *obtaining* a number. On the last day of trial, however, a federal officer inquired whether Little Bird of the Snow already had a Social Security number; he learned that a number had been assigned—under first name "Little," middle name "Bird of the Snow," and last name "Roy."

The Government at this point suggested that the case had become moot because, under Roy's beliefs, Little Bird of the Snow's spirit had already been "robbed." Roy, however, was recalled to the stand and testified that her spirit would be robbed only by "use" of the number. Since no known use of the number had yet been made, Roy expressed his belief that her spirit had not been damaged. The District Court concluded that the case was not moot because of Roy's beliefs regarding "use" of the number. ("Roy believes that the establishment of a Social Security number for Little Bird of the Snow, without more, has not 'robbed her spirit,' but widespread use of the Social Security number by the federal or state governments in their computer systems would have that effect").

After hearing all of the testimony, the District Court denied appellees' request for damages and benefits, but granted injunctive relief. Based on the testimony of the Government's experts and the obvious fact that many people share certain names, the District Court found that "[u]tilization in ⊥**698** the computer system of the name of a benefit recipient alone frequently is not sufficient to ensure the proper payment of benefits." The court nevertheless concluded that the public "interest in maintaining an efficient and fraud resistant system can be met without requiring use of a Social Security number for Little Bird of the Snow," elaborating that:

"It appears to the Court that the harm that the Government might suffer if [appellees] prevailed in this case would be, at worst, that one or perhaps a few individuals could fraudulently obtain welfare benefits. Such a result would obtain only if (1) Little Bird of the Snow attempted fraudulently to obtain welfare benefits or someone else attempted fraudulently to obtain such benefits using Little Bird of the Snow's name *and* (2) identification procedures available to the Defendants that do not require utilization of a Social Security number failed to expose the fraud. This possibility appears to the Court to be remote." Citing our decision in *United States* v. *Lee*, the court entered an injunction containing two basic components. *First*, the Secretary of Health and Human Services was "permanently restrained from making any use of the social security number which was issued in the name of Little Bird of the Snow Roy and from disseminating the number to any agency, individual, business entity, or any other third party." *Second*, the federal and state defendants were enjoined until Little Bird of the Snow's 16th birthday from denying Roy cash assistance, medical assistance, and food stamps "because of the [appellees'] refusal to provide a Social Security number for her."

We noted probable jurisdiction and we reverse.

⊥**699** II

Appellees raise a constitutional challenge to two features of the statutory scheme here. They object to Congress's requirement that a state AFDC plan "*must* . . . provide (A) that, *as a condition of eligibility* under the plan, *each* applicant for or recipient of aid *shall* furnish to the State agency his Social Security account number." 42 U.S.C. § 602(a)(25) (emphasis added). They also object to Congress's requirement that "such State agency *shall utilize* such account numbers . . . in the administration of such plan." *Ibid.* (emphasis added). We analyze each of these contentions, turning to the latter contention first.

Our cases have long recognized a distinction between the freedom of individual belief, which is absolute, and the freedom of individual conduct, which is not absolute. This case implicates only the latter concern. Roy objects to the statutory requirement that state agencies "shall utilize" Social Security numbers not because it places any restriction on what he may believe or what he may do, but because he believes the use of the number may harm his daughter's spirit.

Never to our knowledge has the Court interpreted the First Amendment to require the Government *itself* to behave in ways that the individual believes will further his or her spiritual development or that of his or her family. The Free Exercise Clause simply cannot be understood to require the Government to conduct its own internal affairs in ways that comport with the religious beliefs of particular citizens. Just as the Government may not insist that appellees engage in ⊥**700** any set form of religious observance, so appellees may not demand that the Government join in their chosen religious practices by refraining from using a number to identify their daughter. "[T]he Free Exercise Clause is written in terms of what the government cannot do to the individual, not in terms of what the individual can extract from the government." *Sherbert* v. *Verner*, (Douglas, J., concurring).

As a result, Roy may no more prevail on his religious objection to the Government's use of a Social Security number for his daughter than he could on a sincere religious objection to the size or color of the Government's filing cabinets. The Free Exercise Clause affords an individual protection from certain forms of governmental compulsion; it does not afford an individual a right to dictate the conduct of the Government's internal procedures.

As Roy points out, eight years ago Congress passed a Joint Resolution concerning American Indian religious freedom that provides guidance with respect to this case. As currently codified, the Resolution provides: "On and after August 11, 1978, it shall be the policy of the United States to protect and preserve for American Indians their inherent right of freedom to believe, express, and exercise the traditional religions of the American Indian, Eskimo, Aleut, and Native Hawaiians, including but not limited to access to sites, use and possession of sacred objects, and the freedom to worship through ceremonials and traditional rites." 42 U.S.C. § 1996. That Resolution—with its emphasis on protecting the freedom to believe, express, and exercise a religion—accurately identifies the mission of the Free Exercise Clause itself. The Federal Government's use of a Social Security number for Little Bird of the Snow does not itself in any degree impair Roy's "freedom to believe, express, and exercise" his re⊥**701**ligion. Consequently, appellees' objection to the statutory requirement that each State agency "shall utilize" a Social Security number in the administration of its plan is without merit. It follows that their request for an injunction against use of the Social Security number in processing benefit applications should have been rejected. We therefore hold that the portion of the District Court's injunction that permanently restrained the Secretary from making any use of the Social Security number that had been issued in the name of Little Bird of the Snow Roy must be vacated.

III

Roy also challenges Congress' requirement that a state AFDC plan "*must* . . . provide (A) that, *as a condition of eligibility* under the plan, *each* applicant for or recipient of aid *shall furnish* to the State agency his Social Security account number." The ⊥**702** First Amendment's guarantee that "Congress shall make no law . . . prohibiting the free exercise" of religion holds an important place in our scheme of ordered liberty, but the Court has steadfastly maintained that claims of religious conviction do not automatically entitle a person to fix unilaterally the conditions and terms of dealings with the Government. Not all burdens on religion are unconstitutional. This was treated recently in *United States* v. *Lee*: "To maintain an organized society that guarantees religious freedom to a great variety of faiths requires that some religious practices yield to the common good. Religious beliefs can be accommodated, but there is a point at which accommodation would 'radically restrict the operating latitude of the legislature.'"

⊥**703** The statutory requirement that applicants provide a Social Security number is wholly neutral in religious terms and uniformly applicable. There is no claim that there is any attempt by Congress to discriminate invidiously or any covert suppression of particular religious beliefs. The administrative requirement does not create any danger of censorship or place a direct condition or burden on the dissemination of religious views. It does not intrude on the organization of a religious institution or school. It may indeed confront some applicants for benefits with choices, but in no sense does it affirmatively compel appellees, by threat of sanctions, to refrain from religiously motivated conduct or to engage in conduct that they find objectionable for religious reasons. Rather, it is appellees who seek benefits from the Government and who assert that, because of certain religious beliefs, they should be excused from compliance with a condition that is binding on all other persons who seek the same benefits from the Government.

This is far removed from the historical instances of religious persecution and intolerance that gave concern to those who drafted the Free Exercise Clause of the First Amendment. We are not unmindful of the importance of many government benefits today or of the value of sincerely-held religious be⊥**704**liefs. However, while we do not believe that no government compulsion is involved, we cannot ignore the reality that denial of such benefits by a uniformly applicable statute neutral on its face is of a wholly different, less intrusive nature than affirmative compulsion or prohibition, by threat of penal sanctions, for conduct that has religious implications.

This distinction is clearly revealed in the Court's opinions. Decisions rejecting religious-based challenges have often recited the fact that a mere denial of a governmental benefit by a uniformly applicable statute does not constitute infringement of religious liberty. In *Hamilton* v. *Regents of the University of California*, for example, the Court rejected a religious challenge by students to military courses required as part of their curriculum, explaining: "The fact that they are able to pay their way in this university but not in any other institution in California is without significance upon any constitutional or other question here involved. California has not drafted or called them to attend the university. They are seeking education offered by the State and at the same time insisting that they be excluded from the prescribed course solely upon grounds of their religious beliefs and conscientious objections to war. . . ." In cases upholding First Amendment challenges, on the other hand, the Court has often relied on the showing that **compulsion** of certain activity with religious significance was in⊥**705**volved. In *West Virginia Board of Education* v. *Barnette*, for example, the Court distinguished the earlier *Hamilton* holding and upheld a challenge to a flag salute requirement: "Here . . . we are dealing with a compulsion of students to declare a belief. . . . This issue is not prejudiced by the Court's previous holding that where a State, without compelling attendance, extends college facilities to pupils who voluntarily enroll, it may prescribe military training as part of the course without offense to the Constitution. It was held that those who take advantage of its opportunities may not on ground of conscience refuse compliance with such conditions. *Hamilton* v. *Regents*. In the present case attendance is not optional." The distinction between governmental compulsion and conditions relating to governmental benefits contained in these two cases was emphasized by *Justice* BRENNAN in his concurring opinion in *Abington School District* v. *Schempp*: "The different results of [*Hamilton* and *Barnette*] are attributable only in part to a difference in the strength of the particular state interests which the respective statutes were designed to serve. Far more significant is the fact that *Hamilton* dealt with the voluntary attendance at college of young adults, while *Barnette* involved the compelled attendance of young children at elementary and secondary schools. This distinction warrants a difference in constitutional results." ⊥**706** We have repeatedly emphasized this distinction: In rejecting a Free Exercise challenge in *Bob Jones University* v. *United States*, for example, we observed that the "[d]enial of tax benefits will inevitably have a substantial impact on the operation of private religious schools, but will not prevent those schools from observing their religious tenets."

We conclude then that government regulation that indirectly and incidentally calls for a choice between securing a governmental benefit and adherence to religious beliefs is wholly different from governmental action or legislation that criminalizes religiously inspired activity or inescapably compels conduct that some find objectionable for religious reasons. Although the denial of government benefits over religious objection can raise serious Free Exercise problems, these two very different forms of government action are not governed by the same constitutional standard. A governmental burden on religious liberty is not insulated from review simply because it is indirect, *Thomas* v. *Review Board*, ⊥**707** but the nature of the burden is relevant to the standard the Government must meet to justify the burden.

The general governmental interests involved here buttress this conclusion. Governments today grant a broad range of benefits; inescapably at the same time the administration of complex programs requires certain conditions and restrictions. Although in some situations a mechanism for individual consideration will be created, a policy decision by a government that it wishes to treat all applicants alike and that it does not wish to become involved in case-by-case inquiries into the genuineness of each religious objection to such condition or restrictions is entitled to substantial deference. Moreover, legitimate interests are implicated in the need to avoid any appearance of favoring religious over nonreligious applicants.

The test applied in cases like *Wisconsin* v. *Yoder* is not appropriate in this setting. In the enforcement of a facially neutral and uniformly applicable requirement for the administration of welfare programs reaching many millions of people, the Government is entitled to wide latitude. The Government should not be put to the strict test applied by the District Court; that standard required the Government to justify enforcement of the use of Social Security number requirement as the least restrictive means of accomplishing a compelling state interest. Absent proof of an intent to discriminate against particular religious beliefs or against religion in general, the Government ⊥**708** meets its burden when it demonstrates that a challenged requirement for governmental benefits, neutral and uniform in its application, is a reasonable means of promoting a legitimate public interest.

We reject appellees' contention that *Sherbert* and *Thomas* compel affirmance. The statutory conditions at issue in those cases provided that a person was not eligible for unemployment compensation benefits if, "without good cause," he had quit work or refused available work. The "good cause" standard created a mechanism for individualized exemptions. If a state creates a mechanism, its refusal to extend an exemption to an instance of religious hardship suggests a discriminatory intent. Thus, as was urged in *Thomas*, to consider a religiously motivated resignation to be "without good cause" tends to exhibit hostility, not neutrality, towards religion. (*Thomas* and *Sherbert* may be viewed "as a protection against unequal treatment rather than a grant of favored treatment for the members of the religious sect.") In those cases, therefore, it was appropriate to require the State to demonstrate a compelling reason for denying the requested exemption.

Here there is nothing whatever suggesting antagonism by Congress towards religion generally or towards any particular religious beliefs. The requirement that applicants provide a Social Security number is facially neutral and applies to all applicants for the benefits involved. Congress has made no provision for individual exemptions to the requirement in the two statutes in question. Indeed, to the contrary, Congress has specified that a state AFDC plan "*must* . . . provide (A) that, as a *condition of eligibility* under the plan, *each* applicant for or recipient of aid *shall* furnish to the ⊥**709** State agency his Social Security account number," 42 U.S.C. § 602(a)(25) (emphasis added), and that "[s]tate agencies *shall* (1) *require, as a condition of eligibility* for participation in the food stamp program, that *each* household member furnish to the State agency their Social Security account number," 7 U. S. C. § 2025(e) (emphasis added). Nor are these requirements relics from the past; Congress made the requirement mandatory for the food stamp program in 1981. Congress also recently extended to several other aid programs the mandatory requirement that the States use Social Security numbers in verifying eligibility for benefits.

The Social Security number requirement clearly promotes a legitimate and important public interest. No one can doubt that preventing fraud in these benefits programs is an important goal. As Representative Richmond explained in support of the bill that made the Social Security number requirement mandatory for the Food Stamp program, "We know that however generously motivated Americans may be to furnish resources to the poor to enable them to survive, . . . they understandably object if they believe that those resources are being abused or wasted. . . .

"We want to be certain that the food stamp program is run as efficiently and as error-free as possible.

"We want applicants and recipients constantly to be aware that the Congress does not and will not tolerate any refusal to disclose earnings accurately, and underreporting of welfare or other assistance program benefits, any efforts to evade the work requirement or any other attempts to take advantage of the program and dollars intended only for those who completely satisfy the strin⊥**710**gent eligibility requirements set forth in sections 5 and 7 of the Food Stamp Act of 1977 and further tightened this year and in this bill." 127 Cong. Rec. 24783 (1981). We also think it plain that the Social Security number requirement is a reasonable means of promoting that goal. The programs at issue are of truly staggering magnitude. Each year roughly 3.8 million families receive $7.8 billion through federal funded AFDC programs and 20 million persons receive $11 billion in food stamps. The Social Security program itself is the largest domestic governmental program in the United States today, distributing approximately $51 billion monthly to 36 million recipients. Because of the tremendous administrative problems associated with managing programs of this size, the District Court found that "Social Security numbers are used in making the determination that benefits in the programs are properly paid and that there is no duplication of benefits or failure of payment. . . . Utilization in the computer system of the name of a benefit recipient alone frequently is not sufficient to ensure the proper payment of benefits." Social Security numbers are unique numerical identifiers and are used pervasively in these programs. The numbers are used, for example, to keep track of persons no longer entitled to receive food stamps because of past fraud or abuses of the program. Moreover, the existence of this unique numerical identifier creates opportunities for ferreting out fraudulent applications through computer "matching" techniques. One investigation, "Project Match," compared Federal employee files against AFDC and Medicaid files to determine instances of Government employees receiving welfare benefits improperly. Data from 26 states were examined, and 9,000 individuals were identified as receiving duplicate welfare payments. While undoubtedly some fraud escapes detection in spite of such investigations, the President's Private Sector Survey on Cost Control, known more popularly as the "Grace Commis⊥**711**sion," recently reported that matching "is the Federal Government's most cost-effective tool for verification or investigation in the prevention and detection of fraud, waste and abuse." 7 The President's Private Sector Survey on Cost Control, Management Office Selected Issues—Information Gap in the Federal Government 90 (1984).

The importance of the Social Security number to these matching techniques is illustrated by the facts of this case. The District Court found that "efficient operation of these [matching] programs requires the use of computer systems that utilize unique numerical identifiers such as the Social Security number." It further found that exempting even appellees alone from this requirement could result in "one or perhaps a few individuals . . . fraudulently obtain[ing] welfare benefits," a prospect the court termed "remote." The District Court's assessment of this probability seems quite dubious. But in any event, we know of no case obligating the Government to tolerate a slight risk of "one or perhaps a few individuals" fraudulently obtaining benefits in order to satisfy a religious objection to a requirement designed to combat that very risk. Appellees may not use the Free Exercise Clause to demand ⊥**712** Government benefits, but only on their own terms, particularly where that insistence works a demonstrable disadvantage to the Government in the administration of the programs.

As the Court has recognized before, given the diversity of beliefs in our pluralistic society and the necessity of providing governments with sufficient operating latitude, some incidental neutral restraints on the free exercise of religion are inescapable. As a matter of legislative policy, a legislature might decide to make religious accommodations to a general and neutral system of awarding benefits, "[b]ut our concern is not with the wisdom of legislation but with its constitutional limitation." *Braunfeld* v. *Brown*. We conclude that the Congress's refusal to grant appellees a special exemption does not violate the Free Exercise Clause.

The judgment of the District Court is reversed, and the case is remanded for further proceedings consistent with this opinion.

Reversed.

Justice BLACKMUN, concurring in part.

I join only Parts I and II of the opinion written by *The* CHIEF JUSTICE.

In August 1983, appellees Stephen J. Roy and Karen Miller sued to prevent the Government from requiring them to provide a Social Security number for their two-year-old daughter, Little Bird of the Snow, as a condition for obtaining food stamps and welfare benefits for the child. They object to the Social Security number requirement because of their sincere religious conviction that the Government's widespread use of a unique numerical identifier for their daughter will deprive her of spiritual power. After it developed at trial that the Government already had a Social Secu⊥**713**rity number for Little Bird of the Snow, the District Court enjoined the Government not only from denying benefits to her based on her parents' failure to provide a Social Security number, but also from using or disseminating the number already in the Government's possession until the child's 16th birthday.

I agree with the Court that the District Court erred in enjoining the Government's internal use of Little Bird of the Snow's Social Security number. It is easy to understand the rationale for that part of the District Court's injunction: appellees argue plausibly that the Government's threat to put the Social Security number into active use if they apply for benefits for their daughter requires them to choose between the child's physical sustenance and the dictates of their faith, the same dilemma created by the Government's initial requirement that appellees themselves supply a Social Security number for Little Bird of the Snow. They claim that, absent some compelling state interest, the Government should refrain from acting in ways that appellees believe on religious grounds will harm their daughter's spiritual development.

Although this argument has some facial appeal, I conclude, for the reasons stated in Part II of the Court's opinion, that it stretches the Free Exercise Clause too far. Consequently, I agree that the portion of the District Court's judgment that enjoins the Government from using or disseminating the Social Security number already assigned to Little Bird of the Snow must be vacated. I would also vacate the remainder of the judgment and remand the case for further proceedings, because once the injunction against use or dissemination is set aside, it is unclear on the record presently before us whether a justiciable controversy remains with respect to the rest of the relief ordered by the District Court. Roy and Miller evidently objected to the Social Security number requirement primarily because they did not want the *Govern⊥***714***ment* to be able to use a unique numerical identifier for Little Bird of the Snow, and that injury cannot be redressed if, as the Court today holds, the Government cannot be enjoined from using the pre-existing number. It is possible, however, that appellees still would have an independent religious objection to their being forced to cooperate actively with the Government by themselves providing their daughter's Social Security number on benefit applications.

In my view, the record is ambiguous on this score. In rejecting the Government's argument that the existence of the number rendered the case moot, the District Court found that Roy "feels compelled by his religious belief to avoid any use of that number and, to that end, has refused to provide the number to the Defendants in order to receive welfare benefits for Little Bird of the Snow." It is unclear whether the "use" to which the District Court referred included use by Roy and Miller, or just the more extensive use of the number by the Government. And even if the court meant to refer only to use by the Government, it is not clear that appellees do not also have an independent religious objection to the requirement that they provide a Social Security number for their daughter.

On the other hand, even if appellees do have such an objection, vacating the District Court's injunction against governmental use or dissemination of the number may moot this case in other ways. Regardless of whether Roy and Miller are required to provide their daughter's Social Security number on applications for benefits, they may simply be unwilling to apply for benefits without an assurance that the application will not trigger the use of the number. Conversely, it is possible that the Government, in a welcome display of rea⊥**715**sonableness, will decide that since it already has a Social Security number for Little Bird of the Snow, it will not insist that appellees resupply it.

Since the proceedings on remand might well render unnecessary any discussion of whether appellees constitutionally may be required to provide a Social Security number for Little Bird of the Snow in order to obtain government assistance on her behalf, that question could be said not to be properly before us. I nonetheless address it, partly because the rest of the Court has seen fit to do so, and partly because I think it is not the kind of difficult constitutional question that we should refrain from deciding except when absolutely necessary. Indeed, for the reasons expressed by *Justice* O'CONNOR, I think the question requires nothing more than a straightforward application of ⊥**716** *Sherbert, Thomas*, and *Wisconsin* v. *Yoder*. If it proves necessary to reach the issue on remand, I agree with *Justice* O'CONNOR that, on the facts as determined by the District Court, the Government may not deny assistance to Little Bird of the Snow solely because her parents' religious convictions prevent them from supplying the Government with a Social Security number for their daughter.

Justice STEVENS, concurring in part and concurring in the result.

Members of the Abenaki Indian Tribe are unquestionably entitled to the same constitutional protection against governmental action "prohibiting the free exercise" of their religion as are the adherents of other faiths. Our respect for the sincerity of their religious beliefs does not, however, relieve us from the duty to identify the precise character of the two quite different claims that the parents of Little Bird of the Snow have advanced. They claim, first, that they are entitled to an injunction preventing the Government from making any use of a Social Security number assigned to Little Bird of the Snow; and second, they are entitled to receive a full allowance of food stamps and cash assistance for Little Bird of the Snow without providing a Social Security number for her.

As the Court holds in Part II of its opinion, which I join, the first claim must fail because the Free Exercise Clause ⊥**717** does not give an individual the right to dictate the Government's method of recordkeeping. The second claim, I submit, is either moot or not ripe for decision.

I

In order to understand the precise nature and current posture of appellees' claims, it is necessary to emphasize an extremely unusual feature of this case. At the outset of the litigation, the parties assumed—indeed, they stipulated to—a critical fact that was discovered to be inaccurate on the last day of the trial. Although the parties believed that Little Bird of the Snow did not have a Social Security number, the District Court found, and the parties now agree, that she has had a Social Security number since birth. The contrary belief had been central to the parties' perception of the litigation, and to the requested relief. It is thus also central to the state of the record as we find it.

At the state agency administrative hearing on the threatened withdrawal of certain benefits, the issue had been framed as whether to affirm a decision "determining the appellant's daughter, Little Bird of the Snow, ineligible for public assistance and Medical Assistance because the appellant would not apply for a Social Security Number for her." In their complaint, Little Bird's parents alleged that "[t]he sole basis" for the denial of welfare benefits was "Mr. Roy's refusal to obtain a Social Security Number for Little Bird of the Snow" and thus requested injunctive relief, damages, and benefits. In the statement of "undisputed facts," the parties stipulated that Little Bird of the Snow did not have a Social Security number. In the District Court's opinion ⊥**718** denying summary judgment, the Court began its opinion by observing that Roy and Miller "have refused to obtain a Social Security number for their 2-year-old daughter, Little Bird of the Snow, on the ground that doing so would be contrary to their Native Abenaki Indian religious beliefs." At trial, Roy's counsel introduced his case by emphasizing that Little Bird of the Snow, unlike the other members of the family, did not have a Social Security number and thus had not been exposed to the evil that the number represents. In Roy's own testimony, he emphasized the evil that would follow from *obtaining* a number. On the last day of trial, however, in response to questions, a federal official inquired, during a court recess, whether Little Bird of the Snow already had a Social Security number and discovered that she had been assigned a Social Security number at birth.

This discovery had a dramatic impact on the litigation, and on the judgment under review. Because there was no longer any apparent basis for the dispute, the Government ⊥**719** suggested that the case had become moot. Roy, however, responded to the discovery by changing his request for relief and asking for a cancellation of the existing number.

Concluding that the discovery did not moot the case, the District Court denied the request for damages and benefits, but granted injunctive relief. The injunction—the judgment that we are considering—contains two basic components. First, the Secretary of Health and Human Services is "permanently restrained from making any use of the social security number which was issued in the name Little Bird of the Snow Roy and from disseminating the number to any agency, individual, business entity, or any other third party." Second, the federal and state defendants are enjoined until Little Bird of the Snow's 16th birthday from denying Roy cash assistance, medical assistance, and food stamps "because of the Plaintiffs' refusal to provide a social security number for her." Of course, if the injunction preventing the Secretary from making use of the already existing number had not been granted, there would have been no apparent impediment to providing the benefits that had previously been denied.

As the case comes to us, the first question to be decided is whether the District Court erred in effectively canceling the number that had already been issued for Little Bird of the Snow and that established the appellees' eligibility for the benefits in dispute. The Court correctly holds that the Dis⊥**720**trict Court did err and that "the portion of the District Court's injunction that permanently restrained the Secretary from making any use of the Social Security number that had been issued in the name of Little Bird of the Snow Roy must be vacated." Having so held, however, the Court should pause to consider whether any other constitutional issue need be addressed. For, as the Court demonstrates, an objection to the Government's use of a Social Security number, and a possible objection to "providing" the number when the Government already has it, pose very different constitutional problems.

II

Once we vacate the injunction preventing the Government from making routine use of the number that has already been assigned to Little Bird of the Snow, there is nothing disclosed by the record to prevent the appellees from receiving the payments that are in dispute. Indeed, since the Government itself suggested to the District Court that the case had become moot as soon as it was learned that a Social Security number already existed, it is obvious that the Government perceives no difficulty in making the requested payments in the future. The only issue that prevented the case from becoming moot was the claim asserted by Roy that he was entitled to an injunction that effectively canceled the existing number. Since that issue has now been resolved, nothing remains of the case.

Neither Roy nor the Government has pointed to anything in the record suggesting that Roy will be under any further obligation to "provide" a Social Security number for Little Bird of the Snow. Even if one makes the unsupported assumption that Roy may object to filing certain forms in the future, there is a conspicuous lack of evidence and findings concerning the extent to which such requirements might impose a burden either on Roy, or on any other person who finds difficulty in providing information on pertinent forms.

⊥**721** The absence of this information in the record is significant. Current regulations suggest that assistance for such difficulties may well be available in the programs at issue, particularly for those with mental, physical, and linguistic handicaps that prevent completion of the required forms, or other required steps in the application process. To the extent that ⊥**722** other food stamp and welfare applicants are, in fact, offered exceptions and special assistance in response to their inability to "provide" required information, it would seem that a religious inability should be given no less deference. For our recent free exercise cases suggest that religious claims should not be disadvantaged in relation to other claims.

These considerations highlight the fact that, if this case is not moot, it surely is not ripe. The case, as litigated, simply bears no resemblance to the currently abstract question about what the Government may require if it seeks a Social Security number that it already has.

Consistent with our longstanding principles of constitutional adjudication, we should decide nothing more than is actually necessary to dispose of the precise dispute before the Court, and nothing more than is fairly presented by the ⊥**723** record and the factual findings. Because the District Court has not made findings about the extent to which other exceptions and assistance are available for those who cannot, or do not, "provide" required information, and because there is nothing in the record to suggest that the Government will not pay the benefits in dispute as soon as the District Court's injunction against the use of the number has been vacated, I concur in the judgment vacating the remainder of the injunction. No matter how interesting, or how clear their answers may appear to be, however, I would not address the hypothetical questions debated by *The CHIEF JUSTICE* and *Justice* O'CONNOR because they are not properly presented by the record in this case.

⊥**724** *Justice* O'CONNOR, with whom *Justice* BRENNAN *and Justice* MARSHALL join, concurring in part and dissenting in part.

I join Parts I and II of *The CHIEF JUSTICE's* opinion and I would vacate only a portion of the injunction issued by the District Court.

I

I believe that appellees cannot pursue their free exercise claim based solely on the actions of the Government with respect to the use of a Social Security number already in its possession, or with respect to any other identification number the Government may wish to assign and use in connection with its administration of its welfare assistance program. Accordingly, I join parts I and II of *The CHIEF JUSTICE's* opinion, and I would vacate that portion of the District Court's judgment that enjoins the Government from using or disseminating the Social Security number already assigned to Little Bird of the Snow.

In all, eight members of the Court believe that the District Court's injunction was overbroad in preventing the Government from using information already in its possession.

A logical next step on the facts of this case is to consider whether the case is moot. Only two members of the Court ⊥**725** believe that the case is, or may be, moot. I agree with *The CHIEF JUSTICE*, that the case is not moot.

The District Court enjoined the Government not only from disseminating or using the Social Security number already in its possession, but "from denying Plaintiff Roy cash assistance and medical assistance benefits for Little Bird of the Snow for the Plaintiffs' failure to provide a Social Security number for her." Because of this portion of the District Court's injunction, we continue to have before us a live case or controversy. Mr. Roy sought in part an injunction that "restrai[ns the Government] from denying cash assistance and medical assistance to Little Bird of the Snow for failure to provide a Social Security Number." The District Court granted that relief. The Government still refuses to concede that it should now provide welfare benefits to Little Bird of the Snow, even though it now claims to possess Little Bird of the Snow's Social Security number, and even though the Solicitor General has been "advised by the Social Security Administration that the agency itself assigns [Social Security numbers] to persons who are required by federal law to have one but decline to complete an application." Because the Government contests the District Court's decision that the Government may not deny welfare benefits to Little Bird of the Snow despite its acknowledgement of appellees' sincere religious objections, Mr. Roy may properly press his suit. Although the Government properly challenges part of the District Court's injunction as overbroad, it seeks to overturn the rest of the injunction only on the grounds that the District Court improperly applied the substantive standards of the First Amendment.

⊥**726** II

Given that a majority of the Court believes that the Government may use and disseminate information already in its possession, and given that the case is not moot, there is probably less remaining in this case than meets the eye. The interest asserted by the Government before the District Court could be wholly served after accommodating appellee's sincere religious beliefs, and the interests remaining after vacating the overbroad portion of the injunction are certainly no more difficult to pursue.

The Government has identified its goal as preventing fraud and abuse in the welfare system, a goal that is both laudable and compelling. The District Court, however, soundly rejected the Government's assertion that provision of the Social Security number was necessary to prevent such fraud and abuse. Among the means for which the Social Security number is used to reduce such fraud is "cross-matching," in which various computerized lists are compared with the welfare rolls to detect unreported income, individuals claimed as part of more than one household, and other fraudulent practices. As now appears the Government not only has the Social Security number it wants for Little Bird of the Snow, but it can also use it. But even under the erroneous assumption of the District Court that no such number was available for use, that court found as a fact that, while cross-matching is "more difficult" without Social Security numbers, "[t]he file on a particular benefit recipient can be identified and cross-matching performed, if the recipient's full name, date of birth, and parents' names are entered into the computerized systems." The District Court's generalized evaluation of the asserted indispensability of the Social Security number similarly undermines the Government's claim here: "*The government's interest* in preventing Little Bird of the Snow from fraudulently receiving welfare benefits *can be satisfied without requiring a Social Security num*⊥**727***ber* for Little Bird of the Snow." (emphasis added).

Faced with these facts, however, *The CHIEF JUSTICE* not only believes appellees themselves must provide a Social Security number to the Government before receiving benefits, but he also finds it necessary to invoke a new standard to be applied to test the validity of government regulations under the Free Exercise Clause. He would uphold any facially neutral and uniformly applicable governmental requirement if the Government shows its rule to be "a reasonable means of promoting a legitimate public interest." Such a test has no basis in precedent and relegates a serious First Amendment value to the barest level of minimal scrutiny that the Equal Protection Clause already provides. I would apply our long line of precedents to hold that the Government must accommodate a legitimate free exercise claim unless pursuing an especially important interest by narrowly tailored means.

This Court has stated: "Where the state conditions receipt of an important benefit upon conduct proscribed by a religious faith, or where it denies such a benefit because of conduct mandated by religious belief, thereby putting substantial pressure on an adherent to modify his behavior and to violate his beliefs, a burden upon religion exists." *Thomas* v. *Review Board of Indiana Employment Security Division*. Indeed, *The CHIEF JUSTICE* appears to acknowledge at least that the law at issue here involves governmental compulsion. ("We do not believe that no government compulsion is involved"). The Free Exercise Clause is therefore clearly implicated in this case.

⊥**728** Once it has been shown that a governmental regulation burdens the free exercise of religion, "only those interests of the highest order and those not otherwise served can overbalance legitimate claims to the free exercise of religion." *Wisconsin* v. *Yoder*. This Court has consistently asked the Government to demonstrate that unbending application of its regulation to the religious objector "is essential to accomplish an overriding governmental interest," *United States* v. *Lee*, or represents "the least restrictive means of achieving some compelling state interest," *Thomas* v. *Review Board*. Only an especially important governmental interest pursued by narrowly tailored means can justify exacting a sacrifice of First Amendment freedoms as the price for an equal share of the rights, benefits, and privileges enjoyed by other citizens.

Granting an exemption to Little Bird of the Snow, and to the handful of others who can be expected to make a similar religious objection to providing the Social Security number in conjunction with the receipt of welfare benefits, will not demonstrably diminish the Government's ability to combat welfare fraud. The District Court found that the governmental appellants had hardly shown that a significant number of other individuals were likely to make a claim similar to that at issue here: "There have been four reported cases involving challenges to the Social Security number requirement for welfare benefits based upon the contention that the number violates sincerely held religious beliefs of the welfare recipient." The danger that a religious exemption would invite or encourage fraudulent applications seek⊥**729**ing to avoid cross-matching performed with the use of Social Security numbers is remote on the facts as found by the District Court: few would-be lawbreakers would risk arousing suspicion by requesting an exemption granted only to a very few. And the sincerity of the appellees' religious beliefs is here undisputed. There is therefore no reason to believe that our previous standard for determining whether the Government must accommodate a free exercise claim does not apply.

Bob Jones University v. *United States* does not support *The CHIEF JUSTICE's* analysis. The Court states in that case: "The governmental interest at stake here is compelling. . . . [T]he Government has a fundamental, overriding interest in eradicating racial discrimination in education—discrimination that prevailed, with official approval, for the first 165 years of this Nation's constitutional history. That governmental interest substantially outweighs whatever burden denial of tax benefits places on petitioners' exercise of their religious beliefs. The interests asserted by petitioners cannot be accommodated with that compelling governmental interest, see *United States* v. *Lee*, and no 'less restrictive means,' see *Thomas* v. *Review Board of Indiana Employment Security Div.*, are available to achieve the governmental interest." See also *id.* ("'The State may justify a limitation on religious liberty by showing that it is *essential* to accomplish an *overriding* governmental interest'") (emphasis added) (quoting *United States* v. *Lee*). It is clear that the Court in *Bob Jones University* did not adopt anything like the legitimate interest/rational means test propounded by *The CHIEF JUSTICE*, but rather continued to require the Government to show pursuit of an especially important interest by narrowly tailored means. In addition, ⊥**730** the interest that the Court in *Bob Jones University* balanced against asserted religious interests was not merely a compelling governmental interest but a *constitutional* interest. Here, although prevention of welfare fraud is concededly a compelling interest, the Government asserts only administrative efficiency as its reason for refusing to exempt appellees from furnishing the Social Security number. The District Court found that assertion sorely wanting, and our conclusion that part of the resulting injunction was overbroad only makes the Government's assertion less plausible. Surely the fact that the Court was willing in *Bob Jones University* to give overriding weight to the government's interest in eradicating the scourge of racial discrimination does not mean that the Court must also give overriding weight to the unanchored anxieties of the welfare bureaucracy.

Hamilton v. *Regents of the University of California* also fails to support *The CHIEF JUSTICE's* construction of a new test. When the Court decided *Hamilton*, it had not yet applied, and did not in *Hamilton* apply, the Free Exercise Clause to actions of the States. The Court's discussion in *Hamilton* of the state university's decision to require military training is therefore limited to a generalized analysis under the Fourteenth Amendment of whether the state's policy deprived the would-be students of "life, liberty, or property." The Court concluded that no such deprivation was involved when the state "ha[d] not drafted or called [the individuals] to . . . war."

This Court's opinions have never turned on so slender a reed as whether the challenged requirement is merely a "reasonable means of promoting a legitimate public interest." *The CHIEF JUSTICE* appears to believe that the added inconvenience to the State of administering a selective exemption overbalances any burden on individual religious exercise. But this Court ⊥**731** has held that administrative inconvenience is not alone sufficient to justify a burden of free exercise unless it creates problems of substantial magnitude. See *Sherbert* v. *Verner*. And as Part II of *The CHIEF JUSTICE's* opinion makes clear, there is essentially no administrative burden imposed on the Government in this case.

Appellants have rested their case on vague allegations of administrative inconvenience and harm to the public fisc that are wholly unsubstantiated by the record and the findings of the District Court. The Court simply cannot, consistent with its precedents, distinguish this case from the wide variety of factual situations in which the Free Exercise Clause indisputably imposes significant constraints upon government. Indeed, five members of the Court agree that *Sherbert* and *Thomas*, in which the Government was required to accommodate sincere religious beliefs, control the outcome of this case to the extent it is not moot.

The CHIEF JUSTICE's distinction between this case and the Court's previous decisions on free exercise claims —that here "it is appellees who seek benefits from the Government and who assert that . . . they should be excused from compliance with a condition that is binding on all other persons who seek the same benefits from the Government," has been directly rejected. The fact that the underlying dispute involves an award of benefits rather than an exaction of penalties does not grant the Government license to apply a different version of the Constitution: "[Welfare] benefits are a matter of statutory entitlement for persons qualified to receive them. Their termination involves state action that adjudicates important rights. The constitutional challenge cannot be answered by an argument that public assistance benefits are 'a "privilege" and not a "right."' *Shapiro* v. *Thompson*. Relevant constitu⊥**732**tional restraints apply as much to the withdrawal of public assistance benefits as to disqualification for unemployment compensation, *Sherbert* v. *Verner*." *Goldberg* v. *Kelly*. See also *Sherbert* v. *Verner* ("It is too late in the day to doubt that the liberties of religion and expression may be infringed by the denial of or placing of conditions upon a benefit or privilege"). The fact that appellees seek exemption from a precondition that the Government attaches to an award of benefits does not, therefore, generate a meaningful distinction between this case and one where appellees seek an exemption from the Government's imposition of penalties upon them. Even if the Founding Fathers did not live in a society with the "broad range of benefits [and] complex programs" that the Federal Government administers today, they constructed a society in which the Constitution placed express limits upon governmental actions limiting the freedoms of that society's members. The rise of the welfare state was not the fall of the Free Exercise Clause.

Our precedents have long required the Government to show that a compelling state interest is served by its refusal to grant a religious exemption. The Government here has clearly and easily met its burden of showing that the prevention of welfare fraud is a compelling governmental goal. If the Government could meet its compelling needs only by refusing to grant a religious exemption, and chose a narrowly tailored means to do so, then the Government would prevail. But the Government has failed to show that granting a religious exemption to those who legitimately object to providing a Social Security number will do any harm to its compelling interest in preventing welfare fraud.

I would merely vacate that portion of the injunction issued by the District Court that enjoins the Government from ⊥**733** using or disseminating the Social Security number already in its possession.

Justice WHITE, dissenting.

Being of the view that *Thomas* v. *Review Board*, and *Sherbert* v. *Verner*, control this case, I cannot join the Court's opinion and judgment.

O'LONE v. ESTATE OF SHABAZZ

482 U.S. 342
ON WRIT OF CERTIORARI TO THE UNITED STATES COURT OF APPEALS FOR THE THIRD CIRCUIT
Argued March 24, 1987 — Decided June 9, 1987

⊥**344** *Chief Justice REHNQUIST* delivered the opinion of the Court.

This case requires us to consider once again the standard of review for prison regulations claimed to inhibit the exercise of constitutional rights. Respondents, members of the Is⊥**345**lamic faith, were prisoners in New Jersey's Leesburg State Prison. They challenged policies adopted by prison officials which resulted in their inability to attend Jumu'ah, a weekly Muslim congregational service regularly held in the main prison building and in a separate facility known as "the Farm." Jumu'ah is commanded by the Koran and must be held every Friday after the sun reaches its zenith and before the Asr, or afternoon prayer. See Koran 62:9-10. There is no question that respondents' sincerely held religious beliefs compelled attendance at Jumu'ah. We hold that the prison regulations here challenged did not violate respondents' rights under the Free Exercise Clause of the First Amendment to the United States Constitution.

Inmates at Leesburg are placed in one of three custody classifications. Maximum security and "gang minimum" security inmates are housed in the main prison building, and those with the lowest classification—full minimum—live in "the Farm." Both respondents were classified as gang minimum security prisoners when this suit was filed, and respondent Mateen was later classified as full minimum.

Several changes in prison policy prompted this litigation. In April 1983, the New Jersey Department of Corrections issued Standard 853, which provided that inmates could no longer move directly from maximum security to full minimum status, but were instead required to first spend a period of time in the intermediate gang minimum status. This change was designed to redress problems that had arisen when inmates were transferred directly from the restrictive maximum security status to full minimum status, with its markedly higher level of freedom. Because of serious overcrowding in the main building, Standard 853 further mandated that gang minimum inmates ordinarily be assigned jobs outside the main building. These inmates work in details of 8 to 15 persons, supervised by one guard. ⊥**346** Standard 853 also required that full minimum inmates work outside the main institution, whether on or off prison grounds, or in a satellite building such as the Farm.

Corrections officials at Leesburg implemented these policies gradually and, as the District Court noted, with some difficulty. *Shabazz* v. *O'Lone*. In the initial stages of outside work details for gang minimum prisoners, officials apparently allowed some Muslim inmates to work inside the main building on Fridays so that they could attend Jumu'ah. This alternative was eventually eliminated in March 1984, in light of the directive of Standard 853 that all gang minimum inmates work outside the main building.

Significant problems arose with those inmates assigned to outside work details. Some avoided reporting for their assignments, while others found reasons for returning to the main building during the course of the workday (including their desire to attend religious services). Evidence showed that the return of prisoners during the day resulted in security risks and administrative burdens that prison officials found unacceptable. Because details of inmates were supervised by only one guard, the whole detail was forced to return to the main gate when one prisoner desired to return to the facility. The gate was the site of all incoming foot and vehicle traffic during the day, and prison officials viewed it as a high security risk area. When an inmate returned, vehicle traffic was delayed while the inmate was logged in and searched.

In response to these burdens, Leesburg officials took steps to ensure that those assigned to outside details remained there for the whole day. Thus, arrangements were made to have lunch and required medications brought out to the prisoners, and appointments with doctors and social workers were scheduled for the late afternoon. These changes proved insufficient, however, and prison officials began to study alternatives. After consulting with the director of social services, the director of professional services, and the ⊥**347** prison's imam and chaplain, prison officials in March 1984 issued a policy memorandum which prohibited inmates assigned to outside work details from returning to the prison during the day except in the case of emergency.

The prohibition of returns prevented Muslims assigned to outside work details from attending Jumu'ah. Respondents filed suit under 42 U.S.C. § 1983, alleging that the prison policies unconstitutionally denied them their Free Exercise rights under the First Amendment, as applied to the States through the Fourteenth Amendment. The District Court, applying the standards announced in an earlier decision of the Court of Appeals for the Third Circuit, concluded that no constitutional violation had occurred. The District Court decided that Standard 853 and the March 1984 prohibition on returns "plausibly advance" the goals of security, order, and rehabilitation. It rejected alternative arrangements suggested by respondents, finding that "no less restrictive alternative could be adopted without potentially compromising a legitimate institutional objective."

The Court of Appeals, *sua sponte* hearing the case en banc, decided that its earlier decision relied upon by the District Court was not sufficiently protective of prisoners' free exercise rights, and went on to state that prison policies could be sustained only if:

"the state . . . show[s] that the challenged regulations were intended to serve, and do serve, the important penological goal of security, and that no reasonable method exists by which [prisoners'] religious rights can be accommodated without creating bona fide security problems. The expert testimony of prison officials should be given due weight, but such testimony is not dispositive of the issue whether no reasonable adjustment is possible. . . . Where it is found that reasonable methods of accommodation can be adopted without sacrificing either the state's interest in security or the prisoners' interest ⊥**348** in freely exercising their religious rights, the state's refusal to allow the observance of a central religious practice cannot be justified and violates the prisoner's first amendment rights." *Shabazz* v. *O'Lone*. In considering whether a potential method of accommodation is reasonable, the court added, relevant factors include cost, the effects of overcrowding, understaffing, and inmates' demonstrated proclivity to unruly conduct. The case was remanded to the District Court for reconsideration under the standards enumerated in the opinion. We granted certiorari to consider the important federal constitutional issues presented by the Court of Appeals' decision, and to resolve apparent confusion among the Courts of Appeals on the proper standards to be applied in considering prisoners' free exercise claims.

Several general principles guide our consideration of the issues presented here. First, "convicted prisoners do not forfeit all constitutional protections by reason of their conviction and confinement in prison." *Bell* v. *Wolfish*. Inmates clearly retain protections afforded by the First Amendment, *Pell* v. *Procunier*, including its directive that no law shall prohibit the free exercise of religion. Second, "[l]awful incarceration brings about the necessary withdrawal or limitation of many privileges and rights, a retraction justified by the considerations underlying our penal system." *Price* v. *Johnston*. The limitations on the exercise of constitutional rights arise both from the fact of incarceration and from valid penological objectives—including deterrence of crime, rehabilitation of prisoners, and institutional security.

⊥**349** In considering the appropriate balance of these factors, we have often said that evaluation of penological objectives is committed to the considered judgment of prison administrators, "who are actually charged with and trained in the running of the particular institution under examination." *Bell* v. *Wolfish*. To ensure that courts afford appropriate deference to prison officials, we have determined that prison regulations alleged to infringe constitutional rights are judged under a "reasonableness" test less restrictive than that ordinarily applied to alleged infringements of fundamental constitutional rights. We recently restated the proper standard: "[W]hen a prison regulation impinges on inmates' constitutional rights, the regulation is valid if it is reasonably related to legitimate penological interests." *Turner* v. *Safley*. This approach ensures the ability of corrections officials "to anticipate security problems and to adopt innovative solutions to the intractable problems of prison administration," and avoids unnecessary intrusion of the judiciary into problems particu⊥**350**larly ill suited to "resolution by decree."

We think the Court of Appeals decision in this case was wrong when it established a separate burden on prison officials to prove "that no reasonable method exists by which [prisoners'] religious rights can be accommodated without creating bona fide security problems." (Prison officials should be required "to produce convincing evidence that they are unable to satisfy their institutional goals in any way that does not infringe inmates' free exercise rights.") Though the availability of accommodations is relevant to the reasonableness inquiry, we have rejected the notion that "prison officials . . . have to set up and then shoot down every conceivable alternative method of accommodating the claimant's constitutional complaint." *Turner* v. *Safley*. By placing the burden on prison officials to disprove the availability of alternatives, the approach articulated by the Court of Appeals fails to reflect the respect and deference that the United States Constitution allows for the judgment of prison administrators.

Turning to consideration of the policies challenged in this case, we think the findings of the District Court establish clearly that prison officials have acted in a reasonable manner. *Turner* v. *Safley* drew upon our previous decisions to identify several factors relevant to this reasonableness determination. First, a regulation must have a logical connection to legitimate governmental interests invoked to justify it. The policies at issue here clearly meet that standard. The requirement that full minimum and gang minimum prisoners work outside the main facility was justified by concerns of institutional order and security, for the District Court found that it was "at least in part a response to a critical overcrowding in the state's prisons, and . . . at least in part designed to ease tension and drain on the facilities ⊥**351** during that part of the day when the inmates were outside the confines of the main buildings." We think it beyond doubt that the standard is related to this legitimate concern.

The subsequent policy prohibiting returns to the institution during the day also passes muster under this standard. Prison officials testified that the returns from outside work details generated congestion and delays at the main gate, a high risk area in any event. Return requests also placed pressure on guards supervising outside details, who previously were required to "evaluate each reason possibly justifying a return to the facilities and either accept or reject that reason." Rehabilitative concerns further supported the policy; corrections officials sought a simulation of working conditions and responsibilities in society. Chief Deputy Ucci testified "One of the things that society demands or expects is that when you have a job, you show up on time, you put in your eight hours, or whatever hours you are supposed to put in, and you don't get off. . . . If we can show inmates that they're supposed to show up for work and work a full day, then when they get out at least we've done something." These legitimate goals were advanced by the prohibition on returns; it cannot seriously be maintained that "the logical connection between the regulation and the asserted goal is so remote as to render the policy arbitrary or irrational."

Our decision in *Turner* also found it relevant that "alternative means of exercising the right . . . remain open to prison inmates." There are, of course, no alternative means of attending Jumu'ah; respondents' religious beliefs insist that it occur at a particular time. But the very stringent requirements as to the time at which Jumu'ah may be held may make it extraordinarily difficult for prison officials to assure that every Muslim prisoner is able to attend that service. While we in no way minimize the central importance of Jumu'ah to respondents, we are unwilling to hold that prison ⊥**352** officials are required by the Constitution to sacrifice legitimate penological objectives to that end. In *Turner*, we did not look to see whether prisoners had other means of communicating with fellow inmates, but instead examined whether the inmates were deprived of "all means of expression." Here, similarly, we think it appropriate to see whether under these regulations respondents retain the ability to participate in other Muslim religious ceremonies. The record establishes that respondents are not deprived of all forms of religious exercise, but instead freely observe a number of their religious obligations. The right to congregate for prayer or discussion is "virtually unlimited except during working hours," and the state-provided imam has free access to the prison. Muslim prisoners are given different meals whenever pork is served in the prison cafeteria. Special arrangements are also made during the month-long observance of Ramadan, a period of fasting and prayer. During Ramadan, Muslim prisoners are awakened at 4 a.m. for an early breakfast, and receive dinner at 8:30 each evening. We think this ability on the part of respondents to participate in other religious observances of their faith supports the conclusion that the restrictions at issue here were reasonable.

Finally, the case for the validity of these regulations is strengthened by examination of the impact that accommodation of respondents' asserted right would have on other inmates, on prison personnel, and on allocation of prison resources generally. Respondents suggest several accommodations of their practices, including placing all Muslim inmates in one or two inside work details or providing weekend labor for Muslim inmates. As noted by the District Court, however, each of respondents' suggested accommodations would, in the judgment of prison officials, have adverse effects on the institution. Inside work details for gang minimum inmates would be inconsistent with the legitimate con⊥**353**cerns underlying Standard 853, and the District Court found that the extra supervision necessary to establish weekend details for Muslim prisoners "would be a drain on scarce human resources" at the prison. Prison officials determined that the alternatives would also threaten prison security by allowing "affinity groups" in the prison to flourish. Administrator O'Lone testified that "we have found out and think almost every prison administrator knows that any time you put a group of individuals together with one particular affinity interest . . . you wind up with . . . a leadership role and an organizational structure that will almost invariably challenge the institutional authority." Finally, the officials determined that special arrangements for one group would create problems as "other inmates [see] that a certain segment is escaping a rigorous work detail" and perceive favoritism. These concerns of prison administrators provide adequate support for the conclusion that accommodations of respondents' request to attend Jumu'ah would have undesirable results in the institution. These difficulties also make clear that there are no "obvious, easy alternatives to the policy adopted by petitioners." *Turner* v. *Safley*.

We take this opportunity to reaffirm our refusal, even where claims are made under the First Amendment, to "substitute our judgment on . . . difficult and sensitive matters of institutional administration," for the determinations of those charged with the formidable task of running a prison. Here the District Court decided that the regulations alleged to infringe constitutional rights were reasonably related to legitimate penological objectives. We agree with the District Court, and it necessarily follows that the regulations in question do not offend the Free Exercise Clause of the First Amendment to the United States Constitution. The judgment of the Court of Appeals is therefore

Reversed.

⊥**354** *Justice* BRENNAN, with whom *Justice* MARSHALL, *Justice* BLACKMUN, and *Justice* STEVENS join, dissenting.

The religious ceremony that these respondents seek to attend is not presumptively dangerous, and the prison has completely foreclosed respondents' participation in it. I therefore would require prison officials to demonstrate that the restrictions they have imposed are necessary to further an important government interest, and that these restrictions are no greater than necessary to achieve prison objectives. As a result, I would affirm the Court of Appeals' order to remand the case to the District Court, and would require prison officials to make this showing. Even were I to accept the Court's standard of review, however, I would remand the case to the District Court, since that court has not had the opportunity to review respondents' claim under the new standard established by this Court in *Turner*. As the record now stands, the reasonableness of foreclosing respondents' participation in Jumu'ah has not been established.

I

Prisoners are persons whom most of us would rather not think about. Banished from everyday sight, they exist in a shadow world that only dimly enters our awareness. They are members of a "total institution" that controls their daily existence in a way that few of us can imagine:

"[P]rison is a complex of physical arrangements and of measures, all wholly governmental, all wholly performed by agents of government, which determine the total existence of certain human beings (except perhaps in the realm of the spirit, and inevitably there as well) from sundown to sundown, sleeping, waking, speaking, silent, ⊥**355** working, playing, viewing, eating, voiding, reading, alone, with others. It is not so, with members of the general adult population. State governments have not undertaken to require members of the general adult population to rise at a certain hour, retire at a certain hour, eat at certain hours, live for periods with no companionship whatever, wear certain clothing, or submit to oral and anal searches after visiting hours, nor have state governments undertaken to prohibit members of the general adult population from speaking to one another, wearing beards, embracing their spouses, or corresponding with their lovers." *Morales* v. *Schmidt*.

It is thus easy to think of prisoners as members of a separate netherworld, driven by its own demands, ordered by its own customs, ruled by those whose claim to power rests on raw necessity. Nothing can change the fact, however, that the society that these prisoners inhabit is our own. Prisons may exist on the margins of that society, but no act of will can sever them from the body politic. When prisoners emerge from the shadows to press a constitutional claim, they invoke no alien set of principles drawn from a distant culture. Rather, they speak the language of the charter upon which all of us rely to hold official power accountable. They ask us to acknowledge that power exercised in the shadows must be restrained at least as diligently as power that acts in the sunlight.

In reviewing a prisoner's claim of the infringement of a constitutional right, we must therefore begin from the premise that, as members of this society, prisoners retain constitutional rights that limit the exercise of official authority against them. At the same time, we must acknowledge that incarceration by its nature changes an individual's status in society. Prison officials have the difficult and often thankless job of preserving security in a potentially explosive setting, ⊥356 as well as of attempting to provide rehabilitation that prepares some inmates for re-entry into the social mainstream. Both these demands require the curtailment and elimination of certain rights. The challenge for this Court is to determine how best to protect those prisoners' rights that remain. Our objective in selecting a standard of review is therefore not, as the Court declares, "[t]o ensure that courts afford appropriate deference to prison officials." The Constitution was not adopted as a means of enhancing the efficiency with which government officials conduct their affairs, nor as a blueprint for ensuring sufficient reliance on administrative expertise. Rather, it was meant to provide a bulwark against infringements that might otherwise be justified as necessary expedients of governing. The practice of Europe, wrote James Madison, was "charters of liberty . . . granted by power"; of America, "charters of power granted by liberty." While we must give due consideration to the needs of those in power, this Court's role is to ensure that fundamental *restraints* on that power are enforced.

In my view, adoption of "reasonableness" as a standard of review for *all* constitutional challenges by inmates is inadequate to this task. Such a standard is categorically deferential, and does not discriminate among degrees of deprivation. From this perspective, restricting use of the prison library to certain hours warrants the same level of scrutiny as preventing inmates from reading at all. Various "factors" may be weighed differently in each situation, but the message to prison officials is clear: merely act "reasonably" and your actions will be upheld. If a directive that officials act "reasonably" were deemed sufficient to check all exercises of power, the Constitution would hardly be necessary. Yet the Court deems this single standard adequate to restrain any type of conduct in which prison officials might engage.

⊥357 It is true that the degree of deprivation is one of the factors in the Court's reasonableness determination. This by itself does not make the standard of review appropriate, however. If it did, we would need but a single standard for evaluating all constitutional claims, as long as every relevant factor were considered under its rubric. Clearly, we have never followed such an approach. A standard of review frames the terms in which justification may be offered, and thus delineates the boundaries within which argument may take place. The use of differing levels of scrutiny proclaims that on some occasions official power must justify itself in a way that otherwise it need not. A relatively strict standard of review is a signal that a decree prohibiting a political demonstration on the basis of the participants' political beliefs is of more serious concern, and therefore will be scrutinized more closely, than a rule limiting the number of demonstrations that may take place downtown at noon.

Thus, even if the absolute nature of the deprivation may be taken into account in the Court's formulation, it makes a difference that this is merely one factor in determining if official conduct is "reasonable." Once we provide such an elastic and deferential principle of justification, "[t]he principle . . . lies about like a loaded weapon ready for the hand of any authority that can bring forth a plausible claim of an urgent need. Every repetition imbeds that principle more deeply in our law and thinking and expands it to new purposes." *Korematsu* v. *United States*. **⊥358** Mere assertions of exigency have a way of providing a colorable defense for governmental deprivation, and we should be especially wary of expansive delegations of power to those who wield it on the margins of society. Prisons are too often shielded from public view; there is no need to make them virtually invisible.

An approach better suited to the sensitive task of protecting the constitutional rights of inmates is laid out by Judge Kaufman in *Abdul Wali* v. *Coughlin*. That approach maintains that the degree of scrutiny of prison regulations should depend on "the nature of the right being asserted by prisoners, the type of activity in which they seek to engage, and whether the challenged restriction works a total deprivation (as opposed to a mere limitation) on the exercise of that right." Essentially, if the activity in which inmates seek to engage is presumptively dangerous, or if a regulation merely restricts the time, place, or manner in which prisoners may exercise a right, a prison regulation will be invalidated only if there is no reasonable justification for official action. Where exercise of the asserted right is not presumptively dangerous, however, and where the prison has completely deprived an inmate of that right, then prison officials must show that "a particular restriction is necessary to further an important governmental interest, and that the limitations on freedoms occasioned by the restrictions are no greater than necessary to effectuate the governmental objective involved."

The court's analytical framework in *Abdul Wali* recognizes that in many instances it is inappropriate for courts "to substitute our judgments for those of trained professionals with years of firsthand experience." It would thus apply a standard of review identical to the Court's "reasonableness" standard in a significant percentage of cases. At the same time, the *Abdul Wali* approach takes seriously the Constitution's function of requiring that official power be called to account when it completely deprives a person of a right that **⊥359** society regards as basic. In this limited number of cases, it would require more than a demonstration of "reasonableness" to justify such infringement. To the extent that prison is meant to inculcate a respect for social and legal norms, a requirement that prison officials persuasively demonstrate the need for the absolute deprivation of inmate rights is consistent with that end. Furthermore, prison officials are in control of the evidence that is essential to establish the superiority of such deprivation over other alternatives. It is thus only fair for these officials to be held to a stringent standard of review in such extreme cases.

The prison in this case has completely prevented respondent inmates from attending the central religious service of their Muslim faith. I would therefore hold prison officials to the standard articulated in *Abdul Wali*, and would find their proffered justifications wanting. The State has neither demonstrated that the restriction is necessary to further an important objective nor proved that less extreme measures may not serve its purpose. Even if I accepted the Court's standard of review, however, I could not conclude on this record that prison officials have proved that it is reasonable to preclude respondents from attending Jumu'ah. Petitioners have provided mere unsubstantiated assertions that the plausible alternatives proposed by respondents are infeasible.

II

In *Turner*, the Court set forth a framework for reviewing allegations that a constitutional right has been infringed by prison officials. The Court found relevant to that review "whether there are alternative means of exercising the right that remain open to prison inmates." The Court in this case acknowledges that "respondents' sincerely held religious beliefs compe[l] attendance at Jumu'ah," and concedes that there are "no alternative means of attending Jumu'ah." Nonetheless, the Court finds that prison policy does not work a complete ⊥**360** deprivation of respondents' asserted religious right, because respondents have the opportunity to participate in other religious activities. This analysis ignores the fact that, as the District Court found, Jumu'ah is the central religious ceremony of Muslims, "comparable to the Saturday service of the Jewish faith and the Sunday service of the various Christian sects." As with other faiths, this ceremony provides a special time in which Muslims "assert their identity as a community covenanted to God." As a result:

"unlike other Muslim prayers which are performed individually and can be made up if missed, the Jumu'ah is obligatory, cannot be made up, and must be performed in congregation. The Jumu'ah is therefore regarded as the central service of the Muslim religion, and the obligation to attend is commanded by the Qur'an, the central book of the Muslim religion."

Jumu'ah therefore cannot be regarded as one of several essentially fungible religious practices. The ability to engage in other religious activities cannot obscure the fact that the denial at issue in this case is absolute: respondents are completely foreclosed from participating in the core ceremony that reflects their membership in a particular religious community. If a Catholic prisoner were prevented from attending Mass on Sunday, few would regard that deprivation as anything but absolute, even if the prisoner were afforded other opportunities to pray, to discuss the Catholic faith with others, and even to avoid eating meat on Friday if that were a preference. Prison officials in this case therefore cannot show that "'other avenues' remain available for the exercise of the asserted right." Under the Court's approach, as enunciated in *Turner*, the availability of other means of exercising the right in question ⊥**361** counsels considerable deference to prison officials. By the same token, the infliction of an absolute deprivation should require more than mere assertion that such a deprivation is necessary. In particular, "the existence of obvious, easy alternatives may be evidence that the regulation is not reasonable, but is an 'exaggerated response' to prison concerns." In this case, petitioners have not established the reasonableness of their policy, because they have provided only bare assertions that the proposals for accommodation offered by respondents are infeasible. As discussed below, the federal policy of permitting inmates in federal prisons to participate in Jumu'ah, as well as Leesburg's own policy of permitting participation for several years, lends plausibility to respondents' suggestion that their religious practice can be accommodated.

In *Turner*, the Court found that the practices of the Federal Bureau of Prisons were relevant to the availability of reasonable alternatives to the policy under challenge. In upholding a ban on inmate-to-inmate mail, the Court noted that the Bureau had adopted "substantially similar restrictions." In finding that there were alternatives to a stringent restriction on the ability to marry, the Court observed that marriages by inmates in federal prisons were generally permitted absent a threat to security or public safety. In the present case, it is therefore worth noting that Federal Bureau of Prisons regulations require the adjustment of work assignments to permit inmate participation in religious ceremonies, absent a threat to "security, safety, and good order." 28 CFR § 548.14 (1986). The Bureau's Directive implementing the regulations on Religious Beliefs and Practices of Committed Offend⊥**362**ers, 28 CFR §§ 548.10-548.15 (1986), states that, with respect to scheduling religious observances, "[t]he more central the religious activity is to the tenets of the inmate's religious faith, the greater the presumption is for relieving the inmate from the institution program or assignment." Furthermore, the Chaplain Director of the Bureau has spoken directly to the issue of participation of Muslim inmates in Jumu'ah:

"Provision is made, by policy, in all Bureau facilities for the observance of Jumu'ah by all inmates in general population who wish to keep this faith practice. The service is held each Friday afternoon in the general time frame that corresponds to the requirements of Islamic jurisprudence. . . .

"Subject only to restraints of security and good order in the institution all routine and normal work assignments are suspended for the Islamic inmates to ensure freedom to attend such services. . . .

"In those institutions where the outside work details contain Islamic inmates, they are permitted access to the inside of the institution to attend the Jumu'ah."

That Muslim inmates are able to participate in Jumu'ah throughout the entire federal prison system suggests that the practice is, under normal circumstances, compatible with the demands of prison administration. Indeed, the Leesburg State Prison permitted participation in this ceremony for five years, and experienced no threats to security or safety as a result. In light of both standard federal prison practice and Leesburg's own past practice, a reasonableness test in this ⊥**363** case demands at least minimal substantiation by prison officials that alternatives that would permit participation in Jumu'ah are infeasible. Under the standard articulated by the Court in *Turner*, this does not mean that petitioners are responsible for identifying and discrediting these alternatives; "prison officials do not have to set up and then shoot down every conceivable alternative method of accommodating the claimant's constitutional complaint." When prisoners themselves present alternatives, however, and when they fairly call into question official claims that these alternatives are infeasible, we must demand at least some evidence beyond mere assertion that the religious practice at issue cannot be accommodated. Examination of the alternatives proposed in this case indicates that prison officials have not provided such substantiation.

III

Respondents' first proposal is that gang minimum prisoners be assigned to an alternative inside work detail on Friday, as they had been before the recent change in policy. Prison officials testified that the alternative work detail is now restricted to maximum security prisoners, and that they did not wish maximum and minimum security prisoners to ⊥**364** mingle. Even the District Court had difficulty with this assertion, as it commented that "[t]he defendants did not explain why inmates of different security levels are not mixed on work assignments when otherwise they are mixed." The court found, nonetheless, that this alternative would be inconsistent with Standard 853's mandate to move gang minimum inmates to outside work details. This conclusion, however, neglects the fact that the very issue is whether the prison's policy, of which Standard 853 is a part, should be administered so as to accommodate Muslim inmates. The policy itself cannot serve as a justification for its failure to provide reasonable accommodation. The record as it now stands thus does not establish that the Friday alternate work detail would create a problem for the institution.

Respondents' second proposal is that gang minimum inmates be assigned to work details inside the main building on a regular basis. While admitting that the prison used inside details in the kitchen, bakery, and tailor shop, officials stated that these jobs are reserved for the riskiest gang minimum inmates, for whom an outside job might be unwise. Thus, concluded officials, it would be a bad idea to move these inmates outside to make room for Muslim gang minimum inmates. Respondents contend, however, that the prison's own records indicate that there are a significant number of jobs inside the institution that could be performed by inmates posing a lesser security risk. This suggests that it might not be necessary for the riskier gang minimum inmates to be moved outside to make room for the less risky inmates. Officials provided no data on the number of outside jobs available, the number of high-risk gang minimum inmates performing them, the number of Muslim inmates that might seek inside positions, or the number of staff that would be necessary to monitor such an arrangement. Given the plausibility of respondents' claim, prison officials should present at least ⊥**365** this information in substantiating their contention that inside assignments are infeasible.

Third, respondents suggested that gang minimum inmates be assigned to Saturday or Sunday work details, which would allow them to make up any time lost by attending Jumu'ah on Friday. While prison officials admitted the existence of weekend work details, they stated that "[s]ince prison personnel are needed for other programs on weekends, the creation of additional weekend details would be a drain on scarce human resources." The record provides no indication, however, of the number of Muslims that would seek such a work detail, the current number of weekend details, or why it would be infeasible simply to reassign current Saturday or Sunday workers to Friday, rather than create additional details. The prison is able to arrange work schedules so that Jewish inmates may attend services on Saturday and Christian inmates may attend services on Sunday. Despite the fact that virtually all inmates are housed in the main building over the weekend, so that the demand on the facility is greater than at any other time, the prison is able to provide sufficient staff coverage to permit Jewish and Christian inmates to participate in their central religious ceremonies. Given the prison's duty to provide Muslims a "reasonable opportunity of pursuing [their] faith comparable to the opportunity afforded fellow prisoners who adhere to conventional religious precepts," *Cruz v. Beto*, prison officials should be required to provide more than mere assertions of the infeasibility of weekend details for Muslim inmates.

Finally, respondents proposed that minimum security inmates living at the Farm be assigned to jobs either in the Farm building or in its immediate vicinity. Since Standard 853 permits such assignments for full minimum inmates, and since such inmates need not return to prison facilities through the main entrance, this would interfere neither with Standard 853 nor the concern underlying the no-return pol⊥**366**icy. Nonetheless, prison officials stated that such an arrangement might create an "affinity group" of Muslims representing a threat to prison authority. Officials pointed to no such problem in the five years in which Muslim inmates were permitted to assemble for Jumu'ah, and in which the alternative Friday work detail was in existence. Nor could they identify any threat resulting from the fact that during the month of Ramadan all Muslim prisoners participate in both breakfast and dinner at special times. Furthermore, there was no testimony that the concentration of Jewish or Christian inmates on work details or in religious services posed any type of "affinity group" threat. As the record now stands, prison officials have declared that a security risk is created by a grouping of Muslim inmates in the least dangerous security classification, but not by a grouping of maximum security inmates who are concentrated in a work detail inside the main building, and who are the only Muslims assured of participating in Jumu'ah. Surely, prison officials should be required to provide at least some substantiation for this facially implausible contention.

Petitioners also maintained that the assignment of full minimum Muslim inmates to the Farm or its near vicinity might provoke resentment because of other inmates' perception that Muslims were receiving special treatment. Officials pointed to no such perception during the period in which the alternative Friday detail was in existence, nor to any resentment of the fact that Muslims' dietary preferences are accommodated and that Muslims are permitted to operate on a special schedule during the month of Ramadan. Nor do they identify any such problems created by the accommodation of ⊥**367** the religious preferences of inmates of other faiths. Once again, prison officials should be required at a minimum to identify the basis for their assertions.

Despite the plausibility of the alternatives proposed by respondents in light of federal practice and the prison's own past practice, officials have essentially provided mere pronouncements that such alternatives are not workable. If this Court is to take seriously its commitment to the principle that "[p]rison walls do not form a barrier separating prison inmates from the protections of the Constitution," *Turner*, it must demand more than this record provides to justify a Muslim inmate's complete foreclosure from participation in the central religious service of the Muslim faith.

IV

That the record in this case contains little more than assertion is not surprising in light of the fact that the District Court proceeded on the basis of the approach set forth in *St. Claire* v. *Cuyler*. That case held that mere "sincer[e]" and "arguably correct" testimony by prison officials is sufficient to demonstrate the need to limit prisoners' exercise of constitutional rights. This Court in *Turner*, however, set forth a more systematic framework for analyzing challenges to prison regulations. *Turner* directed attention to two factors of particular relevance to this case: the degree of constitutional deprivation and the availability of reasonable alternatives. The respondents in this case have been absolutely foreclosed from participating in the central religious ceremony of their Muslim faith. At least a colorable claim that such a drastic policy is not necessary can be made in light of the ability of federal prisons to accommodate Muslim inmates, Leesburg's own past practice of doing so, and the plausibility of the alternatives proposed by respondents. If the Court's standard of review is to represent anything more than reflexive deference to prison officials, any ⊥**368** finding of reasonableness must rest on firmer ground than the record now presents.

Incarceration by its nature denies a prisoner participation in the larger human community. To deny the opportunity to affirm membership in a spiritual community, however, may extinguish an inmate's last source of hope for dignity and redemption. Such a denial requires more justification than mere assertion that any other course of action is infeasible. While I would prefer that this case be analyzed under the approach set out in Part I, I would at a minimum remand to the District Court for an analysis of respondents' claims in accordance with the standard enunciated by the Court in *Turner* and in this case. I therefore dissent.

LYNG v. NORTHWEST INDIAN CEMETERY PROTECTIVE ASSOCIATION

485 U.S. 439
ON WRIT OF CERTIORARI TO THE UNITED STATES COURT OF APPEALS FOR THE NINTH CIRCUIT
Argued November 30, 1987 — Decided April 19, 1988

⊥**441** *Justice* O'CONNOR delivered the opinion of the Court.

This case requires us to consider whether the First Amendment's Free Exercise Clause forbids the Government from permitting timber harvesting in, or constructing a road through, a portion of a National Forest that has tradi⊥**442**tionally been used for religious purposes by members of three American Indian tribes in northwestern California. We conclude that it does not.

I

As part of a project to create a paved 75-mile road linking two California towns, Gasquet and Orleans, the United States Forest Service has upgraded 49 miles of previously unpaved roads on federal land. In order to complete this project (the G-O road), the Forest Service must build a 6-mile paved segment through the Chimney Rock section of the Six Rivers National Forest. That section of the forest is situated between two other portions of the road that are already complete.

In 1977, the Forest Service issued a draft environmental impact statement that discussed proposals for upgrading an existing unpaved road that runs through the Chimney Rock area. In response to comments on the draft statement, the Forest Service commissioned a study of American Indian cultural and religious sites in the area. The Hoopa Valley Indian reservation adjoins the Six Rivers National Forest, and the Chimney Rock area has historically been used for religious purposes by Yurok, Karok, and Tolowa Indians. The commissioned study, which was completed in 1979, found that the entire area "is significant as an integral and indispensible [sic] part of Indian religious conceptualization and practice." Specific sites are used for certain rituals, and "successful use of the [area] is dependent upon and facilitated by certain qualities of the physical environment, the most important of which are privacy, silence, and an undisturbed natural setting." The study concluded that constructing a road along any of the available routes "would cause serious and irreparable damage to the sacred areas which are an integral and necessary part of the belief systems and lifeway of Northwest California Indian peoples." Accordingly, the report recommended that the G-O road not be completed.

⊥**443** In 1982, the Forest Service decided not to adopt this recommendation, and it prepared a final environmental impact statement for construction of the road. The Regional Forester selected a route that avoided archeological sites and was removed as far as possible from the sites used by contemporary Indians for specific spiritual activities. Alternative routes that would have avoided the Chimney Rock area altogether were rejected because they would have required the acquisition of private land, had serious soil stability problems, and would in any event have traversed areas having ritualistic value to American Indians. At about the same time, the Forest Service adopted a management plan allowing for the harvesting of significant amounts of timber in this area of the forest. The management plan provided for one-half mile protective zones around all the religious sites identified in the report that had been commissioned in connection with the G-O road.

After exhausting their administrative remedies, respondents—an Indian organization, individual Indians, nature organizations and individual members of those organizations, and the State of California—challenged both the road-building and timber-harvesting decisions in the United States District Court for the Northern District of California. Respondents claimed that the Forest Service's decisions violated the Free Exercise Clause, the Federal Water Pollution Control Act (FWPCA), 86 Stat. 896, as amended, 33 U.S.C. § 1251 *et seq.*, the National Environment Policy Act of 1969 (NEPA), 83 Stat. 852, 42 U.S.C. § 4321 *et seq.*, several other federal statutes, and governmental trust responsibilities to Indians living on the Hoopa Valley Reservation.

After a trial, the District Court issued a permanent injunction forbidding the Government from constructing the Chimney Rock section of the G-O road or putting the timber-harvesting management plan into effect. See *Northwest Indian Cemetery Protective Assn.* v. *Peterson*. The court found that both actions would violate ⊥**444** the Free Exercise Clause because they "would seriously damage the salient visual, aural, and environmental qualities of the high country." The court also found that both proposed actions would violate the FWPCA, and that the environmental impact statements for construction of the road were deficient under the National Environmental Policy Act. Finally, the court concluded that both projects would breach the Government's trust responsibilities to protect water and fishing rights reserved to the Hoopa Valley Indians.

While an appeal was pending before the United States Court of Appeals for the Ninth Circuit, Congress enacted the California Wilderness Act of 1984, Pub. L. 98-425, 98 Stat. 1619. Under that statute, much of the property covered by the Forest Service's management plan is now designated a wilderness area, which means that commercial activities such as timber harvesting are forbidden. The statute exempts a narrow strip of land, coinciding with the Forest Service's proposed route for the remaining segment of the G-O road from the wilderness designation. The legislative history indicates that this exemption was adopted "to enable the completion of the Gasquet-Orleans Road project if the responsible authorities so decide." S. Rep. No. 98-582, p. 29 (1984). The existing unpaved section of road, however, lies within the wilderness area and is therefore now closed to general traffic.

A panel of the Ninth Circuit affirmed in part. The panel unanimously rejected the District Court's conclusion that the Government's proposed actions would breach its trust responsibilities to Indians on the Hoopa Valley Reservation. The panel also vacated the injunction to the extent that it had been rendered moot by the California Wilderness Act, which now prevents timber harvesting certain areas covered by the District Court's order. The District Court's decision, to the extent that it rested on statutory grounds, was otherwise unanimously affirmed.

⊥**445** By a divided decision, the District Court's constitutional ruling was also affirmed. Relying primarily on the Forest Service's own commissioned study, the majority found that construction of the Chimney Rock section of the G-O road would have significant, though largely indirect, adverse effects on Indian religious practices. The majority concluded that the Government had failed to demonstrate a compelling interest in the completion of the road, and that it could have abandoned the road without thereby creating "a religious preserve for a single group in violation of the establishment clause." The majority apparently applied the same analysis to logging operations that might be carried out in portions of the Chimney Rock area not covered by the California Wilderness Act. ("Because most of the high country has now been designated by Congress as a wilderness area, the issue of logging becomes less significant, although it does not disappear.")

The dissenting judge argued that certain of the adverse effects on respondents' religious practices could be eliminated by less drastic measures than a ban on building the road, and that other actual or suggested adverse effects did not pose a serious threat to the Indians' religious practices. He also concluded that the injunction against timber harvesting needed to be reconsidered in light of the California Wilderness Act: "It is not clear whether the district court would have issued an injunction based upon the development of the remaining small parcels. Accordingly, I would remand to allow the district court to reevaluate its injunction in light of the Act."

II

We begin by noting that the courts below did not articulate the bases of their decisions with perfect clarity. A fundamental and longstanding principle of judicial restraint requires that courts avoid reaching constitutional questions in advance of the necessity of deciding them. ⊥**446** This principle required the courts below to determine, before addressing the constitutional issue, whether a decision on that question could have entitled respondents to relief beyond that to which they were entitled on their statutory claims. If no additional relief would have been warranted, a constitutional decision would have been unnecessary and therefore inappropriate.

Neither the District Court nor the Court of Appeals explained or expressly articulated the necessity for their constitutional holdings. Were we persuaded that those holdings were unnecessary, we could simply vacate the relevant portions of the judgment below without discussing the merits of the constitutional issue. The structure and wording of the District Court's injunctive order, however, suggests that the statutory holdings would not have supported all the relief granted. The order is divided into four sections. Two of those sections deal with a 31,100 acre tract referred to as the Blue Creek Roadless Area. The injunction forbids the Forest Service from engaging in timber harvesting or road building anywhere on the tract "unless and until" compliance with the NEPA and the FWPCA have been demonstrated. The sections of the injunction dealing with the smaller Chimney Rock area (*i.e.*, the area affected by the First Amendment challenge) are worded differently. The Forest Service is permanently enjoined, without any qualifying language, from constructing the proposed portion of the G-O road "and/or *any alternative route*" through the area; similarly, the injunction forbids timber harvesting or the construction of logging roads in the Chimney Rock area pursuant to the Forest Service's proposed management plan "or *any other land management plan*" ⊥**447** (emphasis added). These differences in wording suggest, without absolutely implying, that an injunction covering the Chimney Rock area would in some way have been conditional, or narrower in scope, if the District Court had not decided the First Amendment issue as it did. Similarly, the silence of the Court of Appeals as to the necessity of reaching the First Amendment issue may have reflected its understanding that the District Court's injunction necessarily rested in part on constitutional grounds.

Because it appears reasonably likely that the First Amendment issue was necessary to the decisions below, we believe that it would be inadvisable to vacate and remand without addressing that issue on the merits. This conclusion is strengthened by considerations of judicial economy. The Government, which petitioned for certiorari on the constitutional issue alone, has informed us that it believes it can cure the statutory defects identified below, intends to do so, and will not challenge the adverse statutory rulings. In this circumstance, it is difficult to see what principle would be vindicated by sending this case on what would almost certainly be a brief road trip to the courts below.

III

A

The Free Exercise Clause of the First Amendment provides that "Congress shall make no law . . . prohibiting the free exercise [of religion]." U. S. Const., Amdt. 1. It is undisputed that the Indian respondents' beliefs are sincere and that the Government's proposed actions will have severe adverse effects on the practice of their religion. Respondents contend that the burden on their religious practices is heavy enough to violate the Free Exercise Clause unless the Government can demonstrate a compelling need to complete the G-O road or to engage in timber harvesting in the Chimney Rock area. We disagree.

⊥**448** In *Bowen* v. *Roy*, we considered a challenge to a federal statute that required the States to use Social Security numbers in administering certain welfare programs. Two applicants for benefits under these programs contended that their religious beliefs prevented them from acceding to the use of a Social Security number for their two-year-old daughter because the use of a numerical identifier would "'rob the spirit' of [their] daughter and prevent her from attaining greater spiritual power." Similarly, in this case, it is said that disruption of the natural environment caused by the G-O road will diminish the sacredness of the area in question and create distractions that will interfere with "training and ongoing religious experience of individuals using [sites within] the area for personal medicine and growth . . . and as integrated parts of a system of religious belief and practice which correlates ascending degrees of personal power with a geographic hierarchy of power." ("Scarred hills and mountains, and disturbed rocks destroy the purity of the sacred areas, and [Indian] consultants repeatedly stressed the need of a training doctor to be undistracted by such disturbance.") The Court rejected this kind of challenge in *Roy*:

"The Free Exercise Clause simply cannot be understood to require the Government to conduct its own internal affairs in ways that comport with the religious beliefs of particular citizens. Just as the Government may not insist that [the Roys] engage in any set form of religious observance, so [they] may not demand that the Government join in their chosen religious practices by refraining from using a number to identify their daughter. . . .

. . . The Free Exercise Clause affords an individual protection from certain forms of governmental compulsion; it does not afford an individual a right to dictate the conduct of the Government's internal procedures."

⊥**449** The building of a road or the harvesting of timber on publicly owned land cannot meaningfully be distinguished from the use of a Social Security number in *Roy*. In both cases, the challenged government action would interfere significantly with private persons' ability to pursue spiritual fulfillment according to their own religious beliefs. In neither case, however, would the affected individuals be coerced by the Government's action into violating their religious beliefs; nor would either governmental action penalize religious activity by denying any person an equal share of the rights, benefits, and privileges enjoyed by other citizens.

We are asked to distinguish this case from *Roy* on the ground that the infringement on religious liberty here is "significantly greater," or on the ground that the government practice in *Roy* was "purely mechanical" whereas this case involves "a case-by-case substantive determination as to how a particular unit of land will be managed." Similarly, we are told that this case can be distinguished from *Roy* because "the government action is not at some physically removed location where it places no restriction on what a practitioner may do." Brief for Respondent State of California 18. The State suggests that the Social Security number in *Roy* "could be characterized as interfering with Roy's religious tenets from a subjective point of view, where the government's conduct of 'its own internal affairs' was known to him only secondhand and did not interfere with his ability to practice his religion." In this case, however, it is said that the proposed road will "physically destro[y] the environmental conditions and the privacy without which the [religious] practices cannot be conducted."

These efforts to distinguish *Roy* are unavailing. This Court cannot determine the truth of the underlying beliefs that led to the religious objections here or in *Roy*, and accordingly cannot weigh the adverse ef⊥**450**fects on the Roys and compare them with the adverse effects on respondents. Without the ability to make such comparisons, we cannot say that the one form of incidental interference with an individual's spiritual activities should be subjected to a different constitutional analysis than the other. Respondents insist, nonetheless, that the courts below properly relied on a factual inquiry into the degree to which the Indians' spiritual practices would become ineffectual if the G-O road were built. They rely on several cases in which this Court has sustained free exercise challenges to government programs that interfered with individuals' ability to practice their religion. See *Wisconsin* v. *Yoder* (compulsory school-attendance law); *Sherbert* v. *Verner* (denial of unemployment benefits to applicant who refused to accept work requiring her to violate the Sabbath); *Thomas* v. *Review Board, Indiana Employment Security Div.* (denial of unemployment benefits to applicant whose religion forbade him to fabricate weapons); *Hobbie* (denial of unemployment benefits to religious convert who resigned position that required her to work on the Sabbath).

Even apart from the inconsistency between *Roy* and respondents' reading of these cases, their interpretation will not withstand analysis. It is true that this Court has repeatedly held that indirect coercion or penalties on the free exercise of religion, not just outright prohibitions, are subject to scrutiny under the First Amendment. Thus, for example, ineligibility for unemployment benefits, based solely on a refusal to violate the Sabbath, has been analogized to a fine imposed on Sabbath worship. *Sherbert*. This does not and cannot imply that incidental effects of government programs, which may make it more difficult to practice certain religions but which have no tendency to coerce individuals into acting contrary to their religious beliefs, require government to bring forward a compelling justifica⊥**451**tion for its otherwise lawful actions. The crucial word in the constitutional text is "prohibit": "For the Free Exercise Clause is written in terms of what the government cannot do to the individual, not in terms of what the individual can exact from the government." (Douglas, J., concurring).

Whatever may be the exact line between unconstitutional prohibitions on the free exercise of religion and the legitimate conduct by government of its own affairs, the location of the line cannot depend on measuring the effects of a governmental action on a religious objector's spiritual development. The Government does not dispute, and we have no reason to doubt, that the logging and roadbuilding projects at issue in this case could have devastating effects on traditional Indian religious practices. Those practices are intimately and inextricably bound up with the unique features of the Chimney Rock area, which is known to the Indians as the "high country." Individual practitioners use this area for personal spiritual development; some of their activities are believed to be critically important in advancing the welfare of the tribe, and indeed, of mankind itself. The Indians use this area, as they have used it for a very long time, to conduct a wide variety of specific rituals that aim to accomplish their religious goals. According to their beliefs, the rituals would not be efficacious if conducted at other sites than the ones traditionally used, and too much disturbance of the area's natural state would clearly render any meaningful continuation of traditional practices impossible. To be sure, the Indians themselves were far from unanimous in opposing the G-O road, and it seems less than certain that construction of the road will be so disruptive that it will doom their religion. Nevertheless, we can assume that the threat to the efficacy of at least some religious practices is extremely grave.

Even if we assume that we should accept the Ninth Circuit's prediction, according to which the G-O road will "virtually destroy the Indians'. . . ability to practice their religion," ⊥**452** the Constitution simply does not provide a principle that could justify upholding respondents' legal claims. However much we might wish that it were otherwise, government simply could not operate if it were required to satisfy every citizen's religious needs and desires. A broad range of government activities—

from social welfare programs to foreign aid to conservation projects—will always be considered essential to the spiritual well-being of some citizens, often on the basis of sincerely held religious beliefs. Others will find the very same activities deeply offensive, and perhaps incompatible with their own search for spiritual fulfillment and with the tenets of their religion. The First Amendment must apply to all citizens alike, and it can give to none of them a veto over public programs that do not prohibit the free exercise of religion. The Constitution does not, and courts cannot, offer to reconcile the various competing demands on government, many of them rooted in sincere religious belief, that inevitably arise in so diverse a society as ours. That task, to the extent that it is feasible, is for the legislatures and other institutions. Cf. The Federalist No. 10 (suggesting that the effects of religious factionalism are best restrained through competition among a multiplicity of religious sects).

One need not look far beyond the present case to see why the analysis in *Roy*, but not respondents' proposed extension of *Sherbert* and its progeny, offers a sound reading of the Constitution. Respondents attempt to stress the limits of the religious servitude that they are now seeking to impose on the Chimney Rock area of the Six Rivers National Forest. While defending an injunction against logging operations and the construction of a road, they apparently do not *at present* object to the area's being used by recreational visitors, other Indians, or forest rangers. Nothing in the principle for which they contend, however, would distinguish this case from another lawsuit in which they (or similarly situated religious objectors) might seek to exclude all human activity but ⊥**453** their own from sacred areas of the public lands. The Indian respondents insist that "*[p]rivacy* during the power quests is required for the practitioners to maintain the purity needed for a successful journey." Brief for Indian Respondents (emphasis added; citation to record omitted). Similarly: "The practices conducted in the high country entail intense meditation and require the practitioner to achieve a profound awareness of the natural environment. Prayer seats are oriented so there is an unobstructed view, and the practitioner must be surrounded by *undisturbed* naturalness" (emphasis added) (citations to record omitted). No disrespect for these practices is implied when one notes that such beliefs could easily require *de facto* beneficial ownership of some rather spacious tracts of public property. Even without anticipating future cases, the diminution of the Government's property rights, and the concomitant subsidy of the Indian religion, would in this case be far from trivial: the District Court's order permanently forbade commercial timber harvesting, or the construction of a two-lane road, anywhere within an area covering a full 27 sections (i.e., more than 17,000 acres) of public land.

The Constitution does not permit government to discriminate against religions that treat particular physical sites as sacred, and a law forbidding the Indian respondents from visiting the Chimney Rock area would raise a different set of constitutional questions. Whatever rights the Indians may have to the use of the area, however, those rights do not divest the Government of its right to use what is, after all, *its* land. (O'Connor, J., concurring in part and dissenting in part) (distinguishing between the Government's use of information in its possession and the Government's requiring an individual to provide such information) (*Bowen* v. *Roy*).

B

Nothing in our opinion should be read to encourage governmental insensitivity to the religious needs of any citizen. ⊥**454** The Government's rights to the use of its own land, for example, need not and should not discourage it from accommodating religious practices like those engaged in by the Indian respondents. It is worth emphasizing, therefore, that the Government has taken numerous steps in this very case to minimize the impact that construction of the G-O road will have on the Indians' religious activities. First, the Forest Service commissioned a comprehensive study of the effects that the project would have on the cultural and religious value of the Chimney Rock area. The resulting 423-page report was so sympathetic to the Indians' interests that it has constituted the principal piece of evidence relied on by respondents' throughout this litigation.

Although the Forest Service did not in the end adopt the report's recommendation that the project be abandoned, many other ameliorative measures were planned. No sites where specific rituals take place were to be disturbed. In fact, a major factor in choosing among alternative routes for the road was the relation of the various routes to religious sites: the route selected by the Regional Forester is, he noted, "the farthest removed from contemporary spiritual sites; thus, the adverse audible intrusions associated with the road would be less than all other alternatives." Nor were the Forest Service's concerns limited to "audible intrusions." As the dissenting judge below observed, ten specific steps were planned to reduce the visual impact of the road on the surrounding country.

Except for abandoning its project entirely, and thereby leaving the two existing segments of road to deadend in the middle of a National Forest, it is difficult to see how the Government could have been more solicitous. Such solicitude accords with "the policy of the United States to protect and preserve for American Indians their inherent right of freedom to believe, express, and exercise the traditional re⊥**455**ligions of the American Indian . . . including but not limited to access to sites, use and possession of sacred objects, and the freedom to worship through ceremonials and traditional rites." American Indian Religious Freedom Act (AIRFA), Pub. L. 95-341, 92 Stat. 469, 42 U.S.C. § 1996.

Respondents, however, suggest that AIRFA goes further and in effect enacts their interpretation of the First Amendment into statutory law. Although this contention was rejected by the District Court, they seek to defend the judgment below by arguing that AIRFA authorizes the injunction against completion of the G-O road. This argument is without merit. After reciting several legislative findings, AIRFA "resolves" upon the policy quoted above. A second section of the statute, 92 Stat. 470, required an evaluation of federal policies and procedures, in consultation with native religious leaders, of changes necessary to protect and preserve the rights and practices in question. The required report dealing with this evaluation was completed and released in 1979. Nowhere in the law is there so much as a hint of any intent to create a cause of action or any judicially enforceable individual rights.

What is obvious from the face of the statute is confirmed by numerous indications in the legislative history. The sponsor of the bill that became AIRFA, Representative Udall, called it "a sense of Congress joint resolution," aimed at ensuring that "the basic right of the Indian people to exercise their traditional religious practices is not infringed without a clear decision on the part of the Congress or the administrators that such religious practices must yield to some higher consideration." 124 Cong. Rec. 21444 (1978). Representative Udall emphasized that the bill would not "confer special religious rights on Indians," would "not change any existing State or Federal law," and in fact "has no teeth in it." *Id.*

⊥456 C

The dissent proposes an approach to the First Amendment that is fundamentally inconsistent with the principles on which our decision rests. Notwithstanding the sympathy that we all must feel for the plight of the Indian respondents, it is plain that the approach taken by the dissent cannot withstand analysis. On the contrary, the path towards which it points us is incompatible with the text of the Constitution, with the precedents of this Court, and with a responsible sense of our own institutional role.

The dissent begins by asserting that the "constitutional guarantee we interpret today . . . is directed against *any* form of government action that frustrates or inhibits religious practice" (emphasis added). The Constitution, however, says no such thing. Rather, it states: "Congress shall make no law . . . *prohibiting* the free exercise [of religion]." U. S. Const., Amdt. 1 (emphasis added).

As we explained above, *Bowen* v. *Roy* rejected a First Amendment challenge to government activities that the religious objectors sincerely believed would "'rob the spirit' of [their] daughter and prevent her from attaining greater spiritual power." The dissent now offers to distinguish that case by saying that the Government was acting there "in a purely internal manner," whereas land-use decisions "are likely to have substantial external effects." Whatever the source or meaning of the dissent's distinction, it has no basis in *Roy*. Robbing the spirit of a child, and preventing her from attaining greater spiritual power, is both a "substantial external effect" and one that is remarkably similar to the injury claimed by respondents in the case before us today. The dissent's reading of *Roy* would effectively overrule that decision, without providing any compelling justification for doing so.

The dissent also misreads *Wisconsin* v. *Yoder*. The statute at issue in that case prohibited the **⊥457** Amish parents, on pain of criminal prosecution, from providing their children with the kind of education required by the Amish religion. The statute directly compelled the Amish to send their children to public high schools "contrary to the Amish religion and way of life." The Court acknowledged that the statute might be constitutional, *despite* its coercive nature, if the State could show with sufficient "particularity how its admittedly strong interest in compulsory education would be adversely affected by granting an exemption to the Amish." The dissent's out-of-context quotations notwithstanding, there is nothing whatsoever in the *Yoder* opinion to support the proposition that the "impact" on the Amish religion would have been constitutionally problematic if the statute at issue had not been coercive in nature.

Perceiving a "stress point in the longstanding conflict between two disparate cultures," the dissent attacks us for declining to "balanc[e] these competing and potentially irreconcilable interests, choosing instead to turn this difficult task over to the federal legislature." Seeing the Court as the arbiter, the dissent proposes a legal test under which it would decide which public lands are "central" or "indispensable" to which religions, and by implication which are "dispensable" or "peripheral," and would then decide which government programs are "compelling" enough to justify "infringement of those practices." We would accordingly be required to weigh the value of every religious belief and practice that is said to be threatened by any government program. Unless a "showing of 'centrality,'" is nothing but an assertion of centrality, the dissent thus offers us the prospect of this Court holding that some sincerely held religious beliefs and practices are not "central" to certain religions, despite protestations to the contrary from the religious objectors who brought the lawsuit. In other words, the dissent's approach would **⊥458** require us to rule that some religious adherents misunderstand their own religious beliefs. We think such an approach cannot be squared with the Constitution or with our precedents, and that it would cast the judiciary in a role that we were never intended to play.

IV

The decision of the court below, according to which the First Amendment precludes the Government from completing the G-O road or from permitting timber harvesting in the Chimney Rock area, is reversed. In order that the District Court's injunction may be reconsidered in light of this holding, and in the light of any other relevant events that may have intervened since the injunction issued, the case is remanded for further proceedings consistent with this opinion.

It is so ordered.

Justice KENNEDY took no part in the consideration or decision of this case.

Justice BRENNAN, with whom *Justice* MARSHALL and *Justice* BLACKMUN join, dissenting.

"'[T]he Free Exercise Clause,'" the Court explains today, "'is written in terms of what the government cannot do to the individual, not in terms of what the individual can exact from the government.'" (quoting *Sherbert* v. *Verner* (Douglas, J., concurring)). Pledging fidelity to this unremarkable constitutional principle, the Court nevertheless concludes that even where the Government uses federal land in a manner that threatens the very existence of a Native American religion, the Government is simply not "doing" anything to the practitioners of that faith. Instead, the Court believes that Native Americans who request that the Government refrain from destroying their religion effectively seek to exact from the Government *de facto* beneficial ownership of federal property. These two astonishing conclusions follow naturally from the Court's deter⊥**459**mination that federal land-use decisions that render the practice of a given religion impossible do not burden that religion in a manner cognizable under the Free Exercise Clause, because such decisions neither coerce conduct inconsistent with religious belief nor penalize religious activity. The constitutional guarantee we interpret today, however, draws no such fine distinctions between types of restraints on religious exercise, but rather is directed against any form of governmental action that frustrates or inhibits religious practice. Because the Court today refuses even to acknowledge the constitutional injury respondents will suffer, and because this refusal essentially leaves Native Americans with absolutely no constitutional protection against perhaps the gravest threat to their religious practices, I dissent.

I

For at least 200 years and probably much longer, the Yurok, Karok, and Tolowa Indians have held sacred an approximately 25 square-mile area of land situated in what is today the Blue Creek Unit of Six Rivers National Forest in northwestern California. As the Government readily concedes, regular visits to this area, known to respondent Indians as the "high country," have played and continue to play a "critical" role in the religious practices and rituals of these Tribes. Those beliefs, only briefly described in the Court's opinion, are crucial to a proper understanding of respondents' claims.

As the Forest Service's commissioned study, the Theodoratus Report, explains, for Native Americans religion is not a discrete sphere of activity separate from all others, and any attempt to isolate the religious aspects of Indian life "is in reality an exercise which forces Indian concepts into non-Indian categories." D. Theodoratus, Cultural Resources of the Chimney Rock Section, Gasquet-Orleans Road, Six Rivers National Forest (1979). Thus, for most Native Americans, "[t]he area of worship cannot be delineated from ⊥**460** social, political, cultur[al], and other areas o[f] Indian lifestyle." American Indian Religious Freedom, Hearings on S. J. Res. 102 before the Senate Select Committee on Indian Affairs, 95th Cong., 2d Sess., 86 (1978) (statement of Barney Old Coyote, Crow Tribe). A pervasive feature of this lifestyle is the individual's relationship with the natural world; this relationship, which can accurately though somewhat incompletely be characterized as one of stewardship, forms the core of what might be called, for want of a better nomenclature, the Indian religious experience. While traditional Western religions view creation as the work of a deity "who institutes natural laws which then govern the operation of physical nature," tribal religions regard creation as an ongoing process in which they are morally and religiously obligated to participate. Native Americans fulfill this duty through ceremonies and rituals designed to preserve and stabilize the earth and to protect humankind from disease and other catastrophes. Failure to conduct these ceremonies in the manner and place specified, adherents believe, will result in great harm to the earth and to the people whose welfare depends upon it.

In marked contrast to traditional Western religions, the belief systems of Native Americans do not rely on doctrines, creeds, or dogmas. Established or universal truths—the mainstay of Western religions—play no part in Indian faith. Ceremonies are communal efforts undertaken for specific purposes in accordance with instructions handed down from generation to generation. Commentaries on or interpretations of the rituals themselves are deemed absolute violations of the ceremonies, whose value lies not in their ability to explain the natural world or to enlighten individual believers but in their efficacy as protectors and enhancers of tribal existence. Where dogma lies at the heart of Western religions, Native American faith is inextricably ⊥**461** bound to the use of land. The site-specific nature of Indian religious practice derives from the Native American perception that land is itself a sacred, living being. Rituals are performed in prescribed locations not merely as a matter of traditional orthodoxy, but because land, like all other living things, is unique, and specific sites possess different spiritual properties and significance. Within this belief system, therefore, land is not fungible; indeed, at the time of the Spanish colonization of the American southwest, "all . . . Indians held in some form a belief in a sacred and indissoluble bond between themselves and the land in which their settlements were located."

For respondent Indians, the most sacred of lands is the high country where, they believe, prehuman spirits moved with the coming of humans to the earth. Because these spirits are seen as the source of religious power, or "medicine," many of the tribes' rituals and practices require frequent journeys to the area. Thus, for example, religious leaders preparing for the complex of ceremonies that underlie the Tribes' World Renewal efforts must travel to specific sites in the high country in order to attain the medicine necessary for successful renewal. Similarly, individual tribe members may seek curative powers for the healing of the sick, or personal medicine for particular purposes such as good luck in singing, hunting, or love. A period of preparation generally precedes such visits, and individuals must select trails in the sacred area according to the medicine they seek and their abilities, gradually moving to increasingly more powerful sites, which are typically located at higher altitudes. Among the most powerful of sites are Chimney Rock, Doctor Rock, and Peak 8, all of which are elevated rock outcroppings.

⊥462 According to the Theodoratus Report, the qualities "of silence, the aesthetic perspective, and the physical attributes, are an extension of the sacredness of [each] particular site." The act of medicine making is akin to meditation: the individual must integrate physical, mental and vocal actions in order to communicate with the prehuman spirits. As a result, "successful use of the high country is dependent upon and facilitated by certain qualities of the physical environment, the most important of which are privacy, silence, and an undisturbed natural setting." Although few tribe members actually make medicine at the most powerful sites, the entire tribe's welfare hinges on the success of the individual practitioners.

Beginning in 1972, the Forest Service began preparing a multiple-use management plan for the Blue Creek Unit. The plan's principal features included the harvesting of 733 million board feet of Douglas fir over an 80-year period and the completion of a 6-mile segment of paved road running between two northern California towns, Gasquet and Orleans (the G-O road). The road's primary purpose was to provide a route for hauling the timber harvested under the management plan; in addition, it would enhance public access to the Six Rivers and other national forests, and allow for more efficient maintenance and fire control by the Forest Service itself. In the mid-1970s, the Forest Service circulated draft environmental impact statements evaluating the effects of several proposed routes for the final segment of the G-O road, including at least two that circumnavigated the high country altogether. Ultimately, however, the Service settled on a route running along the Chimney Rock Corridor, which traverses the Indians' sacred lands.

Respondent Indians brought suit to enjoin implementation of the plan, alleging that the road construction and timber harvesting would impermissibly interfere with their religious practices in violation of the Free Exercise Clause of the First **⊥463** Amendment. Following a trial, the District Court granted the requested injunctive relief. The court found that "use of the high country is essential to [respondents'] 'World Renewal' ceremonies . . . which constitute the heart of the Northwest Indian religious belief system," and that "'[i]ntrusions on the sanctity of the Blue Creek high country are . . . potentially destructive of the very core of Northwest [Indian] religious beliefs and practices.'" Concluding that these burdens on respondents' religious practices were sufficient to trigger the protections of the Free Exercise Clause, the court found that the interests served by the G-O road and the management plan were insufficient to justify those burdens. In particular, the court found that the road would not improve access to timber resources in the Blue Creek Unit and indeed was unnecessary to the harvesting of that timber; that it would not significantly improve the administration of the Six Rivers National Forest; and that it would increase recreational access only marginally, and at the expense of the very pristine environment that makes the area suitable for primitive recreational use in the first place. The court further found that the unconnected segments of the road had independent utility, and that although completion of the **⊥464** Chimney Rock segment would reduce timber hauling costs, it would not generate new jobs but would instead merely shift work from one area of the region to another. Finally, in enjoining the proposed harvesting activities, the court found that the Blue Creek Unit's timber resources were but a small fraction of those located in the entire national forest and that the local timber industry would not suffer seriously if access to this fraction were foreclosed.

While the case was pending on appeal before the Court of Appeals for the Ninth Circuit, Congress passed the California Wilderness Act of 1984, Pub. L. 98-425, 98 Stat. 1619, which designates most of the Blue Creek Unit a wilderness area, and thus precludes logging and all other commercial activities in most of the area covered by the Forest Service's management plan. Thereafter, the Court of Appeals affirmed the District Court's determination that the proposed harvesting and construction activities violated respondents' constitutional rights. Recognizing that the high country is "indispensable" to the religious lives of the approximately 5,000 tribe members who reside in the area, *Northwest Indian Cemetery Protective Assn.* v. *Peterson*, the court concluded "that the proposed government operations would *virtually destroy the . . . Indians' ability to practice their religion*" (emphasis added). Like the lower court, the Court of Appeals found **⊥465** the Government's interests in building the road and permitting limited timber harvesting—interests which of course were considerably undermined by passage of the California Wilderness Act—did not justify the destruction of respondents' religion.

II

The Court does not for a moment suggest that the interests served by the G-O road are in any way compelling, or that they outweigh the destructive effect construction of the road will have on respondents' religious practices. Instead, the Court embraces the Government's contention that its prerogative as landowner should always take precedence over a claim that a particular use of federal property infringes religious practices. Attempting to justify this rule, the Court argues that the First Amendment bars only outright prohibitions, indirect coercion, and penalties on the free exercise of religion. All other "incidental effects of government programs," it concludes, even those "which may make it more difficult to practice certain religions but which have no tendency to coerce individuals into acting contrary to their religious beliefs," simply do not give rise to constitutional concerns. Since our recognition nearly half a century ago that restraints on religious conduct implicate the concerns of the Free Exercise Clause, we have never suggested that the protections of the guarantee are limited to so narrow a range of governmental burdens. The land-use decision challenged here will restrain respondents from practicing their religion as surely and as completely as any of the governmental actions we have struck down in the past, and the Court's efforts simply to define away respondents' in⊥**466**jury as nonconstitutional is both unjustified and ultimately unpersuasive.

A

The Court ostensibly finds support for its narrow formulation of religious burdens in our decisions in *Hobbie* v. *Unemployment Appeals Comm'n of Fla.*, *Thomas* v. *Review Bd.*, *Indiana Employment Security Division*, and *Sherbert* v. *Verner*. In those cases, the laws at issue forced individuals to choose between adhering to specific religious tenets and forfeiting unemployment benefits on the one hand, and accepting work repugnant to their religious beliefs on the other. The religions involved, therefore, lent themselves to the coercion analysis the Court espouses today, for they proscribed certain conduct such as munitions work *(Thomas)* or working on Saturdays *(Sherbert, Hobbie)* that the unemployment benefits laws effectively compelled. In sustaining the challenges to these laws, however, we nowhere suggested that such coercive compulsion exhausted the range of religious burdens recognized under the Free Exercise Clause.

Indeed, in *Wisconsin* v. *Yoder*, we struck down a state compulsory school attendance law on free exercise grounds not so much because of the affirmative coercion the law exerted on individual religious practitioners, but because of "the *impact* that compulsory high school attendance could have on the continued survival of Amish communities." Like respondents here, the Amish view life as pervasively religious and their faith accordingly dictates their entire lifestyle. Detailed as their religious rules are, however, the parents in *Yoder* did not argue that their religion expressly proscribed public education beyond the eighth grade; rather, they objected to the law because "the *values* . . . of the modern secondary school are in sharp conflict with the fundamental *mode of life* mandated by the Amish religion" (emphasis added). By exposing Amish children "to a ⊥**467** 'worldly' influence in conflict with their beliefs," and by removing those children "from their community, physically and emotionally, during the crucial and formative adolescent period of life" when Amish beliefs are inculcated, the compulsory school law posed "a very real threat of undermining the Amish community and religious practice." Admittedly, this threat arose from the compulsory nature of the law at issue, but it was the "impact" on religious practice itself, not the source of that impact, that led us to invalidate the law.

I thus cannot accept the Court's premise that the form of the Government's restraint on religious practice, rather than its effect, controls our constitutional analysis. Respondents here have demonstrated that construction of the G-O road will completely frustrate the practice of their religion, for as the lower courts found, the proposed logging and construction activities will virtually destroy respondents' religion, and will therefore necessarily force them into abandoning those practices altogether. Indeed, the Government's proposed activities will restrain religious practice to a far greater degree here than in any of the cases cited by the Court today. None of the religious adherents in *Hobbie*, *Thomas*, and *Sherbert*, for example, claimed or could have claimed that the denial of unemployment benefits rendered the practice of their religions impossible; at most, the challenged laws made those practices more expensive. Here, in stark contrast, respondents have claimed—and proved—that the desecration of the high country will prevent religious leaders from attaining the religious power or medicine indispensable to the success of virtually all their rituals and ceremonies. Similarly, in *Yoder* the compulsory school law threatened to "undermin[e] the Amish community and religious practice," and thus to force adherents to "abandon belief . . . or . . . to migrate to some other and more tolerant region." Here the threat posed by the desecration of sacred lands that are indisputably essential to ⊥**468** respondents' religious practices is both more direct and more substantial than that raised by a compulsory school law that simply exposed Amish children to an alien value system. And of course respondents here do not even have the option, however unattractive it might be, of migrating to more hospitable locales; the site-specific nature of their belief system renders it nontransportable.

Ultimately, the Court's coercion test turns on a distinction between governmental actions that compel affirmative conduct inconsistent with religious belief, and those governmental actions that prevent conduct consistent with religious belief. In my view, such a distinction is without constitutional significance. The crucial word in the constitutional text, as the Court itself acknowledges, is "prohibit," a comprehensive term that in no way suggests that the intended protection is aimed only at governmental actions that coerce affirmative conduct. Nor does the Court's distinction comport with the principles animating the constitutional guarantee: religious freedom is threatened no less by governmental action that makes the practice of one's chosen faith impossible than by governmental programs that pressure one to engage in conduct inconsistent with religious beliefs. The Court attempts to explain the line it draws by arguing that the protections of the Free Exercise Clause "cannot depend on measuring the effects of a governmental action on a religious objector's spiritual development," ⊥**469** for in a society as diverse as ours, the Government cannot help but offend the "religious needs and desires" of some citizens. While I agree that governmental action that simply offends religious sensibilities may not be challenged under the Clause, we have recognized that laws that affect spiritual development by impeding the integration of children into the religious community or by increasing the expense of adherence to religious principles—in short, laws that frustrate or inhibit religious *practice*—trigger the protections of the constitutional guarantee. Both common sense and our prior cases teach us, therefore, that governmental action that makes the practice of a given faith more difficult necessarily penalizes that practice and thereby tends to prevent adherence to religious belief. The harm to the practitioners is the same regardless of the manner in which the Government restrains their religious expression, and the Court's fear that an "effects" test will permit religious adherents to challenge governmental actions they merely find "offensive" in no way justifies its refusal to recognize the constitutional injury citizens suffer when governmental action not only offends but actually restrains their religious practices. Here, respondents have demonstrated that the Government's proposed activities will completely prevent them from practicing their religion, and such a showing, no less than those made out in *Hobbie*, *Thomas*, *Sherbert*, and *Yoder*, entitles them to the protections of the Free Exercise Clause.

B

Nor can I agree with the Court's assertion that respondents' constitutional claim is foreclosed by our decision in *Bowen* v. *Roy*. There, applicants for certain welfare benefits objected to the use of a Social Security number in connection with the administration of their two-year-old daughter's application for benefits, contending that such use would "rob the [child's] spirit" and thus interfere with her spiritual development. In rejecting that chal⊥**470**lenge, we stated that "[t]he Free Exercise Clause simply cannot be understood to require the Government to conduct its own *internal affairs* in ways that comport with the religious beliefs of particular citizens." (Stevens, J., concurring in part). ("[T]he Free Exercise Clause does not give an individual the right to dictate the Government's method of recordkeeping"). Accordingly, we explained that Roy could "no more prevail on his religious objection to the Government's use of a Social Security number for his daughter than he could on a sincere religious objection to the size or color of the Government's filing cabinets. The Free Exercise Clause affords an individual protection from certain forms of governmental compulsion; it does not afford an individual a right to dictate the conduct of the government's *internal procedures*" (emphasis added).

Today the Court professes an inability to differentiate *Roy* from the present case, suggesting that "[t]he building of a road or the harvesting of timber on publicly owned land cannot meaningfully be distinguished from the use of a Social Security number." I find this inability altogether remarkable. In *Roy*, we repeatedly stressed the "internal" nature of the Government practice at issue: noting that Roy objected to "the widespread use of the social security number by the federal or state governments *in their computer systems*," (citation omitted; internal quotation marks omitted; emphasis added), we likened the use of such recordkeeping numbers to decisions concerning the purchase of office equipment. When the Government processes information, of course, it acts in a purely internal manner, and any free exercise challenge to such internal recordkeeping in effect seeks to dictate how the Government conducts its own affairs.

Federal land-use decisions, by contrast, are likely to have substantial external effects that government decisions con⊥**471**cerning office furniture and information storage obviously will not, and they are correspondingly subject to public scrutiny and public challenge in a host of ways that office equipment purchases are not. Indeed, in the American Indian Religious Freedom Act (AIRFA), 42 U.S.C. § 1996, Congress expressly recognized the adverse impact land-use decisions and other governmental actions frequently have on the site-specific religious practices of Native Americans, and the Act accordingly directs agencies to consult with Native American religious leaders before taking actions that might impair those practices. Although I agree that the Act does not create any judicially enforceable rights, the absence of any private right of action in no way undermines the statute's significance as an express congressional determination that federal land management decisions are not "internal" government "procedures," but are instead governmental actions that can and indeed are likely to burden Native American religious practices. That such decisions should be subject to constitutional challenge, and potential constitutional limitations, should hardly come as a surprise.

The Court today, however, ignores *Roy's* emphasis on the internal nature of the government practice at issue there, ⊥**472** and instead construes that case as further support for the proposition that governmental action that does not coerce conduct inconsistent with religious faith simply does not implicate the concerns of the Free Exercise Clause. That such a reading is wholly untenable, however, is demonstrated by the cruelly surreal result it produces here: governmental action that will virtually destroy a religion is nevertheless deemed not to "burden" that religion. Moreover, in AIRFA Congress explicitly acknowledged that federal "policies and regulations" could and often did "intrud[e] upon [and] interfere with" site-specific Native American religious ceremonies, Pub. L. 95-341, 92 Stat. 469, and in *Roy* we recognized that this Act—"with its emphasis on protecting the freedom to believe, express, and exercise a religion—accurately identifies the mission of the Free Exercise Clause itself." Ultimately, in *Roy* we concluded that, however much the Government's recordkeeping system may have offended Roy's sincere religious sensibilities, he could not challenge that system under the Free Exercise Clause because the Government's practice did not "in any degree impair Roy's 'freedom to believe, express, and *exercise*' his religion" (emphasis added). That determination distinguishes the injury at issue here, which the Court finds so "remarkably similar" to Roy's, for respondents have made an uncontroverted showing that the proposed construction and logging activities will impair their freedom to exercise their religion in the greatest degree imaginable, and Congress has "accurately identifie[d]" such injuries as falling within the scope of the Free Exercise Clause. The Court's reading of *Roy*, therefore, simply cannot be squared with our endorsement—in that very same case—of this congressional determination. More important, it lends no support to the Court's efforts to narrow both the reach and promise of the Free Exercise Clause itself.

⊥**473** C

In the final analysis, the Court's refusal to recognize the constitutional dimension of respondents' injuries stems from its concern that acceptance of respondents' claim could potentially strip the Government of its ability to manage and use vast tracts of federal property. In addition, the nature of respondents' site-specific religious practices raises the specter of future suits in which Native Americans seek to exclude all human activity from such areas. These concededly legitimate concerns lie at the very heart of this case, which represents yet another stress point in the longstanding conflict between two disparate cultures—the dominant western culture, which views land in terms of ownership and use, and that of Native Americans, in which concepts of private property are not only alien, but contrary to a belief system that holds land sacred. Rather than address this conflict in any meaningful fashion, however, the Court disclaims all responsibility for balancing these competing and potentially irreconcilable interests, choosing instead to turn this difficult task over to the federal legislature. Such an abdication is more than merely indefensible as an institutional matter: by defining respondents' injury as "nonconstitutional," the Court has effectively bestowed on one party to this conflict the unilateral authority to resolve all future disputes in its favor, subject only to the Court's toothless exhortation to be "sensitive" to affected religions. In my view, however, Native Americans deserve—and the Constitution demands—more than this.

Prior to today's decision, several Courts of Appeals had attempted to fashion a test that accommodates the competing "demands" placed on federal property by the two cultures. Recognizing that the Government normally enjoys plenary authority over federal lands, the Courts of Appeals required Native Americans to demonstrate that any land-use decisions they challenged involved lands that were "central" or "indispensable" to their religious practices. ⊥**474** Although this requirement limits the potential number of free exercise claims that might be brought to federal land management decisions, and thus forestalls the possibility that the Government will find itself ensnared in a host of Lilliputian lawsuits, it has been criticized as inherently ethnocentric, for it incorrectly assumes that Native American belief systems ascribe religious significance to land in a traditionally western hierarchical manner. It is frequently the case in constitutional litigation, however, that courts are called upon to balance interests that are not readily translated into rough equivalents. At their most absolute, the competing claims that both the Government and Native Americans assert in federal land are fundamentally incompatible, and unless they are tempered by compromise, mutual accommodation will remain impossible.

I believe it appropriate, therefore, to require some showing of "centrality" before the Government can be required either to come forward with a compelling justification for its proposed use of federal land or to forgo that use altogether. "Centrality," however, should not be equated with the survival or extinction of the religion itself. In *Yoder*, for example, we treated the objection to the compulsory school attendance of adolescents as "central" to the Amish faith even though such attendance did not prevent or otherwise render the practice of that religion impossible, and instead simply ⊥**475** threatened to "undermine" that faith. Because of their perceptions of and relationship with the natural world, Native Americans consider all land sacred. Nevertheless, the Theodoratus Report reveals that respondents here deemed certain lands more powerful and more directly related to their religious practices than others. Thus, in my view, while Native Americans need not demonstrate, as respondents did here, that the Government's land-use decision will assuredly eradicate their faith, I do not think it is enough to allege simply that the land in question is held sacred. Rather, adherents challenging a proposed use of federal land should be required to show that the decision poses a substantial and realistic threat of frustrating their religious practices. Once such a showing is made, the burden should shift to the Government to come forward with a compelling state interest sufficient to justify the infringement of those practices.

The Court today suggests that such an approach would place courts in the untenable position of deciding which practices and beliefs are "central" to a given faith and which are not, and invites the prospect of judges advising some religious adherents that they "misunderstand their own religious beliefs." In fact, however, courts need not undertake any such inquiries: like all other religious adherents, Native Americans would be the arbiters of which practices are central to their faith, subject only to the normal requirement that their claims be genuine and sincere. The question for the courts, then, is not whether the Native American claimants understand their own religion, but rather, whether they have discharged their burden of demonstrating, as the Amish did with respect to the compulsory school law in *Yoder*, that the land-use decision poses a substantial and realistic threat of undermining or frustrating their religious practices. Ironically, the Court's apparent solicitude for the integrity of religious belief and its desire to forestall the possibility that courts might second-guess the ⊥**476** claims of religious adherents leads to far greater inequities than those the Court postulates: today's ruling sacrifices a religion at least as old as the Nation itself, along with the spiritual well-being of its approximately 5,000 adherents, so that the Forest Service can build a 6-mile segment of road that two lower courts found had only the most marginal and speculative utility, both to the Government itself and to the private lumber interests that might conceivably use it.

Similarly, the Court's concern that the claims of Native Americans will place "religious servitudes" upon vast tracts of federal property cannot justify its refusal to recognize the constitutional injury respondents will suffer here. It is true, as the Court notes, that respondents' religious use of the high country requires privacy and solitude. The fact remains, however, that respondents have never asked the Forest Service to exclude others from the area. Should respondents or any other group seek to force the Government to protect their religious practices from the interference of private parties, such a demand would implicate not only the concern of the Free Exercise Clause, but those of the Establishment Clause as well. That case, however, is most assuredly not before us today, and in any event cannot justify the Court's refusal to acknowledge that the injuries respondents will suffer as a result of the Government's proposed activities are sufficient to state a constitutional cause of action.

III

Today, the Court holds that a federal land-use decision that promises to destroy an entire religion does not burden the practice of that faith in a manner recognized by the Free Exercise Clause. Having thus stripped respondents and all other Native Americans of any constitutional protection against perhaps the most serious threat to their age-old religious practices, and indeed to their entire way of life, the Court assures us that nothing in its decision "should be read to encourage governmental insensitivity to the religious ⊥**477** needs of any citizen." I find it difficult, however, to imagine conduct more insensitive to religious needs than the Government's determination to build a marginally useful road in the face of uncontradicted evidence that the road will render the practice of respondents' religion impossible. Nor do I believe that respondents will derive any solace from the knowledge that although the practice of their religion will become "more difficult" as a result of the Government's actions, they remain free to maintain their religious beliefs. Given today's ruling, that freedom amounts to nothing more than the right to believe that their religion will be destroyed. The safeguarding of such a hollow freedom not only makes a mockery of the "'policy of the United States to protect and preserve for American Indians their inherent right of freedom to believe, express, and exercise the[ir] traditional religions,'" it fails utterly to accord with the dictates of the First Amendment.

I dissent.

FREE EXERCISE AND PUBLIC EDUCATION

In the landmark *Brown v. Board of Education* school desegregation decision, Chief Justice Warren wrote for a unanimous Court, "Today education is perhaps the most important function of state and local governments." There is no doubt that in pursuance of this function states may enact and enforce compulsory attendance statutes mandating attendance at public or private schools within designated ages.

The compulsory school attendance laws of Wisconsin required children in that state to attend school until they reached age sixteen. Notwithstanding the requirement, the fourteen- and fifteen-year-old children of Jonas Yoder, Wallace Miller, and Adin Yutzy were not enrolled in school, and their parents were convicted of violating the law and fined a nominal amount. Their defense was that their sincerely held religious beliefs as members of the Old Order Amish and Conservative Amish Mennonite Church forbade their sending the children to school past the eighth grade.

The religious group to which Jonas Yoder and his fellow religionists belonged was not one of the new and exotic "cults" of the 1960s. Its history goes back to the sixteenth century, at which time there were many attempts to reform the Roman Catholic church—attempts which resulted in separate "Protestant" groups. The principal leaders of these groups were Martin Luther, Huldreich Zwingli, Henry VIII, and somewhat later, John Calvin. With the exception of the one initiated by Henry VIII, these attempts at reform were theological in nature, i.e., they tried to reform the church by calling it back to what the different reformers considered to be the New Testament form of Christianity.

However, another Protestant group also originated in the sixteenth century: the Anabaptists emerged in 1525 after and because of their disagreements with Zwingli's reforms in Zurich, Switzerland. The Anabaptists were of the opinion that none of the earlier reformers had gone far enough in their break with Rome. Although the reformers had started in the right direction, they had not followed their own ideas to logical conclusions and consequently had not conformed their Christian lives and thought to the New Testament pattern. The Anabaptists attempted to be meticulously faithful to New Testament ideas and styles of faith and thus to take reformatory ideas to completion. Because of their attitudes, the Anabaptists have been labeled by historians as "the Radical Reformation" or "the Left Wing of the Reformation."

Basic to Anabaptist theology was the idea that the "world" was totally evil and corrupt and that their church was a community of saints. Consequently, the faithful should remain as distinct and separate from the world as possible. The Anabaptists demanded that should Christians from any other church want to join their group, they would have to be baptized into the community of saints in order to become separate from the world: believer's baptism by immersion. The saints considered this to be the only true baptism, but their opponents, all of whom believed in infant baptism, believed it was unnecessary rebaptism. Thus the origin of their name: "Anabaptist" means "rebaptizer," a name of derision given them by their detractors.

One of the problems with other churches, including the Protestant movements, was that they were willing to be state churches, thus bringing the church and the world into close contact. The Anabaptists insisted that there should be a separation of church and state, a principle which made them unique in the sixteenth century.

Although not the founder of the movement, Menno Simons, a converted Roman Catholic priest, became the leader of the nonviolent Dutch Anabaptists. Because he exerted such influential leadership the Dutch Anabaptists came to be called "Mennonites."

In order to maintain congregational discipline and personal sainthood, the Mennonites practiced both excommunication, or the "ban," and "shunning." If a member should fail to maintain the strictly righteous life or should violate the congregation's moral standards, that one would, after admonition, be excommunicated and subjected to social ostracism.

Near the end of the seventeenth century the Mennonite group began to lose momentum, partly because of persecution, partly because of acculturation. The rigorous moral discipline of the group began to decline, and the practice of shunning was infrequently exercised. In the 1690s a Swiss Mennonite lamented the decline in internal moral discipline and sought to revive it. Jakob Ammann led a portion of the Mennonites, chiefly in Alsace, in a revival of the old ways, i.e., a reassertion of the ideal of the church as a highly disciplined community of saints, maintained by the practices of excommunication and shunning. This group, called the Amish after Jakob Ammann, has survived as the strictest of all the Mennonite groups, particularly that branch called the Old Order Amish.

Coming to this country as early as 1727, primarily to escape persecution in Europe, the Amish settled in America throughout the eighteenth and the first quarter of the nineteenth centuries. Only in North America have the name and the distinctive theology and practices of the Amish survived. A principal feature of the group has been adherence to custom and extreme reluctance to change; consequently, the Old Order Amish continue to be a virtual carbon copy of their seventeenth-century conservative forebears. Like their ancestors, contemporary Amish have two favorite passages of Scripture: Romans 12:2, "Do not be conformed to this world, but be transformed by the renewal of your mind, that you may prove what is the will of God, what is good and acceptable and perfect" (RSV), and 2 Corinthians 6:14: "Do not be unequally yoked together with unbelievers; for what fellowship does righteousness have with unrighteousness? and what communion does light have with darkness?" (RSV) These passages mean to the Amish that they should not be like other people in the world, and they have striven mightily to maintain their distinctiveness and individuality.

In order to maintain their character as a community of saints in the midst of a pagan world, the Amish have adopted a distinctive life style which self-consciously sets them apart from the rest of the world. The life style is comprehensive, ranging from unique dress and language to avoidance of modern conveniences.

The Amish recognize the need for a basic elementary education even in their simple agricultural pursuits, and do not object to their children attending school through the eighth grade. But to send their children beyond this level of formal education would expose them to ideas and attitudes that are incompatible with the Amish faith and way of life. Thus, they have chosen to limit their children's formal education in order to avoid the corruption which would inevitably come from massive exposure to the thinking of the outside world. The Amish claim they have the right to do so as one of their constitutionally guaranteed religious rights, overruling any state's compulsory school attendance law.[1]

It is interesting that the Amish did not themselves initiate the litigation discussed here. Given their atti-

[1]Three excellent studies of the history and culture of the Amish are William R. Estep, *The Anabaptist Story*, rev. ed.(Grand Rapids, Mich: Wm. B. Eerdmans Publishing Co., 1975); Franklin H. Littell, *The Origins of Sectarian Protestantism: A Study of the Anabaptist View of the Church* (New York: The Macmillan Co., 1964); and John A. Hostetler, *Amish Society*, 3d. ed. (Baltimore: The Johns Hopkins University Press, 1980).

tudes toward education, they obviously had no college graduates or lawyers of their own. In addition, Amish efforts to avoid contact with the corrupting world have meant that they have traditionally participated in the civil processes, including the judicial, as little as possible. The Yoder litigation was initiated by people who were concerned for the right of the Amish to maintain their religious attitudes and life style. The proceedings were supported by an organization called the National Committee for Amish Religious Freedom which solicited funds from the public to finance the proper forwarding of the case. The case for the Amish was argued before the Supreme Court by William B. Ball, a Roman Catholic.

Writing for a unanimous Court (Justice Douglas dissented in part), Chief Justice Burger used the "compelling state interest—no alternative means" applied first for the protection of religious rights in SHERBERT v. VERNER and BRAUNFELD v. BROWN to uphold the claims of Yoder and the other parents that enforcement of Wisconsin's school attendance law against the Amish abridged their free exercise of religion. He said:

> The essence of all that has been said and written on the subject is that only those interests of the highest order and those not otherwise served can overbalance legitimate claims to the free exercise of religion. We can accept it as settled, therefore, that, however strong the State's interest in universal compulsory education, it is by no means absolute to the exclusion or subordination of all other interests (406 U.S. 205, 215).

The Chief Justice emphasized the long and honorable history of the Amish and spoke approvingly of their "qualities of reliability, self reliance, and dedication to work." He made it clear both that the Court did not wish to become a school board or legislative body and that the Court's holding was limited to the self-sufficient Amish who would look after their own.

Justice Douglas dissented "in part" because he felt that the Court had considered only the religious rights of the parents. Only one child had been queried by the Wisconsin courts as to her views toward high school education. Because "children themselves have constitutionally protectible interests," all of the children should be heard to ascertain their preferences with respect to additional education, without which their lives might be "stunted and deformed." Justice Douglas also complained that the Chief Justice's emphasis on the "law and order" record of the Amish was quite irrelevant. "A religion is a religion," he said, "irrespective of what the misdemeanor or felony records of its members might be."

With few exceptions, cases involving religion and education which have been decided by the Supreme Court have related, as *Yoder*, to problems in elementary and secondary schools. In 1981 the Court was confronted with a difficult question at the university level.

As has been noted frequently, the religion clauses of the First Amendment often conflict with rather than complement one another. In COMMITTEE FOR PUBLIC EDUCATION AND RELIGIOUS LIBERTY v. NYQUIST, the Supreme Court itself recognized that "it may often not be possible to promote free exercise without intruding on establishment." The inevitable tension between the clauses often necessitates a balancing of constitutional rights and limitations.

To add further to the Court's dilemma, sometimes, as in WIDMAR v. VINCENT, a third freedom—in this instance free speech—becomes involved. In 1972, the Board of Curators of the University of Missouri at Kansas City adopted a resolution forbidding the use of campus facilities "for purposes of religious worship or religious teaching by either student or nonstudent groups." The Board maintained that such regulation was mandated by the establishment clauses of both the United States and Missouri Constitutions. On the basis of this regulation, Cornerstone, an organization of active Christian students, was denied permission to hold group Bible studies in university facilities. This denial came four years after the group had begun holding such meetings with permission from university authorities.

To members of Cornerstone, this denial represented not a defense of the Establishment Clause but rather a violation of their right to free exercise of religion. Eleven student members brought suit challenging the regulation in federal district court. That court found the regulation not only justifiable but required by the Establishment Clause of the First Amendment. This decision was subsequently reversed by a court of appeals which ruled that the state's interest in achieving the extreme degree of separation sought was not sufficiently compelling to justify "content-based" discrimination against the religious speech of the Cornerstone members.

On appeal to the Supreme Court, Justice Powell wrote the opinion for seven members of the Court. Justice Stevens concurred in the judgment; Justice White dissented alone. The majority opinion stated flatly: "Here the UMKC has discriminated against student groups and speakers based on their desire to use a generally open forum to engage in religious worship and discussion" (454 U.S. 263, 268). As the Court viewed the case, the question was whether the university could exclude a group because of the content of their speech when there was no reason to believe that the "primary effect of the public forum would be to advance religion" or to "confer any imprimatur of state approval on religious sects or practices." The Court found that the university could not so discriminate against religious activity and discussion by enforcing a "content-based exclusion of religious speech." In this instance the need for protection of free exercise of religion and freedom of speech outweighed the university's concept of the demands of the Establishment Clause.

Only one week later the Court made clear, in *Brandon* v. *Board of Education of Guilderland School District*, that it was not prepared to extend the *Widmar* ruling to public high school campuses. The school board at Guilderland High School near Albany, New York, denied permission to a group called Students for Voluntary Prayer to meet each day before classes in an unused classroom. The school board's action was upheld by the Second U.S. Circuit Court of Appeals; and the Supreme Court, without comment, left that ruling intact. The effect of the two decisions was to emphasize that the Court still adhered to the distinction that it first drew in 1971 in TILTON v. RICHARDSON between public colleges and universities on the one hand and elementary and secondary schools on the other when it upheld a federal construction grant to a church-related college that would undoubtedly have been struck down if made to a lower level school. As was seen in Chapter 2, the Court in 1986 in *Bender* v. *Williamsport*, by the narrowest possible vote, again avoided ruling on the merits of the "equal access" question, this time by use of the standing rule.

WISCONSIN v. YODER

406 U.S. 205
ON CERTIORARI TO THE SUPREME COURT
OF WISCONSIN
Argued December 8, 1971 — Decided May 15, 1972

⊥207 Mr. *Chief Justice BURGER* delivered the opinion of the Court.

On petition of the State of Wisconsin, we granted the writ of certiorari in this case to review a decision of the Wisconsin Supreme Court holding that respondents' convictions of violating the State's compulsory school-attendance law were invalid under the Free Exercise Clause of the First Amendment to the United States Constitution made applicable to the States by the Fourteenth Amendment. For the reasons hereafter stated we affirm the judgment of the Supreme Court of Wisconsin.

Respondents Jonas Yoder and Wallace Miller are members of the Old Order Amish religion, and respondent Adin Yutzy is a member of the Conservative Amish Mennonite Church. They and their families are residents of Green County, Wisconsin. Wisconsin's compulsory school-attendance law required them to cause their children to attend public or private school until reaching age 16 but the respondents declined to send their children, ages 14 and 15, to public school after they completed the eighth grade. The children were not enrolled in any private school, or within any recognized exception to the compulsory-attendance law, and they are conceded to be subject to the Wisconsin statute.

⊥208 On complaint of the school district administrator for the public schools, respondents were charged, tried, and convicted of violating the compulsory-attendance law in Green County Court and were fined the sum of $5 each. Respondents defended on the ground that the applica**⊥209**tion of the compulsory-attendance law violated their rights under the First and Fourteenth Amendments. The trial testimony showed that respondents believed, in accordance with the tenets of Old Order Amish communities generally, that their children's attendance at high school, public or private, was contrary to the Amish religion and way of life. They believed that by sending their children to high school, they would not only expose themselves to the danger of the censure of the church community, but, as found by the county court, also endanger their own salvation and that of their children. The State stipulated that respondent's religious beliefs were sincere.

In support of their position, respondents presented as expert witnesses scholars on religion and education whose testimony is uncontradicted. They expressed their opinions on the relationship of the Amish belief concerning school attendance to the more general tenets of their religion, and described the impact that compulsory high school attendance could have on the continued survival of Amish communities as they exist in the United States today. The history of the Amish **⊥210** sect was given in some detail, beginning with the Swiss Anabaptists of the 16th century who rejected institutionalized churches and sought to return to the early, simple, Christian life de-emphasizing material success, rejecting the competitive spirit, and seeking to insulate themselves from the modern world. As a result of their common heritage, Old Order Amish communities today are characterized by a fundamental belief that salvation requires life in a church community separate and apart from the world and worldly influence. This concept of life aloof from the world and its values is central to their faith.

A related feature of Old Order Amish communities is their devotion to a life in harmony with nature and the soil, as exemplified by the simple life of the early Christian era that continued in America during much of our early national life. Amish beliefs require members of the community to make their living by farming or closely related activities. Broadly speaking, the Old Order Amish religion pervades and determines the entire mode of life of its adherents. Their conduct is regulated in great detail by the *Ordnung*, or rules, of the church community. Adult baptism, which occurs in late adolescence, is the time at which Amish young people voluntarily undertake heavy obligations, not unlike the Bar Mitzvah of the Jews, to abide by the rules of the church community.

Amish objection to formal education beyond the eighth grade is firmly grounded in these central religious concepts. They object to the high school, and higher education generally, because the values they teach ⊥211 are in marked variance with Amish values and the Amish way of life; they view secondary school education as an impermissible exposure of their children to a "worldly" influence in conflict with their beliefs. The high school tends to emphasize intellectual and scientific accomplishments, self-distinction, competitiveness, worldly success, and social life with other students. Amish society emphasizes informal learning-through-doing; a life of "goodness," rather than a life of intellect; wisdom, rather than technical knowledge; community welfare, rather than competition; and separation from, rather than integration with, contemporary worldly society.

Formal high school education beyond the eighth grade is contrary to Amish beliefs, not only because it places Amish children in an environment hostile to Amish beliefs with increasing emphasis on competition in class work and sports and with pressure to conform to the styles, manners, and ways of the peer group, but also because it takes them away from their community, physically and emotionally, during the crucial and formative adolescent period of life. During this period, the children must acquire Amish attitudes favoring manual work and self-reliance and the specific skills needed to perform the adult role of an Amish farmer or housewife. They must learn to enjoy physical labor. Once a child has learned basic reading, writing, and elementary mathematics, these traits, skills, and attitudes admittedly fall within the category of those best learned through example and "doing" rather than in a classroom. And, at this time in life, the Amish child must also grow in his faith and his relationship to the Amish community if he is to be prepared to accept the heavy obligations imposed by adult baptism. In short, high school attendance with teachers who are not of the Amish faith—and may even be hostile to it—interposes a serious barrier to the integration of the Amish child ⊥212 into the Amish religious community. Dr. John Hostetler, one of the experts on Amish society, testified that the modern high school is not equipped, in curriculum or social environment, to impart the values promoted by Amish society.

The Amish do not object to elementary education through the first eight grades as a general proposition because they agree that their children must have basic skills in the "three R's" in order to read the Bible, to be good farmers and citizens, and to be able to deal with non-Amish people when necessary in the course of daily affairs. They view such a basic education as acceptable because it does not significantly expose their children to worldly values or interfere with their development in the Amish community during the crucial adolescent period. While Amish accept compulsory elementary education generally, wherever possible they have established their own elementary schools in many respects like the small local schools of the past. In the Amish belief higher learning tends to develop values they reject as influences that alienate man from God.

On the basis of such considerations, Dr. Hostetler testified that compulsory high school attendance could not only result in great psychological harm to Amish children, because of the conflicts it would produce, but would also, in his opinion, ultimately result in the destruction of the Old Order Amish church community as it exists in the United States today. The testimony of Dr. Donald A. Erickson, an expert witness on education, also showed that the Amish succeed in preparing their high school age children to be productive members of the Amish community. He described their system of learning through doing the skills directly relevant to their adult roles in the Amish community as "ideal" and perhaps superior to ordinary high school education. The evidence also showed that the Amish have an excellent ⊥213 record as lawabiding and generally self-sufficient members of society.

Although the trial court in its careful findings determined that the Wisconsin compulsory school-attendance law "does interfere with the freedom of the Defendants to act in accordance with their sincere religious belief" it also concluded that the requirement of high school attendance until age 16 was a "reasonable and constitutional" exercise of governmental power, and therefore denied the motion to dismiss the charges. The Wisconsin Circuit Court affirmed the convictions. The Wisconsin Supreme Court, however, sustained respondents' claim under the Free Exercise Clause of the First Amendment and reversed the convictions. A majority of the court was of the opinion that the State had failed to make an adequate showing that its interest in "establishing and maintaining an educational system overrides the defendants' right to the free exercise of their religion."

I

There is no doubt as to the power of a State, having a high responsibility for education of its citizens, to impose reasonable regulations for the control and duration of basic education. Providing public schools ranks at the very apex of the function of a State. Yet even this paramount responsibility was, in *Pierce*, made to yield to the right of parents to provide an equivalent education in a privately operated system. There the Court held that Oregon's statute compelling attendance in a public school from age eight to age 16 unreasonably interfered with the interest of parents in directing the rearing of their offspring, including their education in church-operated schools. As that case suggests, the values of parental direction of the religious upbringing ⊥214 and education of their children in their early and formative years have a high place in our society. Thus, a State's interest in universal education, however highly we rank it, is not totally free from a balancing process when it impinges on fundamental rights and interests, such as those specifically protected by the Free Exercise Clause of the First Amendment, and the traditional interest of parents with respect to the religious upbringing of their children so long as they, in the words of *Pierce*, "prepare [them] for additional obligations."

It follows that in order for Wisconsin to compel school attendance beyond the eighth grade against a claim that such attendance interferes with the practice of a legitimate religious belief, it must appear either that the State does not deny the free exercise of religious belief by its requirement, or that there is a state interest of sufficient magnitude to override the interest claiming protection under the Free Exercise Clause. Long before there was general acknowledgment of the need for universal formal education, the Religion Clauses had specifically and firmly fixed the right to free exercise of religious beliefs, and buttressing this fundamental right was an equally firm, even if less explicit, prohibition against the establishment of any religion by government. The values underlying these two provisions relating to religion have been zealously protected, sometimes even at the expense of other interests of admittedly high social importance. The invalidation of financial aid to parochial schools by government grants for a salary subsidy for teachers is but one example of the extent to which courts have gone in this regard, notwithstanding that such aid programs were legislatively determined to be in the public interest and the service of sound educational policy by States and by Congress.

⊥215 The essence of all that has been said and written on the subject is that only those interests of the highest order and those not otherwise served can overbalance legitimate claims to the free exercise of religion. We can accept it as settled, therefore, that, however strong the State's interest in universal compulsory education, it is by no means absolute to the exclusion or subordination of all other interests.

II

We come then to the quality of the claims of the respondents concerning the alleged encroachment of Wisconsin's compulsory school-attendance statute on their rights and the rights of their children to the free exercise of the religious beliefs they and their forebears have adhered to for almost three centuries. In evaluating those claims we must be careful to determine whether the Amish religious faith and their mode of life are, as they claim, inseparable and interdependent. A way of life, however virtuous and admirable, may not be interposed as a barrier to reasonable state regulation of education if it is based on purely secular considerations; to have the protection of the Religion Clauses, the claims must be rooted in religious belief. Although a determination of what is "religious" belief or practice entitled to constitutional protection may present a most delicate question, the very concept of ordered liberty precludes **⊥216** allowing every person to make his own standards on matters of conduct in which society as a whole has important interests. Thus, if the Amish asserted their claims because of their subjective evaluation and rejection of the contemporary secular values accepted by the majority, much as Thoreau rejected the social values of his time and isolated himself at Walden Pond, their claims would not rest on a religious basis. Thoreau's choice was philosophical and personal rather than religious, and such belief does not rise to the demands of the Religion Clauses.

Giving no weight to such secular considerations, however, we see that the record in this case abundantly supports the claim that the traditional way of life of the Amish is not merely a matter of personal preference, but one of deep religious conviction, shared by an organized group, and intimately related to daily living. That the Old Order Amish daily life and religious practice stem from their faith is shown by the fact that it is in response to their literal interpretation of the Biblical injunction from the Epistle of Paul to the Romans, "be not conformed to this world. . . ." This command is fundamental to the Amish faith. Moreover, for the Old Order Amish, religion is not simply a matter of theocratic belief. As the expert witnesses explained, the Old Order Amish religion pervades and determines virtually their entire way of life, regulating it with the detail of the Talmudic diet through the strictly enforced rules of the church community.

The record shows that the respondents' religious beliefs and attitude toward life, family, and home have remained constant—perhaps some would say static—in a period of unparalleled progress in human knowledge generally and great changes in education. The re**⊥217**spondents freely concede, and indeed assert as an article of faith, that their religious beliefs and what we would today call "life style" have not altered in fundamentals for centuries. Their way of life in a church-oriented community, separated from the outside world and "worldly" influences, their attachment to nature and the soil, is a way inherently simple and uncomplicated, albeit difficult to preserve against the pressure to conform. Their rejection of telephones, automobiles, radios, and television, their mode of dress, of speech, their habits of manual work do indeed set them apart from much of contemporary society; these customs are both symbolic and practical.

As the society around the Amish has become more populous, urban, industrialized, and complex, particularly in this century, government regulation of human affairs has correspondingly become more detailed and pervasive. The Amish mode of life has thus come into conflict increasingly with requirements of contemporary society exerting a hydraulic insistence on conformity to majoritarian standards. So long as compulsory education laws were confined to eight grades of elementary basic education imparted in a nearby rural schoolhouse, with a large proportion of students of the Amish faith, the Old Order Amish had little basis to fear that school attendance would expose their children to the worldly influence they reject. But modern compulsory secondary education in rural areas is now largely carried on in a consolidated school, often remote from the student's home and alien to his daily home life. As the record so strongly shows, the values and programs of the modern secondary school are in sharp conflict with the fundamental mode of life mandated by the Amish religion; modern laws requiring compulsory secondary education have accordingly engendered great concern and conflict. ⊥**218** The conclusion is inescapable that secondary schooling, by exposing Amish children to worldly influences in terms of attitudes, goals, and values contrary to beliefs, and by substantially interfering with the religious development of the Amish child and his integration into the way of life of the Amish faith community at the crucial adolescent stage of development, contravenes the basic religious tenets and practice of the Amish faith, both as to the parent and the child.

The impact of the compulsory-attendance law on respondents' practice of the Amish religion is not only severe, but inescapable, for the Wisconsin law affirmatively compels them, under threat of criminal sanction, to perform acts undeniably at odds with fundamental tenets of their religious beliefs. Nor is the impact of the compulsory-attendance law confined to grave interference with important Amish religious tenets from a subjective point of view. It carries with it precisely the kind of objective danger to the free exercise of religion that the First Amendment was designed to prevent. As the record shows, compulsory school attendance to age 16 for Amish children carries with it a very real threat of undermining the Amish community and religious practice as they exist today; they must either abandon belief and be assimilated into society at large, or be forced to migrate to some other and more tolerant region.

⊥**219**In sum, the unchallenged testimony of acknowledged experts in education and religious history, almost 300 years of consistent practice, and strong evidence of a sustained faith pervading and regulating respondents' entire mode of life support the claim that enforcement of the State's requirement of compulsory formal education after the eighth grade would gravely endanger if not destroy the free exercise of respondents' religious beliefs.

III

Neither the findings of the trial court nor the Amish claims as to the nature of their faith are challenged in this Court by the State of Wisconsin. Its position is that the State's interest in universal compulsory formal secondary education to age 16 is so great that it is paramount to the undisputed claims of respondents that their mode of preparing their youth for Amish life, after the traditional elementary education, is an essential part of their religious belief and practice. Nor does the State undertake to meet the claim that the Amish mode of life and education is inseparable from and a part of the basic tenets of their religion—indeed, as much a part of their religious belief and practices as baptism, the confessional, or a sabbath may be for others.

Wisconsin concedes that under the Religion Clauses religious beliefs are absolutely free from the State's control, but it argues that "actions," even though religiously grounded, are outside the protection of the First Amendment. But our decisions have rejected the idea that ⊥**220** religiously grounded conduct is always outside the protection of the Free Exercise Clause. It is true that activities of individuals, even when religiously based, are often subject to regulation by the States in the exercise of their undoubted power to promote the health, safety, and general welfare, or the Federal Government in the exercise of its delegated powers. But to agree that religiously grounded conduct must often be subject to the broad police power of the State is not to deny that there are areas of conduct protected by the Free Exercise Clause of the First Amendment and thus beyond the power of the State to control, even under regulations of general applicability. This case, therefore, does not become easier because respondents were convicted for their "actions" in refusing to send their children to the public high school; in this context belief and action cannot be neatly confined in logic-tight compartments.

Nor can this case be disposed of on the grounds that Wisconsin's requirement for school attendance to age 16 applies uniformly to all citizens of the State and does not, on its face, discriminate against religions or a particular religion, or that it is motivated by legitimate secular concerns. A regulation neutral on its face may, in its application, nonetheless offend the constitutional requirement for governmental neutrality if it unduly burdens the free exercise of religion. The Court must not ignore the danger that an exception ⊥**221** from a general obligation of citizenship on religious grounds may run afoul of the Establishment Clause, but that danger cannot be allowed to prevent any exception no matter how vital it may be to the protection of values promoted by the right of free exercise. . . .

We turn, then, to the State's broader contention that its interest in its system of compulsory education is so compelling that even the established religious practices of the Amish must give way. Where fundamental claims of religious freedom are at stake, however, we cannot accept such a sweeping claim; despite its admitted validity in the generality of cases, we must searchingly examine the interests that the State seeks to promote by its requirement for compulsory education to age 16, and the impediment to those objectives that would flow from recognizing the claimed Amish exemption.

The State advances two primary arguments in support of its system of compulsory education. It notes, as Thomas Jefferson pointed out early in our history, that some degree of education is necessary to prepare citizens to participate effectively and intelligently in our open political system if we are to preserve freedom and independence. Further, education prepares individuals to be self-reliant and self-sufficient participants in society. We accept these propositions.

⊥**222** However, the evidence adduced by the Amish in this case is persuasively to the effect that an additional one or two years of formal high school for Amish children in place of their long-established program of informal vocational education would do little to serve those interests. Respondents' experts testified at trial, without challenge, that the value of all education must be assessed in terms of its capacity to prepare the child for life. It is one thing to say that compulsory education for a year or two beyond the eighth grade may be necessary when its goal is the preparation of the child for life in modern society as the majority live, but it is quite another if the goal of education be viewed as the preparation of the child for life in the separated agrarian community that is the keystone of the Amish faith.

The State attacks respondents' position as one fostering "ignorance" from which the child must be protected by the State. No one can question the State's duty to protect children from ignorance but this argument does not square with the facts disclosed in the record. Whatever their idiosyncrasies as seen by the majority, this record strongly shows that the Amish community has been a highly successful social unit within our society, even if apart from the conventional "mainstream." Its members are productive and very law-abiding members of society; they reject public welfare in any of its usual modern forms. The Congress itself recognized their self-sufficiency by authorizing exemption of such groups as the Amish from the obligation to pay social security taxes.

⊥223 It is neither fair nor correct to suggest that the Amish are opposed to education beyond the eighth grade level. What this record shows is that they are opposed to conventional formal education of the type provided by a certified high school because it comes at the child's crucial adolescent period of religious development. Dr. Donald Erickson, for example, testified that their system of learning-by-doing was an "ideal system" of education in terms of preparing Amish children for life as adults in the Amish community, and that "I would be inclined to say they do a better job in this than most of the rest of us do." As he put it, "These people aren't purporting to be learned people, and it seems to me the self-sufficiency of the community is the best evidence I can point to—whatever is being done seems to function well."

We must not forget that in the Middle Ages important values of the civilization of the Western World were preserved by members of religious orders who isolated themselves from all worldly influences against great obstacles. There can be no assumption that today's majority is **⊥224** "right" and the Amish and others like them are "wrong." A way of life that is odd or even erratic but interferes with no rights or interests of others is not to be condemned because it is different.

The State, however, supports its interest in providing an additional one or two years of compulsory high school education to Amish children because of the possibility that some such children will choose to leave the Amish community, and that if this occurs they will be ill-equipped for life. The State argues that if Amish children leave their church they should not be in the position of making their way in the world without the education available in the one or two additional years the State requires. However, on this record, that argument is highly speculative. There is no specific evidence of the loss of Amish adherents by attrition, nor is there any showing that upon leaving the Amish community Amish children, with their practical agricultural training and habits of industry and self-reliance, would become burdens on society because of educational shortcomings. Indeed, this argument of the State appears to rest primarily on the State's mistaken assumption, already noted, that the Amish do not provide any education for their children beyond the eighth grade, but allow them to grow in "ignorance." To the contrary, not only do the Amish accept the necessity for formal schooling through the eighth grade level, but continue to provide what has been characterized by the undisputed testimony of expert educators as an "ideal" vocational education for their children in the adolescent years.

There is nothing in this record to suggest that the Amish qualities of reliability, self-reliance, and dedication to work would fail to find ready markets in today's society. Absent some contrary evidence supporting the **⊥225** State's position, we are unwilling to assume that persons possessing such valuable vocational skills and habits are doomed to become burdens on society should they determine to leave the Amish faith, nor is there any basis in the record to warrant a finding that an additional one or two years of formal school education beyond the eighth grade would serve to eliminate any such problem that might exist.

Insofar as the State's claim rests on the view that a brief additional period of formal education is imperative to enable the Amish to participate effectively and intelligently in our democratic process, it must fall. The Amish alternative to formal secondary school education has enabled them to function effectively in their day-to-day life under self-imposed limitations on relations with the world, and to survive and prosper in contemporary society as a separate, sharply identifiable and highly self-sufficient community for more than 200 years in this country. In itself this is strong evidence that they are capable of fulfilling the social and political responsibilities of citizenship without compelled attendance beyond the eighth grade at the price of jeopardizing their free exercise of religious belief. When Thomas Jefferson emphasized the need for education as a bulwark of a free people against tyranny, there is nothing to indicate he had in mind compulsory education through any fixed age beyond a basic education. Indeed, the Amish communities singularly parallel and reflect many of the virtues of Jefferson's ideal of the "sturdy yeoman" who would form the basis of what he considered as the **⊥226** ideal of a democratic society. Even their idiosyncratic separateness exemplifies the diversity we profess to admire and encourage.

The requirement for compulsory education beyond the eighth grade is a relatively recent development in our history. Less than 60 years ago, the educational requirements of almost all of the States were satisfied by completion of the elementary grades, at least where the child was regularly and lawfully employed. The inde⊥**227**pendence and successful social functioning of the Amish community for a period approaching almost three centuries and more than 200 years in this country are strong evidence that there is at best a speculative gain, in terms of meeting the duties of citizenship, from an additional one or two years of compulsory formal education. Against this background it would require a more particularized showing from the State on this point to justify the severe interference with religious freedom such additional compulsory attendance would entail.

We should also note that compulsory education and child labor laws find their historical origin in common humanitarian instincts, and that the age limits of both laws have been coordinated to achieve their related objectives. In the context of this case, such considera ⊥**228**tions, if anything, support rather than detract from respondents' position. The origins of the requirement for school attendance to age 16, an age falling after the completion of elementary school but before completion of high school, are not entirely clear. But to some extent such laws reflected the movement to prohibit most child labor under age 16 that culminated in the provisions of the Federal Fair Labor Standards Act of 1938. It is true, then, that the 16-year child labor age limit may to some degree derive from a contemporary impression that children should be in school until that age. But at the same time, it cannot be denied that, conversely, the 16-year education limit reflects, in substantial measure, the concern that children under that age not be employed under conditions hazardous to their health, or in work that should be performed by adults.

The requirement of compulsory schooling to age 16 must therefore be viewed as aimed not merely at providing educational opportunities for children, but as an alternative to the equally undesirable consequence of unhealthful child labor displacing adult workers, or, on the other hand, forced idleness. The two kinds of statutes—compulsory school attendance and child labor laws—tend to keep children of certain ages off the labor market and in school; this regimen in turn provides opportunity to prepare for a livelihood of a higher order than that which children could pursue without education and protects their health in adolescence.

In these terms, Wisconsin's interest in compelling the school attendance of Amish children to age 16 emerges as somewhat less substantial than requiring such attend⊥**229**ance for children generally. For, while agricultural employment is not totally outside the legitimate concerns of the child labor laws, employment of children under parental guidance and on the family farm from age 14 to age 16 is an ancient tradition that lies at the periphery of the objectives of such laws. There is no intimation that the Amish employment of their children on family farms is in any way deleterious to their health or that Amish parents exploit children at tender years. Any such inference would be contrary to the record before us. Moreover, employment of Amish children on the family farm does not present the undesirable economic aspects of eliminating jobs that might otherwise be held by adults.

IV

Finally, the State, on authority of *Prince* v. *Massachusetts*, argues that a decision exempting Amish children from the State's requirement fails to recognize the substantive right of the Amish child to a secondary education, and fails to give due regard to the power of the State as *parens patriae* to extend the benefit of secondary education to children regardless of the wishes of their parents. Taken at its broadest sweep, the Court's language in *Prince*, might be read to give support to the State's position. However, the Court was not confronted in *Prince* with a situation comparable to that of the Amish as revealed in this record; this is shown by the ⊥**230** Court's severe characterization of the evils that it thought the legislature could legitimately associate with child labor, even when performed in the company of an adult. The Court later took great care to confine *Prince* to a narrow scope in *Sherbert* v. *Verner*, when it stated: "On the other hand, the Court has rejected challenges under the Free Exercise Clause to governmental regulation of certain overt acts prompted by religious beliefs or principles, for 'even when the action is in accord with one's religious convictions, [it] is not totally free from legislative restrictions.' *Braunfeld* v. *Brown*. The conduct or actions so regulated have invariably posed some substantial threat to public safety, peace or order."

This case, of course, is not one in which any harm to the physical or mental health of the child or to the public safety, peace, order, or welfare has been demonstrated or may be properly inferred. The record is to the contrary, and any reliance on that theory would find no support in the evidence.

Contrary to the suggestion of the dissenting opinion of Mr. *Justice* DOUGLAS, our holding today in no degree depends on the assertion of the religious interest of the child as contrasted with that of the parents. It is the parents who are subject to prosecution here for failing to cause their children to attend school, and it ⊥**231** is their right of free exercise, not that of their children, that must determine Wisconsin's power to impose criminal penalties on the parent. The dissent argues that a child who expresses a desire to attend public high school in conflict with the wishes of his parents should not be prevented from doing so. There is no reason for the Court to consider that point since it is not an issue in the case. The children are not parties to this litigation. The State has at no point tried this case on the theory that respondents were preventing their children from attending school against their expressed desires, and indeed the record is to the contrary. The State's position from the outset has been that it is empowered to apply its compulsory-attendance law to Amish parents in the same manner as to other parents—that is, without regard to the wishes of the child. That is the claim we reject today.

Our holding in no way determines the proper resolution of possible competing interests of parents, children, and the State in an appropriate state court proceeding in which the power of the State is asserted on the theory that Amish parents are preventing their minor children from attending high school despite their expressed desires to the contrary. Recognition of the claim of the State in such a proceeding would, of course, call into question traditional concepts of parental control over the religious upbringing and education of their minor children recognized in this Court's past decisions. It is clear that such an intrusion by a State into family decisions in the area of religious training would give rise to grave questions of religious freedom comparable to those raised here ⊥**232** and those presented in *Pierce* v. *Society of Sisters*. On this record we neither reach nor decide those issues.

The State's argument proceeds without reliance on any actual conflict between the wishes of parents and children. It appears to rest on the potential that exemption of Amish parents from the requirements of the compulsory-education law might allow some parents to act contrary to the best interests of their children by foreclosing their opportunity to make an intelligent choice between the Amish way of life and that of the outside world. The same argument could, of course, be made with respect to all church schools short of college. There is nothing in the record or in the ordinary course of human experience to suggest that non-Amish parents generally consult with children of ages 14-16 if they are placed in a church school of the parents' faith.

Indeed it seems clear that if the State is empowered, as *parens patriae*, to "save" a child from himself or his Amish parents by requiring an additional two years of compulsory formal high school education, the State will in large measure influence, if not determine, the religious future of the child. Even more markedly than in *Prince*, therefore, this case involves the fundamental interest of parents, as contrasted with that of the State, to guide the religious future and education of their children. The history and culture of Western civilization reflect a strong tradition of parental concern for the nurture and upbringing of their children. This primary role of the parents in the upbringing of their children is now established beyond debate as an enduring American tradition. If not the first, perhaps the most significant statements of the Court in this area are found in *Pierce* v. *Society of Sisters*, in which the Court observed: "Under the doctrine of *Meyer* v. *Nebraska*, we think it entirely plain that the Act ⊥**233** of 1922 unreasonably interferes with the liberty of parents and guardians to direct the upbringing and education of children under their control. As often heretofore pointed out, rights guaranteed by the Constitution may not be abridged by legislation which has no reasonable relation to some purpose within the competency of the State. The fundamental theory of liberty upon which all governments in this Union repose excludes any general power of the State to standardize its children by forcing them to accept instruction from public teachers only. The child is not the mere creature of the State; those who nurture him and direct his destiny have the right, coupled with the high duty, to recognize and prepare him for additional obligations."

The duty to prepare the child for "additional obligations," referred to by the Court, must be read to include the inculcation of moral standards, religious beliefs, and elements of good citizenship. *Pierce*, of course, recognized that where nothing more than the general interest of the parent in the nurture and education of his children is involved, it is beyond dispute that the State acts "reasonably" and constitutionally in requiring education to age 16 in some public or private school meeting the standards prescribed by the State.

However read, the Court's holding in *Pierce* stands as a charter of the rights of parents to direct the religious upbringing of their children. And, when the interests of parenthood are combined with a free exercise claim of the nature revealed by this record, more than merely a "reasonable relation to some purpose within the competency of the State" is required to sustain the validity of the State's requirement under the First Amendment. To be sure, the power of the parent, even when linked to a free exercise claim, may be subject to limitation under *Prince* ⊥**234** if it appears that parental decisions will jeopardize the health or safety of the child, or have a potential for significant social burdens. But in this case, the Amish have introduced persuasive evidence undermining the arguments the State has advanced to support its claims in terms of the welfare of the child and society as a whole. The record strongly indicates that accommodating the religious objections of the Amish by foregoing one, or at most two, additional years of compulsory education will not impair the physical or mental health of the child, or result in an inability to be self-supporting or to discharge the duties and responsibilities of citizenship, or in any other way materially detract from the welfare of society.

In the face of our consistent emphasis on the central values underlying the Religion Clauses in our constitutional scheme of government, we cannot accept a *parens patriae* claim of such all-encompassing scope and with such sweeping potential for broad and unforeseeable application as that urged by the State.

V

For the reasons stated we hold, with the Supreme Court of Wisconsin, that the First and Fourteenth Amendments prevent the State from compelling respondents to cause their children to attend formal high school to age 16. Our disposition of this case, however, in no way ⊥**235** alters our recognition of the obvious fact that courts are not school boards or legislatures, and are ill-equipped to determine the "necessity" of discrete aspects of a State's program of compulsory education. This should suggest that courts must move with great circumspection in performing the sensitive and delicate task of weighing a State's legitimate social concern when faced with religious claims for exemption from generally applicable educational requirements. It cannot be overemphasized that we are not dealing with a way of life and mode of education by a group claiming to have recently discovered some "progressive" or more enlightened process for rearing children for modern life.

Aided by a history of three centuries as an identifiable religious sect and a long history as a successful and self-sufficient segment of American society, the Amish in this case have convincingly demonstrated the sincerity of their religious beliefs, the interrelationship of belief with their mode of life, the vital role that belief and daily conduct play in the continued survival of Old Order Amish communities and their religious organization, and the hazards presented by the State's enforcement of a statute generally valid as to others. Beyond this, they have carried the even more difficult burden of demonstrating the adequacy of their alternative mode of continuing informal vocational education in terms of precisely those overall interests that the State advances in support of its program of compulsory high school education. In light of this con⊥**236**vincing showing, one that probably few other religious groups or sects could make, and weighing the minimal difference between what the State would require and what the Amish already accept, it was incumbent on the State to show with more particularity how its admittedly strong interest in compulsory education would be adversely affected by granting an exemption to the Amish.

Nothing we hold is intended to undermine the general applicability of the State's compulsory school-attendance statutes or to limit the power of the State to promulgate reasonable standards that, while not impairing the free exercise of religion, provide for continuing agricultural vocational education under parental and church guidance by the Old Order Amish or others similarly situated. The States have had a long history of amicable and effective relationships with church-sponsored schools, and there is no basis for assuming that, in this related context, reasonable standards cannot be established concerning the content of the continuing vocational education of Amish children under parental guidance, provided always that state regulations are not inconsistent with what we have said in this opinion.

Affirmed.

Mr. *Justice* POWELL and Mr. *Justice* REHNQUIST took no part in the consideration or decision of this case.

⊥**237** Mr. *Justice* STEWART, with whom Mr. *Justice* BRENNAN joins, concurring.

This case involves the constitutionality of imposing criminal punishment upon Amish parents for their religiously based refusal to compel their children to attend public high schools. Wisconsin has sought to brand these parents as criminals for following their religious beliefs, and the Court today rightly holds that Wisconsin cannot constitutionally do so.

This case in no way involves any questions regarding the right of the children of Amish parents to attend public high schools, or any other institutions of learning, if they wish to do so. As the Court points out, there is no suggestion whatever in the record that the religious beliefs of the children here concerned differ in any way from those of their parents. Only one of the children testified. The last two questions and answers on her cross-examination accurately sum up her testimony:

"Q. So I take it then, Frieda, the only reason you are not going to school, and did not go to school since last September, is because of *your* religion?

"A. Yes.

"Q. That is the only reason?

"A. Yes." (Emphasis supplied.)

It is clear to me, therefore, that this record simply does not present the interesting and important issue discussed in Part II of the dissenting opinion of Mr. *Justice* DOUGLAS. With this observation, I join the opinion and the judgment of the Court.

Mr. *Justice* WHITE, with whom Mr. *Justice* BRENNAN and Mr. *Justice* STEWART join, concurring.

Cases such as this one inevitably call for a delicate balancing of important but conflicting interests. I join the opinion and judgment of the Court because I cannot ⊥**238** say that the State's interest in requiring two more years of compulsory education in the ninth and tenth grades outweighs the importance of the concededly sincere Amish religious practice to the survival of that sect.

This would be a very different case for me if respondents' claim were that their religion forbade their children from attending any school at any time and from complying in any way with the educational standards set by the State. Since the Amish children are permitted to acquire the basic tools of literacy to survive in modern society by attending grades one through eight and since the deviation from the State's compulsory-education law is relatively slight, I conclude that respondents' claim must prevail, largely because "religious freedom—the freedom to believe and to practice strange and, it may be, foreign creeds—has classically been one of the highest values of our society." *Braunfeld* v. *Brown*.

The importance of the state interest asserted here cannot be denigrated, however: "Today, education is perhaps the most important function of state and local governments. Compulsory school attendance laws and the great expenditures for education both demonstrate our recognition of the importance of education to our democratic society. It is required in the performance of our most basic public responsibilities, even service in the armed forces. It is the very foundation of good citizenship. Today it is a principal instrument in awakening the child to cultural values, in preparing him for later professional training; and in helping him to adjust normally to his environment." *Brown* v. *Board of Education*.

⊥**239** As recently as last Term, the Court reemphasized the legitimacy of the State's concern for enforcing minimal educational standards, *Lemon* v. *Kurtzman*. *Pierce* v. *Society of Sisters* lends no support to the contention that parents may replace state educational requirements with their own idiosyncratic views of what knowledge a child needs to be a productive and happy member of society; in *Pierce*, both the parochial and military schools were in compliance with all the educational standards that the State had set, and the Court held simply that while a State may posit such standards, it may not pre-empt the educational process by requiring children to attend public schools. In the present case, the State is not concerned with the maintenance of an educational system as an end in itself, it is rather attempting to nurture and develop the human potential of its children, whether Amish or non-Amish: to expand their knowledge, broaden their sensibilities, kindle their imagination, foster a spirit of free inquiry, and increase their human understanding and tolerance. It is possible that most Amish ⊥**240** children will wish to continue living the rural life of their parents, in which case their training at home will adequately equip them for their future role. Others, however, may wish to become nuclear physicists, ballet dancers, computer programmers, or historians, and for these occupations, formal training will be necessary. There is evidence in the record that many children desert the Amish faith when they come of age. A State has a legitimate interest not only in seeking to develop the latent talents of its children but also in seeking to prepare them for the life style that they may later choose, or at least to provide them with an option other than the life they have led in the past. In the circumstances of this case, although the question is close, I am unable to say that the State has demonstrated that Amish children who leave school in the eighth grade will be intellectually stultified or unable to acquire new academic skills later. The statutory minimum school attendance age set by the State is, after all, only 16.

Decision in cases such as this and the administration of an exemption for Old Order Amish from the State's compulsory school-attendance laws will inevitably involve the kind of close and perhaps repeated scrutiny of religious practices, as is exemplified in today's opinion, which the Court has heretofore been anxious to avoid. But such entanglement does not create a forbidden establishment of religion where it is essential to implement free ⊥**241** exercise values threatened by an otherwise neutral program instituted to foster some permissible, non-religious state objective. I join the Court because the sincerity of the Amish religious policy here is uncontested, because the potentially adverse impact of the state requirement is great, and because the State's valid interest in education has already been largely satisfied by the eight years the children have already spent in school.

Mr. Justice DOUGLAS, dissenting in part.

I

I agree with the Court that the religious scruples of the Amish are opposed to the education of their children beyond the grade schools, yet I disagree with the Court's conclusion that the matter is within the dispensation of parents alone. The Court's analysis assumes that the only interests at stake in the case are those of the Amish parents on the one hand, and those of the State on the other. The difficulty with this approach is that, despite the Court's claim, the parents are seeking to vindicate not only their own free exercise claims, but also those of their high-school-age children.

It is argued that the right of the Amish children to religious freedom is not presented by the facts of the case, as the issue before the Court involved only the Amish parents' religious freedom to defy a state criminal statute imposing upon them an affirmative duty to cause their children to attend high school.

First, respondents' motion to dismiss in the trial court expressly asserts, not only the religious liberty of the adults, but also that of the children, as a defense to the prosecutions. It is, of course, beyond question that the parents have standing as defendants in a criminal prosecution to assert the religious interests of their ⊥**242** children as a defense. Although the lower courts and a majority of this Court assume an identity of interest between parent and child, it is clear that they have treated the religious interest of the child as a factor in the analysis.

Second, it is essential to reach the question to decide the case, not only because the question was squarely raised in the motion to dismiss, but also because no analysis of religious-liberty claims can take place in a vacuum. If the parents in this case are allowed a religious exemption, the inevitable effect is to impose the parents' notions of religious duty upon their children. Where the child is mature enough to express potentially conflicting desires, it would be an invasion of the child's rights to permit such an imposition without canvassing his views. As in *Prince* v. *Massachusetts*, it is in imposition resulting from this very litigation. As the child has no other effective forum, it is in this litigation that his rights should be considered. And, if an Amish child desires to attend high school, and is mature enough to have that desire respected, the State may well be able to override the parents' religiously motivated objections.

⊥**243** Religion is an individual experience. It is not necessary, nor even appropriate, for every Amish child to express his views on the subject in a prosecution of a single adult. Crucial, however, are the views of the child whose parent is the subject of the suit. Frieda Yoder has in fact testified that her own religious views are opposed to high-school education. I therefore join the judgment of the Court as to respondent Jonas Yoder. But Frieda Yoder's views may not be those of Vernon Yutzy or Barbara Miller. I must dissent, therefore, as to respondents Adin Yutzy and Wallace Miller as their motion to dismiss also raised the question of their children's religious liberty.

II

This issue has never been squarely presented before today. Our opinions are full of talk about the power of the parents over the child's education. And we have in the past analyzed similar conflicts between parent and State with little regard for the views of the child. Recent cases, however, have clearly held that the children themselves have constitutionally protectible interests.

These children are "persons" within the meaning of the Bill of Rights. We have so held over and over again. In *Haley* v. *Ohio*, we extended the protection of the Fourteenth Amendment in a state trial of a 15-year-old boy. In *In re Gault*, we held that "neither the Fourteenth Amendment nor the Bill of Rights is for adults alone." In *In re Winship*, we held that a 12-year-old boy, when charged with an act which would be a crime if committed by an adult, was entitled to procedural safeguards contained in the Sixth Amendment.

⊥244 In *Tinker* v. *Des Moines School District*, we dealt with 13-year-old, 15-year-old, and 16-year-old students who wore armbands to public schools and were disciplined for doing so. We gave them relief, saying that their First Amendment rights had been abridged.

"Students in school as well as out of school are 'persons' under our Constitution. They are possessed of fundamental rights which the State must respect, just as they themselves must respect their obligations to the State."

In *Board of Education* v. *Barnette*, we held that schoolchildren, whose religious beliefs collided with a school rule requiring them to salute the flag, could not be required to do so. While the sanction included expulsion of the students and prosecution of the parents, the vice of the regime was its interference with the child's free exercise of religion. We said: "Here . . . we are dealing with a compulsion of students to declare a belief."

. . . . .

On this important and vital matter of education, I think the children should be entitled to be heard. While the parents, absent dissent, normally speak for the entire family, the education of the child is a matter on which the child will often have decided views. He may want to be a pianist or an astronaut or an oceanog**⊥245**rapher. To do so he will have to break from the Amish tradition.

It is the future of the student, not the future of the parents, that is imperiled by today's decision. If a parent keeps his child out of school beyond the grade school, then the child will be forever barred from entry into the new and amazing world of diversity that we have today. The child may decide that that is the preferred course, or he may rebel. It is the student's judgment, not his parents', that is essential if we are to give full meaning to what we have said about the Bill of Rights and of the right of students to be masters of their own destiny. If he is harnessed to the Amish way of life **⊥246** by those in authority over him and if his education is truncated, his entire life may be stunted and deformed. The child, therefore, should be given an opportunity to be heard before the State gives the exemption which we honor today.

The views of the two children in question were not canvassed by the Wisconsin courts. The matter should be explicitly reserved so that new hearings can be held on remand of the case.

III

I think the emphasis of the Court on the "law and order" record of this Amish group of people is quite irrelevant. A religion is a religion irrespective of what the misdemeanor or felony records of its members might be. I am not at all sure how the Catholics, Episcopalians, the Baptists, Jehovah's Witnesses, the Unitarians, and my own Presbyterians would make out if subjected to such a test. It is, of course, true that if a group or society was organized to perpetuate crime and if that is its motive, we would have rather startling problems akin to those that were raised when some years back a particular sect was challenged here as operating on a fraudulent basis. But no such factors are present here, and the Amish, whether with a high or low crim**⊥247**inal record, certainly qualify by all historic standards as a religion within the meaning of the First Amendment.

The Court rightly rejects the notion that actions, even though religiously grounded, are always outside the protection of the Free Exercise Clause of the First Amendment. In so ruling, the Court departs from the teaching of *Reynolds* v. *United States*, where it was said concerning the reach of the Free Exercise Clause of the First Amendment, "Congress was deprived of all legislative power over mere opinion, but was left free to reach actions which were in violation of social duties or subversive of good order." In that case it was conceded that polygamy was a part of the religion of the Mormons. Yet the Court said, "It matters not that his belief [in polygamy] was a part of his professed religion: it was still belief, and belief only."

Action, which the Court deemed to be antisocial, could be punished even though it was grounded on deeply held and sincere religious convictions. What we do today, at least in this respect, opens the way to give organized religion a broader base than it has ever enjoyed; and it even promises that in time *Reynolds* will be overruled.

In another way, however, the Court retreats when in reference to Henry Thoreau it says his "choice was philo-

⊥248sophical and personal rather than religious, and such belief does not rise to the demands of the Religion Clauses." That is contrary to what we held in *United States* v. *Seeger*, where we were concerned with the meaning of the words "religious training and belief" in the Selective Service Act, which were the basis of many conscientious objector claims. We said: "Within that phrase would come all sincere religious beliefs which are based upon a power or being, or upon a faith, to which all else is subordinate or upon which all else is ultimately dependent. The test might be stated in these words: A sincere and meaningful belief which occupies in the life of its possessor a place parallel to that filled by the God of those admittedly qualifying for the exemption comes within the statutory definition. This construction avoids imputing to Congress an intent to classify different religious beliefs, exempting some and excluding others, and is in accord with the well-established congressional policy of equal treatment for those whose opposition to service is grounded in their religious tenets. . . ."

⊥249 I adhere to these exalted views of "religion" and see no acceptable alternative to them now that we have become a Nation of many religions and sects, representing all of the diversities of the human race.

WIDMAR v. VINCENT

454 U.S. 263
ON WRIT OF CERTIORARI TO THE UNITED STATES COURT OF APPEALS FOR THE EIGHTH CIRCUIT
Argued October 6, 1981 — Decided December 8, 1981

⊥264 *Justice POWELL* delivered the opinion of the Court.

This case presents the question whether a state university, which makes its facilities generally available for the activities ⊥265 of registered student groups, may close its facilities to a registered student group desiring to use the facilities for religious worship and religious discussion.

I

It is the stated policy of the University of Missouri at Kansas City to encourage the activities of student organizations. The University officially recognizes over 100 student groups. It routinely provides University facilities for the meetings of registered organizations. Students pay an activity fee of $41 per semester (1978-1979) to help defray the costs to the University.

From 1973 until 1977 a registered religious group named Cornerstone regularly sought and received permission to conduct its meetings in University facilities. In 1977, however, the University informed the group that it could no longer meet in University buildings. The exclusion was based on a regulation, adopted by the Board of Curators in 1972, that prohibits the use of University buildings or grounds "for purposes of religious worship or religious teaching."

⊥266 Eleven University students, all members of Cornerstone, brought suit to challenge the regulation in Federal District Court for the Western District of Missouri. They alleged that the University's discrimination against religious activity and discussion violated their rights to free exercise of religion, equal protection, and freedom of speech under the First and Fourteenth Amendments to the Constitution of the United States.

Upon cross motions for summary judgment, the District Court upheld the challenged regulation. *Chess* v. *Widmar*. It found the regulation not only justified, but required, by the Establishment Clause of the Federal Constitution. Under *Tilton* v. *Richardson*, the court reasoned, the State ⊥267 could not provide facilities for religious use without giving prohibited support to an institution of religion. The District Court rejected the argument that the University could not discriminate against religious speech on the basis of its content. It found religious speech entitled to less protection than other types of expression.

The Court of Appeals for the Eighth Circuit reversed. *Chess* v. *Widmar*. Rejecting the analysis of the District Court, it viewed the University regulation as a content-based discrimination against religious speech, for which it could find no compelling justification. The Court held that the Establishment Clause does not bar a policy of equal access, in which facilities are open to groups and speakers of all kinds. According to the Court of Appeals, the "primary effect" of such a policy would not be to advance religion, but rather to further the neutral purpose of developing students' "'social and cultural awareness as well as [their] intellectual curiosity,'" (quoting from the University bulletin's description of the student activities program).

We now affirm.

II

Through its policy of accommodating their meetings, the University has created a forum generally open for use by student groups. Having done so, the University has assumed an obligation to justify its discriminations and exclusions under applicable constitutional norms. The Constitution ⊥268 forbids a State to enforce certain exclusions from a forum generally open to the public, even if it was not required to create the forum in the first place. See, *e.g.*, *City of Madison Joint School District* v. *Wisconsin Public Employment Relations Comm'n* (although a State may conduct business in private session, "where the State has opened a forum for direct citizen involvement," exclusions bear a heavy burden of justification); *Southeastern Promotions, Ltd.* v. *Conrad* (because municipal theater was a public forum, city could not exclude a production without satisfying constitutional safeguards applicable to prior restraints).

The University's institutional mission, which it describes as providing a "*secular* education" to its students, does not exempt its actions from constitutional scrutiny.

With respect to persons entitled to be there, our cases leave no doubt that the First Amendment ⊥**269** rights of speech and association extend to the campuses of state universities. See, *e.g., Healy* v. *James; Tinker* v. *Des Moines Independent School District; Shelton* v. *Tucker*.

Here the University of Missouri has discriminated against student groups and speakers based on their desire to use a generally open forum to engage in religious worship and discussion. These are forms of speech and association protected by the First Amendment. See, *e.g., Heffron* v. *International Soc'y for Krishna Consciousness, Inc.; Niemotko* v. *Maryland; Saia* v. *New York*. In order to justify discrimina⊥**270**tory exclusion from a public forum based on the religious content of a group's intended speech, the University must therefore satisfy the standard of review appropriate to content-based exclusions. It must show that its regulation is necessary to serve a compelling state interest and that it is narrowly drawn to achieve that end. See *Carey* v. *Brown*.

III

In this case the University claims a compelling interest in maintaining strict separation of church and State. It derives this interest from the "Establishment Clauses" of both the Federal and Missouri Constitutions.

A

The University first argues that it cannot offer its facilities to religious groups and speakers on the terms available to ⊥**271** other groups without violating the Establishment Clause of the Constitution of the United States. We agree that the interest of the University in complying with its constitutional obligations may be characterized as compelling. It does not follow, however, that an "equal access" policy would be incompatible with this Court's Establishment Clause cases. Those cases hold that a policy will not offend the Establishment Clause if it can pass a three-pronged test: "First, the [governmental policy] must have a secular legislative purpose; second, its principal or primary effect must be one that neither advances nor inhibits religion . . .; finally, the [policy] must not foster 'an excessive government entanglement with religion.'" *Lemon* v. *Kurtzman*. See *Committee for Public Education* v. *Regan; Roemer* v. *Maryland Public Works Bd.*

In this case two prongs of the test are clearly met. Both the District Court and the Court of Appeals held that an open-forum policy, including nondiscrimination against religious speech, would have a secular purpose and would ⊥**272** avoid entanglement with religion. But the District Court concluded, and the University argues here, that allowing religious groups to share the limited public forum would have the "primary effect" of advancing religion.

⊥**273** The University's argument misconceives the nature of this case. The question is not whether the creation of a religious forum would violate the Establishment Clause. The University has opened its facilities for use by student groups, and the question is whether it can now exclude groups because of the content of their speech. See *Healy* v. *James*. In this context we are unpersuaded that the primary effect of the public forum, open to all forms of discourse, would be to advance religion.

We are not oblivious to the range of an open forum's likely effects. It is possible—perhaps even foreseeable—that religious groups will benefit from access to University facilities. But this Court has explained that a religious organization's enjoyment of merely "incidental" benefits does not violate the prohibition against the "primary advancement" of religion. *Committee for Public Education* v. *Nyquist;* ⊥**274** see, *e.g., Roemer* v. *Board of Public Works; Hunt* v. *McNair; McGowan* v. *Maryland.*

We are satisfied that any religious benefits of an open forum at UMKC would be "incidental" within the meaning of our cases. Two factors are especially relevant.

First, an open forum in a public university does not confer any imprimatur of State approval on religious sects or practices. As the Court of Appeals quite aptly stated, such a policy "would no more commit the University . . . to religious goals," than it is "now committed to the goals of the Students for a Democratic Society, the Young Socialist Alliance," or any other group eligible to use its facilities. *Chess* v. *Widmar*.

Second, the forum is available to a broad class of nonreligious as well as religious speakers; there are over 100 recognized student groups at UMKC. The provision of benefits to so broad a spectrum of groups is an important index of secular effect. See, *e.g., Wolman* v. *Walter; Committee for Public Education* v. *Nyquist*. If the Establishment Clause barred the extension of general benefits to religious groups, "a church could not be protected by the police and fire depart⊥**275**ments, or have its public sidewalk kept in repair." *Roemer* v. *Maryland* (plurality opinion); quoted in *Committee for Public Education* v. *Regan*. At least in the absence of empirical evidence that religious groups will dominate UMKC's open forum, we agree with the Court of Appeals that the advancement of religion would not be the forum's "primary effect."

B

Arguing that the State of Missouri has gone further than the Federal Constitution in proscribing indirect State support for religion, the University claims a compelling interest in complying with the applicable provisions of the Missouri Constitution.

The Missouri courts have not ruled whether a general policy of accommodating student groups, applied equally to those wishing to gather to engage in religious and nonreligious speech, would offend the State Constitution. We need not, however, determine how the Missouri courts would decide this issue. It is also unnecessary for us to decide whether, under the Supremacy Clause, a state interest, derived from its own constitution, could ever outweigh free ⊥276 speech interests protected by the First Amendment. We limit our holding to the case before us.

On one hand, respondents' First Amendment rights are entitled to special constitutional solicitude. Our cases have required the most exacting scrutiny in cases in which a State undertakes to regulate speech on the basis of its content. See, *e.g.*, *Carey* v. *Brown*; *Police Dept.* v. *Mosley*. On the other hand, the state interest asserted here—in achieving greater separation of church and State than is already ensured under the Establishment Clause of the Federal Constitution—is limited by the Free Exercise Clause and in this case by the Free Speech Clause as well. In this constitutional context, we are unable to recognize the State's interest as sufficiently "compelling" to justify content-based discrimination against respondents' religious speech.

IV

Our holding in this case in no way undermines the capacity of the University to establish reasonable time, place, and manner regulations. Nor do we question the right of the University to make academic judgments as to how best to allocate scarce resources or "to determine for itself on academic grounds who may teach, what may be taught, how it shall be taught, and who may be admitted to study." *Sweezy* v. *New Hampshire* (Frankfurter, J., concurring in the judgment); see *Regents of the Univ. of Cal.* v. *Bakke* (opinion of Powell, J., announcing the judgment of the Court). Fi⊥277nally, we affirm the continuing validity of cases, *e.g.*, *Healy* v. *James*, that recognize a University's right to exclude even First Amendment activities that violate reasonable campus rules or substantially interfere with the opportunity of other students to obtain an education.

The basis for our decision is narrow. Having created a forum generally open to student groups, the University seeks to enforce a content-based exclusion of religious speech. Its exclusionary policy violates the fundamental principle that a state regulation of speech should be content-neutral, and the University is unable to justify this violation under applicable constitutional standards.

For this reason, the decision of the Court of Appeals is,

Affirmed.

Justice STEVENS, concurring in the judgment.

As the Court recognizes, every university must "make academic judgments as to how best to allocate scarce resources." The Court appears to hold, however, that those judgments must "serve a compelling state interest" whenever they are based, even in part, on the content of speech. This conclusion apparently flows from the Court's suggestion that a student activities program—from which the public may be excluded—must be managed as though it were a "public forum." In my opinion, the use of the terms "compelling ⊥278 state interest" and "public forum" to analyze the question presented in this case may needlessly undermine the academic freedom of public universities.

Today most major colleges and universities are operated by public authority. Nevertheless, their facilities are not open to the public in the same way that streets and parks are. University facilities—private or public—are maintained primarily for the benefit of the student body and the faculty. In performing their learning and teaching missions, the managers of a university routinely make countless decisions based on the content of communicative materials. They select books for inclusion in the library, they hire professors on the basis of their academic philosophies, they select courses for inclusion in the curriculum, and they reward scholars for what they have written. In addition, in encouraging students to participate in extracurricular activities, they necessarily make decisions concerning the content of those activities.

Because every university's resources are limited, an educational institution must routinely make decisions concerning the use of the time and space that is available for extracurricular activities. In my judgment, it is both necessary and appropriate for those decisions to evaluate the content of a proposed student activity. I should think it obvious, for example, that if two groups of 25 students requested the use of a room at a particular time—one to view Mickey Mouse cartoons and the other to rehearse an amateur performance of Hamlet—the First Amendment would not require that the room be reserved for the group that submitted its application first. Nor do I see why a university should have to establish a "compelling state interest" to defend its decision to permit one group to use the facility and not the other. In my opinion, a university should be allowed to decide for itself whether a program that illuminates the genius of Walt Disney be given precedence over one that may duplicate material adequately covered in the classroom. Judgments of ⊥279 this kind should be made by academicians, not by federal judges, and their standards for decision should not be encumbered with ambiguous phrases like "compelling state interest."

⊥280 Thus, I do not subscribe to the view that a public university has no greater interest in the content of student activities than the police chief has in the content of a soap box oration on Capitol Hill. A university legitimately may regard some subjects as more relevant to its educational mission than others. But the university, like the police officer, may not allow its agreement or disagreement with the viewpoint of a particular speaker to determine whether access to a forum will be granted. If a state university is to deny recognition to a student organization—or is to give it a lesser right to use school facilities than other student groups—it must have a valid reason for doing so. *Healy* v. *James*.

In this case I agree with the Court that the University has not established a sufficient justification for its refusal to allow the Cornerstone group to engage in religious worship on the campus. The primary reason advanced for the discriminatory treatment is the University's fear of violating the Establishment Clause. But since the record discloses no danger ⊥281 that the University will appear to sponsor any particular religion, and since student participation in the Cornerstone meetings is entirely voluntary, the Court properly concludes that the University's fear is groundless. With that justification put to one side, the University has not met the burden that is imposed on it by *Healy*.

Nor does the University's reliance on the Establishment Clause of the Missouri State Constitution provide a sufficient justification for the discriminatory treatment in this case. As I have said, I believe that the University may exercise a measure of control over the agenda for student use of school facilities, preferring some subjects over others, without needing to identify so-called "compelling state interests." Quite obviously, however, the University could not allow a group of Republicans or Presbyterians to meet while denying Democrats or Mormons the same privilege. It seems apparent that the policy under attack would allow groups of young philosophers to meet to discuss their skepticism that a Supreme Being exists, or a group of political scientists to meet to debate the accuracy of the view that religion is the "opium of the people." If school facilities may be used to discuss anti-clerical doctrine, it seems to me that comparable use by a group desiring to express a belief in God must also be permitted. The fact that their expression of faith includes ceremonial conduct is not, in my opinion, a sufficient reason for suppressing their discussion entirely.

Accordingly, although I do not endorse the Court's reasoning, I concur in its judgment.

⊥282 *Justice WHITE*, dissenting.

In affirming the decision of the Court of Appeals, the majority rejects petitioners' argument that the Establishment Clause of the Constitution prohibits the use of university buildings for religious purposes. A state university may permit its property to be used for purely religious services without violating the First and Fourteenth Amendments. With this I agree. See *Committee for Public Education* v. *Nyquist* (White, J., dissenting); *Lemon* v. *Kurtzman* (Opinion of White, J.). The Establishment Clause, however, sets limits only on what the State may do with respect to religious organizations; it does not establish what the State is *required* to do. I have long argued that Establishment Clause limits on state action which incidentally aids religion are not as strict as the Court has held. The step from the permissible to the necessary, however, is a long one. In my view, just as there is room under the Religion Clauses for state policies that may have some beneficial effect on religion, there is also room for state policies that may incidentally burden religion. In other words, I believe the States to be a good deal freer to formulate policies that affect religion in divergent ways than does the majority. See *Sherbert* v. *Verner* (Harlan, J., dissenting). The majority's position will inevitably lead to those contradictions and tensions between the Establishment and Free Exercise Clauses warned against by *Justice STEWART* in *Sherbert* v. *Verner*.

The University regulation at issue here provides in pertinent part: "No University buildings or grounds (except chapels as herein provided) may be used for purposes of religious worship or religious teaching by either student or nonstudent groups. Student congregations of local ⊥283 churches or of recognized denominations or sects, although not technically recognized campus groups, may use the facilities . . . under the same regulations that apply to recognized campus organizations, provided that no University facilities may be used for purposes of religious worship or religious teaching."

Although there may be instances in which it would be difficult to determine whether a religious group used university facilities for "worship" or "religious teaching," rather than for secular ends, this is not such a case. The regulation was applied to respondents' religious group, Cornerstone, only after the group explicitly informed the University that it sought access to the facilities for the purpose of offering prayer, singing hymns, reading scripture, and teaching biblical principles. Cornerstone described their meetings as follows: "Although these meetings would not appear to a casual observer to correspond precisely to a traditional worship service, there is no doubt that worship is an important part of the general atmosphere." The issue here is only whether the University ⊥284 regulation as applied and interpreted in this case is impermissible under the federal Constitution. If it is impermissible, it is because it runs afoul of either the Free Speech or the Free Exercise Clause of the First Amendment.

A large part of respondents' argument, accepted by the court below and accepted by the majority, is founded on the proposition that because religious worship uses speech, it is protected by the Free Speech Clause of the First Amendment. Not only is it protected, they argue, but religious worship *qua* speech is not different from any other variety of protected speech as a matter of constitutional principle. I believe that this proposition is plainly wrong. Were it right, the Religion Clauses would be emptied of any independent meaning in circumstances in which religious practice took the form of speech. Although the majority describes this argument as "novel," I believe it to be clearly supported by our previous cases. Just last term, the Court found it suffi⊥285ciently obvious that the Establishment Clause prohibited a State from posting a copy of the Ten Commandments on the classroom wall that a statute requiring such a posting was summarily struck down. *Stone* v. *Graham*. That case necessarily presumed that the State could not ignore the religious content of the written message, nor was it permitted to treat that content as it would, or must treat, other—secular—messages under the First Amendment's protection of speech. Similarly, the Court's decisions prohibiting prayer in the public schools rest on a content-based distinction between varieties of speech: as a speech act, apart from its content, a prayer is indistinguishable from a biology lesson. See *School District of Abington Township* v. *Schempp*; *Engel* v. *Vitale*. Operation of the Free Exercise Clause is equally dependent, in certain circumstances, on recognition of a content-based distinction between religious and secular speech. Thus, in *Torcaso* v. *Watkins* the Court struck down, as violative of the Free Exercise Clause, a state requirement that made a declaration of belief in God a condition of state employment. A declaration is again a speech act, but it was the content of the speech that brought the case within the scope of the Free Exercise Clause.

If the majority were right that no distinction may be drawn between verbal acts of worship and other verbal acts, all of these cases would have to be reconsidered. Although I agree that the line may be difficult to draw in many cases, surely the majority cannot seriously suggest that no line may ever be drawn. If that were the case, the majority would ⊥**286** have to uphold the University's right to offer a class entitled "Sunday Mass." Under the majority's view, such a class would be—as a matter of constitutional principle—indistinguishable from a class entitled "The History of the Catholic Church."

There may be instances in which a State's attempt to disentangle itself from religious worship would intrude upon secular speech about religion. In such a case, the State's action would be subject to challenge under the Free Speech Clause of the First Amendment. This is not such a case. This case involves religious worship only; the fact that that worship is accomplished through speech does not add anything to respondents' argument. That argument must rely upon the claim that the State's action impermissibly interferes with the free exercise of respondents' religious practices. Although this is a close question, I conclude that it does not.

Plausible analogies on either side suggest themselves. Respondents argue, and the majority agrees, that by permitting any student group to use its facilities for communicative purposes other than religious worship, the University has created a "public forum." With ample ⊥**287** support, they argue that the State may not make content-based distinctions as to what groups may use, or what messages may be conveyed in, such a forum. See *Police Department of Chicago* v. *Mosley*, *Cox* v. *Louisiana*. The right of the religious to nondiscriminatory access to the public forum is well established. See *Niemotko* v. *Maryland; Murdock* v. *Pennsylvania*. Moreover, it is clear that there are bounds beyond which the University could not go in enforcing its regulation: I don't suppose it could prevent students from saying grace before meals in the school cafeteria, or prevent distribution of religious literature on campus.

Petitioners, on the other hand, argue that allowing use of their facilities for religious worship is constitutionally indistinguishable from directly subsidizing such religious services: It would "[fund] a specifically religious activity in an otherwise substantially secular setting." *Hunt* v. *McNair*. They argue that the fact that secular student groups are entitled to the in-kind subsidy at issue here does not establish that a religious group is entitled to the same subsidy. They could convincingly argue, for example, that a state university that pays for basketballs for the basketball team is not thereby required to pay for Bibles for a group like Cornerstone.

⊥**288** A third analogy suggests itself, one that falls between these two extremes. There are a variety of state policies which incidentally benefit religion that this Court has upheld without implying that they were constitutionally required of the State. See *Board of Education* v. *Allen* (state loan of textbooks to parochial school students); *Zorach* v. *Clauson* (release of students from public schools, during school hours, to perform religious activities away from the school grounds); *Everson* v. *Board of Education* (state provision of transportation to parochial school students). Provision of university facilities on a uniform basis to all student groups is not very different from provision of text books or transportation. From this perspective the issue is not whether the State must, or must not, open its facilities to religious worship; rather, it is whether the state may choose not to do so.

Each of these analogies is persuasive. Because they lead to different results, however, they are of limited help in reaching a decision here. They also demonstrate the difficulty in reconciling the various interests expressed in the Religion Clauses. In my view, therefore, resolution of this case is best achieved by returning to first principles. This requires an assessment of the burden on respondents' ability freely to exercise their religious beliefs and practices and of the State's interest in enforcing its regulation.

Respondents complain that compliance with the regulation would require them to meet "about a block and a half" from campus under conditions less comfortable than those previously available on campus. I view this burden on free exer⊥**289**cise as minimal. Because the burden is minimal, the State need do no more than demonstrate that the regulation furthers some permissible state end. The State's interest in avoiding claims that it is financing or otherwise supporting religious worship—in maintaining a definitive separation between church and state—is such an end. That the State truly does mean to act toward this end is amply supported by the treatment of religion in the State Constitution. Thus, I believe the interest of the state is sufficiently strong to justify the imposition of the minimal burden on respondents' ability freely to exercise their religious beliefs.

On these facts, therefore, I cannot find that the application of the regulation to prevent Cornerstone from holding religious worship services in University facilities violates the First and Fourteenth Amendments. I would not hold as the majority does that if a University permits students and others to use its property for secular purposes, it must also furnish facilities to religious groups for the purposes of worship and the practice of their religion. Accordingly, I would reverse the judgment of the Court of Appeals.

FREE EXERCISE AND TAXATION

At any level of government the power to tax is essential to effective operation of that government: without funds government cannot survive. The primary purpose of taxation is therefore correctly perceived to be the raising of revenue. A secondary, and highly significant, objective of taxation may sometimes be regulation of or even prohibition of certain practices thought to be detrimental to society. The taxing power may also be used to encourage or induce individuals or organizations to take positive action to further contemporary governmental objectives.

Even general neutral tax laws and their exemption provisions often raise legal problems as to their applicability to religious organizations. It has for long been argued by some, for example, that the virtually universal policy of exempting church property from taxation is unconstitutional. As will be discussed at a later point, it was not until 1970 that, in WALZ v. TAX COMMISSION, the Supreme Court spoke definitely and positively to that practice with respect to church property used solely for religious worship. Since that time both Congress and the courts have wrestled with related questions concerning property and income of church activities beyond the immediate scope of the decision. Such a question was involved in *St. Martin Evangelical Lutheran Church* v. *South Dakota* (1980). In this case the issue was whether a church must pay unemployment compensation taxes imposed by the Federal Unemployment Tax Act (FUTA) on employees who work in the church's parochial school. The Lutheran church and academy involved in the litigation argued that to subject them to the tax would violate both the Free Exercise and Establishment Clauses.

The statute at bar provided exemption from the taxes with respect to "service performed—(1) in the employ of (A) a church or convention or association of churches, or (B) an organization . . . which is operated, supervised, controlled, or principally supported by a church or a convention or association of churches." The taxing authorities tried to interpret the word "church" to mean only the actual place of worship—the church building—thus making the employees of a church-related school subject to the collection of the FUTA taxes. After reviewing the legislative history of the act, the Court concluded that such a construction contradicted the phrasing of the statute itself: the employees of a church-related school are "in the employ of a church or convention or association of churches" and are thus eligible for exemption under the act from the collection of the contested taxes. The fact that the Court refused to allow such a narrow definition of the words under question is likely to have wide implications since this or very similar language is used in other statutes, particularly in various places in the Internal Revenue Code.

Later that year the Court heard oral arguments in another case requiring the balancing of free exercise claims against congressional power to tax. Edwin D. Lee, self-employed Pennsylvania farmer and carpenter, refused on religious grounds to withhold or to pay Social Security taxes on wages he paid several Old Order Amish employees. Lee, also a member of that religious group, believed that each individual has the responsibility for caring for those in need in his community, and he maintained it was contrary to his religious tenets either to pay Social Security taxes or to accept Social Security benefits.

When the government brought suit for payment of the taxes, a federal district judge upheld Lee's refusal to pay. The judge cited a 1965 federal law exempting self-employed Amish and members of other religious groups whose religious beliefs forbid payment of the tax or receipt of benefits. The government appealed the decision, contending that the law in question applies only to taxes that a self-employed individual would pay on his own income, not to the tax paid on the compensation of his employees.

In February 1982 Chief Justice Burger, writing for a unanimous Court in UNITED STATES v. LEE, upheld the government's contention that the statutory exemption applied only to self-employed individuals, and did not apply to Lee—an employer—and his employees. Burger then turned to the broader question of whether there was a constitutionally required exemption. He agreed that compulsory participation of the Amish in the Social Security system interfered with their free exercise rights, but he noted that "Not all burdens on religion are unconstitutional." Government, he said, may justify a restraint on religious liberty by showing that the limitation is necessary for accomplishment of an overriding government interest.

The Social Security program is a vital nationwide government service and only by mandatory participation can the government be kept fiscally sound. Religious beliefs can be accommodated, but a system forced to accommodate the great variety of religious beliefs in the area of taxation would be difficult if not impossible to administer. Religious practices must sometimes yield to the public good. Said the Chief Justice:

> Congress and the courts have been sensitive to the needs flowing from the Free Exercise Clause, but every person cannot be shielded from all the burdens incident to exercising every aspect of the right to practice religious beliefs. When followers of a particular sect enter into commercial activity as a matter of choice, the limits they accept on their own conduct as a matter of conscience and faith are not to be superimposed on the statutory schemes which are binding on others in that activity (455 U.S. 252, 262).

Justice Stevens concurred in the judgment, but expressed his belief that the heavy burden now imposed upon government to justify the applicability of general neutral laws to individual conscientious objectors should be shifted to the objector to demonstrate that "there is a unique reason for allowing him a special exemption for a valid law of general applicability."[1]

Several cases have in recent years dealt with the issue of the use of tax exemptions to coerce compliance with government policy. In *First Unitarian Church* v. *County of Los Angeles* (1958), the Court considered a California constitutional provision that made as a condition for tax exemption the signing of an oath stating that the applicant for exemption would not advocate overthrow of the government by force, violence, or unlawful means. The First Unitarian Church of Los Angeles refused to sign the oath, claiming that the state had no right to compel the church to sign an oath affirming any doctrine, advocacy, or belief. In reaching its decision, the Court did not deal with the substantive question of whether the state could condition tax exemption upon acceptance of state-defined beliefs or activities. Rather it said simply that, in order to deny the tax exemption, the state would have to demonstrate that a particular church did in fact advocate overthrow of the government. It was not permissible to withhold the exemption merely because a church would not sign the oath.

Christian Echoes National Ministry v. *United States* (1973) also concerned the exemption issue. The ministry of fundamentalist evangelist Billy James Hargis was denied tax exemption by the IRS because the Hargis organization was substantially involved in political activities in violation of IRS regulations. A tax-exempt religious educational organization may not use a substantial part of its activities or assets to influence legislation or to participate in a political campaign on behalf of a candidate. Because the Hargis organization did both, the IRS withdrew its tax exemption. After the federal court of appeals upheld the IRS revocation, the Supreme Court denied certiorari.

In this controversy, the Christian Echoes Ministry was supported by a large number of religious groups across the theological spectrum. They were, and are, concerned about two dimensions of their relationship with the IRS. The first is that "substantial political participation" means whatever the IRS says it means. That is, there are no objective guidelines as to how much a group may engage in political activity or advocacy before it is in danger of losing its tax exemption. The second dimension is the more crucial one. Does the government have the right to set limits on the activities and speech of religious institutions as they address public issues?[2]

---

[1]In 1984 the United States Court of Appeals for the Tenth Circuit agreed with an Oklahoma City minister that his situation differed from that of Lee, an employer. As a minister opposed to public insurance on religious grounds, he would have been entitled to exemption from self-employed taxes had he filed for exemption within the time frame provided in the governing statute. He had not done so, however, so the court upheld the denial of the exemption by the IRS and Tax Court. Such interference with his free exercise of religion as resulted from the tax was overridden by the government's interest in "maintaining the financial stability of the social security system." Congress could, the court observed, constitutionally remove all exemptions from payment of the tax if it so chose. *Ballinger* v. *Commissioner of Internal Revenue* (1984). Two years later, the Bethel Baptist Church, a fundamentalist congregation in Sellersville, Pennsylvania, received the same ruling from a federal district judge when it challenged the constitutionality of the Social Security Act as amended in 1983 and 1984. Prior to the amendments churches could choose to participate in the Social Security system on a voluntary basis. By the 1984 amendment, churches were required to affirmatively choose not to be a part of the system if they did not wish to contribute to social security. If they did elect, for religious reasons, not to participate in the program, their employees would have to pay the tax applicable to self-employed persons—a greater amount than an employee would contribute at the employee rate. The church did not make the election and in 1984 paid $17,795.04 on wages subject to social security taxes. Subsequently the church filed a claim for refund of the amount paid and challenged the constitutionality of the amendments on free exercise, establishment, and equal protection grounds. District Judge Caldwell held, consistent with *Lee* and *Ballinger*, that the government's overriding compelling interest in maintaining the integrity of the revenue system outweighed the religious claims; he similarly found no violation of the Equal Protection of the Laws Clause (*Bethel Baptist Church* v. *United States* (1986)).

[2]In the late 1980s, a case many people thought would be of tremendous significance was brought before a federal district court in New York. If successful, the suit would have revoked the tax exemption of the Roman Catholic Church. The litigation was brought by Abortion Rights Mobilization and twenty other pro-choice groups and individuals against the United States Catholic Conference and National Conference of Catholic Bishops. Their contention was that the Church had violated §501(c)(3) of the tax code, which provides that tax-exempt organizations cannot "participate in, or intervene in . . . any political campaign on behalf of any candidate for public office." Plaintiffs charged that the Church had violated the prohibition through its consistent efforts to support or oppose candidates based on their stance on the abortion issue. The suit was perceived to have grave implications not only for the Roman Catholic Church, but for all churches because of the financial benefit which accrues to them through tax deductibility of contributions. The case went up and down the federal court chain for several years, during which time the Catholic Church was threatened with massive fines for not surrendering documents to the court of record. But it finally ended with a whimper when the Court of Appeals for the Second Circuit ruled that Abortion Rights Mobilization lacked standing to sue the IRS, and the Supreme Court later denied certiorari, April 30, 1990.

The most publicized controversy concerning the use of tax exemption to bring about compliance with government policy involved Bob Jones University. A fundamentalist Christian school in the strictest sense of the word, it affirms a literalistic view of the Bible, assuming the world to be essentially evil and dominated by atheistic, pagan attitudes. Interracial dating and marriages are said to be forbidden by the Bible. Consequently, prior to 1971, the university accepted no black students. After that time, married black people were accepted as students; later, unmarried blacks were admitted. However, rules were introduced that prohibit interracial dating and marriage, upon penalty of being expelled.

In the 1970s, as the result of extended judicial and administrative interpretation of civil rights laws, certain federal officials determined that racially segregated or discriminatory schools, including church-related colleges, should lose federal benefits and/or tax exemption. These policies were applied to Bob Jones University through litigation initiated by various federal agencies, principally the IRS. That agency declared that the school should lose its tax-exempt status because it at first refused to admit black students and, later, did not treat them equally.

Bob Jones University sued to recover tax-exempt status, arguing that its treatment of blacks was a matter of deeply and sincerely held religious faith and thus was protected by the Free Exercise Clause of the First Amendment. Articulated somewhat more broadly, the issue may be described as follows: Government control over admission policies of church schools deprives these institutions of the right to make decisions that may very well rest on theological or ecclesiastical bases. Further, such government policy negates the judgment of a church college regarding the best means to accomplish goals that the college has set for itself.

In litigation against the IRS, the university won at the trial court level but lost in the appeals court (*Bob Jones University* v. *United States* [1980]). When the university asked the Supreme Court to consider its grievance, the case was consolidated with *Goldsboro Christian Schools* v. *United States* (involving a North Carolina school with virtually identical racial theology and tax problems as Bob Jones) and granted a hearing. However, in January 1982 the Reagan administration (by means of a memorandum from the Justice Department to the Supreme Court, requesting that the case be declared moot) announced that the tax exemption for these schools and any others similarly situated was being restored. After a tremendous cry of protest from blacks and other civil rights advocates, the administration promptly retreated from the original announcement. President Ronald Reagan affirmed that he was firmly opposed to racial discrimination and was asking Congress to pass legislation to withdraw tax exemption from racially discriminatory institutions, including church-related schools. Seeking to explain its actions, the Reagan administration announced that public policy should be made by the legislative branch, not by the regulations of executive agencies.

Congress soon indicated, however, that it had no intention of obliging the President. The issue was further complicated when in February the Court of Appeals in the District of Columbia issued an interim order barring the administration from granting exemptions to "any school that unlawfully discriminates on the basis of race." The Justice Department then filed papers with the Supreme Court stating that its earlier request that the *Bob Jones-Goldsboro* case be vacated as moot was no longer appropriate because of the order of the Court of Appeals.

The administration sought permission from the Court to file a brief arguing that there was no basis in congressional legislation for the Internal Revenue Service's eleven-year policy of denying exemptions to schools that discriminate on racial grounds. Meanwhile, Bob Jones University and Goldsboro Christian Schools asked the Court to reverse the federal appeals court ruling. In March the Supreme Court accepted the government brief.

In May 1983 the Court, with only Justice Rehnquist in dissent, affirmed the judgments of the Court of Appeals in the two cases. Chief Justice Burger delivered the opinion for the Court in BOB JONES UNIVERSITY v. UNITED STATES and GOLDSBORO CHRISTIAN SCHOOLS v. UNITED STATES. The Chief Justice interpreted congressional intent with respect to entitlement to tax exemptions provided for in the Internal Revenue Code to mean that entitlement was to depend not only on an institution's falling within one of the designated eight categories set forth, but on "meeting certain common law standards of charity—namely, that an institution seeking tax-exempt status must serve a public purpose and not be contrary to established public policy" (461 U.S. 574, 586).

Racial discrimination is clearly contrary to public policy, and the IRS therefore acted properly in July 1970 when it concluded that tax-exempt status would no longer be granted to private schools practicing racial discrimination, nor would gifts to such schools be treated as charitable deductions for income tax purposes. The immediate responsibility for interpreting the Internal Revenue Code falls upon the administrative agency. Congress obviously has the power to modify improper IRS rulings, but Congress had been "acutely aware" of the controversial determinations for twelve years and by failing to modify them had in effect acquiesced in and ratified the IRS action.

The majority opinion then spoke to the contention that the construction given the code by the IRS violated First Amendment free exercise rights of religious schools engaging in racial discrimination on the basis of "sincerely held religious beliefs." The Chief Justice agreed that the Court recognized that government regulation of religious beliefs was prohibited; however, it had also consistently recognized that not all burdens on actions based on religious beliefs are forbidden. Some government interests are so compelling as to justify regulation of religiously based conduct. Eradication of racial discrimination in education is such a compelling state interest which "substantially outweighs whatever burden denial of tax benefits places on petitioners' exercise of their religious beliefs" (461 U.S. 574, 604).

Justice Powell concurred in the judgment of the Court, but in a separate opinion he expressed his concern with the "broader implications" of the majority opinion. He was particularly troubled by the conformity which the opinion seemed to mandate, as if suggesting that the "primary function of a tax-exempt organization is to act on behalf of the Government in carrying out governmentally approved policies." Powell assumed that one of the important purposes of tax exemption to private nonprofit schools and other groups is to provide alternative choices and "encourage diverse, indeed often sharply conflicting activities and viewpoints." If tax exemption was to be denied, Congress should so provide. "The contours of public policy," he concluded, "should be determined by Congress, not by judges or the IRS."

Justice Rehnquist, in dissent, agreed that there is a strong national policy against racial discrimination and that Congress could legislate to further that policy through denial of tax exemption. The Court had erred, he argued, in assuming that Congress had adopted the 1970 IRS ruling by failure to pass legislation negating it. He, like Justice Powell, maintained that "this Court should not legislate for Congress."[3]

Beginning at least as early as the encounters of the Jehovah's Witnesses with license fees and taxes on income from sale of religious publications in the 1930s, unpopular, unorthodox religious movements have been made painfully aware that the taxing power can be one of the most successful devices used by unfriendly authorities to limit or to harass their efforts. These incidents have most often occurred at the local level, and the courts—at least the appellate courts—have most often come to the rescue of the beleaguered groups.

In the 1970s and 1980s the Unification Church, having met with widespread negative governmental action, has succeeded the Jehovah's Witnesses as today's most litigated religious movement. Numerous cases have been brought in both state and federal courts against, or on behalf of, the "Moonies," as members of the movement are derogatorily designated. The most highly publicized suits have concerned either the alleged "mind control" and "brainwashing" techniques of the Unification Church or the "deprogramming" activities of Ted Patrick and others who gained considerable public attention for their forcible abduction of young, or sometimes not so young, Unification converts followed by strenuous psychological efforts to cause them to recant and return to their former religious commitment and lifestyle.[4]

However, the litigation most costly in terms of time, finance, and leadership has emanated from tax conflicts. For five years the church was involved in a tax battle with New York City. In 1977 that city's tax commission denied the Church's request for real estate tax exemption for three New York properties—which together served as headquarters for the worldwide movement—on the ground that the primary purpose of the Unification Church was political and economic rather than religious. The church appealed to the Appellate Division of the New York Supreme Court which, finding the record insufficient for review, appointed a special referee to acquire the necessary information to ascertain whether the commission had

[3]For further discussion of the case see "*Bob Jones University* v. *United States*: Paying the Price of Prejudice—Loss of Tax Exemption Status," *Mercer Law Review* 35 (Spring 1984): 937-63, and Charles O. Gavin and Neal Devins, "A Tax Policy Analysis of *Bob Jones University* v. *United States*," *Vanderbilt Law Review* 36 (November 1983):1353-82.

[4]See such state and lower federal court cases as *Katz* v. *Superior Court* (1977), *Colombrito* v. *Kelly* (1985), and *Molko and Leal* v. *Holy Spirit Association* (1986). Responding to great public concern about the proliferation of "cults," particularly after the Jonestown tragedy in 1978, investigations of the cult movement were conducted in numerous state legislatures and Congress as well. In response to alleged brainwashing by adherents of the Unification Church, conservatorship bills to allow state appointment of conservators for a person who had fallen under the control of a group to the point that his or her judgment had been impaired were introduced in at least seven legislatures. The New York legislature actually passed such a bill in 1980, which would allow the state to appoint conservators for persons who had "become closely and regularly associated with a group which practices the use of deception in the recruitment of members and which engages in systematic food or sleep deprivation or isolation from family or unusually long work schedules and such persons for whom the temporary conservator is to be appointed has undergone a sudden and radical change in behavior lifestyle, habits and attitudes, and has become unable to care for his welfare and that his judgment has become impaired to the extent that he is unable to understand the need for such care" (11122-A Section 1, New York 25 March 1980). The bill was vetoed by Governor Hugh L. Carey as both unconstitutional and unworkable. Perceptive accounts for the events of the period are found in David G. Bromely and Anson D. Shupe, Jr., *Strange Gods: The Great American Cult Scare* (Boston: Beacon Press, 1981) and James E. Wood, Jr., "Editorial: New Religions and the First Amendment," *Journal of Church and State* 24 (Autumn 1982):457-62.

acted arbitrarily and capriciously in denying the claim for exemption.

The referee determined that while the primary purpose of the Church was religious, the commission had not acted arbitrarily and capriciously because the political motives and activities of the Church were such as to deny exemption. The Appellate Division approved the report of the referee, but rejected his finding that the church's primary purpose was religious.

On further appeal, the Court of Appeals of New York in 1982 reversed the denial of tax exemption and, citing *Watson*, *Barnette*, and *Ballard*, said: "As stated, it is not the province of civil authorities to indulge in such distillation as to what is to be denominated religious and what political or economic. It is for religious bodies themselves, rather than the courts or administrative agencies to define by their teachings and activities what their religion is." *The Holy Spirit Association for the Unification of World Christianity* v. *The Tax Commission of the City of New York* (435 N.E.2d 662, 668 [1982]).

In December 1981 a criminal suit was filed in the United States District Court for the Southern District of New York which soon overshadowed all previous Unification Church litigation, and which caused grave concern on the part of many individuals and church groups not ordinarily sympathetic with the goals and methods of the Unification Church. After a five-year investigation by the IRS, the suit was brought against Reverend Sun Myung Moon, founder and leader of the Church, and his financial aide. They were indicted on thirteen counts relating to federal tax evasion—filing false tax returns, submitting false documents, perjury, obstruction of justice, etc. Because he feared prejudice on the part of most potential jurors, Reverend Moon asked for but was denied a nonjury trial. He was represented by eminent Harvard Law Professor Laurence H. Tribe.

The case revolved primarily around the question of whether bank accounts in a New York bank and stock in a corporation, both held in Moon's name, were for his personal use and financial benefit as the government contended, or whether he held them as a trustee, and living embodiment of the faith, in behalf of the Unification Church (in which case the interest and dividends would be tax exempt).

After a six-week trial, Moon was found guilty on all counts and Judge Gerard L. Goettel, who had carefully sought to keep the trial free from religious overtones, sentenced him to concurrent prison terms of eighteen months and levied a fine of $25,000 plus court costs. The case was appealed to the Court of Appeals for the Second Circuit which upheld the verdict by a two-to-one vote. In 1984 the Supreme Court refused to review the case and Reverend Moon served thirteen months of the eighteen-month sentence.

That the entire proceeding caused great concern to many individuals and religious and civil rights groups is evidenced by the extraordinary number of amici curiae briefs filed in Moon's behalf. Sixteen briefs were filed by forty individuals and religious and civil rights groups as varied as United States Senators Orrin G. Hatch and Eugene J. McCarthy, the National Council of Christ in the U.S.A., the Presbyterian Church (USA), the National Association of Evangelicals, the African Methodist Episcopal Church, The Church of Jesus Christ of Latter-day Saints, the Southern Christian Leadership Conference, and the Catholic League for Religion and Civil Rights.

The briefs objected not only to what their authors regarded as excessive governmental interference in the internal financial procedures of churches but also to the selective prosecution of a controversial religious leader. They pointed out that the practice of a church holding its funds and property in the name of a pastor is not peculiar to the Unification Church. Thus Moon's conviction had ominous forebodings, particularly for those poorer, less highly organized churches where the pastor may be the only paid employee available to handle funds and financial accounting.

Many persons have commented on the selective prosecution aspect of the case. Trial judge Goettel himself recognized the unusual nature of the case against Reverend Moon when he said, "I am not so naive as to believe that if Reverend Moon was a noncontroversial person whose religion was Pollyannish, who nobody took exception to, that the government would not have as much interest in looking at his taxes as they did."[5]

Senator Orrin Hatch, who chaired a Senate subcommittee that looked into the Moon prosecution, expressed his misgivings about the entire proceeding in a letter to attorney Edward Bennett Williams:

> In my opinion, Rev. Moon's is an extremely important religious freedom case. In a very real way, it has sent a message of how present day America deals with unpopular religions seeking sanctuary on our shores. Sadly, the message is not a good one. . . . The Moon case sends a strong signal that if one's views are unpopular enough, this country will find a way not to tolerate, but to convict.[6]

Whatever Reverend Sun Myung Moon's real motives may have been, what happened to him serves once again to emphasize the potential for control of unpopular religious movements that lies in the power to tax.[7]

In January 1990 the Supreme Court decided a case involving the constitutional right of the State of

[5]Quoted in Leo Pfeffer, *Religion, State and the Burger Court* (Buffalo, N.Y.: Prometheus Books, 1984), p. 13.

[6]*Unification News*, September 1985, p. 5.

[7]Cf. Carlton Sherwood, *Inquisition: The Persecution and Prosecution of the Reverend Sun Myung Moon* (Washington, D.C.: Regnery Gateway, 1991).

California to levy sales and use taxes on distribution of religious materials by Jimmy Swaggart Ministries. The Court rendered a decision that greatly limits future constitutional claims for tax exemptions for religious organizations. California requires payment by retailers of a 6% sales tax on in-state sales of tangible personal property and a 6% use tax on such property bought outside the state. No exemption is provided for religious groups.

Jimmy Swaggart Ministries had conducted 23 evangelistic "crusades" in California, during which substantial sales were made of religious books, collections of sermons, tapes, and records. In addition, "non-religious merchandise" such as T-shirts, bowls, plates, and replicas of the ark of the covenant were sold. Mail-order sales were also made to Californians from headquarters in Baton Rouge, Louisiana.

The California Board of Equalization informed Swaggart Ministries in 1980 that religious materials were not exempt and that the group must register and report its sales. The Board's 1981 audit of the Ministries indicated that since 1974 the group had made mail-order sales from Baton Rouge for use in California valued at $1,702,942.00 and California crusade sales at $240,560.00. The total taxes, interest, and penalties amounted to $166,145.10. Swaggart paid the taxes and did not contest those levied on what he considered "nonreligious merchandise." But the Ministries filed a petition for redetermination, claiming that the tax on specifically religious books and recordings violated both the Free Exercise and Establishment Clauses. The Board removed the penalties, but the Ministries brought suit for tax refund in a California state court which upheld collection of the taxes, as did the appeals court. The state supreme court denied review. In its appeal to the United States Supreme Court, the organization primarily rested its claim on the Court's decisions in MURDOCK v. PENNSYLVANIA and *Follett* v. *McCormick*. In these cases the Court had struck down state efforts to tax an evangelist and a bookseller, both Jehovah's Witnesses.

Writing for a unanimous Court, Justice O'Connor distinguished taxes at issue in the earlier cases as "flat license taxes that operated as a prior restraint on the exercise of religious liberty" from the taxes challenged here. In contrast to the taxes invalidated in the Witnesses cases, the California tax was a neutral, nondiscriminatory, generally applicable tax. The state might well decide to grant exemptions from the taxes on religious activities, but there was no constitutional mandate to do so.

The slight burden imposed by increased administrative costs and possible reduced sales was not "constitutionally significant." Justice O'Connor summed up the holding:

> We therefore conclude that the collection and payment of the generally applicable tax in this case imposes no constitutionally significant burden on appellant's religious practices or beliefs. The Free Exercise Clause accordingly does not require the State to grant appellant an exemption from its generally applicable sales and use tax (493 U.S. 378, 392).

The tax as levied clearly had a secular purpose. Citing WALZ v. TAX COMMISSION, the Court also failed to find any excessive entanglement between government and religion, thus negating the Establishment Clause claim.[8]

UNITED STATES v. LEE

455 U.S. 252
ON APPEAL FROM THE UNITED STATES
DISTRICT COURT FOR THE WESTERN
DISTRICT OF PENNSYLVANIA
Argued November 2, 1981 — Decided February 23, 1982

⊥**254** *Chief Justice BURGER* delivered the opinion of the Court.

We noted probable jurisdiction to determine whether imposition of social security taxes is unconstitutional as applied to persons who object on religious grounds to receipt of public insurance benefits and to payment of taxes to support public insurance funds. The District Court concluded that the Free Exercise Clause prohibits forced payment of social security taxes when payment of taxes and receipt of benefits violates the taxpayer's religion. We reverse.

I

Appellee, a member of the Old Order Amish, is a self-employed farmer and carpenter. From 1970 to 1977, appellee employed several other Amish to work on his farm and in his carpentry shop. He failed to file the quarterly social security tax returns required of employers, withhold social security tax from his employees or pay the employer's share of social security taxes.

In 1978, the Internal Revenue Service assessed appellee in excess of $27,000 for unpaid employment taxes; he paid $91—⊥**255** the amount owed for the first quarter of 1973—and then sued in the United States District

[8]Douglas Laycock is quite critical of the Court's decision. He sees it as potentially imposing more restraint on religious activities than Justice O'Connor indicates. In "The Remnants of Free Exercise," *The Supreme Court Review 1990* (Chicago: The University of Chicago Press, 1991), p. 39., he asserts: "*Swaggart* unambiguously eliminates most constitutional claims to tax exemption. The real choices are now up to legislatures and tax authorities. . . . The Court's new rule is that churches are constitutionally immune only from a flat tax that acts as a prior restraint." He agreed that the impact might well be marginal, but the granting of tax exemptions to religious entities was now a political rather than a judicial question.

Court for the Western District of Pennsylvania for a refund, claiming that imposition of the social security taxes violated his First Amendment Free Exercise rights and those of his Amish employees.

The District Court held the statutes requiring appellee to pay social security and unemployment insurance taxes unconstitutional as applied. The court noted that the Amish believe it sinful not to provide for their own elderly and needy and therefore are religiously opposed to the national social security system. The court also accepted appellee's contention that the Amish religion not only prohibits the acceptance of social security benefits, but also bars all contributions by Amish to the social security system. The District Court observed that in light of their beliefs, Congress has accommodated self-employed Amish and self-employed members of other religious groups with similar beliefs by providing exemptions from social security taxes. 26 U. S. C. § 1402(g). The court's holding was based on both ⊥**256** the exemption statute for the self-employed and the First Amendment; appellee and others "who fall within the carefully circumscribed definition provided in 1402(g) are relieved from paying the employer's share of [social security taxes] as it is an unconstitutional infringement upon the free exercise of their religion."

Direct appeal from the judgment of the District Court was taken pursuant to 28 U. S. C. § 1252.

II

The exemption provided by § 1402(g) is available only to self-employed individuals and does not apply to employers or employees. Consequently, appellee and his employees are not within the express provisions of § 1402(g). Thus any exemption from payment of the employer's share of social security taxes must come from a constitutionally-required exemption.

A

The preliminary inquiry in determining the existence of a constitutionally-required exemption is whether the payment ⊥**257** of social security taxes and the receipt of benefits interferes with the Free Exercise rights of the Amish. The Amish believe that there is a religiously based obligation to provide for their fellow members the kind of assistance contemplated by the social security system. Although the government does not challenge the sincerity of this belief, the government does contend that payment of social security taxes will not threaten the integrity of the Amish religious belief or observance. It is not within "the judicial function and judicial competence," however, to determine whether appellee or the government has the proper interpretation of the Amish faith; "[c]ourts are not arbiters of scriptural interpretation." *Thomas* v. *Review Bd. of Indiana Employment Sec.* We therefore accept appellee's contention that both payment and receipt of social security benefits is forbidden by the Amish faith. Because the payment of the taxes or receipt of benefits violates Amish religious beliefs, compulsory participation in the social security system interferes with their Free Exercise rights.

The conclusion that there is a conflict between the Amish faith and the obligations imposed by the social security system is only the beginning, however, and not the end of the inquiry. Not all burdens on religion are unconstitutional. The state may justify a limitation on religious liberty by showing that it is essential to accomplish an overriding governmental inter⊥**258**est.

B

Because the social security system is nationwide, the governmental interest is apparent. The social security system in the United States serves the public interest by providing a comprehensive insurance system with a variety of benefits available to all participants, with costs shared by employers and employees. The social security system is by far the largest domestic governmental program in the United States today, distributing approximately $11 billion monthly to 36 million Americans. The design of the system requires support by mandatory contributions from covered employers and employees. This mandatory participation is indispensable to the fiscal vitality of the social security system. "[W]idespread individual voluntary coverage under social security . . . would undermine the soundness of the social security program." S. Resp. No. 404, 89th Cong., 1st Sess., Pt. III, U. S. Code Cong. & Admin. News (1965), pp. 1943, 2056. Moreover, a comprehensive national social security system providing for voluntary participation would be almost a contradiction in terms and difficult, if not impossible, to administer. Thus, the government's interest in as⊥**259**suring mandatory and continuous participation in and contribution to the social security system is very high.

C

The remaining inquiry is whether accommodating the Amish belief will unduly interfere with fulfillment of the governmental interest. In *Braunfeld* v. *Brown* this Court noted that "to make accommodation between the religious action and an exercise of state authority is a particularly delicate task . . . because resolution in favor of the State results in the choice to the individual of either abandoning his religious principle or facing . . . prosecution." The difficulty in attempting to accommodate religious beliefs in the area of taxation is that "we are a cosmopolitan nation made up of people of almost every conceivable religious preference." *Braunfeld*. The Court has long recognized that balance must be struck between the values of the comprehensive social system, which rests on a complex of actuarial factors, and the consequences of allowing religiously based exemptions. To maintain an organized society that guarantees religious freedom to a great variety of faiths requires that some religious practices yield to the common good. Religious beliefs can be accommodated, but there is a point at which accommodation would "radically restrict the operating latitude of the legislature." *Braunfeld*.

Unlike the situation presented in *Wisconsin* v. *Yoder*, it would be difficult to accommodate the comprehen⊥**260**sive social security system with myriad exceptions flowing from a wide variety of religious beliefs. The obligation to pay the social security tax initially is not fundamentally different from the obligation to pay income taxes; the difference—in theory at least—is that the social security tax revenues are segregated for use only in furtherance of the statutory program. There is no principled way, however, for purposes of this case, to distinguish between general taxes and those imposed under the Social Security Act. If, for example, a religious adherent believes war is a sin, and if a certain percentage of the federal budget can be identified as devoted to war-related activities, such individuals would have a similarly valid claim to be exempt from paying that percentage of the income tax. The tax system could not function if denominations were allowed to challenge the tax system because tax payments were spent in a manner that violates their religious belief. Because the broad public interest in maintaining a sound tax system is of such a high order, religious belief in conflict with the payment of taxes affords no basis for resisting the tax.

III

Congress has accommodated, to the extent compatible with a comprehensive national program, the practices of those who believe it a violation of their faith to participate in the social security system. In § 1402(g) Congress granted an exemption, on religious grounds, to self-employed Amish and others. Confining the § 1402(g) exemption to the self⊥**261**employed provided for a narrow category which was readily identifiable. Self-employed persons in a religious community having its own "welfare" system are distinguishable from the generality of wage earners employed by others.

Congress and the courts have been sensitive to the needs flowing from the Free Exercise Clause, but every person cannot be shielded from all the burdens incident to exercising every aspect of the right to practice religious beliefs. When followers of a particular sect enter into commercial activity as a matter of choice, the limits they accept on their own conduct as a matter of conscience and faith are not to be superimposed on the statutory schemes which are binding on others in that activity. Granting an exemption from social security taxes to an employer operates to impose the employer's religious faith on the employees. Congress drew a line in § 1402(g), exempting the self-employed Amish but not all persons working for an Amish employer. The tax imposed on employers to support the social security system must be uniformly applicable to all, except as Congress provides explicitly otherwise.

Accordingly, the judgment of the District Court is reversed and the case remanded for proceedings consistent with this opinion.

Reversed and remanded.

Justice STEVENS, concurring in the judgment.

The clash between appellee's religious obligation and his civic obligation is irreconcilable. He must violate either an Amish belief or a federal statute. According to the Court, the religious duty must prevail unless the Government shows ⊥**262** that enforcement of the civic duty "is essential to accomplish an overriding governmental interest." That formulation of the constitutional standard suggests that the Government always bears a heavy burden of justifying the application of neutral general laws to individual conscientious objectors. In my opinion, it is the objector who must shoulder the burden of demonstrating that there is a unique reason for allowing him a special exemption from a valid law of general applicability.

Congress already has granted the Amish a limited exemption from social security taxes. As a matter of administration, it would be a relatively simple matter to extend the exemption to the taxes involved in this case. As a matter of fiscal policy, an enlarged exemption probably would benefit the social security system because the nonpayment of these taxes by the Amish would be more than offset by the elimination of their right to collect benefits. In view of the fact that the Amish have demonstrated their capacity to care for their own, the social cost of eliminating this relatively small group of dedicated believers would be minimal. Thus, if we confine the analysis to the Government's interest in rejecting the particular claim to an exemption at stake in this case, the constitutional standard as formulated by the Court has not been met.

The Court rejects the particular claim of this appellee, not because it presents any special problems, but rather because of the risk that a myriad of other claims would be too difficult to process. The Court overstates the magnitude of this risk because the Amish claim applies only to a small religious community with an established welfare system of its own. ⊥**263** Nevertheless, I agree with the Court's conclusion that the difficulties associated with processing other claims to tax exemption on religious grounds justify a rejection of this claim. I believe, however, that this reasoning supports the adoption of a different constitutional standard than the Court purports to apply.

The Court's analysis supports a holding that there is virtually no room for a "constitutionally-required exemption" on religious grounds from a valid tax law that is entirely neutral in its general application. Because I agree with that holding, I concur in the judgment.

BOB JONES UNIVERSITY v. UNITED STATES

GOLDSBORO CHRISTIAN SCHOOLS, INC. v. UNITED STATES

461 U.S. 574
ON WRIT OF CERTIORARI TO THE UNITED STATES COURT OF APPEALS FOR THE FOURTH CIRCUIT
Argued October 12, 1982 — Decided May 24, 1983

⊥**577** *Chief Justice BURGER* delivered the opinion of the Court.

We granted certiorari to decide whether petitioners, nonprofit private schools that prescribe and enforce racially discriminatory admissions standards on the basis of religious doctrine, qualify as tax exempt organizations under § 501(c)(3) of the Internal Revenue Code of 1954.

I

A

Until 1970, the Internal Revenue Service granted tax-exempt status to private schools, without regard to their racial admissions policies, under § 501(c)(3), and granted chari⊥**578**table deductions for contributions to such schools under § 170 of the Code, 26 U.S.C. § 170.

On January 12, 1970 a three-judge District Court for the District of Columbia issued a preliminary injunction prohibiting the IRS from according tax-exempt status to private schools in Mississippi that discriminated as to admissions on the basis of race. *Green* v. *Kennedy*. Thereafter, in July 1970, the IRS concluded that it could "no longer legally justify allowing tax-exempt status [under § 501(c)(3)] to private schools which practice racial discrimination." At the same time, the IRS announced that it could not "treat gifts to such schools as charitable deductions for income tax purposes [under §170]." By letter dated November 30, 1970 the IRS formally notified private schools, including those involved in this case, of this change in policy, "applicable to all private schools in the United States at all levels of education."

On June 30, 1971 the three-judge District Court issued its opinion on the merits of the Mississippi challenge. *Green* v. *Connally*. That court approved the IRS' amended construction of the Tax Code. The court also held that racially discriminatory private schools were not entitled to exemption under § 501(c)(3) and that donors were not entitled to deductions for contributions to such schools under § 170. The court permanently enjoined the Commissioner of ⊥**579** Internal Revenue from approving tax-exempt status for any school in Mississippi that did not publicly maintain a policy of nondiscrimination.

The revised policy on discrimination was formalized in Revenue Ruling 71-447, 1971-2 Cum. Bull. 230: "Both the courts and the Internal Revenue Service have long recognized that the statutory requirement of being 'organized and operated exclusively for religious, charitable, . . . or educational purposes' was intended to express the basic common law concept [of 'charity']. . . . All charitable trusts, educational or otherwise, are subject to the requirement that the purpose of the trust may not be illegal or contrary to public policy." Based on the "national policy to discourage racial discrimination in education," the IRS ruled that "a private school not having a racially nondiscriminatory policy as to students is not 'charitable' within the common law concepts reflected in sections 170 and 501(c)(3) of the Code."

The application of the IRS construction of these provisions to petitioners, two private schools with racially discriminatory admissions policies, is now before us.

B

No. 81-3, Bob Jones University v. United States

Bob Jones University is a nonprofit corporation located in Greenville, South Carolina. Its purpose is "to conduct an institution ⊥**580** of learning . . . , giving special emphasis to the Christian religion and the ethics revealed in the Holy Scriptures." The corporation operates a school with an enrollment of approximately 5,000 students, from kindergarten through college and graduate school. Bob Jones University is not affiliated with any religious denomination, but is dedicated to the teaching and propagation of its fundamentalist Christian religious beliefs. It is both a religious and educational institution. Its teachers are required to be devout Christians, and all courses at the University are taught according to the Bible. Entering students are screened as to their religious beliefs, and their public and private conduct is strictly regulated by standards promulgated by University authorities.

The sponsors of the University genuinely believe that the Bible forbids interracial dating and marriage. To effectuate these views, Negroes were completely excluded until 1971. From 1971 to May 1975, the University accepted no applications from unmarried Negroes, but did accept applications from Negroes married within their race.

Following the decision of the United States Court of Appeals for the Fourth Circuit in *McCrary* v. *Runyon*, prohibiting racial exclusion from private schools, the University revised its policy. Since May 29, 1975, the University has permitted unmarried Negroes to enroll; but a disciplinary rule prohibits interracial dating and marriage. That rule reads: *There is to be no interracial dating.*

1. Students who are partners in an interracial marriage will be expelled.

⊥**581** 2. Students who are members of or affiliated with any group or organization which holds as one of its goals or advocates interracial marriage will be expelled.

3. Students who date outside their own race will be expelled.

4. Students who espouse, promote, or encourage others to violate the University's dating rules and regulations will be expelled.

The University continues to deny admission to applicants engaged in an interracial marriage or known to advocate interracial marriage or dating.

Until 1970, the IRS extended tax-exempt status to Bob Jones University under § 501(c)(3). By the letter of November 30, 1970, that followed the injunction issued in *Green* v. *Kennedy*, the IRS formally notified the University of the change in IRS policy, and announced its intention to challenge the tax-exempt status of private schools practicing racial discrimination in their admissions policies.

After failing to obtain an assurance of tax exemption through administrative means, the University instituted an action in 1971 seeking to enjoin the IRS from revoking the school's tax-exempt status. That suit culminated in *Bob Jones University* v. *Simon*, in which this Court held that the Anti-Injunction Act of the Internal Revenue Code, 26 U.S.C. § 7421(a), prohibited the University from obtaining judicial review by way of injunctive action before the assessment or collection of any tax.

Thereafter, on April 16, 1975, the IRS notified the University of the proposed revocation of its tax-exempt status. On January 19, 1976, the IRS officially revoked the University's tax-exempt status, effective as of December 1, 1970, the day after the University was formally notified of the change in IRS policy. The University subsequently filed returns under the Federal Unemployment Tax Act for the period from December 1, 1970, to December 31, 1975, and paid a tax ⊥**582** totalling $21.00 on one employee for the calendar year of 1975. After its request for a refund was denied, the University instituted the present action, seeking to recover the $21.00 it had paid to the IRS. The Government counterclaimed for unpaid federal unemployment taxes for the taxable years 1971 through 1975, in the amount of $489,675.59, plus interest.

The United States District Court for the District of South Carolina held that revocation of the University's tax-exempt status exceeded the delegated powers of the IRS, was improper under the IRS rulings and procedures, and violated the University's rights under the Religion Clauses of the First Amendment. The court accordingly ordered the IRS to pay the University the $21.00 refund it claimed and rejected the IRS counterclaim.

The Court of Appeals for the Fourth Circuit, in a divided opinion, reversed. Citing *Green* v. *Connally*, with approval, the Court of Appeals concluded that § 501(c)(3) must be read against the background of charitable trust law. To be eligible for an exemption under that section, an institution must be "charitable" in the common law sense, and therefore must not be contrary to public policy. In the court's view, Bob Jones University did not meet this requirement, since its "racial policies violated the clearly defined public policy, rooted in our Constitution, condemning racial discrimination and, more specifically, the government policy against subsidizing racial discrimination in education, public or private." The court held that the IRS acted within its statutory authority in revoking the University's tax-exempt status. Finally, the Court of Appeals rejected petitioner's arguments that the revocation of the tax exemption violated the Free Exercise and Establishment Clauses of the First Amendment. The case was remanded to the District Court with instructions to dismiss the University's claim for a refund and to reinstate the Government's counterclaim.

⊥**583** C
No. 81-1, Goldsboro Christian Schools, Inc. v. United States

Goldsboro Christian Schools is a nonprofit corporation located in Goldsboro, North Carolina. Like Bob Jones University, it was established "to conduct an institution of learning . . . , giving special emphasis to the Christian religion and the ethics revealed in the Holy scriptures." The school offers classes from kindergarten through high school, and since at least 1969 has satisfied the State of North Carolina's requirements for secular education in private schools. The school requires its high school students to take Bible-related courses, and begins each class with prayer.

Since its incorporation in 1963, Goldsboro Christian Schools has maintained a racially discriminatory admissions policy based upon its interpretation of the Bible. Goldsboro has for the most part accepted only Caucasians. On occasion, however, the school has accepted children from racially mixed marriages in which one of the parents is Caucasian.

Goldsboro never received a determination by the IRS that it was an organization entitled to tax exemption under § 501(c)(3). Upon audit of Goldsboro's records for the years 1969 through 1972, the IRS determined that Goldsboro was not an organization described in § 501(c)(3), and therefore was required to pay taxes under the Federal Insurance Contribution Act and the Federal Unemployment Tax Act.

⊥**584** Goldsboro paid the IRS $3,459.93 in withholding, social security, and unemployment taxes with respect to one employee for the years 1969 through 1972. Thereafter, Goldsboro filed a suit seeking refund of that payment, claiming that the school had been improperly denied § 501(c)(3) exempt status. The IRS counterclaimed for $160,073.96 in unpaid social security and unemployment taxes for the years 1969 through 1972, including interest and penalties.

The District Court for the Eastern District of North Carolina decided the action on cross-motions for summary judgment. In addressing the motions for summary judgment, the court assumed that Goldsboro's racially discriminatory admissions policy was based upon a sincerely held religious belief. The court nevertheless rejected Goldsboro's claim to tax-exempt status under § 501(c)(3), finding that "private schools maintaining racially discriminatory admissions policies violate clearly declared federal policy and, therefore, must be denied the federal tax benefits flowing from qualification under Section 501(c)(3)." The court also rejected Goldsboro's arguments that denial of tax-exempt status violated the Free Exercise and Establishment Clauses of the First Amendment. Accordingly, the court entered summary judgment for the Government on its counterclaim.

The Court of Appeals for the Fourth Circuit affirmed. That court found an "identity for present purposes" between the *Goldsboro* case and the *Bob Jones University* case, which had been decided shortly **⊥585** before by another panel of that court, and affirmed for the reasons set forth in *Bob Jones University*.

We granted certiorari in both cases, and we affirm in each.

II

A

In Revenue Ruling 71-447, the IRS formalized the policy first announced in 1970, that § 170 and § 501(c)(3) embrace the common law "charity" concept. Under that view, to qualify for a tax exemption pursuant to § 501(c)(3), an institution must show, first, that it falls within one of the eight categories expressly set forth in that section, and second, that its activity is not contrary to settled public policy.

Section 501(c)(3) provides that "[c]orporations . . . organized and operated exclusively for religious, charitable . . . or educational purposes" are entitled to tax exemption. Petitioners argue that the plain language of the statute guarantees them tax-exempt status. They emphasize the absence of any language in the statute expressly requiring all exempt organizations to be "charitable" in the common law sense, and they contend that the disjunctive "or" separating the categories in § 501(c)(3) precludes such a reading. Instead, they argue that if an institution falls within one or more of **⊥586** the specified categories it is automatically entitled to exemption, without regard to whether it also qualifies as "charitable." The Court of Appeals rejected that contention and concluded that petitioners' interpretation of the statute "tears section 501(c)(3) from its roots." *United States* v. *Bob Jones University*.

It is a well-established canon of statutory construction that a court should go beyond the literal language of a statute if reliance on that language would defeat the plain purpose of the statute: "The general words used in the clause . . . , taken by themselves, and literally construed, without regard to the object in view, would seem to sanction the claim of the plaintiff. But this mode of expounding a statute has never been adopted by any enlightened tribunal—because it is evident that in many cases it would defeat the object which the Legislature intended to accomplish. And it is well settled that, in interpreting a statute, the court will not look merely to a particular clause in which general words may be used, *but will take in connection with it the whole statute . . . and the objects and policy of the law. . . .*" *Brown* v. *Duchesne* (emphasis added).

Section 501(c)(3) therefore must be analyzed and construed within the framework of the Internal Revenue Code and against the background of the congressional purposes. Such an examination reveals unmistakable evidence that, underlying all relevant parts of the Code, is the intent that entitlement to tax exemption depends on meeting certain common law standards of charity—namely, that an institution seeking tax-exempt status must serve a public purpose and not be contrary to established public policy.

This "charitable" concept appears explicitly in § 170 of the Code. That section contains a list of organizations virtually identical to that contained in § 501(c)(3). It is apparent that Congress intended that list to have the same meaning in both **⊥587** sections. In § 170, Congress used the list of organizations in defining the term "charitable contributions." On its face, therefore, § 170 reveals that Congress' intention was to provide tax benefits to organizations serving charitable purposes. The form of § 170 simply makes plain what common sense and history tell us: in enacting both § 170 and **⊥588** § 501(c)(3), Congress sought to provide tax benefits to charitable organizations, to encourage the development of private institutions that serve a useful public purpose or supplement or take the place of public institutions of the same kind.

Tax exemptions for certain institutions thought beneficial to the social order of the country as a whole, or to a particular community, are deeply rooted in our history, as in that of England. The origins of such exemptions lie in the special privileges that have long been extended to charitable trusts.

More than a century ago, this Court announced the caveat that is critical in this case: "[I]t has now become an established principle of American law, that courts of chancery will sustain and protect . . . a gift . . . to public charitable uses, *provided the same is consistent with local laws and public policy. . . .*" *Perin* v. *Carey* (emphasis added). Soon after that, in 1878, the Court commented: "A charitable use, *where neither law nor public policy forbids*, may be applied to almost any thing *that tends to promote the well-doing and well-being of social man.*" *Ould* v. *Washington Hospital for Foundlings* (emphasis added). **⊥589** In 1891, in a restatement of the English law of charity which has long been recognized as a leading authority in this country, Lord MacNaghten stated: "'Charity' in its legal sense comprises four principal divisions: trusts for the relief of poverty; *trusts for the advancement of education*; trusts for the advancement of religion; and trusts for *other purposes beneficial to the community*, not falling under any of the preceding heads." *Commissioners* v. *Pemsel* (emphasis added). These statements clearly reveal the legal background against which Congress enacted the first charitable exemption statute in 1894: charities were to be given preferential treatment because they provide a benefit to society.

What little floor debate occurred on the charitable exemption provision of the 1894 Act and similar sections of later statutes leaves no doubt that Congress deemed the specified organizations entitled to tax benefits because they served desirable public purposes. ⊥**590** In floor debate on a similar provision in 1917, for example, Senator Hollis articulated the rationale: "For every dollar that a man contributes to these public charities, educational, scientific, or otherwise, the public gets 100 percent." In 1924, this Court restated the common understanding of the charitable exemption provision: "Evidently the exemption is made in recognition of the benefit which the public derives from corporate activities of the class named, and is intended to aid them when not conducted for private gain." *Trinidad* v. *Sagrada Orden*.

In enacting the Revenue Act of 1938, Congress expressly reconfirmed this view with respect to the charitable deduction provision: "The exemption from taxation of money and property devoted to charitable and other purposes is based on the theory that the Government is compensated for the loss of revenue by its relief from financial burdens which would otherwise have to be met by appropriations from other public funds, and by the benefits resulting from the promotion of the general welfare."

⊥**591** A corollary to the public benefit principle is the requirement, long recognized in the law of trusts, that the purpose of a charitable trust may not be illegal or violate established public policy. In 1861, this Court stated that a public charitable use must be "consistent with local laws and public policy," *Perin* v. *Carey*. Modern commentators and courts have echoed that view.

When the Government grants exemptions or allows deductions all taxpayers are affected; the very fact of the exemption or deduction for the donor means that other taxpayers can be said to be indirect and vicarious "donors." Charitable exemptions are justified on the basis that the exempt entity confers a public benefit—a benefit which the society or the community may not itself choose or be able to provide, or which supplements and advances the work of public institutions already supported by tax revenues. History but⊥**592**tresses logic to make clear that, to warrant exemption under § 501(c)(3), an institution must fall within a category specified in that section and must demonstrably serve and be in harmony with the public interest. The institution's purpose must not be so at odds with the common community conscience as to undermine any public benefit that might otherwise be conferred.

B

We are bound to approach these questions with full awareness that determinations of public benefit and public policy are sensitive matters with serious implications for the institutions affected; a declaration that a given institution is not "charitable" should be made only where there can be no doubt that the activity involved is contrary to a fundamental public policy. But there can no longer be any doubt that racial discrimination in education violates deeply and widely accepted views of elementary justice. Prior to 1954, public education in many places still was conducted under the pall of ⊥**593** *Plessy* v. *Ferguson*; racial segregation in primary and secondary education prevailed in many parts of the country. This Court's decision in *Brown* v. *Board of Education*, signalled an end to that era. Over the past quarter of a century, every pronouncement of this Court and myriad Acts of Congress and Executive Orders attest a firm national policy to prohibit racial segregation and discrimination in public education.

An unbroken line of cases following *Brown* v. *Board of Education* establishes beyond doubt this Court's view that racial discrimination in education violates a most fundamental national public policy, as well as rights of individuals. "The right of a student not to be segregated on racial grounds in schools . . . is indeed so fundamental and pervasive that it is embraced in the concept of due process of law." *Cooper* v. *Aaron*. In *Norwood* v. *Harrison*, we dealt with a non-public institution: "[A] private school—even one that discriminates—fulfills an important educational function; *however*, . . . *[that] legitimate educational function cannot be isolated from* ⊥**594** *discriminatory practices . . . [D]iscriminatory treatment exerts a pervasive influence on the entire educational process*" (emphasis added).

Congress, in Titles IV and VI of the Civil Rights Act of 1964, clearly expressed its agreement that racial discrimination in education violates a fundamental public policy. Other sections of that Act, and numerous enactments since then, testify to the public policy against racial discrimination.

The Executive Branch has consistently placed its support behind eradication of racial discrimination. Several years before this Court's decision in *Brown* v. *Board of Education*, President Truman issued Executive Orders prohibiting racial discrimination in federal employment decisions and in classifications for the Selective Service. In 1957, President Eisenhower employed military forces to ensure compliance with federal standards in school desegregation programs. And in 1962, President Kennedy announced: "[T]he granting of federal assistance for . . . housing and related facilities from which Americans are excluded because of their race, color, creed, or national origin is unfair, unjust, and inconsistent with the public policy of ⊥**595** the United States as manifested in its Constitution and laws." These are but a few of numerous Executive Orders over the past three decades demonstrating the commitment of the Executive Branch to the fundamental policy of eliminating racial discrimination.

Few social or political issues in our history have been more vigorously debated and more extensively ventilated than the issue of racial discrimination, particularly in education. Given the stress and anguish of the history of efforts to escape from the shackles of the "separate but equal" doctrine of *Plessy* v. *Ferguson*, it cannot be said that educational institutions that, for whatever reasons, practice racial discrimination, are institutions exercising "beneficial and stabilizing influences in community life," *Walz* v. *Tax Commission*, or should be encouraged by having all taxpayers share in their support by way of special tax status.

There can thus be no question that the interpretation of § 170 and § 501(c)(3) announced by the IRS in 1970 was correct. That it may be seen as belated does not undermine its soundness. It would be wholly incompatible with the concepts underlying tax exemption to grant the benefit of tax-exempt status to racially discriminatory educational entities, which "exer[t] a pervasive influence on the entire educational process." *Norwood* v. *Harrison*. Whatever may be the rationale for such private schools' policies, and however sincere the rationale may be, racial discrimination in education is contrary to public policy. Racially discriminatory educational institutions cannot be viewed as conferring a public benefit within the "charitable" concept discussed ear⊥**596**lier, or within the Congressional intent underlying § 170 and § 501(c)(3).

C

Petitioners contend that, regardless of whether the IRS properly concluded that racially discriminatory private schools violate public policy, only Congress can alter the scope of § 170 and § 501(c)(3). Petitioners accordingly argue that the IRS overstepped its lawful bounds in issuing its 1970 and 1971 rulings.

Yet ever since the inception of the tax code, Congress has seen fit to vest in those administering the tax laws very broad authority to interpret those laws. In an area as complex as the tax system, the agency Congress vests with administrative responsibility must be able to exercise its authority to meet changing conditions and new problems. Indeed as early as 1918, Congress expressly authorized the Commissioner "to make all needful rules and regulations for the enforcement" of the tax laws. Revenue Act of 1918, Ch. 18 § 1309, 40 Stat. 1057, 1143 (1919). The same provision, so essential to efficient and fair administration of the tax laws, has appeared in tax codes ever since; and this Court has long recognized the primary authority of the IRS and its predecessors in construing the Internal Revenue Code.

Congress, the source of IRS authority, can modify IRS rulings it considers improper; and courts exercise review over IRS actions. In the first instance, however, the responsibil⊥**597**ity for construing the Code falls to the IRS. Since Congress cannot be expected to anticipate every conceivable problem that can arise or to carry out day-to-day oversight, it relies on the administrators and on the courts to implement the legislative will. Administrators, like judges, are under oath to do so.

In § 170 and § 501(c)(3), Congress has identified categories of traditionally exempt institutions and has specified certain additional requirements for tax exemption. Yet the need for continuing interpretation of those statutes is unavoidable. For more than 60 years, the IRS and its predecessors have constantly been called upon to interpret these and comparable provisions, and in doing so have referred consistently to principles of charitable trust law. In Treas. Reg. 45, art. 517(1) (1921), for example, the IRS denied charitable exemptions on the basis of proscribed political activity before the Congress itself added such conduct as a disqualifying element. In other instances, the IRS has denied charitable exemptions to otherwise qualified entities because they served too limited a class of people and thus did not provide a truly "public" benefit under the common law test. Some years before the issuance of the rulings challenged in these cases, the IRS also ruled that contributions to community recreational facilities would not be deductible and that the facilities themselves would not be entitled to tax-exempt status, unless those facilities were open to all on a racially nondiscriminatory basis. These rulings reflect the Commissioner's continuing duty to interpret and apply the Internal Revenue Code.

Guided, of course, by the Code, the IRS has the responsibility, in the first instance, to determine whether a particu⊥**598**lar entity is "charitable" for purposes of § 170 and § 501(c)(3). This in turn may necessitate later determinations of whether given activities so violate public policy that the entities involved cannot be deemed to provide a public benefit worthy of "charitable" status. We emphasize, however, that these sensitive determinations should be made only where there is no doubt that the organization's activities violate fundamental public policy.

On the record before us, there can be no doubt as to the national policy. In 1970, when the IRS first issued the ruling challenged here, the position of all three branches of the Federal Government was unmistakably clear. The correctness of the Commissioner's conclusion that a racially discriminatory private school "is not 'charitable' within the common law concepts reflected in . . . the Code" is wholly consistent with what Congress, the Executive and the courts had repeatedly declared before 1970. Indeed, it would be anomalous for the Executive, Legislative and Judicial Branches to reach conclusions that add up to a firm public policy on racial discrimination, and at the same time have the IRS blissfully ignore what all three branches of the Federal Government had declared. Clearly an educational institution engaging in ⊥**599** practices affirmatively at odds with this declared position of the whole government cannot be seen as exercising a "beneficial and stabilizing influenc[e] in community life," *Walz* v. *Tax Commission*, and is not "charitable," within the meaning of § 170 and § 501(c)(3). We therefore hold that the IRS did not exceed its authority when it announced its interpretation of § 170 and § 501(c)(3) in 1970 and 1971.

D

The actions of Congress since 1970 leave no doubt that the IRS reached the correct conclusion in exercising its authority. It is, of course, not unknown for independent agencies or the Executive Branch to misconstrue the intent of a statute; Congress can and often does correct such misconceptions, if the courts have not done so. Yet for a dozen years Congress has been made aware—acutely aware—of the IRS rulings of 1970 and 1971. As we noted earlier, few issues have been the subject of more vigorous and widespread debate and discussion in and out of Congress than those related to racial segregation in education. Sincere adherents advocating contrary views have ventilated the subject for well over three decades. Failure of Congress to modify the IRS rulings of 1970 and 1971, of which Congress was, by its own studies and by public discourse, constantly reminded; and Congress' awareness of the denial of tax-exempt status for racially discriminatory schools when enacting other and related legislation make out an unusually strong case of legislative acquiescence in and ratification by implication of the 1970 and 1971 rulings.

⊥**600** Ordinarily, and quite appropriately, courts are slow to attribute significance to the failure of Congress to act on particular legislation. We have observed that "unsuccessful attempts at legislation are not the best of guides to legislative intent," *Red Lion Broadcasting Co.* v. *FCC*. Here, however, we do not have an ordinary claim of legislative acquiescence. Only one month after the IRS announced its position in 1970, Congress held its first hearings on this precise issue. Exhaustive hearings have been held on the issue at various times since then. These include hearings in February 1982, after we granted review in this case.

Non-action by Congress is not often a useful guide, but the non-action here is significant. During the past 12 years there have been no fewer than 13 bills introduced to overturn the IRS interpretation of § 501(c)(3). Not one of these bills has emerged from any committee, although Congress has enacted numerous other amendments to § 501 during this same period, including an amendment to § 501(c)(3) itself. It is hardly conceivable that Congress—and in this setting, any Member of Congress—was not abundantly ⊥**601** aware of what was going on. In view of its prolonged and acute awareness of so important an issue, Congress' failure to act on the bills proposed on this subject provides added support for concluding that Congress acquiesced in the IRS rulings of 1970 and 1971.

The evidence of Congressional approval of the policy embodied in Revenue Ruling 71-447 goes well beyond the failure of Congress to act on legislative proposals. Congress affirmatively manifested its acquiescence in the IRS policy when it enacted the present § 501(i) of the Code. That provision denies tax-exempt status to social clubs whose charters or policy statements provide for "discrimination against any person on the basis of race, color, or religion." Both the House and Senate committee reports on that bill articulated the national policy against granting tax exemptions to racially discriminatory private clubs.

Even more significant is the fact that both reports focus on this Court's affirmance of *Green* v. *Connally*, as having established that "discrimination on account of race is inconsistent with an *educational institution's* tax-exempt status." These references in Congressional committee reports on an enactment denying tax exemptions to racially discriminatory private social clubs cannot be read ⊥**602** other than as indicating approval of the standards applied to racially discriminatory private schools by the IRS subsequent to 1970, and specifically of Revenue Ruling 71-447.

III

Petitioners contend that, even if the Commissioner's policy is valid as to nonreligious private schools, that policy cannot constitutionally be applied to schools that engage in racial discrimination on the basis of sincerely held religious beliefs. ⊥**603** As to such schools, it is argued that the IRS construction of § 170 and § 501(c)(3) violates their free exercise rights under the Religion Clauses of the First Amendment. This contention presents claims not heretofore considered by this Court in precisely this context.

This Court has long held the Free Exercise Clause of the First Amendment to be an absolute prohibition against governmental regulation of religious beliefs. As interpreted by this Court, moreover, the Free Exercise Clause provides substantial protection for lawful conduct grounded in religious belief. However, "[n]ot all burdens on religion are unconstitutional. . . . The state may justify a limitation on religious liberty by showing that it is essential to accomplish an overriding governmental interest." *United States* v. *Lee*.

On occasion this Court has found certain governmental interests so compelling as to allow even regulations prohibiting religiously based conduct. In *Prince* v. *Massachusetts*, for example, the Court held that neutrally cast child labor laws prohibiting sale of printed materials on public streets could be applied to prohibit children from dispensing religious literature. The Court found no constitutional infirmity in "excluding [Jehovah's Witness children] from doing there what no other children may do." Denial of tax benefits will inevitably have a substan⊥**604**tial impact on the operation of private religious schools, but will not prevent those schools from observing their religious tenets.

The governmental interest at stake here is compelling. As discussed in Part II(B), *supra*, the government has a fundamental, overriding interest in eradicating racial discrimination in education—discrimination that prevailed, with official approval, for the first 165 years of this Nation's history. That governmental interest substantially outweighs whatever burden denial of tax benefits places on petitioners' exercise of their religious beliefs. The interests asserted by petitioners cannot be accommodated with that compelling governmental interest; and no "less restrictive means" are available to achieve the governmental interest.

⊥**605** IV

The remaining issue is whether the IRS properly applied its policy to these petitioners. Petitioner Goldsboro

Christian Schools admits that it "maintain[s] racially discriminatory policies," but seeks to justify those policies on grounds we have fully discussed. The IRS properly denied tax-exempt status to Goldsboro Christian Schools.

Petitioner Bob Jones University, however, contends that it is not racially discriminatory. It emphasizes that it now allows all races to enroll, subject only to its restrictions on the conduct of all students, including its prohibitions of association between men and women of different races, and of interracial marriage. Although a ban on intermarriage or interracial dating applies to all races, decisions of this Court firmly establish that discrimination on the basis of racial affiliation and association is a form of racial discrimination. We therefore find that the IRS properly applied Revenue Ruling 71-447 to Bob Jones University.

The judgments of the Court of Appeals are, accordingly, *Affirmed.*

⊥606 *Justice POWELL,* concurring in part and concurring in the judgment.

I join the Court's judgment, along with part III of its opinion holding that the denial of tax exemptions to petitioners does not violate the First Amendment. I write separately because I am troubled by the broader implications of the Court's opinion with respect to the authority of the Internal Revenue Service (IRS) and its construction of §§ 170(c) and 501(c)(3) of the Internal Revenue Code.

I

Federal taxes are not imposed on organizations "operated exclusively for religious, charitable, scientific, testing for public safety, literary, or educational purposes. . . ." 26 U.S.C. § 510(c)(3). The Code also permits a tax deduction for contributions made to these organizations. § 170(c). It is clear that petitioners, organizations incorporated for educational purposes, fall within the language of the statute. It also is clear that the language itself does not mandate refusal of tax-exempt status to any private school that maintains a racially discriminatory admissions policy. Accordingly, there is force in *Justice REHNQUIST's* argument that §§ 170(c) and 501(c)(3) should be construed as setting forth the only criteria Congress has established for qualification as a tax-exempt organization. Indeed, were we writing prior to the history detailed in the Court's opinion, this could well be the construction I would adopt. But there has been a decade of acceptance that is persuasive in the circumstances of this case, and I conclude that there are now sufficient reasons for accepting the IRS's construction of the Code as proscribing **⊥607** tax exemptions for schools that discriminate on the basis of race as a matter of policy.

I cannot say that this construction of the Code, adopted by the IRS in 1970 and upheld by the Court of Appeals below, is without logical support. The statutory terms are not self-defining, and it is plausible that in some instances an organization seeking a tax exemption might act in a manner so clearly contrary to the purposes of our laws that it could not be deemed to serve the enumerated statutory purposes. And, as the Court notes, if any national policy is sufficiently fundamental to constitute such an overriding limitation on the availability of tax-exempt status under § 501(c)(3), it is the policy against racial discrimination in education. Finally, and of critical importance for me, the subsequent actions of Congress present "an unusually strong case of legislative acquiescence in and ratification by implication of the [IRS] 1970 and 1971 rulings" with respect to racially discriminatory schools. In particular, Congress' enactment of § 501(i) in 1976 is strong evidence of agreement with these particular IRS rulings.

⊥608 II

I therefore concur in the Court's judgment that tax-exempt status under §§ 170(c) and 501(c)(3) is not available to private schools that concededly are racially discriminatory. I do not agree, however, with the Court's more general explanation of the justifications for the tax exemptions provided to charitable organizations. The Court states:

"Charitable exemptions are justified on the basis that the exempt entity confers a public benefit—a benefit which the society or the community may not itself choose or be able to provide, or which supplements and advances the work of public institutions already supported by tax revenues. History buttresses logic to make clear that, to warrant exemption under § 501(c)(3), an institution must fall within a category specified in that section and must demonstrably serve and be in harmony with the public interest. The institution's purpose must not be so at odds with the common community conscience as to undermine any public benefit that might otherwise be conferred." Applying this test to petitioners, the Court concludes that "[c]learly an educational institution engaging in practices affirmatively at odds with [the] declared position of the whole government cannot be seen as exercising a 'beneficial and stabilizing influenc[e] in community life,' . . . and is not 'charitable' within the meaning of § 170 and § 501(c)(3)."

With all respect, I am unconvinced that the critical question in determining tax-exempt status is whether an individual organization provides a clear "public benefit" as defined by the Court. Over 106,000 organizations filed § 501(c)(3) returns in 1981. **⊥609** I find it impossible to believe that all or even most of those organizations could prove that they "demonstrably serve and [are] in harmony with the public interest" or that they are "beneficial and stabilizing influences in community life." Nor am I prepared to say that petitioners, because of their racially discriminatory policies, necessarily contribute nothing of benefit to the community. It is clear from the substantially secular character of the curricula and degrees offered that petitioners provide educational benefits.

Even more troubling to me is the element of conformity that appears to inform the Court's analysis. The Court asserts that an exempt organization must "demonstrably serve and be in harmony with the public interest," must have a purpose that comports with "the common community conscience," and must not act in a manner "affirmatively at odds with [the] declared position of the whole government." Taken together, these passages suggest that the primary function of a tax-exempt organization is to act on behalf of the Government in carrying out governmentally approved policies. In my opinion, such a view of § 501(c)(3) ignores the important role played by tax exemptions in encouraging diverse, indeed often sharply conflicting, activities and viewpoints. As *Justice BRENNAN* has observed, private, nonprofit groups receive tax exemptions because "each group contributes to the diversity of association, viewpoint, and enterprise essential to a vigorous, pluralistic society." *Walz* (Brennan, J., concurring). Far from representing an effort to reinforce any perceived "common community conscience," the provision of tax exemptions to nonprofit groups is one indispensable means of limiting the influence of governmental orthodoxy on important areas of community life.

⊥610 Given the importance of our tradition of pluralism, "[t]he interest in preserving an area of untrammeled choice for private philanthropy is very great." *Jackson* v. *Statler Foundation*.

I do not suggest that these considerations always are or should be dispositive. Congress, of course, may find that some organizations do not warrant tax-exempt status. In this case I agree with the Court that Congress has determined that the policy against racial discrimination in education should override the countervailing interest in permitting unorthodox private behavior.

⊥611 I would emphasize, however, that the balancing of these substantial interests is for *Congress* to perform. I am unwilling to join any suggestion that the Internal Revenue Service is invested with authority to decide which public policies are sufficiently "fundamental" to require denial of tax exemptions. Its business is to administer laws designed to produce revenue for the Government, not to promote "public policy." As former IRS commissioner Kurtz has noted, questions concerning religion and civil rights "are far afield from the more typical tasks of tax administrators—determining taxable income." Kurtz, Difficult Definitional Problems in Tax Administration: Religion and Race, 23 Catholic Lawyer 301 (1978). This Court often has expressed concern that the scope of an agency's authorization be limited to those areas in which the agency fairly may be said to have expertise, and this concern applies with special force when the asserted administrative power is one to determine the scope of public policy. As *Justice BLACKMUN* has noted, "where the philanthropic organization is concerned, there appears to be little to circumscribe the almost unfettered power of the Commissioner. This may be very well so long as one subscribes to the particular brand of social policy the Commissioner happens to be advocating **⊥612** at the time . . . , but application of our tax laws should not operate in so fickle a fashion. Surely, social policy in the first instance is a matter for legislative concern." *Commissioner* v. *"Americans United"* (Blackmun, J., dissenting).

III

The Court's decision upholds IRS Revenue Ruling 71-447, and thus resolves the question whether tax-exempt status is available to private schools that openly maintain racially discriminatory admissions policies. There no longer is any justification for *Congress* to hesitate—as it apparently has—in articulating and codifying its desired policy as to tax exemptions for discriminatory organizations. Many questions remain, such as whether organizations that violate other policies should receive tax-exempt status under § 501(c)(3). These should be legislative policy choices. It is not appropriate to leave the IRS "on the cutting edge of developing national policy." The contours of public policy should be determined by Congress, not by judges or the IRS.

Justice REHNQUIST, dissenting.

The Court points out that there is a strong national policy in this country against racial discrimination. To the extent that the Court states that Congress in furtherance of this policy could deny tax-exempt status to educational institutions that promote racial discrimination, I readily agree. But, unlike the Court, I am convinced that Congress simply has failed to take this action and, as this Court has said over and over again, regardless of our view on the propriety of Congress' failure to legislate we are not constitutionally empowered to act for them.

In approaching this statutory construction question the Court quite adeptly avoids the statute it is construing. This I am sure is no accident, for there is nothing in the language **⊥613** of § 501(c)(3) that supports the result obtained by the Court. Section 501(c)(3) provides tax-exempt status for:

"Corporations, and any community chest, fund, or foundation, organized and operated exclusively for religious, charitable, scientific, testing for public safety, literary, or educational purposes, or to foster national or international amateur sports competition (but only if no part of its activities involve the provision of athletic facilities or equipment), or for the prevention of cruelty to children or animals, no part of the net earnings of which inures to the benefit of any private shareholder or individual, no substantial part of the activities of which is carrying on propaganda, or otherwise attempting, to influence legislation (except as otherwise provided in subsection (h)), and which does not participate in, or intervene in (including the publishing or distributing of statements), any political campaign on behalf of any candidate for public office." With undeniable clarity,

Congress has explicitly defined the requirements for § 501(c)(3) status. An entity must be (1) a corporation, or community chest, fund, or foundation, (2) organized for one of the eight enumerated purposes, (3) operated on a nonprofit basis, and (4) free from involvement in lobbying activities and political campaigns. Nowhere is there to be found some additional, undefined public policy requirement.

The Court first seeks refuge from the obvious reading of § 501(c)(3) by turning to § 170 of the Internal Revenue Code which provides a tax deduction for contributions made to § 501(c)(3) organizations. In setting forth the general rule, § 170 states: "There shall be allowed as a deduction any charitable contribution (as defined in subsection (c)) payment of which is made within the taxable year. A charitable contribution shall be allowable as a deduction only if ver⊥**614**ified under regulations prescribed by the Secretary." The Court seizes the words "charitable contribution" and with little discussion concludes that "[o]n its face, therefore, § 170 reveals that Congress' intention was to provide tax benefits to organizations serving charitable purposes," intimating that this implies some unspecified common law charitable trust requirement.

The Court would have been well advised to look to subsection (c) where, as § 170(a)(1) indicates, Congress has defined a "charitable contribution":

"For purposes of this section, the term 'charitable contribution' means a contribution or gift to or for the use of . . . [a] corporation, trust, or community chest, fund, or foundation . . . organized and operated exclusively for religious, charitable, scientific, literary, or educational purposes, or to foster national or international amateur sports competition (but only if no part of its activities involve the provision of athletic facilities or equipment), or for the prevention of cruelty to children or animals; . . . no part of the net earnings of which inures to the benefit of any private shareholder or individual; and . . . which is not disqualified for tax exemption under section 501(c)(3) by reason of attempting to influence legislation, and which does not participate in, or intervene in (including the publishing or distributing of statements), any political campaign on behalf of any candidate for public office." Plainly, § 170(c) simply tracks the requirements set forth in § 501(c)(3). Since § 170 is no more than a mirror of § 501(c)(3) and, as the Court points out, § 170 followed § 501(c)(3) by more than two decades, it is at best of little usefulness in finding the meaning of § 501(c)(3).

Making a more fruitful inquiry, the Court next turns to the legislative history of § 501(c)(3) and finds that Congress in⊥**615**tended in that statute to offer a tax benefit to organizations that Congress believed were providing public benefit. I certainly agree. But then the Court leaps to the conclusion that this history is proof Congress intended that an organization seeking § 501(c)(3) status "must fall within a category specified in that section and *must demonstrably serve and be in harmony with the public interest*" (emphasis added). To the contrary, I think that the legislative history of § 501(c)(3) unmistakably makes clear that *Congress has decided* what organizations are serving a public purpose and providing a public benefit within the meaning of § 501(c)(3) and has clearly set forth in § 501(c)(3) the characteristics of such organizations. In fact, there are few examples which better illustrate Congress' effort to define and re-define the requirements of a legislative act.

The first general income tax law was passed by Congress in the form of the Tariff Act of 1894. A provision of that Act provided an exemption for "corporations, companies, or associations organized and conducted solely for charitable, religious, or educational purposes." Ch. 349, § 32, 28 Stat. 509, 556 (1894). The income tax portion of the 1894 Act was held unconstitutional by this Court, but a similar exemption appeared in the Tariff Act of 1909 which imposed a tax on corporate income. The 1909 Act provided an exemption for "any corporation or association organized and operated exclusively for religious, charitable, or educational purposes, no part of the net income of which inures to the benefit of any private stockholder or individual."

With the ratification of the Sixteenth Amendment, Congress again turned its attention to an individual income tax with the Tariff Act of 1913. And again, in the direct predecessor of § 501(c)(3), a tax exemption was provided for "any corporation or association organized and operated exclusively for religious, charitable, scientific, or educational purposes, ⊥**616** no part of the net income of which inures to the benefit of any private stockholder or individual." In subsequent acts Congress continued to broaden the list of exempt purposes. The Revenue Act of 1918 added an exemption for corporations or associations organized "for the prevention of cruelty to children or animals." The Revenue Act of 1921 expanded the groups to which the exemption applied to include "any community chest, fund, or foundation" and added "literary" endeavors to the list of exempt purposes. The exemption remained unchanged in the Revenue Acts of 1924, 1926, 1928, and 1932. In the Revenue Act of 1934 Congress added the requirement that no substantial part of the activities of any exempt organization can involve the carrying on of "propaganda" or "attempting to influence legislation." Again, the exemption was left unchanged by the Revenue Acts of 1936 and 1938.

The tax laws were overhauled by the Internal Revenue Code of 1939, but this exemption was left unchanged. When the 1939 Code was replaced with the Internal Revenue Code of 1954, the exemption was adopted in full in the present § 501(c)(3) with the addition of "testing for public safety" as an exempt purpose and an additional restriction that tax-exempt organizations could not "participate in, or intervene in (including the publishing or distributing of statements), any political campaign on behalf of any candidate for public office." Then in 1976 the statute was again amended adding to the purposes for which an exemption would be authorized, "to foster national or international ama⊥**617**teur sports competition," provided the activities did not involve the provision of athletic facilities or equipment.

One way to read the opinion handed down by the Court today leads to the conclusion that this long and arduous refining process of § 501(c)(3) was certainly a waste of time, for when enacting the original 1894 statute Congress intended to adopt a common law term of art, and intended that this term of art carry with it all of the common law baggage which defines it. Such a view, however, leads also to the unsupportable idea that Congress spent almost a century adding illustrations simply to clarify an already defined common law term.

Another way to read the Court's opinion leads to the conclusion that even though Congress has set forth *some* of the requirements of a § 501(c)(3) organization, it intended that the IRS additionally require that organizations meet a higher standard of public interest, not stated by Congress, but to be determined and defined by the IRS and the courts. This view I find equally unsupportable. Almost a century of statutory history proves that Congress itself intended to decide what § 501(c)(3) requires. Congress has expressed its decision in the plainest of terms in § 501(c)(3) by providing that tax-exempt status is to be given to any corporation, or community chest, fund, or foundation that is organized for one of the eight enumerated purposes, operated on a nonprofit basis, and uninvolved in lobbying activities or political campaigns. The IRS certainly is empowered to adopt regulations for the enforcement of these specified requirements, and the courts have authority to resolve challenges to the IRS's exercise of this power, but Congress has left it to neither the IRS nor the courts to select or add to the requirements of § 501(c)(3).

The Court suggests that unless its new requirement be added to § 501(c)(3), nonprofit organizations formed to teach pick-pockets and terrorists would necessarily acquire tax-ex⊥**618**empt status. Since the Court does not challenge the characterization of petitioners as "educational" institutions within the meaning of § 501(c)(3), and in fact states several times in the course of its opinion that petitioners are educational institutions, it is difficult to see how this argument advances the Court's reasoning for disposing of petitioners' cases.

But simply because I reject the Court's heavy-handed creation of the requirement that an organization seeking § 501(c)(3) status must "serve and be in harmony with the public interest," does not mean that I would deny to the IRS the usual authority to adopt regulations, further explaining what Congress meant by the term "educational." The IRS has fully exercised that authority in 26 CFR § 1.501(c)(3)-1(d)(3), which provides:

"(3) *Educational defined*—(i)*In general*. The term "educational", as used in section 501(c)(3), relates to—

"(a) The instruction or training of the individual for the purpose of improving or developing his capabilities; or

"(b) The instruction of the public on subjects useful to the individual and beneficial to the community.

"An organization may be educational even though it advocates a particular position or viewpoint so long as it presents a sufficiently full and fair exposition of the pertinent facts as to permit an individual or the public to form an independent opinion or conclusion. On the other hand, an organization is not educational if its principal function is the mere presentation of unsupported opinion.

"(ii) *Examples of educational organizations*. The following are examples of organizations which, if they otherwise meet the requirements of this section, are educational:

⊥**619** "*Example (1)*. An organization, such as a primary or secondary school, a college, or a professional or trade school, which has a regularly scheduled curriculum, a regular faculty, and a regularly enrolled body of students in attendance at a place where the educational activities are regularly carried on.

"*Example (2)*. An organization whose activities consist of presenting public discussion groups, forums, panels, lectures, or other similar programs. Such programs may be on radio or television.

"*Example (3)*. An organization which presents a course of instruction by means of correspondence or through the utilization of television or radio.

"*Example (4)*. Museums, zoos, planetariums, symphony orchestras, and other similar organizations."

I have little doubt that neither the "Fagin School for Pickpockets" nor a school training students for guerrilla warfare and terrorism in other countries would meet the definitions contained in the regulations.

Prior to 1970, when the charted course was abruptly changed, the IRS had continuously interpreted § 501 (c)(3) and its predecessors in accordance with the view I have expressed above. This, of course, is of considerable significance in determining the intended meaning of the statute.

In 1970 the IRS was sued by parents of black public school children seeking to enjoin the IRS from according tax-exempt status under § 501(c)(3) to private schools in Mississippi that discriminated against blacks. The IRS answered, consistent with its long standing position, by maintaining a lack of authority to deny the tax-exemption if the schools met the specified requirements of § 501(c)(3). Then "[i]n the midst of this litigation", *Green* v. *Connally*, aff'd *sub nom. Coit* v. *Green* and in the face of a preliminary injunc⊥**620**-tion, the IRS changed its position and adopted the view of the plaintiffs.

Following the close of the litigation, the IRS published its new position in Revenue Ruling 71-447, stating that "a school asserting a right to the benefits provided for in section 501(c)(3) of the Code as being organized and operated exclusively for educational purposes must be a common law charity in order to be exempt under that section." The IRS then concluded that a school that promotes racial discrimination violates public policy and therefore cannot qualify as a common law charity. The circumstances under which this change in interpretation was made suggest that it is entitled to very little deference. But even if the circumstances were different, the latter-day wisdom of the IRS has no basis in § 501(c)(3).

Perhaps recognizing the lack of support in the statute itself, or in its history, for the 1970 IRS change in interpretation, the Court finds that "[t]he actions of Congress since 1970 leave no doubt that the IRS reached the correct conclusion in exercising its authority," concluding that there is "an unusually strong case of legislative acquiescence in and ratification by implication of the 1970 and 1971 rulings." The Court relies first on several bills introduced to overturn the IRS interpretation of § 501(c)(3). But we have said before, and it is equally applicable here, that this type of congressional inaction is of virtually no weight in determining legislative intent. These bills and related hearings indicate little more than that a vigorous debate has existed in Congress concerning the new IRS position.

The Court next asserts that "Congress affirmatively manifested its acquiescence in the IRS policy when it enacted the present § 501(i) of the Code," a provision that "denies tax exempt status to social clubs whose charters or policy state⊥**621**ments provide for" racial discrimination. Quite to the contrary, it seems to me that in § 501(i) Congress showed that when it wants to add a requirement prohibiting racial discrimination to one of the tax-benefit provisions, it is fully aware of how to do it.

The Court intimates that the Ashbrook and Dornan Amendments also reflect an intent by Congress to acquiesce in the new IRS position. The amendments were passed to limit certain enforcement procedures proposed by the IRS in 1978 and 1979 for determining whether a school operated in a racially nondiscriminatory fashion. The Court points out that in proposing his amendment, Congressman Ashbrook stated: "'My amendment very clearly indicates on its face that all the regulations in existence as of August 22, 1978, would not be touched.'" The Court fails to note that Congressman Ashbrook also said: "The IRS has no authority to create public policy. . . . So long as the Congress has not acted to set forth a national policy respecting denial of tax exemptions to private schools, it is improper for the IRS or any other branch of the Federal Government to seek denial of tax-exempt status. . . . There exists but a single responsibility which is proper for the Internal Revenue Service: To serve as tax collector." In the same debate, Congressman Grassley asserted: "Nobody argues that racial discrimination should receive preferred tax status in the United States. However, the IRS should not be making these decisions on the agency's own discretion. Congress should make these decisions." The same debates are filled with other similar statements. While on the whole these debates do not show conclusively that Congress believed the IRS had exceeded its authority with the 1970 change in position, they likewise are ⊥**622** far less than a showing of acquiescence in and ratification of the new position.

This Court continuously has been hesitant to find ratification through inaction. This is especially true where such a finding "would result in a construction of the statute which not only is at odds with the language of the section in question and the pattern of the statute taken as a whole, but also is extremely far reaching in terms of the virtually untrammeled and unreviewable power it would vest in a regulatory agency." *SEC* v. *Sloan*. Few cases would call for more caution in finding ratification by acquiescence than the present one. The new IRS interpretation is not only far less than a long standing administrative policy, it is at odds with a position maintained by the IRS, and unquestioned by Congress, for several decades prior to 1970. The interpretation is unsupported by the statutory language, it is unsupported by legislative history, the interpretation has led to considerable controversy in and out of Congress, and the interpretation gives to the IRS a broad power which until now Congress had kept for itself. Where in addition to these circumstances Congress has shown time and time again that it is ready to enact positive legislation to change the tax code when it desires, this Court has no business finding that Congress has adopted the new IRS position by failing to enact legislation to reverse it.

I have no disagreement with the Court's finding that there is a strong national policy in this country opposed to racial discrimination. I agree with the Court that Congress has the power to further this policy by denying § 501(c)(3) status to organizations that practice racial discrimination. But as of yet Congress has failed to do so. Whatever the reasons for the failure, this Court should not legislate for Congress.

⊥**623** Petitioners are each organized for the "instruction or training of the individual for the purpose of improving or developing his capabilities," and thus are organized for "educational purposes" within the meaning of § 501(c)(3). Petitioners' nonprofit status is uncontested. There is no indication that either petitioner has been involved in lobbying activities or political campaigns. Therefore, it is my view that unless and until Congress affirmatively amends § 501(c)(3) to require more, the IRS is without authority to deny petitioners § 501(c)(3) status. For this reason, I would reverse the Court of Appeals.

JIMMY SWAGGART MINISTRIES v. BOARD OF EQUALIZATION OF CALIFORNIA

493 U.S. 378

ON APPEAL FROM THE COURT OF APPEAL OF CALIFORNIA, FOURTH APPELLATE DISTRICT

Argued October 31, 1989 — Decided January 17, 1990

⊥**380** *Justice* O'CONNOR delivered the opinion of the Court.

This case presents the question whether the Religion Clauses of the First Amendment prohibit a State from imposing a generally applicable sales and use tax on the distribution of religious materials by a religious organization.

⊥381 I

California's Sales and Use Tax Law requires retailers to pay a sales tax "[f]or the privilege of selling tangible personal property at retail." Cal. Rev. & Tax Code Ann. § 6051 (West 1987). A "sale" includes any transfer of title or possession of tangible personal property for consideration. Cal. Rev. & Tax Code Ann. § 6006(a) (West Supp. 1989).

The use tax, as a complement to the sales tax, reaches out-of-state purchases by residents of the State. It is "imposed on the storage, use, or other consumption in this state of tangible personal property purchased from any retailer," § 6201, at the same rate as the sales tax (6 percent). Although the use tax is imposed on the purchaser, § 6202, it is generally collected by the retailer at the time the sale is made. §§ 6202-6206. Neither the State Constitution nor the State Sales and Use Tax Law exempts religious organizations from the sales and use tax, apart from a limited exemption for the serving of meals by religious organizations, § 6363.5.

During the tax period in question (1974 to 1981), appellant Jimmy Swaggart Ministries was a religious organization incorporated as a Louisiana nonprofit corporation and recognized as such by the Internal Revenue Service pursuant to § 501(c)(3) of the Internal Revenue Code of 1954, as amended, 26 U.S.C. § 501(c)(3)(1982 ed.), and by the California State Controller pursuant to the Inheritance Tax and Gift Tax Laws of the State of California. Appellant's constitution and by-laws provide that it "is called for the purpose of establishing and maintaining an evangelistic outreach for the worship of Almighty God." This outreach is to be performed "by all available means, both at home and in foreign lands," and "shall specifically include evangelistic crusades; missionary endeavors; radio broadcasting (as owner, broadcaster, and placement agency); television broadcasting (both as owner and broadcaster); and audio production and reproduction of music; audio production and re**⊥382**production of preaching, audio production and reproduction of teaching; writing, printing and publishing; and, any and all other individual or mass media methods that presently exist or may be devised in the future to proclaim the good news of Jesus Christ."

From 1974 to 1981, appellant conducted numerous "evangelistic crusades" in auditoriums and arenas across the country in cooperation with local churches. During this period, appellant held 23 crusades in California—each lasting one to three days, with one crusade lasting six days—for a total of 52 days. At the crusades, appellant conducted religious services that included preaching and singing. Some of these services were recorded for later sale or broadcast. Appellant also sold religious books, tapes, records, and other religious and nonreligious merchandise at the crusades. Appellant also published a monthly magazine, "The Evangelist," which was sold nationwide by subscription. The magazine contained articles of a religious nature as well as advertisements for appellant's religious books, tapes, and records. The magazine included an order form listing the various items for sale in the particular issue and their unit price, with spaces for purchasers to fill in the quantity desired and the total price. Appellant also offered its items for sale through radio, television, and cable television broadcasts, including broadcasts through local California stations.

In 1980, appellee Board of Equalization of the State of California (Board) informed appellant that religious materials were not exempt from the sales tax and requested appellant to register as a seller to facilitate reporting and payment of the tax. See Cal. Rev. & Tax Code Ann. §§ 6066-6074 (West 1987 and Supp. 1989) (tax registration requirement). Appellant responded that it was exempt from such taxes under the First Amendment. In 1981, the Board audited appellant and advised appellant that it should register as a seller and report and pay sales tax on all sales made at its **⊥383** California Crusades. The Board also opined that appellant had a sufficient nexus with the State of California to require appellant to collect and report use tax on its sales to California purchasers.

Based on the Board's review of appellant's records, the parties stipulated "that [appellant] sold for use in California tangible personal property for the period April 1, 1974, through December 31, 1981, measured by payment to [appellant] of $1,702,942.00 for mail order sales from Baton Rouge, Louisiana and $240,560.00 for crusade merchandise sales in California." These figures represented the sales and use in California of merchandise with specific religious content—Bibles, Bible study manuals, printed sermons and collections of sermons, audiocassette tapes of sermons, religious books and pamphlets, and religious music in the form of songbooks, tapes, and records. Based on the sales figures for appellant's religious materials, the Board notified appellant that it owed sales and use taxes of $118,294.54, plus interest of $36,021.11, and a penalty of $11,829.45, for a total amount due of $166,145.10. Appellant did not contest the Board's assessment of tax liability for the sale and use of certain nonreligious merchandise, including such items as "T-shirts with JSM logo, mugs, bowls, plates, replicas of crown of thorns, ark of the covenant, Roman coin, candlesticks, Bible stand, pen and pencil sets, prints of religious scenes, bud vase, and communion cups."

Appellant filed a petition for redetermination with the Board, reiterating its view that the tax on religious materials violated the First Amendment. Following a hearing and an appeal to the Board, the Board deleted the penalty but otherwise redetermined the matter without adjustment in the amount of $118,294.54 in taxes owing, plus $65,043.55 in interest. Pursuant to state procedural law, appellant paid the amount and filed a petition for redetermination and refund with the Board. **⊥384** The Board denied appellant's petition, and appellant brought suit in state court, seeking a refund of the tax paid.

The trial court entered judgment for the Board, ruling that appellant was not entitled to a refund of any tax.

The California Court of Appeal affirmed, and the California Supreme Court denied discretionary review. We noted probable jurisdiction pursuant to 28 U.S.C. § 1257(2) (1982 ed.) (amended in 1988), and now affirm.

II

Appellant's central contention is that the State's imposition of sales and use tax liability on its sale of religious materials contravenes the First Amendment's command, made applicable to the States by the Fourteenth Amendment, to "make no law respecting an establishment of religion, or prohibiting the free exercise thereof." Appellant challenges the sales and use tax law under both the Free Exercise and Establishment Clauses.

A

The Free Exercise Clause, we have noted, "withdraws from legislative power, state and federal, the exertion of any restraint on the free exercise of religion. Its purpose is to secure religious liberty in the individual by prohibiting any invasions thereof by civil authority." *Abington School Dist.* v. *Schempp*. Indeed, "[a] regulation neutral on its face may, in its application, nonetheless offend the constitutional requirement for governmental neutrality if it unduly burdens the free exercise of religion." *Wisconsin* v. *Yoder*. Our cases have established that "[t]he free exercise inquiry asks whether government has placed a substantial burden on the observation of a central religious belief or practice and, if so, whether a compelling governmental interest justifies the ⊥**385** burden." *Hernandez* v. *Commissioner*.

Appellant relies almost exclusively on our decisions in *Murdock* v. *Pennsylvania* and *Follett* v. *McCormick* for the proposition that a State may not impose a sales or use tax on the evangelical distribution of religious material by a religious organization. Appellant contends that the State's imposition of use and sales tax liability on it burdens its evangelical distribution of religious materials in a manner identical to the manner in which the evangelists in *Murdock* and *Follett* were burdened.

We reject appellant's expansive reading of *Murdock* and *Follett* as contrary to the decisions themselves. In *Murdock*, we considered the constitutionality of a city ordinance requiring all persons canvassing or soliciting within the city to procure a license by paying a flat fee. Reversing the convictions of Jehovah's Witnesses convicted under the ordinance of soliciting and distributing religious literature without a license, we explained:

"The hand distribution of religious tracts is an age-old form of missionary evangelism . . . [and] has been a potent force in various religious movements down through the years. This form of evangelism is utilized today on a large scale by various sects whose colporteurs carry the Gospel to thousands upon thousands of homes and seek through personal visitations to win adherents to their faith. It is more than preaching, it is more than distribution of religious literature. It is a combination of both. Its purpose is as evangelical as the revival meeting. This form of religious activity occupies the same high estate under the First Amendment as do worship in the churches and preaching in the pulpits." Accordingly, we held that "spreading one's religious beliefs or preaching the Gospel through distribution of religious lit⊥**386**erature and through personal visitations is an age-old type of evangelism with as high a claim to constitutional protection as the more orthodox types."

We extended *Murdock* the following Term by invalidating, as applied to "one who earns his livelihood as an evangelist or preacher in his home town," an ordinance (similar to that involved in *Murdock*) that required all booksellers to pay a flat fee to procure a license to sell books. *Follett* v. *McCormick*. Reaffirming our observation in *Murdock* that "'the power to tax the exercise of a privilege is the power to control or suppress its enjoyment,'" we reasoned that "[t]he protection of the First Amendment is not restricted to orthodox religious practices any more than it is to the expression of orthodox economic views. He who makes a profession of evangelism is not in a less preferred position than the casual worker."

Our decisions in these cases, however, resulted from the particular nature of the challenged taxes—flat license taxes that operated as a prior restraint on the exercise of religious liberty. In *Murdock*, for instance, we emphasized that the tax at issue was "a license tax—a flat tax imposed on the exercise of a privilege granted by the Bill of Rights," and cautioned that "[w]e do not mean to say that religious groups and the press are free from all financial burdens of government. . . . We have here something quite different, for example, from a tax on the income of one who engages in religious activities or a tax on property used or employed in connection with those activities." See also 319 U.S., at 115 ("This tax is not a charge for the enjoyment of a privilege or benefit bestowed by the state.") In *Follett*, we reiterated that a preacher is not "free from all financial burdens of government, including taxes on income ⊥**387** or property" and, "like other citizens, may be subject to *general* taxation" (emphasis added).

Significantly, we noted in both cases that a primary vice of the ordinances at issue was that they operated as prior restraints of constitutionally protected conduct:

"In all of these cases [in which license taxes have been invalidated] the issuance of the permit or license is dependent on the payment of a license tax. And the license tax is fixed in amount and unrelated to the scope of the activities of petitioners or to their realized revenues. It is not a nominal fee imposed as a regulatory measure to defray the expenses of policing the activities in question. It is in no way apportioned. It is a flat license tax levied and collected as a condition to the pursuit of activities whose enjoyment is guaranteed by the First Amendment. Accordingly, *it restrains in advance those constitutional liberties of press and religion and inevitably tends to suppress their exercise*. That is almost uniformly recognized as the inherent vice and evil of this flat license tax." *Murdock* (emphasis added). See also *Follett* ("[t]he exaction of a tax as a condition to the exercise of the great liberties guaranteed by the First Amendment is as obnoxious as the imposition of a censorship or a previous restraint"). Thus, although *Murdock* and *Follett* establish that appellant's form of religious exercise has "as high a claim to constitutional protection as the more orthodox types," *Murdock*, those cases are of no further help to appellant. Our concern in *Murdock* and *Follett*—that a flat license tax would act as a precondition to the free exercise of religious beliefs—is simply not present where a tax applies to all sales and uses of tangible personal property in the State.

Our reading of *Murdock* and *Follett* is confirmed by our decision in *Minnesota Star & Tribune Co.* v. *Minnesota Commissioner of Revenue*, where we con⊥**388**sidered a newspaper's First Amendment challenge to a state use tax on ink and paper products used in the production of periodic publications. In the course of striking down the tax, we rejected the newspaper's suggestion, premised on *Murdock* and *Follett*, that a generally applicable sales tax could not be applied to publications. Construing those cases involving "a flat tax, unrelated to the receipts or income of the speaker or to the expenses of administering a valid regulatory scheme, as a *condition* of the right to speak" (emphasis in original), we noted:

"By imposing the tax as a condition of engaging in protected activity, the defendants in those cases imposed a form of prior restraint on speech, rendering the tax highly susceptible to constitutional challenge. In that regard, the cases cited by Star Tribune do not resemble a generally applicable sales tax. Indeed, our cases have consistently recognized that nondiscriminatory taxes on the receipts or income of newspapers would be permissible." Accord *Arkansas Writer's Project, Inc.* v. *Ragland* ("a genuinely nondiscriminatory tax on the receipts of newspapers would be constitutionally permissible").

We also note that just last Term a plurality of the Court rejected the precise argument appellant now makes. In *Texas Monthly, Inc.* v. *Bullock*, *Justice BRENNAN*, writing for three Justices, held that a state sales tax exemption for religious publications violated the Establishment Clause. In so concluding, the plurality further held that the Free Exercise Clause did not prevent the State from withdrawing its exemption, noting that "[t]o the extent our opinions in *Murdock* and *Follett* might be read . . . to suggest that the State and the Federal Government may never tax the sale of religious or other publications, we reject those dicta." *Justice WHITE*, concurring in the judgment, con⊥**389**cluded that the exemption violated the Free Press Clause because the content of a publication determined its tax-exempt status. *Justice BLACKMUN*, joined by *Justice O'CONNOR*, concurred in the plurality's holding that the tax exemption at issue in that case contravened the Establishment Clause, but reserved the question whether "the Free Exercise Clause requires a tax exemption for the sale of religious literature by a religious organization; in other words, defining the ultimate scope of *Follett* and *Murdock* may be left for another day." In this case, of course, California has not chosen to create a tax exemption for religious materials, and we therefore have no need to revisit the Establishment Clause question presented in *Texas Monthly*.

We do, however, decide the Free Exercise question left open by *Justice BLACKMUN's* concurrence in *Texas Monthly* by limiting *Murdock* and *Follett* to apply only where a flat license tax operates as a prior restraint on the free exercise of religious beliefs. As such, *Murdock* and *Follett* plainly do not support appellant's free exercise claim. California's generally applicable sales and use tax is not a flat tax, represents only a small fraction of any retail sale, and applies neutrally to all retail sales of tangible personal property made in California. California imposes its sales and use tax even if the seller or the purchaser is charitable, religious, nonprofit, or state or local governmental in nature. Thus, the sales and use tax is not a tax on the right to disseminate religious information, ideas, or beliefs *per se*; rather, it is a tax on the privilege of making retail sales of tangible personal property and on the storage, use, or other consumption of tangible personal property in California. For example, ⊥**390** California treats the sale of a Bible by a religious organization just as it would treat the sale of a Bible by a bookstore; as long as both are in-state retail sales of tangible personal property, they are both subject to the tax regardless of the motivation for the sale or the purchase. There is no danger that appellant's religious activity is being singled out for special and burdensome treatment.

Moreover, our concern in *Murdock* and *Follett* that flat license taxes operate as a precondition to the exercise of evangelistic activity is not present in this case, because the registration requirement, see Cal. Rev. & Tax Code Ann. §§ 6066-6074 (West 1987 and Supp. 1989), and the tax itself do not act as prior restraints—no fee is charged for registering, the tax is due regardless of preregistration, and the tax is not imposed as a precondition of disseminating the message. Thus, unlike the license tax in *Murdock*, which was "in no way apportioned" to the "realized revenues" of the itinerant preachers forced to pay the tax, see also *Texas Monthly*, the tax issue in this case is akin to a generally applicable income or property tax, which *Murdock* and *Follett* specifically state may constitutionally be imposed on religious activity.

In addition to appellant's misplaced reliance on *Murdock* and *Follett*, appellant's free exercise claim is also in significant tension with the Court's decision last Term in *Hernandez* v. *Commissioner*, holding that the Government's disallowance of a tax deduction for religious "auditing" and "training" services did not violate the Free Exercise Clause. The Court reasoned that

"[a]ny burden imposed on auditing or training . . . derives solely from the fact that, as a result of the deduction denial, adherents have less money to gain access to such sessions. This burden is no different from that imposed by any public tax or fee; indeed, the burden imposed by the denial of the 'contribution or gift' deduction ⊥**391** would seem to pale by comparison to the overall federal income tax burden on an adherent." There is no evidence in this case that collection and payment of the tax violates appellant's sincere religious beliefs. California's nondiscriminatory sales and use tax law requires only that appellant collect the tax from its California purchasers and remit the tax money to the State. The only burden on appellant is the claimed reduction in income resulting from the presumably lower demand for appellant's wares (caused by the marginally higher price) and from the costs associated with administering the tax. As the Court made clear in *Hernandez*, however, to the extent that imposition of a generally applicable tax merely decreases the amount of money appellant has to spend on its religious activities, any such burden is not constitutionally significant.

Appellant contends that the availability of a deduction (at issue in *Hernandez*) and the imposition of a tax (at issue here) are distinguishable, but in both cases adherents base their claim for an exemption on the argument that an "incrementally larger tax burden interferes with their religious activities." It is precisely this argument—rather than one applicable only to deductions—that the Court rejected in *Hernandez*. At bottom, though we do not doubt the economic cost to appellant of complying with a generally applicable sales and use tax, such a tax is no different from other generally applicable laws and regulations—such as health and safety regulations—to which appellant must adhere.

Finally, because appellant's religious beliefs do not forbid payment of the sales and use tax, appellant's reliance on *Sherbert* v. *Verner* and its progeny is misplaced, because in no sense has the State "'condition[ed] receipt of an important benefit upon conduct proscribed by a ⊥**392** religious faith, or . . . denie[d] such a benefit because of conduct mandated by religious belief, thereby putting substantial pressure on an adherent to modify his behavior and to violate his beliefs.'" *Hobbie* v. *Unemployment Appeals Comm'n of Florida* (quoting *Thomas* v. *Review Board of Indiana Employment Security Div.*). Appellant has never alleged that the mere act of paying the tax, by itself, violates its sincere religious beliefs.

We therefore conclude that the collection and payment of the generally applicable tax in this case imposes no constitutionally significant burden on appellant's religious practices or beliefs. The Free Exercise Clause accordingly does not *require* the State to grant appellant an exemption from its generally applicable sales and use tax. Although it is of course possible to imagine that a more onerous tax rate, even if generally applicable, might effectively choke off an adherent's religious practices, cf. *Murdock* (the burden of a flat tax could render itinerant evangelism "crushed and closed out by the sheer weight of the toll or tribute which is exacted town by town"), we face no such situation in this case. Accordingly, we intimate no views as to whether such a generally applicable tax might violate the Free Exercise Clause.

B

Appellant also contends that application of the sales and use tax to its sale of religious materials violates the Establishment Clause because it fosters "'an excessive government entanglement with religion,'" *Lemon* v. *Kurtzman* (quoting *Walz* v. *Tax Comm'n of New York City*). Appellant alleges, for example, that the present controversy has featured on-site inspections of appellant's evangelistic crusades, lengthy on-site audits, examinations of appellant's books and records, threats of criminal prosecution, and layers of administrative and judicial proceedings.

⊥**393** The Establishment Clause prohibits "sponsorship, financial support, and active involvement of the sovereign in religious activity." *Walz*. The "excessive entanglement" prong of the tripartite purpose-effect-entanglement *Lemon* test requires examination of "the character and purpose of the institutions that are benefited, the nature of the aid that the State provides, and the resulting relationship between the government and the religious authority." See also *Walz* (separate opinion of Harlan, J.) (warning of "programs, whose very nature is apt to entangle the state in details of administration"). Indeed, in *Walz* we held that a tax exemption for "religious organizations for religious properties used solely for religious worship," as part of a general exemption for non-profit institutions, did not violate the Establishment Clause. In upholding the tax exemption, we specifically noted that taxation of religious properties would cause at least as much administrative entanglement between government and religious authorities as did the exemption:

"Either course, taxation of churches or exemption, occasions some degree of involvement with religion. Elimination of some exemption would tend to expand the involvement of government by giving rise to tax valuation of church property, tax liens, tax foreclosures, and the direct confrontations and conflicts that follow in the train of these legal processes.

"Granting tax exemptions to churches necessarily operates to afford an indirect economic benefit and also gives rise to some, but yet a lesser, involvement than taxing them. In analyzing either alternative the questions are whether the involvement is excessive, and whether it is a continuing one calling for official and continuing surveillance leading to an impermissible degree of entanglement." ⊥**394** The issue presented, therefore, is whether the imposition of sales and use tax liability in this case on appellant results in "excessive" involvement between appellant and the State and "continuing surveillance leading to an impermissible degree of entanglement."

At the outset, it is undeniable that a generally applicable tax has a secular purpose and neither advances nor inhibits religion, for the very essence of such a tax is that it is neutral and nondiscriminatory on questions of religious belief. Thus, whatever the precise contours of the Establishment Clause, see *County of Allegheny* v. *American Civil Liberties Union of Pittsburgh* (tracing evolution of Establishment Clause doctrine); cf. *Bowen* v. *Kendrick* (applying but noting criticism of the entanglement prong of the *Lemon* test), its undisputed core values are not even remotely called into question by the generally applicable tax in this case.

Even applying the "excessive entanglement" prong of the *Lemon* test, however, we hold that California's imposition of sales and use tax liability on appellant threatens no excessive entanglement between church and state. First, we note that the evidence of administrative entanglement in this case is thin. Appellant alleges that collection and payment of the sales and use tax impose severe accounting burdens on it. The Court of Appeal, however, expressly found that the record did not support appellant's factual assertions, noting that appellant "had a sophisticated accounting staff and had recently computerized its accounting and that [appellant] in its own books and for purposes of obtaining a federal income tax exemption segregated 'retail sales' and 'donations.'"

Second, even assuming that the tax imposes substantial administrative burdens on appellant, such administrative and recordkeeping burdens do not rise to a constitutionally significant level. Collection and payment of the tax will of course require some contact between appellant and the State, ⊥**395** but we have held that generally applicable administrative and recordkeeping regulations may be imposed on religious organizations without running afoul of the Establishment Clause. See *Hernandez* ("[R]outine regulatory interaction [such as application of neutral tax laws] which involves no inquiries into religious doctrine, . . . no delegation of state power to a religious body, . . . and no 'detailed monitoring and close administrative contact' between secular and religious bodies, . . . does not of itself violate the nonentanglement command"); *Tony and Susan Alamo Foundation* v. *Secretary of Labor*) ("The Establishment Clause does not exempt religious organizations from such secular governmental activity as fire inspections and building and zoning regulations, *Lemon*, and the recordkeeping requirements of the Fair Labor Standards Act, while perhaps more burdensome in terms of paperwork, are not significantly more intrusive into religious affairs"). To be sure, we noted in *Tony and Susan Alamo Foundation* that the recordkeeping requirements at issue in that case "appl[ied] only to commercial activities undertaken with a 'business purpose,' and would therefore have no impact on petitioners' own evangelical activities," but that recognition did not bear on whether the generally applicable regulation was nevertheless "the kind of government surveillance the Court has previously held to pose an intolerable risk of government entanglement with religion."

The fact that appellant must bear the cost of collecting and remitting a generally applicable sales and use tax—even if the financial burden of such costs may vary from religion to religion—does not enmesh government in religious affairs. Contrary to appellant's contentions, the statutory scheme requires neither the involvement of state employees in, nor on-site continuing inspection of, appellant's day-to-day operations. There is no "official and continuing surveillance," *Walz*, by government auditors. The sorts of ⊥**396** government entanglement that we have found to violate the Establishment Clause have been far more invasive than the level of contact created by the administration of neutral tax laws. Cf. *Aguilar* v. *Felton*, *Larkin* v. *Grendel's Den, Inc.*

Most significantly, the imposition of the sales and use tax without an exemption for appellant does not require the State to inquire into the religious content of the items sold or the religious motivation for selling or purchasing the items, because the materials are subject to the tax regardless of content or motive. From the State's point of view, the critical question is not whether the materials are religious, but whether there is a sale or use, a question which involves only a secular determination. Thus, this case stands on firmer ground than *Hernandez*, because appellant offers the items at a stated price, thereby relieving the State of the need to place a monetary value on appellant's religious items. Compare *Hernandez* (where no comparable good or service is sold in the marketplace, Internal Revenue Service looks to cost of providing the good or service), with *id.* (O'Connor, J., dissenting) ("It becomes impossible . . . to compute the 'contribution' portion of a payment to charity where what is received in return is not merely intangible, but an intangible (or, for that matter a tangible) that is not bought and sold except in donative contexts"). Although appellant asserts that donations often accompany payments made for the religious items and that items are sometimes given away without payment (or only nominal payment), it is plain that, in the first case, appellant's use of "order forms" and "price lists" renders illusory any difficulty in separating the two portions and that, in the second case, the question is only whether any particular transfer constitutes a "sale." Ironically, appellant's theory, under which government may not tax "religious core" activities but may tax "nonreligious" activities, would require government to do precisely what appellant asserts the Religion ⊥**397** Clauses prohibit: "determine which expenditures are religious and which are secular." *Lemon*.

Accordingly, because we find no excessive entanglement between government and religion in this case, we hold that the imposition of sales and use tax liability on appellant does not violate the Establishment Clause.

III

Appellant also contends that the State's imposition of use tax liability on it violates the Commerce and Due Process Clauses because, as an out-of-state distributor, it had an insufficient "nexus" to the State. See *National Geographic Society* v. *California Board of Equalization*, *National Bellas Hess, Inc.* v. *Department of Revenue of Illinois*. We decline to reach the merits of this claim, however, because the courts below ruled that the claim was procedurally barred. . . .

⊥**399** The judgment of the California Court of Appeal is affirmed.

It is so ordered.

SOLICITATION BY RELIGIOUS GROUPS

Solicitation of financial contributions door-to-door and in public places by religious groups is clearly subject to reasonable nondiscriminatory regulation by the state or local community as a protection against fraud, injury, or undue violation of privacy. The community may within reason regulate the time, place, and manner of the solicitation. However, regulation must be accomplished through narrowly drawn, nondiscriminatory statutes designed to protect the legitimate interests of the public without unduly interfering with the free exercise of religion.

In too many instances this has not been the primary goal of these regulations. They are sometimes seen as a convenient means to disadvantage or harass currently unpopular religious movements. The statute to be used may already be in place or it may be especially tailored to the characteristics of the targeted group. Even statutes that appear on the surface to be neutral and nondiscriminatory may be administered with a selectively uneven hand when applied to unpopular religious groups.

Many of the early Jehovah's Witnesses cases discussed earlier in this chapter involved efforts to restrain or prohibit fund solicitation by that widely despised group. Few of the measures survived the scrutiny of the Court.

As was true of the doughty Jehovah's Witnesses of the 1940s, members of today's unorthodox, aggressive sects are most likely to be involved in litigation testing the scope of the free exercise guarantee. Members of the International Society for Krishna Consciousness (ISKCON), known also as Hare Krishna, have in recent years attracted much public attention by their unusual dress and persistent efforts to sell religious literature and to solicit donations in public places such as airports.

Hare Krishnas maintain that these actions constitute a ritual (*Sankirtan*) essential to their religion. Because their activities have intimidated and frightened some and irritated many, practitioners have been subjected to various restrictive efforts on the part of state and local authorities. With mixed results, the constitutionality of these regulations has been challenged by ISKCON in state and federal courts.

In 1981, in HEFFRON v. INTERNATIONAL SOCIETY FOR KRISHNA CONSCIOUSNESS, the United States Supreme Court dealt with the problem when it reviewed a decision of the Minnesota Supreme Court. The Minnesota Agriculture Society, which operates a state fair, required all persons, groups, or firms desiring to sell, exhibit, or distribute materials at the fair to do so at a booth rented from the Society. Representatives of organizations were free to move about the fairgrounds and communicate their views orally. The regulation, as applied to Hare Krishna members, was voided by the Minnesota Supreme Court as unconstitutionally restricting their practice of *Sankirtan*. The rule, as the court agreed, was applied without discrimination and did not prevent representatives of organizations involved from moving freely about the fairgrounds to communicate orally their views to patrons of the fair.

The majority opinion of the Supreme Court, written by Justice White, reversed the Minnesota high court. He found the state's interest in orderly movement of crowds and avoidance of congestion sufficient justification for the challenged rule. The case was decided primarily on free speech grounds. Observing that it is settled law that the First Amendment does not guarantee the right to communicate one's views at all times and places in any manner desired, Justice White expressed the view of the Court that the evenhanded rental of booths to all applicants and the freedom allowed the Hare Krishna to propagate their views orally constituted sufficient alternative outlets for expression of ideas.

The sect, said the Court's opinion, gained no special claim to protection as compared to other religious groups merely by ritualizing the process:

> That organization and its ritual of Sankirtan have no special claim to First Amendment protection as compared to that of other religions who also distribute literature and solicit funds. None of our cases suggest that the inclusion of peripatetic solicitation as part of a church ritual entitles church members to solicitation rights in a public forum superior to those of members of other religious groups that raise money but do not purport to ritualize the process (452 U.S. 640, 652).

The opinion stated further that religious groups in general enjoy under present circumstances no greater right to communicate, distribute literature, and solicit than "other organizations having social, political, or other ideological messages to proselytize."

Justice Brennan, joined by Justices Marshall and Stevens, dissented, contending that the state could have drafted a more narrowly drawn restriction to achieve its legitimate interest in crowd control. Justice Blackmun concurred in part and dissented in part.

Another governmental effort to restrict solicitation in public places had enjoyed less success when it went before the Supreme Court the year before the *Heffron* decision in *Village of Schaumburg* v. *Citizens for a Better Environment* (1980). In this case, no specific religious group was involved and the decision was based on the freedom of speech clause. However, Justice White—who later also wrote for the majority in *Heffron*—cited and discussed numerous Jehovah's Witnesses cases of the 1930s and

1940s. The decision invalidated an ordinance which prohibited door-to-door or on-street solicitation of contributions by charitable organizations, including churches, that did not use at least 75 percent of their receipts for charitable purposes. The Court found the 75 percent requirement to be insufficiently related to legitimate government interests in protecting the public against "fraud, crime, and undue annoyance" and held it to be constitutionally overbroad in violation of the First and Fourteenth Amendments. Only Justice Rehnquist would have upheld Schaumburg's ordinance.

Although the decision was based on Establishment Clause and Equal Protection Clause grounds and is therefore discussed in more detail under that heading, LARSON v. VALENTE, decided the next year, also involved Minnesota restrictions on solicitation as applied to another controversial religious movement—the Unification Church—against whom the law had been primarily aimed from its inception. The statute before the Court required registration and disclosure from only those religious organizations that solicited more than one-half of their contributions from nonmembers.

The Court, by a five-to-four vote, with Justice Brennan speaking for the majority, struck down the application of the registration and reporting act to the Unification Church as preferring one religion over another and effecting the "selective legislative imposition of burdens and advantages upon particular denominations" (456 U.S. 228, 254).

In 1983 the city commission of Clearwater, Florida, Western Hemisphere headquarters of the Church of Scientology, enacted an extremely burdensome solicitation ordinance. The broadly drawn ordinance required charitable organizations to register with the city, keep detailed records, disclose the sources and uses of their contributions, and refrain from engaging in fraudulent solicitation practices. On the complaint of ten or more individuals, the soliciting organizations would be required to submit to an investigation by the city attorney. Although the ordinance was rather obviously aimed at the unpopular Church of Scientology, it also applied, of course, to mainstream religious and charitable organizations.

Americans United for Separation of Church and State, joined by the National Council of Churches, the American Jewish Committees, and the Suncoast Baptist Church of Clearwater, attacked the ordinance in a federal district court alleging violation of the Free Exercise and Establishment Clauses as well as free speech, free press, due process, equal protection, the commerce clause, and the right to privacy. The Church of Scientology filed a separate suit. The city commission, responding to the protests, repealed the first ordinance and passed a second less oppressive measure.

The district court held the original ordinance unconstitutional and permanently enjoined its enforcement. It held the second ordinance to be facially constitutional. The two cases were then joined and went to the United States Court of Appeals for the Eleventh Circuit. That court held that the issue of the constitutionality of the repealed ordinance was at the time moot and should not have been heard by the district court. The appellate court also raised serious questions with respect to proof of standing on the part of the challenging organizations and remanded the cases to the district court with instructions that they be dismissed. Though the cases were technically lost by those who brought them, they obviously had a positive effect. The controversy and accompanying publicity caused the city commission to reconsider its action in enacting the harsh solicitation measure, which would not only have had a chilling effect on the activities of all charitable and religious groups in Clearwater but might, if accepted by the courts, have been adopted as a model for other communities desiring to harass unpopular movements.

Two recent cases involving distribution of free religious literature and solicitation by religious groups at airports are *Board of Airport Commissioners* v. *Jews for Jesus* (1987) and *International Society for Krishna Consciousness* v. *Lee* (1992). Although the 1987 case was actually decided on free speech grounds, it involved a minister of the Gospel for Jews for Jesus. He was stopped from distributing free religious literature on the central walkway in the Central Terminal area at Los Angeles International Airport. His religious organization attacked the resolution on which the restraint was based as unconstitutional under both the state and federal constitutions because it banned speech in a public forum and also because it had been used against Jews for Jesus in a discriminatory way. The United States District Court held that the resolution violated the First Amendment, as did the Court of Appeals.

California appealed to the Supreme Court, and that body unanimously held the resolution unconstitutional without speaking to the issue of whether the airport was considered a public or a nonpublic forum. The resolution was unconstitutional on its face, wrote Justice O'Connor for the Court, because it was "substantially overbroad and is not fairly subject to a limiting construction."

In January 1992 the Court granted certiorari from a decision of the Second Court of Appeals involving the International Society of Krishna Consciousness. A Port Authority regulation prohibited in-person solicitation of funds and distribution of literature in New York and New Jersey airport terminals. The Court of Appeals upheld the ban on solicitation of funds, but held invalid the prohibition of distribution of literature in the terminals, a practice the Court found less disruptive to the flow of traffic. Because of the split decision, two suits were sent to the Supreme Court. In *ISKCON* v. *Lee* the Krishna group was asking the Court to declare the prohibition on solicitation of funds unconstitutional so the group would have free reign of the airport terminals, although subject to time, place, and manner restrictions. The Port Authority counter-sued, in *Lee* v. *ISKCON*, asking the Court to reinstate the prohibition of the distribution of literature, thus banning the religious group's access to the airport terminals altogether. On 24 June, 1992, in an opinion by Chief Justice Rehnquist, the Court voted 6-3 to uphold the ban on solicitations in the airports (*ISKCON* v. *Lee*). But, in an unsigned, 5-4, opinion, the Court held that the distribution of literature was all right (*Lee* v. *ISKCON*), thus affirming the opinion of the Court of Appeals in both dimensions of the case.

HEFFRON v. INTERNATIONAL SOCIETY FOR KRISHNA CONSCIOUSNESS

452 U.S. 640
ON WRIT OF CERTIORARI TO THE SUPREME COURT OF THE STATE OF MINNESOTA
Argued April 20, 1981 — Decided June 22, 1981

⊥**642** *Justice WHITE* delivered the opinion of the Court.

The question presented for review is whether a State, consistent with the First and Fourteenth Amendments, may require a religious organization desiring to distribute and sell religious literature and to solicit donations at a state fair to conduct those activities only at an assigned location within the fairgrounds even though application of the rule limits the religious practices of the organization.

I

⊥**643** Each year, the Minnesota Agricultural Society (Society), a public corporation organized under the laws of Minnesota, operates a state fair on a 125-acre state-owned tract located in St. Paul, Minn. The Fair is conducted for the purpose of "exhibiting . . . the agricultural, stock-breeding, horticultural, mining, mechanical, industrial, and other products and resources of the state, including proper exhibits and expositions of the arts, human skills, and sciences." The Fair is a major public event and attracts visitors from all over Minnesota as well as from other parts of the country. During the past 5 years, the average total attendance for the 12-day fair has been 1,320,000 persons. The average daily attendance on weekdays has been 115,000 persons and on Saturdays and Sundays 160,000.

The Society is authorized to make all "bylaws, ordinances, and rules, not inconsistent with law, which it may deem necessary or proper for the government of the fair grounds. . . ." Under this authority, the Society promulgated Minnesota State Fair Rule 6.05 which provides in relevant part that: "Sale or distribution of any merchandise, including printed or written material except under license issued [by] the Society and/or from a duly-licensed location shall be a misdemeanor."

As Rule 6.05 is construed and applied by the Society, "all persons, groups or firms which desire to sell, exhibit or distribute materials during the annual State Fair must do so only from fixed locations on the fairgrounds." Although the Rule does not prevent organizational representatives from walking about the fairgrounds and communicating the organ⊥**644**ization's views with fair patrons in face-to-face discussions, it does require that any exhibitor conduct its sales, distribution, and fund solicitation operations from a booth rented from the Society. Space in the fairgrounds is rented to all comers in a nondiscriminatory fashion on a first-come, first-served basis with the rental charge based on the size and location of the booth. The rule applies alike to nonprofit, charitable, and commercial enterprises.

One day prior to the opening of the 1977 Minnesota State Fair, respondents International Society for Krishna Consciousness, Inc. (ISKCON), an international religious society espousing the views of the Krishna religion, and Joseph Beca, head of the Minneapolis ISKCON temple, filed suit against numerous state officials seeking a declaration that Rule 6.05, both on its face and as applied, violated respondents' rights under the First Amendment, and seeking injunctive relief ⊥**645** prohibiting enforcement of the Rule against ISKCON and its members. Specifically, ISKCON asserted that the Rule would suppress the practice of Sankirtan, one of its religious rituals, which enjoins its members to go into public places to distribute or sell religious literature and to solicit donations for the support of the Krishna religion. The trial court entered temporary orders to govern the conduct of the parties during the 1977 Fair. When that event concluded and after a hearing, the trial court granted the state officials' motion for summary judgment, upholding the constitutionality of Rule 6.05. Relying on the reasoning in *ISKCON* v. *Evans*, the court found that the State's interest "in providing all fair goers and concessionaries with adequate and equal access to each other and in providing a minimum of ⊥**646** congestion of the fairgrounds" was sufficient to sustain Rule 6.05's limitations as applied to respondents. The court, however, provided that respondents were free to "[r]oam throughout those areas of the fairgrounds generally open to the public for the purpose of discussing with others their religious beliefs."

On appeal, the Minnesota Supreme Court reversed, holding that Rule 6.05, as applied to respondents, unconstitutionally restricted the Krishnas' religious practice of Sankirtan. The court rejected the Society's proffered justifications for the Rule as inadequate to warrant the restriction. Furthermore, the application of Rule 6.05 to ISKCON was not essential to the furtherance of the State's interests in that those interests could be served by means less restrictive of respondents' First Amendment rights. We granted the state officials' petition for writ of certiorari in light of the important constitutional issues presented and the conflicting results reached in similar cases in various lower courts.

II

⊥647 The State does not dispute that the oral and written dissemination of the Krishnas' religious views and doctrines is protected by the First Amendment. See *Schneider* v. *State; Lovell* v. *City of Griffin*. Nor does it claim that this protection is lost because the written materials sought to be distributed are sold rather than given away or because contributions or gifts are solicited in the course of propagating the faith. Our cases indicate as much. *Murdock* v. *Pennsylvania, Village of Schaumburg* v. *Citizens for a Better Environment*. See *Cantwell* v. *Connecticut*.

It is also common ground, however, that the First Amendment does not guarantee the right to communicate one's views at all times and places or in any manner that may be desired. *Adderley* v. *Florida; Poulos* v. *New Hampshire;* see *Cox* v. *Louisiana*. As the Minnesota Supreme Court recognized, the activities of ISKCON, like those of others protected by the First Amendment, are subject to reasonable time, place, and manner restrictions. *Grayned* v. *City of Rockford; Adderley* v. *Florida; Kovacs* v. *Cooper; Cox* v. *New Hampshire*. "We have often ap⊥648proved restrictions of that kind provided that they are justified without reference to the content of the regulated speech, that they serve a significant governmental interest, and that in doing so they leave open ample alternative channels for communication of the information." *Virginia State Board of Pharmacy* v. *Virginia Citizens Consumer Council;* see also *Consolidated Edison Co.* v. *Public Service Commission*. The issue here, as it was below, is whether Rule 6.05 is a permissible restriction on the place and manner of communicating the views of the Krishna religion, more specifically, whether the Society may require the members of ISKCON who desire to practice Sankirtan at the State Fair to confine their distribution, sales, and solicitation activities to a fixed location.

A major criterion for a valid time, place and manner restriction is that the restriction "may not be based upon either the content or subject matter of the speech." *Consolidated Edison Co.* v. *Public Service Commission*. Rule 6.05 ⊥649 qualifies in this respect, since as the Supreme Court of Minnesota observed, the Rule applies evenhandedly to all who wish to distribute and sell written materials or to solicit funds. No person or organization, whether commercial or charitable, is permitted to engage in such activities except from a booth rented for those purposes.

Nor does Rule 6.05 suffer from the more covert forms of discrimination that may result when arbitrary discretion is vested in some governmental authority. The method of allocating space is a straightforward first-come, first-served system. The Rule is not open to the kind of arbitrary application that this Court has condemned as inherently inconsistent with a valid time, place, and manner regulation because such discretion has the potential for becoming a means of suppressing a particular point of view. See *Shuttlesworth* v. *Birmingham; Cox* v. *Louisiana; Staub* v. *City of Baxley; Largent* v. *Texas; Cantwell* v. *Connecticut; Schneider* v. *State; Hague* v. *C.I.O.*

A valid time, place, and manner regulation must also "serve a significant governmental interest." *Virginia Board* v. *Citizens Council*. See *Grayned* v. *City of Rockford*. Here, the principal justification asserted by the State in support of Rule 6.05 is the need to maintain the orderly movement of ⊥650 the crowd given the large number of exhibitors and persons attending the Fair.

The fairgrounds comprise a relatively small area of 125 acres, the bulk of which is covered by permanent buildings, temporary structures, parking lots, and connecting thoroughfares. There were some 1,400 exhibitors and concessionaires renting space for the 1977 and 1978 Fairs, chiefly in permanent and temporary buildings. The Fair is designed to exhibit to the public an enormous variety of goods, services, entertainment and other matters of interest. This is accomplished by confining individual exhibitors to fixed locations, with the public moving to and among the booths or other attractions, using streets and open spaces provided for that purpose. Because the Fair attracts large crowds—an average of 115,000 patrons on weekdays and 160,000 on Saturdays and Sundays—it is apparent that the State's interest in the orderly movement and control of such an assembly of persons is a substantial consideration.

As a general matter, it is clear that a State's interest in protecting the "safety and convenience" of persons using a public forum is a valid governmental objective. See *Grayned* v. *City of Rockford; Cox* v. *New Hampshire*. Furthermore, consideration of a forum's special attributes is relevant to the constitutionality of a regulation since the significance of the governmental ⊥651 interest must be assessed in light of the characteristic nature and function of the particular forum involved. See, *e.g.*, *Grayned* v. *City of Rockford; Lehman* v. *City of Shaker Heights*. This observation bears particular import in the present case since respondents make a number of analogies between the fairgrounds and city streets which have "immemorially been held in trust for the use of the public and, . . . have been used for purposes of assembly, communicating thoughts between citizens, and discussing public questions." *Hague* v. *C.I.O.* See *Kunz* v. *New York*. But it is clear that there are significant differences between a street and the fairgrounds. A street is continually open, often uncongested, and constitutes not only a necessary conduit in the daily affairs of a locality's citizens, but also a place where people may enjoy the open air or the company of friends and neighbors in a relaxed environment. The Minnesota Fair, as described above, is a temporary event attracting great numbers of visitors who come to the event for a short period to see and experience the host of exhibits and attractions at the Fair.

The flow of the crowd and demands of safety are more pressing in the context of the Fair. As such, any comparisons to public streets are necessarily inexact.

The Minnesota Supreme Court recognized that the State's interest in the orderly movement of a large crowd and in avoiding congestion was substantial and that Rule 6.05 furthered that interest significantly. Nevertheless, the Minnesota Supreme Court declared that the case did not turn on the "importance of the state's undeniable interest in pre⊥**652**venting the widespread disorder that would surely exist if no regulation such as Rule 6.05 were in effect" but upon the significance of the State's interest in avoiding whatever disorder would likely result from granting members of ISKCON an exemption from the Rule. Approaching the case in this way, the court concluded that although some disruption would occur from such an exemption, it was not of sufficient concern to warrant confining the Krishnas to a booth. The court also concluded that, in any event, the rule was not essential to the furtherance of the State's interest in crowd control, which could adequately be served by less intrusive means.

As we see it, the Minnesota Supreme Court took too narrow a view of the State's interest in avoiding congestion and maintaining the orderly movement of fair patrons on the fairgrounds. The justification for the Rule should not be measured by the disorder that would result from granting an exemption solely to ISKCON. That organization and its ritual of Sankirtan have no special claim to First Amendment protection as compared to that of other religions who also distribute literature and solicit funds. None of our cases suggest that the inclusion of peripatetic solicitation as part of a church ritual entitles church members to solicitation rights in a public forum superior to those of members of other religious groups that raise money but do not purport to ritualize the process. Nor for present purposes do religious organizations enjoy rights to communicate, distribute, and solicit on the fairgrounds superior to those of other organizations having social, political, or other ideological messages to ⊥**653** proselytize. These nonreligious organizations seeking support for their activities are entitled to rights equal to those of religious groups to enter a public forum and spread their views, whether by soliciting funds or by distributing literature.

If Rule 6.05 is an invalid restriction on the activities of ISKCON, it is no more valid with respect to the other social, political, or charitable organizations that have rented booths at the Fair and confined their distribution, sale, and fund solicitation to those locations. Nor would it be valid with respect to other organizations that did not rent booths, either because they were unavailable due to a lack of space or because they chose to avoid the expense involved, but that would in all probability appear in the fairgrounds to distribute, sell, and solicit if they could freely do so. The question would also inevitably arise as to what extent the First Amendment also gives commercial organizations a right to move among the crowd to distribute information about or to sell their wares as respondents claim they may do.

ISKCON desires to proselytize at the fair because it believes it can successfully communicate and raise funds. In its view, this can be done only by intercepting fair patrons as they move about, and if success is achieved, stopping them momentarily or for longer periods as money is given or exchanged for literature. This consequence would be multiplied many times over if Rule 6.05 could not be applied to confine such transactions by ISKCON and others to fixed locations. Indeed, the court below agreed that without Rule 6.05 there would be widespread disorder at the fairgrounds. The court also recognized that some disorder would inevitably result from exempting the Krishnas from the Rule. Obviously, there would be a much larger threat to the State's interest in crowd control if all other religious, nonreligious, and noncommercial organizations could likewise move freely about the fairgrounds distributing and selling literature and soliciting funds at will.

⊥**654** Given these considerations, we hold that the State's interest in confining distribution, selling, and fund solicitation activities to fixed locations is sufficient to satisfy the requirement that a place or manner restriction must serve a substantial state interest. By focusing on the incidental effect of providing an exemption from Rule 6.05 to ISKCON, the Minnesota Supreme Court did not take into effect the fact that any such exemption cannot be meaningfully limited to ISKCON, and as applied to similarly situated groups would prevent the State from furthering its important concern with managing the flow of the crowd. In our view, the Society may apply its Rule and confine the type of transactions at issue to designated locations without violating the First Amendment.

For similar reasons, we cannot agree with the Minnesota Supreme Court that Rule 6.05 is an unnecessary regulation because the State could avoid the threat to its interest posed by ISKCON by less restrictive means, such as penalizing disorder or disruption, limiting the number of solicitors, or putting more narrowly drawn restrictions on the location and movement of ISKCON's representatives. As we have indicated, the inquiry must involve not only ISKCON, but also all other organizations that would be entitled to distribute, sell or solicit if the booth rule may not be enforced with respect to ISKCON. Looked at in this way, it is quite improbable that the alternative means suggested by the Minnesota Supreme Court would deal adequately with the problems posed by the much larger number of distributors and solicitors that would be present on the fairgrounds if the judgment below were affirmed.

For Rule 6.05 to be valid as a place and manner restriction, it must also be sufficiently clear that alternative forums for the expression of respondents' protected speech exist despite the effects of the Rule. Rule 6.05 is not vulnerable on this ground. First, the Rule does not prevent ISKCON from practicing Sankirtan anywhere outside the fairgrounds. More importantly, the Rule has not been shown to deny access within the forum in question. Here, the Rule does not exclude ISKCON from ⊥655 the fairgrounds, nor does it deny that organization the right to conduct any desired activity at some point within the forum. Its members may mingle with the crowd and orally propagate their views. The organization may also arrange for a booth and distribute and sell literature and solicit funds from that location on the fairgrounds itself. The Minnesota State Fair is a limited public forum in that it exists to provide a means for a great number of exhibitors temporarily to present their products or views, be they commercial, religious, or political, to a large number of people in an efficient fashion. Considering the limited functions of the Fair and the combined area within which it operates, we are unwilling to say that Rule 6.05 does not provide ISKCON and other organizations with an adequate means to sell and solicit on the fairgrounds. The First Amendment protects the right of every citizen to "reach the minds of willing listeners and to do so there must be opportunity to win their attention." *Kovacs* v. *Cooper*. Rule 6.05 does not unnecessarily limit that right within the fairgrounds.

⊥656 The judgment of the Supreme Court of Minnesota is reversed and the case is remanded for further proceedings not inconsistent with this opinion.

So ordered.

Justice BRENNAN, with whom *Justice* MARSHALL and *Justice* STEVENS join, concurring in part and dissenting in part.

As the Court recognizes, the issue in this case is whether Minnesota State Fair Rule 6.05 constitutes a reasonable time, place, and manner restriction on respondents' exercise of protected First Amendment rights. See *Schad* v. *Borough of Mt. Ephraim*; *Grayned* v. *City of Rockford*. In deciding this issue, the Court considers, *inter alia*, whether the regulation serves a significant governmental interest and whether that interest can be served by a less intrusive restriction. The Court errs, however, in failing to apply its analysis separately to each of the protected First Amendment activities restricted by Rule 6.05. Thus, the Court fails to recognize that some of the State's restrictions may be reasonable while others may not.

Rule 6.05 restricts three types of protected First Amendment activity: distribution of literature, sale of literature, and solicitation of funds. See *Village of Schaumburg* v. *Citizens for a Better Environment*; *Murdock* v. *Pennsylvania*; *Jamison* v. *Texas*; *Schneider* v. *State*; *Lovell* v. *City of Griffin*. No individual or group is permitted to engage in these activities at the Minnesota State Fair except from preassigned, rented booth locations. Violation of this rule constitutes a misdemeanor, and violators are subject to arrest and expulsion from the fairgrounds.

The State advances three justifications for its booth rule. The justification relied upon by the Court today is the State's ⊥657 interest in maintaining the orderly movement of the crowds at the fair. The second justification, relied upon by the dissenting Justices below, is the State's interest in protecting its fairgoers from fraudulent, deceptive, and misleading solicitation practices. The third justification, based on the "captive audience" doctrine, is the State's interest in protecting its fairgoers from annoyance and harassment.

I quite agree with the Court that the State has a significant interest in maintaining crowd control on its fairgrounds. See *Grayned* v. *City of Rockford*; *Cox* v. *New Hampshire*. I also have no doubt that the State has a significant interest in protecting its fairgoers from fraudulent or deceptive solicitation practices. See *Village of Schaumburg* v. *Citizens for a Better Environment*; *Virginia State Bd. of Pharmacy* v. *Virginia Citizens Consumer Council*. Indeed, because I believe on this record that this latter interest is substantially furthered by a Rule that restricts sales and solicitation activities to fixed booth locations, where the State will have the greatest opportunity to police and prevent possible deceptive practices, I would hold that Rule 6.05's restriction on those particular forms of First Amendment expression is justified as an anti-fraud measure. Accordingly, I join the judgment of the Court insofar as it upholds Rule 6.05's restriction on sales and solicitations. However, because I believe that the booth rule is an overly intrusive means of achieving the State's interest in crowd control, and because I cannot accept the validity of the State's third asserted justification, I dissent from the Court's approval of Rule 6.05's restriction on the distribution of literature.

⊥658 As our cases have long noted, once a governmental regulation is shown to impinge upon basic First Amendment rights, the burden falls on the government to show the validity of its asserted interest and the absence of less intrusive alternatives. See, *e.g.*, *Schneider* v. *State*. The challenged "regulation must be narrowly tailored to further the State's legitimate interest." *Grayned* v. *City of Rockford*. Minnesota's Rule 6.05 does not meet this test.

The Minnesota State Fair is an annual 12-day festival of people and ideas. Located on permanent fairgrounds comprising approximately 125 acres, the fair attracts an average of 115,000 visitors on weekdays and 160,000 on Saturdays and Sundays. Once the fairgoers pay their admission fees, they are permitted to roam the fairgrounds at will, visiting booths, meeting friends, or just milling about. Significantly, each and every fairgoer, whether political candidate, concerned citizen, or member of a religious group, is free to give speeches, engage in face-to-face advocacy, campaign, or proselytize. No restrictions are placed on any fairgoer's right to speak at any time, at any place, or to any person. Thus, if on a given day 5,000 members of ISKCON came to the fair and paid their admission fees, all 5,000 would be permitted to wander throughout the fairgrounds, delivering speeches to ⊥659 whomever they wanted, about whatever they wanted. Moreover, because this right does not rest on Sankirtan or any other religious principle, it can be exercised by every political candidate, partisan advocate, and common citizen who has paid the price of admission. All share the identical **⊥660** right to move peripatetically and speak freely throughout the fairgrounds.

Because of Rule 6.05, however, as soon as a proselytizing member of ISKCON hands out a free copy of the Bhagavad-Gita to an interested listener, or a political candidate distributes his campaign brochure to a potential voter, he becomes subject to arrest and removal from the fairgrounds. This constitutes a significant restriction on First Amendment rights. By prohibiting distribution of literature outside the booths, the fair officials sharply limit the number of fairgoers to whom the proselytizers and candidates can communicate their messages . Only if a fairgoer affirmatively seeks out such information by approaching a booth does Rule 6.05 fully permit potential communicators to exercise their First Amendment rights.

In support of its crowd control justification, the State contends that if fairgoers are permitted to distribute literature, large crowds will gather, blocking traffic lanes and causing safety problems. As counsel for the State asserted at oral argument: "it seems to me that if you had [distribution] activity going on with not just the Krishnas but 10 or 20 or 30 representatives from perhaps 30 to 60 or 70 groups, that inevitably is going to draw more attention and going to cause or create more or less moving pockets or moving congested crowds. . . . If all of a sudden the crowd becomes aware of the fact that dozens of people are walking around passing out materials and they're going to **⊥661** inevitably be attracted by that. Whereas, they wouldn't be if people were just talking."

But the State has failed to provide any support for these assertions. It has made no showing that relaxation of its booth rule would create additional disorder in a fair that is already characterized by the robust and unrestrained participation of hundreds of thousands of wandering fairgoers. See *ISKCON* v. *Barber*. If fairgoers can make speeches, engage in face-to-face proselytizing, and buttonhole prospective supporters, they can surely distribute literature to members of their audience without significantly adding to the State's asserted crowd control problem. Cf. *Martin* v. *City of Struthers* (Murphy, J. concurring) (invalidating ordinance that banned house-to-house distribution of handbills but did not ban house-to-house proselytizing). The record is devoid of any evidence that the 125-acre fairgrounds could not accommodate peripatetic distributors of literature just as easily as it now accommodates peripatetic speechmakers and proselytizers.

⊥662 Relying on a general, speculative fear of disorder, the State of Minnesota has placed a significant restriction on respondents' ability to exercise core First Amendment rights. This restriction is not narrowly drawn to advance the State's interests, and for that reason is unconstitutional. "[U]ndifferentiated fear or apprehension of disturbance is not enough to overcome the right to freedom of expression." *Tinker* v. *Des Moines Ind. Comm. School Dist.* If the State had a reasonable concern that distribution in certain parts of the fairgrounds—for example, entrances and exits—would cause disorder, it could have drafted its rule to prohibit distribution of literature at those points. If the State felt it necessary to limit the number of persons distributing an organization's literature, it could, within reason, have done that as well. It had no right, however, to ban all distribution of literature outside the booths. A State "may serve its legitimate interests, but it must do so by narrowly drawn regulations designed to serve those **⊥663** interests without unnecessarily interfering with First Amendment freedoms. . . . 'Broad prophylactic rules in the area of free expression are suspect. Precision of regulation must be the touchstone. . . .'" *Village of Schaumburg* v. *Citizens for a Better Environment*, quoting *NAACP* v. *Button*. Accord, *Grayned* v. *City of Rockford*.

Because I believe that the State could have drafted a more narrowly-drawn restriction on the right to distribute literature without undermining its interest in maintaining crowd control on the fairgrounds, I would affirm that part of the judgment below that strikes down Rule 6.05 as it applies to distribution of literature.

Justice BLACKMUN, concurring in part and dissenting in part.

For the reasons stated by *Justice* BRENNAN, I believe that Minnesota State Fair Rule 6.05 is unconstitutional as applied to the distribution of literature. I also agree, however, that the Rule is *constitutional* as applied to the sale of literature and the solicitation of funds. I reach this latter conclusion by a different route than does *Justice* BRENNAN for I am not persuaded that, under the Court's precedents, the State's interest in protecting fairgoers from fraudulent solicitation **⊥664** or sales practices justifies Rule 6.05's restrictions of those activities.

In *Village of Schaumburg* v. *Citizens for a Better Environment* the Court stressed that a community's interest in preventing fraudulent solicitations must be met by narrowly drawn regulations that do not unnecessarily interfere with First Amendment freedoms. It there held that possibility of fraud in "door-to-door" or "on-street" solicitations could be countered "by measures less intrusive than a direct prohibition on solicitation," such as disclosure provisions and penal laws prohibiting fraudulent misrepresentations. I see no reason why the same considerations are not applicable here. There is nothing in this record to suggest that it is more difficult to police fairgrounds for fraudulent solicitations than it is to police an entire community's streets; just as fraudulent solicitors may "melt into a crowd" at the fair, so also may door-to-door solicitors quickly move on after consummating several transactions in a particular neighborhood. Indeed, since respondents have offered to wear identifying tags and since the fairgrounds are an enclosed area, it is at least arguable that it is easier to police the fairgrounds than a community's streets.

Nonetheless, I believe that the State's substantial interest in maintaining crowd control and safety on the fairgrounds does justify Rule 6.05's restriction on solicitation and sales activities not conducted from a booth. As the Court points out, "[t]he flow of the crowd and demands of ⊥**665** safety are more pressing in the context of the Fair" than in the context of a typical street. While I agree with *Justice BRENNAN* that the State's interest in order does not justify restrictions upon distribution of literature, I think that common-sense differences between literature distribution, on the one hand, and solicitation and sales, on the other, suggest that the latter activities present greater crowd control problems than the former. The distribution of literature does not require that the recipient stop in order to receive the message the speaker wishes to convey; instead, the recipient is free to read the message at a later time. For this reason, literature distribution may present even fewer crowd control problems than the oral proselytizing that the State already allows upon the fairgrounds. In contrast, as the dissent in the Minnesota Supreme Court observed, sales and the collection of solicited funds not only require the fairgoer to stop, but also "engender additional confusion . . . because they involve acts of exchanging articles for money, fumbling for and dropping money, making change, etc." Rules restricting the exchange of money to booths have been upheld in analogous contexts, see *e.g.*, *International Society for Krishna Consciousness* v. *Eaves* (Atlanta airports), and for similar reasons I would uphold Rule 6.05 insofar as it applies to solicitation and sales.

APPENDIX A

A Bill for Establishing Religious Freedom*

[Jefferson presented this bill to the Virginia Assembly in June 1779. It was adopted by the Assembly in 1785 and became law 16 January 1786.]

Well aware that the opinions and belief of men depend not on their own will, but follow involuntarily the evidence proposed to their own minds; that Almighty God hath created the mind free, and manifested his supreme will that free it shall remain by making it altogether insusceptible of restraint; that all attempts to influence it by temporal punishments, or burthens, or by civil incapacitations, tend only to beget habits of hypocrisy and meanness, and are a departure from the plan of the holy author of our religion, who being lord both of body and mind, yet chose not to propagate it by coercions on either, as was in his Almighty power to do, but to extend it by its influence on reason alone; that the impious presumption of legislators and rulers, civil as well as ecclesiastical, who, being themselves but fallible and uninspired men, have assumed dominion over the faith of others, setting up their own opinions and modes of thinking as the only true and infallible, and as such endeavoring to impose them on others, hath established and maintained false religions over the greatest part of the world and through all time: That to compel a man to furnish contributions of money for the propagation of opinions which he disbelieves and abhors, is sinful and tyrannical; that even the forcing him to support this or that teacher of his own religious persuasion, is depriving him of the comfortable liberty of giving his contributions to the particular pastor whose morals he would make his pattern, and whose powers he feels most persuasive to righteousness; and is withdrawing from the ministry those temporary rewards, which proceeding from an approbation of their personal conduct, are an additional incitement to earnest and unremitting labours for the instruction of mankind; that our civil rights have no dependance on our religious opinions, any more than our opinions in physics or geometry; that therefore the proscribing any citizen as unworthy the public confidence by laying upon him an incapacity of being called to offices of trust and emolument, unless he profess or renounce this or that religious opinion, is depriving him injuriously of those privileges and advantages to which, in common with his fellow citizens, he has a natural right; that it tends also to corrupt the principles of that very religion it is meant to encourage, by bribing, with a monopoly of worldly honours and emoluments, those who will externally profess and conform to it; that though indeed these are criminal who do not withstand such temptation, yet neither are those innocent who lay the bait in their way; that the opinions of men are not the object of civil government, nor under its jurisdiction; that to suffer the civil magistrate to intrude his powers into the field of opinion and to restrain the profession or propagation of principles on supposition of their ill tendency is a dangerous falacy, which at once destroys all religious liberty, because he being of course judge of that tendency will make his opinions the rule of judgment, and approve or condemn the sentiments of others only as they shall square with or differ from his own; that it is time enough for the rightful purposes of civil government for its officers to interfere when principles break out into overt acts against peace and good order; and finally, that truth is great and will prevail if left to herself; that she is the proper and sufficient antagonist to error, and has nothing to fear from the conflict unless by human interposition disarmed of her natural weapons, free argument and debate; errors ceasing to be dangerous when it is permitted freely to contradict them.

We the General Assembly of Virginia do enact that no man shall be compelled to frequent or support any religious worship, place, or ministry whatsoever, nor shall be enforced, restrained, molested, or burthened in his body or goods, nor shall otherwise suffer, on account of his religious opinions or belief; but that all men shall be free to profess, and by argument to maintain, their opinions in matters of religion, and that the same shall in no wise diminish, enlarge, or affect their civil capacities.

And though we well know that this Assembly, elected by the people for the ordinary purposes of

*From *The Papers of Thomas Jefferson*, ed. Julian P. Boyd (Princeton, N.J.: Princeton University Press, 1950-) 2: 545-46. Reprinted by permission of Princeton University Press.

legislation only, have no power to restrain the acts of succeeding Assemblies, constituted with powers equal to our own, and that therefore to declare this act irrevocable would be of no effect in law; yet we are free to declare, and do declare, that the rights hereby asserted are of the natural rights of mankind, and that if any act shall be hereafter passed to repeal the present or to narrow its operation, such act will be an infringement of natural right.

APPENDIX B

A Memorial and Remonstrance Against Religious Assessments*

1785

[This memorial, written by James Madison, was instrumental in the defeat of a proposal in the Virginia House of Delegates to provide assessments to be used for the teaching of religion.]

To the Honorable the General Assembly of the Commonwealth of Virginia
A Memorial and Remonstrance

We the subscribers, citizens of the said Commonwealth, having taken into serious consideration, a Bill printed by order of the last Session of General Assembly, entitled "A Bill establishing a provision for Teachers of the Christian Religion," and conceiving that the same if finally armed with the sanctions of a law, will be a dangerous abuse of power, are bound as faithful members of a free State to remonstrate against it, and to declare the reasons by which we are determined. We remonstrate against the said Bill,

1. Because we hold it for a fundamental and undeniable truth, "that Religion or the duty which we owe to our Creator and the manner of discharging it, can be directed only by reason and conviction, not by force or violence." The Religion then of every man must be left to the conviction and conscience of every man; and it is the right of every man to exercise it as these may dictate. This right is in its nature an unalienable right. It is unalienable, because the opinions of men, depending only on the evidence contemplated by their own minds cannot follow the dictates of other men: It is unalienable also, because what is here a right towards men, is a duty towards the Creator. It is the duty of every man to render to the Creator such homage and such only as he believes to be acceptable to him. This duty is precedent, both in order of time and in degree of obligation, to the claims of Civil Society. Before any man can be considered as a member of Civil Society, he must be considered as a subject of the Governour of the Universe: And if a member of Civil Society, who enters into any subordinate Association, must always do it with a reservation of his duty to the General Authority; much more must every man who becomes a member of any particular Civil Society, do it with a saving of his allegiance to the Universal Sovereign. We maintain therefore that in matters of Religion, no man's right is abridged by the institution of Civil Society and that Religion is wholly exempt from its cognizance. True it is, that no other rule exists, by which any question which may divide a Society, can be ultimately determined, but the will of the majority; but it is also true that the majority may trespass on the rights of the minority.

2. Because if Religion be exempt from the authority of the Society at large, still less can it be subject to that of the Legislative Body. The latter are but the creatures and viceregents of the former. Their jurisdiction is both derivative and limited: it is limited with regard to the co-ordinate departments, more necessarily is it limited with regard to the constituents. The preservation of a free Government requires not merely that the metes and bounds which separate each department of power be invariably maintained; but more especially that neither of them be suffered to overleap the great Barrier which defends the rights of the people. The Rulers who are guilty of such an encroachment exceed the commission from which they derive their authority, and are Tyrants. The People who submit to it are governed by laws made neither by themselves nor by an authority derived from them, and are slaves.

3. Because it is proper to take alarm at the first experiment on our liberties. We hold this prudent jealousy to be the first duty of Citizens, and one of the noblest characteristics of the late Revolution. The free men of America did not wait till usurped power had strengthened itself by exercise, and entangled the question in precedents. They saw all the consequences in the principle, and they avoided the consequences by denying the principle. We revere this lesson too much soon to forget it. Who does not see that the same authority which can establish Christianity, in exclusion of all other Religions, may establish with the same ease any particular sect of Christians, in exclusion of all other Sects? that the same authority which can force a citizen to contribute

*From *The Papers of James Madison*, eds. William T. Hutchinson and William M. E. Rachal (Chicago: University of Chicago Press, 1962-) 8: 298-304.

three pence only of his property for the support of any one establishment, may force him to conform to any other establishment in all cases whatsoever?

4. Because the Bill violates that equality which ought to be the basis of every law, and which is more indispensible, in proportion as the validity or expediency of any law is more liable to be impeached. If "all men are by nature equally free and independent," all men are to be considered as entering into Society on equal conditions; as relinquishing no more, and therefore retaining no less, one than another, of their natural rights. Above all are they to be considered as retaining an "*equal* title to the free exercise of Religion according to the dictates of Conscience." Whilst we assert for ourselves a freedom to embrace, to profess and to observe the Religion which we believe to be of divine origin, we cannot deny an equal freedom to those whose minds have not yet yielded to the evidence which has convinced us. If this freedom be abused, it is an offence against God, not against man: To God, therefore, not to man, must an account of it be rendered. As the Bill violates equality by subjecting some to peculiar burdens, so it violates the same principle, by granting to others peculiar exemptions. Are the Quakers and Menonists the only sects who think a compulsive support of their Religions unnecessary and unwarrantable? Can their piety alone be entrusted with the care of public worship? Ought their Religions to be endowed above all others with extraordinary privileges by which proselytes may be enticed from all others? We think too favorably of the justice and good sense of these denominations to believe that they either covet pre-eminences over their fellow citizens or that they will be seduced by them from the common opposition to the measure.

5. Because the Bill implies either that the Civil Magistrate is a competent Judge of Religious Truth; or that he may employ Religion as an engine of Civil policy. The first is an arrogant pretension falsified by the contradictory opinions of Rulers in all ages, and throughout the world: the second an unhallowed perversion of the means of salvation.

6. Because the establishment proposed by the Bill is not requisite for the support of the Christian Religion. To say that it is, is a contradiction to the Christian Religion itself, for every page of it disavows a dependence on the powers of this world: it is a contradiction to fact; for it is known that this Religion both existed and flourished, not only without the support of human laws, but in spite of every opposition from them, and not only during the period of miraculous aid, but long after it had been left to its own evidence and the ordinary care of Providence. Nay, it is a contradiction in terms; for a Religion not invented by human policy, must have pre-existed and been supported, before it was established by human policy. It is moreover to weaken in those who profess this Religion a pious confidence in its innate excellence and the patronage of its Author; and to foster in those who still reject it, a suspicion that its friends are too conscious of its fallacies to trust it to its own merits.

7. Because experience witnesseth that ecclesiastical establishments, instead of maintaining the purity and efficacy of Religion, have had a contrary operation. During almost fifteen centuries has the legal establishment of Christianity been on trial. What have been its fruits? More or less in all places, pride and indolence in the Clergy, ignorance and servility in the laity, in both, superstition, bigotry and persecution. Enquire of the Teachers of Christianity for the ages in which it appeared in its greatest lustre; those of every sect point to the ages prior to its incorporation with Civil policy. Propose a restoration of this primitive State in which its Teachers depended on the voluntary rewards of their flocks; many of them predict its downfall. On which Side ought their testimony to have greatest weight, when for or when against their interest?

8. Because the establishment in question is not necessary for the support of the Civil Government. If it be urged as necessary for the support of Civil Government only as it is a means of supporting Religion, and it be not necessary for the latter purpose, it cannot be necessary for the former. If Religion be not within the cognizance of Civil Government how can its legal establishment be necessary to Civil Government? What influence in fact have ecclesiastical establishments had on Civil Society? In some instances they have been seen to erect a spiritual tyranny on the ruins of the Civil authority; in many instances they have been seen upholding the thrones of political tyranny: in no instance have they been seen the guardians of the liberties of the people. Rulers who wished to subvert the public liberty, may have found an established Clergy convenient auxiliaries. A just Government, instituted to secure & perpetuate it, needs them not. Such a Government will be best supported by protecting every Citizen in the enjoyment of his Religion with the same equal hand which protects his person and his property; by neither invading the equal rights of any Sect, nor suffering any Sect to invade those of another.

9. Because the proposed establishment is a departure from that generous policy, which, offering an Asylum to the persecuted and oppressed of every Nation and Religion, promised a lustre to our country, and an accession to the number of its citizens. What a melancholy mark is the Bill of sudden degeneracy? Instead of holding forth an Asylum to the persecuted, it is itself a signal of persecution. It degrades from the equal rank of Citizens all those whose opinions in Religion do not bend to those of the Legislative authority. Distant as it may be in its present form from the Inquisition, it differs from it only in degree. The one is the first step, the other the last in the career of intolerance. The magnanimous sufferer under this cruel

scourge in foreign Regions, must view the Bill as a Beacon on our Coast, warning him to seek some other haven, where liberty and philanthrophy in their due extent, may offer a more certain repose from his Troubles.

10. Because it will have a like tendency to banish our Citizens. The allurements presented by other situations are every day thinning their number. To superadd a fresh motive to emigration by revoking the liberty which they now enjoy, would be the same species of folly which has dishonoured and depopulated flourishing kingdoms.

11. Because it will destroy that moderation and harmony which the forbearance of our laws to intermeddle with Religion has produced among its several sects. Torrents of blood have been spilt in the old world, by vain attempts of the secular arm, to extinguish Religious discord, by proscribing all difference in Religious opinion. Time has at length revealed the true remedy. Every relaxation of narrow and rigorous policy, wherever it has been tried, has been found to assuage the disease. The American Theatre has exhibited proofs that equal and compleat liberty, if it does not wholly eradicate it, sufficiently destroys its malignant influence on the health and prosperity of the State. If with the salutary effects of this system under our own eyes, we begin to contract the bounds of Religious freedom, we know no name that will too severely reproach our folly. At least let warning be taken at the first fruits of the threatened innovation. The very appearance of the Bill has transformed "that Christian forbearance, love and charity," which of late mutually prevailed, into animosities and jealousies, which may not soon be appeased. What mischiefs may not be dreaded, should this enemy to the public quiet be armed with the force of a law?

12. Because the policy of the Bill is adverse to the diffusion of the light of Christianity. The first wish of those who enjoy this precious gift ought to be that it may be imparted to the whole race of mankind. Compare the number of those who have as yet received it with the number still remaining under the dominion of false Religions; and how small is the former! Does the policy of the Bill tend to lessen the disproportion? No; it at once discourages those who are strangers to the light of revelation from coming into the Region of it; and countenances by example the nations who continue in darkness, in shutting out those who might convey it to them. Instead of Levelling as far as possible, every obstacle to the victorious progress of Truth, the Bill with an ignoble and unchristian timidity would circumscribe it with a wall of defence against the encroachments of error.

13. Because attempts to enforce by legal sanctions, acts obnoxious to so great a proportion of Citizens, tend to enervate the laws in general, and to slacken the bands of Society. If it be difficult to execute any law which is not generally deemed necessary or salutary, what must be the case, where it is deemed invalid and dangerous? And what may be the effect of so striking an example of impotency in the Government, on its general authority?

14. Because a measure of such singular magnitude and delicacy ought not to be imposed, without the clearest evidence that it is called for by a majority of citizens, and no satisfactory method is yet proposed by which the voice of the majority in this case may be determined, or its influence secured. "The people of the respective counties are indeed requested to signify their opinion respecting the adoption of the Bill to the next Session of Assembly." But the representation must be made equal, before the voice either of the Representatives or of the Counties will be that of the people. Our hope is that neither of the former will, after due consideration, espouse the dangerous principle of the Bill. Should the event disappoint us, it will still leave us in full confidence, that a fair appeal to the latter will reverse the sentence against our liberties.

15. Because finally, "the equal right of every citizen to the free exercise of his Religion according to the dictates of conscience" is held by the same tenure with all our other rights. If we recur to its origin, it is equally the gift of nature; if we weigh its importance, it cannot be less dear to us; if we consult the "Declaration of those rights which pertain to the good people of Virginia, as the basis and foundation of Government," it is enumerated with equal solemnity, or rather studied emphasis. Either then, we must say, that the Will of the Legislature is the only measure of their authority; and that in the plenitude of this authority, they may sweep away all our fundamental rights; or, that they are bound to leave this particular right untouched and sacred: Either we must say, that they may control the freedom of the press, may abolish the Trial by jury, may swallow up the Executive and judiciary Powers of the State; nay that they may despoil us of our very right of suffrage, and erect themselves into an independent and hereditary Assembly or, we must say, that they have no authority to enact into law the Bill under consideration. We the Subscribers say, that the General Assembly of this Commonwealth have no such authority: And that no effort may be omitted on our part against so dangerous an usurpation, we oppose to it, this remonstrance; earnestly praying, as we are in duty bound, that the Supreme Lawgiver of the Universe, by illuminating those to whom it is addressed, may on the one hand, turn their Councils from every act which would affront his holy prerogative, or violate the trust committed to them: and on the other, guide them into every measure which may be worthy of his blessing, may redound to their own praise, and may establish more firmly the liberties, the prosperity and the happiness of the Commonwealth.

APPENDIX C

Religious Freedom Restoration Act

42 U.S.C. §§ 2000bb—2000bb-4 (Supp. V 1993).

This Act may be cited as the "Religious Freedom Restoration Act of 1993."

§ 2000bb. Congressional findings and declaration of purposes

(a) Findings

The Congress finds that—

(1) the framers of the Constitution, recognizing free exercise of religion as an unalienable right, secured its protection in the First Amendment to the Constitution;

(2) laws "neutral" toward religion may burden religious exercise as surely as laws intended to interfere with religious exercise;

(3) governments should not substantially burden religious exercise without compelling justification;

(4) in Employment Division v. Smith, 494 U.S. 872 (1990) the Supreme Court virtually eliminated the requirement that the government justify burdens on religious exercise imposed by laws neutral toward religion; and

(5) the compelling interest test as set forth in prior Federal court rulings is a workable test for striking sensible balances between religious liberty and competing prior governmental interests.

(b) Purposes

The purposes of this chapter are—

(1) to restore the compelling interest test as set forth in Sherbert v. Verner, 374 U.S. 398 (1963) and Wisconsin v. Yoder, 406 U.S. 205 (1972) and to guarantee its application in all cases where free exercise of religion is substantially burdened; and

(2) to provide a claim or defense to persons whose religious exercise is substantially burdened by government.

§ 2000bb-1. Free exercise of religion protected

(a) In General

Government shall not substantially burden a person's exercise of religion even if the burden results from a rule of general applicability, except as provided in subsection (b) of this section.

(b) Exception

Government may substantially burden a person's exercise of religion only if it demonstrates that application of the burden to the person—

(1) is in furtherance of a compelling governmental interest; and

(2) is the least restrictive means of furthering that compelling governmental interest.

(c) Judicial Relief

A person whose religious exercise has been burdened in violation of this section may assert that violation as a claim or defense in a judicial proceeding and obtain appropriate relief against a government. Standing to assert a claim or defense under this section shall be governed by the general rules of standing under article III of the Constitution.

§ 2000bb-2. Definitions

As used in this chapter—

(1) the term "government" includes a branch, department, agency, instrumentality, and official (or other person acting under color of law) of the United States, a State, or a subdivision of a State;

(2) the term "State" includes the District of Columbia, the Commonwealth of Puerto Rico, and each territory and possession of the United States;

(3) the term "demonstrates" means meets the burdens of going forward with the evidence and of persuasion; and

(4) the term "exercise of religion" means the exercise of religion under the First Amendment to the Constitution.

§ 2000-3. Applicability

(a) In General

This chapter applies to all Federal and State law, and the implementation of that law, whether statutory or otherwise, and whether adopted before or after November 16, 1993.

(b) Rule of Construction

Federal statutory law adopted after November 16, 1993, is subject to this chapter unless such law explicitly excludes such application by reference to this chapter.

(c) Religious Belief Unaffected

Nothing in this chapter shall be construed to authorize any government to burden any religious belief.

§ 2000bb-4. Establishment Clause Unaffected

Nothing in this chapter shall be construed to affect, interpret, or in any way address that portion of the First Amendment prohibiting laws respecting an establishment of religion (referred to in this section as the "Establishment Clause"). Granting government funding, benefits, or exemptions, to the extent permissible under the Establishment Clause, shall not constitute a violation of this chapter. As used in this section, the term "granting," used with respect to government funding, benefits, or exemptions, does not include the denial of government funding, benefits, or exemptions.

BIBLIOGRAPHY

BOOKS

Aaron, Henry J., Thomas E. Mann, and Timothy Taylor. *Values and Public Policy*. Washington, DC: Brookings Institution, 1994.

Abraham, Henry J. *Freedom and the Court: Civil Rights and Liberties in the United States*. 5th ed. New York: Oxford University Press, 1988.

____________. *The Judicial Process: An Introductory Analysis of the Courts of the United States, England, and France*. 5th ed. New York: Oxford University Press, 1986.

____________. *Justices and Presidents: A Political History of Appointments to the Supreme Court*. 2d ed. New York: Oxford University Press, 1985.

Adams, Arlin M. and Charles J. Emmerich. *A Nation Dedicated to Religious Liberty: The Constitutional Heritage of the Religion Clauses*. Philadelphia: University of Pennsylvania Press, 1990.

Adams, James L. *The Growing Church Lobby in Washington*. Grand Rapids, MI: William B. Eerdmans Publishing Co., 1970.

Ahlstrom, Sidney E. *A Religious History of the American People*. New Haven, CT: Yale University Press, 1973.

Albanese, Catherine L. *Sons of the Fathers: The Civil Religion of the American Revolution*. Philadelphia, PA: Temple University Press, 1976.

Alfs, Matthew.*The Evocative Religion of Jehovah's Witnesses*. Minneapolis, MN: Old Theology Book House, 1991.

Alley, Robert S., ed. *James Madison on Religious Liberty*. New York: Prometheus Books, 1985.

____________. *School Prayer: The Court, the Congress, and the First Amendment*. Buffalo, NY: Prometheus Books, 1994.

____________. *So Help Me God: Religion and the Presidency, Wilson to Nixon*. Richmond, VA: John Knox Press, 1972.

____________. *The Supreme Court on Church and State*. New York: Oxford University Press, 1988.

____________. *James Madison on Religious Liberty*. Buffalo, NY: Prometheus Books, 1989.

Allitt, Patrick. *Catholic Intellectuals and Conservative Politics in America: 1950-1985*. Ithaca, NY: Cornell University Press, 1993.

Allport, Gordon W. *The Individual and His Religion*. New York: The Macmillan Company, 1962.

American Association of School Administrators. *Religion in the Public Schools*. New York: Harper and Row, 1964.

Antieau, Chester J. *Freedom From Federal Establishment*. Milwaukee, WI: Bruce Publishing, 1964.

Arnold, O. Carroll. *Religious Freedom on Trial*. Valley Forge, PA: Judson Press, 1978.

Askew, Thomas A. and Peter W. Spellman. *The Churches and the American Experience: Ideals and Institutions*. Grand Rapids, MI: Baker Book House, 1984.

Atkins, Stanley and Theodore McConnell, eds. *Churches on the Wrong Road*. Lake Bluff, IL: Gateway Editions, 1986.

Auerbach, Jerold S. *Rabbis and Lawyers: The Journey from Torah to Constitution*. Bloomington: Indiana University Press, 1993.

Baker, John W., ed. *Taxation and the Free Exercise of Religion: Papers and Proceedings of the Sixteenth Religious Liberty Conference, Washington, D.C., October 3-5, 1977*. Washington, DC: Baptist Joint Committee on Public Affairs, 1978.

Balk, Alfred. *The Religion Business*. Richmond, VA: John Knox Press, 1968.

Ball, William Bentley, ed. *In Search of a National Morality: A Manifesto for Evangelicals and Catholics*. Grand Rapids: Ignatius Press, 1992.

Barker, Lucius J. and Twiley W. Barker, Jr., eds. *Civil Liberties and the Constitution: Cases and Commentaries*. Englewood Cliffs, NJ: Prentice-Hall, Inc., 1970.

Barker, Sir Ernest. *Church, State and Education*. Ann Arbor: University of Michigan Press, 1957.

Barr, David L. and Nicholas Piediscalzi, eds. *The Bible in American Education: From Source Book to Textbook*. Philadelphia: Fortress Press, 1982.

Barrett, Patricia. *Religious Liberty and the American Presidency: A Study in Church-State Relations*. New York: Herder and Herder, 1963.

Barron, Bruce. *Heaven on Earth? The Social and Political Agendas of Dominion Theology*. Grand Rapids, MI: Zondervan Publishing House, 1992.

Barth, Karl. *Community, State, and Church*. Garden City, NY: Doubleday & Co., 1960.

Bates, Stephen. *Battleground: One Mother's Crusade, the Religious Right, and the Struggle for Control of Our Classrooms*. New York: Poseidon Press, 1993.

Beach, Bert B. *Bright Candle of Courage*. Boise, ID: Pacific Press Publishing Association, 1989.

Becker, Theodore L. and Malcolm M. Feeley. *The Impact of Supreme Court Decisions*. New York: Oxford University Press, 1973.

Bellah, Robert N. *The Broken Covenant: American Civil Religion in Time of Trial*. New York: Seabury Press, 1975.

____________. and Phillip E. Hammond. *Varieties of Civil Religion*. New York: Harper & Row, 1980.

Benavides, Gustavo and M. W. Daly, eds. *Religion and Political Power*. Albany: State University of New York Press, 1989.

Benson, Peter L. and Dorothy L. Williams. *Religion on Capitol Hill: Myths and Realities*. San Francisco: Harper and Row, 1982.

Berger, Peter L. *The Noise of Solemn Assemblies: Christian Commitment and the Religious Establishment in America*. Garden City, NY: Doubleday & Co., 1961.

Berman, Harold J. *Faith and Order*. Atlanta, GA: Scholars Press, 1993.

____________. *The Interaction of Law and Religion*. Nashville, TN: Abingdon Press, 1974.

Berns, Walter. *The First Amendment and the Future of American Democracy*. New York: Basic Books, Inc., 1976.

Berra, Tim M. *Evolution and the Myth of Creationism: A Basic Guide to the Facts in the Evolution Debate*. Lexington: University of Kentucky Press, 1990.

Beth, Loren P. *The American Theory of Church and State*. Gainesville: University of Florida Press, 1958.

Blackwell, Victor V. *O'er the Ramparts They Watched*. New York: Carlton Press, 1976.

Blanchard, Paul. *Religion and the Schools: The Great Controversy*. Boston: Beacon Press, 1963.

Blau, Joseph L. *Cornerstones of Religious Freedom in America*. Rev. and enl. edition. New York: Harper and Brothers, 1964.

Blum, Virgil C. *Freedom in Education: Federal Aid for All Children*. Garden City, NY: Doubleday & Co., 1965.

Boles, Donald E. *The Bible, Religion, and the Public Schools*. Ames: Iowa State University Press, 1961, 1964.

____________. *The Two Swords: Commentaries and Cases in Religion and Education*. Ames: Iowa State University Press, 1967.

Borden, Morten. *Jews, Turks, and Infidels*. Chapel Hill: University of North Carolina Press, 1984.

Boyd, Julian P., ed. *The Papers of Thomas Jefferson*. 20 vols. Princeton: Princeton University Press, 1950- .

Bradley, Gerard V. *Church-State Relationships in America*. New York: Greenwood Press, 1987.

Bradley, Martha Sontagg. *Kidnapped from that Land: The Government Raids on the Short Creek Polygamists*. Salt Lake City: The University of Utah Press, 1993.

Brady, Joseph H. *Confusion Twice Confounded: The First Amendment and the Supreme Court*. South Orange, NJ: Seton Hall University Press, 1954.

Brauer, Jerald C., ed. *The Lively Experiment Continued*. Macon, GA: Mercer University Press, 1987.

____________, Sidney E. Mead, and Robert N. Bellah. *Religion and the American Revolution*. Philadelphia: Fortress Press, 1976.

Breslauer, S. Daniel. *Judaism and Civil Religion*. Atlanta, GA: Scholars Press, 1993.

Brickman, William and Stanley Lehrer, eds. *Religion, Government and Education*. New York: Society for the Advancement of Education, 1961.

Brock, Peter. *Pacifism in the United States: From the Colonial Era to the First World War*. Princeton, NJ: Princeton University Press, 1968.

Bromley, David G. and Anson Shupe, eds. *New Christian Politics*. Macon, GA: Mercer University Press, 1984.

____________ and ____________. *Strange Gods: The Great American Cult Scare*. Boston: Beacon Press, 1982.

Bromley, David G. and James T. Richardson, eds. *The Brainwashing/Deprogramming Controversy: Sociological, Psychological, Legal and Historical Perspectives*. Lewiston. NY: The Edwin Mellen Press, 1983.

Brown, Nicholas C., ed. *The Study of Religion in the Public Schools: An Appraisal*. Washington, DC: American Council on Education, 1958.

Brown, Robert McAfee. *Saying Yes and Saying No: On Rendering to God and Caesar*. Philadelphia: Westminster Press, 1986.

____________. *Liberation Theology: An Introductory Guide*. New York: Paulist Press, 1993.

Bruce, Steve. *The Rise and Fall of the New Christian Right: Conservative Protestant Politics in America, 1978-1988*. New York: Oxford University Press, 1990.

Bryk, Anthony S., Valerie E. Lee, and Peter B. Holland. *Catholic Schools and the Common Good*. Notre Dame, IN: University of Notre Dame, 1992.

Bryson, Joseph and Samuel H. Houston, Jr. *The Supreme Court and Public Funds for Religious Schools: The Burger Years, 1969-1986*. Jefferson, NC: McFarland and Company, Inc., 1990.

Buarnstein, Abraham. *Law Concerning Religion in the United States*. 2d ed. Dobbs Ferry, NY: Oceana Publications, 1966.

Butts, R. Freeman. *The American Tradition in Religion and Education*. Boston: Beacon Press, 1950.

Buzzard, Lynn R. and Samuel Ericsson. *The Battle for Religious Liberty*. Elgin, IL: David C. Cook Publishing Co., 1982.

Byrnes, Lawrence. *Religion and Public Education*. New York: Harper & Row, 1975.

Byrnes, Timothy and Mary C. Segers, eds. *The Catholic Church and the Politics of Abortion*. Boulder, CO: Westview Press, 1992.

Cady, Linell E. *Religion, Theology and American Public Life*. Albany: State University of New York Press, 1993.

Callahan, Daniel, ed. *Federal Aid and Catholic Schools*. Baltimore, MD: Helicon Press, 1964.

Capps, Walter H. *The New Religious Right: Piety, Patriotism, and Politics*. Columbia: University of South Carolina Press, 1990.

Carey, George W. and James V. Shall, eds. *Essays on Christianity and Political Philosophy*. Lanham, MD: University Press of America, 1984.

Carmody, Denise Lardner and John Tully Carmody. *The Republic of Many Mansions: Foundations of American Religious Thought*. New York: Paragon House, 1990.

Carper, James C. and Thomas C. Hunt. eds. *Religious Schooling in America*. Birmingham, AL: Religious Education Press, 1984.

Carter, Lief. *An Introduction to Constitutional Interpretation: Cases in Law and Religion*. New York: Longman, 1991.

Carter, Paul A., *Politics, Religion and Rockets*. Tucson: The University of Arizona Press, 1991.

Carter, Stephen L. *The Culture of Disbelief: How American Law and Politics Trivialize Religious Devotion*. New York: Basic Books, 1993.

Catterall, James S. *Tuition Tax Credits: Fact and Fiction*. Bloomington, IN: Phi Delta Kappa Education Foundation, 1983.

Chambers, Robert R. *Political Theory and Societal Ethics*. Buffalo, NY: Prometheus Books, 1992.

Chapman, Audrey R. *Faith, Power, and Politics: Political Ministry and Transformation in Mainline Churches*. New York: Pilgrim Press, 1991.

Cherry, Conrad, ed. *God's New Israel: Religious Interpretations of American Destiny*. Englewood Cliffs, NJ: Prentice-Hall, 1971.

Clayton, A. Stafford. *Religion and Schooling: A Comparative Study*. Waltham, MA: Blaisdell Publishing Co., 1969.

Clark, Stephen R. L. *God's World and the Great Awakening*. Oxford: Clarendon Press, 1991.

Cobb, Sanford H. *The Rise of Religious Liberty in America*. New York: Macmillan Co., 1902.

Cogdell, Gaston D. *What Price Parochiaid?* Washington, DC: Americans United for Separation of Church and State, 1970.

Cogley, John, ed. *Religion in America: Original Essays on Religion in a Free Society*. New York: Meridian Books, 1958.

Cohen, Richard. *Sunday in the Sixties*. New York: Public Affairs Committee, 1962.

Colombo, Furio. *God in America: Religion and Politics in the United States*. New York: Columbia University Press, 1984.

Conway, Flo and Jim Siegelman. *Holy Terror: The Fundamentalist War on America's Freedoms in Religion, Politics, and Our Private Lives*. Garden City, NY: Doubleday and Co., 1982.

Cord, Robert L. *Separation of Church and State: Historical Fact and Current Fiction*. New York: Lambeth Press, 1982.

Cornell, Julian. *The Conscientious Objector and the Law*. New York: John Day Co., 1943.

Costanzo, Joseph T., S.J. *This Nation Under God: Church, State and Schools in America*. New York: Herder and Herder, 1964.

Couser, Richard B. *Ministry and the American Legal System: A Guide for Clergy, Lay Workers and Congregations*. Minneapolis, MN: Fortress/Augsburg Press, 1993.

Cousins, Norman, ed., *'In God We Trust': The Religious Beliefs and Ideas of the American Founding Fathers*. New York: Harper and Row, 1958.

Coutin, Susan Bibler. *The Culture of Protest: Religious Activism and the U.S. Sanctuary Movement*. Boulder, CO: Westview Press, 1993.

Cox, Archibald. *The Role of the Supreme Court in American Government*. New York: Oxford University Press, 1976.

Craig, Robert H. *Religion and Radical Politics: An Alternative Christian Tradition in the United States*. Philadelphia, PA: Temple University Press, 1992.

Cromartie, Michael, ed. *No Longer Exiles: The Religious New Right in American Politics*. Washington, DC: Ethics and Public Policy Center, 1992.

Curry, Thomas J. *The First Freedoms: Church and State in America to the Passage of the First Amendment*. New York: Oxford University Press, 1985.

Davis, Derek. *Original Intent: Chief Justice Rehnquist and the Course of American Church-State Relations*. Buffalo, NY: Prometheus Books, 1991.

Dawson, Joseph M. *America's Way in Church, State, and Society*. New York: Macmillan Co., 1953.

____________. *Separate Church and State Now*. New York: Richard R. Smith, 1948.

Dierenfield, R. H. *Religion in American Public Schools*. Washington, DC: Public Affairs Press, 1962.

Doerr, Edd and Albert J. Menendez. *Church Schools and Public Money*. Buffalo, NY: Prometheus Books.

Dolbeare, Kenneth M. and Philip E. Hammond. *The School Prayer Decisions: From Court Policy to Local Practice.* Chicago: University of Chicago Press, 1971.

Dorsen, Norman. ed. *The Rights of Americans: What They Are and What They Should Be.* New York: Pantheon, 1971. (See article by Leo Pfeffer, "The Right to Religious Liberty," pp. 326-47.)

____________. *Religion, the Courts, and Public Policy.* New York: McGraw-Hill Book Co., 1963.

Douglas, William O. *The Bible and the Schools.* Boston: Little, Brown and Co., 1966.

Drakeman, Donald L. *Church-State Constitutional Issues: Making Sense of the Establishment Clause.* New York: Greenwood Press, 1991.

Drazin, Israel and Cecil B. Currey. *For God and Country: The History of a Constitutional Challenge to the Army Chaplaincy.* New York: KTAV, 1995.

Dreisbach, Daniel L. *Real Threat and Mere Shadow: Religious Liberty and the First Amendment.* Westchester, IL: Crossway Books, 1987.

Drinan, Robert F., S.J. *God and Caesar on the Potomac.* Wilmington, DE: Michael Glazier, Inc., 1986.

____________. *Religion, the Courts, and Public Policy.* New York: McGraw-Hill Book Co., 1963.

Duker, Sam. *The Public Schools and Religion: The Legal Context.* New York: Harper & Row, 1966.

Dutile, Fernand N., and Edward McGlynn Gaffney, Jr. *State and Campus: State Regulation of Religiously Affiliated Higher Education.* Notre Dame, IN: University of Notre Dame Press, 1984.

____________. *Stories from the American Soul: A Reader in Ethics and American Policy for the 1990s.* Chicago: Loyola University Press, 1990.

Eastland, Terry, ed. *Religious Liberty in the Supreme Court: The Cases That Define the Debate over Church and State.* Grand Rapids, MI: Wm. B. Eerdmans Publishing Co., 1995.

Ebersole, Luke Eugene. *Church Lobbying in the Nation's Capital.* New York: Macmillan Co., 1951.

Edwards, Newton. *The Courts and the Public Schools.* Chicago: University of Chicago Press, 1971.

Elliot, Jonathan, ed. *The Debates in the Several State Conventions on the Adoption of the Federal Constitution.* 2d ed., 5 vols. Philadelphia: J. P. Lippincott Company, 1891.

Ellison, Tamara. *Religion and the Public Schools: Guidelines for a Growing and Changing Phenomenon for K-12.* New York: Anti-Defamation League of B'nai B'rith, 1992.

Engel, David E. *Religion in Public Education.* New York: Paulist Press, 1974.

Erickson, Donald A., ed. *Public Controls for Nonpublic Schools.* Chicago: University of Chicago Press, 1969.

Ervin, Sam J., Jr. *Preserving the Constitution.* Charlottesville, VA: The Michie Co., 1985.

Esposito, John L. *The Islamic Threat: Myth or Reality?* New York: Oxford University Press, 1992.

Evans, J. Edward. *Freedom of Religion.* Minneapolis, MN: Lerner Publications, 1990.

Fackre, Gabriel. *The Religious Right and Christian Faith.* Grand Rapids, MI: Wm. B. Eerdmans Publishing Company, 1982.

Feldman, Egal. *Dual Destinies: The Jewish Encounter with Protestant America.* Chicago: University of Illinois Press, 1990.

Fellman, David. *Religion in American Public Law.* Boston: Boston University Press, 1974.

____________. ed. *The Supreme Court and Education.* New York: Columbia University Press, 1969.

Fenwick, Lynda Beck. *Should the Children Pray?: A Historical, Judicial, and Political Examination of Public School Prayer.* Waco, TX: Baylor University Press, 1989.

Ferguson, Thomas P. *Catholic and American: The Political Theology of John Courtney Murray.* Kansas City, MO: Sheed and Ward, 1993.

Fetzer, Joel. *Selective Prosecution of Religiously Motivated Offenders in America: Scrutinizing the Myth of Neutrality.* Lewiston, ME: Edwin Mellen Press, 1989.

Finn, James D., ed. *A Conflict of Loyalties: The Case for Selective Conscientious Objection.* New York: Pegasus, 1968.

Finke, Roger and Rodney Starke. *The Churching of America, 1776-1990: Winners and Losers in Our Religious Economy.* New Brunswick, NJ: Rutgers University Press, 1992.

Fisher, Wallace E. *Politics, Poker and Piety: A Perspective on Cultural Religion in America.* Nashville: Abingdon Press, 1972.

Flowers, Ronald B. *Religion in Strange Times: The 1960s and 1970s.* Macon, GA: Mercer University Press, 1984.

____________. *That Godless Court?: Supreme Court Decisions on Church-State Relationships.* Louisville, KY: Westminster/John Knox Press, 1995.

Forcinelli, Joseph. *The Democratization of Religion in America: A Commonwealth of Religious Freedom by Design.* Lewiston, ME: Edwin Mellen Press, 1990.

Forell, George W. and William H. Lazareth. *God's Call to Public Responsibility.* Philadelphia, PA: Fortress Press, 1978.

Fowler, Robert Booth. *A New Engagement: Evangelical Political Thought, 1966-1976.* Grand Rapids, MI: Wm. B. Eerdmans Publishing Co., 1982.

____________. *Religion and Politics in America.* Metuchen, NJ: Scarecrow Press, 1986.

Frankel, Marvin E. *Faith and Freedom.* New York: Hill and Wang, 1994.

Freund, Paul A. and Robert Ulich. *Religion and the Public Schools.* Cambridge, MA: Harvard University Press, 1965.

Friedman, Murray. *The Utopian Dilemma: American Judaism and Public Policy.* Washington, DC: Ethics and Public Policy Center, 1985.

Frommer, Arthur, ed. *The Bible and the Public Schools.* New York: Liberal Arts Press, 1963.

Frost, J. William. *A Perfect Freedom: Religious Liberty in Pennsylvania.* Westport, CT: Greenwood, 1990.

Gaffney, Edward McGlynn, Jr. *Private Schools and the Public Good: Policy Alternatives for the Eighties.* Notre Dame, IN: University of Notre Dame Press, 1981.

____________. and Philip R. Motts. *Government and Campus: Federal Regulation of Religiously Affiliated Higher Education.* Notre Dame, IN: University of Notre Dame Press, 1982.

____________. and Philip C. Sorensen. *Ascending Liability in Religious and Other Nonprofit Organizations.* Macon, GA: Mercer University Press, 1984.

Gaustad, Edwin Scott. *Dissent in American Religion.* Chicago: University of Chicago Press, 1973.

____________. *Faith of Our Fathers: Religion and the New Nation.* San Francisco: Harper and Row, 1987.

____________. *Liberty of Conscience: Roger Williams in America.* Grand Rapids, MI: Wm. B. Eerdmans Publishing Co., 1995.

____________. *Religious Issues in American History.* New York: Harper & Row, 1968.

Gedicks, Federick Mark. *The Rhetoric of Church and State: A Critical Analysis of Religion Clause Jurisprudence.* Durham, NC: Duke University Press, 1995.

____________. and Roger Hendrix. *Choosing the Dream: The Future of Religion in American Public Life.* New York: Greenwood Press, 1991.

Geisler, Norman L., A.F. Brooke II, and Mark J. Keough. *The Creator in the Courtroom: "Scopes II."* Milford, MI: Mott Media, Inc., 1982.

Gellhorn, Walter and R. Kent Greenawalt. *The Sectarian College and the Public Press.* Dobbs Ferry, NY: Oceana, 1970.

Giannella, Donald A., ed. *Religion and the Public Order, No. 5.* Ithaca, NY: Cornell University Press, 1969.

Gibson, William. *Church, State, and Society.* New York: St. Martin's Press, 1992.

Gilkey, Langdon. *Creationism on Trial: Evolution and God at*

Little Rock. Minneapolis: Winston Press, 1985.

Ginsberg, Benjamin. *The Fatal Embrace: Jews and the State*. Chicago: University of Chicago Press, 1993.

Goldberg, George. *Reconsecrating America*. Grand Rapids, MI: Wm. B. Eerdmans Publishing Co., 1984.

Goldwin, Robert A., and Art Kaufman. *How Does the Constitution Protect Religious Freedom?* American Enterprise, 1988.

Gordis, Robert. *Religion and the Schools*. New York: Fund for the Republic, 1959.

Grant, Daniel R. *The Christian and Politics*. Nashville: Broadman Press, 1968.

Greenawalt, Kent. *Religious Convictions and Political Choice*. New York: Oxford University Press, 1988.

Greene, Evarts B. *Religion and the State: The Making and Testing of an American Tradition*. Ithaca, NY: Cornell University Press, 1959.

Griffith, Carol Friedley. *Christianity and Politics: Catholic and Protestant Perspectives*. Washington, DC: Ethics and Public Policy Center. 1981.

Griffiths, William E. *Religion, the Courts, and the Public Schools: A Century of Litigation*. Cincinnati: W. H. Anderson Company, 1966.

Groh, John E. *Facilitators of the Free Exercise of Religion: Air Force Chaplains, 1981-1990*. Washington, DC: Office of the Chief of Chaplains, USAF, 1991.

Guinness, Os. *The American Hour: A Time of Reckoning and the Once and Future Role of Faith*. New York: The Free Press, 1993.

Haddon, Jeffrey K. and Anson Shupe, eds. *Prophetic Religions and Politics: Religion and the Political Order*. New York: Paragon House Publishers, 1986.

Hammar, Richard R. *Pastor, Church and Law*. 2nd edition. Matthews, NC: Christian Ministry Resources, 1991.

Hammond, Phillip E. *Religion and Personal Autonomy: The Third Disestablishment in America*. Columbia, SC: University of South Carolina Press, 1992.

Handy, Robert T. *A Christian America: Protestant Hopes and Historical Realities*. 2d ed. Oxford: Oxford University Press, 1984.

__________. *Undermined Establishment: Church-State Relations in America, 1880-1920*. Princeton, NJ: Princeton University Press, 1991.

Hansen, Klaus J. *Mormonism and the American Experience*. Chicago: University of Chicago Press, 1981.

Hardy, B. Carmon. *Solemn Covenant: The Mormon Polygamous Passage*. Urbana, IL: University of Illinois Press, 1992.

Hart, Stephen. *What Does the Lord Require?: How American Christians Think About Justice*. New York: Oxford University Press, 1992.

Hayes, Carlton J.H. *Nationalism: A Religion*. New York: Macmillan Co., 1960.

Healey, Robert M. *Jefferson on Religion in Public Education*. New Haven: Yale University Press, 1962.

Hefley, James C. and Edward E. Plowman. *Washington: Christians and the Corridors of Power*. Wheaton, IL: Tyndale House Publishers, Inc., 1975.

Henig, Jeffrey R. *Rethinking School Choice: Limits of the Market Metaphor*. Princeton, NJ: Princeton University Press, 1993.

Herberg, Will. *Protestant, Catholic, Jew: An Essay in American Religious Sociology*. Garden City, NY: Doubleday & Co., 1955; rev. ed., 1960.

Hertzke, Allen D. *Echoes of Discontent: Jesse Jackson, Pat Robertson, and the Resurgence of Populism*. Washington, DC: CQ Press, 1993.

__________. *Representing God in Washington: The Role of Religious Lobbies in the American Polity*. Knoxville: The University of Tennessee Press, 1988.

Hessel, Dieter, ed. *The Church's Public Role: Retrospect and Prospect*. Grand Rapids: Wm. B. Eerdmans Publishing Co., 1993.

Hoekema, Anthony A. *The Four Major Cults: Christian Science, Jehovah's Witnesses, Mormonism, Seventh-Day Adventists*. Grand Rapids, MI: Wm. B. Eerdmans Publishing Co., 1963.

Hoffer, Peter Charles. *The Law's Conscience: Equitable Constitutionalism in America*. Chapel Hill, NC: University of North Carolina Press, 1990.

Hogan, John C. *The Schools, the Courts, and the Public Interest*. Lexington, MA: Lexington Books, 1985.

Hook, Sidney. *Religion in a Free Society*. Lincoln: University of Nebraska Press. 1967.

Hostetler, John A. *Amish Society*. Rev. ed. Baltimore: Johns Hopkins University Press, 1968.

Howard, A. E. Dick. *State Aid to Private Higher Education*. Charlottesville, VA: The Michie Co., 1977.

Howe, Mark DeWolfe, ed. *Cases on Church and State in the United States*. Cambridge, MA: Harvard University Press, 1952.

__________. *The Garden and the Wilderness: Religion and the Government in American Constitutional History*. Chicago: University of Chicago Press, 1965.

Hudson, Winthrop S. *The Great Tradition of the American Churches*. New York: Harper & Bros., 1953.

__________. *Religion in America*. New York: Scribner, 1965, 1973, 1981, 1987, 1992.

Hughson, Thomas, S.J. *The Believer as Citizen: John Courtney Murray in a New Context*. New York: Paulist Press, 1993.

Hunt, Robert P. and Kenneth L. Grasso, eds. *John Courtney Murray and the American Civil Conversation*. Grand Rapids: Wm. B. Eerdmans Publishing Co., 1992.

Hunter, James Davison. *Culture Wars: The Struggle to Define America*. New York: Basic Books, 1991.

Hunter, James Davison, and Os Guinness, eds. *Articles of Faith, Articles of Peace: The Religious Liberty Clauses and the American Public Philosophy*. Washington, DC: Brookings Institution, 1990.

Hutcheson, Richard G., Jr. *God in the White House: How Religion Has Changed the Modern Presidency*. New York: Macmillan, 1989.

Ivers, Gregg. *Lowering the Wall: Religion and the Supreme Court in the 1980s*. New York: Anti-Defamation League, 1991.

__________. *Redefining the First Freedom: The Supreme Court and the Consolidation of State Power*. New Brunswick, NJ: Transaction Publishers, 1992.

Jackson, Robert H. *The Supreme Court in the American System of Government*. New York: Harper and Row, 1955.

James, Thomas and Henry M. Levin, eds. *Public Dollars for Private Schools: The Case of Tuition Tax Credits*. Philadelphia: Temple University Press, 1983.

Jelen, Ted G. *The Political Mobilization of Religious Beliefs*. New York: Praeger Publishers, 1991.

Johns, Warren L. *Dateline Sunday, U.S.A.* Mountain View, CA: Pacific Press Publishing Association, 1967.

Johnson, F. Ernest, ed. *American Education and Religion: The Problem of Religion in the Schools*. New York: Harper and Row, 1952.

Johnson, Alvin W. and Frank H. Yost. *Separation of Church and State in the United States*. Minneapolis: University of Minnesota Press, 1948.

Johnson, Richard M. *The Dynamics of Compliance: Supreme Court Decision-Making from a New Perspective*. Evanston, IL: Northwestern University Press, 1967.

Jorstad, Erling. *Being Religious in America: The Deepening Crisis Over Public Faith*. Minneapolis: Augsburg Publishing House, 1986.

__________. *Evangelicals in the White House: The Cultural Maturation of Born Again Christianity, 1960-1981*. New York: Edwin Mellon Press, 1981.

__________. *The Politics of Moralism: The New Christian Right in American Life*. Minneapolis: Augsburg Publishing House, 1981.

Katz, Wilber G. *Religion and American Constitutions*. Evanston, IL: Northwestern University Press, 1963.

Kaufman, Peter I., and John F. Wilson, ed. *Redeeming Politics*. Princeton University Press, 1990.

Kauper, Paul G. *Civil Liberties and the Constitution*. Ann Arbor: University of Michigan Press, 1962.

____________. *Religion and the Constitution*. Baton Rouge: Louisiana State University Press, 1964.

Keim, Albert N., ed. *Compulsory Education and the Amish: The Right Not to Be Modern*. Boston: Beacon Press, 1975.

Kelley, Dean M. *Why Churches Should Not Pay Taxes*. New York: Harper & Row, 1977.

____________. ed. *Government Intervention in Religious Affairs*. New York: Pilgrim Press, 1982.

____________. ed. *Government Intervention in Religious Affairs, II*. New York: Pilgrim Press 1986.

____________. ed. *The Uneasy Boundary: Church and State*. Vol. 44 of The Annals of the American Academy of Political and Social Science (November 1979).

Kelly, George Armstrong. *Politics and Religious Consciousness in America*. New Brunswick, NJ: Transaction Books, 1984.

Kirk, Russell, ed. *The Assault on Religion: Commentaries on the Decline of Religious Liberty*. Lanham, MD: University Press of America, Cumberland, VA: Center for Judicial Studies, 1986.

Kirkpatrick, David W. *Choice in Schooling: A Case for Tuition Vouchers*. Chicago: Loyola University Press, 1990.

Klein, Christa R. and Christian D. von Dehsen. *Politics and Policy: The Genesis and Theology of Social Statements in the Lutheran Church in America*. Minneapolis: Fortress Press, 1989.

Kliebard, Herbert M. *Religion and Education in America: A Documentary History*. Scranton, PA: International Textbook Co., 1969.

Kolbenschlag, Madonna, ed. *Between God and Caesar*. Rumsey, NJ: Paulist Press, 1986.

Kommers, Donald P. and Michael J. Wahoske, eds. *Freedom and Education: Pierce v. Society of Sisters Reconsidered*. Notre Dame, IN: Center for Civil Rights, University of Notre Dame Law School, 1978.

Konefsky, Samuel J., ed. *The Constitutional World of Mr. Justice Frankfurter: Some Representative Opinions*. New York: Macmillan, 1949.

Konvitz, Milton R. *Religious Liberty and Conscience: A Constitutional Inquiry*. New York: Viking Press, 1968.

Koob, C. Albert and Russell Shaw. *S.O.S. for Catholic Schools: A Strategy for Future Service to Church and Nation*. New York: Holt, Rinehart, and Winston, 1970.

Kramnick, Isaac and R. Laurence Moore. *The Goddess Constitution: The Case Against Religious Correctness*. New York: W. W. Norton and Company, 1996.

Krason, Stephen M. *Abortion: Politics, Morality, and the Constitution: A Critical Study of Roe v. Wade and Doe v. Bolton and a Basis for Change*. Lanham, Md.: University Press of America, 1984.

Kraybill, Donald B., ed. *The Amish and the State*. Baltimore, MD: The John Hopkins University Press, 1993.

Krinsky, Fred. *The Politics of Religion in America*. Beverly Hills: Glencoe Press, 1968.

Kurland, Philip B., ed. *Church and State: The Supreme Court and the First Amendment*. Chicago: University of Chicago Press, 1975.

____________. *Religion and the Law: Of Church and State and the Supreme Court*. Chicago: Aldine Publishing Co., 1962.

____________. *Church and State: The Supreme Court and the First Amendment*. Chicago: The University of Chicago Press, 1975.

____________, Gerhard Casper, and Dennis J. Hutchinson, eds. *The Supreme Court Review, 1983*. Chicago: University of Chicago Press, 1983.

Labunski, Richard E. *Religion and the Law: Of Church and State and the Supreme Court*. Chicago: Aldine Publishing Company, 1962.

La Noue, George R., ed. *Educational Vouchers: Concepts and Controversies*. New York: Teachers College, Columbia University Press, 1972.

Lannie, Vincent P. *Public Money for Parochial Education*. Cleveland: Case Western Reserve University Press, 1968.

Larson, Martin and C. Stanley Lowell. *Praise the Lord for Tax Exemption: How the Churches Grow Rich, While the Cities and You Grow Poor*. Washington, DC: Robert B. Luce, 1969.

____________. *The Religious Empire: The Growth and Danger of Tax-Exempt Property in the United States*. Washington, DC: Robert B. Luce Co., Inc., 1976.

Laubach, John H. *School Prayers: Congress, the Courts, and the Public*. Washington, DC: Public Affairs Press, 1969.

Lee, Francis G., ed. *All Imaginable Liberty: The Religious Liberty Clauses and the First Amendment*. Lanham, MD: University Press of America, 1995.

Levy, Leonard Williams. *The Establishment Clause: Religion and the First Amendment*. New York: Macmillan, 1989.

Liebman, Robert C. and Robert Wuthnow, eds. *The New Christian Right: Mobilization and Legitimation*. New York: Aldine Publishing Co., 1983.

Lienesch, Michael. *Redeeming America: Piety and Politics in the New Christian Right*. Chapel Hill: University of North Carolina Press, 1995.

Lincoln, C. Eric. *The Black Muslims in America*. Boston: Beacon Press, 1961, 1973.

Linder, Robert D. and Richard V. Pierard. *Politics: A Case for Christian Action*. Downers Grove, IL: Inter-Varsity Press, 1973.

Littell, Franklin Hamlin. *The Church and the Body Politic*. New York: Seabury Press, 1969.

____________. *From State Church to Pluralism: A Protestant Interpretation of Religion in American History*. New York: Macmillan, 1971.

____________. *The Origins of Sectarian Protestantism: A Study of the Anabaptist View of the Church*. New York: Macmillan, 1964.

Loder, James E. *Religion and the Public Schools*. New York: Association Press, 1965.

Lovin, Robin W. *Religion and American Public Life: Interpretations and Explorations*. Mahwah, NJ: Paulist Press, 1986.

Lunceford, Lloyd J. *The Religion Clauses of the First Amendment*. Baton Rouge, LA: L. J. Lunceford, 1988.

Lunger, Harold L. *A Citizen Under God*. St. Louis: Christian Board of Publication, 1973.

Lynn, Barry, Marc D. Stern and Oliver S. Thomas. *The Right to Religious Liberty: The Basic ACLU Guide to Religious Rights*. Carbondale, IL: Southern Illinois University Press, 1995.

Maddox, Robert L. *Separation of Church and State: Guarantor of Religious Freedom*. New York: Crossroad Publishing Co., 1987.

Malbin, Michael J. *Religion and Politics: The Intentions of the Authors of the First Amendment*. Washington, DC: American Enterprise Institute, 1978.

Manning, Leonard F. *The Law of Church-State Relations in a Nutshell*. St. Paul, MN: West Publishing Co., 1981.

Manwaring, David R. *Religion, Liberty and the State*. Indianapolis: Bobbs-Merrill, 1971.

____________. *Render Unto Caesar: The Flag Salute Controversy*. Chicago: University of Chicago Press, 1962.

Marnell, William H. *The First Amendment: The History of Religious Freedom in America*. Garden City, NY: Doubleday & Co., 1964.

Marty, Martin E.. *The New Shape of American Religion*. New York: Harper & Row, 1958, 1959.

____________. *The Pro & Con Book of Religious America: A Bicentennial Argument*. Waco, Texas: Word Incorporated, 1975.

____________. *The Public Church: Mainline-Evangelical-Catholic*. New York: Crossroad Books, 1981.

———. *Religion and Republic: The American Circumstance.* Boston: Beacon Press, 1987.

McBrien, Richard P. *Caesar's Coin: Religion and Politics in America.* New York: Macmillan, 1987.

McCarthy, Martha M. *A Delicate Balance: Church, State, and the Schools.* Bloomington: Indiana University Press, 1983.

McCarthy, Rockne M., James W. Skillen, and William A. Harper. *Disestablishment a Second Time: Genuine Pluralism for American Schools.* Grand Rapids: Christian University Press, 1982.

McCluskey, Neil G. *Catholic Viewpoint on Education.* Rev. ed. Garden City, NY: Image Books, 1962.

———. *Catholic Education in America.* New York: Teachers College, Columbia University Press, 1964.

McCollister, John. *So Help Me God: The Faith of America's Presidents.* Louisville: Westminster John Knox Press, 1991.

McCollum, Vashti C. *One Woman's Fight.* Boston: Beacon Press, 1951, reissued, Madison, WI: Freedom From Religion Foundation, 1993.

McCuen, Gary E. *Religion and Politics: Issues in Religious Liberty.* Hudson, WI: G. E. McCuen Publications, 1989.

McGrath, Joseph H., ed. *Church and State in American Law.* Milwaukee, WI: Bruce Publishing Co., 1962.

McManus, Edgar J.*Law and Liberty in Early New England: Criminal Justice and Due Process.* Amherst, MA: The University of Massachusetts Press, 1993.

McMillan, Richard C. *Religion in the Public Schools: An Introduction.* Macon, GA: Mercer University Press, 1984.

Mead, Sidney E. *The Lively Experiment: The Shaping of Christianity in America.* New York: Harper & Row, 1963.

———. *The Nation With the Soul of a Church.* New York: Harper & Row, 1975.

———. *The Old Religion in the Brave New World: Reflections on the Relation Between Christendom and the Republic.* Berkeley: University of California Press, 1977.

Mechling, Jay, ed. *Church, State and Public Policy: The New Shape of the Church-State Debate.* Washington, DC: American Enterprise Institute for Public Policy Research, 1978.

Meixner, Linda L. *The Bible in Literature Courses: Successful Lesson Plans.* New York: Praeger, 1991.

Melton, J. Gordon. *The Encyclopedia of American Religions,* 2 vols., Wilmington, NC: McGrath Publishing Co., 1978.

Menendez, Albert J. *The December Dilemma: Christmas in American Public Life.* Silver Spring, MD: Americans United for Separation of Church and State, 1988.

———. *Religious Conflict in America: A Bibliographic Guide.* New York: Garland Publishing, 1984.

———. *Religion and the U.S. Presidency: A Bibliography.* New York: Garland Press, 1986.

———. *School Prayer and Other Issues in American Public Education: An Annotated Bibliography.* New York: Garland Publishing, 1984.

———. *Visions of Reality: What Fundamentalist Schools Really Teach.* Buffalo, NY: Prometheus Books, 1993.

———. and Edd Doerr, eds. *The Great Quotations of Religious Freedom.* Long Beach, CA.: Centerline Press, 1991.

———. and Edd Doerr, eds. *Religion and Public Education: Common Sense and the Law.* Long Beach, CA: Centerline Press, 1991.

Michaelson, Robert. *Piety in the Public School: Trends and Issues in Relationship Between Religion and the Public Schools in the United States.* New York: Macmillan, 1970.

Michnik, Adam. *The Church and the Left.* Chicago: The University of Chicago Press, 1993.

Miller, Glenn T. *Religious Liberty in America: History and Prospects.* Philadelphia: Westminster Press, 1976.

Miller, Richard B. *Interpretations of Conflict: Ethics, Pacifism and the Just-War Tradition.* Chicago: University of Chicago Press, 1991.

Miller, William L., Robert Bellah, Martin Marty, and Arlin Adams. *Religion & the Public Good: A Bicentennial Forum.* Mercer University Press, 1989.

Miller, William Lee. *The First Liberty: Religion and the American Republic.* New York: Alfred A. Knopf, 1987.

———. *The Protestant and Politics.* Philadelphia: Westminster Press, 1958.

Minear, Paul. *I Pledge Allegiance: Patriotism and the Bible.* Philadelphia: The Geneva Press, 1975.

Moehlman, Conrad H. *The Wall of Separation Between Church and State: An Historical Study of Recent Criticism of the Religious Clauses of the First Amendment.* Boston: Beacon Press, 1951.

Moen, Matthew C. *The Transformation of the Christian Right.* Tuscaloosa: The University of Alabama Press, 1992.

Moen, Matthew C. and Lowell S. Gustafson, eds. *The Religious Challenge to the State.* Philadelphia: Temple University Press, 1992.

Molnar, Thomas. *Politics and the State: The Catholic View.* Chicago: Franciscan Herald Press, 1980.

Moltmann, Jurgen, Herbert W. Richardson, Johann Baptist Metz, Willi Oelmuller, and M. Darrol Bryant. *Religion and Political Society.* New York: Harper & Row, 1974.

Monsma, Stephen V. *Positive Neutrality: Letting Religious Freedom Ring.* Westport, CT: Greenwood Press, 1993.

Mooney, Christopher F. *Boundaries Dimly Perceived: Law, Religion, Education, and the Common Good.* Notre Dame, IN: University of Notre Dame Press, 1990.

———. *Public Virtue: Law and the Social Character of Religion.* Notre Dame, IN: University of Notre Dame Press, 1986.

———. *Religion and the American Dream: The Search for Freedom Under God.* Philadelphia: The Westminster Press, 1977.

Moore, R. Laurence. *Religious Outsiders and the Making of Americans.* New York: Oxford University Press, 1985.

Moots, Philip R. and Edward M. Gaffney, Jr. *Church and Campus: Legal Issues in Religiously Affiliated Education.* Notre Dame and London: University of Notre Dame Press, 1979.

Morgan, Edmund S. *Roger Williams: The Church and the State.* New York: Harcourt, Brace & World, 1967.

Morgan, Richard E. *The Politics of Religious Conflict: Church and State in America.* 2d ed. Washington, DC: University Press of America, 1980.

———. *The Supreme Court and Religion.* New York: Free Press, 1972.

Muir, W.K. *Prayer in the Public Schools: Law and Attitude Change.* Chicago: University of Chicago Press, 1967.

Murray, John Courtney, S.J. *We Hold These Truths: Catholic Reflections on the American Proposition.* Garden City, NY: Doubleday & Co., 1964.

Must, Art, Jr. *Why We Still Need Public Schools: Church/State Relations, and Visions of Democracy.* Buffalo, NY: Prometheus Books, 1992.

Neuhaus, Richard J. *America Against Itself: Moral Vision and the Public Order.* Louisville: Westminster/John Knox Press, 1992.

———. *Christian Faith and Public Policy: Thinking and Acting in the Courage of Uncertainty.* Minneapolis: Augsburg Publishing House, 1977.

———. ed. *Democracy and the Renewal of Public Education.* Grand Rapids: Wm. B. Eerdmans Publishing Co., 1987.

———. *The Naked Public Square: Religion and Democracy in America.* Grand Rapids, MI: Wm. B. Eerdmans Publishing Co., 1984.

Newton, Merlin Owen. *Armed with the Constitution: Jehovah's Witnesses in Alabama and the U.S. Supreme Court, 1939-1946.* Tuscaloosa: University of Alabama Press, 1995.

Nicholls, David. *Deity and Domination: Images of God and State in the Nineteenth and Twentieth Centuries.* New York: Routledge, 1994.

Noll, Mark A., Nathan O. Hatch, and George M. Marsden. *The Search for Christian America.* Expanded edition, Colorado Springs: Helmers and Howard, 1989.

____________. *Christians in the American Revolution.* Washington DC: Christian University Press, 1977.

____________. *One Nation Under God?: Christian Faith and Political Action in America.* San Francisco: Harper and Row, 1988.

____________, ed. *Religion and American Politics: From the Colonial Period to the 1980s.* New York: Oxford University Press, 1990.

Noonan, John T. *The Believer and the Powers that Are: Cases, History, and Other Data Bearing on the Relationship of Religion and Government.* New York: Macmillan, 1987.

Nord, Warren A. *Religion and American Education: Rethinking a National Dilemma.* Chapel Hill: The University of North Carolina Press, 1995.

North, Gary and Gary DeMar. *Christian Reconstruction: What It Is, What It Isn't.* Tyler, TX: Institute for Christian Economics, 1991.

Oaks, Dallin H., ed. *The Wall Between Church and State.* Chicago: University of Chicago Press, 1963.

____________. *Trust Doctrines in Church Controversies.* Macon, GA: Mercer University Press, 1984.

O'Brien, David M. *Storm Center: The Supreme Court in American Politics.* New York: W. W. Norton and Co., 1986.

O'Brien, Francis W. *Justice Reed and the First Amendment: The Religion Clauses.* Washington: Georgetown University Press, 1958.

Odegard, Peter H. *Religion and Politics.* New York: Oceana Publications, 1960.

O'Hair, Madalyn Murray. *Freedom Under Siege: The Impact of Organized Religion on Your Liberty and Your Pocketbook.* Los Angeles: J. P. Tarcher, Inc., 1974.

O'Neill, James M. *Religion and Education under the Constitution.* New York: Harper & Bros, 1949.

Palmer, Parker J., Barbara G. Wheeler, and James W. Fowler. *Caring for the Commonweal: Education for Religious and Public Life.* Macon, GA: Mercer University Press, 1990.

Parsons, Wilfrid P. *The First Freedom: Considerations of Church and State in the United States.* Macmillan, 1948.

Pattillo, Manning M., Jr., and Donald M. Mackenzie. *Church-Sponsored Higher Education in the United States.* Washington, DC: American Council on Education, 1966.

Pavlischek, Keith J. *John Courtney Murray and the Dilemma of Religious Toleration.* Kirksville, MO: Thomas Jefferson University Press, 1994.

Peck, Janice. *The Gods of Televangelism: The Crisis of Meaning and the Appeal of Religious Television.* Cresskill, NY: Hampton Press, 1993.

Peele, Gillian. *Revival and Reaction: The Right in Contemporary America.* Oxford: The Clarendon Press, 1984.

Perry, Barbara A. *A "Representative" Supreme Court: The Impact of Race, Religion, and Gender on Appointments.* New York: Greenwood Press, 1991.

Peterson, Merril D. and Robert C. Vaughan, eds. *The Virginia Statute for Religious Freedom: Its Evolution & Consequences in American History.* Cambridge University Press, 1988.

Peterson, Walfred H. *Thy Liberty in Law.* Nashville, TN: Broadman Press, 1978.

Pfeffer, Leo. *Church, State and Freedom.* Rev. and enl. Boston: Beacon Press, 1967.

____________. *God, Caesar, and the Constitution: The Court as Referee of Church-State Confrontation.* Boston: Beacon Press, 1975.

____________. *The Liberties of an American: The Supreme Court Speaks.* Boston: Beacon Press, 1963.

____________. *Religion, State, and the Burger Court.* Buffalo, NY: Prometheus Books, 1985.

____________. *Religious Freedom.* Skokie, IL: National Textbook Co. in conjunction with the American Civil Liberties Union, 1977.

Pierard, Richard V. and Robert D. Linder. *Civil Religion and the Presidency.* Grand Rapids: Zondervan Publishing House, 1988.

Polishook, Irwin H. *Roger Williams, John Cotton and Religious Freedom.* Englewood Cliffs, NJ: Prentice-Hall, 1967.

Poore, Benjamin P., ed. *The Federal and State Constitutions, Colonial Charters, and Other Organic Laws of the United States.* 2 vols. Washington: Government Printing Office, 1978.

Powell, Theodore. *The School Bus Law:A Case Study in Education, Religion and Politics.* Middleton, CT: Wesleyan University Press, 1960.

Power, M. Susan. *Before the Convention: Religion and the Founders.* New York: University Press of America, 1984.

Pritchett, C. Herman. *The American Constitution.* 3d ed. New York: McGraw-Hill Book Co., 1977.

Provenzo, Eugene F. *Religious Fundamentalism and American Education: The Battle for Public Schools.* Albany, NY: State University of New York Press, 1990.

Rader, Stanley R. *Against the Gates of Hell: The Threat to Religious Freedom in America.* New York: Everest House, 1980.

Rahner, Hugo, S.J. *Church and State in Early Christianity.* San Francisco: Ignatius Press, 1992.

Ramsay, William M. *The Wall of Separation: A Primer on Church and State.* Louisville: Westminster/John Knox Press, 1989.

Rankin, William W. *Confidentiality and Clergy: Churches, Ethics, and the Law.* Harrisburg, PA: Morehouse Publishing, 1990.

Regan, Richard J., S.J. *Private Conscience and Public Law: The American Experience.* New York: Fordham University Press, 1972.

Reichley, A. James. *Religion in American Public Life.* Washington, DC: The Brookings Institution, 1985.

Religion and Public Life: The Role of Religious Bodies in Shaping Public Policy. Cincinnati: Xavier University Press, 1986.

Religious Liberty Under the Free Exercise Clause. Washington, DC: Office of Legal Policy, Dept. of Justice, 1988.

Ribuffo, Leo P. *The Old Christian Right: The Protestant Far Right from the Great Depression to the Cold War.* Philadelphia: Temple University Press, 1983.

Rice, Charles E. *The Supreme Court and Public Prayer: The Need for Restraint.* New York: Fordham University Press, 1964.

Richards, David A. J. *Toleration and the Constitution.* New York: Oxford University Press, 1986.

Richey, Russell E. and Donald G. Jones, eds. *American Civil Religion.* New York: Harper & Row, 1974.

Richter, Edward J. and Dulce Berton. *Religion and the Presidency: A Recurring American Problem.* New York: Macmillan, 1962.

Riskin, Shlomo. *Women and Jewish Divorce: The Rebellious Wife, the Agunah and the Right of Women to Initiate Divorce in Jewish Law—A Halakhic Solution.* New York: KTAV Publishing House, Inc., 1989.

Robbins, Thomas and Dick Anthony. *In God We Trust: New Patterns of Religious Pluralism in America.* Rev. ed. New Brunswick, NJ: Transaction Publishers, 1990.

____________. and Roland Robertson, eds. *Church-State Relations: Tensions and Transitions.* New Brunswick, NJ: Transaction Books, 1986.

____________. William C. Shepherd and James McBride, eds. *Cults, Culture and the Law: Perspectives on New Religious Movements.* Chico, Ca.: Scholars Press, 1985.

Robertson, D. B. *Should Churches Be Taxed?* Philadelphia: Westminster Press, 1968.

Rodgers, Harrell R., Jr. *Community Conflict, Public Opinion and the Law: The Amish Dispute in Iowa.* Columbus, Ohio: Charles E. Merrill Publishing Co., 1969.

Rohr, John A. *Prophets Without Honor:Public Policy and the Selective Conscientious Objector.* Nashville: Abingdon Press, 1971.

Rudin, James and Marcia. *Prison or Paradise: The New Religious Cults.* Philadelphia: Fortress Press, 1980.

Rutyna, Richard and John W. Kuehl, eds. *Conceived in Conscience: An Analysis of Contemporary Church-State Relations*. Norfolk, VA: Donning Company, 1983.

Sahliyeh, Emile, ed. *Religious Resurgence and Politics in the Contemporary World*. Albany, NY: State University of New York Press, 1990.

Sandeen, Ernest R., ed. *The Bible and Social Reform*. Philadelphia: Fortress Press, 1982.

Sanders, Thomas G. *Protestant Concepts of Church and State: Historical Backgrounds and Approaches for the Future*. New York: Holt Rinehart and Winston, 1964.

Sandoz, Ellis. *A Government of Laws: Political Theory, Religion, and the American Founding*. Baton Rouge: Louisiana State University Press, 1990.

____________. *Political Sermons of the American Founding Era*. Indianapolis: Liberty Press, 1990.

Sanford, Charles B. *The Religious Life of Thomas Jefferson*. Charlottesville: University of Virginia Press, 1984.

Savage, David G. *Turning Right: The Making of the Rehnquist Supreme Court*. New York: John Wiley & Sons, 1992.

Semonche, John E. *Religion and Constitutional Government in the United States*. Carrboro, NC: Signal Books, 1986.

Sheldon, Garrett Ward. *Religion and Politics: Major Thinkers on the Relation of Church and State*. New York: Peter Lang Publishing, 1990.

Shepherd, David R. *Ronald Reagan: In God I Trust*. Wheaton, IL: Tyndale House Publishers, 1984.

Shepherd, William C. *To Secure the Blessings of Liberty: American Constitutional Law and the New Religious Movements*. New York: The Crossroad Publishing Company and Scholars Press, 1985.

Sherwood, Carlton. *Inquisition: The Persecution and Prosecution of the Reverend Sun Myung Moon*. Washington, DC: Regnery Gateway, 1991.

Sibley, Mulford Q. *The Obligation to Disobey: Conscience and the Law*. New York: Council on Religion and International Affairs, 1970.

____________. and Philip E. Jacob. *Conscription of Conscience: The American State and the Conscientious Objector, 1940-1947*. Ithaca, NY: Cornell University Press, 1952.

Simon, Arthur. *Christian Faith and Public Policy: No Grounds for Divorce*. Grand Rapids, MI: Wm. B. Eerdmans Publishing Co., 1987.

Sizer, Theodore R., ed. *Religion and Public Education*. Boston: Houghton Mifflin Co., 1967; Lanham, Md.: University Press of America, 1982.

Skillen, James W. *The Scattered Voice: Christians At Odds in the Public Square*. Grand Rapids: Zondervan Publishing House, 1990.

Smith, Elwyn A. *Church and State in Your Community*. Philadelphia: Westminster Press, 1963.

____________. ed. *The Religion of the Republic*. Philadelphia: Fortress Press, 1971, 1980.

____________. *Religious Liberty in the United States: The Development of Church-State Thought Since the Revolutionary Era*. Philadelphia: Fortress Press, 1972.

Smith, Rodney K. *Public Prayer and the Constitution: A Case Study in Constitutional Interpretation*. Wilmington, DE: Scholarly Resources, Inc., 1987.

Smith, H. Shelton, Robert T. Handy and Lefferts A. Loetscher. *American Christianity: An Historical Interpretation with Representative Documents*. 2 vols. New York: Charles Scribner's Sons, 1960.

Sorauf, Frank. *The Wall of Separation: The Constitutional Politics of Church-State*. Princeton: Princeton University Press, 1976.

Spicer, George W. *The Supreme Court and Fundamental Freedom*. New York: Appleton Century-Crofts, 1959.

Stedman, Murray S. *Religion and Politics in America*. New York: Harcourt, Brace & World, 1964.

Stokes, Anson Phelps. *Church and State in the United States*. 3 vols. New York: Harper & Bros., 1950.

____________. and Leo Pfeffer. *Church and State in the United States*. Rev. one volume ed. New York: Harper and Row, 1964.

Stroup, Herbert H. *The Jehovah's Witnesses*. New York: Columbia University Press, 1945.

Strout, Cushing. *The New Heavens and the New Earth: Political Religion in America*. New York: Harper & Row, 1974.

Sullivan, Winnifred Fallers. *Paying the Words Extra: Religious Discourse in the Supreme Court of the United States*. Cambridge: Harvard University Press, 1994.

Swartley, Williard M., ed. *The Bible and Law*. Elkhart, IN: Institute of Mennonite Studies, 1982.

Sweet, William W., ed. *Religion in Colonial America*. New York: Charles Scribner's Sons, 1942.

Swomley, John M. Jr. *Religious Liberty and the Secular State: The Constitutional Context*. Buffalo, NY: Prometheus Books, 1987.

____________. *Religion, the State, and the Schools*. New York: Pegasus, 1968.

Tanner, Kathryn. *The Politics of God: Christian Theologies and Social Justice*. Minneapolis: Fortress Press, 1992.

Tarr, B. Alan. *Judicial Impact and State Supreme Courts*. Lexington, MA: D. C. Heath and Co., 1977.

Thiemann, Ronald F. *Religion in Public Life: A Dilemma for Democracy*. Washington, DC: Georgetown University Press, 1996.

Tiemann, William Harold, and John C. Bush. *The Right to Silence: Privileged Clergy Communication and the Law*. Nashville: Abingdon Press, 1983, 1989.

Tinder, Glenn. *The Political Meaning of Christianity: A Prophetic Stance*. San Francisco: Harper San Francisco, 1991.

Tinker, George.*Missionary Conquest: The Gospel and Native American Cultural Genocide*. Minneapolis, MN: Augsburg Fortress Press, 1993.

Torpey, William G. *Judicial Doctrines of Religious Rights in America*. Chapel Hill: University of North Carolina Press, 1948.

Tribe, Laurence H. *American Constitutional Law*. Mineola, NY: The Foundation Press, 1978.

____________. *The Constitutional Protection of Individual Rights: Limits on Government Authority*. Mineola, NY: The Foundation Press, Inc., 1978.

____________. *God Save This Honorable Court: How the Choice of Supreme Court Justices Shapes our History*. New York: Random House, 1985.

Tushnet, Mark V. *Red, White, and Blue: A Critical Analysis of Constitutional Law*. Cambridge, MA: Harvard University Press, 1988.

Tussman, Joseph, ed. *The Supreme Court on Church and State*. New York: Oxford Press, 1962.

Twomley, Dale E. *Parochiaid and the Courts*. Perrier Springs, MI: Andrews University Press, 1981.

Vaux, Kenneth L. *Ethics and the Gulf War: Religion, Rhetoric, and Righteousness*. Boulder, CO: Westview Press, 1992.

Wald, Kenneth D. *Religion and Politics in the United States*. New York: St. Martin's Press, 1987.

Walter, Erich A., ed. *Religion and the State University*. Ann Arbor: University of Michigan Press, 1964.

Walters, Kerry S. *The American Deists: Voices of Reason and Dissent in the Early Republic*. Lawrence, KS: University Press of Kansas, 1992.

Ward, Hiley H. *Space-Age Sunday*. New York: Macmillan Co., 1960.

Watts, Tim J. *Church and Court: Settling Religious Disputes With Secular Law*. Monticello, IL: Vance Bibliographies, 1988.

Weber, Paul J., ed. *Equal Separation: Understanding the Religion Clauses of the First Amendment*. Westport, CT: Greenwood Press, Inc., 1990.

____________. and Dennis A. Gilbert. *Private Churches and Public Money: Church-Government Fiscal Relations*. Westport, CT: Greenwood Press, 1981.

Weigel, George and Robert Royal, eds., *A Century of Catholic Social Thought: Essays on "Rerum Novarum" and Nine Other Key Documents.* Washington, DC: Ethics and Public Policy Center, 1991.
Wells, Ronald A., ed. *The Wars of America: Christian Views.* Macon, GA: Mercer University Press, 1991.
Wenz, Peter S. *Abortion Rights as Religious Freedom.* Philadelphia, PA: Temple University Press, 1992.
White, Ronald C. and Albright G. Zimmerman, eds. *An Unsettled Arena: Religion and the Bill of Rights.* Grand Rapids, MI: Wm. B. Eerdmans Pub. Co., 1990.
Whitehead, John W. *The Rights of Religious Persons in Public Education.* Wheaton, IL.: Crossway Books, 1991.
__________. *The Separation Illusion: A Lawyer Examines the First Amendment.* Milford, MI: Mott Media, 1977.
Wills, Garry. *Under God: Religion and American Politics.* New York: Simon and Schuster, 1990.
Wilson, John F. *Public Religion in American Culture.* Philadelphia: Temple University Press, 1979.
__________. ed. *Church and State in America: A Bibliographical Guide.* New York: Greenwood Press. Vol. 1: *The Colonial and Early National Period,* 1986; Vol. 2: *The Civil War to the Present Day,* 1987.
__________. ed. *Church and State in American History.* Boston: D. C. Heath and Co., 1965, second edition with Donald Drakeman. Boston: Beacon Press, 1987.
Wogaman, Philip. *Protestant Faith and Religious Liberty.* Nashville: Abingdon Press, 1967.
Wolf, Donald J., S.J. *Toward Consensus: Catholic-Protestant Interpretations of Church and State.* Garden City, NY: Doubleday & Co., 1968.
Wood, James E., Jr. *Religion and Politics.* Waco, TX: J. M. Dawson Institute of Church-State Studies, Baylor University Press, 1983.
__________. ed. *Religion, the State, and Education.* Waco, TX: Baylor University Press, 1984.
__________. *Ecumenical Perspectives on Church and State: Protestant, Catholic, and Jewish.* Waco, TX: J. M. Dawson Institute of Church-State Studies, Baylor University, 1988.
__________. *The First Freedom: Religion and the Bill of Rights.* Waco, TX: J. M. Dawson Institute of Church-State Studies, Baylor University, 1990.
__________. *Religion and the State: Essays in Honor of Leo Pfeffer.* Waco, TX: Baylor University Press, 1985.
__________. *The Role of Religion in the Making of Public Policy.* Waco, TX: J. M. Dawson Institute of Church-State Studies, Baylor University, 1991.
__________, Robert T. Miller and E. Bruce Thompson. *Church and State in Scripture, History and Constitutional Law.* Waco, TX: Baylor University Press, 1958.
Worton, Stanley N. *Freedom of Religion.* Rochelle Park, NJ: Hayden Book Co., 1975.
Wunder, John R. *"Retained by the People": A History of American Indians and the Bill of Rights.* New York: Oxford University Press, 1994.
Wuthnow, Robert. *The Restructuring of American Religion.* Princeton: Princeton University Press, 1988.
__________. *The Struggle for America's Soul.* Grand Rapids, MI: Wm. B. Eerdmans, 1989.

Yandian, Bob. *One Nation Under God: The Rise or Fall of a Nation.* Tulsa, OK: Harrison House, 1988.

Zaretsky, I.I. and M.P. Leone, eds. *Religious Movements in Contemporary America.* Princeton: Princeton University Press, 1974.
Zetterbert, J. Peter, ed. *Evolution versus Creationism: The Public Education Controversy.* Phoenix: Oryx Press, 1983.
Zollman, Carl F. *American Church Law.* St. Paul, MN: West Publishing Co., 1933.

ARTICLES

Abraham, Henry J. "Religion, Medicine, and the State: Reflections on Some Contemporary Issues." *Journal of Church and State* 22 (Autumn 1980): 423-36.
__________. "The Status of the First Amendment's Religion Clauses: Some Reflections on Lines and Limits." *Journal of Church and State* 22 (Spring 1980): 215-31.
Adams, Arlin M. and Charles J. Emmerich. "A Heritage of Religious Liberty." *University of Pennsylvania Law Review* 137 (May 1989): 1559-1671.
__________. and Sarah Barringer Gordon. "The Doctrine of Accommodation in the Jurisprudence of the Religion Clauses." *DePaul Law Review* 37 (Spring 1988): 317-45.
__________. and William R. Hanion. "*Jones v. Wolf*: Church Autonomy and the Religion Clauses of the First Amendment." *University of Pennsylvania Law Review* 128 (June 1980): 409-26.
Ahlstrom, Sydney E. "Religion, Revolution and the Rise of Modern Nationalism: Reflections on the American Experience." *Church History* 44 (December 1975): 492-504.
__________. "The Traumatic Years: American Religion and Culture in the '60s and '70s." *Theology Today* 36 (1980): 504-22.
"Aid to Parochial Schools: A Free Exercise Perspective." *Santa Clara Law Review* 21 (Spring 1983): 587-605.
Akins, Nancy. "New Direction in Sacred Land Claims: *Lyng v. Northwest Indian Cemetery Protective Association.*" *Natural Resources Journal* (April 1 1989): 593-605.
"Another Brick in the Wall: Denominational Preferences and Strict Scrutiny Under the Establishment Clause." *Nebraska Law Review* 62 (1983): 359-83.
Anthony, Dick and Thomas Robbins. "Negligence, Coercion, and the Protection of Religious Belief." *Journal of Church and State* 37 (Summer 1995): 509-36.
Araujo, Robert J., S.J. "Christian Social Thought and American Public Policy: A Dialogue Between the Laity and the American State." *Journal of Church and State* 35 (Autumn 1993): 751-80.
Arp, D. Jarrett. "Beyond Mergens: Balancing a Student's Free Speech Right Against the Establishment Clause in Public High School Equal Access Cases." *William & Mary Law Review* 32 (Fall 1990): 127-60.
Ayres, T.D. "Widmar v. Vincent: The Beginning of the End of the Establishment Clause." *Journal of College and University Law* 8 (1981-82): 511-17.

Baer, Richard A., Jr. "The Supreme Court's Discriminatory Use of the Term 'Sectarian.'" *The Journal of Law and Politics* 6 (Spring 1990): 449-68.
Baker, Brent. "The Special Immigrant Exception For Religious Ministers: An Establishment Clause Analysis." *Boston College Third World Law Journal* 7 (Winter 1987): 97-108.
Balitzer, Alfred. "Some Thoughts About Civil Religion." *Journal of Church and State* 16 (Winter 1974): 31-50.
Ball, William Bentley. "The Fault is Not in the Laws." *Report From the Capital* 45 (June 1990): 7.
__________. "Religious Liberty in Our Time: What Has the Supreme Court Said?" In *Freedom of Religion Clauses of the First Amendment: What Do They Mean Today?* Pennsylvania Catholic Conference, 23-24. Erie, PA: Pennsylvania Catholic Conference, 1990.

Basil, Robert J. "Clergy Malpractice: Taking Spiritual Counseling Conflicts Beyond Intentional Tort Analysis." *Rutgers Law Journal* (Winter 1988): 419-50.

Bauer, Janine G. "The Constitutionality of Student Fees for Political Student Groups in the Campus Public Forum: *Galda* v. *Bloustein* and the Right to Associate." *Rutgers Law Journal* 15 (September 1983): 135-84.

Becker, William H. "Creationism: New Dimensions of the Religion Democracy Relation." *Journal of Church and State* 27 (Spring 1985): 315-33.

Bedig, Laurel A. "The Supreme Court Narrows an Employer's Duty to Accommodate an Employee's Religious Practices Under Title VII." *Brooklyn Law Review* 53 (1987): 245-69.

Bellah, Robert N. "Civil Religion in America." *Daedalus* 96 (Winter 1967): 1-21.

Benjamin, Walter W. "Separation of Church and State: Myth and Reality." *Journal of Church and State* 11 (Winter 1969): 93-110.

Bennet, L. Leslie, Jr. and David E. Sumler. "Ethical Policy-making in Higher Education: State Regulation of Religious Colleges in Maryland." *Journal of Church and State* 35 (Summer 1993): 547-57.

Berger, Raoul. "Standing to Sue in Public Actions: Is It a Constitutional Requirement?" *Yale Law Journal* 78 (April 1969): 816-40.

Berman, Harold J. "Religious Freedom and the Challenge of the Modern State." *Emory Law Journal* 65 (Winter 1990): 149-64.

Bertonneau, Brain. "*Estate of Thornton* v. *Caldor, Inc.*: Defining Sabbath Rights in the Workplace." *Hastings Constitutional Law Quarterly* 15 (Spring 1988): 513-32.

Best, James. "*Lynch* v. *Donnelly*: The Rebirth of the Supreme Court's Attitude Towards the Establishment Clause." *Southern University Law Review* 12 (Fall 1987): 97-105.

BeVier, Lillian R. "The Free Exercise Clause: A View from the Public Forum." *William and Mary Law Review* 27 (1987): 963-74.

Birkby, Robert. "The Supreme Court and the Bible Belt: Tennessee Reaction to the Schempp Decision." *Midwest Journal of Political Science* 10 (August 1966): 304-19.

Bjorklun, Eugene C. "The Rites of Spring: Prayers at High School Graduation." *Educational Law Report* 61 (August 30, 1990): 1-9.

Blischak, Matthew P. "*O'Lone* v. *Estate of Shabazz*: The State of Prisoners' Religious Free Exercise Rights." *American University Law Review* (Winter, 1988): 453-86.

Block, Sharon I. "The Establishment Clause in Public Schools: A Model for Future Analysis *Clayton* v. *Place*." *Georgetown Law Journal* 79 (October 1990): 121-40.

Bloostein, Marc J. "The 'Core'–'Periphery' Dichotomy in First Amendment Free Exercise Clause Doctrine: *Goldman* v. *Weinberger*, *Bowen* v. *Roy*, and *O'Lone* v. *Estate of Shabazz*." *Cornell Law Review* 72 (May 1987): 827-55.

Bohner, Robert J., Jr. "Religious Property Disputes and Intrinsically Religious Evidence: Towards a Narrow Application of the Neutral Principles Approach." *Villanova Law Review* 35 (September 1990): 949-81.

Boles, Donald E. "Church and State and the Burger Court: Recent Developments Affecting Parochial Schools." *Journal of Church and State* 18 (Winter 1976): 21-38.

____________. Religion and the Public Schools in Judicial Review." *Journal of Church and State* 26 (Winter 1984): 55-71.

Bolton, S. Charles and Cal Ledbetter, Jr. "Compulsory Bible Reading in Arkansas and the Culture of Southern Fundamentalism." *Social Science Quarterly* 64 (September 1983): 670-76.

Boothby, Lee and R.W. Nixon. "Religious Accommodation: An Often Delicate Task." *The Notre Dame Lawyer* 57 (June 1982): 797-808.

Boston, Rob. "The Day 'Sherbert' Melted." *Church and State* 43 (June 1990): 4-6.

Bowden, Henry Warner. "A Historian's Response to the Concept of American Civil Religion." *Journal of Church and State* 17 (Autumn 1975): 495-505.

Bowman, Margaret B. "The Reburial of Native American Skeletal Remains: Approaches to the Resolution of a Conflict." *Harvard Environmental Law Review* (1989): 147-208.

Bradley, Elizabeth. "A New Approach to NLRB Jurisdiction Over the Employment Practices of Religious Institutions." *University of Chicago Law Review* 54 (Winter, 1987): 243-76.

Bradley, Gerard V. "Beguiled: Free Exercise Exemptions and the Siren Song of Liberalism." *Hofstra Law Review* 20 (Winter 1991): 245-319.

____________. "Church Autonomy in the Constitutional Order: The End of Church and State?" *Louisiana Law Review* (1989): 1057-87.

Braiterman, Marvin and Dean M. Kelley. "When Is Governmental Intervention Legitimate?" In *Government Intervention in Religious Affairs*. ed. Dean M. Kelley, 170-93. New York: The Pilgrim Press, 1982.

Breyer, Chloe Anne. "Religious Liberty in Law and Practice: Vietnamese Home Temples and the First Amendment." *Journal of Church and State* 35 (Spring 1993): 367-401.

Brisbin, Richard A., Jr. "The Rehnquist Court and the Free Exercise of Religion." *Journal of Church and State* 34 (Winter 1992): 57-76.

Brooks, Lee W. "Intentional Infliction of Emotional Distress by Spiritual Counselors: Can Outrageous Conduct Be 'Free Exercise'?" *Michigan Law Review* 84 (May 1986): 1296-1325.

Brothers, Kenneth W. "Church-Affiliated Universities and Labor Board Jurisdiction: An Unholy Union Between Church and State?" *George Washington Law Review* 56 (March 1988): 558-99.

Broyles, Kevin E. "Establishment of Religion and High School Graduation Ceremonies." *Harvard Journal of Law and Public Policy* 16 (Winter 1993): 279-87.

Brudney, Jeffrey L. and Gary W. Copeland. "Evangelicals as a Political Force: Reagan and the 1980 Religious Vote." *Social Science Quarterly* 65 (December 1984): 1072-79.

Buchanan, G. S. "Governmental Aid to Sectarian Schools: A Study in Corrosive Precedents." *Houston Law Review* 15 (May 1978): 783-838.

____________. "Governmental Aid to Religious Entities: The Total Subsidy Position Prevails." *Fordham Law Review* (October 1 1989): 53-85.

Burleson, Bruce "*E.E.O.C.* v. *Mississippi College*: The Applicability of Title VII to Sectarian Schools." *Baylor Law Review* 33 (Spring 1981): 380-91.

Butler, William B. "The Free Exercise Clause: The Supreme Court Avoids Strict Scrutiny and the 'Compelling Governmental Interest' Test—*Employment Division*." *Mitchell Law Review* 17 (Spring 1991): 595-626.

Butler, William J. "The Effect of State Aid to Church Schools on Public Education." *Journal of Church and State* 6 (Winter 1964): 74-84.

Byler, Celia. "Free Access or Free Exercise?: A Choice Between Mineral Development and American Indian Sacred Site Preservation on Public Lands." *Connecticut Law Review* 22 (Winter 1990): 397-435.

Cahn, Edmund. "On Government and Prayer." *New York Law Review* 37 (December 1962): 981-1000.

Canavan, Francis, S.J. "The Impact of Recent Supreme Court Decisions on Religion in the United States." *Journal of Church and State* 16 (Spring 1974): 217-36.

Capps, Kline and Carl H. Esbeck. "The Use of Government Funding and Taxing Power to Regulate Religious Schools." *Journal of Law and Education* 14 (October 1985): 553-74.

Carmella, Angela C. "Houses of Worship and Religious Liberty: Constitutional Limits to Landmark Preservation and Architectural Review." *Villanova Law Review* 36 (1991): 401-515.

____________. "Liberty and Equality: Paradigms for the Protection of Religious Property Use." *Journal of Church and State* 37 (Summer 1995): 573-98.

Carpenter, James G. "State Regulation of Religious Schools." *Journal of Law and Education* 14 (April 1985): 229-49.

Carroll, William A. "The Constitution, the Supreme Court, and Religion." *American Political Science Review* 61 (September 1967): 657-74.

Carter, Stephen L. "Comment: The Resurrection of Religious Freedom?" *Harvard Law Review* 107 (November 1993): 118-42.

____________. "Evolutionism, Creationism, and Treating Religion as a Hobby." *Duke Law Journal* (December 1987): 977-96.

Case, David W. "Resolving the Conflict Between Chapter 13 of the Bankruptcy Code and the Free Exercise Clause—*In Re Green:* A Step in the Wrong Direction." *Mississippi Law Journal* 57 (April 1987): 163-84.

Casino, Bruce J. "'I Know It When I See It': Mail-Order Ministry Tax Fraud and the Problem of a Constitutionally Acceptable Definition of Religion." *American Criminal Law Review* 25 (Summer 1987): 113-64.

Chase, Jonathan B. "Litigating a Nativity Scene Case." *St. Louis University Law Journal* 24 (1980): 237-71.

Choper, Jesse H., "The Establishment Clause and Aid to Parochial Schools—An Update." *California Law Review* 75 (January 1987): 5-14.

____________. "Defining 'Religion' in the First Amendment." *University of Illinois Law Review 1982* (1982): 579-613.

____________. "The Free Exercise Clause: A Structural Overview and an Appraisal of Recent Developments." *William and Mary Law Review* 27 (1987): 943-61.

____________. "Religion in the Public Schools: A Proposed Constitutional Standard." *Minnesota Law Review* 47 (January 1963): 329-416.

____________. "The Religion Clauses of the First Amendment: Reconciling the Conflict." *University of Pittsburgh Law Review* 41 (Summer 1980): 673-701.

____________. "Separation of Church and State: 'New' Directions by the 'New' Supreme Court." *Journal of Church and State* 34 (Spring 1992): 363-75.

Clark, J. Morris. "Guidelines for the Free Exercise Clause." *Harvard Law Review* 83 (December 1969): 327-65.

Clements, Ben. "Defining 'Religion' in the First Amendment: A Functional Approach." *Cornell Law Review* (March 1989): 532-58.

Cline, Christopher P. "Pursuing Native American Rights in International Law Venues: A Jus Cogens Strategy After *Lyng* v. *Northwest Indian Cemetery Protective Association*." *Hastings Law Journal* 42 (January 1991): 591-633.

Collins, Camala. "No More Religious Protection: The Impact of *Lyng* v. *Northwest Indian Cemetery Protection Association*." *Washington University Journal of Urban and Contemporary Law* 38 (Summer 1990): 369-84.

Connolly, John W. III. "*Mueller* v. *Allen:* A New Standard of Scrutiny Applied to Tax Deductions for Educational Expenses." *Duke Law Journal* 1984 (November 1984): 983-1001.

Connor, M. Colleen. "The Constitutionality of Religious Symbols on Government Property: A Suggested Approach." *Journal of Church and State* 37 (Spring 1995): 385-411.

"Constitutional Law—Legislative Prayer and the Establishment Clause: An Exception to the Traditional Analysis—*Marsh* v. *Chambers*." *Creighton Law Review* 17 (1983/1984): 157-85.

"Constitutional Law—The Clash Between the Free Exercise of Religion and the Military's Uniform Regulations—*Goldman* v. *Secretary of Defense*." *Temple Law Quarterly* 58 (Spring 1985): 195-219.

"The Constitutional Dimensions of Student-Initiated Religious Activity in Public High Schools." *Yale Law Journal* 92 (December 1982): 499-519.

"Constitutionality of Student-Initiated Religious Meetings on Public School Grounds." *University of Cincinnati Law Review* 50 (1981): 740-85.

Cook, Theresa. "The Peyote Case: A Return to *Reynolds*." *Denver University Law Review* 68 (Winter 1991): 91-103.

Cord, Robert L. and Howard Ball. "The Separation of Church and State: A Debate." *Utah Law Review* 1987 (1987): 895-925.

____________. "Church-State Separation: Restoring the 'No Preference' Doctrine of the First Amendment." *Harvard Journal of Law and Public Policy* 9 (Winter 1986): 129-72.

Cordes, Mark W. "Where To Pray? Religious Zoning and the First Amendment." *University of Kansas Law Review* 35 (Summer 1987): 697-762.

Cornelius, William J. "Church and State: The Mandate of the Establishment Clause: Wall of Separation or Benign Neutrality?" *St. Mary's Law Journal* 16 (1984): 1-39.

Corwin, E. S. "The Supreme Court as National School Board." *Law and Contemporary Problems* 14 (Winter 1949): 3-22.

Cote, Denise. "Establishment Clause Analysis of Legislative and Administrative Aid to Religion." *Columbia Law Review* 74 (October 1974): 1175-1202.

Crabb, Kelly C. "Religious Symbols, American Traditions and the Constitution." *Brigham Young University Law Review 1984* (1984): 509-62.

Crough, Maureen M. "A Proposal for Extension of the Occupational Safety and Health Act to Indian-Owned Businesses on Reservations." *University of Michigan Journal of Law Reform* 18 (Winter 1985): 473-502.

Crockenberg, Vincent A. "An Argument for the Constitutionality of Direct Aid to Religious Schools." *Journal of Law and Education* 13 (January 1984): 1-18.

Croney, Vance M. "Secondary Right: Protection of the Free Exercise Clause Reduced by *Oregon v. Smith*." *Willamette Law Review* 27 (Winter 1991): 173-96.

Crumpler, M. Greg. "Constitutional Law—Legislative Chaplaincy Program Held Not to Violate the Establishment of Religion Clause—*Marsh* v. *Chambers*." *Campbell Law Review* 6 (Spring 1984): 143-61.

Curry, David P. "The Constitution in the Supreme Court: Civil Rights and Liberties, 1930-1941." *Duke Law Journal* 1987 (November 1987): 800-30.

____________. "The Constitution in the Supreme Court: The Preferred-Position Debate, 1941-1946." *Catholic University Law Review* 37 (Fall 1987): 39-71.

Curry, Patricia E. "James Madison and the Burger Court: Converging Views of Church-State Separation." *Indiana Law Journal* 56 (Summer 1981): 615-36.

Dane, Perry. "Religious Exemptions Under the Free Exercise Clause: A Model of Competing Authorities." *Yale Law Journal* 90 (December 1980): 350-78.

Dankanich, Michael D. "Constitutional Law—State May Ban Religious Solicitation in Public Sports Complex, Since Complex Is Not A Public Forum—*International Society For Krishna Consciousness, Inc.* v. *New Jersey Sports & Exposition Authority*, 691 F.2D 155 (3D CIR. 1982)." *Temple Law Review* 57 (January 1, 1983): 119-33.

Danzig, Richard. "How Questions Begot Answers in Felix Frankfurter's First Flag Salute Opinion." *1977 Supreme Court Review* (1977): 257-74.

"Daily Moments of Silence in Public Schools: A Constitutional Analysis." *New York University Law Review* 58 (May 1983): 364-408.

Darling, Webster. "*Mozert* v. *Hawkins County Board of Education:* The Struggle to Balance Constitutional Interests in the Public School Curricula." *Arkansas Law Review* (April 1, 1989): 519-48.

Davis, Derek H. "Editorial: Assessing the Proposed Religious Equality Amendment." *Journal of Church and State* 37 (Summer 1995): 493-508.

____________. "Editorial: A Commentary on the Proposed 'Religious Equality/Liberties' Amendment." *Journal of Church and State* 38 (Winter 1996): 5-23.

____________. "Editorial: Rebuilding the Wall: Thoughts on Religion and the Supreme Court Under the Clinton Administration." *Journal of Church and State* 35 (Winter 1993): 7-17.

____________. "Editorial: Religion and the American Revolution." *Journal of Church and State* 36 (Autumn 1994): 709-24.

____________. "Editorial: Religious Dimensions of the

Declaration of Independence: Fact and Fiction." *Journal of Church and State* 36 (Summer 1994): 469-82.

____________. "Editorial: Religious Pluralism and the Quest for Unity in American Life." *Journal of Church and State* 36 (Spring 1994): 245-59.

Dean, James J. "Ceremonial Invocations at Public High School Events and the Establishment Clause." *Florida State University Law Review* (April 1, 1989): 1000-31.

de Andrade, David. "The Equal Access Act: The Establishment Clause v. The Free Exercise and Free Speech Clauses." *New York Law School Law Review* 33 (1988): 447-68.

"Defining the Limits of Free Exercise: The Religion Clause Defenses in *United States* v. *Moon*." *Hastings Constitutional Law Quarterly* 12 (Spring 1985): 515-28.

Delgado, Richard. "Religious Totalism: Gentle and Ungentle Persuasion Under the First Amendment." *Southern California Law Review* 51 (November 1977): 1-98.

Dellinger, Walter. "The Sound of Silence: An Epistle on Prayer and the Constitution." *Yale Law Journal* 95 (July 1986): 1631-46.

Denbeaux, Mark P. "The First Word of the First Amendment." *Northwestern University Law Review* 80 (Spring 1986): 1156-1220.

Devins, Neal and Charles O. Galvin. "A Tax Policy Analysis of *Bob Jones University* v. *United States*." *Vanderbilt Law Review* 36 (November 1983): 1353-82.

____________. "Religious Symbols and the Establishment Clause." *Journal of Church and State* 27 (Winter 1985): 19-46.

____________. "State Regulation of Christian Schools." *Journal of Legislation* 10 (Summer 1983): 351-81.

Dodge, Joseph M. II. "The Free Exercise of Religion: A Sociological Approach." *Michigan Law Review* 67 (February 1969): 679-728.

"Does the Wall Still Stand?: Separation of Church and State in the United States." *Baylor Law Review* 37 (Summer 1985): 755-75.

Donahue, Mary Jo. "First Amendment Rights in the Military Context: What Deference Is Due?—*Goldman* v. *Weinberger*." *Creighton Law Review* 20 (1986-87): 85-110.

Doyle, Denis P. "A Din of Inequity: Private Schools Reconsidered." *American Education* 18 (1982): 11-18.

Drakeman, Donald L. "Antidisestablishmentarianism: The Latest (and Longest) Word from the Supreme Court in *Marsh* v. *Chambers*." *Cardozo Law Review* 5 (Fall 1983): 153-81.

Dreisbach, Daniel L. "Thomas Jefferson and Bills Number 82-86 of the Revision of the Laws of Virginia, 1776-1786: New Light on the Jeffersonian Model of Church-State Relations." *North Carolina Law Review* 69 (November 1990): 159-211.

Drennan, William A. "*Bob Jones University* v. *United States*: For Whom Will the Bell Toll." *St. Louis University Law Journal* 29 (1985): 561-96.

____________. "Prayer in the Schools: Is New Jersey's Moment of Silence Constitutional?" *Rutgers Law Review* 35 (Winter 1983): 341-59.

____________. "Religion and the Republic: James Madison and the First Amendment." *Journal of Church and State* 25 (Autumn, 1983): 427-45.

Driggs, Kenneth David. "The Mormon Church-State Confrontation in Nineteenth-Century America." *Journal of Church and State* 30 (Autumn 1988): 273-89.

Drinan, Robert F., S.J. "State and Federal Aid to Parochial Schools." *Journal of Church and State* 7 (Winter 1965): 67-77.

____________ and Jennifer I. Huffman. "Religious Freedom and the *Oregon* v. *Smith* and *Hialeah* Cases." *Journal of Church and State* 35 (Winter 1993): 19-35.

Drucker, Margo R. "*Bowen* v. *Kendrick*: Establishing Chastity at the Expense of Constitutional Prophylactics." *New York University Law Review* (November 1989): 1165-1210.

Dunsford, John E. "Prayer in the Well: Some Heretical Reflections on the Establishment Syndrome." *Utah Law Review* (1984): 1-44.

Durham W. Cole, Jr., "Religious Liberty and the Call of Conscience." *De Paul Law Review* 42 (Fall 1992): 71-88.

Durrant, Matthew B. "Accrediting Church-Related Schools: A First Amendment Analysis." *Journal of Law and Education* 14 (April 1985): 147-79.

Durso, Keith E. "The Voluntary School Prayer Debate: A Separationist Perspective." *Journal of Church and State* 36 (Winter 1994): 79-96.

Edwards, John Evan. "Democracy and Delegation of Legislative Authority: *Bob Jones University* v. *United States*." *Boston College Law Review* 26 (May 1985): 745-78.

Eisgruber, Christopher L. "Madison's Wager: Religious Liberty in the Constitutional Order." *Northwestern University Law Review* 89 (Winter 1995): 347-410.

Eisgruber, Christopher L. and Lawrence G. Sager. "The Vulnerability of Conscience: The Constitutional Basis for Protecting Religious Conduct." *University of Chicago Law Review* 61 (Fall 1994): 1245-1316.

Elifson, Kirk and C. Kirk Hadaway. "Prayer in Public Schools: When Church and State Collide." *Public Opinion Quarterly* 49 (Fall 1985): 317-29.

Ericsson, Samuel E. "Clergy Malpractice: Constitutional and Political Issues." *The Center for Law and Religious Freedom* (May 1981): 1-32.

Esbeck, Carl H. "Government Regulation of Religiously Based Social Services: The First Amendment Considerations." *Hastings Constitutional Law Quarterly* 19 (Winter 1992): 343-412.

____________. "The Establishment Clause and Liquor Sales: The Supreme Court Rushes in Where Angels Fear to Tread—*Larkin* v. *Grendel's Den*." *Washington Law Review* 59 (1983-84): 87-101.

____________. "Establishment Clause Limits on Governmental Interference With Religious Organizations." *Washington and Lee Law Review* 41 (Spring 1984): 347-420.

____________. "The *Lemon* Test: Should It Be Retained, Reformulated or Rejected?" *Notre Dame Journal of Law, Ethics & Public Policy* 4 (1990): 513-48.

____________. "Religion and a Neutral State: Imperative or Impossibility?" *Cumberland Law Review* 15 (1984-1985): 67-88.

____________. "A Restatement of the Supreme Court's Law of Religious Freedom: Coherence, Conflict, or Chaos?" *Notre Dame Law Review* 70 (1995): 581-650.

____________. "Tort Claims Against Churches and Ecclesiastical Officers: The First Amendment Considerations." *West Virginia Law Review* 89 (Fall 1986): 1-114.

____________. "Toward a General Theory of Church-State Relations and the First Amendment." *Public Law Forum* 4 (1985): 325-54.

Evans, Bette Novit. "Contradictory Demands on the First Amendment Religion Clauses: Having It Both Ways." *Journal of Church and State* 30 (Autumn 1988): 463-81.

"Evolution and Creationism in the Public Schools." *Journal of Contemporary Law* 9 (1983): 81-126.

Feder, Benjamin D. "And a Child Shall Lead Them: Justice O'Connor, The Principle of Religious Liberty and Its Practical Application." *Pace Law Review* 8 (Spring 1988): 249-302.

Feigenson, Neal R. "Political Standing and Governmental Endorsement of Religion: An Alternative to Current Establishment Clause Doctrine." *DePaul Law Review* 40 (Fall 1990): 53-114.

Fellman, David. "Religion, the State, and the Public University." *Journal of Church and State* 26 (Winter 1984): 73-90.

Felsen, David. "Developments in Approaches to Establishment Clause Analysis: Consistency for the Future." *American University Law Review* 395 (Winter 1989): 395-428.

Fielder, David A. "Serving God or Caesar: Constitutional Limits on the Regulation of Religious Employers." *Missouri Law Review* 51 (Summer 1986): 779-91.

Fisher, Barry A. "Comment on 'The Free Exercise Clause: A Structural Overview and an Appraisal of Recent Developments.'" *William and Mary Law Review* 27 (1987): 975-84.

Flowers, Ronald B. "Can Churches Discipline Members and Win in Court?" *Journal of Church and State* 27 (Autumn 1985): 483-98.

____________. "Government Accommodation of Religious-Based Conscientious Objection." *Seton Hall Law Review* 24 (1993): 695-735.

____________. "The Supreme Court's Interpretation of the Free Exercise Clause." *Religion in Life* 49 (Fall 1980): 322-35.

____________. "The Supreme Court's Three Tests of the Establishment Clause." *Religion in Life* 45 (Spring 1976): 41-52.

____________. "Withholding Medical Care for Religious Reasons." *Journal of Religion and Health* 23 (Winter 1984): 268-82.

Fordham, Jefferson B. "The Implications of the Supreme Court Decisions Dealing with Religious Practices in the Public Schools." *Journal of Church and State* 6 (Winter 1964): 44-60.

Fox, Richard P. "Conscientious Objection to War: The Background and a Current Appraisal." *Cleveland State Law Review* 31 (Winter 1982): 77-106.

Freed, Mayer G. and Daniel D. Polsby. "Race, Public Policy, and Bob Jones University." *1983 Supreme Court Review* (1983): 1-31.

Freeman, Brain A. "The Supreme Court and First Amendment Rights of Students in the Public School Classroom: A Proposed Model of Analysis." *Hastings Constitutional Law Quarterly* 12 (September 1984): 1-70.

Freund, Paul A. "Public Aid to Parochial Schools." *Harvard Law Review* 82 (June 1969): 1680-92.

Friedland, Jerod A. "Constitutional Issues in Revoking Religious Tax Exemptions: *Church of Scientology of California* v. *Commissioner*." *University of Florida Law Review* 37 (Tax 1985): 565-89.

Fulbright, Linda. "The Great Revenue Forfeiture: Tax Exemption for Religious Property in Texas." In Eugene W. Jones et al. *Practicing Texas Politics*, 4th ed. Boston: Houghton Mifflin Co., (1980): 540-45.

Gaffney, Edward M., Jr. "Political Divisiveness Along Religious Lines: Entanglement of the Court in Sloppy History and Bad Public Policy." *St. Louis University Law Journal* 24 (1980): 205-36.

Galanter, Marc. "Religious Freedoms in the United States: A Turning Point?" *Wisconsin Law Review 1966* (Spring 1966): 217-96.

Galligan, Michael William. "Judicial Resolution of Intrachurch Disputes." *Columbia Law Review* 83 (December 1983): 2007-38.

Galloway, Russell W. "Basic Free Exercise Clause Analysis." *Santa Clara Law Review* 29 (Fall 1989): 865-78.

Garrett, W. Barry. "IRS Proposal Scored." *Church and State* 29 (June 1976): 10-11.

Garrett, James Leo. "The 'Free Exercise' Clause of the First Amendment: Retrospect and Prospect." *Journal of Church and State* 17 (Autumn 1975): 393-98.

Garvey, John H. "Churches and the Free Exercise of Religion." *Notre Dame Journal of Law, Ethics, and Public Policy* 4 (Fall/Winter 1990): 567-89.

____________. "Free Exercise and the Values of Religious Liberty." *Connecticut Law Review* (1981): 193-221.

____________. "Freedom and Equality in the Religion Clauses." *Supreme Court Review 1981* (1981): 193-221.

Gaustad, Edwin Scott. "A Disestablished Society: Origins of the First Amendment." *Journal of Church and State* 11 (Autumn 1969): 409-26.

Gavin, Charles O. and Neal Devins. "A Tax Policy Analysis of *Bob Jones University* v. *United States*." *Vanderbilt Law Review* 36 (November 1983): 1353-82.

Gay, John. "*Bowen* v. *Kendrick*: Establishing a New Relationship Between Church and State." *American University Law Review* (April 1, 1989): 953-992.

Gedicks, Frederick M. "Motivation, Rationality, and Secular Purpose in Establishment Clause Review." *Arizona State Law Journal 1985* (1985): 677-726.

Gershon, Richard. "Tax-Exempt Entities: Achieving and Maintaining Special Status Under the Watchful Eye of the Internal Revenue Service." *Cumberland Law Review* 16 (1985): 301-27.

Gey, Steven G. "Why is Religion Special?: Reconsidering the Accommodation of Religion Under the Religion Clauses of the First Amendment." *University of Pittsburgh Law Review* 52 (Fall 1990): 75-187.

Geyer, Thomas E. "Free Exercise Jurisprudence: A Comment on the Heightened Threshold and the Proposal of the 'burden plus' Standard." *Ohio State Law Journal* 50 (October 1989): 1035-57.

Giannella, Donald A. "Lemon and Tilton: The Bitter and Sweet of Church-State Entanglement." *Supreme Court Review* 147 (1971): 147-200.

____________. "Religious Liberty, Nonestablishment, and Doctrinal Development. Part I. The Religious Liberty Guarantee." *Harvard Law Review* 80 (May 1967): 1381-1431.

Goff, J. Edward. "Constitutional Law—First Amendment—A State Statute that Permits a Tax Deduction for Public as Well as Non-Public School Tuition and Related Expenses Does Not Violate the Establishment Clause of the First Amendment—*Mueller* v. *Allen*." *Villanova Law Review* 29 (April 1984): 505-34.

Goodwin, Glenn. "Would Caesar Tax God? The Constitutionality of Governmental Taxation of Churches." *Drake Law Review* 35 (1985): 383-404.

Gordon, James D. III. "Free Exercise on the Mountaintop." *California Law Review* 79 (1991): 91-116.

Gordon, Sarah B. "Indian Religious Freedom and Governmental Development of Public Lands." *Yale Law Journal* 94 (May 1985): 1447-71.

Gottlieb, Stephen E. "Compelling Governmental Interests: An Adjudication." *Boston University Law Review* 68 (1988): 917-78.

Gould, Diane Brazen. "The First Amendment and the American Indian Religious Freedom Act: An Approach to Protecting Native American Religion." *Iowa Law Review* 71 (March 1986): 869-91.

"Government Neutrality and Separation of Church and State: Tuition Tax Credits." *Harvard Law Review* 92 (January 1979): 696-717.

Govert, Gary R. "Something There Is That Doesn't Love a Wall: Reflections on the History of North Carolina's Religious Test for Public Office." *North Carolina Law Review* 64 (June 1986): 1071-98.

Graham, David. "Balancing the Free Religious Exercise Right Against Governmental Interests." *Hamline Law Review* 9 (July 1986): 649-99.

Grant, Harriet. "*Lynch* v. *Donnelly*: The Disappearing Wall." *North Carolina Law Review* 63 (April 1985): 782-93.

Green, Steven K. "Evangelicals and the Becker Amendment: A Lesson in Church-State Moderation." *Journal of Church and State* 33 (Summer 1991): 541-67.

____________. "The Misnomer of Equality Under the Equal Access Act." *Vermont Law Review* 14 (Winter 1990): 369-400.

Greenawalt, Kent. "Religion as a Concept in Constitutional Law." *California Law Review* 72 (September 1984): 753-816.

____________. "The Participation of Religious Groups in Political Advocacy." *Journal of Church and State* 36 (Winter 1994): 143-60.

____________. "The Role of Religion in a Liberal Democracy: Dilemmas and Possible Resolutions." *Journal of Church and State* 35 (Summer 1993): 503-19.

____________. "The Use of Religious Convictions by Legislators and Judges." *Journal of Church and State* 36 (Summer 1994): 541-55.

Greene, Abner S. "The Political Balance of the Religion Clauses." *Yale Law Journal* 102 (May 1993): 1611-44.

Griggs, Walter S., Jr. "The Selective Conscientious Objector: A Vietnam Legacy." *Journal of Church and State* 21 (Winter 1979): 91-107.

Hafen, Bruce C. "Hazelwood School District and the Role of First Amendment Institutions." *Duke Law Journal* (September 1988): 685-705.

Hall, Timothy L. "The Sacred and the Profane: A First Amendment Definition of Religion." *Texas Law Review* 61 (August 1982): 139-73.

Hamburger, Philip A., "A Constitutional Right of Religious Exemption: An Historical Perspective." *George Washington Law Review* 60 (April 1992): 915-48.

Hammett, Harold D. "Separation of Church and State: By One Wall or Two?" *Journal of Church and State* 7 (Spring 1965): 190-206.

Hammond, Phillip E. and Eric M. Mazur. "Church, State and the Dilemma of Conscience." *Journal of Church and State* 37 (Summer 1995): 555-71.

Hancock, Ralph C. "Religion and the Limits of Limited Government." *Review of Politics* 50 (Fall 1988): 682-703.

Hanrahan, E.M. "Constitutionality of Legislation Denying Tax-Exempt Status to Racially Discriminatory Schools." *The Catholic Lawyer* 28 (Spring 1983): 137-43.

Harkins, James C. "Of Textbooks and Tenets: *Mozert* v. *Hawkins County Board of Education* and the Free Exercise of Religion." *American University Law Review* 37 (Spring 1988): 985-1012.

Harpaz, Leora. "Justice Jackson's Flag Salute Legacy: The Supreme Court Struggles to Protect Intellectual Individualism." *Texas Law Review* 64 (February 1986): 817-914.

Harris, David J. "Respect for the Living and Respect for the Dead: Return of Indian and Other Native American Burial Remains." *Washington University Journal of Urban & Contemporary Law* 39 (Spring 1991): 195-224.

Hatch, Orrin G. "Foreword." *Ohio State Law Journal* 47 (1986): 291-92.

Hayes, B. Douglas. "Secular Humanism in Public School Textbooks: Thou Shalt Have No Other God (Except Thyself)." *Notre Dame Law Review* 63 (1988): 358-79.

Head, Neil W. "Property—Neutral Principles Approach in Interchurch Property Disputes—*Presbytery of Beaver-Butter of the United Presbyterian Church in the United States* v. *Middlesex Presbyterian Church*." *Temple Law Review* 59 (Summer 1986): 789-806.

Heady, Brian D. "Constitutional Law: What Offends a Theist Does Not Offend the Establishment Clause." *San Diego Law Review* (Fall 1988): 153-74.

____________. "First Americans and the First Amendment: American Indians Battle for Religious Freedom." *Southern Illinois University Law Journal* 13 (Summer 1989): 945-74.

Healy, Peggy. "*Lyng* v. *Northwest Indian Cemetery Protective Association*: A Form-Over Effect Standard for the Free Exercise Clause." *Loy University of China Law Journal* (December 1, 1988): 171-96.

Hess, Danielle A. "The Undoing of Mandatory Free Exercise Accommodation—*Employment Division, Department of Human Resources* v. *Smith*." *Washington Law Review* 66 (April 1991): 587-603.

Hill, Alexander D. and Chi-Dooh Li. "A Current Church-State Battleground: Requiring Clergy to Report Child Abuse." *Journal of Church and State* 32 (Autumn 1990): 795-811.

____________. "Religious Speech in Public Schools: A Case Study in Contradictions." *Journal of Church and State* 37 (Summer 1995): 623-40.

Hogue, William M. "The Civil Disability of Ministers of Religion in State Constitutions." *Journal of Church and State* 36 (Spring 1994): 329-55.

Holland, Robert A. "A Theory of Establishment Clause Adjudication: Individualism, Social Contract, and the Significance of Coercion in Identifying Threats to Religious Liberty." *California Law Review* 80 (December 1992): 1595-1694.

Horn, Carl III. "Secularism and Pluralism in Public Education." *Harvard Journal of Law and Public Policy* 7 (Winter 1984): 177-83.

Hostetler, John A. "The Amish and the Law: A Religious Minority and Its Legal Encounters." *Washington and Lee Law Review* 41 (Winter 1984): 33-47.

Howarth, Don and William D. Connell. "Student Rights to Organize and Meet for Religious Purposes in the University Context." *Valparaiso Law Review* 16 (Fall 1981): 103-43.

Hughes, Richard W. "Indian Law." *New Mexico Law Review* (Winter 1988): 403-67.

Hughson, Thomas, S.J. "From James Madison to William Lee Miller: John Courtney and Baptist Theory of the First Amendment." *Journal of Church and State* 37 (Winter 1995): 15-37.

Idleman, Scott C. "The Religious Freedom Restoration Act: Pushing the Limits of Legislative Power." *Texas Law Review* 73 (December 1994): 247-334.

Ignani, Joseph A. "Explaining and Predicting Supreme Court Decision Making: The Burger Court's Establishment Clause Decisions." *Journal of Church and State* 36 (Spring 1994): 301-27.

Ivers, Gregg. "Organized Religion and the Supreme Court." *Journal of Church and State* 32 (Autumn 1990): 775-93.

"I. V. Medical and Counseling Privileges." *Harvard Law Review* 98 (May 1985): 1530.

Johnson, Phillip E. "Concepts and Compromise in First Amendment Religious Doctrine." *California Law Review* 72 (September 1984): 817-46.

Jones, Harry W. "The Constitutional Status of Public Funds for Church Related Schools." *Journal of Church and State* 6 (Winter 1964): 61-73.

Juster, Sara A. "Free Exercise—Or the Lack Thereof?" *Creighton Law Review* 24 (December 1990): 239-65.

Kaplan, Julie B. "Military Mirrors on the Wall: Nonestablishment and the Military Chaplaincy." *Yale Law Journal* 95 (May 1986): 1210-36.

Katz, Wilber and Harold P. Southerland. "Religious Pluralism and the Supreme Court." *Daedalus* 96 (Winter 1967): 180-92.

Kauper, Paul G. "Church Autonomy and the First Amendment: The Presbyterian Church Case." *1969 The Supreme Court Review* (1969): 347-78.

____________. "Church, State, and Freedom: A Review." *Michigan Law Review* 52 (April 1954): 829-48.

____________. "*Everson* v. *Board of Education*: A Product of the Judicial Will." *Arizona Law Review* 15 (1973): 307-26.

____________. "Prayer, Public Schools, and the Supreme Court." *Michigan Law Review* 61 (April 1963): 1031-68.

____________. "Released Time and Religious Liberty: A Further Reply." *Michigan Law Review* 53 (November 1954): 233-36.

Kelley, Dean M. "A Primer for Pastors: What to Do When the FBI Knocks." *Christianity and Crisis* 37 (May 2, 1977): 86-92.

____________. "When Religion Is Paid to be Silent." *Worldview* 16 (April 1973): 32-7.

Kemper, Keith. "Freedom of Religion vs. Public School Reading Curriculum." *University of Puget Sound Law Review* (April 1, 1988): 405-49.

Kerley, John E. "Constitutional Law—Christian Science Malpractice—Illinois Appellate Court Commands: Thou Shalt Not Interfere with Faith Healers." *Southern University Law Journal* (Winter 1989): 411-27.

Killilea, Alfred G. "Privileging Conscientious Dissent: Another Look at *Sherbert* v. *Verner*." *Journal of Church and State* 16 (Spring 1974): 194-216.

Kirby, James C., Jr. "Everson to Meek and Roemer: From Separation to Detente in Church-State Relations." *North Carolina Law Review* 55 (1977): 563-75.

Kliever, Lonnie D. "Academic Freedom and Church-Affiliated Universities" *Texas Law Review* 66 (June 1988): 1477-80.

Knight, Barbara B. "Religion in Prison: Balancing the Free Exercise, No Establishment, and Equal Protection Clauses." *Journal of Church and State* 26 (Autumn 1984): 437-54.

Kurland, Philip B. "Of Church and State and the Supreme Court." *University of Chicago Law Review* 29 (Autumn 1961): 1-96.

__________. "The Rise and Fall of the 'Doctrine' of Separation of Powers." *Michigan Law Review* 85 (December 1986): 592-613.

__________. "The Irrelevance of the Constitution: The Religion Clauses of the First Amendment and the Supreme Court." *Villanova Law Review* 24 (November 1978): 3-27.

__________. "The Religion Clauses and the Burger Court." *Catholic University Law Review* 34 (Fall 1984): 1-19.

Kushner, James A. "Toward the Central Meaning of Religious Liberty: Non-Sunday Sabbatarians and the Sunday Closing Cases Revisited." *Southwestern Law Journal* 35 (June 1981): 557-84.

Kuznicki, Joseph M. "Section 170, Tax Expenditures, and the First Amendment: The Failure of Charitable Religious Contributions for the Return of a Religious Benefit." *Temple Law Review* 61 (Summer 1988): 443-87.

Lam, Eddie. "*Employment Division, Department of Human Resources of Oregon* v. *Smith*: The Limits of the Free Exercise Clause." *Thurgood Marshall Law Review* 16 (Spring 1991): 377-97.

Lardner, Lynford A. "How Far Does the Constitution Separate Church and State?" *American Political Science Review* 45 (March 1951): 110-32.

Latham, Bill. "*Valley Forge Christian College* v. *Americans United for Separation of Church and State*: Taxpayer Standing and the Establishment Clause." *Baylor Law Review* 34 (Fall 1982): 748-62.

Laurence, Robert. "Martinez, Oliphant and Federal Court Review of Tribal Activity Under the Indian Civil Rights Act." *Campbell Law Review* 10 (Summer 1988): 411-38.

Lavi, Terri Jane. "Free Exercise Challenges to Public School Curricula: Are States Creating Enclaves of Totalitarianism Through Compulsory Reading Requirements?" *George Washington Law Review* (December 1988): 301-27.

Lawless, James J., Jr. "*Roy* v. *Cohen*: Social Security Number and the Free Exercise Clause." *American University Law Review* 36 (Fall 1986): 217-42.

"Laws Respecting an Establishment of Religion: An Inquiry into Tuition Tax Benefits." *New York University Law Review* 58 (April 1983): 207-37.

Laycock, Douglas. "Free Exercise and the Religious Freedom Restoration Act." *Fordham Law Review* 62 (February 1994): 883-904.

__________. "The Religious Freedom Restoration Act." *Brigham Young University Law Review* (1993): 221-58.

__________. "RFRA, Congress, and the Ratchet." *Montana Law Review* 56 (Winter 1995): 145-70.

Laycock, Douglas and Oliver S. Thomas. "Interpreting the Religious Freedom Restoration Act." *Texas Law Review* 73 (December 1994): 209-45.

Laycock, Douglas and Susan E. Waelbroeck. "Academic Freedom and the Free Exercise of Religion." *Texas Law Review* 66 (June 1988): 1455-75.

__________. "A Survey of Religious Liberty in the United States." *Ohio State Law Journal* 47 (1986): 409-51.

__________. "Formal, Substantive, and Disaggregated Neutrality Toward Religion." *DePaul Law Review* 39 (Summer 1990): 993-1018.

__________. "'Noncoercive' Support for Religion: Another False Claim About the Establishment Clause." *Valparaiso University Law Review* 26 (Fall 1991): 37-69.

__________. "Peyote, Wine and the First Amendment." *The Christian Century* 106 (October 4, 1989): 876-80.

__________. "Tax Exceptions for Racially Discriminatory Religious Schools." *Texas Law Review* 60 (Fall 1982): 259-77.

__________. "Text, Intent, and the Religion Clauses." *Notre Dame Journal of Law, Ethics, and Public Policy* 4 (Fall/Winter 1990): 683-97.

__________. "The Remnants of Free Exercise." *1991 The Supreme Court Review* (1991): 1-68.

__________. "Watering Down the Free-Exercise Clause." *The Christian Century* 107 (16-23 May 1990): 518-19.

Leavy, Edward N. and Eric A. Raps. "The Judicial Double Standard for State Aid to Church-Affiliated Educational Institutions." *Journal of Church and State* 21 (Spring 1979): 209-22.

Lee, Rex E. "The Religion Clauses: Problems and Prospects." *Brigham Young University Law Review* (1986): 337-47.

"The Legal Relationship of Conscience to Religion: Refusals to Bear Arms." *University of Chicago Law Review* 38 (Spring 1971): 583-611.

Leitch, David G. "The Myth of Religious Neutrality by Separation in Education." *Virginia Law Review* 71 (February 1985): 127-72.

Leventhal, David. "The Free Exercise Clause Gets a Costly Workout in *Employment Division, Department of Human Resources* v. *Smith*." *Pepperdine Law Review* 18 (December 1990): 163-212.

Levit, Nancy. "Creationism, Evolution and the First Amendment: The Limits of Constitutionally Permissible Scientific Inquiry." *Journal of Law and Education* 14 (April 1985): 211-27.

Linder, Robert D. "Civil Religion in Historical Perspective: The Reality That Underlies the Concept." *Journal of Church and State* 17 (Autumn 1975): 399-421.

Little, Sandra Morgan. "Counsel By Clergy: Is It Privileged?" *Family Advocate* 10 (Summer 1987): 24-7.

Lively, Donald E. "The Establishment Clause: Lost Soul of the First Amendment." *Ohio State Law Journal* (June 1, 1989): 681-99.

Loewy, Arnold H. "School Prayer, Neutrality, and the Open Forum: Why We Don't Need a Constitutional Amendment." *North Carolina Law Review* 61 (October 1982): 141-56.

Louisell, David W. and John H. Jackson. "Religion, Theology and Public Higher Education." *California Law Review* 50 (December 1962): 751-99.

Lovin, Robin W. "Rethinking the History of Church and State: The Believer and the Powers that Are." *California Law Review* (October 1988): 1185-98.

Lupu, Ira C. "Free Exercise Exemption and Religious Institutions: The Case of Employment Discrimination." *Boston University Law Review* 67 (May 1987): 391-442.

__________. "Home Education, Religious Liberty, and the Separation of Powers." *Boston University Law Review* 67 (November 1987): 971-90.

__________. "Reconstructing the Establishment Clause: The Case Against Discretionary Accommodation of Religion." *University of Pennsylvania Law Review* 140 (December 1991): 555-612.

__________. "Where Rights Begin: The Problem of Burdens on the Free Exercise of Religion." *Harvard Law Review* (March 1989): 933-90.

"*Lynch* v. *Donnelly*: Our Christmas Will Be Merry Still." *Mercer Law Review* 36 (Fall 1984): 409-20.

Maddigan, Michael M. "The Establishment Clause, Civil Religion and the Public Church." *California Law Review* 81 (January 1993): 293-349.

Magan, Virginia C. "*Employment Division, Department of Human Resources of Oregon* v. *Smith*: Does the Constitutionally Compelled Free Exercise Exemption Have a Prayer?" *Pacific Law Journal* 22 (July 1991): 1415-53.

Manion, Maureen D. "Parental Religious Freedom, the Rights of Children and the Role of the State." *Journal of Church and State* 34 (Winter 1992): 77-92.

Mansfield, John H. "The Religion Clauses of the First Amendment and the Philosophy of the Constitution." *California Law Review* 72 (September 1984): 847-907.

Marin, Kenneth. "*Employment Division* v. *Smith*: The Supreme Court Alters the State of Free Exercise Doctrine." *American University Law Review* 40 (Summer 1991): 1431-76.

"*Marsh* v. *Chambers*: The Supreme Court Takes a New Look at the Establishment Clause." *Pepperdine Law Review* 11 (March 1984): 591-611.

Marshall, William P. "The Case against the Constitutionally Compelled Free Exercise Exemption." *Case Western Reserve Law Review* 40 (Spring 1990): 357-412.

____________. "In Defense of *Smith* and Free Exercise Dilemma: Free Exercise as Expression." *Minnesota Law Review* 67 (1983): 545-94.

____________. "Solving the Free Exercise Dilemma: Free Exercise as Expression." *Minnesota Law Review* 67 (Fall 1983): 545-94.

____________. "'We Know It When We See It': The Supreme Court and Establishment," *Southern California Law Review* 59 (March 1986): 495-550.

____________. and Douglas C. Blomgren. "Regulating Religious Organizations Under the Establishment Clause." *Ohio State Law Journal* 47 (1986): 293-331.

Martin, Christina. "Student-Initiated Religious Expression after *Mergens* and *Weisman*." *University of Chicago Law Review* 61 (Fall 1994): 1565-95.

Marty, Martin E. "On a Medial Moraine: Religious Dimensions of American Constitutionalism." *Emory Law Journal* 39 (Winter 1990): 9-20.

Mauney, Constance. "Religion and First Amendment Protections: An Analysis of Justice Black's Constitutional Interpretation." *Pepperdine Law Review* 10 (January 1983): 377-420.

Mawdsley, Alice S. "Diminished Status of Religious Liberty in Public Education: Interpreting *Mozert* and *Smith*." *West's Education Law Reporter* 46 (1988): 897.

____________. "Has *Wisconsin* v. *Yoder* Been Reversed? Analysis of *Employment Division* v. *Smith* 63 (December 1990): 11-22.

Mawdsley, Ralph D. "Challenges to Religious Liberties: Procedural Traps." *West's Education Law Reporter* 37 (1987): 11.

____________. and Alice L. Mawdsley. "Religious Freedom and Public Schools: Analysis of Important Policy Areas." *West's Education Law Reporter* (1988): 15.

McBride, James. "Capital Punishment as the Unconstitutional Establishment of Religion: A Girardian Reading of the Death Penalty." *Journal of Church and State* 37 (Spring 1995): 263-87.

____________. "'Is Nothing Sacred?': Flag Desecration, The Constitution and the Establishment of Religion." *St. John's Law Review* 65 (Winter 1991): 297-324.

McCaffrey, C. Grace. "*Nally* v. *Grace Community Church of the Valley*: Clergy Malpractice—A Threat to Both Liberty and Life. *Pace Law Review* 11 (Fall 1990): 137-66.

McCarthy, Martha M. "Student Religious Expression: Mixed Messages from the Supreme Court." *West's Education Law Review* 64 (January 1991): 1-13.

McClamorack, David H. "The First Amendment and Public Funding of Religiously Controlled or Affiliated Higher Education." *Journal of College & University Law* 17 (Winter 1991): 381-428.

McConnell, Michael W. "Accommodation of Religion." *Supreme Court Review* (1985): 1-59.

____________. and Richard A. Posner, "An Economic Approach to Issues of Religious Freedom." *University of Chicago Law Review* 1 (Winter 1989): 1-60.

____________. "Free Exercise Revisionism and the *Smith* Decision." *The University of Chicago Law Review* 57 (Fall 1990): 1109-53.

____________. "Neutrality Under the Religion Clauses." *Northwestern University Law Review* 81 (Fall 1986): 146-67.

____________. "The Origins and Historical Understanding of Free Exercise of Religion." *Harvard Law Review* 103 (May 1990): 1410-1517.

____________. "The Religion Clauses of the First Amendment: Where Is the Supreme Court Heading?" *Catholic Lawyer* 32 (Summer 1988): 187-202.

____________. "Religious Freedom: A Surprising Pattern." *Quarterly* 11 (Spring 1990): 4-8.

____________. "Religious Freedom at a Crossroads." *University of Chicago Law Review* 59 (Winter 1992): 115-94.

____________. "A Response to Professor Marshall." *University of Chicago Law Review* 58 (Winter 1991): 329-32.

McCoy, Thomas R. and Gary A. Kurtz. "A Unifying Theory for the Religion Clauses of the First Amendment." *Vanderbilt Law Review* 39 (March 1986): 249-74.

"*McLean* v. *Arkansas Board of Education*: Finding the Science in 'Creation Science.'" *Northwestern University Law Review* 77 (October 1982): 374-402.

Mead, Sidney E. "The Nation with the Soul of a Church." *Church History* 36 (September 1967): 262-83.

____________. "Neither Church nor State: Reflections on James Madison's 'Line of Separation.'" *Journal of Church and State* 10 (Autumn 1968): 349-64.

____________. "The Post-Protestant Concept and America's Two Religions." *Religion in Life* 33 (Spring 1964): 191-204.

____________. "Religion, Constitutional Federalism, Rights, and the Court." *Journal of Church and State* 14 (Spring 1972): 191-210.

Meiklejohn, Donald. "Religion in the Burger Court: The Heritage of Mr. Justice Black." *Indiana Law Review* 10 (1977): 645-74.

Mermann, Debra Ann. "Free Exercise: A 'Hollow Promise' for the Native American in *Employment Division, Department of Human Resources of Oregon* v. *Smith*." *Mercer Law Review* 42 (1991): 1597-1622.

Michaelsen, Robert S. "Is the Miner's Canary Silent? Implications of the Supreme Court's Denial of American Indian Free Exercise of Religion Claims." *Journal of Law and Religion* 6 (1988): 97-114.

____________. "The Public Schools and 'America's Two Religions.'" *Journal of Church and State* 8 (Autumn 1966): 380-400.

____________. "The Supreme Court and Religion in Public Higher Education." *Journal of Public Law* 13 (No. 2 1964): 342-52.

Miles, Judith C. "Beyond *Bob Jones*: Toward the Elimination of Governmental Subsidy of Discrimination by Religious Institutions." *Harvard Women's Law Journal* 8 (Spring 1985): 31-58.

"Military Ban on Yarmulkes: *Goldman* v. *Weinberger*." *Harvard Law Review* 100 (November 1986).

Miller, Charles. "The Navajo-Hopi Relocation Act and the First Amendment Free Exercise Clause." *University of San Francisco Law Review* (October 1, 1988): 97-121.

Miller, Nicholas P. and Nathan Sheers. "Religious Free Exercise under State Constitutions." *Journal of Church and State* 34 (Spring 1992): 303-23.

Mills, Samuel A. "Parochiaid and the Abortion Decisions: Supreme Court Justice William J. Brennan, Jr. versus the U.S. Catholic Hierarchy." *Journal of Church and State* 34 (Autumn 1992): 751-73.

Minker, Debra Gail. "Constitutional Law—First Amendment—State University's Policy of Equal Access to Campus Facilities for All Organizations Including Those of a Religious Character Does Not Violate the Establishment of Religion Clause of the First Amendment *Widmar* v. *Vincent*." *Emory Law Journal* 32 (Winter 1983): 319-48.

Mirsky, Yehudah. "Civil Religion and the Establishment Clause." *Yale Law Journal* 95 (May 1986): 1237-57.

Mitchell, Mary Harter. "Must Clergy Tell? Child Abuse Reporting Requirements Versus the Clergy Privilege and

Free Exercise of Religion." *Minnesota Law Review* 71 (February 1987): 723-825.

____________. "Secularism in Public Education: The Constitutional Issues." *Boston University Law Review* 67 (July 1987): 603-746.

Moen, Matthew C. "School Prayer and the Politics of Lifestyle Concern." *Social Science Quarterly* 65 (December 1984): 1065-71.

Monopoli, Paula A. "Allocating the Costs of Parental Free Exercise: Striking a New Balance Between Sincere Religious Belief and a Child's Right to Medical Treatment." *Pepperdine Law Review* 18 (January 1991): 319-52.

Monsma, Stephen V. "Justice Potter Stewart on Church and State." *Journal of Church and State* 36 (Summer 1994): 557-76.

Moore, Juliana S. "The Edwards Decision: The End of Creationism in Our Public Schools?" *Akron Law Review* 21 (Fall 1987): 255-67.

Morgan, John. "Values Clarification and Religious Neutrality in the Public Schools: The *Smith* v. *Board of School Commissioner* Constitutional Challenge." *Houston Law Review* (October 1988): 1137-77.

Morris, Kenneth R. "Theological Sources of William Penn's Concept of Religious Toleration." *Journal of Church and State* 35 (Winter 1993): 83-111.

Mott, Kenneth F. "The Supreme Court and the Establishment Clause: From Separation to Accommodation and Beyond." *Journal of Law and Education* 14 (April 1985): 111-45.

Moynihan, Daniel P. "What Do You Do When the Supreme Court Is Wrong?" *The Public Interest* 57 (Fall 1979): 3-24.

"*Mueller* v. *Allen*: A Constitutional Crosswalk to Federal Tuition Tax Credits." *Journal of Legislation* 11 (Winter 1984): 163-74.

"*Mueller* v. *Allen*: The Continued Weakening of the Separation Between Church and State." *New England Law Review* 19 (1983/1984): 459-85.

"*Mueller* v. *Allen*: Tuition Tax Relief and the Original Intent." *Harvard Journal of Law and Public Policy* 7 (Fall 1984): 551-79.

Munich, John R. "Religious Activity in Public Schools: A Proposed Standard." *St. Louis University Law Journal* 24 (September, 1980): 379-405.

Murray, John Courtney, S.J. "Law and Prepossessions?" *Law and Contemporary Problems* 14 (Winter 1949): 23-43.

Nagel, Stuart and Robert Erickson. "Editorial Reaction to Supreme Court Decisions on Church and State." *Public Opinion Quarterly* 30 (Winter 1966-67): 647-55.

Nathan, Richard. "Reflections on Pragmatic Jurisprudence: A Case Study of *Bob Jones University* v. *United States*." *American Business Law Journal* 22 (Summer 1984): 227-48.

Nelson, John Stuart. "Native American Religious Freedom and the Peyote Sacrament: The Precarious Balance Between State Interests and the Free Exercise Clause." *Arizona Law Review* 31 (Spring 1989): 423-46.

Nelson, Lawrence J., Brain P. Buggy and Carol J. Weil. "Forced Medical Treatment of Pregnant Women: 'Compelling Each to Live as Seems Good to the Rest.'" *Hastings Law Journal* 37 (May 1986): 703-63.

Neuhaus, Richard John. "Church, State, and Peyote." *National Review* 42 (June 11, 1990): 40-44.

Newell, Lisa M. "Use of Campus Facilities for First Amendment Activity." *Journal of College and University Law* 9 (No. 1, 1982-83): 27-39.

Newton, Nell Jessup. "Enforcing the Federal-Indian Trust Relationship After Mitchell." *Catholic University Law Review* 31 (Summer 1982): 635-83.

Nolan, James L., Jr. "The Supreme Court and the Story of American Freedom." *Journal of Church and State* 38 (Winter 1996): 37-58.

"A Non-Conflict Approach to the First Amendment Religion Clause." *University of Pennsylvania Law Review* 131 (April 1983): 1175-1208.

Noonan, John T., Jr. "The Constitution's Protection of Individual Rights: The Real Role of the Religion Clauses." *University of Pittsburgh Law Review* 49 (Spring 1988): 717-22.

Noone, Michael F. "Rendering Unto Caesar: Legal Responses to Religious Nonconformity in the Armed Forces." *St. Mary's Law Journal* 18 (1987): 1233-94.

Nordin, Virginia Davis and William Lloyd Turner. "Tax Exempt Status of Private Schools: Wright, Green, and Bob Jones." *West's Education Law Reporter* 35 (December 1986): 329-49.

Nowak, John E. "The Supreme Court, the Religion Clauses and the Nationalization of Education." *Northwestern University Law Review* 70 (January-February 1976): 883-909.

Nuger, Kenneth P. "The Religion of Secular Humanism in Public Schools: *Smith* v. *Board of School Commissioners*." *West's Education Law Reporter* 38 (1987): 871.

Oakes, James L. "Tolerance Theory and the First Amendment." *Michigan Law Review* 85 (April-May 1987).

Okamoto, Duane E. "Religious Discrimination and the Title VII Exemption for Religious Organizations: A Basic Values Analysis for the Proper Allocation of Conflicting Rights." *Southern California Law Review* 60 (July 1987): 1375-1427.

O'Hara, Julie U. "State Aid to Sectarian Higher Education." *Journal of Law and Education* 14 (April 1985): 181-209.

Page, Ellen Adair. "The Scope of the Free Exercise Clause: *Lyng* v. *Northwest Indian Cemetery Protective Association*." *North Carolina Law Review* 68 (January 1990): 410-22.

Patric, Gordon. "The Impact of a Court Decision: Aftermath of the McCollum Case." *Journal of Public Law* 6 (Fall 1967): 455-65.

Pavis, John J. "Compulsory Medical Treatment and Religious Freedom: Whose Law Shall Prevail?" *University of San Francisco Law Review* 10 (Summer 1975): 1-15.

Pavlischek, Keith J. "John Courtney Murray, Civil Religion, and the Problem of Political Neutrality." *Journal of Church and State* 34 (Autumn 1992): 729-50.

Pawa, Matt. "When the Supreme Court Restricts Constitutional Rights, Can Congress Save Us? An Examination of Section 5 of the Fourteenth Amendment." *University of Pennsylvania Law Review* 141 (December 1992): 1029-1101.

Pearlman, Kenneth. "Zoning and the Location of Religious Establishments." *Catholic Lawyer* 31 (1988): 314-45.

Pepper, Stephen L. "The Conundrum of the Free Exercise Clause: Some Reflections on Recent Cases." *Northern Kentucky Law Review* 9 (1982): 265-303.

____________. "Reynolds, Yoder & Beyond: Alternatives for the Free Exercise Clause." *Utah Law Review* 1981: 309-78.

____________. "Taking the Free Exercise Clause Seriously." *Brigham Young University Law Review* (1986): 299-336.

Peterson, Walfred H. "The Thwarted Opportunity for Judicial Activism in Church-State Relations: Separation and Accommodation in Precarious Balance." *Journal of Church and State* 22 (Autumn 1980): 437-58.

Pfeffer, Leo. "Court, Constitution, and Prayer." *Rutgers Law Review* 16 (Summer 1962): 735-52.

____________. "Freedom and Separation: America's Contribution to Civilization." *Journal of Church and State* 2 (November 1960): 100-11.

____________. "Freedom and/or Separation: The Constitutional Dilemma of the First Amendment." *Minnesota Law Review* 64 (March 1980): 561-84.

____________. "The Future of the Bill of Rights: Church-State Relations." In*The Future of Our Liberties: Perspectives on the Bill of Rights*. ed. Stephen C. Halpern, 111-29. Westport, CT: Greenwood Press, 1982.

____________. "What Hath God Wrought to Caesar: The Church as Self-Interest Interest Group." *Journal of Church and State* 13 (Winter 1971): 97-112.

____________. "Workers' Sabbath, Religious Belief and Employment." *Civil Liberties Review* 4 (November-December 1977): 52-6.

Phenix, Philip H. "Religion in Public Education: Principles and Issues." *Journal of Church and State* 14 (Autumn 1979): 415-30.

Piele, Philip K. and Stephen M. Pitt. "The Use of School Facilities by Student Groups for Religious Activities." *Journal of Legal Education* 13 (April 1984): 197-207.

Pochop, Sandra Ashton. "*Employment Division, Department of Human Resources of Oregon* v. *Smith*: Religious Peyotism and the 'Purposeful' Erosion of Free Exercise Protections." *South Dakota Law Review* 36 (1991): 358-81.

Polifka, John C. "Use of the Lemon Test in the Review of Public School Curricular Decisions Concerning 'Secular Humanism' Under the Establishment Clause." *South Dakota Law Review* 33 (1987-88): 112-30.

"Political Entanglement as an Independent Test of Constitutionality Under the Establishment Clause." *Fordham Law Review* 52 (May 1984): 1209-41.

Pollak, Louis H. "Public Prayers in Public Schools." *Harvard Law Review* 77 (November 1963): 62-78.

Porth, William C. and Robert P. George. "Trimming the Ivy: A Bicentennial Re-Examination of the Establishment Clause." *West Virginia Law Review* 90 (Fall 1987): 109-70.

Posner, Ethan M. "Public Prayer and the Constitution." *Michigan Law Review* 86 (May 1988): 1294-1301.

Prevost, Robert. "Clergy Malpractice After *Oregon* v. *Smith*." *Journal of Church and State* 34 (Spring 1992): 279-301.

Pritchard, J. Brett. "Conduct and Belief in the Free Exercise Clause: Developments and Deviations in *Lyng* v. *Northwest Indian Cemetery Protective Association*." *Cornell Law Review* 76 (November 1990): 268-96.

"Protecting Religious Exercise: The First Amendment and Legislative Responses to Religious Vandalism." *Harvard Law Review* 97 (December 1983): 547-63.

"Public School Prayer and the First Amendment: Reconciling Constitutional Claims." *Duquesne Law Review* 22 (Winter 1984): 465-78.

Pushaw, Robert J. "Labor Relations Board Regulation of Parochial Schools: A Practical Free Exercise Accommodation." *Yale Law Journal* 97 (November 1987): 135-55.

Rabinowitz, Stephen Lewis. "*Goldman* v. *Secretary of Defense*: Restricting the Religious Rights of Military Servicemembers." *American University Law Review* 34 (Spring 1985): 881-926.

Rains, Rebecca. "Can Religious Practice Be Given Meaningful Protection after *Employment Division* v. *Smith?*" *University of Colorado Law Review* 62 (1991):687-710.

Ratz, Lucy V. "Caesar, God and Mammon: Business and the Religion Clauses." *Gonzaga Law Review* 22 (1986-87): 327.

Raucher, Alan. "Sunday Business and the Decline of Sunday Closing Laws: A Historical Overview." *Journal of Church and State* 36 (Winter 1994): 13-33.

Rawlings, Tom C. "*Employment Division, Department of Human Resources of Oregon* v. *Smith*: The Supreme Court Deserts the Free Exercise Clause." *Georgia Law Review* 25 (Winter 1991): 567-93.

Redlich, Norman. "Separation of Church and State: The Burger Court's Tortuous Journey." *Notre Dame Law Review* 60 (1985): 1094-1149.

Redman, Barbara J. "Strange Bedfellows: Lubavitcher Hasidim and Conservative Christians." *Journal of Church and State* 34 (Summer 1992): 521-48.

"The 'Released Time' Cases Revisited: A Study of Group Decision Making by the Supreme Court." *Yale Law Journal* 83 (May 1974): 1202-36.

Reichley, A. James. "Religion's Role in Democracy: Commitment or Criticism? A Review of Religion in American Public Life." *Northwestern University Law Review* 81 (1985): 349-61.

Reilly, Elizabeth. "'Secure the Blessings of Liberty': A Free Exercise Analysis Inspired by Selective Service Nonregistrants." *Northern Kentucky Law Review* 16 (1988): 79-144.

Reinertsen, Gail and Ken Vinson. "Florida's School Prayer Statute: *Wallace* v. *Jaffree* and a Crumbling Wall of Separation." *Florida Bar Journal* 60 (March 1986): 9-14.

"Reinterpreting the Religion Clauses: Constitutional Construction and Conceptions of the Self." *Harvard Law Review* 97 (April 1984): 1468-86.

"Religion and the Law." *Hastings Law Journal* 26 (1978). (The entire volume is devoted to this topic.)

"Religion and the State." *Harvard Law Review* 100 (May 1987): 1607-1781.

"Religious Expression in the Public School Forum: The High School Student's Right to Free Speech." *Georgia Law Journal* 72 (October 1983): 135-60.

"Religious Liberty in the Public High School: Bible Study Clubs." *The John Marshall Law Review* 17 (Summer 1981): 933-67.

Renahan, Kathryn R. "*Bob Jones University* v. *United States*—No Taxes For Racially Discriminatory Schools—Supreme Court Clarifies Thirteen-Year Policy Imbroglio." *Journal of College and University Law* 11 (Summer 1984): 69-83.

"Restoring School Prayer by Eliminating Judicial Review: An Examination of Congressional Power to Limit Federal Court Jurisdiction." *North Carolina Law Review* 60 (April 1982): 831-52.

"Rethinking the Incorporation of the Establishment Clause: A Federalist View." *Harvard Law Review* 105 (May 1992): 1700-1719.

Reutter, E. Edmund, Jr. "Unclear Signals On Free Exercise Clause: *Bowen* v. *Roy*." *West's Education Law Reporter* 37 (1987): 1.

Rice, Mark G. "The Constitutionality of the Equal Access Act: *Board of Westside Community School District* v. *Mergens*." *Educational Law Report* 64 (February 1991): 609-21.

Rice, Terry. "Re-Evaluating the Balance Between Zoning Regulations and Religious and Educational Uses." *Pace Law Review* (Winter 1988): 1-61.

Richardson, James T. "Cult/Brainwashing Cases and Freedom of Religion." *Journal of Church and State* 33 (Winter 1991): 55-74.

Richardson, James T. and John Dewitt. "Christian Science Spiritual Healing, the Law, and Public Opinion." *Journal of Church and State* 34 (Summer 1992); 549-61.

Riggs, Robert E. "Judicial Doublethink and the Establishment Clause: The Fallacy of Establishment by Inhibition." *Valparaiso University Law Review* 18 (Winter 1984): 285-330.

"The Rights of Student Religious Groups Under the First Amendment to Hold Religious Meetings in the Public University Campus." *Rutgers Law Review* 33 (Summer 1981): 1008-53.

Ripple, Kenneth F. "The Entanglement Test of the Religion Clauses—A Ten Year Assessment." *UCLA Law Review* 27 (August 1980): 1195-1239.

Robbins, Thomas. "New Religious Movements, Brainwashing, and Deprogramming—The View From the Law Journals: A Review Essay and Survey." *Religious Studies Review* 11 (October 1985): 361-70.

Rosen, Ellyn S. "Keeping the Camel's Nose out of the Tent: The Constitutionality of N.L.R.B. Jurisdiction Over Employees of Religious Institutions." *Indiana Law Journal* (October 1, 1989): 1015-1029.

Rosenstein, Steve. "*Employment Division* v. *Smith*: Sacramental Peyote Use and Free Exercise Analysis—Vision Wanted." *University of West Los Angeles Law Review* 22 (1991): 185-220.

Ross, Gary. "Changing the Rules of the Game: How the Peyote Case Changed Your First Amendment Rights." *Liberty* 85 (July/August 1990): 7-8.

Ross, William G. "The Need for an Exclusive and Uniform Application of 'Neutral Principles' in the Adjudication of Church Property Disputes." *St. Louis University Law Journal* 32 (Winter 1987): 263-316.

Rotstein, Andrew. "Good Faith? Religious-Secular Parallelism and the Establishment Clause." *Columbia Law Review* 93 (November 1993): 1763-1806.

Rotz, Brenda J. "The Christmon Cross: *American Civil Liberties Union* v. *City of St. Charles*." *Chicago-Kent Law Review* 63 (May 1, 1987): 369-89.

Rouse, Kelly Beers. "Clergy Malpractice Claims: A New Problem for Religious Organizations." *North Kentucky Law Review* (1989): 383-96.

Rudd, Myron S. "Toward an Understanding of the Landmark Federal Decisions Affecting Relations Between Church and State." *University of Cincinnati Law Review* 36 (Summer 1967): 413-32.

Ruegger, MaryAnn Schlegel. "An Audience for the Amish: A Communication Based Approach to the Development of Law." *Indiana Law Journal* 66 (Summer 1991): 801-23.

Rugg, Janet V. and Andria A. Simone. "The Free Exercise Clause: Inexplicable Departure from the Strict Scrutiny Standard." *St. John's Journal of Legal Commentary* 6 (Spring 1990): 117-41.

Sadat-Keeling, Leila. "Constitutional Law—Supreme Court Finds First Amendment a Barrier to Taxation of the Press." *Tulane Law Review* 58 (March 1984): 1073-89.

Salomone, Rosemary C. "From Widmar to Mergens: The Winding Road of First Amendment Analysis." *Hastings Constitutional Law Quarterly* 18 (Winter 1991): 295-323.

Schachner, Elliot M. "Religion and the Public Treasury After Taxation with Representation of Washington, Mueller, and Bob Jones." *Utah Law Review* 1984 (May 1984): 275-312.

Schaeffer, Sherri. "*Edwards* v. *Aguillard*: Creation Science and Evolution—The Fall of Balanced Treatment Acts in the Public Schools." *San Diego Law Review* (September-October 1988): 829-55.

Sciarrino, Alfred J. "'Free Exercise' Footsteps in the Defamation Forest: Are 'New Religions' Lost?" *The American Journal of Trial Advocacy* 7 (1984) 57-121; 307-46; 517-65.

____________. "*United States* v. *Sun Myung Moon*: Precedent for Tax Fraud Prosecution of Local Pastors?" *Southern Illinois University Law Journal* 1984 (1984): 237-81.

Schmid, Peter D. "Religion, Secular Humanism and the First Amendment." *Southern Illinois University Law Journal* (Winter 1989): 357-93.

Schimmel, David. "Religious Freedom and the Public School Curriculum: An Analysis of Mozert and Hawkins." *West's Education Law Reporter* 42 (1988): 1047.

Schwarz, Stephen. "Recent Developments in Tax-Exempt Organizations." *University of San Francisco Law Review* 19 (Spring 1985): 299-328.

Senn, Stephen. "The Prosecution of Religious Fraud." *Florida State University Law Review* 17 (Winter 1990): 325-52.

Serra, Theresa M. "Invocations and Benedictions—Is the Supreme Court 'Graduating' to a *Marsh* Analysis?" *University of Detroit Law Review* 65 (Summer 1988): 769-98.

Shaman, Jeffrey M. "The Constitution, the Supreme Court, and Creativity." *Hastings Constitutional Law Quarterly* 9 (Winter 1982): 257-78.

Shapiro, Robert N. "'Mind Control' or Intensity of Faith: The Constitutional Protection of Religious Beliefs." *Harvard Civil Rights-Civil Liberties Law Review* 13 (1978): 751-97.

____________. "Of Robots, Persons, and the Protection of Religious Beliefs." *Southern California Law Review* 56 (Spring 1983): 1277-1318.

Sheffer, Martin S. "The Free Exercise of Religion and Selective Conscientious Objection: A Judicial Response to a Moral Problem." *Capital University Law Review* 9 (1979): 7-29.

____________. "The U. S. Supreme Court and the Free Exercise Clause: Are Standards of Adjudication Possible?" *Journal of Church and State* 23 (Autumn 1981): 533-49.

Sherry, Suzanna. "*Lee* v. *Weisman*: Paradox Redux." *1992 Supreme Court Review* (1992): 123-53.

Shobe, Kiply S. "Public Education in Shreds: Religious Challenges to Curricular Decisions." *Indiana Law Journal* (Winter 1988): 111-53.

Shortt, Bruce Nevin. "The Establishment Clause and Religion-Based Categories: Taking Entanglement Seriously." *Hastings Constitutional Law Quarterly* 10 (Fall 1982): 145-85.

Silbiger, Sara L. "Heaven Can Wait: Judicial Interpretation of Title VII's Religious Accommodation Requirement Since *Trans World Airlines* v. *Hardison*." *Fordham Law Review* 5 (March 1985): 839-61.

Simonetti, Louis F., Jr. "The Constitutionality of State Labor Relations Board Jurisdiction over Parochial Schools: *Catholic High School Association* v. *Culvert*." *Catholic Lawyer* 30 (Spring 1986): 162-76.

Simon, Harry. "Rebuilding the Wall Between Church and State: Public Sponsorship of Religious Displays Under the Federal and California Constitutions." *Hastings Law Journal* 37 (January 1986): 499-534.

Simson, Gary J. "The Establishment Clause in the Supreme Court: Rethinking the Court's Approach." *Cornell Law Review* 72 (July 1987): 905-35.

Singleton, Marvin K. "Colonial Virginia as First Amendment Matrix: Henry, Madison, and the Establishment Clause." *Journal of Church and State* 8 (Autumn 1966): 344-64.

Sirico, Louis J., Jr. "Church Property Disputes: Churches as Secular and Alien Institutions." *Fordham Law Review* 55 (December 1986): 335-62.

____________. "The Secular Contribution of Religion to the Political Process: The First Amendment and School Aid." *Missouri Law Review* 50 (Spring 1985): 321-76.

Slack, Reed D. "The Mormon Belief of an Inspired Constitution." *Journal of Church and State* 36 (Winter 1994): 35-56.

Slye, Terry L. "Rendering Unto Caesar: Defining 'Religion' for Purposes of Administering Religion-Based Tax Exemptions." *Harvard Journal of Law and Public Policy* 6 (Summer 1983): 219-94.

Smart, James M. "*Widmar* v. *Vincent* and the Purposes of the Establishment Clause." *Journal of College and University Law* 9 (1982-83): 469-83.

Smith, Michael Clay, and Richard A. Hartneti. "Teaching Bible in the Public Schools." *West's Education Law Reporter* 32 (July 1986).

Smith, Michael E. "The Special Place of Religion in the Constitution." *1983 The Supreme Court Review* (1983): 83-123.

Smith, Michael R. "Emerging Consequences of Financing Private Colleges with Public Funds." *Valparaiso University Law Review* 9 (Summer 1973): 561-610.

Smith, Norman B. "Constitutional Rights of Students, Their Families, and Teachers in the Public Schools." *Campbell Law Review* 10 (Summer 1988): 353-409.

Smith, Rodney K. "Getting Off on the Wrong Foot and Back On Again: A Reexamination of the History of the Framing of the Religion Clauses of the First Amendment and a Critique of the Reynolds and Everson Decisions." *Wake Forest Law Review* 20 (Fall 1984): 569-642.

____________. "Justice Potter Stewart: A Contemporary Jurist's View of Religious Liberty." *North Dakota Law Review* 59 (1983): 183-210.

Smith, Steven D. "Symbols, Perceptions, and Doctrinal Illusions: Establishment Neutrality and the 'No Endorsement' Test." *Michigan Law Review* 86 (November 1987): 266-332.

Smith, W. F. "Some Observations on the Establishment Clause." *Pepperdine Law Review* 11 (March 1984): 457-71.

Sorauf, Frank J. "*Zorach* v. *Clauson*: The Impact of a Supreme Court Decision." *American Political Science Review* 53 (September 1959): 777-91.

Spiro, Daniel A. "The Creation of a Free Marketplace of Religious Ideas: Revisiting the Establishment Clause After the Alabama Secular Humanism Decision." *Alabama Law Review* 39 (Fall 1987): 1-71.

Starr, Kenneth W. "The Establishment Clause." *Oklahoma Law Review* (Fall, 1988): 477-87.

Steinberg, David E. "Church Control of a Municipality: Establishing a First Amendment Institutional Suit." *Stanford Law Review* 38 (May 1986): 1363-1409.

____________. "Religious Exemptions as Affirmative Action." *Emory Law Journal* 40 (Winter 1991): 77-139.

Stern, Nat. "State Action, Establishment Clause, and Defamation: Blueprints for Civil Liberties in the Rehnquist Court." *University of Cincinnati Law Review* (1989): 1175-1242.

Stevens, John V., Sr. and John G. Tulio. "Casenote *United States* v. *Lee*, A Second Look." *Journal of Church and State* 26 (Autumn 1984): 455-72.

Stewart, D. O. "Taking Christ Out of Christmas?" *American Bar Association Journal* 69 (December 1983): 1832-37.

Stone, Geoffrey R. "In Opposition to the School Prayer Amendment." *University of Chicago Law Review* 50 (Spring 1983): 823-48.

Strain, Charles R. "Permissible Accommodation and Inclusive Pluralism: A Response to Judge Arlin Adams." *De Paul Law Review* 37 (Spring 1988): 357-63.

Strossen, Nadine. "'Secular Humanism' and 'Scientific Creationism': Proposed Standards for Reviewing Curricular Decisions Affecting Students' Religious Freedom." *Ohio State Law Journal* 47 (1986): 333-407.

Sullivan, Dwight H. "The Congressional Response to *Goldman* v. *Weinberger*." *Military Law Review* 121 (Summer 1988): 125-52.

Sullivan, Kathleen M. "Religion and Liberal Democracy." 59 (Winter 1992): 195-223.

Swift, Joel H. "To Insure Domestic Tranquility: The Establishment Clause of the First Amendment." *Hofstra Law Review* (Winter 1988): 301-27.

Tager, Evan M. "The Supreme Court, Effect Inquiry, and Aid to Parochial Education." *Stanford Law Review* 37 (November 1984): 219-51.

Tarr, G. Alan. "Church and State in the States." *Washington Law Review* (January 1989): 73-110.

Terrar, Edward. "Was There a Separation Between Church and State in Mid-17th-Century England and Colonial Maryland?" *Journal of Church and State* 35 (Winter 1993): 61-82.

"Their Life Is in the Blood: Jehovah's Witnesses, Blood Transfusions, and the Courts." *Northern Kentucky Law Review* 10 (1983): 281-304.

"The Supreme Court, Effect Inquiry, and Aid to Parochial Education." *Stanford Law Review* 37 (Fall 1984): 219-51.

"The Unconstitutionality of State Statutes Authorizing Moments of Silence in the Public Schools." *Harvard Law Review* 96 (June 1983): 1874-93.

"The United States Military Chaplaincy Program: Another Seam in the Fabric of our Society?" *Notre Dame Law Review* 59 (1983): 181-223.

"The Unseen Regulator: The Role of Characterization in First Amendment Free Exercise Cases." *Notre Dame Law Review* 59 (1984): 978-1004.

Tilewick, Robert. "Constitutional Law—Ritual Silence in Public Schools—*May* v. *Cooperman*, 572 F. Supp. 1561 (D.N.J. 1983), Appeals Docketed, No. 83-5890 (3D Cir. Dec. 16, 1983), No. 84-5126 (3D Cir. Feb. 28, 1984)." *Temple Law Review* 57 (January 1, 1983): 95-118.

Tillotson, David B. "Free Exercise in the 1980s: A Rollback of Protection." *University of San Francisco Law Review* 24 (Spring 1990): 505-40.

Tipton, Steven M. "Republic and Liberal State: The Place of Religion in an Ambiguous Policy." *Emory Law Journal* 39 (Winter 1990): 191-202.

"Title VII and Sectarian Institutions of Higher Education: Congress Shall Make No Law Prohibiting Free Exercise of Religion." *Cumberland Law Review* 14 (1983/1984): 597-641.

Toulouse, Mark G. "*Christianity Today* and American Public Life: A Case Study." *Journal of Church and State* 35 (Spring 1993): 241-84.

"Toward a Constitutional Definition of Religion." *Harvard Law Review* 91 (March 1978): 1056-89.

Torres, Maximilian B. "Free Exercise of Religion." *Harvard Journal of Law and Public Policy* 14 (Winter 1991): 282-92.

Treinan, David. "Religion in the Public Schools." *Northern Kentucky Law Review* 9 (1982): 229-63.

Tribe, Laurence H. "Church and State in the Constitution." In *Government Intervention in Religious Affairs*. ed. Dean M. Kelley, 31-40. New York: The Pilgrim Press, 1982.

____________. "Revising the Rule of Law." *New York University Law Review* (June 1, 1989): 726-31.

Tushnet, Mark V. "Of Church and State and the Supreme Court: Kurland Revisited." *1989 The Supreme Court Review* (1989): 373-402.

____________. "The Constitution of Religion." *Review of Politics* 50 (Fall 1988): 628-58.

____________. "Reflections on the Role of Purpose in the Jurisprudence of the Religion Clauses." *William and Mary Law Review* 27 (1987): 997-1009.

"*United States* v. *Lee*: Has the Retreat Been Sounded for Free Exercise?" *Stetson Law Review* 12 (Spring 1983): 852-64.

Unmack, Fred. "Equality Under the First Amendment: Protecting Native American Religious Practices on Public Lands." *Public Land Law Review* 8 (1987): 165-76.

Valauri, John T. "The Concept of Neutrality in Establishment Clause Doctrine." *University of Pittsburgh Law Review* 48 (Fall 1986): 83-151.

Van Alstyne, William W. "Constitutional Separation of Church and State: The Quest for a Coherent Position." *American Political Science Review* 57 (December 1963): 865-82.

____________. "Trends in the Supreme Court: Mr. Jefferson's Crumbling Wall—A Comment on *Lynch* v. *Donnelly*." *Duke Law Journal* 1984 (September 1984): 770-87.

____________. "What Is 'An Establishment of Religion'?" *North Carolina Law Review* 65 (June 1987): 909-16.

Van Meter-Drew, Linn. "*Stein* v. *Plainwell Community Schools*—The American Civil Religion and the Establishment Clause." *Hastings Constitutional Law Quarterly* 15 (Spring 1988): 533-47.

Van Patten, Jonathan. "In the End Is the Beginning: An Inquiry into the Meaning of the Religion Clauses." *St. Louis University Law Journal* 27 (Fall 1983): 1-93.

Vanden Berge, Douglas P. "The Establishment Clause: Historical Analysis and Current Application to Public Education." *Willamette Law Review* 24 (Spring 1988): 503.

Venable, Giovan Harbour. "Courts Examine Congregationalism." *Stanford Law Review* (February 1989): 719-49.

Walker, Robert S. "What Constitutes a Religious Use for Zoning Purposes?" *The Catholic Lawyer* 27 (Spring 1982): 129-83.

"*Wallace* v. *Jaffree*: The Lemon Test Sweetened." *Houston Law Review* 22 (October 1985): 1273-92.

Wald, Kenneth D. "The Religious Dimension of Anti-Communism." *Journal of Church and State* 36 (Summer 1994): 483-506.

Waldron, Jeremy. "Autonomy and Perfectionism in Raz's Morality of Freedom." *Southern California Law Review* (May 1, 1989): 1097-1152.

Ward, Scott J. "Reconceptualizing Establishment Clause Cases as Free Exercise Class Action." *Yale Law Journal* (June 1, 1989): 1739-59.

Washington, James M. "The Crisis in the Sanctity of Conscience in American Jurisprudence," *De Paul Law Review* 42 (Fall 1992): 11-60.

Watts, Carolyn. "Where There is No Vision: The Death of Public and Private Education in America." *Vital Speeches of the Day* 49 (1983): 215.

Way, Frank and Barbara J. Burt. "Religious Marginality and the Free Exercise Clause." *American Political Science Review* 77 (September 1983): 652-65.

Way, H. Frank. "Religious Disputation and the Civil Courts: Quasi-Establishment and Secular Principles." *Western Political Quarterly* 42 (December 1989): 523.

____________. "Survey Research on Judicial Decisions: The Prayer and Bible Reading Cases." *Western Political Quarterly* 12 (June 1968): 189-205.

Weber, Francis J. "American Church-State Relations: A Catholic View." *Journal of Church and State* 7 (Winter 1965): 10-4.

Weber, T. J. "Constitutional Law—Establishment Clause—Supreme Court Upholds Direct Noncategorical Grants to Church-Affiliated Colleges." *Fordham Law Review* 45 (March 1977): 979-92.

Weiss, Jonathon. "Privilege, Posture and Protection: Religion in the Law." *Yale Law Journal* 73 (March 1964): 593-623.

Wellons, Gregory D. "*Employment Division, Department of Human Resources* v. *Smith*: The Melting of *Sherbert* Means a Chilling Effect on Religion." *University of San Francisco Law Review* 26 (Fall 1991): 149.

West, Ellis. "The Case Against a Right to Religion-Based Exemptions." *Notre Dame Journal of Law, Ethics, and Public Policy* 4 (Fall/Winter 1990): 591-638.

Western, Peter. "'Freedom' and 'Coercion'—Virtue and Vice Words." *Duke Law Journal* 1985 (June 1985): 541-93.

Whitehair, J. Greg. "Teaching the Theories of Evolution and Scientific Creationism in the Public Schools: The First Amendment Religion Clauses and Permissible Relief." *Journal of Law Reform* 15 (Winter 1982): 421-63.

Whitehead, John W. "Accommodation and Equal Treatment of Religion: Federal Funding of Religious Affiliated Child Care Facilities." *Harvard Journal on Legislation* 26 (Summer 1989): 573-90.

____________. "Avoiding Religious Apartheid: Affording Equal Treatment for Student-Initiated Religious Expression in Public Schools." *Pepperdine Law Review* (1989): 229-58.

Wickham, Douglas A. "Prisoner's Rights." *Georgia Law Review* 74 (February 1986): 973-97.

Williams, J. D. "The Separation of Church and State in Mormon Theory and Practice." *Journal of Church and State* 9 (Spring 1967): 238-62.

Wilson, John F. "Church-State Relations and the Law in the United States to 1940." *Affirmation* 2 (Fall 1989): 21-35.

Wilson, John K. "Religion Under the State Constitutions, 1776-1800." *Journal of Church and State* 32 (Autumn 1990): 753-73.

Witte, John, Jr. "Tax Exemption of Church Property: Historical Anomaly or Valid Constitutional Practice?" *Southern California Law Review* 64 (January 1991): 363-415.

____________. "The Theology and Politics of the First Amendment Religion Clauses: A Bicentennial Essay." *Emory Law Journal* 40 (Spring 1991): 489-507.

Wolman, Benson A. "Separation Anxiety: Free Exercise Versus Equal Protection." *Ohio State Law Journal* 47 (1986): 453-74.

Wood, James E., Jr. "Abridging the Free Exercise Clause." *Journal of Church and State* 32 (Autumn 1990): 741-52.

____________. "Church-State Relations in the United States Since 1940." *Affirmation* 2 (Fall 1989): 37-69.

____________. "Editorial: Ceremonial Prayers at Public School Graduations: *Lee* v. *Weisman*." *Journal of Church and State* 34 (Winter 1992): 7-14.

____________. "Editorial: The Branch Davidian Standoff: An American Tragedy." *Journal of Church and State* 35 (Spring 1993): 233-40.

____________. "Editorial: Religion and the U. S. Presidential Election of 1992." *Journal of Church and State* 34 (Autumn 1992): 721-28.

____________. "Editorial: Religious Pluralism and American Society." *Journal of Church and State* 27 (Autumn 1985): 393-401.

____________. "Editorial: The Restoration of the Free Exercise Clause." *Journal of Church and State* 35 (Autumn 1993): 715-22.

____________. "Equal Access: A New Direction in American Public Education." *Journal of Church and State* 27 (Winter 1985): 5-17.

____________. "The Place of Church-State Studies in the University." *Journal of Church and State* 35 (Winter 1993): 131-51.

____________. "Religion and America's Public Schools." *Journal of Church and State* 9 (Winter 1967): 5-16.

____________. "Religion and Education in American Church-State Relations." *Journal of Church and State* 26 (Winter 1982): 421- 63.

____________. "Tax Exemption and the Churches." *Report from the Capital* 31 (April 1976): 2, 4.

Worthing, Sharon L. "The Internal Revenue Service as a Monitor of Church Institutions: The Excessive Entanglement Problem." *Fordham Law Review* 45 (March 1977): 929-48.

____________. "'Religion' and 'Religious Institutions' Under the First Amendment." *Pepperdine Law Review* 7 (1980): 313-53.

____________. "The State and the Church School: The Conflict Over Social Policy." *Journal of Church and State* 26 (Winter 1984): 91-104.

Yarbrough, Tinsley E. "Church, State, and the Rehnquist Court: A Brief for *Lemon*." *Journal of Church and State* 38 (Winter 1996): 59-85.

Yerby, Winton E. "Toward Religious Neutrality in the Public School Curriculum." *University of Chicago Law Review* (April 1, 1989): 899-934.

Young, David J. and Steven W. Tigges. "Discovery and Use of Church Records by Civil Authorities." *Catholic Lawyer* 30 (Autumn 1986): 198-217.

____________. and ____________ "Into the Religious Thicket—Constitutional Limits on Civil Court Jurisdiction over Ecclesiastical Disputes." *Ohio State Law Journal* 47 (1986): 475-99.

Zamora, Omar. "Discriminatory Religious Services: The Exception to Practices Prohibited by Civil Rights Statutes." *American Journal of Trial Advocacy* 10 (Summer 1986): 141-56.

Zerangue, Clare. "Sabbath Observance and the Workplace: Religion Clause Analysis and Title VII's Reasonable Accommodation Rule." *Louisiana Law Review* 46 (July 1986): 1265-88.

"Zoning Ordinances Affecting Churches: A Proposal for Expanded Free Exercise Protection." *University of Pennsylvania Law Review* 132 (June 1984): 1113-62.

Zuckert, Michael P. "Completing the Constitution: The Fourteenth Amendment and Constitutional Rights." *Publius* 22 (Spring 1992): 69-91.

Zwicker, Laura. "The Politics of Toleration: The Establishment Clause and the Act of Toleration Examined." *Indiana Law Journal* 66 (Summer 1991): 773-99.

There are seven regularly published periodicals completely devoted to church-state concerns:

Church and State, published every month except August by Americans United for Separation of Church and State, 1816 Jefferson Place, NW, Washington, DC 20036-7123.

Journal of Church and State, published four times a year by the J.M. Dawson Institute of Church-State Studies, Baylor University, Box 97308, Waco, Texas 76798-7308.

The Journal of Law and Religion, published twice a year at the Hamline University School of Law, 1536 Hewitt Avenue, St. Paul, Minnesota 55104.

LIBERTY: A Magazine of Religious Freedom, published bimonthly by the Review and Herald Publishing Association, 12501 Old Columbia Pike, Silver Spring, Maryland 20904-1608.

Religious Freedom Reporter, published monthly by the Church-State Resource Center of the Norman Adrian Wiggins

School of Law, Campbell University, P.O. Box 505, Buies Creek, North Carolina, 27506 is a compilation of up-to-date information on current litigation and periodical articles in the field.

Report from the Capital, published 24 times per year by the Baptist Joint Committee on Public Affairs, 200 Maryland Avenue, N.E., Washington, DC 20002.

Rutherford, published monthly by The Rutherford Institute, P.O. Box 7482, Charlottesville, VA, 22906-7482.

GLOSSARY OF LEGAL TERMS AND PHRASES

ADVISORY OPINION. An opinion given by a court as to the constitutionality or legal effect of a law although no actual case or controversy is before it. In several statesthe highest court is authorized to give such opinions at the request of the governor or the legislature, but federal judges do not render advisory opinions.

AMICUS CURIAE. "Friend of the court." A person or group that, while not directly involved in the litigation, is granted permission by the court to enter into judicial proceedings before it in order to present information which will aid the court in its decision.

APPEAL. The procedure by which the losing party takes a case to a higher court for review. A superior court is called on to correct error or injustice on the part of a lower court in interpreting or applying a law. Cases brought to the Supreme Court on appeal are a matter of right. Statutes designate the specific grounds for appeal.

APPELLANT. The party that takes an appeal from a lower to a higher court.

APPELLEE. The party in a litigation against which an appeal is taken.

BRIEF. A document prepared by counsel to serve as the basis for argument before a court. It contains the points of law, arguments, and precedents the counsel desires to present in a case before the court.

CERTIORARI, WRIT OF. "To be informed of"; "to be certain in regard to." A writ issued at the discretion of an appellate court ordering a lower court to send up the record of a case for review so that the higher court can make certain that the court correctly applied the law. Issuance of the writ is completely discretionary, and four members of the Supreme Court must agree before the writ will be issued.

CLASS ACTION. A suit brought by one or more persons on behalf of themselves and all other persons similarly situated.

COMMON LAW. That body of Anglo-Saxon law which originated and developed in England. It is to be distinguished from the Roman, or code, law. It is also distinguished from statutory law in that it is judge-made law based on customary law in different parts of England which over the years became common to all England. There is no federal common law, but federal judges apply the state common law in cases involving citizens of different states if there is no applicable federal statutory provision.

DECLARATORY JUDGMENT. A judicial declaration by means of which, in an actual controversy, the legal rights of parties under a law, contract, or other legal document can be determined before a wrong has been committed or is immediately threatened. No declaratory process or specific order follows the determination of the court.

DEFENDANT. The party against which relief or recovery is sought in a case.

DIVERSITY OF CITIZENSHIP. Cases between citizens of different states. By statute, Congress has given state courts exclusive jurisdiction in such cases if less than $10,000 is involved. State and federal courts have concurrent jurisdiction if more than $10,000 is involved in the litigation.

EQUITY. A branch of law which is intended to provide a just remedy when the common law or statute law will not. It includes such remedies as prevention of threatened damage by means of an injunction or the assurance of an action by means of a writ of specific performance.

ERROR, WRIT OF. A writ issued by an appellate court to an inferior court directing that the records of a case in which that court has made final judgment be sent to the higher court for review. This was a frequently used procedure for seeking review by the Supreme Court prior to 1925, but it has not been used since then.

EX REL. "Upon relation or information." Used in title of a case to indicate the person at whose instigation and on the basis of whose information the appropriate public official is acting.

FEDERAL QUESTION. A case which contains an issue involving the United States Constitution, an act of Congress, or a United States treaty.

INDICTMENT. A formal written accusation drawn by the prosecutor and brought by a grand jury charging one or more persons with the commission of a crime.

INJUNCTION. An equity writ ordering a person or group to refrain from performing some specific act.

IN RE. "In the matter of"; "concerning." A judicial proceeding may be thus entitled when there are no adversary parties but rather a thing or object concerning which judicial action is to be taken, such as an estate which is to be probated.

INTER ALIA. "Among other things."

MANDAMUS, WRIT OF. "We command." A court order directing a designated public official, lower court, corporation, or individual to perform a specific act.

OBITER DICTUM. A statement made in a court opinion that is not necessary or pertinent to the decision of the case at hand. In theory, it is not binding on courts in future cases.

PER CURIAM. "By the court." The term is used to distinguish an unsigned opinion of the whole court from an opinion written by a particular member of the court. It is usually very brief.

PETITIONER. The party that brings an action. The party that appeals to a court on a writ of certiorari.

PLAINTIFF. The party that brings an action; the complainant.

PLURALITY OPINION. An opinion that is referred to as the opinion of the court in a case but is actually not the opinion of a majority of the members participating in the decision. Any justice is free to write a separate concurring opinion in which he agrees with the result reached but takes issue with the line of reasoning applied or seeks to clarify the majority holding.

POLITICAL QUESTION. A question which a court refuses to decide because it is held to involve constitutional issues that can be resolved more effectively by the legislative or executive branches. The doctrine is most often advanced when a court decision might result in conflict with the other branches or when it would be difficult to enforce. It may be used to avoid a particularly controversial issue.

RESPONDENT. In appellate jurisdiction, the party that contends against an appeal. The party against which a writ of certiorari is sought.

STANDING TO SUE. In order to be able to bring an action in federal court against a government officer, the plaintiff must show that the interest he presents is personal, substantial, and legally protected, and that his interest has been injured or is in direct danger of injury from government.

TABLE OF SUPREME COURT OPINIONS

This table lists Supreme Court justices who have written opinions printed in this volume. Justices have been listed alphabetically, and cases have been arranged by categories for quick reference. Years in parentheses indicate each justice's period of service on the Court. All opinions listed, except those that have been specifically identified as either concurring or dissenting, were the majority opinions of the Court.

For all justices a reference has been given to biographical information in *The Justices of the United States Supreme Court: Their Lives and Major Opinions*, ed. Leon Friedman and Fred L. Israel, 5 vols. (New York: Chelsea House Publishers, 1995) [Library of Congress Catalogue Number KF8744 .F75 1995]. This source is abbreviated *J.U.S.S.C.* in the table. Another useful source is Clare Cushman, ed., *The Supreme Court Justices: Illustrated Biographies, 1789-1993* (Washington, D.C.: Congressional Quarterly, under the auspices of the Supreme Court Historical Society, 1993) [Library of Congress Catalogue Number KF8744 .S86 1993]. For information concerning new appointments to the Court, the reader should consult the following semi-annually published source: *CQ Guide to Current American Government* (New York: Congressional Quarterly, Inc.) [Library of Congress Catalogue Number JK1 .C14]

BLACK, HUGO L. (1937-1971): *J.U.S.S.C.*, vol. 3, pp. 1152-1179.

Aid to Parochial Schools
Everson v. *Board of Education*
Conscientious Objection
Welsh v. *United States*
Devotional Exercises in Public Schools
Engel v. *Vitale*
Flag Salute
West Virginia Board of Education v. *Barnette* (concurring)
Released Time
McCollum v. *Board of Education*
Zorach v. *Clauson* (dissenting)
Religious Tests
Torcaso v. *Watkins*
Teaching Evolution in Public Schools
Epperson v. *Arkansas*
Textbook Loan
Board of Education v. *Allen* (dissenting)

BLACKMUN, HARRY (1970-1993): *J.U.S.S.C.*, vol. 4, pp. 1607-1629

Aid to Parochial Schools
Committee for Public Education and Religious Liberty v. *Regan* (dissenting)
Roemer v. *Board of Public Works of Maryland*
Wolman v. *Walter*
Zobrest v. *Catalina Hills School District* (dissenting)
Church Exercising a Government Function
Kiryas Joel v. *Grumet* (concurring)
Church Property
Jones v. *Wolf*
Devotional Exercises in Public Schools
Lee v. *Weisman* (concurring)
Labor Relations (including sabbatarian concerns)
Church of Jesus Christ of Latter-day Saints v. *Amos* (concurring in judgment)
Employment Division of Oregon v. *Smith* (dissenting)
Public Funding for Social Services
Bowen v. *Kendrick* (dissenting)
Religion in the Military and Prisons
Goldman v. *Weinberger* (dissenting)
Religious Symbols on Public Property
Allegheny v. *ACLU*
Lynch v. *Donnelly* (dissenting)
Religious Tests for Public Benefits
Bowen v. *Roy* (concurring in part)
Right to Worship
Church of Lukumi Babalu Aye v. *Hialeah* (concurring in judgment)
State Regulation of Church Solicitation
Heffron v. *ISKCON* (concurring and dissenting)
Tax Exemption
Texas Monthly v. *Bullock* (concurring in judgment)

BRENNAN, WILLIAM J. (1956-1990): *J.U.S.S.C.*, vol. 4, pp. 1519-1545.

Aid to Parochial Schools
Aguilar v. *Felton*
Grand Rapids School District v. *Ball*
Lemon v. *Kurtzman* (separate opinion)
Meek v. *Pittenger* (concurring and dissenting)
Roemer v. *Board of Public Works of Maryland* (dissenting)
Wolman v. *Walter* (concurring and dissenting)
Church Property
Presbyterian Church in the United States v. *Mary Elizabeth Blue Hull Memorial Presbyterian Church*
Serbian Eastern Orthodox Diocese v. *Milivojevich*

Church Taxation
Walz v. *Tax Commission* (concurring)
Devotional Exercises in Public Schools
Abington School District v. *Schempp* (concurring)
Labor Relations (including sabbatarian concerns)
Church of Jesus Christ of Latter-day Saints v. *Amos* (concurring in judgment)
Hobbie v. *Unemployment Comm'n of Florida*
NLRB v. *Catholic Bishop of Chicago* (dissenting)
Sherbert v. *Verner*
Prohibition of Ministers in Politics
McDaniel v. *Paty* (concurring)
Religion in the Military and Prisons
Goldman v. *Weinberger* (dissenting)
O'Lone v. *Estate of Shabazz* (dissenting)
Religious Symbols on Public Property
Allegheny v. *ACLU* (concurring and dissenting)
Lynch v. *Donnelly* (dissenting)
Religious Tests for Public Benefits
Lyng v. *Indian Cemetery Assn.* (dissenting)
Standing
Valley Forge Christian College v. *Americans United* (dissenting)
State Regulation of Church Solicitation
Heffron v. *ISKCON* (concurring and dissenting)
Larson v. *Valente*
State Supported Chaplains
Marsh v. *Chambers* (dissenting)
Sunday Closing Laws
Braunfeld v. *Brown* (concurring and dissenting)
Tax Exemption
Texas Monthly v. *Bullock*
Teaching Evolution in Public Schools
Edwards v. *Aguillard*

BURGER, WARREN E. (Chief Justice, 1969-1986): *J.U.S.S.C.*, vol. 4, pp. 1465-1498.
Aid to Parochial Schools
Aguilar v. *Felton* (dissenting)
Committee for Public Education and Religious Liberty v. *Nyquist* (concurring and dissenting)
Grand Rapids School District v. *Ball* (concurring and dissenting)
Lemon v. *Kurtzman*
Meek v. *Pittenger* (concurring and dissenting)
Tilton v. *Richardson*
Church Exercising a Government Function
Larkin v. *Grendel's Den*
Church Taxation
Walz v. *Tax Commission*
Compulsory Education
Wisconsin v. *Yoder*
Devotional Exercises in Public Schools
Wallace v. *Jaffree* (dissenting)
Labor Relations (including sabbatarian concerns)
Thomas v. *Review Board of the Indiana Employment Security Commission*
Thornton v. *Caldor*
Prohibition of Ministers in Politics
McDaniel v. *Paty*
Religious Symbols on Public Property
Lynch v. *Donnelly*
Religious Test for Public Benefits
Bowen v. *Roy*
Standing
Bender v. *Williamsport* (dissenting)
State Supported Chaplains
Marsh v. *Chambers*
Tax Exemption
Bob Jones University v. *United States*
United States v. *Lee*

BUTLER, PIERCE (1922-1939): *J.U.S.S.C.*, vol. 3, pp. 1081-1090.
Conscientious Objection
Hamilton v. *Regents of the University of California*
United States v. *Schwimmer*

CAMPBELL, JOHN A. (1853-1861): *J.U.S.S.C.*, vol. 2, pp. 462-476.
Church Property
Baker v. *Nachtrieb*

CARDOZO, BENJAMIN (1932-1938): *J.U.S.S.C.*, vol. 3, pp. 1130-1151.
Conscientious Objection
Hamilton v. *Regents of the University of California* (concurring)

CLARK, TOM C. (1949-1967): *J.U.S.S.C.*, vol. 4, pp. 1347-1360.
Conscientious Objection
United States v. *Seeger*
Devotional Exercises in Public Schools
Abington School District v. *Schempp*

CLIFFORD, NATHAN (1858-1881): *J.U.S.S.C.*, vol. 2, pp. 477-490.
Church Property
Watson v. *Jones* (dissenting)

DOUGLAS, WILLIAM O. (1939-1975): *J.U.S.S.C.*, vol. 4, pp. 1219-1246.
Aid to Parochial Schools
Lemon v. *Kurtzman* (concurring)
Tilton v. *Richardson* (dissenting in part)
Church Taxation
Walz v. *Tax Commission* (dissenting)
Compulsory Education
Wisconsin v. *Yoder* (dissenting in part)
Conscientious Objection
Gillette v. *United States* (dissenting)
Girouard v. *United States*
United States v. *Seeger* (concurring)
Devotional Exercises in Public Schools

Abington School District v. *Schempp* (concurring)
Engel v. *Vitale* (concurring)
Labor Relations (including sabbatarian concerns)
Sherbert v. *Verner* (concurring)
Proselytizing on Public Property
Murdock v. *Pennsylvania*
Released Time
Zorach v. *Clauson*
Standing
Flast v. *Cohen* (concurring)
Sunday Closing Laws
McGowan v. *Maryland* (dissenting)
Test of Faith
United States v. *Ballard*
Textbook Loan
Board of Education v. *Allen* (dissenting)

FIELD, STEPHEN J. (1863-1897): *J.U.S.S.C.*, vol. 2, pp. 529-550.
Mormon Polygamy
Davis v. *Beason*

FORTAS, ABE (1965-1969): *J.U.S.S.C.*, vol. 4, pp. 1451-1464.
Standing
Flast v. *Cohen* (concurring)
Teaching Evolution in Public Schools
Epperson v. *Arkansas*
Textbook Loan
Board of Education v. *Allen* (dissenting)

FRANKFURTER, FELIX (1939-1962): *J.U.S.S.C.*, vol. 3, pp. 1199-1217.
Church Property
Kedroff v. *St. Nicholas Cathedral* (concurring)
Flag Salute
Minersville School District v. *Gobitis*
West Virginia Board of Education v. *Barnette* (dissenting)
Proselytizing on Public Property
Murdock v. *Pennsylvania* (dissenting)
Released Time
McCollum v. *Board of Education* (separate opinion)
Zorach v. *Clauson* (dissenting)
Sunday Closing Laws
McGowan v. *Maryland* (separate opinion)

GINSBURG, RUTH BADER (1993-): *J.U.S.S.C.*, vol. 5, pp. 1859-1873.
Religious Symbols on Public Property
Capitol Square v. *Pinette* (dissenting)

GOLDBERG, ARTHUR J. (1962-1965): *J.U.S.S.C.*, vol. 4, pp. 1435-1450.
Devotional Exercises in Public Schools
Abington School District v. *Schempp* (concurring)

GRAY, HORACE (1882-1902): *J.U.S.S.C.*, vol. 2, pp. 666-677.
Church Property
Speidel v. *Henrici*

HARLAN, JOHN M. (1955-1971): *J.U.S.S.C.*, vol. 4, pp. 1401-1421.
Taxation
Walz v. *Tax Commission* (concurring)
Conscientious Objection
Welsh v. *United States* (concurring)
Labor Relations (including sabbatarian concerns)
Sherbert v. *Verner* (dissenting)
Standing
Flast v. *Cohen* (dissenting)
Teaching Evolution in Public Schools
Epperson v. *Arkansas* (concurring)
Textbook Loan
Board of Education v. *Allen* (concurring)

HOLMES, OLIVER WENDELL (1902-1932): *J.U.S.S.C.*, vol. 3, pp. 873-882.
Conscientious Objection
United States v. *Schwimmer* (dissenting)

HUGHES, CHARLES EVANS (Assoc. Justice, 1910-1916; Chief Justice, 1930-1941): *J.U.S.S.C.*, vol. 3, pp. 944-967.
Church Property
Order of St. Benedict v. *Steinhauser*
Conscientious Objection
United States v. *Macintosh* (dissenting)
Proselytizing on Public Property
Cox v. *New Hampshire*
Textbook Loan
Cochran v. *Board of Education*

JACKSON, ROBERT H. (1941-1954): *J.U.S.S.C.*, vol. 4, pp. 1282-1311.
Aid to Parochial Schools
Everson v. *Board of Education* (dissenting)
Church Property
Kedroff v. *St. Nicholas Cathedral* (dissenting)
Flag Salute
West Virginia Board of Education v. *Barnette*
Proselytizing on Public Property
Prince v. *Massachusetts* (separate opinion)
Released Time
McCollum v. *Board of Education* (concurring)
Zorach v. *Clauson* (dissenting)
Test of Faith
United States v. *Ballard* (dissenting)

KENNEDY, ANTHONY (1988-): *J.U.S.S.C.*, vol. 5, pp. 1731-1757.
Church Exercising a Government Function

Kiryas Joel v. *Grumet* (concurring in judgment)
Devotional Exercises in Public Schools
Board of Education v. *Mergens* (concurring in part)
Lamb's Chapel v. *Center Moriches School District* (concurring in part)
Lee v. *Weisman*
Public Funding for Social Services
Bowen v. *Kendrick* (concurring)
Religious Publications in Public Institutions
Rosenberger v. *University of Virginia*
Religious Symbols on Public Property
Allegheny v. *ACLU* (concurring and dissenting)
Right to Worship
Church of Lukumi Babalu Aye v. *Hialeah*

McREYNOLDS, JAMES C. (1914-1941): *J.U.S.S.C.*, vol. 3, pp. 1006-1017.
Right of Parochial Schools to Exist
Pierce v. *Society of Sisters*

MARSHALL, THURGOOD (1967-1991): *J.U.S.S.C.*, vol. 4, pp. 1497-1519.
Aid to Parochial Schools
Mueller v. *Allen* (dissenting)
Wolman v. *Walter* (concurring and dissenting)
Aid to Religious Vocations
Witters v. *Washington Department of Services for the Blind*
Conscientious Objection
Gillette v. *United States*
Devotional Exercises in Public Schools
Board of Education v. *Mergens* (concurring in judgment)
Labor Relations (including sabbatarian concerns)
Trans World Airlines, Inc. v. *Hardison* (dissenting)
Tax Exemption
Hernandez v. *Commissioner of Internal Revenue*

MILLER, SAMUEL (1862-1890): *J.U.S.S.C.*, vol. 2, pp. 504-518.
Church Property
Watson v. *Jones*

MURPHY, FRANK (1940-1949): *J.U.S.S.C.*, vol. 4, pp. 1247-1262.
Proselytizing on Public Property
Jones v. *Opelika* (dissenting)
Prince v. *Massachusetts* (dissenting)

O'CONNOR, SANDRA DAY (1981-): *J.U.S.S.C.*, vol. 5, pp. 1758-1805.
Aid to Parochial Schools
Aguilar v. *Felton* (dissenting)
Grand Rapids School District v. *Ball* (concurring and dissenting)
Zobrest v. *Catalina Foothills School District* (dissenting)
Aid to Religious Vocations
Witters v. *Washington Department of Services for the Blind* (concurring)
Church Exercising a Government Function
Kiryas Joel v. *Grumet* (concurring in part and in judgment)
Devotional Exercises in Public Schools
Board of Education v. *Mergens*
Wallace v. *Jaffree* (concurring)
Labor Relations (including sabbatarian concerns)
Church of Jesus Christ of Latter-day Saints v. *Amos* (concurring in judgment)
Employment Division of Oregon v. *Smith* (concurring in judgment)
Thornton v. *Caldor* (concurring)
Public Funding for Social Services
Bowen v. *Kendrick* (concurring)
Religious Publications in Public Institutions
Rosenberger v. *University of Virginia* (concurring)
Religion in the Military and Prisons
Goldman v. *Weinberger* (dissenting)
Religious Symbols on Public Property
Allegheny v. *ACLU* (concurring in judgment)
Capitol Square v. *Pinette* (concurring in part and in judgment)
Lynch v. *Donnelly* (concurring)
Religious Tests for Public Benefits
Bowen v. *Roy* (concurring and dissenting)
Lyng v. *Indian Cemetery Assn.*
Tax Exemption
Davis v. *United States*
Hernandez v. *Commissioner of Internal Revenue* (dissenting)
Jimmy Swaggart Ministries v. *California*

PECKHAM, RUFUS (1896-1909): *J.U.S.S.C.*, vol. 3, pp. 832-852.
Public Funding for Social Services
Bradfield v. *Roberts*

POWELL, LEWIS F. (1971-1987): *J.U.S.S.C.*, vol. 4, pp. 1630-1662.
Aid to Religious Vocations
Witters v. *Washington Department of Services for the Blind* (concurring)
Aid to Parochial Schools
Aguilar v. *Felton* (concurring)
Committee for Public Education and Religious Liberty v. *Nyquist*
Wolman v. *Walter* (concurring and dissenting)
Church Property
Jones v. *Wolf* (dissenting)
Devotional Exercises in Public Schools
Wallace v. *Jaffree* (concurring)
Devotional Exercises in Public Universities
Widmar v. *Vincent*
Labor Relations (including sabbatarian concerns)

Hobbie v. *Unemployment Comm'n of Florida* (concurring in judgment)
Tax Exemption
Bob Jones University v. *United States* (concurring)
Teaching Evolution in Public Schools
Edwards v. *Aguillard* (concurring)

REED, STANLEY (1938-1957): *J.U.S.S.C.*, vol. 3, pp. 1180-1198.
Church Property
Kedroff v. *St. Nicholas Cathedral*
Proselytizing on Public Property
Jones v. *Opelika*
Murdock v. *Pennsylvania* (dissenting)
Released Time
McCollum v. *Board of Education* (dissenting)

REHNQUIST, WILLIAM H. (Assoc. Justice 1971-1986; Chief Justice 1986-): *J.U.S.S.C.*, vol. 5, pp. 1663-1689.
Aid to Parochial Schools
Aguilar v. *Felton* (dissenting)
Grand Rapids School District v. *Ball* (dissenting)
Meek v. *Pittenger* (concurring and dissenting)
Mueller v. *Allen*
Zobrest v. *Catalina Foothills School District*
Church Exercising a Government Function
Larkin v. *Grendel's Den* (dissenting)
Church Property
Serbian Eastern Orthodox Diocese v. *Milivojevich* (dissenting)
Devotional Exercises in Public Schools
Stone v. *Graham* (dissenting)
Wallace v. *Jaffree* (dissenting)
Labor Relations (including sabbatarian concerns)
Hobbie v. *Unemployment Comm'n of Florida* (dissenting)
Thomas v. *Review Board of the Indiana Employment Security Division* (dissenting)
Thornton v. *Caldor* (dissenting without opinion)
Public Funding for Social Services
Bowen v. *Kendrick*
Religion in the Military or Prisons
Goldman v. *Weinberger*
O'Lone v. *Estate of Shabazz*
Standing
Valley Forge Christian College v. *Americans United*
State Regulation of Church Solicitation
Larson v. *Valente* (dissenting)
Tax Exemption
Bob Jones University v. *United States* (dissenting)

ROBERTS, OWEN J. (1930-1945): *J.U.S.S.C.*, vol. 3, pp. 1117-1129.
Proselytizing on Public Property
Cantwell v. *Connecticut*

RUTLEDGE, WILEY (1943-1949): *J.U.S.S.C.*, vol. 4, pp. 1312-1321.
Aid to Parochial Schools
Everson v. *Board of Education* (dissenting)
Proselytizing on Public Property
Prince v. *Massachusetts*

SCALIA, ANTONIN (1986-): *J.U.S.S.C.*, vol. 5, pp. 1714-1730.
Church Exercising a Government Function
Kiryas Joel v. *Grumet* (dissenting)
Devotional Exercises in Public Schools
Lamb's Chapel v. *Center Moriches School District* (concurring in judgment)
Lee v. *Weisman* (dissenting)
Labor Relations (including sabbatarian concerns)
Employment Division of Oregon v. *Smith*
Religious Symbols on Public Property
Capitol Square v. *Pinette*
Right to Worship
Church of Lukumi Babalu Aye v. *Hialeah* (concurring in part)
Teaching Evolution in Public Schools
Edwards v. *Aguillard* (dissenting)
Tax Exemption
Texas Monthly v. *Bullock* (dissenting)

SOUTER, DAVID H. (1990-): *J.U.S.S.C.*, vol. 5, pp. 1806-1828.
Church Exercising a Government Function
Kiryas Joel v. *Grumet*
Devotional Exercises in Public Schools
Lee v. *Weisman* (concurring)
Religious Publications in Public Institutions
Rosenberger v. *University of Virginia* (dissenting)
Religious Symbols on Public Property
Capitol Square v. *Pinette* (concurring in part and in judgment)
Right to Worship
Church of Lukumi Babalu Aye v. *Hialeah* (concurring in part)

STEVENS, JOHN PAUL (1975-): *J.U.S.S.C.*, vol. 5, pp. 1690-1713.
Aid to Parochial Schools
Committee for Public Education and Religious Liberty v. *Regan* (dissenting)
Roemer v. *Board of Public Works of Maryland* (dissenting)
Wolman v. *Walter* (concurring and dissenting)
Church Exercising a Government Function
Kiryas Joel v. *Grumet* (concurring)
Devotional Exercises in Public Schools
Board of Education v. *Mergens* (dissenting)
Wallace v. *Jaffree*
Devotional Exercises in Public Universities

Widmar v. *Vincent* (concurring)
Labor Relations (including sabbatarian concerns)
Hobbie v. *Unemployment Comm'n of Florida* (concurring in judgment)
Religion in the Military and Prisons
Goldman v. *Weinberger* (concurring)
Religious Symbols on Public Property
Allegheny v. *ACLU* (concurring and dissenting)
Capitol Square v. *Pinette* (dissenting)
Religious Tests for Public Benefits
Bowen v. *Roy* (concurring)
Standing
Valley Forge Christian College v. *Americans United* (dissenting)
State Regulation of Church Solicitation
Larson v. *Valente* (concurring)
State Supported Chaplains
Marsh v. *Chambers* (dissenting)
Tax Exemption
United States v. *Lee* (concurring)

STEWART, POTTER (1958-1981): *J.U.S.S.C.*, vol. 4, pp. 1546-1573.
Aid to Parochial Schools
Meek v. *Pittenger*
Roemer v. *Board of Public Works of Maryland* (dissenting)
Compulsory Education
Wisconsin v. *Yoder* (concurring)
Devotional Exercises in Public Schools
Abington School District v. *Schempp* (dissenting)
Engel v. *Vitale* (dissenting)
Labor Relations (including sabbatarian concerns)
Sherbert v. *Verner* (concurring)
Prohibition of Ministers in Politics
McDaniel v. *Paty* (concurring)
Sunday Closing Laws
Braunfeld v. *Brown* (dissenting)
Teaching Evolution in Public Schools
Epperson v. *Arkansas* (concurring)

STONE, HARLAN F. (Assoc. Justice, 1925-1941; Chief Justice, 1941-1946): *J.U.S.S.C.*, Vol. 3, pp. 1099-1116.
Flag Salute
Minersville School District v. *Gobitis* (dissenting)
Proselytizing on Public Property
Jones v. *Opelika* (dissenting)
Test of Faith
United States v. *Ballard* (dissenting)

SUTHERLAND, GEORGE (1922-1938): *J.U.S.S.C.*, vol. 3, pp. 1069-1080.
Conscientious Objection
United States v. *Macintosh*

THOMAS, CLARENCE (1991-): *J.U.S.S.C.*, vol. 5, pp. 1827-1858.
Religious Publications in Public Institutions
Rosenberger v. *University of Virginia* (concurring)
Religious Symbols on Public Property
Capitol Square v. *Pinette* (concurring)

WAITE, MORRISON R. (Chief Justice, 1874-1888): *J.U.S.S.C.*, vol. 2, pp. 610-626.
Mormon Polygamy
Reynolds v. *United States*

WARREN, EARL (Chief Justice, 1953-1969): *J.U.S.S.C.*, vol. 4, pp. 371-1400.
Standing
Flast v. *Cohen*
Sunday Closing Laws
Braunfeld v. *Brown*
McGowan v. *Maryland*

WHITE, BYRON R. (1962-1993): *J.U.S.S.C.*, vol. 4, pp. 1574-1605.
Aid to Religious Vocations
Witters v. *Washington Department of Services for the Blind* (concurring)
Aid to Parochial Schools
Aguilar v. *Felton* (dissenting)
Committee for Public Education and Religious Liberty v. *Nyquist* (dissenting)
Committee for Public Education and Religious Liberty v. *Regan*
Grand Rapids School District v. *Ball* (dissenting)
Lemon v. *Kurtzman* (concurring and dissenting)
Roemer v. *Board of Public Works of Maryland* (concurring)
Church Property
Serbian Eastern Orthodox Diocese v. *Milivojevich* (concurring)
Conscientious Objection
Welsh v. *United States* (dissenting)
Devotional Exercises in Public Schools
Wallace v. *Jaffree* (dissenting)
Lamb's Chapel v. *Center Moriches School District*
Devotional Exercises in Public Universities
Widmar v. *Vincent* (dissenting)
Labor Relations (including sabbatarian concerns)
Church of Jesus Christ of Latter-day Saints v. *Amos*
Frazee v. *Illinois Dept. of Employment Security*
Trans World Airlines, Inc. v. *Hardison*
Prohibition of Ministers in Politics
McDaniel v. *Paty* (concurring)
Religious Tests for Public Benefits
Bowen v. *Roy* (dissenting)
State Regulation of Church Solicitation
Heffron v. *ISKCON*
Larson v. *Valente* (dissenting)
Tax Exemption
Texas Monthly v. *Bullock* (concurring in judgment)
Teaching Evolution in Public Schools
Edwards v. *Aguillard* (concurring in judgment)
Textbook Loan
Board of Education v. *Allen*

TABLES OF CASES

Listed in the following tables are Supreme Court cases printed in this volume (**TITLES IN BOLD, CAPITAL LETTERS**) and the Supreme Court and lower court cases cited by the Court in its church-state decisions. The tables provide readers with the full citations of these legal sources. Page numbers in regular print indicate where cases are referred to in the essay portions or in the cases themselves. A page number in **boldface** indicates the beginning page of each opinion printed herein.

SUPREME COURT CASES

A

B

D

E

F

G

L

M

R

S

LOWER COURT CASES

A

UNITED STATES SUPREME COURT CONSTITUENCY WITH CHURCH/STATE DECISIONS 1856-1996

The question is frequently asked, especially when the Court seems to have taken a different position from a previous similar case, if a change in the justices made a difference in the Court's decision. This chart shows the composition of the Court for each of the decisions reproduced in this book, beginning with ***Baker* v. *Nachtrieb*** in 1856, with a column for each term of the Court. Where there is a time gap between cases, that interval is indicated by both the dates at the top of the column and a heavy vertical line between columns. When the columns represent consecutive terms of the Court, they are separated by a light vertical line. The first time a justice is mentioned, the date when that person took the judicial oath is given under his or her name. The justices always appear in the same position in the column, so it is possible to tell who replaced whom by reading across the columns from left to right. The name of a newly appointed justice appears in bold italic type.

Below the double horizontal line appear the cases that were decided each term. The name of the case is in bold italic type. Then follows the date of the decision, the author of the majority opinion, and the names of the authors of concurring, dissenting, or separate opinions.

1856-1857	1871-1872	1878-1879	1886-1887	1889-1890
Roger B. Taney, C.J. (March 28, 1836)	***Salmon P. Chase, C.J. (December 15, 1864)***	***Morrison R. Waite, C.J. (March 4, 1874)***	Morrison R. Waite, C.J.	***Melville W. Fuller, C.J. (October 8, 1888)***
John McLean (January 11, 1830)	***Noah H. Swayne (January 27, 1862)***	Noah H. Swayne	***William B. Woods (January 5, 1881)***	***David J. Brewer (January 6, 1890)***
James M. Wayne (January 14, 1835)	***Nathan Clifford (January 21, 1858)***	Nathan Clifford	***Horace Gray (January 9, 1882)***	Horace Gray
John Catron (April 1, 1837)	***Samuel F. Miller (July 21, 1862)***	Samuel F. Miller	Samuel F. Miller	Samuel F. Miller
Peter V. Daniel (January 10, 1842)	***David Davis (December 10, 1862)***	***John Marshall Harlan (December 10, 1877)***	John Marshall Harlan	John Marshall Harlan
Samuel Nelson (February 27, 1845)	***Stephen J. Field (May 20, 1863)***	Stephen J. Field	Stephen J. Field	Stephen J. Field
Robert C. Grier (August 10, 1846)	***William Strong (March 14, 1870)***	William Strong	***Stanley Matthews (May 17, 1881)***	***Lucius Q. C. Lamar (January 18, 1888)***
Benjamin R. Curtis (October 10, 1851)	***Joseph P. Bradley (March 23, 1870)***	Joseph P. Bradley	Joseph P. Bradley	Joseph P. Bradley
James A. Campbell (April 11, 1853)	***Samuel Nelson (February 27, 1845)***	***Ward Hunt (January 9, 1873)***	***Samuel Blatchford (April 3, 1882)***	Samuel Blatchford
Baker v. Nachtrieb December 16, 1856 (Campbell)	***Watson v. Jones*** April 15, 1872 (Miller)	***Reynolds v. United States*** January 4, 1879 (Waite)	***Speidel v. Henrici*** March 7, 1887 (Gray)	***Davis v. Beason*** February 3, 1890 (Field)

UNITED STATES SUPREME COURT CONSTITUENCY WITH CHURCH/STATE DECISIONS 1856-1996 (continued)

1899-1900	1913-1914	1924-1925	1928-1929	1929-1930
Melville W. Fuller, C.J.	***Edward Douglass White, C.J. (December 19, 1910)***	***William Howard Taft, C.J. (July 11, 1921)***	William Howard Taft, C.J.	***Charles Evans Hughes, C.J. (February 24, 1930)***
David J. Brewer	***Charles Evans Hughes (October 10, 1910)***	***George Sutherland (October 2, 1922)***	George Sutherland	George Sutherland
Horace Gray	***Oliver Wendell Holmes (December 8, 1902)***	Oliver Wendell Holmes	Oliver Wendell Holmes	Oliver Wendell Holmes
Henry Billings Brown (January 5, 1891)	***Willis Van Devanter (January 3, 1911)***	Willis Van De Vanter	Willis Van Devanter	Willis Van Devanter
John Marshall Harlan	***Mahlon Pitney (March 18, 1912)***	***Edward T. Sanford (February 19, 1923)***	Edward T. Sanford	***Owen J. Roberts (June 2, 1930)***
Joseph McKenna (January 26, 1898)	Joseph McKenna	***Harlan F. Stone (March 2, 1925)***	Harlan F. Stone	Harlan F. Stone
Rufus W. Peckham (January 6, 1896)	***Horace H. Lurton (January 3, 1910)***	***James C. McReynolds (October 12, 1914)***	James C. McReynolds	James C. McReynolds
George Shiras, Jr. (October 10, 1892)	***William Rufus Day (March 2, 1903)***	***Pierce Butler (January 2, 1923)***	Pierce Butler	Pierce Butler
Edward Douglass White (March 12, 1894)	***Joseph R. Lamar (January 3, 1911)***	***Louis D. Brandeis (June 5, 1916)***	Louis D. Brandeis	Louis D. Brandeis
Bradfield v. Roberts December 4, 1899 (Peckham)	***Order of St. Benedict v. Steinhauser*** June 22, 1914 (Hughes)	***Pierce v. Society of Sisters*** June 1, 1925 (McReynolds)	***United States v. Schwimmer*** May 27, 1929 (Butler) (Holmes, dissenting) (Sanford, dissenting)	***Cochran v. Board of Education*** April 28, 1930 (Hughes)

UNITED STATES SUPREME COURT CONSTITUENCY WITH CHURCH/STATE DECISIONS 1856-1996 (continued)

1899-1900	1913-1914	1924-1925	1928-1929	1929-1930
Melville W. Fuller, C.J.	***Edward Douglass White, C.J. (December 19, 1910)***	***William Howard Taft, C.J. (July 11, 1921)***	William Howard Taft, C.J.	***Charles Evans Hughes, C.J. (February 24, 1930)***
David J. Brewer	***Charles Evans Hughes (October 10, 1910)***	***George Sutherland (October 2, 1922)***	George Sutherland	George Sutherland
Horace Gray	***Oliver Wendell Holmes (December 8, 1902)***	Oliver Wendell Holmes	Oliver Wendell Holmes	Oliver Wendell Holmes
Henry Billings Brown (January 5, 1891)	***Willis Van Devanter (January 3, 1911)***	Willis Van De Vanter	Willis Van Devanter	Willis Van Devanter
John Marshall Harlan	***Mahlon Pitney (March 18, 1912)***	***Edward T. Sanford (February 19, 1923)***	Edward T. Sanford	***Owen J. Roberts (June 2, 1930)***
Joseph McKenna (January 26, 1898)	Joseph McKenna	***Harlan F. Stone (March 2, 1925)***	Harlan F. Stone	Harlan F. Stone
Rufus W. Peckham (January 6, 1896)	***Horace H. Lurton (January 3, 1910)***	***James C. McReynolds (October 12, 1914)***	James C. McReynolds	James C. McReynolds
George Shiras, Jr. (October 10, 1892)	***William Rufus Day (March 2, 1903)***	***Pierce Butler (January 2, 1923)***	Pierce Butler	Pierce Butler
Edward Douglass White (March 12, 1894)	***Joseph R. Lamar (January 3, 1911)***	***Louis D. Brandeis (June 5, 1916)***	Louis D. Brandeis	Louis D. Brandeis
Bradfield v. Roberts December 4, 1899 (Peckham)	***Order of St. Benedict v. Steinhauser*** June 22, 1914 (Hughes)	***Pierce v. Society of Sisters*** June 1, 1925 (McReynolds)	***United States v. Schwimmer*** May 27, 1929 (Butler) (Holmes, dissenting) (Sanford, dissenting)	***Cochran v. Board of Education*** April 28, 1930 (Hughes)

UNITED STATES SUPREME COURT CONSTITUENCY WITH CHURCH/STATE DECISIONS 1856-1996 (continued)

1930-1931	1934-1935	1939-1940	1940-1941	1941-1942
Charles Evans Hughes, C.J.	Charles Evans Hughes, C.J.	Charles Evans Hughes, C.J.	Charles Evans Hughes, C.J.	***Harlan F. Stone, C.J. (July 3, 1941)***
George Sutherland	George Sutherland	***Stanley F. Reed (January 31, 1938)***	Stanley F. Reed	Stanley F. Reed
Oliver Wendell Holmes	***Benjamin N. Cardozo (March 14, 1932)***	***Felix Frankfurter (January 30, 1939)***	Felix Frankfurter	Felix Frankfurter
Willis Van Devanter	Willis Van Devanter	***Hugo L. Black (August 19, 1937)***	Hugo L. Black	Hugo L. Black
Owen J. Roberts	Owen J. Roberts	Owen J. Roberts	Owen J. Roberts	Owen J. Roberts
Harlan F. Stone	Harlan F. Stone	Harlan F. Stone	Harlan F. Stone	***Robert H. Jackson (July 11, 1941)***
James C. McReynolds	James C. McReynolds	James C. McReynolds	James C. McReynolds	***James F. Byrnes (July 8, 1941)***
Pierce Butler	Pierce Butler	Pierce Butler	***Frank Murphy (February 5, 1940)***	Frank Murphy
Louis D. Brandeis	Louis D. Brandeis	***William O. Douglas (April 17, 1939)***	William O. Douglas	William O. Douglas
U.S. v. Macintosh May 25, 1931 (Sutherland) (Hughes, dissenting)	***Hamilton v. Regents of the University of California*** December 3, 1934 (Butler) (Cardozo, concurring)	***Cantwell v. Connecticut*** May 20, 1940 (Roberts) ***Minersville School District v. Gobitis*** June 3, 1940 (Frankfurter) (Stone, dissenting)	***Cox v. New Hampshire*** March 31, 1941 (Hughes)	***Jones v. Opelika*** June 8, 1942 (Reed) (Stone, separate) (Murphy, dissenting) (Black, separate)

UNITED STATES SUPREME COURT CONSTITUENCY WITH CHURCH/STATE DECISIONS 1856-1996 (continued)

1942-1943	1943-1944	1945-1946	1946-1947	1947-1948
Harlan F. Stone, C.J. Stanley F. Reed Felix Frankfurter Hugo L. Black Owen J. Roberts Robert H. Jackson ***Wiley B. Rutledge (February 15, 1943)*** Frank Murphy William O. Douglas	Harlan F. Stone, C.J. Stanley F. Reed Felix Frankfurter Hugo L. Black Owen J. Roberts Robert H. Jackson Wiley B. Rutledge Frank Murphy William O. Douglas	Harlan F. Stone, C.J. Stanley F. Reed Felix Frankfurter Hugo L. Black ***Harold H. Burton (October 1, 1945)*** Robert H. Jackson Wiley B. Rutledge Frank Murphy William O. Douglas	***Frederick M. Vinson, C.J. (June 24, 1946)*** Stanley F. Reed Felix Frankfurter Hugo L. Black Harold H. Burton Robert H. Jackson Wiley B. Rutledge Frank Murphy William O. Douglas	Frederick M. Vinson, C.J. Stanley F. Reed Felix Frankfurter Hugo L. Black Harold H. Burton Robert H. Jackson Wiley B. Rutledge Frank Murphy William O. Douglas
Murdock v. Pennsylvania May 3, 1943 (Douglas) (Reed, dissenting) (Frankfurter, dissenting) ***West Virginia State Board of Education v. Barnette*** June 14, 1943 (Jackson) (Black, concurring) (Murphy, concurring) (Frankfurter, dissenting)	***Prince v. Massachusetts*** January 31, 1944 (Rutledge) (Murphy, dissenting) (Jackson, dissenting) ***United States v. Ballard*** April 24, 1944 (Douglas) (Stone, dissenting) (Jackson, dissenting)	***Girouard v. United States*** April 22, 1946 (Douglas) (Stone, dissenting)	***Everson v. Board of Education*** February 10, 1947 (Black) (Jackson, dissenting) (Rutledge, dissenting)	***McCollum v. Board of Education*** March 8, 1948 (Black) (Frankfurter, separate) (Jackson, concurring) (Reed, dissenting)

UNITED STATES SUPREME COURT CONSTITUENCY WITH CHURCH/STATE DECISIONS 1856-1996 (continued)

1951-1952	1952-1953	1960-1961	1961-1962	1962-1963
Frederick M. Vinson, C.J.	Frederick M. Vinson, C.J.	***Earl Warren, C.J.* *(October 5, 1953)***	Earl Warren, C.J.	Earl Warren, C.J.
Stanley F. Reed	Stanley F. Reed	***Charles E. Whittaker* *(March 25, 1957)***	***Byron R. White* *(April 16, 1962)***	Byron R. White
Felix Frankfurter	Felix Frankfurter	Felix Frankfurter	Felix Frankfurter	***Arthur Goldberg* *(October 1, 1962)***
Hugo L. Black	Hugo L. Black	Hugo L. Black	Hugo L. Black	Hugo L. Black
Harold H. Burton	Harold H. Burton	***Potter Stewart* *(October 14, 1958)***	Potter Stewart	Potter Stewart
Robert H. Jackson	Robert H. Jackson	***John Marshall Harlan* *(March 28, 1955)***	John Marshall Harlan	John Marshall Harlan
Sherman Minton* *(October 12, 1949)	Sherman Minton	***William Brennan, Jr.* *(October 16, 1956)***	William Brennan, Jr.	William Brennan, Jr.
Tom C. Clark* *(August 24, 1949)	Tom C. Clark	Tom C. Clark	Tom C. Clark	Tom C. Clark
William O. Douglas	William O. Douglas	William O. Douglas	William O. Douglas	William O. Douglas
Zorach v. Clauson April 12, 1952 (Douglas) (Black, dissenting) (Frankfurter, dissenting) (Jackson, dissenting)	***Kedroff v. Saint Nicholas Cathedral*** November 24, 1952 (Reed) (Frankfurter, concurring) (Jackson, dissenting)	***McGowan v. Maryland*** May 29, 1961 (Warren) (Frankfurter, separate) (Douglas, dissenting) ***Braunfeld v. Brown*** May 29, 1961 (Warren) (Brennan, concurring and dissenting) (Stewart, dissenting) ***Torcaso v. Watkins*** June 19, 1961 (Black)	***Engel v. Vitale*** June 25, 1962 (Black) (Douglas, concurring) (Stewart, dissenting)	***Abington Township School District v. Schempp*** June 17, 1963 (Clark) (Douglas, concurring) (Brennan, concurring) (Goldberg, concurring) (Stewart, dissenting)

UNITED STATES SUPREME COURT CONSTITUENCY WITH CHURCH/STATE DECISIONS 1856-1996 (continued)

1964-1965	1967-1968	1968-1969	1969-1970	1970-1971
Earl Warren, C.J. Byron R. White Arthur Goldberg Hugo L. Black Potter Stewart John Marshall Harlan William Brennan, Jr. Tom C. Clark William O. Douglas	Earl Warren, C.J. Byron R. White ***Abe Fortas (October 4, 1965)*** Hugo L. Black Potter Stewart John Marshall Harlan William Brennan, Jr. ***Thurgood Marshall (October 2, 1967)*** William O. Douglas	Earl Warren, C.J. Byron R. White Abe Fortas Hugo L. Black Potter Stewart John Marshall Harlan William Brennan, Jr. Thurgood Marshall William O. Douglas	***Warren E. Burger, C.J. (June 23, 1969)*** Byron R. White ***Harry A. Blackmun (June 9, 1970)*** Hugo L. Black Potter Stewart John Marshall Harlan William Brennan, Jr. Thurgood Marshall William O. Douglas	Warren E. Burger, C.J. Byron R. White Harry A. Blackmun Hugo L. Black Potter Stewart John Marshall Harlan William Brennan, Jr. Thurgood Marshall William O. Douglas
United States v. Seeger March 8, 1965 (Clark) (Douglas, concurring)	***Board of Education v. Allen*** June 10, 1968 (White) (Harlan, concurring) (Douglas, dissenting) (Fortas, dissenting) ***Flast v. Cohen*** June 10, 1968 (Warren) (Douglas, concurring) (Stewart, concurring) (Fortas, concurring) (Harlan, dissenting)	***Epperson v. Arkansas*** November 12, 1968 (Fortas) (Black, concurring) (Harlan, concurring) (Stewart, concurring) ***Presbyterian Church v. Hull Memorial Presbyterian Church*** January 27, 1969 (Brennan)	***Walz v. Tax Commission*** May 4, 1970 (Burger) (Brennan, concurring) (Douglas, dissenting) ***Welsh v. United States*** June 15, 1970 (Black) (Harlan, concurring) (White, dissenting)	***Gillette v. United States*** March 8, 1971 (Marshall) (Douglas, dissenting) ***Lemon v. Kurtzman*** June 28, 1971 (Burger) (Douglas, concurring) (Brennan, concurring and dissenting) (White, concurring and dissenting) ***Tilton v. Richardson*** June 28, 1971 (Burger) (Douglas, dissenting in part)

UNITED STATES SUPREME COURT CONSTITUENCY WITH CHURCH/STATE DECISIONS 1856-1996 (continued)

1971-1972	1972-1973	1974-1975	1975-1976	1976-1977
Warren E. Burger, C.J. Byron R. White Harry A. Blackmun ***Lewis F. Powell, Jr. (January 7, 1972)*** Potter Stewart ***William H. Rehnquist (January 7, 1972)*** William Brennan, Jr. Thurgood Marshall William O. Douglas	Warren E. Burger, C.J. Byron R. White Harry A. Blackmun Lewis F. Powell, Jr. Potter Stewart William H. Rehnquist William Brennan, Jr. Thurgood Marshall William O. Douglas	Warren E. Burger, C.J. Byron R. White Harry A. Blackmun Lewis F. Powell, Jr. Potter Stewart William H. Rehnquist William Brennan, Jr. Thurgood Marshall William O. Douglas	Warren E. Burger, C.J. Byron R. White Harry A. Blackmun Lewis F. Powell, Jr. Potter Stewart William H. Rehnquist William Brennan, Jr. Thurgood Marshall ***John Paul Stevens (December 19, 1975)***	Warren E. Burger, C.J. Byron R. White Harry A. Blackmun Lewis F. Powell, Jr. Potter Stewart William H. Rehnquist William Brennan, Jr. Thurgood Marshall John Paul Stevens
Wisconsin v. Yoder May 15, 1972 (Burger) (Stewart, concurring) (White, concurring) (Douglas, dissenting in part)	***Committee for Public Education & Religious Liberty v. Nyquist*** June 25, 1973 (Powell) (Burger, concurring and dissenting) (White, dissenting) (Rehnquist, dissenting in part)	***Meek v. Pittenger*** May 19, 1975 (Stewart) (Brennan, concurring and dissenting)	***Roemer v. Board of Public Works of Maryland*** June 21, 1976 (Blackmun) (White, concurring) (Brennan, dissenting) (Stewart, dissenting) (Stevens, dissenting) ***Serbian Eastern Orthodox Diocese v. Milivojevich*** June 21, 1976 (Brennan) (White, concurring) (Rehnquist, dissenting)	***Trans World Airlines v. Hardison*** June 16, 1977 (White) (Marshall, dissenting) ***Wolman v. Walter*** June 24, 1977 (Blackmun) (Brennan, concurring and dissenting) (Marshall, concurring and dissenting) (Powell, concurring and dissenting) (Stevens, concurring and dissenting)

UNITED STATES SUPREME COURT CONSTITUENCY WITH CHURCH/STATE DECISIONS 1856-1996 (continued)

1977-1978	1978-1979	1979-1980	1980-1981	1981-1982
Warren E. Burger, C.J. Byron R. White Harry A. Blackmun Lewis F. Powell, Jr. Potter Stewart William H. Rehnquist William Brennan, Jr. Thurgood Marshall John Paul Stevens	Warren E. Burger, C.J. Byron R. White Harry A. Blackmun Lewis F. Powell, Jr. Potter Stewart William H. Rehnquist William Brennan, Jr. Thurgood Marshall John Paul Stevens	Warren E. Burger, C.J. Byron R. White Harry A. Blackmun Lewis F. Powell, Jr. Potter Stewart William H. Rehnquist William Brennan, Jr. Thurgood Marshall John Paul Stevens	Warren E. Burger, C.J. Byron R. White Harry A. Blackmun Lewis F. Powell, Jr. Potter Stewart William H. Rehnquist William Brennan, Jr. Thurgood Marshall John Paul Stevens	Warren E. Burger, C.J. Byron R. White Harry A. Blackmun Lewis F. Powell, Jr. ***Sandra Day O'Connor (September 26, 1981)*** William H. Rehnquist William Brennan, Jr. Thurgood Marshall John Paul Stevens
McDaniel v. Paty April 19, 1978 (Burger) (Brennan, concurring) (Stewart, concurring) (White, concurring)	***National Labor Relations Board v. Catholic Bishop of Chicago*** March 21, 1979 (Burger) (Brennan, dissenting) ***Jones v. Wolf*** July 2, 1979 (Blackmun) (Powell, dissenting)	***Committee for Public Education and Religious Liberty v. Regan*** February 20, 1980 (White) (Blackmun, dissenting) (Stevens, dissenting)	***Stone v. Graham*** November 17, 1980 (Per Curiam) (Rehnquist, dissenting) ***Thomas v. Review Board of Indiana Employment Security Division*** April 6, 1981 (Burger) (Rehnquist, dissenting) ***Heffron v. International Society of Krishna Consciousness*** June 22, 1981 (White) (Brennan, concurring and dissenting) (Blackmun, concurring and dissenting)	***Widmar v. Vincent*** December 8, 1981 (Powell) (Stevens, concurring) (White, dissenting) ***Valley Forge Christian College v. Americans United for Separation of Church and State*** January 12, 1982 (Rehnquist) (Brennan, dissenting) (Stevens, dissenting) ***United States v. Lee*** February 23, 1982 (Burger) (Stevens, concurring) ***Larson v. Valente*** April 21, 1982 (Brennan) (Stevens, concurring) (White, dissenting) (Rehnquist, dissenting)

UNITED STATES SUPREME COURT CONSTITUENCY WITH CHURCH/STATE DECISIONS 1856-1996 (continued)

1982-1983	1983-1984	1984-1985	1985-1986	1986-1987
Warren E. Burger, C.J. Byron R. White Harry A. Blackmun Lewis F. Powell, Jr. Sandra Day O'Connor William H. Rehnquist William Brennan, Jr. Thurgood Marshall John Paul Stevens	Warren E. Burger, C.J. Byron R. White Harry A. Blackmun Lewis F. Powell, Jr. Sandra Day O'Connor William H. Rehnquist William Brennan, Jr. Thurgood Marshall John Paul Stevens	Warren E. Burger, C.J. Byron R. White Harry A. Blackmun Lewis F. Powell, Jr. Sandra Day O'Connor William H. Rehnquist William Brennan, Jr. Thurgood Marshall John Paul Stevens	Warren E. Burger, C.J. Byron R. White Harry A. Blackmun Lewis F. Powell, Jr. Sandra Day O'Connor William H. Rehnquist William Brennan, Jr. Thurgood Marshall John Paul Stevens	***William H. Rehnquist, C.J. (September 26, 1986)*** Byron R. White Harry A. Blackmun Lewis F. Powell, Jr. Sandra Day O'Connor ***Antonin Scalia (September 26, 1986)*** William Brennan, Jr. Thurgood Marshall John Paul Stevens
Larkin v. Grendel's Den December13, 1982 (Burger) (Rehnquist, dissenting) ***Bob Jones University v. United States*** May 24, 1983 (Burger) (Powell, concurring) (Rehnquist, dissenting) ***Mueller v. Allen*** June 29, 1983 (Rehnquist) (Marshall, dissenting) ***Marsh v. Chambers*** July 5, 1983 (Burger) (Brennan, dissenting (Stevens, dissenting)	***Lynch v. Donnelly*** March 5, 1984 (Burger) (O'Connor, concurring) (Brennan, dissenting) (Blackmun, dissenting)	***Wallace v. Jaffree*** June 4, 1985 (Stevens) (Powell, concurring) (O'Connor, concurring) (Burger, dissenting) (White, dissenting) (Rehnquist, dissenting) ***Estate of Thornton v. Caldor*** June 21, 1985 (Burger) (O'Connor, concurring) ***Aguilar v. Felton*** July 1, 1985 (Brennan) (Powell, concurring) (Burger, dissenting) (Rehnquist, dissenting) (O'Connor, dissenting) ***Grand Rapids School District v. Ball*** July 1, 1985 (Brennan) (Burger, concurring and dissenting) (O'Connor, concurring and dissenting) (White, dissenting)	***Witters v. Washington Department of Services for the Blind*** January 27, 1986 (Marshall) (White, concurring) (Powell, concurring) (O'Connor, concurring) ***Goldman v. Weinberger*** March 25, 1986 (Rehnquist) (Stevens, concurring) (Brennan, dissenting) (Blackmun, dissenting) (O'Connor, dissenting) ***Bowen v. Roy*** (June 11, 1986 (Burger) (Blackmun, concurring) (Stevens, concurring) (O'Connor, concurring and dissenting) (White, dissenting)	***Hobbie v. Unemployment Appeals Commission*** February 25, 1987 (Brennan) (Powell, concurring) (Stevens, concuring) (Rehnquist, dissenting) ***O'Lone v. Estate of Shabazz*** June 9, 1987 (Rehnquist) (Brennan, dissenting) ***Edwards v. Aguillard*** June 19, 1987 (Brennan) (Powell, concurring) (White, concurring) (Scalia, dissenting) ***Church of Jesus Christ of Latter-Day Saints v. Amos*** June 24, 1987 (White) (Brennan, concurring) (Blackmun, concurring) (O'Connor, concurring)

UNITED STATES SUPREME COURT CONSTITUENCY WITH CHURCH/STATE DECISIONS 1856-1996 (continued)

1987-1988	1988-1989	1989-1990	1991-1992	1992-1993
William H. Rehnquist, C.J. Byron R. White Harry A. Blackmun ***Anthony Kennedy (February 18, 1988)*** Sandra Day O'Connor Antonin Scalia William Brennan, Jr. Thurgood Marshall John Paul Stevens	William H. Rehnquist, C.J. Byron R. White Harry A. Blackmun Anthony Kennedy Sandra Day O'Connor Antonin Scalia William Brennan, Jr. Thurgood Marshall John Paul Stevens	William H. Rehnquist, C.J. Byron R. White Harry A. Blackmun Anthony Kennedy Sandra Day O'Connor Antonin Scalia William Brennan, Jr. Thurgood Marshall John Paul Stevens	William H. Rehnquist, C.J. Byron R. White Harry A. Blackmun Anthony Kennedy Sandra Day O'Connor Antonin Scalia ***David H. Souter (October 9, 1990)*** ***Clarence Thomas (October 23, 1991)*** John Paul Stevens	William H. Rehnquist, C.J. Byron R. White Harry A. Blackmun Anthony Kennedy Sandra Day O'Connor Antonin Scalia David H. Souter Clarence Thomas John Paul Stevens
Lyng v. Northwest Indian Cemetery Protective Association April 19, 1988 (O'Connor) (Brennan, dissenting) ***Bowen v. Kendrick*** June 29, 1988 (Rehnquist) (Kennedy, concurring) (O'Connor, concurring) (Blackmun, dissenting)	***Texas Monthly v. Bullock*** February 21, 1989 (Brennan) (White, concurring) (Blackmun, concurring) (Scalia, dissenting) ***Frazee v. Illinois Department of Employment Security*** March 29, 1989 (White) ***Hernandez v. Commissioner of Internal Revenue*** June 5, 1989 (Marshall) (O'Connor, dissenting) ***Allegheny v. ACLU of Pittsburgh*** July 3, 1989 (Blackmun) (O'Connor, concurring) (Brennan, concurring and dissenting) (Stevens, concurring and dissenting) (Kennedy, concurring and dissenting)	***Jimmy Swaggart Ministries v. Board of Equalization of California*** January 17, 1990 (O'Connor) ***Employment Division, Department of Human Resources of Oregon v. Smith*** April 17, 1990 (Scalia) (O'Connor, concurring) (Blackmun, dissenting) ***Davis v. United States*** May 21, 1990 (O'Connor) ***Board of Education v. Mergens*** June 4, 1990 (O'Connor) (Kennedy, concurring) (Marshall, concurring) (Stevens, dissenting)	***Lee v. Weisman*** June 24, 1992 (Kennedy) (Blackmun, concurring) (Souter, concurring) (Scalia, dissenting)	***Lamb's Chapel v. Center Moriches School District*** June 7, 1993 (White) (Scalia, concurring) (Kennedy, concurring) ***Church of the Lukumi Babalu Aye v. Hialeah*** June 11, 1993 (Kennedy) (Scalia, concurring) (Souter, concurring) (Blackmun, concurring) ***Zobrest v. Catalina Foothills School District*** June 18, 1993 (Rehnquist) (Blackmun, dissenting)

UNITED STATES SUPREME COURT CONSTITUENCY WITH CHURCH/STATE DECISIONS 1856-1996 (continued)

1993-1994	1994-1995	1995-1996		
William H. Rehnquist, C.J. ***Ruth Bader Ginsburg (August 10, 1993)*** Harry A. Blackmun Anthony Kennedy Sandra Day O'Connor Antonin Scalia David H. Souter Clarence Thomas John Paul Stevens	William H. Rehnquist, C.J. Ruth Bader Ginsburg ***Stephen G. Breyer (September 30, 1994)*** Anthony Kennedy Sandra Day O'Connor Antonin Scalia David H. Souter Clarence Thomas John Paul Stevens	William H. Rehnquist, C.J. Ruth Bader Ginsburg Stephen G. Breyer Anthony Kennedy Sandra Day O'Connor Antonin Scalia David H. Souter Clarence Thomas John Paul Stevens		
Board of Education of Kiryas Joel v. Grumet June 27, 1994 (Souter) (Blackmun, concurring) (Stevens, concurring) (O'Connor, concurring) (Kennedy, concurring) (Scalia, dissenting)	***Rosenberger v. University Of Virginia*** June 29, 1995 (Kennedy) (O'Connor , concurring) (Thomas , concurring) (Souter, dissenting) ***Capital Square Review Board v. Pinette*** June 29, 1995 (Scalia) (Thomas, concurring) (O'Connor, concurring) (Souter, concurring) (Stevens, dissenting) (Ginsberg, dissenting)			